The Good Pub Guide 1991

The Good Pub Guide 1991

Edited by Alisdair Aird

Deputy Editor: Fiona May
Research Officer: Martin Hamilton

EBURY PRESS · LONDON

First published by Ebury Press
an imprint of the Random Century Group
Random Century House
20 Vauxhall Bridge Road
London SW1V 2SA

The Good Pub Guide.—1991.
    1. Hotels, taverns, etc.—Great Britain—
Directories   2. Restaurants, lunchrooms etc.
    —Great Britain—Directories
    1.Aird, Alisdair   II. Consumers' Association
    647'.9541'05   TX910.G7

ISBN 0 85223 839 8

Typeset in Linotron/Sabon from authors disk by Saxon Printing Limited, Derby
Printed and bound in Great Britain by Richard Clay Limited, Bungay, Suffolk

Contents

Introduction

THE SEARCH FOR LOWER PRICES

This year we focus attention on prices, and value for money, for two particular reasons. The main one is that in the last few months we have seen some startling increases in pub prices for drink and food: so we've been searching out the best bargains (fortunately there are plenty of them). And the second is the introduction of regulations intended to reduce the monopoly power of the big brewers, and make the beer/pub market more competitive: we've been investigating their effect in practice.

In May 1990 the first stage of the Government's attempt to weaken the big brewers' monopoly took effect. Tenants of tied pubs, and landlords of the high proportion of free houses which are in effect tied to the big brewers by a loan agreement, are now free to buy a different real ale from another source (and to get wines, spirits, soft drinks and so forth from a different supplier). The theory is that this will increase the choice of drinks available and – by exposing the big brewers to competition in their own pubs from market-hungry independent brewers – will help to keep prices down.

In a survey of prices and beer brands in over 1,000 pubs across the country, we've been checking on the effects in practice. Of course it's very early days yet, but what we found suggests little hope of any fundamental change.

First, we found that less than 40% of the nationally tied pubs keep or even plan to keep any 'guest beer'. Moreover, even when they do, it is generally supplied not by some independent brewer but by the national brewery the pub is tied to. The big brewers have been putting together portfolios of smaller breweries' beers, which they advertise and sell to their tied houses alongside their own national brands. For example, in our survey Whitbreads pubs stood out among the nationals for being the most likely to stock an outside beer. But when we looked into the details this commonly turned out to be Marstons Pedigree; Whitbreads have had a distribution deal with Marstons since 1988 (and have a substantial shareholding in Marstons, too). Along with Marstons Pedigree, Wadworths 6X is probably the most prominent independent beer in national brewers' distribution schemes. There are plenty of other examples: it's now typical for a national brewer to have a portfolio of a dozen or more independent beers which it sells to its tied pubs, giving the pubs in any one region a choice between say two out of this list.

Naturally, independent brewers who've been able to strike these sorts of deals with the nationals are pleased, as it does increase their market. But does the customer benefit? After all, these schemes leave the national brewers more or less in control of pricing. The practical test of whether the new guest beer law is doing anything to make prices keener is the comparison between what tied pubs charge for guest beers and what they charge for the beers produced by their national brewer.

In our survey, we found that when nationally tied pubs stock a guest beer they generally sell it at a *higher* price than their basic national beer. We found only one in nine sold the guest beer more cheaply, with another one in eight selling it at the same price. But the independent breweries' own prices are actually *lower* than those of the nationals. When we compared beer prices in pubs tied to independent brewers with those in pubs tied to national ones, we found that the independents on average charge about 7p a pint *less* than the nationals. The conclusion is inescapable: these distribution schemes are letting the national breweries overprice the independent beers they supply to their tied pubs, and thus preventing serious price competition against their own brands. Certainly, our survey shows that customers are generally getting no financial benefit from the wider introduction of independent guest beers into tied pubs.

In our view, these distribution schemes run counter to the 1989 recommendations of the Monopolies and Mergers Commission that the supply of beer should become less monopolistic. We shall be emphasising this point (backed by the detail of our survey research findings) to the Director General of Fair Trading, who has been asked by the Government to monitor the effects of this and other regulations designed to open up the beer market.

An important incidental point is that it's clear from their reports to us that many readers are unaware of the way in which the big national brewers sell beers that sound from their names as if they come from small independent brewers but are in fact brewed in one of their own breweries. Names commonly used by Allied include ABC, Arrols, Benskins, Fergusons, Friary Meux, Halls, Holt Plant & Deakins, Ind Coope, Taylor Walker, Tetleys, Tetley Walker and Walkers. Bass use the names Charrington, Hancocks, Highgate, Mitchells & Butlers (M & B), Springfield, Stones, Tennents and Worthington. Courage have just one alias – John Smiths. Scottish & Newcastle (S & N) include Home, Matthew Browns, McEwans, Theakstons and Youngers. Watneys, part of Grand Metropolitan, have Ruddles, Trumans, Ushers, Websters and Wilsons, and use other names such as Manns and Norwich on pub signs. Whitbreads include Bentleys, Boddingtons, Chesters, Flowers, Fremlins, Higsons and Wethereds.

Customer choice would become a good deal clearer if brewers had to disclose the real identities underlying these aliases at the point of sale – the pub itself. We would like to see a requirement that pubs tied to brewers should carry on their signs the name of the parent group and not just the subsidiary brewery. And brewers should be required to label their beers with the parent group name, too, on pumps, cans and so forth – in good-sized print. We are putting this proposal to the OFT and the Department of Trade and Industry.

Another weapon in the Government's attempt to open up the pub/beer market is the new regulation under which the big brewers will either have to cut their pub estates to under 2,000 over this next year (Bass currently has over 7,000), or 'untie' a large part of their estates if they do keep more pubs. The brewers have been working on various clever defensive measures. The most prominent plan has been the proposal under which Grand Metropolitan would transfer all its Watneys brewing interests to Courage, while Courage would hand over its pubs to Grand Met. This huge new group, not brewing its own beer, would escape the effects of the 2,000-limit regulation virtually entirely. It would be free to buy all its beers from the new enlarged Courage brewing operation, which would count as an outside supplier (Grand Met has already drawn up a 10-year supply deal with Courage). This new group would dominate the pub scene in some areas: the enlarged Grand Met estate would control around a third of all London pubs, for example, and nearly a quarter of all the pubs in the rest of the south east. Though it's hard to see this particular scheme getting approval of the Monopolies & Mergers Commission (they were due to report just as we went to press), it is a clear example of the determined ingenuity the brewers are using to escape the intended effects of the new regulations. So developments over the next year or so will be tremendously important for pub customers. We'll be keeping a careful watch for threats to the interests of pub users, so that we can represent those interests most strongly to the OFT, MMC and Government.

Drinks prices

Two years ago the idea of the £1 pint was almost a joke. It's now a widespread reality. Our national price survey shows that pub drinks prices have been rising faster than inflation, and in the country as a whole the price of a pint now averages over 110p. This overall figure masks wide differences between different parts of the country, and between individual pubs and brewers.

Central London stands out as the most expensive area for pub drinks: on average it's nearly 20p a pint more expensive than the country-wide norm, and on present trends we predict that the £1.50 pint will have become quite common in London by the end of 1991. Elsewhere, Surrey takes the biscuit for high drinks prices – more expensive even than outer London. Next most costly are Sussex, Buckinghamshire, Hampshire, Kent and Berkshire.

The Channel Islands, particularly Jersey, have the lowest prices of all (so much so that we excluded pubs here from the analysis of our main price survey). On the mainland, Lancashire (including Greater Manchester and Merseyside) is now home of the country's cheapest pints; drinkers there pay 30p a pint less than in central London. It's followed very closely indeed by Yorkshire, Cheshire, Cumbria, Derbyshire/Staffordshire, Humberside and Northumbria. Shropshire, Herefordshire and Worcestershire and the Midlands (including Northamptonshire and Warwickshire) are nearly as cheap.

Overall, prices in free houses are close to average, prices in pubs tied to the nationals are rather higher, and prices in pubs tied to smaller regional or locals breweries are rather lower. On average, a pint from one of these smaller breweries' pubs costs about 7p less than a pint from one of the nationals' pubs.

Among the nationals, drinks prices in Allied, Courage and Whitbreads pubs tend to be a few pence higher than in Bass pubs, which are actually no higher than the overall average. Scottish & Newcastle stands out as the cheapest national brewer, with prices well below the country-wide average. The detail of our survey suggests that this is largely because pubs belonging to breweries that they have taken over in recent years (Matthew Browns, Theakstons and in particular Home of Nottingham) used to be low-priced in their independent days, and their prices have not yet climbed to national brewery levels.

Among the main regional breweries, Banks's and Hansons of Wolverhampton and Dudley (very cheap indeed) and Robinsons of Stockport stand out as particularly good value – still easily below the £1 a pint barrier. Even the least cheap of the regional brewers (Camerons/Brent Walker, Devenish and Greene King) rarely price their beers higher than the overall countrywide average. (We had no survey information on Mansfield, one of the regional brewers.) It's worth noting too that we found free houses tend to have the lowest prices if they get their beers from a nearish regional brewer.

Among smaller more local breweries, we found the lowest prices with Holts (Manchester – oustanding), Bathams (West Midlands, also very cheap indeed), Lees (Manchester), Timothy Taylors (W Yorks), Maclays (lowland Scotland), Mitchells (Lancs), Clarks (W Yorks), Smiles (Bristol), Hardys & Hansons (Nottingham), Donnington and Hook Norton (Oxon), Hoskins (Leicester), Jennings (Cumbria), St Austell (Cornwall), Cotleigh (Devon) and Ridleys (Essex). All these undercut the country-wide average by at least 10p a pint.

Pubs which brew their own beers are as cheap as these bargain brewers. Own-brew pubs are growing in number (there were 25 in our price survey); good news for customers, as we found their prices generally at least 10p below the average of other pubs in their areas. Among them, we found one outstanding bargain – our year's *Best Buy for Bottom-Price Beer* – the Old Swan in Netherton (Midlands).

Among pubs supplied from more orthodox sources, our *Top Ten for Low Priced Pints* are, in rough order, the Yew Tree at Cauldon (Staffs), Crooked House in Himley (W Midlands), Green Man at Fownhope (Herefs and Worcs), Mount Skip at Midgley (Yorks), Marble Arch in Manchester, Wharf in Old Hill (W Midlands), Anchor at Oldbury on Severn (Avon), Little Mill at Rowarth (Derbys), Fat Cat in Sheffield and Cornish Arms at St Merryn (Cornwall).

FOOD BARGAINS

In a check on the prices of some 10,000 pub meals, we've found wide variations between areas.

Hunting for bargains, we set two arbitrary price limits. We looked for decent snacks for under £1; and we looked for worthwhile main dishes for under £3. In most parts of the south east we found these targets too tough for about nine out of ten pubs, though Essex and Hertfordshire scored better than most of the region. By contrast, London itself with its staggeringly high drinks prices was quite respectable for pub food: about twice as many pubs meeting our targets. The difference of course is that the level of drinks prices in London is set largely by the big nationals, who own over half the pubs there; food pricing depends much more on the individual publican's judgement.

Scotland, Wales and Derbyshire/Staffordshire stand out as the best areas for pub food bargains – both snacks and main dishes. Here, one in three pubs or more met our low price targets. Humberside and Lancashire are as good as these for bargain main dishes – but much less so for cheap light snacks (maybe appetites there are simply too hearty).

This year, our *Cheap Meal Champion* is the Greyhound in Penkhull (Staffs). Close runners-up are the Olde White Hart in Hull (Humberside), the Cap & Stocking at Kegworth (Leics), the Elephant & Castle at Bloxham (Oxon), the Pack Horse at South Stoke (Avon), the Cricketers in Dorking (Surrey), the Six Bells at Chiddingly (Sussex), the Red Lion at Langthwaite, Whitelocks in Leeds, Fat Cat in Sheffield and Staff of Life in Todmorden (all Yorks), and the Rowan Tree in Uddingston (Scotland).

OTHER TOP PUBS

More and more pubs are now serving really interesting and imaginative food, with fresh ingredients and often introducing foreign influences (Turkish, creole, Polynesian, Chinese, Thai, Greek, Indian) that combine with pub food traditions to create a novel and very refreshing style of eating out. Good examples include the Swan at Inkpen (Berks), the Walnut Tree at Fawley (Bucks), the Cholmondeley Arms near Bickley Moss (Cheshire), the Bay Horse at Ulverston (Cumbria), the Manor House at Carterway Heads (Northumbria), the Roebuck at Brimfield (Herefs & Worcs), the Black Horse at Walcote (Leics), the Old Hall at Threshfield (Yorks), the Druid at Birchover (Derbys) and the Druidstone at Broad Haven (Wales). Currently, the *Best Inventive Cooking* is to be found at the Crown in Southwold (Suffolk).

Our four *Food Discoveries of the Year* – making their debut in this edition of the *Guide* – are the Drewe Arms at Broadhembury in Devon (interesting fish cooking in character surroundings), the Kings Arms at Broomfield in Essex (careful cooking, good ingredients), the Three Crowns at Brinkworth in Wiltshire (a well judged combination of novelties and traditional dishes), and the Rock & Fountain at Clydach in Wales (ambitious, inventive cooking).

Fresh fish is increasingly a pub speciality. The best English examples are currently the Sloop at Bantham and Start Bay at Torcross (Devon), the Three Horseshoes at Powerstock and Ilchester Arms at Symondsbury (Dorset), the Crown at Blockley (Gloucs), the New Inn at Shalfleet (Isle of Wight), the

Brown Trout at Lamberhurst, Sankeys at the Gate in Tunbridge Wells and Pearsons in Whitstable (Kent), the Waterford Arms in Seaton Sluice (Northumbria), the Woodcock at Felbridge (Surrey), and the Frog & Parrot in Sheffield (Yorks). Scotland's west coast has a great wealth of fine fish cooking: it's there that we found our *Fish Pub of the Year*, the Morefield Motel in Ullapool.

Cheese is the long-standing staple of traditional pub food. A great many new British cheese-makers are now getting their often interesting products into local and even distant pubs, which is adding a touch of novelty to this old favourite. The Cock at Broom (Beds), Nobody Inn at Doddiscombsleigh (Devon), La Galoche in Tunbridge Wells (Kent) and Mark Addy and Royal Oak in Manchester all offer formidable value cheese lunches. But we pick as *Cheese Pub of the Year* the Shepherds at Melmerby (Cumbria), for its wide, inventive and perfectly ripened choice.

This year over twice as many pubs as last are making loaf-sized Yorkshire puddings with rich gravy fillings – but so far none of the newcomers can seriously challenge our *Champion Yorkshire Pudding Pub*, the Half Moon at Skidby (Humberside).

At a price, some pubs can now easily beat restaurants at their own game. The Italianate Walnut Tree at Llandewi Skirrid (Wales) is the nonpareil: for the second year running it reigns supreme for *luxury pub food*. Runners-up are the Royal Oak at Yattendon (Berks), Sir Charles Napier near Chinnor (Oxon) and Silver Plough at Pitton (Wilts).

There are a great many contenders now for the title of best all-round dining pub. We are looking for not just good food but also a really enjoyable atmosphere and surroundings. It was with considerable difficulty that we whittled our final shortlist down to the Pheasant at Keyston (Cambs), the White Horse at Scales (Cumbria), the Old Rydon at Kingsteignton (Devon), the Green Dragon at Cowley (Gloucs), the Wykeham Arms in Winchester (Hants), the George at Newnham (Kent), the Moorcock at Blacko (Lancs), the Falcon at Fotheringhay (Midlands), the Beehive at Horringer (Suffolk), the Five Horseshoes at Maidensgrove and Home Sweet Home at Roke (Oxon), the Wenlock Edge Inn on Wenlock Edge and Stables at Hope (Shrops), the Strode Arms at Cranmore and Notley Arms at Monksilver (Somerset), the Horseguards at Tillington (Sussex), the Lamb at Hindon (Wilts) and the Riverside at Canonbie, Crown at Portpatrick and Wheatsheaf at Swinton (Scotland). Particularly bearing in mind its lovely atmosphere, our final choice for *Dining Pub of the Year* is the George at Newnham in Kent.

Cellarman of the Year is Albert Kitchin of the Hoop at Stock (Essex); he keeps a wide range of interesting beers in top condition – with a quite unrivalled choice on the May Day weekend. We choose as *Brew Pub of the Year* the Burton Bridge Brewery in Burton-on-Trent (Staffs) – a new entry this year, where Jeff Plumb brews an interesting range of fine beers for his engaging no-frills town local. The Richmond Arms at West Ashling (Sussex) earns the title of *Beer Taster's Delight*, for Roger and Julie Jackson's unwearying search for an ever-changing range of eclectic cask and bottled beers.

Wine in pubs is becoming increasingly respectable – and many more pubs can now rival decent wine bars in the quality of what they serve. Particularly good examples include the Cholmondeley Arms near Bickley Moss (Cheshire), the Nobody Inn at Doddiscombsleigh (Devon), the New Inn at Cerne Abbas and Ilchester Arms at Symondsbury (Dorset), the Wykeham Arms in Winchester (Hants), the Ship at Conyer Quay – a tremendous choice of spirits, too – and La Galoche in Tunbridge Wells (Kent), the George in Stamford (Lincs), the Snooty Fox at Lowick (Midlands), the Red Lion at Steeple Aston

(Oxon), the Crown in Southwold (Suffolk), the Plough at Blackbrook (Surrey), the Angel at Hetton (Yorks), and the Olde Bulls Head in Beaumaris (Wales). Though it's a close-cut thing, from these we choose as *Wine Pub of the Year* the Wykeham Arms in Winchester, where the Jamesons have a really interesting choice by the glass, in good condition. And for Roger Berman's careful choice of locally grown wines we choose as *English Wines Pub of the Year* the Jack Fullers at Oxleys Green (Sussex), an attractive dining pub that makes its *Guide* debut this year.

Among a good few pubs that have now amassed collections of hundreds of whiskies, the Cragg Lodge at Wormald Green (Yorks) stands out as unrivalled: it is our *Whisky Pub of the Year.*

Nicholas Borst-Smith of the Nobody Inn at Doddiscombsleigh (Devon) has perhaps the best of all pub wine cellars, besides a good range of beers and a tremendous choice of whiskies and other drinks. On top of that, he's made the Nobody an exceptionally attractive inn, with good food and a great deal of character: he is our *Landlord of the Year.*

Our *Discovery of the Year* is the Eliot Arms at Tregadillet in Cornwall; other exceptionally attractive new finds are the Sun at Bentworth (Hants), the Duke of York at Iddesleigh (Devon), the Fleur de Lys at Lowsonford (Midlands) and the Malt Shovel at Brearton (Yorks).

The year's *Most Welcoming Pub* is Richard and Di Stockton's Griffin at Llyswen in Wales. Our *Favourite Country Pub* is Jack Eddleston's White Horse, the Pub With No Name, up on the downs near Petersfield (Hants). The year's *Best Village Pub* is John and Hazel Milligan's Falkland Arms at Great Tew (Oxon); the year's *Best Town Bar* is I W Frazers Bow Bar in Edinburgh – a new entry, owned by Ian Whyte. The year's *Most Interesting Pub* is Alan East's Yew Tree at Cauldon (Staffs), a remarkable living museum.

Our award for *Best New Pub* goes to the Shiremoor House Farm at New York on the outskirts of Newcastle-upon-Tyne, a brilliant conversion of former Tyneside farm buildings, designed by Alan Simpson; the *Best Pub Restoration* is the local Lees brewery's painstaking refurbishment, now at last complete, of the ancient Olde Boars Head in Middleton (Gtr Manchester); the *Most Attractive Refurbishment* is that done by the Thwaites brewery of the Waggon & Horses in Brierfield (Lancs).

FAMILIES IN PUBS

Family Pub of the Year is the Seabrights Barn at Great Baddow (Essex); an object-lesson in how to cater for families with children. Most of the pubs in this book now allow children. The proportion has grown quickly since our first edition eight years ago. In theory, some of the pubs that do allow children are breaking the law, as it is illegal for children under 14 to be in a room in which alcohol is served. The practice seems to vary depending on how the local magistrates interpret the law (it seems common for example to count a distance of 14 feet from the serving counter as being out of the room), and on how the local police enforce it. Readers' experience shows that these local variations are most perplexing in practice – and can be very upsetting indeed for people with children.

As we go to press it seems likely that amendments to the Scottish licensing law will at some time during 1991 allow children into Scottish pubs much more generally. If the changes in the law go ahead, they will allow Scottish pubs to get Children's Certificates if the local licensing board judges them suitable; these Certificates will allow children into any part of a pub up until 8pm, so long as they are eating and with an adult.

It's high time for a review of the law on children in pubs in England and Wales, and we will be pressing the case for this on the Home Secretary. There is a good case for a Certificate scheme. But if one is introduced in England and Wales it will be important to build into the law some specification of what qualities make a pub suitable for certification and what characteristics disqualify it. This would ensure that the judgement was a sound and rational one, consistent across the country and perhaps subject to appeal, rather than depending on the personal views of the licensing magistrates. Moreover, the suggested 8pm evening time limit may not be universally appropriate (it would certainly be laughed out of court in European equivalents of the British pub).

ALL DAY OPENING

All day opening is relatively recent for pubs in England and Wales: the law was changed in 1988. This year we found that one in four pubs are now staying open, on at least some days (sometimes summer only). This is a slightly higher proportion than we found last year, with the numbers dribbling up by ones and twos almost everywhere – as the Special Interest List at the end of the book shows. The increase in afternoon opening has been most marked in Cumbria, Lancashire, Northumbria and Yorkshire; in the north as a whole, more than one in three pubs now open all day (more than half in Lancashire). The proportion is as high as this in Cornwall, the Isle of Wight and Wales. As we predicted when the law was changed, it does look as if the level of all day opening is gradually starting a climb towards the level now prevailing in Scotland – where all day opening has been allowed for 15 years, and where at least two-thirds of pubs stay open all day. In London (and other big cities) all day opening is now the general rule.

NO SMOKING

As most pub customers are now non-smokers, we decided this year to do a special survey to see how many pubs provide for non-smokers. We expected a virtually nil result. It came as a real surprise to find that one in eight pubs are now setting aside at least some area as no smoking – even in cities like London. We found the highest proportion in Cumbria, Dorset and Norfolk, where one in three or four pubs now have some sort of no smoking area. Given this start, we'd expect the process to snowball. As customers discover that at least some pubs have taken an initiative to suit the non-smoking majority, and as other pubs see that their competitors are doing it, many of these other pubs will no doubt follow suit. So this year we've added a new section to the Special Interest Lists at the end of the book: pubs making at least some sort of provision for non smokers.

Using the *Guide*

THE COUNTIES

England has been split alphabetically into counties, mainly to make it easier for people scanning through the book to find pubs near them. Each chapter starts by picking out pubs that are specially attractive for one reason or another.

Occasionally, counties have been grouped together into a single chapter, and metropolitan areas have been included in the counties around them – for example, Merseyside in Lancashire. When there's any risk of confusion, we have put a note about where to find a county at the place in the book where you'd probably look for it. But if in doubt, check the Contents: note that this year the north-eastern chapter, grouping together Durham, Northumberland, Cleveland and Tyne & Wear, has been called Northumbria.

Scotland and Wales have each been covered in single chapters, and London appears immediately before them at the end of England. Except in London (which is split into Central, North, South, West and East), pubs are listed alphabetically under the name of the town or village where they are. If the village is so small that you probably wouldn't find it on a road map, we've listed it under the name of the nearest sizeable village or town instead. The maps use the same town and village names, and additionally include a few big cities that don't have any listed pubs – for orientation.

We always list pubs in their true locations – so if a village is actually in Buckinghamshire that's where we list it, even if its postal address is via some town in Oxfordshire. Just once or twice, while the village itself is in one county the pub is just over the border in the next-door county. We then use the village county, not the pub one.

STARS

Specially good pubs are picked out with a star after their name. In a few cases, pubs have two stars: these are the aristocrats among pubs, really worth going out of your way to find. And just two pubs have three stars – the tops. The stars do NOT signify extra luxury or specially good food. The detailed description of each pub shows what its special appeal is, and it's that that the stars refer to.

FOOD AND STAY AWARDS: 🔪 🛏

The knife-and-fork rosette shows those pubs where food is outstanding. The bed symbol shows pubs which we know to be good as places to stay in – bearing in mind the price of the rooms (obviously you can't expect the same level of luxury at £12 a head as you'd get for £30 a head).

RECOMMENDERS

At the end of each main entry we include the names of readers who have recently recommended that pub (unless they've asked us not to). Important note: the description of the pub and the comments on it are our own and *not* the recommenders'; they are based on our own personal inspections and on later verification of facts with each pub. As some recommenders' names appear quite often, you can get an extra idea of what a pub is like by seeing which other pubs those recommenders have approved.

LUCKY DIPS

At the end of each county chapter we include brief descriptions of pubs that have been recommended by readers, with the readers' names in brackets. The name Lucky Dip is now a bit of a misnomer. When we started this system a few years ago we had so few reports from readers, on so few pubs, that it was a fair description. Now, the flood of reports from readers has given us a great deal of solid information about thousands of pubs, well worth trying, with descriptions often reflecting the balanced judgement of a number of different readers. They have't usually been inspected by us, unless the recommenders include the initials LYM or BB. LYM means the pub was in a previous edition of the *Guide*. The usual reason that it's no longer a main entry is that, although we've heard nothing really condemnatory about it, we've not had enough favourable reports to be sure that it's still ahead of the local competition. BB means that, although the pub has never been a main entry, we have inspected it, and found nothing against it. In both these cases, the description is our own; in others, it's based on the readers' reports.

Lucky Dip pubs marked with a ☆ are ones where the information we have (either from our own inspections or from trusted reader/reporters) suggests a firm recommendation. Roughly speaking, we'd say that these pubs are as much worth considering, at least for the virtues described for them, as many of the main entries themselves. Note that in the Dips we always commend food if we have information supporting a positive recommendation. So a bare mention that food is served shouldn't be taken to imply a recommendation of the food. The same is true of accommodation and so forth.

The Lucky Dips (particularly, of course, the starred ones) are under consideration for inspection for a future edition – so please let us have any comments you can make on them. You can use the report forms at the end of the book, the report card which should be included in it, or just write direct (no stamp needed if posted in the UK). Our address is *The Good Pub Guide*, FREEPOST, London SW10 0BR.

MAP REFERENCES

All pubs are given four-figure map references. On the main entries, it looks like this: SX5678 Map 1. Map 1 means that it's on the first map at the end of the book. SX means it's in the square labelled SX on that map. The first figure, 5, tells you to look along the grid at the top and bottom of the SX square for the figure 5. The *third* figure, 7, tells you to look down he grid at the side of the square to find the figure 7. Imaginary lines drawn down and across the square from these figures should intersect near the pub itself.

The second and fourth figures, the 6 and the 8, are for more precise pin-pointing, and are really for use with larger-scale maps such as road atlases or the Ordnance Survey 1:50,000 maps, which use exactly the same map reference system. On the relevant Ordnance Survey map, instead of finding the 5 marker on the top grid you'd find the 56 one; instead of the 7 on the side grid you'd look for the 78 marker. This makes it very easy to locate even the smallest village.

Where a pub is exceptionally difficult to find, we include a six-figure reference in the directions, such as OS Sheet 102 reference 654783. This refers to Sheet 102 of the Ordnance Survey 1:50,000 maps, which explain how to use the six-figure references to pin-point a pub to the nearest 100 metres.

MOTORWAY PUBS

If a pub is within four or five miles of a motorway junction, and reaching it doesn't involve much slow traffic, we give special directions for finding it from the motorway. And the Special Interest Lists at the end of the book include a list of these pubs, motorway by motorway.

PRICES AND OTHER FACTUAL DETAILS

The *Guide* went to press during the summer of 1990. As late as possible before that, each pub was sent a checking sheet to get up-to-date food, drink and bedroom prices and other factual information. In the last year, we've found that prices have tended to increase by up to around 15% over the year – so you should expect that sort of increase by summer 1991. But if you find a significantly different price (with a few pubs this last year, some prices have jumped by over 30%) *please let us know*. Not every pub returned the sheet to us (if it didn't, we don't show a licensee's name after the brewery name at the end of the entry), and in some cases those that did omitted some prices. In such cases we ourselves were usually able to gather the information – especially prices – anyway. But where details are missing, that is the explanation. Again, this is something we'd particularly welcome readers' reports on.

Breweries to which pubs are 'tied' are named at the beginning of the italic-print rubric after each main entry. That means the pub has to get most if not all of its drinks from that brewery. If the brewery is not an independent one but just part of a combine, we name the combine in brackets.

Free houses are pubs not tied to a brewery, so in theory they can shop around to get the drinks their customers want, at the best prices they can find. But in practice many free houses have loans from the big brewers, on terms that bind them to sell those breweries' beers – indeed, about half of all the beer sold in free houses is supplied by the big national brewery combines to free houses that have these loan ties. So don't be too surprised to find that so-called free houses may be stocking just as restricted a range of beers as openly tied pubs.

Real ale is used by us to mean beer that has been maturing naturally in its cask. We do not count as real ale beer which has been pasteurised or filtered to remove its natural yeasts. If it is kept under a blanket of carbon dioxide ('blanket pressure') to preserve it, we still generally mention it – as long as the pressure is too light for you to notice any extra fizz, it's hard to tell the difference. But we say that the carbon dioxide blanket is there.

Other drinks: we paid particular attention to picking out those pubs where the quality or range of *wines* is above the general pub average (gradually improving, though still well below what it should be). We're always particularly grateful to readers for reports on wine quality in pubs. We've also looked out particularly for pubs doing enterprising non-alcoholic drinks (including good tea or coffee), interesting spirits (especially malt whiskies), country wines (elderflower and the like) and good farm ciders. So many pubs now stock one of the main brands of draught cider that we normally mention cider only if the pub keeps quite a range, or one of the less common farm-made ciders.

Meals refers to what is sold in the bar, not in any separate restaurant. It means that pub sells food in its bar substantial enough to do as a proper meal – something you'd sit down to with knife and fork. It doesn't necessarily mean you can get three separate courses.

Snacks means sandwiches, ploughman's, pies and so forth, rather than pork scratchings or packets of crisps. We always mention sandwiches in the text if we know that a pub does them – if you don't see them mentioned, assume you can't get them.

The food listed in the description of each pub is an example of the sort of thing you'd find served in the bar on a normal day. We try to indicate any difference we know of between lunchtime and evening, and between summer and winter (on the whole stressing summer food more). In winter, many pubs tend to have a more restricted range, particularly of salads, and then to do more in the way of filled baked potatoes, casseroles and hot pies. We always mention barbecues if we know a pub does them. Food quality and variety may be affected by holidays – particularly in a small pub, where the licensees do the cooking themselves (May and early June seems to be a popular time for licensees to take their holidays).

Any separate *restaurant* is mentioned, and we give a telephone number if tables can be booked. We also note any pubs which told us they'd be keeping their restaurant open into Sunday afternoons (when, in England and Wales, they have to close their bars). But in general all comments on the type of food served, and in particular all the other details about meals and snacks at the end of each entry, relate to the pub food and not to the restaurant food.

Children under 14 are now allowed into at least some part of most of the pubs included in this *Guide* (there is no legal restriction on 14-year-olds going into the bar, though only 18-year-olds can get alcohol there). As we went to press, we asked pubs a series of detailed questions about their rules. *Children welcome* means the pub has told us that it simply lets them come in, with no special restrictions. In other cases we report exactly what arrangements pubs say they make for children. However, we have to note that in readers' experience some pubs set a time limit (say, no children after 8pm) that they haven't told us about, while others may impose some other rule (children only if eating, for example). If you come across this, please let us know, so that we can clarify the information for the pub concerned in the next edition. Even if we don't mention children at all, it is worth asking: one or two pubs told us frankly that they do welcome children but don't want to advertise the fact, for fear of being penalised. All but one or two pubs (we mention these in the text) allow children in their garden or on their terrace, if they have one. Note that in Scotland the law may change during 1991, allowing children more freely into pubs so long as they are eating (and with an adult).

Dogs, cats and other animals are mentioned in the text if we know either that they are likely to be present or that they are specifically excluded – we depend chiefly on readers and partly on our own inspections for this information.

If an entry says something like 'on *Good Walks Guide* Walk 22' (or, in the Lucky Dips, 'on GWG Walk 22'), the pub is on one of the walks described in the book of that name by Tim Locke, published by Consumers' Association and Hodder & Stoughton.

Parking is not mentioned if you should normally be able to park outside the pub, or in a private car park, without difficulty. But if we know that parking space is limited or metered, we say so.

Opening hours are for summer weekdays. If these show a pub stays open until 11pm, it will close at 10.30pm in winter unless we say *all year*. And in winter some pubs open an hour or so later, too; we mention this where we know of it. In the country, many pubs may open rather later and close earlier than their details show unless there are plenty of customers around (if you come across this, please let us know – with details). Unless we say otherwise for a particular county or pub, pubs generally stay open until 11pm on Friday and Saturday evening. Since 1988, pubs in England and Wales have been allowed to stay open all day Mondays to Saturdays, from 11am (earlier, if the area's licensing magistrates have permitted) till 11pm; Scottish pubs have been allowed to do this since 1976, and all-day opening is far more generally common there – outside cities, it's still quite rare in England and Wales, where pubs are still experimenting with the new hours. Again, we'd be very grateful to hear of any differences from the hours we quote. You are allowed 20 minutes' drinking-up time after the quoted hours – half an hour if you've been having a meal in the pub.

Sunday hours are standard for all English and Welsh pubs that open on that day: 12–3, 7–10.30. In Scotland, a few pubs close on Sundays (we specify those that we know of), most are open 12.30–2.30 and 6.30–11, and some stay open all day. If we know of a pub closing for any day of the week or part of the year, we say so. The few pubs which we say stay closed on Monday do open on Bank Holiday Mondays.

Bedroom prices normally include full English breakfasts (if these are available, which they usually are), VAT and any automatic service charge that we know about. If we give just one price, it is the total price for two people sharing a double or twin-bedded room for one night. Otherwise, prices before the / are for single occupancy, prices after it for double. A capital B against the price means that it includes a private bathroom, a capital S a private shower. As all this coding packs in quite a lot of information, some examples may help to explain it:

£30 on its own means that's the total bill for two people sharing a twin or double room without private bath; the pub has no rooms with private bath, and a single person might have to pay that full price

£30B means exactly the same – but all the rooms have private bath

£30(£35B) means rooms with private baths cost £5 extra

£18/£30(£35B) means the same as the last example, but also shows that there are single rooms for £18, none of which have private bathrooms

If there's a choice of rooms at different prices, we normally give the cheapest. If there are seasonal price variations, we give the summer price (the highest). This winter – 1990–91 – many inns, particularly in the country, will have special cheaper rates. And at other times, especially in holiday areas, you will often find prices cheaper if you stay for several nights. On weekends, inns that aren't in obvious weekending areas often have bargain rates for two- or three-night stays.

MEAL TIMES

As bar food service has become such a normal part of a pub's operations, pubs have become more consistent in the times at which they serve it. Commonly, it's served from 12–2 and 7–9, at least from Monday to Saturday (food service often stops a bit earlier on Sundays). If we don't give a time against the meals and snacks note at the bottom of a main entry, that means that you should be able to get bar food at those times. However, we do spell out the times if we know that bar food service starts after 12.15 or after 7.15; if it stops before 2 or before 8.45; or if food is served for significantly longer than usual (say, till 2.30 or 9.45).

Though we note days when pubs have told us they don't do food, experience suggests that you should play safe on Sundays and check first with any pub before planning an expedition that depends on getting a meal there. Also, out-of-the-way pubs often cut down on cooking during the week if they're quiet – as they tend to be, except at holiday times. Please let us know if you find anything different from what we say!

NO SMOKING (NEW THIS YEAR)

We say in the text of each entry what if any provision a pub makes for non-smokers. Pubs setting aside at least some sort of no smoking area are also listed county by county in the Special Interest Lists at the back of the book.

CHANGES DURING THE YEAR – PLEASE TELL US

Changes are inevitable, during the course of the year. Landlords change, and so do their policies. And, as we've said, not all returned our fact-checking sheets. We very much hope that you will find everything just as we say. But if you find anything different, please let us know, using the tear-out card in the middle of the book (which doesn't need an envelope), the report forms here, or just a letter. You don't need a stamp: the address is *The Good Pub Guide*, FREEPOST, London SW10 0BR.

Author's acknowledgements

We owe a great deal to the many readers who report, often regularly, on pubs – thanks to you all. In particular, we are deeply in debt to a small group of readers who have each over the years told us about several hundred pubs, often in meticulous detail: Gwen and Peter Andrews, Len Beattie, S V Bishop, Wayne Brindle, PLC, Lyn and Bill Capper, Dr and Mrs A K Clarke, Frank Cummins, Nick Dowson and Alison Hayward, Gordon and Daphne, Phil and Sally Gorton, Lee Goulding, Tim and Sue Halstead, Steve and Carolyn Harvey, Richard Houghton, Roger Huggins, WHBM, Brian and Anna Marsden, Joan Olivier, E G Parish, Ian Phillips, Heather Sharland, Jon Wainwright and Patrick Young.

Readers giving us particular help with this edition have been Andy and Jill Kassube, Brian Jones, Derek and Sylvia Stephenson, Thomas Nott, Chris Raisin, Graham Gibson, Nigel Gibbs, Steve Mitcheson and Caroline Collins, Graham Bush, Peter Griffiths, TBB, Jenny and Brian Seller, H K Dyson, John Baker, Tony and Lynne Stark, Ewan McCall, Tom McLean, Dave Braisted, John Evans, Peter Corris, Robert Lester, Reg Nelson, Michael and Alison Sandy, Mike and Wendy Proctor, Simon Collett-Jones, A T Langton, Comus Elliott, A J Skull, Richard Sanders, Syd and Wyn Donald, Simon Turner, Dr and Mrs I W Muir, BKA, S J A Velate, Mr and Mrs J H Adam and David and Flo Wallington.

Warm thanks to Pat Taylor Chalmers for meticulous proof reading under pressure of very tight deadlines; to David Perrott for his care with the maps; and to Bridget Warrington for additional research.

England

Avon   *see* Somerset

Bedfordshire   *see* Cambridgeshire

Berkshire

This is one of the more expensive parts of England for pubs; on the drinks side, it's worth looking out for the fairly local Brakspears and, particularly, Morlands, as we found these generally cheaper here than other beers. With food, it's now hard here finding good snacks under £1 or decent main dishes under £3 – but it can be done, for instance in the charming Old Bell at Aldworth, the horse-country Crown & Horns in East Ilsley, the peacefully rusticated Pot Kiln at Frilsham, the warmly friendly Queen Victoria at Hare Hatch (a new entry in this edition) and the Rising Sun at Woolhampton (which has a fine range of well kept real ales). Though above these particular price barriers, the Four Points at Aldworth serves monumentally large helpings. And other pubs which come down firmly on the customer's side of the price / quality equation are the Pheasant near Great Shefford (handy for the M4), the White Hart at Hamstead Marshall (more main dishes than snacks, with an Italian flavour – a nice place to stay), the Swan at Inkpen (try its Singapore specialities), the Bird in Hand at Knowl Hill (a splendid buffet), the comfortable Red House at Marsh Benham (approaching a food award now), the Little Angel at Remenham (pricey, but smart, with some emphasis on seafood), the cottagey Old Boot (good value right up and down the price scale) and the friendly Bull (a new entry this year – the soups are excellent) both at Stanford Dingley, and the Royal Oak at Yattendon (by no means cheap, but easily the best bar food in Berkshire, and better value than many good restaurants – another very pleasant place to stay). Special points to pick out about other main entries here this year include the popular newish licensees at the Blue Boar near Chieveley, the remarkable continuing stylish refinement of the Bel & the Dragon in Cookham, the handsome layout of the elegantly refurbished Swan in East Ilsley, the continuing rise in readers' affections of the tucked-away Dew Drop above Hurley, the remarkable wines to be had at the Dundas Arms at Kintbury (nice to see the nearby Kennet & Avon Canal reopened now), and the splendid way the Bull in Sonning has been keeping up its picturesquely old-fashioned charm. In the Lucky Dip section at the end of the chapter, pubs currently showing well are the Pineapple at Brimpton, Ibex in Chaddleworth, New Inn at Hampstead Norreys, Castle in Hurst, Union in Old Windsor, and Bell at Waltham St Lawrence.

ALDWORTH   SU5579 Map 2

Bell ★

A329 Reading–Wallingford; left on to B4009 at Streatley

At Christmas local mummers perform in the road outside this old-fashioned place, by the ancient well-head (the shaft is sunk 400 feet through the chalk); steaming jugs of hot punch and mince pies are handed round afterwards, and a little of that heady atmosphere seems to linger all year. There's a cheerful beamed bar, with benches built around the panelled walls and into the gaps left by a big disused fireplace and bread oven – though there's still a woodburning stove. The very well kept Arkells BBB and Kingsdown, Badger Best and Morrells (all on handpump) are handed through a small hatch in the central servery. Fresh hot crusty rolls are filled with cheddar, ham, pâté or stilton (70p), turkey, corned beef or tongue (80p), and smoked salmon (£1.20); darts, shove-ha'penny, cribbage, dominoes, chess and Aunt Sally. The quiet garden is at its best in summer, when it's filled with roses, mallows and lavender. Close to the Ridgeway, the pub is popular with walkers on Sundays, and quieter on weekday lunchtimes. *(Recommended by Gordon and Daphne, Richard Houghton, Bev and Doug Warwick, A T Langton, Dr Stewart Rae, Neville Burke)*

Free house   Licensee Mrs H E Macaulay   Real ale   Snacks   Children in tap room Open 11–3, 6–11; closed Mon (not Bank Hols) and 25 Dec

Four Points ☺

B4009 towards Hampstead Norreys

This chatty and welcoming old thatched pub has simple red leatherette furniture on the red-tiled floor, china in a corner cupboard, a big log fire, and vases of flowers in the main area, with a partly panelled carpeted room to one side; sensibly placed darts here. The award is primarily for outstanding value – normal helpings are so prodigious that there are also optional smaller ones. Depending on what Mrs Gillas fancies cooking that day, this might include sandwiches (from 90p, substantial bacon and mushroom or prawn £2.50), a lunchtime selection such as omelettes, smoked oysters or curried prawns (around £2.50), ploughman's with imaginatively presented salads (£2.45), hare or rabbit pies (£3.95 – the animals are often donated by local farmers), lasagne, moussaka or shepherd's pie (£3.95), and steaks (from £6.95); croûtons are set out on the thick-topped wooden tables, and on Sundays there are extra nibbles such as prawns, cheese and celery and poppadums. Well kept Charrington, Courage Directors, Morlands and Wadworths 6X on handpump, and a well chosen selection of wines. The building dates from the early 17th century, and in summer is colourfully enlivened by hanging baskets and flower tubs; the garden across the road has climbing frames, a little-old-lady shoe house and so forth. *(Recommended by Keith and Sian Mitchell, David Warrellow, Gordon and Daphne, Lyn and Bill Capper, HNJ, PEJ, Richard and Dilys Smith, David Wallington, Stan Edwards)*

Free house   Licensees John and Audrey Gillas   Real ale   Meals and snacks   Children welcome   Open 11–2.30, 5.30–11

BRAY   SU9079   Map 2

Crown

1 ¾ miles from M4 junction 9; A308 towards Windsor, then left at Bray signpost on to B3028

Decent bar food in this friendly timbered pub includes, at lunchtime, sandwiches on request, a choice of well filled rolls (90p), pâté (£2.20), quiche (£3.20), Chinese barbecued pork (£4.50), and home-made puddings like Gaelic coffee trifle, mousses or apple pie (£1.85); in the evening the selection is more elaborate – lobster soup (£3.50), avocado and seafood (£4.50), frogs' legs in garlic (£5.50), duck (£10.75), and steaks (from £11); vegetables are grown in their kitchen garden; summer Sunday barbecues. The main bar is softly lit and partly panelled, with low beams, old timbers conveniently left at elbow height where walls have been knocked through, leather-backed seats around copper-topped or wooden tables, and a cosy winter fire; some caricatures by Spy and his competitors on the walls, guns, pistols, and stuffed animals; well kept Courage Best tapped from the cask, and a fair choice of wines; piped music and a lively atmosphere. The large back garden has tables under cocktail parasols here, and there are more tables and benches in the flagstoned courtyard and vine arbour. *(Recommended by Graham Bush, TBB, J P Cinnamond, JMC, W J Wonham, W A Gardiner)*

Courage   Licensee Hugh Whitton   Real ale   Meals (not Sat lunchtime, or Sun – but see above for barbecues) and lunchtime snacks (12.30–2, 7.30–10)   Well behaved children welcome   Restaurant tel Maidenhead (0628) 21936; closed Sun   Open 10.30–3, 5.30–11

CHIEVELEY SU4774 Map 2

Blue Boar

4 miles from M4 junction 13: A34 N towards Abingdon, first left into Chieveley, bear left and keep on until T-junction with B4494 – turn right towards Wantage, pub on right

Standing on the picturesquely stunted ancient oak outside this thatched inn is the Blue Sandstone Boar, said to have been presented by Cromwell who stayed here in 1644 on the eve of the Battle of Newbury. The atmosphere these days in the three rambling rooms of the beamed bar is a good deal more civilised than it must have been then – but still attractively old-fashioned, with furnishings such as plush or brocaded cushioned stools, high-backed settles, Windsor chairs and polished tables, as well as a variety of heavy harness (including a massive collar), hunting prints and photographs. The middle room has an unusual inglenook seat, and the left-hand room a seat built into the sunny bow window with a fine view over unspoilt fields, and a roaring log fire. Adnams and Wadworths 6X on handpump, 60 types of whisky, cocktails, and several liqueur coffees; piped music. Bar food includes soup (£1.80), sandwiches (from £2.15; fillet steak £4.95), ploughman's (£3.95), pasta of the day (£5.45), home-made burger (£4.95), salads (from £4.95), beef curry or steak and kidney pie (£5.95), and puddings (from £2); Sunday roast (£7.95). There are tables among tubs and flowerbeds on the rough front cobbles. The landlord, who took over towards the end of 1989, has been warmly received by readers. (*Recommended by Gordon and Daphne, Simon Collett-Jones, C R Ball, L G and D L Smith; more reports please*)

Free house Licensee Mr Bachelor Real ale Meals and snacks Restaurant Well behaved children welcome Open 11–3, 6–11 Bedrooms tel Chieveley (0635) 248236; £50B/£65B

COOKHAM SU8884 Map 2

Bel & the Dragon ★

High Street; B4447 N of Maidenhead

This stretch of the Thames is by no means cheap as far as pubs are concerned, and although this quietly up-market and restful old place is no exception, it's considerably better value than most. Three atmospheric communicating lounge rooms have oak panelling, old oak settles, deep, comfortable leather chairs, and pewter tankards hanging from heavy Tudor beams. A smartly dressed and grave but friendly barman behind the very low zinc-topped bar counter serves well kept Brakspears PA and Old and Wethereds Bitter tapped from the cask, wines including decent ports and champagne, and cocktails made with the proper ingredients. There are often free peanuts and home-made crisps, as well as home-made soup or quiche (£2.25), sandwiches (from £2.25, prawn £3.75, smoked salmon £5.25; toasties £3), home-made pizza (£3.75), slimmer's salad (including walnuts and fresh fruit – £5), steak and kidney pie (£5.75), and puddings (£2); the eating area of the bar is no-smoking. In summer and good weather snacks (and indeed restaurant meals) are also served in the garden or on the terrace, furnished as pleasantly as the pub itself. The Stanley Spencer Gallery is almost opposite. (*Recommended by Alison Hayward, Nick Dowson, Ian Phillips, TBB, BKA, Richard Houghton, John Day*)

Free house Owners Mr and Mrs F E Stuber, Mr and Mrs H Schlatter Real ale Bar snacks Restaurant tel Bourne End (06285) 21263 Children in eating area of bar only Open 11–2.30, 6–10.30; closed evening 25 Dec

COOKHAM RISE SU8984 Map 2

Swan Uppers

B4447 Cookham–Maidenhead

There's a particularly cosy atmosphere here, with cream walls over a shiny black panelled dado, heavy black beams, and broad worn flagstones throughout, even in the restaurant area which rambles off on the right. Two or three quieter dark blue plush booths are around on the left, and there are also cushioned wall benches and stools, railway-lantern lamps, blow-ups of sepia cartes-de-visite and other Victorian photographs; an old bread oven is set in the side of the bigger fireplace over on the left. Well kept Eldridge Pope Best and Royal Oak, Marstons Pedigree and Palmers Best on handpump, with a dozen or so decent malts; maybe unusual piped music in some areas. Good bar food includes sandwiches (from £1.30), ploughman's (from £2.25), braised ham and celery (£4.25), popular fresh haddock, stir-fried chicken or liver and bacon (all £4.50), and puddings (from £2). Tables are set out on a fairy-lit back terrace, with some wooden ones at the front by the village road. There are two poodles, Lanson and Podge. *(Recommended by Nick Dowson, Alison Hayward, TBB, Simon Collett-Jones; more reports please)*

Free house Licensee J Waring Real ale Meals and snacks (12–2, 7.30–10) Restaurant (not Sun evening) Children welcome Open 11–3, 6–11; closed evening 25 Dec Bedrooms tel Bourne End (062 85) 21324; £25/36

EAST ILSLEY SU4981 Map 2

Crown & Horns

A34, about 5 miles N of M4 Junction 13

Very much in horse-training country, this interesting building is decorated with racing prints and photographs in the partly panelled and beamed main bar, and the TV is on for the racing in a side bar. Bar food includes sandwiches and main meals such as good value, tasty venison pie, lasagne or liver and bacon casserole (£2.95), moussaka (£3.25), duck in a honey and orange sauce (£4.75), and steak (£8.75); friendly service. There's an attractive range of rotating real ales, which typically includes Arkells BBB, Bass, Brakspears SB, Fullers London Pride, Morlands Old Master, Theakstons Old Peculier and Wadworths 6X, on handpump; a collection of 170 whiskies spans most of the world – even Morocco, Korea, Japan, China, Spain and New Zealand; skittle alley, darts, pool, bar billiards, shove-ha'penny, dominoes, cribbage, pinball, fruit machine, juke box and piped music. The pretty paved stable yard has tables under two chestnut trees. *(Recommended by Mrs G L Carlisle, Mr and Mrs D A P Grattan; more reports please)*

Free house Licensees Chris and Jane Bexx Real ale Meals and snacks (12–2, 6–10) Children in eating area, restaurant and TV room Open 11–3, 6–11 Bedrooms tel East Ilsley (063 528) 205/545; £17.50(£26B)/£27.50(£36B)

Swan 🖙

Dating back largely to the 17th century, this fine pub was taken over in the 1840s by Morlands, who at the time brewed in nearby West Ilsley – the Morlands Bitter and Old Masters are well kept on handpump. Particularly well refurbished in open-plan style, the bar is a stylish assortment of irregularly shaped nooks and corners, divided by low walls topped with broad polished woodwork; one area down by an elegantly arched 1930s fireplace is mainly for drinkers – the fact that the serving counter's right over on the opposite side somehow seems to help the quietly thriving overall atmosphere; the main area has a mix of diners and chatting other customers, with bentwood tables and armed chairs on an elegant pastel flowery carpet; there are some pub cartoons in the lower area, and lots of local photographs in the main part; darts, cribbage, dominoes, unobtrusive fruit machine, faint piped music. Good value home-made bar food includes sandwiches (from £1.20; prawn £2.50), several ploughman's (from £2.10), spaghetti with a bolognese or vegetarian sauce (£3), cottage pie (£3.20), with at least 20 further choices from a daily blackboard, such as roast lamb or fish pie (£3.65), fresh 16oz plaice (£4.50), gammon (£5.75), and several home-made puddings; good friendly service. There are picnic-table sets on a prettily trellised back terrace, and on a sheltered lawn with a play area. *(Recommended by Richard Houghton, Stan Edwards, S A Starkey, A T Langton)*

Morlands Licensees Michael and Jenny Connolly Real ale Meals and snacks Restaurant Children in eating area and restaurant Open 10.30–2.30, 6–11 Bedrooms tel East Ilsley (063 528) 238; £17.50(£28B)/£35(£45S)

FRILSHAM SU5473 Map 2
Pot Kiln

From Yattendon follow Frilsham signpost, but just after crossing motorway go straight on towards Bucklebury when Frilsham is signposted right

The fine rural setting – sheltering woods and peaceable pastures – is best appreciated on a summer evening in the newly extended garden, where there are suntrap tables and folding garden chairs. The pub is a striking brick affair, with bare benches and pews, wooden floorboards, and a good log fire; it's popular with locals, and the atmosphere is attractively unspoilt and old-fashioned. Well kept Arkells BBB, Morlands, Ringwood Fortyniner and a guest beer, all on handpump, are served from a hatch in the panelled entrance lobby – which just has room for one bar stool. Good bar food includes filled hot rolls (from 80p), home-made soup (£1.10), a decent ploughman's (£2.10), lots of vegetarian dishes such as curry (£2.65) or spinach and mushroom lasagne (£3.85), smoked trout salad (£5.25), and steak (£6.95); friendly service, though there may be delays at busy times. The public bar has darts, dominoes, shove-ha'penny and cribbage; informal folk music on Sunday evenings – people get up to play more or less as the mood takes them. It's good dog-walking country, though they don't actually allow them in the main bar. (*Recommended by Ian Phillips, Keith and Sian Mitchell, Gordon and Daphne, TBB, Lyn and Bill Capper, Jon Wainwright, H N and P E Jeffery, Richard and Dilys Smith*)

Free house Licensee Mrs Gent Real ale Meals (not Sun) and snacks Well behaved children in one bar Folk singing Sun Open 12–2.30, 6.30–11

GREAT SHEFFORD SU3875 Map 2
Pheasant ⊘

Under half a mile from M4 junction 14; A338 towards Wantage, then first left (pub visible from main road, and actually at Shefford Woodland, S of the village itself)

This atmospheric, white-painted tile-hung house pub has four neat communicating room areas with cut-away cask seats, wall pews and other chairs on their Turkey carpet, and racehorse prints on the walls. The home-made bar food is good value – sandwiches, interesting soups (from £1.10, with a speciality one such as courgette and coriander or carrot with citrus and ginger at £1.65), ploughman's (from £2.25; in winter they do it combined with soup for £2.75), chilli con carne (£5), steak and kidney pie (£5.50), steaks (from £9), with popular puddings (£2). Though it's very conveniently placed for stop-offs from the M4, service can be very slow – so if you want to eat on a quick motorway break, it's a good idea to ask how long a meal is likely to take. Well kept Courage Best and Wadworths IPA and 6X on handpump, decent coffee; darts, cribbage, dominoes, ring the bull – very popular – and fruit machine in the public bar; piped music. Rustic tables in a smallish garden look over the fields. Mr Jones also runs the Royal Oak at Wootton Rivers (see Wilts). (*Recommended by Stan Edwards, Greg Parston, BKA, Mr and Mrs H W Clayton, Graham and Glenis Watkins, John and Pat Smyth; more reports on service please*)

Free house Licensees John and Rosa Jones Real ale Meals and snacks Small restaurant tel Great Shefford (0488) 39284 Children in restaurant Open 10.30–2.30, 5.30–11

HAMSTEAD MARSHALL SU4165 Map 2
White Hart ⊘ ⇌

Village signposted from A4 W of Newbury

The extension of the dining room into the bar area reflects the deserved growth in popularity for the home-made food in this fine Georgian country inn; beyond soup and pâté with bread they bake themselves, there's not much in the way of simple snacks, but the choice of main dishes is very good: authentic pasta (from £4.90) such as lasagne, cannelloni, fettucini and gnocchi, mushrooms stuffed with ham, herbs and garlic (£5.90), meatballs stuffed with mozzarella and braised in a wine, mushroom and tomato sauce, spare ribs (£6.90), crispy roast duck (£8.50), and a lot of fish brought fresh from Billingsgate, such as mussels in wine and tomato (£6.90), bass or turbot (around £8); they make their own cassata (Mr Aromando, from Italy, does most of the cooking; his wife Dorothy does the puddings, including a popular concoction they call tirami su). The atmosphere is unpretentious but civilised; the low-ceilinged, L-shaped bar has red plush seats built into the bow windows, red-cushioned chairs around oak and other tables, a copper-topped bar counter, steeplechasing and other horse prints on its ochre walls, and a central log fire. Well kept Badger Best and Eldridge Pope Royal Oak on handpump; politely friendly service. No dogs (their own Welsh setter's called Sam, and the pony's called Solo). The flower-bordered and walled lawn is shaded by a lime tree, ancient pear tree and much younger eucalyptus. The bedrooms are in a converted barn across the courtyard. *(Recommended by Lyn and Bill Capper, Margaet Dyke, Mr J C Bell, John Tyzack, Gordon and Daphne, GB, CH)*

Free house   Licensee Mr Nicola Aromando   Real ale   Meals and snacks (not Sun) Restaurant (not Sun)   Children in restaurant   Open 12–2.30, 6.30–11; closed Sun, 25–26 Dec and 2 weeks Aug   Bedrooms tel Kintbury (0488) 58201; £40B/£55B

HARE HATCH

Queen Victoria

Blakes Lane, The Holt; just N of A4 Reading–Maidenhead, 3 miles W of exit roundabout from A423(M) – keep your eyes skinned for the turning

The specials are the things to go for here, often adventurous and always good value (most around £3): steak and kidney casserole, beef and Guinness stew, baked leeks au gratin with hunky bread. Soups of the day are often a bargain, such as a mushroom soup so full of mushrooms that one reader found it hard to prise his spoon in; other dishes include ploughman's or spicy sausage (£1.95), filled baked potatoes, steak sandwich, cheese and nut croquette (£2.65), beef taco shells (£2.95), tandoori chicken or pork and pineapple curry (£3.95), maybe pheasant casserole (£4.25) and steak (£5.95). The pub's a warmly friendly two-roomed local, low-beamed, with sturdy furnishings, a stuffed sparrowhawk, a Delft shelf lined with Beaujolais bottles and lots of games from a fruit machine and video game to darts, cribbage, dominoes, solitaire and three-dimensional noughts and crosses; well kept Brakspears PA, SB, Mild and Old on handpump, a notably welcoming landlord. There's a robust table or two in front by the car park. *(Recommended by Ian Phillips, Comus Elliott, David Warrellow, D C and R J Deeming)*

Brakspears   Licensee Ronald Rossington   Real ale   Meals and snacks (11.30–2.30, 6.30–10.30)   Children welcome   Open 11–3, 5.30–11

HOLYPORT   SU8977 Map 2

Belgian Arms

1 1/2 miles from M4 junction 8/9; take A308(M) then at terminal roundabout follow Holyport signpost along A330 towards Bracknell; in village turn left on to big green, then left again at War Memorial shelter

The L-shaped, low-ceilinged bar in this homely village pub has a variety of chairs around a few small tables on the carpet, good prints and framed postcards of Belgian military uniforms on the walls, a china cupboard in one corner, and a winter log fire; generally well kept Brakspears PA, SB and in winter Old on handpump. Tasty, simple bar food includes sandwiches, plain or toasted (from £1.10; the open prawn one at £3 is excellent, and the toasted 'special' is very popular – ham, cheese, sweetcorn, peppers, onion and mushroom £1.65), a range of daily specials (£3.50), seafood platter or home-cooked ham and eggs (£4.40), and steaks (from £8.50). The pleasant conservatory is used as a restaurant in the evening, but at lunchtime you can take bar food there; polite service. The charming garden has a flag-iris pond, and beyond, a pen of goats and hens. *(Recommended by Keith and Sian Mitchell, Lyn and Bill Capper, William D Cissna, Peter Blood, TBB, Simon Collett-Jones, G Shannon)*

Brakspears   Licensee Alfred Morgan   Real ale   Meals and snacks (not Sun)   Small conservatory restaurant (not Sun, nor summer) tel Maidenhead (0628) 34468   Open 11–2.30, 5.30 (7.30 winter Sat)–11

nr HURLEY   SU8283   Map 2

Dew Drop ★

Just W of Hurley on A423 turn left up Honey Lane – look out for the IGAP sign; at small red post-box after large farm, fork right – the pub is down a right-hand turn-off at the first cluster of little houses

This genuinely secluded brick and flint cottage has quite a loyal following among readers – it's a welcoming place with friendly locals, simple furnishings that include a log fire at each end of the main bar, and generous helpings of good bar food, such as soup (£1.10), jumbo sausage, ploughman's, pâté, garlic mushrooms on toast (£2.50), substantial gammon with egg, home-made steak, kidney and mushroom pie in Guinness or lamb rogan josh (all £4.50), and puddings such as jam roly-poly or pecan pie. Well kept Brakspears PA and Old on handpump and some good malt whiskies; shove-ha'penny and darts. It's a lovely place in summer, when you can sit on seats in the attractively wild sloping garden, looking down to where white doves strut on the pub's red tiles, above tubs of bright flowers; there's a children's play area. From his conversation and from the pictures on the wall, it's not difficult to discover the landlord's passion – golf. Popular with dog owners. *(Recommended by Ian Phillips, R J Walden, Nick Dowson, TBB, Chris Raisin, Graham Doyle, Richard Houghton, David Wallington)*

Brakspears   Licensee Michael Morris   Real ale   Meals and snacks (not Mon or Sun evening)   Open 11.30–2.30, 6–11

HURST   SU7972   Map 2

Green Man

Hinton Road; A321 Twyford–Wokingham, turn right into B3030, then NE just S of filling station in village centre

This popular but unspoilt pub serves good bar food, from rolls (from £1), superb stilton ploughman's (£2.45) and burgers (from £1.30), to main dishes such as good prawn curry (£3.75), home-made pies like steak and kidney, pigeon or game (all £4.65), evening vegetarian dishes like nut roast Portuguese (£6.85), and steaks (from £8). The low-beamed, atmospheric bar has tapestried wall seats and wheelback chairs around brass-topped tables on the green carpet, lots of alcoves and country pictures, black standing timbers, horsebrasses and brass stirrups, and an open fire at both ends (neatly closed in summer by black-and-brass folding doors). Some black japanned milkchurns serve as seats around the counter, which dispenses well kept Brakspears PA and SB and Old tapped from the cask. Dominoes, cribbage and piped music (maybe loudish Radio 1). Trivia on Mondays, boules, Aunt Sally and a golf society; garden behind. *(Recommended by Gordon and Daphne, S J Curtis, Chris Raisin, Graham Doyle, Ian Phillips, Mrs Caroline Gibbins)*

Brakspears   Licensee Allen Hayward   Real ale   Meals and snacks (12–2, 7–10; not Sun, not Mon evening)   Marquee restaurant (not Sun) tel Reading (0734) 342599 Open 11–2.30, 6–11

INKPEN   SU3564   Map 2

Swan ⊘

Lower Inkpen; coming from A338 in Hungerford, take Park Street (first left after railway bridge, coming from A4); Inkpen is then signposted from Hungerford Common

First impressions suggest nothing extraordinary about this tiled, white-painted brick pub: a long, rambling row of rooms, with well waxed flowery-cushioned pews and tables on the muted beige and brown carpet, some traditional black-painted wall settles, log fires (including a big old fireplace with an oak mantlebeam between the bar counter and the restaurant area), and at the bottom, heavily-beamed end neat blond dining chairs and tables with a woodburning stove. However the licensee's Singapore-Chinese influence quickly emerges, not least in the bar menu and its selection of fresh and fragrantly flavoured food: prawns marinated in beer and wine then deep-fried (£3.70), satay (£3.95), nasi goreng (£4.45), Singapore noodles (£4.75), popular chicken with cashew nuts (£5.35), chilli crab claws (£5.50) and pork in ginger and pineapple sauce (£6.50); in the evening the only western-style dishes available are lamb cutlets or steaks, though there's a wider range at lunchtime – home-made pâté, quiche, beef and venison pie and so forth, as well as children's helpings; friendly service. The Singapore connection shows in one or two other ways, too: a wicked gin sling, for instance, and deeply chilled foreign lagers (as well as well kept Brakspears, Flowers Original and Hook Norton on handpump); a dice game called balut (as well as darts, shove-ha'penny and a fruit machine); and the magazines in one snug alcove up a couple of steps. The house claret is chateau-bottled for them by a friend with a house in Bordeaux – the licensees have recently bought a hotel and restaurant with them on the River Garonne. There are flowers out in front by the picnic-table sets, which are raised above the quiet village road. (*Recommended by Gordon and Daphne, A W Dickinson, Mr and Mrs C Austin, Chris Payne, Joan and John Calvert, Michael Thomson*)

Free house   Licensees John and Esther Scothorne   Real ale   Meals and snacks (12–1.45, 7–9.30, not Sun evening, Tues lunchtime or Mon)   Restaurant tel Inkpen (048 84) 326   Children in restaurant and bottom end of bar lunchtime and early evening   Open 11.30–2.30, 6.30–11; closed all day Mon, Tues lunchtime

KINTBURY   SU3866   Map 2

Dundas Arms 🛏

A4 Newbury–Hungerford; don't take the first signposted turning to Kintbury, but continue through Halfway, then take first left after about a mile; pub is after the River Kennet, but just before the Kennet and Avon Canal and the village itself

The comprehensive bar menu in this old-fashioned, waterside inn includes sandwiches (from £1.50), soup (£1.75), smoked salmon pâté (£3.50), crab au gratin (£3.30), smoked salmon quiche (£4), gammon and egg (£4.30), smoked haddock with poached eggs (£4.60), steak and kidney pie (£4.80), home-made gravadlax (£5.50), and steak (£8.50); good breakfasts. The partly panelled and carpeted bar has cream walls, one of which is covered with an outstanding array of blue and white plates. Well kept Adnams Bitter, Eldridge Hardy (new last year, to commemorate Hardy's 150th anniversary), and Morlands Bitter on handpump. There's a remarkable range of clarets in the good evening restaurant. The bedrooms are in converted ex-barge-horse stables, and their French windows open on to a secluded terrace. Erected early last century for the canal builders, the pub is set between a quiet pool of the River Kennet and the Kennet and Avon Canal, which reopened last year after 40 years of restoration; there's a lock just beyond the hump-backed bridge. (*Recommended by Lyn and Bill Capper, John C Baker, Tony and Louise Clarke, Alan Skull, M G Richards, Mr and Mrs D A P Grattan, David Wallington*)

Free house   Licensee David Dalzell-Piper   Real ale   Meals and snacks   Restaurant (not Sun)   Children in eating area of bar   Open 11–2.30, 6–11; closed Christmas to New Year   Bedrooms tel Kintbury (0488) 58263; £50B/£60B

KNOWL HILL   SU8279   Map 2

Bird in Hand 🔍

About 8 miles along A4 Reading–Maidenhead

The spacious main bar in this roadside inn is decidedly smart and civilised – for some readers more like a hotel; but the atmosphere is still relaxed, friendly and generally pubby, with well kept Brakspears PA and Old, and Youngs Special on handpump, several wines and a few good malt whiskies, including the Macallan. There are cosy alcoves, beams, some attractive Victorian stained glass in one big bow window, dark brown panelling with a high shelf of willow-pattern plates, a red Turkey carpet on polished oak parquet, and a log fire. There's a centuries-older side bar, and a snug well padded back cocktail bar. Generous helpings of good home-made food include an excellent lunchtime cold buffet laid out in a no-smoking area (£4.95 for as much as you want), with good cold salt beef, salami, ham, three other cold meats, four or five fish and shellfish dishes, and lots of fresh and imaginative salads such as apple, celery and peanut, or carrot and leek strips in a lemon-juice dressing. There's also home-made soup (£1.50), sandwiches (from £2, smoked salmon open sandwich £4.25, sirloin steak £4.75), filled baked potatoes (from £2.25), chicken tikka (£3.50), changing daily hot dishes such as popular steak and kidney pudding, game casserole, chicken with tarragon in a white wine sauce or haddock in a chive and mussel sauce (all £4.95), and good home-made puddings such as sherry trifle or lemon meringue pie (£2); efficient, professional service. The garden at the side is roomy and neatly kept. *(Recommended by John Baker, david Warrellow, Dr J C Harrison, Gary Scott, Hilary Robinson, Peter Maden, Lindsey Shaw Radley, Simon Collett-Jones)*

Free house   Licensee Jack Shone   Real ale   Meals and snacks (12–2.30, 6–10.30) Children in eating area and restaurant   Restaurant   Open 11–3, 6–11   Bedrooms tel *Littlewick Green (062 882) 2781/6622; £60B/£80B*

LITTLEWICK GREEN   SU8379   Map 2
Cricketers

3 3/4 miles from M4 junction 9: A423(M) then left on to A4, from which village is signposted on left

The landlord here is indeed a cricketer – in summer he captains his cricket team (matches every weekend, some weekdays) on the attractive village green opposite. The cheerful and well kept lounge has maroon plush window seats and stools, lots of Windsor chairs, cricketing prints, books and assorted memorabilia, cartoons and a prominent old factory clocking-in clock. Adnams, Eldridge Pope Hardy, Morlands and Wadworths 6X on handpump; cribbage, a fruit machine and piped music. Bar food includes sandwiches (from £1.40; toasties from £1.50), ploughman's (£3.50), good chilli con carne with potato skins, sour cream and chives (£3.75), vegetarian or meaty lasagne or chicken curry (£4), home-made steak and kidney pie (£4.25), tasty smoked haddock pasta with prawns and mushrooms (£4.50), and puddings like hot treacle tart (£1.50); dishes are archly given cricketing pun names. The sway-backed pub is in good walking country – the National Trust's Maidenhead Thicket is just east on the A4, and there are woods along the A404 towards Marlow. *(Recommended by TBB, A W Dickinson, Peter Maden, Hilary Robinson, Dr J C Harrison, J P Day, Ian Phillips, David Young, Simon Collett-Jones)*

Free house   Licensees John and Adrienne Hammond   Real ale   Meals and snacks Children welcome   Open 11–3, 5.30–11; 11–11 Sat; closed 26 Dec

MARSH BENHAM   SU4267   Map 2
Red House

Village signposted from A4 W of Newbury

Recent restrained refurbishment in this popular, friendly pub has left much of the old-fashioned atmosphere intact: the two rooms of the comfortable bar, separated by an arch with a fine formal flower arrangement, have deeply carved Victorian gothick settles (and some older ones), and attractive prints (including some Cecil Aldin village scenes). Imaginative and plentiful food, well presented and brought to your table by efficient, uniformed waitresses, typically includes home-made soup (£1), sandwiches (from £1.50, smoked salmon £2.95), steak and kidney pie (£3.75), ploughman's (from £2.75; stilton in port £3.25), gammon (£3.50), spicy lamb with mango chutney (£4.25), and lamb cutlets or ox tongue in a madeira sauce (£4.50); vegetables are fresh and seasonal; puddings such as home-made ice cream (from £1.75). It fills up for food very quickly at weekends – readers advise getting there before 12.30 if you want a seat at one of the glossily varnished tables: seating arrangements – apart from this squeeze – are good. Well kept – they've installed a cooling system in the cellar since last year – Brakspears PA and SPA, Flowers Original and Marstons Pedigree on handpump, and good wines by the glass. An attractive garden by the side of the thatched brick building has a wooden sun house, and a butterfly reserve. Handy for the reopened Kennet & Avon canal. *(Recommended by Margaret Dyke, Dr J C Harrison, Dr and Mrs R E S Tanner, Angus and Rosemary Campbell, Gordon and Daphne, Alan Skull, David and Christine Foulkes, John C Baker, T Galligan, HNJ, PEJ, Sheila Keene, Stephen Goodchild, Henry Midwinter)*

Free house   Licensees John Goodman, Michael Hoskins   Real ale   Meals and snacks (12–2, 6.30–9.30)   Restaurant tel Newbury (0635) 41637   Children in restaurant Open 10.30–3, 6–11

PEASEMORE   SU4577   Map 2

Fox & Hounds

Village signposted from B4494 Newbury–Wantage

Good home-made bar food in this unaffected downland pub includes soups such as celery and tomato (£1.95), a proper ploughman's with real as opposed to plastic-wrapped butter (from £2.50), filled baked potatoes (from £2.50), home-made pizzas (from £3.50), several pies such as beef in beer or tuna and sweetcorn (£4.50), chicken breast marinated in yoghurt and charcoal-grilled (£5.95) and steaks (from 8oz rump £8.95); they even do lunch on Christmas day. A new side extension has been added, shifting the L-shaped bar over to the left, and making more space for the restaurant and the bar servery; there are brocaded stripped wall settles, chairs and stools around shiny wooden tables, and a log-effect gas fire open to both the new and the old bar. The popularity of horse-racing locally is reflected in a full set of Somerville's entertaining *Slipper's ABC of Fox-Hunting* prints, and one stripped-brick wall has a row of flat-capped fox masks. Well kept Courage Best, John Smiths and Eldridge Pope Best on handpump at prices that are notably low for the county, with a reasonable choice of wines; quick, friendly service; darts, cribbage, pool table, video and fruit machines and discreet juke box in the new bar. A few picnic-table sets in front, by the quiet lane, look over to the rolling fields. *(HNJ, PEJ; more reports please)*

Free house   Licensees David and Loretta Smith   Real ale   Meals and snacks Restaurant tel Chieveley (0635) 248252   Children welcome   Open 11–3, 6–11, maybe longer summer afternoons; closed evening 25 Dec

REMENHAM   SU7683   Map 2

Little Angel ⚤

A423, just over bridge E of Henley

The major attraction here is the choice of food, which from the bar menu might typically include home-made soup (£2.50), vegetarian chow mein (£4), mussels in black bean sauce (£4.50), seafood tagliatelle (£5.50), beef in oyster sauce (£7), braised duck (£7.50), six jumbo prawns (£9), steak (£8.50) and Dover sole (£14); there's a 10% service charge. There's quite an emphasis on seafood in the restaurant – they collect from Billingsgate several times a week, and there are special food events, particularly during the Henley Regatta, when it's best to book well ahead. Brakspears PA and Old on handpump, a wide range of reasonably priced wines, and kirs. The main part of the stylish bar is decorated in deep glossy red and black, matching the little tiles of the bar counter and the carpet; leading off is the candlelit Garden Room (and restaurant), which is more given over to eating. The terrace behind (its name, the Champagne Garden, gives some idea of the style of this pub) has tables and pink umbrellas and is floodlit at night. It can get very crowded at peak times; wooden tables and benches outside. *(Recommended by Lindsey Shaw Radley; more reports please)*

Brakspears   Licensee Paul Southwood   Real ale   Meals and snacks (12–2, 7–11)

Children welcome   Restaurant tel *Henley-on-Thames (0491) 574165   Open 11–2.30, 6–11*

SONNING   SU7575 Map 2
Bull

Village signposted on A4 E of Reading; off B478, in village

This wisteria-covered, black and white timbered and unpretentious pub has beams in the low ceilings of the two communicating rooms of the bar, cosy alcoves (one with a set of books), cushioned antique settles and low wooden chairs, newspapers on racks, inglenook fireplaces, and a penny-farthing; warmly atmospheric, with chatty staff. Well kept Flowers Original, Marstons Pedigree, and Wethereds SPA on handpump; soft piped music. Lunchtime bar food includes a good cold buffet with salads such as pork pie and mixed meats (£4.20), and pies or quiche (£3.80). The courtyard outside is particularly attractive, with tubs of flowers and a rose pergola – though at busy times it may be packed with cars. If you bear left through the ivy-clad churchyard opposite, then turn left along the bank of the river Thames, you come to a very pretty lock. (*Recommended by Dick Brown, Cdr W S D Hendry, Gethin Lewis, Brian and Jenny Seller, Chris Raisin, Graham Doyle, Margaret Dyke, TBB, JMC, Mr and Mrs H L Malhotra, Ian Phillips, Lindsey Shaw Radley, Alison Hayward, Nick Dowson, John Knighton, Simon Collett-Jones*)

Wethereds (Whitbreads)   Licensee Dennis Catton   Real ale   Lunchtime meals and snacks   Restaurant   Children in restaurant   Open 10–2.30, 5.30–11; closed evening 25 Dec   Bedrooms tel *Reading (0734) 693901; £31.05/£62.10*

STANFORD DINGLEY   SU5771 Map 2
Bull

From M4 junction 12, W on A4, then right at roundabout on to A340 towards Pangbourne; first left to Bradfield, where left, then Stanford Dingley signposted on right

Relaxed and friendly, the little left-hand bar in this attractive 15th-century red brick country pub is partly divided into two by a couple of standing timbers hung with horse-brasses. One side has heavy black beams, red quarry tiles, some red-cushioned seats carved out of barrels, a cushioned window settle and wheelback chairs, and an old brick fireplace; the other side is similarly furnished but carpeted, and decorations include an old station clock, some corn dollies and a few old prints. The big bowls of piping hot soup have come in for particular praise: French onion (£1.55), creamy carrot and orange (£1.95) and Stilton (£2.10). They also do sandwiches on request (from £1.10), filled baked potatoes (from £1.65), ploughman's (from £2.20), savoury pancakes with a vegetarian or salmon and shrimp filling (£3.70), chilli con carne (£4.05), chicken provençale (£5.20), steaks (from £5.99), daily specials such as leek and potato pie (£3.70), lamb and rosemary (£4.50), excellent beef in Guinness (£5.20), and puddings like fruit crumble (£1.50). Well kept Bass, Brakspears, Charrington IPA, and Eldridge Pope Hardy on handpump; ring-the-bull, occasional classical or easy listening music. There's also a simpler saloon bar with plush grey semi-circular banquettes and wheelback chairs, a tiny barrel-like bar counter, and another brick fireplace. In front of the building are some big rustic tables and benches, and to the side is a small garden with a few more seats. (*Recommended by R E Osborne, Angus and Rosemary Campbell, David Warrellow, Keith and Sian Mitchell, Keith and Dorothy Pickering, Comus Elliott*)

Free House   Licensees Patrick and Trudi Langdon   Real ale   Meals and snacks (not Mon lunchtime)   Children in saloon bar lunchtime and early evening (not Sat)   Open 12–3, 7–11; closed Mon lunchtime and 25 Dec

Old Boot 🕮

There's quite an emphasis on tasty, well presented bar food in this quiet but popular village pub, with sandwiches, home-made soup (£1.50), lots of ploughman's (from £2.25), good home-made 8-oz burgers (from £2.80), chilli con carne (£2.95), popular garlic mushrooms with bacon and granary toast (£3), smoked salmon and scrambled eggs on croûtons (£3.30), salads (from £3.30), ham and egg (£4.35), lemon sole stuffed with crabmeat (£4.95), some vegetarian dishes such as vegetable and blue cheese dip (£3), and changing daily specials such as home-made cottage pie, chicken and Stilton roulade or roast pork (£3–4); the chef may be willing to prepare particular dishes on request; good, cheerful service. The neat bar has a couple of highly polished built-in settles, wheelback chairs with red plush cushions, pews, two carved and other tables, thoughtfully chosen pictures (the one of the yacht on the open sea is striking), a few beams and wall timbers, and an inglenook fireplace; up a couple of steps and through some French window-style doors – which have attractive fabrics for the old-fashioned wooden-ring curtains – is the pretty little restaurant. There's also a simple locals bar. Well kept Brakspears, Eldridge Pope Royal Oak, Flowers IPA and Whitbreads Castle Eden on handpump; darts and piped music. There are flowers in white tubs in front of the building, with white garden furniture on a secluded back terrace and picnic-table sets in the big country garden. *(Recommended by Mike Tucker, Syd and Wyn Donald, Keith and Sian Mitchell, Gordon and Daphne, Dr and Mrs R E S Tanner, M S Hancock, TBB, J Charles, Dr Stewart Rae, Comus Elliott, Barry and Anne, H N and P E Jeffery, Richard and Dilys Smith)*

Free house   Licensee Anthony Howells   Real ale   Meals and snacks (12–2, 6–10) Restaurant tel Reading (0734) 744292   Children in eating area and restaurant   Open 11–2.30, 6–11; closed evening 25 and 26 Dec

WARGRAVE   SU7878   Map 2

Bull

Village off A321 Henley-On-Thames–Twyford; pub on High Street

This diminutive and low-beamed fifteenth-century brick inn has a traditional but neatly modernised and relaxing bar, with lots of plain chairs and tables, and collections of baseball caps, horse brasses and china bulls. Leading off is a room with French windows opening on to a sheltered back terrace with rustic tables and benches among flowering shrubs; another area has a huge log fireplace. Good value lunchtime bar food includes sandwiches (from £1.20), home-made soup (£1.75), ploughman's (£2.75), vegetarian lasagne (£3.75), and daily specials like steak and kidney pie or curries (£3.75); in the evening this changes to scallops (£2.75), savoury crêpe (£3), marinated Barnsley chop in a red wine sauce (£4.95), Norfolk duckling with almonds and orange (£6.95), and steaks (from £6.25); friendly, speedy service. Well kept Brakspears PA and SB on handpump, and a decent collection of other drinks including several wines by the glass and Pimms by the half-pint. *(Recommended by K H Miller, TBB, Ian Phillips, Simon Collett-Jones, Comus Elliott; more reports please)*

Brakspears   Licensee Noel Harman   Real ale   Meals and snacks (not Sun evening) Children in restaurant   Open 11–2.30, 6–11   Bedrooms tel Wargrave (0734) 403120; £18/£30

WEST ILSLEY   SU4782   Map 2

Harrow

Signposted at East Ilsley slip road off A34 Newbury–Abingdon

Bar food in this little tiled white house ranges from snacks like filled granary French bread (from £1.50), cream of onion soup with oatmeal (£1.50), ploughman's (from £3) and devilled kidneys (£2.50), to main dishes like home-made rabbit pie with lemon and herbs (£3.75) or steak and kidney (£3.95), home-baked gammon (£4.25), seafood casserole or lamb's liver with coriander and orange (£6.25), steaks (£7.50), and home-made puddings like treacle tart or chocolate and rum trifle (£2). The simply furnished bar has a well worn and homely feel, with its red leatherette wall seats and bucket chairs, and is decorated with cricket team and other local photographs; darts, cribbage and piped music. Morlands, who started brewing in this village before they moved to Abingdon, still supply the Bitter and Old Masters, kept well on handpump. Picnic-table sets and other tables under cocktail parasols look out over the duck pond and cricket green, and a spacious children's garden has a notable play area with a big climber, swings, rocker and so forth – not to mention ducks, fowls, canaries, rabbits, goats and a donkey. The pub can be surprisingly lively – on show days, say, or if there's a cricket match going on. There are lots of walks nearby – the Ridgeway is just a mile away. Note they no longer do bedrooms. (*Recommended by Richard Houghton, A T Langton, TBB*)

Morlands   Licensee Mrs Heather Humphreys   Real ale   Meals and snacks (not Sun evening in winter)   Restaurant (not Sun evening) tel East Ilsley (063 528) 260 Children in eating area   Open 11–2.30 (3 Sat), 6–11

WICKHAM   SU3971 Map 2

Five Bells 🍺

3 miles from M4 junction 14; A338 towards Wantage, then first right into B4000

At one end of the long, open-plan carpeted bar in this comfortable pub there are wheelback chairs around polished tables, and patio doors that lead out to a garden with plenty more tables, as well as a very well equipped children's play area with a swimming pool. At the other end inside, beyond brick pillars, there's a huge log fire, with tables set for meals; a stripped brick dado runs along the walls. The servery extends back into the low eaves, hung with all sorts of bric-a-brac: brass blowlamps, an antique muller, copper whisking bowl, old bottles and so forth; pictures throughout reflect that this is racing country – there's also a separate TV room to keep up with the latest results. Home-made bar food includes sandwiches (from £1.20), soup (£2.25), pâté (£2.50), good ploughman's (£2.75), jumbo sausages or vegetarian spring roll (£3), very popular steak and kidney pie or tasty gammon (£5), a choice of salads (from £3.75), and steaks (from £7.50); daily specials (around £5), and a choice of puddings (from £2.25). Well kept Ushers Best, Ruddles County, and Websters Yorkshire on handpump, and a good choice of spirits; lively bar staff and a chatty licensee, pool, dominoes, juke box, fruit machine. (*Recommended by Paul Evans, HNJ, PEJ, John and Pat Smyth*)

Ushers (Watneys)   Licensee Mrs Dorothy Channing-Williams   Real ale   Meals and snacks   Children in eating area of bar   Restaurant   Open 10.30–2.30, 5.30–11 Bedrooms tel Boxford (048 838) 242; £30/£40

WINTERBOURNE   SU4572 Map 2

Winterbourne Arms

Not far from M4 junction 13; village signposted from B4494 Newbury–Wantage

This pretty black-and-white brick house has had its name changed since our last edition – from the New Inn. It's an individual sort of place, very much a local, with a pleasant clutter of decorations – old bottles on strings, plates, smoothing-irons and lots of small pictures on the cream walls, and a slow-ticking wall-clock; off on the right you can find bar billiards (popular with regulars). There are brocaded small settles, chairs and stools on the flowery red carpet, and a log fire. Generous helpings of home-made bar food include, at lunchtime, filled rolls (from £1.50), a range of ploughman's (from £2.95, tuna or sausage £3.95, maybe a useful winter combination with soup), baked potato filled with cheese (£3.25), several home-made daily specials, and gammon (£5.75); in the evening prices are slightly higher, with extra dishes such as chicken (£5.25) and steak (£8.25). Well kept Brakspears, Flowers Original, Marstons Pedigree and Wethereds Bitter and SPA on handpump; darts, cribbage, a tucked-away fruit machine, piped music. As the road is slightly sunken between the pub's two lawns, you can't actually see it from inside the bar – so the view from the big windows is rather peaceful. Picnic-table sets, and a big weeping willow outside. Under the New Inn name, but the same management, the pub was noted for its cheery atmosphere and quick service; we trust the slowdown found by one reader last spring, shortly before this report was written, was a temporary interruption. (*Recommended by HNJ, PEJ; more reports please*)

Free house   Licensees Tony and Janet Tratt   Real ale   Meals and snacks (not Sun, Mon or Tues evenings)   Restaurant (not Sun evening) tel Chieveley (0635) 248200   Children in restaurant; none under 14 in bar   Open 11.30–2.30, 6 (7 winter)–11; closed 25 and 26 Dec

WOOLHAMPTON   SU5767   Map 2

Rising Sun

A4, nearly a mile E of village

Though weather-beaten outside, the rambling red and black lounge here is warm and comfortable, and decorated with small reproduction coaching prints; the public bar has darts, bar billiards, dominoes, cribbage, fruit machine and piped music. Popular, reasonably priced bar food includes filled baked potatoes (from £1), sandwiches (from £1.20), a range of ploughman's (from £2.10), cottage pie (£2.90), curry (£2.95), steak and Guinness pie (£3.10), lasagne (£3.25), scampi (£3.60), chicken Kiev (£5.75), and steaks (from £7.65); friendly service. The fine selection of real ales on handpump changes regularly, and might include Arkells BBB, Gales HSB, Marstons Pedigree, Morlands, Ringwood Old Thumper, Theakstons XB, and Youngers IPA; several malts. Seats outside at the back, where there's a swing. They're planning bedrooms for 1991. *(Recommended by Chris Fluck, E H and R F Warner, R Houghton, Phil Smith, John Baker)*

Free house   Licensee Peter Head   Real ale   Meals and snacks (till 10 on Wed to Sat evening sessions)   Restaurant tel Woolhampton (0734) 712717   Children in restaurant   Open 11.15–2.30 (3 Sat), 6–11

YATTENDON   SU5574   Map 2

Royal Oak ★ ⊘ ⇌

The Square; B4009 NE from Newbury; turn right at Hampstead Norreys, village signposted on left

Though there's a certain school of thought that pubs should confine themselves to simple meals for a pound or two, the overwhelming majority of readers are highly enthusiastic about the emphasis on sophisticated, restauranty food in this comfortable and stylish old inn. The selection changes daily and includes filled rolls (if they're not too busy – they don't like to do them unless they've time to make them really well), home-made soups such as creamy mushroom (£2.75), salad of warm duck livers with spring onions or grilled calves kidneys and black pudding with green herb mustard sauce (£3.75 as a starter or £7.50 as a main course – they have two prices for several dishes), avocado and seafood salad (£4.95 or £7.50), ploughman's with an unusual selection of farmhouse cheeses (£4.50), salad with honey-baked ham or cold roast beef (£5), crispy duck and salad frisée (£4.75 or £6.95), supreme of chicken with oyster mushrooms and creamy curry sauce (£8.50), and grilled fillet of monkfish with scallops and saffron sauce (around £9.75); home-made puddings such as fresh mango (£3) and apple and raspberry crumble (£4), and good vegetables; for bar lunches you have to book a table. However food isn't the only draw – the lounge and prettily decorated panelled bar have an extremely pleasant atmosphere, log fires in winter, and a good range of well kept beers – Adnams, Badger Tanglefoot, and Wadworths 6X on handpump; they'll also open any bottle of wine on their bar wine list if customers wish to have half a bottle. The pretty garden is primarily for the use of residents and restaurant guests, but is available on busy days for those in the bar. The village – where Robert Bridges lived for many years – is very attractive. *(Recommended by Dr Sheila Smith, R J Walden, Simon Barber, Mike and Jill Dixon and friends, Gordon and Daphne, John and Pat Smyth, W C M Jones, Bev and Doug Warrick, Henry Midwinter, A T Langton, J E Thompson, Dr Stewart Rae, TBB, Mr and Mrs D A P Grattan)*

Free house   Licensees Richard and Kate Smith   Real ale   Meals and snacks   Well behaved children in eating area   Restaurant (closed Sun evenings)   Occasional jazz evenings   Open 11–2.30, 6–11   Bedrooms tel Hermitage (0635) 201325; £50(£60B)/£60(£70B)

Lucky Dip

Besides the fully inspected pubs, you might like to try these Lucky Dips recommended to us and described by readers (if you do, please send us reports):

Ascot [High St; SU9268], *Stag*: Lively and welcoming traditional pub with well kept Friary Meux and Tetleys, bar food, slick service, piped music *(Simon Collett-Jones)*

Ashampstead [SU5676], *Fleece & Feathers*: Attractively refurbished free house on quiet country road, pleasantly furnished bar with polished dark tables, settles, Windsor chairs etc; friendly licensees and dog, wide food choice inc steaks and less usual items such as chicken in black bean sauce; Wadworths 6X *(Stan Edwards)*

Aston [Ferry Lane; back rd through Remenham; SU7884], *Flower Pot*: Edwardian hotel a short stroll from Thames, with comfortable welcoming lounge bar, well kept Brakspears, well presented bar food from sandwiches or ploughman's to main dishes such as trout, friendly service; good garden with views over meadows to cottages and far side of river; on GWG68 *(Ian Phillips, Brian and Jenny Seller)*

Bagnor [SU4569], *Blackbird*: Particularly popular lunchtimes for good food, esp cauliflower cheese and steak sandwich, at very reasonable prices; nr Watermill Theatre *(David and Christine Foulkes)*

☆ **Binfield** [B3034 from Windsor; SU8471], *Stag & Hounds*: Low beams in several interconnecting rooms, real fires, imaginative menu in wine bar/bistro, good atmosphere, friendly service, well kept Courage Best and Directors *(Alan Symes, Simon Collett-Jones)*

Binfield [Terrace Rd North; SU8471], *Victoria Arms*: Attractive mix of old and new in comfortably laid out Fullers pub with good choice of seating areas, well kept real ales, reasonably priced bar food; children's room, summer barbecues in sheltered garden *(LYM)*

Bisham [SU8484], *Bull*: Free house with pubby main bar, though emphasis on restaurant; quiet and relaxing even though popular, friendly uniformed staff, and well kept local real ales; tidy lavatories; large car park *(Richard Houghton)*

Bracknell [London Rd; SU8769], *Royal Oak*: Very busy place, rather like an old city pub with lively atmosphere and mixed customers; well kept Courage beers, and friendly, fast service despite the crowds *(Richard Houghton)*

Bradfield [A4; SU6072], *Queens Head*: Well run and comfortable, with good atmosphere *(Comus Elliott)*

Bray [SU9079], *Hinds Head*: Decidedly civilised upmarket pub in handsome building, smart and beautifully kept with leather armchairs, high-backed settles, early Tudor beams, oak panelling, good log fires, Wethereds real ale; seats outside, attractive upstairs restaurant — which is what they concentrate on *(LYM)*; [Windsor Rd (2 miles S)], *Queens Head*: Cosy, low-ceilinged old

pub, popular with people from the film studios — lots of photos and mementoes; nice atmosphere, friendly landlord and well kept Friary Meux and Tetleys on handpump *(Nick Dowson)*

☆ **Brimpton** [Brimpton Common; B3051, W of Heath End; SU5564], *Pineapple*: Popular thatched country pub, heavy low beams, stripped brick and timbering, rustic furniture on the tiled floor, rocking-chair by the fire; food inc sandwiches, pies, lots of filled baked potatoes, steaks, well kept Flowers Original, Wethereds and Whitbreads Pompey Royal and a good range of other drinks, side games area, maybe piped pop music; lots of tables on sheltered lawn, play area; open all day; children in eating area *(R M Sparkes, LYM — more reports please)*

Bucklebury [Chapel Row; SU5570], *Blade Bone*: Comfortable pub, piped music in public bar, friendly service and good bar food *(Lyn and Bill Capper)*

☆ **Chaddleworth** [SU4177], *Ibex*: Pleasantly old-fashioned layout for comfortably civilised village pub in horse-racing country, good bar food including often interesting choice of daily specials, all well presented and quite quickly served, well kept Courage, friendly licensee and staff, attractive garden *(Dr M Ian Crichton, HNJ, PEJ, Barbara McHugh, LYM)*

Cheapside [Cheapside Rd; SU9469], *Thatched Tavern*: Small, low-beamed smart pub with good atmosphere, limited choice of beer and excellent food (not cheap) *(Anon)*

☆ **Chieveley** [East Lane; SU4774], *Hare & Hounds*: Well kept beer, very friendly atmosphere, good food inc real chips at remarkably low prices in low-beamed bar full of amazing collectors' items but not a speck of dust; enjoyable skittle evenings (with food, by arrangement) *(John and Pat Smyth, A T Langton)*

Chieveley [East Lane], *Red Lion*: Much refurbished main-road free house, a useful stop for travellers, with reasonable welcome, Courage Best and usual bar food *(Ian Phillips)*

Cippenham [Lower Cippenham Lane; SU9480], *Kings Head*: Pleasantly placed in village centre by duck pond; lovely cosy atmosphere, very busy but friendly staff cope well; well kept Wethereds, good food choice, big garden; open all day *(R Houghton)*; [Cippenham Lane; SU9480], *Long Barn*: Interesting and attractively converted old raftered barn with Courage Best and John Smiths on handpump, cheerful atmosphere — popular with young people; upstairs restaurant, pleasant terrace *(Nick Dowson, Alison Hayward, Mayur Shah)*

☆ **Cockpole Green** [signed off A4 W of Maidenhead; SU7981], *Old Hatch Gate*: Has been a remarkable survivor, very basic and genuinely rustic, with cheap well kept

Brakspears in a flagstoned tap room which like its customers has seemed scarcely to change from decade to decade; *(Ian Phillips, TBB, Nick Dowson, R Houghton, David Warrellow, LYM)*

Compton [E end, just off Streatley rd; SU5279], *Red Lion*: First-rate under newish management, with well kept Morlands beers and above-average food range *(Stan Edwards)*

Cookham [SU8884], *Ferry*: Splendid riverside position is the plus for what's now become a Harvester restaurant, thoroughly modernised, with good Thames views from its two big-windowed floors and spacious waterside terrace; pricey bar food and Watneys-related real ales, impersonal decor *(LYM)*; [High St], *Royal Exchange*: Pleasantly cosy, ivy-covered Benskins village pub with low ceiling and dark panelling; useful back garden; bar food, decent real ale, though prices on the high side *(Nick Dowson, Alison Hayward)*

Cookham Dean [SU8785], *Chequers*: Good bar snacks *(R S Eades)* [Church Lane; SU8785], *Jolly Farmer*: Pretty 18th-century cottage pub in nice spot opp church, bought three years ago by consortium of 60 regulars who wanted to keep it as it was; open fire in low-beamed bar, snug, good bar food (grilled sardines, curry, trout, rare beef all recommended), Courage ales; traditional English food in cosy restaurant; garden *(R S Eades)*

Cookham Dean Common [Harding Green; SU8785], *Uncle Toms Cabin*: Quaintly basic old-fashioned pub, quiet on weekdays; small bars with numerous oil lamps, friendly licensee and locals, pleasant atmosphere, well kept Benskins Best, home-made bar food and clean outside lavatories *(Richard Houghton)*

☆ **Crazies Hill** [from A4, take Warren Row Rd at Cockpole Green signpost just E of Knowle Hill, then past Warren Row follow Crazies Hill signposts; also signed off A321 Wargrave—Henley — OS Sheet 175 map reference 799809; SU7980], *Horns*: Odd little unassuming village pub with basic furnishings, but well kept Brakspears PA and SB on handpump, decent wines, good collection of spirits, and food which can rise clear out of the ordinary (notable South-East Asian cooking sometimes, fine two-nut hazelnut/walnut cauliflower cheese, maybe Lebanese lamb; meals limited Sun and Mon evenings); pleasant seats outside; quiet children may be allowed in small bistro area until 7.30 *(TBB, Jack Lalor, Ian Phillips, LYM — more reports please)*

Crazies Hill [SU7980], *Frog & Toad*: French landlord — the finest glass of red wine you're likely to find in the three counties; good omelettes *(R S Eades)*

Curridge [OS Sheet 174 map reference 492723; SU4871], *Bunk*: Uncommon real ales, and some concentration now on recently extended back restaurant — good food *(A T Langton)*

Datchet [The Green; not far from M4 junction 5; SU9876], *Royal Stag*: Friendly old local with well kept Ind Coope real ales, bar food lunchtime and evening, good service; interesting wood panels, pictures and nick-nacks; overlooks graveyard *(Dr and Mrs A K Clarke, Richard Houghton)*

East Ilsley [leaving village southwards; SU4981], *Star*: Tudor building of character, with beams, lots of black woodwork, fine inglenook log fire, simple traditional furnishings and big windows overlooking village; well kept Watneys-related and other real ales, attractively priced food from sandwiches through fry-ups to scampi and salads, faint piped music, garden behind with picnic-table sets and big play boot-house; plans for bedrooms *(BB)*

Eton [Bridge St; SU9678], *Watermans Arms*: Striking rowing and other decorations in lively local nr the Thames (and nr Eton Coll rowing club), well kept Courage Best and Directors on handpump, straightforward bar food *(LYM)*

Grazeley [The Green; SU6966], *Old Bell*: Well kept ales, very professional and friendly service and good atmosphere in what is predominantly a food pub *(Richard Houghton)*; *Wheatsheaf*: Welcoming, clean and efficient little one-room pub with the original half-timbered building behind it in cornfields; tweed-covered stools and benches, a brownish patterned carpet and plain walls with a few agricultural memorabilia; Courage Best and straightforward bar food; nice people, no machines, fire, quiet piped music and spotless lavatories *(Ian Phillips)*

☆ **Great Shefford** [2 miles from M4 junction 14 — A338 towards Wantage; SU3875], *Swan*: Pleasant restaurant overlooks tree-hung stream with ducks, as do tables on quiet lawn and terrace — with summer barbecues; games and piped music in public bar, comfortable lounge, bar food from sandwiches to quite an extensive range of often imaginative dishes (not Sun evening), well kept Courage Best and Directors; children in eating areas *(Dennis and Pat Jones, Stan Edwards, LYM — more reports on the newish regime please)*

Halfway [A4 Hungerford—Newbury; SU4168], *Halfway*: Pleasant pub, recently converted to Harmony Steak House — popular, and has a good atmosphere so worth knowing *(L G and D L Smith)*

Hampstead Norreys [Yattendon Rd; SU5376], *New Inn*: One of the most spacious pub gardens around here, inc play area and feature goldfish pond; comfortable low-beamed back lounge with log fire, games in simple, lively public bar; good value food from sandwiches and ploughman's to steak and kidney pie or seafood platter, with more elaborate dishes evenings (not Mon or Tues); well kept Morlands Mild, Bitter and Best under light blanket pressure, friendly and efficient licensee; children welcome; bedrooms *(Gordon and Daphne, LYM — more reports please)*

Hermitage [2 1/2 miles from M4 junction 13; village slip road off A34 just N of exit roundabout; SU5073], *Fox*: Handily placed, with wide choice of bar food from open sandwiches, decent ham and egg and many other snacks to steaks; Morlands, Tetleys or Eldridge Pope Royal Oak and Websters Yorkshire on handpump, comfortable bar with games machines, prettily decorated plush lounge as anteroom to separate restaurant, recently renovated terrace and attractive garden; children welcome; open all day Fri–Sat *(Tom Evans, R Houghton, David and Christine Foulkes, Jon Wainwright, LYM)*

Holyport [The Green; SU8977], *George*: Busy old pub with open-plan layout (some readers feel the low ceilings and sensibly laid out furniture and partitions compensate for the loss of separate small rooms, others don't); decent home cooking shows at its best in excellent Sunday beef, friendly efficient service, Courage beers *(R Houghton, TBB)*

Hungerford [Charnham St; 3 miles from M4 junction 14; town signposted at junction; SU3368], *Bear*: Has been popular for civilised traditional bar overlooking charming courtyard, with nice touches like unusual newspapers to read — and ornate lavatories; still decidedly upmarket, but recently the feeling of leisured spaciousness has been missed, with doubts about bar food value (quality still usually good) and service speed; well kept Morlands; bedrooms comfortable and attractive, though expensive *(R Elliott, Andrea and Guy Bradley, Roger Huggins, LYM)*; [Bridge St, A338], *John o' Gaunt*: Old inn, recently refurbished, with bar food lunchtime and (more interesting dishes) evening, Courage Best and Wadworths 6X; dogs allowed; bedrooms *(Dr and Mrs R E S Tanner, Chris Payne, LYM)*; [113 High St], *Plume*: Lunchtime bar food such as good ham and eggs; evening restaurant; bedrooms *(G M K Donkin)*; [1 Station Rd], *Railway*: Recently refurbished, friendly pub with railway theme and well kept beer *(Dr and Mrs A K Clarke)*; [Charnham St (A4/A338 roundabout)], *Red Lion*: Basic pub with good helpings of simple food and good beers; juke box can be loud; bedrooms *(Jenny and Michael Back)*; [top of main st going towards Sarum], *Tuttiman*: Pleasantly refurbished pub with really friendly newish landlord and canal/agricultural theme; decent beer *(Dr and Mrs A K Clarke)*

Hurley [SU8283], *Olde Bell*: Civilised and old-fashioned partly beamed bar with old theatre posters, cosy atmosphere and friendly, efficient service in handsome timbered inn with Norman doorway and window, fine gardens, restaurant; not cheap; bedrooms *(Simon Collett-Jones, LYM)*

☆ **Hurst** [opp church; SU7972], *Castle*: Handsome and warmly welcoming traditional brick-built village inn with picnic-table sets overlooking its own bowling green; its three bar rooms inc little back dining parlour still have very cottagey air, especially in winter with roaring fires; friendly staff, well kept Courage ales and good coffee, generous, decent home-cooked food such as memorable Welsh rarebit or boiled beef and carrots, with wonderful imaginative puddings; bedrooms *(Ian Phillips, Comus Elliott)* ; [Davis St], *Jolly Farmer*: Intimate little pub, comfortable rather than smart, with large lawn with tables and umbrellas; reasonable menu inc specials *(Anon)*

☆ **Knowl Hill** [Bath Rd (A4 Reading—Maidenhead); SU8279], *Seven Stars*: Promisingly helpful and enterprising newish licensee and pleasant recent decorations — fairly smart, with extensive panelling, log fire, civilised and relaxed atmosphere; well kept and cheap Brakspears Mild, PA and Old, wide choice of wines, good range of simple bar food up to steaks inc vegetarian dishes, full range of sandwiches and useful soup/bread/cheese combination, professional service, fruit machine; large well laid out garden with busy summer barbecue and play-house; a couple of attractive dogs; children's room *(Simon Collett-Jones, Ian Phillips, TBB, Alison Hayward, Nick Dowson)*

Knowl Hill [A4], *Old Devil*: Free house with large one-bar area sensibly divided to create comfortable, relaxed atmosphere; smartly dressed bar staff, obliging service, several real ales, wide range of cheap bar food, restaurant *(Richard Houghton)*

Lambourn [Lambourn Woodlands; B4000, 2 1/2 miles towards Newbury; SU3278], *Hare & Hounds*: Under new regime, old and unpretentious with modern extension; spacious bars, good choice of beers, extensive range of good value food from ploughman's to scampi and various grills, with home-made specials such as liver and bacon and children's dishes; attentive and quick service, carpeted dining area with dozen tables, unobtrusive piped music and easy parking *(HNJ, PEJ)*

Littlewick Green [3 miles from M4 junction 9; A423(M) then left on to A4; SU8379], *Shire Horse*: Worth visiting for Courage's interesting adjoining Shire Horse Centre (Mar-Oct); spacious and comfortable open-plan beamed lounge bar, well kept Courage ales, piped music, bar food; tea house, play area by big side lawn *(LYM)*

Maidenhead [Bridge St (former A4); SU8783], *Albion*: Old two-bar pub with friendly landlord, pleasant atmosphere, well kept Courage Best, extensive range of reasonably priced bar food and nearby public car park *(Richard Houghton)*; [Queen St], *Jack of Both Sides*: Rather large and unassuming, but warm, clean and friendly, with reasonable bar food inc good value daily special, acceptable Wethereds ales — and excellent gents' *(Anon)*

☆ **nr Maidenhead** [Pinkneys Green (A308 N); SU8582], *Golden Ball*: Well organised Brewers Fayre pub with pleasant decor, cosy atmosphere, well kept Whitbreads-related real ales, good food (steak and kidney pie recommended) and service; much refurbished, though the low-ceilinged bit by the open fire still has a rustic air; seats on peaceful lawn, open all day; a family place, though popular with businessmen weekday lunchtimes *(Sybil Baker, Simon Collett-Jones, TBB, LYM)*

☆ *nr* **Maidenhead** [Marion Rd (A308 N)], *Robin Hood*: Friendly old low-ceilinged pub with no piped music, bar food inc good omelettes (shame about the cold plate), well kept Courage, garden with play area, new car park *(Anon)*; [Pinkneys Green], *Stag & Hounds*: Plain and basic two-room pub, not very comfortable, but worth knowing in this expensive area for its wide range of simple good value food inc cheap minestrone; children welcome *(Anon)*

Maidens Green [Winkfield Rd; signs to Winkfield Plain W of Winkfield off A330; SU8972], *Cottage*: Lovely cosy old pub with flagstone floor; service with a real welcome, well kept Badger Best tapped from the cask; nice atmosphere, if dominated by locals; considerable emphasis on its popular restaurant *(R Houghton)*; *Stirrups*: Country-house hotel, though bar is quite pub-like, with good if fairly expensive food *(TBB)*

Moneyrow Green [B3024 — OS Sheet 175 map reference 889768; SU8977], *Jolly Gardener*: Refurbished with relaxing atmosphere, well kept Youngers, good bar and service *(R Houghton)*

Newbury [Market Pl; SU4666], *Old Waggon & Horses*: Back on form this last year or so, with pleasant views of Kennet from beamed and partly flagstoned riverside lounge bar, old fishing rods and stuffed fish behind counter, courteous, friendly service, unhurried civilised atmosphere; Courage beers, food from beef sandwiches to gammon, juke box, fruit machine *(Simon Collett-Jones, LYM)*; [Stroud Green], *Plough*: Small refurbished pub with servery for outdoor tables, Courage Directors on handpump, partitioned-off darts area *(Paul Corbett)*; [Greenham Rd], *Railway*: Pleasant little hotel with railway theme, decent real ale and friendly landlord; the A43 — which we had to cross to get to it — is horrendous *(Dr and Mrs A K Clarke)*

Oakley Green [B3024; SU9276], *Olde Red Lion*: Lovely old pub, cosy interior; well kept Friary Meux, pleasant service, restaurant *(R Houghton)*

☆ **Old Windsor** [17 Crimp Hill; between River Thames and Savill Gardens; SU9874], *Union*: Spotlessly clean and friendly pub, very popular for its good value food — in bar and restaurant, which is attractively priced by local standards; film-star photographs, lovely lavatories with waiting area provided with quality newspapers; good choice of real ales such as Theakstons; tables on front terrace; bedrooms also good value, small but newly furnished and decorated to high standard, with own bathrooms and good breakfasts *(Ian Phillips, Shirley Pielou, D W Boydell, TBB)*

Old Windsor [Burghfield Rd], *Fox & Castle*: Attractive pub with cosy, comfortable interior; friendly staff, reasonable Courage beer, good-sized car park *(Richard Houghton)*; [Crimp Hill], *Oxford Blue*: Nice jolly atmosphere, very well patronised; good lunchtime food such as delicious ham and egg with bubble and squeak, served pleasantly in garden-room extension *(Shirley Pielou)*

Paley Street [B3024; SU8675], *Royal Oak*: Characterful original part (not enhanced by extension), very friendly locals, nice landlord, good service, Fullers beers *(Anon)*

Pangbourne [opp Church; SU6376], *Cross Keys*: Simple but comfortable lounge with aviation photographs and intimate, friendly atmosphere; Courage ales and decent bar food from sandwiches to steaks; popular Sun lunchtime barbecues on excellent largely covered back terrace, with decorative Japanese bridge over little stream; two interconnecting family rooms with suitable furniture *(Keith and Sian Mitchell, Ian Phillips)*; [Shooters Hill], *Swan*: Interesting genuinely ancient pub in lovely Thames setting, comfortable and welcoming with considerable atmosphere — well worth a visit, though price/quality considerations may deter you from sampling the bar food *(Ian Phillips, A Goodman)*

☆ **Reading** [Kennet Side; SU7272], *Fishermans Cottage*: Has moved up-market in recent years, and now strikes some as perhaps a bit impersonal and yuppified, with atmosphere a cross between that of a pub and a wine bar, but much enjoyed for its position by a lock on the Kennet, and lovely back garden; character decor includes pleasant stone snug behind fireplace with wood-burning cast-iron range, bar counter like side of a boat; light and airy conservatory has cane furniture, marble standing tables and lampposts; well kept Fullers Chiswick, ESB and London Pride, small selection of wines, food (chilli con carne etc) ready to serve and cooked to order, pleasant service, small darts room *(Simon Collett-Jones, Stephen King, Richard Houghton, Ian Phillips)*

Reading [35 Blagrave St], *Blagrave Arms*: Pleasant Courage pub, very popular with central office workers for good snack meals, especially the special — hot beef sandwich of immense proportions with salad; lots of seats *(Ian Phillips)*; [29 Market Pl], *Coopers*: Big open-plan bar with upper gallery and vast carved oak fireplace in panelled alcove; Courage ales and short choice of straightforward bar food; wine bar on far side of original coach entry *(Ian Phillips)*; [Mount Pleasant], *Greyhound*: Worth noting for its home-made pizzas *(Kev and Caron Holmes)*; [next to elevated section of inner ring road], *Hook & Tackle*: Pleasant free house, recently refurbished pub in 'traditional' style which works well *(Nick Dowson)*; [316 Kennetside], *Jolly Anglers*: Good unspoiled canalside local with couple of picnic-set tables on towpath; warm welcome, very reasonable food, Courage

beers *(Ian Phillips)* ; [8 Gt John St], *Retreat*:
Basic 1960ish local, very much a man's
place, with warm welcome, friendly
atmosphere, well kept Whitbreads-related
real ales, good simple food, bar billiards —
well worth a visit to see what pubs were like
before the Dralon revolution *(Richard
Houghton)*; [Castle St], *Sun*: Large,
many-roomed pub with two bars and
various levels; good decorative order,
carpeted throughout and some genuine as
well as reproduction beams; Courage Bitter
and quite a range of straightforward snacks
(Ian Phillips); [London Rd], *Turks Head*:
Free house with hard chairs on bare boards,
well kept Tetleys and Wadworths 6X, good
value food, and young, pleasant and efficient
staff *(Richard Houghton)*; [King St],
Warwick Arms: Recently refurbished, very
good choice of real ales, decent food; quite
busy town-centre pub *(Simon Weinberger)*;
[Abbey St], *White Lion*: Civilised modern
Morlands house with impressive carved
limestone heraldic lion as its sign; spotless
mixture of Byzantine pillars, stainless steel
girders, wooden trellises and plastic ivy;
calm and comfortable atmosphere, limited
but well presented bar food, piped music,
pleasant terrace *(Ian Phillips)*; [110 Kings
Rd], *Wynford Arms*: Clean and welcoming
with efficient service and reasonable prices;
one bar with pool table, juke box and fruit
machine, the other serving good, simple,
well prepared bar food; parking nearby may
be difficult *(Ian Phillips)*

Sandhurst [Yorktown Rd; SU8361],
Wellington Arms: Well kept popular local
with excellent Brakspears, small choice of
bar meals, pleasant staff; garden, car park
(Peter Turl)

☆ **Sindlesham** [Bearwood Rd; signposted
Sindlesham from B3349; SU7769], *Walter
Arms*: Comfortable dining pub — not a
place for just a drink — with wide choice of
good quickly served bar food, well kept
Courage Best and Directors, cheerful
welcome; pleasant bedrooms, with
substantial well cooked breakfasts *(LYM —
more reports please)*

Slough [Church St; SU9779], *Coachmakers*:
Lively town-centre local with one bar, well
kept Courage, friendly and efficient service
(RH); [Stoke Rd], *Printers Devil*:
Comfortable, with well kept Benskins, polite
uniformed bar staff *(Richard Houghton)*;
[Windsor Rd], *Rising Sun*: Pleasant
open-plan town local, busy but not
boisterous; friendly service, well kept Bass,
Charrington IPA and a guest beer;
reasonable bar food Mon–Fri *(Richard
Houghton)* [Albert St], *Wheatsheaf*: Fullers
well kept on handpump; popular for lunch
and with younger people in evening;
spacious, oak-beamed bar, smallish sun-trap
back garden; filled rolls from bar, hot meals
and salads down steps *(A W Dickinson)*

☆ **Streatley** [SU5980], *Bull*: Busy traditional
pub with well kept Watneys-related real ales
on handpump, good sensibly priced food in
bar and restaurant; nr GWG97 *(A T
Langton)*

Streatley, *Swan*: Smart hotel/timeshare
complex with comfortable and
big-windowed boathouse-theme bar
adjoining fitness centre, original bar
adjoining restaurant; well kept real ales, well
made bar food (limited to soup and
sandwiches Sun), light evening meals (not
Sun) in college rowing-club state barge,
good service, traditional games, children *(Dr
and Mrs A K Clarke)*

Tilehurst [Oxford Rd; SU6673],
Restoration: Pleasant, plum-coloured,
Victorian-style interior with comfortable
tables and chairs; friendly barmaids,
excellent home-made hot pies and
sandwiches, and beers like Tetleys and
Wadworths (though seems to be owned by
Halls/Allied); games bar, car park *(Geoffrey
Medcalf, Richard Purser)*

Twyford [High St; SU7876], *Duke of
Wellington*: Most congenial, with noisy,
friendly bar and quiet lounge; well kept
Brakspears SB *(John Baker)* [A4; SU7876],
Horse & Groom: Steakhouse-style pub
worth knowing for warm welcome and good
bar snacks *(Ian Phillips)*

Upper Basildon [village signposted from
Pangbourne and A417

Pangbourne—Streetley; SU5976], *Beehive*:
Blond furniture in knocked-through
black-beamed bar with cushioned booths
around tables, good range of real ales on
handpump, straightforward bar food,
swings and seats in small garden *(LYM)*

☆ **Waltham St Lawrence** [SU8276], *Bell*:
Handsome and interesting 16th-century pub
owned by local charity, in centre of pretty
village; two nicely restored bars, open fires,
oak beams, longcase clock and other
antiques, straightforward bar food (not Sun)
and separate restaurant, well kept and
decently priced Brakspears, Tetleys and
Wadworths, wide choice of whiskies, maybe
piped music; pleasant back lawn; ladies' out
by kitchen door, parking not always easy
*(Ian Phillips, Dawn and Phil Garside, Comus
Elliott, Margaret Dyke, Simon Collett-Jones,
LYM)*

Waltham St Lawrence [West End, well
outside the village], *Plough*: Has been a
notable calm and civilised old country pub,
with good if a bit pricey food and fine
Morlands tapped straight from the cask, but
reports have been mixed since the recent
retirement of its very long-serving landlady
— more news please *(LYM)*

Warfield [Cricketers Lane; SU8872],
Cricketers: Good atmosphere, pleasant staff
and half-a-dozen well kept real ales; average
bar food, pretty restaurant *(TBB, Steve
Huggins)*; [Church Lane (corner Bracknell rd
with Maidenhead—Windsor rd)], *Plough &
Harrow*: Unimpressive decor, but bar staff
(especially Moggie) very friendly, well kept
Morlands Best, short choice of very cheap
home-cooked bar meals in good helpings *(D
J and P M Taylor)*; [Church Lane], *Yorkshire
Rose*: Former tea house, now a
pub/restaurant with two separate areas; pub

part is cosy with low beams and nice atmosphere, with many different age groups, good service from uniformed staff, Brakspears and a guest beer; good-sized car park, super gents' *(Richard Houghton, TBB)*

☆ **Wargrave** [High St; SU7878], *White Hart*: Spacious but cheerfully bustling low-beamed lounge bar decorated to suit its 18th-century character, good value bar food, well kept Whitbreads-related real ales maybe inc Pompey Royal; restaurant, good-sized car park behind *(Richard Houghton, TBB, LYM)*

☆ **Windsor** [Castle Hill, opposite Henry VIII Gate; SU9676], *Horse & Groom*: Friendly little partly Tudor pub, nicest near the door; relaxed staff, well done straightforward cheap food, well kept Courage Best and Directors; surprisingly uncrowded, maybe loud radio music *(Gary Scott, Dr and Mrs A K Clarke, BB)*

☆ **Windsor** [Datchet Rd — opp Riverside Stn, nr Castle], *Royal Oak*: Clean, well run and spacious; beams, joists, some fine stained-glass screens, half panelling, red plush seating and armed Windsor chairs, old and well-lit prints, and brick fireplace dividing off another similar room; airy eating room with large food serving counter — good choice of reasonably priced bar snacks and full meals; very efficient friendly service, maybe some traffic noise; white furniture in L-shaped concreted garden; under same ownership as Greyhound in Chalfont St Peter *(John and Heather Dwane, Mrs A Crowhurst, Dr and Mrs A K Clarke, BB)*

Windsor [Thames St; SU9676], *Adam & Eve*: Bustling young people's pub by theatre, well kept Bass and Charrington IPA, occasional barbecues in little back yard; forget about trying to park nearby *(Sidney and Erna Wells, LYM)*; [Kings Rd, on outskirts], *Prince Christian*: Pleasant free house, well kept Brakspears, Fullers and Ruddles; good service, comfortable furnishings, reasonably priced food *(R Houghton)*; [Park St, off High St next to Mews], *Two Brewers*: Courage house in Georgian street close to castle; Armoury bar on left, lounge with Windsor chairs on right, food servery nr entrance; good home-made lunchtime bar food, wooden benches on pavement outside; open all day summer *(JMC)*

☆ **Winkfield** [Lovel Rd; A330 just W of junction with B3034, turning off at Fleur de Lis — OS Sheet 175 map reference 921715; SU9071], *Slug & Lettuce*: Attractive and locally popular pastiche of old-world tavern — all bare bricks, low beams, black oak timbers, shelves of books, antiqued cottagey furnishings, log-effect gas fires; good bar food (not Sun eve — other evenings served only if you find seat in restaurant), but prices high (helpings not large, veg extra), barbecues, well kept real ales such as Boddingtons, Brakspears, Courage Best and Theakstons Old Peculier; friendly labrador and Siamese cats, Radio-1-style piped music (can be obtrusive); may be full of young

people at weekends; children in restaurant; part no-smoking *(KC, Simon Collett-Jones, M Rising, TBB, Dr M Owton, LYM)*

Winkfield [towards Windsor on B3022], *Hernes Oak*: Welcoming well run local, pleasant staff, enterprising choice of spirits, bar food, children allowed in back room *(LYM)* ; [Church Rd (A330)], *White Hart*: Relaxed and neatly modernised Tudor pub with some fine old beams in ex-bakery bar and ex-courthouse weekend restaurant; Courage real ale, friendly and efficient service; sizeable garden — though may not have outside seating *(TBB, LYM)*

☆ **Wokingham** [from Wokingham inner ring rd left into Easthampstead Rd just after A329 Bracknell turn off; turn right at White Horse, then left into Honey Hill — OS Sheet 175 map reference 826668; SU8068], *Crooked Billet*: Jolly and homely atmosphere in sprucely furnished weatherboarded country pub — pews, tiles, brick serving counter, crooked black joists; particularly well kept Brakspears PA, SB, and Old on handpump, simple cheap food, nice mix of customers, communicating restaurant area (not Sun — bar food very limited Sun evening); seats and swings outside; children in restaurant; has been open all day *(Philip Harrison, W Bailey, Steve Waters, Mrs A Crowhurst, Ian Phillips, LYM)*

Wokingham [222 London Rd], *Three Frogs*: Old pub bigger inside than it looks; cosy atmosphere, bar nibbles Sun lunchtime, big car park *(Richard Houghton)*

☆ **Woodside** [off A322 Windsor—Ascot — look for blue/gold board; SU9270], *Duke of Edinburgh*: Pleasant, cosy atmosphere, well kept Arkells or Courage, friendly service, good bar food — especially fish, but cauliflower cheese and bacon and cheesecake also recommended; small garden, shame about the juke box *(R Houghton, TBB, Robert Kimberley)*

Woolhampton [Bath Rd (A4); SU5767], *Falmouth Arms*: Quite an imposing pub with good modern decor, well kept Eldridge Pope, friendly service, tables outside, clean lavatories *(Dr and Mrs A K Clarke)* [off A4; SU5767], *Rowbarge*: Country pub nr recently reopened Kennet & Avon Canal, with lots of tables outside, friendly beamed bar, panelled family room, big French-windowed dining room, tables in cottage garden; good small choice of bar food inc freshly made sandwiches and Sun roasts; well behaved dogs allowed *(Dr and Mrs R E S Tanner, LYM)*

Wraysbury [29 Wraysbury Rd; TQ0174], *George*: Two bars with light wood beams and wall panelling, and stripped pine, farmhouse-style furniture; friendly service, Courage Best and Directors and John Smiths, and extensive range of continental-style bar food *(Simon Collett-Jones)*; [Coppermill Rd], *Green Man*: Fairly old with bright interior; well kept Friary Meux and Ind Coope Burton, welcoming and obliging staff, good popular food, big car park *(Richard Houghton)*

Buckinghamshire

A high proportion of this county's good pubs are in or close to beautiful countryside – and the area stands out for a high standard of cleanliness, even in its most unassuming and old-fashioned pubs. However, pub prices are on average nearly 10% higher than the national average, so it's worth looking for the bargains – we've picked out a good many pubs, and individual dishes that they serve, for food value; four pubs to praise for relatively low drinks prices are the George in Great Missenden, Old Sun at Lane End, Shoulder of Mutton at Little Horwood and White Swan in Whitchurch. Pubs here that seem on an upward trend at the moment include the Kings Arms in Amersham (a good atmosphere in a lovely old building), the Bottle & Glass near Aylesbury (strengthening its image as a dining pub of character), the Old Hare in Beaconsfield and Bull at Bellingdon (both new main entries – the Bull's food is particularly promising), the civilised old Lions of Bledlow, the Walnut Tree at Fawley (probably the best pub food in the area), the Chequers at Fingest (unusual dishes, and a lovely garden), the Yew Tree at Frieth (good food, nice Austrian touches), the George in Great Missenden (wide choice of food), the Fox at Ibstone (a successful move up-market), the cheerful Pink & Lily near Lacey Green, the quaint old Shoulder of Mutton at Little Horwood, the neat and simple Red Lion on the outskirts of Princes Risborough, the friendly New Zealand-run Red Lion at Stoke Green, the lovely old George & Dragon in West Wycombe, the very friendly White Swan in Whitchurch and the strikingly pretty Clifden Arms at Worminghall. At the end of the chapter, Lucky Dip entries that won't surprise us if they soon come knocking at the main-entry door include the Five Bells at Botley, Dinton Hermit at Ford, Hampden Arms at Great Hampden, Jolly Woodman on Littleworth Common, Hit or Miss at Penn Street, Kings Arms at Skirmett, White Lion at St Leonards and Falcon at Wooburn Moor (all of them notable country pubs); the neat Seven Stars at Dinton (good value food); the highly nautical little Ship in Marlow; the canalside Black Horse at Great Linford, White Lion at Marsworth and New Inn at New Bradwell; and the civilised Red Lion at Chenies, Angel in Long Crendon, Stag at Mentmore and Cock & Rabbit at The Lee (all these have decent food – Italian at the last).

ADSTOCK SP7330 Map 4

Old Thatched Inn

Just N of A413, 4 miles SE of Buckingham

This pretty thatched village pub has a well kept, comfortable bar with flagstones by the bar counter, stripped beams and timbers and wheelback chairs and bays of green plush button-back banquettes in carpeted areas leading off. The walls are decorated with antique hunting prints, copper and brassware, and there are potted plants, fresh flowers and an open winter fire (with a log-effect gas fire in summer). Good helpings of bar food include home-made soup (£1.75), open sandwiches (from £2), ploughman's (from £2.50), gammon with pineapple or home-made lasagne (£4.50), home-made steak and kidney pie or Malaysian chicken (£5) and

8oz sirloin steak (£7); efficient staff. Well kept Adnams, Ruddles County and Tetleys on handpump, with Morrells under light blanket pressure – and as a useful alternative, as much tea or coffee as you can drink for 75p; dominoes, piped music. A new dining conservatory which is attached to the restaurant has been built over the back garden. (*Recommended by Marjorie and David Lamb, Mr and Mrs T F Marshall, M O'Driscoll; more reports please*)

Free house   Licensee Ian Tring   Real ale   Meals and snacks (not Sun evening) Restaurant tel Winslow (029 671) 2584; not Sun evening   Children in restaurant Open 12–2.30 (till 3 Sat), 6–11; closed 25 Dec

AKELEY   SP7037 Map 4
Bull & Butcher

The Square; just off A413

In the small dining room of this friendly village pub there's a popular lunchtime buffet with a wide range of decently made help-yourself salads, home-cooked beef or honey-roast ham, and home-made quiches and pies (around £4 to £6). There's also an evening steak bar (8oz rump £11 – which includes pudding and coffee; other dishes too, such as large salmon steaks, 8oz lamb noisettes and scampi). Well kept Hook Norton Best, Marstons Pedigree and a guest beer from handpump, good value wines by the bottle, several malt whiskies and farm cider. The long open-plan bar has red plush button-back banquettes, the rough-cast walls are decorated with drawings of well known customers and on each side of a massive central stone chimney there are fires, with a third down at the end; the curved beams in this wood-floored lower bar area are unusual. Darts, shove-ha'penny, cribbage, dominoes, Sunday evening bridge club, piped music. Pleasant beer garden. (*Recommended by A M Neal, B A Law, Dr T MacLennan, B M Eldridge*)

Free house   Licensee Harry Dyson   Real ale   Lunchtime meals and snacks (not Sun) Steak bar tel Lillingstone Dayrell (028 06) 257 (not Sun or Mon)   Children in eating areas   Occasional live entertainment   Open 12–3, 6 (6.30 Sat)–11

AMERSHAM   SU9597 Map 4
Kings Arms

High Street; A413

The atmosphere in the bar of this handsome rambling Tudor inn is particularly bustling and friendly. There are heavy beams, a big inglenook, high-backed antique settles, quaint old-fashioned chairs and other seats – you can usually find a seat even though it tends to get busy at lunchtime – and lots of snug alcoves. Simple bar food includes toasted ham and cheese sandwich (£1.30), home-made soup (£1.35), jumbo sausage in French bread (£1.75), ploughman's (£2.25), open prawn sandwich (£2.75), chilli con carne (£3.50), Hungarian goulash or turkey salad (£3.70), and blackboard specials and puddings; they also do cream teas between 3 and 5pm. Benskins Best and Greene King IPA on handpump, with Ind Coope Burton tapped from the cask behind the bar counter; friendly efficient service. Dominoes, cribbage and two popular monthly quiz competitions. In an attractive little flower-filled courtyard and coachyard there are seats, with more tables and a climbing frame beyond, on a tree-sheltered lawn; the goat is called Jocelyn. (*Recommended by Michael and Alison Sandy, M Saunders, R M Savage, Jim and Becky Bryson, M J Dyke, Mr and Mrs D M Norton*)

Benskins (Allied)   Licensee John Jennison   Real ale   Meals and snacks (all day until 9pm)   Restaurant (not Sun evening or Mon – no pipes or cigars, and they ask other smokers to be considerate) tel Amersham (0494) 726333   Children in eating area of bar until 8pm   Open 11–11

nr AMERSHAM   SU9495 Map 4
Queens Head

Whielden Gate; pub in sight just off A404, 1 1/2 miles towards High Wycombe at Winchmore Hill turn-off; OS Sheet 165 map reference 941957

Refreshingly unpretentious, this pretty little 18th-century country cottage has simple traditional furnishings, low beams and flagstones by the big inglenook fireplace (which still has the old-fashioned wooden built-in wall seat curving around right in beside the woodburning stove – with plenty of space under the seat for log storage). Decorations include a good cigarette card collection, horsebrasses, lots of brass spigots, a stuffed albino pheasant, and old guns; there's also a tabby cat and Monty, the friendly dalmatian. Home-made bar food includes soup (£1.50), omelettes (£2.50), seafood pancakes (£3.95), pheasant or pigeon pie or salmon steak (£4.50), and lots of pizzas (from £3). Well kept Benskins Best and Ind Coope Burton on handpump; darts, shove-ha'penny, dominoes, cribbage, fruit machine, space game, trivia and piped music. There are often summer barbecues in the garden behind – plump conifers, a small pond, attractive tubs of flowers on the terrace, swings and a climber. *(Recommended by Jill Hampton, Brian Metherell, J H Walker, Simon Collett-Jones)*

Benskins (Allied)   Licensees Les and Mary Anne Robbins   Real ale   Meals and snacks   Children in family room   Live music once a month   Open 11–2.30, 5.30–11 (Sat evening opening 6)

ASTWOOD   SP9547 Map 4
Swan

Main Road; village signposted from A422 Milton Keynes–Bedford

Though it's open-plan, the bar in this partly thatched early 17th-century pub has a thoroughly old-fashioned and warmly welcoming atmosphere. There are low oak beams, antique seats and tables and a log fire in the handsome inglenook. Bar food includes good home-made soup (£1), a choice of ploughman's (from £1.75), good quiche (£2.50), harvest pie (£2.80), steak sandwich in a freshly baked roll (£2.95), salads (from £2.95), roast chicken or scampi (£2.95), and 8oz steak (£6 – in the restaurant their steaks run up to 2lb). Well kept Brakspears SB, Flowers Original, Marstons Pedigree, Wethereds and Whitbreads Castle Eden on handpump; friendly service; darts, shove-ha'penny, cribbage, dominoes, unobtrusive piped pop music. The quiet lawn at the back has tables under old fruit trees, and there are more seats out in front; handy for Stagsden Bird Gardens. *(Recommended by Lyn and Bill Capper, Mr and Mrs J M Elden, Philip King, Mr and Mrs H W Clayton, TBB)*

Free house   Licensees Jim and Diane Niklen and Paul Cribb   Real ale   Meals and snacks (not Sun evening)   Restaurant   Children in one part of bar and restaurant Open 11–2.30, 6–11 – maybe all day on Bank Hols and special occasions   Two bedrooms tel North Crawley (023 065) 272; £25S/£35S

nr AYLESBURY   SP8213 Map 4
Bottle & Glass ✪

Gibraltar – A418 some miles towards Thame, beyond Stone; OS Sheet 165 map reference 758108

Rather than traditional bar snacks, the food in this thatched white dining pub tends to lean more to main meals, though they do soup (£2.25), ploughman's (£2.50), and home-made pâtés (£3), generous salads (from £5), pancakes filled with a light vegetable curry and served with a mint and turmeric yoghurt dip or seafood crumble (£6.50), beef and baby sweetcorn casserole (£6.95), fillet of pork in a coriander and orange sauce (£7.95) and Aberdeen Angus steaks (from £8.50); puddings such as bread and butter pudding or raspberry mousse (from £2.25). Besides well kept ABC and Tetleys Bitter on handpump, they do notably good wines. On the right, there's a very cosy little alcovey bar decorated in deep green – walls, ceiling, seating, and sofa that nestles in the former fireplace; only the flooring tiles are red. The green mood does filter through to the left side, too (as do the red tiles), but stops short of the main dining room. This has well spaced tables, some big old photographs on its panelled walls, and a high Delft shelf; it opens into an airy extension, which itself leads out to a terrace and neat lawn with more tables. Well reproduced blues, jazz or pop music; no dogs. (*Recommended by Mr and Mrs T F Marshall; more reports please*)

ABC (Allied) *Licensee Tim Supple Real ale Meals and snacks (12–2.15, 7–10; not Sun evening) Well behaved children welcome Possible live music Sun evenings Open 12–2.30, 6–11*

BEACONSFIELD SU9490 Map 2

Old Hare

A mile from M40 junction 2; 41 Aylesbury End, Old Beaconsfield

The hardworking staff at this busy, well run pub cope with the hordes of people queuing for the good, varied and often imaginative food with cheerful efficiency. At lunchtime, dishes may include cream of cauliflower soup (£1.75), filled wholemeal bap or French bread (from £1.50 for spicy sausage to £4.75 for 6oz rump steak with garlic mushrooms), ploughman's (£2.75), salads (from £3.25), very good and piping hot beef, Guinness and mushroom pie or vegetable curry with minted tomato and onion salad (£3.45), decent burgers (from £3.45), prawns and white fish creole (£3.65) and 8oz rump steak (£6.95); evening extras like fillet of haddock with onions, celery and watercress in an orange and cider sauce (£4.75) or medaillons of lamb marinaded in fresh lime juice and garlic and finished with Pernod (£5.75), and blackboard specials such as their green and gold salad (avocado, egg and croûtons in Tabasco sauce and topped with parmesan (£2.95) or meatballs in Chinese sauce on noodles (£3.95); vegetables are extra; winter Sunday roast lunch and summer Sunday lunchtime barbecues. Well kept Benskins Best, Ind Coope Burton and Tetleys Yorkshire on handpump, and a dozen malt whiskies; no machines or music. Several bars ramble about: to the right of the door a dimly lit end room has a big, very high-backed antique settle as well as more straightforward furniture (and a serving hatch); a lighter room has a big inglenook with a copper hood and a mix of chairs and stools; the rooms by the odd-angled bar counter are decorated with prints of hares, photographs and prints of the pub, and furnished with armed wheelback chairs and built-in wall benches; the veneered ceiling is unusual. The big, sunny back garden has lots of white plastic garden furniture and a couple of picnic-table sets and was packed on our warm lunchtime visit with local business people and ladies lunching. (*Recommended by Andy and Jill Kassube, Richard Houghton, Ian Phillips, Pat and Dennis Jones, Tony Marshall*)

Benskins (Allied) *Licensees J E A Godrich and A M Reed Real ale Meals and snacks (12–2, 7.30–10); no food Sun evenings Open 11–2.30, 5.30–11; closed evening May 10 for annual street fair*

BELLINGDON SP9405 Map 4

Bull

Signposted off A416 in Chesham; on Bellingdon Rd on N side of village

The Steers – who previously ran the Swan at Ley Hill, where they won warm praise from readers for their food – have now moved to this small, attractive old brick cottage. It's neatly kept and friendly, with built-in planked dark wood and red plush-cushioned wall seats, a few nice old dining chairs and plush stools, a mix of small wooden tables with little vases of fresh flowers, and a bow window with a highly polished round table and built-in seats. There are beams in the slightly sloping ceiling, several attractive display cases, a big clock and barrel tops on the walls, an inglenook fireplace with horsebrasses on the mantlebeam, and a tiny room up some steps with quite a few old cattle prints. Our initial impressions of their bar food are very promising, and we'd expect that a food award will be in order, though it's such early days that we've so far had too few reports to confirm this. It includes blackboard specials such as caesar salad (£2), cottage pie (£3.75), water chestnuts and vegetables in a sweet and sour sauce (£4), sautéed kidneys in red wine and mushrooms (£5), salmon and mushroom pancake, and pork stroganoff (£6); also, home-made soups (£1.20), mushrooms cooked in cider and tomato sauce (£1.75), sandwiches or filled baked potatoes (from £1.75), ploughman's (from £1.95), tagliatelle with bacon and mushrooms in a hot chilli sauce (£3.25), beef, Guinness and mushroom pie or broccoli, leek and nut lasagne (£3.50), and rump steak (£6.95); puddings like treacle tart or special ice-creams. Well kept Benskins Best, Ind Coope Burton and either Adnams or Greene King on handpump, and Addlestone's cider served from the dark wood-planked bar counter; the friendly retriever is called Oscar. The front garden (which was being prettily planted on our visit) has picnic-table sets, attractive barrels of flowers and a swing; there are a few enamel signs on the wall by the car park, and a bus stop just outside. D H Lawrence and actress Hermione Baddeley are said to have been regular visitors. (*Recommended by Stephen King*)

Benskins (Allied)   Licensees Jeff and Sue Steers   Real ale   Meals and snacks   Open 11–2.30, 6–11; closed 25 Dec

BLEDLOW   SP7702   Map 4

Lions of Bledlow ★

From B4009 from Chinnor towards Princes Risborough, take first right after Chinnor into West Lane, or take next turn on right signposted Bledlow Ridge and first right into village outside Chinnor goes straight to the pub; from the second, wider right turn, turn right through village

From the bay windows in the inglenook bar of this 16th-century Chilterns pub there are marvellous views over a small quiet green to the plain stretched out below. Attractive oak stalls are built into one partly panelled wall, there are other seats including an antique settle on its deeply polished ancient tiles, and lots of heavy low beams. Freshly cooked food includes soup (£1.50), filled French bread (from £1.75) and ploughman's (from £2.25), as well as changing daily specials like chicken stir-fry (£3.20), mushrooms and bacon sautéed in a garlicky sauce (£3.75), chicken goujons in home-made spicy breadcrumbs (£3.95), moussaka (£4.25), a tender mixed grill and good puddings such as lemon meringue pie or treacle tart. Well kept Courage Directors, Wadworths 6X, Wethereds and Youngs on handpump, with a guest beer such as Badger Tanglefoot; log fires; one of the two cottagey side rooms has a space game. It's perched on a steep slope, and beyond a sheltered crazy-paved terrace and a series of small sloping lawns, you can walk straight up into the hills and the steep beechwoods beyond. (*Recommended by Margaret and Trevor Errington, Tony and Lynne Stark, TBB, Dr J C Harrison, Gwen and Peter Andrews, Lyn and Bill Capper, Mary Claire, Mick and Hannah Jones, Nick Dowson, Alison Hayward*)

Free house   Licensee F J McKeown   Real ale   Meals and snacks (not Sun evening) Restaurant (not Sun evening) tel Princes Risborough (084 44) 3345   Children in side rooms and restaurant   Open 11–3, 6–11; closed evening 25 Dec

BOLTER END   SU7992   Map 4

Peacock

Just over 4 miles from M40 junction 5; A40 to Stokenchurch, then B482

Cheerfully well kept, this popular place has a good log fire in one alcove of its rambling but brightly modernised bar, and a wide range of efficiently served food such as good sausages in French bread with chips (£2.20), ploughman's (£2.50), deep-pan pizzas (from £2.80 or £5.25, depending on size and filling), vegetarian dishes with Basmati rice (from £3.25), tasty curried beef and vegetable pie (£3.75), seafood Mornay (£4.50), prawn fritters with a sweet and sour dip (£4.75), steaks from 12oz rump (£8.25), lots of popular puddings (£1.50), and dishes of the day such as pork satay done for them by a Thai cook, or fish fresh from Billingsgate on Thursdays. ABC and Bass on handpump, decent wines, good cider; darts, piped music; with food cooked to order, there may be a delay if they're busy. In summer there are seats around a low stone table and picnic-table sets in the neatly kept roadside garden. (*Recommended by Margaret Dyke, A W Dickinson, C A Holloway, A C Morrison, Ian Phillips*)

ABC (Allied)   Licensee Peter Hodges   Real ale   Meals and snacks (12–2, 7–10, not Sun evening)   Open 11–2.30, 6–11

BRILL   SP6513   Map 4
Pheasant

Windmill Rd; village signposted from B4011 Bicester–Long Crendon

Many buildings in this village are older than their brick faces suggest – this one is 17th-century. It's perched 600 feet up by one of the oldest post windmills still in working order. Inside, the neatly kept bar has been quietly modernised: comfortable russet leatherette button-back banquettes in bays around its tables, a woodburning stove and a step up to a dining area which is decorated with attractively framed Alken hunting prints – and which has the view. Bar food includes sandwiches (from £1.20), tagliatelle (£2.40), popular burgers (from £2.95), a notable ploughman's (£3.60), home-cooked honey-roast ham with two eggs (£3.95), cod steak (£5.75), trout stuffed with cashew nuts (£6.50), scampi provençale (£6.95), steaks (from £9.40), and blackboard specials like home-made soup (£1.40), home-made lasagne (£3.95) or roast rack of English lamb (£7.80); puddings such as home-made cheesecake (£1.60). Well kept Ind Coope Burton and Tetleys on handpump; no dogs (they have a friendly golden retriever themselves). Picnic-table sets in the small, sheltered back garden look down towards Oxfordshire fading into a great distance. (*Recommended by Mike O'Driscoll, Mrs M Lawrence; more reports please*)

Halls (Allied)   Licensee Mike Carr   Real ale   Meals and snacks   Restaurant tel Kingston Blount (0844) 237104   Children in restaurant   Open 11–3, 5.30 (6.30 Sat)–11; closed 25 Dec

CHALFONT ST PETER   SU9990   Map 3
Greyhound

High Street; A413

Smartly modernised but dating back to the 14th century, this friendly, well kept inn has a long and low-beamed open-plan bar with brasses on the lantern-lit dark panelling, plenty of deep red plush seats and a huge winter log fire in a handsome fireplace. Bar food includes sandwiches (from £1.20), home-made soup (£1.30), ploughman's (from £2.25), filled baked potatoes (from £2.30), chilli con carne (£3.50), salads (from £3.50), home-made shepherd's pie (£3.95), daily specials such as steak and kidney pie (£3.95) and a roast of the day from their carvery (£4.95); summer weekend barbecues. Well kept Courage Best and Directors and John Smiths on handpump, from a good long counter; piped pop music at one end, fruit machine. There are tables among flower tubs in the pretty front courtyard, with more on a sheltered lawn by the little River Misbourne. The same people also run the Royal Oak in Windsor. (*Recommended by A M S Jeeves, JM, PM, D C Horwood; more reports please*)

Courage   Manager Mr Mea   Real ale   Meals and snacks (12–2.30, 7–9.30 – till 10 weekends)   Restaurant (midnight supper licence)   Children in eating area and restaurant   Open 11–3, 5.30–11; 11–11 Sat   Bedrooms tel Gerrards Cross (0753) 883404; £39/£49

CHESHAM   SP9502   Map 4
Black Horse

The Vale; leaving Chesham on A416 towards Berkhamsted fork left at Hawridge 3, Colesbury 3 1/2 signpost

The small black-beamed original core in this pretty white-painted brick pub has an inglenook big enough to hold two tables; this opens into an extension with lots of heavy dark-lacquered tables, wheelback chairs and high-backed winged rustic settles; there are little country pictures on the rough-plastered white walls, black beams and joists in the ceiling. There's also a separate heavy-raftered barn with shelves of interesting old books. They specialise in home-made pies, with eight from beef, Guinness and orange to wild rabbit and tarragon with soft green peppercorns or chicken with leeks and walnuts (£4.25); other generously served, good value bar food includes sandwiches (from 95p), soup (95p), ploughman's (£2.25), filled baked potatoes (from £2.25), salads (from £3.50), smoked trout fillets (£3.75), cold poached salmon with lemon mayonnaise or gammon and egg (£4.25) and sirloin steak (£5.75); good Sunday roast. Well kept Benskins Best, Friary Meux Best, Ind Coope Burton and a guest beer such as Youngs Special on handpump; speedy, cheerful service; unobtrusive piped music. There are lots of well spaced picnic-table sets and a climbing frame on the big back lawn, with more tables under cocktail parasols in front. They now also own the White Lion at Marsworth. *(Recommended by Lyn and Bill Capper, Richard Houghton, Jan and Ian Alcock, JM, PM)*

Benskins (Allied)   Licensee Roger Wordley   Real ale   Meals and snacks (12–2, 6–9.30)   Open 11–2.30, 6–11

COLNBROOK   TQ0277 Map 3
Ostrich

1 1/4 miles from M4, junction 5; A4 towards Hounslow, then first right on to B3378 – at start of village where main road bends sharply to right keep straight on into Access Only village High Street

A former Norman house which became a hospice for the Abbey of Abingdon, this pub was rebuilt in Elizabethan times (though a large part of the building is much more modern, and even more has disappeared altogether). It's still well worth a visit for its striking timbered facade, jettied out over the village street. Inside, the two carpeted communicating rooms of the front bar have heavy beams, timbered ochre walls decorated with guns, swords and old pictures of the pub, a grandfather clock and splendid log fires. It has specialised in up-market fresh seafood, with other bar food (not cheap) such as cheeses, stuffed mushrooms, home-made steak and kidney pie, salads and vegetarian dishes, with well kept if rather pricey Courage Best and Directors on handpump and some interesting wines – in 1990, it's changed hands and we regret to say that the new manageress has felt unable to discuss her future catering plans with us. Maybe discreet piped music. There are picnic-table sets under cocktail parasols in the back car park. Close to Heathrow's Terminal Four, it's just the ticket for giving foreign visitors a quick glimpse of the classic English pub. *(Recommended by TBB, Ian Phillips, John Gould, Gwen and Peter Andrews, Graham Bush, Dennis and Pat Jones)*

Free house   Real ale   Meals and snacks   Restaurant tel Slough (0753) 682628   Open 11–2.30, 6–11; has been closed Dec 25–26

FAWLEY   SU7586 Map 2
Walnut Tree ★ ⊘

Village signposted off A4155 and off B480, N of Henley

Apart from its most attractive setting, what marks this friendly Chilterns pub out as special is the the range of generously served, imaginative bar food: starters like smoked Welsh lamb with a mustard and caper dip or Stilton beignets with chilli and mint yoghurt (£3.20), giant kiwi mussels grilled with basil, garlic and parmesan cheese (£3.40), and prawns in garlic and raspberry vinegar (£3.60), with main courses such as Greek-style lamb (£6.25), grilled pink trout almondine or calves liver with tomatoes, sage and mushrooms (£6.95), Scotch sirloin steak (£7.85), and grilled Dover sole (£8.75); the puddings are good, too. Well kept Brakspears PA and SB on handpump, a good range of wines (including local English ones), and decent malt whiskies; pleasant and helpful service. Attractively simple furniture, a winter log fire and a warm welcome for walkers – though not a great deal of room; darts, dominoes, cribbage, fruit machine, juke box. The big lawn around the front car park has some well spaced rustic tables, with some seats in a covered terrace extension – and a hitching rail for riders. *(Recommended by TBB, Jill Hampton, Brian Metherell, Margaret Dyke, Dr J C Harrison, TBB, Roger and Lynda Pilgrim, Mrs A Sheard, Gordon Hewitt)*

Brakspears   Licensee Geoffrey W Knight   Real ale   Meals and snacks (12–2, 7–10) Restaurant   Children in eating area of public bar and in restaurant   Open 11–3 (2.30 in winter), 6–11   Bedrooms tel Turville Heath (049 163) 360; I £45S

FINGEST   SU7791   Map 2

Chequers ⊗

Village signposted off B482 Marlow–Stokenchurch

French windows lead from a sunny lounge with comfortable easy chairs into the spacious garden – marvellous in summer with lots of tables under cocktail parasols among flowerbeds; beyond this, quiet pastures slope up to beechwoods, and there are views right down the Hambleden valley. An inner room is decorated with pistols, antique guns and swords, toby jugs, pewter mugs and decorative plates; there are some seats built into its black-painted wooden dado, an 18th-century oak settle, other chairs of varying ages from ancient to modern, and a big log fire. The no-smoking area is popular with readers. Highly praised food from an efficiently run servery includes sandwiches (from £1.40), ploughman's (from £2.25), home-made soup such as fennel and almond soup or local spicy sausages (£2.50), cottage pie, lasagne or chicken and game pie (£4.50), steak and kidney pie (£4.75 – a special favourite here), roast lamb or liver and bacon (£4.95), hot avocado and prawns in cheese sauce or freshly caught trout (£6.50), and vegetarian dishes like vegetable and nut bake or spinach and mushroom lasagne; there's also a romantic restaurant. Well kept Brakspears PA, SB and in season Old Ale on handpump; polite service can be slow when under pressure; dominoes, cribbage, backgammon. Over the road is a unique Norman twin-roofed church tower – probably the nave of the original church. *(Recommended by M Saunders, Tony and Lynne Stark, Simon Collett-Jones, Maureen Hobbs, Margaret Dyke, Mr and Mrs T F Marshall, Richard Houghton, Mr and Mrs H W Clayton, A M S Jeeves, John and Karen Day, Robert Kimberley, Dr and Mrs James Stewart, Roger and Lynda Pilgrim, TBB)*

Brakspears   Licensee Bryan Heasman   Real ale   Meals and snacks (not Sun evening) Restaurant tel Turville Heath (049 163) 335   Children in eating area and restaurant Open 11–3, 6–11; closed evening 25 Dec

FORTY GREEN   SU9292   Map 2

Royal Standard of England

3 1/2 miles from M40 junction 2, via A40 to Beaconsfield, then follow sign to Forty Green, off B474 3/4 mile N of New Beaconsfield

This ancient pub used to be called the Ship until after the Battle of Worcester in 1651, when Charles II hid in the high rafters of what is now its food bar. It's best visited on weekday lunchtimes (at weekends – even in winter – it gets extremely busy), when there's a chance to enjoy the fine collection of ancient pewter and pottery tankards, old rifles, powder-flasks and bugles, lots of brass and copper, needlework samplers, oak settles, finely carved antique panelling, and stained glass. The open fires have handsomely decorated iron firebacks – including one from Edmund Burke's old home nearby. The food bar includes a good soup of the day (£1.25), ploughman's (£2.75), sausages and chips (£3.50), chicken (£4.25), a range of home-made pies including venison or pigeon (from £4.25), hot dishes such as plaice, fritto misto or vegetarian flan (£4.50), crab (£5) and salmon (£5.50). Well kept Brakspears SB, Huntsman Royal Oak and Marstons Pedigree and Owd Rodger (the beer was originally brewed here, until the pub passed the recipe on to Marstons), and another beer brewed for the pub, on handpump. There are seats outside in a neatly hedged front rose garden, or in the shade of a tree.

(Recommended by Marjorie and David Lamb, A M S Jeeves, A W Dickinson, Chris Raisin, Philip Orbell, Jim and Becky Bryson, Tony and Lynne Stark, Andy and Jill Kassube, Peter Watkins, Pam Stanley, JM, PM, Dr J C Harrison, Gary Scott, Lindsey Shaw Radley, Mr and Mrs D Norton, BKA, Chris Raisin, Graham Doyle, Richard Houghton, Mrs E M Thompson)

Free house Licensees Philip Eldridge and Alan Wainwright Real ale Meals and snacks (12–2.30, 6–10) Children in area alongside Candle Bar Open 11–3, 5.30–11; closed evening 25 Dec

FRIETH SU7990 Map 2

Yew Tree ✪

Village, signposted off B482 N of Marlow, is in Bucks though it has an Oxon postal address

Readers warmly praise the particularly good and unusual food and eclectic choice of drinks in this 400-year-old free house. Mr Aitzetmuller comes from Austria and his bar food might include vegetarian pancakes (£2.95), home-made sausages (£3.95), stuffed peppers, pork goulash or delicious ham and mushroom strudel (£3.95), steamed skate (£4.25), Wiener brathuhn, and a dish of the day like stuffed shoulder of veal or lamb casserole (£4.95); puddings such as bread and butter pudding (£1.95). Besides well kept Arkells, Ruddles County, Theakstons Old Peculier and Websters Yorkshire on handpump, they do gluhwein and several interesting punches, maybe including schnapps, honey and spices in the hot winter ones, and squeezing fresh fruit for delightful cold ones in summer – including non-alcoholic ones; their wines and coffee are good; friendly service. The bar is smart and comfortable with stripped beams and joists, animal and sporting pictures (look out for the entertaining fishing engravings by F Naumann), china and glass sparkling in corner cupboards, horsebrasses and guns over the log fires at each end. The neat front garden has tables on its lawn and small terrace – they serve out here too; there's also tethering space for horseriding clubs. *(Recommended by R M Savage, TBB, A W Dickinson, Simon Collett-Jones, Margaret Dyke, David Wallington, Mr and Mrs D Norton)*

Free house Licensees Franz Aitzetmuller and Annie Beckett Real ale Meals (12–2, 5.30–10.30) Children in eating area of bar and restaurant Restaurant tel High Wycombe (0494) 882330; closed Sun evening Open 10.30–2.30, 5.30–11; winter evening opening 6

GREAT BRICKHILL SP9030 Map 4

Old Red Lion

There's a comfortable villagey atmosphere in the two gently refurbished and carpeted bars here, with fresh flowers on the tables and a log fire in the smaller one. Attractively presented and promptly served bar food includes soup (£1), sandwiches (from £1.20; steak in a crusty roll £2.75), ploughman's (£2.50), vegetarian moussaka (£3.25), salads (from £3.50), cottage pie (£3.75), good lamb steak with rosemary or grilled salmon fillet (£5.50), and steaks (from £6.25). Well kept Flowers Original, Marstons Pedigree and Wethereds on handpump, decent wines and coffee; dominoes, cribbage, fruit machine, unobtrusive piped music. The prettily kept walled back garden has picnic-table sets and swings, and a superb view over Buckinghamshire and far beyond; the Ouzel Valley falls away steeply below. *(Recommended by Geoff Roynon, Ted George, Lyn and Bill Capper, Mrs M E Lawrence; more reports please)*

Whitbreads Licensee Andrew McCollin Real ale Meals and snacks (12–2, 7–10; not Sun evening) Children in eating area Open 11–2.30, 5.30–11; 11–3, 6.30–11 Sat

GREAT MISSENDEN SP8900 Map 4

George ★ ✪

94 High St

Built in 1483 as a hospice for the nearby Abbey, this busy, friendly pub has a cosy two-roomed bar with a high mantlepiece holding Staffordshire and other figurines over the big log fire, timbered walls decorated with prints, attractively moulded heavy beams and little alcoves (including one with an attractively carved box settle – just room for two – under a fine early 17th-century oak panel). A snug inner room has a sofa, little settles and a smaller coal fire. The popular food is served in a more straightforward (but spaciously comfortable) room. It runs from onion bhajis with cucumber and yoghurt raita (£2.45), through pasta (£3.50) or fresh fish, to 8oz gammon (£5.70), several curries (£5.95), 10oz Scotch rump steak (£7.50), and duck with orange sauce (£9.95), with children's dishes (from 95p) and good puddings that change daily like profiteroles, summer pudding or strawberry shortcake (from £1.20). Vegetarian dishes include thick vegetable soup (£1.25), crunchy mixed vegetables (£1.50, weekday lunchtimes), fresh pasta (£3.50), cheese and nut croquettes (£4.60), and vegetable Stroganof (£5.60). On weekday lunchtimes there are also chips with a dip (85p), sandwiches (from £1.20), filled baked potatoes (from £1.25), and ploughman's (£2.25). They do two sittings in the evenings (you should now book a few days before for Friday and Saturday evening, and for Sunday lunchtime – when you can order a whole joint to carve yourself, and take home anything left). Well kept ABC, Bass, Wadworths 6X and a guest beer on handpump (under light blanket pressure), mulled wine in winter, tea, coffee and so forth; obliging service; shove-ha'penny, cribbage, trivia and piped light music. *(Recommended by Jill Hampton, Brian Metherell, Peter Watkins, Pam Stanely, JM, PM, Dennis and Pat Jones, BKA, Mr and Mrs T F Marshall, Richard Houghton, Douglas Bail, Mrs J Kingsbury, E J and J W Cutting, J N Phillips, J P Day)*

Halls (Allied)   Licensees Guy and Sally Smith   Real ale   Snacks (weekday lunchtimes) and meals (not Sun evening; 12–2, 7–9.45)   Restaurant Fri–Sat evenings, Sun lunch tel Great Missenden (024 06) 2084   Children in eating area and restaurant   Open 11–2.30 (3 Sat), 6–11; closed evening 25 Dec–evening 26 Dec

HAMBLEDEN   SU7886   Map 2
Stag & Huntsman

Village signposted from A4155

Set on the far edge of one of the prettiest Chilterns villages, this small inn has two busy bars – the low-ceilinged lounge with upholstered seating and wooden chairs on its carpet and the attractively simple public bar with a fruit machine. Home-made bar food includes soup (£2.15), good ploughman's (from £2.40), smoked salmon pâté (£2.60), chilli nachos (£3.10), tagliatelle (£4.35), evening steaks from the good village butcher (£8.50) and puddings (from £2); at really busy times the choice may be much curtailed. Brakspears PA and SPA, Flowers Original, locally brewed Luxters Barn Ale, and Wadworths 6X on handpump, with a guest beer. The pretty and neatly kept country garden backs directly on to the Chilterns beechwoods. *(Recommended by Harry Blood, T Galligan, TBB, David Warrellow, Margaret Dyke, Margaret and Trevor Errington, Alison Hayward, Nick Dowson)*

Free house   Licensees Mike and Janet Matthews   Real ale   Meals and snacks (not Sun evening)   Restaurant   Children no longer allowed   Open 11–2.30, 6–11; closed evening 25 Dec   Bedrooms (tel) Henley (0491) 571227; £39.50S/£39.50S

HAWRIDGE COMMON   SP9406   Map 4
Full Moon

Follow Hawridge sign off A416 N of Chesham and keep on towards Cholesbury; OS Sheet 165 map reference 945062

We hope this report will not prove to have been an 'obituary notice' for yet another fine old country pub which has been closed down and turned into a private house, or – worse still – turned into some vile mass-catering operation. The sword of Damocles hanging over it as we go to press is Wally Pope's imminent retirement. As tenant, he's kept it marvellously old-fashioned, unspoilt and friendly – a fine place to finish a walk. The snug core of the pretty red-tiled white pub has ancient dark beams, shiny black built-in floor-to-ceiling settles and ancient polished flagstones and flooring tiles; the hunting prints are genuine, and there's a good log fire in the inglenook. A couple of more modern little rooms lead off; it can get smoky if it's busy. Simple but wholesome food has included pasties (£1.20), ploughman's (from £1.90), salads (from £2.60), and maybe one or two hot dishes such as soup (90p), lasagne or steak and kidney pudding (£2.50); of course, all that may change in this coming year. Well kept Flowers and Wethereds SPA on handpump, with Winter Royal when it's available; well priced Rombouts coffee. Picnic-table sets and rustic seats are set out among fruit trees on a spacious side lawn with roses along its low flint wall. *(Recommended by Stephen King; more reports please)*

Whitbreads   Real ale   Meals (weekday lunchtimes) and snacks (lunchtime, not Sun; these times may change)   Open 11.30–2.30, 6–11; has been closed evening 25 and 26 Dec

IBSTONE   SU7593   Map 4

Fox ⇔

1 3/4 miles from M40 junction 5: unclassified lane leading S from motorway exit roundabout; pub is on Ibstone Common

In summer there are decent cook-it-yourself barbecues outside this considerably extended country inn, and beyond the neat rose garden – prettily lit by old lamps – the wilder common leads eventually to rolling fields and the Chilterns oak and beech woods. The comfortable lounge bar has high-backed settles and country seats under the low, 17th-century beams, there are old village photographs on the walls and log fires. In the public bar – which still has shove-ha'penny, dominoes, cribbage and maybe unobtrusive piped music – the pine settles and tables match the woodblock floor. Home-made bar food includes sandwiches (from £1.20), several ploughman's (from £2.75), fish (from £3.95), pasta dishes (from £4), steak and kidney or turkey and mushroom pies (from £4.50), beef or lamb steaks (from £6.95), and home-made puddings (£1.65); there's also a smart restaurant. Well kept Brakspears PA and SB and a couple of guest beers such as Adnams, Flowers Original, Greene King Abbot or Tetleys on handpump, with several imported bottled lagers, Weston's farm cider, and decent wines by the glass; friendly service. The pub overlooks the village common and its cricket ground. *(Recommended by Marjorie and David Lamb, A M S Jeeves, Dave Braisted, Dr J C Harrison, Mayur Shah, AP)*

Free house   Licensees Ann and David Banks   Real ale   Meals and snacks (12–2, 7–10)   Restaurant   Children in eating area   Bedrooms tel Turville Heath (049 163) 289/722; £57S/£70S   Open 11–3, 6–11

LACEY GREEN   SP8100   Map 4

Pink & Lily

Parslow's Hillock; from A4010 High Wycombe–Princes Risborough follow Loosley Row signpost, and in that village follow Great Hampden, Great Missenden signpost; OS Sheet 165 map reference 826019

A Spanish-style extension with big arches and white garden furniture has been added to this airy, modernised dining pub. The little tap room has been preserved very much as it used to be in the days when this was a favourite of Rupert Brooke's: red flooring tiles, built-in wall benches, the old wooden ham-rack hanging from the ceiling and the broad inglenook with its low mantelpiece – as well as darts, shove-ha'penny, dominoes, cribbage and ring the bull. The airy main bar has low pink plush seats, with more intimate side areas and an open fire. Popular home-cooked food includes sandwiches (from £1.25), steak (£3.25), filled baked potatoes (from £1.95), macaroni cheese (£2.95), steak and kidney pie or lasagne (£3.50), daily specials such as goulash or chicken casserole (£3.95), puddings like rhubarb crumble or jam roly-poly (£1.50), and Sunday roast beef (£4.50). Well kept Bass, Brakspears PA and SB, Flowers Original, Glenny Hobgoblin, Ruddles County, Wadworths 6X and Wethereds on handpump; good friendly service. The garden has rustic tables and seats. *(Recommended by Tony and Lynne Stark, Mike Tucker, Richard Houghton, Mr and Mrs T F Marshall, Nick Dowson, Alison Hayward, Roger and Lynda Pilgrim, A D Button)*

Free house   Licensees Clive and Marion Mason   Real ale   Meals and snacks (not Sun evenings)   Well behaved children in eating area till 8   Open 11.45 (11 Sat)–3, 6–11

LANE END   SU7991   Map 2

Old Sun

B482 Marlow–Stokenchurch

In the centre of quite a lively village, this cream-painted tiled house with dark green woodwork has a warmly welcoming atmosphere. The three traditional communicating areas have cushioned vertical-panelled-back wall benches, a round table and bench seating in the big 400-year-old chimney, a low shiny ochre ceiling, brasses, old prints and cartoons on the walls, two winter log fires, and snug recesses. Good value bar food includes plain or toasted sandwiches (£1.20), ploughman's (£2.50), mozzarella fingers (£3.25), goujons of plaice, stuffed turkey nuggets or a bowl of hot chilli (£3.50), smoked haddock pasta (£3.75), and Irish filled potato skins (£3.95). Well kept Boddingtons Bitter, Flowers Original, Wethereds and a guest beer such as Marstons Pedigree on handpump, and quite a few Irish whiskies; darts, shove-ha'penny, table skittles, cribbage, dominoes, chess, puzzles, fruit machine, trivia, unobtrusive piped pop music, and garden games. It's pretty outside, with seats to the left of the pub on a grassy flat which gradually slopes down to a safe children's play area with slides, swings, climbing frame and so forth, and overlooks the nearby woods; there's also a quieter part with picnic-table sets under cocktail parasols. *(Recommended by A M S Jeeves, Algis and Lesley Kuliukas, Richard Houghton)*

Wethereds   Licensee Malcolm Raven   Real ale   Meals and snacks (12–2, 6–9; not Sun or Mon evenings)   Well behaved children welcome (unless pub very busy)   Live entertainment every 2–3 weeks   Open 11–2.30 (till 3 Fri–Sun), 6–11; Fri and Sat evening opening 5.30; Bank Hols as Sun opening hours; closed 25 Dec

LEY HILL   SP9802   Map 4

Swan ✪

Village signposted from A416 in Chesham

New licensees have taken over this pub since our last edition went to press, and have introduced a new menu (including a children's menu with proper food), summer barbecues, and hope to set up a children's animal farm. The rambling main bar has snugs and alcoves with cushioned window and wall seats around country tables, low heavy black beams, black oak props, an old kitchen range with a club fireguard and another big fireplace; part of the room is no-smoking. Bar food includes sandwiches (from £1.55 – you can choose your own relish), ploughman's (£2.25 – you can choose your own fruit, pickle or type of bread), filled baked potatoes (£2.25), fish or chicken and asparagus pies or lasagne (£3.50), steak and kidney pudding (£3.65), game pie in port that's been marinated for 24 hours (£3.95), fresh trout (£5.20), salmon steak (£6.50), and steaks (from £6.95); they do 'half-hour specials' for people in a hurry such as chilli con carne or macaroni cheese (£2.90), puddings like old English trifle, summer pudding or crumbles, children's dishes (from 50p) and barbecues that include curried chicken and spare ribs (around £3.50). Well kept Benskins Best, Ind Coope, Tetleys and Youngs Special on handpump. There are picnic-table sets on the front and back terraces and side lawn, as well as pretty hanging baskets, tubs of flowers and a climbing frame; the pub faces the cricket field and common. *(Recommended by R C Vincent, TBB, Stephen King, D C Bail, Lyn and Bill Capper)*

Benskins (Allied)   Licensees Matthew and Teresa Lock   Real ale   Meals and snacks (not Sun evening or 25 Dec)   Children welcome away from bar   Open 11–2.30, 5.30–11; all day Sat

LITTLE HAMPDEN   SP8503   Map 4

Rising Sun 🏵

Village signposted from back road (ie W of A413) Great Missenden – Stoke Mandeville; pub at end of village lane; OS Sheet 165 map reference 856040

As we went to press, this secluded place was refurbishing the opened-up bar and moving towards becoming even more of a smart country dining pub: comfortable blue patterned plush chairs and bench seating, cream and blue floral curtains, stripped pine panelling, and a woodburning stove. The very good, imaginative food includes lunchtime sandwiches (not Sunday), home-made soup (£1.65), crispy mushrooms with garlic mayonnaise or avocado and prawn salad (£2.95), tandoori chicken with cucumber raita and garlic bread (£3.45), savoury macaroni crunch (smoked turkey sausage, sweet peppers and mushrooms £3.95), spinach and mushroom pancake (£4.95), sweet and sour pork in batter (£5.95), grilled rump steak (£7.95), and changing puddings (though food service stops so punctually that you may find you are unable to order one). They do a monthly changing fixed dinner menu (£12.95) and three-course Sunday roast lunch (£8.95 – no other food then). Well kept Adnams, Eldridge Pope Royal Oak, Marstons Pedigree, and Sam Smiths OB on handpump, with Addlestone's cider and Hacker-Pschorr lager from Munich. There are some tables on the terrace by the sloping front grass; tracks lead on through the woods in various directions, and the pub's on *Good Walks Guide* Walk 71, which takes in Hampden House and Coombe Hill (National Trust – with fine views). Muddy boots and dogs must be left outside. (*Recommended by Stephen King, Andrea and Guy Bradley, Geoffrey and Sylvia Donald, John Hawley, Michael and Alison Sandy, Colin Price, Mark Evans, Asher and Sarah Rickayzen, BKA, Lindsey Shaw Radley, Lyn and Bill Capper, Mr and Mrs T F Marshall, D J Cooke, Ken and Barbara Turner, J N Phillips, Mark Evans, Nick Dowson, Alison Hayward*)

Free house   Licensee Rory Dawson   Real ale   Meals and snacks (not Sun evening, not Mon)   Restaurant tel High Wycombe (0494) 488393/488360; not Sun evening   Open 11.30–2.30, 6.30–11; Tues/Weds evening hours 7–10.30; closed Sun evening, all day Mon (which includes Bank Hols) and may close over/after Christmas

LITTLE HORWOOD   SP7930   Map 4

Shoulder of Mutton

Church St; back road 1 mile S of A421 Buckingham–Bletchley

Below an unusual hinge-up shutter, one window in this half-timbered partly thatched 14th-century pub looks out on the back garden with plenty of tables, and there's a quiet churchyard beside it. The T-shaped bar has sturdy seats around chunky rustic tables, quarry-tiles, a showcase of china swans, and a huge fireplace at one end with a woodburning stove. At weekends and in the evenings the atmosphere gets very lively; the friendly Alsatian is called Benjamin. Bar food includes sandwiches (from 90p), a decent ploughman's, hot snacks (from £1.50), home-cooked main dishes and daily specials such as a filling bacon and onion dumpling (from £2.90), and steaks (from £6.90). Well kept ABC Best and Wadworths 6X on handpump; pleasant, friendly service; shove-ha'penny, cribbage, dominoes, and fruit machine in the games area, and piped music. From the north, the car park entrance is tricky. (*Recommended by Ian Phillips, Lyn and Bill Capper, Nick Dowson, Alison Hayward; more reports please*)

ABC (Allied)   Licensee June Fessey   Real ale   Meals and snacks (not Mon or Sun evenings)   Restaurant tel Winslow (029 671) 2514; closed Sun evening   Children in eating area of bar until 9pm   Open 11–2.30 (3 Sat), 6–11; closed Mon lunchtime

MARLOW   SU8586   Map 2

Two Brewers

St Peter Street; at double roundabout approaching bridge turn into Station Road, then first right

The T-shaped bar in this quietly placed, popular pub has low beams, shiny black woodwork, nautical pictures, gleaming brassware and a pleasant atmosphere. A wide choice of bar food includes sandwiches (from £1.30), filled baked potatoes (£3.20), chilli con carne (£3.40), ploughman's (£3.50), decent salads (from £3.50), plaice fingers (£5.30) and good moules marinière (£5.80); well kept Flowers Original, Marstons Pedigree and Wethereds on handpump, traditional cider, decent wines, tea and coffee; maybe piped music. The former function room is a no-smoking restaurant area. A sheltered back courtyard has rustic seats and benches in front give a glimpse of the Thames. Please note they no longer do bedrooms. (*Recommended by Philip Harrison, Jon Wainwright, Richard Houghton, W J G Wingate*)

Whitbreads   Licensee F W J Boxall   Real ale   Meals and snacks   Restaurant (not Sun evening in winter)   Children in restaurant unless pub too busy   Open 11–3, 5.30–11; may open all day Sat and Bank Hols

MARSH GIBBON   SP6423 Map 4
Greyhound

Back road about 4 miles E of Bicester; pub SW of village, towards A41 and Blackthorn

Largely rebuilt in 1740 after a 'terable fire', this quietly old-fashioned pub was originally Tudor. The walls are stripped back to golden-grey stone, there are unusual hexagonal flooring tiles, stripped beams, a finely ornamented iron stove, comfortable heavy-armed seats and tables with old Singer sewing machine bases. The new licensee places a lot of emphasis on the wide choice of home-made food: filled French bread (from £1), soup (£1.50), meaty or vegetarian lasagne (£3.45), meat ploughman's or goulash (£3.50), venison in red wine (£3.75), steak in Guinness pie or popular chicken Kiev (£4.20), and puddings like chocolate sponge or cheesecake (from £1.50). Well kept Fullers London Pride, Greene King Abbot and IPA, Hook Norton Best and Theakstons Best on handpump; dominoes, cribbage, piped music. There's a small but pretty front garden with silvery stone tables, and a more spacious garden at the back, with swings and a climbing frame tucked among the trees. (*Recommended by Lyn and Bill Capper, Marjorie and David Lamb, Nick Dowson, Alison Hayward, Brian and Anna Marsden, Janet and Gary Amos, Alan Skull, P J Taylor*)

Free house   Licensee Richard Kiam   Real ale   Meals and snacks (not Sun evening) Restaurant tel Stratton Audley (086 97) 365   Children allowed   Open 11–3, 6–11

MEDMENHAM   SU8084 Map 2
Dog & Badger

A4155 Henley–Marlow

Nell Gwynn was supposed to have sold her wares here, and as late as 1899 the Medmenham Parish Clerk used to announce the banns of marriage in this pub before they were published in the church. The big, busy bar is comfortably modernised and neatly kept, with banquettes and stools around the tables, low oak beams (some dating back to the 15th century), soft lighting, brasses, patterned carpet and an open fire (as well as an illuminated oven). Attractively presented bar food includes good sandwiches or rolls (from £1.10), enterprising filled baked potatoes or several versions along the ploughman's theme (from £3.25), pizza (£3.65), salads (from £3.85), tagliatelle (£3.95), steak and kidney pie (£4.65), and rump steak (£4.85); well kept Boddingtons, Flowers Original, and Wethereds on handpump, and quite a few whiskies; unobtrusive piped pop music, trivia; efficient service. A pleasant short walk takes you down to the Thames. (*Recommended by T Galligan, Lyn and Bill Capper, Mr and Mrs D Norton, Alison Hayward, Nick Dowson; more reports please*)

Whitbreads   Licensee W F Farrell   Real ale   Meals and snacks   Restaurant tel Henley-on-Thames (0491) 571362   Children in eating area of bar   Open 11–3, 5.30–11

NORTHEND   SU7392 Map 4
White Hart

Off B4009 in Watlington, via Christmas Common, and up on to the Chilterns

In an area popular with walkers, this pub has hatch service in summer to the attractive, sheltered garden – where there's a children's play area. The cosy, unspoilt bar has some panelling, very low handsomely carved oak beams, good log fires (one in a vast fireplace), and comfortable window seats. Bar food includes good home-made chicken soup, sandwiches (£1.15), several ploughman's with pickles (from £2.50), filled pancakes (£3.50), salads (from £3.90), liver and bacon (£4.30), beef and cider or lamb and mustard pies (£4.95), gammon (£5.75), and sirloin steak (£7.35); they do a few things for those with small appetites (£1.75). Well kept Brakspears PA, SB and Old on handpump; friendly service. *(Recommended by TBB, Dr and Mrs Peter Crosby, Roger and Lynda Pilgrim, BHP, Michael Thomson; more reports please)*

Brakspears   Licensees Frank and Barbara Nolan   Real ale   Meals and snacks (12–2, 7–10, though on Sat and Bank Hols and on summer weekdays food served noon–10) Children in top room (lunchtime only)   Open 11–11 Mar–Sept, and Sat all year; 11.30–2.30, 6.30–11 winter weekdays   Bedrooms tel Henley-on-Thames (0491) 63353; £30/£40

PENN   SU9193 Map 4
Crown

B474

Fine views from the back terraces of this creeper-covered Chef & Brewer pub – on a ridge over 500 feet high – look out over rolling pastures and woodland. Tables among pretty roses face the 14th-century church in front, and there are slides, swings, climbing frames and a wooden horse and cart for children; in summer they've had mid-week barbecues. Inside, it's neat and comfortable, with an olde-worlde decor and well preserved medieval flooring tiles in one room. Efficiently served bar food includes home-made soup (£1.75), ploughman's (from £2.50), salads (around £3.60), and hot dishes such as chicken in tarragon, steak and mushroom pie or lasagne (from £3.35); quite a few tables tend to have been reserved. Well kept Ruddles Best and County and Websters Yorkshire on handpump; fruit machine, trivia, juke box or piped music; can be busy evenings and weekend lunchtimes. *(Recommended by A M S Jeeves, Chris Raisin, Mr and Mrs F W Sturch; more reports please)*

Trumans (Watneys)   Real ale   Bar meals and snacks (lunchtime; also evening July–Aug)   Restaurant tel Penn (049 481) 2640 – open noon–9 Sun   Children in eating area and restaurant – also weekday family room   Open 11.30–2.30, 6–11

nr PRINCES RISBOROUGH   SP8003 Map 4
Red Lion

Upper Icknield Way, Whiteleaf; village signposted off A4010 towards Aylesbury; OS Sheet 165 map reference 817040

Quiet on weekday lunchtimes, this 17th-century inn is very popular with local people in the evenings and with walkers at weekends. It's neatly kept and simply furnished, and the low-ceilinged small bar has an alcove of cream-painted antique winged settles, small prints on the walls, vases of flowers, and a log fire that the big golden labrador is fond of. Good bar food includes sandwiches (from £1), filled baked potatoes (from £1.90), excellent omelettes (from £2.50), home-made cottage pie (£3.95) or lasagne (£4.50), and a popular four-course Sunday lunch (£8.95); super chips. Well kept Brakspears PA and SB, Morlands PA and Hook Norton Best on handpump; cribbage, dominoes, cards, and piped music. The pub is tucked up a quiet village lane close to Whiteleaf Fields (National Trust); it has a couple of rustic tables on the neat little side lawn. *(Recommended by David Wallington, Ian Phillips; more reports please)*

*Free house   Licensee R T Howard   Real ale   Meals and snacks (12–2, 6–9; not Sun)
Restaurant (not Sun evening)   Children in restaurant   Open 11.30–3, 5.30 (6
Sat)–11   Bedrooms tel Princes Risborough (084 44) 4476; £20/£30*

SKIRMETT   SU7790 Map 2
Old Crown ★ ⊘

High St; from A4155 NE of Henley take Hambleden turn and keep on; or from B482
Stokenchurch–Marlow take Turville turn and keep on

Unless you make a reservation, you may find all the tables in this unspoilt village
pub booked up by people keen to enjoy the constantly changing, home-made bar
food: very good soup such as tomato and coriander (£2.20), deep-fried camembert
with gooseberry conserve (£3.25), smoked Scotch salmon roulade (£3.85), steak,
kidney and mushroom pie (£5.65), breast of chicken stuffed with cream cheese and
asparagus (£7), seafood au gratin (£7.95), and puddings like banoffi pie (£2.25).
The small central room and larger one leading off have Windsor chairs, tankards
hanging from the beams, and logs burning in the big fireplace; the little
white-painted tap room has trestle tables and an old-fashioned settle by its
inglenook fireplace. There are over 700 bric-a-brac items, paintings, antiques,
bottles and tools. Well kept Brakspears PA, SB and Old Ale are tapped from casks
in a still room, and served though a hatch; good value wine; dominoes, cribbage,
and trivia. A sheltered front terrace has flower tubs, and there are picnic-table sets
under cocktail parasols on the big back lawn. Note that children under 10 are not
allowed even in the garden. The alsatian's called Bruno; no car park. (*Recommended
by TBB, Simon Collett-Jonesw, Richard Houghton, Miss J Powell, Norman Foot, John Day, J
Maloney, Dennis and Pat Jones*)

*Brakspears   Licensees Peter and Liz Mumby   Real ale   Meals and snacks (not Mon)
Restaurant (not Mon) tel Turville Heath (049 163) 435   Well behaved children over 10
in restaurant   Open 10.30–2.30, 6–11; closed 25 Dec*

STOKE GREEN   SU9882 Map 2
Red Lion

1 mile S of Stoke Poges, off B416 signposted to Wexham and George Green; OS Sheet
175 map reference 986824

This attractive early Georgian ex-farmhouse is charmingly run by a friendly New
Zealand couple, who serve good value bar lunches in a no-smoking pantry bar
(though the food may be eaten anywhere in the pub): filled French bread (from
£1.60), a choice of ploughman's (from £2.20), salads (from £3.50) and hot dishes
such as sweet and sour pork, seafood mornay, meaty or vegetable lasagne and
chilli con carne (£3.75–3.95). In the evening most food is served in the back
Stables restaurant (where they have a 'sizzles' menu – things you cook yourself on
a sizzling-hot stone that's brought to your table); this is decorated in a lively rustic
style, and connected to the main pub by a covered walkway. The main bar has
robust high-backed settles forming alcoves, inglenook seats, lots of bric-a-brac, big
antique prints and mezzotints including a good Alken steeplechasing series, and
fresh flowers. Well kept Bass and Charrington IPA from a chest-high bar counter,
lots of lagers, a good choice of wines, winter hot toddies, and tea or coffee;
dominoes, cribbage, fruit machine, maybe piped music. There are picnic-table sets
under cocktail parasols on the roundel of lawn in front of this attractive
wisteria-covered tiled house, and they have summer barbecues on the sheltered
back terrace. (*Recommended by Lindsey Shaw Radley, A W Dickinson, TBB; more reports
please*)

*Charringtons   Licensees Brian and Denize O'Connor   Real ale   Meals and snacks
(11.30–2.30)   Restaurant tel Slough (0753) 21739; not Sat lunchtime; open till 3 Sun
afternoon   Children in pantry bar (not evening) and restaurant   Open 11–2.30,
5.30–11; 11–11 Thurs–Sat; closed evening 25 Dec*

nr THE LEE SP8904 Map 4
Old Swan

Swan Bottom; back road 3/4 mile N of The Lee; OS map 165 reference 902055

The popular bar food here includes lunchtime sandwiches (from £1.40), soup (£1.65), ploughman's (£2.95 – there's a good honey-roast ham version, too), bangers and mash (£3.45) and chicken and mushroom pie (£3.75), and they often have fish dishes such as big grilled sardines or good moules marinière (£3.25), dressed crab (£3.95), seafood pancake (£4.50), and salmon in a fresh dill, wine and cream sauce (£4.75); good puddings such as plum and apple crumble with cinnamon topping (£1.95). On Sundays, there's a winter roast (£5.95) or summer barbecue. The four low-beamed interconnecting rooms have high-backed antique settles and window seats as well as more modern dining chairs, an attractive mixture of carpet and flooring tiles, and a melodious wall clock; in winter logs burn in the old iron cooking range of the 16th-century inglenook fireplace. The cosy dining area was once the stables. Well kept Adnams, Bass, Marstons Burton, and Wadworths 6X on handpump; friendly service. Muddy boots are unwelcome, though the pub's dogs may appear. The spreading back garden has plenty of tables among shrubs and flowerbeds (and a play area), with more seats in front of the pretty tiled white pub. (*Recommended by JM, PM, Mark Evans, Gordon Davico, Richard Houghton, Alan Skull, David Wallington, BKA*)

Free house   Licensee Sean Michaelson-Yeates   Real ale   Meals and snacks (not Sun or Mon evenings)   Restaurant tel The Lee (024 020) 239   Children in restaurant   Open 12–3, 6–11; 12–11 Fri and Sat

TURVILLE SU7690 Map 2
Bull & Butcher

Off B482 at Bolter End; or can be reached via Hambleden and Skirmett from A4155 W of Medmenham

Set among cottages sheltering in a wooded Chilterns valley, this busy but welcoming black-and-white timbered pub has tables on a lawn by fruit trees and a neatly umbrella-shaped hawthorn; Sunday barbecues out here when it's fine (£4.25). Partly divided into two areas, the comfortable low-ceilinged bar is liberally decorated with big motor-racing prints, other photographs, and yachting and photographic bric-a-brac, and there are cushioned wall settles and an old-fashioned high-backed settle by one log fire; a stable half-door lets in a breeze on warm summer days. Bar food includes home-made soups and pâtés, baked potatoes with a range of fillings (winter only, from £3.50), summer salads (from £3.50), a vegetarian dish of the day (from £3.95), Somerset pork in cider (£4.50), minted lamb casserole (£4.75), and beef in ale pie (£4.95). On winter Sundays they do a roast lunch (£4.95) and vegetarian nut roast (£4.25). Well kept Brakspears PA, SB and Old Ale on handpump, and farm cider; dominoes, cribbage and video game. Walkers are welcome, and the inseparable black labrador and little Jack Russell are amusing. (*Recommended by Ian Phillips, TBB, A M S Jeeves, Richard Houghton, Chris Raisin, Graham Doyle, John Day*)

Brakspears   Licensees Sandie Watson, Peter Wright   Real ale   Meals and snacks (12–2, 7.30–10)   Live entertainment every other Thurs   Open 11–2.30, 6–11

WEST WYCOMBE SU8394 Map 4
George & Dragon ✿

London Road; A40 W of High Wycombe

Dating from the 15th century, this handsome inn has massive oak beams, sloping walls, a big log fire and a magnificent oak staircase (haunted by a wronged girl – there's also a poltergeist that hides things which turn up unexpectedly in odd places). The rambling, comfortably modernised bar has Windsor chairs and comfortable wall seats around the many wood or copper-topped tables.

Consistently good bar food using fresh ingredients includes toasted sandwiches (from £1), home-made soup (£1.50), ploughman's with a choice of cheeses (from £2.50), home-made game pâté (£2.70), gratin of seafood, whitefish and shellfish in a wine sauce (£3.45), beef curry (£3.85), excellent home-made pies like ham, leek and cider (£3.95), salmon steak with prawn paste in puff pastry and served with sour cream (£5.95), sirloin steak (£8.95), and home-made puddings such as ice-creams (£1.95) or chocolate roulade (£2.25). It's very popular at weekends – you have to get there early for a seat, though the cheerful service is still usually fairly prompt. Courage Best and Directors and guest beers on handpump, and a good range of whiskies; dominoes, cribbage; the back-to-front clock in spite of appearances does keep good time. The arched and cobbled coach entry leads to a spacious, peaceful garden with picnic-table sets, a climbing frame and slides; the pub is on *Good Walks Guide* Walk 70. Note the rare and elegantly mounted lead inn sign which spans much of the street in this National Trust village. We'd be particularly grateful for reports on the bedrooms here – we've no reason to think that the inn does not deserve our place-to-stay award, but have never heard from readers who've stayed here. (*Recommended by K Leist, Hilarie Miles-Sharp, Ian Phillips, Barbara Hatfield, Prof and Mrs Keith Patchett, Simon Collett-Jones*)

Courage   Licensee Philip Todd   Real ale   Meals and snacks (12–2, 6–9.30; snacks served all day Sat; not Sun or Bank Hol Mon evenings)   Children in separate small room   Bedrooms tel High Wycombe (0494) 464414; £37S(£40B)/£47S(£50B)   Open 11–2.30, 5.30–11; 11–11 Sat; closed evenings 25–26 Dec

WHITCHURCH   SP8020   Map 4

White Swan ★   ⊘

10 High Street; A413 Aylesbury–Buckingham

This partly thatched homely old building has an odd-shaped saloon bar with seats built into squared honey-coloured oak panelling below a Delft shelf, a few venerable leather dining chairs and a carved Gothick settle around its chunky elm tables; there's a longcase clock, fresh flowers, pretty wall lamps and a small open fire. This room's named for Charlie, the pub's yellow labrador – there are also three cats called Thomas, TC and Pi. A wide range of good value, wholesome bar food includes soup (£1.10), a huge choice of well made sandwiches and toasties (from 80p, triple-deckers from £1.65, good hot salt beef with dill £2, smoked salmon and salad £3.25), lots of ploughman's (from £2.25), good hors d'oeuvres (£3), salads (from £2.75, ham and peach £4, mixed seafood £5), breakfast grill (£3.20), a variety of superb omelettes (from £3), vegetable lasagne (£3.75), steak and kidney pie or seafood au gratin (£4), tasty gammon and eggs (£4.75), evening rump steak (£7), and puddings; courteous and helpful service. Well kept ABC Best, Bass and Wadworths 6X on handpump, cheap help-yourself coffee; sensibly placed darts, shove-ha'penny, dominoes, cribbage and piped music. Behind the pub, a rambling informal garden has picnic-table sets under trees. (*Recommended by Marjorie and David Lamb, John Whitehead, R C Gandy, Mr and Mrs Allan Chapman, Lyn and Bill Capper, Alan Skull, Nick Dowson, Alison Hayward, M J Morgan*)

ABC (Allied)   Licensees Rex and Janet Tucker   Real ale   Meals and snacks (12–2, 6–9.45; Sun 12–1.45, not Sun evening)   Children in dining room   Open 11–2.30, 6–11

WORMINGHALL   SP6308   Map 4

Clifden Arms

Off A40 E of Oxford; take Wheatley turn off, then Old London Road off A418 (sign easiest to see heading east) on outskirts of Wheatley; pub signed off road in village

The garden of this particularly pretty and very friendly black and white 16th-century timbered cottage loops around behind the house, with picnic-table sets in the orchard, a sheltered flower garden with roses, an ancient pump and well, a run of fancy poultry, a large pond with resident turtle, and donkeys; the big play area has slides, a boot house, log fort and giant red indian. Inside, a cosy little lounge has quite a forest of interesting bottles, brass powder-flasks, black iron vices and tools (it's worth asking the landlord what the unfamiliar ones are for), milk-yokes and so forth hanging from its heavy beams, old-fashioned seats, squint-timbered ochre walls and a roaring log fire in its big fireplace. A cheerful lino-floored bar, also beamed, has a second fire, and opens into a pool room; darts, shove-ha'penny, fruit machine, space game, ring-the-bull (with real horns), maybe piped music. This year, there's a new no-smoking restaurant. Good value bar food includes sandwiches (from £1.30; steak £2.45, a monumental club sandwich named for a neighbouring American £4.40), marvellous home-made soup (£1.65), burger (£2.75), filled baked potatoes (from £2.75), salmon fishcakes (£3), a breakfast grill (£3.25), a hefty ploughman's with five cheeses (£3.85), plaice or omelettes (£4.40), salads (from £5.50), trout (£6) and sirloin steak (£10.15), with specials such as butterfly prawns with garlic mayonnaise (£3), liver casserole, poached salmon, a vegetarian dish like good vegetable curry, a 16oz T-bone steak (£11.55), children's helpings on request, and puddings like home-made fruit pie or banana boat (from £1.75). Well kept Halls Harvest, Ind Coope Burton and Tetleys on handpump, decent coffee. The Jack Russell is called Porty. The picturesque village has almshouses built in 1675, and the Norman church has a 15th-century tower and 14th-century chancel. Nearby Waterperry Gardens are worth a visit. *(Recommended by Mrs S Fergy, TBB, Michael Thomson, Lyn and Bill Capper)*

Halls (Allied)   Licensees Bob and Gwen Spencer   Real ale   Meals and snacks (11–3, 6–10)   No-smoking restaurant tel Ickford (0844) 339273   Children in restaurant Open 11–3, 6–11; open all day Sat; closed 25 Dec

Lucky Dip

Besides the fully inspected pubs, you might like to try these Lucky Dips recommended to us and described by readers (if you do, please send us reports):

Amersham [High St (A413); SU9597], *Eagle*: New licensees have transformed into pleasant place with large open bar, tiled and partly carpeted, low beams — ventilation could perhaps be improved; darts, soft piped music, fruit machine; Adnams as well as Benskins beers, usual bar food *(Lyn and Bill Capper)*; [High St], *Elephant & Castle*: Low beams, china, velvet and brasses in popular Whitbreads food pub with fine U-shaped bar counter, piped music; Wethereds on handpump *(LYM)*; [The Broadway], *Griffin*: Ancient inn with cobbled yard, log fires in wrought-iron fire basket, old stone beer bottles (and a stone hot-water bottle) on mantlepiece, decent bar menu *(R M Savage)*
Ashley Green [A416 Chesham—Berkhamsted; SP9705], *Golden Eagle*: Pleasant, timbered pub with clean and welcoming bars; Ind Coope Burton, good bar food at reasonable prices; may be pet rabbits in small inner courtyard *(Douglas Bail)*
Aylesbury [Temple Sq; SP8213], *Queens Head*: Small corner pub on quiet square away from main shopping area; warmly welcoming with notably low-priced food such as gammon and eggs, salads, ploughman's and sandwiches; main and back bar and dining area all with waitress service *(Ian Phillips)*
Beaconsfield [Aylesbury End, Old Beaconsfield; SU9490], *Charles Dickens*: Modernised old pub with quiet relaxed atmosphere and formal, polite service; impressive furniture, well kept Flowers Original and Marstons Pedigree on handpump; good wine list *(Richard*

Houghton);
Beaconsfield [London Rd; SU9490], *Royal Saracens Head*: Striking timbered facade, and massive beams and timbers in one corner of the spreading open-plan bar — much modernised, with lots of artificial plants, books and nick-nacks; Wethereds real ale, Beefeater steak bar, attractive sheltered courtyard, long history *(Simon Collett-Jones, Andy and Jill Kassube, LYM)*
Bletchley [Wilton Ave, off Buckingham Rd; SP8733], *Eight Bells*: Pleasant modern-style pub popular with young people; friendly staff serving Flowers IPA and Wethereds; peculiarly shaped pool table and usual machines in L-shaped bar *(Keith Houlgate)*
☆ **Botley** [Tylers Hill Rd; SP9702], *Five Bells*: Remote country pub, clean, pleasant and quiet, with inglenook fireplaces, good pubby atmosphere, friendly landlord, good service; notable range of well kept real ales, good value lunchtime bar food; children in eating area; may be changing hands *(Mr and Mrs F W Sturch, Richard Houghton, LYM; more reports please)*
Botley, *Hen & Chickens*: Pretty open-plan pub with nice atmosphere; pleasant, efficient service; well kept Benskins and Adnams *(Richard Houghton)*
Bourne End [Cores End Rd; SU8985], *Heart in Hand*: Pleasant, vibrant atmosphere with predominantly young customers, comfortable interior and well kept Whitbreads *(Richard Houghton)*; [Hedsor Rd], *Old Red Lion*: Renamed Masons by its present friendly and helpful owners, now a good popular pub/restaurant *(Simon Collett-Jones)*

☆ **Brill** [Windmill St; SP6513], *Sun*: New
landlord arrived some months ago after
extensive refurbishment, inc bedrooms; food
now excellent in bar (good soups and soused
herrings) and restaurant *(John Wheeler)*

☆ **Burnham** [Hawthorn Lane, Burnham
Beeches; SU9381], *Stag*: Reopened under
new management in splendid style after a
couple of years' dereliction — leather-look
sofas, cottagey tables and chairs,
conservatory, bar food from sandwiches to
steaks, well kept Brakspears, Flowers
Original, Wethereds and a guest such as
Boddingtons, jazz Weds, restaurant upstairs;
service very friendly and polite; open all day,
right on the edge of the Beeches *(Richard
Houghton)*

Burnham [High St], *Crispin*: Very much a
regulars' local, but visitors made welcome
by pleasant atmosphere; well kept Bass and
Charringtons IPA, bar food, large car park
(Richard Houghton)

☆ **Cadmore End** [B482 towards Stokenchurch;
SU7892], *Blue Flag*: Recently extended old
beamed pub attached to small modern hotel,
with several bar areas divided by wall
partitions and standing timbers; brocaded
cushioned wall settles, purple leatherette
brass-studded chairs around a mix of
wooden tables, horse brasses, brewery and
Coca-Cola mirrors and Schweppes prints on
walls, and half-barrels built into bar
counter; huge blackboard menu with very
wide choice of well prepared food; changing
well kept real ales such as Adnams
Southwold, Morlands, Theakstons XB and
Wadworths 6X on handpump; attractive
little restaurant; piped Radio 1, efficient
rather than friendly service, and a rather
barky dog called Colonel *(Dr J C Harrison, D
C Ball, Richard Houghton, BB)*

Cadmore End [B482 — OS Sheet 175 map
reference 785927], *Old Ship*: Unspoilt and
old-fashioned simple little country pub,
almost like having a drink in someone's
front room; well kept Brakspears straight
from the cellar, friendly and informal service
— appealing if you like this
fast-disappearing very basic style of rural
pub *(Roger and Lynda Pilgrim)*

Cadsden [Lower Cadsden — OS Sheet 165
map reference 825045; SP8204], *Plough*:
Attractively refurbished with warm Turkey
carpets, dark oak tables and chintz curtains;
Benskins Best, Friary Meux and Ind Coope
Burton, wide choice of wines inc mulled
wine; has had good rustic atmosphere,
friendly and efficient staff and excellent
range of attractively presented food, but
we've not heard enough since a recent
. management change to give a firm rating —
more reports please; on GWG71 *(R M
Savage, D J Cooke)*

Chalfont Common [TQ0092], *Dumb Bell*:
Comfortably refurbished country pub with
good value simple food and well kept
Courage *(LYM)*

Chalfont St Giles [High St; village
signposted off A413; SU9893], *Feathers*:
Cosy and cheerful low-beamed local, handy

for Milton's cottage, with well kept
Whitbreads-related real ales, comfortable
settees, good open fires and seats outside
(LYM)

Chalfont St Giles [London Rd; SU9893], *Ivy
House*: Benskins house, successfully
converted to brasserie with French-style
decor; friendly staff, no fruit machines, and
– at prices higher than when it was a pub –
wonderful, imaginative bar food *(Dennis
and Pat Jones)*

Pheasant: Seventeenth-century Benskins pub
carefully and comfortably restored to bring
out its age, with massive oak beams, three
faithfully recreated stone fireplaces and a
country sporting theme; generous helpings
of well prepared varied bar food and
wide-ranging reataurant dishes inc game and
fresh veg (no-smoking dining room),
moderate prices, efficient friendly service *(R
M Savage, Mr and Mrs T F Marshall)*

Cheddington [SP9217], *Duke of Wellington*:
By canal bridge, with good value food inc
super ploughman's, so generous we needed
doggy bag *(Margaret and Trevor Errington)*;
[High St], *Old Swan*: Traditional well kept
old pub with two bars and restaurant, now
semi open-plan but tastefully done; well kept
ABC Best, Tetleys and Wadworths 6X,
lovely atmosphere with two real fireplaces
— very pleasant and relaxing; efficient
uniformed staff, large car park *(Richard
Houghton)*

☆ **Chenies** [Chesham Rd; TQ0198], *Red Lion*:
Lavishly refurbished pub, increasingly
popular, with good chatty atmosphere in
spotless U-shaped main bar (look out for the
long step which rather merges into the
carpet), small back snug, dining room with
wide and interesting choice of good value
well presented bar food from wholemeal
baps (inc a fine roast beef one) to steak, well
kept Benskins Best, Ind Coope Burton and
Tetleys; no piped music or fruit machines;
decent pictures, smiling landlord; dogs
allowed; convenient for Chenies Manor
which is open 2–5 Weds, Thurs Apr–Oct
*(Mr and Mrs R P Begg, R M Savage, Lyn and
Bill Capper, David Wallington, Tony and
Lynne Stark, B R Shiner)*

Chesham [SP9501], *George & Dragon*:
Extensively refurbished 17th-century pub
with low thick beams, pokey little alcoves
leading off, period pictures and fine
fireplace; Benskins, Ind Coope and Tetleys
real ales, standard bar food, maybe copies of
Beano in the gents'; pity about the piped
music *(Gwen and Peter Andrews)*;
[Waterside], *Pheasant*: Well kept, pleasant
open-planned pub with riverside garden
(David Wallington); [Church St], *Queens
Head*: Quaint and friendly town local with
well kept Brakspears *(Tony and Lynne Stark)*

Coleshill [SU9495], *Magpies*: Welcoming
licensee, good warm mix of customers, no
juke box; well kept Benskins, range of bar
food at reasonable prices, clean lavatories,
large car park *(Richard Houghton)*; [Village
Road; SU9495], *Red Lion*: Pleasantly placed
off the beaten track, well furnished, with

excellent atmosphere and friendly staff; good range of real ales inc Burtons, excellent reasonably priced bar food Mon–Sat, separate dining room *(John Hawley)*
Colnbrook [High St; TQ0277], *Star & Garter*: Good atmosphere and service in small cosy low-ceilinged bar, with genuine welcome even for strangers; good helpings of nicely prepared reasonably priced food from limited bar menu — but plenty of sandwiches; well kept Courage Best and John Smiths, coal-effect fire, pleasant riverside garden *(Richard Houghton)*

☆ **Cuddington** [Upper Church St; village signposted from A418 Thame—Aylesbury; SP7311], *Red Lion*: Olive-green plush chairs, stools and sofa and dimpled copper tables in discreetly chintzy small lounge with big inglenook fireplace, well kept ABC Best and maybe Bass on handpump, and rewarding restaurant food inc a good choice of vegetarian, fish, chicken and steak dishes; also lots of starters, and bar food such as soup, sandwiches, ploughman's and hot dishes; piped music, garden with play area *(Don and Margaret Wrattan, Mike O'Driscoll, Lyn and Bill Capper, BB)*

☆ **Denham** [3/4 mile from M40 junction 1; follow Denham Village signs; TQ0486], *Swan*: Neatly renovated and comfortable bar with friendly staff, well kept Courage and John Smiths real ales, bar food often including interesting daily specials; wide range of sandwiches, salad bar and good hot salt beef rolls, coal fire, maybe piped music; extensive floodlit garden with children's play house *(Ian Phillips, Lynn and Bill Capper, TBB, Henry Midwinter, Michael and Alison Sandy, LYM)*

☆ **Dinton** [Stars Lane; take New Road signed Dinton off A418 SW of Aylesbury at Gibraltar; SP7611], *Seven Stars*: Pretty white pub tucked away in quiet village, popular for attractively priced bar food from soup, sandwiches and ploughman's to home-made pies and salads, with specials such as ham and egg or pork schnitzel; neat carpeted lounge with recently exposed beams, more interesting public bar with glossily varnished ancient built-in settles by vast stone inglenook, well kept ABC Best and Tetleys on handpump, maybe unobtrusive piped music, tables on sheltered terrace and lawn, restaurant; immaculate lavatories *(Lyn and Bill Capper, BB)*
Dorney [Village Rd; SU9278], *Palmers Arms*: Very comfortable dining pub with lots of varied seating around modern reproduction pine tables; wide choice of good food lunchtime and evening — smoked bacon and mushrooms in garlic sauce, chicken dishes and sirloin steak filled with brie all recommended, though prices of main dishes run up to £7 or more; Bass and Charrington IPA, large car park, pleasant garden; close to Dorney Court *(Ian Phillips)*; [Lake End Rd; SU9278], *Pineapple*: Not smart, but popular and friendly with a certain old-fashioned pub feel *(TBB)*
Downley [OS Sheet 165 map reference

849959; SU8594], *Le De Spencer*: Unpretentious pub hidden away on common, fairy-lit loggia overlooking lawn, friendly landlord, Wethereds SPA on handpump, snacks *(LYM)*
Eton Wick [17 Eton Wick Rd; SU9478], *Shepherds Hut*: Welcoming licensees, simple but comfortable bar, well kept Friary Meux Best, good bar food, reasonable prices, large car park *(Richard Houghton)*
Farnham Royal [Farnham Rd; SU9583], *Dukes Head*: Pleasant atmosphere, well kept Courage, good food at acceptable prices, friendly service *(Richard Houghton)*; [Blackpond Lane], *Emperor of India*: Popular with businessmen for decent bar food at lunchtime, a proper local in the evening; two separate bars, one quiet, one with darts; well kept Whitbreads-related beers, large car park; used to be called the King of Prussia *(Richard Houghton)*

☆ **Ford** [village signposted between A418 and B4009, SW of Aylesbury; SP7709], *Dinton Hermit*: Good atmosphere in neatly kept snug stone cottage with good value food (not Sun or Mon) such as toasted sandwiches, ploughman's, baked potatoes, salads and fish and other main-course dishes, lots of puddings, well kept ABC Best, Bass and Tetleys on handpump, friendly efficient service; comfortable log-fire lounge on right, more interesting scrubbed-table public bar with huge inglenook (and darts) on left, attractive sheltered country garden with play area *(Lyn and Bill Capper, BB)*
Gayhurst [B526; SP8446], *Sir Francis Drake*: Some specialisation in freshly made curries besides more conventional bar food in charmingly incongruous Gothick traceried and pinnacled building, cosy inside, strong on spirits and cocktails; picnic-table sets under cocktail parasols in neat garden *(LYM)*
Gerrards Cross [A40, E; TQ0087], *Apple Tree*: Comfortable atmosphere and pleasant, attentive staff; usual Whitbreads ales and good variable range of bar snacks; Beefeater restaurant *(AP)*

☆ **Great Hampden** [corner of Hampden Common — OS Sheet 165 map reference 845015; SP8401], *Hampden Arms*: Friendly efficient service from promising new young licensees this last year, in pleasant and comfortable country pub with just two rooms, one very small — well positioned for walkers and adjacent to common often used for cricket; good choice of well presented reasonably priced bar food inc very good fisherman's platter *(Margaret Dyke, Mrs Olive Way, Marjorie and David Lamb, Maureen Hobbs)*
Great Kimble [Risborough Rd (A4010); SP8206], *Bernard Arms*: Cheerful atmosphere and reasonably priced food in neatly refurbished Benskins pub; promising new management this last year — more reports please *(Gordon Leighton)*

☆ **Great Linford** [4 1/2 miles from M1, junction 14; from Newport Pagnell take Wolverton Rd towards Stony Stratford;

SP8542], *Black Horse*: Particularly notable for position just below Grand Union Canal embankment — drinks can be taken out on the towpath, and garden has biggish play area; spacious and rambling, with genuinely pubby atmosphere, very well kept ABC Best, Ind Coope Burton and another beer such as Everards Tiger on handpump, good range of popular bar food, large garden inc biggish play area; pleasant walk here (weather permitting) along canal from New Inn at New Bradwell, 1 1/2 miles away — see below; children allowed in restaurant *(Jonathan and Jane Hagger, Geoff Roynon, Dave Braisted, LYM)*

☆ **Great Missenden** [High St; SP8901], *Cross Keys*: Genuine old-fashioned atmosphere with nice old settles, beams, open fire, welcoming staff — warm and friendly though not exactly spacious; well kept ABC Best, Bass Ind Coope Burton and Tetleys on handpump, good range of home-cooked and waitress-served food inc cold buffet in separate eating area, clean lavatories *(Richard Houghton, Michael and Alison Sandy, Norman Foot, JM, PM, V H Balchin)*

Great Missenden [62 High St], *Red Lion*: Previously popular for its good range of fresh fish and other food, comfortable Victorian-style decor and well kept real ales, this inn has now closed, with plans for redevelopment as offices *(LYM)*

Hawridge [The Vale; village signposted from A416 N of Chesham — OS Sheet 165 map reference 960050; SP9505], *Rose & Crown*: Country pub with around eight real ales on handpump (attracting lots of young people in the evening — maybe with loud music then), masses of whiskies, bar food (may be no evening nor dishes, and service may be slow); big log fire in spaciously refurbished open-plan bar, broad terrace with lawn dropping down beyond giving good views, play area; children allowed *(Stephen King, Tony and Lynne Stark, LYM)*

☆ **Hedgerley** [One Pin Lane; SE of M40 junction 2; junction Parish Lane/Collum Green Rd — OS Sheet 175 map reference 968863; SU9686], *One Pin*: Cheerfully welcoming family-run pub with good value, straightforward and freshly prepared bar food, good service, well kept Courage ales *(AP)*

High Wycombe [Frogmore (A4128); SU8593], *Bell*: Popular with young people, polite and well organised staff, well kept Fullers; low lights and a nice buzz of conversation *(Richard Houghton)*

Holmer Green [Earl Howe Rd; SU9097], *Earl Howe*: Honest, down-to-earth local, friendly, unspoilt and spotless; acceptable real ale, simple but good value food *(Anon)*; [New Pond Rd], *Valiant Trooper*: Cosy pub in village centre; well kept ales and good food in bar and restaurant *(J N Phillips)*

Hyde Heath [village signposted off B485 Great Missenden—Chesham; SU9399], *Plough*: Prettily placed little pub with chatty local atmosphere in freshly furnished long bar, fairly priced food, well kept Benskins

Best and Ind Coope Burton, open fires, bar food *(LYM)*

Iver [146 Swallow St; TQ0381], *Oddfellows Arms*: Large old local divided into small areas, good open fire and cosy atmosphere; well kept Courage and Youngs beers, extensive lunchtime bar food (not Sun; also trying Fri and Sat evenings), dominoes and cribbage, large car park; standards maintained despite some management changes *(James M Goode, Richard Houghton)*

Little Chalfont [White Lion Rd; A404 Chorleywood—Amersham; SU9997], *White Lion*: Warm, comfortable country pub with carpeted bars and traditional furniture, Courage Best and Directors, and a wide range of fairly priced bar and restaurant food; quick, friendly service *(R M Savage)*

Little Kingshill [Hare La; SU8999], *Full Moon*: Very homely and almost cottagey, with a real welcome; plenty of regulars, young and old, but visitors feel at home; comfortably modernised with an abundance of horse brasses, copper and riding crops, with well kept Benskins Best and Tetleys on handpump and Adnams as a guest beer, and bar food; pleasant garden, small car park; last year's licensees have moved to the Bricklayers Arms in Flaunden — see Herts main entries *(Richard Houghton, J N Phillips, Mr and Mrs T F Marshall)*

Little Marlow [Church Rd; off A4155 about two miles E of Marlow, pub signed off main rd; SU8786], *Kings Head*: Quiet, relaxing and cosy low-beamed local with dark oak panelling in lounge — used virtually wholly as dining area weekday lunchtime; welcoming licensees, well kept Wethereds and other Whitbreads-related beers, real fire, quick service *(Richard Houghton)*

Little Missenden [SU9298], *Crown*: Pleasant little pub, almost like a private house; local flavour but no especial notice taken of visitors; friendly and obliging landlord and landlady; very well kept Morrells, Hook Norton and Marstons Pedigree; small car park, but easy to park on the road *(Joel Dobris, Richard Houghton)*; *Red Lion*: Simple country pub with large coal fire and attractive old kitchen range, friendly staff, real ales and fresh, home-cooked bar food at reasonable prices *(R J Groves)*

☆ **Littleworth Common** [2 miles from M40 junction 2; off A355; SU9487], *Jolly Woodman*: Fairly large pub, but beamed and pleasantly cottagey, with welcoming atmosphere, big seating area, long bar, central fireplace; attractive range of reasonably priced freshly cooked food, as well as cold salads and meat, from separate counter; Flowers Original and Wethereds on handpump, open all day; alone on the edge off Burnham Beeches — looks slightly continental among the trees *(Christian Leigh, Barbara Hatfield, P Gillbe, LYM)*

Littleworth Common [Common Lane — turn L by Jolly Woodman, then 1st R], *Blackwood Arms*: Tranquil atmosphere, even Sun lunchtimes, with a new area for diners, changing well kept real ales, pleasant service (though they could sometimes do with more people behind the bar on busy weekends), good-sized car park (*Barbara Hatfield*)

☆ **Long Crendon** [Bicester Rd (B4011); SP6808], *Angel*: Pleasantly refurbished partly 17th-century pub, warm and spotless, with fresh atmosphere, young welcoming staff, decent range of real ales, and fine range of generously if not quickly served good food inc fish delivered fresh thrice a week, and tender meats cooked just so; not cheap but good value (*D B Delany, Dr and Mrs R E S Tanner, Roger & Lynda Pilgrim*)

Long Crendon [Bicester Rd (B4011)], *Chandos Arms*: Thatched roof with peacock and beer jug designs; two communicating carpeted bars with low-beamed ceilings, wooden settles, chairs, tables and lots of brass and copperware; Wethereds and Whitbreads, no piped music, friendly and efficient service and well presented reasonably priced bar food; log fire, darts and shove-ha'penny in one bar (*Lyn and Bill Capper*)

☆ **Marlow** [West St; A4155 towards Henley; SU8586], *Ship*: Low-beamed town local with genuinely interesting collection of warship photographs and nautical equipment in twin side-by-side bars, straightfoward bar lunches from sandwiches upwards, well kept Marstons Pedigree, Wethereds, SPA and Winter Royal on handpump, cosy atmosphere, pleasant staff, piped music, tables on back terrace, evening restaurant; open all day Fri–Sat, and popular with young people on weekend evenings; children in restaurant (*Jon Wainwright, LYM*)

☆ **Marlow** [further along A4155 towards Henley], *Hare & Hounds*: Ivy-clad cottage on outskirts with calm, almost club-like atmosphere with restrained elegance but warm welcome for strangers, dove-grey carpeted bar on different levels, two log-effect gas fires; charming licensee, Wethereds, decent coffee, wide choice of good bar food, popular restaurant, small garden, large car park (*Ian Phillips*)

Marlow [A4155 a mile W of bridge; SU8586], *Bull*: Said to date from around 1250, and present building combines architectural beauty with a very luxurious interior: heraldic stained-glass bar window, real ale, comfortable seats and pleasant service (*E G Parish*); [High St], *Chequers*: popular roadside pub with two bars – one small and quiet, the other with rock music and young people, excellent food, friendly service, table on pavement, open all day; also own Highwayman, Woodcote (*Cdr W S D Hendry*); [Quoiting Sq], *Clayton Arms*: Eccentric local with exceptionally long-serving licensee, pre-war side lounge, excellent Brakspears and incredibly friendly customers inc local farmers, pensioners and archetypal darts players (*Jon Wainwright*); *Coach & Horses*: Large choice of good freshly cooked food, decent beer, reasonable prices (*Anon*)

☆ **Marsworth** [Startops End — village signed off B489 Dunstable—Aylesbury; SP9214], *White Lion*: Canalside pub which has had good food in bar and restaurant and well kept Marstons Pedigree; recently taken over as free house by licensee of the Black Horse, Chesham (see main entries), which promises particularly well for the future — should be well worth knowing; on GWG110 (*Reports please*)

Marsworth [Vicarage Rd], *Red Lion*: Partly thatched simple and unfussy pub close to impressive flight of canal locks, basic traditional furnishings and lively games area in tiled-floor main bar with two open fires, steps up to cosy parlour, straightforward food from back buttery (not Sun), well kept real ales such as ABC Best, Bass and Wadworths 6X, decent wines; tables in front, and in small sheltered back garden; children in games area until 8.30 (*Janet and Gary Amos, LYM*)

☆ **Mentmore** [SP9119], *Stag*: Small carpeted lounge bar with sturdy green leatherette seats around low oak tables, attractive fresh flower arrangements, open fire, and restaurant leading off; sturdily furnished public bar; good value well presented bar food from sandwiches to main dishes, with wider choice in the evenings; well kept Charles Wells Eagle, polite well dressed staff (service relaxed rather than speedy), charming sloping garden with floodlit pear tree; prices match the unusually civilised ambience (*Michael and Alison Sandy, BB*)

Milton Keynes [Exchange House; Midsummer Boulevard; SP8938], *Houstons*: More restaurant than pub, with expensive drinks, but fun (and includes night club, swimming pool and winter gardens); one large room divided into smoking and non-smoking areas, decorations inc an old petrol pump, a spaceman, an indian, an old bird cage hanging from the ceiling, and an old station clock bracketed on to the red brick wall; rectangular counter with stained glass around the top, piped music (*Roger Huggins*); [just below the Point, by garden centre], *Old Barn*: Well kept Flowers, usual good quality steak-house food (*Andrea and Guy Bradley*)

Naphill [SU8497], *Black Lion*: Small, quiet local with dining extension, Courage beers, and good value food from large menu; picnic-table sets on side lawn (*Geoff Lee, LYM*)

☆ **New Bradwell** [2 Bradwell Rd; SP8341], *New Inn*: Comfortable local by Grand Union Canal with some waterside tables, serving perfectly kept Charles Wells Eagle and Bombardier; food well prepared, with usual selection and a few more exciting dishes; dogs allowed (*John Baker, Geoff Roynon*)

Oving [off A413 Winslow rd out of Whitchurch; SP7821], *Black Boy*: Early 17th-century pub at end of superb green with panoramic view from terrace over plain towards Buckingham; warm and comfortable atmosphere, well kept Ind

Coope Burton, good choice of well prepared food in bar and (evenings Tues–Sat) restaurant *(J N Phillips)*

Owlswick [SP7806], *Hare & Hounds*: Beautifully placed free house by old village green; nice atmosphere in public bar and lounge; changing range of decent beers; service faultless, clean lavatories, large car park *(Richard Houghton)*

Penn [SU9193], *Horse & Jockey*: Pleasant local with changing Ind Coope-related beers such as Tetleys, and good food served till 10pm all week — lamb and pork gratin recommended *(Mike Tucker)*; [Elm Rd], *Red Lion*: Overlooks pleasant, well kept green with large duck pond; comfortable lounge, separate games room, unobtrusive piped music; Flowers, Wethereds and Whitbreads, good range of good value hot and cold bar food inc sandwiches and daily specials, efficient service; run by welcoming Liverpudlian couple *(Lyn and Bill Capper and others)*

☆ **Penn Street** [SU9295], *Hit or Miss*: Imaginative — and imaginatively described — food from sandwiches up in bar and restaurant of comfortably modernised low-beamed pub with own cricket ground, and good cricket memorabilia; open fire, no piped music or fruit machines; Hook Norton and Marstons Pedigree, wines by the glass, spacious restaurant, car park over rd *(Lyn and Bill Capper, BKA)*

Saunderton [SU8198], *Rose & Crown*: Feels (and looks) more like someone's lounge with helpful, friendly and somewhat eccentric service; well kept Morlands, Morrells and Wethereds, a good few whiskies and bar food with an emphasis on seafood; jolly atmosphere, separate restaurant *(Simon Collet-Jones)*

Shabbington [SP6607], *Old Fisherman*: Comfortable old pub with just the right amount of modernisation and delightful, rural, spacious grounds running down to small river with benches and tables; satisfactory Morrells Bitter, low-key friendliness from staff *(Dr Paul Kitchener)*

☆ **Skirmett** [Fingest rd off B482 at Bolter End, then follow Skirmett signs; SU7790], *Kings Arms*: Country pub in quiet and attractive valley, with inglenook fireplace and log fire in traditionally furnished high-beamed bar with more modern extension, wide range of bar food (not Sun evening) inc unusual as well as traditional dishes, using fresh vegetables and maybe herbs from the garden, small restaurant; well kept Brakspears and Whitbreads-related real ales, decent wine list, good service; seats on side lawn, attractive if not spacious (and quite pricey) bedrooms; children in eating area and restaurant *(Mrs A M S Jeeves, Sandra Kempson, LYM)*

☆ **Speen** [Flowers Bottom Lane; rd towards Lacey Green and Saunderton Stn — OS Sheet 165 map reference 835995; SU8399], *Old Plow*: Enchanting position, tucked in a deep fold of the Chilterns and surrounded by orchards, with oak beams, brick fireplaces,

horse brasses and harness in crisply cottagey interior; has had several changes of ownership in the last few years, but recent reports are of excellent though pricey food, with bar snacks as well as the restaurant side which has tended to dominate; well kept Brakspears, a good choice of wines; bedrooms *(R M Savage, JMC, Michael Thomson)*

Speen [Hampden Rd], *King William IV*: Now more country restaurant than pub, with whole of lounge as well as original no-smoking dining room now also given over to tables for eating, and only a restaurant menu — food good and well served, but not cheap; still has real ales such as Flowers and Ruddles, and is well run and spotless *(Mr and Mrs T F Marshall, R M Savage)*

☆ **St Leonards** [edge of Buckland Common — village signed off A4011 Wendover—Tring; SP9107], *White Lion*: Simple but neat open-plan Chilterns pub with old black beams, cushioned seats, log-effect gas fire; good value home cooking from sandwiches, filled baked potatoes and ploughman's to salads, sausage and egg, shepherd's pie and so forth (no hot main dishes Sat, no food Sun); well kept Benskins Best, Friary Meux Best and Ind Coope Burton on handpump, friendly service, unobtrusive piped music, small but attractive sheltered garden; provision for children *(David Wallington, BB)*

Stewkley [High St South; junction of Wing and Dunton rds; SP8526], *Carpenters Arms*: Promising new management in attractive old pub with sensible recent refurbishments inc back room opened into bar; bar food (also small restaurant in converted railway carriage), well kept Benskins and guest beers, pleasant service, warm atmosphere *(S V Bishop, LYM — more reports please)*

Stoke Goldington [SP8348], *White Hart*: Thatched pub with friendly staff, well kept Charles Wells and enterprising choice of other drinks, bar food; beams and quarry tiles in saloon, comfortable plush lounge, lively public bar, sheltered back lawn *(LYM)*

Stoke Hammond [SP8829], *Three Locks*: By popular section of Grand Union Canal (and large public car park), so can be very busy at holiday times; carpeted bar with food counter at one end, comprehensive range of bar food *(Lyn and Bill Capper)*

Stoke Poges [Gerrards Cross Rd (B416, Stoke Common) — OS Sheet 175 map reference 982857; SU9885], *Fox & Pheasant*: Popular for its Chef & Brewer carvery restaurant; the bar is smartly well appointed, a bit like a cocktail bar, but welcoming, with a relaxed atmosphere and good service; Watneys-related real ales (drinks not cheap here), decent straightforward bar food *(AP)*; [Hollybush Hill], *Rose & Crown*: Pleasant Courage pub with good decor and excellent atmosphere in small bar; picnic-table sets by good-sized car park *(Richard Houghton)*

Stokenchurch [nr M40 junction 5; SU7695],

Kings Arms: Popular, with generous bar snacks throughout opening hours; occasional evening entertainment *(Roger and Lynda Pilgrim)*

Stony Stratford [High St; SP7840], *Bull*: Vaults Bar considered as separate entity from hotel side (which has its own bar — and bedrooms), with good atmosphere; interesting display of articles on bar and hanging from ceiling, mostly agricultural or mechanical; good beer range such as ABC, Bass, Brakspears, Fullers London Pride, Marstons Pedigree, Theakstons and Wadworths 6X; food available; good opening hours, busy at weekends, live folk Sun *(Dominic Woodfield, LYM)*; [72 High St], *Cock*: Quiet, old-fashioned and unpretentious hotel with handsome old oak settles in otherwise straightforward bar, Adnams and Courage Directors, good choice of lunchtime bar food, attentive service; bedrooms *(LYM)*

☆ **Taplow** [Station Rd; SU9082], *Oak & Saw*: Popular and friendly pub in quiet village with old photographs of area, good mix of customers; good value food, pleasant staff, well kept Courage, separate eating area *(TBB, Richard Houghton)*

☆ **The Lee** [back roads 2 1/2 miles N of Great Missenden, E of A413; SP8904], *Cock & Rabbit*: Stylish and comfortable Italian-owned pub, with imaginative and attractively served food, all home-made, using local produce; friendly staff, real ales such as Flowers, Morlands and Wethereds, decent wines, and big garden with tables on verandah, terraces and lawn; well worth knowing, though bar food prices (not Sun or Mon evening) are rather high for a pub, and the character of the place is closer to a country restaurant; children in eating area and restaurant *(Peter Watkins, Pam Stanley, Andrea and Guy Bradley, AP, LYM)*

The Lee [Lee Common], *Gate*: Pleasant situation, reasonable food and good beer, especially Wadworths Farmers Glory; can get a bit crowded some evenings *(Mark Evans)*

Thornborough [4 miles E of Buckingham on A421 outside village — pub name on OS165; SP7433], *Lone Tree*: Quite small and cosy ABC pub, with dining tables at one end; good menu — prawns, game pie, steaks and puddings all recommended *(Hazel Church)*

Twyford [SP6626], *Red Lion*: 17th-century pub in quiet, pretty setting at end of cul-de-sac; nice old-fashioned atmosphere, friendly landlord, ABC and Ind Coope Burton ales, and good choice of hot dishes; picnic-table sets on front lawn *(Lyn and Bill Capper)*

Wavendon [not far from M1 junctions 13 and 14; SP9137], *Plough*: Pretty village pub with friendly mix of locals and business people, good value bar food (not Sun, nor Mon and Tues evening) *(Monica Darlington)*

Wendover [High St; SP8607], *Red Lion*: Pleasant staff, good food and choice of real ales in beamed hotel bar and restaurant; bedrooms *(Dennis and Pat Jones)*

Whaddon [SP8034], *Lowndes Arms*: Friendly place with well kept ABC beers; main attraction the food, particularly the good value steaks in a range of sizes *(Virginia Jones)*

☆ **Wheelerend Common** [just off A40; SU8093], *Brickmakers Arms*: Spacious, panelled pub in attractive spot, with interesting shortish walks nearby; comfortable seats and tables, friendly, helpful staff, good value food, particularly steak and kidney pudding, decent range of beers; large garden, popular in summer, with children's play area; good-sized car park *(Dr Paul Kitchener, A J Vere)*

Wheelerend Common [about 1/2 mile from Lane End], *Chequers*: Pleasant old free house, welcoming licensee, well kept beer, wide range of bar food from sandwiches up *(Richard Houghton)*

☆ **Winchmore Hill** [The Hill; SU9394], *Plough*: Clean and comfortably modernised spacious bar overlooking green, several interconnecting areas, some interesting nick-nacks, wide choice of reasonably priced and generously served bar food, well kept real ales such as Theakstons and Youngers Scotch and IPA, neat helpful staff, piped music, tables on lawn with wishing well; restaurant named after landlady Barbara Windsor *(Richard Houghton, BB)*

Winslow [Market Sq; SP7627], *Bell*: Under new management, this elegant black and white timbered inn has a plush lounge, restaurant-style bar food, good Sun lunch, well kept Adnams, Marstons Pedigree and Wadworths 6X on handpump, and decent wines; piped music; restaurant, tables in pleasant inner courtyard; sadly, the little 18th-century tap room has now gone; bedrooms *(S V Bishop, Sidney and Erna Wells, Mr and Mrs Allan Chapman, M J Morgan, Michael and Alison Sandy, LYM)*

Wooburn Common [Wooburn Common Rd; about 3 1/2 miles from M40 junction 2; SU9387], *Royal Standard*: Cleanly decorated and civilised pub, popular particularly on weekend evenings, with well kept Whitbreads-related real ales, pleasant atmosphere, reasonably priced bar food, seats out behind; children welcome *(Nick Dowson, Alison Hayward, LYM)*

☆ **Wooburn Moor** [Watery Lane — OS Sheet 175 map reference 913898; SU9189], *Falcon*: Friendly, small, low-beamed pub with relaxing atmosphere, good variety of customers, well kept Flowers Original, Wethereds and another Whitbreads-related guest beer such as Fremlins; lovely, well kept garden, big car park *(Nick Dowson, Alison Hayward, Richard Houghton)*

Cambridgeshire and Bedfordshire

This is a relatively expensive area for pubs, with both drinks and food prices above the national average. But the Three Tuns at Biddenham and that lovely little pub the Cock at Broom both set a fine example for bargain food and drink, selling beers at least 10p a pint below the area's average, and comfortably beating our £1 target for decent snacks and the £3 target for more substantial dishes. It's worth noting that we find pubs tied to regional or local breweries here (and in practice that most often tends to mean Greene King) tend to be cheaper than free houses, and substantially cheaper than pubs tied to the national combines. Interesting new entries here this year include the Anchor and the Mill, both in attractive spots in Cambridge itself, and recently refurbished each in a quite different style that successfully catches the mood of the times; the John Barleycorn at Duxford (a comfortable well run place, popular for eating out); and the Queens Head at Fowlmere, kept deliberately simple yet welcoming, with a fine approach to cheeses as a pub staple (and a fair-minded attitude to wine pricing). Though it's by no means difficult to find a good pub meal here, especially good food's currently to be had at the Crafty Fox out on the fens near Chatteris, the Pheasant at Keyston (its bar has been extended this year, and a conservatory's been added) and the Anchor in its fine riverside position at Sutton Gault, while the Queens Head at Newton – like the Cock at Broom – shows that food doesn't need to be smart or expensive to be really good. Changes are under way at the Olde Ferry Boat at Holywell (a young and enthusiastic landlord – though the pub has ancient roots it's not seeming such an antique nowadays) and the grand old Haycock at Wansford – which seems to sprout yet another wing every time we see it, yet always seems to preserve its attractive blend of character and civility. Another place always worth a visit to catch up on the latest development is the Bell at Stilton; gradual careful restoration continues at this handsome old coaching inn which originally popularised the cheese named after the village – though not coming from there. In the Lucky Dip section at the end of the chapter, Cambridge stands out as increasingly rewarding to the pub lover, with 20 recommended pubs there as well as the six in the main section. Elsewhere, Lucky Dip pubs notching up particularly promising popularity scores in the last few months include the Hardwicke Arms at Arrington, Millstone at Barnack, Royal Oak at Hail Weston, Three Horseshoes at Madingley, Pike & Eel near Needingworth, Rose & Crown at Ridgmont, Red Lion at Swaffham Prior, and Three Cranes at Turvey. The substantial refurbishment of the Red Lion at Grantchester sounds a success; and it's really only a shortage of readers' reports which has kept the Racehorse at Catworth, Kings Head at Dullingham, George & Dragon at Elsworth, Pheasant at Great Chishill, John o' Gaunt at Sutton and

Three Blackbirds at Woodditton – all of them known to us as good pubs – out of the main entries this year.

BARRINGTON (Cambs) TL3949 Map 5
Royal Oak

From M11 junction 11, take A10 for Royston; village signposted on right after 3 1/2 miles

This thatched and heavily timbered pub is attractively positioned across from the village's unusually long green, where you can sit under cocktail parasols in summer. Good bar food, served by friendly staff, includes sandwiches (from £1.45), soup (£1.75), ploughman's (£2.75), omelettes (£3.35), salads (from around £3), home-made steak and kidney pie (£4.20), a good selection of vegetarian dishes like a hazelnut, pineapple and pepper pancake, popular moussaka, pasta, nut cutlet, walnut roulade with a sweet and sour sauce or Challis cottage crumble (from £3.90 to £4.20), and 8oz sirloin steak (£7.75); puddings such as home-made apple strudel (£2). The tile-floored rooms ramble into each other, and are decorated with brass, copper, antlers and harness. The building itself dates back to the 14th century – look out for the fine Tudor brickwork above a mantlebeam in the large central chimney, now opened up as a sort of connecting lobby. Well kept Adnams and Greene King IPA and Abbot on handpump; fruit machine, piped music and skittle alley. One of the restaurant areas is no-smoking. *(Recommended by Drs M and K Parier, Paul Harrop, Derek Patey, Gordon Theaker, Nigel Gibbs, Sandra Cook, NAC)*

Free house   Licensees Robert and Elizabeth Nicholls   Real ale   Meals and snacks (12–2, 6.30–10.30)   Restaurant tel Cambridge (0223) 870791   Children in eating areas   Open 11.30–2.30, 6.30–11

BIDDENHAM (Beds) TL0249 Map 5
Three Tuns

57 Main Road; village signposted from A428 just W of Bedford

There's an attractively wide range of bar food in this stone village pub, ranging from sandwiches (from 90p), excellent home-made soup (95p; they also do soup and a choice of sandwich for £1.55 – an idea it would be nice if other pubs copied) and pâté (£1.50), through several ploughman's (£1.80), burgers (from £2.30) and salads (£2.30; prawn £3.20), to various hot dishes such as quiche, lasagne or chilli con carne (£2.90), home-made chicken casserole or steak and kidney pie (£3.50), evening steaks (£6), and specials such as excellent seafood gratin; children's menu (£1.30). Beneath the thatch and the low beams in the comfortable lounge there are country paintings on the walls. Table skittles as well as darts, dominoes, fruit machine, and piped music in the livelier public bar; very well kept Greene King IPA and Abbot on handpump. The big garden, popular with families, has doves and a dovecote. *(Recommended by Richard Dolphin, Colleen Holiday, J Morley, Pete Storey, Wayne Brindle; more reports please)*

Greene King   Licensees Alan and Tina Wilkins   Real ale   Meals and snacks (not Sun)   Children in small dining room   Open 11.30–2.30, 6–11

BOLNHURST (Beds) TL0859 Map 5
Olde Plough

B660 Bedford–Kimbolton

Last year's hopes that this ancient cottage would re-open after fire damage sadly weren't fulfilled, but the careful refurbishment that's been going on for some time now *should* almost certainly have been completed by the end of 1990. The carpeted lounge bar will have black beams, little armchairs around low tables, a leather sofa and a leather armchair, and a log fire in the big stone fireplace; a room leading off here has some dining tables. The public bar will have two refectory tables, a pair of settles and other seats on the flagstones, a big woodburning stove, and darts, dominoes, cribbage, Trivial Pursuit, pool, hood skittles and fruit machine; the cats are called Chubbs, Blacky and Titch. Bar food should be along traditional lines – home-made soup, ploughman's, steak and kidney pie and so forth. The pretty garden has an established rock bank (where there's the remains of a moat under trees), as well as rustic seats and tables, and a long crazy-paved terrace. *(More reports please)*

Free house   Licensee M J Horridge   Real ale   Meals and snacks (not 25 Dec) Restaurant tel Colmworth (023 062) 274   Well behaved children till 9pm   Open 12–2.30 (3 Sat), 7–11; closed 25 Dec

BROOM (Beds)   TL1743   Map 5

Cock ★ ⊘

23 High Street; from A1 opposite northernmost Biggleswade turnoff follow Old Warden 3, Aerodrome 2 signpost, and take first left signposted Broom

It's the combination of rustic simplicity and outstanding management that so consistently charms readers in this fine old pub overlooking the village green. There's no bar counter – the very well kept Greene King IPA and Abbot are tapped straight from the cask in the cellar – and each of the four rooms only has two or three tables, some with fresh flowers on neat gingham tablecloths. The layout is attractively old-fashioned: antique tile floors, low ochre ceilings, stripped panelling and built-in furnishings – cupboards, uncushioned wall benches and simple latch doors. A central corridor runs down the middle of the building, with the sink for washing glasses on one side (pewter mugs hang over it) and on the other steps down to the cellar. Bar food is highly praised for its freshness and presentation; though they also serve a good, filling game or onion soup (80p), sandwiches (from 95p, toasties from 75p), salads (£2.95), pork and rabbit, game or shepherd's pies (£2.95), they keep around twenty different cheeses in fine condition – mostly English. These come in sandwiches or in variations on the ploughman's theme, from the simplest (£1.65) to several tailored to the taste of an individual cheese (£1.95–2.95), and even a sweet dessert cheese (£1.35); service is most friendly. Winter log fires, hood skittles, darts, shove-ha'penny, cribbage, and dominoes in one front room, unobtrusive piped music; it can be extremely busy at weekends. There are picnic-table sets on the terrace by the back lawn; the pétanque pitch out here is new. *(Recommended by Pete Storey, Mr and Mrs Gwyse, Colleen Holiday, J D Maplethorpe, Gwen and Peter Andrews, M B P Carpenter, Barbara and Norman Wells, J S Rutter, J R Smylie, K Leist, G L Tong, Tony and Lynne Stark, Roger Danes, Nigel Paine, Janet and Gary Amos, M J Horridge, S J Curtis, Trevor Rule, John Baker)*

Greene King   Licensees Martin and Brenda Murphy   Real ale   Meals and snacks (not evenings Sun or Bank Holidays)   Children away from area where drinks dispensed Open 12–2.30, 6–11

CAMBRIDGE   TL4658   Map 5

Anchor

Silver St

In a marvellous spot right by the river (where there are punts for hire – with a boatman if needed), this lively pub, popular with students, is set out on several levels. The downstairs cafe-bar (open all day) has settles, farmhouse chairs, hefty stools and round wooden tables on the bare boards, and a workmanlike brass footrail along the bar counter (where there's also a glass food cabinet). Steps take you down to a similar though simpler flagstoned room with picnic-table sets and display cabinets to do with brewing; french windows lead out to a suntrap terrace with more picnic-table sets and some tubs of flowers. An area by the entrance has leatherette armchairs and a brick fire at one end, and a chesterfield, a couple of stools and another brick fireplace at the other; there's a mix of college and local photographs on the walls, and a few plants. The upstairs bar (closed in the afternoon) has ceiling fans and a huge domed glass light, a wooden bar counter with a modern glass and brass gantry, and bar stools by stained-glass shelves that look over a plusher area; the windows here have good riverside views. Bar food includes sausage roll (60p), pasty (£1.10), sandwiches (from £1.15), ploughman's (£2.95), and scampi (£3.95), with specials like meaty or vegetarian lasagne (from £2.75) and Sunday roast (£3.50); they serve doughnuts (55p) and cheesecake (£1.25) throughout the afternoon. Well kept Flowers Original, Wethereds and Whitbreads Castle Eden on handpump; cheerful young service, piped music, various trivia and fruit machines. *(Recommended by Wayne Brindle, Alan and Ruth Woodhouse)*

Whitbreads Licensee Kevin Atkins Real ale Meals (12–2) and snacks (11–2.15); not evenings Children welcome until 7 Live jazz Tues and Thurs evenings Open 11–11 Mon-Sat; open all Sun afternoon for tea and cakes

Boathouse

14 Chesterton Road; one-way section of ring road, by A10 Ely turn-off

Looking across to Jesus Green, with barges moored between the pub and a nearby lock, this is a most attractive – and popular – spot in summer. The bar itself consists of little partitioned snugs by net-curtained etched-glass windows on the roadside, a U-shaped serving counter, paisley-pattern wallpaper and dark Anaglypta, bookshelves and small prints, and steps up to an airier part – hung with oars and inverted sections of boats – with big windows overlooking the riverside garden and its picnic tables. Adnams, Boddingtons, Flowers IPA and Original, Greene King Abbot, Marstons Pedigree and Whitbreads Castle Eden on handpump; piped jazz, two fruit machines. Bar food is quickly served from a side counter and includes soup (£1.40), filled baked potatoes (from £1.80), hot beef sandwiches (£1.90), salads (from £2.20), steak and kidney pie (£3.85) and 8oz rump steak (£6), with four or five specials such as aubergine and parmesan bake (£3.55) and chicken Madras (£3.85), with Sunday lunches, and filled rolls normally available through the afternoon. Formerly the Rob Roy, this was closed and virtually derelict until Whitbreads reopened it a couple of years ago. *(Recommended by Wayne Brindle, Ben Wimpenny, Steve Waters; more reports please)*

Whitbreads Real ale Meals and snacks Jazz Sun evening Open 11–11

Cambridge Blue

85 Gwydir Street

Leased to Banks & Taylors by the owners of the Free Press, this attractively straightforward pub is favoured for its fine range of real ales, well kept on handpump: Banks & Taylors Shefford, SOS, SOD, and a variety of guest beers, as well as Weston's scrumpy. They're complemented by a good choice of home-made pies and cold meats served with as many salads as you like (from £3.30), soup (£1.30), quiche (£2.95), macaroni cheese (£2.50), and curries, vegetarian or meaty lasagne or nut roast (£2.95); Sunday roast lunch. The two small, low-ceilinged rooms (one of them no-smoking) are simply furnished with stripped kitchen chairs and some cushioned built-in wall benches around a medley of tables on dark red linoleum, and on the buttery Anaglypta walls there are lots of university sports photographs and paintings for sale by local artists; shove-ha'penny, cribbage, dominoes; the atmosphere is warmly pubby, and often busy. French windows open on to a sheltered terrace, with picnic-table sets among some shrubs, and a children's climbing frame; pétanque and barbecues in summer. *(Recommended by Michael Spriggs, Drs M and K Parier, Wayne Brindle, Steve Waters, Yvonne Lahaise, John Bromell, Alan and Ruth Woodhouse, Catherine Allerton)*

Banks & Taylors Managers Nick Winnington and Mandy Cant Real ale Meals and snacks (12–2, 6–9.30; not Sun evening) Open 12–2.30(3.30 Sat), 6–11; closed evening 25 Dec

Free Press

Prospect Row

A particular distinction in this traditional and busy back-street place is that it's the only pub we know of that doubles as a boat club – so it can show off its collection of oars and rowing photographs with more legitimacy than most Cambridge pubs. Well kept Greene King IPA and Abbot on handpump – one room is served from a hatch; furnishings are simple but authentic; the snug – which doubles as the eating area – is no-smoking. Good, wholesome bar food includes soup such as curried parsley or carrot and orange (£1), chilli con carne (£2), lemon chicken (£3.55), and cold dishes such as pies, quiches or vegetarian pâtés with interesting salads such as pear with mayonnaise and a dash of tabasco or marinated carrot and parsnip (£2.90-£4.10); puddings such as home-made treacle tart or raspberry shortcakes (from £1.30); you're advised to get there early if you want a seat. The sheltered and paved garden at the rear is quite a sun trap. *(Recommended by Michael Spriggs, P Argent, Alan and Ruth Woodhouse, W H Bland, Wayne Brindle, Drs M and K Parier, Pete Storey, Steve Waters, Nigel Gibbs, Richard Sanders)*

Greene King Licensees Chris and Debbie Lloyd Real ale Meals and snacks (12–2, 6–8.30) Children welcome Open 12–2.30, 6–11

Mill

Mill Lane

During the first half of 1990, this popular riverside pub served 106 different well kept real ales. On handpump and chalked up on a board, these included on our visit Camerons Strongarm, Crouch Vale Best and SAS, Nethergate Bitter, Palmers IPA, Robinsons Best and Smiles Best, though they change constantly; they also have farm ciders and English country wines. The relaxed but busy U-shaped bar has a small area at one end with built-in planked wall benches, an open brick fireplace, a display case with clay pipes, lots of photographs of college games teams, and a glass food cabinet. Kitchen chairs, chunky stools, settles and a mix of wooden tables sit on the bare boards (or ancient quarry tiles) of the rest of the bar, oars with past names of Pembroke College rowers are nailed to the beams, and there are photographs of brewing tuns, display cases of brewery taps and slings, and shelves of miscellaneous jars, tins and old bottles. Bar food includes sandwiches (from £1.25, doorsteps from £1.95), filled baked potatoes (from £1.75), giant Yorkshire puddings filled with sausage and beans or stew (£2.85), salads (from £2.95), daily specials such as shepherd's pie or a vegetarian dish (£2.95) and a huge ploughman's with grapes, an apple, pickles and so forth (£3.80); they serve buns and sandwiches till 6pm. Pleasant and efficient male staff; dominoes, cribbage, shove-ha'penny, bar skittles and piped pop music. The hanging baskets and window boxes are pretty in summer, and the main punt station is next door. There are a few other pubs, mainly in the North of England, in this chain of Tap & Spile back-to-basics real ale pubs, which Camerons started up in Byker. *(Recommended by W H Bland, Graham and Glenis Watkins, Frank Cummins)*

Free house Licensee J H Gibbs Real ale Meals and snacks (12–2, though buns and sandwiches till 6pm) Children welcome at lunchtime Open 11–11

Old Spring

Ferry Path (pub's car park is on Chesterton Road)

The decor and furnishings here look considerably older than they actually are – the bare boards, earth-coloured rough plaster walls, cushioned small settles, pews, stools and traditional tables are all the result of a well executed renovation of recent years. The gas lighting (electricity is more or less confined to lighting some of the countryside and romantic pictures) makes the atmosphere attractively subdued, but also rather hot if it's busy. A newer conservatory/restaurant blends in well with the core of the pub. Well kept Greene King IPA and Abbot and Rayments on handpump, two fruit machines and a couple of open fires. Bar food includes ploughman's (£2.75), Greek dips with pitta bread (£3.55), sausage and tomato pie, chilli con carne or vegetarian pasta bake (all around £4), steak (£6.50), and fish such as shark or swordfish; Sunday roast, and summer barbecues. *(Recommended by Wayne Brindle; more up-to-date reports please)*

Greene King Real ale Meals and snacks (11–3, 5.30–9.30) Restaurant tel Cambridge (0223) 357228 Children in conservatory Open 11–3, 5.30–11; open all day Sat nr CHATTERIS (Cambs)   TL3883 Map 5

Crafty Fox 🏮

Pickle Fen; B1050 towards St Ives

It's the attention to detail in the almost entirely home-made range of food that so distinguishes this country pub – such as, in summer, asparagus with butter that the licensee gets from his parents in Jersey, or gammon, cooked overnight in cider and mustard then glazed with honey; there's also winter soup, sandwiches on request at lunchtime, cockles and garlic bread (£2.25), mushrooms in wine (£2.50), interesting vegetarian dishes such as courgette and walnut bake (£4.45), chicken and lime chilli or beef and mushroom lasagne (£5.45), and more expensive dishes such as crab thermidor (£6.45), steaks (from £7.95), and king prawns (£8.25), with crisp, zestily dressed side salads; puddings such as chocolate brandy cake or apple crumble (£1.50); though there's a lot of flexibility in the arrangements – so, for example, they may be willing to make up a starter into more of a main course if you just want a light lunch – they do stress that it's best to phone ahead to book: it's a small, remote and popular place. The eating area is charmingly atmospheric, with soft lighting (some candles at night), fresh flowers and a mix of country kitchen chairs around its half-dozen tables; an attractive wall seat is built into a corner by the stone fireplace; fieldmouse paintings, avocet and hunting prints and a plan of the Spithead royal fleet review of 1977 decorate the walls. A more or less open screen divides off the main area from a small corner around the serving bar, from which you can see into the spotless kitchen. In summer the pub's great pride is an extensive conservatory terrace shaded by properly cared-for grape vines, with a small fountain, coloured lights, and a barbecue for Sunday lunchtimes (though if you book in advance, they will arrange a do-it-yourself barbecue in the week); the shade netting is a useful idea. Note, though, that if the terrace is being used for a private function the kitchens won't be doing any food for the rest of the pub – another reason for phoning if you want to eat. Well kept Adnams Bitter, Wadworths 6X and maybe a guest on handpump, Weizenthaler (proper lager imported from Germany) on draught, and decent wines; cribbage, dominoes, draughts, backgammon, chess, and faint piped music. The licensee (Tim Lough) is a retired submariner. *(Recommended by Frank Gadbois, Alan and Ruth Woodhouse)*

Free house   Licensees Tim Lough and David Skeggs   Real ale   Meals and snacks (bookings Chatteris (035 43) 2266; after 9.30pm if booked in advance; no food 25 Dec, 1 Jan or Bank Holiday evenings)   Well behaved children in eating area (not after their bedtime)   Open 11–3, 6–11

COTON (Cambs)   TL4058 Map 5

Plough 🏮

Under a mile from M11 junction 13; left on to A1303, then village signposted left – once on this side road don't turn off right at the Village, Church signpost; though this junction is exit only northbound and entrance only southbound, you can quickly get back to the motorway by heading straight on past the pub to the nearby junction 12 – which also gives signposted access to the village if you're heading south on the M11

At edge of village; clean white walls with big windows, comfortable leatherette dining and bucket chairs, ladderback chairs, wheelback chairs and brocaded wall banquettes; woodburning stove; patterned red carpet. One way of reaching this attractive country pub is by taking the Wimpole Way footpath from the centre of Cambridge. The bar itself is in a large, modern bright extension, with comfortable seats and long machine tapestry-upholstered banquettes around polished tables on either side of an arched dividing wall, and a woodburning stove. The front part of the building, with its fine beams, is largely given over to the restaurant. However it's also possible to enjoy much of the food in the bar, where the choice, praised for its freshness and presentation, ranges from sandwiches (from £1.20), decent home-made soups (£1.40), ploughman's (£2.20) and salads (from £4.30, beef £5.30), to quite a lot of fish such as grilled trout or lemon sole (£4.50) or fresh Scotch salmon (£5.80), gammon (£5) and steaks (from £8.20), with specials such as excellent dressed Cromer crab (£5); service is attentive and efficient; the restaurant is held in some esteem by readers. Well kept Flowers Original on handpump, and fresh orange juice; piped music. The delightful back garden has a summer house and some groups of seats among the trees and shrubs. *(Recommended by John Tyzack, Margaret White, Dr and Mrs R E S Tanner, M and J Back, E A George, Frank Cummins, Mrs E M Thompson, G F Scott)*

Whitbreads   Licensees Mr and Mrs Barrie Ashworth   Real ale   Meals and snacks (not 25 or 26 Dec)   Restaurant tel Madingley (0954) 210489   Children in eating area Open 11–2.30, 6–11

DUXFORD (Cambs)   TL4745 Map 5

John Barleycorn ⊘

Moorfield Rd; village signposted off A1301; pub at far end of village

The front of this low, early 17th-century thatched pub is exceptionally pretty in summer when the hanging baskets, tubs and flowerbeds are a mass of colour. There are a couple of picnic-table sets out here, with more in the back garden along a little grass area surrounded by roses and flowering shrubs, and filled with bird-song; a converted barn with ancient timbers has some back-to-back seats, and there's a brick barbecue. Inside, the dimly lit bar is attractively furnished with high-backed booth-type oak settles, some wheelback chairs and chunky country tables, autumnal-coloured curtains to match the cushions, a raised brick fireplace with horsebrasses hung along the mantlebeam and a shotgun on the wall above, and a mix of old prints, decorative plates (including game ones), photographs of the pub, brass lamps, a ship's clock and some scales, horse bits and reins, and a stuffed hooded crow; the room is broken up by a brick pillar and a couple of standing timbers, and the atmosphere is quietly chatty (though there is piped light jazz piano), with the emphasis very much on food. Popular with local business people at lunchtime, this includes toasties (from £1.70), filled baked potatoes (£2.05), generous ploughman's (from £2.50), spare ribs (£4.30), very good Turkish lamb with nuts and fruit (£4.90), spiced beef with dumplings (£5), casseroled pigeon (£5.10), salads (from £5.10), smoked haddock with poached eggs (£5.20), and poached salmon (£7.40). Well kept Greene King Abbot, IPA and XX and KK on handpump, several decent wines by the glass, and very efficient, courteous service. Dominoes, cribbage, shove-ha'penny. *(Recommended by Nigel Gibbs, Sandra Cook, Joy Heatherley)*

Greene King   Licensee Henry Sewell   Real ale   Meals and snacks (12–2, 7–10) Morris dancers 2 or 3 times during summer   Open 11.30–2.30, 6.30–11; closed 25 Dec

ELTISLEY (Cambs)   TL2659 Map 5

Leeds Arms ⇔

The Green; village signposted off A45

This straightforward but well kept white brick house overlooks the large and peaceful village green (a fine place to spend a drowsy afternoon); the beamed lounge bar consists of two rooms knocked together, with a third, recently refurbished, down some steps and dominated by tables with cushioned wheelback chairs. There are also red plush stools, pew-like cushioned wall benches, and a huge winter log fire with brass hunting horns and decorative plates on the mantlepiece. Well kept Greene King IPA on handpump; darts, shove-ha'penny, dominoes, a fruit machine sensibly set aside in an alcove, and piped music; they also sell confectionery. Good value bar food includes sandwiches (from £1), home-made soup (£1), ploughman's (£1.60), home-made curry or chilli con carne (£3), trout (£3.50), salads (from £4), home-made steak and kidney or chicken pie (£3.75), scampi (£4.25), and steaks (from £7.75); puddings include home-made apple pie (£1); good, friendly service. The garden is well provisioned with swings, slides and picnic-table sets among the silver birches on the lawn. The bedrooms, plainly furnished but comfortable and well equipped, are in a separate block beyond the garden. *(Recommended by Simon Collet-Jones, Wayne Brindle, Barry and Anne, P J and S E Robbins, M McCrum)*

Free house   Licensee George Cottrell   Real ale   Meals and snacks (12–2, 7–9.45)
Restaurant (not Sun evening)   Children in restaurant   Open 11.30–2.30, 6.30–11
Bedrooms tel Croxton (048 087) 283; £32.50B/£40B

ETTON (Cambs)   TF1406   Map 5

Golden Pheasant

Village just off B1443, just E of Helpston level crossing; and will no doubt be signposted
from near N end of new A15 Peterborough bypass

Described by one reader as like the drawing room of an hospitable lord of the
manor, the bar here runs across the whole front of the square stone-built house;
furnishings are comfortable, with high-backed button-back maroon plush settles
built against the walls and around the corners, some spindleback chairs, and Lloyd
Loom chairs around glass-topped cane tables in the airy, glass-walled side room;
there's also quite a high burnt ochre Anaglypta ceiling, a patterned red carpet and
little gilt fringe-shaded wall lamps. Open fire, fruit machine, well reproduced and
chosen piped pop music, Adnams, Batemans XXXB, Courage Directors, Greene
King IPA, Marstons Pedigree, and two guest beers each week on handpump, and
some decent malt whiskies. Good value bar food includes French onion soup
(£1.40), ploughman's (from £2.50), chicken tikka (£4), beef stroganoff (£5.25) and
pork massala or rump steak (£7); barbecue summer Sunday lunchtimes. The
stone-walled garden, surrounded by tall trees, looks out across flat countryside;
pétanque is played here in summer. The big paddock is safe for children.
(Recommended by John Baker, Nic James; more reports on service please)

Free house   Real ale   Meals and snacks (12–2, 6–9.30; not Sun evening)   Restaurant
tel Peterborough (0733) 252387   Children in conservatory   Open 11.30–3.30,
5.30–11 (all day Fri, Sat)

FEN DRAYTON (Cambs)   TL3368   Map 5

Three Tuns 🅐

High Street; village signposted off A604 NW of Cambridge

Consistently praised bar food in this attractive thatched pub includes sandwiches
with a choice of brown, white or French bread (from £1), home-made soup
(£1.80), home-made chicken liver and bacon pâté (£1.90), Greek dips (£2.20),
ploughman's (£2.50), home-made dishes such as meaty or vegetarian lasagne or
chicken curry (£3.20), salads (from £3), gammon with pineapple (£4.40), chicken
Kiev (£5.30), 8oz rump steak (£6.50), and puddings like home-made apple pie
(from £1.20); lovely garlic bread; friendly service. Beneath the moulded and very
heavy early Tudor beams there are cushioned settles and an interesting variety of
chairs, big portraits and old photographs of local scenes, brass plates on the
timbered walls, old crockery in a corner dresser, and two inglenook fireplaces, one
of which should always be alight. Greene King XX, IPA and Abbot on air pressure,
a range of malt whiskies, sensibly placed darts, shove-ha'penny, dominoes,
cribbage, and fruit machine. A well tended lawn at the back has tables under
cocktail parasols, apple and flowering cherry trees, and some children's play
equipment. The unusual inn sign consists of three tiny barrels sitting on a pole, and
the building may have been the medieval guild hall for the pretty village. It can get
very crowded. *(Recommended by Gordon Theaker, M D Hare, Wayne Brindle, Frank
Cummins, Mrs E M Thompson; more reports please)*

Greene King   Licensee Michael Nugent   Meals and snacks (12–2, 7–10; not Sun evening)
Children in eating area before 8pm   Open 11–2.30, 6.30–11; closed evening 25 Dec

FOWLMERE (Cambs)   TL4245   Map 5

Chequers

B1368

This 16th-century former coaching inn has two comfortably furnished communicating rooms; upstairs there are beams, wall timbering and some interesting moulded plasterwork above the fireplace, and downstairs has prints and photographs of Spitfires and Mustangs flown from Fowlmere aerodrome; open log fire. The garden is particularly well looked after, with white tables under cocktail parasols among the flowers and shrub roses. Tolly on handpump, freshly squeezed orange juice, a good choice of vintage and late-bottled ports by the glass and an excellent range of fine brandies and liqueurs; there's a cruover machine so that fine wines can be kept in perfect condition for serving by the glass. Bar food — which has regained readers' confidence after a blip last year — isn't cheap but it is ambitious and original: stilton and walnut pâté (£2.80), soft herring roes with black butter and capers (£3.10), bacon and prawn salad (£4.40) and tacos (£4.40). Look out for the priest's hole above the bar. The atmosphere is discreet, civilised and friendly. *(Recommended by BHP, Nigel Gibbs, Sandra Cook, John Evans, Drs M and K Parier, J P Cinnamond, Henry Midwinter, John Tyzack, M Fisher, Joy Heatherley)*

Tolly   Licensee Norman Rushton   Real ale   Meals and snacks (12–2, 7–10) Children welcome   Restaurant tel Fowlmere (076 382) 369   Open 12–2.30, 6–11; closed 25 Dec

Queens Head

Long Lane; turn left by war memorial, pub on corner

After considerable much-needed refurbishments, this pretty thatched 17th-century cottage has been re-opened by the new, hard-working licensees. In the main room they've uncovered some panelling along one wall and around the bar, opened up the brick fireplace, and furnished it simply with farmhouse chairs and brocaded stools around wooden tables, some attractive old portrait photographs, a photograph of the pub and a couple of decorative plates, and a few horsebrasses along a beam; on two shelves to one side of the fireplace are some books, an old clock, and shove-ha'penny, dominoes, cribbage and shut-the-box; also darts, fruit machine, a pop quiz competition schedule — they are hoping to install ring-the-bull. The cosy little beamed lounge bar (where families are allowed) has wheelbacks and other similar furniture, half-panelled walls and bar counter, another brick fireplace, and walls decorated with some prints, plates and horsebrasses. They specialise in cheeses (£2.20 – doggy bags provided) which come with a choice of breads such as granary, herb and onion, mild garlic, wholemeal rye and wholemeal walnut: farmhouse cheddar, brie, blue stilton, edam, white cheshire, smoked bavarian, Nutcracker (cheddar with walnuts), popular gouda with nettles, wensleydale, Celebration, Bellshire and rutland. Other bar food includes home-made soups like butterbean and tomato or creamed stilton and onion (£1.30), doorstep sandwiches made with wholemeal bread (from £1.20; they do a take-away service, too – £1.10) and pâté (£2.20). Greene King IPA and Abbot on handpump, attractively priced wines, coffee. The sizeable garden (half of which was under construction as we went to press) has picnic-table sets; they plan to add a non-working 1953 Fordson tractor for children to play on. *(More reports please)*

Greene King   Licensees Howard and Sue Gascoyne   Real ale   Meals and snacks (12–2, 5.30–7.30; 12–2.30 weekends)   Children welcome   Open 12–2.30, 5.30–11; 12–4, 7–11 Sat – may open longer if trade demands

HEYDON (Cambs)   TL4340 Map 5

King William IV

Village signposted from A505 W of M11 junction 10; bear right in village

The quantity of agricultural implements in the rambling rooms of this village pub borders on the overwhelming — the standing props, wall timbers and dark oak beams are covered with ploughshares, yokes, iron tools, cowbells, beer steins, samovars, cut-glass, brass or black wrought-iron lamps, copper-bound casks and milk ewers, harness, horsebrasses, smith's bellows and decorative plates. It even spills out into the pretty garden, where there are pieces of old farming machinery as well as a paddock with Jacob sheep, a donkey, geese, rabbit, guinea pigs and fan tail doves. Some tables in the bar are made of great slabs of wood slung on black chains from the ceiling. Bar food includes soup (£1.30), sandwiches (from £2.15), mushrooms in lager batter (£2.65), filled baked potatoes (from £2.75), ploughman's (£3.25), steak and mushroom pie, goulash or Wiener Schnitzel (£3.95); well kept Adnams, Flowers Original and IPA, Greene King IPA, Ruddles and Wethereds on handpump; fruit machine, trivia and piped music. The Wood Green Animal Shelter is nearby. *(Recommended by Gwen and Peter Andrews, Colleen Holiday, Nigel Gibbs, Sandra Cook, Drs M and K Parier, J P Cinnamond, Sidney and Erna Wells, GP, N Barker, Dennis Royles, Derek and Sylvia Stephenson, Christopher Knowles-Fitton)*

Free house   Real ale   Meals and snacks   Restaurant   Children in restaurant and eating area of bar   Open 12–3, 7–11   Bedrooms tel Royston (0763) 838773; £30S/£55(£52S)

HOLYWELL (Cambs)   TL3370   Map 5
Olde Ferry Boat

Village and pub both signposted (keep your eyes skinned!) off A1123 in Needingworth

Attractively set on the edge of the Great Ouse in a remote part of the Fens, this thatched, wisteria-covered old building is actually one of the oldest inns in the country – it dates back to the 10th century, and was originally a monastic ferry house. The licensees who took over in the summer of 1989 have spent over £100,000 in refurbishments – adding a new kitchen and some bedrooms, and modernising the bars and restaurant; but there's still a rambling and old-fashioned atmosphere in the four bar areas – two of which are no-smoking – with their low-beamed ceilings, timbered or panelled walls, red leather settees, river-view window seats and a pretty little carved settle; one of the four open fires has a fish and an eel among rushes moulded on its chimney beam. Well kept Adnams Broadside, Bass, Greene King Abbot and IPA, Marstons Pedigree and a guest on handpump. Bar food – which changes every three months or so – includes home-made soup (£1.75), rolls (£2), stilton and lamb pâté (£2.95), lunchtime ploughman's (£3.95), omelettes (£4.50), vegetable risotto or quiche (£4.95), sausage, kidney and mushroom pie (£5.25), lasagne (from £5.50), and steak (£7.50); children's dishes (from £2.50); occasional food theme evenings; note that they only do hot dishes in the evening; friendly, attentive service. The front terrace has tables under cocktail parasols, with more on a side rose lawn along the river. In the middle of the bar there's a stone marking the site of a 900-year-old grave; the ghost, Juliette, reputedly rises on March 17. *(Recommended by Miss R Murdoch, Chris Raisin, Michael and Betty Hall, M S Hancock, Ted George, Alison and Tony Godfrey, Andy Hick, J P Cinnamond, Simon Scott, Frank W Gadbois, E Kinnersly, John Baker, Nigel Gibbs; more reports please)*

Free house   Licensee Richard Jeffrey   Real ale   Meals and snacks (12–2, 7–10) Children welcome   Restaurant (not Sun evening)   Open 10.30–3, 6–11   7 bedrooms tel St Ives (0480) 63227; £32.50B/£39.50B

HORNINGSEA (Cambs)   TL4962   Map 5
Plough & Fleece ★ ∅

Just NE of Cambridge: first slip-road off A45 heading E after A10, then left at T; or take B1047 Fen Ditton road off A1303

The extensive range of home-cooked and imaginatively prepared food in this small but rambling country pub includes home-made soup (£1.40), home-made pâté (£2.25), devilled crab (£2.50), cottage pie (£2.90), omelettes (£3.80), salads such as home-cooked ham (£4), Suffolk ham hot-pot (£4), fish pie (£4.75), Romany rabbit (£6.25), honey-roast guinea fowl (£6.75), Scotch salmon poached in white wine and topped with a smoked salmon and prawn sauce (£8.25), sirloin steak (£8.50) and beef Wellington (£9.25). In the evenings, when the menu also includes a vegetarian dish with asparagus, eggs, cheese and almonds (£5.20), the hot dishes all cost slightly more. At lunchtimes only there are also sandwiches (from £1.20,

toasties from £1.40), ploughman's or hot snacks such as sausage and bacon flan
(£2.25), and home-cooked ham and egg (£3.20); good puddings such as Norfolk
treacle tart or home-made ginger and brandy ice cream and a potent chocolate
pudding (£1.75); efficient service even under pressure. Amidst the continuing
chorus of warm praise for the food from readers, there have been one or two
voices of dissent, but we're keeping our fingers crossed that this is just a temporary
blip. There's a genuinely homely atmosphere, particularly in the black-beamed
public bar, with its high-backed settles and plain seats on the red tiled floor, plain
wooden tables – including an enormously long slab of elm (with an equally long
pew to match it) – butter-yellow walls, a stuffed parrot, and a stuffed fox by the
log fire. Well kept Greene King IPA and Abbot on handpump, half-a-dozen good
malt whiskies and a couple of vintage ports; dominoes and cribbage. The mix of
wild and cultivated flowers in the garden is a nice touch; picnic-table sets beyond
the car park, and beyond a herbaceous border is a children's play area with a rope
ladder climbing into an old pear tree. *(Recommended by E B Warrington, A T Langton,
Alan and Ruth Woodhouse, Barry and Anne, Drs M and K Parier, Wayne Brindle, Robert and
Elizabeth Scott, John Tyzack, Nick Dowson, Alison Hayward, KC, J P Cinnamond, Mrs E M
Thompson, Nigel Gibbs, Gordon Theaker, R C Vincent, Mrs R Green)*

*Greene King   Licensee Kenneth Grimes   Real ale   Meals and snacks (not Sun or Mon
evening)   Open 11.30–2.30, 7–11; closed evenings 25 and 26 Dec*

KENNETT (Cambs)   TL6968 Map 5

Bell

Bury Road; crossroads B1506/B1085, through Kentford on the Newmarket slip-road
just off A45 Bury St Edmunds–Cambridge

The decent choice of tasty bar food from an attractive and efficient servery includes
good home-made soup (£1.50), winter filled baked potatoes, filled French bread
(from £1.50), smoked salmon sandwich (£2.75), ploughman's (from £3.25), a
help-yourself salad bar (from £1.50), home-made quiche or Newmarket sausage
(£3.75), steak and stout pie (£4.25), and several more expensive dishes such as
steaks (from £9.95) and Dover sole (£11.95); obliging service. Beneath the wealth
of heavy oak beams in the rambling, Turkey-carpeted bar there are lots of stripped
country tables with Windsor armchairs and cushioned dining chairs, a brick
inglenook and a freestanding fireplace; a tiled-floor room, serving as a wine and
oyster bar, leads off; occasional theme evenings here. There should always be seven
real ales, well kept on handpump: three regulars – Adnams, Hook Norton and
Nethergate – and guests such as John Smiths, Marstons Old Peculier or Charles
Wells Bombardier; Marstons Owd Rodger in winter; fruit machine, juke box, and
piped music. *(Recommended by Frank W Gadbois, John Behle, G L Tong, Sybil Baker, Rona
Murdoch, Paul Sexton, Sue Harrison)*

*Free house   Licensees Mr and Mrs Colin Hayling   Real ale   Meals and snacks (12–2,
7–9.45)   Restaurant   Children in restaurant at lunchtime   Jazz Tues evenings   Open
11.30–2.30, 6–11; open from 11 and 5 if racing at Newmarket; closed evenings 25 and
26 Dec   Bedrooms tel Newmarket (0638) 750286; £25B/£35B*

KEYSOE (Beds)   TL0762 Map 5

Chequers

B660 N of Bedford

The two beamed bars in this charming pub are comfortably modernised and have a
particularly welcoming feel. Well kept Hook Norton and guest beers such as
Badger Tanglefoot, Eldridge Pope Hardy or Wadworths 6X, all from handpumps
on the stone bar counter, some malts, and Kellercup – a blend of stawberries and
hock. Good bar food includes home-made soup (£1.20), sandwiches (from £1.20),
good ploughman's (£3), tasty home-made steak pie or scampi (£4.50), chicken
stuffed with Stilton and chives (£6), trout in an almond and cream sauce (£6.50)
and home-made puddings (£1.75); Sunday roast lunch (£3.50); children's helpings
(from £1.60); the pub is often full, particularly at lunchtime, when food may finish

early because of the heavy demand. A central feature – though not always lit – is the unusual stone-pillared log fireplace; fruit machine, video game, piped music. The terrace on the small front lawn looks across the village; there are more tables at the back, on the grass around the car park, and a children's play area. *(Recommended by Dr R J A Jones, Michael and Jenny Back, Roger Danesark; more reports please)*

Free house   Licensee Jeffrey Kearns   Real ale   Meals and snacks (12–2, 7–9.45; not Mon)   Children in eating area   Open 11–2.30, 6.30–11; closed Mondays, except Bank Holidays, and 25 and 26 Dec

KEYSTON (Cambs)   TL0475   Map 5

Pheasant ⊘

Village loop road; from A604 SE of Thrapston, right on to B663

Part of this well tended and thatched white building, now one of Ivo Vannocci's Poste Hotels, used to be the village smithy, as the heavy-horse harness on the high rafters, and an old horse-drawn harrow still suggest. The main bar, recently extended, has lower beams and a comfortable atmosphere, with leather slung stools and a heavily carved wooden armchair among the Windsor chairs; the walls are decorated with old photographs of the pub. There's a distinct emphasis on fresh, imaginative and home-cooked food; dishes recently praised include the small selection of Thai dishes – such as spicy spring chicken or sweet and sour pork (£5.50), the home-made beefburgers and the puddings, such as melon with raspberry sorbet or fruit brûlée (£2); there's also soup (£1.50), pigeon or chicken liver pâté (£2.50), smoked mackerel salad (£3.45), crab mornay or gravadlax (£3.95), lasagne, seafood pancake or spare ribs (£4.95), loin of pork with orange sauce (£5.50), and steaks (£7.50); in season local pheasant is used in pâtés and casseroles. Well kept Adnams, Banks & Taylors Shefford and SOS and Batemans XXXB on handpump, and a good selection of wines by the bottle or from a Canadian Wine Machine; friendly, efficient service. Some tables under cocktail parasols at the front are laid with tablecloths. No dogs. *(Recommended by Rita Horridge, John and Tessa Rainsford, John Baker, Dr M V Jones, Rita Horridge, C R Cooke, John Baker)*

Free house   Licensee William Bennett   Meals and snacks   Children welcome Restaurant Bythorn (080 14) 241   Open 10.30–2.30, 6–11

NEWTON (Cambs)   TL4349   Map 5

Queens Head ⊘

2 1/2 miles from M11 junction 11; A10 towards Royston, then left on to B1368

There's an unchanging and pleasantly straightforward atmosphere in this vine-covered brick village tavern; furnishings in the main bar are traditional, with bare wooden benches and seats built into the walls and bow windows, a curved high backed settle on the yellow tiled floor, unusual seats in the fireplace, a loudly ticking clock, and paintings on the cream walls. The little carpeted saloon is broadly similar but cosier. Darts in a side room, with shove-ha'penny, table skittles, dominoes, cribbage, nine men's morris and a fruit machine. On the food front, the licensees have stuck to a policy of simplicity and freshness, and have scored well for both integrity and quality; the range includes a good choice of sandwiches (from £1.20, smoked salmon £1.70), superb home-made soup or baked potato with cheese (£1.40); in the evening and on Sunday lunchtime they serve plates of excellent quality cold meat, smoked salmon, cheeses and pâté (from £2). Well kept Adnams Bitter and Broadside tapped from the cask, with Old Ale in winter; elderflower wine; efficient service may be stretched at busy times. Belinda the goose, now a long-standing feature (she patrols the car park day and night), features on the pub sign, painted by the landlord and his father. Seats at the front outside. *(Recommended by Tony and Lynne Stark, Alan and Ruth Woodhouse, Pete Storey, Drs M and K Parier, Dr Mark Stocker, Steve Waters, GP, Richard Sanders)*

Free house　Licensee David Short　Real ale　Snacks (12–2, 6–10)　Children in games room　Open 11.30 (11 Sat)–2.30, 6–11; closed 25 Dec

SOUTHILL (Beds)　TL1542　Map 5
White Horse

From A603 E of Bedford, right on to B658; village signposted on right after 4 miles

Pleasantly isolated in the countryside, this friendly and well kept pub is an obvious draw for families, not least because of its spacious garden, which has a garden shop, a children's games and play area, and a 7 1/4-inch gauge railway with diesel engines, bridges and a tunnel. Children's rides are 20p; the steam engines have moved on now, but steam enthusiasts are encouraged to bring their own locomotives. Inside, the main lounge is comfortable and decorated with 1930s cigarette picture cards, framed old English currency notes, and cricketing prints on the cream walls; a smaller public bar has plain seats and settles in front of a big woodburning stove, and comic railway pictures and prints among the harness on the terracotta-coloured walls. There's an interesting spotlit well in the dining room; Flowers IPA and Wethereds on handpump, darts, shove-ha'penny, dominoes, cribbage, table skittles, fruit machine and piped music. Bar food may include sandwiches (from £1.20), ploughman's (from £2.75), sausages or ham and egg (£3), burgers (£3.50), scampi (£3.75), salads (from £4.90), and children's meals (£1.50); Sunday roasts. The licensees have enlarged the car park and converted an old stable block into a function room. Handy for the Shuttleworth Collection of old cars and early aeroplanes. *(Recommended by Roger Danes, Mrs E M Thompson; more up-to-date reports please)*

Whitbreads　Real ale　Meals and snacks (12–2.30, 6.30–10; not Sun evening) Children in eating areas　Restaurant tel Hitchin (0462) 813364; closed Sun evening Open 11–3, 6.30–11

STILTON (Cambs)　TL1689　Map 5
Bell

High Street; village signposted from A1 S of Peterborough

Until a few years ago this handsomely rambling old coaching inn was almost completely derelict; the licensees have been gradually changing this, and their ambitious programme of restoration and modernisation is almost complete. The two opened-up rooms of the bar have flagstones, floor tiles, big prints of sailing and winter coaching scenes on the partly stripped walls, plush-cushioned button-back banquettes built around the walls and bow windows, other sturdy upright wooden seats, and a large log fire in the fine stone fireplace. Well kept Courage Directors, Ind Coope Burton, Marstons Pedigree and Tetleys on handpump; dominoes, backgammon, cards, Mastermind. Stilton the cheese got its name originally from being sold to the inn's coaching customers and thus widely travelled around the country, though until then it had been known as the Quenby cheese and was actually made in Little Dalby and Wymondham up near Melton Mowbray; it's therefore no surprise that it still features prominently on the bar menu: soup (£1.30), excellent pâté (£1.90) and ploughman's (£2.65) and with plum bread (£2.75). Other food from a menu that changes daily includes good sandwiches (from £1.20), rabbit pie (£4.50), oak-smoked trout with lemon dressing (£4.65), and honey roast gammon (£4.45). The sheltered cobbled and flagstoned back courtyard has some tables; a bedroom extension is also out here. The inn sign is a large and stately affair – a curlicued gantry and a coach-arch, with distances to cities carved on the courtyard side. *(Recommended by Mr and Mrs P A Jones, M Morgan, Martin, Jane and Simon Bailey, Chris Raisin, W H Bland, Kathleen Morley, A Jarman, Barry and Anne, F J Robinson, Eleanor Wallis, Alison and Tony Godfrey, D A Wilcock, Miss C M Davidson, Dr J R Hamilton)*

Free house　Licensees John and Liam McGivern　Real ale　Meals and snacks Children in eating area until 7pm　Restaurant　Open 11–2.30, 6–11　Bedrooms tel Peterborough (0733) 241066; £55B/£70B

SUTTON GAULT (Cambs)   TL4279 Map 5

Anchor ✪

Village signed off B1381 in Sutton

This pub on the Old Bedford River has four heavily timbered, old-fashioned rooms, one of them recently created from the old kitchen (actually the oldest part of the building), and each furnished with antique settles (including one elaborately Gothick, and another with an attractively curved high back), dining or kitchen chairs and well spaced, stripped and scrubbed deal tables; sloping floors, good lithographs and big prints on the walls, candles and gas lighting (from swan's-neck gas lamps), and three log fires. There's an emphasis – not at the expense of the pubby atmosphere – on consistently attractive, home-made bar food, including fish chowder (£1.95), smoked mackerel pâté (£2.10), egg and prawn in garlic mayonnaise or mushrooms in cream and garlic (£2.25), smoked Scotch salmon (£3.60), tagliatelle with mushrooms, cream and bacon or blue cheese (£4.50), vegetarian curried nut loaf with tomato and basil sauce or ratatouille (£4.95), chicken Elizabeth (cold chicken in a lightly curried mayonnaise with grapes) or really rare roast beef (£5.95), fresh poached salmon with hollandaise (£7.50), and steak (£8.50; with king prawns £11.50); home-made puddings such as lemon soufflé, mixed fruit crumble or chocolate roulade (£1.75, with cream); service is cheerful and charming. Well kept Tolly Bitter and Original tapped from the cask, good wine list, winter hot punch; they also do freshly squeezed orange juice (£1.10 a glass). Shove-ha'penny, dominoes, cribbage, well reproduced classical music at lunchtime, middle-of-the-road in the evening; the rough-haired dachshund now has a son. Tables outside by the river, with fine views across the unspoilt countryside. No dogs. *(Recommended by Mrs V Constable, Mrs C Fairweather, R C Wiles, Gary Melnyk, J P Cinnamond, Wayne Brindle, Julian Holland)*

Free house   Licensees A P and J R F Stretton-Downes   Real ale   Meals (not Sun evening)   Restaurant tel Ely (0353) 778537   Children in restaurant till 9pm   Open 12–2.30, 6–11; closed 25 Dec

SWAVESEY (Cambs)   TL3668 Map 5

Trinity Foot

A604, N side; to reach it from the westbound carriageway, take Swavesey, Fen Drayton turnoff

Though this comfortable pub actually dates mainly from 1957, it's named for the foot-followers of Trinity College's beagles, who hunted here from the 1880s. The wide choice of consistently good and nicely presented bar food includes sandwiches, ploughman's or pâté , fish dishes, lamb cutlets, mixed grill, daily specials which might include oysters, steak and kidney pie, and good Sunday roasts; tables are well set out, with fresh flowers. Flowers Original and Wethereds on handpump; nicely made Pimms with bergamot flower; efficient, friendly service. The enclosed garden of shrubs, trees and lawns is pleasant. *(Recommended by Annette and John Kenny, Wayne Brindle, Mrs E M Thompson, Janet Goodjohn; more up-to-date reports please)*

Whitbreads   Real ale   Meals and snacks (12–2, 6–9.30; not Sun evening)   Children in eating area   Open 11–2.30, 6–11; closed 25 and 26 Dec

UFFORD (Cambs)   TF0904 Map 5

Olde White Hart

From A15 N of Peterborough, left on to B1443; village signposted at unmarked road on left after about 4 miles

The lounge bar in this late 17th-century building has pewter tankards hanging from the beam over the bar counter, wheelback chairs around dark tripod tables, and Boris the stuffed tarantula; an attractive stone chimney divides the room into two. In the carpeted public bar there are old-fashioned settles and dark tables. Well kept Home Bitter, Theakstons XB and Old Peculier, Youngers Scotch, and guest beers on handpump, and several wines by the glass; darts, cribbage, and dominoes. Bar food includes rolls (90p), steak and mushroom pie or lasagne (£4.35), and weekly changing specials such as chicken goujons with garlic sauce (£4.35), vegetarian tortellini (£4.40), fresh Cromer crab salad (£4.85), poached salmon (£6), and fillet steak Torpel (stuffed with Stilton, with a herb and port sauce, £8.80); on Sunday lunchtime they do hot roast beef rolls (£1.30), and Sunday roast lunch; imaginative puddings; barbecues Thursday, Friday and Saturday evenings. The sunny terrace has white metal seats and an electric canopy (for theme nights in summer and on wet days), and there's a big, pretty garden with two tethered goats and a children's play area with swings, slides and so forth. The pub was actually a farm until the middle of last century. *(Recommended by Sarah Bullard, M Morgan; more reports please)*

Home (S & N)   Real ale   Meals and snacks (12–2, 6–9.30; not Sun evening or Mon) Restaurant tel Stamford (0780) 740250   Children in eating area   Open 11–3 (till 4 Sat), 6–11; closed 25 Dec

WANSFORD (Cambs)   TL0799   Map 5

Haycock ★ ⊘ ⇌

Village clearly signposted from A1 W of Peterborough

Since the last edition of the *Guide* a sizeable extension – larger than the original part of the building – has opened in this golden-stone inn, with around 30 new bedrooms and a business centre with its own ballroom; we'd expect that this would have some effect on the overall tone of the place, but the core remains warmly pubby. Beyond the flagstoned main entry hall, with its antique seats and longcase clock, the lively but civilised panelled main bar overlooks tables in a charming cobbled courtyard. On the other side of the servery is a quieter lounge with plush sofas and easy chairs, hunting or steeplechasing prints, wallpaper to match the long flowery curtains, and a good winter log fire. The buffet table, in another well kept lounge overlooking the garden, has a good range of cold meats and salads (£2.95 for a side salad, around £6.95 otherwise); other home-made food – not cheap – includes sandwiches, soup (£2.45), chicken liver pâté (£3.65), escalope of pork or baked pepper stuffed with chilli beef (£6.50), salmon and haddock pancake (£6.75), and chicken breast stuffed with stilton, or beef curry with rice (£6.95); a good choice of puddings, and weekend barbecues; the waitress service is formal but friendly; part of the eating area is no-smoking. Well kept Bass, Ruddles Best and County and Tolly Original on handpump, a good range of decent wines by the glass – the cruover machine allows them to keep a dozen or so in very good condition – and properly mature vintage ports by the glass. The attractive and spacious walled formal garden opens on to its own cricket field by the stately bridge over the River Nene; there's also an extensive pétanque court and fishing. One of Ivo Vannocci's Poste Hotels. *(Recommended by Philip Orbell, Tony Gayfer, Tony Bland, Rosalind Russell, R C Wiles, John Baker, Roger Bellingham, Wayne Brindle)*

Free House   Manager Richard Neale   Real ale   Meals and snacks (12–2.30, 6.30–10.30)   Children welcome   Restaurant   Open 10–2.30 (till 3 Sat), 5.30–11 Bedrooms tel Stamford (0780) 782223; £60B/£85B

Lucky Dip

Besides the fully inspected pubs, you might like to try these Lucky Dips recommended to us and described by readers (if you do, please send us reports):

Abbots Ripton, Cambs [TL2378], *Three Horseshoes:* Lovely refurbished pink-washed thatched pub with warm low-beamed lounge *(Wayne Brindle)* **Alconbury,** Cambs [TL1875], *White Hart:* Popular local free house with

Watneys-related real ales, wide range of bar food from sausage and egg to steaks and mixed grills — handy for A1, at lower than A1 prices *(Michael and Jenny Back)* **Alwalton,** Cambs [Oundle Rd; TL1396], *Wheatsheaf:* Popular village pub with well kept Allied real ales and good food *(T Mansell)*

☆ **Arrington**, Cambs [TL3250], *Hardwicke Arms*: Quaint creeper-covered coaching inn currently doing well, with elegant beamed and panelled lounge, high-ceilinged further room, friendly helpful service, good often imaginative lunchtime bar food, well kept Adnams, Bass and Greene King real ales; games room, tables in spacious outside area; next to Wimpole Hall; bedrooms *(Tom Evans, Mrs D M LLewellyn, LYM)*

Babraham, Cambs [just off A1307; TL5150], *George*: No recent reports on this old pub, well liked by readers in past editions for pleasant atmosphere, friendly landlord and interesting food in bar and restaurant *(More news please)*

☆ **Balsham**, Cambs [High St; TL5850], *Black Bull*: Attractive beamed bar with cheerful log fire, spacious eating area serving wide range of food inc interesting daily specials, well kept Sam Smiths OB, separate evening restaurant *(Philip and Diana Nicholson, Stuart Watkinson)*

☆ **Barnack**, Cambs [Millstone Lane; off B1443 SE of Stamford; turn off School Lane nr the Fox; TF0704], *Millstone*: Well kept Adnams, Everards Tiger and Old Original and Fullers ESB in strongly traditional bar with wall timbers and high beams weighed down with harness, and a really good woodburning stove; good choice of decent bar food from soup and sandwiches through omelettes and pies to gammon and trout, served apart in side area with pews; fruit machine, piped music *(M J Morgan, Nic James, A G Purkis, M V Jones, BB)*

Bartlow, Cambs [TL5845], *Three Hills*: Good friendly rural pub with well kept Greene King IPA and Abbot, good home-cooked food, log fire *(Barbara and Norman Wells)*

Bedford, Beds [St Mary's St; TL0449], *Kings Arms*: Well kept recently refurbished open-plan town-centre pub, popular for wide range of food and well kept Greene King real ales; huge anachronistic pubby painting in smaller carpeted side area *(Roger Danes, Michael and Alison Sandy, Steve Waters, LYM)*

Bletsoe, Beds [TL0258], *Falcon*: Pleasant coaching inn dating from 17th century, with big riverside garden; bar food from sandwiches up, restaurant, Charles Wells real ale *(Mrs E M Thompson)*

Bottisham, Cambs [TL5560], *White Swan*: Simple pub taking lots of pride in its food, with beautiful range of innovative cooking inc wonderful puddings; well kept Paines EG on handpump *(Paul Evans)*

Boxworth, Cambs [TL3464], *Golden Ball*: Pleasant, spacious and well appointed village pub with good service; comprehensive, straightforward menu and separate children's meals *(D B Haunch)*

Brampton, Cambs [TL2170], *Black Bull*: Olde-worlde pub full of character, with low ceiling, separate public and lounge bars, and good if slightly pricey evening food *(Chris*

Fluck); [Broomholme Lane], *Old Mill*: Old converted watermill in beautiful spot, attractively floodlit at night; busy atmosphere, wide range of often interesting real ales, excellent farm cider and upper-level restaurant *(Wayne Brindle)*

☆ **Cambridge** [Mawson Rd], *Live & Let Live*: Lively young customers in cosy and friendly street-corner local, with antiques, nick-nacks, panelling, pine furniture and changing beers such as Marstons Pedigree, Nethergate, Theakstons and Wadworths 6X; good staff, tasty food *(Nigel Gibbs, Sandra Cook, Tony and Lynne Stark, Wayne Brindle)*

☆ **Cambridge** [Tenison Rd], *Salisbury Arms*: It's the dozen or so well kept real ales, and perhaps the good no-smoking area, which attract crowds of predominantly young customers to the surprisingly high-ceilinged and spacious back bar, with its brewing posters and lively chatty atmosphere; lunchtime bar food inc ploughman's and hot dish, good staff, pub games, farm cider, smaller front public bar *(Steve Waters, Drs M and K Parier, Nigel Gibbs, Tony and Lynne Stark, Wayne Brindle, LYM)*

Cambridge [Napier St; next to Grafton Centre], *Ancient Druids*: Ultra-modern air-conditioned pub with interesting own-brewed Kite, Druids Special and Merlin, and good value food (not Sun evening); you can see the brewing from the street *(Wayne Brindle)*; [19 Bridge St], *Baron of Beef*: Unspoilt busy pub with very long bar counter, lots of character, panelled partition dividing two bars, wide range of customers, Greene King under pressure, simple good value food from help-yourself buffet, friendly landlord *(Barry and Anne, Wayne Brindle, Ben Wimpenny)*; [Bene't St], *Bath*: Very popular with students, especially at weekends, with good pizzas, well kept Marstons Pedigree, and excellent CD juke box *(Julian Holland)*; [4 King St], *Cambridge Arms*: Spacious and comfortable modern conversion of former brewery, giving unusual interesting layout; young, lively atmosphere, Greene King IPA and Abbot, rather good food, sheltered courtyard, maybe jazz nights *(Richard Sanders, Tony and Lynne Stark, Wayne Brindle, LYM)*; [Clarendon St], *Clarendon Arms*: Tucked away behind Parkers Piece and doing a roaring trade in simple bar food specialising in spicy soups and massive crusty sandwiches — you look straight into the kitchen; very mixed clientele, helpful friendly staff, well kept reasonably priced Greene King beers, nice back courtyard; open all day *(Wayne Brindle)*; [Elm St], *Elm Tree*: Pleasant backstreet pub which has had unusual Thai bar food *(P A Jennings)*; [Thoday St], *Empress*: Genuine no-nonsense local with friendly landlord, well kept Marstons and Whitbreads ales, and wide choice of interesting snacks; pool, darts (keen team), and mix of young and old customers; terraced garden; busy most evenings *(Nigel Gibbs, Sandra Cook)*;

[Midsummer Common], *Fort St George*: Comfortably renovated riverside pub in charming waterside position on Midsummer Common, interesting core dating back to Tudor times, Greene King real ales, bar food, games in public bar; can get very crowded; very atmospheric on the terrace in summer *(Wayne Brindle, LYM)*; [Barton Rd/Kings Rd], *Hat & Feathers*: Friendly three-roomed local with good atmosphere, lots of tables in raised balconied area; Tolly ales, popular lunchtime and evening bar food, garden *(JMC)*; [nr Grafton Centre], *Hop Bine & Barley Ear*: Quiet modernised end-of-terrace pub with well kept Greene King ales and imaginative lunchtime food *(Peter Corris, Wayne Brindle)*; [Panton St], *Panton Arms*: Formerly a brewery with two interesting bars and an interesting atmosphere *(Dr and Mrs A K Clarke)*; [Magdelene St], *Pickerel*: Olde-worlde, very atmospheric street; spacious free house with several adjoining areas, friendly staff, juke box and fruit machines; Greene King, Ruddles Best and County, hot dishes and salad bar *(Alan and Ruth Woodhouse)*; [110 Water St, Chesterton], *Pike & Eel*: Spacious and plush riverside pub with lovely views but high bar prices *(Wayne Brindle)*; [Thompsons Lane, next to Jesus Common], *Spade & Becket*: River views from conservatory, balcony and waterside terrace; good choice of bar food, popular with young people on summer weekends, comfortable when quiet *(Wayne Brindle, Richard Sanders)*; [Dover St (off East Rd)], *Tram Depot*: Clever conversion of old tram depot, with glazed mezzanine, long central skylight, bare brick walls and stone floor, old furniture that fits in nicely; popular home-made bar food; under same ownership as Victoria, Earl Soham (see Suffolk main entries), with good beers brewed at that pub *(Howard and Sue Gascoyne)*; [Regent St], *University Arms*: Free house with friendly, cheerful licensees and locals; fairly basic decor, wide range of well kept real ales, interesting bar food; bedrooms *(John Baker, F Teare)*; [James St, Newmarket Rd], *Zebra*: Nice, friendly pub away from tourist area, reasonably priced food *(Wayne Brindle)*

☆ **Castor**, Cambs [24 Peterborough Rd; TL1298], *Royal Oak*: Old thatched pub with good value home cooking, well kept Allied real ales inc particularly good Burton, several open fires, small traditional bar areas and sociable landlord — should benefit hugely from new bypass; very busy weekends *(A G Purkis, T Mansell, LYM)*
Castor, *Fitzwilliam Arms*: Popular long, thatched dining pub with well kept Allied real ales and varied range of good food *(T Mansell)*; [Peterborough Rd], *Prince of Wales*: Pleasant old beamed pub with good open fire and limited range of well cooked lunchtime and evening bar food *(D J Brighouse)*; [Peterborough Rd], *Wheatsheaf*: Small village pub with pool table, darts and good bar food served all day *(D J Brighouse)*

☆ **Catworth**, Cambs [High St; B660 between A45 (Kimbolton) and A604; TL0873], *Racehorse*: An odd dearth of recent reports is all that keeps this well run and rather elegant village pub out of the main entries; richly decorated with flat-racing photographs and genealogies, it has lots of whiskies, well kept Adnams and Courage Directors on handpump, log fire, piped classical music, bar food from soup and sandwiches to steaks and mixed grill, restaurant; games in public bar, tables outside, stables behind; children welcome *(Fiona and Chris Brown, L F Turner, LYM — more reports please)*

Clayhithe, Cambs [TL5064], *Bridge*: Interestingly furnished beamed and timbered bar, and pretty garden by the River Cam; good log fire, well kept Everards, bar food, usually friendly service; bedrooms in motel extension *(P G Evans, A D Fisher, E Kinnersly, LYM)*

Colmworth, Beds [Wilden Rd; TL1058], *Wheatsheaf*: Old beamed pub with changing real ales such as Adnams, Everards and Marstons Pedigree, bar and restaurant food, open fire; garden *(Nigel Gibbs, Sandra Cook)*

Conington, Cambs [Boxworth Rd; TL3266], *White Swan*: Friendly pub with good atmosphere, well kept Greene King Abbot, big garden, and ample parking *(J D Maplethorpe, Wayne Brindle, Gordon Theaker)*

Cotton End, Beds [A600 Bedford—Baldock; TL0745], *Bell*: Timbered Whitbreads pub near British Airship Industries base, its two rooms and linking bar full of photographs of airships of different eras, comfortable red settles and chairs, and friendly, welcoming landlord; well kept Whitbreads Castle Eden and good bar food — especially sausage sandwiches and toasties; very cosy beamed back room *(Pete Storey)*

Croxton, Cambs [TL2459], *Spread Eagle*: Welcoming pub with bar food maybe inc good game pie, Greene King ales *(R Aitken)*

Croydon, Cambs [TL3149], *Queen Adelaide*: Cosy rural pub with nicely decorated big bar, quiet piped music; consistently well kept Adnams Southwold, Marstons Pedigree, Youngers IPA and guest beers, good bar food all week, friendly service; restaurant; children's room, large paddock with climbing frames *(Mr and Mrs Geoffrey Perryman, Nigel Gibbs)*

Downham, Cambs [Main St; sometimes known as Little Downham — the one near Ely; TL5283], *Plough*: Real Fenland village local with lots of atmosphere, walls covered with pictures of pub outings and local events; tremendous choice of whiskies, well prepared food — soups and specials recommended *(John Baker)*

Dry Drayton, Cambs [Park St; TL3862], *Black Horse*: Very friendly with good freshly cooked food inc plenty for vegetarians, good beers; attractive dining room with flowers on lovely table; snooker, darts, garden *(J Kingsbury)*

☆ **Dullingham**, Cambs [50 Station Rd; TL6357], *Kings Head*: Cosy dining pub, popular for a wide range of freshly made food from sandwiches through omelettes or celery and cashew risotto to splendid duck, with lots of puddings; open fires, well kept Tolly and Original, friendly staff, fairy-lit seats out above the broad village green; children in family area *(J P Cinnamond, M Morgan, LYM)*

Earith, Cambs [TL3874], *Riverview*: Traditional country pub by Great Ouse with brass platters on walls, candles on tables and good atmosphere; good range of well kept ales such as Adnams, Arkells BBB, Batemans XXXB, Courage Directors, Greene King IPA and Marstons Pedigree; good bar food and service, separate restaurant *(Dave and Kate Buckley)*

East Hyde, Beds [Lower Luton Rd (B653); TL1217], *Leather Bottle*: Small two-bar pub with rather brown-Windsor decor, worth knowing for character landlord, well kept Whitbreads-related real ales, bar food inc fresh fish and meat dish of the day during the week *(D L Johnson)*

Eaton Bray, Beds [SP9620], *White Horse*: Clean place with good atmosphere, above-average food, pleasant position, and nice customers and staff; lovely in summer *(ILP)*

☆ **Eaton Socon**, Cambs [Old Great North Rd; village signposted from A1 nr St Neots; TL1658], *White Horse*: Good value food served quickly in rambling series of well kept low-beamed rooms inc one with high-backed traditional settles around fine log fire, several well kept Whitbreads-related real ales on handpump, relaxed chatty atmosphere (reasonably unsmoky), play area in back garden; children in eating areas; good parking; bedrooms *(David Young, Nigel Gibbs, Sandra Cook, Wayne Brindle, LYM)*

☆ **Eaton Socon**, *Crown*: Cosy little pub with two low-beamed bars, good range of beers such as Brains SA and Bitter, Hook Norton Best and Tetleys; moderately priced bar food (not Sun), open fire, restaurant; no T-shirts *(Nigel Gibbs, Sandra Cook, Genie and Brian Smart, Wayne Brindle)*

Eaton Socon, *Waggon & Horses*: Comfortable and roomy open-plan beamed bar; good range of moderately priced hot and cold bar food, Tolly and other real ales, good mix of customers *(G T Rhys, Nigel Gibbs, Sandra Cook)*

☆ **Elsworth**, Cambs [TL3163], *George & Dragon*: Good atmosphere in pleasantly indiosyncratic pub with attractively furnished and decorated panelled main bar and quieter back dining area by garden, wide choice of decent food, Tolly real ales, nice terraces, play area in garden, restaurant *(Wayne Brindle, LYM)*

Elsworth, *Poacher*: Small, cosy, thatched pub with friendly atmosphere *(Wayne Brindle)*

☆ **Elton**, Cambs [Duck St; TL0893], *Crown*: Opposite green in small, beautiful village, rebuilt and modernised with taste and real character since 1984 fire; well kept real ales including Greene King IPA and Marstons Pedigree, particularly good varied food in bar, conservatory and upstairs restaurant *(T Mansell)*

Elton, *Black Horse*: Pleasant old stone pub with homely lounge and separate dining area *(T Mansell)*

Ely, Cambs [Annesdale; TL5380], *Cutter*: Superb spot on river, enormous meals at sensible prices, friendly and helpful staff, good choice of beers, good parking and mooring; shame about the juke box in the riverside bar *(Peter and Jacqueline Petts, Tony and Lynne Stark)*; [St Marys St], *Kings Arms*: Pleasant pub with friendly bar staff, well kept Watneys-related real ales, wide choice of very good food; satellite TV *(Julian Holland)*

☆ **Fen Ditton**, Cambs [High St; TL4860], *Ancient Shepherds*: Cosy village pub with armchairs and sofas in pleasant lounge; decent restaurant food, served in bar too, pleasant friendly staff, well kept decent Tolly *(R Wiles, Wayne Brindle)*

Fen Ditton [Green End], *Plough*: Comfortable Brewers Fayre refurbishment with attractive riverside gardens — nice walk across meadows from town *(Howard and Sue Gascoyne, LYM)*

Fenstanton, Cambs [High St; off A604 near St Ives; TL3168], *King William IV*: Attractive cottage-style pub with wide choice of excellent food and well kept Tolly; car parking can be awkward if busy *(J D Maplethorpe)*

Fowlmere, Cambs [High St], *Swan House*: Busy village pub with good selection of food and Greene King ales *(Nigel Gibbs, Sandra Cook)*

Glinton, Cambs [TF1505], *Blue Bell*: Atmosphere cosy and relaxed, staff friendly, beer well kept, limited choice of straightforward but good food; huge back garden full of families in summer *(Jacquie and Jon Payne)*

☆ **Godmanchester**, Cambs [London Rd; TL2470], *Exhibition*: Interesting decor, good choice of excellent bar food, well kept Watneys-related real ales *(E Robinson, Derek Patey)*

Gorefield, Cambs [TF4111], *Woodmans Cottage*: Spacious modernised open-plan bar rambling around central servery, leatherette stools and banquettes, beams and open fires, welcoming staff and lively atmosphere, good value bar food, tables on front verandah *(BB)*

☆ **Grantchester**, Cambs [TL4455], *Red Lion*: Pleasant atmosphere in bright and cheerful bar of comfortable and spacious food pub, handsomely refurbished during long 1989 closure; restaurant, sheltered terrace and good-sized lawn; the village is pretty, a short stroll from lovely riverside meadows *(R C Wiles, Wayne Brindle, LYM)*

Grantchester, *Green Man*: Attractively laid-out pub in pretty village with individual furnishings; Tolly ales, bar food inc unusual salad bar *(E Kinnersly, LYM)*; [junction Coton rd with Cambridge—Trumpington rd

— OS Sheet 154 map reference 433557], *Rupert Brooke*: Whitbreads refurbishment, with Rupert Brooke allusions alongside the usual imported beamery, brickwork, old bottles and farm tools; well kept Whitbreads-related real ales, somewhat pricey bar food, cheerful young bar staff, unobtrusive piped music, back lawn and shrubbery *(Frank Cummins, Robert and Elizabeth Scott)*

☆ **Great Chishill**, Cambs [TL4239], *Pheasant*: Good atmosphere in friendly, cosy and comfortable local with sound selection of good food (not Sun lunchtime or Mon — nice fish), well kept Adnams and Greene King beers; charming garden; closed Mon lunchtime *(Nigel Gibbs, Sandra Cook, LYM)*

Great Eversden, Cambs [off A603; TL3653], *Hoops*: Friendly village pub; bedrooms *(Ron Gentry, Geoff Lee)*

Great Wilbraham, Cambs [10 High St; TL5558], *Carpenter Arms*: Two-room village local with well kept Greene King IPA and Abbot on handpump, good value ploughman's and hot dishes, evening food Weds-Sat, open fires; pétanque in summer *(Richard Sanders)*

Guyhirn, Cambs [High Rd; TF3903], *Oliver Twist*: Free house with wide choice of beers, reasonably priced bar food and separate dining room serving excellent evening meals; a good place to stay *(E Robinson, M Morgan)*

☆ **Hail Weston**, Cambs [just off A45, not far from A1 St Neots bypass; TL1662], *Royal Oak*: Picturesque thatched and beamed pub in quiet village, well suited to families, with nice big garden; good value food from sandwiches and ploughman's up, cosy fire in winter, well kept Charles Wells Eagle and Bombardier, welcoming locals; handy for Grafham Water *(Andy and Jill Kassube, J D Maplethorpe)*

Harlington, Beds [Sundon Rd; handy for M1 junction 12; TL0330], *Carpenters Arms*: Good village pub with pleasant lounge, not smart but spacious and comfortable; interesting dishes among more usual bar food (more limited Sun), ambitious restaurant *(Michael and Alison Sandy)*

Harrold, Beds [SP9456], *Oakley Arms*: Large, thatched village pub, comfortable and welcoming; real ale and varied choice of home-made bar food *(F M Williams)*

Harston, Cambs [48 Royston Rd (A10); nr M11 junction 11; TL4251], *Queens Head*: Solid, reliable local with decent food and Greene King ales; no-smoking area car park *(Nigel Gibbs, Sandra Cook, Mr and Mrs K J Morris)*

Hartford, Cambs [TL2572], *Barley Mow*: Pleasant stone pub with open-plan bar, well kept Charles Wells beer, good lunchtime food, and particularly jovial landlord *(Chris Fluck)*

Hexton, Beds [Pegsdon; B655 a mile E of Hexton; TL1230], *Live & Let Live*: Snug little pub with lovely garden below the Chilterns, two rooms opening off tiled and panelled taproom, well kept Greene King

IPA and Abbot, reasonable well presented food, good service, amiable dog and entertaining African Grey parrot *(Colleen Holiday, John & Margaret Estdale, LYM)*

Hildersham, Cambs [High St; TL5448], *Pear Tree*: Friendly little village local, good bar food *(Stuart Watkinson)*

Hinxton, Cambs [High St; TL4945], *Red Lion*: Warm, friendly and cosy, with a good range of changing beers and fine choice of good value, unusual freshly prepared food — more a diners' than a drinkers' place; various artefacts on walls and in alcoves *(Nigel Gibbs, Sandra Cook, John Baker)*

Histon, Cambs [TL4363], *Red Lion*: Clean, warm and friendly, with excellent food (especially the seafood pie) and several real ales such as Adnams, Greene King and maybe superb Timothy Taylors Landlord *(Graham and Glenis Watkins)*

Holme, Cambs [Station Rd; TL1987], *Admiral Wells*: Large, characterful pub with good beer brewed for it by Woodfordes; popular restaurant *(John Baker)*

Houghton, Cambs [TL2872], *Jolly Butchers*: Traditional black and white pub with beams and brasses; quiet family atmosphere, good bar food inc Sun lunches, tables outside, occasional barbecues; children's play area *(Simon Scott)*; *Three Horseshoes*: French windows into garden from comfortable lounge, locals' bar with black beams and inglenook, well kept Watneys-related real ales, bar food (not Sun evening) inc lunchtime cold buffet *(Wayne Brindle, LYM)*

Huntingdon, Cambs [TL2371], *George*: Elegant and spacious Georgian lounge bar in comfortable THF inn, popular for bar food; restaurant; comfortable bedrooms overlook galleried central courtyard where Shakespeare play performed during last fortnight or so of June *(LYM)*; [Cromwell Walk], *Territorial*: Large, pleasant pub with well kept Charles Wells ales and super value bar food *(Chris Fluck)*; [Victoria Sq], *Victoria*: Welcoming local, well kept real ales, farm cider, good value imaginative bar food *(Wayne Brindle)*

Isleham, Cambs [TL6474], *Griffin*: Pleasant local atmosphere, well kept Adnams *(Graham & Glenis Watkins)*

Leighton Bromswold, Cambs [TL1175], *Green Man*: Neatly modernised open-plan village pub with hundreds of good horse brasses on heavy low beams, bar food, well kept Tolly, sensible games area *(LYM)*

Linton, Cambs [TL5646], *Dog & Duck*: Lovely pub with excellent food; nice to sit outside and feed the motley collection of ducks *(Jenny Cantle)*

Littleport, Cambs [Sandhill Rd; TL5686], *Black Horse*: Smartish lounge with high-backed chairs, restaurant area with nice view of river, bar with pool tables; Watneys-related real ales, new licensees have extended the range of bar food; tables on terrace *(M and J Back)*

☆ **Madingley**, Cambs [TL3960], *Three Horseshoes*: Upmarket thatched place, more restaurant than pub with prices to match, comfortable furnishings and elegant garden; food includes popular summer buffet and good charcoal-grilled fish; nicely decorated small bar dining area, very clean, with Tolly and Original on handpump; children welcome *(R E Horner, Frank W Gadbois, R Wiles, JMC, Rita Horridge, Mrs E M Thompson, LYM)*

March, Cambs [Acre Rd; turn off B1101 opp Royal Exchange pub on corner of Market Sq; TL4195], *Acre*: Busy at lunchtime for its good value food, this pub separated by a narrow stretch of meadow from the River Nene has an airy main bar with blond captains' chairs and blue plush stools around the tables, more tables in a smaller side bar with unusual horizontal planks for the backs of its wall seats, and tables out on a verandah and terrace; keg Greene King; can be very quiet in the evenings *(R H Inns, BB)*; [Stonea; B1098 Chatteris—Upwell, E of town], *Golden Lion*: Pleasant oasis in rather bleak part of fens, with well kept Greene King IPA, freshly cut sandwiches and children's play area *(John Baker)*; [Nene Parade], *Ship*: Good varied and reasonably priced food, separate dining room *(R P Fisher)*

Marholm, Cambs [TF1402], *Fitzwilliam Arms*: Old, floodlit thatched pub in small village, well kept Allied real ales, three open fires in large front bar, good food inc home-made pizzas served in bar and back extension, friendly service; good big garden; also known as Green Man because of the way the tree by the front entrance has been shaped *(T Mansell, Mike Prentice, M Morgan, Nic James)*

Milton Bryan, Beds [off B528 S of Woburn; SP9730], *Red Lion*: Excellent unspoilt country inn, good detour from M1; well kept Whitbreads beers, friendly landlord, restaurant *(Comus Elliott)*

Moggerhanger, Beds [off A1; TL1449], *Guinea*: Pleasant, homely atmosphere in clean and attractive pub with Charles Wells beers on handpump, bar food *(Comus Elliot)*

Needingworth, Cambs [Overcote Lane; pub signposted from A1123; TL3472], *Pike & Eel*: Marvellous peaceful riverside location, with spacious lawns and marina; roomy plush bar, easy chairs and big open fire in smaller room on left, and ambitious extensive glass-walled restaurant (food confined to this, but does include some bar-food things); well kept Adnams, Bass, and Greene King Abbot, friendly and obliging landlord, provision for children; pleasant if basic bedrooms, good breakfasts *(Ted George, Alison and Tony Godfrey, Mr and Mrs J D Cranston, Betsy Coury, Frank W Gadbois, LYM)*

Odell, Beds [Horsefair Lane; SP9658], *Bell*: Lovely old pub with good Greene King beer and excellent value bar food inc home-cooked pies, decent range of vegetarian dishes and children's dishes; garden backing on to River Ouse *(Mrs E M Thompson)*

Odsey, Cambs [A505 NE of Baldock, by Ashwell & Morden stn; TL2938], *Jester*: Rural spot by railway, large, comfortable, open-plan pub with pleasant atmosphere, friendly licensees, three real ales, bar food, restaurant *(Jim Froggatt, Denise Plummer)*

Old Warden, Beds [TL1343], *Hare & Hounds*: Cosy, popular old local in charming village, with friendly, comfortable lounge, wide choice of generously served bar food, Charles Wells beers, restaurant, garden with children's play area; handy for the Shuttleworth Collection *(Colleen Holiday)*

Peakirk, Cambs [TF1606], *Ruddy Duck*: Stone-built low-beamed village pub, very clean and comfortable; good choice of very good quite reasonably priced food, pleasant waitress service, Watneys-related beers, restaurant; could get busy in summer as very close to Wildfowl Trust sanctuary *(C E Power)*

Peterborough, Cambs [465 Oundle Rd; off A605 in Woodston; TL1897], *Botolph Arms*: Sam Smiths pub with interesting interior, predominantly stone floors; popular with business people at lunchtime *(Wayne Brindle)*; [Oundle Rd, Woodston], *Cherry Tree*: Unspoilt pub run by local jazz musician, with Allied real ales, live music Fri and Sat evenings and Sun lunchtime jazz club; food only occasional Fri lunchtimes *(Nic James)*

☆ **Ridgmont**, Beds [SP9736], *Rose & Crown*: Unchanging over the last few years, just the same good value somewhat chippy food, warm welcome, well kept Charles Wells Eagle and Bombardier on handpump; open fire in traditional low-ceilinged public bar, smarter lounge with masses of *Rupert Annual* covers, well laid out to take a good few people; games inc darts and pool, maybe rabbits in attractive back garden, stables restaurant (not Mon or Tues evenings); children allowed in bar eating area; easy parking, good wheelchair access *(Nick Holmes, L M Miall, Michael and Alison Sandy, D J Braisted, LYM)*

Riseley, Beds [High St; off A6; TL0362], *Fox & Hounds*: 16th-century pub with good bar food inc renowned charcoal-grilled steaks using properly hung beef; beamed restaurant *(Dr R J A Jones)*

Salford, Beds [not far from M1 junction 13 — left off A5140; SP9339], *Swan*: A friendly welcome and good beer *(Comus Elliott)*

Sandy, Beds [Deepdale; B1042 towards Potton and Cambridge; TL1749], *Locomotive*: Reasonable pub food (not Sun) inc good specials, well kept Charles Wells Eagle and Bombardier, lots of railway memorabilia, big garden with views, new restaurant area; handy for RSPB headquarters, can get very busy (and smoky); children allowed in eating area *(P Lloyd, Miss K Bamford, Paul Gore, John C Baker, LYM)*

Sawston, Cambs [Cambridge Rd; TL4849], *Greyhound*: Old weatherboarded local, recently tastefully refurbished; Marstons and Whitbreads beers, friendly, helpful staff, good food lunchtime and evening, big garden; new restaurant *(Nigel Gibbs, Sandra Cook, S R Gilbert)*; [Pampisford Rd], *University Arms*: Ordinary building, curiously done up inside with cemented-in bottles used Spanish-style as part of the structure; but enthusiastic choice of real ales such as Brains, Felinfoel Double Dragon, Hook Norton Best, Marstons Pedigree, Mitchells Mild and Websters, good range of bar food (some tables in no-smoking area), weekend and evening restaurant; live bands sometimes *(M and J Back, John C Baker, Alan and Ruth Woodhouse)*

Sharnbrook, Beds [SP9959], *Swan With Two Nicks*: Popular locals' pub in picturesque village; friendly welcome and well kept Charles Wells Eagle *(John Baker)*

Shefford, Beds [Deadmans Cross; A600 towards Bedford; TL1141], *White Horse*: Welcoming, comfortable pub with excellent Banks & Taylors ales brewed locally, decent wine list, friendly landlady, and lounge with cosy inglenook fire, armchairs and bookcases; good food, family room, play area, large cottage-style restaurant *(Pete Storey, Roger Danes)*

St Ives, Cambs [Ramsey Rd; TL3171], *Slepe Hall*: Plush hotel bar with friendly service and reasonably priced food; bedrooms *(Wayne Brindle)*

Steppingley, Beds [TL0135], *French Horn*: 16th-century pub with wide choice of real ales such as ABC, Bass, Everards Tiger, Ind Coope Burton and Wadworths 6X, good food in bar and restaurant, garden *(Howard Barclay)*

☆ **Stretham**, Cambs [Cambridge Rd, Elford Closes (off A10 S of Stretham roundabout); TL5072], *Lazy Otter*: Riverside family pub, homely decor in large pleasant bar and conservatory, helpful staff, well kept Adnams and Greene King, good value imaginative bar food, restaurant; waterside garden with family theme days and evening barbecues, boat moorings *(Nigel Gibbs)*

Studham, Beds [Dunstable Rd; TL0215], *Bell*: Welcoming staff, well presented drinks and good bar food *(Karen Elton)*; *Red Lion*: Handy for Whipsnade Zoo, in attractive spot with tables outside looking up to grassy common; cheerful modernish decor, good value bar food (not Sun), decent real ales *(Michael Sandy, Gary Scott, LYM)*

☆ **Sutton**, Beds [village signposted off B1040 Biggleswade—Potton; TL2247], *John o' Gaunt*: Cosy low-beamed bar with easy chairs and low settles around copper-topped tables, enterprising bar food inc imaginative seafood dishes, well kept Greene King IPA, pretty flowers; lovely pink-washed low building with larch and apple trees around garden, near fine 14th-century packhorse bridge with shallow ford taking cars past it; service friendly and attentive *(GB, CH, Joan and Tony Walker, LYM)*

☆ **Swaffham Prior**, Cambs [B1102 NE of Cambridge; TL5764], *Red Lion*: Lovely village local with welcoming and very

friendly staff, well kept Tolly Original, and maybe Old Strong tapped from cask on bar, wide range of food from ploughman's to steaks, separate dining lounge; unusually plush gents' *(Wayne Brindle, M and J Back, John and Tessa Rainsford)*

Swineshead, Beds [Main St; TL0565], *Wheatsheaf*: Recently refurbished by welcoming new landlord, with very good bedrooms (and breakfast); real ale *(G T and J Barnes)*

☆ **Tempsford**, Beds [TL1652], *Anchor*: Extensive roadhouse with lots for children, included as a useful break from A1, and notable for its big riverside gardens with outdoor chess and draughts, boules, fishing on the River Ouse; quickly served straightforward food, restaurant *(Wayne Brindle, LYM)*

The Turves, Cambs [W of March; TL3396], *Three Horseshoes*: Externally looks more like a large village post office, but internally very comfortable with conservatory for families; well kept Greene King IPA and full range of bar food from burgers to quails in brandy and mushrooms, cooked by francophile licensee/chef *(John Baker)*

Toddington, Beds [64 High St; all 3 pubs here handy for M1 junction 12; TL0028], *Bedford Arms*: Well preserved and not over-decorated Tudor pub with particularly well kept Charles Wells Eagle; good provision for families, adequate car parking *(John C Baker)*; *Oddfellows Arms*: Very welcoming staff and roaring coal fires in the two bars; varied range of reasonably priced food such as home-made beef broth and excellent kidneys, liver and bacon; used mostly by business men at lunchtime; Watneys-related beers *(Ken Krober)*; *Sow & Pigs*: Interesting local with pig ornaments all over the place, two open fires, landlord of great character and well kept Greene King IPA and Abbot; much used by classical musicians in transit, especially as it's open all day *(M C Howells)*

Trumpington, Cambs [High St (A1309); TL4454], *Coach & Horses*: Picturesque old pub, comfortably furnished, with lounge, restaurant and grill; well kept beer on handpump, wide choice from good hot and cold buffet — huge helpings; garden, no piped music *(I S Thomson, Charles Bardswell)*

☆ **Turvey**, Beds [Bridge St; A428 NW of Bedford — at W end of village; SP9452], *Three Fyshes*: Great appeal for those who like unfussy, even basic, pubbiness and good beer — they brew their own, and have several good ales from other breweries, as well as farm ciders; good sandwiches and big crusty rolls, hot dishes from vegetarian specialities to steaks and venison — a bit pricey; traditional games, summer barbecues, inglenook fires, dogs and cats; open all day Sat; children welcome *(R C Gandy, Ted George, Roger Danes, LYM)*

☆ **Turvey** [off A428, by church], *Three Cranes*: Particularly friendly and welcoming, decorated with African art and landlady's own paintings; well kept beer, limited but well prepared and reasonably priced bar food, good restaurant; seating outside in pleasant village street, in front verandah and secluded back garden, which has occasional summer jazz and barbecues; fruit machine, piped music (particularly Simon and Garfunkel), newspapers *(Jonathan and Jane Hagger, W H King, F M Williams, Michael and Alison Sandy)*

Waresley, Cambs [TL2454], *Duncombe Arms*: Tudor building which has undergone numerous transformations over the years; busy but comfortable atmosphere, well kept Greene King, interesting bar food such as scampi in fresh tomato, garlic and basil sauce *(John Baker)*

Weston Colville, Cambs [Weston Green; TL6153], *Fox & Hounds*: Welcoming and comfortable, with excellent, unusual food inc English and some delicious Portuguese or even Angolan dishes *(D T Richards, Alan and Ruth Woodhouse)*

Whipsnade, Beds [B4540 E; TL0117], *Old Hunters Lodge*: No recent reports on this, well liked by readers in past editions for good food from sandwiches up, particularly inc fish dishes, and well kept Greene King Abbot, in nice smallish bar; popular restaurant; children welcome *(More news please)*

Whittlesey, Cambs [Ramsey Rd; TL2696], *Boat*: Small remote riverside pub with well kept Elgoods, decent bar food, good value restaurant, helpful landlord *(N W James);* [B1040 N], *Old Dog in a Doublet*: Isolated spot by River Nene, and a former haunt of the great Fenland skaters; large, comfortably furnished bar with good range of beer inc Adnams and Greene King, good bar food generously served and at reasonable prices, separate restaurant, outside seating; fairly close to bronze age site at Flag Fen *(R D Norman)*

Whittlesford, Cambs [off B1379 S of Cambridge; handy for M10 junction 10, via A505; TL4748], *Tickell Arms*: (Sadly the landlord of this interestingly furnished pub died in summer 1990; his flamboyant character is what made it so special, so we'd be glad of more news) *(Tony and Lynne Stark, Peter Hall, Noel Sephton, Nigel Gibbs, Sandra Cook, LYM)*

Whittlesford [nr stn], *Red Lion*: Rambling timbered pub with relaxed atmosphere, Bass beer, lovely summer garden, restaurant *(Nigel Gibbs, Sandra Cook)*

Wisbech, Cambs [North Brink; TF4609], *Red Lion*: Small, friendly pub on River Nene; excellent home-cooked food prepared by landlord; well kept local Elgoods; plenty of parking *(Mr and Mrs I J W Ferguson)*

Woburn, Beds [1 Bedford St; SP9433], *Black Horse*: Refurbished and opened up pub, handy for the Abbey, with tables out in a sheltered garden, friendly service from newish licensees; concentration now on food from sandwiches and baked potatoes up, with two new restaurants rather specialising in fish and in steaks cooked in front of you, also children's and vegetarian dishes and lots of summer barbecues; well kept Courage on handpump; open all day summer Sat and Bank Hols; children in eating area and restaurant *(Lyn and Bill Capper, C A Holloway, Michael and Alison Sandy, John Baker, LYM; more reports please);* [Hockcliffe Rd], *Royal Oak*: Pleasant but small — basic public area, smaller lounge and a little, restauranty area at the end where you can reserve one of the four tables; very pleasant and friendly, drinks (Greene King) noticeably cheap and food decent if ordinary; very full in summer; smallish garden with barbecues and lots of flowers *(Anon)*

☆ **Woodditton**, Cambs [Ditton Green; village signed off B1063 at Cheveley; TL6659], *Three Blackbirds*: Two snug bars in pretty thatched village pub, friendly and efficient service, well kept Tolly Bitter and Original, popular good value bar food from sandwiches and lunchtime ploughman's through home-cooked ham to good steaks and Sun roasts; piped music, pretty garden, restaurant Tues-Sat — where children allowed *(Mr and Mrs J Back, LYM; more reports please)*

Wootton, Beds [Hall End; TL0045], *Chequers*: Warm and cosy 15th-century pub of character, popular with locals and visitors, with friendly, helpful service; very good food in bar and restaurant *(Mrs Jenny Clark)*

Cheshire

Notable new entries here, or places back among the main entries after an absence, include the fine old Blue Bell at Bell o th Hill in the south of the county (often listed under nearby Tushingham), the Badger at Church Minshull (straightforward surroundings, very popular food — and friendly), the smartly decorated and furnished Whipping Stocks at Over Peover, the spacious Golden Pheasant at Plumley (doing well under its new licensees), the civilised White Lion at Weston (very handy for the M6 — but has its own bowling green, and a good bedroom block) and the Swan at Wybunbury (promising food and a relaxed, unpretentious atmosphere). The Sutton Hall Hotel, formerly listed by us under Sutton, will now be found under Macclesfield — easier to find it from there. Other pubs doing specially well here at the moment include the Cholmondeley Arms near Bickley Moss (unanimous praise for the inventive food in this interestingly converted Victorian schoolhouse — we'd expect good things of the newish bedrooms too, though have not yet heard from readers about these), the Stanley Arms up on the moors at Bottom of the Oven (substantial food helpings), the Spinner & Bergamot at Comberbach (particularly welcoming), the Pheasant at Higher Burwardsley (its bedrooms have glorious views, and the new conservatory is an asset), the isolated Leathers Smithy up at Langley (very well placed for walkers), the Bells of Peover at Lower Peover (a growing groundswell of approval for the changes by the newish licensees at this starred entry), the really welcoming Dun Cow at Ollerton, the beautifully placed Highwayman up at Rainow (good beer and food) and the cosy Rising Sun in Tarporley. The Holly Bush at Little Leigh has been one of the very few surviving highly traditional old-fashioned farm-pubs, but with the retirement of its long-serving tenant the brewery has been talking of dramatic changes, perhaps even closure; we have written to the brewery (and to the local planning authority) pointing out readers' particular delight in the pub's unique and so far unchanging qualities, but as we go to press do not yet know the outcome. Drinks in the area are decidedly cheaper than the national average. They are kept down by the competitive strength here of a number of thriving regional and local breweries — particularly Greenalls, also Burtonwood, Marstons, Robinsons and Thwaites (and though Boddingtons has now been swallowed by Whitbreads its pubs' prices have not yet climbed to the national level of Whitbreads' other pubs). These set the area's low-price trend, and our records of local prices show that pubs tied to the national brewing combines tend to match the other breweries' low prices here — though free houses here more often drift above that price level. Two main entries, the Golden Pheasant at Plumley and Dog at Peover Heath, stand out as having particularly low drinks prices. On the food side, relatively few pubs here can beat our £1 target for really cheap snacks — the White Lions at Alvanley and Weston, and perhaps the filling soup at the Copper Mine at Fullers Moor. But a good few Cheshire pubs sell heartier food at bargain prices – particularly the Blue Bell at Bell o th Hill, Badger at Church Minshull, Crown at Goostrey (lunchtime), Olde Red Lion there, Leathers Smithy at Langley, Highwayman at Rainow (pizzas), Rising Sun at Tarporley and those two White Lions again. At all of these we found decent main dishes at under £3.

ALVANLEY   SJ4974 Map 7

White Lion

2 ¹/₂ miles from M56, junction 14; A5117 towards Helsby, bear left into A56 then quickly turn right, following village signpost; in village, turn right into Manley Road

This attractive little black and white pub, opposite the village church, can be surprisingly popular – there may even be queues before opening time. Generous helpings of well presented food range from soup (90p), sandwiches (from £1, toasties from £1.20, steak barm-cake £1.60) and quite a wide variety of ploughman's (from £1.80), through home-made hot-pot or cottage pie (£1.60) and salads (from £2.90), to specials like home-made steak pie (£3.25) or chicken chasseur (£3.90); puddings (£1.50); polite and friendly service. The low-ceilinged lounge has decorative plates on the walls, softly cushioned red plush seats and wall banquettes, and beer-steins, pistols, copper jugs and so forth hanging from its moulded black beams; piped music. The smaller public bar has darts, dominoes, fruit machine and space game; Greenalls Mild and Bitter on handpump. Outside, there are rustic picnic-table sets on the grass by the play area (which has an assault course and sand-floored fortress), white tables and chairs under cocktail parasols, and attractive hanging baskets; an adjacent field has various ducks, geese and sheep. *(Recommended by J W Sutton, Mr and Mrs J H Adam, Brian and Anna Marsden, Geoff Halson; more reports please)*

Greenalls   Licensees Keith and Brenda Morris   Real ale   Meals and snacks (12–2, 6–9.30; not 25 or 26 Dec)   Children welcome   Open 11.30–3, 5.30–11

BARTHOMLEY   SJ7752 Map 7

White Lion ★

Village link signposted from M6 junction 16 exit towards Crewe

There's a peaceable view of the attractive village from the tables under the old yew tree or on the front cobbles beside this black and white timbered and thatched 17th-century pub. The simply furnished main room has heavy oak beams in the low ceiling (one big enough to house quite a collection of plates), attractively moulded black panelling, Cheshire watercolours and prints, an open fire and latticed windows; up some steps, a second room has more oak panelling, a high-backed winged settle, a paraffin lamp hinged to the wall, another open fire, and sensibly placed darts, shove-ha'penny and dominoes. Limited, cheap bar snacks run to hot pies, excellent ham, beef or cheese salad rolls, and soup at lunchtime; well kept Burtonwood Bitter on handpump. It can get very busy at weekends – readers recommend an evening mid-week in which to appreciate the particularly friendly and unspoilt atmosphere. The early 15th-century red sandstone church of St Bertiline across the road is worth a visit. *(Recommended by Mike and Wendy Proctor, Sue Holland, Dave Webster, L M Miall, William Rodgers, Martin Aust, Denis Mann, Theo Schofield, Ewan McCall)*

Burtonwood   Real ale   Snacks (not Sun evening)   Children at lunchtime only   Open 11–3, 6–11

BELL O TH HILL   SJ5245 Map 7

Blue Bell

Signed just off A41 N of Whitchurch

Opposite a farm and with cows and maybe a donkey or two around it, this black and white timbered building – with a massive central chimney – has an entrance calculated to raise the pub-lover's spirits. Through a great oak door by a mounting-block, you find yourself in a small quarry-tiled hallway, with stairs up, and another formidable oak door on your right. This leads into three very heavily beamed communicating rooms, two served by hatch, with a cheerful mix of furnishings from comfortable plush wall seats and stripped country-kitchen tables (with bunches of flowers) to a nice little antique settle; there are a few decorative plates, one or two dog or hunting prints and some strange curios on the walls, and each room has an open fire – the main bar's in an inglenook with an attractively moulded black oak mantlebeam. Quickly served good value bar food includes sandwiches (£1), burgers (£1.20), soup (£1.25), steak sandwich or pizza (£2.50), ploughman's or simple hot dishes (£2.95), steak and kidney pie (£3.35), 8oz scampi, Cumberland sausage mixed grill or lasagne (£3.40) and steaks (from £6.40), with several specials such as deep-fried feta cheese (£1.50), pork done with apple, fresh sage and cider or smoked cod and prawn cheesebake (£3.60). Greenalls and Original on handpump, dominoes, quiet piped music, friendly service. There are picnic-table sets among flowers on the front grass. *(Recommended by Chris Raisin)*

Greenalls   Licensee Mark Sumner   Real ale   Meals and snacks (12–2, 6.30–10) Children welcome   Open 12–3, 6.30–11; closed Mon lunchtime

BICKLEY MOSS   SJ5549   Map 7

Cholmondeley Arms ★ 🍷

Cholmondeley; A49 5 1/2 miles N of Whitchurch

It takes a moment to adjust here – it's not every day you go to an old Victorian schoolhouse for a drink. Readers' enthusiasm for the food is unanimous, with the home-made pies (£4.50) emerging as a particular favourite; other food includes sandwiches (from £2.25; they may also make them up on request), several children's dishes (£2.50), ploughman's (£3), a complicated terrine (£3.20), garlic mushrooms with bacon (£3.50), hot crab pâté (£3.20), omelettes (£3.75), good stuffed pancakes (£4.25), devilled kidneys on toast (£4.75), salads with home-made mayonnaise (£4.50), hot beef curry (£4.80), gammon (£5.25), steaks (from £8.10) and grilled king prawns and chicken with satay sauce (£8.20); a very wide choice of home-made puddings such as very good syrup sponge or bananas in cream and brandy (from £2). An old blackboard lists ten or so interesting and often uncommon wines by the glass, including a decent champagne; well kept Marstons Burton and Pedigree on handpump, with a guest such as Border; big (4 cup) pot of coffee. The cross-shaped and high-ceilinged bar is furnished with anything from cane and bentwood to pews and carved oak, with some of the old school desks above the bar on a gantry; there are masses of Victorian pictures (especially portraits and military subjects), patterned paper on the shutters to match the curtains, an open fire, and a great stag's head over one of the side arches; well reproduced taped music; a fresh and airy atmosphere. There are seats out on a sizeable lawn, and Cholmondeley Castle and gardens are close by. The manager, John Radford, was with the licensees in their days at the Crown in Hopton Wafers. *(Recommended by W C M Jones, Mike Beiley, J Scarisbrick, I T Parry, Susan Palmer, Laurence Manning, G A Price, Mr and Mrs J E Rycroft, Celia and David Watt, Wayne Brindle, J M Shaw, George Jonas, M A and W R Proctor, Philip Riding, Philip Williams, Martin Aust, M and J Godfrey, C F Walling, Jon Wainwright)*

Free house   Licensees Julian and Ginny Harrison   Real ale   Meals and snacks (12–2.15, 6ish–10)   Children welcome   Open 11–3, 6.30(6 Sat)–11; winter evening opening 7 (6.30 Sat); closed 25 Dec   Bedrooms tel Cholmondeley (0829) 720300; £30S/£40S

BOLLINGTON SJ9377 Map 7

Vale

29 Adlington Road; off B5091 on road heading N by railway viaduct; OS Sheet 118 map reference 931781

Originally three terraced houses, this very relaxing and surprisingly quiet pub retains much of that homely atmosphere. The open-plan bar is unobtrusively modernised, with tapestried wall seats, wheelback chairs, and tables set with cheery red tablecloths at lunchtime. There are also heavy dark green velvet curtains, brass platters on the end stripped-stone wall, some racehorse prints and 1936 Gallaghers cricketer cigarette cards, a log fire in the stone fireplace (as well as central heating), and a couple of big stone supporting pillars with internal arches. Well kept Thwaites Bitter and Mild, and Timothy Taylors Landlord on handpump from the substantial timber-topped and stone-built corner counter; fruit machine, good pop music. Food includes home-made soup or sandwiches (£1), ploughman's (£3.30), home-made dishes such as chilli con carne (£3.30) and steak and kidney pie or lasagne (£3.50), half a chicken (£4.40), and fish dishes such as cod, plaice or haddock (£3), seafood platter (£3.60) and scampi (£4.40); the beef and ham are home-cooked. The garden is a neat little lawn with picnic-table sets, by the edge of a wood, and there are swings, a slide, a rocking horse, climbing frame and paddling pool. A bowling green, cricket field, play-park and tennis courts are all nearby, and the charming and well preserved village itself is close to the start of *Good Walks Guide* Walk 73. *(Recommended by Lee Goulding, Tony and Pat Young, Brian and Anna Marsden, Paul Wreglesworth; more reports please)*

Free house   Licensee Mrs Patricia Capper   Real ale   Lunchtime meals and snacks (12–2, 6.30–9.30; not Mon lunchtime except Bank Hols)   Open 11.30–3, 5.30–11; closed Mon lunchtime except Bank Holidays

BOTTOM OF THE OVEN SJ9872 Map 7

Stanley Arms ⚑

From A537 Buxton–Macclesfield heading towards Macclesfield, take first left turn (not signposted) after Cat & Fiddle; OS Sheet 118 map reference 980723

Bar food in this isolated and unspoilt moorland pub comes in remarkably substantial helpings; at lunchtime it includes sandwiches (from £1.40, not Sunday), home-made soup (£1.40), good ploughman's (£3.50), and tasty lasagne (£3.80); in the evening there are more elaborate main dishes such as outstanding salads (up to £6.40 for ham), chicken in a bacon, mushroom and wine sauce or beef cooked in Guinness (£5.95), halibut steak with caviare and prawns (£7.95), half a duckling with orange sauce (£8.75), and a daily special; friendly service. Two of the three snug rooms have lots of shiny black lacquered woodwork, subdued red and black flowery plush wall settles and stools, some dark blue seats, and low dimpled copper tables on the grey carpets; the third is laid out as a dining room, with pretty pastel tablecloths; bunches of flowers in summer, open fires in winter, little landscape watercolours on the ochre walls and piped Vivaldi. Well kept Marstons Burton and Pedigree on handpump, and a good range of spirits; it can get busy at the weekend. There are fine views out to the steep pastures that rise towards Shuttlingsloe; picnic-table sets on the grass behind. *(Recommended by Paul and Margaret Baker, Jill and Peter Brickley, Janet and Gary Amos, P J and S E Robbins, Laurence Manning, T Galligan, Philip Riding, Paul Wreglesworth, Mr and Mrs B Hobden, Alan Skull, Graham Gibson)*

Marstons   Licensees Mr and Mrs Alan Harvey   Real ale   Lunchtime snacks and meals (12–2.30, 7–10)   Restaurant tel Sutton (02605) 2414   Children in eating area and restaurant   Open 11.30–3, 7–11; closed 25 Dec

BRERETON GREEN   SJ7864 Map 7

Bears Head 🛏

1 3/4 miles from M6, junction 17; fork left from Congleton road almost immediately, then left on to A50; also from junction 18, via Holmes Chapel

The series of rambling rooms here has masses of heavy black beams and timbers, some traditional oak panel-back settles, ladder-back rush seats, some Windsor armchairs, a corner cupboard full of Venetian glass, and in a room at the back a modern, reconstructed fireplace with a brick back and a high front mantlebeam forming an inglenook; there are two serving bars, though only one is normally in use. A section of wall in one room (under glass for protection) has had the plaster removed to show the construction of timber underneath; civilised and atmospheric. Bar food consists of home-made soup (£1.40), sandwiches (from £1.60, excellent steak and onion £4.60), home-made pâtés (from £3) salads (£4.50, poached fresh Scotch salmon £4.65), and daily hot dishes such as gammon with egg or pineapple, roast chicken or fried fillet of plaice (all £4.35), and sirloin steak (£7.50); home-made puddings such as chocolate roulade (£2); courteous service from smart uniformed staff. Bass and Burtonwood Bitter on handpump, kept in fine deep cellars; fruit machine, soothing piped music. A pretty side terrace by the black-and-white timbered inn has white cast-iron tables and chairs under cocktail parasols, big black cast-iron lamp clusters and a central fountain. *(Recommended by Laurence Manning, Margaret and Roy Randle, David Shillitoe, John and Pat Smyth, Robert and Vicky Tod)*

Free house   Licensees Mr and Mrs Roberto Tarquini   Real ale   Meals and snacks (12–2, 7–10)   Restaurant (not Sun evening)   Children in eating area   Open 11–3, 7–11   Bedrooms tel Holmes Chapel (0477) 35251; £41.50S/£49.50S

CHESTER   SJ4166 Map 7

Boot

Eastgate Row North

Over the past few years this pub has expanded considerably from its original upstairs bar, which used to open, via a long corridor, on to the balconied shopping arcade above the street. Now you can enter directly from the street, into a carefully refurbished, split-level bar downstairs; there's lots of beams, exposed wattle and daub behind glass panels, oak flooring and flagstones, solidly built-in wooden furniture, heavy beams and woodwork, the brewery's Yorkshire-rose emblem worked into stained-glass panels in the latticed windows, and a couple of framed Victorian newspapers; fruit machine, piped music. A handsome staircase takes you to an oak-panelled function room; beyond the food serving room is another lounge, with a black-leaded kitchen range and a collection of glass and pot boots. Well kept Sam Smiths OB (delivered bright from the brewery) and Museum tapped from cask downstairs; notably good service. Bar food includes filled rolls, soup, pâté or hot beef sandwich, and ploughman's, filled baked potatoes, and quiche. The attractively landscaped zoo to the north of the city is entertaining. *(Recommended by Graham Gibson, Jon Wainwright, Mr and Mrs P A Jones, H K Dyson, Mr and Mrs J H Adam, Dennis Royles)*

Sam Smiths   Licensees Anne and Peter Kinsey   Real ale   Snacks (not evenings)   No nearby parking   Open 11–4, 5(6 Sat)–11; closed 25 and 26 Dec

Falcon

Lower Bridge Street

First mentioned in local records in 1602, this handsome timbered building didn't actually become a pub until the end of the 18th century; it was taken over by a textile firm about a century later, and its current late-Victorian style is the result of recent and concerted refurbishment. The quiet, airy room upstairs (available for functions in the early part of the week) has a fine range of latticed windows looking over the street, and there's some interesting quatrefoil. Well kept Sam

Smiths OB and Museum on handpump; soft drinks may be on the pricey side; fruit machine, piped music. Bar food includes open sandwiches, various salads and daily hot dishes such as casseroles, steak and kidney pie or moussaka; the bar staff wear uniforms (it's that sort of place). It can get very crowded on Friday and Saturday evenings. *(Recommended by Jenny and Brian Seller, P Corris, H K Dyson, Celia and David Watt, Dennis Royles; more reports please)*

Sam Smiths   Licensees Gail and Andrew Waller   Real ale   Meals and snacks (lunchtime, not Sun)   Children in upstairs bar lunchtime only   Parking may be difficult   Jazz once a month   Open 11–3, 5–11; all day Sat

CHURCH MINSHULL   SJ6661 Map 7
Badger

B5074 Nantwich–Winsford

It's the very friendly atmosphere and interesting beers which readers have particularly delighted in here, though the food's good too – filled baps (from £1.95), plaice (£2.75), several vegetarian dishes (£2.95), fine quiches and home-made pies such as turkey and ham or steak and kidney (£3.50), baked halibut (£4.95), steaks (from £5.50) and several children's dishes (£1.25). Puddings are good, especially the authentic rice pudding and the treacle tart. The beers, well kept on handpump, are Marstons Mild, Best and Pedigree, and Oak Best, Double Dagger, Old Oak and Wobbly Bob; they also have several malt whiskies on optic including Macallan and Smiths. The bar has straightforward, largely modern furnishings, though lots of stuffed animals lurking in nooks and crannies (particularly in the bar counter itself – and there's a badger peering out of a hole in a big wooden cask) give an unusual touch. The bare-boards public bar has pool, sensibly placed darts, dominoes, cards, a fruit machine that takes 2p pieces, and a piano; coal fires, piped music, helpful service. There are picnic-table sets under cocktail parasols in the neat garden below the handsome village church, sheltered by shrubs and a flowering cherry, with some seats on a back verandah; besides a sundial and swings there may be rabbits. This is one of the very few pubs we know with the village post office under the same roof. *(Recommended by Derek and Sylvia Stephenson, John Scarisbrick, Chris Raisin, C F Walling, E G Parish, Charles Hall, G T Jones)*

Free house   Licensee Bernard Conwell   Real ale   Meals and snacks   Restaurant tel Church Minshull (027 071) 607   Children welcome   Open 11.30–3, 5.30–11; 11.30–11 Sat

COMBERBACH   SJ6477 Map 7
Spinner & Bergamot ⊘

Village signposted from A553 and A559 NW or Northwich; pub towards Great Budworth

There's a particularly welcoming atmosphere in the front bar of this slated and pebbledashed pub, with its red plush button-back built-in wall banquettes, some toby jugs hanging from the beams, and one or two hunting prints on the cream textured walls. The softly lit back dining room has country-kitchen furniture (some of oak), pretty curtains, and a big brick inglenook with a stripped high mantelbeam; brocaded wall seats in the neat red-tiled public bar; each room has an open fire, lit with logs in winter. Well kept Greenalls on handpump; darts, dominoes, piped music, and a bowling green outside at the back – bowls can be hired. Generously served, home-cooked bar food includes sandwiches (from £1.40), soup (£1.20), several other starters such as deep-fried mushrooms filled with pâté (£2.20), steak and kidney pie (£3.80), good salads, gammon and egg (£4.50), fresh cod or plaice (£5.50), excellent scampi in home-made batter (£6), steaks (from 8oz rump £7.50) and dishes of the day such as potted shrimps (£2.50) or lasagne (£4.50); cheerful, efficient service. A hatch in the front lobby serves the white tables out on a sloping lawn, which has swings, a climber and assorted rabbits and birds; there are lots of flower tubs and hanging baskets outside, bunches of fresh flowers inside. *(Recommended by C F Walling, Simon Turner, Tony and*

Pat Young, A F C Young, G T Jones, Syd and Wyn Donald, G Eyre-Rodger, Dr and Mrs S G Donald)

Greenalls   Licensees Doug and Mavis Hughes   Real ale   Meals and snacks (not Sun evening)   Open 11.30–3.30, 5.30–11

FADDILEY   SJ5953   Map 7
Tollemache Arms

A534 Nantwich–Wrexham

Though from the map the road here looks like a busy through route to North Wales, it's actually a quiet country scene, with fields of cows around this black and white, thatched and timbered 15th-century little pub. The two rooms on the right have rather cottagey decorations – copper utensils, houseplants and so forth – with re-upholstered, built-in wall settles and leatherette-cushioned cask seats around gleaming copper tables, dark glossy beams, and an open fire; the inner room, up a couple of steps, is the snugger of the two. The room on the left is laid up more conventionally, but like the others has lots of brass and copper, and shiny beams. Well kept Greenalls Cask on handpump; darts and dominoes in the back public bar; piped music. The decent range of bar food includes sandwiches, home-made soup (£1.20), a mixed ploughman's (£2.75), home-made quiche (£2.95), steak and mushroom pie (£3.25), chicken breast in stilton, celery and apple sauce or cod in parsley sauce (£3.50), vegetable lasagne, gammon (£4.25), mixed grill (£5.95) and steaks (from £6.50); puddings (from £1.60). The neat small lawn, with a couple of substantial yew trees guarding the gate in its picket fence, has picnic-table sets. The pub is floodlit at night. (Recommended by P Corris, Graham Gibson; more reports please)

Greenalls   Licensees Janice Brindley and Andy Babbington   Real ale   Meals and snacks (not Mon)   Children in eating area   Open 12–3, 7–11; closed Mon lunchtime

FULLERS MOOR   SJ4954   Map 7
Copper Mine

A534 Wrexham–Nantwich, about a mile E of A41 junction

A pleasant base for exploring the local countryside – there are good walks to Bickerton and Larkton Hills; the pub itself has spacious grounds, and in season you can watch the house martins nesting in the eaves from the picnic-table sets under cocktail parasols; summer barbecues. Highly praised bar food includes soup (95p), pancake rolls (£1.95), cottage pie or a curry of the day (£3.75), steak and mushroom pie (£3.95), a good selection of help-yourself salads (from £4.50), vegetarian lasagne (£3.95), honey-grilled pork ribs (£4.75), steaks (from 4oz sirloin £3.95 to 16oz £8.50), and specials like fresh salmon or seafood platter; occasional Spanish, Italian or Turkish theme nights. The well kept, softly lit and low-ceilinged bars, divided into separate seating areas, have stripped beams and timbering, blacked stove doors set into the dividing wall, and prettily papered walls covered with masses of copper-mining mementoes – blasting explosives and fuses, old lamps, and photographic tableaux of more-or-less tense moments in local mining history. Well kept Boddingtons Bitter and Mild and Burtonwood on handpump; juke box, rack of magazines, good open fires. (Recommended by Eric Locker, Laurence Manning, Graham Gibson, Mr and Mrs J H Adam, Dr P Webb, BHP, Peter Corris)

Boddingtons (Whitbreads)   Licensees Dave and Gill Furmston   Real ale   Meals and · snacks   Chidren welcome   Open 11.30–3, 6.30(6 Sat)–11; all day on Bank Holidays, and may open longer in afternoon

GOOSTREY   SJ7870   Map 7
Crown

111 Main Road; village signposted from A50 and A535

This comfortable and civilised pub, originally a farmhouse, serves freshly prepared food, including sandwiches (from £1.10, delicious and generous open prawn

£3.25; toasties such as ham and pineapple £1.20), excellent Stilton ploughman's (£2.50), chilli con carne (£2.95), Southern fried chicken (£3.20), and a lunchtime special (£2.95); in the evening, there are extra dishes such as rack of lamb or rump steak (£4.95), and duckling, king prawns or veal (£5.95) in the back bistro dining room; bookings are essential here at weekends – it usually secures the table for all or most of the evening; in any event it's best to get there early to be sure of a place. An upstairs room can be booked for dinner parties, preferably not on Saturdays, and is otherwise available for diners. In the two communicating rooms of the lounge bar there's a chaise longue and cushioned settles as well as more conventional seats, prints of some of Lowry's less well known paintings, and open fires. The smaller and brighter taproom is plain and traditional, with darts, dominoes, and cribbage; piped music; well kept Marstons Pedigree on handpump. Seats on the front terrace face the village road. *(Recommended by Simon Turner, H B Vanstone, Steve Mitcheson, Anne Collins, J Scarisbrick, Roger Huggins, Laurence Manning, Robert and Vicky Tod, Dennis Royles, David Young)*

Marstons   Licensee Peter McGrath   Real ale   Meals and snacks (not Mon, not Sun evening)   Restaurant (not Sun evening)   Children in eating area of bar   Jazz or folk Sun evening   Open 11.30–3, 5.30–11   Bedrooms tel Holmes Chapel (0477) 32128; £15/£20

Olde Red Lion

Station Road; closer to A535

The open-plan bar in this attractively modernised pub, at the bottom of a steep dell, has cushioned banquettes built in against the floral wallpapered walls; Tetleys on handpump; darts, fruit machine, and piped music. Decent bar food includes baked potatoes (from £1.35), pies (£1.55), sandwiches (from £2.10; toasties £1.45), ploughman's (£2.25), bratwurst (£2.45), and Yorkshire puddings filled with chicken and sweetcorn (£2.50); service stays efficient under pressure. There are some white tables on a small lawn in the pretty garden with a children's play area. *(Recommended by Roger Braithwaite, Steve Mitcheson, Anne Collins, G D and J A Amos; more reports please)*

Tetleys (Allied)   Manager Michael Reavey   Real ale   Meals and snacks (12–2, 7–10) Children welcome   Restaurant tel Holmes Chapel (0477) 32033   Open 11.30–3, 7–11; closed evening 25 Dec

GREAT BUDWORTH   SJ6778   Map 7

George & Dragon

4 1/2 miles from M6, junction 19; from A556 towards Northwich, turn right into B5391 almost at once; then fork right at signpost to Aston-by-Budworth, Arley Hall & Gardens

The rambling and panelled lounge in this picturesque 17th-century pub has red plush button-back banquettes and older settles on its Turkey carpet, plenty of nooks and alcoves, copper jugs hanging from the beams, and a fine big mirror with horsebrasses on the wooden pillars of its frame. The public bar has a lively atmosphere and is simply furnished; darts, dominoes, and fruit machine; the piped music may sometimes be loud. Popular and well presented bar food includes sandwiches (from £1.30), ploughman's (£2.75), vegetarian lasagne or roast meats (£3.50), fish (from £3.25; lemon sole £4.25), salads from a self-service lunchtime cold table on the bar (from £3.50), and steaks (from £6.50); children's menu (£1.20), and Sunday roast £3.75). Ind Coope Burton, Tetleys Mild and Bitter on handpump, and some malt whiskies. The 11th-century church and village stocks are opposite the fine wrought-iron gantry that serves for an inn sign. *(Recommended by Derek and Sylvia Stephenson, Alan and Marlene Radford, TBB, C F Walling, Dr P Webb)*

Tetleys (Allied)   Licensees Malcolm and Lynne Curtin   Real ale   Meals and snacks Upstairs restaurant tel Comberbach (0606) 891317   Children in eating area at lunchtime, restaurant in evening   Open 11.30–3, 7–11

HIGHER BURWARDSLEY   SJ5256 Map 7

Pheasant ⇐

Burwardsley signposted from Tattenhall (which itself is signposted off A41 S of Chester) and from Harthill (reached by turning off A534 Natnwich–Holt at the Copper Mine); follow pub's signpost on up hill from Post Office; OS Sheet 117 map reference 523566

Well placed for walks along the Peckforton Hills (and at the start of *Good Walks Guide* Walk 72), and overlooking the Cheshire Plain and the Wirral, this 17th-century, half-timbered and sandstone building has a most attractive bar: large colour engravings of Victorian officials of the North Cheshire Hunt, a stuffed pheasant (as well as a picture of one), a set of whimsical little cock-fighting pictures done in real feathers, foreign banknotes on the beams, and plates over the high stone mantlepiece of the see-through fireplace – said to house the biggest log fire in the county. There's a tall leather-cushioned fender around the fire and a fine variety of other seats on its Turkey carpet, ranging from red leatherette or plush wall seats to one or two antique oak settles. Good bar food includes home-made soup (£1.75), nicely presented sandwiches (from £1.30, home-cooked topside £1.65, smoked Scotch salmon £2.75), ploughman's (£2.85), several salads (from £2.40 for Scotch egg, £3.30 for game pie, £4.90 prawn), lasagne or home-made steak and kidney pie (£3.30), chicken and Stilton roulades or pheasant casserole (£4.50), and sirloin steak (£7); children's menu (£1.60). Well kept Bass on handpump, and quite a few wines; friendly staff. Darts, fruit machine (not in main bar) and piped music. The conservatory, aimed primarily at families, is built over the old terrace, and the dining room specialises in game and beef dishes – the pub's own Highland cattle herd have won several prizes at the Royal Show and other major shows. The bedrooms – two of which are new this year – are in an attractively and very comfortably converted sandstone-built barn, and all have views. Picnic-table sets on a big side lawn. *(Recommended by D W Huebner, David and Eloise Smaylen, Laurence Manning, Martin Aust, Mark Evans, David Waterhouse, Neil and Angela Huxter; more reports please)*

Free house   Licensee David Greenhaugh   Real ale   Meals and snacks   Restaurant   Children in conservatory lunchtime only   Horses welcomed, and horse-and-trap rides can be arranged   Open 12–3, 7–11   Bedrooms tel Tattenhall (0829) 70434; £35B/£45B

LANGLEY   SJ9471 Map 7

Leathers Smithy

From Macclesfield, heading S from centre on A523 turn left into Byrons Lane at Langley, Wincle signpost; in Langley follow main road forking left at church into Clarke Lane – keep on towards the moors; OS Sheet 118 map reference 952715

The views across to the Ridgegate Reservoir from a comfortable bay window seat, or to the mountains from the back garden are most attractive in this isolated pub, surrounded by rich upland sheep pastures. The agreeable range of bar food includes sandwiches (from £1.10), beef pie (£1.80), king rib steaklet (£1.90), ploughman's (from £2.10), lasagne or vegetarian mung bean biriani (£2.70), tasty steak and kidney pie (£3.25), good salads, and gammon and egg (£3.70); delicious puddings such as butterscotch and walnut fudge cake (£1.20). The lively, partly flagstoned right-hand bar has bow window seats or wheelback chairs, and gin traps, farrier's pincers, a hay basket and other ironwork on the roughcast cream walls. On the left, there are more wheelback chairs around cast-iron-framed tables on Turkey carpet, little country pictures and drawings of Cheshire buildings, Wills steam engine cigarette cards and a locomotive name-plate curving over one of the two open fires, and faint piped music. Ind Coope Burton, Jennings Bitter, and Tetleys Bitter and Mild on handpump, hot mulled wine in winter (imported from Germany) served from a polished copper salamander, and a decent collection of spirits, including several malt whiskies; dominoes, fruit machine. The pub is popular with walkers. *(Recommended by Christian Leigh, Mike and Wendy Proctor; more reports please)*

Tetleys (Allied)   Licensee Paul Hadfield   Real ale   Meals and snacks (not Mon evening)   Children in own room Sat & Sun lunchtime only   Occasional pianola music   Open 12–3, 7–11

LITTLE LEIGH   SJ6276   Map 7

Holly Bush

4 1/2 miles from M56 junction 10: A49 towards Northwich, pub just S of A533 junction

This may be a private house by the time the *Guide* appears – though it won't have been without a concerted campaign to save it by the local farming community, CAMRA, the press and others. One of Cheshire's oldest pubs, it's actually a fine timber-framed and thatched, old-fashioned farmhouse, with varnished wall benches with sloping panelled backs around waxed and polished country tables, two naval pictures on the wall, and a warm open fire; there's no bar – the Greenalls and Mild (on handpump) are served from the open doorway of a little back tap room. Its survival as a mainstay of traditional English rural life has been due largely to its being in the same family for as long as anyone can remember – Albert Cowap retired at the age of 70 last May and his son took over. However when we last heard Greenalls had applied for planning permission to change it to an ordinary house, on the grounds that it would be too costly to refurbish – even though to have it changed in any way is the last thing anyone wants. We're keeping our fingers crossed, but we fear the worst. *(Recommended by Graham Gibson; more reports please)*

Greenalls   Licensee Albert Cowap   Real ale   Snacks   Children in small snug, not after 9pm   Open 11–3, 5.30–11

LOWER PEOVER   SJ7474   Map 7

Bells of Peover ★

From B5081 take short cobbled lane signposted to church

The slight wobble in readers' reports following the changes instigated by the new licensees in summer 1989 has now settled down to a clear groundswell of warm approval – there seems little danger of this elegant wisteria-covered pub being anything other than a long-standing favourite. Much in fact is unchanged: the little tiled bar with Toby jugs, comic Victorian prints, and side hatches for its serving counter, and the general style of the original lounge with its antique settles, antique china in the dresser, high-backed Windsor armchairs, spacious window seat, and pictures above the panelling; sadly both fireplaces have been removed and replaced by smaller grates, now coal-lit. The old kitchen is now a second similar lounge, there's Turkey carpeting throughout, and the restaurant is even smarter than before – jacket and tie are advised. Bar food includes home-made soup (£1), good, fresh sandwiches (from £1.20; open or salmon £2.50), home-made lasagne (£3.50), steak and kidney pie (£3.60), home-made quiche such as celery and broccoli or smoked salmon (£3.85), baked potatoes with interesting fillings, good daily specials, and several puddings (£1.40); friendly and efficient service; there has been some indication that the new kitchens haven't always been able to cope with the demands of bar and restaurant, but we're keeping our fingers crossed that this has just been a question of teething problems. Very well kept Greenalls Best on handpump; dominoes; good, modern lavatories. The sheltered crazy-paved terrace in front of the pub faces a beautiful black and white timbered church (mainly 14th-century, with lovely woodwork inside; the stone tower is 16th-century); a spacious lawn beyond the old coachyard at the side spreads down through trees and rose pergolas to a little stream. The Barkers used to run the Maypole at Acton Bridge (where they were voted top licensees by their brewery), but Mrs Barker's great-grandfather George Bell ran this place for half a century (and also gave it its name) – so in a sense they've come home. *(Recommended by Simon Turner, Brian and Anna Marsden, John and Tessa Rainsford, Tony and Pat Young, H B Vanstone, Keith Mills, Tony and Lynne Stark, Graham Gibson, RT, J F Kent, Audrey and Brian Green, A F C Young, Steve Dark, Ralph A Raimi, John Atherton, Robert and Vicky Tod, John Broughton, Chris Cooke, Paul Wreglesworth, Laurence Manning)*

Greenalls   *Licensee Dave Barker   Real ale   Meals and snacks   Restaurant* tel *Lower Peover* (056 581) 2269 *(closed Sun evening, Mon)   Open 11–3, 5.30(6 Sat)–11; closed evening 25 Dec*

LOWER WHITLEY   SJ6179   Map 7

Chetwode Arms

2 1/4 miles from M 56, junction 10; village signposted from A49 Whitchurch road

The beautifully kept bowling green is a delight in summer, while the roaring coal fires (as well as the central heating) complement the natural warmth of this traditional country pub. Wholesome food includes home-made soup (£1.10), sandwiches (from £1.10), vegetarian quiche (£3.25), salads (from £3.25), kofta curry (£3.50), steak and kidney pie (£3.75), fresh fillet of plaice (£5), and steaks (£6.25); also specials like chicken tikka or tandoori (£4.95); children's dishes on request. By the small central servery is a snug little room with a settle and some chairs, and three more carpeted rooms leading off – one with a handsome heavy seat built right around its walls. The locals' bar is on the right, served by a hatch, with old green-cushioned settles, heavy mahogany tables, and darts and dominoes. There's some farm equipment such as a miniature harrow and plough, horsebrasses, little country pictures on the walls, and a collection of china teapots and so forth. Greenalls on electric pump; darts, pool, dominoes, piped music. *(Recommended by G T Jones, Andy and Jill Kassube, Syd and Wyn Donald, C F Walling, Dennis Royles, Wayne Brindle, Dr and Mrs S G Donald; more reports please)*

Greenalls   *Licensees Robert and Anita Southerton   Real ale   Meals and snacks (12–2.30, 6–9.30)   Children welcome   Organist Wed evening   Open 11.30–3, 5.30–11; all day Sat*

MACCLESFIELD   SJ9271   Map 7

Sutton Hall Hotel   ★   ⊘   🛏

Leaving Macclesfield southwards on A523, turn left into Byrons Lane signposted Langley, Wincle, then just before canal viaduct fork right into Bullocks Lane; OS Sheet 118 map reference 925715

The range of bar food in this smart and secluded country hotel is neither wide nor particularly unusual, but it wins full marks for fine cooking and stylish presentation: home-made soup (£1.25), open sandwiches (from £1.75), chicken liver pâté (£2.65 starter, £4.65 main course), pasta with prawns, vegetarian lasagne, tasty moussaka, steak and kidney pie or very good meat kebabs (all £4.65), steak (£7.95), and puddings (£1.75); really friendly service. With the exception of one black-and-white wing (with some worn figures carved into the timbering), the building is stone-built; the bar is decidedly characterful, with an enormous bronze bell for calling time, a brass cigar-lighting gas taper on the bar counter itself, antique squared oak panelling, lightly patterned art nouveau stained glass windows, and an open fire, raised a couple of feet, at the end of the bar counter (which is surrounded by broad flagstones – there's carpet elsewhere); there's also a longcase clock, a suit of armour by another substantial stone fireplace, and raj fans circling slowly in the lofty ceiling. Tall black timbers divide the separate areas and furnishings are mainly straightforward ladderback chairs around sturdy thick-topped cast-iron-framed tables; the atmosphere is at the up-market end of civilised, but still warmly welcoming. Well kept Bass and Mild, Marstons Burton and Stones Best on handpump, decent wines. There are tables on a tree-sheltered lawn. We've listed this in previous editions under Sutton, but as Macclesfield is the nearest point of reference we've changed to that this year. *(Recommended by Laurence Manning, D W Huebner, Brian and Anna Marsden, Keith Mills)*

Free house   *Licensee Robert Bradshaw   Real ale   Meals and snacks   Restaurant Children welcome weekend and Bank Holiday lunchtimes only   Four-poster bedrooms* tel *Sutton* (026 05) 3211; £55.95B/£73B   *Open all day*

MOBBERLEY   SJ7879 Map 7
Bird in Hand

B5085 towards Alderley

Good bar food in this atmospheric and relaxed ancient place ranges from home-made soup (£1.30), sandwiches (from £1.30; open sandwiches such as cottage cheese with fresh fruit £2.65) and ploughman's (£2.80), through home-made pâté (£3.30), salads (from £3.50, fresh crab £4.75), and home-made specials like steak and onion pie, Welsh rarebit or fresh battered haddock (£4.15), to puddings such as home-made deep-filled treacle tart (£1.50); filled rolls only on Sunday, when there are also chunks of strong cheddar cheese and bowls of biscuits on the bar. Rambling off the central servery is a series of low-ceilinged little rooms, with small pictures on the attractive Victorian wallpaper, Toby jugs and other china on a high shelf, comfortably cushioned heavy wooden seats and so forth, wood panelling in the cosy snug, and a blazing winter fire. Sam Smiths OB and Museum on handpump, and several malt whiskies; darts, dominoes and fruit machine. It can get crowded; seats outside. (*Recommended by Paul Wreglesworth, Brian and Anna Marsden, David and Karina Stanley, Alan Skull, E V Walder; more reports please*)

Sam Smiths   Licensees Mr and Mrs Andrew Towers   Real ale   Meals and snacks (not Mon or Sun evening)   Children in eating area of bar   Open 11–3, 5.30–11; all day Sat

OLLERTON   SJ7877 Map 7
Dun Cow

A537 SE of Knutsford

One of a minority of pubs that are warmly and instantly welcoming – not least in the low-ceilinged lounge, sheltered by a wooden draught screen, and with the sort of atmosphere that seems to mature over the years; two blazing fires here, with a low wicker-seat chair (like a nursing chair with arms) by one of them. An oak settle is squeezed into a little alcove, and a corner snug has small pictures and nice little oak chairs and tables. There are also traditional dark wood built-in seats, a couple of longcase clocks, a polished chest by the entry, and some large embroidered panels (particularly the one on the way through to the restaurant). The small tap room has darts, dominoes, and bar billiards; well kept Greenalls Bitter and Original on handpump. Good value bar food includes soup (£1), sandwiches (from £1; on Sunday this is all they do in the bar), home-made steak and kidney pie (£3.30), deep fried plaice (£4), steaks (from £4.50), and daily specials. A few picnic-tables under the oak trees in front of the building. As we went to press we heard that the landlord was about to retire, so things may change. (*Recommended by Paul Wreglesworth, J E Rycroft, Steve Mitcheson, Anne Collins, John Broughton, Ian Blackwell, Roger Huggins, Graham Gibson, Peter and Moyna Lynch, J H M Broughton*)

Greenalls   Licensee Geoffrey Tilling   Real ale   Meals and snacks (not Sun–Tues evenings)   Restaurant tel Knutsford (0565) 3093   Children in eating area and in restaurant   Open 11–11; closed evening 25 Dec

OVER PEOVER   SJ7674 Map 7
Whipping Stocks

Stocks Lane; just off and easily seen from A50 S of Knutsford

Substantial and so well built that it feels a good deal older than it really is, this comfortable and relaxing pub has been doing well under the licensees who took over in 1989. Several rooms, each with a distinct style of its own, open off the fairly spacious central bar area; there's a good deal of oak panelling, and the bar counter itself is staunchly oaken – with fine elbow and foot rests. Seats range from small linenfold wooden chairs to sturdy wall settles upholstered in rather a 1930s plush fabric; most rooms have neat fireplaces. Popular waitress-served home-made bar food includes sandwiches (from £1.20), rollmop (£1.50), quiche (£3.10) and scampi or haddock (£3.25), with lunchtime extras such as filled baked potatoes (from £1.95), ploughman's (£2.30) and steak and kidney pie (£3.25); in the evening the basic menu is extended to gammon (£3.55) and sirloin steak (£5.95). Sam Smiths OB on handpump is well kept; fruit machine, well chosen and reproduced piped music, welcoming landlord. There are picnic-table sets in quite a spacious tree-sheltered garden with a barbecue and safe play area; this is attractive, level countryside, with a pretty walk through to the church and hall. The grey and white cat is called Smudge. *(Recommended by Mr and Mrs J H Adam, Brian and Anna Marsden, Miss R Murdoch, Graham Gibson, G T Jones)*

Sam Smiths   Licensee John Eadie   Real ale   Meals and snacks (not Sun or Mon evenings)   Older children allowed till early evening   Open 11–3, 5.30–11

PEOVER HEATH   SJ7973   Map 7

Dog

Off A50 N of Holmes Chapel at the Whippings Stocks, keep on past Parkgate into Wellbank Lane; OS Sheet 118 map reference 794735; note that this village is called Peover Heath on the OS map and shown under that name on many road maps, but the pub is often listed under Over Peover instead

There's something of a canine motif in this relaxed and rambling inn: it used to be called the Gay Dog, and there are big dog cartouches on the red carpet, Staffordshire dogs in the china cupboard. Around the main bar is an engaging series of small areas, with logs burning in one old-fashioned black grate, and a coal fire opposite it flanked by two wood-backed built-in fireside seats. Other seats range from a little rocking chair, through rust-coloured cloth wall seats (one built into a snug alcove around an oak table), to the handsome ribbed banquettes in the quiet and spacious dining room on the left. Well kept Boddingtons Bitter, Chesters, Flowers IPA, Marstons Pedigree and Whitbreads Castle Eden on handpump; darts, pool and a juke box in the tap room, and a tucked-away fruit machine. Bar food has included interesting soups, ploughman's and enterprising fish dishes, but as we went to press there was a change of licensees and we gather things may have changed under them – we'd appreciate more news in this respect. There are picnic-table sets out on the quiet lane. *(Recommended by Mr and Mrs A B Taylor, Laurence Manning, D M Moss, Simon Turner, G T Jones, Mrs T A Uthwatt)*

Free house   Real ale   Meals and snacks (not Sun evenings or all day Mon)   Children in family room   Live music Wed evening   Open 11.30–3, 5.30(7 Sat)–11   Bedrooms tel Chilford (0625) 861421; £23B/£46B

PLUMLEY   SJ7175   Map 7

Golden Pheasant

Plumley Moor Lane; signposted Plumley off A556 by the Smoker – see next entry

New licensees have gained readers' enthusiasm for the welcome they extend to strangers in this comfortably modernised and spacious pub. In the open-plan rooms there are one or two antiques – an odd sofa, a fine longcase clock – among the more conventional furnishings; also a couple of elaborate antique flower prints and wooden partitions with stained glass inserts, and the built-in wall seats are more attractively upholstered than usual; open fire. Bar food includes soup (£1.10), sandwiches (from £1.20, prawn £2.25), chilli con carne or lasagne (£3.25), and steak and kidney pie or a fish dish (£3.75); Sunday roast (£4.25); staff are smart and efficient. Lees Bitter and Mild; darts, juke box, fruit machine, with pool in a separate games room. The sizeable garden, which still has a neatly kept bowling green, has picnic-table sets under cocktail parasols, and a climbing frame. Plans are afoot for extra bedrooms this year; the rates are about ten pounds cheaper at the weekend. *(Recommended by C F Walling, Richard Houghton, John Broughton, Mr and Mrs J H Adam)*

Lees   Licensee Mrs Murphy   Real ale   Meals and snacks   Restaurant   Open 11–3, 6–11   Bedrooms tel Lower Peover (056 581) 2261; £39B/49B

Smoker

2 1/2 miles from M6 junction 19: A556 towards Northwich and Chester

The three communicating rooms here are well decorated with military prints on dark panelling in one room, a glass case containing a remnant from the Houses of Parliament salavaged after it was hit by a bomb in World War II, an Edwardian print by Goodwin Kilburne of a hunt meeting outside the pub, and a large collection of copper kettles. There are also comfortable deep sofas, cushioned settles, Windsor chairs, some rush-seat dining chairs, and open fires in impressive period fireplaces; a warm and affable atmosphere. Well kept Robinsons Best and Mild on electric pump; 25 single malt whiskies and a decent choice of wines by the bottle. Reliable home-made bar food includes sandwiches (from £1.10), home-made soup (£1), salads (from £3.25), lasagne or kofta curry (£3.55), fresh plaice (£3.95), home-made steak and kidney pie, gammon or roast sirloin (£4.25), and rump steak (£5.95); children's dishes (£1.65). Around this 16th-century thatched building are a cobbled front area and a sizeable side lawn with roses and flowerbeds. They're considering setting up a no-smoking area. *(Recommended by Graham Gibson, A Wright, Audrey and Brian Green, Michael and Joan Melling, J H M Broughton, W C M Jones, Mr and Mrs J H Adam)*

Robinsons   Licensees John and Diana Bailey   Real ale   Meals and snacks (12–2.30, 6.30–10)   Restaurant tel Lower Peover (056 581) 2338 (not Sun evening)   Children in eating area and restaurant   Open 11–3, 5.30–11

RAINOW   SJ9576   Map 7

Highwayman ★

A mile above village, NE along A5002 Macclesfield–Whaley Bridge

It's the combination of a fine position (good views over the Cheshire Plain), well kept beer (Thwaites on handpump) and decent food that attracts readers here. The bar menu includes home-made soup (£1.20), sandwiches and filled barm cakes (from £1.20), black pudding (£1.50), savoury pancake rolls (£2.75), a choice of half a dozen freshly made pizzas (£2.50; the seafood one is recommended), and breaded plaice, freshly roasted chicken or scampi (£3.50). The cosy little rooms (each with its own winter coal fire) have low beams, some antique settles and simpler cushioned seats around rustic wooden tables; the high bar counter is attractively covered with copper; darts, fruit machine. On fine summer evenings or weekends it gets quite crowded, and nearby parking may be difficult. There's a terrace in front of this early-17th-century, small-windowed building. *(Recommended by Derek and Sylvia Stephenson, Janet and Gary Amos, Ian Briggs, G T Jones, H B Vanstone, Wayne Brindle, Dennis Royles, Steve Mitcheson, Anne Collins)*

Thwaites   Licensee Frank Jones   Real ale   Meals and snacks   Children in snug Open 12–3, 6–11; closed 25 Dec evening

TARPORLEY   SJ5563   Map 7

Rising Sun

High St; village signposted off A51 Nantwich–Chester

It's not unknown for readers to drive 30 miles to enjoy the atmosphere in this village pub, warmed to cosiness by three open fires. The low-ceilinged and beamed rooms have character seats including creaky 19th-century mahogany and oak settles around the well chosen tables, an attractively blacked iron kitchen range, a big oriental rug in the back room, and sporting and other old-fashioned prints. Well kept Robinsons Best and Mild on handpump; fruit machine, maybe unobtrusive background music. Reasonably priced lunchtime bar food includes sandwiches (from £1.20), filled baked potatoes (from £1.25), home-made cottage pie (£1.80), steak and kidney pie (£2.75), scampi (£3.25), salads (from £2.50), good home-made quiche, gammon and egg (£3.50) and chicken chasseur (£3.75); in the evening they concentrate more on full meals, with starters such as pâté-stuffed mushrooms (£1.85) and main dishes like seafood platter (£3.50), a tasty chicken Kiev, game casserole (£5.50), steaks (from £5.50), and a huge mixed grill (£6.25); friendly service. It's a popular haunt of local cricketers and the bowls team. *(Recommended by Mike Tucker, Joan Goodwin, KC)*

Robinsons   Licensee Alec Robertson   Real ale   Meals and snacks (12–2, 6–9.30; not in back bar evenings)   Children in restaurant lunchtime   Restaurant tel Tarporley (082 93) 2423   Open 11.30–3, 5.30–11

WESTON   SJ7352   Map 7

White Lion 🛏

3 1/2 miles from M6 junction 16; A500 towards Crewe, then village signposted on right

The comfortable hotel part here is discreetly built out behind – from the road you still get the impression of a little black-and-white timbered inn, and that's very much the style of the bar itself. The black-beamed main room, on the right, is divided into small areas by very gnarled black oak standing timbers, with a very varied mix of seats from orange-cushioned modern settles to ancient oak ones, with plenty of smaller chairs. The best settles are in a smaller room on the left – three of them, well carved in 18th-century style. Bar food includes good sandwiches (from 90p), soup (95p), pâtés (£1.95) and other starters, toasted sandwiches (£1.20, huge speciality ones £2.95), broccoli quiche (£2.75), ploughman's, salads and a lunchtime dish of the day such as cottage pie (£2.95), scampi or plaice (£3.25), good steaks (£6.50) and – a favourite of several readers – cold Dee salmon (£5.95). Well kept Ind Coope Burton and Tetleys on handpump, piped music, friendly service by smartly dressed staff; two no-smoking areas. Picnic-table sets shelter on neat grass behind, by the pub's own bowling green. *(Recommended by E G Parish, Laurence Manning, Geoff Lee)*

Free house   Licensee Mrs A J Davies   Real ale   Meals and snacks (not 25 or 26 Dec or 1 Jan evenings)   Restaurant   Open 11–3, 6.30–11; winter evening opening 7 Children in eating area   Bedrooms tel Crewe (0270) 500303; £42.50B/£52.50B

WYBUNBURY   SJ6950   Map 7

Swan

B5071; signposted off A500 (still shown as A52 on most maps) and A51, E of Nantwich

Doing particularly well at the moment under its friendly young chef-patron, this pretty and companionable pub has a mass of bric-a-brac in its two-room bar. The ceiling joists are liberally hung with wooden farm tools, pewter tankards, small cartwheels and harness, one window has a horn gramophone with that His Master's Voice dog beside it, the big fireplace (with a good winter fire) has a copper kettle and even an anvil, and some of the lamps are splendidly ornate. A wide choice of good value bar food, all home-made, includes soup (£1.10), sandwiches (from £1.40), garlic mushrooms (£1.75) and a good few other starters, cheeseburger (£2.90), moussaka or vegetarian lasagne (£3.25), Mexican pork (£4.50), halibut basquaise or rack of lamb (£5), mixed grill (£5.50) and pepper steak or scampi Newburg (£7.50), with children's dishes (£1.20) and a good Sunday choice. Comfortable seats include good bays built into the windows – which overlook the village church tower standing among statuesque lime trees (the rest of the church collapsed in a storm). Well kept Theakstons Best, Youngers Scotch and McEwans 80/- on handpump; piped music – Simon and Garfunkel, say – and cribbage, dominoes, fruit machine and space game. There are picnic-table sets under cocktail parasols in a neat garden with a big tree-playhouse, with a couple more in the sheltered back yard. The restaurant is no-smoking. *(Recommended by Graham Gibson, Mr and Mrs J H Adam, Martin Aust; more reports please)*

Scottish & Newcastle   Licensee Richard Staveley   Real ale   Meals and snacks (not Sun evening)   Restaurant (12–9 Sun)   Children in eating area and restaurant   Open 12–3(3.30 Sat), 7–11   Bedrooms tel Crewe (0270) 841280; £24B/£32B

Lucky Dip

Besides the fully inspected pubs, you might like to try these Lucky Dips recommended to us and described by readers (if you do, please send us reports):

☆ **Acton Bridge** [Hilltop Rd; take B5153 off A49 in Weaverham; then right towards Acton Cliff; SJ5975], *Maypole*: Spacious and archetypally well-heeled Cheshire beamed pub, some antique settles as well as more modern comfortable furnishings, decent food, friendly service, two coal fires, Greenalls Bitter and Mild on handpump, gentle piped music, seats outside, orchard behind (*Geoff Halson, Wayne Brindle, G T Jones, Syd and Wyn Donald, LYM*)

Alderley Edge [about 250 yds past Royal Oak, off Heyes Lane (which is off A34); SJ8478], *Moss Rose*: Tucked-away terraced pub, enlarged a few years ago by incorporating some neighbouring cottages, and with its own bowling green; bar food (*Graham Gibson*); [The Sidings, London Rd; off A34 by stn; SJ8478], *Queensgate*: Unique Chef & Brewer done up with cobbled row of mock shops, cocktail bar and restaurant; fine wood panelling, ornate ceiling, some fine wall prints, and brass foot rest around the bar; Ruddles Best and County on handpump, bar food, spotless lavatories (*Graham Gibson*)

Alsager [Linley Lane; SJ8154], *Linley*: Recently renovated, with friendly landlord and some very good food (*Joan Goodwin*); [Crewe Rd], *Lodge*: Friendly, well run local with good atmosphere and decent mix of customers; well kept Tetleys Bitter and Ansells or Tetleys Mild on handpump, snack lunches including generously filled rolls, good coffee (*Sue Holland, Dave Webster*); [Sandbach Rd N], *Wilbraham Arms*: Food good, particularly the special salads, and Robinsons well kept, in tidy and spacious building with fine seats and fittings, pretty little restaurant and large garden with goat; efficient staff (*Laurence Manning*)

Appleton [not far from M6 junction 20; B5356 Stretton Rd, junction Arley Rd; SJ6484], *Thorn*: Pleasant, modern, clean roadside pub, comfortable furnishings, wide choice of bar food (*Tim Brierly*)

Aston [Wrenbury Rd (off A530); SJ6147], *Bhurtpore*: Once the epitome of a traditional country pub, this has now been thoroughly altered and a restaurant has been added; interesting food inc chicken noodle soup, gravadlax and smoked trout madras; Boddingtons and Tetleys on handpump, maybe Marstons Pedigree (*Graham Gibson*)

Audlem [The Square; junction A529/A525; SJ6644], *Lord Combermere*: Nice rambling pub done up without losing all its character; friendly locals and staff, well kept Courage Directors and John Smiths (*Derek and Sylvia Stephenson*); [Audlem Wharf — OS Sheet 118 map reference 658436], *Shroppie Fly*: Named after the narrow-boats using the Shropshire Union canal, and superbly placed by one of the long flight of locks here;

mainly modern furnishings, one bar shaped like a barge, good canal photographs, collection of brightly painted bargees' china and bric-a-brac, seats on waterside terrace; simple food, well kept Springfield on handpump, children in room off bar and in restaurant (*Derek and Sylvia Stephenson, LYM*)

☆ **Barbridge** [off A51 some 3/4 miles N of Nantwich; SJ6156], *Barbridge Inn*: Popular refurbished pub on Shropshire Union Canal, with generous helpings of good value food in bar and restaurant; children's room, well kept Boddingtons and Higsons, maybe Oldham Mild, large canalside garden with play area (*Chris Raisin, Graham Gibson, Derek and Sylvia Stephenson, P Lloyd, Miss K Bamford, Martin Aust*)

☆ **Barton** [A534 E of Farndon; SJ4554], *Cock*: Handsome sandstone country pub with log fires, traditional furnishings including high-backed built-in settles, black beams, snug alcoves, hunting and ornamental fowl prints, well kept McEwans 80/- and Youngers Scotch, bar food from soup and sandwiches to steak; tables outside with separate summer soft drinks snack servery; closed Mon lunchtime; kept out of main entries only by lack of current reports (*Philip Riding, LYM*)

Beeston [Bunbury Heath (A49 S of Tarporley); SJ5459], *Beeston Castle*: Standard pub, jolly licensee, interesting range of food inc fine smoked goose breast, enormous open sandwiches, Greek dishes; country and western and quiz evenings (*M and J Godfrey, D T Taylor*)

☆ **Bickerton** [Bulkeley — A534 E of junction with A41; SJ5052], *Bickerton Poacher*: Attractive barbecue extension around sheltered courtyard (summer Fri and Sat evenings, Sun lunchtime), with lots of live music and special events; good atmosphere — despite the skeleton — in traditionally furnished comfortable rambling rooms in main part, with poacher theme (and a lot of game dishes); up to five Marstons and Border or Burtonwood real ales kept well, adequate bar food and recently refurbished bistro; children welcome (*Martin Aust, Mr and Mrs L G Smith, Brian and Anna Marsden, Peter Corris, Dr P D Putwain, Simon J Barber, LYM*)

Bollington [SJ9377], *Church House*: Friendly local with cosy atmosphere, well kept Theakstons and Wadworths 6X, good simple bar food (*Dr and Mrs R J Ashleigh, Graham Gibson*)

Bunbury [SJ5758], *Dysart Arms*: Attractive pub next to church with decent bar food and Thwaites on handpump (*Derek and Sylvia Stephenson*)

Burleydam [A525 Whitchurch—Audlem; SJ6143], *Combermere Arms*: Rural pub, supposedly 450 years old and haunted; lots of fine woodwork, leaded windows, comfortable wall seating and other chairs and pretty carpet; Bass, Marstons Pedigree, Springfield and Youngers on handpump, bar food from sandwiches to steaks, restaurant *(M A and W R Proctor)*

Burtonwood [Alder Lane; 3 miles from M62 junct 9, signposted from A49 towards Newton-le-Willows — OS Sheet 108 map reference 585930; SJ5692], *Fiddle i'th' Bag*: Nicely placed in unusually peaceful setting by canal and riverside, three open-plan sections with brassware, pottery and numerous stuffed animals; keg Greenalls, reasonably priced standard pub food; popular Sun lunchtimes; seats outside *(Lee Goulding)*

☆ **Butley Town** [A523 Macclesfield—Stockport; SJ9177], *Ash Tree*: Small-roomed pub well converted by Boddingtons into a 'Henry's Table' family pub/restaurant, and tastefully refurbished in keeping with original structure and layout; friendly staff, good range of well cooked bar food inc splendid lunchtime buffet with fine ploughman's, hot dishes, daily specials; popular restaurant; nice winter coal fires, well kept Boddingtons on handpump, comfortable atmosphere *(Andy and Jill Kassube, Tony and Pat Young, Paul Wreglesworth)*

☆ **Chester** [Watergate St], *Custom House*: Interesting and consistently popular old three-roomed pub opposite the original custom house with good evening atmosphere, lunchtime snacks, well kept Border Exhibition and Marstons Mild, Bitter and Pedigree, efficient service; shame about the fruit machine in the lounge *(Sue Holland and Dave Webster, Mr and Mrs P A Jones, Mr and Mrs J H Adam, Jon Wainwright)*

☆ **Chester** [Tower Wharf, Raymond St — behind Northgate St, nr rly], *Telfords Warehouse*: Popular converted warehouse credited architecturally to Thomas Telford, with big windows overlooking Shrops Union Canal basin; pleasing new-wood furniture, well kept Theakstons XB, Youngers IPA and Scotch, bar food served at tables when your name is called by loudspeaker — up to three dozen different cheeses at lunchtime inc recherché British ones; steps down to cellar winebar (with decent wines), steps up to restaurant area; trad jazz Sun lunchtime and Tues evening *(Graham Gibson, Derek and Sylvia Stephenson)*

☆ **Chester** [Park St (by Roman Walls, off Albion St)], *Albion*: Interesting three-roomed Victorian pub alongside city wall, recently smartened up without losing its character — even the new wallpaper keeps the dark green floral pattern dear to the regulars' hearts; good value lunchtime food, generously served, well kept Greenalls ales, masses of wartime memorabilia *(Mr and Mrs P A Jones, Jon Wainwright, Derek and Sylvia Stephenson)*

Chester [94 Lower Bridge St], *Bear & Billet*: Good-looking black and white riverside pub of considerable potential, with way-out customers and rock discos Thurs and Sat evenings; simple lunchtime meals upstairs, Tetleys on handpump *(Graham Gibson, John Gould, Jon Wainwright)*; [Garden Lane (off A540)], *Bouverie*: Bustling, friendly local, Greenalls on handpump *(Jon Wainwright)*; [Upper Northgate St (by bus stn)], *Bull & Stirrup*: Impressive and tastefully modernised Victorian hotel with high-ceilinged rooms; lunchtime food, Boddingtons Mild and Higsons Mild and Bitter on handpump *(Mr and Mrs P A Jones)*; [Foregate St/Frodsham St], *City Arms*: Bright, clean shop-theme pub — bookshop, toys and apothecary and haberdashers behind bar; well kept Greenalls Bitter and Original, reasonably good value lunchtime bar food; can get very lively in the evenings *(Mr and Mrs J H Adam, Mr and Mrs P A Jones)*; [Lower Bridge St], *Clavertons*: More wine bar than pub, but has well kept Lees Bitter and Moonraker as well as good range of well priced wines; impressive Georgian columned entrance leads also to antique market; wide range of well priced wines by the glass, heavy beams, lots of nooks and crannies, interesting choice of bar food inc vegetarian dishes; fast service, juke box or piped music, open all day — popular with young people particularly at weekends *(John C Gould, Mr and Mrs J H Adam, Jon Wainwright)*; [behind the Deva, Westgate Row — top of Watergate St], *Commercial*: Pleasantly refurbished pub in hidden paved square, occasional folk evenings in walled, paved area, good atmosphere, lunchtime food, well kept Greenalls; bedrooms *(Mr and Mrs P A Jones)*; [Westgate Row N], *Deva*: Pleasantly refurbished and well kept long close-carpeted lounge bar in fine medieval building *(Graham Gibson)*; [Lower Bridge St], *Kings Head*: Black and white timbered Greenalls house dating back to 17th century; original woodwork, Davenports on handpump; open all day, can get crowded evenings; eight bedrooms, some with four-posters *(John Gould, Patrick Godfrey)*; [99 Boughton (A51)], *Little Oak*: Narrow pub with public bar and slightly partitioned lounge bar; popular despite 10-minute walk from town centre *(Jon Wainwright)*; [Frodsham St], *Oddfellows Arms*: Good if visiting Chester by canal, and handy for city centre; well kept Greenalls on handpump *(Mr and Mrs P A Jones)*; [1 Russell St (off City Rd, by canal)], *Old Harkers Arms*: Promising free house with six well kept real ales such as Batemans XXXB, Boddingtons, Everards Tiger, Oak Best, Pilgrims Progress and Marstons Pedigree; interesting menu with things like pear and watercress soup *(Graham Gibson)*; [Northgate St], *Pied Bull*: Atmospheric pub with well kept Greenalls Original and particularly good beef and Guinness casserole *(G T Jones)*; [Sandy Lane (B5130)], *Red House*: Chief attraction is setting by River Dee — big garden with jetty where there are boats for hire in season; brightly comfortable inside in current Bass style — typical wallpaper, Raj fans and pictures; food lunchtime and evening, Bass on handpump *(Graham Gibson)*; [George St], *Ship Victory*: Isolated pub with pleasant, simple decor; Jennings and Tetleys beers *(Jon Wainwright)*

Christleton [Plough Lane — OS Sheet 117 map reference 454653; SJ4466], *Plough*: Curious window-seat (the former entrance) in older part, with clocking-on timepiece, wooden partitioning and lots of horse brasses; new part with tapestried wall seats and benches on stone floor; ebullient landlord, darts, connect-4, good lunchtime food, tables on terrace, children's play area *(Mr and Mrs J H Adam)*

Congleton [off A34 S; SJ8663], *Great Moreton Hall*: Beautifully kept hotel and restaurant in marvellous handsomely restored building with attractive spacious grounds, comfortable bedrooms; high bar prices, but worth a visit *(Graham Gibson)*

Cotebrook [junction A49/B5152 N of Tarporley; SJ5765], *Alvanley Arms*: Handsome old creeper-covered Georgian inn with fairly close-set tables and big open fire in high-beamed main lounge bar, quieter room with nice prints and china across chintzy hall, well kept Robinsons Mild, Best and Old Tom on handpump, long bar menu from sandwiches up, restaurant; bedrooms; readers' reports not yet entirely settled down since change of management late 1989 — more news please *(Robert and Kate Hodkinson, LYM)*; [A49], *Fox & Barrel*: Friendly staff, welcoming fire, genuine hunting decorations, cosy corners and larger rooms, and discreet piped music; Greenalls Bitter tapped from the cask, good range of bar food such as steak and mushroom pie or vegetarian pancake, flamboyant puddings, excellent blue cheshire cheese; big car park *(F and J Hamer)*

Cranage [Allostock; B5082, off A50 N; SJ7471], *Three Greyhounds*: Pleasant, unpretentious beamed pub with cretonne cushions and curtains, good inexpensive bar food, friendly locals *(Robert and Vicky Tod)*

Crewe [Sydney; just off A534 towards M6 junction 17; SJ7256], *Hunters Lodge*: Comfortable bar in attractive hotel, a former farmhouse; decent choice of well kept real ales on handpump, good bar food at moderate prices, first-class service, Tudor-style restaurant; bedrooms *(E G Parish)*; [Middlewich Rd (A530)], *Rising Sun*: Popular pub recently refurbished to high standard with log fires, well kept Wem Best on handpump, good bar food, well organised bar service, big car park; bedrooms comfortable *(E G Parish, Martin Aust)*

Croft [Hill St; SJ6393], *Heathcote Arms*: Pleasantly situated village local with Everards Tiger, Old and Original, and guest beers on handpump; good value bar snacks *(Andy and Jill Kassube)*; [left just after the Noggin, right at next T-junction; SJ6393], *Horseshoe*: Good service, tremendous range of good food spanning a wide price range; pity there's no real ale *(Simon Turner)*

Dean Row [SJ8781], *Unicorn*: Generous helpings of good home-cooked food, well kept Boddingtons, pleasant staff and comfortable seating *(Mr and Mrs B Hobden)*

☆ **Delamere** [A54/B5152; SJ5669], *Fishpool*: Bright, comfortable and attractive country pub divided into small rooms, some with open fires; bottle collection behind bar, plates and brasses around walls; one really low door; good range of bar food inc interesting dishes; Greenalls Mild and Bitter on handpump; pleasantly placed nr Delamere Forest *(Graham Gibson, Mr and Mrs J H Adam)*

Disley [Buxton Rd; E end of village, opp school; SJ9784], *Crescent*: Comfortable, friendly and homely local with good value, simple bar food served generously all week — steak pie strongly tipped; well kept Robinsons on handpump, small garden overlooking railway *(Keith Mills)*; [Buxton Rd], *Dandy Cock*: Remarkably clean pub with lots of brass and militaria, backing on to spectacular valley; Robinsons ales and good value bar food; restaurant; children welcome *(John Hayward)*; [up side road by Rams Head Hotel], *White Horse*: Well kept Robinsons on handpump, good food made with fresh ingredients *(A F C Young)*

Duddon [A51 NW of Tarporley; SJ5265], *Headless Woman*: Attractive interior with the impression of lots of little rooms, old timbers worked into the walls, Greenalls Bitter, and pool table; very much an eating house, with good varied bar food *(Graham Gibson, R H Sawyer)*

Eaton [A536 Congleton—Macclesfield; SU8765], *Plough*: Well kept Banks's Bitter and Mild on handpump, wide choice of good value bar food *(Paul Wreglesworth)*

Elworth [London Rd; SJ7462], *Fox*: Well modernised open-plan village pub with enterprising bar food and Tetleys and maybe Ind Coope Burton on handpump *(Jon Wainwright)*

☆ **Gawsworth** [nr Macclesfield; SJ8969], *Harrington Arms*: Basic farm pub with tree-trunk tables outside and rudimentary comforts in; by popular demand recently 'de-improved' to restore original character of wood-screened narrow roomlets with fine carved bar counter; well kept Robinsons Best and Best Mild on handpump, food very simple but unmistakeably home-made *(LYM)*

Gorstage [Millington Lane; off A49 W of Northwich; SJ6173], *Oaklands*: Tucked away in countryside and surrounded by fair amount of land; building most attractive with country-house feel to it; Greenalls Bitter and Original, meals and banquets available; big unmarked car park; bedrooms *(Graham Gibson)*

Grappenhall [Church Lane; off A50; SJ6486], *Rams Head*: Attractive sandstone building not far from Bridgewater Canal, with elaborate wrought-iron sign and sun dial; lots of fine wood panelling, leaded windows, wall seats and carved heads; Greenalls on handpump *(Graham Gibson)*

Halton [Castle Rd; SJ5482], *Castle*: Fine views over Runcorn and Widnes, lovely when all the street lights are on (it's said that on a fine day you can see seven counties); stone-built, with royal coat of arms above door, prints of country pursuits, lunchtime food, Greenalls on handpump, maybe live music upstairs; nr ruined Halton Castle *(Graham Gibson)*

Handforth [30 Wilmslow Rd; SJ8583], *Bulls Head*: Reopened as Watneys Country Carvery, with big bar, family restaurant, conservatory, beer garden, big car park; new but has old paintings and so forth; Ruddles County well priced on handpump, good value food, helpful staff *(John Gould)*

Hankelow [A529 Audlem—Nantwich; SJ6745], *White Lion*: Well organised, comfortable pub with open fires, pool table at one end and clean, friendly atmosphere; excellent food, fresh veg *(Dr G B Whitaker)*

Hartford [Chester Rd; opp stn; SJ6472], *Coachmans*: Pleasant 300-year-old local with friendly regulars, darts, dominoes, Greenalls Mild and Bitter on handpump *(Graham Gibson)*

Hatchmere [B5152, off A556 at Abbey Arms; SJ5672], *Carriers*: Country pub overlooking Hatchmere Lake (where pike can be caught), and useful for walks in Delamere Forest; tap room and two-level lounge, well kept Burtonwood Bitter and Mild on handpump, decent straightforward food inc good value Sun lunch, notably friendly landlord *(Mr and Mrs J H Adam, G T Jones, Graham Gibson)*

Hatton [Hatton Lane; SJ6082], *Hatton Arms*: Comfortable, old-fashioned village local in area where too many like it have been 'modernised'; welcoming, homely lounge with real winter fire; adjoining tap room with darts, dominoes, cribbage, endless chat; Greenalls on handpump; pleasant service, interesting locals *(Robert Timmis, Ian and Sue Brocklebank)*

High Legh [A50; SJ7084], *Bears Paw*: Really good atmosphere, Greenalls ales and barbecue area in partly covered back area *(G T Jones)*

Higher Whitley [1 1/4 miles from M56 junction 10; A559 towards Northwich; SJ6280], *Birch & Bottle*: Extended recently, with first-rate fittings, and new restaurant in attractively furnished conservatory — but this may have lost it much of the cosy atmosphere which made the snug alcoves of its original dining area so welcoming; mixed reports in the last year or so on staff, and on food from hot and cold buffet in main part of pub, served by man in chef's garb; decent wines, Greenalls Mild, Bitter and Original, fresh orange juice, open fires; children allowed if eating, till 8.30 *(Hugh Saddington, M J Ridgway, Andy and Jill Kassube, LYM)*

Hollins Green [just off A57 Manchester—Warrington, 3 miles from M6 junction 21; SJ6991], *Black Swan*: Attractively furnished low-ceilinged old building, with nooks and crannies on different levels; particularly noted for its Christmas decorations, which draw visitors from a wide radius; new licensee last year has kept up the tradition, and food is now good, inc specials such as roast beef freshly cut from the joint; Tetleys beers, piped noisy Musak; lavatories notably clean *(G T Jones, Peter Corris)*

Hooton [A41; SJ3678], *Chimneys*: Fine gothic-style hotel, giant fork and spoon hanging from beams and clock shaped like key in public bar; Bass, Stones Best and Boddingtons on handpump, grill room, dining room for residents *(Mr and Mrs J H Adam)*

Houghton Green [fairly handy for M62 junction 9 (so also M6 junction 10); SJ6292], *Nags Head*: Tiny old country pub with most acceptable if fairly conventional food cooked by landlord's wife and served by his daughter; decent wine *(W C M Jones)*

Kelsall [SJ5268], *Morris Dancers*: Newish Spanish landlord has now extended into added tapas bar, small restaurant and reception suite; bar food (at a price), well kept Greenalls *(More reports please)*

Knutsford [Mobberley Rd; SJ7578], *Builders Arms*: Lively and attractive terraced building with good windows; Marstons Burton and Pedigree *(Jon Wainwright)*

☆ nr **Langley** [Higher Sutton; village signed off A54 beside Fourways Motel — OS Sheet 118 map reference 952696; SJ9471], *Hanging Gate*: Cosy little low-beamed country pub with lovely views, big coal fires, attractive old photographs of Cheshire towns; reasonably priced bar food from sandwiches and soup through vegetarian dishes and steak and kidney pie to game, well kept Border Bitter and Marstons Pedigree, winter mulled wine, friendly atmosphere; seats on crazy-paved terrace; kept out of main entries only by lack of recent reports; children allowed *(C F Walling, Mike and Wendy Proctor, LYM)*

☆ **Little Bollington** [2 miles from M56 junction 7: A56 towards Lymm, then first right at Stamford Arms into Park Lane — use A556 to get back on to M56 westbound; SJ7286], *Swan With Two Nicks*: Village pub richly decorated with brass and copperware and other bric-a-brac, antique settles in back room, snug alcoves, log fire, good home-cooked bar food (lunchtime, not Sun), well kept Whitbreads-related real ales at fair prices, tables outside, attractive surroundings inc Dunham Hall deer park; no dogs or children *(Simon Turner, Dr P Webb, RT, LYM)*

Little Bollington [A56], *Olde No 3*: Ancient canalside pub, with promising atmosphere and food and good service under new landlord; John Smiths beer *(G T Jones)*

Little Budworth [SJ5966], *Red Lion*: Pleasant little pub with comfortable lounge bar, decent bar food, quick service *(Mr and Mrs P W Dryland)*; [A54; SJ5966], *Shrewsbury Arms*: Clean and comfortable, Robinsons beer, well presented and generously served bar food, pleasant outside area *(C F Walling)*

✗ **Little Leigh** [A49 by swing bridge; SJ6276], *Leigh Arms*: Popular very mock-Tudor pub in pleasant waterside setting with limited choice of tasty and inexpensive bar food inc vegetarian dishes and steaks; friendly service, well kept Burtonwood, country wines; organ music Sun, quiz night Wed, country and western duo Thurs; children allowed in eating area *(C F Walling, G T Jones)*

Lower Peover [Crown Lane (B5081, off A50); SJ7474], *Crown*: Charming and popular country pub with pleasant landlord and locals, relaxing atmosphere in L-shaped bar and two rooms leading off; wide choice of bar food, efficient friendly service *(Steve Mitcheson, Anne Collins, C F Walling, Wayne Brindle)*

✗ **Lymm** [Eagle Brow — nr M6 junction 20; SJ6787], *Spread Eagle*: Big, well furnished village pub of quite some character; Lees Bitter and winter Moonraker, lots of friendly regulars, good range of bar food; quiet midweek, and small room nr entrance has no piped music; weekly jazz; parking may be difficult *(Simon Turner, Alan and Marlene Radford)*

Lymm [A6144 — OS Sheet 109 map reference 684874; SJ6787], *Bulls Head*: Reasonably priced straightforward bar food in clean and rather smart pub with well kept Hydes Mild and Bitter, friendly service; has been open all day — popular with canal users in summer *(Geoff Lee, Dennis Royles)*

✗ nr **Macclesfield** [A537 some miles out towards Buxton — OS Sheet 119 map reference 001719; SK0071], *Cat & Fiddle*: Britain's 2nd-highest pub, surrounded by spectacular moorland (though on a trunk road), with magnificent views across Cheshire; spacious spotlessly kept lounge, roomy flagstoned public bar, Robinsons real ales, bar food inc good value scampi; gets busy lunchtime in summer *(F Teare, P A Crossland, D A Cawley, LYM)*

Macclesfield [Congleton Rd; junction Pack Lane/Ivy Lane; SJ9273], *Flower Pot*: Good choice of lunchtime hot and cold food laid out on counter, well kept Robinsons; in the evenings more of a young person's meeting place *(Paul Wreglesworth)*

Malpas [High St; SJ4947], *Red Lion*: Hotel with pool room and even a sauna; Bass and Oak Best on handpump, juke box; bedrooms *(Graham Gibson)*

Marbury [OS Sheet 117 map reference 562457; SJ5645], *Swan*: Friendly and efficient service and good bar food, especially the daily specials, excellent veg and fine choice of tempting puddings, in busy rustic dining pub *(W C M Jones, Mr and Mrs K Virgin)*

✗ **Mobberley** [Town Lane; down hill from sharp bend on B5185 at E edge of 30mph limit; SJ7879], *Roebuck*: Spacious and pleasant open-plan bar with long pews on richly polished floorboards, well kept Watneys-related real ales from the handsome bar counter, generously served

good value bar food, attentive service, restaurant, seats in cobbled courtyard and garden behind, play area; the popular licensee is French, his Cheshire wife does the cooking; children welcome *(Neil and Elspeth Fearn, Simon J Barber, LYM)*

Mobberley [Wilsons Mill Lane], *Bulls Head*: Friendly and comfortable low-beamed village pub with soft lighting, well kept Tetleys real ale, folk-singing landlord and own immaculate bowling green *(BB)*

Moulton [Whitlow Lane; SJ6569], *Travellers Rest*: Very popular three-room village pub with lots of bric-a-brac, good choice of well kept Whitbreads-related real ales, welcoming atmosphere and separate restaurant *(Peter Corris, Graham Gibson)*

Mow Cop [Station Rd — OS Sheet 118 map reference 854574; SJ8557], *Cheshire View*: What marks out this friendly and simply furnished pub is its tremendous bird's-eye view of the Cheshire Plain; Marstons real ales, bar food *(Mike and Wendy Proctor, LYM)*

☆ **Nantwich** [Hospital St — by side passage to central church; SJ6552], *Lamb*: Fine flower-decked old pub with pillared entrance, lamb etched in glass just through the door; comfortably sedate and beautifully kept bar with lots of seating, real ale, nicely presented quickly served bar food *(W C M Jones, Graham Gibson)*

Nantwich [The Gullet], *Bowling Green*: Superb position — secluded yet in the centre of town; well kept Watneys-related beers, food all day, small restaurant *(Nick and Karen Boughton)*; [High St — centre almost opp W end of church], *Crown*: Striking timbered and jettied Elizabethan inn with rambling beamed and timbered bar, comfortably modernised; Chesters and Marstons Pedigree on handpump, bar food, video juke box (a draw for lots of young people in the evening), restaurant; bedrooms *(LYM)*; [97 Welsh Row], *Oddfellows Arms*: Well kept Tetleys Bitter and Mild, good value food inc excellent chicken curry; small and cosy with open fires and warm welcome; nice garden *(Nick and Karen Boughton)*

Norley [Pytchleys Hollow — OS Sheet 117 map reference 572727; SJ5773], *Tigers Head*: Pleasantly refurbished 17th-century inn nr Delamere Forest, well run by friendly and energetic licensees; good range of bar food, Burtonwood ale *(Mr and Mrs J H Adam)*

Over Peover [off A50 S of Knutsford; SJ7674], *Parkgate*: Attractive collection of small rooms, agreeable licensee with very friendly style of management, above-average bar food; nice walk to village and Peover Hall *(John Broughton, G T Jones)*

Over Tabley [Chester Rd (A556), by M6 junction 19; SJ7280], *Windmill*: Little rooms to explore, well kept beers, good fires *(Denis Mann)*

Overton [Bellemonte Rd; just over 2 miles from M56 junction 12; SJ5277], *Ring o' Bells*: We've heard nothing against this friendly many-roomed early 17th-century pub — the only reason we haven't kept it in the main entries is a lack of reader reports this year; there's a good deal to look at inside, and a view down past the church to the distant Mersey; decent lunchtime bar food from sandwiches to some interesting hot dishes, well kept Greenalls Bitter and Original, lots of malt whiskies, piped music; children allowed away from the old-fashioned hatch-like servery *(G J Lewis, Mary Anne Cameron, LYM)*

Parkgate [The Parade; SJ2878], *Boathouse*: Tastefully restored bright room looking over Dee estuary to N Wales; good range of bar food, evening restaurant, Greenalls real ale *(Mr and Mrs J H Adam)*

Parkgate [The Parade; SJ2878], *Red Lion*: Friendly local in attractive waterfront position, with characterful landlady, well kept Tetleys, Victorian paintings and atmosphere; good value sandwiches with masses of salad *(Tony and Lynne Stark, Jenny and Brian Seller)*

Pott Shrigley [from B5091 out of Bollington at Turners Arms fork straight ahead into Ingersley Rd towards Rainow, then up hill turn left at Pott Shrigley sign; OS Sheet 118 map reference 945782; SJ9479], *Cheshire Hunt*: This charming and very popular small-roomed country dining pub, a former farmhouse, closed in early spring 1990; we hope it may be reopened *(Reports please)*

Prestbury [SJ9077], *Admiral Rodney*: Welcoming, comfortable pub with well kept Robinsons ales and good range of modestly priced quickly served bar food *(Canon Gerald Hollis)*

Puddington [Woodbank; A540 nr A550; SJ3373], *Yacht*: Pleasant atmosphere, well kept Greenalls and even wider choice of decent bar food than before, in newly extended pub with nicely decorated lounge bar *(Mr and Mrs J H Adam, E G Parish)*

Risley [Gorse Covert Shopping Precinct; nr M62 junction 11; SJ6592], *Poacher*: Large, modern but comfortable Tetleys house, good lunchtime bar food inc help-yourself salad bar; can get very busy Fri lunchtime and in winter *(Simon Turner)*

Sandbach [Market Sq (handy for M6 junction 17); SJ7661], *Lower Chequer*: Picturesque pub, comfortably modernised, good bar food and accommodating staff *(Wayne Brindle)*; [Betchton (A533 towards Rode); SJ7959], *New Inn*: Small and popular roadside pub with public bar, lounge and recent dining room extension; reliably good bar food — especially specials, steak sandwiches and home-made pies; well kept Marstons Burton and Pedigree; garden and play area on other side of road; Ginge the cat is very fond of chicken *(Sue Holland, Dave Webster)*; [Newcastle Rd (very handy for M6 junction 17), *Old Hall*: Handsome black and white timbered building with Jacobean panelling and big garden; under new management by late 1989, and so emphasising its smart hotel-and-restaurant side (without the real ales, for instance, and

with less of a public bar) that it's hardly appropriate now for a main entry — though no less appealing as a place to stay; bedrooms comfortable and well equipped *(Richard Phillips, LYM)*

Smallwood [SJ8160], *Bulls Head*: Lovely country pub with lots of different rooms, nooks and crannies, assorted furniture; Tetleys on handpump, consistently good and imaginative bar food, especially fish and salads, generously served by friendly staff *(Sue Holland and Dave Webster)*

Stoak [Little Stanney Lane — OS Sheet 117 map reference 423734; SJ4273], *Bunbury Arms*: Good Higsons pub, popular at lunchtime for its good value food and well kept handpumped beer; nice atmosphere, friendly locals, lawn with seating; a short walk for canal users, from bridge 136 or 138 *(Mr and Mrs P A Jones)*

Stretton [just off M56 junction 10; A559 towards Northwich; SJ6283], *Ring o' Bells*: Immaculate three-roomed country pub with glistening brasses, plenty of prints, plates and pewter jugs; well kept Greenalls *(Graham Gibson)*

Styal [B5166 nr Ringway Airport; SJ8383], *Old Ship*: Friendly welcome from cheerful staff and well kept Watneys-related real ales; open all day — useful for this National Trust village with nice walks in the riverside woods to the south; nr start GWG74 *(Len Beattie)*

Sutton [Higher Sutton — outside Macclesfield; SJ9271], *Ryles Arms*: Attractive and welcoming stone country pub, variety of comfortable chairs and settees, popular reasonably priced food; pretty garden *(Mike and Wendy Proctor)*

☆ **Swettenham** [off A54 Congleton—Holmes Chapel or A535 Chelford—Holmes Chapel; SJ8067], *Swettenham Arms*: Carefully restored big beamed family bar divided into several sections with old-fashioned furnishings, in pretty position behind church of tucked-away village; well kept Watneys-related real ales with a guest such as Banks's, decent coffee, good value bar food, seats in big garden; may be closed weekday lunchtimes *(Comus Elliott, Robert and Vicky Tod, Mr and Mrs S Turner, LYM)*

☆ **Tarporley** [High St — village signposted off A49; SJ5563], *Swan*: Georgian inn recently extensively and very comfortably refurbished, though there are those who preferred the easy-going old flagstoned kitchen bar to the modern comfort; well kept Greenalls on handpump, wide choice of bar food including good soup, reasonable open sandwiches and filled warm fresh rolls, restaurant, tables in pleasant garden, provision for children; comfortable and well equipped bedrooms *(Mr and Mrs P A Jones, I Coburn, KC, W C M Jones, LYM)*

Tarvin [High St; SJ4967], *George & Dragon*: Bright, interesting and spacious lounge on two levels with fairy lights around the higher one, a mural depicting Tarvin in the 19th century, lots of brasses and plates, a barometer/clock, and a parakeet; red furnishings, well kept Banks's beers *(Graham Gibson)*

Tattenhall [Broxton; junction A41/A534, 3 miles S — OS Sheet 117 map reference 480532; SJ4858], *Egerton Arms*: Black and white pub with popular food, well kept Burtonwood beers, cosy atmosphere, good restaurant; bedrooms *(GG)*

Thurstaston [SJ2584], *Cottage Loaf*: Popular roadhouse open all day, which manages to keep its Whitbreads Castle Eden cool even in hot weather; friendly staff, tables outside, clean lavatories *(Jenny and Brian Seller)*

Tilston [SJ4652], *Carden Arms*: Lively pub with reasonably priced lunchtime and evening bar food, Greenalls beers, interesting inn sign *(P Corris)*; *Fox & Hounds*: Quiet village-centre pub with Border beers and lunchtime and evening food; lounge and public bars *(P Corris)*

☆ **Walker Barn** [A537 Macclesfield—Buxton; SJ9573], *Setter Dog*: Remote and attractive extended moorland pub with fine bleak and windswept view; plain but pleasant inside, with well kept Marstons, reasonable choice of good food in small bar and restaurant, good service, roaring fire; handy for Teggs Nose Country Park *(G T Jones, P Grimshaw)*

Warmingham [Middlewich Rd; SJ7161], *Bears Paw*: Country pub with well kept Chesters Best, Marstons Pedigree and Whitbreads on handpump, solid wooden bar counter, nicely varnished wooden ceiling; usual bar food *(Graham Gibson)*

Warrington [Golden Sq; SJ6188], *Barley Mow*: Striking Tudor building in modern shopping precinct, open all day for coffee, tea and so forth; low beams, flagstones, nooks and crannies, but also strong leanings towards the current library style of refurbishment; Tetleys and Ind Coope Burton on handpump, hot bar food from servery; can get crowded *(Graham Gibson)*; [Old Hall Rd, Bewsey; off A57/A574 NW of town; SJ5989], *Bewsey Farm*: Attractive open-plan bar, part carpeted and part flagstones, with Boddingtons and Higsons on handpump, sensibly placed darts, tables outside *(Graham Gibson)*; [Ballater Dr, Cinnamon Brow, New Town], *Millhouse*: Modern estate pub with traditional layout of public bar and big lounge, lunchtime meals, garden for children, Holts Mild and Bitter at prices to make southerners green with envy *(P Corris)*

nr **Warrington** [Fiddlers Ferry; leaving Warrington on A562 towards Widnes, keep eyes open as you pass Harris Carpets in Penketh then turn left by Red Lion Cavalier Restaurant (Tetleys); in Tannery Lane turn left again into Station Rd, park by rly and walk across — about 50 yds — OS Sheet 108 map reference 560863], *Ferry*: Picturesquely isolated between Manchester Ship Canal and Mersey, with comfortable easy chairs, old-fashioned settle and sofa as well as more modern seats in nautically

decorated low-beamed bar, buffet bar food lunchtimes and Fri–Sat evenings, good river views, tables outside; provision for children, well kept Watneys-related real ales on handpump *(Graham Gibson, Alan and Marlene Radford, LYM)*

Wettenhall [SJ6261], *Boot & Slipper*: Recently wholly refurbished country pub, very small, with nicely served if fairly conventional food — snacks in bar, meals in dining room — roast duck is the general favourite *(W C M Jones)*

☆ **Whiteley Green** [OS Sheet 118 map reference 924789; SJ9278], *Windmill*: Big lawn prettily planted with shrub and flower borders, summer bar and barbecues — idyllic on a fine afternoon, in attractive countryside; comfortable seats around well spaced tables in spaciously modernised lounge with friendly helpful staff, good lunchtime bar food (children allowed in good carvery/bistro area, open 12-7 Mon–Sat, 12-9.30 Sun), well kept Boddingtons and Marstons Burton and Pedigree, capuccino coffee, fruit machine; close to Middlewood Way *(David Waterhouse, BB)*

☆ **Willaston** [Wistaston Rd — OS Sheet 117 map reference 329777; SJ3378], *Pollards*: Striking building with two sandstone wings, central whitewashed part, biggish lawns and gardens — originally 14th-century farmhouse; comfortable stone-floored bar on left has beams and high shelves, nice cushioned wall seats with some stone armrests; conservatory/lounge extension looks on to pleasant garden; Davenports and Greenalls Original on handpump; wide choice of good bar food, restaurant on right; bedrooms *(Mr and Mrs J H Adam, Mr and Mrs J C MacGregor)*

Willaston [87 Wistaston Rd — nr Pollards], *Nags Head*: Very popular with local regulars, good food inc some unusual dishes such as shark in barbecue sauce; well kept Marstons ales *(E G Parish, K H Miller)*

Wilmslow [Altrincham Rd; SJ8481], *Boddington Arms*: Spacious and comfortably refurbished Boddingtons house with helpful young staff, well kept ales on handpump, good value 'Henry's Table' bar food and separate restaurant, outside seating; close to Lindon Common *(John Gould, David Waterhouse)*; [Chapel Lane (off A34)], *Farmers Arms*: Attractive little black and white painted pub with beautiful etched windows and several rooms, with lots of brass, plates, guns, clocks and barometers, even a trumpet (and a piano which is played Sun evenings); lunchtime food (not Sun), well kept Boddingtons Mild and Bitter on handpump *(Graham Gibson)*

☆ **Wincle** [SU9666], *Ship*: Friendly 16th-century free house tucked away in scenic countryside; small, quaint and snug lounge and bar, stone walls some eighteen inches thick, well kept Marstons Pedigree, good value bar food (mackerel pâté tipped), coal fire and tables in garden; get there early for a seat at weekends; nr start GWG103 *(M A and W R Proctor, Tim Locke, D W Crossley; more reports on the new regime please)*

☆ **Wrenbury** [signed off A530 Nantwich—Whitchurch; SJ5948], *Dusty Miller*: Attractively placed in peaceful spot by Llangollen Canal, with big windows and tables outside making the most of the position; much modernised mill conversion, wide choice of quickly served bar food, good no-smoking area by windows, well kept

Robinsons Best, piped music, upstairs restaurant (not Sun evening); open noon—11, shorter winter hours; children in restaurant *(Laurence Manning, Dawn and Phil Garside, Catherine and Andrew Brian, Dave and Becky Killick, B and D Sowter, Robert and Kate Hodkinson, LYM)*

Wrenbury [SJ5948], *Cotton Arms*: Beamed and timbered pub with friendly owners, good value bar food, Greenalls ales and open fire; may be closed Mon lunchtime *(P Lloyd, Miss K Bamford)*

Cleveland *see* Northumbria

Cornwall

A good few new main entries here – or pubs back after an absence – include a real star: the Eliot Arms in Tregadillett, a remarkable treasure-trove of antiques in interesting rambling rooms, with good food. Others are the Trengilly Wartha near Constantine, an interesting conversion out in the country, doing well under newish licensees; the Old Inn up at St Breward – cheap food in interesting very old-fashioned surroundings; the cheerful Min Pin near Tintagel, brewing its own beers; and the very neatly kept Wheel by the water at Tresillian. Several important changes include new licensees at the Maltsters Arms, the popular food pub at Chapel Amble, the Ship at Lerryn (good reports on its complete refurbishment), and the quaint Admiral Benbow in Penzance; we're very glad to report that the landlord of the Roseland at Philleigh is staying on – as we said in the last edition, there was the possibility that his brewery would not renew the tenancy. Cornish pubs doing specially well at the moment include the cheerfully interesting Cobweb in Boscastle, the nice old Carpenters Arms at Metherell, the Ship in Mousehole, the Turks Head in Penzance, the snug little Blue Peter in Polperro, the Port Gaverne Hotel near Port Isaac, the Ship in Porthleven and the Logan Rock at Treen – virtually all close to the sea, though for position the Pandora near Mylor Bridge is perhaps hardest of all to beat. Pub prices here are a bit below the national average; for drinks, the Maltsters Arms at Chapel Amble, London Inn in Padstow, Royal Oak at Perranwell, Port Gaverne Hotel near Port Isaac and Cornish Arms at St Merryn are worthy price-fighters, while both bargain snacks and cheap hot dishes are to be had at the Royal Oak in Lostwithiel, Blue Peter in Polperro and Old Inn at St Breward. Pubs making strong headway among the starred Lucky Dip entries at the end of the chapter include the Old Ferry at Bodinnick, Napoleon in Boscastle, Seahorse and others in Falmouth, Ship in Fowey, Fishermans Arms at Golant, Bird in Hand in Hayle, Lugger at Polruan, Lugger at Portloe, Preston Gate at Poughill, Who'd Have Thought It at St Dominick, Star in St Just, St Kew Inn, White Hart at St Teath, Long Cross at Trelights and Bowgie at West Pentire; the two hottest current tips on the Isles of Scilly are the Turks Head on St Agnes and the St Martins Hotel.

BOSCASTLE SX0990 Map 1

Cobweb

B3263, just E of harbour

A lively mix of locals and visitors gather under the hundreds of old bottles that hang from the heavy beams in the big bar of this interesting village pub; there are flagstones, a log fire in cool weather, two or three curved high-backed winged settles against the dark stone walls, and a few leatherette dining chairs. Quickly served, good value bar food includes sandwiches (from 90p), hot chicken salad, and either roast beef or vegetarian or meaty lasagne (£3). Well kept St Austell Tinners, HSD and Wadworths 6X on handpump, with occasional guest beers and Inch's cider; friendly service. Good juke box, darts, dominoes, pool table (keen players here), and fruit machine; the big communicating family room has an enormous armchair carved out of a tree trunk as well as its more conventional Windsor armchairs, and another cosy winter fire. Opening off this a good-sized children's room has a second pool table, and more machines. The tiny steeply-cut harbour nearby is very attractive, as is the main village climbing up above. *(Recommended by Helena and Arthur Harbottle, Brian and Genie Smart, ACP, Richard Houghton, Mrs R Horridge, William D Cissna, C M Whitehouse, Nick Dowson, Alison Hayward, P Miller, John Branford, Linda Duncan, Tim and Lynne Crawford, Steve Dark)*

Free house   Licensee Alfred 'Ivor' Bright   Real ale   Meals and snacks   Restaurant Boscastle (084 05) 278 (not Sun evening)   Children in own room   Folk, country and western or modern music Sat   Open 11–11 (till midnight Sat); 11–3, 6–11 in winter

CHAPEL AMBLE   SW9975   Map 1
Maltsters Arms
Village signposted from A39 NE of Wadebridge; and from B3314

The Pollards, who left this friendly 16th-century pub in spring 1989 after a successful 18 months, have now come back. They've rebuilt the kitchen, extended and refurbished the family room, and introduced a new wine list as well as a range of cheeses from the region. With an emphasis on fresh local produce, the frequently changing menu might include home-made stilton and celery soup (£1.75), ploughman's (from £1.90), sirloin steak in bread with horseradish (£2.50), aubergine, spinach, nut and tomato layer (£3.75), home-made beef, Guinness and smoked oyster pie (£4.75), fresh dressed crab salad (£5.25), good whole fresh lemon sole (£6.95), and whole lobster (choose your own from their live lobster tank £12.50); evening extras such as popular pork in cider, Cornish mead and cream (£5.75). There are puddings like home-made bread and butter pudding or crumbles (from £1.50), cheeses (from £1.90), and children's dishes (from £1.50 – until 8pm); they don't take table reservations. Devenish Cornish Original, Ruddles County, Ushers Best and a changing guest beer on handpump, kept under light blanket pressure, and several malt whiskies. Darts, pool, fruit machine, winter Sunday quizzes, and piped music. The rooms of the busy main bar have heavy wooden tables on the partly carpeted big flagstones, black oak joists in the white ceiling, partly panelled stripped stone walls, and a large stone fireplace; there's also a side room with Windsor chairs. Benches outside in a sheltered sunny corner. The local hunt meets here twice a year. *(Recommended by A K Ogilvie, C M Whitehouse, Iain and Penny Muir, C L Ives, Tim and Lynne Crawford, Giles and Fiona Ebbutt, R F Warner)*

Free house   Licensees Jeffrey Pollard and Michael Munds   Real ale   Meals and snacks (12–2.30, 7–10)   Children in eating area of bar   Open 11–3, 5.30–11

CONSTANTINE   SW7229   Map 1
Trengilly Wartha
Constantine signposted from B3291 Penryn–Gweek; in village turn right just before Minimarket (towards Gweek); in nearly a mile pub signposted left; at Nancenoy, OS sheet 204, map reference 731282

Since the present licensees took over this country inn in November 1988, they have served over 50 different real ales – a surprisingly good run for the area. A typical batch might consist of Courage Directors, Exmoor, Fullers, St Austell and Theakstons tapped from the cask; they also list over 80 wines, a couple of dozen whiskies, overproof rums and many 'guest' drinks. Modern high-backed settles face each other across polished heavy wooden tables in the low-beamed bar, there's an open woodburning stove with a built-in curved settle beside it, and – up a step – an eating area with some winged settles and tables. Bar food includes home-made soup or pasties (£1.40), filled baked potatoes (from £1.60), lunchtime ploughman's with home-pickled vegetables (from £2.80), raised vegetable pie (£3.50), salads (from £3.80; whole local crab £4), 10oz sirloin steak (£8), and daily specials such as tortellini (£3.80), and mussels in wine (£4); home-made puddings (from £1.70), Sunday buffet lunch and Saturday lunchtime/Sunday evening barbecues, weather permitting. A cosy lounge has machine-tapestried wall benches, a log fire and some harness; a spacious front games room has darts, pool, fruit machine, video game, shove-ha'penny, cribbage, shut-the-box and backgammon. The attractive garden has some picnic-table sets, and the Helford River is close by. (*Recommended by Tom Bowen, George Atkinson, Charles and Mary Winpenny, Richard Houghton, R and Mrs P F Shelton, Drs M and K Parier, Mr and Mrs B E Witcher*)

Free house   Licensees Nigel Logan and Michael Maguire   Real ale   Meals and snacks (12–2.30, 6.30–9.30 – may be slightly shorter in winter)   Restaurant (evening) Children in family room and eating area of bar   Occasional live music Fri/Sat in winter   Open 11–2.30, 6–11   Bedrooms tel Falmouth (0326) 40332; £29.34(£32.37B)/£35.38(£40.45B)

CROWS NEST   SX2669 Map1

Crows Nest

Signposted off B3264 N of Liskeard; or pleasant drive from A30 by Siblyback/St Cleer rd from Bolventor, turning left at Common Moor, Siblyback signpost, then forking right to Darite; OS Sheet 201 map reference 263692

Tucked away in a small village up in a fold of the moors, this old-fashioned stripped stone 17th-century pub has an unusually long black wall settle by the big fireplace, with more orthodox seats around polished tables. Its bowed dark oak beams are hung with lots of stirrups, bits and spurs. On the right, and divided by a balustered partition, is a similar area with old local photographs and maybe flowers on the tablecloths. Bar food includes home-made specials like cottage pie (£2.20), seafood pie (£2.75), steak and kidney pie (£2.95), beef curry (£3.50), and a huge mixed grill (£9.50). Well kept St Austell Tinners and HSD on handpump; darts, dominoes, euchre, juke box, fruit machine, and piped music; quick and pleasant service. The terrace by the quiet lane has picnic-table sets. (*Recommended by David and Sarah Gilmore, R L Turnham, Charles and Mary Winpenny*)

St Austell   Licensee T W C Rosser   Real ale   Meals and snacks (not Mon evening) Open 11–11; 11–3.30, 6–11 in winter

HELFORD   SW7526 Map 1

Shipwrights Arms ★ ✍

On summer evenings, this lovely waterside pub holds barbecues with prawns and steaks, and burgers for children on the terraces. It's partly these terraces – which drop down among flowers and palm trees to the creek's edge – which make the pub so special. The top part of the terrace is roofed over with Perspex. Inside, there are lots of ship models and navigation lamps, sea pictures, drawings of lifeboat coxswains, and (live) yachtsmen congregating under the low shiny ochre ceiling by the bar counter. At the other end, a dining area has oak settles, tables and waitress service; an open fire in winter. Home-made bar food – not cheap for the area – includes pasties (£1.35), home-made soup (£1.65), ploughman's (from £2.95, with crab £4.25), a winter home-made daily special (£4), and very good summer salads (from £4; fresh local crab £5.75), with evening dishes like mushrooms in garlic butter or pâté (£2.35), half a roast spring chicken or beef cooked in red wine (£5.75), local scallops or monkfish provençal in white wine (£7.25), sirloin steak (£6.75) and lobster (from £8.50); home-made puddings (from £1.90). Well kept John Devenish and Cornish Original on handpump; chilled white wine. Dominoes, cribbage, euchre, piped music. It does get very busy at peak times. (*Recommended by Ewan and Moira McCall, Wayne Stockton, Brian Skelcher, Nick Dowson, Alison Hayward, Cliff and Karen Spooner, Steve Dark, Joan and Michael Melling, Drs M and K Parier, David Wallington, G Smith, S A Robbins, David Pearman, Gwen and Peter Andrews*)

Cornish Brewery   Licensees Brandon Flynn and Charles Herbert   Real ale   Meals and snacks (not Sun or Mon evenings in winter) tel Manaccan (032 623) 235   Children in eating area   Parking only right outside the village in summer   Open 11–2.30, 6–11

HELSTON SW6527 Map 1
Blue Anchor
50 Coinagehall Street

Probably the oldest brewing house in the country, this thatched town local dates back to the 15th century, when it was a monks' rest house; it carried on brewing as a pub after the dissolution of the monasteries, right through to modern times. The ancient brewhouse is still used to produce the Medium, Best, 'Spingo' Special and Extra Special ales at very reasonable prices – you are usually welcome to look around the brewhouse and cellar at lunchtime. A series of small, low-ceilinged rooms open off the central corridor with flagstones, simple old-fashioned furniture, interesting old prints, some bared stone walls, and in one room a fine inglenook fireplace; a family room has several space games and a fruit machine. Past this, and an old stone bench in the sheltered little terrace area, is a skittle alley which has its own bar at busy times. The nearby Flambards Triple Theme Park has a lot of family attractions, and Godolphin House is well worth visiting. *(Recommended by Carol Mason, Richard Houghton, Nick Dowson, Alison Hayward, Nigel Gibbs, Sandra Cook, David and Sarah Gilmore, Reg Nelson, Cliff Blakemore, Theo Schofield, Gwen and Peter Andrews)*

Own brew   Real ale   Snacks   Children in family room   Parking sometimes difficult Open 10.30–3, 6–11, though they may open longer at busy times

LAMORNA SW4424 Map 1
Lamorna Wink
Signposted off B3315 SW of Penzance

After a bracing walk along the coastal path – the pub is near *Good Walks Guide* Walk 3 and an attractive little cove – this popular, neatly kept country local makes a welcome lunchtime break. It's simply furnished, and has one of the best collections of warship mementoes, sea photographs and nautical brassware in the county. Bar food includes sandwiches, home-made quiches (£2.50), local seafood (from £3) and home-made fruit pies with clotted cream (£1.50). Well kept Devenish Cornish Original and JD on handpump, kept under light blanket pressure; piped music. Pool, trivia, one-armed bandit, and juke box in separate outside games room; darts, cribbage, and fruit machine inside. There are benches outside where you can just hear the sound of the sea and the burble of the stream behind – one reader swears you can catch trout in it. *(Recommended by Richard Gibbs, Peter Sutton, Bobby Goodale, Paul Smith, Neil and Anita Christopher, James and Marion Seeley, C T and J M Laffin, Gwen and Peter Andrews, Russell and Christina Jones)*

Cornish Brewery   Licensee Bob Drennan   Real ale   Meals and snacks (11–2.30, 6–9)   Children in own outside room   Open 11–11

LANNER SW7240 Map 1
Fox & Hounds
Comford; junction A393/B3293; OS sheet 204 map reference 734399

Several red-carpeted areas in this pretty white house ramble around with greeny gold plush or deep pink cloth banquettes, some stripped stonework and dark panelling, black beams and joists, and comical 1920s prints by Lawson Wood; in one granite fireplace there's a woodburning stove, with logs burning in another, and lots of flowers in summer. A good range of bar food, served quickly except at peak times, includes good soup (90p), sandwiches (from £1), salads (from £3; local crab in season), plaice (£3.25), gammon (£5.75), sirloin steak (£6.75), and daily specials (£3.50). Well kept Bass and St Austell BB and HSD tapped from the cask; darts, fruit machine, space game, juke box and piped music. Outside is pretty, with hanging baskets and tubs of flowers, picnic-table sets on the front terrace, and more by swings and a climber on a sheltered and neatly kept back lawn. *(Recommended by Charles and Mary Winpenny, David and Sarah Gilmore, J C Proud, D J Devey, TBB)*

St Austell   Licensee Coral Snipp   Real ale   Meals and snacks (12–2, 7–10)   Children in eating area of bar and restaurant   Restaurant tel St Day (0209) 820251   Open 11–3, 6–11; 11–11 mid July–mid Sept; closed evening 25 Dec

LANREATH   SX1757   Map 1

Punch Bowl   🍺

Village signposted off B3359

This early 17th-century inn has a big stone fireplace, built-in red leatherette wall seats and sturdy wooden tables in the two-roomed flagstoned Farmers' Kitchen. The Turkey-carpeted Visitors' Kitchen has some high-backed antique black settles, a couple of flamboyant red velveteen chaises longues, a Delft shelf above the squared black panelling, and a longcase clock; piped music. Bar food includes filled sandwiches, ploughman's (from £1.80), home-made curry (£3.25), and seafood lasagne (£3.95); very well kept Bass, St Austell HSD and Theakstons Old Peculier on handpump, local farm cider, and a good choice of malt whiskies, bourbons and brandies. Darts, dominoes, fruit machine, space game, and juke box in the games bar. The tucked-away village has a farm museum, and an attractive church with a fine set of bells. *(Recommended by J C Proud, Charles and Mary Winpenny; more reports please)*

Free house   Licensee Harvey Frith   Real ale   Meals and snacks   Restaurant Children in restaurant and own room   Open 11–3, 6–11   Bedrooms tel Lanreath (0503) 20218; £17.50(£24)/£35(£48B)

LERRYN   SX1457   Map 1

Ship

Village signposted from A390 in Lostwithiel

The new landlord has completely refurbished this attractively placed pub. The public bar and games room have old slate floors (a curious change of role for the one in the public bar – it used to be a water tank). The extended, partly no-smoking lounge bar is now carpeted and has old village photographs and trophies, as well as photographs of the Seagull-engined small boat race that's held in December; the winner's the first back to ring the pub's ship's bell. There are brasses on beams, and a locally made grandfather clock; an old settle and table are virtually reserved for their longest-serving customer. Home-made bar food includes sandwiches, watercress quiche, pumpkin crumble or cheese and leek pie (£4) and mariner's or steak and oyster pie or beef escoril (£4.50). Well kept Courage Best and Directors and regularly changing guest beers on handpump or tapped from the cask, and local farm cider; a separate room has sensibly placed darts, pool, dominoes, cribbage, fruit machines, and piped music. In front of the stone building, among flower borders, tubs and hanging baskets, there are some picnic-table sets, with more on a sheltered back lawn which also has a children's play area. You can walk along the bank of the River Lerryn, or through National Trust woodland nearby. *(Recommended by Peter Watkins, Pam Stanley, R Elliott, J C Proud, Patrick Young, R L Turnham, A B Sykes, Ted George)*

Free house   Licensee Howard Packer   Real ale   Meals and snacks (11–2, 6–10) Restaurant tel Bodmin (0208) 872374   Children welcome   Open 11–3 (2.30 in winter), 6–11

LOSTWITHIEL   SX1059   Map 1

Royal Oak

Duke St; pub easily visible from A390 in centre

There's a tale that a smugglers' underground tunnel links this 13th-century pub's cellar to the dungeons in the courtyard of Restormel Castle. It's a friendly place, with an unusual range of real ales for Cornwall: Bass, Flowers Original and IPA, Fullers London Pride, Marstons Pedigree and two or three guest beers on handpump; they also have a good choice of bottled beers, and draught ciders. The well kept lounge has walls stripped back to the old reddish granite, a couple of wooden armchairs by the gas-effect log fire, and captain's chairs and brown leatherette button-back banquettes on its patterned carpet. There's also a Delft china shelf, with a small dresser in one inner alcove; piped music. Generous helpings of reliable bar food include sandwiches (from 90p), soup (£1), pâté (£2), ploughman's (from £2.20), basket meals (from £2.95), very good scallops in cheese and white wine sauce (£2.90), tasty curries (£3.25), summer salads (from £2.95), and specials like stuffed mushrooms (£2), broccoli and cream cheese pie (£3.25) or barbary duck (£7.50); children's menu (from £1.35). The flagstoned back public bar has darts, dominoes, cribbage, fruit machine and juke box, and younger customers. On a raised terrace by the car park, lined with cordylines, are some picnic-table sets. *(Recommended by WHBM, Charles and Mary Winpenny, J M Fletcher, Peter Watkins, Pam Stanley, Roy McNeill, S A Robbins, Ian Shaw, Lindsey Shaw Radley, JM, PM)*

Free house   Licensees Malcolm and Eileen Hine   Real ale   Meals and snacks (12–2, 6.30–10)   Restaurant   Children in restaurant   Open 11–3, 5.30–11   Bedrooms tel Bodmin (0208) 872552; £25B/£42B

MALPAS   SW8442 Map 1

Heron

Village signposted from A39 at main Truro roundabout

The sunny slate-paved front terrace has a lovely view over the wooded creek far below, making this a very appealing place in summer. Inside, the long, rectangular bar has brasses, bric-a-brac, an excellent collection of late 19th-century photographs of Truro and the surrounding countryside, and winter log fires. Good bar food includes generously filled sandwiches (from £1.30; crab £2.95), soup (£1.65), liver, bacon and mushroom kebab with garlic bread or macaroni cheese (£2.95), ploughman's (from £2.95), home-made steak pie (£3.95), lasagne (£4.35), and sirloin steak and scampi (£5.95), with evening dishes like gammon with egg and pineapple (£6.95), pork marsala (£7.55) and fillet steak (£8.50); daily specials, puddings, and children's menu (£1.95). Well kept St Austell Tinners and HSD on handpump; fruit machine, space game, trivia and piped music. At weekends and in other busy periods, the pub can get exceedingly crowded – when nearby parking may not be easy (especially as there are double yellow lines outside the building); service still copes well then. *(Recommended by Patrick Young, Peter Corris, S A Robbins; more reports please)*

St Austell   Licensees Calvin and Anne Kneebone   Real ale   Meals and snacks Children in eating area of bar   Occasional live entertainment Sat evenings   Open 11–3.30, 6–11; 11.30–2.30, 7–10.30 in winter

MANACCAN   SW7625 Map 1

New ★

Down hill signposted to Gillan and St Keverne

In a sleepy coastal village on the south side of the Helford River, this old thatched local has a cosy and simply furnished double-room bar with a beam and plank ceiling, pictures on the walls, individually chosen chairs, traditional built-in wall seats, and a well-heeled clientele; attractive touches include hops around the windows, freshly-cut flowers, and oriental rugs. Bar food is good, with dishes like very tasty home-made soups such as puréed local vegetable and curry or chilled pea and mint (£1.20), home-made pasty (winter only), sandwiches (£1.50; delicious crab £2), good crab or smoked salmon pâté (£1.75), ploughman's (£3), kidney turbigo (£4), home-baked ham in cider (£4.50), lovely leek and courgette flan, fresh poached salmon (£6.50), sirloin steak (£7.50), and puddings like good treacle tart or excellent bread and butter pudding (£2); they may have home-cooked locally caught fish dishes (depending on availability). Well kept Devenish JD and Cornish Original tapped from the cask; dominoes, cribbage, euchre, chess, backgammon and yahtzee. A sheltered lawn with picnic-table sets slopes up behind the pub. The outside lavatories are not the place to linger on a cold day. *(Recommended by W Bailey, Nick Dowson, Alison Hayward, Cliff and Karen Spooner, Ewan and Moira McCall, Gwen and Peter Andrews, ACP, Robert Brown, Ian Shaw, Lindsey Shaw Radley, David Wallington, Cliff Blakemore, JM, PM, Sue Carlyle, Dr and Mrs A K Clarke, Russell and Christina Jones)*

Cornish Brewery   Licensee Patrick Cullinan   Real ale   Meals and snacks   Children in eating area of bar until 8pm   Parking may be difficult in summer   Open 10.30–3, 6–11

METHERELL   SX4069   Map 1

Carpenters Arms

Village signposted from Honicombe, which itself is signposted from St Ann's Chapel, just W of Gunnislake on A390; pub signposted in village, OS Sheet 201, map reference 408694

Huge polished flagstones, tiny windows, massive stone walls and heavy black beams suggest the age of this village inn – some 500 years. The friendly bar has winged high-backed red leatherette settles in the various alcoves, brasses, a large slowly ticking clock, and lots of succulent plants. A wide choice of bar food includes home-made soup (£1.25), sandwiches (from £1.20; toasties from £1.35), ploughman's (from £2.25), excellent omelettes (from £2.75), salads (from £3) fresh whole mackerel with tomato sauce (£3.40), vegetable curry or Chinese bean casserole (£3.75), good home-made steak and kidney pie (£4), gammon with egg or pineapple (£4.20), steaks (from £5.75), puddings like home-made blackcurrant cake (£1.35), and children's dishes (£1.30). Well kept Bass, Flowers Original, Wadworths 6X and Whitbreads Best, with guests like Cotleigh Tawny or Marstons Pedigree on handpump or tapped from casks behind the bar; good farm ciders and decent house white wine; piped music, sensibly placed darts, and fruit machine. Outside, by an old well, there are some sheltered tables. Cotehele, the lovely National Trust Tudor house by the head of the Tamar estuary, is a couple of miles further on through these narrow lanes. Please note, they no longer do bedrooms. *(Recommended by Philip and Trisha Ferris, Mrs B Barnes, John Kirk, Ewan and Moira McCall; more reports please)*

Free house   Licensees Douglas and Jill Brace   Real ale   Meals and snacks   Children in eating area of bar   Open 11.30–2.30, 6.30–11

MITHIAN   SW7450   Map 1

Miners Arms ★

Between B3284 and B3285, E of St Agnes

This year, what had been a small dining room has become a cosy refurbished additional lounge with a decorative low ceiling, lots of books and quite a few interesting ornaments. The atmospheric little back bar has bulging squint walls (one with a fine old wall painting of Elizabeth I), irregular beam and plank ceiling, and a wood block floor. A lot of this character spills over into the comfortable and spacious main lounge; there's also a stone-built cellar lounge and darts room. Good, popular bar food includes sandwiches, soup (from 95p, wonderful home-made tomato soup with toasted garlic bread £1.80), tasty locally-made pasty (£2.05), exceptionally good ploughman's (from £2.65), a pot of pâté with tomato bread (£2.25), home-made cottage pie (£3.50), vegetarian devilled layer (£3.65), home-made steak and kidney pie (£3.95), and sirloin steak (£7.95); home-made puddings like farmhouse crumble (from £1.50), Sunday lunch (£4.95 – booking essential). Well kept Cornish Original and Devenish JD on handpump, farm cider; table skittles, fruit machine and piped music; good winter fire. There are benches on the sheltered front cobbled terrace. Please note that they have stopped doing accommodation. *(Recommended by WHBM, Margo and Peter Thomas, Patrick Young, David and Sarah Gilmore, M P Hallewell, JM, PM, James and Marion Seeley, Mrs L Cantelo, Steve Dark)*

Cornish Brewery   Licensee Peter Andrew   Real ale   Meals and snacks   Restaurant
tel *St Agnes (087 255) 2375*   Children in cellar lounge and eating area of bar   Open
11–3, 6–11

MORWENSTOW   SS2015 Map 1
Bush

Village signposted off A39 N of Kilkhampton

In lovely walking country, this homely and highly idiosyncratic little pub was once
a monastic rest house on a pilgrim route between Wales and Spain. Part of it dates
back just over 1,000 years (a Celtic piscina carved from serpentine stone is still set
in one wall), and it has a strong claim to be one of the very oldest (and most
haunted) pubs in Britain. There are ancient built-in settles, a big stone fireplace,
and a cosy side area with antique seats, a lovely old elm trestle table, and a wooden
propeller from a 1930 De Havilland Gipsy. An upper bar, opened at busy times,
has built-in settles, and is decorated with antique knife-grinding wheels, miners'
lamps, casks, funnels, and so forth. Well kept St Austell HSD and guest beers such
as Bass, Cotleigh Old Buzzard, Wadworths 6X and Farmers Glory on handpump
or tapped from the cask behind the wood-topped stone bar counter (with pewter
tankards lining the beams above it); quite a few malt whiskies, and Inch's cider.
Simple bar food includes sandwiches, home-made soup (90p), good home-made
pasties, quiche or home-made steak and kidney pie (£1.50), and home-made stew
or ploughman's with a bowl of home-made pickle (£1.75). Darts, cribbage,
dominoes and fruit machine; the landlord is firmly against piped music and dogs or
children in the bar. Seats outside shelter in the slightly sunken yard. Vicarage Cliff,
one of the grandest parts of the Cornish coast – with 400ft precipices – is a
ten-minute walk away. *(Recommended by Gary Phillips, William D Cissna, Nick Dowson,
Alison Hayward, Steve Dark, R Del Mar)*

*Free house   Licensee J H Gregory   Real ale   Meals and snacks (not Sun)   Open
12–2.30, 7–11; closed Mon Oct–Mar and 25 Dec*

MOUSEHOLE   SW4726 Map 1
Ship

Off B3315 SW of Penzance

One reader who has known this pub off and on since 1938 was delighted to find it
still very much the friendly local – yet welcoming to visitors as well. The L-shaped
main bar has built-in wooden wall benches and stools around low tables, rough
granite and bare board floor, black beams and panelling, sailors' rope fancywork,
and an open fire. In winter they bring a pool table and dart board into a
communicating bar. Bar food includes sandwiches (from £1.40, excellent crab
£2.50), fisherman's lunch (£2.50), smokey fish bake or lasagne (£3.50), crab salad
(£5.50) and steaks; well kept St Austell BB, HSD and Tinners on handpump, and
several malt whiskies; friendly staff. The beautiful village does get packed in
summer and over the Christmas period (when the elaborate harbour lights are a
special draw). *(Recommended by Gwen and Peter Andrews, Margaret and Roy Randle,
Richard Gibbs, Patrick Stapley, Paul Smith, Bobby Goodale, Peter Sutton, Gwyneth and Salvo
Spadaro-Dutturi, John Branford, Linda Duncan, Steve Mitcheson, Anne Collins)*

*St Austell   Licensees Michael and Tracey Maddern   Meals and snacks (12–2.30,
6–9.30; not winter evenings)   Children in eating area of bar   Summer parking can be
difficult   Open 10.30–11; 10.30–2.30, 6–11 in winter   Bedrooms tel Penzance (0736)
731234; /£35B*

nr MYLOR BRIDGE   SW8036 Map 1
Pandora ★ ★

Restronguet Passage: from A39 in Penryn, take turning signposted Mylor Church,
Mylor Bridge, Flushing and go straight through Mylor Bridge following Restronguet

Passage signs; or from A39 further N, at or near Perranarworthal, take turning signposted Mylor, Restronguet, then follow Restronguet Weir signs, but turn left down hill at Restronguet Passage sign

At high tide on a quiet day, this thatched medieval pub looks particularly fine. There are lots of picnic-table sets in front and on a long floating jetty – where food and drink are served (weather permitting); quite a few people arrive by boat – there are showers for visiting yachtsmen. Inside, several rambling, interconnecting rooms have cosy alcoves with leatherette benches built into the walls, beautifully polished big flagstones, low wooden ceilings (mind your head on some of the beams), a kitchen range, and a log fire in a high hearth (to protect it against tidal floods); one area is no-smoking. Bar food includes home-made soup (£1 or £1.20), sandwiches (from £1.75; local crab with cucumber and lettuce £3.75), cauliflower cheese (£2.75), fish pie (£3.75), salads (from £4.50), evening sirloin steak (£7.95), puddings like home-made lemon meringue pie (from £1.75), and children's dishes (from £1.25). Bass, St Austell Tinners, HSD and Bosun on handpump from a temperature controlled cellar, and ten malt whiskies; winter pool. It does get very crowded in summer, and parking is difficult at peak times. *(Recommended by Gwen and Peter Andrews, Malcolm Littler, WHBM, Michael Bechley, Gethin Lewis, R J Walden, Nick Dowson, Alison Hayward, W Bailey, S P Bobeldijk, Richard Houghton, Carol Mason, Patrick Young, J C Proud, David Wallington, Annie Taylor, Cdr W S D Hendry, Steve Dark, Joy Heatherley, David Pearman)*

St Austell   Licensees Roger and Helen Hough   Real ale   Meals and snacks   Evening restaurant tel Falmouth (0326) 72678; closed winter Sun evenings   Children in eating area of bar and restaurant   Open 11–11; 12–10.30 Sun; 11–2.30, 6.30–11 winter weekdays

PADSTOW   SW9175   Map 1

London Inn

Lanadwell Street

This bustling side-street pub was originally three fishermen's cottages, and is close to the attractive working harbour. The two friendly and neatly nautical rooms have lots of red and cream woodwork, an oak parquet floor, new and more comfortable furniture, and brass ships' instruments and sea photographs. Bar food includes delicious sandwiches (from £1, good crab and prawn £1.60), ploughman's (£2), filled baked potatoes (from £2.50), omelettes, salads (from £3, crab and prawn £5), a roast (£3.75), and a variety of fresh seafood. Well kept St Austell BB, Tinners and HSD on handpump, and quite a few malts; darts, shove-ha'penny, dominoes, cribbage, euchre, fruit machine and piped music. For vigorous walks you might try the old railway line as well as the coast path. It can get very busy in summer. There is a good bird garden nearby. *(Recommended by Iain and Penny Muir, J C Proud, Ted George, Cdr W S D Hendry; more reports please)*

St Austell   Licensee Clive Lean   Real ale   Meals and snacks   Restaurant   Children in restaurant and eating area of bar (12–2.30 lunchtime, until 9pm evening   Open 11–4, 6–11   3 bedrooms (not Christmas week) tel Padstow (0841) 532554; £16/£28

PELYNT   SX2055   Map 1

Jubilee ⏎

B3359 NW of Looe

An inner area of the lounge in this rather smart and comfortable old place is decorated with mementoes of Queen Victoria – making it clear which Jubilee is in question. The main part has neatly squared oak beams, an early 18th-century Derbyshire oak armchair, brown leather and red fabric cushioned wall and window seats, Windsor armchairs, magazines stacked under the oak tables, and a good winter log fire under a copper hood in the big stone fireplace. The flagstoned entry is separated from this room by an attractively old-fangled glass-paned partition. There are more handsome flagstones in the public bar, and pool, sensibly placed darts, dominoes, cribbage, fruit machine, space game, trivia, juke box, piped music, football game and a mechanical animal in the garden for children. Quickly served, decent bar food includes a good choice of lunchtime sandwiches (from £1.50, local crab £2.90), home-made soup (£1.60), ploughman's (£2.80), mushrooms in batter with a devilled sauce (£3.60), good barbecued spare ribs (£4), home-baked ham and eggs (£4.70), local plaice (£4.90), salads (from £5.10, £6.40 for local crab), steaks (from £8.30), daily specials like good roast lamb with home-made mint sauce, and puddings (£2.20). Well kept Fergusons Dartmoor Pride (known as Jubilee Original here) on handpump, several malt whiskies, and quite a few wines. A crazy-paved central courtyard has barbecues (weather permitting), and there's a well equipped children's play area. *(Recommended by E A Simmons, Mrs D M Hacker, D C Bail, D P Ryan, Mr and Mrs Simon Turner, J A Scott, J C Proud, Joy Heatherley, R F Warner)*

Fergusons (Allied)   Licensee Frank Williams   Real ale   Meals and snacks   Restaurant (not Sun evening)   Children in eating area of bar only if eating   Jazz Fri evenings Open 11–3, 6–11; 11–11 Sat   Bedrooms tel Lanreath (0503) 20312; £23.50B/£47B

PENDOGGETT   SX0279 Map 1

Cornish Arms 🚫 🛏

B3314

As we went to press there was the possibility that this 16th-century pub might change hands; this could of course mean other changes, but we should make the point that past changes of ownership have done nothing to dim this fine pub's appeal. A lunchtime bar menu (not Sunday) has included sandwiches (from £1.40), ploughman's (£2.15), king prawns in garlic butter (£2.60), a good value cold buffet (from £3 – the beef has been delicious), breaded scampi (£3.95), grilled shark steak coated in a fennel and parsley sauce (£4.25), grilled lemon sole (£5.95), and steak chasseur (£6.95). You could also eat from the restaurant menu: chopped mushrooms and bacon with mixed herbs and double cream (£2.95), hors d'oeuvres (£5.35), kidney kebab (£6.50), salads (from £6.50), roast duck in a morello cherry and red wine sauce (£8.45), steaks (from £8.95), fresh local lobster (£17), vegetarian dishes and home-made puddings. Sunday lunch is £7. Well kept Bass tapped from the cask, and Pendoggett Special brewed for the pub on handpump. Good wines – the extensive list is carefully thought out, with some eminences and some attractive bargains; farm ciders, a dozen malt whiskies, and lots of liqueurs. The two panelled rooms of the front bar (one of which is no-smoking at lunchtime) have high-backed built-in oak settles surrounding solid old wooden tables on the Delabole slate floor, fresh flowers, and a warm atmosphere. The big, lively locals' bar has high-backed settles around stripped deal tables, a big woodburning stove, and darts, dominoes, cribbage, euchre, fruit machine, maybe a portable television, and occasional piped music. Tables out on a corner terrace have a sea view down the valley. *(Recommended by Brian Skelcher, Paul Smith, I S Wilson, C Vallely, Rosalind Russell, Charles and Mary Winpenny, Steve Dark, Graham Tayar; more reports please)*

Free house   Licensees Mervyn Gilmour, Paul Stewart   Real ale   Meals and snacks (12.15–2.30, 6–10.30)   Restaurant   Children in coffee room (lunchtimes) and restaurant Sun lunch and evenings   Pianist most Sat evenings   Open 11–11 Bedrooms tel Bodmin (0208) 880263; £36(£38B)/£46(£49B)

PENZANCE   SW4730 Map 1

Admiral Benbow

Chapel St; turn off top of main street, by big domed building (Lloyds Bank)

Lots of nautical memorabilia fill the low-beamed, upstairs bar here: fancy carving, figureheads, wreck charts (including a nice one with Gillespie drawings), lots of shiny paintwork, elaborate balustered pillars, engine-room telegraphs, model ships in glass cases, a lovely brass cannon, navigation lanterns and so forth, and ropes neatly wound in and out all over the place. The various alcoves have red plush seats around the tables, and there are lots of mirrors and plants. A plainer back room – with less atmosphere – has a pool table and lots of seats. Bar food includes sandwiches, beef and Guinness pie and lasagne (£3.50). Devenish Cornish Original and Wadworths 6X on electric pump; darts, fruit machine and piped music. The pub is popular with young people in the evenings. *(Recommended by Gwen and Peter Andrews, Carol Mason, Peter Corris, WMS; more reports on the new regime please)*

Free house Licensee Stephen Stoyles Real ale Meals and snacks Restaurant tel Penzance (0736) 63448 Children welcome Live entertainment Open 11–11; 11–3, 6–11 in winter

Turks Head

At top of main street, by big domed building (Lloyds Bank), turn left down Chapel Street Popular with locals and visitors, this busy, friendly pub has old flat-irons, jugs and so forth hanging from the beams, pottery above the wood-effect panelling, wall seats and tables, and a couple of elbow rests around central pillars; a smaller side room is set out for eating, as is the downstairs cellar room (which has been a bar for several hundred years). A wide choice of seafood includes crab soup (£1.30), excellent grilled sardines, mussels in wine, tomato and garlic (£3.95), crevettes (from £3.95), crab salad (mixed meat £4.70, white meat £5.95), and cold seafood platter (£7.20); there's also plenty of non-seafood variety, such as lunchtime sandwiches (from £1), home-made soup (from £1.10), filled baked potatoes (from £1.65), ploughman's (from £2.75), ratatouille topped with cheese (£2.45), good chilli con carne (£3.20), meaty or vegetarian lasagne (£3.65), gammon steak (£4.95), and very good charcoal-grilled steaks (from £7.50). Devenish Royal Wessex, Cornish Original and Steam on handpump, country wines, quite a few cocktails, and winter hot punch; pleasant, helpful service; fruit machine, piped music; in the evening there can be quite a lively young crowd. The sun-trap back garden has big urns of flowers. *(Recommended by Pat and Malcolm Rudlin, Mr and Mrs M A Smith, Neil and Anita Christopher, Patrick Stapley, Richard Gibbs, RAB, Bobby Goodale)*

Cornish Brewery Licensee William Morris Real ale Meals and snacks (11–2.30, 6–9.30, till 10 summer) Restaurant tel Penzance (0736) 63093 Children in cellar dining room Open 11–3, 5.30–11; 11–11 Fri and Sat in summer

PERRANWELL SW7839 Map 1

Royal Oak

Village signposted off A393 Redruth–Falmouth and A39 Falmouth–Truro

This friendly and pretty stone-built village pub has horsebrasses and pewter and china mugs on black beams and joists, foxhunting decorations, red-cushioned seats around the tables on the red carpet, and lots of brassware around the stone fireplace – the bar rambles around into a snug little nook of a room behind this, with a prettily filled Delft shelf. An attractively laid out lunchtime cold buffet gives generous helpings of such things as smoked mackerel or quiche (£3.05), home-cooked gammon (£4.10), roast beef (£5.20) or crab and prawn (£5.70); they also do soup (£1.10), filled baked potatoes (£1.65), ploughman's (from £1.95), omelettes (from £2.20), plaice (£2.75), scampi (£3.85) and a seafood platter, with similar hot dishes in the evening running up to steaks. Well kept Devenish JD and Royal Wessex on handpump, piped pop music. There are some picnic-table sets outside, by the quiet village lane. *(Recommended by Margo and Peter Thomas, J C Proud)*

Cornish Brewery Licensee Adrian Fitzgerald Real ale Meals and snacks Children in eating area area behind fireplace Open 11–2.30, 5–11

PHILLEIGH SW8639 Map 1

Roseland ★ ⊘

Between A3078 Truro–St Mawes and B3269

Charming inside and out, this 17th-century pub has a pretty paved front courtyard with flowers among its attractive tables and chairs. The carefully chosen bar furnishings include a lovely oak settle and old-fashioned seats around the sturdy tables on the flagstones, lots of old sporting prints and other pictures under the low beams, an old wall clock, and attractive bunches of fresh flowers; good winter fire. Home-made bar food includes sandwiches (from £1.10, toasties £1.25, fresh local crab £3.50), vegetable soup (£1.50), generous ploughman's (£2.75), home-made cheese and asparagus quiche (£3.25), tasty seafood mornay or egg mayonnaise with prawns (£3.50), lasagne (£3.75), beef in beer pie or kedgeree (£4), and puddings like chocolate biscuit cake or teacle tart with cream (£1.75). Well kept Devenish JD and Cornish Original on handpump from a temperature-controlled cellar, and winter hot toddies; dominoes, cribbage. The quiet lane leads on to the little half-hourly *King Harry* car ferry across a pretty wooded channel, with Trelissick Gardens on the far side. *(Recommended by Charles and Mary Winpenny, Brian Skelcher, Patrick Young, Iain and Penny Muir, David and Sarah Gilmore, Robert Brown, T Galligan, JM, PM, Dr C J Weir, Mary Rayner, Russell and Christina Jones)*

Cornish Brewery Licensee Desmond Sinnott Real ale Meals and snacks (not 25 Dec) Children in lounge Open 11.30–2.30, 6–11; winter evening hours 7–10.30

POLKERRIS SX0952 Map 1

Rashleigh

The setting could hardly be bettered: an isolated beach and attractively restored jetty, overlooked by tables on the stone terrace (and by the figurehead which presides over it); there are barbecues here in summer. Inside, the front part of the bar has comfortably cushioned seats, with local photographs on the brown panelling of a more simply furnished back area. Food includes an extensive lunchtime cold buffet (from £5), also soup (£1), sandwiches (from £1), ploughman's (£3), prawns (£6), seafood cocottes (£6.50), and chargrilled steaks (£8). Fergusons Bolsters Bitter and St Austell HSD on handpump; dominoes, cribbage, fruit machine and piped music. This section of the Cornish coast path includes striking scenery, and there are safe moorings for small yachts in the cove. Though parking space next to the pub is limited, there's a large village car park. *(Recommended by Margo and Peter Thomas, J M Fletcher, David and Sarah Gilmore, ACP, Roy McNeill, David Wallington, Joy Heatherley, Barbara Want)*

Free house Licensee Bernard Smith Real ale Meals and snacks (11–2, 6–10) Restaurant tel Par (072 681) 3991 (Weds-Sat, though buffet/bar meals served here Sun) Children in eating area of bar Pianist Fri and Sat evenings Open 11–11

POLPERRO SX2051 Map 1

Blue Peter ★ ⊘

The Quay; on the right-hand side as you go round the harbour – a brisk 10-minute walk from the public car park

Hearty food in this welcoming pub – overlooking the small working harbour – includes sandwiches (from 95p, local crab £1.95), pasty (£1.50), home-made soup (£1.20), filled baked potatoes (from £1.50), platters (a mixture between a ploughman's and a salad, from £2.75, local crab £3.95), pizzas freshly cooked on the premises (from £2.50), and home-made hot dishes like beef and Guinness pie (£3.75) and Rangoon chicken curry with basmati rice and poppadum or deep ocean bake (£3.95). Daily specials might include fresh local trout grilled with garlic, a good, really hot chilli con carne and fresh seafood – depending on what the local fishermen caught that morning, maybe monkfish kebabs, scallops or a seafood platter; puddings (from £1.75), children's menu (from £1.35), vegetarian dishes and winter Sunday roasts. Well kept St Austell Tinners and HSD, a beer brewed for the pub and a guest beer such as Brains SA or Gibbs Mew Bishops Tipple on handpump, as well as strong farm cider. The cosy low-beamed bar has a small winged settle, a polished pew, and a seat cut from a big cask (as well as more ordinary seats), fishing nets, some boat pictures, and a huge naval shell by the coal fire. One window seat looks down on the harbour, another looks out past rocks to the sea. Darts, shove-ha'penny, cribbage, dominoes, fruit machine, space game, trivia and piped jazz and blues. The small V-shaped terrace at the top of the flight of steps up to the door has some slat seats. Near *Good Walks Guide* Walk 9. *(Recommended by Steve Dark, M Rowlinson, Ian Shaw, Lindsey Shaw Radley, Rosalind Russell, John Branford, Linda Duncan, Tim and Lynne Crawford; more reports please)*

Free house   Licensees Tim Horn, Jennie Craig-Hallam, Terry Bicknell   Real ale Meals and snacks (12–2.30, 6–9.30)   Children in two upstairs family rooms   Jazz Sun lunchtime all year, light rock/blues Thurs Oct–May   Open 11–11; closed evening 25 Dec

PORTHLEVEN   SW6225 Map 1

Ship ★

Signposted off A394 Helston–Penzance

To get into this old fisherman's pub, set into steep rocks above a working harbour which is interestingly floodlit at night, you have to climb a flight of rough stone steps. The knocked-through bar has genuine character, with cosy alcove window seats giving good sea views, big log fires in capacious stone fireplaces, and very friendly staff. There's also a summer cellar bar. Very good, nicely presented bar food – served in the candle-lit dining room, with excellent views – includes filled hot crusty bread (£1.50), tasty fish pie, lasagne, cottage pie or moussaka (all £3.90), salads (from £4, crab claws £5.25), rump steak (£6.95) and seafood platter (£9.75), with specials like an excellent big bowl of mushrooms in garlic (£2.50) or fresh mackerel cooked in cider and stuffed with apple (£2.95); well kept Courage Best and Directors and John Smiths on handpump; good, fast service; dominoes, cribbage, fruit machine and piped music; terraced garden. *(Recommended by E A George, Tom Evans, David and Sarah Gilmore, Mr and Mrs B E Witcher, Clifford Blakemore, Annie Taylor, Tim and Lynne Crawford, S A Robbins)*

Courage   Licensee Colin Oakden   Real ale   Meals and snacks (not winter Sun evenings)   Children in family room   Parking can be difficult in summer   Open 11.30–11; 11.30–2.30, 7–11 in winter

nr PORT ISAAC   SX0080 Map 1

Port Gaverne Hotel ★ 🛏

Port Gaverne signposted from Port Isaac, and from B3314 E of Pendoggett

In a lovely spot, just back from the sea and close to splendid clifftop walks, this civilised, early 17th-century inn has been run by the same friendly licensees for over 20 years. The well kept bars have low beams, some exposed stone, flagstones where they're not carpeted, a collection of antique cruets, an enormous marine chronometer, and big log fires. In spring the lounge is filled with pictures from the local art society's annual exhibition in aid of the Royal National Lifeboat Institution (the pub also takes part in the annual costumed four-legged race in aid of the same organization); at other times there are interesting antique local photographs. Many people praise the bar food, though the choice is not wide: sandwiches (from £1, excellent crab £2.25), home-made soup (from £1.05, crab £1.95), pâté (£1.85), ploughman's (from £1.95), home-made cottage pie (£2.35), salads (from £3, half a lobster £8.75), home-made steak and kidney pie or a daily special (£4.75), with evening extras such as burger (£1.80), deep fried local plaice (£3.65) and sirloin steak; Sunday roast lunch is £4.95. From Spring Bank Holiday until the end of October food is served buffet-style in the dining room at lunchtime, and there is the same arrangement for Sunday lunchtime (when food stops at 1.30 sharp) throughout the year, but otherwise it's served in the bar or 'Captain's Cabin' – a little room where everything except an antique admiral's hat is shrunk to scale (old oak chest, model sailing ship, even the prints on the white stone walls). Well kept Flowers IPA and St Austell HSD on handpump, a good bin-end wine list, a very good choice of whiskies and other spirits, and around three dozen liqueurs; quick, efficient service. Dominoes and cribbage, with darts, pool and a fruit machine in the renovated Green Door Club across the lane, which also has a big diarama of Port Isaac. A raised terrace outside has a good sea view (the bar does not). Each year, a costumed raft race is held here. *(Recommended by Iain and Penny Muir, C M Whitehouse, Andrea and Guy Bradley, Steve Dark, C T and J M Laffin, Lyn and Bill Capper, Lesley Underhill, Mr and Mrs M V Melling, Paul Smith, Mr and Mrs D M Norton, Sue Carlyle, David Pearman, Peter Corris, George Jonas, Graham Tayar)*

Free house   Licensee Frederick Ross   Real ale   Meals and snacks (12–2, 7–10)   Restaurant   Children in restaurant (though under 6 only until 8pm) and in Captain's Cabin in evening (please reserve)   Open 11–3, 5.30–11; closed 13 Jan to 16 Feb   Bedrooms tel Bodmin (0208) 880244; £39B/£78B; canine guests £2, food not provided; also restored 18th-century self-contained cottages

SCORRIER   SW7244 Map 1

Fox & Hounds ✪

Village signposted from A30; B3298 Falmouth road

The often inventive food here is locally so popular that it's wise to arrive early for a table. Served by uniformed waitresses, dishes might include soup (£1.50), sandwiches (toasties from £1.85, open sandwiches from £2.10), filled baked potatoes (from £2.10), ploughman's (£2.20), several vegetarian dishes (£3.30), home-made curry or Lebanese kofta (£3.30), cold prawns in a curried mayonnaise (£3.95) and 8oz sirloin steak (£6.40), with evening extras like fresh local trout (£4.10), chicken Kiev (£4.50), lamb in an orange and ginger sauce (£5.95), lemon sole in mushrooms and white wine £6.10) and daily specials such as lamb goulash or beef with fresh chillis and peppers (around £3.35). There are delicious puddings like lockshen (a Jewish version of bread and butter pudding but made with noodles, £1.55), pavlovas, crumbles or a chocolate swiss roll filled with strawberry jelly, whipped cream, chunks of chocolate and fresh strawberries (£1.65); Sunday roast lunch is £3.35. Well kept Devenish JD and Cornish Original on handpump; warmly friendly service. The long bar is divided into sections by a partition wall and low screens. It's comfortably furnished, with red plush seats around dimpled copper tables, creaky joists in the red ceiling, some vertical panelling, some stripped stonework, hunting prints, a stuffed fox, a fox mask, and big log fires. There is more seating in a no-smoking front extension, formerly a verandah; fruit machine, piped nostalgic music. The long, low white building – well set back from the road – is prettily decorated with hanging baskets and window-boxes, and has picnic-table sets under cocktail parasols in front. *(Recommended by Gwen and Peter Andrews, Pat and Malcolm Rudlin; more reports please)*

Cornish Brewery   Licensee D J Halfpenny   Real ale   Meals and snacks (12–2, 7–10; not Mon evening except Bank Hols)   Open 11–2.30, 6–11; Sat evening opening 6.30; closed 26 Dec

ST AGNES   SW7250 Map 1

Railway

Vicarage Rd; from centre follow B3277 signs for Porthtowan and Truro

One reader feels that over the ten years he's been coming here, this busy little pub has remained as pleasant as ever. It's almost like a museum, and has a remarkable collection of shoes – minute or giant, made of strange skins, fur, leather, wood, mother-of-pearl, or embroidered with gold and silver, from Turkey, Persia, China or Japan and worn by ordinary people or famous men. There's also some splendid brasswork (including one of the finest original horsebrass collections in the country), and a notable collection of naval memorabilia from model sailing ships and rope fancywork to the texts of Admiralty messages at important historical moments. Bar food includes burger or home-made soup (£1.20), sandwiches (from £1.35), ploughman's (from £2.40), chicken (£3.35), scampi (£3.75), and a daily special such as fresh mussels in garlic with crusty bread (£3.25), a pasta dish (£3.50) and 8oz sirloin steak (£5.95). Well kept Devenish JD and Cornish Original tapped from the cask; darts, shove-ha'penny, dominoes, fruit machine and piped music. When the locals are there in force it can get pretty crowded. *(Recommended by Iain and Penny Muir, JM, PM, Peter Corris, Cdr W S D Hendry; more reports please)*

Cornish Brewery   Licensee Christopher O'Brien   Real ale   Meals and snacks
Children in family room   Open 11–3, 6–11 weekdays (though may stay open longer if
trade demands); 11–5, 6–11 Fri and Sat

ST BREWARD   SX0977 Map 1
Old Inn

Old Town; village signposted off B3266 S of Camelford

One of Cornwall's highest pubs, this quietly friendly old place shares its hilltop
with a church whose tower is a landmark for miles around; behind is open
moorland, and cattle and sheep wander into the village. The two-roomed bar has
fine broad slate flagstones, plates hanging on stripped stonework, banknotes and
horsebrasses on the low oak joists that support the ochre upstairs floorboards. Its
inner room, with cushioned wall benches and chairs around its tables, naif
paintings on slate by a local artist (for sale cheaply), and a good log fire, has a glass
panel showing a separate games room with pool table, fruit machine and space
game. The outer room has fewer tables (old ones, of character), a woodburning
stove in the big granite fireplace, a piano and sensibly placed darts – the ladies'
team are hot stuff; also, dominoes, cribbage, juke box and piped music. Bargain
bar food includes sandwiches (from 85p, egg and bacon bap £1), local pasties
(£2.45), salads (from £2.60), local ham and eggs (£2.65), home-made curry
(£3.30), devilled lamb chops (£4.25) and mixed grill (£5.20), with dishes of the day
such as pork in cider or beef in red wine (£4.25), and puddings like blackberry and
apple crumble (£1.30); well kept Ruddles County and Ushers Best on handpump,
cheap but decent coffee. Picnic-table sets outside are protected by low stone walls.
(Recommended by Mr and Mrs R P Begg, D L Parkhurst)

Free house   Licensee Derek Judd   Real ale   Meals and snacks (12–2, 7–10)
Restaurant tel Bodmin (0208) 850711   Children in eating areas and pool room   Open
11.30–3, 6–11

ST EWE   SW9746 Map 1
Crown

Village signposted from B3287; easy to find from Mevagissey

Traditional furnishings in this friendly and attractive cottage include a very
high-backed curved old settle with flowery cushions, long shiny wooden tables,
16th-century flagstones, and a roaring winter log fire with an ancient
weight-driven working spit; shelves beside the fire have plates, a brass teapot and
jug. The eating area has a burgundy-coloured carpet, velvet curtains, and matching
cushions on the old church pews. Good bar food includes tasty pasties (70p), egg
mayonnaise (£1), traditional and open sandwiches (from £1, local crab in season
£2.50), home-made soup (£1.20), ploughman's (from £2), filled baked potatoes
(from £2.50), salads (from £3.50, fresh crab in season £5.50), gammon and egg
(£6.20), tasty steaks (from £7), and home-made puddings like fruit or mincemeat
and brandy pies (from £1) and their special ice-cream (£2); large, wholesome
breakfasts. Well kept St Austell BB on handpump, several malt whiskies and local
wine; darts, pool, dominoes, fruit machine, space game and piped music. There are
several picnic-table sets on a raised back lawn, with a family room out at the back
too. *(Recommended by Gwen and Peter Andrews, Charles and Mary Winpenny, Michael and
Alison Sandy, Peter Watkins, Pam Stanley, David and Sarah Gilmore, Iain and Penny Muir,
Philip and Trisha Ferris, T Galligan, Joy Heatherley, Peter Corris, Harry Stirling)*

*St Austell   Licensee Norman Jeffery   Real ale   Meals and snacks (12.30–2,
7.30–9.45)   Restaurant   Children in family room and restaurant   Open 11–3, 6–11;
closed evening 25 Dec   Bedrooms tel Mevagissey (0726) 843322; /£30*

ST MAWES   SW8537 Map 1

Rising Sun 🍺

The St Austell brewery has taken over the running of this busy, small hotel, formerly privately run, and have installed a manager. There have been changes on the food side: bar food might include broccoli and fennel soup (£1.20), sandwiches (from £1.75, crab £3.95), filled baked potatoes (from £1.85), ploughman's or salads (from £2.75), lamb curry (£3.10), scallop mornay (£5.50), and puddings like chocolate mousse (£1.10). The position remains outstanding, just over the lane from the sea wall, overlooking one of England's prettiest anchorages. An attractive conservatory bar has cane furniture, lots of brass, and white boarding; and the pubby front bar – popular with locals – has simple furnishings, and a big window seat overlooking the sea. Well kept St Austell BB and HSD on handpump, and several malt whiskies; fruit machine, winter darts. The crazy-paved harbourside terrace has sturdy slate-topped tables, with a low stone wall to sit on when those are full. (*Recommended by Carol Mason, Robert Brown, T Galligan, C T and J M Laffin, Joan and Michael Melling, Mary Rayner*)

St Austell   Manager Trevor Hitchings   Real ale   Lunchtime meals and snacks Evening restaurant (they do Sun lunch)   Children in restaurant and eating area of bar Open 11–11; 11–2.30, 6–10.30 in winter   Bedrooms tel St Mawes (0326) 270233; £42(£42B)/£76(£76B)

ST MERRYN   SW8874 Map 1

Cornish Arms

Church Town; B3276 towards Padstow

The last 68 years have seen only three landlords at this low stone building – and this year, Mr Fitter has celebrated his 20th year here. The bar dates back to the 12th or 13th century and has fine Delabole slate flagstones, neatly exposed ancient stonework, a sturdy mahogany serving counter, and a shining copper footrail. It's simply furnished, with leatherette-cushioned oak wall settles and dining chairs around wooden tables, framed monthly rainfall figures for the past 20-odd years, and photographs of local lighthouses facing a striking print of a lifeboat launch. Simple bar food includes good pasties, sandwiches, ploughman's (£2.10), home-made cottage pie or beef curry (£2.95), chicken (£2.95), plaice (£3.10) and steaks (from £7.20); well kept St Austell Tinners on handpump, and most attractively priced wines; coal-effect gas fire, maybe piped music; quietly friendly service, and a warmly welcoming atmosphere. On the left, there's a thickly carpeted ply-panelled games bar with pool, darts, cribbage, dominoes, fruit machines and a juke box. Picnic-table sets under cocktail parasols in front of this pretty cottage face the stone-built church; this can be a breezy spot. (*Recommended by Iain and Penny Muir, Christopher and Heather Barton, David Wallington, Cdr W S D Hendry*)

St Austell   Licensee Peter Fitter   Real ale   Meals and snacks (not Jan–Mar)   Children over 6 in eating area of bar   Open 11–2.30, 6–11; 11–11 July–Aug

TINTAGEL   SX0587 Map 1

Min Pin

Tregatta (B3263 S)

The beers brewed here by Stephanie Hall (the young daughter of the family) use malt extract, but are very appetising, with a good clean finish: the pale, fragrant and well rounded Legend, and the hefty Brown Willy, named for Cornwall's highest hill. The family come from Brighton, and have made this ex-farmhouse a sunnily homely place, with cheerful piped music, and pictures of their prize-winning toy terriers and other dogs on the bobbly white walls – Min Pin, incidentally, stands for miniature pinscher. Even the handsome slate gravestone commemorating an early 18th-century owner, which now forms the hearth for the small fire, seems to strike an unexpectedly friendly note. There are well padded modern seats around the sturdy dark elm and other tables on the brightly patterned carpet of the main bar, with red leatherette furniture and a big open fireplace in the family room on the left, and a restaurant beyond. Bar food includes soup with bread (£1.50), garlic mushrooms, ploughman's or big filled sandwiches (£2.50), home-made lasagne or vegetable goulash, filled Yorkshire puddings, and prawn creole, with evening trout, pies and steaks; there are white plastic tables and chairs in the front garden, lined by a small rookery in summer. *(Recommended by Tim and Lynne Crawford, Sue Hallam, Richard Houghton)*

Own brew   Licensees Keith, Marie and Stephanie Hall   Real ale   Meals and snacks Children in family room if eating   Restaurant   Open 11–3, 6.30–11; weekends only in winter   Bedrooms tel Tintagel (0840) 770241; £16S/£32S

TREBARWITH   SX0585 Map 1

Mill House Inn   🏠

Signposted from B3263 and B3314 SE of Tintagel

In its own wooded combe running down to the sea, this family-run, 17th-century converted watermill has a big friendly main bar with some stripped pine settles, pews, handle-back chairs and oak tables on its Delabole slate floor; an airy communicating extension has pine tables in side stalls. Home-made bar food can be eaten in the bar, small restaurant or out on the terrace: sandwiches (from 85p), home-made soup (£1.20), basket meals (from £1.50), ploughman's (from £2.50), salads (from £3.50), gammon (£4.95), and 8oz steak (£6.75), with daily specials like home-made pasties (£3.20) or chicken in a mushroom and cream sauce (£3.35); home-made puddings (from £1.25) and children's menu (£1.75). Well kept Flowers IPA and Original, Whitbreads Best and a weekly changing guest beer on handpump; darts, pool, shove-ha'penny, dominoes, cribbage, fruit machine, ring the bull, draughts and piped music. The garden has terraces, waterfalls and a children's play area. *(Recommended by Richard Houghton, Peter Brabbs, ACP, Dr and Mrs B D Smith, Drs M and K Parier, C M Whitehouse, Iain and Penny Muir)*

Free house   Licensee Kevin Howard   Real ale   Meals and snacks (12–2.30, 6.30–10)   Evening restaurant   Children in family room   Live band Mon/Weds/Fri evenings in main bar (not too loud)   Open 11–11 (till midnight Tues and Sat); 11–3, 6–11 in winter   Bedrooms tel Camelford (0840) 770200; £22.50B/£45B

Logan Rock

Off B3283 Penzance–Land's End coast road

Caring and very friendly staff, an easy-going atmosphere and popular home-made food make this well run and cosy stone pub appeal to both visitors and regulars alike. The low-beamed main bar has old prints on the partly panelled walls, telling the story of the Logan Rock – an 80-ton teetering boulder which someone once tipped from its clifftop fulcrum to show off his strength, and then had to pay a small fortune to have it hauled up the cliff again; also, high-backed modern oak settles, wall seats, tables, and a really warm coal fire. Bar food includes sandwiches (from 90p, local crab £2.60), good pasties (£1), wholesome soup (£1.35), vegetarian quiche (£2.50), salads (from £3.25, crab £5.25), lasagne or a popular fish and egg dish they call the Seafarer (£3), scampi (£4), and good charcoal-grilled steaks (from £6); specials such as slightly spiced prawn pasta or curry (£3), puddings like home-made blackberry and apple pie (£1.75) and children's menu (£1). They will heat baby foods on request. Well kept St Austell Tinners and HSD on handpump, with XXXX tapped from the cask and kept under light blanket pressure, farm cider and several malt whiskies; darts, table skittles, dominoes, cribbage, fruit machine and piped music, with space and video games, juke box, pool table and another fruit machine in the family room across the way. Dogs are allowed if on a lead. There are some tables in a small but attractive wall-sheltered garden, looking over fields, with more in the front court. *(Recommended by Ewan and Moira McCall, David and Sarah Gilmore, Cliff and Karen Spooner, Patrick Stapley, Richard Gibbs, RAB, Bobby Goodale, Peter Sutton, Paul Smith)*

St Austell   Licensees Peter and Anita George   Real ale   Meals and snacks
Restaurant tel St Buryan (0736) 810495 (table service winter only)   Children in family
room   Open 10.30–3, 5.30–11; 11–11 July–Aug; 10.30–2.30, 6–11 in winter

TREGADILLETT   SX2940 Map 1

Eliot Arms ★

Village signposted off A30 at junction with A395, W end of Launceston bypass

The bar of this creeper-covered old house consists of a delightful warren of little softly lit rooms, with every inch of wall camouflaged with old prints, if we counted right no less than 62 antique clocks including seven grandfathers, many hundreds of horsebrasses, old postcards or cigarette cards grouped in frames, shelves of books and china. The furniture's a fine old mix, too, from high-backed built-in curved settles, through plush Victorian dining chairs, armed seats, chaises longues and mahogany housekeeper's chairs, to more modern seats; flower-printed cushions match the curtains, and the slate floors are partly carpeted. The atmosphere is quietly cosy, with flowers on most tables, efficient yet friendly and pleasant staff, and inoffensive piped music. A wide choice of food in generous helpings includes several ploughman's (from £2.25), daunting open sandwiches including a massive slab of rib of beef (£2.95 – £3.60 with chips), salads (from £3.25), home-made curries (from £3.75), cheese and nut croquettes or home-made vegetable moussaka (£3.95), lots of speciality charcoal grills (from £5.95), poached seafood platter in a creamy crab sauce (£6.95), Greek-style pork kebab (£7.75), and specials such as cheese, ham and potato pie (£3.15), fresh herring (£3.25), lamb and orange goulash (£4.25) and a big pork chop with stilton and apple (£4.95). Well kept Devenish Cornish Original and Royal Wessex on handpump, Bulmers traditional cider, and open fires; darts, bar billiards, fruit machine and trivia. A garden beyond the car park has picnic-table sets, a good climbing frame, swing and playhouse. We've not yet heard from any readers who have stayed here, but would expect good value. *(Recommended by M and C Hardwick, Iain and Penny Muir, Alan and Audrey Chatting)*

Cornish Brewery   Licensee John Cook   Real ale   Meals and snacks (not 25 Dec)
Children in eating area of bar   Open 11–2.30, 6–11   Bedrooms tel Launceston (0566)
772051; £15/£28

TRELEIGH   SW7043 Map 1

Inn for all Seasons ⊘

From A30, take easternmost Scorrier turn-off, then immediate right on A3047 towards Camborne

The licensees have now left the pub they used to run in tandem – the Rising Sun at St Mawes – so that they can concentrate on this restful and very different place; it now has bedrooms. The spacious and stylish lounge bar has carefully staggered booths along the walls, quiet recesses and separate islands with small easy chairs, plush banquettes, and black-lacquered chairs well spaced around solid dark tables. The colours are deep purples, soft pinks, and gentle greys and browns, the lighting (and the well reproduced piped music) is gentle, and the few old prints on the textured walls are carefully chosen. Very good food includes soup with home-made roll (£1.50), sandwiches (from £1.50), filled baked potatoes (£2.25), lentil and wild mushroom terrine (£2.75), ploughman's (£2.95), stir-fried chicken with waterchestnuts (£3.45), home-baked honey ham with salad (£3.95), poached monkfish with shellfish sauce (£4.50), pheasant casserole (£5.25), sirloin steak (£7.25), and home-made puddings like apricot and hazelnut roulade, fresh fruit pavlova and sticky toffee pudding (from £1.50). Wadworths 6X served under light blanket pressure, and a wide range of drinks from the long and elegant bar counter; good coffee; friendly, correct service. Broad windows, and white tables under cocktail parasols in front, look beyond the busy dual carriageway a couple of hundred yards away to distant rolling hills. *(More reports please)*

Free house   Licensees John Milan and Frank Atherley   Meals and snacks   Restaurant (evenings Mon–Sat, Sun lunch)   Children in restaurant and eating area of bar   Open 11–3, 5.30–11   Bedrooms tel Redruth (0209) 219511; £35B/£50B

TRESILLIAN   SW8646   Map 1
Wheel

A39 Truro–St Austell

With a history going back to the 14th century, this spick-and-span pub with its distinctive wheel worked into the thatch of the roof is still owned by Lord Falmouth. Watch for the low door as you go in. The two carpeted original room areas are cosy, traditional and softly lit, with leatherette wall seats, low ceiling joists, some timbering and stripped stonework, and steps from one part to another (though access for the disabled is quite reasonable); there's a further lighter and more spacious room. Bar food includes soup (95p), large filled rolls (from £1.50), hot smoked mackerel (£1.50), ploughman's (from £1.90), vegetarian dishes (from £2.50), ham and cheese pizza (£2.70), home-made daily specials, basket meals (from £2.90), Sunday roasts, gammon (£4.60), steaks (from 8oz fillet £7.50), children's dishes (from £1; also small helpings off main menu) and several home-made puddings (£1.20). Well kept Devenish JD, Cornish Original and Royal Wessex on handpump; piped music; the pub can get very busy. The neat garden stretches down to a tidal stretch of the River Fal, and has a play area. *(Recommended by Cdr W S D Hendry, Richard Houghton)*

Devenish   Licensee David Hulson   Real ale   Meals and snacks (till 10 – 9.30 Sun) Children in further room   Open 11–2.30 (3 Sat or if busy), 6–11

Lucky Dip

Besides the fully inspected pubs, you might like to try these Lucky Dips recommended to us and described by readers (if you do, please send us reports):

Albaston [OS Sheet 201 map reference 423704; SX4270], *Queens Head*: Rather off the tourist track, with very friendly welcome, well kept, cheap Courage beer, and interesting collection of industrial memorabilia *(Phil Gorton)*
Angarrack [SW5838], *Angarrack*: Welcoming St Austell pub just off A30 with well kept beer and good food (even Sun evening) inc big gammon steaks; pleasant setting *(Iain and Penny Muir)*
Blisland [SX1073], *Royal Oak*: Two-bar village local overlooking village green — real rarity in Cornwall; Bass and two other real ales, bar meals, and friendly atmosphere with many farmer-type locals *(Iain and Penny Muir)*
☆ **Bodinnick** [across the water from Fowey; SX1352], *Old Ferry*: Lovely situation looking over water for cosy old inn with public rooms stepped steeply back up the rocky hillside, basic bar food inc home-made pasties, well kept St Austell real ale and decent wine by the glass; good evening restaurant; children in good games room and eating area; bedrooms comfortable if simply furnished, some with big window overlooking river and ferry, proper breakfast with splendid kippers *(David Wallington, E A Simmons, LYM)*
☆ **Bodmin** [Dunmere, A389 NW; SX0467], *Borough Arms*: Neatly kept, with stripped stonework, lots of harness hanging from low joists, open fire, side room packed with old railway photographs and posters, decent piped music, fruit machine; big helpings of wholesome bar food with specials such as fresh fish and pork with a cream and mushroom sauce, well kept Devenish Cornish Original and Steam on handpump; picnic-table sets out among fruit trees, some traffic noise; can get very busy at lunchtime in season *(Andrea and Guy Bradley, Mr and Mrs A J Land, Iain and Penny Muir, BB)*
Bodmin [centre], *Hole in the Wall*: Friendly local with dark beamed lounge, interesting helmets, swords, model ships and other militaria; two other bars, usual bar food, fruit machines *(Cdr W S D Hendry)*
Bolingey [Penwartha Rd (off B3284); SW7653], *Bolingey*: Quiet, picturesque and unspoiled local in small village; cosy atmosphere, well kept Devenish beers on handpump, lunchtime bar food, outside seating; handy for Perranporth but away from the tourists *(Peter Corris, Iain and Penny Muir)*
☆ **Boscastle** [SX0990], *Napoleon*: Small beamed rooms and alcoves in cosy partly 16th-century pub at top of very steep village, which some like more than the Cobweb; good mainly home-cooked bar food inc vegetarian dishes (service may not be brisk, and menu may be very limited at quiet times), lots of interesting Napoleon prints inc rare ones, well kept Bass and St Austell

real ale, decent wines, darts, pool, sheltered terrace; has had Celtic folk music Mon and Weds, though piped music can otherwise be intrusive; children allowed in eating area *(Iain and Penny Muir, Nick Dowson, Alison Hayward, Louise Donovan, R Del Mar, LYM)*

Botallack [SW3633], *Queens Arms*: Friendly pub with big open fireplace, Devenish ales, fabulous huge pasties and garden; wonderful country walks along clifftop — nr start GWG4 *(Charlie Salt)*

Botusfleming [SX4061], *Rising Sun*: Becoming less dilapidated as the young brother-and-sister licensees (grandchildren of the previous landlord) are slowly renovating the building; still has unspoilt character, however, albeit in a very spartan way *(Phil Gorton, David and Sarah Gilmore)*

Cadgwith [SW7214], *Cadgwith Cove*: Excellent, friendly pub in dreamlike village with a good mix of local crab fishermen and visitors, and good value, simple bar food (drinks could be cheaper); locals raise the roof with their singing on Fri nights (anyone can join in) *(Vic and Reba Longhorn, M D Hare)*

☆ **Callington** [Newport Sq (A388 towards Launceston); SX3669], *Coachmakers Arms*: Reliable bar food from sandwiches through salmon and crab pâté, omelettes or ham and egg to gammon done with honey, mustard and pineapple or mixed grill, Bass on handpump, decent wines and efficient service in irregularly shaped timbered bar with appropriate old local advertisements; children in eating area and restaurant; bedrooms *(John Kirk, Brian Horner, H W and A B Tuffill, Miss P A Barfield, LYM)*

Calstock [SX4368], *Boot*: Locally popular free house in picturesque village on the Tamar, friendly licensees, good selection of beers, good Duboeuf wines by the glass; fair-priced sandwiches and other bar snacks in generous helpings; excellent, reasonably priced restaurant upstairs, all food cooked to order; a pub with a difference in every way; bedrooms *(John and Tessa Rainsford*

Camborne [B3303 towards Helston; SW6440], *Old Shire*: Comfortable, homely pub with friendly staff, good range of beers, interesting good value bar food, summer barbecues, popular help-yourself carvery/buffet, children's area, garden; five bedrooms *(Pat and Malcolm Rudlin, Gwen Cranfield)*

Crafthole [village signposted off A574; SX3654], *Finnygook*: Good friendly welcome in much modernised spacious lounge bar with wide choice of good value straightforward food, efficient service; pleasant restaurant, good sea views from residents' lounge; bedrooms small but very comfortable, beautifully warm — very good value *(Geoffrey Thompson, BB)*

Crantock [SW7960], *Old Albion*: Pleasantly placed thatched and pink-washed village pub with old-fashioned dark-beamed bars, Courage Best and Directors on handpump, good bar lunches; smuggling background *(Mike Dick, LYM)*

Cremyll [SX4553], *Mount Edgecombe*: Well kept Courage in pub due for refurbishment *(J C Proud)*

Cripples Ease [SW5036], *Engine*: Former counting house of old tin mine, popular with locals, with well kept beer and bar food; superb moorland location with views of the sea on all sides from nearby hill; bedrooms good value *(John Branford, Linda Duncan)*

Cubert [Trebellan; SW7858], *Smugglers Den*: Enormous inglenook and friendly staff; usual bar food, well cooked, from soup and ploughman's to steaks, also quiet restaurant, children's room with jukebox, space game and fruit machine, pool, picnic tables, coarse fishing, campsite *(Margo and Peter Thomas, Charles and Mary Winpenny)*; *Treetops*: Good value food inc very good quiche salad; big, pleasant bar, family room and beer garden; own cocktails *(T J Howe)*

Devoran [SW7939], *Old Quay*: Small, unpretentious pub in nice position overlooking Carnon River; excellent sandwiches and good range of other food, well kept Devenish Cornish Original, and pleasant, small, sheltered terraced garden at back *(M W Turner)*

☆ **Falmouth** [Maenporth Beach; SW8032], *Seahorse*: Extensively modernised, enterprisingly run and increasingly popular pub, almost a continental cafe/bar, with super view over beach and Fal estuary through smoked glass facade or from terrace tables; Watneys-related real ales, chilled foreign beers, good value bar food with various ethnic themes (the paella's good); new upstairs restaurant; part of new holiday complex *(M P Hallewell, J C Proud)*

☆ **Falmouth** [Custom House Quay], *Chain Locker*: Strongly nautical harbourside pub, popular with locals and visitors alike; good choice of well kept real ales inc Devenish Cornish Original, pleasant buffet, quick service and lovely views from dining area; open all day at least in summer, waterside tables outside *(Rona Murdoch, Colin Gooch, LYM)*

☆ **Falmouth** [Prinslow Lane, Swanvale], *Boslowick*: Reliably good reasonably priced bar food running up to steaks and mixed grills, consistently well kept Courage Best and Directors, and courteous staff, in fine old black and white beamed and panelled manor house; plenty of seats including plush sofas, log-effect gas fires; children's playpark *(M P Hallewell, J C Proud)*

Falmouth [Killgrew St], *Kimberley Arms*: Fishermen's bar and more comfortable lounge, lots of fascinating objects on the walls, good choice of food, pleasantly served freshly brewed coffee *(Gwen and Peter Andrews)*; [Church St], *Kings Head*: Pleasant mix of soft settees, easy chairs and firmer dining chairs in rambling bar with long thin serving counter that's done out like the front of an old-fashioned shop; old plates and engravings, well kept Devenish real ales, bar food, winter log fire, piped music *(LYM; up-to-date reports please)*; [The Moor], *Seven Stars*: Warmly welcoming old-fashioned pub with well kept Bass, Flowers Original and St Austell HSD tapped from the cask, simple snacks, tables on courtyard behind flower tubs; run as it has been for generations *(Phil Gorton, BB)*; [Trevethan Hill (from centre follow High St straight on up hill)], *Sportsmans Arms*: Exceptional harbour views and well kept Devenish real ales in pleasant local *(LYM)*

☆ Fowey [SX1252], *Ship*: Good, well worn atmosphere with cosy fire and lighting, and good mix of locals and visitors, young and old; notably friendly licensee, separate pool room, well kept St Austell Tinners, simple bar food with daily home-made specials such as scallops in garlic butter, gammon with parsley sauce or leek and ham pie, and efficient service; lovely hanging baskets in summer, pleasant children's room *(David Wallington, Iain and Penny Muir, Ian Blackwell)*

Fowey [Town Quay], *King of Prussia*: Still popular for superb location, with harbour view from bow windows of upstairs bar and St Austell real ales; mixed views on some other aspects *(John Branford, Linda Duncan, E H and R F Warner, Iain and Penny Muir, LYM)*; [from centre follow Car Ferry signs], *Riverside*: Splendid spot with comfortable hotelish lounge overlooking river and boats, more workmanlike streetside public bar; bedrooms comfortable *(BB)*

Fraddon [SW9158], *Blue Anchor*: Large roadside pub with attractive lounge bar, well kept St Austell, big range of bar food, car park *(Cdr W S D Hendry)*

☆ Golant [difficult approach from B3269; SX1155], *Fishermans Arms*: Superb spot with view of estuary from bar window and terrace looking down on garden; pleasant newish licensees, interesting copper, brass and old photographs; well kept St Austell Tinners, excellent sandwiches with thick-cut roast beef *(David Wallington, WHBM)*

Goldsithney [SW5430], *Trevelyan Arms*: Comfortable and friendly, good value food in generous helpings, well kept beer; children welcome *(Mr and Mrs R W Mair)*

☆ Hayle [Bird Paradise Park; SW5536], *Bird in Hand*: Barn-like place aimed at family groups visiting the Bird Park (lunchtime Easter–end Oct, evenings not Sun July–early Sept), with own-brewed Paradise Bitter and strong Artists Ale, three or four guest beers, decent food bar, evening pizzas and sometimes do-it-yourself barbecues; interesting upstairs four-table pool room, garden, play area, helpful staff; children welcome *(Nigel Gibbs, Sandra Cook, Brian Horner, Iain and Penny Muir, David and Sarah Gilmore)*

Helford Passage [SW7627], *Ferry Boat*: Somewhat brash atmosphere but wide range of food (at a price) and afternoon teas in spacious and friendly modern bar excellently placed to overlook boating estuary — can get packed in summer; worth walking along riverside lane to small private beach; children welcome *(Ian Shaw, Lindsey Shaw Radley, M D Hare, BB)*

Helston [SW6527], *Fitzsimmons Arms*: Tastefully preserved, with lots of interesting little corners, smart prints and classy bric-a-brac everywhere; boxing memorabilia in one corner celebrates Helston-born Bob Fitzsimmons *(Reg Nelson)*; *Red Lion*: Characterful mock olde-worlde pub with vibrant personality and real ale *(Reg Nelson)*

nr **Helston** [Gunwalloe (signposted off A3083, S); SW6522], *Halzephron*: Pleasant and welcoming traditional pub looking over clifftop fields to sea; well kept Devenish beers, standard pub food, good log fire, tables with cocktail parasols outside; children welcome; bedrooms *(Cliff Blakemore, LYM)*

Hessenford [A387 Looe—Torpoint; SX3057], *Copley Arms*: Lovely riverside spot, comfortable furnishings, St Austell Tinners on handpump, lunchtime and evening bar food, restaurant, garden *(Peter Corris)*

Kilkhampton [SS2511], *New Inn*: Spacious well kept local with rambling interconnecting rooms, some traditional furnishings, fine woodburner, bar food, well kept Bass; children in good games room *(LYM)*

☆ Kingsand [Fore St; towards Cawsand — OS Sheet 201 map reference 434505; SX4350], *Halfway House*: So named because it marks the pre-1835 dividing line between between Cornwall and Devon; cosy, dimly lit, neat, clean and simple, with low ceilings, huge central fireplace, unobtrusive piped music, Bass, Charrington and Worthington, reasonable house wines and good value food — mixed grill and liver and bacon recommended; handy for Mount Edgcumbe and marvellous cliff walks on Rame Head *(Joy Heatherley)*

Lands End [SW3425], *Lands End*: Rather smart if darkish bar with big picture windows overlooking terrace and sea beyond, light and airy conservatory with light cane chairs and cushioned seats, circular tables, plants and ship pictures; children in conservatory *(Anon)*; *State House*: Comfortable well run bar with Theakstons Old Peculier and a beer named for the pub; food particularly good value for the setting; bedrooms good value too *(HEG)*

☆ Lanlivery [SX0759], *Crown*: Pleasant neatly kept pub with well kept Bass, good waitress-served lunchtime bar food (pasties and pâté recommended) and evening restaurant, friendly staff; bedrooms *(David Wallington, Mr and Mrs Owen)*

Lelant [Fore St; SW5437], *Badger*: Recently attractively refurbished; St Austell Tinners and other beers, food inc good filled baked potatoes and smoked mackerel salad, friendly and efficient service *(D H and M C Watkinson)*

☆ Lizard [SW7712], *Top House*: Comfortable and genuine village pub, with strong maritime theme highlighting local lifeboat service, exposed timber rafters and log fire; pleasant efficient service, well kept real ales inc Devenish Steam; wide range of attractively presented, quickly served bar food inc notable ploughman's, crab sandwiches and vegetarian dishes; fruit machine; tables on attractive terrace *(Colin Gooch, Cliff Blakemore)*

Longrock [old coast rd Penzance—Marazion; SW5031], *Mexico*: Imaginative reasonably priced bar food with most dishes prepared to order so service not fast, but worth waiting for; Bass and St Austell ales *(Pat and Malcolm Rudlin)*

Looe [quayside West Looe, nr main bridge; SX2553], *Harbour Moon*: Old pub with modern picture windows overlooking harbour; well kept Courage Best on handpump, good lunchtime and evening bar food; children's room *(Peter Corris)*; [West Looe, just off quayside], *Jolly Sailors*: Old, unusually planned pub with various nooks and crannies; Watneys-related real ales on handpump, good value bar food *(Peter Corris)*

☆ **Ludgvan** [Churchtown; off A30 Penzance—Hayle at Crowlas — OS Sheet 203 map reference 505330; SW5033], *White Hart*: Reconstructed 19th-century pub, dark, snug and cottagey, with beams, small rooms, faded wallpaper, oil-type lamps, lots of mugs and jugs glinting in corner, and no piped music — so good place to talk; well kept beer and good, simple food *(WMS)*

Luxulyan [SX0558], *Kings Arms*: Simple, friendly local with good value food such as toasted sandwiches, ploughman's, basket chicken and ham and egg; juke box, darts, games machines *(Mr and Mrs A J Land)*

Marazion [The Square; SW5231], *Cutty Sark*: Nothing special to look at, but really friendly pub, with two fine cats; well kept Cornish beers, decent wine, big helpings of food, easy-going service, good value restaurant and bedrooms *(Helen Emmitt, Rosalind Russell, Reg Nelson)*; *Kings Arms*: Well preserved, smartish pub with real ale *(Reg Nelson)*

☆ **Marhamchurch** [off A39 just S of Bude; SS2203], *Bullers Arms*: Friendly L-shaped bar with half a dozen well kept real ales and quickly served if conventional bar food from sandwiches and ploughman's through fresh fish to steaks; darts in flagstoned back part; separate pool room and 1930s-style cocktail bar; piped pop music (maybe loud); a mile's walk to the sea; restaurant; children welcome; at its best when full enough to be lively, not so full that it's noisy; bedrooms *(Richard Cole, Mrs R Horridge, Mandy and Michael Challis, Dr R Trigwell, LYM)*

Mawgan [SW7125], *Old Court House*: Has been largely preserved as former court house; well kept Devenish beers, pleasant service, friendly locals, good choice of lunchtime and evening food *(Richard Houghton)*; *Ship*: Devenish pub down steep lane with welcoming Cornish landlord; popular with locals, well kept beer and good, piping hot pasties; outside ladies' *(Gwen and Peter Andrews)*

Mawnan Smith [SW7728], *Red Lion*: Good value simple food in welcoming thatched village pub with warm woodburning stove in high-ceilinged lounge (pianist Fri), spacious locals' public bar, well kept Devenish real ales; children in big family room *(Ewan and Moira McCall, BB)*

Mevagissey [Fore St, nr harbour; SX0145], *Ship*: Old stone building refurbished in nautical style; St Austell Bosuns and HSD on handpump, good lunchtime and evening bar food with seafood specials; children welcome *(Peter Corris)*; [quayside], *Sharks Fin*: Rather smart and well kept place on pretty harbour with fairly priced, decent food, excellent smiling service; bedrooms *(Colin Laffan)*

☆ **Mitchell** [A30 Bodmin—Redruth; SW8654], *Plume of Feathers*: Lots of bric-a-brac and even a well in friendly and comfortable rambling bar with huge bank open fire; sandwiches, choice of ploughman's, pies, curries and casseroles, Cornish Original and Devenish JD on handpump, good coffee, piped music, darts and winter pool; tables outside, with adventure playground and farm animals; children welcome *(Iain and Penny Muir, Gwen and Peter Andrews, LYM; more reports please)*

Mullion [SW6719], *Old Inn*: Shipwreck mementoes and crabbing pictures in long lantern-lit bar of thatched village inn, big inglenook fireplace, well kept Cornish Original and Devenish JD on handpump, quickly served home-cooked bar food inc choice of pizzas and often local fish, summer barbecues Tues—Sat, good games area (pool in winter), TV and small aviary in children's room, seats outside; bedrooms, and self-catering cottages *(M D Hare, Wayne Stockton, David Pearman, LYM)*

Newbridge [A3071 Penzance—St Just; OS Sheet 203 map reference 424316; SW4232], *Fountain*: Warm, dark and friendly local with winter log fire, simple, comfortable alcoves, armchairs *(WMS)*

Newlyn [SW4628], *Dolphin*: Though no real ale, there's an amazing collection of curios; smart prints and discreet corners *(Reg Nelson)*; [Fore St (coast rd)], *Fishermans Arms*: Gem of an ancient fisherman's inn with superb nautical memorabilia, real ale, and wonderful views of Mounts Bay and Marazion Sands *(Reg Nelson)*; *Red Lion*: Real ale, nautical memorabilia — lovely views again *(Reg Nelson)*; *Swordfish*: A locals' favourite and full of character; real ale, too *(Reg Nelson)*

Newquay [Bank St; up alley by Newquay Arms; SW8161], *Malt & Hops*: Spacious family holiday pub with rustic-style decor, videos, piped pop music, Devenish beers, attentive staff; surprisingly quiet atmosphere *(Colin Gooch)*

Padstow [Lanadwell St; SW9175], *Golden Lion*: Friendly local with pleasant black-beamed front bar, high-raftered back lounge with russet plush banquettes against the ancient white stone walls; good value lunches from soup and sandwiches through freshly caught local fish, ham and egg, scampi and so forth to evening steaks; well kept Devenish JD and Cornish Original on handpump, piped music, juke box, fruit machines; three decent bedrooms *(Cdr W S D Hendry, BB)*; [South Quay], *Old Custom House*: St Austell real ale in spacious and comfortably modernised split-level bar; pub food, steak bar; pretty spot on waterfront; bedrooms *(LYM)*; [Mill Sq, just off North Quay/Broad St], *Old Ship*: Tables on front courtyard of simple hotel tucked away behind harbour, bustling open-plan bar with well kept Flowers IPA on handpump, usual bar food, fruit machines, juke box or piped music (live music Weds and Sat), more tables in Perspex-roofed inner courtyard; children's room; bedrooms *(Cdr W S D Hendry, BB)*; [North Quay; SW9175], *Shipwrights*: Stripped-brick St Austell pub popular for its quayside position, fruit machines and bar billiards, bar food inc decent sandwiches, juke box — may be loud; tables and chairs outside *(Iain and Penny Muir, LYM)*

Pendeen [SW3834], *Radjel*: Local photographs on stripped walls of simple local with bar food, St Austell Tinners, darts, pool, jukebox; children in eating area; nr GWG4 *(LYM)*

Penelewey [Feock Downs; B3291; SW8240], *Punch Bowl & Ladle*: Large Cornish Brewery house decorated with old farm implements, carpentry tools and other bric-a-brac — much as others in this chain; cosy lounge with armchairs, lively and interesting atmosphere (Bishop of Truro's local); handy for Trelissick Gardens; children allowed if eating *(Charles and Mary Winpenny, WHBM, Peter Corris)*

Penryn [SW7834], *Seven Stars*: Cosy and popular Devenish pub notable for its exceptional collection of sparkling-clean brass platters and ornaments — perhaps the biggest in the country *(BB)*

Penzance [Barbican; Newlyn rd; opp harbour after swing-bridge; SW4730], *Dolphin*: Extensively refurbished pub with big windows overlooking harbour, well done maritime decor reflecting the pub's interesting early naval history, quickly served good bar food (home-made treacle tart strongly tipped), St Austell ales under light CO2 blanket, big pool room with jukebox etc; children in room off main bar *(Derek Patey, Reg Nelson, LYM)*; *Farmers Arms*: Town-centre local with genuine atmosphere and real ale *(Reg Nelson)*; *Longboat*: Given the full Cornish Breweries theme refurbishment — full of bric-a-brac; this one has atmosphere, and the Devenish real ale is well kept *(Reg Nelson)*; *Navy*: Interesting historic house with atmosphere, though space for drinkers severely limited in favour of those eating *(Reg Nelson)*; [Market Jew St], *Star*: Low beams, red plush wall seats, ship pictures and nautical memorabilia, some stripped stone and panelling; notable for splendid two-storey indoor children's play area overlooked by family room; home-made bar food inc

bookings-only Sun lunch; Devenish real ale *(Reg Nelson)*; *Union*: Interesting old place with atmosphere, though given over largely to people eating *(Reg Nelson)*; *White Lion*: Town-centre local with some atmosphere and well kept real ale *(Reg Nelson)*

Perranarworthal [A39 Truro—Penryn; SW7839], *Norway*: Elaborately done out in old-fashioned style, with a more or less parlourish mood in most of the little beamed room-areas that ramble around the central bar, and lots of country bygones, china, stuffed birds and fish, fishing-rods and so forth, with masses of pictures; lunchtime bar food — soup, ploughman's, big filled rolls, a few hot dishes; restaurant (evenings too); Devenish real ales; tables outside; very popular since the refurbishment — though a couple of readers with long memories regret the lost genuine intimacy of the former panelled back bar *(Lt Cdr G J Cardew, BB)*

☆ **Perranuthnoe** [signed off A394 Penzance—Helston; SW5329], *Victoria*: A stroll up from Mounts Bay, village pub with some stripped stonework, local coastal and wreck photographs; booth seating in family area, games area; generous if not cheap bar food from sandwiches and filled baked potatoes to steaks, well kept Courage Best and Directors and John Smiths on handpump, welcoming landlord, picnic-table sets outside; children allowed in dining room; good value bedrooms *(Cliff Blakemore, Jim Turnbull, Theo Schofield, LYM)*

Phillack [Church Town Rd; SW5638], *Bucket of Blood*: Cheerful pub with well kept St Austell beers and entertainingly gruesome ghost stories *(LYM)*

Pillaton [SX3664], *Weary Friar*: Dating back to 12th century, with two big rooms linked at reception, both furnished attractively and in character; well kept Courage Best and Directors, good coffee; staff pleasant, and as the year or so since new owners took over has worn on, reports have begun to suggest that the bar food deserves attention as plentiful and well presented — there's also an attractive restaurant; bedrooms comfortable *(M P Hallewell, Ted George, LYM — more views please)*

Pityme [Pityme Farm Rd; SW9576], *Pityme*: Conversion and extension of former farmhouse — modern in style, but worth knowing for food and has St Austell real ales *(Roy and Barbara Longman)*

Polgooth [SW9950], *Polgooth*: Large and noisy rustic inn with own farmyard; favoured by younger people for popular bar meals and exceedingly well kept St Austell real ales; bedrooms *(Iain and Penny Muir, LYM)*

Polperro [bear R approaching harbour; SX2051], *Noughts & Crosses*: Cosy with low beams and panelling; little bar with darts and fruit machine has stairs up to family room and steps down to softly lit riverside bar with comfortable banquettes, pool table and fruit machines; good atmosphere especially for young people, Courage beers, piped music, usual bar food *(Mayur Shah)*; [by the harbour], *Three Pilchards*: Good, basic, informal pub, with often imaginative bar food and pleasant young staff *(Ian Shaw, Lindsey Shaw Radley, K and E Leist)*

☆ **Polruan** [The Quay; SX1251], *Lugger*: Lively and charmingly nautical two-bar pub up steep flight of stone steps just a few yards from quay of delightful village on steep hill overlooking River Fowey; well kept St Austell and Worthington beers, appetising traditional food and friendly welcome — from licensees who earned many friends among readers at their last pub, the Mermaid at Hugh Town in the Isles of Scilly *(Iain and Penny Muir, Ian Blackwell; more reports please)*

Polzeath [SW9378], *Doom*: Excellent views, cosy atmosphere *(J D Shaw)*

Ponsanooth [A393 Penryn—Redruth; SW7537], *Stag Hunt*: Busy village pub with unpretentious bar, attractive stone-walled back dining room (bargain Sun lunch), well kept Devenish real ales; has had very good value bar food under its former splendid landlord Colin Gilham, but he's now left (we'd be very grateful for news of him — there's a rumour that he may now have a pub up in Cumbria), and it's too soon for us to be able to rate the new regime *(LYM)*

Pool [SW6641], *Plume of Feathers*: Ex-village local which has now had the Cornish Breweries treatment and looks like all the rest inside; old atmosphere has gone but it's convenient and pleasant, with well kept Devenish Cornish Original and Steam and a guest such as Marstons Pedigree on handpump *(Charles and Mary Winpenny)*

☆ **Porthleven** [Peverell Terr; SW6225], *Atlantic*: Stunning setting overlooking sea; large, open-plan lounge with alcoves, pleasant open log fire in granite fireplace, well kept Devenish real ales, wide choice of bar food with emphasis on local seafood *(Cliff Blakemore, Patrick Young)*

Porthleven, *Harbour*: Tastefully modernised harbourside pub, St Austell Bosuns and HSD on handpump, restaurant ; children in restaurant; bedrooms *(Peter Corris)*

☆ **Port Isaac** [SX0080], *Golden Lion*: Old pub high over harbour in lovely steep village, nice view from the seat by the window; simple but good atmosphere, old pictures and photographs, good value lunchtime snacks (esp local pasties, fresh crab sandwiches and crab ploughman's), well kept St Austell Tinners and HSD; if anything at its best out of season, but in summer there's an extra downstairs bar — and both bars have terraces; good stopping-off point on North Cornwall Coastal Footpath, and currently on particularly good form *(David and Sarah Gilmore, Iain and Penny Muir, John and Jane Horn, LYM)*

Port Isaac, *Slipway*: Built into side of cliff on several floors with pleasant bar, helpful staff and excellent seafood in restaurant; bedrooms very small *(Mrs A Crowhurst)*

☆ **Portloe** [SW9339], *Lugger*: Beautiful pub in tiny cove approached on narrow roads; tasteful furnishings, spotlessly clean, friendly staff, excellent bar food inc outstanding crab sandwiches and prawns; sea views from terrace and attractive bedrooms *(Joan and Michael Melling; more reports please)*

Portmellon Cove [has been closed Oct–Mar; SX0144], *Rising Sun*: Small lower bar and big upper summer bar overlooking sandy cove near Mevagissey, bar food, St Austell real ales; open for morning coffee and afternoon cream teas; some live music; children in restaurant and family room *(David and Sarah Gilmore, LYM)*

Portscatho [SW8735], *Plume of Feathers*: Clean, lively and friendly pub in pretty fishing village; good value food, inc take-aways, from hatch in corner of main bar; small eating area, side locals' bar, well kept St Austell Tinners; well reproduced loudish pop music; very popular with summer visitors; on South Cornwall Coastal path *(Iain and Penny Muir, David and Sarah Gilmore, WHBM, LYM)*

☆ **Poughill** [SS2207], *Preston Gate*: Current licensees doing well in this 1980s conversion of two cottages — he's an ex-seaman, and the attractive partly flagstoned bar has a fine model galleon made by him; pews, mahogany tables and log fires, good value bar food, well kept Watneys-related real ales from impressive cellar, some seats outside; village is pronounced 'Poffle' *(Audrey and Keith Patchett, LYM)*

Probus [Fore St; SW8947], *Hawkins Arms*: St Austell pub with big garden serving good real ale; bar food inc generously filled, big baked potatoes; bedrooms *(Iain and Penny Muir)*

Rilla Mill [SW2973], *Manor House*: Homely bar with excellent food; pleasant gardens; licensee used to own Coachmakers Arms at Callington *(John Kirk)*

☆ **Roche** [SW9860], *Victoria*: Useful A30 stop — snug low-ceilinged bar, antique oak settles, oak panelling and a carved doorway, old ship furniture and farm tools, brass pots, mugs, measures and guns, even a man trap; popular food inc excellent home-made pasties, well kept St Austell ales, panelled children's room, cheery service, restaurant *(Patrick Young, John Hayward, LYM)*

Sennen [SW3525], *First & Last*: Good atmosphere, welcoming licensees, bar food inc excellent pasties, eating steaks; dogs allowed if on lead; children's room *(Gwyneth and Salvo Spadaro-Dutturi)*

☆ **Sennen Cove** [SW3526], *Old Success*: 17th-century fisherman's local in glorious spot beside big beach — view along Whitesand Bay is magnificent, esp outside the main holiday season; refurbished but new decor blends in well, set off by fishing paraphernalia and photographs of the lifeboat and shipwrecks in the bay; friendly staff and good quickly served food (seafood particularly praised), good range of real ales inc Bass; probably at its best out of season; nr GWG2; pleasantly furnished bedrooms

— good value winter weekends (*Gwyneth and Salvo Spadaro-Dutturi, David and Sarah Gilmore*)

St Agnes [SW7250], *St Agnes Hotel*: Two wood-planked bars with ships' wheels, model ships, navigation and storm lamps, photographs, chronometers, an old-fashioned diver's helmet, and shell cases — the Wrecks Bar is shaped like a cabin with photographs of wrecks on the walls (and a slot machine); bar food inc sandwiches, home-cooked ham, green-lipped mussels, friendly licensee, piped music, small restaurant (popular for Sun lunch); bedrooms (*Lyn and Bill Capper*)

St Buryan [SW4025], *St Buryan*: Simple pub with two bars and friendly landlord; part lino-tiled, part carpeted, solid-fuel stove, tractor seats by bar, kitchen chairs and a few plain tables; horse collars and brass on modern stone wall, TV and plastic flowers; well kept Courage Best; juke box, darts, fruit machine (*RAB*)

St Columb Major [Market Sq, Bank St; SW9163], *Ring o' Bells*: Friendly town pub with simple food and decent real ale in several simply furnished rooms going back from narrow road frontage (*BB*)

☆ **St Dominick** [Saltash; SX3967], *Who'd Have Thought It*: Consistently good and often out-of-the-ordinary food such as tasty chicken and broccoli crumble and ham and leek crumble, in entertainingly unCornish bar — flock wallpaper, tasselled plush seats, Gothick tables, gleaming pottery and copper; well kept Bass and Courage Directors, decent wine by the glass, friendly Jack Russell terriers (*E A Simmons, John Kirk, David and Sarah Gilmore, LYM*)

St Issey [SW9271], *Ring o' Bells*: Cheerful well modernised village inn with good value well cooked if not unusual food, inc good chips, fresh veg and small helpings of some dishes (not puddings) for children; well kept Courage real ale; service could sometimes be quicker; bedrooms (*Christopher and Heather Barton, LYM*)

St Ives [Fore St; SW5441], *Castle*: Comfortable pub, popular with locals; original pine panelling, old photographs of town and various maritime memorabilia such as ship lamps; good value bar food (*Donn and Jess Barrett, Reg Nelson*); *Three Ferrets*: Tasteful mock-character place with vibrant atmosphere and real ale (*Reg Nelson*); *Union*: Interesting decor, good atmosphere (*Reg Nelson*)

☆ **St Just in Penwith** [SW3631], *Star*: Honest-to-goodness village local in windswept town not far from Lands End; plenty of interesting mining artefacts and ornaments, low beams, thick walls, good company and happy atmosphere; well kept St Austell ales tapped from the cask, satisfactory food inc good steak rolls, excellent 1950s and 1960s music on juke box; little TV parlour, seats in small courtyard — which leads straight through to a farmyard; bedrooms comfortable, with huge breakfast served in delightful snug

(*WMS, WHBM, R Fieldhouse, Charlie Salt, Tim and Lynne Crawford, Steve Waters, LYM*)

☆ **St Kew** [signposted from A39 NE of Wadebridge; SX0276], *St Kew Inn*: Friendly unpretentious local, a special favourite of some readers, tucked away in small, sheltered village; winged high-backed settles on broad slate flagstones, logs burning in kitchen range, well kept St Austell Tinners and HSD tapped from the cask, fine evening steaks (not Sun) though service can be slow, good home-made puddings such as treacle tart with clotted cream (*M K C Wills, Iain and Penny Muir, Steve Dark, I S Wilson, Nick Dowson, Alison Hayward, Roy and Barbara Longman, LYM*)

St Mawes [SW8533], *Victory*: Lots of sailing and other sea photographs in unpretentious bar, warmly welcoming even to dripping-wet yachtsmen; well kept Devenish JD on handpump, simple bar food; seats out in the alley, a few steep yards up from the harbour; bedrooms simple but good value (don't expect an early night) (*W Bailey, LYM*)

St Mawgan [village signposted from A30; SW8765], *Falcon*: Wisteria-covered stone inn with sun-trap seats in most attractive sheltered garden, in pretty village; well kept St Austell Bosuns and Tinners, usual bar food (not sandwiches); bedrooms (*Charles and Mary Winpenny, LYM*)

St Neot [N of A38 Liskeard—Bodmin; SX1867], *London*: Imaginative home-made bar food inc excellent soup and pâtés (*Pat and Malcolm Rudlin*)

☆ **St Teath** [B3267; signposted off A39 SW of Camelford; SX0680], *White Hart*: Good steaks in companionable village pub with snug slate-floored main bar, comfortable eating bar and lively games bar with darts, pool and juke box; other bar food from good sandwiches to chicken or gammon, well kept Ruddles County and Ushers Best, naval and marines memorabilia, open fire; a nice pub — more reports on it please; bedrooms (*C M Whitehouse, Iain and Penny Muir, L A Mills, Roy and Barbara Longman, LYM*)

Stithians [Frogpool; NE of A393 — ie opp side to Stithians; SW7640], *Cornish Arms*: Good value bar food and steak dinners in friendly village pub with well kept Devenish real ales, cheerful local atmosphere and comfortable sitting areas (*BB*)

Stratton [SS2406], *Tree*: Rambling 17th-century building with great gate for arched coach entry — off yard bars include pleasant lounge with flagstone floor, log fire, genuine old furniture and beams, well kept Bass and St Austell Tinners, reasonable range of bar food (simple at lunchtime); up for sale (*Prof H G Allen, Mayur Shah, William D Cissna*)

Threemilestone [SW7844], *Victoria*: Friendly, comfortable pub, well kept St Austell Tinners on handpump, lunchtime and evening restaurant; children welcome (*Peter Corris*)

Tideford [SX3459], *Rod & Line*: Unspoilt

and evidently totally unchanging single-roomed pub with low, bowed, ochre ceiling and Victorian cash register; children welcome *(Phil Gorton)*

Tintagel [Fore St; SX0588], *Tintagel Arms*: This hotel has been enjoyed for its small bar partitioned off to from Zorba's Taverna, serving good value Greek-based meals — but came up for sale last year; bedrooms *(Iain and Penny Muir)*

Tregony [SW9245], *Kings Arms*: Substantial recently refurbished pub in wide street of prosperous village, welcoming atmosphere *(WHBM)*

☆ **Trelights** [signposted off B3314 Wadebridge—Delabole; SW9979], *Long Cross*: Spotless plush-and-varnish furnishings in modern bar with Victorian stained-glass panels, unusual heptagonal bench around small stone pool, restrained maybe classical piped music, good house wines, well kept St Austell Tinners, good value bar food such as ploughman's, baked potatoes, burgers, salads and chicken; family room, further dining bar, cream teas; picnic-table sets around pool outside, excellent play area; owners slowly restoring what now seems to be the best garden on this exposed coast — well worth a visit (small charge), with lots of attractive ideas and some sweeping coast views; bedrooms comfortable and well furnished, many with good views *(Mrs R F Warner, BB)*

Trespin [A3076 N of Truro; SW8450], *Trespin*: Lively local with excellent choice of real ales — five plus a weekly guest; pool table, juke box; the new 22 year old is the youngest female licensee in Cornwall; good parking *(Cdr W S D Hendry)*

Trevarrian [B3276 NE of Newquay; SW8566], *Travellers Rest*: 18th-century or older local on spectacular coastal route; not pretentious but traditional, with big collection of unusual jugs; bar food, inc Sun lunch, usually very good; separate dining room but food can be eaten in other rooms; well kept St Austell beers, family room with pool table; ample parking *(Brian Skelcher)*

Trevaunance Cove [The Beach; SW7251], *Driftwood Spars*: Scarcely an ancient pub despite its huge beams, thick stone walls, and winter log fires, but well worth knowing for its particularly good food in bar and restaurant; well kept ales, an extensive malt whisky collection, and just moments from the sea; bedrooms excellent *(Mr and Mrs A C Goundry)*

☆ **Truro** [Frances St; SW8244], *Globe*: Several rooms around central serving area, thoroughly Devenishised — but attractively so, with lots of old panelling and beams, bottle-glass screens, a medley of furniture inc deep buttoned leather armchairs and sofas, numerous Christies hat boxes, stuffed fish, hunting trophies and old prints; good value help-yourself home-made bar food lunchtime and evening, well kept Devenish real ales *(Patrick Young, Pat and Malcolm Rudlin)*

☆ **Truro** [Kenwyn St], *William IV*: Particularly notable for nice conservatory dining room opening into garden, but busy dark-panelled bar popular too, with slightly secluded raised areas, lots of chamberpots, bottles, scales, ewers and basins; good value buffet food inc daily hot specials, well kept St Austell beers, maybe large-screen music video weekday lunchtimes; plenty of tables and chairs outside, and front absolutely bedecked with tubs and pots of plants *(Sue Hallam, B H Stamp, Margo and Peter Thomas, Ian Shaw, Lindsey Shaw Radley, Patrick Young)*

Truro [Lemon Quay, by central car park], *Market*: Cosy and intimate refurbishment — lots of oak, bentwood chairs, well kept Devenish Cornish Original and GBH on handpump, and currently has particularly good bar food *(Patrick Young, LYM)*

Tywardreath [off A3082; SX0854], *New Inn*: Well kept Bass and St Austells ales in friendly and very informal pub, converted from a private house; nice village setting; bedrooms *(BB)*

Upton Cross [B3254 N of Liskeard; SX2872], *Caradon*: Welcoming two-bar free house with Flowers Original, St Austell HSD and Wadworths 6X, and good bar food — home-made steak and kidney pie and daily specials recommended *(Iain and Penny Muir)*

Veryan [SW9139], *New Inn*: Spotless, quiet and welcoming pub with particularly well kept St Austell BB and Tinners tapped from the cask, and attractive bar food; bedrooms *(Iain and Penny Muir, David and Sarah Gilmore)*

☆ **West Pentire** [SW7760], *Bowgie*: Friendly atmosphere in hotelish lounge bar looking out over the rolling lawns of this magnificent headland to Crantock beach and the sea; good if not cheap beer (Flowers IPA and Original, a guest such as Marstons Pedigree) and food, newspapers and magazines available, soundproofed family room, good play area; children allowed in main part lunchtime; bedrooms well appointed — good value *(S P Bobeldijk, Charles and Mary Winpenny)*

Zennor [SW4538], *Tinners Arms*: Fingers crossed for this simple but comfortable stripped-panelling pub near a fine part of the Coast Path, with bar food and well kept St Austells real ales; up for sale earlier this year, it could be a winner if it gets the good licensee it deserves *(Brian Skelcher, John Branford, Linda Duncan, Neil and Anita Christopher, Nick Dowson, Alison Hayward, LYM)*

ISLES OF SCILLY

Bryher [SV8715], *Hell Bay*: Comfortable hotel with tables in lovely garden; small stone-walled bar with friendly service and good range of drinks and snacks inc good crab sandwiches, delicious gateaux; bedrooms *(Margaret and Roy Randle, John Evans)*

St Marys — Hugh Town [The Strand;

SV9010], *Atlantic*: Very large newly refurbished low-beamed bar almost lapped by high tide, all sorts of spars, lamps, marine nick-nacks and wreck and other photographs; substantial helpings of bar food such as huge pasties, ham and egg, scampi, fresh fish, mixed grill, children's dishes; friendly staff, St Austell Tinners and HSD; small terrace also overlooks harbour; separate restaurant, adjacent hotel *(Neil and Anita Christopher)*; [Silver St (A3110)], *Bishop & Wolf*: Reasonably priced straightforward food (crab sandwiches particularly recommended) in clean and comfortable bar bedecked with nets, oars, lamps and so forth, friendly staff, St Austell ales, pool, fruit machine, unobtrusive piped music; decent upstairs restaurant with second bar; open all day *(Neil and Anita Christopher, Derek Patey, TBB, Margaret and Roy Randle, GCS)*; [The Quay], *Mermaid*: Fine view of harbour from picture-window bar done up with maritime relics, rough wood, stone floor, large winter stove and dim lighting; pool table and video juke box upstairs, well kept Devenish real ales, swift service, bar food; recent reports suggest that the atmosphere's now recovering from the major changes reported in the last edition *(Angie and Dave Parkes, Keith and Sian Mitchell, Margaret and Roy Randle, Derek Patey, Brian Barefoot)*; [Garrison Hill], *Star Castle*: Hotel (not pub) in star-shaped Elizabethan castle, worth knowing for wonderful views from ramparts; basic lunchtime bar snacks such as pasties and ploughman's up here and in dungeon bar which housed illustrious prisoners transferred from Tower of London *(Neil and Anita Christopher)*

☆ **St Agnes** [The Quay; SV8807], *Turks Head*: Currently readers' most warmly recommended pub on the islands; small but friendly pine-panelled bar in idyllic surroundings, affable and efficient service, good range of drinks — though not real ale — and snacks at fair prices; the home-made pasties are the things to go for, with large crab rolls a close second, and a noted ice-cream pie (food stops 8pm); magnificent sea and island views from the garden terrace; boats from St Marys most nights during season (pub closed afternoons), but pub opens only one night a week in winter; singsongs Sun and Thurs; ideal stop-off after trip to Bishop Rock *(Peter and Rose Flower, John Evans, Pat and Malcolm Rudlin, Angie and Dave Parkes, Brian Barefoot, GCS, Margaret and Roy Randle, Derek Patey, Keith and Sian Mitchell)*

☆ **St Martins** [SV9215], *St Martins*: Good choice of reasonably priced bar snacks inc delicious quiches, sea views and friendly service in comfortable Laura Ashleyesque lounge or on lawn of newish plush hotel sympathetically built like row of cottages, in idyllic spot looking across to Tresco; Devenish Steam real ale; yachtsmen may like to know that there's no charge for using the showers in the lavatories *(Neil and Anita Christopher, Gwen and Peter Andrews, Angus and Rosemary Campbell, John Evans)*

St Martins, *Seven Stones*: Worth knowing that there is a pub here too, but it doubles as the village hall and looks it; cheerful loud service, pasties, sandwiches and toasties, no real ale — but a lovely spot, with beautiful views from seats outside *(John Evans, Brian Barefoot, Neil and Anita Christopher)* ;

☆ **Tresco** [New Grimsby; SV8915], *New Inn*: Old cottage-style inn with decent bars, good choice of bar lunches such as sandwiches, soup and pizzas, more interesting evening food, pool table; caring staff, nice garden, small swimming pool; comfortable bedrooms *(George Atkinson, Neil and Anita Christopher)*

Cumbria

The Lake District now has a mass of good value comfortable bedroom accommodation in attractive pubs and inns – among the main entries, we'd particularly mention the civilised Barbon Inn at Barbon, the Pheasant by Bassenthwaite Lake with its delightfully old-fashioned bar, the Wheatsheaf at Beetham, the Sun looking down over Coniston (under new licensees this year), the very successful Britannia by Elterwater, the stylish Bower House at Eskdale Green, the cosy String of Horses up at Faugh, the very smart Wordsworth Hotel in Grasmere (we've really included it for its friendly little separate Dove & Olive bar – surprisingly cheap), the Kings Arms in Hawkshead, the Three Shires in Little Langdale, the Old Dungeon Ghyll in a particularly grand spot over the hill in Langdale itself, and the similarly grandly sited Wasdale Head Inn up at Wasdale Head. Among the large number of inns and pubs with bedrooms in the Lucky Dip section at the end of the chapter we have confident recommendations for accommodation – spanning a very wide range of prices – at the Unicorn in Ambleside, Queens Head at Askham, St Patricks Well at Bampton, George & Dragon at Garrigill, Swan and Travellers Rest in Grasmere, Old Crown up at Hesket Newmarket, George in Keswick, Scale Hill by Loweswater, Kings Head over in Ravenstonedale, Dalesman in Sedbergh, Beech Hill by Windermere, Tarn End at Talkin, Church House at Torver and Bay Horse at Winton. Interesting new entries this year (or pubs returning to the Guide under new licensees after a break) include the Punch Bowl at Askham (good imaginative food), the Sun at Bassenthwaite (a very popular Italian licensee in this quaint little village pub), the Punch Bowl at Crosthwaite (a remarkable refurbishment of a fine old inn), the Outgate Inn at Outgate (most welcoming and well run) and the Queens Head at Tirril (currently on fine traditional form). Important changes at other main entries include popular new licensees at the Hare & Hounds at Levens, new microbreweries at the charmingly placed Sun in Dent and at the Masons Arms on Cartmel Fell (already one of the most popular pubs in the country), and a decision to do bar lunches at the Bay Horse at Ulverston (the restaurant here is outstanding – so this innovation is particularly welcome). Drinks prices up here are substantially lower than the national average – Lakeland drinkers are now saving nearly 10p on every pint. This is largely because local breweries (Jennings, Mitchells and Yates), and Hartleys, the local arm of the regional brewer Robinsons, have relatively low prices in their tied pubs. This in turn seems to be helping to hold down prices not just in free houses but even in pubs tied to the national combines. Generally, these last have the highest drinks prices here. For food, there's no doubt that many Lakeland pubs score high marks for quality – and that Cumbrian trademark, really big helpings. However, we've been disappointed to see this year that it's now become virtually impossible in Cumbria to find a decent pub snack – say a good sandwich – for under £1; and it's hard to find

*a filling and well presented main dish at under £3. But it can be done.
Pubs which have been beating that £3 target are the Wheatsheaf at
Beetham, New Inn at Brampton, Sun at Dent, Blue Bell at
Heversham, Outgate Inn (cheap sandwiches here, too), Kings Arms at
Stainton and Wasdale Head Inn.*

AMBLESIDE   NY3804 Map 9

Golden Rule

Smithy Brow; follow Kirkstone Pass signpost from A591 on N side of town

This popular pub is a fine sight in summer, when its window boxes are a riot of
colour. Inside there are lots of local country pictures and a few fox masks on the
butter-coloured walls, horsebrasses on the black beams, built-in leatherette wall
seats, and cast-iron-framed tables. The room on the left has darts, a fruit machine
and dominoes; the one down a few steps on the right is a quieter sitting room. The
Hartleys Bitter and XB are attentively well kept on handpump – one reader was
given a free pint because he had to wait when the beer ran off; good baps, filled
French sticks and some meals; friendly service. The pub's name refers to a brass
measuring yard mounted over the bar counter. Near the start of *Good Walks
Guide* Walk 130. *(Recommended by H K Dyson, W H Bland, K Hollywood, Andrew and
Ruth Triggs, A Parsons, Andy and Jill Kassube, Steve Waters, Peter Corris)*

*Hartleys (Robinsons)   Licensee John Lockley   Real ale   Meals and snacks   Children
welcome   Nearby parking virtually out of the question   Open 11–11*

APPLEBY   NY6921 Map 10

Royal Oak 🦮 🛏

Bongate; B6542 on S edge of town

There's considerable attention to detail with the fresh home-made bar food in this
popular and comfortable inn; the full, reasonably priced range was being changed
as we went to press, but typically includes superb soup (£1), lunchtime sandwiches
such as home-cooked ham and beef (£1), Cumberland sausage (made by hand by
the local butcher's wife) or traditional ploughman's (£2.15), hot pancakes stuffed
with apple and stilton (£2.50), vegetarian dishes such as savoury crumble (£3.80),
fresh white fish or salads (from £3.25), fish and meat hors d'oeuvres or pie of the
day (£3.55), local lamb cutlets (£4.50); adventurous daily specials, children's meals
(from £1.40), puddings (from £1.30), and local cheeses (£1.65); the breakfasts are
gigantic; service may be stretched when it's very busy – at weekends or on bank
holidays, say. The beamed lounge has some armchairs and a carved settle, old
pictures on the timbered walls, and a panelling-and-glass snug enclosing the bar
counter; there's a good open fire in the smaller, oak-panelled public bar. Well kept
McEwans 70/- and local Yates on handpump, with guest beers like Brakspears,
Broughton Merlins, Huntsman and Wadworths; several malt whiskies, and a
carefully chosen wine list; dominoes. Seats on the front terrace, among masses of
flowers in tubs, troughs and hanging baskets, overlook the red stone church; the
building itself is based on a partly 14th-century posting house. The bedrooms are
being refurbished. *(Recommended by Caroline Wright, Kathryn Ogden, George Hunt,
Roger Etherington, David Young, Andy and Jill Kassube, Michael and Joan Melling, Mike
Beiley, R F Plater, A C and S J Beardsley, Jill and Paul Ormrod, John Honnor, Carol and
Philip Seddon)*

*Free house   Licensees Colin and Hilary Cheyne   Real ale   Meals and snacks
Restaurant   Children in eating area of bar   Open 11–3, 6–11   Bedrooms tel Appleby
(0930) 51463; £27B/£45B*

ASKHAM   NY5123 Map 9

Punch Bowl

Village signposted on right from A6 4 miles S of Penrith

The licensees who took over some time ago – in summer 1988 – have established a loyal following among readers, not least for the good selection of imaginative bar food; this includes lunchtime sandwiches, smokies (£2.45), deep-fried stilton (£2.95), turkey bake (£4.10), fritters (£4.30), and steak (£6.10). A further major attraction is the pub's position – at the bottom of the lovely lower village green, and facing the wall of the Lowther estate. There's a mix of interesting furnishings in the rambling beamed bar, with Chippendale dining chairs and rushwork ladder-back seats around the sturdy wooden tables, an antique settle by an open log fire, and well cushioned window seats in the white-painted thick stone walls, decorated with local photographs and prints of Askham; the old-fashioned woodburning stove, with its gleaming stainless chimney in the big main fireplace, is now largely decorative. Well kept Whitbreads Castle Eden and a monthly guest beer on handpump; dominoes and piped pop music, and in the separate public bar darts, fruit machine, trivia and juke box. There are tables out on a gravelled side terrace. *(Recommended by W H Bland, Mr and Mrs G W Hodgson, Mrs P Cardy, D J Milner, Sue Holland, Dave Webster, PLC)*

Whitbreads   Licensees David and Frances Riley   Real ale   Snacks (lunchtime) and meals   Restaurant   Children only when food served   Live entertainment Friday evening   Open 11–3, 6(6.30 Sat)–11; 12–3, 7–11 winter   Bedrooms tel Hackthorpe (093 12) 443; £17.50/£35

BARBON   SD6383   Map 10

Barbon Inn   ★   🛏

Village signposted off A683 Kirkby Lonsdale–Sedbergh; OS Sheet 97, map reference 628826

Each of the small rooms leading off the main bar in this civilised and welcoming inn is individually and comfortably furnished, with carved 18th-century oak settles, deep chintzy sofas and armchairs, and lots of fresh flowers. Well kept Theakstons Best and Old Peculier on handpump, and quite a few wines; dominoes and piped music. Home-made bar food includes sandwiches (from £1.10), soup (£1.25), tasty Morecambe Bay potted shrimps (£2.95), ploughman's (from £2.95), duck and chicken liver pâté (£2.50), Cumberland sausage (£3.50), home-baked ham or a vegetarian dish of the day (£3.95), home-made steak and kidney pie (£4.50), sirloin steak (£7.95), and puddings like home-made fruit pie (£1.30). The neatly kept, sheltered garden is very prettily planted and floodlit at night, with some paths and tracks leading up to the fells. *(Recommended by Barbara Wensworth, Ben Wimpenny, Hayward Wane, H K Dyson, M A and W R Proctor, Jill and Paul Ormrod, Mike Tucker, John and Joan Wyatt, Mr and Mrs J E Rycroft, Steve Dark)*

Free house   Licensee L MacDiarmid   Real ale   Meals and snacks   Restaurant Children welcome   Open 12–3ish, 6.30–11   Bedrooms tel Barbon (046 836) 233; £21.50/£41

BASSENTHWAITE   NY2332   Map 9

Sun

Village itself, signposted off A591 a few miles NW of Keswick

In their few short years here the licensees – he's Italian, she's from the Lakes – have made this village pub quite a favourite among Lakeland readers. Though it looks tiny from outside, its bar rambles around into areas that stretch usefully back on both sides of the servery. There are low 17th-century black oak beams, lots of brasses, built-in wall seats and plush stools around heavy wooden tables, and a good stone fireplace with big logs burning in winter. The favourite dish here is meaty or vegetarian lasagne with lashings of garlic bread (£4.50), as well as minestrone soup (£1), salads (from £3.50), Cumberland or steak and kidney pie (£4), gammon (£4.50), pork in mushroom sauce (£5), and steak (£7), with puddings such as walnut and honey £1.50); the range is suprisingly wide for such a tucked-away place. Well kept Jennings on handpump; truly welcoming service; juke box (never heard playing, on our own visit or readers' visits), and in winter darts, dominoes and pool; no dogs. There are a few tables in the front yard by a neighbour's blackcurrant patch, in the heart of this charmingly close huddle of white houses looking up to Skiddaw and other high fells. *(Recommended by Mr and Mrs L D Rainger, Michael Wadsworth, D P Ryan, M A and W R Proctor, P J and S E Robbins, C A Holloway, Nigel Pritchard)*

Jennings   Licensees Giuseppe and Josephine Scopelliti   Real ale   Meals and snacks (12–1.30, 6.30–8.30ish; not Sun evening)   Children in family room next to bar   Open 11–3ish, 6–11; winter 12–2.30ish, 6.30–11

BASSENTHWAITE LAKE   NY2228   Map 9

Pheasant ★ ⇔

Follow Wythop Mill signpost at N end of dual carriageway stretch of A66 by Bassenthwaite Lake

There's a certain school of thought that this would be more worthy just of a hotel guide; and indeed some of the prices – for afternoon tea, say – are a good indication of what to expect. Nonetheless the distinct pubiness of the bar – for one reader one of the best in England – is well worth seeking out. The two rooms, linked by a fine wood-framed arch, have an old-fashioned and welcoming atmosphere; the hatch at the low serving counter leads to the entry corridor through a traditional wood-and-glass partition, and there are rush-seat chairs, library seats, cushioned settles, and hunting prints and photographs on the fine ochre walls. Good, freshly made lunchtime bar food includes soup (95p), ploughman's or tasty pâté (£2.25), quail eggs with hazelnut mayonnaise (£2.55), vegetable and nut terrine (£2.85), cold Cumberland sausage platter (£2.65), smoked lamb with melon or prawns with lobster sauce (£3.10), sweet smoked chicken (£3.25), and smoked Scotch salmon (£4.80); they do main dishes in the dining room (which is no-smoking). Well kept Bass and Theakstons Best on handpump. A large and airy beamed lounge at the back has easy chairs on its polished parquet floor and a big log fire on cool days; there are also some chintzy sitting rooms with antique furniture. You can walk into the attractive beechwoods from the garden. *(Recommended by W H Bland, M Box, Mr and Mrs Simon Turner, Hayward Wane, Richard Holloway, Mr and Mrs J E Rycroft, M A and W R Proctor, Simon Bates, D T Taylor, Dennis and Pat Jones, John and Anne McIver, Lord Evans of Claughton, Dr R H M Stewart, Dr J R Hamilton, PLC)*

Free house   Licensee W E Barrington Wilson   Real ale   Lunchtime snacks Restaurant   Children in lounge and restaurant weekdays (not Sun)   Open 11–3, 5.30–10.30; till 11 Friday and Saturday   Bedrooms tel Bassenthwaite Lake (059 681) 234; £38B/£68B

BEETHAM   SD5079   Map 7

Wheatsheaf ⇔

Village (and inn) signposted just off A6 S of Milnthorpe

There's a fine black-and-white timbered cornerpiece on this old-fashioned building – a glorified two-storey set of gabled oriel windows jettied out from the corner and into the quiet village street. The lounge bar has lots of exposed beams and joists, a massive antique carved oak armchair, attractive built-in wall settles, tapestry-cushioned chairs, a cabinet filled with foreign costume dolls, fox mask and brush, and a calm old golden labrador. There's also a little central snug, and beyond that a tiled-floor bar with darts, dominoes and fruit machine; piped music. Bar food includes home-made soup (85p), sandwiches (from £1.15), good home-made pies such as cheese (£2.30), cottage with cheesy topping (£2.40) or steak and onion (£3.10), fresh fish of the day (£3.35), salads (from £2.90), and steaks (from £5.95); Sunday lunch (£5.50) and a set evening menu in the dining room (£7.50); agreeable service. Thwaites Bitter on handpump, and quite a few malt whiskies and wines. *(Recommended by P Lloyd, Kathleen Morley, Maurice and Gill McMahon, Barbara M McHugh, Miss K Bamford, Dr R Fuller, JM, PM, Mrs H D Astley, A T Langton)*

Free house   Licensee Mrs Florence Miller   Real ale   Meals and snacks   Restaurant   Children in eating area till 8.30   Open 11–3, 6–11; closed 25 Dec evening   Bedrooms   tel Milnthorpe (05395) 62123; £25B/£35B

BIGGAR   SD1965   Map 7

Queens Arms

On Isle of Walney; follow A590 or A5087 into Barrow-in-Furness centre, then Walney signposted through Vickerstown – bear left on the island

Tracking down this pub is an entertaining expedition: the road threads past a series of gigantic shipyard gates, weaves across a couple of great drawbridges, then tracks down the island. The pub itself – in what looks like a little huddle of black-trimmed white farm buildings – is right next to a large and sunny beach, which may well be virtually empty, with only the curlews and wading birds for company. The snug little bar has a good deal of brown varnish, wheelback chairs and tapestried built-in banquettes, a Delft shelf, and an open fire in its stone fireplace. Rustic seats and tables shelter in the yard, and opening off this there's a smallish eating room with high-backed settles forming booths around the tables and a more spacious restaurant. Good value bar food includes home-made soup (95p), sandwiches (from £1.20), moules marinières (£2.75), salads (from £3.95), home-made steak and kidney pie or lasagne (£4.20), Cumberland game pie (£4.50), and steak (£7.95). Hartleys XB and Whitbreads Boddingtons and Castle Eden on handpump or tapped from the cask. There's a nature reserve to the south. *(Recommended by TBB, Brian Jones; more reports please)*

Whitbreads   Licensee Cyril Whiteside   Real ale   Meals and snacks (11.45–2, 6.45–9.30)   Restaurant tel Barrow-in-Furness (0229) 41113   Children in eating area of bar and restaurant   Open 11.30–3, 6.30–11.30

BOOT   NY1801   Map 9

Burnmoor

Village signposted just off the Wrynose/Hardknott Pass road, OS Sheet 89 map reference 175010

In a pretty and outstandingly peaceful hamlet close to Dalegarth Station (the top terminus of the Ravenglass and Eskdale light steam railway), this partly 16th-century, family-run pub has a beamed and carpeted white-painted bar with an open fire, red leatherette seats and small metal tables. Well kept Jennings on handpump; dominoes, juke box, pool room. Generous helpings of quickly served bar food include delicious soup (90p), ploughman's or wholemeal cheese and onion flan (£2.60), breaded haddock (£3.20), cold beef or ham (£3.30), Cumberland game pie (£4.40), Wienerschnitzel (£4.90), sirloin steak (£6.40), and puddings (£1.10); children's menu (£2.10); they grow a lot of the vegetables themselves, and keep hens and pigs. The landlord shepherded for years on the hills around here and can suggest good walks – of which there is no lack, such as up along Whillan Beck to Burnmoor Tarn; and *Good Walks Guide* Walk 125 is nearby. There are seats outside on the sheltered front lawn. *(Recommended by Comus Elliott, A M Neal, Steve and Maureen Collins, Roger Huggins)*

Free house   Licensees Tony and Heidi Foster   Real ale   Meals and snacks (12–2, 6–9)   Restaurant   Children welcome till 9   Open 11–3, 5–11; 11–2.30, 5–11 in winter   Bedrooms tel Eskdale (094 03) 224; £15.50(£17.50B)/£31(£35B)

BOWLAND BRIDGE   SD4289   Map 9

Hare & Hounds   🛏

Village signposted from A5074; OS Sheet 97 map reference 417895

Popular bar food in this white-painted and tiled pub includes sandwiches (from £1.30), soup (£1.20), pâté (£2.50), ploughman's (£2.95), pizzas (from £3.50), salads (from £3.50), roast chicken or cold meats (£4.50), and steaks (from £7.95);

prompt, very friendly service. The comfortably modernised bar has been enlarged and opened out into the pool room; there are ladder-back chairs around dark wood tables on its Turkey carpet, and open fires; some stub walls divide it into smaller areas; decorations include blue and white china, reproduction hunting prints and a stuffed pheasant; dominoes. The landlord used to play for Liverpool and England – as the team photographs and caps on the wall testify. Well kept Greenalls on handpump, from a long bar counter with a cushioned red leatherette elbow rest for people using the sensible backrest-type bar stools; the Stable Bar is now a residents' lounge, and a bedroom extension has just been built. The pub is down by the bridge itself, and has geraniums in hanging baskets and climbing roses on the walls; picnic-table sets in the spacious garden at one side. *(Recommended by N F Calver, Peter Barnsley, TBB, Carol and Richard Glover, H K Dyson, Brian Jones, A T Langton, David Heath, Lee Goulding, Diane Hall)*

Free house   Licensee Peter Thompson   Real ale   Meals and snacks   Children welcome   Open 11–3, 5.30–11   Bedrooms tel Crosthwaite (044 88) 333; £18(£18S)/£36(48S)

BRAMPTON   NY6723   Map 10

New Inn

Off A66 N of Appleby – follow Long Marton 1 signpost then turn right at church; village also signposted off B6542 at N end of Appleby

The two small rooms of the bar in this eighteenth-century black and white slated building are a cosy affair, with a medley of seats including panelled oak settles and a nice little oak chair. There's a mass of local pictures, mainly sheep and wildlife; a stuffed fox is curled on top of the corner TV, and a red squirrel pokes out of a little hole in the dividing wall. In the second week of June the Committee of the Appleby Horse Fair pretty much uses the inn as its base, so it tends to get packed – especially in the dining room, which becomes the special preserve of the gipsy women. It's a well proportioned, flagstoned room with horsebrasses on its low black beams, well spaced tables, and a splendid original black cooking range at one end, separated from the door by an immensely sturdy old oak built-in settle. Notably good value home cooking is served here and includes soup (£1), garlic mushrooms (£1.60), potted shrimps (£2.20), with main dishes such as pizzas (from £2.30), Cumberland sausage (£2.75), nut roast (£3.30), plaice or steak and kidney pie (£3.50) and 10oz sirloin steak (£6.95). They also do lunchtime sandwiches (from 90p; steak £2.20) and ploughman's (£2.50); on Sundays, besides three-course lunches, there's a more limited choice. Well kept Theakstons Bitter and XB, Whitbreads Castle Eden and Youngers Scotch on handpump; a good choice of whiskies with some eminent malts; friendly service, and no games other than dominoes. No dogs in bedrooms. *(Recommended by Dave Braisted; more reports please)*

Free house   Licensees Roger and Anne Cranswick   Real ale   Meals and snacks (not Tues winter)   Restaurant   Children till 9pm   Open 11–3, 6–11; 11–2, 7–11 winter; closed Tues lunchtime winter   Bedrooms tel Kirkby Thore (07683) 51231; £15/£30

CARTMEL FELL   SD4288   Map 9

Masons Arms ★ ★

Strawberry Bank, a few miles S of Windermere between A592 and A5074; perhaps the simplest way of finding the pub is to go uphill W from Bowland Bridge (which is signposted off A5074) towards Newby Bridge and keep right then left at the staggered crossroads – it's then on your right, below Gummer's How; OS Sheet 97 ref 413895

There are various explanations as to why this is one of the most popular pubs in the country. High on anybody's list must be its unrivalled setting, overlooking the Winster Valley to the woods below Whitbarrow Scar; a good terrace, with rustic benches and tables, makes the most of the view. Then there are the bars themselves, old-fashioned and very well preserved; the main bar has country chairs and plain wooden tables on polished flagstones, low black beams in a bowed ceiling, needlework samplers and country pictures, a big log fire, and by it a grandly Gothick seat with snarling dogs as its arms. A small lounge has oak tables and settles to match its fine Jacobean panelling, and a plain little room beyond the serving counter has more pictures and a fire in an open range; the family room has an old-parlourish atmosphere; dominoes, piped music. A third virtue is the staggering range of drinks, with some 200 bottled beers from all over the world, including thirty or so from all over Britain; a helpful and comprehensive leaflet pre-empts at least some of the inevitable confusion. It's also one of the few pubs we know that has real German beer on draught – Furstenburg Export and Antonio, and Weizenthaler. Besides these, they keep Batemans XB, Thwaites Bitter, and Yates Bitter, with guest beers from all over the country – anything up to 100 a year. New this year is their own micro-brewery, producing Amazon – light and hoppy but quite strong, and named for Arthur Ransome, the author of *Swallows and Amazons*, who used to live in the area; also interesting farm ciders and perrys and country wines. Food, plentiful and wholesome though not cheap, includes soup (from £1.40), sandwiches (from £1.80), ploughman's (£3.60), fisherman's pie (£4.25), and Cumberland sausage and cider casserole (£5.50), with specials (several for vegetarians) such as fennel and cashew nut crumble or broccoli and brie lasagne (£4.25), beef burritos (£4.95) and gravadlax (£5.50); puddings (£2). They also sell leaflets outlining local walks of varying lengths and difficulty. There are good self-catering flats in an adjoining stone barn. The stream of customers is inevitably at its heaviest at weekends and high season; it's often much quieter mid-week. (*Recommended by R J Yates, Mr and Mrs Simon Turner, Dave Braisted, Andy and Jill Kassube, Graham Bush, A Parsons, Paul Wreglesworth, M H Box, Simon Bates, Mrs V A Middlebrook, Barbara Wensworth, Terry Glendenning, Janet and John Towers, A M Neal, GB, J Scarisbrick, M A and W R Proctor, Steve and Maureen Collins, BKA, TBB, Jill and Paul Ormrod, Mr and Mrs D M Norton, Dennis Royles, Steve and Carolyn Harvey, P Lloyd, K Bamford, A T Langton, Carol and Richard Glover, Brian and Anna Marsden, Roger Bellingham, David Heath, S J Willmot, Steve Dark, Lee Goulding*)

Own brew Licensees Helen and Nigel Stevenson Real ale Meals and snacks (12–2, 6–8.45) Children welcome Open 11–3, 6–11 Self-catering flats tel Crosthwaite (044 88) 486

CASTERTON SD6379 Map 7

Pheasant

A683 about a mile N of junction with A65, by Kirkby Lonsdale

The bar food in this neat and civilised white-painted inn has come in for particular praise recently; the good range includes some unusual home-made soups such as cream of mussel (£1.50), sandwiches, Morecambe Bay shrimps (£2.50), main dishes such as a very good Cumberland sausage with apple sauce (£3.75), steak and kidney pie (£4.50), Cumberland ham with cheese and pineapple or eggs (£5), steaks (from £8), and adventurous specials like goat's cheese salad with pine kernels (£2), cauliflower, almond and tomato bake (£3.50) and braised wood pigeon in Irish whiskey (£6); puddings (£2). The two comfortably modernised rooms of the main bar have ladder-back chairs and antique tables, newspapers and magazines to read, and an open log fire in a nicely arched bare stone fireplace. Well kept Theakstons Old Peculier and Youngers Scotch on handpump, and several wines; friendly staff; dominoes; the dining room and garden lounge are no-smoking. There are some tables with cocktail parasols outside by the road. The nearby church (built for the girls' school of Brontë fame here) has some attractive pre-Raphaelite stained glass and paintings. (*Recommended by Mr and Mrs M V Melling, Thelma and George Clarke, TBB, P Lloyd, Miss K Bamford, Jill and Paul Ormrod*)

Free house Licensees David Seed Hesmondhalgh Real ale Meals and snacks Restaurant Children welcome Open 11–3, 6–11 (12–2.30, 6–10.30 winter); closed some Mondays Jan and Feb Bedrooms tel Kirkby Lonsdale (05242) 71230; £35B/£55B

CONISTON   SD3098 Map 9

Sun ⊘ ⇐

Inn signposted from centre

As it's out of the centre of Coniston, this substantial stone inn is a deal less touristy than most (and may explain why we've been getting so few reports on it), but is still spectacularly positioned, with bare fells all around, and tracks from the lane leading straight up to the Old Man of Coniston. Fishing, riding and shooting can all be arranged for residents, and the start of *Good Walks Guide* Walk 126 is nearby. Inside, the back bar has some cask seats (one pair remarkably heavy) as well as cushioned spindleback chairs and brown plush built-in wall benches around the traditional cast-iron-framed tables, lots of Lakeland colour photographs and some recalling Donald Campbell (this was his HQ during his final attempt on the world water speed record), and a small but very warm log fire; the floors are part carpeted, part handsome polished flagstones. Home-made bar food includes a soup of the day such as tomato and tarragon (£1.10), sandwiches (from £1.10), pâté (£2.75), ploughman's (from £2.95), Cumberland sausage (£3), two baked potatoes with interesting daily fillings (£3.25), home-cooked gammon salad (£3.95), and gammon steak (£3.75); puddings such as sticky toffee or real bread and butter pudding. Jennings, Marstons Pedigree and Tetleys on handpump, from the deep 16th-century granite cellar, and lots of rare malt whiskies; darts, dominoes, piped music. The restaurant is no-smoking. There are white tables out on the terrace, and a big, tree-sheltered garden runs down to a steep little beck. *(Recommended by Doug Kennedy, Robert and Vicky Tod, Heather Sharland, Nicola Plummer; more up-to-date reports on the new regime please)*

Free house   Licensees the Elson Family   Real ale   Meals and snacks (12–2, 6(7 Sun)–9)   Restaurant   Children in eating area till 9   Open 11–11   Bedrooms tel Coniston (053 94) 41248; £30B/£60B

CROSTHWAITE   SD4491 Map 9

Punch Bowl

Village signposted off A5074 SE of Windermere

Though the heavy-slated white inn's been here by the church in this charming fold of the hills since the 16th century, its bar has been imaginatively reworked to give a lot of space in several separate areas. By the serving counter a high-raftered central area has an upper gallery on either side, with steps down into a couple of small dimly lit rooms on the right, and a doorway through into two more airy rooms on the left. Through here the furnishings are particularly comfortable, with well spaced tables, good hunting prints and open fires giving a relaxed feel. It's all spick and span, with close-fitted carpets, and the staff are smartly dressed (yet friendly). Generously served lunchtime bar food includes sandwiches (from £1.50), fried mushrooms with a good dip (£2.75), ploughman's (£3.50), salads (from £3.50), Cumberland sausage or steak pie (£4.25), home-made lasagne (£4.50; vegetarian £4.25), plaice (£4.75), children's dishes (£2.50) and good puddings such as spiced apple crumble (£1.50); in the evenings, and from Friday onwards, the choice widens to include more fish, steaks and so forth, and there are specials such as asparagus and ham crêpe (£2.75, £5.50 as a main course) and pork chop normande (£5.50). Well kept Theakstons Best and summer guest beers on handpump, darts, pool, dominoes, unobtrusive piped music, fruit machine and juke box (tucked away down at the lower end). There are some tables on a terrace stepped into the hillside; dogs allowed. The bedrooms have four-posters. The pub is a meeting place for vintage-car enthusiasts about four times a year. *(Recommended by C Trows, Stephen K Holman, Anne and Tim Neale, Robert and Vicky Tod, Barbara McHugh)*

Free house   Licensee Anita L Crompton   Real ale   Meals and snacks   Children welcome away from bar   Open 11.30–2.30(3 Sat), 6.30(6 Sat)–11; closed 3 days in Jan   Bedrooms tel Crosthwaite (044 88) 237; £25B/£35B

DENT   SD7187 Map 10

Sun

Village signposted from Sedbergh; and from Barbon, off A683

There's a nice, traditional feel in this little inn – one of the prettiest buildings in an attractive village – with its fine old oak timbers and beams (studded with coins), dark armed chairs, brown leatherette wall benches, and a coal fire; the walls are decorated with lots of local snapshots and old Schweppes advertisements; one of the areas is no-smoking. Through the arch to the left are banquettes upholstered to match the carpet (as are the curtains). The pub's own Dent Brewery, set up in a converted barn some three miles up in the Dale, started production (about 1,000 gallons a week) early last year, and supplies its Bitter and Ramsbottom to some other pubs and breweries in the area; they're also available here, of course, together with well kept Theakstons XB and Youngers Scotch on handpump. Generous helpings of good value bar food include home-made minestrone soup (95p), sandwiches (from £1.05), filled baked potato (£1.25), home-made pasties (£2.35), vegetarian or meaty lasagne (£2.75), 12oz Cumberland sausage (£2.95), 10oz gammon steak with pineapple (£3.35), and rump steak (£3.75); children's portions, enormous breakfasts; friendly service; darts, pool, dominoes, fruit machine, and juke box (in the pool room). There are rustic seats and tables outside, and barbecues in summer – when it can get very busy. *(Recommended by H K Dyson, Ruth Humphrey, Wayne Brindle, Helena and Arthur Harbottle, Alan Hall, Jenny Cantle)*

Own brew   Licensees Jacky and Martin Stafford   Real ale   Meals and snacks (not 25 Dec)   Children welcome until 9pm   Open 11–2.30, 6.15–11, all day Sat and during school holidays; 12–2, 7–11 in winter   Bedrooms tel Dent (058 75) 208; £12.50/£25

ELTERWATER   NY3305 Map 9

Britannia Inn ★ 🛏

Off B5343

As it's so well placed in the heart of the Lake District, close to Langdale and the central lakes and with tracks over the fells to Grasmere and Easedale, it's no surprise that this fine inn is popular with ramblers – and indeed actively encourages them; the welcome is perhaps at its warmest in the traditionally furnished, small beamed bar at the back. It's at its most popular in summer, when people flock to watch Morris and Step and Garland Dancers on the pretty village green. The front bar has a couple of window seats looking across to Elterwater itself through the trees on the far side, as well as settles, oak benches, Windsor chairs and winter coal fires; there's also a comfortable lounge. This year the forecourt has been terraced with local slate and fitted out with chairs and slate-topped tables. Well kept Hartleys XB and Bitter, Jennings Bitter and Mild, and Marstons Pedigree on handpump, Bulmers cider, several malt whiskies, a well chosen, good value wine list, and country wines; darts, dominoes and cribbage. Good home-cooked bar food includes home-made soup (£1), lunchtime filled wholemeal baps (£1), cheese burger (£1.60), filled baked potato (from £1.50), lunchtime ploughman's (£2.95), cheese and onion quiche (£3.95), salads or steak and kidney pie (£4.25), and rainbow trout (£4.25); puddings (£1.60), children's dishes (from £1.60); friendly, efficient service; the restaurant is no-smoking. It's one of the best pubs to stay at around here, and we hope that the addition of private bathrooms to two more of the bedrooms will have resolved one or two complaints we've had about the rooms being a little on the small side. Near the start of the *Good Walks Guide* Walk 128. *(Recommended by W H Bland, M Box, Ian Clayton, Hilary Thorpe, John Fazakerley, Andy and Jill Kassube, H K Dyson, Tim Locke, Mary and Lionel Tonks, M A and W R Proctor, Simon Bates, J Scarisbrick, BKA, Raymond Palmer, D J Cooke, David and Christine Foulkes, Steve Dark, Barbara Wensworth, Mike Beiley, Rosalind Russell, Steve Waters, Steve and Carolyn Harvey, KC, P Lloyd, K Bamford, M J Lawson, Brian Jones, Dr and Mrs Peter Dykes, Ewan McCall, C A Holloway, J A Edwards)*

Free house   David Fry   Real ale   Meals and snacks   Restaurant   Occasional Morris dancing   Summer parking may be difficult   Open 11–11; closed 25 Dec and evening 26 Dec   Bedrooms tel Langdale (096 67) 210 or 382 (from 1991: 05394 37210 or 37382);   £37.50(£43S)/£42.50(£48S)

ESKDALE GREEN   NY1400   Map 9

Bower House   🍺

1/2 mile W of village towards Santon Bridge

Good value bar food in this comfortable and welcoming isolated inn includes sandwiches, pâté, Cumberland sausage (£3.25), lasagne or steak and kidney pie (£4.25), gammon and egg (£3.95), vegetarian dishes such as hazelnut and lentil loaf or spinach and walnut lasagne, guinea fowl in cranberry sauce, pheasant or venison (£6), and home-made puddings such as sticky toffee or bread and butter (1.60); the restaurant is no-smoking. The lounge bar has a good winter fire, as well as cushioned settles and Windsor chairs that blend in well with the original beamed and alcoved nucleus around the serving counter; there's also a separate lounge with easy chairs and sofas; dominoes, playing cards. Well kept Hartleys, Theakstons, and Youngers on handpump; reasonably priced wine list. The sheltered lawn and garden are particularly well tended; close to *Good Walks Guide* Walk 125. Some bedrooms are in the annexe across the garden. *(Recommended by Graham Bush, Simon Turner, Tim and Sue Halstead, Michael Brookes, Simon Baker, Peter Watkins, Pam Stanley, Andy and Jill Kassube, J A Edwards, Steve Dark, GB)*

Free house   Licensee Derek Connor   Real ale   Meals and snacks (12–2, 6.30–9.30)   Restaurant   Children welcome   Open 11–3, 6–11   Bedrooms tel Eskdale (094 03) 244 (or 337/308/395);   £35B/£48B

FAUGH   NY5155   Map 9

String of Horses   🍺

From A69 in Warwick Bridge, turn off at Heads Nook, Castle Carrock signpost, then follow Faugh signs – if you have to ask the way, it's pronounced Faff

The walls of the several cosy communicating rooms of the open-plan bar in this 17th-century inn are panelled or covered with Laura Ashley wallpaper. There are heavy beams, fine old settles and elaborately carved Gothick seats and tables, as well as simpler Windsor and other chairs, and log fires in cool weather (which may even mean a summer evening); decorations include brass pots and warming pans, and some interesting antique prints on the cream walls. Bar food includes sandwiches, home-made soup (£1.25), filled Yorkshire puddings or lunchtime ploughman's (£2.75), Cumberland sausage (£3.50), salads (from £3.95), steak and mushroom pie or chicken tikka (£4.95), gammon with peach and cottage cheese (£4.95); also, daily specials like Hungarian goulash or sweet and sour pork fillet, good home-made puddings (£1.75), and Sunday roast lunch. Several malt whiskies and an extensive wine list; fruit machine, trivia and piped music. Outside, it's pretty, with Dutch blinds and lanterns, and more lanterns and neat wrought iron among the greenery of the sheltered terrace. Residents have the use of a Jacuzzi, sauna, solarium and small outdoor heated pool. *(Recommended by John and Anne McIver, Richard Holloway, Dr R H M Stewart, Steve Dark; more reports please)*

Free house   Licensees Anne and Eric Tasker   Meals and snacks (12–2.30, 7–10)   Restaurant   Children welcome   Occasional live music in restaurant Sat   Open 11.30–3, 5.30–11   Bedrooms tel Hayton (0228) 70297 or 70509; £55B/£62B

GRASMERE   NY3406   Map 9

Wordsworth Hotel   🍺

In village itself

For such a touristy village, the little beamed bar – the Dove & Olive – in this up-market hotel is unpretentious and local in its atmosphere. Good value, simple bar food includes home-made soup (£1.25), filled wheatmeal rolls (£1.25), generously filled baked potatoes (£1.75), vegetarian lasagne (£2.50), and shepherd's pie or ploughman's (£3.25). There are stuffed fish, fox masks and brushes, sea and sporting prints, and photographs of the local fell races on the walls; a good winter log fire, big bare beams with nice plates, and mate's chairs and attractively cushioned built-in seats around cast-iron-framed tables on the slate floor. Well kept Bass Special on handpump, and a good hot toddy. There are sturdy old teak seats in a slate-floored verandah leading out of the bar, and the hotel gardens are very neat; near the start of *Good Walks Guide* Walk 129. *(Recommended by Lesley Sones, Geralyn Meyler, Mary Ann Cameron; more reports please)*

Free house   Licensee Robin Lees   Real ale   Lunchtime meals and snacks Restaurant   No children under 14   Open 11–3(4 Sat), 6–11   Bedrooms tel Grasmere (096 65) 592; £42B/£84B

nr HAWKSHEAD   SD3598 Map 9

Drunken Duck

Barngates; the hamlet is signposted from B5286 Hawkshead–Ambleside, opposite the Outgate Inn; OS Sheet 90 map reference 350013

This old white pub, completely remote in peaceful hill country, is popular (notably at weekends and holiday times) for its home-made bar food; chalked up on a board and changing daily, this includes filled rolls (£1.25), soup such as curried parsnip (£1.50), pâtés such as celery and nut or tuna, dill and garlic (£2.75), ploughman's (£3.25), red bean casserole or stuffed vine leaves (£3.75), ricotta, stilton and apple cannelloni (£4), chilli con carne, chicken in a paprika cream sauce or a selection of pies (all £4.25), and lots of puddings such as jam or syrup roly poly or sticky toffee pudding (£1.75); friendly service. There's an unchanging atmosphere in the several pubby rooms, furnished with ladderback country chairs, blond pews, cushioned old settles, and tapestried stools on fitted Turkey carpet; there are also beams, good fires, lots of landscapes, Cecil Aldin prints, and a big longcase clock. Well kept Marstons Pedigree, Tetleys Bitter, Theakstons XB and Old Peculier, and Yates Bitter on handpump; over 70 whiskies and their own-label wine; darts, dominoes. Seats on the front verandah look across to Lake Windermere in the distance; to the side there are quite a few rustic wooden chairs and tables, sheltered by a stone wall with alpine plants along its top, and the pub has fishing in two private tarns behind. The bedrooms have been refurbished in a chintzy and Laura Ashley style; good breakfasts. Dogs welcome. *(Recommended by A T Longton, Dave Braisted, W A and S Rinaldi-Butcher, Tim and Sue Halstead, Viv Middlebrook, C F Walling, Andy and Jill Kassube, Andrew and Ruth Triggs, Simon Bates, H K Dyson, Cathy Long, Bev and Doug Warrick, Brian and Anna Marsden, Steve and Carolyn Harvey, Greg Parston)*

Free house   Licensee Peter Barton   Real ale   Meals and snacks (12–2, 6.30–9.30) Restaurant (open to residents only on Sun)   Children in rooms away from main bar Open 11.30–3, 6–11   Bedrooms tel Hawkshead (096 66) 347; £30B/£52.50B

HAWKSHEAD   SD3598 Map 9

Kings Arms 🛏

Overlooking the central square of the delightful Elizabethan village, the terrace here is a fine place to sit, with its old-fashioned teak seats and oak cask tables around the roses. The low-ceilinged bar has an open fire, red-cushioned wall and window seats and red plush stools on the Turkey carpet; open fire. Bar food includes home-made soup (£1.10), lunchtime sandwiches (from £1.30), ploughman's (from £3.10), Cumberland sausage (£3.30), salads (from £2.80; prawn £5.75), half a herby chicken (£3.85), home-made steak and kidney pie or lasagne (£3.95), and 8oz sirloin steak (£6.45), with specials like mushroom stroganoff or honey roast ham with peaches; puddings and children's meals (£2.10); the restaurant is no-smoking. Matthew Browns Mild and Tetleys on handpump, with Theakstons Best and Old Peculier under light blanket pressure; darts, dominoes, fruit machine and piped pop music. The coins embedded in the oak beams of some of the bedrooms are very much in keeping with the picturesque old-fashionedness of the inn. They supply free permits to guests for the nearby public car park. *(Recommended by N E Bushby, W H Bland, H K Dyson, Brian and Anna Marsden, Gary Scott; more reports on food service please)*

Free house   Licensee Rosalie Johnson   Real ale   Meals and snacks (12–2, 6–9.30) Restaurant   Well behaved children welcome   Open 11–11   Bedrooms tel Hawkshead (096 66) 372;   £19.50(£22B)/£32(£39B)

Queens Head

The village – a charming and virtually car-free network of stone-paved alleys winding through huddles of whitewashed cottages – very much adds to the atmosphere of this busy pub. Popular bar food includes home-made soup (£1.20), lunchtime sandwiches (from £1.25, bacon and egg brunch bap £2.50, open sandwiches from £2.75), pâté (£2.75), ploughman's (£3.50), salads (from £4), Cumberland sausage (£3.95), tagliatelle carbonara (£4.50), beef goulash (£4.75), grilled gammon with egg or pineapple (£5.25), and steaks (from £6.50); puddings (£1.95); the dining room is no-smoking. The low-ceilinged, open-plan bar has heavy bowed black beams, red leatherette wall seats and plush stools around heavy traditional tables – mostly used by diners – on the discreetly patterned red carpet, a few plates decorating one panelled wall, and a snug little room leading off. Well kept Hartleys XB and Robinsons Bitter on handpump. *(Recommended by James and Libby Cane, W H Bland, Viv Middlebrook, Dennis and Pat Jones, N E Bushby, E J Knight, BKA, R H Sawyer, M A Watts, H K Dyson, Mary Ann Cameron, Gary Scott, S J Willmot, Ewan McCall)*

Hartleys (Robinsons)   Licensee Tony Merrick   Real ale   Meals and snacks (12–2.30, 6.15–9.30)   Restaurant (closed Sun lunchtime)   Children in restaurant and eating area of bar   Open 11–11   Bedrooms tel Hawkshead (096 66) 271; £23.50(£30)/£39(£46B)

HEVERSHAM   SD4983 Map 9

Blue Bell

A6 (now a relatively very quiet road here)

Over the years this dazzlingly white and partly black-timbered inn has quietly expanded at the back and out of its vicarage roots; and as it's on a slight hill, it very much dominates the surrounding, modest fields. Inside, there are pewter platters hanging from the beams in the bay-windowed lounge bar, and small antique sporting prints on the partly panelled walls, an antique carved settle, comfortable cushioned Windsor armchairs and upholstered stools on the flowery carpet; in cool weather there's an open fire. One big bay-windowed area has been divided off as a children's room, and the long, tiled-floor, quieter public bar has darts and dominoes. Bar food, still relatively good value, includes home-made soup (£1.10), open sandwiches (from £1.20, smoked salmon £2.90), locally baked steak and kidney pie (£2.20), tasty Morecambe Bay potted shrimps (£2.25), home-made quiche (£2.40), home-made cottage pie (£2.60) and salads (from £4.75, fresh salmon £5.25). Well kept Sam Smiths OB and Museum on handpump; helpful staff; darts, dominoes and cribbage. Crossing over the A6 into the village itself, you come to a picturesque church with a rambling little graveyard; if you walk through this and on to the hills beyond, there's a fine view across to the estuary of the River Kent; the estuary itself is a short walk from the pub, down the country road that runs by its side. *(Recommended by Pamela E Roper, D J Cooke, Raymond Palmer, D T Taylor, Dr T W Hoskins, Bev and Doug Warrick, Roger Bellingham, D Singleton)*

Sam Smiths   Licensee Christopher Bates   Real ale   Meals and snacks   Restaurant Children in own room   Occasional live music   Open 11–3, 6–11   Bedrooms tel Milnthorpe (05395) 62018; £30(£40S)/£55B

KESWICK NY2624 Map 9
Dog & Gun

Lake Road; off top end of Market Square

The open-plan bar in this lively old place has a long serving counter with a slate floor in front of it, and the carpeted back area has upholstered settles, a cast-iron stove, and old beams taken from a local pub undergoing renovation. In one room there are low beams studded with coins, wheelback chairs and upholstered, high-backed settles on the bare floorboards, and an open fire; a fine collection of striking mountain photograpahs by the local firm G P Abrahams are hung on the walls. Popular, reasonably priced bar food includes home-made French onion soup (£1), sandwiches (from £1.25), and hot home-roasted ham with garlic bread, fresh Borrowdale trout, home-made Hungarian goulash and hot roast poussin (all £4.25). Well kept Theakstons Best, XB and Old Peculier on handpump; dominoes, fruit machine and piped music. On Friday and Saturday evenings they have a doorman who may turn away groups of young men. *(Recommended by W H Bland, Ben Wimpenny, H K Dyson, W H Bland, Andrew and Ruth Triggs, Dick Brown, D J Cooke, Pat and Dennis Jones, Simon Bates, Steve Waters, R F Plater)*

Matthew Browns (S&N)   Licensee Frank Hughes   Real ale   Meals and snacks (12–2.30, 6–9.30)   Children in eating area of bar lunchtime and early evening   Open 11–11 (11–5, 6–11 Sat, 11–3, 6–11 winter); closed 25 Dec

KIRKBY LONSDALE SD6278 Map 7
Sun 🛏

Market St (B6254)

Generous and popular helpings of homely bar food in this atmospheric little inn include sandwiches, local Cumberland sausage or haddock, pizzas (£3.50), beef and Guinness casserole (£3.95), home-made chicken Kiev or filled with ham and cheese (£4.95), and steak (£7.95). The several comfortably modernised and rambling rooms have low beams, green plush cushioned seats, captain's and spindleback chairs on the red carpet, and winter fires; also, a large collection of some three hundred banknotes, maps, old engravings, and battleaxes on the walls, some of which are stripped to bare stone or have panelled dados; the stools by the long bar counter in the front room have good backrests. The restaurant has now been refurbished, but against their hopes they haven't been able to incorporate the 16th-century arched cellar. Well kept Boddingtons, Marstons Pedigree, Whitbreads Castle Eden and Youngers Scotch and No 3 on handpump, and several malt whiskies; quick, cheerful service; dominoes and piped music. There's an unusual pillared porch outside in the cobbled alley. *(Recommended by Mr and Mrs R P Begg, Michael Marlow, Sarah Bullard, Jill and Paul Ormrod)*

Free house   Licensees Andrew and Belinda Wilkinson   Real ale   Meals and snacks (12–2, 6–10)   Restaurant   Children welcome   Open 11–11   Bedrooms tel Kirkby Lonsdale (05242) 71965;   £18.50(£18.50B)/£32.50(£37.50B)

LANGDALE NY2906 Map 9
Old Dungeon Ghyll 🛏

B5343

This inn, dramatically surrounded by fells – including the Langdale Pikes flanking the Dungeon Ghyll Force waterfall which inspired Wordsworth's poem 'The Idle Shepherd Boys' – has a cosy and characterful bar, with a simplicity to its furnishings that really appeals to readers. It's particularly adapted to the needs of the walkers and climbers who use it most, with window seats cut into the enormously thick stone walls, a huge fire, and a grand view of the Pike of Blisco rising behind Kettle Crag. Hartleys Mild, Marstons Pedigree, Theakstons Old Peculier, Yates Bitter and guest beers on handpump; a choice of snuffs; darts, cribbage, shove-ha'penny and dominoes. Good value bar food includes home-made soup with home-made bread (£1.20), Cumberland sausage (£3.80), and lasagne or chilli con carne (£3.95); book if you want a full evening meal. It can get really lively on a Saturday night. *(Recommended by Steve Dark, Andy and Jill Kassube, H K Dyson, Andrew and Ruth Triggs, Mike Beiley, R E Horner, BKA, Lesley Sones, Geralyn Meyler, A C and S J Beardsley, Steve Waters, Steve and Carolyn Harvey, M J Lawson, Brian and Anna Marsden, Andrew McKeand)*

Free house Licensee Neil Walmsley Real ale Meals (12–2, 6–8.30) Evening restaurant Children welcome Open 11–11 Bedrooms tel Langdale (096 67) 272; £19.75(£23B)/£39.50(£46B)

LEVENS SD4886 Map 7
Hare & Hounds

Village signposted from A590; since completion of dual carriageway link, best approach is following route signposted for high vehicles

The low-beamed, carpeted lounge bar in this village pub is furnished with a wicker-backed Jacobean-style armchair and antique settle on its sloping floor, as well as old-fashioned brown leatherette dining seats and red-cushioned seats built into the partly panelled walls. The tap room at the front is a snug place, and has darts, cribbage and dominoes; there's a golden-oldie juke box and a fruit machine in the separate pool room, down some steps. Vaux Samson and Lorimers Best Scotch on handpump, with Wards Bitter on electric pump. Bar food includes soup (£1), lunchtime sandwiches (from £1.05) or ploughman's (£2.45), plaice or wheat and walnut casserole (£3.35), steak and kidney pie (£3.45), salads (from £3.50), with extra dishes in the evening such as gammon (£5.20) and steak (£6.55). The new licensees who took over at the end of 1989 have kept most of the staff. *(Recommended by Edward and Jean Rycroft, Mr and Mrs Simon Turner, Ruth Humphrey, Simon Bates, Dr R Fuller, D T Taylor, J Scarisbrick, Steve Waters, Roger Bellingham, Margaret and Roy Randle; more reports on the new regime please)*

Vaux Licensees Pat and Maggie Dolan Real ale Meals and snacks; no food Sun-Tues evenings Nov-Mar Children in eating area of bar lunchtime and 7–8pm Open 11–3, 6–11

LITTLE LANGDALE NY3204 Map 9
Three Shires 🏠

From A593 3 miles W of Ambleside take small road signposted The Langdales, Wrynose Pass; then bear left at first fork

This comfortable stone-built inn has an extended back bar with antique oak carved settles, country kitchen chairs and stools on its big dark slate flagstones, local photographs on the walls, and a coal fire in cool weather. Ruddles County and Websters Yorkshire on handpump, lots of malt whiskies and a comprehensive wine list; darts, dominoes. Bar food includes soup (£1.20), lunchtime sandwiches (from £1.20), good ploughman's (from £3.20), salads (from £3.50), Cumberland sausage (£3.85), home-made steak and kidney pie or a vegetarian dish of the day (£4), local trout (£5), and sirloin steak (£6.75); in the evening, dishes are slightly more expensive; good breakfasts. There are lovely views from the terrace out over the valley to the partly wooded hills below Tilberthwaite Fells, and there are more seats on a well kept lawn behind the car park, backed by a small oak wood. The pub is on *Good Walks Guide* Walk 128. *(Recommended by M A Watts, R C Watkins, M H Box, H W and A B Tuffill, Lt G I Mitchell, David Goldstone)*

Free house Licensee Ian Stephenson Real ale Meals and snacks (no food in evening, Dec and Jan) Restaurant (closed Sun lunchtime) Children in eating area of bar if eating – till 9pm Open 11–11; 11.30–2.30, 8–10.30 in winter; closed 25 Dec Bedrooms tel Langdale (096 67) 215; £22(£26B)/£44(£52B)

LOWESWATER NY1222 Map 9
Kirkstile

From B5289 follow signs to Loweswater Lake; OS Sheet 89, map reference 140210

Between Loweswater and Crummock Water, this popular little country inn is surrounded by arresting peaks and fells, best appreciated from the big bow windows in one of the rooms off the main bar. The bar itself is low-beamed and carpeted, with partly stripped stone walls, comfortably cushioned small settles and pews, and a big log fire. Well kept Jennings on handpump, and a good choice of malt whiskies; darts, dominoes, chess and a slate shove-ha'penny board; a side games room called the Little Barn has pool, fruit machine, space game and juke box. Bar food includes home-made filled rolls (from £1.10), good soup (£1.35), filled baked potatoes (from £1.80), ploughman's (£2.60), omelettes (from £3.20), vegetarian casserole (£3.25), and steak (£7.95), with weekend specials; good breakfasts, morning coffee. There are picnic-table sets on the lawn. (*Recommended by Michael Brookes, Dr and Mrs A K Clarke, Simon J Barber, Caroline Wright, P J and S E Robbins, Simon Bates, Jon and Jacquie Payne*)

Free house   Licensees Ken and Shirley Gorley   Real ale   Meals and snacks Restaurant (closed Sun lunchtime)   Children welcome   Open 11–11   Bedrooms tel Lorton (090 085) 219; £24.50(£32.50B)/£32.50(£39.50B)

LOWICK GREEN SD2985 Map 9
Farmers Arms

A590 N from Ulverston, then left on to A5092 after about 4 miles

A few miles south of Coniston Water, this busy, rambling old hotel has a heavy-beamed public bar with huge flagstones and a handsome fireplace with a big open fire; some seats are in cosy side alcoves. The hotel itself is across the yard, with its own plusher lounge bar, and a preserved spinning gallery. Bar food includes home-made soup (£1.75), sandwiches (from £1.95; open £4.50), Morecambe Bay potted shrimps (£2.95), ploughman's (£3.75), salads (£4.50), home-made steak and kidney pie in stout (£4.50), and sirloin steak (£6.50). Youngers on handpump, and a decent wine list; dominoes, fruit and trivia machines, juke box, and piped music; also pool room and darts alley. (*Recommended by Raymond Palmer, Mary and Lionel Tonks, Simon Bates*)

Scottish & Newcastle   Licensee Alan Lockwell   Real ale   Meals and snacks Restaurant   Children welcome   Open 11–11; closed 25 Dec and 1 Jan   Bedrooms tel Greenodd (0229) 861376 or 861277; £24(£35B)/£48B

MELMERBY NY6237 Map 10
Shepherds ⊘

About halfway along A686 Penrith–Alston

For some readers who use it regularly, the quality of the food here is the standard by which they judge other pubs. Only local produce (and local butchers) is used where possible, and there are nice touches such as home-made rolls; the wide range includes home-made pasties, soup (£1.30), pork and port pâté (£2.60), ploughman's with over 20 good cheeses to choose from – the mature cheddar is *really* mature – (from £2.60), home-cooked ham (£3.70), plaice (£3.90), flavoursome Cumberland sausage and egg (£3.80), chicken curry or lasagne (£4.90), steak and kidney pie (£5), beef goulash, very tender spiced lamb with yoghurt or chicken breast Leoni (all £5.50), and steaks (from £7.80); lots of daily specials, vegetarian dishes such as chestnut and mushroom pie or ratatouille pancakes (£4.90), surprise starters like pasta with strong gorgonzola, Sunday roast lunch (£4) and tasty home-made puddings (£1.50); good, friendly table service. The red-sandstone pub itself is spacious, with cushioned wall seats, sunny window seats, sensible tables and chairs, light-panelling, lots of pot plants, and an open fire. A games bar has darts, pool, shove-ha'penny, table skittles, dominoes and fruit machine. Well kept Marstons Burton, Pedigree, Merrie Monk and Owd Rodger on handpump, as well as 40 malt whiskies. Hartside Nursery Garden, a noted alpine and primula plant specialist, is just over the Hartside Pass, and there are fine views across the green to the Pennines. *(Recommended by PLC, Richard Holloway, Janet and John Towers, Andy and Jill Kassube, W H Bland, David Morrell, Simon Ward, L D Rainger, Mr and Mrs M Wall, E V Walder, R J Yates, M A and W R Proctor, GB)*

Marstons   Licensee Martin Baucutt   Real ale   Meals and snacks (11–2.30, 6–9.45; 12–2, 7–9.45 Sun)   Children in eating area lunchtime and till 8.30   Open 11.30–3, 6–11; closed 25 Dec

NEAR SAWREY   SD3796   Map 9
Tower Bank Arms

B5285 towards the Windermere ferry

The traditionally furnished, low-beamed main bar here has local hunting photographs, a grandfather clock, high-backed settles on the rough slate floor, a big cooking range with a lovely log fire, and maybe Emma, Maxwell or Nelson the pub's labradors. Matthew Browns Mild, Theakstons Best, XB and Old Peculier, and Youngers Scotch on handpump, as well as several malt whiskies and wine bottled for the pub; darts, shove-ha'penny, dominoes and cribbage. Lunchtime bar food includes home-made soup (£1.20), filled brown rolls (from £1.20), ploughman's (£2.90), home-made quiche (£3.50), and a home-made pie of the day (£3.75); more substantial evening main meals such as grilled gammon and eggs or Esthwaite trout (£5), and steaks; good, sticky puddings; helpful service. It does get crowded in summer. The black and white pub is owned by the National Trust, and there are good views outside of the wooded Claife Heights. Beatrix Potter's farm is just behind. *(Recommended by D T Taylor, Mr and Mrs Simon Turner, Ben Wimpenny, A T Langton, James and Libby Cane, Michael Brookes, Ruth Humphrey, Steve and Carolyn Harvey, Steve Waters, Gary Scott)*

Free house   Licensee Philip Broadley   Real ale   Meals and lunchtime snacks (not 25 Dec)   Restaurant   Children in eating area of bar lunchtime, in restaurant lunchtime and evening   11–3, 6–11   Bedrooms tel Hawkshead (096 66) 334; £21B/£32B

OUTGATE   SD3699   Map 9
Outgate Inn

B5286 Ambleside–Hawkshead

Comfortably modernised and well kept, this clean roadside pub has three neatly carpeted communicating room areas. All have local photographs and country prints, often carefully lit, but the decor and furnishings vary from each to each – button-back wall banquettes as opposed to country-kitchen and housekeeper's chairs, exposed joists rather than plaster ceiling, an alcovey feel with shelves of books and oddments in a cosy corner instead of big windows looking out through the beech trees to steep pastures. Popular bar food includes sandwiches (from 95p; open prawn £3.50), soup or a bowl of chips (£1), herrings in sour cream (£1.95), burgers or haddock (£2.95), gammon and egg (£3.75), home-made steak and kidney pie (£3.95), 8oz sirloin steak (£6.75) and several children's dishes (from £1.20); well kept Hartleys XB and Robinsons on handpump, friendly service, open fires, darts, dominoes, cards, maybe restrained piped music. There are a couple of tables in front. *(Recommended by H Carline, Denzil Taylor, A T Langton, G J S May, Terry Glendenning, Ben Winpenny, Kathleen Morley)*

Hartleys (Robinsons)   Licensees Ian and Katrina Kirsopp   Real ale   Meals and snacks   Children welcome till 9   Jazz Fri   Open 11–3, 6–11   Bedrooms tel Hawkshead (096 66) 413; £15/£30

SCALES NY3427 Map 9

White Horse ⊘

A66 1 1/2 miles E of Threlkeld: keep your eyes skinned – it looks like a farmhouse up on a slope

From this isolated cluster of pub and farm buildings, tracks lead up into the splendidly daunting and rocky fells around Blencathra – which have names like Foule Crag and Sharp Edge. The unanimously praised bar food is made mainly from local produce, and there are no convenience foods; the range at lunchtime (when it's advisable to get there early) includes home-made soup such as spinach, cream and nutmeg (£1.25), savoury flan or peach halves filled with garlic and herb cream cheese (£2.95), a good ploughman's (£3.25), potted shrimps with hot garlic bread or prawn open sandwich (£3.75), Waberthwaite Cumberland sausage with mushrooms (£4.75), and superb Waberthwaite Cumberland ham with two eggs (£4.75); in the evenings (when booking is advisable and often pretty much essential – Threlkeld (059 683) 241) – there are dishes like good poached Borrowdale trout (£5.95), pork fillet with sherry and mushroom sauce (£7.50), steaks (£8.25), and seasonal specials like local salmon, grouse, venison and muscovy duck; tasty puddings such as home-made brown bread and honey ice-cream or fresh strawberry cheesecake (from £1.95). The beamed bar, which extends into the old kitchen (now no-smoking), has quite a hunting theme – hunting pictures and local hunting cartoons on the walls, and a growing range of locally mounted animals and birds native to the area; there's also dark oak high-backed settle-style seating upholstered in deep red, an unusual textured wall hanging showing a white horse on the fells, warm winter fires, and candles and flowers on the tables; a cosy little snug is installed in what used to be the dairy. Well kept Jennings on handpump, some malts; cheery, efficient service; dominoes. There are wooden settles, flower boxes and tubs outside. The inn sign is new this year. *(Recommended by Graham Bush, Mr and Mrs Simon Turner, Stephanie Sowerby, Pat and Dennis Jones, A M Neal, Lesley Sones, Geralyn Meyler, Caroline Wright, Mary and Lionel Tonks, Sue Holland, Dave Webster, Hayward Wane, Mr and Mrs M Wall, H W and A B Tuffill, PLC)*

Free house   Licensees Laurence and Judith Slattery   Real ale   Meals and lunchtime snacks   Children over 5 in eating area   Open 11–3, 6–11; 12–2, 7–11 in winter; closed 25 Dec

STAINTON NY4928 Map 10

Kings Arms

1 3/4 miles from M6 junction 40: village signposted from A66 towards Keswick, though quickest to fork left at A592 roundabout then turn first right

The open-plan bar in this modernised old pub has leatherette wall banquettes, stools and armchairs, wood-effect tables, brasses on the black beams and swirly cream walls; piped music. Good value bar food includes soup (90p), sandwiches (from £1, open sandwiches from £2), filled baked potato (£1.30), home-made steak and kidney pie (£2.80), Cumberland sausage with egg (£2.90), salads (from £2.90), home roast ham (£3), spinach and walnut lasagne (£3.30), local trout (£3.50), delicious farmhouse gammon with egg or pineapple (£3.60), and sirloin steak (£5.50). Well kept Whitbreads Castle Eden on handpump; pleasant staff. Sensibly placed darts, dominoes, fruit machine, fairly quiet juke box, piped music. Quiet on a weekday lunchtime, it's probably at its best in the evenings, when there's a good mix of locals and visitors. There are tables outside on the side terrace and a small lawn. *(Recommended by R F Plater, Richard Dolphin, Mr and Mrs J H Adam, Cdr J W Hackett, Simon Ward; more reports please)*

Whitbreads   Licensee Raymond Tweddle   Real ale   Meals and snacks   Children welcome if eating   Country and Western Sun evening once a month   Open 11–3, 6(7 winter)–11

TIRRIL   NY5126   Map 10

Queens Head

3 1/2 miles from M6 junction 40; take A66 towards Brough, A6 towards Shap, then B5320 towards Ullswater

Up until a few years ago this was Italian run, with quite an emphasis on an open-plan, modern pizzeria behind the bar area. A change of brewery and licensee led to considerable redevelopment, both in the restaurant and upstairs, where there are now bedrooms. The main bar area at the front is more or less unchanged, with low bare beams, black panelling, old-fashioned high-backed settles and some armchairs and sofas, and a roomy inglenook fireplace (once a cupboard for smoking hams); under the flowery carpet is raw rock which was quarried out as the inn's floor in the early 18th century; a friendly, old-fashioned atmosphere. The comprehensive range of bar food includes soup (£1.10), lunchtime sandwiches (from £1.30), Cumberland sausage (£2.95), salads (from £3.50), home-made pies such as vegetable or beef and venison (£3.50), with extra evening dishes such as chicken (£4.50), rack of lamb (£4.95) and steak (£5.95); puddings (from £1.25) and children's menu (£1.95). Matthew Browns Lion Bitter on handpump; piped music, darts, pool, dominoes, fruit and trivia machine, space game and juke box in the back part. Part of the restaurant is no-smoking. *(Recommended by Gwen and Peter Andrews, Martin Ragg, SS, Wayne Brindle, Tim Halstead, Brian and Anna Marsden, Gary Wilkes)*

Matthew Browns (S & N)   Licensee Paul Louis   Real ale   Meals and snacks (11.30–2.30, 6.30–9.30)   Restaurant   Children welcome   Open 11–3, 6–11 Bedrooms tel Penrith (0768) 63219; £20.50/£28(£33B)

ULVERSTON   SD2978   Map 7

Bay Horse ⊘

Canal Foot

The range of food here is select, imaginative and decidedly restauranty; however since becoming a free house last May they do now serve food at lunchtimes in the bar itself. The selection here gives you some idea of what to expect of the restaurant: as well as home-made baps (£1.20) and soup (£1.25), there's home-made herb and cheese pâté (£3.75), melon with Cumbrian air-dried ham and damson cheese tartlet (£3.95), Cumberland sausage with onion and red pepper marmalade and apple sauce or meat and potato pie (£4.50), minced lamb with tomato and almonds topped with egg custard or barbecue spare ribs (£4.95), cod with mushroom pâté and spinach purée in a cheese and brandy sauce (£5.50), and Scotch salmon in a white wine and herb cream sauce (£6.25). Also new this year is the grill, with well hung Scotch steaks (from £10.50); three-course set lunch in the no-smoking restaurant (£11.50) – the view from here across to Morecambe Bay is outstanding. The civilised but pubby smallish bar has black beams and props with lots of horsebrasses, attractive wooden armchairs, glossy hardwood traditional tables, some pale green plush built-in wall banquettes, blue plates on a Delft shelf, and a huge but elegant stone horse's head. Besides well kept Mitchells ESB and guests such as Marstons Pedigree and local Yates on handpump, there's a decent choice of spirits, and a wine list with a strong emphasis on New-World wines (the sweet Morris Old Liqueur Muscat from Australia, sold by the glass, is recommended). Magazines are dotted about; there's a handsomely marbled green granite fireplace, and decently reproduced piped music; dominoes, chess, bagatelle, cribbage and draughts. There are picnic-table sets out on the terrace. The owners also run an outstanding restaurant at their Miller Howe hotel on Windermere. *(Recommended by Steve and Maureen Collins and others; more reports please)*

Free house   Licensee Robert Lyons   Real ale   Lunchtime meals and snacks (not Mon)   Restaurant Ulverston (0229) 53972 (not Sun; closed Jan and Feb)   Children in eating area   Open 11–3, 6–11

WASDALE HEAD NY1808 Map 9

Wasdale Head Inn 🍺

To NE of lake; signposted from Gosforth

This gabled old hotel is actually named after its first landlord, Will Ritson, who for his tall stories was reputed to be the world's biggest liar; in his memory they still hold liar competitions here towards the end of November. The high-ceilinged, spacious main bar has a polished slate floor, shiny panelling, cushioned settles, fine George Abraham photographs on the walls, and a log-effect gas fire; there's an adjoining pool room, as well as a panelled and comfortably old-fashioned residents' bar and lounge. Well kept Jennings, Theakstons Best and Old Peculier and Yates on handpump, and a good selection of malt whiskies; dominoes, cribbage. Home-made bar food includes soup (95p), locally potted shrimps (£1.90), cheese and onion flan (£2.10), steak and kidney pie (£2.75), ploughman's (from £2.75), chicken casserole (£3.20) and mixed locally smoked meat salad (£3.80); also daily specials and huge breakfasts. There's a self-catering cottage and two flats in converted inn buildings nearby. As it's well away from the main tourist areas and surrounded by steep fells, it makes an excellent base for walking and climbing; and Wastwater – the most severely grand of all the lakes – is nearby, surrounded by towering screes. *(Recommended by Comus Elliott, Kathleen Morley, Simon Bates, T Galligan, Graham Bush, A C and S J Beardsley, R K Smith, Doug Kennedy)*

Free house   Licensee Jaspar Carr   Real ale   Meals and snacks (11–3, 6–10) Restaurant   Children in own room   Open 11–11; mid Nov–mid March only open Fri evening, Sat, and Sun lunchtime   Bedrooms (they only do dinner, bed and breakfast; no accommodation mid Nov–mid March (except 28 Dec–mid Jan) tel Wasdale (094 67) 26229; £39B/£74B 7

Lucky Dip

Besides the fully inspected pubs, you might like to try these Lucky Dips recommended to us and described by readers (if you do, please send us reports):

Allithwaite [B5277 SW of Grange Over Sands; SD3976], *Guide Over Sands*: Whitbreads house — used to be called Royal Oak but recently refurbished and facilities improved; lunchtime and evening meals very good, Hartleys XB too *(A T Langton)*

Alston [Main St; NY7246], *Angel*: Lively 17th-century pub with good jolly atmosphere, well kept McEwans 70/-, pleasant staff and enjoyable food — open prawn sandwich a meal in itself; good steak and kidney pie, children's helpings; village close to Pennine Way; children welcome; bedrooms *(R J Yates, Len Beattie)*

☆ **Ambleside** [North Rd; NY3804], *Unicorn*: Small backstreet village local with friendly landlord and staff, well kept Hartleys and Robinsons, occasional jazz band, good value food; bedrooms newly refurbished, nice and quiet, with good breakfasts — excellent value *(Andrew and Ruth Triggs, H K Dyson)*

nr **Ambleside** [A592 N of Troutbeck; NY4009], *Kirkstone Pass*: Remote roadside mountain inn — the highest in Lakeland — with wide choice of whiskies, well kept beer, open fire, lively amusements, cheery atmosphere, cheap simple food (all-day summer cafe), fine surrounding scenery; a useful shelter in bad weather, and at its best in winter; bedrooms *(Steve Waters, Simon Bates, LYM)*

Appleby [by stn; NY6921], *Midland*: Worth knowing especially for railway buffs, as this severe-looking building is right by the station on the famous Settle—Carlisle line, with railway memorabilia in its two smallish bars; Marstons Pedigree on handpump *(John and Joan Wyatt)*

Arnside [SD4678], *Albion*: Plain corner pub in fine site on quiet, attractive estuary seafront with great views from bar and waterside tables; tidy, basic interior, pool table, well kept beer, good simple bar food — no pop music; nr start GWG124 *(Graham Bush, MGBD)*

☆ **Askham** [village crossroads by lower green; NY5123], *Queens Head*: Still very popular, though the impressive model railway's gone (there's a pond instead); gleaming copper and brass, Vaux and Wards, friendly staff, bar food inc good steaks on sizzling platters; children in back bar until 9; bedrooms comfortable *(Richard Holloway, Roger Broadie, P Corris, John Atherton, Roger Etherington, LYM)*

Bampton [NY5118], *St Patricks Well*: Friendly welcome, well kept beer, quickly served home-cooked bar food; bedrooms excellent value, with basic facilities and good breakfasts *(Dr and Mrs R J Ashleigh, C A Holloway)*

Bardsea [SD3074], *Bradylls Arms*: Popular, pleasant village pub overlooking Morecambe Bay, bar food in extended dining lounge now the main focus *(Raymond Palmer)*

Barrow in Furness [Holbeck Park Ave, Roose; SD2069], *Crofters*: Converted farmhouse with barbecue park, well kept Thwaites on handpump, bar food *(Anon)*

Borrowdale [Ravenscraig; NY2515], *Sca Fell*: Remote hotel with good Riverside Bar, just right for walkers *(Graham Bush)*

☆ **Bowness on Windermere** [SD4097], *Hole in t' Wall*: Ancient pub with farm tools, smith's bellows, ploughshares etc in slate-floored lower bar (which can get crowded), handsome if simply furnished panelled upper room with fine plaster ceiling, simple lunchtime food, well kept Hartleys XB on handpump, quick service; lots of pow, zap and bleep from pool room games machines, intensive juke box; rustic tables in nice flagstoned courtyard *(Steve Waters, E J Knight, Andy and Jill Kassube, Roy Butler, LYM)*

Bowness on Windermere [Rayrigg Rd], *John Peel*: Friendly atmosphere, well kept Theakstons Best, XB and Old Peculier, reasonably priced food; open all day *(Dennis and Pat Jones); Royal Oak*: Decent local just out of tourist mainstream; well kept Castle Eden *(Peter Barnsley)*

☆ **Braithwaite** [NY2324], *Coledale*: Comfortable and popular, with busy lounge bar and dining room and friendly, efficient service; wide range of food ideal for hungry hikers, with children's specials; attractive setting; may be out (even from garden) by 9.30 *(Mr and Mrs D J Nash, KC)*

Brigsteer [OS Sheet 97 map reference 481896; SD4889], *Wheatsheaf*: Well kept Castle Eden, good bar food — especially soups, gammon sandwiches and Cumberland sausages with proper sauce *(A T Langton)*

Brough Sowerby [A685; NY7913], *Black Bull*: Well kept beer and good, decent food in quiet pub with separate dining area; very clean, with welcoming licensees *(K H Frostick)*

Broughton in Furness [Foxfield Rd; SD2187], *Eccle Riggs*: Well kept real ale, good value bar food, extensive Sun lunchtime buffet, children's menu (they can use the small but pleasant indoor swimming pool free if they eat here); food service may be leisurely; bedrooms *(Brian Jones);* [A595 towards Millom], *High Cross*: Free house under newish licensees, with well kept Websters, good bar and restaurant meals; bedrooms *(A T Langton)*

☆ **Buttermere** [NY1817], *Bridge*: Good lunchtime bar food in simply furnished but comfortable lounge bar of extended stone hotel, well kept Theakstons Best, XB and Old Peculier on handpump, tables on flagstoned terrace; in a lovely spot, handy for Crummock Water and Buttermere — the pretty little village, at the start of GWG135, fills with walkers in summer (though they don't allow boots or walking gear here); evening restaurant; prices not low, but helpings generous; a black mark is that you can't order just a starter on its own as a light snack, and their exclusion of vinegar — they say it might spoil the beer — seems a trifle

high-handed; bedrooms *(Graham Bush, Mr and Mrs Simon Turner, Ben Wimpenny, H K Dyson, G J Lewis, Richard Holloway, LYM)*

☆ **Cark in Cartmel** [SD3776], *Engine*: Friendly and comfortably modernised with lots of brasses and flowers, good open fire, friendly and attentive newish landlord, well kept Bass, good range of whiskies, piped music; tables out by little stream. *(A T Langton, LYM)*

Cartmel [off main sq; SD3879], *Cavendish Arms*: Well kept Bass, good bar food inc particularly good freshly made sandwiches, prompt polite service *(A T Langton, Mr and Mrs J H Bloom);* [The Square], *Kings Arms*: Picturesque and friendly pub nicely placed at the head of the attractive town square — rambling bar with heavy beams but clean and bright decor, bar food (they're generous with the prawns, and soup's been enjoyed), well kept Whitbreads Castle Eden; popular with young locals; children welcome till 8.30 *(Ruth Humphrey, J Scarisbrick, TBB, Mrs H D Astley, Malcolm Ramsay, LYM);* [The Square], *Royal Oak*: Decent bar food, good garden *(J Scarisbrick)*

☆ **Chapel Stile** [B5343; NY3205], *Wainwrights*: Pleasant and comfortable, in fine setting, with generous helpings of good value food inc children's dishes, well kept Theakstons XB and Old Peculier on handpump, good friendly atmosphere; service usually though not infallibly quick *(J A Edwards, Dave Braisted, H K Dyson, Edward and Jean Rycroft, KC)*

Clifton [A6, S end; NY5327], *George & Dragon*: Small free house with three interlinking rooms, well kept Tetleys, and good value, simple food; games room has darts, pool, and so forth; bedrooms *(Michael Brookes)*

Cockermouth [NY1231], *Trout*: Chintz and red plush in comfortable bar of solid old hotel, well kept restaurant, garden by River Cocker; bedrooms *(Raymond Palmer, P J and S E Robbins, BB; more reports on new regime please)*

Coniston [SD3098], *Crown*: Quickly served bar food, well kept Hartleys on handpump, pictures of the late Sir Donald Campbell; bedrooms *(Roger Huggins)*

☆ **Crosby Ravensworth** [NY6215], *Butchers Arms*: Good value simple food from sandwiches and pizzas through beef in beer, game pie or vegetarian lasagne to steaks, splendidly sticky puddings, well kept Marstons Pedigree, Yates and Youngers Scotch on handpump, very friendly young licensees (as is Sam the spaniel), simple but comfortable furnishings, interesting mountain photographs; this village, like its neighbour Maulds Meaburn, is very pretty indeed; children welcome *(BB)*

Dalton in Furness [Goose Green; SD2273], *Brown Cow*: Lively and busy locals' pub with sensibly knocked-together rooms; a few wooden tables on front terrace *(Brian Jones)*

Dent [SD7187], *Stone Close*: Pleasant and well kept pub in outstandingly pretty mountain village *(D T Taylor)*

Dockray [NY3921], *Royal*: Unpretentious

bar and lounge with seats outside in summer; good food using local produce, especially game pie, Cumberland sausage; very popular with walkers; bedrooms *(Raymond Palmer)*

Dufton [NY6925], *Stag*: Small, basic pub in lovely village; no food, keg beer *(Len Beattie)*

Eamont Bridge [A6, a mile S of A66; handy for M6 junction 40; NY5328], *Beehive*: One-room village pub with Hartleys and Whitbreads, good helpings of bar food; children allowed in for meals, separate play area; interesting inn sign *(P Corris)*; *Crown*: Welcoming pubby lounge bar in hotel, open to non-residents; well cooked, fairly priced food — even a choice of mustards; bedrooms *(Alan Jones)*

Eskdale [Bleabeck; midway between Boot and Hard Knott Pass; NY1400], *Woolpack*: Comfortable roadside inn with small lounge and larger bar with pool table; well kept Youngers IPA on handpump, bar food inc good value sirloin steak; ideal for walkers; bedrooms *(P LLoyd, K Bamford)*

☆ **Eskdale Green** [NY1400], *George IV*: Many-roomed, oak-beamed pub with wide range of good value food, well kept Marstons Pedigree and Theakstons on handpump; over 100 malt whiskies, decent wines; family room, pool, table skittles, fruit machine, and juke box; on GWG125; three bedrooms; has been on the market recently — news please *(Roy Goodwin, P Lloyd, K Bamford)*

☆ **Far Sawrey** [SD3893], *Sawrey*: Interesting if overtly basic Claife Crier stable bar preferred to hotel lounge; wooden stalls dividing tables, harness on rough white walls, good simple food inc wide choice of sandwiches and fine ploughman's, well kept Jennings and Theakstons real ales, staff (and cat) very friendly, service quick; seats on nice lawn look up to Claife Heights, which have good views of Lake Windermere; nr GWG127; bedrooms — attractive special family rates *(Mr and Mrs Simon Turner, Greg Parston, Heather Sharp)*

☆ **Garrigill** [NY7441], *George & Dragon*: 17th-century village pub with friendly and informal welcome in flagstoned bar of genuine character, good ale, good value well presented bar food, unexpectedly comprehensive menu in part stripped-stone, part panelled dining room, running up to duck and pheasant but all freshly cooked; faultless service; on dead-end road in beautiful scenery; bedrooms small but comfortable and clean — good value *(Richard Hooker)*

Glenridding [back of main car park, top of road; NY3917], *Travellers Rest*: Keg beers, but food ideal for hungry youth hostellers and walkers; generous helpings of main dishes, puddings with cream; comfortable and popular, but limited parking; nr start GWG138, nr GWG132 *(KC)*

☆ **Grasmere** [main bypass rd; NY3406], *Swan*: Good home-made bar food in relaxing and attractively old-fashioned lounge of spacious THF hotel, popular with walkers even though it's short on 'local' feel — certainly a

comfortable base for the fells which rise behind; darts in small public bar, well kept Tetleys on handpump, decent range of simple but well prepared bar food inc fine sandwiches, oak beams, inglenook log fires, friendly staff, tables in garden; comfortable bedrooms *(John Gould, Steve Dark)*

Grasmere [on main bypass rd; NY3406], *Travellers Rest*: Wide choice of home-cooked bar meals in homely old roadside pub with Websters real ale, thick carpet stretching from games room through plainly furnished lounge to family dining room, open fire, gentle piped music, tables in small area outside; nr start GWG129; bedrooms comfortable *(Phil Taylor, Janet and Paul Waring, Steve and Carolyn Harvey, BB)*

Great Urswick [SD2775], *General Burgoyne*: Small village pub overlooking small tarn; bar and lounge with open log fires, Hartleys ale and simple bar food *(N M Williams)*

Haverthwaite [A590 Barrow rd — OS Sheet 97 map reference 328842; SD3484], *Dicksons Arms*: Well kept Bass, good bar lunches *(A T Langton)*

Hawkshead [SD3598], *Red Lion*: Comfortably modernised 16th-century inn with old-fashioned touches, lively atmosphere, well kept Ruddles, reasonable bar food; bedrooms *(H K Dyson, BKA, LYM)*

Helton [NY5122], *Helton*: Basic, rural local popular with walkers; friendly welcome, well kept Theakstons on handpump and good, reasonably priced lunchtime and evening bar food *(Andy and Jill Kassube)*

☆ **Hesket Newmarket** [NY3438], *Old Crown*: Small and friendly, with well kept real ales inc their own Blencathra Bitter brewed here; wide range of food, games from shove-ha'penny and dominoes to modern, three-dimensional wooden puzzles, and small lending library (10p a book, for benefit of guide dogs for the blind); bedrooms good value *(Nicola MacLeod)*

Ireby [NY2439], *Sun*: Clean and welcoming, with beams, brasses, horsey bric-a-brac and flowers; reasonable choice of bar meals with several good puddings, woodburning stove *(M A and W R Proctor, Marc and Margaret Wall)*

☆ **Kendal** [Highgate; SD5293], *Olde Fleece*: The best choice here — smart and tastefully refurbished without destroying its olde-worlde character, nice atmosphere in long front and back bars, well kept Youngers real ales, pleasant service, good helpings of useful bar food *(R A Nelson, BKA, Len Beattie)*

☆ **Keswick** [St John's St; NY2624], *George*: Interesting inside, with well worn flagstones, old beams, old-fashioned furnishings as well as modern banquettes in bustling main bar; snug black-panelled side bar with log fire (interesting Wordsworth associations), well kept Theakstons and Yates, good if sometimes rather noisy atmosphere; good value bar food, more upmarket restaurant; trout fishing; bedrooms comfortable *(Graham Bush, Dick Brown, Simon Bates,*

Dick Brown, P Miller, LYM)
Keswick [Main St], *Bank*: Popular local with decent straightforward bar meals, good beer, agreeable licensees, attractive sitting-out area right in the busiest part of town *(Dick Brown)*; [Lake Rd], *Four in Hand*: Small and cosy hotel bar with warm welcome, open fire, lots of bric-a-brac such as horsebrasses and bridles, banknotes, old pictures of Keswick and area, good range of reasonably priced bar food; bedrooms *(Carol and Richard Glover)*; [off Market Sq, behind Queens Hotel], *Old Queens Head*: Modernised olde-worlde pub, large open-plan downstairs bar with low beams, exposed stone, some flagstones, red plush seating, big fire, bric-a-brac on walls, pool table; upstairs room with juke box; warm welcome, good range of bar food *(Carol and Richard Glover)*; [off Market Sq, behind Lloyds Bank], *Pack Horse*: Snug and likeable low-beamed town pub in attractive alley courtyard, well kept Jennings *(LYM)*

☆ **nr Keswick** [Newlands Valley — OS Sheet 90 map reference 242217], *Swinside*: Clean and friendly country inn in peaceful valley surrounded by marvellous crags and fells — tables outside, and picture-window upstairs dining room, make the most of the view; wide choice of bar food from good sandwiches and massive ploughman's to generous main dishes — but maybe no soup; Jennings Mild and Bitter, good parking; bedrooms *(KC, Margaret and Roy Randle, LYM)*

☆ **Kirkby Lonsdale** [Main St; B6254; SD6278], *Snooty Fox*: Attractive character bar with splendid harness, old prints and lots more elaborate 'de-modernisation'; well kept Hartleys XB and Youngers Scotch on handpump, open fires; some rather mixed reports on food and service recently, though as 1990 wore on it seemed as if things were getting back to normal — which for this pub is to say good; children welcome; open all day summer; bedrooms *(Jill and Paul Ormrod, Fiona Mutch, Mr and Mrs R P Begg, Hayward Wane, Miss K Bamford, LYM — more reports please)*
Kirkby Lonsdale [SD6278], *Red Dragon*: Popular and well kept pub with pleasant decor, good atmosphere, wide choice of good value foods, friendly licensees *(Yvonne and Don John, W P Haigh)*

☆ **Kirkby Stephen** [NY7808], *Kings Arms*: Solid comfort in cosy if rather formal oak-panelled lounge bar, darts and dominoes in easy-going main bar, friendly welcome for strangers, pleasant service, bar food inc well filled sandwiches with local cheese, popular lunchtime cold table with assorted meats, some enterprising evening dishes; well kept Whitbreads Trophy, tables in walled garden; children allowed in restaurant; bedrooms *(Brian Barefoot, Anne Morris, LYM)*
Kirkby Stephen, *Pennine*: Attractively placed in this fine old hill town, with well kept Marstons Pedigree and Whitbreads on handpump, decent simple food at attractive prices, plainly furnished small lounge and busy public bar (the pinball competition on

Mon and Weds is an attraction), upstairs restaurant, a few tables in front by the square *(BB)*
Langdale [NY2906], *New Dungeon Ghyll*: Large barn with dim lighting and tiled floor, popular with walkers down from the Langdale Pikes; open all day in summer, food at standard times, real ale *(Ewan McCall)*; [by car park for Stickle Ghyll], *Stickle Barn*: Useful pub with bunk-barn accommodation and well kept Ruddles County *(Len Beattie)*
Levens [Sedgwick Rd, nr entrance to Sizergh Castle — OS Sheet 97 map reference 500872; SD5087], *Strickland Arms*: Pleasant, clean and comfortable stone-built local named after the family at the castle; friendly staff, well kept Theakstons Best, popular bar food, piped music *(A T Langton, M A and W R Proctor, Roger Bellingham)*
Lindale [OS Sheet 97 map reference 419805; SD4280], *Lindale*: Good bar food inc quickly served Sun lunch *(A T Langton)*

☆ **Little Bampton** [NY2755], *Tam o' Shanter*: Good village pub doing well after extensive alterations by new licensees — comfortable, with excellent food and friendly service *(Mr and Mrs L D Rainger)*
Loweswater [unclassified Loweswater rd off B5289 Cockermouth—Buttermere; NY1421], *Scale Hill*: Old-fashioned hotel full of cosy corners and cats; nothing pretentious, but unusually snug with a reassuringly competent air; bedrooms a bit plain, but good value, with lovely views at the back *(Tim Locke)*
Metal Bridge [A74 Carlisle—Gretna; NY3565], *Metal Bridge*: Friendly staff, good bar food; nice river view from sun lounge *(A M Lewery)*

☆ **Middleton** [A683 Kirkby Lonsdale—Sedbergh; SD6386], *Middleton Fells*: Comfortable open-plan oak-beamed bar, lots of brasswork (some made by the landlord), open fire, green plush seating, new barn extension; popular home-made food from filled warm crusty rolls through dressed crab and seafood pasta to duck or big steaks, friendly service, well kept Tetleys and Youngers Scotch; games and juke box; neatly kept garden, charming countryside; children welcome till 8.30; closed winter Mon lunchtimes exc Bank Hols; kept from main entries this year by lack of reader reports *(Richard and Sarah Elwell, LYM)*

☆ **Middleton** [A683 Kirkby Lonsdale—Sedbergh; SD6386], *Swan*: Good news is that this quaint little inn, which closed in 1988, has reopened; before the hiatus it was a popular main entry, much appreciated by readers for its homely charm, well kept beer and interesting food — and the initial impression is that the new management will keep up that standard *(Mrs R S Young, LYM — more reports please)*

☆ **Mungrisdale** [village signed off A66 Penrith—Keswick, a bit over a mile W of A5091 Ullswater rd — OS Sheet 90 map reference 363302; NY3731], *Mill Inn*: Notable for its position in lovely secluded valley hamlet surrounded by soaring fells — one of the nicest spots of any Cumbrian pub; tables on gravel forecourt and neat lawn sloping to little river, simple bar, bar food and afternoon teas, Theakstons Best, lots of malt whiskies, friendly staff, separate restaurant; can arrange salmon and sea trout fishing on River Eden; new licensees this last year; seven bedrooms (note that there's a quite separate Mill Hotel here) (*Mr and Mrs L D Rainger, LYM; more reports on new regime please*)

Nether Wasdale [between Gosforth and Wasdale Head — OS Sheet 89 map reference 125041; NY1204], *Screes*: Comfortable and relaxed pub well placed in spectacular valley, off the usual tourist track; well kept Theakstons Best and Old Peculier and Yates, good choice of malt whiskies, decent food; five bedrooms (*Anon*); *Strands*: Good value food just right for hungry hikers, well kept Hartleys and Robinsons, friendly atmosphere both from holiday makers in summer and locals in winter; efficient service, piped music (can be on the loud side), neat lavatories; bedrooms (*KC, Mr and Mrs Simon Turner, Mr and Mrs D Johnson, T Galligan*)

Newby Bridge [SD3786], *Swan*: Cosy fire, friendly atmosphere and well kept Theakstons in straightforward lounge of large hotel (*Brian Marsden, Kathleen Morley*)

☆ **Oxen Park** [OS Sheet 97 map reference 316873; SD3287], *Manor House*: Spotless, quiet and comfortably refurbished beamed pub with friendly licensees, good coal fire, well kept Hartleys XB on handpump; really good home-cooked food at reasonable prices — even tasty home-made profiteroles; nostalgic music — no juke box; children welcome (*Terry Glendenning, Brian and Anna Marsden*)

Oxenholme [SD5389], *Station*: Well run and quiet unspoilt country pub, with log fire, limited choice of simple food inc excellent soup and sandwiches, long-serving landlord, Whitbreads beers; no music except Sat night piano (*MGBD*)

Patterdale [NY3916], *White Lion*: Cheerful atmosphere, well kept beer, bar food; nr GWG132; bedrooms basic (*Dr and Mrs R J Ashleigh*)

☆ **Penrith** [NY5130], *George*: Well run and substantial hotel with old-fashioned lounge hall — oak panelling and beams, handsome plasterwork, oak settles and easy chairs around good open fire, big bow windows; reasonably priced lunchtime bar food, well kept Marstons Pedigree, lively back bar, restaurant; bedrooms (*LYM*)

Penrith [Cromwell Rd/Castlegate — first roundabout coming from M6], *Agricultural*: Friendly and old-fashioned, with well kept Marstons, large helpings of good bar food — Cumberland sausage in French bread particularly good (*R G Ollier, Barbara Wensworth*)

Pooley Bridge [NY4724], *Sun*: Warm, cosy bar with well kept Marstons Pedigree on handpump, good value generously served bar food, separate restaurant (*Mike Beiley*)

Ravenglass [SD0996], *Ratty Arms*:

Ex-railway bar (terminus for England's oldest narrow-gauge steam railway) with pool table in crowded public bar, well kept beer, good value restaurant, low prices (*Comus Elliott, LYM*)

Ravenstonedale [village and pub signposted off A685 W of Kirkby Stephen; NY7204], *Kings Head*: Carefully refurbished beamed bar, log fires, well kept beer, good food, warm welcome; bedrooms being refurbished 1990 (*Michael Marlow, LYM*)

☆ **Rockcliffe** [NY3661], *Crown & Thistle*: Nice pub doing particularly well under most obliging new licensees, good food in generous helpings served quickly even at busy times (*Mr and Mrs L D Rainger*)

Rosthwaite [NY2615], *Scafell*: Simple food at lunchtime, sandwiches 7-8, and well kept Theakstons XB in very plain riverside hikers' bar tucked away behind kitchens of smart hotel; verandah overlooks river at back (*Graham Bush*)

☆ **Sandside** [B5282 OS Sheet 97 map reference 478808; SD4781], *Ship*: Extensive modernised pub with glorious view over the broad Kent estuary to the Lakeland hills; bar food, well kept Youngers real ales, summer barbecues, notably good children's play area; children allowed in eating area; bedrooms (*Brian Jones, LYM*)

☆ **Seathwaite** [Duddon Valley, nr Ulpha (ie not Seathwaite in Borrowdale); SD2396], *Newfield*: Friendly welcome in good clean local, popular with walkers — no feeling that boots and bags are unwanted; good service, good straightforward bar food — particularly steaks; clean lavatories (*G L Daltry, D J Cooke*)

Seatoller [NY2414], *Yew Tree*: More restaurant than pub, with lovely low-ceilinged 17th-century Lakeland dining room; nr start GWG134, and has been widely praised for food (and well kept Jennings), but former landlord has moved to bigger premises nr Keswick (*More reports please*)

☆ **Sedbergh** [Main St; SD6692], *Dalesman*: Well renovated free house with clean and attractive bar, good service and atmosphere, friendly staff, good choice of excellent food; bedrooms very comfortable (*Yvonne and Don Johnson*)

Sedbergh [Finkle St; A683], *Red Lion*: Cheerful local bar with stuffed gamebirds and sporting dog prints, Marstons Mild, Burton and Pedigree on handpump, bar food from sandwiches through cottage pie and omelettes to steak, games in back area; bedrooms (*Gwen and Peter Andrews, BB*)

☆ **nr Sedbergh** [A683 halfway between Sedbergh and Kirkby Stephen], *Fat Lamb*: Alone on the moors, pews and piped music in two-room bar with some red flock wallpaper and brightly patterned carpet, but also open fire in traditional black kitchen range and good photographs of steam trains and local beagles; usual bar food, maybe piped classical music, restaurant, seats outside by sheep pastures; bedrooms with own bathrooms (*Gwen and Peter Andrews, BB*)

Silecroft [SD1382], *Miners Arms*:

Moderately priced lunchtime and evening bar food inc take-aways, tables out on shrub-bordered terrace with barbecue *(Mrs M Brown, Dick Brown)*

Southwaite [Broad Field — away from village; NY4244], *Crown*: Welcoming and friendly, well kept Theakstons and a guest beer, good value food well served *(Charles Holloway)*

Spark Bridge [SD3185], *Royal Oak*: Large riverside pub with raftered upper bar, large pool room; well kept Hartleys XB and Thwaites Mild and Bitter; children welcome *(Kathleen Morley, Brian and Anna Marsden)*

☆ **Staveley** [SD4798], *Eagle & Child*: Very good value simple food inc cheap steak-in-a-bun and nice home-cooked ham or Cumberland sausage — generous helpings; bright but comfortable little modern front lounge and more spacious carpeted bar; well kept, with small neat garden; bedrooms quite cheap *(Barbara M McHugh, BB)*

Swarthmoor [Fox St; SD2777], *Miners Arms*: Small village pub, well kept Hartleys tapped from the cask, good bar food, friendly service, maybe live music *(M W Woodburn)*

Talkin [village signed off B6413 S of Brampton; NY5557], *Blacksmiths Arms*: Attractive decor somewhat reminiscent of a German Gasthof — clean, bright and cheerful; Theakstons Best and Old Peculier on handpump, food plentiful and good (fish done in beer recommended), open fire; friendly newish licensees; five bedrooms *(Russell Hafter, Mr and Mrs L D Rainger)*; *Hare & Hounds*: The Stewarts who made this village inn such a cheery and chatty place to stay in have now sold it; [Talkin Tarn], *Tarn End*: 19th-century family-run lakeside farmhouse, with two boats for residents; praised in previous editions for particularly good fresh food, often unusual, in bar and evening restaurant, for really friendly service with a good welcome for children, and for good value well equipped bedrooms — but no recent news *(More reports please)*

Temple Sowerby [NY6127], *Kings Arms*: Cosily comfortable hotelish lounge and bigger L-shaped lounge bar with lots of window seats, in handsome well run red sandstone inn; bedrooms *(M J Morgan, LYM)*

☆ **Threlkeld** [old main rd, bypassed by A66; NY3325], *Salutation*: Friendly small village local used by fell-walkers, with lots of connecting rooms; open fire, cards and dominoes; big helpings of excellent food inc the formidable Sally (a no-holds-barred beefburger), well kept Matthew Browns and Theakstons Old Peculier on handpump, welcoming staff; can get crowded; large upstairs children's room with pool table and juke box (oldies) *(C A Holloway, P J and S E Robbins)*

☆ **Torver** [A593 S of Coniston; SD2894], *Church House*: Cosy low-beamed bar — open all day at least in summer — with splendid views over surrounding hills, large garden; reasonably priced good bar meals, small restaurant, well kept Tetleys or Whitbreads Castle Eden and local Manor beer, large garden; children welcome; spacious, airy bedrooms *(Tony Hodge, Lisa Wilson, Nigel B Pritchard, Dr and Mrs A K Clarke)*

☆ **Troutbeck** [NY4103], *Mortal Man*: Warm, clean inn with wide choice of good value bar food in generous helpings; main bar more attractive than rather sombre second room; friendly welcoming service, well kept Youngers Scotch, restaurant; on GWG130; bedrooms *(M J Morgan, Mrs W Knowles, Raymond Palmer, M Box)*

Troutbeck [NY4103], *Queens Head*: Busily popular heavily beamed tourist pub with rambling alcoves — lots of oddities and antique carvings (even a massive Elizabethan four-poster as bar counter), interesting fireplace; lively atmosphere, fine views from seats outside, Watneys-related real ales, bar food (not cheap), darts; nr GWG130; bedrooms *(Ben Wimpenny, Simon Bates, LYM)*

Ulverston [King St; SD2978], *Rose & Crown*: Interesting old building with wide choice of food, well kept Hartleys *(Anon)*

Underbarrow [SD4792], *Punchbowl*: Pleasant exterior, clean interior; friendly staff, well kept beer *(D T Taylor)*

☆ **Warwick on Eden** [2 miles from M6, junction 43; A69 towards Hexham, then village signposted; NY4657], *Queens Arms*: Friendly two-room bar, with well kept Marstons Pedigree, Tetleys and Theakstons, some interesting wines, farm cider, generous helpings of home-cooked bar food (not winter Sun evening) from good sandwiches and baked potatoes to gammon and egg and so forth, roaring log fires, model cars, trains and vintage car pictures; tables in neat side garden, good play area; open all day Sat; children allowed till 9.30; bedrooms *(Michael Davis, J and A Prince, Lesley Jones, Geralyn Meyler, Neil and Angela Huxter, Mr and Mrs L D Rainger, LYM)*

Wigton [West St; NY2648], *Hare & Hounds*: Busy pub, attentive and helpful licensees, excellent food *(Mr and Mrs L D Rainger)*

Windermere [Newby Bridge Rd (A592 4 miles S of Bowness) SD4109], *Beech Hill*: THF hotel on shore of lake; two bars, helicopter pad, big garden with jetty; great for walkers, with good bar food and restaurant; children welcome; bedrooms comfortable *(John Gould)* ; [Lake Rd], *Brookside*: Attractive pub in fine surroundings, with good beer, company and conversation (Peter Barnsley); *Greys*: Pleasant bar adjoining hotel, with generous helpings of good food running up to steaks and huge mixed grills, sensible prices; pool, darts, dominoes, juke box and fruit machine (Steve and Carolyn Harvey)

☆ **Winton** [just off A683; NY7810], *Bay Horse*: Friendly little village local in lovely moorland setting, two low-ceilinged rooms decorated with Pennine photographs and local fly-tying, good value bar food running up to local pheasant, well kept McEwans 80/-, Youngers and guest real ales; pool in games room; clean good value bedrooms *(Alan Hall, LYM)*

Derbyshire and Staffordshire

This is a notably rewarding area for eating out in pubs; throughout, there are plenty of pubs of real character serving good substantial main dishes at under £3, or worthwhile bar snacks at under £1 – or both. Drinks are in general priced below the national average, too, and there are more pubs here than in most areas offering a really wide and interesting choice of unusual beers. Particular bargains are often to be found in pubs brewing their own ales – notably the civilised John Thompson near Melbourne, lively Rising Sun at Shraleybrook and (a new entry this year) the no-frills Burton Bridge Brewery in Burton itself. The outstanding place for low prices is Alan East's Yew Tree at Cauldon – and what makes it doubly remarkable is that this is also probably the country's most interesting pub. Other places doing particularly well here at the moment are the charming George at Alstonefield, the Druid at Birchover (a runaway success on the food side, yet the landlord always seems to have time for a friendly word), the Brunswick in Derby (really rewarding real ales – and make a note in your diary of their October 1991 beer festival), the Maynard Arms at Grindleford (a comfortable dining pub – and good value as a place to stay), the cosy little Packhorse at Little Longstone, the Royal Oak at Millthorpe (friendly and full of character), the Monsal Head Hotel in its fine position on the Head itself, the friendly and relaxed Lathkil at Over Haddon, the Greyhound in Penkhull (real bargains in food), the homely Greyhound at Warslow, the nice old Mainwaring Arms at Whitmore and the neat and tidy Crown at Wrinehill. Pubs winning their spurs by gaining a new main entry this year include the Lazy Landlord at Foolow (interesting food in relaxed surroundings), the Robin Hood at Holmesfield (go-ahead new licensees), the Poachers at Rudyard (quickly gaining a firm reputation for good straightforward food under new licensees who won much praise from readers at their last pub, the Red Lion at Ipstones), the Hoskins Wharf at Shardlow (a lovely position for this substantial and handsomely restored listed canal building) and the Bulls Head at Wardlow (very popular for eating out under its new licensee). At the end of the chapter, Lucky Dip entries which have been attracting particular attention recently – often because of promising new licensees – include the Ashford Inn at Ashford in the Water, Olde Cheshire Cheese and Olde Nags Head in Castleton and Poachers Arms nearby at Hope, Lamb at Chinley, Green Man at Clifton Campville, Swan at Fradley, Queen Anne at Great Hucklow, Barley Mow at Kirk Ireton, Three Horseshoes at Longlane, Colvile Arms at Lullington, Star in Penkridge and White Horse at Woolley.

ALREWAS (Staffs)   SK1714   Map 7

George & Dragon 🛏

High St; bypassed village signposted from A38 and A513

Opening off the central servery, the three busy, snug rooms of this attractive village inn have low black beams, flagstones, homely decorations such as family photographs (they've been here over 40 years) and a large number of brass candlesticks on the remarkably long inglenook mantlepiece. A big room at one side has a splendid collection of commemorative royal china. Good value bar food includes sandwiches (from £1), ploughman's or cold meat with crusty bread (£2.20), a wide choice of hot dishes such as omelettes (from £2.20), salads (from £2.65), vegetarian dishes (from £2.85), home-made pies (£3.10), gammon with egg or pineapple (£4.60) and sirloin steak (£7.70), with a choice of baked potatoes or chips; efficient service. Very well kept Marstons Pedigree on handpump; dominoes, cribbage, fruit machine, piped music. The attractive, partly covered garden has a terrace (where there are occasional barbecues), an aviary with cockatiels and other birds, white doves strutting along the tops of the walls and roofs, and a well serviced children's play area, with a swing, playboat and a play elephant called Eric. The modern bedrooms are in a separate block. (*Recommended by Alison and Tony Godfrey, Helen and Wal Burns, Dave Braisted, N P Hopkins, Christopher Knowles-Fitton*)

Marstons Licensees Ray and Mary Stanbrook Real ale Meals and snacks (till 10 evening, not Sun or 25 Dec) Evening restaurant – though they do Sun lunch Open 11–2.30, 6–11 Bedrooms tel Burton-on-Trent (0283) 790202; £31B/£40B

ALSTONEFIELD (Staffs) SK1355 Map 7
George

Village signposted from A515 Ashbourne–Buxton

In a quiet, stone-built farming hamlet, this charming and friendly 16th-century inn has pewter tankards hanging by the copper-topped bar counter (where there may be a box of greeting cards, some depicting the pub, reproduced from paintings by a local artist), a fine collection of old Peak District photographs and drawings on the darkening cream walls, foreign banknotes on the beams in the low-butter-coloured ceiling and a warm winter coal fire. A more spacious family room is full of wheelback chairs around tables. Popular, good value food is ordered at the kitchen door: soup or sandwiches (£1.25), ploughman's (£2.75), home-made Spanish quiche (£3.75), smoked trout (£3.95), meat and potato pie or lasagne (£3.85), and fillet steak (£5.20); considerate service. Well kept Ansells and Ind Coope Burton on handpump; darts, dominoes, fruit machine. The pretty rockery in the sheltered and spacious back stableyard has picnic seats, and there are some stone seats beneath the pretty inn sign at the front. It's good walking territory, and you can arrange with the landlord to camp on the croft. (*Recommended by A M Neal, Chris Raisin, Simon Velate, G T and J Barnes, Mike and Wendy Proctor, DC, Graham Bush, Steve Mitcheson, Anne Collins, Andrew Turnbull, Mrs Lili Lomas, T Galligan, C McDowall, Peter Walker, Jon Wainwright, Keith Mills, E J Alcock, P Miller*)

Allied Licensees Richard and Sue Grandjean Real ale Meals and snacks (till 10 evening) Open 11–2.30, 6–11; winter evening opening 7, closed 25 Dec

BAMFORD (Derbys) SK2083 Map 7
Derwent

Main St (A6013)

The carpeted hall in this relaxed Upper Derwent inn does duty as the bar servery, and there's an old cushioned settle and books on its bookshelves. Several rooms lead off, one of which has large sunny windows, lots of wooden tables and big pictures on its wood-effect panelling. Another has yokes, heavy-horse harness and trace shafts on the partly panelled walls, two more bay windows, and an old-fashioned green plush wall seat curving all around it. There are usually lots of fresh flowers and potted plants. The games bar (with its local team photographs) has darts, table skittles, pool, fruit machine, shove-ha'penny, cribbage, shut-the-box; piped music. Well kept Bass, Ruddles Best, Stones Best, and Wards Sheffield Best on handpump. Bar food ranges from soup (£1.20), sandwiches (from £1.25), ploughman's or a delicious cheese platter (£2.75), through steak and kidney pie or lasagne (£3) and chicken breast in a wine sauce (£4.25), to steaks (from £5.25); home-made puddings (£1.25). The charming little dining room has stripped-pine panelling. There are seats in the garden. *(Recommended by Len Beattie, A M Neal, Jenny Cantle, Sue Holland, Dave Webster, Andy and Jill Kassube, Neville Kenyon, Lee Goulding, Steve Mitcheson, Anne Collins, KC, Mr and Mrs H Hearnshaw)*

Free house   Licensees David and Angela Ryan   Real ale   Meals and snacks   Children welcome   Restaurant   Open 11–11   Bedrooms tel Hope Valley (0433) 51395; £21(£27.50B)/£34(£39B)

BIRCH VALE (Derbys)   SK0287 Map 7

Sycamore 🛏

From A6015 take Station Road towards Thornsett

The downstairs bar in this popular food pub has an indoor fountain and is set aside for drinkers. Upstairs, the main bar area is primarily for eaters – you can book and there's a sensible table-queue system with a 'waiting board' for busy times. Four connecting carpeted rooms, which have a warm and friendly atmosphere, are furnished with a variety of seats including wheelback chairs, pews, button-back red plush wall banquettes, mate's chairs, high seats by eating-ledges, and settees. There's a wide choice of bar food, including home-made soup (£1.25), sandwiches (from £1.45), braised steak £2.85), ploughman's (£2.75), vegetarian nut roast (£3.25), lambs liver and onions (£3.45), home-made steak and mushroom pie (£3.55), chicken breast marinated with special yoghurt and spices (£4.75), a good range of steaks including those you cook yourself on a grillstone (from £6.45), with children's dishes (from £1.25) and lots of rich puddings (from £1.55). In fine weather, there are do-it-yourself summer barbecues on the high terrace, while below the pub (where you can also find the main car park), there are some attractively spacious valley gardens by a stream; also, solid swings, seesaw, and a climbing frame made of trunks and logs, a play-tree, canaries in an aviary, rabbits, and a summer drinks-and-ice-cream bar. Disco in downstairs bar on Fridays and Sundays; no dogs. *(Recommended by M A and W R Proctor, Steve Mitcheson, Anne Collins, KC, Alan Skull, David Waterhouse)*

Free house   Licensees Malcolm and Christine Nash   Meals and snacks (12–2, 7–10) Restaurant – open all day Sun   Children welcome   Open 12–3, 6–11; 12–10.30 Sun Bedrooms tel New Mills (0663) 42715; £35B/£45B

BIRCHOVER (Derbys)   SK2462 Map 7

Druid 🗫

Village signposted from B5056

An unusually wide range of excellent, interesting – and in some cases award-winning – food draws readers to this remote, creeper-covered gritstone house. Chalked up on three large blackboards, the choice might include soups (£1.60), Yugoslavian Ajwar with peppers, aubergines and garlic (£3.20), peppered mushrooms in a cream sauce on a bed of rice (£3.30), prawns in hot garlic butter with apple and celery (£3.50), and a generous three-cheese ploughman's with fresh fruit and pickle (£3.90); main courses like steamed Chinese vegetables with sweet and sour sauce (£4.40), apricot and hazelnuts on a bed of spinach and spaghetti with a tomato and garlic topping (£4.50), steak and mussel pie (£4.60), Greek moussaka (£4.70), very good half pheasant with cranberry sauce, lamb cooked Turkish-style with apricot, hazelnuts, cumin, cardamom, red peppers, and garlic and served with a cool yoghurt, cucumber and mint sauce (£6.60), Creole-style rabbit fricassée (£7.20), brace of quail tandoori-style, stuffed with rice and glazed in honey (£7.90), and steaks (from £8.20; with local Stilton sauce £8.80); enterprising puddings such as bakewell pudding, fruit and sherry trifle or fresh lemon torte (all at £2.25); half-price helpings for children. In the evenings and at weekends, when it's often very crowded, it may be advisable to book for meals. The bar itself is small and plain, with green plush-upholstered wooden wall benches, small dining chairs and stools around strightforward tables, and a little coal fire. The spacious and airy two-storey dining extension, candlelit at night, has pink plush seats on olive-green carpet and pepper-grinders and sea salt on all the tables. Well kept Marstons Pedigree on handpump and a good collection of malt whiskies; a small public bar has darts, dominoes, cribbage; well reproduced classical music. The pub's name was reputedly inspired, during the 18th-century craze for druids, by a strange cave behind it, among the beech trees sprouting from the Row Tor. There are picnic-table sets in front. *(Recommended by Simon Velate, Curt and Lois Stevens, Hilary Sargeant, Norman Clarke, John Scarisbrick, P A Crossland, D A Cawley, Mike and Wendy Proctor, A F C Young, John and Christine Simpson, Pat and Norman Godley, Alan Skull, Keith Bloomfield, Jim Wiltshire, Brian and Genie Smart, Dennis and Janet Johnson)*

Free house   Licensee Brian Bunce   Real ale   Meals and snacks (not 25 Dec or evening 26 Dec)   Bookings tel Winster (062 988) 302   Children in bar until 8, and must be eating   Open 12–3, 7–11; closed 25 Dec

BRASSINGTON (Derbys)   SK2354 Map 7
Olde Gate

Village signposted off B5056 and B5035 NE of Ashbourne

Though the date outside this creeper-covered pub is 1874, it was built in 1616, of magnesian limestone and timbers salvaged from Armada wrecks and exchanged for lead mined here. The public bar on the right is traditionally furnished with rush-seated old chairs, antique settles (one ancient, partly reframed, and made of solid black oak), pewter mugs hanging from one beam, embossed Doulton stoneware flagons on a side shelf, and an ancient wall clock; there's also a lovely old kitchen range with lots of gleaming copper pots, stone-mullioned windows that look across the garden to small silvery-walled pastures, and a pleasantly relaxed atmosphere. On the left of a small hatch-served lobby, another beamed room has stripped panelled settles, tables with scrubbed tops, and a fire under a huge mantlebeam. Good value bar food changing day by day includes open sandwiches such as prawns or crab (from £2.75), salads, hot dishes such as home-made steak and kidney pie in ale (£3.95), game pie, tandoori chicken or Barnsley chops (£4.25), barbecued steaks, and puddings like good lemon mousses or traditional English puddings with custard; they don't do chips; well kept Marstons Pedigree on handpump and 20 malt whiskies; darts, cribbage, dominoes. The small front yard has a couple of benches – a nice spot in summer to listen to the village bell-ringers practising on Friday evenings (best from 8 to 9, as it's learners earlier). The Carsington reservoir is being developed to provide water sports and so forth. *(Recommended by John and Christine Simpson, Andy and Jill Kassube, Chris Raisin, Graham Doyle, Lynne Sheridan, Bob West, Derek and Sylvia Stephenson)*

Marstons   Licensee Paul Scott Burlinson   Real ale   Meals and snacks (not Mon evening)   Children in old kitchen room; under 12 up to 9pm   Open 11.30–3, 6–11; winter lunchtime opening 12

BURTON ON TRENT (Staffs)   SK2423 Map 7
Albion

Shobnall Rd (close to Marstons Brewery, out by A38 flyover)

As you'd expect from the position, the Marstons Pedigree on handpump in this attractively modernised family pub is in excellent condition. The huge carpeted lounge has stained-glass entrance doors, with the motto *Through this wide-opening gate none too early come, none return too late*, and the good solid furnishings include deep maroon swagged velvet curtains, nice Victorian reproductions on the flowery-papered walls, a long and efficiently staffed bar counter, and a side area, slightly raised behind a balustrade, with a button-back leather settee, great winged armchair and other more parlourish furnishings. It opens into a conservatory – popular with families – with cane chairs around marble-topped tables, which in turn leads out into a spacious fairy-lit garden with swings, a children's bar, a yew walk and a fenced-off stream. The big public bar is comfortable and well decorated too, with pool, darts, fruit machine and juke box.

Bar food includes rolls (from 70p, hot meat ones £1.50), ploughman's (from £1.70), salads (£2.65), curry or steak and kidney pie (£2.75) and a roast of the day (£3.60); summer barbecues. *(Recommended by Richard Sanders, Dr and Mrs C D E Morris; more reports please)*

Marstons   Licensee Malcolm Wink   Real ale   Lunchtime meals and snacks Children's room   Open 10.30–2.30, 5.30–11

Burton Bridge Brewery

23 Bridge St (A50)

Those in the know head for the little front bar in this friendly, basic local, which is where the beers the pub brews itself are beautifully kept on handpump: Bridge Bitter (the one we sampled: well structured, with a clean, hoppy finish), Burton Bridge XL Bitter, Porter, Festive Ale and Old Expensive. The plain walls are hung with notices, awards and brewery memorabilia, simple furnishings include pews and plain tables and there's an open fire; even when it's quiet people tend to spill out into the corridor. Bar snacks such as good filled cobs (from 55p), chip butties (80p), ploughman's (£1.80), filled Yorkshire puddings (from £1.50), and beef in Porter casserole (£2.20). Upstairs there's a skittle alley and a Thursday jazz club. The brewery is actually down at the back in a long, very old-fashioned yard. *(Recommended by Derek and Sylvia Stephenson, Chris Raisin, Graham Doyle, Richard Sanders, Matt Pringle, T R G Alcock, Colin Dowse)*

Own Brew   Licensee Jeff Plumb   Real ale   Meals and snacks   Open 11.30–3, 5.30–11

BUTTERTON (Staffs)   SK0756   Map 7

Black Lion ★ 🛏

Village signposted from B5053

Butterton has now been declared a conservation village so some of the changes this unspoilt and warmly friendly 18th-century stone inn has made this year (such as building new stone walls next to the car park) have been done under the direction of the Peak Park Planning Board. They've also refurbished the bedrooms and completely redesigned the dining room – which now offers a carvery Friday and Saturday evenings and Sunday lunchtimes. The rambling bar is made up of several homely rooms: one has well polished mahogany and other tables, a fine old red leatherette settle curling around its walls, comfortable old bar stools with backrests, lots of brassware and china, a low black beam-and-board ceiling and a good log fire. Off to the left, there are red plush button-back banquettes around sewing-machine tables and Victorian prints. An inner room has a parakeet called Sergeant Bilko who squawks loudly at regular intervals, a Liberty-print sofa and a fine old kitchen range. Good value bar food includes home-made soup (£1.20), sandwiches (from £1.20), huge lunchtime ploughman's (£3), steak and kidney pie (£3.75), vegetarian lasagne or tasty chicken curry (£3.95), and good 10oz rump steak (£5.50), as well as daily specials such as liver, bacon and onions or Cumberland bake (£3.50), beef in red wine (£3.95), good stews and ham off the bone, and puddings of the day; friendly service. McEwans 70/- and 80/-, Theakstons Best and Youngers No 3 on handpump and several malt whiskies; darts, bar billiards, shove-ha'penny, dominoes, cribbage, space game, fruit machine, and separate well lit pool room; piped music. Picnic-table sets and rustic seats on the prettily planted terrace look up to the tall and elegant spire of the local church, and across to the surrounding hills. *(Recommended by Kevin Fields, Graham Bush, Alan and Ruth Woodhouse, Gwen and Peter Andrews, Chris Raisin, Graham Doyle, E Chivers, Simon Velate, J Scarisbrick, Mike and Wendy Proctor, A Wright, Mrs J Edwards, T Galligan, Steve Mitcheson, Anne Collins, D R and J A Munford, David Eversley, E J Waller, Jon Wainwright)*

Free house   Licensee Ron Smith   Real ale   Meals and snacks   Restaurant (not Sun evening)   Children welcome   Monthly live entertainment Thurs/Fri evenings; impromptu Sat evenings   Open 12–3, 7–11; closed Weds lunchtime   Bedrooms tel Onecote (053 88) 232; £18.15B/£34.50B nr BUXTON (Derbys)   SK0673   Map 7

Bull i'th' Thorn ★

Ashbourne Road (A515) six miles S of Buxton, nr Hurdlow; OS Sheet 119 map reference 128665

The core of this extended roadhouse is a striking 14th-century hall with handsome panelling, old flagstones stepping gently down to a big open fire, a massive central beam among a forest of smaller ones, an ornately carved hunting chair, and fine long settles and panelled window seats in the embrasures of the thick stone walls; also, a longcase clock, a powder-horn, armour that includes 17th-century German helmets, swords, and blunderbusses and so forth. The straightforward bar food includes sandwiches (from 60p), soup (80p), ploughman's (£2), sausages (£1.50), salads (from £2), cottage pie (£2.20), steak and kidney pie or scampi (£2.75), and sirloin steak (£5); children's dishes (£1) and a Sunday roast lunch (£3.30); friendly service. An adjoining room has darts, pool, dominoes, fruit machine, juke box and piped music; well kept Robinsons Best on handpump. The family room opens on to a terrace and big lawn, with swings, and there are more tables in a sheltered angle in front – where a lively carving over the main entrance depicts a bull caught in a thornbush; there are others of an eagle with a freshly caught hare, and some spaniels chasing a rabbit. *(Recommended by Helen and Wal Burns, Mike and Wendy Proctor, Margaret and Trevor Errington, Simon Velate, Gwen and Peter Andrews, Steve Mitcheson, Anne Collins, Roy and Margaret Randle, Mrs M Price)*

Robinsons   Licensees Bob and Judith Haywood   Real ale   Meals and snacks Children in family room   Open 11–3, 6.30–11   Two bedrooms tel Longnor (029 883) 348; £12/£22

CAULDON (Staffs)   SK0749   Map 7

Yew Tree ★ ★ ★

Village signposted from A523 and A52 about 8 miles W of Ashbourne; OS Sheet 119 map reference 075493

A uniquely splendid place for lovers of the unusual, this remarkable pub has several cluttered, old-fashioned and dimly lit rooms full of 18th-century settles, soggily sprung sofas (not a place for those who like crisp cushion covers and wall-to-wall carpets), ancient guns and pistols, several penny-farthings, an old sit-and-stride boneshaker, a rocking horse, swordfish blades and even a fine marquetry cabinet crammed with notable early Staffordshire pottery; this year they've added a four-person oak church choir seat with carved heads which came from St Mary's church in Stafford. Above the bar is an odd iron dog-carrier (don't ask how it works!) The most unusual things are the working Polyphons and Symphonions – 19th-century developments of the musical box, often taller than a person, each with quite a repertoire of tunes and of the most elaborate sound-effects; go with plenty of 2p pieces to work them. There's also an expanding set of fine (and vociferous) longcase clocks in the gallery just above the entrance, a pianola with an excellent collection of piano rolls, a working vintage valve radio set, a crank-handle telephone and a sinuous medieval wind instrument made of leather. The atmosphere is basic but very friendly, and prices for the hot sausage rolls (25p), big pork pies (40p), big filled baps (from 60p), quiche and smoked mackerel (£1.50) are remarkably low, as they are for the drinks – including Bass, Burton Bridge and M & B Mild on handpump or tapped from the cask, and some interesting malt whiskies such as overproof Glenfarclas. Darts, shove-ha'penny, table skittles (taken very seriously here), dominoes and cribbage. The old brick pub, hiding behind a big yew tree, is difficult to spot – unless a veteran bus is parked outside. Dovedale and the Manifold Valley are not far away. *(Recommended by Graham Bush, A M Neal, Simon Velate, Laurence Manning, Sarah Bullard, J Scarisbrick, Mike and Wendy Proctor, John and Chris Simpson, T Galligan, Tom McLean, Ewan McCall, Roger Huggins, Heather Sharland, Tim Locke, Sue Holland, Dave Webster, Chris Raisin, Graham Doyle, Hazel Morgan, Steve Mitcheson, Anne Collins, Margaret and*

Roy Randle, WHBM, David and Flo Wallington, Steve and Carolyn Harvey, Alan Skull, Klaus and Elizabeth Leist, Richard Sanders)

Free house   Licensee Alan East   Real ale   Snacks (generally something to eat any time they're open)   Children in Polyphon room   Pianola most nights – played by the landlord   Open 10–3 (4 if needed on Sat), 6–11

CONSALL (Staffs)   SJ9748   Map 7
Black Lion

Consallforge; from A522 just S of Wetley Rocks (which is E of Stoke-on-Trent) follow Consall turn-off right through village, then turn right into Nature Park, with easy access to the pub from its car park; OS Sheets 118 and 119, map reference 000491

In a peaceful and pleasantly remote spot by the Caldon Canal and the weir on the River Churnet, this simple and unspoilt pub has cafe seats and Formica tables, plain brick walls, a good coal fire on cool days, and bar food such as sandwiches (70p), egg and chips (£1.10), omelette (£1.95), chicken (£2.50), gammon (£3) and sirloin steak (£4.50); it's popular at weekends. Although there's an access road, the two traditional walks to it – from the footpath sign just past the Old Hall on the village road, or along the canal from Cheddleton – are still well worth making. Marstons Pedigree and Ruddles County on handpump; sensibly placed darts at one end, also dominoes, cribbage, and piped music. *(Recommended by R J Whiston, J Scarisbrick, Richard Sanders; more reports please)*

Free house   Licensee Mrs Ethel Morris   Real ale   Meals and snacks   Restaurant tel Stoke-on-Trent (0782) 550294   Children welcome   Open 11–3, 6–11

DERBY   SK3438   Map 7
Abbey Inn

Darley Street; coming in from A38/A6 roundabout, take first left signposted Darley Abbey, then left into Old Road signposted to toll bridge, turning right just before the bridge itself

Parts of this smallish pub are all that's left of what used to be a powerful 11th-century monastery, covering much of this area. It's been thoughtfully restored, and the downstairs bar has a brick floor, some massive stonework (leaning, in the case of the outer wall), studded oak doors, a refectory table and some shiny elm ones, William Morrisish brocaded stools and benches, a long pew, and a big brick inglenook with stone chimneypiece. A new spiral stone staircase leads up to a bigger and quieter bar where the restored stonework is more notable, especially in the modelling of the windows; into the wall they've built the bow of a Viking longship and there are handsome reconstructed high oak rafters and trusses, and neat cushioned pews built into stalls around the tables. Lunchtime bar food includes home-made soup (£1.50), a cold buffet (from £2.50), lemon sole (£2.65), pies like pork and apple in cider or rabbit in sherry (£2.80), vegetarian dishes, and curries (from £3). Well kept Sam Smiths Museum and Old Brewery on handpump; darts, shove-ha'penny, cribbage, dominoes, piped music (reproduced much better upstairs than down on our visit), and quiz team every other Wednesday; quietly relaxed atmosphere. Besides a couple of sturdy teak seats outside, there are stone side-steps to sit on, and a stone well-head; customers tend to stray into the park opposite, by a weir on the Derwent. The pub has a cricket and football team and a sort of Viking Association (anyone can join) which holds occasional mock-battles. *(Recommended by Chris Raisin)*

Sam Smiths   Licensees Christine and Simon Meyers   Real ale   Meals and snacks (lunchtime, not Sun)   Children in eating area of bar until 7pm   Occasional keyboard vocalist   Open 11–2.30, 6–11; 11–11 summer Sats

Brunswick

1 Railway Terrace; close to Derby Midland railway station

Originally one of England's oldest railway pubs (built in 1842), this is popular with real ale enthusiasts for its remarkable range of well kept beers, and since opening in October 1987 they have served over 250 different ones. Regularly available are Adnams Bitter, Bass, Batemans Mild (they always have a Mild on offer), Burton Bridge Bitter, Hook Norton Old Hookey, Marstons Pedigree, Theakstons XB, Timothy Taylors Landlord, Wards Kirby and Sheffield and Youngers No 3 on handpump, with Theakstons Old Peculier tapped from the cask; ever-changing forthcoming beers are listed on a blackboard. The building work on their own brewery has been slightly delayed as a well was discovered – the water may be used for brewing later on. Over four days around 3 October (the anniversary of their opening) they have a beer festival, with many more ales on offer. A couple of farm ciders are always available, tapped from the cask. Careful renovations have made the most of the rather unusual floor-plan, and downstairs there are original flagstones throughout. The high-ceilinged serving bar has heavy, well padded leatherette seats, whisky-water jugs above the dado, and a dark blue ceiling and upper wall, with squared dark panelling below. The no-smoking room is decorated with little old-fashioned prints and swan's neck lamps, there's a high-backed wall settle, and a coal fire; behind a curved glazed partition wall is a quietly chatty family parlour narrowing to the apex of the triangular building. Darts, cribbage, dominoes, fruit machine, occasional piped music; good friendly service. Bar food includes filled rolls (the hot beef ones are good), chilli con carne (£2.10), home-made steak and kidney pie (£2.85) and beef in Hook Norton Old Hookey (£3); the dining room is used for evening functions, with buffets and occasional live bands. There are seats in the terrace area behind. (*Recommended by Andrew Stephenson, Derek and Sylvia Stephenson, Graham Bush, Carl Southwell, Angie and Dave Parkes, Chris Raisin, Richard Sanders*)

Free house　Licensee Trevor Harris　Real ale　Lunchtime meals and snacks (rolls only Sun)　Restaurant tel Derby (0332) 290677 (not Sun)‾ Children in family parlour Upstairs folk club alternate Suns, jazz Mon evenings　Open 11–11 – though closed between 2.30–5.30 on Sat when Derby County Football Club play at home

FENNY BENTLEY (Derbys)　SK1750　Map 7
Coach & Horses

A515 N of Ashbourne

The nice little back room in this former 17th-century coaching inn has comfortable, ribbed green built-in wall banquettes, old prints and engravings on the dark green leafy Victorian wallpaper, and a quietly welcoming atmosphere. There are more old prints in the front bar, which has waggonwheels hanging from the black beams, horsebrasses and pewter mugs, flowery-cushioned wall settles and library chairs around the dark tables on its Turkey carpet, and a huge mirror. Quickly served good value bar food includes filled baps (from 85p), soup (90p), sandwiches (£1.20), burgers or filled baked potatoes (from £1.50), choice of ploughman's (£2.50), salads (£3.20), home-made pies such as steak and kidney (£3.50), gammon and egg (£4.95) and steaks running up to generously accompanied 16oz ones (from £7.50 – they give you a free pint if you eat your plate clean). Well kept Bass on handpump, good coffee, unobtrusive piped music. There are picnic-table sets on the back grass by an elder tree, with rustic benches and white tables and chairs under cocktail parasols on the terrace in front of this pretty rendered stone house. (*Recommended by A J Woodhouse, Denzil Taylor, Mike and Proctor*)

Bass　Licensee Edward Anderson　Real ale　Meals and snacks　Restaurant tel Thorpe Cloud (033 529) 246　Open 11–2.30, 6.30–11

FOOLOW (Derbys)　SK1976　Map 7
Lazy Landlord ⊘

Village signposted off A623 Chesterfield–Chapel en le Frith

The most interesting dishes here tend to be the half dozen or so specials of the day – a typical selection might include goat's milk cheesecake with chives (£2.50), sea bream with a herby crust (£6.25), lamb done with mint and green peppercorns (£6.50), veal with a fresh orange sauce (£7.75), duck breast with fresh nectarine sauce (£7.95) and a coconut and raspberry tart (£1.50). The basic choice runs from sandwiches (from £1.30), soup (£1.50) and starters such as potted shrimps (£2.50) through vegetable crumble (£4.25) and steak and kidney pie (£4.50) to steaks (from £8); Sunday roast with two joints (£4.75); vegetables are fresh, cooked al dente. Steps from the simply furnished central bar lead down into a quietly relaxed room with a comfortable variety of seats including lots of maroon plush small dining chairs, pleasant tables with inlaid brass number-plates, harness on stripped stone walls, an open fire and unusually high ceiling joists. On the other side, a dining room with more stripped stone has tables in snug individual stalls. Well kept Wards Sheffield Best and Darleys Thorne on handpump, welcoming service (the pub's run by two brothers and their father), very quiet piped music. There are three picnic-table sets in front of the maroon-shuttered pub, which has fine Victorian etched and cut glass windows. Rolling moorland pasture surrounds the pretty village, its modern houses toning in well with the older ones around the pond and green. *(Recommended by Colin Price, Simon Velate, Dorothy and David Young, Neville Kenyon, Brian and Anna Marsden)*

Free house   Licensees D W, M D and K G Holden   Real ale   Meals and snacks (12–2, 6–10)   Bookings Hope Valley (0433) 30873   Well behaved children welcome lunchtime and early evening   Open 11–3, 6–11; closed 25 Dec

nr FOOLOW (Derbys)   SK1976   Map 7
Barrel

Bretton; signposted from Foolow which itself is signposted from A623 just E of junction with B6465 to Bakewell

Stubs of massive knocked-through stone walls divide the beamed bar in this friendly, traditional pub into several areas – the cosiest of which is at the far end, with a leather-cushioned settle and built-in corner wall-bench by an antique oak table in front of the open fire. The cream walls are decorated with local maps, an aerial photograph, a rack of clay pipes, poems about the pub and a clock which moves in an anti-clockwise direction, the varied seating includes some old barrels, and a Delft shelf has lots of old glass and china bottles. Bar food includes sandwiches (from 85p – the crab are very good; toasties from £1.25), and prawn or smoked salmon baps or duck and apricot or beef and ale pies (all £2.50). A good choice of whiskies; darts, dominoes. From the breezy front terrace there are fine views to the pastures below the high ridge. *(Recommended by Helen and Wal Burns, Simon Velate, Wayne Brindle, Brian and Anna Marsden, Peter and Moyna Lynch, M A and W R Proctor)*

Bass   Licensee Edward Walsh   Meals and snacks   Children in eating area of bar lunchtime only   Open 12–3, 6.30–11

FROGGATT EDGE (Derbys)   SK2477   Map 7
Chequers

B6054, off A623 N of Bakewell; Ordnance Survey Sheet 119, map reference 247761

The Edge itself is up through the woods behind this old-fashioned and comfortable inn, which has tables on the back terrace, and white benches at the front that look out over an attractive valley. Inside, there are antique prints on the white walls (partly stripped back to big dark stone blocks), library chairs or small high-backed winged settles on the well waxed floorboards, an attractive, richly varnished beam-and-board ceiling, and a big solid-fuel stove. One corner has a big grandfather clock, another a nicely carved oak cupboard, and the Siamese cat is friendly. Well kept Wards Sheffield Best on handpump, a good range of wines and 86 malt whiskies. Bar food includes a generous soup (£1.50), good home-cooked meat sandwiches (£1.45; prawn £3), ploughman's (£2.95), salads (from £2.95), chilli con carne (£3.25), steak and mushroom pie (£3.50), sirloin steak (£6.50) and puddings (£1.50). Fruit machine, juke box and piped music. *(Recommended by*

Simon Velate, Drs M and K Parier, Mr and Mrs A Gray, Frazer and Louise Smith, Tim and
Lynne Crawford, E J Waller, Alan Skull)

*Wards (Vaux)   Licensee Ian McLeod   Real ale   Meals and snacks (12–2, 6–9; not
Sun evening)   Children in family room   Open 11–3, 6–11   Bedrooms tel Hope
Valley (0433) 30231; £25/£35*

GRINDLEFORD (Derbys)   SK2478 Map 7

Maynard Arms ⇦

B6521 N of village

Popular bar food here includes a Yorkshire pudding filled with roast beef and
gravy, turkey or stew (£3.25, not Sunday lunchtime), as well as soup (85p), filled
cobs or sandwiches (£1), a traditional breakfast (£2.50, served lunchtime and
evening), fish and chips (£2.95), curry (£3.25), vegetable lasagne (£3.50), seafood
pancakes (£3.60), home-made steak, kidney and mushroom pie (£3.75, with a
twenty-minute wait), 8oz steaks (£6.25), home-made puddings (90p), daily specials
and children's dishes; when it's busy there can be considerable delays. The spacious
and recently refurbished main bar has some dark panelling, tapestry wall hangings,
comfortable blue-coloured plush seats on the blue patterned carpet, silver tankards
above the bar, and a high ceiling. Off the hall there's a smaller green plush bar.
Stones on handpump; piped music, darts and dominoes; friendly service. The
restaurant looks out over the neatly kept garden to the valley. *(Recommended by
Mike and Wendy Proctor, Harry Stirling, Simon Velate, D J and P M Taylor, Wayne Brindle,
Win and Gordon Lambert, T Galligan, Peter and Moyna Lynch, WTF)*

*Bass   Licensees Bob Graham and Helen Siddall   Real ale   Meals and snacks (12–2,
5.30–9.30)   Restaurant   Children in eating area if eating and in restaurant   Open
11–3, 5.30–11; 11–11 Sat   Bedrooms tel Hope Valley (0433) 30321; £48B/£58B*

GRINDON (Staffs)   SK0854 Map 7

Cavalier

Village signposted from B5033 just over two miles N of junction with A523

Popular with walkers and cyclists, this small stone village house has an engaging
rustic garden with swings, and is just a mile from the Manifold Valley. The two
rooms are simply and traditionally furnished, with some Turkey carpet on the old
flooring tiles and a high beam-and-plank ceiling. Decorations include old guns and
other ancient weapons, tiny shoes, lots of brass round one of the open fires, iron
tools, harness with horsebrasses and decorative plates. Bar food includes
sandwiches, beef casseroled in ginger, lamb and apricot pie (£4.25), local trout or
pheasant in wine, brandy and honey (£5.75), prawn creole (£6), and a big mixed
grill (£9). Well kept Marstons Pedigree, Ruddles County and guest beers on
handpump, as well as unusual bottled foreign beers and malt whiskies; darts, pool,
dominoes, piped music. This 16th-century building was once an undertakers' (the
ghost's said to be most active in summer). *(Recommended by Simon Velate, J Scarisbrick,
Steve Mitcheson, Anne Collins, Chris Raisin, Lee Goulding, Diane Hall, Tim and Lynne
Crawford, Mike and Wendy Proctor)*

*Free house   Licensee Lynda Blunden   Real ale   Meals and snacks (not Mon
lunchtime)   Restaurant tel Onecote (0538) 8285 (not Sun Evening)   Children inside
family room and restaurant   Live entertainment some Sat evenings   Open 12 (11.30
Sat)–3.30, 7–11; closed Mon lunchtime*

HARDWICK HALL (Derbys)   SK4663 Map 7

Hardwick Inn

4 1/2 miles from M1 junction 29: A617 towards Mansfield, then in Glapwell turn right
at Hardwick Hall signpost and keep on to the far side of the park; can also be reached
from A6010 via Stainsby The several separate rooms in this golden stone house have a
relaxed, old-fashioned atmosphere. The carpeted lounge has varnished wooden tables,

comfortably upholstered wall settles, tub chairs and stools, and stone-mullioned latticed windows. Bar food includes sandwiches, soup (90p), ploughman's (from £2.40), Lincolnshire sausage with egg (£2.50), home-made steak and kidney pie (£2.95), plaice or haddock (£3.15), a daily vegetarian dish (£3.25), salads (from £3.65), gammon and egg or pineapple (£3.75) and steaks (from £5.95); a daily special, puddings (£1.30), and children's menu (from £1.50). Well kept Theakstons XB and Youngers Scotch on handpump. This 17th-century building, originally the lodge for the nearby Elizabethan Hall, is now owned by the National Trust; the park is splendid, and the lawns extensive. *(Recommended by Alan Skull, Dr Keith Bloomfield, Mike and Mandy Challis, J Harvey Hallam, Thomas Nott, Richard Sanders, B M Eldridge, Jane and Niall, Tim and Lynne Crawford)*

Free house Licensees Peter and Pauline Batty Real ale Meals and snacks (not Sun evening) Carvery restaurant (Tues-Sat, Sun lunchtime) tel Chesterfield (0246) 850245; not Sun evening Children in restaurant and family room Open 11.30–3, 6.30–11

nr HARTINGTON (Derbys) SK1360 Map 7
Jug & Glass

Newhaven; on A515 about 1 mile N of junction with A5012; OS Sheet 119 map reference 156614

The emphasis in the cosy bar of this remote moorland pub is very much on its fine range of beers: Banks's Bitter and Mild, Hardys and Hansons Best and Best Mild, Marstons Pedigree and Owd Rodger, Ruddles Best and County, Theakstons XB and a weekly guest beer from all over the country on handpump; on the second Wednesday of July they hold a mini-beer festival, with all beers at half price. There's a cuckoo clock, a piano, lots of flowery china hanging from low beams, simple furnishings, winter coal fires (as well as central heating), and a friendly atmosphere. Another room with flock wallpaper takes the overflow when the small main bar gets too crowded. In the attractive no-smoking dining room there's a stone-pillared fireplace with an old oak mantlebeam. Bar food includes home-made soup (95p), ploughman's (£2.50), breaded haddock or vegetable lasagne (£3.25), gammon with egg, pineapple and sausage (£5), steaks (from 7oz sirloin £6.25), and specials; they use local meat, and at 24 hours' notice will do a full leg of lamb, loin of pork or rib of beef to carve yourself (£7.50 each including starters, puddings and coffee, minimum four people – you can take home what's left; if you wish the landlord to carve there's a nominal charge of half-a-pint!) Darts, dominoes, cribbage, fruit machine, juke box; piped music. There are tables outside under cocktail parasols on the terrace. *(Recommended by Simon Velate, Mike and Wendy Proctor, John and Joan Wyatt, JMC, Richard Sanders, Jon Wainright)*

Free house Licensee John Bryan Real ale Meals and snacks (11.30–2.30, 7–9.30) Restaurant tel Hartington (0298) 84224 Children welcome Open 11–4, 6–11 (winter evening opening 7)

HOLMESFIELD (Derbys) SK3277 Map 7
Robin Hood

Lydgate; B6054 towards Hathersage

As we went to press, we heard that the lounge/restaurant area in this friendly, rambling ex-farmhouse was being extended and refurbished, and that bedrooms were to be opened up. There are exposed beams, open fires, chintz and paisley curtains, plush button-back wall banquettes around wood-effect tables and partly carpeted flagstone floors. Popular bar food from a varied menu includes home-made soup (£1.25), sandwiches (from £2.25, with chips and salad), hot roast beef bap (£2.75), ploughman's (from £3.50), vegetarian quiche or spiced beef salad (£4.45), home-cooked ham (£4.50), steak and kidney pie (£4.65), steaks (from £7.95), and daily specials such as mushrooms and prawns in garlic or spare ribs (£1.95), vegetable moussaka (£4.25), Lancashire hot-pot (£4.65), tandoori chicken (£5.25), seafood pancake (£5.25), pork in cream and sherry sauce (£5.95), and swordfish steak (£6.95); puddings such as apple and raspberry pie, strawberry and kiwi pavlova (from £1.75). Though booking is advisable at weekends, only half the tables are booked out at any time; piped music. Outside on the cobbled front courtyard there are stone tables. *(Recommended by Mike Tucker, Dave Braisted)*

Free house   Licensees Chris and Julie Hughes   Meals and snacks (12–2.30, 6–9.30)
Children in eating areas   Open 11.30–3, 6–11; winter evening opening 6.30
Bedrooms under construction as we went to press tel Sheffield (0742) 890360; \£40

LITTLE HUCKLOW (Derbys)   SK1678 Map 7

Old Bulls Head ★

Pub signposted from B6049

Scrupulously neat and tidy, the two small rooms in this popular village pub have thickly cushioned built-in settles, old oak beams, interesting collections of locally mined semi-precious stones, antique brass and iron household tools; there's a coal fire in a neatly restored stone hearth. One room is served from a hatch, the other over a polished bar counter. Well kept Wards Sheffield Best from carved handpumps; bar snacks are simple and consist of sandwiches (£1.10) and ploughman's (£2); well reproduced classical music, dominoes. In the well tended, dry-stone-walled garden there's a fine collection of well restored and attractively painted old farm machinery. Note the restricted winter opening hours. The quiet village is surrounded by upland sheep pastures. *(Recommended by Mike and Wendy Proctor, Alan and Eileen Bowker, H K Dyson, W P P Clarke, Steve Mitcheson, Anne Collins, Steve and Sandra Hampson)*

Free house   Licensee Geoff Hawketts   Real ale   Snacks (lunchtime)   Children welcome   Open 12–2, 7–11; closed winter weekday lunchtimes

LITTLE LONGSTONE (Derbys)   SK1971 Map 7

Packhorse

Monsal Dale and Ashford Village signposted off A6 NW of Bakewell; follow Monsal Dale signposts, then turn right into Little Longstone at Monsal Head Hotel

First mentioned as a pub in a census of 1787, this enjoyable little cottagey tavern is cosily placed in a village terrace. The two small rooms are individually but discreetly decorated with prettily hung decorative mugs, a collection of brass spigots, attractive landscape photographs by Steve Riley, blow-ups of older local photographs and the odd cornet or trumpet. Simple furnishings range from country-kitchen chairs and cloth-cushioned settles to an odd almost batwinged corner chair; there's a beam-and-plank ceiling and open fires. Good value bar food might include sandwiches (from 90p), soup (£1.10), baps spread with dripping and generously filled with hot well hung beef or with hot pork, apple sauce and stuffing (£1.20), starters like spare ribs (which are a meal in themselves), prawn provençale or Stilton garlic mushrooms (all £1.95), ploughman's with a selection of cheeses, main courses such as cauliflower and leek bake, meat salad, chilli con carne or very tasty, filling steak and kidney pie (all £3.45), marinated chicken (£4.25), duck with Cumberland sauce (£5.50), sirloin steak (£5.75), and puddings (£1.35). Well kept Marstons Burton and Pedigree on handpump; darts, dominoes, cribbage. In the steep little garden there are goats and rabbits. Please note, they no longer do bedrooms. *(Recommended by Mike and Wendy Proctor, Neville Kenyon, Simon Velate, D W Crossley, Dennis and Janet Johnson, Derek and Sylvia Stephenson, Mrs D M Everard)*

Marstons   Licensees Sandra and Mark Lythgoe   Real ale   Meals and snacks   Well behaved children in eating area until 9pm   Open 11–3, 5–11; closed 25 Dec evening

nr MELBOURNE (Derbys)   SK3825 Map 7

John Thompson

Ingleby; village signposted from A514 at Swarkestone

This large, busy pub takes its name from the man who both owns it and brews its highly praised beer, and you can buy their home-brew kits; there's also Marstons

Pedigree on handpump. In the spacious, modernised lounge there are some old oak settles, button-back leather seats, sturdy oak tables, ceiling joists, antique prints and paintings, and a log-effect gas fire; a couple of smaller cosier rooms open off; there is a no-smoking area. Good but straightforward bar food consists of soup (£1), sandwiches (£1 – nothing else on Sundays; the beef is excellent), a cold buffet (£3), hot roast beef (£4.25 – not Mon) and puddings (£1). The surroundings are attractive: well kept lawns and flowerbeds running down to the rich watermeadows along the River Trent, lots of tables on the upper lawn, and a partly covered outside terrace with its own serving bar. *(Recommended by Pete Storey, Dr Keith Bloomfield, Matt Pringle, Tim and Lynne Crawford, Jon Wainwright, Richard Sanders)*

Own brew   Licensee John Thompson   Real ale   Meals (lunchtime, not Sun; cold buffet only, Mon) and snacks   Children in separate room   Open 10.30–2.30, 7–11

MILLTHORPE (Derbys)   SK3276   Map 7
Royal Oak

B6051

There's a lot of character in the main room of this well run and very friendly 17th-century stone pub which has bare stone walls, solid furnishings under the old oak beams and a winter log fire. The main room opens into a small, more comfortable and quieter lounge. Well kept and well priced Darleys Thorne and Wards Sheffield Best on handpump; selection of malt whiskies and quite a few spirits and liqueurs. Good value home-made food includes toasties and sandwiches such as bacon and black pudding (85p-£1.25), a wide choice of ploughman's (from £2.20), cottage pie (£2.30), ratatouille (£2.75), meaty or vegetarian lasagne or chicken pie (£2.95), and seafood Mornay (£3.25), with Cumberland sausage (£2.75), mixed grill or 8oz steak (£3.95), and game pie (£4.50) on winter evenings; puddings like bread and butter pudding or fruit crumble (from £1). The crazy-paved terrace under hawthorn, ash and other trees, has picnic-table sets – as does a side lawn further up; several good walks in the area. *(Recommended by J D Baines, M M Baines, Andrew Turnbull, Peter Mitchell, Lynn Higginson; more reports please)*

Free house   Licensees Harry and Elaine Wills   Real ale   Meals and snacks (not Sat-Sun evenings)   Open 11.30–3, 5.30–11 (11.30–4, 6–11 Sat); closed Mon lunchtime, except Bank Holidays

MONSAL HEAD (Derbys)   SK1871   Map 7
Monsal Head Hotel

B6465

Popular with locals and walkers, the attractive all-day bar here is housed in the old stables. It's a lively flagstoned room with cushioned oak pews around flowery-clothed tables in the stripped timber horse-stalls, which are decked out with harness, horsey brassware, farm tools, and railway signs and lamps from a local disused station, and there's a a big woodburning stove in an inglenook; steps lead up into a crafts gallery. The spacious high-ceilinged main front bar is set out more as a wine bar, with dining chairs around big tables; it's partitioned off from the restaurant area. Bar food includes sandwiches (from £1.10), and good soup (£1.40), and there's a carvery in the lounge (from £3.25), as well as scampi or lasagne (£3.25), vegetarian dishes, home-made steak and kidney pie (£3.60), salads (from £3.75), and in the evenings gammon (£4.65), and steak or chicken Kiev (£6.25). Well kept John Smiths, Theakstons Old Peculier, a beer brewed for the pub and a regularly changing guest beer such as Greene King Abbot on handpump, as well as Westons Old Rosie cider; darts, shove-ha'penny, table skittles, dominoes and cribbage; quiet (and free) juke box. The pub's position above the steep valley of the River Wye is marvellous and gives good views from its balconies and the big windows of its lounge, though perhaps the best place for them is the terrace by the front car park. Both the restaurant and the bedrooms are decorated in authentically Victorian style. The back garden has a play area and animals; on *Good Walks Guide* Walk 82. The bedrooms have been upgraded. (*Recommended by Simon Velate, Matt Pringle, Michael Thomson, Derek Patey, Dr Paul Kitchener, Gill and Neil Patrick, Mike and Wendy Proctor, G W Kerby, Giles Quick, L G and D L Smith, Wayne Brindle, Derek and Sylvia Stephenson, Peter and Moyna Lynch, Steve Waters, M A and W R Proctor*)

Free house   Licensee Nicholas Smith   Real ale   Meals and snacks   Restaurant Children in eating area and restaurant   Open 11–11; closed 25 Dec   Bedrooms tel *Great Longstone (062 987) 250; £45S(50B)*

ONECOTE (Staffs)   SK0555 Map 7

Jervis Arms

B5053, off A523 Leek–Ashbourne

The neat riverside lawn beside this 17th-century pub has picnic-table sets under cocktail parasols, assault climber and an enchanted tree with slide, swing and rope, a little shrubby rockery behind, and lots of sheltering ash trees; a footbridge leads to the car park. Inside, the irregularly shaped main bar has window-seats, wheelback chairs, two or three unusually low plush chairs and white planks over shiny black beams; the walls are hung with little hunting prints and there are Toby jugs and decorative plates on the high mantlepiece of its big stone fireplace. A similar if slightly simpler inner room has a fruit machine, and there are two family rooms (as well as high chairs and a mother and baby room). Quickly served good bar food includes soup (£1), ham, beef or cheese rolls (£1.25), tasty baked potatoes filled with chilli or home-made shepherd's pie (£2.50), ploughman's or generous home-cooked ham (£3), roast chicken (quarter £3.50, half £5), vegetarian dishes such as curried nut, fruit and vegetable pie or savoury cheesecake (£3.75), and 12oz sirloin steak (£7); puddings (from £1.25), children's helpings (from £1). Well kept Banks's Bitter, Bass, Ruddles County, Stones Best, Theakstons XB and Old Peculier on handpump; friendly service; dominoes, cribbage, fruit machine and juke box or piped pop music. A spacious barn behind the pub has been converted to self-catering accommodation. There are lovely moorland pastures above the village. It does get busy at weekends. (*Recommended by J Scarisbrick, Mike and Wendy Proctor, Geoffrey and Nora Cleaver, Chris Raisin, John Beeken, John Beeken, Steve Mitcheson, Anne Collins, Jon Wainwright*)

Free house   Licensees Peter and Julie Wilkinson   Real ale   Meals and snacks (till 10 evening)   Children welcome   Open 12–3, 7–11; closed 25 and 26 Dec   Self-catering barn (with two bedrooms) tel *Onecote (053 88) 206; £25 for the whole unit*

OVER HADDON (Derbys)   SK2066 Map 7

Lathkil ⊘ ⟸

Village and inn signposted from B5055 just SW of Bakewell

Memorable views from this inn sweep over the wooded slopes of Lathkill Dale, Youlgreave church tower and the village of Stanton in Peak, and if you follow the footpath to the east of the pub you can see the River Lathkill far below flowing over a series of weirs. It's a warmly welcoming, informal place and the airy room on the right has a cheery fire in the attractively carved fireplace, black beams, old-fashioned settles with upholstered cushions or plain wooden chairs, a Delft shelf of blue and white plates on one white wall, original prints and photographs and big windows. On the left is the spacious and sunny family dining area, which doubles as a restaurant in the evenings; at lunchtime the highly praised bar food is served here and includes home-made soup (£1.20), filled cobs (from £1.20), smoked mackerel salad (£2.80), lamb curry or quiche (£3.45), lasagne (£3.50), steak and kidney pie or beef and mushroom casserole (£3.75), smoked trout (£3.75), and a help-yourself cold buffet (£3.95); home-made puddings (from £1.25). Well kept Wards Darleys Best Mild and Sheffield Best on handpump and good breakfasts; piped classical music or jazz, shove-ha'penny, dominoes, cribbage. The pub is popular with walkers and there's even a place in the lobby to leave muddy boots. *(Recommended by Curt and Lois Stevens, Mike and Wendy Proctor, Gordon Theaker, Sarah Bullard, Paul and Margaret Baker, Simon Velate, John and Joan Wyatt, Michael Thomson, Steve Mitcheson, Anne Collins, Andrew Stephenson, D J Milner, Kelvin and Janet Lawton, F C Price, Brian and Anna Marsden, Richard Sanders)*

Free house   Licensee Robert Grigor-Taylor   Real ale   Lunchtime meals and snacks Evening restaurant (not Sun)   Children in eating area of bar at lunchtime and in restaurant in evening   Open 11.30–3, 6–11; closed 25 Dec evening   Bedrooms tel Bakewell (0629) 812501; £32.50S/£60B

PENKHULL (Staffs)   SJ8644   Map 7
Greyhound

Leaving Newcastle centre on A34 for Stafford, look out for the first left turn after two hospital signposts and a stretch of parkland; turn into this Newcastle Lane to find village centre at top of hill; pub in Manor Court St, opposite church; OS Sheet 118 map reference 868448

One of the oldest Potteries pubs in the area, this pretty 16th-century place is genuinely friendly and its rooms traditionally furnished: one has red plush seats around massive old-fashioned gilt tables, tiny pictures on its white walls and a neat and cosy inglenook fireplace (filled with flowers in summer). The other has more of a 1940s atmosphere, with seats built into its darkening Anaglypta walls, elaborate gas-style wall lamps, an organ and dark panelling elsewhere. A decent range of good value bar food – depending on the weather – might include filled baps (from 50p), soup (60p), filled baked potatoes (from 80p), a choice of omelettes (£1.85), ploughman's (£2.10), and home-made specials such as hot-pot (£1.95), chicken casserole, cottage pie or pork steaks (£2.25); puddings (from 80p). Ansells Bitter, Ind Coope Burton and Tetleys on handpump; table skittles, football table, darts, cribbage, dominoes, and CD juke box. A couple of picnic-table sets on the front pavement face the churchyard of the charming village, with more behind – where there's a barbecue; they are hoping to redecorate the outside of the building in the near future. *(Recommended by Mike and Wendy Proctor, Dr and Mrs G J Sutton; more reports please)*

Ansells (Allied)   Licensees Mr and Mrs John Chadwick   Real ale   Lunchtime meals and snacks (lunchtime, not Sun)   Children if eating, lunchtime   Open 12–3, 6.30–11; closed 25 Dec evening

ROWARTH (Derbys)   SK0189   Map 7
Little Mill

Turn off A626 at Mellor signpost (in steep dip at Marple Bridge); fork left at Rowarth signpost, then follow Little Mill signpost; OS Sheet 110 map reference 011889

Roses, honeysuckle and tubs of flowers decorate the front terrace of this isolated but popular stone-slated white house and there are little lawns with ash trees, seats, swings and a climbing frame. Inside, the open-plan bar has stub walls, bare brick pillars, and simple furniture, and bar food includes soup (85p), sandwiches (from £1.10), black pudding (£1.20), tasty deep-fried mushrooms, doner kebab (from £2.10), ploughman's (£3), and home-made dishes such as lasagne (£2.45), steak and kidney pie (£3.25), lamb or chicken curry (£3.45), and puddings (£1.25). Banks's, Batemans, Hansons, Robinsons Best Mild and Bitter on handpump and quite a few malt whiskies; darts, pool, dominoes, cribbage, fruit and trivia machine, juke box and piped music. The 1932 Pullman railway dining car (called the Deryshire Belle) is converted into three well appointed bedrooms. The pub is tucked away down tricky roads in good walking country. *(Recommended by H B Vanstone, Steve Mitcheson, Anne Collins, A M Neal)*

Free house   Licensee Christopher Barnes   Real ale   Meals and snacks (all day) Upstairs restaurant   Children welcome   Jazz Suns, blues Weds evenings   Bedrooms tel New Mills (0663) 743178; £25B/£35B; they also have two self-contained cottages Open 12–11

RUDYARD (Staffs)   SJ9558   Map 7

Poachers 🅟

Village sigposted off A523 just N of Leek

Reminiscent in character of the licensees' former pub, the Red Lion over at Ipstones (a great favourite with readers in their day), this has a spreading dining lounge with lots of well spaced (and well polished) tables and wheelback chairs. The room rambles around the central servery, and parts have a pretty view over steep pastures to Leek (it's an easy walk to Rudyard Park). The atmosphere's comfortable and relaxed, but the main thing is the food, which includes lunchtime ploughman's (£2.50) and salads (from £2.75), and soup (90p), chicken crunch or steak and kidney pie (£3.25), pork Italiano (£3.95), gammon and eggs or vegetarian dishes like butter bean and vegetable au gratin (£4.50), halibut steak with a tomato, mushroom, white wine and cream sauce (£4.95), and steaks (£6.95 – special sauce £1.50 extra); specials such as lemon sole filled with crabmeat (£4.95) or Barnsley chop with mint sauce (£5.95), children's meals (£1.95, not Saturday evening). Service is efficient even at busy times (notably, weekends). Behind the sturdy rather imposing gritstone building is a terrace with tables under yew trees, and more in a spacious newish loggia – where swallows nest under the eaves. Well kept Bass and Worthington PA on handpump, decent wines. The restaurant is smart. *(Recommended by John Scarisbrick; more reports please)*

Bass   Licensees Anne and Graham Yates   Real ale   Meals and snacks   Restaurant tel Rudyard (053 833) 294; closed Sun-Tues evenings   Children welcome   Open 12–2.30, 7–11

SANDONBANK (Staffs)   SJ9428   Map 7

Seven Stars

4 1/2 miles from M6 junction 14; A34 link road towards Stone but at first roundabout continue on A518 ring road, then turn left on to B5066; alternatively from A51 in Sandon, follow signpost B5066, Stafford

There are several cosy corners in the open-plan bar of this popular white house, as well as an array of pink plush stools and cushioned captain's chairs, little country prints, lots of polished brass and two large open fires. Steps lead down to a lower wood-panelled lounge with comfortable chairs and thick-pile carpet. Popular with businessmen at lunchtime, the bar food includes sandwiches, ploughman's (lunchtime only, from £1.95), beef curry (£3.50), a selection of chicken dishes (from £3.50; with crabmeat and prawns £4.75), plaice (£3.75), vegetarian dishes (£3.95), lamb cutlets (£4), gammon or seafood provençale (£4.50), steaks (from £6.75) and daily specials such as a large beef pie. They only take credit cards for orders over ten pounds. Burtonwood and Dark Mild on handpump; two pool tables (used in winter only), piped music. Outside there are picnic-table sets at the front, and a swing on the grass at the back. *(Recommended by J Scarisbrick, TBB, Mike and Wendy Proctor, Dr C D E Morris, Pamela E Roper, Paul and Margaret Baker, Laurence Manning, Dave Braisted)*

Burtonwood   Licensee Mrs A D Jackson   Real ale   Meals and snacks (till 9.45 evening)   Restaurant tel Sandon (088 97) 316   Children welcome   Open 11.30–3, 6.30–11

SEIGHFORD (Staffs)   SJ8725   Map 7

Holly Bush

3 miles from M6 junction 14: A5013 towards Eccleshall, left on to B5405 in Great Bridgeford, then first left signposted Seighford

The licensee who has taken over this country pub since our last edition used to run the Seven Stars at Sandonbank – another long-standing main entry. He's redecorated the bars and the pub is even more geared to serving food than before. The spacious and airy black-beamed bar has wheelback chairs and comfortable settles around the varnished rustic tables, big windows, ivy-leaf chintz curtains and light modern prints of landscapes; there's also an interesting collection of antique bric-a-brac, brass cooking instruments and foreign coins – these are stuck on the mirrors around the attractively carved inglenook fireplace. The lounge bar is no-smoking. Bar food includes home-made soup (£1), home-made pâté (£1.95), lunchtime ploughman's (£2.35) or open sandwiches (£2.75), lasagne (£3.75), salads (£4.50), very good gammon with egg or pineapple or vegetarian dishes (£4.75), steaks (from £6.50), and daily specials; children's menu (£1.50 – up till 8pm). Well kept Tetleys on handpump and several vintage ports. The neat back rose garden has seats on a terrace, in a vine arbour, and on the spacious lawn. (*Recommended by J Scarisbrick, A G Roby, Richard Dolphin, Peter Watkins, Pam Stanley, Caroline Wright, Helen and Wal Burns, R P Fisher*)

Ansells (Allied) Licensee Ron Roestenburg Real ale Meals and snacks (till 10 evening) Restaurant tel Seighford (0785) 282280 Children welcome Open 11–3, 6–11

SHARDLOW (Derbys) SK4330 Map 7

Hoskins Wharf

3 1/2 miles from M1 junction 24; A6 towards Derby, pub on left

A neat and unfussy conversion of an imposing late 18th-century canal warehouse – very striking because of the way that one branch of the canal plunges through a sweeping arch in the building's centre. You reach the bar by a counter-weighted drawbridge: inside is not large, with simple furniture, stripped brickwork, heavy beams, brick flooring, some colourful narrow-boat nameplates, a picture window overlooking the canal basin – and plenty of chat. Outside there are picnic-table sets among weeping willows (and an unusually big dragon's-claw willow) on a grassy promontory between the canal branches, with more by a children's mini-adventure playground on a bigger stretch of grass behind; a very pretty spot. An upstairs restaurant shares the view (where there's a bargain 3-course meal at £4.99); lunchtime bar food includes soup (85p), filled French sticks (from £1), jumbo sausage (£1.95), ploughman's and cold meat salads (£2.25), breaded plaice (£2.50), and lasagne or steak and kidney pie (£2.85). Well kept Hoskins Bitter, Penns and Premium on handpump, with a changing guest beer such as Vaux Samson, several malt whiskies and a farm cider; dominoes, fruit machine, maybe darts, and piped music. (*Recommended by Carl Southwell, Steve Waters, Andrew Stephenson, Jon Wainwright, Derek and Sylvia Stephenson, Mr and Mrs P A Jones, Andy and Jill Kassube, Dr P H Mitchell*)

Hoskins Licensee Ray Theobald Real ale Lunchtime meals and snacks Restaurant Open 11.30–2.30, 6.15–11; 11.30–11 Thurs-Sat in summer; bedrooms should be open during 1991, tel Derby (0332) 792844

Malt Shovel ✿

Directions as above, then in Shardlow itself turn down Wilne Lane at Great Wilne signpost, then left after crossing canal

Right by the Trent and Mersey Canal, this friendly 18th-century pub used to be a maltings – hence its varying ceiling heights and odd angled walls. There's lots to look at such as jugs, mugs, plates, swords, brewery and tobacco mirrors and advertisements, cartoons and other pictures and cigarette cards. Good window seats overlook the busy canal, with more tables out beside it, and there's a good winter log fire. Tasty lunchtime bar food includes soup (80p), sandwiches (from 90p), basket meals (from £1.70), ploughman's (£1.80), sausage and egg (£2.25), chilli con carne (£2.50), steak and kidney pie or superb beef casserole (£2.50), salads (from £2.90), ham and pineapple (£3.75), and steaks (from £5), with more unusual daily specials like salmon and prawn pie (£3.60), pork in Pernod or beef whirls (£4.30), and lamb with cheese-mint or Mediterranean chicken (£4.50); puddings (£1); good, helpful service, even when busy. Well kept Marstons Burton, Pedigree and Mercian Mild on handpump and a few malt whiskies; piped music. The nearby marina has a museum of canalboat life, and the Castle Donington collection of historic racing cars is not far. No motor-cyclists. (*Recommended by Jane and Calum Maclean, K W Mills, Richard and Ann Jenkins, J D Andrews, Tony Bland, Dr Paul Kitchener, Carol and Richard Glover, T Nott, Mr and Mrs P A Jones, J D Roberts, Ted George, Roger Bellingham, Steve Waters, Jon Wainwright, Genie and Brian Smart, Richard Sanders, Wayne Brindle, Jane and Niall, G Bloxsom*)

Marstons   Licensees Peter and Gillian Morton-Harrison   Real ale   Lunchtime meals and snacks (not Sun)   Children welcome if eating   Open 11.30–3, 5.30–11; closed evenings 25 and 26 Dec

SHRALEYBROOK (Staffs)   SJ7850   Map 7

Rising Sun

3 miles from M6 junction 16; from A500 towards Stoke take first right turn signposted Alsager, Audley; in Audley turn right on the road still shown on many maps as A52, but now in fact a B, signposted Balterley, Nantwich; pub then signposted on left (at the T-junction look out for the Watneys Red Barrel)

As well as their own-brew beer produced in the brewery behind the pub – Rising, Setting and Sunstroke Bitters and a more powerful brew appropriately called Total Eclipse – they keep half a dozen on handpump, rotating weekly from a cellar of around 30, and typically including Adnams, Badger, Batemans XXXB, Courage Directors, Eagle, Hadrian Gladiator and Centurion, Mansfield, Pitfield Dark Star, Robinwood Old Fart, and Titanic; they also have around 110 malts and 100 liqueurs, and Thatcher's and Westons Special Vintage ciders. The friendly, gently lit bar has shiny black panelling and beams and timbers in the ochre walls, red leatherette seats tucked into the timberwork and cosy alcoves, brasses and some netting and a warm open fire. A wide choice of bar food includes sandwiches, soup (90p), burgers (£1.55), vegetarian sausage (£2), breaded plaice (£3), lots of vegetarian meals or beef in ale casserole (£4.20), and chicken Kiev or sirloin steak (£6). Dominoes, fruit machine and piped music. There may be a minibus service to get you home. (*Recommended by Mike and Wendy Proctor, Dr M Owton, John Scarisbrick, Sue Holland, Dave Webster, Pamela E Roper, Len Beattie, Martin Aust*)

Own brew   Licensee Mrs Gillian Holland   Real ale   Meals and snacks (12–2.30, 6.30–10.30)   Restaurant tel Stoke on Trent (0782) 720600   Children welcome Occasional live entertainment Fri and Sat evenings in upstairs function room   Open 12–3.30, 6.30–11; all day Sat

TUTBURY (Staffs)   SK2028   Map 7

Olde Dog & Partridge 🛏

A50 N of Burton on Trent; bypass is being built around the attractive small town

This extended white-fronted Tudor coaching inn was a centre for bull-running until the practice was abolished in 1778. It's now popular for its very spacious carvery (where there's a no-smoking area): soup (£1.35), a choice of pâtés (£2.20) and lots of other starters, steak pie done in Owd Rodger (£4.85), a help-yourself cold table (from £4.95), spit-roasts (from £5.20), roasts (from £5.85) and puddings (from £1.50); a pianist performs here each evening. The well kept and civilised bar has two warm Turkey-carpeted rooms, one with red plush banquettes and rather close-set studded leather chairs, sporting pictures, stags' heads and a sizeable tapestry, the other with a plush-cushioned oak settle, an attractive built-in window seat, brocaded stools and a couple of Cecil Aldin hunting prints. Well kept Marstons Pedigree from the small oak bar counter; lunchtime snacks, including sandwiches (from £1.40); efficient service. The neat garden has white cast-iron seats and tables under cocktail parasols, with stone steps between its lawns, bedding plants, roses and trees. The bedrooms are very comfortable and they have planning permission to add quite a few more. (*Recommended by Stephen Goodchild, B M Eldridge; more reports please!*)

Free house   Licensee Mrs Yvette Martindale   Real ale   Lunchtime snacks (not Sun) Carvery and (not Sun) small evening restaurant   Children welcome   Evening pianist Open 10.30–3, 6–11; closed 25 and 26 Dec   Bedrooms tel Tutbury (0283) 813030; £54B/£66B

WARDLOW (Derbys)   SK1874 Map 7

Bulls Head

B6465; village signposted off A623 W of Chesterfield

A passing glance from the road might misleadingly suggest that this heavy-slated white house opposite the farm is a basic village local, but in fact it's decidedly a dining pub, its close-set tables filled with cheerful people enjoying a night out. It's doing well under the couple who took it over in 1989. The front part has deep green walls and plush button-back built-in wall banquettes, Turkey carpet, a lot of exposed stonework, some harness, and a coal-effect gas fire; behind is a no-smoking red-carpeted room, with its tables more intimately set between winged settles forming individual stalls. Bar food includes soup (£1), tasty potted shrimps (£2.25), popular cottage pie with red cabbage, a good seafood Mornay or steak and kidney pie (£3.95), evening steaks (from 8oz rump £6.95; also Sunday lunch) and dishes of the day such as plaice or chicken with asparagus (£7.25); there's a minimum charge of £3. Well kept Mansfield and Wards Sheffield Best on handpump; efficient service, piped music. There are tables on a small flagstoned terrace in front, and a couple on grass by sycamores behind; stone-walled small pastures stretch away on all sides. (*Recommended by Dennis Royles, MP, Mrs D M Everard, Derek and Sylvia Stephenson, D W Crossley*)

Free house   Licensees Brian and Lynn Wetherall   Real ale   Meals (12–2, 6–9.30; booking strongly advised Fri-Sun)   Restaurant   Children in eating area of bar   Open 11–3, 6.30–11   Bedrooms tel Tideswell (0298) 871431; no prices available as we went to press

Three Stags Heads

Wardlow Mires

A small, no-smoking dining parlour with a full licence, bookable tables and original fireplace has been opened in this white-painted stone cottage. The unspoilt little parlour bar has flagstones, a cast-iron kitchen range which is kept alight in winter, old leathercloth seats, a couple of antique settles with flowery cushions, two high-backed Windsor armchairs and simple oak tables; also, a double rack of pots (made in the barn which is a pottery workshop – they also make the majority of the plates used in the pub), a petrified cat in a glass case, and three live dogs. Food is served all day from a regularly changing menu and home-made dishes include humous or crudités, black pudding, courgette and tomato casserole with cheese dumplings (£4), gnocchi verde with rich tomato sauce (£4.50), and rabbit pie or lamb and apricot tagine with cous-cous (£6). Matthew Browns Mild, Theakstons Old Peculier and Youngers Scotch and No 3 on handpump; cribbage, dominoes, spoof, chess, and nine men's morris. The front terrace outside looks across the main road to the distant hills. Walkers – and their boots – are welcome. Car park. (*Recommended by Simon Velate, Matt Pringle, Wayne Brindle*)

Free house   Licensees Geoff and Pat Fuller   Real ale   Meals and snacks (12–10; 12–2.30, 7–9.30 Sun)   Restaurant tel Tideswell (0298) 872268   Children in eating area of bar before 8.30pm   Live folk/traditional blues Sat evening and Sun lunchtime Open 11–11; closed lunchtime winter Mons (not Bank Hols) when evening opening is 7

WARSLOW (Staffs)   SK0858 Map 7

Greyhound 🏚

B5053 S of Buxton

It's the homely, friendly atmosphere in this slated stone building that has particularly pleased readers. The long beamed bar has elm-topped stools and cushioned oak antique settles, some quite elegant, on its carpet, a log fire, and quietly restrained landscapes on the cream walls; the windows, with both curtains and net curtains, are decorated with houseplants and there's now a yard ale. Good home-made bar food includes soup (£1), sandwiches or home-baked rolls (from £1 – they home-cook their meat), ploughman's (from £2.55), cheesey vegetable flan

(£2.75), Indonesian curried pork and peaches (£3.55), chicken fillet in cheese and cider sauce or gammon and pineapple (£3.95), sirloin steak (£5.50), and daily specials that are chalked up on a board; puddings (from £1.10), children's menu (£1.50), traditional Sunday lunch (£3.25) – best to get there early then (and on Saturday evening); good breakfasts. Well kept Bass and a guest beer on handpump and a log fire; pool room, with darts, dominoes, fruit machine and table skittles; piped music from Bros to Beethoven. There are rustic seats out in front, with picnic-table sets under ash trees in the side garden. The village is just a short stroll from the Manifold Valley, and quite well placed for other Peak District features. The simple bedrooms are comfortable and clean and there are local information leaflets in the foyer. *(Recommended by Mike and Wendy Proctor, Martin and Amy Evans, Steve Mitcheson, Anne Collins, M G Clark, Mr and Mrs M Knowles, Mr and Mrs R Armit)*

Free house   Licensees Bob Charlton and Colin Cook   Real ale   Meals and snacks (12–2.15, 6.30–10 – 9.30 Sat)   Children until 9pm in pool room and tap room   Live music Sat (usually singer and guitarist)   Open 11.30–3, 6.30–11 (till 11.45 Sat); 12–2.30, 7–11 in winter (till 11.45 Sat)   Bedrooms tel Buxton (0298) 84249; £13l£26

WETTON (Staffs)   SK1055 Map 7

Olde Royal Oak

Just as you enter this white-painted and shuttered stone village pub there's an old part with black beams supporting white ceiling boards, an oak corner cupboard, small dining chairs around rustic tables and a log fire in the stone fireplace. This extends into a more modern-feeling area, with another fire and a door into a carpeted sun lounge, which looks on to the small garden. The new licensees have changed the bar food: sandwiches (from 90p), ploughman's (from £2.50 – the cheese for the Stilton version is made in nearby Hartington), and main dishes like sausages (£2.25), local gammon and egg (£3.50), home-made steak and kidney pie (£3.75), and rump steak (£5.95); traditional fish and chips on Friday and Saturday evenings and main course Sunday roast (£3.25). Ruddles County and Rutland and Theakstons XB on handpump and several malt whiskies; darts, dominoes. It's set in National Trust and walking country, with places like Wetton Hill and the Manifold Valley nearby. Behind the pub is a croft suitable for caravans and tents. *(Recommended by Tony and Pat Young, Dr Keith Bloomfield, John Scarisbrick, Simon Velate, J H G Owen, Steve Mitcheson, Anne Collins, T Galligan, JMC, Dennis Royles, A C and S J Beardsley, Jon Wainwright)*

Free house   Licensees George and Barbara Burgess   Real ale   Meals and snacks (not winter Sun evenings)   Children in sun lounge   Open 11.30–2.30, 7–11 (11–3, 6.30–11 summer Sats); closed evening 25 Dec

WHITMORE (Staffs)   SJ8141 Map 7

Mainwaring Arms ★

3 miles from M6 junction 15; follow signs for Market Drayton, Shrewsbury, on to A53

Though a new licensee has taken over this lovely stone building, little has changed – a new menu has been introduced and a barbecue area at the back has been cobbled. Inside, the interconnecting oak-beamed rooms ramble up and down in and out, with some old-fashioned settles among comfortable, more modern seats, reproduction memorial brasses on the walls and three open fires, one in a capacious stone fireplace in the lower room. Home-made bar food includes soup (95p), sandwiches (from 95p), ploughman's (from £2.50), a good summer cold buffet with salads and a choice of meats (£3.75), cottage or steak and kidney pie, plaice mornay or chicken in a tomato sauce (all £3.25), gammon with egg or pineapple (£3.75), steaks (£6), and puddings like sherry trifle, chocolate fudge cake or hot cheesecake (£1.50). Well kept Bass, Boddingtons, and Marstons Pedigree on handpump. There are seats outside, opposite the idyllic village church. The pub is named after the family that has owned it (and most other things around here) since the 11th century. The local hunt may use it for gatherings. *(Recommended by J Scarisbrick, Mike and Wendy Proctor, T Nott, TBB, Niall and Jane, Laurence Manning, D J Braisted)*

Free house   Licensee Peter Slack   Real ale   Meals and snacks   Children in eating area, lunchtime   Open 11–2.30 (3 Sat), 5.30–11

WRINEHILL (Staffs)   SJ7547 Map 7
Crown

Den Lane; pub signed just off A531 Newcastle-under-Lyme–Nantwich

Spreading comfortably around the brick-built serving bar (which has some nice hand-painted stained glass behind it), this civilised and neatly kept country pub has been in the same hands for 14 years. It's been carefully refurbished with red plush wall settles, banquettes and stools around the dark cast-iron-framed tables on its carpet, patterned curtains on rings on rails, and attractive pictures ranging from little etchings of pottery kilns to big landscapes and old prints. At one end, there's a flagstoned inglenook with plush side seats and at the other, a second open fire in a stripped brick fireplace with black-iron side oven. Generously served, good value bar food includes lasagne or plaice (£3.25), scampi (£3.60), vegetarian dishes and steaks from sirloin (£5.95) to 16oz T-bone (£6.95), with good home-made ice-creams; well kept Bass and Marstons Pedigree on handpump; dominoes, well reproduced pop music, friendly service. *(Recommended by Catherine and Andrew Brian, Laurence Manning)*

Free house   Licensees Charles and Sue Davenhill   Real ale   Meals (not weekday lunchtimes, not Sun evening)   Children in eating area of bar until mid-evening   Open 6–11 weekdays (closed lunch, except Bank Hols), 12–3, 7–11 Sat; usual Sun hours

Lucky Dip

Besides the fully inspected pubs, you might like to try these Lucky Dips recommended to us and described by readers (if you do, please send us reports):

Abbots Bromley, Staffs [SK0724], *Bagots Arms*: Popular local *(M A Robinson)*; [High St], *Coach & Horses*: Attractive low-beamed bar with friendly atmosphere, wide range of customers; lunchtime food, well kept Ind Coope Burton; three comfortable bedrooms *(M A Robinson)*; *Crown*: Bass pub, worth knowing as a good value place to stay; the much-modernised lounge bar is plain but comfortable; games — and a big wall painting of the village's very ancient Sept horn dance — in bright public bar; bar food served till 10; children welcome; bedrooms airy and decently equipped *(S G Game, David Barnes, LYM)*; *Goats Head*: Very attractive timbered building overlooking centre of picturesque village; reasonable choice of food *(M A and W R Proctor)*; [High St], *Royal Oak*: Friendly welcome and high standard of cheap, varied bar food; popular, interesting Oak Room restaurant *(Fiona Carrey, M A Robinson)*

Alrewas, Staffs [King William IV Rd; off main st; SK1714], *King William IV*: Weekly changing specials particularly praised — tables can be reserved in separate raised eating area; no food Sun-Wed evenings *(Mike and Mandy Challis, Hilary Sargeant, Norman Clarke)*

☆ **Alstonefield**, Staffs [Hopedale; SK1355], *Watts Russell Arms*: Simple welcoming pub, light and airy, with usual range of bar food decently prepared, well kept Marstons Burton and Pedigree on handpump, open fire, chatty staff, piped radio music; tables on small terrace by quiet lane, handy for Dovedale and Manifold valleys; opens noon; two recently added bedrooms *(Jon Wainwright, A C Lang, Steve Mitcheson, Anne Collins, G T and J Barnes, BB)*

Amington, Staffs [Tamworth Rd; SK2304], *Gate*: Recently refurbished and partly rebuilt; well kept beer inc consistently good Marstons Pedigree, superb range of bar food at affordable prices, small garden, car park, canal mooring; very busy weekends and summer, no dogs; children allowed in conservatory *(Colin Gooch, J Jewitt)*

Anslow, Staffs [Bramhill Rd; SK2125], *Brickmakers Arms*: Small and unpretentiously friendly local, well kept Marstons Pedigree, good value bar lunches in generous helpings, inc old-fashioned home-made puddings *(M A and W R Proctor)*

Apperknowle, Derbys [SK3878], *Yellow Lion*: Charming lounge with plenty of country character; well kept Burton Bitter and others; good, reasonably priced food at all times; children allowed in dining room *(Rory and Elizabeth Cunningham)*

Ashbourne, Derbys [Ashbourne Green; top of hill on way to Matlock; SK1846], *Bowling Green*: Reasonably priced food with good choice inc vegetarian dishes is the attraction at this fairly plain pub, with good friendly atmosphere and weekly guest beer; bedrooms clean and pleasant *(M A and W R Proctor, P Da Silva, Richard Sanders)*; [St Johns St], *Smiths*: Narrow bar in clean and appealing town pub; steps up to small lounge area (just a couple of tables here), which leads to dining room with some fine antique furniture; hearty helpings of usual bar food, Marstons Pedigree *(Simon Velate, Dorothy and David Young, Richard Sanders)*

☆ **Ashford in the Water**, Derbys [SK1969], *Ashford Inn*: Clean, comfortably refurbished and well kept, with loads of gleaming brass, pleasant staff, good helpings of well prepared bar food with fresh veg, upmarket restaurant with emphasis on healthy eating; get there early to be sure of the good specials; Bass and Stones on handpump; bedrooms inc at least one four-poster; picturesque village, pleasant staff *(Neville Kenyon, Cdr H R Spedding, P A Crossland, D A Cawley, BB)*

Ashford in the Water, *Black Bull*: Comfortable, smartly done out lounge with friendly welcome, good service and home-made food including imaginative dishes, well kept Marstons *(Dr and Mrs James Stewart, David Heath, Mrs Carolyn Smith, DC)*

☆ **Ashley**, Staffs [signposted from A53 NE of Market Drayton; SJ7636], *Peel Arms*: Well run refurbished pub in pretty village, with interconnecting rooms, plush seating and large cooking-range fire; well kept Marstons Pedigree, attractive garden overlooking fields *(Philip Williams, G T and J Barnes)*

☆ **Ashley** [Lower Rd (towards B5026)], *Robin Hood*: Olde-worlde decor, oak beams, open fire, brown leather seating in both lounge and bar, unobtrusive piped music, well kept McEwans 70/- and 80/-, good bar snacks at attractive prices, Sun lunches, keen young staff and jovial licensees; separate dining room, well behaved children allowed *(G T and J Barnes)*

Ashley, *Meynell Arms*: Village pub with deep sofa, cast-iron stove and other old-fashioned touches in timbered, panelled and stripped stone lounge with wolf pictures and ram's head in corner; games inc darts and table skittles in comfortable public bar, well kept Bass on handpump, bar food, children in eating area *(G T and J Barnes, LYM)*

Ashover, Derbys [Church St; SK3564], *Black Swan*: Very friendly Bass pub with nicely furnished one-room bar, separate eating area at one end, big open fire; well kept beer, friendly atmosphere, good service, and interesting food; children's room *(Derek and Sylvia Stephenson); Red Lion*: Spacious and gracious pub on windy corner of unspoilt village — a glorious rural spot; free house with Mansfield and Youngs and good food *(Robert Caldwell)*

Bagnall, Staffs [SJ9251], *Stafford Arms*: Pleasant village setting for picturesque pub with real fires in beamed bar and stripped-stone lounge converted from former stables; restaurant extension, new landlord

Bakewell, Derbys [Market Pl; SK2168], *Peacock*: Lovely stone building outside, clean and bright modern furnishings inside; Wards ales, no food Sun evening *(Steve Mitcheson, Anne Collins); [Market Pl], Red*

Lion: Panelled lounge with atmosphere of a market-town pub, well kept Marstons Pedigree, straightforward bar food upstairs inc good Bakewell tart *(Steve Mitcheson, Anne Collins, Sidney and Erna Wells);* [The Square], *Rutland Arms*: Worth knowing for the calm atmosphere of its well kept bar, though it's predominantly a hotel *(Steve Mitcheson, Anne Collins, BB)*

Baldwins Gate, Staffs [Whitmore Rd; SJ7940], *Sheet Anchor*: Large roadside Davenports house with naval theme and pine, country-style furniture; Mild and Bitter *(Sue Holland, Dave Webster)*

☆ **Balterley**, Staffs [Newcastle Rd; SJ7650], *Broughton Arms*: Pleasant rural pub with airy bar, everything clean and well presented; quick service, well kept Greenalls, sensible choice of well served bar food inc good value steaks *(Catherine and Andrew Brian, S R Lear)*

☆ **Bamford**, Derbys [Taggs Knoll — main rd; SK2083], *Anglers Rest*: Large, spotlessly clean pub with revolving door and warm atmosphere; wide choice of good value bar food, quick service *(Steve Mitcheson, Anne Collins, Joan and John Calvert)*

Bamford [main rd], *Marquis of Granby*: Substantial old hotel with unsurprising large bar — but worth knowing for its Derwentside garden and smaller cocktail bar furnished with sumptuous panelling etc salvaged from *Titanic's* sister-ship *(Steve Mitcheson, Anne Collins, LYM)*

Barlborough, Derbys [SK4878], *Royal Oak*: Worth visiting for the 1920s room with cane seating, nostalgic silhouettes and black and white photographs *(Robert Caldwell)*

☆ **Baslow**, Derbys [SK2572], *Devonshire Arms*: Pleasantly refurbished inn nr Chatsworth, clean and well run, with particularly good furnishings, attractive nick-nacks and good value food centring on excellent sausages and seven-inch filled Yorkshire puddings; Shipstones and Marstons Pedigree *(ILP, Dr Keith Bloomfield)*

☆ **Beeley**, Derbys [SK2667], *Devonshire Arms*: Black oak beams and stripped stone- and slate-work in clean and spacious pub also handy for Chatsworth, with well kept Theakstons and Wards real ales, big log fires, straightforward food in bar and nice separate dining room — best to arrive early for good seats, and decidedly overpopular at really busy times; attractive rolling scenery; children welcome, with upstairs family room and own menu *(Keith Bloomfield, M A and W R Proctor, Simon Velate)*

Birchover, Derbys [SK2462], *Red Lion*: Welcoming, friendly local with lots of atmosphere; sandwiches only *(C J and L M Elston)*

Bobbington, Staffs [A458 Bridgnorth—Stourbridge; SO8090], *Six Ashes*: Pleasant low building, friendly staff, well kept Banks's, good bar food inc fine beef and pasta casserole *(Dave Braisted)*

Bottom House, Staffs [A523 SE of Leek; SK0452], *Forge*: Friendly warm service with good choice of well kept beer and good home-made food; Tudor-style decor, spacious *(Colin D Rivis)*

Boylestone, Derbys [Harehill; signed off A515, N of A50 junction; SK1735], *Rose & Crown*: Bar quite original, with tongue and groove walls, inglenook, tiled very 1950s fireplace and red tiled floor; lounge cosier; well kept Marstons Pedigree — a friendly place *(Chris Raisin)*

☆ **Bradley**, Staffs [SJ8718], *Red Lion*: Friendly 16th-century pub with particularly good value food and well kept drink; really good garden centre nearby *(Nigel Hopkins)*

Bradwell, Derbys [Smalldale (off B6049); SK1781], *Bowling Green*: Good views from terrace outside much-modernised village pub with lots of malt whiskies *(LYM)*

Brewood, Staffs [SK8808], *Admiral Rodney*: Welcoming pseudo-Victorian atmosphere, good choice of well kept ales and good value food — especially steaks *(Patrick and Mary McDermott)*

Brocton, Staffs [Cannock Rd; SJ9619], *Chetwyn Arms*: Good, reasonably priced bar food from wide-ranging menu, well kept Banks's, cordial atmosphere *(G C Hixon)*

Burnhill Green, Staffs [Snowdon Rd; SJ7900], *Dartmouth Arms*: Charming pub at end of village street, tastefully extended, with good food and service *(Dave Braisted)*

☆ **Burton on Trent**, Staffs [Cross St — a no entry — heading N down Station St, pass Bass Brewery then turn left into Milton St (from which pub has a back entrance; SK2423], *Coopers Tavern*: Highly traditional back tap room with chatty landlord and notably well kept Bass straight from the imposing row of casks, accompanied by appropriate food such as cheap and nourishing hot filled cobs, pie and chips and so forth virtually throughout opening hours; the nearby Bass brewing museum is well worth a visit — and the pub is a very fine example of its type, we wish we had more reports on it; children welcome *(Chris Raisin, Graham Doyle, Richard Sanders, LYM)*

Burton on Trent [Moor St], *Black Horse*: Quiet but friendly Marstons house with plates from around the world in lounge, comfortable seating, piped music, pool table in bar, well kept Pedigree on handpump, good value filled rolls *(B M Eldridge)* ; [349 Anglesey Rd], *New Talbot*: Friendly Marstons pub with outstanding Pedigree on handpump, juke box and pool table in bar, piped music in lounge, filled rolls *(B M Eldridge)*

☆ **Buxton**, Derbys [Hurdlow Town; A515 Ashbourne Rd, about half a mile from the Bull i'th' Thorn; SK1166], *Duke of York*: Friendly, helpful landlord and good bar food, served all day Sun — soups and steak sandwich particularly recommended; also children's menu; Robinsons real ale; can get very busy indeed on holidays *(Steve Mitcheson, Anne Collins, R D Llewellyn, A J Francis)*

Buxton, Derbys [West Rd; SK0673], *Bakers Arms*: Good, homely, terraced local with

welcoming comfortable atmosphere and good mix of customers *(Jon Wainwright)*; [High St], *Cheshire Cheese*: Pleasant low-ceilinged open-plan pub with dark timber and stained glass, well kept Hardy & Hansons, decent malt whisky, warm welcome and decent attractively priced food in bar and restaurant; piped music; barbecues in newish back beer garden; jazz Sun, Mon and Weds *(Brian Smart, Genie Krakowska Smart)*

☆ **Castleton** Derbys [SK1583], *Olde Cheshire Cheese*: Two comfortable communicating bar areas in slated white timbered pub; wide choice of generously served bar food (the daily specials, pies such as rabbit or chicken, and the chips are well recommended), sensibly placed darts, leatherette seats around wooden tables, particularly affable licensee, piped jazz; popular with young people; bedrooms *(Lorna Koskela, Sidney and Erna Wells, Peter and Moyna Lynch, David and Rebecca Killick, Steve Mitcheson, Anne Collins, Dr B A W Perkins, BB)*

☆ **Castleton** [Cross St], *Olde Nags Head*: Village hotel renovated to preserve character, welcoming and spacious with open fires, antique furniture, well presented traditional bar food, good service, restaurant; bedrooms warm and comfortable *(Peter and Moyna Lynch, Richard Fawcett, Angela Nowill)*

Castleton [Cross St], *Bulls Head*: Unspoilt village pub, food inc fine Yorkshire puddings, honest landlady, warm fires, separate pool room and well kept Robinsons *(Matt Pringle, Robin and Christine Harman)*; [High St at junction with Castle St], *Castle*: More hotel than pub, but an interesting attractively sited place, with handsome flagstones, beams and stripped stonework in its plush bars, and some strange tales to tell; fruit machine and noisy trivia, food in bar and restaurant, well equipped if rather pricey bedrooms in recent extension, open all day in summer, with tables outside — but a recent run of mixed reports leaves us hoping for more news of this long-standing main entry; on GWG81 *(Steve Mitcheson, Anne Collins, A S Clements, Dorothy and David Young, LYM)*; *George*: Well kept Bass *(Steve Mitcheson, Anne Collins)*; [How Lane], *Peak*: Tetleys local with two bar areas, one comfortable and tidy, the other more homely and welcoming *(Steve Mitcheson, Anne Collins)*

☆ **Cheddleton**, Staffs [Basford Bridge Lane, off A520; SJ9651], *Boat*: Cheerful pub just above canal, low plank ceilings, well kept Marstons real ales; handy for North Staffs Steam Railway Museum *(M A and W R Proctor, LYM)*

Chesterfield, Derbys [Baslow Rd; SK3871], *Highwayman*: Steakhouse-type pub with good, cheap food, friendly service and good value comfortable bedrooms in hotel wing *(MN)* ; *Nelson*: Friendly staff, good lunchtime bar food inc vegetarian dishes *(Lorna Koskela)*

☆ **Chinley**, Derbys [A624 towards Hayfield;

SK0482], *Lamb*: Interesting old stone-built moorland free house, long and low, with row of three small rooms, the middle containing bar counter and chess table; fine stone fireplace; good friendly atmosphere, well prepared reasonably priced bar food served quickly once you order (though you may have to wait a while for a table), famous crown green bowler as licensee, Bass and Chesters on handpump; children allowed till 7 *(P A Crossland, D A Cawley, Steve Mitcheson, Anne Collins, Wayne Brindle)*
Chinley, Derbys [SK0482], *Old Hall*: Stone-built, ivy-clad pub with good Marstons Pedigree and fine good value restaurant; bedrooms very comfortable *(Andy and Jill Kassube)*
Chunal, Derbys [A624 a mile S of Glossop; SK0391], *Grouse*: Pleasant open-plan but cosy moorland pub with spectacular views of Glossop, real fires, old photographs of surrounding countryside, traditional furnishings and candlelit tables; friendly service, well kept Thwaites, decent bar food, restaurant upstairs where children allowed *(Lee Goulding, Gwen and Peter Andrews)*
Church Broughton, Derbys [OS Sheet 128 map reference 205337; SK2033], *Holly Bush*: Neatly refurbished brick village pub with well kept Marstons Pedigree; popular for home-made food — simple but good; separate dining room, good value Sun, a couple of friendly labradors (staff will move them if they bother you) *(Chris Raisin)*
Clayton, Staffs [Westbury Rd, Westbury Park; very nr M6 junction 15; SJ8542], *Westbury*: Good atmosphere and service, good value well presented bar food *(Catherine and Andrew Brian)*
☆ **Clifton Campville**, Staffs [SK2510], *Green Man*: Spick-and-span 15th-century village pub with friendly atmosphere and kind, efficient service; low beams, inglenook and chubby armchair in public bar, airy lounge, well kept Ind Coope and Tetleys and good value bar food inc fine sandwiches — especially the steak one; children in snug and family room, garden with donkeys, rabbits, fishpond, aviary and swings; good-sized car park *(Pete Storey, Chris Raisin, Graham Richardson, M A and W R Proctor, LYM)*
Colton, Staffs [SK0520], *Greyhound*: Well kept Banks's, courteous and efficient service, good bar food inc salmon in pastry — worth booking *(G C Hixon, Tim and Lynne Crawford)*
Coven, Staffs [off A449 Wolverhampton—Stafford; SJ9006], *Anchor*: Canalside pub with good moorings, well kept beers and reasonably priced food; Porterhouse restaurant with good grills *(Patrick and Mary McDermott)*; [A449], *Harrows*: Attractive, friendly roadside pub with quality interior, well kept beer and good bar food *(Denzil Taylor)*
Cromford, Derbys [SK2956], *Greyhound*: Attractive, spacious old-style bars in centre of pleasant market town; well kept Home Bitter; close to Via Gellia, dynamited around 1830 out of the fantastic rocks here *(Robert Caldwell)*
Derby [Siddals Rd], *Alexandra*: Imposing white-painted Victorian pub gently refurbished; good Batemans beers, cheery staff, snacks, bare boards *(Chris Raisin)*; [13 Exeter Pl], *Exeter Arms*: Low-ceilinged, beamed and traditional city-centre pub with recent extension but, on left of entrance, lovely little snug with built-in settles, black and white tiled floor, black lead and brass range, glowing fire and wonderfully cosy atmosphere; Marstons Burton, Pedigree and Merrie Monk on handpump, good sandwiches *(Angie and Dave Parkes, Chris Raisin, Carl Southwell)*; [Arleston La, Sinfin], *Ferrers Arms*: Modern, purpose-built pub with remarkably plush split-level bar, open fires in lounge, Everards on handpump and occasional guest beer *(Carl Southwell)*; [Queen St, nr cathedral], *Olde Dolphin*: In the oldest part and city's oldest pub, one room dedicated to the old Offilers brewery with photographs, bottles, and beermats; beamed and timbered bar, cosy snug, separate lounge, upstairs 'tearoom' with good value snacks all day; Bass, Springfield Bitter and Mild on handpump *(Angie and Dave Parkes, Steve Waters, Carl Southwell)*; [204 Abbey St], *Olde Spa*: Friendly old local built on spa, tiled floor and cast-iron fireplace (with coal-effect gas fire) alongside comfortable new built-in settles; refreshing mixture of young and old customers, locals and visitors; Ind Coope Burton on handpump, separate games room, garden with fountain *(Carl Southwell)*; [The Morlege], *Wardwick*: Atmospheric early 18th-century town pub with basic furnishings and floorboards, eating area on raised level; ABC Best, Ind Coope Burton and Tetleys on handpump, good value food; very popular with young people in the evening *(Carl Southwell)*
Dovedale, Staffs [Thorpe—Ilam rd; Ilam signposted off A52, Thorpe off A515, NW of Ashbourne; SK1452], *Izaak Walton*: Low-beamed bar with some distinctive antique oak settles and chairs and massive central stone chimney for the good log fire; Ind Coope Burton on handpump, bar food, restaurant, morning coffee, afternoon tea; seats outside; alone in fine position on the peaceful sloping pastures of Bunster Hill; nr start GWG84; bedrooms comfortable *(M A and W R Proctor, Dr Keith Bloomfield, LYM)*
Doveridge, Derbys [SK1134], *Cavendish Arms*: Nice relaxing pub with well kept Marstons Burton, wonderful warming fire *(Jon Wainwright)*
Draycott in the Clay, Staffs [SK1528], *Roebuck*: Simple roadside pub with big inglenook and well kept Marstons *(BB)*
Eckington, Derbys [SK4379], *Prince of Wales*: Quaint lounge, games room and good garden with swings for children, also drinks and sweets for them; well kept Marstons Best and Pedigree on handpump; good home-made food *(Rory and Elizabeth Cunningham)*
Edale, Derbys [SK1285], *Old Nags Head*:

Popular and spaciously high-raftered walkers' pub at start of Pennine Way; efficiently served substantial basic cheap food, open fire, well kept real ales; children in airy back family room with several space games; can get busy during walking season — lovely countryside around this village; nr start GWG83 *(Helen and John Thompson, Steve Mitcheson, Anne Collins, MN, Len Beattie, LYM)*

Ednaston, Derbys [SK2442], *Yew Tree*: Unusual pub with four separate rooms served from central bar, separate games room out by car park; best room overlooks garden through large bay window and has wall seats, large round table, dark beams and open fire; Bass on handpump, good bar food *(Chris Raisin)*

Egginton, Derbys [SK2628], *White Swan*: Warm welcome, well kept beer and particularly good value food; children's play area *(P Da Silva)*

Elmton, Derbys [SK5073], *Elm Tree*: Very popular softly lit rural pub with consistently well kept Bass, good pianist (ballads, oldies) Weds and Sat, bar food *(R A Caldwell)*

Endon, Staffs [Leek Rd (A53); SJ9253], *Plough*: Pleasant village pub, cheerfully renovated; separate restaurant and carvery, good car park *(D Brighouse)*

Etruria, Staffs [Etruria Rd (A53); SJ8647], *Rose & Crown*: Warm and friendly local devoting increasing space to dining — reasonably priced food; lots of old photographs and radios; Ansells, Ind Coope and other real ales *(M A and W R Proctor)*

Eyam, Derbys [Water Lane; SK2276], *Miners Arms*: Cheerful and helpful service and nice atmosphere in comfortably modernised dining pub, with pleasant and unhurried set lunch — good fresh ingredients; bedrooms *(LYM)*; *Rose & Crown*: Clean and well organised, popular with locals, well kept beer, good food and obliging service *(G C Hixon, Dave Braisted)*

☆ **Farnah Green**, Derbys [follow Hazelwood signpost off A517 in Blackbrook, W edge of Belper; SK3346], *Bluebell*: Good meals from omelettes, home-baked ham salads and steak and kidney pies to steaks in smartly kept dining pub with plushly furnished and discreetly decorated small rooms, and sturdy tables out on terrace and in quiet gently sloping spacious side garden; watchful staff, smart restaurant with inventive cooking; well kept Bass *(Wendy and Ian Phillips, BB)*

Flagg, Derbys [off A515 S of Buxton, at Duke of York; SK1368], *Plough*: Homely and very friendly stone pub in beautiful Peak District village; real fire, welcoming service, well kept Tetleys on handpump and well cooked reasonably priced bar food *(D M Moss)*

Flash, Staffs [SK0267], *New Inn*: Real little pub with good community feel, fabulous views, well kept Bass, pleasant service and reasonable bar food *(Sue Holland, Dave Webster)*; [A53 Buxton—Leek], *Travellers Rest*: Isolated hill pub on main road — Britain's third-highest; astonishing array of

beers with probably the largest number of pumps and taps in the country (most keg, not all on); old pennies embedded in table-tops are fun, though the decor doesn't appeal to everyone; juke box and/or TV can be loud, and there's no shortage of amusement machines; nice views over Longnor and beyond from back terrace, simple snacks; has been open all day *(Patrick Godfrey, Lee Goulding, Diane Hall, LYM)*

☆ **Fradley**, Staffs [canal junction, off A38 — OS Sheet 139 map reference 140140; SK1513], *Swan*: On junction of the Trent-Mersey canal and Birmingham Navigation system, doing well under new licensees — very popular with canal enthusiasts, and locals; well kept Ansells Bitter and Mild and Ind Coope Burton on handpump, decent bar food inc good Sun lunch; children welcome *(Clifford Blakemore, Dr and Mrs C D E Morris, Hilary Sargeant, Norman Clarke)*

Glossop, Derbys [Manor Park Rd; SK0394], *Commercial*: Welcoming and reliably friendly local, attentive licensees; darts, pool table, juke box and well kept Chesters; new dining area serving good food including hot roast beef sandwiches cut from joint Sat evenings *(Steve Mitcheson, Anne Collins)*; [off High St], *Fleece*: Extended street-corner local with functional furnishings and half a dozen ever-changing real ales (Tetleys always on); quiet atmosphere, except when there's live music (inc regular jazz); simple bar food; cheap *(Lee Goulding)*; [Norfolk St, opp rly stn], *Winston*: Busy, but warm and friendly pub with pleasant tropical fish tank; well kept Ruddles, good value bar food; comfortable bedrooms *(Steve Mitcheson, Anne Collins)*

☆ **Great Hucklow**, Derbys [SK1878], *Queen Anne*: Charming and clean family-run pub with Tetleys beers and freshly-squeezed orange juice from amazing American 1950s-style machine; interesting bar food with imaginative starters and daily specials such as Brazilian duck; large tables in comfortable, beamed bar with gleaming copper and open fire in winter, and two other rooms, one with French windows on to small terrace and pleasant garden with idyllic views; particularly neat lavatories; children welcome *(Francesca Lopez, Neville Kenyon)*

Hanley, Staffs [65 Lichfield St; SJ8747], *Coachmakers Arms*: Largely unaltered town-centre pub with lots of rooms leading off central corridor; lots of character, friendly atmosphere, good beer; outside gents *(Len Beattie)*

Hartshill, Staffs [296 Hartshill Rd (A52); SJ8545], *Jolly Potters*: Busy and friendly with several rooms; good beer *(Len Beattie)*; *New Victoria*: Actually a theatre, but its two bars open even when no plays are showing; choice of real ales inc guests, small self-service restaurant *(M A and W R Proctor)*

Hassop, Derbys [SK2272], *Eyre Arms*: Attractive creeper-covered stone building, L-shaped lounge bar dominated by painted coat of arms above stone fireplace, cushioned settles around the walls, low red velveteen chairs, lots of brass and copper; small public bar has darts; Stones on electric pump, bar food *(Simon Velate)*

Hathersage, Derbys [SK2381], *George*: Substantial old inn, picturesque outside, comfortable modernity in; a nice place to stay — they look after you well (the back bedrooms are the quiet ones); popular lunchtime bar food, neat flagstoned back terrace by rose garden; nr start GWG80 *(LYM)*; [side rd], *Scotsmans Pack*: Spacious and pleasant separate rooms with attractive woodwork, opposite interesting school building — attracts locals and walkers, with darts in back room, bar food lunchtime and evening, Bass on handpump and Stones on electric pump; nr Little John's reputed grave *(Matt Pringle)*

nr **Hathersage** [A625 about 2 1/2 miles E], *Fox House*: Handsome 18th-century stone pub worth knowing for its well kept Bass and nice moorland location; cheap food, piped Sinatra, simple furnishings *(BB)*

☆ **Hayfield**, Derbys [Church St; SK0387], *George*: Impressive village pub on picturesque main street, with stream nearby; comfortable, relaxing and cosy, particularly around roaring coal fire — there's another airier room; lots of local photographs, lunchtime food, well kept Burtonwood beers, small front terrace *(Lee Goulding, Steve Mitcheson, Anne Collins, M A and W R Proctor)*

☆ **Hayfield** [Little Hayfield; A625 N of Hayfield; SK0388], *Lantern Pike*: Friendly little village inn, cosy and homely, with very friendly and relaxed landlord, open fire in front room, back dining room (children allowed), bargains steaks — service may be slow; fine hill views from back terrace, served by window at side of bar; Blezards real ale; good value bedrooms *(P A Crossland, D A Cawley, Steve Mitcheson, Anne Collins)*

Hayfield [Market St; off A624 Glossop—Chapel-en-le-Frith], *Pack Horse*: Busy dining pub — generous helpings; well behaved children welcome till 8, no dogs *(Steve Mitcheson, Anne Collins, David Waterhouse)*; [SK0387], *Royal*: Notably friendly and relaxed atmosphere in former vicarage, now large riverside hotel; part-panelled bar, good side room full of curios and Toby jugs, real fires, lunchtime and evening food, good beers inc Websters Choice; bedrooms *(Lee Goulding, M A and W R Proctor)*; [Kinder Rd], *Sportsman*: Traditional, friendly, roomy pub, two coal fires, well kept Thwaites beers, wide choice of decent food inc well presented Sun roast *(Simon Barber)*; [close to Pack Horse], *Tipsy Pheasant*: Light and airy continental cafe-bar, popular with young people; loud rock music, space game, Stones beer *(Steve Mitcheson, Anne Collins)*

Heath, Derbys [just off M1 junction 29; A6175 towards Clay Cross, then first right; SK4466], *Elm Tree*: Very simple but good

meals — home-made and extremely reasonably priced; staff really friendly, Mansfield beers *(Geoff Lee)*

Hednesford, Staffs [Hill St; SJ9913], *Queens Arms*: Spotless pub with superb, cosy atmosphere in both lounge and bar; subdued lighting, lots of horse brasses and mining memorabilia, consistently well kept Bass, darts *(Tony Southall)*; [Mount St], *West Cannock*: Don't be misled by external appearances — cosy Victorian-style parlour on left, functional bar on right; friendly and attentive licensees, pool table, well kept Bass beers, good value food lunchtime and evening, beer garden *(John and Christine Simpson)*

High Offley, Staffs [SJ7826], *Anchor*: Homely and basic one-room pub on banks of Shropshire Union Canal; Marstons Pedigree and Owd Rodger and Wadworths 6x brought up from cellar, eleven different ciders, two perries and two scrumpies; snacks only *(P Lloyd, Miss K Bamford)*

Hilton, Derbys [Egginton Rd (A5132); SK2430], *White Swan*: Late 17th-century building with original beams, modern facilities; well kept Bass, good value grill-type bar food, garden with quite a menagerie of friendly animals; children's play area; *(Roger Ife)*

☆ **Hope**, Derbys [out towards Castleton; SK1783], *Poachers Arms*: Village pub with several welcoming bars, good decor, efficient service, generous helpings of interesting and varied well cooked food inc adventurous vegetarian dishes; Fri evening electric organ a real conversation-stopper; children welcome; bedrooms *(Dr B A W Perkins, D W Crossley, Mrs R M Morris, D J and P M Taylor)*

Hope [Edale Rd], *Cheshire Cheese*: Little up-and-down oak-beamed rooms — though not a lot of space when it's busy — in 16th-century stone-built village pub with lots of old local photographs and prints, abundant coal fires, well kept Wards Sheffield Best and Darleys Best, bar food (not Sun evening); children allowed in eating area; nr start GWG81; bedrooms inc cottage over the road; has changed hands several times in recent years *(Patrick Godfrey, Dr B A W Perkins, LYM)*

Hopwas, Staffs [SK1704], *Chequers*: Well kept open-plan pub near canal; frequent discos and live music *(Graham Richardson, LYM)*

Huddlesford, Staffs [off A38 2 miles E of Lichfield — OS Sheet 139 map reference 152097; SK1509], *Plough*: Extended old brick free house on Birmingham and Fazely canal; warm friendly atmosphere, well kept beer, good helpings of really good honest food, waterside tables *(Dave Braisted, Patrick and Mary McDermott)*

Hulme End, Staffs [SK1059], *Manifold Valley*: Stone hotel, close to river in open countryside; large lounge bar with good atmosphere, open fire and skittles; well kept Darleys Dark, Thorne Best and Wards Sheffield Best, separate dining room serving generous helpings of bar food and Sun lunches; children up to 2 allowed in bar, above that in dining room (*J Scarisbrick, BB*)

Hyde Lea, Staffs [just S of Stafford; SJ9120], *Crown*: Warm, friendly pub doing well under new licensees — good service and well kept Bass beers (*John and Christine Simpson*)

☆ **Ipstones**, Staffs [B5053 (village signposted from A52 and from A523); SK0249], *Red Lion*: Gentle colour scheme and comfortable seats in friendly and well run pub overlooking valley, well kept Burtonwood Best on handpump, reliably good value bar food, games area, piped music (*Patrick Godfrey, SJC, Jon Wainwright, LYM*)

Kings Bromley, Staffs [SK1216], *Royal Oak*: Basic but cosy bar with very enjoyable atmosphere, pleasant dining room and good choice of food — nothing fancy, but well prepared and agreeably presented; may be donkeys behind garden (*Graham Richardson*)

Kings Newton, Derbys [nr M1 junction 24; SK3826], *Hardinge Arms*: Rambling front bar with interestingly carved counter, handsome wall clock and attractive bow window, opening into stylish dining lounge with good food; well kept Marstons real ale, restaurant; children welcome (*E E Hemmings, LYM*)

☆ **Kinver**, Staffs [A449; SO8483], *Whittington*: Striking black and white timbered Tudor house 300 yds from Staffs and Worcs Canal and built by Dick Whittington's family, fine garden with pétanque, old-fashioned bar, decent bar food, real ales, cheerful attentive staff (*Dr and Mrs C D E Morris, Neil and Anita Christopher, LYM*)

Kirk Hallam, Derbys [Kenilworth Dr; SK4540], *Nottingham Castle*: Excellent exterior, good bar, friendly locals and well kept beer (*Russell Allen*)

☆ **Kirk Ireton**, Derbys [SK2650], *Barley Mow*: Range of well kept real ales tapped from the cask in unspoilt and basic series of interconnecting rooms — no frills, lots of woodwork (*Richard Sanders, Andrew Turnbull*)

☆ **Ladybower Reservoir**, Derbys [A57 Sheffield—Glossop, at junction with A6013; SK1986], *Ladybower*: Impressive stone pub nestling in sharp-sided valley with menacing boulders perched above; clean and comfortable open-plan layout inside, with well kept Tetleys, Theakstons and Wilsons, popular food in eating area, fox masks; stone settles outside, good views of reservoir and surrounding moorlands (many walks nearby) (*Steve Mitcheson, Anne Collins, P A Crossland, D A Cawley*)

Leek, Staffs [outskirts; SJ9856], *Abbey*: Lovely rural spot, well bulding with large raised terrace; well kept Bass, good lunchtime and evening bar food (*J Scarisbrick*); [17 Osbourne Rd], *Blue Mugge*: Excellent local with central counter and four rooms, each dedicated to an historic figure such as Queen Victoria or Winston Churchill; genuine atmosphere, friendly service, well kept Bass (*Sue Holland, Dave Webster*)

☆ **Lichfield**, Staffs [Market St; one of the central pedestrian-only streets; SK1109], *Scales*: Old-fashioned two-room pub with big etched window, Delft shelf over dark oak panelling, Bass and M&B Springfield on electric pump, attractively planted suntrap back courtyard; bar food (lunchtime, not Sun) inc attractive cold table, friendly service, good coffee; small restaurant; children welcome (*K and E Leist, Graham Richardson, LYM*)

☆ **Lichfield** [London Rd, just before A38 bypass], *Shoulder of Mutton*: Large uncrowded pub, recently handsomely refurbished to give comfortable separate areas inc conservatory and reading room; good food bar with generous carvery and self-service vegetables; good choice of non-beer and low-alcohol drinks, pleasant service (*Dave Braisted, Brian and Genie Smart*)

Lichfield [Birmingham Rd/Tamworth Rd], *Bald Buck*: Smartly comfortable and spacious town-edge pub with well kept Banks's, food, friendly service; easy parking nearby (*Patrick Godfrey, BB*); [Tamworth St], *Pig & Truffle*: Changing choice of good lunchtime food inc wide range of fresh fish; waitress service couldn't be faulted; well kept real ales, good coffee, friendly atmosphere, lavatories exceptionally clean (*J and B Grove*)

Little Bridgeford, Staffs [nr M6 junction 14; turn right off A5013 at Little Bridgeford; SJ8727], *Worston Mill*: Fine building — former watermill, with wheel and gear still preserved, ducks on millpond and millstream in well laid out garden with play area, attractive conservatory; popular bar food, well kept real ale, restaurant (*Tom McLean, Roger Huggins, LYM*)

Little Hay, Staffs [SK1202], *Holly Bush*: Though part of the Porterhouse chain a pleasant pub; good value bar snacks, quick service, well kept Ansells and Tetleys (*Dave Braisted*)

☆ **Litton**, Derbys [SK1675], *Red Lion*: Food — a mixture of solid provincial and bistro French with British country cooking — is the main thing at this cosy and pretty partly panelled village pub almost wholely given over to close-set bookable tables (not open weekday lunchtimes); snug low-ceilinged front rooms with warm open fires, bigger back room with stripped stone and antique prints; good service (*LYM*)

☆ **Longlane**, Derbys [SK2538], *Three Horseshoes*: Bought 1989 by group of locals wanting to keep it simple and traditional; a successful start, with well kept Marstons Pedigree and a guest such as Woodfordes or Burton Bridge, friendly welcome, open fire, no juke box (*Derek Stephenson, Chris Raisin*)

Longnor, Staffs [SK0965], *Olde Cheshire Cheese*: Wide range of well prepared home-cooked bar food, well kept Robinsons ales (*G C Hixon*)

Longsdon, Staffs [Denford; SJ9655], *Hollybush*: Canalside pub in pretty spot with cosy, cottagey interior; Ind Coope Burton, good bar food inc reasonably priced filled French sticks, friendly service, waterside tables *(Sue Holland, Dave Webster)*; [Leek Rd (A53)], *Wheel*: Old, beamed pub with coal fire; good choice of lunchtime and evening bar food, upstairs restaurant; small car park *(D Brighouse)*

☆ **Lullington**, Derbys [SK2513], *Colvile Arms*: Fine pub doing well under friendly and able new landlord, with big built-in settle and serving hatch in nice unspoilt bar, comfortably modernised lounge; good atmosphere, well kept beer, bar snacks, big pretty garden *(David Gaunt, Chris Raisin)*

Mackworth, Derbys [Ashbourne Rd; A52 Ashbourne—Derby; SK3137], *Mundy Arms*: Refurbished main-road pub, recently extended with new restaurant and comfortable chalet-type bedrooms, built to match original stable block; comfortable bar with plush banquettes and framed prints, good food generously served *(Chris Raisin)*

Makeney, Derbys [Holly Bush Lane; SK3544], *Holly Bush*: Traditional flagstoned and stone-walled free house, real ale served by jug, open fire, small games room, terrace behind; quiet village *(Richard Sanders, Derek and Sylvia Stephenson)*

Marston Montgomery, Derbys [SK1338], *Crown*: Hospitable licensees, cheerful atmosphere with open fire (even at breakfast), well kept beer on handpump, imaginatively presented bar food and reasonable prices; bedrooms large and comfortable with easy chairs and televisions *(Thomas Newton)*; [A515, N of A50 junction], *Rose & Crown*: Large, imposing brick building reached by terrace surrounded by flowers; lounge with dark green plush wall banquettes, well kept Vaux, promising food *(Chris Raisin)*

Matlock Bath, Derbys [Matlock Rd; SK2958], *County & Station*: Particularly well kept Marstons Pedigree, guest beers *(J D Shaw)*

Meerbrook, Staffs [SJ9961], *Lazy Trout*: Cosy lounge, Ind Coope Burton, wide choice of bar food inc local Staffordshire oatcakes with various fillings, or trout from the nearby Tittesworth Reservoir with its superb adventure playground *(J Scarisbrick)*

☆ **Melbourne**, Derbys [SK3825], *White Swan*: Strikingly restored to show ancient structure though interestingly there's a slightly modern feel to it — ambitious food inc good Sun lunch and popular puddings, attractive decorations, comfortable seats, chatty landlord, well kept Marstons Pedigree; pleasant narrow garden; children welcome *(Jon Wainwright, Eileen and Alan Bowker, LYM)*

Muckley Corner, Staffs [A5/A461; SK0806], *Muckley Corner*: Well run, friendly atmosphere and service, pleasant decor, separate dining area, sensibly priced food, well kept beer; children allowed in dining room *(Graham Richardson)*

New Mills, Derbys [Brook Bottom; SJ9886], *Fox*: Clean, well cared for and friendly pub

with reasonable, well prepared, simple and varied menu; Robinsons Bitter very well kept; good for walkers *(Maurice and Gill McMahon)*

Newcastle under Lyme, Staffs [Hassell St; SJ8445], *Slug & Lettuce*: Welcome oasis in small market town, well modernised with lots of wood panelling and pine furniture; good range of Ind Coope beers inc good Brown Slug Mild, varied choice of bar food such as filling 'door-stop' sandwiches served with imaginative salads, excellent garlic mushrooms, cauliflower cheese, various pasta dishes and super coffee *(Sue Holland, Dave Webster)*

Norbury Junction, Staffs [SJ7922], *Junction*: Busy pub with good value food inc bargain steaks, well kept beer *(John and Christine Simpson)*

Oakamoor, Staffs [B5417 E of Cheadle; SK0544], *Admiral Jervis*: Well placed for Alton Towers and the Peak District; pleasant interior split into two, with separate dining room; bar meals, restaurant menu *(M A and W R Proctor)*

Oakerthorpe, Derbys [B6013 Belper—Claycross; SK3955], *Anchor*: Well kept Bass and Marstons Pedigree on handpump, good and often inventive reasonably priced bar food, restaurant *(Alan and Eileen Bowker)*

Ockbrook, Derbys [SK4236], *White Swan*: Small, clean, pretty pub, friendly licensee, well kept real ale *(Brian and Genie Smart)*

Old Glossop, Derbys [SK0494], *Wheatsheaf*: Impressively renovated Whitbreads pub, with comfortable and cosy surroundings and decent food inc good value Sun lunch *(Deborah Clark)*

Osmaston, Derbys [off A52 SE of Ashbourne; SK1944], *Shoulder of Mutton*: Snug and inviting pub with well kept Bass, friendly bar staff, filled baps home-baked by landlady's father; pub owned by local lord of manor who also owns village and most of surrounding countryside *(Tony and Pat Young, Graham Richardson)*

Padfield, Derbys [SK0396], *Peels Arms*: Stone village pub with split-level lounge and cosy public bar, three real fires, games room, well kept Youngers real ales, friendly service; special certificate if you can squeeze through the tiny hole in the lounge wall *(Steve Mitcheson, Anne Collins)*

☆ **Penkridge**, Staffs [SJ9214], *Star*: Recently refurbished village pub with friendly atmosphere, good licensees, well kept cheap Banks's ales and fine lunchtime bar food — filled rolls and steak and kidney pie tipped; single bar with lots of old beams and nooks; very busy at lunchtimes, but open all day — handy for M6 junctions 12/13 *(Colin Chattoe, John and Christine Simpson)*

Penkridge [Filiance Bridge; off A449], *Cross Keys*: By Staffordshire and Worcestershire canal with garden next to towpath; bar snacks and hot meals *(Patrick and Mary McDermott)*

Pilsley, Derbys [SK2471], *Devonshire Arms*: Welcoming and cosy little free house with

Mansfield and Stones on electric pump, quickly served good food from short menu *(Dr and Mrs S G Donald)*

Ramshaw Rocks, Staffs [A53 Leek—Buxton; SK0262], *Winking Man*: More restaurant than pub, busy at weekends; very generous helpings of beef salad or gammon, gorgeous puddings, and other more ambitious dishes from menu that changes daily; nice furnishings, pleasant staff *(Margaret and Trevor Errington)*

Rowsley, Derbys [SK2566], *Grouse & Claret*: Large but friendly pub on busy junction close to Chatsworth; well kept beers, hearty food, extended opening hours; 'novelty' events *(H Claridge)*; *Peacock*: Civilised and upmarket small hotel, with long history and distinguished character; has had a pleasantly old-fashioned inner bar, more spacious comfortable lounge, decent lunchtime bar food (not Sun) and well kept real ales, but we have not kept it in the main entries this year as Embassy Hotels, of which it is part, was being sold as we went to press; nr GWG79; bedrooms comfortable — a nice place to stay, with attractive gardens *(J S Rutter, J Wiltshire, LYM)*

☆ **Shardlow**, Derbys [Aston Rd (A6); SK4330], *Dog & Duck*: Pleasant and cosy old pub with central serving area opening into large lounge with open fire and small low-beamed games room; warm, cosy atmosphere, well kept Marstons ales on handpump, marvellous collection of cigarette cards, classic traditional games room with bar billiards, children allowed in simply furnished extension; spacious back garden with play equipment, big aviary, geese, a donkey and picnic-table sets *(Andrew Stephenson, Jon Wainwright, Carl Southwell)*

Shardlow [London Rd (A6 about 1/2 mile E — even handier for M1 junction 24)], *Cavendish Arms*: Well kept Wards, Darleys and Vaux, bar food *(Mr and Mrs J H Adam)*; [A6], *Shakespeare*: Well kept Home ales and bar food inc good value rolls *(Dave Braisted)*

Snelston Common, Derbys [B5033, about 1 1/2 miles W of A515 — S of Ashbourne; SK1541], *Queen Adelaide*: Victorian house in a field; decor unusual — brick-effect wallpaper, stone-effect in inglenook, Indian arch over Formica serving counter, plastic-covered wooden tables, nice curved settle; second room has piano and huge case of stuffed birds and animals; outstanding Marstons Pedigree *(Chris Raisin, Graham Doyle)*

☆ **Sparrowpit**, Derbys [nr Chapel en le Frith; SK0980], *Wanted Inn*: Marvellous, rugged stone building with two real fires, lots of photographs of spectacular surrounding countryside, welcoming licensees and good home-cooked food *(Steve Mitcheson, Anne Collins)*

Stafford, Staffs [SJ9223], *Garth*: Large, fresh, good value, hot and cold buffet with friendly service *(John and Ruth Roberts)*; [A34/A449 central roundabout; take Access Only rd past service stn], *Malt & Hops*: Lively rambling pub with real ales such as

Holdens, Marstons Pedigree and McEwans 80/-, popular at lunchtime for low-priced food, though in the evenings the clientele's much younger, concentrating more on the lagers and the loud video juke box — with Thurs-Sat discos when it stays open till 1am (midnight other nights); provision for children *(LYM)*; [Forebridge (Lichfield rd, opp Borough Library)], *Sun*: Busy town-centre pub; well kept Bass, cheap bar food *(John and Christine Simpson)*

Stone, Staffs [21 Stafford St; A520; SJ9034], *Star*: Canal photographs and exposed joists in intimate public bar, snug lounge and family room of simple eighteenth-century pub in attractive canalside setting; well kept Bass and M&B Springfield, friendly welcome, basic food, open fire in one room *(Jon Wainwright, LYM)*

Stourton, Staffs [Bridgnorth Rd; SO8585], *Fox*: Pleasant, airy well renovated pub with conservatory and large garden; imaginative bar snacks — try the BLT — and well kept real ales such as Banks's and Batemans; in countryside nr Kinver Edge *(E J Alcock, Dave Braisted)*

Sudbury, Derbys [off A50; SK1632], *Vernon Arms*: 17th-century free house in village once famed for its drinkers — a rector back then was accused of getting drunk in taverns here and keeping fish in his font; well kept Marstons, good value bar food *(Richard Sanders)*

Swinscoe, Derbys [A52 3 miles W of Ashbourne; SK1348], *Dog & Partridge*: 17th-century coaching inn with comfortable motel accommodation attached — a convenient base for the Derbyshire peaks; efficient landlady *(Col and Mrs L N Smyth)*

Swynnerton, Staffs [SJ8535], *Fitzherbert Arms*: Pleasant and tastefully modernised, with decent bar food and well kept Bass; bedrooms *(Dave Braisted)*

Taddington, Derbys [SK1472], *Queens Arms*: Good food in well kept comfortable pub *(G C Hixon)*

Tamworth, Staffs [Albert Rd/Victoria Rd; SK2004], *Tweeddale Arms*: Traditional and homely with well kept Bass in town, limited range of bar food, fruit machine, juke box *(Colin Gooch)*

Tansley, Derbys [A615 Matlock—Mansfield; SK3259], *Royal Oak*: Well kept Hardys & Hansons, limited choice of excellent value plain and unpretentious food inc Sun roast *(Michael and Rachel Brookes)*

Tatenhill, Staffs [off A38 W of Burton; SK2021], *Horseshoe*: Large and tastefully decorated with friendly service, well kept Marstons Pedigree, and well prepared, reasonably priced bar food *(Eric Locker)*

☆ **Ticknall**, Derbys [B5006 towards Ashby de la Zouch; SK3423], *Chequers*: Good fire in enormous inglenook fireplace of clean and cosy 16th-century pub with well kept Bass tapped from the cask, unusual spirits, good lunchtime filled baps and ploughman's (not Sun), seats in sizeable garden; nearby Calke Abbey is worth visiting *(Mrs D M Everard,*

Graham Richardson, LYM); Staff of Life: Good atmosphere, excellent range of real ales inc three or four guest beers, and enormous slices of gammon, well cooked and good value for those with appetites *(Eric Locker);* [A514], *Wheel*: Pleasant, welcoming landlord, well kept Bass, friendly service of simple but well prepared hot food; nr entrance to Calke Abbey (NT) *(E A Turner)*

☆ **Tideswell**, Derbys [SK1575], *George*: Wall benches and small chairs in plain bar with coal fire, toby jugs on Delft shelf and puddings display cabinet; small tile-floored snug, pool room beyond with loud juke box; good value piping hot bar food inc well recommended steak and kidney pie, well kept Hardys & Hansons Best on handpump; good value bedrooms — pretty village with end-June well-dressing *(Matt Pringle, D Ainsworth, Simon Velate, BB)*

Tintwistle, Derbys [off A628, N side; SK0297], *Bulls Head*: Pleasant, relaxing place with good views over Glossop to the south; open-plan but with cosy alcove by open fire; food, particularly well kept Bass and Stones; quiet, friendly atmosphere; car park *(Lee Goulding)*

Upper Hulme, Staffs [A53 Leek—Buxton; SK0161], *Winking Man*: Large bar with red plush upholstery, open fire and local photographs; usual bar food inc good range of specials, vegetarian dishes and children's menu, piped radio; huge car park, with ballroom behind *(Neil and Anita Christopher)*

Waterhouses, Staffs [SK0850], *Olde Crown*: Cosy tidy bar in Tetleys pub with red seats, horse brasses, food, decent coffee; bedrooms in attached cottages *(Graham Bush)*

Wensley, Derbys [SK2661], *Crown*: Stone-built 17th-century village pub, well kept Bass and good range of other beers, helpful staff, wide choice of bar food inc vegetarian dishes, in big helpings and fairly priced; garden behind with play area *(G and M Armstrong) D7/89*

☆ **Whittington Moor**, Derbys [Sheffield Rd (off A61 1 1/2 miles N of Chesterfield centre)], *Derby Tup*: Friendly no-frills basic pub with

small snug, large lounge, and emphasis on wide range of superbly kept real ales such as Batemans XXXB, Ruddles County, Timothy Taylors Landlord, Tetleys, Theakstons XB and Old Peculier, Wards Sheffield Best and Whitbreads Castle Eden; range of pub games, but no food *(Richard Sanders)*

Willington, Derbys [The Green; SK2928], *Green Dragon*: Pleasant pub with attractive, L-shaped bar and friendly, relaxed atmosphere *(Jon Wainwright)*

Winster, Derbys [A5012 / B5056; SK2460], *Miners Standard*: Welcoming, friendly local with good reasonably priced food till 10, well kept Marstons Pedigree and Theakstons, cheerful service, big open fires *(B O Jones, C J and L M Elston); Winster Hall*: Dated 1628, the grandest of a number of superb three-storeyed stone buildings lining the main street; inside straightforwardly pubby, with well kept Mansfield Old Baily on handpump, cheap, cheerful bar food; bedrooms *(Simon Velate)*

Wirksworth, Derbys [Market Pl; SK2854], *Hope & Anchor*: Interesting old pub with friendly welcome from new licensee, pleasant decor with old prints and curios, generously filled baps and separate restaurant *(Sue Holland, Dave Webster)*

☆ **Woolley**, Derbys [Badger Lane; off B6014, Woolley Moor; SK3760], *White Horse*: Friendly country pub with well kept Bass and a guest, and particularly good value home-cooked food (not Sun evening) — difficult to believe how low prices are for a good evening meal; handy for Ogston Reservoir, with good Amber Valley views and playground for children *(Derek and Sylvia Stephenson, R Caldwell)*

Wrinehill, Staffs [Main Rd; SJ7547], *Hand & Trumpet*: Welcoming and comfortable with large, back room for families; well cooked good value food, splendid garden with duck pond *(Joy Heatherley)*

Yoxall, Staffs [Main St; SK1319], *Crown*: Typical English village pub with high standard of reasonably priced food; very cheerful atmosphere and Marstons beers *(Dr and Mrs G J Sutton, B M Eldridge)*

Devon

*Over the last few years there's been a striking increase in the number
of Devon pubs with good value bedroom accommodation. Main
entries worth picking out particularly for this include the busy Sloop
at Bantham (excellent fresh fish), the charmingly placed old Fountain
Head at Branscombe (self-catering), the ancient thatched New Inn at
Coleford, the Exmoor Sandpiper at Countisbury, the Cott at
Dartington (back to normal after its bad thatch fire), the Royal Castle
overlooking the water in Dartmouth, the Nobody Inn at
Doddiscombsleigh (our most popular west country pub, with
amazing wines and up to 40 cheeses at a time), the White Hart in
Exeter (a lovely old place – normally our own first choice as a Devon
base), the 15th-century George in Hatherleigh, the strongly
food-oriented Rock at Haytor Vale below Dartmoor, the friendly and
very ancient Church House at Holne, the very relaxed Masons Arms
at Knowstone on Exmoor, the Castle close to the beautiful gorge at
Lydford, the Rising Sun in its magnificent harbourside setting at
Lynmouth, the White Hart at Moretonhampstead (a comfortable
Dartmoor base), the friendly Half Moon at Sheepwash (ideal for
fishermen), the Blue Ball at Sidford (in the same family for 75 years –
very hospitable), the stately Oxenham Arms at South Zeal, the nice
little Golden Lion at Tipton St John, the Globe near the water in
Topsham, and the Black Horse in Torrington (handy for the Royal
Horticultural Society's Rosemoor garden). Many of these inns have
particularly good food. Around another 50 of the Lucky Dip entries
at the end of the chapter also have bedrooms, spanning a tremendous
range of prices and grandeur – many particularly recommended by
readers as places to stay. One of this year's new main entries, the
Duke of York at Iddesleigh, has good bedrooms – and really good
food; other newcomers include the Drewe Arms at Broadhembury,
delightfully refurbished by licensees who won fame among readers for
their food at the Pickerel at Ixworth (over in Suffolk), the Hunters
Lodge at Cornworthy (notable food in most unpretentious
surroundings), the Sir Walter Raleigh in lovely East Budleigh, the
Tally Ho in Hatherleigh (the charming Italian owner brews his own
beer), and the Maltsters Arms at Tuckenhay (a lovely spot – and its
new owner's reputation as a food writer and broadcaster has brought
it a talented team of chefs). These newcomers underline Devon's
growing success as an area for really good pub food; apart from pubs
already mentioned, we'd also pick out the villagey Butterleigh Inn at
Butterleigh, the very good value Old Thatch at Cheriton Bishop, the
Tuckers Arms at Dalwood (interesting), the handsome little Cherub
in Dartmouth (fresh fish), the Pyne Arms at East Down, the Swans
Nest at Exminster, the Church House at Harberton (particularly its
daily specials), the beautifully isolated Elephants Nest at Horndon,
the Old Rydon at Kingsteignton (interesting food – and pub), the
homely Who'd Have Thought It at Miltoncombe, the Peter Tavy Inn
at Peter Tavy (good vegetarian dishes), the Kings Arms at Stockland,*

*and the Start Bay at Torcross (fresh fish). Prices here are generally
around the national norm – a shade higher, if anything. But there is a
very wide spread of prices around this general average. Very few
Devon pubs now do decent snacks at under £1 (the Olde Globe at
Berrynarbor, Poltimore Arms at Brayford and Old Thatch at
Cheriton Bishop all have something), but around a quarter of the
main entries here can still beat our £3 target for a bargain main dish.
For drinks, the Drewe Arms at Broadhembury, Butterleigh Inn,
Church House at Holne, Oxenham Arms at South Zeal, Globe in
Topsham and, particularly, Royal at Horsebridge stand out as much
cheaper than usual; the last brews its own beers, and in most of the
others it's locally brewed beers that keep the prices down.*

ASHBURTON SX7569 Map 1

London Hotel

11 West St

The beers they brew in this rather grand old three-storey coaching inn – Bitter and
IPA (served on handpump under light blanket pressure) – can also be sampled in
Plymouth at the Mutton Cove, which Mr Thompson also runs. The big
Turkey-carpeted lounge spreads back into a softly lit dining area with one wall
curtained in red velvet, and furnishings include little brocaded or red leatherette
armchairs and other seats around the copper-topped casks they use as tables; the
clean white walls are largely stripped back to stone, and there's a central fireplace.
Fruit machine. Bar food includes home-made soup (£1.20), sandwiches (from
£1.30), ploughman's (from £1.75), omelettes or salads (from £3.50), fresh local
trout (£6), chicken cordon bleu (£7.40), steaks (from £7.75), and puddings like
home-made apple pie (£1.25). There are no bedrooms despite the pub's name.
*(Recommended by R J Walden, M G Richards, Richard and Dilys Smith, J R Carey; more
reports please)*

Own brew   Licensee D F Thompson   Real ale   Meals and snacks   Restaurant
tel *Ashburton (0364) 52478   Children in eating area of bar   Open 11–2.30, 5–11*

ASHPRINGTON SX8156 Map 1

Durant Arms

Village signposted off A381 S of Totnes; OS Sheet 202 map reference 819571

This extensively renovated, pretty gable-ended cottage has received praise from
readers for its home-made bar food. As well as the memorable Brown Pot – filled
with bacon, kidney and vegetables, cooked in stout and topped with pastry (£3.30)
– there's also sandwiches, chicken curry (£3), whole plaice (£5), chicken (£5.50),
and whole lemon sole (£6.95). Bass, Ind Coope Burton, Palmers IPA, and Tetleys
on handpump, several malt whiskies and Luscombe cider (summer only); friendly
service. Popular with families, the lower carpeted lounge has settles, tables, chairs,
red velvet curtains and a winter fire. The old-fashioned upper bar has unusual
cutaway barrel seats and a bay window overlooking the village street. In the simply
furnished games bar there are darts, dominoes, cribbage and piped music. George
the black labrador is the epitome of the pub dog (he'll even carry ladies' handbags
into the pub), and an oil painting of him now occupies pride of place in one of the
bars. There are tables in the sheltered back garden. *(Recommended by M V and
J Melling, R H Martyn, David Wallington, H K Dyson, Mr and Mrs L W Norcott, S V Bishop,
G and M Stewart, Robert and Linda Carew, Col G D Stafford)*

*Free house   Licensees John and Gill Diprose   Real ale   Meals and snacks
(11.30–2.30. 6–11)   Children in eating area of bar – no pushchairs   Open 11.30–2.30,
6–11*

Watermans Arms

Bow Bridge, on Tuckenhay road

Well run by friendly and efficient licensees, this popular waterside pub has high-backed settles and built-in black wall benches in the flagstoned front area of the bar, with more tables in a comfortable carpeted oak-beamed inner area. Good value, generously served bar food includes soup (different ones each day, £1.30), well filled sandwiches (from £1.50), ploughman's with a choice of cheeses (from £2.35), lunchtime hot dishes such as cottage pie, home-made steak and kidney or trout (£4.50), grilled fresh sardines, salads (from £4.50), seafood platter (£5.50) and steaks (from £7.95). Palmers IPA on handpump; piped music. Across the road there are tables by the little Harbourne River where you can watch the ducks pottering about, and maybe a heron in the tidal creek to the right. (*Recommended by David and Ann Stranack, Verity Kemp, Richard Mills, M Box, S V Bishop, Peter York, John Knighton, Alan Merricks, JAH, J K Cuneen, T R Norris*)

Free house   Licensee Terry Wing   Real ale   Meals and snacks (6.30–10 evening) Children in family room   Restaurant tel Harbertonford (080 423) 214   Open 11–2.30, 6–11

AXMOUTH   SY2591   Map 1

Harbour

Much bigger inside than it looks from outside, this thatched pub has a huge inglenook fireplace with fat pots hanging from pot-irons in its Harbour Bar, as well as black oak beams and joists, a high-backed oak settle, brass-bound cask seats and an antique wall clock. A central lounge has more cask seats and settles, and over on the left another room is divided from the dining room by a two-way log fireplace. At the back, a big flagstoned lobby with sturdy seats leads on to a very spacious simply furnished family bar, and there are tables in the neat flower garden behind. Bar food includes home-made soup (£1.25), sandwiches (from £1.75), a good few other snacks or starters such as garlic bread and cheese (£1.75), ploughman's (from £2.25), a vegetarian special like vegetable quiche or cauliflower and Stilton bake (£3.50), home-cooked ham and egg (£3.95), steak and kidney pie (£4), salads (from £4), local fresh fish (when available) for dishes like crispy cod bake (£4), crab salad (£5.50), and lemon sole (£6.50), and evening grills running up to rump steak (£6.75); children's helpings of many dishes. Well kept Bass and Devenish Royal Wessex on handpump, farm cider; efficient service; darts, winter skittle alley, cribbage, maybe unobtrusive piped music. They have a lavatory for disabled people, and general access is good. The church opposite has some fine stone gargoyles. (*Recommended by Brian and Anna Marsden, Mrs Caroline Ginnins, Andrew and Michele Wells, Joan and Ian Wilson*)

Free house   Licensees Dave and Pat Squire   Real ale   Meals and snacks (not Mon, not winter Sun evenings, not 25 Dec)   Children in family area   Open 11–2.30, 6–11

BANTHAM   SX6643   Map 1

Sloop 🚫 🛏

Cheerful and busy, this 16th-century village inn has an atmospheric black-beamed bar with stripped stone walls, flagstones, country chairs around wooden tables, and easy chairs in a quieter side area – lots of varnished marine ply gives this part a nautical atmosphere. Bar food includes very popular fresh fish such as grilled sardines or garlic prawns (£2.95), crab claws (£3.20), red gurnard (£3.95), superb giant cod (£5.35), excellent skate or whole plaice (£5.95), and john dory (£6.60); there's also pasties (85p), tasty home-made turkey broth (£1.10), granary-bread sandwiches (from £1.25, good fresh crab £2.40), basket meals (from £1.95), ploughman's (£2.60), a good range of salads (from £3.90, superb seafood £5.85) and good steaks (from £6.95). Home-made puddings like hot chocolate fudge cake (£1.60) or raspberry Pavlova (£1.80); hearty breakfasts for residents. There are delays at busy times. Well kept Bass, Flowers IPA and Ushers Best on handpump,

Churchward's cider from Paignton and a decent range of malts. Darts, dominoes, cribbage, table skittles, fruit machine, space game, and trivia. Around a wishing well in the yard behind, there are some seats. The sandy beach – one of the best for surfing on the south coast – is only a few hundred yards over the dunes; the coast path runs past here. *(Recommended by David Wallington, Janet and Paul Waring, R W Stanbury, Hilary Roberts, M V and J Melling, N P Cox, David and Ann Stranack, G Malcolm Pearce, W C M Jones, Mr and Mrs L W Norcott, G Malcolm Pearce, N P Cox, Mrs A Turner, Roy Isaac, Paul and Janet Waring, JS, BS, John Tyzack, Col G D Stafford, David Barnes, John Barker, Amanda Dauncey, Ann and David Stranack, D P Darby)*

Free house   Licensee Neil Girling   Real ale   Meals and snacks (till 10 evening) Restaurant   Children in restaurant and eating area of bar   Open 11–2.30, 6–11 (winter evening opening 6.30)   Bedrooms tel Kingsbridge (0548) 560489/560215; £19.50(£20B)/£29(£40B); they also have self-catering cottages

BERRYNARBOR   SS5646 Map 1

Olde Globe ★

Village signposted from A399 E of Ilfracombe

Besides genuinely old pictures, this friendly seventeenth-century pub (converted from three 13th-century cottages) is decorated with a profusion of priests (fish-coshes), thatcher's knives, sheep shears, gin traps, pitchforks, antlers, copper warming pans and lots of cutlasses, swords, shields and fine powder flasks. The rambling, dimly lit and homely rooms and alcoves have curved walls, darkened to a deep ochre, that bulge unevenly in places, low ceilings, and floors of flagstones or of ancient lime-ash (with silver coins embedded in them); there are old high-backed oak settles (some carved) and red leatherette cushioned cask seats around antique tables. Bar food includes sandwiches (from 85p), steak and kidney pie or pasties (£1.90), ploughman's (£1.95), salads (from £2.70), home-made pizza (£2.75), spaghetti bolognese (£3), lasagne or plaice (£3.10), scampi (£3.45), gammon (£4.50), rump steak (£5.50) and 16oz T-bone (£8), with children's meals (£1.50); good, traditional Sunday lunch (£5.25 – you have to book). Well kept Ushers Best on handpump, and several country wines; sensibly placed darts, skittle alley, pool room, dominoes, shove-ha'penny, cribbage, fruit machine, piped music. The crazy-paved front terrace has old-fashioned garden seats, with an attractive garden beside it (which won them first prize in a brewery competition). *(Recommended by P M Bisby, Mr and Mrs S Harvey, John Drummond, Leonard Tivey; more reports please)*

Free house   Licensees Lynne and Phil Bridle   Real ale   Meals and snacks (till 10 evening)   Gaslit restaurant Combe Martin (027 188) 2465   Children in kitchen bar and family room   Children's night, Thurs   Open 11.30–2.30, 6–11 (winter evening opening 7)

BRANSCOMBE   SY1988 Map1

Fountain Head ⇌

Upper village, above the robust old church; village signposted off A3052 Sidmouth–Seaton

Prettily situated up a narrow winding lane past the church, this pleasantly relaxed, quiet, 14th-century stone house has seats out on the front loggia and terrace, a cart, and a little stream rustling under the flagstoned path. The room on the left – formerly a smithy – has a log fire in the original raised firebed with its tall central chimney, cushioned pews and mates' chairs around wooden tables and walls of stripped uncoursed stone; its high oak beams are hung with horseshoes and forge tools. On the right, an irregularly shaped, more orthodox snug room has a white-painted plank ceiling with an unusual carved ceiling-rose, brown-varnished panelled walls, rugs on its flagstone-and-lime-ash floor and another log fire. Good value bar food includes cockles or mussels (75p), soup (£1), sandwiches (from £1.25, fresh crab £1.50), ploughman's (£1.75), home-made shepherd's or fish pies or vegetarian lasagne (£2.50), home-made steak and kidney pie (£3.25), salads (from £3.25, fresh crab £5), kebabs (£4) and steaks (from £6.25), with children's dishes (from £1.50). Well kept Badger Best and Tanglefoot and Devenish Royal Wessex on handpump; friendly quick service and an amiable dog; darts, cribbage, dominoes. Our place-to-stay award is for the self-catering flat and adjacent cottage; they don't have ordinary letting bedrooms. (*Recommended by Dewi Jones, Patrick Freeman, Gordon and Daphne, A S Clements, Philip and Sheila Hanley, Jenny and Michael Back, A C Earl*)

Free house   Licensee Mrs Catherine Luxton   Real ale   Meals and snacks (not Wed evenings; Sun lunchtime service stops 1.30; no food winter evenings unless arranged ahead)   Children in small children's room   Open 11–2.30, 6.30–11; closes half-hour earlier winter   Self-catering tel Branscombe (029 780) 359

BRAYFORD   SS6834   Map 1

Poltimore Arms

Yarde Down – three miles from village, towards Simonsbath; OS Sheet 180 map reference 724356

The main bar of this straightforward Exmoor pub has an inglenook fireplace with a woodburning stove, old leather-seated chairs with carved or slatted backs, cushioned wall settles, a little window seat, some interesting tables, and a beam in the slightly sagging cream ceiling with another over the small serving counter; also, photos of hunt meetings, and hunting cartoons. The decent range of bar food includes sandwiches (from 80p, toasties 10p extra), home-made soup or curried eggs (90p), omelettes (£1.25), ploughman's (from £2.30), salads (from £2.50), home-made steak and kidney pie, lasagne or vegetarian nut croquette (£2.75), and steaks (from £5.80), with extra evening dishes such as their speciality noisettes of lamb (£4), fresh fish (from £4) and mixed grills (£6.50). Ushers on handpump, Cotleigh Tawny tapped from the cask. The lounge bar has a mix of chairs and a settle, Guinness and Fry's Chocolate prints, plants and a small brick open fire; a plainly decorated games room has pool, darts, shove-ha'penny, cribbage, fruit machine and juke box; friendly cat. In the side garden there are picnic-table sets and a grill for barbecues. The pub has its own cricket team. (*Recommended by B M Eldridge; more reports please*)

Free house   Licensees Mike and Mella Wright   Real ale   Meals and snacks   Children's room   Open 11.30–2.30, 6.30–11 (6 Sat)

BROADHEMBURY   ST1004   Map 1

Drewe Arms ★ ✪

The licensees who made the Pickerel at Ixworth in Suffolk so successful for exceptional value food have now come right across country to take over this very pretty – and very small – thatched 15th-century village inn. They specialise in fresh local fish (£5.95-£9.95) which includes whole plaice, sole, brill, John Dory, turbot, Lyme Bay scallops, smoked eel, monkfish, interesting salmon dishes, spider crabs, and whole lobster (grilled with tarragon or as a ploughman's); also, open sandwiches (rare beef, prawns or smoked venison from £2.95), always two meat dishes like local venison or fillet steak, puddings such as nectarines in cognac, chocolate marquise or treacle tart with ginger (from £1.95), and cream teas (2.30–5.30 Tues-Sat, 4–5.30 Sun) – they grow some of their produce. Well kept Barrons Exe Valley, Bass, Cotleigh Tawny and Old Buzzard, and Wadworths 6X tapped from the cask, and a comprehensive wine list (with good value house wine); shove-ha'penny, cribbage and skittle alley. The flagstoned entry has a narrow corridor of a room by the servery with a couple of tables. As you come into the bar, a high-backed stripped settle on the left separates off a little room with three tables, a mix of chairs, flowers on sturdy country tables, plank-panelled walls painted brown below and yellow above with attractive engravings and prints, and a big black-painted fireplace with bric-a-brac on a high mantelpiece. There are neatly carved beams in the high ceiling, handsome stone-mullioned windows (one with a small carved roundabout horse), a piece of 15th-century linenfold panelling, and a warm, friendly atmosphere. A flower-filled lawn with picnic-table sets and under cocktail parasols stretches back under the shadow of chestnuts towards a church which has a singularly melodious hour-bell. This is an attractive village of cream-coloured thatched cottages. (*Recommended by Mr and Mrs G W Hodgson, Dr and Mrs R J Williams*)

Free house   Licensees Kerstin and Nigel Burge   Real ale   Meals and snacks (not Sun evening Sept-May)   Well behaved children allowed   Open 11–11; 11–2.30, 6–11 in winter

BURGH ISLAND   SX6443 Map 1

Pilchard

Park in Bigbury-on-Sea and walk about 300 yards across the sands, which are covered for between six and eight hours of the twelve-hour tide; in summer use the Tractor, a unique bus-on-stilts which beats the tide by its eight-foot-high 'deck'

Owned by the licensees, this small island has an attractive art deco hotel (where Agatha Christie used to write and which the Duke of Windsor reputedly visited) and this atmospheric 12th-century pub. The small L-shaped bar has thick-walled embrasures and storm-shuttered windows which give a snug view of the tide inching across the sands, low chairs, settles edged with rope and others with high backs, cosy snug booths and lots of bare wood and stripped stone; lighting is by big ships' lamps hanging from the beam-and-plank ceiling and there's a good – though not always lit – log fire. The white-plastered back bar has darts, shove-ha'penny and dominoes. Bar food (sporadically available) might include soup, home-made pasties, filled baked potatoes, open sandwiches, and salads; Ruddles County and Ushers on handpump, farm cider; darts, dominoes, maybe piped music. It can be very popular in season and there's an outside terrace overlooking the beach. (*Recommended by H K Dyson, David and Sarah Gilmore, John Knighton, Alan and Audrey Chatting, Peter Adcock, Doug Kennedy*)

Free house   Real ale   Meals and snacks   Evening seafood and salad bistro, bookings only tel Kingsbridge (0548) 810344   Children in back bar and bistro   £1 car parking in Bigbury   Open 11–11

BUTTERLEIGH   SS9708 Map 1

Butterleigh Inn ✿

Village signposted off A398 in Bickleigh; or in Cullompton take turning by Manor House Hotel – it's the old Tiverton road, with the village eventually signposted off on the left

Relaxed and friendly, this 16th-century village inn has an unassuming series of little rooms with comfortable, well worn furnishings: an attractive elm trestle table and sensibly placed darts in one, old dining chairs around country kitchen tables in another and prettily upholstered settles around the four tables that just fit into the cosy back snug. There are topographical prints and watercolours, pictures of birds and dogs, a fine embroidery of the Devonshire Regiment's coat-of-arms and plates hanging by one big fireplace. Very good bar food includes large granary rolls (from £1.50), home-made burgers (£2.95), two or three vegetarian dishes such as peanut and lentil bake (£2.95), chilli sausages (£3.25), grilled quail with port sauce (£5.50), 8oz fillet steak glazed with stilton or 16oz T-bone steak (£7.95) and puddings like chocolate and brandy pots, bread pudding and treacle tart (£1.25). Well kept Cotleigh Tawny, Harrier and Old Buzzard on handpump and local farm cider; attentive service. Shove-ha'penny, cribbage, dominoes, chess, piped music; jars of snuff on the bar. There are tables on a sheltered terrace and neat small lawn with a log cabin for children. (*Recommended by Gordon and Daphne, Alan and Eileen Bowker, Patrick Young, Michael and Alison Sandy, Graham and Glenis Watkins, Gill Graham, Steve and Carolyn Harvey, J R Carey, J Stronach*)

Free house   Licensees Mike and Penny Wolter   Real ale   Meals and snacks   Open 12–2.30 (3 Sat and Sun), 6 (5 Fri)–11   Bedrooms tel Bickleigh (088 45) 407; £14.50/£21; also cottage sleeping four

CHERITON BISHOP SX7793 Map 1

Old Thatch ⊗

Village signposted from A30

Attractive old pub in Dartmoor's sprawling National Park and popular with drivers from the A30 for its wide range of good value, home-made bar food: good home-made soup (90p), sandwiches and toasties, imaginative starters such as sautéed kidneys with herbs, bacon and mushrooms (£1.75) or Scotch rabbit (actually a kipper dish, £2.20), ploughman's (£1.90), salads (£3.30), and good hot dishes like Boston dry hash (£2.50), steak and kidney pudding or a curry of the day served with cucumber raita, mango chutney and a poppadom (£3.50), braised stuffed hearts (£3.95), beef bourguignonne (£4.50), pan-fried fish of the day (£4.75), excellent, large mixed grill (£4.25), steak (£6.30), and enterprising puddings such as spiced bread pudding made with Guinness (£1.40), or ginger cake trifle (£1.60); pleasant, friendly service. Tables are bookable. The rambling, beamed bar is separated from the lounge by a large open stone fireplace, lit in the cooler months. Bass Triangle, Dartmoor Best Bitter, and Wadworths 6X on handpump; dominoes, cribbage, piped music. (*Recommended by Mrs R F Warner, John O'Gorman, Dr Sheila Smith, Nigel Paine, JS, BS*)

Free house   Licensee Brian Bryon-Edmond   Real ale   Meals and snacks (12–2, 6.30–9.30)   Open 12–3, 6.30 (6 Sat)–11 (Mon–Thurs winter evening opening 7); closed first two weeks Nov   Bedrooms tel Cheriton Bishop (064 724) 204; £26.50B/£37.50B

CHURCHSTOW SX7145 Map 1

Church House

A379 NW of Kingsbridge

This fine medieval pub – once a Benedictine hospice – has an atmospheric bar with cushioned seats cut into the deep window embrasures of the stripped stone walls, low and heavy black oak beams and a great stone fireplace with side bread oven. The long, cosy room is neatly kept and comfortable, with an antique curved high-backed settle as well as the many smaller red-cushioned ones by the black tables on its Turkey carpet, and a line of stools – each with its own brass coathook – along the long glossy black serving counter. Just inside the back entrance there's a conservatory area with a floodlit well in the centre. Bass, Ruddles County and Ushers Best on handpump; dominoes, darts, cribbage, euchre, fruit machine. Bar food, served at the curtained-off end of the bar, includes sandwiches (from £1.10), home-made soup (£1.35), ploughman's (from £1.75), haddock (£2.85 or £3.25 depending on size), home-made dishes such as cottage pie (£2.95) or devilled chicken (£3.45), salads (from £3.45), mixed grill (£5.75), rump steak (£6.45) and puddings like good bread and butter pudding (from £1.60); the carvery – fine roasts, help-yourself vegetables – is good value (£6.50 including home-made puddings), and you're advised to book. There are seats outside. (*Recommended by Carol Mason, Margaret and Trevor Errington, Mrs A Turner, Ann and David Stranack, John Barker, Harry Stirling*)

Free house   Licensee Nick Nicholson   Real ale   Meals and snacks (not 25 or 26 Dec)   Carvery Wed–Sat evenings, Sun lunch tel Kingsbridge (0548) 852237   Children welcome   Open 11–2.30, 6–11

COCKWOOD SX9780 Map 1

Anchor

Off, but visible from, A379 Exeter–Torbay

Tables on a sheltered verandah here look over a quiet lane to yachts and crabbing boats in the landlocked harbour. Inside, a series of communicating small rooms have black panelling, low ceilings, good-sized tables in various alcoves, and a cheerful winter coal fire in the snug; even when it's busy, there's still a good local atmosphere. Bar food includes quite a few fish dishes: Torbay crab sandwiches

(£2.45), crab and brandy soup (£2.65), local mussels in cream, wine and garlic (3.95), grilled whole plaice (£4.75), seafood in cheese sauce (£5.65), and local crab platter (£5.75); there's also sandwiches (from £1.30), home-made soup (£1.55), various platters (from £2.85, home-baked ham £3.95), and home-made cottage pie (£3.85). Well kept Bass, Flowers Original and Huntsman Royal Oak on handpump, with quite a few wines by the glass and farm cider; darts, shove-ha'penny, dominoes, cribbage, fruit machine. Nearby parking may be difficult on a busy evening. *(Recommended by Mike Hallewell, M Box, Nigel Hopkins, D J and K Cooke, George Jonas)*

Heavitree (who no longer brew)   Licensee P Reynolds   Real ale   Meals and snacks (12–2, 6–10)   Restaurant tel Starcross (0626) 890203   Children in eating area and restaurant   Open 11–11; 11–2.30 6–11 in winter

COLEFORD   SS7701   Map 1

New Inn 🖙

Just off A377 Crediton–Barnstaple

Four interestingly furnished areas spiral around the central servery in the big rambling bar of this ancient, thatched inn. There are some character tables – a pheasant worked into the grain of one – carved dressers and chests, ancient and modern settles, spindleback chairs, low dark green velour armchairs and plush-cushioned stone wall seats. The white walls are hung with paraffin lamps, antique prints and old guns, with landscape plates on one of the beams and pewter tankards on another; the resident parrot is still keeping customers entertained. The servery itself has modern settles forming stalls around tables on the russet carpet, and there's a winter log fire. A good range of home-made bar food (using fresh local produce where possible) can be eaten anywhere in the pub. This might include cream of celery soup (£1.50), stilton and walnut pâté (£2.30), tagliatelle with mushrooms and Stilton or tomato and garlic sauce, leek and ham mornay, curries or courgette provençal (all £3.50), mussels in garlic and cream (£3.95), lamb tagine with spiced rice or natural oak-smoked haddock (£6.25), steaks (from £7.95), and home-made puddings such as summer pudding, chocolate and mandarin roulade or treacle tart (£1.80). Flowers IPA and Original, Wadworths 6X and a guest beer such as Brakspears on handpump, and a decent range of wines by the glass; fruit machine (out of the way up by the door), darts, shove-ha'penny and piped music. Attractive courtyard and small garden by stream. *(Recommended by C M Andrews, Lawrence Manning, Mrs K J Betts, Ian Blackwell, Joseph Melling)*

Free house   Licensee Paul Butt   Real ale   Meals and snacks (12–2, 7–10)   Restaurant   Children in eating area of bar   Open 11.30–2.30, 6–11   Bedrooms tel Copplestone (0363) 84242; £20(£27B)/£30(£38B)

COLYTON   SY2493   Map 1

Kingfisher

Dolphin St; village signposted off A35 and A3052 E of Sidmouth, in village follow Axminster, Shute, Taunton signpost

The range of well kept beers in this warmly welcoming, homely village pub includes Badger Best, Flowers IPA, and guests such as Cotleigh Kingfisher, Whitbreads Pompey Royal, Wiltshire Old Grumble and Youngs Special on handpump; they also have Farmer John's cider, from along the Exeter road a bit (the cider farm's open for visits). The bar has blue plush cushioned window seats, stools, sturdy elm wing settles and rustic tables, a big open fireplace and walls stripped back to stone. Glasses slotted into the two waggon-wheels hanging above the bar swing in unison when someone in the upstairs family room (where there's a useful box of toys) walks above the beamed ceiling. Bar food includes sandwiches (from £1, speciality prawn £2.10), filled baked potatoes (£2.25), various meals from sausages (£2.20) to scampi (£3.75), home-made cheesecakes and fruit pies (from £1.30), and children's menu (£1.50); sensibly placed darts, dominoes, cribbage, fruit machine, trivia and skittle alley. The terrace (where there are tables under cocktail parasols) has been extended this year to include a pergola, flower beds and water features; there's also a lawn and climbing frame for children. *(Recommended by Brian and Anna Marsden, Dr D M Forsyth, Quentin Williamson, Richard and Ann Jenkins, John and Heather Dwane, Dr Stewart Rae, J R Carey)*

Free house   Licensees Graeme and Cherry Sutherland   Real ale   Meals and snacks (till 10 evening)   Children in family room   Open 11–2.30, 6–11

COMBEINTEIGNHEAD   SX9071 Map 1
Coombe Cellars

Pub signposted off B3195 Newton Abbot–Shaldon

A new licensee has taken over this popular estuary pub and has made quite a few changes. There are now pontoons and jetties with tables overlooking the water, extensive new terraces and a newly turfed garden area, and a safe, fenced-in children's playground with a huge play galleon. Inside, the long main bar is decorated with nautical bric-a-brac and captain's chairs, with compasses set into the couch, and very large windows along its left-hand side giving a superb view up the River Teign. There's a family area off one end, three log-effect gas fires, and a Porthole bar (which was the original bar and is used by skiers and windsurfers – open all day at weekends) with barrel seats and tables, and more nautical bric-a-brac. The restaurant, which also overlooks the river, is being extended and new kitchens have been added. Bar food includes home-made soup (£1.20, fish soup £2.95, seafood chowder £3.25), sandwiches (from £1.50), basket meals (from £2.25, home-made burger £2.65), several ploughman's (£2.65), pork spare ribs in a sweet sauce on rice (£2.75), tagliatelli Alfredo or a pot of prawns with garlic mayonnaise (£2.95), three vegetarian dishes (£3.95), salads (from £4.50), pan-fried lemon sole fillets (£5.95), steaks (from £6.95), monkfish provençal (£7), rack of English lamb (£7.25), and guinea fowl in white wine, cream and asparagus (£7.95). Well kept Bass, Fergusons Dartmoor and Strong and Tetleys on handpump, an extensive wine list, 10 malt whiskies, and farm cider on handpump; fruit machine, space game, juke box and piped music. At low tide, innumerable busy wading birds join the shelducks, mergansers, herons, cormorants and gulls to pick over the shiny mudflats. There are lots of water-sports facilities – the pub is the base for the South Devon Water Sports Association – and day boat trips up to Coombe Cellars. *(Recommended by W Bailey, David and Sarah Gilmore, Steve Huggins)*

Free house   Licensee Simon Tyler   Real ale   Meals and snacks (11–2.15, 6–10.15) Restaurant tel Newton Abbot (0626) 872423   Children in family room   Open 11–3, 5.30–11 (Porthole bar open all day at weekends)

CORNWORTHY   SX8255 Map 1
Hunters Lodge ✪

Off A381 Totnes–Kingsbridge ½ mile S of Harbertonford, turning left at Washbourne; can also be reached direct from Totnes, on the Ashprington–Dittisham road

Though Keith Floyd's pub just up the road gets the media attention, it's this simple and quietly friendly village inn which in-the-know Devon gourmets track down. And so did we – on a day which turned out to be the very height of the January 1990 gales, with virtually all roads in the area blocked and all power lines down. So the choice of food was severely curtailed – but 'they'd see what they could do'. Some time later, what a memorable steak and kidney pie emerged, with no less than six vegetables including fine sauté potatoes, remarkable crisp cabbage evidently stir-fried with a splash of stock, vinegar and soy sauce, and a most individualistic lightly cheesy bubble-and-squeakish spinach – all for £3.50. The normal menu covers a remarkable range, with popular examples running from soup (£1), sardines (£1.70) and local pasties (£1.80) through stuffed mushrooms (£3.25), sweet and sour crispy cod or garlicky prawns (£3.95) and gammon and egg or mixed grill (£4.50), to plaice (£5.50), various steaks (£6.50), salmon (£6.95), pheasant (£7.25), a seafood mixed grill (£8.25) and halibut served with crab claws and prawns (£8.50); helpings verge on the titanic. Despite these culinary riches, the atmosphere's very firmly that of an unpretentious country local. The two rooms of the little low-ceilinged bar have red plush wall seats and captain's chairs around heavy elm tables – scarcely more than half a dozen, though, so there could well be pressure on space at holiday times. There's also a small and pretty cottagey dining room with a good log fire in its big 17th-century stone fireplace. Well kept and attractively priced Blackawton Special and Ushers Best on handpump, with local Beenleigh Manor farm cider; cribbage, dominoes, table skittles, a selection of games for adults and children, books, fruit machine and piped music, with euchre on Tuesday and Sunday winter evenings; the amiable alsatian is called Misty and other dogs are welcome. There are picnic-table sets on a big lawn stretching up behind the car park, with swings, a climbing frame and summer barbecues. We've not yet heard from any reader who's stayed here. *(Recommended by M G Richards, C J Parsons, Brian Marsden)*

Free house Licensee Robin Thorns Real ale Meals and snacks (12–2, 7–10) Cottagey restaurant tel Harbertonford (080423) 204 Children in restaurant and eating area of bar Open 11.30 (11 Sat)–3, 6.30 (6 Sat)–11

COUNTISBURY SS7449 Map 1

Exmoor Sandpiper 🡄

A39, two or three miles E of Lynton on the Porlock road

Four or five rooms ramble around this big low white inn: ancient bumpy plaster walls, low ceilings, some heavy black beams and antique dining chairs and settles. There are fox and badger masks, an antique fortune-telling machine and darts, pool, dominoes, board games and fruit machine in the games area; piped music. Particularly recommended on the food side is their ham, smoked on the premises in the chimneys of the four log fires – look out for the ones hanging among the pots, cauldrons and kettles of the great central fire. It features prominently in the good range of large salads (from £4.95); other dishes include soup (£1.25), good sandwiches (from £1.25), and ploughman's (£2.50). Well kept Bass, Boddingtons, and Charringtons IPA on handpump, and a good range of unusual whiskies. The pub is tucked into the hillside opposite a moorland church and is well placed for Exmoor and the National Trust Watersmeet estate; on *Good Walks Guide* Walk 22. *(Recommended by J P Berryman, Lynne Sheridan, Bob West, Maj and Mrs I McKillop, Henry Midwinter)*

Free house Licensee A Vickery Real ale Meals and snacks Book-lined restaurant Children welcome Open 11–3, 5.30–11 (may open longer, afternoon) Bedrooms tel Brendon (059 87) 263; £40.25B/£64.40B

DALWOOD ST2400 Map 1

Tuckers Arms 🕸

Village signposted off A35 Axminster–Honiton

Perhaps the most popular dish in this recently refurbished, thatched medieval longhouse is their 'tiddy': a big puff pastry with a changing home-made filling, such as ham, cauliflower and blue cheese (£4.95) or layers of salmon and asparagus topped with a white wine sauce (£5.75). Other enterprising bar food includes home-made soup, potato skins with interesting dips (from £1.95), prawns in garlic mayonnaise (£2.75), lasagne (£4.25), home-made beef curry (£4.55), pan-fried veal schnitzel (£5.25), braised duck in a rich spicey apricot sauce or whole sole with rich seafood filling and dill sauce (£5.95), steaks (from £6.45), puddings like home-made apple tart (£1.55), daily specials, and children's menu (until 7.30pm – £1.55). The informally furnished bar has a random mixture of dining chairs, a funky armchair, window-seats, a pew and a high-backed winged black settle. The oak stripped beams and flagstones are original and there's both a big inglenook log fireplace and a woodburning stove. A side lounge with shiny black woodwork has a couple of cushioned oak armchairs and other comfortable but unpretentious seats. Well kept Boddingtons, Flowers Original, Marstons Pedigree, Whitbreads Pompey Royal, and Wadworths 6X on handpump, and quite a few malt whiskies; cribbage, fruit machine, piped music, and skittle alley. The inn is prettily decked with hanging baskets and big pots of flowers and there are some picnic-table sets; this year a terrace has been added. Careful parking will keep the villagers happy. (*Recommended by Dr D M Forsyth, Chris Raisin, Gordon and Daphne, Major and Mrs J V Rees, J R Carey*)

Free house   Licensees David and Kate Beck   Real ale   Meals and snacks (till 10pm)
Children in eating area of bar and in own room   Live music most Sat evenings   Open
11–3, 6.30–11   Bedrooms tel Stockland (040 488) 342; £18.50S/£33S

DARTINGTON   SX7762 Map 1

Cott 🏷️ 🛏️

In hamlet with the same name, signposted off A385 W of Totnes opposite A384 turn-off

Though a bad fire destroyed nearly three-quarters of the top floor of this picturesque inn in August 1989, things are now very much back to normal. Its outstanding feature is the thatched roof – at 183 feet one of the longest in the south of England – which is best admired from the benches in the crazy-paved courtyard where there are also attractive buckets of flowers. The heavy-beamed bar generally lives up to the expectations aroused by this traditional exterior: the communicating rooms have lots of polished brass and horse-harnesses on the white-washed walls, big open fires, some flagstone flooring, and traditional carved cast-iron, copper-topped round tables in front of sturdy high-backed settles, some elaborately carved. A small area is set aside for non-smokers. Good bar food includes sandwiches, fillet of cod with prawns and cheese or roast loin of pork (£4.25), braised duck leg with cranberry gravy (£4.50), and local scallops with smoked bacon (£10.50); friendly, courteous service. Well kept Bass and Tetleys on handpump; Churchward's cider, a good range of wines by the glass and several armagnacs. There are good walks through the grounds of nearby Dartington Hall, and it's good touring country – particularly for the popular Dartington craft centre, the Totnes–Buckfastleigh steam railway and one of the prettiest towns in the West Country, Totnes. (*Recommended by Patrick Freeman, Jim and Maggie Cowell, H K Dyson, Mr and Mrs Simon Turner, Caroline Wright, S V Bishop, Susan Turner, Wayne Brindle, Roy McIsaac, Dr C I Haines, W C M Jones, J and J Payne, Mrs L Grant, Heather Sharland, Ann and David Stranack, W A Gardiner, P R Truelove, Mr and Mrs I Blackwell, John Barker*)

Free house   Licensees Stephen and Gillian Culverhouse   Real ale   Meals and snacks
(12–2, 6.30–9.30)   Restaurant   Open 11–2.30, 6–11   Bedrooms tel Totnes (0803)
863777; £45(£55B)/£50(£60B)

DARTMOUTH   SX8751 Map 1

Cherub 🏷️

Higher Street

This is one of the very few British pubs listed officially as Grade I. It dates from about 1380 and was built mainly from ship's timbers. When it became an inn in 1972, it was named after a type of locally built wool-carrying boat, the Cherub. The cosy, atmospheric bar has tapestried seats under creaky heavy beams, red-curtained leaded-light windows and an open stove in the big stone fireplace. Consistently good bar food includes sandwiches (from £1.35; toasties from £1.45), soup (£1.40), French onion £1.50), filled baked potatoes or ploughman's (from £2.45), smoked haddock in a white wine and cheese sauce (£2.50), spaghetti bolognese or chilli con carne (£3.75), ratatouille (£3.95), smoked chicken with broccoli and ham (£4.50), seafood pasta (£4.95) and half-a-dozen fresh fish specials such as poached salmon in orange butter (£8.95) or John Dory in a Pernod and chive sauce (£9.50). Bass, Blackawton and Flowers IPA and Original on handpump, and 52 malt whiskies. Each of the two heavily timbered upper floors just further out than the one below. (*Recommended by David and Ann Stranack, Mr and Mrs L W Norcott, John Knighton, Carol Mason, John R Jones, Roy McIsaac, Margaret and Trevor Errington, D I Baddeley, Mrs A Turner, A E Melven, H K Dyson, Margaret and*

206   Devon

Trevor Errington, Sue Carlyle, George Jonas, Paul and Janet Waring)

Free house   Licensees John and Janet Hill   Real ale   Meals and snacks (12–2, 7–10)
Restaurant tel Dartmouth (080 43) 2571   Children in restaurant   Open 11–3, 5–11

Royal Castle 🛏

11 The Quay

Some of the oak beams in this 350-year-old waterside hotel reputedly came from the wreckage of the Spanish Armada. The lively, left-hand, local bar is decorated with navigation lanterns, glass net-floats and old local ship photographs, and big windows overlook the inner harbour and beyond to the bigger boats in the main one. A mix of tables ranges from scrubbed deal to polished mahogany and there are stripped pine country kitchen chairs and stools, mate's chairs and a couple of interesting old settles; one wall is stripped to the original stonework and there's a big log fire. On the right in the more sedate Turkey-carpeted bar, they spit-roast joints over the open range (pork over apple wood on Monday, lamb over sycamore on Tuesday evening and beef over oak Wednesday lunchtime); there's also a Tudor fireplace with copper jugs and kettles (beside which are the remains of a spiral staircase) and plush furnishings, including some Jacobean-style chairs, and in one alcove swords and heraldic shields on the wall. The range of generously served bar food includes lunchtime sandwiches (from £1.25, prawn or crab £2.75), and a choice of ploughman's (from £2.45), as well as home-made soup (£1.25), baked potatoes with hot or cold fillings (from £2.50), vegetable curry or chilli con carne (£3.25), home-made steak and kidney pie or locally made lamb, bacon and garlic sausages with apple and mint chutney (£4.25), whole plaice or a curry of the day (£4.75), steaks (from £7.25), daily specials, and puddings such as home-made apple pie (£1.65); may be evening bar nibbles. Well kept Bass, Flowers IPA and guests such as Marstons Pedigree and a local beer on handpump, and quite a few malt whiskies; welcoming staff; darts, cribbage, dominoes, and trivia. A regular newsletter can be forwarded to guests on request. *(Recommended by M V and J Melling, H K Dyson, Gwen and Peter Andrews, Mr and Mrs L W Norcott, John Knighton)*

Free house   Licensees Nigel and Anne Way   Real ale   Meals and snacks (12–9.45)
Restaurant   Children in eating areas   Folk music in public bar Weds and Sun, jazz in back of lounge bar Thurs   Open 11–11   Bedrooms tel Dartmouth (0803) 833033; £40B/£64B

DITTISHAM   SX8654 Map 1
Ferry Boat

Follow Ferry sign (sharp right turn), park in main car park and walk down narrow steep lane to water's edge; or at low tide keep straight on past Ferry sign, park down by playing fields and walk along foreshore to pub; or even come up on the little passenger ferry from Dartmouth

New licensees have taken over this little pub and have introduced a menu which includes sandwiches (from £1.65), home-made pasties (£1.20), ploughman's (from £2.50), fresh local crab, plaice, salmon and scallops (from £6.95), and in winter, home-made soups, old-fashioned meat puddings and game pies. Simple seats in the big picture window have fine views of boats on the wide river, and there's a ship's bell (with another outside which you can use to call the ferry to take you across the river to Dartmouth), brass gear and a ship's clock over the coal fire, ship's badges over the serving counter, and photographs of boats and ships; they chalk the tide times up on the wall. Courage Best and Directors on handpump, and quite a few malt whiskies; dominoes, cribbage, euchre and winter musical evenings. There are some seats outside. *(Recommended by H K Dyson, Helen Emmitt, David and Ann Stranack, Margaret and Trevor Errington)*

Courage   Licensee A M Tyrrell-Smith   Real ale   Meals and snacks   Open 11–3, 6–11

DODDISCOMBSLEIGH SX8586 Map 1

Nobody Inn ★ ★ ⊘ ⇆

Village signposted off B3193, opposite northernmost Christow turn-off

We get more rounded praise about this friendly, 16th-century pub than almost any other in the Guide, and as we went to press the licensees celebrated their 20th year here. The two rooms of the lounge bar are highly atmospheric, the bar food pleasing and surprisingly good value, and drinks include a remarkable choice of 700 well cellared wines by the bottle, 15 by the glass kept oxidation-free, properly mulled wine in winter, and twice-monthly tutored tastings in winter (they also do a retail trade, and the good tasting-notes in their detailed list are worth the £2.50 it costs – anyway refunded if you buy more than £20-worth); there's also a choice of 220 whiskies, Gray's Farm cider and usually well kept Bass, Flowers IPA, Eldridge Pope Royal Oak and Youngs on handpump or tapped straight from the cask. Attractive furnishings include handsomely carved antique settles, Windsor and wheelback chairs, red leatherette benches and carriage lanterns hanging from the beams (some of which are original). A snug area by one of the big inglenook fireplaces is decorated with guns and hunting prints. The wide range of efficiently served bar food includes sandwiches (from £1, made to order; good crab), home-made soup (£1.30), coarse home-made calves liver pâté (£1.90), sausage and mash or hot pitta salad (£2.20), good butterbean casserole (£2.30), macaroni cheese with ham (£2.40), good, enormous ploughman's (£2.50), and excellent rare beef salad (£3.90); daily specials such as fish or chicken pie or vegetarian shepherd's pie, and interesting puddings like ice-cream sprinkled with raisins and marinaded in Australian Muscat wine (£1.50), first rate fruit flan (£1.70), outstanding chocolate mousse and a selection of anything from 15 to 40 local cheeses to eat here or take away (£2.50). They serve baskets of fresh vegetables with the main dishes (or to have on their own), and also sell local honey and clotted Jersey cream. There are picnic-table sets in the charming garden, with views of the surrounding wooded hill pastures. The medieval stained glass in the local church is some of the best in the West Country. *(Recommended by D M and D E Livesley, Chris Raisin, R J Walden, John and Christine Simpson, Elisabeth Kemp, David and Ann Stranack, Hilary Roberts, David Wallington, Ian Whitlock, Gwen and Peter Andrews, WHBM, Tim and Ann Newell, Laurence Manning, W Bailey, Steve Dark, Mrs Lili Lomas, Andrea and Guy Bradley, Gethin Lewis, Charles Gurney, Ewan and Moira McCall, Wayne Brindle, M D Hare, John D Blaylock, Lyn and Bill Capper, Sybil Baker, C Vallely, WTF, David and Jane Russell, Peter Donahue, Christopher Knowles-Fitton, D Rowden)*

Free house   Licensee Nicholas Borst-Smith   Real ale   Meals and snacks (till 10 evening)   Open 12–2.30, 6–11 (winter evening opening 7); closed 25 Dec   Evening restaurant (Wed–Sat)   Children in restaurant   Bedrooms (some in distinguished 18th-century house 150yds away) tel Christow (0647) 52394; £13(£25B)/£32(£43B) Restaurant and bedrooms closed second week Jan

DREWSTEIGNTON SX7390 Map 1

Drewe Arms

Mabel Mudge, the landlady, has been running this thatched village alehouse for 71 years and is the oldest licensee in the country. Its genuine simplicity is not for everyone: basic built-in wooden benches face each other across plain tables, ochre walls have local team photographs and advertisements tacked to them, and there's no serving counter – the well kept real ale (typically Wadworths 6X and Whitbreads) and draught cider, which you can draw yourself, are kept on racks in the tap room at the back. There's a third room which is used occasionally; friendly locals. Note the herringbone-pattern Elizabethan brick floor. Though nearby Castle Drogo (open for visits) looks medieval, it was built earlier this century. Near the start of *Good Walks Guide* Walk 19. *(Recommended by Gordon and Daphne, Nick Dowson, Alison Hayward, Phil Gorton, Robert Humphreys, Chris Raisin, Graham Doyle, Joseph Melling)*

Free house   Real ale   Snacks   Open 10.30–2.30, 6–11 all year

EAST BUDLEIGH   SY0684   Map 1

Sir Walter Raleigh 🛏

Village signposted off A3052 Exeter–Sidmouth; then follow Village Centre sign

Just the right sort of pub for this delightful thatch-and-cob village, crowned by a fine church with a unique collection of carved oak bench ends (the man with the grotesquely large tongue could well have been working up a thirst for the pub's well kept Devenish JD and Wessex, on handpump). The simple bar has leatherette wall seats and wheelback chairs around the tables on its brightly patterned carpet, with a step down to a neat dining area; good bar food includes a fine home-made steak and kidney pie, 3-egg omelette (£3.50), chicken à là crème (£6.95), huge steaks cut by the landlord, specials such as lamb rissoles (£3.25), lots of fish such as cod (£4.25), scampi tails (£4.25), fresh crab (£4.95), grilled langoustines, salmon with asparagus sauce or lemon sole (£8.95) and half a fresh lobster (£10.95), and home-made puddings (£1.75); the herbs used in the cooking come from the licensee's garden, and there are regular special evenings with a French or Italian menu. Service is helpful and attentive, the landlord is friendly (as is Cracker the fluffy golden retriever); maybe piped pop music. There are old-fashioned slat and cast-iron benches outside the thatched house. (Recommended by J R Carey, Gordon and Daphne, Mr and Mrs Foruria, P Gillbe)

Devenish   Licensee David Rogers   Real ale   Meals and snacks   Restaurant
Children welcome   Open 11–3, 6–11   Bedrooms tel Budleigh Salterton (039 54)
2510; £12/£24

EAST DOWN   SS5941   Map 1

Pyne Arms ✿

Off A39 Barnstaple–Lynton; OS sheet 180, map reference 600415

The low-beamed, L-shaped bar of this busy food pub has lots of nooks and crannies, a very high-backed curved settle by the door (as well as more ordinary pub seating), some copper jugs, big barrels and a woodburning stove with horse harness and farm tools on the wall above it; the red walls are hung with horse-racing prints and Guinness and Martell placards, and up some steps is a small galleried loft with more tables and chairs. Reasonably priced bar food includes home-made soup (£1), filled rolls and sandwiches (from £1.25), ploughman's (£2.25), home-made pâté (£2.35), home-cooked ham and egg (£2.95), mussels in season prepared in four different ways (£4.75), scampi provençal (£5.95), several veal dishes (£6.95), steaks (from £6.95), beef Stroganoff (£7.35), and a range of puddings made in their own bakery (from £1.45). A flagstoned games area has pine-plank wall benches, a shelf with old soda syphons, handbells, and a clock, some swan-necked wall lamps, antlers, racing and hunting prints and a piano; pool table, darts, shove-ha'penny, table skittles, cribbage, dominoes and fruit machine; juke box. Well kept Flowers IPA on handpump, 5 wines by the glass, and quick, friendly service. The boisterous Doberman is popular with visitors, though he isn't allowed in the bar. The Black Venus at Challacombe and the Station House at Blackmoor Gate are under the same management. Arlington Court is close by. (Recommended by Steve and Carolyn Harvey, David Wallington, Nicholas Kingsley, G W Warren, Mr and Mrs P C Clark, H J Hooper, Paul and Joanna Pearson, Maj and Mrs I McKillop)

Free house   Licensees Jurgen and Elisabeth Kempf   Real ale   Meals and snacks (12–2, 7–10)   No children under 5 and those over that age in the small galleried loft only
Open 11–2.30, 6–11

EXETER   SX9292   Map 1

Double Locks ★

Canal Banks, Alphington; from A30 take main Exeter turn-off (A377/396) then next right into Marsh Barton Industrial Estate and follow Refuse Incinerator signs; when road bends round in front of the factory-like incinerator, take narrow dead end track over humpy bridge, cross narrow canal swing bridge and follow track along canal; much quicker than it sounds, and a very worthwhile diversion from the final M5 junction

The atmosphere in this ancient and remote lockhouse is marvellously relaxed and easy going and the staff particularly friendly. The bar resembles the interior of a retired seafarer's cottage, with nautical furnishings that include ship's lamps and model ships. Service is very friendly and the generous helpings of simple, home-made food include sandwiches (from £1), soup, a generous mushrooms on toast, hot dishes such as leek and macaroni bake, turkey and mushroom or cottage pie and tasty lasagne (all £2.40), good ploughman's (£2.50), daily specials (from £2.70), and salads (from £3.50), with good home-made ices and puddings (from £1.40); summer weekend barbecues (from £2.20). Well kept Everards Old Original, Exmoor, Greene King Abbot, Eldridge Pope Royal Oak, Marstons Pedigree and Owd Rodger, Wadsworth 6X and a guest beer on handpump or tapped from the cask, a decent range of Irish whiskies, hot toddies in winter and Pimms in summer; darts, shove-ha'penny, dominoes in the main bar, bar billiards in another; piped music and trivia. There are picnic-table sets and a well provisioned play area, with an old steam train and swings, out on the grass. *(Recommended by Cliff and Karen Spooner, Mrs F Smith, Simon Weinberger, Ruth Humphrey, Sue Hallam, Andrea and Guy Bradley, Lt Cdr G R D Jackson, Ian Phillips, Dr and Mrs B D Smith, Steve and Caroyln Harvey, David Pearman)*

Free house   Licensee Jamie Stuart   Real ale   Meals and snacks (available all day on weekdays)   Children welcome   Jazz 1st and 3rd Thurs of the month, and occasional other bands   Open 11–11

White Hart ★ 🛏

66 South Street; 4 rather slow miles from M5 junction 30; follow City Centre signs via A379, B3182; straight towards centre if you're coming from A377 Topsham Road

A popular meeting place for centuries, this splendid, well run 14th-century inn has a rambling main bar with big Windsor armchairs and built-in winged settles with latticed glass tops to their high backs, oak tables on the bare oak floorboards (carpet in the quieter lower area) and a log fire in one great fireplace with long-barrelled rifles above it; big copper jugs hang from heavy bowed beams in the dark ochre terracotta ceiling, the walls are decorated with pictorial plates, old copper and brass platters (on which the antique lantern lights glisten) and a wall cabinet holds some silver and copper. In one of the bay windows, there's a set of fine old brass beer engines. From the latticed windows, with their stained-glass coats-of-arms, one can look out on the cobbled courtyard – lovely when the wisteria is flowering in May. The Tap Bar, across the yard, with flagstones, candles in bottles and a more wine-barish feel, serves soup (£1.25), sandwiches (from £1.70), baked potato with cheese and anchovy topping (£1.95), dish of prawns (£2.10), cold meats (from £3.95), chicken and chestnut pie (£4.85), steak and kidney pie (£4.95), rib of beef steak (£7.50) and sirloin steak (£7.95). There is yet another bar, called Bottlescreu Bill's, even more dimly candlelit, with bare stone walls and sawdust on the floor. It serves much the same food, as well as a respectable range of Davy's wines and pint jugs of vintage port from the wood or tankards of bucks fizz, and in summer does lunchtime barbecue grills in a second, sheltered courtyard. On Sundays both these bars are closed. Bass and Davy's Old Wallop (served in pewter tankards in Bottlescreu Bill's) on handpump. Bedrooms are in a separate modern block. *(Recommended by Ruth Humphrey, WMS, Genie and Brian Smart, Steve and Carolyn Harvey; more reports please)*

Free house   Licensee Graham Frederick Stone   Real ale   Meals and snacks (not Sun)   Restaurant   Children in restaurant and eating area of bar   Open 11–3.30, 5–11 (all day Thurs–Sat); closed 25 and 26 Dec   Bedrooms tel Exeter (0392) 79897; £33(£48B)/£70B

EXMINSTER   SX9487 Map 1

Swans Nest ★ ⊘

Pub signposted from A379 S of village

Very much a food pub – though it's kept its pubby atmosphere – this popular place has a sensible no-smoking area extending from the long food servery: the wide range of food includes soup, sandwiches (not Saturday evening or Sunday lunchtime), home-made steak and kidney pie (£5.25), a good choice of salads (from £4.85), chef's specials such as rabbit casserole or roast haunch of venison in a red wine sauce (£4.50), roast pheasant (when available, £4.95), fillet steak rossini (£5.95), and an attractive carvery (£5.95); interesting puddings, and children's menu (£3). Bass, Tetleys, and Wadworths 6X on handpump, and country wines; friendly service. The decidedly rambling bar has groups of sofas and armchairs, some carved old-fashioned settles, lots of wheelback chairs, high-backed winged settles (set out as booths around the tables), heavy beams, grandfather clocks, high shelves of willow-pattern platters and so on; skittle alley. In the vast but charmingly landscaped car park they ask you to drive forwards into the bays, to prevent exhaust damage to their fine shrubs. (*Recommended by Andrea and Guy Bradley, T Galligan, P and M Rudlin, Gerald Gilling, Patrick Young*)

Free house   Licensees D W Major, A Amatruda   Real ale   Meals and snacks (12–2, 6–10)   Children in eating area of bar only   Live entertainment Fri–Sat evenings Open 11–2.30, 6–11; closed 26 Dec

Turf ★

Continue past the Swans Nest (see previous entry) to end of track, by gates; park, and walk right along canal towpath – nearly a mile

From the bay windows of this isolated inn's connected series of airy high-ceilinged rooms, there's a fine seaview out to the mudflats at low tide, full of gulls and waders. There are fresh flowers on low varnished tables, flagstones or broad bare floorboards, a woodburning stove and canal photographs and big bright shorebird prints by John Tennent on the white walls. Bar food is straightforward (though the new licensees are planning to introduce a more ambitious menu): sandwiches and toasties (from £1.10; home-cooked beef with horseradish £1.40), home-made soup (£1.25), filled baked potatoes (from £1.60), cottage pie or vegetable cassoulet (£1.95), ham and eggs (£2.30), ploughman's and platters (from £2.50), salads, and steak and Guinness pie (£3.25); also, puddings and a cook-yourself barbecue (from £1.25); friendly, efficient service. The dining room is no-smoking. Well kept Flowers IPA and Marstons Pedigree on handpump or tapped from the cask; darts, shove-ha'penny, trivia. Below, on the big lawn running down to the shore, you can play French boules; there are also log seats, picnic-table sets and a beached cabin boat for children to play in. The walk along the ship canal to its end by the pub takes about twenty minutes or you can take a 40-minute ride from Countess Wear in their own boat, the *Water Mongoose* (bar on board; £2 return, charter for up to 56 people £85). They welcome animals. (*Recommended by P and M Rudlin, Chris Raisin, Graham Doyle, D J and K Cooke*)

Free house   Licensees Clive and Ginny Redfern   Real ale   Meals and snacks Children in eating area of bar only   Open 11–2.30, 6–11; 11–11 summer Sats Bedrooms tel Exeter (0392) 833128; £15/£30

HARBERTON   SX7758 Map 1

Church House ⊘

Village signposted from A381 just S of Totnes

The latticed glass on the back wall of the open-plan bar by the entrance to this ancient pub was in a window which had been walled off (probably to evade window tax) until Victorian times; it's almost 700 years old, and one of the earliest examples of non-ecclesiastical glass in the country. Similarly, the magnificent medieval oak panelling was only discovered behind some plaster when renovations were carried out in 1950. Furnishings include attractive 17th-and 18th-century pews and settles, the bar counter originally came from a bank, and there's a large inglenook fireplace with a woodburning stove; one half of the room is set out for eating. The wide range of popular bar food (there may be delays on a busy evening) includes sandwiches (from £1.10), home-made soup (£1.30, crab £1.80), sausages (£1.95), ploughman's (from £2.15), fillet of plaice (£3.50, whole £4.95), gammon or three lamb cutlets (£4.95), steaks (from £6.25), and puddings (from £1.20). Lots of daily specials are chalked up on a board: seafood provençal (£1.95), deep fried brie wrapped in bacon and served with a spicy redcurrant jelly (£2.95), vegetarian dishes, local roast guinea fowl in port, rosemary and redcurrant sauce (£7.50), and special fresh local fish and shellfish dishes on Wednesdays and Thursdays. Bass, Courage Best and Directors, and a guest beer such as Greene King Abbot, Charrington IPA, Devenish Steam, Eldridge Pope Royal Oak, Exmoor or Marstons Pedigree on handpump, as well as Churchward's farm cider and Georges Duboeuf wines; efficient and friendly service; dominoes, cribbage. The pub is in a steep little twisting village, pretty and surrounded by hills. *(Recommended by WMS, David Wallington, David and Ann Stranack, Philip and Trisha Ferris, Mrs D B Broadhurst, John Walker, Roy Scott)*

Free house   Licensee Mrs Jennifer Wright   Real ale   Meals and snacks   Restaurant tel Totnes (0803) 863707   Children in family room   Local Morris team and local amateur jazz band   Open 11.30–2.30 (3 Sat), 6–11; winter lunchtime opening 12; closed evening 25 Dec

HATHERLEIGH   SS5404 Map 1

George 🛏

The little front bar – mainly for residents – in the original part of this pleasant, 15th-century inn has an enormous fireplace, tremendous oak beams, stone walls two or three feet thick, and easy chairs, sofas and antique cushioned settles. Across the corridor from this there's an even smaller, and very simple bar, which is only open on market day (Tuesday). The spacious L-shaped main bar was built from the wreck of the inn's old brewhouse and coachmen's loft, and has beams, a woodburning stove and antique settles around sewing-machine treadle tables; a quieter no-smoking extension, with more modern furnishings, leads off this. Straightforward, efficiently served bar food ranges from sandwiches (from £1.20, clubs £2.25), home-made soup (£1.30), filled baked potatoes (from £1.75) and ploughman's (from £1.90), through lasagne (£3), spinach and mushroom roulade, plaice or steak and kidney pie (£3.50), fry-up (£3.75) and steaks (£6.50), to puddings (£1.75); daily specials are chalked up on a board. Well kept Barrons Exe Valley, Bass, Wadworths 6X and Whitbreads Castle Eden and Pompey Royal on handpump, a good range of Spey and Islay malt whiskies, and farm ciders; darts, pool, cribbage, dominoes and piped music. In the flood-lit courtyard there are hanging baskets and window-boxes on the black and white timbering, and rustic wooden seats and tables on its cobblestones. A small heated swimming pool is well screened by the car park. *(Recommended by Helena and Arthur Harbottle, Cliff and Karen Spooner, G W Warren, David Wallington, Roy and Barbara Longman)*

Free house   Licensees Veronica Devereux and John Dunbar-Ainley   Real ale   Meals and snacks (12–2, 6–9.30)   Restaurant (closed Sun)   Children welcome   Open 11–11 (10am opening Mon/Tues)   Bedrooms tel Okehampton (0837) 810454; £27(£36B)/£36(£47B)

Tally Ho

Market St (A386)

So English, this venerable village pub with its heavy beams, beer brewed on the premises, and hospitable pipe-smoking cardigan-wearing landlord – the surprise is that he's actually an Italian, an engineer who fell in love with both the area and the pub as an institution while on holiday with his family here a few years ago. There are indeed Italian touches here: the good-value Wednesday pizza night, the old brass and copper espresso machine on the counter, Verdi and Rossini arias at a midsummer garden concert (but that appropriate Flanders and Swan song *Gianni's Cellar* too). Yet the pub's character is perfectly preserved: sturdy old oak and elm tables on the partly carpeted brick floor, candles in bottles, fresh flowers, two woodburning stoves (an armchair by one, the other in a very high-mantled smoking-chamber of a hearth, with a fox mask above it), decorative plates between the wall timbers, shelves of old bottles and pottery. Firmly home-made bar food includes pasties (£1.25), sandwiches (from £1.75), ploughman's (from £2), omelette (from £2.15), home-made soup or sausages (£2.20), lasagne (£3.50), devilled crab (£3.80), a vegetarian dish, fritto misto (£6.50), sirloin steak (£7.50), puddings (from £1.40) and lots of dishes of the day such as cannelloni (£3.25); on Wednesday evenings in summer there are barbecues; darts, shove-ha'penny, cribbage, dominoes, fruit machine, trivia, maybe unobtrusive piped pop radio. You can view the spotless new copper brewing equipment through a big window in one building of the former back coach yard; besides their own deep-coloured quite strongly hopped Potboiler with its sturdily appetising finish, they have a couple of well kept guest beers such as Butcombe and Eldridge Pope Royal Oak on handpump, a fine range of Italian wines, and a dozen malt whiskies. The friendly boxer is called Boris. There are tables in the sheltered garden. The atmospheric little back dining room specialises in Italian dishes. We've not yet heard from readers who've stayed here, but would expect the licensees to look after you well. Mr Scoz is a keen fisherman and fishing can be arranged on about 8 miles of the Torridge. *(Recommended by R J Walden, J R Carey, Cliff and Karen Spooner)*

Own brew   Licensees Gianni and Annamaria Scoz   Real ale   Meals and snacks   Restaurant   Open 11–2.30, 6–11; 11–11 Tues (market day)   Children in eating area of bar   Bedrooms tel Hatherleigh (0837) 810306; £20B/£38B

HAYTOR VALE   SX7677   Map 1

Rock ★ ∅ ⇒

Haytor signposted off B3344 just W of Bovey Tracey, on good moorland road to Widecombe

Highly praised, the wide choice of bar food in this civilised Dartmoor inn includes pasty (95p), home-made soup (£1.25), sandwiches (from £1.25, ham, asparagus and pineapple £3.95), filled baked potato (£1.95), omelettes made with local free-range eggs or ploughman's (£2.75), vegetarian dishes (from £3.25), rabbit surprise (£3.55), lasagne, curries, steak and kidney pudding or plaice stuffed with garlic butter (all £3.95), grilled lamb chops (£5.95), steaks (from £6.25), grilled fresh brill (£7.95), and a good range of puddings such as rapsberry montiechristie, treacle tart, bread and butter pudding and steamed puddings (all £1.35); they warn of delays at busy periods. Bass and Eldridge Pope Dorchester and Royal Oak on handpump; helpful, friendly service. The relaxed, partly panelled bar has polished antique tables, easy chairs, oak Windsor armchairs and high-backed settles. In the two communicating rooms there are flowers in summer, good log fires in winter (the main fireplace has a fine Stuart fireback), and old-fashioned prints and decorative plates on the walls. The winter Friday-night break – you pay for a meal for two in the restaurant and get free overnight accommodation – is good value. The village itself is just inside the National Park, and the inn is well positioned for golf, horse riding and fishing. The big garden is pretty and well kept. *(Recommended by M Saunders, Helena and Arthur Harbottle, Bob Smith, D M and D E Livesley, Mr and Mrs Simon Turner, Tony and Alison Sims, D I Baddeley, J A Harrison, Peter Donahue, D K and H M Brenchley, Steve Huggins, Hilary Robinson, Peter Maden, W A Gardiner)*

Free house   Licensee Christopher Graves   Real ale   Snacks (not Sun or Bank Hol)   No-smoking restaurant (residents only on Sun)   Children in restaurant   Open 11–2.30, 6.30–11 (winter evening opening 7)   Bedrooms tel Haytor (036 46) 305; £25(£35.50B)/£40(£49.50B)

HENNOCK SX8380 Map 1

Palk Arms

Village signposted from B3193; also good road first right turn after leaving Chudleigh Knighton on B3344 for Bovey Tracey

The restaurant in this 16th-century inn has been repositioned and makes even more of the magnificent views over the spread of the Teign Valley. New kitchens have been installed, too, and food now includes sandwiches, fresh and smoked salmon dishes (from £2.50), salads (from £3.50), hot dishes such as steak and kidney pie, curries or pasta (from £4.15), fresh Brixham plaice (£4.75), and steaks (£7.15); very good breakfasts, and welcoming, helpful staff. The main bar has a large log fire in a stone fireplace and downstairs from the lounge bar is an attractive bread oven. Fergusons Dartmoor on handpump; darts, dominoes, cribbage, fruit machine, juke box, and piped music. Picnic-table sets on the back lawn enjoy the view. Close to the Hennock reservoirs which are good for fly-fishing. *(Recommended by Hu' and Eve Deverson, Julia Bowder; more reports please)*

Free house Licensees Jim and Judith Young Real ale Meals and snacks (not Sun evening) Restaurant (closed Sun evening) Children in restaurant Open 11–2.30, 6–11 (12–2.30, 7–11 winter); closed Mon morning Nov–end April Bedrooms tel *Bovey Tracey (0626) 833027; £12.50/£25*

HOLNE SX7069 Map 1

Church House ⊘ ⇌

Perhaps the nicest way of getting to this Grade II-listed medieval inn is the quarter-hour walk from the Newbridge National Trust car park; there are many other attractive walks nearby, up on to Dartmoor as well as along the wooded Dart valley – and fine moorland views from the pillared porch (popular with regulars). The lower bar has stripped pine panelling, and an atmospheric carpeted lounge bar has a 16th-century heavy oak partition and an 18th-century curved elm settle. They use fresh local produce (organic if possible) in their food, which at lunchtime includes ploughman's or filled baked potatoes (from £2.50), cauliflower cheese or lasagne (£3.25), omelettes (from £3.25), salads (from £4), large, tasty steak and kidney pie (£4.25), and puddings (from £1.50), with evening starters such as salmon mousse, mushrooms in garlic or greek salad and feta cheese (from £1.50), and main courses like a vegetarian dish (£3.75), roasts (from £4.25), Devon lamb in cider or venison in red wine (from £4.75), and grills (from £5). Blackawton Bitter and 44 and Fergusons Dartmoor on handpump, and Addlestones cask conditioned cider; friendly staff. Darts, dominoes, and table skittles in the public bar. Charles Kingsley (of *Water Babies* fame) was born in this village – which is surprisingly untouristy. *(Recommended by David and Shirley Way, Mrs A Crowhurst, Wayne Brindle, Mr and Mrs D Hampton, M D Hare, Mrs J Fellowes, Mr and Mrs I Blackwell, David and Flo Wallington)*

Free house Licensees N E and W J Bevan Real ale Snacks (not evening) and meals No-smoking restaurant Children in eating area of bar Local folk groups and instrumentalists last Fri in month Open 12–2.30 (3 Sat), 6.30–11; 11.30–2, 6.30–10.30 (11 Fri and Sat) in winter; closed evening 25 Dec Bedrooms tel *Poundsgate (036 43) 208; £17.50(£22.50B)/£30(£43B)*

HORNDON SX5280 Map 1

Elephant's Nest ★ ★ ⊘

If coming from Okehampton on A386 turn left at Mary Tavy inn, then left after about 1/2 mile; pub signposted beside Mary Tavy Inn, then Horndon signposted; on the Ordnance Survey Outdoor Leisure Map it's named as the New Inn

Some changes this year to this 400-year-old pub include a new room created from the old beer cellar which will act as a dining or function room or just an overspill from the bar on busy nights, and which has views over the garden and beyond to the moors, and new wooden benches and tables for the lawn. The friendly bar has an amusing elephant mural, large rugs and flagstones, a beams-and-board ceiling, cushioned stone seats built into the windows, captain's chairs around the tables, and a good log fire on cool days. Bar food is chalked up on a board and at lunchtime includes good home-made soup (£1.10), sandwiches, five good ploughman's (from £2.20), chilli con carne (£2.60), a generous home-made steak and kidney pie (£3.50), game pie (£4), and good sticky puddings (from £1.60), with evening dishes like curry (£3.50), a tandoori dish (£4.50), gammon (£4.80), local trout (£5), steaks (from £7.60), three vegetarian dishes, and seven changing daily specials; fresh vegetables are 80p extra. Well kept Boddingtons, Palmers IPA, St Austell HSD and Websters Yorkshire on handpump, with up to 32 summer guests; several wines, a few country wines and Inch's cider on handpump; sensibly placed darts, cribbage, dominoes, fruit machine and piped music; efficient service. There are several dogs. Though you can walk from here straight on to the moor or Black Down, a better start (army exercises permitting) might be to drive past Wapsworthy to the end of the lane, at OS Sheet 191 map reference 546805. *(Recommended by N W Acton, Jacquie and Jon Payne, Mayur Shah, Harry Stirling, Mr and Mrs Simon Turner, Brian Jones, J C Proud, Wayne Brindle, Helena and Arthur Harbottle, Heather Sharland, Richard Cole, TBB, Hilary Robinson, Peter Maden)*

Free house   Licensees Nick and Gill Hamer and Peta Hughes   Real ale   Meals and snacks (11.30–2, 7–10)   Children in dining area and areas away from bar   Occasional live entertainment   Open 11.30–2.30 (3 Sat), 6.30–11   Bedrooms tel Mary Tavy (0822) 810273; l£27

HORSEBRIDGE   SX3975 Map 1

Royal ★

Village signposted off A384 Tavistock–Launceston

The covered area in the garden, presided over by Fred, the resident jackdaw, has now been taken over by budgies, finches, cockatiels and so forth, and a new big terrace with seats, a rose arbour and hanging baskets has been built. Inside, you get the impression that the simple, old-fashioned bar can't have changed much since Turner slept on a settle in front of the fire, so that he could slip out early to paint the bridge. In the right-hand room there are vertically panelled cushioned stall seats around neat old tables, some mate's chairs and wheelback chairs, and harness and brasses on the stripped stone walls; the one on the left has cushioned casks and benches around three tables on the slate floor, and bar billiards, sensibly placed darts and piped music. There's another small room, called the Drip Tray, for the overflow at busy times. Besides the beers brewed on the premises – Tamar, Horsebridge Best and the more powerful Heller – they also keep Bass, Greene King Abbot and Marstons Pedigree on handpump. Good bar food includes a wide choice of lunchtime ploughman's (£2, with home-made herby bread), pot meals like moussaka or sausage (£2.25), beef and oyster pie (£3), tandoori drumsticks (£3.25), venison in port (£4.25) and duck in orange (£4.75), a decent range of vegetarian dishes such as nut roast, onion bhaji or samosa (£3) and some unusual puddings (£1.35); food service stops promptly at 2. The bridge from which the village takes its name has remarkably exact unmortared masonry, and was the first over the River Tamar, built by monks in 1437 – not long before they built this inn, which is about fifty yards away. It was originally called the Packhorse, and got its present name for services rendered to Charles I (whose seal is carved in the doorstep). *(Recommended by Richard Houghton, Graham and Glenis Watkins, Phil Gorton, David and Sarah Gilmore, Mr and Mrs Simon Turner, Paul and Heather Bettesworth, M L Hooper-Immins, Charles and Mary Winpenny, H W and A B Tuffill, John and Pat Smyth, PB, HB)*

Own brew   Licensees T G and J H Wood   Real ale   Meals and snacks (12–2, 7.15–9.30; not Sun evening)   Open 12–2.30, 7–11

IDDESLEIGH SS5708 Map 1

Duke of York 🅿️ 🛏️

B3217 Exbourne–Dolton

The licensees who took over in 1988 have made this largely 14th-century thatched pub a splendidly relaxed and welcoming place, both for strangers and for the locals who drop in so casually for a chat (with their dogs maybe looking forward to a treat from the landlord, maybe just winking sheepishly at Poppy the ginger cat). Well spaced stripped country tables have flowers and lit candles in bottles, there's a housekeeper's chair by one big high-mantled stone fireplace – where logs may be burning even in summer. Generously served truly home-made bar food is chalked up on a blackboard and includes filled baked potatoes (from £2), a fair ploughman's (from £2.50), pasta with pesto or a choice of interesting speciality sausages (£2.75), ham and egg (£3.25), several enterprising specials such as beef and wild mushroom casserole (£3.50), cauliflower and courgette crumble with pistachios (£3.75) and devilled crab (£4.50), maybe a splendid help-yourself buffet (£5), and children's dishes (£1.75); the sticky toffee pudding is particularly good, as is the brown sugar meringue with raspberry sauce – both with clotted cream, of course (£1.75). We don't usually mention ice-creams, but their strawberry one is worth breaking the rule for. Well kept Cotleigh Tawny, Wadworths 6X and various guests tapped from the cask, Inch's farm ciders, several malt whiskies, old-fashioned cordials; shove-ha'penny, cribbage, dominoes, backgammon, Trivial Pursuit, various books and magazines and sensibly placed darts. Through a small coach arch is a little back garden with some picnic-table sets under cocktail parasols, with a slide, and a rabbit hutch in the owners' part. Good fishing nearby; and if you stay you're well placed to take particular advantage of dinner in the charming little dining room – fine, interesting cooking. *(Recommended by Mr and Mrs J D Cranston, G R Cleaver, David Wallington, J R Carey, Mrs S Andrews, R W Stanbury)*

Free house   Licensees Trish and John Colvill   Real ale   Meals and snacks   Restaurant (Tues–Sat evenings; must book before noon)   Children in eating area of bar and in restaurant for Sunday buffet   Morris dancers and occasional country storytellers   Open 11–3, 6.30–11; closed evening 25 Dec   Bedrooms tel Hatherleigh (0837) 810253; £17.50(£20B)/£35(£40B)

KINGSKERSWELL SX8767 Map 1

Barn Owl

Aller Road; just off A380 Newton Abbot–Torquay – inn-sign on main road opposite RAC post

As we went to press, the outside of this pub was being redecorated, a new entrance, reception area, lavatories and residents' lounge were under construction, and new en-suite bedrooms had just been completed. One public room has grand furnishings such as a couple of carved oak settles and old-fashioned dining chairs around the handsome polished tables on its flowery carpet, antique dark oak panelling, a decorative wooden chimney piece and an elaborate ornamental plaster ceiling. Two other rooms have been stripped back to low black oak beams, with polished flagstones and a kitchen range in one. The wide choice of bar food ranges from soup (£1), sandwiches (from £1.80, crab £3), filled baked potatoes (from £2.15), ploughman's (from £2.60), quite a few salads (from £3.95; fresh local salmon £6.50), fresh fillet of plaice (£3.95), fresh fillet of sole (£4.25), gammon with pineapple (£4.35), a grill or steaks (from £7.50), and home-made specials like liver and bacon casserole, prawn and mushroom pancakes, chicken marengo and fresh fish. Janners on handpump and several malt whiskies; log fires throughout. There are picnic-table sets in a small sheltered garden. *(Recommended by D I Baddeley, M Saunders, B A Cox)*

Free house   Licensees Derek and Margaret Warner   Real ale   Meals and snacks (till 10 evening)   Restaurant Mon–Sat evenings and Sun lunchtime; best to book and they prefer you not to smoke   Open 11.30–2.30, 7–11   Bedrooms tel Kingskerswell (0803) 872130; £45B/£55B

KINGSTEIGNTON   SX8773   Map 1

Old Rydon ★ ⊘

Rydon Rd; from A381 Teignmouth turn off A380, take first real right turn (Longford Lane), go straight on to the bottom of the hill, then next right turn into Rydon Road following Council Office signpost; pub is just past the school, OS Sheet 192 map reference 872739

This friendly, characterful little former farmhouse is particularly popular for its unusual home-made bar food. The menu changes daily depending on what fresh ingredients they've bought, but might include soup (£1.10), creamy garlic and herb dip (£1.65), seafood pancake (£2.45), with main dishes like vegetarian butterbean hotpot with cheddar topping and garlic bread (£3.45), Normandy pork in cider and cream or Bami Goreng (an Indonesian dish with pork and noodles £4.25), fisherman's pie with crumble topping (£4.50), an outstanding fish salad with crab, prawns, salmon and red mullet, and puddings like bread and butter pudding or tiramisu (£1.60); local game and fresh mussels in winter. Well kept Bass, Janners Devon Special (called Old Rydon Ale here) and Wadworths 6X on handpump; prompt service. The small, cosy bar has cask seats and upholstered seats built against the white-painted stone walls, a heavy beam-and-plank ceiling with lots of beer mugs hanging from them, and a big winter log fire in a raised fireplace. There are a few more seats in an upper former cider loft, now a gallery facing the antlers and antelope horns on one high white wall. On a covered side terrace are some seats, with more in a nice biggish sheltered garden, which has a swing. *(Recommended by M Saunders, J C Proud, B A Cox, E H and R F Warner, Tom Evans, Rita Horridge, MKW, JMW, P Miller, Steve Higgins)*

Free house   Licensees Hermann and Miranda Hruby   Real ale   Meals and snacks Restaurant tel Newton Abbot (0626) 54626; closed Sun   Children in restaurant at lunchtime, and upstairs till 8pm   Open 11–3, 6–11; closed 25 Dec

KINGSTON   SX6347   Map 1

Dolphin

The cheerfully informal bar of this yellow-shuttered 16th-century house is made up of several knocked-through beamed rooms, with rustic tables and cushioned seats and settles around their bared stone walls. Popular, generously served bar food includes home-made soup (£1.20), lunchtime sandwiches and ploughman's (from £1.35, local crab £2.25), cottage pie, chilli, or sausages, ham and egg (£2.95), steak and kidney pie or chicken curry (£4.25), and local crab salad (£5.50), with additional evening dishes like chicken breast (£5.25), and steaks (from £7.95); puddings such as treacle tart or home-made chocolate truffle cake (from £1.75), children's dishes (£1.50), and Sunday roast beef (£3.50, children £2.25). The menu is more limited on Sunday and Monday evenings, when the prices are lower. Well kept Courage Best and guests like Devenish Steam and Marstons Pedigree on handpump. There are tables, swings, a children's summer snack bar and summer barbecues in the garden. Half a dozen tracks lead down to the sea, and unspoilt Wonwell Beach, about a mile and a half away. *(Recommended by Jane and Mark Hayward, D and B Carron; more reports please)*

Courage   Licensee Barry Fryer   Real ale   Meals and snacks (12–2, 7–10)   Children in family room and eating area of bar until 9pm   Open 11–3, 6–11

KNOWLE   SS4938   Map 1

Ebrington Arms

Pub signposted just off A361, in village two miles N of Braunton

A good mix of customers come to this busy pub to enjoy the wide-ranging bar food: home-made soup (£1.60), ploughman's (from £2.45), smoked trout (£2.50), chilli con carne or turkey curry (£2.80), cottage pie (£3.15), vegetarian lasagne or fettucine (£3.25), steak casserole in Guinness (£4.15), and popular cockles, mussels and prawns in white wine and cream (£4.25). There's a candlelit dining area up one or two steps at one end – highly spoken of by readers. The two opened-up rooms of the carpeted lounge have red plush stools around low tables, some pews, cushioned seats built into the stripped-stone outer walls (the inner ones are white), a copper-plated chimney breast, and a friendly atmosphere; the walls and black joists are decorated with lots of brass, prints, plates and pewter mugs. A snug bar has darts, shove-ha'penny, cribbage, space game and a fruit machine; separate pool room. Bass on handpump; juke box and piped music. Tess the dog is warmly welcoming. Note that if you choose something from the diningroom menu, you can't eat it in the bar (and vice versa). *(Recommended by Richard Fawcett, E V Walder, Philip and Trisha Ferris, John Drummond, Alan P Carr, Pamela and Merlyn Horswell, Mrs Nina Elliott)*

Free house   Licensees Alex and Nancy Coombs   Real ale   Meals and snacks Restaurant area tel Braunton (0271) 812166   Children in eating area   Open 11–2.30, 6–11

KNOWSTONE   SS8223   Map 1

Masons Arms ★ ★ ⊘ ⇌

Village signposted off A361 Bampton–South Molton

This simple but very hospitable thatched 13th-century stone inn has substantial rustic furniture on the stone floor of its small main bar, farm tools on the walls, ancient bottles of all shapes and sizes hanging from the heavy medieval black beams, and a fine open fireplace with a big log fire and side bread oven. A small lower sitting room has pinkish plush chairs around a low table in front of the fire and bar billiards. The locals are chatty, and the landlord is most helpful about places to visit and so forth – and likely to remember your name on a second visit. (It's important to note that the house style here is engagingly homely and almost soporifically relaxed.) Good, farmhousey bar food includes widely praised home-made soup (£1.25) and pâté (£1.75 – the walnut and cheese one is quite special), ploughman's with good fresh cheese and butter in a pot (from £2.05), fried plaice (£2.95), salads (from £2.95), home-made pies, varying from day to day, like cheese and leek or rabbit and venison (£3.25), meat salads (£3.25), home-made curry (£4.20), fritto misto (£4.95), sirloin steak (£7.95) and puddings like excellent toffee pudding (from £1.25); specials such as moules marinières with garlic bread (£2.50), Devonshire cassoulet (£4.50) or tiramisu (£1.50), very good value Sunday lunch (main course £3.50, 3 courses £6), and a popular Thursday curry night with half-a-dozen to choose from, along with 5 or 6 sambals. They often sell home-made marmalades, fruit breads or hot gooseberry chutney over the counter. Well kept Hook Norton and Badger Best, Cotleigh Tawny and Wadworths 6x tapped from the cask, farm cider and a small but well chosen wine list; several snuffs on the counter; darts, shove-ha'penny, table skittles, dominoes, cribbage, and a Sunday and Bank Holiday weekend trivia quiz (proceeds to charity). Charlie the engaging bearded collie likes to join you on a walk – at least part of the way; the cats are called Archie and Allie. The pub is attractively placed opposite the church. We should make clear that the place-to-stay award reflects the distinctive character of the pub, much enjoyed by many readers who have stayed here – and by us; the level of comfort and sometimes of housekeeping is not however up to everyone's expectations. *(Recommended by Steve and Carolyn Harvey, Michael and Joan Melling, Alan and Julie Wear, G W Warren, Virginia Jones, Prof M P Furmston, Cliff and Karen Spooner, Audrey and Roger Adcock, David Wallington, Mrs S Andrews, T J Maddison, Sarah Vickers, John Evans, Mr and Mrs D M Norton, Ann and David Stranack, Rita Horridge, Chris Raisin, Graham Doyle, Peter Adcock, Isobel and Lindy May and William Stapley)*

Free house   Licensees David and Elizabeth Todd   Real ale   Meals and snacks No-smoking restaurant (closed Sun evening)   Children in restaurant and eating areas Occasional live entertainment such as a summer jazz night or spontaneous acoustic guitar   Open 11–3, 7–11; lunchtime closing 2.30 in winter; closed evening 25 Dec Bedrooms tel Anstey Mills (039 84) 231; £19.50(£24S)/£39(£48S)

LUSTLEIGH   SX7881 Map 1

Cleave

Village signposted off A382 Bovey Tracey–Moretonhampstead

In an attractive out-of-the-way village, this thatched white 15th-century inn is surrounded by a neat and pretty sheltered garden, where you may meet strolling peacocks. Inside, the cosy low-ceilinged lounge bar has fresh flowers in summer and big log fires in winter, and attractive antique high-backed settles, pale leatherette bucket chairs, red-cushioned wall seats and wheelback chairs around the tables on its patterned carpet. A traditionally furnished second bar has darts, dominoes, cribbage, and a fruit machine; piped music. The real ale changes regularly, typically including Bass, Flowers IPA and a guest beer on handpump. Reasonably priced, tasty bar food includes home-made soup (£1.50), large filled plaited bread rolls (£2.50), ploughman's (from £2.95), home-made cheese and onion flan (£2.95), home-cooked ham (£3.10), home-made lasagne (£3.95), home-made steak, kidney and Guinness pie (£4.75), and puddings (£1.60), with evening dishes like snails (£2.75), hot home-made chilli con carne (£3.95), salads (from £4.95), and 12oz sirloin steak (£9.10); generous breakfasts for residents; friendly service. It's near *Good Walks Guide* Walk 18. *(Recommended by S J Breame, Steve Huggins, Genie Krakowska Smart, Paul and Janet Waring, Ann and David Stranack, Hilary Robinson, Peter Maden, Rita Horridge, Henry Hooper, John Knighton, Mr and Mrs B Hobden, W A Gardiner)*

Heavitree (who no longer brew)   Licensees A and A Perring   Real ale   Meals and snacks   No-smoking restaurant   Open 11–11; 11–2.30, 7–11 winter   Children in family room; under 10 until 9pm   Parking may be difficult   Three bedrooms tel Lustleigh (064 77) 223; £17.50/£35

LUTTON   SX5959 Map 1

Mountain

Pub signposted from Cornwood–Sparkwell road

A window seat in the beamed bar here looks over the lower slopes of Dartmoor; there are also some walls stripped back to the bare stone, a high-backed settle by the log fire and Windsor chairs around old-fashioned polished tables in a larger connecting room. Well kept Burton Ind Coope, Fergusons Dartmoor and Exmoor and Tetleys on handpump, and local farm cider; darts, dominoes. Generous helpings of straightforward bar food include French bread filled generously with beef and generous, thick-cut cider-baked ham (£3.30), as well as sandwiches (from £1.30, prawn £2.25), chilli con carne or curries (£2.40), home-made beef and vegetable or courgette and Stilton soup with nearly half-a-pound cheese and a roll, ploughman's (£3.30), lasagne, game casserole or beef stroganoff, and apple pie with more apple than pie. There are seats on the terrace under a vine. *(Recommended by Jack and Mark Hayward, D J K Waltho, Philip and Trisha Ferris; more reports please)*

Free house   Licensees Charles and Margaret Bullock   Real ale   Meals and snacks (till 10 evening)   Children in eating area and small family room   Open 11–3, 6–11; winter Sun–Thurs evening opening 7

LYDFORD   SX5184 Map 1

Castle ★ 🛏

In a village that was one of the four strong-points developed by Alfred the Great as a defence against the Danes, it's the daunting medieval tower that gives its name to this charming pink-washed Tudor inn. The twin-roomed bar is furnished with country kitchen chairs, high-backed winged settles and old captain's chairs around mahogany tripod tables on big slate flagstones; unusual stained-glass doors. One room, where the bar food is served, has masses of brightly decorated plates, some Hogarth prints, an attractive grandfather clock, low lamp-lit beams, a sizeable open fire and near the serving-counter seven Lydford pennies hammered out in the old Saxon mint in the reign of Ethelred the Unready, in the 10th-century; the second room has an interesting collection of antique stallion posters. Courage Best and Directors and Wadworths 6X on handpump; sensibly placed darts, shove-ha'penny, cribbage, piped music. The imaginative lunchtime cold buffet table (£5), available every day in summer and at weekends in winter, has a good choice of salads with the meats, home-made pies and scotch eggs, salmon, trout, cold tandoori chicken and so forth; other bar food typically includes chicken, poultry pie, seafood risotto, daily fresh fish or curry (£3.75-£4) and steak and kidney pie (£4); Sunday roasts. The well kept garden has an adventure playground and barbecue area. The Jack Russell is called Podge and the two cats, Harvey and JR. The pub is close to a beautiful river gorge (owned by the National Trust). *(Recommended by P M Rowntree, Mr and Mrs Simon Turner, J A Scott, R W Stanbury, Nick Dowson, Alison Hayward, Drs M and K Parier, Wayne Brindle, Mr and Mrs P C Clark, Col G D Stafford, David Wallington, Henry Hooper, Mrs K Currie, TBB, Frances Mansbridge, Phil and Sally Gorton, Charles and Mary Winpenny)*

Free house   Licensees David and Susan Grey   Real ale   Snacks (not Sun) and meals (12–2.30, 6–9.30)   Restaurant (part of which is no-smoking)   Well behaved, quiet children welcome   Open 11–3, 6–11; closed 25 Dec   Bedrooms tel Lydford (082 282) 242; £25(£33B)/£35(£45B)

LYNMOUTH   SS7249 Map 1

Rising Sun 🛏

Mars Hill; down by harbour

The setting of this thatched 14th-century inn is lovely – looking over boats in the little harbour to the sea and in its own residential garden. The steep walk up the Lyn valley to Watersmeet (National Trust) and Exmoor is particularly pleasant. The modernised panelled bar has uneven oak floors, black beams in the crooked ceiling, some stripped stone at the fireplace end, cushioned built-in stall-seats, and latticed windows facing the harbour. Good lunchtime bar food includes home-made soup (£1.50), filled baked potatoes (£1.95), open Danish sandwiches (from £1.95, crab, prawns or smoked salmon £2.95), steak, mushroom and Guinness pie (£3.25), spicy sausages and eggs (£3.50), 6oz rump steak (£4.95), seafood platter (£5.25), and puddings; the best place to eat in is the small oak-panelled diningroom. Ushers Best on handpump; friendly service; piped music. Near *Good Walks Guide* Walk 20. The bedrooms are mostly up the hill in the adjoining cottages, in one of which Shelley reputedly spent his honeymoon with his 16-year old bride, Harriet. *(Recommended by Carol Mason, J A Scott, Jean and Hugo Thomas, D R Tyler, N C Dickerson, John Drummond, Dr R Trigwell, Steve Dark, Rita Horridge, Mrs J R T Mosesson, E G Parish)*

Free house   Licensee Hugo Jeune   Real ale   Lunchtime meals and snacks No-smoking restaurant   Children in restaurant   Open 11–3, 5.30–11   Bedrooms tel Lynton (0598) 53223; £37B/£64B

MILTONCOMBE   SX4865 Map 1

Who'd Have Thought It ★ 🏵

Village signposted from A386 S of Tavistock

The painting over the entrance to this attractive, white-painted pub with its tulip-filled window boxes, depicts it in the 16th century. The cheerfully atmospheric bar has colourful plates on a big black dresser, cushioned high-backed winged settles around a woodburning stove in the big stone fireplace, rapiers and other weapons on its walls, and black panelling; two other rooms have seats made from barrels. Generous helpings of popular bar food include granary bread sandwiches (from £1.20, good crab £1.85), generous ploughman's (lunchtime only, from £2.40), basket meals (from £2.30), cod (£2.95), platters (from £4.40), grills (from £5.20), and puddings like cherry or blackcurrant pie with clotted cream (£1.40); specials like chilli con carne (£2.50), steak and kidney pie or chicken curry (£3.50), and braised steak in red wine or good duck casserole (£5.25). On Sunday lunchtimes the menu is restricted to sandwiches, ploughman's and basket meals. Well kept Bass, Eldridge Pope Royal Oak, Exmoor, Fullers ESB, and Wadworths 6X on handpump, with Bulmers and Inch's ciders; efficient, friendly staff. Darts, dominoes, cribbage, fruit machine, and piped music. There are picnic-table sets on a terrace with hanging baskets, by the little stream. It's handy for the lovely gardens of the Garden House at Buckland Monachorum and for Buckland Abbey. (*Recommended by Gwen and Peter Andrews, Hilary Roberts, Helena and Arthur Harbottle, R J Walden, Andy and Jill Kassube, Mr and Mrs Simon Turner, Wayne Brindle, Heather Sharland, Tom Evans, John Barker, Jutta Whitley, John Knighton, K and E Leist)*

Free house   Licensees Keith Yeo and Gary Rager   Real ale   Meals and snacks (restricted Sun lunchtime)   Folk club Sun evening in lower bar   Open 11.30–2.30 (3 Sat), 6.30–11

MORETONHAMPSTEAD   SX7585 Map 1

White Hart 🛏

Well placed for Dartmoor, this friendly, neatly kept hotel has a hind rather than a hart over its entrance. The spacious lounge bar has armchairs, plush seats, stools and oak pews from the parish church on its Turkey carpet; the hall has a splendidly large-scale 1827 map of Devon by Greenwood. Decent bar food includes soup or home-made pasty (£1.50), lunchtime sandwiches (from £1.50) and ploughman's (£3.25), vegetable quiche, home-cooked ham, lasagne or spicy pasta shells Italienne (all £3.25), salads, home-made chicken and ham pie or curry (£3.95), scampi (£4.50) and puddings like good treacle tart with clotted cream (from £1.75), with evening grills such as local trout (£6.95), lamb chops (£7.95) or steaks (£8.50); Sunday roasts. The lively public bar has leatherette seats and settles under a white beam-and-plank ceiling; darts, cribbage, dominoes and shove-ha'penny. Well kept Bass and Fergusons Dartmoor on handpump, and local farm dry cider. You can sit on a pew among the flowers in the small back courtyard. Comfortable bedrooms. (*Recommended by Steve Short, Chris Short and friends, David Wallington, Henry Hooper, P Miller)*

Free house   Licensee Peter Morgan   Real ale   Meals and snacks (12–2, 7–8.30); afternoon cream teas   Restaurant and evening grill room   Children in restaurant and eating area of bar   May have to park in the public car park, a short walk away   Open 11–11   Bedrooms tel Moretonhampstead (0647) 40406; £33B/£53B

NEWTON ST CYRES   SX8798 Map 1

Beer Engine

Sweetham; from Newton St Cyres on A377 follow St Cyres Station, Thorverton signpost

From the downstairs cellar bar, you can see the stainless brewhouse which turns out the pub's own Rail Ale, Piston Bitter, and the very strong Sleeper. The spacious main bar has partitioning alcoves, Windsor chairs and some button-back banquettes around dark varnished tables on its red carpet. There's a simple range of food, including sandwiches, speciality sausages (£2.75), steak and kidney or cod and prawn pies (£2.95), gammon or grilled trout (£4.25), and 8oz rump steak (£6.45). Darts, shove-ha'penny, dominoes and cribbage; fruit machine and space game in the downstairs lobby. There's a real ale / real train link-up with Exeter at the weekends. This is an old station hotel and is popular with young people at weekends. The licensee also runs the Sleeper at the Royal Clarence Hotel in Seaton. (*Recommended by R Houghton, P A Jennings; more reports please)*

Own brew   Licensee Peter Hawksley   Real ale   Meals and snacks   Children in eating area of bar   Rock and blues Fri and Sat evenings (when cellar bar open till midnight) and folk and jazz some Sun lunchtimes   Open 11.30–3, 6–11 (11.30–11 Sat and Bank Hols)

NORTH BOVEY SX7483 Map 1
Ring of Bells

Outside this 13th-century village inn are seats on a terrace well sheltered by the mossily-thatched white buildings around it, and on the attractively bordered lawn there are summer lawn skittles and a good children's play area. The simply furnished, opened up, carpeted main bar has bulgy white walls and horsebrasses on its beams, and bar food ranges from good parsnip soup (£1.75), a generous ploughman's and a summer salad bar (from around £2.50), to main dishes like curry or lasagne (£3.75), steak and kidney pie (£4.50) and specials such as brill, John Dory, local trout or pheasant (£7.50). Well kept Fergusons Dartmoor, Ind Coope Burton, Tetleys, Wadworths 6X and Whitbreads Trophy and occasional guest beers on handpump or tapped from the cask; also Gray's farm cider in summer and a selection of wines; darts, cribbage, pool in winter, fruit machine and piped music. It's set back from the village green – a lively place during the traditional mid-July Saturday fair. Fishing, shooting and pony-trekking can be arranged for guests, and the inn is well placed for some of the most interesting parts of Dartmoor. (*Recommended by Gwen and Peter Andrews, Janet and Paul Waring, TSS, Cliff and Karen Spooner, D J Devey, David and Christine Foulkes, Mr and Mrs Simon Turner, Ruth Humphrey, Paul and Heather Bettesworth, John Knighton, Helena and Arthur Harbottle, Steve Huggins, PB, HB, Hilary Robinson, Peter Maden, Henry Hooper*)

Free house Licensee Anthony Rix Real ale Meals and snacks Restaurant Children welcome Open 11–3, 6–11 Bedrooms tel Moretonhampstead (0647) 40375; £25B/£45B

PAIGNTON SX8960 Map 1
Inn on the Green

27 Esplanade Road

This airy and popular family inn serves an incredibly wide choice of bar food: home-made soup (£1.25), filled baked potatoes (£1.95), sandwiches (from £1.95, double decker with smoked salmon and prawns £3.75), ploughman's (from £2.75), home-made jumbo sausages (£2.75), home-made macaroni cheese (£2.95), spit-roast chicken or 4-egg omelettes (from £2.95), home-made burgers (£3.25), home-made chilli or curry (£3.95), several vegetarian dishes such as aubergine and mushroom lasagne (£4.25), steak and kidney, mushroom and Guinness pie (£4.35), a range of fish dishes like seafood au gratin (£4.35) or local poached halibut (£5.55), and charcoal grills (from £4.95, steaks from £7.75, a huge mixed grill £7.95). The very popular Sunday lunchtime carvery has a choice of five roasts (£3.95, children £2.95), there are children's dishes (from £1.25), and puddings served with clotted cream (£1.95). The lounge bar spreads around the enormously long serving counter and through a succession of arches where lots of blond cane chairs and cane-framed tables match the soft colour-scheme of peachy beige plush banquettes, pink and buff swagged curtains in the many bay windows, and marbled creamy-yellow wallpaper. There's a small dance-floor, pool table and juke box in the family room; fruit machine in lobby; Ruddles County, Ushers Best and Websters Yorkshire on handpump. Seats on the front terrace among cordylines, pampas-grass and hydrangeas look out over the green towards the sea. (*Recommended by Carol Mason, Alan and Audrey Chatting*)

Free house Licensees Brian Shone and Anthony Blackaby Real ale Meals and snacks (12–3, 6.30–12) Restaurant Children in eating area and family room with free juke box, dance foor and giant screen video Live music nightly Open 11–midnight Self-catering apartments tel Paignton (0803) 557841; from £11B per person per night

PETER TAVY SX5177 Map 1
Peter Tavy ★ ⊗

Interesting vegetarian dishes, a good range of real ales, and a relaxed, welcoming atmosphere cause this pub to fill up very quickly, even on a mid-week lunchtime in winter. Friendly staff serve the bar food that includes things like creamy cashew nut fingers (£1.10) or pancakes stuffed with spinach and garlic (£2.25), with a choice of unusual salads; on the meat side there's excellent beef pepper pot, and pork fillet stuffed with sage and onion or plaice stuffed with prawns in a cheese sauce (£7.25); the home-made soups and puddings are good, too. Well kept Bass, Butcombe, Eldridge Pope Royal Oak, Exmoor Gold, Fergusons Dartmoor and Marstons Pedigree tapped from the cask; fruit wines. The particularly atmospheric low-beamed bar has high-backed settles on the black flagstones by the big stone fireplace (which usually has a good log fire on cold days), smaller settles in stone-mullioned windows, entertaining DIY grafitti on the low beams, and a snug side dining area; darts. Picnic-table sets among fruit trees in a small raised garden have peaceful views of the moor rising above nearby pastures. As we went to press a big new restaurant and kitchen extension opened (with what we trust was a momentary hiccup in what's otherwise been commendably consistent cooking quality). *(Recommended by Wayne Brindle, Peter Maden, Hilary Robinson, Cliff and Karen Spooner, Amanda Dauncey, R J Walden, Steve Dark, Simon Turner, Annie Taylor, Helen Crookston, Jackie and Jon Payne, C H and W A Harbottle, Steve Huggins)*

Free house   Licensees Mr and Mrs P J Hawkins   Real ale   Meals and snacks (not 25 Dec)   Restaurant tel Mary Tavy (082 281) 348   Children in restaurant and eating area of bar   Nearby parking often difficult   Open 11.30–2.30 (3 Sat), 6.30–11; closed evening 25 Dec

nr POSTBRIDGE   SX6579   Map 1

Warren House

B3212 1 3/4 miles NE of Postbridge

The fire at one end of the bar in this remote pub, alone on Dartmoor, is said to have been kept continuously alight since 1845. Simple furnishings include easy chairs and rustic settles under a beamed ochre ceiling, wild animal pictures on the partly panelled stone walls, and dim lighting (fuelled by the pub's own generator); even in high season it keeps quite a local atmosphere as it's something of a focus for this scattered moorland community. Bar food consists of soup, good pasties, sandwiches, ploughman's and fish and chips; Flowers IPA and Original and Marstons Pedigree on handpump, farm cider and a range of country wines. Darts, dominoes, cribbage, pool, space game, fruit machine, piped music. This road is worth knowing, as a good little-used route westward through fine scenery. *(Recommended by Elisabeth Kemp, WMS; more reports please)*

Free house   Licensee Peter Parsons   Real ale   Meals and snacks   Children in family room   Open 11–11 (11–2.30, 5.30–11 winter)

RATTERY   SX7461   Map 1

Church House

Village signposted from A385 W of Totnes, and A38 S of Buckfastleigh

The original building here probably housed the craftsmen who built the Norman church, and may then have served as a hostel for passing monks. Parts of that ancient church house still survive in this fine old pub – notably, the flight of spiral stone steps behind a little stone doorway on your left as you go in. They probably date from about 1030, making this one of the oldest pub buildings in Britain. The open-plan bar has massive oak beams and standing timbers, large fireplaces (one with a little cosy nook partitioned off around it), Windsor armchairs, comfortable leather bucket seats and window seats, and prints on the plain white walls; the dining room is separated from this room by heavy curtains. Courage Best and Directors and a weekly guest beer on handpump, quite a few wines, 25 malt whiskies and farm cider. Bar food includes home-made soup (£1.60), filled granary rolls (£2.25), ploughman's with good cheeses (from £2.60), vegetarian fry-up (£3.25), salads (from £3.25), excellent home-made quiche (£3.50), good value smoked salmon (£3.75), tasty steak and kidney pie (£4.50), smoked chicken and leek pie (£5.25), steaks (from £5.70), roast duckling (£5.95), daily specials, and good home-made puddings (£1.60); there may be some delays when it's busy. Outside, there are peaceful views of the partly wooded surrounding hills from picnic-table sets on a hedged courtyard by the churchyard. *(Recommended by John Evans, Mr and Mrs L W Norcott, H K Dyson, S V Bishop, Heather Sharland, W A Gardiner, C A Gurney, Jean and Roger Davis, Ann and David Stranack, Paul and Janet Waring)*

Free house   Licensees Mr B and Mrs J J Evans   Real ale   Meals and snacks   Dining room tel Buckfastleigh (0364) 42220   Children in dining room and eating area of bar Open 11–2.30, 6–11; winter morning opening 11.30; closed evenings 25 and 26 Dec

SANDY PARK   SX7189   Map 1

Sandy Park Inn

Just off A382 N of Moretonhampstead

With no intrusions by machines or music, the atmosphere in the small black-beamed bar here is relaxed and chatty. The country-style furnishings are simple: two or three stripped tables on the composition floor, built-in pale brown varnished wall seats, lots of postcards pinned above the crackling log fire, newspapers, and attractively arranged fresh flowers; a small back area has three or four cast-iron-framed tables and one wall stripped to bare stone. The original doorway is blocked by the greyhound's huge wicker basket. Lunchtime bar food consists of pasties (£1.10), home-made soup in winter (£1.20), ploughman's (from £2), smoked trout or smoked chicken with salad (from £2.50), cottage pie (£3), lasagne or pork and apple pie (£3.50), and home-made puddings (from £1.80); in the evening they do roasts (from £4), a dish of the day such as chicken breasts in sauce (£4.50) or guinea fowl. Well kept Eldridge Pope Royal Oak, Exe Valley, and Marstons Pedigree on handpump, and Palmers IPA tapped from the cask; decent wines, a good selection of spirits; shove-ha'penny, cribbage, and dominoes. Sturdy benches beside the honeysuckle outside the thatched white house look out to the pretty surrounding wooded hills. *(Recommended by Nick Dowson, Alison Hayward, Paul and Heather Bettesworth, Peter Donahue)*

Free house   Licensee Marion Weir   Real ale   Meals and snacks   Small restaurant Children in restaurant and in snug   Open 11–11; 11–3, 5–11 in winter   Bedrooms tel Chagford (064 73) 3538; £12.50/£25

SHEEPWASH   SS4806   Map 1

Half Moon   ⇦

The fine inn sign (a curving salmon neatly interlocking with a crescent moon), hints at the inn's fishing reputation: salmon or trout fishing can be arranged on the Torridge for non-residents as well as residents. The neatly-kept and friendly carpeted main bar has solid old furniture under the beams, lots of fishing pictures on the white walls, and a big log fire fronted by slate flagstones. Bass and Courage Best on handpump (well kept in a temperature-controlled cellar), a fine choice of spirits and a good wine list; darts, fruit machine and a separate pool room. Lunchtime bar food is attractively straightforward, including sandwiches (£1.25, toasted £1.50), soup or pasty (£1.50), ploughman's (£2.50) and salads (£3.50). The buff-painted and civilised building takes up one whole side of the colourful village square – blue, pink, white, cream and olive thatched or slate-roofed cottages. *(Recommended by David Wallington, Peter Bisby, R J Walden, J W Dixon)*

Free house   Licensees Benjamin Robert Inniss and Charles Inniss   Real ale   Snacks (lunchtime)   Evening restaurant (must book)   Children till 7.30   Open 11.30–2.30 (3.30 Sat), 6–11   Bedrooms tel Black Torrington (040 923) 376; £23(£25B)/£40(46B)

SIDFORD   SY1390   Map 1

Blue Ball   ★   ⊘   ⇦

A3052 just N of Sidmouth

Run by the same family for over 75 years, this well kept and friendly 14th-century

thatched village inn displays its food (particularly fresh local fish on crushed ice)
enticingly at the back of the bar area; it includes good crusty white or wholemeal
sandwiches (from £1.20, crab £2), a very generous ploughman's (from £2.60),
omelettes (£3.50), cheese and asparagus flan (£3.75), home-made steak and kidney
pie (£4.25), salads (from £3.50) and good steaks (from 8oz rump £7.50); puddings
(£1.60), traditional roasts on Sunday and Thursday lunchtimes and evenings, and
very good breakfasts (with free papers); efficient service. The low, partly-panelled
lounge bar has a lovely winter log fire in the stone fireplace (there are two other
open fires as well), Windsor chairs and upholstered wall benches under the heavy
beams, and Devenish JD, Royal Wessex, Steam and Vallances on handpump, kept
well in a temperature-controlled cellar; a plainer public bar has darts, dominoes,
cribbage and a fruit machine; piped music. Tables on a terrace look out over a
colourful walled front flower garden, with more on a bigger back lawn, where
there are summer barbecues; also a safe swing, see saw and play house.
*(Recommended by Neil and Anita Christopher, Mr and Mrs D A P Grattan, E Mitchelmore,
Gordon and Daphne, Brian and Anna Marsden, E A George, Gwen Cranfield, JAH, Philip and
Sheila Hanley, W C M Jones, A C Earl)*

*Devenish   Licensee R H Newton   Real ale   Meals and snacks (10.30–2, 6.30–10,
though they also serve breakfasts to anyone from 8.30–10)   Well behaved children in
eating area and family room   Open 10.30–2.30, 5.30–11   Bedrooms tel Sidmouth
(0395) 514062; £19/£30*

SLAPTON   SX8244   Map 1

Tower

A fine range of real ales, good food and a happy welcoming atmosphere continue
to draw people to this fine 14th-century inn. On handpump, the ten real ales
include Badger Tanglefoot, Blackawton, Gibbs Mew Bishops Tipple, Exe Valley,
Exmoor, Eldridge Pope Royal Oak, Palmers IPA, Ruddles County and Best and
Wadworths 6X. The Italian licensee's pasta dishes are popular – lasagne, broccoli
pasta or spaghetti bolognese (£3.80) and al mare (£3.95; de luxe seafood £6.95);
there are also sandwiches, basket meals, pizzas (from £3.80), fresh sole, and
chicken in tomatoes and red pepper (£4.95); there's also a buffet, new this year.
The low-ceilinged bar has small armchairs, low-backed settles and some furniture
made from casks on the flagstones, and on cool days a woodburning stove and a
log fire in one stripped stone wall; pool, dominoes, fruit machine, space game and
piped music. There are picnic-table sets on the quiet back lawn, which is overhung
by the ivy-covered ruin of a 14th-century chantry. The narrow lane up to the pub
is tortuous. *(Recommended by G W Warren, R J Walden, R W Stanbury, Steve Dark,
Amanda Dauncey, David and Ann Stranack, Richard and Dilys Smith, John Knighton)*

*Free house   Licensees Keith and Kim Romp, Jan Khan, Carlo Cascianelli   Real ale
Meals and snacks (12–2.30, 6.30–9.30)   Restaurant   Children in eating area and
family room   Open 11.30–2.30, 6–11   Bedrooms tel Kingsbridge (0548) 580216;
£15.50/£31*

SOURTON   SX5390   Map 1

Highwayman   ★

A386 SW of Okehampton; a short detour from the A30

The sheer eccentricity of this pub's remarkable design will take your breath away.
It's been meticulously carried out using first-class materials by the licensees – who
themselves have character to match this exuberant decor. A nobleman's carriage of
a porch leads into a warren of dimly lit stonework and flagstone-floored burrows
and alcoves, richly fitted out with red plush seats discreetly cut into the
higgledy-piggledy walls, elaborately carved pews, a leather porter's chair,
Jacobean-style wicker chairs, and seats in quaintly bulging small-paned bow
windows; the ceiling in one part, where there's an array of stuffed animals, gives
the impression of being underneath a tree, roots and all. The separate Rita Jones'
Locker is a make-believe sailing galleon, full of intricate woodwork and splendid

timber baulks, with red-check tables in the embrasures that might have held cannons. Outside, there's a play area in similar style for children (who aren't allowed in the pub itself) with little black-and-white roundabouts like a Victorian fairground, a fairy-tale pumpkin house and an old-lady-who-lived-in-the-shoe house. They don't do real ale, but specialise in farm cider; food is confined to a range of pasties (95p); old-fashioned penny fruit machine. (*Recommended by Peter Woods, Mayur Shah, Jutta Whitley*)

Free house   Licensees Buster and Rita Jones   Snacks (10–1.45, 6–10)   Open 10–2, 6–10.30; closed 25 and 26 Dec   Bedrooms tel Bridestowe (083 786) 243; £15/£30

SOUTH POOL SX7740 Map 1

Millbrook

The enterprising can find their way here by water – it's 45 minutes by hired boat from Salcombe, and a few moments' stroll from Southpool Creek. It's one of the tiniest pubs in the book, so the little back bar fills up quickly at peak times. There are drawings and paintings (and a chart) on its cream walls, handsome Windsor chairs, a chintz easy chair, and fresh flowers. Bar food under the new licensees includes home-made soup such as celery and apple (£1.25), sandwiches (from £1.25, crab £3), filled baked potatoes (from £2.50), ploughman's with mature cheddar or stilton (£2.50), quiche, fish pie (£2.75), and puddings such as apple cider cake or treacle tart (£1.65). Bass tapped from the cask, and Churchward's cider; darts and euchre in the public bar; piped music. There are seats out in front, on a sheltered flowery terrace. (*Recommended by Roy McIsaac, Margaret and Trevor Errington, John Knighton, Margaret and Trevor Errington, Major and Mrs J V Rees, David and Ann Stranack; more reports on the new regime please*)

Free house   Licensees Arthur and Cindy Spedding   Real ale   Meals and snacks (12–2, 6–9.30)   Children in front bar   Nearby parking may be difficult   Open 11–3, 5.30–11; may open longer in summer to cover high tide

SOUTH ZEAL SX6593 Map 1

Oxenham Arms ★ 🛏️ 🕰️

Village signposted from A30 at A382 roundabout and B3260 Okehampton turnoff

As one reader put it – everything feels as if it belongs. It's a lovely old pub with a marvellously relaxed atmosphere and particularly friendly staff and locals. The beamed and partly panelled bar has Windsor armchairs around low oak tables and built-in wall seats, as well as elegant mullioned windows and Stuart fireplaces. Consistently good bar food includes tasty soup (£1.25), sandwiches (from £1.45; the rare roast beef are particularly good), a generous ploughman's (£2.50), fish and chips (from £3), excellent home-made steak, kidney, mushroom and Guinness pie (£3.95), salads (from £3), grilled trout (£4.75), and good daily specials such as lamb, good tuna bake (£3.25), barbecued chicken (£3.95), and local venison. Bass and St Austell Tinners tapped from the cask, Gray's farm cider and decent wines; darts, shove-ha'penny, dominoes and cribbage. The inn was originally a Norman monastery, built here to combat the pagan power of the neolithic standing stone that still forms part of the wall in the family TV room behind the bar (there are actually twenty more feet of stone below the floor). There's further monastic evidence in the imposing curved stone steps leading up to the garden, and a sloping spread of lawn. The courtyard is now a car park for residents. (*Recommended by Peter Sutton, Janet and Paul Waring, Tom Espley, John and Christine Simpson, Diane Duane-Smyth, Joel Dobris, Patrick Stapley, Laurence Manning, S P Bobeldijk, Jonathan N C Jensen, Peter Morwood, Joel Dobris, Neil and Anita Christopher, William Rodgers, Mary Rayner, Ian Shaw, Lindsay Shaw Radley, Andrew and Michel Wells, Col G D Stafford, Paul Smith, Sue Carlyle, Peter Donahue, Henry Hooper, HEG*)

Free house   Licensee James Henry   Real ale   Meals and snacks   Restaurant Children in eating area   Open 11–2.30, 6–11   Bedrooms tel Okehampton (0837) 840244; £34.50B/£45B

STAVERTON   SX7964   Map 1

Sea Trout

Village signposted from A384 NW of Totnes

The pretty garden of this friendly village pub has seats and tables on crazy paving among stone-walled flower borders, with a rock pool under a weeping willow. They can arrange fishing for you on the River Dart, and a station for the Torbay Steam Railway is not far away. The neatly kept rambling lounge bar has salmon and seatrout flies, stuffed fish on the walls (some of which are stripped back to bare granite), a stag's head above the fireplace, beams, and cushioned settles and stools on its carpet; the main bar has low banquettes, soft lighting and an open fire; a good range of real ales on handpump – Bass, Fergusons Dartmoor, Ruddles and Wadworths 6X, as well as farm ciders. There's also a public bar, popular with locals, with a pool table, darts, trivia and fruit machines and juke box. Good bar food includes home-made soup (£1), sandwiches (from £1.40), burgers (from £2.20), ploughman's (from £2.50), superb home-made pork sausages with herb or apple (£2.95), home-cooked ham (£3.65), home-made steak and kidney pie (£3.95), salads (from £4.25), local trout or gammon (£4.50), and steaks (from £6.25); children's dishes (from £1.95). The bedrooms have been refurbished and up-graded. *(Recommended by S V Bishop, W C M Jones, Mrs Joan Harris, Mr and Mrs M A Stockman, Charlie Salt, Ann and David Stranack, JAH, Geoffrey Thompson)*

Free house   Licensee Andrew Mooford   Real ale   Meals and snacks (12–2, 7–10)   Children in eating area   Acoustic guitarist Wed evening   Open 11–3, 6–11   Bedrooms tel Staverton (080 426) 274; £35B/£44B

STOCKLAND   ST2404   Map 1

Kings Arms 🕸

Village signposted from A30 Honiton–Chard

This friendly, 16th-century former coaching inn is popular with people from miles around for its very wide choice of mouth-watering food, served in the small but elegant dining lounge. Carefully described by the manager, these dishes might include grilled sardines (£2.50), tricolori salad (£2.50), Pacific prawns in garlic and white wine sauce (£4.50), beef Stroganoff (but using cream and pickled dill cucumber instead of soured cream; £6.50), chicken supreme flamed in brandy, poached in sherry, and reduced with thick cream (£7), darne of wild salmon in lobster and dill sauce (£7.50) or crispy slow-roasted duck (£8.50), and puddings like apple strudel or zabaglione; booking is essential. At lunchtime there are simpler snacks as well, including a basket of chips 75p), sandwiches (from £1), ploughman's (from £2), burger (£2.50), omelettes or steak and kidney pie (£3.50) and salads (from £4); on Sundays there's a traditional lunch instead (small children half-price). This lounge has a medieval oak screen dividing it into two, dark beams, attractive landscapes, solid refectory tables, and a great stone fireplace across almost the whole width of one end. At the back, a flagstoned bar has leatherette chairs and seats built into the stripped high dado of its bare stone walls; it leads on to a carpeted darts room with two boards, another room with dark beige plush armchairs and settees (and a fruit machine), and a neat ten-pin skittle alley (the pub fields six teams, Monday, Wednesday and Friday in winter; on Thursdays there's a keep-fit class). There are tables under cocktail parasols on the terrace in front of the cream-faced thatched pub, with more by a weeping willow in the sheltered back garden. Well kept Badger Best and Exmoor, decent wines and brandies, a good choice of whiskies – particularly strong on island single malts; cribbage, dominoes, darts, space game, and pervasive piped classical music; well behaved dogs allowed. We'd be grateful for up-to-date bedrooms reports, as we have no reason to doubt that this would be a nice place to stay. *(Recommended by G W Warren, D Baddeley, Mayur Shah, W L B Reed, David Gaunt, J W and E K Scropes)*

Free house   Licensees Heinz Kiefer and Paul Diviani   Real ale   Snacks (lunchtime) and meals   Restaurant (12–1.45 Sun)   Well behaved children welcome   Open 12–3, 6.30–11 (all day Spring Bank Hol); closed 25 Dec   Bedrooms tel Stockland (040 488) 361; £20B/£30B

STOKE GABRIEL   SX8457 Map 1

Church House ★

Village signposted from A385 just W of junction with A3022, in Collaton St Mary; can also be reached from nearer Totnes; nearby parking not easy

Displayed in the bar of this 14th-century, flower-covered pub is a case containing a mummified cat, probably about 200 years old, found during restoration of the roof space in the verger's cottage three doors up the lane – one of a handful found in the West Country and believed to have been a talisman against evil spirits. The lounge has a lovely beam and plank ceiling, a black oak partition wall, a huge fireplace still used in winter to cook the stew, window seats cut into the thick butter-colour walls, decorative plates and vases of flowers on a dresser. Bar food includes home-made soup (£1.10), sandwiches (from £1.10, salmon £2.50), baked potato filled with prawns (£2.50), a variety of ploughman's (from around £2.50), home-made cottage pie (£3.25) and Dart salmon (£6.50, possibly caught by the licensee's son-in-law). Darts, dominoes, cribbage, euchre and fruit machine in the little public bar; piped music. The Bass on handpump is particularly well kept, unusually fed from a temperature-controlled cellar at a higher level, or tapped from the cask. There are picnic-table sets on the little terrace in front of the pub. Relations with the Church of England (which still owns it) go back a long way – witness the priest hole, dating from the Reformation, visible from outside the pub. *Recommended by Mrs A Turner, R H Martyn, John Knighton, B A Cox, W A Gardiner, H K Dyson)*

Bass   Licensee G W Bradford   Real ale   Meals and snacks; cream teas in summer Open 11–11; winter 11–3, 6–11

TIPTON ST JOHN   SY0991 Map 1

Golden Lion 🍺

Pub signposted off B3176 Sidmouth–Ottery St Mary

Over the years, the licensees (now in their 20th year here) have worked hard to turn what was originally a straightforward railway box inn into a thriving village local. The softly-lit bar has an attractive Gothic carved box settle, a comfortable old settee, red leatherette built-in wall banquettes, a carved dresser, a longcase clock and a pleasantly relaxed atmosphere; also, lots of guns, little kegs, a brass cauldron and other brassware, bottles and jars along a Delft shelf, and plenty of fresh flowers. A wide choice of reasonably priced home-cooked bar food here includes home-made soup (£1.05; good crab bisque £1.20), sandwiches (from £1.80), ploughman's (from £2.25), quiche, lasagne or chilli con carne (£3.25) and salads (from £4.95), with grills such as gammon (£5.95) and steaks (from £7.50); home-made puddings (from £1.55); friendly service. Well kept Bass and Flowers IPA and Original on handpump; dominoes, piped music, open fire. There are a few picnic-table sets on the side lawn, and a terrace with summer barbecues and food-theme evenings. The restaurant is no-smoking. *(Recommended by Gordon and Daphne, Dr D M Forsyth, Michael and Alison Sandy, Shirley Pielou, John and Ruth Roberts, Graham and Glenis Watkins, J R Carey)*

Heavitree (who no longer brew)   Real ale   Meals and snacks   Small restaurant, best to book   Open 11–3, 6–11   Two bedrooms tel Ottery St Mary (0404) 812881; £16.70S/£33.35S

TOPSHAM   SX9688 Map 1

Bridge ★

2 1/4 miles from M5 junction 30: Topsham signposted from exit roundabout; in Topsham follow signpost (A376) Exmouth on the Elmgrove Road

Voted cellarman of the year in our 1990 book, Mrs Cheffers continues to run this eccentric 16th-century pub in an unchanging, old-fashioned way. The wonderful choice of real ales – tapped from the cask in the cosy inner sanctum where only the most regular of regulars sit – might include less common ones, such as Blackawton Headstrong, Gibbs Mew Bishops Tipple, Marstons Owd Rodger, Theakstons Old Peculier, Wadworths Old Timer and Wiltshire Old Devil, as well as Badger Tanglefoot, Bass, Blackawton, Courage Directors, Eldridge Pope Royal Oak, Exmoor Bitter and Gold, Fullers ESB, Marstons Pedigree, Wadworths 6X and Youngs Special. The cosy little parlour, partitioned off from an inner corridor with leaded lights let into the curved high back of one settle, is decorated with a booming grandfather clock, crossed guns, swords, country pictures and rowing cartoons, and mugs hanging from the beams; a bigger room is opened at busy times. Food is confined to pasties (75p), sandwiches (£1) and ploughman's (from £1.75, ham or stilton £2.25). *(Recommended by Gordon and Daphne, P Argent, Dr M I Crichton, Caroline Gibbins, Annie Taylor)*

Free house   Licensee Mrs Phyllis Cheffers   Real ale   Snacks   Children welcome Open 12–2, 6–10.30 (11 Fri and Sat)

Globe 🛏

2 miles from M5 junction 30: Topsham signposted from exit roundabout; in Topsham, keep straight on into Fore Street where the inn has a small car park

This relaxed and civilised 16th-century coaching inn has a heavy-beamed bar comfortably furnished with red leatherette seats around the big bow window, a big panel-back settle, heavy wooden armchairs, and good sporting prints on the dark oak panelling, with an open fire under the attractive wooden mantelpiece. Good value bar food includes smokies (£1.20), ploughman's (£1.75), whitebait, home-made pies such as rabbit or steak and kidney (£2.75) and bacon, egg and kidneys (£2.75); beside the main restaurant there's a snug little eating room with its own fire; friendly service. Well kept Bass and Ushers Best on handpump. There are seats out in a small sheltered and partly covered courtyard. *(Recommended by Gordon and Daphne, L and J, Gethin Lewis, Graham and Glenis Watkins)*

Free house   Licensee D G L Price   Real ale   Meals and snacks   Restaurant Children in eating area   Open 11–11   Bedrooms tel Topsham (0392) 873471; £28B/£38B

TORCROSS   SX8241 Map 1

Start Bay ★ ⌀

A379 S of Dartmouth

Just behind this popular old thatched pub is the freshwater wildlife lagoon of Slapton Ley, and there are picnic-table sets on the terrace that look out over the three-mile pebble beach. People often queue outside before the pub opens to make sure they get an early choice of the large selection of very fresh and generously served seafood: cod and haddock come in three sizes – medium (£2.80 or £2.90), large (£3.45 or £3.55) and jumbo (£4.25 or £4.35 – truly enormous); plaice (caught in season by the licensee and his manager) is served in medium (£2.80) and large (£3.60) varieties; there's also skate (£3.75) and a much praised seafood platter, with prawns or crab, shrimps, cockles, mussels and smoked mackerel (£5.95); other food includes sandwiches (from £1.20), ploughman's (£2.50), home-made spinach and mushroom lasagne (£3.10), gammon (£4.50) and steaks (from £6.50); they warn of delays at peak times. Well kept Flowers IPA and Marstons Pedigree on handpump, and Addlestones cider. The unpretentious, busy main bar has photographs of storms buffeting the pub and country pictures on its cream walls, wheelback chairs around plenty of dark tables or (round a corner) back-to-back settles forming booths, and a winter coal fire; a small chatty drinking area by the counter has a brass ship's clock and barometer. The good winter games room has pool, darts, shove-ha'penny, dominoes and space game; there's more booth seating in a family room with sailing boat pictures. Fruit machine in the lobby, piped music. *(Recommended by Richard and Ann Jenkins, David and Ann Stranack, Joan and Michael Melling, Chris Short and friends, D I Baddeley, David and Ann Stranack, Helena and Arthur Harbottle, JAH, Gordon Hewitt)*

Heavitree (who no longer brew)   Licensee Paul Stubbs   Real ale   Meals and snacks (11.30–2, 6–10)   Children over 14 in eating room   Open 11.30–2.30 (3 Bank Hols), 6–11; 25 Dec no food and open only 11.30–1.30

TORRINGTON SS4919 Map 1

Black Horse 🛏

High Street

Though the overhanging upper storeys are dated 1616, this pretty twin-gabled building goes back to the 15th century. A lounge on the right has a striking ancient black oak partition wall, a couple of attractive oak seats, muted plush easy chairs and a settee. The bar on the left has a couple of fat black beams, an oak counter, a comfortable seat running right along its full-width window, and chunky elm tables; the restaurant is oak-panelled. Generously served home-cooked bar food includes sandwiches (from 75p), soup (£1), ploughman's or salads (from £1.85), chicken and mushroom pie or chilli con carne (£2.45), home-made steak and kidney pie (£2.75) and steaks (from £5.45); well kept Ruddles County and Ushers Best on handpump; darts, shove-ha'penny, cribbage, dominoes, fruit machine, trivia; well reproduced piped music. Though the inn is reputed to have collected at least one ghost, the licensees – a notably friendly couple – haven't seen anything, though they're convinced their dogs have. A black horse in a cut-out silhouette prances along the inn-sign's gantry. Handy for the RHS Rosemoor garden. *(Recommended by K R Harris, Miss J Metherell, A R Gale, D J Wallington; more reports please)*

Ushers   Licensees David and Val Sawyer   Real ale   Meals and snacks (not Sun evening)   Restaurant   Children in lounge and restaurant (no young children in restaurant, evening)   Open 11–3, 6(6.30 Sat)–11   Bedrooms tel Torrington (0805) 22121; £14B/£24B

TOTNES SX8060 Map 1

Kingsbridge Inn

Leechwell Street; going up the old town's main one-way street, bear left into Leechwell Street approaching the top

Mentioned in the Domesday Book, this busy old pub has a rambling bar with bare stone or black and white timbering, low heavy beams, broad stripped plank panelling, and comfortable peach plush seats and wheelbacks around rustic tables on the clover and peach carpet; new licensees have changed some of the furniture, painted the ceiling and introduced fresh flowers in the bar. There's an elaborately carved bench in one intimate little alcove, an antique water pump and a log-effect gas fire. Lunchtime bar food includes soup (£1.25), sandwiches or filled French bread (from £1.25), fish and vegetarian dishes (from £2.95), with more elaborate dishes running up to steaks (from £7.45) in the evening; home-made puddings such as green figs in wine and honey or brandy and vanilla ice cream. Courage Best and guest beers on handpump; friendly service. *(Recommended by David Wallington, P Argent, H K Dyson, Carol Mason, Joseph J Lewy, Ian Blackwell, Ann and David Stranack, R F Warner; more reports please)*

Free house   Licensees Paul and Rosemary Triggs, Martyn and Jane Canevali   Real ale   Meals and snacks (11–2, 6–10)   Children in eating area   Local groups Wed evening, harpist Sat evening or Sun lunchtime   Open 11–2.30, 5.30–11

TRUSHAM SX8582 Map 1

Cridford Inn

Village and pub signposted from B3193 NW of Chudleigh, just N of big ARC works; 1½ very narrow miles

The sun-trap front terrace in front of this 14th-century oak-beamed longhouse (which, oddly, has a corrugated iron roof) has sturdy rustic benches and tables under cocktail parasols, and a small play area. Inside, there are stout standing timbers, old hunting prints, a couple of guns and display cases of cartridges on white-painted uncoursed stone walls, rugs on flagstones, cushioned window-seats, pews and chapel chairs around kitchen and pub tables, some stained glass in the windows, and a big woodburning stove in the stone fireplace; the atmosphere is delightfully relaxed. Good value bar food includes sandwiches (from £1.10), filled baked potatoes (from £1.30), big home-made pasties (£1.65), kipper pâté (£1.75), macaroni cheese, liver and bacon casserole or home-made pork pie (£2.50), speciality sausages (£3), and dishes from the restaurant menu such as trout (£6), venison casserole (£6.50) and steak (£8.50); well kept Exmoor on handpump, Bass, Cotleigh Old Buzzard and an interesting weekly guest beer such as Smiles Best tapped from the cask, and Reddaway's farm ciders from over near Ideford. Darts, dominoes, fruit machine, trivia and juke box in the end family room. The little hamlet is largely modern. *(Recommended by Gordon and Daphne, Mayur Shah, Sarah and David Read; more reports please – we've heard nothing yet about the bedrooms)*

Free house   Licensees Tony and Mick Shepherd   Real ale   Meals and snacks (12–2, 7–10)   Children welcome (till 8 evening)   Open 11–3, 6(7 winter)–11   Bedrooms tel Chudleigh (0626) 853694; £30B/£40B

TUCKENHAY   SX8156   Map 1

Maltsters Arms ⊘

From A381 S of Totnes take Ashprington road in Harbertonford, then after 3 miles turn right over river to pass Watermans Arms; or take Ashprington road out of Totnes, keeping on past Watermans Arms

A popular broadcaster and cookery writer has taken over this waterside pub and created five areas from the former big open-plan bar – a refreshing change from the usual over-enthusiasm for knocking through. On the left, there's a wood-floored room with red-painted vertical panelled seats and stripped kitchen tables, lots of small fish prints three-to-a-frame, and a model sailing ship over the log fire. At the other end is a snug little room with a couple of fat leather armchairs (which the young ginger cat favours), a sofa, other chairs and small tables, more Victorian fish prints, some stuffed fish in glass cabinets, a cabinet of vintage Barrie & Jenkins fishing books, and a second fire. These rooms are linked by the long, narrow bar with its stools, fishing rods on the ceiling, and jars of cockles, pickled eggs, mint imperials and jelly babies on the counter; there are tempting glimpses of the light and airy restaurant alongside – which has commandeered the picture windows (and the view, of a particularly attractive stretch of wooded creek). Even in the bar the food's won quick approval and everything including the bread, mayonnaise and pastries is home-made. A short choice of snacks might include soup (£2), rare beef sandwich (£2.80), terrine (£3.50), 'bread and cheese' that, besides four different cheeses and French bread, came with biscuits, grapes, dates, pickle and chunks of butter (all £3.50), cold poached salmon (£5.85), six Helford oysters (£6), and maybe occasional dishes from the fine restaurant; puddings such as five-inch French apple tarts with lashings of clotted cream or crispy tulip brandysnap with chocolate mousse (from £2.50). Ansells Bitter, Exmoor and (pump-assisted) Bass, Blackawton, Fergusons Dartmoor and Flowers on handpump, decent wines, a wide selection of malts, and an interesting brandy list; friendly service; dominoes, cribbage, and lots of board games, including Trivial Pursuit. No bedrooms, but there's a smart B & B next door in a converted wine warehouse. You can reach the pub by boat. *(Recommended by W C M Jones, S V Bishop, David and Ann Stranack, Dennis Heatley, Alan Merricks, David Wallington)*

Free house   Manager/chef Christophe Novelli; owner Keith Floyd   Real ale   Meals and snacks (12–2.30, 7–10)   Restaurant tel Harbertonford (080423) 350   Open 11–3, 6–11

UGBOROUGH   SX6755 Map 1

Anchor

On B3210; village signposted from Ivybridge (just off A38 E of Plymouth)

In an attractive village, unusual for its spacious central square, this well kept pub serves good food, more restaurant under the new licensees: sandwiches (from £1, prawn £3; toasted at the same price), home-made soup (£1.30), ploughman's (from £2), basket meals (from £2), salads (from £2.75), gammon (£4), seafood platter (£4) and steaks (from £8), with specials such as wild rabbit or do-it-yourself grills. The oak-beamed public bar has wall settles and seats around the wooden tables on the polished woodblock floor, and a log fire in its stone fireplace. There are Windsor armchairs in the comfortable carpeted lounge; well kept Bass and Wadworths 6X tapped from the cask; darts, cribbage, dominoes, fruit machine and piped music. There are now more bedrooms, well appointed in converted outbuildings. *(Recommended by M J Clifford, C T and J M Caffan, John Evans, Mayur Shah, R J Walden, Peter Woods, F J Robinson, John Bowdler; more reports on the new regime please)*

Free house   Licensees Sheelagh and Ken Jeffreys-Simmons   Real ale   Meals and snacks   Restaurant   Children in eating area and restaurant   Live entertainment alternate Mons   Open 11.30–11   Bedrooms tel Plymouth (0752) 892283; £30B/£35B

WINKLEIGH   SS6308 Map 1

Kings Arms

Off B3220, in village centre

The attractive flagstoned main bar in this old-fashioned, thatched pub is more or less divided into two by the staircase. There are some old-fashioned built-in wall settles, scrubbed pine tables and benches, beams, dim lighting, a log fire in a cavernous fireplace, and a couple of large fish tanks (with some real rarities) over by the lunchtime salad bar. They've uncovered some ancient stonework and constructed a two-way fireplace with a woodburning stove which separates the bar from the new no-smoking restaurant (where they've found the original well). Home-made bar food includes vegetable soup (£1.50), crab pâté (£2.25), ploughman's (£2.55), omelette or lasagne (£3.25), a help-yourself lunchtime summer salad bar or game pie (£3.50), venison pie (£4.50), chicken breast in curry sauce (£4.95), daily specials (£4), and puddings like sticky toffee pudding (£2.25). Ruddles Best and Ushers Best and occasionally Websters Yorkshire on handpump from a temperature-controlled cold room, and Gray's farm cider; friendly service; well reproduced piped pop music. There are a couple of white tables by a small pool in the little side courtyard, sheltered by large shrubs. It's appealingly placed on the edge of the village square. *(Recommended by Jonathan N C Jensen, Karen Spooner, Michael and Joan Melling, John D Blaylock, John Evans)*

Free house   Licensee Nigel Rickard   Meals and snacks (11.30–2.15, 6–10, not Mon)   Restaurant Tues–Sat evenings, Sun lunch   Children over 6 in eating area and restaurant   Open 11–2.30, 6–11; closed Mon, but open Bank Hol lunchtimes   Bedrooms in self-contained cottage tel Winkleigh (0837) 83384; £12.50B/£25B

WOODBURY SALTERTON   SY0189 Map 1

Digger's Rest ★

3 ½ miles from M5 junction 30: A3052 towards Sidmouth, village signposted on right about ½ mile after Clyst St Mary; also signposted from B3179 SE of Exeter

Named after a former Australian landlord, this friendly thatched Tudor pub has a terrace garden with views of the countryside. Inside, the main bar has heavy black oak beams, a dark oak Jacobean screen, comfortable old-fashioned country chairs and settles around polished antique tables, a grandfather clock, and plates decorating the walls of one alcove; there's a log fire at one end and an ornate solid fuel stove at the other. Families can entertain themselves in the big skittles alley (open for them in July and August) and games room. Well kept Bass and Flowers IPA on ancient handpumps, and a good selection of farmhouse ciders; sensibly placed darts, and dominoes, in the small brick-walled public bar. Decent bar food includes home-made soup (£1.15), sandwiches (from £1.50, local crab £1.85), ploughman's (from £2.45), prawns in garlic (£2.75), home-made curry, turkey pie or cold gammon (all £3.50), scampi (£4.35), a daily special such as lasagne or steak and kidney pie (£3.50) and puddings that also include a daily special (£1.45). (Recommended by John D Blaylock, Michael and Alison Sandy, Heather Sharland, Brian and Anna Marsden, Peter Finzi)

Free house   Licensee Sally Pratt   Real ale   Meals and snacks (12–1.45, 7–10)
Children in family room   Open 11–2.30, 6.30–11

Lucky Dip

Besides the fully inspected pubs, you might like to try these Lucky Dips recommended to us and described by readers (if you do, please send us reports):

Alswear [A373 South Molton—Tiverton; SS7222], Butchers Arms: Friendly, neat and tidy public bar with beams, flagstones, stripped stonework, huge inglenook log fire, chiming grandmother clock; Bass and Flowers, generous helpings of usual food; also brightly decorated lounge, small restaurant, regular music nights; children allowed in basic pool room with juke box, fruit machine, sensibly placed darts; bedrooms (Steve and Carolyn Harvey, J R Carey)

Appledore [Irsha St (N end of village); SS4630], Royal George: Relaxed atmosphere in three-bar pub, one with big windows overlooking water, one with stripped pine furniture, board floor and lots of prints, a third with pool table (children allowed); popular with locals and visitors, cheerful young local staff, a couple of picnic-table sets by sea wall; doing well under newish licensees (Colin Humphries, Lindy May)

Ashburton [West St; SX7569], Exeter: Immediately appealing old pub, cheerful licensee, Ruddles ale, good value bar food (Phil Stone)

Avonwick [B3210 1/2 mile from A38; SX7157], Mill: Friendly service and big helpings of reasonably priced light bar meals in recently extended lively and very popular dining pub; Bass on handpump, attractive surroundings, busy carvery, children's area, big car park (J S Evans, Geoffrey Thompson)

Axmouth [SY2591], Ship: Polite, comfortable pub with lots of folk-costume dolls, Devenish JD and Royal Wessex, rather good food with strong seafood emphasis inc excellent crab salad or seafood surprise; attractive garden a sort of convalescent home for owls and other birds from Newbury Wildlife Hospital, three cuddly and loving samoyeds; has been found closed Fri (Brian and Anna Marsden, LYM)

Beer [Fore St; ST2389], Anchor: Clean and friendly with well kept beer and notable bar food in separate area inc excellent fresh fish; bedrooms (P Gillbe); [B3174 2 miles N], Bovey House: 16th-century Inglenook Bar in former manor house which belonged to

Katherine Parr; beams, flagstones, warm hospitality, Flowers on handpump, fine wines, extensive grounds; bedrooms (E G Parish)

Beesands [SX8140], Cricket: Friendly local on beach of fishing village with comfortably affable landlord (WMS)

Belstone [SX6293], Tors: Enjoyable country pub on the edge of Dartmoor; good reasonably priced food, well kept beer, local atmosphere (PB, HB)

Berry Head [SX9456], Berry Head: Well furnished bars, reasonably priced Bass on handpump, good range of bar food, excellent clifftop terrace (P L Jackson)

Bickington [SX7972], Dartmoor Half Way: Warm welcome, good Flowers, wide range of bar food (Steve Huggins)

Bickleigh [A396, N of junction with A3072; SS9407], Trout: Comfortable individual furnishings in plush and remarkably spacious dining lounge with wide choice from efficient food counter inc good help-yourself salads; well kept real ales such as Ruddles County, restaurant, tables on pretty lawn (road can be noisy), provision for children; good-sized well equipped bedrooms (Laurence Manning, LYM)

Bigbury [St Anns Chapel; B3392 N; SX6647], Pickwick: Main bar with traditionally rustic feel, well kept Bass, Flowers and maybe Palmers, local Stancombe cider tapped from the cask, usual bar food inc marvellously fresh prawn sandwiches, friendly bar staff, piped music; pool and other games in spacious newer and plainer family extension which brings lots of children to the pub; restaurant; bedrooms (Amanda Dauncey, LYM)

☆ Bishops Tawton [A377 S of Barnstaple; SS5630], Chichester Arms: Picturesque 15th-century cob and thatch pub, with pleasant olde-worlde atmosphere, small windows, very low sagging beams, interesting old local photographs, large stone fireplace, well kept Ushers on handpump, bar food and small garden with terrace by village green (J R Carey)

☆ Blackawton [SX8050], Normandy Arms: Quaint and pleasant 15th-century pub in remote, pretty village, doing particularly well under warmly welcoming newish licensees; interesting bars hark strongly back to World War II (when this village was used as secret rehearsal ground for Normandy landings); log fire, several well kept ales such as Bass and Wadworths 6X, excellent bar food, good restaurant concentrating on fresh food especially local fish, friendly staff; well-mannered dogs welcomed; good value bedrooms, clean and comfortable if not smartly decorated *(Roger Sims, W Bailey, Gordon Hewitt, Dr C I Haines)*

☆ **Blackmoor Gate** [SS6443], *Old Station House*: Recently turned into pub by same family as at Pyne Arms, East Down (see main entries); church pews, altar and rail, wide choice of good value food served all day (at least in summer), so generously that an extra children's helping could be syphoned off — there's a small children's menu too; big no-smoking eating area (no under-fives here, but allowed in small family room, games room with two pool tables); picnic-table sets outside with splendid views over rolling countryside *(Steve and Carolyn Harvey, J A Scott)*

☆ **Blagdon** [Higher Blagdon; pub (and Aircraft Museum) signed off A385 leaving Paignton; SX8561], *Barton Pines*: Sadly too few readers have reported on this interesting place for us to keep it among the main entries — though we should stress that we've heard nothing against it; it's a spaciously converted mock-Elizabethan 19th-century mansion, with extensive provision for families, a wide range of decent food from sandwiches to mixed grills, real ale, grand gardens giving views out to sea and over to Dartmoor *(LYM)*

Bovey Tracey [High St; SX8278], *King of Prussia*: Traditional pub, friendly landlady and son, amiable locals, fruit machine, darts, well kept Bass and farm cider, maybe sandwich or pasties *(Charlie Salt)*

Brandis Corner [A3072 Hatherleigh—Holsworthy; SS4103], *Bickford Arms*: Wide range of consistently good worth-waiting-for bar food under newish licensees, Bass and Flowers on handpump; games in separate building *(Keith Houlgate, David and Sarah Gilmore)*

☆ **Branscombe** [lower village; signed off A3052 Sidmouth—Seaton; SY1988], *Masons Arms*: Rambling low-beamed bar in very busy 14th-century inn, in lovely sheltered combe just up from the sea, not far from interesting donkey sanctuary, and attractive in summer for its pretty tables outside and in winter for its roaring log fire, sometimes used for spit-roasts; well kept Bass, Badger Best and Tanglefoot, bar food, restaurant (evenings/Sun lunch); bedrooms comfortable and attractive, though not cheap; the many reports we get on the inn have been rather mixed in the last couple of years, and children are not welcome inside *(Mr and Mrs W E Potter, D M Forsyth, S J Rice, Laurence Manning, Mrs Caroline Gibbins, Graham and Glenis Watkins, D Baddeley, A C Earl, LYM)*

Bratton Fleming [SS6437], *White Hart*: Bass, Flowers IPA and farm cider in lively traditionally furnished village pub with big inglenook fire and lots of other alcoves; bar food (not Sun lunchtime), pub games in one side area, some seats outside; children welcome *(B M Eldridge, LYM — more reports on new regime please)*

Brixham [SX9255], *Quayside*: Well kept beer, good wines, enterprising range of bar food, maybe Sun lunchtime jazz; bedrooms *(George Jonas)*

☆ **Broadclyst** [Whimple Rd; SX9897], *New Inn*: Friendly service in isolated converted farmhouse with cushioned milk churns as bar stools, stripped brickwork, panelled bar ceiling, three old fireplaces, one with roaring log fire and circled by comfortable chairs, genuine saws, harnesses and hunting horn, back issues of *Horse & Hound*, low doorways; particularly good bar food, unusual and varied, with fresh ingredients, home-made bread, and vegetables which all readers have singled out as superb; well kept real ales, decent wines, palatial skittle alley *(J R Carey, Mrs Barbara Andrews)*

Broadclyst [B3121, by church], *Red Lion*: Semi-rustic free house on village green, renovated to expose old bricks and beams, log fire, good choice of hot and cold bar food *(E V M Whiteway, K R Harris)*

Buckfastleigh [SX7366], *Dartbridge*: Ideally situated for Dart Valley Steam Railway, butterfly farm, otter sanctuary and abbey; large pub with big central bar, dark mock beams, panelling, sepia Devon views; good choice of food from self-service salad carvery, Bass and Flowers real ales, afternoon teas; large outside area with seats, attractive flowers, shack with games machines, small adventure playground; letting chalets with swimming pool *(Keith Widdowson, Gwen and Peter Andrews)*

☆ **Buckland Brewer** [OS Sheet 190 map reference 423206; SS4220], *Coach & Horses*: Not enough reports this year to keep this friendly thatched pub in the main entries — but it's well worth knowing for its attractively furnished heavy-beamed bar, with inglenook log fire, Flowers IPA on handpump, pub games, decent food from sandwiches to off-the-bone ham, local trout and steaks, and obliging service; restaurant, tables in pretty garden; children in eating area; bedrooms *(John Bowdler, LYM)*

Buckland Monachorum [SX4868], *Drakes Manor*: Old beamed pub full of copper and china, with orange banquettes, Courage real ales, cheap and generously served home-cooked food inc fried dishes, good roast beef and fine ploughman's, fruit machines; in Dartmoor-edge village with notable garden — the Garden House *(Jutta Whitley, PB, HB, Dorothy and Charles Morley)*

Budleigh Salterton [High St; SY0682], *King William*: Attractive exterior, warm welcome, Devenish on handpump, wide choice of bar food, good service; bedrooms

(E G Parish)

☆ **Budleigh Salterton** [Chapel St; SY0682], *Salterton Arms*: Increasingly popular in last three years, clean and comfortable, with train pictures, nautical mementoes, open stairway to railed gallery and small side room — bookable tables and children allowed up here; good value food (lasagne, vegetarian dishes and — not so cheap — seafood recommended, also children's dishes though they don't advertise them, and lunchtime snacks), well kept Courage Best and Directors and maybe other beers on handpump, friendly waitresses *(Brian Jones, Mrs Joan Harris, Simon Collett-Jones, Michael and Alison Sandy)*

Burlescombe [A38 some way E of village turning; ST0716], *Poachers Pocket*: Simple food in quiet and comfortably modernised lounge bar of well kept inn, handy for M5 junction 27, with children's dishes, well kept real ale, restaurant, skittle alley *(Alan Carr, LYM)*

Calverleigh [B3221 Tiverton—Rackenford; SS9214], *Rose & Crown*: Quiet and welcoming, not usually crowded; well kept beers, food all week at modest prices, nicely served in big helpings; skittle alley *(Audrey and Roger Adcock)*

Chagford [Mill St; SX7087], *Bullers Arms*: Old-fashioned local, unpretentious almost to a fault; three changing well kept real ales, basic but plentiful and very cheap food, log fires, collection of militaria, friendly welcome; summer barbecues in yard *(Robert Humphreys, LYM); Globe*: Friendly atmosphere, real ale, generous helpings of bar food (specials such as veal chop recommended), picnics to order; bedrooms *(Neil and Anita Christopher); Ring o' Bells*: Busy old black-and-white local, spacious and comfortable, log-effect gas fire, friendly licensee, well kept Wadworths 6X and farm cider on handpump, good home-made bar food, restaurant *(Peter Donahue)*

☆ **Challacombe** [B3358 Blackmoor Gate—Simonsbath — OS Sheet 180 map reference 695411; SS6941], *Black Venus*: Friendly pub in same family as Pyne Arms, East Down (see main entries), in impressive valley spot; well kept real ales, good reasonably priced bar food inc locally caught fish, side games room, occasional live entertainment; bedrooms *(Simon Reed, Irene and Peter Cranston, Mrs J Fellowes, Steve and Carolyn Harvey, B M Eldridge)*

☆ **Chardstock** [off A358 Chard—Axminster; ST3004], *George*: Charming old-world mainly flint and thatch pub in idyllic village surrounded by hills, tables out in front and in new flint-cobbled back courtyard; old panelling, framed local poems, dried hops on beams in the series of bars (one of which has piped music), well kept Flowers and Whitbreads PA, good range of whiskies, decent wines, particularly good bar food from sandwiches through pizzas big enough to share to steaks, small restaurant with baby grand; four splendid bedrooms *(Fiona Easeman, C Collins)*

☆ **Chillington** [SX7942], *Chillington Inn*: 17th-century village inn doing particularly well under current owner, very good food in old-world atmosphere; small restaurant; comfortable bedrooms, bargain breaks *(Mr and Mrs T A Towers, David and Ann Stranack)*

☆ **Chittlehamholt** [off A377 Barnstaple—Crediton, and B3226 SW of South Molton; SS6521], *Exeter Inn*: Bright and recently completely redecorated beamed bar in 16th-century thatched inn, a couple of cask armchairs by the fire as well as mate's chairs and so forth, matchbox and foreign banknote collections, well kept Ushers Best and Websters Yorkshire on handpump, Hancock's farm cider, bar food from sandwiches and ploughman's through local trout, children allowed in eating area; restaurant; comfortable bedrooms *(Steve Dark, LYM; more reports please)*

☆ **Christow** [Village Rd; SX8385], *Artichoke*: Pleasant little thatched local built lengthways down hillside, so open-plan bars are on different levels, with water flowing from bank behind into grotto; friendly, talkative landlord; close to lovely Canonteign Waterfalls and Country Park; bedrooms *(Gordon and Daphne)*

Chudleigh Knighton [SX8477], *Clay Cutters Arms*: Big helpings of simple food in thatched village local with big winter log fires, Flowers IPA and Eldridge Pope Royal Oak, popular games area, seats on side terrace and in orchard; bedrooms *(LYM)*

Chulmleigh [South Molton Rd; SS6814], *Fortescue Arms*: Fishing inn with fresh flowers in simple, pleasant bar, Bass, home-cooked food that may include game or freshly caught fish, dining room; service may not be the briskest; bedrooms *(BB)*

Clayhidon [ST1615], *Half Moon*: Miles from anywhere, with magnificent position and views; interesting reasonably priced food inc excellent Sunday spread, well kept beers; recent extensions; children welcome *(Alastair and Alison Riley); Harriers*: Friendly pub, local real ales, good lunchtime bar food, big garden; good picnic/walking area *(Derek Patey)*

Clearbrook [off A386 Tavistock—Plymouth; SX5265], *Skylark*: Pleasant and popular Dartmoor-edge pub with two large lounge-cum-bar areas, children's room off car park; good beer, large platefuls of nice bar food (particularly good garlic bread); views across the moor *(Ted George, Charles Gurney)*

Clovelly [Steep St; SS3225], *New Inn*: Medieval inn handsomely rebuilt in 1914 (hotel and pub part divided by cobbled lane); old dark oak timbers, timbered balcony above little terrace; cosy bar (and tea room) have fine old village photographs, well kept Burton ale, and decent food inc home-made pasties and filled rolls; nice garden; bedrooms *(J R Carey); Red Lion*: Stupendous setting built into harbour wall; rather spartan bar with some fine old photographs, and quay to sit out on;

Land-Rover will ferry people who can't face steep climb back up hill; bedrooms *(J R Carey)*

Clyst St Mary [nr M5 junction 30; SX9790], *Half Moon*: Very old inn with good bar food inc delicious home-cooked ham and home-made sausages *(Mrs G M Wight)*

Cockington [SX8963], *Drum*: Thatched though not really old, in rustic village; large bar with exposed beams and settles, stools and Windsor chairs around tables, Fergusons real ale, usual bar food, piped music, juke box; skittle alley, front terrace and superb gardens *(Steve Huggins)*

Coffinswell [SX8968], *Linny*: Very relaxed atmosphere, friendly staff and tasty food such as vegetarian lasagne *(J and J Payne)*

Colyford [A3052 Sidmouth—Lyme Regis — OS Sheet 192 map reference 253925; SY2492], *Wheelwright*: Thatched 17th-century pub with long, narrow neatly kept stonebuilt lounge bar, plenty of tables, comfortably busy feel; extensive good value fresh bar and restaurant food, well kept real ales such as Bass and Charrington IPA, good coffee; tables on narrow lawn *(Gwen and Peter Andrews, W L B and J Reed)*

Colyton [by church; SY2493], *Gerrards Arms*: Pleasant, friendly local with well kept Boddingtons, interesting food, hospitable landlord *(Robert and Vicky Tod)*

Combe Martin [SS5847], *Dolphin*: Pleasant location with wide range of beers inc Exmoor, local farm cider, good choice of bar food served till quite late *(Richard and Ann Jenkins)*

☆ **Croyde** [off B3231 NW of Braunton; SS4439], *Whiteleaf*: Not a pub but a guest house — included here because it's where readers have followed the Wallingtons, still famous among pub lovers from their time some years ago building the reputation of the Rhydspence, Whitney on Wye (Hereford & Worcester); the Whiteleaf is a firm recommendation if you want to be pampered at surprisingly modest cost for a few days, with truly imaginative all-fresh food and good wines in comfortable surroundings; dogs accepted *(Mr and Mrs Norman Edwardes and others)*

☆ **Croyde**, *Thatched Barn*: Highly commercial extended thatched inn near fine surfing beach, interesting original features still to be found in rambling but largely modernised bar, well kept Courage ales, largely home-made bar food inc local fish and good puddings, loud piped music, provision for children, morning coffee served from 10am, restaurant *(Pamela and Merlyn Horswell, H F H Barclay, Prof H G Allen, Rita Horridge, LYM)*

☆ **Dartmouth** [Smith St; SX8751], *Seven Stars*: Good atmosphere in busy long black-beamed oak-panelled bar with leatherette settles around rustic elm tables, well kept Courage Best and Directors, piped pop music and fruit machine; upstairs restaurant, children's room, efficiently served and well priced popular food *(H K Dyson, John Barker, BB)*

Dartmouth [Sandquay], *Floating Bridge*: Clean and friendly with decent beer, reasonable bar snacks *(H K Dyson)*

Denbury [SX8268], *Union*: Good, clean, welcoming 15th-century village pub with well kept Flowers and Whitbreads, good value home-cooked food inc unusual puddings, stripped stonework, log fires, live music three times a week; big garden *(Caroline Wright)*

Devonport [6 Cornwall St; SX4555], *Swan*: Riverside local with great atmosphere, nightly live music, midnight closing; over a dozen real ales inc Gibbs Mew Bishops Tipple and Wadworths 6X, good chunky sandwiches and chilli con carne *(Amanda Dauncey)*

Dog Village [B3185; SX9896], *Hungry Fox*: Comfortably furnished free house with wide range of beers and wines, good choice of rewarding hot and cold bar food, large car park *(E V M Whiteway)*

☆ **Drewsteignton** [Fingle Bridge — OS Sheet 191 map reference 743899; SX7390], *Anglers Rest*: Sprucely airy and spacious bar, in idyllic wooded valley by 16th-century packhorse bridge; reliable pub food, well kept Cotleigh and Courage or John Smiths real ales, brisk summer business in tourist souvenirs; winter opening times more restricted; easy parking; nr GWG19 *(Helena and Arthur Harbottle, Helen Crookston, LYM)*

Dunsford [OS Sheet 191 map reference 813891; SX8189], *Royal Oak*: Good value bar food inc fine sandwiches and vegetarian dishes, in light and airy lounge bar of village inn, well kept Wadworths on handpump, pleasant landlord, wonderful red setter, games in public bar, small restaurant, provision for children, Fri barbecues on terrace, good value bedrooms *(LYM)*

East Budleigh [SY0684], *Rolle Arms*: Simple decor, excellent food generously if not always quickly served; curry and giant mixed grill particularly recommended *(Mrs Joan Harris)*

East Prawle [SX7836], *Providence*: Very welcoming and uncommercialised small 18th-century pub with decent lunchtime sandwiches, ploughman's and small range of hot meals, Plympton real ale, Rombouts coffee *(Peter Woods)*

Ermington [SX6353], *Crooked Spire*: Friendly service, nice atmosphere, good hearty food inc excellent steaks in restaurant *(John Evans)*

Exbourne [SX6002], *Red Lion*: Promising new regime, with well kept Flowers Original and greatly improved layout and decor *(R J Walden)*

Exeter [Cowley Bridge Rd; SX9292], *Artful Dodger*: Heavily restored, lots of separate areas, darts and pool separated off; a useful refuge despite loud piped music, with friendly atmosphere and usual bar food from sandwiches or filled baked potatoes to steaks *(IP)*; [Topsham Rd (B3181 ring rd roundabout)], *Countess Wear Lodge*: Worth knowing for quickly served good value food in Reillys Bar, Ushers real ale, restaurant, big car park; bedrooms good value too (*E V M Whiteway*); [The Quay], *Prospect*: Lovely relatively quiet spot on terrace over River Exe next to newly renovated quay, handy for ferry to Maritime Museum; congenial main bar area with settles around panelled walls, wide range of food in large dining area up a few steps, helpful staff (*Michael and Alison Sandy, Helen Crookston*); [Martins Lane], *Ship*: Photogenic 14th-century pub just off cathedral close, with well kept Bass, Flowers IPA and Original on handpump, bar lunches from filled baked potatoes and good pasties up, fish inc good Torbay sole (*HEG, LYM*); [High St North], *Turks Head*: Where Dickens found the original of Joe, the Pickwick Papers' fat boy, forever nodding off; now a Beefeater, with a long two-level book-lined lounge bar, wide choice of bar food, Flowers Original on handpump, polite staff; restaurant (*LYM*); [Union Rd, Pennsylvania], *Victoria*: Suburban pub remodelled with genuine old timbers, furniture and pictures; good choice of beers inc Devenish, wide range of bar food such as pizzas and fish, filter coffee (*E Whiteway*); [The Close], *Well House*: Most notable for its lovely position, with big windows looking over close to cathedral (though trees partly block the view in summer); open-plan bar divided by inner walls and partitions, lots of Victorian prints, popular with local business people for good value bar lunches; Bass, Flowers, Exe Valley and guests such as Ma Pardoes and Wiltshire Weedkiller on handpump (*R Hodgins, BB*)

Exmouth [The Beacon; SY0080], *Beacon Vaults*: Pleasant pub, worth knowing (*Graham and Glenis Watkins*)

☆ **Filleigh** [off A361 N Devon link rd; SS6627], *Stags Head*: Family-run 16th-century free house doing particularly well under current regime; good range of quality food for people with big appetites, well kept Bass and wide range of other beers; most friendly atmosphere, home of local cricket team; bedrooms comfortable and good value (*Graham and Jane Smithard, J R Carey*)

Folly Gate [A386 Hatherleigh—Okehampton; SX5797], *Crossways*: Small, well run pub with Bass and Charrington IPA on handpump; food well worth the wait — very popular in tourist season; children allowed in quieter parts (*Keith Houlgate*)

Galmpton [Maypool; off A3022 at Greenway Quay signpost, then bear left to Maypool; SX8856], *Lost & Found*: Idyllic setting overlooking Torbay Steam Railway, with well kept Flowers and good bar food inc fine sandwiches — hotel/restaurant licence, so you can drink only if you eat; restaurant has attractive dining terrace; comfortable bedrooms (*Margaret and Trevor Errington*)

☆ **Georgeham** [Rock Hill; above village — OS Sheet 180 map reference 466399; SS4639], *Rock*: Oak beams, old red quarry tiles, open fire, pleasant mix of country furniture inc

traditional wall seats, good chatty atmosphere, with well kept Watneys-related real ales, local farm cider and limited but good range of home-made bar food inc good soup, filled French bread, home-cooked dishes; darts, fruit machine, unobtrusive piped music; further room with pool and food cabinet, tables under cocktail parasols on front terrace, pretty hanging baskets; doing well under new regime (*David Wallington, J R Carey, Henry Midwinter, Lindy May, RAB*)

Gittisham [Gittisham Common; SY1398], *Hare & Hounds*: Convenient spot; spacious pub with warm, friendly welcome and good choice of great ales (*Graham and Glenis Watkins*)

Great Torrington [SS4919], *Puffing Billy*: Old railway station with bar and lounge 'on the platform'; good food and beer, restaurant; tables in garden, walk along old railway line being developed (*Mr and Mrs D Hampton*)

Grenofen [SX4971], *Halfway House*: Wide variety of decent bar food from sandwiches to steak (*John O'Gorman*)

Gulworthy [Chipshop — 1 1/2 miles N, towards Lamerton; SX4375], *Chipshop Inn*: A chip shop is what it isn't — most interesting choice of beers, wholesome well presented bar food (*Peter Skinnard*)

Hartland Quay [SS2522], *Hartland Quay*: Included for remarkable, isolated position by derelict quay at foot of cliffs, with waves crashing over rocks; room by bar with odd collection of clocks, St Austell Tinners, moderately priced bar food; could be crowded at peak holiday times (*Prof H G Allen*)

Hawkchurch [ST3400], *Fairwater Head*: Not really a pub, but a small and very well appointed hotel — worth knowing for its excellent food and service, and really magnificent views; may be closed winter (*Anon*); *Old Inn*: Charming old pub in lovely village centre; modernised thoughtfully to keep atmosphere, straightforward food in informal surroundings, dogs welcome; seats outside, large car park (*Anon*)

Hemerdon [SX5657], *Miners Arms*: Friendly licensees in nice low-beamed pub, wide range of well kept beers such as Bass, Marstons Pedigree, Ruddles, Sam Smiths, good service, big garden, decent car park (*Neil Spink, C A Gurney*)

Heybrook Bay [SX4948], *Eddystone*: Clean, bright pub with good service and lunchtime and evening bar food at reasonable prices (*Geoffrey Thompson*)

Highampton [A3072 W of Hatherleigh; SS4804], *Golden*: Attractive and homely 16th-century thatched free house, low-beamed lounge with alcoves, padded barrel stools, long high-backed upholstered settle among other seats, brasses, watercolours, farm tools, stove in big stone fireplace; Courage Best, John Smiths and Worthington tapped from the cask, bar food inc sandwiches, basket meals and more

substantial evening dishes; pool room, back garden with view of Dartmoor Tors *(Helena and Arthur Harbottle)*
Holbeton [Fore St; SX6150], *Dartmoor Union*: Very clean and friendly pub under newish ex-Sussex landlord, with good fresh fish and well kept Bass; in picturesque village *(Graham and Glenis Watkins)*; *Mildmay Colours*: Popular, with good cheerful service, lots of atmosphere; wide choice of good value bar food (inc vegetarian dishes), evening carvery about three times a week and Sun lunch in upstairs restaurant (best to book); front terrace has lovely views *(Susan and Derek Lockyer)*
nr **Honiton** [Fenny Bridges (A30 4 miles W); ST1500], *Fenny Bridges*: Pleasant well kept bar with kindly, quick bar staff; good choice of real ales, wide choice of food lunchtime and evening, restaurant; garden *(W R Porter, Ninka Sharland)*; [Fenny Bridges], *Greyhound*: Big well run thatched roadhouse, now a Chef & Brewer, with droves of red plush dining chairs and banquettes in its heavily beamed rambling bar, and deliberately old-fashioned style; quickly served good value food in bar and carvery, Ushers on handpump, comfortable well equipped games room; bedrooms *(Dr D M Forsyth, Mr and Mrs F W Sturch, J S Clements, LYM)*; [Putts Corner; A375 S, junction with B3174; SY1496], *Hare & Hounds*: Impressive stone building, large, plush and smart; spacious lounge bar, smaller popular wood-and-tiles tap room, comfortable sofas as well as more normal furnishings, stuffed birds, four changing well kept beers, good range of roasts and other dishes, restaurant *(Michael and Alison Sandy)*
Hope Cove [SX6640], *Hope & Anchor*: Simple seaside inn with local flavour, pleasant staff and cheap bedrooms *(Margaret and Trevor Errington, LYM)*
Horns Cross [A39 Clovelly—Bideford — OS Sheet 190 map reference 385233; SS3823], *Hoops*: Ancient thatched inn, very well ordered, with home-made bar food, Flowers IPA and Original, log fires in big inglenooks, oak beams; neatly refurbished to cope with many diners; comfortable bedrooms *(Colin and Evelyn Turner, LYM)*
Hunters Inn [SS6548]: see under Lynton
Ideford [SX8977], *Royal Oak*: Small, olde-worlde thatched local, one bar crammed with Victorian and turn-of-the-century regalia and old flags; friendly character landlord, particularly well kept Bass, raised log fire *(Steve Huggins)*
Ilfracombe [Broad St (just by harbour); SS5147], *Royal Britannia*: Pleasant, friendly pub/hotel with comfortable lounge — low seats and armchairs; very reasonably priced food, well kept Courage, John Smiths and Websters Yorkshire; bedrooms *(B M Eldridge)*
Ipplepen [Poplar Terrace; SX8366], *Plough*: Friendly staff, two real ales, food even Sun evening; darts, games machine, small garden; plenty of room for children *(Peter Turl)*

Ivybridge [High St; SX6356], *Exchange*: Large friendly pub, interesting old farm and smithy tools; Websters Yorkshire, good food, darts; tables on balcony over river *(P Bromley)*; [Western Rd], *Imperial*: Interesting choice of good food, generous well served helpings; pub small, so get there early or book a table; friendly staff *(Alan and Audrey Chatting)*
Kenn [not far off A38; SX9285], *Ley Arms*: Nice old village pub dating back to 13th century, big inglenook, good choice of occasionally changing well kept beers on handpump such as Bass, Flowers, Halls Harvest and Dartmoor Strong; bar food inc good value children's dishes (or they can have half-price helpings of other dishes), carvery *(Brian Jones, Gordon and Daphne)*
☆ **Kentisbeare** [3 1/2 miles from M5 junction 28, via A373; ST0608], *Wyndham Arms*: Bustling and well run village local, friendly to strangers, with daily papers for the settee by the big log fire, tables tucked into walls of long beamed main bar and out in sheltered courtyard; candlelit restaurant and games room leading off, also skittle alley; good value bar food such as sandwiches, ploughman's, home-made steak and kidney pie, local ham and egg, salads; well kept Flowers IPA and Original *(David Gaunt, Margaret and Roy Randle, BB)*
☆ **Kilmington** [A35; SY2797], *Old Inn*: Friendly and welcoming thatched village local with character bar, comfortable inglenook lounge, good value bar food (children's dishes attractively priced), Bass and Charrington, open fires, traditional games and skittle alley, restaurant, children's play area in nice garden *(Brian and Anna Marsden, Pauline Williams, David Gaunt, LYM)*
☆ **Kingsbridge** [edge of town; SX7344], *Crabshell*: Currently on an upswing, in pleasant estuary-side spot with delightful view over moorings; friendly atmosphere, well kept Bass and Charrington IPA, warm winter fire, good bar food — particularly ploughman's, filled rolls and crab sandwiches *(Amanda Dauncey, M Box, WMS, Ann and David Stranack)*
Kingswear [SX8851], *Ship*: Good atmosphere in genuine warmly welcoming beamed local, Whitbreads-related real ales, bar food *(John Knighton, H K Dyson)*; *Steam Packet*: Pleasant narrow-roomed little pub, decent beer *(H K Dyson)*
Lee [SS4846], *Grampus*: Attractive 14th-century pub with nice quiet garden, just a stroll up through the village from the sea; well kept Flowers, good sheep-cheese ploughman's *(C Elliott, B M Eldridge, LYM)*
Littlehempston [A381; SX8162], *Pig & Whistle*: Large no-smoking area, good food and service *(JAH)*; *Tally Ho!*: Superb pub off beaten track with warm welcome, well kept Palmers Tally Ho and fine food *(Alan Merricks)*
☆ **Lower Ashton** [off B3193; SX8484], *Manor*: Generous helpings of good simple home-made non-fried food (not Mon),

usually three well kept real ales tapped from the cask, in small but popular and friendly two-bar pub; garden overlooking Teign Valley *(R Hodgins, P Cowlard, David and Flo Wallington)*

Luton [Haldon Moor; SX9076], *Elizabethan*: Comfortable and welcoming, pleasing decor, conscientious staff, wide choice of good attractively priced food; Devenish and other real ales, unobtrusive piped music, big car park *(G Marchant, Mr and Mrs M A Garraway)*

Lympstone [Exmouth Rd; SX9984], *Nutwell Lodge*: Large open-plan pub neatly divided into alcoves and separate areas, part no-smoking; immaculately decorated, black beams, beautiful furnishings, armchairs and settees; huge helpings of food in daily carvery, vegetarian dishes and marvellous choice of puddings; huge car park, a shame about the jolly piped music *(Pat Woodward)*

Lynmouth [SS7249], *Rock House*: Small warm and cosy hotel bar with lots of ship/naval memorabilia, good range of usual bar food, friendly, efficient bar staff; piped music; bedrooms *(Prof H G Allen)*

☆ nr **Lynton** [Rockford; Lynton—Simonsbath rd, off B2332 — OS Sheet 180 map reference 755477; SS7547], *Rockford Inn*: Very friendly licensees in traditional village local on the East Lyn; beamed split-level bar attractively decorated with farm tools and prints of Lynmouth through the years; well kept real ales such as Cotleigh Tawny, Courage Best and Directors, good bar food such as local trout (meals rather than snacks in the evening); beautiful Exmoor spot nr Doone valley, on GWG22 and nr NT walks at Watersmeet; nearly two miles of Exe fishing; limited parking; six bedrooms *(Derek and Sue Hammond, Steve and Carolyn Harvey)*

nr **Lynton** [Martinhoe, towards Heddons Mouth — OS Sheet 180 map reference 654482], *Hunters Inn*: Popular pub, well kept Eldridge Pope Dorset, bar meals (rather than snacks) inc help-yourself salads, cheerful service, garden with peacocks; good parking point for walk to coast through NT land — start of GWG21 *(Anon)*

☆ **Malborough** [SX7039], *Old Inn*: Village pub, quiet yet full of life, with quick polite service, good choice of reasonably priced bar food inc fine mussels and smart puddings; ample parking; children's room *(Margaret and Trevor Errington, Michael Halsted, Mr Forester)*

☆ **Manaton** [SX7581], *Kestor*: Smartly refurbished, clean and comfortable, with surprisingly chic decor for this splendid Dartmoor-edge location; Exmoor, Flowers and Marstons Pedigree, wide range of good value, wholesome and often imaginative bar food inc excellent open sandwiches, cheerful and helpful service; attractive bedrooms *(Murray J Daffern, Genie and Brian Smart, Eric Locker, Peter Maden, Hilary Robinson)*

☆ **Meavy** [SX5467], *Royal Oak*: Lovely old country pub, preserved against modernity by the fact that it's one of England's only two

pubs owned by their parish councils; attractive spot on green of Dartmoor village, comfortable L-shaped main bar with rustic tables, smaller attractively traditional public bar, good atmosphere, simple home-made food, well kept Bass and Ushers Best on handpump *(Jutta Whitley, PB, HB, LYM)*

Meeth [A386 Hatherleigh—Torrington; SS5408], *Bull & Dragon*: Stone and thatch pub flourishing under new and enthusiastic young licensees, Devenish and other real ales, decent wines, Macallan on optic, regularly changing menu with specials on blackboard; cosy restaurant partitioned off from bar; bedrooms well modernised after drastic thatch fire *(Peter Bisby)*

Merrivale [SX5475], *Dartmoor*: Refurbished pub with Courage and a guest real ale on handpump, good choice of country wines, open fire, good value lunchtime bar food, maybe early morning coffee, efficient service, roadside garden; handy for the nearby Dartmoor bronze-age hut circles and stone rows; at start of GWG15 *(Cliff and Karen Spooner, Margaret and Trevor Errington, Geoffrey Thompson)*

☆ **Monkton** [A30 NE of Honiton; ST1803], *Monkton Court*: Well refurbished in 1989, with roomy and attractively laid out beamed main bar, snug side areas, efficient friendly service, well kept Courage, good choice of reliable bar food (ham sandwiches and curry particularly recommended); provision for children, spacious relaxing garden; bedrooms *(Mrs Joan Harris, Mr and Mrs J W Gibson, LYM)*

☆ **Mortehoe** [free parking by church; village signed with Woolacombe from A361 Ilfracombe—Braunton; SS4545], *Ship Aground*: Pleasing village pub by church, in good coastal walking country (Morte Point, Bull Point, Lee, Woolacombe Warren); open-plan, with leatherette wall seating, massive tree-trunk tables, lots of nautical brassware, log fire; well kept Flowers Original, Exmoor and a guest beer, good if not cheap bar food (sandwiches, soup, curry, seafood all recommended), friendly staff; piped music may be loud; children in restaurant and games room; has been open all day in summer *(Christopher and Heather Barton, P Miller, WHBM, J A Scott, LYM)*

Muddiford [B3230 Barnstaple—Ilfracombe; SS5638], *Muddiford*: Large, lively village pub, willing young staff; food good and well presented in no-smoking area *(K R Harris)*

Musbury [corner A358 with Lyme Regis rd; SY2794], *Golden Hind*: Friendly stone-floored pub with cosy rural atmosphere; good Bass *(Quentin Williamson)*

Newton Abbot [East St; SX8671], *Old Cider Bar*: Good range of well kept ciders in very basic unchanging locals' pub, decent ham rolls *(WMS)*

☆ nr **Newton Abbot** [Abbotskerswell; A381 2 miles S; SX8671], *Two Mile Oak*: Well kept Bass and Charrington IPA, good log fires, beams, lounge with secluded candlelit alcoves, black-panelled traditional public bar with lots of brasses, generous helpings of

straightforward bar food from filled rolls through ploughman's with local cheeses to steaks, seats on back terrace and nicely planted garden; children not allowed in *(K and E Leist, Steve Huggins, Charlie Salt, LYM)*
Newton Ferrers [Riverside Rd East; SX5448], *Dolphin*: Nice waterside pub, small but comfortable, in very pretty village, looking over River Yealm to Noss Mayo; friendly staff, particularly well kept Bass on handpump from barrels racked at back of bar, reasonably priced bar food *(Graham and Glenis Watkins, Paul Hussell)*
No Mans land [B3131 Tiverton—South Molton; SS8313], *Mountpleasant*: Cheerful roadside pub with friendly staff, well kept Butcombe on handpump, good bar food; children's room *(D W Backhouse)*
North Bovey [SX7483], *Manor House*: Well kept and comfortable *(Henry Hooper)*
North Tawton [SS6601], *Copper Key*: Comfortably furnished pub with local atmosphere; friendly service, well kept Marstons Pedigree, decent bar food *(Andrew and Michele Wells, R J Walden)*
Noss Mayo [SX5447], *Old Ship*: 16th-century pub notable for its delightful position on edge of creek, with terrace on own quay, in lovely village; jolly staff, well kept Bass, restaurant, coffee lounge *(J R Carey, S J Rice)*
Okehampton [Main Rd (just off A30); SX5895], *Fountain*: Varied menu with locally caught fish; a lot of atmosphere; restaurant; bedrooms good value *(Mandy and Michael Challis)*
Ottery St Mary [Gold St; SY0995], *London*: Well kept old pub with plenty of tables, quick friendly service, welcoming atmosphere, Ushers and two ciders on draught, and good range of hot and cold bar food from sandwiches up *(E V M Whiteway, Dr D M Forsyth, JAH)*
Parkham [SS3821], *Bell*: Plain thatched village local with simple reasonably priced food running up to steaks, Bass and Flowers IPA and Original tapped from the cask *(Steve and Carolyn Harvey, LYM)*
☆ **Parracombe** [off A39 Blackmoor Gate—Lynton — OS Sheet 180 map reference 668448; SS6644], *Fox & Goose*: Small local with amazing range of good food in comfortable and unspoilt atmosphere — a dozen blackboards of menu inc half pheasant, honey-roast duck, swordfish, four kinds of ploughman's, range of sandwiches, omelettes and steaks; friendly, unrushed service, Flowers IPA *(Dick Brown)*
Plymouth [Old George St; Derrys Cross, behind Theatre Royal; SX4755], *Bank*: Attractive conversion of Edwardian bank, varying levels with dark wood railings, conservatory, upstairs coffee shop; usual bar food, well kept Plympton Best, lively young licensees with own jazz band; busy with lunchtime yuppies and after theatre *(H Paulinski, Ian Phillips, Ted George, Andy Kassube, Jenny Shephard)*; [Barbican], *Distillery*: Previous gin distillery, nicely converted to slick modern town pub with

wrought iron and palm trees; children welcome in more rustic stone-floored entrance area, good basic pub food *(J R Carey)*; [Mutley Plain], *Fortescue*: Popular at lunchtime for good salads and hot dishes; well kept Plympton Best and Pride and Fergusons Dartmoor; lovely outside roof garden *(Amanda Dauncey)*; [The Hoe], *Mayflower*: Warm and friendly Boston Bar in THF Post House hotel, very clean and well run with excellent Bass; good reasonably priced bar snacks, fantastic view over the Hoe, parking — very handy in Plymouth; bedrooms comfortable if far from cheap *(Graham and Glenis Watkins)*; [The Quay, Barbican], *Ship*: Good, filling and cheap food in upstairs Watneys Country Carvery; good range of beers and wine downstairs (drinks can be taken upstairs); good furnishings, pleasant atmosphere *(Chris Wilcox)*; [172 Devonport Rd, Stoke], *Stopford Arms*: Decent back-street pub with well kept Courage, good juke box, and formidable but excellent Bass *(John Nicholson)*; [Harwell St, off Western Approach], *Town House*: Courage house with predominantly wood interior, friendly service, good range of bar food inc superb omelettes, plenty of seafood and steaks, pleasant atmosphere, well kept beer; small car park *(Mr and Mrs Simon Turner)*; [New George St/Eastlake St], *Unity*: Friendly pub open all day right in the shopping area — ideal for waiting males; well kept Plympton ales *(Graham and Glenis Watkins)*; [Saltram Pl — back of Plymouth Hoe, behind Moat House], *Yard Arm*: Pleasant naval-theme pub popular with businessmen at lunchtime; well kept Courage beers, friendly licensees, good bar food *(C A Gurney, George Jonas)*
Plympton [Station Rd; central shopping area; SX5356], *Joshua Reynolds*: Busy pub with generously served fresh food, attractive prices *(Royal Bromell)*
☆ **Postbridge** [B3212; SX6579], *East Dart*: Cheerful family bar in central Dartmoor hotel by pretty river — it has some 30 miles of fishing; efficiently served bar food, choice of real ales on handpump, farm cider; children welcome; bedrooms *(BB)*
Poundsgate [SX7072], *Tavistock*: Ancient Dartmoor pub with original flagstone floors and fireplaces, well worth a summer visit for its prize-winning gardens; extensive menu inc good home-prepared dishes, also open for breakfast, afternoon tea (May-Sept); very popular in summer, when service may slow — a proper local out of season *(Philip and Trisha Ferris)*
Princetown [SX5873], *Plume of Feathers*: Oldest building in Princetown with two log fires and excellent welcome; well kept Bass and St Austell HSD and Tinners, freshly cooked good value food; bedrooms, bunkhouse and camping facilities *(Gwyneth and Salvo Spadaro-Dutturi)*; *Prince of Wales*: Good value food at candlelit tables, Flowers and Ruddles on handpump, huge fires in two rooms, lots of rugs draped on the walls; cheerful warders from Dartmoor Prison

chatting and joking; owned by the Duchy of Cornwall — when its namesake last visited he said his ambition was to have a free drink in every bar named after him *(BB)*

☆ **Rackenford** [SS8518], *Stag*: Largely early 13th-century, with massive walls, stone-flagged entrance passage, settles around large open fire; full of atmosphere under new management, with well kept Cotleigh on handpump; food in bar and dining room — we've not yet had reports on this *(Audrey and Roger Adcock, D W Backhouse, BB)*

☆ **Ringmore** [SX6545], *Journeys End*: Interesting old-fashioned furnishings in panelled lounge of friendly and unusual partly medieval inn, comfortable new back conservatory overlooking attractively planted garden; wide range of generously served bar food, over half a dozen well kept real ales, farm cider, helpful service; evening restaurant; not far from the sea; could do with rather fewer written notices; bedrooms comfortable and well equipped *(John Knighton, A D Atienza, LYM)*

Roborough [off B3217 N of Winkleigh; SS5717], *Old Inne*: Up to half a dozen or more real ales, changing constantly, are the draw at this tucked-away village pub — maybe Adnams Mild, Devenish Steam, Exmoor Gold, Felinfoel Double Dragon, Greene King IPA and Ringwood Best; cheery, with basic furnishings, welcoming young couple, farm cider, country wines, sensibly placed darts, some tables outside; folk Tues, jazz Thurs, maybe events Sat (for which it may open all day); decent simple food from doorstep sandwiches to steak; children not allowed — but can sit in small garden *(G R Cleaver, R Hodgins, C M Andrews, BB)*

Rockford, see under Lynton

Salcombe [off Fore St nr Portlemouth Ferry; SX7338], *Ferry*: It's the setting which attracts here, with three storeys of stripped-stone bars (not all open out of season) looking out over the sheltered flagstoned waterside terrace to the picturesque estuary; Palmers real ales, bar food, restaurant, games bar — and of course holiday crowds, which can slow food service and give it a very seasidey atmosphere; the many steps make it unsuitable for disabled people, and some prices are on the high side *(Tim and Lynne Crawford, S J Curtis, R H Inns, LYM)*; [Union St], *Fortescue*: Useful well kept pub *(GSS)*; [Fore St], *Kings Arms*: Good family pub; Courage ales, good budget-priced food in restaurant *(Amanda Dauncey)*; [Fore St], *Shipwrights*: Comfortable, with well kept Courage, good value seafood, delightfully floral sheltered back terrace — perhaps the best pub here *(S J Curtis, Eric Locker)*

Sampford Courtenay [B3072 Crediton—Holsworthy; SS6301], *New Inn*: Recently open-planned 16th-century thatched free house, low beams, brasses, black and white prints, open fires, very friendly staff, cheerful atmosphere, well kept Bass, Flowers IPA and Original, varied menu inc good toasties, ploughman's, children's helpings; pleasant garden with swings and playhouse, lovely flower-filled village *(Helena and Arthur Harbottle, Tessa Stuart)*

☆ **Sampford Peverell** [16 Lower Town; a mile from M5 junction 27, village signed from Tiverton turn-off; ST0214], *Globe*: Spacious and comfortably modernised bar with food from sandwiches through salads and chippy things to steaks, popular Sun lunch, well kept Flowers IPA and Original, piped music, games in public bar, pool room, skittle alley, tables in front; open all day; children allowed in eating area and family room *(K R Harris, Richard Dolphin, Steve and Carolyn Harvey, Margaret Dyke, LYM)*

Scorriton [SX7068], *Tradesmans Arms*: Very clean open-plan bar with end snug, excellent views of Dartmoor-edge hills; friendly landlord, real ale, decent low-priced food; car park; large children's room; bedrooms *(Ted George)*

Seaton [Queen St; SY2490], *Old George*: Large open-plan bar, various levels connected by ramps; black-beamed ceiling, pine dado, Victorian pictures and prints, Devenish and Websters on handpump, good range of bar food; has been open all day summer, and winter Sats *(Michael and Alison Sandy)*

Shaldon [just past harbour; SX9372], *Ferryboat*: Rough and ready jolly fisherman's pub with lively, talkative locals crowded at bar, well kept Courage, wholesome-looking food *(Tom Evans)*; [SX9372], *London*: Superb Sun lunches worth booking — ample helpings of very reasonably priced home cooking; maybe remarkable beef sandwiches on Mon *(Bob and Joan Rosier)*; [Ringmore Rd (B3195 to Newton Abbot)], *Shipwrights Arms*: Friendly village local with reasonably priced food inc good crab sandwiches, warmly chatty atmosphere, river views from back garden *(LYM)*

Shaugh Prior [SX5363], *Whitethorn*: Pleasant-looking, comfortable pub with Courage Best and Directors and good 1950s piped music *(Mr and Mrs Simon Turner)*

Shebbear [SS4409], *Devils Stone*: Friendly country village pub with good value cheap bedrooms, simple bar food, well kept Flowers Original *(LYM)*

☆ **Sidmouth** [Old Fore St; SY1287], *Old Ship*: A lot of character in partly 14th-century pub with shiny black timber and panelling, close-set tables and ship pictures in its three opened-together rooms, and a roomier raftered upstairs bar; fair-priced food inc sandwiches, pizzas, grills, fish, well kept real ales such as Boddingtons, Marstons Pedigree, Wadworths 6X; dogs allowed; just moments from the sea, so can get crowded in summer; bedrooms *(Graham and Glenis Watkins, Robert and Vicky Tod, Prof H G Allen, BB)*

Sidmouth, *Anchor*: Devenish ales, all-day food; comfortable seating, children's play

area and garden, back car park (*E G Parish*);
[Fore St], *Black Horse*: Attractive
flower-covered exterior, comfortable,
spacious and well designed inside;
Whitbreads on handpump, good range of
bar food at reasonable prices (*E G Parish*)

☆ **nr Sidmouth** [Bowd Cross; junction
B3176/A3052; SY1089], *Bowd*: Thatched
dining pub with one of the best gardens in
the region, clean, warm and comfortable
inside, with soft lighting, an expanse of
Turkey carpet, soothing maybe classical
piped music and nice family room; well kept
Devenish and a guest beer, plenty of space,
rather an up-market feel and some
interesting furnishings, though character is
not perhaps its strong suit; has been open all
day; big car park (*Gordon and Daphne, Dr D
M Forsyth, Brian and Anna Marsden, LYM*)

Silverton [14 Exeter Rd; SS9502], *Three
Tuns*: Picturesque and welcoming old
thatched pub, long beamed bar with
pleasant window alcoves, log fire, good
choice of real ales such as Exe Valley,
Eldridge Pope Dorchester and Wadworths
6X, popular food (*J R Carey*)

South Brent [Exeter Rd; SX6960], *London*:
Courage pub with wide choice of very good
value varied food, cheerful and efficient
service (*P and M Rudlin*)

South Tawton [off A30 at A382 roundabout
or Okehampton exit, then signed from
Sticklepath; SX6594], *Seven Stars*:
Unpretentious village pub in quiet
countryside, good helpings of decent bar
food, well kept real ales such as Ind Coope
Burton, Palmers and Wadworths 6X, farm
cider; pool and other bar games, a couple of
good-natured dogs, folk club last Sun in
month; restaurant (closed Sun and Mon
evenings winter); children welcome;
bedrooms (*PB, HB, HEG, LYM*)

☆ **Spreyton** [SX6996], *Tom Cobbley*:
Atmospheric village local, small and warmly
welcoming, with good home-cooked food
inc special curry evenings (booking needed),
and will cook to order if notified in advance;
well kept Cotleigh Tawny and occasional
guest beers, darts and cards, lovely garden
with summer barbecues; busy at weekends;
spotless bedrooms (*Charlie Salt and others*)

Sticklepath [village signposted from A30 at
A382 roundabout and B3260 Okehampton
exit; SX6494], *Devonshire*: 16th-century
thatched village inn of potential, with big log
fire, well kept real ales inc Courage and
Ushers, traditional games, usual bar food
served quickly, restaurant, provision for
children; bedrooms (*LYM*)

Stockland [a mile or so towards Chard;
ST2404], *Longbridge*: Lively typical local,
small choice of beers; good value bar food,
connecting restaurant (*Mayur Shah*)

☆ **Stoke Fleming** [SX8648], *Green Dragon*:
Friendly old pub in small village with beams,
panelling, and leaded windows; well kept
Bass and Flowers, really good value bar food
(soups, filled potato skins and Texan pie all
recommended), enterprising choice of
take-away picnics, good service (*Mark

Jackson, Louise Mee, RS, AS*)
Stokeinteignhead [SX9170], *Chasers Arms*:
Delightful 16th-century thatched longhouse
in lovely village down deep combe; more
restaurant than pub, with well kept Eldridge
Pope Dorset IPA, splendid house wines,
quick friendly service and particularly good
food inc outstanding steak and kidney pie (*J
R Carey*); *Church House*: Extremely
picturesque recently restored 13th-century
thatched inn, snug Farmers Bar, spacious
beamed lounge with high-backed settles,
well kept Bass, Flowers IPA and Marstons
Pedigree on handpump, good food (*J R
Carey*)

☆ **Stokenham** [opp church, just off A379
Dartmouth—Kingsbridge; SX8042], *Church
House*: Busy, lively food pub with wide
range of well presented bar food, especially
local fish, seafood, remarkable range of
filled baked potatoes and own-grown
vegetables; steak, curries and gammon also
praised; children allowed in small dining
room with games machine (tables can be
booked here); well kept Bass, friendly
landlord, garden with tables, chairs and
swings (*Steve Huggins, M J Chapman, David
and Ann Stranack*)

☆ **Stokenham**, *Tradesmans Arms*: Noted for a
fine range of malt whiskies, with Bass and a
couple of other real ales, this pretty thatched
cottage has plenty of neatly set antique
tables, piped classical music, and bar food
strong on fresh fish — the honey-baked
gammon and Madras curry are popular,
too; picnic-table sets outside (nice
surroundings), restaurant, no provision for
children (*R J Walden, Ann and David
Stranack, Steve Huggins, S J Curtis, LYM*)

Tedburn St Mary [village signposted from
A30 W of Exeter; SX8193], *Kings Arms*:
Old inn showing promise since changing
hands late 1989, long cosy open-plan bar
with big log fire, generally good if not cheap
food (not Sun evening) in eating area at one
end, games area around corner at other end,
a couple of well kept real ales, local cider;
children allowed in eating area; bedrooms
(*Cdr W S D Hendry, LYM*)

Thelbridge Cross [OS Sheet 180 map
reference 790120; SS7912], *Thelbridge
Cross*: Friendly atmosphere and particularly
good food in welcoming recently extended
pub; restaurant (*Mr and Mrs F Elliott and
others*)

Thornbury [village signposted from A3072
E of Holsworthy; SS4008], *Woodcott Arms*:
First impressions are of a private house with
its own drive; bar with pictures, wood
panels and copperware, games room,
Flowers IPA, good reasonably priced food in
small restaurant (*Keith Houlgate*)

☆ **Thorverton** [SS9202], *Dolphin*: Engaging
village inn run by cheerful brother and sister,
simple bar with sensibly placed darts and
pool, heavily velvet-curtained lounge
spreading from conventionally furnished bar
area through low easy chairs and
comfortable settees into cosy dining room;
bar food inc sandwiches and hot dishes such

as lasagne and notable steak and kidney pie, Flowers IPA and Original and Wethereds Winter Royal on handpump; winning dogs and cat, entertaining special evenings, tables out under ancient wisteria and in small garden; bedrooms good value (*J R Carey, Paul and Margaret Baker, BB*)

Thorverton, *Exeter*: Old local (though friendly towards strangers) with beams, old weapons, clocks and bygones, and 30ft glass-covered well by the bar; well kept Courage Best and Directors and John Smiths (*Paul and Margaret Baker*)

Tiverton [Market Pl; SS9512], *Half Moon*: Busy town pub with genuinely home-cooked bar lunches, well kept real ales and friendly service; open all day (*Patrick Godfrey*)

☆ **Topsham** [Ferry Rd; SX9688], *Passage*: Not enough reports this year to keep this attractive waterside pub in the main entries; honest bar food (not Sun evening) from lunchtime sandwiches or ploughman's through Exe salmon and often other fish dishes to steaks, Bass and Flowers IPA and Original, plank panelling, black oak beams, flagstones, seats on a shoreside terrace, restaurant; open all day Sat (*LYM*)

Topsham, *Lighter*: Spacious and well kept comfortably refurbished quayside pub with red plush seats in panelled alcoves and by long windows looking out over the lock-keepers' cottage and the tidal flats; efficient food bar and good Badger real ales; good choice of board games; bedrooms (*J R Carey, Klaus and Elizabeth Leist, BB*); [Monmouth Hill], *Steam Packet*: Flagstones, scrubbed boards, panelling, stripped stonework and brick, bar food, well kept Bass, Flowers Original and Whitbreads; on boat-builders' quay (*LYM*)

☆ **Torbryan** [most easily reached from A381 Newton Abbot—Totnes via Ipplepen; SX8266], *Old Church House*: Almost too many real ales — up to around 20 — in thatched pub with several comfortable and discreetly lit lounge areas on the left, and snug Tudor-panelled bar on the right; well presented bar food from sandwiches to salads and hot dishes such as curry or trout, friendly staff, piped music, imposing log fires, evening restaurant; children allowed in family room (*Peter Turl, J A Harrison, Steve Huggins, LYM — more reports please*)

Torquay [Alpine Rd; SX9264], *Alpine*: Friendly, small community pub with welcoming locals and staff; well kept Courage Best on handpump; lively games night Fri (pool and darts) (*Glenn Bonnell*)

Totnes [Fore St, The Plains; SX8060], *Royal Seven Stars*: Decent beer in airy hotel bar (*H K Dyson, P Argent*)

Two Bridges [B3357/B3212 across Dartmoor; SX6175], *Two Bridges*: Well kept real ales inc Flowers and good value food, esp filled rolls, soup, stilton ploughman's; bedrooms (*Andrew Hudson*)

Tytherleigh [A358 Chard—Axminster; ST3103], *Tytherleigh Arms*: Friendly pub in attractive village with good cheap range of bar food inc home-made soups, pies, local

fish and steaks, Eldridge Pope real ales, padded settles and armchairs; restaurant; children allowed if eating (*Tim Brierly*)

Uppottery [ST2007], *Sidmouth Arms*: Fine old Devon pub, tastefully furnished without spoiling its character, with well kept beer and good food (*PB, Dr D Forsyth, HB*)

☆ **Welcombe** [SS2218], *Old Smithy*: Pretty thatched country pub with charming garden and setting — a good choice for meals outside on a sunny day; well kept real ales inc Ushers, comfortable open-plan bar with log fires, juke box and so forth, bar food, pleasant family room; nearby Welcombe Mouth is an attractive rocky cove; bedrooms (*Christopher and Heather Barton, William D Cissna, LYM*)

Wembury [SX5248], *Langdon Court*: Very comfortable and welcoming hotel bar, good choice of beers and excellent straightforward food; bedrooms (*A D Atienza*); *Odd Wheel*: Friendly pub with good value food, facilities for children inside and out in garden (*D J Fisher*)

West Alvington [SX7243], *Ring o' Bells*: Sunny balcony for eating out, with views over Kingsbridge; bar snacks, restaurant area and carvery; spotlessly clean throughout; no dogs; four double bedrooms, all with views (*Philip and Trisha Ferris*)

Westcott [B3181 S of Cullompton; ST0104], *Merry Harriers*: Good food, good beer and friendly service (*T J Miles*)

Westleigh [1/2 mile off A39 Bideford—Instow; SS4628], *Westleigh*: Friendly village pub included for the gorgeous views down over the Torridge estuary from its neatly kept garden (*LYM*)

Weston [ST1200], *Otter*: Spacious yet interesting foody pub with very friendly landlord and bar staff, log fire, oak beams, wide range of pleasant bar food, customers of all ages (*Gordon and Daphne, Dr D M Forsyth*)

Whiddon Down [A30; SX6992], *Post*: Old coaching inn with china and masses of horsebrasses, big helpings of food from extensive menu inc huge puddings with clotted cream, Flowers Original and guest ale, family room, skittle alley, small garden (*Neil and Anita Christopher, K R Harris,*)

Whimple [off A30 Exeter—Honiton; SY4097], *New Fountain*: A remarkable success in previous editions, civilised and snug, with simple lunchtime bar food but transforming in the evening into a serious though delightfully cottagey restaurant — imaginative cooking, all fresh ingredients; but the brewery has now sold the pub, and its tenants (with their goats, angora rabbits and cats) have moved to the Springhead at Sutton Poyntz in Dorset (*C T and JM Laffin, LYM*)

☆ **Widecombe** [SX7176], *Old Inne*: Lovely old pub, comfortably rebuilt in the 1970s, with good friendly service, well kept beer, interesting reasonably priced food inc some unusual things, enormous salads, vegetarian and children's dishes and a good range of home-made puddings; good garden; the beauty-spot village is a magnet for visitors, so in summer the pub's very busy indeed — out of season the lovely open fire's an added attraction (*J and M Larrive, Henry Hooper, LYM*)

☆ **Widecombe** [turning opposite Olde Inn, down hill past long church house — OS Sheet 191 map reference 720765], *Rugglestone*: Unspoilt and welcoming little basic pub in beautiful setting, with landlady who sits in bar with the locals and goes out and gets their well kept reasonably priced Bass for them — if she isn't around, they bang the table with their empty glasses; little stream runs under the road and past front of the pub (*Gordon and Daphne, Paul Hussell*)

Yealmpton [SX5751], *Rose & Crown*:

Friendly, huge helpings of tasty food, good decor, atmosphere perhaps more that of a hotel bar than a pub (*Mr & Mrs S Turner, Mr and Mrs C D Mason*)

Yelverton [by roundabout on A386 halfway between Plymouth and Tavistock; SX5267], *Rock*: Real ales inc well kept Flowers Original and St Austell HSD, quick bar service, comfortable seats and no piped music (but fruit machine), welcoming staff; bedrooms (*Mr and Mrs Simon Turner*)

Yeoford [SX7898], *Mare & Foal*: Friendly Edwardian-looking pub with wide choice of beer, reasonable sandwiches, good value steak, comfortable lounge, parquet-floored games bar, good log fires, upstairs sauna; good parking (*BB*)

Dorset

Interesting pubs making their debut in the Guide this year are the Inn in the Park in Branksome Park (looks like a small residential seaside hotel, but turns out to be perhaps the most widely appealing pub in the Bournemouth area), the Saxon at Child Okeford (unpretentiously relaxing, an engaging collection of animals), the stylish Museum at Farnham (good food in attractive surroundings) and the pleasantly chatty Drovers at Gussage All Saints. Other pubs on a current upswing include the Ilchester Arms in Abbotsbury (decent food under new licensees, and redecorated bedrooms), the Spyway at Askerswell (a food award this year, for its honest and rewarding straightforward cooking), the New Inn in Cerne Abbas (another pub winning that food award; good wines by the glass, too, and a comfortable place to stay), the friendly and informal Weld Arms at East Lulworth (enjoyable food), the Elm Tree at Langton Herring (interesting, varied and thoughtful food, with good vegetarian dishes), the Marquis of Lorne at Nettlecombe (a popular place for a weekend stay), the Shave Cross Inn at Shave Cross (its fine ploughman's on top form), the pleasant New Inn at Stoke Abbott (good food, with a good vegetarian choice), and the Ilchester Arms at Symondsbury (good food, especially fish, with good wines by the glass; the licensees have been thinking of moving on, though). Quite a few pubs in the Lucky Dip section at the end of the chapter are particularly worth attention, too: our current pick of the bunch would be the George in Bridport, Gaggle of Geese at Buckland Newton, White Horse at Hinton St Mary, Scott Arms at Kingston, Bakers Arms at Lytchett Minster, Crown at Marnhull, Hambro Arms at Milton Abbas, Red Lion in Sturminster Newton, Springhead at Sutton Poyntz, Crown at Uploders and Coach & Horses at Winterbourne Abbas. Pub prices in Dorset tend to be quite close to the national average. On food, very few Dorset pubs can now produce a decent snack for under £1. Their strength is instead increasingly in good value main dishes. We found more – about one in four – able to meet our under £3 target for bargain main dishes. The best drinks bargains, saving you a few pennies a glass, tend to be found in pubs tied to regional or local brewers – notably Eldridge Pope (often good wines in their pubs, too), Palmers, Badger or Devenish. It was in a Devenish pub, the Ilchester Arms at Symondsbury, that we found our cheapest Dorset pint of the year.

ABBOTSBURY   SY5785 Map 2

Ilchester Arms 🛏

B3157

In a delightful village of golden stone and thatch, this handsome old inn is handy for the coast, the Abbey, and the sheltered 20-acre gardens (closed winter) with their unusual tender plants and peacocks; lanes lead from behind the pub into the countryside. The nearby swannery, famous for centuries for its hundreds of nesting pairs, prompts the profusion of swan pictures in the three main sitting areas, which have red plush button-back seats and spindleback chairs around cast-iron-framed and other tables on Turkey carpets, some brocaded armchairs in front of the open log fire, stirrups, horsebrasses, and hunting horns on the beams, a stag's head, some stuffed fish, and lots of hunting prints; there's also a sizeable and attractive no-smoking conservatory. Bar food includes soup (£1.50), ploughman's and salads (from £2.75), cod or Cumberland sausage (£2.95), home-made curry (£3.50), very good roast of the day (£3.95), deep-fried fresh chicken with bacon (£4.25), 120z gammon steak (£6), and steaks (from £7.95), and home-made puddings (£1.95). Well kept Devenish Royal Wessex and Wadworths 6X on handpump, red wine bin ends, and malt whiskies; darts, dominoes, fruit machine, board games and piped music. The bedrooms have been redecorated this year and are named after flowers; in summer, breakfasts are served in the conservatory. *(Recommended by G W H Kerby, I R Pinnock, Pat Woodward, Mr and Mrs J H Adam, Carol Mason, Mrs A Turner, Maggie and Bruce Clarke, Heather Sharland)*

Devenish   Licensee Maureen Davidson   Real ale   Meals and snacks   Restaurant Children in eating area of bar and conservatory   60s and country singing every second Friday   Open 11–11   Bedrooms tel Dorchester (0305) 871243; £45B/£55B (4-poster £60B)

ASKERSWELL   SY5292   Map 2

Spyway ★ ⊘

Village signposted N of A35 Bridport–Dorchester; inn signposted locally; OS Sheet 194 map reference 529933

Quick and friendly service, cosy little rooms of undoubted character and a fine position up in the coastal hills add up to such a draw that it's wise to get here early if you want a seat – even out by the ducks and other pets in the pretty back garden in fine weather, as it's a lovely peaceful summer viewpoint. Inside, furnishings include old-fashioned high-backed settles, cushioned wall and window seats, a longcase clock, fine decorative china, harness and a milkmaid's yoke; a new family eating area has been opened. Favourite food values are the fine choice of generous ploughman's such as hot sausages and tomato pickle (£1.95) or home-cooked ham with sweet pickle (£2.50), three-egg omelettes (£2.10), haddock or plaice (£2.40), salads (from £2.75), and specials like sausage and onion, country or game pies, and lasagne or curry; evening dishes like gammon and egg (£4.25) and steaks (£6.50), and puddings such as home-made crumble or cheesecake (from £1.20). Well kept Ruddles County, Ushers Best and Websters Yorkshire on handpump, as well as country wines, and around 40 whiskies; darts, shove-ha'penny, table skittles, dominoes and cribbage; play area outside, and lots of good walks nearby. *(Recommended by Mrs J A Gardner, Olive Carroll, Caroline Wright, Mr and Mrs B E Witcher, John Fazakerley, WMS, John and Chris Simpson, R B Crail, Alan Skull, Mr and Mrs M Woodger, Mrs S A Bishop, Margaret and Trevor Errington, Y M Healey, Shirley Pielou, David Pearman, Mrs L Saumarez Smith, Freddy Costello)*

Free house   Licensees Don and Jackie Roderick   Real ale   Meals and snacks Children in eating area of bar   Open 10–2.30, 6–11

BISHOPS CAUNDLE   ST6913   Map 2

White Hart

A3030

Though it's quite a size, the irregular shape of this popular dining pub's lounge bar gives it a genuinely companionable feel. The furnishings are relaxing, too: a good variety of seats and tables in decent wood, handsomely moulded low beams, ancient panelling, dark red curtains and nice lamps. Under the new licensees, the mostly home-made bar food includes sandwiches (from £1.20), home-made soup (£1.50), ploughman's (from £2.65), home-made pies like steak and kidney or fisherman's (from £3.45), vegetarian dishes (from £3.65), steaks (from £6.15), local trout (£6.20), daily specials like sausage, onion and tomato pie topped with cheese (£3.75), puddings (from £1.30), and children's menu (from £1.75, though they can have smaller helpings of adult food); they serve fresh vegetables. Well kept Badger Best and Tanglefoot on handpump; darts, dominoes, cribbage, chess, draughts, fruit machine and piped music. The biggish garden – floodlit at night – has a children's play area with trampolines, a playhouse with slides, and pet rabbits; there's a skittle alley. (Recommended by Laurie Nutton, L Walker, B A Chambers, John Fazakerley, Mr and Mrs J H Adam, W F C Phillips)

Badger   Licensees Geoff and Beverley Maxted   Real ale   Meals and snacks (11–2, 6.30–10)   Children in eating area   Open 11–2.30, 6.30–11

BOURTON   ST7430   Map 2

White Lion ⚲

Pub signposted off A303

Beams, broad flagstones, 18th-century woodwork, a warm woodburner and jolly locals – combine this old-fashioned setting (not to mention the proximity to Stourhead) with warmly welcoming helpful service and good cooking, and you get a rare recipe for popularity. There's even said to be a ghost: easiest to imagine him sitting on a quiet winter's night by the old oak table in front of the big fire in the side room, with its Turkey rugs on the stone floor; or maybe in the tiny traditional village bar across the entrance corridor. Yet another room, up a couple of steps, is set out for eating and has been extended this year – it's partly no-smoking; built-in settles around a medley of tables. The food concentrates on fresh local ingredients – there's been most praise recently for home-cooked ham and egg (£2.65), the vegetarian dishes such as spinach and walnut lasagne or beans and peppers simmered in a spicy coconut sauce (£3.25), beef in red wine with sautéed vegetables (£3.25), fresh Scotch salmon in a prawn, grape and cream sauce (£6.65), evening Scotch steak with brandy sauce, puddings such as torte or jam roly-poly (£1.10), and the three-course Sunday lunch (booking advisable). Helpings could hardly be more generous, they take obvious pride in their vegetables, and a good choice of other things includes sandwiches (from 90p), home-made soup (£1.20), a wide range of ploughman's (from £2.20), salads (from £3), steak and kidney or pork and apple pie (£3.45), fresh local trout (£4.75) and at least three other fresh fish dishes. Well kept Ruddles Best and County and Ushers Best on handpump, with guests like Bass, Smiles and Wadworths 6X; farm ciders and perry; shove-ha'penny, cribbage, dominoes, fruit machine, and quiet piped music. There are picnic-table sets in the several attractive garden areas which surround the rose- and clematis-covered old stone pub; regular weekend lunchtime barbecues. (Recommended by Mr and Mrs B E Witcher, R J Walden, S V Bishop, Ewan and Moira McCall, Hazel Morgan, Dorothy Leith, M D Hare, Stephen Lambert, R W Stanbury, T Galligan, John and Joan Nash, WHBM, S V Bishop)

Ushers (Watneys: leashold)   Licensee Christopher Frowde   Real ale   Meals and snacks   Partly no-smoking evening restaurant tel Gillingham (0747) 840866   Children in eating areas (till 8, unless over 14)   Occasional live entertainment Sat evenings or barbecue nights   Open 10.30–3, 6–11; 11–11 Sat   Holiday flat for up to 6 planned

BRANKSOME PARK   SZ0590   Map 2

Inn in the Park ⇐

Pinewood Road; from A338, at big roundabout just after coming into Poole from Bournemouth, follow Alum Chine, Branksome Chine (and brown Compton Acres sign) into The Avenue; after traffic lights take first left into Tower Road, which leads into Pinewood Road

An unlikely find, this small hotel in a quiet pine-filled residential area – but its bar is a real oasis. Not exactly pubby in character, with its toning shades of brown plush, Venetian red walls, flowery dark blue carpet and fresh atmosphere, but it's genuinely welcoming, with well kept Ringwood Best and Wadworths IPA and 6X on handpump, and good value bar food (there's an attractive flowery-wallpapered dining room on the left): sandwiches (from £1.20), ploughman's (from £2.25), salads (from £3.50 for home-made quiche to £4.50 for prawn), scampi (£3.95), puddings like home-made cheesecake (£1.30), and children's menu (£1.95); there's a more extensive menu on Friday and Saturday evenings. Piped music. A smallish terrace has seats among neatly kept roses. The road leads on down to Branksome Chine and the sea; and the hotel is almost opposite the entrance to the car park for Branksome Dene Chine, with a pleasant if steep walk down through low sandy cliffs to the beach. (*Recommended by WHBM, Steve Pratt*)

Free house Licensee Alan Potter Real ale Meals and snacks (not Sun evening) Evening restaurant (not Sun evening) Children in restaurant Open 11–2.30, 5.30(6 Sat)–11 Bedrooms tel Bournemouth (0202) 761318; £30B/£45B

CERNE ABBAS ST6601 Map 2

New Inn ⊘ ⇌

14 Long Street

Seats in the stone-mullioned windows of the friendly and comfortable high-beamed lounge bar have a fine view down the main street of this attractive stone-built village: just the place to embark on a lazy wine-tasting session. Eldridge Pope landlords tend to set a good example in the wines they keep, but here the choice by the glass is quite exceptional – maybe ten or more in good condition – often unusual, attractively priced and changing weekly; the list won the licensee his brewery's 1990 award for Vintner of the Year. Real care is taken over the food, too, which comes in big helpings and includes sandwiches (from £1.40), home-made soup (£1.65), watercress and mushroom mousse (£1.95), French bread with good cold meats (£1.85), ploughman's (from £2.20), cheese and broccoli quiche (from £2.10), three-egg omelettes (from £2.35), sausage and egg (£3.10), battered cod fillet (£3.75), meats and fish with help-yourself salads (£5.25), gammon with egg or pineapple or lamb with garlic and cream (£5.95 – particularly praised), steaks (from £7.75), puddings (from £1.55), and daily specials such as wine and nut pâté (£2.95), devilled beef (£4.25), fillet of cod Orkney style (£4.50), or spinach and almond cannelloni (£4.80). Eldridge Pope Hardy, Royal Oak, and Best on electric pump, and ten malt whiskies; considerate service; piped music. The inn's credentials as a really comfortable place to stay go back some 500 years, when it served as a guest house for the Benedictine Abbey; the bedrooms have been redecorated this year, and there are a couple of four-posters. It's on *Good Walks Guide* Walk 29, which focuses on the Cerne Giant above the village. Behind the old coachyard there are tables on a sheltered lawn, and being enclosed, it's safe for children. (*Recommended by John Evans, J R Williams, M L Hooper-Immins, Pat Woodwood, R J Walden, John Evans, A P Hudson, Carol Mason, Cathy Long, R W Stanbury, Joanna and Ian Chisholm, Chris Raisin, Graham Doyle*)

Eldridge Pope Licensee Paul Edmunds Real ale Meals and snacks (till 10 Fri and Sat) Children in eating area of bar Open 11–11; 11–2.30, 6–11 winter Bedrooms tel Cerne Abbas (030 03) 274; £20/£36

Royal Oak

Long Street

No problems getting to the bar here: the counter serving the row of three communicating rooms is uncommonly long. From outside, the very steep roof of massive stone slabs firmly says Tudor, and inside there are sturdy oak beams, flagstones, neat courses of stonework decked out with antique china, brasses and farm tools, lots of shiny black panelling, and big log fires. Carefully prepared home-made bar food includes winter soup (£1), sandwiches (from £1), omelettes (from £2.25), lasagne (£3.50), steak and kidney pie (£3.75), minute steak (£4.50), gammon (£5.25) and good sirloin steak (£6.50), with specials such as goujons of lemon sole or vegetarian harvest pie (£3.50) or smoked salmon (£3.75). Well kept Devenish JD and Royal Wessex and Marstons Pedigree on handpump; a happily relaxed atmosphere; piped music. There are seats outside. The pub is on *Good*

Walks Guide Walk 29. (Recommended by A P Hudson, Gordon and Daphne; more reports please)

Devenish   Licensee Barry Holmes   Real ale   Meals and snacks   Open 11–2.30, 6–11; closed evening 25 Dec

CHEDINGTON   ST4805 Map 1

Winyards Gap

A356 Dorchester–Crewkerne

New licensees taking over in early 1990 show promising signs of building on the reputation founded so firmly by the Pezaros, now retired. They've changed little inside: plenty of seating in the comfortably modernised beamed bar, decorated with lots of pottery, brasses and copper. Tables by the windows make the most of the far-reaching view down from this unspoilt National Trust hillside over the little rolling fields far below. Bar food includes home-made soup (£1.10), crispy mushrooms with garlic dip (£1.95), ploughman's (from £2.60), Lyme Bay bake (smoked fish and flaked white fish in cheesy sauce) or savoury mince in a herby pastry topping (both £3.95), pies like steak and kidney (£4.50) or local venison, beef and game cooked in elderberry wine (£6.40), and home-made puddings like jam roly poly or treacle tart (£1.75). Well kept Bass, Exmoor, Hook Norton and a guest ale on handpump, and country wines; pleasant staff. Darts, pool, and a spacious and comfortably furnished skittle alley. There are cast-iron tables on the terrace in front, with more seats in the attractively planted and more sheltered garden. The stroll from behind the pub to the monument is pleasant, and you can walk on through the woods to the village itself. *(Recommended by G T Rhys; more reports on the new regime please)*

Free house   Licensees Clive and Pam Martin   Real ale   Meals and snacks (12–1.45, 7–9.30)   Children in restaurant   Country and western/folk Sun evenings   Open 11.30–3, 7–11   Self-catering flats in converted barn tel Corscombe (093 589) 244

CHESIL   SY6873 Map 2

Cove House

Entering Portland on A354, bear right following Chiswell Only signs: keep eyes skinned for pub, up Big Ope entry on right

It's hard to quarrel with this pub's position: it's cornered an impressive spot looking down the miles of that pebble-spotter's paradise, Chesil Beach – the sunsets can be glorious. The bar on the right is warmly friendly, with a welcome from Ben and Sam the golden retrievers; it's simply furnished, with the polished floorboards and local shipwreck photographs gently underlining the maritime feel, and opens into a dining room on the left. Bar food includes good piping hot soups such as tomato and fennel or winter vegetable (£1.25), sandwiches (from £1.25, crab £2.25), ploughman's (from £2), stuffed mushrooms with spicy dip (£2.25), aubergine casserole or cauliflower and courgette bake (£2.95), cottage pie (£3.25), turkey and fruit curry or lasagne (£3.95), chicken provençal (£5.25), fresh crab salad (£4.95), fresh fish (from £5), savoury baked crab (£5.95). Well kept Devenish JD, Royal Wessex and Steam, Marstons Pedigree and Wadworths 6X on handpump; helpful service, piped music, darts, dominoes, cribbage, trivia, fruit machine, and lots of board games. There are tables under parasols out on the sea-wall promenade. If you go out by the gents' at the back you can see the massive masonry which has let the pub stand up to the storms. *(Recommended by Roger Huggins, Ian Phillips, Denise Plummer, Jim Froggatt; more reports please)*

Devenish   Licensee Sean Durkin   Real ale   Meals and snacks (12–2, 6.30–10) Restaurant tel Portland (0305) 820895   Children welcome   Open 12–3(11–2.30 winter), 6–11; 11–11 summer Sats

nr CHIDEOCK   SY4292 Map 2

Anchor

Seatown; signposted off A35 from Chideock

Below a 617-ft high cliff pinnacle used as a smugglers' signalling point, this friendly little pub has a grand cove virtually to itself, with sheep grazing the pastures that swell steeply up towards the cliffs on the far side. The two bars have simple but comfortable seats around neat tables, low white-planked ceilings and some sea pictures; there's a busily unpretentious family seaside atmosphere in summer, a quieter charm in winter with roaring log fires; one table is no-smoking. Bar food includes home-made soup (£1.20), sandwiches (from £1.20, crab £2.30), ploughman's (from £2.45), ham and egg or curry (£2.75), pizzas (from £3.25), steak and mushroom pie (£3.75), and evening steak (£6.95), with daily specials such as avocado with crab and grilled cheese or seafood lasagne (£3.75) or venison pie (£4.75); afternoon clotted cream teas in summer. Palmers BB, IPA and Tally Ho on handpump, kept under light top pressure during the winter; freshly squeezed orange juice, and a decent little wine list; darts, table skittles, dominoes, fruit machine, boules and piped music. There are tables out on the front terraces, above a shallow stream bisecting the beach. The thatched cottage next door can be rented, tel *Bridport (0308) 22396*. (*Recommended by Neil and Anita Christopher, Ian Phillips, David Pearman, Fiona Easeman; more reports please*)

Palmers   Licensee David Miles   Real ale   Snacks (served all afternoon in summer) and meals (no food winter Sun evenings)   Children in family room   Occasional folk/blues winter Sat evenings   Open 11–11; 11–2.30, 7–11 in winter; closed evening 25 Dec

CHILD OKEFORD   ST8313 Map 2

Saxon

Gold Hill; village signposted off A350 Blandford Forum–Shaftesbury and A357 Blandford–Sherborne; from centre follow Gillingham, Manston signpost

Set back from the village lane behind other cottages, this quietly clubby little pub's approach is best summed up by the notice in its bar: *There are no strangers here, only friends yet to meet*. The small bar, with its own log fire, leads through a lethally low-beamed doorway into a rather more spacious side room with plank-panelled dado, a big woodburning stove in its brick and stone fireplace, and among other tables an attractive mahogany one in the centre. Bar food's simple but neatly presented and good value, including lots of sandwiches (from 90p), filled baked potatoes (£1.35), ploughman's (from £2.45), a wide choice of hot dishes such as shepherd's pie (£2.95), filled Yorkshire puddings (from £3.50), a vegetarian dish, home-made steak and kidney pie (£4.25) and steaks (from 8oz rump £6.95), with several dishes of the day such as cheese and asparagus flan (£3.50) and lemon sole filled with crab (£4.25); children's menu (from £1.20). Well kept Bass and Charrington IPA on handpump; maybe quite well reproduced piped music – medleys of the 50s and 60s on our visit – shove-ha'penny, cribbage, dominoes. Besides their dogs (Bass, a golden retriever and Sebastian, a bearded collie) and cats (William, Henry, and Thomas), they allow dry dogs on leads. The back garden has an attractively planted border, slide and swings, contented rabbits in neat hutches, goldfish, a couple of small paddocks with an entertainingly wide variety of fowls from khaki campbells to vociferous geese, and two goats called Polly and Thea. (*Recommended by Crawford Reid, Brian Chambers, WHBM*)

Bass   Licensees Roger and Hilary Pendleton   Real ale   Meals and snacks (11.45–1.45, 7–9.30); not Sun or Tues evenings   Children welcome in top bar   Open 11.30–2.30, 7–11   Two bedrooms tel Child Okeford (0258) 860310; £12/£24

COLEHILL   SU0201 Map 2

Barley Mow

Village signposted from A31 E of Wimborne Minster, and also from Wimborne Minster itself; in village take Colehill Lane opposite big church among pine trees; OS Sheet 195 map reference 032024

Lovely in summer, with tables among the tubs of flowers in front, and more flowers in hanging baskets set off vividly against the whitewash, this thatched country pub also has a back lawn sheltered by oak trees. In winter there's a good fire in the huge fireplace of the comfortable beamed main bar, which is decorated with some Hogarth prints and attractively moulded oak panelling. Pick of the good value bar food may be the salads, with home-cooked meats, generous salads and crisp warm French bread (£3.50), though the sandwiches (£1.40) and moussaka (£2.60) have their champions; other dishes include home-made soup (£1.25), filled baked potatoes (£2.30), ploughman's (from £2.50), cottage pie (£2.60), home-made steak and kidney pie (£3.20), gammon steak (£4.30) and steaks (from £6). Badger Best and Tanglefoot and Charles Wells on handpump; darts and pool. *(Recommended by WHBM, John and Heather Dwane, John Nash; more reports please)*

Badger   Licensee David Parker   Real ale   Meals and snacks (12–2, 6–9.30) Children in family room   Open 11–3, 5.30–11

CORFE CASTLE (Isle of Purbeck)   SY9681 Map 2

Fox

West Street, off A351; from town centre, follow dead-end Car Park sign behind church

Behind this cosy and unspoilt old pub is an attractive sun-trap garden – divided into secluded areas by flowerbeds and a twisted pear tree – that's reached by a pretty flower-hung side entrance, and has good views of the ruined castle. Inside, the tiny front bar scarcely has room for the single heavy oak table and the cushioned wall benches which surround it; it's served by a hatch, lit by one old-fashioned lamp, and among other pictures above the ochre panelling is a good old engraving of the ruined castle. A back lounge is more comfortable, though less atmospheric. Generous helpings of fresh bar food include sandwiches like fresh crab (£1.60), ploughman's (from £2.20), quiches such as ham and pineapple, smoked mackerel or quiche Lorraine (£2.50), crab salad (£4.50), and puddings like home-made bread pudding with custard (from 60p). Well kept Flowers Original, Fremlins and Whitbreads Pompey Royal tapped from the cask; good dry white wine. The surrounding countryside is very fine and the pub is on *Good Walks Guide* Walk 25. There's a local museum opposite. *(Recommended by Steve and Carolyn Harvey, Ian Phillips, Stephen King, M E Hughes, Steve Huggins)*

Whitbreads   Licensee Miss A L Brown   Real ale   Lunchtime snacks   Open 11–2.30, 6(7 Sats and in winter)–11; closed 25 Dec

Greyhound

A351

Well placed just below the castle, this old-fashioned pub has mellowed oak panelling and old photographs of the town on the walls of the three small low-ceilinged areas of the main bar; there's also a no-smoking family area. Fresh local seafood is the speciality here: excellent Poole cockles, hot local crab quiche (£3), Mediterranean prawns sautéed in garlic (£4), very good fresh crab salad, and fresh lobster or mixed seafood platter (£7); other bar food includes large filled rolls (from 70p), home-made soup, a good choice of filled baked potatoes (from £2), lasagne or fisherman's pies (£2.70), and salads (from £3); daily specials and seafood are chalked up on a blackboard. Well kept Flowers Original, Whitbreads Strong Country and a guest beer on handpump; friendly service; darts sensibly placed in the back room, pool (winter only), fruit machine, space game, trivia, and juke box. There are benches outside. *(Recommended by J P Cinnamond, Mrs R F Warner, Barbara and Norman Wells, M E Hughes, Klaus and Elizabeth Leist, WHBM, Mrs A M Viney)*

Whitbreads   Licensee R A Wild   Real ale   Meals and snacks (11.30–2, 6.30–9; not 25 Dec)   Children in family area   Open 11–3, 6–11; winter evening opening 6.30

CRANBORNE SU0513 Map 2

Fleur-de-Lys 🛏

B3078 N of Wimborne Minster

Thomas Hardy stayed here for part of the time that he was writing *Tess of the d'Urbervilles*, and if you fork left past the church you can follow the downland track that Hardy must have visualised Tess taking home to 'Trentridge' (actually Pentridge), after dancing here. There's an attractively modernised, oak-panelled lounge bar and a more simply furnished beamed public bar. Bar food includes sandwiches, half pint of prawns (£3.75), chicken and mushroom pie (£4.15), home-made steak pie (£4.25), and vegetarian dishes like creamy leek crumble, nutty mushroom layer and cream cheese and spinach cannelloni (£4.15); home-made puddings and daily specials. Well kept Badger Best and Tanglefoot on handpump, farm cider, and some malt whiskies; darts, shove-ha'penny, dominoes, cribbage, fruit machine, and juke box. There are swings and a slide on the lawn behind the car park. The attractive rolling farmland round the village marks its closeness to the New Forest with occasional ancient oaks and yews. *(Recommended by John and Anne McIver, Roy McIsaac, Mrs J A Gardner, Hank Hotchkiss, G Shannon; more reports please)*

Badger Licensee Charles Hancock Real ale Meals and snacks (not 25 Dec or evening 26 Dec) Children in eating area of bar Open 10.30–2.30, 6–11 Bedrooms tel Cranborne (072 54) 282; £21(£25B)/£33(£38B)

EAST CHALDON SY7983 Map 2

Sailors Return

Village signposted from A352 Wareham–Dorchester; from village green, follow Dorchester, Weymouth signpost; note that the village is also known as Chaldon Herring; Ordnance Survey sheet 194, map reference 790834

In a very pretty, peaceful spot, this extensively renovated old pub has carefully kept its original character – the low-ceilinged stone-floored core now serves as a coffee house. The newer part has open beams showing the roof above, uncompromisingly plain and simple furnishings, and old notices for decoration; the dining area has solid old tables in nooks and crannies. Bar food includes sandwiches (from 95p, filled French stick from £1.20), home-made soup (£1.15), filled baked potatoes (from £1.75), home-made steak and kidney pie (£2.45), ploughman's (from £2.45), home-cooked ham and egg (£2.65), salads (from £2.75), scampi (£3.65), and steaks (from £6.15); also, fresh local fish or daily specials like chicken and asparagus lasagne (£3.25) or whole local plaice (£3.50), and children's meals (from £1.10). Well kept Eldridge Pope Royal Oak and guests beers on handpump, country wines, and farm cider; pleasant service. Darts, bar billiards, shove-ha'penny, table skittles, dominoes, and piped music. Benches, picnic-table sets and log seats on the grass in front look down over cow pastures to the village, which is set in a wide hollow below Chaldon Down; from nearby West Chaldon a bridleway leads across to join the Dorset Coast Path by the National Trust cliffs above Ringstead Bay. *(Recommended by Nic James, Jonathan and Helen Palmer, Marjorie and David Lamb, Mrs A M Viney, A V Lewis)*

Free house Licensees Mr and Mrs C E Groves Real ale Meals and snacks (11–2, 7–10) Partly no-smoking restaurant tel Dorchester (0305) 853847 Children in restaurant Open 11–2.30, 7–11

EAST LULWORTH SY8581 Map 2

Weld Arms 🍺

B3070

There are some assorted easy chairs by the fireplace in the homely and relaxed main bar, where there are likely to be fresh flowers from the rambling garden in summer, and where you may be able to roast your own chestnuts in winter (donations to RNLI). As well as more regular seats, there are a couple of long oak-panelled settles and a pair of pews, and some big oak tables. Reflecting the enthusiasm of the licensee (who's a single-handed Transatlantic man) are the ensigns which drape the yellowing ceiling, and newspaper sailing clippings, yacht pennants and nautical charts behind the bar. Lunchtime bar food includes home-made soup, prawn or crab sandwiches (£2), home-made cottage pie (£2.20), steak rolls (£2.50), and delicious chick pea and fennel casserole or steak and kidney pie; the changing but distinctive evening menu may include pizzas (from £1.90), mushroom fritters or pheasant pieces casseroled in red wine (£2.50), crevettes (£3.70), pigeon casseroled with bacon, celery, mushroom and sultanas, half rack of lamb in an Asian marinade, roasted and served with a nutty sauce, or sea trout (£7.30), and good home-made puddings. Well kept Devenish JD and Royal Wessex on handpump; courteous service. There's a smaller, snugger bar on the left (not always open) and a back family room, with darts, table skittles, shove-ha'penny, dominoes, cribbage, fruit machine, juke box, and decent unobtrusive piped music. There are picnic-table sets behind the thatched white house, as well as swings and a climbing frame. (Recommended by Keith and Sian Mitchell, David and Marjorie Lamb, Denise Plummer, Jim Froggatt, Gavin Udall, J N Hanson; more reports please)

Devenish   Licensee Peter Crowther   Real ale   Meals and snacks   Children in eating area of bar   Open 11.30 (11 Sat)–2.30, 6.30–11   Bedrooms tel West Lulworth (092 941) 211; £14/£25

FARNHAM   ST9515 Map 2

Museum ✿

Village signposted off A354 Blandford Forum–Salisbury

A solid brick building in a rustic village that's otherwise largely thatch and flint, this faces a line of venerable beech trees. The Coopers Bar is the one to head for: civilised, with green cloth-cushioned seats set into walls and windows, inglenook fireplace, local pictures by Robin Davidson, piped classical music (Brahms on our visit), and a calm atmosphere. Though they do sandwiches and ploughman's, most visitors seem to go for the main menu, even if they find enough from just a starter such as avocado and prawns, oysters, asparagus or smoked salmon; main dishes are around £4.50–£6, with a dish of the day such as steak and kidney pudding (done properly – with oysters in the recipe) or chicken curry, again with the proper accompaniments. Besides particularly well kept Badger Best and a couple of guest beers such as Greene King Abbot, Marstons Pedigree and Wadworths 6X on handpump, they keep decent wines, local country wines and some malt whiskies; darts, pool, fruit machine, juke box and piped music. There's a most attractive small brick-walled dining conservatory, leading out to a sheltered terrace with white tables under cocktail parasols, and beyond an arched wall is a garden with swings and a colourful tractor. The lavatories get top marks; the four bedrooms are in a neatly and recently converted former stables – we've not yet heard from readers who've stayed, but would expect good value. The green-corrugated locals' side bar has darts and a fruit machine. (Recommended by WHBM, Nigel Paine)

Free house   Licensee John Barnes   Real ale   Meals and snacks (12–1.45, 7–9.30) Children in restaurant   Occasional live entertainment   Open 11–3, 6–11; closed 25 Dec   Bedrooms tel Tollard Royal (072 56) 261; £35B/£45B

GODMANSTONE   SY6697 Map 2

Smiths Arms

A352 N of Dorchester

The little bar in this 15th-century ex-smithy has a warm atmosphere, and some antique waxed and polished small pews around the walls, one elegant little high-backed settle, high leather bar stools with comfortable backrests, and National Hunt racing pictures. Well kept Devenish Royal Wessex tapped from casks behind the bar; polite, helpful staff; darts, dominoes, backgammon, and shut the box. Food includes sandwiches, home-made steak and kidney pie or spaghetti marinara, home-cooked ham, and home-made bread pudding. You can sit outside on a crazy-paved terrace or on a grassy mound by the narrow River Cerne – and from here you can walk over Cowdon Hill to the River Piddle, one of the rivers the devil is supposed to have pissed around Dorchester. *(Recommended by Carol Mason, Gethin Lewis; more reports please)*

Free house   Licensees John and Linda Foster   Real ale   Meals and snacks (12–2, 6–9.30)   Open 11–3, 6–11; winter evening opening 6.30

GUSSAGE ALL SAINTS   SU0010 Map 2
Drovers

Village signposted off B3078 Wimborne Minster–Cranborne at Horton Inn; pub then signposted

Friendly and chatty under its newish young and welcoming landlady, this popular partly thatched village pub looks out past the picnic-table sets on its front lawn to low rolling farmland. It's pleasantly laid out, part quarry-tiled and part carpeted, with the big brick fireplace dividing it into two main areas; sturdy country chairs around the tables, beams, pink-shaded wall lamps, a few pictures, plates and guns on the white walls. Good value home-made bar food, particularly popular on Sunday lunchtimes, includes soup (£1.20), sandwiches (from £1.35), ploughman's (from £2.65), omelettes (from £3.45), steak and mushroom pie (£4.95), trout (£5.75), various steaks (from 8oz rump £7.50) and several dishes of the day such as grilled sardines (£2.; 95) and spinach and walnut lasagne (£4.25). Well kept Courage Directors, Flowers Original, Marstons Pedigree, Ringwood Fortyniner, Wadworths 6X and Whitbreads Best and Pompey Royal on handpump; maybe piped radio. There's a good children's play area outside. *(Recommended by WHBM, Roy McIsaac, E W B and M G Wauton)*

Free house   Licensee Gilly Long   Real ale   Meals and snacks   Ragtime pianist some Tues   Open 11–3, 6–11

HURN   SZ1397 Map 2
Avon Causeway 🍺

Hurn signposted off A338, then at Hurn roundabout follow Avon, Sopley, Mutchams singpost

Until it was abandoned in 1935, this was originally a station, and they've kept the old platform with its traditional toothed-edge canopy (now supporting bright hanging baskets) and sturdy old mahogany station seats (which now face a Pullman carriage – a restaurant). Interesting decorations include old local timetables and scale drawings of steam locomotives, posters, uniforms and photographs. An expansively comfortable and spacious lounge bar is divided into several separate rambling areas by the layout of the button-back plush seats, with sturdy pale wood tables and substantial standard lamp globes standing sentinel here and there, and spreads into an airy Moroccan-theme family room complete with palm trees. There's a fine range of well kept real ales on handpump kept under light blanket pressure – up to eleven, such as Adnams, Marstons Pedigree, Merrie Monk and Owd Rodger, Ringwood Best, Fortyniner and Old Thumper, Wadworths 6X and Farmers Glory and Youngers IPA. Under the new licensees, the bar food includes sandwiches (from £1.40), filled baked potatoes, basket meals or ploughman's (from £2.05), salads (from £3.50), steak and kidney pie (£3.85), cod or home-cooked ham and egg (£4.15), weekend roasts (£4.75), steaks (from £6.95), and children's dishes. Unobtrusive piped music, fruit machine, space game, trivia. There are also lots of picnic-table sets under cocktail parasols and the pub is surrounded by quiet woodland. *(Recommended by Bernard Phillips, Ian and Catherine Harvey, Michael and Rachel Brookes, Tony Triggle)*

Free house   Licensees Peter May and Meline Anstice   Real ale   Meals and snacks Indian restaurant in Pullman carriage   Children in family room   Jazz Sun evenings Open 11–11   Bedrooms tel Christchurch (0202) 482714; £35(£45B)/£49(£55B)

LANGTON HERRING   SY6182   Map 2

Elm Tree ⊗

Village signposted off B3157

A wide choice of very good, inventive home-made food in this popular dining pub includes sandwiches (from 95p), home-made soup (£1.80), ploughman's (from £2.85), smoked mackerel pâté (£3.50), vegetable and peanut loaf or celery, apple and walnut roulade (£3.95), excellent spicy beef casserole (£4.50), quiches like prawn and stilton, bacon and pineapple or spinach and mushroom (from £4.75), prawn-stuffed garlic bread (£5.25), salads with home-cooked ham or beef (from £4.65), mixed grill (£6.50), steaks (from £6.50), lots of daily specials, and home-made ice-creams like banana and butterscotch, apricot and roasted almond or chocolate and nougat (£1.85), with puddings chalked up on a board (from £2.50). Devenish Royal Wessex on handpump kept under light top pressure; special liqueur coffees; piped music. The two main carpeted rooms have cushioned window seats, red leatherette stools, Windsor chairs, lots of tables, and beams and walls festooned with copper, brass and bellows; there is a central circular modern fireplace in one room, an older inglenook (and some old-fashioned settles) in the other. There's also a traditionally furnished extension. The pretty flower-filled sunken garden has colourful hanging baskets, flower tubs, and tables; a track leads down to the Dorset Coast Path, which here skirts the eight-mile lagoon enclosed by Chesil Beach. *(Recommended by W J Wonham, Cathy Long, D K and H M Brenchley, W F C Phillips, Peter Hall, Carol Mason, K Leist, John and Joan Nash)*

Devenish   Licensees Anthony and Karen Guarraci   Real ale   Meals and snacks Children welcome   Open 11–2.30, 6.30–11

LYME REGIS   SY3492   Map 1

Pilot Boat ⊗

Bridge Street

The light, airy bar in this old smugglers' pub has comfortable blue plush seating and decorations such as local pictures, Navy and helicopter photographs, lobster-pot lamps, sharks' heads, an interesting collection of local fossils, a model of one of the last sailing ships to use the harbour, and a notable collection of sailors' hat ribands. At the back, there's a long and narrow lounge bar overlooking the little River Lym. Good, popular waitress served food includes a decent range of vegetarian dishes as well as sandwiches (from £1, delicious crab £1.95; open sandwiches from £2.25), home-made soup (£1.20), excellent huge ploughman's or a popular Norwegian mushroom dish (£2.50), steak and kidney pie or vegetable moussaka (£3.95), salads (from £4.50, home-cooked ham £4.75, local crab £5.95), mixed grill (£6.50), steaks (from £6.95), puddings such as lemon meringue pie, treacle tart or bread pudding, and a children's menu (from £1.95); specials and fresh fish are chalked up on a blackboard. Well kept Palmers Bridport, IPA and Tally Ho on handpump, and a decent wine and liqueur list. Darts, dominoes, cribbage. *(Recommended by Michael and Alison Sandy, Stan Edwards, Jon and Jacquie Payne, Patrick Freeman, Cdr G F Barnett, Marjorie and David Lamb, M L Hooper-Immins, Brian and Anna Marsden, Richard Parr, Peter Argent, Steve and Carolyn Harvey, E G Parish)*

Palmers   Licensee W C Wiscombe   Real ale   Meals and snacks (12–2.30, 6–10 in summer)   No-smoking restaurant tel Lyme Regis (029 74) 3157   Children welcome if well behaved and sitting down   Occasional live entertainment   Open 11–11; 11–2.30, 7–11

MARNHULL   ST7718   Map 2

Blackmore Vale ⊗

Burton Street; quiet side street

Decorated with 14 guns and rifles, keys, a few horsebrasses and old brass spigots on the beams, this friendly pub has a carpeted and comfortably modernised lounge bar with a log fire, and well kept Badger Best and Tanglefoot on handpump; also, farm cider and a decent wine list. A wide choice of bar food includes home-made soup (£1.20), sandwiches (from £1.20), ploughman's (from £2.80), several pies like beef and venison or an unusual crab one done with whisky, cheese and cream (from £3.20), vegetarian dishes (from £3.30), home-cooked ham (£3.60), trout with celery and walnut filling (£5.75), salmon en croûte (£6.30), guinea fowl (£6.95), and quite a few steaks (from £6.95, 26oz T-bone £11.50); they will bring your food to the garden. Darts, cribbage, dominoes, shove-ha'penny, fruit machine, piped music, and a skittle alley. There's an extensive range of purpose-built wooden children's play equipment, and a dovecote. (*Recommended by Roy McIsaac, Mrs J A Gardner, Dr John Innes, Richard Dolphin, H J Stirling, Lyn and Bill Capper, WHBM*)

Badger   Licensees Roger and Marion Hiron   Real ale   Meals and snacks (till 10pm) Children in small bar only   Open 11–2.30, 6.30–11

NETTLECOMBE   SY5195 Map 2

Marquis of Lorne 🚫 🛏️

Close to Powerstock and can be found by following the routes described under the entry included for that village – see below

This charming, well kept 16th-century pub with its pretty baskets of summer flowers and lovely view is a very popular place to stay. The warmly friendly main bar has a log fire, green plush button-back small settles, round green stools and highly varnished tables on a flowery blue carpet, and Doberman and Rottweiler photographs; a similar side room decorated in shades of brown opens off it. Generous helpings of bar food includes sandwiches (from £1.10), home-made soup or sandwiches (from £1.40), filled, deep fried mushrooms with mayonnaise dip (£2.25 starter, £3.75 main course), basket meals (from £2.95), ploughman's (£3.25), spaghetti bolognese (£3.50), salads (from £3.95), home-cooked ham and egg (£4.25), plaice (£4.55), grilled gammon with pineapple (£6.50), chicken Mexican (£8.50), half honey roast duck (£9.50), and T-bone steak (£10.95), with puddings like home-made sherry trifle (£1.95), and specials such as sea bass, scallops or lobster (caught by local fishermen) or rabbit fillets (bagged by the landlord); superb Sunday lunch. Well kept Palmers Bridport and IPA on handpump; darts, shove-ha'penny, dominoes, cribbage, table skittles, trivia and piped music. The big garden has masses of swings, climbing frames and so forth among the picnic-table sets under its apple trees. The earth-fort of Eggardon Hill is close by.(*Recommended by Heather Sharland, Maureen Hobbs, C A Hall, D S Moxham, Stephen Goodchild, Gordon Hewitt, Freddy Costello, John Nash, R C Blatch, Joan and John Calvert*)

Palmers   Licensee Robert Bone   Real ale   Meals and snacks   Partly no-smoking restaurant   Children welcome   Open 11–2.30, 6–11; closed 25 Dec   Bedrooms tel Powerstock (030 885) 236; £19(£20.50B)/£38(£41B)

OSMINGTON MILLS   SY7341 Map 2

Smugglers

Village signposted off A353 NE of Wareham

Though this well run, partly thatched stone-built pub is big, shiny black panelling and woodwork divide the bar into lots of cosy, friendly areas. There are stormy sea pictures, big wooden blocks and tackle, soft red lantern-light and logs burning in an open stove; some seats are tucked into alcoves and window embrasures, and one is part of an upended boat. Good value and efficiently served bar food includes soup (£1), filled French bread (£2.20), ploughman's (£2.80), quiche (£3), filled baked potatoes (£3.20), a changing vegetarian dish (£3.50), steak and kidney pie (£4), and children's dishes (£2), with more elaborate main dishes in a pleasantly cottagey dining area which opens off on the right: seafood terrine with raspberry coulis (£1.75), Cambozola fritters (£2.20), steaks (from £7), and seafood platter (£15). Pool, fruit machine, space game and trivia are well segregated, dominoes and cribbage, and piped pop or light classical music. Well kept Courage Best and Directors and Ringwood Old Thumper on handpump, several wines and country wines, and a good choice of liqueurs. There are picnic-table sets out on crazy paving by a little stream, with a thatched summer bar and a good play area over on a steep lawn; the coast path goes by, and the sea is just moments away – a stroll down through the pretty combe. It gets very busy in high season (there's a holiday settlement just up the lane). (*Recommended by Brian Chambers, P A Barfield, David Fowles, Sidney Wells, Barbara M McHugh, Barbara and Norman Wells, C D Gill, Alan and Janet Pearson, H W and A B Tuffill*)

Free house   Licensee Bill Bishop   Real ale   Meals and snacks   Partly no-smoking restaurant   Children in eating area of bar   Open 11–11; 11–2.30, 6.30–11 winter   Bedrooms tel Preston (0305) 833125; £25B/£48B

PLUSH   ST7102   Map 2

Brace of Pheasants

Village signposted from B3143 N of Dorchester at Piddletrenthide

Originally a row of cottages that included the village forge, this long, low 16th-century thatched pub is charmingly placed in a fold of the hills surrounding the Piddle Valley, and lies alongside Plush Brook. The well run and very friendly beamed bar has fresh flowers, a heavy-beamed inglenook at one end (which has a woodburning stove), with a good log fire at the other, good solid tables on the flowery carpet, and some good oak window seats as well as the Windsor chairs. Popular bar food includes home-made soup (£1.50), crab savoury (£2.75), ploughman's (from £2.75), smoked pheasant pâté (£2.95), salads (from £5.50), steak, kidney and mushroom pie or gammon and pineapple (£5.50), fish pie (£5.75), grilled local trout with almonds and prawns (£7.25), pheasant in red wine (£7.95), char-grilled steaks (from £8.25), and duck with apple and calvados (£8.95); specials like scallops and mussels in pastry, pernod and cream (£3.25), or chicken and coconut curry (£4.50), and children's menu (from £1.50). Well kept Bass and Charrington IPA on handpump; darts, alley and table skittles, and dominoes. The golden retriever is called Scallywag and the labradors Becky and Tilly. There's a good size play garden with swings and an aviary, or you can sit on a lawn which slopes up towards a rookery in this quiet, sheltered valley; and there's an attractive bridleway walk behind, to the left of the wood, over to Church Hill. Keith Andrew's orchid nursery is next door. (*Recommended by Michael Pritchard, John Knighton, Caroline Wright, P A Barfield, John Kirk, Mrs Vivien Warrington, David and Eloise Smaylen, K Leist, J M Watkinson, Mrs E M Thompson, Mr and Mrs J D Cranston*)

Free house   Licensees Jane and Geoffrey Knights   Real ale   Meals and snacks (till 10 in evening)   No-smoking restaurant tel Piddletrenthide (030 04) 357   Children in family room and restaurant   Open 11.30–2.30, 6(7 winter)–11

POOLE   SZ0190   Map 2

Angel

28 Market Street; opposite Guildhall which is signposted off A348 in centre – parking at the pub

This year, a restaurant has been added on to the back of this well run pub and bedrooms opened. The spacious relaxed lounge has carefully decorated green walls hung with turn-of-the-century prints, magazine covers and advertisements including ones by Toulouse-Lautrec and Mocha, naughty 1920s seaside postcards and some interesting old local photographs; cushioned banquettes form bays around pale wood tables, and there are a couple of sofas. Bar food from a separate efficient servery includes sandwiches, a vegetarian dish (£2.95), tagliatelle carbonara (£3.25), and fresh fish bake or steak and Guinness pie (£3.50). Well kept Ushers Best and Ruddles Best and County on handpump; fruit machine, trivia, and piped music; cricket team and football team. There are picnic-table sets in the back courtyard, with summer barbecues. The handsome 18th-century in the back courtyard, with summer barbecues. The handsome 18th-century Guildhall is a museum of the town's development. *(Recommended by J S Rutter; more reports please)*

Ushers (Watneys)   Licensee David McGuigan   Real ale   Meals and snacks   Children in restaurant and eating area of bar until 6   Open 11–11; 11–4, 5–11 in winter; Bedrooms tel Poole (0202) 675354; £15B/£30B

POWERSTOCK   SY5196   Map 2

Three Horseshoes ⊗ 🛏

Can be reached by taking Askerswell turn off A35 then keeping uphill past the Spyway Inn, and bearing left all the way round Eggardon Hill – a lovely drive, but steep narrow roads; a better road is signposted West Milton off the A3066 Beaminster–Bridport, then take Powerstock road

Good bar food in this secluded stone-and-thatch pub concentrates on fresh fish, such as grilled sardines (£3.75), a properly made fresh fish soup (£4.50), local codling baked in a light cheese sauce (£6.75), crab or tuna steak with herb butter (£8.50), monkfish in wine and cream or poached halibut fillet (£9.50), and stir-fried king prawns (£12); other food includes spinach pancake with cheese sauce or cannelloni with bacon and mushrooms (£3.75), carbonnade of beef (£5.50), Dorset lamb (£8.75), and puddings like apricot and almond tart or chocolate mousse (£2.75). Good breakfasts with home-made marmalade. Well kept Palmers Bridport and IPA on handpump. The comfortable L-shaped bar has country-style chairs around the polished tables, pictures on the stripped panelled walls, warm fires, and a friendly atmosphere. On the neat lawn perched steeply above the pub there are charming views, as well as swings and a climbing frame. Our stay award is for the larger rooms, which have their own bathrooms. You can book six-hour fishing trips, there are nearby trout ponds, and plenty of beach casting. *(Recommended by Heather Sharland, Mrs M T Garden, Mr and Mrs G Turner, Rosemary Flower, John and Joan Nash, Jackie and Jon Payne, Amelia Thorpe, Ken and Barbara Turner, H W and A B Tuffill, David Pearman, Freddy Costello)*

Palmers   Licensee P W Ferguson   Real ale   Meals and snacks (not Sun or Mon evenings)   No-smoking restaurant   Children welcome   Open 11–3, 6–11   Bedrooms tel Powerstock (030 885) 328; £20(£25B)/£50(£60B)

RAMPISHAM   ST5602   Map 2

Tigers Head 🛏

Pub (and village) signposted off A356 Dorchester–Crewkerne; OS Sheet 194 map reference 561023

Delightfully old-fashioned, this relaxed and welcoming old pub has two little rooms with carefully chosen hunting prints of all ages, photographs of ships brought in by ex-Navy locals, and comfortable old settles and a sofa; countless competition award rosettes above the bar confirm that riding's a particular interest of the licensees (Mrs Austin judges at horse shows, too), who with notice can arrange riding, clay-pigeon shooting or fishing for residents. The Siamese cat is friendly, though customers' favourite is Gladys the bulldog (a seasoned TV personality). Bar food, all home-made and largely using local ingredients and fresh vegetables, includes carrot, tomato and orange soup or sandwiches, steak and kidney pie, excellent rabbit pie or a range of vegetarian dishes, venison casserole, and steaks. Well kept Bass, Butcombe, Greene King Abbot and Wadworths 6X tapped from casks behind the bar, local farm cider, and country wines. There's darts, shove-ha'penny, dominoes, table skittles and a skittle alley. An attractive sheltered back garden has picnic-table sets; this is pleasant walking country. The owner of the village has proposed that the pub should be moved from its present building to another building some way away; this proposal has been resisted by the licensees and users of the pub, and as we go to press the outcome is uncertain. Naturally, we'd hope such a fine old place is left untouched. *(Recommended by Heather Sharland, Roy McIsaac, D K and H M Brenchley, Heather Sharland, Charles Bardswell, Michael and Alison Sandy, MCG, Peter Jones)*

Free house   Licensees Mike and Pat Austin   Real ale   Meals and snacks   Children's room   Restaurant   Two bedrooms tel Evershot (093 583) 244; £18/£36   Open 11–3, 7–11; closed Tues lunchtimes in mid-winter

SANDFORD ORCAS   ST6220 Map 2

Mitre

Village signposted off B3148 and B3145 N of Sherborne

Very relaxed and friendly, this white rustic village pub has red leatherette wall benches, big flagstones, a big fireplace, with a side bread oven, for the woodburning stove, and the pub's four unusually personable whippets and three amiable cats; readers have even found wool being spun on some occasions; there's a no-smoking area. The L-shaped dining room carries through the same mood, with plain tables on the flagstones, cream walls, and a big woodburning stove set in the stripped-brick end wall. Popular bar food includes omelettes (from £2.25), ploughman's (£2.50), roast chicken (£2.75), home-roast ham and egg (£3.25), steak and kidney pie (£3.95), salads (from £3.75), vegetable curry (£3.75), tagliatelli (£4.25), beef curry (£4.50), puddings like sticky toffee pudding (£1.60), and specials such as rack of lamb or salmon en croute. This is one place you can be sure the venison isn't a freezer pack, as they themselves joint all the venison they use; they also butcher their own sheep, though they're killed elsewhere. Butcombe on handpump, cider made in the village, and decent house wines; piped music. There are picnic-table sets up on the grass above the car park, and they have Hebridean, Manx and Jacobs sheep that were originally just to keep their own steep acre under control, but have now expanded to other pastures such as the cricket green at Over Compton and an orchard at Trent. (Recommended by D A B and J V Llewelyn, Jonathan and Helen Palmer, Paul and Monica Mann, D Baddeley, Mrs Frances Smith, Mrs J A Gardner, R M Savage)

Free house   Licensees Philip and Brenda Hayes   Real ale   Meals and snacks (12–2, 7–10)   Restaurant tel Corton Denham (096 322) 271   Children welcome   Open 11.30–2.30, 7–11

SHAFTESBURY   ST8622 Map 2

Ship

Bleke Street; you pass pub on main entrance to town from N

This unpretentious 17th-century pub has seats built into the snug black-panelled alcove facing the main bar counter, and on the left there's a panelled but similarly furnished room. Well kept Badger Best and Tanglefoot on handpump; darts, pool, cribbage, dominoes, fruit machine, backgammon, chess, dice games, and piped music. Under the new licensees, the bar food includes sandwiches, lasagne (£3), steak and kidney pie (£3.50), salmon kiev (£4.50), and daily specials. (Recommended by Ian Phillips, Gordon and Daphne, Mr and Mrs J H Adam, Alan Skull)

Badger   Licensees Rene and Karen Broers   Real ale   Meals and snacks (11–2.15, 6.30–10.15)   Children in eating area of bar   Open 11–3, 6.30–11; all day Thurs–Sat

SHAVE CROSS   SY4198 Map 1

Shave Cross Inn ★ ⊘

On back lane Bridport–Marshwood, signposted locally; OS Sheet 193, ref 415980

Apart from an excellent ploughman's (£1.95), the good bar food in this thatched partly 14th-century pub includes pâté (£2.20), basket meals (from £2.30), steak sandwich (£2.95), daily specials like lamb and apricot pie, meaty or vegetable lasagne, chicken, ham and leek pie or vegetarian chilli (all £3.35), salads that include home-cooked ham (from £3.15), evening chargrilled steaks (£7.25), puddings such as Dorset apple cake or seasonal fruit pies, and children's meals (from £1.70). Well kept Badger Best, Bass and Eldridge Pope Royal Oak on handpump, cider in summer, and country wines. The original timbered bar is a lovely flagstoned room with one big table in the middle, a smaller one by the window seat, a row of chintz-cushioned Windsor chairs, and an enormous inglenook fireplace with plates hanging from the chimney breast. The larger carpeted side lounge has a dresser at one end set with plates, and modern rustic light-coloured seats making booths around the tables; friendly, polite staff. Darts, table and alley skittles, dominoes, cribbage and space game. The pretty flower-filled sheltered garden has a thatched wishing-well and a goldfish pool. There's a children's adventure playground, and a small secluded campsite for touring caravans and campers. *(Recommended by Patrick Freeman, Mr and Mrs B E Witcher, Mrs Sue Fergy, Barbara M McHugh, Gethan Lewis, Dr Stewart Rae, Margaret and Trevor Errington)*

Free house   Licensees Bill and Ruth Slade   Real ale   Meals and snacks (not Mon, except Bank Hols)   Children in own area   Open 12–3 7–11; closed Mon (except Bank Hols)

STOKE ABBOTT   ST4500   Map 1

New Inn

Village signposted from B3162 and B3163 W of Beaminster

A good choice of home-made vegetarian dishes here includes cheese and onion quiche (£3.25), stilton and cheese flan (£3.50), vegetable lasagne (£3.95), and mushroom tettrazini or spinach and walnut cannelloni (£4.50); other home-made food such as pizza (£3.25), salads (from £3.50), steak and kidney pie (£3.95), chicken cacciatore (£4.25), chicken or prawn curry (from £4.50), scampi (£4.95), and sirloin steak (£8.25). On the beams of the carpeted bar, there's the licensees' own collection of over 200 horse brasses, old coins framed on the walls, and wheelback chairs and cushioned built-in settles around its simple wooden tables, and a settle built into a snug stripped stone alcove beside the big log fireplace. Well kept Palmers Bridport, IPA and Tally Ho on handpump kept under light blanket pressure; darts, table skittles, piped music, and pleasant, helpful service. Sheltering behind a golden stone wall which merges into an attractively planted rockery, the well kept garden here has long gnarled silvery logs to sit on, wooden benches by the tables, and swings. *(Recommended by G Parker, Leo Black, Felicity Vincent, C S Kirk)*

Palmers   Licensee Graham Gibbs   Real ale   Meals and snacks (not Mon evenings except Bank Hols)   Children in no-smoking dining room   Open 12–2.30, 7–11   Bedrooms tel Broadwindsor (0308) 68333; £15/£30

SYMONDSBURY   SY4493   Map 1

Ilchester Arms ⊘ ⇌

Village signposted from A35 just W of Bridport

In a quiet hamlet, down a country lane, this pretty old thatched inn is well run by very friendly, attentive licensees (though as we went to press, we heard that they may be moving on). One side of the open-plan bar has rustic benches and tables, seats in the mullioned windows, and a high-backed settle built into the bar counter next to the big inglenook fireplace; the other side, also with an open fire, has candle-lit tables and is used mainly for dining in the evening and at weekends. They specialise in fresh fish such as crab, lobster, scallops, grouper, red snapper, pan-fried calamares, fresh sardines with a lime sauce, and whole fresh baby shark (all from around £5); there's an excellent range of other food chalked up on all available beams and woodwork such as home-made chicken pâté or marsh samphire with smoked bacon and crispy croûtons (£3.95), thali of fresh vegetables with hot garlic bread or sweet and sour tart (£4.95), roast English lamb with redcurrant, orange and mint sauce (£5.50), chicken tandoori (£6.95), roast quail with blueberry and gin sauce (£8.95), and puddings like home-made Dorset apple cake or banana and caramel crunch (£1.95); booking essential. Very good breakfasts. Well kept Devenish JD and Royal Wessex on handpump, ten wines and champagne by the glass, and freshly squeezed orange juice. Darts, dominoes, cribbage, fruit machine, and a separate skittle alley (with tables). The Burmese cats are called Eric and George. There are tables outside in a quiet back garden by a stream. The high-hedged lanes which twist deeply through the sandstone behind this village of pretty stone houses lead to good walks through the wooded low hills above the Marshwood Vale. *(Recommended by Jean Paul and Solange Desgain, G T Rhys, Neil and Anita Christopher, Anne Wallbank, Mrs F Smith, Mrs Sue Fergy, Mr and Mrs R G Ing, Freddy Costello, Don Easton, C S Kirk, Mr and Mrs M Woodger, Denis Waters, Steve Huggins)*

Devenish   Licensees Terry and Margaret Flenley   Real ale   Meals and snacks (not Mon)   Restaurant   Well behaved children welcome   Open 11–2.30, 6–11; winter evening opening 7   Bedrooms tel Bridport (0308) 22600; l£32

TARRANT MONKTON   ST9408   Map 2

Langton Arms

Village signposted from A354, then head for church

Reached by driving through a shallow ford, this warm and friendly 17th-century pub is popular with a good mix of people. The main bar has settles forming a couple of secluded booths around tables at the carpeted end, window seats, and another table or two at the serving end where the floor's tiled. Bar food includes lentil and onion soup (£1.20), ploughman's (£2.10), steak and kidney pudding or chicken and vegetable curry (£2.95), gammon steak (£4.50), steaks (from £6), puddings (£1.20), and specials such as garlic prawns, moules marinières, lamb with orange and tarragon, and oxtail in Guinness; most evenings have special food themes – Chinese, French, pizza, curry, and bangers and mash. To be sure of a table, it's best to get there early. The public bar, with a big inglenook fireplace, has darts, pool, shove-ha'penny, cribbage and juke box, while a skittle alley with its own bar and more tables has a space game and fruit machine. Well kept Adnams Broadside, Bass, Greene King Abbot and Wadworths 6X, with weekly guest beers on handpump or tapped from the cask; sangria and Pimms in summer, mulled wine in winter, quite a few wines, and malt whiskies. There's a barbecue in the pretty garden. On the end of the building, they have opened a village/craft/delicatessen shop and post office. There are tracks leading up to Crichel Down above the village, and Badbury Rings, a hill fort by the B3082 just south of here, is very striking. *(Recommended by Jerry and Alison Oakes, Mrs R F Warner, C T and J M Laffin, M J D Inskip, E M Brandwood, Bernard Phillips, M D Hare, Gavin Udall, R F K Hutchings)*

Free house   Licensees Chris and Diane Goodinge   Real ale   Meals and snacks (12–2, 6–10.30)   Restaurant   Children welcome   Occasional live music   Open 11.30–2.30, 6–11   Bedrooms tel Tarrant Hinton (025 889) 225; £28B/£42B

WEST BEXINGTON   SY5387   Map 2

Manor Hotel ⊘ ⇌

Village signposted off B3157 SE of Bridport, opposite the Bull in Swyre

From the handsome flagstoned and Jacobean carved-oak-panelled hall in this well kept hotel, you go down a flight of steps to get to the busy, pubby Cellar bar: black beams and joists, heavy harness over the log fire, small country pictures and good leather-mounted horse brasses on the walls, red leatherette stools, low-backed chairs (with one fat seat carved from a beer cask), and soft lighting. A handsome no-smoking Victorian-style conservatory has airy furnishings and lots of plants. Very good bar food includes home-made soup (£1.45), sandwiches (from £1.85), ploughman's (from £2.85), salads (from £4.35, smoked salmon, prawn and crab £6.75), filled baked potatoes (from £4.45), omelettes (£4.55), home-made steak and kidney pie or cottage pie (£4.65), courgette and tomato lasagne (£5.15), casserole of rabbit or grilled liver and bacon (£5.25), pheasant stuffed with pâté and chestnuts (£5.75), monkfish in green pepper sauce or West Bay scallops and bacon (£7.95), steaks (from £8.65), puddings like strawberry pavlova, summer pudding or lemon mousse, and children's dishes (from £2.75); espresso, cappuccino, and hot chococlate. Well kept Eldridge Pope Royal Oak, Palmers

Bridport (which here carries the pub's name) and Wadworths 6X on handpump; skittle alley, trivia and piped music. The spreading south-sloping garden has picnic-table sets on a small lawn with flowerbeds lining the low sheltering walls, and there's a much bigger side lawn with a children's play area. The sea is just a stroll away (past the bungalows which make up most of this village), and the walks along the cliff are bracing. *(Recommended by Marjorie and David Lamb, Richard Parr, Lynne Sheridan, Bob West, W F C Phillips, I R Pinnock, M Aston, Heather Sharland, K Leist, Nigel Williamson, Bernard Phillips, TOH)*

Free house   Licensee Richard Childs   Real ale   Meals and snacks (till 10pm) Restaurant   Children welcome   Open 10.30–2.30, 6–11   Bedrooms tel Burton Bradstock (0308) 897616; £28.95B/£51B

WEST LULWORTH   SY8280   Map 2

Castle 🛏

B3070

The lively public bar in this friendly thatched white house has polished flagstones and button-back leatherette seats that form a maze of booths around the tables. The comfortably furnished lounge bar is cosy, though more modern-feeling, with blue banquettes under the countryside prints on the walls, and pewter tankards hanging from one beam. Good, popular bar food includes sandwiches (from 80p), ploughman's (from £1.90, with good ham £2.20), chilli con carne (£2.80), home-made pies (from £3), beef stroganoff (£3.80), and rabbit and pork casserole with apple or pigeon and bacon casserole (£5); excellent breakfasts. Well kept Devenish JD, Royal Wessex and Steam on handpump, helpful staff; darts, shove-ha'penny, table skittles, dominoes, cribbage, fruit machine, trivia, outdoor chess, and piped music. On the lawn above steeply terraced rose beds, there's a barbecue area. Best to walk down to Lulworth Cove from here, as the car park at the bottom is expensive; there are lots of fine walks in the area (the inn is near the start of *Good Walks Guide* Walk 27), usually with splendid views. *(Recommended by M E Hughes, J P Cinnamond, Richard Dolphin, Nic James, Jenny and Michael Back, Richard Dolphin, Fiona Holt, Denise Plummer, Jim Froggatt, W C M Jones, Steve and Carolyn Harvey, David Pearman)*

Devenish   Licensee Graham Halliday   Real ale   Meals and snacks, served all the time the pub is open   Restaurant   Children in restaurant and eating area of bar   Very occasional live music   Open 11–2.30, 7–11   Bedrooms tel West Lulworth (092 941) 311; £19(£25B)/£32(£38B)

WORTH MATRAVERS   SY9777   (Isle of Purbeck) Map 2

Square & Compass

At fork of both roads signposted to village from B3069

Sticking firmly to tradition, the old-fashioned main bar here has wall benches around the elbow-polished old tables on the flagstones, and interesting local pictures under its low ceilings. Whitbreads Pompey Royal and Strong Country is tapped from a row of casks behind a couple of hatches in the flagstoned corridor (local fossils back here, and various curios inside the servery), which leads to a more conventional summer bar. Reasonably priced bar snacks include crab sandwiches, home-made pasties or filled rolls and ploughman's; shove-ha'penny, dominoes. There are seats outside on a side lawn that looks down over the village rooftops to the sea showing between the East Man and the West Man (hills that guard the sea approach); on summer evenings you can watch the sun set beyond Portland Bill. The pub is at the start of an OS Walkers Britain walk and on *Good Walks Guide* Walk 25. *(Recommended by Barbara and Norman Wells, Derek Patey, Steve and Carolyn Harvey, Phil and Sally Gorton, David Pearman)*

Whitbreads   Licensee Ray Newman   Real ale   Snacks   Children welcome Occasional live music   Open 11–3, 6–11

Lucky dip

Besides the fully inspected pubs, you might like to try these Lucky Dips recommended to us and described by readers (if you do, please send us reports):

Alderholt [back rd Fordingbridge–Cranborne;[SU1212], *Churchill Arms*: Well furnished local with pub games, quick friendly service, Badger beer, wide range of reasonably priced bar food, garden, swimming pool; children's room; big car park *(Canon G Hollis)*

☆ **Almer** [just off A31 Wimborne Minster—Bere Regis; SY9097], *Worlds End*: Charming 15th-century L-shaped thatched pub with Badger real ales, well renovated red tiles, horsebrasses, wide choice of good value food in eating area decorated with hats and fans (children allowed here), friendly atmosphere; tables out in former stone sheep pen, big well equipped play area; very handy for this stretch of the road *(WHBM)*

☆ **Ansty** [Higher Ansty; ST7603], *Fox*: Notable particularly for its interesting collection of some 800 toby jugs, also lots of colourful plates; cold table and carvery-style food, wide choice of puddings, well equipped children's bar with games and pool table, skittle alley with own bar, piped pop music (can be intrusive); strong local beer brewed for the pub, under pressure but interesting; small swimming pool, caravan site nearby; bedrooms (generous breakfasts) *(Keith and Sian Mitchell, H W and A B Tuffill, LYM)*

Ashley Heath [SU1105], *Struan*: Good straightforward bar food, decent drinks, highly efficient service; bedrooms *(J M Watkinson)*

Beaminster [Clay Lane; ST4701], *Knapp*: Village pub at end of cottage row, with Butcombe and Watneys-related real ales, generously served good value bar snacks and meals inc particularly good vegetarian choice *(G and M Armstrong)*; [Market Sq], *Red Lion*: 17th-century family hotel, small but efficient, with very pleasant staff; Bass, Tetleys and Worthington real ales, substantial bar snacks all day; bedrooms pleasant, clean and comfortable — good value *(G and M Armstrong)*

☆ **Bere Regis** [West St; SY8494], *Royal Oak*: Down-to-earth friendly pub with well kept open-plan modernised bar, good range of low-priced and well made bar food, Flowers Original and Whitbreads Strong Country on handpump, woodburning stove, sensibly placed darts, cribbage, fruit machine; dining room; open all day Fri and Sat; bedrooms *(R Wilson, Mrs Nina Elliott, Nigel Williamson, BB)*

Bournemouth [423 Charminster Rd; SZ0991], *Fiveways*: Busy, friendly pre-war town pub, well updated, with wide choice of usual pub food, Eldridge Pope real ales, no-smoking area, good games room *(Nigel Williamson)*; [6 Ravine Rd, Canford Cliffs], *Nightjar*: Friendly Bass pub with winter log fires, no music, and good value

straightforward bar food — very busy at lunchtime *(John Mason)*

☆ **Bridport** [4 South St; SY4692], *George*: Why don't we get more reports on this civilised and consistently friendly old-fashioned town local? The bar food runs to local fish fresh daily, home-made pies and puddings, decent sandwiches and fine sauté kidneys, they do freshly squeezed orange or grapefruit juice and good applejuice from a local cider farm as well as well kept Palmers real ales, and are open all day — from 8.30 for coffee and croissants; children allowed in dining room; bedrooms *(C M Whitehouse, Ian Phillips, LYM)*

☆ **Broadstone** [Waterloo Rd; junction A349/B3074; SZ0095], *Darbys Corner*: Large comfortably refurbished and well ventilated pub with three areas (one no-smoking) radiating from central bar; big helpings of decent food with bargain lunchtime prices for OAPs, pleasant atmosphere, Badger Best and Tanglefoot *(WHBM, Mr and Mrs R Harrington, Win and Reg Harrington)*

☆ **Buckhorn Weston** [ST7524], *Stapleton Arms*: Spacious pub with comfortable lounge, snug, well equipped carpeted games bar (two pool tables) and nicely furnished restaurant; piped classical music, wide choice of reasonably priced food inc children's helpings and good Sun lunches, friendly locals and landlord, good choice of real ales such as Exmoor, Palmers, Wadworths 6X and Wethereds on handpump, plenty of tables in back garden *(Mr and Mrs B E Witcher, D A B and J V Llewelyn)*

☆ **Buckland Newton** [ST6904], *Gaggle of Geese*: Quiet free house in secluded village, welcoming licensees (formerly making the Eclipse in Winchester a popular main entry), well kept real ale, bar food, elegant bar with distinguished furnishings, spacious pool/snooker and skittle rooms; attractive garden with pond and big play area; goose auction twice a year, other country events; five new bedrooms *(Robert and Elizabeth Scott, N J Hogg)*

☆ **Burton Bradstock** [SY4889], *Three Horseshoes*: Attractive and popular thatched inn with comfortable carpeted lounge, Palmers real ales inc Tally Ho, pleasant and willing staff, good choice of bar food from sandwiches up, inc children's dishes, also separate restaurant; clean lavatories, no piped music, pleasant shingle beach a few minutes' drive away (with NT car park); nice atmosphere; bedrooms *(F Costello)*

Burton Bradstock, *Anchor*: Friendly pub in unspoilt village setting, big helpings of home-made food inc good puddings *(R Wilson)*

Cashmoor [A354 6 miles E of Blandford;

ST9713], *Cashmoor*: Small well run former coaching inn, not over-modernised; fair-sized bar with wishing well, Badger beers, over 60 whiskies, friendly obliging staff, wide range of reasonably priced bar food, restaurant (where children allowed); proclaims itself Pub of the Year 1887 *(WHBM)*

☆ Cerne Abbas [Main St; ST6601], *Red Lion*: Cosy, picturesque and friendly oak-beamed pub, pleasantly refurbished, with well kept real ales such as Wadworths 6X, good atmosphere, generous helpings of good uncomplicated food inc perfectly cooked vegetables, quick service; good value bedrooms *(D K and H M Brenchley, Chris Raisin, Marjorie and David Lamb, J L and S J Power)*

☆ Charlton Marshall [A350 Poole—Blandford; ST9004], *Charlton*: Attractively refurbished country-style bars with wide choice of generously served food, Badger Best and Tanglefoot, quick friendly service, unobtrusive piped music *(Richard Dolphin, S Watkins)*

☆ Charminster [A352 N of Dorchester; SY6793], *Three Compasses*: Friendly village pub with well kept Devenish Royal Wessex, good value food, skittle alley, family room with colour TV; bedrooms *(Nigel Pritchard, Stan Edwards)*

☆ Chetnole [ST6007], *Chetnole Arms*: Small comfortable local in very quiet village, generous helpings of straightforward bar food, well kept real ale, no piped music, genial landlord *(A P Hudson)*
Chickerell [Lower Putton Lane; off B3157; SY6480], *Fishermans Arms*: Two small, comfortable bars with copper-topped tables, aquarium, maps and stuffed swordfish; friendly licensee, well kept Devenish Cornish Original tapped from the cask, restaurant *(Denise Plummer, Jim Froggatt)*; [East St], *Turks Head*: Hotel-restaurant with huge helpings of attractively presented bar food such as massive sandwiches with interesting salads; ploughman's and hot dishes too *(Ian Phillips)*

☆ Chideock [A35 Bridport—Lyme Regis; SY4292], *George*: Thatched 17th-century pub with plush seats in simple dark-beamed lounge, wide choice of straightforward bar food, well kept Palmers real ales, big log fire, family room with pool, darts and other games, various household pets, juke box, tables in back garden; nr GWG23; bedrooms *(John Kirk, Win and Gordon Lambert, Neil and Anita Christopher, Brian and Anna Marsden, LYM)*
Chideock [A35], *Clock*: Attractive thatched village inn with pleasant mix of styles and furnishings in open-plan bar, popular straightforward food, well kept Devenish Wessex, table skittles, brightly lit pool table; restaurant, simple bedrooms; nr GWG23 *(Neil and Anita Christopher, BB)*

☆ Child Okeford [on lane entering village from A357 Sturminster Newton—Blandford], *Union Arms*: Claret-coloured furnishings in bar and restaurant extension from original

traditional core, where high-backed settles huddle around woodburning stove in big stone fireplace; well kept Hook Norton Best and a couple of interesting guest beers on handpump, discreet piped music, lunchtime bar food, some concentration on restaurant; pleasant licensees *(D A B and J V Llewelyn, Nigel Paine, LYM)*
Christchurch [Walkford Rd — OS Sheet 195 map reference 222943; SZ1593], *Amberwood Arms*: Big straightforward but warm and comfortable open-plan bar, good value bar food and restaurant meals, well kept Badger beers on handpump; interesting collection of electric spiders, fruit machines; children welcome *(Mike Beiley)*

☆ Church Knowle [SY9481], *New Inn*: Partly thatched pub looking over the Purbeck hills, can get very busy in summer; stripped stone and high rafters in spacious public bar, cosy lounge, well kept Devenish real ales, decent wines, wide choice of good bar food inc attractive dishes of the day, skittle alley and children's room in separate building *(John Kirk, L Walker, Steve and Carolyn Harvey, Mrs P Powis, LYM)*
Colehill [SU0201], *Horns*: Small pub in heart of country with Badger beers and good choice of food *(John Kirk)*

☆ Corscombe [off A356 Dorchester—Crewkerne; outskirts, towards Halstock; ST5105], *Fox*: Lots of interesting things in idiosyncratic pub with obvious horse and hunting connections, old-fashioned furnishings, well kept real ales such as Devenish JD and Exmoor tapped from the cask, short choice of bar food; seats across quiet lane on streamside lawn *(MCG, Olive Carroll, L Walker, Chris Raisin, Heather Sharland, LYM)*
Cranborne [SU0513], *Sheaf of Arrows*: Very welcoming pub with somewhat old-fashioned decor; bar food inc good roast beef lunch; children welcome *(Susan Wilkie)*
Dewlish [SY7798], *Royal Oak*: Archetypal country local with well kept beer, good basic bar food inc good gammon steaks prepared by landlord himself *(PB, HB)*

☆ Dorchester [Monmouth Rd], *Bakers Arms*: Bar dominated by tiled wall with two big steel-doored ovens — used to be combination bakery/off licence; well presented simple home-made food from sandwiches to steaks, at fair prices, well kept Eldridge Pope ales, friendly landlord, enjoyable atmosphere *(Nic James, Steve Huggins)*

☆ Dorchester [High East St], *Kings Arms*: Smart and comfortable hotel bar with well kept Eldridge Pope ales and wide choice of freshly prepared bar food inc roasts and vegetarian dishes; close associations with Nelson and Hardy's *Mayor of Casterbridge*; bedrooms *(A P Hudson, LYM)*

☆ Dorchester [20 High West St], *Royal Oak*: Busy central pub, simple, warm and clean with comfortable atmosphere, bar with dining area up a few steps, another across hallway; pleasant quick service, good value straightforward bar food *(B A Chambers, R*

Blatch)

Dorchester [High West St], *Old Ship*: Simply furnished, with good value bar food inc vegetarian dishes, well kept Eldridge Pope real ales *(David Pearman)*; [A352 towards Wareham], *Trumpet Major*: Large pub with sporting-theme public bar and dining room off, lounge, restaurant; well kept beer, wide choice of good value food inc excellent mixed grills, tables on pleasant terrace, spacious garden with good play area *(Stan Edwards)*

Easton [SY6870], *New Inn*: Basic pub, but well decorated, with plenty of locals, warm welcome, helpful service, good bar food *(Richard Dolphin)*

☆ **Evershot** [off A37 8 miles S of Yeovil; ST5704], *Acorn*: Decent wines and several changing real ales, some kept under light blanket pressure, in comfortable L-shaped bar with stripped stone, fine old fireplaces, somewhat frilly furnishings; games in public bar; bar food from sandwiches to fish and steaks, piped music; good Hardy walking country; children in skittle alley (plans to change this into bar extension) and restaurant; bedrooms comfortable *(David Pearman, Jonathan and Helen Palmer, John Nash, Mr and Mrs J H Adam, Heather Sharland, Roy McIsaac, Shirley Pielou, LYM)*

Ferndown [A31; SU0700], *Smugglers Haunt*: A Roast Inn, with some concentration on restaurant, though bar food good value; Whitbreads Pompey Royal *(Nigel Pritchard)*

☆ **Fiddleford** [A357 Sturminster Newton—Blandford Forum; ST8013], *Fiddleford Inn*: Pleasant and attractive old pub with vast flagstones in nicely furnished bar, wide choice of bar food (not cheap), interesting well kept real ales inc guest beers, good garden with play area; bedrooms clean and comfortable, with substantial breakfasts *(Kenneth Philpot, Richard Dolphin, LYM)*

Hilfield [ST6305], *Good Hope*: Attractive pub in isolated scenic spot, friendly licensees and attentive staff, unusual choice of good food in bar and restaurant *(Henry and Margaret Midwinter)*

☆ **Hinton St Mary** [just off B3092 a mile N of Sturminster; ST7816], *White Horse*: Popular and attractive country inn doing well under current regime, with good fish and wide choice of other fresh food served quickly and generously in light and cheerful extended lounge bar with cushioned settles and chairs; darts in larger public bar, no piped music, Wadworths 6X; booking recommended for good restaurant Sun lunch; quiet village with superb manor house and medieval tithe barn *(Donald Smith, Barbara M McHugh, S Watkins, Brian Chambers)*

Holywell [A37 Yeovil—Dorchester; ST5904], *Strangways Arms*: Large, quiet family-run village pub with clean and comfortable bars and good range of well cooked good value food; very helpful staff; bedrooms *(K R Harris)*

☆ **Kingston** [B3069; SY9579], *Scott Arms*: Well worth knowing for the superb view of Corfe Castle from the garden, and the rambling layout of the original part is interesting; this part is now largely devoted to efficient fast food service for families, with drinks served in modern Barn Bar extension; on GWG25, in beautiful village; bedrooms comfortable *(John Fazakerley, C M Whitehouse, R J Walden, P A Barfield, Ken and Barbara Turner, Adrian M Kelly, M E Hughes, Barbara and Norman Wells, W J Wonham, LYM)*

☆ **Knap Corner** [B3092 S of Gillingham; 1/2 mile N of East Stour A30 Shaftesbury—Sherborne; ST8023], *Crown*: Small, delightful pub with gorgeous log fire in stone fireplace at one end, bar at other end; friendly licensees and locals, two labradors, unobtrusive instrumental piped music, Wiltshire Stonehenge, Old Grumble and Old Devil on handpump and good choice of decent food *(Nigel Paine)*

Leigh [the one nr Sherborne; ST6208], *Carpenters Arms*: Charming country inn recently extensively renovated, unusual central fireplace in lounge, reasonably priced bar food; skittle alley, public bar with snooker and pool tables; plans to convert wing into bedrooms *(B A Chambers)*

Longham [A348 Ferndown—Poole; SZ0698], *Angel*: Good lively family place with wide choice of food (may be just barbecued burgers Mon evening), piped music *(Nigel Pritchard)*; *White Hart*: Low, snug and comfortable open-plan cottage-style pub with two fireplaces, two collies, lots of high-backed Windsor-type chairs; good range of food from ploughman's to steak (there may be a wait); newspapers available, lots of locals *(Ian Phillips)*

Lyme Regis [The Cobb; SY3492], *Olde Ship*: Set almost on the Cobb itself, with a small sea-view balcony *(F Costello)*; [25 Marine Parade, The Cobb], *Royal Standard*: Friendly and popular little pub leading to beach through suntrap walled and partly canvas-roofed courtyard; well kept Palmers, quickly served home-made bar food inc fresh crab sandwiches *(R Fieldhouse)*

☆ **Lytchett Minster** [Dorchester Rd; SY9593], *Bakers Arms*: Lively holiday atmosphere in well run efficient pub, very much bigger than you'd guess from its thatched facade; extraordinary collections from Elton John's 1940s Wurlitzer juke box to a working glass beehive; reliable food from soup and sandwiches through basket meals and help-yourself salads to steaks, well kept Flowers Original and Wadworths 6X, piped music, games, skittle alley; children in eating area — and adventure playground outside *(Jenny and Michael Back, Denise Plummer, Jim Froggatt, Nigel Gibbs, Stan Edwards, LYM)*

☆ **Marnhull** [B3092; ST7718], *Crown*: It's a long time since we've had a report on this attractive thatched inn, with its oak beams, old settles and elm tables, broad flagstones and big log fire much as they were when Hardy modelled the Pure Drop at Marlott

on it, in *Tess of the d'Urbervilles;* small more modern lounge, reasonably priced bar food from sandwiches through generous omelettes to steak, well kept Badger Best and Tanglefoot; children in eating area; also restaurant; bedrooms good value *(LYM)*
Marshwood [SY3799], *Bottle:* Simple country pub with well kept Ushers, traditional games and skittle alley; usually has reasonably priced bar food and is handy for pretty walking country *(David Pearman, LYM)*
☆ **Melbury Osmond** [Roman Rd, Drive End; ST5707], *Rest & Welcome:* Clean, cosy, warm and welcoming little pub; limited but good choice of straightforward food, well kept beer, good service *(T Billington, H J Stephens)*
☆ **Milton Abbas** [ST8001], *Hambro Arms:* Like the beautifully landscaped 18th-century village, this pretty inn is a powerful draw in the tourist season, but even then service in the airy opened-up bar is normally quick and friendly; wide choice of good bar food (sandwiches, steak and kidney pudding, game pie, sweet and sour pork, chicken and plaice recommended), well kept Devenish JD and Royal Wessex on handpump; on GWG24; neat bedrooms, inc at least one four-poster *(Shirley Pielou, J R Williams, Mr and Mrs J H Adam, E A George, N Paine, Bernard Phillips, LYM)*
Morden [off B3075, between A35 and A31 E of Bere Regis; SY9195], *Cock & Bottle:* Friendly country local with easy mix of regulars and strangers; clean and neat, with good basic food prepared by landlord's wife; Badger Best and Tanglefoot *(WHBM)*
Mosterton [High St; ST4505], *Admiral Hood:* Wide range of food, especially fish, in quiet and popular dining pub with neatly furnished spacious L-shaped bar, well kept Watneys-related real ales on handpump, coal fire in handsome stone fireplace, quick service, simple skittle alley behind the thatched 18th-century stone building *(R A and D M Hill, BB)*
☆ **Mudeford** [beyond huge seaside car park at Mudeford Pier — OS Sheet 195 map reference 182916; SZ1891], *Haven House:* Quaint old part-flagstoned heart to much-extended seaside pub with Devenish ales and good value bar food from sandwiches to crab salad; family cafeteria, tables on sheltered terrace; you can walk by the sea for miles from here *(WHBM, Ian Phillips, LYM)*
Pamphill [OS Sheet 195 map reference 995003; ST9900], *Vine:* Tiny, simple pub in rural surroundings run by the same family for three or four generations; well cared-for feel, Whitbreads Strong Country on handpump and simple bar food inc fresh sandwiches and ploughman's; handy for Kingston Lacy (NT) *(WHBM)*
☆ **Piddlehinton** [SY7197], *Thimble:* Lovely old listed thatched pub, creeper-clad and quite small inside, doing well under newish regime; glistening bar with collection of thimbles above, good wooden tables and

chairs, well kept Badger Best and Tanglefoot, Marstons Pedigree and Devenish Steam on handpump, wide range of food inc good sandwiches and huge puddings, helpful service; stream alongside with little bridge, friendly goat in garden; homely good value bedrooms, with decent breakfasts *(WHBM, Caroline Wright, Freddy Costello)*
☆ **Poole** [The Quay; SZ0190], *Lord Nelson:* Large friendly waterside pub with nautical theme and maritime relics and artefacts, but a genuine feel of being used by fishermen, too, with interesting little corners, friendly staff, well kept Badger and Gales beers on handpump, and lunchtime food; lively and busy at lunchtime and later evening (when there may be a band); outside seats *(Nigel Gibbs, R A Nelson)*
Poole [Sandbanks Rd, Lilliput], *Beehive:* Pleasant family pub with good atmosphere, enormous eating area for those with children, good food (not cheap, but worth it), well kept beer, garden with big sensibly segregated play area and barbecue *(Mr and Mrs Edwicker, Mr and Mrs A P Reeves);* [The Quay], *Jolly Sailor:* Waterfront pub with good atmosphere and some unusual dishes; busy at lunchtime and in late evening; outside seats *(Nigel Gibbs);* [Quayside], *Poole Arms:* Magnificent green-tiled facade of waterfront local looking across harbour to Brownsea Island; handy for Poole Aquarium, with lively evening atmosphere, Whitbreads Strong Country, good ladies' darts team Thurs *(LYM);* [Longfleet Rd/Fernside Rd], *Shah of Persia:* Good atmosphere, wide choice of generous good food at reasonable prices — especially steak and kidney pie; Eldridge Pope beers; children welcome *(Mr and Mrs A P Reeves)*
☆ **Portland Bill** [SY6870], *Pulpit:* Pleasant and comfortably refurbished pub in interesting spot near Pulpit Rock, with great sea views; well kept Gibbs Mew real ales, friendly obliging staff, piped music, food in bar and restaurant *(Philip Whitehead, Sidney Wells, Denise Plummer, Jim Froggatt)*
☆ **Shaftesbury** [The Commons; ST8622], *Grosvenor:* Old wisteria-covered coaching house (now THF), with small fish pond in front; public bar used by locals, with cheap bar food inc soup, large ploughman's, one or two hot dishes and help-yourself salads; ask Reception if you can see the magnificently carved oak 19th-century Chevy Chase sideboard in the first-floor lounge (not always possible as used for private meetings); bedrooms *(B A Chambers, Barbara M McHugh)*
Sherborne [Greenhill; ST6316], *Antelope:* Good home-cooked and generously served interesting food in both bar and restaurant *(SJE);* [Cooks Lane (nr abbey)], *Digby Tap:* Simple, lively town-centre pub with plenty of character and seats outside; has been popular for interesting real ales such as Smiles, farm cider, and bar food, but no recent reports *(News please);* [Higher Cheap St], *George:* Eldridge Pope pub, brightened

up under new regime; full range of beers and enterprising bar food inc traditional dishes, well cooked and generously served *(Joan and Michel Hooper-Immins)*; [Horsecastles], *Skippers*: More locals than tourists, and imaginative bar food inc red snapper, vegetable pie, good local and other cheeses; small restaurant, King & Barnes and other small-brewery guest beers *(Robert W Buckle)*

Sixpenny Handley [B3081; ST9917], *Star*: Welcoming and well kept village pub good real ales, bar food, seats outside *(Anon)*

Southbourne [Broadway; OS Sheet 195 map reference 155914; SZ1591], *Saxon King*: Large and clean, with efficient friendly service, Eldridge Pope Dorchester, Dorset and Royal Oak; food inc sandwiches and ploughman's as well as hot dishes, with separate dining room; second bar with pool, darts and juke box; handy for Hengistbury Head *(Keith Widdowson)*

☆ **Studland** [SZ0382], *Bankes Arms*: The special feature is the wonderful peaceful spot above one of England's best beaches, giving good views of Poole Harbour and Bournemouth Bay; homely atmosphere in modest but friendly bar, good choice of simple bar food served generously, welcoming staff, well kept Marstons Pedigree; nr start GWG26 and south-western Coast Path; bedrooms clean and comfortable *(E G Parish, Barbara and Norman Wells, Mrs H M T Carpenter, Barbara Hatfield)*

Studland [Beach Rd], *Manor House*: Good sandwiches with cheerful and homely atmosphere, but strictly not a pub — a comfortable country house hotel; bedrooms *(E G Parish)*

Sturminster Marshall [SY9499], *Black Horse*: Good, friendly service, pleasant atmosphere, well kept Badger ales, bar food; handy for NT Kingston Lacey *(Theo Schofield)*

☆ **Sturminster Newton** [A357; ST7814], *Red Lion*: Small, homely and cosy, with warmly welcoming staff, pleasant unhurried service, relaxing atmosphere, well kept beers, good reasonably priced food, log fire *(John Knighton)*

Sturminster Newton [Market Sq], *White Hart*: Clean, friendly and pleasant old pub in centre of small market town with good range of nicely presented food (home-made soup) and Badger beers *(K R Harris)*

☆ **Sutton Poyntz** [SY7083], *Springhead*: Pat and Debbie Jackson who made the New Fountain at Whimple in Devon such a civilised and attractive pub, with simple lunchtime bar food and remarkable evening meals using all fresh ingredients, well kept beers and interesting wines, moved to this airy and cleanly refurbished place with its stunning views in summer 1990 — too late for us to inspect as a potential main entry for this new edition, but an obvious candidate *(News please)*

Swanage [1 Burlington Rd; SZ0278], *Pines*: Good, reasonably priced food, courteous service and coffee room with view of bay;

bedrooms *(N M Glover)*; [High St], *Purbeck*: Friendly welcome in warm softly lit stone-walled pub *(Derek Patey)*

Swyre [B3157; SY5288], *Bull*: Pleasantly redecorated lounge bar with good range of well kept beers inc Wadworths 6X, and good reasonably priced food from ploughman's to steaks *(Mr and Mrs N Palfrey)*

Sydling St Nicholas [SY6399], *Greyhound*: Recently reopened after refurb, tasteful renovation; well kept beer and promising food *(J L and S J Power)*

☆ **Tarrant Gunville** [Tarrant Hinton; ST9212], *Bugle Horn*: Well furnished country pub with pleasant and welcoming licensees, tasteful and comfortably furnished lounge bar, Ringwood and Wadworths 6X, usual bar food, seats in garden *(Barbara M McHugh, Brian Chambers, JM, PM)*

Tolpuddle [SY7994], *Martyrs*: Large, tidy and straightforward roadside pub, friendly staff, well kept Badger and good value varied bar food *(John Hayward)*

Trent [ST5918], *Rose & Crown*: Converted farmhouse by beautiful old country church, relaxed atmosphere, books over the log fire, flagstone floors, original bar counter, good oak settles, some nice pictures and lots of freshly cut flowers; well cooked good value food specialising in fresh local fish, real ales such as Hook Norton and Wadworths 6X tapped from the cask *(Freddy Costello)*

☆ **Uploders** [SY5093], *Crown*: Recently extended, with and adjoining former beamed stable tastefully decorated and fitted out with good wooden tables and chairs; good food from cheese salad or lasagne to baked halibut with prawns or Dover sole with an elaborate sauce, and home-made puddings like cherry pie and jam roly-poly — oven cooking, no microwave; well kept Badgers, hard-working young licensees, tables on small back lawn *(Jon and Jacquie Payne, J L Simpson, Barbara M McHugh)*

☆ **Upwey** [B3159, nr junction A354 — OS Sheet 194 map reference 666845; SY6684], *Masons Arms*: Fine atmosphere in largely unspoilt bar decorated with photos of submarines and *Ark Royal*, fine collection of caps, shillelaghs and all sorts of plates, prints, fox brushes and oddments; Devenish ales, particularly good value bar food inc fine salads, skittle alley; attractive garden, big children's play area *(Wendy and Ian Phillips)*

Upwey [A354 N of Weymouth, away from village], *Old Ship*: Good bar food in old pub known to have been used by Thomas Hardy; character bar with big fireplace, skittle alley, well kept beer, garden *(John Hayward)*

☆ **Wareham** [South St; SY9287], *Quay*: Pub in charming quayside spot, with two spacious stripped-stone bars, open fire, friendly young staff, well presented generous bar food inc vegetarian dishes, trendy music, good beer; parking nearby can be difficult *(Jacquie and Jon Payne, WHBM)*

Wareham [41 North St; A351, N end of

town], *Kings Arms*: Flagstoned central corridor to back serving counter divides the two traditonal bars of this thatched town pub; Whitbreads Strong Country and Pompey Royal well kept, reasonably priced bar food (not Fri—Sun evenings), back garden *(LYM)*

☆ **West Knighton** [SY7387], *New Inn*: Clean and well managed refurbished Devenish pub, full of character, warm welcome; attractive home cooking in bar and reasonably priced restaurant, Devenish Royal Wessex on handpump, country wines, skittle alley, garden; children's room *(Charles Bardswell, C A Hall, R B Crail)*

☆ **West Stafford** [SY7289], *Wise Man*: Comfortable thatched two-bar pub with lots of toby jugs hanging from beams in lounge; clean and tidy, great welcome, super beer and excellent, cheap and well presented food inc good country ham and eggs and some vegetarian dishes, in big helpings; nr Hardy's cottage *(John Voos, Nic James)*

West Stour [ST7822], *Ship*: Small well kept 18th-century local with big log fire, intimate split-level restaurant, garden behind and comfortable bedrooms; has been praised for well kept real ales, good value nicely presented food and attentive service, but no recent reports *(News please)*

Weymouth [85 The Esplanade; SY6778], *Cork & Bottle*: Pleasantly old-fashioned cellar bar with bare boards and lots of interesting jugs and pots hanging from ceiling and walls; well kept Marstons Pedigree and Wadworths 6X, simple bar food inc freshly prepared pizzas *(Peter Griffiths)*; [Custom House Quay], *George*: Quayside pub, still attractive after modernisation and extension; Badger Best and Tanglefoot, tasty good value bar food *(Joan and Michel Hooper-Immins)*; [Dorchester Rd], *Old Ship*: Spotless, with nautical theme; particularly good

home-baked ham; [outskirts], *Spa*: Friendly and pleasant inside, with good value food, friendly staff, surprisingly big play area behind *(Stan Edwards)*

Wimborne Minster [SZ0199], *Dormers*: Completely refurbished with large, light conservatory, well kept beer, and comprehensive menu inc Poole cockles; pleasant gardens *(John Kirk)*; [The Square], *Kings Head*: Friendly, warm atmosphere; restaurant particularly good, with well cooked food and fast service; comfortable bedrooms *(B C and E L Armstrong)*; [Uddens Cross; former A31, some way eastwards], *Old Thatch*: Pleasant spot, attractive thatched building recently renovated in Beefeater style; clean and modern, ample seating, one big bar with no-smoking eating area, Flowers Original and Wadworths 6X, standard menu from sandwiches to steak, pleasant service, piped music, big car park and outside seats; children's area *(Anon)*

Winterborne Zelston [A31 Wimborne—Dorchester; SY8997], *Botany Bay*: Free house with good choice of beers; good food inc home-made pies, many vegetarian dishes and more unusual dishes such as avocado and Poole crab; restaurant *(John Kirk)*

☆ **Winterbourne Abbas** [A35 W of Dorchester; SY6190], *Coach & Horses*: Spacious recently refurbished pub, big on food, with reasonable prices and wide choice from rolls, sandwiches and ploughman's through good help-yourself salads to huge 20oz T-bone steaks and carvery with succulent joints; really welcoming atmosphere, brasses, hunting horns and pictures, stools with saddle seats, lots of barrel tables and comfortable chairs, also restaurant; generous helpings; attentive licensee, polite staff; bedrooms *(T Muston, Mrs S A Bishop, Sidney Drury)*

Durham *see* Northumbria

Essex

New entries here this year include the Kings Arms at Broomfield (the licensees have moved here with much of their former team from the Eight Bells in Saffron Walden – where they gained a great reputation for good food), the Seabrights Barn at Great Baddow (an outstanding family pub), the White Hart at Great Saling with its oaken Tudor gallery, and the cosy and friendly White Horse at Pleshey. New licensees are ringing the changes at the Three Horseshoes at Bannister Green, the Anchor at Danbury and the Dolphin at Stisted; at all, preliminary reports are promising. Among other main entries, pubs doing especially well at the moment include the Axe & Compasses at Arkesden (good food, in a pretty village), the Half Moon at Belchamp St Paul (its temperature-controlled cellar is a success – and, unusually, it keeps real German lager), the Bell at Castle Hedingham (its one-acre garden has been particularly pretty this last summer), the Swan well placed by the striking Victorian viaduct at Chappel, the riverside Swan (or Henny Swan, as they're punningly calling it now) near Great Henny, the heavy-beamed White Hart at Great Yeldham, the Rainbow & Dove at Hastingwood (so handy for the motorway), the sporting Bell at Horndon on the Hill, the Crooked Billet by the water at Leigh on Sea, the cosy Green Man at Little Braxted, the Gardeners Arms in Loughton, the Viper by the woods at Mill Green, the Bell on its rare Essex hill at Purleigh, the Hoop at Stock (outstanding for real ales), the delightfully cosy Cap & Feathers at Tillingham, and the Cats at Woodham Walter (a good summer pub). Particularly promising pubs in the Lucky Dip section at the end of the chapter include the Cock at Beazley End, Lion & Lamb at Canfield End, Cricketers at Clavering, several possibilities in and around Coggeshall – a marvellous village for good pubs, the Square & Compasses at Fuller Street, Plough at Great Chesterford, Moreton Massey at Moreton, Alma Arms at Navestock, Ferryboat at North Fambridge, Eight Bells at Saffron Walden under its new regime, Swan at Stanway, Swan at Thaxted, Volunteer near Waltham Abbey and Fleur de Lys at Widdington. Pub prices in Essex are a shade higher than the national average, perhaps partly because of the way that the big national brewing combines control more pubs than usual here. Though we found drinks prices in pubs tied to regional or local breweries here dramatically lower, there simply aren't enough of these to put a significant dent in the county's pub prices – drinks prices in free houses here are just a few pence lower than in the national breweries' tied houses. The Three Horseshoes at Bannister Green and Dolphin at Stisted stand out for cheap drinks. The Three Horseshoes again, and the Green Man at Little Braxted, Viper at Mill Green, Bell at Purleigh and Hoop at Stock, deserve special credit for giving a choice between decent snacks at under £1 and bargain main dishes at under £3; the Old Anchor at Feering and Cap & Feathers at Tillingham are also good for really cheap snacks.

ARKESDEN   TL4834 Map 5

Axe & Compasses ★ ⊘

Village signposted from B1038 – but B1039 from Wendens Ambo, then forking left, is prettier; OS Sheet 154 map reference 482344

The range of food in this pretty village pub is at its best in the evening, when there's a different theme depending on the day: on Monday, a vegetarian menu (£4.50); Tuesday, fresh fish and scampi from Lowestoft (from £4.95); Wednesday, an £8.50 meal with steak or plaice as the main course, including a glass of wine or pint of bitter; Thursdays traditional English cooking – sausages, cottage pie, steak and kidney pie or lamb cutlets (from £3.25); Fridays and Saturdays a grander range of full meals (£16) as well as bar snacks; Sundays, roast lunches (£9.50) and evening pasta (£5.50). At lunchtime the food includes very good home-made soup such as tomato or minestrone (£1), generous wholemeal sandwiches (from £1.50), various ploughman's (from £2.50; the Stilton one is good), sausages, fish and grills with good, big chips, and home-made daily specials – steak and kidney pie, beef and mushroom hot pot, vegetarian dishes, a different roast three times a week, and so forth (around £4), and puddings that include moist chocolate rum gateau, lovely lemon soufflé or home-made ice-cream specialities (from £1.95). They also do a big Christmas lunch (bookable up to nine months in advance). The rambling and comfortable carpeted saloon bar is distinctively furnished with cushioned oak and elm seats, quite a few easy chairs, old wooden tables, lots of brasses on the walls, a bright coal fire, and a particularly happy atmosphere. The smaller public bar, with cosy built-in settles, has sensibly placed darts, shove-ha'penny, dominoes, cribbage and a fruit machine. Greene King BBA ('Rayments') and IPA on handpump, good house wines, and several malts; part of the bar is set aside for non-alcoholic drinks. There are seats outside, on a side terrace with colourful hanging baskets; there's a popular barbecue here too on Saturday and Sunday lunchtimes – weather permitting. The village is pretty. (Recommended by Gwen and Peter Andrews, TBB, Sidney and Erna Wells, SJC, Derek Patey, R P Hastings, A M Kelly, J S B Vereker, Dennis Royles, WTF, Mrs P Russell, R L Turnham)

Greene King   Licensee Jerry Roberts   Real ale   Meals and snacks (not Mon evening) Restaurant tel Saffron Walden (0799) 550272   Children in restaurant   Open 11–2.30, 6–11; closed evening 25 Dec

BANNISTER GREEN   TL6920 Map 5

Three Horseshoes

Village signposted with Felsted from A131 Chelmsford–Braintree opposite St Annes Castle pub; also signposted from B1417, off A120 Dunmow–Braintree at Felsted signpost

New licensees seem to have kept things on an even keel in this atmospheric place; the extended saloon bar on the right has an interesting collection of pewter mugs hanging over the counter, horse brasses, and big fireplace. The bar on the left has a low 17th-century beam-and-plank ceiling, a high brown panelled dado, dark plush ribbed wall banquettes and spindleback chairs around neat tables, and lots of brass and a musket decorating its brick fireplace. Lunchtime bar food now includes sandwiches (from 75p, toasties from 95p), filled baked potatoes (from £1), ploughman's (from £1.90), salads (from £1.95), omelettes (from £2.15), and plaice (£2.85); in the evening the emphasis is on main dishes, with soup (85p), lasagne (£2.50), chargrilled chicken (£4.50), and steak (£6). Ridleys on handpump, and a good choice of whiskies; darts, fruit machine, shove-ha'penny, dominoes, cribbage and ring-the-bull (rare in Essex). The neat garden to the side of this low, dormer-windowed and tiled white building has picnic-table sets under cocktail parasols among fruit trees, and there are tables out on the big, quiet village green. (Recommended by Gwen and Peter Andrews, Barbara and Norman Wells, Graham Oddey, J H Walker; reports on the new regime please)

Ridleys   Licensees Liam and Diane MacVeigh   Real ale   Meals and snacks (not Mon evening)   Children welcome   Open 11–3, 6–11, all day Sat (not winter)

BELCHAMP ST PAUL TL7942 Map 5

Half Moon

Cole Green; Belchamp St Paul is on good back road Great Yeldham–Cavendish; the Belchamps are quite well signposted within the Sudbury–Clare–Sible Hedingham triangle

The beamed lounge area in this pretty 16th-century place has cushioned built-in wall benches and Windsor chairs on the dark red carpet, a glass-fronted solid fuel stove, and a snug cubby by the serving counter. The lively locals' bar has darts, dominoes, fruit machine, and piped music; in summer, a bar in the back beer garden serves soft drinks and so forth. Bar snacks range from sandwiches on request (from £1.35), home-made soup (£1.55), and ham or mixed cheese ploughman's (£2.95), and locally made sausages (£2.75), to more substantial meals (particularly in the evening) such as vegetarian pancakes (£4.75), chicken in a cream and champagne sauce (£7.25), and peppered sirloin steak (£7.95); puddings (from £1.30); with 36 hours' notice they'll prepare more elaborate dishes. Adnams Southwold, Greene King IPA and Abbot and Nethergate Bitter on handpump from the temperature-controlled cellar, with Old Growler in winter; they also have Hackerpschorr, a full-flavoured real lager from Munich. The village green, close to this white thatched building, is very attractive. (*Recommended by Barbara and Norman Wells; more reports please*)

Free house   Licensees Bob and Deni Horsfield   Real ale   Meals and snacks (12–2, 7.30–10; not Mon or Tues evenings)   Restaurant tel Clare (0787) 277402   Well behaved children welcome; Fri or Sat evenings if parents have booked   Open 11.30–3, 7–11; closed evening 25 Dec

BROOMFIELD TL7010 Map 5

Kings Arms ✪

A130 N of Chelmsford

Mr Moore used to run the Eight Bells in Saffron Walden, which has been a popular main entry with very good food. He's now moved to this half-timbered village pub, bringing his manager and several other staff too. The two heavy-beamed and dimly lit rooms of the bar are divided by a central brick chimney with arched brick fireplaces on either side (one with an unusual shuttered painting of the pub above it) and have brocade-cushioned reddish country chairs, some plush built-in window seats, and a mix of tables including a rather fine one built around a central standing timber; one side is more set out for eating – pleasantly so, with flowers on the tables. The atmosphere throughout is quietly relaxed and chatty, and the staff pleasant and helpful. Good bar food from a menu that changes daily includes home-made soup (£1.75), giant French baguette (£2.25), home-made chicken liver and brandy pâté or ploughman's (£2.95), guacamole (£3.25), vegetarian dishes such as stilton-topped mushrooms baked in cider and thyme with garlic bread (£4.50), tagliatelle with cream, smoked ham, mushrooms and garlic or braised beef in ale with garlic croûtons (£4.95), fresh fillet of plaice with a cream and tarragon sauce (£5.95), fresh Thaxted duckling with a herb and black cherry sauce (£6.50), steaks (from £9.95), fresh lobster mayonnaise (£12.95), and home-made puddings such as rich chocolate and brandy pot or apple and apricot crumble (£1.95); children's meals (from £1.50 – they will try to do half adult helpings where possible if preferred). Well kept Tetleys and a guest beer like Adnams, Greene King IPA or Nethergate on handpump, good wines by the glass or bottle, and several malt whiskies, ports, armagnacs and sherries, as well as regular coffee, cappuccino with whipped cream and espresso, and hot chocolate with whipped cream; fruit machine, quiet piped music. There are some picnic-table sets in front of the pub by particularly pretty tubs and hanging baskets, though the road that runs alongside is very busy. (*Recommended by Gwen and Peter Andrews*)

Ind Coope (Allied)   Licensee Robin Moore   Real ale   Meals and snacks (12–2, 6.30–9.30 or 10 Sat; not Sun or Mon evenings)   Children in eating area only   Open 11–2.30, 6.30–11; closed 25 and 26 Dec

CASTLE HEDINGHAM   TL7835 Map 5

Bell

B1058 E of Sible Hedingham, towards Sudbury

In the popular, beamed and timbered saloon bar here there are Jacobean-style seats and Windsor chairs around oak tables; a few steps, beyond the standing timbers left from a knocked-through wall, lead up to a little gallery. A games room behind the traditionally furnished public bar has dominoes and cribbage; piped pop music. Bar food includes sausage bap (£2), ploughman's (£2.20), half pint of smoked prawns with garlic dip (£2.75), lasagne (£3.30), steak and Guinness pie or lamb hot pot (£3.50), and hot treacle tart (£1.60); well kept Greene King IPA and Abbot tapped from the cask. Besides seats on a small terrace in the car park, there's a fine big walled garden behind the pub – an acre or so, with grass, trees and shrubs. Lucia the Great Dane may be ambling around. *(Recommended by Barbara and Norman Wells, David Cardy, Gwen and Peter Andrews, R M Sparkes)*

Grays (who no longer brew)   Licensee Mrs Sandra Ferguson   Real ale   Meals and snacks (12–2, 7–10, till 9.30 Sun; not Mon evening except Bank Holidays)   Children welcome (not in public bar)   Open 11.30–2.30(3 Sat), 6.15–11; closed evening 25 Dec

CHAPPEL   TL8927 Map 5

Swan

Wakes Colne; pub visible just off A604 Colchester–Halstead

Just below the garden of this lovely old pub is a splendid Victorian viaduct, which carries the Colne Valley Steam Railway; the Railway Centre itself, a must for steam enthusiasts, is only ¼ mile away. The bar area is a spacious, rambling and low-beamed affair, with banquettes around lots of dark tables, red velvet curtains on brass rings hanging from wooden curtain rails, and one or two swan pictures and plates on the white and partly panelled walls; some standing oak timbers divide off side areas, and there are a few attractive tiles above the very big fireplace (log fires in winter, lots of plants in summer); good, relaxing atmosphere. Bar food includes filled French rolls (£1.25), sandwiches (from £1.25), ploughman's (from £2.50), home-cooked ham, gammon steak and pineapple, cod or home-made steak and kidney pie (all £3.45), and sirloin steak (£7.95). Greene King IPA and Mauldons Bitter on handpump, and a good selection of wines by the glass; faint piped music; pool, cribbage, fruit machine, space game and juke box in the biggish well furnished public bar. The very sheltered suntrap cobbled courtyard has a slightly continental flavour, with its big tubs overflowing with flowers, parasols and French street signs; it's flanked on one side by the glass wall of the restaurant extension. The garden (through which runs the River Colne) has picnic-tables sets on grass stretching away from the big car park. *(Recommended by Barbara and Norman Wells, Gwen and Peter Andrews, John Evans)*

Free house   Licensees Terence and Frances Martin   Real ale   Meals and snacks (11.30–2.30, 6.30–10; not 25 or 26 Dec)   Restaurant (no bookings)   Children in restaurant and eating area of bar   Open 11–3, 6–11

DANBURY   TL7805 Map 5

Anchor

Runsell Green; just off A414 Chelmsford–Maldon

The open-plan, heavily beamed and sturdily timbered bar here, popular with locals, is furnished with comfortable plush settles and stools around simple modern oak tables, and has masses of brass and copper around its fireplaces (including an engaging clock with a tinkling chime), and decorative plates on the cream walls; the no-smoking conservatory/family room becomes a restaurant in the evening. Well kept Adnams, Bass and Charrington IPA on handpump, and an extensive wine list; fruit machine and juke box in a side room. Bar food includes sandwiches (£1), soup (£1.50), ploughman's (£2.35), home-made pâté (£2.75), pan fried mussels in garlic butter or devilled whitebait (£2.65), steak, kidney and mushroom pie in Guinness, pork with apple sauce (£6.25), schnitzel (£6.95) and steaks. The raised lawn in front of this listed building (which was probably originally a yeoman farmer's in the 15th century) has picnic-table sets; swings behind. The new licensees have been described as outgoing by readers. *(Recommended by Gwen and Peter Andrews, Quentin Williamson, Shirley Pielou, Derek Patey, Tony Tucker, Peter Griffiths; more reports on the new regime please)*

Charringtons (Bass)   Licensee Mr Aris   Real ale   Meals and snacks   Evening restaurant tel Danbury (024 541) 2457   Children in conservatory   Open 11–3(4 Sat), 6–11

DEDHAM   TM0533   Map 5

Marlborough Head ⊗

Consistently good bar food includes outstanding soup (£1.20), sandwiches (from £1.20, £2 for sweetcure ham with cream cheese, walnut and onion), baked potato with cheese (£1.10, with crunchy salad £1.50), ploughman's with home-made chutney (£2.50), smoked salmon pâté (£2.75), bacon, mushroom and tomato quiche (£3.50), lentil croquettes with a tomato sauce (£3.50), home-made Scotch egg (£3.75), rabbit in mustard sauce (£4.40), Aga-roasted back bacon steak with peaches (£4.75), lamb chops with Cumberland sauce (£5), and steak (£8); puddings – such as home-made treacle tart (£1.75) or sherry trifle (£2.25) – are popular; get there early if you want a table. There's a wealth of finely carved woodwork in the cheerful central lounge; the refurbished beamed and timbered Constable bar is popular for eating, with many tables (which have a numbered pebble for ordering food) in wooden alcoves around its plum-coloured carpet. Well kept Adnams and Benskins on handpump; friendly service. The timbered pub is opposite Constable's old school. Seats in the garden at the back. *(Recommended by Gwen and Peter Andrews, R C Morgan, Barbara and Norman Wells, David Cardy, Tony Gayfer, Jenny Cantle, Helen Crookston, Jan and Ian Alcock, M J Morgan, E J Knight, NIP)*

Ind Coope (Allied)   Licensee Brian Wills   Real ale   Meals and snacks   Children in family room and Royal Square Room   Open 11–2.30, 6–11; closed 25 and 26 Dec evening   Bedrooms tel Colchester (0206) 323250 or 323124; £23S/£41S

FEERING   TL8720   Map 5

Old Anchor

B1024; take Kelvedon turn off A12 Chelsmford–Colchester and keep on right through Kelvedon

An old half-timbered village inn based on a pair of Tudor farm cottages, this has been extensively modernised inside to give a big rambling bar. It's comfortable and neatly kept, with plenty of bottle-green plush seats around black tables, various snug corners and alcoves – including one tiny cubicle like a confessional – and pictures of old Essex on the walls. There's a well lit pool table round to the right, where the beams are heavier and lower, and where there's some black panelling and an attractive china cabinet; log fire, fruit machines, trivia machine; unobtrusive, well reproduced piped music. Bar food includes filled French bread (from 60p), filled baked potatoes (from £1.30), a popular help-yourself salad bar (from £2.70), and a daily hot dish such as steak and kidney pie (£3.85) or Chinese beef; Ruddles Best and County and Websters Yorkshire on handpump from the long serving counter, and a reasonable choice of malt whiskies. There are tables in the sheltered garden. *(Recommended by Gwen and Peter Andrews, Mrs P J Pearce, Paul Barker, Alison Findlay, Brian Wood; more reports please)*

Trumans   Licensees Mr and Mrs Martin Hopwood   Real ale   Meals and snacks   Restaurant   Open 11–2.30(3 Fri), 6–11; all day Sat   Bedrooms tel Kelvedon (0376) 70684; £18.50/£27.50

FYFIELD　TL5606　Map 5
Black Bull

B184, N end of village

Particularly popular at lunchtime with businessmen and older people for its wide choice of food, this tiled white village pub serves guacamole or good chicken satay with peanut sauce (£2.20), smokies (£2.35), chicken tikka (£2.65), chilli con carne (£2.85), spinach and mushroom lasagne (£2.65), steak and kidney pie (£3.15), Mediterranean prawns and squid (£6), steaks (from £6), pheasant in a red wine and mushroom sauce (£6.25) and duck breast with honey and lemon (£6.50); vegetables, salad or bread are extra. The several communicating but separate areas more or less make up an H-shaped layout, and all have low ceilings, big black beams, standing timbers, and cushioned wheelback chairs and modern settles on the muted maroon carpet. Well kept Bass and Charrington IPA on handpump, piped music, fruit machine. By the car park, an aviary under a fairy-lit arbour has budgerigars and cockatiels, and there are picnic-table sets on a stretch of grass further back, and to the side of the building. *(Recommended by Derek Patey, Alan and Ruth Woodhouse, Caroline Wright; more reports please)*

Charringtons (Bass)　Licensee Alan Smith　Real ale　Meals and snacks (12–1.45, 7–9.30)　Open 11–2.30, 6.30–11; may be closed 25 Dec

nr GREAT HENNY　TL8637　Map 5
Henny Swan

Henny Street; A131 from Sudbury, left at Middleton road at foot of Ballingdon hill; OS Sheet 155 map reference 879384

Right by a weir on the River Stour, this small pub was once a barge-house. In the cosy L-shaped and timbered lounge there are well cushioned seats and a big fireplace with a log-effect gas fire; a Victorian-style conservatory leads on to a terrace in the garden, where there's a pond and rustic benches among the willows on a riverside lawn. Greene King IPA and Abbot on handpump; maybe Radio Chiltern. The good selection of bar food includes sandwiches (from £1.10), good home-made soup (£1.20), pâté (£1.95), scampi (£3.95), sole or trout (£5.90), steaks (from £7.25), half a roast duck (£6.50), pheasant (in season, £8), and daily specials like home-made steak and kidney pie, moussaka, crab salad, lamb curry or guinea fowl (from £2.95). Fishing permits are available and barbecues are held on Sundays and Wednesday evenings in fine weather. The pub tends to get very popular on Saturday evenings and on fine days. *(Recommended by Barbara and Norman Wells, John Evans, Mrs E J Pateman, Alison Findlay, John Branford, Joy Heatherley, Gwen and Peter Andrews)*

Greene King　Licensee P A Underhill　Real ale　Meals (not Sun evening) and snacks Restaurant tel Twinstead (0787) 269238 (not Sun evening)　Children in eating area of bar until 9pm　Open 11–3, 6–11; closed evening 25 Dec

GREAT BADDOW　TL7204　Map 5
Seabrights Barn

From A12 Chelmsford bypass, take A1007 to Galleywood; turn right at lights and go right through village – pub on right

Particularly popular with families, this is a fine conversion of a derelict 16th-century barn. It's airy and spacious with the original high raftered and beamed ceiling, and furnished with very high-backed farmhouse and other sturdy plush cushioned chairs, tractor-seat stools along the brick, wooden-topped bar counter, and rustic decorations – we liked the cheerfully painted wooden animals best. At one end there's an upper gallery, at the other a small cosy area separated from the main room by standing timbers; bright artificial hanging baskets. There's a decent no-smoking conservatory-style family room off the main bar with cane plush-cushioned seating, ceiling fans, trivia and a television with cartoons. Across the corridor is an attractive little dining room; a big restaurant was being added as we went to press. Bar food includes home-made soup (£1.10), filled potato skins (from £1.95), ham, cheese or quiche ploughman's, barbecued spare ribs or hot dog and onions (£2.95), filled baguettes (from £3.15), curry (£3.75), salads (from £3.95), vegetarian dishes like ratatouille casserole or omelettes (from £3.95), fish dishes such as swordfish steak, sea trout or salmon salad (from £4.95), spicy cajun chicken (£7.25), steaks (from £7.85), puddings (from £1.95), and children's dishes (from £2.75); Saturday and Sunday barbecues, when there may be a bouncy castle for children. Well kept Adnams and Broadside, Greene King IPA and Abbot and Ridleys IPA on handpump, a good choice of wines. Fruit machine, space game, CD juke box, piped music. The terrace has picnic-table sets, umbrellas, two football tables and a barbecue, and leads to a very well equipped children's play area and a pets' corner with six goats (the three Angora ones are called Light, Bitter and Willi) and other creatures. It gets very busy at weekends; big car park. *(Recommended by Gwen and Peter Andrews)*

Free house   Licensees Stephen Gormley and Ian Jones   Real ale   Meals and snacks (12–2.30, 6–10.30)   No-smoking restaurant tel Chelmsford (0245) 478033; open all day Sat and Sun   Children welcome   Live entertainment inc Sun lunch magician for children, Weds evening magician for adults, jazz Mon evening, singer some Fri evenings   Open 12–3, 6–11; 12–11 Sat

GREAT SALING   TL7025 Map 5
White Hart

Village signposted from A120

The attractive timbered lounge bar of this flower-decked Tudor pub has Windsor chairs on its antique tiles, guns hanging behind the bar, and a stairway up to a little gallery with roughly timbered walls and easy chairs on its wide oak floorboards. Well kept Adnams Extra and Ridleys on handpump; darts, dominoes and a fruit machine in the public bar. Bar food is marked out by the generous giant huffer sandwiches, a long-standing speciality and much loved by readers; also rollmops, home-made pâté and more conventional sandwiches; cheerful service. As well as the usual picnic-set tables outside, there's a bench right round the trunk of a fine lime tree. *(Recommended by Denny Lyster, James Turner, A L and J W Taylor, J S Rowe)*

Ridleys   Real ale   Snacks   Open 11–3, 6–11

GREAT YELDHAM   TL7638 Map 5
White Hart

Poole Street; A604 Halstead–Haverhill

This striking, black-and-white tiled Tudor house was built in 1505 – though the only original flooring left is in what was originally built as a cell for prisoners on their way to Chelmsford Jail in the late 17th century. The heavy-beamed and oak-panelled bar, popular but cosy, is furnished with winged easy chairs, settees and wall settles, as well as attractive antique Morland prints and a log fire; it opens into an extension, giving the feel of three separate room areas; Nethergate on handpump; a friendly, civilised atmosphere. Bar food consists of sandwiches (from £1), home-made soup (£1.75), French bread with three sausages (£2.75), ploughman's with a choice of English cheeses (£2.75), omelettes (from £2.75), a proper chilli con carne (£3.50), salads (from £3.50), and a dish of the day such as loin of pork marinated in saffron, cumin, five-spice and pineapple juice (£3.95). The timbered and jettied building is surrounded by well kept lawns, where white cast-iron tables stand among lots of trees and shrubs; Samuel Pepys is said to have endorsed the original licence application. *(Recommended by Barbara and Norman Wells, Mrs Elizabeth Willis)*

Free house   Licensee David Smillie   Real ale   Meals and snacks (not Sun evening) Restaurant (not Sun evening) tel Great Yeldham (0787) 237250   Children welcome Open 11–3, 6.30–11; closed Sun evening

HASTINGWOOD TL4807 Map 5

Rainbow & Dove

1/4 mile from M11, junction 7; Hastingwood signposted from exit roundabout

Handy for the motorway, this rose-covered, tiled cottage is popular at lunchtime for its simple bar food – sandwiches, ploughman's (from £2.50), home-made sausages (£2.60), moussaka or lasagne (£3.10), ham off the bone (£3.20), scampi (£3.85), and steak (£7.50). Three small low-beamed rooms open off the main bar area; the one on the left is particularly snug and beamy, with the lower part of the wall stripped back to bare brick and decorated with old golf clubs, brass pistols and plates. Elsewhere, there are big brass platters, brass horseshoes and so forth, with horse-collars, the odd halberd and boomerang, and even a collection of garden ornaments in one fireplace. Picnic-table sets under cocktail parasols, on a stretch of grass hedged off from the car park, are bordered by an 18-hole putting course and a paddock; there may be a children's summer bar out here at busy times (weekends, say), and there are summer Sunday evening barbecues. *(Recommended by Derek Patey, Billy Dee, Nicky Morris, L M Miall, Col A H N Reade, Joy Heatherley, Steve Waters; more reports please)*

Ind Coope (Allied)   Licensee A R Bird   Meals (not Mon evening or Sun lunchtime) and snacks (12–2, 7–9.45)   Children in eating area   Open 11.30–2.30, 6.30(7 winter)–11

HIGH EASTER TL6214 Map 5

Cock & Bell

The Easters are signposted from the Rodings, on B184/A1060 The heavily oak-beamed lounge bar in this timbered, black and white 14th-century house – free since the end of 1989 – is furnished with comfortably cushioned Windsor chairs and vases of fresh flowers. A cheerful second bar has the oldest dragon-beam ceiling in Essex, as well as a log fire; the atmosphere throughout is pleasantly local – the pub is in the centre of the village, and is quite a draw. Well kept, regularly changing beers such as Mauldons and Shepherd Neame Bitter and Old on handpump, and a decent choice of wines; piped music. Generously served, restaurany bar food – not cheap – includes home-made soup (£1.95), pâté (£2.95), mixed fried fish (£6.75), chicken breast in mushroom sauce and puff pastry (£6.95), a cold plate of home-cooked ham, cheddar, prawns, caviar and langoustine or supreme of chicken poached in white wine and herbs with Stilton and brandy sauce (£7.25), pork cutlets in cider and apple (£7.45), salmon steak in campari and white wine (£8.75) and steaks (from £7.45); puddings such as home-made cheesecake (from £1.65); three-course Sunday lunch (£8.95, booking advisable). They have occasional Dickensian evenings in winter and barbecues with a marquee in summer. There's a terrace and garden with a play area outside. *(Recommended by Caroline Wright, WTF, Derek Patey, R P Hastings)*

Free house   Licensee Barrie Day   Real ale   Meals and snacks   Children welcome   Restaurant tel Chelmsford (0245) 31296   Open 12–2.30, 7–11

HORNDON ON THE HILL TQ6683 Map 3

Bell

M25 junction 30 into A13, then left into B1007 after 7 miles

This relaxing and friendly country pub is quite a centre for sporting activities: they have a ski club, a team in the London to Brighton cycle ride, and are coming up to their 15th year of the monthly Fun Runs, which take place every second Wednesday in summer (7pm start); the village cricket team were the Essex winners of the National Village Competition recently. Seats in a bow window at the back of the open-plan bar have views over the fields, and there are some antique high-backed settles, plush burgundy stools and benches, flagstones or highly-polished oak floorboards, and timbering and panelling; the fossilised objects hanging from the ceiling are hot-cross buns – collected, one a year, since 1900, though perhaps the wood carvings hanging from a block on the panelling and collected over much the same period are more edifying. Well kept Bass and Charrington IPA on handpump, and a good selection of wines – listed on a blackboard with notes on what to drink with your food. Good bar food includes sandwiches, ploughman's (£1.50), steak and kidney or pork, plum and celery pie (£4.25), lamb with mushroom sauce (£5.75), and steak (£8.95); up to ten changing dishes, freshly made each day, are chalked up on a blackboard. The sheltered back yard has picnic-table sets, pretty hanging baskets, old mangles used as flower pots, and a fountain. On the last weekend in June the High Road outside is closed (by Royal Charter) for period-costume festivities and a crafts fair; the pub holds a feast then. *(Recommended by Graham Bush, Ian Phillips, Derek Patey, J P Day, David Cardy, E G Parish, Graham Oddey)*

Charringtons (Bass)   Licensee John Vereker   Real ale   Meals and snacks Restaurant   Children in restaurant and eating area of bar   Open 11–2.30(3 Sat), 6–11   Bedrooms in house two doors away tel Stanford-le-Hope (0375) 673154; I£40B

LAMARSH   TL8835   Map 5
Red Lion

From Bures on B1508 Sudbury–Colchester take Station Road, passing station; Lamarsh then signposted

There's a welcoming atmosphere in the softly lit, timbered bar in this small, tiled white house, especially when huge logs smoulder in the big brick 16th-century fireplace. Tables and small pews are set by the front windows, in stalls with red velvet curtain dividers, and a timbered-off area has pool and darts; maybe unobtrusive piped music; well kept Adnams and Greene King IPA on handpump. Good value bar food shows some eclectic touches such as a pea and bacon soup (£1) or the Greek-style tuna salad with feta cheese (£3.25), as well as sandwiches (from £1.10), filled baked potato (£1.50), ploughman's (from £2.15), spaghetti bolognese, ham and egg or pork loin and mushroom sauce (£3.25), a substantial double burger (£3.80), mixed grill (£5.50) and steaks (rump £7.50), with good rare roast beef on Sundays; the restaurant is in a former barn. There are swings in the biggish sheltered sloping garden. The pub is in a fairly hilly part of Essex, overlooking the undulating fields and colour-washed houses of the Stour valley. *(Recommended by Gwen and Peter Andrews, Denis Korn; more reports please)*

Free house   Licensees John and Angela O'Sullivan   Real ale   Meals and snacks Restaurant (Thurs–Sat evenings, Sun lunch) tel Bures (0787) 227918   Children in eating area and restaurant (not after early evening)   Open 11–3, 6–11

LEIGH ON SEA   TQ8385   Map 3
Crooked Billet

51 High St; from A13 follow signpost to station, then cross bridge over railway towards waterside

The pub's big terrace, by the ancient wooden salt store and the sea wall, makes the most of its position – overlooking the shellfish boats in the old-fashioned working harbour. They don't mind you eating cockles, shrimps or jellied eels out here, from Ivy Osborne's marvellous stall, just down the lane (it shuts at 10pm). The unspoilt lounge bar has two big bay windows, cushioned seats facing into the room built in around the walls, shiny yellowing walls decorated with photographs of local cockle smacks, and a solid fuel stove; on the left, the bare-floored public bar has a huge log fire, more photographs, and sensibly placed darts, shove-ha'penny, and cribbage. Well kept Ind Coope Burton, Taylor-Walker, and Tetleys on handpump; straightforward snacks such as filled rolls (£1; prawn £1.80), ploughman's (£2.25), chilli con carne and hot pots (from £2.75). *(Recommended by Jenny Cantle, Ian Phillips; more reports please)*

Ind Coope (Allied)   Licensee Alan Downing   Real ale   Meals and snacks (lunchtime, not Sun, and quiet evenings)   Open 11.30–3, 6–11; longer afternoon opening in fine weather

LITTLE BRAXTED   TL8314   Map 5

Green Man

Kelvedon Road; village signposted off B1389 by NE end of A12 Witham bypass – keep
on patiently

The pleasantness of this pub's almost complete isolation (tucked away on a very
quiet lane) is equalled only by the cosiness of the atmosphere in the little traditional
lounge, with its collection of 200 horse brasses and some harness, as well as mugs
hanging from a beam, a lovely copper urn, and an open fire. Well kept Ridleys is
dispensed from handpumps in the form of 40mm brass cannon shells, and there
are several malt whiskies; piped music. The tiled public bar leads to a games room
with darts, shove-ha'penny, dominoes, cribbage, and video game. Good value bar
food includes sandwiches (from 95p, good steak), filled baked potatoes (from
£1.60), hot locally-baked French bread filled with ham off the bone, sardines,
chicken, turkey, beef or even meaty haggis brought from Scotland (from £1.25),
pâté (£1.75), ploughman's (from £2.15), lasagne, beef curry or chilli con carne
(£2.80), and salads (from £4.40). There are picnic-set tables in the sheltered garden
behind this pretty tiled brick house. *(Recommended by Alan and Ruth Woodhouse,
Anthony Barnes, John and Karen Day)*

*Ridleys   Licensee Eion MacGregor   Real ale   Meals and snacks (12–2, 7.30–10.15)
Open 11–3, 6–11; winter evening opening 6.30*

LOUGHTON   TQ4296   Map 5

Gardeners Arms

2 1/4 miles from M11, junction 5; in Loughton, turn left on to A121, then right at war
memorial and Kings Head on right; 103 York Hill

On one of the highest hills in Essex, this tiled and weatherboarded house has
spreading views to parts of Epping Forest from the picnic-table sets on the side
terrace; there's also a little front verandah. Bar food includes sandwiches (from
£1.20, toasties from £1.30, steak £3.35), ploughman's (£2.30), omelettes (£2.70),
lasagne (£3.75), home-cooked ham and eggs (£3.95), salads (from £3.25), steak,
kidney and mushroom pie (£4.75), and steak (£7.25); daily specials are chalked up
on a blackboard; as it's all freshly cooked, they warn of delays of 20–30 minutes
with some dishes. The spacious open-plan bar, with its low lighting and ceilings
(except in one place, where it soars up to the full height of the pitched roof), has an
intimate and civilised atmosphere, and is well decorated with prints, engravings
and pencil drawings of this and other picturesque old inns (including some by Cecil
Aldin), two or three Delft shelves, some figured plates on the walls, an aged kitchen
clock, guns above the beam where the bar opens into the restaurant area, and a
couple of open fires. Ruddles County and Websters Yorkshire on handpump.
(Recommended by Joy Heatherley; more reports please)

*Watneys   Licensee Robert Worrell   Real ale   Lunchtime meals and snacks (not Sun)
Restaurant tel 081–508 1655   Children in restaurant   Open 11–2.30(3 Sat), 6–11*

MILL GREEN   TL6400   Map 5

Viper

Mill Green Rd; from Fryerning (which is signposted off *north-east bound* A12
Ingatestone bypass) follow Writtle signposts; OS Sheet 167 map reference 640019

The immediate surroundings of this homely little pub are almost Arcadian: the
garden has masses of nasturtiums, foxgloves, geraniums and lathyrus around the
tables on a neat lawn, with honeysuckle and overflowing hanging baskets and
window boxes on the pub itself; and all around is an oak wood, leading off to a
bank of sweet chestnuts. Bar snacks include soup (£1), good sandwiches (from
90p, toasties from £1), Hawaiian toast (£2), chilli con carne (£2.20), and
ploughman's (from £2.20). The two little rooms of the lounge have a low ochre
ceiling, pale hessian walls (the log fireplace is in a stripped brick wall), spindleback
seats, armed country kitchen chairs, and tapestried wall seats around neat little old

tables, vases of flowers in summer, and maybe the pub cat. The parquet-floored tap room (where booted walkers are directed) is more simply furnished with shiny wooden traditional wall seats, and beyond there's another room with country kitchen chairs and sensibly placed darts. Well kept Ruddles Best and County on handpump from the oak-panelled bar counter; shove-ha'penny, dominoes, cribbage and a fruit machine. Popular with walkers. *(Recommended by Derek Patey, WTF, J S Rutter, Graham Oddey, Roy Clark, Nigel Paine)*

Trumans (Watneys) Licensee Fred Beard Real ale Snacks Open 11–2.30(3 Sat), 6–11

NEWNEY GREEN TL6507 Map 5

Duck

Village signposted off A414 W of Chelmsford

The cosily atmospheric beamed bar here (large enough to cope comfortably with considerable numbers of people) is attractively furnished with wheelback chairs, lots of tables tucked between high-backed booth seats, and some more unusual seating such as the great curved high-backed settle in one of the alcoves; there are also ancient-looking pictures and old farm and garden tools on the partly dark-panelled and partly timbered walls, a wind-up gramophone, and a coal-effect gas fire in a big two-faced brick fireplace draped with hop bines. Well kept Adnams, Crouch Vale Best and Greene King Abbot and IPA on handpump; also, several malt whiskies and cocktails. Food from a servery by the bar includes filled baps or sandwiches (from £1.50) and ploughman's (£2.75 – both these at lunchtime only), chicken hot pot pie (£4.50), gammon and pineapple or good vegetarian lasagne (£5), salads (£5.25), poached whole trout (£5.50), venison casserole (£6), roast half duck (£7), and puddings (from £1.75); you're given a big wooden duck with your number on when you order. The garden by the huge car park has tables under cocktail parasols, lit by old streetlamps; there are two big lily-ponds (with anti-heron defences for the goldfish) in a rockery, and a hollow play tree with swings for children, a slide and a treehouse. *(Recommended by Gwen and Peter Andrews, R C Morgan, Jenny Cantle, John Baker, P Miller)*

Free house Licensee Gerald Ambrose Real ale Snacks (lunchtime) and meals (not Sun evening) Open 11.30–3, 6.30–11; closed Mon and 25 Dec

PELDON TL9916 Map 5

Rose

B1025 Colchester–Mersea, at junction with southernmost turn-off to Peldon

The cosy, cream-walled bar in this well preserved and popular pub, not far from the coast, is furnished mostly with antique mahogany and the occasional, rather creaky, close-set table; one or two standing timbers support the low ceiling with its dark bowed oak beams, brass and copper decorate the mantlepiece of the Gothick-arched brick fireplace, and there are chintz curtains in the leaded-light windows; the large conservatory is a no-smoking area. The food servery, beside a stripped pine dresser on an old-fashioned brick floor, does winter Dutch pea or Hungarian goulash soup, sandwiches, beef curry, lasagne, steak and kidney pie or Italian chicken, steaks, and Sunday roast beef; other alcovey areas lead off here. Adnams on handpump and quite a few wines. The garden outside this pink-washed house has good teak seats, a swing and a see-saw, as well as two ponds – the ducks have been known to wander expectantly among the tables. *(Recommended by Gwen and Peter Andrews, Mr and Mrs T F Marshall, Alison Findlay; more reports please)*

Free house Licensees Ariette and Alan Everett Real ale Meals and snacks (12–2, 7–10) Restaurant; only Fri and Sat evening Open 11–2.30, 5.30–11 Bedrooms tel Peldon (020 635) 248; £30/£60

PLESHEY   TL6614   Map 5
White Horse

Signposted with Howe Street off A130 Dunmow–Chelmsford

Several cosy areas with shiny ochre ceilings make up the bar in this relaxed and very friendly 15th-century pub. By the tiny bar counter, a snug room has brick and beamed walls, a comfortable sofa, some bar stools and a table with magazines on the brick floor, and a sonorous clock. Brick and half-timbered walls divide the main rooms which are furnished with wheelback and other chairs and a mix of dark wooden tables, and decorated with jugs, tankards, antlers, miscellaneous brass items, a ship's bell, a shelf of books and old bottles, and several prints; one fireplace has a woodburning stove, another big brick one has horse-brasses along the mantlebeam, and yet another has an unusual curtain-like fireguard. Popular bar food includes huffers (from £1.50), ploughman's or lots of filled baked potatoes (from £2), a tasty pie named after the pub (£3), lasagne (£3.50), vegetarian dishes such as lentil crumble or spinach and mushroom lasagne (£3.60), curry (£4), 6oz fillet steak (£7), and puddings like spotted dick and custard (£1.60). Well kept Boddingtons, Marstons Pedigree, Nethergate and Ridleys on handpump, good wines and several brandies; fruit machine. A large dining room has sturdy furniture, lots of plants, glass cabinets with over 1,500 miniatures, and an old-fashioned stove in the brick fireplace. Doors from here open on to a terrace with white plastic garden furniture, a grass area with similar seating and a few picnic-table sets, and a children's play area with slide, swings and a see-saw. The hanging baskets and flowering tubs are lovely. The cat is called Tigger.
(Recommended by Caroline Wright, Gwen and Peter Andrews, Tony Beaulah)

Free house   Licensees John and Helen Thorburn   Real ale   Meals and snacks (12–3, 7–10.30)   Restaurant tel (024537) 281   Well behaved children allowed   Open 11–3, 6–11

PURLEIGH   TL8401   Map 5
Bell

A414 E from Chelmsford, then right into B1010 after 5 miles; village signposted on right, pub by church at top of hill

Set on the only hill for miles (and with good views from its bow window over hedged flatlands to the Blackwater estuary), this popular and well kept pub serves good food, including sandwiches (from 80p, toasties 10p extra), pizza (£1.65), ploughman's (£1.60), ham and egg (£2.20), salads (from £2.30), plaice (£2.60) and scampi (£3); anyone not using the bar will have a 50p service charge added to the price of their food; friendly service. The rambling main bar has heavy black beams and timbers, cushioned wall banquettes and Windsor chairs on the carpet, and a huge log fire. Well kept Adnams and Benskins Best on handpump (the landlord encourages moderate drinking for drivers); dominoes, cribbage, trivia. Picnic-set tables on the side grass also have estuary views; New Hall Vineyard is closeby.
(Recommended by Derek Patey, Graham Bush, Alison Findlay, Quentin Williamson)

Ind Coope (Allied)   Licensee Robert A Cooke   Real ale   Lunchtime meals (not Sun) and snacks   Open 11–3, 6–11

STISTED   TL7924   Map 5
Dolphin

A120 E of Braintree

This roadside pub has a softly lit, heavily beamed and timbered room with comfortable banquettes on the black wood floor, and an open fire; Adnams Extra and Ridleys PA are tapped from wooden casks behind the bar; cheerful staff; darts, dominoes, cribbage, fruit machine, and piped music. Straightforward bar food includes sandwiches or rolls (from £1; good ham off the bone), ploughman's (from £2.50), lamb chop, chicken or scampi (£3), pork chop (£4) and steaks (from £6). There's a play area in the garden. The new licensee has been described as friendly and efficient by readers. *(Recommended by Gwen and Peter Andrews, C M Vipond, Alison Findlay; more reports on the new regime please)*

Ridleys   Licensee George Jame   Real ale   Meals and snacks   Children in eating area of bar   Open 10.30–3, 5.30–11; 10.30am–11pm Sat

STOCK   TQ6998 Map 5

Hoop

B1007; from A12 Chelmsford bypass take Galleywood, Billericay turn-off

There's an outstanding range of real ales here – they normally have at least Adnams Bitter and Mild, Boddingtons, Hook Norton Old Hooky, Marstons Pedigree and Owd Rodger, Nethergate, Theakstons Old Peculier and Wadworths 6X on handpump or more likely tapped from the cask, with Timothy Taylors Landlord every fortnight, and two or three guest beers such as Brains Red Dragon, Robinsons Mild and Palmers Tally Ho; however the best time to catch it is on the May Day weekend, when around a hundred real ales are available; also farm cider, decent wines by the glass, and mulled wine in winter. To the left there are brocaded wall seats around dimpled copper tables, with a cluster of brocaded stools on the right – where there's a coal-effect gas fire in the big brick fireplace. Sensibly placed darts (the heavy black beams are studded with hundreds of darts flights), cribbage and dominoes. Good value bar food, available all day, includes sandwiches (from 70p), soup (£1), filled baked potatoes (from £1), ploughman's (£2), omelettes (from £1.50), quiche or home-cooked ham and egg (£2), steak and kidney pie (£3), meaty grilled trout (caught by the licensee or his friends from their local reservoir), specials like Lanchashire hot pot or braised oxtail with dumplings (£3), and puddings (£1). There are lots of picnic-table sets in the big sheltered back garden, which is prettily bordered with flowers and where they have occasional summer barbecues and maybe croquet (or boules on the front gravel). The dog is called Misty and the cat Thomas. *(Recommended by Patrick Young, Jenny Cantle, Graham Oddey, Gwen and Peter Andrews, Quentin Williamson, Nigel Paine)*

Free house   Licensee Albert Kitchin   Real ale   Meals and snacks (all day)   Open 10am–11pm

TILLINGHAM   TL9903 Map 5

Cap & Feathers ★

B1027 N of Southminster

Bar food in this splendidly relaxing, tiled and white clapboarded village pub features the succulent and distinctively flavoured products of their own smokery – thinly sliced beef as a starter (£2.50), cod (£4.30), trout (£4.60) and specials such as pheasant (£4.60); the smoked mackerel is not local. Other home-cooked dishes include sandwiches (from 95p), hearty soup, burgers (from £1.30, vegetarian £1.40), ploughman's (from £2.75), fish pie (ingredients caught by the landlord, if he's been lucky – £3.95), a couple of vegetarian dishes, steak and ale pie (£4.25), good steaks (from 8oz sirloin £6.50) and a generous mixed grill (£6.65); puddings are traditional – fruit crumble, rice pudding and so forth – and breakfast includes home-smoked kippers. The bar, divided into three snug areas, has uneven low beams, timbers, sturdy wall seats (including a venerable built-in floor-to-ceiling settle), little wheelback chairs with arms, a homely dresser and a formidable woodburning stove; one parquet-floored part has bar billiards, sensibly placed darts, and table skittles – there's another set in the attractive family room, and they have shove-ha'penny, cribbage and dominoes. The atmosphere throughout is decidedly warm, with notably friendly service. The fine range of drinks includes well kept Crouch Vale Woodham, Best, SAS, Essex Porter and in winter Willie Warmer, with Thatcher's farm cider, decent wines by the glass, and good coffee. There are a few picnic-table sets under birch trees on a small side terrace. *(Recommended by Gwen and Peter Andrews, Peter Seddon, P Cammiade, Simon Wilmshurst)*

Crouch Vale   Licensees Olly and Carol Graham   Real ale   Meals and snacks

Children in family room – which can be 'hired' for free   Folk music first Sun in month (the landlord plays the spoons)   Open 11–3(4 Sat), 6–11   Three bedrooms tel Tillingham (0621) 779212; £15/£30

WOODHAM WALTER   TL8006 Map 5

Bell

A414 E from Chelmsford; village signposted on left after about 6 miles

The lounge bar in this lovely tiled and timbered Elizabethan building is neatly kept, but friendly and informal, and divided into irregularly-shaped alcoves on various levels, with old timbers and beams, comfortable seats and a log fire. The bar food is standard – sandwiches, soup, sausage in French bread, ploughman's, salads, and daily specials; there's a prettily decorated dining room in a partly panelled gallery up steps from the main bar. Benskins Best on handpump. *(Recommended by Mayur Shah, Gwen and Peter Andrews, Helen and John Thompson, Alison Findlay; more reports please)*

Ind Coope (Allied)   Real ale   Meals (not Sun evening) and snacks   Well behaved children welcome   Restaurant Danbury (024 541) 3437 (not Sun or Mon evenings) Open 11–3, 6–11

Cats

Back road to Curling Tye and Maldon, from N end of village

The well kept garden, looking out over quiet fields, makes this pretty, black and white cottage – its roof decorated with prowling stone cats – an attractive place in summer; it's often busy, even on a Monday evening. The L-shaped bar is a rambling affair, full of interesting nooks and crannies and traditionally decorated, with button-back red leatherette seats, black beams and timbering set off well by neat white paintwork, and a collection of china cats on the mantlepiece over the open fire. The food is very simple and straightforward, and the Adnams, Greene King IPA and Abbot and Mauldons on handpump particularly well kept; they have another real ale, brewed specially for them, called Cats Piss; friendly service. *(Recommended by Gwen and Peter Andrews, Quentin Williamson, Jenny Cantle)*

Free house   Real ale   Snacks   Open 10.30–2, 6.30ish–11; closed Mon, Tues, Weds, though maybe only in winter

---

Lucky Dip

Besides the fully inspected pubs, you might like to try these Lucky Dips recommended to us and described by readers (if you do, please send us reports):

Abridge [TQ4696], *Maltsters Arms*: Crockery all over the ceiling, well kept Greene King and Youngs, basic lunchtime bar food; busy at weekends *(MN)*; [Market Pl; TQ4696], *White Hart*: Well kept Bass and Flowers IPA, good value food *(R P Hastings)*

Aldham [Ford St (A604 2 miles W of A12); TL9125], *Queens Head*: Large collection of water jugs hanging from beams, seven beers on draught, bar food inc marvellous toasties, restaurant *(Paul Barker)*; *Shoulder of Mutton*: 14th-century inn with very pleasant atmosphere, Taylor Walker Best on handpump, good value bar snacks *(Mr and Mrs L G Smith)*

☆ **Althorne** [TQ9199], *Huntsman & Hounds*: Popular country local — enlarged thatched cottage, long bar and L-shaped extensions at each end with open fire, low beams decorated with brasses, plates, mugs and foreign bank notes; well kept Greene King

IPA and Abbot, good bar food, friendly staff, unobtrusive piped music, decent garden *(Peter Seddon, Gwen and Peter Andrews, LYM)*

Althorne, *Black Lion*: Pleasant atmosphere and good varied menu in recently refurbished and comfortably equipped pub *(T G Saul)*

☆ **Ardleigh** [Harwich Rd; A137 — actually towards Colchester; TM0529], *Wooden Fender*: Comfortably modernised open-plan beamed bar with freshly prepared bar food, straightforward but tasty, and good Sun lunch; well kept Adnams, Greene King IPA and Abbot and Marstons Pedigree on handpump, prompt service, log fire, piped music, restaurant allowing children, a pool in back garden *(John Baker, M Morgan, E G Parish, LYM)*

Ashdon [back rd Saffron Walden—Haverhill; TL5842], *Rose & Crown*: 17th-century pub with small rooms, original gothic lettering and geometric patterns decorating one; big helpings of good food in bar and restaurant, real fire, Greene King Abbot, resident dogs; pool room *(Adrian Pitts, J Johnson)*

Battlesbridge [Hawk Hill; TQ7894], *Barge*: Old-fashioned cottagey pub with low ceilings, cosy rooms, barge pictures, well kept Taylor-Walker, appetising lunchtime snacks strong on fried food, more seating in outbuilding; art and craft centre here *(Jenny Cantle, B R Wood)*; *Hawk*: Friendly, welcoming staff, Charrington ales, ample helpings of interesting lunchtime food *(B R Wood)*

☆ **Beazley End** [off B1053 N of Braintree; TL7428], *Cock*: Neat and spacious beamed lounge with quiet relaxing atmosphere, open fire and fascinating clock, village bar with pool and darts, restaurant decorated with corn dollies; well kept Adnams, Beazley (brewed for them by Mauldons) and Crouch Vale on handpump, farm cider, good choice of decent bar food, welcoming licensees and piped music; no dogs *(Gwen and Peter Andrews)*

☆ **Birchanger** [nr M11 junction 8 — right turn off A120 to Bishops Stortford; TL5022], *Three Willows*: Small pub doing well under current regime, with well kept Greene King IPA and Abbot and Rayments, cheap wines, and wide range of bar food good enough to forgive the menu's cricketing puns — Tues fresh fish particularly good *(M J Morgan, P Thorogood)*

Blackmore [Paslow Wood Common; TL6001], *Black Horse*: One-bar beamed and timbered country pub with friendly staff and good atmosphere; Greene King Abbot and Fullers ESB on handpump *(Robert Lester)*; [nr church], *Bull*: Friendly two-bar pub with snug, lively public bar with darts, plush lounge; good atmosphere, decent bar food, Ind Coope beers *(Robert Lester)*; [The Green], *Leather Bottle*: Small, quiet and friendly two-bar pub with back garden and Benskins Best *(Robert Lester)*; [The Green], *Prince Albert*: Pleasant pub with friendly, welcoming landlord, brass tankards hanging from ceiling, log fires, and separate snug area with darts; Bass and Charrington IPA on handpump, good bar food inc some vegetarian dishes *(Derek Patey, Robert Lester)*

Bradwell [A120 Braintree—Colchester; TL8022], *Swan*: Friendly service, bar food from 6.30 — usefully early *(Dave Braisted)*

Bradwell on Sea [Waterside; TM0006], *Green Man*: Interestingly furnished flagstoned 15th-century pub with games room and garden, nr former village one-man lockup and ancient church; footpath to sea; new licensees this last year *(E G Parish, LYM)*; *Kings Head*: Popular and comfortable pub by coast, well kept with lots of pictures, pleasant fire, big helpings of good food; good garden with facilities for children *(Alison Findlay, K Leist)*

Braintree [Bradford St, Bocking; TL7524], *Old Court*: Nice atmosphere in Chef & Brewer with friendly service, good food

including some unusual dishes, well kept beer; bedrooms *(Barbara and Norman Wells)*

Broxted [TL5726], *Prince of Wales*: Friendly, cosy, and nicely furnished inn with good value food and Ruddles Best and County and Websters Yorkshire on handpump; opens early *(P Lloyd, Miss K Bamford)*

Buckhurst Hill [Buckhurst Way; TQ4193], *Monkhams*: Carvery pub with reasonable snacks and separate restaurant; Flowers and a monthly guest beer on handpump; open all day, very popular in summer — new landlord trying hard *(Robin Harman)*

Bulphan [TQ6485], *Harrow*: Good value simple bar food *(Derek Patey)*

☆ **Burnham on Crouch** [The Quay; TQ9596], *White Harte*: Nice staying here, to be lulled asleep by the clacking of rigging on the masts of the anchored boats; the public rooms have the style and atmosphere of an old-fashioned yachting inn — high ceilings, oak tables, polished parquet, sea pictures, panelling and stripped brickwork; bar food from sandwiches to boiled ham, lamb chops and so forth, well kept Adnams and Tolly, restaurant, children allowed in eating area; bedrooms *(LYM)*

☆ **Canfield End** [Little Canfield; A120 Bishops Stortford—Dunmow; TL5821], *Lion & Lamb*: Grandly refurbished comfortable open-plan pub, welcoming and relaxed with well kept Adnams and Ridleys, good home-cooked bar food inc fresh generously filled sandwiches, good vegetarian dishes, children's dishes; central red-brick fireplace, imposing grandfather clock; sizeable restaurant, efficient service, tables on terrace and in family garden; beware the steps between the different levels in the bar *(Mrs M C Lutyens, M J Morgan, Gwen and Peter Andrews, T G Saul)*

Chelmsford [Cooksmill Green; A414 5 miles W; TL6306], *Fox & Goose*: Plushly well kept extended dining pub with lots of tables, lively but not boisterous evening atmosphere, well kept Trumans Best and Websters Yorkshire on handpump, popular bar food, friendly efficient service *(Robert Lester, LYM)*; [Roxwell Rd; TL7006], *Horse & Groom*: Popular mock-Tudor pub, friendly and busy but relaxed, consistently good reasonably priced food inc lots of salads (not Sun), Watneys-related real ales, good furnishings and decor; benches outside *(Roy Clark, M Morgan)*; [Lower Anchor St], *Orange Tree*: Cheerful, orderly and spacious but cosy pub with pleasant efficient service, good value lunchtime bar food (not Sun) inc good huffers, pleasant terrace with climbing plants and waterfall; easy access for wheelchairs; darts, gas fires, unobtrusive piped music, occasional live music *(Brian Quentin)*

☆ **Chignall Smealy** [TL6711], *Pig & Whistle*: Pleasant country pub with coal fire, brasses and farm tools, well kept Adnams on handpump, guest beers tapped from the cask, straightforward bar food (ham rolls recommended) *(Gwen and Peter Andrews,*

Derek Patey)

Chigwell [High Rd (A113); TQ4693], *King William IV*: New spaciously split-level pub with darts and Charrington IPA and Tolly Original on handpump *(Robert Lester)*

☆ Clavering [B1038 Newport—Buntingford, Newport end of village; TL4731], *Cricketers*: Spacious yet cosy and attractive L-shaped bar with low beams and two open fires; well kept Flowers and Wethereds on handpump, wide choice of good well presented food inc help-yourself salads, some imaginative dishes and often roast beef carved from big dome-lidded trolley, restaurant, outside tables; accent very much on food — even bar tables can be booked; prices not low, but worth it *(Michael Prentice, A M Kelly, Mr and Mrs E J Smith, Dorothy and Jack Rayner)*

Cock Clarks [off B1010; TL8102], *Fox & Hounds*: Light and cheerful bar, popular with locals but welcoming to visitors also; well kept Ridleys and Adnams Extra on handpump *(Gwen and Peter Andrews)*

☆ Coggeshall [91 Church St; turn off main st opp Post Office and Barclays Bank, then bear right], *Woolpack*: Particularly handsome timber-framed Tudor inn with attractive softly lit period lounge, good value home-cooked bar food, well kept Adnams and Ind Coope related real ales and other decent drinks, log fire, friendly landlord, maybe unobtrusive piped Radio 2; children welcome; bedrooms comfortable *(Gwen and Peter Andrews, Barbara and Norman Wells, LYM)*

☆ Coggeshall [West St (towards Braintree)], *Fleece*: Handsome Elizabethan pub next to Paycocke's (lovely timber-framed house open pm summer Weds, Thurs and Sun)], grand fireplace, finely carved beams, well kept Greene King IPA and Abbot on handpump, decent wine, good straightforward pub food (not Tues evening), warm and friendly local atmosphere with plenty of leg-pulling yet a real welcome for strangers; play area in spacious sheltered garden; provision for children; has been open all day Mon-Fri *(Gwen and Peter Andrews, Barbara and Norman Wells, LYM)*

☆ Coggeshall [main st], *White Hart*: 15th-century inn with lots of low dark beams, library chairs and one or two attractive antique settles around oak tables, seats in bow windows, flower prints and fishing trophies on cream walls, good bar lunches, well kept Adnams, freshly squeezed orange juice and decent wines and coffee; promising reports on pleasant newish young licensees *(More news please)*

Coggeshall [7 West St], *Cricketers*: Small local with pleasant landlady popular for good helpings of plain home cooking inc good value burgers, cosy log fire *(Alison Findlay, M Morgan)*

☆ nr Coggeshall [Pattiswick (signed from A120 about 2 miles W of Coggeshall — OS Sheet 168 map reference 820247)], *Compasses*: Secluded country pub surrounded by farmland with comfortable and attractively decorated spacious rooms inc restaurant, beams, flooring tiles, brasses; wide range of attractively priced agreeable bar food every evening and lunchtimes Weds-Sat, Greene King IPA and Abbot and Mauldons (named for the pub) on handpump, kept well under light blanket pressure; traditional pub games, fruit machine, piped music; spreading lawns, orchard, play area; very quiet weekday lunchtimes, perhaps at its best evenings and weekends *(Gwen and Peter Andrews, Barbara and Norman Wells, David Cardy, Martin and Debbie Chester, LYM)*

☆ Colchester [East St; TM0025], *Rose & Crown*: Carefully modernised handsome Tudor inn, timbered and jettied, parts of a former gaol preserved in its rambling beamed bar, good value bar food, Tolly real ale; comfortable bedrooms *(Barbara and Norman Wells, M J Morgan, LYM)*

Colchester [Trinity St], *Clarendon*: Wide choice of reasonably priced food inc good salads and vegetarian dishes; no-smoking area, friendly service, well kept beer, coffee *(Betty and Tony Croot);* [Lexden Rd], *Hospital Arms*: Well kept pub with active staff and good value plentiful food; home of Colchester RC *(A L Latham, M J Morgan);* [High St], *Red Lion*: Vestiges of former Tudor grandeur survive in what is now a bussinessman's comfortable central hotel, with Greene King ales and a popular variety of eateries from coffee shop through burger and pizza bar to steakhouse *(LYM);* [North Hill], *Wig & Pen*: Pleasant pub with Greene King IPA and good range of bar snacks; excellent staff; restaurant *(M J Morgan)*

Copford Green [TL9222], *Alma*: Attractively refurbished brick pub with well kept Greene King IPA and Abbot, decent wine and good value bar food *(Brian and Pam Cowling)*

Crays Hill [TQ7192], *Shepherd & Dog*: Off the beaten track and usually a good meeting place; central-island bar with well kept Ind Coope/Allied beers; food in bar and dining extension, popular quiz night Weds *(Graham Bush, Helen and John Thompson)*

Cressing [TL7920], *Willows*: Very pretty, cosy pub with lots of ornaments and nick-nacks and lovely floral displays, good range of bar food, friendly staff, extended separate restaurant *(Alison Findlay)*

Debden Estate [1168 The Broadway; TQ4398], *Sir Winston Churchill*: Friendly, recently refurbished two-bar pub with pool table in each bar (darts in public), and Watneys-related real ales on handpump *(Robert Lester)*

Dedham [TM0533], *Sun*: Nicely carved beams and wood panelling in spacious and comfortably modernised Tudor pub, popular with locals; friendly, attentive staff, wide choice of bar food from hefty sandwiches and burgers to steaks, restaurant; bedrooms *(Barbara and Norman Wells, LYM)*

☆ Easthorpe [village signposted from A12;

TL9121], *House Without A Name*: Heavy standing timbers and low beams in recently extended Tudor pub with good choice of real ales inc Mauldons (sold under the pub's name), good log fire, usual pub food, friendly service, restaurant, seats in small garden; piped music may be loud; provision for children *(Simon Bates, M Morgan, LYM)*

Epping [Ivy Chimneys; TL4500], *Spotted Dog*: Refurbished pub with leather armchairs, panelling, restaurant, good choice of food and well kept Flowers Original and Wethereds; garden with barbecue and well equipped children's play area *(Robert Lester)*

Fiddlers Hamlet [Stewards Green Rd; TL4700], *Merry Fiddlers*: Quiet, friendly pub with good bar food and well kept Benskins and Ind Coope real ales *(Robert Lester, Robin and Christine Harman)*

Ford End [set well back from A130; TL6716], *Swan*: Quaint and friendly little low-beamed pub with brasses, farm tools, fine clock over counter; well kept Ridleys, decent coffee, home-made bar food (Sun lunch must be booked), darts, pool, unobtrusive piped music *(Gwen and Peter Andrews)*

Fordstreet [TL9126], *Queens Head*: Tastefully furnished place with good value bar meals and restaurant *(Sylvia Findlay)*

☆ Fuller Street [The Green (off A131 Chelmsford—Braintree, towards Fairstead); TL7416], *Square & Compasses*: Old converted cottage with lots of brass, exposed beams, well kept Ridleys, good reasonably priced home-cooked bar food inc popular pies — not fast food; piped folk music (live first Fri of month), maybe Morris dancing; on Essex Way, very popular with CAMRA members *(Gwen and Peter Andrews, Roy Clark, John Gunby, Mr and Mrs M P Loy)*

Furneux Pelham [TL4327], *Brewery Tap*: Very friendly, with good, reasonably priced traditional pub food and outstanding garden — spacious, with neat lawns and superb flowerbeds *(Sidney and Erna Wells)*

☆ Gestingthorpe [OS Sheet 155 map reference 813375; TL8138], *Pheasant*: Simple country pub with attractive old-fashioned furnishings, popular and often interesting lunchtime food, well kept Adnams, Batemans XXXB, Greene King IPA, Nethergate and a guest beer, open fire; on the up-and-up under outgoing newish licensees; children welcome *(Gwen and Peter Andrews, LYM)*

☆ Gosfield [TL7829], *Green Man*: A mix of styles, with lovely old brick fireplace rubbing shoulders with pictures of World War II planes — not to mention the piranha; two restaurant areas lead off the spacious bar, bar food from sandwiches through beef, cod, scampi and so forth is well presented; warm welcome, well kept Greene King IPA and Abbot on handpump, good wines and coffee; garden *(Gwen and Peter Andrews)*

Gosfield [A1017 Braintree—Halstead], *Kings Head*: Extraordinary collection of police uniforms on full-size dummies,

truncheons, handcuffs, and so forth — well worth a look if you're nearby, and the licensees' dog has a prize-winning repertoire of over 40 tricks; decent bar food, coffee; good value bedrooms *(Gwen and Peter Andrews, Barbara and Norman Wells)*

☆ Great Chesterford [High St; 2 miles E of M11 junction 9; TL5143], *Plough*: Classic village pub with open fire, old beams, friendly and relaxed atmosphere, better than average bar food, well kept Greene King IPA and Abbot on handpump or direct from the cask in the cellar — doing well under new licensee, worth watching; lovely garden with farm animals, peaceful village *(John Baker, P Thorogood, Barbara and Norman Wells)*

Great Horkesley [TL9730], *Rose & Crown*: Recently sympathetically restored pub with restaurant; good bar food, real ale and better-than-average wine list; no music *(Richard Goss)*

Great Sampford [TL6435], *Red Lion*: Friendly 18th-century village pub, hard-working licensees, spacious but cosy beamed bar decorated with brasses and framed music-hall song sheets; decent bar food, well kept Ridleys, pleasant service, small restaurant; five bedrooms

Great Stambridge [TQ9091], *Cherry Tree*: Good choice of well cooked food at reasonable prices inc bargain three-course suppers Mon-Thurs, well kept Watneys-related real ales, spacious conservatory — attractive year-round *(C Sharpe, Peter Griffiths);* [Stambridge Mills], *Royal Oak*: Good food, inc Sun evening *(C Sharpe)*

Great Wakering [High St; TQ9487], *White Hart*: Nice, quiet Watneys pub with friendly atmosphere, attractive furniture made from barrels, jugs hanging from ceiling *(N J Clark)*

Great Waltham [A130, about 3/4 mile from Ash Tree Corner junction with A131; TL6913], *Free House*: Spotless 16th-century pub with well kept real ales such as Boddingtons, Brakspears, Fullers ESB, Hook Norton, Eldridge Pope Royal Oak and King & Barnes Festive, good choice of malt whiskies; good lunchtime bar food, ghost said to use gents' *(Mr and Mrs M Knowles)*

Great Warley Street [TQ5890], *Headley Arms*: Smartly modernised open-plan Watneys pub with carvery restaurant upstairs, real ale; extensive refurbishment early 1990; nice position between duckpond and Warley Gap woods *(Robert Lester)*; *Thatchers Arms*: Pretty pub by village green incorporating Chef & Brewer restaurant; well kept Watneys-related real ales, good atmosphere, varied choice of decent food; good parking *(A M Kelly, Derek Patey)*

Hadstock [B1052; TL5544], *Kings Head*: Simple but warmly welcoming beamed pub in historic village, well kept Tolly real ales; good bar food (not Mon) from snacks to steaks, bar billiards; closed Mon lunchtime *(Geoff and Sarah Schrecker)*

Harlow [Three Horseshoes Rd; TL4510], *Cock*: Pleasant and attentive staff, good bar food *(Gerald Roll)*

Hatfield Broad Oak [TL5416], *Dukes Head*: Interesting and unusual food in old dining pub with friendly atmosphere, homely and attractive decor inc well furnished conservatory; close to Hatfield Forest — and Stansted Airport *(Alan and Ruth Woodhouse)*

☆ **Hatfield Heath** [overlooks biggest village green in Essex, junction of several roads; TL5215], *White Horse*: Friendly village pub on big green; dining area off main lounge opens on to pleasant lawn; solid wooden benches and a mix of interesting tables; Greene King ales, decent wines by the glass, bar food *(R P Hastings)*

☆ **Herongate** [Dunton Rd — turn off A128 Brentford—Grays at big sign for Boars Head; TQ6391], *Old Dog*: Long traditional bar with dark-beamed ceiling, open fire, relaxed atmosphere, comfortable new back lounge, well kept though not cheap Adnams Extra, Greene King IPA and Abbot, Ridleys PA and Ruddles County on handpump, with lots of guest beers such as Mauldons, three types of Arkells and Morlands tapped from the cask; lunchtime bar food popular with Ford staff (only snacks weekends); picnic-table sets on front terrace and in neat sheltered side garden *(Graham Bush, LYM)*

Heybridge Basin [TL8707], *Old Ship*: Good cheap food — and they don't mind if you just have a coffee; wonderful view of canal, lock and estuary *(Margaret and Trevor Errington)*

High Ongar [The Street, just off A414 Chipping Ongar—Chelmsford; TL5603], *Foresters Arms*: Free house with delightful low-beamed bar, good range of well kept real ales inc Adnams Southwold, Greene King Abbot and Mauldons on handpump *(Robert Lester)*; [King St, Nine Ashes], *Wheatsheaf*: Small two-bar country pub with 'coffin-lid' tables, back garden and Wethereds on handpump *(Robert Lester)*

Howe Street [TL6914], *Green Man*: Beamed pub with decent Ridleys ales and wines by the glass, usual bar food, restaurant (must book Sun lunch); piped music could be quieter *(SJC)*

Ingatestone [High St; TQ6499], *Bell*: Rather stylishly done up to look older than it is, with well kept Bass and Charrington IPA *(Dr and Mrs A K Clarke, P Thorogood)*; [High St], *Star*: Small and completely unpretentious — like going back 30 years; enormous winter log fire, well kept Greene King IPA and Abbot, interesting hat collection, friendly landlord *(Gerry and Beverley Markham, Dr and Mrs A K Clarke)*

Kirby Le Soken [TM2221], *Ship*: Old pink-washed beamed building with very friendly service; tables can be booked for wide choice of food with good range of prices — steak and kidney pie and enormous ploughman's tipped *(Margaret and Trevor Errington)*

Knowl Green [TL7841], *Cherry Tree*: Doing well under new licensees — welcoming and unspoilt atmosphere, real ales, good home-made bar food, no piped music *(Mrs M Mackintosh)*

Leigh on Sea [Old Leigh; TQ8385], *Peter Boat*: Friendly, cosy pub by harbour, well kept beers and good, cheap bar food *(Quentin Williamson)*

Little Baddow [The Ridge; minor rd Hatfield Peverel—Danbury; TL7807], *Generals Arms*: Well kept Bass and Charrington IPA, decent wines, bar food and (Thurs–Sat evening, Sun lunch) restaurant in friendly neatly kept local with new licensees; big lawn with tables and play area; we heard it was up for sale as we went to press – more news please *(Gwen and Peter Andrews, LYM)*; [North Hill (towards Hatfield Peverel)], *Rodney*: Low-beamed pub doing well under new licensees, with friendly welcome, sparkling brasses, coal fire, reasonably priced home-made bar food, well kept Adnams and Tetleys on handpump; small terrace and garden *(Gwen and Peter Andrews)*

Little Walden [B1052; TL5441], *Crown*: Highly rated in last year's Dip (and Egon Ronay's pub of the year in 1987), but we've heard nothing of it since it closed in 1989 *(News please)*

☆ **Littlebury** [TL5139], *Queens Head*: Very congenial inside, with connecting areas and exposed beams; good bar food, now expanded from the ploughman's recommended in last year's edition to dishes such as mushrooms with garlic and bacon, crispy duck with orange and salad, really fresh strawberries, splendid baked bananas in a creamy sauce; well kept Adnams, Marstons Pedigree and Websters Yorkshire, restaurant *(Robert Mitchell, Joyce and Norman Bailey)*

Loughton [99 Smarts Lane; TQ4296], *Carpenters Arms*: Town pub with boxing memorabilia and carpenters' tools in cosy lounge and public bars; Flowers Original and Wethereds on handpump *(Robert Lester)*; [2 Church Hill (A121)], *Kings Head*: Plush lounge bar, wood-decorated public, good friendly atmosphere; Watneys-related real ales on handpump; restaurant *(Robert Lester)*; [15 York Hill], *Wheatsheaf*: Small, friendly open-plan beamed local with Bass and Charrington IPA on handpump; best to get there early *(Robert Lester)*

Lower Mayland [back rd Latchingdon—Bradwell-on-Sea; TL9101], *Mayland*: Pleasantly refurbished 16th-century pub with one long bar and restaurant annexe; plenty of tables, food home-made, steaks well cooked *(Gwen and Peter Andrews)*

Maldon [Silver St; TL8506], *Blue Boar*: Pleasantly placed, with good seafood, well kept Adnams, pleasant service; bedrooms *(Peter Burton)*; [The Quay], *Jolly Sailor*: Cosy old pub on quay beside medieval church; slightly elevated position gives views over stackies — the Thames sailing barges once used to take hay stacks to London; bar food, Watneys-related real ales *(Quentin Williamson)*

☆ **Margaretting Tye** [TL6800], *White Hart*:

Secluded pub in quiet surroundings by village green, with lots of tables in well kept garden, barbecue, ponies in adjoining paddock; wide choice of good value simple food served generously, well kept Adnams and Broadside, Mauldons, Greene King IPA and a guest beer on handpump, friendly staff, good mix of customers; some live music *(Gwen and Peter Andrews, Mike Beiley)*

☆ Matching Tye [TL5111], *Fox*: Very comfortable and friendly low-beamed 17th-century building, with simple but wholesome food — mainly various ploughman's and interesting choice of filled baked potatoes; lots of fox pictures, peaceful garden in lovely rural surroundings *(Alan and Ruth Woodhouse)*

Monk Street [TL6128], *Greyhound*: Pleasant welcome, well kept Adnams Southwold, Rombouts coffee, usual bar food *(Gwen and Peter Andrews)*

☆ Moreton [TL5307], *Moreton Massey*: Large and attractive open-plan beamed pub, comfortably furnished and well run, with good imaginative bar food; well kept changing real ales such as Bass, Greene King, Marstons and Thwaites, good choice of wines inc Chilean ones (the drinks don't stand out as cheap), plenty of seating — though it does fill up; restaurant *(Alan and Ruth Woodhouse, Robert Lester)*

Mountnessing [TQ6297], *Prince of Wales*: Straightforwardly furnished pub with consistently well kept Ridleys, small but unusual selection of malt whiskies, well placed bar food, reasonably good-natured Doberman *(J H Walker, P Thorogood)*

☆ Navestock [Horsemans Side (off B175); TQ5397], *Alma Arms*: Popular, comfortable, low-beamed free house with emphasis on bar food, but also serving well kept ales such as Adnams, Greene King IPA and Abbot, Rayments BBA and Youngs Special; busy but unspoilt atmosphere, good service *(R Houghton, Derek Patey, Peter Andrews)*

Navestock [Tamhouse Lane; Horsemanside—Sabines Green], *King William IV*: Small, tucked-away clapboard pub, cosy and well decorated, with real fire, Thelwell drawings illustrating pub names, Watneys-related ales, friendly atmosphere; good gardens with serving hatch in summer *(Quentin Williamson, Gerry and Beverley Markham)*

Navestock Side [TQ5697], *Green Man*: Pleasant spot by cricket pitch; well kept Ind Coope Burton and decent wines, cheerful lounge (may be closed for functions), darker middle bar, pricey restaurant (not Mon) in adjoining barn; may be Sunday bar nibbles *(Gwen and Peter Andrews)*

☆ North Fambridge [The Quay; TQ8597], *Ferryboat*: Quaint little weatherboarded pub in remote riverside spot, with low beams, flagstones, old benches, old-fashioned atmosphere and lighting that gives a romantic feel; well kept Tetleys, cheap bar food and friendly mix of locals and (particularly in summer) Londoners and yachtsmen *(Quentin Williamson, Graham Bush)*

☆ North Shoebury [Frobisher Way (behind ASDA); TQ9485], *Parsons Barn*: Attractively olde-worlde reworking of former barn, with five real ales on handpump and Adnams tapped from the cask (a Watneys development, but run as a free house); good value bar food, friendly service *(MN, Peter Seddon)*

☆ Paglesham [TQ9293], *Plough & Sail*: Good value food pub in pretty spot near the marshes — attractive building with warm and friendly atmosphere, well kept Watneys-related beers, quick helpful service, good choice of decent bar food (all day at least in summer) inc oysters, also carvery; can get crowded on warm summer evenings, but pleasant even then *(MN, Jenny Cantle, C Sharpe)*

Paglesham [East End], *Punchbowl*: Pretty and beautifully kept pub, with very good food *(Jenny Cantle, C Sharpe)*

Peldon [TL9916], *Plough*: Pretty little tiled and white-boarded unpretentious village local, popular for genuinely fresh fish and seafood; cheerfully busy in the evenings and at weekends *(Jan and Ian Alcock, BB)*

Pilgrims Hatch [Ongar Rd; TQ5895], *Black Horse*: Good value bar food *(Derek Patey)*

Purfleet [TQ5578], *Royal*: Beefeater steak bar with fine Thames views from outside tables, good range of lunchtime bar food; restaurant *(B R Wood)*

Radley Green [TL6205], *Thatchers Arms*: Secluded, friendly and snug open-plan country local with Adnams Extra and Ridleys Bitter and Old Bob on handpump; beer garden, own football pitch *(Robert Lester)*

Rayleigh [High St; TQ8190], *Paul Pry*: Good local atmosphere without being unfriendly, small snugs with Ruddles Best and County, big garden with barbecue *(Graham Bush)*

Rettendon [Southend Rd; A130 S; TQ7698], *Plough & Sail*: Much-extended roadside pub with big conservatory, good choice of beers inc Greene King IPA as well as Watneys-related ones, good value bar food, separate carvery; children's area *(M J Morgan)*

☆ Rickling Green [B1383 Stansted—Newport; TL5029], *Cricketers Arms*: Delightful pub with friendly licensees, staff and even dogs, good fresh bar food all home-made inc relaxed Sun lunches, well kept Greene King IPA and Abbot and a guest beer, piped music catering for all tastes, delicious coffee; near charming cricket pavilion *(Caroline Wright, Kevin Perkins)*

Ridgewell [A604 Haverhill—Halstead; TL7340], *Kings Head*: Simply furnished pub with Tudor beams and big brick fireplace, but otherwise much modernised, with good value bar food in dining area of small lounge, well kept Greene King IPA and Abbot on handpump, local World War II memorabilia inc Dambusters print, signed James Stewart photograph, huge brass shellcases; pool and other games in airy public bar, piped music, a few tables in roadside garden *(Patrick Young, BB)*

Rochford [North St; TQ8790], *Golden Lion*: Homely and intimate pub (so small that it's quite a pack at busy times); welcoming licensee, excellent choice of real ales such as Crouch Vale Bitter and SAS, Fullers London Pride, Greene King Abbot, Mauldons Mild, Sam Smiths OB and Theakstons Old Peculier, lunchtime bar snacks, basic outside lavatories *(Graham Bush, MN)*

Rowhedge [Quay; TM0021], *Anchor*: Splendid position overlooking River Colne with its swans, gulls and yachts; well kept Watneys-related real ales, fishing bric-a-brac, good atmosphere, ample helpings of good value food such as fresh plaice, restaurant *(J H Walker, Tony Tucker)*

Roydon [42 High St; TL4109], *Crusader*: Large, smart open-plan pub with McMullens AK Mild and Bitter on handpump *(Robert Lester);* [High St (B181)], *White Hart*: Pleasant, cosy bar with Greene King Abbot and Rayments BBA on handpump *(Mrs E M Thompson)*

☆ **Saffron Walden** [Bridge St; B184 towards Cambridge; TL5438], *Eight Bells*: The Moores, who made this a very popular main entry with their reliably good food, especially fresh fish from Lowestoft, well kept real ales and a notable collection of decent wines by the glass, have now moved — with some key staff — to the Kings Arms at Broomfield (see main entries); Benskins have put a manager into this handsome Tudor pub, and first reports are that it's still well worth knowing as a place to eat, with adventurous food still, cheerful service and well kept Adnams and Tetleys; nr start GWG107; bedrooms *(Gwen and Peter Andrews, John Baker, ASM, MEM, LYM — more reports on the new regime please)*

South Fambridge [TQ8596], *Anchor*: Always popular and welcoming; interesting guest beers such as Theakstons Old Peculier and the very strong Willy Warmer *(Jenny Cantle)*

South Hanningfield [TQ7497], *Windmill*: Staff friendly, carvery worth knowing; handy for Hanningfield reservoir *(S Corrigan)*

☆ **South Weald** [Weald Rd (off A12); TQ5793], *Tower Arms*: Well kept beers such as Adnams, Greene King IPA and Abbot and Youngs Special, good gardens, and pleasant village setting; attractive conservatory restaurant, friendly staff *(Gerry and Beverley Markham, P Thorogood, Derek Patey)*

Stansted [Silver St; TL5124], *Cock*: Pleasant atmosphere, good cheap food *(Mrs C Wardell); Kings Arms*: Good food in simple dining room — proper cooking with good sauces and crisp vegetables; decent house wine *(Alison Graham)*

☆ **Stanway** [London Rd; TL9324], *Swan*: Very big yet friendly local with well kept beer and several oak-beamed rooms inc pretty

restaurant (where children are allowed) used at lunchtime as servery for wide range of good hot and cold bar food; cheerful generous service, big open fire *(Alison Findlay, Barbara and Norman Wells, John and Ruth Bell)*

☆ **Stock** [The Square (just off village st); TQ6998], *Bear*: Pleasant bars with warm and cosy atmosphere and lots of character, well kept Allied beers, good bar food, friendly landlord and helpful service; restaurant; links with Essex CCC *(Graham Oddey)*

☆ **Stock** [B1007 towards Galleywood — OS Sheet 167 map reference 704004], *Ship*: Particularly good food from choice of dainty or doorstep sandwiches through omelettes to mixed grill in old plastered building concealed behind a bank of trees, with oak furniture in beamed original bar, modern flock-wallpaper and wrought-iron-fitted addition; Paines EG and Tolly Original on handpump, restaurant *(Patrick Young)*

Stock [Common Rd; just off B1007 Chelmsford—Billericay], *Bakers Arms*: Popular local with pleasant garden, good atmosphere, genial landlord, straightforward bar food and Watneys-related real ales; provision for children *(Gwen and Peter Andrews, Graham Oddey)*

☆ **Thaxted** [Bullring; TL6130], *Swan*: Four-gabled late 15th-century inn reopened after longish closure and complete renovation; partly carpeted slate-floored circular bar, well refurbished, with plain wooden chairs and settles, soft lighting, good piped music; Greene King IPA and Abbot and several well kept guest beers such as Courage Directors and Eldridge Pope Royal Oak; pleasantly pubby atmosphere, with lots of regulars; sandwiches in bar, other food in cellar restaurant; bedrooms comfortably modernised, all with own bathroom *(Gwen and Peter Andrews)*

Thaxted [Mill End], *Star*: Old beams, well kept Ind Coope Burton, pleasant staff, decent straightforward food *(Richard Houghton)*

Theydon Bois [Station Rd (off B172); TQ4599], *Railway Arms*: Small and friendly recently refurbished village local, with prints of old steam engines; well kept Flowers and Wethereds on handpump *(Robert Lester)*

Tillingham [TL9903], *Fox & Hounds*: Friendly and well kept timbered bar with eating area, open fire, pub games, Greene King IPA on handpump, good coffee *(Gwen and Peter Andrews)*

Tolleshunt Knights [B1023 Tiptree—Tolleshunt D'Arcy; TL9114], *Rose & Crown*: Beamed bars with brass and plates on walls, well kept Crouch Vale Willie Warmer, Greene King IPA and Abbot and Tolly on handpump; bar food every day, restaurant lunchtime (not Mon); friendly staff *(Gwen and Peter Andrews)*

☆ **Toot Hill** [village signed off A113 S of Ongar and from A414 W of Ongar; TL5102], *Green Man*: A most enlightened attitude to wines — with a tremendous choice from a good variety of merchants, inc dozens of champagnes — lifts this simply furnished dining pub out of the ordinary, and the food (which does include bar snacks and sandwiches) runs to some quite ambitious cooking; pretty front terrace, tables in back garden; staff could perhaps be more obliging sometimes; children over 10 allowed *(MN, Helen Crookston, Joy Heatherley, P R Davis, Alan and Ruth Woodhouse, Derek Patey, LYM)*

Toppesfield [TL7337], *Crawley Arms*: Friendly little pub in pretty unspoilt village off the beaten track; nicely decorated, with fresh flowers, chintzy curtains *(Alison Findlay)*

☆ nr **Waltham Abbey** [very handy for M25 junction 26; A121 towards Waltham Abbey, then follow Epping, Loughton sign from exit roundabout; TL3800], *Volunteer*: Nicely placed on the edge of Epping Forest; substantial roadhouse with pretty hanging baskets and so forth, very spacious inside — big open-plan bar with several separate areas and attractive conservatory, interesting decorations; bar food includes lots of chow mein dishes and big pancake rolls prepared by Chinese landlady, alongside usual things, in enormous helpings; McMullens beer, some tables on side terrace, lots of staff; can get very busy at weekends *(Alan and Ruth Woodhouse, Joy and Peter Heatherley, Comus Elliott, Kevin Perkins)*

Waltham Abbey [Crooked Mile/Sun St (B194)], *New*: Smart, roomy open-plan pub with lively atmosphere, Benskins Best on handpump, restaurant *(Robert Lester)*; [High Bridge St (A121)], *Old English Gentleman*: Town pub by River Lea; spacious, with friendly atmosphere and staff, well kept McMullen AK Mild and Country Bitter *(Robert Lester)*; [Honey Lane; handy for M25 junction 26 — via A121], *Woodbine*: Pleasantly refurbished, keeping Victorian/Edwardian character in spite of fruit machines and juke box; central fireplace, small conservatory, some seats outside (well tended window boxes, even in winter); cheerful staff, decent food inc good sandwiches, well kept Ind Coope Burton, palatable house wine, darts *(Joy Heatherley)*

☆ **Widdington** [High St; TL5331], *Fleur de Lys*: Clean and unpretentious village pub, spacious and nicely decorated low-beamed bar, good log fire in fine old fireplace, well kept Adnams Broadside and Southwold, Greene King IPA, Mauldons and Nethergate on handpump, pleasant young staff, small snooker and darts room, wide choice of reasonably priced bar food from sandwiches (good rare beef) and a fine stilton ploughman's to venison steaks, restaurant (children allowed here), tables outside; handy for Widdington Wildlife Park *(Gwen and Peter Andrews, Joyce and Norman Bailey, Alan and Ruth Woodhouse)*

☆ **Witham** [113 Hatfield Rd (B1389); TL8214], *Jack & Jenny*: Well run family pub, open all day, with late afternoon teas; spacious L-shaped bar, comfortable chairs and sofas, pool table at one end, good mix of customers, attentive service even when busy, and relaxing atmosphere; well kept Courage Best and Directors, John Smiths and a guest real ale such as Fullers ESB on handpump, Symonds cider, standard bar food at reasonable prices, exuberantly decorated new conservatory, garden *(Gwen and Peter Andrews)*

Wivenhoe [TM0321], *Rose & Crown*: Friendly quayside pub with traditional welcome and warm winter fire; seafood stall outside in summer and good fish and chip shop nearby — so you can eat and drink on quayside; warm fire in winter *(Jan and Ian Alcock)*

Woodham Mortimer [TL8104], *Hurdlemakers Arms*: Quiet tucked-away local looking like a cosy house, open fire in simply furnished flagstoned lounge with cushioned settles, low ceiling and timbered walls; well kept Greene King IPA and Abbot, good darts alley in public bar, picnic-table sets well spaced among trees and shrubs outside *(Gwen Andrews, BB)*

Youngs End [A131 Braintree—Chelmsford, nr Essex Show Ground; TL7319], *Green Dragon*: Cosy bars with plush seats and smaller snug, big beamed barn restaurant; well kept Greene King IPA and Abbot and winter Willie Warmer on handpump, decent wines; nicely served swordfish steaks; neat and pleasant staff; children's play area, and green dragon by car park, some barbecues *(Gwen and Peter Andrews)*

Gloucestershire

Masses of new main entries here include the Black Horse perched on a steep hillside in Amberley, the unspoilt Boat by the Severn at Ashleworth Quay (in the same family for centuries), the well restored Bear in the striking stone village of Bisley, the simple and friendly Brockweir Inn at Brockweir, the distinctive Seven Tuns at Chedworth (another lovely village), the relaxed Ebrington Arms at Ebrington (handy for Hidcote), the lively and attractively reshaped Royal Oak at Gretton, the Thames Head near Kemble (a new venture from the same stable as the Swan at Southrop), the Royal Spring in a remarkably fine position at Lower Lydbrook in the Forest of Dean, the friendly Horse & Groom at Oddington (run by two young brothers), and the rambling, chatty old Greyhound at Siddington. Several of these have notable food, and other pubs in the county to pick out for this include the relaxed Gardeners Arms at Alderton (bargain lunchtime sandwiches, good evening restaurant), the Kings Head at Bledington (a nice place to stay, too), the Crown at Blockley (civilised, with lots of fresh fish), the relaxed Bakers Arms in Broad Campden, the Green Dragon at Cowley (a great favourite for food), the rambling Hunters Hall near Kingscote (good atmosphere), the Hobnails at Little Washbourne (lots of huge and interesting filled baps), the Black Horse at Naunton, the Swan at Southrop, and the Ram at Woodchester (approaching a star award now). Though they don't have our food award, all these attractive pubs are now pushing towards it: the Village Pub at Barnsley, the Crown at Frampton Mansell (good cold buffet), the Lamb at Great Rissington (a good place to stay), the Trout on the Thames near Lechlade, the Weighbridge near Nailsworth (especially its two-in-one pies), the Coach & Horses near Stow-on-the-Wold (doing particularly well under its very young licensees), and the Mill Inn at Withington. Prices in the area are close to the national average, but a number of pubs stand out as notably cheap: for drinks, the Ebrington Arms at Ebrington, Mount at Stanton, Coach & Horses near Stow-on-the-Wold and Daneway at Sapperton (all these are supplied by local breweries – Donnington in particular can always be relied on for low prices here); for bargain snacks, the Gardeners Arms at Alderton, Lygon Arms at Chipping Campden and that lively real-ale inn the New Inn near North Nibley (we found something under £1 at all three); and for main dishes (our target was something decent under £3) the Crown of Crucis at Ampney Crucis, Bear at Bisley, Seven Tuns at Chedworth, Thames Head at Kemble, Weighbridge near Nailsworth, New Inn near North Nibley again, Boat at Redbrook, George at St Briavels, Greyhound at Siddington, Queens Head in Stow-on-the-Wold and Coach & Horses just outside. In the Lucky Dip section at the end of the chapter, pubs and inns to mark your card with include the Craven Arms at Brockhampton, Plough at Cold Aston, Colesbourne Inn, Wild Duck at Ewen, Fox at Great Barrington, Canning Arms at Hartpury, Kilkenny Inn, Royal Oak at

*Leighterton, Kings Arms at Mickleton, Apple Tree at Minsterworth,
Egypt Mill in Nailsworth, Ostrich at Newland, Woodman at
Parkend, Bell at Sapperton, Snowshill Arms, and Corner Cupboard in
Winchcombe.*

ALDERTON   SP0033 Map 4

Gardeners Arms ✪

Village signposted from A438 Tewkesbury–Stow-on-the-Wold

This thatched and timbered, black-and-white Tudor house has a smart,
old-fashioned, L-shaped bar with high-backed antique settles and other good solid
seats, old mugs and tankards hanging from its sturdy beams, and a fine collection
of interesting 19th-century prints on its cream walls – sporting, political, and
scurrilous French literary ones by J-J Granville; good winter log fire, a relaxed
atmosphere, and two friendly labradors called Sally (yellow) and Captain
(chocolate). The more straightforward public bar has sensibly placed darts,
shove-ha'penny, dominoes, cribbage, fruit machine and juke box; well kept
Flowers Original, Wadworths 6X and Whitbreads West Country PA on
handpump. Good lunchtime bar snacks include sandwiches (from 95p),
ploughman's (from £2.50), home-made pâté (£2.95), salads (from £3.25),
delicious melon filled with prawns (£3.75), and lovely fresh sardines (£3.50);
however, the landlord-chef saves most of his culinary energy for the evening
restaurant, which specialises in local game and good meats (contrary to our usual
practice, it's this that the food award refers to). There are tables outside, where a
partly covered crazy-paved back courtyard and a second terrace open on to a well
kept garden. *(Recommended by PADEMLUC, Dick Brown, Chris Raisin, A Triggs, Denny
Lyster, Laurence Manning, Michael and Harriet Robinson)*

*Whitbreads   Licensee Jack Terry   Real ale   Snacks (lunchtime, not Sun or Mon) and
Sun roast lunch   Evening restaurant (Tues–Sat), though they do Sun roast lunch
tel Alderton (024 262) 257   Children welcome   Singer-guitarist Thurs evening   Open
11–2 (2.30 Sat), 6.30–11; closed evening 25 Dec*

AMBERLEY   SO8401 Map 4

Black Horse

Village signposted off A46 Stroud–Nailsworth; as you pass village name take first very
sharp left turn (before Amberley Inn) then bear steeply right – pub on your left

The carpeted bar is simply furnished, with wheelback chairs, green-cushioned
window seats, just a few prints on the plain cream walls, a fire in a small stone
fireplace; one window gives a striking panoramic view of the woods and stone
villages tucked into the steep folds of the hillside opposite. The well kept real ales
come from far afield (mainly north): Davenports, Fullers ESB, Moorhouses Pendle
Witches Brew, Tetleys and Timothy Taylors Landlord. Bar food's a bit different
from the usual run, too, including interesting fillings for toasted French bread
(£2.95), pies such as lamb and apricot (£4.25) or beef with venison (£4.50) as well
as steak and kidney, kippers (£4.50) and Japanese prawns (£6.95); also sandwiches
(£1.50), ploughman's (£2.75), filled baked potatoes (£3) and so forth; darts. Teak
seats and picnic-table sets on a back terrace (with barbecue) have the same glorious
view, as does a conservatory extension of the neat and rather promisingly
ambitious restaurant. On the other side a lawn with pretty flowers and
honeysuckle has more picnic-table sets. The pub's on the edge of Minchinhampton
Common – a unique high cow-grazed plateau dotted with buildings (and
prehistoric remains), enjoying remarkable views of the much more crumpled and
folded surrounding hills. *(Recommended by Heather Sharland, P Freeman, Tom McLean,
Roger Huggins, Ewan McCall, Roger Entwistle)*

*Free house   Manager Mark Lennox   Real ale   Meals and snacks (12.30–2.30, 7–11)
Restaurant tel Amberley (0453) 872556   Children welcome   Open 11–3(Sat 3.30),
6–11*

AMPNEY CRUCIS   SP0602   Map 4

Crown of Crucis

A417 E of Cirencester

Even when this refurbished food pub is very busy (at weekends, particularly Sunday lunchtime), the service remains cheerful and efficient. Popular bar food includes home-made soup (£1), sandwiches (from £1.05, toasties from £1.20), ploughman's (£2), basket meals (from £2.05), salads (from £3.55), herb pancakes filled with mushroom, spinach and nuts or lasagne (£3.65), marinated beef, lamb and sausage kebabs (£3.70), home-made beef curry (£3.85), seafood bake (£4.25), and steaks (from £6.20); home-made puddings (£1.50), children's dishes (from £1.50). The spacious bar is sympathetically and comfortably modernised, and serves well kept Archers Village, Marstons Pedigree and Tetleys on handpump. There are lots of tables on the grass at the back, by a stream with ducks and maybe swans. *(Recommended by M J B Pearson, E Davies, Mr and Mrs J H Adam, Patrick Freeman, Barbara M McHugh, Mr and Mrs P B Dowsett, John and Pat Smyth, P and R Woods, Patrick Freeman, Henry Midwinter, CEP, Peter Scillitoe)*

Free house   Licensee R K Mills   Real ale   Meals and snacks (12–2.30, 6–10) Restaurant   Children in restaurant and eating area of bar until 8pm   Open 11–11; 10.30–2.30, 6–11 in winter; closed 25 Dec   Bedrooms tel Poulton (0285) 851806; £43B/£54B

ASHLEWORTH QUAY   SO8125   Map 4

Boat

Ashleworth signposted off A417 N of Gloucester; Quay signed from village

In the same family since it was originally licensed by Royal Charter (we believe this is a record for continuous pub ownership), this delightful 15th-century riverside cottage's timeless quality is beautifully preserved by the two ladies who've been running it in exactly the same charming way – with help now from a friendly younger girl – for so many years. A pair of flower-cushioned antique settles face each other in the back room where Arkells, Smiles and a full range of Westons farm ciders are tapped from the cask, while the front parlour has a great built-in settle by a long scrubbed deal table facing an old-fashioned open kitchen range with a side bread oven and a couple of elderly fireside chairs. There are rush mats on the scrubbed flagstones, houseplants in the window, fresh garden flowers, and old magazines to read. A back parlour with rugs on its red tiles has plump overstuffed chairs and a sofa, a grandfather clock and dresser, a big dog basket in front of the fire, cribbage, dominoes and lots of board games (the front room has darts). They do lunchtime rolls. A sun-trap crazy-paved front courtyard, bright with plant tubs in summer, has a couple of picnic-table sets under cocktail parasols, with more seats and tables under cover at the sides. It's set back from the embankment of this peaceful curve of the River Severn,

which has a good slipway here; the medieval tithe barn nearby is striking. A very special place. *(Recommended by Ewan McCall, Tom McLean, Roger Huggins, BOB)*

Free house   Licensees Irene and Sybil Jelf   Real ale   Lunchtime snacks   Children welcome   Occasional Morris Men in summer   Open 11–2.30, 6–11; closed evening 25 Dec

AWRE   SO7108   Map 4

Red Hart

Village signposted off A48 S of Newnham

Surprisingly tall, this red tiled, three-storey, 16th-century pub is set in a quiet farming hamlet, close to the River Severn. The L-shaped bar has big prints on the walls, a deep glass-covered well, a stuffed pheasant on the mantlepiece over the good log fire, and a back area where a bale of straw swings from pitched rafters; fruit machine. The new licensee has introduced a different menu: home-made soup

(£1.30), sandwiches (from £1.30), ploughman's (from £1.95), omelettes (from £2.25), cottage pie (£3.95), gammon and egg (£5), sirloin steak (£7.50), daily specials, and home-made puddings (£1.35). Well kept Banks's on handpump, several malt whiskies and freshly squeezed orange juice; friendly service. There are picnic-table sets on the sheltered back lawn, with more out in front. *(Recommended by Gwynne Harper, Susi Joynes; more reports please)*

Free house Licensee John Bailes Real ale Meals and snacks 12–2, 7–10 Restaurant tel Dean (0594) 510220; midnight supper licence; closed Sun evening (except Bank Hol weekends) Children welcome Pianist Sat evening and pianist/organist Sun evening Open 11–2.30, 7–11

BARNSLEY SP0705 Map 4
Village Pub

A433 Cirencester–Burford

Despite the many visitors, this busy, friendly pub manages to retain a good local atmosphere. The comfortable, communicating rooms have plush chairs, stools and window settles around the polished tables on the carpet, low ceilings, and walls (some stripped back to bare stone) decorated with gin-traps, scythes and other farm tools; several winter log fires. Well kept Flowers IPA and Wadworths 6X on handpump, and a range of country wines; cribbage, dominoes, piped pop music. Good, varied bar food includes sandwiches (£1.50), home-made soup, ploughman's (£2.50), steak and kidney pie or decent sausages (£3.95), salads (from £4.25), bean and vegetable casserole (£4.50), local pink trout (£4.95), 10oz charcoal-grilled sirloin steak (£7.25), and daily specials such as herrings in cream sauce (£2.95), very spicy lamb creole or beef in elderberry wine (around £4.95); good puddings. The sheltered back courtyard has plenty of tables, and its own outside servery. *(Recommended by L Walker, Mrs J A Gardner, D J Cooke, Sidney Wells, David and Christine Foulkes, John Broughton, P and R Woods, Caroline Wright, Alan Skull, N P Cox, Tom McLean, Ewan McCall, Roger Huggins, Jean and Edward Rycroft, Philip King, B and J Derry, P H King, Laurence Manning, Mrs J Oakes, John and Pat Smyth, Dr M V Jones)*

Free house Licensee Miss S Stevens Real ale Meals and snacks (not 25 Dec) Restaurant Children in eating area and restaurant Open 10.30–3, 6–11; closed 25 Dec Bedrooms tel Bibury (028 574) 421; £25B/£38B

BISLEY SO9005 Map 4
Bear

Village signposted off A419 just E of Stroud

For its first 300 years the Bear served as the courthouse for this striking stone-built steep village – well off the beaten track, so one of the Cotswolds' more hidden treasures. The meandering L-shaped bar has a long shiny black built-in settle and a smaller but even sturdier oak settle by the front entrance, facing an enormously wide recently opened-up stone fireplace (not very high – the ochre ceiling's too low for that). At the back there's a tropical fish tank facing the bar counter, which has well kept Flowers IPA and Original, Wadworths 6X and Whitbreads Pompey Royal on handpump; several malt whiskies. Bar food includes sandwiches (from 75p), filled baked potatoes (£1.30), ploughman's (from £2.35), cottage pie (£2.60), chilli con carne (£2.65), basket meals such as chicken (£3.40) and evening steaks (from 8oz rump £7.25); there's a separate stripped-stone no-smoking dining area. The atmosphere is homely and relaxed, the landlord welcoming and interesting; table skittles, shove-ha'penny, dominoes, cribbage, trivia machine, quoits, and faint piped music. A small front colonnade supports the upper floor, and the sheltered little flagstoned courtyard made by this has a traditional bench (and a dog water-bowl); there's a re-done garden, and quite a collection of stone mounting-blocks. *(Recommended by Roger Huggins, Ewan McCall, Tom McLean, A H J Sale)*

Flowers (Whitbreads) Licensee D Stevenson Real ale Meals and snacks (till 1.45;

not Sun or Mon evenings) Open 11–2.30 (3 Sat), 6–11 – they may stay open longer in the afternoon if busy; closed 25 and 26 Dec and 1 Jan

BLEDINGTON SP2422 Map 4

Kings Head ✪ ⟳

B4450

Tables on terraces at the front of this 15th-century inn look over the attractive village green with its ducks and stream, and in summer months Morris Dancers regularly perform in the courtyard; the landscaped garden has a children's play area. Inside, the central main bar has some beams – including a heavy vertical one next to the serving counter – high-backed wooden settles, gateleg or pedestal tables, and a cheery log fire in the stone inglenook, in which hangs a big black kettle. The lounge looks on to the garden. Popular bar food (the menu varies twice daily) includes at lunchtime, excellent soup (£1.50), sausages (£2.25), delicious hot roast beef sandwich (£2.95), aubergine au gratin or a good grilled red mullet (£3.95), tasty spare ribs (£5.25), and steak and wine pie (£5.50); in the evening they have chilli prawns and pasta or hot black pudding with apple and bacon (£2.95), kidneys braised in red wine bacon and parsley (£4.95), local trout stuffed with herbs and prawns (£6.25), steaks (from £7.95), fruity lamb (£8.50), and blackboard specials such as lasagne (£4.95), roast poussin in lemon sauce (£7.95), and venison steak in whisky and orange sauce (£9.50). Well kept Hook Norton, Tetleys, Wadworths 6X and guest beers on handpump from the antique bar counter, and a good choice of malt whiskies; piped music. The public bar has pool, bar billiards, shove-ha'penny, dominoes, fruit machine, and juke box, with Aunt Sally in the garden. The continuing steady flow of warm enthusiasm from readers for this pub has in the last year or so been somewhat diluted by a cooler trickle of concern about service – over-strict timekeeping for ending Sunday food service, for instance, or one unhappy incident over getting the wrong bedroom. We hope further reports will confirm that everything is firmly back on track. *(Recommended by Dr Sheila Smith, Alan Skull, Roger and Jenny Huggins, Laurence Manning, S V Bishop, Stephen King, Mrs E M Thompson, C F Walling)*

Free house Licensees Michael and Annette Royce Real ale Meals and snacks Partly no-smoking restaurant – closed Sun evenings Children in restaurant Open 11–2.30, 6–11 Bedrooms tel Kingham (060 871) 365; £26B/£45B

BLOCKLEY SP1634 Map 4

Crown ★ ⟳

High Street

Smart and civilised, this golden stone Elizabethan inn specialises in lots of fresh fish dishes: sea bream, Cornish megrin, plaice, monkfish, eel, red and grey mullet, sardines, trout, shark, lobster, green-lipped mussels from New Zealand, and maybe tiger prawns (from around £6). Other food includes sandwiches (from £1.50), home-made soup (£1.60), home-made chicken liver terrine (£2.95), delicious fresh asparagus, tagliatelli (£4.75), steak and kidney pie (£5.95), steaks, and good home-made puddings (£1.60); Sunday lunch. The public bar has an antique settle and more recent furnishings, and off this is the snug carpeted lounge with an attractive window seat, Windsor chairs around traditional cast-iron-framed tables, a winter log fire, and steps up into a little sitting room with easy chairs. This in turn leads through to a spacious dining room. Well kept Butcombe, Courage Directors, Marstons Pedigree, Wadworths 6X and a guest beer on handpump and a good selection of wines; you can sit out in front and have your drinks handed down from the window by the bar counter. Fruit machine and piped music. Close to Batsford Park Arboretum. *(Recommended by Mrs M E Lawrence, Ted George, Robert and Vicky Tod, Mrs J A Gardner, Cynth and Malc Pollard, William D Cissna, Laurence Manning, Dennis Royles, E V Walder, Derek and Sylvia Stephenson, G Eyre-Rodger)*

Free house   Licensees Jim and Betty Champion   Real ale   Meals and snacks (till 10 evening)   Restaurant   Children over 12 in eating area of bar   Open 11–2.30 (3 Sat), 6–11   Bedrooms tel Blockley (0386) 700245; £49.50S/£72.50S

BOURTON ON THE HILL   SP1732 Map 4

Horse & Groom 🛏

A44 W of Moreton-in-Marsh

Handy both for the Batsford arboretum and for Sezincote, this quiet, roadside pub has an attractive little lounge bar with high beams, stripped-stone walls, flowery-cushioned easy chairs, cricketing cartoons and steeplechasing photographs, and a large log fire. There's a local atmosphere in the bigger, orthodoxly furnished public bar; sensibly placed darts, dominoes and fruit machine; Bass on handpump. Bar food includes soup (95p), sandwiches (from 1.15), pâté or ploughman's (£2.75), omelettes (£2.95), home-made cannelloni, gammon (£5.25) and steak (£5.95). *(Recommended by Barry and Anne, Joan Morgan, Wayne Brindle)*

Free house   Licensee J L Aizpuru   Real ale   Meals and snacks   Restaurant (not Sun or Mon evenings)   Children over 10 only   Open 11–2.30, 6.30–11   Double bedrooms tel Evesham (0386) 700413; /£32S

BROAD CAMPDEN   SP1637 Map 4

Bakers Arms ✪

Village signposted from B4081 in Chipping Campden

In a tranquil village, this atmospheric ex-granary has a warmly friendly bar with beams in the dark ceiling, a pleasantly mixed bag of tables and seats around the walls (which are stripped back to bare stone), a log fire under a big black iron canopy at one end with a rocking chair beside it and a tank of shimmering tropical fish on a shelf above it, and another log fire at the other end. The oak bar counter is attractive, and there's a big framed rugwork picture of the pub. Well kept Flowers IPA and Original, Marstons Pedigree, and Wadworths 6X on handpump, with a guest beer like Theakstons Old Peculier or XB; a growing range of malt whiskies; darts, cribbage, dominoes. Nicely presented food includes herby tomato soup (95p), excellent garlic bread (a whole stick, £1.50), ploughman's (£1.50), omelette (from £2), salads (from £2.50, generous prawn £3.95), chilli con carne or chicken curry (£2.75), a selection of lasagnes (£2.95), chicken Kiev (£4) and good vegetarian dishes (sensibly marked out on the menu) such as chilli (£2.75) or mushroom and nut fettucini (£2.95); in the evenings they serve fresh vegetables. There are white tables under cocktail parasols by flower tubs on a side terrace, some seats under a fairy-lit arbour, and they've extended the garden behind to include more seats under cocktail parasols and plan to extend the well provisioned play area; Aunt Sally. *(Recommended by Marjorie and David Lamb, Richard Parr, Joan Morgan, Joy and Peter Heatherley, Caroline Wright, Gethin Lewis, Ted George, Bernard Phillips, Mr and Mrs W Dermott, PADEMLUC)*

Flowers (Whitbreads)   Licensees Carolyn and Tony Perry   Real ale   Meals and snacks (noon–9.45 Spring Bank Hol–Sept when they do afternoon teas from 3–6; 12–2, 6.30–9.45 winter; till 8.45 Suns; not 25 or 26 Dec)   Children in eating area   Folk music 3rd Tues of month   Open 11.30–11; 12–10.30 Sun, though they close the bar between 3 and 7; 11.30–2.30, 6.30–11 winter; closed 25 Dec and evening 26 Dec

BROCKWEIR   SO5401 Map 4

Brockweir

Village signposted just off A466 Chepstow–Monmouth

From this simple and friendly Wye Valley pub you can walk up steep sheep-pastures to Offa's Dyke Path and the Devil's Pulpit, with views over the Wye and Tintern Abbey. Canoeing, horse riding and salmon fishing are available locally. The bare-stone-walled main bar has sturdy settles on quarry tiles in the front part, and brocaded seats and copper-topped tables in a series of carpeted alcoves at the back; there are lots of community notices and a local atmosphere. The bare-floored public bar is traditionally furnished, and has darts, pool, dominoes, and cribbage; piped music. Well kept Boddingtons, Hook Norton and Theakstons XB on handpump, and farm cider. Simple bar food includes sandwiches, home-made soup, and lasagne, fettucini, and spicy chilli (£3.25). A covered courtyard at the back opens into a sheltered terrace. *(Recommended by Jacqueline Davis, David Young, D and B Carron, Drs M and K Parier)*

Free house   Licensee George Jones   Real ale   Meals and snacks   Children in eating area   Open 11.30–2.30 (3 Sat), 7–11   Bedrooms tel Tintern (02918) 548; £20/£35

CHEDWORTH   SP0511   Map 4

Seven Tuns

Queen Street, Upper Chedworth; village signposted off A429 NE of Cirencester; then take second signposted right turn and bear left towards church

It's the lounge on the right which most readers prefer: quite smart but cosy, with a good winter log fire in the big stone fireplace, sizeable antique prints, tankards hanging from the beam over the serving bar, a partly boarded ceiling, comfortable seats, decent tables and a quiet and peaceful atmosphere. The basic bar on the left is OK for people in wellies or with children, and opens into a games room with darts, dominoes, juke box, pool, and fruit machine; there's also a skittle alley (which can be hired). Both the house pâtés (from £1.10) such as stilton with herbs and the puddings (from £1) such as jam roly-poly, apple and blackberry pie and profiteroles come in for special praise; main dishes include a vegetarian dish (£3.20), a good steak and kidney pie (£3.50), and dishes of the day such as chicken satay (£1.90), basket meals (from £2.20), seafood gratin (£2.40) and smoked mackerel or moussaka (£3.40); sandwiches (from 70p), ploughman's (£2.50) and children's basket meals (£1.80). Well kept Courage Best and Directors on handpump; service is normally most welcoming. There are picnic-table sets under cocktail parasols on a side terrace, and older tables and seats over the lane in a little walled raised terrace with a stream running through it and forming a miniature waterfall outside; this steep collection of stone houses does seem to collect a lot of water and in wet weather the car park can be a bit mucky. *(Recommended by Roger Huggins, Ewan McCall, Tom McLean, J M Potter, Mrs A M Stephenson, Mr and Mrs P B Dowsett, A H J Sale)*

Courage   Licensees Barbara and Brian Eacott   Real ale   Meals and snacks (not winter Mon lunchtime, not 25 Dec)   Children welcome, but not in lounge bar   Occasional Morris Men or Mummers   Open 11.45–3, 6 (6.30 in winter)–11; closed winter Mon lunchtime, and may close 2.30 if licensees have a lot to do

CHIPPING CAMPDEN   SP1539   Map 4

Lygon Arms

Popular with young locals, this friendly place has a variety of horse photographs and hunting plates on the stripped stone walls of the small bar, stripped high-backed settles and green plush stools around the dimpled copper tables on the flowery carpet, and a curious stone-slate roof over the stone-built bar counter. Bar food includes filled rolls (from 80p) and sandwiches (from £1), sausage and egg (£2.50), home-made chicken liver pâté (£2.85), salads with home-made quiche and home-boiled ham (from £3.25), home-made hot dishes such as chilli con carne (£4), lasagne (£4.50), and steak and kidney pie (£4.65), and 8oz rump £7.75). Donnington SBA, Hook Norton Best, Ruddles Best and Wadworths 6X on handpump; some interesting wines by the glass. Darts and skittle alley. A few white cast-iron tables are set out in the sheltered inner courtyard. *(Recommended by Richard Parr, Lynne Sheridan, Bob West, Barry and Anne)*

Free house   Licensee I G Potter   Real ale   Meals and snacks (11.30–2.30, 6–10) Evening raftered steak-and-wine bar   Children in good family room and in eating area of bar   Folk music Sun evening   Open 11–2.30, 6–11   Bedrooms tel Evesham (0386) 840318; £20/£35

Noel Arms 🍺

Charles II is said to have stayed at this engaging old inn on his flight after the Battle of Worcester. The atmospheric bar has farm tools, horseshoes and gin traps on the bare stone walls, casks hanging from its beams, attractive old tables, seats and settles among the Windsor chairs, and a coal fire; a dining conservatory has been added. The small lounge areas are comfortable and traditionally furnished, and the reception area is interestingly decorated with armour and leopard skins. Bar menu includes sandwiches (from £1.40), soup (£1.45), filled baked potatoes (from £2.25), ploughman's (£2.75), cottage pie (£3.50), and steak and kidney pie or chicken Kiev (£4.25). Bass, Ruddles Best and Theakstons XB on handpump, and a good choice of malt whiskies; in the bar you can choose from the restaurant wine list. There are seats in the coachyard. *(Recommended by A Triggs, Roy Bromell; more reports please)*

Free house   Licensee David Feasey   Real ale   Meals and lunchtime snacks Restaurant   Children in restaurant and eating area of bar   Open 11–11; 11–3, 5.30–11 in winter   Bedrooms tel Evesham (0386) 840317; £45B/£65B

CIRENCESTER SP0201 Map 4
Slug & Lettuce

West Market Place

Several atmospheric communicating areas, large and small, have a lot of stripped pine, stonework and flagstones, large rugs on bare boards, long cushioned pews or country kitchen chairs as well as a superannuated consulting couch, an enormous banqueting table, shelves and cases filled with books, and big log fires. They keep decent wines, and there are old wine bottles or labels, claret case ends and vineyard charts. They don't serve sandwiches or ploughman's, but bar food includes chicken liver pâté with cointreau (£2.95), a couple of tagliatelle dishes (£3.50), broccoli and stilton quiche (£3.75), barbecued ribs (£4.25), home-made salmon fishcakes (£4.65), chicken breast with avocado and garlic (£5.75), and specials. Well kept Courage Best and Directors and John Smiths on handpump; piped music. There are tables in a well protected central courtyard. The pub was called the Crown until a few years ago. *(Recommended by Ewan McCall, Roger Huggins, Tom McLean, Patrick Freeman, Mr and Mrs A G Gillanders, Joy Heatherley)*

Courage   Licensee Miss Samantha Howell   Real ale   Meals (till 10 evening) Bookings tel Cirencester (0285) 653206/652454   Children welcome   Open 11.30–2.30, 6–11; closed 25 Dec

COATES SO9700 Map 4
Tunnel House

Village signposted off A419 W of Cirencester; in village follow Tarlton signposts, turning right then left; pub up track on right just after railway bridge; OS Sheet 163 map reference 965005

Guarding one entry to the derelict tunnel which carried the old Thames and Severn Canal over two miles to Sapperton, this lively bow-fronted stone house has an unusual mix of furnishings: massive rustic benches and seats built into the sunny windows, a haphazard mixture of easy chairs, a sofa, little spindleback seats, a well carved wooden fireplace for one of the several open fires, and lots of enamel advertising signs, race tickets, air travel labels, and dried flowers hanging from its beams; there's also a python – called Pythagoras – secured in a glass case by the bar, and several friendly dogs and cats. Bar food includes bacon or sausage butties (£1.40), ploughman's or cauliflower cheese (£2.60), and chilli con carne (£3.80). Well kept Archers Best, Tetleys and Wadworths 6X on handpump; darts, pinball, dominoes, space game, fruit machine and juke box (there may be a TV on). The pub is popular with students from the Royal Agricultural College in Cirencester.

(*Recommended by Jim and Becky Bryson, Patrick Freeman, A J H Sale, Mrs Lili Lomas, Caroline Wright, Peter and Rose Flower*)

Free house   Licensee Chris Kite   Real ale   Meals and snacks (12–2, 7–10)   Children welcome   Open 11–3, 7–11; 11–11 Sat

nr COWLEY   SO9614   Map 4

Green Dragon ★ ⊘

Cockleford; pub signposted from A435 about 1 1/2 miles S of junction with A436 – or follow Elkstone turn-off; OS Sheet 163 map reference 969142

Particularly good service, interesting food, and a fine range of well kept real ales continue to draw readers to this attractive stone-fronted pub. Changing every week, the menu might include salmon and cucumber pâté (£1.95), good soup such as cream of celery and onion or cream of lobster and brandy (from £1.50), tuna and apple flan (£1.95), ploughman's (from £2.25), whole prawns with dill mayonnaise or vegetarian quiche (£2.50), lambs sweetbreads (£3.75), mushroom curry or pork and pineapple curry (£4), a Burmese lemon sole dish or beef and mushrooms in Guinness (£4.50), chargrilled steaks (from £8), and puddings such as banoffi pie (especially popular) or orange and chocolate mousse (from £1.50); it fills up quickly so it's best to get there early for a table. There's a lunchtime family carvery on Sundays and Bank Holiday Mondays. Badger Tanglefoot, Bass, Boddingtons, Butcombe, Flowers Original, Hook Norton, Theakstons Old Peculier and Wadworths 6X on handpump or tapped from the cask; wines that include a local one, and farm cider. The bar has country kitchen chairs and tables, big flagstones as well as some red carpet, a collection of foreign banknotes pinned to some of the beams, logs burning all year in a spacious stone fireplace, and a woodburning stove in a big stone fireplace. They ask customers to dress decently. The skittle alley is a self-contained function room which is available for hire. There are seats outside on the terrace in front of the building. The Cotswold Way with lovely walks is not far off. (*Recommended by BKA, John and Joan Wyatt, Owen Barder, Eleanor Grey, Martin Richards, Maureen and Pat Campbell, John Matthews, C E Power, A J H Sale, Mrs Lili Lomas, Christopher and Heather Barton, G D Collier, Mrs Y M Healey, Mrs Joan Harris, Alan Skull, R and S Bentley, N P Cox, Frank Cummins, Simon Ward, J S Taylor, Frank Gadbois, Laurence Manning, Patrick Freeman*)

Free house   Licensees Barry and Susan Hinton   Real ale   Meals and snacks (11.15–2, 6.15–10 Mon–Sat; 12–2 (2.30 carvery), 7.15–10 Sun   Children in restaurant and in carvery for Sun lunch   Jazz Mon evening, folk Wed evenings   Open 11–2.30, 6–11

EBRINGTON   SP1840   Map 4

Ebrington Arms

Signposted from B4035 E of Chipping Campden; and from A429 N of Moreton-in-Marsh

Handy for Hidcote and Kiftsgate, this well run small village inn does quickly (and generously) served decent simple bar food including sandwiches (£1.25, sirloin steak baguette £3.25), hearty soups (£1.35), egg and chips (£1.75), ratatouille (£2.50), omelettes (from £2.75), lasagne (£2.95), fresh cod (£4.25), gammon and eggs (£4.35), a good steak and kidney pie (£4.75) and steaks (from 8oz sirloin £8.95). The nice little flagstoned and low-beamed bar has a big stone fireplace (with a roaring fire in winter), a slightly raised woodfloored area, and recently made sturdy traditional furnishings – including seats built into the airy bow window. A lower room, also beamed and flagstoned, has stripped country-kitchen furnishings and another enormous log fireplace. Particularly well kept Donnington SBA, Hook Norton Best and Theakstons XB on handpump, Bulmer's farm cider, decent coffee; absolutely no piped music or games machines – just an old-fashioned harmonium, dominoes, cribbage and darts. The two friendly Welsh springers (not allowed in during food times) are called Cymro and Rhys. An arched stone wall shelters a terrace with picnic-table sets under cocktail parasols; the village is quiet, and pretty. You can count on good breakfasts if you stay; we'd expect from the helpfulness of the staff and the efficient housekeeping that this new entry will deserve our place-to-stay award, but have not yet heard from enough readers about this aspect. *(Recommended by E V Walder, D A Wilcock, Miss C M Davidson, Hugh Patterson, P J Brooks, Margaret and Trevor Errington; more reports please)*

Free house Licensees Mr and Mrs Richards Real ale Meals and snacks (not Sun evening) Children in dining room Open 11–2.30, 6–11; closed 25 Dec Bedrooms tel Paxford (038 678) 223; /£30B

FORD SP0829 Map 4

Plough ★

B4077

Between April and June, this ancient, rambling inn holds popular asparagus feasts (£8) – one reader arrived to find them preparing a sitting for 64; other bar food includes sandwiches (from £1), soup (£1.25), mushrooms on toast (£2.25), ploughman's (£2.75), home-made pies (£4.75), and winter pheasant (£7.50 or so), with seafood every other Thursday evening (around £7.50 depending on availability). The beamed and stripped-stone bar has old settles and benches around the big tables on its uneven flagstones, oak tables in a snug alcove, and log fires; the atmosphere is frequently enlivened by Reg and his (not always well tuned) piano. Well kept Donnington BB and SBA on handpump; service can be slow when it's busy. Darts, shove-ha'penny, dominoes. There are benches in front, with rustic tables and chairs on grass by white lilacs and fairy lights. The inn used to be the local court house – and what's now the cellar was the gaol. *(Recommended by PLC, Gordon and Daphne, Victoria Logue, A Triggs, P B Dowsett, G D Collier, Mrs S McGreevy, E V Walder, Gwyneth and Salvo Spadaro-Dutturi, Derek and Sylvia Stephenson, W L Congreve, Dr J M Jackson, Simon Ward, Dr M V Jones, A T Langton)*

Donnington Licensee Leslie Carter Real ale Meals and snacks (12–2.30, 7–10) Children welcome Pianist Open 10.30–3, 5.30–11 Twin bedrooms tel Stanton (038 673) 215; /£30

FRAMPTON MANSELL SO9102 Map 4

Crown

Village signposted off A419 Cirencester–Stroud

Overlooking a steep wooded valley and set above the stone-built village, this friendly Cotswold inn has an extremely good cold buffet, served by uniformed waitresses; there's a range of salads, from ham or chicken to beef (around £3.50–6.50), as well as soup (£1.25) and ploughman's (from £2.20). The main bar has a traditional settle alongside more up-to-date cushioned wall benches and ladder-back rush seats on the patterned carpet, stripped stonework, a dark beam-and-plank ceiling, and little mullioned windows; there's a simpler public bar. Archers Village and Wadworths 6X on handpump, darts, piped music. Good teak seats outside overlook the valley. *(Recommended by Mrs Lili Lomas, John Bowdler, Mrs J Oakes)*

Free house Licensee Ernest Sykes Real ale Meals and snacks Restaurant (not Sun evening, except for residents) Children in eating area of bar only Open 11.30–2, 6–10.30 (11 Sat) Bedrooms tel Frampton Mansell (028 576) 601; £40B/£50B

GREAT RISSINGTON SP1917 Map 4

Lamb 🛏

On the walls of the cosy two-room bar here, there's a plaque donated by the only survivor of a bomber that crashed in the back garden in 1943, photographs of the 13 guide dogs that the inn and customers have raised money for, a history of the village, and plates, pictures and an interesting collection of old cigarette and tobacco tins; wheelback and tub chairs with cushioned seats are grouped around polished tables on the light brown carpet, there's a nook under the stairs with a settle and table, and a log-effect gas fire in the stone fireplace. Bar food is truly home-made (apart from one pudding) and includes sandwiches (from £1.30, huge open prawn £3.50), thick vegetable soup (£1.50), ploughman's or pâtés such as chicken liver (£2.50), fish pie with light flaky pastry lid (£3.80), lamb and apricot casserole or beef and mushroom pie in Guinness (£4.40), chicken filled with cream cheese, mushrooms and garlic, king prawns in garlic (£4.65), and puddings like sherry trifle, lemon cheesecake or banoffi pie (£1.75); on Sunday the menu is limited to a roast lunch and ploughman's. We strongly suspect the food here is becoming so good as to deserve our Food Award – and we'd be very grateful for more reports on this aspect. Well kept Flowers Original, Wadworths 6X and guest beers such as Hook Norton on handpump; a decent wine list, country wines, and farm cider. The sheltered hillside garden has a play area and aviary. One of the chintzy bedrooms in the warren of small stairs and doors has a four-poster carved by the landlord; there's an indoor swimming pool. You can walk from here, via disused gravel pits that are now a habitat for water birds, to Bourton on the Water. *(Recommended by A Y Drummond, H K Dyson, Frank Cummins, Tom McLean, Roger Huggins, Ewan McCall, Patrick and Mary McDermott)*

Free house   Licensees Richard and Kate Cleverly   Real ale   Meals and snacks Restaurant (not Sun evening)   Children in eating area of bar   Open 11–2.30, 6.30–11; closed 25 and 26 Dec   Bedrooms tel Cotswold (0451) 20388; £25(£28B)/£32(£36B)

GRETTON   SP0131 Map 4
Royal Oak

Village signposted off what is now officially B4077 (still often mapped and even signed as A438), E of Tewkesbury; keep on through village

An enterprising conversion of a pair of old stone-built cottages, carefully extended in keeping and given an airy conservatory dining room, this is given a warm and lively atmosphere by its young landlord. Pub-keeping clearly runs in the family – on our inspection his two-year-old son was correctly pointing out exactly which handpump dispensed each of the well kept Courage Best and Directors, John Smiths and Wadworths 6X; around 70 whiskies. The long series of bare-boarded or flagstoned rooms have soft lighting (including candles in bottles on the mix of stripped oak and pine tables), dark ochre walls, beams (some hung with tankards, hop bines, chamber-pots), old prints, and a medley of pews and various chairs. The dining conservatory has a solid roof (keeping it cool in summer, warm in winter), stripped country furnishings, and a broad view over farmland to Alderton and Dumbleton Hills. Enterprising bar food includes a good few starters such as garlic mushrooms (£2.50), herring roes on toast, prawns with crab and grilled mussels in a tasty combination with stilton (£2.75), ploughman's with a good choice of cheeses or filled baked potatoes (£3), and lots of main dishes such as Arnold Bennett omelette (with smoked haddock) or chilli con carne (£3.75), gammon and peaches or smoked chicken (£5.25), duck with plum sauce or nicely done guineafowl (£6.50) and steaks (from 8oz sirloin £7.50 – their mustard sauce is good); pleasant staff; darts, shove-ha'penny, piped music, fruit machine. The cat is called Alice and the English setters, George and Freddy. There are picnic-table sets on a terrace with hanging baskets and clematis and out under a giant pear tree; a neatly kept big lawn runs down past a small hen-run to a play area. At weekends and on Bank Holidays, the Great Western Steam Railway runs from Toddington to Winchcombe station and then stops at the bottom of the garden here; eventually the line will go on to Cheltenham.

Free house   Licensees Bob and Kathy Willison   Real ale   Meals and snacks Restaurant tel Cheltenham (0242) 602477   Folk music Wed evening   Open 11–2.30, 6.30–11; closed 25 and 26 Dec

GUITING POWER SP0924 Map 4

Olde Inne

Village signposted off B4068 SW of Stow-on-the-Wold (still called A436 on many maps)

This snug stone cottage pub, also known as Th'Ollow Bottom, has a jovial, helpful licensee – the white cat is friendly, too. The gently lit bar has a winter log fire in an unusual pillar-supported stone fireplace, attractive built-in wall and window seats (including one, near the serving counter, that's the height of the bar stools) and small brocaded armchairs. Turkey carpet sweeps from here into a more spacious dining room with winged settles and wheelback chairs around neat tables. The public bar is furnished like the main bar but has flagstones and stripped stone masonry, as well as sensibly placed darts, fruit machine, and space game. Bar food includes ploughman's (from £2.25), cod or haddock (£3.50), lasagne (£3.75), home-cooked ham or home-made steak and kidney pie (£4.25), and rump steak (£7.50), with specials such as vegetable curry or butterbean bake (£3.95), delicious Victorian chicken pie (£4.25), beef stroganoff (£4.95) or baked trout (£5.75). Hook Norton, Theakstons, and Wadworths 6X on handpump, and a selection of malt whiskies. Tables on a strip of gravel in front look over the quiet lane to a gentle slope of field, and at the back the pleasant garden overlooks more fields. (*Recommended by R W Grey, Derek and Sylvia Stephenson, HNJ, PEJ, M A and C R Starling, PADEMLUC*)

Free house   Licensees Kenneth and Paula Thouless-Meyrick   Real ale   Meals and snacks (not Mon evening Sept–April)   Restaurant (not Sun evening)   Children in eating area and restaurant   Open 11.30–2.30, 5.30–11

HYDE SO8801 Map 4

Ragged Cot

Burnt Ash; Hyde signposted with Minchinhampton from A419 E of Stroud; or (better road) follow Minchinhampton, Aston Down signposted from A419 at Aston Down airfield; OS Sheet 162 map reference 886012

Rambling around a longish serving counter, with a newish no-smoking restaurant area off to the right near the kitchen, the bar in this relaxed and chatty old place has stripped stone and black beams, a traditional dark wood wall settle by the end fire, and red cushioned window-seats overlooking the garden and its line of chestnut trees. Home-made bar food includes onion soup (£1.25), pizzas (£2.20), pâté (£2.50), cauliflower cheese or omelettes (£2.95), steak and kidney pie (£4.50), gammon (£4.95) and steaks (from £7.95); well kept Boddingtons, Marstons Pedigree, Theakstons Best, Uley Old Spot and Youngers IPA on handpump. Service is kind and quick. There are picnic-table sets outside, and at holiday times a pavilion-like garden bar may be used. This year they have opened letting bedrooms in an adjacent converted barn. (*Recommended by John Broughton, Ewan McCall, Roger Huggins, Tom McLean, Margaret Dyke, Patrick Freeman*)

Free house   Licensees Mr and Mrs M Case   Real ale   Meals and snacks (not 25 Dec) Restaurant   Open 11–2.30, 6–11; closed evening 25 Dec   Bedrooms tel Brimscombe (0453) 884643; £39B/£55B (4-poster £65B)

KEMBLE ST9898 Map 4

Thames Head ⊗

A433 Cirencester–Tetbury – away from village itself, which is over on A429

Now with close connections to the Swan at Southrop, this new main entry has recently come on in leaps and bounds. What earns its food award is primarily the interesting choice in the back bar, which – closely echoing the Swan – in the evening includes unusual soups (tomato with orange and mint, say, at £1.80), several good pâtés such as crab or mushroom with lentils and hazelnuts (£2.35), deep-fried camembert with cranberry and orange sauce (£2.35), charcoal-grilled chicken tikka (£2.75), mediterranean chicken casserole (£5.50), fresh pasta with seafood or bacon and tomato (£6.25), sirloin steak (£7) and beef Wellington

(£7.25); also children's dishes. The front bar has a more straightforward value-based evening choice including half a chicken (£2.75), ploughman's (£2.85), cottage pie or sausage and ham with chips (£3); lunchtime dishes in both bars concentrate on that sort of thing, with one or two of the evening specialities at attractive prices (bacon and mushrooms in an oatmeal pancake for £3.50, say). Puddings are delicious. The back bar has William Morris prints for its curtains and cushions, stripped stone walls, mahogany-varnished tables, pews and wheelback chairs, with a log-effect gas fire in a big stone fireplace; it opens into a country-look dining room with another imposing log-effect gas fire. The front bar is more what you'd expect from outside this main-road pub – red plush, bobbly white walls, louder music, sensibly placed darts, dominoes, fruit machine; it opens into a small pool room. Well kept Arkells Bitter, 3B on handpump; pleasant and efficient young staff. There are some picnic-table sets outside, with swings; also a skittle alley for hire; exemplary lavatories. You won't now find any water at what used to be the nearby source of the Thames. (*Recommended by Roger Huggins, Frank Gadbois, Neil and Anita Christopher*)

Arkells   Licensee Mr P Keen   Real ale   Meals and snacks   Children welcome   Open 11–3, 6.30 (7 in winter)–11

KINGSCOTE   ST8196   Map 4

Hunters Hall ★ Ⓟ

A4135 Dursley–Tetbury

There's usually plenty of space in this pretty, creeper-covered building – which has had a continuous licence for 500 years – even when the local hunt, a wedding party, and large group of ramblers crowd in. The elegant series of high-beamed connecting rooms have a comfortable miscellany of easy chairs, sofas and a fine old box settle as well as some more elementary seats, velvet curtains, exposed stone walls and good winter log fires; there's more space to eat in the Gallery upstairs. The lower-ceilinged public bar has sturdy settles and oak tables on the flagstones in front of another big log fire, and a back room – relatively untouched – is popular with local lads playing pool; darts, shove-ha'penny, and fruit machine. Bar food, generally served from a buffet in an airy end room, includes lunchtime sandwiches (not Sunday), mussels in white wine, smoked trout, very good steak and kidney pie (£3.90), turkey and ham pie or seafood pancakes (£4.75), salads such as rare beef or mixed meats (£5.50), charcoal-grilled steaks (from £6.35), and salmon (£6.50). Bass, Hook Norton, Smiles Best and Uley Old Spot on handpump, and quite a few wines by the glass. The big garden has weekend summer barbecues and is good for families with a big play area at the far end with a fortress of thatched whisky-kegs linked by timber catwalks, as well as a climber and swings. (*Recommended by Roger Huggins, Barry and Anne, Alastair Campbell, G D Collier, Alastair Campbell, Cherry Knott, D A B and J V Llewelyn, N P Cox, Peter and Rose Flower, Heather Sharland, BKA, Patrick Freeman, Mrs J Oakes, Dr M V Jones, Adrian Kelly*)

Free house   Licensee David Barnett-Roberts   Real ale   Meals and snacks   Restaurant (à la carte menu not available Sun)   Children in eating area of bar, restaurant and family room   Open 11–2.30, 6.30 (6 Sat)–11; closed 25 Dec   Bedrooms tel Dursley (0453) 860393; £44B/£54B

nr LECHLADE   SU2199   Map 4

Trout

St John's Bridge; 1 mile E of Lechlade on A417

Around 1220, the old wooden bridge over the Thames here was replaced by a stone one, and to house the workmen an almshouse was founded; when the main Priory was dissolved by Edward VI in 1472 the almshouse continued as an inn known as 'Ye Sygne of St John Baptist Head' until 1704 when the name was changed to Trout. Ancient fishery rights are still held by the pub. The low-beamed main bar is partly panelled and decorated with trout and stuffed pike, and there's a flagstoned part by the serving counter which has Courage Best and Directors and

Websters Yorkshire on handpump; darts and Aunt Sally. A snug area, once the ground-floor cellar, opens off here, and is furnished with wooden tables and settles, with fishing prints on the walls. A third bar leads on to the spacious garden, which has plenty of tables by the old walnut tree, a summer bar and marquee; there are fine views from here over the meadows towards Lechlade. Good, varied bar food includes home-made soup (£2.25), ploughman's (£2.95), home-made pâté (£3.75), excellent moussaka, vegetarian lasagne or home-made seafood crumble (£4.50), fresh local trout (£7.20) and 10oz rump steak (£9.95), with daily specials and children's dishes (from £1.75); quick, courteous service, and the friendly pointer is called Blucher. *(Recommended by Lyn and Bill Capper, Joan Olivier, S V Bishop, Alastair Campbell, Wayne Brindle, P B Dowsett, Patrick Freeman)*

Courage   Licensee R G Warren   Real ale   Meals and snacks (12–2, 7–10) Restaurant tel Faringdon (0367) 52313; closed Sun   Children in restaurant   Jazz on winter Tues evenings and in marquee in summer   Open 11–2.30, 6–11; 11–11 summer Sats

LITTLE WASHBOURNE   SO9933   Map 4

Hobnails ✪

A438 Tewkesbury–Stow-on-the-Wold; 7 1/2 miles E of M5 junction 9

Run by the same family since 1743, this cheerful, partly 15th-century pub specialises in a wide range of large and generously filled baps, which range from sausage and fried egg (£1.45), through liver and onions (£2.40) and chicken and mushroom in creamy sauce (£3.40), to steak with egg and mushrooms (£4.95); there's also a choice of tasty soups (£1.50) and other starters, a large bowl of salad (£1.90) and a wide range of home-made puddings including several based on liqueurs (from £1.90). The snug little front bar has low sway-backed beams hung with pewter tankards and old wall benches by a couple of tables on its quarry-tiled floor, and there's a more modern, carpeted back bar with comfortable button-back leatherette banquettes. Flowers IPA and Original, Wadworths 6X and Whitbreads West Country PA on handpump; darts, shove-ha'penny, fruit machine, piped music. A separate skittle alley (with tables) is for hire Monday to Friday evenings. Between the two buildings, and beside a small lawn and flowerbed, there's a terrace with tables. *(Recommended by Michael and Alison Sandy, Andrew and Barbara Sykes, Derek and Sylvia Stephenson, G and M Hollis, Ted George, E V Walder; more reports please)*

Flowers (Whitbreads)   Licensee Stephen Farbrother   Real ale   Meals and snacks (12–2, 6.45–10.30)   Restaurant tel Alderton (024 262) 237   Children in eating area and restaurant   Open 11–2.30, 6–11

LOWER LYDBROOK   SO5916   Map 4

Royal Spring ✪

Vention Lane – which with the pub is signed off B4228 at NE edge of village

Tucked away in a steep coombe on the edge of the Forest of Dean, this old pub has been transformed over the last few years. The most has been made of the lovely position, building a garden around the waterfalls of a little stream that eventually drops down to the River Wye at the bottom of the lane. Behind the little white house (and a sizeable pigeon-house) are rustic tables up among the trees, a play area, and a pets' corner with a well stocked aviary (the peacock cries echo vividly around the peaceful valley). Below the house and over the lane are more rustic seats and tables under cocktail parasols, on a lawn by an orchard. A back Perspex-roofed terrace has yet more tables. There's a carefully restored 18th-century lime kiln up on the left. Inside, a long lounge looking down the valley has pews, high-backed black modern settles and other seats on its carpets; the beams are thickly hung with old bottles and earthenware flagons. Bar food runs from good mushroom soup (£1.25), deep-fried camembert (£2.30), broccoli and macaroni cheese, stuffed mushrooms (£2.50) and ploughman's (£2.75) through lasagne, moussaka, sweet and sour chicken and so forth (£4.50) to local seasonal game such as pheasant casserole or Wye salmon mornay; children's helpings are half price and there's also a menu for them (£1.95). A back extension has a fruit machine and juke box, and there's dominoes, cribbage and winter darts; several readers feel it's a shame they do no real ale. Our inspection shortly after the new licensees had taken over suggested the high standards of their predecessors has been kept up – hence the food award. *(Recommended by Sybil Baker, John Miles, Frank Cummins, Neil and Anita Christopher, D O Morris, VL)*

Free house   Licensees May and Phil Crawley   Meals and snacks   Children welcome Folk Thurs evening, middle-of-road Sun evening   Open 12–3, 7–11

NAILSWORTH   ST8499 Map 4
Weighbridge

B4014 towards Tetbury

Relaxed and friendly even when it's very busy, this stone-built Cotswolds pub has three little downstairs rooms, with walls either crisply white or stripped to bare stone, and attractive antique settles and small country chairs; the one on the left has its black beam-and-plank ceiling thickly festooned with black ironware – sheepshears, gintraps, lamps, cauldrons, bellows; there are log fires in each. Up some steps is a raftered loft with candles in bottles on an engaging mix of more or less rustic tables, and some unexpected decorations such as a wooden butcher's block. You can walk from here into the sheltered garden rising behind the pub, with swings and picnic-table sets under cocktail parasols. An unusual feature of the bar menu is the popular two-in-one pies with steak on one side and cauliflower cheese on the other, say (£3.90 large, £2.90 small), also shepherd's (£2.80), steak and mushroom or turkey, sweetcorn and pepper (£2.90); other bar food includes cottage rolls or toasties (from £1.20), filled baked potatoes (from £1.40), ploughman's (from £2.40), tasty hot pizzas, and salads (from £2.70). Well kept Courage Best and Directors and Wadworths 6X on handpump, and reasonably priced wines. *(Recommended by Roger Huggins, Tom McLean, Ewan McCall, BKA, John Broughton, Capt and Mrs D S Kirkland, G D Collier, Alan Skull, E A George, Janet Tomalin, BKA, Klaus and Elizabeth Leist)*

Free house   Licensee J M Kulesza   Real ale   Meals and snacks   Children in two rooms away from bar   Open 11–2.30, 7 (6.30 Sat)–11

NAUNTON   SP1123 Map 4
Black Horse ⊘ ⊨

Village signposted from B4068 (shown as A436 on older maps) W of Stow-on-the-Wold

The unpretentiously furnished bar in this L-shaped little inn has simple country-kitchen chairs and built-in oak pews, polished elm cast-iron-framed tables, flagstones and flooring tiles, black beams and some stripped stonework, a big woodburning stove, and a sophisticated atmosphere. A good range of food includes home-made soup (£1.25), pâté (£2), ploughman's (from £2.25), salads (from £3.50), home-cooked cold ham, chicken breast or seafood platter (£4), tasty gammon with egg or pineapple (£5.50) and succulent Scotch steak (£7.50), with specials such as marinated herring fillets (£2), beef casserole (£4), fresh seasonal salmon salad (£6), half a delicious roast duckling (£7), and puddings like lemon brûlée or chocolate trufito (£2); chips are crisp; last orders for Sunday lunch 1.30 prompt. Well kept Donnington BB and SBA, several wines, shove-ha'penny, cribbage, dominoes, sensibly placed darts, fruit machine and juke box; some tables outside. Note that they don't allow children. *(Recommended by Andy and Jill Kassube, Maureen and Pat Campbell, Mrs Carol A Riddick, Simon Ward, Henry Midwinter)*

Donnington   Licensees Adrian and Jennie Bowen-Jones   Real ale   Meals and snacks (not 25 Dec)   Restaurant   Open 11–2.30, 6–11   Two bedrooms tel Guiting Power (0451) 850378; £17/£30

NORTH NIBLEY   ST7496   Map 4

New Inn ★ ⇥

Waterley Bottom, which is quite well signposted from surrounding lanes; inn signposted from the Bottom itself; one route is from A4135 S of Dursley, via lane with red sign saying Steep Hill, 1 in 5 (just SE of Stinchcombe Golf Course turn-off), turning right when you get to the bottom; another is to follow Waterley Bottom signpost from previous main entry, keeping eyes skinned for small low signpost to inn; OS Sheet 162 map reference 758963

Picture windows in the carpeted lounge bar look out on to a beautifully kept rose terrace, the garden beyond, and then a bowl of quiet pastures, rising to a fringe of woods; at the far end of the garden, there's a small orchard with swings, slides and a timber tree-house. Inside, there's a fine collection of breweriana – particularly antique handpump beer engines, including the ones actually used to dispense the well kept real ales: Cotleigh Tawny, Greene King Abbot, Smiles Best and Exhibition, Theakstons Old Peculier, and WB (a bitter brewed for the pub by Cotleigh), as well as guests. Also, Inch's cider and a good range of malt whiskies. Furnishings such as cushioned Windsor chairs and varnished high-backed settles against the partly stripped stone walls, and sensibly placed darts, dominoes, shove-ha'penny, cribbage, and quiz games in the simple public bar; piped music. The home-made bar food is good value, with filled brown baps (from 50p), toasted sandwiches (from 85p), ploughman's (from £2), chilli con carne (£2.75), tasty steak and onion pie (£2.95), and lasagne (£3.10), with puddings like peach and banana crumble. To stay here (it's pleasant walking country) you have to book a long way ahead – and best not to arrive outside opening hours. This year, the bedrooms have been refurbished and the bathroom modernised. *(Recommended by Alan Skull, Drs M and K Parier, Nigel Cant, Patrick Freeman, Roger Huggins, Mr and Mrs J D Cranston, Cynthia McDowall, Dr and Mrs A K Clarke, Peter and Rose Flower)*

Free house   Licensee Ruby Sainty   Real ale   Meals and snacks   Open 12–2.30, 7–11   Two bedrooms tel Dursley (0453) 3659; £15/£30

ODDINGTON   SP2225   Map 4

Horse & Groom ⇥

Upper Oddington; signposted from A436 E of Stow-on-the-Wold

Understated tradition here: pale polished flagstones, stripped stone walls with some harness and a few brass platters, a handsome antique oak box settle among other more modern seats, decent tables, a big log fire, just a few horsebrasses on the dark 16th-century oak beams in the ochre ceiling, hunting-print curtains for smallish windows. Good value bar food includes lunchtime sandwiches (from £1.20) and ploughman's (£2.95), and soup such as fresh white onion (£1.45), quiche, lasagne, tagliatelli or vegetarian dishes (£3.95), lamb and cherry casserole, steak and kidney pie or a pie of the day such as chicken with sweetcorn and mushrooms (£4.50), trout (£4.75), children's dishes and good puddings such as oranges in Drambuie; Hook Norton Best and Old Hookey and Wadworths 6X on handpump; Taunton cider. A quarry-tiled side area with a fine old polished woodburner has pool; also, darts, dominoes and piped music. There are picnic-table sets on the neat lawn below the car park, with apple trees, a fine play area including an enormous log climber, a budgerigar aviary, a hut housing fat rabbits, and maybe Aunt Sally; beyond a rose hedge is a pretty water-garden where there are large trout. The bedrooms are not large, but quaint and comfortable, and the candlelit dining room is pretty. *(Recommended by Sir Nigel Foulkes, Mr and Mrs T A Towers, Derek and Sue Hammond, Tim Brierly)*

Free house   Licensees Russell and Stephen Gainford   Real ale   Meals and snacks Restaurant   Children in eating area of bar and in restaurant   Open 11.30–2.30, 6–11; winter evening opening 6.30; closed 25 and 26 Dec   Bedrooms tel Cotswold (0451) 30584; £24.50B/£39B

PAINSWICK   SO8609   Map 4

Royal Oak

St Mary's St

In the centre of a charming small hillside town of old stone buildings, narrow alleys and antique shops, this popular pub has a friendly lounge bar with seats and copper-topped tables made from barrels, an elegant oak settle (and lovely panelled oak door), some walls stripped back to silvery stone, and an open fire in the massive chimney which divides the room into two parts. There's a second bar on the left, and a small sun lounge facing a sheltered suntrap courtyard with wisteria and colourful pots of geraniums and calceolarias. Good bar food ranges from sandwiches (from £1.10, very good fresh salmon £2), home-made soup (£1.25) and ploughman's (from £2.20), through home-made pâté (£2) and salads (around £4.50, salmon £5), to an enterprising range of hot dishes, changing every day, but typically including fresh haddock with two poached eggs or large grilled sardines (£4), chicken breast stuffed with cheese and mustard or chicken Kiev (£4.95), and steaks (from £9); well kept Flowers Original and Whitbreads PA on handpump. Handy for St Mary's churchyard with its 99 yew trees. *(Recommended by Shirley Allen, Cherry Knott, Barbara M McHugh, BKA, Mr and Mrs G Turner, R and S Bentley, Tom Evans, David and Ruth Hollands, Dr M V Jones, Helena and Arthur Harbottle)*

Flowers (Whitbreads)   Licensee Mr Morris   Real ale   Meals and snacks (not Sun; till 10pm for snacks)   Children welcome   Nearby parking may be difficult   Open 11–3, 6–11; closed 25 Dec

REDBROOK   SO5410   Map 4

Boat

Pub's inconspicuously signed car park in village on A466 Chepstow–Monmouth; from here 100-yard footbridge crosses Wye (pub actually in Penallt in Wales – but much easier to find this way); OS Sheet 162 map reference 534097

This endearingly take-us-as-you-find-us pub is in a marvellous position by an old bridge on the banks of the River Wye, and there are splendid views of the valley from the steep terraced garden (prettily lit at night), which has tables among little waterfalls, and a pond cut into the rocks. The bar has a tiled floor, a woodburning stove with a huge pile of logs in a corner, miscellaneous framed historical documents on the walls, a wall settle, a grey-painted piano, and a relaxed, friendly atmosphere. The well kept real ales, tapped straight from casks behind the long curved bar counter usually include three guest beers weekly, as well as the regular Bass, Greene King Abbot, Hook Norton Old Hookey, Marstons Pedigree, Theakstons Best, XB and Old Peculier and Wadworths 6X; also farmhouse cider; cribbage, dominoes and a space game. Bar food includes pasty and pickle (£1.15), filled baked potatoes (from £1.25), ploughman's (£2.10), vegetable curry, mushroom and barley bake, pan haggerty or chilli con carne (all £3), lasagne (£3.20), good value beef rogan josh or lamb hot pot (£3.50), and smoked salmon salad (£4.10). We might rate this even higher when they do something about the lavatories – which frankly don't match the appeal of the rest of the pub. *(Recommended by Jacqueline Davis, Tony and Lynne Stark, Tom Evans, PB, HB, S P Bobeldijk, Brian and Anna Marsden, P B Dowsett, Frank Cummins, R W Stanbury, R P Taylor, Paul S McPherson, Dave Braisted, P L Duncan, D Godden, Ian Clay)*

Free house   Licensee Brian Beck   Real ale   Meals and snacks (12–2.30, 6–10)   Children in family room   Folk music Tues, jazz Thurs   Open 11–3, 6–11

SAPPERTON   SO9403   Map 4

Daneway

Village signposted from A419 Stroud–Cirencester; from village centre follow Edgeworth, Bisley signpost; OS Sheet 163 map reference 939034

The heavy-horse harness and brasses in the traditionally furnished lounge here recall the days when this was a popular bargees' pub, frequented particularly by 'leggers' – men who lay on top of the canal-boats and pushed them through the two-and-a-quarter-mile tunnel, using their legs against the tunnel roof; the canal fell into disuse around 1930, though it's now being partially restored by a canal trust. There's a remarkably grand and dominating fireplace, elaborately carved oak from floor to ceiling, and racing and hunting prints on the attractively papered walls. Lunchtime bar food includes filled rolls (75p, not Sundays; bacon and mushroom £1.50), tasty garlic bread, ploughman's (from £1.85), filled baked potatoes (£1.90), lasagne (£2.95), and steak and kidney pie (£3.95), with evening extras like gammon steak (£4.95) and rump steak (£6.95); puddings (£1.25). Well kept Archers Best and a beer brewed locally for the pub on handpump and electric pump, Wadworths IPA on handpump, and 6X tapped from the cask, also regular guest beers and local farm cider. Darts, dominoes, shove-ha'penny, and ring-the-bull in the public bar, which has a big inglenook fireplace; quoits; friendly, cheerful service. Lots of bench/table sets on a sloping lawn bright with flowerbeds and a rose trellis look down over the remains of the canal and the valley of the little River Frome. The pub's car park is built over what used to be one of its locks – you can still see the corner-stone of the lock gates. It's on *Good Walks Guide* Walk 89. *(Recommended by A Y Drummond, Mrs Lili Lomas, Barry and Anne, Chris Raisin, Tom McLean, Ewan McCall, Roger Huggins, HNJ, PEJ, Patrick Freeman)*

Free house   Managers Liz and Richard Goodfellow   Real ale   Meals and snacks Children in small family room off lounge   Open 11–2.30 (3 Sat), 6.30–11

SIDDINGTON   SU0399   Map 4
Greyhound

Ashton Rd; village signposted from industrial estate roundabout in Cirencester through-traffic system; and from A419 (northbound only)

The cheerful and helpful newish licensees make this interesting pub a warmly welcoming place. The biggish lounge bar on the right has an old herringbone brick floor, carpeted at the far end, with a red plush wing armchair by one of its two big log fires, but otherwise a happily heterogeneous mix of high-backed winged settles, high dining chairs, chapel seats and so forth, and good tables – mainly stripped pine, but one fine circular mahogany one. There's lots of copper and brass on the beams and ochre walls, with a few hunting prints, Edwardian hat feathers, some black-lacquered farm tools, china and other bric-a-brac – but the dominant impression is of chatty geniality. A wide choice of good value bar food includes filled rolls (from £1.85), soup or garlic mushrooms (£1.85), omelettes (from £2.05), filled baked potatoes (from £2.20 – cheese, onion and bacon recommended), ploughman's (from £2.85), garlic prawns (£2.95), meat salads (from £3.50), vegetable gratin (£3.95), lasagne (£4.35), curry (£4.45) and steaks (from 8oz rump £9.25), with crisp sauté potatoes, good salad garnishes and fresh puddings such as chocolate fudge Pavlova; well kept Wadworths IPA and 6X and a guest such as Badger Tanglefoot on handpump; the public bar has darts, table skittles and fruit machine; piped music. There are picnic-table sets and older seats among lilacs, apple trees, flower borders and short stone walls behind the car park. *(Recommended by Mrs Lili Lomas, John and Joan Wyatt, Tom McLean, Ewan McCall, Roger Huggins)*

Wadworths   Licensee R E Flaxman   Real ale   Meals and snacks (11.30–2, 7–10.30) Open 11.30–2.30, 6.30–11; evening opening Sat–Mon 7; closed 25 Dec and evenings 26 Dec, 1 Jan

SOUTHROP   SP1903   Map 4
Swan ✪

Village signposted from A417 and A361, near Lechlade

The choice of enterprising and home-made bar food in this popular dining pub is more restauranty in the evening, when it might include traditional French fish or Stilton and onion soups (£1.95), mushroom, lentil and hazlenut pâté (£2.35), charcoal grilled chicken tikka with yoghurt, cucumber and mint (£2.75), and a

good range of main dishes such as fresh pasta with mushrooms in a pesto sauce
(£6.25), roast duck breast with orange or black cherry sauce (£6.95) or beef
Wellington (£7.50); at lunchtime there's a bigger choice of light snacks,
ploughman's (£2.50), as well as a selection of the evening dishes at markedly lower
prices, and cottage pie or sausages (£2.50), moussaka (£3.75), seafood pasta
(£4.50) and charcoal grilled sirloin steak (£6); puddings (£1.50). The extended
low-ceilinged front lounge has cottagey wall seats and chairs, and winter log fires,
and beyond it is a spacious stripped-stone-wall skittle alley, well modernised, with
plenty of tables on the carpeted part, and its own bar service at busy times; Arkells
and Morlands PA on handpump, and a fair selection of wines by the bottle; fruit
machine and trivia in the public bar. There are tables in the sheltered garden
behind. *(Recommended by Alan Skull, Margaret Dyke, Paul Harrop, Tom McLean, Ewan
McCall, Roger Huggins, A J H Sale, Jenny and Brian Seller, P B Dowsett, Frank W Gadbois,
Patrick Freeman, HNJ, PEJ)*

*Free house   Licensee Patrick Keen   Real ale   Meals and snacks (not Sun evening)
Restaurant tel Southrop (036 785) 205; closed Sun evening   Children welcome   Open
12–2.30, 7–11*

ST BRIAVELS   SO5605 Map 4

George 🛏

A Celtic coffin lid dating from 1070, discovered when a fireplace was removed, is
mounted next to the bar counter here. The three rambling rooms have
green-cushioned small settles, old-fashioned built-in wall seats, some booth
seating, Toby jugs and antique bottles on black beams over the servery, and a large
stone open fireplace. Bar food includes sandwiches (from £1.30), filled baked
potatoes (from £1.50), salads (from £1.50), burgers (from £1.60), ploughman's
(from £2), three home-made pork sausages and garlic bread (£2.50), vegetable
lasagne (£3.30), and fresh locally caught trout or home-made steak and kidney pie;
their speciality is what they call an oriental steamboat with fresh prawns, squid,
diced fish, meats, quails eggs and oriental fruits (4 people and they need 48 hours'
notice). Marstons Pedigree and Wadworths 6X and guests such as Bass or Badger
Tanglefoot on handpump; darts, cribbage, dominoes, trivia, piped music. Outside
the pub there are tables on a flagstoned terrace at the back that overlook a grassy
former moat to a silvery stone 12th-century castle built as a fortification against
the Welsh, and later used by King John as a hunting lodge; there are more tables
among roses and shrubs and there's an outdoor chess board. *(Recommended by
Donald Godden, BKA, G B Pugh, J F and M Sayers; more reports please)*

*Free house   Licensees Maurice and Cherry Day   Real ale   Meals and snacks (12.30–3,
7.30–9.30; last orders Sun lunchtime 2.30)   Children in eating area of bar up till 9 pm
Open 12–3, 7–11   Bedrooms tel Dean (0594) 530228; £28/£35*

STANTON   SO0634 Map 4

Mount

Village signposted off B4632 (the old A46) SW of Broadway; Old Snowshill Road – take
no-through road up hill and bear left

The terrace gives the best view from this popular Cotswold pub – looking back
down the steep hill over the lovely golden stone village and across to the Welsh
mountains. The atmospheric original bar has black beams, cask seats on big
flagstones, heavy-horse harness and racing photographs, and a big fireplace. A
spacious extension with comfortable oak wall seats, cigarette cards of Derby and
Grand National winners, and an aquarium of goldfish and angel fish, also has
some big picture windows. Well kept, reasonably priced Donnington BB on
handpump, and farm cider; friendly staff. Darts, dominoes, shove-ha'penny,
cribbage, fruit and space machine and piped music. Good bar food includes
sandwiches (from £1.50), tasty toasties £2.50), ploughman's (from £3.25), their
own large cow pie (£3.50), chicken and broccoli lasagne (£3.75), daily specials,
and puddings (£1.25). You can play boules on the lawn; on *Good Walks Guide*

Walk 88. It does get very busy at peak times. *(Recommended by Miss P de Earthe Bond, A C Morrison, David Young, Bob Smith, Laurence Manning, Michael and Alison Sandy; more reports please)*

Donnington   Licensee Colin Johns   Real ale   Meals and snacks (not Sun evening)   Children welcome if well behaved   Open 11–3, 6–11; 11–11 Sat; closed 25 Dec

nr STOW ON THE WOLD   SP1925   Map 4
Coach & Horses

Ganborough; A424 2 1/2 miles N of Stow; OS Sheet 163 map reference 172292

The cheerful young licensees in this welcoming and popular Cotswold stone pub took over from Mrs Morris's father just three years ago, and the genuinely home-made bar food is now in such demand that they may build an extension. From an attractive range this includes soup (£1.35), sandwiches (from £1.35; toasties from £1.50), cottage pie (£1.75), lasagne, seafood scallop or a vegetarian dish (£2.50), basket meals or filled baked potatoes (from £2.40), ploughman's (from £2.55), chicken Kiev or steak and kidney pie (£4.20), local trout (£4.95), and steak (£6.45), with specials such as winter stew made with Donnington beer (£2.95), and quiche Lorraine or rib of beef (£3.75); puddings (from £1.30); occasional barbecues summer Sunday evenings and on Bank Holidays. Being so close to the brewery, the Donnington XXX, BB and SBA is well kept on handpump. The bar area has leatherette wall benches, stools and Windsor chairs on the flagstone floor, and steps up to a carpeted part with high-backed settles around the tables; it's decorated with good wildlife photographs and coach horns on its ceiling joists, there's a winter log fire in the central chimney-piece, and the atmosphere is welcoming. Darts, dominoes, fruit machine, space game and juke box. There are seats outside, on a terrace and a narrow lawn. The attached field is where their German Shepherd, Candy, and their very likeable but not-very-bright Irish Wolfhound, Kelly, play; they also have a goat and occasional horse, and are a site for Caravan Club members; slide and swings for children. *(Recommended by Mr and Mrs A G Gillanders, G T and J Barnes, John and Joan Wyatt)*

Donnington   Licensees Andy and Sarah Morris   Real ale   Meals and snacks (not Sun evening)   Children in eating area   Occasional duo pop/country during summer, and always on New Years Eve   Open 11–3, 6–11; winter lunchtime closing 2.30; closed 25 Dec

STOW ON THE WOLD   SP1925   Map 4
Queens Head

The Square

At lunchtime, the busy stripped-stone front lounge – packed with small tables, little Windsor armchairs and brocaded wall banquettes – is popular with a mixture of tourists and local businessmen. The spacious flagstoned back bar, which has a couple of attractive high-backed settles as well as wheelback chairs, lots of beams, public school football team colours on a back wall, and a big log fire in the stone fireplace, is the best place to sample the local atmosphere; piped opera in here (not in front), darts, shove-ha'penny and fruit machine. Bar food includes sandwiches (from £1.20), very good soup or filled baked potatoes (£1.50), broccoli flan (£2.75), ploughman's (£2.25), chilli con carne or faggots (£2.75), good sirloin steak and puddings such as delicious apricot crumble or toffee pudding; Donnington BB and SBA are particularly well kept on handpump. A green bench in front of this charming building, under the climbing rose and the hanging baskets, looks across the pretty square, and in a back courtyard, there are some white tables. Two dogs. *(Recommended by Jim and Becky Bryson, Andy and Jill Kassube, Sheila Keene, A Triggs, N P Cox, Michael and Alison Sandy, David and Jane Russell)*

Donnington   Licensee Timothy Eager   Real ale   Meals and snacks (not Sun evening)   Children in back bar   Occasional jazz Sun, sometimes guitarist in week   Open 11–2.30, 6–11

WITHINGTON   SP0315 Map 4

Mill Inn   ★

Village signposted from A436, and from A40; from village centre follow sign towards Roman villa (but don't be tempted astray by villa signs *before* you reach the village!)

Much of the masonry of this mossy-roofed old stone inn came from the former Northleach House of Correction, and the site of the original mill from which the pub takes its name is now an island in the garden, connected by a stone bridge. Little side rooms open off the rambling carpeted bar, which is full of little nooks and corners, with antique high-backed settles and big cut-away barrel seats under its beams, an attractive bay window seat, old china and pewter on a high delft shelf, and good log fires in its stone fireplace. Decent bar food, ordered at the bar and served by waitresses, includes various starters (from £1.25), ploughman's (£2.50), basket meals (from £2.20), and main dishes like curry (£3.25), trout (£3.75), home-made steak and mushroom pie (£4.20) and steaks (£7.40). Sam Smiths OB and Museum on handpump; darts, shove-ha'penny, cribbage, dominoes, fruit machine, space game and trivia in the games bar; piped music. The location is marvellous; it stands virtually alone in a little valley surrounded by beech and chestnut trees and a rookery, and its neatly kept gardens. The Roman villa is a good walk away. On fine weekends, even in winter, the pub does get very busy. *(Recommended by Mrs Lili Lomas, G D Collier, Paul Harrop, Ann Marie Stephenson, Ewan McCall, Tom McLean, Roger Huggins, P B Dowsett, Gordon and Daphne, Margaret and Roy Randle, Dr and Mrs James Stewart, M A and C R Starling, Graham and Glenis Watkins, Simon Ward, HNJ, PEJ, G and M Hollis, Leith Stuart, Mrs J Oakes, John Branford)*

Sam Smiths   Licensee David Foley   Real ale   Meals and snacks (till 10 evening) Children welcome away from bar area   Open 11.30–2.30 (3 Sat), 6.30–11   Bedrooms tel Cheltenham (0242) 89204; £35/£60

WOODCHESTER   SO8302 Map 4

Ram   ⊘

South Woodchester, which is signposted off A46 Stroud–Nailsworth

There are spectacular views down the steep and pretty valley from picnic-table sets on the terrace by tubs of flowers and an unusually big hibiscus. Inside, furnishings in the attractive L-shaped bar range from country-kitchen chairs to several cushioned antique panelled settles around a variety of country tables, and built-in wall and window seats; there's a nice combination of crisp white walls, some stripped stonework, beams and three open fires. The range of well kept real ales on handpump is enterprising, with Archers Village, Boddingtons, Holdens, Hook Norton Old Hookey, the local Uley Bitter and Old Spot and two guest beers each week; good, friendly staff; sensibly placed darts, table skittles, fruit machine. The extensive, consistently good and very popular bar food includes ploughman's, prawns with garlic dip and main dishes such as home-cooked pizza (£2.50), beef and oyster pie (£4.05), chicken tikka, herb and spinach roulade or chilli burgers (all £4.25), and supreme of chicken stuffed with crab mousse and lobster brandy sauce (£6.50); puddings such as bread and butter pudding. *(Recommended by Margaret Dyke, Maureen Hobbs, M Rowlinson, Colleen Holiday, Pete and Rose Flower, BKA, Mrs Lili Lomas, John and Joan Wyatt, G D Collier, M A and C R Starling, Tom McLean, Ewan McCall, Roger Huggins, Robert and Vicky Tod, Patrick Freeman)*

Free house   Licensees Stuart and Teresa Callaway   Real ale   Meals and snacks (12–2, 6.30–9.30)   Children in eating area of bar   Impromptu piano   Open 11–3 (4 Sat), 6–11

Lucky Dip

Besides the fully inspected pubs, you might like to try these Lucky Dips recommended to us and described by readers (if you do, please send us reports):

Aldsworth [A433 Oxford—Cirencester; SP1510], *Sherborne Arms*: Typical Cotswold pub with friendly, helpful licensee, rustic atmosphere, well kept beer, decent food and log fire (*K R Harris, P B Dowsett, Mrs M Price*)

Amberley [SO8401], *Amberley Arms*: Impressive building in attractive spot, with good restaurant, pleasant service and comfortable bedrooms (*Mrs J Oakes, Patrick Freeman*)

Ampney Crucis [turn left at the Crown of Crucis and veer left at triangle — OS Sheet 163 map reference 069024; SP0602], *Butchers Arms*: Small pub concentrating more and more on food under new licensees; large helpings, seasonally-changing menu, decent wines and beers, no fruit machines or piped music (*D H and M C Watkinson, Mr and Mrs P B Dowsett*)

Ampney St Peter [OS Sheet 163 map reference 089013; SP0801], *Red Lion*: A favourite local with delightful atmosphere and lots of entertaining chat, very unpretentious (*Ewan McCall, Roger Huggins, Tom McLean*)

Apperley [SO8628], *Farmers Arms*: Well run pleasant old beamed Cotswold family pub with wide choice of good food, well kept Flowers, open fire, garden; children welcome (*J H C Peters*)

Ashleworth [village signposted off A417 at Hartpury; SO8125], *Arkle*: Unpretentious and remarkably welcoming Donnington village local, large entrance hall with skittle alley, darts and fruit machines, bar opening off with flock wallpaper and mock stone decor; warm and clean, with well kept XXX, BB and SBA on handpump, simple but tasty freshly filled evening rolls, bar billiards; closes early lunchtime (*Peter Scillitoe*)

Berkeley [ST6899], *Berkeley Arms*: Riverside pub with character — L-shaped room with high-backed settles (*Tom McLean, Ewan McCall, Roger Huggins*); *Berkeley Hunt*: Quaint serving bar between two rooms, pleasant atmosphere (*Tom McLean, Ewan McCall, Roger Huggins*); [bottom of main rd through village], *Mariners Arms*: 15th-century pub with delicious home-made food, Whitbreads ales, tables outside (*Mrs Carol Mason*)

Berry Hill [SO5713], *Pike House*: Warm welcome and wide range of particularly good value food (*Brenda Turner, John Turner*)

Bibury [SP1106], *Catherine Wheel*: Busy Courage pub in pleasant spot, with well kept Courage Best and good choice of well cooked food, not cheap but served almost too generously; fruit machine and piped music can be obtrusive, but quiet, attractive garden; good-sized car park (*Roger Huggins, Tom McLean, Ewan McCall, Dr M I Crichton, Wayne Brindle, Jim and Becky Bryson, Mr and Mrs P B Dowsett, Margaret Dyke*)

Birdlip [A417/A436 roundabout—OS Sheet 163 map reference 935162; SO9316], *Air Balloon*: Worth knowing chiefly for its good play area, maybe with pets, in one of the two garden areas, and for staying open later into the afternoon than most around here; open-plan inside, with piped music and fast-food catering — can get very busy (*Tom McLean, Roger Huggins, Ewan McCall, BKA*)

Bisley [SO9005], *Stirrup Cup*: Busy, lively and friendly L-shaped bar in village local (*Ewan McCall, Tom McLean*)

Bourton on the Water [SP1620], *Duke of Wellington*: Interesting food in pub with bar, garden and wine-bar/dining room, beers and decor good (*Andy and Jill Kassube*)

Brimpsfield [Nettleton Bottom—A417 Birdlip—Cirencester at start of village bypass; SO9312], *Golden Heart*: Formerly a popular main entry, with a wide and interesting range of real ales tapped from the cask, a short choice of genuine home cooking (not your usual pub food), friendly staff and simple old-fashioned surroundings — but in late summer 1990 the licensees moved to the Canning Arms in Hartpury, planning the same sort of thing there; there may be major changes here, and a more conventional pub-food operation; there's a sheltered little terrace (*LYM*)

☆ **Broadoak** [SO7013], *White Hart*: Spacious and comfortable beamed bar, large evening restaurant, terrace overlooking River Severn; well kept Flowers and Whitbreads Pompey Royal, wide range of cold dishes, some hot food — good helpings; fruit machine and quiet piped music (not pop), quick friendly service, though busy at weekends; children welcome (*Lyn and Bill Capper, Paul McPherson*)

Broadwell [off A429 2 miles N of Stow-on-the-Wold; SP2027], *Fox*: Civilised — some might say almost clinical — village pub in lovely spot opposite spreading village green, with flagstones, three local Donnington beers on handpump, and good home-cooked food inc lunchtime sandwiches and ploughman's as well as hot dishes; bedrooms (*P and R Woods*)

☆ **Brockhampton** [the one between Andoversford and Winchcombe — OS Sheet 163 map reference 035223; SP0322], *Craven Arms*: Pleasant, comfortable and popular 17th-century pub, with several spotless and spacious rooms — log fire, low beams, stripped stonework, mainly pine furniture, but undeniably modernised, and can get crowded weekends; efficient cheerful service, well kept Butcombe and Hook Norton on handpump, good bar food inc excellent Sun lunches, nice puddings and in season bargain asparagus; pleasant garden (*John Haig, John and Joan Wyatt, Alan Skull, PADEMLUC, Mrs Joan Harris, Derek and Sylvia Stephenson*)

Cam [High St; ST7599], *Berkeley Arms*: Great local with good atmosphere (*J R Jewitt*)

Cambridge [3 miles from M5 junction 13 — A38 towards Bristol; SO7403], *George*: Busy and popular dining pub with attractive decor inc old sewing machines; good value bar food inc good puddings trolley, well kept Marstons Pedigree, pleasant table staff; separate restaurant, tables outside (and barbecues), summer caravan site; best to book at weekends; neatly framed graffiti in gents'; children's play area *(Neil and Anita Christopher, W C M Jones, Tom Evans)*

Chalford [France Lynch — OS Sheet 163 map reference 904036; SO9002], *Kings Head*: Good country local with great views, friendly atmosphere, well kept beer, wide range of bar food even Sun lunchtime, garden *(Roger Entwistle)*

Charlton Kings [Cirencester Rd; SO9620], *Clock Tower*: Well kept and cheap Banks's Mild and Bitter and Hansons, in spacious and attractive converted ex-stable block of former Lilleybrook Hotel, with comfortable if brightly upholstered armchairs and sofas and other darker wooden furniture, potted palms, memorabilia on walls; substantial lunchtime bar food *(John and Joan Wyatt)*

Cheltenham [behind bus stn; SO9422], *Bay Tree*: Friendly back-street pub with good Wadworths 6X and piped jazz *(John Nicholson)*; [London Rd (A40 towards Charlton Kings, nr junction A435); SO9422], *Beaufort Arms*: Well kept Wadworths Old Timer from the barrel, IPA and 6X on handpump; good value crusty filled rolls at lunchtime; friendly landlord *(John and Joan Wyatt)*; [Portland St], *Cotswold*: Warm and welcoming atmosphere in easy-going pub with Victorian prints on flock-papered walls; well kept Wadworths IPA, 6X and Farmers Pride on handpump, variety of good home-cooked food inc Sun lunches, pleasant staff; open all day *(Alan Skull, Paul Harrop)*; [North Pl], *Duck & Pheasant*: Spacious, with good choice of well presented bar food *(Shirley Pielou)*; [37 High St], *Old Swan*: Pleasant, quiet and spacious town pub with generous helpings of well presented good value home-made lunchtime food, decent beers, tea or coffee and scones served all day, comfortable conservatory; friendly service *(G D Collier and others)*; [Montpellier Walk; SO9422], *Rotunda*: Well kept Smiles, Tetleys and Wadworths 6X, bar snacks and good piped music; open all day Sat *(Salvo and Gwyneth Spadaro-Dutturi)*

☆ **Chipping Campden**, [Main St; SP1539], *Kings Arms*: Civilised small hotel with good, well presented food at reasonable prices, helpful and friendly staff and good log fire in its comfortable and old-fashioned bar; bedrooms stylish and comfortable *(Mr and Mrs W Dermott, LYM)*

Chipping Campden *Greenstocks*: Tastefully decorated bar, cheerful service, good reasonably priced food *(John Bowdler)*

Cirencester [SP0201], *Drillmans Arms*: Decent, friendly enough local with Archers Best and ASB, Flowers IPA and a guest beer *(Tom McLean, Ewan McCall, Roger Huggins)*; [between church and Corinium Museum], *Golden Cross*: Very small and busy local, with quite a good range of very cheap food *(Margaret and Trevor Errington)*

☆ **Clearwell** [B4231 — OS Sheet 162 map reference 572081; SO5708], *Wyndham Arms*: Primarily a hotel and restaurant, but with a good bar, smart and well kept, with stone walls, decorative beams, big open fireplace, well kept Bass on handpump, lots of malt whiskies, pleasant service; attractive countryside nr Wye and Forest of Dean; bedrooms comfortable, in new extension *(Frank Cummins, M A Watts, LYM)*

Coberley [A436 Brockworth—Andoversford, just SW of junction with A435 Cheltenham—Cirencester; SO9516], *Seven Springs*: Unusual and comfortable if somewhat impersonal reworking of lofty and spacious stone barn, with airy food area, more interesting side areas and sloping pond-side garden; Courage beers, maybe a pianist or organist; children allowed during daytime — has been open all day *(Neil and Anita Christopher, John Miles)*

☆ **Cold Aston** [maybe under Aston Blank; signed from A436 (was B4068) and A429 SW of Stow-on-the-Wold; SP1219], *Plough*: Snug is almost too ample a word for this diminutive 17th-century village pub, with its low black beams, flagstones, old-fashioned simple furnishings, open fire, well kept Wadworths IPA on handpump, Norbury farm cider and generous helpings of decent bar food from home-baked rolls or well filled baked potatoes to hot dishes and salad; friendly service, piped music, traditional games, seats outside; children allowed in eating area; bedrooms *(Patrick Freeman, G and M Brooke-Williams, Alan Skull, Craig and Suzanne Everhart, LYM — more news of this nice pub please)*

Coleford [Joyford; from Coleford, follow Ross signs, then first right after A4136 crossroads; from B4228 just S of English Bicknor take narrow rd going S; either way, look for easy-to-miss sign to pub up narrow side lane screened by thick hedge — OS Sheet 162 map reference 580134; SO5813], *Dog & Muffler*: Small furnished foyer leads into cosy bar with long conservatory along back wall, overlooking verandah and secluded lawn surrounded by high hedges; tables with linen and fresh flowers, nicely cooked and presented straightforward food, well kept Sam Smiths on handpump, service friendly and welcoming, log-effect gas fire *(Frank Cummins)*

☆ **Colesbourne** [A435; SO9913], *Colesbourne Inn*: Good, comfortably refurbished pub/hotel with friendly landlord, huge log fire, good atmosphere, settles and oak tables; well kept beer, wide range of good value though not low-priced bar food inc fresh salmon, pheasant and pigeon, smart waitresses *(Laurence Manning, Patrick Freeman)*

Coln St Aldwyns [SP1405], *New Inn*: Latest news is that in spite of closure and plans for redevelopment as flats a determined local campaign has won a new lease of life for this prettily placed Cotswold inn, which was formerly so popular for its snug series of 17th-century rooms and comfortable bedrooms; it's to be part inn, part small country-house hotel/restaurant *(LYM — reports please)*

Cranham [SO8912], *Royal William*: Popular, spacious Whitbread Brewers Fayre pub with friendly staff, well kept Flowers Original and IPA, fair choice of bar food; nr Cotswold Way *(Neil and Anita Christopher, Barbara M McHugh)*

Duntisbourne Abbots [A417 N of Cirencester — OS Sheet 163 map reference 978091; SO9709], *Five Mile House*: A really old-fashioned locals' local, with room for only a couple of tables in the flagstoned bay-windowed bar, high settles forming a snug in the partly partitioned-off entrance hall; well kept Courage tapped from the barrel *(Tom McLean, Ewan McCall, Roger Huggins)*

Dursley [May Lane; ST7598], *Happy Pig*: Large range of well kept beers — Bass, Smiles, Timothy Taylors, Theakstons, Robinsons, Courage Best, Banks's and a guest *(Nigel Cant)*; [Kingshill], *Kingshill*: Attractively decorated, with Whitbreads beers and food served all day *(Alastair Campbell)*

Dymock [SO7031], *Beauchamp Arms*: Flowers Original and Marstons Pedigree on handpump, interesting range of lunchtime bar food, reasonably priced; obliging staff, small, pleasant garden with pond; bedrooms *(John and Joan Wyatt, Neil and Anita Christopher)*

Eastleach Turville [SP1905], *Victoria*: Pleasantly remodelled lounge, second simpler bar, food such as ham salad, king prawns, butterfly prawns, smoked salmon salad and interesting puddings, well kept Arkells beers; beautiful village, with daffodils along the river *(R C Watkins)*

Edge [A4173 N of Stroud; SO8509], *Edgemoor*: Modernised food pub notable for the striking valley views through its big picture windows; Whitbreads-related ales under light carbon dioxide blanket, unobtrusive piped music, children in eating area *(Barry and Anne, LYM)*

☆ **Elkstone** [Beechpike; A417 6 miles N of Cirencester — OS Sheet 163 map reference 966108; SO9610], *Highwayman*: A surprise for this busy trunk road — a rambling warren of low beams, stripped stone, alcoves, antique settles among more modern furnishings, log fires; popular food running up to steaks, with a wide choice of lunchtime open sandwiches and ploughman's, children's dishes, friendly staff, Arkells on handpump, piped music; outside play area; children in eating area, two family rooms and restaurant *(Jon Wainwright, Jane and Calum, Ian and James Phillips, LYM)*

☆ **Ewen** [signed from A429 S of Cirencester; SU0097], *Wild Duck*: Small 16th-century hotel with attractive old-fashioned furnishings in high-beamed main bar, soberly civilised atmosphere, stylish cooking even for the bar food — which like the drinks is not cheap; Bass and Wadworths 6X on handpump, shove-ha'penny, piped music, tables in sheltered and charming garden; can get very busy, dogs allowed; bedrooms comfortable and pleasantly furnished, if rather pricey *(M J Dyke, Mrs Lili Lomas, M A and C R Starling, Peter and Rose Flower, Patrick Freeman, Roger Huggins, Tom McLean, Ewan McCall, Neville Kenyon, Robert and Vicky Tod, Laurence Manning, Alastair Campbell, Alan Skull, LYM)*

Fairford [Market Pl; SP1501], *Bull*: Very friendly, good value food, nice spot nr 15th-century church and river walk; comfortable bedrooms *(Jim and Becky Bryson)*

Foss Cross [SP0609], *Hare & Hounds*: Small roadside pub with well kept Hook Norton Best and Wadworths 6X, nice open log fire, special eating area for families (pub especially welcoming to families), good restaurant popular for Sun lunch; nice area outside, good car park *(John Drummond)*

☆ **Fossebridge** [A429 Cirencester—Stow-on-the-Wold; SP0811], *Fossebridge Inn*: Handsome Georgian inn with much older two-room bar at the back, attractively furnished in old-fashioned style with more modern side area; under new ownership early 1990, and preliminary reports suggested that the quality/price/service equation had gone a bit awry as far as the ambitious bar food was concerned; tables out on streamside terrace and spacious lawn, restaurant; children welcome; comfortable bedrooms *(LYM)*

☆ **Glasshouse** [by Newent Woods; first right turn off A40 going W from junction with A4136 — OS Sheet 162 map reference 710213; SO7122], *Glasshouse*: Carefully preserved as basic country tavern, with decorative plates, fine British Match poster and open fires in cavernous hearth of kitchen bar, changing well kept real ales such as Butcombe and Flowers or Theakstons tapped from a rack of casks, ploughman's and plain basket meals, seats on grass outside; fine nearby woodland walks *(Peter Scillitoe, LYM)*

☆ **Gloucester** [Bristol Rd], *Linden Tree*: Attractive decor, good welcoming atmosphere, good range of well kept real ales such as Butcombe, Hook Norton, Marstons Pedigree and Wadworths 6X, well prepared reasonably priced food *(Chris Payne)*

Gloucester [Southgate St], *County*: Panelling and solid furniture, several well kept real ales, particularly good value bar food; bedrooms *(Tom Evans)*; [100 Westgate St], *Dick Whittingtons House*: Unusual in being listed Grade I — Georgian facade but 14th-century inside — probably former guild hall and mansion house; an atmospheric place for a quiet early-evening drink *(Pamela and Merlyn Horswell)*; [Westgate St], *Tailor of Gloucester*: Formerly the Union Inn, but recently refurbished and enlarged by taking over the building next door — nicely done, and now a comfortable town-centre pub; well kept beers inc Marstons Pedigree, decent bar food such as cheap steak sandwich, gammon and egg, mixed grill *(Nicholas Kingsley)*

☆ **Great Barrington** [signed off A40 Burford—Northleach; SP2013], *Fox:* Simple little Cotswold inn, stripped stonework, rustic furniture, and long-serving licensees who've kept it determinedly unspoilt; plain bar food, Donnington beers, skittle alley, sheltered terrace by River Windrush — its appeal is to people who don't want to be cosseted and prefer the old-fashioned lack of airs and graces here; bedrooms *(HNJ, PEJ, Robert Timmis, Alan Skull, Stephen King, Simon Ward, EML, LYM)*

Gretton [SP0131], *Bugatti:* Well kept pub with good meals and friendly service *(E A Donnan)*

Hardwicke [Sellars Bridge; SO7912], *Pilot:* Pleasantly furnished long, busy bar looking out over canal lock, good atmosphere, well kept Flowers Original, Wethereds and Whitbreads Pompey Royal, smiling prompt service, bar food *(Gwen and Peter Andrews, Tom Evans)*

☆ **Hartpury** [Ledbury Rd; SO7924], *Canning Arms:* Has been doing well — attractive, cheerful and welcoming with good value bar food inc vegetarian dishes, decent beer and wine; garden great for children; as we went to press we heard that the licensees who made a success of the Golden Heart at Brimpfield (great choice of real ales, unaffected surroundings and genuine home cooking) were planning to move here *(Mr and Mrs P Pitt, Chris Richardson, G T Doyle — reports on the new regime please)*

Hartbury [Hamms Lane], *Rising Sun:* Friendly atmosphere, good, cheap bar food — particularly specials and Sun roast; children welcome, with swings and so forth outside; good value bedrooms *(Mae and Brian Postlethwaite)*

☆ **Kilkenny** [A436 nr Cheltenham — OS Sheet 163 map reference 007187; SP0019], *Kilkenny Inn:* Small, comfortable country pub, pleasant atmosphere, lunchtime and evening bar food – the reason for the star rating is that it's recently been bought by the licensees who originally built up the reputations of the Boat at Redbrook, Green Dragon at Cowley and (in its original palmy days) Seven Springs at Coberley, so should be well worth investigating *(Neil and Anita Christopher)*

Kineton [village signposted from B4068 and B4077 W of Stow-on-the-Wold; SP0926], *Halfway House:* Unpretentiously traditional but squeaky-clean and polished Donnington pub, with well kept and attractively priced beer from that local brewery, simple bar food from sandwiches to steaks, pub games (and juke box), tables on narrow front terrace and sheltered back lawn, restaurant; children allowed lunchtime; if we had a more regular flow of reports on this it would probably be a regular rather than intermittent main entry; bedrooms *(HJN, PEJ, Mrs N Lawson, Colin Scott-Morton, LYM)*

☆ **Lechlade** [The Square; SU2199], *New Inn:* Very comfortable lounge bar in largish hotel, extremely popular at lunchtime for really good value bar food; choice of beers, big open fire, restaurant, superb Thames-side garden (mooring allowed); bedrooms *(Wayne Brindle, P B Dowsett)*

☆ **Lechlade**, *Red Lion:* Good range of reasonably priced food, quiet, pleasant and efficient service, well kept Arkells (but beware a fake handpump dispensing keg BBB) *(Derek and Sylvia Stephenson, Marjorie and David Lamb)*

☆ **Leighterton** [off A46 S of Nailsworth; ST8291], *Royal Oak:* Old country pub in beautiful countryside; good, simple bar food at reasonable prices, running up to steaks and local trout; well kept real ales inc Hook Norton and Uley, friendly landlord; quite handy for Westonbirt Arboretum *(Peter and Rose Flower, Margaret Dyke, P and R Woods)*

Littledean [A4151 E of Cinderford; SO6714], *George:* Old-fashioned pub with rambling rooms, Whitbreads ales and bar food; garden with pleasant view of Forest of Dean and Severn Vale *(Dave Braisted)*

Longhope [Ross Rd (A40); SO6919], *Farmers Boy:* Popular with readers in former editions as comfortable old pub with nice choice of good food, decent wines and beer, room for teenagers, pleasant owners — but we've had no recent reports *(More reports please)*

☆ **Lower Swell** [B4068 W of Stow-on-the-Wold (sometimes still called A436 on maps); SP1725], *Golden Ball:* Neat and simple local inn — no pretensions to much atmosphere — with well kept Donnington BB, SBA and XXX Mild from the pretty brewery just 20 minutes' walk away, generously served bar food from soup, ploughman's, filled baked potatoes, decent cottage pie and imaginative salads to steak and a memorable game pie, good service; games area behind log fireplace, occasional barbecues, Aunt Sally and quoits in pleasant streamside garden; evening restaurant, no food Sun evening; very clean simple bedrooms, good value; bedrooms *(Jon Wainwright, M H Box, B S Bourne, John and Joan Wyatt, C A Holloway, LYM)*

Lower Swell [SP1725], *Old Farm House:* Not strictly a pub, but worth knowing for good lunchtime bar snacks and pleasant peaceful atmosphere *(Mrs E M Thompson)*

Lower Wick [ST7196], *Pickwick:* Comfortably refurbished free house with changing choice of good home-cooked food, choice of fresh fish (inc some unusual ones); well kept Butcombe and Theakstons *(Nigel Cant)*

Meysey Hampton [SU1199], *Masons Arms:* Recently reopened after extensive alterations, with friendly landlord, particularly well kept Ash Vine, spare decor *(Mr and Mrs P B Dowsett, Ewan McCall, Roger Huggins, Tom McLean)*

☆ **Mickleton** [fairly handy for Stratford; SP1543], *Kings Arms:* Comfortable and relaxed L-shaped lounge bar with rugs on

parquet, plush-cushioned window seats and small settles, brocaded chairs and stools, well spaced tables; popular for admirable choice of low-cost snacks and particularly good value filled home-baked rolls inc hot beef on Sun and baked cheese and onion; also two or three good hot dishes, puddings; pleasant staff, Flowers IPA and Original on handpump, some tables outside, relaxing at lunchtime when it's particularly popular with older people; handy for Hidcote and Kiftsgate, even Stratford; opens 10, closes earlyish *(Hope Chenhalls, A C Morrison, BB)*
Mickleton, *Butchers Arms*: Clean and tidy, with friendly atmosphere, good beer, big helpings of good hot food; lawn outside with benches, tables, and fishpond *(R W Grey)*

☆ **Minchinhampton** [Minchinhampton Common; Nailsworth—Brimscombe — on common fork left at pub's sign], *Old Lodge*: Partly 16th-century, superbly placed on high National Trust commons, with a good range of interesting real ales, friendly service, and food which can be imaginative and good value; recent reports suggest that some refurbishment would be welcome *(Patrick Freeman, LYM)*

☆ **Minchinhampton**, *Crown*: Happy, welcoming Cotswold-stone pub on market sq of historic village, well kept Flowers Original on handpump, decent wines, good hot and cold bar food, open fires, darts and dominoes *(Gethin Lewis, W H Bland)*

☆ **Minsterworth** [A48 S of Gloucester; SO7716], *Apple Tree*: Originally 17th-century farmhouse, recently extended and refurbished by Whitbreads keeping oak beams, open fires, comfortable assorted seating; friendly service, unobtrusive piped music, well kept Flowers Original, Marstons Pedigree and Wadworths 6X, wide choice of usual food presented well, big garden ideal for children with safe enclosed play area; open all day — lane beside leads down to the Severn, a good way of avoiding east bank crowds on a Bore weekend *(David Gethyn-Jones, G D Collier, Christopher and Heather Barton, Jacquie and Jon Payne)*
Miserden [OS Sheet 163 map reference 936089; SE9308], *Carpenters Arms*: Food good inc formidable help-yourself buffet, but not cheap; closed Mon except Bank Hols; strictly no children *(Roger Bellingham, Gordon and Kathy Lewis, Mrs Lili Lomas)*

☆ **Moreton in Marsh** [SP2032], *Redesdale Arms*: Well renovated and comfortable bar and buttery in old-fashioned but lively country-town hotel with good log fires, well kept Courage Directors; food, though not cheap, above normal pub standards inc first-class veg and home-made ice-cream, served by helpful staff; bedrooms *(Wayne Brindle, P Knight, Dr and Mrs A K Clarke, E V Walder)*

☆ **Nailsworth** [ST8499], *Egypt Mill*: Former mill tastefully converted to pub, with working mill wheel in one room, static machinery in second area, Ind Coope Burton and Wadworths 6X on handpump, good bar food, quick service, upstairs restaurant; can get crowded at weekends, and car park — with little bridge to pub — could do with resurfacing; occasional jazz evenings; children welcome, but no dogs *(Roger Huggins, Tom McLean, Ewan McColl)*

☆ **Newland** [OS Sheet 162 map reference 555096; SO5509], *Ostrich*: Lovely little low-ceilinged 17th-century pub in charming old village close to River Wye; friendly and spacious bar with well kept Flowers IPA and Original, Marstons Pedigree and Wadworths 6X on handpump, good food in bar (not Sun) and restaurant, big log fire, maybe subdued piped radio, Sunday newspapers; service pleasant without being effusive; bedrooms pleasant, with huge breakfasts *(Frank Cummins, Dr John Innes)*
Newnham [SO7012], *Victoria*: Friendly service, good, reasonably priced food, good atmosphere, open fire *(W L Congreve)*
Newport [A38; ST7098], *Stagecoach*: Traditional place with interesting fireplace, horsebrasses, beams, coach supports; well kept Flowers Original, Hook Norton, Marstons Pedigree, John Smiths and Wadworths 6X on handpump, variety of food in small bar and larger carvery restaurant; garden with play area *(A C Lang)*

☆ **North Cerney** [A435 Cirencester—Cheltenham; SP0208], *Bathurst Arms*: High-backed antique settles and nice window seats in beamed and black-panelled bar, splendid stone fireplace, fine range of over half a dozen real ales, welcoming staff, goodish if somewhat pricey and restaurany bar food — though the regulars can sometimes rather hog the atmosphere; barbecues most summer weekends, lunchtime and evening, on the pretty streamside front lawn; restaurant; children allowed in eating area; bedrooms *(Russell and Christina Jones, R Gardner, Jane and Calum, A L Willey, LYM)*

☆ **North Nibley** [B4060; ST7496], *Black Horse*: Straightforward but neatly kept pub with Flowers Original, Whitbreads PA and a guest beer on handpump, bar food from sandwiches through chilli con carne and so forth to steaks, decent puddings — served till 10; restaurant Tues–Sat evenings, Sun lunchtime, tables outside; bedrooms not large, but clean and comfortable, most with shower and private lavatory *(JM, PM, WHBM, Mr and Mrs Stevens, LYM)*
Northleach [Square; SP1114], *Red Lion*: Comfortable room with raised open fireplace and simple bar food, reasonably priced and well presented; close to World of Mechanical Music — polyphons, musical boxes, autopianos, clocks *(E V Walder)*; [Square], *Union*: Doing well under current licensees, with decor and layout improved yet keeping traditional Cotswold atmosphere; attractive food; bedrooms *(Sidney and Erna Wells)*
Nympsfield [SO8000], *Rose & Crown*: Wide choice of beers on handpump, farm cider, attractive village setting, friendly staff, good value food in big helpings inc fine

ploughman's, bar games; seats outside; bedrooms (*Alastair Campbell*)

☆ **Oakridge Lynch** [SO9102], *Butchers Arms*: Above a particularly steep and twisty village — luckily the good-sized car park is on the level top road; big neatly modernised rambling carpeted bar with low beams, big fireplace, some stripped stonework, and good range of well kept real ales such as Archers, Butcombe, Ind Coope Burton, Ruddles Best and County; lunchtime bar food, very friendly atmosphere, skittle alley (*Ewan McCall, Roger Huggins, Tom McLean, Mrs A Crowhurst, Mrs Lili Lomas, BB*)

☆ **Parkend** [SO6208], *Woodman*: Welcoming Forest of Dean pub doing particularly well under current regime, with long heavy-beamed bar, wide choice of good value food from sandwiches through several vegetarian dishes to steaks, children's menu and Sun lunch; well kept Flowers Original, Marstons Pedigree and Bulmers cider on handpump, two fireplaces (flowers in one), saws and blades on the wall, pleasant and helpful service; darts, fruit machine, juke box; children and small dogs at one end; bedrooms (*Frank Cummins, R P Taylor, Paul and Heather Bettesworth, Annette Keith*)

Paxford [B4479; SP1837], *Churchill*: Flagstoned bar originally two tiny rooms, simple tables, spindlebacked chairs, former commode (full of old books), big open fireplace with small darts alcove tucked in by chimney breast; welcoming licensees, well kept Hook Norton Best and Old Hookey, simple range of bar food, small garden with picnic-set tables (*E V Walder*)

☆ **Prestbury** [Mill St; SO9624], *Plough*: Unspoilt thatched village pub with well kept Flowers and Whitbreads tapped from the cask and good bar food; the back part is best, with its grandfather clock, wooden benches and tables, stone floor and big open fireplace; there's also a lounge for those who don't know what a village pub is for; pleasant back garden (*B M Eldridge, P J Simmons*)

Purton [just upstream from Sharpness village on left bank of Severn estuary — ie not the pub of this name in nearby Berkeley; SO6904], *Berkeley Arms*: Marvellous estuary pub — no food, no noise, a lovely settle in the main bar (*N W Acton*)

Redmarley [Playley Green (A417 just off M50 exit 2); SO7531], *Rose & Crown*: Friendly pub with good food in bar and in carefully decorated restaurant (former skittle alley); charming licensees (*Rex Sargent, B Walton*)

☆ **Sapperton** [OS Sheet 163 map reference 948033; SO9403], *Bell*: Well kept Flowers Original, Whitbreads PA and other beers such as Bass, Marstons Pedigree or Wadworths 6X, and now a wider choice of good value straightforward food in recently extended lounge and in roomy L-shaped bar with big tables, wall and window settles and Windsor chairs; darts, quoits, fruit machine, log fire, tables on small front lawn; fine walks from here — it's on GWG89 ; well

behaved children welcome — a popular family pub at weekends (*Roger Huggins, Ewan McCall, Tom McLean, John Miles, Cliff and Karen Spooner, Mrs Lili Lomas*)

☆ **Selsley** [just SW of Stroud; SO8304], *Bell*: Attractive pub on common, popular with walkers of the Cotswold Way; small and tidy but welcoming and relaxed, friendly staff and locals, wide range of reasonably priced home-cooked bar food, particularly the home-made pies, specials and puddings such as jam roly-poly with nice custard; Flowers beer, some live music (*S Rochford, Cherry Knott, Margaret Dyke*)

☆ **Sheepscombe** [village signposted from B4070 NE of Stroud, and A46 N of Painswick; SO8910], *Butchers Arms*: This simple village inn has been very popular in previous editions, and would in this edition have been a main entry for its cheerful atmosphere, low prices, well kept Flowers Original and Whitbreads PA under light carbon dioxide blanket, plain lunchtime bar food (only light ploughman's on Sun), and fine views from bay windows and seats outside; also very simple bedrooms, good value in summer; but the landlord tells us he is leaving, as Whitbreads may be selling the pub as a private house (*More news please*)

Shipton Oliffe [SP0318], *Frogmill*: Manages to absorb crowds and still appear uncrowded; good service, bar snacks and Flowers beers; bedrooms (*Dave Braisted*)

Shurdington [Shurdington Rd; SO8318], *Bell*: Very friendly landlord and staff welcome everyone, prices are reasonable, and beer inc Wadworths 6X consistently well kept (*K Matthews*)

Slad [SO8707], *Woolpack*: Small pub, very much a local — Laurie Lee's local, indeed — but landlord welcoming and helpful, Marstons Pedigree and Wadworths 6X well kept, and good range of bar food decently priced (*Ewan McCall, Roger Huggins, Tom McLean, BKA*)

Sling [SO5807], *Montague*: Well run pub with well kept beer and good bar food; small restaurant — be early or book (*Sybil Baker*); *Orepool*: Doing well under current regime, extended in keeping with original building; friendly welcome, good beer and food; children welcome and properly catered for so that they don't inconvenience others (*PB, HB*)

☆ **Snowshill** [SP0934], *Snowshill Arms*: Well kept Donnington BB and SBA, open fire, efficiently served popular food (inc Tannoy system for back garden, which has a good play area — and a skittle alley); more airy inside than many Cotswold pubs, with charming village views from bow windows; cheery atmosphere, helpful Italian licensee and English wife, prices notably low for the Cotswolds — and, a nice touch for this tourist area, at least one table kept clear for the locals; children welcome if eating (*Peter Scillitoe, P Knight, Mr and Mrs W Dermott, Caroline Wright, Mrs Lili Lomas, Mrs E M Thompson, Richard Parr, William D Cissna, Curt and Lois Stevens, LYM*)

Stow on the Wold [SP1925], *Grapevine*: Beautiful conservatory with 120-year-old vine, good, cheap food and helpful staff; comfortable bedrooms *(Mr and Mrs W Dermott)*; [The Square], *Old Stocks*: Good value bedrooms in well run simple hotel with small comfortable bar, seats on pavement and in sheltered garden *(BB)*; [The Square], *White Hart*: Cheery atmosphere (it's next to the YHA) in front bar with heavy rustic furniture, some easy chairs and log-effect gas fire; green plush seats in plainer back lounge with tables set for bar lunches — the food's good and attractively priced; clean and well kept, no music, keg beer; bedrooms *(Alastair Campbell, BB)*

Stroud [1 Bath Rd; SO8504], *Clothiers Arms*: Popular pub with one big bar divided into two areas, decorated with penny-farthing bicycle, spinning wheels, weaving frames, old sewing-machine tables, 19th-century bobbins and carding combs, framed embroidered greetings cards, fish tank and two modern settles; bar food, well kept Archers ASB and Village, Smiles, and Wadworths *(BKA)*

Tetbury [Market Pl; ST8893], *Crown*: Wide choice of bar food from sandwiches to steaks in long front bar, back conservatory used as evening restaurant (and bar lunch overflow); friendly service, no piped music or fruit machines; Flowers and Whitbreads beers; bedrooms *(Lyn and Bill Capper)*; [London Rd], *Priory*: More eating house than pub, with well presented food — and worth knowing for clean and comfortable bedrooms *(Joy Matthews, N Matthews)*; [Market Pl], *Snooty Fox*: Modernised hotel lounge; welcoming, especially during happy hour *(Dr and Mrs A K Clarke)*

Tetbury [A433 towards Cirencester, nr Cherington; ST8893], *Trouble House*: Homely 17th-century pub with basic bar, cosy lounge with open fire and fruit machine, further room leading off for bar billiards, darts and juke box; well kept Wadworths on handpump, simple low-priced bar food from sandwiches and rolls to chilli con carne or scampi; name of pub dates back to Civil War *(Roger Huggins, Tom McLean)*

Tewkesbury [52 Church St; SO8932], *Bell*: Comfortable plush lounge with some neat William and Mary oak panelling, black oak timbers, medieval leaf-and-fruit frescoes and big log fire; lunchtime food counter, garden above Severnside walk near lovely weir; bedrooms *(Wayne Brindle, BB)*; *Plough*: Welcome as pleasant retreat from town bustle *(Wayne Brindle)*

Toddington [A46 Broadway—Winchcombe, junction with A438 and B4077; SP0432], *Pheasant*: Halls house with lots of malt whiskies, choice of hot and cold bar food, friendly staff, tables in garden with children's play area; close to Gloucs & Warwicks Railway *(Joan Olivier)*

☆ **Twyning** [SO8936], *Village Inn*: Pleasant and popular village pub, with good atmosphere, helpful staff, interesting locals, good if not cheap bar food especially local sausages (may be limited Mon and Tues); beer and wines good, dogs allowed; pretty garden *(W C M Jones, Robert and Vicky Tod)*

Uley [The Street; ST7898], *Kings Head*: Early 18th-century stuccoed pub, spick and span inside, with well kept Wadworths Devizes and 6X on handpump, good value food such as home-made moussaka, lively down-to-earth atmosphere, friendly landlord; open all day Sat *(John and Joan Wyatt, Alastair Campbell)*; [The Street], *Old Crown*: Unpretentious, cosy Whitbreads pub in pleasant spot overlooking village green, doing well under current regime; now with local Uley Best as well as Marstons Pedigree and Whitbreads PA on handpump, and fairly big helpings of tasty home-cooked bar food (steak and onion pie recommended) *(Alastair Campbell, Alan Frankland, Sarah Mellor)*

Up Hatherley [Alma Rd; SO9120], *Bass House*: Comfortable and friendly estate pub, well kept Bass, very efficient service *(G D Collier)*

Viney Hill [off A48 Blakeney—Lydney; SO6606], *New Inn*: Well kept beer and excellent food in recently refurbished pub, comfortable and tremendously friendly; children most welcome *(Mrs Sybil Baker)*

Westbury on Severn [Grange Court — off A48; SO7114], *Junction*: Filled with railway memorabilia — the inn-sign comes from the now-closed station, no longer a junction; Theakstons as a guest beer and tasty, substantial food with some interesting dishes; piped music *(John and Joan Wyatt)*; [Popes Hill], *White House*: Good pub with perfect views, not open weekday lunchtimes; children allowed in restaurant *(Sybil Baker)*

Westonbirt [ST8589], *Hare & Hounds*: Rather smart family-run country hotel next to Westonbirt arboretum; really good pubby atmosphere in altogether more regular bar, good interesting food, well kept Wadworths Devizes and 6X and Websters Yorkshire; bedrooms good *(Gordon Theaker, Ewan McCall, Roger Huggins, Tom McLean)*

☆ **Whitminster** [A38 1 1/2 miles N of M5 junction 13; SO7708], *Old Forge*: Pleasant and friendly old beamed pub with small restaurant; good choice of beers and wines, very good home-made bar food with fresh veg *(M C and D H Watkinson, Joan Olivier, Richard and Ann Jenkins)*

☆ **Winchcombe** [High St; SP0228], *Corner Cupboard*: Attractive Cotswold pub with pleasant atmosphere if limited seating in two simply furnished bars; five real ales, particularly good wines, simple bar food, altogether more adventurous and rewarding if not cheap suppers relying wholly on fresh local produce in the small restaurant *(David Gethyn-Jones, Mrs Joan Harris, David and Flo Wallington, Mr and Mrs J H Adam)*

Woodmancote [Stockwell Lane; SO9727], *Apple Tree*: Very good value food from extensive menu, plenty of places to sit, pleasant service *(Miss P de Earthe Bond)*

Hampshire

Pub-users here are generally paying at least 10p a pint more than the national average. The two cheapest main-entry pubs we found, the Olde Whyte Harte in Hamble and the Wykeham Arms in Winchester, are both tied to relatively small breweries operating in this area (Gales and Eldridge Pope); as we've found elsewhere, drinks prices in pubs tied to local and regional breweries do tend to undercut those tied to the nationals, and quite often work out lower than prices in free houses, too. The Royal Oak at Langstone (tied to Whitbreads) had lower drinks prices than most nationally-tied pubs here. Food prices also tend to be higher than average here. But we did find several pubs breaking our bargain targets of decent snacks for under £1 or main dishes for under £3 – the Coach & Horses at Rotherwick and Red Lion in Southampton (both); the White Horse near Petersfield (cheap sandwiches) and the Olde Whyte Harte in Hamble again (bargain main dishes). As we've found repeatedly elsewhere, paying less certainly doesn't mean getting lower quality. Among these pubs we've mentioned for cheapness, the White Horse stands out as one of England's best examples of an unspoilt country pub; the Wykeham Arms, also a particular favourite with readers, is the best we've found in the county for wines, and has particularly good food; the Royal Oak has an exceptionally attractive waterside position; the Olde Whyte Harte, delightfully old-fashioned and in well-heeled yachting territory, is just the sort of place you'd expect to charge extra instead of less; and both the Coach & Horses (with good value food) and Red Lion are rewarding places, of considerable interest. A good many changes in the area this year include bedrooms becoming available at that downland favourite, Milbury's at Beauworth, our discovery of the splendidly unspoilt Sun tucked away in Bentworth (good value food), a wider choice of food under new Spanish licensees at the interesting Fox & Hounds at Crawley, a popular new regime for the White Horse at Droxford (bringing it into the main entries), the return of the unusual Cart & Horses in Kings Worthy to the main entries, a £250,000 rebuilding at the beautifully placed High Corner near Linwood after a bad fire late last year, a new landlord at the Bush in its charming Itchen valley position at Ovington (good early reports), friendly new Scots licensees at the stylish Luzborough House near Romsey, the addition of a second pub in Steep to the main entries (the Cricketers – really well run, good value food, and a comfortable place to stay), the transformation of the former restaurant at the attractive little Boot near Vernham Dean into a family dining room, a particularly promising new team taking over the Chequers at Well – and yet another change of licensees at the Eclipse in Winchester. Pubs that haven't overtly changed but seem on specially good form at the moment include the lively Hobler at Battramsley (good big helpings of food), the Red Lion at Boldre (good food, nice atmosphere), the New Forest Inn at Emery Down (particularly warm welcome, close attention to detail, good food, a nice place to stay), and the simple Travellers Rest at Newtown (strong on fresh ingredients). Among the Lucky Dip entries at the end of the chapter, pubs currently showing particular promise include the Master Builders House at Bucklers Hard, Flower Pots at Cheriton, Fox & Hounds at Bursledon (the Jolly Sailor there is worth a visit, too), Hampshire Bowman at Dundridge, Rose & Crown at Farringdon, Foresters at Frogham, Bugle at Twyford and Thomas Lord at West Meon. Though the Three Lions at Stuckton is now too restaurantish to be included among the main entries, it's well worth knowing for good food.*

ALRESFORD   SU5832 Map 2

Horse & Groom

Broad St; town signposted from new A31 bypass

An open-plan yet atmospherically secluded place, this has several rambling nooks and crannies to suit different moods – the tables in the three bow windows on the right, looking out over the broad street, are an enjoyable place to sit. Elsewhere there's neat settles and Windsor chairs, black beams and timbered walls partly stripped to brickwork, old local photographs and shelves of earthenware jugs and bottles. Well kept Flowers Original, Fremlins, Marstons Pedigree and Whitbreads Strong Country on handpump; coal-effect gas fire. Bar food includes sandwiches (from £1.60; prawn £2.30), soup (£1.50), good ploughman's (from £2.50), sausages (£3.25), salads (from £4.25), tasty home-made steak and kidney pie (£3.95), gammon (£5.75) and steaks (from £7.25); they warn of some delays at busy periods. *(Recommended by Canon Kenneth Wills, BKA, Bernard Phillips; more reports please)*

Whitbreads   Licensees Robin and Kate Howard   Real ale   Meals and snacks (12–2, 7–10)   Open 11–2.30(3 Sat), 6–11

BATTRAMSLEY   SZ3099 Map 2

Hobler

A337 a couple of miles S of Brockenhurst; OS Sheet 196 map reference 307990

Bar food, praised for generosity at attractive prices, includes filled baked potatoes (from £2.50), ploughman's (from around £2), salads (from £3.50), devilled liver (£3.95), steak and kidney pie (£4.95), seafood such as red snapper (£6.95) or fresh lobster, half a shoulder of lamb (£6.95), steaks (from £7.95) and lots of daily specials; the format of the menu itself changes every few weeks, and may be punctuated with broad-minded jokes. It is very popular, so get there early for a table in the main building (many are booked in the evening). The distinctively lively black-beamed bar, divided by the massive stub of an ancient wall, is furnished with lots of tables with red leatherette bucket seats, pews, little dining chairs and a comfortable bow-window seat, and there are guns, china, New-Forest saws, the odd big engraving, and several customer photographs on the walls, some of which are stripped back to timbered brick. The cosy area on the left is black-panelled and full of books. Well kept Flowers Original, Wadworths 6X and a high-gravity guest such as Bunces Old Smokey on handpump, and a good range of malt whiskies and wines (including some expensive bargains by the bottle); friendly golden labrador. There's more seating out in a comfortable alpine-style log cabin with a hefty woodburning stove, and in summer a spacious forest-edge lawn has a summer bar and marquee, a huge timber climbing fort for the good play area, and a good few picnic-table sets, beside a paddock with ponies, donkeys and hens. *(Recommended by Andrew Gale, Paul Brown, John and Chris Simpson, Dick Brown, John and Christine Simpson, Michael and Rachael Brookes, Mr and Mrs D A P Grattan, Barbara Hatfield)*

Whitbreads   Licensee Pip Steven   Real ale   Meals and snacks (11–2, 6–11)   Jazz Tues   Open 10.30–2.30, 6–11

BEAULIEU   SU3802   Map 2

Montagu Arms ⊘ ⇦

Before the climate cooled down in the 13th century there were a good few
vineyards in south Hampshire; there's a long tradition that a nearby ruined
building served as a wine press for a vineyard more or less on this spot – though
apart from a short-lived experiment in the 18th century it's only in the last 30 years
that a vineyard has again become a feature of Beaulieu. It's appropriate, therefore,
that the semi-circular bar counter here is shaped like part of a wine press, and that
the wine list is unusually interesting. Divided into quiet separate areas by low
curtain-topped partitions and sweeping arches, the bar has stylishly comfortable
furnishings, an understated colour-scheme of cool greens, and a big Cecil Aldin
hunting print as well as attractive little local landscapes. Bar food includes soup
(£1.50), filled baked potatoes (from £2.50), ploughman's (£3.50), a couple of daily
specials (including a vegetarian one) such as beef goulash or chilli con carne
(around £4.50), a good selection of salads (£4.95), seafood platter (£4.95) and
steak (£8.95); quick, friendly service; the dining area is no-smoking. Well kept if
not cheap Flowers, Marstons Pedigree and Wadworths 6X on handpump, decent
coffee; unobtrusive piped pop music (and loudspeaker food announcements). The
inn, very solidly built in the early 1920s and decorously comfortable and well run,
is off to one side, with a pretty lake just beyond it. Picnic-table sets in the front
courtyard look down to the Palace gates. (*Recommended by S Watkins, M E Hughes,
Mrs A Turner, Mrs E M Thompson, E G Parish*)

*Free house   Licensee N Walford   Real ale   Meals and snacks   Restaurant   Children
in eating area, lunchtime   Open 11–3, 6–11; 11–11 Sat   Bedrooms tel Beaulieu (0590)
612324; £60B/£75B*

BEAUWORTH   SU5726   Map 2

Milbury's

Turn off A272 Winchester/Petersfield at Beauworth 3/4, Bishops Waltham 6 signpost,
then continue straight on past village

One of the more interesting features of this carefully restored, cheerful pub is the
well in a side area overlooked by a little timber gallery (and safely grille-covered);
probably dug 600 years ago, it is cut nearly 300 feet into the chalk and carefully
spot-lit so that in its narrow depths you see the twinkle of water reflections. The
massive treadwheel beside it used to be worked by a donkey; in the war, when the
landlord had to give up the animal, he found it took him 678 paces to wind up the
original 18-gallon water cask. There are also broad flagstones, sturdy beams,
stripped masonry and massive open fireplaces (with good winter log fires);
furnishings inside and out in the garden are in character with the pub's age. Well
kept Courage Best and Directors, Gales HSB and John Smiths on handpump; some
malt whiskies and a range of over 100 wines. Bar food, largely home-made using
local ingredients, includes home-made soup (£1.10), sandwiches (from £1.50), a
choice of ploughman's (£2.60), salads (from £3.25), prawn and spinach pancake
(£3.65), steak and mushroom pie (£3.80), gammon (£4.60), and steak (from
£5.65), with children's dishes (£2), a good choice of home-made puddings (from
£1.10 and Sunday roasts. Sunday brunch (£4.50, served 9.30–11.15) comes with
Sunday papers; weekend summer barbecues; efficient, cheerful service. They're
planning a skittle alley for this year. The pub used to be called the Fox & Hounds
– Milbury's was originally its nickname, from a Bronze Age cemetery surrounding
it – the Millbarrow, briefly famous back in 1833 when a Norman hoard of 6,000
silver coins was found here. (*Recommended by E U Broadbent, Michael Bechley, W J
Wonham, Jerry and Alison Oakes, Lynn Sharpless, Bob Eardley, Roger Mallard, Donald
Godden, John and Chris Simpson, Patrick and Mary McDermott, Prof A N Black, Bev and
Doug Warrick, Jacquie and Jon Payne, HNJ, PEJ, Gordon and Daphne, Stephen Goodchild,
Margaret Dyke, Bernard Phillips, Tom McLean, Ewan McCall, Roger Huggins, W A
Gardiner, John and Margaret Estdale*)

Free house   Licensees Jan and Len Larden   Real ale   Meals and snacks (till 10.30 Fri and Sat evening)   Restaurant   Children in eating area and restaurant   Open 11–3, 6–11   Bedrooms tel Bramdean (096 279) 248; £27.50B/£37.50

BENTLEY   SU7844   Map 2
Bull

A31 Farnham–Alton, W of village and accessible from both directions at W end of dual carriageway Farnham bypass

Well placed for Alice Holt Forest, this little tiled white pub has two low-beamed rooms, traditionally furnished with tapestried wall seats and stools; besides country and old master prints, there are several comical prewar Bonzo prints – particularly in the left-hand room, which has a dimly lit back alcove with a tapestried pew built around a nice mahogany table, and a log-effect gas fire in a big old fireplace. Bar food ranges from sandwiches (from £1.25), home-made soup (£1.40) and ploughman's (from £2.50), through basket meals (from £2.25), salads (from £3.45), lasagne (£3.75) and home-made steak and kidney pie (£3.95), to steaks (from £8.75) and puddings (from £1.75). Courage Best and Directors on handpump; darts, shove-ha'penny, fruit machine, piped music. There are tables on the side terrace, by a fairy-lit Wendy house on stilts. It's under the same management as one of our Lucky Dip entries, the Hen & Chicken down the road at Froyle. *(Recommended by John and Heather Dwane, S J Rice, WHBM, Tim and Ann Newell, Dr John Innes)*

Courage   Licensees Peter and Mary Holmes   Real ale   Meals and snacks (till 10, Sun–Thurs evening, 10.30 Fri and Sat)   Restaurant tel Bentley (0420) 22156; not Sun evening   Children in eating area and restaurant   Open 11–2.30, 6–11

BENTWORTH   SU6640   Map 2
Sun

Sun Hill; from the A339 coming from Alton the first turning takes you there direct; or in village follow Shalden 2 1/4, Alton 4 1/4 signpost

Delightfully unspoilt, this tucked-away early 17th-century pub has just two little communicating rooms – brick-tiled floor and lacy tablecloths on the right (but not at all twee), bare boards and scrubbed deal tables on the left. Both low-beamed rooms have fat woodburning stoves in big fireplaces, seats mix high-backed antique settles with pews and schoolroom chairs, and there are olde-worlde prints, corn dollies and blacksmith's tools (the smith always asks for the coldest drink when he's in). There's a lively local atmosphere, and service is quick and friendly. Bar food in generous helpings is good and fresh, including sandwiches (from £1.30, steak £3.45), ploughman's (from £2.25), omelettes (£2.75), filled baked potatoes (£3.25), plaice, ham and egg (lots of juicy ham), cottage pie, lasagne and vegetarian dishes (£3.95), trout (£5.95) and 8oz sirloin steak (£6.95); well kept Bass, Bunces, Gales HSB, Marstons Pedigree and a guest beer such as King & Barnes Broadwood on handpump, country wines; shove-ha'penny, table skittles, cribbage and dominoes. Zulu the black collie cross will be a friend for life if you play chase the matchstick; the jack russell is called Datchet. There are a couple of picnic-table sets under cocktail parasols by the quiet lane. *(Recommended by Gordon and Daphne, Richard Houghton)*

Free house   Licensee Jeremy McKay   Real ale   Meals and snacks (12–2, 6–9.30)   Open 11–3, 6–11; closed 25 Dec

BOLDRE   SZ3298   Map 2
Red Lion ★ ☯

Village signposted from A337 N of Lymington

The bar area in this thoroughly enticing and atmospheric pub consists of a row of four, black-beamed rooms. The carpeted bar on the left has several pictures – small local landscapes or hunting prints – heavy-horse harness, lots of ferocious gin traps – two are man-traps – and a good winter log fire. Next is a small flagstoned sitting room, with more gin traps decorating its big fireplace, and more hunting pictures. The third room has quite a few tables on its carpet, hunting prints, and chamber pots hanging from its beams. The end room, with a second serving bar, has pews, wheelback chairs and tapestried stools, and a pretty collection of old bottles and glasses in the window by the counter. Consistently popular bar food includes home-made soup (£1.50), well made sandwiches (from £1.60), ploughman's or avocado and prawns (£2.50), smoked salmon (£3.50), and salads (from £4.20); for once even the basket meals are something special, and include marinated pork chops (£4.50), and half a duck with fresh orange soaked in wine (£4.90); notably friendly and efficient service; it's advisable to get there early if you want a table – it really does fill up, especially at weekends. Well kept Eldridge Pope Dorchester and Royal Oak on handpump. The pub is conveniently placed on the fringes of the New Forest and near the Lymington River; in summer the area in front of it is a riot of colourful flowerbeds. Mr Fenge, who used to run the Red Lion with the Bicknells, retired last year. *(Recommended by John and Christine Simpson, Mr and Mrs A Dean, Jane Buekett, John Mason, Paul Brown, Mrs J A Gardener, M C Howells, B A Cox, Dick Brown, M E Hughes, Mr and Mrs J A Oxley, Ken and Barbara Turner, H K Dyson, P L Jackson, Bernard Phillips, Philip and Sheila Hanley, Mrs E M Brandwood, R M Sparkes, Jenny and Michael Back)*

Eldridge Pope   Licensees John and Penny Bicknell   Real ale   Meals and snacks (11–2.15, 6–10.15)   Restaurant tel Lymington (0590) 673177   Open 10.30–3, 6–11

BRAMDEAN   SU6128   Map 2

Fox

A272 Winchester–Petersfield

There's quite an emphasis on food in this early 17th-century (but much modernised) white weather-boarded pub – many of the tables may be laid out for diners; the range includes sandwiches (from £1.95), good soup (£1.95 or £2.25), ploughman's (£2.75), locally smoked trout (£3.95), king prawns with mayonnaise (£4.25), mussels and prawns in sherry and garlic butter (£4.95), cauliflower cheese or battered cod (£5.25), and beef Stroganoff (£6.95); original touches, in the ingredients and presentation, lift it out of the ordin ry; attentive, friendly service. The well kept black-beamed open-plan bar has tall stools with proper backrests around its L-shaped counter, and comfortably cushioned wall pews and wheelback chairs; the fox motif shows in a big painting over the fireplace, and on much of the decorative china. Well kept Marstons Burton and Pedigree on handpump, decent coffee, friendly service; sensibly placed darts in the games room, fruit machine, unobtrusive piped music. At the back there's a walled-in patio area, and a spacious lawn spreading among the fruit trees, with a really good play area – trampoline as well as swings and a see-saw; children like the hens in the neat run alongside. *(Recommended by Mr and Mrs Foreman, Nigel Gibbs, John H Walker, Alan Skull, R Elliott, Colin Laffan, Prof A N Black)*

Marstons   Licensee Mrs Jane Inder   Real ale   Meals and snacks   Open 10.30–2.30(3 Sat), 6–11; closed 25 Dec

CHALTON   SU7315   Map 2

Red Lion

Village signposted E of A3 Petersfield–Horndean

In a lovely position beneath the village church and overlooking the South Downs, this ancient (licensed in 1503 but dating back partly to 1150) thatched pub has a heavy-beamed and panelled bar furnished with high-backed traditional settles and elm tables, and an ancient inglenook fireplace, with a frieze of burnished threepenny bits set into its mantlebeam. A more modern extension, completed by the new licensees, leads off. Gales BBB and HSB on handpump, and a variety of country wines; reasonably priced bar food such as toasted sandwiches or filled rolls, Stilton ploughman's and steak and mushroom pie (there's no really separate eating area); tables outside. It's popular with walkers and riders, and fairly close to the extensive Queen Elizabeth Country Park, which includes a working reconstruction of an Iron Age farming settlement. (*Recommended by N J Clark, Jacqueline Davis, John and Chris Simpson, Barry and Anne, A J Blackler, G B Longden, Diana Cussons, R Houghton, Charles Turner; more reports on the new regime please*)

Gales   Licensee Mr Worth   Real ale   Meals and snacks   Open 10.30–2.30, 6–11

CRAWLEY SU4234 Map 2

Fox & Hounds

Village signposted from A272 Winchester–Stockbridge and B3420 Winchester–Andover

From the outside this is a striking sight, with each timbered upper storey successively jutting further out, lots of pegged structural timbers in the neat brickwork (especially around the latticed windows), and elaborately carved steep gable-ends. The meticulous workmanship continues inside, with oak parquet, latticed windows, and an elegant black timber arch in the small lounge, and neatly panelled black wall benches around the polished copper tables of the beamed main bar. There are fires in both rooms – real logs in the lounge, log-effect gas in the other. The Spanish licensees who took over with their son and daughter-in-law in the summer of 1989 have expanded the bar and restaurant menus considerably, and with enough notice they'll cook pretty much anything you want; the range includes home-made soup, hot stilton, celery and apple bake or smokies (£2.85), very good ham and asparagus pancake and chicken provençale, baked crab au gratin (£3.60), mixed bean casserole (£4.95), home-made steak and kidney pie, courgettes stuffed with salmon and prawns or seafood pancake (£5.75), and whole lemon sole (£7.25). Well kept Gales BBB and Wadworths 6X on handpump. The pub's architectural qualities are maintained in the rest of the village, which also has a pretty duckpond. (*Recommended by Peter Hall, Dr and Mrs A K Clarke, Michael Thomson, G Shannon, Joan and John Calvert, W A Gardiner, R A Bellingham; more reports please*)

Free house   Licensees Doreen and Luis Sanz-Diez   Real ale   Meals and snacks
Restaurant (closed Sun evening)   Children in restaurant   Open 11.30–2.30, 6–11
Bedrooms tel Sparsholt (0962) 72285; l£50B

DROXFORD SU6018 Map 2

White Horse

4 miles along A32 from Wickham

After a long absence from these pages, and more than one change of management, this fine old pub has very recently come firmly back into the reckoning. Mr Higgins is proving very welcoming, and the rambling bar has been attractively and comfortably refurnished, while keeping the low beams, bow windows, alcoves and log fires. The lounge bar, which dates back to the 16th century, is a series of small, intimate rooms; the public bar is larger and more straightforward, with cribbage, dominoes, pool, fruit machine, space game and piped music. The interesting bar menu includes sandwiches (from £1.30), soup (£1.75), ploughman's (from £2.35), salads (from £3.55), some good vegetarian dishes or cod (£4.05), gammon (£4.95), brace of smoked quail (£5.50), steak (£8.75) and puddings (from £1.10). Well kept Courage Directors, Gales HSB, Marstons Pedigree, Morlands Old Masters, Shepherd Neame Old and Wadworths 6X on handpump; they're about 5p cheaper in the public bar. The back courtyard, sheltered by the building's back wings, is a good place to linger, and there's a terrace. This old coaching inn is handy for Portsmouth or even Southampton. (*Recommended by Mel and Phil Lloyd, A D Bulmer, Mrs Y M Healey, HEG*)

Free house   Licensee Sidney Higgins   Real ale   Meals and snacks (11–2, 7–9.45)
Children in family room and restaurant   Occasional Morris dancers   Open 11–2.30,
6–11; public bar 11–11 Sat   Bedrooms tel Droxford (0489) 877490; l£40B(£50B)

DUMMER   SU5846   Map 2

Queen

Half a mile from M3, junction 7; take Dummer slip road

Quickly served, good value food includes some magnificent sandwiches (from £1.75, going up to whopper club ones £3.95), home-made soup (£1.75), pâté (£2.50), salads (from £4.95), and generous helpings of hot dishes such as chilli con carne or lasagne (£5.95), grilled plaice (£6.95) and char-grilled steaks (from £9.95); cheerful service. Though the bar is open-plan, it has a pleasantly alcovey feel, with a liberal use of timbered brick and plaster partition walls, as well as beams and joists and an open fire. There are built-in padded seats, cushioned spindleback chairs and stools around the tables on the dark blue patterned carpet, and it's decorated with pictures of queens, old photographs, small steeplechase prints and advertisements. Well kept Courage Best and Directors, John Smiths and Wadworths 6X on handpump; bar billiards and fruit machine in one corner, well reproduced pop music. There are picnic-table sets under cocktail parasols on the terrace and in a neat little sheltered back garden. (Recommended by Jutta Whitley, Richard Gibbs, KC, WHBM)

Courage   Licensee John Holland   Real ale   Meals and snacks (12–2, 6.30–10) Restaurant area tel Dummer (025 675) 367   Children in restaurant area   Open 11–3, 5.30–11; closed 25 Dec and 1 Jan

EMERY DOWN   SU2808   Map 2

New Forest Inn ★ ⊘ ⇌

Village signposted off A35 just W of Lyndhurst

A strong favourite with readers, who pick out the warmth of the welcome and the attention to detail with the food as particular points for praise. The big, softly lit open-plan bar is often busy, but a friendly atmosphere prevails; it's furnished with good solid tables, russet plush settles and wall seats, and smaller chairs, and decorated with antlers, fox masks, a big china owl and smaller china forest animals, country prints and old photographs of the area; a couple of log fires. Flowers Original, Wadworths 6X and Whitbreads Strong Country on handpump; good coffee. The good choice of food includes soup (£1.75), various ploughman's with warm cottage loaves (from £2.50), particularly good mushrooms in a garlic and tomato sauce (£3.25), Cumberland sausage (£3.25), chicken curry with poppadoms or a daily pasta dish (£4.75), avocado and bacon or fresh fruit and cottage cheese salad (£4.75), gammon (£5.75), pork fillet in a green peppercorn sauce (£6.75) and steaks (from £7.75); puddings (£1.95); vegetables are properly cooked, and the sauces are interesting. Daily specials – so popular that they're often gone by 1 o'clock – run to such dishes as giant prawns wrapped in bacon with cheese and garlic, salmon in champagne sauce or beef in stilton and celery. The sloping back lawn is a hive of animal activity, with white rabbits, a pony looking over the post-and-rails fence, maybe lambs or kids in the side stables, perhaps the Old English sheepdog's latest litter. (Recommended by Tom Espley, GB, CH, Mr Cowell, Mike and Jill Dixon, Jacquie and Jon Payne, Mrs J A Gardner, Peter Hall, M E Hughes, Dr John Innes, Dick Brown, M and C Hardwick, Roy McIsaac, David Goldstone, Kenneth Sharp, Sybil Baker, John Derbyshire, Roger Knight, Peter Adcock, Mr and Mrs D A P Grattan, Heather Sharland, Ian Phillips, Nigel Pritchard, Norman Foot)

Whitbreads   Licensees Sue and Nick Emberley   Real ale   Meals and snacks (11.30–2.30, 6–9.30; 12–1.30, 7–9 Sun)   Children welcome   Bedrooms tel Lyndhurst (0703) 282329; £20B/£40B   Open 11–2.30, 6–11 (10.30 winter)

nr FAWLEY   SU4503   Map 2

Jolly Sailor

Ashlett Creek; from A326 turn left into School Road, signposted Fawley ½; at Falcon pub crossroads take Calshot road, then fork left almost at once.

The comfortably modernised bar here has soft banquettes, red velvet curtains and a central flame-effect fire, with lots of photographs of Southampton liners on the walls. Bar food under the new licensees includes soup (£1.15), sandwiches (from £1.50), ploughman's (£2.95), salads (from £3.35), lasagne (£3.55), steak and kidney pie (£3.75), gammon and egg (£4.45), and steak (£6.75). Flowers Original and Wadworths 6X on handpump; darts, fruit machine, trivia, piped music. The restaurant overlooks the busy shipping channel, where curlews and sandpipers strut at low water, and beyond to the distant bustle of Southampton Water; picnic-table sets on the side lawn have a similar view.

(Recommended by Richard Marjoram, W C M Jones, Mike and Jill Dixon, John and Joan Calvert, Bernard Phillips, Tony Triggle; more reports on the new regime please)

Whitbreads   Licensee Ian R Morrison   Real ale   Meals and snacks (not Sun evening)   Restaurant tel Fawley (0703) 891305 (not Sun)   Children in eating area Open 11–11

HAMBLE   SU4806   Map 2
Olde Whyte Harte

3 miles from M27 junction 8; on B3397 (High Street)

This genuinely ancient place (the three-foot-thick wall at the back may even go back to the 12th century) has settles and Windsor chairs on the flagstones of the main white-panelled low-ceilinged bar, a fine inglenook fireplace with the Charles I coat-of-arms on its iron fireback, Tudor ship's timbers serving as beams (you can still see some of their original fastenings), and old maps and charts, rope fancywork, mugs and copper pans. Astonishingly good value bar food includes sandwiches and toasties, home-made shepherd's pie (£2), home-made steak and kidney pie (£3.50), and lots of specials (from £2). Gales BBB, HSB and XXXL Mild on handpump, and lots of country wines; dominoes, cribbage, fruit machine, juke box. Besides barrel seats on the small front terrace, there is a back terrace by the sheltered lawn and garden. Popular with yachtsmen at the weekends.
(Recommended by Dr J D Bassett, Mr Cowell, Ian Phillips; more reports please)

Gales   Licensee D Kerans   Real ale   Meals and snacks   Children in eating area Open 11–2.30, 6–11

IBSLEY   SU1509   Map 2
Old Beams

A338 Ringwood–Salisbury

The oak-beamed main room here is a spacious affair, divided by wooden panelling and a canopied log-effect gas fire; the U-shaped bar counter serves Eldridge Pope Royal Oak, Gibbs Mew Bishops Tipple, Ringwood Best and Wadworths 6X on handpump, a decent choice of wines by the glass and some foreign bottled beers; there are lots of varnished wooden tables and country-kitchen chairs under the good oak beams; the front half of the pub is no-smoking. The emphasis is fairly strongly on food – well prepared and popular dishes, including soup (90p), sandwiches (from £1.55), ploughman's (from £2), and lots of hot dishes such as chilli con carne, scampi, or lasagne (£3.55), rabbit casserole (£3.95), veal casserole or lamb chops (£4.70), pork chop in cider (£4.85), venison in red wine (£5.55) and braised steak (£5.85). The garden behind has picnic-table sets among its trees. The same family also owns the Swans Nest at Exminster (Devon) and Bakers Arms near Lytchett Minster (Dorset), both featured in the *Guide*. *(Recommended by Mrs A Turner, Ian Phillips, Mr and Mrs G Turner, J M Norton, E M Brandwood; more reports please)*

Free house   Licensees R Major and C Newell   Real ale   Meals and snacks (12–2, 7–10)   Restaurant tel Ringwood (0425) 473387   Children welcome   Open 11–2.30, 6–11

KINGS WORTHY   SU4933   Map 2

Cart & Horses

A3090 E of Winchester, just off A33

This picturesque pub, attractively decorated with window boxes, has a public bar with cushioned settles and some milk-churn seats in its various rambling alcoves, old enamel advertising placards on the walls, and darts and bar billiards – there's also a separate skittle alley. The spacious, comfortable lounge is largely given over to eating – the range includes soup, filled baked potatoes (from £2.75), a fry-up (£3.50), battered cod or lasagne (£3.75), pasta (£3.95), pies such as steak and kidney or cod and prawn (£4.95), local trout (£4.95), stir-fry beef or pork (£5.25), gammon (£5.95) and steaks (from £5.95); children's dishes (£1.50). Well kept Marstons Burton, Pedigree and Owd Rodger on handpump, and Bulmer's cider; friendly, efficient service. There are heavy wooden tables in front of the pub, with more in the sheltered garden behind, which has a play area with several trampolines, a see-saw and a Wendy house; summer barbecues. (Recommended by Keith Houlgate, David Shillitoe, Mr and Mrs Foreman, Ian Phillips)

Marstons   Licensee David Lee Smith   Real ale   Meals and snacks   Restaurant tel Winchester (0962) 882360   Children in family and dining rooms   Open 11–3, 5.30–11

LANGSTONE   SU7105   Map 2

Royal Oak

High Street; last turn left off A3023 (confusingly called A324 on some signs) before Hayling Island bridge

This lovely pub is charmingly placed on the edge of a landlocked natural harbour, with fine views from waterside benches and seats in the bow windows. The flagstoned bar is simply furnished, with Windsor chairs around old wooden tables on the wooden parquet and ancient flagstones, and two open fires in winter. Bar food includes soup, ploughman's (£2.95), home-made hot dishes such as lasagne (£3.55), seafood mornay (£3.85), chicken and ham pie (£3.95), goulash (£4.50), a few vegetarian dishes, rib of beef (£4.75), and rump steak (£6.95). Well kept Flowers Original, Gales HSB, Marstons Pedigree and Whitbreads Strong Country on handpump, as well as Bulmer's cider; smartly dressed staff. At high water swans come right up to the pub, and at low tide the saltings between here and Hayling Island fill with wading birds; more animal diversions are provided at the back of the pub, where the pets' corner has goats and rabbits. (Recommended by Phil and Sally Gorton, D J Cooke, Jacqueline Davis, J H Walker; more reports please)

Whitbreads   Licensee Hilary Wallace   Real ale   Meals and snacks   Restaurant tel Portsmouth (0705) 483125   Children in eating area   Parking at all close may be very difficult   Open 11–11

nr LINWOOD   SU1910   Map 2

High Corner

Linwood signposted via Moyles Court from A338 (and also from A31); follow road straight up on to heath and eventually pub signposted left down a gravelled track; OS Sheet 195 ref 196107

At the end of 1989 fire gutted the oldest, thatched part of this New Forest inn, destroying the lower beamed bar, bedrooms, restaurant and main kitchens; a £250,000 restoration has happily returned everything as much as possible to its original, atmospheric state. A series of rooms rambles beyond the main serving bar, and there's a family room, glazed verandah lounge and a separate stable bar. Bar food includes home-made soup (£1.40), sandwiches (from £1.65), ploughman's (from £2.50), chicken or vegetable curry (£3.75), plaice or scampi (£3.95), home-made steak, kidney and mushroom pie or trout (£4.75), a choice of steaks (from £7.50), and children's dishes (from £1.75). Well kept Flowers Original, Wadworths 6X and Whitbreads Best on handpump; darts, shove-ha'penny, dominoes, cribbage, fruit and trivia machine, space game, unobtrusive piped music, squash court. Though it feels remote out of season, it can get very busy – even on the big neatly kept woodside lawn, which with well spaced picnic-table sets and a sizeable children's play area is a great draw in summer, when they have cook-yourself barbecues (or you can pay a little extra and they'll do the cooking). Close to *Good Walks Guide* Walk 40. *(Recommended by Steve Dark, Mr and Mrs A P Reeves, Jacquie and Jon Payne, M Rising, Peter Adcock, Celia and David Watt, H W and A B Tuffill, WHBM)*

Free house   Licensees Lin and Roger Kernan   Real ale   Meals and snacks (12–2, 7–10)   Restaurant (all day Sun)   Children in four eating areas   Open 11–3, 6–11 (11–11 Sat; winter evening opening 7)   Bedrooms tel Ringwood (0425) 473973; £41.50B/£59.50B

LONGPARISH   SU4344   Map 2
Plough

B3048 – off A303 just E of Andover

Though there is a small pubby part, much of the open-plan lounge in this village pub has a restaurant feel. The menu includes sandwiches and a choice of ploughman's (around £2.70), as well as good watercress soup (£1.25), chicken casserole, steak and kidney pie or gammon (all £6.75), tasty smoked trout, a choice of two or three fresh fish dishes (from £7 – the grilled bream is recommended), rump steak (£7.50) and puddings (£1.75). On Sunday there's either a three-course roast lunch (£8.75) or ploughman's and sandwiches; recent reports have warned of service delays and some staff shortages; it's often best to book. Well kept Boddingtons, Flowers Original and Whitbreads Strong Country on handpump. What used to be the spacious garden is now a car park. *(Recommended by John Evans, D I Baddeley, HNJ, PEJ, Mary Springer, S A Robbins, R Elliott; more reports please)*

Whitbreads   Licensee Trevor Colgate   Real ale   Meals (limited on Sun lunchtime – see above) and snacks   Restaurant tel Andover (0264) 72358   Children over 4 in restaurant   Open 11–3, 6–11; closed 25 Dec and 26 Dec evening

MATTINGLEY   SU7358   Map 2
Leather Bottle

3 miles from M3, junction 5; in Hook, turn right-and-left on to B3349 Reading Road (former A32)

The main, beamed front bar in this warmly welcoming place has brocaded built-in wall seats and little curved low-backed wooden chairs, some sabres on the cream wall, red plush bar stools, red velvet curtains, and good inglenook fireplaces – one with a ticking metal clock over it. The cottagey second bar at the back (which used to be the restaurant) is characterful, with country pictures on the walls (some stripped to brick), lantern lighting, lots of black beams, an antique clock, a red carpet on bare floorboards, and sturdy inlaid tables with seats to suit. Well kept Courage Best tapped from the cask and Directors on handpump, decent coffee; fruit machine, maybe unobtrusive piped music. Good value bar food includes sandwiches (from £1, toasted ham and egg – named a Tom Special for one of the regulars – £2.20, steak £3.60), soup (£1.50), lots of ploughman's (£2.50), sweetcorn and mushroom pizza (£3.80), salads (from £4.50), ham and egg (£4.50), 8oz burgers (£4.30), lemon sole (£4.80), tacos (£5.20), char-grilled half-chicken (£5.50), and steaks (from 8oz sirloin £8.40). There's a riot of colour outside this brick-and-tiled pub in summer – tubs and baskets of bright flowers, wisteria, honeysuckle and roses, and a neat, tree-sheltered garden. The licensees now run another pub in Hampshire, the Swan at North in Warnborough. *(Recommended by Jack Lalor, Simon Collett-Jones, KC, Dawn and Phil Garside)*

Courage   Licensees Richard and Pauline Moore   Real ale   Meals and snacks (12–2, 7–10)   Children in eating area   Open 11–3, 6–11

MINLEY   SU8357   Map 2

Crown & Cushion

From A30 take B3013 towards Fleet, then first left turn signposted Minley, Cove, Farnborough

Since its conversion to a Chef & Brewer, this tiled and timbered pub has expanded its efficient food counter, which serves a good range of home-cooked meats and fresh salads (from £2.50–£3.95), ploughman's (£2.75), and at lunchtime a varied choice of hot dishes such as generous cuts from a huge joint, with three vegetables (£3.95, not Sunday). In the evening they add toasted sandwiches (from £2.50, served with chips), basket meals (from £3.15), burgers (from £3.20) and plaice (£3.50). Perhaps the most interesting part to visit is the 'Meade Hall' at the back – a lively pastiche of an ancient feasting place, with two very long communal refectory tables, smaller candlelit tables in intimate side stalls, broad flagstones, a huge log fire, and a veritable armoury of scythes, pitchforks and other rustic ironmongery festooning its rafters and timbers (it also has anachronistic piped music and slot machines). The separate original pub part is comfortable, and has darts, dominoes, cribbage and a fruit machine. Gales HSB, Ruddles County and Websters Yorkshire on handpump, with country wines, mead and a couple of draught ciders. The pub's name commemorates the closest that anyone has come to stealing the Crown Jewels – Colonel Blood from nearby Minley Warren was caught here in 1671 with them in his saddlebags, after a subtle raid on the Tower of London. The yew tree outside – if you look hard enough – is cut in the shape of a cushioned crown; there are picnic-table sets across from it. (*Recommended by Dr R Fuller, John Baker; more reports please*)

Phoenix (Watneys)   Real ale   Meals (not Sun) and snacks   Bar open 5–11 Mon-Fri, 11–11 Sat and usual hours on Sun; Meade Hall 11.30–2.30, 7–11, 11–11 Sat

NEWTOWN   SU6113   Map 2

Travellers Rest ✪

Church Road – E of village, which is signposted off A32 N of Wickham

Bar food in this uncomplicated and traditional pub includes sandwiches, ploughman's and simple hot dishes such as ham and egg (£2.60) or plaice (£3.20); but it's more than complemented by the dish of the day, which in winter is usually game (half a roast pheasant, say, at £4.50, or quail or venison) and in summer tends towards fresh seafood (running up to a whole lobster salad); they do their best to keep up a supply of their own vegetables for whatever's on offer. The two small rooms of the bar have unfussy old furnishings – well cushioned housekeeper's chairs, a winged settle, leatherette armed chairs, and built-in cushioned wall seats; darts, dominoes, fruit machine, piano, and a particularly chatty atmosphere warmly fuelled by locals and friendly licensees (and their two large cats). Well kept Gibbs Mew Wiltshire, Salisbury and Bishops Tipple on handpump. The pretty back garden, floodlit at night, is notably well tended. (*Recommended by Richard Houghton, Mr Cowell, Melvyn Payne, J A Jones; more reports please*)

Gibbs Mew   Licensee Peter Redman   Real ale   Meals and snacks (12–2.15, 7.30–10.15)   Monthly gatherings for piano singalongs, Irish or folk music, and occasional Morris dancers   Open 11–3, 6–11

OVINGTON   SU5531   Map 2

Bush ★

Village signposted from A31 on Winchester side of Alresford

It's the comfortable, unpretentious and secluded atmosphere here which so appeals to readers, and which on first reports is being well maintained by the new licensee. The dimly lit, green-walled and low-ceilinged bar has cushioned high-backed settles, elm tables with pews and kitchen chairs, masses of old pictures in heavy gilt frames, and a roaring fire on one side, with an antique solid fuel stove opposite; it can get really busy. Boddingtons, Flowers, Gales HSB, Wadworths 6X, Whitbreads Strong Country and one or two guests on handpump; a good selection of wines. Bar food includes home-made soup, sandwiches (from £1.25), ploughman's (from £2.30), steak and kidney pie or mussels in garlic butter (£4.95), trout (£5.95) and a seafood platter (£8.75); puddings (from 95p), children's dishes (£1.95) and a roast Sunday lunch (when the choice of other dishes may be more limited); it's worth booking on summer weekends. The tree-sheltered pergola dining terrace outside has white wrought-iron tables by a good-sized fountain pool, and there are quiet walks along the river; handy for the A31 – though the pub itself is peacefully placed in the Itchen valley. *(Recommended by Richard Houghton, R Heaton, Ian Phillips, S J Rice, John Branford, Linda Duncan, Robert and Elizabeth Scott, W A Gardiner, John and Chris Simpson, Gordon and Daphne, HEG; more reports on the new regime please)*

Free house   Licensee Robert Middleton   Real ale   Meals and snacks   Restaurant (not Sun) tel Alresford (0962) 732764   Nearby parking may be difficult   Children in restaurant   Open 11–2.30, 6–11; closed 25 and 26 Dec

nr PETERSFIELD   SU7423   Map 2

White Horse ★ ★ ★

Priors Dean – but don't follow Priors Dean signposts: simplest route is from Petersfield, leaving centre on A272 towards Winchester, take right turn at roundabout after level crossing, towards Steep, and keep on for four miles or so, up on to the downs, passing another pub on your right (and not turning off into Steep there); at last, at crossroads signposted East Tisted/Privett, turn right towards East Tisted, then almost at once turn right on to second gravel track (the first just goes into a field); there's no inn sign; alternatively, from A32 5 miles S of Alton, take road by bus lay-by signposted Steep, then, after 1 3/4 miles, turn off as above – though obviously left this time – at East Tisted/Privett crossroads; OS Sheet 197 coming from Petersfield (Sheet 186 is better the other way), map reference 715290

As ever, we should advise initiates to the ever-growing band of enthusiasts about what *not* to expect of this remote 17th-century pub – namely elegance, conventional comforts or a five-star kind of luxury; its outstanding pubiness is in a sense against all that. Instead you get a *Weltanschauung* that is as unassuming as it is unpolished – so however far you've come (and dedicated loyalists travel considerable distances) you won't be treated with any more deference than the regular locals; as the Pub With No Name (the nickname it gets from its lack of a sign) it doesn't lead anyone to expect more from it than it aims to give. From the outside it doesn't look special, and some of the furnishings testify to their popularity in times gone by. The two charming and highly idiosyncratic parlour rooms, with their old pictures, farm tools, rugs and drop-leaf tables, look as if they've always looked as they do – which is precisely their attraction. If the old cat's not asleep on one of the oak settles, it'll probably be on the fireside rocking-chair. If the stuffed antelope heads were missing or the longcase clock stopped ticking, hundreds of people would feel they'd lost a friend. It simply wouldn't be the same without the dozing dog. Above all there's the atmosphere – unhurried and happy, and largely generated by the dedication of Jack Eddleston – licensee now for 18 years. Then there's the range of beers – a dozen or so good real ales, including their own very strong White Horse No Name, as well as Ballards, Bass, Courage Best, Eldridge Pope Royal Oak, King & Barnes Broadwood, Festive, Mild and Bitter, Ringwood Fortyniner and Ruddles; lots of interesting country wines are tapped from small china kegs; shove-ha'penny, dominoes, cribbage. Bar food includes sandwiches (from 70p, prawn £2.20), home-made soup (recommended – the stock's usually done overnight on the Aga), good baked potatoes, ploughman's (from £2.20), salads (from £3.25), and a selection of home-made hot dishes most days, such as hot-pot (£3.50; as Jack comes from Lancashire, it's genuine), vegetarian lasagne (£3.50), cheesy Cumberland cottage pie or beef and ale pie (£3.85); be warned that the cook has to go home at two, so you won't be able to get something to eat then; but they've usually got local eggs for sale, including organic free range ones, and in season pheasants too. There are of course times (not always predictable, with Sundays – even in winter – often busier than Saturdays) when the place does get packed. The rustic seats outside (which include chunks of tree-trunk) have been joined this year by a terrace (popular with the older locals), and there are caravan facilities in the nearby field, which is regularly used for pony club meetings – or maybe for the odd tiger-moth plane to land in. As this is one of the highest spots in the county it can be quite breezy. *(Recommended by Mrs Lili Lomas, Steve and Carolyn Harvey, Gordon Mott, TBB, Steve Dark, Jutta Whitley, Henry Midwinter, Robert and Elizabeth Scott, Mr and Mrs D M Norton, John and Chris Simpson, Ian Phillips, Canon K C A Wills and M K C Wills, Tom McLean, Ewan McCall, Roger Huggins, Matt Pringle, Chris Raisin, Graham Doyle, Jacqueline Davis, Alan Skull, W A Gardiner, Celia and David Watt, Gordon and Daphne, Tim and Ann Newell, M Rising)*

Free house   Licensee Jack Eddleston   Real ale   Meals (sandwiches only Sun and Bank Holidays) and snacks   Children over 14 allowed   Open 11–2.30 (3 Sat), 6–11

ROCKBOURNE   SU1118   Map 2
Rose & Thistle

Village signposted from B3078 Fordingbridge–Cranborne

The civilised lounge bar in this thatched, 17th-century pub has prettily upholstered stools and small settles around close-set tables, old engravings, sparkling brass and a good log fire; in the public bar there are tables arranged more in the style of booths. Well kept Whitbread Strong Country and Pompey Royal on handpump, piped music. Bar food includes a good selection of seafood, fresh each day – the Dover sole (£10.50), big as well as tasty, is recommended, and there's also lemon sole (£8.50), plump moules marinières in winter, and smoked salmon sandwiches (£2). Other food ranges from home-made soup (£1.20) through taramasalata (£2.40) or steak and kidney pie (£5.50) to Dorset crab and lobster (around £10). There are tables by a thatched dovecot in the neat front garden, and the charming village has the excavated remains of a Roman villa. *(Recommended by B A Cox, WHBM, J M Watkinson, E U Broadbent)*

Whitbreads   Licensee Norman Toombs   Real ale   Meals and snacks   Open 11–3, 6–11; closed 25 Dec evening

nr ROMSEY   SU3521   Map 2
Luzborough House

3 miles from M27 junction 3; A3057 towards Romsey, but turn right at A27

Though a large pub, the variety of smaller rooms gives a feeling of intimacy, while the large high-raftered main bar is bright and attractive with plenty of space to stand around the bar; there are also high-backed stools by ledges around stripped-brick pillars, a sofa and easy chairs. The popular, elegant cream-panelled 18th-century dining room is decorated with attractive landscapes, and has a neat conservatory with white cast-iron tables opening off it. The snug 16th-century country kitchen has low beams, and a huge woodburning stove in its inglenook fireplace. Throughout, careful attention's been paid to the lighting. Well kept Flowers Original, Whitbreads Strong Country and Pompey Royal on handpump. Bar food under the new licensees includes soup (£1.25), sandwiches (from £2.25) ploughman's (from £2.55), plaice (£3.15), steak and kidney pie (£3.45), gammon (£4.45), steak (£8.25), and a substantial mixed grill (£8.95). There are picnic-table sets under cocktail parasols in the spacious walled lawn, as well as a slide and sprung rockers. *(Recommended by T Galligan, Jackie and Jon Payne, E U Broadbent; more reports on the new regime please)*

Whitbreads   Licensees Jim and Joyce Noonan   Real ale   Meals and snacks (12–10)   Restaurant   Children in conservatory and restaurant   Open 11–11

ROTHERWICK SU7156 Map 2
Coach & Horses 🏮

4 miles from M3, junction 5; follow Newnham signpost from exit roundabout, then
Rotherwick signpost, then turn right at Mattingley, Heckfield signpost; village also
signposted from A32 N of Hook

Well cooked, attractively priced and straightforward bar food in this cheerful
village pub includes sandwiches (from 90p, open prawn £2.35), ploughman's
(from £1.95), smoked trout pâté (£1.95), home-made burger (£2.25), a variety of
home-made pizzas (from £2.15), chilli con carne (£2.75), gammon and egg
(£4.45), mixed grill (£6.45) and steaks (from £6.25); on Sundays there's a good
carvery – though it isn't cheap; efficient, attentive service. The two small beamed
front rooms, one carpeted and the other with neat red and black flooring tiles,
have interesting furniture such as oak chairs and a giant rattan one, and a fine
assortment of attractive pictures; there's a stripped brick open fireplace in each
room; popular with local business people. The wide choice of well kept real ales on
handpump, dispensed at the servery in the parquet-floored inner area, may include
Arkells Kingsdown, Badger Best, Eldridge Pope Dorset and Royal Oak, Fullers
London Pride, Marstons Pedigree, Palmers BB, Ringwood Old Thumper,
Theakstons Old Peculier, a guest beer and one or two others. The partly
creeper-covered, 16th-century building is surrounded by tubs and baskets of
flowers in summer, and there are rustic seats and picnic-table sets under cocktail
parasols. *(Recommended by G and M Stewart, Susan Grossman, Patrick Freeman, WHBM,
TBB, KC, R Houghton, Patrick and Mary McDermott, Gordon Theaker, Gordon and
Daphne, M Rising, Ian Phillips, Dr and Mrs Crichton, John and Christine Simpson)*

*Free house Licensee Mrs Terry Williams Real ale Meals and snacks (12–2, 7–10;
carvery only, Sun lunchtime) Restaurant tel Rotherwick (0256) 762542 Children in
eating area Open 11–2.30, 5.30–11*

SETLEY SU3000 Map 2
Filly

A337 Brockenhurst–Lymington

Neatly well run, this New Forest pub's a good deal bigger inside than you'd
imagine from the road. Dark red walls, dark ochre ceilings, dim lighting and
capacious fireplaces make for a warm feel. The beams are liberally decorated with
horsebrasses, and there are little wooden kegs, cork and glass net-floats, tackle
blocks and antlers; one area has long cushioned antique settles and built-in pews,
the other has spindle-back chairs around oak tables with a couple of cosy alcoves.
Popular bar food includes sandwiches (from £1.25, toasted from £1.50), filled
baked potatoes (from £1.75), ploughman's (from £2.95), home-made lasagne or
chilli con carne (£3.25), salads (from £3.95), steak and kidney pie, seafood platter
or scampi (£4.25), a decent choice of vegetarian dishes, and steaks (from £6.95);
food orders are announced over a loud-speaker system. The interesting range of
beers – Bass, Palmers IPA, Ringwood Old Thumper and Wadworths 6X – is well
kept on handpump; the Alsatian's called Tess. There are a few picnic-table sets on
neat grass at the back. *(Recommended by Mr and Mrs J A Oxley, Dick Brown, Trevor
Rule, Paul and Margaret Baker, Jacquie and Jon Payne)*

*Free house Licensees Tony and Lynn Bargrove Real ale Meals and snacks (till 10
evening) Children in eating area Open 11–2.30, 6–11; closed 25 and 26 Dec*

SOBERTON SU6116 Map 2
White Lion

Village signposted off A32 S of Droxford

Bar food in this pleasant but lively, tiled and white-painted pub is carefully cooked
and attractively presented; it ranges from home-made soup (£1.25), filled French
bread (from £1.45), and ploughman's (from £2.30), through filled baked potatoes

(from £2.40), lots of pasta dishes (from £3.45), omelettes (from £3.35), steak and kidney pie (£4.30), poached trout (£4.90) and steaks (from £8.50), to dishes of the day such as stir-fry beef (£5.45) or moules marinières (£5.70); there's a Sunday buffet; friendly service. The carpeted bar on the right, a rambling affair, is simply furnished with red-cushioned pews and scrubbed tables, with a woodburning stove and in a lower area a big photograph of HMS *Soberton*. The irregularly shaped public bar has more pews with built-in wooden wall seats, and darts. Flowers Original, Fremlins, Marstons Pedigree, Whitbreads Strong Country and Pompey Royal, Wadworths 6X; occasional theme nights. There are attractive views over the quiet green to the tall trees of the churchyard, and picnic-table sets in a sheltered garden with swings, a slide and climbing bars, and on a sun-trap fairy-lit terrace; they roast pigs on Bank Holidays out here (if it rains, there's an awning for the terrace), and may have children's entertainment in the afternoon then. It tends to get busy at weekends. *(Recommended by J H Walker, Mr Cowell, M K C Wills, Michael Bechley, Mel and Phil Lloyd, J A Jones, ML)*

Whitbreads   Licensees Rod and Joanie Johnson   Real ale   Meals and snacks Restaurant (open noon–10.30 Sun) tel Droxford (0489) 877346   Children in eating area and restaurant   Open 11–2.30(3 Sat), 6–11

SOUTHAMPTON   SU4212 Map 2

Red Lion

55 High Street; turning off inner ring road, in S of city

Something of an unexpected gem inside an unpromising, modern-city exterior – it's actually a medieval hall, with dark Tudor panelling, lofty and steeply pitched oak rafters, and timbered walls decorated with arms, armour and even a flag reputed to have been presented to the city by Elizabeth I in 1585. Ruddles Best and County and Websters Yorkshire on handpump; fruit machine and trivia, piped music. Straightforward bar food, served in the lower-ceilinged back bar below the creaky upper gallery, includes filled rolls (from 65p) and sandwiches (from 85p), filled baked potatoes (from £1), ploughman's (from £1.90), basket meals (from £2.20), home-made lasagne or vegetarian dishes (£2.65), salads (from £3.25), cod or plaice (£3.25), home-made steak and kidney pie (£3.25), scampi (£4.95) and steak (from £6.45). *(Recommended by Ian Phillips, John and Christine Simpson, Mr and Mrs M Hanson, Steve Waters, Paul Corbett)*

Phoenix (Watneys)   Licensee Ian J Williams   Real ale   Meals and snacks (12 noon–9.30)   Restaurant tel Southampton (0703) 333595 (closed Sun)   Children in restaurant   Daytime parking nearby difficult   Open 10–11; closed 25 Dec

STEEP   SU7425 Map 2

Cricketers 🍽

Church Rd; from A272 leaving Petersfield towards Winchester take right turn at roundabout after level crossing; or from A325 in Sheet (outskirts of Petersfield) follow Steep signpost and keep right on beyond village

An object-lesson in what an enthusiastic family can do to transform a straightforward modern roadside pub into a place really worth knowing – so long as you don't want to take children there. Service is unfailingly friendly and helpful, the furnishings (chiefly beige plush chairs, sturdy settles and banquettes in the spacious and airy carpeted lounge) are solidly comfortable, everything's spick-and-span, and both food and drinks are enterprising and memorable enough to bring you back. The wide choice of food, fresh and home-cooked, includes ploughman's, lots of starters that would also do as light snacks such as macaroni cheese (£2.10) or garlic mushrooms (£2.25), and main dishes such as cottage pie (£2.70), filled baked potatoes, haddock or omelettes (£3.25), large burgers (£3.40), lamb and apricot pie (£3.50), steak sandwich (£4.25) and steaks (from 8oz rump £7); in the evenings there are extra things like trout done with lemon and rosemary (£6.10), gammon and egg (£6.50) and veal cordon bleu (£7.10). Well over 100 malt whiskies, well kept Gales Butser, Best and HSB on handpump, country wines;

log fire, fruit machine, unobtrusive piped music. A separate comfortable public bar has sensibly placed darts, round pool table, cribbage, dominoes, connect–4 and shut-the-box. The mother-and-daughter Siamese cats are Jessica and Minty. There are sturdy picnic-table sets under cocktail parasols on a back lawn around a big flowering cherry, with tall swings and a play-house on stilts. *(Recommended by HEG, Graham Dale, John Sterry, M G Rapley)*

Gales Licensee William Turnbull Real ale Meals and snacks Open 11.45–3, 5.15–11.30; Sat 11.30–3.30, 6–11.30; closed 26 Dec, evening 25 Dec Bedrooms (no children) tel Petersfield (0730) 61035; £25B/£30B

HARROW ⊘

Simplest to follow Steep signpost off A325 opp Sheet church NE on outskirts of Petersfield

This diminutive, cottagey pub has a terrific unspoilt and unchanging style – there's almost an Edwardian atmosphere in the little tiled-floor public bar, with its built-in wall benches around scrubbed deal tables, tiled floor, a good log fire in the big inglenook, stripped pine wallboards, and lots of summery cornflowers and drying wildflowers; dominoes, cribbage. A major draw for the many people who visit it, apart from its total lack of airs and graces, is the devastating helpings of simple home-cooked food – you may even have difficulties getting through a whole round of sandwiches (from £1.10) after the excellent soup, overflowing from an old-fashioned bowl (£1.60). Other choices include outstanding home-made Scotch eggs (£1), huge ploughman's (from £2.70), lasagne (£3.80), meat loaf (£4) and salads (from £4.50, served on an enormous carving plate); even the bread's normally baked on the premises. Flowers Original and Whitbreads Best and Strong Country tapped from casks behind the counter, country wines and a praiseworthy choice of soft drinks including locally made apple juice. The big, free-flowering and pleasantly unkempt garden has lots of tables; children are allowed only here. *(Recommended by Michael Simmonds, Pat and Derek Westcott, Steve and Carolyn Harvey, Gordon and Daphne, Ian Phillips, D Godden, Jean T Crosley, Henry Midwinter, Chris Raisin, Graham Doyle)*

Whitbreads Licensee Edward C McCutcheon Real ale Meals and snacks Open 10.30–2.30 (3 Sat), 6–11

STOCKBRIDGE   SU3535   Map 2

Vine

High St (A30)

There's quite an emphasis on eating here – many of the tables may be laid for eating, and it's often advisable to book at the weekend. However the atmosphere in the open-plan bar, with its interesting combination of woodwork, brickwork and papered walls, is still distinctly pubby; there are also gold velvet curtains, and a Delft shelf of china and pewter. Generously served, good value bar food includes sandwiches (from £1.20; open from £2.95), soup (£1.20), ploughman's (from £2.65), five-egg omelettes (from £2.75), quiche (£3.25), lasagne verdi (£3.95), good grilled fresh sardines (£4.50), gammon and egg, local trout or fresh plaice (£4.95) and seasonal fish specials. Mr Harding the licensee is also the chef, and if it's his day off there may not be any specials; they also warn of delays with some dishes. Flowers Original, Marstons Pedigree and Whitbreads Best on handpump, and a small but decent wine list; friendly, helpful service. The garden behind runs down to a carrier of the River Test. *(Recommended by T Galligan, Ron Gentry, W C M Jones, Norman Foot, John Baxter, Celia and David Watt, Joan and John Calvert)*

Whitbreads Licensees Michael and Vanessa Harding Real Ale Meals and snacks (12–2.30, 7–10; not Sun evening) Restaurant (closed Sun evening) Children welcome Bedrooms tel Andover (0264) 810652; £17.50/£27.50 Open 11–3.30, 6–11

White Hart

Bottom end of High Street; junction roundabout A272/A3057

Its irregular shape and the brick pillars supporting its low ochre ceiling divide the bar of this old coaching inn into plenty of separate little areas, which have tables with oak pews, wheelback chairs and low rustic elm stools, small antique prints on the walls, and a collection of shaving mugs hanging over the bar counter; there's lots of china on the beams in the small side restaurant. Bar food includes sandwiches (from £1.10), ploughman's or smoked local trout (£3), home-made curry or chilli con carne (£3.30) and steaks; good Sunday lunches, and cook-yourself summer barbecues. Bass and Charrington IPA on handpump and a range of country wines; shove-ha'penny. There's also a back wine bar. Front benches shelter under the unusually deep overhang of the pillared upper storey. *(Recommended by John Baxter, Jan and Ian Alcock, Joan and John Calvert, D Godden, Barry and Anne, O E Hole; more reports please)*

Free house   Licensee Peter Curtis   Real ale   Meals (in restaurant only, Sun lunchtime) and snacks (till 10 evening)   Restaurant (not Mon)   Children in restaurant   Open 11–2.30 (3 Sat), 6–11   Bedrooms tel Andover (0264) 810475; £20(£30B)/£37.50(£47.50B)

TICHBORNE   SU5630   Map 2

Tichborne Arms ⊘

Village signed off A31 just W of Alresford

The comfortable, square-panelled room on the right here has wheelback chairs and settles (one very long), latticed windows with flowery curtains, fresh flowers, and a log fire in an attractive stone fireplace; pictures and documents on the walls recall the bizarre Tichborne Case – when a mystery man from Australia claimed fraudulently to be the heir to this estate. On the left, a larger and livelier room, partly panelled and also carpeted, has sensibly placed darts, shove-ha'penny, cribbage and a fruit machine; well kept Courage Best and Directors, John Smiths and Wadworths 6X tapped from the cask; friendly service. Good value, attractively straightforward and fresh bar food includes home-made soup (£1.25), bacon sandwiches with local watercress (£1.35; others from £1.15), liver and bacon nibbles with a home-made dip (£1.75), ploughman's (from £2), baked potatoes with a fine range of fillings (from £2.85), salads (from £3.75), a range of home-made daily specials such as stilton and brocolli quiche (£3.50), chicken and peach casserole or turkey and leek pie (£4.25) and plenty of home-made puddings such as golden syrup sponge with custard and fudge, walnut flan with cream or a dense chocolate cake (£1.25); they warn of delays at busy times. There are picnic-table sets outside this attractive thatched building, in the big well kept garden. *(Recommended by Richard Sachs, Steve and Carolyn Harvey, SJC, Lynn Sharpless, Bob Eardley, Dr C S Shaw, PLC, W A Gardiner, John and Heather Dwane, Gordon P Hewitt, Mr and Mrs G Turner, Richard Parr, H G Allen)*

Free house   Licensees Chris and Peter Byron   Real ale   Meals and snacks (12–1.45, 6.30–9.45)   Open 11.30–2.30, 6–11

TURGIS GREEN   SU6959   Map 2

Jekyll & Hyde

A33 Reading–Basingstoke

A spread of muted brown carpet in this rambling pub unifies the various areas opening off each other; there are black beams and joists, wheelback chairs around rather rustic oak tables, some more individual furnishings, and cream-painted walls. The dining area up a few steps looks down into the main bar area through timbered openings, and a back room has a fine winged and high-backed settle among more modern furnishings, and big Morland and Landseer prints. Adnams Southwold, Badger Best and Tanglefoot, Gales HSB and Wadworths 6X on handpump. Well presented bar food includes sandwiches, ploughman's (£3.25), spinach and bacon au gratin (£2.85), filled baked potatoes (from £2.50), mixed bean casserole (£3.85), good lasagne (£4.35), salads (from £4), steaks (from £8.95), and plenty of puddings; children's dishes (£1.95). There are lots of picnic-table sets under cocktail parasols in the sheltered and attractively planted garden, with swings, a slide and a climber, as well as lots of games – cricket, swingball, rounders and so forth. *(Recommended by R M Sparkes, Simon Collett-Jones, Roger Mallard, Ian Phillips, Patrick and Mary McDermott, KC, E U Broadbent; more reports please)*

Free house   Licensees Tracy and David Hunter   Real ale   Meals and snacks (12–2, 6.30–10; till 9 Sun)   Children in eating area   Open 11–2.30 (3 Sat), 6–11

nr VERNHAM DEAN   SU3558   Map 2

Boot

Littledown; on Upton side of Vernham Dean follow Vernham Street signposts

It's really enjoyable sitting outside this downland flint pub – under the spreading sycamore in the lovely garden, say; there's an old paddock, now used as a children's play area, and tables on a terrace. Inside it's charmingly small (despite a side extension), with an original low-beamed white-panelled bar – where there's barely space for a pair of tables by the attractive inglenook fireplace; maybe piped music. The conservatory has darts, dominoes, cribbage, table skittles and shove-ha'penny, and there's a collection of model boots and shoes in a corner cupboard. Now that they no longer have a restaurant (which is now a family room and overflow for the conservatory), they've expanded the decent range of bar food to include a weekly specials board, with such dishes as spicy sausage stew or ratatouille (£3.50), local venison or pheasant casseroles or lamb (£5), and lots of puddings (£1.35); the permanent menu includes sandwiches (from £1.25; good ham with brown bread and mustard £1.50), ploughman's or basket meals (from £3), and steaks. Besides Badger Best, Hook Norton Old Hookey, Marstons Burton and Pedigree and Wadworths 6X tapped from casks on trestles, they keep a good range of malt whiskies. *(Recommended by Gordon and Daphne, Dr M Ian Crichton, Margaret Dyke, Ewan McCall, Roger Huggins, Tom McLean, Mrs Maureen Hobbs, HNJ, PEJ)*

Free house   Licensees Neale and Helen Baker   Real ale   Meals and snacks   Children in dining room and conservatory   Open 12–3, 6–11; 12–2.30, 7–11 winter; closed Mon except Bank Holidays

VERNHAM DEAN   SU3456   Map 2

George

On the old coach road going NW from Hurstbourne Tarrant; follow Upton signpost from A343; or from A338 5 miles S of Hungerford follow Oxenwood signpost and keep on

The smooth curve of the roof over the first-floor windows gives this old timbered brick and flint building a raised-eyebrows look. Inside it's relaxed and friendly, with a rambling open-plan beamed bar which has a log fire in its big inglenook fireplace, a lovely polished elm table, traditional black wall seats built into the panelled dado, and some easy chairs. Good value bar food includes sizeable toasted sandwiches (£1.60), soup with home-made stock (£1.50), a range of ploughman's, and daily hot dishes such as corned beef hash or winter rabbit stew. Well kept Marstons Burton and Pedigree on handpump; cribbage, dominoes and fruit machine. There are tables in the pretty garden behind. The landlady used to run the Cricketers at Tangley, a popular *Guide* entry under her regime. *(Recommended by L Walker, HNJ, PEJ, Gordon and Daphne, M J Whitehouse; more reports please)*

Marstons   Licensees Mary and Philip Perry   Real ale   Meals and snacks (limited menu, Sunday)   Well behaved children in family room, lunchtime   Open 11–2.30 (3 Sat), 6–11

WELL SU7646 Map2

Chequers

5 miles W of Farnham; off A287 via Crondall, or A31 via Froyle and Lower Froyle (easier if longer than via Bentley); from A32 S of Odiham, go via Long Sutton; OS Sheet 186 map reference 761467

Somewhere between an English pub and a French bistro (until a few years ago it was actually French-run) this snug little pub, nicely remote below the North Downs, has a back-to-basics bar full of alcoves, low beams, antique settles, heavily comfortable seats and stools, and lots of farm tools and brasses; good winter log fires. Flowers, Wadworths 6X and Whitbreads on handpump. Enterprising bar food includes pasta or grilled avocado with hot cheshire cheese (£3.50), salads such as warm bacon, apple and walnut (£3.60) and scrambled eggs and smoked salmon (£4.40). There are tables under cocktail parasols in the garden at the back, and at the front a rather idyllic, fairy-lit vine-covered front arbour. (*Recommended by Michael Bareau, KC, E H and R F Warner, Mr and Mrs P Wilkins, GSS; more reports on the new regime please*)

Free house Licensees Christopher Phillips and Hugh Stanford Real ale Meals and snacks (12-2.30, 7-10) Restaurant tel Basingstoke (0256) 862605 Children in restaurant Open 11-3, 5.30-11

nr WHERWELL SU3941 Map 2

Mayfly

Testcombe; A3057 SE of Andover, between B3420 turn-off and Leckford where road crosses River Test

Bar food in this fine old pub is popular -- particularly the excellent range of cheeses, served with fresh crusty wholemeal bread (£2.50) from a separate counter; there's also soup (£1.50), daily hot dishes, and a selection of cold meats such as chicken tandoori or topside of beef, served with a good choice of attractive salads (which are charged extra, 60p each); in the winter there are extra dishes such as braised oxtails or steak and vegetable pie (from £3.90); service remains good-tempered under pressure. The spacious, beamed and carpeted bar has Windsor chairs around lots of tables, fishing pictures and bric-a-brac on the cream walls above its dark wood dado, two woodburning stoves, and bow windows overlooking the water. Well kept Flowers Original, Wadworths 6X, Whitbreads Best and Strong Country on handpump. The views from the peaceful tables by the fast-flowing River Test are memorable, and much loved by readers. There may be crowds on fine summer days -- when it's advisable to arrive early if you want to eat. (*Recommended by R M Young, T Nott, Dr and Mrs A K Clarke, R J Walden, Brian Barefoot, H W and A B Tuffill, M J Dyke, TBB, Roy McIsaac, Roger Mallard, Mrs L Saumarez Smith, Jan and Ian Alcock, Dr Peter Donahue, R Elliott, Mr and Mrs D W Fisher*)

Whitbreads Licensees Barry and Julie Lane Real ale Meals and snacks Children welcome Open 11--11

WINCHESTER SU4829 Map 2

Eclipse

The Square; between High Street and Cathedral

The diminutive, heavy-beamed front bar in this picturesque, 14th-century pub has oak settles, mugs hanging from the ceiling, and timbers where walls have been knocked through -- including one running vertically, to the right of the fireplace, and around which the original building was built. Flowers Original and Whitbreads Pompey Royal and Strong Country on handpump under light blanket pressure; shove-ha'penny, cribbage, dominoes, piped music. Bar food includes sandwiches (from £1.10, toasted 15p extra), ravioli (£1.68), ploughman's (from £1.75), good filled baked potatoes (from £1.70), plaice (£3.15), home-made steak and kidney or game pie (£3.52) and scampi (£3.62). New licensees took over at the start of last year, and seem to have maintained standards all round. There are benches out on the pavement, under the overhang of the jettied black-and-white timbered upper part. *(Recommended by Lynn Sharpless, Bob Eardley, Joan and John Calvert, R Elliott, T C and A R Newell; more reports on the new regime please)*

Whitbreads   Licensee Roy Skeats   Real ale   Meals and snacks   Children in back room   Folk music Wed once a month   Daytime parking nearby may be difficult   Open 11–11 (11–3, 5.30–11 winter); closed 25 and 26 Dec

Wykeham Arms ★ 🚫 🛏

75 Kingsgate Street (Kingsgate Arch and College Street are now closed to traffic; there is access via Canon Street)

Highly praised lunchtime bar food in this popular and professionally run town inn includes sandwiches, soup, ploughman's, stilton and quince pâté (£2.95), and cauliflower cheese, mushroom bake or cottage pie (£3.95), with changing evening dishes such as creamed leek and stilton mille feuilles (£5.50), pan-fried pigeon breast with blackcurrant cream and cassis sauce (£8.25), and rack of lamb (£9.25); puddings such as brown bread ice cream or rhubarb fool (£2.25); service is notably friendly and helpful. The stylish series of rooms radiating from the central bar includes a snug no-smoking one at the back, known as the Watchmakers and decorated with a set of Ronald Searle 'Winespeak' prints; a second one is panelled, and all of them have a log fire. Among the more interesting furnishings are 19th-century oak desks retired from nearby Winchester College, a redundant pew from the same source, kitchen chairs and candlelit deal tables; the big windows have swagged paisley curtains, the piano carries quite a load of houseplants, and there are abundant quantities of fresh flowers; two thirds of all the bar area are no-smoking after 8pm on Friday and Saturday. The award-winning range of wines by the glass runs to over 20, and the Eldridge Pope Dorchester, Hardy and Royal Oak on handpump are well kept. There are tables on a covered back terrace, with more on a small but sheltered lawn. Residents have the use of a sauna; the inn is very handy for the Cathedral. *(Recommended by Robert and Elizabeth Scott, Barbara M McHugh, Quentin Williamson, Steve and Carolyn Harvey, Ann Stranack, John Moate, Dr C S Shaw, Steve Goodchild, Cdr J W Hackett, Tony and Lynne Stark, Gordon Mott, Lynn Sharpless, Bob Eardley, H W and A B Tuffill, David Young, Alison Hayward, Nick Dowson, R W Stanbury)*

Eldridge Pope   Licensees Mr and Mrs Graeme Jameson   Real ale   Meals and snacks (not Mon evening or Sun)   If the small car park is full local parking may be difficult – don't be tempted to block up Kingsgate Street itself   Open 11–11; closed 25 Dec evening   Bedrooms tel Winchester (0962) 53834; £55B/£65B

Lucky Dip

Besides the fully inspected pubs, you might like to try these Lucky Dips recommended to us and described by readers (if you do, please send us reports):

☆ **Alresford** [The Soke, Broad St (extreme lower end); SU5832], *Globe*: Attractive spot in quiet street, with lovely view of 12th-century ponds from back windows and garden; good if not particularly cheap bar food such as ploughman's, grilled trout and salads till 10, well kept Gales HSB and Watneys-related real ales on handpump, friendly staff, quite a lot of local or historical display material; shame about the piped music; open all day, nearby parking can be difficult *(John Kimber, Dave Braisted, Tim and Ann Newell)*

Alresford [West St], *Swan*: Straightforward place, comfortably refurbished this last year, with decent reasonably priced salad bar; parking in side st or at stn; bedrooms *(R E Stratton, Philip and Trisha Ferris)*

☆ **Alton** [Church St; SU7139], *Eight Bells*: Attractive, often busy low-ceilinged olde-worlde bar full of bric-a-brac, inc chamber-pots hanging from beam; five well kept Allied and guest beers on handpump, friendly barman *(Dr John Innes, Derek Patey, Tim and Ann Newell)*

Alton [Market St], *Kings Head*: Welcoming atmosphere, friendly bar staff, cheap home-cooked bar food, play area in enclosed garden *(Miss L Canham, M White)*

Ampfield [A31 Winchester–Romsey; SU4023], *White Horse*: New landlord making special effort in pleasant wayside pub *(Dr and Mrs Tony Clarke)*

☆ **Ball Hill** [Hatt Common; leaving Newbury on A343 turn right towards East Woodhay — OS Sheet 174 map reference 423631; SU4263], *Furze Bush*: Clean and airy decor, pews and pine tables, well kept real ales inc Bass and Marstons Pedigree on handpump, decent wines by the bottle, tables on terrace and in good-sized sheltered lawn and orchard with play area; usual bar food (not cheap, and service may be slow), restaurant; well behaved children allowed, no-smoking area in dining room *(HNJ, PEJ, LYM)*

Barton on Sea [SZ2393], *Ventana*: Small pub/hotel on cliff opp the Needles with exceptionally wide choice of genuine bar food, well kept Flowers and Wadworths 6X and friendly, helpful staff; can be a real sun-trap; games room *(WHBM)*

☆ **Basing** [Bartons Lane (attached to Bartons Mill Restaurant); SU6653], *Millstone*: Remarkable choice of well kept real ales tapped from the cask in unusual, busy converted mill in lovely setting by River Lodden; good ploughman's and salads, well cooked hot dishes such as lasagne, civil service, big garden; sometimes crowded with young people *(Bernard Phillips, Patrick and Mary McDermott)*

Bighton [OS Sheet 185 map reference 615344; SU6134], *Three Horseshoes*: Traditional country pub doing well under friendly newish licensees; well kept Gales beers, wide range of fruit wines, good simple food in two fairly small comfortable bars *(Lynn Sharpless, Bob Eardley)*

Binsted [SU7741], *Cedars*: Homely local with big, lively public bar (and huge bear's head), quieter sitting-roomish lounge bar, well kept Courage ales, good freshly prepared food *(W A Gardiner, BB)*

☆ **Bishops Sutton** [former A31 on Alton side of Alresford — now bypassed; SU6031], *Ship*: Friendly, pleasant and cosy local with relaxed atmosphere, good varied bar food quickly served, discreet piped music *(G and M Stewart, LYM)*

Bishops Waltham [Church St; SU5517], *Bunch of Grapes*: Friendly and old-fashioned pub, very basic, in lovely village lane, with emphasis on conversation, not food; welcoming licensees (pub in same family for many years), well kept Courage Best tapped from the cask with Directors at Christmas; small garden *(Melvyn Payne, SJC)*; [The Square], *Crown*: Attractive period pub, refurbished (not excessively) as Whitbreads Brewers Fayre pub; straightforward bar food, friendly staff, small terrace; parking for five disabled drivers next to pub, main car park across rd *(Michael Bechley)*

Bishopstoke [SU4619], *River*: Big, popular family pub, plenty of places for children to sit and play; atmosphere and food rather impersonal, though some interesting nick-nacks inc dolls, Brooke Bond cards, replica Crown Jewels *(Mel and Phil Lloyd)*

Blacknest [OS Sheet 186 map reference 798416; SU7941], *Jolly Farmer*: Recommended in previous editions as popular country pub with skittle alley, choice of real ales, good bar food and pleasant garden; but destroyed by explosion treated by the police as deliberate (chef killed — culprit not yet found as we go to press); should have been rebuilt by the time this edition is published, with new family room added *(G and M Stewart, Peter Turl; reports please)*

☆ **Botley** [The Square; SU5112], *Bugle*: Well decorated beamed bar with Flowers and Whitbreads Strong County on handpump,

good bar food inc good fresh seafood, steaks, curries and so forth, quick pleasant service; restaurant *(C D Gill, John and Christine Simpson)*

☆ **Braishfield** [Newport Lane; SU3725], *Newport*: Very unassuming, with down-to-earth landlord, but popular, with good comfortable atmosphere in two old-fashioned bars; well kept Gales, good range of country wines, decent coffee, simple quickly served food such as sandwiches and ploughman's; pleasant garden with animals *(Lynn Sharpless, Bob Eardley, H W and A B Tuffill)*

☆ **Bransgore** [Highcliffe Rd; SZ1897], *Three Tuns*: Friendly, comfortable and attractive pub in older part of village, with open fire, well kept beer, good bar lunches, evening restaurant *(WHBM)*

Brockenhurst [Lyndhurst Rd; SU2902], *Snakecatcher*: Friendly local, Eldridge Pope Royal Oak and IPA, wide choice of decent wines by the glass, good bar food with some interesting dishes *(WHBM)*

☆ **Bucklers Hard** [SU4000], *Master Builders House*: Lovely spot by the water in carefully preserved Montagu-estate village; beamed and timbered bar with big log fire, good self-service food bar in separate room, friendly service, well kept Ind Coope Burton — reports increasingly favourable over the past year or so; can get crowded, part of a substantial hotel complex *(Y M Healey, WHBM, R W Stanbury, Patrick Young, Leith Stuart, Barbara Hatfield, LYM)*

☆ **Burghclere** [off A34 — OS Sheet 174 map reference 462608; SU4761], *Carpenters Arms*: Well kept and friendly pub, small and busy, with big helpings of reasonably priced bar food inc vegetarian dishes, Watneys-related real ales, unobtrusive piped music, fruit machine, garden; small evening fixed-price restaurant; opp Sandham Memorial Chapel (NT), Stanley Spencer's masterwork *(D J Cooke, Robert and Elizabeth Scott, Dennis and Pat Jones)*

☆ **Buriton** [OS Sheet 197 map reference 735205; SU7420], *Five Bells*: Doing particularly well after recent tasteful refurbishments; lots of character, very wide choice of decent food inc straightforward regular dishes and interesting specials; Allied real ales on handpump *(Peter Ames, Ian and Wendy McCaw)*

Buriton, *Master Robert*: Very pleasantly decorated, wide choice of good food *(Alan and Sharron Todd)*

Burley [on back rd Ringwood—Lymington; SU2003], *Queens Head*: Tudor pub with flagstones, low beams, timbering, panelling, good log fire; has had masses of bric-a-brac, usual bar food (not winter evenings), well kept Whitbreads-related real ales and provision for children, but we've had no reports since 1990 closure for major alterations *(LYM; news please)*

☆ **Bursledon** [Hungerford Bottom], *Fox & Hounds*: Chef & Brewer popular especially with young people for handsomely rebuilt ancient Lone Barn behind — long oak-trunk table, lantern-lit side stalls, jolly rustic atmosphere and lots of interesting farm tools and equipment, food bar, well kept Watneys-related real ales with a guest beer such as Gales; seats out in sheltered fairy-lit flagstone courtyard with electric ride and small pets' corner; games and juke box in main pub, which has 16th-century cooking spit; children in Lone Barn; big car park *(John and Christine Simpson, Keith Houlgate, LYM)*

☆ **Bursledon** [2 miles from M27 junction 8; A27 towards Fareham, then right towards Bursledon Stn — best to park there (free) and walk up hill on left; beware long steep steps down from lane], *Jolly Sailor*: Superb position by yacht harbour makes this popular; tables out by the water with a children's bar at busy times, good views from the nautical-mood airy front bar, pews and settles by the fire in the beams-and-flagstones back bar, full range of Badger and Gales ales well kept on handpump, expanded range of bar food inc wide choice of fish, restaurant, welcoming staff; thorough refurbishment 1990 — very clean throughout now, with impeccable lavatories; children in eating area and restaurant *(Michael Bechley, J H Walker, Mr Cowell, Leith Stuart, Peter Adcock, LYM)*

☆ **Cadnam** [by M27, junction 1; SU2913], *Sir John Barleycorn*: Lovely thatched pub said to date in part to 12th century, with two big open fires in spotless, cosily divided long open-plan bar; pot plants, hunting and game prints, popular snacks and meals (not cheap but home-made and generous), well kept Flowers Original and Whitbreads Strong Country on handpump, friendly staff; garden with barbecue *(Mike and Jill Dixon, Dennis and Pat Jones)*

Chandlers Ford [SU4320], *Cleveland Bay*: Particularly well kept Badger Tanglefoot, Wadworths Farmers Glory and guest beers such as Timothy Taylors Landlord, bar food, attractive layout and furnishings *(Jacquie and Jon Payne)*

☆ **Cheriton** [just off B3046 towards Beauworth — OS Sheet 185 map reference 581282; SU5828], *Flower Pots*: Unspoilt take-us-as-you-find-us village local with homely parlourish bar, well kept Flowers Original and Whitbreads Strong Country, cheap sandwiches and ploughman's, traditional games in public bar, old-fashioned seats on front grass, long-established landlady; bedrooms good value though very simple; good breakfasts *(R Elliott, Richard Parr, Ian Phillips, R Blatch, D C Kennedy, Lynn Sharpless, Bob Eardley, LYM)*

Crondall [SU7948], *Hampshire Arms*: Welcoming, good food *(Michael Bareau)*; [Bowling Alley, N of village just off A287 Farnham—Basingstoke — OS Sheet 186 map reference 798502], *Horn*: Remarkably clean, with well kept Watneys-related real ales, good food, courteous service *(D S Male)*

☆ **Denmead** [Forest Rd, Worlds End; SU6211], *Chairmakers Arms*: Well kept Gales BBB, HSB, and XXXL and (from separate counter) wide choice of bar food from spectacular sandwiches to steaks in spacious communicating rooms of simply decorated but comfortable pub surrounded by paddocks and farmland; friendly service, no music *(Mel and Phil Lloyd, H and P Jeffery, Richard Houghton, LYM)*

Denmead [Hambledon Rd (B2150)], *Forest of Bere*: Village local with small cosy lounge, lively public bar; well kept Allied real ales, good choice of reasonably priced food from sandwiches to full meals, nice welcome from friendly regulars *(Richard Houghton)*

Downton [SZ2793], *Royal Oak*: Cheerful staff and consistently good food inc good fish pies; clean lavatories *(John Kirk)*

Droxford [SU6018], *Hurdles*: Friendly service, well kept beer and good choice of food including excellent vegetarian dishes at reasonable prices in bustling fast-food pub, small share-a-table bar, separate restaurant *(John and Margaret Estdale)*

☆ **Dundridge** [Dundridge Lane; off B3035 towards Droxford, Swanmore, then right towards Bishops Waltham — OS Sheet 185 map reference 579185; SU5718], *Hampshire Bowman*: Simple isolated downland pub, cosy and unspoilt, with well kept Archers and Gales ales tapped from the cask maybe under light blanket pressure, good plain food inc good chilli con carne, friendly civilised service; tables on spacious lawn; children welcome *(A R and B E Sayer, Derek and Sylvia Stephenson, ML, SJC, LYM)*

East End [back rd Lymington—Beaulieu, parallel to B3054 — keep on past Lymington ferry; SZ3697], *East End Arms*: Doing well under new owner; cosy lounge with easy chairs around a big open log fire, good locals' bar, reasonably priced home-cooked food, very good Christmas programme, pleasant tables outside *(L Tapsell)*

☆ **East Meon** [Church St; signed off A272 W of Petersfield, and off A32 in West Meon; SU6822], *George*: Massive slabs of timber make up some of the furnishings in the cosy areas which loop around the central servery — up to three log fires, candlelit dining room, scrubbed deal, beams and saddlery; the bar food servery, spick and span, opens off, and has given good value from sandwiches through several home-made specials to steaks — though we'd like more reports on the current newish regime; Ind Coope, Gales and other real ales *(Charles Turner, J S Rutter, R Houghton, Jacqueline Davis, LYM)*

East Meon, *Izaak Walton*: Friendly staff, well kept Gales HSB and Watneys-related real ales, bar food *(Richard Houghton)*

East Stratton [SU5439], *Plough*: Above-average simply decorated village pub with courteous, efficient staff *(Dr J L Innes, R and E Harfield)*

East Tytherley [SU2929], *Star*: Comfortable lounge, well kept Gales *(H W and A B Tuffill)*

East Worldham [Caters Land (B3004); TV6199], *Three Horseshoes*: Pleasant beamed building with relaxed atmosphere, polite efficient service, well kept Gales, and decent helpings of well presented popular food *(Richard Houghton)*

Emery Down [SU2808], *Green Dragon*: Busy pub with good mix of customers, well kept beer, bar counter surrounds interestingly veneered with different woods from named Forest localities, quickly served bar food, garden; HQ of the commoners' pony and cattle association *(WHBM)*

Emsworth [South St; SU7406], *Coal Exchange*: Welcoming new licensee, friendly locals, basic interior but plenty of character and atmosphere, well kept Gales and good cheap food inc local cockles *(Richard Houghton)*; [New Brighton Rd], *Fairfield*: Substantial and discreetly comfortable Regency building with two bars, delightful separate dining area and proper pub atmosphere; well kept Gales, good value bar food, friendly service *(Richard Houghton)*; [North St], *Scalywags*: Pleasantly plush, with well kept Gibbs Mew and Watneys-related real ales, friendly staff, decent helpings of good value food *(Richard Houghton)*; [Main St], *Ship*: Decent simple food from sandwiches to local fish and well kept Bass and Charrington IPA in plain but comfortable well kept local, pleasant tables in pretty little back yard *(LYM)*; [2 West St], *Town Brewery*: Interesting home-brew pub with sawdust on the bare boards, basic furniture, but cosy atmosphere, friendly licensee, generous good value food cooked by his wife; open all day *(Phil and Sally Gorton, Richard Houghton)*

Eversley [A327; SU7762], *Toad & Stumps*: Friendly local with interesting food, Courage Directors, some live music *(Dr M Owton)*

☆ **Everton** [SZ2994], *Crown*: Good, traditional, two-bar local with good service, decent bar lunches in eating area, well kept Whitbreads-related real ales; but whisky is the special drink here, and the friendly landlord (who has sampled over 4,000) will guide your choice *(Comus Elliott, WHMB)*

Exton [signposted from A32; SU6121], *Shoe*: Clean partly panelled pub in pleasant riverside spot, Allied real ales, usual range of decent bar food, good puddings *(Mrs S A Bishop, Lynn Sharpless, Bob Eardley)*

Faccombe [SU3858], *Jack Russell*: Hilltop village free house opposite pond, lovely views nearby; small but spotless bar, pleasant young licensees, usual range of bar food done nicely, with interesting extras like home-cured ham and eggs and pheasant casserole — fish specially good; closed Tues; bedrooms *(HNJ, PEJ)*

☆ **Farnborough** [Rectory Rd; nr Farnborough North stn; SU8753], *Prince of Wales*: Unpretentious local, Edwardian with some more recent antiquing, notable for exceptional range of particularly well kept changing real ales such as Fullers London Pride, Eldridge Pope Royal Oak, Hoskins & Oldfields Navigation, King & Barnes Broadwood, Marstons Owd Rodger and Wadworths 6X, also reasonable choice of malt whiskies; good helpings of decent bar food inc interesting filled French sticks, warm management and staff, good mix of customers, clean lavatories *(Dr R Fuller, Peter Griffiths, Richard Houghton)*

☆ **Farringdon** [Crows Lane, Upper Farringdon (follow Church sign off A32 S of Alton); SU7135], *Rose & Crown*: Clean, bright and very friendly local doing well under new owners, with old saws and other tools on ceiling joists, simple mainly modern bar furnishings, back dining room, well kept Flowers Original, Gales HSB, Marstons Mild, Burton and Pedigree and Owd Rodger and Ringwood Old Thumper on handpump, decent wines, well prepared sandwiches, ploughman's, pizzas, filled baked potatoes and children's dishes, good value restaurant food such as salmon-dressed crab; tables,

swings and bouncy ride in neat back garden *(Gordon and Daphne, Robert Crail, HEG, BB)*

Farringdon [A32 S of Alton], *Royal Oak*: Attractive interior, with relaxed atmosphere and local jokes chalked on beams; friendly efficient staff, good choice of bar food at reasonable prices, coffee served on small tray with sugar basin and cream jug *(TOH)*

☆ **Fordingbridge** [14 Bridge St; SU1414], *George*: Outstanding waterside position, with tables out on terrace and in new sun lounge; bar recently smartened-up too, with warm welcome, good rather upmarket bar food with some concentration on salad bar, attentive service *(WHBM, Margaret and Geoffrey Tobin, Roy McIsaac)*

☆ **Fritham** [SU2314], *Royal Oak*: Thatched New Forest pub, Flowers and Whitbreads Strong Country tapped from the cask for two quite unspoilt and decidedly basic — even untidy — bars, one with high-backed settles and chairs, pots and kettles hanging in wide old chimney; outside seats, tables, climbers and maybe a couple of friendly sheep, with cows, ponies and even pigs wandering nearby; no food beyond pickled eggs, but your own sandwiches welcome; children in back room; start GWG40 *(Charlie Salt, WHBM, LYM)*

☆ **Frogham** [SU1713], *Foresters*: Busy forest-edge local, doing well under new young management, with good value food now from sandwiches and ploughman's up; good, friendly atmosphere, interesting changing choice of well kept real ales such as Hook Norton, Ringwood Best and Fortyniner and Hoskins & Oldfields Navigation; farm cider, wooden settles *(WHBM, Charlie Salt)*

Froxfield Green [Alton—Petersfield rd; SU7025], *Trooper*: Well kept Flowers and Wadworths, interesting choice of inexpensive wines and cheap, simple and freshly prepared bar food *(HEG)*

☆ **Froyle** [Upper Froyle; A31 Alton—Farnham; SU7542], *Hen & Chicken*: Popular for wide choice of bar food, not cheap and verging on the approach of a restaurant rather than of a pub, but generously served (till 10), and including at a price sandwiches or interesting filled baked potatoes as well as things running up to local game, steaks and lobster; good value Sun lunch (booking recommended); beside more modern furnishings there are antique settles and oak tables by the huge fireplace; good choice of well kept real ales such as Adnams Broadside, Brakspears SB, Courage Best and Wadworths 6X on handpump, efficient helpful service, unobtrusive piped music, tables outside; children very welcome in eating area and small panelled restaurant; play area *(Hazel Morgan, S J Rice, Quentin Williamson, Patrick and Mary McDermott, E G Parish, Caroline Wright, Tim Neale, L A Dormer, HEG)*

☆ **Grateley** [SU2741], *Plough*: Typical old village local with helpful and friendly staff, good choice (particularly evening) of generous nicely presented bar food served quickly in smart little candlelit dining area off good-sized lounge, big open fire, well kept Gibbs Mew Wiltshire and Salisbury, subdued piped music *(H and P Jeffery, R Elliott)*

Greywell [M3 junction 5; A287 toward Odiham, then first right; SU7151], *Fox & Goose*: Small, friendly village pub with well kept Courage beers and good bar food (not Sun evenings); open fire, family room, garden *(Patrick and Mary McDermott)*

Hamble [High St; 3 miles from M27 junction 8; SU4806], *Bugle*: Varied bar food, range of real ales and expensive river-view restaurant in very extended pub, popular for its *Howards Way* position *(A J Castle, LYM)*

☆ Hambledon [Broadhalfpenny Down; about 2 miles E towards Clanfield; SU6414], *Bat & Ball*: Recently refurbished dining pub in attractive spot, with decent food and Allied real ales, relaxing atmosphere, pleasant log fire and real cricketing history — lots of memorabilia in the popular restaurant *(GSS, N J Clark, Jacqueline Davis, LYM)*

☆ Hambledon [West St], *Vine*: Welcoming well furnished old pub with two bars, nice prints, lots of farm tools, old banknotes and so forth; well prepared straightforward food from filled baps, home-made pasties and ploughman's up, well kept ales such as Courage, Gales, Morlands, Marstons and Wadworths, purpose-built shove-ha'penny board, darts, good lavatories *(Ian and James Phillips, Richard Houghton)*

Hambledon, *Horse & Jockey*: Busy at lunchtimes for good food; clean and civilised, good service, attractive spot *(D S Male)*

Hartley Wintney [B3011; SU7656], *Shoulder of Mutton*: Well kept Courage ales on handpump, wide choice of good value straightforward food (most tables set for this), pleasant staff, unexceptional piped music, nice sunny garden looking out over countryside *(Aleister and Geraldine Martin)*

Havant [6 Homewell, just off shopping mall; SU7106], *Robin Hood*: Proper cosy old town pub with well kept Gales tapped from the cask and quickly prepared, reasonably priced good food, pleasant staff *(Richard Houghton)*

Hayling Island [9 Havant Rd (A3023); SY7201], *Maypole*: Friendly license, well kept Gales, good food *(Richard Houghton)*; [Havant Rd (A3023)], *Yew Tree*: Pleasant atmosphere in recently renovated open-plan bar, good realistically priced food, limited choice of well kept ales *(Chris Fluck)*

☆ Heckfield [B3349 Hook—Reading (still called A32 on some maps); SU7260], *New Inn*: Wide range of food running up to steaks in very extensive rambling open-plan bar, some traditional furniture and a couple of good log fires as well as the many well spaced dining tables, warm welcome and friendly atmosphere, well kept Badger Best and Tanglefoot and Courage Best; restaurant (not Sun); bedrooms in comfortable and well equipped new extension *(Ian Phillips, Dr R Fuller, DJ, JJ, LYM)*

☆ Highclere [Andover Rd; A343 S of village; SU4360], *Yew Tree*: Good straightforward bar food from soup and sandwiches to shoulder of lamb and steaks in spruce plushly refurbished bar with big log fire, Wadworths 6X and Whitbreads-related real ales on handpump, decent wines, discreet piped music, friendly staff; children in area off bar; bedrooms *(R M Sparkes, Brian and Genie Smart, LYM)*

Hill Head [Hill Head Rd; SU5402], *Osborne View*: Relaxed, modernised pub with superb view over Solent and Isle of Wight; full range of Badger real ales kept well, bar food, friendly service *(Jacqueline Davis; more reports on new regime please)*

☆ Hook [London Rd — about a mile E; SU7254], *Crooked Billet*: Spaciously welcoming refurbished pub with homely open fires, good atmosphere, well kept beer and good range of soft drinks, wide choice of good bar food from sandwiches to steaks all day; superb spot with stream, ducks, garden (some traffic noise out here); children welcome, dogs may be allowed *(Mrs Sue Mills, WHBM, J S Rutter)*

☆ Horndean [London Rd; SU7013], *Ship & Bell*: Tastefully refurbished, quiet, clean and relaxed, with pleasant town-pub atmosphere; friendly service, good choice of reasonably priced bar food, well kept Gales beers from the brewery next door; bedrooms *(R Houghton, Jacqueline Davis, Nigel Gibbs)*

Horsebridge [about a mile SW of Kings Somborne — OS Sheet 185 map reference 346303; SU3430], *John o' Gaunt*: Well prepared fresh food — very popular on fine weekends *(H W and A B Tuffill)*

Hursley [A31 Winchester—Romsey; SU4225], *Dolphin*: Well run, good bar food inc fine ploughman's *(GSS)*; *Kings Head*: Polite, efficient service, Bass and other well kept real ales, wide range of good reasonably priced snacks; popular lunchtime with IBM staff *(Jon and Jacquie Payne, Gethin Lewis, GSS)*

Hythe [Hart Hill, off Frost Lane; SU4207], *Travellers Rest*: Friendly, quiet local with Whitbreads beers *(Dr M Owton)*

☆ Keyhaven [SZ3091], *Gun*: Wide choice of good value simple bar food and well kept Whitbreads-related real ales in busy villagey pub, dating back to 17th century and overlooking boatyard; garden, good walk along spit to Hurst Castle with Isle of Wight views; pay & display parking *(Barbara Hatfield, Comus Elliott, John Mason)*

☆ Kingsclere [SU5258], *Crown*: Long comfortable partly panelled lounge with central log fire, Courage real ales, games in simpler public bar, pleasant atmosphere; very popular for somewhat pricey home cooking; children in family room; bedrooms comfortable *(Gordon and Daphne, LYM)*

☆ Langstone [A3023; SU7105], *Ship*: Spacious pub in attractive spot by sea, with cheerful log fire, wide choice of appetising food at reasonable prices, efficient pleasant service, well kept Gales *(Mrs J A Blanks)*

☆ Lasham [SU6742], *Royal Oak*: Comfortable, friendly country pub in attractive spot nr gliding centre, with Courage Best, Eldridge Pope Royal Oak, Marstons Pedigree and Wadworths 6X; wide choice of popular though not cheap food in bar and restaurant (ham and eggs and home-made apple pie particularly good); tables outside, big car park *(Patrick and Mary McDermott, Nigel Gibbs, Derek Patey)*

Lee on the Solent [Crofton Ave/Sea Lane, off Stubbington Lane; SU5600], *Swordfish*: Big terrace with Solent views, Watneys-related beers; children's area with swings, swingboat and slide, friendly staff, popular food in bar and restaurant, open all day weekends at least in summer; big car park *(Keith Houlgate)*

Linwood [signposted from A338 via Moyles Court, and from A31; go on up heath — OS Sheet 195 map reference 186094; SU1910], *Red Shoot*: Now tied to Wadworths, but with Bass and Badger Tanglefoot too; doing well, with usual bar food from sandwiches and filled baked potatoes up, good pubby atmosphere; service could sometimes be quicker *(WHBM)*

Lower Farringdon [Gosport Rd (A32); SU7035], *Royal Oak*: Good value bar food, served almost instantly; friendly staff, reasonable Courage; big car park *(Richard Houghton)*

☆ **Lower Froyle** [SU7544], *Anchor*: Popular, clean and brightly lit pub said to date to 14th century, with well in bar; good service, good range of beers, piped music, friendly atmosphere, good varied straightforward bar food from well made sandwiches up; good restaurant *(W A Gardiner, R G E Mallin, John and Heather Dwane)*

Lower Swanwick [SU4909], *Ship*: By Hamble boatyard and loaded with marine artefacts and ship models; lounge with dark-wood panelling, matching chairs and settees and good view of river; good variety of quality food served in separate area with its own bar; friendly service, Gales on handpump *(Robert and Elizabeth Scott)*

Lower Wield [SU6340], *Yew Tree*: Remote family-run pub with welcoming landlord, small but imaginative choice of bar food (not Mon), from small kitchen — so can be slow; well kept Marstons Pedigree *(Gordon Smith)*

Lyde Green [SU7057], *Fox*: Isolated but lively no-frills country local, central fireplace, bar food; children's play area *(Gordon and Daphne)*

Lymington [High St; SZ3295], *Angel*: Largely home-made food in spacious darkly decorated modernised hotel bar with Eldridge Pope Dorchester, Dorset and Royal Oak on handpump — and reputedly a collection of ghosts that includes one of the very few Naval ones; children in Tuck bar; clean bedrooms *(M E Hughes, Edwin H Bradshaw, LYM)*; [centre], *Black Cat*: Good town pub, open all day; nice atmosphere, good beer *(Comus Elliott)*; [Quay Hill], *Kings Head*: Interesting pewter tankards and glasses hung from beams of attractive, cottagey bar with comfortable settles, good atmosphere, pleasant licensee and Whitbreads Pompey Royal and Strong Country on handpump *(E G Parish)*; [Southampton Rd (A337)], *Toll House*: Friendly, with good value food from sandwiches to steaks *(Mrs Poolman, W H Mecham)*; [nr pier], *Wagon & Horses*: Well kept real ale and good choice of well cooked and presented food *(J H C Peters)*

Lyndhurst [High St; SU2908], *Fox & Hounds*: Much modernised with lots of exposed brickwork, dried flowers in fireplaces, standing timbers dividing it into four areas, family room beyond former coach entry, Whitbreads-related real ales, usual bar food from ploughman's to steaks

(Ian Phillips)

Lyndhurst Road Station [A35 Southampton—Lyndhurst, on edge of Ashurst; SU3310], *New Forest*: Useful spacious family pub, big garden (terrace and lawn) with play area inc bouncing castle, some goats and other animals; Courage Directors, reasonable range of fairly priced food; children in conservatory area; nr big caravan park *(Nigel Pritchard)*

Marchwood [Beaulieu Rd; off A326 Southampton—Fawley at Twiggs La; SU3810], *Bold Forester*: Watneys Country Carvery restaurant, in quiet spot on border of New Forest; Watneys-related real ales, reliable food, darts, skittle alley and fruit machines *(Paul Corbett)*

☆ **Mattingley** [B3011 on Hazeley Heath; SU7459], *Shoulder of Mutton*: Popular pub well off beaten track, impeccable service, well kept Courage, good if not cheap food, pleasant atmosphere with quiet piped music; arrive early to get a table *(G and M Stewart)*

Meonstoke [SU6119], *Bucks Head*: Neat, middle-sized old pub in pleasant spot; warm and welcoming atmosphere, good value bar food *(E Manning)*

Milford on Sea [SZ2891], *Smugglers*: Nice smart pub, good food and drink *(Comus Elliott)*; *White Horse*: Friendly well kept pub *(Comus Elliott)*

Monxton [SU3144], *Black Swan*: Pretty pub in village of thatched rose-covered cottages; wide range of pub food from sandwiches or baked potatoes to steaks in big back extension, Whitbreads-related beers; tables in courtyard and garden with play area, barbecue and slow-flowing stream *(Ian Phillips)*

☆ **Mortimer West End** [off Aldermaston rd at Silchester sign; SU6363], *Red Lion*: Country pub with beams, panelling, timbers, stripped masonry, wide range of real ales though now tied to Badger, bar food inc lots of home-made pies, seats outside; changed hands 1990, reports on new regime not yet conclusive enough to confirm its former position as main entry *(Dr and Mrs R E S Tanner, LYM)*

☆ **Nether Wallop** [village signed from A30 or B2084 W of Stockbridge; SU3036], *Five Bells*: Simple village inn with good value food, well kept Marstons real ales on handpump inc Mild, long cushioned settles and good log fire in beamed bar, pictures of helicopter aerobatics, friendly licensee; bar billiards and other traditional games in locals' bar, small restaurant, seats outside, provision for children *(Philip and Trisha Ferris, Mrs Ann Sugden, Alan Skull, LYM)*

New Milton [SZ2495], *Speckled Trout*: Good lunchtime food, big car park *(R E Stratton)*

North Warnborough [nr M3 junction 5; SU7351], *Swan*: Interesting enjoyable atmosphere, good beer and bar food *(Patrick and Mary McDermott)*

Oakhanger [off A325 Farnham—Petersfield; SU7635], *Red Lion*: Friendly and comfortable, good food, clean lavatories *(Ian Phillips)*

☆ **Odiham** [Church Sq; SU7450], *Bell*: Lovely little welcoming local attractively placed in pretty square opp church and stocks; walls and ceiling festooned with bric-a-brac, good food in bar and restaurant, well kept Courage Best and Directors *(Ian Phillips)*

Odiham [High St (A287)], *George*: Well kept Courage Best and Directors and John Smiths and bar food in well furnished and civilised old-fashioned bar; pleasant staff; bedrooms *(E G Parish, LYM)*; [Colt Hill Wharf, signed off High St], *Water Witch*: Attractive-looking and comfortable pub, pleasant welcome but rather impersonal atmosphere; big garden leading to Odiham basin of Basingstoke Canal; gets very busy weekends and Bank Hols; bar food from sandwiches to steaks, Watneys-related real ales *(Patrick and Mary McDermott)*

☆ **Owslebury** [SU5123], *Ship*: The O'Neills, who in the last decade built a really firm following among readers across two continents for this friendly and unspoilt downland village pub, left in spring 1990 — they'll be much missed; it's got terrific views from the two peaceful garden areas, and has had well kept Marstons real ale and good value bar food, so we hope to hear that the new licensees are keeping up its fine traditions *(LYM — reports on the new regime please)*

☆ **Pennington** [Ridgeway Lane; marked dead end from A337 roundabout W of Lymington by White Hart; SZ3194], *Chequers*: Tucked-away yachtsmen's local, simple yet stylish — attractive pictures, plain chairs and pews, polished floorboards and quarry tiles; bar food, a real cut above the average, is served till 10 and changes daily depending on what's been bought fresh; five well kept real ales such as Flowers Original, Gales HSB and Wadworths 6X, well reproduced pop music, pub games, tables out in courtyard and neat garden; children in eating area; restaurant; open all day Sat *(Dr C S Shaw, John Mason, LYM — more news of this fine pub please)*

Pennington [Milford Rd; SZ3194], *White Hart*: Good country local with well kept Marstons Pedigree, bar food, friendly landlord, terrace and garden *(Comus Elliott)*

☆ **Petersfield** [College St; SU7423], *Good Intent*: Welcoming and spotlessly kept 16th-century beamed and timbered local, clean, comfortable and thickly carpeted throughout; probably best in winter, with log fires; well cooked and presented bar food, efficient service, cosy restaurant *(Paul and Margaret Baker, Phil and Sally Gorton)*

Portchester [White Hart Lane; SU6105], *Wicor Mill*: Welcoming licensees, pleasant locals, well kept Bass, particularly good value food; building itself not special *(Richard Houghton)*

Portsea [84 Queen St; SU6400], *George*: One-room nautical pub with pubby leather seats and panelling in front, more comfortably plush at back, with glass-topped well and piano; friendly staff, regulars and cats, well kept Flowers Original, Marstons Pedigree, Merrie Monk and Owd Roger on handpump, excellent fish dishes; handy for Naval Heritage Centre, open all day Thurs and Fri; bedrooms *(Matt Pringle)*

Portsmouth [Canber Dock; SU6501], *Bridge*: Included for its position on the busy quay of the old harbour, opposite Isle of Wight ferry and fishing-boat quay; done up

with pine tables and paving-slab floors, quite a good choice of help-yourself salads, baked potatoes and ploughman's, Marstons Pedigree *(Ian Phillips)*; [Bath Sq], *Coal Exchange*: Small unpretentious corner building with good harbour views, oak tables, log-effect gas fire, Whitbreads ales, friendly service; upstairs lounge *(Jacqueline Davis)*; [High St], *Dolphin*: Spacious and well run highly refurbished Whitbreads pub (with Wadworths 6X too), wide range of hot and cold food, video games *(E A George)*; [58 Cromwell Rd, Gastney], *Royal Marines Artillery*: Local with main public bar and small lounge; good mix of people, well kept Gales, country wines, good value lunchtime bar food, good service, Sun lunch in back restaurant *(N J Clark)*; [High St, Old Town], *Sally Port*: Big bar recently gutted and reopened with nautical theme; Whitbreads, related and other real ales, bar food; in street full of character, opp cathedral and nr HMS *Victory*, HMS *Warrior* and dockyard heritage centre; bedrooms *(Nigel Gibbs)*; [Bath Sq], *Still & West*: Included for marvellous position, with upstairs windows, terrace and new roof terrace seeming almost within touching distance of the boats and ships fighting the strong tides in the narrow harbour mouth; upstairs and downstairs bars recently done out in touristic nautical theme, family room, Gales ales *(J H Walker, Nigel Gibbs, Mayur Shah, LYM)*; [Copnor Rd], *Swan*: Spacious straightforward pub with warm welcome, well kept Bass, good, cheap food; small car park *(Richard Houghton)*; [London Rd, North End], *Tap*: Free house with eight changing well kept real ales, thriving lunchtime atmosphere, genuine service, good choice of bar food inc king-sized sandwiches *(Richard Houghton)*; [London Rd, North End], *Thatched House*: Welcoming old town-centre pub with relaxing atmosphere, lots of bric-a-brac, good service, well kept beer inc Whitbreads Pompey Royal *(Richard Houghton)*; [off Grand Parade, Old Town], *Wellington*: Friendly and popular little traditional pub with good mix of customers, well kept beer and ciders, bar food, juke box, limited street parking *(Colin Gooch, Andy and Jill Kassube)*

Purbrook [SU6707], *Hampshire Rose*: Wide choice of food and friendly, helpful service in roomy, comfortable surroundings *(F Haworth)*

☆ **Ringwood** [A31 W of town — OS Sheet 195 map reference 140050; SU1505], *Fish*: Friendly and comfortably modernised main-road Whitbreads pub with properly pubby atmosphere in clean, pleasant and restful bar with woodburning stove and open fire burning three-foot logs, plain eating area where children allowed, lawn by River Avon; good value straightforward freshly prepared food from sandwiches up, discreet fruit machines; a useful stop *(Ian Phillips, Nigel Williamson, LYM)*

Ringwood [The Furlong; behind Woolworths; SU1505], *Inn on the Furlong*: Tastefully refurbished mixing 17th-century brickwork and oak with 19th-century pine panelling; pleasant landlord and staff, particularly good real ale (Ringwood Brewery's only tied house), bar food *(R Houghton)*

☆ **Rockford** [OS Sheet 195 map reference 160081; SU1608], *Alice Lisle*: Cheerful open-plan bar with well kept Gales HSB, XXXXX and BBB, guest beers such as Ringwood Fortyniner and Wadworths 6X; bar food inc good salads, large and popular conservatory-style eating area, good service even when busy; log cabins, slides and so forth in garden; attractive position on green, on outskirts of New Forest *(Jon and Jacquie Payne, David Eversley, BB)*

☆ **Romsey** [Middlebridge St; SU3521], *Three Tuns*: Cosy olde-worlde pub, popular at lunchtime for good choice of modestly priced bar food; friendly and experienced staff, well kept Marstons Pedigree and Whitbreads-related real ales *(H W and A B Tuffill, Joan and John Calvert, WHBM, Chris Fluck)*

Romsey [Church St], *Abbey*: Good choice of food, efficient service, well kept Courage Best and Directors *(P Argent, R N Haygarth)*; [Station Rd], *Fleming Arms*: Friendly welcome in two spacious bars *(Patrick Godfrey)*; *Old House At Home*: Spotlessly clean pub with good value well served food *(Anon)*; [The Hundred], *Romsey*: Smart, bright, clean and up-to-date, with well kept range of beers, tasty food generously served *(Quentin Williamson)*

☆ **Sarisbury** [Sarisbury Green; 2 1/2 miles from M27 junction 8 — left on A27; SU5008], *Bat & Ball*: Well laid-out family pub, spaciously and comfortably modern, with settees, library chairs, solid country dining furniture, efficient bar and food service, Legoland playroom and outdoor play area, tables on sheltered back terrace; well kept Flowers Original and Whitbreads Pompey Royal on handpump, fruit machine, unobtrusive piped music; a Whitbreads Brewers Fayre pub, with afternoon teas too *(Keith Houlgate, BB)*

☆ **Selborne** [SU7433], *Queens*: Friendly if not brisk service, well kept Courage Best and Directors and limited choice of good, generous bar food in main bar (due for some refurbishment) and lounge bar with log fire or portable gas heater; children's area in garden, pleasant walks in picturesque countryside nearby; bedrooms good value, with decent breakfasts *(Eric Locker, Yvonne Warren, Tim and Ann Newell, A T Langton, LYM)*

Shawford [SU4624], *Bridge*: Good range of tasty food, Watneys-related real ales on handpump; good facilities for children *(Joan and John Calvert)*

Sherfield on Loddon [SU6857], *White Hart*: Long, low 17th-century inn, extensively refurbished but some relics of coaching days inc message rack over big inglenook fireplace and attractive bow window seat where ostlers and coachmen used to sit; wide choice of food (especially in the restaurant on the left), well kept Courage Best and Directors, big garden with play area *(Gordon and Daphne, LYM)*

Sopley [B3347 N of Christchurch; SZ1597], *Woolpack*: Local with rambling low-beamed bar, conservatory looking down on little stream, bridge across to play area; Whitbreads real ales, bottled foreign beers, bar food from sandwiches and baked potatoes to home-made curries, casseroles, pizzas and so forth, pub games, unobtrusive piped music; children in eating area and family room *(LYM)*

☆ **Southampton** [Oxford St; SU4212], *Grapes*: Roaring log fire, pianola played by dummy in tails, authentic Victorian prints and vases, small round tables with red-fringed tablecloths to the floor; well kept Flowers Original, quick, pleasant waitress service, good range of reasonably priced hot and cold food; live music some nights — not for sensitive ears; parking on nearby meters can be virtually impossible at lunchtime when pub is popular with local business people — busy evenings too *(Michael Bechley, Jim and Becky Bryson)*

Southampton [Commercial Rd], *Buds*: Spacious, modern pub well aimed at 18-35s, with cool grey and beige furnishings, unobtrusive piped music and wide range of bar food with emphasis on hamburgers *(Ian Phillips)*; [The Avenue], *Cowherd*: Long, low Toby Inn pleasantly set on common, well restyled to give numerous alcoves and rooms with individual decor, lots of Victorian photographs of Sunday-school outings and rustic scenes, carpets on polished boards, lots of fireplaces; simple bar food, Bass ales, efficient staff, restaurant, tables outside *(Ian Phillips)*; [45 St Mary St], *Masons Arms*: Small and friendly with Gales ales, good, basic bar food and live music from the landlord and his friends Sun lunchtimes *(Peter Adcock)*; [Town Quay, by Mayflower Park and IOW ferry terminal], *Royal Pier*: Lofty building with upper floor reached by spiral staircase; relaxed atmosphere, well kept Flowers, good range of reasonably priced bar food served by efficient waitresses; popular lunchtimes with businessmen, late evening takes on more the feel of a night club; sheltered sun-trap terrace, ample parking; children welcome *(Ian Phillips)*

☆ **Southsea** [Albert Rd; opp Kings Theatre; SZ6498], *Wine Vaults*: A real-ale drinkers' dream, with broadside of a dozen handpumps dispensing two new own brews and tantalising choice of other changing beers such as Boddingtons, Burts, Gales, Glenny Wychwood, Marstons Pedigree, Morlands Old Masters, Palmers Bitter and Tally Ho, Ringwood Fortyniner and Old Thumper; big bar with simple unpretentious decor, upstairs wine bar/restaurant serving very reasonably priced food from sandwiches up, with strong vegetarian/wholefood leanings *(Andy and Jill Kassube, Nigel Gibbs)*

Southsea [15 Eldon St], *Eldon Arms*: Ornately green-tiled large pub with adjoining restaurant serving lunchtime and evening meals with good choice at reasonable prices; good choice of wines, well kept Eldridge Pope beers and guests such as Palmers Bitter, darts and cricket teams; popular with Polytechnic students *(Nigel Gibbs)*; [The Parade], *Parade*: Tiled pub with polished wooden floors, panels with engraved glass, wood and marble tables, brass footrail and immaculate decor; Flowers, Wadworths 6X and Whitbreads Pompey Royal on handpump, good food; shame about the piped music *(A R Lord)*

Southwick [High St; SU6208], *Red Lion*:

Popular with businessmen and locals, with well kept Gales, good choice of home-made bar food, prompt courteous service *(R Houghton, D S Male)*

Sparsholt [SU4331], *Plough*: Consistently good lunchtime bar food, with weekend menu concentrating on quickly prepared dishes as they are so busy; well kept Flowers, good facilities for young children (popular with retired people too), plenty of outside tables *(Joan and John Calvert)*

☆ **St Mary Bourne** [SU4250], *Bourne Valley*: Pleasant, roomy pub with comfortable, airy bar, good seating and friendly bar staff; good range of standard bar food at moderate prices, good small restaurant, large wild garden at back and smaller one at side; can get busy lunchtime; well equipped bedrooms *(HNJ, PEJ)*

☆ **St Mary Bourne**, *Coronation Arms*: Friendly neatly kept village local with welcoming landlord, well kept Marstons real ale, usual pub food, set lunches on Sun — when there may be free cockles and mussels on the counter; handy for Test Way walks; clean lavatories; bedrooms *(Maureen Hobbs, Margaret Dyke, BB)*

Stockbridge [High St; SU3535], *Grosvenor*: Elegant old country-town hotel with big well kept garden behind, friendly bar service, decent bar food (we can't speak for the restaurant), piped music; bedrooms *(WHBM, John Baxter, BB)*

☆ **Stratfield Saye** [SU6861], *New Inn*: Remote, simple pub with very friendly bar staff, good range of changing real ales such as Adnams, Badger and Wadworths, good wholesome food — even bar snacks for children and dogs; big car park *(Richard Houghton, R E C Griffith)*

Stratfield Turgis [SU6960], *Wellington Arms*: Quiet, tastefully decorated bar; Badger ale and bar food inc good beef sandwiches *(Col G D Stafford)*

Stubbington [Stubbington Lane; SU5503], *Golden Bowler*: Well run local with Bass and Wadworths 6X on handpump, bar snacks and back restaurant, welcoming licensees, tables outside; on rainy days children allowed in small bar till 8; big car park *(Keith Houlgate)*

☆ **Stuckton** [village signposted S of Fordingbridge, by A338/B3078 junction; SU1613], *Three Lions*: Pub-restaurant with wide choice of interesting and unusual food, great service, good wines and well kept Halls Harvest, Ind Coope Burton and Wadworths 6X on handpump; now chiefly a restaurant rather than a pub, which is why we no longer include it as a main entry, but the neat and airy bar, with lots of fresh flowers, has a good choice of really enterprising though not cheap lunchtime snacks (not Mon); closed Sun evening and Mon in winter, maybe two weeks' summer hol *(C N Cairns, Hope Chenhalls, LYM)*

☆ **Swanwick** [Swanwick Lane (A3051); handy for M27 junction 9 — OS Sheet 196 map reference 515097; SU5109], *Elm Tree*: Old, much enlarged pub, Watneys-related real ales, wide range of good food (steak and kidney pie strongly recommended), quick friendly service; restaurant; children welcome *(J H Walker, R C Blatch, John and Christine Simpson)*

Sway [SZ2798], *Hare & Hounds*: Well spaced tables in comfortable and agreeable New Forest pub with real ales, decent food and service, big garden; very pretty in summer *(WHBM)*

☆ **Tangley** [SU3252], *Fox*: Small, smart pub with well kept Courage ale, extensive wine list, friendly licensees, quick service, wide choice of good home-cooked food in bar and pleasant restaurant — booking needed here *(P M Wray, HNJ, PEJ)*

Tangley [Tangley Bottom; towards the Chutes — OS Sheet 185 map reference 326528], *Cricketers Arms*: Extended village pub owned by MP for Romsey, with good cricketing prints and fine fireplace in stylishly simple small original bar, L-shaped extension bar with tiled fireplace, dark woodwork, colonial-style furnishings — cricketing theme here too; well kept Flowers Original and Whitbreads Strong Country on handpump, bar food inc a couple of hot dishes (not Thurs lunchtime), rustic seats outside *(LYM)*

☆ **Timsbury** [Michelmersh (A3057 towards Stockbridge); SU3423], *Bear & Ragged Staff*: Spacious country pub, formerly tenanted and a main entry, taken back into management by Whitbreads; as this edition goes to press it is being closed for extensive refurbishment, so we don't yet know what will become of its black-beamed bar with heavy elm tables and log fire; it's had tables in gardens front and back, with a play area, and been popular for bar food from sandwiches and help-yourself salads to steaks, with Whitbreads-related real ales *(H W and A B Tuffill, Roy McIsaac, Dr C S Shaw, Joan and John Calvert, W A Gardiner, LYM; news please)*

Totford [B3046 Basingstoke—Alresford; SU5738], *Woolpack*: Pleasant and interesting pub in attractive isolated spot, rambling comfortable bar with stripped brickwork and pitched ceiling, real ales such as Eldridge Pope Dorchester, bar food (not Sun or Mon), restaurant extension, skittle barn; bedrooms in nearby block, with own showers *(Philip and Trisha Ferris)*

☆ **Twyford** [SU4724], *Bugle*: Plenty of widely spaced tables in big U-shaped bar, lovely bustle of activity, very wide choice of food inc unusual dishes of the day, lots of different pancakes and omelettes; a good many wines by the glass; big car park *(Ian Phillips, Joan and John Calvert, Barbara M McHugh)*

☆ **Upham** [Shoe Lane — village signposted from B2177 (former A333) and from Winchester— Bishops Waltham downs rd; SU5320], *Brushmakers Arms*: Friendly and comfortably modernised L-shaped bar with dark red wall settles and other stools, good value home-cooked bar food, well kept Bass and a guest beer such as Morlands Old Masters on handpump, big woodburning stove, lots of ethnic brushes as decoration, tables in sheltered smallish garden, fruit machine *(John and Joan Calvert, BB)*

☆ **Upton Grey** [SU6948], *Hoddington Arms*: Good local to match its very upmarket village, good though not cheap food, well kept Courage Best and Directors; high marks for welcome and atmosphere *(H W and A B Tuffill, G and M Stewart, PLC)*

Walhampton [W edge of Lymington; SZ3395], *Waggon & Horses*: Good waterside pub with good range of beers and efficient service, even on busy Sat lunchtime; good value generous bar food (*A J Vere*)

☆ **Warnford** [A32; SU6223], *George & Falcon*: Popular, spacious and comfortable country pub with wide range of beers and extensive choice of good food (lasagne recommended) served generously and promptly by friendly staff; piped light classical music; big car park (*Colin Gooch, Alan and Sharron Todd*)

Warsash [Fleet End Rd — OS Sheet 196 map reference 509062; SU4906], *Jolly Farmer*: Friendly efficient staff, reasonably priced and generously served good bar food, comfortable restaurant; good-sized garden with adventure playground and barbecue, big car park (*N E Bushby, W Atkins, D Bushby*)

☆ **West Meon** [High St; SU6424], *Thomas Lord*: Attractive village local with strong cricketing influence and welcoming family atmosphere; well kept Flowers and Whitbreads, good simple range of generously served, tasty and modestly priced food inc delicious fish, helpful service (*M K C Wills, Dr and Mrs A K Clarke, Mr and Mrs D Barnes*)

West Wellow [nr M27 junction 2; A36 2 miles N of junction with A431; SU2919], *Red Rover*: Pleasant, welcoming pub, good choice of well cooked and presented bar food, range of beers (*K R Harris*)

☆ **Weyhill** [signposted off A303; SU3146], *Weyhill Fair*: Lively local popular for its Morrells and other well kept real ales on handpump, with weekly guest beers such as Batemans Mild tapped from the cask in the cellar, and for swiftly served good value straightforward food; spacious lounge with easy chairs around wood-burner, other solid furnishings, prints of stamp designs, old advertisements and poster for eponymous fair, pleasant atmosphere; smaller family room away from bar (*HEG, Michael and Alison Sandy, P M Wray, R Elliott, LYM*)

Wherwell [SU3941], *White Lion*: Cosy pub with good atmosphere, pleasant staff and tasty food at reasonable prices (*Anon*)

☆ **Whitsbury** [follow Rockbourne sign off A354 SW of Salisbury, turning left just before village; or head W off A338 at S end of Breamore, or in Upper Burgate; SU1219], *Cartwheel*: Pleasantly placed good country pub with horse-racing theme, wide choice of well prepared and generously served home-cooked food; good range of some half-dozen regularly changing beers in top condition; children allowed in restaurant when not in use; start GWG37 (*Richard Houghton, R H Inns, Roy McIsaac*)

☆ **Wickham** [Wickham Sq; SU5711], *Kings Head*: Interesting building with two main

bars, Gales ales and nearly 150 whiskies, warm atmosphere with pleasant log fire, friendly and helpful licensees, good range of bar food — not many tables, so get there early; further bar behind skittle alley; opens 4.45 evening (*Barry and Anne, J Clarke*)

Wickham [A32], *Roebuck*: Good food and beer (*Adrian Kelly*); [Station Rd], *White Lion*: Flock wallpaper, prize-winning floral decorations, Allied real ales, reasonably priced straightforward bar food; normally friendly and welcoming (*Mel and Phil Lloyd*)

Winchester [off 22 High St; down passage to right of Barclays Bank], *Bakers Arms*: Good bar snacks from sandwiches to chilli con carne in busy central pub (*S Corrigan*); [Wharf Hill], *Black Boy*: Wide range of real ales inc interesting guest beers, usual lunchtime bar food (may be limited weekends), good juke box (or occasional discos) making it lively in the evening; bays of button-back banquettes in main L-shaped bar, separate rustic barn bar open busy evenings, seats outside (*Alison Hayward, Nick Dowson, LYM*); [Southgate St], *Exchange*: Plain but comfortable, well organised for food from ploughman's to steaks, well kept Courage ales; open all day (*Matt Pringle*); *Jolly Farmer*: Smart, with emphasis on food but real ales too (*Dr and Mrs A K Clarke*); [Eastgate St], *Mash Tun*: Fairly unspoilt, with scrubbed tables, entertaining customers, pool table and particularly well kept beer (*Dr and Mrs A K Clarke*); [34 The Square], *Old Market*: Good food and drink promptly served in expensively refurbished Whitbreads corner pub with soft piped music; handy for cathedral (*Celia and David Watt, LYM*); [Alresford Rd (by Winchester exit from A31)], *Percy Hobbs*: Homely and warm with comfortable settles and chairs, well kept Flowers on handpump, good bar food including an authentic ploughman's and quiet, efficient service (*E G Parish*); [57 Stockbridge Rd], *Roebuck*: Comfortably furnished and attractive, with good service, Marstons real ales, food from sandwiches and ploughman's to steaks (*Philip and Trisha Ferris*); [Royal Oak Passage, off pedestrian part of High St], *Royal Oak*: Cheerful town pub included for its no-smoking cellar bar (not always open in the evenings), visually not special, but its massive 12th-century beams and even a Saxon wall give it some claim to be the country's oldest drinking spot; well kept Whitbreads-related real ales and maybe a guest such as Wadworths 6X, usual bar food (not winter evenings) (*Ian Phillips, T Nott, LYM*)

Wolverton [Towns End, off A339; SU5558], *George & Dragon*: Pleasant open-plan, low-beamed pub in open countryside; well prepared simple bar food, helpful staff, well kept beers (*Chris Fluck, J V Dadswell*)

Hereford & Worcester

Very rewarding for people who like good pubs, this area takes you through fine scenery to find often rewarding food in attractive surroundings. A good many recent new main entries include as this year's crop the Roebuck at Brimfield (by no means cheap, but really good food, about as home-made as you can get – even using honey from their own hives), the Feathers in Ledbury (the new owners have made the bedrooms delightful, and remodelled the bar most successfully; the only place we know where you cut out your own chunk of cheese for a ploughman's), the Olde Salutation in Weobley (keen young licensees – and one of the area's prettiest villages) and the Crown at Woolhope (very popular licensees, good food). Other pubs doing particularly well at the moment include the Little Pack Horse in Bewdley (probably the best of the Little chain), the relaxed Pandy at Dorstone (good home cooking), the historic Green Man at Fownhope (increasingly popular as a place to stay), the atmospheric and unspoilt Three Kings at Hanley Castle (they do bedrooms now), the friendly Kings Arms at Ombersley, the rather smart Ancient Camp in a lovely spot at Ruckhall Common (good food, good bedrooms), the Loughpool at Sellack (a particularly warm flow of recent reports on this fine food pub), the Rhydspence at Whitney on Wye (lovely atmosphere, very good food), the neat Sun down the road at Winforton, the busy Farriers Arms in Worcester (good value food) and the Anchor at Wyre Piddle (simple but really decent food, a lovely spot in summer). The Monkey House at Defford, unique as an unsigned utterly traditional cider house, has pleased a good few readers since finding its way into our pages, and the chatty little Huntsman at Kempsey is well worth knowing. We should note that there are new licensees at the pleasant and interesting Talbot at Knightwick (good reports still on its food, atmosphere and bedrooms), and at the fascinating old Fleece at Bretforton. Among the Lucky Dip pubs at the end of the chapter, the White Swan at Eardisland, Talbot in Leominster, Slip at Much Marcle and Bell at Pensax are currently showing particular promise; and the Coach & Horses at Weatheroak Hill is specially notable for its fine range of real ales. Beer prices in the area are rather below the national average – far below it at the Butchers Arms at Woolhope, Three Kings at Hanley Castle, New Inn at Pembridge (special praise for this Whitbreads pub, reversing the usual trend for pubs tied to the national chains to work out most expensive), and, particularly, the Green Man at Fownhope. The Three Kings also serves bargain main dishes at below our £3 target, and we found these price-busters at the Bretforton Fleece and Worcester Farriers Arms too.

BEWDLEY   SO7875   Map 4

Little Pack Horse ★

High Street; no nearby parking – best to park in main car park, cross A4117 Cleobury road, and keep walking on down narrowing High Street; can park in Lax Lane car park

The epitome of an old-fashioned traditional pub, this is probably the best of Mr O'Rourke's eccentric chain of 'Little' pubs. The small rooms have roughly plastered white walls, low beams, pews, red leatherette wall settles, and a mixed bag of tables on the red-tiled floor, and lots of old photographs and advertisements, clocks, wood-working tools, Indian clubs, a fireman's helmet, an old car horn, an incendiary bomb, and a wall-mounted wooden pig's mask that's used in the pub's idiosyncratic game of swinging a weighted string to knock a coin off its ear or snout; the atmosphere is chatty and relaxed. Good value bar food includes home-made soup (£1.25), large filled baked potatoes (£2.45), lasagne (£2.95), prawns (half-pint £2.95), omelettes or chilli con carne (£3.25), the hefty Desperate Dan pie (£3.95), and sirloin steak (£5.25). Well kept Ind Coope Burton and the good value strong Lumphammer ale that's brewed for the chain (even non-beer-drinkers seem to like it) on handpump, house wine, and well made coffee; woodburning stove; darts, dominoes, fruit machine and sweet box for children. Dogs allowed (one unfailing visitor is a good-natured Alsatian cross called Pepper). This quiet riverside town is full of attractive buildings. *(Recommended by Wayne Brindle, Jamie and Sarah Allan, Roger Taylor; more reports please)*

Free house   Licensee Peter D'Amery   Real ale   Meals and snacks (12–2, 6–10)
Children at the back of the rooms away from the bar   Open 11–3, 6–11

BISHOPS FROME   SO6648 Map 4

Green Dragon

Just off village centre, which is on B4214 Bromyard–Ledbury

The impressive range of well kept real ales in this heavily beamed old pub might include Bass, Caledonian 80/-, Courage Directors, Exmoor Best, Hook Norton and Old Hookey, Robinsons Old Tom, Theakstons Old Peculier, Timothy Taylors Bitter, Landlord and Ram Tam in winter, and Wadworths 6X. Generous helpings of good value basic bar food include sandwiches (from £1.20, steak £3.20), eight or nine starters (from around £1.30), ploughman's (£2), omelettes (from £2.50), hot dishes from good home-cooked pies such as gammon and apple (£3) through curries (£3.50) or steak and kidney (£3.55) to steaks (from £7). The main bar is simply furnished with pews, settles and wall benches on the polished flagstones or flooring tiles, and there's a good log fire in the big stone fireplace; a separate newer games bar has darts, dominoes, pool, cribbage, pinball and fruit machine; juke box. You can sit under apple trees on a small raised side lawn bordered by flowers. *(Recommended by Cliff and Karen Spooner, R P Taylor, Derek and Sylvia Stephenson, David and Eloise Smaylen, G T Rhys, W L Congreve, Roger Huggins, Tom McLean, Ewan McCall, PADEMLUC, Jason Caulkin, Gordon and Daphne, Alan and Audrey Chatting)*

Free house   Licensees John and Anna Maria Pinto   Real ale   Meals and snacks
Restaurant tel Munderfield (0885) 490607   Children welcome   Open 12–3, 5.30–11,
11–11 Sat; closed 25 Dec

BREDON   SO9236 Map 4

Fox & Hounds

4 1/2 miles from M5 junction 9; A438 to Northway, left at B4079, then in Bredon follow To-church-and-river signpost on right

This neatly thatched, modernised house has a spacious and comfortable main bar with swirly white-plastered walls, stripped timbers, maroon plush and wheelback chairs around attractive mahogany and cast-iron-framed tables, and elegant wall lamps. A smaller side bar has red leatherette wall seats, with more in its inglenook. Popular food includes home-made soup (£1.45), ploughman's (from £2.50), salads (from £2.95 for vegetarian quiche), braised faggots (£3.25), chicken curry (£3.95), smoked haddock and mushroom mornay (£4.25), steak and kidney pie (£4.50), daily specials and good puddings. Well kept Flowers IPA and Original and Marstons Pedigree on handpump; prompt friendly service; darts, shove-ha'penny, dominoes, fruit machine and piped music. Beside the pub with its colourful hanging baskets are picnic-table sets, some under Perspex, a barbecue and thatched

Wendy house. Dogs allowed – the pub has two terriers of its own. *(Recommended by A Triggs, Ms P Woodward, Richard Parr, Brian and Anna Marsden, Robert and Vicky Tod, M H Davis)*

Flowers (Whitbreads)   Licensee Michael Hardwick   Real ale   Meals and snacks (12–2, 7–10; not Sun evening)   Restaurant   Children welcome   Open 11–3, 6.30–11

BRETFORTON   SP0943 Map 4

Fleece ★ ★

B4035 E of Evesham: turn S off this road into village; pub is in centre square by church; there's a sizeable car park at one side of the church

This exceptional pub, wrapped in its time warp, has unique, original – and in some cases quite priceless – furniture that belonged to the family which owned this house for nearly 500 years until 1977, when it was bequeathed to the National Trust. A great oak dresser holds a 48-piece set of Stuart pewter, there's a fine grandfather clock, ancient kitchen chairs, curved high-backed settles, a rocking chair, and a rack of heavy pointed iron shafts, probably for spit roasting, in one of the huge inglenook fireplaces. Also, massive beams and exposed timbers, worn and crazed flagstones (scored with marks to keep out demons), and many more antiques such as a great cheese-press and set of cheese moulds, and a rare dough-proving table. The room with the pewter is no-smoking. In summer, when it gets very busy, they make the most of the extensive orchard, with seats on the goat-cropped grass that spreads around the beautifully restored thatched and timbered barn, among the fruit trees, and at the front by the stone pump-trough. There's also an adventure playground, a display of farm engines, barbecues, and maybe anything from Morris dancing, a vintage car rally or a sheep-shearing, spinning and weaving demonstration to the merriment of their Friday-to-Sunday festival on the first weekend in July, with up to 30 real ales, bands and pony-rides. In previous editions of the *Guide* this has had three stars, and we've been used to seeing virtually universal approval for that exceptional high rating from the many readers who make the expedition to come here. This last year, though enthusiasm for the building itself and contents is undimmed, there's been a significant undertone of concern that the atmosphere isn't always as perfect as it clearly should be in a three-star pub. So we would urge you as strongly as ever to make even a cross-country pilgrimage here if you want to see the finest, truly traditional old country pub in Britain; but after much deliberation we have concluded that two stars – still an exceptionally high rating – probably gives the truest current indication of the Fleece's overall style and atmosphere. Well kept Hook Norton Best, M & B Brew XI, Uley Pigs Ear and a changing guest beer on handpump; maybe farm ciders. Bar food includes sandwiches (from 90p), ploughman's (from £2.20), chilli con carne (£2.30), Gloucester sausages (£2.40), plaice (£2.80), steak and kidney pie (£3.10) and locally cured gammon (£4). Darts, dominoes, or shove-ha'penny. *(Recommended by Tony and Lynne Stark, Andy and Jill Kassube, Helen and Wal Burns, Lynne Sheridan, Bob West, Alison and Tony Godfrey, Joan Olivier, Michael and Alison Sandy, Mr and Mrs C Moncreiffe, D Godden, Cynth and Malc Pollard, A Triggs, Philip Orbell, N P Cox, J M M Hill, Barbara Wensworth, BKA, Chris Raisin, Graham Doyle, Mrs E M Thompson, H K Dyson, G and M Hollis, Pamela and Merlyn Horswell, Simon Ward, Steve Mitcheson, Anne Collins, Peter and Rose Flower, Laurence Manning, H W and A B Tuffill, Dennis Royles, M Rising, Graham and Glenis Watkins, Denis Mann, Nick Dowson, Alison Hayward, Alan Skull, Steve and Carolyn Harvey)*

Free house   Licensee Norman Griffiths   Real ale   Meals and snacks (not Mon evening)   Open 10–2.30, 6–11; winter morning opening 11

BRIMFIELD   SO5368 Map 4

Roebuck ⊘ ⇔

Village signposted just off A49 Shrewsbury–Leominster

Though most people eating here head for the cool modern elegance of the big-windowed side restaurant, the food is also noteworthy – though by no means cheap – in the quiet and traditional little back lounge bar with its dimpled copper-topped cask tables, decorative plates mounted over dark ply panelling and small open fire. It includes good soups (£1.75), starters or light snacks such as crab pot (£4.20), ploughman's with home-made organic bread and their own pickled walnuts, onions and cabbage or avocado gratin with nuts (£4.50) or scallops with a pretty salad of three contrasting types of lettuce, mange-tout, croutons, bacon strips and fresh dill (£5.50), and main dishes such as steak and kidney pie (£5.20), pigeon in red wine (£5.50), poussin – very lemony in parts, very rosemaryish in other parts (£7) and salmon baked in cream (£7.50); vegetables are good, they do children's helpings, Matilda the pet hen provides the eggs which they pickle, and they keep bees which they use in their home-made mustard and in their honey and lavender ice-cream (£3.25). You get an idea of the style of the place from the fact that they serve olives and friandises (good ones) before your bar meal comes. The pleasant staff may ask you rather too often whether you're enjoying your meal – but are so nice about it that it's easy to forgive them. The wine list is remarkably good, particularly strong on the better burgundy and rhône growers and éleveurs, and New World wines; chilled Ansells on handpump under light pressure; several malt whiskies, good coffee. A little panelled front snug leads through to a public bar with pool and darts; fruit machine, trivia, juke box, cribbage, dominoes and quoits. The bedrooms are a new departure this last year. Incidentally, there's a family connection with the Walnut Tree at Llandewi Skirrid. *(Recommended by Paul McPherson, Cynthia McDowall, D Mayall; more reports please)*

Free house   Licensees John and Carole Evans   Meals and snacks (not Sun, Mon or 25 and 26 Dec) ̄ No-smoking restaurant (closed 2 weeks Feb, 1 week Oct)   Children welcome (they will provide a highchair)   Open 11–3, 6–11   Bedrooms tel Brimfield (058 472) 230; £35B/£60B

CAREY   SO5631 Map 4

Cottage of Content 🅰 🛏

Village, and for most of the way pub itself, signposted from good road through Hoarwithy

Very quiet on a weekday lunchtime, this out-of-the-way and very pretty little inn has two attractive and comfortable bar rooms – connected by an alcove with an antique settle: dark beams, some timbering and panelling, rugs on the wooden floor, more antique settles, fresh flowers and plants, and an open coal-burning range. Consistently good bar food includes soup (£1.25), sandwiches (from £1), mussels in garlic butter (£2), ploughman's (from £2.50), and hot dishes such as a fine vegetable crumble or vegetable croquettes in apricot sauce (£3), lasagne (£3.25), plaice (£3.50), good home-made pies (£3.75), gammon (£4.50) and 10oz rump steak (£7.50); good breakfasts. Well kept Hook Norton Mild, Best and Old Hookey and Marstons Pedigree on handpump, with good farm ciders; darts, dominoes and cribbage. Tables on a back terrace look up to a steep expanse of lawn, and there are a couple more on the front terrace facing a little stream and the very quiet village lane. *(Recommended by Peter and Rose Flower, Patrick Freeman, Cliff and Karen Spooner, Col D G Stafford, John and Joan Wyatt, Mr and Mrs M Wall, Tony and Lynne Stark, M J Penford, Andrew Hudson, S J A Velate, David and Eloise Smaylen, John and Pat Smyth, Nick Dowson, Alison Hayward, Allan Slimming)*

Free house   Licensee M J Wainford   Real ale   Meals and snacks   ̄ Children welcome   Open 12–2.30, 7–11 (Fri and Sat summer evening opening 6)   Bedrooms tel Carey (043 270) 242; £27.50B/£38B

DEFFORD   SO9143 Map 4

Monkey House

Woodmancote; A4104 towards Upton – immediately after passing Oak public house on right, there's a small group of cottages, of which this is the last

A really traditional cider house quite unmarked by any inn-sign – it doesn't even have a bar. Beside the door, there's a hatch where very cheap Bulmer's Medium or

Special Dry cider, tapped from wooden barrels, is poured by jug into pottery mugs. In good weather, you stand outside the pretty black-and-white thatched cottage with the bull terrier and the hens and cockerels that wander in from an adjacent collection of caravans and sheds; they now have two horses called Murphy and Mandy. Or you can retreat to a small side outbuilding with a couple of plain tables, a settle and an open fire. They don't serve food (except crisps and nuts), but allow customers to bring their own. It's set back from the road behind a small garden with one or two fruit trees. The name came from a drunken customer some years ago who fell into bramble bushes and insisted he was attacked by monkeys. *(Recommended by Peter and Rose Flower, T Nott)*

Free house   Licensee Graham Collins   Open 11–2.30, 6–10.30 (11 Sat); closed Mon evening, Tues

DORSTONE   SO3141   Map 6

Pandy ✪

Pub signed off B4348 E of Hay-on-Wye

Built in 1185 for Richard de Brico's workers while they were building the church here, in atonement for his part in the murder of Thomas à Becket, this fine half-timbered building is Herefordshire's oldest inn. It's very much the focus for the village community, and the main room – on the right as you go in – has upright chairs on its broad worn flagstones and in its various alcoves, heavy beams in the ochre ceiling, stout timbers, a vast open fireplace with logs, and a friendly, relaxed atmosphere. Bar food varies every day, and in summer when they have enough customers to allow a wider choice than in winter, it's often inventive: sandwiches, ploughman's, soup such as watercress and onion (£1.25), smoked salmon mousse (£2.95), pie in the sky (£4.25), various fresh pasta dishes like cannelloni with ricotta and spinach (£4.50), home-smoked prawns or sole stuffed with crab and scallops, gammon with as many eggs as you want (£5.95), and guinea fowl in a red wine sauce or king prawns in garlic and white wine (£6.95); the big helpings make the prices good value. Very well kept Bass, Brains SA and a guest beer on handpump, most Scotch whiskies and all major Irish ones, and unlimited coffee. A games area with stripped stone walls and a big woodburning stove has pool, darts, shove-ha'penny, cribbage, dominoes, quoits, old-fashioned juke box, trivia and fruit machine; a side extension has been kept more or less in character. There are picnic-table sets and a play area in the neat side garden (which has a play area). The surrounding, partly wooded gentle hills are most attractive. *(Recommended by Mrs Joan Harris, Miss S Le Huray, Cliff and Karen Spooner, D Morris, Adrian Pitts, Patrick Freeman, David and Eloise Smaylen, Paul McPherson, Cdr J W Hackett, M E A Horler, Mr and Mrs P W Dryland, Mrs Nina Elliott)*

Free house   Licensees Chris and Margaret Burtonwood   Real ale   Meals and snacks Children welcome   Visiting Morris Dancers and ceilidh band in summer, other occasional live entertainment   Open 12–3 (4 Sat), 7–11; closed winter Tues lunchtime

DUNHAMPSTEAD   SO9160   Map 4

Firs

3 1/2 miles from M5 junction 6; A4538 towards Droitwich, first right signposted Offerton, Smite, then after Pear Tree first right signposted Oddingley, next left, next right signposted Dunhampstead, Trench Lane, then at T-junction right towards Sale Green; OS Sheet 150 map reference 919600

This is a lovely spot in summer with lots of hanging baskets, a pretty flower-filled terrace with white tables under cocktail parasols, and towpaths by the nearby Worcs & Birmingham Canal to stroll along. The two rooms of the relaxed bar – partly divided by timber uprights – have flowers on the cast-iron-framed tables, Victorian prints over the dark pink dado, and people reading newspapers or chatting by the bar; the inner part which leads through to a restaurant area has bentwood chairs (like the rest of the pub), and armchairs and settees around the open fire. Good bar food at average prices includes filled baked potatoes (£2.75), omelettes (from £3.85), lasagne (£2.50), steak and kidney pie (£4.35), steaks (£6.95), and interesting daily specials. Well kept Bass on handpump, piped piano music, fruit machine in a dark-panelled side area (and juke box, rarely used). Pleasant service; the dogs are called William (the doberman) and Oscar (less easily classified). *(Recommended by R E and L J Rosier, Barbara M McHugh, Doreen and Ray Whiteoak, Robert and Vicky Tod, Michael Thomson, Craig and Suzanne Everhart, Michael and Harriet Robinson)*

Free house   Licensees Mr and Mrs T S Forster   Real ale   Meals and snacks Restaurant tel Droitwich (0905) 774094   Well behaved children have been allowed Has been open 11.30–2.30, 6–11, closed 25 and 26 Dec

FOWNHOPE   SO5834 Map 4

Green Man 🛏

B4224

The quiet garden behind this striking black-and-white Tudor inn has robust benches and seats around slatted tables among the trees and flowerbeds of the big back lawn, where they serve coffee and afternoon tea in good weather; there's also a play area. Inside, the rather stately lounge has comfortable armchairs under its high oak beams, long cushioned settles agains the timbered ochre walls (which are hung with small pictures and brasses), seats set into tall latticed windows, and a big log fire. A second smaller but broadly similar bar is named after the judges who used this as their Petty Sessions court in the 18th and 19th centuries, and has darts and dominoes; piped music. Good value bar food in generous helpings includes sandwiches (from £1, toasties £2.30), soup (£1.20), ploughman's (£2.40), salads (from £2.75), local chicken (£2.80), lasagne (£3.40), home-made steak pie or trout with almonds (£4.25), rump steak (£6.25), puddings (£1.30) and children's menu (£2.25). Well kept and attractively priced Hook Norton Best, Marstons Pedigree and Sam Smiths OB on handpump, and local ciders. The residents' lounge is no-smoking. *(Recommended by Patrick Godfrey, Peter and Rose Flower, D I Baddeley, Cliff and Karen Spooner, Col D G Stafford, Helen and John Thompson, M J Penford, Mrs K J Betts, Paul McPherson, S J A Velate)*

Free house   Licensees Arthur and Margaret Williams   Real ale   Meals and snacks (till 10 evening)   Two restaurants   Children in eating area of bar   Open 11–2.30, 6–11 Bedrooms tel Fownhope (043 277) 243 – will probably change to (0432) 860243; £28B/£39.50B

HANLEY CASTLE   SO8442 Map 4

Three Kings

Pub signposted (not prominently) off B4211 opposite castle gates, N of Upton upon Severn

Combining a quaint black-and-white half-timbered cottage with another faced in Georgian brick, this pretty country pub has several atmospheric little rooms. On the right, there's a little tiled-floor tap room, separated off from the entrance corridor by the monumental built-in settle which faces its equally vast inglenook fireplace. The hatch here serves well kept and low-priced Butcombe Bitter, Theakstons Best and Wadworths 6X on handpump, and maybe farm cider. The left-hand room is decorated with lots of small locomotive pictures, has darts and cribbage, and opens into a pool room beyond. A separate entrance leads to the comfortable timbered lounge with little leatherette armchairs and spindleback chairs arounds its tables, another antique winged and high-backed settle, a neatly blacked kitchen range and an unchanging atmosphere. Good value home-cooked bar food includes soup, omelettes (from £1 to £1.75), toasted bacon sandwich (£1.25), ploughman's (from £1.50), good chicken en croûte with soft cheese, pork chop or gammon and egg (£3.25) and hefty steaks (from £5.25), with more challenging specials which may take half an hour or so to do. Bow windows in the three main rooms, and old-fashioned wood-and-iron seats on the front terrace, look across to the great cedar which shades the tiny green. *(Recommended by*

PADEMLUC, *Frank Gadbois, David Braisted, Derek and Sylvia Stephenson)*

Free house   Licensee Mrs Sheila Roberts   Real ale   Meals and snacks (not Sun evening)   Children in side room   Live music Sun evening, folk club alternate Thurs Open 11–2.30, 7–11   Bedrooms tel Upton upon Severn (068 46) 2686; £15B/£27.50

KEMPSEY   SO8548   Map 4

Huntsman

Green Street Village – signposted down Post Office Lane off A38 S of Worcester, in Kempsey; OS Sheet 150 map reference 869491

The two small rooms on the right in this well kept and unaffected village local have horse and games pictures on the plain swirly plaster walls, a small fire in the stone fireplace, well cushioned oak seats around attractive old waxed kitchen tables in window alcoves, hop bines over the small corner bar counter, and a chatty, cosy atmosphere; beyond is a dining area appropriately named the Rookery Nook. On the left a lower room has lots of little leatherette armchairs around its walls, and a trivia machine; there's a full-size skittle alley. Bar food includes sandwiches, ploughman's (from £2), gammon and egg (£4.95), chicken, leek and Stilton sauce (£5.95), and steaks (from £6.25); well kept Banks's or Donnington on handpump. Under cocktail parasols on the side lawn, there are rustic slabby benches and picnic-table sets; the calmly friendly great dane is called Sam. (*Recommended by PADEMLUC; more reports please*)

Free house   Licensees Neil Harris   Real ale   Meals and snacks (not Sun or Mon evenings)   Restaurant tel Worcester (0905) 820336   Children welcome   Open 12–3, 7–11; closed 25 Dec, evening 26 Dec

KIDDERMINSTER   SO8376   Map 4

Little Tumbling Sailor ⊘

42 Mill Lane; from Mill St, which is signposted off ring road by A442 Bridgnorth exit, fork right at General Hospital up narrow lane

New licensees have taken over this entertaining maritime pub. There's a particularly rich collection of naval photographs on the navy-blue walls of the bar with the relevant sailor's hat riband for each ship, masses of other ship pictures, ship's wheels and badges, nautical brassware, net-floats, hammocks, anchors, oars, a naughty figurehead, model ships and rope fancywork. The several rooms that radiate from the central servery have red and blue leatherette seats around cast-iron-framed tables. We hope they haven't changed the food, which is probably the most interesting in this small and idiosyncratic chain of 'Little' pubs. It includes seafood dishes such as smoked oysters with garlic mayonnaise (£1.75), Boatman pie (a huge fish pie), salmon steak (£3.95), and fresh fish of the day, as well as soup (£1.25), filled baked potatoes (£2.75), vegetarian lasagne (£2.95), curries (from £3.15), home-baked ham (£3.75), Desperate Dan pie (£3.95), rump steak (£5.25), and puddings like jam roly poly (£1.25). Well kept Ind Coope Burton and the chain's own Lumphammer on handpump, and house wine; fruit machine, trivia machine, and piped pop music. They sell their own pink seaside rock, key rings, printed T-shirts, and edited paper *The Lark*. The little sheltered garden has a trawler's deckhouse, wave-making machine, sand pit and even a substantial mock-up of a lighthouse for children. (*Recommended by Roger Taylor, Roy Bromell, Peter Scillitoe, E J Alcock; more reports please*)

Free house   Licensee John Baxter   Real ale   Meals and snacks (12–2, 6–10, not 25 Dec)   Children welcome   Music night Mon (from 50s and 60s to Folk and Irish) Open 11–3, 6–11; closed 25 Dec

KNIGHTWICK   SO7355   Map 4

Talbot ⊘ 🛏

Knightsford Bridge; B4197 just off A44 Worcester–Bromyard

Attractively placed by the old bridge over the River Teme, this quiet and pleasant

14th-century inn has a big rambling lounge with entertaining and rather distinguished coaching and sporting prints and paintings on its butter-coloured walls, a variety of interesting seats from small carved or leatherette armchairs to the winged settles by the tall bow windows, heavy beams, and a vast stove which squats in the big central stone hearth; there's another log fire, too – in cold weather it's best to get close to one or the other. The inventive food (the same as is served in the small restaurant) includes excellent carrot and coriander soup, filled rolls (from £1), fresh sardines or vegetarian kebabs (£1.95), pork and prune pâté or tagliatelle Italienne (£2.50), ploughman's (from £2.50), spinach and nut turnovers or lasagne (£3.50), liver and bacon (£3.95), good steak and kidney pie (£4.75), lamb noisettes with mint and yoghurt (£5.50), roast duck and peach gravy (£7.50), sirloin steak (£8.50), and puddings like sticky date or apple crumble (from £1.50); the fresh vegetables are well cooked. The well furnished back public bar has darts, dominoes, cribbage, pool on a raised side area, fruit machine, space game and juke box; well kept Bass and Flowers IPA on handpump – and, more cheaply, Banks's, though there may not be a visible label; polite, unassuming service. Well behaved dogs welcome. Some of the bedrooms, clean and spacious, are above the bar. There are some old-fashioned seats outside, in front, with more on a good-sized lawn over the lane (they serve out here too). This settlement is mentioned in the Domesday book. *(Recommended by Peter Burton, Robert and Vicky Tod, Nigel Gibbs, Dr M Owton, C M Whitehouse, T Nott, John Bowdler, Gwen and Peter Andrews, John Gillett, Mr and Mrs J M Elden, John Bowdler, John Gillett, C M Whitehouse, Jason Caulkin, Philip Riding, D S Fowles, PADEMLUC)*

Free house   Licensee J P P Clift   Real ale   Meals and snacks   Restaurant   Children welcome   Open 11–11; closed 25 Dec evening   Bedrooms tel Knightwick (0886) 21235; £20(£25B)/£35(£47.50B)

LEDBURY   SO7138 Map 4

Feathers 🢀

High Street; A417

The marvellous black and white timbering of this hotel dates mainly from 1521, though the top floor – you can see the differences if you look closely – was added later in Jacobean times. Inside, the spreading beamed and timbered Fuggles Bar is broken up into areas by attractive brick pillars, and has some blond squared panelling, pleasantly individual cloth banquettes built into bays, one or two old oak panelled settles, comfortable upholstered seats, and fresh flowers on a variety of solid tables; the atmosphere is relaxed and there are decorations such as 19th-century caricatures, fowl prints on the stripped brick chimney breast, hop bines draped liberally over the beams, some country antiques, and soft lighting from picture lamps, one or two tablelamps and old-fashioned wall lamps. Big curtained windows look over the rather narrow coachyard. There's also a more formal lounge by the reception area with high-sided armchairs and settees. Good bar food includes home-made soup (£1.80), starters which can also be eaten as a main course such as smoked duck breast or avocado and wood pigeon (£2.75), a traditional ploughman's with apple, pickles and freshly baked bread (you cut your own cheese from a whole one, £3.25), and main courses such as Arbroath smokies or scallops of pork with ham and cheese (£4.95), salmon in filo pastry (£6.50), and daily specials such as steak pie or lasagne (around £4.25). Bass, Felinfoel Double Dragon and M & B Brew XI and a guest beer, and afternoon teas; quick, efficient service. *(Recommended by John Bowdler, S J A Velate, D J Cooke, Ninka Sharland; more reports please)*

Mitchells & Butlers (Bass)   Licensee Manson Malcolm   Real ale   Meals and snacks (and afternoon teas)   Restaurant   Children welcome   Open 10.30–2.30, 5.30–11; closed evening 25 Dec   Bedrooms tel Ledbury (0531) 5266; £49.50B/£69.50B

OMBERSLEY   SO8463 Map 4

Crown & Sandys Arms ✆

Coming into the village from the A433, turn left at the roundabout, into the 'Dead End' road

Imaginative home-made daily specials in this pretty Dutch-gabled white house might include fresh seasonal fish, fresh curries, rabbit pie, oxtail and other casseroles, and at least two daily vegetarian dishes (from £3.85); other dishes include very good soups, (£1.10), sandwiches (from £1, toasties from £1.25), ploughman's (from £1.95), cold sugar-baked ham or quiche (£3.85), steak and kidney pie (£4.50), gammon (£5.25) and 10oz local sirloin steak (£7.75), with puddings like treacle tart, and children's dishes (£1.25). The black-beamed lounge bar has comfortable Windsor armchairs, antique settles, a couple of easy chairs and plush built-in wall seats on the partly flagstoned floor, old prints, maps and ornamental clocks (which are for sale) on its timbered walls, and log fires; no smoking at a couple of tables. Well kept Bass, Hook Norton Best and Old Hookey and a range of guest beers like Badger Tanglefoot, Ruddles County, Uley Old Spot and so forth on handpump, and decent wines; dominoes, cribbage. There are picnic-table sets in the garden behind the building. The antique shop and picture framer's in the back stables opens on Tuesday, Friday and Saturday. *(Recommended by Peter Burton, Roy McIsaac, Brian and Anna Marsden, Robert and Vicky Tod, Michel Hooper-Immins, J S Rutter, Barbara M McHugh, Alan and Marlene Radford, John Bowdler, Kenneth Krober, E J Alcock, John Baker, W C M Jones, PLC)*

Free house   Licensee R E Ransome   Real ale   Meals and snacks (12–2.30, 5.30–10 Mon–Sat; Sun evening start 6.30)   Restaurant   Well behaved children allowed until 8pm (no prams, push-chairs or carrycots)   Open 11.30–2.30, 5.30–11; closed 25 and 26 Dec   Bedrooms tel Worcester (0905) 620252; £16(£25B)/£40B

Kings Arms ✆

The rambling friendly rooms of this comfortable black-beamed and timbered Tudor pub have various nooks and crannies populated with stuffed animals and birds, and a collection of rustic bric-a-brac. One room has Charles II's coat of arms moulded into its decorated plaster ceiling; he's reputed to have been here in 1651. A wide choice of enterprising and regularly-changing home-made bar food includes sandwiches (from £1.25, weekday lunchtime), appetising home-made soup (£1.65 or very good fish soup with croûtons £1.95), home-made pâtés that include a vegetarian cream cheese and cashew nut one (£2.50), and main dishes like home-made steak and kidney pie (£4.25), broccoli and cauliflower mornay with walnuts or cold meats (£4.50), grilled gammon with egg and pineapple or fresh trout (£5.95), sirloin steak (£7.25), and quite a few excellent puddings such as the best lemon meringue pie one reader has had for a very long time, lovely ginger trifle and very good treacle tart (£1.75); specials might include delicious salmon and asparagus quiche with a fascinating salad, interesting bean, smoked haddock and prawn casserole or tasty turkey and leek pie (from £4.95). Well kept Bass on handpump; two good log fires (one in an inglenook); quick friendly service; no dogs. A pretty tree-sheltered courtyard has tables under cocktail parasols. *(Recommended by PLC, W C M Jones, A C Morrison, Frank Cummins, C M Whitehouse, Robert and Vicky Tod, Barbara M McHugh, Hilary Sargeant, Norman Clarke, PADEMLUC, Brian Jones, PLC, Mr and Mrs D M Norton)*

Mitchells & Butlers (Bass)   Licensees Chris and Judy Blundell   Real ale   Meals and snacks (12.15–2.15, 6–10 Mon–Sat, noon–10 Sun)   Children over 6 welcome up to 8.30pm   Open 11–3, 5.30–11

PEMBRIDGE   SO3958 Map 6

New Inn

Market Square; A44

Very old indeed, this inn has massive stones below the black and white timbered walls that date back some seven hundred years, and it used to house the Petty

Sessions court and jail. Elderly traditional furnishings include a fine antique curved-back settle on the worn flagstones, as well as aged oak peg-latch doors, and heavy beams, timbering, and a substantial log fire. Bar food served on old willow china plates includes sandwiches, deep-fried brie and cranberry sauce or avocado and crispy bacon (£2.75), stir-fried vegetables in a peanut dressing or chicken in cider (£3.50), steak in lager and whisky (£7.50), and puddings such as chocolate and mint roulade (£1.25). Flowers Original, Marstons Pedigree and Whitbreads West Country PA on handpump or tapped from the cask, and a few malt whiskies; darts, shove-ha'penny, dominoes and quoits. There are tables on the cobblestones between the pub and the open-sided 16th-century former wool market behind it. *(Recommended by B M McHugh, Brian and Anna Marsden, C M Whitehouse, Barbara M McHugh, Cliff and Karen Spooner, Brian Skelcher, R W Stanbury, PLC, M E A Horler)*

Whitbreads   Licensee Jane Melvin   Real ale   Meals and snacks   Evening restaurant   Children in eating area of bar   Open 11–3 (4 Sat), 6–11; 11–2.30, 6.30–11 in winter   Bedrooms tel Pembridge (054 47) 427; £14l£28

RUCKHALL COMMON   SO4539   Map 4

Ancient Camp ⊘ ⇐

Ruckhall signposted off A465 W of Hereford at Belmont Abbey; then pub signed, down narrow country lanes and finally a rough track

This quite remote but rather smart little country inn has a long front terrace right on the edge of the steep bluff with white tables and chairs among roses that look down on a picturesque rustic landscape with the River Wye curling gently through the foreground. The central beamed and flagstoned bar is simply but thoughtfully furnished with comfortably solid green-upholstered settles and library chairs around nice old elm tables. On the left, a green-carpeted room has a big Victorian architectural drawing of the imposing Ram Mills in Oldham (the family firm), a good few sailing pictures, matching sofas around the walls, and kitchen chairs around tripod tables. On the right, there are simple dining chairs around stripped kitchen tables on a brown carpet, and stripped stonework. The food, all home-made, is quite something, including sandwiches (from £1.35), soup (£1.50), ploughman's (from £2.75), taramasalata or good garlic mushrooms (£2.95), stuffed peppers (£4.25), Greek shepherd's pie (£4.95), cannelloni with ricotta cheese and spinach or with spicy meat filling (£4.95), steak baguette (£5.25) and pan fried garlic chicken (£5.75). On Sundays there's a cold buffet with original salads, and one hot dish such as pheasant casserole. Well kept Whitbreads West Country PA and Woods Parish on handpump, decent wines and spirits, kind service; good log fires, maybe unobtrusive piped music. When you set off for a walk, Jack the hunt terrier may come part of the way. *(Recommended by Denny Lyster, Peter and Rose Flower, John and Ann Prince, Jamie Lyons, Ruth Harrison, Maryon and David Beer, Fiona Hellowell, PLC, Paul McPherson, Allan Slimming, David and Eloise Smaylen)*

Free house   Licensees David and Nova Hague   Real ale   Meals and snacks (not Sun evening, not Mon)   Restaurant – closed Sun and Mon   Children in eating area of bar at lunchtime, in restaurant if over 8   Open 12–2.30, 6–11; closed Mon lunchtime (all day Mon Nov–Feb)   Bedrooms tel Golden Valley (0981) 250449; £30Sl£42.50S

SELLACK   SO5627   Map 4

Loughpool ★ ⊘

Back road Hoarwithy–Ross on Wye; OS Sheet 162 map reference 558268

In a lovely country setting, this attractive black-and-white timbered cottage is popular with readers for the friendly welcome and very good home-made food. This might include soup (£1.35), pâté (£1.95), Stilton pancake (£2.45), sausages (£2.75), nut roast with orange sauce (£3.75), good macaroni and leek cheese (£3.95), moussaka (£4), chicken curry (£4.25), chilli bean pork (£5.25), tasty beef in apricot and toasted almond sauce (£5.95), and stuffed trout with bacon, almonds and mushrooms (£6). The beamed and largely flagstoned main room has a log fire at each end, kitchen chairs and cushioned window seats around plain wooden tables, and sporting prints and bunches of dried flowers. Other rooms lead off, with attractive individual furnishings and nice touches like the dresser of patterned plates. Well kept Bass, M & B Springfield and Wye Valley Hereford on handpump. The neat front lawn has plenty of picnic-table sets. *(Recommended by PLC, Jacqueline Davis, Helen and Wal Burns, D L Evans, Caroline Wright, Cliff and Karen Spooner, Pamela and Merlyn Horswell, Mrs Joan Harris, Peter and Rose Flower, Audrey and Brian Green, I J McDowall, J Penford, Gwyneth and Salvo Spadaro-Dutturi, John Bowdler, S J A Velate, B Walton, David and Eloise Smaylen, P L Jackson, Paul McPherson, Allan Slimming, M A and C R Starling, Mrs Nina Elliott, Nick Dowson, Alison Hayward)*

Free house   Licensees Paul and Karen Whitford   Real ale   Meals and snacks   Restaurant tel Harewood End (098 987) 236   Children in restaurant   Open 12–2.30, 7–11

UPTON UPON SEVERN   SO8540 Map 4

Swan

Riverside

Civilised and comfortable, this Severn-side pub has beams, sofas, easy chairs, antique settles and Windsor chairs, and a big open fire at one end. From the side food bar, imaginative bar meals – reasonably priced considering the high quality – include haddock in a cream and cheese sauce (£3.50), home-made chicken, ham and mushroom pie or lasagne (£3.95), seafood gratinée or home-made steak, kidney and mushroom pie (£4.50), home-cured gravadlax (£5.25) and fresh salmon mayonnaise or medallions of fillet steak (£6.25). Well kept Bass, Butcombe and Wadworths 6X on handpump, and decent wines. There are tables on a waterside lawn (where the pub has its own moorings) across the quiet lane – with waitress service out here too. *(Recommended by EML, A Triggs, Gethin Lewis, A R Sayer, Mrs Nina Elliott, Paul McPherson)*

Free house   Licensees Peter and Sue Davies   Real ale   Meals (not Sun or Mon) Evening bistro, Tues–Sat   tel Upton upon Severn (068 46) 2601   Children over 12 Open 11.30–2.30, 6–11   Bedrooms planned

WEOBLEY   SO4052 Map 6

Olde Salutation

Village signposted from A4112 SW of Leominster; and from A44 NW of Hereford (there's also a good back road direct from Hereford – straight out past S side of racecourse

The best pub in this picture-book village, it looks straight down the broad village street – and has friendly licensees, and decent food and drink. The quiet lounge, its two areas separated by a few steps and standing timbers, has a couple of big cut-away cask seats, brocaded modern winged settles and smaller seats, a hop bine over the bar counter, wildlife decorations, and logs burning in a big stone fireplace; it's divided by more standing timbers from a neat restaurant area (where there's piped music), and there's a separate smaller parquet-floored public bar with sensibly placed darts, fruit machine, space game and juke box; dominoes and cribbage. Bar food includes soups such as cream of broccoli (£1.25), Cumberland sausage with cranberry sauce or chilli con carne (£3.50), lasagne (£3.70), smoked trout (£4), beef casserole or chicken curry (£4.25) and home-made fruit pies, with good specials such as prawn crêpinette (£4.50), mousseline of avocado and salmon (£4.75), pork with an interesting old-fashioned sage and raisin sauce (£7.50) and duck with cherry sauce (£10.50). The three-course Sunday lunch (£5.95) is a bargain. Well kept Hook Norton Best and Marstons Pedigree on handpump, Weston's ciders, and quite a good collection of whiskies. There are picnic-table sets under cocktail parasols on a sheltered back terrace. *(Recommended by J Harvey Hallam, Andrew and Valerie Dixon, Mrs B Warburton, Brian and Anna Marsden, G Richardson)*

Free house   Licensees Chris and Frances Anthony   Real ale   Meals and snacks (till 10

*in evening; not Sun evening or Mon lunchtime)　Restaurant　Children welcome
Open 11–3, 7–11; closed 25 Dec　Bedrooms tel (0544) 318443; £20B/£26(£36B),
4-poster £40B*

WHITNEY ON WYE　SO2747 Map 6

Rhydspence ★ ⊘ 🛏

Pub signposted off A438 about 1 1/2 miles W of Whitney

A popular new restaurant looks out over the new terrace and lawns of the tidied
up garden here, and across to the lovely Wye Valley and hills beyond. This is a
striking timbered building with a homely, friendly atmosphere and rambling
beamed rooms furnished with old library chairs and cushioned wall benches built
into the heavily timbered walls, and a fine big stone fireplace in the central bar;
magazines and newspapers are set out to read. Particularly good bar food which
changes every three months includes soup (£1.95), filled baked potatoes (£2.95),
ploughman's (from £3.10), home-made burger (£3.25), the Landlord's Favourites
('Hammy' or 'Fishy' from £3.25), spinach pie or Devon farm sausages such as pork
and garlic or venison and bacon (£4.25), beef curry (£4.65), steak and kidney pie
(£5.95), and specials like grilled sardines (£3.75) or Mediterranean prawns in
garlic and white wine (£4.50); the delicious puddings such as chocolate roulade,
Norwegian cream or Maron Mont Blanc are especially popular in the evenings and
on Sunday lunchtimes. There's also a pretty cottagey dining room; big breakfasts.
Well kept Marstons Pedigree and Robinsons Best on handpump, decent wines, ten
malt whiskies, and farm cider on handpump; darts, dominoes, shove-ha'penny and
cribbage; no dogs. Full marks for the get-you-home service for locals.
*(Recommended by Jacqueline Davis, Colin Laffan, Cliff and Karen Spooner, John Bowdler,
Robert and Kate Hodkinson, Tony and Lynne Stark, Helen and John Thompson, M J Penford,
Gary Phillips, Frank Cummins, P Miller, George Atkinson, P L Jackson, G and M
Brooke-Williams, Mrs E M Thompson, Ninka Sharland, John and Ruth Bell, Laurence
Manning, John Baker)*

*Free house　Licensees Peter and Pam Glover　Real ale　Meals and snacks
Restaurant　Children welcome　Open 11–2.30, 7–11　Bedrooms tel Clifford (049 73)
262; £23B/£46B*

WINFORTON　SO2947 Map 6

Sun

Popular with locals, this neatly kept, friendly pub has a central servery flanked by
two rather red-lit beamed areas. These have an individual assortment of
comfortable country-kitchen chairs, high-backed settles and good solid wooden
tables, two log-burning stoves, and heavy-horse harness, brasses and old farm tools
on the mainly stripped stone walls. Generous helpings of good, tasty bar food
include starters like watercress soup (£1.45), cajun chicken kebabs (£2.60) or
mousseline of pike (£4.15), and main courses such as good steak and Guinness pie
(£4.99), stuffed shoulder of lamb with a mint and orange sauce (£5.60), oxtail
braised in cider (£6.60), half a butter-roast Guinea fowl in port wine sauce (£7.35),
and poached salmon with a black bean sauce (£7.85); good vegetables. Well kept
Buckleys, Felinfoel, and Robinsons on handpump, and quite a few malt whiskies;
sensibly placed darts, cribbage, dominoes, and piped music. The neat garden, with
some sheltered tables, also has a good timbery play area. *(Recommended by Barry and
Anne, Cliff and Karen Spooner, Mrs Joan Harris, N W Kingsley, Mike Tucker, Frank
Cummins, PLC)*

*Free house　Licensees Brian and Wendy Hibbard　Real ale　Meals and snacks (not
Tues)　Children in eating area of bar　Open 11–3, 6.30–11.30; closed Tues*

WOOLHOPE　SO6136 Map 4

Butchers Arms 🛏

Signposted from B4224 in Fownhope; carry straight on past Woolhope village

Tucked away down a country lane through a gentle wood-rimmed valley, this 14th-century inn has welcoming twin bars, each with a big sedately ticking clock, log fire, simple but traditional furnishings, and some old pictures and engravings. Using good fresh ingredients, the bar food includes lunchtime sandwiches, home-made soup (£1.25), ploughman's (£2.25 – they do their own apple chutney and pickles), deep fried cod (£2.75), cheese, onion and herb quiche (£3.35), salads (from £3.75), tasty rabbit and bacon pie cooked in local cider or chicken curry (£4.25), gammon with pineapple (£4.95), local 10oz rump steak (£7.95) and puddings (£1.25). Well kept Hook Norton Best and Old Hookey and Marstons Pedigree on handpump, Weston's farm cider, decent coffee; generous breakfasts; friendly cat – dogs not welcome. Sliding French windows behind the tiled and timbered house lead out to a charming terrace by a tiny willow-lined brook. The bowl of fruit in the spotless bedrooms is a nice touch. *(Recommended by Jacqueline Davis, Patrick Freeman, F A Owens, Tony and Lynne Stark, EML, M and J Back, Simon Reynolds, Elisabeth Kemp, J and A Prince, Caroline and Colin, Helen and John Thompson, John and Ruth Bell, Paul McPherson, Kat Wilson, S J A Velate, Henry Midwinter, David and Eloise Smaylen, John and Helen Thompson, John Baker, Graham and Glenis Watkins, Mrs Nina Elliott, Pamela and Merlyn Horswell)*

Free house   Licensee Bill Griffiths   Real ale   Meals and snacks (11.30–2, 7–10) Restaurant (Wed–Sat evenings)   Children in restaurant   Open 11.30–2.30, 6–11 (winter evening opening 7)   Bedrooms tel Fownhope (043 277) 281; will change to (0432) 860281; £20.50/£33

Crown 🍺

In village centre

In their three years here the pleasant young licensees have notched up such a good local reputation for their straightforward but well prepared and faultlessly presented food that the pub starts filling with prospective diners well before 7. Bar food includes soup (£1.20), several starters or light snacks such as potted stilton or smoked mackerel fillet (£1.90), and a very wide choice of main dishes including plaice (£3.35), broccoli baked with noodles and cream or spinach and cheese quiche (£3.55), scampi, curry, seafood vol au vent or steak and kidney pie (£3.95), pork chop, gammon or trout (£4.95) and mixed grill (£6.80). Among the home-made puddings (£1.25) – which change every 8 weeks and are made by the landlady – creme brûlée, treacle sponge, chocolate marquise, lemon mousse, chocolate and Cointreau mousse, liqueur cheesecake and raspberry clo-clo, have each been recommended to us in recent months by different readers – an impressive list of favourites. The lounge bar is light and airy, with dark burgundy plush button-back built-in wall banquettes and stools, a timbered divider strung with hop bines, stripped pine dado, good wildlife photographs and little country pictures on the cream walls, and open fires; very quiet piped music. Well kept Hook Norton Best and Smiles Best on handpump, Weston's and maybe Stowford Press farm cider, decent wines; good service; picnic-table sets under cocktail parasols on the neat front lawn; darts, summer quoits (though it's difficult to imagine the bar being empty enough to use them). *(Recommended by Derek and Sylvia Stephenson, B H Stamp, O M Bisby, D G and J M Moore, Cliff and Karen Spooner, A S Maxted, Hilary Beggs, M J Penford)*

Free house   Licensees Neil and Sally Gordon   Real ale   Meals and snacks (till 10; not 25 Dec)   Bookings tel Fownhope (043 277) 468   Well behaved children allowed Open 12–2.30, 6.30–11; winter evening opening 7; closed evening 25 Dec

WORCESTER   SO8555   Map 4

Farriers Arms 🍺

Fish Street; off pedestrian High Street, just N of the cathedral

Handy for the cathedral, this welcoming, busy 17th-century pub has a snug little black-beamed lounge bar with some copper-topped tables and attractive old seats, supplies of the landlady's book on pressed flowers, and a grandfather clock carved with writhing lizards; piped music. The more rambling and simpler public bar has sensibly placed darts, shove-ha'penny, dominoes, cribbage, an old penny arcade machine (which works with 2p pieces), a fruit machine, and juke box. Tasty and decidedly well priced home-cooked food includes soup (£1), hummus with hot pitta bread (£1.40), ploughman's (£2), a vegetarian dish of the day (£2.25), lasagne or beef and mushroom pie (£2.75), honey-roast ham (£3.25), puddings like tipsy trifle (£1.25) or treacle tart flavoured with lemon and ginger (£1.45), and a daily special (from £2.75). The Courage Best and Directors on handpump is well kept. Dogs allowed. Tables on the sheltered terrace have their own summer servery. (*Recommended by Peter Burton, G T Rhys, C H Stride, Col G D Stafford, Klaus and Elizabeth Leist*)

Courage   Licensee Nona Pettersen   Real ale   Meals and snacks (11–9, with a half-hour gap between 2.30–3)   Open 10.30–11

WYRE PIDDLE   SO9647   Map 4

Anchor ⊗

B4084 NW of Evesham

A particular summer attraction of this relaxing 17th-century pub is the big lawn sloping steeply down to the River Avon and the barge moorings. The view beyond spreads over the Vale of Evesham as far as the Cotswolds, the

Malverns and Bredon Hill. An airy room with big wildfowl prints looks out on this, but in winter the snuggest place is the little lounge with a good log fire in its attractively restored inglenook fireplace, comfortably upholstered chairs and settles, and two beams in the shiny ceiling. Good value simple home-made food includes sandwiches (from £1.40), substantial soup (£1.20), an honest ploughman's (from £2.25), good West Country gammon with egg or pineapple, or whole fresh trout (£3.75), omelettes or locally smoked chicken with their own apricot chutney (£3.95), Scotch beef salad (£4.25) and steaks (from £6.35); puddings include good home-made meringue concoctions (£1.40) and lovely hot stuffed peaches (£1.60). Well kept Flowers IPA and Original on handpump; cheerful, efficient service; occasional unobtrusive Radio 2 or 4. (*Recommended by Rachel Waterhouse, John Bowdler, Frank Cummins, Dr and Mrs K J Lower, PADEMLUC, J C Proud, P Bramhall, Paul McPherson, PLC, GB*)

Whitbreads   Licensees G N and J Jordan   Real ale   Meals and snacks (not Sun evening)   River-view lunchtime restaurant tel Pershore (0386) 552799   Children in restaurant and eating area of bar   Open 11–2.30, 6–11

Lucky Dip

Besides the fully inspected pubs, you might like to try these Lucky Dips recommended to us and described by readers (if you do, please send us reports):

Abberley [SO7667], *Manor Arms*: Friendly place to stay, with comfortable and attractive bedrooms, decent breakfasts, food in bar and restaurant, Banks's beers (*NWN, Mr and Mrs W H Crowther*)

☆ **Abbey Dore** [SO3830], *Neville Arms*: Tastefully furnished old building with very Victorian extension; upmarket lounge bar, welcoming and enjoyable country bar, beautiful views of the Golden Valley, friendly landlord, well produced generous bar food, well kept Welsh beers and good coffee (*Caroline Wright, Canon K Wills*)

Ashton under Hill [Elmley Rd — OS Sheet 150 map reference 997378; SO9938], *Star*: Bar itself interesting, with decent food, simple home cooking generously served, welcomingly quiet music, Flowers and Marstons real ale (*P J Brooks, PADEMLUC*)

Astley [The Burf — E of B4196, S of Stourport; SO8167], *Hampstall*: Unique spot overlooking River Severn; big building

with cheap Davenports Mild and Bitter, good value bar food from double-decker sandwiches and filled baked potatoes to T-bone steaks; terrace and children's play area; car park big, but cars still queue to get in on summer weekends (*Pat and Malcolm Rudlin*)

☆ **Aston Crews** [B4222 — village signposted off A40 at Lea; SO6723], *Penny Farthing*: Good value food, especially baked potatoes with wide range of imaginative fillings, in series of modernised rooms with rather bright carpet, some stripped stonework, easy chairs around low dimpled copper tables, one table formed from glass-topped floodlit deep well, and more orthodox dining tables; well kept Bass and Hook Norton Old Hookey on handpump, matter-of-fact service, rather muffled piped pop music; airy big-windowed restaurant, pretty valley views from garden tables, even better views from comfortable bedrooms; children in top bar *(P L Jackson, John Miles, BB)*

Aston Crews [off B4222; village signed off A40 at Lea; SO6723], *White Hart*: Hilltop village pub with easy chairs among other seats in low-beamed sloping bar dominated by huge fireplace, other rooms leading off; Banks's and Wadworths 6X on handpump, bar food, pub games, tables in attractive surroundings outside *(LYM)*

Badsey [2 miles E of Evesham on B4035; SP0743], *Round of Gras*: Though not all readers welcome the extension and refurbishment, the longer flagstoned and comfortably pink-furnished bar and dining area give more space for the good bargain asparagus suppers (in season); other food home-cooked too; friendly and efficient service, Flowers real ale, fruit machines, maybe pop music; no dogs now *(Robert and Vicky Tod, Dr and Mrs G J Sutton, Steve Mitcheson, Anne Collins, BB)*

Baughton [SO8741], *Gay Dog*: Well furnished free house with friendly atmosphere; two comfortable bedrooms — good value *(T G Saul)*

Beckford [SO9735], *Beckford*: Good welcome, well kept beer and good bar food *(L D Cartwright)*

Belbroughton [High St (off A491); SO9277], *Queens*: Interesting and comfortable pub in lovely village; busy at lunchtimes, with appetising food, well kept Marstons and friendly staff *(Dave Braisted, Robert and Vicky Tod)*

☆ **Berrow** [A438 Tewkesbury—Ledbury just E of junction with B4208; SO7934], *Duke of York*: Friendly dining pub, older than it looks from outside, with two connected bar areas and a small back restaurant, Flowers real ales, popular good value food especially Wed to Sun, from pâté through good salads to Severn salmon and fine steaks, with good fresh vegetables; attentive licensees, log fire in winter and big summer lawn *(G and M Hollis, H B Walton, BB)*

Bewdley [50 Wyre Hill (off A456); SO7875], *Black Boy*: Immaculately kept, comfortable, quiet and welcoming, with limited bar food and impressive militaria *(PADEMLUC, Brian Skelcher)*; [B4194 2 1/2 miles NW; SO7477], *Buttonoak*: Good helpings of home-made bar food inc bargain Sun lunch under newish licensees, in two linked rooms, one with small stove in inglenook; well kept Banks's Bitter and Mild on electric pump, decent wine, fruit machine; service hatch to garden with good sized lawn, flowerbeds and picnic tables *(Frank Cummins)*

Birtsmorton [off B4208; SO7935], *Farmers Arms*: Attractive black-and-white timbered village pub with outside skittles pitch, delightfully low beams at one end; decidedly a local *(Roger Huggins, Tom McLean, Ewan McCall, BB)*

☆ **Bishops Frome** [B4214; SO6648], *Chase*: Attractively decorated bar, warm welcome, well kept Hook Norton, limited range of good home-made bar food inc good steaks, restaurant; seats on terrace and in garden;

children welcome; three comfortable bedrooms *(PLC)*

Bliss Gate [signposted off A456 about 3 miles W of Bewdley; SO7572], *Bliss Gate*: Good village local, with fine choice of a couple of dozen malt whiskies, Marstons beers, tiled-floor public bar with darts and fruit machine, simple lounge; play area in back garden; no food, at least as we go to press *(Anon)*

Bodenham [just off A417 at Bodenham turn-off, about 6 miles S of Leominster; SO5351], *Englands Gate*: Well kept Davenports on handpump, good variety of bar food at reasonable prices *(J H C Peters)*

☆ **Bournheath** [Dodford Rd — OS Sheet 139 map reference 935735; SO9474], *Gate*: Attractive and very popular food pub — good value in bar and restaurant, with good range of beer and friendly service; some Louisiana specialities; can get very busy, especially in summer *(Brian Jones, Dave Braisted)*

Bradley Green [B4090 E of Droitwich; SP9862], *M A D O'Rourkes Kipper Factory*: One of the latest — and biggest — in this chain, with a fishing boat and double-decker bus outside *(Dave Braisted)*: [SP9862], *Red Lion*: Pleasant staff, good food at reasonable prices and big car park; handy for NT Hanbury Hall *(Denzil Taylor)*

Bransford [SO7852], *Bear & Ragged Staff*: Popular dining pub with pleasantly decorated series of rooms, with open fire, friendly licensees, well kept Flowers on handpump; restaurant *(EML)*

Bretforton [Main St; SP0943], *Victoria Arms*: Clean and well laid out pub with friendly atmosphere, good pool table and pleasant back garden *(Steve Mitcheson, Anne Collins)*

☆ **Broadway** [Main St (A44); SP0937], *Lygon Arms*: Stately Cotswold hotel, owned by the Savoy group, well worth visiting for the strikingly handsome building itself, with interesting old rooms rambling away from the attractive if pricey oak-panelled bar; sandwiches available all day, and in adjoining Goblets wine bar food is imaginative; tables in prettily planted courtyard, well kept gardens; children allowed away from bar; bedrooms smart and comfortable; open all day in summer *(Laurence Manning, Ms P Woodward, A Triggs, LYM)*

Broadway, *Horse & Hound*: Spacious old Cotswold pub with comfortable armchairs and quiet, modern piped music in lounge; good-sized public bars, pleasant helpful staff, Flowers IPA and Original, varied choice of good bar food from ploughman's to steaks, courteous service *(MR Williamson, Mr and Mrs W W Matthews)*; [Main St (A44)], *Swan*: Attractive pub — part of a Beefeater Steakhouse — at end of long, busy main street, with pleasant staff and real ales *(Alastair Campbell)*

☆ **Broughton Hackett** [A422 Worcester—Alcester — OS Sheet 150 map reference 923543; SO9254], *March Hare*: Well cushioned stripped pews, country-kitchen chairs and tables, wing armchair, and rugs on tiled floor, glass-covered deep floodlit well; notably good bar food inc some unusual dishes such as the combination of taramasalata, hummus, tsatsiki and pitta bread, well kept Flowers Original, Hook Norton Best and Ruddles County on handpump, good wines by the glass; good public bar with games inc pool, big steak restaurant (not Sun evening), tables in garden with corner water feature, more with assault climber by car park; pleasant businesslike service, immaculate lavatories, provision for children *(EML, Norman Clarke, Hilary Sargeant, H R Bevan)*

Chaddesley Corbett [off A448 Bromsgrove—Kidderminster; SO8973], *Swan*: Well kept Bathams Bitter *(Dave Braisted)*; [OS Sheet 139 map reference 892736], *Talbot*: Decent bar food inc good fish pie and ham with parsley sauce *(Brian and Genie Smart)*

Childswickham [signed off A44 and A46 W of Broadway; SP0738], *Childswickham*: Pleasant pub, Whitbreads ales, separate dining room *(Dave Braisted)*

☆ **Claines** [3 miles from M5 junction 6; A449 towards Ombersley, then leave dual carriageway at second exit for Worcester; village signposted from here, and park in Cornmeadow Lane; SO8558], *Mug House*: Ancient pub actually inside the country churchyard, decidedly plain and simple decor, low doorways, heavy oak beams, well kept cheap Banks's Bitter and Mild, minimal choice of basic but generous snacks (not Sun), sizeable garden merging into farmland with view of the Malvern Hills; children allowed in snug away from servery *(E J Alcock, PADEMLUC, LYM)*

Clifford [B4350 N of Hay-on-Wye; SO2445], *Castlefield*: Delightfully peaceful traditional country pub in lovely countryside overlooking River Wye and close to the Black Mountains; good reasonably priced food inc summer cold table with interesting salads; back orchard with caravan facilities *(Mrs B Warburton)*

Clifton upon Teme [SO7162], *Red Lion*: Clean and civilised old pub in attractive village; lounge with central fireplace, separate public bar, pleasant service; lovely beamed bedrooms *(Gordon and Daphne)*

Clows Top [Tenbury Rd (A456); SO7172], *Colliers Arms*: Tastefully modernised dining pub with open fire, Ansells beer, good food inc excellent dish of the day, pleasant service *(G and M Hollis)*

Colwall [SO7342], *Crown*: Cottagey pub, with attractive frontage and hanging baskets; welcoming atmosphere, bar food, restaurant *(E G Parish)*; *Horse & Jockey*: Tasty Ansells, good, plain sandwiches and clean lavatories *(D J Cooke)*

☆ **Conderton** [southern slope of Bredon Hill — OS Sheet 150 map reference 960370; SO9637], *Yew Tree*: Relaxing and unspoilt pub with stone floors, beams and so forth, well kept Marstons Pedigree and Weston's farm cider on handpump, bar food *(Derek and Sylvia Stephenson)*

Cradley [A4103 3 miles W of Gt Malvern; SO7347], *Red Lion*: Cosy, oak-beamed old pub doing well under current regime, with generous helpings of good value food inc children's dishes, cheerful service, well kept Banks's, Courage Directors, Ind Coope and John Smiths, and beautifully kept garden; big car park *(Tom Rhys)*

Craswall [about 6 miles S of Hay on Wye — OS Sheet 161 map reference 278360; SO2736], *Bulls Head*: Old and remote, with many original features inc beams, stone floors, original 19th-century prints; Flowers and Greenalls served through hole in the wall, sandwiches and ploughman's *(Salvo and Gwyneth Spadaro-Dutturi)*

Crowle [SO9256], *Old Chequers*: Considerably enlarged and refurbished, so less cosy, but undeniably comfortable, and popular (though not cheap) for consistently good food inc imaginative specials, with friendly staff and super-efficient service *(Norman Clarke and Hilary Sargeant, Mrs V A Middlebrook, PADEMLUC)*

☆ **Cutnall Green** [SO8768], *Live & Let Live*: Simple, small and narrow, with wide range of good reasonably priced home-made food (even frozen take-aways); the Shed in the pretty garden can be booked for parties *(NWN, R E and L J Rosier)*;

Cutnall Green *New Inn*: Atmosphere cheerful and friendly, very pleasant landlord and staff, well kept Marstons Burton, popular freshly produced bar food *(John Baker)*

Defford [SO9143], *Defford Arms*: Well kept Davenports, interesting choice of food in friendly and pleasant extended pub; spacious, interesting garden *(Derek and Sylvia Stephenson)*

Drakes Broughton [A44 Pershore—Worcester; SO9248], *Plough & Harrow*: Friendly and attractive rambling lounge, well kept Flowers, wide range of food inc good salads and Sun lunch; lovely garden; open all day *(Richard Parr)*

Droitwich [Rashwood Hill; A38 1/2 mile W of M5 junction 5; SO9063], *Robin Hood*: Useful for generous helpings of reasonably priced food inc good cold meat platter and home-made steak and kidney pie, well kept M&B beers *(Mr and Mrs I M Howden, M B P Carpenter)*

Dunley [A451 S of Stourport; SO7969], *Dog*: Helpful licensee and staff, good reasonably priced bar food running up to venison pie, mixed grill and T-bone steaks; garden, bowling green, big car park, but keg beer; bedrooms *(Pat and Malcolm Rudlin)*

☆ **Eardisland** [A44; SO4258], *White Swan*: Delightful pub in picturesque black and white village, with pleasant atmosphere, old oak beams, gleaming copper, good winter log fires, magazines and books to read; cosy dining room, good value food (not Tues) inc wonderful home-made steak pie, fine veg, excellent puddings — no bookings, get there early; well kept Marstons Pedigree, good garden behind with retired tractor for children to play on *(James and Marion Seeley,*

Mrs B Warburton, Ian Phillips, H H Richards, Cliff and Karen Spooner)

☆ **Elmley Castle** [village signposted off A44 and A435, not far from Evesham; SO9841], *Queen Elizabeth*: Ancient rambling locals' local, in pretty and old-fashioned village below Bredon Hill; attractive old-fashioned tap room, haphazard medley of periods in decoration and furnishings, friendly licensee and locals, well kept Marstons real ales, piped classical music *(A L Willey, Derek and Sylvia Stephenson, Chris Raisin, LYM)*

Elmley Castle [Mill Lane], *Old Mill*: Former mill house in pleasant millpond surroundings just outside the village, with good range of bar food, good service and well kept Hook Norton Best and Old Hookey and Marstons Pedigree on handpump; neat L-shaped lounge, children allowed in eating area; tables on well kept lawn looking over village cricket pitch to Bredon Hill *(Dr J M Jackson, Derek and Sylvia Stephenson, LYM)*

Elsdon [SO3254], *Bird in Bush*: Well kept McEwans 80/- and sandwiches crammed with well cooked, tender meat *(Mr and Mrs M D Jones)*

Fladbury [Chequers Lane — OS Sheet 150 map reference 996461; SO9946], *Chequers*: Popular but not overcrowded pub, pleasant and comfortable; friendly and helpful staff, well kept Banks's Bitter, good bar food inc sandwiches; big car park, newish bedroom extension in former stable/kitchen block *(Andrew Cooke, PADEMLUC)*

Fownhope [SO5834], *Ferry & Forge*: Basic village pub with friendly landlord; well kept real ales inc local rarities *(John Baker)*

Frith Common [SO6969], *Paul Pry*: Pleasant trip down narrow lanes; free house with Banks's, Courage and Websters, bar food *(Dave Braisted)*

Goodrich [SO5719], *Hostelrie*: Village pub upgraded to small hotel with unusual turreted Gothic extension, but keeping the bar; pleasant friendly service, generous helpings of bar food, garden; nr Goodrich Castle and Wye Valley Walk *(Neil and Anita Christopher)*

Grafton [A49 2 miles S of Hereford; SO5038], *Grafton*: Nicely decorated bars, pleasant staff, above-average food *(G B Pugh)*

Great Malvern [outskirts, by junction B4211 to Rhydd Green with B4208 to Malvern Wells Showground; SO7845], *Bluebell*: Marstons pub set back from road with low beamed bar divided into lounge and public areas; prompt service, Marstons beers on handpump, and generous helpings of food promptly served on hot plates; tables outside *(M and J Back)*

Greet [Evesham Rd; B4078 N of Winchcombe; SP0230], *Harvest Home*: Friendly Whitbreads village pub with good choice of good pub food in big dining area, quick service *(A H Denman)*

Hanbury [SO9663], *Gate Hangs Well*: Busy, comfortable and very popular; warm welcome and good bar food at prices that can be ridiculously low — eg bargain rump

steak *(R E and L J Rosier)*

Harewood End [A49 Hereford—Ross; SO5327], *Harewood End*: Warm welcome, good bar food inc fine steak and kidney pie, quick service in modernised country pub *(Dawn Ross, S J Willmot)*

Hereford, *Bowling Green*: Black and white pub with well kept Marstons Pedigree, friendly staff, classy music; outside tables; bowling green *(Gwyneth and Salvo Spadaro-Dutturi)*; [Commercial Rd], *Hop Pole*: Very busy city centre pub with good bar and restaurant food at reasonable prices *(S J Willmot)*; [Bridge St/King St], *Orange Tree*: Reopened after tasteful refurbishment retaining some old panelling; promising start *(Cdr John Hackett)*

☆ **Hoarwithy** [signposted off A49 Hereford—Ross on Wye; SO5429], *New Harp*: Friendly and well kept, not pretentious, in attractive village below unusual Italianate church close to River Wye; nice bow-window seats, little country pictures on plain white walls, area around corner with pool, darts and fruit machine; good simple food at attractive prices from bacon and mushroom bap through good home-cooked ham to steaks, well kept Flowers Original and Whitbreads Castle Eden on handpump, picnic-table sets on yew-sheltered lawn beside pretty flower garden; children welcome; bedrooms good value, in cottage across road *(S J A Velate, Caroline Wright, R P Taylor, E A George, BB)*

☆ **Inkberrow** [A422 Worcester—Alcester; set well back — OS Sheet 150 map reference 015573; SP0157], *Old Bull*: Handsome black and white Tudor pub with big inglenook log fire, flagstones, oak beams and trusses, and some old-fashioned high-backed settles among the predominantly more modern furnishings; the model for the Archers' Bull in Ambridge; Whitbreads-related real ales and a guest such as Marstons Pedigree on handpump, bar lunches from sandwiches and ploughman's to gammon and egg, prawn stir-fry and so forth; seats outside; children allowed in eating area; open all day summer, with afternoon tea *(H K Dyson, PADEMLUC, Barbara M McHugh, A Triggs, Frank Cummins, LYM)*

☆ **Kidderminster** [Comberton Hill, in stn; SO8376], *King & Castle*: Good value food from wide menu, half a dozen well kept changing real ales, and railway memorabilia; what with its location by the Severn Valley Steam Railway, has very much the atmosphere of a 1920s station bar — a clean one *(Mrs P Lawrence, SJP, Richard Sanders)*

Kingsland [SO4561], *Angel*: Old, beamed pub with inglenook fireplace, pleasant chairs, settles and tables, soft piped music and delightful atmosphere; standard bar food served generously with good daily specials and puddings; restaurant *(Mrs Colbatch Clark, B H Stamp)*

☆ **Kington** [Church Rd (A44); note this is the Herefs one, handy for Hergest Croft Garden, Hergest Ridge and Offa's Dyke

Path, at SO3057], *Swan*: Border town inn with ceiling fans in attractively redesigned airy bar overlooking square and main street; efficient and welcoming service, good value food (inc well filled toasted sandwiches and excellent ploughman's), well kept Ansells and Tetleys, good evening restaurant; children welcome; at start of GWG93; bedrooms clean and simple, with good breakfasts *(Alison and Tony Godfrey, Neil and Anita Christopher)*

Kington [Victoria Rd], *Olde Tavern*: In a 1900 time-warp — plain parlour with ochre walls and ceiling, dark brown woodwork, commemorative china, no counter — beer brought from fine bank of handpumps in back stillroom *(Tim Locke)*; [Church Rd], *Royal Oak*: Several bars, friendly landlord, well kept Marstons ales, bar food and restaurant; seats in front and in back garden, camping available; bedrooms *(Tim Thomas, Alison and Tony Godfrey)*

Kinnersley [Letton rd (off A4112 Hay—Leominster — OS Sheet 148 map reference 341487; SO3449], *Kinnersley Arms*: Pleasant country local with lounge (no dogs) and public bar (dogs and boots welcome); well kept Bass on handpump, varied bar food, small restaurant, games room; friendly, sleepy black and white cat; tables in big garden; bedrooms *(Frank Cummins, Brian and Anna Marsden)*

Ledbury [New St; SO7138], *Olde Talbot*: Modernised ancient building with quietly friendly atmosphere under newish licensees, no juke box, real fire, well kept beer and cider, good bar food; said to be haunted by a benign poltergeist; bedrooms *(J H C Peters, LYM)*

☆ Leominster [West St; SO4959], *Talbot*: Attractive hotel with carpeted and polished wood floors, heavy oak beams and gleaming copper everywhere, and delightful entrance bar — bay windows either side, armchairs, stools and settles (one impressively carved), and log fires in carved fireplaces; bedrooms *(David Wallington, S J A Velate)*

Leominster, *Barons Court*: Good views from public and lounge bars and from tables outside; cheap beers, good food and cheerful licensee *(A L Willey)*; [Broad St], *Grape Vaults*: Warm, clean and cheerful atmosphere in imaginatively refurbished old pub — two roaring fires, gleaming brass and copperware, and interesting three-sided back bar cleverly decorated with old nick-nacks; agreeable staff, lunchtime bar food *(Ninka Sharland)*; [South St], *Royal Oak*: Rambling coaching inn with good home-made food and real ales such as Woods; bedrooms *(John Baker)*

Lingen [OS Sheet 149 map reference 367670; SO3767], *Royal George*: Spacious and interesting, with varied choice of good reasonably priced food, Three Tuns and Woods real ales, Weston's farm cider; big garden with yew tree, tables and open views *(Tim Thomas)*

Longley Green [OS Sheet 150 map reference 731503; SO7350], *Nelson*: Pleasant and comfortable lounge bar, friendly staff, Flowers, Hook Norton and Ruddles, and reasonable range of bar food, well cooked and presented *(Mr and Mrs W H Crowther)*

☆ Lyonshall [SO3355], *Royal George*: Clean, bright and cheerful, with three bars opening off central servery; good standard bar menu with masses of daily specials — excellent quality (especially meat) and quantity, and well presented; no-smoking dining area, well kept Flowers, friendly, helpful staff, no music *(CEP, M E A Horler)*

Malvern [British Camp, Wynds Pt; SO7641], *Malvern Hills*: Bass and good lunchtime buffet in comfortable oak-panelled hotel lounge; good bedrooms *(BKA)*; [Graham Rd], *Royal Malvern*: Friendly, with interesting bar food inc vegetarian dishes; Woods on handpump *(Chris Draper, Anna Jeffery)*

Mamble [just off A456 Bewdley—Tenbury Wells; SO6971], *Dog & Duck*: Old country pub doing well under newish regime, with emphasis on good, unusual home-cooked food such as turnip soup or hot avocado filled with port and topped with grilled stilton; well kept Hook Norton beers, nice view from lounge; closed Sun evening and all Mon, with late lunch Sat and Sun *(Dave Braisted)*

Martley [B4197; SO7559], *Crown*: Friendly, with decent bar food inc good value pork and stuffing roll; Banks's Bitter *(Dave Braisted)*

☆ Mathon [SO7345], *Cliffe Arms*: Clean and cosy old black and white timbered pub in pleasant spot, tiny low-beamed rooms full of nooks and crannies; well kept Flowers, Hook Norton and Marstons Pedigree, good bar food (not Sun or Mon, not Tues evening) — ham off bone, vegetarian quiche, lasagne, salads, braised pigeon, treacle tart all recommended; also newish evening restaurant (Weds–Sat evening, Sun lunch; bookings only); streamside garden *(EML)*

Michaelchurch Escley [OS Sheet 161 map reference 318341; SO3134], *Bridge*: Remote stone-roofed pub in idyllic spot by brook with jumping fish, good beer and food; being sensitively refurbished *(J Penford)*

Much Birch [Ross Rd (A49 S of Hereford); SO5131], *Axe & Cleaver*: Neatly kept small bar with open fire leading to larger dining area; friendly staff, imaginative well cooked and presented bar food inc several daily specials, more formal and more expensive evening menu; well kept beer *(Horace Hipkiss, G and M Hollis)*

☆ Much Marcle [off A449 SW of Ledbury; take Woolhope turning at village stores, then right at pub sign; SO6633], *Slip*: Quite outstanding flower garden around secluded country pub among the orchards of the Weston's cider village, also new conservatory; pleasantly chatty atmosphere, small choice of carefully cooked bar food inc good value specials, well kept Flowers Original and local cider; straightforwardly furnished neat lounge on left angling around to family area, fruit machine in public bar, unobtrusive piped music; very popular with older people at lunchtime, more villagey in the evening; service can slow down at peak times, and booking recommended (*W L Congreve, Paul McPherson, G and M Hollis, John and Bridget Dean, Sybil Baker, A T Langton, BB*)

Much Marcle [off A449 Ross-on-Wye—Ledbury], *Royal Oak*: Superb rural spot with magnificent views, pleasant lounge with stools around small round tables and open fire, bar with pool table, large back dining area; Flowers IPA, Whitbreads PA and Weston's very local cider, bar food from sandwiches up (*S J A Velate*)

☆ **Munsley** [Trumpet; A438 Hereford—Ledbury; SO6641], *Verzons*: 19th-century hotel and restaurant doing well under new regime, serving good choice of food in long bar-cum-bistro on left (also full-blown restaurant on right); well kept Hook Norton and friendly atmosphere (*J H C Peters, Paul S McPherson*)

Newtown [A4103 Hereford—Worcester, junction with A417; SO6145], *Newtown*: Clean decor, attentive licensee, well kept beer and good food — especially lamb shanks; very popular with older people, not a lot of space though (*Maggie and Bruce Clarke, SJC*)

Oddingley [Smite Hill; nr M5 junction 6 — A4538 towards Droitwich, then first right — OS Sheet 150 map reference 901589; SO9059], *Pear Tree*: Deceptively large, divided into multitude of nooks and crannies; good choice of bar food especially seafood (*E J Alcock, J S Rutter*)

Orleton [SO4967], *Boot*: 15th-century black-and-white building converted into dining pub, with good if not cheap food inc unusual dishes such as delicious elderflower fritters; Ruddles real ale, no dogs, pleasant garden (*Robert and Vicky Tod*)

☆ **Pensax** [B4202 Abberley—Clows Top; SO7269], *Bell*: Consistently good interesting food in unspoilt and warmly welcoming 19th-century pub with changing well kept real ales such as Everards, Hook Norton, Ruddles, Timothy Taylors, open fires and cheerful service; dining room extension with good view over hills towards Wyre Forest, opening on to wooden sun deck; children welcome (*PLC, Tony Ritson, Paul Denham, Nicola Denham-Brown*)

Peopleton [SO9350], *Crown*: Masses of flowers around the tables outside this pretty Whitbreads pub — welcoming inside, with good range of bar food (*PADEMLUC, Paul McPherson*)

Pershore [Bridge St; SO9445], *Millers Arms*: A young people's pub in the evenings, well worth knowing for its fine range of Wadworths and guest beers, and good value food in big helpings — omelettes, casseroles, cannelloni and pork chop in cider all recommended (*R J Yates, Derek and Sylvia Stephenson*); [Newlands], *Talbot*: Pleasant local with guest beer and pub games (*Dr and Mrs A K Clarke*)

Pixley [SO6639], *Trumpet*: Pleasant old pub, popular at lunchtimes, with attractively

timbered rambling bars, bar food (*Barbara M McHugh*)

Rashwood [A38, just S of M5 junction 5; SO9165], *Robin Hood*: Pleasant pub, not over-crowded despite proximity to motorway; good meals at reasonable prices, M&B beers (*Dave Braisted*)

Risbury [OS Sheet 149 map reference 560549; SO5555], *Hop Pole*: Hidden down a track and with no sign, this farmhouse pub has two adjacent rooms; quarry tiles, seats from an old motor coach, and a blue leatherette bar; real ale, chatty landlord (*PG*)

Rock Hill [SO9569], *Greyhound*: Refurbished pub with well kept Flowers and good value bar food inc interesting and individual dishes (*Dave Braisted*)

Romsley [B4551 towards Halesowen; SO9679], *Sun*: Good food, drink and atmosphere, but food service can be slow (*Dave Braisted*)

☆ **Ross on Wye** [Riverside; coming in from A40 W side, 1st left after bridge; SO6024], *Hope & Anchor*: Notable for its position by the river, with big-windowed family extension looking out on flower-lined waterside lawns; boating theme in cheery main bar, snugger Victorian-style upstairs lounge and dining room, bar food inc children's helpings, well kept M&B Springfield and Marstons Pedigree on handpump, silver band summer Sun evenings (*John Honnor, M J Penford, LYM*)

Ross on Wye [Edde Cross St], *King Charles II*: Huge helpings of good home-cooked lunchtime bar food (*Cathy Long*); [High St], *Kings Head*: Good atmosphere in comfortable pub, good food inc Sun lunch (*Paul McPherson*); [High St (car park nr top of hill)], *Man of Ross*: Two bars, the lounge with interesting documents on the walls; well kept Flowers Original and good, home-made bar food inc range of salads and steak and kidney pie; open all day (not Sun) (*Adrian Pitts*)

Rye Street [SO7835], *Duke of York*: Pleasant, welcoming atmosphere, Flowers IPA and good range of food inc good curry; subdued piped music (*PADEMLUC*)

Severn Stoke [A38 S of Worcester; SO8544], *Rose & Crown*: Old white, low-beamed pub by green; Ansells, Banks's and Marstons; pizzas recommended (*Dave Braisted*)

Shatterford [Bridgenorth Rd; SO7981], *Red Lion*: Friendly free house serving Banks's, Bathams and Robinsons; bar food inc good 'drunken bull' — beef casserole with garlic bread; restaurant (*Dave Braisted*)

Spetchley [Evesham Rd; SO8953], *Berkeley Arms*: Pleasant pub with real ales, good range of home-cooked bar food and friendly, helpful staff (*K R Harris*); *Berkeley Knot*: Comfortable and welcoming dining pub with wide range of good bar food, pleasantly served by waitresses; well kept Bass (*PADEMLUC*)

St Margarets [SO3533], *Sun*: This pub recommended in previous editions has now closed

St Owens Cross [SO5425], *New Inn*:

15th-century coaching inn of considerable potential — first pub of friendly young owners who've been renovating it attractively over the last few years; not entirely unmixed reports so far, but readers who've had good food from sandwiches to steaks and sea bass suggest that it's well worth watching; bedrooms give you a lot for your money — on main rd, but double glazing helps *(Gina Randall, Jamie Lyons, Ruth Harrison, Mrs Nina Elliott)*

Staplow [B4214 Ledbury—Bromyard; SO6941], *Oak*: Well kept Flowers Original and IPA, good range of imaginative bar food *(J H C Peters)*

Staunton on Wye [SO3645], *Worlds End Lodge*: One of the few licensed Youth Hostels; well kept Marstons Pedigree, farm cider, good vegetarian and vegan menu, prices from reasonable to cheap, games room; part of an outdoor centre, remarkable mix of customers; bedrooms basic but cheap and comfortable, with good breakfasts *(Philip Thomas, D Morris)*

Stiffords Bridge [SO7348], *Red Lion*: Very friendly small pub with good, interesting food in restaurant area *(Jason Caulkin)*

☆ **Stoke Lacy** [A465 Bromyard—Hereford, just N of village; SO6249], *Plough*: Modernised pub by Symonds' cider plant, comfortable and clean, with friendly service, good range of generously served home-made bar food inc fresh veg in bar and restaurant (fried brie, rabbit in cider, steak and kidney pie, peach crunch, treacle tart all recommended); Greenalls real ales, choice of ciders, restaurant *(Dave Braisted, M A Watts, Anthony Nelson-Smith)*

☆ **Stoke Pound** [Sugarbrook Lane; SO9667], *Queens Head*: Large modern — air-conditioned — locally popular canalside pub with wide choice of beers, friendly atmosphere, good straightforward bar food inc seafood specialities, evening carvery, restaurant; service quick even when busy *(F H Sommer, C H Stride)*

Stoke Prior [off A49 or A44 1 mile SE of Leominster; SO5256], *Lamb*: Well kept Flowers IPA on handpump, good choice of reasonably priced bar food *(J H C Peters)*

☆ **Stoke Works** [Shaw Lane; a mile from M5 Junction 5 — OS Sheet 150 map reference 938656; SO9365], *Bowling Green*: Excellent drinking pub with well kept Banks's Bitter and Mild, good atmosphere and friendly service — but also short choice of particularly good value food, well cooked and presented, inc good sandwiches and children's dishes; attractive building with big though not pretty garden, and its own bowling green; very handy for Worcester—Birmingham Canal *(Brian Jones, Barry and Anne)*

Stourport on Severn [Canalside; SO8171], *Black Star*: Good old-fashioned pub with warm welcome, friendly local atmosphere, well kept real ales, good value home-cooked food, occasional live music *(Paul and Sue Tanser)*; [Walshes Meadow, by swimming pool just over bridge towards Gt Whitley],

Old Beams: Comfortable and attractive pub divided into areas by stub walls with arched timbered openings, smart food in eating area at one end, Flowers Original on handpump, piped music; has been open all day in summer *(Roger Huggins)*; [The River Basin], *Tontine*: Large historic pub alongside Staffs & Worcs canal basin, gardens overlooking River Severn; good food, well kept Banks's *(Steve J Pratt)*

Symonds Yat [Symonds Yat West; SO5616], *Old Ferre*: Lively and attractive pub overlooking river, with its own hand-pulled ferry; real ale, good value restaurant meals inc huge mixed grill; nr start GWG90; has small boat for 30-min river trips *(Ian Clay, Lynne Sheridan, Bob West)*

Tardebigge [SO9969], *Tardebigge*: Big recently refurbished Edwardian dining pub with sensible tables, comfortable chairs, pleasant waiters and waitresses, good choice of meals; well kept ale; can be lively Sat evenings *(Roy Bromell, Jim Whitaker)*

☆ **Tenbury Wells** [Worcester Rd (A456 about 2 miles E); SO5968], *Peacock*: Warm, attractive, olde-worlde pub with friendly landlord and staff, real fire, well kept beer, straightforward but above-average good value food — no chips; restaurant *(Mrs B Wooldridge, Jamie and Sarah Allan)*

☆ **Tenbury Wells** [High St], *Ship*: Lots of dark wood, well kept Ansells, wide range of good reasonably priced bar meals concentrating on seafood, rather nice semi-separate dining room (smarter yet more intimate), notable Sun lunch, good coffee, attentive service, warm atmosphere; good back bar with pool and so forth; bedrooms comfortable *(M B P Carpenter)*

Tenbury Wells [A4112], *Fountain*: Quaint, crooked, black and white pub with fountain in front, on quiet main road; real fire, cosy atmosphere, rather good bar menu with good choice of puddings, unobtrusive piped music; restaurant behind *(Wendy Proctor, Carole Hall)*

Ullingswick [SO5949], *Three Crowns*: Unspoilt, with candles on tables, good food and beer (Tetleys and Burton), friendly landlord; small attractive lawn with good views in summer; a nice place to stay *(J Penford)*

Upper Arley [nr stn; SO7680], *Harbour*: Cosy, compactly charming old pub with good range of bar food, large dining room where children welcome and good-sized garden with play area and livestock; close to Severn Valley steam rly, and Worcester Way *(E J Alcock)*

Upper Sapey [B4203 Bromyard—Great Witley; SO6863], *Baiting House*: Two small bars, old fireplace, well kept Banks's and Flowers, good bar food; in good spot with fine views *(Dave Braisted)*

☆ **Upper Wyche** [from Walwyn Rd (B4218) heading W, first left turn after hilltop, on right-hand bend, on to Chase Rd; SO7643], *Chase*: Small country pub nestling on western side of Malvern Hills, well kept Donnington BB and SBA and Wye Valley real ales, limited but good and often interesting bar food ranging from rolls through omelettes to steaks, with good fresh vegetables; fine views from charming lounge; closed Tues *(Derek and Sylvia Stephenson)*

☆ **Upton upon Severn** [far end High St; SO8540], *Little Upton Muggery*: Another of the Little pubs; warm atmosphere, pine tables and sawdust on floor, hundreds of mugs hanging from ceiling; enjoyable food from the Muggery Grubbery, well kept beers inc the usual Lumphammer *(Dave Braisted, Ron and Audrey Davidson)*

Upton upon Severn [High St], *Olde Anchor*: Picturesque 16th-century pub with old-fashioned furnishings, old black timbers propping its low ceiling, lots of copper, brass and pewter; Watneys-related real ales, straightforward bar food; has been open all day summer — useful for visiting this charming Severnside village — but no longer has provision for children (nor does it have live music) *(A Triggs, WHBM, E J Knight, Wayne Brindle, PLC, Laurence Manning, Alan Skull, LYM)*

Wadborough [Station Rd; SO9047], *Masons Arms*: Has been favoured as friendly and unpretentious village pub with good food — particularly fine sandwiches — and well kept Banks's ales, but we've had no recent news *(More reports please)*

Warndon [just off M5 junction 6; SO8856], *Haywain*: Interesting barn conversion with bar at far side of restaurant, bar food (service can be slow); Banks's beers *(Dave Braisted)*

☆ **Weatheroak Hill** [Icknield St — coming S on A435 from Wythall roundabout, filter right off dual carriageway a mile S, then in village turn left towards Alvechurch; SP0674], *Coach & Horses*: Plush-seated two-level lounge bar and tiled-floor public bar in country pub notable for its well kept and interesting range of real ales — usually ten or so on handpump, inc relative rarities; decent range of cheap simple food inc speciality main-course onion soup (tables can be booked, which means some may stay empty even when pub busy), good chatty atmosphere, piped music, good garden with plenty of seats on lawns and upper terrace; service usually quick; children allowed in eating area *(Derek and Sylvia Stephenson, Lynne Sheridan, Bob West, Mike and Wendy Proctor, Frank Cummins, LYM)*

Welland [A4104; SO7940], *Marlbank*: Good value straightforward food, friendly bar staff, clean lavatories *(Margaret Dyke)*

Wellington Heath [SO7141], *Farmers Arms*: Cleanly kept, comfortable and surprisingly spacious, with friendly atmosphere, good range of well served bar food; tables on sunny terrace overlooking pretty wooded valley *(Mr and Mrs W H Crowther, P J Brooks)*

☆ **Whitney on Wye** [SO2747], *Boat*: Large and beautifully kept redbrick pub, well furnished, warm and friendly; big windows make the most of its delightful riverbank position; very ample home-cooked bar food, with fine puddings; bedrooms *(Paul McPherson)*

☆ **Wigmore** [SO4169], *Olde Oaken Bucket*: Olde-worlde front bar, elegant candlelit back lounge with shelves housing collection of butter dishes; good choice of good value food inc steaks, back garden *(Shirley Allen, Paul McPherson)*

☆ **Willersey** [hotel signed off A44 about 2 miles E of Broadway; SP1238], *Dormy House*: In a beautiful and peaceful setting, this smart hotel has a cosy Cotswold bar and eating area in original 17th-century farmhouse core, which opens into inner courtyard with tables under cocktail parasols, more tables on front terrace; short choice of good bar food (not cheap, but worth it), decent house wine, good coffee, young keen staff, excellent lavatories; attractive and extensive garden overlooks golf course and distant hills *(JMC, S V Bishop, Roy Bromell)*

Wolverley [SO8279], *Lock*: Pleasant canalside pub with adventurous food, homely lounge bar, well kept Banks's, good wine list *(Steve J Pratt)*

☆ **Worcester** [London Rd, about 1/2 mile from centre], *Little Worcester Sauce Factory*: The exuberantly over-the-top decor that marks this small chain, with sauce bottles as the theme; good value food along the lines of others in the chain, well kept beers *(Dave Braisted, PLC)*

Worcester [Oldbury Rd, St Johns], *Coppertops*: Modern, recently refurbished M&B pub popular with locals; bar food, seats in garden, good parking *(E G Parish)*; *Foresters Arms*: Pleasant, bright atmosphere, bare-knuckle boxing pictures, quick, courteous service; imaginative, reasonably priced, well cooked and presented food *(Edward J Elsey)*; *Fownes*: A hotel — ingenious and well equipped conversion of a former glass factory — worth knowing for its Tilleys Brasserie, which has an attractive pub atmosphere, tempting food and jazz on Fri evenings; bedrooms comfortable *(Bernard Phillips)*; [Lowesmoor], *Jolly Roger*: Unpretentious, roomy home-brew pub with random collection of comfortable furniture; good range of excellent beer, good value straightforward bar food *(Geoffrey and Nora Cleaver)*

Wychbold [A38 towards Bromsgrove; part of Webbs Garden Centre — open 10–5 — OS Sheet 150 map reference 929670; SO9265], *Thatch*: Good range of well cooked and presented snacks and meals in pleasant and really clean surroundings; not a pub (part of Webbs Garden Centre, open 10–5, with wine licence) but worth noting for value for money *(Mr and Mrs W H Crowther)*

Yarpole [SO4765], *Bell*: Friendly and pleasantly done-up village pub with impressive wood and brasswork, lots of bric-a-brac in big rambling lounge, pseudo-classical piped music; wide range of usual food (not cheap); well kept Woods Special, children's play area, animals in field, three stabled horses; nr Croft Castle and Berrington Hall *(Norman Foot, Brian and Anna Marsden)*

Hertfordshire

The Green Man at Great Offley, continuing its marked progress, this year gains a star award for its happy combination of decent food, pleasant and individual surroundings, and notably skilful management. The two other fine pubs which it joins to make up the county's top three are the Fox & Hounds at Barley (a wide choice of home-cooked food in interesting and lively surroundings – and very cheap beer, brewed on the premises) and the George & Dragon at Watton-at-Stone (the county's best pub food, without losing the unpretentious welcome of a true local – and it's one of the rare places in the south east where we found bargain snacks at under £1). Two new entries, under new licensees, look extremely promising: the Bricklayers Arms at Flaunden has been taken on by people who previously won quite a following for the Full Moon at Little Kingshill (at this Flaunden pub, they've changed the layout to allow interesting developments for diners without sacrificing the strength of its local appeal); the Moon & Stars at Rushden has been reworked very sympathetically, and now serves rather rewarding food. On the question of food, we should mention the White Hart at Puckeridge (quite an emphasis on seafood on the good value menu in this well run family pub); the Valiant Trooper at Aldbury (not a wide choice, but good – a nice pub, in attractive walking country); and, for keeping food prices below the highish local average, the civilised Rose & Crown in St Albans (some bargain main dishes) and the cheerful Sow & Pigs near Wadesmill (cheap snacks, most notably in the form of their pauper's lunch – one of the cheapest bar snacks we've found in the whole country). Drinks prices in the area are generally rather above the national average, too. The Valiant Trooper at Aldbury and Brocket Arms at Ayot St Lawrence, relatively cheap for drinks, are both free houses stocking a good choice of beers from smallish breweries; we found that it was pubs tied to the national brewing combines which tended to have the highest drinks prices here. Promising pubs in the Lucky Dip section at the end of the chapter – all of which should be particularly worth a visit – include the Boat at Berkhamsted, Two Brewers at Chipperfield, Green Dragon at Flaunden, Bull at Much Hadham, Holly Bush at Potters Crouch, Cabinet at Reed, Yew Tree at Walkern, Eagle & Child at Whitwell; several interesting entries in St Albans; and, under newish licensees, the Elephant & Castle at Amwell and Plume of Feathers at Tewin.

ALDBURY   SP9612 Map 4

Valiant Trooper

Village signposted from Tring and under a mile E of Tring railway station; Trooper Road (towards Aldbury Common)

This partly white-painted, tiled brick house serves a fairly limited but good value selection of bar food – sandwiches, home-made soup, filled baked potatoes, pork chop in a mushroom and wine sauce, gammon and pineapple or liver and bacon casserole (all £3.80), roast lamb or beef, fresh local trout, and mixed grill (£4.20); friendly service. The lively first room, beamed and tiled in red and black, has built-in wall benches, a pew and small dining chairs around the attractive country tables, and a woodburning stove in its inglenook fireplace. In the brown-carpeted middle room there's some exposed brick work and spindleback chairs, and the far room has nice country kitchen chairs around individually chosen tables, and a brick fireplace; decorations are mostly antique prints of cavalrymen. Well kept and well priced Fullers London Pride and ESB, Greene King Abbot, Hook Norton, and Marstons Pedigree on handpump, and cheap spirits; darts, shove-ha'penny, dominoes, cribbage; dogs welcome. There are some tables in the small, prettily flowered garden at the back. The pub is in good walking country – it's on *Good Walks Guide* Walk 109. (*Recommended by Sidney and Erna Wells, Ted George, BKA, Mrs M Lawrence, Stephen King, Peter Adcock; more reports please*)

Free house   Licensee Dorothy Eileen O'Gorman   Real ale   Meals and snacks (12.30–2, 6.30–8.30; not Sun or Mon, or Sat evening)   Restaurant tel Aldbury Common (044 285) 203 (not Sun evening)   Children in restaurant and eating area of bar (lunchtime only)   Open 12–3, 6–11; 12–11 Sat; closed Mon lunchtime, Oct–Jun

AYOT ST LAWRENCE   TL1916 Map 5

Brocket Arms

B651 N of St Albans for about 6 miles; village signposted on right after Wheathampstead and Marshall's Heath golf course; or B653 NE of Luton, then right on to B651

This white-painted and tiled 14th-century brick pub is close to the house George Bernard Shaw lived in from 1904 until his death in 1950 (when his ashes were scattered in the garden; it's now owned by the National Trust, and kept exactly as he left it). The two atmospheric and old-fashioned rooms have orange lanterns hanging from the sturdy oak beams, a big inglenook fireplace, a long built-in wall settle in one parquet-floored room, and a wide choice of piped music from Bach to pop. Bar food includes soup (£1), ploughman's (£2.50), pâté (£3), salads, shepherd's pie, scampi or plaice (£3.50), and coq au vin, tagliatelle or fish pie; winter Sunday roast lunch. A wide range of beers on handpump such as Banks & Taylors SOD, Greene King IPA and Abbot, Gales HSB, Gibbs Mew Bishops Tipple, Marstons Pedigree and Wadworths 6X, as well as Zum Zider; darts, cribbage and dominoes. The walled gardens behind are especially safe for children; on *Good Walks Guide* Walk 108. Just over the road are the romantic ivy-hung ruins of a medieval church. (*Recommended by Barbara Wensworth, Michael and Alison Sandy, Gary Scott, Tony and Lynne Stark; more reports please*)

Free house   Licensee Toby Wingfield Digby   Real ale   Meals and snacks No-smoking restaurant   Children in restaurant   Open 11–2, 6–11   Bedrooms tel Stevenage (0438) 820250; l£35

BARLEY   TL3938 Map 5

Fox & Hounds ★ ⊘

Junction 10 of M11 then A505 towards Royston, then left on to B1368 after 4 miles

The bar food in this 15th-century locals' pub is mostly home-made, and popular with readers; the substantial selection includes sandwiches, generous whitebait (£2.30), garlic mushrooms (£1.95), spare ribs (£2.95), vegetable provençale (£3.25), curries (from £3.25), lasagne (£3.50), steak and kidney or chicken, ham and sweetcorn pies (£3.95), scallops, prawns and mushrooms in white wine (£4.45), poached salmon and prawns, whole plaice or chicken Kiev (£4.95), and steaks (from £5.95); meaty and vegetarian specials, and theme evenings such as fish; service holds up under pressure. The low ceilinged and alcovey rambling rooms are well furnished – one of the stripped wood tables has a brightly-painted cast iron base which used to be a wringer; there are substantial log fires on both sides of a massive central chimney, and a friendly cat. The dining area with its odd-shaped nooks and crannies was originally the kitchen and cellar; the conservatory is no-smoking. A big bonus is the fact that they brew their own, attractively priced beers – Old Dragon and Flame Thrower, as well as serving beers on seven handpumps from all over the country on continual rotation; farm cider, malt whiskies, and a good selection of wines by the glass or bottle. There's also a fine range of games, from darts (two league darts teams), bar billiards and dominoes (two schools), to cribbage, fruit machine and juke box; also a league football team. The garden is well equipped for children, and there's a skittle alley and a barbecue area. They run a mini-bus service for customers who may or may not be over the limit. *(Recommended by Colin and Evelyn Turner, TTB, David Eversley, Charles Bardswell, SJC, Colleen Holiday, Nigel Gibbs, Sandra Cook, Tony and Lynne Stark, Olive Carroll, Alan Whelan, Gwen and Peter Andrews, Denise Plummer, Jim Froggatt, Jill Hampton)*

Own brew　Licensee Rita Nicholson　Real ale　Meals and snacks (12–2, 6.30–10) Children welcome (not too late Sats)　Open 12–3, 6–11

FLAUNDEN　TL0100　Map 5

Bricklayers Arms

Village signposted from Bovingdon, on B4505 Hemel Hempstead–Chesham; Hogpits Bottom – from village centre follow Boxmoor, Bovingdon road and turn right at Belsize, Watford signpost

Almost cottage-like and covered with Virginia creeper, this well refurbished, low brick and tiled pub is a peaceful spot in summer, with picnic-table seats and older tables and chairs under big apple trees on a lawn surrounded by foxgloves along its sheltering hawthorn and ivy hedges. In the low-beamed bar the stubs of the knocked-through oak-timbered walls give a snug feeling to the three original rooms; buff leatherette armchairs and dark brown painted traditional wooden wall seats sit on the bright carpet; open fires in winter. A dining room has been added at the back, leaving the atmosphere in the bars nicely local, particularly at weekends. A good choice of bar food includes soup (£1.40), sandwiches (from £1.50), ploughman's (from £1.80), filled baked potatoes (from £2.50), chilli con carne (£3), trout (£5.75), and steaks (£6.95). Adnams, Brakspears, Fullers London Pride and two guests on handpump; piped music. Just up the Belsize road there's a path on the left, through woods, to more Forestry Commission woods around Hollow Hedge. Until fairly recently the licensees ran the Full Moon at Little Kingshill in Buckinghamshire. *(Recommended by T Kenny, R M Savage, D B Delany, BKA, Douglas Bail, Mr and Mrs F W Sturch)*

Free house　Licensee A P Power　Real ale　Meals and snacks (not Sun evening) Open 11–2.30(3 Sat), 5.30(6 Sat)–11; winter evening opening 6

GREAT OFFLEY　TL1427　Map 5

Green Man ★

Village signposted off A505 Luton–Hitchin

Curlicued iron tables and chairs on the flagstoned terrace in this popular country pub have a grand view beyond the lawn with its rockery, pond and little waterfall, to the flatter land below, stretching for miles to the east. There's a profusion of flowers in hanging baskets and tubs of flowers, and a couple of ponies may be stretching their necks over the stile at the end of the lawn – in which case children are asked to sit out in front, where there are swings and a slide. Inside, the rambling bars have wheelback and spindleback chairs around simple country tables, stripped brick, low moulded beams, lots of antique farm-tool illustrations, and a woodburning stove and fruit machine on the left. The larger and more airy right-hand room has lots of little countryside prints and one or two larger pictures, a cabinet of trophies, cushioned built-in wall seats as well as the chairs around its tables, another big woodburner (with a row of brass spigots decorating the chimneypiece), and fruit machine. Highly praised bar food includes soup (£1.10), generous sandwiches and large filled rolls (from £1.65), filled baked potatoes (from £1.75), ploughman's (from £2.25), cottage or chicken and mushroom pie (£3.75), a good lunchtime spread of help-yourself salads (from £4.75), and gammon with pineapple (£5.15); the meat is supplied by the local butcher and the turkeys come from a local farm; service stays firm and friendly under pressure. Well kept Flowers IPA and Original, Ruddles County, Websters Yorkshire and (unusual down here) Whitbreads Castle Eden on handpump under light blanket pressure, with a decent choice of wines by the glass; friendly cat, piped music. The licensee runs another pub (and fish restaurant) round the corner, the Prince Henry. *(Recommended by Michael and Alison Sandy, Lyn and Bill Capper, Peter and Jacqueline Petts, R A Reeves, David Shillitoe, K and J Morris, D L Johnson, George Mitchell, Roger Broadie, Sidney and Erna Wells)*

Free house   Licensee Raymond H Scarbrow   Real ale   Meals and snacks (11.30–11) Restaurant tel Offley (046 276) 256   Children welcome   Open 10.30–11

NEWGATE STREET   TL3005 Map 5
Coach & Horses

B153 W of Cuffley then first right just outside village

This engaging country house, covered in a profusion of ivy, is handy for walks in nearby rolling fields (there are lots of paths), or in vast woods such as the Great Wood country park (from the Northaw road, take the B157 towards Brookmans Park). The remains of some wall ends in the open-plan bar create an illusion of separate little rooms, with a relaxing mix of carpet and large flagstones, cosy built-in wall settles, good winter fires at either end, subdued lighting and perhaps piped music or Radio Essex. Well kept Benskins Best and Ind Coope Burton on handpump; cribbage, shove-ha'penny, dominoes, fruit machine, trivia and piped music. Good bar food includes a wide range of sandwiches or toasties (from £1.20; Reg's Special £2.45), ploughman's (from £3), and home-made specials like steak and kidney or chicken pie, macaroni cheese or beef curry (£3.75); vegetarian dishes. There are tables on a lawn with high trees around it, and more on the forecourt. *(Recommended by John Day, Alan and Ruth Woodhouse, Gwen and Peter Andrews; more reports please)*

Benskins (Allied)   Licensee Reg Newcombe   Real ale   Meals and snacks (12–2, 6–9; not Sun)   Children in family room   Open 11–3, 5.30–11

PUCKERIDGE   TL3823 Map 5
White Hart 🏮

Village signposted from A10 and A120

There's quite an emphasis on seafood on the good value menu in this well run family pub: crab sandwiches (£1.75), fresh prawns (from £1.95), spicy crab pâté (£2.50), insalata di mare (octopus, squid, prawns and mussels, £2.75), Mediterranean prawns (from £4.70), delicious hot Arbroath smokie (£4.95), whole baked plaice stuffed with prawns (£5.75), and cold seafood platter (£5.95) – a gigantic concoction which comes with a full salad; if you eat it all (unaided) they'll give you a voucher for £5.95, to be deducted from your next meal. Other food includes sandwiches (from £1), ploughman's (from £2.30), home-made venison pâté (£2.50), home-made moussaka or fresh oven-roasted turkey (£4.95), lots of vegetarian dishes like lentil crumble or home-made tomato pancakes (£4.95), steaks (from £7.95), and a children's menu; meals can be taken in either the bar or the dining room. The heavy beamed, rambling bar has lots of wooden armchairs, wheelback chairs and button-back banquettes, and traditional decorations such as pewter tankards, horse brasses and coach horns; the fireplace has a massive carved mantlebeam. Well kept McMullens Bitter and AK Mild on handpump; shove-ha'penny, cribbage, fruit machine, trivia and piped music. There are seats and swings in the floodlit garden by a paddock with chickens, roosters, ducks, goats, rabbits, sheep and ponies, and more under a thatched shelter built around a spreading tree. *(Recommended by Stephen King, Colin and Evelyn Turner, Jill Hampton, Brian Metherell, Derek and Sylvia Stephenson)*

McMullens   Licensees Colin and Rita Boom   Real ale   Meals and snacks (12–2, 6.30–9.30)   Restaurant tel Ware (0920) 821309 (not Sun evening)   Children in eating area of bar and restaurant   Open 10.30–2.30, 5.30–11; closed evenings 25 and 26 Dec

RUSHDEN　TL3031 Map 5

Moon & Stars

Village signposted from A507 Baldock–Buntingford, about 1 mile W of Cottered

Since taking over at the start of 1989 the young licensee has made considerable changes to this pretty tiled country pub, while maintaining its unspoilt and cottagey atmosphere. The villagey public bar has been left as before, with its heavy-beamed low ceiling and vast inglenook fireplace, but it now connects at the front with the lounge bar, which has lots of tables; there's a shiny new kitchen at the back, providing a decent selection of bar food including sandwiches (from 85p), filled baked potatoes (£1.60), ploughman's (from £2.45), huge Yorkshire puddings with big fillings (£2.95), omelettes (from £2.50), ham and egg (£2.85), gammon (£4.95) and steak (£5.75); on Saturday night there's a family hour from 6 to 7 with a children's menu (children have to be out by 7.30), and on Wednesday night there's particular emphasis on the Yorkshire puddings and filled potatoes; a hot dish of the day, small, decent wine list. Greene King IPA, Abbot and KK Mild on handpump; darts, dominoes, shove-ha'penny, cribbage and a fruit machine, maybe piped music; lively pub dog. A garden at the back has tables, a climbing frame and swings; also benches in front. The pub was originally a row of three cottages. *(Recommended by Charles Bardswell, John Whitehead; more up-to-date reports please)*

Greene King　Licensee Robbie Davidson　Real ale　Meals and snacks (not Sun evening)　Children over 5 in lounge if eating　Open 11.30–2.30, 5.30(6 Sat)–11; winter evening opening 6 (7 Sat)

ST ALBANS　TL1507 Map 5

Garibaldi

61 Albert Street; off Holywell Hill below White Hart Hotel – some parking at end of street

A surprisingly wide vista of a pub behind an unassuming backstreet facade, this well kept, refurbished Victorian place centres round the island servery, visible from the little tiled-floor snug up some steps; a separate food counter on a lower level opens out into a neat and cosy little no-smoking conservatory. It's often notably lively, not least when a fairly regular crowd of mainly youngish people gathers there. Good value home-made bar food includes sandwiches (from £1.10), soup (£1.30), ploughman's (£2.75), salads (from around £3), steak pie laced with ESB (£4.40), and other changing hot dishes such as spicy meatballs (£2.50), fresh vegetable and pasta bake (£2.85), Barnsley chop done with red wine and rosemary (£3.80) and chicken Kiev (£4.40); friendly service. Well kept Fullers Chiswick, London Pride and ESB; cribbage, dominoes, trivia machine, fruit machine, decent piped pop music; they have their own cricket team. There are a few picnic-table sets in the side yard. *(Recommended by David Fowles, Michael and Alison Sandy; more reports please)*

Fullers　Real ale　Meals and snacks　Children allowed away from bar if quiet, till about 7.30　Open 11–3, 5–11; all day Fri and Sat

Goat

Sopwell Lane; a No Entry beside Strutt and Parker estate agents on Holywell Hill, the main southwards exit from town – by car, take the next lane down and go round the block

In the 18th century this fine old pub had the most extensive stables of any inn in the area; these days they provide shelter for the tables on the neat lawn-and-gravel back yard. The network of linked rooms contains a profusion of eye-catching decorations – stuffed birds, chamber pots, books and prints. Bar food ranges from soup (£1.20) and good value, tasty sandwiches, through pizzas (from £2.50), steak and mushroom pie (£3.25), tagliatelli carbonara (£3.60) and burgers (from £3.60), to steaks and home-made puddings. The wide selection of fairly priced real ales includes Boddingtons, Fullers London Pride, Greene King Abbot, Hook Norton

Best and Old Hookey, Marstons Pedigree, and Wadworths 6X on handpump. Dominoes, fruit machine, trivia and piped music. *(Recommended by N Barker, K W Mills, BKA, Richard and Dilys Smith, David Goldstone and others)*

Free house (though now owned by Inn Leisure/Devenish)   Real ale   Meals and snacks (12–2, 6.30–9.30; not Sun evening)   Children in eating area of bar   Jazz Sun lunchtime   Nearby parking may be rather difficult   Open 11–2.30, 5.30–11 (all day Sat); closed 25 Dec

Rose & Crown

St Michaels Street; from town centre follow George Street down past the Abbey towards the Roman town

Good value, filling lunchtime bar food in this thoroughly antique and elegantly facaded pub includes plain or toasted sandwiches on request, home-made soup (£1.40), cheesey potato pie (£2.25), ploughman's, curries (£2.95), beef stew with dumplings, pork in cider or venison in red wine with juniper berries (£3.50), lots of home-made vegetarian dishes, and puddings. The beamed public bars have unevenly timbered walls, old-fashioned wall benches, a pile of old coffee-table magazines, black cauldrons in a deep fireplace, and an engaging atmosphere. Well kept Adnams, Benskins, Ind Coope Burton and Tetleys on handpump, and farm ciders, some whiskies, lots of country wines and winter hot punch; unusual crisps and a selection of snuffs; friendly service. Darts (placed sensibly to one side), shove-ha'penny, dominoes, cribbage, fruit machine, video game, and juke box. There's always a selection of books for sale – proceeds go towards buying guide dogs. *(Recommended by Richard Houghton, A W Dickinson, Michael and Alison Sandy, Christian Leigh)*

Benskins (Allied)   Licensee John Milligan   Real ale   Lunchtime snacks (11.30–2.15) Folk music Thurs   Evening parking may be difficult   Open 11.15–2.30(3 Sat), 5.30(6 Sat)–11

WADESMILL   TL3517 Map 5

Sow & Pigs

Thundridge (the village where it's actually situated – but not marked on many road maps, which is why we list it under nearby Wadesmill); A10 just S of Wadesmill, towards Ware

The natural focus of this unassuming, well run and comfortable pub is the central serving bar – small, traditional and plank-panelled, with a rustic table supported by two barrels in the bay of the cosy window seat, lots of little piggies in a glass cabinet by the bar, an attractive wall clock, and a small ship's wheel and binnacle under a collection of military badges. More spacious rooms lead off on both sides – on the right the dining room, with big copper urns hanging from dark beams, massive rustic tables and a big nautical chart; the area on the left has a timber part divider, and a couple of steps halfway along, helping to break it up. Well kept Adnams, Benskins Best and Ind Coope Burton on handpump or tapped from the cask. They really know how to make sandwiches – the roast beef done with dripping (£1.25), smoked salmon (£2) and steak (£2.80) are all recommended. Other well priced bar food includes a pauper's lunch (30p), good home-made soup (£1.15), ploughman's (£1.85), steak and kidney pie (£3), tasty bacon and leek roly-poly and a bargain three-course steak lunch (£5.50). There are picnic-table sets under cocktail parasols, with their own service hatch, on a smallish fairylit grass area behind by the car park, sheltered by tall oaks and chestnut trees. The landlord has a cheerful constitution. *(Recommended by M B P Carpenter, John Whitehead, C A Holloway, R C Vincent)*

Benskins (Allied)   Licensee Willie Morgan   Real ale   Snacks (any time during opening hours) and meals   Restaurant tel Ware (0920) 463281   Children in restaurant   Open 11–2.30, 6–11

WATTON AT STONE   TL3019   Map 5

George & Dragon ★ ✍

Village signposted off A602 about 5 miles S of Stevenage, on B1001; High St

There's been a strong vote of confidence from readers in this pub, praised for maintaining the unpretentious welcome of a local while having a decidedly unparochial outlook on food. The imaginative menu – which changes every two months or so – typically includes thick tasty soup (£1.25; Corsican fish soup £3), sandwiches (from 80p), ploughman's (£2.50), herring roes in butter and fresh lime or endive and mixed lettuce salad (£2.75), an evening hot snack (£3.25), a lunchtime dish of the day (£4), salads (from £3.30), stuffed mushrooms or flaked smoked haddock topped with tomato concassé gratinated and grilled (£3.75), locally smoked salmon (£6), fillet steak in a bread roll (from £6), prawns with spring onions, ginger and garlic (£6.50) and puddings (£1.50); they only take credit cards on bills over ten pounds. Proper napkins, good house wines by half-pint or pint carafes, and a selected house claret; the good restaurant doesn't impinge on the pub itself. There's also an official dress code – it's best if you at least wear shirts with sleeves; be warned that it's likely to be crowded by 12.30. The carpeted main bar has country kitchen armchairs around attractive old tables, dark blue cloth-upholstered seats in its bay windows, an interesting mix of antique and modern prints on the partly timbered ochre walls, and a big inglenook fireplace. A quieter room off, with spindleback chairs and wall settles cushioned to match the green floral curtains, has a nice set of Cruikshank anti-drink engravings above its panelled dado. Greene King beers under air pressure; friendly, efficient service, and daily papers set out to read at lunchtime; fruit machine. There are picnic-table sets in a small shrub-screened garden, and the pub is handy for Benington Lordship Gardens. *(Recommended by Charles Bardswell, A C Morrison, Alan and Ruth Woodhouse, C A Holloway, Neville Kenyon, David Shillitoe, Barbara Wensworth and others)*

Greene King   Licensee Kevin Dinnin   Meals and snacks (12–2, 7.15–10; not Sun) Restaurant tel Ware (0920) 830285 (not Sun)   Children in restaurant   Open 11–2.30, 6–11; closed 25 and 26 Dec evenings

WESTMILL   TL3626   Map 5

Sword in Hand

Village signposted W of A10, about 1 mile S of Buntingford

One of the prettiest buildings in a particularly pretty village (rows of tiled or thatched cottages), this friendly pub takes its name from the crest of a local landowner – the first licensee, a blacksmith, used to make tools for his Caribbean sugar plantations. The comfortable bar has lots of photographs of classic cars and local houses, and pictures of local scenes on the black and white timbered walls, cushioned seats on the Turkey carpet, and a log fire. Well kept Benskins on handpump, with Greene King Abbot and Ind Coope Burton tapped from the cask; however the pub was just turning into a free house as we went to press, and they plan to expand their range. Darts, shove-ha'penny, dominoes, cribbage, fruit machine, trivia and piped music; the playful little dog is called Scruffy. The good range of home-made bar food includes French onion soup (£1.50), pâté with Cointreau and orange (£2.25), ploughman's (from £2.25), smoked salmon mousse (£2.50), seafood or meaty lasagne (£3.95), pies with flaky pastry (the speciality here – lamb and rosemary £3.95, steak and kidney or chicken, gammon and mushroom £4.15), stuffed baked trout wrapped in vine leaves (£6.50), steaks (from £6.95), and puddings like caramel delight or spotted dick (£1.95). There are tables on a partly crazy-paved sheltered side garden under the pear tree. The licensee, a classic-car enthusiast, holds regular shows in the spacious two-acre back garden in summer and meetings in the pub in winter. *(Recommended by R F Plater, Colleen Holiday, Sidney and Erna Wells; more reports please)*

Now free   Licensees David and Heather Hopperton   Real ale   Meals and snacks Restaurant tel Royston (0763) 71356   Well behaved children allowed   Open 11–2.30(3 Sat), 6–11; they may stay open longer in afternoon if there are customers

Lucky Dip

Besides the fully inspected pubs, you might like to try these Lucky Dips recommended to us and described by readers (if you do, please send us reports):

Abbots Langley [TL0902], *Compasses*: Very friendly; good food inc pork fillet in red wine, garlic king prawns, steaks stuffed with stilton; wide choice of malt whiskies *(R A Reeves)*

☆ **Amwell** [village signposted SW from Wheathampstead; TL1613], *Elephant & Castle*: Particularly nice in summer for its spacious and attractive floodlit gardens, with barbecues; low-beamed ancient pub, well run, with inglenook fireplace, panelling, stripped brickwork, 200-ft well shaft in bar — open layout, with eating area; usual bar food (not Sun) gradually being extended by promising new licensee, with several hand-raised pies; well kept Benskins Best, Ind Coope Burton and Tetleys (served with a northern head) on handpump, maybe a guest such as Adnams or Youngs; children in eating area *(Michael and Alison Sandy, Mr and Mrs F E M Hardy, Fay Reid, David Shillitoe, LYM)*

Ardeley [OS Sheet 166 map reference 310272; TL3027], *Jolly Waggoner*: Genuine, rustic and friendly pub with two unspoilt bars, one for eating which is extended into adjoining cottage, with wide range of good home-cooked bar food; well kept Greene King ales *(Charles Bardswell)*

Ashwell [beside the Church; TL2639], *Bushel & Strike*: Character building in old village, well kept Charles Wells beer, good food *(Tony and Lynne Stark)*; [69 High St], *Rose & Crown*: Good pub with decent well presented food, good bar, spotless lavatories; ample parking *(N S Holmes, Sidney and Erna Wells)*

Aspenden [off A10 nr Buntingford; TL3528], *Fox*: Popular village pub under new regime, small bars, traditional locals' dominoes bar, 19th-century pews, benches and piano in main bar; well kept Greene King Abbot and IPA, lunchtime bar food, big back garden suitable for children *(Adrian Pitts)*

Ayot Green [TL2213], *Waggoners*: Pleasant, well maintained interior with shiny tables, carpets, lots of mugs hanging from low ceiling in bar; good bar food inc outstanding moussaka served on Wedgwood china, separate eating area, young and friendly staff; on GWG 108 *(GB, CH)*

☆ **Berkhamsted** [Gravel Path; SP9807], *Boat*: Pleasantly decorated newish Fullers pub in delightful canalside setting, friendly atmosphere, good value lunchtime bar food (not Sun), well kept Fullers Chiswick, London Pride and ESB, obliging licensees; tables on waterside terrace with weekend barbecues, shrubs and hanging baskets *(Stephen King, A D Clench, David Oakes, John Wright, Michael Ansell, O Travers, E J Mooring)*

Berkhamsted [High St], *George*: Pleasant town pub with rambling rooms; saloon full of interesting prints and two large, comfortable leather chairs; well kept Ruddles Best and County, and Wethereds, good, cheap bar food, pinball machine unobtrusively placed in back room, no music *(Anon)*

Bishops Stortford [London Rd; TL4820], *Old Bulls Head*: Extremely well kept beer, friendly landlord and staff, well prepared food (not cheap, but good helpings) inc speciality curries and home-made sausages; barbecues on summer weekends; really nice garden overlooks River Stort *(SJC)*

Bourne End [Winkwell — down narrow leafy lane next to garage off A41 towards Berkhamsted; TL0206], *Three Horseshoes*: Idyllic setting by canal swingbridge; 16th-century, with stripped brickwork, harness, low lighting; Benskins Best, Ind Coope Burton and Tetleys on handpump, seats outside; no food Sun *(Gary Scott, Mr and Mrs J Wyatt)*

Bovingdon [Hempstead Rd; TL0103], *Halfway House*: Popular extended Benskins pub, reasonably priced food all week, separate eating area, pleasant garden, big car park *(D C Horwood)*; *Wheatsheaf*: Cosy pub with beamed ceilings, settles with cushioned seats and stools around tables, open fires; Whitbreads-related real ales, reasonably priced food from sandwiches up, friendly service; fruit machine, piped pop music and darts in upper extension *(Lyn and Bill Capper, Richard Dolphin)*

Braughing [B1368; TL3925], *Axe & Compasses*: Cricket-oriented pub with two lovely bars, the left one corner-shaped; pleasant seating, good generous daily specials *(Alan and Ruth Woodhouse)*

Bushey [High St; TQ1395], *Red Lion*: Friendly, competent service, Bass and Benskins Best on handpump, reasonable wine by the glass and good bar food *(D C Bail)*; [42 Sparrows Herne], *Royal Oak*: Well kept Charles Wells and a couple of guests such as Adnams Broadside and Marstons Pedigree; good choice of generously served food in pleasant timbered bar or adjoining dining room *(Stan Edwards, Richard Houghton)*

☆ **Chandlers Cross** [TQ0698], *Clarendon Arms*: Good atmosphere in large, popular bar with plenty of tables, friendly staff and locals, cheap plain bar food (not Sun) lunchtime — when it may be full of young people; Brakspears, Websters Yorkshire and Youngs, help-yourself coffee; best in summer, for its nice setting and pleasant covered verandah *(BKA)*

Chapmore End [off B158

Hertford—Wadesmill; TL3216], *Woodman*: Tiny but welcoming two-room village pub by pond with well kept Greene King beer tapped from the cask, big garden with fowls *(Tony and Lynne Stark, Helen and John

Thompson)

Charlton [TL1727], *Windmill*: Attractive spot, busy pub even midweek lunchtimes, attentive and obliging service *(G L Tong)*

☆ **Chipperfield** [The Common; TL0401], *Two Brewers*: It's a THF, but hard to believe from the relaxed and genuinely pubby atmosphere of the spacious dark-beamed main bar, with its cushioned antique settles and half a dozen or so well kept real ales on handpump such as Bass, Greene King IPA and Abbot, Marstons Pedigree and Youngers Scotch; lunchtime bar food (not Sun) from the comfortable bow-windowed lounge includes a good buffet, and the long, low inn overlooks a pretty tree-flanked cricket green; children allowed in lounge and restaurant; open all day Sat *(Lyn and Bill Capper, TBB, D L Johnson, David Oakes, Dr Mark Stocker, R C Morgan, LYM)*

Chipperfield [Tower Hill], *Boot*: Welcoming with immaculate interior, open fires and warm atmosphere; good food from simple range, well kept Allied real ales on handpump *(Anon)*; *Royal Oak*: Two small well kept bars, log fire, soft piped music, no juke box and relaxed atmosphere; good bar food at reasonable prices *(Mrs Olive Way)*

Chipping [off A10; TL3532], *Countryman*: Beams and timbering, traditional settles, open fire, farm tools, wide choice of bar food, restaurant, well kept Adnams, Courage Best, Marstons Pedigree and Ruddles County from elaborately carved bar counter, piped music; in summer (when the pub's been open all day Sats) the big pleasant garden is a plus; children in restaurant *(Alan and Ruth Woodhouse, LYM)*

Chiswell Green [TL1304], *Three Hammers*: Handsomely renovated in good solid style with several different areas; food good basic English, reasonably priced *(Ian Phillips)*

☆ **Chorleywood** [Long Lane — follow Heronsgate signpost from M25 junction 17 exit roundabout; TQ0295], *Land of Liberty, Peace & Plenty*: Spotlessly kept pub with good range of substantial bar food (especially at lunchtime); friendly staff, well kept Courage and John Smiths, decent coffee, maybe unobtrusive piped music; children's play area, several pub dogs *(Mr and Mrs F W Sturch, G S Landa, G and M Stewart)*

Chorleywood [Chorleywood Bottom], *Old Shepherd*: Quaint old exterior, very much a welcoming local inside; two bars, well kept Allied real ales; plenty of parking *(R Houghton)*; [Station Approach; opp main entrance to stn; handy for M25 junction 18], *Sportsman*: An unusually spacious and well ordered 19th-century hotel with panelled public bar and upper lounge leading into conservatory; reasonably priced food from upper bar and grill room, Bass, Charrington IPA and Worthington, efficient, friendly service; family room leading to garden with big play area; bedrooms attractively furnished *(R M Savage)*; [Long Lane — just off M25 junction 17; Heronsgate Rd, The Swillet], *Stag*: Benskins pub transformed by

refurbishment; pleasant, airy atmosphere — one big bar area with comfortable seating; prompt service, real ales inc Ind Coope Burton and Best, and good, straightforward food; bigger car park *(Lyn and Bill Capper, Douglas Bail)*

Codicote [High St; TL2118], *Bell*: Comfortably modernised old Whitbreads pub with terrace bar behind lounge, generous helpings of good bar food from separate counter (and handsome restaurant), well kept Flowers and Wethereds on handpump, piped music, fruit machine; bedrooms *(John Whitehead, Lyn and Bill Capper, D L Johnson)*

Coleman Green [TL1812], *John Bunyan*: Well run with very pleasant atmosphere; tables on front lawn *(Mr and Mrs F E M Hardy)*

☆ **Colney Heath** [TL2005], *Crooked Billet*: Good range of well kept real ales and lots of unusual bottled beers in traditional tiled bar and comfortably modernised lounge — no frills, but friendly service, straightforward bar food, summer barbecues, pets' corner in garden, maybe children's ponies to ride in summer; partly covered terrace *(David Fowles, John Whitehead, LYM)*

Cottered [TL3129], *Bell*: Recently rethatched Benskins pub with well kept Ind Coope Burton, friendly landlord and wide choice of bar food inc carefully cooked main dishes and traditional English puddings; welcoming fire *(Charles Bardswell, Gwen and Peter Andrews, Sidney Wells)*; [TL3129], *Bull*: Well run and popular *(Charles Bardswell)*

Croxley Green [Rickmansworth Rd (A412); junction Watford Rd / Baldwins Lane — OS Sheet 176 map reference 087959; TQ0795], *Two Bridges*: Has been popular as comfortably refurbished and relaxing place with attractive muted decor, sofas, easy chairs, books and so forth, and has had well kept Allied real ales and efficiently served bar food; but closed 1990, and we await further news *(LYM)*

Dane End [Great Munden; from Dane End go two miles past the Boot — OS Sheet 166 map reference 352234; TL3321], *Plough*: Included for the unique full-size Compton theatre organ in the comfortable and lofty lounge extension that's been built specially to house it; otherwise, usual bar food, well kept Greene King IPA and Abbot and Rayments, pleasant staff, local atmosphere — very busy weekend evenings *(J P Day, LYM)*

☆ **Datchworth** [Bramfield Rd, Bulls Grn; TL2717], *Horns*: Pretty 15th-century country pub, well cared for and decorated interestingly to show its age, with attractive rugs on brickwork floor, big inglenook, low beams or high rafters, seats out among roses on the crazy paving; good pub food worth waiting for, well kept Flowers Original and Wethereds on handpump, good cider and coffee *(John Whitehead, LYM)*

Datchworth [1 Watton Rd; TL2718], *Inn on the Green*: Friendly, clean and quite smart, with several well kept real ales but particularly strong on food, with quite a wide choice and much space set aside for eating; relaxed and comfortable, though piped music could perhaps be a shade quieter; tables outside, big car park *(John Whitehead)*

☆ Essendon [West End Lane — off B158, which with Essendon and B1455 is signposted off A414 Hatfield—Hertford; TL2708], *Candlestick*: Friendly local alone in the countryside, plenty of seats outside; comfortable two-room mock-Tudor lounge, brightly lit public bar with games; generous helpings of good value simple food at low, low prices lunchtimes and Tues–Fri evenings, well kept McMullens Bitter and AK Mild, log fires, good service; note — still shuts 2pm Sun *(Alan and Ruth Woodhouse, John Whitehead, BB)*

Essendon, *Salisbury Crest*: Attractive pub with decent food which at Christmas runs up to splendid seven-course lunches; good atmosphere *(Mr and Mrs F E M Hardy)*

Flamstead [High St; TL0714], *Three Blackbirds*: Low-beamed pub with two real fires, good value bar food, well kept Watneys-related real ales, friendly service; good place for walks *(David Shillitoe)*

☆ Flaunden [TL0100], *Green Dragon*: Neat and comfortable partly panelled pub with traditional untouched tap bar, well kept Marstons Pedigree and other real ales such as Theakstons and maybe Burton Bridge, wide choice of reasonably priced bar food from soups to steaks; darts and shove-ha'penny, spotless lavatories; charming well kept garden with summer-house and aviaries *(Capt and Mrs Gardner, David Wallington, Richard Houghton, LYM)*

☆ Frithsden [from Berkhamsted take unmarked rd towards Potten End, pass Potten End turning on right then take next left towards Ashridge College; TL0110], *Alford Arms*: Whitbreads-related and other real ales inc two or three brewed on the premises (the tiny brewhouse is worth a look in daylight); simple bar food, local atmosphere, good service even when it gets busy, attractive country surroundings which make it a splendid summer pub — tables in front; piped music (not obtrusive) in games area, massive cactus in public bar; live music Weds, open all day Sat *(Lyn and Bill Capper, R Houghton, LYM)*

Great Offley [TL1427], *Prince Henry*: Done up with fountains outside, comfortable cane and brass inside, all 20s-style; Greene King beers, good value bar food at all times, mainly grills, also good fish and chip restaurant at back; can get full *(Michael and Alison Sandy)*, *Red Lion*: Good food cooked by creative chef, friendly staff, pleasant surroundings; recently refurbished bedrooms *(Billy Dee, Nicky Morris)*

Harpenden [High St/Station Rd; TL1314], *Harpenden Arms*: Well decorated with Victorian-style wallpaper, pictures, tiles and plants, and plenty of small tables and chairs in the airy and spacious food area; well kept

Fullers, wide range of good value food inc good filled baked potatoes *(Michael and Alison Sandy)*

Hatfield [89 Great North Rd; off A414; TL2309], *Wrestlers*: Busy pub, attractive and well kept, with brassware and bric-a-brac; friendly staff, well kept beer, good bar food, wide range of customers *(M Thompson)*

Hazel End [shown as Hazeland on some maps — just N of Bishops Stortford; TL4924], *Five Horseshoes*: Delightful spot, good food and pleasant garden *(S Pollock-Hill)*

nr Hemel Hempstead [Briden's Camp; leaving on A4146, right at Flamstead/Markyate signpost opp Red Lion — OS Sheet 166 map reference 044111; TL0506], *Crown & Sceptre*: Country pub which still has some character, with three rooms, roaring fire, well kept Greene King and Rayments BBA, friendly staff, basic food *(D L Johnson, R Houghton, BKA, LYM)*

☆ Hertford [Fore St], *Salisbury Arms*: Cocktail bar, public bar with machines, darts etc and lounge with lots of tables, in comfortably traditional English country-town hotel, with good Chinese food alongside more usual bar food inc outstanding sandwiches; well kept McMullens ales inc AK Mild, friendly waitress service; bedrooms *(K and E Leist)*

Hertford [The Folly; TL3213], *Old Barge*: Comfortably renovated canalside pub with good, welcoming atmosphere, friendly efficient staff, well kept Benskins and good home-baked baguettes filled with ham or seafood *(Colin Dourish, LYM)*; [Castle St], *White Horse*: Small intimate no-frills free house with friendly atmosphere and several real ales *(David Fowles)*; [Old Cross], *Woolpack*: Large McMullens house next to brewery with bare floorboards, wooden tables and chairs and open fire; impressive range of home-made, good value lunchtime bar food *(David Fowles)*

Hitchin [Bucklersbury; TL1929], *George*: Named for George Washington; interesting decor, rather homely comfort, friendly service, Benskins and Tetleys; popular with local business people for good variety of sandwiches and salad bar; some tables in adjoining alleyway; no under-21s allowed *(Coleen Holiday, Wayne Brindle)*

Hunton Bridge [Bridge Rd; just off A41 N of Watford; TL0800], *Kings Head*: Outstanding children's play area, plenty of grass, three slides and other equipment, and Grand Union Canal at the end; good bar food, well kept Benskins beers *(Stan Edwards)*

Ickleford [TL1831], *Cricketers*: Comfortable old timbered village pub doing particularly well under current regime, with rotating real ales such as Adnams, Banks & Taylors SOS, Boddingtons, Hook Norton, Timothy Taylors Landlord, Wiltshire Dark Star; unusual specials eg filled Yorkshire puddings, neat terrace; open till 4.30 Fri and Sat; bedrooms *(Sidney and Erna Wells)*; *Old George*: Rambling heavy-beamed Tudor

pub by churchyard, good value simple but
substantial food pleasantly served, Greene
King beers; very quiet midweek lunchtime
(*G L Tong, LYM*)

Kings Langley [60 High St; TL0702], *Rose
& Crown*: Popualr and welcoming, with
jazz/live bands four nights a week and Sun
lunchtime; tied to Benskins, but also several
well kept guest beers such as Adnams Mild
and Broadside, Gibbs Mew Bishops Tipple,
Marstons Merrie Monk and Pedigree
(*Gordon Leighton*)

Langley [off B656 S of Hitchin; TL2122],
Farmers Boy: Welcoming village pub with
well kept Greene King ales, and big helpings
of food (*Peter Watkins, Pam Stanley*)

☆ **Lemsford** [A6129 towards
Wheathampstead; TL2111], *Crooked
Chimney*: Roomy and comfortable
open-plan dining pub with central feature
fireplace, Allied real ales, restaurant and
garden by fields (*John Whitehead, LYM*)

Lemsford, *Long Arm & Short Arm*:
Particularly good value Sun lunch — get
there early (*Margaret and Trevor Errington*)

☆ **Letchmore Heath** [2 miles from M1 junction
5; A41 towards Harrow, first left towards
Aldenham, then signed right; TQ1597],
Three Horseshoes: Though so handy for the
M1 this cottagey little low-ceilinged local
sits opposite a duck pond on a serenely
tree-shaded green; a wide choice of the usual
lunchtime bar food (not Sun), well kept
Benskins Best and Ind Coope Burton on
handpump, maybe faint piped music, white
tables outside the pretty flower-decked pub;
can get crowded (*Hope Chenhalls, Philip
Harrison, Olive Carroll, A C Morrison, LYM*)

☆ **Little Hadham** [The Ford; TL4422], *Nags
Head*: Well kept Greene King and Rayments
real ales and good food using fresh
ingredients in friendly 16th-century country
local — the puddings are specially good;
restaurant; children welcome (*P Gillbe,
LYM*)

☆ **London Colney** [Waterside; just off main st
by bridge at S end; TL1704], *Green Dragon*:
Immaculately kept, with friendly
atmosphere, good value straightforward
lunchtime bar food (not Sun), well kept
Benskins Best, lots of beams and brasses,
tables outside by quiet riverside green (*Mr
and Mrs H L Malhotra, LYM*)

London Colney, *Bull*: Jolly, active pub with
good atmosphere, lounge and lively bar, well
kept beer and friendly, helpful staff (*Dr and
Mrs A K Clarke*)

Long Marston [38 Tring Rd — OS Sheet
165 map reference 899157; SP8915],
Queens Head: Wide range of good value
food from sandwiches up in three-sided bar
with stone floors, open log fire and plenty of
olde-worlde charm; ABC Best, Bass,
Everards Tiger and Ind Coope Burton on
handpump, wide range of bar food, small
garden; children's room (*Margaret and
Trevor Errington*)

Markyate [TL0616], *Sun*: Low-beamed old
pub with inglenook, small range of simple
lunchtime snacks, seats in garden (*LYM*)

☆ **Much Hadham** [B1004; TL4319], *Bull*:
Simple proper pub food in the attractively
straightforward inglenook public bar and a
much wider choice in the comfortable
brocade-banquette lounge and cosy back
family dining room — inc half-price
children's helpings and rich puddings; well
kept Benskins Best and Ind Coope Burton on
handpump, a respectable choice of wines,
rustic seats dotted around spacious informal
back garden (*R C Vincent, WTF, M and J
Back, LYM*)

Much Hadham [Hertford Rd, about 1/4 mile
outside], *Jolly Waggoners*: Well furnished
traditional pub, good atmosphere, pleasant
service and high standard of bar food inc
children's dishes and bargain senior citizens'
lunch Weds; play area for children, maybe
sheep in adjoining paddock; live music Sun
(*T G Saul*)

Northaw [A121; TL2802], *Two Brewers*:
Well furnished pub in pretty village with
good choice of food and well kept Benskins
(*A M Kelly*)

Oxhey [108 Villiers Rd; off Pinner Rd
nearly opp Bushey & Oxhey Stn, towards
Watford—Bushey rd; TQ1195], *Villiers
Arms*: Enjoyable bar lunches in genuine pub
(*Stan Edwards*)

Pepperstock [nr M1 junction 10; TL0817],
Half Moon: Friendly, popular and attractive
Brewers Fayre refurbishment, with wide
range of reasonably priced bar food inc good
puddings, Whitbreads-related real ales; big
bookcase of old books (*Margaret and Trevor
Errington*)

Perry Green [TL4317], *Hoops*: Popular
local, reasonable choice of beers, good bar
food and pleasant surroundings (*R C
Vincent, Mrs C Wardell*)

Pirton [TL1431], *Cat & Fiddle*: Homely pub
facing village green, well kept Charles Wells
real ales, bar food, swing on back lawn
(*Colleen Holiday, LYM*); *Motte & Bailey*:
Cosy pub with log fire, Marstons and
Ruddles, and big helpings of good,
interesting food (*SJC*)

☆ **Potters Crouch** [leaving St Albans on
Watford rd via Chiswell Green, turn right
after M10 — OS Sheet 166 map reference
116052; TL1105], *Holly Bush*: Small
whitewashed pub with highly polished good
biggish tables and other dark wood
furniture, lots of pictures, plates, brasses and
antlers, old-fashioned lighting; Benskins Best
and Ind Coope Burton, reasonable simple
food, efficient service, big garden with
picnic-table sets; gets very popular (*Michael
and Alison Sandy, Christian Leigh, BKA*)

Redbourn [Redbourn Rd (A5183); nr M1
junction 9; TL1012], *Chequers*: Roomy old
oak-beamed Chef & Brewer pub in
attractive open countryside; popular for
good atmosphere, good value food (inc wide
choice of specials), well kept
Watneys-related real ales; back terrace and
big garden by stream, nice restaurant;
children welcome (*P Marsh, John Whitehead,
Mr and Mrs H L Malhotra, Mr and Mrs D
Gritten*)

☆ **Reed** [High St; TL3636], *Cabinet*: Friendly and relaxed tiled and weatherboarded house, a pub for centuries; parlourish inside with spacious lounge extension, nice garden out, wide choice of well kept real ales such as Adnams, Greene King Abbot, Hook Norton, Mauldons and Nethergate tapped from the cask, reasonably priced bar food, children's summer bar in charming garden, warm welcome *(LYM)*

☆ **Rickmansworth** [TQ0594], *Scotsbridge Mill*: Tasteful Beefeater conversion of old water mill — River Chess runs through building and through grounds crossed with narrow bridges; carpeted bar with comfortable chairs and tables, Whitbreads-related real ales, salads, hot dishes and puddings; extensive menu in big rambling two-floor restaurant; tables out behind — spacious site in nice countryside, with big car park *(Lyn and Bill Capper)*

Rickmansworth [Woodcock Hill; Harefield rd, off A404 at Batchworth], *Rose & Crown*: Beamed building with cosy bar and separate eating area; very mixed clientele, fast friendly service, well kept Allied beers; big car park *(Richard Houghton)*

Ridge [Crossoaks Lane; TL2100], *Old Guinea*: Small and friendly with rustic atmosphere; tasty reasonably priced bar food, accommodating for wheelchair *(Mr and Mrs G Sparrow)*

Sandridge [High St; TL1610], *Rose & Crown*: Pleasant 15th-century pub with several rooms, four well kept real ales, welcoming mainly young staff, wide choice of fair-priced and generously served food showing some imagination; very clean, with quiet and relaxed friendly atmosphere *(John Whitehead)*

Sarratt [The Green; TQ0499], *Cricketers*: Pleasant comfortable atmosphere in popular low-beamed lounge bar with well laid-out eating area, quickly served good bar food from sandwiches up even on Sun, well kept Courage and Jon Smiths beers, fruit machine and darts in public bar, no piped music; tables out facing green; good parking *(Lyn and Bill Capper, Quentin Williamson)*

Sawbridgeworth [TL4814], *White Lion*: Lively and popular without being rowdy; attractively furnished and decorated, big hearth filled with dried flowers and so forth, well kept Greene King, friendly staff, good service, good choice of reasonably priced bar food *(Alan and Ruth Woodhouse)*

Spellbrook [TL4817], *Three Horseshoes*: Good choice of meals served in reasonable quantities at acceptable prices; good range of beers *(R C Vincent)*

☆ **St Albans** [Holywell Hill; TL1507], *White Hart*: Friendly but civilised hotel with considerable character and charm, and long and entertaining history; comfortable bar with antique panelling, handsome fireplaces and furnishings; bar food and accommodating restaurant, Benskins Best, Ind Coope Burton and Tetleys on handpump; bedrooms *(Gordon Mott, David Goldstone, Michael and Alison Sandy, LYM)*

☆ **St Albans** [off George St; through abbey gateway — you can drive down but then may find difficulty parking], *Fighting Cocks*: Odd-shaped former abbey gatehouse, much modernised inside but still showing the sunken area which was a Stuart cockpit, some low and heavy beams, an inglenook log fire, and pleasant nooks, corners and window alcoves; the garden's attractive, and beyond is a waterside park and then the Roman city; lunchtime bar food, friendly service, well kept Benskins Best, Ind Coope Burton and Tetleys, open all day summer *(David Goldstone, Gary Scott, A W Dickinson, LYM)*

☆ **St Albans** [36 Fishpool St], *Lower Red Lion*: Back-street free house in conservation area of the old city; lively atmosphere, good mix of customers, well kept Adnams, Fullers London Pride, Greene King Abbot and Youngs Special on handpump in beamed bars with log-effect gas fires, plenty of seating, and friendly atmosphere; good value interesting bar food inc big steak sandwiches; pretty garden, but parking not brilliant; bedrooms reasonably priced, though share bathrooms; huge breakfast *(Michael and Alison Sandy, Richard Houghton, Neil Tallantire)*

St Albans [32 Lower Dagnall St], *Farriers Arms*: Very plain but welcoming little back-street local in no-frills old area of city; well kept McMullens; customers' bicycles seem chained to all the lampposts in the area *(David Fowles, Christian Leigh)*; [6 London Rd], *Peahen*: Big pub, extensively refurbished, with lots of comfortable seats, long, low Victorian-style bar, display cases of Victoriana, toys, a wedding dress, and so forth; decent bar food inc help-yourself salads, well kept McMullens AK and Bitter, and piped Radio 1; good old-fashioned public bar round the corner with tiled floor, Formica-topped tables *(Michael and Alison Sandy)*; [Lower Dagnall St], *Verulam Arms*: One-room corner Benskins pub in conservation area; welcoming and attentive licensees, well kept beer, nicely prepared food — tasty and attractively priced *(David Fowles)*

nr **St Albans** [Tyttenhanger Green; TL1805], *Plough*: Clean and friendly; good range of beers inc Fullers London Pride and Greene King Abbot, and cheap, wholesome and good value for money bar food (no Sun lunch) *(M B Porter)*

Stevenage [High St, Old Stevenage; TL2324], *White Lion*: Friendly, warm and welcoming place with attractive, exposed beamed lounge; well kept Greene King IPA and Abbot, and good, reasonably priced bar food; restaurant *(Mr and Mrs D Heath)*

☆ **Tewin** [Upper Green Rd; TL2714], *Plume of Feathers*: Newish licensee has made this pleasant Benskins pub very much a place to be reckoned with on the food side, with reliable cooking and really good ingredients (particularly good meat), for both bar and the restaurant which is now attracting a high proportion of customers *(D L Johnson, John Whitehead)*

☆ **Thorley Street** [A1184
Sawbridgeworth—Bishops Stortford;
TL4718], *Coach & Horses*: Generous
helpings of good value bar food and quick,
pleasant service in tastefully furnished and
extended dining area; Sun lunch especially
popular; homely atmosphere, friendly
welcoming staff, Benskins beer and generous
glasses of decent wine; children's play area,
maybe special bouncing castle Bank Hols
(R C Vincent, T G Saul)

Tring [London Rd (A41); SP9211], *Cow
Roast*: Efficient service, cheerful welcome,
and skilled cooking in the up-market
restaurant; decent choice of good value bar
food, too *(R M Savage)*; [King St], *Kings
Arms*: Pleasant backstreet local with pine
furniture inc pews and old chairs; well kept
Greene King Abbot and IPA, King &
Barnes, Wadworths 6X and guest beers such
as Fullers, big helpings of cheap interesting
bar food, pleasant garden *(Mark Evans)*

☆ **Walkern** [TL2826], *Yew Tree*: Welcoming
pub with clean bar, McMullens ale, well
presented bar food from sandwiches up inc
good puddings, and outstanding steaks
which amaze even American visitors;
landlord was a butcher, and it shows
(Charles Bardswell)

Walkern, *White Lion*: Comfortable and
welcoming old pub, sensitively restored
outside, popular for bar food and small
restaurant, cosy alcoves and low beams, nice
inglenook *(Charles Bardswell, LYM)*

Water End [B197 N of Potters Bar;
TL2214], *Woodman*: Two cosily decorated
bars, traditional furniture and good fires at
either end; well kept Adnams, Marstons and
Sam Smiths, home-cooked bar food *(Alan
and Ruth Woodhouse)*

Watford [Stamford Rd; TQ1196], *Nascot
Arms*: Two bars, refurbished in salmon and
avocado colours; popular lunchtimes with
local office staff for good value bar food
(Stan Edwards)

Wheathampstead [TL1716], *Swan*: Friendly
old pub with quick service even when

crowded, good range of decent food at
reasonable prices inc help-yourself salads
(Margaret and Trevor Errington)

nr **Wheathampstead** [Gustard Wood, off
B651 1 1/2 miles N, towards Shaws Corner],
Cross Keys: Unspoilt easy-going open-plan
pub alone in countryside, well kept Benskins
real ales, very reasonably priced bar food,
friendly service; picnic-table sets out in
orchard (watch out for greedy chickens)
(Geoff Lee, LYM); [Gustard Wood; poor
approach rd off B651], *Tin Pot*: Good
welcome from long-serving licensee, good,
pubby atmosphere, decent food; can get
crowded, when service may slow *(D L
Johnson)*; [Nomansland Common; B651 1/2
mile S], *Wicked Lady*: Whitbreads Brewers
Fayre pub with several areas inc a
no-smoking one, separate food servery,
family conservatory extension; fruit
machines and piped music, well kept
Whitbreads-related real ales; perhaps now
worth knowing most for the big lawn with
good play area *(John Whitehead, Lyn and Bill
Capper, Peter Watkins, Pam Stanley, LYM)*

☆ **Whitwell** [B651; TL1820], *Eagle & Child*:
Currently doing well, with good bar food
such as superb poached salmon; cosy lounge
with attractive inglenook fireplace,
handsomely moulded beams with queen
post, Whitbreads-related real ales, darts in
snugly clubby public bar; good play area in
back garden *(Fay Reid, Sidney Wells, LYM)*

Whitwell [67 High St (B651); TL1820],
Maidens Head: Atmospheric pub with
amusing and friendly staff, interesting
collection of key-rings, well kept McMullens
tapped from the cask, good food, and decent
choice of spirits; seats in garden *(A J
Jennings)*

Woolmer Green [London Rd; TL2518],
Chequers: More big restaurant than pub,
with plain pine tables and chairs — but
worth knowing for fine choice of good food,
especially fish on Tues and Weds, and good
puddings *(DLJ)*

Humberside

Both food and drinks prices here are markedly lower than the national average – beer about 10p a pint cheaper, for instance, and plenty of pubs beating our £3 target for a bargain main dish. Some pubs to pick out in particular here include the Triton at Sledmere, a fine old small coaching inn, back in these pages after a break; it's doing well under a new licensee. There are new licensees too at the White Horse in Beverley (they're emphasising its highly traditional and unchanging character) and the Gold Cup in Low Catton (they're doing good food). Currently, the pubs doing best of all here are the Olde White Harte in Hull (a glorious old building, with very cheap food), the Half Moon at Skidby (bargain food, including amazing Yorkshire puddings – a new sister pub in Beverley, the Beaver, should be worth investigating), the Seabirds at Flamborough (warm appreciation of its low-priced food, which gains a Food Award this year) and the Plough at Allerthorpe (just what a village pub should be). The Minerva on the Hull waterfront deserves a special word for its own-brewed beer (and cheap food); another two pubs with food prices even lower than the area's low average are the Dacre Arms at Brandesburton and Three Cups at Stamford Bridge. Among the Lucky Dip entries at the end of the chapter, the Tiger at Cottingham and Star at North Dalton currently look particularly promising.

ALLERTHORPE   SE7847 Map 7
Plough

Off A1079 nr Pocklington

This pretty white house, handy for the attractive lily-pond gardens and stuffed sporting trophies of Burnby Hall, has a friendly two-room lounge bar with hunting prints, some wartime RAF and RCAF photographs (squadrons of both were stationed here), snug alcoves (including one big bay window), and open fires. Good value, home-made bar food includes daily specials such as game pie, as well as soup or light Yorkshire pudding with onion gravy (£1.10), open sandwiches (from £1.10), ploughman's (from £2.20), spare ribs, beef and mushroom pie or curry (£3.25), salads such as home-cooked beef or ham (£3.50), lasagne (£3.50), steaks (from £5.75), children's dishes (from £1.10), and puddings (from £1.50); Sunday roast lunch (best to book), charcoal grills on Friday and Saturday nights and vegetarian dishes on request. The games – pool, dominoes, shove-ha'penny, cribbage, fruit machine, trivia game and juke box – are in an extension. Well kept Theakstons Best, XB and Old Peculier, Youngers IPA and occasional guest beers on handpump; piped music. There are tables on the grass outside. (Recommended by Roger A Bellingham, Andy and Jill Kassube, David Gaunt, M Suther, Eddie Palker; more reports please)

Free house   Licensee David Banks   Real ale   Meals and snacks; not 25 Dec   Restaurant (closed Sun evenings) tel   Pocklington (0759) 302349   Children welcome   Open 12–3, 7–11; closed for annual holidays (dates not given)

BEVERLEY   TA0340 Map 8
White Horse ('Nellies')

Hengate, close to the imposing Church of St Mary's; runs off North Bar Within
Dating from around 1425, this fine unspoilt pub has a carefully preserved

Victorian feel – quite without frills. The small rooms have bare floorboards, brown leatherette seats (with high-backed settles in one little snug), a gas-lit pulley-controlled chandelier, a deeply reverberating chiming clock, antique cartoons and sentimental engravings, and open fires – one with an attractively tiled fireplace. Well kept Sam Smiths OB and Museum on handpump, and remarkably cheap food – sandwiches (55p), fish and chips or chicken and mushroom pie (£2.25), and ploughman's (£2.50); darts, dominoes, and trivia. (*Recommended by Andy and Jill Kassube, Paul Harrop, DC*)

Sam Smiths   Licensee Mr Southern   Real ale   Lunchtime meals and snacks   Evening restaurant tel Hull (0482) 861973   Children welcome   Folk music Mon, Jazz Wed Open 11–3, 5–11; 11–11 Sat

BRANDESBURTON   TA1247 Map 8

Dacre Arms

Village signposted from A165 N of Beverley and Hornsea turn-offs

Roomy and comfortable, the rambling rough-plastered bar in this modernised Georgian posting house is vividly furnished with plenty of tables, and the snug area on the right once housed the local Court of Justices. A wide range of reasonably priced bar food includes sandwiches, soup (£1.10), Yorkshire puddings (from £1.35 with onion gravy, from £2.75 with choice of meats), home-made pâté (£1.80), basket meals (from £2.10), ploughman's (£2.65), fried mixed seafood (£3.50), and salads (from £3.65), with specialities like steak and kidney pie (from £2.20), lasagne (£3.85), smoked haddock with prawns (£4.85), and steaks (from £6.20); puddings such as apple strudel with ice cream (from £1.35); children's dishes. Well kept Tetleys Bitter, Theakstons Best and Old Peculier, and Youngers Scotch on handpump; fruit machine, space game and piped music. The cobbled yard outside once had stabling for up to 50 horses. (*Recommended by M B P Carpenter, Stan Edwards; more reports please*)

Free house   Licensee B C Jefferson   Real ale   Meals and snacks (12–2, 7–10.30) Restaurant tel Hornsea (0964) 542392   Children in eating area of bar and restaurant Open 11–2.30, 6.30–11 (6 Sat)

FLAMBOROUGH   TA2270 Map 8

Seabirds ✸

Junction of B1255 and B1229

Readers have been warm in their praise this year for the friendly service and very good value food – with particular emphasis on the fish: sandwiches, ploughman's, good soup (£1.25), warm potted shrimps on a toasted crumpet (£2.25), omelettes (from £2.50), delicious fresh local haddock or deep-fried seafood platter (£3), grilled fish of the day, chicken Kiev (£5), rack of lamb or roast duckling with apple sauce and giblet gravy (£6), and steak (from £7.25); daily specials such as home-made fish pie, fresh crab or salmon salads or lobster thermidor (in season). Camerons Strongarm on handpump; over 35 wines, hot mulled wine and a large selection of whiskies and liqueurs; friendly staff. The public bar is full of shipping paraphernalia, scowling toby jugs, and old framed photographs of Flamborough, and leading off this is the lounge, which has pictures and paintings of the local landscape, a mirror glazed with grape vines, and a woodburning stove; there's also a whole case of stuffed seabirds along one wall. Darts, dominoes, fruit machine and piped music. There's now a family room in the garden. (*Recommended by D J Milner, Tony and Penny Burton, Jan and Ian Alcock, Syd and Wyn Donald, Roger Bellingham, David and Rebecca Killick, Prof S Barnett, Tony and Penny Burton*)

Camerons   Licensee Keith Rostron   Real ale   Meals and snacks (not Sun or Mon evenings in winter)   Restaurant tel Bridlington (0262) 850242 (not Sun evening) Children in eating area of bar and restaurant   Open 11–3, 6–11

HULL   TA0927 Map 8

Minerva

From A63 Castle Street/Garrison Road, turn into Queen Street towards piers at central traffic lights; some metered parking here; pub is in pedestrianised Nelson Street, at far end

The floor of this picturesque pub – built in 1809 on reclaimed land – is raised a few feet above ground level, though the windows are down at normal height – so the view over the attractive old waterfront is unusually good. Several thoughtfully refurbished rooms ramble all the way around a central servery: comfortable seats, interesting photographs and pictures of old Hull (with two attractive wash drawings by Roger Davis), a big chart of the Humber, a tiny snug with room for just three people, and a back room (which looks out to the marina basin, and has darts) with a profusion of varnished woodwork. Besides well kept Tetleys Bitter on handpump, the pub brews its own Pilots Pride (you can see into the microbrewery from the street). Lunchtime bar food includes sandwiches, meaty or vegetarian lasagne, chicken curry or chilli (all £2.75), and home-made beef cobbler or steak and potato pie (£2.95); in the evening there are burgers, plaice or scampi, chicken Kiev, gammon and steaks. Darts, dominoes, and fruit machine. Piped music from the fine reproduction Wurlitzer juke box (the real 'works', with the records, are actually in a completely different place) is loud and clear. A broad prettily paved pedestrian walkway separates the pub, just around the corner from the Pilot Office, from the Humber. *(More reports please)*

Own brew (Tetleys – Allied)   Licensee John Harris McCue   Real ale   Meals and snacks (12–2, 6–8; not Sun evening)   Children in eating area of bar only   Open 11–11 in summer; 11–4, 6–11 Mon–Thurs in winter; closed 25 Dec

Olde White Harte ★

Off 25 Silver Street, a continuation of Whitefriargate (see previous entry); pub is up narrow passage beside the jewellers' Barnby and Rust, and should not be confused with the much more modern White Hart nearby

It's on quiet weekday evenings that you get the best chance to appreciate this ancient tavern's fine features: carved heavy beams supporting black ceiling boards, attractive stained glass windows over the bow window-seat, polished flooring tiles, and brocaded Jacobean-style chairs in the inglenook by a fireplace decorated with Delft tiles. The curved copper-topped counter serves well kept Youngers IPA and No 3, Theakstons XB on handpump and 14 malt whiskies. Simple, traditional bar food includes sandwiches (from 65p, hot beef £1.30), made to order salads (from £1.50), a wide range of ploughman's (from £1.50), and lasagne (£2.05); Sunday lunch; courteous, speedy service. A handsome old oak staircase takes you up past a grandfather clock to a heavily panelled room where on St George's Day 1642 Sir John Hotham, the town's Governor, decided to lock the gate at the far end of Whitefriargate against King Charles, depriving him of the town's arsenal – a fateful start to the Civil War. There are seats in the courtyard outside. *(Recommended by J D Shaw, Steve Waters; more reports please)*

Youngers (S & N)   Licensees Gary and Anne Sowden   Real ale   Meals and snacks 11.30–2   Lunchtime restaurant tel Hull (0482) 26363   Children in restaurant   No nearby parking   Open 11–11 Mon to Fri, 11–4, 6–11 Sat

LOW CATTON   SE7053 Map 7

Gold Cup ✪

Village signposted with High Catton off A166 in Stamford Bridge or A1079 at Kexby Bridge

People come out from York for the bar food here, and under the new licensees this includes soup (£1.10), sandwiches (from £1.10), giant Yorkshire pudding sandwich (£3.25), scrumpy spiced ham, grilled gammon or steak pie (£3.50), scampi (£4.20), chicken Kiev (£4.50) and a vegetarian selection (from £3.50); well kept John Smiths and Tetleys on handpump and maybe a guest such as Old Mill, good coffee with real cream, decent wines; friendly service. The three communicating rooms of the comfortable lounge have red plush wall seats and stools around good solid tables, flowery curtains, some decorative plates and brasswork on the walls, soft red lighting, open fires at each end, and a relaxed and unforced atmosphere. The back games bar is comfortable too, with a well lit pool table, darts, dominoes, quiz game, fruit machine and well reproduced music. The restaurant is very popular, so it's best to book, particularly for Sunday lunch. The fat geese in the pub's back paddock came originally from the farm next door, and Shetland ponies keep them company. *(Recommended by Ray Wharram, Tim Gilroy, N P Hodgson, Roger Bellingham)*

Free house Licensees Raymond and Patricia Ann Hales Real ale Snacks (not Fri or Sat evenings) and meals (11.30–1.30, 7–9.30) Restaurant (not Sun evenings) tel Stamford Bridge (0759) 71354 Children welcome Open 11.30–3.30, 7–11; closed Monday lunch (except Bank Hols) and 25 Dec

MILLINGTON SE8352 Map 7

Gate

Village signposted from Pocklington

As we went to press, we heard that new licensees were to take over this unpretentious and welcoming village pub. There are modern simple furnishings as well as an antique settle with wings and a high back to keep the draught out, black beams supporting the ochre planks of the ceiling, and a big stone fireplace. Plates decorate the main beam over an opening through to another room furnished entirely in yew wood (the age of the trees used has been put at 1,500 years, though the pub itself is 16th-century); this room has a set of antlers above its log fire. Cheap and well kept Bass and Tetleys and Molton Brewery (from a small local independent brewery) on handpump, and the good value food has included sandwiches, home-made meat or rabbit pies, maybe pheasant, hare or wild duck in season, gammon, and steaks. Darts, pool, and trivia in a back room; piped music. There are good Wolds walks and remarkable East Riding views from just up the hill. *(More reports on the new regime, please)*

Free house Real ale Meals and snacks (not Thurs) Restaurant under construction Children in eating area of bar Open 12–2.30, 6.30–12 Bedrooms tel Pocklington (0759) 302045; £8/£16

SKIDBY TA0133 Map 8

Half Moon ⊘

Main Street; off A164

The speciality here is a series of loaf-sized but feather-light Yorkshire puddings with various fillings from £1.70 for onion and gravy, £2.25 with vegetarian gravy, £3.50 for roast beef – so popular that they're said to get through 60,000 eggs and 7,000lb of flour a year. Other food, efficiently served, includes soup (95p), 4oz burgers (from £1.65), ploughman's (£2.20), chilli con carne (£2.80), steak and kidney pie (£2.95); they serve afternoon sandwiches (3–5.30, not Sun); friendly staff. There's an old-fashioned partly panelled front tap room with a tiled floor, long cushioned wall benches, old elm tables, a little high shelf of foreign beer bottles and miniatures, and a coal fire. The more spacious communicating back rooms have a lighter and airier atmosphere, and an unusually big clock. Darts, bar billiards, dominoes, cribbage, fruit machine, piped music; John Smiths on handpump. The landscaped garden area beside the car park has a children's play area with a suspended net maze, and there are plans for a family room, terrace and barbecue area. A black and white windmill is nearby. The licensees have taken over the Beaver in Beverley, where they are doing similarly enterprising food. *(Recommended by Andy and Jill Kassube, PLC, Philip Riding; more reports please)*

John Smiths (Courage) Licensees Peter and Diane Madeley Meals and snacks (12–2, 7–10; till 2.30 Sun lunchtimes; afternoon sandwiches 3–5.50) Children welcome; no under 14s after 8.30 Country and Western Tues from 9 Open 11–11

SLEDMERE   SE9365   Map 8

Triton 🛏️

Junction of B1252 and B1253 NW of Great Driffield

On an old posting road that strides over fine open rolling country and by the walls of Sledmere House, this welcoming 18th-century inn still bears the notice outside which says 'Licensed to let post horses'. Inside, the attractive traditional lounge bar has stately high-backed cushioned settles, a roaring winter fire, and a quiet, pleasant atmosphere; well kept Tetleys and Youngers Scotch on handpump. The menu includes soup, sandwiches, ploughman's (£1.95), lasagne (£2.95), pigeon casserole (£3.95) or rump steak (£6.95); Sunday lunch and enormous breakfasts. The public bar has darts, dominoes, table skittles, fruit machine, juke box. *(Recommended by T Nott, Gwen and Peter Andrews, M A and W R Proctor)*

Free house   Licensee C Emmett   Real ale   Meals and snacks (not Mon lunchtime) Restaurant   Children welcome   Live entertainment every 6 weeks   Open 11.30–3, 6.30–11   Bedrooms tel Driffield (0377) 86644; £15/£30(£42B)

SOUTH DALTON   SE9645   Map 8

Pipe & Glass

Village signposted off B1248 NW of Beverley

The entrance to the main bar of this tiled white pub is done up as a replica of a stage-coach door; both bars have beams, leather seats around the walls and in the bow windows, some high-backed settles, old prints, and log fires. There's also a conservatory. The popular, good value food changes daily, and a typical menu might include sandwiches (£1.35), watercress and potato soup (£1.50), garlic mushrooms (£2.50), lasagne, home-made steak and mushroom pie or chicken piri piri (£3.95), prawn madras or grilled loin of pork with mustard sauce or dressed crab salad (£4.50), and grilled rump steak chasseur (£6.25); on Sundays they stick to sandwiches and salads, with a carvery in the old separate stable block. Castle Eden Best Bitter and Websters Yorkshire Bitter on handpump; the choice of wines is very good for the area; darts and piped music. In summer, the hanging baskets are charming, and there are tables on a quiet lawn by the edge of Dalton Park, with a children's play area, flower borders, a very fine yew tree, ginger cats and maybe kittens. The village itself is best found by aiming for the unusually tall and elegant spire of the church, visible for miles around. *(Recommended by J C Proud, PLC; more reports please)*

Free house   Licensee Malcolm Crease   Real ale   Meals and snacks until 10 (not Mon)   Restaurant tel Dalton Holme (0430) 810246 (not Sun)   Children welcome Open 11.30–2.30, 7–11; closed Mon

STAMFORD BRIDGE   SE7155   Map 7

Three Cups

A166, W end of town; as it's actually over the Derwent Bridge it is just inside the N Yorks border

There's a rare annotated *Vanity Fair* cartoon of the nobs at Newmarket in 1885 in the spacious bar area of this busy ex-farmhouse; also, lots of bare ochre brick walls (including an arched stripped partition dividing the two rooms), oak beams, extensive panelling, and green banquettes, library chairs, stools and low armchairs around dark rustic tables. In the pleasant alcove at one end there are shelves of books, sepia photographs, and an open fire with a hand-turned bellows machine. Popular bar food includes a carvery (Tues–Sun, £3.95), as well as soup (95p), filled rolls (£1.35), burgers (from £2.20), ploughman's (from £2.50), home-made lasagne, daily curry or vegetarian dish (£2.95), gammon with egg or pineapple, (£3.95), steaks (from £5.95), and puddings (£1.35); children's meals (from £1.50). Well kept Bass and Stones on handpump. Rustic tables run along the front terrace, with more tables on the back lawn, swings and a big shoe house. *(Recommended by J C Proud, S V Bishop; more reports please)*

Bass   Licensees Ian and Gill McEnaney   Real ale   Meals and snacks (12–2, 7–10)
No-smoking restaurant   Children in eating area of bar and restaurant till 9pm   Open
11–2.30, 6–11; winter evening opening 6.30   Bedrooms tel Stamford Bridge (0759)
71396; /£30S

Lucky Dip

Besides the fully inspected pubs, you might like to try these Lucky Dips recommended to
us and described by readers (if you do, please send us reports):

Aldbrough [1 High St; TA2438], *George &
Dragon*: Friendly 500-year-old local, focal
point of sleepy village on unspoilt coastline;
two simple but stylish rooms with lots of
potted plants, log fire, good service,
Youngers beers, bar food, loudish CD juke
box, children's play area; bedrooms (*Lee
Goulding*)
☆ **Barnetby le Wold** [close to M180 junction 8,
opp rly stn; SE0509], *Station*: Pleasantly
remote; comfortable and congenial lounge
with charcoal drawings of steam
locomotives and old railway train prints;
particularly well kept Wards inc Dark Mild
on handpump, interesting good value bar
food lunchtime and evening (*John Baker, D
W Stokes*)
☆ **Beverley** [TA0340], *Beverley Arms*:
Comfortable and well kept THF hotel with
spacious and traditional oak-panelled bar,
well kept real ales, choice of several places to
eat inc covered former coachyard, now very
much an internal part of the building with
an impressive bank of former kitchen
ranges; good bedrooms (*LYM*)
Beverley [North Bar Within; TA0340],
Beaver: Recently taken over by the licensees
of the Half Moon at Skidby; doing similarly
enterprising food, inc the Half Moon's
famous Yorkshire puddings (*News please*);
[Hull Bridge (A1035 towards Leven)],
Crown & Anchor: Pleasant pub by River
Hull with outside tables and good, simple
bar food (*Roger Bellingham*); [Saturday
Mkt], *Kings Head*: Good choice of hot and
cold food from buffet display, fine puddings
trolley, generous helpings — usefully on Sun
lunchtime too; spacious L-shaped bar in
listed building, opening into two smaller
dining rooms; Mansfield Riding and
Marksman on handpump; bedrooms (*G T
Rhys, DC*); [Flemingate, next to Minster],
Sun: Cosy old pub doing well under current
regime, with well kept beer and good value
food (*Michael Swallow*)
Bishop Burton [A1079 Beverley—York;
SE9939], *Altisidora*: Recently extended pub
with good value bar food (not Sun, if the
restaurant on which they're increasingly
concentrating is busy) inc big well filled
sandwiches, in low-beamed modernised
lounge with comfortable alcoves, games in
saloon bar, seats out by neatly kept
flowerbeds looking over to ducks on pretty
pond in lovely village green (*G C and M D
Dickinson, Dr and Mrs S G Donald, LYM*)
Brandesburton [TA1247], *Black Swan*:
Spacious and attractively refurbished pub
which has been popular with readers for

good choice of beers inc Batemans and
Mansfield, and efficiently served good bar
lunches — but we've had no recent reports
(*News please*)
☆ **Bridlington** [184 Kingsgate (A165, just
outside); TA1867], *Broadacres*: Large,
popular pub with Watneys-related real ales
on handpump, good log fires, well planned
layout inc snack bar, Watneys Country
Carvery restaurant and children's room;
good food inc superb local haddock,
excellent service (*Roger Bellingham*)
Bridlington [Market Pl], *Packhorse*: Clean,
well cared for and welcoming, with cosy
polished decor and particularly good value
home-cooked food, good choice of drinks;
children welcome, with soft drinks bar in
separate room where they're allowed
unaccompanied (*W B Gray*)
Burton Fleming [TA0872], *Burton Arms*:
Solidly built, traditional pub in unspoilt
Wolds village; two cosy and cheerful bars
with down-to-earth friendliness — one
mainly for young people with darts, music
and conversational hubbub, the other more
sedate with a spacious, ingle-nooky
restaurant leading off (*G T Rhys*)
☆ **Cottingham** [TA0633], *Tiger*: Very popular
comfortably refurbished pub, with friendly
landlord and staff, well kept Bass on
handpump, generous helpings of reasonably
priced good hot and cold bar food — soups,
pheasant or turkey sandwiches, steak and
kidney pie all recommended (*David Gaunt,
Mr and Mrs Harry McCann*)
Ellerker [SE9229], *Black Horse*: This
attractively cottagey and cosy low-beamed
pub has become much more of a restaurant
now — worth knowing though, as a nice
place for a good value meal out (*DG, PM,
LYM*)
☆ **Ellerton** [signed off B1228 — OS Sheet 105
map reference 705398; SE7039], *Boot &
Shoe*: The only reason this low-beamed
16th-century cottage drops out of the main
entries this year is our lack of recent reports
on it; well worth knowing for its
comfortable and friendly old bar, fair-priced
standard evening bar food (not Mon, but
Sun lunch too — when it can get crowded),
well kept Old Mill and Tetleys on
handpump and three winter log fires; pub
games, good-sized garden behind with a
couple of retired goods vans, restaurant;
children till 9; has been closed weekday
lunchtime, winter Sat lunchtime (*Andy and
Jill Kassube, LYM*)
☆ **Etton** [3 ½ miles N of Beverley, off B1248;
SE9843], *Light Dragoon*: Two roomy,

comfortable bars with wide range of good value bar food inc generous sandwiches, good ham and eggs and steak pie; well kept Youngers real ales, inglenook fireplace; garden with children's play area *(Ann Griffiths, LYM)*

☆ **Flamborough** [junction B1255/B1229; TA2270], *Royal Dog & Duck*: Warm and welcoming bar with cosy, homely atmosphere in snug back bar and several other rambling rooms; generous helpings of popular food in efficient restaurant, inc good home-made soups and puddings, fresh veg; keg beers; children warmly welcomed, lots of amusements for them in courtyard; bedrooms *(Tony and Penny Burton, Barbara and Norman Wells, LYM)*

☆ **Grimsby** [Brighowgate; TA2609], *County*: Good value popular bar with well kept Youngers and terrific breakfasts throughout the morning; bedrooms comfortable and reasonably priced *(Stephen Merson)*

Harpham [TA0961], *St Quintons Arms*: Small, cosy and welcoming inn with good value home-made food inc excellent steaks; well kept Courage Directors and Sam Smiths; bedrooms *(I S Morley)*

☆ **Hedon** [TA1928], *Shakespeare*: Cosy village local, small L-shaped bar with thousands of beermats on beams, old framed brewery advertisements, real fire; friendly service, at least five real ales inc Darleys, Vaux Samson and Wards, juke box; gets very busy; bedrooms *(Lee Goulding)*

☆ **Hull** [Land of Green Ginger, Old Town; TA0927], *George*: Only lack of recent reports keeps this handsomely traditional long Victorian bar out of the main entries; plenty of oak, mahogany and copper, cheap bar lunches, well kept Bass and Stones on handpump, thriving atmosphere, piped music; handy for the fine Docks Museum; children allowed in plush upstairs dining room; open all day *(LYM)*

☆ **Hull** [150 High St (in Old Town to S of centre, quite near Olde White Harte], *Olde Black Boy*: Historic pub associated with naval press gangs and slavers; little black-panelled low-ceilinged front smoke room, lofty 18th-century back vaults bar (with juke box strong on golden oldies, fruit machine, TV); well kept Tetleys Mild and Bitter, bar food, friendly staff *(BB)*

☆ **Hull** [alley off Lowgate; look out for huge blue bell over pavement], *Olde Blue Bell*: Well kept Sam Smiths OB on handpump and good value simple lunchtime food inc traditional Sunday lunch, in old pub refurbished in traditional style, with three snug rooms; near market *(J D Shaw, BB)*

Kirkburn [signed off A163 SW of Great Driffield; SE9855], *Queens Head*: Under new regime has usual bar food with a lunchtime summer carvery, well kept Watneys-related real ales, decent wines, tables among flowers and fruit-trees in pretty garden, galleried restaurant (Sun lunchtime, Tues–Sat evenings); children welcome; open all day summer *(LYM)*

Langtoft [just off B1249, about a mile N of village — OS Sheet 101 map reference 007680; TA0167], *Old Mill*: Quiet, remote pub, friendly service, John Smiths beer, bar food inc some interesting dishes, restaurant *(Dave Braisted)*

Little Driffield [Downe Arms; TA0158], *Downe Arms*: Friendly village pub with attractive decor and good reasonably priced food from a varied menu; restaurant *(Mrs Barbara Head)*

☆ **North Dalton** [SE9352], *Star*: Upmarket village pub overlooking big pond, enthusiastically run by young licensees; well kept Tetleys on handpump, good food in bar and restaurant inc excellent range of fixed price meals; comfortable bedrooms; *(J C Proud, PLC)*

North Frodingham [TA1053], *Blue Post*: Airy but unspoilt village pub with locals' Farm Bar and small peaceful lounge across the ex-beer-barrels serving counter; simple home-cooked food in bar and restaurant, Watneys-related real ales, friendly service *(Lee Goulding)*

North Newbald [SE9136], *Tiger*: Attractively refurbished village pub on big green surrounded by rolling hills; has been popular for generous helpings of excellent value bar food, upstairs restaurant, but we've had no recent reports *(LYM; news please)*

☆ **Pocklington** [SE8049], *Feathers*: Comfortable and popular open-plan lounge, good solid bar food, well kept Youngers real ales, friendly service, children welcome; comfortable motel-style bedrooms *(LYM)*

Rawcliffe [High St; SE6823], *Neptune*: Cheerful and helpful staff, reasonably priced and reliably good standard food — particularly fish (bar food Sun lunchtime too), ageing overstuffed furniture, Mansfield beers *(DWC)*

Ryhill [a mile off A1033 Hull—Withernsea; TA2225], *Crooked Billet*: Isolated but very popular old smugglers' pub, with nautical public bar, lounge, open fires, relaxed atmosphere; well kept Tetleys beers, lunchtime food Tues–Thurs (unless pub closed) *(Lee Goulding)*

Scawby [A15 S of Brigg; SE9605], *King William IV*: Cosy little pub with quiet, relaxing atmosphere and equestrian decorations inc some brasses; Wards on handpump, bar snacks *(Andy and Jill Kassube)*

Skerne [Wansford Rd; TA0455], *Eagle*: Rarely unspoilt and unpretentious village local with real fires in both its spartan yet cosy rooms; no counter — drinks poured in tiny mezzanine cellar and brought to your table by friendly landlady; the Camerons real ales are dispensed by Victorian cash-register-style handpumps; no food or music — just a warm welcome in a pub full of character *(Lee Goulding)*

☆ **Snaith** [10 Pontefract Rd; SE6422], *Brewers Arms*: Recent solid mill conversion, with exposed joists, brick and timber bar counter, mock skeleton in old well, local photographs, light conservatory-style dining area with pine ceiling, green plush chairs,

Turkey carpet and lots of plants; notable for the fine Old Mill and Bullion from their own brewery; bedrooms *(T Nott)*

South Cave [SE9231], *Fox & Coney*: Popular old white pub with single traditional bar, old settles, treadle sewing tables, lots of hunting bric-a-brac; Youngers real ale, bar food, good walks nearby inc Wolds Way *(Lee Goulding)*

Stamford Bridge [SE7155], *Swordsman*: Well kept real ales in riverside pub with half the bar tables laid for lunch *(G T Rhys)*

☆ **Sutton upon Derwent** [B1228 SE of York; SE7047], *St Vincent Arms*: The pleasant atmosphere of this cosy old pub has survived several changes of licensee over the last few years, as has the wide choice of wines by the bottle — unusual for the area; a panelled front parlour with high-backed old settles, brass, copper and plates opens into another lounge, dining room and restaurant, then a big garden; popular if rather pricey bar food till 10, real ales such as Courage Best; children welcome; has been open all day Sat in summer *(Gwen and Peter Andrews, LYM)*

Ulceby [TA1014], *Brocklesby Ox*: Good old pub with nice atmosphere, well kept beer and good food inc fine fish and chips *(David Gaunt)*

☆ **Walkington** [B1230; SE9937], *Ferguson Fawsitt Arms*: Attractive mock-Tudor bars with wide choice of home-cooked hot dishes from buffet, inc unusual puddings, in airy flagstone-floored food bar, tables on outside terrace, games bar with pool table *(LYM)*

Waltham [High St; TA2603], *Kings Head*: Popular local with courteous staff, wide variety of good value food, hugely successful new year's party *(Mrs K Jackson, P Selby)*

☆ **Welton** [village signposted from A63 just E of Hull outskirts; SE9627], *Green Dragon*: Spacious and comfortably refurbished, with good range of reasonably priced bar food inc children's dishes, evening restaurant; notable as the real-life scene of the arrest of Dick Turpin *(LYM)*

Winterton [SE9318], *Butchers Arms*: John Smiths house with very friendly landlord and staff, attractively priced good bar food *(David Gaunt)*

Isle of Wight

As the spring wore into summer, and as we shifted from inspecting new pubs to preparing this edition of the Guide for printing, our postbag signalled two hot tips on the island – not yet main entries, as the good news came too late for us to act on it and inspect. They are the Red Lion at Freshwater and Crown at Shorwell, and on the basis of several reliable readers' recommendations we'd rate these as highly as the island's firm main entries. These include as particular favourites the lively Clarendon at Chale (or rather its Wight Mouse pub side), the well run White Lion at Arreton, the Bonchurch Inn at Bonchurch – Italian-run, with really good value pizzas, yet pleasantly traditional in other ways (back in these pages after quite a break), and the cosy Fishermans Cottage in its splendid position on the beach below Shanklin Chine (cheap food here – beating our £1 target for snacks and £3 for main dishes). Other Dip entries that look particularly promising include the Crab & Lobster at Bembridge, Hare & Hounds at Downend, Buddle at Niton, Seaview Hotel at Seaview (smart food, a good place to stay) and Spyglass in Ventnor. In Yarmouth, the Bugle and the George are running virtually neck-and-neck in readers' current ratings. For low drinks prices on the island, head for the Burts sign: the island's own brewery is a dedicated price-buster, and we found its beers much cheaper than the national average – whereas other, mainland drinks sold on the island now tend to work out more expensive than the national average.

ARRETON   SZ5486 Map 2

White Lion

A3056 Newport–Sandown

Popular with walkers and visitors moving between Arreton and Haseley Manors (the former houses the National Wireless Museum), this comfortable white house serves good value and filling helpings of home-made food – English cheeses and home-made pâtés, sandwiches, good ploughman's, home-made quiches, pies, curries, broths, pasta and chilli con carne. The communicating rooms of the roomy, beamed lounge bar have partly panelled walls decorated with guns, brass and horse-harness, and cushioned Windsor chairs on the brown carpet. The smaller, plainer public bar has dominoes and winter darts; readers have praised the welcoming atmosphere generated by attentive staff. Whitbreads Strong Country and Flowers Original tapped from casks behind the bar with an interesting cask-levelling device; piped music and a fruit machine. There's a family Cabin Bar, full of old farm tools, in the pleasing garden, and you can also sit out in front by the tubs of flowers. The village church is 12th century and houses the Isle of Wight Brass Rubbing Centre; a craft village nearby. *(Recommended by Charles Owens, T Nott, Roger Danes, John and Pat Smyth, Mr and Mrs P C Clark)*

Whitbreads   Licensees David and Maureen James   Real ale   Meals and snacks (12–3, 6–10.30)   Children in family room and eating area   Open 11–4, 6.30–11; winter closing 3 and evening opening 7

BONCHURCH   SZ5778 Map 2

Bonchurch Inn

Bonchurch Shute; from A3055 E of Ventnor turn down to Old Bonchurch opposite Leconfield Hotel

There's the undertone of a continental cafe in the atmosphere here – the licensee (who runs it with his English wife) is Italian and there are several food and wine specialities from his native country. But it's properly pubby, too, with Burts Real Ale and Marstons Pedigree tapped from the cask, darts, bar billiards, shove-ha'penny, dominoes and cribbage. The high-ceilinged and friendly public bar is partly cut into the steep rocks of the Shute, and conjures up an image of salvaged shipwrecks with its floor of narrow-planked ship's decking, folding chairs of the sort that old-fashioned steamers used to have and solid fuel stove in one corner; there's also a smaller saloon. Other bar food includes sandwiches (from £1.20, toasties 20p extra), home-made minestrone soup (£1.40), Pizza Napoletana (£2.60), quiche Lorraine or ploughman's with a choice of Cheddar or pâté (£2.85), deep fried squid (£3.10) cold salad platter (from £3.50), antipasto with meats, prawns and pâté (£3.85), 8oz steak or chicken Kiev or grilled halibut steak (£5.50), cannelloni, lasagne or grilled fillet of plaice (£3.50), venison and port wine (£6), and puddings (from £1.75) including zabaglione (£1.95). The old stone inn used to be stables for the nearby manor house; another converted stable, with a splendid arched entrance and across the cobbled courtyard, is now a cafe. (Recommended by Roger Danes, Andrew Stephenson, HNJ, PEJ, D J Perry)

Free house   Licensees Nino and Gillian Besozzi   Real ale   Meals and snacks 11.30–2.30, 6–10.30   Restaurant (7–9 Sun)   Children in eating area   Open 11–3, 6–11; closed 26 Dec   Bedrooms tel Ventnor (0983) 852611; £16/£32

CHALE   SZ4877   Map 2

Clarendon / Wight Mouse ★

In village, on B3399, but now has access road directly off A3055

For many readers the place to head for is the Wight Mouse bar – a notably perky place shaped a bit like a dumb-bell, with the narrow bar-counter part joining two more spacious areas; there's a huge collection of musical instruments hanging from the ceiling and an outstanding choice of around 365 whiskies – one for every day of the year – as well as some uncommon brandies, madeiras and country wines; live music every night of the week, but at a volume that still lets you chat companionably. The bar area is complemented by the collection of family areas – including a popular dining section that's open all afternoon – and of course by the hotel itself which is small, comfortable and well furnished. Big helpings of locally produced and home-made bar food include sandwiches (from £1.20, fresh crab £2.40, toasties 25p extra), home-made soup (£1.25), ploughman's (from £2.00), burgers (from £2.90), ham and eggs (£3.10), salads (from £3.10), home-made pizzas (from £3.95) and scampi or Mexican hot chilli con carne in taco shells (£3.95), Wiener schnitzel (£4.30), fisherman's platter or gravadlax (£5.30), giant mixed grill (£5.85) and steaks (from £7.40) and a range of vegetarian dishes (from £2.50); puddings such as home-made meringue nests filled with fruit, cream, ice-cream and nuts (£1.45); there's also a children's menu and service is friendly and efficient. Well kept and decently priced Burts Island Ale, Gales HSB, Marstons Pedigree and Whitbreads Strong Country on handpump; darts at one end, dominoes, fruit machine, piped music; an adjoining games/family room has pool, space game, and a juke box. Picnic-table sets on a side lawn, many more on the big back lawn looking over the fields to the sea and for children, swings, slide, see-saw, rabbits, and chickens. They run a pick-you-up and drop-you-home mini-bus service for four or more people (£2 per person). The hotel is named after a ship which was wrecked just off shore here in the Great Storm of 1836. (Recommended by Alan Skull, GB, CH, Pat and Derek Westcott, M W Barratt, Alan and Sharron Tod, Paul Sweetman, John Farmer, A Sweatman, R G Tickner, Andrew Stephenson, Mr and Mrs P C Clark, Alan and Audrey Chatting, Richard and Dilys Smith, Charles Owens, Roger Danes)

Free house   Licensees John and Jean Bradshaw   Real ale   Meals and snacks 12–10 all day, (12–3, 7–10.30 Sun)   Restaurant   Children in eating areas and three family rooms   Live music every night   Open 11am–midnight   Bedrooms tel Niton (0983) 730431; £19(£21B)/£38(£42B)

nr COWES (EAST)   SZ5095 Map 2
Folly

Folly Lane – which is signposted off A3021 just S of Whippingham

This was originally based on a sea-going barge beached here in the early 1700s – the roof still includes part of the original barge deck. It was first recorded as a proper building in 1792, but the nautical (and these days yachting) connection is still there – effects include a VHF radio-telephone, a wind speed indicator, a barometer and a chronometer, and big windows look out over the boats, as do picnic-table sets on the water's-edge terrace. Around the old wood timbered walls are venerable wooden chairs and refectory-type tables, shelves of old books and plates, railway bric-a-brac and farm tools, old pictures, and brass lights. They even have their own mail collection boxes, showers and a launderette. Bar food includes vegetable crumble (£2.75), chicken curry (£3), beef and ale or seafood pie (3.95), and a pint of prawns (£4). Marstons Pedigree, Pompey Royal and Whitbreads Strong Country on handpump and a wide choice of rums such as West Indian amber; darts, pool, space game, trivia game, a fruit machine and piped music. There's a good children's playroom, and a landscaped garden. Close to Osborne House. *(Recommended by Ian Phillips, W E Parker, John and Pat Smyth, Alan and Audrey Chatting)*

Whitbreads   Licensees Peter and Barbara Handtschoewercker   Real ale   Meals and snacks   Restaurant tel Isle of Wight (0983) 297171   Children in eating area and family room   Live entertainment Tues, Thurs, Sat, Sun   Open 11–3, 6.30–11; closes 4 Sat; winter evenings open 7

SHALFLEET   SZ4189 Map 2
New Inn

A3054 Newport–Yarmouth

The partly panelled, flagstoned public bar in this dining pub has a boarded ceiling, scrubbed deal tables, a cushioned built-in settle and Windsor chairs, a boarded ceiling, and on cold days a roaring log fire in the big stone hearth, which has guns and an ale yard hanging above it; in the lounge bar there are Windsor chairs and wall banquettes around the stone walls and under the beams. Bar food includes soup, sandwiches to order, five different ploughman's, lasagne, red hot chilli con carne, crab salad, 8oz sirloin steak, and a daily changing blackboard menu. There's also a lot of fresh fish, bought from the previous landlord, who owns his own small trawler and lobster boat; the selection might include prawns, prawn curry, poacher's pie, and Dover sole, and fresh crab and lobster when available; in winter there are live mussels and oysters. Flowers Original, Fremlins, Whitbreads Pompey Royal, and guests such as Gales HSB and Marstons Pedigree tapped from the cask. There are rustic tables outside by the road, and a garden. *(Recommended by Mr and Mrs P C Clark, T Nott, Peter Adcock, Mrs J A Blanks, Anne and Tim Neale, B S Bourne, Alan and Audrey Chatting; more reports especially on food please)*

Whitbreads   Real ale   Meals (12–6, 7–10) and snacks (12–6)   Restaurant tel Calbourne (098 378) 314   Children in restaurant   Open 11–11; may well close winter afternoons

SHANKLIN   SZ5881 Map 2
Fishermans Cottage

Bottom of Shanklin Chine

Picturesquely tucked into the cliffs on Appley beach, this thatched cottage feels more isolated than it actually is – just a short and well signposted walk from the esplanade. The low-beamed, flagstoned rooms have photographs, paintings and drawings of the pub on their stripped stone walls, bowls of fresh flowers, and a friendly atmosphere. Good value bar food includes sandwiches (from 95p), sausages (£1.80), ploughman's (from £1.95), half pint of prawns (summer only

£2.50), scampi (£2.95), crab salad (summer only £3.95) and in winter there are daily specials. Coffee is served from 10.30 and there are a range of country wines; darts, cribbage, a fruit machine and piped music. From the seats on the terrace you can look straight out onto the beach. Though you can drive to the pub, a path (for which there's a charge in season) zigzags down the picturesquely steep and sinuous Chine. (Recommended by Mr and Mrs P C Clark, T Nott, Andrew Stephenson, Tony and Penny Burton, Roger Danes)

Free house   Licensees Mrs A P P Springman and Duncan McDonald   Meals and snacks (12–2.30, 7–9.30)   Children in eating area winter only   Occasional live music in summer   Open 11–3, 7–11

Lucky Dip

Besides the fully inspected pubs, you might like to try these Lucky Dips recommended to us and described by readers (if you do, please send us reports):

☆ Bembridge [Forelands, off Howgate Lane — look for sign into Foreland Fields Rd; OS Sheet 196 map reference 655873; SZ6587], *Crab & Lobster*: Solent (and, more prominently, coastguard station) views from front window of recently refurbished pub — a pretty if rather genteel parlour effect; usual bar food, not cheap considering the size of the helpings, with some emphasis on cheese and local seafood, good club sandwiches, better than average choice of puddings; friendly service, well kept Whitbreads beers, 1950s piped music — rather loud in the lavatories; if you get there early or late you'll avoid coach tours; bedrooms (T Nott, Roger Danes, J H C Peters)

☆ Cowes [25 High St; SZ4896], *Pier View*: Victorian pub with efficient pleasant service, fresh flowers on tables, unobtrusive piped music, prints of sailing ships, plates and keys on the walls; well kept Flowers and Marstons Pedigree, good choice of house wines, original bar food such as fresh prawns with Greek salad or duck with morello cherry sauce (Dr J R Hamilton)

Cowes, *Harbour Lights*: Recently refitted as pizza-pub (good value pizzas), with large windows overlooking harbour; popular with wind-surfers who make trip from mainland for lunch and with families (Anon)

☆ Downend [B3056, at crossroads; SZ5387], *Hare & Hounds*: Excellent food and service in charming and inviting thatched Burts pub with interesting local bar and more orthodox modern extension behind; nice and warm in winter, and handy for Robin Hill Country Park (Tony Bland, A J Woodhouse)

Fishbourne [SZ5592], *Fishbourne Inn*: Pleasant surroundings, atmosphere and friendly service; good food with tempting reasonably priced puddings (Alan and Audrey Chatting)

☆ Freshwater [Church Pl — OS Sheet 196 map reference 347873; SZ3484], *Red Lion*: Delightful atmosphere, with flagstone floors, scrubbed kitchen tables, comfortable chesterfields, reproduction antique settles — a careful and successful Whitbreads refurbishment; friendly and helpful licensees, impressive bar food inc outstanding beef

sandwiches, good daily specials such as smoked haddock pasta with mushrooms and prawns, and wide choice of filled baked potatoes (W E Taylor, J P Berryman, T Nott, Pat and Derek Westcott)

Freshwater Bay [SZ3484], *Albion*: Large room overlooking bay with outside terrace; bright and efficient service by white-jacketed staff, generous fresh salads and hot meals, well kept Bass (Mrs M R Sale)

Godshill [Newport Rd; SZ5282], *Griffin*: Haven of peace and sanity — refuge from teashops and tourists; good garden, service, food and drink (U W Bankes)

Hulverstone [B3399 — OS Sheet 196 map reference 398840; SZ3984], *Sun*: Thatched Whitbreads village pub worth knowing for pleasant well kept gardens looking over to the sea, and play area; very simple menu appealing to families, ordinary interior (T Nott)

Newchurch [OS Sheet 196 map reference 562855; SZ5685], *Pointer*: Friendly helpful service in two-bar village local close to church, pleasant and well kept, with comfortable lounge bar, cheerful staff, relaxed atmosphere; decent bar food, good range of low-alcohol and soft drinks, well kept lavatories (Mrs C Spence, T Nott)

Newport [High St; SZ4988], *Castle*: Old flagstones, massive end wall, and a lot of more recent antiquery; friendly service with good luncht menu from varied menu, well kept Whitbreads real ales, piped music (Alan and Audrey Chatting)

Ningwood [A3054 Newport—Yarmouth, a mile W of Shalfleet — OS Sheet 196 map reference 399892; SZ3989], *Horse & Groom*: Big Whitbreads pub, fairly busy at weekends; fossils in partly stripped limestone wall, new olde-worlde settles, Windsor chairs, brocaded banquettes, bare brickwork, black-stained rough woodwork, limited choice of well prepared pub food with some emphasis on chargrill, Flowers under pressure; garden (Charles Owens, T Nott, Peter Adcock)

☆ Niton [towards St Catherines Point; A3055 Ventnor rd through Niton, then right after BP garage; SZ5076], *Buddle*: Original beams and flagstones, considerably more modern comfortable refurbishment and extension (as you'd expect, not all agree about the appropriateness of this), also family Smugglers Barn; good range of well kept Whitbreads real ales with a guest, friendly service, fresh good value bar food — there's a very modern display cabinet and servery in the L-shaped entrance area; garden with ride-on machines for children, open all day (*Mrs M R Sale, Tim Brierly, T Nott, Roger Danes, LYM*)

☆ Seaview [High St; SZ6291], *Seaview Hotel*: Reasonably priced bar food a decided cut above the average, inc some things from the highly thought-of restaurant as well as more routine pubby dishes — fresh fish a strong point, and the hot crab ramekin specially recommended; the two Edwardian-style bars and courtyard attract plenty of people; bedrooms very comfortable — a good place to stay (*J P Berryman, Mrs J A Blanks, John and Margaret Estdale*)

Seaview [Esplanade; B3340, just off B3330 Ryde—Brading], *Old Fort*: Good value buffet with generous helpings of decent food, well served in pleasant atmosphere (*Pat and Derek Westcott*)

☆ Shanklin [Chine Hill; SZ5881], *Chine*: Interesting timbered pub in lovely wooded setting on side of chine with good views over chine, beach and sea; three bars seem caught in a 30-year time-warp with their unassuming furnishings, also large conservatory family area with magnificent fruiting grapevine; wide range of straightforward bar food all week, well kept cheap Burts ales; no juke box, fruit machines or pool table (darts in locals' bar); children allowed away from bar (*Andrew Stephenson, Glenn Thorpe*)

Shanklin [High St Old Town; A3055 towards Ventnor], *Crab*: Thatched outside, but inside now refitted in high-ceilinged rather urban style; lunchtime sandwiches, salads and hot dishes, well kept Flowers Original and Whitbreads Strong Country on handpump, games and children's room; open all day, very popular with tourists (*M C Howells, W E Taylor, LYM*)

☆ Shorwell [OS Sheet 196 map reference 456829; SZ4582], *Crown*: Comfortable and attractively furnished old pub with pleasant atmosphere, unspoilt decor, comfortable wooden settles and tables, real fire, friendly staff, no piped music; as it's a bit off the beaten track it keeps a pleasantly local touch; consistently good food at reasonable prices inc interesting vegetarian dishes and

good home-cooked veg instead of chips and peas, well kept Flowers and Whitbreads Strong County tapped from the cask, friendly staff, beautifully kept garden with trout stream and willow trees (*Anne and Tim Neale, T Nott, Lyn Jolliffe, Andrew Grant, HNJ, PEJ, Alan and Audrey Chatting*)

☆ Ventnor [Esplanade, SW end; SZ5577], *Spyglass*: Cleverly designed to give genuine atmosphere and varied, balanced decor, with lots of nautical memorabilia; nice range of well prepared and presented food, a beer brewed for the pub and Coopers (from Ringwood), with another beer such as Gibbs Mew Bishops Tipple, seafood dishes as well as more usual pub food; good-sized terrace overlooking sea, children welcome, regular lunchtime piano (*T Nott, Reg Tickner*)

Ventnor [Pier St], *Rose & Crown*: Old, pleasant and spacious, with good food and attractive outside area (*Miss E Waller*)

Whitwell [SZ5277], *White Horse*: Country-style decor, good busy atmosphere, friendly efficient staff, well kept Flowers Original and Whitbreads Strong Country, adequate choice of well presented bar food, darts (*Reg Tickner*)

Wootton [A3054 Ryde—Newport; SZ5492], *Cedar*: Cedars in garden, large public bar with darts, good-sized lounge bar with gas fireplace used for spit-roasting; Whitbreads Strong Country and another real ale, decent food; handy for Isle of Wight Steam Railway; children's room (*Keith Widdowson*)

Wootton Bridge [SZ5492], *Sloop*: Busy, but service efficient and friendly; usual range of bar food prepared and presented well (*Alan and Audrey Chatting*)

☆ Yarmouth [St James' Sq; SZ3589], *Bugle*: The nautical theme in the lively bar runs to a wall-length photograph of the harbour and a bar counter like the stern of a galleon, with food from well filled sandwiches to grills and seafood salads; well kept Flowers Original and Marstons Pedigree on handpump, restaurant, children's room, sizeable garden which may have impressive summer barbecues; nr GWG40; bedrooms — ask for one that's not over the bar (*Pat and Derek Westcott, Peter Adcock, P A Barfield, LYM*)

☆ Yarmouth [Quay St], *George*: Good food swiftly and courteously served, a nice relaxing new bar with nautical theme, and intelligent, friendly staff; bedrooms (*Tessa Stuart, Tim Brierly*)

Kent

Pub food in the county is increasingly good – especially as more and more pubs here are searching out supplies of freshly landed fish. Pre-eminent among these are the Brown Trout just outside Lamberhurst, Sankeys at the Gate in Tunbridge Wells and Pearsons in Whitstable, all of which rival good fish restaurants for the freshness of their ingredients – at considerably lower prices. Other places here currently particularly good for food include the delightful George at Newnham (full of character), the Dering Arms at Pluckley (good fish specials), the tucked-away Ringlestone at Ringlestone (good choice of beers, too; and its barn has just been fitted out to sell crafts and country wines), the popular White Lion at Selling, the Cliffe Tavern Hotel at St Margarets At Cliffe (a useful place to stay if you're catching an early ferry), the friendly Black Lion at Southfleet (a new main entry), the Galoche in Tunbridge Wells (outstanding cheeses) and the quaint Pepper Box at Ulcombe (another new main entry). Pubs here currently doing notably well in other ways include the Little Gem in Aylesford (the county's smallest pub – lots of real ales), the Flying Horse at Boughton Aluph (a pleasant place to stay), the Gate by the marshes at Boyden Gate (an entertaining country local), the Castle in the lovely village of Chiddingstone, the White Horse in its rather larger-scale rival for beauty, Chilham (a new main entry; the new licensee at the other good pub here, the Woolpack, is promising), the creekside Ship at Conyer Quay (nice atmosphere, amazing collection of drinks – back as a main entry after quite a break), the simple Dove in its lovely garden at Dargate, the very unspoilt Mounted Rifleman at Luddenham (celebrating its new status as a free house – it's no longer tied to Whitbreads, but after a lifetime of learning how to keep Fremlins so well the landlord will go on selling it), the Spotted Dog just outside Penshurst (new licensees bringing this beautifully placed pub back into these pages, on top form), the handsome old George & Dragon at Speldhurst, and the quiet and relaxing Tiger, out in the country at Stowting. Pubs to pick out particularly in the Lucky Dip section at the end of the chapter (either former main entries which we've not heard enough of recently, or 'coming' pubs which are currently showing special promise) include the William IV at Benenden, White Horse at Boughton Street, Little Brown Jug at Chiddingstone Causeway, Griffins Head at Chillenden, Oak & Ivy in Hawkhurst, Gun & Spitroast at Horsmonden, Fayreness in Kingsgate, Star at St Mary in the Marsh, Grove Ferry at Upstreet, St Crispin at Worth, Bull at Wrotham and Tickled Trout and New Flying Horse in Wye; there are several interesting possibilities in or just outside Penshurst. This is by no means a cheap county. Pubs here tend to charge around 10p more than the national average for drinks. Our price survey showed that your best general chance of good value drinks is in pubs tied to the local brewer, Shepherd Neame. These consistently tended to work out a few pence cheaper than either free houses or the national chains. The cheapest *drinks we found were in the Gate at Boyden Gate. This was also the only main-entry pub here where we found decent snacks for less than £1 and main dishes for under £3 – a sharp contrast with pubs up in the north, say, where that sort of pricing is still the rule rather than the exception.*

AYLESFORD TQ7359 Map 3

Little Gem

3 miles from M2 junction 3; A229 towards Maidstone, then first right turn, following signposts to village. Also 1 3/4 miles from M20 junction 6; A229 towards Maidstone, then follow Aylesford signpost; 19 High Street

One of this quaint and ancient little pub's chief attractions is its unusually enterprising choice of real ales on handpump or tapped from the cask: Bass, Everards Old Original, Fullers London Pride, Greene King Abbot, King & Barnes Festive, Marstons Owd Rodger, Theakstons Old Peculier, Wadworths 6X, Youngers IPA, Youngs Special, and a guest ale; local cider, Irish whiskies. There's a cosy, friendly atmosphere, heavy timbers, a big open fire, interesting oddments including a history of the pub, and an unusual high pitched ceiling following the line of the roof; an open staircase leads to a mezzanine floor, a bit like a minstrels gallery, with a few tables. Bar food includes doorstep sandwiches (£1.50), ploughman's (from £1.75), vegetarian lasagne or curry (from £2.50), scampi or seafood platter (from £3); piped music. It claims to be Kent's smallest pub. *(Recommended by Peter Neate; more reports please)*

Free house Licensee Mrs Sandra Brenchley Real ale Snacks and lunchtime meals Children in eating area of bar Open 11–3, 6–11

nr BIDDENDEN TQ8538 Map 3

Three Chimneys ★

A262, a mile W of village

Radiating from the central bar counter in this characterful country pub is a series of small, very traditionally furnished rooms with old settles, some harness and sporting prints on the walls, low oak beams, and good winter log fires. Bar food, from a choice of four starters or four main courses, might include leek and bacon tartlet or tomato and celeriac soup (£1.85), ham and parmesan pancakes (£2.80), a quiche such as tuna and mushroom (£3.95), turkey curry (£5.15), Russian fish pie (£5.45), and duck and pheasant casserole (£5.75); there are puddings like banoffi pie (£1.95) or chocolate and orange mousse (£2.25), all with Jersey cream. They usually have a couple of vegetarian dishes, such as vegetable crumble (£4.10). There is a useful overspill Garden Room, popular with families, where you can book tables (Biddenden (0580) 291472); as this part isn't licensed you have to carry your drinks in from the main bar. Besides a range of well kept real ales tapped from the cask, including Adnams Best, Fremlins, Goachers (from Maidstone), Harveys Best, Hook Norton Old Hookey and Marstons Pedigree (and in winter Harveys Old Ale), they keep local cider, several malt whiskies, and their sensible wine list includes several half bottles. The simple public bar has darts, shove ha'penny, dominoes and cribbage. The garden is another plus: careful plantings of flowering shrubs and shrub roses shelter the neatly kept lawn in a series of gentle curves. Just down the road from Sissinghurst. *(Recommended by John Evans, Terry Buckland, R and E Harfield, Norman Foot, John Highley, William D Cissna, T Galligan, Mr Stoner, Mrs C Hartley, John and Joan Nash, Mr and Mrs D M Norton, Jill and Paul Ormond, Stephen Goodchild, Mrs E M Thompson, K Leist, Dr T H M Mackenzie, Mike Dixon, C Trows, G Smith, Miss A Tress, Peter Hall, Paul Sexton, Sue Harrison, Theo Schofield, S A Robbins)*

Free house Licensees C F W Sayers and G A Sheepwash Real ale Meals and snacks (11.30–2, 6.30–10) Restaurant (see above) Children in Garden Room Open 11–2.30, 6–11; closed 25 and 26 Dec

BOUGH BEECH   TQ4846 Map 3

Wheatsheaf

B2027, S of reservoir

Partly tile-hung and partly clad with weather boarding and roses, this quiet old pub has a smart bar with a massive stone fireplace and an unusually high-ceiling with lofty timbers. A couple of lower rooms lead off and are divided from the central part by standing timbers. Decorations include a stag's head, cigarette cards, swordfish spears, and – over the massive stone fireplace which separates off the public bar – a mysterious 1607 inscription reading *Foxy Galumpy*. Bar food includes sandwiches (from £1, toasties 5p extra), soup (£1.15), home-made pâté (£1.25), omelettes (from £1.60), ploughman's (from £2.15), home-cooked ham with egg or deep-fried seafood platter (£3.20), and steaks (£6.95); home-made puddings such as walnut, apple and raisin steamed pudding (£1.50), and children's dish (£1.70). Well kept Fremlins and Flowers on handpump. The public bar has an attractive old settle carved with wheatsheaves, buffalo horns over its fire, and shove-ha'penny, dominoes, cribbage, fruit machine, trivia and sensibly placed darts; piped music. A pretty sheltered lawn with flowerbeds, fruit trees, roses, flowering shrubs, and a children's rustic cottage stretches behind the building. *(Recommended by Heather Martin, R Bennett, L M Miall, Joy Heatherley; more reports please)*

Fremlins (Whitbreads)   Licensee Ron Smith   Real ale   Meals and snacks (not Wed or Sun evenings)   Children in area set aside for them by public bar   Open 10 (10.30 Sat)–2.30, 6–11

BOUGHTON ALUPH   TR0247 Map 3

Flying Horse 🛏

Boughton Lees; just off A251 N of Ashford

On the ancient Pilgrims' Way to Canterbury, this friendly 15th-century pub faces the broad cricket green (weekly matches in summer). The open-plan bar has comfortable upholstered modern wall benches, fresh flowers on many tables and hop bines around the serving area, horse brasses, stone animals on either side of the blazing log fire, and lots of standing space. Further inside, age shows in the shiny old black panelling and the arched windows (though they are a later Gothic addition). Good bar food includes sandwiches, home-made steak and kidney pie (£4), first-class cold meat salad, home-made lasagne (£4.20), and lemon sole stuffed with salmon mousse or poached fresh salmon (£4.75). Well kept Courage Best and Directors on handpump, and they are hoping to include others; a good wine list that includes their own labelled house wine. Darts, shove-ha'penny, cribbage, dominoes, fruit machine and piped music. You can sit outside in the rose garden. *(Recommended by Werner Arend, David Gaunt, Mrs A Crowhurst, Gwen and Peter Andrews, D N Lane, John McGee, Jenny and Brian Seller)*

Courage   Licensees Howard and Christine Smith   Real ale   Meals and snacks Children in dining room only   Occasional jazz nights   Open 11–3, 6–11; 11–11 summer Sats   Bedrooms tel Ashford (0233) 620914; £18(£20S)/£29(£27S)

BOYDEN GATE   TR2265 Map 3

Gate Inn ★

Off A299 Herne Bay–Ramsgate – follow Chislet, Upstreet signpost opposite Roman Gallery; Chislet also signposted off A28 Canterbury–Margate at Upstreet – after turning right into Chislet main street keep right on to Boyden; the pub gives its address as Marshside, though Boyden Gate seems more usual on maps

This charming country local is right on the edge of the marshes, and if you sit outside at the picnic-table sets on the sheltered side lawn on a fine summer's evening, the air is filled with the contented quacking of a million ducks and geese (they sell duck food inside – 5p a bag). The bar has hop bines hanging from the beams, attractively etched windows, pews with flowery cushions around tables of considerable character, and a good winter log fire (which serves both quarry-tiled rooms); there are photographs on the walls – some ancient sepia ones, others new ('MCC' here stands for Marshside Cricket Club – the pub is a focus for many other games, too), and part of the area is no-smoking. Bar food consists of sandwiches and enterprising toasties (from 95p), ploughman's with home-boiled bacon (£2.50), home-made ratatouille flan (£2.70), filled baked potatoes or home-made bean and pepper hot pot (£2.95), and puddings like prize-winning bread pudding (95p). Well kept Shepherd Neame Bitter, Bishops Finger and Old tapped from the cask; sensibly placed darts, as well as shove-ha'penny, dominoes, cribbage, and trivia. *(Recommended by L M Miall; more reports please)*

Shepherd Neame Licensee Christopher Smith Real ale Meals and snacks (available during all opening hours) Children welcome (family room) Piano Sun, folk music Wed Open 11–2.30(3 Sat), 6–11

CHIDDINGSTONE   TQ4944 Map 3
Castle

Village signposted from B2027 Tonbridge–Edenbridge

Like the rest of the beautiful village, this ancient building – an inn since 1730 – is owned by the National Trust. The neatly modernised beamed bar has well made settles forming booths around the tables on its partly carpeted oak floor, cushioned sturdy wall benches, an attractive mullioned window seat in one small alcove, and latticed windows. Bar food includes home-made soup (£1.95), open sandwiches (from £2.50), filled baked potatoes (from £2.80), ploughman's (from £3.40), very hot chilli con carne or beef in ale pie (£4.35), and salads (from £6.55). Well kept King & Barnes Bitter, Larkins Sovereign and Shepherd Neame Old on handpump; over 140 wines (including house wines) by the bottle, and liqueur coffees. The public bar – popular with locals – has darts, shove-ha'penny, dominoes and cribbage. The back garden is pretty, with a small pool and fountain set in a rockery, and tables on a brick terrace and neat lawn; there's also a barbecue bar here. *(Recommended by Mrs C Hartley, Neil Barker, Terry Buckland, Ruth Humphrey, Richard Houghton, Cynth and Malc Pollard, Christian Leigh, L D Glazer, Heather Martin, Mr and Mrs R C Abbott)*

Free house Licensee Nigel Lucas Real ale Meals and snacks (11–2.45, 6–10.45) Restaurant tel Penshurst (0892) 870247 Children in eating area of bar Open 11–3, 6–11

CHILHAM   TR0753 Map 3
White Horse

Village signposted off A252/A28 W of Canterbury; pub in centre

This old pub's special feature is its position in the prettiest village square in Kent: a couple of white tables out on the corner give a perfect view of the timber-framed Tudor houses. The comfortably modernised open-plan lounge bar, which spreads around the neat central bar servery, has a massive fireplace with the Lancastrian rose carved at the end of its mantlebeam – a relic of the Wars of the Roses, uncovered only in 1966, during refurbishments. The handsomely carved ceiling beams are as old, and there's a theory that two skeletons found under the floor were victims of a skirmish in the 14th-century Peasants' Revolt. Bar food includes sandwiches, and home-made dishes that include curries (from £3.30). Flowers, Fremlins and Marstons Pedigree on handpump; sensibly placed darts, piped music. The grand park of nearby Chilham Castle makes a good outing. *(Recommended by Robert and Elizabeth Scott, S V Bishop, Simon Bates, Simon Collett-Jones)*

Whitbreads Licensee L R Terry Real ale Meals and snacks (not Tues evening) Restaurant tel Canterbury (0227) 730355 Open 11–11; 11–2.30, 6–11 winter weekdays

Woolpack 🛏

Best approached from the signposted village road at junction A28/A252, which leads straight to the inn

This comfortably renovated old timbered pub has a busy, friendly bar with little brocaded armchairs, a sofa, pews and wall seats, lots of copper urns hanging from a high beam, and a row of jugs, flagons and kegs; it's dominated by a cavernous fireplace with a big log fire, and they are opening up the inglenook in the restaurant. Bar food includes sandwiches (from £1.15, the prawn is tasty), ploughman's (£2.60), good dressed crab, and hot food such as beef bourguignon, steak and kidney pie or Woolpack platter (from £2.85). Well kept Shepherd Neame Bishops Finger and Old on handpump; pleasant service; unobtrusive piped music. The bedrooms are in an attractively converted former stable buildings behind, and the beautiful medieval square which has made the village famous is just up the lane. (Recommended by Simon Bates, S V Bishop, John and Tessa Rainsford, Simon Collett-Jones, John and Joan Nash, Paul and Margaret Baker, Graham and Glenis Watkins)

Shepherd Neame   Licensee Glyn Ford   Real ale   Meals and snacks (till 10 in evening on Sat)   Restaurant   Children in restaurant lunchtime and early evening   Open 11–3, 6–11   Bedrooms tel Canterbury (0227) 730208; £37.50B/£45B; 4-posters £55

CHIPSTEAD   TQ4956 Map 3

George & Dragon

39 High Street; 1 1/4 miles from M25 junction 5: A21 S, then A25 towards Sevenoaks, then first left

The atmosphere in this popular dining pub is relaxed and friendly and the furnishings in the open-plan bar, though modern, do tone in with the heavy black beams (some of them nicely carved), oak tables and Windsor chairs on the geometric carpet; upright timbers divide the room into smaller, cosier areas, two of which have open fires. The new licensees have changed the menu, which now includes at lunchtime, soup, sandwiches (from £1.20), ploughman's (from £2.35), ham and egg (£3.30), home-made steak and kidney pie (£4.20), a farmhouse grill, and chicken Kiev (£4.75), with evening dishes such as mussels in garlic or Mediterranean prawns (from £2.20), supreme of chicken (£5.85) and lots of Scotch steaks (from £8.40); daily specials like fresh cod, haddock or trout and beef strogonoff (from around £4). Well kept Courage Best and Directors and Younger Bitter on handpump; fruit machine, piped music. There are tables on neatly kept grass beside roses and tall trees, behind the car park. (Recommended by E G Parish, K Widdowson, Dave Braisted; more reports please)

Courage   Licensees Mr and Mrs F J Varley   Real ale   Meals and snacks (12–2.30, 7–9.45)   Open 11–3, 5.30–11

COBHAM   TQ6768 Map 3

Leather Bottle

2 1/2 miles from M2 junction 1; village signposted from A2 (towards London) on B2009

The Dickens connection is very strong in this ancient half-timbered house, as he often used to end up here after strolling through the park of Cobham Hall, and mentions it fondly in Pickwick Papers as 'clean and commodious'. In amongst all the decorations you'd expect, there are some truly interesting prints of Dickens characters, including early postcards and teacards. The large, open-plan bar serves sandwiches (from £1.20), ploughman's (£3.95), good value cold meat salads (£4.25) and a daily hot dish such as lasagne, pies or roasts, as well as Ruddles County and Websters Yorkshire; friendly staff. Tables are laid out on the extended back lawn and in the orchard at the bottom there's a large fish pond with a children's play area and an outdoors summer tuck shop. The village itself is pretty, with medieval almshouses, and outstanding brasses in the church. *(Recommended by Hank Hotchkiss, Brendan Moran, M Rising, Peter Griffiths)*

Trumans (Watneys)   Licensee Michael Eakins   Real ale   Meals and snacks (not Sun evening)   Restaurant   Children in eating area and in restaurant   Open 11–11; closed winter lunchtimes but open 5.30–11   Bedrooms tel Meopham (0474) 814327; £33/£48(£64.50B)

CONYER QUAY   TQ9665 Map 3
Ship

From A2 Sittingbourne–Faversham turn off towards Deerton Stn (signposted) then at T-junction turn right signposted Teynham, Sittingbourne; Conyer signposted from Teynham

Tables on a narrow gravel terrace here face the edge of a creek packed with small boats. Inside, the rambling and cosy little rooms have wooden floors, wall boards, a planked ceiling, various nautical nick-nacks and a notice-board with boating advertisements. Flowers and Fremlins are well kept on handpump (they have a happy hour every night between 6 and 7 – 7–8 Sundays – when doubles are priced as singles and pints of beer or cider are 10p cheaper), and an incredible range of more than 150 malt whiskies (they have a Whisky trail with prizes) plus a further 100 blended scotches, Irish whiskies and bourbons, more than 160 wines (14 by the glass or carafe and 14 half bottles), over 100 liqueurs, 25 rums, 20 ports, and 25 cognacs, Armagnacs and brandies. Lots of liqueur coffees. Bar food includes toasties (from £1.20), soup (£1.95), ploughman's (from £2.45), burgers (from £2.50), salads (from £3.50), basket meals or home-made pies like leek and apricot or steak and kidney (£3.75), and lasagne (£4.25). Shove-ha'penny, dominoes, cribbage, various board and card games, and a quiz each Tuesday evening at 8.30; also piped music. Used paperbacks are sold and exchanged – proceeds to charity, and there are reference books and magazines for use whilst in the pub. During opening hours they can supply you with groceries. *(Recommended by L M Miall, H Paulinski)*

Whitbreads   Licensee Alec Heard   Real ale   Meals and snacks (12–2.30, 7–10.30)   Restaurant tel Teynham (0795) 521404   Children in restaurant   Open 11–3, 6–11

DARGATE   TR0761 Map 3
Dove

Village signposted from A299

The garden around this pretty and friendly honeysuckle-clad brick house is lovely: picnic-table sets under pear trees, a dovecot with white doves, roses, lilacs, paeonies and many other flowers, and a swing; this year they've added a rockery and pool, and plan to have a barbecue. A bridlepath leads up into Blean Wood. Inside, it's carefully refurbished, there's a good winter log fire, and well kept Shepherd Neame Old on handpump (which can also be served by the jug), and some malt whiskies; unobtrusive piped music. Mostly home-made food includes sandwiches (from 95p), soup (£1.20), ploughman's (from £2.25), excellent lasagne (£2.45), cauliflower cheese with prawns and sweetcorn (£3.25), supreme of chicken or stuffed pork chop (£6.50), lemon sole (£6.75), steaks (from £7.95), and winter game dishes like rabbit chasseur (£7.25) or roast venison (£7.50). *(Recommended by S D Samuels, Gary Scott, L M Miall; more reports please)*

Shepherd Neame   Licensees Peter and Susan Smith   Real ale   Meals (not Sun evening) and lunchtime snacks   Restaurant tel Canterbury (0227) 751360   Children in restaurant and eating area of bar   Open 11–3, 6–11; closed 25 Dec

FORDWICH   TR1759 Map 3
Fordwich Arms

Village signposted off A28 in Sturry, just on Canterbury side of level crossing

On the flagstoned terrace outside this strikingly well built pub are some white tables, chairs and cocktail parasols, and there's a spacious garden by the River Stour – in Roman times sea-going ships came up this far. The dark green hessian walls of the bar are hung with small country prints and a few old local photographs, a high Delft shelf holds some plates, and there are comfortable golden yellow corduroy plush button-back banquettes on the oak parquet floor that sweep in bays around the room, brick mullions for the handsomely crafted arched windows, and copper pots (some with plants in), antique soda-syphons, pewter jugs and dried flowers. The new licensees have introduced a different menu: home-made soup (£1.35), sandwiches (from £1.50), large double filled rolls (from £1.85), filled baked potatoes or ploughman's (from £2.75), salads (£4.25), and specials such as spinach and mushroom lasagne (£3.95), beef stew and dumplings or bacon and onion pudding (£4.25), and prawn and mussels au gratin (£5.25). Well kept Boddingtons, Fremlins and Marstons Pedigree on handpump; jugs of Pimms. The lovely little herringbone-brick half-timbered medieval town hall opposite is said to be the smallest and perhaps the oldest in Britain. Parking can be difficult if the car park is full. *(Recommended by Mayur Shah; more reports please)*

Whitbreads   Licensees Nigel and Patsy Thompson   Real ale   Meals and snacks (12–2, 6–10; not Sun)   Children in dining room/lounge   Open 11–2.30, 6–11

GROOMBRIDGE   TQ5337   Map 3

Crown

B2110

This pretty tile-hung Elizabethan house has several old-fashioned rambling rooms. The one most popular with drinkers has a long copper-topped serving bar, a relaxed, chatty atmosphere, masses of old teapots, pewter tankards and so forth, and logs burning in the big brick inglenook. The end room, normally for eaters, has fairly close-spaced tables with a variety of good solid chairs, a log-effect gas fire in a big fireplace, and an arch through to the food ordering area. The walls, mostly rough yellowing plaster with some squared panelling and some timbering, are decorated with lots of small topographical, game and sporting prints (often in pretty maple frames), and a circular large-scale map with the pub at its centre; some of the beams have horsebrasses. Quickly served on an entertaining assortment of plates old and new, the tasty food includes home-made soup, moussaka (£3.50), chicken curry with a poppadum or roast duck (£4), steak and mushroom pie or chicken in a white wine sauce with parma ham and tagliatelle (£4.25), and poached salmon with tarragon mayonnaise (£4.50); excellent breakfasts. Well kept Brakspears SB, Harveys PA and Marstons Pedigree on handpump, good value house wines, and farm cider; friendly service, shove-ha'penny, cribbage. The nicest place to sit outside is at the picnic-table sets on the sunny front brick terrace or on the steep, neatly kept village green. *(Recommended by Maggie and Derek Washington, Mrs C Hartley, Dr T H M Mackenzie, S J A Velate, Mr and Mrs J H Adam, Philip and Sheila Hanley, Gwen and Peter Andrews)*

Free house   Licensees Bill and Vivienne Rhodes   Real ale   Meals and snacks (not Sun evening)   Restaurant tel Tunbridge Wells (0892) 864742; not Sun evening   Children in eating area of bar and in snug bar   Open 11–2.30(3 Sat), 6–11   Bedrooms tel Groombridge (0892 864) 742; £15/£25

nr HADLOW   TQ6349   Map 3

Artichoke

Hamptons; from Hadlow–Plaxtol road take first right (signposted West Peckham – the pub too is discreetly signposted, on an oak tree); OS Sheet 188, map reference 627524

The two softly lit rooms in this pretty 13th-century cottage have cushioned high-backed wooden settles, wooden farmhouse-kitchen chairs, upholstered wrought-iron stools matching unusual wrought-iron, glass-topped tables on its Turkey carpet, and beams in the low ceilings. One room has an inglenook fireplace and is decked out with jugs, kettles, pots, pans and plates, and the other has a woodburning range. Decorations include lots of gleaming brass, country pictures (mainly hunting scenes), some antique umbrellas and old storm lamps. Bar food includes ploughman's (£2.95), jumbo pork sausage (£3.25), home-made quiche Lorraine (£4.25), home-made lasagne (£4.75), home-made steak and kidney pie or mixed grill (£5.25), prawn salad or chicken Kiev (£6.25), and sirloin steak (£8.75), with specials such as Barnsley lamb chop (£5.95) and winter casseroles. Fullers London Pride, Marstons Pedigree, and Youngs Special on handpump, with a good range of spirits; friendly rather than speedy service. There are seats on a fairy-lit front terrace with a striped awning, and more built around a tall lime tree across the lane. *(Recommended by Norman Foot, Peter and Joy Heatherley, Maurice Southon, Peter Neate; more reports please)*

Free house   Licensees Terence and Barbara Simmonds   Real ale   Meals and snacks (not winter Sun evenings)   Restaurant (Fri and Sat evenings) tel Plaxtol (0732) 810763   Children in eating area of bar   Open 11.30–2.30, 6.30–11; they may close 10.30 at weekends; closed winter Sun evenings

LAMBERHURST   TQ6635 Map 3

Brown Trout ✇

B2169, just off A21 S of village nearly opposite entrance to Scotney Castle

The food in this dining pub is so popular that you have to book weeks ahead for a Saturday evening meal. The menu is strongest on fish with starters such as soft roes on toast (£2.50), a heap of mussels (Sept–March £3), six oysters (£4), and Mediterranean prawns in garlic butter (£4.50), and main courses like an 8–10oz fresh fillet of plaice (£3.75), wing of skate (£5.50), dressed crab with prawns (£5.95), 16/18oz Dover sole (£9.50), and whole lobster (from £11.50); there are non-fishy dishes like soup (£1.75), chicken (£3.95), escalope of veal à la crème (£5.75), and steaks (from £7.50). The remarkable value daily specials may include fresh huss (£3.25), grilled trout in herb butter (£3.50), and a pair of gammon steaks or white crab meat with prawns (£4.25); pleasant, efficient and hard-working staff. The serving counter is still decidedly the centre of the bar, which has beams thickly hung with copper and brass, small country prints, mainly of trout fishing, on the russet hessian walls, and a thoroughly unstuffy and relaxed atmosphere. With only eight or nine tables in the small bar itself, in summer they certainly need the overflow into the biggish extension dining room; on the way through, there's a big and remarkably well stocked aquarium. Well kept Flowers IPA and Marstons Pedigree on handpump, and a large choice of wines; side fruit machine, faint piped music. Even in winter the pub is bright with hanging baskets and tubs of pansies – and very pretty in summer, with picnic-table sets under cocktail parasols on the sloping front grass, opposite a big converted oast house with unusually tall black-rendered brick kiln roofs. *(Recommended by A J Castle, Robert and Elizabeth Scott, Mrs C Hartley, Mrs Carol A Riddick, Robert M Deeley, Dave Braisted, Win and Reg Harrington, S J A Velate, Mrs E M Thompson, E J and J W Cutting)*

Whitbreads   Licensee Joseph Stringer   Real ale   Meals and snacks (11–2, 6–10) Restaurant tel Tunbridge Wells (0892) 890312   Children in restaurant and eating area of bar   Open 11–3, 6–11

LUDDENHAM   TQ9862 Map 3

Mounted Rifleman

3 1/2 miles from M2 junction 6; follow Faversham signpost to A2, turn left on to A2, then follow Oare, Luddenham signpost; take first left turn (signposted Buckland, Luddenham), then turn right just before railway crossing; OS Sheet 178 map reference 981627 – hamlet marked as Elverton

The truly old-fashioned standard of welcoming hospitality here includes your well-kept Fremlins being tapped in the cellar and brought up on a tray, and summer sandwiches served with home-pickled onions and eggs. The two simply furnished, communicating rooms have bare benches, kitchen chairs and the like on their bare floorboards, and some hunting prints on the ochre walls; behind the bar is the former scullery with stone sink, Aga and kitchen table; darts, dominoes and cribbage. There are a couple of tables out behind, by the roses on the way to the vegetable patch. *(More reports please)*

Free house   Licensee Bob Jarrett   Real ale   Snacks   Open 11–3, 6–11

NEWNHAM   TQ9557 Map 3

George ★ ⊘

44 The Street; village signposted from A2 just W of Ospringe, outside Faversham

Varied and interesting food in this distinctive 16th-century pub might include sandwiches (from 90p), delicious soup (£1.25), cheese-topped cottage pie (£2.50), a good variety of ploughman's and salads (from £3, avocado and prawns £5), pasta of the day (£3.50), steak and kidney pie or pudding (£4.65), with, in the evening, grills and fish, and a good many specials such as taramasalata cheesecake (£2.75), pan-fried wild mushrooms and bacon (£3), fresh ducks' livers with cheese on a crouton (£3.25), chicken and ham pie (£4.75), oxtail casserole (£5.90), boiled mutton and caper sauce with a root vegetable purée (£7), and four-fish brochette with Alsacienne sauce (£7.80). Puddings like nursery delight (£1.90), apple and calvados pancake or rich chocolate slice (£2); game in season, vegetarian dishes. The spreading series of rooms is filled with individually chosen and cared for things: prettily upholstered mahogany settles, dining chairs and leather carving chairs around candlelit tables, rugs on the waxed floorboards, table lamps and gas-type ceiling chandeliers, a cabinet of fine rummers and other glassware, early nineteenth-century prints (Dominica negroes, Oxford academics, politicians), and a collection of British butterflies and moths; the flower arrangements are beautiful, hop bines hang from the beams, and there are open fires. Well kept Shepherd Neame Best and Old on handpump, four wines by the glass, and unobtrusive, well reproduced and interesting piped music; shove-ha'penny, cribbage, dominoes, fruit machine. There are picnic-table sets in a spacious sheltered garden with a fine spreading cobnut tree, below the slopes of the sheep pastures. Dogs allowed. *(Recommended by Mrs D M Hacker, S Blaxland, Simon Reynolds)*

Shepherd Neame   Licensee Simon Barnes   Real ale   Meals and snacks (not Sun evening, not Mon; 12–2, 7.30–10)   Children in eating area of bar   Occasional impromptu pianist   Open 10.30–3, 6–11; closed 25 Dec and evening 26 Dec

OARE   TR0062 Map 3

Shipwrights Arms ★

Ham Road, Hollow Shore; from A2 just W of Faversham, follow Oare–Luddenham signpost; fork right at Oare–Harty Ferry signpost, drive straight through Oare (don't turn off to Harty Ferry), then left into Ham Street on the outskirts of Faversham, following pub signpost

Lighting in this isolated 17th-century cottage is by generator (and water is pumped from a well), so the three original and cosy little bars are remarkably dimly lit. They are separated by standing timbers and wood part-partitions or narrow door arches and filled with a medley of seats from tapestry cushioned stools and chairs through some big Windsor armchairs to black wood-panelled built-in settles forming little booths; hops and pewter tankards hang over the bar counter, there are copper kettles, boating pictures, flags or boating pennants on the ceilings, several brick fireplaces, and a woodburning stove. Bar food, chalked up on a blackboard, includes filled rolls (£1.35), two soups (£1.50), various ploughman's (£2.85), sausage and bean stew (£2.95), corn beef hash or fish crumble (£3.25) and beef in beer (£5.25). Well kept Adnams Broadside, Batemans Mild and XXXB, Shepherd Neame Old, Youngers IPA and No 3 and Youngs Special tapped from casks behind the counter; farm ciders, including their own called Looney Juice; cribbage and piped music. A larger room with less atmosphere but considerably more light has a food hatch where a loudspeaker tells you your food is ready. The lane, across the marshes, is long and extremely bumpy, and the small front and back gardens outside the white weather-boarded and tiled pub lead up a bank to the path above the creek where lots of boats are moored. *(Recommended by M Rising, Jill and Paul Ormrod, C Trows, Ann and David Stranack, S A Robbins; more reports please)*

Free house   Licensees Mr and Mrs N Rye   Real ale   Meals and snacks   Children welcome   Mid-stream disco Fri nights, guitarist Sun   Open 10.30–3, 6–11; 11–11 Sat; closed evening 25 Dec

PENSHURST   TQ5243 Map 3

Spotted Dog

Smart's Hill; going S from village centre on B2188, fork right up hill at telephone box: in just under 1/2 mile the pub is on your left

Readers feel the hardworking new licensees are steering this quaint tiled and white weatherboarded house firmly back on course. The heavily beamed and timbered bar, licensed since 1520, has a fine brick inglenook fireplace, attractive moulded panelling in one alcove, and some antique settles as well as the wheelback chairs on its rugs and tiles. Home-made bar food includes open sandwiches, filled baked potatoes (from £2.95), very good local Speldhurst sausages (£3.15), ploughman's (from £3.25), vegetable curry and other vegetarian dishes (£3.50), lasagne or tagliatelli (£3.95), pies like steak and kidney, fisherman's or cottage (£4.25), and puddings such as bread and butter pudding, spotted dick, or apple pie (£1.75). Flowers, Fremlins, Marstons Pedigree and Whitbreads Pompey Royal on handpump, and local Penshurst wine; piped music. From the rustic tables and benches on the split-level terrace outside the pub, there's an idyllic summer view: 20 miles of countryside, with the lush Medway valley curling round towards medieval Penshurst Place. *(Recommended by James Cross; more reports on the new regime, please)*

Whitbreads   Paul Keasey   Real ale   Meals and snacks (till 10pm)   Restaurant tel Penshurst (0892) 870253   Children in restaurant and eating area of bar   Open 11–2.30, 6–11

PLUCKLEY   TQ9243 Map 3

Dering Arms 🏮 🛏

Near station, which is signposted from B2077 in village

Originally built as a hunting lodge for the Dering estate, this striking old Dutch-gabled pub has simply but attractively decorated bars, with a good variety of solid wooden furniture on the wood and stone floors, log fires, and a relaxed, friendly atmosphere. Good bar food includes sandwiches (from 80p, toasties 10p extra), home-made soup (£1.65), sausage (£2.25), various ploughman's (£2.65), home-made pie of the day (£3.65), local panfried trout with lemon and hazelnuts (£6.75), rump steak (£7.45), and puddings like fruit crumble or banana pancake (£1.95); the Food Award is chiefly for the specials which are chalked up on a board – a vegetarian dish, potted crab (£2.65), scallop and brill mousseline (£3.95), 6 oysters (£4.95), supreme of chicken in port and green peppercorn sauce or fillet of sea bream (£7.45), halibut cutlet with hollandaise sauce (£8.95), and turbot, sea bass or lobster when available. They also have gourmet evenings every six weeks. Well kept Adnams Best, Goachers Maidstone Light, a beer they brew for the pub, and winter Old, Shepherd Neame Old and Youngs Special on handpump or tapped from the cask, a large wine list, and local cider; darts, bar billiards, dominoes, and juke box. *(Recommended by Theo Schofield, Geoff and Sarah Schrecker; more reports please)*

Free house   Licensee James Buss   Real ale   Meals and snacks   Restaurant; closed Sun evening   Children in eating area of bar and in games room   Occasional live music   Open 11.30–2.30(3 Sat), 6–11   Bedrooms tel Pluckley (023 384) 371; £25/£32

RINGLESTONE TQ8755 Map 3

Ringlestone ✪

Ringlestone Road; village normally signposted off B2163; heading towards Sittingbourne from Hollingbourne, turn right towards Doddington at top of hill above Hollingbourne, by water tower, and follow road for a couple of miles; OS Sheet 178 map reference 879558

Built in 1533, and originally a hospice used to shelter monks, this popular country pub keeps lots of changing well kept real ales tapped from casks behind the bar or on handpump and chalked up on a board: Adnams, Archers Headbanger, Brakspears, Felinfoel Double Dragon, Fremlins, Flowers IPA, Gales BBB and HSB, Mitchells ESB, Shepherd Neame Bishops Finger and Spitfire (for each barrel of Spitfire, the brewery donate £10 to the RAF Benevolent Fund), and a beer from the local brewers Goachers (although they sometimes use a guest beer) called Ringlestone; they can be quite pricey; local cider, and over 24 country wines (including sparkling ones). Good bar food includes a help-yourself hot and cold lunchtime buffet: good soup (£2.25), filled baked potatoes (£2.45), ploughman's with four cheeses (£3.25), crab pâté with lemon mayonnaise (£3.75), lasagne (£4.45), lamb and coconut curry or chicken casserole (£4.75), good speciality home-made pies (chicken and bacon, vegetarian or game with Madeira, from £5.50), fresh trout in lemon, almonds and oatmeal (£6.95), rump steak (£8.25), and puddings like home-made cheesecake or fruit crumble (£2.50); vegetables or potatoes of the day £2 extra; no chips or fried food. The central room has farmhouse chairs and cushioned wall settles on the brick floor, tables with candle lanterns set into ropework centrepieces, old-fashioned brass and glass lamps on the bare brick walls, and a woodburning stove and small bread oven in an inglenook fireplace. An arch from here through a wall – rather like the *outside* of a house, windows and all – opens into a long, quieter room with cushioned wall benches, tiny farmhouse chairs, three old carved settles (one rather fine and dated 1620), similar tables, and etchings of country folk on its walls (bare brick too). Regulars tend to sit at the wood-panelled bar counter, or liven up a little wood-floored side room. Cribbage and piped pop music. There are picnic table sets on the large raised lawn above a rockery with waterfalls and a fountain, and troughs of pretty flowers along the pub walls. The ladies' lavatory has been thoughtfully smartened up with antique mirrors, early 20th-century prints and unusual West African tiles. They hope to convert the barn into an English Country Wine and Craft Centre. *(Recommended by Tony and Lynne Stark, E G Parish, Dave Braisted, David Cardy)*

Free house   Licensee Michael Buck   Real ale   Meals and snacks   Restaurant tel Maidstone (0622) 859900   Children welcome (under gentle supervision)   Occasional Morris Dancers in summer   Open 11–3, 6.30–11; may stay open longer in afternoon if trade demands; closed evening 25 Dec   Bedrooms planned

ST MARGARET'S AT CLIFFE TR3644 Map 3

Cliffe Tavern Hotel 🛏

High Street

The 17th-century series of Kentish clapboarded buildings that make up this popular hotel is in a high part of town, back from the National Trust coastal cliffs and near *Good Walks Guide* Walk 43. It's a comfortable and friendly place, with settles, several prints, and a striking picture of a World War II aerial dogfight above the village in the bar; there's also a larger open-plan lounge. Good, often imaginative food includes sandwiches, home-made soups like spinach, pea and mint or carrot, orange and coriander (£1.95), chicken satay with peanut sauce, home-made pies such as steak and kidney, cottage or chicken (£3.75), fresh salmon and sorrel twist (£4.50), several vegetarian dishes like aubergine and red bean goulash with sour cream or vegetable korma with roasted sesame seeds (£4.75), whole lemon sole or halibut (£6.50), and puddings; there's a dining area next to the back bar. Well kept Adnams, Ruddles County, and Shepherd Neame Best on handpump; helpful, courteous staff; fruit machine. On the quiet back lawn, sheltered by sycamores and a rose-covered flint wall, are some tables. Most of the bedrooms are in two little cottages across the yard from the main building. *(Recommended by Hank Hotchkiss, John and Joan Nash, Mrs K J Betts, Margaret Dyke, Jane Palmer, Bernard Phillips)*

Free house   Licensee Christopher Waring Westby   Real ale   Meals and snacks Children in dining room   Open 11.15–3, 6–11, though they may stay open longer in afternoon if trade demands   Bedrooms tel Dover (0304) 852749 or 852400; £33B/£45B

SELLING   TR0456 Map 3

White Lion

3 1/2 miles from M2 junction 7; village signposted from exit roundabout; village also signposted off A251 S of Faversham

The atmosphere in this 17th-century ex-coaching inn is friendly and homely, there are two huge brick fireplaces (with a spit over the right-hand one), pews on stripped floorboards, and an unusual semi-circular bar counter. Generous helpings of bar food include sandwiches (from 75p), home-made soup (£1.75), delicious garlic and herb pâté (£2.50), ploughman's (from £2.50, the Stilton has been praised), scampi (£3.95), salads (from £4), chicken coconut curry (£4.95), home-made vegetarian Stilton and sweetcorn quiche (£5), steaks (from £6.75), lunchtime specials such as traditional beef pudding or steak, kidney and mushroom pie (£3.75), puddings (£1.95), and very popular Sunday roasts (£4). Well kept Shepherd Neame Old on handpump, with decent wines by the glass; fruit machine, space game, maybe quiet piped music – the landlord's a trumpet-player. The garden has a thriving community of budgerigars, canaries, zebra finches, button quail, golden pheasants, rabbits and guineapigs, with their young, and two cats called Timmy and Remi. *(Recommended by TBB, Paul Harrop, Colleen Holiday, Comus Elliott, Quentin Williamson)*

Shepherd Neame   Licensee Anthony Richards   Real ale   Meals and snacks Restaurant tel Canterbury (0227) 752211   Children welcome (own room)   Jazz Tues evening   Open 11–3, 6.30–11, though they may stay open longer in afternoon if there are customers; midnight supper licence; closed 25 Dec

nr SMARDEN   TQ8842 Map 3

Bell ★

From Smarden follow lane between church and The Chequers, then turn left at T-junction; or from A274 take unsignposted turn E a mile N of B2077 to Smarden

The snug little back rooms in this popular, friendly pub have low beams, pews and the like around the simple candlelit tables, bare brick or ochre plastered walls, brick or flagstone floors, and an inglenook fireplace. Part of the lively front bar is set aside for families with children, and also has darts, pool, shove-ha'penny, dominoes, fruit machine, trivia and juke box. One bar is no-smoking. Good bar food includes home-made soup (£1.10), sandwiches (from £1.20, toasties from £1.30; rump steak £2.75), home-made pâté (£1.90), ploughman's or pizza (from £2.15), home-made shepherd's pie or basket meals (£2.75), salads (from £3.75), home-made steak and kidney pie (£3.95), gammon steak with pineapple (£4.55), steaks – including perfectly cooked fillet (from £6.95), and daily specials such as fish mornay or cumberland pie; puddings like home-made chocolate crunch cake (£1.30). They only do light snacks on Sunday lunchtimes. Well kept Flowers Original, Fremlins, Fullers London Pride, Goachers Maidstone, Harveys, Shepherd Neame, and Ringwood Old Thumper on handpump; also, six wines by the glass, and local cider. You can sit out at the side, among fruit trees and shrubs, admiring the pub, which is hung with fancy tiles and covered with roses. Every second Sunday in the month at midday, there is a gathering of vintage and classic cars (the pub is packed then). Basic continental breakfasts only. *(Recommended by Mr and Mrs J H Adam, Peter Scillitoe, Mrs C Hartley, J Maloney, Theo Schofield; more reports please)*

Free house   Licensee Ian Turner   Real ale   Meals and snacks (12–2, 6.30–10 or even

10.30 Fri and Sat)   Children in front family area of bar   Open 11.30 (11 Sat)–2.30, 6–11; closed 25 Dec   Bedrooms tel Smarden (023 377) 283; £16/£28

SPELDHURST   TQ5541   Map 3

George & Dragon

Village signposted from A264 W of Tunbridge Wells

This big half-timbered house is one of the oldest pubs in the south of England. It's based on a manorial great hall dating back to 1212, and there are some of the biggest flagstones you can find anywhere, heavy beams (installed during 'modernisation' in 1589 – until then the room went up to the roof), panelling, snug alcoves, antique cushioned settles and Windsor chairs, and a massive stone fireplace. Bar food includes sandwiches, various ploughman's (£2.50), Speldhurst sausages (£2.70), sautéed lambs liver and bacon with onion gravy (£3.55), gammon with fresh pineapple and barbecue sauce (£3.70), grilled fillets of plaice with prawns and capers (£3.75), steak and kidney pie or pudding (£3.80). Well kept Harveys XX, BB and winter Old, King & Barnes, Larkins Bitter and Marstons Pedigree on handpump, and lots of malt whiskies; cribbage. It can get very crowded at weekends, especially in the evenings. The striking first-floor restaurant under the original massive roof timbers serves good but expensive food and is served by a quite splendid wine cellar – a place for special occasions. There are white tables and chairs on the neat little lawn, ringed with flowers, in front of the building. *(Recommended by Heather Martin, Prof and Mrs C G Wall, S D Samuels, Mrs C Hartley, Brian and Jenny Seller, Nigel Williamson, Joy Heatherley, Alan Skull, Peter Neate, Richard Gibbs)*

Free house   Licensee Mrs Jennifer Sankey   Real ale   Meals and snacks   Restaurant tel Langton (0892 86) 3125; closed Sun evening   Children in restaurant and eating area of bar   Open 11–2.30, 6–11

SOUTHFLEET   TQ6171   Map 3

Black Lion

Signposted off A20 just W of Gravesend; follow signs into village then fork left into Red Street at The Ship

This long thatched village pub has a thriving local atmosphere – very warm and welcoming, with notably helpful staff. The main bar has two room areas opened together, through the remains of a timbered wall, with a mix of furnishings, including some shiny copper tables and a carpet on the quarry tiles of the quieter part away from the serving counter – and one particularly comfortable tubby little easy chair by the raised open fire over there on the right. There is a second smaller bar on the left, with steps up to a handsome restaurant. Generously and quickly served decent bar food includes soup (£1.30), ploughman's (£2.50), chilli con carne (£4.30), lamb and mango curry or lasagne (£4.50), home-baked ham and chips (£4.60), plaice stuffed with prawns and mushrooms or steak and kidney pie (£4.70), szechuan chilli prawns (£4.80), sirloin steak (£8), a couple of daily specials such as pork chop or smoked chicken salad, and puddings such as home-made apple pie or spotted dick (£2). Well kept Ruddles Best and County and Websters Yorkshire on handpump; fruit machine, maybe unobtrusive piped music; Harry the friendly airedale may wander in towards closing time. Though most of the cooking is pretty robust, they do pick out some 'heart-friendly' dishes. The big shrub-sheltered back garden has a pleasant variety of well spaced seating, with a good barbecue; it's backed by open fields. *(Recommended by Peter Griffiths, Geoffrey and Teresa Salt)*

Watneys   Licensees Bill Ray and Colette O'Flaherty   Real ale   Meals and snacks (till 10)   Restaurant Tues–Sat tel Southfleet (047 483) 2386   Children allowed if eating   Open 11–2.30, 6–11

STAPLE TR2756 Map 3

Black Pig

Barnsole Road, follow signs to village hall; pub signposted from Wingham–Sandwich back road through Staple, on the Sandwich side of the village

New licensees have taken over this ancient half-timbered pub and plan to have the garden developed to include herbs and shrubs, more seats for eating, and some amusements for children. Inside, the rambling main bar has a heavy beam-and-plank ceiling, comfortable chairs on the carpet, an unusual fireplace with a sort of semi-inglenook which may originally have been a smoking cabinet, and a homely atmosphere. Bar food includes sandwiches (from £2.25), lasagne (£3.95), steak and kidney pie (£4.25), pheasant in port (£5.25), and fresh seasonal fish; Sunday roast lunch. Well kept Adnams, Flowers Original and quite a few guest beers on handpump, local cider, guest house wines, and local wine from Staple Vineyard; darts, pool and snooker, fruit machine, trivia, juke box, piped music, and bat and trap in the garden. (*Recommended by Cynth and Malc Pollard, Mr and Mrs J H Adam, John Knighton, M Y Simon, L M Miall*)

Free house   Licensees Graham and Clair Gould and Adrian Hawkes   Real ale   Meals and snacks   Restaurant – with dance floor – tel Dover (0304) 812361   Children welcome away from bar servery   Occasional jazz summer Sats in garden   Open 11–11; 11–2.30, 6.30(6 Sat)–11 in winter

STOWTING TR1242 Map 3

Tiger

The simplest route if coming from S is to turn left off B2068 signposted Stowting, straight across crossroads, then fork right after 1/4 mile and pub is on right; coming from N, follow Brabourne, Wye, Ashford signpost to right at fork, then turn left towards Posting and Lyminge at T-junction

Simple furnishings in this peaceful old country pub consist of plain chairs and dark pews built in against the walls, candles stuck into bottles, faded rugs on the dark floorboards, and some floor-to-ceiling plank panelling. There are shelves of little kegs, stone jugs and copper pots, an abundance of hop bines draped from the high ceiling, and an open fire at each end of the main bar. Good home-made bar food includes sandwiches, lovely soup, ploughman's with good ham, prawns (from £2.45), tasty baked potato filled with Stilton, vegetarian dishes (from £3.75), home-made pies (£4.50), whole local plaice (£4.75), whole local trout (£5.25) and weekly specials. Well kept Everards Tiger, Fremlins, Ind Coope Burton, King & Barnes, Tetleys, and Wadworths 6X on handpump, and farm cider; darts, dominoes, cribbage, and piped music. Outside, picnic-table sets and other tables sit on the front terrace, some under a thinly planted arbour. (*Recommended by Brian and Jenny Seller, Mr and Mrs J H Adam, David and Diana Livesley*)

Free house   Licensees Alan and Linda Harris   Real ale   Meals and snacks (12–2, 7–10)   Restaurant tel Lyminge (0303) 862130   Jazz Mon evening   Open 12–3, 6.30 (6 Sat)–11

TUNBRIDGE WELLS TQ5839 Map 3

La Galoche ⊘ ⇌

Mount Edgcumbe House Hotel, The Common

A friendly place to drop in for a drink, this little bar (actually part of a small, well-run hotel on the Common) has a good deal of character. It's built into the rock, and has a tiny cavern-like area to one side, a long built-in slatted pine wall seat, solid pine tables, bar stools against the slatted pine bar counter (where on Sundays there may be prawns and mussels to pick at and newspapers to read), bright modern prints and cartoons, and newspapers to read. The small two-roomed restaurant is most attractive and overlooks the Common. Good home-made bar food from a menu that changes daily might include charcuterie with tomato and onion salad (£3.38), oyster mushrooms in herb and garlic butter (£3.94), steak and kidney pie, lambs liver and bacon or vegetarian Stilton and nut roast (all £5.63), good minute steak (£5.91), pojarski smitane (meatballs with herbs and garlic and a sour cream, mushroom and white wine sauce, £6.19), devilled grey mullet (£6.75), guinea fowl in red wine and crabapple sauce (£8.44), and grilled Dover sole (£9.56); puddings (from £2.81), and an excellent cheeseboard includes 30 different French cheeses (£3.38 for French bread and as many as you want to taste); these prices include the 12 1/2 per cent service charge they add, unless you ask them not to. Occasional 'special' weeks feature food and wine from particular areas, together with tutored tastings. Well kept Bass on handpump, and up to 20 wines (including champagne) by the glass. (Recommended by Peter Neate, Patrick Stapley, RAB, the May families, Mrs J A Blanks, Mrs C Hartley)

Free house   Licensees David and Susan Barnard   Real ale   Meals and snacks (12–2, 7–10)   Restaurant   Children Sat and Sun mornings only   Open 12–3, 6.30–11 Bedrooms tel Tunbridge Wells (0892) 26823; £36S/£62S

Sankeys at the Gate ⊘

39 Mount Ephraim (A26 just N of junction with A267)

There are plans to make the downstairs area in this Victorian house more of a bistro/bar with a no-smoking area and decorations such as Spy and fish prints, old maps and bottles; this will lead to the garden where there are seats. Bar food specialises in fish which is bought direct from source (wherever possible) or kept in their seawater tank: fish soup with rouille and gruyere (£3.50), fresh calamari salad (£4), stuffed Cornish clams (£4.50), baby clams with bacon, wine, tomato and chorizo or spaghetti with fresh shellfish (£5), Mediterranean prawns (hot or cold with home-made mayonnaise £8.50), Loch Fyne salmon (en croute, poached or cold £10), turbot (£13), fillet of monkfish roasted with garlic (£12.50), dressed Cornish cock crab or Dover sole (£14.50), a whole lobster (hot or cold, from £20), and puddings such as chocolate brandy cake or lemon and ginger crunch (£3.50). Well kept Harveys from an antique beer engine, and a decent wine list. (Recommended by Kit Read, R G and S Bentley, Heather Sharland)

Free house   Licensee Guy Sankey   Real ale   Meals and snacks (12–2, 7–10; not Sun)   Restaurant tel Tunbridge Wells (0892) 511422; closed Sun   Children welcome Open 11–3, 6–11; closed Sun, Bank Holiday Mons, and 25 and 26 Dec

ULCOMBE   TQ8550   Map 3

Pepper Box

Fairbourne Heath (signposted from A20 in Harrietsham; or follow Ulcombe signpost from A20, then turn left at crossroads with sign to pub)

Looking out over a great plateau of rolling arable farmland, this cottagey country pub has good value home-cooked food, particularly fish, with daily additions such as crab pâté (£3), grilled whole plaice (£4.80) or lemon sole (£5.50) joining the regular choice of smoked mackerel (£2.50), fresh taramasalata (£3), fish pie (£4.25) and plaice fillets wrapped around prawns (£5). Other dishes include sandwiches (from £1), soup (£1.25), ploughman's (from £2.30), lasagne (£3.50), salads (from £3.50), ham and eggs (£3.60), stir-fried chicken (£4), shredded beef with hot chilli (£4.50) and steaks (from £6.50); on summer Sundays it's cold food only. The cosy little low-beamed hop-strung bar has a homely feel, with flock wallpaper, some very low-seated Windsor chairs, wing armchairs and a sofa by the huge inglenook log fire, and copper kettles and pans on window sills and standing timbers. A side area (with enticing puddings in a cold cabinet at one end) is more functionally furnished for eating; there's a separate rustic little dining room, very snug and ideal for dinner-parties (booking (0622) 842558). The atmosphere is friendly and quietly chatty; well kept Shepherd Neame (under light blanket pressure) and Bishops Finger tapped from the cask. The garden (with a caravan beside it) has tables among trees, shrubs, flowerbeds, a small pond and a swing; even if you don't catch a glimpse of the deer that come up, you may meet Jones the tabby tom, the other two cats, or Boots the plump collie. (Recommended by Jenny and Brian Seller, Derek and Sylvia Stephenson)

Shepherd Neame   Licensees Geoff and Sarah Pemble   Real ale   Meals and snacks (till 10)   Open 11–3, 6.30–11; closed 25 Dec, evening 26 Dec

WHITSTABLE   TR1166 Map 3

Pearsons ☺

Sea Wall; follow main road into centre as far as you can, turning L into Horsebridge Rd; pub opposite Royal Free Fishers & Dredgers; parking limited

Served in a lively, friendly atmosphere, the consistently good, very fresh seafood here consists of cockles (£1.10), rollmops or delicious crab sandwiches (£1.50), prawn or smoked salmon sandwiches or smoked mackerel (£1.75), peeled prawns (£1.95), king prawns (£4.75), local oysters in season (three £3, six £6), and seafood platter (£7.95), with changing fresh fish or shellfish specials; also, other sandwiches (from 95p) and ploughman's (£1.95). Small areas of the downstairs bar are divided by stripped brickwork, and decorated with sea paintings, old local photographs, a ship's wheel, and lobster pots; a lower flagstoned part gets most of its submarine light from a huge lobster tank. Well kept Flowers Original, Fremlins, and a cask-conditioned version of Whitbreads Best on handpump; decent house wines, piped pop music, fruit machine. Upstairs, in two or three pleasantly close-packed dining rooms, there's a wider choice (as well as a sea view from some tables – downstairs the sea wall gets in the way); efficient, cheerful service. There are some picnic-table sets outside between the pub and the sea. *(Recommended by Mayur Shah, J Harvey Hallam, L M Miall, Theo Schofield; more reports please)*

Whitbreads   Licensee Michael Wingrove   Real ale   Meals and snacks   Restaurant tel Whitstable (0227) 272005;   Children in restaurant   Open 11–3, 6–11

Lucky Dip

Besides the fully inspected pubs, you might like to try these Lucky Dips recommended to us and described by readers (if you do, please send us reports):

☆ **Aldington** [TR0736], *Walnut Tree*: New licensees in old smugglers' pub dating back to early 14th century with interestingly old-fashioned kitchen bar and lively local public bar; home-made bar food from sandwiches up, well kept Shepherd Neame on handpump, sheltered garden with pool and summer barbecues; children allowed in eating area and restaurant *(LYM — reports on new regime please)*

Appledore [Station; TQ9529], *Railway*: Wide choice of good bar food in family pub with range of well kept real ales, good log fires, friendly atmosphere *(Gordon Smith)*; [The Street], *Red Lion*: Friendly pub with partitioned eating area; good food inc vegetarian dishes, Courage beers, freshly squeezed orange juice, good coffee; comfortable bedrooms *(Sandra Kempson)*

Aylesford [High St; TQ7359], *Chequers*: Warm and comfortable though sparely decorated 16th-century pub in fine riverside position with superb views, good range of beers, large helpings of food, welcoming staff; fruit machines, car park some way off *(P B Godfrey, W Stockton)*

Barham [Elham Valley Rd (B2065); TR2050], *Dolls House*: Extensively refurbished pub/restaurant with home-cooked food; closed Tues *(Reports please)*; [The Street], *Duke of Cumberland*: Pleasant atmosphere and plenty of tables in two-bar local with Whitbreads-related real ales, big helpings of good value straightforward lunchtime food; bedrooms,

caravan site *(L M Miall)*

Bearsted [TQ7955], *Bull*: Hospitable pub with well kept beer and generously served bar food inc generous tempting sandwiches; fruit machine *(J D Martin)*; [Weavering St], *Fox & Goose*: Consistently well kept Courage and John Smiths in recently extended local with French cooking in little restaurant *(Comus Elliott)*

☆ **Benenden** [The Street (B2086); TQ8033], *King William IV*: Carefully unsophisticated but upmarket low-ceilinged village local with flowers on its few tables, cushioned pews, kitchen chairs and a good log fire; some readers have felt unwanted, though most have enjoyed the limited but often imaginative bar food (the duck liver pâté is a long-standing favourite), well kept Shepherd Neame and Mild, and good wines by the glass; games in public bar, small garden; no food Mon evening or Sun *(Mrs M E Lawrence, Joy Heatherley, Mr Stoner, L M Miall, Mrs C Hartley, LYM)*

Botolphs Bridge [Lower Wall Rd; TR1233], *Botolphs Bridge*: Recently refurbished open-plan pub overlooking Romney Marsh and fields of grazing sheep; pleasant and attentive licensees, enjoyable bar food (not Sun, not Fri/Sat evenings), small restaurant with midnight supper licence Tues—Sat evenings, live music Sun evening, darts, small garden with occasional barbecues; children in restaurant *(Peter Davies)*

☆ **Boughton Street** [3/4 mile from M2 junction 7, off A2 — note that this is called Boughton

Street on most maps, though most people just call it Boughton; TR0559], *White Horse*: Little more than a minute from the motorway, this carefully restored inn is open from 7 for breakfast; there's a lot to look at in its cosy dark-beamed bars, which lead through into the restaurant area; decent bar food served throughout the day runs from sandwiches through a good choice of omelettes to steak, with well kept Shepherd Neame on handpump and tables in the garden; children allowed; bedrooms comfortable and well equipped *(LYM — more news of this good pub please)*

Boxley [nestling under M20; TQ7759], *Yew Tree*: Smart little pub in pretty village with attractive church, tucked beneath Kentish Downs, with easy parking opposite; has been popular for well kept Shepherd Neame and good sandwiches, but no recent reports *(News please)*

☆ Brasted [High St (A25), 3 miles from M25 (Sevenoaks junction) — OS Sheet 188 map reference 469550; TQ4654], *Bull*: Friendly local doing well under new licensees, with smiling service, well kept Shepherd Neame Best, Old and Stock, good choice of excellent home-made food with wide selection of vegetarian dishes in cosy dining lounge, separate public bar with darts and maybe skittles; tables in garden; children welcome *(Keith Widdowson, R J and F J Ambroziak)*

☆ Brasted [A25], *White Hart*: Friendly and efficient staff and relaxed weekday atmosphere in spacious lounge and sun lounge (it can get very busy at weekends); well kept Bass and Charrington IPA in Battle of Britain bar with signatures and mementoes of Biggin Hill fighter pilots, big neatly kept garden; generous helpings of reasonably priced bar food, restaurant; children welcome; bedrooms very clean if rather old-fashioned *(C A Holloway, LYM)*

Brasted [A25], *Kings Arms*: Has been popular — particularly with musicians — for nice traditional furnishings, lunchtime food, evening snacks, well kept Shepherd Neame and friendly welcome, but no recent reports *(News please)*

Brenchley [High St; TQ6741], *Bull*: Clean and friendly pub with big helpings of home-cooked food, in lovely village *(R Jones, Gary Rottman)*; *Rose & Crown*: Sturdily timbered old inn with comfortable seats around rustic tables, straightforward home-made bar food inc good home-cured ham, choice of real ales, friendly licensees, piped music; children in eating area, restaurant and family room, seats on terrace, garden play area; bedrooms well equipped *(LYM)*

☆ Bridge [TR1854], *White Horse*: Smart series of spick and span, comfortable rooms, Fremlins and Whitbreads on handpump, daily papers in tasteful lounge with good collection of guns on walls; bar food inc good ham ploughman's, well kept restaurant with food such as pike quenelles with prawn sauce; clean lavatories, good car park, pleasant village now bypassed by A2 *(Peter Robinson, Brian and Jenny Seller)*

Broadoak [TR1661], *Royal Oak*: Really friendly local with lovely pre-Christmas atmosphere *(Comus Elliott)*

Broadstairs [TR3967], *Tartar Frigate*: Comfortable without being plush, decorated with fishing nick-nacks, overlooking bay; popular with locals, friendly landlord; quayside car park *(E J Alcock)*

Brookland [just off and signed from A259 about 1/2 mile out of village; TQ9825], *Woolpack*: Attractive low-beamed 14th-century pub with friendly and relaxed atmosphere, well kept Shepherd Neame on handpump, good straightforward food inc ploughman's with home-baked bread, streamside garden *(Geoff and Sarah Schrecker)*

☆ Burham [Church St (nr M2 junction 3); TQ7361], *Golden Eagle*: Notable for inventive, freshly cooked and nicely presented Malaysian and other bar food at reasonable prices; good friendly atmosphere, welcoming landlord, well kept Whitbreads-related real ales, attractive North Downs view; lots of jugs and mugs hanging from impressive beams, seating rather 1960ish *(Peter Griffiths)*

Burham [Burham Common, just W of Blue Bell Hill], *Robin Hood*: Lovely, welcome haven on undeveloped part of North Downs Way; neat and homely interior, Courage Directors, big garden with plenty of seating, clean lavatories, big car park; bar food (maybe not in winter unless local shoot meeting) *(Brian and Jenny Seller)*

Canterbury [North Lane], *Falstaff*: Good ploughman's, pies, filled baked potatoes and other reasonably priced weekday lunchtime bar food in clean and friendly old pub nicely refurbished in style of basic ale-and-cider house, with stripped panelling, hop bines, old coins, and plenty of gingham-tablecloth tables in dining area; well kept Whitbreads-related real ales, cheery staff (even trendy — maybe a mohican-haircut barman); music can be a bit on the loud side; closed Sun lunchtime; note that this is different from the Falstaff Hotel in St Dunstans St — good, but decidedly not a pub *(Brian and Jenny Seller, Simon Collett-Jones; hotel recommended by Paul and Margaret Baker)*; [St Stephens], *Olde Beverlie*: Spacious, clean and warm with cheerful, comfortable atmosphere; attractive red stone floor; no food evenings *(TBB)*; [162 New Dover Rd], *Olde Tate*: Bright and clean 18th-century inn with exceptionally friendly licensee; varied menu, real ales on handpump, dining area full of locals; bedrooms *(John Murphy)*; [67 Old Dover Rd], *Phoenix*: Good value lunches, well kept real ales such as Adnams and Greene King *(Richard Sanders)*; [Watling St], *Three Tuns*: 16th-century, with comfortable beamed bar areas, sloping floors, conservatory, usual bar food, real ale, piped music, children's room; bedrooms generously sized; but a big black mark for their ban on military personnel *(L Russell, Sidney Wells)*

☆ Capel le Ferne [A20 towards Folkestone; TR2439], *Valiant Sailor*: Big neatly kept roadside pub, warm welcome, well kept Flowers Original, generous good value lunchtime food inc fine steak and kidney pie, comfortable separate lounge with settees and armchairs; spotless lavatories; they ask for respectable dress; useful stop on North Downs Way *(Brian and Jenny Seller, G A*

Broughton)
Challock [Church Lane; TR0050],
Chequers: Tastefully modernised country
pub, and inn since 1700; reasonable range of
good value bar food (Tues—Sat), nice spot,
terrace *(Miss M Byrne)*
Charing Heath [TQ9249], *Red Lion*:
Splendid country pub, friendly and unspoilt
with no juke box and Shepherd Neame beers
(Comus Elliott)
Chatham [Railway St; TQ7567], *Prince of
Wales*: Town-centre pub, popular with
business people at lunchtime, but more
cosmopolitan in evenings; friendly welcome,
cheerful staff, good lunchtime bar food,
popular upstairs restaurant *(A W Spencer)*
☆ **Chiddingstone Causeway** [B2027;
TQ5146], *Little Brown Jug*: Good
welcoming atmosphere in comfortably
modernised country pub, pleasant landlord
(LSO trombonist — also plays jazz), half a
dozen well kept real ales, wide choice of
good bar food which can be eaten in small
restaurant, cheerful if not always speedy
service; children allowed in public side;
attractive garden with children's play tree
and so forth; interesting to watch cricket
balls being produced by hand at Duke's
factory nearby *(J A Snell)*
☆ **Chillenden** [TR2653], *Griffins Head*:
Unpretentious rural pub in attractive, quiet
spot, original stone floor, beams, big
fireplace with roaring winter fire, two other
rooms, restaurant; good range of beers,
good bar food such as veal escalopes and
firm vegetables, decent cutlery and crockery,
very good service *(Ian Whitlock, L M Miall)*
Chislet [TR2264], *Six Bells*: Proper
old-fashioned unspoilt country free house
with wooden floorboards, good choice of
beers, nice, inexpensive, simple bar food;
tables in garden *(C Elliott)*
Claygate [B2162 Yalding—Lamberhurst;
TQ7144], *White Hart*: Clean, well kept pub
with good choice of bar food and friendly
service; children in restaurant *(S Watkins)*
Cowden [junction B2026 with Markbeech
rd; TQ4640], *Queens Arms*: Has been well
liked by readers for its friendly and very
old-fashioned atmosphere, well kept
Whitbreads, pride in not selling lagers, and
mammoth helpings of cheap bread, cheese
and pickle; but no recent reports *(News
please)*; [Holtye Common (A264 S of village
— actually just over border in Sussex)],
White Horse: Old free house, tastefully
enlarged, with King & Barnes and Pilgrims,
and good value bar food *(Dave Braisted)*
Cranbrook [TQ7735], *Duke of York*:
Unpretentious refurbished pub, with warm
welcome and bargain food *(Joy Hardwick)*
Detling [TQ7958], *Cock Horse*: Friendly
atmosphere, well kept Whitbreads-related
real ales, good value bar food, separate
restaurant; pleasant outside seating areas,
clean lavatories *(Brian and Jenny Seller)*
Dungeness [TR0916], *Pilot*: Free house right
on the beach, with enormous helpings of
good freshly cooked fish dishes at
reasonable prices; close to RSPB sanctuary,
Hythe Dymchurch railway and Dungeness
lighthouse; get there early as it's very
popular *(Mrs M Pybus)*
Dunks Green [Silver Hill; TQ6152], *Kentish
Rifleman*: Recently decorated 16th-century

inn on the Greensand Way; pretty garden
with tables and umbrellas *(JS, BS)*
☆ **Eastling** [off A251 S of M2 junction 6, via
Painters Forstal; TQ9656], *Carpenters
Arms*: Lace tablecloths, an abundance of
cottagey decorations, oak beams and big
fireplaces front and back, with warm
welcome, food (not Sun evening) in bar and
restaurant, well kept Shepherd Neame Old,
decent wines, and some seats outside the
pretty house; children allowed in eating area
and restaurant; has been open all day
(Anthony Barnes, LYM)
☆ **Edenbridge** [TQ4446], *Crown*: Cheerful
local with Tudor origins and not
over-modernised, popular for
straightforward bar food, with good service,
real ales such as Friary Meux Best; one of
the last pubs to have kept its 'gallows'
inn-sign stretching right across the road
(Andy and Jill Kassube, LYM)
Edenbridge [on edge], *Swan*: Popular pub
with spectacular gardens; unspoilt inside,
with stone fireplace, floral upholstery and
curtains, copper and brasses, willow-pattern
plates; friendly attentive licensee, well kept
Friary Meux Best and Ind Coope Burton,
good bar food (limited Sun) *(Heather
Sharland, E G Parish)*
Etchinghill [TR1639], *New Inn*: Large,
fairly old pub with nicely laid out interior,
helpful licensees, Whitbreads-related real
ales on handpump, well cooked
locally-caught grilled sole; small restaurant
popular in evenings *(Brian and Jenny Seller)*
☆ **Eynsford** [TQ5365], *Malt Shovel*: Popular
Victorian local with interesting decor (and
reputed ghost), well kept Courage Best and
Directors, good choice of generously served
excellent value bar food (maybe not if
restaurant busy eg Sun lunchtime); friendly
staff *(P Gillbe)*
Faversham [10 West St; TR0161], *Sun*:
Rambling old-world 15th-century town pub
which has been praised by readers for good
atmosphere, unpretentious furnishings, good
value lunchtime bar food and well kept
Shepherd Neame; but no recent reports
(News please)
☆ **Finglesham** [The Street; just off A258
Sandwich—Deal; TR3353], *Crown*:
Country free house with pleasant
atmosphere, helpful and friendly staff, wide
choice of reasonably priced bar food,
popular olde-worlde restaurant with
inglenook fireplace and flagstones; huge car
park *(M Roberts, Mrs P Williams)*
Folkestone [Tontine St; TR2336], *Brewery
Tap*: Attractive murals, above-average hot
and cold bar food, pub games, car park
behind *(E G Parish)*; [42 North St], *Lifeboat*:
Friendly staff, half-a-dozen or more well
kept and interesting real ales, good bar food;
tables outside *(Andy and Jill Kassube)*
Four Elms [B2027/B269 E of Edenbridge;
TQ4648], *Four Elms*: Well kept Courage
Directors, amazing range of bar food,
generously served and reasonably priced;
restaurant *(Paul Evans)*
Gillingham [15 Garden St, Brompton;
TQ7768], *Cannon*: Welcoming and relaxed,
Allied real ales, good bar food; local
cartoons in snug, meeting place for sports
clubs; bedrooms good value *(A W Spencer)*;
[Court Lodge Rd], *Ship*: Nicely modernised

Friary Meux pub overlooking mudflats and moorings, distant views dominated by big power station; pretty, steep-tiled roof and weatherboarded walls, new conservatory extension and terrace; bar food from sandwiches up, inc speciality home-made pies *(Ian Phillips)*

Goathurst Common [TQ4952], *Woodman*: Lots of beams and much bare brickwork giving olde-worlde effect to extended Berni steak house — but they still have a wide choice of real ales, and food from sandwiches up, in the large split-level bar with several distinct areas *(S J A Velate, A H Denman)*

☆ **Goudhurst**, *Star & Eagle*: Striking medieval inn with settles and Jacobean-style seats in heavily beamed open-plan bar, well kept Whitbreads-related real ales on handpump, decent bar food, tables behind with pretty views; polite service; now too much of a tourist hotel (in pricing and atmosphere) for the main listings; children welcome; lovely character bedrooms, well furnished and comfortable; parking can be difficult *(Mike Dixon, Jas E Cross, Mr and Mrs Foruria, LYM)*

☆ **Goudhurst** [A262 W of village], *Green Cross*: Good, interesting home-cooked bar food, good choice of real ales inc distant rarities (though atmosphere not really very pubby); beamed dining room for residents; bedrooms light and airy, good value *(Jas E Cross)*

Gravesend [Queen St/Milton Rd; A226; TQ6473], *New Inn*: Pleasant town-centre pub with separate lounge and public bars and a good local atmosphere; regular sing-songs, good Whitbreads-related real ales *(Dave Webster)*

☆ **Hadlow** [Ashes Lane (off A26 Tonbridge Rd); TQ6349], *Rose Revived*: Friendly and attractive 16th-century pub with decent choice of well kept beers inc Harveys and King & Barnes, good bar food inc well filled fresh sandwiches *(Kit Read)*

Hadlow [Three Elms Lane (pub signposted from A26)], *Carpenters Arms*: Delightful pub, friendly licensees, generously served good value bar food in attractive dining room; pretty garden with goat and other animals; convenient for Medway walks *(W J Wonham)*

Harrietsham [Warren St; TQ8652], *Harrow*: Pleasant, relaxed and civilised atmosphere, choice of country wines, good food and very polite service; a good place to stay *(Mr and Mrs J R Graham)*

Harvel [TQ6563], *Amazon & Tiger*: Friendly, with good if not cheap choice of real ales, good food (inc Sun); in beautiful countryside *(G F Scott)*

☆ **Hawkhurst** [A268 towards Rye; TQ7730], *Oak & Ivy*: Comfortable and traditional old panelled pub with good atmosphere, friendly and efficient staff, generously served good value bar food (plaice and locally smoked chicken recommended), well kept Whitbreads-related real ales and roaring log fires; attractive restaurant *(Alan Merricks, C T and J M Laffan)*

Herne Bay [Sea Front; TR1768], *Bun Penny*: Friendly three-bar pub overlooking sea, well kept Shepherd Neame, good cheap bar food, outside seating; dogs on leads

allowed *(Brian and Pam Cowling)*

Hever [TQ4744], *Henry VIII*: Country pub refurbished for people visiting Hever Castle; not cheap, but worth knowing, particularly for its big pondside lawn and Boleyn connections *(C A Holloway, LYM)*

Hildenborough [TQ5648], *Plough*: Carefully extended country pub praised by readers for its big log fire, wide choice of real ales and good value food in bar and Barn carvery; but no recent reports *(News please)*

☆ **Hodsoll Street** [TQ6263], *Green Man*: Attractive and well kept recently extended pub by village green; well prepared interesting food inc good value cold buffet, very friendly staff, log fire, well kept Flowers and Fremlins on handpump *(Dr B A W Perkins, A S Maxted)*

☆ **Hollingbourne** [Eyhorne St (B2163, off A20 — OS Sheet 188 map reference 833547); TQ8454], *Windmill*: Interesting and friendly pub with comfortable and welcoming bar — half-a-dozen different levels and nooks around the central servery; helpful staff, good food, well kept Whitbreads-related real ales, sunny garden with children's play area *(Roger Taylor)*

Hollingbourne [A20], *Park Gate*: Interesting 16th-century pub, neat and clean, with friendly staff, four well kept real ales, well presented bar food (not Sun evening), big car park; handy for Leeds Castle *(Mayur Shah, Richard Houghton)*; *Pilgrims Rest*: Cosy, warm and inviting with good range of real ales inc distant rarities, good value ploughman's with excellent wholemeal bread; on North Downs Way *(Brian and Jenny Seller)*

☆ **Horsmonden** [TQ7040], *Gun & Spitroast*: Attractive up-market pub, overlooking village green, with very comfortable, spotless and spacious lounge, wide choice of good value bar food inc generous hot or cold sandwiches carved in front of you, spit roasts on alternate days, well kept Ind Coope Burton; restaurant; friendly, smart and efficient service *(Gordon Smith)*

Ickham [TR2257], *Duke William*: Fine local in pretty village with wide choice of beers and tempting food *(Comus Elliott)*

☆ **Ide Hill** [off B2042 SW of Sevenoaks; TQ4851], *Cock*: Pretty old pub, comfortably modernised inside, on charming village green, with decent straightforward bar food from sandwiches to steak (not Sun evening, only snacks Sun lunchtime), well kept Friary Meux, Ind Coope Burton and Gales HSB on handpump, good log fire, bar billiards, piped music, brisk rather than friendly service, some seats out in front; handy for Chartwell and nearby walks — so gets busy, with nearby parking sometimes out of the question *(Miss M Byrne, TOH, Norman Foot, M D Hare, J A Snell, LYM)*

Ide Hill, *Crown*: Simple take-us-as-you-find-us local with hot and cold food prepared to order, Belhaven and Tetleys ales, unobtrusive piped jazz, darts, small back garden with picnic-table sets; seats on attractive village green with seats *(Lyn and Bill Capper, Ian Blackwell)*

Iden Green [Benenden Rd; TQ8032], *Royal Oak*: Friendly and popular pub, attractive inside, with cheerful rather than speedy service, big helpings of usually good reasonably priced food inc vegetarian dishes, real ales such as Batemans, Harveys and King & Barnes (*W J Wonham, Dave Braisted*)

☆ **Ightham Common** [Common Rd; TQ5755], *Harrow*: Modest-looking but comfortable two-bar pub with notable well presented bar food, substantial and varied — fresh wherever possible (fish pie and chicken and asparagus pie strongly recommended); well kept Fremlins and King & Barnes Sussex on handpump, endless coffee; separate restaurant evenings and Sun; bedrooms (*Derek and Sylvia Stephenson*)

☆ **nr Ivy Hatch** [Stone Street; TQ5754], *Rose & Crown*: Good value bar food inc outstanding Italian puddings in pleasant bar with some stripped masonry and fine collection of jugs hanging from ceiling; well kept Whitbreads-related real ales, decent wines, restaurant overlooking orchards; can get booked up, with long waits for a table; spacious garden with Fri evening summer barbecues, children's room in barn; on GWG49 (*Derek and Sylvia Stephenson, LYM*)

☆ **Kingsgate** [Kingsgate Ave; TR3870], *Fayrence*: Outstandingly beautiful setting right by the shingle beach, warm welcome, consistently good bar food and well kept Youngs in efficient and professional pub; can get crowded (*D S Fowles, Mr and Mrs J H Adam, JG*)

☆ **Lamberhurst** [B2100; TQ6735], *Horse & Groom*: Pleasant and welcoming two-bar local, well kept Shepherd Neame, good food in bar and restaurant area, darts, massive tie collection; bedrooms (*Gordon Smith, Richard Gibbs, M Box*)

Lamberhurst [School Hill], *Chequers*: Well kept and pleasant inn; bedrooms (*William D Cissna*); [High St], *George & Dragon*: Keen newish management, decent choice of restaurant food and reasonable bar food, real ales; bedrooms quietest at back (*A J Castle*)

nr Lamberhurst [Hook Green (B2169); TQ6535], *Elephants Head*: Spotless old pub nr Bayham Abbey and Owl House, well kept Harveys, polite service, good choice of bar food inc fresh sandwiches, pleasant country views (*E G Parish, B H Pinsent, LYM*)

☆ **Larkfield** [New Hythe Lane (nr M20 junction 3); TQ7058], *Monks Head*: Olde-worlde low-beamed local dating back to 16th century; four small bar areas, one up steps, with two big fireplaces; well kept Courage Best and Directors on handpump, good really interesting bar food, particularly during the week (*Peter Griffiths*)

Leeds [A20; TQ8253], *Park Gate*: Spotless oak-beamed 16th-century free house with good log fire, usual bar food (*F J Robinson*)

☆ **Leigh** [Powder Mills — OS Sheet 188 map reference 568469; TQ5446], *Plough*: Well kept and popular timbered country pub with cosy atmosphere, huge log fire, variety of seating places in huge old barn, good range of real ales, consistently good bar food; juke box — and Bank Holiday crowds (*Peter Neate, Mr and Mrs G Lacey, Audrey and Brian Green*)

Linton [A229 S of Maidstone; TQ7550], *Bull*: 17th-century pub looking the part, well kept Whitbreads-related real ales, friendly staff, good food esp freshly caught fish;

superb garden, with well maintained lawns and flowerbeds, and wonderful views; clean lavatories, big car park (*Jenny and Brian Seller*)

Lower Hardres [TR1552], *Three Horseshoes*: Old-fashioned furnishings in idiosyncratic country pub with Papas prints of Canterbury, choice of real ales, bar food inc wide choice of cheeses for ploughman's (*Comus Elliott, LYM*)

Luddesdown [TQ6766], *Golden Lion*: Simple pub with big woodburning stove as well as open fire, Watneys-related real ales, bar food (not Sun, nor Mon—Thurs evenings); handy for M2 junction 2, yet in lovely peaceful valley (*D Thomas, LYM*)

Maidstone [Penenden Heath Rd; 1/4 mile from M20, junction 7, on Maidstone rd; TQ7656], *Chiltern Hundreds*: Well kept and warm, with comfortable furnishings in airy well renovated lounge bar, good value hot dishes and filled crusty rolls, well kept Courage Directors, friendly efficient service, seats on terrace and in conservatory (*BB*); [9 Fairmeadow (off A20/A229)], *Drakes*: Old-world feel in crab and oyster house with good bar food, well kept beer (*Dr and Mrs A K Clarke*); [1 Perry St], *Wheelers Arms*: Very popular local with well kept Shepherd Neame beer and good bar food (*James Young*)

Markbeech [TQ4742], *Kentish Horse*: Good home cooking in attractive pub, very colourful in summer; nr GWG50 (*D Thomas*)

☆ **Martin** [TR3346], *Old Lantern*: Popular old-world 17th-century pub with comfortable lounge, good log fire, well kept Watneys-related real ales and another beer such as Shepherd Neame Old (not cheap), food usually good and reasonably priced, service usually cheerful and friendly; plenty of tables in attractive gardens; at its best at quiet times (*Mr and Mrs J H Adam, A Y Drummond*)

Matfield [TQ6541], *Wheelwrights Arms*: Attractive old building, part white-washed brick and part weatherboarded, simple furnishings, lots of horse brasses and yokes on walls and beams; Whitbreads-related real ales on handpump, bar food from big sandwiches and ploughman's to steaks (*S J A Velate*)

Meopham [Meopham Green; TQ6466], *Cricketers*: Good pub with long cricketing tradition, facing cricketgreen; good beer and food (*David Gaunt*); *Station*: Pleasant commuter-belt country pub with separate attractive lounge; tasty food, especially potato pie (*Wayne Brindle*)

Minster [2 High St; the one nr Ramsgate, at TR3164], *Bell*: Has been praised by readers for character and atmosphere, comfortable old wooden settles, well kept Whitbreads-related real ales and good value bar food; but no recent reports (*News please*)

Newenden [A268; TQ8227], *White Hart*: Attractive 16th-century pub with low beams, timbers and inglenook log fire, good food from snacks to Scotch steaks in bar and restaurant, well kept beer, decent house wine, helpful service (*BB*)

Old Romney [TR0325], *Rose & Crown*: Village free house with quiet, peaceful atmosphere and good bar food; good base for the coast and SE Kent; well equipped bedrooms in separate block, good breakfasts *(Mrs M Pybus)*

☆ Otford [TQ5359], *Bull*: Really professionally run, with well kept Courage Best and Directors, bar food, pleasant young staff, attractive garden, good family room; nr GWG47 *(John McGee, GS, K Leist)*

Pembury [TQ6240], *Black Horse*: Interesting combination of pub and wine bar, with good food and decent wine *(Brian Smith)*

☆ Penshurst [village centre; TQ5243], *Leicester Arms*: Pleasant atmosphere in well kept hotel bar with quiet corners and spacious eating area for high standard, averagely priced bar food (particularly good bread and butter pudding); good service, restaurant; on GWG50; bedrooms *(Colin Laffan, Win and Reg Harrington, Jas E Cross)*

☆ nr Penshurst [Coldharbour Lane, Smarts Hill; following Smarts Hill signpost off B2188, bear right towards Chiddingstone and Cowden], *Bottle House*: Fine atmosphere in cosy and friendly family-run pub, wide choice of particularly good attractively priced food inc good value daily specials, good service; comfortable and attractive restaurant, garden *(Keith Walton, Cynth and Mak Pollard, Ian Whitlock)*

☆ nr Penshurst [Hoath Corner; first R off B2188 S of village, then right again — OS Sheet 188 map reference 497431], *Rock*: Ancient beamed pub with inglenook, well kept Fremlins and Marstons Pedigree, bar food inc outstandingly generous ploughman's (all they do on Sun) with good cheddar or sausages; ring the bull — the horn's sported by a well worn buffalo head; tables out in front and in garden, big car park; on GWG50 *(Jenny and Brian Seller)*

Petham [Stone St; TR1251], *Slippery Sams*: Clean old beamed pub with friendly, cosy atmosphere; well kept Shepherd Neame, wide choice of well prepared food in candlelit restaurant *(Paul and Margaret Baker)*

☆ Pett Bottom [off B2068 S of Canterbury, via Lower Hardres — OS Sheet 179 map reference 161521; TR1552], *Duck*: Remote tile-hung cottage with two small rooms, big 17th-century fireplace, plain furnishings — can be packed out for expensive bar food inc interesting pies; Shepherd Neame and a couple of guest beers, decent wines by the glass, local cider, piped music; side restaurant; tables in sizeable garden; children allowed in smaller room *(Paul and Margaret Baker, Gwen and Peter Andrews, LMM, LYM)*

☆ nr Plaxtol [Sheet Hill; from Plaxtol, take Tree Lane from war memorial and church, straight through Yopps Green; from A227 nearly a mile S of Ightham, take unmarked turning beside lonely white cottage Bewley Bar, then right at oast house signposted Plaxtol; TQ6053], *Golding Hop*: Secluded and idiosyncratic country pub with sun-trap lawn fenced off from small stream, well kept real ales such as Adnams Best and Broadside, Batemans XXXB, King & Barnes Festive and Youngs Special tapped from the cask, choice of good farm ciders (it's even made its own; its own-brewed beer is served under heavy top pressure), simple bar food

(not Mon evening), straightforward country furniture; music can be loud, may have spit-roast pig on Bank Hols — when it gets very busy; children not allowed in (even to use lavatory) *(Derek and Sylvia Stephenson, Maureen Preston, Joy Heatherley, LYM)*

☆ Pluckley [TQ9245], *Black Horse*: Cosy and busy old low-beamed local, reputedly haunted, with interesting rounded-top Dering windows, vast inglenook with unusual brazier-type fire, dark oak settles; friendly staff, huge amiable black cat, good if rather pricey home-made bar food inc excellent puddings, well kept Whitbreads-related and Marstons real ales, clean lavatories; big area given over to restaurant serving tasty business lunches; reputedly haunted, nicely laid out garden *(Geoff and Sarah Schrecker, Jenny and Brian Seller)*

Ramsgate [Harbour Parade; TR3865], *Queens Head*: Lots of fishing gear, drawings, nets, maps, figureheads, and lamps — even a small rowing boat above the bar, and binnacles etc bolted to the floor; Whitbreads ales, good busy atmosphere; open all day *(Steve Mitcheson, Anne Collins)*

Ripple [TR3449], *Plough*: Attractive olde-worlde pub with cosy flagstoned rooms, well kept changing real ales, decent bar food, friendly service *(Mr and Mrs J H Adam)*

☆ Rochester [10 St Margarets St; TQ7467], *Coopers Arms*: Interesting and comfortable old local, spotlessly kept, with quaint, friendly atmosphere; pleasant decor, brisk lunchtime trade for tasty bar meals; handy for castle and cathedral *(Dr and Mrs S G Donald, Gordon Mott, Barbara Hatfield)*

Rochester, *Under the Clock*: Basic atmospheric pub below street level, with interesting choice of real ales *(Wayne Brindle)*

Ruckinge [TR0233], *Blue Anchor*: Well kept Whitbreads-related and Marstons real ales, wide choice of rather pricey bar food; very popular with young people on Sun lunchtimes, when they may have hot chips in baskets on bar; car park, outside tables *(Jenny and Brian Seller)*

Ryarsh [The Street; TQ6659], *Duke of Wellington*: Good bar food in well kept refurbished Tudor pub *(D Thomas)*

☆ Sandgate [Brewers Lane — main rd towards Hythe, then 100 yds or so after it emerges on to sea front park opp telephone box on R (beware high tides) and walk up steep cobbled track beside it; TR2035], *Clarendon*: Sparely furnished tucked-away pub with friendly licensees, consistently well kept Shepherd Neame, bar food inc delicious clams, splendid dog *(Terry Buckland, Tim Locke, Andy and Jill Kassube)*

Sandgate [High St], *Ship*: Small unpretentious front bar with friendly atmosphere; genuinely old furnishings; passage to another small back room; very good value home-made food, good service, well kept Allied real ales, seats outside *(Hugh Williams, Andy and Jill Kassube)*

Sandhurst [Rye Rd; TQ7928], *Harrier*: Good value home-made bar food (not winter evenings Mon—Wed) inc children's menu, summer barbecues, Sun roasts; darts, round pool table; children's play area *(Linda Barnes)*

Sandwich [Strand St (A257); TR3358],
Admiral Owen: Clean and welcoming,
characterful French licensee; interesting
nick-nacks on walls, good lunchtime and
evening food *(Mr and Mrs A J Winthorpe)*;
[Market St], *Market*: Small, cosy pub in
centre of this attractive old-world town,
with good value food *(E J Alcock)*;
[Cattlemarket], *Red Cow*: Ancient beamed
pub also in centre, with warm atmosphere;
evening meals (not Mon), welcoming
licensees, pleasant back garden *(N J D
Bodiam)*
Sarre [TR2565], *Crown*: Interesting old
place also known as the Old Cherry Brandy
House, recently reopened after careful
refurbishment by Shepherd Neame — now a
delightful country inn; particularly well kept
Master Brew *(Comus Elliott)*
Sevenoaks [Godden Green, just E; TQ5355],
Bucks Head: Idyllic spot by duckpond on
green, good standard bar food, prompt
cheerful service, well kept Courage ales,
decent wines, very cosy and atmosphere
pleasant (unless there's a crowd of young
lager-drinkers); nr GWG49, handy for
Knole Park (NT) *(TOH, Norman Foot)*;
[A225 just S (note that this is different from
the next-door Royal Oak Hotel], *Royal Oak
Tap*: Pleasant pub with restaurant, almost
opp entrance to Knole Park, which has been
popular for good value bar food, good
service and well kept Watneys-related and
other real ales; but no recent reports *(News
please)*; [Bessels Green, just off A21], *Kings
Head*: Has been particularly praised as
welcoming, friendly and clean, with reliably
good food in bar and restaurant and
colourful garden — but again no recent
reports *(News please)*
Shatterling [Pedding Hill; A257
Ash—Wingham; TR2658], *Green Man*:
Good atmosphere, lively bar, restaurant
with varied wholesome menu at reasonable
prices *(Mr and Mrs J H Adam)*
Shepherdswell [North Downs Way;
TR2648], *Old Bell*: Pretty little pub, on
village green with commemorative seat;
friendly licensee, well kept
Whitbreads-related and Marstons real ales,
bar food inc good value ploughman's; on
North Downs Way *(Brian and Jenny Seller)*
Smarden [TQ8842], *Chequers*: Pleasant
atmosphere, Courage beers and good food;
bedrooms *(Comus Elliott)*; [B2077], *Flying
Horse*: Good atmosphere, friendly landlord,
good beer and bar food *(David Gaunt)*
Snargate [Romney Marsh; B2080
Appledore—Brenzett — OS Sheet 189 map
reference 990285; TQ9828], *Red Lion*:
Genuinely unspoilt and old-fashioned, but
warm and cosy (with newly opened-up
fireplace) despite plain furnishings; well kept
Batemans and Shepherd Neame real ales
(Phil and Sally Gorton)
☆ **Sole Street** [the one above Wye; TR0949],
Compasses: Largely unspoilt 16th-century
country pub with big attractive garden,
rustic atmosphere, good service, friendly
landlord, wide choice of good value bar
food, Shepherd Neame real ales, choice of
local farm ciders, log-effect gas fires, bar
billiards, piped music *(Judy and Martin
Corson, Miss M L Margetts, LYM)*
☆ **Southfleet** [High Cross Rd, Westwood;

coming from A2, keep on B262 into
Betsham where you turn left — or coming
through Southfleet keep straight ahead past
The Ship], *Wheatsheaf*: Thatched and
beamed Tudor pub kept simple inside —
padded barrel chairs, traditional
high-backed settles, sloping heavy beams,
inglenook with big woodburner; well kept
Courage Best and Directors, simple bar
lunches (not weekends) such as ploughman's
and fry-ups, spontaneous folk musicians,
occasional Morris dancers; big lawn above
car park, and tables around sizeable softly
floodlit pond *(Peter Griffiths, Des Thomas,
BB)*
☆ **St Mary in the Marsh** [TR0628], *Star*:
Remote recently renovated pub by small,
attractive church, with good bar food at
moderate prices, friendly family service,
Shepherd Neame tapped from the cask and
other real ales on handpump; nice
bedrooms, with views of Romney Marsh
(Jim Froggatt, Denise Plummer, Robert Crail)
Stone in Oxney [TQ9427], *Ferry*: Former
smugglers' pub, genuinely old-fashioned,
with pleasantly well worn feel, good
welcome, decent reasonably priced bar food;
big garden *(Phil and Sally Gorton)*
Tenterden [High St; TQ8833], *Eight Bells*:
Old building with friendly atmosphere,
family room and bar food *(Joan Olivier)*;
[High St], *White Lion*: Substantial early
16th-century inn with lots of atmosphere,
pleasant bar, good range of beers on
handpump inc Bass, wide choice of
restaurant food, streetside terrace; bedrooms
delightful *(R B Crail)*; *William Caxton*:
Pretty refurbished pub with
Whitbreads-related ales on handpump,
moderately priced good bar food, small
restaurant, garden; bedrooms *(R B Crail)*
Tilmanstone [A256; TR3051], *Plough &
Harrow*: Well kept Courage, Gales HSB and
Shepherd Neame beers, simple food *(Derek
and Sylvia Stephenson)*
Tonbridge [High St; TQ5946], *Castle*:
Attractive building with pleasant riverside
terrace; busy atmosphere, friendly service,
well kept Courage Directors; bedrooms
(Paul Evans)
Trottiscliffe [TQ6460], *George*: Unspoilt,
basic free house with table skittles *(D
Thomas)*
Tudeley [TQ6244], *Carpenters Arms*: Quiet
on a midweek lunchtime, very friendly,
pleasant service, decent bar food *(HMM)*
Tunbridge Wells [Mount Ephraim; behind
Royal Wells Hotel; TQ5839], *Beau Nash*:
Promising new lease of life under new
regime for popular refurbished pub with
good atmosphere, decent food, tables in
paved garden with leafy corners *(E G Parish,
William D Cissna)*; [Bells Yew Green; SE, by
B2169], *Brennock Arms*: Well kept real ales
inc Harveys Mild, friendly welcome, polite
service, bar food inc fine stilton
ploughman's *(Graeme Pilcher)*; [Spa Hotel,
Mt Ephraim], *Equestrian Bar*: Long, light
and comfortable room with unusual
equestrian floor-tile painting and
steeplechasing pictures; wicker and velveteen
furnishings, friendly uniformed staff, good
lunch snacks, well kept Fremlins and King
& Barnes on handpump; bedrooms *(LYM)*;
[Mount Ephraim], *Royal Wells*:

Refurbished, well lit hotel bar with comfortable settees and chairs, cosy corners, well kept Courage Directors and Shepherd Neame Old on handpump, food inc decent meat dishes with fresh vegetables, good service by pleasant young staff; adjoining public bar; bedrooms *(E G Parish, Peter Neate);* [Denny Bottom], *Toad Rock:* Pleasant little pub with well kept Whitbreads-related real ales, good value bar food inc vegetarian dishes, clean lavatories, tables and chairs outside; nr the Toad Rock itself *(Brian and Jenny Seller)*

Under River [SE of Sevenoaks, off B245; TQ5551], *White Rock:* Small, two-bar village pub, off the beaten track; choice of real ales, good range of bar food, children truly welcome, good garden *(J A Snell)*

Upnor [29 High St; Upper Upnor; TQ7571], *Tudor Rose:* Old-fashioned, friendly free house with good choice of beer *(Comus Elliott)*

Upper Halling [TQ6964], *Black Boy:* Spotless listed building with gleaming brass, well kept Courage ales; no meals Sun (maybe a good sandwich then, though) *(Brian and Jenny Seller)*

☆ **Upstreet** [Grove Ferry; off A28 towards Preston; TR2263], *Grove Ferry:* Neatly kept pub in lovely position, with big front and back gardens — the back one by the river; two nicely decorated bars with nautical brass and copperware, full-length windows looking out on the water, wide choice of generously served good bar food, restaurant, good Sun lunchtime carvery; well kept Courage Directors and a beer named for the pub on handpump; spotless lavatories; very popular in good weather *(D Savage, W P Ford)*

Walderslade [nr Bluebell Hill — and M2 junction 3; TQ7663], *Lower Bell:* Busy, old-fashioned pub with live music, Courage Best on handpump; no Sun food *(Jenny and Brian Seller)*

☆ **Warren Street** [just off A20 at top of North Downs — OS Sheet 189 map reference 926529; TQ9253], *Harrow:* Immaculate dining pub with extensive comfortably modernised low-beamed bar, very neatly furnished, with quietly low-key atmosphere, flowers and candles on the tables, faint piped music, big woodburner; attentive service and generous helpings of well cooked food — by no means cheap, but worth it, with particularly good vegetables and lots of dishes of the day; Shepherd Neame and a guest beer such as Youngs on handpump; big car park; bedrooms *(Mr and Mrs Graham, Jane Palmer, BB)*

Wateringbury [TQ6853], *Duke Without A Head:* Warm, friendly pub with three main areas; good service, generous helpings of good food (can book tables); snooker room *(J D Martin)*

☆ **Weald** [village signposted off A21; in centre, turn left into Scabharbour Rd; TQ5450], *Chequer Tree:* Spacious and neatly modernised country pub with a notable garden — fairy-lit terraces, quite a big pond, lots of room up on the spreading lawns among trees and shrubs, and summer barbecues; bar food such as sandwiches, good omelettes, ham and egg and steak and kidney pie (till 10; not Sun or Mon

evenings), well kept Watneys-related real ales on handpump, flagstoned games area, restaurant (not Sun evening); children allowed in eating area and restaurant; big car park *(K Widdowson, Simon Velate, Michael Thomson, LYM)*

Weald [Sevenoaks Rd], *Prince of Wales:* Interesting, friendly place with unusual real ales such as Wiltshire Stonehenge tapped from the cask, good value ploughman's, and biscuits and peanuts on the counter; very nice garden with own serving counter and wandering ducks *(Jenny and Brian Seller)*

West Peckham [TQ6452], *Swan:* Beautiful setting facing village cricket green and by church with Saxon tower and 14th-century aisle; friendly inside, with Courage beers and good value ploughman's *(BS, JS)*

Westerham [Market Sq; TQ4454], *George & Dragon:* Welcoming licensees in Chef & Brewer pub with old cinema programmes and advertisements in comfortable lounge with excellent pubby atmosphere, good service, Watneys-related real ales, food from good sandwiches to decent traditional Sun lunches *(E G Parish, Andy and Jill Kassube);* [4 The Green; TQ4454], *Grasshopper:* Old village free house with first-class service, well kept beers inc Courage Best, King & Barnes and guests, lots of bric-a-brac and royal pictures in open-plan bar with three areas; nr start GWG48 *(Richard Houghton)*

☆ **Wickhambreaux** [TR2158], *Rose:* Attractive old building both inside and out, friendly atmosphere, well kept beer, good bar food inc fine sandwiches and ploughman's; pretty village *(G A Broughton)*

Wingham [High St (A257); TR2457], *Anchor:* Traditional beamed pub with good reasonably priced bar food, warm service *(L Russell, Mr and Mrs J H Adam);* [High St], *Red Lion:* Comfortably modernised inn — part of a college founded here 600 years ago by Archbishop of Canterbury; pleasant, friendly atmosphere, neatly attractive decor, good varied bar food, well kept Whitbreads-related real ales on handpump; restaurant; bedrooms *(LYM)*

☆ **Worth** [The Street; TR3356], *St Crispin:* Busy but relaxed and friendly partly 15th-century village pub, completely refurbished, with well kept beer inc guests, reasonably priced good bar food, restaurant, nice waitresses; pleasant garden, nice spot nr beach and golf courses *(Mrs R Horridge, J D Martin, Comus Elliott)*

☆ **Wrotham** [signposted 1 ¾ miles from M20, junction 2; TQ6159], *Bull:* Civilised food all day at linen-covered tables in character room with three log fires; good lunchtime snacks served from bar inc wide choice of fettucini, omelettes, steak pie, moules marinières; imaginative restaurant dishes (at prices to match); well kept Whitbreads-related real ales, friendly landlady, children welcome; though it's now more a restaurant than a bar readers still enjoy it — and the village, like the inn, is attractive; bedrooms, ample parking *(M J Brooks, TOH, Dr James Haworth, Jenny and Brian Seller, LYM)*

Wrotham [The Square], *Three Post Boys:* Simple local under new landlord, with log-burning stove, pool table, decent value food *(Ian Phillips, Joy Heatherley)*

☆ **Wye** [village signed off A28 NE of Ashford; TR0546], *Tickled Trout*: Charming riverside spot, with tables out on waterside lawn and newish conservatory/restaurant; bar done out with heavy timbering, stripped brickwork and copper tables, decent straightforward bar food from sandwiches and filled baked potatoes to steaks, Whitbreads-related and Marstons real ales on handpump; children allowed in eating area and restaurant; nr start GWG46 *(Brian and Jenny Seller, TBB, L M Miall, LYM)*

☆ **Wye** [Upper Bridge St], *New Flying Horse*: Comfortably modernised 17th-century beamed inn, pleasantly light, friendly atmosphere, locals at bar; wide choice of substantial bar food, well kept Shepherd Neame ales inc Old, good service, popular restaurant; attractive garden with Japanese influence; bedrooms pleasant — especially those in converted outbuildings — with good breakfasts *(Heather Sharland, E G Parish, Stephen Goodchild)*

☆ **Yalding** [Yalding Hill; TQ7050], *Walnut Tree*: Ancient beams, inglenook, antiques and interesting pictures, with good bar food inc fine ploughman's, well kept Whitbreads-related real ales, restaurant, immaculate lavatories; bedrooms *(Jenny and Brian Seller)*

Lancashire
(including Greater Manchester
and Merseyside)

*Pubs currently doing particularly well here include the Moorcock up
on the moors at Blacko (its food is a big pull), the Waggon & Horses
in Brierfield (a delightful new entry), the White Horse up on
Blackstone Edge (good helpings of homely bar food), the welcoming
Old Rosins near Darwen (doing bedrooms now), the Strawbury
Duck at Entwistle (in a good walking area – isolated, but right by
where a local train from Blackburn and Bolton stops), Th'Owd
Tithebarn in Garstang (bubbling with atmosphere), the Bushells
Arms at Goosnargh (impressive range of food), the palatial
Philharmonic in Liverpool, the Mark Addy and Royal Oak in
Manchester (incredible value cheese lunches), the lively Lass o'
Gowrie and the Marble Arch there (both more for beer lovers), the
Olde Boars Head in Middleton (remarkable restoration of a fine old
building – a new entry), the very rustic Tandle Hill Tavern there, the
Hark to Bounty at Slaidburn (doing well under new management),
and the Inn at Whitewell (lots going on in this fine stone inn, the most
rewarding pub in the area). There's new management at the
interesting Station Inn in Broadbottom (preliminary reports are
promising), the Coal Clough House in Burnley (more foody now, and
open all day) and the quaint Golden Ball at Heaton with Oxcliffe
(planning water sports). Outstanding for low prices, the area deserves
a footnote in economic history books as the last place to hold out
against the £1 pint. It was as recently as July 1990 that we finally saw
the average price of the Lancashire pint reach the £1 mark, and even
now you can still find beer costing well under that here. The reason
for low drinks prices here is partly the local market strength of
relatively small breweries, setting a low-price trend. Holts is
outstanding for this; the powerful regional brewers Greenalls,
Robinsons and Thwaites, and several local ones such as Lees, Hydes,
Mitchells and Moorhouses, all play a useful part. Even though two
other important regional breweries have now become tied to national
combines (Matthew Browns has been bought by Scottish &
Newcastle, Boddingtons is now tied to Whitbreads), prices in their
pubs have so far not yet fallen into line with the higher national
average. Pub landlords have more personal control over food prices
than drinks prices, so the area's particularly low food prices are a
significant tribute to the determination of Lancashire landlords to
give good value. We found plenty selling decent snacks (most often a
bowl of good soup with a roll) for under £1, though some other
counties drew a complete blank for this. Over one in three served
substantial main dishes at under – sometimes well under – our £3
target for bargain meals. Besides the many main entries here,
particularly promising pubs in the Lucky Dip section at the end of the*

418

chapter currently include the White Bear at Adlington, Black Dog up at Belmont, Howcroft in Bolton, Hesketh Arms at Churchtown (the Merseyside one), Rams Head at Denshaw, Pump House in Liverpool, perhaps the Griffin at Heaton Mersey pre-eminent among several strong contenders in Manchester and Stockport, Cemetery in Rochdale and Owd Betts on the hills above it.

nr BALDERSTONE (Lancs)   SD6332   Map 7

Myerscough Hotel

2 miles from M6 junction 31; A59 towards Skipton

This softly lit, beamed pub, quietly strong on atmosphere, has well made oak settles around dimpled copper or heavy cast-iron-framed tables, lots of brass and copper, ink and pen drawings of local scenes, and a painting of the month by a local artist; the serving counter has a nice padded elbow rest. Good value, well kept Robinsons Best and Mild on handpump. The bar menu changes slightly in the evening, when it's also more expensive (but still good value for the ample portions); at lunchtime it's very popular with businessmen and workers from the aircraft factory over the road; the range includes home-made soup (85p), sandwiches (95p; £1.20 for open in the evening), ploughman's (£2.10; evening £2.40), delicious grilled steak barm cake (£2.10 or £2.40), home-made steak and kidney in gravy (£2.60 or £2.95), salads (from £2.85), a daily roast (£2.95 or £3.50), sirloin steak (£5.50), and specials such as liver and bacon, beef curry or sweet and sour pork. There are picnic-table sets, bantams and their chicks, and rabbits in the garden. *(Recommended by George Hunt, Mr and Mrs J H Adam, Lee Goulding, Len Beattie)*

Robinsons   Licensees John and Carol Pedder   Real ale   Meals and snacks (12–2, 6.30–8.30; not Sun evening)   Well behaved children away from bar till 8.30   Open 11.30–3, 5.30–11

BILSBORROW (Lancs)   SD5139   Map 7

Owd Nells

St Michaels Road; at S end of village (which is on A6 N of Preston) take Myerscough College of Agriculture turn

This thatched canalside pub, popular with the owners of the boats that moor nearby, serves a good selection of decent bar food, including home-made soup (95p), cheese and pickles (£1.95), local potted shrimps (£2), hot roast beef sandwich (from £2.30), fresh Fleetwood fish and chips (£3.40), steak and kidney pudding (£3.50) and minute steak (£4.60), with several dishes of the day such as black pudding, liver and onion and beef salad. They also do afternoon sandwiches (from £1.60), and late-evening snacks such as deep-fried courgette strips (£1.60), mussel casserole (£2.20) and fresh prawns (£2.85); efficient waitress service. The spacious three or four communicating room areas have high pitched rafters at either end, lower beams (and flagstones) by the bar counter in the middle, and a mix of brocaded button-back banquettes, stable-stall seating, library chairs and other seats; the atmosphere is old-fashioned, though in fact the pub is fairly new. Well kept Boddingtons, Chesters, Whitbreads Castle Eden and a beer named for the pub, with guest beers such as Flowers Original, Hartleys XB or Wethereds, and maybe good chunks of a cheese such as red leicester as bar nibbles; decent wines including a bargain house champagne, tea, coffee, hot chocolate; space game, fruit machine, table football and TV in one area, with unobtrusive piped pop music. There are colourful seats out on this large white house's terrace, part of which is covered by a thatched roof; a small walled-in play area has a timber castle. New this year are the bedrooms, in a substantial motel complex, which may also have affected the layout of the bars. *(Recommended by F Teare, Graham Bush, G J Lewis; more reports please)*

Free house   Real ale   Meals (12–8) and snacks (all day)   Next-door restaurant; open all day inc Sun   Children in eating area of bar   Open 11–11; closed 25 Dec   Bedrooms tel (0995) 40010/40020; £29.50B per room

BLACKO (Lancs)   SD8541   Map 7

Moorcock ⊗

A682; N of village towards Gisburn

This consistently popular moorland pub draws visitors across considerable distances just to sample its outstandingly good and almost entirely home-made food; there's quite a continental theme, with garlicky Italian and Austrian dishes such as excellent bratwürst (£2.95), authentic goulash (£3.75) and schweinschnitzel (£3.95), as well as soup (£1.10), a substantial ploughman's (from £2.75, with proper little pots of butter), pâté (£1.95), burger or steak sandwich (£3), savoury pancakes (£3.25), vegetable biriani (£3.75), steak and kidney pie or whole ham shank in a mustard sauce (£3.85), halibut mornay (£4.25), steaks (£7), and lots of daily specials; puddings such as cheesecake or good fruit pies (£1.25) and fresh Sunday roasts (£3.95); friendly, speedy service. The bar is spaciously comfortable, with cream walls hung with brass ornaments, lofty ceiling, and breath-taking views from the big picture windows. Well kept Thwaites Bitter and Best Mild on handpump; friendly sheepdog. The attractively landscaped back garden is very busy at weekends, though quieter during the week. They no longer do bedrooms. *(Recommended by John Hayward, Gwen and Peter Andrews, Andy and Jill Kassube, Kathryn Ogden, George Hunt, Simon Bates, Derek and Sylvia Stephenson, Michael and Joan Melling, Andrew Stephenson, Dr and Mrs S G Donald, Len Beattie)*

Thwaites   Licensees Elizabeth and Peter Holt   Real ale   Meals and snacks (12–2.30, 7–11; noon–11 Sun)   Restaurant   Children welcome   Open 12–2.30, 6.45–11; open all day Sun

BLACKSTONE EDGE (Gtr Manchester)   SD9716   Map 7

White House

A58 Ripponden–Littleborough, just W of B6138

Good helpings of homely bar food in this imposing, stone-built moorland pub include home-made vegetable soup (90p), sandwiches (from £1.20, steak £1.40), Cumberland sausage with egg (£2), quiche Lorraine (£2.20), lasagne (£2.50), home-made steak and kidney pie (£2.75), salads (from £2.75), and 8oz sirloin steak (£5.75); also, daily specials and home-made apple pie (80p). The cosy main bar, a regular haunt of hikers and walkers, has a blazing coal fire in front of a Turkey carpet and under a large-scale map of the area; the snug Pennine Room opens off here, with brightly coloured antimacassars on its small soft settees. To the left, a spacious room has a big horseshoe window that looks out over the moors, comfortable seats around its tables, and coloured pins on a map of the world showing where foreign visitors have come from. Well kept Clarks Hammerhead, Exmoor Gold, John Smiths, Moorhouses Pendle Witches Brew and Robinwood Old Fart on handpump; trivia, fruit machine. *(Recommended by John Branford, Linda Duncan, Carol and Richard Glover, Comus Elliott, Andrew Hazeldine)*

Free house   Licensee Neville Marney   Real ale   Meals and snacks (11.30–2, 7–10)   Restaurant tel Littleborough (0706) 78456   Children allowed until 9pm   Open 11.30–3, 7–11

BRIERFIELD (Lancs)   SD8435   Map 7

Waggon & Horses

Just over 1/2 mile from M65 junction 12; A682 signposted Brierfield, pub on left

Unpromising from the busy road, this turns out to be a real find inside: lovingly and painstakingly restored to an idealised vision of a prosperous late Victorian local, yet with a warm and genuine atmosphere – very much alive, a chatty and thoroughly welcoming place. The high-ceilinged carpeted central area has plush stools, some cream tilework, heavy maroon woodwork and attractively cut and etched glass, especially around the servery itself. But the real delight is in the small rooms leading off. Our own favourite is the one at the back on the left: heavy button-back wall seats in old gold plush, a couple of elegant Regency-striped chairs, ochre Anaglypta walls with good reproductions of Renoir nudes, soft gas lighting, thick flowered curtains, dark red ceiling, a figured walnut piano and a coal fire in a period fireplace with decorative tiles. Three other small rooms, also with fires, each have their own devotees (and one has darts). Well kept Thwaites Bitter and Mild on handpump (at bargain prices early Tuesday and Wednesday evenings); some tables out on a side terrace; fruit machine. Good value lunchtime bar food includes cheese burgers (£1.15), Lancashire hot pot (£1.90), shepherd's pie (£1.95), mixed grill (£2.20), chicken kiev (£2.50) and scampi (£2.60); service is friendly and efficient. The Pyrenean mountain dog (like a white donkey, according to the licensees) is called Sebastian, and the pub is a short stroll from the Leeds to Liverpool canal. (*Recommended by Brian Jones, Dr Thomas Mackenzie*)

Thwaites   Licensee Kevin D Edwards   Real ale   Meals and snacks (lunchtime)
Children in side rooms at lunchtime   Open 11–2.30, 5–11.30; 11–11 Fri and Sat

BROADBOTTOM (Gtr Manchester)   SJ9993 Map 7
Station

Just E of present end of M67; village signposted off A57 in Mottram; the train from Manchester Piccadilly (every half-hour, more often in rush hours) takes 25 minutes

Enjoying the solid comforts of this attractive stone building, it's difficult to remember that a few years ago it was a virtually derelict station. The railway influence remains, notably in one of the (no-smoking) restaurant areas, done up as a dining car on the Orient Express, down to details like the curved and lofted carriage roof, tulip lamps, masses of little vertical mirrors and a showy slave-lampholder. The bar itself, which opens straight on to the platform, has a similar Victorian style, with a sturdy brass footrest and elbow rest for the bar counter, patterned carpeting, blue-and-pink walls with Anaglypta dado and inset bookshelves, prints large and small, elaborate brass lamps, and blue curtains on fat wooden rails. Stairs (which divide the bar roughly into two) lead up to a second, galleried restaurant area, with banquette seating in booths, and a striking art deco stained-glass ceiling. Bar food under the new licensees includes soup (90p), sandwiches (from £1.10), pâté (£2.25), spare ribs (£2.50), ploughman's (£3.50), salads (from £3), steak and kidney pie (£3.25), and vegetarian dishes (£4.95), with children's dishes (£1.95) and puddings (£1.50); black-and-white uniformed staff. Banks's Mild and Bitter on handpump (and coffee or tea). It's at its liveliest on a Thursday evening, when there's a disco, quizzes and so forth. (*Recommended by Steve Mitcheson, Anne Collins, P A Crossland, D A Cawley, Keith Mills; more reports on the new regime please*)

Free house   Licensees Larry and Irene Duggan   Real ale   Meals and snacks
Restaurants tel Mottram (0457) 63327; open all day Sun   Children welcome   Live
music Thurs evening   Open 11.30–3, 5.30–11; all day Sun

nr BROUGHTON (Lancs)   SD5235 Map 7
Plough at Eaves

4 1/2 miles from M6, junction 32: take M55 turn-off, then A6 N, then after about 1 mile N of Broughton traffic lights, first left into Station Lane; after canal bridge bear right at junction, then left at fork; pub on the right; OS Sheet 102 map refererence 495374

A simple, uncluttered old country pub, with two bars that have rush-seat chairs around dark wooden tripod tables, lots of wooden casks, an antique oak linen chest and corner cupboard, a couple of guns over one good copper-hooded open fire with a row of Royal Doulton figurines above another, very low dark beams, and little latticed windows. Well kept Thwaites Bitter on handpump; darts, dominoes, fruit machine, trivia and quiet piped music. As we went to press the bar menu was changing from a Thwaites-operated Daniels Kitchen to the pub's own selection; it should include soup (90p), sandwiches (from £1.50), ploughman's (around £2.50), steak and kidney pie (£2.95), gammon or a vegetarian dish such as spinach, mushroom and walnut pancake (£3.95), roast beef (£3.99), cod steaks (£4.25), and steak (£6.95); children's menu (£1.35). There's a well equipped children's play area at the back, and metal and wood-slat seats and cast-iron-framed tables running along the front by the quiet lane. *(Recommended by L M Miall, John Atherton, Derek and Sylvia Stephenson, Graham Bush, Philip Riding, Jon and Jacquie Payne)*

Thwaites   Licensee David Atherton   Real ale   Meals and snacks (12–2.30, 6.30–9.30)   Restaurant tel Catforth (0772) 690233   Children in eating area   Open 12–3, 6.30–11

BURNLEY (Lancs)   SD8332   Map 7
Coal Clough House

Coal Clough Lane; between Burnham Gate (B6239) and A646; OS Sheet 103, map reference 830818

Since last year this elegant Victorian house has become much more foody under the new licensee – following a general face-lift most of the bar area has been opened up for dining. The notably well decorated lounge has antique prints, an elaborately moulded high plaster ceiling, a lovely carved mantlepiece around the big open fireplace, and lots of oak panelling; the front sun lounge is popular, particularly with lunchtime businessmen. The conservatory and part of the family room are no-smoking. Bar food, from the new Millers Kitchen, includes soup (80p), sandwiches (from £1.30), ploughman's (from £2.75), scampi or vegetable lasagne (£3.25), steak, kidney and mushroom pie (£3.45), sirloin steak (£5.25), and children's meals (99p); efficient service from well dressed bar staff; fruit machine, piped music. There are tables outside on the terrace by the wisteria, and beside the roses and mature trees on the lawn. *(Recommended by Len Beattie, Carol and Richard Glover, John Atherton, Andrew Stephenson; more reports on the new regime please)*

Greenalls   Licensee Stephen Hayes   Meals and snacks (12–2.30, 6–9.30; 6–10 Fri and Sat, all day Sun)   Children in family room   Open 11.30–11

CLAYTON LE MOORS (Lancs)   SE7430   Map 7
Dunk Inn 🖙

1/2 mile from junction 7 M65; A6185 towards Clitheroe, then first left A678 towards Rishton, then first left into Dunkenhalgh Hotel

Standing in extensive mature grounds, this castellated Gothick country house is predominantly a hotel; but tucked away at the back is a converted stable block, with a properly pubby atmosphere and laden with heavy brown beams and stripped masonry; there are mates' chairs around dark wooden tables on Turkey carpet, an open fire, and cosy barrel-vaulted side sections (one with pool and darts); conservatory-style window bays look out past the sunken entry court to the sloping grass and shrubs beyond. Lunchtime bar food is from a popular, help-yourself buffet (£3.25), with more main dishes in the evening; fruit machine, trivia, CD juke box and piped music. In the days before the thriving local community started expanding, the hotel used to stand in over 600 acres of grounds; these days it still has a handsome 17, through which the River Hyndburn flows. *(Recommended by Len Beattie; more reports please)*

Free house   Licensee John Smith   Meals and snacks (not Mon evening)   Restaurant Children in restaurant   Singer Weds, organist Thurs, disco Fri–Sun   Open 11–3, 6–11   Bedrooms tel Accrington (0254) 398021; £55B/£65B

nr DARWEN (Lancs)   SD6922 Map 7

Old Rosins

Pickup Bank, Hoddlesden; from B6232 Haslingden–Belthorn, turn off towards Edgeworth opposite the Grey Mare – pub then signposted off to the right; OS Sheet 103 map reference 722227

In a fine wooded valley and surrounded by moors, this warmly welcoming place has an extensive open-plan lounge furnished with comfortable red plush built-in button-back banquettes, and stools and small wooden chairs around dark cast-iron-framed tables; decorations include mugs, whisky-water jugs and so forth hanging from the high joists, and small prints, plates and old farm tools on the walls; big picture windows make the most of the view, and there's a good log fire. Boddingtons, Flowers and Whitbreads Bentleys Yorkshire on handpump; fruit machine and piped music. Good value, interesting food ranges from home-made soup (90p), sandwiches (from £1.25) and ploughman's (£2.50), through home-made pizzas (from £2.95), salads (£2.95) and chicken tikka or paella (£3.25), to steak (£5.95). There are picnic-table sets on a spacious crazy-paved terrace, with see-saws, swings and a climber on the lawn; summer barbecues out here on Friday evenings and Sunday lunchtimes. There may be sheep wandering in the car park. They now do bedrooms. *(Recommended by G J Lewis, Len Beattie, Alan Holden, Carol and Richard Glover)*

Free house   Licensee Bryan Hankinson   Real ale   Meals and snacks (12–10.30, till 10 Sun)   Restaurant   Children welcome   Open 11–11   Bedrooms tel Darwen (0254) 771264; £42B/£52B

nr DELPH (Gtr Manchester)   SD9808 Map 7

Horse & Jockey

Junction of A62 and A670

Alone on the moors, two snug and dimly lit rooms with a good deal of character: just the place to tell tall tales, or – with the logs flickering and flaring and stormy weather outside – maybe a ghost story. It's comfortably furnished with settees, easy chairs and Windsor chairs, and one room is panelled and served from a high hatch. A good range of well kept, changing real ales on handpump runs through Clarks, Everards, Marstons, Mitchells, Moorhouses Pendle Witches Brew, Oak Best from Cheshire, Timothy Taylors and Vaux Sunderland. There are lovely views over the high moors, and good local walks, including one down to the site of a Roman fort by Castleshaw reservoir; the Pennine Way is not far away. *(Recommended by Gary Scott, Len Beattie, Andrew Triggs; more reports please)*

Free house   Real ale   No food   Open 7–11; 1–2.30, 7.30–11 Sat

DOWNHAM (Lancs)   SD7844 Map 7

Assheton Arms

From A59 NE of Clitheroe turn off into Chatburn (signposted); in Chatburn follow Downham signpost; OS Sheet 103 map reference 785443

The stonebuilt village, spreading out along a duck-inhabited stream, is charmingly preserved in traditional style by the Asshetons – the family of Lord Clitheroe – who've been here since 1558. The pub itself nestles on a pastoral slope opposite the church, and has a rambling, beamed and red-carpeted bar with olive plush-cushioned winged settles around attractive grainy oak tables, some cushioned window seats, and two grenadier busts on the mantlepiece over a massive stone fireplace (that helps to divide the separate areas). Well kept Marstons Pedigree, Whitbreads Bentleys Yorkshire and Castle Eden on handpump; piped music; young, helpful staff. A wide choice of good, popular bar food includes home-made soup (£1.25), sandwiches (from £1.75 – not Saturday evening or Sunday lunchtime), Stilton or chicken liver pâté (£2.25), delicious potted Morecambe Bay shrimps (£3.10), steak and kidney pie (£3.95), plaice (£4.50), grilled ham with free-range eggs (£4.75), game pie (£5.25) and sirloin steak (£6.75), with several children's dishes (£1.75). There are picnic-table sets under cocktail parasols outside. *(Recommended by Michael and Joan Melling, Robert and Vicky Tod, Mr and Mrs Harry McCann)*

Whitbreads   Licensees David and Wendy Busby   Real ale   Meals and snacks (12–2, 7–10)   Children welcome   Open 12–3, 7–11

EDGWORTH (Lancs)   SD7416 Map 7
White Horse

A676 N of Bolton, then left onto B6391; village signposted on right about ¹/₂ mile after Turton Tower; pub on Bury St

Comfortable and friendly in a villagey sort of way, this place has a lovely interior with a profusion of highly lacquered, carved dark brown oak panelling, lots of copper jugs and so forth hanging from the beams, a brass ship's clock and barometer, a couple of log fires (not always lit), and plush button-back wall banquettes curved around wooden or dimpled copper tables. Well kept Matthew Browns Mild and Bitter, Theakstons XB and Youngers IPA and No 3 on handpump; darts, pool, cribbage, dominoes, fruit machine, space game, trivia and juke box. Bar food includes good home-made steak or chicken and mushroom pie (£2.85), meaty or seafood lasagne or home-made curries (£3) and steak (£4.95). Garden outside. *(Recommended by G T Jones, Ben Wimpenny, R C Gandy, Roger Huggins; more reports please)*

Matthew Browns (S & N)   Licensee Alan Parry   Real ale   Meals and snacks (not Sat evening)   Children welcome   Disco Thurs evening   Open 12–3, 7–11; 11–11 Sat; closed Mon and Tues lunchtime

ENTWISTLE (Lancs)   SD7217 Map 7
Strawbury Duck

Village signposted down narrow lane from Blackburn Rd N of Edgworth; or take Batridge Rd off B6391 N of Chapeltown and take pretty ³/₄ mile walk from park at Entwistle reservoir; OS Sheet 109 map reference 726177

Isolated in an area of the moors popular with hikers and ramblers, this has a cosy flagstoned L-shaped bar with Victorian pictures on its partly timbered, partly rough-stone walls, a variety of seats, stools, little settees and pews, stuffed birds (and in the dining room a stuffed mongoose struggling with a cobra), a mounted gun, and ceiling beams – the one over the servery is very low; one of the tables seems to be made from a big cheese press. Darts, fruit machine, space game, juke box and a pool table in the flagstoned tap room. Bar food includes sandwiches (£1.25), soup (75p), filled baked potato (from £1.25), ploughman's (£1.95), steak and kidney pie or chilli con carne (£3.25), vegetarian dishes (£3.50), and steaks (from £7). There's also a popular choice of well kept real ales such as Flowers Original, Harveys, Marstons Pedigree, Timothy Taylors Bitter, Mild, and Landlord, and regular guest beers all on handpump; also Furstenberg Bavarian lager. Outside, tables are perched high over the cutting of the little railway line which brings occasional trains (and customers) from Blackburn or Bolton. Hikers are welcome – you leave your boots in the porch. *(Recommended by Keith Mills, Ben Wimpenny, Brian and Anna Marsden, John Fazakerley, Mr and Mrs Harry McCann, Denis Mann, Sandra Kempson, K Sharp)*

Free house   Licensee James B Speakman   Real ale   Meals and snacks (12–2, 7–10; 12–10 Sat, 12–9.30 Sun; not Mon lunchtime)   Restaurant   Children allowed till 8.30   Folk/jazz Thurs evening   Open 12–3, 7–11; 12–11 Sat, 12–10.30 Sun; closed Mon lunchtime (except on Bank Hol)   Bedrooms tel Turton (0204) 852013; £28B/£37B

GARSTANG (Lancs)   SD4845   Map 7

Th'Owd Tithebarn ★

Signposted off Church Street; turn left off one-way system at Farmers Arms

Loved by readers for its Lancastrian welcome and atmosphere, this converted, creeper-covered barn is well placed by a canal basin, with a big stone terrace where you can sit watching the boats and ducks (which you can feed if they've got some bread left over). Inside, the dining area is particularly pleasant – more like a farmhouse kitchen parlour really, with an old kitchen range, prints of agricultural equipment on the walls, low beams – and waitresses in period costume with mob-caps. The rest of the bar has masses of antique farm tools, stuffed animals and birds, and pews and glossy tables spaced out on the flagstones under the high rafters. Popular, good value food includes home-made soup with a good hunk of bread (£1.40), pâté (£1.35), ploughman's (£2.25), Lancashire hot-pot (£2.85), steak and kidney pie (£3.55), salads (from £3.60), a choice of roast meats (£3.90) and ham and eggs (£4.15); lots of puddings (£1.50), and a good children's menu (from 80p). Country wines, and a fine antique bar billiards machine that takes shillings. It can get very busy at weekends. *(Recommended by John Branford, Linda Duncan, Carol and Richard Glover, G A Worthington, Graham Bush, M A and W R Proctor, John Fazakerley, Mr and Mrs D J Nash, John and Christine Simpson, Russell Hafter, J P Cinnamond)*

Free house   Licensees Kerry and Eunice Matthews   Meals and snacks (12–2.30, 7–10; not Mon)   Children in dining area   Open 11–3, 7(6 Sat)–11; closed Mon (though not lunchtime Bank Hol Mons)

GOOSNARGH (Lancs)   SD5537   Map 7

Bushells Arms ✪

4 miles from M6 junction 32; A6 towards Garstang, turn right at Broughton traffic lights (the first ones you come to), then left at Goosnargh Village signpost (it's pretty insignificant – the turn's more or less opposite Whittingham Post Office)

The enormously impressive range of bar food continues to be the draw here; it's served with skill, imagination and engagingly warm courtesy – one reader's explanation of his dietary problems led to an offer of a special meal that wasn't on the menu. Starters, which like other dishes have a Greek and Levantine undertone, include humous or taramasalata with hot pitta bread (£1), falafel or crispy samosas (£1.80), duck pâté (£2), spicy chicken wings (£2.25), with more main dishes such as ploughman's or an authentic chilli con carne (£3.50), an elaborate fish pie or Malayan-style pork curry (£5), very popular steak and kidney pie (£4.50), chicken fillet with smoked bacon, asparagus, fresh chervil and hollandaise sauce in puff pastry (£5.50), local sirloin steak (£7), several dishes of the day, and a good choice of vegetarian dishes (from £3.50 – they also have rennet-free cream for the sumptuous puddings like strawberry pavlova or sponge envelope filled with fresh fruit and cream £1.30); crisp and fresh vegetables include tasty potatoes, done with garlic, cream, peppers and parmesan. They will do sandwiches if they're not busy, serve some children's things (£1.75) or child-size helpings, and make the traditional local shortbread flavoured with caraway seeds and known as Goosnargh cakes (the place is pronounced Goozner, incidentally); they warn of delays at peak periods – mainly Saturday night. The spacious, modernised and green-carpeted bar – much of which is no-smoking – has lots of snug bays, each holding not more than two or three tables and often faced with big chunks of sandstone (plastic plants and spotlit bare boughs heighten the rockery effect); also soft red plush button-back banquettes, with flagstones by the bar; fruit machine, and maybe piped 1960ish music. Boddingtons Bitter on handpump, a good choice of wines (including some New World ones), and several malt whiskies. The licensees have produced their own book on pub catering. *(Recommended by P J and S E Robbins, C J McFeeters, M B P Carpenter, Col A H N Reade, Alan and Marlene Radford, Miss E J Thickett, R H Sawyer, M A Watts, Roy Butler)*

Whitbreads   Licensees David and Glynis Best   Real ale   Meals and snacks (12–2.30, 7–10)   Children in eating area of bar   Open 12–3, 6–11

HASLINGDEN (Lancs)   SD7823   Map 7

Duke of Wellington

Grane Road; B6232 signed from Haslingden centre – OS Sheet 103 map reference
767228

Surprisingly strong on creature comforts considering its moorland isolation, this
spacious pub has built its reputation to quite an extent on the welcome it gives to
families; the playground, fenced off in the garden, is notably well equipped. Bar
food includes soup (90p), sandwiches (from £1.40), Cumberland sausage and egg
(£2.70), steak and kidney pie (£3), cold platters with salad (from around £3),
gammon with egg or pineapple (£3.50), 8oz sirloin steak (£6), daily specials, and
imaginative ice creams; service can be slow when it's busy (Sunday lunchtime, say),
but they do warn you. The softly lit main room, divided up by balustered wood
and black cast-iron screens, has a plethora of polished dark woodwork, the odd
button-back leather sofa, button-back pink cloth settees and slat-back chairs
around its tables, quiet country pictures on the muted pink-papered walls, deco
lamps, and bookshelves. Well kept Boddingtons and Hartleys XB on handpump.
The picnic tables outside have panoramic views. *(Recommended by Len Beattie, Lee
Goulding, Carol and Richard Glover; more reports please)*

Whitbreads   Real ale   Meals and snacks   Restaurant tel *Rossendale (0706) 215610
Children in restaurant   Open 11.30–3, 6–11; 11–11 Sat*

HEATON WITH OXCLIFFE (Lancs)   SD4460   Map 7

Golden Ball

Lancaster Road; coming from Lancaster on B5273, turn left by sandy wasteland where
sign warns road liable to be underwater at high tide (should also be signposted Overton)

Liable to get crowded in summer because of its fine position overlooking the boats
on the River Lune, this welcoming pub consists of several little low-beamed rooms
furnished with cushioned antique settles, old-fashioned upright chairs, and built-in
benches around cask tables; good winter fires. Mitchells Bitter on handpump and
served from a hatch; darts, fruit machine and space game. Bar food includes baked
potatoes (from £1), home-made soup (90p), sandwiches (£1.60; toasted £1.75),
meat and potato pie (£1.45), salads (£2.85), toad in the hole (£2.90), and a roast
of the day (£3.15). There are old-fashioned teak seats on a raised terrace in front.
The new licensee plans to establish more watersports facilities. *(Recommended by
Alison and Tony Godfrey, Jon Wainwright; more reports on the new regime please)*

Mitchells   Licensee Steve Blane   Real ale   Meals and snacks   Evening restaurant
tel *Morecambe (0524) 63317   Children welcome   Open 11–3, 6–11; 11–11 Sat
(normal hours in winter)*

LIVERPOOL   SJ4395   Map 7

Philharmonic ★

36 Hope Street; corner of Hardman Street

This extravagant and well maintained and restored 19th-century gin palace is one
of the few entries in the *Guide* whose gents' is worth seeking out as more than a
functional attraction – a remarkable period piece, all red marble and opulent
glinting mosaics, it was featured fairly recently in the BBC's *Forty Minutes* series.
The physical and social centre is the mosaic-faced serving counter, from which
heavily carved and polished mahogany partitions radiate under the intricate
plasterwork high ceiling, dividing off cosy little cubicles from the echoing main
hall. This is decorated by a huge mosaic floor, rich panelling, and stained glass
including contemporary portraits of Boer War heroes such as Baden-Powell and
Lord Roberts; above the fireplace is an alcove with copper panels of musicians.
Well kept Ind Coope Burton, Jennings Bitter and Tetleys Bitter and Mild on
handpump, and some malt whiskies; fruit machine, piped music, and quizzes.
Home-made bar food that includes sandwiches, and main dishes such as chicken

chasseur, liver and bacon, steak and mushroom pie or chilli con carne (all £2.50), is served in a splendid Grecian room decorated with half-naked art nouveau plaster goddesses reclining high above the squared panelling. There are two plushly comfortable sitting rooms, and a function room on the first floor. The pub's full name is the Philharmonic Dining Rooms. *(Recommended by Richard Sanders, R Elliott, Ian Phillips, Kevin Fields, D P Herlihy, Steve Waters, Steve Mitcheson, Anne Collins)*

Tetley-Walkers (Allied)   Licensee John Draper   Real ale   Lunchtime meals and snacks   Metered parking nearby   Open 11.30–11 weekdays; 11.30–3, 6–11 Sat

LYTHAM (Lancs)   SD3627 Map 7
Captains Cabin

A584 S of Blackpool; Henry Street – in centre, one street in from West Beach

Good value, simple lunchtime bar food in this comfortable place includes soup (75p), sandwiches (from £1.10, toasties £1.65), filled baked potatoes (£1), and cold platters (from £2.15), with hot daily specials like steak and kidney pie or quiche Lorraine. The modest little bar is decorated in Victorian style, with quite a bit of stained glass decoration – in the solid wood screens which divide up the central area, and in the main windows, which have good freestyle stained inserts of fish and gulls; there are also dark pink button-back plush seats and captain's chairs in bays around the sides, well chosen pictures – including local boats – on the muted bird-of-paradise wallpaper, open fires, and a coal-effect gas fire between two built-in bookcases at one end. Well kept Boddingtons Bitter, Chesters Best Mild, Marstons Pedigree and Whitbreads Castle Eden and Trophy on handpump; two fruit machines, trivia, juke box and piped music. *(Recommended by D C Turner, F Teare, Simon Bates, Carol and Richard Glover, Graham Bush; more reports please)*

Whitbreads   Licensee John Rollo   Real ale   Lunchtime meals and snacks (not 25 or 26 Dec)   Children in eating area   Open 11–11

MANCHESTER   SJ8398 Map 7
Lass o' Gowrie

36 Charles Street; off Oxford Street at BBC

A point of interest in this busy city pub is the mini-brewery in the cellar – seats around a sort of glass cage in one part give a view of the brewing process of LOG35 and LOG42, malt-extract beers named for their original gravity (strength); the former is quite lightly flavoured and slips down very easily, the latter is meatier; there's also well kept Boddingtons Bitter on handpump. The bare-floorboarded and gas-lit longish tall room is mainly stripped back to varnished bricks, with big windows in its richly tiled arched brown facade, and hop-sacks draping the ceiling; there are seats around lower tables on a cosier carpeted dais at one end, and quite high stools against ledges or higher tables. Good value home-made food from a separate side servery includes ploughman's (£1.95), and beef casserole, mince and onion pie, lamb hotpot or savoury pork (all £2.20); friendly, efficient service. The volume of the piped pop music really depends on the volume and youth of the customers – so it may be at its loudest on a term-time Friday or Saturday night, when it's popular with students. *(Recommended by Steve Mitcheson, Anne Collins, Paul Evans, Brian and Anna Marsden, Virginia Jones, RT, Andy and Jill Kassube, Len Beattie)*

Whitbreads/Own brew   Licensee Joe Fylan   Real ale   Lunchtime meals and snacks (no hot food Sat or Sun)   Children in small side room and raised area   Open 11.30–11 weekdays; 11.30–3, 6.15–11 Sat

Marble Arch

73 Rochdale Rd (A664), Ancoats; corner of Gould St, just E of Victoria Station

Taking its name from its porphyry entrance pillars, this chatty place has a Victorian feel to it, with its rag-rolled walls, magnificently restored glazed brick lightly barrel-vaulted high ceiling, and marble and tiling throughout – particularly the frieze advertising various spirits, and the chimney breast above the carved wooden mantlepiece; this year the serving counter has been moved down to the far end of the bar to give more room, the false floor has been removed to reveal the original, sloping mosaic floor, and parts of the walls have been stripped back to the glazed brick. Readers are consistently drawn by the outstanding range of regularly changing beers on handpump, such as Fullers London Pride, Hydes Anvil, Marstons Pedigree, Moorhouses Pendle Witches Brew, Oak Wobbly Bob, Ruddles, Timothy Taylors Landlord, and rarities such as Goachers from Kent; there's also a good choice of bottled beers – such as Belgian Trappist beers – and a selection of country wines. Bar food, served in the new lounge extension at the back, includes filled barm cakes, a huge ploughman's, salads or a daily vegetarian dish (£1.95), and hot dishes such as hot beef curry or real ale stew (£2.50); dominoes, cribbage, fruit machine, trivia and juke box. *(Recommended by Brian and Anna Marsden, Steve Mitcheson, Anne Collins, Colin Dowse, P Corris, R C Gandy)*

Free house   Licensee Vance de Bechevel   Real ale   Meals and snacks (not Sat or Sun)   Children in eating area of bar   R & B or jazz some Thurs   Open 12–11; closed Sun and Bank Hol lunchtimes, and 25 and 26 Dec

Mark Addy ✦

Stanley Street, Salford, Manchester 3; look out not for a pub but for what looks like a smoked glass modernist subway entrance

The bar food in this very smart waterside place is outstanding provided you like cheese – there are over 50 of them at any one time, from all over Britain and Europe; they come with granary bread (£2) and it's unlikely you'll be able to finish your helping – a doggy-bag is thoughtfully provided; there's also a choice of pâté s including a vegetarian one (£2), and soup in winter. The pub itself is attractively converted from waiting rooms for boat passengers, and consists of a series of barrel-vaulted brick bays, with russet or dove plush seats and upholstered stalls, wide glassed-in brick arches, cast-iron pillars, and a flagstone floor. Photographs around the walls show the River Irwell in the 19th century: a sluggish open sewer from which a Mr Mark Addy rescued over 50 people from drowning. Well kept Boddingtons and Marstons Pedigree on handpump, and quite a few wines; piped music; service stays efficient under pressure. The canalside courtyard has tubs of flowers around its tables, from which you can watch the home-bred ducks. The strict dress code has now been relaxed. *(Recommended by A M Neal, Len Beattie, Keith Mills, Denis Mann, Steve Mitcheson, Anne Collins, Virginia Jones)*

Free house   Manager John Edwards   Real ale   Snacks   Children welcome   Open 11.30–11

Peveril of the Peak

127 Great Bridgewater Street

With less of an overt appeal than some of its Mancunian rivals, this homely, quaint-shaped green tiled building is nonetheless strong on understated virtues. Three separate small rooms lead off the central servery, which has various hatches and counters, a profusion of mahogany and stained glass, and framed Victorian song-covers and ancient prints of obscure village games such as sack-jumping; traditional furnishings include red leatherette built-in button-back wall settles, or sturdy red plush ones. Well kept Websters Yorkshire and Choice and Wilsons Original and Mild on handpump; sensibly placed darts, pool, dominoes, fruit machine, juke box and (rarity of rarities now) bar football table. Food consists of sandwiches, hot pies such as steak and kidney or cheese and onion, and pork pie (all 65p). In summer, there are some seats outside on the terrace. Duke, the pub dog, is fond of Mild. *(Recommended by Andy and Jill Kassube, Virginia Jones, Denis Mann, Steve Mitcheson, Anne Collins; more reports please)*

Wilsons (Watneys)   Licensee Teresa Swanick   Real ale   Snacks (not Sun)   Children welcome   Open 11.30–3, 5.30(7 Sat)–11

Royal Oak ✦

729 Wilmslow Road, Didsbury, Manchester 20

This very busy end-of-terrace pub is simply furnished with theatrical handbills, porcelain spirit casks, coronation mugs, and old-fashioned brass anti-spill rims around the heavy cast-iron-framed tables; there's a quieter snug bar. The full range of cheeses, tracked down with great enthusiasm by the landlord over the last 30-odd years, is probably the widest you can find anywhere in the country – it's unusual to be served with less than a pound of cheese, even the rarer ones, with a substantial chunk of bread, salad and extras such as beetroot and pickled onions (£2; take-away bags provided); there are also pâtés; service is almost military in its efficiency, but friendly and chatty too. Well kept Marstons Burton, Pedigree and Mercian Mild on handpump, and some wines from the wood. There are some seats outside. *(Recommended by Richard Sanders, Keith Mills, RT, Jon Wainwright, Simon Turner, Simon Barber, Paul Evans, Mrs Simon Turner)*

Marstons   Licensee Arthur Gosling   Real ale   Lunchtime snacks (not Sat or Sun) Open 11–3, 5–11; 11–11 Sat; closed evening 25 Dec

Sinclairs Oyster Bar

Shambles Square, Manchester 3; in Arndale Centre between Deansgate and Corporation Street, opposite Exchange Street

Incongruously positioned in the middle of a modern shopping complex, this low-ceilinged, late 18th-century pub is traditionally furnished with small-backed stools that run along a tall old-fashioned marble-topped eating (and no-smoking) bar, squared oak panelling, and, in the larger room upstairs, low old-fashioned wall settles, and a scrolly old leather settee; there are also pictures of old Manchester up here, and a lunchtime food bar serving decent bar food, including ploughman's (£1.75), steak pie (£2.75), roast beef, gammon or turkey (£3), beef and oyster pie (£3.50), seafood platter (£3.70), and of course oysters (£4.50 the half-dozen), with sandwiches (hot gammon £1.50), rolls (75p) and side salads upstairs; friendly service from neatly-uniformed barmaids; the dining areas are also no-smoking. Well kept Sam Smiths OB and Museum on handpump kept under light blanket pressure, chess, dominoes, fruit machine, and piped music. There are picnic-table sets outside in the pedestrians-only square. *(Recommended by Steve Mitcheson, Len Beattie, Anne Collins, Virginia Jones, BKA, P Miller, Brian and Anna Marsden)*

Sam Smiths   Licensee Darren Coles   Real ale   Lunchtime meals and snacks (not Sun)   Nearby parking difficult   Open 11–11

Tommy Ducks

East Street, Manchester 2

We have to admit that the exclamations of dismay about the demise of this pub's knicker collection haven't been universal; most were donated to charity after a recent refurbishment, though enthusiasts can still gaze at the selected few that remain in a glass cabinet. Other changes have been mainly cosmetic, leaving the overall plan and character unchanged. In the bar there are plush button-back banquettes with gold fringes, antique theatrical posters, photographs and music hall cards on the mirrored walls, heavy swagged red curtains, and in one of its communicating rooms, a big old-fashioned black cooking range. Bar food includes sandwiches, beef in beer, curries, lasagne, and sweet and sour chicken (all around £2.75). Well kept Greenalls Local and Original on handpump, and a good few whiskies; fruit machine, juke box; very busy on weekday lunchtimes. From the outside – a black-and-white Victorian building surrounded by towering new prestige office-blocks – it's quite a sight. The street outside has been blocked off and there are picnic-table sets on the paving; handy for the exhibition centre in the former Central Station. *(Recommended by Howard and Sue Gascoyne, Steve Mitcheson, Anne Collins, Brian Marsden, Matt Pringle; more up-to-date reports please)*

Greenalls   Licensee Keith Shaw-Moores   Real ale   Lunchtime meals and snacks (not Sat or Sun)   Children in eating area of bar – not evenings   Open 11.30–11 weekdays; 11.30–3, 7.15–11 Sat

MERECLOUGH (Lancs)   SD8332   Map 7

Kettledrum

302 Red Lees Road; from A646 Burnley–Halifax, quickest route is turnoff between Walk Mill and Holme Chapel, signposted Over Town, Worsethorne; OS Sheet 103 map reference 873305

The extension to the bar area – pushing it through to where the dining room used to be – in this lively little place has been done with some discretion, preserving and increasing the attractive collection of artefacts – wooden and copper masks, buffalo horns, gruesome-looking knives by the dozen, and sparkling brass – shovels, knockers, measures, corkscrews, keys, scales, weights, spigots, fancy boot-horns, imps, toasting forks, and warming pans. Furnishings include some sensible angled and padded bottom-rests, tapestried wall seats, dimpled copper tables, and a solid-fuel stove. The (gas-lit) dining room is now upstairs. Well kept Courage Directors, John Smiths Bitter and Magnet, and Theakstons Best, XB and Old Peculier; several malt whiskies; darts, space game, and piped music. A wide choice of food includes soup (95p), sandwiches (from £1.25), good vegetarian dishes such as stuffed vine leaves or chilli casserole (from £1.90), omelettes (£2.45), ploughman's (£2.75), gammon with egg (£3.25), salads (from £3.25), home-made steak and kidney pie or good home-made chilli con carne (£3.50), trout (£4.25), a substantial mixed grill (£4.95) and 16oz T-bone steak (£7.25), with home-made puddings and children's dishes (from £1.25). Seats outside look over a low stone wall beyond the quiet road, to Burnley and its surrounding moors. *(Recommended by Comus Elliott, Andy and Jill Kassube, Len Beattie, Dr Thomas Mackenzie)*

Free house   Licensee Roy Ratcliffe   Real ale   Meals and snacks (12–2, 6–10.30) Restaurant tel Burnley (0282) 24591   Children in restaurant till 7.30   Open 11–3, 5.30–11; closed evening 25 Dec

MIDDLETON (Gtr Manchester)   SD8606   Map 7

Olde Boars Head

Just under 2 miles from M62 junction 19; A664 into Middleton (Long Street – pub on right)

Full marks to the brewery, John Willie Lees, for their noble restoration of this landmark building, so quaintly timbered and gabled. It dates back to the 12th century, though most of the current building is Elizabethan. Inside, a long central servery is backed by a flagstoned spinal corridor, leading out of a kitchen area with an open range in its massive chimney and hops strung from its high rafters. One of two small and cosily furnished parlours back here is named for Sam Bamford, a 19th-century weaver who, captivated by Homer, educated (and 'bettered') himself, was unjustly implicated in the events leading to the Peterloo massacre, and used to give readings of his pretty dire verse here. Other rooms include one on the left with standard lamps lighting the chairs and tables on its Turkey carpet; a spacious and rather grandly decorated sessions room at the opposite end, with a woodburning stove in its fine fireplace (and a little hatch to the servery, just about showing the top of the barmaid's head if you bend down enough); and two long front rooms comfortably fitted out with navy blue leatherette button-back built-in wall banquettes. There's no end of faded oak beams and timbers, with some fine ancient door frames. Simple bar food consists of soup (85p), sandwiches (from £1.25), a few hot dishes such as lamb stew, chicken and leek pie and lasagne (£2.95) and a bowl of chips (50p); well kept Lees Bitter and GB Mild on handpump; decently reproduced piped pop music; a warm, thoroughly pubby atmosphere, with good service. Picnic-table sets in a small sheltered back courtyard catch the evening sun; good parking (with TV surveillance). *(Recommended by Carol and Richard Glover)*

Lees   Licensee Martin T Reeves   Real ale   Meals and snacks (lunchtime)   Children in eating area till 8   Quiz/folk music Mon, jazz Thurs   Open 11.30(12 Sat)–3, 5.30 (7 Sat)–11

Tandle Hill Tavern

Thornham Lane, Slattocks; this, with Thornham Old Road, is a largely unmade track between A664 and A671 just S of (but not quickly accessible from) M62 junction 20; OS Sheet 109 map reference 899090

You'd never guess that this pub – down a rough track which burrows into really rustic countryside – was within the Manchester built-up area; it's actually part of a farm. The two snug rooms have spindleback chairs around dimpled copper tables, and lots of brass candlesticks on the mantlepiece above the coal fire. Well kept Lees ales on handpump; darts, cribbage, dominoes, and piped music. Cheap bar food includes soup, toasties, pie, and minute steak. There are some benches outside among the ducks, ponies and ageing tractors. Paths lead off on all sides, and it's handy for the Tandle Hill Country Park. *(Recommended by Carol and Richard Glover, Comus Elliott, David Butcher)*

Lees   Real ale   Snacks (12–2, 7–10)   Children welcome   Open 12.30–3, 7–11; 12–4, 7–11 Sat; closed lunchtime on winter weekdays

NEWTON (Lancs)   SD6950   Map 7

Parkers Arms

B6478 7 miles N of Clitheroe

The bar inside this black and white pub has a cheerful and friendly atmosphere, as well as red plush button-back banquettes around dimpled copper tables on a flowery blue carpet, one or two pictures on the white Anaglypta walls, lots of copper and brass kettles, candlesticks and an urn on the neat stone mantlepiece. Beyond an arch is a similar area with sensibly placed darts, pool, dominoes, fruit and trivia machines, and discreet piped music; an unobtrusive black labrador may wander in – or escort you in friendly fashion back to your car. Straightforward bar food includes soup, sandwiches, home-made steak and kidney pie, gammon and egg, fresh salmon and so forth; they do Sunday teas in the airy restaurant; good service. Flowers on handpump. There are pretty window boxes outside, and well spaced picnic-table sets on the big lawn, looking down towards the village's river, and beyond to the hills. *(Recommended by P Devitt, Colin and Caroline Maxwell, F and J Hamer, Len Beattie, Logan Petch; more reports please)*

Whitbreads   Licensee Henry Rhodes   Real ale   Meals and snacks (12–9 on Sun in summer)   Children welcome   Open 11–3, 6–11   Bedrooms tel Slaidburn (020 06) 236; £20/£32

RABY (Merseyside)   SJ3180   Map 7

Wheatsheaf

The Green, Rabymere Road; off A540 S of Heswall

An original 17th-century country-hamlet alehouse in a quiet village, this is furnished and decorated in traditional fashion, with thatch and timbering outside, and low beams and red tiles inside; the central room has an old wall clock and homely black kitchen shelves, and a nice snug formed by antique settles built in around its fine old fireplace. A second, more spacious room has upholstered wall seats around the tables, small hunting prints on the cream walls and a smaller coal fire. Well kept real ales on handpump include Flowers IPA, Higsons, Ind Coope Burton, Tetleys, Thwaites and Youngers Scotch and No 3, and there's a good choice of malt whiskies. *(Recommended by Tony and Lynne Stark, M J B Pearson, Mr and Mrs J H Adam, P Miller; more reports please)*

Free house   Real ale   Lunchtime meals and snacks (not Sun)   Open 11.30–3, 5.30–10.30

SLAIDBURN (Lancs)   SD7152 Map 7

Hark to Bounty

Since taking over just as last year's *Guide* went to press, the new management has inspired strong enthusiasm from readers, who have consistently praised standards of food and service, and the bedrooms, with comparisons running up to a French provincial hotel. The cream-walled lounge bar, comfortable and cosy, is decorated with big Victorian engravings, a few Victorian fashion plates, brass and copper over the open fire, and local photographs; furnishings range from an antique settee and a Victorian settle, to one or two easy chairs and neat armed dining chairs. The wide range of popular bar food includes home-made soup (£1.15), lunchtime sandwiches (from £1.30; not Sun), ploughman's (£2.95), Cumberland sausage with a tasty stuffing and apple sauce (£3.55), salads (from £3.75), home-made steak and kidney pie (£3.95), chicken (£4.45), good daily specials such as monkfish or venison casserole, and cooked as well as cream afternoon teas (3–5pm, including Sundays); professional service. The restaurant has a small but praised menu. Well kept Theakstons Best and Old Peculier and Youngers Scotch on hand or electric pump. There's lots of room to sit outside – on high days and feast days they may even have a fairground organ. Beyond the gently rolling wooded hills around here there are high fells and fly fishing can be arranged on the nearby Stocks Reservoir; a steam traction rally is held annually on the first weekend in June. The village itself, tucked away in the Forest of Bowland, is gauntly handsome. (*Recommended by John Atherton, Comus Elliott, Len Beattie, J E Cross, R D and H M Bromley, Graham Bush, Geofrrey Carew, Alan and Marlene Radford, Lesley Wood, Sean Hilton, Mr and Mrs J E Rycroft, G Dobson*)

Scottish & Newcastle   Manager Henry Lynch   Real ale   Meals and snacks Restaurant   Children welcome   Open 11–11; closed 25 Dec   Bedrooms tel Slaidburn (020 06) 246; £18B/£36B

STALYBRIDGE (Gtr Manchester)   SJ9698 Map 7

Stalybridge Station Buffet

A delightful elaboration of what remains firmly a working station buffet, this friendly place still serves traditional cafe stand-bys – cheap snacks like delicious black-eyed peas (35p), sandwiches (52p), hot or cold pies with black peas (85p), and tea made freshly by the pot. But there's also very well kept Moorhouses Premier and three guest beers (almost changing daily) from all over the country (including from home-brew pubs) on handpump, and occasional farm ciders. Lovingly well kept, it's splendidly Victorian in a very basic way that recalls the days when there was still a third class on the railways – lots of railway memorabilia, including barge and railway pictures set into the red bar counter, and more railway pictures and some old station signs on the high walls; the beermats are interesting; trivia. Proceeds from a paperback library on the piano beside the open fire go to a guide-dog charity. (*Recommended by Gary Scott, Andy and Jill Kassube, P A Crossland, D A Cawley, Dennis Jones, Steve Mitcheson, Anne Collins, M A and W R Proctor; more reports please*)

Free house   Licensee Ken Redfern   Real ale   Snacks   Children welcome   Folk singers Sat evening   Open 12–3, 5(7 Sat)–11; closed Sun, Mon, and Tues lunchtime

THORNTON HOUGH (Merseyside)   SJ3081 Map 7

Seven Stars

Church Road; B5136 in village centre

Quite a food pub, this has a well kept and popular bar area of two rooms with cushioned wheelback chairs and button-back wall banquettes, easy chairs and a sofa by the fireplace; plastic plants hang along the ceiling trusses, and there are framed accounts on the walls of local history. Bar food is brought to your table, and includes soup (80p), sandwiches (from £1.20), ploughman's (£1.95), pork satay (£1.75), a daily vegetarian dish (£3.25), gammon (£4.25), and steaks (from

£5.95, T-bone £7.95); they also now do more specials – anything from Turkish or Indian dishes to quail or local rabbit stew; puddings (from £1.50); good service from the uniformed waitresses; some of the tables are no-smoking. Well kept Boddingtons or Whitbreads Castle Eden on handpump, gentle piped music. Seats on the terrace and in the small garden look across to the neighbouring twin churches. *(Recommended by Christian Leigh, M J B Pearson, Alan and Marlene Radford, Drs M and K Parier, Mr and Mrs J H Adam)*

Whitbreads Licensee Mrs C E Nelson Real ale Snacks (lunchtime) and meals Restaurant tel Liverpool (051) 336 4574 Open 11.30–11; 11–3, 5–11 Oct-Apr; closed 25 Dec

TOCKHOLES (Lancs) SD6623 Map 7
Royal Arms

Village signposted from A6062 on S edge of Blackburn; though not signposted, good route on pretty moorland road about 1 1/2 miles N of Belmont, just past AA telephone box (and on opposite side of road) – this is then the first pub you come to

The views from the sheltered terrace here are mainly of the woods in the surrounding rolling countryside, but if you look hard on a clear day you can make out Blackpool Tower. The four little rooms of the bar, old-fashioned and countrified, have rustic decorations on the panelling-effect walls, cushioned wall settles, and big log fires in handsome stone fireplaces. Well kept Thwaites Bitter and Best Mild on handpump, dominoes, fruit machine, juke box and well reproduced easy-listening classics. Bar food includes sandwiches, ploughman's, salads, home-made steak and kidney pie, scampi, and maybe steaks done over one of the open fires; friendly service. There's a play area in the garden, white doves in a dovecote, geese in the field behind, and a nature trail opposite. *(Recommended by Len Beattie, Ben Wimpenny, G T Jones, Denis Mann, Geoff Halson; more reports please)*

Thwaites Real ale Meals and snacks Children welcome Open 12–3, 7–11

UPPERMILL (Gtr Manchester) SD9905 Map 7
Cross Keys

Runninghill Gate; from A670 in Uppermill turn into New Street, by a zebra crossing close to the chapel; this is the most practical-looking of the lanes towards the high moors and leads directly into Runninghill Gate

The decent choice of bar food in this rambling pub includes soup (80p), sandwiches (from 80p, toasties from 90p), and a wide range of dishes such as liver and bacon casserole, Hungarian goulash, chilli con carne, scampi, Chinese spring roll, and salads (all £3), with puddings like apricot crumble or apple and blackberry pancake (from 90p). The several connecting rooms of the bars have low beams, pews, settles, flagstones, and an original cooking range. Well kept Lees Bitter and Mild on handpump; darts, dominoes, cribbage and fruit machine, and Bridge school Monday and Friday evenings and Saturday lunchtime. There's a side terrace and a stylish flagstoned back terrace with bright flowers sheltered by a dry stone wall; next to it are swings, a slide and a climbing frame. Since it's headquarters of the Oldham Mountain Rescue Team and various outdoor sports clubs, the sporting connections are strong: they're annual sponsors of the road running or fell races in the first week in June and on the last Saturday in August (there are lots of colourful photographs of these among the interesting older prints on the walls), and the Saddleworth Clog and Garland Girls practise regularly here. Tracks from behind the pub lead straight up towards Broadstone Hill and Dick Hill. *(Recommended by Steve Mitcheson, Anne Collins, Michael Rooke, P A Crossland, D A Cawley, Pamela and Merlyn Horswell; more reports please)*

Lees Licensee Philip Kay Real ale Meals and snacks Children in eating area of bar Jazz and clog dancing Mon evenings, folk Wed evenings Open 11–11; 11–3, 6.30–11 in winter

WHARLES (Lancs)   SD4435   Map 7
Eagle & Child

Church Road; from B5268 W of Broughton turn left into Higham Side Road at HMS Inskip sign; OS Sheet 102 map reference 448356

The attention to antique detail is considerable here; highlights include a magnificent, elaborately carved Jacobean settle which came originally from Aston Hall in Birmingham, now part of a whole collection of antique oak seats; those in the alcove of the L-shaped bar are really elaborately carved, with two handsome 17th-century oak armchairs; there's also a carved oak chimneypiece, and a couple of fine longcase clocks. The plain cream walls are hung with modern advertising mirrors and some older mirrors, and there are exotic knives, carpentry tools and so forth on the plastered structural beams; even when it's not particularly cold, there should be a good fire burning in the elaborate cast-iron stove. Well kept Boddingtons on handpump, with several guest beers such as Mansfield Bitter and Old Baily and Wadworths 6X, on handpump; darts in a sensible side area; juke box, friendly ginger cat. One or two picnic-table sets outside. As we say, it's closed on weekday lunchtimes. *(Recommended by Graham Bush, Simon Bates, Jon Wainwright)*

Free house   Licensees Brian and Angela Tatham   Real ale   No food   Open 7–11 (and 12–3 Sat; usual Sun hours)

WHEATLEY LANE (Lancs)   SD8338   Map 7
Old Sparrow Hawk

Towards E end of village road which runs N of and parallel to A6068; one way of reaching it is to follow Fence, Newchurch 1 3/4 signpost, then turn off at Barrowford 3/4 signpost

Finely positioned – with Pendle Hill rising beyond and views over to the moors behind Nelson and Colne – this bustling pub has dark oak panelling, stripped stonework, and an unusual stained glass ceiling dome in its big semi-circular bar; also studded leather seats and long button-back banquettes, and three stuffed sparrowhawks and an owl above the gleaming copper hoods of the log-effect gas fires; a small room leads off. Well kept Bass, Bass Special and Mild on handpump; good coffee. Served from an efficient food servery, the food includes a good range of sandwiches (from £1, double deckers from £1.95; toasties from £1.25, steak £2.85), soup (£1.35), ploughman's (£2.10), and lots of attractively presented salads or cold plates including smoked or roast ham, roast meats and smoked salmon, and a range of at least five hot home-made daily specials such as chilli con carne (£3.50), steak and kidney or chicken and leek pie (£3.95), and sirloin steak (£5.95). A mock-Tudor carvery serves good roasts (lunch, not Saturday, £8.95; dinner 3 courses £9.95). There are tables outside on the good-sized terrace. *(Recommended by Mike Tucker, John Hayward, Len Beattie, Jon Wainwright)*

Bass   Licensee Don Butterworth   Real ale   Meals and snacks (11.30–11)   Restaurant tel Burnley (0282) 64126; 12–3, 4.30–10.30 Sun   Children in eating area and restaurant   Open 11.30–11

WHITEWELL (Lancs)   SD6546   Map 7
Inn at Whitewell ★ ★ 🛏

Most easily reached by B6246 from Whalley; road through Dunsop Bridge from B6478 is also good

This long, low stone inn, alone by a church and surrounded by well wooded rolling hills set off against higher moors, is the focal point for much activity – it also houses a wine merchant (hence the unusually wide range of wines available – the claret is recommended), an art gallery, and a shop selling cashmere, shoes and so forth, and owns six miles of trout, salmon and sea trout fishing on the Hodder; with notice they'll arrange shooting. Lunchtime bar food includes soup (£1.20), fish pâté (£3.30), ploughman's (£4.30), Cumberland sausage, steak kidney and mushroom or fish pie (all £4.30), and salads (from £4.50); in the evenings there's also half a melon with prawns (£3.50), seafood pancakes (£4.30), home-made gravadlax with dill mayonnaise, trout or fillet steak sandwich (£5); also, popular home-made puddings like summer or bread and butter puddings, fresh fruit jellies, and ice-creams (£1.80); they serve coffee and cream teas all day. The bar itself, old-fashioned and country-house in feel, has antique settles, oak gateleg tables, sonorous clocks, heavy curtains on sturdy wooden rails, old cricketing and sporting prints, and log fires (the lounge has a particularly attractive stone fireplace); one area has a selection of newspapers, local maps and guide books. The public bar has darts, pool, shove-ha'penny, dominoes, and juke box, with a 1920s game-of-skill slot machine; there's a piano for anyone who wants to play. Well kept Moorhouses Premier and Pendle Witches Brew on handpump. The seats outside are in a pleasant sun-trap. The bedrooms have been upgraded. *(Recommended by Len Beattie, Douglas Cohen, C F Walling, Kathleen Morley, Denis Mann, A M Neal, Mr and Mrs J E Rycroft, Andrew Stephenson, John and Anna McIver, Mr and Mrs Harry McCann)*

Free house   Licensee Richard Bowman   Real ale   Meals and snacks (not Sat evening if a big function is on)   Restaurant (not Sun lunchtime)   Children welcome   Pianist Fri and Sat evenings   Open 11–3, 6–11   Bedrooms tel Dunsop Bridge (020 08) 222; £29B/£43B

Lucky Dip

Besides the fully inspected pubs, you might like to try these Lucky Dips recommended to us and described by readers (if you do, please send us reports):

☆ **Adlington**, Lancs [5A Market St; SD5912], *White Bear*: Small very quiet village pub doing well under newish landlord, recently stripped back to pretty external stonework, with hanging baskets and potted shrubs, and tastefully decorated inside, with flowers and plants in the corners, open fire in one room, juke box in other, pool table in back room, children's play area in garden behind; growing reputation for exceptionally cheap good food, with quick friendly service; Theakstons XB, Best and Old Peculier well kept; parking difficult *(Debbie Jackson, R J Yates, G T Jones)*

Affetside, Gtr Manchester [Watling St; SD7513], *Pack Horse*: Attractive moorland local on outskirts of Bolton *(Denis Mann, Michael Rooke)*

Ainsworth, Gtr Manchester [off B6196 E of Bolton — down rough rd beside churchyard; SD7610], *Prince William*: Small comfortable pub with helpful staff, imaginative menu (especially black pudding starter); separate dining room *(E J Alcock)*

Altrincham, Gtr Manchester [Stamford St; SJ7788], *Malt Shovels*: Lively and spacious consistently good Sam Smiths pub with focal staircase, big games room at side, Fri jazz *(Jon Wainwright)*; [42 Victoria St], *Old Roebuck*: Pleasant Wilsons pub with good layout and plenty of space *(Jon Wainwright)*; [Old Market Pl], *Orange Tree*: Handsome central bar, cosy back room, pleasant furnishings, Watneys-related real ales on handpump *(Jon Wainwright)*

Ashton under Lyne, Lancs [Mossley Rd; SJ9399], *Heroes of Waterloo*: Pleasant, clean and spacious, with good, old-fashioned bar food from sandwiches up, good service *(N Hesketh, Steve Mitcheson, Anne Collins, Dennis Jones)*; [52 Old St], *Wychwood*: Refurbished but still unpretentious and friendly, popular for uncommonly wide choice of well kept real

ales, which landlord is very knowledgeable about — and for Sat live bands, sometimes heavy metal, sometimes not so loud (afternoons are best if you want relative quiet) *(P A Crossland, D A Cawley, Dennis Jones, Steve Mitcheson, Anne Collins)*

Atherton, Gtr Manchester [Bolton Old Rd; SD6703], *Bay Horse*: Archetypal mining-town local full of character(s) — flat caps, beer bellies and whippets abound — not for the faint-hearted; smoky lounge, peaceful pool room, vibrant vault, busy, efficient staff *(Lee Goulding)*

Audenshaw, Gtr Manchester [Audenshaw Rd (B6390), Guide Bridge; SJ8896], *Boundary*: Good value low-priced food inc children's dishes and good puddings, served until late evening; very busy — they tell approximately how long your order will take; can be smoky, get there early for a seat; helpful licensee, barge trips with meals on board; children allowed in dining room *(P A Crossland, D A Cawley, Steve Mitcheson, Anne Collins)*

Bamber Bridge, Lancs [Preston Rd (old A6), nr M6 junction 29; SD5625], *Halfway House*: Banks's house with very reasonably priced restaurant *(D J Brighouse)*

Barley, Lancs [OS Sheet 103 map reference 821405; SD8240], *Pendle*: Nice village in shadow of Pendle Hill (in fact the best place from which to attempt the hill); lovely less strenuous walks nearby; adequate meals in comfortable surroundings, Bass beers *(Len Beattie)*

Barnston, Merseyside [Barnston Rd (A551); SJ2883], *Fox & Hounds*: Nicely refurbished country pub with good food weekday lunchtimes, pianist Sun lunchtime, well kept Watneys-related real ales *(Mr and Mrs J H Adam)*

Barrow, Lancs [OS Sheet 103 map reference 735375; SD7338], *Dog & Partridge*: Always welcoming and chatty; good range of beers and generously served home-made food *(Hugh Geddes); Spread Eagle*: Spacious well kept pub with wide choice of generously served food and helpful staff, but busy weekends when service may slow; no piped music *(KC)*

Barrowford, Lancs [Gisburn Road (A682); SD8539], *White Bear*: Good friendly small-town pub, with cheap, excellent sandwiches, cosy atmosphere, well kept Bass and Stones; children welcome *(Comus Elliott)*

Barton, Lancs [A6 Preston—Garstang; SD5137], *White Horse*: Willing and courteous staff, well kept Theakstons on handpump, and very good reasonably priced straightforward food *(Jim and Maggie Colvell)*

☆ **Bashall Eaves**, Lancs [SD6943], *Red Pump*: Beautifully situated, warm, consistently friendly and not too crowded, though busy at weekends, with reasonably priced better-than-average food *(Dr P H Mitchell, F and J Hamer, Andrew Stephenson)*

☆ **Belmont**, Lancs [A675; SD6716], *Black Dog*: Moorland village pub with traditional communicating rooms, warm open fires, decor from railwaymen's lamps and chamber-pots to landscape paintings, also picture-window extension lounge; bar food from sandwiches and winter broth to steaks (service may be slow), well kept and remarkably cheap Holts Bitter and Mild; lively and friendly, with piped classical music; good walks; open till 4, closed Sun evening; children welcome; bedrooms *(Denis Mann, Michael Rooke, Ben Wimpenny, G T Jones, LYM — more reports please)*

Belthorn, Lancs [Elton Rd (B6232 S); SD7225], *Grey Mare*: Typical Thwaites out-of-town pub, with well kept Bitter and Mild on handpump, good value food lunchtime and evening; on Oswaldtwistle Moor, with fine views across to Blackburn, Preston and Blackpool *(P Corris)*

Birkenhead, Merseyside [Arrowe Park Rd; SJ3289], *Arrowe Park*: Nicely cared for and decorated, very popular with local Rotary Club, Women's Guilds and so forth, for its bar food *(E G Parish)*; [Claughton Firs, Oxton], *Shrewsbury Arms*: Delightful pub with atmosphere, in villagey area; public bar, big lounge, fine Higsons on handpump, seats on terrace *(P Corris)*

Bispham Green, Lancs [Chorley Rd — turn off B5246 N of Parbold at sign for Chorley, Leyland, Mawdesley, Eccleston; SD4914], *Farmers Arms*: Pleasant, friendly Burtonwood house with several bars, family room and dining room; comfortable banquettes, mock timbering, usual bar food; children's play area *(T Nott)*

Blackburn, Lancs [Accrington Rd; SD6828], *Wharf*: Converted warehouse, part wooden and part carpeted floors, lots of windows overlooking canal; wine-bar-style drinks and food, not cheap *(Wayne Brindle)*

☆ **Blackpool**, Lancs [35 Clifton St, just behind Town Hall; SD3035], *St Martins Tavern*: Stylish cafe-bar with marble, columns, statues, lofty coffered ceiling, good swivel seats, solid ash bar counter in central sunken area, tasty reasonably priced home-made lunchtime food, keg beers, espresso machine, rather assertive piped music; used to be a

bank, now a popular evening meeting place; open all day *(I Coburn, Carol and Richard Glover, John Hayward, Graham Bush, LYM)*

☆ **Blackpool** [Whitegate Dr, Marton; SD3435], *Saddle*: A rare find, with original bar, etched and stained glass, tiles, snugs, open fires, signed pictures of personalities from the 30s, 40s and 50s; good atmosphere though it gets very busy, well kept Bass Mild and Special on draught, no food — and rather a male preserve in the later evening; the hope is that the rumours of impending modernisation are unfounded *(Graham Bush, Brian and Anna Marsden)*

Blackpool [Corporation St], *Grapes*: Town-centre pub nr Tower, with original snugs and central-island bar, Tetleys on electric pump; cheap for the area *(Graham Bush)*; [Leamington Rd], *Raikes Hall*: Smart, tidy bar and vaults with red plush seating and Laura Ashley wallpaper; jazz Weds (and rock some summer nights) in upstairs function room, well kept Bass and Stones, straightforward food, garden by neat terrace overlooking crown bowling green (customers can play) *(Graham Bush)*; [204 Talbot Rd], *Ramsden Arms*: Notably warm pubby atmosphere with friendly licensee and well kept Jennings on handpump *(Kenneth Wilkinson)*; [Vicarage Lane/Cherry Tree Rd, Marton], *Welcome*: Spacious and lively holiday pub with pink-and-plastic-plants decor, well kept Burtonwood and generous helpings of bar food now showing the benefits of the recent kitchen refurbishments; unusual conservatory bar, discos in lounge bar, garden/playroom very popular with young families at weekends *(Graham Bush)*

☆ **Blacksnape**, Lancs [Old Roman Rd; SD7121], *Red Lion*: Doing well under current regime, with well kept Burtonwood ales and generous helpings of traditional bar food inc good pizzas and interesting set lunches *(Jeremy and Margaret Wallington)*

Blacksnape [Grimehills — Old Roman Rd], *Crown & Thistle*: Isolated little low-beamed moorland dining pub, on such a steep hill that its rooms are on different levels; good atmosphere, lots of brass on the stone walls, clean and smart furnishings in dining room, wide choice of home-cooked food, Thwaites Bitter and Mild *(More reports please)*

☆ **Bolton**, Gtr Manchester [Pool St; SD7108], *Howcroft*: Beautifully preserved friendly old local tucked away in modern housing development by old people's home; lots of small, screened-off rooms, plenty of games inc pin-table, darts, bar billiards, well kept Allied real ales, Addlestone's cider; bowling green *(Jon Wainwright, Ben Wimpenny, Denis Mann)*

Bolton [606 Halliwell Rd], *Ainsworth Arms*: Lively local, very busy in evenings, but there's always a seat in the smoke room; food lunchtimes inc Sun, well kept Walkers, very quick service *(Andrew Hazeldine)*

☆ **Bolton by Bowland**, Lancs [SD7849], *Coach & Horses*: Delightful neatly kept village pub in lovely spot, comfortable and clean with coal fires and welcoming atmosphere; well kept Whitbreads Castle Eden, good home-made bar food (not usually Tues) inc imaginative dishes; get there early weekends for a table *(Dr and Mrs Gavin, Dr Fuller)*

Bowdon, Gtr Manchester [SJ7686], *Phoenix*: Large, attractive pub with good atmosphere and decor, big fires, Watneys-related beers, bar food; strikes happy medium between diner and drinker *(Jon Wainwright)*

☆ **Brindle**, Lancs [B5256, off A6 from M6 junction 29; SD6024], *Cavendish Arms*: Tidy and attractive extended whitewashed pub by church of pleasant moorland village, with tiny bar, plush lounge, little snugs, coal fires, stained-glass windows throughout (even the inn-sign), ornate almost ecclesiastical bar gantry, well kept Burtonwood real ales, darts; good car park *(Graham Bush)*

Burnley, Lancs [Manchester Rd; Habergham Eves, a mile or so S; SD8133], *Bull & Butcher*: Recently completely renovated main-road pub, open-plan with plush seating, decent food in attractive former barn, now a buttery, family room with satellite TV etc, baby-changing facilities, play area outside; well kept Allied beers, big back car park *(Carol and Richard Glover, George Day)*; [Brownside, Pike Hill; SD8632], *Thornton Arms*: Converted from old barn by the man whose name it bears; well kept Youngers IPA, popular meals *(Len Beattie)*; [Manchester Rd, out on moors], *Waggoners*: Warm and welcoming open-plan pub with red plush seating in one flagstoned area, two more simply furnished areas with sewing-machine tables; plain walls covered with bric-a-brac, saddles, brasses etc, huge bellows over open fire; good reasonably priced bar menu (not Tues evening), Courage beers, decent wine list, unobtrusive piped music; fine views *(Carol and Richard Glover)*

Burscough, Lancs [SD4310], *Briars Hall*: Friendly, efficient service, good Allied beers; extraordinarily cheap bar food, and plenty of it; restaurant *(Comus Elliott)*

Bury, Gtr Manchester [Castle Hill Rd, Birtle; SD8313], *Church*: Family-owned pub-restaurant tucked away behind Birtle church; quaint 17th-century building with more modern extensions; good beers and food *(Don Kirkpatrick)*; [pub signposted E off A56 N of Bury], *Lord Raglan*: Family-owned 17th-century building high on moors overlooking Bury; fine antique furniture and fixtures, good choice of beers; larger adjoining restaurant *(Don Kirkpatrick)*; [Manchester Old Rd], *Rose & Crown*: Excellent little pub just out of centre with six well kept real ales on handpump inc Boddingtons and Thwaites; good-value filling lunchtime snacks *(Andy and Jill Kassube)*

Catforth, Lancs [SD4736], *Running Pump*: Quiet roadside pub looking over fields to hills; island bar, long thin room, snug and lounge (with red-topped pool table); Robinsons Bitter and Mild, lunchtime food, piped music, and very big home-packed bags of nuts; friendly local atmosphere *(Graham Bush)*

Caton, Lancs [A683, E of M6 junction 34; SD5364], *Station*: large, clean local with two bars, games room and family room; decent choice of very generously served good value food and well kept Mitchells real ales; bowling green; children welcome *(John*

Hayward, Andrew Hazeldine)

Chatburn, Lancs [SD7644], *Brown Cow*: Pleasant atmosphere, real ale, good range of bar food, attentive staff *(R Gosling)*

Cheadle, Gtr Manchester [1a Cheadle Rd (A5149); SJ8688], *Village*: New hotel/sports club/bar/restaurant complex, one of a small chain up here; attractive bar areas with plenty of seating, conservatory area, Boddingtons on handpump, food (not cheap but decent value) from hot counter and salad bar lunchtime and till 10 every evening; popular with the younger local smart set *(Michael Sandy)*

Cheadle Hulme, Gtr Manchester [Church Rd/Ravenoak Rd; SJ8787], *Church*: Two busy and lively beamed and partly panelled rooms, huge brass plates and simple old furnishings in small overflow room; lunchtime food, very well kept Robinsons on handpump *(Lee Goulding)*

Chipping, Lancs [Windy St; SD6243], *Sun*: Simple stone local with three small snug rooms, one with pool table, another darts, old TV, and very old juke box, and a third tables, sports trophies, a fire, and papers and magazines; well kept Boddingtons on handpump facing the central hall (an underground stream cools the cellar) *(Graham Bush, Andy and Jill Kassube, D J Cooke)*

☆ nr **Chipping** [Hesketh Lane Village; crossroads Chipping—Longridge with Inglewhite—Clitheroe — OS Sheet 103 map reference 619413], *Dog & Partridge*: Comfortable little lounge bar with easy chairs around low tables and log fire, very smooth and genteel, generous home-made bar food except Sat evening and Sun lunchtime, Tetleys on electric pump, restaurant; attractive country setting *(G T Jones, LYM)*

nr **Chipping** [minor rd to Doeford Bridge — OS Sheet 103 map reference 638425], *Gibbon Bridge*: Country-house hotel with spacious lounge bar, dining room, conservatory and coffee lounge; good traditional midday lunch and more expensive evening menu; big garden with terrace, rock garden, lawn, stream, and view of Longridge Fell *(F and J Hamer)*

☆ nr **Chorley**, Lancs [White Coppice; 2 miles from M61 junction 8; signposted from A674 towards Blackburn; SD6118], *Railway*: Simple comfort by the North-West Pennine Recreational Park, well kept Matthew Browns Bitter and Mild, bar food with half-price children's helpings; weekend cricket on the green, clay pigeon shoots winter Suns, fine cigarette card collection, Sat evening live entertainment in winter, monthly in summer *(G T Jones, LYM)*

Chorley, Lancs [Chapel St, nr mkt; SD5817], *Crown*: Good food and Theakstons beers *(D J Brighouse)*

☆ **Churchtown**, Merseyside [off A565 from Preston, taking B5244 at Southport; SD3618], *Hesketh Arms*: Attractive thatched pub sheltered by trees, off flagstoned village lane; spacious bar with central servery, pretty dark wood and blue wallpaper decor, good freshly prepared food from chip butties to outstanding roast beef and Yorkshire pudding, Tetleys on handpump; close to botanical gardens *(Ian*

Phillips, A T Langton)

☆ **Churchtown**, the different Lancs one [nr church, off A586 Garstang—St Michaels-on-Wyre; SD4843], *Punchbowl*: Tetleys pub/restaurant in small and attractive peaceful village; stained glass, wood panelling, lots of stuffed animals in mock-Tudor bar with friendly staff, reasonably priced good food, well kept real ale, good fires; lavatory for disabled people *(Graham Bush)*

Churchtown [the Lancs one again, on A586], *Horns*: Recent complete refurbishment perhaps less of an attraction than the wide choice of bar food; table service, real ale, wine by the glass *(Dr James Haworth)*

☆ **Clayton Green**, Lancs [just off B5256, not far from M1 junction 29; SD5723], *Lord Nelson*: Friendly, busy local, nice and spacious inside with plenty of stripped stonework and pictures; good atmosphere, well kept Matthew Browns ales and good but limited bar food served quickly and cheerfully *(Col G D Stafford, Kathleen Morley)*

Clitheroe, Lancs [Station Rd; SD7441], *Castle*: Food inc French and Italian in rather American-style surroundings, full range of Matthew Brown beers, small car park in larger public car parks nearby *(F and J Hamer)*

☆ **nr Clitheroe** [Higher Hodder Bridge; nr Chaigley on old Clitheroe—Longbridge high rd, parallel to B6243 — OS Sheet 103 map reference 699412], *Hodder Bridge*: Alone by the pretty River Hodder, with terraces looking down to the river — the hotel has its own fishing; panelled back lounge, bar food from home-made soup and sandwiches through steak and kidney pie and gammon and eggs to steaks, generous Sun carvery, Websters and Wilsons on handpump, river-view restaurant; has been open till 5 weekends; children welcome; bedrooms quiet and comfortable *(Len Beattie, LYM)*

nr Clitheroe, [Chaigley, out on Chipping rd; SD6941], *Craven Heifer*: Well run pub in Ribble Valley; very good restaurant meals (with speciality black pudding) and bar service, well kept real ales *(Dr James Haworth)*

Cowan Bridge, Lancs [Burrow-by-Burrow; A65 towards Kirkby Lonsdale; SD6477], *Whoop Hall*: Spruced-up but comfortable decor and layout, quick food service at buttery bar, well kept Tetleys and Youngers Scotch and No 3 on handpump, tables outside with play area; children allowed in eating area *(Andy and Jill Kassube, LYM)*

Croston, Lancs [Westhead Rd; SD4818], *Black Horse*: Doing well under current regime, with good value bar food lunchtimes and evenings, Bass, Thwaites Mild, and three changing guest beers; small restaurant Thurs–Sun evenings with limited but good menu *(P Lloyd, Miss K Bamford)*; *Highfield*: Good low-priced bar food inc excellent cottage pie with fresh vegetables; real coffee *(Anon)*

Delph, Gtr Manchester [OS Sheet 109 map reference 980070; SD9808], *Cross Keys*: Good food inc tasty beef pie, real chips *(G C and M D Dickinson)*

☆ **Denshaw**, Gtr Manchester [2 miles from

M62 junction 2; A672 towards Oldham, pub N of village; SD9710], *Rams Head*: Comfortable moorland pub, part of a farm; traditional settles, beams, panelling, log fires and small rooms, with well kept Theakstons and usually a guest beer tapped from the cask via a big metal jug, unobtrusive piped music and simple food Fri–Sun lunchtimes; lovely views, good walking; closed lunchtimes (except Sun); a fine pub *(Alan Holden, Gary Scott, Steve Mitcheson, Anne Collins, LYM)*

Denshaw, *Junction*: Nice cosy pub with bar, lounge and back dining area; comfortable furnishings, roaring fire, pool table, fruit machine, juke box, Lees Bitter and genuinely thoughtful landlady *(Jon Wainwright)*

Denton, Gtr Manchester [Stockport Rd; SJ9295], *Fletchers Arms*: Spaciously refurbished beamed bar with well kept Robinsons, decent wine and good plentiful food, bookcases, striking fairy-lit garden with fountain, pond and lots of room for children to play *(Steve Mitcheson, Anne Collins)*

☆ **Diggle**, Gtr Manchester [Diglea Hamlet, Sam Rd; village signed off A670 just N of Dobcross; SE0008], *Diggle Hotel*: Three modernised open-plan rooms used mainly by diners — food from sandwiches or a choice of ploughman's through home-made steak and kidney pie to steaks, with children's dishes; well kept Boddingtons, Oldham Bitter and maybe Mild, and Timothy Taylors Golden Best and Landlord, decent wines, good choice of malt whiskies, good coffee, soft piped music, really welcoming service; rustic fairy-lit tables among the trees in front of this dark stone house — it's a nice spot just below the moors, by the mouth of the long railway tunnel (and the now-disused canal tunnel); opens noon *(Steve Mitcheson, Anne Collins, Jon Wainwright, BB)*

Dobcross, Gtr Manchester [SD9906], *Swan*: Fine stone-built Bass house with series of cosy rooms *(Steve Mitcheson, Anne Collins)*

Dunham Woodhouses, Gtr Manchester [B5160 — OS Sheet 109 map reference 724880; SJ7288], *Vine*: Surprisingly unspoilt village inn considering proximity of ritzier end of Manchester; Mischa the rotweiler seems friendly *(G T Jones)*

☆ **Eccles**, Gtr Manchester [33 Regent St (A57 — handy for M602 junction 2); SJ7798], *Lamb*: Large pub, down to earth but still steeped in Edwardian splendour and character, with etched windows, nice woodwork and furnishings, and very unusual bar counter; separate tap room accessible only from outside; well kept Holts, possibly the only pub in Manchester with a full-size snooker table *(Steve Mitcheson, Anne Collins, J P Glew, Richard Sanders, Michael Rooke)*

Eccles [Church St (A57)], *Duke of York*: Redecorated high-ceilinged Victorian pub with open fires in two rooms, no-smoking room; changing well kept Whitbreads-related and other often interesting real ales, Bulmers cider on handpump, good value home-made lunchtime bar food from separate servery, unobtrusive piped music, darts and juke box; has been open all day Sat *(Mr and Mrs*

Harry McCann, Steve Mitcheson, Anne Collins); [off A57], *Hare & Hounds:* In a shopping street full of pubs — clean and friendly *(Steve Mitcheson, Anne Collins);* [133 Liverpool Rd, Patricroft (a mile from M63 junction 2); SJ7698], *White Lion:* Busy, popular three-roomed street-corner pub with 50-year-old inn-sign, etched windows and passageway servery — recent changes haven't spoilt the character; well kept Holts *(Richard Sanders, Steve Mitcheson, Anne Collins, Michael Rooke)*

Eccleston, Lancs [Towngate; SD5117], *Farmers Arms:* Good choice of very reasonably priced food, good service; very popular; bedrooms *(Jill and Des Monk)*

Edenfield, Lancs [Bury Rd; SD7919], *Duckworth Arms:* Refurbished Whitbreads Brewers Fayre dining pub, lively and popular, with quickly served decent food *(Carol and Richard Glover)*

Elswick, Lancs [High St; SD4238], *Ship:* Distinguished by particularly well kept Boddingtons and good garden for children *(Graham Bush)*

Failsworth, Gtr Manchester [Wrigley Head; corner of Oldham Rd (A62); SD9002], *Old Pack Horse:* Characterful old stone building with several unspoilt, rambling rooms, one with book collection, one with real fire and all with old photographs; Marstons beers, service friendly and fast *(Lee Goulding)*

☆ **Fence**, Lancs [2 3/4 miles from M65 junction 12 — follow Nelson, Brierfield sign, then right at roundabout, then right at traffic lights; in Fence turn right at T-junction, first left into Harpers Lane, OS Sheet 103 map reference 828376; SD8237], *Harpers:* Spaciously comfortable and handsomely modernised lounge bar with balustraded restaurant area (food all day Sun), bar food from soup and sandwiches through steak and kidney pie and so forth to steaks, well kept Thwaites Mild and Bitter, decent choice of wines, piped music — a thriving friendly atmosphere; children in eating area *(Len Beattie, Carol and Richard Glover, LYM — more reports please)*

☆ **Fence** [300 Wheatley Lane Rd], *White Swan:* The fine collection of about a dozen well kept real ales is the main attraction of this friendly and lively village pub with simple comfortable furnishings and roaring fires in all three separate communicating areas; horsey decorations inc jockey's silks, impressive collection of whiskies; pub may not open before 1pm weekdays *(Jon Wainwright, Andrew Stephenson, Derek and Sylvia Stephenson, John Hayward, LYM)*

Fence [Wheatley Lane Rd], *Bay Horse:* Big dining area, with decent food inc good salads; efficient service *(KC)*

Foulridge, Lancs [SD8842], *Hole In The Wall:* Simple pub in picturesque village close to E entrance to Foulridge Tunnel on Leeds & Liverpool canal; picture on wall shows cow which fell into canal at far end of tunnel, swam through and was revived by brandy at the pub; friendly service from husband-and-wife team (she does the cooking — food excellent value and in big helpings); well kept Bass Special and Mild on handpump; children at least at lunchtime *(Brian Jones)*

Freckleton, Lancs [off A584 opp The

Plough; towards Naze Lane Ind Est, then right into Bunker St; SD4228], *Ship:* Oldest pub on the Fylde, with big windows looking out over the watermeadows — and maybe fighters zapping close by from the Warton aerodrome; roomy main bar has had bar food inc sandwiches, hot specials and salads (not Mon evening), Boddingtons on handpump, tables outside; and there's been an airy upstairs carvery and buffet; children provided for *(Graham Bush, LYM — more reports please)*

Galgate, Lancs [A6 S of Lancaster; handy for M6 junction 33; SD4755], *Plough:* Attractive roadside inn run by pleasant young couple eager to succeed; menu small but meals large, fresh and competitively priced; well kept Boddingtons on handpump; open all day *(C C Kenny-Levick)*

Garstang, Lancs [northbound section of one-way system; SD4845], *Wheatsheaf:* Small and cosy, low beams and creaky ceiling-planks, gleaming copper and brass, little plush-cushioned black settles and dining chairs; has been recommended in previous editions for warm atmosphere, good service, food inc notable dishes of the day, from mussels in garlic butter to grilled halibut with prawn sauce or even lobster, but no recent reports *(News please)*

Gisburn, Lancs [SD8248], *White Bull:* Excellent atmosphere, good food quickly served *(Sidney and Erna Wells)*

Godley, Gtr Manchester [signposted from A57, off Station Rd; SJ9595], *Godley Hall:* Low ceilings, plush seating, lots of brasses, lots of character and friendly, welcoming atmosphere *(Steve Mitcheson, Anne Collins)*

Goosnargh, Lancs [SD5537], *Grapes:* Friendly local, with cheap and generous straightforward food such as haddock and a foot-long Cumberland sausage; Tetleys beers, maybe Jennings; interesting collection of water-jugs and telephones *(Andrew Hazeldine, Pamela and Merlyn Horswell);* [pub signposted from village], *Horns:* Interesting, family-run old pub close to Bleasdale Fell with shining brasses and blazing fires in cold weather; fine home-cooked food (not Sun lunchtime) inc speciality duck and soups *(Mr and Mrs M V Melling)*

Greasby, Merseyside [Greasby Rd; off B5139 in centre; SJ2587], *Greave Dunning:* Spacious revamp of 18th-century farm, lofty brightly lit main lounge with upper gallery, cushioned pews in flagstoned locals' bar with cosy snugs leading off, real ales such as Bass, Boddingtons, Tetleys and Websters Yorkshire, games room *(Tony and Lynne Stark, LYM);* [Greasby Rd], *Twelfth Man:* Refurbished pub, part of the Boddingtons Henry's Table chain, and popular with local organisations and business people *(E G Parish)*

Great Eccleston, Lancs [Market Pl; just off A586 — OS Sheet 102 map reference 428402; SD4240], *White Bull:* Bass Special on handpump, simple bar food inc sandwiches under new regime, good varied live music Weds, occasional quiz nights; can be very quiet *(John Atherton)*

Great Mitton, Lancs [B6246 — OS Sheet 103 map reference 716377; SD7139], *Aspinall Arms:* Popular pub with big beer

garden overlooking River Ribble; good
Whitbreads Castle Eden and bar food;
children in separate areas away from bar
(Len Beattie)

Haigh, Gtr Manchester [SD6009], *Red
Lion*: Well refurbished by Greenalls *(T Nott)*

Hapton, Lancs [outside village; nr M65
junction 9 — exit from eastbound only —
OS Sheet 103 map reference 803318;
SD7932], *Bentley Wood Farm*: Former
farmhouse, now a steakhouse, busy and
friendly with upholstered settles and
wheelback chairs, mix of old and new decor,
partly plastered walls, some beams;
Thwaites real ales *(Len Beattie)*

☆ **Hawk Green**, Lancs [SU9687], *Crown*:
Extensive and popular food pub extended
into adjoining barn, lively atmosphere, well
kept Robinsons, wide choice of food in bar
and well laid out restaurant, friendly
waitresses *(John Gould, Steve Mitcheson,
Anne Collins)*

Heskin Green, Lancs [Barmskin Lane;
SD5315], *Brook House*: Isolated Greenalls
pub with cosy interior, genuine staff,
restaurant and bar snacks in big helpings *(D
Bryan)*

Heswall, Merseyside [Pensby Rd; SJ2782],
Harvest Mouse: Open-plan, modern
Greenalls pub; good food at very reasonable
prices; children allowed *(George Mitchell)*

Heywood, Gtr Manchester [Pilsworth Rd;
SD8612], *Three Arrows*: Recently totally
rebuilt, greatly enlarged and open-plan,
more traditional at front, more modern
(tastefully so) at the back — an odd mixture;
well kept Lees beers *(Carol and Richard
Glover)*

☆ **nr Heywood** [off narrow Ashworth Rd; pub
itself signposted off B6222 on Bury side of N
Heywood], *Egerton Arms*: Alone by
moorland church, with lovely views all
around, especially from tables on terrace;
comfortable sofas and easy chairs in plush
lounge used mainly by people dining in the
smart restaurant (which serves huge steaks),
more simply furnished bar with cosy coal
fire even in summer, big-windowed small
extension, bar food from sandwiches and
local black pudding through a variant on
moules marinières to tagliatelle or steak and
kidney pie *(Carol and Richard Glover, BB)*

High Lane, Gtr Manchester [A6
Stockport—Disley; SJ9585], *Bulls Head*:
Friendly Boddingtons local with good
home-cooked food, friendly service and
three cosy rooms *(Steve Mitcheson, Anne
Collins)*

Holden, Lancs [the one up by Bolton by
Bowland — OS Sheet 103 map reference
777494; SD7749], *Copy Nook*: Pleasant
pub in lovely countryside with welcoming
atmosphere and decent food *(G T Jones)*

Holme Chapel, Lancs [A646
Burnley—Todmorden; SD8829], *Ram*:
Much modernised old coaching inn with
well kept Bass, good choice of bar food
ordered at kitchen door; well placed for
ascent of Thieveley Pike with views of
Pendle, Ingleborough; big car park *(G T
Jones)*

Hornby, Lancs [SD5869], *Royal Oak*: Well
decorated and efficiently run pub with fast
service, well kept beer and good range of
cheap bar food *(P J Taylor)*

Hoylake, Merseyside [Market St; SJ2289],
Ship: Unspoilt pub with well kept
Whitbreads beers and good, varied and
reasonably priced lunchtime bar food;
friendly, pleasant atmosphere, genial
landlord *(L W Norcott)*

Hutton, Lancs [A59 Longton roundabout,
just S of Hutton; SD4826], *Anchor*: Popular
for good value bar food inc good
ploughman's *(R H Sawyer)*

Irby, Merseyside [Irby Mill Hill; SJ2684],
Irby Mill: Popular 18th-century sandstone
mill with real fires in two main lounges,
flagstoned floor and dark oak furniture;
cosy atmosphere, friendly bar staff,
Boddingtons and Higsons ales *(Mrs Margaret
Naylor)*

☆ **Lancaster** [Canal Side; parking in Aldcliffe
Rd behind Royal Lancaster Infirmary, off
A6 — cross canal by pub's footbridge],
Water Witch: Pitch-pine panelling,
flagstones, bare masonry and rafters in
simply furnished conversion of 18th-century
waterside barge-horse stabling, with hearty
bar food, summer barbecues on terrace, and
hot beverages as well as cheap wines and
Tetleys, Thwaites and McEwans 70/-; games
room, juke box; run as a Yates Wine Lodge;
open all day Sat; children allowed in eating
areas *(Keith Mills, Peter Corris, Comus Elliott,
G J Lewis, LYM)*

☆ **Lancaster** [Green Lane — heading N on A6,
last turn on right leaving speed restriction],
Howe Ghyll: Neat and spacious conversion
of former mansion in most attractive
grounds on edge of town, well kept
Mitchells real ales, efficient quick-service
lunchtime food counter, games in public
bar; children in family room *(LYM)*

Lancaster [Brewery Lane (next to Mitchells
Brewery/Dukes Arts Centre)], *Golden Lion*:
Lively traditional town-centre Matthew
Browns pub with no-smoking room, several
small bars, good atmosphere, Theakstons
and lunchtime pies *(Graham Bush)*; [centre],
John of Gaunt: Tetleys pub with remarkable
beermat collection *(Peter Corris)*; [Prospect
St], *Park*: Cosy local with open fire in
red-decorated lounge bar, public bar with
darts; lively, young atmosphere, non-disco
juke box *(Graham Bush)*; [St Georges Quay],
Wagon & Horses: Likeable atmosphere in
relatively basic drinkers' pub, good choice of
beers, good service *(Jon Wainwright)*

Leigh, Gtr Manchester [78 Chapel St;
SJ6699], *Eagle & Hawk*: Large pleasantly
refurbished pub, friendly staff *(Dr and Mrs A
K Clarke)*

Leyland, Lancs [Dunkirk Lane; western
outskirts, by bypass; SD5422], *Dunkirk
Hall*: Farmhouse converted to pub, tastefully
furnished and decorated, with food
lunchtime and evening, John Smiths beers *(P
Corris)*

Litherland, Merseyside [Sefton Rd; SJ3397],
Priory: Modernised but cosy, with good
value lunchtime bar food (inc Sun roast), Ind
Coope Burton and Walkers Mild, Bitter and
Winter Warmer on handpump; Addlestone's
cider *(P Lloyd, Miss K Bamford)*

Littleborough, Gtr Manchester [A58
towards Halifax, on right; SD9316], *Rake*:
Said to be haunted — while we were there
one of the ornaments fell to the ground after
some shaking in the ghost's area *(John*

Branford, Linda Duncan)

☆ **Liverpool** [Albert Dock Complex], *Pump House*: Interesting conversion in fine waterside spot; lots of polished dark wood, renovated old brickwork, sunken area in busy ground floor, mezzanine, upper area with exposed roof trusses; marble counter with bulbous beer engines and brass rail supported by elephants' heads, tall chimney; bar food mainly very generous helpings of 10 cheeses and bread with pickle, etc; some hot food such as cheap pork and chestnut pie; friendly, efficient service but no real ale; tables outside overlook museum of shipping, dock and Liver building; good lavatories *(John Fazakerley, Ian Phillips, Howard and Sue Gascoyne, Jim and Becky Bryson)*

☆ **Liverpool** [4 Hackins Hey, off Dale St], *Hole in Ye Wall*: Smallish pub recently sold by Allied to Belhaven; well restored, with several different areas in pleasant panelled bar; friendly staff, beer unusually fed by gravity via pillars from upstairs cellar; side food servery popular at lunchtime with local businessmen; uncertain evening opening hours *(Richard Sanders, Jon Wainwright — more news of the new regime please)*

☆ **Liverpool** [67 Moorfields], *Lion*: Splendidly preserved pub with etched glass and serving hatches in central bar, curious wallpaper, big mirrors, panelling and tilework, fine domed structure behind, well kept beer, cheap lunchtime bar food much appreciated by businessmen, well kept Walkers Bitter and Mild; at its best when not too full *(Richard Sanders, Jon Wainwright)*

☆ **Liverpool** [Ranelagh St; opp Central Stn], *Central Commercial*: Mahogany woodwork, sumptuous engraved glass, marble pillars and elaborately moulded domed ceiling in Victorian pub with attractively priced hot and cold buffet, well kept Ind Coope-related real ales, busy atmosphere, good but loud juke box *(Steve Mitcheson, Anne Collins, LYM)*

Liverpool [Regent Rd, Sandhills], *Atlantic*: Docks pub, plain and clean decor, good atmosphere, Boddingtons and Whitbreads on handpump, live folk or jazz most nights *(P Corris)*; [33a Wapping], *Baltic Fleet*: Typical Merseyside pub with lots of atmosphere and good choice of real ale; opp Albert Dock *(Comus Elliott)*; [Tarleton St], *Carnarvon Castle*: Neat and welcoming city-centre pub next to main shopping area; fairly small, with one main bar and back lounge; cabinet of Dinky toys, well kept Boddingtons and Higsons on handpump, lunchtime bar snacks *(P Corris, Jon Wainwright)*; [Quarry St, Woolton], *Cobden*: Lively sporty bar, excellent cottagey atmosphere in lounge with Toby jugs and lots of other ornaments; well kept John Smiths on handpump *(Peter Corris)*; [13 Rice St], *Cracke*: Attractively basic students' pub with bare boards, walls covered with posters for local events and pictures of local buildings; largest room has unusual Beatles diorama; juke box and TV, simple sandwiches, well kept Marstons *(Steve Mitcheson, Anne Collins, Jon Wainwright)*; [Matthew St], *Grapes*: Good, lively pub with Beatles associations, recently sympathetically refitted, still with cottagey decor and flagstoned floor — but more

open-plan, with bar counter more central; consistently well kept Boddingtons and Higsons on handpump, good service, bar lunches maybe more standardised and less abundant than before but still good value; open all day, closed Sun *(P Corris, Jon Wainwright)*; [Roscoe St], *Roscoe Head*: Small, clean Tetleys pub, often very busy, with fine atmosphere and maybe well kept Jennings *(Peter Corris)*; [Wood St], *Swan*: Bare-boarded no-frills big room with well equipped bar, juke box and fruit machine; Marstons Owd Rodger, standard range of bar food inc Cumberland sausage *(Steve Mitcheson, Anne Collins)*; [off Matthew St], *White Star*: Sensitively refurbished pub with particularly well kept Bass *(Jon Wainwright)*

Longridge, Lancs [Thornley; 1 1/2 miles N on back rd to Chipping — OS Sheet 103 map reference 607393; SD6039], *Derby Arms*: Stone-built pub with barn converted to restaurant; small entrance bar and small darts room off with poultry cigarette cards, other rooms given over to dining; good Greenalls on handpump, decent wine, good pub lunches, can be crowded with diners weekend evenings — food-oriented but not exclusively so *(John Fazakerley)*

Lowton, Gtr Manchester [Southworth Rd; SJ6297], *Bulls Head*: Well kept beer, good bar food *(David Halton)*; [Newton Rd], *Red Lion*: Clean and well furnished, well kept Greenalls, restaurant serving excellent steaks and good choice of home-made puddings *(E E Hemmings)*

Lydiate, Merseyside [Bells Lane; SD3604], *Running Horses*: Canalside pub with cosy family room and lounge, reasonably priced lunchtime food and consistently well kept Walkers ales; waterside terrace, garden with farm animals, Bank Hol fun days *(P Corris)*

Lytham, Lancs [Church Rd; SD3627], *County*: Large revamped Boddingtons food pub, well kept beer *(Graham Bush, Simon Bates)*; [Forest Dr], *Hole-in-One*: Good modern estate local with pool, darts, juke box and well kept Thwaites in plain bar; cosy mock-library opening into larger, general lounge area *(Graham Bush, Simon Bates)*

☆ **Manchester** [50 Great Bridgewater St; corner of Lower Mosley St], *Britons Protection*: Fine tilework and solid woodwork in smallish rather plush front bar, attractive softly lit inner lounge with coal-effect gas fire, battle murals in passage leading to it; well kept though not cheap Ind Coope Burton, Jennings and Tetleys, popular at lunchtime for its simple well prepared food, quiet evenings; handy for GMEX centre; rumours of brewery plans to redevelop it as hotel *(Brian and Anna Marsden, Steve Mitcheson, Anne Collins, BB)*

☆ **Manchester** [6 Angel St, off Rochdale Rd], *Beer House*: True free house with up to ten regularly changing well kept real ales, also farm ciders and good range of bottled foreign beers; lively atmosphere, simple inexpensive bar food, unpretentious basic decor, good juke box with part of the beer-wise landlord's collection of blues records; very popular, especially with nearby Co-op Head Office workers, lunchtime and early evening *(Lee Goulding, Matthew Pringle, Brian and Anna Marsden, Richard*

Sanders, Andy and Jill Kassube)

☆ **Manchester** [Cateaton St (nr cathedral and Arndale Centre)], *Chesters Pie & Ale House*: Whitbreads pastiche of Victorian alehouse, big bare-boarded main bar and smaller area up steps; stripped walls, beams with anti-spitting notices, Victoriana such as clay pipes, old bottles, posters, plumbing taps — good period feel in spite of piped pop music; stools by counter overlooking street, Chesters, Marstons Pedigree and Thwaites, decent wines, pies and other well prepared food, reasonable prices, service friendly for city centre, often fairly quiet *(Steve Mitcheson, Anne Collins)*

Manchester [Oldham St], *Dry 201*: Latest venture of MICR's Factory Records — minimalist bar appealing to alternative types of all ages; two big rooms with bare floors and pillars, ideal for posing; choice of continental lagers, Marstons Pedigree and genuine Russian vodkas; mixture of hip hop and other alternative music at bearable volume; smart, designer-aproned staff *(Lee Goulding)*

☆ **Manchester** [Shambles Sq; behind Arndale off Market St in centre], *Old Wellington*: The only timber-framed building of its age to survive in the centre — flagstones and gnarled oak timbers, well kept Bass and Stones on handpump, oak-panelled bar; bar food (from noon, not Sun) with hot beef sandwiches a speciality, small upstairs Toby carvery (closed Mon–Wed evenings and all day Sun); often packed lunchtime *(Steve Mitcheson, Anne Collins, Len Beattie, BB)*

☆ **Manchester** [682 Wilmslow Rd], *Station*: Unspoilt two-roomed local of character — very unusual for the area — full of old railway nick-nacks, cigarette cards, photos and prints of the old Liverpool & Manchester Railway; British Rail wooden seats, a long ticket from Llanfairpwllgwyng YYL, particularly well kept Marstons ales on handpump, and friendly staff; recent back games extension, seats outside among lovely floral displays *(Lee Goulding, Michael Cochrane)*

Manchester, [Albert Hill Rd; off Wilmslow Rd, Didsbury], *Albert*: Clean and quite cosy traditional layout with three main rooms, big central area, smallish bar counter at far end; friendly service, well kept Hydes beers, surprisingly cheap simple lunchtime food (ploughman's particularly good value), good collections of cigarette cards, film-star photographs and caricatures *(Michael Cochrane, RT)*; [Monton], *Bargee*: Canalside free house, well decorated and furnished, good range of real ales inc Boddingtons, Hartleys Mild, Bitter and XB on handpump, good bar food, upstairs restaurant *(Mr and Mrs Harry McCann)*; [1235 Chester Rd (A56), Stretford], *Bass Drum*: Modern — and round as a drum, with flat roof; comfortably furnished lounge and bar, Bass, outside tables and chairs with parasols *(Steve Mitcheson, Anne Collins)*; [Gt Ducie St (next to Boddingtons Brewery)], *Brewers Arms*: Very clean Boddingtons show pub, with a nice character for such a new pub; enormous, cheap helpings of decent food, friendly service *(Steve Mitcheson and Anne Collins)*; [86 Portland St], *Circus*: Tiny character pub with two cosy panelled rooms, wall seating, minuscule bar counter with well kept cheapish Tetleys; weekend evening opening 8 — so popular that they may shut the door when full *(Steve Mitcheson, Anne Collins)*; [Windsor Crescent (A6); opp Salford University], *Crescent*: Four-room pub with three serving bars, basic decor, good pubby atmosphere (not studenty — though so close to the University); good range of real ales, mini beer festivals; piped laidback 1970s rock music *(Richard Sanders)*; [41 Hilton St — off Newton St nr Piccadilly], *Crown & Anchor*: Well decorated, atmospheric pub with good choice of Whitbreads-related and other real ales such as Timothy Taylors Landlord on handpump, good value lunchtime food, efficient friendly service even when busy *(P Corris, Brian and Anna Marsden)*; [Collier St — off Greengate, Salford], *Eagle*: Seems untouched since the 1950s, absolutely no frills, well kept Holts ales at old-fashioned prices — a particularly fine example of the unspoilt and unaffected *(Richard Sanders)*; [Portland St — nr Piccadilly], *Grey Horse*: Little Hydes pub with well kept beer, some unusual malt whiskies, popular for lunchtime food *(Steve Mitcheson, Anne Collins)*; [47 Ducie St], *Jolly Angler*: Archetypal CAMRA pub, small and cosy, with low-priced well kept Hydes and a warm welcome *(Richard Sanders, Andy and Jill Kassube, BB)*; [4a Helmshaw Walk — nr Upper Brook St (A34), off Kincardine Rd/Whitekirk Cl], *Kings Arms*: Nicely renovated Victorian pub tucked away in rather run-down 60s council estate, with quiet games vault and lively lounge, both rather spare and bright in style; friendly staff and lunchtime food, but included particularly for the pub's new local brews, Dobbins Mild, Bitter, Guiltless Stout and the very strong Special Bitter *(Brian and Anna Marsden, Lee Goulding)*; [Hyde Rd, Gorton — nr Tan Yard Brown], *Lord Nelson*: Surprisingly cottagey pub set well back, with cosy, dimly lit lounge and plainer back overspill room; friendly welcome, Wilsons real ales, bar food *(Steve Mitcheson, Anne Collins)*; [Francis St], *Mawson*: Welcoming, traditional, multi-roomed pub with well kept Ind Coope Burton and Tetleys Mild and Bitter *(Brian Marsden)*; [52 Cross St], *Mr Thomas Chop House*: Tiled-floor Victorian-style pub popular lunchtime and early evening for home-made food such as braised lamb's liver and onions, grilled lamb, pork chops, roast beef with Yorkshire pudding and above all pies and hot beef sandwiches; good choice of well kept real ales inc Boddingtons and Thwaites *(Andy and Jill Kassube)*; [Green Lane, Heaton Norris], *Nursery*: Well preserved pub at end of cobbled street, three rooms and big lobby with central bar serving Hydes ales; attractive good value food inc good three-egg omelettes; children's room, back bowling green; pub saw foundation of Stockport CFC *(Claire Meakin)*; [Bloom St — by Charlton St National Express Coach Stn], *Paddys Goose*: Small pub with surprisingly ornate interior, well kept Websters, short choice of food *(Wayne Brindle, Steve Mitcheson, Anne Collins)*; [Park Lane, Whitefield], *Parkfield*: Well refurbished

Whitbreads estate pub with split-level main bar and games room (darts and two pool tables); lively atmosphere, juke box in background, good food, reasonable beer, efficient service; big car park *(Hilary Robinson, Peter Maden);* [Honey St — off Red Bank, nr Victoria Stn], *Queens Arms:* Attractively renovated, quiet but atmospheric, always welcoming single bar with bar billiards, good juke box and bottle collection; well kept Theakstons and three changing guest beers, simple lunchtime and evening bar food; pleasant back garden sloping down towards the Ire Valley and its railway complex *(Lee Goulding, P Corris);* [Wilmslow Rd, Withington], *Red Lion:* Very big pub with quaint, atmospheric front rooms and big back bar with raised and plushly furnished area; bare-boarded food area (no food Sun evenings), and well kept Marstons Pedigree; lots of outside seating around the pub's own bowling green *(Gary Scott);* [Bury New Rd, Prestwich], *Red Lion:* Friendly local with good Holts beer, lunchtime bar food, and pleasant decor; occasional sixties nights *(Mr and Mrs D Johnson);* [Sackville St], *Rembrandt:* Unusual, modern furnishings, juke box and fruit machine; no food Sat *(Steve Mitcheson, Anne Collins);* [Leigh St, off Oxford Rd], *Salisbury Ale House:* Cosy atmosphere, wooden floors; popular with young people *(Steve Mitcheson, Anne Collins);* [8 Corporation St, opp Marks & Spencer], *Seftons:* Big room with dark wood and plush carpeting, relaxing atmosphere, variety of tempting food, efficient uniformed staff, juke box; upstairs restaurant *(Steve Mitcheson, Anne Collins);* [Bootle St, off Deansgate], *Sir Ralph Abercrombie:* Clean, popular for food; Australian landlady *(Steve Mitcheson, Anne Collins);* [Errwood Rd, Burnage], *Sun in September:* Useful for the area *(RT);* [Kirk St, Gorton], *Vale Cottage:* Three cosy rooms in interesting and unusual almost country-type pub, full of bits and pieces; friendly welcome, well kept Watneys-related real ales, freshly squeezed orange juice, big helpings of reasonably priced bar food, nice tree-lined terrace; closed-circuit TV shows what's going on in car park; opens noon *(Steve Mitcheson, Anne Collins);* [Kennedy St], *Vine:* Young people's pub, bright but interesting decor, Courage ales, popular cellar food bar *(Steve Mitcheson, Anne Collins);* [120 Regent Rd, Salford], *Wellington:* Clean and tidy, attractive stained glass, good value food *(T R G Alcock, Brian and Anna Marsden);* [Oxford Rd], *Whitworth:* Lively spot, with formidable pâté or cheese sandwiches at lunchtime *(Peter Race)*

☆ **Marple**, Gtr Manchester [130 Church Lane; by canal, Bridge 2 — OS Sheet 109 map reference 960884; SJ9588], *Ring o' Bells:* Big welcoming village pub close to working Macclesfield Canal (trips arranged; 16 locks raise it 210ft through Marple, and the towpath walk is very picturesque); good helpings of good value food served very efficiently (it's becoming very much a dining pub), well kept Robinsons, reasonable wine, lots of canal and barge pictures; small garden with summer barbecues and tables overlooking canal — but piped music even

out here; children welcome *(P A Crossland, D A Cawley, K J Letchford, Steve Mitcheson, Anne Collins)*

☆ **Marple** [Ridge End; off A626 via Church Lane, following The Ridge signposts — OS Sheet 109 map reference 965867], *Romper:* Comfortably furnished and busy food pub with softly lit knocked-through oak-beamed rooms, well kept real ales such as Tetleys, Theakstons Best and Old Peculier, Timothy Taylors Landlord and Wadworths 6X, helpful staff, wide choice of food; superb setting alone on steep side of Goyt Valley; opens noon *(Steve Mitcheson, Anne Collins, RT, LYM)*

Marple Bridge, Gtr Manchester [Ley Lane; SJ9689], *Hare & Hounds:* Comfortable and generally quiet, with good country-pub atmosphere in superb attractive spot — a surprise to find a pub here at all, let alone a good one; open fire, shining brasses and beautiful setting; welcoming owner, good varied bar food, Robinsons beers, garden behind; may be open all day Bank Hols *(Lee Goulding, Steve Mitcheson, Anne Collins);* [48 Town St], *Royal Scot:* Pleasant small local with lots of Manchester City FC memorabilia, unsmoky bar, helpful licensees, good atmosphere, efficient service, well kept beer, no juke box or fruit machine, three curling stones by the fire *(Steve Mitcheson, Anne Collins)*

Mawdesley, Lancs [Bluestone Lane; Croston—Eccleston road, N of village — keep going! OS Sheet 108 map reference 505164; SD4915], *Robin Hood:* Well refurbished and extended, with three open bars and upstairs restaurant, well kept Whitbreads-related real ales on handpump, limited choice of simple good value bar food, well presented and quickly served; popular weekday lunchtimes, restaurant *(Thomas Nott, Peter Corris)*

☆ **Mellor**, Gtr Manchester [Longhurst Lane; this is the Mellor S of Manchester; SJ9888], *Devonshire Arms:* Comfortable, attractive and well kept rustic pub in attractive Pennine village; bright bar full of antiques which attracts wide range of affluent locals, and second, smaller bar, darker than first and with oddly colourful wallpaper; attractively priced food from interesting menu, open fires, quick, friendly service, well kept Robinsons ales; outside gents' (watch the step) *(Lee Goulding, Steve Mitcheson, Anne Collins)*

Mellor [Shiloh Rd, same village], *Moorfield Arms:* Sandblasted former chapel, high in the hills, with beams, stonework and original panelling, good views all around, coal fire, well kept Boddingtons, decent wine, food, sunny garden *(Steve Mitcheson, Anne Collins)*

Morecambe, Lancs [Marine Dr; SD4565], *Midland:* Hotel with good view over bay; spacious bar, big lounge open all day, helpful staff, big car park; children welcome; bedrooms comfortable *(John Gould);* [Lord St], *Morecambe:* Clean Tetleys pub, consistently good, with oak beams, lots of polished brass, ships' bells and open fire; friendly staff, good bar snacks and big garden *(Dave and Kate Buckley)*

☆ **Mossley**, Gtr Manchester [Manchester Rd (A635 N); SD9802], *Roaches Lock:*

Beautifully kept stripped-stone free house, particularly welcoming licensee, well laid out interior with long bar, fans, hunting-horn, tropical fish; four real ales inc well kept Marstons Pedigree, over a hundred whiskies, food inc good value three-course Sun lunch, quick service; tables out by Huddersfield Canal (Steve Mitcheson, Anne Collins)

Mottram, Gtr Manchester [SJ9995], Waggon: Wide choice of particularly good food inc interesting daily specials such as mint-glazed lamb and phenomenal puddings; brass, copper, old weapons and farm tools on walls, central log-effect gas fire; very friendly and efficient staff, juke box, fruit machine and trivia machine; restaurant (Dennis Jones)

Newburgh, Lancs [SD4710], Red Lion: Friendly low-beamed village pub with cosy lounge bar, popular as a Stocks Tavern for good range of pleasantly presented bar food (chequered table cloths); pool and games room, well kept Burtonwood on handpump, separate upstairs restaurant, garden with swings; children welcome; bedrooms (Comus Elliott, Howard and Sue Gascoyne)

Newton, Lancs [A583 Kirkham—Preston; SD4431], Highgate: Straightforward pub majoring on straightforward food for Blackpool-bound tourists — cheap, and of excellent quality (GB)

Oldham, Gtr Manchester [Manchester Rd (A62); opp Werneth Pk; SD9305], Auld Lang Syne: Three-roomed pub with down-to-earth atmosphere, popular with locals, real ale buffs and families at weekends; several regularly changing real ales, bar food inc three-course Sun lunch, 1960s/70s juke box; open all day, and linked to Manchester Beer House (Lee Goulding); [Manchester Rd (A62), Hollinwood; opp Bower Lane; SD9002], Hat & Feathers: Unspoilt terraced local with two rooms — small one is best, full of interesting, friendly people; very welcoming landlady, cheap well kept Marstons beers (Lee Goulding); [Hollins Rd], King George: Pleasant and comfortable with mixed clientele, real ales inc Boddingtons and Oldham, reasonably priced home-cooked bar food, restaurant (Lee Goulding, Diane Hall); [Springhead; SD9504], Peels Arms: Good Boddingtons and Sam Smiths, warm friendly atmosphere, cheap, plentiful and delicious simple food; landlord leader of the Dooleys, gold discs framed over bar (Dennis Jones)

☆ nr Oldham [Grains Bar (A672/B6197); SD9608], Bulls Head: Gleaming brass and copper in snug two-room moorland pub with well kept Bass, Bass Special and Mild on handpump, and nostalgic singalongs to theatre organ played with gusto by Mr Wilson the landlord on Wed, Fri, Sat and Sun evenings (Dr Thomas Mackenzie, LYM)

Ormskirk, Lancs [Burscough St; SD4108], Buck i'th Vine: Very pleasant old pub with lots of rooms and nooks and crannies; good food (particularly chilli con carne) well kept Walkers on handpump, nice outside in summer (Dave Cargill); [Aughton (A59, S edge of town); SD3905], Royal Oak: Well run pub with good service, well kept Ind Coope Burton on handpump (landlord may show you cellar if not busy), bar food (Gordon Smith)

Oswaldtwistle, Lancs [Haslingden Old Rd; A677/B6231; SD7327], Britannia: Solidly traditional old-fashioned furnishings and fittings inc log-burning ranges in friendly bar, Daniels Kitchen family restaurant, bar food from soup and lunchtime sandwiches to steaks with some emphasis on fresh fish, well kept Thwaites and Mild; sun-trap back terrace and play area; food all day Sun; children in family room and restaurant (Wayne Brindle, LYM — more reports please)

Over Hulton, Lancs [A6/A579; SD6805], Red Lion: Old, grey-stone roadside inn mostly given over to food, in separate restaurant; pub part is lounge down steps from central bar area, with lots of prints and sofas, subdued, conservative decor; food from sandwiches to multi-course main meals, Jennings on handpump; restaurant down steps too, with own bar; open all day (Lee Goulding)

☆ Parbold, Lancs [A5209; SD4911], Wiggin Tree: Comfortable and locally popular Brewers Fayre pub, good friendly service, tasty reasonably priced food inc particularly wide choice of puddings, well kept Whitbreads-related and maybe other real ales, wines on tap; magnificent view (Geoff Halson)

Parbold, Lancs [SD4911], Railway: Nice and comfortable, with railway memorabilia etc (Comus Elliott) ; [Alder Lane], Stocks Tun: Efficient service, well kept Tetleys, good bar food — gets very busy in the evenings (Comus Elliott)

Port Sunlight, Merseyside [Bolton Rd; SJ3485], Olde Bridge: Tetleys pub, interesting as early 20th-century architect's vision of Old Village Inn, though recent refurbishments importing milk and butter churns, old casks and so forth add a different note; interesting old Lever Bros advertisements, real ales, limited but well prepared and presented bar food (Ian Phillips, TN)

Poulton le Fylde, Lancs [Ball St; SD3439], Thatched House: Lively open-plan pub doing well under new regime, with well kept real ales inc Boddingtons, cosy front area, bar snacks, pool table, fruit machine; adjacent churchyard a sea of crocuses in spring (Graham Bush); [The Square], Town Hall: Busy newish pub in former town hall, friendly atmosphere, well kept beer, good value food, efficient service (G J Lewis)

Preesall, Lancs [Park Lane; SD3647], Saracens Head: Friendly staff, cheerful — mainly local — customers, reasonably priced home-made food, particularly well kept Thwaites Bitter; pianist Fri; bedrooms (John Atherton)

Preston, Lancs [Watery La (A583); SD5530], New Ship: Former dockland pub reopened after refurbishment; cheap filling food, Greenalls on handpump, big side music room with Fri/Sat discos — landlord as DJ; handy for Merseyside—Blackpool coaches (Glenn Bonnell); [Fishergate (by Ringway)], Old Black Bull: Included really for its outside appearance — lovely corner building with period tiling and stained glass; not so special inside, but tidy, with particularly well kept Boddingtons (and pool table) (GB); [114 Church St], Olde Blue

Bell: Busy Sam Smiths pub, popular for its well kept beer *(Jon Wainwright, Andy and Jill Kassube, Graham Bush)*

Rawtenstall, Lancs [371 Bury Old Rd (A56 towards Edenfield) — OS Sheet 103 map reference 803217; SD8123], *Whitchaff*: Large open-plan pub with partly stone-stripped walls and open fire; olde-worlde character, bric-a-brac and household bygones on walls and shelves, framed cigarette cards, unusual stone table, unobtrusive piped music; good varied menu inc good value gammon and egg, restaurant, tables outside *(Carol and Richard Glover)*

Ribchester, Lancs [Main St (B6245); SD6435], *Black Bull*: Utterly unpretentious, honest local opp interesting Museum of Childhood; good generous food, well kept Thwaites *(Sue Holland, Dave Webster)*; [B6245], *Ribchester Arms*: Long lounge with main eating area on different level — food includes particularly good ploughman's; well kept Flowers IPA, friendly staff *(Len Beattie)*; [Church St; sharp turn off B6245 at Black Bull; SD6435], *White Bull*: Refurbished village pub, popular for food, with Whitbreads-related real ales; its porch is supported by 1,900-year-old Tuscan pillars recycled centuries ago from the Roman camp here — the second-oldest component of any pub we know *(Len Beattie, LYM)*

Rishton, Lancs [High St; SD7230], *Roebuck*: Excellent value food, inc good Sun lunch; good service *(D J Barden)*

Roby Mill, Lancs [not far from M6 junction 26; off A577 at Up Holland; SD5107], *Fox*: Two-roomed, black and white inn with good value food, Greenalls ales, pool and darts (competitions too), weekly quizzes; restaurant *(P Lloyd, Miss K Bamford, Kathleen Morley)*

☆ **Rochdale**, Gtr Manchester [470 Bury Rd; A6222, junction with A6452 continuation — OS Sheet 109 map reference 881130; SD8913], *Cemetery*: Splendidly old-fashioned four-room pub, its tiled facade (with etched windows advertising the old Bury Crown Ales) raising it well above the road; numerous bottled beers and over half-a-dozen real ales such as Boddingtons, Old Mill Bullion, Ruddles, Timothy Taylors Best and Landlord and Thwaites Mild and Bitter, with one brewed for the pub; good bare-boarded parlour, two comfortable little Victorian-style lounges, interesting collection of customers *(Steve Mitcheson, Anne Collins, Dr and Mrs A K Clarke, N Burke)*

Rochdale, *Alpine*: Swiss chalet-type building with old-fashioned balconies; soft piped music and good value food, particularly carvery *(Mrs J McCluskey)*

☆ **nr Rochdale** [Cheesden, Ashworth Moor; A680 — OS Sheet 109 map reference 831161], *Owd Betts*: Isolated moorland pub with great views over Ashworth Reservoir and right across to Bury and beyond; lots of tables in three cosy low-beamed areas, dark oak settles, stripped stonework, brasses and china cabinet; friendly service, well kept Greenalls Bitter and Mild on handpump, bar food from steak barm cake to steak and kidney pie, pizza and plaice, open fires *(Carol and Richard Glover, Steve Mitcheson,*

Anne Collins, BB)

☆ **nr Rochdale**, [Oldham Rd, Thornham], *Yew Tree*: Cosy rooms with stripped stone walls and relaxed country atmosphere; well kept Sam Smiths, good value food in bar and Pullman railway-carriage dining room *(Alan and Marlene Radford, LYM)*

☆ **Romiley**, Gtr Manchester [Stockport Rd (B6104); SJ9390], *Duke of York*: Cheap John Smiths on handpump in older building with friendly atmosphere, lots of woodwork, some brasses, bar area opening into two smaller rooms, one of which, up a couple of steps, has creaky floorboards and is served by hatch, also back vaults bar — can get smoky when busy; good value lunchtime and evening bar food, good upstairs restaurant (not Suns in Advent) *(Mr and Mrs Simon Turner, RT, Steve Mitcheson, Anne Collins)*

Rossendale, Lancs [Burnley Rd, Love Clough; SD8127], *Huntsman*: Excellent rural position, with attractive scenery behind; good beer and food *(George Day)*

Salwick, Lancs [N of Salwick Stn, towards Inskip; SD4535], *Hand & Dagger*: Canalside pub with lively local atmosphere and various rooms full of old benches, mirrors and bric-a-brac; bar food, Greenalls Bitter, Original, Mild, good coffee *(Graham Bush)*

Slyne, Lancs [A6 a couple of miles N of Lancaster; SD4866], *Cross Keys*: Big, well decorated and comfortable Matthew Browns pub with well kept Theakstons Best and Youngers on handpump, good service, very good value food especially Sun lunch *(A E Alcock)*

Southport, Merseyside [Union St; SD3316], *Guest House*: Good art nouveau facade, lovely figured oak panelling in both main rooms, some original oak tables; Boddingtons and Higsons ales *(Tony Harrison)*; [Kingsway], *Two Brewers*: Spacious, comfortable bar with interesting furniture and friendly atmosphere; Tetleys, wide range of good bar food, restaurant with continental menu; open all day *(Mr and Mrs J H Adam)*; [Seabank Rd], *Windmill*: Nicely kept pub with plenty of antiques on walls, well kept Matthew Browns Mild and Bitter and Theakstons XB and Old Peculier on handpump, good bar food inc fine steak sandwich, lunchtime and early evening; big outside area with relayed juke box music *(Dave Cargill)*

St Annes, Lancs [Church Rd; SD3129], *Victoria*: Particularly well kept Boddingtons in lofty-roomed local with lively lounge bar, public bar with pool table, pizza stall; originally designed by Mr Boddington the brewer as his own local, in the days when St Annes was a new town *(Graham Bush, F Teare)*

Stalmine, Lancs [SD3745], *Seven Stars*: Real local with unpretentious roomy bar, bright and clean with good coal fire; well kept Greenalls, good bar food inc meaty pies and good sandwiches *(D J Cooke)*

Stalybridge, Gtr Manchester [Mottram Rd; SJ9698], *Hare & Hounds*: Country-pub feel, with good Bass on handpump, good lunchtime food pleasantly served — prawns larger than usual, beef always fresh and lean *(Neville Kenyon)*; [Astley St], *Old 13th*

Cheshire Astley Volunteer Rifleman Corps: Walls covered with old regimental pictures; friendly locals, homely atmosphere, pool table, juke box, well kept Wilsons *(Steve Mitcheson, Anne Collins)*

☆ **Standish**, Gtr Manchester [4 miles from M6 junction 27; A5209, straight on into B5239 as you go through Standish, then at T-junction turn left into Worthington, then left into Platt Lane; SD5610], *Crown*: Chesterfields, armchairs, panelling, fresh flowers and an open fire in comfortable pub with wide range of good value bar food and well kept real ales such as Bass and Bass Mild and Boddingtons on rather splendid handpumps; may be summer barbecues out by the pub's own bowling green; children allowed away from bar *(Comus Elliott, R J Yates, LYM — more reports please)*

☆ **Stockport** [552 Didsbury Rd (off A5145), Heaton Mersey; SJ8691], *Griffin*: Outstandingly popular with real ale enthusiasts for its remarkably cheap and well kept Holts Bitter and Mild, in unpretentious — even basic — surroundings and thriving local atmosphere; four Victorian rooms open off central servery with largely original curved-glass gantry, no piped music, basic lunchtime snacks; seats outside *(Michael Cochrane, Colin Dowse, Derek and Sylvia Stephenson, RT, Graham Bush, BB)*

☆ **Stockport**, Gtr Manchester [14 Middle Hillgate], *Red Bull*: Substantial settles and seats, beams, flagstones, open fires, lots of pictures and brassware, and a traditional island servery; good value bar lunches (not Sun), well kept Robinsons Best and Best Mild, notably friendly atmosphere — quiet at lunchtime, can get crowded in the evening *(M A Robinson, Steve Mitcheson, Anne Collins, LYM)*

Stockport, Gtr Manchester [Millgate; SJ8991], *Arden Arms*: Full of character but pleasantly quiet with two rooms, grandfather clocks, aquarium, old and restored wall seats, plants; well kept Robinsons served through doorway, lunchtime bar food, good landlord, garden; parking difficult *(Lee Goulding, Diane Hall, Steve Mitcheson, Anne Collins)*; [Market Pl], *Bakers Vaults*: Good food and well kept Robinsons in good unpretentious town-centre local with evening live music; children welcome *(Peter Adcock, Steve Mitcheson, Anne Collins)*; [154 Heaton La, Heaton Norris], *Crown*: Pleasant town pub under arch of vast viaduct; partly open-plan but with several cosy areas, stylish modern decor; well kept Boddingtons Mild and Bitter and Higsons Bitter, lunchtime bar food, open all day *(Lee Goulding, Diane Hall)*; [Heaton Moor Rd], *Elizabethan*: Very comfortably refurbished, with good food from soup and sandwiches to steaks, also more unusual dishes; good cappuccino, good service *(Mr and Mrs W Middleton)*; [Wellington St, off Wellington Rd S (A6)], *Little Jack Horners*: Small pub on several levels with separate restaurant area; varied menu at reasonable prices (not Sat) *(Steve Mitcheson, Anne Collins)*; [263 Newbridge Lane], *Midway*: Clean pub doing well under newish licensees, with good home-cooked food generously served (not Sat–Mon

evenings); chiming longcase clock, suit of armour, unusual brasses and copperware, beautifully carved settle; pleasant garden with tree and wishing well; children allowed in dining area *(Steve Mitcheson, Anne Collins, P A Barratt)*; [King St W/Chatham St, nr back entrance Stockport Edgeley Stn], *Old Queen Vic*: Small, homely free house popular with locals for good range of real ales such as Bass, Brains, Tetleys, Timothy Taylors Landlord and Wadworths 6X *(Keith Mills)*; [Market Pl], *Pack Horse*: Welcoming mock-Tudor pub close to centre with three bars inc pool room; brasses, hunting prints, well kept Tetleys, bar food *(Lee Goulding, Diane Hall)*; [82 Heaton Moor Rd, Heaton Moor], *Plough*: Spacious comfortably refurbished pub with antique furnishings, bric-a-brac, polished wood, open fire, well kept Tetleys and Jennings, particularly good bar food *(J C Gould, RT)*; [Little Underbank], *Queens Head*: Friendly atmosphere in long and narrow old pub with standing-room front bar, small snug, back dining area; well kept Sam Smiths on handpump, rare brass cordials fountain; the former gents (still in use alongside the new lavatories) is the smallest in Britain; no car park *(John Gould, Steve and Sandra Hampson)*

Timperley, Gtr Manchester [Bloomsbury Lane; SJ7988], *Quarry Bank*: Friendly village local with very cheap well kept Hydes Bitter and Mild on electric pump *(W Ryan)*

☆ **Tockholes**, Lancs [Brokenstones Rd, Livesey; between Tockholes and Blackburn — OS Sheet 103 map reference 666247; SD6623], *Black Bull*: Comfortably modernised and consistently welcoming food pub in good walking country, with good views from big windows; good straightforward bar food inc good home-made pizzas, well kept Thwaites Bitter and Mild on handpump, fine old slate-bed snooker table in side room, some seats outside; dogs allowed, and children at lunchtime *(Len Beattie, Dennis Royles, Philip Riding, LYM)*

☆ **Tockholes** [330 yds N of village — OS Sheet 103 map reference 663233], *Rock*: Particularly comfortable swivel bar stools and more cottagey furniture, lots of brass and china, tasteful prints, crossed sabres over bar; affable landlord, substantial helpings of good bar food (not Mon, but all day Sun) from sandwiches to steaks, inc Cumberland sausages made specially for them and daily specials cooked by the landlady, well kept Thwaites and Mild on handpump, open fire, unobtrusive piped music; tables on small terrace, good views, especially from the car park; children allowed in two rooms, quiet public playground nearby *(John Fazakerley, Graham Bush)*

☆ **Tockholes** [in village], *Victoria*: Good value bar food (not Mon evening) in comfortable and friendly moorland pub with tables in snug alcoves, partly stripped stone walls, woodburning stove, well kept Matthew Browns and Theakstons; Italian-oriented restaurant with midnight supper licence; children welcome *(Len Beattie, Denis Mann, LYM)*

Town of Lowton, Gtr Manchester [OS Sheet 109 map reference 610962; SJ6096], *Travellers Rest*: Greenalls pub with lots of alcoves, friendly and efficient service by uniformed staff, restaurant and garden *(G T Jones)*

☆ **Uppermill**, Gtr Manchester [Runninghill Gate, nr Dick Hill; SD9905], *Church*: Well kept Theakstons and other real ales and small range of well prepared generously served bar food in clean and comfortable partly stripped-stone old pub on steep moorland slope by isolated church; eager young waitresses, local drawings, annual gurning championship, carefully chosen piped music; downstairs restaurant *(Steve Mitcheson, Anne Collins, LYM)*

Warton, Lancs [the one nr Freckleton; Bryning Lance, off A584 towards Lytham; SD4028], *Birley Arms*: Rustic pub with large, high entrance hall and flagstones; good atmosphere, Greenalls, cheap food; separate dining room with big fire and hemispherical extension *(Graham Bush)*

Warton, Lancs [the one nr Carnforth, not far from M6 junction 35; SD5072], *Black Bull*: Quiet and comfortable, with decent food and no juke box; decor much as it might have been in the 1930s *(MGBD)*

Weeton, Lancs [B5260; SD3834], *Eagle & Child*: Spacious and well kept village local with decent food and beer garden *(Simon Bates, F Teare)*

☆ **Werneth Low**, Gtr Manchester [Werneth Low Rd; from A560 Stockport Rd in Hyde take Joel Lane, turn right at top; SJ9592], *Hare & Hounds*: Large, popular hilltop pub in former farmhouse with lots of beams and stripped stone, good views; well kept Boddingtons, generous helpings of good value Henry's Table food in two eating areas (one no-smoking) *(David Waterhouse, Simon and Caroline Turner, John Gould)*

West Bradford, Lancs [SD7444], *Three Millstones*: Most congenial atmosphere, friendly welcome, good range of good bar food, particularly home-made hot-pot and apple pie *(J E Cross)*

Westhoughton, Gtr Manchester [2 Market St (A58); SD6505], *White Lion*: Classic rough-and-ready pub with good cheap Holts — you have to bend down to see barmaid's face *(Denis Mann)*

White Stake, Lancs [Wham Lane; not far from M6 junction 29; SD5126], *Farmers Arms*: Smartly furnished and decorated bar with Whitbreads-related real ales on handpump; popular with young people in the evening; busy restaurant, big car park *(John Fazakerley)*

Whitebirk, Lancs [SD7028], *Red Lion*: Quiet and friendly 18th-century pub with dimly lit alcoves, Matthew Browns and Theakstons *(Len Beattie)*

Wigan, Gtr Manchester [Standishgate; SD5805], *Millstone*: Small and comfortable Thwaites house; can be busy, but very friendly with good service *(Comus Elliott)*; *Pear Tree*: Good cheap bar snacks *(Comus Elliott)*

Woodford, Gtr Manchester [550 Chester Rd — opp British Aerospace; SJ8982], *Davenport Arms*: Highly traditional with lots of aeronautical memorabilia, good atmosphere, roaring fires, Robinsons beers, good mix of customers; outside gents' could do with heating in winter *(Lee Goulding)*

Woodley, Gtr Manchester [A560 Stockport—Hyde; SJ9392], *White Hart*: Stripped pine, log fire, etched mirrors and eye-catching stained-glass ceiling creating apex; well kept Stones on handpump, darts, juke box and fruit machine *(Steve Mitcheson, Anne Collins)*

Worsthorne, Lancs [SD8732], *Crooked Billet*: Attractive village setting and reasonable if limited choice of low-priced food inc good soup, fish and chips and chicken and mushroom pie; good service, very clean lavatory (also disabled one) *(KC)*

Wrea Green, Lancs [Station Rd; SD3931], *Grapes*: Large recently refurbished open-plan village local doing well under new landlord, with Boddingtons beers, open fire, bar food and popular restaurant; picturesque neighbouring church and open green *(Graham Bush, Jon Wainwright)*

Wrightington Bar, Lancs [Highmoor Lane, 2 miles from M6 junction 27; SD5313], *High Moor*: Remote but comfortable and unpretentious, with good helpful service; primarily a restaurant, noted for good imaginative freshly-cooked food, inc excellent vegetables *(John Fairhurst)*; [Whittle Lane, High Moor — nr above entry], *Rigbye Arms*: Pleasant spot, recently refurbished pub with oak beams, log fires in winter, well kept Tetleys on handpump, good value lunchtime bar food (only sandwiches in evening) and bowling green *(John Fairhurst)*

Yealand Conyers, Lancs [not far from M6 junction 35A; SD5074], *New Inn*: Main bar with good fire, friendly local atmosphere, nick-nacks inc deer and fox heads and two ancient cash registers; plainer back pool room (which is where they normally expect children to go); well kept Hartleys XB, decent bar food *(Brian and Anna Marsden)*

Leicestershire, Lincolnshire and Nottinghamshire

A good *few new entries here, or pubs back in the Guide after an absence, include the friendly and unpretentious Eagle in Boston (good real ales, cheap food), the interesting old Leagate near Coningsby (good value food), the spacious traditional Fox & Hounds at Exton (doing well since becoming a free house), the Black Horse at Grimston (masses of cricket memorabilia), the friendly Dovecote in interesting surroundings at Laxton, the well run Nevill Arms by its little stream at Medbourne, the Market in Ordsall on the outskirts of Retford (masses of interesting real ales), and the Olde Red Lion by the towering maypole in Wellow (generous helpings of cheap food). The area's pubs are slightly cheaper than average for drinks (usually a few pence a pint below the national average – and significantly cheaper than average at the Old Kings Arms in Newark, Sir John Borlase Warren in Nottingham and Black Horse at Walcote). And food is now often a real bargain here. More than one in three of the area's pubs comfortably met our target of £1 for bargain snacks or £3 for a good main dish – or often both; this is a far higher proportion than in most areas. In particular, most pubs here still do decent sandwiches or filled cobs or baps; elsewhere, all too many publicans frown on the sandwich as being insufficiently profit-worthy. Pubs doing particularly well here currently include the Bell at Coleby (good food using local produce), the White Horse at Empingham (flourishing under new licensees), the Old Barn at Glooston (good all round), the Bewicke Arms at Hallaton (very warm atmosphere, good food), the Cap & Stocking at Kegworth (idiosyncratic and unspoilt, with appetising home cooking), the Wig & Mitre in Lincoln (very popular for its food served all day), the Old Kings Arms in Newark (good beers, food using a lot of organic produce), the Red Lion at Newton (popular new licensee, good food and drink), the Fellows Clayton & Morton in Nottingham (another new licensee doing well; the beers brewed on the premises seem on top form), the Crown at Old Dalby (wide choice of beers and imaginative if not cheap food in interesting surroundings), the friendly King William at Scaftworth (decent food), the White Hart at Tetford (another warmly friendly place, with decent food) and the Cross Keys at Upton (interesting cooking). Among the Lucky Dip entries at the end of the chapter, pubs with a particular claim to attention include the Tally Ho at Aswarby, Wishing Well at Dyke, Five Bells at Edenhamn, Boat at Hayton, Brownlow Arms at Hough on the Hill, Jolly Brewer and several other pubs in Lincoln, Lincolnshire Poacher and several others in Nottingham, Fox & Hounds at Preston, Nickerson Arms at Rothwell, Vine on the edge of Skegness, Ram Jam at Stretton, Royal Arms at Sutton Cheney, Wheatsheaf at Thurcaston and Rutland Arms at Woolsthorpe.*

BOSTON (Lincs) TF3244 Map 8

Eagle

West Street; from centre towards railway station

Notable for its fine choice of well kept real ales, this cheerful and simple corner pub has Adnams Mild, Extra and Broadside, Marstons Pedigree, Timothy Taylors Landlord and a guest such as Courage Directors on handpump – and they have fairly regular mini beer festivals (tel Boston (0205) 61116 for dates) with a dozen or more ales, with jazz and barbecues); farm cider. The plain L-shaped bar has red and black lino floor, workmanlike furnishings, darts, shove-ha'penny, cribbage, dominoes, fruit machine, trivia and piped pop music, and there's a fire in the small red plush lounge. Simple bar food includes good value specials such as bacon with cabbage, potatoes and gravy (£1.75) and other dishes like filled jumbo rolls (from 95p), home-made chilli con carne or sausage and mash (£1.95); there are roast Sunday lunches in the upstairs dining room (3 courses £4.25); some seats outside. *(Recommended by Peter Donahue, Andy and Jill Kassube, Michael Rooke)*

Free house   Licensees Andrew Watson and Antony Eastwood   Real ale   Meals and snacks (lunchtime)   Children in small area of bar 11–2.30 only   Local folk club and other occasional groups   Open 11–2.30, 6 (5 Thurs and Fri)–11; 11–11 Sat; closed evening 25 Dec

BURROUGH ON THE HILL (Leics) SK7510 Map 7

Stag & Hounds

Village signposted from B6047 in Twyford, 6 miles S of Melton Mowbray

The strong point of this friendly and comfortable little village pub is the licensee's cooking: sandwiches (from 75p), soup (£1.25), ploughman's (£1.95), smoked mackerel in a Stilton sauce (£2.25), Yorkshire pudding with gravy, vegetable or meaty lasagne, local Rutland trout (£4.99), beef in one of the Parish ales (£5.99), huge peppered steaks, venison in season, and the landlord's personal special, duck in port and redcurrant sauce (£6.99); the three-course Sunday lunch is excellent value at £4.25. The pub's former owner has kept the brewery which is just across the road – it's one of Britain's smallest – and supplies the pub's 'own brews' which include Parish Bitter, Mild and Poachers, and Baz's Bonce Blower which is the second-strongest handpumped real ale we've ever come across, and not a beer to be trifled with – much stronger than wine and with a taste more reminiscent of port than of ale; there are also guests from other breweries. To make the most of the beer, groups of 12 or more can book a supper that includes a brewery tour and as much beer as you want all evening – £12.50. Fruit and video machines, juke box; open fires and a friendly black cat. There are seats in the garden, with a children's play area; not far from *Good Walks Guide* Walk 112. *(Recommended by M L Hooper-Immins, Mel and Phil Lloyd, Nigel Gibbs, Ian Blackwell, Julian Holland)*

Free house   Licensees Peter and Sue Ierston   Real ale   Meals and snacks   Restaurant tel Somerby (066 477) 375   Well behaved children welcome until 9   Live music every other Thurs   Open 12–2.30 (3 Sat, Sun), 7–11; closed Mon–Tues lunchtimes and Sun evening

COLEBY (Lincs) SK9760 Map 8

Bell

Far Lane; village signposted off A607 S of Lincoln

The row of three communicating carpeted rooms in this popular dining pub has low black joists, open fires, pale brown plank-panelling, and a variety of small prints. The considerable range of bar food includes a good cold carvery with good salads (from £3.75), as well as sandwiches (lunchtimes, not Sunday), home-made soup (£1.25), basket meals (from £2.25), grilled prawns (£2.75), vegetarian lasagne (£4.50), steak, mushroom and Guinness pie or pan-fried whole plaice (£4.75), steaks (from £6.75), and a specials board featuring fresh fish and local produce: local leg of lamb steaks with a mint wine and lavender sauce (£5.25), roast pork fillet in a cider and sultana sauce (£5.95) or a pair of red mullet in a lemon butter and wine sauce (£6.50). Well kept Camerons Strongarm, Everards Old Original and Marstons Pedigree on handpump, decent wines, faint piped music or juke box, efficient service. There's a cosy and quite separate pool room, and a couple of picnic-table sets outside. *(Recommended by Richard Trigwell, Dave Braisted, Andy and Jill Kassube, J D Maplethorpe, A and J Heaphy; more reports please)*

Camerons Licensees Mick and Gail Aram Real ale Meals and snacks (till 10 evening) Restaurant tel Lincoln (0522) 810240 Children welcome Open 10.30–3, 7–11

CONINGSBY (Lincs) TF2458 Map 8

Leagate

B1192; off A153 NE of village

Before the fens were drained this old place stood by one of the perilous tracks through the marshes: it's the last of the fenland guide houses to survive. Three separate cosy and softly lit areas link together around the corner bar counter, attractively furnished with a variety of tables and chairs including antique oak settles with hunting-print cushions and two great high-backed settles making a snug around the biggest of the fireplaces. Another fireplace has an interesting cast-iron fireplate depicting the Last Supper above it; there are heavy black beams supporting ochre boards, and a collection of game-bird decorative plates in one cabinet. Bar food includes nicely presented sandwiches (from 80p), soup (£1.10), garlic mushrooms (£1.55), burgers (from £1.60), ploughman's or Lincolnshire sausage (£2.50), a good chilli con carne made with fresh chillis (£3), fresh fish or steak and kidney pie (£3.30), several fresh summer salads (£3.75), 6oz sirloin steak (£6) and dishes of the day such as smoked pork loin (£3.75). Well kept Marstons Pedigree, Timothy Taylors Landlord and Whitbreads Castle Eden on handpump; piped jazz or pop music, fruit machine. The pretty garden has rustic seats and white modern furniture on the lawn, with more on a paved terrace and under a big yew tree; there's a play shoe and swings in an enclosed area, and beyond a rockery is their koi carp centre – they sell the fish. *(Recommended by Frank Cummins, J D Maplethorpe, Peter Donahue, Andy and Jill Kassube)*

Free house Licensee Brian Dennison Real ale Meals and snacks (till 10 in evening) Restaurant tel Coningsby (0526) 42370 Children only if eating, up to 9pm Open 11.30–2.30, 7–11

DRAKEHOLES (Notts) SK7090 Map 7

Griff Inn ⇨

Village signposted from A631 in Everton, between Bawtry and Gainsborough

Once a staging post for mail coaches, this civilised and much refurbished 18th-century inn hums with life in the evenings, though it can be quieter at lunchtime. The neat and carefully colour-matched main lounge bar has small plush seats around its tables, and little landscape prints on silky-papered walls; besides the main restaurant, there's a more airy brasserie-style summer restaurant and a cosy cocktail bar. A wide range of bar food including things such as soup, sandwiches, ploughman's, salads, scampi, seafood platter and steak, ranges from £1.50 to £6.75; there's also an exceptional value lunchtime carvery, Sunday lunch, and substantial breakfasts. Tetleys and Whitbreads Castle Eden on handpump; good service; trivia and piped music. In summer, people head for the well kept gardens, with their pretty view down over the Idle valley – and what was a loading basin, reached from the former Chesterfield Canal by tunnel under the road. *(Recommended by D L Parkhurst, David and Rebecca Killick, Col and Mrs L N Smyth, David and Ruth Hollands; more reports please)*

Free house Licensees Michael and Barbara Edmanson Meals and snacks (till 10 evening) No-smoking restaurant Children welcome Open 12–3, 7–11; closed winter Mons (except for residents) Bedrooms tel Retford (0777) 817206; £35B/£50B

EMPINGHAM (Leics)   SK9408   Map 4

White Horse ⊘ ⇨

Main Street; A606 Stamford–Oakham

So handy for Rutland Water, this busy, extensively refurbished inn has an open-plan lounge bar with russet plush wall seats, stools and armchairs with little silver scatter-cushions around dark tables, lovely flower arrangements, and a big log fire below an unusual free-standing chimney-funnel; one side area is no-smoking. As we went to press, the new licensee and chef were to change the menu slightly, but it still included soup (£1.35), pâtés (£1.95), ploughman's with a good choice of cheese including local Stilton (£3.95), a fine steak and kidney pie (£4.60), pizza or Grimsby cod (£4.65), salads (from £4.95), and oriental seafood stir-fry or pork with mushrooms, bacon and cider (£5.25); puddings that include some unusual Scottish ones (from £1.50), small helpings for children, and fine breakfasts. Friendly, efficient service; well kept Courage Directors and John Smiths Magnet on handpump, and good wines; dominoes, fruit machine and piped music. They serve coffee and croissants from 8am and may do cream teas. Bedrooms include some in a delightfully converted back stable block, away from the main road. In front of the inn are some rustic tables among urns of flowers. *(Recommended by E J Cutting, Gwen and Peter Andrews, Mr and Mrs J H Adam, Tim and Lynne Crawford, David Eversley, David Oakes, John and Christine Simpson, Roy Butler, W H Bland, B R Shiner, M J Morgan, Janet and Gary Amos)*

John Smiths (Courage)   Licensee Roger Bourne   Real ale   Meals and snacks (till 10 evening)   Restaurant   Well behaved children allowed   Open 11–midnight; open from 8am for breakfast etc; closed except for residents evening 25 Dec and 26 Dec   Bedrooms tel Empingham (078 086) 221/521; £21.50(£32.50B)/£29.50(£42.50B)

EXTON (Leics)   SK9211   Map 8

Fox & Hounds

The unusual village green makes a fine setting for this strikingly tall stone building – which owes its grandeur largely to the fact that the quiet back road was once the main Oakham coach route. The elegant high-ceilinged rooms of the lounge bar have hunting and striking military prints on the walls, some dark red plush easy chairs as well as wheelback seats around lots of dark tables, and a winter log fire in a big stone fireplace. Good bar food includes soup (£1.25), sandwiches (from £1.25), ploughman's (from £1.80), lasagne (£3.95) and home-made pies such as steak and kidney (£4.25) at lunchtime, with scampi or gammon (£4.95) and rump steak (£7.75) in the evenings. On Sundays at lunchtime there's a choice between ploughman's and a traditional roast lunch (£7.50). Well kept Marstons Pedigree and Sam Smiths OB on handpump, unobtrusive piped music. The lively and quite separate public bar has darts, pool, dominoes, cribbage, juke box, fruit machine, and space game. There are seats among large rose beds on the well kept back lawn, overlooking paddocks. Rutland Water is about two miles away. *(Recommended by E J and J W Cutting, Dr Keith Bloomfield; more reports please)*

Free house   Licensee David Hillier   Real ale   Meals (not Mon lunchtime) and snacks (not Mon)   Restaurant   Children in eating areas   Open 11–2.30, 6–11; winter evening opening 6.45   Bedrooms tel Oakham (0572) 812403; £18/£32

GLOOSTON (Leics)   SP7595   Map 4

Old Barn ★ ⊘ ⇨

From B6047 in Tur Langton follow Hallaton signpost, then fork left following Glooston signpost

Warmly friendly and most attractively restored, this 16th-century pub has a tremendous range of well kept real ales on handpump. They only serve three or four at any one time, but from a selection of over a dozen: Adnams Broadside, Batemans XXXB, Flowers, Greene King IPA and Abbot, Hook Norton Old

Hookey, Mauldons Suffolk Punch, Theakstons XB and Old Peculier, Wadworths 6X, and so forth. The servery is between the very small and charming restaurant with its attendant bar, and the lower main bar, which has stripped kitchen tables and country chairs on its green Turkey carpet, pewter plates on a beam, Players cricketer cigarette cards, and an open fire; up steps, a snug corner has easy chairs and attractive country prints. The lighting's very sympathetic. Freshly made bar food includes mushrooms in cream and garlic on granary toast (£3.25), sandwiches that include hot beef (£4.50), home-made venison and chicken pie with apricots (£6.25), and supreme of chicken and bean shoots with lemon and lime glaze; good breakfasts may include local ham. There are a few old-fashioned teak seats in front, with picnic-table sets by roses under the trees behind. *(Recommended by L Walker, Jill Hampton, Brian Metherell, Philip Orbell, Chris Raisin, W H Bland, Mel and Phil Lloyd, Derek and Sylvia Stephenson, Mike Prentice, Gary Scott, Helen May, D R and J A Munford, M and J Black, Pamela and Merlyn Horswell)*

Free house Licensees Charles Edmondson-Jones and Stuart Sturge Real ale Meals and snacks Restaurant (not Sun evening) Well behaved children allowed Open 12–2.30, 7–11; closed Sun evening and Mon morning Bedrooms tel East Langton (085 884) 215; £32.50B/£39.50B

GRANTHAM (Lincs)   SK9135 Map 7
Beehive

Castlegate; from main street turn down Finkin Street opposite the George Hotel

Mounted in a lime tree outside this friendly pub is a unique inn-sign. It's a hive, complete with live bees, and has been the pub's sign since certainly 1830, and probably the 18th century – making this one of the oldest populations of bees in the world. An old rhyme mentions it:

Grantham, now two rarities are thine:
A lofty steeple and a living sign,...

The pub itself is pleasantly straightforward, and serves a good value basic ploughman's with cheese or ham (from £1.90 – or a small version from just £1.20); the present licensee's father has a fair claim to have invented the ploughman's lunch, serving it first under this name nearly 30 years ago. Other attractively priced bar food includes a wide choice of freshly cut sandwiches (from 85p), filled baked potatoes (from £1.20), home-made soup (£1.25), home-made chilli con carne or ham and egg (£1.95), pâté (£2.10), salads (from £2.65), and specials like cold country pie (£2.50), home-made steak and kidney pie (£2.95), and puddings (£1.35). Mansfield Riding and Old Baily, and a guest beer on handpump, under light blanket pressure; a few malt whiskies; fruit machine, space game and good juke box. *(Recommended by T Mansell; more reports please)*

Free house Licensee John Bull Real ale Meals and snacks (12–2, 5.30–8, not Sun) Open 11–3 (5 Sat), 5 (7 Sat)–11

GRIMSTON (Leics)   SK6821 Map 7
Black Horse

Village signposted off A6006 W of Melton Mowbray

This pretty flower-decked white house above a small green is a must for cricket enthusiasts. A remarkable collection of memorabilia runs from the (signed) bat with which Joe Hardstaff scored 1750 runs for Notts and England in 1936 through interesting Larwood mementoes to Desmond Lilley's headband, and among the hundreds of Test and other cricketers' signatures on dozens of bats we ourselves had a moment of delighted surprise when we found the faded signature of a childhood friend, Harry Altham. More general virtues here include good freshly cooked bar food served with decent vegetables – the steak pie (£4.40) and poussin (£4.60) are both particularly recommended, and there's also sandwiches (from 95p), home-made soup (£1.20), ploughman's (£1.95), fresh haddock and plaice (£4.40), gammon with egg or pineapple (£4.60), steaks (from £7.50), and home-made puddings such as pavlovas and apple pie (£1.45); well kept Marstons Pedigree on handpump; efficient service; and a good open fire. Furnishings are straightforwardly comfortable – built-in green plush wall seats and so forth, with neat tables; piped music. *(Recommended by Norman Edwardes, Jane Palmer, R J Haerdi, Andrew Stephenson)*

Free house   Licensees Bert and Doss Pooley   Real ale   Meals and snacks (12–1.45, 7.30–9.45; not Sun or Mon)   Open 12–2.30, 7–11; closed Sun evening and Mon

HALLATON (Leics)   SP7896   (Map 5)

Bewicke Arms ★

On good fast back road across open rolling countryside between Uppingham and Kibworth; village signposted from B6047 in Tur Langton and from B664 SW of Uppingham

Readers are unanimous in their warm approval of this newly thatched pub, not just for its well kept beers and excellent food but for the vibrantly friendly atmosphere and good service as well. The two small oddly shaped rooms of the unpretentious beamed main bar have farming implements and deer heads on the walls, pokerwork seats, old-fashioned settles (including some with high backs and wings), wall benches, and stripped oak tables, and four copper kettles gleaming over one of the log fires; the bottom room is no-smoking during the week. Bar food includes sandwiches (from £1.20), a huge crock of help-yourself soup (£1.50), ploughman's (from £2.60), daily fish specials like large and tasty New Zealand mussels in a very good sauce, chilli con carne (£4.30), tasty smoked haddock and mushroom pancake, lasagne (£4.50), beery beef casserole (£5.20), swordfish steaks (£5.60), chicken Boursin (£6.20), chicken breast with bacon, mushrooms in a port, fresh rosemary and cream sauce (£6.80), gammon and steaks, popular puddings like hot sticky toffee pudding, excellent lemon cheesecake or pavlovas, and daily specials that change with the season; children's menu or small helpings of adult food. Bar meals can be booked on Saturday evening. Very well kept Marstons Pedigree, Ruddles Best and County and Websters Yorkshire on handpump; coffee; darts, and a fruit machine in the side corridor; piped music. Picnic-table sets on a crazy-paved terrace behind the whitewashed pub look over the ex-stableyard car park to the hills behind. There's Morris dancing in summer on the village green, and a cheery traditional Easter Monday 'bottle-kicking' race (they actually use miniature barrels). No dogs. *(Recommended by Mel and Phil Lloyd, Chris Raisin, Philip Orbell, Mr and Mrs J Back, Andrew Stephenson, Mrs M Lawrence, Michael Prentice)*

Free house   Licensee Neil Spiers   Real ale   Meals and snacks   Restaurant tel Hallaton (085 889) 217   Well behaved children allowed   Open 12–2.30, 7–11 Big self-catering flat for 8/10 people from £400 per week

HECKINGTON (Lincs)   TF1444   Map 8

Nags Head

High Street; village signposted from A17 Sleaford–Boston

The right-hand part of the cosy two-room bar in this picturesque 17th-century village inn has red plush button-back built-in wall banquettes, small spindleback chairs, a clock and an attractive bronze statuette-lamp on the mantelpiece of its coal fire, and a fruit machine. On the left, there's a another coal fire below the shiny black wooden chimney-piece in what must once have been a great inglenook, curving into the corner and taking up the whole of one end of the small room – it now houses three tables, one of them of beaten brass; also, a lively watercolour of a horse-race finish (the horses racing straight towards you), and a modern sporting print of a problematic gun dog. Bar food changes daily, and besides well filled sandwiches, might typically give a choice of oxtail soup (£1.20), avocado and prawn hot-pot (£2.95), steak and kidney pie or lasagne (£3.25), gammon and pineapple or haddock (£3.50), and puddings (£1.75); Sunday roast lunch. Well kept Ruddles Best and County and Websters Yorkshire on handpump, obliging service, newspapers and magazines set out, and shove-ha'penny, dominoes, trivia and juke box. There are picnic-table sets in the garden behind. (*Recommended by Anthony Golds, Patrick Clarke, Andy and Jill Kassube; more reports please*)

Manns (Watneys)   Licensee Bruce Pickworth   Real ale   Meals and snacks (till 10 evening)   Children in eating area of bar at lunchtime   Open 11–3, 7–11   Bedrooms tel Sleaford (0529) 60218; £22S/£32S

HOSE (Leics)   SK7329   Map 7
Rose & Crown

Bolton Lane

Changing frequently and mainly on handpump, the interesting range of about half-a-dozen real ales in this comfortably modernised village pub often comes from smaller breweries in the west country or up north as well as including more local heroes such as Batemans XXXB or Hoskins & Oldfields Old Navigation. A wide range of bar food includes filled baps (from 95p), ploughman's (from £3), home-made pies (£4.95), good fresh salads (from £5), lots of steaks (from £5.95), fresh seafood platter (£6.75), and daily specials such as beef cobbler (£4.95); quiet, homely service. The neat beamed lounge bar, separated into two areas by three broad steps, has green plush seats around dimpled copper tables. The simpler public bar has pool, a fruit machine, space game and juke box. There are tables on a fairy-lit sheltered terrace behind the building. (*Recommended by Chris Raisin, R J Haerdi; more reports please*)

Free house   Licensees Carl and Carmel Routh   Real Ale   Meals and snacks Restaurant tel Bingham (0949) 60424   Children in restaurant (lunchtimes) and eating area   Open 11.30–2.30, 7–11

HOUGHTON ON THE HILL (Leics)   SK6703   Map 4
Rose & Crown

69 Uppingham Road; A47 Leicester–Uppingham

Italian-run, this comfortably plush main-road pub serves lunchtime sandwiches, soup (£1.20), several home-made pasta dishes (from £3.60), pizzas (from £3.80), grills (from £5.30), help-yourself salads (from £5.50), puddings (£1.60), and children's menu (from £1.60). The lounge bar, with gilt-trimmed panelling, has purple bucket armchairs and button-back wall banquettes, with Bass on electric pump. There are good summer weekend barbecues. Beware that lunchtime food service stops promptly at 2pm. (*Recommended by Howard and Sue Gascoyne; more reports please*)

M & B (Bass)   Licensees Tienno and Elaine Vandelli   Real ale   Meals and snacks (not Sun or Mon evenings)   Well behaved children allowed till 8.30   Open 11–2.30, 6–11

ILLSTON ON THE HILL (Leics)   SP7099   Map 4
Fox & Goose

Village signposted off B6047 Market Harborough–Melton Mowbray, 3 miles S of A47

Amusing and unusual, this tiled-floor pub is crammed full of fox masks and brushes, gamecocks, a badger head and squirrel, and even a human skull; Jubilee celebration photographs, Fernie hunt pictures and commemorative plates, lots of McLachlan original cartoons, and gin traps, gas masks, helmets, and ancient bottles. The small and simple bar serves well kept Adnams Bitter and Everards Tiger on handpump; there's a warm winter coal fire in here, and in the cosy sitting-roomish front lounge; darts and piped music. They serve filled rolls and cobs at weekends. Both ourselves and readers have found the pub very quiet, but a poltergeist is said to liven it up from time to time. (*Recommended by Gary Scott; more reports please*)

Everards   Licensee Marilyn Kendall   Real ale   Snacks (not weekdays)   Open 7–11 (and 11–2 Sat and Sun)

KEGWORTH (Leics)   SK4826 Map 7

Cap & Stocking ★

Under a mile from M1 junction 24: follow A6 towards Loughborough; in village, turn left at chemists' down one-way Dragwall opposite High Street, then left and left again, into Borough Street

Despite extensions and other changes, the two front rooms here remain staunchly traditional. Each has a coal fire, and on the right are fabric-covered wall benches and heavy cast-iron-framed tables, lots of etched glass, big cases of stuffed birds and locally caught fish, and a cast-iron range; the back room has French windows to the garden. Well kept and reasonably priced Bass, Highgate Mild, Worthington BB, and a regularly changing guest beer tapped from the cask; Thatcher's cider and several malt whiskies. Very good value bar food includes filled cobs (from 55p, home-cooked beef 70p), home-made soup (75p), burgers (from £1.20), ploughman's (from £1.75), chilli con carne or vegetarian spaghetti (£2.25), Lancashire hot-pot or beef carbonnade (£2.50), and home-made specials such as liver and bacon casserole, rogan josh or Balinese beef; dominoes, cribbage, fruit machine, and old juke box. There's a sheltered garden and terrace where they play péanque. *(Recommended by Graham Bush, Andrew Stephenson, Wayne Brindle, Andy and Jill Kassube, Neil and Elspeth Fearn, Richard Sanders, Jon Wainwright, Jane and Niall)*

Bass   Licensees Bil and Linda Poynton   Real ale   Meals and snacks (12–2, 7–8; not Mon evening)   Open 11.30–3, 6–11

KIBWORTH HARCOURT (Leics)   SP6894 Map 4

Three Horseshoes

Main Street; just off A6 in village centre

In a quiet village street, this neat cream-painted brick and slate house has a big open-plan bar, well-kept by lots of cheerful staff. There are bays of comfortable tawny plush button-back built-in wall banquettes in the part by the serving counter, bookable tables set with wheelback chairs in two side areas, illustrated maps of hunting territory, and several elaborate table paraffin lamps converted to electricity. Bar food includes sandwiches, quite a few snacks, home-made pies (from £4.50), fillet steak (£7.95), puddings like home-made fruit crumble (£1.50), and several daily specials; well kept Marstons Pedigree on handpump, and own-label house wine; piped music. You'd never guess that Smoky the amiable cat is getting on for 14. *(More reports please)*

Free house   Licensee Barrie Sutton   Real ale   Meals and snacks (not Sun evening) Restaurant tel Leicester (0533) 793303 (not Sun evening)   Children in restaurant and eating area of bar   Open 11–2.30, 6.30–11

LAXTON (Notts)   SK7267 Map 7

Dovecote

Signposted off A6075 E of Ollerton

In a former stable block behind this redbrick village house is a walk-round visitor centre explaining the three huge medieval fields here, a unique survival. The unfenced and unmarked strips of farmland within the fields are individually owned, and photographs in the pub show the villagers meeting there for the Court Baron which still administers the system, and walking the fields on the original grassy sykes which visitors too can use. The pub itself is warmly welcoming. A central room by the bar has brocaded button-back built-in corner seats, stools and chairs, a coal-effect gas fire, wild-rose wallpaper, and a window looking over the village to the church tower; it opens through a small bay which was the original entry into another similar room. Around the other side a simpler room with some entertaining Lawson Wood 1930s tourist cartoons leads through to a pool room with darts, juke box and fruit machine; also, cribbage, dominoes, and piped music. Attractively presented home-cooked food includes sandwiches (from £1.25, chip buttie 85p), soup (£1.20), crudités (£2.30), ploughman's (£2.50), salads (from £2.50), steak and kidney pie (£3.75), lasagne (£3.95), several fish dishes from plaice (£4.35) to salmon (£6), gammon (£4.95), 9oz sirloin steak (£6.45), children's dishes (from £1.75), and puddings (from £1.25); well kept Mansfield Old Baily and Whitbreads Castle Eden on handpump, decent coffee (as well as quite a few liqueur coffees); helpful service. There are white tables and chairs on a small front terrace by a sloping garden with a disused white dovecote. *(Recommended by Alan Frankland, Sarah Mellor, Alan and Eileen Bowker, Derek and Sylvia Stephenson)*

Free house   Licensees John and Elizabeth Waters   Real ale   Meals and snacks till 10 Children welcome   Open 11.30–3, 6.30–11; 11–3.30, 6.30–11 Sat

LEICESTER   SK5804   Map 4

Tom Hoskins

131 Beaumanor Rd; from A6 at Red Hill Circle (huge roundabout N of centre) follow Motorway, Burton, Coventry sign into Abbey Lane (A5131), take second left into Wade St – pub on left at next crossroads

Part of the small Hoskins brewery (you can arrange to be shown round the late Victorian brewhouse (*tel* Leicester (0533) 661122), this backstreet pub has a comfortable partly flagstoned and panelled lounge bar that's been converted from the brewery's former malt loft, and decorated with old brewing equipment; piped music. The original and much plainer wood-floored tap room has a smokily masculine and chatty atmosphere, varnished pews around cast-iron-framed tables, and flagstones by the servery; Bitter, Mild, Penns, and in summer Premium on handpump, and dominoes, darts and cribbage. A small range of straightforward lunchtime bar food includes filled cobs (from 65p), ploughman's (£2.35) and scampi (£2.95); beer prices (they also keep a changing choice of other brewers' real ales) are low. *(Recommended by Pete Storey, Richard Sanders, Peter Donahue, Dave Braisted; more reports please)*

Hoskins   Licensees Roy and Maureen Allen   Real ale   Meals and snacks (lunchtime, not Sun)   Open 11.30–3, 5.30 (6 Sat)–11

LINCOLN   SK9872   Map 8

Wig & Mitre ★ ⊘

29 Steep Hill; just below cathedral

Perhaps best enjoyed out of season when it's not so crowded, this attractively restored 14th-century building is on two floors. Downstairs, the cheerful, simpler bar has pews and other more straightforward furniture on its tiles, and a couple of window tables on either side of the entrance; the upstairs dining room has settees, elegant small settles, Victorian armchairs, shelves of old books, and an open fire. It's decorated with antique prints and more modern caricatures of lawyers and clerics, and by the stairs you can see some of the original medieval wattle-and-daub; the oak rafters are exposed, too. Served all day (with last orders around 11pm) and changed twice during that time, the food covers a remarkable range. Besides sandwiches (from £2), ploughman's (£2.45), and all-day breakfast dishes (full fried breakfast £3.50), there are usually two or three soups (from £1.50), a choice of pâtés (from £3.25), ratatouille with garlic toast (£3.50), main dishes like pork in cider, apples and sage (£4.25), gammon and eggs (£4.65), roast fillet of cod with parsley sauce (£5.50), medallions of salmon with quenelles and saffron (£10.25), and puddings like poached pears in chocolate sauce or tiramisu (£2.25). You can also choose from the less quickly changing restaurant menu, which includes more expensive dishes such as chicken breast with parma ham baked in pastry (£8.95) and fillet of beef with fresh basil and tomatoes (£12.95). A very wide though not cheap choice of wines by the glass, many more by the bottle,

Sam Smiths OB and Museum on handpump, and lots of liqueurs and spirits; good coffee; newspapers and magazines to read. A small sheltered back terrace has seats by a small pool and fountain. *(Recommended by ILP, Jill Hampton, Brian Metherell, Barry and Anne, Mr and Mrs P A Jones, Sue Holland, Dave Webster, John and Joan Wyatt, Andy and Jill Kassube, Helen and Wal Burns, Reg Nelson, BKA, Michael and Alison Sandy, Paul McPherson, Peter Donahue, J D Maplethorpe, M A and W R Proctor, Michael Quine, E Krakowska Smart, B Smart, Gary Scott)*

Sam Smiths   Licensees Michael and Valerie Hope   Real ale   Meals and snacks (8–midnight)   Restaurant tel Lincoln (0522) 535190/537482/523705   Children in eating area and restaurant   Open 8am–11pm, including Sunday; closed 25 Dec

LYDDINGTON (Leics)   SP8797   Map 4
Marquess of Exeter

Village signposted off A6003 N of Corby

In a charming village long owned by the Burghley family, this handsome and friendly stone inn – now part of a hotel group – has a rambling beamed lounge, plushly furnished in red, with a good log fire in its well built stone fireplace. Served by neatly uniformed staff, the good bar food includes soup (£1.25), sandwiches (from £1.25), smokies (£2.45), chicken pancake (£3.75), lasagne (£3.95), a pie (£4.75), and home-made specials. Well kept Ruddles and Theakstons XB on handpump, and some malt whiskies; piped music. *(Recommended by H D Spottiswoode, Neil Tungate, W H Bland, Jamie and Sarah Allen, Derek and Sylvia Stephenson)*

Free house   Licensees R M Morrell and L S Evitt   Real ale   Meals and snacks (12.15–1.45, 7.15–10)   Restaurant (not Sun evening)   Children in eating area of bar   Occasional live entertainment   Open 11.30–3, 6.30–11   Bedrooms tel Uppingham (0572) 822477; £50B/£64B, though prices are cheaper at weekends

MARKET DEEPING (Lincs)   TF1310   Map 8
Bull

Market Place

There's plenty of room for finding quiet, snug spots in the low-ceilinged alcoves and little corridors of the cheerful and lively bars here. Down some steps is the Dugout Bar – a long cellar-like narrow room with heavy black beams and roughly plastered walls made from enormous blocks of ancient stone – surely much older than the early Georgian facade. Well kept Adnams, Everards Tiger and Old Original and a guest beer on handpump. Decent bar food, lunchtime sandwiches, mushrooms in garlic butter (£1.85), home-made steak and kidney pie (£4.45), peppered steak (£6.26), 24oz T-bone (£11), and puddings (£1.40); 3-course Sunday lunch (£6.75, children £4.25) – best to book. Fruit machine, trivia and piped music. There are seats in a pretty back coachyard. *(Recommended by M J Morgan; more reports please)*

Everards   Licensee David Dye   Real ale   Meals and snacks (11–2, 7–10; not Sun or Mon evening)   Restaurant (not Sun evening)   Children in restaurant and eating area of bar   Nearby daytime parking may be difficult   Monthly jazz Sun evening and monthly party nights (and on Bank Hols)   Open 11–3, 5.30–11; 11–11 Fri and Sat   Bedrooms tel Market Deeping (0778) 343320; £18/£30

MEDBOURNE   SP7993   Map 4
Nevill Arms

B664 Market Harborough–Uppingham

A footbridge takes you over a stream to this village-centre pub with its handsome stonework and latticed mullioned windows. Through the arched doorway the main bar has chairs and small wall settles around its tables – warm in winter with its two log fires, cool in summer as its dark-joisted ceiling is quite lofty. A spacious back room by the former coachyard has pews around more tables – much needed in summer when the old coach roads striding over the rolling surrounding countryside bring plenty of visitors. There are tables out on the grass by the stream then, too (and they may give you old bread for the ducks); and there's a freshly painted dovecot. Bar food includes sandwiches, cheese and vegetable bake (£4.25), steak and kidney pie, chicken in stilton and leek sauce or pork, apricot and almond casserole (£4.50), and home-made puddings such as treacle tart or bread and butter pudding. Well kept Adnams, Hook Norton Best, Marstons Pedigree and Ruddles County on handpump; freshly squeezed orange juice; friendly service. Darts, shove-ha'penny, table skittles, cribbage, dominoes, and fruit machine, with carpet bowls, Devil Among the Tailors, and Captain's Mistress available for organised functions. The pub dogs, not normally in evidence, include a stately great dane. *(Recommended by Rona Murdoch, Brian and Genie Smart, Dr Peter Donahue, Eric Locker; more reports please)*

Free house   Licensees E F Hall and Partners   Real ale   Meals and snacks   Children in eating area of bar   Open 12–2.30 (3 Sat), 7–11   Bedrooms should be ready by Autumn 1990 tel Medbourne Green (085 883) 288; £25B/£35B

NEWARK (Notts)   SK8054   Map 7
Old Kings Arms

19 Kirkgate; follow To The Market Place signpost opposite Maltby agricultural engineers on A46

This very popular pub, with its warm and lively atmosphere, has a refurbished upstairs eating area which is open all day (from 9.30 for morning coffee; they also do afternoon teas till 5). The bar has a vaulted ceiling, plain stripped deal tables, and traditional wall benches and so forth. Using free-range eggs, free-range, organically fed meat and poultry, and fresh (and sometimes organically grown) vegetables, the good home-made food includes sandwiches, soup (95p), ploughman's (from £1.80), two sizes of dishes like chilli con carne or lasagne (from £1.80), ratatouille (from £2.10), and chicken curry (from £2.80), salads (from £2.90), beef in Guinness (£3.30), 8–10oz steak (£5.50), and puddings such as fruit crumble or pie (80p); daily specials like nut roast, braised liver and onions, tuna and peanut risotto or pork in cider (all £3). Marstons Burton, Exhibition, Merrie Monk, Pedigree, and Owd Rodger on handpump are notably well kept, and service helpful. Dominoes, cribbage, shove-ha'penny, a fruit machine, trivia and juke box (which can be loud). A small terrace has some tables and chairs, and the castle ruins are just a stroll away. *(Recommended by Brian and Genie Smart, Mr and Mrs P A Jones, Nigel Hopkins, Andy and Jill Kassube, T M McMillan, Richard Sanders)*

Marstons   Licensee Christopher Holmes   Real ale   Meals and snacks (9.30am–7.30pm)   Partly no-smoking restaurant tel Newark (0636) 703416   Children in upstairs restaurant   Trad jazz Mon, folk Fri   Restricted nearby parking   Open 10.30–3, 5–11

NEWTON (Lincs)   TF0436   Map 8
Red Lion ★ ⊘

Village signposted from A52 E of Grantham; at village road turn right towards Haceby and Braceby; pub itself also discreetly signed off A52 closer to Grantham

It's the imaginatively displayed and served food which is the highlight for most people visiting this quietly civilised village pub. You choose as much as you like from an attractive and individual display of salads, with four different types of fish such as fresh salmon, cold meats, and pies; a small helping is £5.50, normal £6, and large £7.50, with children's helpings £1. The winter soups are also very good, as are the one or two local specialities such as stuffed chine of pork or spicy Lincolnshire sausages, and the rich puddings; they'll do sandwiches. The communicating rooms have a Gothick carved settle, old-fashioned oak and elm seats and cushioned wall benches built into the cream-rendered or bare stone walls; these are profusely decorated with farm tools, malters' wooden shovels, a stuffed fox, stag's head and green woodpecker, pictures made from pressed flowers, a dresser full of china, and hunting and coaching prints – a stuffed rat hangs above the serving-counter, and there's even a penny-farthing cycle. Very well kept Batemans XXXB on handpump, good coffee and good value champagne, fresh flowers, unobtrusive but well reproduced piped music, and friendly, relaxed service. Fruit machine, and during the day and at weekends two squash courts run by the pub can be used by non-members (there's also pool and video here). The neat, well sheltered back garden has some seats on the grass and on a terrace, and there are pleasant walks in the surrounding countryside. *(Recommended by David and Ruth Hollands, Steve Dark, Tim and Lynne Crawford, Edward and Diane Everest, M J Morgan, Pete Storey, Neil and Angela Huxter)*

Free house   Licensee Graham Watkin   Real ale   Meals and snacks (12–2, 7–10; not Sun or Mon evenings   Children in eating area of bar   Open 11–2.30 (3 Sat), 6–11; closed 25 Dec

NOTTINGHAM   SK5640 Map 7

Bell

18 Angel Row; off Old Market Square

In the same family since 1898, this very popular 15th-century building has three downstairs bars – the nicest of which is probably the low-beamed Elizabethan Bar with its half-panelled walls and comfortable high-backed armchairs; they've uncovered some of the original timbers in here and in the Tudor Bar. Upstairs, the Belfry is usually quieter in the evenings (especially in term-time when it can get really busy downstairs) and at the back you can see the rafters of the 15th-century crown post roof or look down on the busy street at the front; at lunchtime, when there's a fairly priced hot and cold buffet, this functions as a family restaurant. Bar food includes filled cobs, soup (90p), ploughman's (£2.50), salads (from £2.65), steak and kidney pie (£2.85), mixed grill (£4.75), steaks (from £5.50), and puddings (£1.20). Bass, Greene King Abbot, Jennings Bitter, Marstons Pedigree, Theakstons XB and Old Peculier and weekly guest beers on handpump (from cellars 30 feet down in the sandstone rock – groups may be able to arrange tours); good value wines, and quite a few malt whiskies; they also have a variety of wine tastings and history talks for groups. Fruit machine, piped music. In summer there's waiter service to the tables on the pavement outside. *(Recommended by Graham Bush, BKA, Nigel Gibbs, Dr Keith Bloomfield, P Miller, A C and S J Beardsley, Steve Waters, Richard Sanders; more reports please)*

Free house   Licensees David, Simon and Paul Jackson, Manager Richard Jackson Real ale   Lunchtime meals and snacks (not Sun, though they do lunchtime rolls then) Restaurant (closed Sun)   Children in restaurant lunchtimes   Trad jazz Sun lunchtime and evening, Mon and Tues evenings   Open 10.30–11 weekdays; 10.30–2.30, 5.30–11 Sat

Fellows Clayton & Morton

Canal Street (part of inner ring road)

From the quarry-tiled glassed-in back area which looks towards the canal here, cast-iron steps take you up to a big window into the brewery where they produce their own creamily malty gently hopped Samuel Fellows and stronger Matthew Claytons – well kept on handpump, as is the Whitbreads Castle Eden (they also have decent wines). It's a softly lit, careful conversion of a former canal building with dark blue plush seats built into its alcoves, copper-topped tables, some seats up two or three steps in a side gallery, screens of wood and stained glass, some bric-a-brac on the shelf just below the glossy dark green high ceiling, and a quietly friendly pubby atmosphere that appeals to shoppers and a wide mix of working people alike. Under the new licensee, the bar food has changed: filled cobs (from 70p; very good hot beef at lunchtime £1.10), good soup (95p), ploughman's (from £1.75), vegetarian dishes (from £2), steak and kidney pie or curry (from £2.50), fish and chips (the house special, £3.25), and rump steak (£4.95); welcoming, quick service. Well reproduced nostalgic pop music, trivia machine, and maybe newspapers on a rack. This year they've added a new terrace with seats and tables.

The canal museum is nearby, and Nottingham station is just a short walk away. *(Recommended by D L Parkhurst, Dr Keith Bloomfield, BKA, Nick Dowson, Alison Hayward, Alan and Eileen Bowker, Wayne Brindle, Nigel Gibbs, Derek and Sylvia Stephenson)*

Own brew   Licensee Les Howard   Real ale   Meals and snacks   Restaurant   tel Nottingham (0602) 506795   Children in restaurant   Open 11–11

Olde Trip to Jerusalem ★

Brewhouse Yard; from inner ring road follow The North, A6005 Long Eaton signpost until you are in Castle Boulevard then almost at once turn right into Castle Road; pub is up on the left

Hardys & Hansons have taken over this quaint old pub and installed new licensees. The building is mainly 17th century, and the star award is for the unique upstairs bar: it's cut into the sandstone rock below the castle, and the walls, panelled at the bottom, soar steeply up into remote and shadowy heights, with cosy simply furnished hollowed-out side alcoves (it's often closed at lunchtime). The friendly downstairs bar – popular with young people – is also mainly carved from the rock, with leatherette-cushioned settles built into the dark panelling, barrel tables on tiles or flagstones, and more low-ceilinged rock alcoves. Bar food includes cobs and sandwiches (toasties 90p, egg, bacon, sausage, and tomato or beans in a giant bun £1.50), filled baked potatoes, ploughman's (£2.75), a game or a vegetarian pie, and daily specials. These caverns may have served as cellarage for an early medieval castle brewhouse which stood here, and they still keep the Kimberley Bitter and Marstons Pedigree Bass. Several whiskies and wines. Fruit machine, ring-the-bull; seats outside. *(Recommended by Helen and Wal Burns, Graham Bush, Ian Phillips, Richard Sanders, Nick Dowson, Alison Hayward, Mr and Mrs P A Jones, Wayne Brindle, Jon Wainwright, M A and W R Proctor, Barry; more reports on the new regime, please)*

Hardys & Hansons   Licensees Brian and Janet Palethorpe   Real ale   Lunchtime meals and snacks   Open 11–3 (4 Sat), 5.30–11; closed 25 Dec

Sir John Borlase Warren

Canning Circus (A52 towards Derby – pub faces you as you come up the hill from city centre)

Full of the friendly buzz of conversation, the half-a-dozen communicating rooms in this civilised, traditional pub have all the old-fashioned trappings: swagged russet curtains with net lower curtains in the three big bay windows, comfortable parlourish seating, swirly Victorian acanthus-leaf wallpaper, dark brown anaglypta dado, sturdy brass lamps, Delft shelf, etched mirrors, engraved glass, and pictures ranging from little Victorian cartoons to the big chromolithograph of Queen Victoria's Diamond Jubilee procession or the various prints commemorating Sir John, who defeated an attempted French invasion of Ireland off Kilkenna in 1798. Bar food, from a counter in the downstairs room, is slightly different under the new licensee: filled cobs (from 55p), filled baked potatoes (from £1.20), ploughman's (from £1.65), salads (from £2.20), a vegetarian dish (£2.40), scampi (£2.50), and daily specials. Cheap and well kept Shipstones Mild and Bitter on handpump; fruit machine, trivia, piped music. The pub is attractively placed opposite Georgian almshouses and there are tables sheltering under an old tree behind. *(Recommended by Andrew Stephenson, Ian Phillips, Nigel Gibbs)*

Shipstones (Greenalls)   Licensee David Astley   Real ale   Meals and snacks (12–2, 5.30–9); not Sun evening   Live entertainment Wed evening   Open 11–11

OLD DALBY (Leics)   SK6723 Map 7

Crown ★   ★   ⊘

By school in village centre turn into Longcliff Hill then left into Debdale Hill

The three or four little rooms in this hidden-away converted farmhouse have been refurbished this year, and the homely furnishings that include easy chairs now have Sanderson loose covers and there are William Morris curtains; also, black beams, hunting and other rustic prints, one or two antique oak settles and Windsor armchairs, fresh flowers, open fires, and a relaxed, unspoilt atmosphere. The two small and cottagey rooms of the restaurant have also been refurbished, and the front-house staff now wear uniforms of black and white with red silk ties. A wide range of real ales tapped from the cask includes Badger Tanglefoot, Exmoor Gold, Kimberley Best, Marstons Pedigree, Merrie Monk and Owd Rodger, Ringwood Fortyniner, Theakstons Old Peculier, Woodfordes Wherry and Phoenix, and rotating guests such as Adnams, Batemans XXXB, Greene King IPA and Abbot, and Timothy Taylors Porter; 20 malt whiskies, several brandies and Italian liqueurs. Fresh, interesting, though not cheap, food (there are no freezers, microwaves or chips) includes soup (£2), sandwiches and rolls (from £2, 4oz steak £3.95), oven baked tomatoes stuffed with cheese, walnuts and sweetcorn, topped with thyme butter and served with melba toast (£3.75), a bumper ploughman's with home-made pickle or black pudding and fried apple on a creamy mustard sauce (£5.50), vegetable lasagne or fresh tagliatelle with a sauce of wild mushrooms, smoked bacon, egg yolks, cream and fresh parmesan (£5.95), pan-fried, marinated pork with a light plum sauce (£6.95), fresh king prawns with onions and fennel (£7.95), and freshly-made puddings (£2.50); Sunday lunch; no credit cards. It can get very full (especially in the evenings and at weekends). One room has darts, dominoes, cribbage and table skittles. There are plenty of tables on a terrace, with a big, sheltered lawn (where you can play pétanque) sloping down among roses and fruit trees. The two stars make this one of the region's top pubs, reflecting the great enthusiasm of most readers who've been. But we should point out that there is a minority who feel it could do better at the prices – and it can feel cramped at busy times. *(Recommended by Helen and Wal Burns, Nigel Hopkins, Mr and Mrs G Gittings, Mel and Phil Lloyd, Sue Corrigan, L M Miall, Philip Orbell, WTF, Ken and Barbara Turner, G and M Brooke-Williams, P Miller, A C and S J Beardsley, Tim and Lynne Crawford, Roger Entwistle, Richard Dolphin, Graham Oddey, Syd and Wyn Donald, Peter Donahue, A and J Heaphy, Steve Dark, Derek and Sylvia Stephenson)*

Free house Licensees Lynne Bryan and Salvatore Inguanta   Real Ale   Meals and snacks (not Sun evenings)   Restaurant tel Melton Mowbray (0664) 823134; not Sun evening   Children in eating area of bar   Open 12–2.30, 6–11

RETFORD (Notts)   SH7079 Map 7

Market

West Carr Road, Ordsall; follow Retford Leisure Centre sign off A620 W, then after West Carr Road Industrial Estate sign on your right take first left turning up track which – if you look closely – is signed for the pub; or, on foot, from Retford Rly Stn follow footpath under S of frontage, turn R at end; note that there is a quite separate Market Hotel in Retford itself

A most unlikely find among these factories, this comfortable place has a long, cosy bar with green plush wall banquettes and dimpled copper or dark wood tables, pantiles over the bar servery, over the open fire at one end and over a little blue plush snug at the other; a spacious new conservatory dining room opens off (it can get very warm on a sunny summer's day), and in turn gives on to a small terrace with white tables. A remarkable choice of well kept real ales on handpump runs to Adnams Bitter and Broadside, that wonderfully silky deceiver Batemans Victory, Everards Tiger, Exmoor, Marstons Pedigree, Tetleys, Theakstons Best and XB, Timothy Taylors Landlord, Youngers Scotch and a guest beer such as Robinwood Old Fart; Stolichnaya is the house vodka. A simple range of good home-cooked food gives real value – as does the service (they'll ask how hot you want your chilli, for instance). The friendly young landlord's father ran the pub before him. *(Recommended by Maureen and Steve Collins, John C Baker, Derek and Sylvia Stephenson, Mr and Mrs P A Jones, Michael Rooke)*

Free house   Real ale   Meals and snacks   Open 11–3, 5.30–11; all day Sat

SCAFTWORTH (Notts)   SK6692   Map 7

King William

Village signposted (not prominently) off A631 Bawtry—Everton

The three connecting rooms of the bar in this peaceful, friendly pub have a pleasant variety of seats such as a sofa and high-backed settles, as well as plainer chairs around tables, hunting and other prints above the stripped dado, a wall filled with entertaining photographs, old farm tools, Delft shelves of nick-nacks, and masses of brasses; in summer there are bunches of flowers, in winter generous open fires, and the end room is no-smoking. Imaginative bar food includes home-made soup (£1.45), ploughman's, salads, fish casserole in a spiced coconut sauce or chilli con carne (£4.30), and a good many interestingly flavoured pies (you can choose between white or wholemeal pastry or a stuffing crumble topping) such as rabbit and tomato, chicken, bacon and mushroom, steak in old ale or vegetarian (all (£4.50). Well kept Everards Old Original, Marstons Pedigree, Tolly Original and Whitbreads Castle Eden on handpump, over 52 malt whiskies, decent wines and an espresso coffee machine; darts, shove-ha'penny, dominoes, cribbage, fruit machine, pinball (very rare in pubs nowadays, sadly), unobtrusive piped music. Down a corridor a clean, light and airy family room, with milk-churns as seats, leads through French windows to the sheltered garden. This runs down to the River Idle, with cows grazing beyond; it's sheltered and well planted with shrubs and young trees, with plenty of well spaced tables, swings, slides, a climber, a covered barbecue area, and amiable ginger cats, rootling chickens, and preening peacocks. *(Recommended by Mrs I L Phillipson, Mrs R M Morris; more reports please)*

Free house   Licensee Michael Wright   Real ale   Meals and snacks (12–2.30, 7–10, but see opening hours below)   Children in eating area of bar, in dining room and in family room   Morris men in summer   Open 12–3, 6.30–11; closed lunchtime Mon and Tues in summer and Mon—Wed lunchtimes in winter; open Bank Hol Mons

SIBSON (Leics)   SK3500   Map 4

Cock

A444 N of Nuneaton

Owned by the Church until just before the war (it got a Sunday licence only in 1954), this charming thatched and timbered black-and-white pub dates back in part to 1250. There are heavy black beams, ancient wall timbers, genuine latticed windows, and unusually low doorways. The room on the right has seats built in to what was once an immense fireplace, with other comfortable seats around cast-iron-framed tables. The room on the left has country kitchen chairs around wooden tables. Good value car food cooked by the new manager and his wife includes sandwiches (from 75p), home-made soup (£1), salads (from £2), vegetable au gratin (£3.50), home-made steak and kidney pie or lasagne (£3.75) and steaks (from £6), with children's dishes (£2). Well kept Bass and M & B Brew XI; bar billiards, piped music. There are tables on the lawn behind. The restaurant (in a former stable block) is popular. They have a caravan field (certified with the Caravan Club). *(Recommended by Dave Braisted, Graham Bush, Graham Richardson, Genie and Brian Smart, Mike and Wendy Proctor)*

M & B (Bass)   Manager Graham Lindsay   Real ale   Meals and snacks (not Sun) Restaurant (not Sun evening) tel Tamworth (0827) 880357   Children in eating area and restaurant   Open 11.30–2.30, 7–11

STAMFORD (Lincs)   TF0207   Map 8

Bull & Swan

High St, St Martins; B1081 leaving town southwards

The three spacious but cosy rooms of the comfortable bar in this old stone pub are divided by shallow steps and wooden partition walls. There are low and heavy beams hung with lots of highly polished copper kettles and brassware, velvet-cushioned armchairs all around its walls, log-effect gas fires, and a good atmosphere throughout. A wide choice of bar food, all home-made, includes sandwiches (from £1.20, steak £3.95), soup (£1.20), filled baked potatoes (from £1.50), a choice of ploughman's (from £2.20), steak and mushroom pie (£3.90), trout in a sweet and sour sauce (£3.85), a mixed grill (£6), a good few puddings (£1.40) and attractively priced daily specials such as lemon sole mornay (from £3). Well kept Camerons Strongarm, with maybe Whitbreads or Courage beers too; good friendly service; unobtrusive piped music. There are tables in the coachyard behind. *(Recommended by T Mansell, Michael and Margaret Slater, John Whitehead, Jamie and Sarah Allan, J D Maplethorpe; more reports please)*

Tolly (Brent Walker)   Licensee Maurice de Sadeleer   Real ale   Meals and snacks (11.45–2, 6.30–10; till 10.30 Sat, 7–9 Sun)   Restaurant   Children in separate room Open 11–2.30, 6–11   Bedrooms tel Stamford (0780) 63558; £30(£32B)/£36(£38B)

George ★ ★ ⊘ ⇌

71 St Martins

This handsome and beautifully preserved sizeable hotel was built in 1597 for Lord Burghley (whose splendid nearby Elizabethan house is well worth visiting). It includes parts of a much older Norman pilgrims' hospice, and a crypt under the present cocktail bar may be more than 1,000 years old. There are several interesting and decidedly pubby bars. The central lounge has sturdy timbers, broad flagstones, heavy beams, and massive stonework, and the 18th-century panelled front rooms – named for the London and York coaches, up to 20 a day each way, which changed horses here – have a medley of seats ranging from sturdy bar settles through leather, cane and antique wicker to soft settees and easy chairs. The nicest place for lunch (if it's not a sunny day) is the indoor Garden Lounge, with well spaced white cast-iron furniture on herringbone glazed bricks around a central tropical grove, and a splendidly tempting help-yourself buffet (from £7.95). Bar food includes soup (£2.95), Danish open sandwiches (from £4.80), stir-fried vegetables in black-bean sauce or three Lincolnshire sausages in a mushroom and red wine sauce with smoked bacon (£4.95), fresh pasta (the sauce changes daily) or lasagne (£5.95), paella Valenciana (£6.95), char-grilled rump steak (£8.95), and whole lemon sole with parsley butter (£9.95); good puddings (£3.25). The cobbled courtyard at the back is lovely in summer, with comfortable chairs and tables among attractive plant tubs and colourful hanging baskets; waiter drinks service. The best drinks are the Italian wines, many of which are good value (they don't sell real ales), and they sell ten by the glass; filter, espresso or cappuccino coffee. Besides the courtyard, there's a well kept walled garden, with a sunken lawn where croquet is often played. This is the headquarters of Ivo Vannocci's small but reliably good chain of Poste Hotels. *(Recommended by John Evans, Margaret Dyke, Pete Storey, F Teare, Dr and Mrs S G Donald, Gordon Theaker, T Mansell, F M Wand-Tetley; more reports please)*

Free house   Licensees Ivo Vannocci and Chris Pitman   Meals and snacks (noon–11) Restaurant   Children welcome   Open 11–11   Bedrooms tel Stamford (0780) 55171; £62.50B/£86B

SWITHLAND (Leics)   SK5413   Map 7

Griffin

Village signposted from A6 Leicester–Loughborough

This year, the three communicating rooms of this warmly welcoming modernised country pub have been refurbished; the furniture is now covered with deep red plush material and there are new chintz drapes in the windows; also, beams, some modern panelling, and carpet or parquet flooring. The end room is usually quietest, with seats by its fire, and there's a nice children's room; one area is no-smoking. Good fresh bar snacks that include toasties, sausage and chips and gammon and egg, and well kept Adnams Bitter and Everards Beacon, Mild, Tiger and Old Original, and a guest beer on handpump. Darts, dominoes, cribbage, fruit machine and piped music, with a skittle alley in the quite separate back Stable Bar (which was being refurbished as we went to press). Handy for Bradgate Country Park, with walks in Swithland woods. *(Recommended by Barry and Anne, Richard Sanders, T Nott; more reports please)*

Everards   Licensees Norman and Brenda Jefferson   Real ale   Meals and snacks (not Sun)   Children in own room   Open 11–2.30, 6–11

TETFORD (Lincs)   TF3374   Map 8

White Hart

Village signposted from Greetham–Belchford road off A158 Horncastle–Skegness, and from Scamblesby–South Ormsby road between A153 and A16 S of Louth; inn near centre of this straggly village – OS Sheet 122 map reference 333748

In attractive Wolds countryside, this white-rendered village inn has a cosily traditional red-tiled bar with slabby elm tables, hunting-print cushions on some settles, china and pewter hanging from one black beam, and a high-backed curved oak settle by a big brick inglenook fireplace hung with brass plaques and horsebrasses; darts, dominoes, quiet piped music, a chatty welcome and friendly service. A bigger extension opening off is more simply furnished with plenty of tables and chairs, and line ink drawings of the village. There's also a small, no-smoking snug. Cheap bar food includes soup, ploughman's (from £1.95), lasagne (£2), lamb cutlets, good pork chops with apple sauce, cottage or steak and kidney pies (all £3.75), good grilled lemon sole, and steak; puddings like superb crumble. Well kept Batemans XB and XXXB and Marstons Pedigree on handpump. The sheltered back lawn has seats and swings, and the pub is near *Good Walks Guide* Walk 114. *(Recommended by Derek and Sylvia Stephenson, Tim and Sue Holstead, T Nott, Anthony Barnes, Sidney and Erna Wells; more reports please)*

Free house   Licensee Stuart Dick   Real ale   Meals and snacks (not Mon, except Bank Hols)   Restaurant   Children in eating area of bar   Open 12–3, 7–11; closed Mon lunchtime (not Bank Holidays)   Bedrooms tel Tetford (065 883) 255; £21/£28

UPTON (Notts)   SK7354   Map 7

Cross Keys   ★   ⊘

Main Street (A612 towards Southwell)

Service is efficient and friendly, even when this heavy-beamed 17th-century pub is busy, and the very good, generously served bar food might include cream of pea soup, stuffed mushrooms or spiced chicken wings (£2.75), vegetarian dishes such as mushroom and leek stroganoff or lentil and couscous bake (£3.85), excellent lasagne, lambs' kidneys Forestière or fish or steak and mushroom pies (£3.95), lamb noisettes in port and redcurrant jelly, as well as lunchtime sandwiches and ploughman's; inventive puddings; they don't do chips, and the menu changes day by day. The restaurant is in the old dovecote. Well kept Batemans XXXB, Boddingtons Bitter, Marstons Pedigree and Whitbreads Castle Eden on handpump, with regular guest beers. The bar rambles around a central two-way log fireplace and in and out of various alcoves, with decorative plates and metalwork in one corner, and lots of pictures from sporting cartoons to local watercolours. An extension room has carved pews from Newark church. Darts, dominoes and piped music; the dog's well behaved. Half a dozen tables are strung out in bays of the neatly plant-lined fence behind. *(Recommended by Helen and Wal Burns, Miss Karen Ann Ross, Philip Wood, Paul Harrop, D P Ryan, Maureen and Steve Collin, Tony Gayfer, Derek and Sylvia Stephenson, Mr and Mrs M O Jones, George Mitchell, Dr Keith Bloomfield, J D Maplethorpe, Mike Tucker, Mrs M E Collins, Angie and Dave Parkes, Peter Burton)*

Free house   Licensee Michael Kirrage   Real ale   Snacks (lunchtime) and meals (till 10 evening)   Restaurant tel Southwell (0636) 813269   Children in new extension room lunchtimes only and in restaurant   Folk/roots music Sun evening Sept–May   Open 11.30–2.30, 6–11; closed evening 25 Dec

French Horn

A612

The neat and comfortable open-plan bar here has cushioned captain's chairs, wall banquettes around glossy tables, and friendly and efficient service; they often have a show by local painters. Generous helpings of home-made food include filled rolls (from 75p), soup (from £1.10), ploughman's (from £2.95), stir-fry dishes (from £3.25), open sandwiches (£3.50), vegetarian dishes (from £3.50), hot tossed chicken with salad (£4.25), Cumberland lamb cobbler (£4.95), salmon with lime and herb butter (£5.75), and lots of puddings such as olde English trifle with mead and macaroons or hot sticky toffee pudding (from £1.75). The choice is wider in the upstairs brasserie. Well kept John Smiths and an occasional guest beer on handpump, and a good choice of decent wines by the glass. The big sloping back paddock, with picnic-table sets, looks over farmland. *(Recommended by Mr and Mrs B H James, Andy and Jill Kassube, Pat and Norman Godley; more reports please)*

John Smiths (Courage)   Licensees Graham and Linda Mills   Real ale   Meals and snacks (12–2, 6.30–10)   Restaurant tel Southwell (0636) 812394; not Sun evening Children welcome   Open 11–3, 6.30–11; closed evenings 25 and 26 Dec

WAINFLEET (Lincs)   TF5058   Map 8
Angel

High St (A52 Skegness–Boston)

The former home of the Barkham family, who sent a Lord Mayor to London in 1621, this Georgian-fronted building has been an inn since the 18th century. The neatly kept lounge bar has prints on its cream-painted walls, dark red plush-cushioned sturdy settles, smaller seats and stools on its red carpet, and traditional cast-iron-framed tables. The new licensee has changed what was the restaurant into a snooker/children's room with video. Reliably good bar food includes sandwiches (75p), burgers (£1), tasty omelettes like tuna and tomato (£2.25), good meaty or vegetarian lasagne or chilli con carne (£2.95), and rump steak (£5.95). Well kept Bass and a guest beer such as Batemans on handpump, and tea or coffee; friendly service; coal fire; darts. *(Recommended by D I Baddeley, Derek and Sylvia Stephenson, Richard Sanders; more reports please)*

Bass   Licensee Steven Williams   Real ale   Meals and snacks   Well behaved children allowed   Open 11–3, 7–11

WALCOTE (Leics)   SP5683   Map 4
Black Horse ⊘

1 1/2 miles from M1 junction 20; A427 towards Market Harborough

The real surprise in this unsurprising-looking pub is that the bar food is exclusively Thai – the landlady, who does the cooking, comes from Thailand. You can choose one of the half spicy and half savoury dishes such as strips of beef in oyster sauce or khao mu daeng (marinated pork – all £3), phat khing (stir-fry meat or prawn with ginger and onion or with garlic, chilli and special hot basil herbs, all from £3), a Thai mixed grill (£3.50), and various Thai curries such as kaeng pla (fish, £3.50) or kaeng kai (chicken, £4). A fine choice of drinks includes well kept Hook Norton Best and Old Hookey, Hoskins & Oldfields HOB, Timothy Taylors Landlord, and guest beers on handpump, an eclectic range of bottled beers that runs to Singha from Thailand, and country wines. It's furnished with russet plush button-back built-in wall banquettes, cast-iron and other heavy tables, more booth-like seats at the side, and pale mate's chairs in an airier section up steps; the atmosphere is quietly chatty, there's an open fire, and (for summer) seats out behind. *(Recommended by Dick Brown, J D Cranston, John and Joan Wyatt, Jim Aitkenhead, Hilary Sargeant, Norman Clarke)*

Free house   Licensee Mrs Saovanee Tinker   Real ale   Meals   Children in eating areas   Open 11–2.30, 5.30 (6 Sat)–11; closed Tues lunchtime

WELLOW (Notts)   SK6766 Map 7

Olde Red Lion

Eakring Road; pub visible from A616 E of Ollerton

Get here early if you want to eat: though there are several small rooms they fill up quickly as the food has a great local reputation for value – a combination of low prices and big helpings. It includes good doorstep sandwiches (from 85p), soup (90p), squid rings or garlic mushrooms (£1.95), salads (from £2.35), hot-pot or steak and kidney pie (£2.95), vegetarian dishes such as sweet and sour almonds (£3.65), tandoori chicken (£4.25), steaks (from £6.95) and children's dishes (from £1.85); bookings are recommended for Sunday lunch (Mansfield (0623) 861000). The low-beamed front room has old-fashioned button-back built-in wall seats as well as captain's chairs and stools, all in red plush, around its dark cast-iron-framed tables, and looks out on a tremendously tall brightly spiral-painted maypole (where Spring Bank Holiday Monday celebrations take place). Beyond a snug little Turkey-carpeted drinking bar are two further rooms (the dining room is no-smoking); well kept Marstons Pedigree and Ruddles Best and a couple of guest beers on handpump; several liqueur coffees; quick service; dominoes, fairly unobtrusive piped pop music. An L-shaped strip of grass above the car park has picnic-table sets under cocktail parasols, and a set of swings. *(Recommended by Colin Wright, Derek and Sylvia Stephenson)*

Free house   Licensees John and Carol Henshaw   Real ale   Meals and snacks (12–2, 7.30–10)   Open 11.30–3, 5.30–11; closed evening 25 Dec

WEST LEAKE (Notts)   SK5226 Map 7

Star

Village signposted from A6006

The prints on the ochre walls of the bar in this old village pub recall the days when cockfights were held here – the reason it's still known as the Pit House. The beamed public bar is traditionally furnished with sturdy settles and oak tables on the tiled floor, with harness, whips, and foxes' masks on the walls, quite a collection of cats, and a warm welcome from behind the bar. The Adnams and Bass on handpump is well kept (your money's just put in a wooden tray). The partly panelled lounge on the right has comfortable armed chairs and a good log fire. Good value simple food includes soup (70p), salads (from £3), a daily hot dish (around £3) and puddings (75p). There are picnic-table sets by the quiet lane in front. *(Recommended by Helen and Wal Burns, Pete Storey, John Wainwright, Richard Sanders)*

Bass   Licensee F Whatnall   Real ale   Meals and snacks (lunchtime, not Sat or Sun)   Children in eating area   Open 10.30–2.30, 6–11

WHITWELL (Leics)   SK9208 Map 8

Noel Arms

The bar the locals go for and the one with the really warm atmosphere is in the original part of this thatched inn: two tiny characterful rooms, with things like the odd contraption in which they keep the pot plants (it's actually the local pattern of spit-roaster, turning on a vertical axis in front of the fire), and the box for fishermen on Rutland Water to note what they've caught. There's much more room in the spacious and plushly comfortable back extension, where there may be piped music. Good, waitress-served home-made bar food at lunchtime includes sandwiches, vegetable soup (£1.95), ploughman's (£2.85), sausage and egg (£3.25), quiche Lorraine (£3.95), lasagne or seafood pancakes (£4.50), and steak and kidney pie or cold mixed meat salad (£4.75), with evening extras such as Mediterranean prawns (£4.95), grilled fresh halibut (£6.50), and steaks (from £6.95); home-made puddings (£2.50). Well kept Ansells, and Ruddles Best and County on electric pump, and an extensive wine list; fruit machine; they do afternoon teas (not Mondays). There are tables on the south-facing slope behind,

with occasional barbecues. Residents have to book for the restaurant.
(Recommended by W H Bland; more reports please)

*Free house   Licensee Sam Healey   Real ale   Meals and snacks (till 10 evening)
Restaurant   Children welcome   Open 10–3, 6–11   Bedrooms tel Empingham (078
086) 334; £28(£35B)/£39(£47B)*

WILSON (Leics)   SK4024   Map 7

Bulls Head

On side road Breedon on the Hill–Melbourne; village signposted from A453 Ashby de la
Zouch–Castle Donington

Comfortably modernised, this well run and friendly country pub is popular for its
fresh and reasonably priced bar food: soup (95p), sandwiches (from £1.25),
ploughman's (from £2.50), a daily special (£4), hot roast beef (£5), and attractively
presented salads from the buffet counter (from £3.75), with seafood such as
dressed crab, cold fresh salmon or freshly sliced smoked salmon (£5.75). Very
good Sunday lunch. The beamed bar has maroon plush banquettes and settles
around neat black tables, smart and cheerfully efficient mature barmaids, and
several quiet alcoves decorated with old sepia racing-car photographs (Donington
race track is nearby) and some striking modern prints of immensely magnified
insects; piped music. Well kept Ind Coope Burton on handpump. *(Recommended by
Pete Storey, Neil and Angela Huxter, Paul and Janet Waring, A C and S J Beardsley, T Nott,
Chris Raisin; more reports please)*

*Ind Coope   Licensee Michael Johnson   Real ale   Meals and snacks (12–2, 6–10; not
Sun or Mon evenings)   Children in eating area   Open 11–2.30, 6–11*

Lucky Dip

Besides the fully inspected pubs, you might like to try these Lucky Dips recommended to
us and described by readers (if you do, please send us reports):

Alford, Lincs [West St (A1004); TF4576],
Half Moon: Large pub with several rooms,
simple bar food, Bass and Bass Mild,
Batemans XB and XXXB, and a guest beer
such as Wards on handpump; nice garden;
children welcome *(Derek and Sylvia
Stephenson, Keith Day)*; *White Horse*:
Picturesque and comfortable 16th-century
pub, carefully restored over the years, with
interesting pictures, local real ales, good
reasonably priced bar food, good restaurant,
ample parking; bedrooms tastefully chintzy,
good value *(Paulina Blowes)*
Ancaster, Lincs [High St (B6403); SK9843],
Ermine Way: Bar and lounge/restaurant
recently tastefully refurbished; wide choice
of good reasonably priced bar food, big car
park; bedrooms *(J D Maplethorpe)*
Anstey, Leics [Bradgate Rd; SK5408], *Hare
& Hounds*: Good local atmosphere, friendly
and efficient licensees, several tastefully
refurbished rooms, wide range of
home-made food, well kept Marstons
Pedigree *(Paul and Janet Waring)*
Ashby de la Zouch, Leics [Market St;
SK3516], *Queens Head*: Good choice of
reasonably priced bar food inc generous Sun
lunch (also restaurant); good choice of other
bar food at reasonable prices; homely
atmosphere *(Mr and Mrs Kilburn)*
Ashby Folville, Leics [SK7011], *Carrington
Arms*: Spacious, comfortable bar in not
over-done-up Edwardian pub; friendly
landlord, good choice of well kept real ale
inc Everards on handpump, reasonably

priced bar food inc proper omelettes *(John
and Joan Wyatt, Dr and Mrs A K Clarke)*
☆ **Aswarby**, Lincs [A15
Folkingham—Sleaford; TF0639], *Tally Ho*:
Well kept country pub with two friendly
rooms; country prints, big log fire and
woodburning stove, oak beams, simple
traditional furnishings; well kept Adnams,
Batemans XB and a guest beer on
handpump, straightforward bar food,
welcoming service; tables and timber play
fort on grass behind, by sheep meadow;
bedrooms comfortable and well equipped, in
neatly converted block behind *(Mrs Pamela
Dumenil, J D Maplethorpe, A and J Heaphy,
BB)*
Aubourn, Lincs [SK9262], *Royal Oak*:
Cheerful family-run country pub with
welcoming open fire, good filling food in
quantity, and Batemans XB and XXXB,
Sam Smiths, and a guest beer on handpump;
nice garden *(Andy and Jill Kassube, Derek and
Sylvia Stephenson, J D Maplethorpe)*
Bagthorpe, Notts [Lower Bagthorpe; 2 miles
from M1 junction 27, off A608 towards
Eastwood; SK4751], *Dixies Arms*:
Traditional mining village pub with plenty
of character; tiny snug, quaint public bar
with interesting china collection, plush small
Victorian lounge; filled rolls, well kept beer,
wonderful atmosphere; blazing coal fire in
winter; big car park *(Mr and Mrs P B
Dowsett)*; [Upper Bagthorpe; 2 miles from
M1 junction 27: A608 towards Eastwood,
first right, then right at T-junction, then first

left], *Shepherds Rest*: Traditional mining pub, alone in pretty surroundings, with plenty of seats in big front garden; welcoming and comfortable *(Mr and Mrs P B Dowsett)*

Barholm, Lincs [TF0810], *Five Horseshoes*: Well kept Adnams, Batemans and guest beers in homely easy-going village local with horsey connections and paddocks behind the garden tables *(M Morgan, LYM)*

☆ **Barrow upon Soar**, Leics [Mill Lane, off South St (B5328); SK5717], *Navigation*: Picturesque two-roomed extended split-level pub by Grand Union Canal, based on former barge-horse stabling, popular at weekends for good value straightforward lunchtime bar food and well kept John Smiths, Marstons Pedigree and Shipstones Mild and Bitter on handpump; skittle alley, small back terrace by boat moorings, car park over small humped-back bridge *(Mr and Mrs P A Jones, Richard Sanders)*

Barrow upon Soar, *Soar Bridge*: Collection of old cast signs, local railway pictures and canal memorabilia; popular good value food, well kept Everards Beacon and Old Original, lots of country wines; short walk behind to river *(Mr and Mrs P A Jones)*

Barrowden, Leics [Main St; just off A47 Uppingham—Peterborough; SK9400], *Exeter Arms*: In picturesque village overlooking duck pond; well kept Batemans and two guest beers, good food in bar and busy restaurant area *(Nic James)*

Bassingham, Lincs [High St; SK9160], *Five Bells*: Immaculate pub brimming with brass, beams and nick-nacks; warm and friendly atmosphere, roaring fire, well kept Allied real ales, decent wine *(A and J Heaphy, Andy and Jill Kassube)*

Baston, Lincs [Church St; TF1113], *Spinning Wheel*: Good choice of beers inc Bass, good value food in bar and restaurant *(M Morgan)*

Belmesthorpe, Leics [Shepherds Walk; TF0410], *Bluebell*: Olde-worlde pub with lively atmosphere and entertaining landlord; well kept Marstons Pedigree and Ruddles County, good value lunchtime bar food (not Sun) *(M Morgan)*

☆ **Bicker**, Lincs [A52 NE of Donnington; TF2237], *Red Lion*: Well kept Adnams Broadside, Bass, Ind Coope Burton, Tetleys and two guest beers on handpump in simply modernised 17th-century pub with masses of china hanging from bowed black beams, huge fireplace, bar food inc good mixed grill and inventive pancakes, tables on terrace and tree-shaded lawn; interesting area — formerly a sea inlet, with remains of Roman sea fishery *(J D Maplethorpe, D C Hawkins, David and Ruth Hollands, LYM)*

☆ **Blidworth**, Notts [SK5956], *Bird in Hand*: Friendly local with probably the best view in Notts over Sherwood Forest; one comfortable U-shaped room, well kept Mansfield Riding and Old Baily on handpump, good cheap bar food, good mix of customers (a special welcome for wheelchair patients from nearby nursing home), big garden *(Angie and Dave Parkes, Derek and Sylvia Stephenson, Maureen and Steve Collin)*

Blyth, Notts [SK6287], *Angel*: Cheerful much-modernised coaching inn with comfortable and quite lively lounge, well kept Hardys & Hansons real ales on electric pump, nice coal fire, piped music; public bar and pool room, seats in garden; bar food straightforward (ham salad recommended), but usefully served on Sun too (rare around here) — so handy for A1; children welcome; bedrooms very simple, though OK for a stopover *(Roger Broadie, LYM)*; *White Swan*: Attractive pub, friendly landlord, well kept beer, good bar food *(C Elliott)*

☆ **Boston**, Lincs [Witham St; TF3244], *Carpenters Arms*: Traditional very friendly backstreet inn, vibrant with locals and young people (landlord's young too), well kept Batemans Mild and XB, enterprising home-cooked lunchtime food; bedrooms reasonably priced *(Richard Sanders, Michael Rooke)*

Boston [Wainfleet Rd (A52)], *Burton House*: Smart and comfortable lounge bar in pleasant hotel, bar food inc good special with local fresh vegetables, fresh fish, home-made puddings; Bass and Batemans XB on handpump; bedrooms *(Andy and Jill Kassube)*; [Horncastle Rd (B1183)], *Kings Arms*: Small redbrick town inn refurbished under new licensees, airy and light front bar with shining brass and warm atmosphere looking over road to canal and striking tall working windmill; neat smaller red plush back bar, well kept Batemans, fair-priced bar food; bedrooms modern and comfortable with cheery furnishings; good value *(Paulina Blowes, BB)*

Bramcote, Notts [Derby Rd; SK5037], *Sherwin Arms*: Lively and friendly black and white local with comfortable cottagey atmosphere, well kept beer, freshly prepared and reasonably priced bar food *(B R Shiner, Roger Taylor)*

☆ **Brandy Wharf**, Lincs [B1205 SE of Scunthorpe; TF0197], *Hankerin*: Traditional riverside pub with sense of space, popular with boating people as there are good moorings and slipways; jovial licensee, remarkable choice of dozens of farm ciders (with summer 'Sydre Shoppe'), standard choice of good cheap nicely served bar food inc excellent curry; the buildings look lucky to have survived, and the unusual decor is perhaps not the main attraction; clean outside lavatories; closed Christmas, New Year and Mon winter lunchtimes *(Andy and Jill Kassube, T Nott)*

Branston, Leics [Main St; SK8129], *Wheel*: Free house in beautiful area with friendly atmosphere, Batemans and John Smiths, reasonably priced bar food especially schnitzels and stilton-based dishes, juke box *(Keith Bloomfield, Richard Sanders)*

☆ **Braunston**, Leics [off A606 in Oakham; SK8306], *Old Plough*: There's some concentration now on the elegant back dining conservatory, though the good range of bar food runs from filled rolls and ploughman's to salmon and huge tender steaks; the black-beamed lounge has brocaded seats around its traditional pub tables, a clean and pleasant atmosphere, and Pimms by the jug in summer as well as well kept John Smiths on handpump; seats in sheltered garden; children allowed in restaurant *(CEP, RJH, LYM — more reports please)*

Burbage, Leics [SP4294], *Cross Keys*: Good atmosphere in pleasant building with two bars and snug; well kept Marstons, open fire, long garden with separate children's room and cricket pitch at end *(Graham Bush)*

Carlton on Trent, Notts [SK7964], *Great Northern*: Pub with two bars and family conservatory, in long-closed station; railway memorabilia, good-humoured landlord, good value standard bar food inc good prawn omelette, unusual beers and cider, quiet piped music, pool table; Inter-City trains belt past every so often *(Michael Thomson, RAF)*

Castle Bytham, Lincs [SK9818], *Castle*: Charming licensee and consistently good bar food (not Tues) *(D R Uphill, Andy and Jill Kassube)*

☆ **Castle Donington**, Leics [Kings Mills; SK4427], *Priest House*: Rambling beamed building with medieval tower, in attractive spot by River Trent, which has had well kept Watneys-related real ales, friendly service, games room, hearty snacks, play area and decent separate bedroom block; we've heard nothing recent of their plans to move towards a more restaurant-oriented operation *(Martin Aust, LYM — news please)*

☆ **Castle Donington** [90 Bondgate (B6504)], *Cross Keys*: Well kept Vaux Samson and Wards Best, attractive atmosphere, good fire and good mix of customers *(Richard Sanders)*

☆ **Catthorpe**, Leics [just off A5 S of Gibbet Island; SP5578], *Cherry Tree*: Cosy village inn doing particularly well under cheerful new young licensees; tastefully furnished, very clean, well kept Bass, promising food Fri to Sun lunchtimes, open fire; closed Mon–Thurs lunchtime, small car park *(Ted George)*

Caythorpe, Lincs [SK9348], *Red Lion*: Well positioned 400-year-old pub; reasonably priced bar food, Everards Tiger, Ruddles County, Marstons Pedigree and guest beers *(Andy and Jill Kassube)*

Chapel St Leonards, Lincs [Sea Rd — N of centre; TF5572], *Ship*: Old, comfortable and welcoming pub stands aloof from the gaudy holiday village; well kept Batemans Mild, XB, XXXB and good, inexpensive food; sometimes opening hours are extended *(Michael Rooke)*

Church Langton, Leics [B6047 about 3 miles N of Mkt Harborough, just off A6; SP7293], *Langton Arms*: Wide choice of bar food, quick waitress service, plenty of space in two big bars; garden *(Jack and Barbara Smale)*

☆ **Clayworth**, Notts [High St; SK7388], *Blacksmiths Arms*: Interesting and very popular old village local with comfortable lounge area, more basic bar area with settles and upright chairs and prints for sale; well kept Bass and Tetleys, good value wines, country wines, and freshly squeezed orange juice; good straightforward bar food inc excellent wholemeal ham sandwiches, good value back restaurant *(Dr A E Hanwell, Mr and Mrs P A Jones)*

☆ **Clipstone**, Notts [Old Clipstone; B6030 Mansfield—Ollerton — OS Sheet 120 map reference 606647; SK6064], *Dog & Duck*: Comfortably modernised and friendly three-roomed pub doing well under current regime, with good home-made hot meals and well kept Home ales; not far from Center Parc at Rufford; children's room *(Alan and Marlene Radford)*

Coalville, Leics [SK4214], *Bull*: Friendly atmosphere with helpful, courteous service, good decor, well kept Burton and good food *(P Miller)*

Collingham, Notts [High St; SK8361], *Royal Oak*: Cheerful, rambling pub in pleasant village; well kept John Smiths served in tight-headed northern manner *(John Baker)*

Colston Bassett, Notts [SK7033], *Martins Arms*: Rustic local in charming village, with imposing wood-carved fireplace and matching bar, well kept Bass and Ruddles on handpump, bowling green; has been closed Sun; as we went to press we heard it was up for sale — more news please *(Chris Raisin)*

☆ **Copt Oak**, Leics [nr M1 junc 22; A50 towards Leics, then B587; SK4812], *Copt Oak*: Well refurbished in 1920s style, with concentration on wide choice of reasonably priced good food in big new dining area, efficiently run with good waitress service; lush green plants in profusion and stunning views over the Charnwood Forest; big car park *(J D Martin, C E Power)*

Cotes, Leics [A60 Loughborough—Nottingham; SK5520], *Cotes Mill*: This substantial converted watermill has a great deal of potential, with its garden by the mill pond, waterwheel view from the foyer, simple but spacious white-walled bar and upstairs dining area; our most recent news is of straightforward food, well kept Banks's beers and a landlord keen on stock-cars and all-day opening, but the rate of change here has tended to be rather brisk *(Martin Aust, Derek and Sylvia Stephenson, Mr and Mrs P A Jones, Richard Sanders, Andrew Stephenson, Andy and Jill Kassube, LYM — more reports please)*

☆ **Cottesmore**, Leics [Main St; SK9013], *Sun*: Very popular for bar food — soup, wrapped baps and several same-price hot dishes such as rabbit casserole or ham and egg; decent sporting prints and plush button-back banquettes in modernised bar with hot fire in stone inglenook, quieter side rooms, piped music and fruit machine, tables in garden; children welcome *(BB)*

Cropston, Leics [15 Station Rd (B5328); SK5510], *Bradgate Arms*: Good range of Hoskins real ales with interesting well kept guest beers (the cellar's been redone) and Weston's cider in completely refurbished village pub with family area, skittle alley and biggish garden *(Mr and Mrs P A Jones, Richard R Dolphin, LYM)*

Cropwell Bishop, Notts [SK6835], *Wheatsheaf*: Notably well kept Home Bitter *(Nigel Hopkins)*

Cuckney, Notts [SK5671], *Greendale Oak*: Charming, spacious, and comfortable rural pub with intelligent, personable locals, well kept Home Bitter, and unobtrusive piped music; easy car parking *(R A Caldwell)*

Dadlington, Leics [SP4097], *Dog & Hedgehog*: Comfortably extended dining pub with particularly good enormous grills *(Ken and Barbara Turner)*

☆ **Diseworth**, Leics [street opp churchyard; nr East Midlands Airport, and new M1 junction 23A; SK4524], *Plough*: Happy pub — new extensions and attractive refurbishment have not impaired its character, with a pleasant mix of locals and aviation people, and pictures of Orion Airways aircraft (one reader recalls this airport when autopilot meant knowing where to tie the string on the DC3 controls); well kept Bass, good range of bar food, weekday lunchtime closing 2.30 (*T Nott, Harry Blood*)

Diseworth, Leics [nr East Midlands Airport; SK4524], *Bull & Swan*: Well kept Shipstones, good bar food (*Dave Braisted*)

☆ **Donington on Bain**, Lincs [TF2382], *Black Horse*: A pub with character, good reasonably priced food, well kept Watneys-related real ales (*Jack and Barbara Smale*)

☆ **Dyke**, Lincs [21 Main St; off A15 N of Bourne; TF1022], *Wishing Well*: Imaginatively refurbished village inn, its long open-plan main bar full of heavy beams, dark stone, candlelight, brasswork and even a wishing well; good value home-cooked bar food inc toasted sandwiches, ploughman's, good steak and kidney pie and other hot dishes Mon—Sat, with a three-course Sunday lunch — and small dining room serving superb steaks; well kept Adnams, Greene King IPA and Abbot and Marstons Pedigree on handpump, games in plain public bar, relaxed atmosphere with a pleasant but not effusive welcome; bedrooms simple but good value (don't expect the bar to quieten down early) (*R F Plater, M Morgan, Anthony Barnes, Giles Quick, LYM — more reports please*)

☆ **East Langton**, Leics [the Langtons signed off A6 n of Mkt Harborough, E Langton also off B6047; SP7292], *Bell*: Pretty and civilised white pub that's been a popular main entry for its outstanding food, in elegant and comfortable surroundings with pink-painted beams, stone walls, winter log fire and carefully chosen piped music; though — besides decent wines and good coffee — it does have Ruddles under light blanket pressure, it has lately under its new landlord now become so much a restaurant rather than a pub that you can scarcely drop in just for a drink any more, which is why this year we've relegated it to the Dips (*RJH, LYM*)

Eastville, Lincs [TF4057], *Wheat Sheaf*: Clean, basic, Fenland pub with well kept Batemans, friendly, helpful licensees; worth knowing the good cheap nearby fish and chip shop (*John Baker*)

☆ **Edenham**, Lincs [A151; TF0621], *Five Bells*: Currently doing particularly well, with friendly landlord, waitresses and locals, wide choice of usual bar food served quickly, well kept Camerons Original and Strongarm and Tolly Best; busy but spacious modernised lounge with neatly ranged tables, log fire, piped music, lots of foreign banknotes, soft lighting; new restaurant/function room behind, good play area in garden; children welcome (*A and J Heaphy, Mr and Mrs J Barnes, Geoff Halson, LYM*)

☆ **Elkesley**, Notts [just off A1 S of Blyth; SK6975], *Robin Hood*: Tidy pub, very useful for the A1 as it has particularly good bar food — especially home-made soups, ratatouille with wholemeal bread, garlic mushrooms, hot and spicy home-made chilli and curry, imaginative daily specials; well kept Marstons Pedigree and Whitbreads Castle Eden, excellent service, nice restaurant (*Andy and Jill Kassube, Gordon Smith*)

☆ **Elston**, Notts [A47 S of Lincoln; SK7548], *Coeur de Lion*: Extraordinary building like a small Iberian summer palace — pinnacles, domes, lancet windows, steep roofs, tall chimneys, elevated terraces; decorous panelled bar with soft russet plush seats, country prints and engravings, neatly uniformed careful staff; good bar food served under domed silver covers, decent spirits, free peanuts; two candlelit dining rooms, one upstairs with soaring pitched and raftered ceiling (*David and Ruth Hollands, BB*)

☆ **Epperstone**, Notts [SK6548], *Cross Keys*: Particularly friendly village pub with well kept Hardys & Hansons on handpump, copious helpings of excellent value bar food (*Dr Keith Bloomfield, Derek and Sylvia Stephenson, David Carnill*)

☆ **Ewerby**, Lincs [TF1247], *Finch Hatton Arms*: Substantial and solidly built and furnished mock-Tudor pub, very neat, with red plush button-back seating, pegged rafters, Delft shelf of china, some rustic bygones, efficient staff; popular bar food from sandwiches up, well kept Stones Best and Wards Sheffield Best on handpump, coal fire, smart restaurant area, comfortable back locals' bar, a couple of rustic seats outside (*A and J Heaphy, J D Maplethorpe, Andy and Jill Kassube, BB*)

Farnsfield, Notts [SK6456], *White Post*: Spacious, comfortable pub with good value bar food and restaurant (*R A Caldwell*)

Fiskerton, Notts [SK7351], *Bromley Arms*: Popular local, especially for families and fishermen, on River Trent (car park gives river access); well kept Hardys & Hansons, bar food inc good sandwiches (*John Baker*)

Foxton, Leics [off A6 N of Market Harborough; SP7090], *Shoulder of Mutton*: Cosy pine interior, small good value restaurant (best to book) with particularly good service; no food Sun or Mon (*C T H Wickham*)

Frampton, Lincs [signposted off A16 S of Boston; TF3239], *Moers Arms*: Attractive old free house with beamed lounge, well kept Adnams on handpump, simple home-made bar food from sandwiches up, big garden; busy Sun lunchtime (*Peter Donahue*)

Frisby in the Wreake, Leics [Main St; SK6917], *Bell*: Reasonably priced bar food running up to steaks, inc good home-made fruit pies; obliging staff, fair range of wines, piped music, weekend evening dining room, tables outside (*RJH*)

Gedney, Lincs [Chapelgate; TF4024], *Old Black Lion*: Good food, homely atmosphere, warm welcome and good service (*R Pinch*)

☆ **Glaston**, Leics [SK8900], *Monkton Arms*: Remarkably wide choice of good if not cheap bar food in informal, very friendly surroundings, inc good steaks, fresh fish, spare ribs and home-made puddings; well kept real ales inc Theakstons XB, good range of wines (B J A King, M L Hooper-Immins)

☆ **Gotham**, Notts [SK5330], *Star*: Licensees who made the Old Plough, Sutton Bonington a popular main entry have now made this a very pleasant place, with good welcome and excellent value food, though no real ale *(Pete Storey)*

☆ **Grantham**, Lincs [High St; SK9135], *Angel & Royal*: The stone facade of this THF hotel (much extended behind) is quite unique, with carvings done 600 years ago to honour the visit by King Edward III to what was then a Commandery of the Knights Templar; the plush hotel bar on left of coach entry still has interesting oriel window, and high-beamed main bar opp has massive inglenook — tremendous potential for the historically minded; well kept Bass and occasional guest beers *(T Mansell, LYM)*

☆ **Grantham** [Vine St], *Blue Pig*: Ancient, attractive half-timbered corner pub, with several cosy and atmospheric beamed drinking areas, lots of prints and photographs of old Grantham on the walls; well kept Whitbreads-related real ales on handpump, bar food served quickly and in generous helpings, friendly staff; pretty hanging baskets in summer *(Howard and Sue Gascoyne, T Mansell)*

☆ **Great Casterton**, Lincs [village signed off A1; TF0009], *Crown*: High-backed booth seating in neat bar with walls stripped to bare stone above the white-painted wainscoting, good value bar food from soup, bacon sandwiches and ploughman's to hefty gammon and steaks with cheap daily specials, well kept Camerons and Tolly Original on handpump, log fire in inglenook; simpler back bar popular with the Young Farmers; old-fashioned seats in pretty little garden opposite attractive church; Post Office in car park *(Stan Edwards, BB)*

Greatford, Lincs [TF0811], *Hare & Hounds*: Small, comfortable and homely lounge with roaring fire, well kept Adnams Broadside, Charles Wells Eagle and Bombardier, and Riding, and good, properly cooked food (worth the wait); separate public bar *(M and Mrs J Back)*

☆ **Greetham**, Leics [B668 Stretton—Cottesmore; SK9214], *Wheatsheaf*: Good value bar food served till late evening, from lunchtime sandwiches and ploughman's through cheap charcoal-grilled burgers to steaks; simply furnished L-shaped series of communicating rooms, coal fire, nautical charts, well kept Camerons Bitter and Strongarm Premium on handpump; pool and other games in end room, restaurant, tables on side grass *(M and J Back, BB)*

Grimsthorpe, Lincs [A151; TF0422], *Black Horse*: More hotel and restaurant than pub, but worth knowing — well kept Camerons in main lounge bar with settles and tables; armchairs, chairs and stools in smaller Pheasantry bar, good home-cooked snacks in Buttery, good traditional English food in dining room *(M Morgan)*

Halam, Notts [SK6754], *Wagon & Horses*: Locally popular and immaculate village dining pub, with good bar food, well kept Marstons Pedigree on handpump, few

wooden tables at front, small car park *(Tim and Lynne Crawford, Dr Keith Bloomfield, Derek and Sylvia Stephenson)*

Haltham, Lincs [loop off A163 Horncastle—Coningsby; TF2463], *Marmion Arms*: Small and spotless thatched pub with good Shipstones on handpump, reasonably priced home-made bar food, friendly landlady, 60s piped pop; garden, good parking *(Terry Glendenning)*

☆ **Halton Holegate**, Lincs [TF4165], *Bell*: Pretty tiled white-painted house with hanging baskets and passion-flower near the church in quiet village where the rolling Wolds slope down into the fens; simple but comfortable furnishings, aircraft pictures (the Lancaster bomber flying over the pub on the inn-sign commemorates 207 and 44 Squadrons, stationed nearby), decent home-made food from soup and sandwiches through chicken breasts and gammon to steaks; well kept Batemans XB on handpump, good coffee, friendly landlord (ditto Sam, the sleek black dog) *(Bert Dowty, BB)*

☆ **Hayton**, Notts [Main St (B1403) — OS Sheet 120 map reference 728852; SK7384], *Boat*: White-painted free house backing on to quiet stretch of Chesterfield Canal, with comfortable furnishings, big log fire, very friendly atmosphere, obliging landlord; garden with tables, swings, play area and summer help-yourself barbecue; good food from hot or cold beef or pork roll to carvery and good puddings — get there early to eat; separate restaurant, booking essential; well kept Bass, Marstons Pedigree and a couple of other real ales; moorings, bedrooms in separate cottage block — good value, with good breakfasts *(Mr and Mrs P A Jones, Denise Plummer, Jim Froggatt)*

Hinckley, Leics [New Buildings; SP4294], *Greyhound*: Good young people's pub, with live trad jazz Weds, be-bop, mainstream and contemporary Thurs *(Graham Bush)*; [Coventry Rd (not far from M69 junction 1)], *Wharf*: Unspoilt many-roomed pub with collection of Toby jugs in pleasant lounge, basic bar area, old-world snug with beams and brasses; well kept Marstons Burton and Pedigree *(Graham Bush)*

Hoby, Leics [SK6717], *Blue Bell*: Tastefully modernised thatched pub, very friendly, with well kept Everards *(Dr and Mrs A K Clarke)*

☆ **Horbling**, Lincs [4 Spring Lane (off B1177); TF1135], *Plough*: Almost unique in being owned by Parish Council; currently doing well, with cheap well presented bar food from toasted sandwiches to mixed grills, well kept Greene King IPA and Abbot and guest beers on handpump, cosy and friendly comfortable lounge with log fire, darts and other games in lively public bar; children in eating area; bedrooms cheap but comfortable *(Nic James, Anthony Barnes, A B Barton, LYM)*

Horncastle, Lincs [Bull Ring; TF2669], *Bull*: Part of a country-town hotel (with separate carvery), the comfortable L-shaped pub part has green leatherette wall settles, oak armchairs, stools, and varnished oval tables; exceptionally pleasant bar and food service, well kept Bass and Stones on handpump, decent straightforward food inc omelettes, curry, steak and specials *(Frank Cummins)*

Hose, Leics [Bolton Lane; SK7329], *Black Horse*: A beer-drinkers' favourite, with particularly well kept Home Bitter and Mild in classic no-frills village local; three rooms — usually two in use, both with roaring coal fires; settles on red-tiled floor, crisps kept in ancient Beeston Crisp Co tins (no proper bar food), back skittle alley and garden *(Richard Sanders, Dr C T Ankcorn)*

☆ **Hough on the Hill**, Lincs [SK9246], *Brownlow Arms*: Attractive pub in peaceful picturesque village; sofas and comfortable chairs in relaxing lounge, separate bar, wide range of good value well cooked and presented food in bar and restaurant, friendly welcome, efficient service; attractive bedrooms with lovely breakfasts, reasonable prices *(Andy and Jill Kassube, Mrs Anne Brown)*

Hoveringham, Notts [Main St (off A612); SK6946], *Marquis of Granby*: Warmly welcoming village local with fresh home cooking, also sandwiches, salads and ploughman's, Marstons Pedigree and guest beers *(Andy and Jill Kassube)*

Hungarton, Leics [SK6807], *Black Boy*: Pleasant, rustic local with lunchtime and evening bar food inc home-made specials, grills and choice of filled cobs *(A R M Moate)*

Husbands Bosworth, Leics [A427 Market Harborough—Lutterworth, junction A50; SP6484], *Bell*: Pleasantly decorated L-shaped bar in clean pub with lots of brass, log fire, friendly helpful staff, Ansells Mild and Ind Coope Burton, freshly cooked and liberally served food from sandwiches to steaks *(A E Alcock)*

Huthwaite, Notts [Woodend, N of village; SK4560], *Woodend*: Popular pub with high-backed settles, unusual bottle collection, friendly atmosphere; cheap Stones beer, massive helpings of good bar food, big car park *(Mr and Mrs P B Dowsett)*

Ingham, Lincs [off B1398; SK9483], *Black Horse*: 200-year-old former cottages, with good attractively priced food from sandwiches up in lounge, till 10pm, well kept Marstons Pedigree and Tolly; traditional public bar with fruit machine and juke box; garden *(Melvyn Payne)*; [High St], *Inn on the Green*: Fully refurbished on village green, wide choice of bar food inc game pie, home-made Mexican, Chinese and Indian dishes, good steaks; wise to book Sat *(Andy and Jill Kassube)*

Ketton, Leics [SK9704], *Northwick Arms*: Friendly local, bar food inc huge helpings of fish and chips *(Margaret and Trevor Errington)*

Kilby Bridge, Leics [A50 S of Leicester; SP6097], *Navigation*: Well maintained pub with friendly atmosphere, good furniture and huge fish in tank in lounge; Burton ale and good, reasonably priced bar food *(Mel and Phil Lloyd)*

Kneesall, Notts [SK7064], *Angel*: Two roomy and comfortably done-up connecting bars, Whitbreads Castle Eden on handpump, interesting bar food at reasonable prices *(Denise Plummer, Jim Froggatt)*

Knipton, Leics [SK8231], *Red House*: Beautifully proportioned former hunting lodge looking over pretty village close to Belvoir Castle; orthodox bar furnishings, but good value food from soup, bacon sandwiches and decent ploughman's through curries with basmati rice or venison and juniper pie to steaks; well kept Ind Coope Burton and Marstons Pedigree on handpump, unobtrusive piped music, a welcoming tribe of dogs; restaurant *(BB)*

☆ **Lambley**, Notts [Church St; SK6245], *Woodlark*: Well preserved and interestingly laid out, with a cheerful welcome for strangers and outstanding value cheap snacks, relaxing and quiet; well kept Home ales, navy memorabilia, wide range of pub games inc pool room, table skittles and skittle alley; children in annexe *(BB)*

Laneham, Notts [SK8076], *Butchers Arms*: Old pub with two lounges, bar with pool table and so forth, and beams, gleaming furniture and copper, old photographs, horse brasses, and inglenook fireplace; Ind Coope Burton, Marstons Pedigree and Tetleys on handpump and tasty, good helpings of straightforward bar food *(David and Ruth Hollands)*

Langham, Leics [Bridge St; SK8411], *Noel Arms*: Well kept Ruddles beers from the neighbouring Watneys-owned brewery and bar food inc help-yourself buffet laid out on long table in comfortable low-ceilinged lounge divided by log fire; smart covered terrace, restaurant *(LYM)*

Leadenham, Lincs [High St; A17 Newark—Sleaford; SK9552], *George*: Remarkable range of several hundred whiskies, a good choice of wines by the glass inc their own direct German imports, and well kept Greene King IPA, Ruddles County and Theakstons Old Peculier on handpump, fair-priced and quickly served food from sandwiches to steaks in unassuming bar, side games room, piped music, restaurant; maybe weekend disco in adjoining barn; bedrooms plain but good value; good breakfasts, for non-residents too *(Andy and Jill Kassube, LYM — more reports please)*

☆ **Leicester** [Silver St], *Globe*: Period features inc gas lighting and original woodwork, but rather more comfort than the original; reasonably priced lunchtime food upstairs, well kept Everards real ale with a guest beer such as Adnams *(Steve Waters, Andy and Jill Kassube, Richard Sanders, LYM)*

☆ **Leicester** [Melton Rd (A607 N, corner of Gipsy Rd); edge of city], *Melton*: Large well run Asian-owned Victorian pub with interesting back Simba grill (Thurs—Sun evenings, 7—11), where chef from Bombay, working in front of you and using proper tandoori oven, cooks authentic good food inc tikkas, excellent nan, chilli dishes and kebabs with traditional sauces; no cutlery — use right hand for eating; well kept Marstons Burton, Pedigree and Border Mild on handpump *(Mr and Mrs P A Jones)*

☆ **Leicester** [Belgrave Gate (nr flyover)], *Black Swan*: Recently refurbished by Hoskins, with lots of pine furniture, sawdust on floor and little overt comfort — but pleasant atmosphere; welcoming licensees, full range of Hoskins ales and guest beers such as Camerons; two games machines, basic food *(Mr and Mrs P A Jones, Joan and Michel Hooper-Immins)*

Leicester [Belgrave Rd (A6, N)], *Balmoral*: Asian-owned pub with good kebabs in lounge from back Simba grill; no cutlery — use right hand for eating; keg beer *(Lorna and Ashley Feroze)*; [Welford Rd], *Bricklayers Arms*: Busy, lively pub with well kept beer *(Richard Sanders)*; [Newarke St, opp Phoenix Theatre], *Magazine*: Front bar with panelled lobby entrance, back bar with food and occasional folk music; oldish decor and posters on walls from various theatre/local productions; Bass tapped from the cask, tables in courtyard, parking in multi-storey car park *(Graham Bush)*; [Melton Rd (A607 N)], *Owl & the Pussycat*: Recently de-open-planned, with locals' bar and comfortable lounge; cobs and snacks Sat lunchtime, successful weekday business lunches, well kept Shipstones Bitter and Mild on handpump *(Mr and Mrs P A Jones)*; [Duns Gate (nr Polytechnic)], *Pump & Tap*: Sawdust on floor, plain tables, chairs and benches, very lively young atmosphere, foreign bottled beers, Allied real ales on handpump, piped rock and jazz, occasional live bands *(Graham Bush)*; [Charles St], *Rainbow & Dove*: Large brightly decorated open-plan bar divided into two, with full range of Hoskins beers and a guest such as Wadworths 6X, all kept well, and a couple of ciders; staff decked out in brewery aprons, weekday lunchtime bar food improving under new landlord; popular with students, parking difficult *(M L Hooper-Immins, Richard Sanders, Mel and Phil Lloyd, Pete Storey)*; [Leire St/Harrison Rd], *Victoria Jubilee*: Local with simple front bar (dominoes and darts) and comfortable lounge (occasional live music); consistently well kept Marstons Burton, Pedigree, Merrie Monk, Border Mild and winter Owd Rodger; no bar food, though Asian barbecues in summer in large, flagstoned back yard — excellent value *(Mr and Mrs P A Jones)*

☆ **Lincoln** [26 Broadgate], *Jolly Brewer*: Fascinating art deco pub given real atmosphere by its enthusiastic owners; vibrantly popular, with good choice of real ales — Everards Tiger and Old Original, Home, McEwans; bar food; busy Sat night, quiet on a Sun lunchtime *(Mr and Mrs P A Jones, N J D Bodiam, Reg Nelson)*

☆ **Lincoln** [Moor St (off A57 Sheffield rd nr racecourse)], *Queen in the West*: Pleasant back-street pub converted from farmhouse with military prints and miniatures in well decorated lounge, interesting sporting prints in public bar, welcoming atmosphere, well kept Marstons Pedigree, Theakstons XB and Old Peculier, Timothy Taylors Landlord, Wards Sheffield, reasonably priced simply home cooking *(Andy and Jill Kassube, BKA)*

☆ **Lincoln** [Steep Hill], *Browns Pie Shop*: Not a pub, as you can get a drink only if you're eating — but they do have Everards Tiger and Ruddles Best, and the food's very much worth knowing — home-made soup and pâté, spectacular pies (actually small casseroles with puff-pastry lids), vegetarian dishes, Sun lunch, good puddings especially bread and butter; helpful staff, pleasant traditional atmosphere *(Derek and Sylvia Stephenson, BKA, D L Parkhurst)*

☆ **Lincoln** [Union Rd; behind Castle], *Victoria*: Classic backstreet down-to-earth real ale drinkers' pub, with few concessions to luxury — just relaxed and warmly friendly, with half a dozen or more changing well kept real ales on handpump inc as regulars Batemans and Timothy Taylors, country wines, cheap and cheerful bargain lunchtime food changing daily — a no-frills pub with a heart of gold *(Sue Holland, Dave Webster, David and Ruth Hollands, Andy and Jill Kassube, Richard Sanders, Michael Rooke, Reg Nelson, Derek and Sylvia Stephenson)*

☆ **Lincoln** [2 Alfred St; off High St nr Jaguar garage], *City Vaults*: Hatch service of particularly well kept Wards ales, inc Mild, in simple but welcoming backstreet local, a former police house; lounge recently and attractively modernised in dark brown and cream with ornate red-on-cream tiles; separate dining area, cheap and nicely presented lunchtime food inc filled Yorkshire puddings, good atmosphere *(Sue Holland, Dave Webster, Andy and Jill Kassube, Richard Sanders, Reg Nelson, BB)*

Lincoln [25 Lindum Rd; (Wragby rd)], *Adam & Eve*: Large unspoilt pub tucked behind cathedral with two low-beamed atmospheric bars, smart prints, and curios; popular with young and old locals *(Reg Nelson, BKA)*; [44 Bailgate], *Duke William*: Converted row of oak-beamed cottages close to cathedral with friendly weekday evening atmosphere (can be busier weekends), lunchtime bar food, restaurant; new bedrooms *(Reg Nelson, Andy Kassube)*; [21 High St], *Golden Eagle*: Welcoming pub with well kept Batemans and decent bar food *(Richard Sanders)*; [Waterside North], *Green Dragon*: Noble waterside Tudor building — carved 16th-century facade gave its homelier name 'The Cat Garret'; modernised but attractively timbered and beamed bar, with John Smiths real ale, worth a look at quiet times (but fruit machines could be more discreetly placed, and tends to get crowded with young people in evening); locally popular restaurant *(Reg Nelson, LYM)*; [Broadgate], *Lindum*: Very basic 60s-style local — could do with some renovation, but good atmosphere; well kept Marstons Pedigree, McEwans 80/- and Wards on handpump; video juke box seems rather out of place *(Mr and Mrs P A Jones)*; [Bailgate], *Lion & Snake*: Reputedly the city's oldest pub, tastefully refurbished, nice atmosphere, real ale *(Reg Nelson)*; [Greetwell Gate], *Morning Star*: Friendly atmosphere in plain but well scrubbed and comfortable pub with well kept reasonably priced beer *(J D Maplethorpe)*; [Clasketgate, opp Theatre Royal], *Olde Crowne*: Lots of signed publicity shots, young lively customers, real ale *(Reg Nelson)*; [centre, off High St], *Still*: Interesting restored woodwork; very popular with young people weekend evenings; Mansfield ales on handpump *(Mr and Mrs P A Jones)*; [The Strait], *Straits*: Pleasant pub with polished wood floors and fire in winter; well kept Adnams Bitter, Everards Tiger and Old Original, well presented bar food, upstairs restaurant *(Andy Kassube)*; [83 Westgate], *Strugglers*: Old-fashioned basic two-roomed local; jolly atmosphere, well kept Bass on handpump *(Sue Holland, Dave Webster, Richard*

Sanders); [High St], *Treaty of Commerce*: Tudor building with oak beams, grand old stained glass, real etchings, lively pubby atmosphere, real ale, enthusiastic ladies' darts team *(Reg Nelson)*

Lissington, Lincs [TF1183], *White Hart*: Typical English pub with a lot of character, with usual bar meals, well kept Bass on handpump; can be very busy weekends *(Andy and Jill Kassube)*

Little Bowden, Leics [Kettering Rd (A6); SP7487], *Greyhound*: Pleasantly decorated bar, lounge and small smoking room; well kept Watneys-related real ales on handpump, reasonably priced bar food, restaurant, terrace and garden, car park *(A E Alcock)*

Little Bytham, Lincs [TF0118], *Willoughby Arms*: Free house with good simple food and pleasant garden overlooking fields *(E J and J W Cutting)*

☆ **Long Whatton**, Leics [SK4723], *Falcon*: Big comfortable bays of seats under stuffed animals and birds and other bric-a-brac; relaxing atmosphere, friendly, efficient service, good choice of bar food from well filled cobs to fine steaks, well kept Everards Old Original and Tiger; good restaurant area stepped up from lounge (booking advisable), coffee lounge *(Howard and Sue Gascoyne, Paul and Janet Waring)*

☆ **Loughborough**, Leics [The Rushes (A6); SK5319], *Swan in the Rushes*: No-frills town pub with outstanding range of well kept real ales such as Batemans Mild and XXXB, Border Exhibition, Darleys Dark Mild, Gales XXXD Mild, Hardys & Hansons Best Mild, Hull Mild, Marstons Pedigree and Merrie Monk, Tetleys and changing guest beers, also good range of foreign bottled beers; good value straightforward bar food, open fire, three high-ceilinged rooms, some entertaining domestic strife cartoons, down-to-earth chatty atmosphere — popular with students *(M L Hooper-Immins, Pete Storey, D P Ryan, John Laing, Andy and Jill Kassube, Richard Sanders, BB)*

☆ **Loughborough** [canal bank, about ¼ mile from Loughborough Wharf], *Albion*: Busy, welcoming, canalside local with friendly licensees, two rooms and central bar, white-washed walls, brasses and mirrors; well kept Banks's Mild and Bitter, Batemans Mild, Hoskins & Oldfields HOB and Old Navigation and Sam Smiths OB; good value bar food inc steak and kidney pie, lovely home-cooked beef rolls and occasional barbecues; friendly staff; wonderful budgie aviary in big courtyard; children welcome *(Pete Storey, Mr and Mrs P A Jones, Richard Sanders)*

Loughborough [Sparrow Hill], *Windmill*: Improved greatly by recent costly refurbishment, but has kept its atmosphere; Ansells and Ind Coope Burton on handpump *(Mr and Mrs P A Jones)*

Lount, Leics [A453 NE of Ashby de la Zouch; SK3819], *Ferrier Arms*: Consistently good even though building slightly over-restored *(Dave Braisted)*

Louth, Lincs [Westgate; TF3387], *Wheatsheaf*: Well kept pub with decent food and drink, good atmosphere *(John Bowdler)*

Lowdham, Notts [Plough Lane; SK6646],

Worlds End: Small, clean and friendly two-bar village pub, coal fire in lounge, some original features inc beams, well kept Marstons Pedigree on handpump; filled rolls lunchtime *(Karen Ann Ross, Philip Wood)*

Mansfield, Notts [Nottingham Rd (a mile from centre); SK5561], *Talbot*: Extensively refurbished open-plan pub raised dining area, rather trendy atmosphere as evening wears on — but still some quiet corners, good range of bar food inc casseroles and excellent puddings, particularly at lunchtime; well kept Shipstones *(Derek and Sylvia Stephenson)*

Maplebeck, Notts [signposted from A616/A617; SK7160], *Beehive*: Deep in the country, snug little beamed bar, clean and tidy but basic, with plain traditional furnishings; tables on small terrace with grassy bank running down to small stream, open fire, Mansfield real ale on handpump, free juke box; an idyllic spot *(Tim and Lynne Crawford, LYM)*

☆ **Mareham le Fen**, Lincs [A115; TF2861], *Royal Oak*: Beams and brasses in tastefully refurbished pub with pleasant atmosphere, open fire, friendly staff; well kept Batemans XB, XXB and XXXB, decent coffee, limited but good bar food in small restaurant *(R F Plater, Derek and Sylvia Stephenson, Michael Rooke)*

Market Bosworth, Leics [1 Park St; from centre follow Leicester and Hinckley signs; SK4003], *Olde Red Lion*: Chiefly notable for the good range of Hoskins beers, with other guest beers, this take-us-as-you-find-us L-shaped town bar also does fair-priced bar food from filled cobs and ploughman's to steaks (not Sun evening); bar billiards, piped music, tables and play area in sheltered courtyard, jazz 3rd Thurs of month; open all day; children welcome; bedrooms *(Mike and Wendy Proctor, Richard Sanders, E J Alcock, LYM)*

Market Deeping, Lincs [Bridge Foot; TF1310], *Old Coach House*: Good range of particularly well kept beers inc Batemans XXXB, Greene King IPA and Abbot and Marstons Pedigree on handpump; good bar food *(Nic James)*

Marston, Lincs [2 miles E of A1 just N of Grantham; SK8943], *Thorold Arms*: Straightforward pub with well kept Batemans XXXB, limited choice of good value bar food; children welcome *(Stan Edwards, Derek Patey)*

Moorgreen, Notts [SK4847], *Horse & Groom*: Recent alterations tastefully completed; pleasant atmosphere, efficient staff, well kept Hardys & Hansons, good bar food *(Alan Gough)*

Navenby, Lincs [car park behind is off East Rd; SK9858], *Kings Head*: Quiet, charming little pub with particularly nice lounge; good, home-cooked bar food, good restaurant *(Andy and Jill Kassube)*

Nettleham, Lincs [The Green; TF0075], *Plough*: Comfortable low-beamed village pub; hot and cold bar lunches — home-made pies a speciality; particularly well kept Batemans *(Andy and Jill Kassube)*

☆ **Newark**, Notts [Northgate; SK8054], *Malt Shovel*: Small but comfortably refurbished old-fashioned local, green-tiled outside, notable for well kept Timothy Taylors

Landlord, Wards Sheffield Best and regular guest beers; good lunchtime hot dishes, thick crusty sandwiches and Sun lunches, friendly welcome; nearby parking not easy *(Maureen and Steve Collins, Andy and Jill Kassube, Mr and Mrs P A Jones)*

Newark, *Queens Head*: Good atmosphere, friendly service, well kept John Smiths and wide choice of bar food *(Prof S Barnett)*

Normanton on Soar, Notts [A6006; SK5123], *Rose & Crown*: Nicely laid out waterside pub with Watneys-related real ales on handpump, good value food; popular with boating people *(Peter Corris)*

Normanton on Trent, Notts [SK7969], *Square & Compass*: Cosy village pub with pleasant atmosphere, friendly licensees, good value straightforward bar food from sandwiches up inc generous home-made steak and kidney pie and children's dishes; Mansfield Bitter and Mild, Stones, Theakstons, and Whitbreads Trophy; bedrooms *(Norman Edwardes)*

North Hykeham, Lincs [Lincoln Rd; SK9466], *Lincoln Green*: Large, popular pub with comfortable lounge, Home Bitter, good value lunchtime bar food generously served (not Sun) *(Andy and Jill Kassube)*

North Kilworth, Leics [4 1/2 miles from M1 junction 20; A427 towards Mkt Harborough; SP6183], *White Lion*: Pleasant, welcoming atmosphere, well kept Marstons Pedigree, good food inc decent home-made soups, excellent steak and onions in beer *(J P Cinnamond)*; [SP6184], *White Swan*: Pleasant canalside pub with good atmosphere, Watneys-related real ales, good range of bar food *(Gordon Theaker)*

North Luffenham, Leics [12 Church St; SK9303], *Horse & Pannier*: Pleasant but basic village pub with warm friendly atmosphere in listed building dating back to 1640, known locally as Nag 'n' Bag; good range of real ales *(Nic James)*

☆ **North Muskham**, Notts [Ferry Lane — just off A1 about 3 miles N of Newark; SK7958], *Muskham Ferry*: Lovely spot by River Trent, friendly efficient staff, good bar food, cold buffet and restaurant; flower-girt terrace, garden with play area, own moorings, slipway, private fishing; big car park *(PJP, Barbara and Norman Wells)*

Norton Disney, Lincs [Main St (off A46); SK8859], *St Vincent Arms*: Quiet little country pub with real fire, Adnams, Everards Old Original and guest beers on handpump, bar food inc good lamb and apricot pie and steaks, big back garden inc well equipped play area *(Andy and Jill Kassube)*

☆ **Nottingham** [Mansfield Rd], *Lincolnshire Poacher*: Several basic but well refurbished bar areas inc small wood-panelled snug and conservatory; particularly well kept Batemans and four or five guest real ales, good ciders, Continental lagers, bar food, very mixed clientele of all ages — as it's not big it can get crowded; open all day *(Richard Sanders, John L Laing, Roger Taylor, D P Ryan, Derek and Sylvia Stephenson, Wayne Brindle)*

☆ **Nottingham** [40 Broad St; corner of Lower Parliament St, on inner ring rd], *New Market*: The austerely neo-classical facade could be that of a bank — and you can save money here, on the commendably low drinks prices; only a lack of recent reports from readers has put this well kept pub out of the main entries this year — its food is simple and cheap, its Home Mild and Bitter and Youngers IPA and No 3 in perfect condition, its back bar comfortable and its utilitarian front bar worth a look; dogs allowed; children welcome; closed only 4.30—5.30 weekdays *(Richard Sanders, Wayne Brindle, LYM — more reports please)*

☆ **Nottingham** [Gt Northern Cl; just off London Rd (A60), opp junction with Station Rd], *Grand Central*: Imaginative conversion of former railway building, good atmosphere in two roomy railway-arch areas — one cocktailish, one pubbier with cold but well conditioned Ind Coope Burton and Tetleys on handpump; steps up to little row of snug booths in mock-up of Orient Express, bar food and rather elegant side dining area, some interesting cigarette cards, well reproduced pop music, good mix of ages; tables on tank-engine terrace *(BB)*

Nottingham [Wollaton Rd, Wollaton; SK5139], *Admiral Rodney*: Large panelled pub in 'village' enveloped by suburbs of Nottingham, with Home Mild and Bitter, limited but popular weekday lunchtime food Mon—Friday (not that cheap for area), morning coffee *(Nigel Gibbs)*; [Hucknall Lane, Bulwell; SK5344], *Apollo*: Warm, friendly welcome under new regime; good bar, well kept Home Bitter, good range of bar food *(Russell Allen)*; [Parliament St], *Blue Bell*: Well run with well kept Home ales, good value food, pleasant staff, jazz nights *(Richard Sanders)*; [Balloon Wood, Wollaton; SK5139], *Gondola*: Hearty welcome, good bar food inc special evenings *(Russell Allen)*; [Canal St], *Narrow Boat*: Island serving counter, portholes decor, entrance corridor with original prewar green tiles, pool and TV rooms; well kept Shipstones *(Graham Bush, Richard Sanders)*; [Mansfield Rd], *Peacock*: Nothing special about the character, but comfortably quiet, with well kept Home ales *(Wayne Brindle, Richard Sanders)*; [Nuthall Rd, Cinderhill; SK5343], *Red Lion*: Warm welcome from staff and locals, good range of wines and beers and good home-cooked bar food *(Russell Allen)*; [Castle Gate], *Royal Children*: Well kept Home ales, lovely original decor not smartened up; now has bar billiards as well as darts *(Graham Bush)*; [Sherwood Rise (B682)], *Royal Oak*: Friendly welcome, good service, good bar food; lively special games evenings with darts and outdoor skittles — mentally handicapped and others encouraged to join in, free food laid on *(Colin Rivis)*; [Maid Marion Way], *Salutation*: Plush modern front, but attractive genuinely ancient beamed and flagstoned back part; Whitbreads-related real ales and Marstons Pedigree, reasonably priced bar food — inc snacks even late evening; can get smoky when it's crowded; the old rock cellars can be visited at quiet times by arrangement *(Wayne Brindle, Ian Phillips, BB)*; [Market Pl], *Talbot*: Massive unpretentious Yates Wine Lodge, run extremely efficiently, with very good lively atmosphere — full of vibrant young people out for a good time;

good value ports (*Wayne Brindle, Mr and Mrs P A Jones*); [402 Derby Rd], *Three Wheatsheaves*: Rambling old pub with flagstones, traditional furnishings, somewhat basic feel but good atmosphere; bar food, well kept Shipstones, summer lunchtime barbecues daily in big garden; good parking (*Andrew Stephenson, LYM*); [Trent Bridge], *Trent Bridge*: Has been popular for well kept Allied real ales, dining area with several decent hot dishes, and corner bar with cricket memorabilia (especially Larwood), but as we went to press in summer 1990 had been closed for restyling in conjunction with building of new adjoining cricket-ground stand (*BKA, Andy and Jill Kassube — more reports please*); [Upper Parliament St], *Turf*: Traditional simple single room with well kept Shipstones; tiled facade (*Graham Bush*)

Oakham, Leics [North St; SK8508], *Wheatsheaf*: Two-part, town-centre pub with open fire in comfortable lounge; well kept Adnams on handpump, changing menu of tasty food, friendly licensee (*Julian Holland*)

☆ **Old Somerby**, Lincs [SK9633], *Fox & Hounds*: Attractive pub, warm welcome, well kept real ales such as Marstons Pedigree and Merrie Monk and Ruddles County on handpump, good range of reasonably priced bar food inc spectacular long filled rolls called submarines; several rooms with copper-topped tables and hunting-print wall banquettes (*Derek and Sylvia Stephenson*)

Ollerton, Notts [Market Pl, off A614; SK6667], *White Hart*: Refurbished local with attentive landlord, good food and well kept beer; handy for Sherwood Forest area (*M Bevan*)

Osbaston, Leics [A447; SK4204], *Gate*: Recently attractively refurbished country pub, pretty wallpaper and comfortable chairs and sofas; good freshly made sandwiches from a decent reasonably priced menu, very popular family Sun lunches, Marstons beers (*Brian and Genie Smart*)

Plumtree, Notts [just off A606 S of Nottingham; SK6132], *Griffin*: Ample helpings of good value straightforward food in clean pub with good beer; piped music could be quieter, and even follows you into the lavatories (*E J Cutting, R J Haerdi*)

☆ **Potterhanworth**, Lincs [Cross St; TF0565], *Chequers*: Pleasant village free house, cheerful licensees, wide range of good value bar food, creamy Mansfield Old Baily; piano in lounge bar (*J D Maplethorpe, Andy and Jill Kassube*)

☆ **Preston**, Leics [High St; SK8602], *Fox & Hounds*: Well kept 16th-century free house with plenty of character in delightful stone village; nicely presented and generously served good food inc three soups, lots of vegetarian dishes, bargain children's helpings; several real ales inc Adnams, chatty licensee; plenty of tables in garden — also amiable great dane and rabbit (*R Grey, S T L Coupland, Eric Locker*)

Quorndon, Leics [Meeting St; SK5616], *Blacksmiths Arms*: Popular two-roomed old pub, low ceilings, well kept Marstons Pedigree, lunchtime bar food (*Richard Sanders*); [corner Meeting St/A6], *Royal Oak*: Popular pub with small snug at front,

particularly well kept Bass and M & B Mild, bar food (*Richard Sanders*); [Main St (A6)], *White Hart*: Pleasant little pub with slightly limited but good value food, real ale on handpump; can get a bit crowded in evening (*Andy and Jill Kassube*)

Ratby, Leics [Boroughs Rd; SK5105], *Plough*: Cheerful unpretentious village pub with lively Fri night sing-alongs, well kept Marstons real ales, simple cheap lunchtime food and good play area in big back garden; decidedly a local, though (*Janet and Paul Waring, LYM*)

Ratcliffe Culey, Leics [SP3299], *Gate*: Very friendly, cosy village pub with two bars and eating area, low ceilings, open fires, fish tank and baby grand; Ind Coope Burton on handpump, good range of good value food from vegetarian dishes to bargain monster steaks; swings in garden; children welcome (*Karen Bettesworth, Chris Down*)

Redmile, Leics [SK8036], *Olde Windmill*: Friendly village pub with pleasant ex-miner landlord, good range of well kept real ales such as Hook Norton Old Hookey, Mansfield Riding and Marstons Pedigree, plain but good value bar food; small restaurant, back terrace (*Dr Keith Bloomfield*); [Main St], *Peacock*: Friendly village pub with well kept real ales such as Marstons, Ruddles and Timothy Taylors, good choice of decent reasonably priced food from scrupulously clean kitchen; stripped pine woodwork, open fires, tasteful ornaments and pictures, piped music, and friendly, efficient service; good value restaurant, tables outside; children in no-smoking family room; both these pubs are in a quiet village close to Belvoir Castle (*S Wooler, Dr and Mrs A M Evans*)

Rolleston, Notts [SK7452], *Crown*: Fine old building with lots of beams in lounge, well kept Marstons Pedigree, popular food (not after 1.30 Sun) (*John C Baker*)

Rothley, Leics [The Green; SK5812], *Royal Oak*: Large village pub on green with wide choice of good value lunchtime food, Adnams, Everards Tiger and Mild and a guest beer on handpump, and occasional live folk music; ample car parking; handy for steam rly, chapel of Knights Templar and Bradgate Park (*Mr and Mrs P A Jones*)

☆ **Rothwell**, Lincs [Caistor Rd (A46); TF1599], *Nickerson Arms*: Very pleasant relaxed atmosphere in friendly and pleasantly decorated stone-built village local, good choice of well kept ales inc Batemans, Tetleys, Timothy Taylors Landlord and regular guest beers, simple but good weekday lunchtime bar food inc fine steak and kidney pie with fresh vegetables, and decent trifle; children's room, outside seating (*Andy and Jill Kassube, Derek and Sylvia Stephenson*)

Ruddington, Notts [off A60 S of Nottingham, N edge of village; SK5733], *Victoria*: Village local, recently tastefully refurbished, with well kept Bass (*Chris Raisin*)

Salmonby, Lincs [TF3273], *Crossed Keys*: Green leatherette banquettes in bays of simply decorated lounge extending back into bigger dining area, pool and other games in public bar, big windows, Ruddles Best on handpump, unobtrusive piped pop music, cheap simple food with bargain steaks Wed evening, friendly staff, tables and play area in garden behind; bedrooms cheap, clean and comfortable, with big breakfasts *(BB)*

☆ **Saxilby**, Lincs [Canal Side (A57); SK8975], *Bridge*: Welcoming canalside pub with good home-made food from particularly good value big brown rolls filled with hot roast beef, salad and blue cheese dressing to hot pies, fresh trout, haddock and so forth, also good steak and seafood restaurant; well kept Marstons Pedigree and Ruddles Best and County, good well kept garden *(Mr and Mrs P A Jones, Andy and Jill Kassube)*

Saxilby, *Sun*: Recently refurbished open-plan Whitbreads pub with well kept Marstons Pedigree and Whitbreads Castle Eden on handpump; specialises in Indian dishes such as beef Madras, rogan josh, tandoori mixed grill, as well as usual pub food; River Witham just over rd *(Mr and Mrs J B Jones)*

Scotter, Lincs [High St; SE8801], *Gamekeeper*: Old pub, with five connecting rooms on different levels — beams, panelling, Delft shelves and abundant china, stuffed birds and animals, varied seating; has been popular for well kept Darleys, Wards and Youngers on handpump and wide choice of food from sandwiches up, but no recent reports *(News please)*; [The Green], *White Swan*: Friendly staff, tasty bar food, extension inc restaurant with bedrooms above; jazz Mon *(J A Calvert)*

Seaton, Leics [off B672 Caldecott—S Luffenham; SP9098], *George & Dragon*: Small village free house with guest beers such as Greene King IPA, Marstons Pedigree and Youngers IPA, wide range of attractively priced bar food cooked to order and generously served, very clean lavatories *(Michael and Jenny Back)*

Sewstern, Leics [just off B767 Colsterworth—Melton Mowbray; SK8821], *Blue Dog*: Small but comfortable lounge bar, good range of home-cooked food, John Smiths and Marstons Pedigree; bedrooms *(M and J Back)*

Shackerstone, Leics [SK3706], *Rising Sun*: Peaceful village pub with panelled lounge, restaurant in converted barn, exposed brickwork, well kept Marstons; very busy at peak times; car park; nr Steam Rly Centre *(Graham Richardson)*

Sharnford, Leics [B4114; SP4791], *Falconer*: Well kept Ansells Mild and Bitter and Tetleys on handpump, wide choice of good value food, quieter tables in wine-bar area behind bar *(Ted George, BB)*

☆ **Shawell**, Leics [not far from M6 junction 1; village signed off A5/A427 roundabout — turn right in village; SP5480], *White Swan*: Oak panelling, royal blue upholstery, coal fire and two log-effect gas fires in bar, separate lounge and games room; good range of well kept real ales inc Adnams Broadside and Banks's, good well presented food (very popular for this at weekends), friendly staff *(Ted George, Cdr Patrick Tailyour)*

Shearsby, Leics [A50 Leicester—Northampton; SP6290], *Chandlers Arms*: Friendly modernised pub in delightful village, Adnams, Boddingtons, Marstons Pedigree, good value food

lunchtime and evenings, with quite a few curries *(Mel and Phil Lloyd)*

☆ **Sheepy Magna**, Leics [Main St (B4116); SK3201], *Black Horse*: Decently kept village pub with generous helpings of good value bar food inc good cheapish steaks, generous home-made steak and kidney pie and wide choice of cheeses for ploughman's; well kept Marstons Pedigree and Border on handpump, games in lively public bar, family area, tables outside, plenty of parking *(Geoff Lee, Mr and Mrs J Back, LYM)*

Shepshed, Leics [6 Ashby Rd; SK4719], *Delisle Arms*: Warm, friendly pub with receptive locals; consistently good food, live music each Thursday fortnight *(Alex Slack)*

Sibson, Leics [A444 N; SK3500], *Millers*: Much modernised, with pleasant rustle of water from slowly turning millwheel; bar food seven days — not cheap, but very generously served *(Genie and Brian Smart)*

☆ **Sileby**, Leics [Swan St; SK6015], *White Swan*: Comfortable and welcoming book-lined dining lounge with generous helpings of enterprising bar food (not Sun or Mon) inc home-made bread, good pies, casseroles and puddings, with a particularly wide evening choice *(SJ)*

☆ **Skegness**, Lincs [Vine Rd, Seacroft (off Drummond Rd); TF5660], *Vine*: Pleasant, relaxing bar with good atmosphere in well run 17th-century inn where Lord Tennyson stayed; well kept Batemans XB and XXXB, good but limited bar food from dining room (macaroni cheese, ham and turkey salad, fish pie, charlotte russe all recommended); pictures of variety artistes who've stayed here while playing Skeg; bedrooms *(Derek and Sylvia Stephenson)*

Somerby, Leics [Main St; SK7710], *Stilton Cheese*: Good, friendly service, food inc good Sun lunch with bargain price for children and OAPs *(Genie and Brian Smart)*

South Kilworth, Leics [Rugby Rd; SP6081], *White Hart*: Well kept, plain little pub with good simple home-cooked food at reasonable prices, well kept Banks's Bitter; small dining room *(Cdr Patrick Tailyour)*

☆ **South Luffenham**, Leics [10 The Street; off A6121 at Halfway House, then first right; SK9402], *Boot & Shoe*: Friendly village local with comfortable, rambling stripped-stone bar, good log fire, well kept Greene King Abbot and Tolly, friendly service, steps up to softly lit no-smoking eating area with limited choice of bar food from soup and starters to gammon steaks; also more upmarket evening restaurant (not Mon) run as quite separate operation; seats in neat small garden, pool in public bar; no dogs — friendly pub alsatian called Bruno; children welcome; four simple bedrooms, sharing two bathrooms — good breakfasts *(M and J Back, Gwen and Peter Andrews, D P and M E Cartwright, Michael Thomson, BB)*

☆ **South Rauceby**, Lincs [Main St; TF0245], *Bustard*: Nice old stone building, much modernised inside with red plush seating, crossed sabres, decorative plates, copper and brass houseplant holders, pretty little pencil sketches of birds — and of course some bustard pictures; appealing bar food from doorstep sandwiches using home-baked bread to steaks, quite quickly served, with good choice of puddings; log fires, well kept

Ruddles Best and County on handpump, maybe local Martins; pleasant piped music — operatic highlights and so forth; attractive sheltered garden *(A and J Heaphy, Philip Harrison, Andy and Jill Kassube, P Williams, S Berrisford, BB)*

South Thoresby, Lincs [(about a mile off A16); TF4077], *Vine*: Pleasant, welcoming pub with reasonably priced food inc nice home-made pies; Batemans XB and guests such as Timothy Taylors Landlord and Woodforde Norfolk Pride on handpump; children in dining room; bedrooms *(Derek and Sylvia Stephenson)*

Southrey, Lincs [TF1366], *Riverside*: Nice family pub close to River Wirham; good value meals inc good steaks, small restaurant (booking advised) *(Andy and Jill Kassube)*

☆ **Southwell**, Notts [Church St (A612); SK6953], *Bramley Apple*: Recently pleasantly refurbished on bramley apple theme, inc a specially made carpet with an apple-and-blossom carpet; bar and restaurant sensibly divided by stained-glass screens; good value food such as roast beef carved from the joint, fish, ham and steaks; Batemans XB and XXXB and Marstons Pedigree on handpump *(Dr Keith Bloomfield, Derek and Sylvia Stephenson)*

☆ **Southwell**, *Saracens Head*: Interesting old THF hotel (where Charles I spent his last free night), with well kept John Smiths on handpump, straightforward bar lunches in main beamed Smoke Room bar which has a good deal of character, pleasant young Italian staff; children in eating area or restaurant; bedrooms comfortable and well kept, though some are small and none are cheap (but no extra charge for room service) *(ILP, Andy and Jill Kassube, LYM)*

Spalding, Lincs [TF2422], *Bull*: Large and modern with comfortable red plush furnishings; very friendly bar staff, good food, popular with locals *(Sidney and Erna Wells)*

Spilsby, Lincs [High St; TF4066], *White Hart*: Well kept Bass and Stones and short reasonably priced choice of decent fresh bar food inc Grimsby fish, in typical market-town hotel comfortably done out in pink plush *(Frank Cummins)*

☆ **Stamford**, Lincs [Broad St; TF0207], *Lord Burghley*: Bubbling atmosphere in well laid out and splendidly furnished town-centre pub with well kept Adnams, Greene King Abbot and IPA and a guest such as Fullers London Pride, good choice of attractively priced bar food inc well filled lunchtime rolls and good steak sandwich, friendly efficient service, small sheltered garden with summer barbecues; no dogs — except Jess, the huge pub dog *(T Mansell, M L Hooper-Immins, Wayne Brindle)*

Stamford [High St, St Martins], *Anchor*: Old stone inn next to river bridge, tastefully modernised with one long bar, good service, well kept beer, bar food; bedrooms *(T Mansell)*; *Hole in the Wall*: Small, friendly L-shaped bar with old tables, chairs and settles, good choice of beers inc Marstons Pedigree and Owd Rodger, good wine list at reasonable prices, good choice of food, consistently pleasant service *(M Morgan)*

Stanton under Bardon, Leics [Main St; 1 1/2 miles from M1 junction 22, off A50 towards Coalville; SK4610], *Old Thatched*: Large, friendly open-plan thatched pub divided into various areas, one with open fire; well kept Marstons Pedigree and Border Mild on handpump, bar food inc good grills (Mon to Sat; Sun lunch if booked) *(Richard Sanders)*

☆ **Staunton in the Vale**, Notts [SK8043], *Staunton Arms*: Attractive open-plan refurbishment, with interesting partitions, raised dining area with good reasonably priced food; well kept Marstons Pedigree, Tetleys and guest beer such as Ringwood, good service *(Derek and Sylvia Stephenson)*

Stoke Golding, Leics [High St; SP3997], *Three Horseshoes*: Roomy canalside bar (also cocktail bar and restaurant) which has been liked for friendly staff, good value well cooked bar food even Sun evening, well kept Watneys-related real ales and Marstons Pedigree, and a welcome for children; but no recent reports *(News please)*

Stoney Stanton, Leics [Long St; SP4894], *Blue Bell*: Popular, comfortable and welcoming local with well kept Everards Bitter, Tiger and Old Original on handpump, good value straightforward food running up to hefty steaks lunchtime and early evening; busy at weekends *(Mike Tucker)*; *Farmers Arms*: Local with lots of curios and stuffed animals in lounge, large bar with live rock music Fri, well kept Marstons beers *(Graham Bush)*

☆ **Stragglethorpe**, Notts [off A52 Nottingham—Radcliffe-on-Trent; SK6437], *Shepherds*: Large thatched Brewers Fayre family pub-restaurant with usual food and Whitbreads beers; notable for splendid facilities for children — family room has fenced-off play area well equipped with books and toys, garden has two separate good play areas, for different age-groups *(Roy Y Bromell, Graham Bush)*

☆ **Stretton**, Leics [Great North Rd (actually on A1); SK9416], *Ram Jam*: Outstanding value as civilised immediate escape from A1: smart all-day continental-style snack bar from breakfast-time on, with good value well chosen and well prepared snacks, fresh-ground coffee, fresh-squeezed orange and so forth, impressive service; for licensed hours, comfortably airy modern lounge bar — again, a civilised continental feel, not that of a traditional pub — with good choice of food served quickly from buffet counter, Ruddles Best and County on handpump, teak seats on terrace; adjoining restaurant; bedrooms comfortable and well equipped *(Tony Bland, BB)*

☆ **Stretton**, [village signed off A1], *Jackson Stops*: Very handy for the A1, yet tucked away in a quiet village; idiosyncratic and informal, with homely furnishings and a pleasantly mixed bag of rustic bygones, antlers and stuffed animal heads, well kept Ruddles Best and County and Sam Smiths OB on handpump, decent wines, open fires; even though service has not been uniformly welcoming and willing, and food (from lunchtime sandwiches to steaks) has not recently been such a high point as to justify in everyone's eyes the seating preference they give to diners, we do still rate this as a most appealing pub *(Lyn and Bill Capper, A S Maxted, LYM — more reports please)*

Stretton, *Shires*: Welcoming and well run

pub, of some character *(P F Dakin)*

Surfleet, Lincs [A16 nearby; TF2528], *Mermaid*: Well kept ales inc Ruddles and Shipstones, wide choice of food inc speciality filled crêpes; interesting church nearby, with leaning tower; bedrooms *(Dr Keith Bloomfield)*

Sutton Bonington, Leics, *Old Plough*: The licensees who made this roomy modern Shipstones pub very popular with readers have now moved to the Star in Gotham

☆ **Sutton Cheney**, Leics [Main St — off A447 3 miles S of Mkt Bosworth; SK4100], *Royal Arms*: Imposing village pub, friendly inside, with central bar, three smallish low-ceilinged rooms around it, two open fires, well kept Marstons and Shipstones on handpump, wide choice of bar food (not cheap, but worth it) inc masses of changing specials; can get smoky when busy at weekends; upstairs restaurant, family conservatory with wishing well, garden with children's play area *(Ken and Barbara Turner, J Beeken, Mandy and Mike Challis, Graham Richardson)*

☆ **Sutton Cheney** [Main St], *Hercules*: Wide range of frequently changing real ales inc rarities and one or two brewed for the pub, in cheerful refurbished bar; piped music, friendly licensees, dining area *(LYM)*

Sutton in Ashfield, Notts [Alfreton Rd; off M1 junction 28; SK5059], *Duke of Sussex*: Useful motorway break *(Angie and David Parkes)*

☆ **Sutton in the Elms**, Leics [Coventry Rd; B581/B4114 nr M69 junction 2 — OS Sheet 140 map reference 509937; SP5194], *Mill on the Soar*: Buoyant and friendly atmosphere in huge, bustling conversion of substantial watermill — stripped brickwork, some rugs and carpet on the flagstones, brown beams and joists festooned with china and copper, conservatory area, river views from upstairs restaurant, quickly served bar food until 10 (9.30 Sat) from sandwiches through popular hot dishes, Everards and guest ales, lots of space and interest outside; children welcome; bedrooms in separate comfortably modern block *(Theo Schofield, LYM — more reports please)*

Swayfield, Lincs [SK9922], *Royal Oak*: Friendly pub in small village, lots of character and big choice of usual bar food from ploughman's to steaks, generously served *(Andy and Jill Kassube)*

Syston, Leics [SK6311], *Gate Hangs Well*: Large pub with several small, snug rooms, traditional bar, old-fashioned conservatory overlooking terrace, big garden with tables looking over Wreake Valley; well kept Everards Tiger, Old Original, Beacon and guest beer, big skittle alley in former stables by disused canal *(Mr and Mrs P A Jones)*

☆ **Tattershall Thorpe**, Lincs [TF2259], *Blue Bell*: Attractive outside and in, very friendly landlord, good value bar food *(J D Maplethorpe, Andy and Jill Kassube)*

☆ **Thurcaston**, Leics [Leicester Rd; SK5610], *Wheatsheaf*: The Marshalls who made the Wheatsheaf at Woodhouse Eaves so popular with readers have now moved here: comfortable, clean and welcoming, well kept John Smiths, decent bar food from filled rolls to good specials and fine fresh steak and kidney pie *(Peter and Anne Storer, A G Norwell)*

Thurgarton, Notts [Southwell Rd; SK6949], *Red Lion*: Pleasant surroundings, friendly licensee, well kept John Smiths on handpump, good reasonably priced bar food *(E E Hemmings)*

Torksey, Lincs [Torksey Lock; SK8478], *White Swan*: Pretty country pub with hanging baskets, big front terrace with tables under yellow cocktail parasols; comfortable red plush seating and polished tables in dark-beamed main room with Turkey carpet, old photographs, golden-tiled serving area; friendly owner, decent piped music, welcoming atmosphere, attentive service, bar food inc good fresh sandwiches and spicy moussaka *(GB, CH)*

☆ **Tugby**, Leics [Main St; village signposted off A47 E of Leicester, bear right in village; SK7600], *Black Horse*: Good value home-made evening meals in cosy and attractively traditional small rooms of picturesque black-and-white thatched village pub, Ansells on handpump, friendly service, log fire; children welcome; closed lunchtime *(LYM)*

Tur Langton, Leics [off B6047; follow Kibworth signpost from village centre; SP7194], *Crown*: Well kept Bass, Marstons Pedigree and Shipstones in distinctive pub with attractive furnishings from an antique curved settle to the chintzy and unpubby lounge on the left; tables on pleasantly planted terraces and in sheltered back courtyard; restaurant; closed weekday lunchtimes *(LYM)*

Twycross, Leics [SK3305], *Curzon Arms*: Now very much a dining pub, with extensive choice of reasonably priced food; friendly staff, very popular in summer for its spacious lawn *(Mandy and Michael Challis)*

Underwood, Notts [nr M1 junction 27 via A608 towards Eastwood; SK4750], *Hole in the Wall*: Modernised hotel in mining village — comfortable, with good bar food, good beer and coal fires in winter; good adjoining restaurant; piped music can be loud, big car park; bedrooms *(Mr and Mrs P B Dowsett)*

☆ **Upper Hambleton**, Leics [village signposted from A606 on E edge of Oakham; SK9007], *Finches Arms*: Dining pub perched above Rutland Water (which now covers what used to be Lower Hambleton), with built-in button-back leatherette banquettes and open fire in knocked-through front bar, velvet curtain to restaurant extension with picture windows, tables on gravel terrace; good choice of well prepared bar food from sandwiches up, well kept Darleys Thorne, Wards Sheffield Best and Kirby and Vaux Samson on handpump *(M Morgan, Julian Holland, LYM)*

Uppingham, Leics [High St; SP8699], *Vaults*: Reasonably priced decent food in pleasant little beamed pub on village square; Marstons Pedigree, Tetleys; reasonably priced, decent food *(Dr John Innes)*

Wainfleet, Lincs [39 High St; TF5058], *Woolpack*: Friendly, obliging landlord, well kept Batemans Mild and XB (favoured here even by Mr and Mrs B themselves), good value bar food *(Dr K Bloomfield)*

Walkeringham, Notts [off B1403 — formerly the Brickmakers Arms); SK7792], *Brickmakers*: Popular, friendly place with homely decor, hard-working licensees, good fairly priced food from sandwiches up to fine restaurant dishes, well kept Tetleys Bitter and Mild, Bass Special and Stones; new bedrooms, with private baths *(Norman Edwardes)*

☆ **Waltham on the Wolds**, Leics [A607; SK8024], *Royal Horseshoes*: Not enough recent readers' reports to keep this sturdily furnished stone-built inn in the main entries; help-yourself carvery/buffet and other bar food (residents only, Sun evening) — some cheaper snacks would be welcome; well kept John Smiths on handpump, decent wines, a fair range of malts, piped music, three open fires, seats outside; children allowed in eating area; bedrooms comfortable, tidy and well equipped *(G Smith, Miss A Tress, LYM)*

Washingborough, Lincs [TF0270], *Ferry Boat*: Friendly village pub with reconstructed mill wheel; Watneys-related real ales, separate eating area with own bar and salad bar *(Andy and Jill Kassube)*

Welton, Lincs [Main St; TF0179], *Black Bull*: Old pub with RAF pictures, well kept Ansells and Tetleys on handpump; popular for its good steaks inc giant porterhouse and T-bone *(Andy and Jill Kassube)*

West Stockwith, Notts [SK7995], *Waterfront*: Superbly refurbished waterside pub with interesting good value food, decent beers *(Mr and Mrs P A Jones)*

Whitwick, Leics [SK4316], *Belfry*: Pleasant free house, nice spot *(Martin Aust)*

Wilford, Notts [Main Rd; SK5637], *Ferry*: large, popular pub by River Trent, view of Nottingham Castle; plush lounge, pleasant beamed and tiled main bar, well kept Shipstones, bar food *(Graham Bush)*

☆ **Wing**, Leics [Top St; signed off A6003 S of Oakham; SK8903], *Kings Arms*: Simple early 17th-century stonebuilt inn, refurbished by new owners last year; has had wide choice of home-cooked food from sandwiches to steaks, mixed grills and giant prawns, several well kept real ales inc Batemans and Greene King on handpump, and good log fires; small but interesting medieval turf maze nearby *(LYM — reports on new regime please)*

Woodborough, Notts [Main St; SK6347], *Nags Head*: Delightful olde worlde village pub with quiet, comfortable atmosphere, good service and wide choice of bar food *(TWG)*

Woodhall Spa, Lincs [Kirkstead; Tattersall Rd (B1192 Woodhall Spa—Coningsby); TF1963], *Abbey Lodge*: Attractively if rather darkly decorated warm and cosy food pub with good sized tasty bar meals, restaurant *(A and J Heaphy, J D Maplethorpe, Patrick Godfrey)*

☆ **Woodhouse Eaves**, Leics [off B591 S of Loughborough; SK5214], *Bulls Head*: Popular pub, nicely decorated and furnished, well placed in attractive village; big hot and cold food display with wide range of attractive salads, sandwiches on granary bread, hot roast beef, fresh salmon, home-made puddings and so forth; good table service by friendly staff, clean lavatories, big car park *(J and B Grove, Martin Aust)*

Woodhouse Eaves [Brand Hill, leading up past the end of Main St], *Wheatsheaf*: Civilised open-plan country pub with good open fires, plush seating, lots of sporting prints, tables out in floodlit former coachyard; rated well in previous editions for decent bar food and well kept real ales, but the former tenants are now operating instead at the Wheatsheaf, Thurcaston and Black Swan in Ashover (Derbys) *(LYM)*

☆ **Woolsthorpe**, Lincs [the one nr Belvoir; signposted off A52 Grantham—Nottingham; SK8435], *Rutland Arms*: Quite large welcoming pub, also known as the Dirty Duck, in quiet Vale of Belvoir setting by disused Grantham Canal; smart, relaxed lounge with some high-backed settles, hunting prints and brasses, very popular midweek with older people; family extension with old furniture, open fire, video juke box, bric-a-brac on walls and windows; quite good range of reasonably priced bar food, well kept Whitbreads Castle Eden on handpump, two pool tables in annexe; play equipment on large lawn *(Howard and Sue Gascoyne, Dr Keith Bloomfield, Gary Phillips)*

Wrangle, Lincs [TF4251], *Angel*: Popular but not overcrowded country pub, recently refurbished, with clean, warm atmosphere, good value food, good choice of local beers inc Batemans; children's play area out by pony paddock outside; attractive bedrooms — residents made to feel part of the family, with mammoth breakfasts *(Mr and Mrs J M Luckett)*

Wymondham, Leics [off B676 E of Melton Mowbray; SK8518], *Hunters*: Good roadside pub with open fire and cosy atmosphere; well kept Bass, Greene King IPA and Abbot, good food in bar and restaurant *(Ian Pendlebury)*

Wysall, Notts [off A60 at Costock, or A6006 at Wymeswold; SK6027], *Plough*: Popular, friendly village pub with witty young landlady; cosy, with built-in cushioned wall seats, wrought-iron tables, assorted wood chairs, log fire, old glass ceiling lights and lovely oak beams; well kept McEwans 70/- and Shipstones (Mr S said to drink here), French doors on to terrace and lawn above road; occasional Morris dancing *(Chris Raisin)*

Lincolnshire *see* Leicestershire

Midlands (Northamptonshire, Warwickshire and West Midlands)

Free houses and pubs tied to the big national brewing combines both generally work out a few pence cheaper for drinks here than the national average. But the real bargains here tend to be found in pubs tied to smaller regional or local breweries, based in or just outside the area – such as Banks's and Hansons, Batemans, Bathams, Donnington, Everards, Hook Norton and Hoskins. Aside from the fabulously cheap own-brews from the Old Swan in Netherton, it was a Banks's pub (the very quaint and aptly named Crooked House in Himley) which gave us our cheapest pint in the area – followed closely by the Brewery in Langley, which is indeed the brewery for two of the beers sold by a small local chain called Holt Plant & Deakins (actually part of the Allied national combine, but with quite a distinctive identity). Food prices here are low, too: we found one in three pubs comfortably within our £1 target for cheap snacks or our £3 target for bargain main dishes – or more usually both. Pub food here often scores highly on quality, as at the rambling Bell at Alderminster, the civilised Falcon in Fotheringhay, the sensitively restored Snooty Fox at Lowick (a new main entry), the pleasantly civilised canalside Fleur de Lys at Lowsonford (serving food all day in summer – another new main entry), the lively Slug & Lettuce in Stratford, the friendly stone-built Three Conies at Thorpe Mandeville, and the cheerful Pheasant at Withybrook. Other newcomers in this edition of the Guide include the welcoming old Bulls Head at Clipston, the Red Lion at Crick (very useful for the motorway), the cheery canalside Navigation at Lapworth, the vibrant old Ship in Oundle (wearing its years very lightly) and the relaxing and notably well run Falcon in Priors Marston; all these also have good value food – in very varying styles. Several other pubs to note particularly this year include the Old Coach House at Ashby St Ledgers (a pub which has polarised readers sharply in past years – the new licensees look like bringing it firmly down on the right side of the fence); the Vine in Brierley Hill (refurbishment of this classic – and cheap – Black Country brewery tap seems to be widening its appeal without spoiling it); the Case is Altered at Five Ways (a time-warp gem); the Red Lion at Little Compton (simple but civilised – good value as a place to stay); the Wharf at Old Hill (chatty and warm-hearted, with a good assembly of S&N and some other beers); and the own-brew Old Swan at Netherton (its new landlady was popular when she ran the Wharf before S&N took that pub over). The Little pubs are always good fun; besides the main entry at Netherton, there are several of this expanding small chain dotted through the Lucky Dip entries at *the end of the chapter. Other Dips currently of particular note include the Montagu Arms at Barnwell, Golden Cross at Bearley, Dog & Doublet at Bodymoor Heath, Navigation at Cosgrove, Old Windmill in Coventry, British Oak among others in Dudley, White Lion at Hampton in Arden, reopened Holly Bush at Priors Marston, Rose & Crown at Ratley, Tom o' the Wood at Rowington, Beacon in Sedgley, Vane Arms at Sudborough, Blue Boar at Temple Grafton, Crossroads at Weedon and Old Watling at Willey; the patrician Shakespeare is probably the current pick of several strong Stratford contenders.*

ALDERMINSTER (War) SP2348 Map 4
Bell ⊗

A34 Oxford–Stratford

The menu, much praised by readers, changes frequently in this friendly Cotswold pub; typically it might include sandwiches, soup such as bortsch or pea and mint (£1.95), various pâtés (£3.50), ploughman's (£3.25), seafood and mushroom scallop (£3.95), salads (from £5), and lots of changing specials such as braised sausage in red wine (£5), fresh fish (from £6.50), creamy lamb and almond casserole, chicken in tarragon or steak, kidney and oyster pie (all £6.75), and calves liver in cream and herbs (£7.95), with several puddings such as peach and almond tart (£2.50); they only use fresh produce and have no fried food at all. But it's also a pleasant place just for a drink – the communicating areas of the spacious bar, well refurbished in recent years and stripped back to their original flagstones and wooden floors, have small landscape prints and swan's-neck brass-and-globe lamps on the cream walls, plenty of stripped slatback chairs around wooden tables (each with a plant on it), a panelled oak settle, little vases of flowers, and a solid fuel stove in a stripped brick inglenook. Flowers IPA and Original on handpump, and a good range of wines (from Berry Bros & Rudd); good service; dominoes. There are tables under cocktail parasols on the sheltered grass, and a large car park; four miles from Stratford. Half the restaurant is no-smoking. *(Recommended by M A and C R Starling, Sarah Bullard, Mr and Mrs G J Rice, Brian Skelcher, Joy and Peter Heatherley, John Bowdler, S V Bishop, MC, John Knighton, Laurence Manning, J Harvey Hallam, Mrs Simon Turner, C A Holloway)*

Free house   Licensees Keith and Vanessa Brewer   Real ale   Meals and snacks (12–2, 7–10)   Restaurant tel Alderminster (078 987) 414   Children welcome   Open 12–2.30, 7–11; closed most evenings 26 Dec–3 Jan, inc 31 Dec

ASHBY ST LEDGERS (Northants) SP5768 Map 4
Old Coach House

4 miles from M1, junction 18; A5 S to Kilsby, then A361 S towards Daventry; village is signposted left

We're hoping that the new licensees who took over early in 1990 will be sweeping things clean – both literally and metaphorically. Certainly the groundswell of reports is such that we've little hesitation in keeping in this snug, comfortable and rambling place: several little rooms, with high-backed winged settles on polished black and red tiles, a big winter log fire, old kitchen tables, harness on a few standing timbers, and hunting pictures (often of the Pytchley, which sometimes meets outside) and Thelwell prints. A front room has darts, pool, trivia and piped music. Well kept Everards Old Original and Tiger, Flowers Original and Marstons Pedigree on handpump. Bar food includes home-made soup (£1.40), ploughman's (£2.25), chilli con carne (£2.50), lasagne (£2.75), breakfast (£2.85, served lunchtime and evening), giant prawns (£2.95), home-made pies such as steak and mushroom or chicken and bacon (£3.75), pork kebabs (£4.95), steaks (£5.95), and children's dishes (from 60p); daily buffet. There are seats among fruit trees and under a fairy-lit arbour, with a climbing frame, slide and swings. The attractive village is full of thatched stone houses, and has wide grass verges running down to the lane; the nearby manor house was owned by one of the gunpowder plotters. *(Recommended by Lesley Jones, Tony Bland, D and B Carron, Lesley Jones, Geralyn Meyler, Dr Paul Kitchener, Mr and Mrs J M Elden, H W and A B Tuffill, E J Alcock, Curt and Lois Stevens, Olive Carroll, Alan Whelan, Richard Dolphin, Alan Skull, Wayne Brindle, Hilary Robinson, Peter Maden, J W Dixon; more reports on the new regime please)*

Free house   Licensees Brian and Philippa McCabe   Real ale   Meals and snacks Children allowed till 8pm   Open 12–2.30, 6–11   Bedrooms (four-posters in all rooms) tel Rugby (0788) 890349; £32.50B/£38B

BERKSWELL (W Midlands)   SP2479 Map 4
Bear

Spencer Lane; village signposted from A452

In a pretty village with a church that's well worth a visit, this timbered pub is popular for its bar food: rolls (from £1), and hot dishes such as steak and kidney or turkey and ham pie, lasagne, beef stroganoff or cod mornay (all £3.50); on weekday lunchtimes they have a cold table with quiches, cold meats and cheese and help-yourself salads (£3.10). Ruddles Best and County and Websters Yorkshire on handpump; piped music; tables and chairs out on the tree-sheltered back lawn. The cannon in front of the building is a veteran of the Crimean War – and blasted nearby buildings when it was fired with blank ammunition during local festivities some years ago. *(Recommended by Sheila Keene, H R Bevan, Graham Richardson, Brian Skelcher, R P Hastings; more reports please)*

Manns (Watneys)   Licensees Mr and Mrs John D'Arcy   Real ale   Meals and snacks Restaurant tel Berkswell (0676) 33202 (closed Sun evening)   Open 11–2.30, 6–11

BIRMINGHAM   SP0786 Map 4
Bartons Arms   ★

2 miles from M6 junction 6; leave junction on A38(M) towards city centre but take first exit, going right at exit roundabout into Victoria Road, and left at next big roundabout into Aston High Street – A34 towards city centre; pub on the next corner at Park Lane (B4144); car park just past pub on opposite side of road; or take junction 7 of M6 – pub an unmissable landmark on A34 going N from town centre

There's been a drinking house here since 1840, though this magnificent Edwardian building was built in 1901; it's easily recognised by its domed clock tower, and inside the eclectic series of rooms – from palatial salons to cosy snugs – are strikingly decorated with richly coloured and painted elaborate tilework; there are also lots of highly polished mahogany and rosewood, sparkling cut glass mirrors and stained glass, plush seating, heavy brass hanging lamps, and of course a full set of painted cut-glass snob screens – little swivelling panels that you open when you want a drink and shut when you want privacy. M & B Mild and Brew XI on handpump; fruit machine, dominoes, juke box – and a lively atmosphere. Well priced bar food includes rolls (50p) sandwiches (from 60p), ploughman's (£1.90), scampi (£2), and steak and kidney pie, lasagne or cottage pie (all £2.50); roasts and stews in winter. *(Recommended by Dr and Mrs C D E Morris, E J Alcock, Kevin Fields, Patrick and Mary McDermott, Len Beattie, Lynne Sheridan and Bob West; more reports please)*

M & B (Bass)   Manageress Christine Evans   Real ale   Lunchtime meals and snacks (not Sat or Sun)   Children allowed lunchtime   Open 11.30(11 Sat)–2.30, 6–11

BRIERLEY HILL (W Midlands)   SO9187 Map 4
Vine

Delph Rd; B4172 between A461 and A4100, near A4100

Much refurbished in the last year, this friendly and lively Black Country pub now has brass chandliers, re-covered seats and fresh wallpaper in the rear bar, and the side yard is now covered over as far as the much-improved lavatories. In the front bar there are wall benches and simple leatherette-topped oak stools; a snug on the left has solidly built red plush seats. Benefiting from being right next to the brewery, it serves very well kept and priced Bitter and Mild (dark, unusually full-flavoured with a touch of hops, and outstanding value) on handpump, with Delph Strong in winter. Good, fresh snacks include old-fashioned sandwiches (from 85p), and salads with home-cooked ham (£1.70) or beef (£1.90). Darts, cribbage, dominoes, space game, trivia and piano. *(Recommended by E J Alcock, Dave Braisted, J S Rutter, Michael Rooke, Kevin Fields, Brian Jones, Matt Pringle, Tony Gayfer; more reports please)*

Bathams   Licensee Melvyn Wood   Real ale   Lunchtime snacks (not Sun) Children in own room   Rock Sun, Jazz or folk Mon   Open 12–4, 6–11 Mon–Thurs, 12–11 Fri and Sat

CHARLTON (Northants)   SP5236 Map 4
Rose & Crown

Village signposted from A41 at W edge of Aynho, and from Kings Sutton

Bar food in this villagey, thatched pub ranges from sandwiches, through beef salad, home-baked ham, chilli con carne or lasagne (£4), gammon or Barnsley chop (£4.50), to excellent Angus steak (from £7.50), and four-course Sunday lunch (£9 – bookings only). In the beamed bar there are some good prints on the walls, mainly stripped back to carefully coursed masonry, as well as a sofa, winged armchairs and seats that match the sturdy country-kitchen tables, and shelves of books by the big open fireplace; the quiet collie is called Boltby. This year a new dining room's been added – the old one should now be a no-smoking lounge. The commendable choice of real ales on handpump includes Marstons Burton and Pedigree, Morlands Bitter and Old Masters, Wadworths 6X and Whitbreads Castle Eden; also, some carefully chosen malt whiskies among the better known ones, Dows Vintage Port, and good value wine. There are a couple of picnic-table sets on a small front terrace by the village lane, with a few more on gravel behind. *(Recommended by Sir Nigel Foulkes, Elizabeth and Klaus Leist, M O'Driscoll, David and Jane Russell, Roy Bamford; more reports please)*

Free house   Licensees Peter and Brenda Reeves   Real ale   Meals and snacks (12.30–3, 7.15–9.30; not Sun evening)   Restaurant; till 3 Sun   Children allowed till 7.30 in small room away from bar   Open 12–3, 5–11; Sat evening opening 6, 6.30 winter; closed 25 and 26 Dec evenings   Bedrooms should be ready by 1991 – tel Banbury (0295) 811317; £25.50B/£40B

CLIPSTON (Northants)   SP7181 Map 4
Bulls Head

B4036 S of Market Harborough

The countless coins glistening in the black beams of the lounge bar – cosily divided into three snug areas leading down from the servery – continue an odd tradition started by US airmen based nearby in World War II; they used to wedge the money waiting for their next drink in cracks and crannies of the ancient woodwork. The atmosphere's very friendly and relaxed, largely local in the evenings – but with a warm welcome for visitors. Seats are mainly comfortable and sturdy small settles and stools upholstered in red plush. Decent bar food includes lots of light snacks and starters such as steak sandwich or burger (£1) and soup (£1.20), with main dishes majoring on several speciality pies (£3.95); also gammon, scampi, fresh summer salads or farmhouse grill at the same price, lasagne (£3.40), chicken Kiev (£4.35) and steaks (from £5.75), with good puddings. Well kept Everards, Hook Norton Old Hookey, Moorhouses Pendle Witches Brew and Ruddles Best and County on handpump, and a very impressive choice of malt whiskies. The long back games bar, lively in the evenings, has darts, pool, table skittles, cribbage,

dominoes, fruit machine and juke box; there are a few white tables under cocktail parasols on the terrace that stretches back beside it, with a barbecue.
(Recommended by M and J Back, David Butcher, Cdr Patrick Tailyour)

Manns (Watneys)   Licensees Colin and Jenny Smith   Real ale   Meals and snacks (till 9.45; not Sun or Mon evenings)   Children welcome   Occasional live entertainment, esp around Christmas and Bank Hols   Open 11.30–2.30, 6.30–11; closed 25 Dec

CRICK (Northants)   SP5872   Map 4

Red Lion

A mile from M1 junction 18; A428

A pleasantly chatty and relaxed refuge from the motorway, this thatched stone inn has soft lighting, stripped stonework and good log fires in winter (in summer the two ornamental stone fireplaces are bright with big copper dishes and brassware); it's quietest and snuggest in the inner part of the bar – but there's freedom from piped music throughout. Bar food includes chicken or gammon (£4.50), scampi (£4.75), trout (£5) and steaks (from £6.50) in the evening, with lunchtime sandwiches (85p), ploughman's (£2), lasagne, steak and kidney pie and so forth (£3) and steak (£6); well kept Ruddles Best and Websters Yorkshire on handpump; fruit machine in side room. Families can use a Perspex-roofed sheltered terrace in the old coach yard, with lots of pretty summer hanging baskets; there are a few picnic-table sets under cocktail parasols on grass by the car park.
(Recommended by Gordon Theaker, Denis Waters, David Gaunt)

Manns (Watneys)   Licensees Tom and Mary Marks   Real ale   Meals and snacks (till 1.45; not Wed evening, not Sun)   Open 11.30–2.30, 6.30–11

EAST HADDON (Northants)   SP6668   Map 4

Red Lion 🛏

High St; village signposted off A428 (turn right in village) and off A50 N of Northampton

This solid, golden stone small hotel has a civilised, panelled lounge bar decorated in comfortably subdued colours – patterned dark flowery carpet, brown velvet curtains, dark brown ceiling; it's well furnished with oak panelled settles, library chairs, soft modern dining chairs and a mix of oak, mahogany and cast-iron-framed tables, as well as recessed china cabinets, old prints and pewter; a couple of beams are hung sparingly with little kegs, brass pots, swords and so forth. There are sturdy old-fashioned red leather seats in the small public bar; well kept Charles Wells Eagle on handpump. Good bar food includes sandwiches (£1.75, open from £2.95), ploughman's (£3.25), and hot dishes such as chicken chasseur (£4.50), haddock and prawn rissotto (£4.75), home-made faggots or steak and kidney pie (£4.95), with a popular cold table (from £4.75) and a good choice of home-made puddings; attentive service. The walled side garden has lilac, fruit trees, roses and neat little flower beds, and leads back to the bigger lawn, where there are well spaced picnic-table sets; a small side terrace has white tables under cocktail parasols. A big copper beech shades the gravel car park.
(Recommended by David Gaunt, J M Norton, Cdr Patrick Tailyour, H W and A B Tuffill; more reports please)

Charles Wells   Licensees Mr and Mrs Ian Kennedy   Real ale   Meals and snacks (not over the Christmas period)   Pretty restaurant (evenings, Sun lunch)   Open 11–2.30, 6–11   Bedrooms tel Northampton (0604) 770223; £35/£48

EASTCOTE (Northants)   SP6753   Map 4

Eastcote Arms

Gayton Rd; village signposted from A5 3 miles N of Towcester

The wealth of pictures above the dark brown wooden dado here reflects a particularly individual taste – cricket, fishing and other sports, militia, as well as the pub and its history. The bustling bar is traditionally furnished, and has two winter log fires, flowery curtains, and fresh flowers; dominoes and unobtrusive piped music. Good value food includes rolls (80p), soup (£1), good fresh sandwiches (from around £1), very good big home-made pasty with gravy (£1.70), ploughman's (£2), and daily specials like lasagne, tasty goulash or steak and kidney pie. The well kept real ales include a fine fragrant beer brewed by Banks & Taylors especially for them (though now sold elsewhere too), as well as Adnams Extra, Marstons Pedigree, Sam Smiths OB and a guest beer changing monthly. There are picnic-table sets and other tables in an attractive back garden, with roses, geraniums and so forth around the neat lawn. Up until the mid-seventies – when the current licensees took over – the pub was known as the Rose & Crown. *(Recommended by John Baker, Mrs M E Lawrence, Nick Dowson, Alison Hayward, R D and S A Mackay; more reports please)*

Free house Licensees Mike and Sheila Manning Real ale Lunchtime snacks (not Sun or Mon) Open 12–2.30, 6–10.30(11 Sat); closed Mon lunchtime, except Bank Holidays

ETTINGTON (War) SP2749 Map 4
Chequers

A422 Banbury–Stratford

The main lounge bar is at the back here, and is furnished and decorated with brown leatherette wall seats and modern chairs, and attractive Ros Goody Barbour-jacket-era sporting prints; the front bar is more straightforward, and has sensibly placed darts, shove-ha'penny, dominoes, trivia machine and juke box. Well kept Adnams Southwold, M & B Brew XI and Marstons Pedigree on handpump; pool room, and a spacious conservatory with garden tables and chairs. The good choice of food includes lunchtime sandwiches or ploughman's, soup (£1.45), vegetable au gratin, moussaka or lasagne (£4.15), help-yourself salads (£4.95), home-made pies (£5.45), buttered poussin (£6.75), and steaks (from £9.15); puddings (from £1.55). There are tables out on the neat back lawn and on an awninged terrace, with lots of hanging baskets. Customers' dogs are welcome in the bar and garden, but not in the lounge. *(Recommended by Frank Cummins, Ted George, Mike and Wendy Proctor, P R Davis, KC, Andy and Jill Kassube; more reports please)*

Free house Licensee Mrs Jan Williams Real ale Meals and snacks (12–2, 6–9.30; not 25 Dec) Well behaved children in eating area Occasional live entertainment, particularly in July Open 10.30–2.30, 6–11

FIVE WAYS (Warwicks) SP2270 Map 4
Case is Altered

Follow Rowington signposts from A41 at junction roundabout with A4177 N of Warwick

A tiled white-painted brick cottage on a quiet lane, this is a real gem of a place, in which you're likely to experience some kind of time-warp. The small main bar is very unspoilt and only has a few, sturdy and old-fashioned tables, with a couple of leather-covered sturdy settles facing each other over the spotless tiles; it's decorated with a fine old poster showing the Lucas Blackwell & Arkwright brewery (now flats), and a clock with its hours spelling out Thornleys, another defunct brewery. From here you reach the homely lounge (usually open only on Friday and Saturday evenings) through a door lit up on either side. A door at the back of the building leads into a simple little room, usually empty on weekday lunchtimes, with a rug on its tiled floor and a bar billiards table protected by an ancient leather cover (it takes pre-decimal sixpences). But what makes it all special is the warmth of the welcome – from the landlady (probably sitting chatting to customers), and from the regulars themselves. Well kept Ansells Mild and Flowers Original served by rare miniature pumps mounted on the casks that are stilled behind the counter, maybe good lunchtime sandwiches. Behind a wrought-iron gate is a little brick-paved courtyard with a stone table under a chestnut tree. *(Recommended by*

Gordon and Daphne, Mark Evans, Brian Jones, Karen Bettesworth, Chris Down, Judith Steinert)

Free house   Licensee Gwen Jones   Real ale   Snacks (lunchtime)   Open 11–2.30, 6–11

FOTHERINGHAY (Northants)   TL0593   Map 5
Falcon ⊘

Village signposted off A605 on Peterborough side of Oundle

Good, imaginative and very popular bar food includes home-made soups like French onion or iced gazpacho (£1.90), home-made pâtés like mackerel and whisky or smoked salmon (from £2), ploughman's (£2), sweet spiced herring salad (£2.50), steak and kidney pie (£3.90), good salads with proper dressing, baked sugar-glazed ham with peaches (£5.60), roast duckling with apple and rosemary stuffing (£6), jumbo prawns (£7.50), and puddings (£1.80); prices are slightly cheaper at lunchtime. The comfortable lounge has cushioned slatback armchairs and bucket chairs, winter log fires in stone fireplaces at each end, antique engravings on its cream walls, and a hum of quiet conversation. There is a simpler public bar which the landlord prefers to keep for the locals. Well kept Elgoods Bitter and Greyhound and Greene King IPA and Abbot on handpump; darts, shove-ha'penny, dominoes, cribbage, magazines to read. There are seats on the terrace and in the neat garden by this fine stone building. It also carries the sign of the Yorkist falcon – which, gilded, tops the striking lantern tower of the vast church (well worth a visit) just behind it. *(Recommended by B M Eldridge, Mrs J A Blanks, John Cox, J P Cinnamond, Mrs E M Thompson)*

Free house   Licensee Alan Stewart   Real ale   Meals (not Mon) and snacks (not Mon evening)   Children welcome   Open 10–3, 6–11; may close Mon evening in winter

GREAT WOLFORD (War)   SP2434   Map 4
Fox & Hounds

Village signposted on right on A34 3 miles S of Shipston on Stour

The cosy, low-beamed and old-fashioned open-plan bar in this Cotswold pub has a pair of high-backed old settles and other comfortable armchairish seats around a nice collection of old tables on its flagstones, well cushioned wall benches and a window seat, and old hunting prints on the walls, which are partly stripped back to the bare stone. There's a large stone fireplace with a good winter log fire (which may smoke if it's windy) by the fine old bread oven, and a small tap room serving Flowers IPA, Marstons Pedigree and Whitbreads Castle Eden and Pompey Royal on handpump, as well as quite a few malt whiskies and country wines; darts, shove-ha'penny, dominoes, chess, draughts, cards, (all in the tap room), with classical piped music in the main bar. Bar food includes sandwiches, soup (£1.10), pâté (£1.95), garlic mushrooms (£2.20), ploughman's, lasagne (£3.10), salads (£3.60), steak and kidney pie (£4.50), Turkish-style lamb (£4.50), sirloin steak in red wine sauce (£6.75), and puddings like spotted dick with custard or chocolate mousse (£1.50); the dining room doubles as the restaurant at weekends. Outside, there's a terrace with a well. *(Recommended by Laurence Manning, G P Beckett, JM, PM, Mrs Lili Lomas)*

Free house   Licensees David and Joan Hawker   Real ale   Meals and snacks (12–2, 7–10)   Weekend restaurant (not Sun evening) tel Barton-on-the-Heath (0608 74) 220   Children in eating area of bar (must be seated)   Open 12–2.30(3 Sat), 7–11

HIMLEY (W Midlands – though see below)   SO8889   Map 4
Crooked House ★

Pub signposted from B4176 Gornalwood–Himley, OS Sheet 139 map reference 896908; Readers have got so used to thinking of the pub as being near Kingswinford in the

Midlands (though Himley is actually in Staffs) that we still include it in this chapter – the pub itself is virtually smack on the county boundary. Until recently this country pub was known as the Glynne Arms; the current title says everything about the results of local mining – even getting the doors open is an uphill struggle, the walls and floors slope very steeply, and on one table a bottle on its side actually rolls 'upwards' against the apparent direction of the slope. A large, level and more modern extension with local antiques is at the back. Well kept cheap Banks's Bitter or Mild (on electric pump); dominoes, fruit machine and piped music. Bar food includes sandwiches, smokies (£1.95), home-made faggots (£2.25), scampi, home-made steak and kidney pie (£2.95) and rump steak. It can get busy if there's a local clay-pigeon shoot outside. The terrace is spacious. *(Recommended by Richard Sanders, Brian Jones, Patrick and Mary McDermott, Matt Pringle, Audrey and Brian Green, Kevin Fields)*

Banks's   Licensee Gary Ensor   Real ale   Lunchtime meals and snacks   Open 11–11; 11.30–2.30, 6–11 winter

KENILWORTH (War)   SP2871 Map 4
Virgins & Castle

High St; opposite A429 Coventry Rd at junction with A452

The inner flagstones-and-beams servery in this old-fashioned town pub has several rooms radiating off it. Down a couple of steps, a large room has heavy beams, a big rug on ancient red tiles, and matching seat and stool covers. A couple of simply furnished small snugs – one with flagstones and the other with rugs on its bare boards – flank the entrance corridor, and there's a carpeted lounge with more beams, some little booths, hatch service, a good warm coal fire and fruit machine (there's another in a lobby). Popular, good value bar food includes well filled rolls and sandwiches, ploughman's, salads, gammon and pineapple, rump steak and daily specials; well kept Davenports and Wem Special on handpump, and farm cider. There are seats outside in a sheltered garden. *(Recommended by Brian Jones, Graham Richardson, Brian Skelcher, Quentin Williamson; more reports please)*

Davenports (Greenalls)   Real ale   Meals and snacks   Live music Tues   Open 11–2.30, 6–11

LANGLEY (W Midlands)   SO9788 Map 4
Brewery ★

1 1/2 miles from M5, junction 2; from A4034 to W Bromwich and Oldbury take first right turn signposted Junction 2 Ind Estate then bear left past Albright & Wilson into Station Rd

Though none of the decor is older than 1984, there's a degree of authenticity to the Victorian feel in this own-brew subsidiary of Allied Breweries, the Ind Coope empire; the Parlour on the left, lit by brass swan's neck wall lamps, has a coal fire in a tiled Victorian fireplace with china on the overmantle, a corner china cabinet, plates and old engravings on the walls, and dining chairs or sturdy built-in settles around four good solid tables. A red-tiled kitchen, divided off by shelves of Staffordshire pottery and old books, is similarly furnished, with the addition of lots of copper pans around its big black range. The more simple Tap Bar serves their own Entire – full-flavoured, quite strong and much loved by readers – as well as Bitter and Mild, both brewed up in Warrington. Simple bar food includes exceptionally good value sandwiches – double deckers, and tasty hot beef, pork or roast ham in thick doorsteps of bread (90p-£1.10), and faggots (£1.10). Tractor seats in a back corridor give a view into the brewhouse through a big picture window; darts, dominoes, cribbage, trivia and piped music. *(Recommended by Brian Jones, T Henwood, J S Rutter, E J Alcock, Richard Sanders, John and Christine Simpson, Dave Braisted, Mike and Wendy Proctor, T R G Alcock, Frank Cummins)*

Holt, Plant & Deakins (Allied)   Licensee Tony Stanton   Real ale   Snacks (not Sun) Children in eating area of bar   Open 11–2.30, 6–11

LAPWORTH (Warwicks) SP1670 Map 4

Navigation

Old Warwick Rd (B4439 Warwick–Hockley Heath)

A bustling local doubling as a canal-users' pub, this consistently friendly little pub has good value simple food, and well kept beers on handpump – Bass, M&B Bitter and Mild, and a guest beer such as Titanic Premium. The lively flagstoned bar has newish high-backed winged settles, seats built around its window bay and a coal fire in its high-mantled inglenook; it's decorated with brightly painted canal ware (you can buy horseshoes in this style here, in aid of cot death research), and cases of stuffed fish. A second quieter room has tables on its board-and-carpet floor – and a dresser with dominoes, cribbage and board games. Generous straightforward bar food, cheap for the area and pleasantly served, includes well filled cottage rolls (lunchtime, and Sat evening; £1), double giant sausage or double burger with egg and chips (£2.95), lasagne (£3.65), scampi or chilli con carne (£3.85) and gammon and egg, chicken, lamb curry or steak and kidney pie (£3.95); fruit machine. There are tables on a back terrace and sheltered canalside lawn, edged with flowers, with outside hatch service and lit at night. *(Recommended by Brian Jones, C H Stride, D P Cartwright)*

M & B (Bass)   Licensee A C Kimber   Real ale   Meals (not Mon evening or Sun) and snacks (not Mon evening); 12–2, 6–9, no food winter evenings Sun–Wed   Children in inner room   Occasional folk dancing   Open 11–2.30(3 Sat), 5.30(6 Sat)–11; maybe longer if busy; closed evening 25/26 Dec

LITTLE COMPTON (War) SP2630 Map 4

Red Lion 🛏

Off A44 Moreton-in-Marsh–Chipping Norton

This simple but civilised low-beamed Cotswold-stone inn has snug alcoves, a couple of little tables by the open fire, with a settee facing it, some window seats, and attractive etchings on the stripped stone walls. The plainer public bar has darts, dominoes, fruit machine, juke box and Aunt Sally. Well kept Donnington BB and SBA on handpump; piped music. Good bar food, served in the dining area leading off the lounge, includes ploughman's (from £3), celery, apple and prawn salad (£3.20), home-cooked ham and egg, chicken breast in a bacon, mushroom, cream and wine sauce (£4.95), venison casserole (£5.25), and lots of steaks (from 8oz rump £9.50), with changing home-made specials like soup, chicken liver pâté with brandy and port and so forth. In the garden there's a walled-off play area with climber, swings and tunnels made from giant piping. The bedrooms are good value. *(Recommended by Barry and Anne; more reports please)*

Donnington   Licensee David Smith   Real ale   Meals and snacks (not Mon in Jan or 25 Dec)   Children in eating area and restaurant   Occasional live entertainment   Open 11–2.30, 6–11   Bedrooms tel Barton on the Heath (0608 74) 397; £14/26

LOWICK (Northants) SP9780 Map 4

Snooty Fox ⊘

Village signposted off A6116 Corby–Raunds

Sympathetically restored, this imposing 17th-century inn has a spacious two-room lounge with handsomely moulded dark oak beams, and stripped stone walls decorated with hunt caricatures, Monarch of the Glen lithographs and old prints of ornamental pheasants – there's a stuffed Lady Amherst's pheasant on the carved mantlebeam of the big stone log fireplace. There are neat and attractive dining chairs around the well spaced tables – with plenty of space too along the formidable monumentally carved bar counter. Bar food is good value and carefully cooked, including spicy sausages (£2.95), lasagne (£4.20), lots of fresh Whitby fish such as cod (£4.95), crispy chicken or steak and Guinness pie (£5.50), giant garlic prawns, enormous helpings of gammon or daily fresh dressed crab with prawns

(£5.95), rump steak (£6.50) and dishes of the day such as baked ham (£4.75); though you can eat anywhere, they may suggest you use the restaurant at the other end – similar in style, but more intimately lit. At lunchtime there is more choice at the lower end, including pâté, ploughman's or cheese plate (£1.95), and omelettes and other hot dishes (from £2.50). Well kept Adnams, Marstons Pedigree, Ruddles Best and County and a changing guest beer from Yorkshire on handpump, with lots of malt whiskies and carefully chosen wines (from a wide choice by the bottle, the bin-end burgundies tend to be particularly rewarding). Service is friendly and efficient, and they're good to children (with high chairs and so forth). The picnic-table sets softly floodlit on the front grass are very inviting on a warm evening. (*Recommended by M J Horridge, T N de Bray, Richard and James Groome, Mr and Mrs M K Triebwasser*)

Free house   Licensee John Lewis   Real ale   Meals and lunchtime snacks (11.30–2.30, 7–10)   Children welcome   Open 11.30–2.30, 7–11   Bedrooms planned   tel Thrapston (080 12) 3434

LOWSONFORD (Warwicks)   SP1868 Map 4
Fleur de Lys ✿

Village signposted off B4439 Hockley Heath–Warwick; can be reached too from B4095 via Preston Bagot

One of the best canalside pubs, combining a lovely location with interesting and civilised old-fashioned surroundings – and it does rather imaginative food all day. The spreading bar has rugs on flagstones and antique tiles; it's at its most parlourish on the left, with a sofa and some bookshelves, and at its most dining-roomish down steps on the right, where there are flowers on polished tables, and cushioned plush button-back built-in wall banquettes. Elsewhere, most seats around the well spaced tables are brocade-cushioned mate's, wheelback and dining chairs; the butter-coloured ceiling has lots of low black beams. The changing bar food might include carrot and orange soup or open sandwiches (from £1.50), starters or light snacks such as pork-filled pasta or mushrooms with gammon (£2.50), crab pâté (£2.75) and gravadlax with melon and avocado (£3.95), salads (from £3.75) and tuna, prawn and celery lasagne (£5.75), turkey done with a chilli feta sauce (£5.95), goulash (£6.25), 8oz rump steak (£6.95) and salmon in filo pastry with mango (£7.25); the middle area is no-smoking. Well kept Boddingtons, Flowers Original, Marstons Pedigree and Wadworths 6X on handpump, decent wines including good New World ones, proper cider, several open fires, newspapers and magazines, piped classical music; good staff. The family room is unusually elegant; plush dining chairs, and a red-ceilinged raftered upper gallery – there's a children's menu. Down on the grass among tall weeping willows by the Stratford-upon-Avon Canal are picnic-table sets, with a very good safely fenced and well equipped play area. (*Recommended by Brian Jones, Jonathan and Jane Hagger, A J Young, Daphne and David Carter, H R Bevan, Brian Skelcher*)

Whitbreads   Licensee S Pedersen   Real ale   Meals and snacks (12–9; winter 12–2.30, 6–9.30)   Children in family room and away from bar   Open 11–11

NETHERTON (W Midlands)   SO9387 Map 4
Little Dry Dock

Windmill End, Bumble Hole; you really need an A-Z street map to find it – or OS Sheet 139 map reference 953881

This diminutive canalside pub is no exception to the idiosyncrasy that so characterizes Mr O'Rourke's small chain of Black Country pubs (see also main entries in Bewdley and Kidderminster (Hereford and Worcester), and several in the Lucky Dips). Vividly painted in red, white and blue and with a green-planked ceiling, it has quite a nautical theme – a huge model boat in one front transom-style window, marine windows, winches and barge rudders flanking the door, and lots of brightly coloured bargees' water pots, lanterns, jugs and lifebuoys; and then of course there's an entire narrow-boat somehow squeezed into the right-hand bar and used as the servery (its engine is in the room on the left); lively piped music, fruit machine. High point of the menu is the Desperate Dan Pie, complete with horns (£4.45), with other generous food served from the end galley such as soup (£1.45), sandwiches (from £1.15), pâté (£1.95), filled baked potatoes (from £1.65), vegetarian lasagne or curry, ham salad (£4.25), swordfish steak (£4.95), and daily specials. In common with the other pubs in the chain, they have their own Little Lumphammer ale as well as Ind Coope Burton, and their own wine, Chateau Ballykilferret. (Recommended by R P Taylor, J S Rutter, Sue Holland, Dave Webster, Peter Scillitoe, A Parsons, Brian Jones, Dr M A Thomas, E V Walder, Steve J Pratt, David and Eloise Smaylen, Patrick and Mary McDermott)

Free house   Licensee Julie Mincher   Real ale   Meals and snacks (available all opening hours)   Children welcome   Open 11–2.30, 6–11; 11–11 Sat, may open longer afternoons if demand

Old Swan

Halesowen Road; A459 towards Halesowen just S of Netherton centre

Long before the current fad for home-brew pubs, this place was held in affection for its traditional brewing methods – and is still known as Ma Pardoe's after the lady who ran it. The home-brew is still good – fresh and fragrant – and there's also Wiltshire Stonehenge, Old Grumble and Old Devil, and a Mild. The original bar is traditionally furnished, with mirrors behind the bar engraved with the swan design, an old-fashioned cylinder stove with its chimney angling away to the wall, and a lovely patterned ceiling with a big swan centrepiece. 'Ma Pardoe's Bar' itself is decorated with 1920s bric-a-brac, though fitted out very much in keeping with the rest of the building, using recycled bricks and woodwork, and even matching etched window panels; darts, dominoes, fruit machine and piped music. Bar food includes large breakfast baps (sausage, egg and bacon – 85p), black pudding and cheese, and home-made pies such as steak and mushroom (£2.55). There's a good car park at the back of the pub. (Recommended by Sue Holland, Michael Rooke, Dave Webster, Patrick and Mary McDermott, Steve J Pratt, E J Alcock; more reports please)

Own brew (Wiltshire)   Licensee Mandy Collins   Real ale   Meals and snacks Restaurant tel Dudley (0384) 253075   Children in snug   Folk club Sat evening   Open 12–3, 6.30–11

NEWBOLD ON STOUR (War)   SP2446 Map 4

White Hart

A34 Shipston on Stour–Stratford

Reliable bar food here, well presented and reasonably priced, includes soup, garlic mushrooms in cream and herbs, a prawn and smoked haddock dish (£2.25), moules marinières (£2.50), chicken in a tarragon and cream sauce (£4.35), and salmon fishcakes or curried prawns with fresh pineapple (£4.95); good choice of puddings. The airy, beamed and quarry-tiled main bar, partly divided up by stub walls and the chimney, has gleaming copper-topped tables, reddish russet cord plush cushions for the modern high-backed winged settles, seats set into big bay windows, a fair amount of brass, and a gun hanging over the log fire in one big stone fireplace. The roomy back public bar has darts, pool, dominoes, fruit machine and juke box; Bass and maybe a guest beer on handpump; there seems to be no objection to well behaved dogs. There are some picnic-table sets under cocktail parasols in front of the pub, with its well tended hanging baskets. (Recommended by A C Morrison; more reports please)

M & B (Bass)   Licensees Mr and Mrs J C Cruttwell   Real ale   Meals and snacks (not Sun evening)   Restaurant tel Stratford upon Avon (0789) 87205; not Sun evening Children welcome   Open 11–2.30(3 Sat), 6–11

OLD HILL (W Midlands)   SO9685 Map 4

Wharf

Station Road, which is between Gorsythill Road (A459) and Halesowen Road (A459) in

Cradley Heath; this entrance involves a hideously steep wooden canal bridge – the back way into the car park, from Grange Road off Waterfall Lane, is much easier

In a good position by the largely disused Dudley Canal, this popular, chatty drinking pub dispenses a good range of well kept real ales on handpump, chalked up on a board (with another board showing what will be available the following week) and including Home Bitter and Mild, Hoskins & Oldfields Premium, Theakstons XB, Youngers IPA and No 3 (relatively rare for the Midlands), and maybe the very uncommon Maidens Ruin. The quarry-tiled and well kept front room has red leatherette settles, a fruit machine, and the carpeted back room has tapestry-cushioned mate's chairs around black tables, and a plum-coloured fabric ceiling. Stripped brick arches open between the two, as does a gas-effect coal fire, and there are old-fashioned little touches like the curly brass and etched glass wall lamps; shove-ha'penny, dominoes, pool, space game, trivia, juke box, and piped music. Bar food includes sandwiches (70p), curry (£2.15), scampi (£3), steak and kidney pie (£3.05), stuffed plaice (£3.25) and steaks (from £4.95; T-bone £6.95). There are picnic-table sets in a sheltered side garden which has a good children's play area with a fort and drawbridge. The pub – pretty and cottagey to look at – is reputed to be the oldest surviving farm building in the district. *(Recommended by Brian Jones, J S Rutter, R P Taylor, Steve J Pratt, David and Eloise Smaylen, Roger Huggins)*

Scottish & Newcastle   Licensee Janice Williams   Real ale   Meals and snacks Children in family room   Occasional music   Open 11.30–3, 6–11; may open all day some Sats and Bank Hols

OUNDLE (Northants)   TL0388   Map 5
Ship

West St

This small town preserves great traditional character, even elegance, in its buildings, yet has lots of life – and the Ship is a perfect paradigm of the larger whole. Off the central corridor, the very heavily beamed lounge bar on the left is split into three rooms: down one end a panelled no-smoking snug with button-back leather seats built in around it; up by the street a mix of leather and other seats including a very flowery piano stool (and its piano), with sturdy tables and a log fire in a stone inglenook. In between, the landlord and his son with great efficiency and good humour dispense well kept Bass, Greene King IPA, Marstons Pedigree and Theakstons XB to what on a Friday evening can seem like half the town; a warmly lively yet relaxing atmosphere. Bar food includes soup (£1), pâté (£2) and ploughman's, salads or smoked mackerel (£2.50), with enormous winter Sunday lunches and summer lunchtime cold buffet; cribbage, dominoes; maybe free Sunday nuts and crisps on the bar. The tiled-floor public side has darts, juke box or piped music and fruit machine. A series of small sheltered terraces strung out behind has wooden tables and chairs, lit at night. Several of the bedrooms are in a new extension. *(Recommended by Monica Darlington, David Brown, Nic James)*

Free house   Licensee Frank Langridge   Real ale   Meals and snacks   Children welcome   Live bands winter Fri and Sat   Open 11–3, 6–11 (all day Sat; closed evening 25 Dec)   Bedrooms tel Oundle (0832) 273918; £35B/$27.50(£45B)

PRESTON BAGOT (War)   SP1765   Map 4
Olde Crab Mill

B4095 Henley-in-Arden–Warwick

A comfortable old timbered and beamed roadside pub, this has lots of cosy nooks and crannies in the comfortable, low-ochre-ceilinged communicating rooms, with cushioned antique carved settles, chintz-cushioned wicker easy chairs and other seats (similarly upholstered), antique prints, old-fashioned small-paned windows, and two log fires. Flowers IPA and Original, Marstons Pedigree and Wadworths 6X on handpump; piped music, newspapers and magazines to read. Bar food includes soup (95p), steak sandwich (£2.45), ploughman's (£2.95), lasagne (£3.45), steak and kidney pie or Cumberland sausage (£3.75), salads (from £3.95), gammon and egg (£4.45), and steak (£7.95); children's dishes (£1.75). Outside there are some sheltered seats, and a children's tree-giant. *(Recommended by Brian Jones, H R Bevan, M O'Driscoll, Ted George, C H Stride, Kevin Fields, David and Eloise Smaylen, Olive Carroll)*

Whitbreads   Licensee David P Tye   Real ale   Meals and snacks (not Sun evening) Children in own area   Open 11(12 winter)–11

PRIORS MARSTON (Warwicks)   SP4857 Map 4

Falcon

Hellidon Rd; village signposted off A425 Daventry Rd in Southam; and from A361 S of Daventry

The civilised, relaxing atmosphere of this handsome and neatly kept 17th-century golden stone pub owes a lot to the landlord's obviously welcoming attitude to all his customers. The main bar rambles around into an L beyond the log fire in the big high-mantled stone fireplace, with well padded high-backed winged settles on its cheerfully patterned carpet; a couple of big framed mirrors alongside the country pictures give a feeling of extra space. Well presented bar food in generous helpings includes sandwiches (from £1.45), barbecued smoked chicken wings (£3.25), 8oz burger (£3.75), chilli con carne or scampi (£3.95), lasagne or chicken tagliatelle (£4.25), gammon and egg (£4.45), lamb kebabs (£5.25) and steaks (from £6.45); there's a choice of chips, new or baked potatoes. Well kept Everards Tiger, Hook Norton Best, John Smiths and Moorhouses Pendle Witches Brew on handpump, decent wine; unobtrusive piped music; cribbage, dominoes. *(Recommended by Sylvia and Len Henderson, David Gittins, CEP, WHBM, Richard and Maria Gillespie, Lynne Sheridan, Bob West, Alexandra Gunther, Michael Schofield)*

Free house   Licensees Stephen and Jane Richards   Real ale   Meals and snacks (till 10)   Restaurant tel Daventry (0327) 60562   Well behaved children allowed   Open 12–3, 7–11; closed evening 25 Dec

SAMBOURNE (War)   SP0561 Map 4

Green Dragon

A435 N of Alcester, then left fork onto A448 just before Studley; village signposted on left soon after

Prettily covered in season with roses climbing against its shuttered and timbered façade, this village-green pub serves good value bar food including sandwiches (from £1), home-made soup (£1.10), pâté (£1.95), ploughman's (from £2.50), sausage and egg (£3.50), omelettes (from £3.30), a fish dish of the day (£3.95), home-made steak and kidney pie (£4.25), gammon (£4.50), salads (from £4.50), and steaks (from £7.50). The modernised beamed communicating rooms have little armed seats, some small settles, and open fires; Bass, M & B Brew XI and Springfield on handpump. There are picnic-table sets and teak seats among flowering cherries on a side courtyard, by the car park. *(Recommended by A J Woodhouse, S V Bishop, J E Rycroft, John Bowdler, Andrew Hudson, David and Eloise Smaylen, K and E Leist; more reports please)*

Bass   Licensee Phil Burke   Real ale   Meals and snacks (12–2, 7–10; not Sun) Restaurant tel Astwood Bank (052 789) 2465   Children welcome   Open 11–3, 6–11

SHIPSTON ON STOUR (War)   SP2540 Map 4

White Bear

High Street

This fine old coaching inn, popular with a wide range of people, serves imaginative food from a varied menu: soup such as tomato and basil (£2), cream of fennel with coriander (£2.35), sardines with lemon and garlic (£2.75 or £5.25), tagliatelle (£3.95), warm salad of black pudding, apple and celery (£4.25 or £7.75), Scotch langoustines (£4.95 or £8.95), steak, kidney and Guinness pudding (£5.25), fish crumble (£5.95), pastry puff of baby leeks and oyster mushrooms in a truffle sauce (£7.25), and Aberdeen Angus steak (£9.50), with puddings such as spotted dick (£2.50); the breakfasts are recommended; part of the main eating area is no-smoking. A separate bar on the right has a woodburning stove in a big painted stone fireplace, with a fruit machine round at the back; the narrow front bar on the left has massive stripped settles, attractive lamps on the rag-rolled walls, newspapers out for customers, and interesting pictures: charming pen and wash drawing of Paris cafe society, and sporting and other cartoons from Alken through Lawson Wood to bright modern ones by Tibb. The back lounge is more plainly furnished and decorated, with comfortable modern furniture, and big Toulouse-Lautrec and other prints of French music-hall life. Well kept Bass and M & B Brew XI on handpump, with decent wines; darts, shove-ha'penny, dominoes, cribbage; maybe dogs. There are some white cast-iron tables in a small back yard, and benches face the street. Note that it can get very busy, sometimes with most tables taken by noon. *(Recommended by S V Bishop, A C Morrison, JM, PM, John Bowdler, W H Bland)*

M & B (Bass)   Licensee Suzanne Roberts   Real ale   Meals and snacks   Restaurant   Children welcome   Open 11–3, 6–11   Bedrooms tel Shipston on Stour (0608) 61558; £33B/£45B

SHUSTOKE (War)   SP2290 Map 4
Griffin

5 miles from M6, junction 4; A446 towards Tamworth, then right on to B4114 and go straight through Coleshill; pub is at Church End, past Shustoke centre

On the edge of a playing field, this charming brick house has a low-beamed, L-shaped bar with an old-fashioned settle and cushioned cafe seats (some quite closely packed), sturdily elm-topped sewing trestles, lots of old jugs on the beams, and log fires in both stone fireplaces (one's a big inglenook). The good range of well kept real ales on handpump typically includes Batemans XXXB, Burton Bridge, Eldridge Pope Royal Oak, Hook Norton Old Hooky, Marstons Pedigree, Pendle Witches Brew, Theakstons Old Peculier and Wadworths 6X, all from a servery under a very low, thick beam. Good value lunchtime bar food includes appetising sandwiches, ham and egg or chilli con carne (£3), and home-made steak and kidney pie, lasagne or curry (all £3.30); local fresh eggs, and leeks and cauliflower in season, for sale. Terrace outside, and old-fashioned seats and tables on the back grass. The new roomy conservatory is a handy addition for families. *(Recommended by Brian Jones, J Harvey Hallam, M Rowlinson, J S Rutter, Derek and Sylvia Stephenson, Frank Cummins, Ian Blackwell, E J Alcock; more reports please)*

Free house   Licensees Michael Pugh and S Wedge   Real ale   Lunchtime meals and snacks (not Sun)   Children in conservatory   Open 12–2.30, 7–11

SOUTHAM (War)   SP4161 Map 4
Old Mint

Coventry Street; A423, towards Coventry

Originally a monks' hospice, this medieval stone building has an interestingly-shaped, heavy-beamed and two-roomed bar, with walls peppered with antique guns, powder flasks, rapiers, sabres, cutlasses and pikes, masses of Toby jugs behind the serving counter, sturdy old seats and settles, two cosy little alcoves, and an open fire. Well kept Batemans XXXB, Hook Norton, Flowers Original, Marstons Pedigree, Theakstons XB, Wadworths 6X and occasional guest beers on handpump; friendly service. Good bar food includes sandwiches, filled baked potatoes (from £1.50), filled Yorkshire puddings (from £2.50), cottage pie (£3), lasagne or vegetarian dishes (£3.50) and three-course Sunday lunch (£6.50); pleasant, courteous service. Through the medieval arch of the back door there are tables and chairs in the sheltered, extended garden here, with more on the cobbles and laid bricks of a sheltered yard, which has clematis on a side wall and is fairy-lit at night. *(Recommended by Roy Bromell, B R Shiner, A Parsons, Peter Watkins, Pam Stanley, Philip Orbell, T Nott)*

Free house   Licensee Geoffrey G Wright   Real ale   Meals and snacks (12–2, 7–10; not winter Sun evening)   Restaurant tel Southam (092 681) 2339; not winter Sun evening   Children allowed, but only in garden at busy periods   Open 11–2.30, 5.30–11; 11–11 Fri and Sat; winter opening 11–2.30, 6.30–11; 11–3, 6–11 Sat

STOKE BRUERNE (Northants)   SP7450 Map 4

Boat

3 1/2 miles from M1 junction 15: A508 towards Stony Stratford, then Stoke Bruerne signposted on the right

Owned and run by the same family for over a century, this old-fashioned place is well positioned by the Grand Union Canal: from tables outside by the neatly painted double locks you can watch the colourful narrowboats, and on the other side there's an interesting canal museum in a handsome row of 18th-century warehouses. The low-ceilinged and tiled-floor bar and tap room, which can get very crowded, are brightly painted with simple vignettes of barges and barge life; a spacious lounge at the back is perfectly comfortable though less special; a good, rustic atmosphere. Everards Old Original, Marstons Burton and Pedigree, Sam Smiths OB and Theakstons OB on handpump; dominoes, cribbage, fruit machine, trivia, piped music, and a separate alley for hood skittles. Sandwiches (£1.25; toasted £1.40), ploughman's (from £1.65), burgers (from £1.75), basket meals (from £1.95), vegetarian quiche (£3.25), or crumble (£3.45), home-made lasagne (£3.45), salads (£3.75), mini grill (£4.25) and steak (£6.50); there are also canalside tea rooms. A narrowboat is available for party or individual hire. *(Recommended by Mrs M E Lawrence, Tim and Sue Halstead, Carol and Richard Glover, Gordon Theaker, Sue Corrigan, Jim Aitkenhead, Mike and Sue Wheeler)*

Free house   Licensee John Woodward   Real ale   Meals and snacks (11.30–2.30, 7–9.30; tea room open 9.30–6)   Restaurant tel Roade (0604) 862428; not Sun evening   Children in eating area, restaurant and tea room   Cabaret Nov and Dec, local canal music throughout the year, and by arrangement at other times   Parking may be difficult at peak holiday times   Open 11–3, 6–11, though may open longer in afternoon if trade demands; all day Sat

STRATFORD UPON AVON (War)   SP2055 Map 4

Garrick

High Street; close to Town Hall

This elaborately timbered building has small and often irregularly shaped rooms, with heavy wall timbers, high ceiling beams, some walls stripped back to bare stone and others heavily plastered with posters, sawdust on the wood floor, long upholstered settles and stools, and maybe a talking mynah bird; the back bar centres on an open fire with a conical brass hood. Flowers IPA and Original on handpump, kept under light blanket pressure; a fruit machine and thoughtfully chosen piped music. Bar food includes filled rolls, ploughman's, steak and kidney pie, game pie and cottage pie or lasagne. The name Garrick originates from 1769 when the actor David Garrick visited Stratford and inaugurated the Stratford Festival. *(Recommended by Mr and Mrs J H Adam, Andy and Jill Kassube, David and Eloise Smaylen, Sheila Keene; more reports please)*

Flowers (Whitbreads)   Real ale   Lunchtime meals (not Sun or Mon) and snacks   Children in dining room Tues–Sat lunchtimes only   Nearby daytime parking difficult   Open 10.30–2.30, 5.30ish–11

Slug & Lettuce ⊗

38 Guild Street, corner of Union Street

You can see some of the bar food being prepared at one end of the long L-shaped bar counter in this civilised place; the enterprising range is being maintained under the new licensees, with such dishes as home-made celery and almond soup (£1.75), salad niçoise (£3.50), chicken livers sautéed in garlic and sage (£4), chicken breast baked with avocado and garlic (£6.75), and lemon sole with prawns in a cream and white wine sauce. The bar itself, popular with theatre-goers, has pine kitchen tables and chairs on rugs and flagstones, a few period prints on stripped squared panelling, sprays of flowers on the tables, a newspaper rack, and a solid fuel fire. The good range of well kept beers on handpump includes Ansells, Ind Coope Burton, Tetleys, two other Ind Coope-related beers named for the pub, and a guest such as Holts; decent wine list, a good range of spirits, and they do a good Pimms. The small flagstoned terrace at the back, floodlit at night, has lots of flower boxes and sturdy teak tables under cocktail parasols, with more up steps. *(Recommended by Mrs E M Thompson, John Moate, Mr and Mrs G J Rice, Brian Skelcher, Roy Bromell, Brian Jones, Len Beattie, T Nott, Frank Cummins; more reports on the new regime please)*

Ansells (Allied)   Licensee Tim Hunter   Real ale   Meals and snacks (noon–10 Mon–Sat, normal hours Sun)   Children in eating area lunchtime   Open 11–11; closed 1 Jan

White Swan

Rother Street; leads into the A34

Best entered by a cobbled sideway, the bar itself in this THF hotel is an old-fashioned affair, with cushioned leather armchairs, carved ancient oak settles, plush smaller seats, a nice window seat, heavy beams, and highly polished Jacobean oak panelling throughout; one fireplace has a handsomely carved chimney piece, another smaller one an attractive marquetry surround. Well kept Marstons Pedigree, Wadworths 6X and a guest on handpump. A staffed food counter outside serves home-made soup (£1.50), ploughman's (£3), a daily hot dish (£3.85), quiche (£4.35), cold meat platter (£4.65), and puddings (from £1.40); friendly service. Look out for the wall painting of Tobias and the Angel with the miraculous fish – painted in 1560 but not discovered until 1927. *(Recommended by Len Beattie, T C W Moody; more reports please)*

Free house (THF)   Manager Philip Bellamy   Real ale   Lunchtime snacks Restaurant   Children in eating area   Open 11–2.30, 6–11   Bedrooms tel Stratford-upon-Avon (0789) 297022; £72B/£87B

THORPE MANDEVILLE (Northants)   SP5344 Map 4
Three Conies

In village, just off B4525 Banbury–Northampton

Close to Sulgrave Manor (George Washington's ancestral home) and Canons Ashby House (the Dryden family home), this 17th-century stone pub is popular with readers for its genuinely home-made food, which ranges from sandwiches (from £1), soup (the jet-black mushroom one is recommended), ploughman's, sausages (£2.15), mushrooms in a garlic and cream sauce, chicken breast (£3.85), salads (£4.40), steaks, and daily specials such as chilli con carne or steak and kidney pie (from around £3.20); puddings such as home-made ice-creams, sherry trifle or chocolate éclairs (from £1.65), and Sunday roast lunch; the evening menu has a different selection, though the friendly Cockney licensee may let you have something from it at lunchtime. The low-beamed lounge bar is well furnished with tapestried built-in settles and spindleback chairs around tables on its patterned carpet, little hunting prints and polished brass on the walls (which are partly stripped back to golden stone), and horsebrasses around the open fireplace. Beyond the servery, the public bar has bigger pictures on its stripped stone walls, and a pool table. Well kept Hook Norton Best and Old Hookey on handpump and a good selection of wines and spirits. There are old-fashioned teak and curly iron seats on a lawn with a fruit tree. *(Recommended by Ted George, JM, PM, Pete Storey, Lyn and Bill Capper, Dave Braisted, M O'Driscoll, J E Rycroft)*

Hook Norton   Licensees John and Maureen Day   Real ale   Meals and snacks Restaurant tel Banbury (0295) 711025; not Sun   Children welcome   Open 11–3, 6–11

TWYWELL (Northants)   SP9478 Map 4

Old Friar

Village signposted from A604 about 2 miles W of Thrapston

The good range of bar food in this dining pub – most of the tables are set for eating – includes sandwiches, soup (£1.55), oriental parcels (£2.45), lasagne or lamb moussaka (£4.25), vegetarian dishes (£3.95), home-made pies (£4.75), gammon (£7.25) and steaks (from £8.45), a hot and cold carvery (£5.95); part of the dining area is no-smoking. The bar is attractively furnished with plain wooden tables, tub chairs and settles; both the beams and the brick fireplaces have wooden carvings of friars. Well kept Ruddles Best and County, and Websters Yorkshire on handpump served from the brick bar counter; shove-ha'penny, dominoes, fruit machine and piped music. No dogs. *(Recommended by L Walker; more reports please)*

Manns (Watneys)   Licensees David and Yvonne Crisp   Real ale   Meals and snacks (12–1.45, 7–9.45; 10 Sat)   Restaurant tel Thrapston (080 12) 2625   Children welcome   Open 11–2.30(3 Sat), 6–11

WARMINGTON (War)   SP4147 Map 4

Plough

Village just off A41 N of Banbury

The softly lit bar in this little golden ironstone pub, dating from the early 1600s, has a cosy atmosphere, with small settee, an old high-backed winged settle, leatherette-cushioned wall seats and lots of comfortable Deco small armed chairs and library chairs, and good winter log fires; on the walls, largely stripped back to the stone, there are old photographs of the village and locals. Well kept Hook Norton Best, Marstons Pedigree and Merrie Monk, and Wadworths 6X on handpump, and several malt whiskies; Aunt Sally shy, maybe faint piped pop music. Straightforward but generously served lunchtime bar food includes good minestrone soup, sandwiches, ploughman's, good minced beef pie, salads (from £3), flavoursome home-baked ham (£3.50), and home-cooked daily specials (from £2). From the outside the pub is at its prettiest when the creeper that covers it turns crimson. *(Recommended by Ted George, M Rising, Derek and Sylvia Stephenson, H R Bevan, K and E Leist, C P Scott-Malden)*

Free house   Licensees E J and D L Wilson   Real ale   Meals and snacks (lunchtime, not Sun)   Children in eating area of bar   Occasional live music   Open 11.30–2.30, 6–11

WARWICK (War)   SP2865 Map 4

Saxon Mill

Guy's Cliffe; A429 N of town

Attractively positioned across from the Avon weir, this cottagey and old-fashioned place (actually a Harvester Family Restaurant) has as its centre piece a great wheel turning slowly behind glass, and a mill race rushing under a glass floor panel (for decorative purposes only these days – it hasn't worked as a watermill since 1938). Elsewhere in the pine-clad, partly beamed and flagstoned bar rooms there are brasses, open fireplaces and bookshelves. The standard range of bar food, Courage Best and Directors on handpump, and gentle piped music. There are picnic-table sets on a terrace below and out under the surrounding trees, a fishing club (anyone can join), weekend barbecues (weather permitting), and a children's play area with slides, swings and so forth. *(Recommended by Auriol and Paul McLoughlin, Miss R Murdoch; more reports please)*

Free house (THF)   Real ale   Lunchtime meals and snacks   Restaurant tel Warwick (0926) 492255   Children welcome   Rock music Tues, jazz Thurs, Country & Western Sun   Open 11–11 Mon–Sat, 12–3, 7–11 Sun

WELFORD ON AVON (War)   SP1452 Map 4

Bell

High Street; village signposted from A439

The comfortable, beamed lounge bar here has sober seats and tables to match the dark timbering, open fireplaces (one with a real fire, one with electric), and a low ceiling; the flagstoned public bar has another open fire. Bar food includes sandwiches, steak and kidney pie (£3.80), plaice stuffed with mushrooms and prawns (£4.70), chicken kiev or cold Scotch salmon (£4.75), and good gammon and eggs; Sunday lunch, and several types of liqueur coffee. Flowers Original and IPA on handpump; darts, pool, cribbage, fruit machine, trivia, juke box and piped music; seats in the pretty garden area and back courtyard. The riverside village, with its church and thatched black and white cottages, is pretty. (*Recommended by CEP, Mrs R Heaton, Paul and Margaret Baker, S V Bishop; more reports please*)

Whitbreads   Licensee Mike Eynon   Real ale   Meals and snacks (12–2.30, 7–10) Restaurant tel *Stratford-upon-Avon (0789) 750353   Children in centrally heated, furnished and enclosed terrace   Open 11–3, 6–11*

WEST BROMWICH (W Midlands)   SP0091 Map 4

Manor House

2 miles from M6, junction 9; from A461 towards Wednesbury take first left into Woden Rd East; at T-junction, left into Crankhall Lane; at eventual roundabout, right into Hall Green Rd

This small manor house dates from the 13th century, though something was on its site centuries earlier – it's listed in the Domesday Book as being held by William Fitz Ansculph, Baron of Dudley. It's still a remarkable place: you enter through the ancient gatehouse, across the moat, and inside, the main bar is actually a great flagstoned hall, where massive oak trusses support the soaring pitched roof (the central one, eliminating any need for supporting pillars, is probably unique), and a fine old sliding door opens on to stairs leading up to a series of smaller and cosier timbered upper rooms, including a medieval Solar, which again have lovely oak trusses supporting their pitched ceiling beams; there are blue carpets, and plenty of tables, and upstairs comfortably cushioned seats and stools around small tables, with the occasional settle; a snug Parlour Bar is tucked in beneath the Solar. Well kept Banks's Bitter and Mild and Hansons on electric pump; friendly service, piped music, space game, and fruit machines. Bar food, served from a side bar, includes soup (90p), ploughman's or salads (£2.50), a vegetarian dish (£2.75) and half-a-dozen hot dishes such as steak and kidney or cottage pie (£3) and roasts (£3.50); there are also banquets in the hall about once a month. A broad stretch of grass leads away behind the moat, and a car park is sensitively tucked away behind some modern ancillary buildings. (*Recommended by Drs M and K Parier, Roger Huggins, J S Rutter, Len Beattie, Andrew Triggs, Dr and Mrs C D E Morris, E J Alcock, Dave Braisted*)

Banks's   Manager Mr Carter   Real ale   Meals and snacks   Restaurant tel *Birmingham (021) 588 2035; not Sun evening   Children in restaurant and eating area of bar   Open 11.30–2.30, 6–11*

WHATCOTE (War)   SP2944 Map 4

Royal Oak

Village signposted from A34 N of Shipston on Stour; and from A422 Banbury–Stratford, via Oxhill

Originally a commissary for the builders of the 12th-century village church, this charming stone building, popular with readers, has low ceilings in the small rooms of the original bar, a huge inglenook fireplace with rungs leading up to a chamber on the right (originally either a priest's hiding hole, or a smoking chamber for hams), a miscellany of stools, cushioned pews and other seats, old local photographs, brasses, a sword, and a stuffed peewit on the walls, and coins, bookmatches and foreign banknotes on the beams behind the high copper bar counter. A larger, and less elaborately decorated bar is on the left. Well kept Flowers Original, Marstons Pedigree and Wethereds Winter Royal; darts (winter), dominoes, fruit machine and piped music; Shadow the German shepherd is friendly. A wide choice of bar food includes sandwiches (if they're not busy), home-made soup (£1.25), ploughman's (£3), tasty cold ham (£3.30), trout (£3.70), chicken kiev (£5.80), sirloin steak (£7) and imaginative specials such as vegetable lasagne (£3.60), game dishes in season (from £3.50), shark steak (£4.50), and chicken with crab and peppercorns (£5). The front terrace has some picnic-tables sets, and there are more on grass at the side. Around 20–30 October the Sealed Knots re-enact the Battle of Edgehill, and come to the pub in period costume for lunch – in 1642 Cromwell used it as temporary quarters, and there's a tradition that he came back here after the battle for drinks. *(Recommended by Mrs V A Middlebrook, Barry and Anne, M O'Driscoll, Mrs Nina Elliott, P R Davis, C A Holloway, Frank Cummins, Wayne Brindle, John Bowdler, Sir Nigel Foulkes, Brian Skelcher)*

Free house   Licensee Mrs Catherine Matthews   Real ale   Meals and snacks (12–2, 6–10.30)   Children in eating area of bar   Open 10.30–2.30, 6–11

WITHYBROOK (War)   SP4384 Map 4

Pheasant

4 miles from M6, junction 2; follow Ansty, Shilton signpost; bear right in Shilton towards Wolvey then take first right signposted Withybrook – or, longer but wider, second right into B4112 to Withybrook

Much liked by readers for its cheerful standards of service and extensive and generous choice of food, this well kept pub has a spacious lounge with a serving counter flanked by well polished rocky flagstones, lots of plush-cushioned wheelback chairs and dark tables on the patterned carpet, a few farm tools on its cream walls, and good winter fires; well kept Courage Directors on handpump, with John Smiths on electric pump; a fruit machine in the lobby, and piped music. The bar food itself includes sandwiches (from 95p), soup (£1), a cheesy ploughman's (£2.25), omelettes (from £3.50), home-made lasagne, steak and kidney pie, fresh quiches or braised liver and onions (all £3.75), salads (from £3.50), vegetarian dishes such as pie or lentil and mushroom lasagne (£3.95), tasty seafood vol-au-vent (£4.75), braised guinea fowl royale (£5.75), steaks (from £7.45), and puddings (£1.50); Sunday lunch in restaurant £7.25. They take your name when you arrive, and sit you down in order (a good idea), giving you time to relax with a drink early beforehand – though readers do warn that it really is popular for food. There are tables under fairy lights on a brookside terrace, and the bank opposite is prettily planted with flowers and shrubs. The Ankor Morris Men come a few times a year. *(Recommended by Graham Bush, Brian and Genie Smart, Mike and Wendy Proctor, Tim Newell, David and Sarah Gilmore, Brian and Anna Marsden, Harry Stirling, Thomas Nott, A Parsons, Wayne Brindle, Geoff Lee, Paul Wreglesworth, Dave Braisted, Ken and Barbara Turner, Olive Carroll)*

Free house   Licensees Derek Guy, Mr and Mrs Alan Bean   Real ale   Meals and snacks (12–2, 6.30–10)   Restaurant Hinkley (0455) 220480   Children welcome Open 11–2.30(3 Sat), 6.30–11; closed evenings 25 and 26 Dec

Lucky Dip

Besides the fully inspected pubs, you might like to try these Lucky Dips recommended to us and described by readers (if you do, please send us reports):

Alcester, War [Stratford Rd; SP0857], *Cross Keys*: Doing well under current regime, with good choice of traditional bar food, well kept Ansells, Banks's Mild and Tetleys *(A J Woodhouse)*; [High St; next to PO], *Royal Oak*: Modernised old-world pub with large well-appointed back dining room, reasonably priced generous helpings of good bar food, Davenports ales; friendly staff *(G

Lawrence)*
☆ **Alveston**, War [SP2356], *Ferry*: Should be well worth knowing, as the Russons who made the Howard Arms at Ilmington an extremely well favoured main entry were to move here shortly after this edition went to press *(Reports please)*
Ansty, War [Ansty—Shilton rd, E of Coventry; between M6 junction 2 and

B4029; SP3983], *Crown*: Pleasant atmosphere and well kept beers in busy local *(Tim Newell)*

☆ **Ardens Grafton**, War [on edge of village, towards Wixford — OS Sheet 150 map reference 114538; SP1153], *Golden Cross*: Masses of ancient and modern dolls, of all sizes and descriptions, wearing costumes made by the landlady, in pleasant, carpeted L-shaped room with low ceiling, decorative beams and tables set for meals on one side; generous helpings of good bar food, separate restaurant menu, well kept Whitbreads-related real ales on handpump, warm welcome, efficient service, unobstrusive piped music, fruit machine; seats outside *(Frank Cummins, Mr and Mrs F Egerton, E J Alcock)*

Arthingworth, Northants [SP7581], *Bulls Head*: Pleasant atmosphere, log fires, good bar menu with wide choice of vegetarian dishes; small restaurant with good but not exotic food; attentive service *(Mr and Mrs P Crane)*

☆ **Aston Cantlow**, War [SP1359], *Kings Head*: Beautifully timbered village pub not far from Mary Arden's house in Wilmcote, nicely restored with flagstones, inglenook, cheery log fire and settles; grandfather clock in low-beamed room on left, snug on right, well kept Flowers IPA and Original, good value home-made bar food, good atmosphere, friendly service *(Brian Jones, Brian Skelcher, LYM)*

Atherstone, War [Long St; SP3097], *Cloisters*: Warm friendly atmosphere in bar with good range of drinks inc farm cider; nice staff, reasonably priced bar food; folk music weekly *(Matthew Gough)*

Austrey, War [Church Lane (A453); SK2906], *Bird in Hand*: Reputably one of the oldest pubs in the area, prettily thatched, and inc old ships' timbers as beams; decidedly a local, with well kept Marstons Pedigree on handpump, traditional games, pleasant coal fire *(C Davies)*

Aynho, Northants [SP5133], *Cartwright Arms*: 16th-century inn, now become a Kings Steakhouse — big helpings of reasonable food in new restaurant, but no longer the country pub recommended in previous editions; bedrooms comfortable *(Bob and Val Collman, BB)*; [Wharf Base (B4031 W)], *Great Western Arms*: Friendly bar staff, well kept beer on handpump and bar food inc good big ploughman's *(Graham Oddey)*

Badby, Northants [village signposted off A361 Daventry—Banbury; SP5559], *Maltsters Arms*: Character pub with interesting locals and pleasant service *(J V Dadswell)*; *Windmill*: Fundamentally refurbished thatched stone village inn, now more upmarket restaurant-with-bedrooms than pub — but well kept Hook Norton Best, Theakstons XB and Youngers IPA in bar nicely furnished with scrubbed deal tables — small lounge across passage more in keeping with hotel image *(Ted George, LYM)*

☆ **Balsall Common**, W Mid [SP2377], *Saracens Head*: Rambling 16th-century character pub, several interconnecting rooms, some with beams and flagstones, good straightforward bar food, newspapers out to read, muted piped rock music, well kept Ansells Mild and Bitter, Ind Coope Burton, Tetleys and maybe Marstons Pedigree; polite service, restaurant *(Brian Jones, Dr J A Benbow)*

Barford, War [SP2760], *Joseph Arch*: Well kept Flowers Original on handpump and good reasonably priced bar food in pub named for founder of agricultural workers' union *(W H Bland)*

☆ **Barnacle**, War [village signed off B4029 in Shilton, nr M6 junction 2; SP3884], *Red Lion*: Quiet pub with two rooms, one small, the other long with a leather bench seat around edge and collection of plates; Bass and M&B, ample cheap bar food (not Sun lunchtime); seats out in covered front area *(Ted George, Geoff Lee)*

☆ **Barnwell**, Northants [TL0484], *Montagu Arms*: Popular old pub with low beams and flagstones in original part, extension bar and restaurant; well kept Greene King IPA, Marstons Pedigree and Charles Wells on handpump, guest beers such as Batemans XXXB, simple reasonably priced but imaginatively presented lunchtime bar food inc good puddings, more extensive evening menu; waitress service, good atmosphere; bedrooms and self-catering accommodation in recently converted outbuildings *(Mr and Mrs J Barnes, M and J Back, Eric Locker)*

Barton, War [pub signed off B4085, just S of Bidford-on-Avon; SP1051], *Cottage of Content*: Cosy flagstoned bar with simple traditional furnishings, solid fuel stove in inglenook, low black beams, short choice of simple bar food from soup and sandwiches up, well kept Flowers IPA and Original on handpump, piped music, restaurant; picnic-tables sets in front of the pretty house, touring caravan site with good play area behind; day fishing on River Avon here *(BB)*

☆ **Bearley**, War [A34 N of Stratford; SP1860], *Golden Cross*: Friendly and welcoming atmosphere in lovely old timbered bar with open fireplaces, soft lighting; increasingly popular for good generous bar food, wide range of beers, wine on tap, helpful staff; small restaurant *(A J Woodhouse, Dr J A Benbow, Wayne Brindle)*

Bidford on Avon, War [High St; SP1051], *White Lion*: Pleasant inn with good food and atmosphere; bedrooms *(H R Bevan)*

Binley Woods, War [A428 Coventry—Warwicks; SP3977], *Cocked Hat*: Popular with businessmen during the week, nice relaxed atmosphere at weekends, with good food inc vegetarian dishes in restaurant; comfortable bedrooms *(Sandra Kempson)*

Birmingham [back bar of Midland Hotel, Stephenson St, off New St], *Atkinson Bar*: Clearly enjoyed its heyday in the first decade of the century — echoes of faded glory in hushed bar lined with bookshelves; a nice place to ponder what has been and what might be again, over a peaceful glass of well kept real ale (good range on handpump, inc Holdens) and fresh French bread sandwich *(Ann Griffiths, John C Baker)*; [Wheelers Lane, Kings Heath; SP0781], *Billesley*: Quiet and friendly with reasonably priced good food; bedrooms *(Anon)*; [Cambrian Wharf; Kingston Row, off Broad St], *Longboat*: Modern city-centre pub with terrace and balcony over canal; well kept beers, efficient service, very popular lunchtime for straightforward bar food, quiet evenings; juke box, fruit machines *(Patrick and Mary McDermott);* [Lea End Lane/Icknield St], *Peacock:* Picturesque setting for small isolated pub with homely atmosphere, low ceilings and pub games; picnic-table sets in quiet garden — yet only mins from centre *(E J Alcock);* [St Pauls Sq, Hockley], *Rope Walk:* One of several new pubs springing up in this quiet business area — lots of glass, wood and atmosphere, well kept beers, wide choice of good value food, friendly if not always speedy service; piped music and fruit machine; parking nearby, open all day; nr Science Museum *(Colin Gooch);* [Aston St, nr Gosta Green triangle], *Sacks of Potatoes:* Recently refurbished, popular with Aston students for well kept Bass, M&B Mild and Springfield on handpump, good varied cheap bar food *(Gary Phillips, Hilary Sargeant, N P Clarke);* [120 Bridge St], *Wharf:* Newish well run Beefeater in relaxing canalside setting nr centre; decent bar or restaurant food served in or out, friendly, attentive service, no music, clean lavatories *(RJH);* [Edmund St], *White Swan:* Clean, smart, split-level pub with large front bar and back food area; Edwardian furnishings, gas lamps, heavy wallpaper, stained-glass screens creating small booths, pillars with shelf tables, comfortable banquettes; Brew XI, good sandwiches, ploughman's and pâté, sundae-type puddings; covered yard with white cast-iron tables and chairs; children welcome *(Ian Phillips)*

☆ **Blakesley**, Northants [High St (Woodend rd); SP6250], *Bartholomew Arms:* Two pleasantly cosy beamed bars cluttered with nick-nacks, friendly staff, well kept Watneys-related real ales and Marstons Pedigree, cheap filled rolls and hot dishes, sun-trap garden with summerhouse *(L Walker, Nick Dowson, Alison Hayward)*

☆ **Bodymoor Heath**, War [Dog Lane; SP2096], *Dog & Doublet:* Canalside pub which can get packed at weekends, and it's a shame that they let you eat only snacks in the pleasant garden, with its dovecote (children aren't allowed inside); but well worth knowing for its setting close to Kingsbury Water Park, for the reasonably priced good bar food inc meals in a separate dining room, and for the general character of the place — beams, brasses, bargees' painted ware, well kept M&B, comfortable seats, several open fires *(Colin Gooch)*

Braunston, Northants [on canal, about a mile from the village; SP5466], *Admiral Nelson:* Large, modernised waterside pub with good atmosphere, piped music, Watneys-related real ales, good range of well cooked bar food — more meals than snacks; a nice summer pub *(Gordon Theaker, JWGG, EAG);* [A45 at canal junction], *Boatman:* Large waterside pub with Watneys-related real ales on handpump, big back lounge, games room at front, wide range of usual bar food; children allowed in restaurant by canal; bedrooms *(Mike and Sue Wheeler, Ted George)*

Bretford, War [A428 Coventry—Rugby — OS Sheet 140 map reference 431772;

SP4377], *Queens Head:* Large, spacious and airy pub, with big helpings of reasonably priced good straightforward bar food; big garden *(Mike and Wendy Proctor, Geoff Lee)*

Brierley Hill, W Mid [Delph Rd; SO9187], *Tenth Lock:* Virtually at bottom of Delph Flight of locks, with Banks's beers and reasonable, traditional food *(Dave Braisted)*

Brinklow, War [Fosse Way; A427, fairly handy for M6 junction 2; SP4379], *Raven:* Pleasant location, beams, friendly staff, and good choice of reasonably priced bar food inc vegetarian dishes *(M A and W R Proctor)*

Broom, War [SP0853], *Broom Hall:* Good choice of reasonably priced food, and real ales, in comfortable and relaxing lounge bar; bedrooms *(JM, PM)*

Bubbenhall, War [SP3672], *Malt Shovel:* Clean and tidy olde-worlde pub with friendly staff, well kept Allied real ales, wide range of bar food, spacious garden with seats in summer, two bowling greens and big car park *(Ted George)*

☆ **Bulwick**, Northants [Main St; just off A43 Kettering—Duddington; SP9694], *Queens Head:* Beautiful listed 17th-century beamed stone pub, with genuine atmosphere, friendly landlord, well kept Batemans XXXB and two changing guest beers; cheap snacks (sandwiches and especially baked potatoes recommended), good value restaurant; no juke box *(Nic James, Geoff Lee)*

Chadwick End, War [A41; SP2073], *Orange Tree:* Well refurbished, comfortable and ingeniously laid out Whitbreads Brewers Fayre pub; Marstons Pedigree and Whitbreads-related real ales, well prepared standard bar food, piped music; no-smoking family room has high chairs, children's food, games, even baby wipes *(Dave Braisted, Mr and Mrs M D Jones)*

Church Lawford, War [OS Sheet 140 map reference 450765; SP4476], *White Lion:* Mellow oak beams, horsebrasses, food inc interesting very hot West African curry; tables out among roses, in small and attractive village *(Geoff Lee)*

☆ **Churchover**, War [handy for M6 junction 1, off A426; SP5180], *Haywaggon:* Carefully modernised old pub on edge of quiet village in lovely countryside, with two small separate eating areas leading off bar, friendly pubby atmosphere, efficient staff, good range of beer inc Badger Best, Bass, Courage Best and Directors, Marstons, Ruddles County and regular guest beers, good straightforward bar food *(Ted George, Aleister and Geraldine Martin, BB)*

☆ **Claverdon**, War [SP1964], *Red Lion:* Clean and spacious back saloon (where children allowed) opening on to sheltered garden with tables on terrace and play area; small plush front L-shaped lounge; popular for quickly served reliable food from ploughman's through dishes such as Arbroath smokies, lamb and leek or steak and kidney pie to attractively priced steaks; well kept Flowers IPA and Original on handpump, open fire *(Geoff Lee, Mrs R Heaton, Brian Jones, BB)*

Clay Coton, Northants [off B5414 nr Stanford Hall; SP5977], *Fox & Hounds:* Fine country pub, tastefully furnished, with two log fires, well kept Adnams, Hook

Norton Old Hookey, Marstons Pedigree and Theakstons XB, good generously served bar food; big car park *(Ted George)*

Clifton upon Dunsmore, War [B5414 NE of Rugby; SP5376], *Black Bull*: Popular, cosy village local, separate dining room *(Wayne Brindle)*

☆ **Coleshill**, War [High St; not far from M6 junction 4; SP1989], *George & Dragon*: Well decorated and clean, with well kept M&B on handpump and good value bar food; big front public bar packed on Sat night, people waiting for tables in dining lounge — not then the place for a quiet meal, but astonishingly good value, with remarkably cheap steaks *(Brian Jones)*

Coleshill, *Wheatsheaf*: Spotless M&B pub with relaxing, friendly atmosphere, good staff, wide choice of food and well kept beer *(S Ziaja)*

Corley, War [A51 Coventry—Tamworth; SP2985], *Horse & Jockey*: Good Chef & Brewer pub with decent lunchtime specials and well kept Watneys-related real ales *(Dave Braisted)*

☆ **Cosgrove**, Northants [Thrupp Wharf, towards Castlethorpe; SP7942], *Navigation*: Mellow stone pub, very popular in summer for rural setting on Grand Union Canal, cosy in winter with coal-effect gas fires; inexpensive good straightforward food, good choice of real ales, with unusual guests — regulars are Banks & Taylors SOD, Charrington IPA and Greene King and Marstons beers; lots of dining tables in tidy lounge, pool and games in public bar, elevated back verandah-terrace, spacious garden and children's area by canal, own moorings *(Dominic Woodfield, Michael and Alison Sandy, BB)*

☆ **Coventry**, W Mid [Spon St; SP3379], *Old Windmill*: Still known as Ma Brown's after a former landlady, this quaint and popular timber-framed 16th-century pub is all nooks and crannies with no big room; fine ancient fireplace, good atmosphere in lots of small rooms, one with carved oak seats and flagstones; generous helpings of simple but extraordinarily cheap lunchtime food (chips and beans loom large) served quickly from the kitchen door, well kept Watneys-related real ales; very busy Fri and Sat evening; one of the few buildings which started its life in this interesting street, to which other ancient survivors of wartime bombing have now been moved *(Geoff Lee, Dr J R Hamilton, Syd and Wyn Donald, Dawn and Phil Garside)*

☆ **Coventry**, W Mid [Sutton Stop, Aldermans Green/Hawkesbury; close to M6 junction 3, via Black Horse Rd off B4113 Coventry Rd], *Greyhound*: Good food at attractive prices inc particularly good pies, well kept Bass and Brew XI on electric pump, waterside tables in delightful garden at junction of Coventry and Oxford Canals, interesting collection of ties, odd little donkey-box (tiny snug); last year they were in the spotlight for charging 55p for a glass of tap water *(C Davies, T R G Alcock)*

Coventry, W Mid [Craven St, Chapel Fields], *Coombe Abbey*: Particularly friendly, with small, busy lounge; well kept Bass, good value bar food; occasional folk music, terrace *(Clive Davies)*; [Walsgrave Rd; nr M6 junction 2 — left at A4600 roundabout into Coventry], *Mount Pleasant*: A nice place, with good range of good value food — refurbished as a Marstons Tavern Table *(Geoff Lee)*; [Bond St, behind Coventry Theatre], *Town Wall*: Compact recently brightened up Victorian pub, with original Atkinsons engraved windows, open fire in small lounge, simpler bar, tiny snug and flower-filled back yard; has had well kept Bass and enterprising good value bar food even running to goat stew lunchtime and early evening, but we've had no recent reports *(News please)*; [1059 Foleshill Rd], *William IV*: Unassuming, suburban two-lounge M&B pub with mock timbering outside, plush banquettes and flock wallpaper; the notable thing about it is its excellent authentic Indian food (the pub's Asian-run), reasonably priced and well up to restaurant standard; gets very busy, even early evening midweek *(E V Walder)*

☆ **Cradley Heath**, W Mid [St Annes Rd, Five Ways; SO9486], *Sausage Works*: One of the Little Pubs chain, with good food featuring a variety of interesting sausage dishes — and over-the-top decor to match; well kept real ales inc Little Lumphammer *(Steve J Pratt, E J Alcock, Dave Braisted)*

Cradley Heath [Halesowen Rd], *Hadden Cross*: Good value bar food, well kept Banks's *(Dave Braisted)*; [Halesowen/Dudley Rd], *Rose & Crown*: Friendly pub with good value bar snacks and Bass beers *(Dave Braisted)*; [Cradley Forge], *Waggon & Horses*: Old building tastefully extended; good value bar snacks such as quiche and filled baked potatoes, well kept reasonably priced real ales inc Hansons *(Dave Braisted)*; [135 Station Rd], *Wharf*: Imaginative, reasonably priced food, good choice of beers inc well kept Home, friendly staff and attractive original canalside setting *(Russell Allen)*

Crick, Northants [A428, a mile from M1 junction 18; SP5872], *Old Royal Oak*: Lovely old village pub, two cosy log fires, friendly licensees, good food in restaurant *(Ted George)*

Darlaston, W Mid [Cemetery Rd; nr M6 junctions 9 and 10; SO9796], *Railway*: Popular local, in unattractive area two mins from M6; friendly staff, bar food, extrovert landlady at her best on quiz nights *(Sun and Wed)* *(E J Alcock)*

☆ **Deppers Bridge**, War [SP4059], *Great Western*: Decorated in old GWR theme — lots of railway features and posters, even a model railway running around the ceiling; clean and comfortable, with friendly staff, unobtrusive piped music, well kept Allied beers on handpump, good choice of wines, liberal helpings of good value food from starters and burgers to steaks — amazing choice inc vegetarian and children's dishes (they have high chairs, too); tiled terrace with plenty of seats and big play area, good car park *(A E and T R G Alcock, G H Gall)*

Dorridge, W Mid [SP1775], *Railway*: Very much a local, though very friendly; well kept M&B Brew XI, nice garden *(Ian Phillips)*

☆ **Dudley**, W Mid [Salop St, Eve Hill; SO9390], *British Oak*: Simply decorated pub, full of local characters and atmosphere; brews its own good value beers inc Castle Ruin, Eve and maybe in winter Dungeon and Old Jones, has made its own cider; also Ansells, Tetleys and Wadworths on handpump, with a guest beer such as Boddingtons, a good few whiskies, generous helpings of simple but very low-priced food inc good value Sun roast, piped music, fruit machine; handy for Dudley Zoo and Black Country Museum *(T R G and A E Alcock, J S Rutter, Ian Holden, Dave Braisted)*

☆ Dudley [Black Country Museum], *Bottle & Glass*: Friendly, old-fashioned atmosphere in Victorian pub reconstructed in village of Black Country Museum (well worth a visit — it also includes working trams and trip up canal tunnel); well kept Hansons on handpump, good sandwiches; open lunchtimes only *(PLC)*

☆ Dudley [Blowers Green Rd (A461/A454)], *Lamp*: Friendly Black Country pub doing well under current regime, with well kept Bathams Mild and Bitter, good value food (burger with egg recommended), fine choice of malt whiskies (sold by the bottle, too), good view from terrace *(Dave Braisted)*

☆ Dunchurch, War [very handy for M45 junction 1; SP4871], *Dun Cow*: Classic coaching-inn layout with big central courtyard; pubby front bars (linked by hallway with settles and antiques) have heavy beams, brasses, warm fires in inglenooks, old-fashioned furnishings, panelling; good atmosphere, particularly in evenings; bedrooms *(LYM)*

☆ Dunchurch [Daventry Rd], *Green Man*: Pleasant village local doing well under young and welcoming new licensees, dining area with home-cooked food from basket meals to steaks, tables in garden; bedrooms, with big breakfasts *(Mr and Mrs R Berresford, Wayne Brindle)*

☆ Eathorpe, War [car park off Fosse Way; SP3868], *Plough*: Small pub of some character, just off Fosse Way; two piranha tanks in rugby-theme bar, good value bar food or more substantial and distinctive meals in long, narrow restaurant; friendly staff, well kept Ansells *(Roy J Bromell, Dr and Mrs A K Clarke, Clive Davies)*

Ecton, Northants [Ecton Rd; A45 Northampton—Wellingborough;SP8263], *Worlds End*: Recently refurbished pub with big bar and restaurant, good value meals (service may slow on busy weekends), family room, play area; big car park *(D C Horwood)*

☆ Edge Hill, War [SP3747], *Castle*: Notable for terrific garden perched over steep slope of Edge Hill, with lovely views through the trees; and for the building itself, a battlemented folly of great potential; internally, the bar, like the turreted lavatories, is rather basic, with straightforward bar food and Hook Norton real ales *(LYM)*

Ettington, War [Banbury Rd (A422 S of Stratford); SP2749], *Houndshill*: Family-run traditional inn with good range of decent value bar food, restaurant, friendly service; children's play area in spacious garden; bedrooms *(Roy Y Bromell)*

Eydon, Northants [Lime Ave; village signed off A361 Daventry—Banbury, and from B4525; SP5450], *Royal Oak*: Idiosyncratic low-beamed village local with several small rooms opening off central corridor-room

with its own serving hatch; well kept Banks's and Hook Norton on handpump, with guest beers such as Hansons, but little or no bar food — and found closed on one summer 1990 visit; considerable potential *(Nick Dowson, Alison Hayward, LYM; more reports please)*

☆ Farnborough, War [off A423 N of Banbury; SP4349], *Butchers Arms*: Farmhouse-style main lounge bar with pews and stout deal tables, country furnishings in timbered and flagstoned extension, usual bar food, Flowers IPA and Original on handpump; play area on safely fenced front lawn, more tables on flower-edged lawn sloping up behind *(Ken and Barbara Turner, C Aydon, R F Plater, Mrs E M Thompson, LYM)*

Farthingstone, Northants [SP6155], *Kings Arms*: Excellent olde-worlde pub full of atmosphere, pictures, tempting food, well kept Hook Norton *(Comus Elliott)*

Fenny Compton, War [SP4152], *George & Dragon*: Friendly canalside pub with real ales, good bar food; piped music *(Gordon Theaker)*

Gaydon, War [B4451, just off A41 Banbury—Warwick; SP3654], *Malt Shovel*: Modernised pub with pleasant atmosphere, good service, well kept Flowers IPA and Original, good value bar food *(M J Morgan)*

Gayton, Northants [High St; SP7054], *Eykyn Arms*: Lively little skittles bar, more spacious and comfortable lounge with flowered seating, plainer back bar, and well kept Charles Wells Eagle on handpump; pretty hanging baskets *(Nick Dowson)*; *Queen Victoria*: Refurbished village pub with hunting prints in comfortable back lounge, some emphasis on food running up to steaks from modern servery area, darts and hood skittles in lively front public bar, pool room, real ales *(Nick Dowson, LYM)*

Great Brington, Northants [SP6664], *Fox & Hounds*: Sandstone pub in charming village: open fire, cottage chairs on flagstone floor, low beams, separate games room with table skittles; Watneys-related beers; entertaining talkative parrot *(Philip Orbell)*

☆ Great Houghton, Northants [up No Through Road just before the White Hart; SP7958], *Old Cherry Tree*: Cosy low-beamed old pub, renovated but interesting, with single servery for two alcovey areas, well kept Charles Wells Eagle and Bombardier on handpump, bar food inc good value filled French bread *(Dr and Mrs A K Clarke)*

Great Houghton [off A428 Northampton—Bedford], *White Hart*: Attractive thatched pub, pleasant inside (mainly stools and copper-topped tables), bar food inc splendid choice of good value pies, well kept Watneys-related real ales, friendly staff *(Jim Aitkenhead)*

Great Oxendon, Northants [SP7383], *George*: Consistently good imaginative bar food, pleasant service, and good choice of beers and wines *(M Ruskin)*

Grendon, Northants [SP8760], *Crown*: Pleasant bar, lounge and restaurant, friendly staff, well kept Adnams, Marstons Pedigree and guest beer, good straightforward food *(Philip Orbell)*; [just off A5, NW end Atherstone bypass], *Kings Head*: Small, friendly, two-roomed canalside pub with well kept beer on handpump, good value bar food inc big filled Yorkshire puddings and Sun lunch *(Mike and Mandy Challis)*

☆ **Halesowen**, W Mid [Cowley Gate Rd; just off A458 to Stourbridge, at Cradley Heath — OS Sheet 139 map reference 941847; SO9683], *Little White Lion*: A prime light-hearted example of the Little pubs, with bright red and blue paintwork, white lions all over the place, cask tables, six-foot papier-mâché bear, windows painted as if stained glass; good value freshly made bar food in massive helpings, consistently well kept Allied real ales inc Mild, and Little Lumphammer, good service; live music Tues, otherwise quiet piped nostalgic pop *(Brian Jones)*

Halesowen [Stourbridge Rd; next to Halesowen FC], *King Edward VII*: Popular for home-cooked bar lunches and well kept Ansells; lots of stained glass above bar and around partitioning *(Dave Braisted)*; [Furnace Hill], *Loyal Lodge*: New pub, already popular for good bar lunches *(Dave Braisted)*; [Hagley Rd, Hasbury], *Rose & Crown*: Pleasant, friendly pub; bar food, well kept Holt, Plant & Deakins real ales *(Dave Braisted)*

☆ **Hampton in Arden**, W Mid [High St; SP2081], *White Lion*: Attractive stuccoed village pub, friendly and genuine, with good atmosphere; well kept M&B, good food inc lunchtime buffet and fine interestingly filled baps, quick friendly service, log fire; quite handy for National Exhibition Centre; children's room *(Dave Braisted, Gwyneth and Salvo Spadaro-Dutturi, Audrey and Brian Green)*

Hampton Lucy, War [SP2557], *Boars Head*: Pleasant, unspoilt village pub with log fire, brasses and friendly atmosphere; Flowers ale, simple, reasonably priced bar food and prompt service *(T Nott, M Box)*

☆ **Harborne**, W Mid [not far from M5 junction 3; SP0284], *Bell*: Lovely little pub in Botanical Gardens area, with servery by passageway at foot of stairs, much of snug (served by hatch) actually within chimneybreast of former vast open fireplace; large, comfortable lounge, well kept M&B Mild, full range of reasonably priced lunchtime bar food; seats outside, wooden balcony overlooking bowling green *(Ian Phillips)*

Harbury, War [Chapel St; SP3759], *Gamecock*: Particularly good choice of well cooked reasonably priced food, so popular with older regulars that you may need to book; warm and friendly, with well kept beer and decent wine *(Elisabeth Kemp)*; *Shakespeare*: Well kept beer, good value food, friendly atmosphere *(Peter Watkins, Pam Stanley)*

Harlestone, Northants [A428; SP7064], *Fox & Hounds*: Two popular carpeted bars with wide range of hot and cold food, Watneys-related real ales, good choice of wines, fruit machine in one room, piped music; no dogs, motorcyclists or (except out on terrace) children; handy for Althorp *(Lyn and Bill Capper)*

☆ **Harpole**, Northants [High St; nr M1 junction 16; SP6860], *Bull*: Pleasant, clean and friendly pub with good choice of cheap food in generous portions; friendly, helpful service *(Virginia Jones)*

☆ **Hatton**, War [SP2467], *Waterman*: Wide choice of often interesting food inc vegetarian and children's dishes, in generous helpings, Davenports-related beers; well placed next to Hatton flight of locks on Grand Union Canal, with huge garden; very popular Sun lunchtime; children welcome *(Patrick and Mary McDermott, Kenneth Krober)*

Hawkesbury, W Mid [Blackhorse Rd, nr M6 junction 3 — OS Sheet 140 map reference 358846; SP3684], *Boat*: Restrained refurbishment of 1850 canal pub in interesting spot nr junction; well kept real ale, three coal fires, good mix of locals and canal people, traditional games, imaginative bar food *(Geoff Lee)*

Hellidon, Northants [off A425 W of Daventry; SP5158], *Red Lion*: Three connecting rooms around bar, very good bar food and good value fixed-price three-course meal in big but cosy restaurant; Davenports and Courage Best and Directors, skittle table away from main room; picturesque village-green setting, good car park *(Ted George)*

Henley in Arden, War [High St; SP1466], *Blue Bell*: Impressive timber-framed beamed building with fine gateway to former coachyard; well kept Flowers, friendly service, good value straightforward food, modern furnishings *(Brian Skelcher)*

☆ **Hockley Heath**, W Mid [Stratford Rd; A34 Birmingham—Henley-in-Arden; SP1573], *Barn*: Beefeater motel, the rambling bar/restaurant side tricked out with lots of beams and even brick-and-tile miniature houses and canopies over dining tables on various levels stepped up from the big serving counter; hums with activity, and worth knowing for decent standard range of food up to steaks, well kept Marstons Pedigree and Whitbreads-related real ales on handpump, cheerful friendly service, and a really genuine welcome for children; bedrooms satisfactory *(Dr R Fuller)*

Hockley Heath [Stratford Rd], *Wharf*: Spacious Chef & Brewer with reasonably priced straightforward bar food from sandwiches up, piped music, fruit machines; service friendly, garden and terrace overlooking Stratford Canal, lavatory for disabled *(Joan Olivier, P M Elliott, Ian Phillips)*

☆ **Ilmington**, War [SP2143], *Howard Arms*: Whitbreads were planning to put this handsome golden stone village pub on the market as this edition went to press; this has meant that the Russons, who during their tenancy here gained one of our food awards, have had to move on — to the Ferry at Alveston; so we know nothing of the new regime, but heavy beams, rugs on polished flagstones, good log fires (one in a big inglenook screened off by a built-in settle), the village-green view, and the attractive garden are all plusses *(LYM; news please)*

Kenilworth, War [Castle Hill; SP2871], *Clarendon Arms*: Recently upgraded pub now serving good bar meals in small downstairs dining room or slightly more expensive larger upstairs restaurant with waitress service; pleasant atmosphere, Courage Directors *(Roger Braithwaite, A*

Parsons); [High St], *Clarendon House*: Painstakingly restored and interestingly decorated to make the most of its long history; has been praised for good range of drinks inc Flowers and Hook Norton real ales, and reasonably priced lunchtime bar food, but no recent reports; restaurant, bedrooms *(News please)*

Kilsby, Northants [A5; SP5671], *George*: Tastefully decorated oak-panelled lounge with hunting prints and plush seating; Bass on handpump, darts and pool, good choice of bar food from sandwiches to steak, pleasant garden *(J H Adam)*

Kings Sutton, Northants [SP4936], *Butchers Arms*: Charming stone building with good village atmosphere, well kept Hook Norton on handpump, cheerful and friendly licensees, popular simple bar food, play area *(John Baker)*

Knowle, W Mid [SP1876], *Red Lion*: Large, modern and comfortable local; good food, very friendly *(Sidney and Erna Wells)*

☆ **Ladbroke**, War [A423 S of Southam; SP4158], *Bell*: Pleasant surroundings, tables in garden, well kept Davenports and wide range of well served grilled and fried food, superb value for money; very busy at weekends *(Michael Brookes)*

Lapworth, War [Old Warwick Rd (B4439); SP1670], *Boot*: Food is unchanging good value, in big helpings; competent bar staff, cheerful and obliging waitresses, pleasant canalside position; nr GWG105 *(John Bowdler)*

Leamington Spa, War [Sydenham Dr, Sydenham; SP3165], *Fusiliers*: Friendly, happy pub close to Grand Union Canal; two large bars with darts, pool and snooker, separate lounge, good bar food; children welcome *(Sarah Baker)*

☆ **Lilbourne**, Northants [Rugby Rd; 4 miles from M1 junction 18 — A5 N, then first right; SP5677], *Bell*: Spaciously comfortable clean and modern lounge bar well worth knowing as a motorway stopoff, with low-priced quickly served good value simple bar food, seats outside (and climbing frame); children welcome *(Graham and Glenis Watkins, Wayne Brindle, LYM)*

Litchborough, Northants [B4525 Banbury—Northampton; SP6353], *Red Lion*: Pleasant and cheerful, with home-cooked bar food, well kept Watneys-related real ales, done-up inglenook *(Comus Elliott)*

☆ **Little Addington**, Northants [SP9573], *Bell*: Popular village pub with beams and exposed stone in long, comfortable lounge bar, well kept Adnams and Allied real ales, food in bar and good value restaurant, inc imaginative puddings; barbecues in pleasant garden *(Roderic Plinston)*

☆ **Little Brington**, Northants [also signed from A428; 4 1/2 miles from M1 junction 16; first right off A45 to Daventry; SP6663], *Saracens Head*: Old-fashioned village pub, harking back to an idealised memory of the 1950s — spick-and-span brass and copper, cosy seats by the lounge fireside, games in big L-shaped public bar (a log fire here too), tables in neat back garden overlooking quiet fields; friendly service and reasonably priced, well cooked and presented bar food, piano singalong Sat evening,

Watneys-related real ale *(Dudley Fromant, LYM)*

☆ **Long Itchington**, War [Church Rd; SP4165], *Harvester*: Clean pub with straightforward furnishings, well kept Hook Norton and Wadworths 6X on handpump, good value bar food, very reasonably priced meals in small, relaxed restaurant, friendly staff *(Ted George)*

Long Itchington [off A423], *Two Boats*: Neat little canalside pub with good moorings on Grand Union Canal, has been praised for well kept Flowers Original, good value food, welcome for children and friendly staff, but no recent reports *(News please)*

☆ **Lower Boddington**, Northants [off A361 Banbury—Daventry — OS Sheet 151 map reference 481521; SP4852], *Carpenters Arms*: Solidly traditional rural local with warmly welcoming licensees, particularly well kept Hook Norton beers, wide range of lunchtime bar food inc good fry-ups *(Joan and Michel Hooper-Immins)*

☆ **Lower Quinton**, War [off A46 Stratford—Broadway; SP1847], *College Arms*: Whitbreads pub with large open-plan lounge, unusual table in former fireplace, stripped stone walls, heavy beams, partly carpeted parquet floor; wide range of bar food from sandwiches up *(E V Walder, Brian Skelcher)*

Ludstone, W Mid [Upper Ludstone; B4176 Dudley to Telford — OS Sheet 138 map reference 802953; SO8094], *Boycott Arms*: Large, pleasant Banks's pub, good value home cooking *(Dave Braisted)*

☆ **Lye**, W Mid [Pedmore Rd; SO9284], *Shovel Inn*: Friendly refurbished town-centre pub with good range of changing well kept real ales such as Bathams, Everards Tiger and Old Original and Hook Norton Old Hookey, good value home-cooked bar food inc good steaks; pleasant lounge, basic bar — small, can get very crowded *(Steve J Pratt, Dave Braisted, Brian Jones)*

Marston St Lawrence, Northants [off A422 Banbury—Brackley; SP5342], *Marston*: This formerly quite unspoilt village house has changed hands and now been done up, but still has well kept Hook Norton beers *(LYM)*

Meer End, W Mid [SP2474], *Tipperary*: Friendly comfortable pub with bar snacks, Davenports real ale, enormous goldfish in piano-aquarium, tables in garden *(Brian Skelcher, LYM)*

Middleton, War [OS Sheet 139 map reference 175984; SP1798], *Green Man*: Pleasant family pub with good value bar food, helpful service *(J M Norton)*

Minworth, W Mid [SP1592], *Boat*: Good canalside pub with Ansells beer, good value food in new restaurant *(J Jewitt)*

☆ **Monks Kirby**, War [Bell Lane, just off A427 W of Pailton; SP4683], *Bell*: Good generous bar food inc interesting Spanish cooking with some emphasis on fish, as well as ambitious range of traditional dishes; quiet open-plan beamed and timbered bar divided into separate areas, with slabbed and cobbled floor, woodburning stove; relaxed service, restaurant *(Ted George, Geoff Lee, Roy Bromell)*

Moreton Pinkney, Northants [SP5749], *Red*

Lion: 16th-century small-roomed pub, charming though due for some redecoration, with cheerful landlady helped by two daughters, well kept Banks's beer, good home-cooked food, reasonable prices; seats outside *(KL, EL)*

☆ **Napton**, War [A425 Daventry—Leamington; SP4661], *Napton Bridge*: Well run, busy canal pub with well kept Davenports and particularly good plain but hearty food at reasonable prices from sandwiches to steaks, inc quite outstanding pasta specials (landlord's wife is Italian); former stable for bargees' horses is now a skittle alley *(Cdr W S D Hendry, WHBM)*

Napton, *Kings Head*: Reasonable pub with Ansells beer, bar food, pub games *(Dave Braisted)*

☆ **Nassington**, Northants [Fotheringhay Rd; TL0696], *Black Horse*: Particularly ambitious if not cheap food inc sophisticated specialities, and well kept real ales such as Adnams, Greene King IPA and Wadworths 6X; two comfortable beamed dining rooms linked by bar servery, with striking stone fireplace, panelling from Rufford Abbey, easy chairs and small settees; children allowed in eating area; restaurant; seats on sheltered lawn *(Drs M and K Parier, LYM)*

Nether Heyford, Northants [close to M1 junction 16; SP6558], *Old Sun*: Small, clean pub with amazing collection of old signs and brasses; good generous bar food *(Jan and Ian Alcock)*

Netherton, W Mid [Woodside Rd, not far from Merry Hill shopping centre; SO9387], *Woodside*: Welcoming art deco pub with home-cooked food and Timothy Taylors ales *(SJP)*

☆ **Newbold on Avon**, War [SP4777], *Barley Mow*: Small, straightforward pub particularly nice in summer for its pretty canalside terrace and garden; good value bar food from sandwiches to tender steaks inc children's dishes, well kept beer, good friendly service *(Mr and Mrs C H Stride, E J Alcock, M Morgan)*

☆ **Newbold on Avon** [B4112], *Boat*: Clean extended three-bar canalside pub with small but reasonable choice of good value food — steaks and mixed grill recommended; Davenports Bitter and Mild on handpump, plush seats, open fire between dining area and bar, table skittles, darts *(M Morgan, E J and T R G Alcock)*

Newnham, Northants [SP5859], *Romer Arms*: Popular free house on green, friendly, relaxed atmosphere, bar food; has brewed its own beer *(Dr Paul Kitchener)*

☆ **Northampton** [Wellingborough Rd], *Abington Park*: Big own-brew pub in elegant building nr Abington Park and Northants CC, with brewery tours by arrangement, and choice running to Cricketers, Cobblers, Lionhearts Porter, Abington Extra, Celebration and Headspinner — they may give you free sips to try; several bars inc a spacious Victorian lounge, good hot and cold lunchtime bar food (pie tipped), friendly, helpful staff, restaurant *(Nigel Gibbs)*

☆ **Northampton** [3 ¾ miles from M1 junction 15; A508, then A428 towards Bedford, then right just after roundabout], *Britannia*: Open-plan beamed and flagstoned bar with rambling roomy alcoves and Victorian-style decorations, side room done out as attractive 18th-century kitchen with original cooking range and washing copper still intact; Watneys-related real ales, straightforward lunchtime bar food, carvery, conservatory facing River Nene; disco Sun, Tues, Thurs *(Jim Aitkenhead, Virginia Jones, Michael and Alison Sandy, LYM)*

Northampton [London Rd], *Queen Eleanor*: Smart 1930s pub, lively with lots of games and reasonable food *(Dr and Mrs A K Clarke)*

☆ **Offchurch**, War [off A425 Radford Semele; SP3565], *Stags Head*: 16th-century thatched dining pub with concentration on food service — varied choice of well prepared dishes, help-yourself salad bar, good vegetarian food, nice choice of puddings; helpful, efficient staff *(C H Stride, Curt and Lois Stevens)*

Old Hill, W Mid [Waterfall Lane, nr M5 junction 2; SO9685], *Waterfall*: Rejuvenated by enthusiastic licensees, ten changing beers, good choice of well prepared and served bar food *(E J Alcock)*

Oldbury, W Mid [nr Savacentre; SO9888], *Waggon & Horses*: Impressive tiled Edwardian bar, with separate dining area — food inc super hot pork sandwiches *(Hilary Sargeant, Norman Clarke)*

Princethorpe, War [B4453 towards Cubbington; SP4070], *Woodhouse*: Pleasant hotel lounge, well kept Watneys-related real ales, good help-yourself buffet, big car park; bedrooms *(Ted George)*

Priors Hardwick, War [SP4756], *Butchers Arms*: Fine old place with medieval oak beams, panelling, flagstones, antiques, log fire and country garden; run now as good upmarket restaurant, with prices to match, and the inglenook bar is really just an adjunct *(Graham Bush, Gordon Theaker)*

☆ **Priors Marston** [from village centre follow Shuckburgh signpost, but still in village take first R by telephone box], *Holly Bush*: Rambling and unusual ancient golden stone house reopened under new management after longish closure, with interesting stripped-stone decor, good log fire in main room, darts and table skittles in smaller one, friendly new licensees, well kept Marstons Pedigree and other real ales, and new dining-room extension (no news of this yet as we go to press) *(G P Beckett, Peter Watkins, Pam Stanley, R C Gandy, LYM)*

☆ **Pytchley**, Northants [SP8574], *Overstone Arms*: Delightful pub and garden in attractive countryside, friendly professional service, good changing choice of bar food inc speciality pies and puddings in spacious lounge with dining area, good Pimms, Watneys-related real ales, games room *(J M Norton, Roy Y Bromell)*

☆ **Quarry Bank**, W Mid [High St; SO9390], *Church Tavern*: Pleasantly renovated homely pub with welcoming landlord, good value traditional Black Country bar food, reasonably priced well kept local Holt, Plant & Deakins beer *(SJP, Dave Braisted)*

Quarry Bank, W Mid [Saltwells Lane; signed off Coppice Lane, off A4036 nr Merry Hill Centre — OS Sheet 139 map reference 934868; SO9386], *Saltwells*: Surprisingly modern hotel at end of rough lane through nature reserve — books on shelves in carefully refurbished main lounge, family room, garden with play area; has been praised for cheap straightforward bar food and Banks's and Hansons ales, but no recent reports; bedrooms (News please)

☆ Radford Semele, War [A425 2 miles E of Leamington Spa — OS Sheet 151 map reference 343645; SP3464], White Lion: Good generously served cheap food inc speciality ploughman's in straightforward old pub, cheerful staff, Davenports ales, garden (G H Gall)

☆ Ratley, War [OS Sheet 151 map reference 384473; SP3847], Rose & Crown: New owners drumming up support for handsome old local of golden Hornton stone, nr lovely church in small sleepy village; quickly served good food inc curries, moussaka, steaks, lots of death-by-chocolate-type puddings and so forth in small eating area, well kept real ales such as Arkells Kingsdown, Badger Tanglefoot, Batemans, Burton Bridge Festival, Donnington SBA, Greene King Abbot, Hook Norton Best and Morlands Old Master; woodburning stove in flagstoned bar on right, big log fireplace in carpeted area on left, lots of cricket memorabilia, quick service; small back terrace, steep steps from car park (Mark Evans, P R Davis, Ted George)

☆ Rockingham, Northants [SP8691], Sondes Arms: Nice welcoming and civilised old pub with friendly service, good home-made food (sandwiches, mackerel bake, curries and puddings all praised) and well kept Charles Wells Bombardier and Eagle on handpump (EML)

☆ Rowington, War [Finwood Rd; off B4439 N of Rowington, following Lowsonford sign; SP2069], Tom o' the Wood: Decent food from sandwiches to steaks (grilled plaice recommended) in several comfortably modernised communicating rooms, well kept Whitbreads-related real ales on handpump, fruit machine, piped music, picnic-table sets on terrace and neat side lawn; service may slow when busy; handsome Elizabethan ceiling in upstairs restaurant, provision for children lunchtime; nice spot, big car park (Brian Jones, H R Bevan, C E Power, Cdr W S D Hendry, LYM)

Rugby, War [Hilmorton Wharf, Crick Rd; SP5075], Old Royal Oak: Comfortable canalside pub with several softly lit alcoves, well kept beer, tasty bar food; popular with young people (Wayne Brindle)

Rushall, W Mid [Park Lane; off A461; SK0301], Manor Arms: Old low-beamed pub by Rushall Canal, with several rooms in contrasting styles; no bar (pumps are fixed to the walls), big inglenook fireplace, generous helpings of basic pub food, canalside garden; can get crowded early at weekends (E J Alcock)

Salfords Priors, War [A435 W of Bidford; SP0751], Queens Head: Family pub with friendly, welcoming landlord, flagstoned bar with log fire, well kept Flowers Original and Marstons Pedigree on handpump, good food with interesting specials such as pigeon in wine; family room with blackboard; children welcome (the menu includes jellies) (Keith and Ann Dibble)

☆ Sedgley, W Mid [Bilston St (A463); SO9193], Beacon: Attractive restoration of Victorian pub with original fittings and furnishings in five distinct drinking areas, inc a family room, radiating from tiny serving area with hatches; well kept Holdens Special and M&B Springfield, their own interesting and potent Sarah Hughes Dark Ruby Mild brewed in a restored small tower brewery behind, and a guest beer that changes every second day; seats on terrace; good atmosphere, very mixed clientele (Richard Sanders, Colin Dowse)

Sedgley [Kent St (A459)], Pig on the Wall: Tastefully refurbished free house with Ansells, Banks's and British Oak Castle Ruin, good value food — when friendly staff say sauce is hot, they mean it! (Dave Braisted)

Shrewley, War [off B4439 Hockley Heath—Warwick; SP2167], Durham Ox: This otherwise straightforward pub gains its place for its spacious garden, with beer-barrel dovecotes on telegraph poles housing a flight of white doves — canal, railway and the new M40 extension nearby; cheap basic snacks (not Sun lunchtime), M&B beers (LYM)

Shustoke, War [B4114 Nuneaton—Coleshill; SP2290], Plough: Good atmosphere, friendly service, beer that's cheap for the locality (Dave Braisted)

☆ Shuttington, War [SK2505], Wolferstan Arms: Recently attractively refurbished panoramic lounge and spacious restaurant with views over lake; nicely cooked reasonably priced straightforward food, pleasant waitress service, well kept Marstons Pedigree on handpump, tropical fishtank; big car park — pub busy with families at weekends; garden with children's play areas (Graham Richardson)

Smethwick, W Mid [Waterloo Rd (A457/A4136/A4092); SP0288], Waterloo: Well worth a visit for the splendid Victorian tilework in the decidedly unpretentious public bar, and for the old-fashioned mosaic-floored tiled basement dining room, with good choice of steaks and vegetables, well served, from the open grill; cheap M&B and Springfield ales, more orthodox comfortable lounge (FC, LYM)

Smethwick [Uplands/Meadow Rd], Old Chapel: Small M&B beamed local, separate bars and lounges served from one counter; bright M&B Springfield and Brew XI on handpump, sandwiches inc hot pork, short choice of cooked dishes such as lasagne and rice, friendly landlord, tables on sheltered back terrace (Frank Cummins)

Stockton, War [off A426 Southam—Rugby; SP4363], Barley Mow: Nice friendly clean pub with two-level high-ceilinged lounge decorated with plates and photographs, well kept beer, and decent well served food; good upstairs grill room (Ted George)

Stonnall, W Mid [Main St; SK0503], Royal Oak: Refurbished local with popular hot and cold lunchtime food, good range of beers on handpump (Clifford Blakemore)

☆ Stourbridge, W Mid [Amblecote Rd (A491); SO8984], Moorings: Large, busy pub by canal spur, doing well under new owners (same chain as Wharf in Old Hill); good changing choice of real ales, fair choice of reasonably priced bar food, pleasant back terrace (E J Alcock, Dave Braisted)

☆ **Stratford upon Avon**, War [Chapel St; SP2055], *Shakespeare*: Smart THF hotel based on handsome lavishly modernised Tudor merchants' houses, stylish public rooms and accommodation, patrician rather than plebeian atmosphere and customers; also comfortable Froth & Elbow bar with settles and armchairs, good choice of interesting and well kept Courage Directors and Hook Norton Best on handpump, bar food inc reliable cold table and hot dishes of the day, pleasant service; tables in back courtyard; three mins' walk from theatre; bedrooms comfortable and well equipped, though not cheap *(Frank Cummins, Auriol and Paul McLoughlin, Andy and Jill Kassube, LYM)*

☆ **Stratford upon Avon** [Southern Way], *Black Swan*: Clean 16th-century pub known as the Dirty Duck, in delightful position with attractive terrace looking over the riverside public gardens; usual bar food at moderate prices, Flowers IPA and Original, signed RSC photographs, children allowed in restaurant; quietest during — rather than before or after — a performance at the nearby Memorial Theatre *(Philip King, T Nott, Dr T W Hoskins, Jonathan and Jane Hagger)*

Stratford upon Avon, *Falcon*: Original core, with two bars and restaurant, is atmospheric and friendly; piped music; bedrooms (can be noisy in old part, functional in modern wing) *(John Evans)*; [Rother St (opp United Reform Church, handy for Friday Market)], *Lamplighters*: Big pub with long softly lit bar, log-effect gas fire, well kept if cold Tetleys; reasonably priced food, limited Sun *(Sheila Keene, Andy and Jill Kassube, Lynne Sheridan, Bob West)*; [Shipston Rd (A34)], *Old Tramway*: Recently renovated — pleasant decor, calm and relaxed atmosphere, and good value drinks inc unusual beers, farm cider *(P R Davis)*; [Ely St], *Queens Head*: Well run genuine local, good atmosphere, real fire, good barman, well kept M&B, bar food inc good toasted sandwiches *(Sheila Keene)*; [Warwick Rd, opp Midland Red bus depot], *Red Lion*: Roast Hog pub with big area for bar snacks, another for main carvery meals — reduced food prices for OAPs *(A H Denman)*

☆ **Studley**, War [Icknield St Dr; left turn off A435, going N from B4093 roundabout; SP0763], *Old Washford Mill*: Pretty waterside gardens with good play area, by extensive and popular watermill conversion with old mill machinery, lots of different levels inc quiet alcoves, variety of catering, provision for children, real fire *(LYM)* **Studley** [Alcester Rd (A435)], *Little Lark*: Yet another of the Little pubs, with a newspaper theme *(Dave Braisted)*

☆ **Sudborough**, Northants [High St; SP9682], *Vane Arms*: Usually seven to ten regularly changing well kept real ales in nice thatched inn with good fair-priced freshly cooked bar food inc fine steak and kidney pie, more unusual dishes and lots of puddings; cheerful service; fine walking country; children welcome; bedroom block *(Michel Hooper-Immins, Ashley Jordan, Bob Allan, T N de Bray)*

Sutton Bassett, Northants [SP7790], *Queens Head*: Doing well under current regime,

with well kept Marstons Pedigree and a guest beer on handpump, good food inc excellent value steaks; upstairs restaurant *(M B P Carpenter)*

☆ **Temple Grafton**, War [a mile E, towards Binton; off A422 W of Stratford; SP1255], *Blue Boar*: New regime doing well in popular extended pub with open fire in softly lit stripped-stone bar, communicating dining room; good service by natural, pleasant and obliging staff, consistently good reasonably priced bar food with well prepared fresh veg, well kept Flowers, darts in flagstoned area; parking can be difficult when busy *(S V Bishop, Brian Skelcher, John Bowdler)*

Thornby, Northants [Welford Rd — A50 Northampton—Leicester; SP6775], *Red Lion*: Attractive decor and furnishings inc deep leather armchairs and sofa, old-fashioned lamps, lots of decorative china plates, jugs and steins, woodburning stove; rather a decidedly local atmosphere under its new regime; bar food, Marstons real ales, seats outside *(LYM)*

Thorpe Waterville, Northants [A605 Thrapston—Oundle; TL0281], *Fox*: Big helpings of well prepared straightforward food at reasonable prices, coal fire, space for children, genial Irish landlord, real ales such as Adnams Broadside and Charles Wells *(Mr and Mrs J Back)*

☆ **Tipton**, W Mid [Hurst Lane, Dudley Rd; towards Wednesbury, junction A457/A4037 — look for the Irish flag; SO9592], *M A D O'Rourkes Pie Factory*: One of the liveliest and roomiest Little pubs, with a vivid meat-processing theme, all sorts of interesting ancient equipment, not to mention strings of model hams, sausages, pigs' heads and so forth; good value food (you may be warned of delays when it's busy) from black pudding thermidor to gargantuan Desperate Dan cow pie, complete with pastry horns, also traditional puddings, well kept Ind Coope-related real ales and their own Lumphammer, piped or live jazz or folk music; children welcome if eating; good car park *(R P Taylor, Brian Jones, J S Rutter, Dave Braisted, J Overton, E J Alcock, E V Walder, M A and W R Proctor)*

☆ **Tipton** [Lower Church Lane, opp Police Stn], *Old Court House*: Well run but basic beer-lovers' local included chiefly for its half-dozen interesting and often far-flung real ales; generous helpings of good value bar food inc Black Country specials *(R P Taylor, Russell Allen)*

Tipton [Owen St], *Fountain*: Friendly, snug, quiet and well kept old-fashioned pub, Holt, Plant & Deakins real ales *(J Overton)*

☆ **Titchmarsh**, Northants [village signed from A604 and A605, just E of Thrapston; TL0279], *Wheatsheaf*: Good value home-made bar food and Allied real ales in comfortably extended village pub with friendly service, pool room, restaurant; children allowed in eating areas; has been closed Mon, and Tues—Fri lunchtimes *(LYM)*

☆ **Tredington**, War [SP2543], *White Lion*: Clean, comfortable pub, good food at very attractive prices *(R G Watts, P R Davis)* **Ufton**, War [White Hart Lane; just off A425 Daventry—Leamington, towards Bascote; SP3761], *White Hart*: Relaxed stone-built pub in pretty spot nr top of hill above Avon Vale; large main lounge, smaller lower bar, prompt service, well kept Davenports, good bar food up to big steaks, traditional puddings *(Mike O'Driscoll)*

☆ **Upper Benefield**, Northants [SP9889], *Wheatsheaf*: Wide choice of interesting bar food, not cheap but good and generously served, in attractive and well run upmarket pub/hotel/restaurant; comfortable bedrooms *(Cdr Patrick Tailyour, Geoff Lee)*

☆ **Upper Brailes**, War [SP3039], *Gate*: Attractive village pub with genuine old-world atmosphere, pleasantly free from pretentious over-decoration; good bar food inc wide range of sandwiches, good service, genial landlord, log fires, low beams, extensive gardens *(Sir Nigel Foulkes)*

Wadenhoe, Northants [Church St; TL0083], *Kings Head*: 17th-century thatched pub with small quarry-tiled and beamed bar, friendly licensees, well kept Batemans XXX, Courage Directors, Marstons Pedigree and a guest beer, bar food inc good home-made winter pheasant soup; table skittles, big garden by River Nene, outside gents' *(Ian K Chitty)*

Wakerley, Northants [SP9599], *Exeter Arms*: Pleasantly set out tables in bar for wide range of good well cooked food; well kept Batemans XXX, Flowers Best, Hook Norton Old Hookey, McEwans Export and Youngers IPA, side room beyond fireplace with games and juke box *(Mr and Mrs J Back)*

Walsall, W Mid [John St; SP0198], *Pretty Bricks*: Well kept Allied real ales and good value lunchtime and evening bar food (not Sun evening), inc good Sun lunch; juke box *(Paul Noble)*

☆ **Warley**, W Mid [Church St, Oldbury; SO9987], *Waggon & Horses*: Handsome well refurbished Edwardian tiled bar, good range of well kept real ales inc Bathams on handpump; good bar food from sandwiches through omelettes, home-made pies and curries to steaks lunchtime and evening, inc weekends, friendly staff *(David and Eloise Smaylen)*

☆ **Warmington**, War [A41 towards Shotteswell; SP4147], *Wobbly Wheel*: Warm welcome, attractive lounge and bar, enterprising food, real ales, pleasant situation *(M J Morgan, M Dolbear)*

☆ **Warwick** [11 Church St], *Zetland Arms*: Good value simple food, well kept Davenports on handpump, lively conversation around the bar but quieter areas too; delightful and well kept sheltered back garden *(Geoff Lee, R N Haygarth, Roger Taylor, LYM)*

☆ **Warwick**, [Birmingham Rd; A41, opp Sainsburys nr racecourse], *Black Horse*: Neatly kept lounge and public bar in welcoming pub with plentiful good food, well kept beers; bedrooms reasonably cheap, with decent breakfasts *(Patrick and Mary McDermott, Brian Jones, BB)*

Warwick [St Nicholas Church St], *Barn*: Converted barn with beams, exposed brickwork and flagstones, sewing-machine trestle tables with candles and fresh flowers, stripped wood chairs, tractor-seat bar stools, old farm tools, open fire; tables in courtyard with well; has been popular for food, but no

recent reports *(News please)*; *Tilted Wig*: Friendly and comfortable central pub with imaginative and good if not uniformly cheap meals *(Hilary Sargeant, N P Clarke)*

☆ **Weedon**, Northants [3 miles from M1 junction 16; A45 towards Daventry; on A5 junction; SP6259], *Crossroads*: Main bar of this modern main-road hotel much enjoyed for its unusual and flamboyant decor, with lots of interest inc serving-counters made from antique mahogany chemist's-shop fittings; light and airy separate coffee parlour a useful all-day motorway break, also a restaurant; bar food rather pricey, well kept Bass and Watneys-related real ales, freshly squeezed orange juice; children welcome; bedrooms comfortable and attractive *(Mrs C Smith, H W and A B Tuffill, Dennis and Janet Johnson, Penny Zweep, Robert Kimberley, Lynne Sheridan and Bob West, R Elliott, Philip Orbell, Barbara and Norman Wells, LYM — more reports please)*

☆ **Weedon** [Stowe Hill (A5, S)], *Narrow Boat*: Spacious terrace and big garden with pheasants and peacocks sweeping down to Grand Union Canal, good canal photographs in busy main bar, high-raftered ex-kitchen family room, home-made bar food, summer barbecues, Cantonese specialities in restaurant (Mon–Sat, traditional Sun lunch); well kept Charles Wells real ales; very busy in summer *(D C Horwood, LYM)*

Weedon [junction A5/A45], *Globe*: Pleasant old pub in centre of village, good choice of beers, good lunchtime and evening bar food, occasional live music; bedrooms *(Mike and Sue Wheeler)*

Welford, Northants [SP6480], *Shoulder of Mutton*: Friendly pub with Watneys-related real ales and good bar food; about half a mile from canal *(Gordon Theaker)*

☆ **Welford on Avon**, War [Maypole; SP1452], *Shakespeare*: Very popular for food, with considerable concentration on this, and good range of wines; stunning displays of bedding plants and hanging baskets in summer *(Brian Skelcher)*

Wellesbourne, War [out towards Walton; SP2755], *Stags Head*: Good atmosphere and welcoming service in beamed lounge bar, generous helpings of home-cooked food inc good steak and kidney pie; lovely setting in group of Elizabethan cottages *(Mr and Mrs W M Abruzzi)*

☆ **West Bromwich**, W Mid [High St; SP0091], *Old Hop Pole*: Cosy local with good atmosphere, lots of old nick-nacks, roaring fire in black-leaded grate, well kept Holt, Plant & Deakins ales, superb doorstep sandwiches — especially the local speciality, hot pork; Sun lunchtime lots of dominoes-players *(Roger Taylor, J S Rutter)*

West Haddon, Northants [about 3 miles from M1 junction 18; A428 towards Northampton; SP6272], *Wheatsheaf*: Comfortably snug and tasteful upstairs lounge, good bar meals and wide choice of courteously presented good food and wines in big candelit restaurant; pool table in small cosy downstairs bar *(H W and A B Tuffill)*

☆ **Weston**, Northants [the one N of Brackley; SP5846], *Crown*: Good food and range of ales inc Hook Norton and Wadworths 6X in warmly welcoming and attractive flagstoned village pub with highwayman connections; handy for NT Canons Ashby *(C A Gurney)*

Whilton, Northants [SP6365], *Locks*: Large, modern and comfortable, popular at lunchtime with local office people for its good range of bar food; back terrace with picnic-table sets, nr four locks of Grand Union Canal (not picturesque here) *(Michael and Alison Sandy)*

Wilby, Northants [A45; SP8666], *George*: Comfortable Turkey-carpeted and partly panelled lounge with spacious beamed dining area, locally popular for food (not Tues evening or Sun); small front bar, basic public bar, Watneys-related real ales on handpump, big garden with seats looking on to farmland *(Michael and Alison Sandy)*

☆ **Willey**, War [just off A5, N of A427 junction; SP4984], *Old Watling*: Formerly the Sarah Mansfield, renamed and refurbished under current regime — neat, cosy and popular blend of polished flagstones, stripped masonry and open fire with modern comfort; big helpings of good value bar food, well kept Adnams, Banks's, Courage and John Smiths; big car park *(Dave Braisted, Ted George)*

☆ **Wixford**, War [B4085 Alcester—Bidford — OS Sheet 150 map reference 085546; SP0954], *Fish*: Tastefully refurbished roomy L-shaped bar and snug, beams, polished panelling, carpets over flagstones, well kept Bass on handpump, reasonably priced bar food, pleasant, efficient service *(JM, PM)*

Wollaston, W Mid [High St; SO8984], *Bulls Head*: Largish, very pleasant and relaxing panelled lounge — a surprise for the area *(E J Alcock)*

Wolvey, War [near M65 junction 1; SP4287], *Blue Pig*: Friendly olde-worlde local with nice atmosphere, reasonably priced bar food inc good chargrills, good mix of customers; busy weekends *(Comus Elliott, Ian Blackwell)*

Wolvey Heath, War [OS Sheet 140 map reference 436890; SP4390], *Axe & Compass*: Very popular dining pub with wide choice from bar snacks up to big steaks; good restaurant, pleasant garden *(Ken and Barbara Turner)*

Woodford Halse, Northants [SP5452], *Fleur de Lys*: Old-fashioned stone-built village local with fairly big bar, basic furnishings, bench seats, wooden stools and wood-panelled counter; lively, friendly atmosphere, welcoming, efficient bar staff, well kept Hook Norton Best and Marstons Pedigree on handpump; children's room *(Mike O'Driscoll)*

Woolaston, W Mid [Bridgnorth Rd (A458); SO8984], *Forresters Arms*: Pleasant service, friendly atmosphere, good food, and Allied Brewery beers; gets very busy lunchtime *(Dave Braisted)*

☆ **Wootton Wawen**, War [N side of village; SP1563], *Bulls Head*: 18th-century or older black-and-white pub with massive timber uprights in low-ceilinged and heavily oak-beamed L-shaped lounge, good bar food (there may be a wait), friendly staff, popular restaurant; M&B Springfield and Brew XI, garden *(Geoff Lee, Nigel B Pritchard)*

☆ **Yarwell**, Northants [Main St; TL0697], *Angel*: Quaint and cosy old two-roomed village pub off the beaten track; well kept Youngers on handpump, notable food at reasonable prices (not Thurs), friendly and welcoming owners; children's room and garden with play area and maybe pets *(N W James, Andrew Taylor)*

Norfolk

Norfolk now has a good many well run pubs of considerable individuality; ones currently on an upward trend include the bustling Kings Arms in Blakeney (good value food), the civilised Buckinghamshire Arms in its fine spot at Blickling (new managers upgrading the food), the Ship by the water at Brandon Creek (popular new licensees), the quaint Lord Nelson at Burnham Thorpe (it seems to get more individual each year), the Hare & Hounds at Hempstead (good imaginative food; note that this pub has previously been listed under Baconsthorpe – closer, but in fact a different parish), the Bluebell at Hunworth (a classic country pub all-rounder), the Kings Head at Letheringsett (now under the same ownership), the Broads-side Ferry at Reedham (increasingly popular food), the well run Gin Trap at Ringstead (good food), the wonderful old Scole Inn at Scole (new licensee), the Red Lion at Upper Sheringham (really interesting food in this simple place), the Horseshoes at Warham (another unspoilt place with tasty food) and the notably friendly Fishermans Return at Winterton-on-Sea. More than in past years, this wealth of individuality is echoed in the Lucky Dip section at the end of the chapter. For years Watneys the big brewing combine has dominated the pub scene here, but have now been selling many of their East Anglian pubs, since publication of the Monopolies and Mergers Commission's report proposing action to make brewers' pub ownership less monopolistic (and Government adoption of at least some of the proposals). This is adding yet another impetus to the increasing interest and diversity of pubs here – even when it's been another brewer such as Whitbreads that has taken the pubs over. With all this going on, it's no surprise that there are a good few promising prospects among the Lucky Dip entries at the end of the chapter, notably the Crown at Colkirk, Feathers at Dersingham, Pilgrims Reach at Docking, both the Bell and the very cut-off Berney Arms near Great Yarmouth, Hill House at Happisburgh, Tudor Rose in Kings Lynn, Crown at Mundford, Jolly Farmers at North Creake, Old Brewery House at Reepham, Hare Arms at Stow Bardolph, reopened Chequers at Thompson, Kings Head at Thornham and Bull at Walsingham. Pub prices in the area are rather above the national average. Drinks tend to cost a few pence more here, especially when the pub's tied to a national brewer (still usually Watneys, despite the sell-offs; the Fishermans Return at Winterton deserves special praise for selling a local beer at a lower price, despite its Watneys tie); the cheapest drinks we found were in the Ostrich at Castle Acre, tied to the regional brewer Greene King – it was one of the cheapest places for food, too.

BLAKENEY   TG0243 Map 8

Kings Arms

West Gate St

As it's not far from the harbour, this pretty white cottage can get crowded at peak times. It's a bustling place with three simply furnished, knocked-together rooms decorated with some interesting photographs of the licencees' theatrical careers on the walls (as well as framed reprints of old Schweppes advertisements); one of the other small rooms is no-smoking. The atmosphere is relaxed and friendly and the staff are helpful and efficient. Tasty bar food at lunchtime includes sandwiches (from 90p, local crab in season £1.75), lots of filled baked potatoes (from £1.75), a wide choice of ploughman's (from £2.75, locally smoked ham (£3.75), fresh local mussels (£3.25), locally caught fresh haddock or cod (£3.75), and puddings like home-made crumble (£1.95), with evening salads (from £4.25, the seasonal local crab is lovely £5.20) and grills (from £4.95). Well kept Ruddles County, Websters Yorkshire and a guest beer on handpump; darts, dominoes and fruit machine. The large garden has lots of tables and chairs and a separate, equipped children's area. *(Recommended by Margaret Dyke, Margaret White, Norman Hill, BKA, Charles Bardswell, Mrs Russell Davis, Paul Sexton, Sue Harrison, L Walker, Wayne Brindle)*

Manns (Watneys)   Licensee Howard Davies   Meals and snacks (12–2.30, 6–9.30, though served all day at weekends and school hols)   Children welcome   Open 11–11

BLICKLING   TG1728 Map 8

Buckinghamshire Arms 🛏

Off B1354 N of Aylsham

Readers enjoy the civilised and relaxed atmosphere of this handsome Jacobean inn, owned by the National Trust. The small front snug is simply furnished with fabric cushioned banquettes, some brass tack above the open fire, and an antique seed-sowing machine in an alcove. The bigger lounge has landscapes and cockfighting prints, neatly built-in pews, and stripped deal tables. The new licensees are planning to up-grade the bar food to include freshly-made, home-made dishes: steak and mushroom, rabbit or chicken pies (£4) and fresh fish, including crab; decent breakfasts. Well kept Adnams, Greene King IPA and Woodfordes Wherry on handpump. Picnic-table sets shelter under cocktail parasols on the lawn (they serve food from an out-building here in summer), and there's a wide stretch of neatly raked gravel between the inn and a splendid Dutch-gabled stable block; climbing frame, slide and swing. Neighbouring National Trust Blickling Hall is open from April to mid-October only, and closed Mondays and Thursdays, though you can walk through the park at any time. The inn can get packed. *(Recommended by Peter Burton, R C Vincent, P Thorogood, Joy Heatherley, David Oakes, Geoff Halson, Charles Bardswell, Jack Taylor, M A and W R Proctor)*

Free house   Managers John and Judith Summers   Real ale   Meals and snacks Restaurant   Children in restaurant   Open 11–2.30, 6–11   Three double bedrooms tel Aylsham (0263) 732133; £38/£48

BRANCASTER STAITHE   TF7743 Map 8

Jolly Sailors

This country pub is on the edge of thousands of acres of National Trust dunes and salt flats. The three small pleasant rooms have shorebird pictures, small but intricately detailed colour prints of Georgian naval uniforms, and three stuffed albino birds in a glass case on the white-painted rough stone walls, some modern seats as well as a worn black oak settle and another with a roof and carved wings, and stripped deal or mahogany tables on the red-tiled floor. The log fire has one of those old-fashioned sturdy guards to sit on. The winter mussels, baked with garlic butter or white wine and cream, come from the anchorage just across the road that's protected by Scolt Head Island nature reserve. Other home-made bar food –

served all day in summer – includes sandwiches, soup (from 90p), ploughman's and salads (from £3.20), quiche or vegetarian lasagne (£3.70), chicken and mushroom pie (£4.50), seafood pancake (£4.60), home-made puddings like trifle or cheesecake (from £1.20), and children's dishes (from £1.80). Well kept Greene King Abbot and IPA on handpump, and an award-winning wine list; happy hour 6–7pm Friday and Saturday in winter. Sensibly placed darts in one room, also shove-ha'penny, dominoes, table skittles, and warri. There are seats by flowering shrubs on a sheltered lawn, or on a canopied side terrace, a hard tennis court (which can be booked at the bar), and a children's play house and slides. *(Recommended by Bev and Doug Warrick, Charles Bardswell, Geoff Halson, Joy Heatherley, Peter Griffiths, M A and W R Proctor, James Cane; more reports please)*

Free house   Licensee Alister Borthwick   Real ale   Meals and snacks (11am–10pm July/August and Bank Hols; not 25 Dec)   Partly no-smoking restaurant   tel Brancaster (0485) 210314   Children in eating areas   Open 11–11; 11–3, 7 (6 Fri and Sat)–11 in winter; closed 25 Dec   Local bed and breakfast can be arranged

BRANDON CREEK   TL6091 Map 5

Ship

A10 Ely–Downham Market

At the junction of the creek with the high-banked Great Ouse, this bow-windowed pink-washed pub has some tables by its own moorings. Inside, the comfortable and spacious bar has soft lighting, slatback chairs and one or two upholstered settles, some interesting black and white photographs, and an open fire at one end, with a woodburning stove at the other; from here, steps drop down into a sunken area that was a working forge until not long ago (as the massive stone masonry and photographs on the walls show). The very long bar-counter is decorated above with shepherds' crooks made from intricately plaited corn stalks. The new licensees have introduced home-made bar food which changes daily and includes soup (£1.30), pâtés (£2.30), vegetarian dishes like zucchini bake or lasagne (£3.75), steak and kidney pie or quiche (£3.80), steaks (from £8.50), and puddings like muesli crumble cake, apple pie or cheesecakes (£1.50). Well kept Ruddles Best and County, and Websters Yorkshire on handpump; friendly staff. *(Recommended by Frank Gadbois, Wayne Brindle; more reports please)*

Manns (Watneys)   Licensees Marion and Trevor Cook   Real ale   Meals and lunchtime snacks   Restaurant tel Brandon Creek (035 376) 228   Children in eating area of bar till 8.30 and in restaurant   Occasional Sun evening entertainment in summer and monthly Fri evening country music in winter   Open 10.30–3, 6.30–11; they also have a supper license

BURNHAM THORPE   TF8541 Map 8

Lord Nelson

Village signposted from B1155 and B1355, near Burnham Market

A delicious and extremely popular rum and, we think, curaçao-based concoction called Nelson's Blood is made to a secret recipe by the landlord here. It's a delightfully unspoilt place with some 60 pictures on show connected with Nelson, though this is just part of the knowledgeable licensee's fine collection of over 200 items. These line the entrance corridor as well as the bar itself – a small room with well waxed antique settles on the worn red flooring tiles, a sheathed cutlass on one beam, and a cabinet of miniature bottles. Well kept Greene King IPA and Abbot is tapped from the cask in a back stillroom; the glasses are simply stacked by the spotless sink, separated off from the rest of the room by two high settle-backs. You are asked not to smoke. *(Recommended by Robert Harman, Derek and Sylvia Stephenson, Kevin Fields, Charles Bardswell, James Cane, M A and W R Proctor)*

Greene King   Licensee Les Winter   Real ale   No food   Open 11.30–3, 7–11

CASTLE ACRE   TF8115 Map 8
Ostrich

Stocks Green; village signposted from A1065 N of Swaffham; OS Sheet 144 map reference 815153

On the tree-lined green near to the ruins of a Norman castle, this largely 18th-century inn has a strong local atmosphere in its back room: a very high pitched ceiling with exposed oak beams and trusses, an end wall with exposed 16th-century masonry, and a good log fire. The L-shaped front bar has big photographs of the local sites on hessian walls, a low ceiling, a huge old fireplace with a swinging potyard below its low mantlebeam (which may be used in winter for cooking soups and hams), and straightforward furnishings. Decent bar food includes sandwiches (from 70p, crab and smoked salmon double-decker £2.45), various basket meals (from £1.20), pizzas (from £1.40), a wide range of ploughman's (from £1.70), omelettes (from £2), salads (from £3), rainbow trout (£4), daily specials such as vegetarian ratatouille crumble (£2.80) or squid and prawn salad (£3.50). Well kept Greene King IPA, Abbot and XX Mild on handpump; fruit machine, piped music, and picnic-table sets in the sheltered garden, where you can play boules. There's a Cluniac monastery in the village. *(Recommended by R P Hastings, P Thorogood, Derek Pascall, Nigel Gibbs, Sandra Cook, Geoff Halson, Dave Braisted, Joy Heatherley, J D Maplethorpe, Graham and Glenis Watkins, L Walker)*

Greene King   Licensee Ray Wakelen   Real ale   Meals and snacks (12–2, 7–10.30; not 25 Dec)   Children in decent adjacent family room   Jazz every other Tues, Folk/Blues last Wed in month   Open 11–3, 6–11; closed evening 25 Dec   Bedrooms (single only) tel Swaffham (0760) 755398; £12

HEMPSTEAD   TG1236 Map 8
Hare & Hounds

Towards Baconsthorpe – and actually closer to that village, though just inside the Hempstead parish boundary; village signposted from A148 in Holt; OS Sheet 133 map reference 115372

Carefully demodernised, this small pantiled flint cottage has a couple of friendly little bars with rugs on old red flooring tiles, a casual mix of chairs and cushioned pews around plain deal or cast-iron-framed tables, several sets of Lawson Wood cartoons on the beige walls, dog-breed cigarette cards, pewter tankards hanging from one beam, earthenware flagons on the deep sills of the small windows, and a big woodburning stove in the broad low-beamed fireplace below a pendulum clock. Interestingly done bar food might include vegetarian parsley andd watercress roulade, leek, bacon and potato bake, Normandy fish casserole, lamb biriani, beef bourguignonne, and game pie (all £4.25); well kept Adnams, Bass and Batemans on handpump, with a full-bodied and fragrantly fruity best bitter brewed for the pub by Woodfordes, guest beers, and decent wines. There are some picnic-table sets on the side grass, facing a pond and rockery; also a children's play area. *(More reports please)*

Free house   Licensee J M D Hobson   Real ale   Meals and snacks   Small children's room   Open 11.30–2.30, 7–11   Self-contained cottage for 5 £200pw

HUNWORTH   TG0635 Map 8
Bluebell

Village signposted off B roads S of Holt

The hard-working staff are friendly and pleasant even when the locals and visitors crowd in. The cosy L-shaped bar has Norfolk watercolours and pictures for sale hanging above the panelling dado, Windsor chairs around dark wooden tables, and comfortable settees, some of which are grouped around the log fire. Generous helpings of good value bar food include filled baked potatoes (from £1), sandwiches (from £1.10), good crab cocktail, ploughman's (from £2), salads (from

£2.50, local crab £3.50), plaice (£3.20), home-made steak and kidney pie or good home-cooked ham (£3.75), gammon and pineapple (£4.50), sirloin steak (£6.50), and a daily special such as leek and ham mornay. Real ales include particularly well kept Woodfordes Wherry, as well as Adnams, Bass, and Greene King Abbot; darts, and fruit machine. In good weather there's bar service to the tables under cocktail parasols on the back lawn where there are fruit trees – heavily laden in summer. They also own the Kings Head, Letheringsett. *(Recommended by Norman Hill, F A Owens, Derek and Sylvia Stephenson, David Oakes, Laurie Walker, Mr and Mrs K H Frostick, Charles Bardswell, Paul Sexton, Sue Harrison)*

Free house   Licensee Sally King   Real ale   Meals and snacks   Children in eating area of bar   Open 11–3, 6–11

LETHERINGSETT   TG0538   Map 8

Kings Head

A148 just W of Holt

Attractively decorated, the main bar in this country-house-like pub is decorated with a signed John Betjeman poem, picturesque advertisements, lots of Battle of Britain pictures especially involving East Anglia, a panoramic view of Edward VII's first opening of Parliament, and jokey French pictures of naughty dogs. There's also a small plush lounge, and a separate games room with darts, pool, dominoes, cribbage, pinball (a rarity nowadays), and fruit machines. Reasonably priced bar food includes sandwiches (from 90p, crab £1.50, evening toasties £1.50), home-made pasty (£2.95), salads (from £2.95, local crab in season £3.50), home-cooked ham or steak and kidney pie (£3.50), a huge and tasty pork chop, steaks (from £6.50, evening only), a daily special, and vegetarian dishes. Adnams, Bass and Greene King IPA and Abbot on handpump. Two decorative cats, no dogs. The pub is surrounded by a spacious lawn with lots of picnic-table sets and there are some interesting wild birds; park and paddock slope up beyond a post-and-rails fence. The church over the road has an unusual round tower, and nearby Letheringsett water mill is worth a visit. The licensee also owns the Bluebell at Hunworth. *(Recommended by Norman Hill, R C Vincent, F A Owens, Charles Bardswell, Geoff Halson, Charles Bardswell, David and Ruth Hollands)*

Free house   Licensee Thomas King   Real ale   Meals and snacks   Restaurant tel Holt (0263) 712691; not Sun evening   Children in eating area of bar during food serving times   Country and Western Mon   Open 11–3, 6–11

NORWICH   TG2308   Map 5

Adam & Eve

Bishopgate; follow Palace Street from Tombland N of the Cathedral

A favourite of one reader since his schooldays for its traditionally furnished bars: old-fashioned high-backed settles, one handsomely carved, cushioned benches built into partly panelled walls, and tiled or parquet floors. It's Norwich's oldest pub and parts of it date back to 1249; the snug is no-smoking at lunchtime. Generous helpings of good home-made bar food include sandwiches or filled French bread (from £1.25, excellent prawn £1.95), ploughman's (from £2.20), salads (from £2.30), chicken curry (£2.80), shepherd's pie or vegetable bake (£2.90), fish pie (£3.10), and casserole of pork in cider and rosemary or scampi (£3.20); puddings like home-made bread and butter pudding (£1.10), and daily specials (£3.30). Ruddles Best and Websters Yorkshire on handpump from a serving counter with a fine range of pewter tankards, several malt whiskies, and around 34 different wines; prompt, friendly service. There are seats on the quiet terrace – pretty in summer with clematis and baskets of flowers. *(Recommended by Sidney and Erna Wells, Margaret White, Ian Phillips, Wayne Brindle, Audrey and Brian Green, J S Rutter, D I Baddeley, Paul Sexton, Sue Harrison, Geoff Lee)*

Manns (Watneys)   Licensee Colin Burgess   Real ale   Lunchtime meals and snacks   Children in eating area of bar   Open 11–11

REEDHAM TG4101 Map 5

Ferry 🐾

B1140 Beccles–Acle; the ferry here holds only two cars but goes back and forth continuously till 10pm, taking only a minute or so to cross – fare £1.50, 10p passengers, 30p pedestrians

Popular with holidaymakers cruising the Broads, this little pub has good moorings (the fee is refundable against what you buy in the pub), and solid tables spaced well apart on the neatly kept grass that look out over the River Yare. Inside, the long front bar has comfortable banquettes lining the big picture windows, robust rustic tables carved from slabs of tree-trunk, and space game, trivia and fruit machines. The back bar, secluded and relaxing, has a good deal of traditional character, antique rifles, copper and brass, and a fine log fire. Generous helpings of good bar food include sandwiches (from £1.10), home-made soup (£1.60), ploughman's or steak sandwich (£3.25), salads (from £3.75), lasagne (£4.25), home-made steak and kidney pie (£4.75), good beef curry, medallions of pork fillet in white wine, cream and mushroom sauce (£5.25), char-grilled sirloin steak (£7.50), home-made puddings like good treacle tart, and children's dishes (£1.50), even arrangements for baby food (and changing facilities in the ladies' lavatory). Well kept Adnams Bitter and Woodfordes Wherry on handpump, lots of whiskies, and fruit wines; good cheerful service, piped music; showers in the lavatories for the boaters moored here. The woodturner's shop next door is interesting. (*Recommended by Gordon Theaker, Mr and Mrs P A Jones, T Nott, R Aitken*)

Free house   Licensee David Archer   Real ale   Meals and snacks (till 10 in evening) Children in eating area of bar   Open 11–3, 6.30–11; 11–2.30, 7–11 in winter

RINGSTEAD TF7040 Map 8

Gin Trap

Village signposted off A149 near Hunstanton; OS Sheet 132 map reference 707403

The comfortable and very neatly kept open-plan bar in this friendly white painted pub has captain's chairs with machine-tapestried cushions, built-in window seats and cast-iron-framed tables on the green and white patterned motif carpet, copper kettles, carpenters' tools, cartwheels, and bottles hanging from the beams in the lower part of the bar, toasting forks above an open fire (which has dried flowers in summer), and lots of traps (some converted to electric candle-effect wall lights); the tortoiseshell cat is called Whisky. A small no-smoking room laid out for eating has quite a few chamber pots hanging from the ceiling and high-backed pine settles, and is bookable on Saturday evening (048525 264). Well kept Adnams Bitter, Bass, Greene King Abbot, Woodfordes Baldric and a beer brewed by Woodfordes for the pub on handpump; efficient staff; trivia, piped music. Good home-made bar food includes lunchtimes sandwiches, winter soup, excellent Norfolk pie, very good lasagne or steak and kidney pie (£4), good home-cooked ham, trout (£5.25), steaks (from £6.60), and at least three daily specials; on Fridays they do fresh fish dishes (from £3.75). There are free prawns croutons, cheese, or cockles on the bar counter on Sunday lunchtimes. This year, the walled back garden has new seats on the grass or small paved area, new fencing and lots more flowers to join the pretty tubs. The pub is close to the Peddar's Way and hikers and walkers welcome (but not their muddy boots). There's an art gallery next door. (*Recommended by Margaret Bull, Charles Bardwell, Derek Pascall, Denise Plummer, Jim Froggatt, JMC, James Cane, Patrick Stapley*)

Free house   Licensees Brian and Margaret Harmes   Real ale   Meals and snacks (12–2, 7–9.30; till 10 Fri and Sat; not winter Sun evenings)   Well behaved children in dining area of bar   Occasional country dancing   Open 11.30–2.30, 6.30/7–11

SCOLE   TM1576   Map 5

Scole Inn ★ 🛏

A140 just N of A143

Built in 1655 by John Peck, a wealthy Norwich wool merchant, this stately building, with its magnificently rounded Dutch gables, later became an important stopping place for up to 40 horse drawn coaches a day and was famous for its enormous round bed that could sleep 30 people at a time (feet to the middle). It's one of only a handful of pubs or inns to have a Grade I preservation listing. The high-beamed lounge bar has antique settles, leather-cushioned seats and benches around oak refectory tables on its Turkey carpets, a handsomely carved oak mantle-beam, a big fireplace with a coat-of-arms iron fireback, and a 17th-century iron-studded oak door. In the bare-boarded public bar there's another good open fire, and stripped high-backed settles and kitchen chairs around oak tables. Waitress-served bar food – popular with businessmen at lunchtime – includes home-made soup, sandwiches (from £1.30), good ploughman's, fish pie (£3.95), salads including dressed crab (from £3.95), and steak and kidney pie or pan-fried liver and onions (£4.25). Well kept Adnams Broadside, Charringtons IPA, and Greene King Abbot on handpump, and over 30 malt whiskies; piped music. The ladies' must be one of the only ones in the country with such a grand fireplace. The gate half-way up the great oak staircase was to stop people riding their horses up and down (as John Belcher the highwayman is said to have done over 200 years ago). *(Recommended by Mike and Jill Dixon and friends, WTF, J G Simpson, T Nott, P Thorogood, Simon Bates, Jane Palmer, E J Waller, Richard Fawcett, Geoff Halson, Rona Murdoch, Paul Sexton, Sue Harrison)*

Free house   Licensee Fergie MacDonald   Real ale   Meals and snacks (12–2.15, 6–9.15)   Restaurant   Children in eating area of bar until 8.30   Open 11–11 Bedrooms tel Diss (0379) 740481; £45B/£62B

SNETTISHAM   TF6834   Map 8

Rose & Crown

Old Church Rd; just off A149 in centre

At the front of this cosy and pretty fourteenth-century pub is an old-fashioned beamed bar with cushioned black settles on the red tiled floor, lots of carpentry and farm tools, and a great pile of logs by the fire in the vast fireplace (which has a gleaming black japanned side oven). Beside this, an airy carpeted room has plush seats around tables with matching tablecloths, and pictures for sale on the wall. The cosy locals' bar at the back has perhaps the nicest atmosphere, with tapestried seats around cast-iron-framed tables, and a big log fire. There's also an extensive modern summer bar with a clean Scandinavian look: bentwood chairs and tractor seats on its tiled floor, bare brick walls, and narrow-planked ceilings. Very good, quickly served bar food includes soup (£1.30), ploughman's (£2.50), open baps (with home-cooked honey roast ham or excellent rare topside of beef £2.95), gammon with pineapple or eggs or pork chop (£5.75), salads (£5.95), steaks (from £6.95), and cold seafood (£7.50); also, vegetarian dishes, a daily special like steak and mushroom pie (£2.95), lemon sole (£6.25), or Chinese-style beef (£8.95), puddings such as home-made apple pie (£1.60), children's dishes (£1.50) and a barbecue menu. Bass (called Rose & Crown here), Adnams Bitter and Broadside, Greene King IPA and Abbot and Woodfordes Wherry on handpump, with freshly squeezed orange juice and own-label house wines; friendly service, even when pushed; piped music in some rooms, an old-fashioned penny slot game. There are picnic-table sets on a neat sheltered lawn and terrace; children's play area. No dogs. *(Recommended by Peter Corris, Derek and Sylvia Stephenson, Peter Griffiths, L Walker, R J Haerdi; more reports please)*

Free house   Licensee Margaret Trafford   Real ale   Meals and snacks (12–2, 7–10; not winter Sun evenings)   Restaurant tel Dersingham (0485) 541382; not Sun evening; two tables are no-smoking   Children welcome (own room)   Open 11–3, 5.30–11; closed 25 Dec

THORNHAM   TF7343 Map 8

Lifeboat ★

Turn off A149 by Kings Head, then take first left turn

This atmospheric and welcoming old place – on the edge of remote coastal salt
flats – has several cosy rooms. Two on the left of the door are popular with locals;
one of them has just three tables, machine-tapestried wall pews and a few
wheelback chairs, a small brick fireplace and guns and swords on the walls. The
main bar has low settles, window seats, pews, and carved oak tables on the rugs on
the tiled floor, panelling, great oak beams hung with romantic antique lamps
(which are still lit) and traps and yokes, shelves of china, and masses of guns,
swords, black metal mattocks, reed-slashers and other antique farm tools. The
atmosphere is chatty and relaxed, and there are no fewer than five fires – one with
an elaborately carved wood overmantle. A simple conservatory (which is very
popular with families) has benches and tables, an old-fashioned stove, a flourishing
vine, and a hatch for ordering the popular, home-made food. This includes soup
(£1.75), sandwiches (from £1.20) various ploughman's (£3.25), hot mussels with
wine and cream or home-made pies (£4.95), fresh fish (from around £5.50),
vegetarian dishes, steaks (£8.95), and home-made puddings like ginger sponge;
children's dishes, too. The quaint and pretty little restaurant does a good value set
menu with some choice; booking recommended. Well kept Adnams, Greene King
IPA and Abbot, and guest beers on handpump, with a wide range of wines;
efficient, helpful staff. Shove-ha'penny and an antique penny-in-the-hole bench. Up
some steps from the conservatory is a terrace with picnic-table sets, a climbing
frame, and a slide. The pub – which can get very busy, even out of season – is near
Good Walks Guide Walk 116. Large car park (which some readers feel obliterates
the view of the marsh). A barn conversion and extension has provided more
bedrooms, most with views of the salt marshes and sea; the restaurant has been
enlarged, too. They also own the Sculthorpe Mill at Sculthorpe near Fakenham.
*(Recommended by Peter Griffiths, M Morgan, Margaret White, Paulina Blowes, Charles
Bardswell, WHBM, Derek and Sylvia Stephenson, David and Ruth Hollands, M A and W R
Proctor, James Cane, M J Morgan, Wayne Brindle; more reports please)*

*Free house   Licensees Nicholas and Lynn Handley   Real ale   Meals and snacks
(12–2.30, 7–10)   Restaurant; not Sun lunch   Children welcome   Occasional folk
singer   Open 11–3, 5.30–11 (11–11 high summer)   Bedrooms tel Thornham (048
526) 236; £37B/£55B*

TITCHWELL   TF7543 Map 8

Manor Hotel 🛏

A149 E of Hunstanton

This newly refurbished hotel keeps a good naturalists' record of the wildlife in the
nearby RSPB reserve – which draws many people here. In the main part of the
building, a small bar has pretty patterned beige wallpaper, blue plush wall
banquettes, small round tables, and Impressionist prints. Another room – right
over on the right – is rather like a farmhouse kitchen with pine furniture, a Welsh
dresser with unusual mustards and pickles on it, and a collection of baskets and
bric-a-brac; children are allowed in here. There's also a pretty restaurant with
French windows that open on to a sizeable and sheltered neatly kept lawn with
sturdy white garden seats. Bar food, served in the pine room, includes home-made
soup, sandwiches, fresh mussels, crab or lobster in season (from £3.95), lambs
kidneys Dijonaise (£4.50), and pot-roasted venison with red wine and juniper (£5).
Greene King IPA and Abbot on handpump. *(More reports please)*

*Free house   Licensees G I and M M Snaith   Real ale   Meals and snacks   Children
welcome   Open 12–2.30, 6.30–11   Bedrooms tel Brancaster (0485) 210221;
£34B/£62B*

TIVETSHALL ST MARY TM1686 Map 5

Old Ram

Ipswich Rd; A140 15 miles S of Norwich

Several individually refurbished areas have been created in this big well run food pub. The spacious main room, ringed by cosier side areas, some carpeted, has standing-timber dividers, stripped beams and brick floors, a huge log fire in the brick hearth, a longcase clock, lots of Lawson Wood 1920s humorous prints, and antique craftsmen's tools on the ceiling; other rooms ramble off and there are pretty lamps and Sanderson fabrics. An attractive, intimate dining room with pews, an open woodburning stove and big sentimental engravings leads up to a gallery set out with pictures for sale, Victorian copper and brassware and sofas for idle contemplation; another (new) dining room is no-smoking. The emphasis is very much on food, with some tables reserved on weekdays. It includes burgers (£1.50), filled rolls (from £1.65), ploughman's (£3.25), home-made aubergine and mushroom bake, lasagne or steak and kidney pie (from £4.25), salads (from £4.50), jumbo-sized fresh cod fillet in home-made golden batter (£5.25), gammon and pineapple (£5.95), steaks (from £7.95), and formidable puddings. Well kept Adnams, Greene King Abbot, Ruddles County, Websters Yorkshire and a guest beer, decent house wines, several malt whiskies, good coffee, freshly squeezed orange juice; unobtrusive fruit machine, piped music. There are seats on the sheltered, flower-filled terrace and lawn behind. It can get very busy at weekends. No dogs. (*Recommended by Mrs M E Beard, Edward and Jean Rycroft, R G Tennant; more reports please*)

Free house   Licensee John Trafford   Real ale   Meals and snacks (11.30–10 Mon–Sat, till 9.30 Sun)   Children welcome   Open 11–11

UPPER SHERINGHAM TG1441 Map 8

Red Lion ⊗

B1157; village signposted off A148 Cromer–Holt, and the A149 just W of Sheringham

Very simply furnished, the two small bars of this traditional-looking flint cottage have red tiles or bare boards on the floor, stripped high-backed settles and country-kitchen chairs, plain off-white walls and ceiling, a big woodburning stove, a rack of newspapers, and little bunches of country flowers. Interesting, home-made bar food which changes daily might include cream of mushroom soup (£1.20), smoked mackerel pâté (£2.25), vegetarian cheese and tomato quiche (as a starter £2.35, main course £3.50), fresh salmon (as starter £2.95, main course £5.50), lasagne or meaty Cromer crab (£3.75), home-baked hot ham (which they then eat cold, £3.75), lambs liver and bacon (£3.95), grilled whole plaice or lemon sole, fresh every morning (£4.95), seafood pancakes, and lots of puddings like apple crumble or treacle tart (£1.60). They do a winter three-course meal every Wednesday evening, a winter feast night every second Tuesday with a French theme or roast duck and so forth, steaks and fresh salmon on Friday or Saturday evenings, a home-baked and glazed ham on Saturday lunchtime, and a traditional Sunday roast lunch (both around £4.25). They keep quite the best range of malt whiskies we've come across in this area (around 120), including a good few rarities; also well kept Adnams Bitter and Broadside and a guest like Marstons Pedigree on handpump, and decent wines; cribbage, dominoes. There is sometimes an albino cockatiel in one room, and the atmosphere's good. Dogs welcome. (*Recommended by Mr and Mrs J D Cranston, Derek and Sylvia Stephenson, Heather Sharland, WHBM, J Bord*)

Free house   Licensee Ian Bryson   Real ale   Meals and snacks   Children welcome Open 11–3, 6–11; winter evening opening 7   Bedrooms tel Sheringham (0263) 825408; £15/£30

WARHAM TF9441 Map 8

Horseshoes

Warham All Saints; village signposted from A149 Wells-next-the-Sea–Blakeney, and from B1105 S of Wells

This plain two-room village pub is determinedly unspoilt and old-fashioned: sturdy red leatherette settles built around the yellowing beige walls, stripped deal or mahogany tables (one marked for shove-ha'penny), gas lighting (with an electric lamp for the darts), an antique American Mills one-arm bandit still in working order, a big longcase clock with a clear piping strike, a pianola, and a small but cheerful log fire. Particularly good value and tasty bar food includes soup such as seafood broth (90p), sandwiches (from £1), potted meat on toast (£1.40), filled baked potatoes (£1.50), shrimps or local cockles in a cream sauce (£2), huge double cheese ploughman's (£2.25), local rollmops (£2.80), local crab salad (£3.80), popular specials such as chanterelles on toast (£1.10) or chicken and mushroom casserole (£3), and especially good puddings like home-made fruit pie (£1.10). There are decent house wines as well as the well kept Greene King IPA on handpump and Abbot and Woodfordes Wherry tapped from the cask (also, tea or coffee). A separate games room has darts, pool, shove-ha'penny, cribbage, dominoes, fruit machine and juke box, and one of the outbuildings houses a wind-up gramophone museum – opened on request. There are rustic tables out on the side grass, and the lavatories are outside. *(Recommended by Peter Griffiths, Derek and Sylvia Stephenson, Peter Griffiths, J E Cooper, R E Tennant, RCL, B Parkins)*

Free house   Licensee Iain Salmon   Real ale   Meals and snacks (12–2, 7–8.30; not Sun–Weds evenings)   Restaurant   Children in eating area of bar and games room   Pianola every other Saturday night   Open 11–3, 7–11   Bedrooms tel Fakenham (0328) 710547; £15/£30

WELLS NEXT THE SEA TF9143 Map 8

Crown 🛏️

The Buttlands

There's a thriving local atmosphere – especially in the front part of the bar of this well kept, big black-and-white Georgian-faced inn. The two rooms at the back are often quieter (that's where the black cat snoozes in front of the roaring log fire), and have some worthwhile pictures – including several big Nelson prints, maps showing the town in the eighteenth and nineteenth centuries, and local photographs a good deal more interesting than those decorating most pubs; one of these rooms is no-smoking. Good value bar food served efficiently by neat waitresses includes sandwiches (from £1), soup (£1.50), ploughman's (£2.75), three-egg omelettes or vegetarian tagliatelle with mixed vegetables (£3), ham and egg (£3.25), steak and kidney pie (£3.75), salads (from £3.50, crab £3.75), and rump steak (£8.75), with children's dishes (£2). Adnams, Marstons Pedigree and Tetleys on handpump; log fire; darts, fruit machine, space game and piped music. A neat conservatory with small modern settles around the tables looks over the back garden. The central square of quiet Georgian houses is most attractive. *(Recommended by Denzil T Taylor, M Morgan, Derek Pascall, Peter Griffiths, Gordon Pitt, Sandra Kempson, M J Morgan)*

Free house   Licensee Wilfred Foyers   Real ale   Meals and snacks   Restaurant   Children in own room   Open 11–2.30, 6–11; closed evening 25 Dec   Bedrooms tel Fakenham (0328) 710209; £33(£40B)/£43(£50B)

WINTERTON-ON-SEA TG4919 Map 8

Fishermans Return 🛏️

From B1159 turn into village at church on bend, then turn right into The Lane

In a quiet village not far from a sandy beach, this pretty and very friendly brick inn has a white-painted, panelled lounge bar with neat brass-studded red leatherette seats, a good winter log fire, and a cosy, relaxed atmosphere. The panelled public bar has low ceilings and a glossily varnished nautical air. There's also a separate serving counter in the back bar, which opens on to a terrace and good-sized sheltered garden; more seats face the quiet village lane. Good bar food includes toasted sandwiches (from £1), taramasalata with pitta bread or ploughman's with a choice of cheeses (£2.25), fish pie (£2.50), burgers (from £2.50), chilli con carne (£3), salads (from £3), omelettes (from £3.50), seafood platter with their own special sauce (£4), Dover sole (£7.50), and steaks (from £7.50), with daily specials, children's dishes (£1.50) and puddings like fruit crumble (£1.25); excellent breakfasts. Well kept Adnams Bitter, Ruddles Best and Websters Yorkshire on handpump, and own label by the glass or bottle; good service; darts, dominoes, cribbage, and piped music (CD). (Recommended by Derek and Irene Cranston, G T and J Barnes, W R Porter, M A and W R Proctor, M B Batley)

Manns (Watneys)   Licensee John Findlay   Real ale   Meals and snacks (11.30–2, 6.30–9.30; from 7 in winter; no food 25 Dec)   Children in dining room and garden room   Open 11–2.30 (3 Sat), 6–11; 11–2.30, 7–11 in winter   Bedrooms tel Winterton-on-Sea (049 376) 305; £20/£35

Lucky Dip

Besides the fully inspected pubs, you might like to try these Lucky Dips recommended to us and described by readers (if you do, please send us reports):

Bawburgh [TG1508], Kings Head: Pleasant lounge, lovely raftered upper room, open fire, good, reasonably priced food inc vegetarian dishes; bar with music and machines (Lyn Jolliffe)

Billingford [Bintree Rd; TG0124], Forge: Converted forge with well kept ales inc Greene King Abbot and good value home-made bar food; children welcome (David Oakes)

Blakeney [TG0243], White Horse: Good spot close to harbour; friendly little hotel bar with Watneys-related real ales, good buffet, RSPB display; bedrooms (BKA, Paul Sexton, Sue Harrison)

Bodham Street [TG1240], Red Hart: Pleasant pub with well kept Whitbreads-related real ales, bar food (R P Hastings)

Brancaster Staithe [TF7743], White Horse: Marvellous view across harbour and coastline to Scolt Head island from dining room behind bar, with big helpings of home-made food lunchtime (recently expanded menu) and evening, helpful waitress service, Watneys-related real ales on handpump, big wine list (M and J Back, Mr and Mrs J Barnes)

Bressingham [Thetford Rd; TM0781], Garden House: Cheerful, rambling pub, with original beams in one part; well kept Adnams Bitter, basic but popular bar food; five minutes' walk to Bressingham Gardens (John Baker)

☆ Briston [B1354, Aylsham end of village; TG0532], John H Stracey: Attractive pub with genial licensee, good choice of beers inc local Reepham Rapier, good food in bar and popular restaurant (R C Vincent)

Brockdish [TM2179], Greyhound: Well run, welcoming free house, pleasantly modernised, with well kept beers, good home-cooked and well presented food; subdued piped music of unusually high quality; spotless bedrooms, well furnished and equipped (Richard and Barbara Philpott)

Broome [village edge — actually just over Suffolk border; TM3491], Oaksmere: Popular, beamed bar in oldest part of country-house pub, well kept Adnams Bitter, good restaurant (John Baker)

☆ Brundall [Station Rd — OS Sheet 134 map reference 328079; TG3208], Yare: Busy, popular pub near river; wattled hurdles on ceiling, navigation lamps, ship's curios, good photographs of boats; generous helpings of well presented pub food inc reliable crab salads, real ales such as Boddingtons, Sam Smiths and Woodefordes, splendid log fire; children's room (R Aitken, T Nott)

Burnham Market [The Green; B1155; TF8342], Capt Sir William Hoste: Comfortable bow-windowed inn overlooking green, interesting old-fashioned touches in lounge though also things like gun ports over the bar, bar food from soup through steak and mushroom pie or help-yourself salads to steaks, maybe inc generous helpings of good local mussels, well kept Adnams Broadside, Greene King IPA and Ruddles County, decent wines; naval pictures in black-panelled side room, restaurant; children allowed in family room; bedrooms (Peter Griffiths, M A and W R Proctor, LYM); Lord Nelson: Small pub, locally popular for good fish cooking by ex-bank-manager landlord (Charles Bardswell)

Buxton [TG2322], Mill: Recently opened, traditionally yet comfortably furnished pub with real ale inc guests, good bar and restaurant food (Anon)

☆ Caistor St Edmunds [Caistor Lane; TG2303], Caistor Hall: Originally a hotel and country club, now quiet and comfortable pub/restaurant in lovely grounds; bar (counter an 18th-century shop front) leads into lounge looking on to sweeping lawns, cedar trees etc; also an original library, and tables on terrace; bar food from good sandwiches up, decent wine (Ian Phillips)

☆ **Castle Rising** [TF6624], *Black Horse*: Well run and comfortable family pub notable not so much for atmosphere as for generous helpings of well presented good bar food inc sandwiches, notable ploughman's, local seafood, children's dishes, attractive puddings; well kept Adnams and Charrington IPA on handpump, cheerful smiling service, unobtrusive pop music; restaurant and carvery; very popular at weekends *(Mr and Mrs K H Frostick, M J Morgan, Derek Pascall, Charles Bardswell, Laurie Walker)*

☆ **Cawston** [Eastgate — OS Sheet 133 map reference 144225; TG1425], *Ratcatchers*: Pleasant and friendly old-style pub with well kept Adnams and Woodfordes, wide choice of enterprising bar food particularly strong on starters, fresh fish, steaks, vegetarian dishes and puddings (not Tues); restaurant (due to be extended); quaint front balcony facing sunset *(P S Galbraith, R P Hastings)*

Cley Next the Sea [nr church, overlooking green; TG0443], *Three Swallows*: Two-bar pub with popular food inc freshly fried dishes, Whitbreads-related real ales, very friendly bar staff *(K R Harris, R P Hastings)*

☆ **Colkirk** [TF9126], *Crown*: Unpretentious but well furnished Greene King pub in pleasant village, good bar food inc fine grilled lemon sole, friendly landlord, well kept IPA and Abbot on handpump, decent wines, good choice of other drinks; restaurant, own bowling green behind, big car park *(Gwen and Peter Andrews, Mrs Margaret Dennis, P Thorogood)*

Coltishall [TG2719], *Rising Sun*: Superb spot on pretty bend of River Bure; well presented food inc good value ploughman's, courteous satff, real ales, waterside and other outside tables, family room *(LYM)*

☆ **Cromer** [Promenade; TG2142], *Bath House*: Welcoming inn right down on the seafront — below the cliff the town's built on; lots of dark wood, friendly staff, well kept Greene King Abbot and an interesting guest real ale such as Burton Bridge Porter on handpump; bar food from good sandwiches and ploughman's (lunchtime) through good range of salads to steaks, in eating area up steps; tables out on prom; bedrooms *(Michael and Alison Sandy, T R G Alcock)*

Cromer [Tucker St; off A149], *Red Lion*: Refurbished pub, with bar food inc good filled rolls, well kept real ale; bedrooms *(R P Hastings)*

☆ **Dersingham** [Manor Rd (B1440 out towards Sandringham); TF6830], *Feathers*: Solidly handsome dark sandstone seventeenth-century inn with relaxed and comfortably modernised dark-panelled bars opening on to attractive garden with play area; well kept Charrington and maybe Adnams on handpump, pleasant service, reasonably priced bar food, restaurant (not Sun evening); can get very busy in season; children welcome; comfortable well furnished bedrooms *(Jack and Barbara Smale, Charles Bardswell, Peter Corris, LYM)*

☆ **Diss** [9 St Nicholas St; town centre, off B1077; TM1179], *Greyhound*: Some handsome Tudor features such as the high moulded beams in welcoming and comfortably refurbished carpeted lounge,

with big brick fireplace, well kept Watneys-related real ales, popular reasonably priced bar food, games in public bar; children in eating area *(K A V Read, LYM)*

☆ **Docking** [centre; TF7637], *Pilgrims Reach*: Particularly good food in pleasant and friendly pub currently doing well, with Adnams and Everards real ales, tables in sheltered and attractive terrace garden; restaurant *(Mr and Mrs D J Hancock, James Cane)*

East Barsham [B1105 3 miles N of Fakenham on Wells road; TF9133], *White Horse*: Large open fireplace with log fire, good choice of well kept beers including Woodfordes, good range of attractive reasonably priced bar food inc local fish, piped music *(M J Morgan, Derek Pascall)*

☆ **East Harling** [High St; TL9986], *Swan*: Quiet, comfortable and welcoming old-fashioned village pub with circular bar, tiled floor, low dark beams, lots of small pictures (mostly of ships); plush chairs and settles in lounge, pool table in separate alcove, well kept Watneys-related real ales, good home-cooked food, decent dining room *(Gwen and Peter Andrews, K R Harris)*

Erpingham [OS Sheet 133 map reference 191319; TG1931], *Spread Eagle*: Well worth a visit for its full range of fine Woodfordes beers which used to be brewed here, but now come from Woodbastwick; otherwise it's not so special, apart from terraced garden facing bowling green; children allowed in games room *(Derek and Sylvia Stephenson, WHBM)*

Foulden [TL7698], *White Hart*: Pleasant local with good home-cooked food and decent beer at reasonable prices *(Paul F Milner)*

Framingham Earl [B1332; TG2702], *Railway*: Well kept open-plan modern dining pub with character and relaxing atmosphere — more of a restaurant now, for good sit-down meals; well kept Watneys-related real ales *(TN)*

Fritton [Beccles Rd (A143); TG4600], *Fritton Decoy*: Good atmosphere, courteous and helpful licensee, good variety of reasonably priced bar food, juke box, tables in garden *(M J and P Watts)*

Gillingham [TM4091], *Swan*: Well furnished inn with pleasant staff, well kept Adnams and other beers, good value wines, beautifully presented bar food inc fine lemon sole in cream sauce topped with prawns, outstanding lavatories; comfortable bedrooms — good centre for Broads *(Mrs M E Beard)*

☆ **Great Cressingham** [OS Sheet 144 map reference 849016; TF8501], *Windmill*: Friendly and cosy, with several rooms opening off either side of main bar area; good value food, quick service, Adnams, Ruddles and Sam Smiths, good mix of locals and visitors, lots of farm tools; conservatory for families, well kept big garden *(R P Hastings)*

Great Ryburgh [TF9527], *Boar*: Friendly, comfortable atmosphere, good food, well kept Adnams and Tolly *(Mrs Margaret Dennis)*

Great Yarmouth [South Quay; TG5207], *Gallon Can*: True dockside pub, very plain and simple Bass house just over the road from ocean-going ships, with maybe a couple of lascars playing pool, and other harbour customers; limited but nicely presented cheap food *(T Nott)*

☆ **nr Great Yarmouth** [St Olaves; A143 towards Beccles, where it crosses R Waveney — OS Sheet 134 map reference 458994], *Bell*: Attractive Tudor herringbone brickwork and heavy oak timbering underline its claim to be the oldest Broads pub; spacious and comfortably modernised inside, with efficient service, good bar food (salmon and roast beef recommended), Whitbreads-related real ales on handpump, games in public bar, two attractive open fires; barbecues and good children's play area in riverside garden with free moorings; children in restaurant *(R Aitken, A T Langton, M J and P Watts, LYM)*

☆ **nr Great Yarmouth** [Berney Arms Stn; 8-min train trip from Gt Yarmouth — out 11.10 (not Sun) or 12, return about 3.45 (earlier Sun); OS Sheet 134 map reference 464049], *Berney Arms*: Only safe mooring between Reedham and Gt Yarmouth on River Yare, and accessible only by water or by rail Gt Yarmouth—Norwich; interesting building with flagstone floors, woodburning stove, fishing nets and lamps, settles made from barrel staves; well kept Adnams and Courage, decent straightforward bar food inc good sausages, cheerful service; closed winter; nearby windmill worth visiting *(R P Hastings, R Aitken)*

Gressenhall [TF9515], *Swan*: Friendly service with limited choice of well-cooked bar food, popular with locals; Whitbreads-related real ales; beer garden *(M and J Black)*

Guist [Guist Bottom; A1067 SE of Fakenham; TF9826], *Ordnance Arms*: Free house notable mainly for its good, unusual Thai food *(Paul McPherson)*

☆ **Happisburgh** [by village church; TG3830], *Hill House*: Very pleasant pub with friendly atmosphere, doing particularly well under current regime; well kept Woodfordes Wherry on handpump, also Adnams, well presented reasonably priced tasty bar food from sandwiches up, inc particularly good interesting salads, good smoked haddock fries; good restaurant for Sun lunch; children's room separate from pub, well equipped with toys; bedrooms *(Derek and Sylvia Stephenson, Denzil Taylor)*

Happisburgh [Lower St], *Victoria*: Well run pub on country road with lots of old pictures, good choice of beers, friendly staff, uncomplicated bar food inc good ploughman's; garden with fishpond and swings *(R Grey, S T L Coupland)*

Harleston [The Thoroughfare; TM2483], *Swan*: Tudor bar and restaurant, warm welcome from new licensees, good value carvery; comfortable Georgian bedrooms *(David Morrell)*

☆ **Hethersett** [TG1505], *Kings Head*: Homely and cheerful pub with enjoyable lunchtime bar food, comfortable carpeted lounge, friendly and courteous welcome, traditional games in cosy public bar, attractive and spacious back lawn; well kept Watneys-related real ales *(Dr R Fuller, LYM)*

Hethersett [Henstead Rd], *Greyhound*:

Traditional, simple village pub, strong on atmosphere; Watneys-related real ales, decent wines, good home-made bar food, good garden *(O C Winterbottom)*

☆ **Heydon** [village signposted from B1149; TG1127], *Earle Arms*: Flagstones, bare boards, well kept Adnams tapped from the cask and served through a hatch — and absolutely no pretensions or concessions to current fashions in pub design; readers who like it say proudly that 'basic' is an understatement, though others find it much too primitive for them; bedrooms (cheap and simple); pub faces interestingly unspoilt village green — and still has stables in use behind *(LYM)*

☆ **Hillborough** [A1065; TF8100], *Swan*: Pretty pink cottage pub, dated 1718, simple but comfortable and welcoming, with obliging staff, well kept Adnams, Batemans, Greene King Abbot and IPA and Marstons Pedigree, and good value food inc home-made soup, open doorstep sandwiches, good choice of ploughman's, hot dishes cooked to order — so service can't be quick when it's busy; tables on sheltered lawn *(Peter Griffiths, Joy Heatherley, Charles Bardswell)*

Hingham [TG0202], *White Hart*: Elegant stuccoed Georgian facade with white hart over handsome portico, in pretty village; smartly renovated inside, with woodburning stove in big brick fireplace, vibrant carpet and mirror-fronted bar; bar food *(Ian Phillips)*

☆ **Holkham** [A149 nr Holkham Hall; TF8943], *Victoria*: Several simply furnished but comfortable hotelish bar rooms in pleasantly informal coastal inn by entry to Holkham Hall, with bar food from generous sandwiches to sirloin steak, Tolly real ale; tables in former stableyard and on front terrace; handy for Holkham Hall, beaches and nature reserves a half-mile away; nr start GWG118; children welcome; bedrooms *(LYM)*

Holme Next the Sea [TF7043], *White Horse*: Pleasant pub with remarkably generous good bar food inc bargain lunchtime sandwiches and salads *(Margaret Bull)*

Holt [main st; TG0738], *Feathers*: Reliably well run and welcoming Berni Inn with Watneys-related real ales on handpump, bar food from double-decker sandwiches up, attractive restaurant; bedrooms *(David and Ruth Hollands)*; [Bull St], *Kings Head*: Relaxed atmosphere and pleasant staff, with limited choice of good value food *(K R Harris)*

Horning [TG3417], *Ferry*: Riverside Chef & Brewer with well kept ales and friendly service, even when busy *(MN)*; *New Inn*: Old, well maintained Chef & Brewer pub with tiled floors, panelled bar, big collection of old farm tools, four separate eating areas inc conservatory-style extension with terrace overlooking lawns to river *(R Aitken)*; [Lower St], *Swan*: Riverside Berni Inn perfectly placed on banks of Broads with waterside lawn; well kept Watneys-related real ales on handpump, rather pricey but decent food in bar and restaurant, pleasant service; bedrooms — not cheap but comfortable *(R Aitken, Peter Corris, G M K Donkin)*

Hoveton [TG3018], *Black Horse*: Two comfortable, clean bars with friendly atmosphere, good reasonably priced home-cooked bar food *(H R Edwards)*

☆ **Kings Lynn** [St Nicholas St; TF6220], *Tudor Rose*: Attractive 15th-century pub with wide choice of wines, whiskies and beers (inc well kept Adnams, Bass and Batemans), good bar food inc vegetarian dishes, friendly atmosphere, efficient service, restaurant; bedrooms good value, with private baths and very big breakfasts *(N and J D Bailey, Mr and Mrs K E P Wohl)*

Kirby Bedon [Woods End Rd; off A146 SE of Norwich; TG2805], *Bramerton Woodsend*: Quiet, clean waterside Chef & Brewer pub on south side of River Yare; panelled bar leads to bar food servery with doors to outside terrace, lawns and river view; wholesome, well cooked good value food with help-yourself salads, very pleasant staff *(J D Cranston)*

Litcham [TF8817], *Bull*: Delightful genuine village pub with well kept Watneys-related real ales, bar food inc good home-made pies *(Robert Mitchell)*

Little Dunham [off A47 E of Swaffham; TF8612], *Black Swan*: Big bar area with restaurant sections to left and right, tables in front bar; nice decor, old pictures, brass and copper; Adnams, M&B and guests on handpump; good helpings of food from soup to fish platter and wider evening choice inc steaks — popular then with locals; obliging landlord *(Mr and Mrs J Back)*

Little Melton [off B1108 4 miles W of Norwich; TG1606], *Village Inn*: Recently expanded with plenty of space; efficient service, substantial helpings of good food; good parking *(Col and Mrs L N Smyth)*

Lyng [TG0617], *Fox & Hounds*: Very friendly local on River Wensum, huge helpings of bar food inc delicious steak and mushroom pie *(Margaret and Trevor Errington)*

☆ **Mundford** [Crown St; TL8093], *Crown*: Ancient posting inn rebuilt in 18th century, in charming village, attractive choice of good value main dishes (sandwiches and ploughman's less obviously low-priced, but also good), very welcoming staff, happy atmosphere, well kept real ale; bedrooms good *(Caroline Wright, R P Hastings, E A George, Norman Hill)*

☆ **Neatishead** [TG3420], *White Horse*: Small, quiet and homely with lounge bar resembling one's own front room; Greene King, good reasonably priced home-cooked food, friendly service; only a few minutes' walk from the staithe *(Tim and Anne Neale, J D Maplethorpe)*

☆ **New Buckenham** [TM0890], *George*: Pleasant village-green pub with well kept Courage Best and Directors, Flowers and Wethereds on handpump, generous helpings of decent bar food inc huge ploughman's and well cooked hot dishes in dining room set out as restaurant; bar, lively games area with juke box; a pleasant place, on corner of the village green *(M and J Back)*

Newton [A1065 by Castle Acre; TF8315], *George & Dragon*: Good choice of reasonably priced food inc good fruity curry and other often specially good dishes, friendly staff, pleasant surroundings, well kept Watneys-related real ales, unobtrusive piped music; children in small restaurant area and games bar; small caravan site *(Bill and Wendy Burge, R P Hastings)*

☆ **North Creake** [TF8538], *Jolly Farmers*: Simple and unspoilt, but welcoming — and doing well under current regime, with good local food, well cooked and genially served; the makings of a very pleasant little restaurant *(W F Coghill, Charles Bardswell)*

North Walsham [B1150 a mile NW — OS Sheet 133 map reference 292311; TG2730], *Blue Bell*: Modern but pleasant, well kept real ales, eating area with huge helpings of good value food — wide choice; play area in garden *(R P Hastings)*

☆ **Norwich** [10 Dereham Rd; TG2308], *Reindeer*: Own-brew pub producing three good ales, Bills Bevy, Reindeer and Red Nose — you can see the brewery through back window; about five guest beers too, lively bare-boards-and-casks atmosphere, can get crowded and smoky; big helpings of hearty food, occasional folk bands *(Matthew Pringle, Maureen and Steve Collin, Frank Gadbois)*

Norwich [57 Bethel St], *Coach & Horses*: Good welcome, comfortable atmosphere, imaginative range of bar food from ploughman's up, well presented, reasonably priced and served till 10, inc fresh scampi and wonderful puddings; decent red wine *(Ian Phillips)*; [Tombland, opp cathedral], *Edith Cavell*: Entertaining pub — former teashop, small, comfortable and friendly, with good value food (till 7); Watneys-related real ales, piped music can be loud in evenings *(WJGW, Wayne Brindle)*; [King St], *Ferryboat*: Traditional beamed old-fashioned front part, spacious raftered and flagstoned back area where you may find pianist in action, kitchen alcove complete with baking oven, well kept and attractively priced Greene King IPA and Abbot and Woodfordes, refurbished restaurant; slide and climbing frame in riverside garden with barbecue; children welcome *(LYM — more reports please)*; [Timber Hill], *Gardeners Arms*: Good big town-centre pub with old beams, panels and kitchen alcove complete with baking oven; Adnams, Tetleys and Woodfordes Best, bar food; piped pop music can be loud in evening *(R P Hastings, Graham and Glenis Watkins)*; [Heigham St], *Gibraltar Gardens*: Well kept beer, good reasonably priced food, excellent garden; good parking; children welcome *(P Gillbe)*; [St Leonards Rd (Thorpe Hamlet)], *Jubilee*: Victorian town pub on outskirts; meals well presented and inexpensive, up to ten real ales inc Jubilee Bitter brewed at the pub *(Nic James)*; [Tombland], *Louis Marchen*: Named after member of first Round Table; civilised pub with cheap food, unobtrusive juke box, Watneys-related real ales *(WJGW)*; *Mischief*: Superbly renovated ale and wine vaults next to river with good Watneys-related real ales, good value food; brilliant atmosphere with live music some nights; restaurant *(Wayne Brindle)*; [131 Earlham Rd], *Mitre*: Good home-cooked straightforward bar food, friendly atmosphere, well kept beer *(C J Bartlett)*; [King St], *Nags Head*: Big straightforward Courage pub with separate dining section, pleasant and friendly atmosphere; bar food inc very good value well filled fresh baps *(Ian Phillips)*; *Rib of Beef*: Fairly attractive city-centre riverside pub, unpretentious, basic split-level interior, splendid range of real ales inc unusual Norfolk beers, informative and friendly bar staff *(William McKenzie)*; [Rosary Rd], *Rosary*: Friendly local with good range of beers, bar billiards — hope they've levelled the table by now *(Maureen and Steve Collin)*; [Newmarket St/Bury St], *Unthank Arms*: Refurbished old pub with good atmosphere, open fires, well kept real ales, choice of wines and good range of inexpensive food *(Dr Paul Conn)*; [St Martin, nr Palace Plain — opp cathedral], *Wig & Pen*: Lots of prints of Vanity Fair lawyers and judges, pleasant and homely worn leather banquettes, roaring stove with horsebrasses on overmantle; bar food, popular with newspapermen *(Ian Phillips)*; [St George St], *Wild Man*: Gets busy for consistently good value lunchtime food and well kept beer *(K R Harris)*

nr **Norwich** [Thorpe St Andrew (A47 towards Gt Yarmouth); TG2609], *Buck*: Long building with four different roof levels in front of village church; friendly atmosphere and good value food; River Yare over rd *(Peter Corris)*; [36 Yarmouth Rd (A47), Thorpe St Andrew — OS Sheet 134 map reference 257085], *Kings Head*: Attractive mixture of buildings all uniformly painted; welcoming bar, bar food, interesting fish restaurant where chef cooks in view of diners, riverside garden, free moorings *(R Aitken)*

Old Hunstanton [TF6842], *Ancient Mariner*: Interesting old pub with bare bricks and flagstones, several little areas inc upstairs room overlooking bar, and big counter with locals sitting around three sides; well kept Adnams Bitter and Broadside, Bass and Charrington IPA, good bar food *(Denise Plummer, Jim Froggatt)*

Ormesby St Michael [TG4614], *Eels Foot*: Beautifully sited Whitbreads Broads pub with spacious waterside lawn, comfortably refurbished inside, with good bar food and civilised efficient service *(LYM)*

Overstrand [High St; TG2440], *White Horse*: Good honest very friendly local with well kept Whitbreads-related real ales, limited choice of well cooked inexpensive meals *(R P Hastings)*

Potter Heigham [A1065 Wroxham Rd — OS Sheet 134 map reference 413191; TG4119], *Falsgate*: Unpretentious local with neat open-plan dining area, curiously homely unsmart lounge with lots of houseplants, simple bar, pool room; limited choice of food inc any combination of four pastas with four sauces — wholewheat ravioli carbonara and spinach and walnut with real bolognese both very tasty; Courage Directors and John Smiths on handpump *(T Nott)*

Ranworth [village signposted from B1140 Norwich—Acle; TG3514], *Maltsters*: Included for its fine position across quiet lane from Ranworth Broad; straightforward bar food *(Tim and Anne Neale, LYM)*

☆ **Reepham** [Market Sq; TG0922], *Old Brewery House*: Attractive Georgian house

overlooking market sq with prominent sundial over door and wellhouse in adjacent yard; friendly and cosy but windowless bar, good choice of well kept beers inc Adnams, helpful service, wide range of reasonably priced and generously served straightforward bar food in dining area, restaurant; bedrooms comfortable and attractive *(Geoff Lee, Ian Phillips, R P Hastings)*

☆ **Salhouse** [Bell Lane; TG3014], *Bell*: Pleasant and friendly, with well kept real ales and limited choice of inexpensive food *(A T Langton, J H C Peters)*

Sculthorpe [A148 2 miles W of Fakenham; TF8930], *Sculthorpe Mill*: Licensees of the very highly rated Lifeboat at Thornham (see main entries) have now opened this converted watermill — should be well worth investigating *(News please)*

Sheringham [Cromer Rd; TG1543], *Dunstable Arms*: Two pleasant fires in lounge of good honest pub, Watneys-related real ales, good value straightforward bar food *(R C Vincent)*; *Two Lifeboats*: Well kept beer and reasonably priced food inc good ploughman's; bedrooms *(R P Hastings)*; *Windham Arms*: Friendly pub on sea front, popular with locals out of season; good range of bar food *(Gordon Theaker)*

Smallburgh [TG3225], *Crown*: Good atmosphere in free house, very useful for the area, with good value bar food inc home-made steak and mushroom pie with fresh vegetables; restaurant *(R C Watkins)*

South Walsham [TG3713], *Ship*: Well kept real ale, good ploughman's, pleasant staff *(David and Genevieve Benest)*

Stalham [High St; TG3725], *Kingfisher*: In a very popular village, the tiny bar here has good food at very reasonable prices and well kept Adnams; bedrooms *(R P Hastings)*

☆ **Stokesby** [TG4310], *Ferry House*: Fairly basic traditional pub on River Bure with plenty of character, good service, generous helpings of good food, choice of real ales inc well kept Adnams Extra and Flowers on handpump; very popular with boating holidaymakers (free moorings); children welcome *(Peter Seddon)*

☆ **Stow Bardolph** [TF6205], *Hare Arms*: Pleasantly refurbished country pub opposite Stow Hall, with reasonably priced and quickly served good lunchtime bar food from sandwiches up — inc generous puddings; cheerful licensees, well kept Greene King IPA and Abbot, separate elegant evening restaurant (food then not cheap but good), conservatory for children *(Derek and Sylvia Stephenson, A E Clay, Mr and Mrs Clark)*

☆ **Stradsett** [A134/A1122; TF6604], *Fouldgate*: Long timbered bar with plenty of tables and comfortable seats, big helpings of reasonably priced traditional pub food inc good salads, Watneys-related real ales on handpump, good white wine; pleasant, efficient staff, fresh flowers, juke box, big car park *(Gwen and Peter Andrews, Bill and Wendy Burge)*

☆ **Surlingham** [TG3206], *Coldham Hall*: Beautiful waterside setting on edge of Broads with attractive, well kept gardens; generous helpings of good bar food, well kept beer and cider, friendly service, family room *(J E Cooper)*

☆ **Surlingham** [from village head N; pub on bumpy track into which both village roads fork], *Ferry House*: Spaciously comfortable if dimly lit modernised bar with good views of the river (there's still a rowing-boat ferry); usual range of bar food from big filled granary rolls to steaks, several vegetarian dishes, Watneys-related real ales on handpump, traditional bar games, piped music, restaurant, free mooring for 24 hours; children welcome, with own menu; has opened 8pm winter *(LYM)*

☆ **Sutton Staithe** [village signposted from A149 S of Stalham; TG3823], *Sutton Staithe*: The great attraction is the position, in a particularly unspoilt part of the Broads; little alcoves, built-in seats and an antique settle among more modern furnishings, well kept Adnams and sometimes other real ales tapped from the cask, usual bar food from sandwiches to steaks inc children's menu, restaurant; good nearby moorings; children allowed in eating areas; has been open all day summer; bedrooms *(M W Atkinson, Jason Caulkin, LYM)*

Swaffham [Market Pl, London Rd; TF8109], *White Hart*: Formerly the Breckland, now refurbished under new management; decent bars and bar food, good restaurant *(Mr and Mrs Douglas Parker)*

Swannington [TG1318], *Swannington Arms*: Converted from a moated mansion in the middle of nowhere; real ales, bar snacks, summer barbecue; some concentration on restaurant side *(Nic James)*

Swanton Abbot [off B1150 11 miles N of Norwich — OS Sheet 133 map reference 265254; TG2625], *Weavers Arms*: Pleasant, rural pub with clean, homely atmosphere; bar with pool and family rooms off, all decorated with old farm tools; separate lounge with small adjoining restaurant; well kept Whitbreads-related real ales and Marstons Pedigree on handpump, good home-made bar food *(Michael Dixon)*

☆ **Swanton Morley** [B1147, E end of village; TG0216], *Darbys*: Short choice of food in cosy beamed country pub, tractor seats with potato sacks as cushions at bar, well kept Adnams and Broadside and Woodfordes Best, warm welcome, winter log fire; children's room, upstairs restaurant *(Mr and Mrs J D Cranston, Derek and Sylvia Stephenson; more reports please)*

☆ **Thetford** [King St; TL8783], *Bell*: Clean, tidy and pleasant beamed and timbered Tudor bar with well kept Adnams and Greene King real ales and generously served bar food in THF hotel which is otherwise spaciously modern *(BB)*

☆ **Thetford** [White Hart St], *Thomas Paine*: Well kept Adnams and Tolly Original in friendly, spacious and comfortable hotel lounge bar, good value bar food from fine range of sandwiches to hot dishes; good service, small fire in big fireplace; children welcome *(LYM)*

Thetford, *Ark*: Good range of bar food, separate restaurant and barbecues in garden when seasonable; children's climbing area *(Anon)*; [Castle St], *Bridge*: Good food at reasonable prices, Watneys-related real ales, riverside garden with play area; plenty of parking *(Mrs M E Beard)*

☆ **Thompson** [Griston Rd — OS Sheet 144 map reference 923969; TL9196], *Chequers*: Latest news is that this long, low and picturesque 15th-century thatched house, its series of quaint rooms reopened last year after a longish closure, is recovering its atmosphere and again serving good food *(Pamela Goodwyn, Mr and Mrs Douglas Parker, LYM — more reports please)*

☆ **Thornham** [Church St; TF7343], *Kings Head*: Cosy atmosphere in lovely old white-fronted pub converted from village cottages; two attractive bars with low dark beams and lots of brass; darts in wider tiled part, narrower no-smoking part with carvery and tables and banquettes in well lit alcoves; big helpings of good food, interesting landlord, friendly staff; real ales inc Greene King Abbot on handpump; nr GWG116; bedrooms *(Gwen and Peter Andrews, Mrs D K Rae, Peter Griffiths, Peter Corris)*

Titchwell [A149; TF7543], *Three Horseshoes*: Relatively modern pub, arranged and run well, with well kept beer, good food inc evening carvery, family room *(Charles Bardswell)*

Walpole Cross Keys [A17 8 miles W of Kings Lynn; TF5119], *Woolpack*: Attractive family-run pub with friendly service, good choice of home-cooked food inc sandwiches, vegetarian dishes and children's meals; well kept Adnams on handpump, restaurant, garden with play area *(G G Calderwood, Derek and Sylvia Stephenson)*

☆ **Walsingham** [Common Place/Shire Hall Plain; TF9236], *Bull*: A short walk from the shrine, and no visit to Walsingham complete without an hour or so here — good Watneys-related real ales, simple bar food, very friendly service and friendly company; what's more, if you go in in a dog collar, the locals don't choke over their drink, and the staff just ask 'What are you going to drink, Father?' *(Canon Kenneth Wills)*

Walsingham [Friday Market Pl], *Black Lion*: 14th-century free house, pleasant lounge, wide choice of well presented bar food; bedrooms *(Miss E Judge)*

Watton [TF9100], *Crown*: Well worth knowing for the area, as staff and landlord most obliging, Adnams well kept and choice of food good and very reasonably priced indeed; bedrooms *(Ian Phillips)*

West Beckham [Bodham Rd; TG1339], *Wheatsheaf*: Well kept beer, friendly service and good food at reasonable prices; bedrooms *(Revd John Cooper, P Thorogood)*

West Runton [TG1842], *Village Inn*: Beautifully placed in village centre, fine food inc delightful lunchtime cold table; real ales on handpump, tables on front lawn *(Peter Corris)*

☆ **West Somerton** [B1159/B1152; TG4619], *Lion*: It's the genuinely warm and friendly welcome which pulls this airy and comfortable roadside pub out of the average; good value efficiently served bar food, well kept Greene King and guest real ales; handy for Martham Broad; children in family room *(LYM)*

☆ **Wighton** [TF9340], *Sandpiper*: A real well-scrubbed modest East Anglian country pub with well kept Tolly and guest beers, bar food, friendly hardworking licensees;

games room; garden with play area, animals on green opposite; attractive village; children welcome; good value bedrooms *(John Baker)*

Wiveton [TG0342], *Bell*: Popular old pub overlooking village green and church; much modernised inside with three well kept real ales and good straightforward bar food; tables out in front, more in attractive back garden *(R P Hastings)*

Wortwell [TM2784], *Dove*: Good bar food, good Sun lunch *(Brian MacIvor)*

Wreningham [TM1598], *Bird in Hand*: Recently refurbished and extended pub, cleanly refurbished, with local bygones and Lotus car photographs (local company), good range of reasonably priced meals, and Flowers, Marstons Pedigree and Woodfordes ales; big car park *(Nigel Gibbs)*

☆ nr **Wroxham** [Rackheath; A1151 towards Norwich; TG2917], *Green Man*: Notable for its beautifully kept bowling green, but

well kept and comfortable inside too — easy chairs, plush banquettes and other seats in open-plan bar, log fires, popular bar food (mainly fish in the evening), real ales, piped music; children allowed in eating area *(LYM)*

Wymondham [Market Pl; TG1101], *Cross Keys*: Friendly staff, pleasant atmosphere, bar food inc good value ploughman's and ham off bone — full of locals at lunchtime *(Audrey and Brian Green);* [Town Green], *Feathers*: Lots of character, enthusiastic staff and properly kept ales (especially Tickler named for the pub by Woodfordes); bar food *(John Baker);* [Church St], *Green Dragon*: Fine 17th-century inn with solid beams in lounge bar, Tudor mantlepiece in quaint old snug; good value bar food, Courage Directors, Flowers and John Smiths tapped from the cask; behind the abbey *(Frank Gadbois)*

Northamptonshire *see* Midlands

Northumberland *see* Northumbria

Northumbria (including Durham, Northumberland, Cleveland and Tyne & Wear)

A pub renaissance up here is bringing a good deal of interest into this section of the Guide. Old pubs are being refurbished top to toe: besides many examples brightening up the Lucky Dip section at the end of the chapter, two new main entries show two different approaches to this. The Tap & Spile in Newcastle, formerly the Prince of Wales, has been remodelled by the brewery owning it (Camerons, now part of the Brent Walker group) as an attractive pastiche of how it's nice to imagine pubs used to be a few decades ago – assuming a heftily rose-tinted pair of spectacles. An important point is that in spite of the brewery ownership it's run as a free house, with a fine choice of beers. The concept is spreading; good news. The Cook & Barker Arms at Newton on the Moor shows what can be done by a genuine free house, deftly updated to cater comfortably for strangers using the nearby A1 during the day, yet particularly in the evening still preserving vigorous local roots. A third new entry – the Shiremoor House Farm at New York – shows a third approach: an entirely new pub developed from buildings (in this case derelict) which previously served quite a different purpose. At least in this case, the approach is such a complete success that it comes straight into the main entries with a star award – and has quickly become one of the most enjoyable and relaxing pubs in the north east. Other main entries currently on top form include the Manor House at Carterway Heads (lovely food, gradual good refurbishment), the civilised Fox & Hounds at Cotherstone (good genuine food), the prettily placed Jolly Fisherman at Craster (remarkably cheap snacks), the attractive Three Tuns at Eggleston (decent honest food), the thriving Tankerville Arms at Eglingham, the handsome old Crown Posada in Newcastle (yet another new entry), the George at Piercebridge (doing well under newish licensees), the Rose & Crown at Romaldkirk (another place flourishing under new licensees) and the Warenford Lodge at Warenford (very interesting food – and virtually right on the A1). Lucky Dip entries of particular current interest include the Lord Crewe Arms at Bamburgh, Percy Arms at Chatton, Duke of York at Fir Tree, Milecastle near Haltwhistle, General Havelock at Haydon Bridge, High Force Hotel at High Force, both entries at Rennington, Ship at Saltburn by the Sea and Seven Stars at Shincliffe. A great feature of pubs throughout the area is sheer value for money. In our national price survey we found that drinkers here are now usually paying around 10p a pint less than the countrywide average (two attractive country pubs, the Black Bull at Etal and the Feathers at Hedley on the Hill, stood out as particularly cheap). And we found that pub food here also costs much less than the national average, with getting on for half the pubs meeting our bargain targets – decent

snacks for under £1, or substantial main dishes for under £3;
Tyneside pubs in particular stand out as giving good food value.

BEAMISH (Durham)   NZ2254 Map 10
Shepherd & Shepherdess
By main gate of Open Air Museum

Efficiently served bar food in this well managed and neatly refurbished pub includes sandwiches, cheese and asparagus quiche, lasagne or plaice (£2.85), vegetarian dishes and salads (from £2.85), steak and kidney pie (£2.95), seafood platter (£3.50), gammon (£3.75), rump steak (£5.35), and farmhouse grill (£5.15). Well kept Vaux Samson and Wards Sheffield Best on handpump. The spacious lounge has been refurbished this year, with new covers for the plush button-back built-in wall banquettes and small comfortable chairs on the carpet; a hand-painted mural showing local places of interest and beauty has been added above the substantial mahogany-fitted servery area, a spinning wheel now sits in one corner and lots more decorative plates and pleasant reproductions of Victorian pictures have been hung on the walls; there's an attractive Victorian fireplace. Fruit machine, space game, piped 1970s pop music. There are tables outside the slate-roofed white house. (*Recommended by Mr and Mrs M D Jones, Mr and Mrs G D Amos, John Oddey; more reports please*)

Vaux   Licensee William Dean   Real ale   Meals and snacks (till 10 in evening)
Children welcome   Open 11–11; 11–3, 6.30–11 in winter

Sun
Open Air Museum; note that you have to enter the museum (1989 adult fee £4), and the pub is then on the far side of the 260-acre site – so the point of going is to visit the museum, and not just the pub

Part of a remarkable living museum, this happily bustling pub – moved lock, stock and barrel from Bishop Auckland – has two smallish rooms with a real turn-of-the-century feel: bare boards, Victorian-style wallpaper, a varnished panelled dado, sturdy settles, antique coat rails, service bell-pushes, advertisements, and stuffed birds, antlers and stags' heads. It has well kept McEwans 80/- and Youngers No 3 on handpump, bits of black pudding as nibbles on the bar counter and filled barm cakes – only the prices are today's. Big etched and cut-glass windows look out over the cobbled street (past the vintage tram and 1913 Daimler bus which can take you free around the site) to a drapers' and Co-op moved here from nearby Annfield Plain, fitted out inside with Edwardian goods, with shop assistants dressed to match and even a working Edwardian upstairs cafe. The same little street includes a row of Georgian houses fitted out with a 1920s dentist's, stationers' and solicitor's; other thoroughly functional 'antiques' – the place is growing all the time – include a row of period miners' cottages with busily house-proud 'miners' wives', a turn-of-the-century station (with steam trains), a working colliery, smithy and farm (with a local cheesemaker using traditional equipment to make Dales-type cheeses). Pervading everything is that nostalgic pre-smokeless smell of burning coal fires. In the yard behind the pub, you'll find the Scottish & Newcastle Clydesdale dray horses stabled, with an immaculate period tack room. (*Recommended by Andy and Jill Kassube, Derek Patey, Comus Elliott*)

Youngers   Real ale   Snacks   Children welcome   Open 11–5

BLANCHLAND (Northumberland)   NY9750 Map 10
Lord Crewe Arms
This ancient inn was built originally in 1235 as part of the guest-house of a Premonstratensian monastery. Part of the cloister still stands in the neatly terraced gardens, and one bar is down in a crypt – simply furnished, with pews against massive stone walls under a barrel-vaulted ceiling. Upstairs, the Derwent Room has old settles, low beams and sepia photographs on its walls. There's also a

priest's hole next to a striking 13th-century fireplace where the Jacobite Tom Forster (part of the family who had owned the building before it was sold to the formidable Lord Crewe, Bishop of Durham) is said to have hidden after escaping from prison in London, on his way to exile in France. Simple bar food includes soup (£1.20), filled granary rolls (£1.50), ploughman's (£2.75), salads (from £3), grilled fillet of cod (£3.70), breadcrumbed supreme of chicken with tagliatelli, crushed tomato and mozzarella (£3.85), and puddings (£1.20); Vaux Samson on handpump; friendly, helpful licensees; darts. (*Recommended by Sidney and Erna Wells, Simon Baker, David Oakes, Stephanie Sowerby, Mrs E M Thompson*)

Free house Licensees Mr and Mrs Gingell, A Todd Real ale Lunchtime meals and snacks Evening restaurant, though they do Sun lunch Children in eating area of bar and in room off main bar Open 11–3, 6–11 (all day in summer if very busy) Bedrooms tel Hexham (0434) 675251; £54B/£76B

CARTERWAY HEADS (Northumberland) NZ0552 Map 10

Manor House 🏅

A68 just N of B6278, near Derwent Reservoir

A friendly and enthusiastic young couple, together with the licensee's sister, run this simple stone building which has quickly become popular for its daily-changing bar food: carrot and parsnip soup (£1.50), filled French bread, ploughman's (£3.25), Tuscan bean stew (£3.50), warm courgette and cheese tart or filled leek and mushroom pancake (£3.75), pigeon casserole (£4.25), and hot sticky toffee pudding, gooseberry Betty or home-made ice-creams like rhubarb (£1.50). The straightforward lounge bar has big photographs of sheep, lambs and Muscovy duck, flowers and houseplants in its red-velvet-curtained windows, and red plush button-back built-in wall banquettes and other seats around its tables; the beamed locals' bar has been refurbished this year with pine tables, chairs and stools, old oak pews, and a new mahogany bar. Darts, dominoes, and piped music; well kept Vaux Double Maxim and Wards Sheffield Best on handpump, half-a-dozen malt whiskies, and decent coffee. The evening restaurant has its own comfortable lounge, with sofas and so forth. Rustic tables out on a small side terrace and lawn have a pleasant view south over moorland pastures. (*Recommended by John Oddey, Graham Oddey, Lesley Jones, Geralyn Meyler, M B P Carpenter, Dr R H M Stewart, G G Calderwood*)

Free house Licensees Anthony and Jane Pelly, Miss E J C Pelly Real ale Meals and snacks (12–2.30, 7–9.30; not winter Mon lunchtime) Restaurant tel Consett (0207) 55268 Tues–Sat (Thurs–Sat Jan 7–Easter) Children in eating area until 8.30 Open 11–3, 6–11; closed Mon lunch 1 Jan–31 March

COTHERSTONE (Durham) NZ0119 Map 10

Fox & Hounds 🏅

B6277 – incidentally a good quiet route to Scotland, through interesting scenery

Civilised and friendly, this white-painted house serves very good, imaginative home-made bar food in its L-shaped lounge bar. This might consist at lunchtime of open home-made rolls (from £1.95) and ploughman's (£3.25), as well as meat and vegetable broth (£1.45), chicken liver pâté with walnut toast (£2.45), a farmhouse grill (£3.65), good steak and kidney pie (£4.45), chicken and mushroom pancake or chicken with fresh pineapple and walnuts in a light curry mayonnaise (£5.25), and steak (£7.95), with specials such as fresh mussel and white wine soup (£2.95), game pie (£4.25), vegetable crumble (£4.95) or fresh plaice and prawn gratinée (£6.95); home-made puddings like chocolate cream crunch or fresh strawberry and hazelnut pavlova (from £2.25), and children's meals (£2); attentive service. The same menu – with the same prices – is used in the restaurant. Comfortable furnishings in the various alcoves and recesses of the bar include thickly cushioned wall seats, and there are beams, local photographs and country pictures, and a winter open fire. John Smiths on handpump, and quite a few wines. The pub overlooks a picturesque little village green. (*Recommended by Roger Broadie, Simon Baker, Robert Kimberley, the Atherton family, Margaret and Roy Randle, E R Thompson*)

Free house   Licensees Patrick and Jenny Crawley   Real ale   Snacks (lunchtime, not Sun) and meals   Restaurant   Children in eating area and restaurant   Open 11.30–2.30, 6.30–11; may close Mon lunchtimes in winter   Bedrooms tel Teesdale (0833) 50241; £30B/£40B

CRASTER (Northumberland)   NU2620 Map 10

Jolly Fisherman ★

Off B1339 NE of Alnwick

The atmospheric original bar, particularly the snug by the entrance, is the place to sit in this unpretentious place, popular with workers from the kippering shed opposite and the working harbour just below; there are good sea views from the big picture window in the airy extension, and it's close to a splendid clifftop walk – *Good Walks Guide* Walk 145 – to Dunstanburgh Castle. The pleasantly simple (and cheap) food includes burgers (90p), home-made pizzas (£1), and highly praised local crab and salmon sandwiches (£1.25); obliging service. Well kept Wards Sheffield Bitter on handpump; darts, shove-ha'penny, dominoes, cribbage, juke box, fruit machine, trivia and space game. *(Recommended by Helen and Roy Sumner, BKA, Mr and Mrs P R Lynch, Ann Marie Stephenson, Dr and Mrs Frank Rackow, David Oakes, Simon Baker, Linda Sewell, Derek Patey, Mr and Mrs G D Amos, Mike Tucker, A C and S J Beardsley)*

Vaux   Licensee A George   Real ale   Snacks (available during opening hours)   Children welcome   Open 11–3, 6–11

DURHAM   NZ2743 Map 10

Shakespeare

Sadler Street

This half-timbered building is small and cosy, with an almost vibrantly welcoming atmosphere in the busy, unpretentious main front bar, charming panelled snug, and further back room – and popular with a happy mix of well behaved students, the cathedral choir, local business people and tourists. A good range of well kept real ales might typically include McEwans 80/-, Theakstons Best and XB and Youngers No 3, lots of malt whiskies, simple good value bar snacks such as good freshly made sandwiches and toasties (60p), and friendly efficient service. The pub is nicely placed on a pedestrians-only street between the old market square and the cathedral; you can hire boats on the river. *(Recommended by Helen and Roy Sumner, SJC, Ian and Sue Brocklebank, John Tyzack, Sue Holland, Dave Webster, Jon Dewhirst)*

Scottish & Newcastle   Licensee Miss Karen Tims   Real ale   Snacks (not Sun)   Children welcome   Open 11–11

EGGLESTON (Durham)   NY9924 Map 10

Three Tuns ✪

Big windows in the Teesdale Room here look out past the terrace and garden to open fields and the Tees valley; the room itself is used for bar meals (first come, first served for the window seats). The relaxed and friendly beamed bar has old oak settles, one with amusingly horrific Gothick carving, as well as Windsor armchairs and the like, and a log fire. A decent range of food includes home-made soup (£1.50), ploughman's or home-made game pâté with coleslaw and pickle (£2.35), through home-made cottage pie (£2.75), three-egg omelettes made with their own free range eggs (£3.15), locally smoked chicken with yoghurt and garlic dressing (£3.75), roast duck with orange (£4.85), and steaks (£6.25), with daily specials such as very popular pheasant casserole; Sunday lunch (booking essential); six decent house wines by the glass or carafe; dominoes. The licensees have been here 21 years. There are some fine moorland roads – the B6282, B6278 and B6279 – close by. *(Recommended by E R Thompson, Rosalind Russell; more reports please)*

Free house   Licensees James and Christine Dykes   Meals and snacks (not Sun evening, not Mon – except Bank Hols)   *Restaurant Sun lunch and Tues–Sat evenings, bookings only by previous day Teesdale (0833) 50289   Children in eating area and restaurant Open 11.30–2.30, 7–11; closed Mon (except Bank Hols) and 25 Dec*

EGLINGHAM (Northumberland)   NU1019 Map 10

Tankerville Arms

B6346 NW of Alnwick

Busy in the evening with chatty locals, this long stonebuilt village pub has black joists, some walls stripped to bare stone, red plush banquettes and captain's chairs around cast-iron-framed tables on the Turkey carpet, and coal fires at each end; there's a snug no-smoking area. Good, well presented bar food includes sandwiches, smoked fish or steak and kidney pies, gammon and peaches or fresh smoked trout and Aberdeen Angus steaks; service, usually good and friendly, can get hurried at busy times. Decent wines; fruit machine and piped music. The garden is to have new furniture. *(Recommended by E R Thompson, Dr T H M Mackenzie, Hazel Church)*

Free house   Licensee George Heydon   Meals and snacks (11–2.15, 6–9.30) Restaurant tel Powburn (066 578) 444   Children welcome   Open 11–3, 6–12

ETAL (Northumberland)   NT9339 Map 10

Black Bull

Off B6354, SW from Berwick

A three-mile light railway has been constructed and trains run between Heatherslaw (where there's a working watermill from which you can buy flour ground on the premises) and the bare ruins of Etal Castle on the banks of the River Till at the far end of this particularly picturesque village. The pub is a white-painted and thatched cottage with a roomy, modernised lounge bar: Windsor chairs around the tables on its carpet and glossily varnished beams. Good value, straightforward bar food includes filled rolls and sandwiches (from 75p), soup (80p), ploughman's (£2.30), haddock (£2.80), vegetarian dishes like cheese and herb puff parcels or tagliatelle rosa (around £4), farm-cured gammon (£4.85), Tweed salmon salad (£5.80) and rump steak (£6.80); children's helpings. Well kept Lorrimers Scotch on handpump; darts, dominoes, cribbage, fruit machine. The village's offspring, New Etal, a diminutive hamlet across the river, was originally conceived to replace Etal when it was destroyed by Border marauders. *(Recommended by P J and S E Robbins, Andy and Jill Kassube, Martin and Carol Fincham, Mr and Mrs M O Jones, Alan Hall, Mr and Mrs G D Amos)*

Vaux   Licensee Thomas Hailes   Real ale   Meals and snacks   Children in eating area only, away from the bar   Open 12–3, 7–11

GRETA BRIDGE (Durham)   NZ0813 Map 10

Morritt Arms 🛏

Hotel signposted off A66 W of Scotch Corner

A lively, lifesize Pickwickian mural runs right the way round the high-ceilinged Dickens Bar of this quiet hotel (which is the sole survivor of three 18th-century coaching inns, in one of which Dickens stayed on his way to Barnard Castle in January 1838 to begin his research for *Nicholas Nickleby*). Sturdy green-plush-seated oak settles and big Windsor armchairs cluster around traditional cast-iron-framed tables and the big windows look out on the extensive lawn. The adjacent green bar has dark grey leatherette wall seats, a stag's head and a big case of stuffed black game; there's also a fine big model traction engine in one of the lounges. Well kept Theakstons Best on handpump; good open fires. A proper old shove-ha'penny board, with raisable brass rails to check the lie of the coins, and in the separate public bar, darts, dominoes and a juke box. Bar food includes soup (lunchtime), sandwiches (evening), and ploughman's (£3.10), pork cutlets (£4.50), rack of lamb with rosemary (£4.75), and fresh salmon salad (£6.25). The decoration here (particularly Gilroy's signed mural, painted in 1946) has always been popular, but the time is perhaps coming when some decoration will be needed. There are picnic-table sets and swings at the far end, and teak tables in a pretty side area look along to the graceful old bridge by the stately gates to Rokeby Park. (*Recommended by Simon Baker, Mrs E M Thompson*)

Free house   Licensees David and John Mulley   Real ale   Meals and snacks (lunchtime; sandwiches and soup in evening)   Restaurant   Children welcome Open 11–3, 6–11   Bedrooms tel Teesdale (0833) 27232/27392; £40B/£62B

HEDLEY ON THE HILL (Northumberland)   NZ0859 Map 10

Feathers

Village signposted from New Ridley, which is signposted from B6309 N of Consett; OS Sheet 88 map reference 078592

The three friendly, Turkey-carpeted bars in this traditional village local have beams, stripped stonework, solid brown leatherette settles, woodburning stoves, and country pictures. Weekend lunchtime home-made bar food includes sandwiches, soup (£1), smokies (£2.95), and a main dish like Greek casserole (£3.35). Well kept Marstons Pedigree, Ruddles Best and a regular weekly guest beer on handpump, and around twenty malt whiskies; darts, shove-ha'penny, table skittles, dominoes and space game. (*Recommended by Simon Baker, John Oddey; more reports please*)

Free house   Licensees Marina and Colin Atkinson   Real ale   Snacks (Sat and Sun, but see above)   Children welcome until 8.30   Open 6–11 weekdays; 12–3, 6–11 Sat; 12–3 Sun)

LONGFRAMLINGTON (Northumberland)   NU1301 Map 10

Granby ⊘ ⇐

A697

In the evening, when there's quite an emphasis on food, most people come to eat rather than to drink in this small modernised 18th-century inn. Well prepared, the wide range includes soup (£1.25, not evenings), sandwiches (from £2.15, steak £2.55), moules marinières (£2.65), cod or plaice (£3.55), home-made steak and kidney pie (lunchtime only, £3.65), salads (from £5.10), chicken Kiev (£6.25), roast duckling with orange sauce (£7.65), good steaks (from £7.55), and puddings (from £1.30); substantial breakfasts, with large kippers, for residents; friendly service. The two rooms of the bar have copper and whisky-water jars and ushers' lamps hanging from the black joists, red brocaded wall settles and stools around the white walls and in the bay windows, brown wooden tables, a copper-covered little fireplace in one room, and faint piped music; they keep 27 malt whiskies. There are some picnic tables on the small front terrace. (*Recommended by R Johnstone, John Oddey, Richard Dolphin, Comus Elliott*)

Bass   Licensee Anne Bright   Meals and snacks   Restaurant   Children over 8 in lounge lunchtime only   Open 11–3, 6–11   Bedrooms tel Longframlington (066 570) 228; £20.50(£21.50B)/£43B

LONGHORSLEY (Northumberland)   NZ1597 Map 10

Linden Pub ⇐

Part of Linden Hall Hotel; down long drive, and past the hotel itself

Behind a smartly restored country house hotel, this pub is a two-storey conversion of the stone granary. It's comfortable and airy, and the red-carpeted bar has lots of light-coloured woodwork and bare stone, a log-effect gas fire in a large round central hearth and a remarkable collection of old enamel advertising signs, with stairs to the partly no-smoking galleried upper part. The courtyard is to be revamped, new flagstones laid, and new wooden cask-type tables and seats added. Bar food at lunchtime, served from a side counter, includes sandwiches, good broth (£1.25), leek and pasta crumble (£3.25), salads (from £3.25), steak and kidney pie (£3.75), and grilled lamb cutlets (£4.15), with evening dishes like supreme of chicken (£4.45), trout fillets in a pancake with fresh tomato and herb sauce (£4.75), and steak (£6.25); puddings (from £1.25); helpful service. Theakstons Best and guests like Big Lamp Prince Bishop and McEwans 80/- on handpump; darts, pool (both sensibly placed), dominoes, cribbage, fruit machine and piped music. Garden draughts are played out in the yard, where barbecues are organised in good weather, and there is a good outdoor games area in the spacious grounds of the adjoining hotel, as well as the play area by the pub. *(Recommended by Mr and Mrs P Mackey, J H Tate, GB; more reports please)*

Free house   Licensee I M Moore   Real ale   Meals and snacks   Children upstairs Open 11–3, 6–11   Bedrooms and restaurant in the hotel tel Morpeth (0670) 516611, Telex 538224; £82.50B/£99.50B

MOORSHOLM (Cleveland)   NZ6914 Map 8

Jolly Sailor

A171 nearly 1 mile E of Moorsholm village turn-off

There are tables (and some children's playthings) outside this stone-built pub, looking over the moorland pasture to heather and bracken rising beyond. Inside, the long, friendly bar is cosy but spacious, with lots of comfortably upholstered little booths around the solid black tables, ceiling beams, and some heavy horse harness on the stripped stone walls. Bar food includes sandwiches (£1.25), ploughman's (£3.25), Whitby haddock or home-made steak and kidney pie (£4.20), gammon (£4.25) and steaks (from £7.50); also a good range of vegetarian dishes such as spinach and mushroom lasagne, mushroom and nut pasta or lentil crumble (£4.35); Sunday lunch (£5.95, £4 children); children's menu (£2); friendly service. Well equipped family room; juke box, darts on request. *(Recommended by Alan and Ruth Woodhouse; more reports please)*

Free house   Licensee Mrs Elaine Ford   Meals and snacks (served during opening hours)   Restaurant tel Castleton (0287) 60270   Children in family room   Open 11.30–3, 6–11 (all day Sat and Bank Holidays); closed weekday lunchtimes Oct–Apr

NEWCASTLE UPON TYNE (Tyne & Wear)   NZ2266 Map 10

Bridge Hotel

Castle Square (in local A-Z street atlas index as Castle Garth); right in centre, just off Nicholas St (A6215) at start of High Level Bridge; only a few parking meters nearby, but evening parking easy

The imposing, neatly kept Victorian lounge in this Grade-II listed building has a massive mahogany carved fireplace, a bar counter equipped with unusual pull-down slatted snob screens, decorative mirrors, brown leather banquettes and elegant small chairs on its rust carpet, and high ceilings; depending on the time of day or week, it can get noisy, though service remains friendly and welcoming. In the public bar, which has some cheerful stained glass, there's a good juke box, pool, dominoes and fruit machine (with a second in the lounge lobby). Well kept Tetleys Bitter, Theakstons Best and XB and a weekly guest beer on handpump; simple bar snacks include toasted sandwiches (65p) and stottie cakes with meat and salad (70p). Some picnic-table sets on the flagstoned back terrace by the remains of the city wall look down over the Tyne and the bridges. The Thursday folk club here is one of the country's oldest. *(Recommended by Andy and Jill Kassube, Dave Braisted, Brian and Anna Marsden, Michael and Rachel Brookes, Simon Baker, Graham Oddey, J F Thorndike)*

Free house   Licensee Dave Shipley   Real ale   Snacks   Blues club Tues, folk club Thurs   Open 11.30–3, 5.30 (6 Sat)–11; closed 25 Dec, 1 Jan

Cooperage

32 The Close, Quayside; immediately below and just to the W of the High Level Bridge; parking across road limited lunchtime, easy evening

As the name implies, casks were indeed once made in this wonky timbered Tudor house. It's a popular place with locals and businessmen at lunchtime and students in the evening for its range of real ales. On handpump, these include regulars such as Ind Coope Burton, Marstons Owd Rodger and Pedigree and Tetleys Bitter, as well as three guests from an extremely extensive list, like Ansells Mild, Flowers Original, Fullers ESB, Greene King Abbot, Ruddles County or Timothy Taylors Landlord; also hand-pulled Addlestones and Coates farm cider. The bustling bar has heavy Tudor oak beams and exposed stonework, and there's extra seating in the lounge area by the pool room; fruit and trivia machines, space game and juke box. Good value bar food includes soup (80p), burger or cheese and tomato omelette (£1.80), hot beef stottie (£1.90), vegetarian casserole (£2.10), chicken and mushroom curry (£2.95), sirloin steak (£5.30), with specials such as kedgeree (£2.90), and rabbit casserole or steak and beer pie (£3.25); puddings (85p). It's actually one of Newcastle's oldest buildings. *(Recommended by Andy and Jill Kassube, Brian and Anna Marsden, W H Bland, Simon Baker, Julian Holland)*

Free house   Licensee Michael Westwell   Real ale   Meals and snacks   Restaurant tel Newcastle (091) 232 8286; not Sun evening   Children in eating area of bar   Open 11–11; closed 25 Dec

Crown Posada

31 The Side; off Dean Street, between and below the two high central bridges (A6125 and A6127)

At night the pre-Raphaelite stained-glass windows catch the eye from across this steep street, and by day the golden crown adds grandeur to an already imposing carved stone facade. The architectural charm continues inside – an elaborate coffered ceiling in cream and dusky pink, a line of gilt mirrors each with a tulip lamp on a curly brass mount matching the great ceiling candelabra, the Victorian flowered wallpaper above the brown dado (with its fat heating pipes along the bottom – a popular footrest when the east wind brings the rain off the North Sea), the mellifluous carved mahogany of the bar gantry, more stained glass in the counter screens. But this is first and foremost a friendly, bustling city pub – though on weekday evenings you can find it quiet, with regulars reading the papers put out in the front snug. It's very long and narrow, making quite a bottleneck by the serving counter; beyond that, a long soft green built-in leatherette wall seat is flanked by narrow tables. Well kept Big Lamp and Hadrian Gladiator (both local), and McEwans 80/- and Timothy Taylors Landlord on handpump; lunchtime rolls and toasties (60p); friendly barmen, chatty customers; fruit machine. *(Recommended by GB, CH, Michael Brookes, Brian Marsden)*

Free house   Licensee Mrs M Butterfield   Real ale   Snacks (lunchtime)   Open 11–3, 5.30(7 Sat)–11; all day Fri

Tap & Spile

33 Shields Road, Byker; from central motorway (A6127(M)) take A193/A187 Wallsend road, then fork off left into Shields Road Shopping Centre

The model for other pubs in this growing small chain under the Camerons (now Brent Walker) umbrella, this combines a wide and rapidly changing choice of interesting and well kept real ales at attractive prices with a return to simple yet perfectly clean and comfortable furnishings. On our visit the beers, coming from as far as Dorset, Oxfordshire, Wales and Scotland, ran to Badger Best, Bull Mastiff, Glenny Witney, the local Hadrian Gladiator, Harviestoun Waverley, Mitchells ESB and Timothy Taylors Landlord, with Westons Old Rosie farm cider and country wines; Camerons Strongarm and Everards Old Original are regulars. If there's a distant beer you'd particularly like, they'll try to get it for you. The nicer room is at the back: stripped brickwork, bare boards, big modern windows, sturdy built-in wall seats, stripped chairs, even tractor seats around one corner table – quiet and relaxed. There are lots of old brewery pictures, cases of taps and spiles, models of cask slings and so forth. The front bar has pool, darts and fruit machine. Good value bar food includes winter soup and toasties, home-made lasagne, chilli con carne and curries (£2.20), gammon and pineapple (£2.30), scampi (£2.30), and a daily special such as giant Yorkshire pudding with sausage and onion gravy or savoury mince (£1.95); they plan Sunday lunches. (*Recommended by Julian Holland, W H Bland*)

Free house   Licensees Rob and Sara Barraclough   Real ale   Meals and snacks (12–2, 5.30–7.30; no weekend evening food)   Open 11–3, 5.30–11; all day Fri and Sat

NEWTON ON THE MOOR (Northumberland)   NU1605 Map 10

Cook & Barker Arms

Village signposted from A1 Alnwick–Felton

Hardworking, friendly new licensees have taken over this pub since it was last in the *Guide*. They've completely refurbished it, trying to stick to the original traditional style. The long beamed bar has freshly stripped, partly panelled walls, brocade-seated settles around oak-topped tables, paintings by local artists, brasses, a highly polished oak servery, and a coal fire at one end with a coal-effect gas fire at the other. They've opened up the old storeroom, added tables and chairs (and kept the original settle), and put in darts – this room is popular with locals; there's also a games room with pool table, fruit machine, space game, juke box and dominoes; French windows from here lead to the terrace. Home-made lunchtime bar food (they don't serve evening bar meals, preferring to keep the place for drinkers only, then) includes sandwiches (from £1, popular open sandwiches like avocado and prawns and so forth from £3.25), steak and kidney pie (£3.95), mixed grill or gammon (£5.75), and changing daily specials like stir-fried beef with soy vegetables, baked potato filled with sweet and sour pork or flans (from around £2.75). The restaurant – which was a blacksmith's shop and dates in parts back to the 1700s – has been carefully renovated to reveal stone walls and exposed roof timbers. Well kept Theakstons Best on handpump, and quite a few wines. (*Recommended by John Oddey, Ron and Marjorie Bishop*)

Free house   Licensees Lynn and Phil Farmer   Real ale   Lunchtime meals and snacks   Restaurant tel Shilbottle (066 575) 234   Children in eating area of bar and in pool room   Open 11–3, 6–11

NEW YORK (Tyne & Wear)   NZ3370 Map 10

Shiremoor House Farm ★ ⊘

Middle Engine Lane/Norham Road; from A1 going N from Tyne Tunnel, right into A1058 then next left signposted New York, then left at end of speed limit (pub signed); or at W end of New York A191 bypass turn S into Norham Road, then first right (pub signed)

'Stunning' is how one reader describes this new conversion of formerly derelict farm steadings, and we'd agree that its designer Alan Simpson deserves top marks. The understated references to the building's origins are very pleasing: the conical rafters of the former gin-gan over the main bar's serving counter, gentle lighting picking up the surface modelling of the pale stone and beam ends, just a few farm tools, good rustic pictures (mid-West prints, big crisp black-and-white photographs of country people, modern Greek bull sketches), perhaps above all the warmly colourful farmhouse paintwork of the chunky bar counter and of some tables. It's well divided into separate areas, with a good variety of interesting and extremely comfortable furniture, and in one place a big kelim rug on the flagstones; the atmosphere is very relaxed. Interesting bar food includes good soups (£1.30), several starters such as cheese and walnut pâté (£2.50), scallops in bacon (£2.95) and salmon pâté (£3.10) and main dishes such as poached haddock bonne femme (£3.25), liver stroganoff (£3.50), stuffed aubergines (£5.75), Brazilian chicken (£8.25), Spanish pork steak (£8.75) and good steaks (from £9.95); the lightly cooked vegetables keep their fresh taste, helpings are generous and the home-made puddings are tempting. Well kept McEwans 80/-, local Big Lamp Prince Bishops, Stones Best, Timothy Taylors Landlord and Theakstons Best and Old Peculier on handpump, decent wines by the glass, polite and efficient young staff – and no music or games machines. A separate bar serves the equally attractive rather smart restaurant. It's already a very popular place, particularly at weekday lunchtimes. There are picnic-table sets on neat grass at the edge of the flagstoned farm courtyard, by tubs and a manger filled with flowers. *(Recommended by John Oddey, W H Bland, GB, Brian and Pam Cowling, GB)*

Free house   Licensees M W Garrett and C W Kerridge   Real ale   Meals and snacks (12–3, 6–9)   Restaurant tel 091–257 6302   An extension is being built which will allow children   Open 11–11

NORTH SHIELDS (Tyne & Wear)   NZ3468 Map 10
Chain Locker

New Quay

New licensees have taken over this turn-of-the-century pub: the bar's been extended, but has kept its relaxed atmosphere. There are nautical pictures and navigational charts and maps on the walls (some giving a detailed account of the Falklands campaign), local literature and arts information, stools and wooden wall benches around small tables – the one on your left as you go in, built over a radiator, is prized in winter – and an open fire. Well kept Ruddles Best and County, Websters Choice and Yorkshire, and three weekly guest beers on handpump; malt whiskies; dominoes. Bar food includes lunchtime sandwiches, chilli con carne (£2.60), steak and kidney pie (£2.95), steak (£4.95), and local fresh fish every day: rock turbot in cider or smoked fish pie (£2.75) or cod and chips (£2.95); Sunday lunch. *(Recommended by Michael and Rachel Brookes, Brian and Anna Marsden, Simon Baker, E V Walder, Graham Oddey, GB)*

Free house   Licensee W A Kelly   Real ale   Meals and snacks (12–2.30, 6–9.30; not Sun evening)   Restaurant (Thurs–Sat evening, and Sun lunch)   Children in eating area of bar   Mon sing-along, Folk Fri   Open 11.30–3, 6–11; all day Fri and Sat

PIERCEBRIDGE (Co Durham)   NZ2116 Map 10
George

B6275 over bridge just S of village

This is said to be where the clock *stopped short, never to go again, when the old man died*. Three bars have solid wood furniture, and Chesterfields in the lounge (which overlooks the river), plates, pictures and old farming equipment on the walls, and no less than five open fires in one room or another. Well worth a visit is the Ballroom Bar – just that, a bar inside a fully-fitted ballroom (open only for special functions or during barbecues). A wide choice of bar food includes breakfast (£4.25), quite a few starters like good soup, tuna and cucumber savoury or garlic mushrooms on toast (£1.45), vegetarian dishes such as kebabs, curry or stroganoff (£4.25), quite a few meaty dishes with orange, Stilton or pepper sauces (from around £4.25), gammon (£5), and steaks (from £7.95). John Smiths and Websters Yorkshire on handpump, and decent wines; good, friendly service. Fruit machine and piped music. A fine garden runs down to the River Tees, and this former coaching inn is attractively positioned on the alternative, scenic route between Scotch Corner and Edinburgh. *(Recommended by Robert Kimberley, Philip Harrison, Dr and Mrs Frank Rackow, Simon Baker, John and Anne McIver, Dr R H M Stewart, R F Plater, Mr and Mrs Norman Edwardes)*

Free house   Licensees Mr and Mrs Wayne   Real ale   Meals and snacks (available all day)   Restaurant (open all day)   Children in eating area   Open 7am–midnight   Bedrooms tel Piercebridge (0325) 374576; £35B/45B

ROMALDKIRK (Durham)   NY9922 Map 10

Rose & Crown 🚫 ⛻

Just off B6277

Careful redecoration has taken place over the last year in this comfortable coaching inn, and the beamed, traditionally furnished bar has cream walls decorated with lots of gin traps, some old farm tools, and black and white pictures of Romaldkirk at the turn of the century, a Jacobean oak settle, a grandfather clock, lots of brass and copper, and old-fashioned seats facing the log fire. The Crown Room, where bar food is served, now has original coloured etchings of hunting scenes, farm implements, and more brass and copper, the restaurant has been completely refurbished and the old oak panelling renovated, a resident's lounge has been created in what was the second dining room, and the hall hung with wine maps, and other interesting prints. Bar food at lunchtime includes sandwiches (from £1.65) and ploughman's with their own pickled onions and chutney (£2.95), starters such as home-made soup (£1.35), pasta tossed in cream with mushrooms and smoked bacon (£2.35) or locally smoked chicken with a herb mayonnaise (£3.25), main courses like sautéed chicken livers in a cream, sherry and walnut sauce on a granary crouton (£3.95), cold meats and salads (£4), steak and mushroom in ale pie (£4.40), sautéed rosettes of fillet of pork with a cream and green peppercorn sauce (£5.25) and pan-fried sirloin steak (£7.95), with evening extras such as hot gratin of crab (£3.25), breast of chicken stuffed with garlic, lemon and parsley butter (£4.95), and venison, smoked bacon and walnut casserole (£5.25); apple and spice pie, sticky walnut tart and lots of other puddings (£1.75), and daily specials that include scallop soup baked under a pastry crust, fresh langoustines sautéed in garlic butter (£3.85), chicken, leek and prune pie (£4.85), grilled plaice (£5), and poached salmon with hollandaise (£6.85). Theakstons Best and Old Peculier and Youngers No 3 on handpump; dominoes, occasional piped music. The village is close to the Bowes Museum and the High Force waterfall. (*Recommended by Simon Baker, Robert Kimberley, Andy and Jill Kassube, Peter Barnsley, Mr and Mrs J F Stalley, K Leist, Jim Whitaker, Rosalind Russell, Stephanie Sowerby, Sandra Kempson, Sue Carlyle, Mrs E M Thompson*)

Free house   Licensees Christopher and Alison Davy   Real ale   Meals and snacks Restaurant (not Sun evening)   Children welcome   Open 11–3, 5.30–11; closed 25 and 26 Dec   Bedrooms tel Teesdale (0833) 50213; £40B/£55B

SEAHOUSES (Northumberland)   NU2232 Map 10

Olde Ship ★ ⛻

B1340 coast road

The one clear window in the busy saloon bar of this seaside inn looks out over the harbour to the Farne Islands (the rest have stained-glass sea pictures). The floor is scrubbed ship's decking, and the walls are packed with good sea pictures and ship's models, including a fine one of the North Sunderland lifeboat, finely polished brass and other ship's instruments and equipment given up by local sailors, and a knotted anchor made by local fishermen. There is another low-beamed snug bar, and a family room at the back. Throughout, teak and mahogany woodwork, shiny brass fittings and small rooms feel almost more like a ship than a building. An anemometer is connected to the top of the chimney. The atmosphere is authentically local, with sailors as many of the regulars. Bar food includes home-made soups such as vegetable (£1) or crab (£1.50), filled rolls and sandwiches, ploughman's, and salads such as crab (£3), with three or four lunchtime hot dishes, changing daily, like popular mince and dumplings, fillet of two fish and sauce, beef in beer, and fish stew (all £3); no chips. The hotel dining room does a Sunday roast lunch (as well as good meals in the evening, when only sandwiches are served in the bar). McEwans 70/- and Theakstons Best and XB on handpump, whiskies that include several malts, a hot toddy and mulled wine in winter, and some uncommon bottled beers. Open fire, dominoes, space game and trivia. Pews surround barrel tables in the back courtyard, and a battlemented side terrace with a sun lounge looks out on the harbour. You can book boat trips to the Farne Islands Bird Sanctuary at the harbour, and there are bracing coastal walks, particularly to Bamburgh, Grace Darling's birthplace. They've up-graded the bedrooms this year. (*Recommended by Mr and Mrs P A Jones, BKA, Mrs E M Everard, W H Bland, Janet and Paul Waring, M and J Dixon, Mr and Mrs P R Lynch, Helen and Roy Sumner, Sidney and Erna Wells, Andrew and Michele Wells, A C and S J Beardsley, Christopher Knowles-Fitton, Z Cumberpatch, E E Hemmings*)

Free house   Licensees Alan and Jean Glen   Real ale   Meals (lunchtime) and snacks (sandwiches only, evening)   Restaurant   Children in restaurant   Open 11–3, 6–11 Bedrooms tel Seahouses (0665) 720200; £25B/£50B

SEATON SLUICE (Northumberland)   NZ3477 Map 10

Waterford Arms ⊗

Just off A193 N of Whitley Bay

The main reason for including this comfortably modernised pub is its profusion of local fish from the harbour just down the road. Served in vast helpings and priced according to size – small, medium or large – this includes lemon sole, cod or haddock (£3.95–£8.25); other food such as home-made soup (£1), sandwiches (from £1.15), sausage, mash and gravy (£3.25), leek pudding with mince or ploughman's (£3.95), home-made steak and kidney pie (£4.25), a generous seafood platter (£8.30), steaks (from £8.15), and puddings like home-made treacle or jam sponge (£1.50); for those in a hurry, it may be best to check how long the wait is likely to be; large breakfasts, with home-made jams, for residents. The bar has spacious green plush banquettes in its roomy bays, and bright paintings in one high-ceilinged room, and brown plush furnishings and a big children's rocking machine in another. Well kept Vaux Samson on handpump; pool in the back lobby. (*Recommended by Michael and Rachel Brookes, Mr and Mrs M O Jones, R Johnstone, Barbara and Norman Wells, Richard Dolphin, Helen and Roy Sumner*)

Vaux   Licensee Mrs Patrica Charlton   Real ale   Meals and snacks   Children in eating area   Open 11–3.30, 6.30–11; 11–4, 6.30–10 Sat   Bedrooms tel Tyneside (091) 237 0450; £20S/£40S

TYNEMOUTH (Tyne & Wear)   NZ3468 Map 10

Tynemouth Lodge

Tynemouth Road (A193); 1/2 mile W of Tynemouth Metro station

On the edge of Northumberland Park, this friendly and clean little pub has a good range of very well kept real ales, including Belhaven 80/-, Marstons Pedigree, Theakstons Best and Wards Sheffield Best on handpump; Merrydown and Thatcher's ciders; most of the customers are men. Bar food is straightforward, with stottie sandwiches (75p) and pot meals such as chilli con carne or lamb hot-pot (£2.20). The bar has copper-topped cast-iron tables, and button-back green leatherette seats built against the walls (which have stylish bird-of-paradise wallpaper); there's a winter coal fire in the neat Victorian tiled fireplace; tables beyond the car park. The licensee also owns the Wolsington House in North Shields. (*Recommended by Brian and Anna Marsden; more reports please*)

Free house   Licensee Hugh Price   Real ale   Lunchtime meals and snacks (11–3.30; not Sun)   Open 11–11 all year

Wooden Doll

103 Hudson Street; from Tyne Tunnel, follow A187 into town centre; keep straight ahead (when the A187 turns off left) until, approaching the sea, you can see the pub in Hudson Street on your right

From this unassuming pub (with new licensees this year) there's a fine view over the bustling boats and warehouses of the Shields Fish Quay immediately below, harbour derricks and gantries beyond, and then the sweep of the outer harbour with its long piers, headlands, and low Black Middens rocks. The three bars are simply but comfortably furnished with brown and green leatherette chairs, a brown plush long settle and Formica-topped cast-iron tables, flame-effect gas fire, and paintings by local artists for sale; fine views from the covered glassed-in verandah. There's a good range of well kept real ales, with Arkells 80/-, Ansells Mild, Friary Meux, Halls Harvest, Ind Coope Burton, Tetleys Bitter, and Youngers No 3 on handpump or tapped from the cask. Home-made bar food includes filled baps (from £1.30), winter soup, chilli con carne (£2.75), fresh fish (around £3.15), steak and kidney pie or lasagne (£3.25), cod and prawn bake (£3.95), their special seafood platter (£4.85) and puddings like cherry pie or cheesecake (from £1.25). Dominoes, fruit machine, trivia, and piped music. *(Recommended by Linda Sewell, Michael and Rachel Brookes, Brian and Anna Marsden, Dr T H M Mackenzie, Mr and Mrs Allan Chapman, Simon Baker, Graham Oddey, GB, Mr and Mrs G D Amos)*

Free house   Licensee Mrs R A Holliday   Real ale   Lunchtime meals and snacks Children in eating area until 5.30   Live entertainment every evening, with classical quartet Sun evening, sing-along Fri and Sat   Open 11–11

WARENFORD   NU1429 Map 10

Warenford Lodge ♀

Just off A1 Alnwick–Belford, on village loop road

The choice of interesting, home-made bar food here is consistently well prepared and attractively presented; the menu varies seasonally, but it might typically include home-made soup (£1.15), Syrian lamb roll stuffed with pine-nuts or grilled mussels topped with fresh herbed butter (£2.50), sausage, egg and tomato pie, home-cooked ham with pease pudding or a black bean casserole with white rice garnished with orange, onion and egg (£3.50), woodpigeon casserole (£4.90), tanrogan pie (a traditional Manx dish with king scallops and mushrooms £5.50), and steaks (£9.90); puddings like apricot crumble flan or bitter chocolate mousse (£1.95); decent selection of wines. Though it's quite old, the bar has a relaxed up-to-date feel, with cushioned wooden seats, a big stone fireplace, and some stripped stone walls; steps lead up to an extension which has comfortable easy chairs and settees around low tables, and a big woodburning stove. *(Recommended by A J Powell, A H Doran; more reports please)*

Free house   Licensee Raymond Matthewman   Meals and snacks (not Mon lunchtime)   Evening restaurant tel Belford (0668) 213453   Children in restaurant Open 12–2, 7–11; closed Tues lunchtime and all day Mon Oct–Easter

---

Lucky Dip

Besides the fully inspected pubs, you might like to try these Lucky Dips recommended to us and described by readers (if you do, please send us reports):

☆ **Acomb**, Northumberland [NY9366], *Miners Arms*: Small, friendly old pub, charming character, huge open fire, welcoming licensee and locals; unusual and well kept real ales, home-cooked bar food; children in dining room *(John Oddey)*
Allenheads, Northumberland [NY8545], *Allenheads*: Olde-worlde pub in delightful village, has been open all day; good home-cooked bar food, good walking area; bedrooms *(E R Thompson)*
Alnwick, Northumberland [Bondgate Without; NU1913], *Fleece*: Friendly Tetleys town pub with handpumped beers, good food, pleasant service; children welcome *(Mr and Mrs M O Jones)*; *Market Tavern*: Not to everyone's taste structurally, but the three bars (selling various beers) lead into a large, plain dining area with good food inc Sun lunch at unmissable prices; play tree area for children behind dining area *(P J and S E*

Robbins); [South Rd], *Oaks*: Small new licensed hotel locally popular for well kept beer in pristine lounge (everything almost clinically spotless), and for good bar food in charming dining room; friendly helpful staff; bedrooms *(John Oddey)*; [Narrowgate], *Oddfellows Arms*: Pleasant and spotlessly clean lounge with coal fire and well kept Vaux Samson and Lorimers Best Scotch on handpump; nr start GWG142; bedrooms *(I T Glendenning)*; [Narrowgate], *Olde Cross*: Interesting and unpretentious old place, with ancient bottles in low window, friendly locals, dominoes, good beer on handpump, low-priced bar food *(Sidney and Erna Wells)*; [Market St], *Queens Head*: Unpretentious, but roomy and dignified, with well kept Ind Coope Burton and very friendly helpful staff; bar food; bedrooms good value *(Neil and Angela Huxter, Paul McPherson)*; [Hotspur St], *Tanners Arms*: Small single-bar character pub with friendly atmosphere, flagstones and bare stone walls, pleasant staff, well kept Belhaven 70/- and 80/- on handpump, good juke box *(Mr and Mrs P A Jones)*

Alwinton, Northumberland [NT9206], *Star & Thistle*: Working farm pub with basic seating in main room painted deep blue; good lunches; pool table *(Dave Webster, Sue Holland)*

☆ **Bamburgh**, Northumberland [NU1835], *Lord Crewe Arms*: Relaxing and comfortable old inn, beautifully placed in charming coastal village below magnificent Norman castle; back cocktail bar, with entertaining bric-a-brac and log fire, is the one to go for; generously served straightforward food in bar and grill room, good service, children in side bar; bedrooms comfortable, good breakfasts and dinners; dogs allowed *(Rosalind Russell, Mrs J Roberts, Mrs S Major, WTA, LYM)*

Bardon Mill, Northumberland [Military Rd (B6318); NY7864], *Thrice Brewed*: Large pub with good choice of real ales and malt whiskies, imaginative food, friendly bar staff; well placed for fell-walkers, and major Wall sites; bedrooms rather spartan but warm and cheap *(A Nelson-Smith)*

☆ **Barnard Castle**, Durham [Market Pl; NZ0617], *Golden Lion*: Warm and comfortable old pub with two sizeable bars, big helpings of good value, pleasantly served lunchtime food inc cheap but generous children's helpings and good filling home-made soup; friendly service even when busy, keg beers, children's room *(RAF, P J and S E Robbins)*

☆ **Belford**, Northumberland [Market Pl; village signed off A1 S of Berwick; NU1134], *Blue Bell*: Comfortable, stylish and relaxing lounge; plentiful bar food inc children's dishes served mainly in family bar in former stables, with harness, saddlery and so forth, Theakstons Best on handpump, darts, pool and piped music; pleasantly old-fashioned dining room overlooking attractive garden, which produces some of the vegetables and fruit they use — there may be a surcharge if you have bar food served out here; polite and friendly service; children in eating areas; comfortably refurbished bedrooms *(Mr and Mrs G D Amos, Helen and Roy Sumner, GB, LYM)*

Belsay, Northumberland [NZ1079], *Highlander*: Consistently good bar meals in busy, comfortably straightforward pub; popular evening restaurant *(Rosalind Russell, Ann Marie Stephenson)*

☆ **Berwick upon Tweed**, Northumberland [Tweed St, nr rly stn; NU0053], *Tweed View*: Former convent, with good bar food in lounge overlooking grand Tweed bridges — views from terrace too; bedrooms *(P J and S E Robbins)*

☆ **Berwick upon Tweed** [A1 N of town], *Meadow House*: Friendly atmosphere and good service in big, popular eating area with simple good value bar food; Vaux Lorimers Best Scotch on handpump *(A H Doran)*

Berwick upon Tweed [The Green], *Pilot*: Small bar full of nautical nick-nacks, comfortable lounge, well kept Greenmantle, lunchtime snacks, welcoming landlord *(William Dryburgh)*

nr Berwick upon Tweed [B6461 towards Paxton — OS Sheet 75 map reference 959526], *Cantys Brig*: Nice modern place with upstairs dining room overlooking Whiteadder River, tables out on lawn running down to it; decent food under newish licensees *(Paul McPherson)*; [Aller Dean; NT9847], *Plough*: Remote pub on crossroads with farm, chapel and sheep fields, old and comfortable with open fire in small main bar, Burmese cats, games room, well kept beer, attentive service, good value restaurant *(Mike Tucker)*

☆ **Billy Row**, Durham [Old White Lea, off A689; NZ1638], *Dun Cow*: After a good walk off the beaten track, this is like stepping back in time — cosy front room with warming range, comfortable wall settles, photographs of local football teams since the year dot; bar in back room serving well kept Camerons and Vaux Double Maxim, friendly pub dog *(Ian and Sue Brocklebank)*

Boldon, Tyne & Wear [Front St (A184), E Boldon; NZ3661], *Black Bull*: Open-plan lounge bar with good-sized tables, welcoming licensees, well kept Vaux Samson, good whiskies, excellent lunchtime bar food; soft piped music, garden with children's play area; big car park *(E R Thompson)*

☆ **Bowes**, Durham [NY9914], *Ancient Unicorn*: Welcoming open-plan modernised bar, good honest bar food, comfortable bedrooms in well converted stables block, in coaching inn with *Nicholas Nickleby* connection *(Mr and Mrs L G Smith, LYM)*

☆ **Byrness**, Northumberland [A68 Otterburn—Jedburgh; NT7602], *Byrness Inn*: Particularly useful for the Pennine Way, with big open fire in small rather dark but cheerful bar, limited choice of nicely prepared food, friendly cat; bedrooms *(John Oddey, Len Beattie, M J Lawson)*

☆ **Chatton**, Northumberland [B6348 E of Wooler; NU0628], *Percy Arms*: Good value straightforward home-made food from soup and ploughman's to evening steaks, with children's dishes, in neat and comfortable carpeted lounge with brocaded seats and family area through stone-faced arch; well kept Theakstons XB on handpump, fair choice of malt whiskies, open fire, picnic-table sets outside; big good value bedrooms *(Dennis Heatley, Dr P D Smart, Paul McPherson, GB, BB)*

☆ **Coatham Mundeville**, Durham [part of Hallgarth Hotel; from A1(M) turn towards Brafferton off A167 Darlington rd on hill; NZ2920], *Stables*: Converted from stone outbuildings with high ceilings, lots of seating, separate no-smoking eating area behind, good choice of well prepared bar food and Sun lunches, well kept McEwans 80/- and Theakstons Best, Old Peculier and XB; side conservatory for families; bedrooms *(R J Walden)*

Coatham Mundeville [Brafferton Lane; off A68, ¼ mile from A1(M)], *Foresters Arms*: Big pub with well kept Theakstons and pleasant, attentive staff *(John Tyzack)*

Corbridge, Northumberland [main street; NY9964], *Black Bull*: Attractively renovated, with plenty of space and character, lots of cosy nooks and crannies

under low beams, comfortable settles and chairs; cheerful and helpful staff, good range of bar food from soup and sandwiches up (*John Oddey*); [Bridge End — OS Sheet 87 map reference 998640], *Lion*: Warm welcome in straightforward bar with Theakstons beer and good value home-made bar food inc fresh fish; children welcome; bedrooms (*Mr and Mrs G D Amos*); [St Helens St], *Wheatsheaf*: Very welcoming stylishly refurbished lounge, good choice of familiar bar food, Vaux beers on handpump, lovely pictures; bedrooms comfortable and attractive (*Andy and Jill Kassube*)
Cornsay, Durham [Old Cornsay; NZ1443], *Black Horse*: Good food and drink, welcoming licensees, pleasant area (*Mr and Mrs P Crosby*)

☆ **Cramlington**, Northumberland [NZ2777], *Plough*: Cavernous open-plan pub converted from farm buildings, with original stone, woodwork and impressive beams; wide choice of real ales such as McEwans 80/- or Youngers No 3, Marstons Pedigree and Stones, good value bar food inc fine freshly-made pizzas with thin bases and thick toppings, friendly, helpful staff (*Graham and Karen Oddey, John Oddey*)
Crook, Durham [off A68, W of Crook; NZ1236], *Helm Park Hall*: Hotel with good bar meals in very pleasant surroundings with magnificent views of Weardale (*J H Tate*)
Crookham, Northumberland [A697 Wooler—Cornwall; NT9238], *Blue Bell*: Well kept McEwans 80/- on handpump and well presented food inc good steaks and seafood platter (*Mr and Mrs M D Jones*)

☆ **Dunstan**, Northumberland [NU2520], *Cottage*: Attractive layout, well stocked bar, pleasant dining room and terrace, good imaginative bar food with some concentration on seafood, decent wines; bargain three-course dinner — free conveyance for parties of four or more within 12 miles (*B Isserlin*)
Durham [Old Elvet; NZ2743], *Dun Cow*: Traditional pub in pretty black-and-white timbered cottage; good value cheap snacks, well kept Whitbreads Castle Eden, maybe rapper dancing; children welcome (*Andy and Jill Kassube, LYM*); [Elvet Bridge], *Swan & Three Cygnets*: Well placed above river, with good bar lunches inc very generous cheese and pâté; well kept Sam Smiths OB; friendly and busy (piped music may be loud, with evening doormen); open all day Sat (*More reports please*); [86 Hallgarth St (A177 nr Dunelm House)], *Victoria*: Unspoilt Victorian family pub with Theakstons and McEwans 80/-, over 60 whiskies, sandwiches and toasties all day (open 11-11); under the same management as the Sun at Beamish Open Air Museum; bedrooms (*Anon*)
East Ord, Northumberland [NT9952], *Salmon*: Small Vaux pub with friendly licensees and good simple bar food; children welcome (*Mr and Mrs M O Jones*)

☆ **Eastgate**, Durham [signposted from A689 W of Stanhope; NY9638], *Horsley Hall*: Lovely old manor house-type building with comfortable modern bar and beautiful original restaurant; huge helpings of very good value food, splendid views (*John Tyzack*)

☆ **Egglescliffe**, Cleveland [663 Yarm Rd (A67); NZ4213], *Blue Bell*: Simple lunchtime bar food (not Sun) inc good sandwiches in spacious big-windowed bar, seats on terrace by goat-cropped grass sloping down to the River Tees with fine view of the great 1849 railway viaduct — it's the position that's the particular attraction; friendly service, restaurant; children welcome (*D J Cooke, LYM*)
Egglescliffe, *Pot & Glass*: Popular local in nice setting, with friendly helpful staff, good value food and well kept Bass; garden good for children (*Richard Burt, Jon Dewhirst*)

☆ **Elwick**, Northumberland [off A1/A19 just N of Belford; NU1237], *Spotted Cow*: Pleasantly placed on village green, old but refurbished pub with red plush lounge and separate dining room; wide choice of good value bar food from sandwiches or burgers to breaded plaice stuffed with crabmeat, Camerons Strongarm and Everards Old Original (*Dr Keith Bloomfield, W H Bland*)
Esh, Durham [off B6302/A691 W of Durham; NZ1944], *George*: Outstandingly cheap bar food in unmodernised but comfortable pub with good atmosphere in small rooms, pool table, well kept beer; hillside spot overlooking former mining valley (*Linda Sewell*)

☆ **Fir Tree**, Durham [A68 West Auckland—Tow Law; NZ1434], *Duke of York*: Plain but comfortable dining lounge with decent solid furnishings, racing prints, Delft shelf; wide choice of reasonably priced bar food, Greenalls Original on handpump; cosy wing-chair bar on left leading into dining room; cheerful uniformed waitresses, children welcome, seats on grass between car park and paddock (*John Tyzack, V R Flint, Mr and Mrs K Charlton, A J Powell, BB*)

☆ **Framwellgate Moor**, Durham [Front St; NZ2745], *Tap & Spile*: Refurbished pub run largely as free house, and like others under the same name most popular for its quickly changing choice of eight well kept real ales; simply but comfortably decorated series of four main rooms, one used for pool and fruit machines, another for board games; friendly atmosphere (*I W and P J Muir, Maureen and Steve Collin*)
Fulwell, Tyne & Wear [Sea Rd; B1291; NZ3959], *Sunderland Flying Boat*: Recently renovated one-room pub with brasses and flying-boat memorabilia; good reasonably priced lunches (no chips), well kept Marstons Pedigree, Tetleys and guest beers (*Andy and Jill Kassube*)
Gateshead, Tyne & Wear [Eighton Banks, Low Fell; NZ2758], *Lambton Arms*: Consistently good food over past few years, pleasant helpful staff, well kept beer and good coffee (*AKC*)

☆ **Great Stainton**, Durham [NZ3422], *Kings Head*: Popular well run pub with comfortable chairs, stools and settles around tables in big saloon, friendly locals' bar with darts and so forth, well kept Whitbreads Castle Eden and good, imaginative food; restaurant (*Jon Dewhirst*)

☆ **nr Haltwhistle**, Northumberland [Military Rd; B6318 — OS Sheet 86 map reference 715660; NY7164], *Milecastle*: Heavily refurbished, but comfortable and attractive, with lots of brasses in cosy, warm bar with good coal fire — posh, but walkers welcome; plentiful and interesting good value food running up to pheasant or salmon pie, welcoming service, Watneys-related real ales on handpump, local leaflets on mantlepiece; restaurant — best to book *(Russell Hafter, E R Thompson, Kay Johnson, Mrs Wendy Loncaster, David and Flo Wallington)*

☆ **Haydon Bridge**, Northumberland [NY8464], *General Havelock*: Lovely four-course meals in most attractive stripped-stone back dining room overlooking garden, River Tyne and hill sheep pastures; very attentive landlord and staff — a great place to eat, meat, seafood and pastry consistently good *(M B P Carpenter, Dr Kenneth Miller)*

Heighington, Durham [Heighington Lane; a mile W, off A167 at Aycliffe; NZ2522], *Locomotion One*: Former station where Stephenson launched steam locomotion in 1825, converted to popular pub with good inexpensive straightforward food from open sandwiches and filled baked potatoes up, in bar and upstairs restaurant, fine choice of real ales *(Andy and Jill Kassube)*

☆ **Hexham**, Northumberland [Priestpopple; E end of main st, on left entering from Newcastle; NY9464], *County*: Reliable place, popular for straightforward bar lunches (though like other northern places they could do with more variety and vegetarian alternatives — and a better wine by the glass); friendly and considerate service; over the years has stood out in readers' reports as the best place here; bedrooms *(Dr R H M Stewart, Mrs P Brown)*

Hexham [Battle Hill], *Tap & Spile*: Formerly 'Criterion', now very similar in down-to-earth furnishings and decor to others of same name; a joy to visit for its half dozen well kept changing real ales on handpump, with Camerons Strongarm as a regular *(W H Bland)*

☆ **High Force**, Durham [B6277 about 4 miles NW of Middleton-in-Teesdale; NY8728], *High Force*: Though several women readers recommend this walkers' inn, so handy for the moors (and England's highest waterfall, for which it's named), others have noted that it's a far from feminine place, with robustly basic furnishings and food (from sandwiches to steaks, not winter Mon evenings); good range of malt whiskies, cheerful bar; children allowed, though restricted evenings; bedrooms comfortable — extra charge for morning teatray was a surprise *(M J Lawson, Sue Carlyle, Helen and Roy Sumner, T N Brooke, LYM)*

Hilton, Cleveland [just off A19 S of Middlesbrough; NZ4611], *Falcon*: Large rather chintzy dining pub, very popular for its wide choice of good, interesting food inc half a dozen vegetarian dishes *(Alan and Ruth Woodhouse)*

Holy Island, Northumberland [check tides before visiting — the causeway is covered at high tide; NU1343], *Lindisfarne*: Friendly, cafe-like pub with good value simple bar food inc fine crab sandwiches, also morning coffee, afternoon and high teas; welcoming, helpful licensees, friendly locals in the evening; well tended gardens; handy for the nature reserve; children always welcome; bedrooms good value *(Mr and Mrs Purcell, Mr and Mrs G D Amos)*; *Northumberland Arms*: Doing well under friendly new licensees, well kept sensibly priced beers inc McEwans 80/- and Theakstons Best on handpump and Newcastle Exhibition and Youngers Scotch tapped from the cask; five reasonably priced bedrooms *(Julian Holland)*

☆ **Horsley**, Northumberland [this is the one just off A69 Newcastle—Hexham; NZ0966], *Lion & Lamb*: Comfortable stone dining pub with open fire, well kept Whitbreads Castle Eden, decent wine and pleasant young staff; concentration now on the restaurant side, inc good Sun lunches, but bar snacks too *(Dr P D Smart, Michael Brookes)*

Humshaugh, Northumberland [NY9272], *Kings Head*: Small village pub with warm welcome from keen licensees; good simple food; bedrooms *(Sidney and Erna Wells)*

Lanchester, Durham [NZ1647], *Queens Head*: Comfortable and enjoyable village pub, heraldic shields, lofty ceilings, good choice of well prepared bar food at affordable prices; well kept Vaux beers *(Iain and Penny Muir)*

Langdon Beck, Durham [B6277 Middleton—Alston; NY8631], *Langdon Beck*: Good, cheap and filling bar meals and well kept Youngers Scotch in homely parlourish bar, popular with local farmers, those staying in nearby youth hostel, and Pennine Way walkers; bedrooms *(M J Lawson)*

☆ nr **Langley on Tyne**, Northumberland [A686 S; NY8361], *Carts Bog*: Quickly served bar food and well kept Tetleys and Marstons Pedigree or Theakstons in cosy beamed bar and lounge allowing children; open fire, welcoming service, friendly cat, limited choice of bar food, pool and other games, summer barbecues out by the moors; may be closed weekday lunchtimes *(John Oddey, LYM)*

Longbenton, Tyne & Wear [Front St (A191); NZ2769], *Ship*: Nice, friendly, three-roomed pub with bell-push service, Theakstons and McEwans 80/- on handpump, and pub games *(Michael Brookes)*

☆ **Longframlington**, Northumberland [Wheldon Bridge; NU1301], *Anglers Arms*: Imaginative lunchtime food inc fresh local fish — the rather dark and austere decor features fish, too; well kept Wards Sheffield Best, good table service *(Comus Elliott)*

Longframlington *New Inn*: Good drinking pub *(Comus Elliott)*

Lowick, Northumberland [NY0239], *Black Bull*: Well kept McEwans on handpump, nice quiet back snug, lively locals' bar, friendly landlord; bar food inc good local salmon — may need to book weekends *(Mr and Mrs M D Jones)*

☆ **Marsden**, Tyne & Wear [signposted passage to lift in A183 car park, just before entering Marsden coming from Whitburn; NZ4164], *Grotto*: Notable for its unique and atmospheric position, partly built into cliff caverns: you take a lift down to the two floors — upper pink plush, lower brown varnish; Vaux Samson real ales, food in bar and restaurant *(John Oddey)*

☆ **Matfen**, Northumberland [NZ0372], *Black Bull*: Comfortable, spotless and relaxed country pub in idyllic surroundings facing village green, with well kept Theakstons, good sensibly priced bar food, very good restaurant, friendly welcome, helpful staff *(John Whitehead)*

Middlesbrough, Cleveland [Grange Rd (central); NZ4919], *Strand*: Polite and friendly service, good well price food particularly steak pie *(Robin White)*

☆ **Middleton in Teesdale**, Durham [Market Pl; NY9526], *Teesdale*: Wide range of customers in reliably welcoming, clean, comfortable and well furnished pub with well kept John Smiths and Tetleys and good food — sumptuously so in restaurant; occasional unobtrusive piped music; bedrooms well equipped and comfortable *(Stephanie Sowerby)*

Middleton One Row, Durham [NZ3612], *Devonport*: Pub looking over green to Tees valley; has been praised for good food inc excellent sandwiches, but no recent reports; bedrooms *(News please)*

Mitford, Northumberland [just off A1 Morpeth bypass; NZ1786], *Plough*: Friendly pub in small village with decent bar food, restaurant *(Ken Smith)*

Morpeth, Northumberland [Manchester St; NZ2086], *Tap & Spile*: Stripped pine furniture, interesting old photographs, lovingly kept real ale — always Camerons Strongman and Everards Old Original, plus six guests (inc customers' requests) *(W H Bland)*

Netherton, Northumberland [OS Sheet 81 map reference 989077; NT9807], *Star*: Spartan local, pared to the essentials — notably, excellent beer tapped from the cask; no food *(Dave Webster, Sue Holland)*

☆ **Newcastle upon Tyne** [High Bridge], *Duke of Wellington*: Attractive softly lit horseshoe bar with red-upholstered seats around small tables, lots of 19th-century prints and documents, many connected with the Iron Duke, real ales inc Marstons Pedigree, Tetleys and Timothy Taylors, good range of reasonably priced bar food; open all day, gets very lively on weekday evenings *(Michael and Rachel Brookes, Ken Smith, Andy and Jill Kassube, Julian Holland)*

☆ **Newcastle upon Tyne** [Broad Chare; by river], *Baltic Tavern*: Spacious and comfortably converted warehouse, lots of stripped brick and flagstones or bare boards (as well as plusher carpeted parts) in warren of separate areas, good value bar food, well kept Whitbreads Castle Eden and Durham *(Michael and Rachel Brookes, LYM)*

Newcastle upon Tyne [City Rd; nr quayside], *Barley Mow*: Spruce-looking local, fairly spare, with nostalgic gas streetlamps opp bar counter, small garden overlooking Tyne quayside, wide range of local and other ales, food served through hatch, real fire; juke box may be loud, and rock bands play live here *(GB, K A Topping)*; [Clayton St W/Westmoreland Rd, nr Central Stn], *Dog & Parrot*: Busy pub, popular with students, with lots of seating and standing space, loud juke box, and beers which it brews on the premises (malt extract); may have November beer festival *(J F Thorndike, Michael and Rachel Brookes)*; [Pilgrim St],

Market Lane: Warm and welcoming with wide choice of beer and good food (especially good value lunchtime snacks); darts matches, good juke box, happy hour till 8 Fri and Sat; lots of toy monkeys *(K A Topping)*; [Cloth Market; down alley past Pumphreys Bar], *Old George*: Old coaching inn with splendid wood panelling, beams and attractive fireplace; well kept Bass and Stones on handpump, good lunches *(Andy and Jill Kassube)*; [Groat Mkt/Bigg Mkt], *Robinsons*: Very friendly, clean bar with lots of pine; Camerons and Whitbreads ales, pop video screens on some walls; popular with young people *(R P Taylor)*; [Gt North Rd, Gosforth; NZ2468], *Three Mile*: On the outskirts, large, recently refurbished hotel-like bar with almost palatial decor, Youngers and Theakstons ales; restaurant *(Ken Smith)*; [Osborne Rd, Jesmond; NZ2567], *Trotters*: Lively pub named for local MP, with lots of nick-nacks from 1950s film memorabilia to Zurich car registration plates; traditional bar fitting, several real ales inc Robinsons, tables outside; very popular, especially with young people; trivia quiz Mon evenings *(R P Taylor)*; [off Groat Mkt], *Turks Head*: Recently refurbished airy bar with lots of pine furniture; bar food *(R P Taylor)*

☆ **Newton**, Cleveland [A173; NZ5713], *Kings Head*: Sprucely refurbished old pub with wide choice of good value food from hefty club sandwiches to three-course lunch (cut price for children); lots of alcoves in nicely furnished spacious lounge, good dining area with outside terrace, soft piped music, good service, John Smiths real ale; below Roseberry Topping, a beauty spot for walks *(E R Thompson)*

Newton Aycliffe, Durham [Main rd; NZ2825], *North Britain*: Good, cheap bar food; keg beer *(E E Hemmings)*

☆ **Newton by the Sea**, Northumberland [The Square, Low Newton; NU2426], *Ship*: Unspoilt, idyllic spot in little cluster of cottages around green, looking out to sandy beach with lots of wildlife and sailing boats; basic knocked-through bar, friendly, helpful licensees, a wide choice of beers and local seafood specialities inc good crab and salmon sandwiches; good ploughman's and soup too; keg Drybroughs, tea; children welcome *(Mrs Rina McIvor, Mr and Mrs G D Amos)*

☆ **North Hylton**, Tyne & Wear [Ferryboat Lane; N bank of River Wear almost under the A19 bridge — OS Sheet 88 map reference 350570; NZ4057], *Shipwright*: Olde-worlde refurbishment, river views, homely welcome, lovely coal fire, soft piped music, fruit machine; Vaux beer, extensive range of good bar food at reasonable prices, restaurant; open longer at weekends *(E R Thompson)*

☆ **North Shields**, Tyne & Wear [Burdon Main Row, off A187 Howdon Rd — by Appledore ship repair yard; NZ3470], *Wolsington House*: Unspoilt Edwardian docklands pub with thoroughly masculine big lofty-ceilinged bar, family lounge decorated in period style with two coal fires (children allowed here), recently stripped panelling, cheap bar food lunchtime and early evening, well kept Hartleys XB,

Warsteiner real Pilsener, farm cider; open all day, free live music most nights inc Tues jazz, good free Sun lunchtime bar snacks (*E V Walder*)

North Shields [Ferry Landing, New Quay], *Lady Eleanors*: Unusual surroundings with view of river; service first-class from very pleasant, helpful staff; good proper food — no chips (*R Sandford*); [Preston Grange; NZ3470], *Pheasant*: Good food and service — a lot of table cooking (*R Riccalton*)

☆ **Otterburn**, Northumberland [NY8992], *Tower*: 1830s castellated hotel built around original 13th-century pele tower, doing well under present owners, unusual and imposing — something of a Hammer-horror atmosphere with suits of armour, crossbows and stuffed birds, but friendly; limited range of decent bar meals and morning coffee or afternoon tea in plush lounge, rather wildernessy stately grounds fun to explore; neat public bar, own fishing on 3 1/2 mile stretch of River Rede; bedrooms comfortable and good value, with good breakfasts (*Syd and Wyn Donald and others, LYM*)

Penshaw, Tyne & Wear [nr Monument; NZ3254], *Grey Horse*: Cosy though surprisingly spacious pub with low ceilings, nice decor, and welcoming atmosphere; good traditional English bar meals (*Ken Smith*)

☆ **Rennington**, Northumberland [Stamford Cott; B1340 NE of Alnwick; NU2119], *Masons Arms*: Generous helpings of quickly served good bar food — game pie, steak sandwich and steaks tipped strongly; well kept Tetleys on handpump, comfortable lounge bar decorated with heavy-horse photographs, piped music, games in public bar, tables on front terrace, cheery licensees; children welcome; open all day — so useful as an A1 detour; bedrooms clean and tidy, with decent breakfasts (*Mr and Mrs G D Amos, BKA, Dave Braisted, Sue Holland, Dave Webster, John Tyzack, John Whitehead, Helen and Roy Sumner, A C and S J Beardsley, LYM*)

☆ **Rennington**, *Horseshoes*: Clean and comfortable flagstoned pub, popular and welcoming, with happy and helpful staff, good helpings of reasonably priced freshly cooked straightforward food, S&N keg beers, friendly dogs, tables outside; attractive village well placed for coast (*Alan Hall, GB, Dave Braisted, Helen and Roy Sumner, P J and S E Robbins, C A Thomas*)

Ridsdale, Northumberland [A68 S of Otterburn; NY9184], *Gun*: Plain pub in isolated hamlet built by Lord Armstrong to people his arms foundry; friendly new owners keep it spotlessly clean and serve limited range of decent home-cooked food; lots of shell cases, photographs of old guns being tested etc; warm and comfortable, friendly cat (*John Oddey*)

☆ **Rochester**, Northumberland [A68 3 miles W of Otterburn; NY8398], *Redesdale Arms*: Convenient old coaching inn on the old hill road to Scotland, with well kept 80/-, friendly atmosphere and reasonably priced nourishing bar food inc good venison casserole; a good base for the Kielder Forest and Borders area — bedrooms good value (*PLC, Dennis Heatley, Bernard Phillips*)

Roker, Tyne & Wear [Harbour View

(A183); NZ4159], *Pilot Cutter*: Popular pub with several well kept handpumped beers, bar lunches, and good views over seafront and Sunderland from outside drinking area (*Andy and Jill Kassube*)

Romaldkirk, Durham [NY9922], *Kirk*: Friendly free house with imaginatively and generously presented food (spare ribs especially good) and well kept real ales inc Whitbreads Castle Eden (*David and Christine Foulkes*)

Rothbury, Northumberland [NU0602], *Queens Head*: Stone-built village pub popular with bell-ringers visiting Rothbury church with its fine eight-bell peal; comfortable and welcoming carpeted bars, with limited choice of simple but very popular bar food from new chef; well kept Vaux Samson on handpump; good value bedrooms (*W H Bland*)

Sacriston, Durham [off B6532 NW of Durham; NZ2447], *Travellers Rest*: Several real ales on handpump, usually inc Theakstons XB; bar food good, with interesting changing menus; meals served in attractive, airy and south-facing conservatory (*W H Bland*)

☆ **Saltburn by the Sea**, Cleveland [A174 towards Whitby; NZ6722], *Ship*: Magnificent position right on the beach (and Cleveland Way long-distance path) with splendid sea views from original nautical-style black-beamed bars and big plainer summer dining lounge; good range of speedily served bar food (poached cod recommended); cheerful friendly service, restaurant, children's room, seats on terrace by the beached fishing boats; busy at holiday times (*Syd and Wyn Donald, Walter and Susan Rinaldi-Butcher, John Tyzack, Sue Corrigan, LYM*)

☆ **Seahouses**, Northumberland [NU2232], *Lodge*: Pleasant atmosphere and friendly staff in bar of Scandinavian-style hotel with nice atmosphere, specialising in seafood but inc particularly good ploughman's and other conventional bar food; keg beer, restaurant; bedrooms (*Lyn Sharpless, Bob Eardley*)

Seahouses, [above harbour], *Bamburgh Castle*: Spectacular site right on harbour and overlooking Farne Islands gives great potential; upstairs lounge (mainly for residents) has had better reports than the Gallery Bar; keg beers, big fires, shelves of books, straightforward food; bedrooms a bit basic, but generally judged good value given the price, with good generous breakfasts (*Mr and Mrs D Pybus*); [Union St], *Black Swan*: Tucked away but overlooking harbour, friendly atmosphere with roaring fire, warm welcome, Theakstons XB; interesting name board from the Scottish wreck whose survivors were saved by local heroine Grace Darling (also copy of court ruling allowing pub to keep the sign) (*Denise Plummer, Jim Froggat*)

Shadforth, Durham [off B1283 Durham—Peterlee; NZ3441], *Plough*: Cosy pub, locals' bar and lounge with open fire and no juke box; friendly licensee, well kept Stones on handpump, good value simple bar food (*Jon Dewhirst*)

☆ **Shincliffe**, Durham [A177 a mile S of Durham; NZ2941], *Seven Stars*: Delightful semi-rural pub in attractive village, small but comfortable, traditionally furnished in one half, with a remarkable fireplace in the other; friendly staff, amiable pug, quiet atmosphere, good substantial fairly plain food in bar and restaurant, well kept Vaux ales; nice in summer, with some seats outside; bedrooms (*I W Muir, Andy and Jill Kassube, Maureen and Steve Collin, John Tyzack*)

Shincliffe, Durham [NZ2941], *Rose Tree*: Clean and comfortable, if simply furnished, Vaux pub; decent meals promptly served, well kept Vaux Double Maxim (*Iain and Penny Muir, Andy and Jill Kassube*)

☆ **Slaley**, Northumberland [NY9858], *Rose & Crown*: Friendly welcome in cleanly refurbished and locally popular pub with good plain home-cooked bar food in tastefully railed-off eating area, and more upmarket evening menu; well kept McEwans 70/- and Youngers No 3, efficient unobtrusive service; rather spartan decor (*John Oddey*)

☆ **South Shields**, Tyne & Wear [South Foreshore; beach rd towards Marsden; NZ3766], *Marsden Rattler*: A decided curiosity, made up of two railway carriages mounted on their tracks and joined by a bar, also a glass conservatory with plants; all-day tea, coffee and cakes, evening restaurant (*Gary Scott, Andy and Jill Kassube*)

South Shields [100 Greens Pl], *Beacon*: Nicely renovated little pub with superb view over mouth of River Tyne; warm welcome, well kept Wards and Vaux Samson, good home-cooked food (*Andy and Jill Kassube*); [Mill Dam], *Steamboat*: Old-fashioned nautical pub full of photos and ship models, plenty of authentic atmosphere, Vaux ales, bar food (*Andy and Jill Kassube*)

Stamfordham, Northumberland [NZ0872], *Bay Horse*: Large, clean and comfortable pub on village green, with good value ample bar food — a useful lunch stop (*John Whitehead*)

☆ **Stannersburn**, Northumberland [NY7286], *Pheasant*: Friendly 17th-century pub in small scenic village with good choice of beers inc McEwans and Theakstons, and excellent, home-cooked food in bar and restaurant; bedrooms comfortable (*Andrew Triggs, John Haig*)

☆ **nr Stannersburn** [Greystead; on Kielder Water rd from Bellingham, past Birks — OS Sheet 80 map reference 768856], *Moorcock*: Plain and unspoilt but comfortable country pub on way to Kielder Water, welcoming landlord, well kept Tetleys, attractive old-fashioned fireplaces, short choice of excellent lunchtime bar food — all home-cooked; children welcome, with sweets if they finish their food; well equipped bedrooms in new wing (*John Oddey, Mr and Mrs M O Jones*)

☆ **Stockton on Tees**, Cleveland [Hartburn; southern outskirts, NZ4218], *Masham Arms*: Four small rooms, each with its own character, from black and gold flock wallpaper to panelling, with showy chandeliers; well kept Bass, good cheap baps and sandwiches, and garden with aviary and children's play area backing on to paddock (*Jon Dewhirst*)

Stockton on Tees, *Hardwick Hall*: Comfortable hotel bar, popular with locals; welcoming staff, good choice of decent food; bedrooms (*John Tyzack*)

Tanfield, Durham [NZ1956], *Pack Horse*: Super, reasonably priced food, friendly staff, good service (*Janet and David Baldock*)

Tantobie, Durham [NZ1855], *Oak Tree*: Very good evening meals, helpful staff; comfortable and well equipped bedrooms in cottage annexe (*Mr and Mrs L G Smith*)

☆ **Thropton**, Northumberland [NU0302], *Cross Keys*: Traditional stone-built three-bar village pub, handy for Cragside and Coquet Valley; open fires in cosy beamed main lounge, attractive garden with panoramic view over village to Cheviots, well kept Bass and now a post-MMC guest beer (*W H Bland, LYM*)

Tynemouth, Tyne & Wear [Broadway; NZ3468], *Broadway*: Recently refurbished, good bar food served all day (*Mrs R Sandford*)

☆ **Upsall**, Cleveland [A171; NZ5616], *Cross Keys*: Good choice of S&N ales; fast, cafeteria-style food service of good value, well cooked meals inc good puddings, also salad and snack bar; children welcome at lunchtime (*E A Turner*)

Wall, Northumberland [NY9269], *Hadrian*: Very good food in 16th-century house with cosy, comfortable atmosphere in Jacobean-style bars, good service; bedrooms (*Jean and Theodore Rowland-Entwistle*)

Warden, Northumberland [1/2m N of A69; NY9267], *Boatside*: Bass, McEwans and Stones, choice of wines and good value food in bar or restaurant, freshly prepared and generous, inc good puddings; spacious pub by River Tyne, closed Mon lunchtime (*E R Thompson*)

Wark, Northumberland [NY8677], *Black Bull*: Genuine basic no-frills local with entertaining clientele even on quiet lunchtime — New Year with Northumbrian pipes is something else again! (*Linda Sewell*)

Warkworth, Northumberland [Castle St; NU2506], *Masons Arms*: Unpretentious pub with new lounge, cheerful newish management, well kept McEwans 80/- on handpump, straightforward bar food (*Terry Glendenning*); [6 Castle Terr], *Sun*: Homely, welcoming 17th-century hotel, obliging licensee most helpful with disabled people, wide choice of reasonably priced good food from home-cooked ham sandwiches to local sole, McEwans and Theakstons; children welcome; bedrooms (*E R Thompson*)

West Auckland, Durham [A68; NZ1926], *Blacksmiths Arms*: Oak-beamed room with central bar counter, log fire and extensive range of bar food including sandwiches and home-made dishes (*Mike and Mandy Challis*)

☆ **West Woodburn**, Northumberland [NY8987], *Bay Horse*: Refurbished inn well placed on the hill road to Scotland, and looking up under current regime, with friendly welcome, good service, good value food in clean and comfortable bar; comfortable bedrooms (*John Whitehead, LYM*)

Whitley Bay, Tyne & Wear [Sea Front; NZ3672], *Briar Dene*: Warm, pleasant atmosphere in recently refurnished pub with properly cooked and presented good bar food such as lemon sole, good service — particularly good value (*Mrs R Sandford*);

[Whitley Lodge], *Kittiwake*: Huge helpings of good value individually prepared varied bar food, good service *(Mrs R Sandford)*

☆ **Wooler**, Northumberland [Ryecroft Way (off A697)], *Ryecroft*: Busy lounge bar of well run and friendly family hotel, locally popular for well kept real ales such as Caledonian, Marstons Pedigree and Yates; open fire, imaginative restaurant food; bedrooms comfortable and good value *(Andy and Jill Kassube)*

Yarm, Cleveland [High St; NZ4213], *Ketton Ox*: One of village's oldest and most historic buildings, the windowless upper floor once being a cockpit; unpretentiously friendly, Vaux Samson and Wards on handpump, back pool room, fruit machines, no juke box; children welcome *(Martin Thomas)*

Nottinghamshire   *see* Leicestershire

Oxfordshire

Not a cheap county, this: most pubs drifted over the £1 mark for snacks and the £3 level for main dishes long ago. But we did find bargain cheap snacks at the Elephant & Castle at Bloxham, Three Tuns in Henley, Trout at Tadpole Bridge and – outstandingly so – King William IV at Hailey; and particularly cheap main dishes at the Bottle & Glass at Binfield Heath, Red Lion at Steeple Aston (winter), and again the Elephant & Castle. Oxfordshire pub-goers are paying about 5p extra in the £ for their drinks, compared with the national average. Overall, there were on average few differences in pricing here between free houses, pubs tied to national brewing combines, and those tied to smaller breweries. However, the best value pubs we found for drinkers – the Elephant & Castle at Bloxham, Red Lion at Steeple Aston, Falkland Arms at Great Tew, Gate Hangs High near Hook Norton and Bell at Shenington – all sold beers from the local brewers Hook Norton or Donnington, or were tied to them. These two brewers in particular stand out as good value; the county's main local brewer, Brakspears, is now notable more for the many delightful pubs in its estate than for particularly low prices. New main entries to note here this year include the Abingdon Arms at Beckley (lovely garden, decent food), the Mermaid in Burford (notable food in olde-worlde surroundings), the very civilised Peacock at Henton (a nice place to stay) and the very welcoming Gate Hangs High right out in open country near Hook Norton. Other important changes include new licensees at the quaint Bottle & Glass at Binfield Heath, the Clanfield Tavern at Clanfield, the Bell in Faringdon, the Bell at Shenington, the smart Lamb at Shipton-under-Wychwood (they've kept the chef – the food's still especially good), Harcourt Arms at Stanton Harcourt, the charmingly old-fashioned Crooked Billet at Stoke Row (much more adventurous food now) and the Trout in its specially attractive position at Tadpole Bridge on the Thames; on all these, early reports are favourable, with general approval of changes that have been made or are under way. The Wheatsheaf at East Hendred has stopped letting bedrooms; but the Mason Arms at South Leigh has started letting them. The bedrooms at the Old Swan at Minster Lovell have been handsomely refurbished (much more expensive now, though), as have those at the Beetle & Wedge in Moulsford. This increasingly upmarket pub does some of the best food here now – pricey and restauranty rather than cheap pub fare; other pubs currently outstanding for good food here include the Sir Charles Napier near Chinnor (pricey), the Five Horseshoes at Maidensgrove, the cottagey Home Sweet Home at Roke, and the Chequers at Watlington (though the licensee has changed, he's the brother-in-law of the old one, and there's no perceptible change in style here). Other special favourites include the charmingly traditional and old-fashioned Lamb in Burford, the friendly and rustic Woodman at Fernham, the Falkland Arms at Great Tew (one of the finest examples there is anywhere of a quaint and unspoilt country *pub), the civilised Crown at Pishill, and the Red Lion at Steeple Aston (good lunchtime food, shipping their own wines from France). Among the Lucky Dip entries at the end of the chapter, pubs currently showing notably well include the Fox at Bix, Duke of Cumberlands Head at Clifton, Queens Head at Crowmarsh, Crown in Faringdon, Bell at Great Milton, Pear Tree in Hook Norton, Nut Tree at Murcott, Beehive at Russells Water, Wykham Arms at Sibford Gower, Fish at Sutton Courtenay and Gardiners Arms at Tackley.*

BECKLEY   SP5611 Map 4
Abingdon Arms

Village signposted off B4027

On a warm summer evening the garden makes this a very special place: from a gently floodlit terrace and small formal flower-edged lawn just behind the stone-built pub it drops quietly and spaciously away into the shadows of groves of fruit trees, willows and other shrubs and trees, with well spaced tables, a summer-house, a little tinkling fountain. By day, there are enticing views over the Otmoor wilderness, just beyond. The comfortably modernised simple lounge has cloth-cushioned seats built around the wall; a smaller public bar on the right has a couple of antique carved settles (one for just one person), and bar billiards. Food, varying from season to season, is imaginative. In summer it's mainly cold food such as a selection of cheeses (from £2.25), pasta salad or avocado with tomato and basil (£3.25), Greek salad with taramasalata (£3.95), smoked chicken (£5.30), prawns with chilli mayonnaise (£5.75) and strips of rare roast beef or cold poached salmon (£5.95). In winter, besides some of these dishes, there's a splendid bouillabaisse, chicken curry and so forth. Well kept Wadworths 6X and a guest beer such as Adnams Extra on handpump, decent wines, log fire, bar billiards, cribbage, dominoes, no music or games machines. Service is usually friendly and efficient, but can seem low-key; there may sometimes be a wait for food. *(Recommended by Mike O'Driscoll, KL, EL, Sir Nigel Foulkes, A T Langton, Margaret and Roy Randle, Annie Taylor, Henry Midwinter, A M Ranklin)*

Free house   Licensee Hugh B Greatbatch   Real ale   Meals and snacks (12.15–1.45, 7.15–9.30, not Sun evening)   Open 11–2.30, 6.30–11; closed 25 Dec evening

BINFIELD HEATH   SU7478 Map 2
Bottle & Glass ★

Village signposted off A4155 at Shiplake; from village centre turn into Kiln Lane – pub at end, on Harpsden Road (Henley–Reading back road)

The attractively flagstoned bar here is furnished with spindleback chairs, a bench built into black squared panelling, and very heavily scrubbed, ancient tables under the low beams; there are huge logs in the big fireplace. The side room, similarly decorated, has a window with diamond-scratched family records of earlier landlords; Brakspears Bitter, SB and Old on handpump; dominoes. The good selection of bar food, chalked on the blackboard, includes lunchtime sandwiches, home-made soup (£1.50), home-made chicken and duck pâté (£1.95), chicken livers with bacon, garlic and cream or vegetable curry (£2.95), Cumberland sausage, chilli con carne, ham and egg or pasta (all £3.50), steak and Guiness pie (£3.95), gammon (£4.25), pheasant (£5.25), and steak (£7.80); service stays cheerful under pressure. In the garden by this thatched, black-and-white timbered 15th-century building there are old-fashioned wooden seats and tables under little thatched roofs, and an open-sided shed like a rustic pavilion. *(Recommended by Henry Midwinter, Ian Phillips, Lindsey Shaw Radley, Chris Raisin, Graham Doyle)*

Brakspears   Licensees Mike and Anne Robinson   Real ale   Meals and snacks (not Sun)   Open 11–2.30(3 Sat), 6–11

BLOXHAM SP4235 Map 4
Elephant & Castle

Humber Street; off A361

Remarkably good value food in this fine old building includes a ploughman's for just £1.10; there's also soup (75p), good sandwiches (from 60p; toasted from 85p), sausage or ham with eggs (£1.60 or £2), steak and kidney pie (£2.30), salads (from £2.50), scampi (£2.60), and rump steak (£4.50); children's dishes (from £1). The beer is decently priced too – very well kept Hook Norton Best and Old Hookey on handpump; malt whiskies. The building itself consists of an elegantly simple public bar with a striking 17th-century stone fireplace and a strip wood floor, and a comfortable lounge, divided into two by a very thick wall and which also has a good winter log fire in the massive fireplace; the atmosphere is relaxed and friendly. Sensibly placed darts, dominoes, cribbage, a fruit machine, and shove-ha'penny – the board is over a century old. In the flower-filled yard there's an Aunt Sally pitch, which they use just in the summer. The pub is in a street of thatched stone-built cottages in this imposing Cotswold village. *(Recommended by Marjorie and David Lamb, Tom Evans, Lyn and Bill Capper, Stephen King)*

Hook Norton   Licensee Chas Finch   Real ale   Lunchtime meals and snacks (not Sun)   Restaurant tel Banbury (0295) 720383; closed Sun   Children in eating area Open 10.30–2.30, 6–11

BRIGHTWELL BALDWIN SU6595 Map 4
Lord Nelson ✿

Brightwell signposted off B480 at Oxford end of Cuxham or B4009 Benson–Watlington

Prettily placed on a very quiet lane opposite the church, this was originally called the Admiral Nelson until the man himself got his peerage in 1797. His presence is still very much felt – particularly in the bar on the left, where the plain white walls are decorated with pictures and prints of the sea and ships, there are some ship design plans, and a naval sword hangs over the big brick fireplace in the wall (which divides off a further room). It's comfortably modernised, with wheelback chairs (some armed), country kitchen and dining chairs around the tables on its Turkey carpet, candles in coloured glasses, orange lanterns on the walls, and pretty fresh flowers; piped music. On the food front, the menu covers the bar and restaurant (though in the evening the restaurant has its own menu), and includes home-made soup (£2), duck liver and pork pâté (£2.75), garlic mushrooms with crispy bacon or prawn and peach cocktail with a brandy cocktail sauce (£3.25), popular and substantial lunchtime Welsh rarebit (£4.75), steak and kidney pie (£5.95), fettucine al pesto (£5.75), salads (from £6.50), duck in orange pie or casserole of scallops, prawns and monkfish (£6.95), and puddings such as fruit crumble (£2.25) or raspberry meringue (£2.75); Sunday lunch (from £9.50); friendly waitress service. Tables are not bookable (except in the restaurant), so it's best to get here early at weekends. Brakspears PA on handpump, and a decent wine list, including a good range of cheaper French wines. There's a verandah at the front, and tables on a back terrace by the attractive garden or under its big weeping willow, beside the colourful herbaceous border. *(Recommended by Joan Olivier, Henry Midwinter, AP, R and E Harfield, A T Langton, Sir Nigel Foulkes, PLC)*

Free house   Licensees Peter Neal, Richard Britcliffe, Ann Neal   Real ale   Meals and snacks (12–2, 7–10)   Restaurant tel Watlington (049 161) 2497   Children by arrangement   Open 11.30–3, 6.30–11.20 (late supper licence); closed evening 25 Dec, all day 26 Dec

BURFORD SP2512 Map 4
Lamb ★ ★ 🛏

Sheep Street; A40 W of Oxford

An excellent place to stop – as it was in the 18th century, when the village boasted so many inns that it was a popular place for a 'Burford bait' for coach travellers (a euphemism for having a lot to drink). This inn is three centuries older than the phrase, and is charmingly traditional and old-fashioned. The spacious beamed main lounge has distinguished old seats including a chintzy high-winged settle, ancient cushioned wooden armchairs, easy chairs, and seats built into its stone-mullioned windows, as well as bunches of flowers on polished oak and elm tables. There are oriental rugs on the wide flagstones and polished oak floorboards, attractive pictures, shelves of plates and other antique decorations, a grandfather clock, a writing desk, and a good winter log fire under its elegant mantlepiece. The public bar has high-backed settles and old chairs on flagstones in front of its fire; the bedrooms are in similar style – simple, old-fashioned, chintzy. The well kept Wadworths IPA, 6X and winter Old Timer are dispensed from an antique handpump beer engine in a glassed-in cubicle. Well presented bar lunches, rotating on a daily basis, should typically include soup (£1.50), sandwiches (from £1.45, smoked salmon £2.50), ploughman's (£2.75), grilled sardines or ham salad (£3.95), duck casserole, sautéed lamb's kidneys or gammon (£4.50), smoked salmon salad (£5.95), and delicious puddings such as fruit pie or paw paw flan (£1.75); free dips at Sunday lunchtime. A pretty terrace leads down to small neatly-kept lawns surrounded by flowers, flowering shrubs and small trees, and the garden itself can be really sunny, enclosed as it is by the warm stone of the surrounding buildings. Dogs welcome. (*Recommended by Stephen Goodchild, Adam and Elizabeth Duff, Chris Raisin, Syd and Wyn Donald, J P Bowdler, Robert and Elizabeth Scott, Simon Collett-Jones, Mr and Mrs G Turner, Peter Scillitoe, Brian Jones, WHBM, Henry Midwinter, P B Dowsett, Alan Skull, Gordon and Daphne, J M M Hill, Bev and Doug Warwick, John and Anne Mciver, Patrick Freeman, David and Jane Russell*)

Free house   Licensee Richard de Wolf   Real ale   Meals and snacks (lunchtime, not Sun)   Restaurant   Children welcome   Open 11–2.30, 6–11; closed 25 and 26 Dec Bedrooms tel Burford (099 382) 3155; £32.50(£45B)/£60B

Mermaid 🏮

High St

Though the picnic-table sets under cocktail parasols out on the broad pavement of the famously picturesque sloping Cotswold street are an undeniable attraction in fine weather, the main draw here is the food (it regularly brings the pub into the national finals of a trade competition run by *Pub Caterer*). It includes good sandwiches (from £1.80), superb soups such as stilton and spicy tomato or lentil, carrot and avocado (£2.20), lots of other starters such as chicken wings with garlic and fresh ginger (£4.25), ploughman's or Cumberland sausage with red cabbage (£2.95), bacon and black pudding or baked mackerel (£3.95), over half-a-dozen vegetarian dishes such as vegetable hot-pot (£4.95), scampi, steak and kidney pie or an unusually tasty cottage pie (£4.95), kidneys and bacon (£5.50), gammon hot-pot (£5.95), a fine curry (£6.50), plaice (£8.95), seasonal dishes such as cold wild duck pie with an orange summer salad (£8.95) and steaks (from 10oz rump £9.95); vegetables are good. Note that some of these prices will be higher if you eat in the beamed restaurant area, on the right and upstairs, instead of in the attractive if rather dark bar. This is flagstoned, long and narrow, with brocaded seats in bays around the single row of tables down one side – each softly lit by a red-fringed lamp. The inner end, with a figurehead over the fireplace and toby jugs hanging from the beams, is panelled, the rest has stripped stonework. Courage Best and Directors on handpump, friendly and helpful service (food comes quickly, though there may be a wait at the bar). (*Recommended by Mike O'Driscoll, Brian Jones, Alastair Campbell, John Kimber, B Lambert, B Williams, Robert and Vicky Tod, Lindsey Shaw Radley*)

Courage   Licensees John and Lynda Titcombe   Real ale   Meals and snacks (12–2.30, 6–10)   Restaurant tel Burford (099382) 2193   Children in restaurant   Maybe no nearby parking   Open 11–11 nr CHINNOR SP7500 Map 4

Sir Charles Napier ✿

Spriggs Alley; from B4009 follow Bledlow Ridge sign from Chinnor; then, up beech wood hill, fork right (signposted Radnage and Sprigg Alley); OS Sheet 165 map reference 763983

Readers need to be distinctly prepared for the idiosyncracies of this place, which only just qualifies for an entry by our calculated stretching of the definition of a pub – which is actually a back-handed compliment to this one's high standards. From the outside a plain and slightly dishevelled Chilterns pub, inside it's almost wholly dedicated to a stylish restaurant, decorated with works by two local artists – sketches of Francis Bacon by Claire Shenstone, commissioned by him to do his portrait, and sculpture by Michael Cooper; at weekends, there's little point in going unless you do want a restaurant meal (which could easily cost you £50 a head); Sunday lunch, at around £25 a head, is distinctly fashionable – in summer it's served in the crazy-paved back courtyard with rustic tables by an arbour of vines, honeysuckle and wisteria (lit at night by candles in terracotta lamps). But through the week, when it's quieter and there's more room in the original small front bar, you're more likely to find something cheaper to eat with a straightforward drink; the short menu includes soup such as chilled cucumber and mint (£3), warm artichoke with dill hollandaise (£3.50), a salad of salami, parma ham, olives and avocado with walnut dressing, or poached eggs and ham (£4), shellfish marinière (£4.50), chicken with lemon, cream and herbs (£7.50), and baked haddock with parsley butter or braised Welsh lamb with caper sauce (£8.50). There are homely furnishings such as armchairs, narrow spartan benches by the wall, and highly polished tables on the plain wood-block or tiled floor, with bare oak boards in the low ceiling, and a good winter log fire, which has gleaming copper pipes running from the back boiler. Well kept Wadworths IPA tapped from the cask, champagne on draught, well chosen wines by the bottle, freshly squeezed orange juice, Russian vodkas and a few malt whiskies; piped music well reproduced by the huge loudspeakers; service is relaxed and friendly. The croquet lawn and paddocks by the beech woods drop steeply away to the Chilterns. (*Recommended by TBB, A J Young, M A and C R Starling, Patrick Freeman, Roger and Lynda Pilgrim*)

Free house   Licensee Mrs Julie Griffiths   Real ale   Lunchtime bar meals (not Sun or Mon)   Restaurant tel Radnage (0494) 483011; not Sun evening   Children welcome lunchtimes; in evenings if over 7   Open 11.45–4, 6.30–12 Tues–Sat; closed Sun evening and Mon

CHRISTMAS COMMON SU7193 Map 4
Fox & Hounds

Hill Rd from B4009 in Watlington; or village signposted from B480 at junction with B481

This unspoilt tiny cottage is covered with an Albéric Barbier rose, and there are old-fashioned garden seats and sitting-logs by the roses and buddleia on the front grass beyond a small gravel drive, with picnic-table sets under a sumac beside the house. The beamed bar on the left is simply furnished with three tables and wooden wall benches or bow-window seats, a framed Ordnance Survey walker's map on one cream wall, a little carpet down on the red-and-black flooring tiles, and two sturdy logs to sit on in the big inglenook – which has a fire burning even in summer; the room on the right is popular with locals and pretty much for drinking only; the Alsatian is friendly. Lunchtime food includes soup (£1), sandwiches (from £1), ham and eggs (£3.50) and scampi (£4.50); they only do soup and sandwiches on Sundays and Mondays; good coffee. Well kept Brakspears PA tapped from the cask in a back still room; darts, shove-ha'penny, dominoes, cribbage. The pub is in good Chilterns walking country. (*Recommended by Ian Phillips, Joan Olivier, Chris Raisin, Graham Doyle, Mayur Shah, WHBM*)

Brakspears   Licensee Mr K Moran   Real ale   Snacks (lunchtime)   Children in games room off one bar   Open 12–2.30, 6–11

CLANFIELD   SP2801 Map 4

Clanfield Tavern

A4095 5 miles S of Witney

Since taking over in 1989 the licensees have been greeted with enthusiasm by readers, who like their chatty and attentive manner. Imaginative, home-made bar food includes soup (£1.30), sandwiches, ploughman's, vegetable stroganoff (£3.50), burgers (from £3.75), and rump steak (around £6), with specials like roast quail (£4.20), chicken breast (£4.75) and Scotch salmon in a cream and wine sauce (£5.20). Several flagstoned, heavy-beamed and stone-walled small rooms lead off the main bar, and are furnished with various chairs and seats cut from casks and settles around the tables, as well as brass platters, hunting prints, and a handsome open stone fireplace with a big log fire and 17th-century plasterwork panel above it. Well kept Hook Norton Best, Morlands Bitter and Morrells Varsity on handpump, and quite a few bin end wines; darts, dominoes, shove-ha'penny, cribbage, piped music, fruit machine and trivia, and there is a proper skittles alley. Tables on a flower-bordered small lawn look across to the village green and pond. *(Recommended by Mr and Mrs P J Hardy, Jack and Barbara Smale, Mrs M E Lawrence, Maj R A Colville, Patrick Freeman)*

Free house   Licensees Keith and Anne Gill   Real ale   Meals and snacks (12–2, 6–10)   Cottagey restaurant   Children welcome   Open 11.30–2.30, 6–11   Bedrooms tel Clanfield (036 781) 223; £15/£30

CLIFTON HAMPDEN   SU5495 Map 4

Barley Mow

Back road S of A415 towards Long Wittenham

Considered by Jerome K Jerome the quaintest and most old-world inn on the Thames, this 13th-century place has a well furnished lounge, with antique oak high-backed settles, as well as ship's timbers for its end wall, low beams, and old engravings on the walls. The black-flagstoned public bar is broadly similar, and the side family room has handsome squared oak panelling. Ruddles County, Ushers Best and Websters Yorkshire on handpump; dominoes, cribbage, fruit machine. Decent bar food includes ploughman's (£2.10), a buffet table (£3.50), daily specials, a roast of the day (£4; £4.50 Sunday), and puddings like apple or fruit pies (£1.50). The well tended, sheltered lawn has rustic seats, and the Thames bridge is nearby. *(Recommended by R C Gandy, Marjorie and David Lamb, Gethin Lewis, TBB, M J Dyke, R Houghton)*

Ushers (Watneys)   Licensee Margaret Welch   Real ale   Meals and snacks Restaurant; closed Sun evening   Children in oak room   Open 11–2.30, 6–11 Bedrooms tel Clifton Hampden (086 730) 7847; £32/£50 (own lavatories)

CROPREDY   SP4646 Map 4

Red Lion

Off A423 4 miles N of Banbury

Opposite a raised churchyard and a short stroll from the Oxford Canal, this simply furnished place has high-backed settles under its beams, brasses on the walls, a fish tank, and a winter open fire. The good selection of drinks includes well kept Arkells BBB, Tetleys, and Wadworths 6X on handpump, decent wines with special offers on a blackboard, properly mixed Pimms or bloody Mary, and summer and winter punches; darts, dominoes, cribbage, pool, fruit machine, and juke box. Bar food includes sandwiches (from £1.30), home-made soup (£1.95), garlic mushrooms (£2.65), ploughman's (£2.95), lamb cutlets (£4.95), steak (£6.75), and excellent king prawns in garlic (£8.35), with puddings such as chocolate biscuit gateau or hot chocolate fudge cake (£2). There are seats in the back garden. *(Recommended by J Charles, Patrick and Mary McDermott, Graham Oddey; more reports please)*

*Free house   Licensee Jeremy Hunt   Real ale   Meals and snacks   Children welcome
Parking may be difficult in summer   Open 11–3.30, 6–11; winter afternoon closing
2.30*

CUMNOR   SP4603   Map 4

Bear & Ragged Staff

*19 Appleton Road; village signposted from A420: follow one-way system into village,
bear left into High St then left again into Appleton Road – signposted Eaton, Appleton*

One of the 'Buccaneer Inns', this largely 16th-century pub serves a good choice of
food (though the portions may not always satisfy the very hungry): ploughman's
(£2.75), salads with pâté (£4), locally smoked Eynsham trout (£4.60),
home-cooked beef or ham (£5.20), hot dishes such as vegetarian flan or prawn and
asparagus quiche (£3.85), lasagne (£4.35), veal and liver stir-fry (£4.65), a daily
roast (from £4.65), lamb and mushroom casserole or fisherman's pie (£4.95),
braised rib of beef (£5.20), and four or five puddings; one of the eating areas is
no-smoking. The comfortably rambling, softly lit bar has easy chairs, sofas and
more orthodox cushioned seats and wall banquettes, and polished black flagstones
in one part, with Turkey carpet elsewhere; it can get very busy at weekends. Well
kept Morrells and Varsity on handpump, a decent wine list, and malt whiskies;
friendly service. There's a children's play area, with a swing and climbing frame at
the back by the car park. This twin-gabled farmhouse is named for the three-foot
model of a Warwick heraldic bear which guards the large open fire. *(Recommended
by Mr and Mrs D A P Grattan, Nigel Gibbs, Mike Tucker, Lynda and Howard Dix, Dr C S
Shaw, Henry Midwinter)*

*Morrells   Licensee Michael Kerridge   Real ale   Meals (12–2, 7–9.30) and snacks
(12–2.30, 6.30–10)   Restaurant tel Oxford (0865) 862329   Children in eating area of
bar lunchtime and early evening   Open 11–3, 5.30–11*

DORCHESTER   SU5794   Map 4

George 🛏

Village signposted from A423

This 15th-century timber and tile inn has old-fashioned, comfortable furnishings –
cushioned settles and leather chairs – as well as beams, a big fireplace, and carpet
on the woodblock floor of the bar; the atmosphere is civilised and welcoming.
Brakspears on handpump, good wine by the glass. Lunchtime food includes
home-made soup (£2.50), a little pot of prawns and mushrooms (£3.25), open
sandwiches (from £3.55), omelettes made with free-range eggs (£4.50), lasagne,
Cornish fish pie or a daily special (£4.95), grilled calves liver and bacon (£5.50),
and home-made puddings (£2.50). It was originally built as a brewhouse for the
Norman abbey – which still stands opposite – before being used as a posting and
then a coaching inn; close to *Good Walks Guide* Walk 96. *(Recommended by Roger
Bellingham, JMC; more reports please)*

*Free house   Manager Mark Stott   Real ale   Lunchtime meals and snacks (not Sun)
Restaurant   Children in restaurant   Open 11–3, 6–11; closed Christmas week
Bedrooms tel Oxford (0865) 340404; £54B/£72B*

EAST HENDRED   SU4588   Map 2

Wheatsheaf

Chapel Square; village signposted from A417

In a fine village just below the Downs, this busy black and white timbered pub has
high-backed settles and stools around tables on quarry tiles by a log-burning stove,
a tiny parquet-floored triangular platform by the bar, some wall panelling, and
cork wall tiles; low, stripped deal settles form booths around tables in a carpeted
area up some broad steps. Well kept Morlands Bitter and Old Masters on
handpump, a few malt whiskies and country wines; piped music, and maybe Ben,

the golden labrador (who's lost some weight, the licensees tell us). Bar food – quite adventurous in its range and almost restaurant in its aspirations – includes sandwiches (from £1, big baps from £1.70), soup (£1.25), sausages (£2.10), vegetarian curry or kedgeree (£3.25), pasta or gammon steak (£3.95), rack of lamb (£5.95), steaks (from 5oz rump £3.95; 10oz sirloin £9.95), trout (£4.95), chicken supreme (£5.95), and puddings (£1.75); the emphasis on food is greater at lunchtime – there's more room for darts, dominoes and Aunt Sally in the evening. A budgerigar aviary and play area for children with swings and so forth enliven the back grass area, colourful with roses and other flowers, conifers and silver birches. The nearby church is interesting – its Tudor clock has elaborate chimes but no hands. Note that they no longer do bedrooms. (Recommended by A T Langton, R Oxfordshire and E Harfield, M J Dyke, R C Watkins, Lyn and Bill Capper, P B Dowsett, David Young, Dr Stewart Rae, Henry Midwinter)

Morlands   Licensees Liz and Neil Kennedy   Real ale   Meals and snacks (not Mon evening)   Children in eating area   Open 11–3, 6–11

FARINGDON   SU2895   Map 4

Bell

Market Place; A420 SW of Oxford, then right into A417

The cobbled and paved yard here, sheltered by the back wings of the old coaching inn, has wooden seats and tables among tubs of flowers. Inside there's a comfortably faded feel, with red leather settles, Cecil Aldin hunting prints, some unusual fragments of a very old mural, and, notably, a 17th-century carved oak chimney-piece over the splendid inglenook fireplace, as well as an ancient glazed screen through which customers would watch the coaches trundling through the alley to the back coach yard – now the hallway. Badger Tanglefoot and Wadworths IPA on handpump. Bar food under the new management includes soup (£1.25), sandwiches (£1.50), baked mussels, king prawns or ploughman's (all £2.95), steak and kidney or beef and Guinness pie (£3.45), grilled plaice (£4.05), steak (£6.25), and puddings (£1.50). (Recommended by Mr and Mrs P B Dowsett, Gordon and Daphne, M B P Carpenter, Mr and Mrs J H Adam, B and J Derry, Patrick Freeman; more reports please)

Wadworths   Manager Ian Wardell   Real ale   Meals and snacks   Restaurant Children welcome   Open 10.30–3, 5.30–11; 11–11 Sat; closed 25 Dec   Bedrooms tel Faringdon (0367) 240534; £32.50B/£45B)

FERNHAM   SU2992   Map 4

Woodman ★

A420 SW of Oxford, then left into B4508 after about 11 miles; village a further 6 miles on

A long-standing favourite with some readers, this friendly rustic place is strong on individual touches – such as the clay pipes ready-filled for smoking, hot saki, the big central log fire that sometimes has a hot-pot simmering over it in winter, or the collection of over a hundred hats above the bar. Bar food, served at your table, includes ploughman's (£2), hot-pot or chilli con carne (£3.20), vegetarian dishes such as couscous or pasta with aubergines (£3.40), fish pie or smoked haddock and sweetcorn crumble (£3.50), home-made steak and kidney pie (£3.75), chicken and broccoli lasagne, and various puddings such as hot chocolate fudge cake (£1.50). The heavily beamed and roughly plastered rooms are well decorated with milkmaids' yokes, leather tack, coach horns, an old screw press, and good black and white photographs of horses, and there are cushioned benches built into the rough plaster walls, pews, Windsor chairs, and candle-lit tables made simply from old casks; the barn, once a games room, is now another bar area. Well kept Hook Norton, Morlands PA and Old Masters, Morrells Graduate, Theakstons Old Peculier and a guest beer tapped from casks behind the bar, and country wines; regular OAPs get a very substantial discount; country wines; friendly dog. (Recommended by W Bailey, Margaret Dyke, Gordon and Daphne, Margaret and Roy Randle, V Collman, Patrick Freeman, Marjorie and David Lamb, P B Dowsett, HNJ, PEJ)

Free house   Licensee John Lane   Real ale   Meals and snacks (not Mon)   Children in eating area of bar   Live music Fri or Sat every few weeks   Open 12–2.30, 6.30–11, though may open longer in afternoons if trade demands

FYFIELD   SU4298   Map 4
White Hart

In village, off A420 8 miles SW of Oxford

This was originally built for Sir John Golafre in about 1450 to house priests who would pray for his soul for ever; the atmosphere may be less pious these days, but it's still impressive – the main room is a hall with soaring eaves, huge stone-flanked window embrasures, and an attractive carpeted upper gallery looking down into it. A low-ceilinged side bar has an inglenook fireplace with a huge black urn hanging over the grate, and a framed history of the pub on the wall. The priests' room is now a dining area, as is the barrel-vaulted cellar. There's a wide choice of bar food, such as soup (£1.50), pâté (£2.25), ploughman's (from £2.25), vegetarian lasagne or curry (£3.55), Indonesian chicken or scampi (£4.25), a range of home-made pies (from £3.75), and steaks (£6.95); daily specials are usually available; one or two readers have been disappointed in the service. The attractively large range of well kept real ales, which changes from time to time, usually includes Boddingtons Bitter, Gibbs Mew Bishops Tipple, Morlands Bitter, Ruddles County, Theakstons Old Peculier, Wadworths 6X and Farmers Glory, and guest beers on handpump or tapped from the cask; Weston's cider. Dominoes, cribbage, shove-ha'penny, fruit machine and piped music. A heavy wooden door leads out to the rambling, sheltered and flowery back lawn; close to Pusey House, with its fine gardens. *(Recommended by V Collman, Dr and Mrs A K Clarke, Jill Hampton, Brian Metherell, Roger Bellingham, Margaret Dyke, Dick Brown; more reports please)*

Free house   Licensees Edward and John Howard   Real ale   Meals and snacks (12–2, 7–10)   Restaurant tel Oxford (0865) 390585; closed Sun   Children in three or four rooms   Open 11–2.30, 6.30–11; closed evening 25 Dec and all day 26 Dec

GORING HEATH   SU6579   Map 2
King Charles Head

Goring Heath signposted off A4074 NW of Reading, and B4526 E of Goring

Nicely isolated in woodlands, this warmly atmospheric brick cottage is within walking distance of Holly Copse and the Thames itself, by Mapledurham Country Park; it's close to *Good Walks Guide* Walk 98. Inside, small rooms ramble around a solidly built central servery, with comfortable floral-print wall banquettes and other seats, glossy plain tables, decorative plates and small country pictures on the white walls, and logs burning in a back stove and the open fire on the right. The wide choice of well cooked and generously served food includes sandwiches (from £1), home-made soup (£1.50), ploughman's (£2.50), attractively presented fresh salads (£2.75), lasagne (£3.75), grilled sardines (£3.95), steak and kidney casserole (£4) and steak (£7.75); during the summer there are extra lunchtime dishes such as mushroom and cashewnut rissotto (£3.95) or poached salmon (£6.50). Well kept Adnams, Brakspears PA and Mild, Glenny Hobgoblin and Wychwood, Hook Norton Best, Marstons Pedigree and Wadworths 6X on handpump; darts, cribbage, fruit machine. A more modern back extension opens into the charmingly meandering garden, which blends into the surrounding tall beech woods; there are lots of tables under cocktail parasols on a terrace and on the grass, with a timber climber and tyre swings. *(Recommended by James Cane, Bob Timmis, Steve Huggins, Henry Midwinter and others; more reports please)*

Free house   Licensees David, Christine and A Glyn Lawton   Real ale   Meals and snacks (not Sun evening)   Children in eating area   Open 11.15–2.45, 6–11; closed 25 Dec

GREAT TEW SP3929 Map 4

Falkland Arms ★ ★ 🛏

Off B4022 about 5 miles E of Chipping Norton

Until fairly recently, the eccentric Lord of the Manor who owned Great Tew kept the rents as low as 50p a week and left the village resolutely unimproved; though action eventually had to be taken to prevent some buildings from collapsing, a sense of unimproved timelessness does still prevail in the cluster of thatched and honey-coloured stone buildings which nestle around the village green. Nowhere is this more true than in the inn itself, Grade I listed, partly thatched and wisteria-covered (though no longer in such abundance since the new roof was put on). The partly panelled bar has shutters for the stone-mullioned latticed windows, a wonderful inglenook fireplace, high-backed settles and a diversity of stools around plain stripped tables on flagstones and bare boards, one, two and three handled mugs hanging from the beam-and-board ceiling, and dim converted oil lamps. The bar counter, decorated with antique Doulton jugs, mugs and tobacco jars, always serves several reasonably priced and well kept guest beers, as well as the regular Badger Tanglefoot, Donnington BB, Hook Norton Best and Wadworths 6X; also country wines and farm ciders, hot punch in winter, clay pipes filled ready to smoke, some 50 different snuffs, and handkerchiefs for sale. Lunchtime bar food – naturally taking a back seat given the pub's tremendous appeal in other respects – is home-made and includes sandwiches, a range of ploughman's (from £1.50), and daily specials like stuffed peppers (£3.80), vegetable lasagne, hot-pot, lamb mornay or mince and tomato crumble (all £3.90), and pork and stilton pie (£4); they use their own duck and chicken eggs for the Scotch eggs and bubble and squeak; friendly and cheerful service; darts, shove-ha'penny, dominoes, cribbage, and table skittles. The front terrace, with wooden seats among roses, doves cooing among the lumpy cushions of moss on the heavy stone roof-slabs, and maybe some ducks and geese wandering contentedly, can feel quite special. Note that as they can't do any 'improvements' to the building, the lavatories are a couple of doors down the lane. The manor itself belonged to the Falkland family until the end of the 17th century; the fifth Viscount Falkland, who was treasurer of the Navy in 1690, gave his name to the Falkland Islands, as well as to the inn. *(Recommended by Robert Gomme, Andy and Jill Kassube, Syd and Wyn Donald, Bernard Phillips, Pete Storey, Dennis and Pat Jones, Diane Duane-Smyth, Mr and Mrs J D Cranston, David Young, Simon Collett-Jones, Kevin Myers, Nick Dowson, Mrs S McGreevy, Ian Phillips, Su and Andy Hill, John Bowdler, Mrs E M Bartholomew, Richard Houghton, Richard Sanders, Tony and Lynne Stark, Gordon and Daphne, Dr and Mrs James Stewart, Dick Brown, Mr and Mrs J H Adam, Paul Corbett, Denis Mann, Christopher Knowles-Fitton, A M Kelly, HNJ, PEJ, Alan and Ruth Woodhouse, Chris Raisin, Graham Doyle)*

Free house Licensee John Milligan Real ale Lunchtime meals and snacks (not Sun or Mon) Children in eating area of bar Folk music Sun evening Open 11.30–2.30, 6–11; closed Mon lunchtime Three bedrooms tel Great Tew (060 883) 653; £30/£34S(£38B) (double rooms only)

HAILEY SU6485 Map 2

King William IV ★

Note – this is the hamlet of Hailey, near Ipsden (not the larger Hailey over in west Oxon); signposted with Ipsden from A4074 S of Wallingford; can also be reached from A423; OS Sheet 175 map reference 641859

Quiet and cosy in winter, busy and cheerful in summer, this country museum-piece of a Chilterns pub serves popular filled rolls such as ham, cheese and pickle, corned beef (from 50p – the only evening food), and pies, pasties or Stilton ploughman's with home-made soup (from £2.70). The beamed bar is dominated by the well restored farm implements, all with details of their age, use and maker, and festooning the timbered bare brick walls; there are root cutters, forks, ratchets, shovels, crooks, grabbers, man-traps, wicker sieves, full-size carts, ploughs, and a pitching prong; the big winter log fire still has its original faggot oven, with good sturdy furniture on the tiled floor in front of it. Two broadly similar carpeted areas open off. Well kept and reasonably priced Brakspears PA, SB, XXXX Old and Mild tapped from casks behind the bar. The back lawn of this white house, which overlooks rolling pastures, has seats among smartly painted veteran farm equipment such as cake-breakers and chaff cutters. A friend of the landlord's operates horse and wagon rides from Nettlebed to the pub where you then have a ploughman's or supper and gently return through the woods and via Stoke Row back to Nettlebed (£8.50 a head; phone Ian Smith on 0491–641364); the pub's own Shire horse – popular with children – pulls a brewer's dray. *(Recommended by Keith and Sian Mitchell, David Warrellow, Bob Timmis, Lyn and Bill Capper, Col A H N Reade, Nick Dowson, Dr Stewart Rae, Chris Raisin, Graham Doyle, David Marshall)*

Brakspears Licensee Brian Penney Real ale Snacks Children in eating area Open 11–2.30, 6–11

HENLEY-ON-THAMES SU7682 Map 2

Besides Lucky Dip entries listed under this town, you might like to see entries listed under Remenham – just over the Thames bridge, and therefore in Berkshire

Three Tuns

5 Market Place

Quite a traditional place, with an old-fashioned central servery and a good, friendly atmosphere. The heavily beamed buttery is notably cosy, with a central chimney and log-effect gas fire dividing off its back part. Two small rooms open off the long tiled and panelled corridor and are decorated with several cast-iron, pre-nationalisation railway company notices on the walls. The panelled front public bar has dominoes, cribbage, shove-ha'penny and fruit machine. Well kept Brakspears PA and SB on handpump, with Mild and Old tapped from the cask, and reasonably priced doubles; piped music. Bar food, priced eccentrically with a complete disregard for the decimal system, includes soup (90p), sandwiches (from £1.04, two-rasher bacon, lettuce and tomato £1.82, hot salt beef £2.37), home-made chicken liver pâté (£1.79), ploughman's (from £2.09), vegetarian lasagne (£3), egg, bacon, sausage and tomato (£3.22), meaty lasagne (£3.34), a pie of the day (£3.61), gammon with egg or pineapple (£5.29), mixed seafood (£5.51), and 6oz sirloin steak (£7.83). There's a small terrace at the back; close to *Good Walks Guide* Walk 68. *(Recommended by Gary Scott, David Warrellow, R S Laws, Ian Phillips, David and Eloise Smaylen, Chris Payne, Sheila Keene, Richard Sanders)*

Brakspears Licensees Jack and Gillian Knowles Real ale Meals and snacks (10–9.30 Mon–Fri, noon–9 Sun) Children in rear part of buttery Open 10–11; closed evening 25 Dec

HENTON SP7602 Map 4

Peacock 🍺

From B4445 SE of Thame, left on to B4009, village signposted on left after about 1 mile

There are indeed peacocks around this quaint black and white thatched and timbered house and its back bedroom block. From the front courtyard with its little goldfish pool and fountain you make your way into a civilised and comfortable beamed bar, with guns above the good log fire in its big brick fireplace, a few swords on the wall, and plush wall banquettes and wheelback chairs or winged low settles and dining chairs around close-set tables. A wide choice of well served bar food includes lots of starters (which make decent lunchtime snacks) such as soup (£2.25), calamares (£3.25), avocado with smoked salmon (£3.75) and prawns, mushroom and cheese (£4), as well as soup (£2.25), open sandwiches (from £2.50), vegetable curry (£5.95), chicken supreme (£5.95), and several speciality seafood, duck and steak dishes – the restaurant area round on the left rather concentrates on these. Well kept Brakspears PA and maybe Hook Norton Best on handpump, winter mulled wine, smart and courteous measured service, unobtrusive piped music. *(Recommended by BKA, Richard Houghton)*

Free house   Licensee Bert Good   Real ale   Lunchtime meals and snacks
Restaurant   Children if eating   Open 10.30–2.30, 6–11   Bedrooms tel Kingston
Blount (0844) 53519; £45B/£55B

nr HOOK NORTON   SP3533   Map 4
Gate Hangs High

Banbury Rd; a mile N of village towards Sibford, at Banbury–Rollright crossroads

In summer this isolated country pub's garden is a pleasant place for a drink, with
its broad lawn under holly and apple trees, swings for children to play on, and
view down over a plump quilt of rolling fields and pastures. Inside it's clean and
welcoming, with joists in the long, low ceiling, a brick bar counter, a gleaming
copper hood over the hearth in the inglenook fireplace, stools and assorted chairs
on the carpet, and some tables set for diners. The good choice of reasonably priced
bar food, from a blackboard that changes daily, typically includes soup (£1.20),
paté (£1.95), lasagne, chilli con carne or sweet and sour pork (all £3.95), beef in
beer (£4.50), steak and kidney pie with lots of fresh vegetables (£4.95), and steaks
(£7.50), as well as a salad bar; the emphasis tends to be on meals rather than
snacks; good, friendly service. Well kept Hook Norton Best on handpump,
dominoes. (Recommended by Sir Nigel Foulkes, Barbara M McHugh, VL, Joy and Peter
Heatherley, Iain Hewitt, Frank Cummins, Alan and Julie Wear; more reports please)

Hook Norton   Licensee Stuart Rust   Real ale   Meals and snacks (not Sun and Tues
evenings)   Restaurant tel Chipping Norton (0608) 737387   Children in restaurant
Open 11.30–3, 6.30–11

LITTLE MILTON   SP6100   Map 4
Lamb

3 miles from M40, junction 7; A329 towards Wallingford

Set in rolling farmland, this honey-coloured, thatched pub has little windows in the
stripped stone walls of the beamed bar that are so low you have to stoop to look
out; there are also lots of tables with wheelback chairs, and soft lighting. Halls
Harvest, Ind Coope Burton and Tetleys on handpump; fruit machine, piped music.
The range of home-made food includes sandwiches (from £1.25), ploughman's
with warmed bread (£2.50), ham or beef salad (£5.45), and hot main dishes such
as rabbit and prunes, lamb and courgette casserole, chicken in tarragon or grilled
Portuguese sardines (£5.35), venison in red wine (£5.85), Guinea fowl (£6.25), and
steaks (from £8.35); there are lots of puddings such as lemon charlotte (£1.85).
The quiet garden has swings, roses, a herbaceous border and fruit trees; in summer
there are hanging baskets and tubs of flowers. (Recommended by Joan Olivier, Dr J R
Hamilton, D L Johnson, A T Langton)

Halls (Allied)   Licensee David Bowell   Real ale   Meals and snacks (12–2, 7–10);
bookings tel Great Milton (0844) 279527   Open 11–2.30, 6.30–11; closed 25 and 26
Dec evening

MAIDENSGROVE   SU7288   Map 2
Five Horseshoes 🚫

W of village, which is signposted from B480 and B481; OS Sheet 175, map reference
711890

Popular with walkers – with a separate bar where boots are welcome – this
isolated Chilterns pub is strong on food (there's often a queue for tables at the
weekend); the enterprising range includes home-made soup (from £1.75),
ploughman's (from £2.75), baked potatoes with interesting fillings (from £2.95),
home-made pâtés like smoked trout or avocado and walnut (mostly £3.50), chilli
con carne (£3.95), steak and kidney pie (£4.50), outstanding calf's liver, a casserole
of the day, seafood lasagne (£5.95), stir-fried beef (£5.95), Scotch salmon (£6.50),
and Scotch steak (from £9); specials include vegetable lasagne (£4.50), breaded

butterfly prawns (£5.50) or giant New Zealand mussels (£6.50). In the main area of the rambling bar the low ceiling is covered in bank notes from all over the world, mainly donated by customers; furnishings are modern for the most part – wheelback chairs around shiny dark wooden tables – though there are some attractive older seats and a big baluster-leg table, as well as a good log fire in winter. Well kept Brakspears PA and SB on handpump; courteous, helpful service. There are picnic-set tables on the sheltered lawn and under a fairylit Perspex arbour, and the surrounding common is covered in beech trees. *(Recommended by Mrs R M Thomas, David Warrellow, Gordon and Daphne, Lyn and Bill Capper, Jane and Calum Maclean, Richard and Dilys Smith)*

Brakspears   Licensees Graham and Mary Cromack   Real ale   Meals and snacks (not Sun evening)   Children over 14   Open 11–2.30, 6–11

MINSTER LOVELL   SP3111   Map 4

Old Swan ★ 🍺

Just N of B4047; follow Old Minster signs

In an historic village by the sleepy little River Windrush, this ancient Cotswold inn has a notably good garden, with a lily pond, flowers and shrubs, and some shade from chestnut and sycamore trees for the seats on the neat lawn. Inside, a few smartly modernised and attractive low-beamed rooms open off the small central bar, furnished and decorated with Liberty-print easy chairs, good china in corner cupboards, an antique box settle, Turkey carpets on the polished flagstones, and big log fires in huge fireplaces. Lunchtime bar food includes soup (£1.40), sandwiches (from £1.40), home-made pâtés (from £2.50), a well presented ploughman's (£2.75), a slimmer's salad (£3.30), and prawns in a spicy dip (£3.80); well kept Ind Coope Burton and Tetleys on handpump pulled by a neatly dressed barman. The restaurant is housed in what used to be the brewhouse, and there's a medieval well on the way out to the garden. The bedrooms have been substantially refurbished. *(Recommended by C R Ball, B Lambert, Tim and Sue Halstead, B Williams, Ann Marie Stephenson, Patrick Freeman, A T Langton, John Branford, E G Parish, Jill Hampton, Brian Metherell, Richard Dolphin, Roger Huggins; more reports please)*

Halls (Allied)   Real ale   Lunchtime snacks (not Sun)   Restaurant; not Sun evening Children welcome   Open 11–11   Bedrooms tel Witney (0993) 774441; £94B/£120B

MOULSFORD   SU5983   Map 2

Beetle & Wedge 🍴 🍺

Ferry Lane; off A329, 1 1/2 miles N of Streatley

This fine Thameside inn has very much gone up market in the past couple of years; under the same ownership as the Royal Oak at Yattendon (one of Berkshire's classiest pubs for food, and another main entry in the *Guide*), its atmosphere is quite hotelish – not just in the lounge, but also in the pubby part in the Boathouse by the river, where there's a leisured, almost Edwardian feel – a mix of old chairs, some armchairs, bar stools, a ten-foot Edwardian sofa, polished wooden tables, oak saddle-beams, a tiled floor, and flint and brick walls, all done in a calming mixture of tortoiseshell, green and brown; you can also sit in the flagstoned conservatory. Considerable importance is attached to the food, which *is* expensive but correspondingly imaginative; the range includes soup such as summer gazpacho (£3.25), crispy duck with frisée salad (£4.75 or £7.50), cods roe pâté or avocado salad with smoked chicken and prawns (£4.75 or £7.50), ploughman's with local farm cheeses (£5), salad of skate, squid and prawns or lightly curried chicken (£7.25), maybe fillet of red mullet with queen scallops and saffron sauce, sirloin steak (£10.50), and half a lobster (£15); there's a charcoal grill for steaks. Well kept Adnams Bitter, Badger Tanglefoot, and Wadworths 6X on handpump; friendly service. The waterside lawn, flanked by roses, has robustly old-fashioned garden furniture. Moorings are available at £15 per boat per night, refundable on food in the bar or restaurant, and there should be a ferry running from here on summer weekends. The hotel is a popular attraction in literature – Jerome K Jerome's *Three Men* called in, and H G Wells' Mr Polly thought it an automatic choice for a jaunt up the river; near the start of *Good Walks Guide* Walk 97. *(Recommended by Dr Stewart Rae, Dick Brown, Kathy King, John Knighton, TOH, W C M Jones; more reports please)*

Free house   Licensees Richard and Kate Smith   Real ale   Meals and snacks (12.30–2, 7.30–10)   Restaurant   Well behaved children welcome   Occasional jazz nights   Open 11–2.30, 6–11   Bedrooms tel Cholsey (0491) 651381; £65B/£75B

NETTLEBED   SU6986   Map 2

Carpenters Arms

Crocker End; hamlet signposted from A423 on W edge of Nettlebed

The carpeted main room in this traditional little brick cottage has burgundy upholstered dark small pews, wheelback chairs, and country pictures on the cream walls; the partly panelled side saloon bar has been refurbished, with more wheelbacks and pews; the hooks on the ceiling here were originally used to hang up cooked pigs – regulars were handed a knife with their pint and helped themselves. Well kept Brakspears PA and SB on handpump; darts, shove-ha'penny, dominoes, cribbage, and piped music; winter log fires. The good choice of bar food includes home-made soup (£1.50), several ploughman's (from £2.95), lemon sole or mushroom stroganoff (£4.25), home-made steak pie or prawn fritters in sweet and sour sauce (£4.50), specials such as grilled sardines (£3.25), lasagne (£3.75), and steaks (from £7.95), with good puddings like bread and butter pudding soaked in whisky (£1.50); they advise bookings at weekends. There are wooden tables and benches on the bright front terrace. *(Recommended by John and Karen Day, C G and B Mason, Sheila Keene, Joan Olivier)*

Brakspears   Licensees David and Debbie Taylor   Real ale   Meals and snacks (12–2.30, 7–9.30, 7–10 weekends; not Tues evening)   Restaurant tel Nettlebed (0491) 641477   Children over 14   Open 11–3, 6–11 all year

White Hart

A423, in centre

A large brick and flint house, this has a rambling open-plan, beamed lounge bar with several seating areas, with cosy leather easy chairs, and other old-fashioned seats and settles; a snug area has a good winter log fire, another has a highly polished grand piano, and there's a big Act of Parliament wall clock. Brakspears PA and SB on handpump; shove-ha'penny, backgammon and chess; tables and benches outside. Bar food includes sandwiches, mushrooms in a Stilton sauce, home-made charcoal grilled burgers, pies and nut cutlets or vegetarian salads; children's helpings available. *(Recommended by Robert Timmis, Colin and Caroline Maxwell, Roderic Plinston; more reports please)*

Brakspears   Real ale   Meals and snacks   Restaurant   Children welcome   Open 11–2.30, 6–11   Bedrooms tel Nettlebed (0491) 641245; £22/£34

NEWBRIDGE   SP4101   Map 4

Rose Revived

A415 7 miles S of Witney

On a quiet reach of the upper Thames, this large stone inn, used as a drinking house since the 18th century, has lots of Victoriana in the bar area – rose patterned wallpaper, rose pictures, polished flagstones, glass lamps, marble tables and so forth. In the dining room there's a 16th-century stone fireplace – not always lit, even on a cold day – with an oak mantlebeam. The buffet bar serves sandwiches, ploughman's (from £2.50), salads (from £2.95) and hot dishes such as lasagne or steak and kidney pie (from around £3.25); the area off here is no-smoking. Morlands Bitter and Old Masters on handpump; fruit machine and piped music. The spacious garden, lit up at night by retired street lamps, has a long lawn, crazy-paved paths, weeping willows, spring bulbs or a colourful summer herbaceous border. *(Recommended by R C Gandy, Joan Olivier, A T Langton, Mr and Mrs P B Dowsett, W H Bland; more reports please)*

*Morlands   Licensee Alan Jefferson   Real ale   Meals and snacks   Restaurant
Children in eating area and restaurant   Jazz Sun evening   Open 11–11   Bedrooms*
tel *Oxford (0865) 300221; £30(£35B)/£40(£45B)*

NOKE   SP5413   Map 4
Plough

Village signposted from B4027, NE of Oxford

Close to Otmoor, this relaxed and unhurried place has a bar of three knocked-together, dark-beamed and brown-carpeted rooms with settles and other closely spaced seats, lots of brightly pictorial plates, and a few dogs and cats; the kitchen end of the bar is no-smoking. Decent helpings of attractively simple bar food include sandwiches (if they're not too busy), home-made French onion soup (£1), ploughman's (from £1.50), sausages and egg (£1.75), good value fry-up, home-made steak and kidney pie or charcoal roasted ham with egg (all £3), scampi (£3.75), lamb chops or gammon (£4), steak braised in Guinness gravy (£4.50), and filling puddings such as fruit pie (from £1); orders are taken from a hatch to the kitchen; perky service. Courage Best and Directors on handpump; piped music. In summer – when it can get busy on Sunday lunchtimes – there are plenty of seats out in the pretty garden, which backs on to farmland. *(Recommended by Margaret Dyke, Mrs E Ellis, Hazel J Church, Joan Olivier, Margaret and Roy Randle, C G and B Mason, Dr and Mrs James Stewart)*

*Courage   Licensee Peter Broadbent   Real ale   Meals and snacks (not Wed evening)
Well behaved children at kitchen end of bar   Country music Tues, folk 3rd Sun of the
month   Open 12–2.30(3 Sat), 7–11*

OXFORD   SP5106   Map 4
Oxford Brewhouse

14 Gloucester St; by central car park and Gloucester Green bus station

The changing selection of around nine real ales is quite a draw in this spacious, wood and brick corner pub; typically there's Archers Village, Arkells BBB, Burton Bridge Porter, Fullers London Pride, Glenny Wychwood Best, Hook Norton Old Hookey, and Wadworths 6X. The split-level bar – with a rambling main area and a cosier pit – has lots of basic junk-shop-style chairs, rocking chairs, pews and tables, and a big woodburning stove; piped music. Bar food includes sandwiches, soup with cheese and bread, ploughman's, and several hot meals like tagliatelle, a vegetarian dish, home-made quiche, curry or steak pie. A small courtyard at the back has picnic-table sets under a tall ash tree. *(Recommended by Jenny and Brian Seller, Paul Harrop, Simon Collett-Jones, A W Dickinson, Steve and Carolyn Harvey, P Miller, M O'Driscoll, David Fowles, Duncan and Lucy Gardener, Michael and Alison Sandy, R H Inns, Roy Gawne, RCL; more reports please)*

*Halls (Allied)   Real ale   Meals and snacks (not Sat or Sun evenings)   Children in
upper levels   Live music once a month   Open 10.30–2.30, 5.30–11*

Turf Tavern

Bath Place; via St Helen's Passage, between Holywell Street and New College Lane

One of Oxford's most busy pubs – and to some extent on the sightseeing trail, though popular with students too – this rambling but secluded building is still much as described by Hardy a century ago, when Jude the Obscure came to Christminster with such high aspirations. One of the city's oldest buildings, and partly surrounded by the ancient city wall, it has lots of dark beams, low ceilings with doors to match, and flagstoned or gravel courtyards. Bar food includes home-made soup (£1.15), a good selection of vegetarian meals (from around £3), and beef and beer pie or lasagne (£3.75); you usually have to queue when it's busy and service is put under pressure. Well kept Archers Headbanger, Flowers Original, Glenny Hobgoblin and Witney, Greene King Abbot, Uley Pigor Mortis and Whitbreads Castle Eden on handpump, with mulled wine in winter; trivia machine. It's very close to the Bodleian and the Sheldonian theatre. (*Recommended by Nigel Gibbs, Paul Harrop, Steve and Carolyn Harvey, John and Joan Wyatt, Wayne Brindle, Davis Fowles, Michael and Alison Sandy, Gordon and Daphne, R G Ollier, JMC, RCL, John Hill, P Miller, M O'Driscoll, Richard Sanders*)

Whitbreads   Licensee Stephen Shelley   Real ale   Meals and snacks   No nearby parking   Open 11–11

PISHILL   SU7389   Map 2

Crown

B480 N of Henley

In a peaceful valley, this wisteria-covered building has a calming and civilised atmosphere in the latticed-window bar, with its elegant corner cabinet of decorated plates, old photographs on the partly panelled walls in the front area, and a central black-beamed and red-and-gold carpeted part with little blocky country chairs and stools around wooden tables. The rear section is knocked-through, with standing oak timbers; three fine fireplaces all blaze in winter. Well kept Brakspears, Flowers Original, Marstons Pedigree and Wethereds Bitter on handpump. Relatively expensive but good home-made bar food includes sandwiches (weekday lunchtimes only), tasty soup (£1.75), filled baked potatoes (from £2.75), ploughman's or deep-fried mushrooms with a garlic dip (£2.50), ratatouille topped with cheese (£3.75), steak, kidney and mushroom pie or lasagne (£4.50), creamy prawn curry or beef stroganoff (£5.25), and sirloin steak (£6.50). Though the red brick and flint pub is relatively modern, records of a monastic building on this site go back to the 11th century, and the thatched barn they use for parties and functions is some 500 years old. There are picnic table sets on the attractive side lawn. (*Recommended by Ian Phillips, D Mackay, P M Johnson, Richard Houghton, Tony and Lynne Stark, TBB, Dick Brown, J P Day, M J Dyke, Derek and Sylvia Stephenson*)

Free house   Licensee Jeremy Capon   Real ale   Meals and snacks (12–2, 7–10) Restaurant tel Turville Heath (049 163) 364   Children in restaurant Sun lunchtime only   Open 11.30–2.30, 6–11   Bedrooms tel Henley-on-Thames (0491) 63364 in separate cottage; £65B

ROKE   SU6293   Map 2

Home Sweet Home 🏆

Village signposted off B4009 Benson–Watlington

The selection of home-made food in this civilised dining pub is at its widest – and most exalted – in the pretty restaurant; however it is possible to eat in the bar from it. The bar menu ranges from sandwiches (from £1.25), soup (£1.40), ploughman's (from £2.25), lots of filled baked potatoes (from £2.25) and omelettes (£3.25), through burgers (from £2.95), salads (from £3.65), creamy baked prawns or ham and egg (£3.95), scallops provençale (£4.35), smoked duck breast (£4.25), to dishes of the day such as stuffed mushrooms with prawn and cream cheese salad, garlicky and herby chicken, turkey breast and a well flavoured game pie with very light pastry; they have a notable range of good vegetarian dishes (£1.60–£4.95); roast Sunday lunch (£4.50). The two smallish, bare-boarded and stone-walled rooms of the quietly welcoming main bar have heavy stripped beams, leather armed chairs, just a few horsey or game pictures such as a nice Thorburn print of snipe, and big log fires – one with a great high-backed settle facing it across a hefty slab of a rustic table. On the right, a carpeted room with low settees and armchairs, and an attractive corner glass cupboard, leads through to the restaurant. Well kept Brakspears and Eldridge Pope Hardy on handpump, a good choice of malt whiskies, interesting wines; friendly service. The low-walled garden at the front of this thatched and tiled old house looks on to the quiet hamlet, and has lots of flowers around the tables out by the well. The licensees also run another of our main entries, the Old Boot at Stanford Dingley in Berkshire. *(Recommended by Lyn and Bill Capper, TBB, Maureen Hobbs; more reports please)*

Free house   Licensees Jill Madle, Peter and Irene Mountford   Real ale   Meals and snacks (12–2.30, 5.30–10)   Restaurant tel Wallingford (0491) 38249   Children in restaurant and snug   Open 11–3, 5.30–11; closed evening 25 Dec

SHENINGTON   SP3742 Map 4
Bell

Village signposted from A422 W of Banbury

Part of a row of little golden Hornton stone cottages, this 300-year-old pub is steadily building up a reputation for food; the bar menu currently includes sandwiches, stilton with black and white grapes, apple, celery and biscuits, home-made lasagne (£3.75), cod in celery sauce or pork chop in mushroom sauce (£5.75), beef and orange casserole (£5.95), and duck breast in apricot (£7.50); food is available until late evening. The heavy-beamed and carpeted lounge has old maps and documents on the cream wall, brown cloth-cushioned wall seats and window seats, and tables with vases of flowers; the wall in the flagstoned area on the left is stripped to stone and decorated with heavy-horse harness; the right side opens into a neat little pine-panelled room (popular with locals) with decorated plates on its walls. Well kept Courage Directors and Hook Norton Best on handpump, and a good choice of wines from Berry Bros; quick, efficient service; darts. The selection of animals includes two tortoiseshell cats (Myrtle and Mittens), a labrador called Katie and a West Highland terrier, Lucy. The tables at the front look across to the green. *(Recommended by John Bowdler, J Bramley, Sheila and Len Wallis, Joy and Peter Heatherley, Gordon and Daphne, G and M Brooke-Williams, N W Kingsley, Ted George, Mrs Lili Lomas, Su and Andy Hill)*

Free house   Licensees Jennifer and Stephen Dixon and Sylvia Baggott   Real ale   Meals and snacks (not Sun evening)   Children in eating area of bar only   Open 12–3, 7–12 (supper licence)   Bedrooms tel Edge Hill (0295) 87274; £15/£36B

SHIPTON-UNDER-WYCHWOOD   SP2717 Map 4
Lamb 🏆 🛏

Just off A361 to Burford

Since the last edition of the *Guide*, this old-fashioned, relaxing and rather up-market inn has been sold; but as the new licensees have kept the old chef on, and as it remains a firm favourite with readers, we feel confident in maintaining both its awards. Bar food includes a good summer cold buffet, home-made soup, duck and orange pâté (£3), and main dishes such as gravadlax (£4.50) or smoked salmon (£4.75), Cotswold pie or chicken with asparagus and tarragon sauce (£5.50), poached salmon and shrimp sauce (£7.50), and puddings such as treacle tart or marmalade cheesecake (£1.75); vegetables are well presented, salads well dressed; friendly service. The beamed bar has a fine oak-panelled settle, long pews, a solid oak bar counter, and flowery curtains in the small windows of the old partly bared stone walls; maybe newspapers to read. Well kept Hook Norton Best on handpump; good wines and several malt whiskies. In summer, you can sit at tables among the roses at the back. The restaurant is no-smoking. *(Recommended by Sidney and Erna Wells, Charles Turner, Colin Pearson, Adam and Elizabeth Duff, P B Dowsett, Mr and Mrs J W Gibson, A M Ranklin, J R Smylie, A J Madel, Robin Hillman, Charles Bardswell)*

Free house   Licensees Mr and Mrs L Valenta   Real ale   Meals and snacks   Restaurant; not Sun evening   Children over 14 in restaurant   Open 11–2.30, 6–11   Bedrooms tel Shipton-under-Wychwood (0993) 830465; /£58B (double rooms only)

Shaven Crown

This heavily stone-roofed pub is perhaps best appreciated from the courtyard garden, with its own lily pool, roses, and old-fashioned seats set out on the stone cobbles and crazy paving. Beyond it is a fine beamed bar with a relief of the 1146 Battle of Evesham, as well as seats forming little stalls around the tables and upholstered benches built into the walls. The decent range of bar food, served here, includes soup (£1.35), ploughman's (£2.35), Canadian-style potato skins (£2.50), bobotie (£3.95), lightly curried prawns (£4.85), sirloin steak, and puddings like treacle tart (£1.50); good cream teas, even on a Sunday. At the front, the magnificent double-collar braced hall roof and the lounge, with its lofty beams and sweeping double stairway down the stone wall, are part of the original Tudor building – said to have been used as a hunting lodge by Elizabeth I. Flowers Original and Hook Norton on handpump; the pub has its own bowling green. One reader felt that his twin bedroom was a little cramped. (Recommended by Joy and Peter Heatherley, Paul Harrop, Marjorie and David Lamb, Robert and Elizabeth Scott, Tim Briely, Mrs Lili Lomas, Stephen King, R G Bentley, Frank Cummins)

Free house   Licensee Trevor Brookes   Real ale   Meals and snacks   Restaurant Children in eating area of bar   Open 12–2.30, 7–11   Bedrooms tel Shipton-under-Wychwood (0993) 830330; £27B/£59B

SOUTH LEIGH   SP3908   Map 4

Mason Arms

Village signposted from A40 Witney–Eynsham

This polished, thatched 15th-century village pub has a pretty garden lively with peacocks and chickens – and there should be some Cotswold sheep in the small field by the car park; picnic-set tables shelter in a small grove. Inside, the flagstone lounge, separated into two halves by a wrought-iron divider, has built-in cushioned settles curving around the corners, an open fire with stone hearth at one end, and a log-effect gas fire at the other. Bar food includes home-made soup (£1.50), sandwiches (from £1.60), ploughman's (£3), vegetable pasta or seafood pancake (£3.90), salads (from £4), steak, kidney and Guinness pie (£4.60), and steak (£7.95). Hook Norton Best and a beer named for the pub on handpump, a good range of cognacs and malt whiskies, and lots of wines. They now do bedrooms. (Recommended by TBB, Ian Phillips, Edward Hibbert)

Free house   Licensee Geoff Waters   Real ale   Meals and snacks (not Sun evening, not Mon)   Restaurant (not Sun evening)   Children in restaurant   Open 11–2.30, 6.30–11; closed Mon (except Bank Hols)   Bedrooms tel Witney (0993) 702485; £27.50B/£46B

SOUTH STOKE   SU5983   Map 2

Perch & Pike

Off B4009 2 miles N of Goring

This busy flint pub has a low-beamed, brick-floored bar with a slight piscatorial theme – stuffed perch and pike on the shiny orange walls, a collection of plates painted with fish. Bar food, cooked with fresh herbs, includes French bread rolls (from £1.75), steak roll (£1.95), soup such as Stilton and watercress (£2.40), mixed ploughman's (£3.20), ham and egg (£3.50), beef, Guinness and orange casserole (£5.95), chicken in tarragon and white wine (£6.50), steaks (£9.50), and puddings such as real cheesecake. Brakspears PA, SB and maybe Old on handpump; darts, bar billiards, shove-ha'penny, dominoes, cribbage, fruit machine, boules, Aunt Sally and piped music. Past a black wooden barn, the large flower-bordered lawn has a slide, see-saw and swings, and there are benches by tubs of flowers and honeysuckle; occasional summer barbecues. The landlord was a professional guitarist, and now plays and sings in the bar on Saturday evenings. The pub is just a field away from the Thames, and has fishing rights – tickets available at around £2 a day. (Recommended by Col A H N Reade, T Galligan, David and Diane Livesley, Keith and Sian Mitchell, Gordon and Daphne)

Brakspears   Licensees Susie and Roy Mason-Apps   Real ale   Meals and snacks (limited Sun and Mon evenings in summer; no food then in winter)   Restaurant tel Goring (0491) 872415   Children in restaurant   Assorted guest musicians Thurs *evening, singing guitarist landlord Sat evening   Open 10.30–3(4ish Sat), 6–11; may open longer in afternoon if trade demands*

STANTON HARCOURT   SP4105 Map 4
Harcourt Arms

B4449 S of Eynsham

Since a change of ownership in 1989, readers have been divided in their opinions about this village pub – the greater emphasis on food has disappointed those who expect a more straightforwardly pubby atmosphere; but there's still enthusiastic support – notably for the warm welcome, the attractive surroundings, and of course for the food itself. The range includes sandwiches (from £1.50), soup (£1.95), home-made pâté (£2.20), ploughman's (from £2.75), grilled king prawns (from £3.50), steak sandwich (£3.50), spicy sausages (£4.95), trout with orange butter (£5.25), steak and kidney pie (£5.50), and chicken tikka (£6.95); three-course high teas in summer (£8.25), Sunday lunch (£9.50); maybe summer barbecues. The three dining areas are simply furnished with spindle-back chairs around wooden tables, and the annex room has Windsor-back chairs and framed Ape and Spy caricatures from *Vanity Fair*, and massive stone fireplaces; around 100 wines; piped music. The side lawn has now made way for a car park, but there's a garden at the rear and tables with parasols in front. *(Recommended by Lynda and Howard Dix, Mr and Mrs Peter Woods, BKA, Henry Midwinter, Mr and Mrs N W Briggs, Patrick Freeman, Mrs D M Hacker, JMC; more reports on the new regime please)*

Free house   Licensee J Mouncey   Meals and snacks (12–2.30, 6–10.30)   Restaurant tel Oxford (0865) 881931   Children welcome   Open 11.30–3, 6–11

STANTON ST JOHN   SP5709 Map 4
Star

Pub signposted off B4027; village is signposted off A40 heading E of Oxford (heading W, the road's signposted Forest Hill, Islip instead)

The original part of this well lit pub centres on two little low-beamed rooms, one of which has ancient brick flooring tiles and the other carpet and quite close-set tables. A well refurbished and no-smoking extension is up a flight of stairs, with old-fashioned dining chairs and an interesting mix of dark oak and elm tables, shelves of good pewter, terracotta-coloured walls with a portrait in oils, a stuffed ermine, pairs of bookshelves on each side of an attractive new inglenook fireplace, and rugs on flagstones. Badger Tanglefoot, Wadworths IPA, Farmers Glory and 6X on handpump, hot toddies and hot chocolate; behind the bars is a display of brewery ties, beer bottles and so forth; shove-ha'penny, dominoes, cribbage, piped music, and Aunt Sally. Bar food includes sandwiches (from £1.30), soup (£1.60), pâté or half a pint of prawns (£2.50), ploughman's (from £2.50), quiche (£3.45), specials such as coq au vin (£3.60), beef and Guinness or pork and cider pie or bulghar wheat and walnut casserole (£3.75), and various chicken dishes (£5.25); puddings such as home-made bread pudding (£1.25); children's meals (from £1.70). The walled garden has picnic-table sets among the rockeries, and swings and a sandpit. *(Recommended by TBB, Sir Denis Wright, Edward Hibbert, Dave Braisted, John Day, R M Sparkes, Ian Phillips, Michael Thomson; more reports please)*

Wadworths   Licensees Nigel and Suzanne Tucker   Real ale   Meals and snacks (12–2, 7–10)   Children in eating area   Open 11–2.30, 6.30–11; closed 25 and 26 Dec

STEEPLE ASTON   SP4725 Map 4
Red Lion

Off A423 12 miles N of Oxford

The good selection of lunchtime bar food in this comfortable and friendly little stone place includes tasty stockpot soup (£1), sandwiches (from £1.25), ploughman's with local crusty bread (from £1.95), pâté or home-made taramasalata (£2.50), summer salads such as fresh salmon (around £4.15), and in winter varying hot-pots (around £2.80). The beamed bar has good furnishings such as an antique settle, as well as dark hessian above its panelling, and a collection of rather crossword-oriented books. Well kept Badger Tanglefoot, Hook Norton Best and Wadworths 6X on handpump, a choice of sixty or so malt whiskies, and around 100 good wines in the restaurant (they ship their own wines from France). The terrace is quite a sun-trap. *(Recommended by Nick Dowson, Alison Hayward, Pete Storey, Richard Sanders, Jill Hampton, Brian Metherell, E J Waller, J Charles, V Collman, J P Cinnamond, John Bowdler, TBB, Gordon and Daphne)*

Free house   Licensee Colin Mead   Real ale   Lunchtime meals and snacks (not Sun) Restaurant tel Steeple Aston (0869) 40225; not Sun   Open 11–3, 6–11; closed 25 Dec evening

STOKE ROW   SU6784 Map 2

Crooked Billet

Newlands Lane; B481 N from Reading, village signposted on left at Highmoor Cross, after about 7 miles

Since the change of ownership in Christmas 1989, there have been some changes to this distinctively old-fashioned place – mainly to the food, which now changes more or less daily, but typically includes soup such as vichyssoise (£2.70), adventurous starters like salad of wild mushrooms, green peppercorns and rabbit (£3.75), and main dishes such as lamb chops with parsley butter and watercress (£5.95), chicken breast in hoi sin sauce and oyster mushrooms (£6.60), skate with capers and lemon sauce (£6.65), halibut in a prawn and mussel sauce (£6.85), steaks (from £7.50), and calves liver pan-fried with bacon (£8.95); puddings such as lemon cheesecake or treacle tart (£2.75); Sunday lunch (£11.95). Otherwise it's been a question of tidying up the attractively atmospheric bar area; at its heart is the little wood-panelled parlour, with a big table under a single lamp hanging from the bowed beam, and a log fire with an attractive rug in front of it; the public bar has a couple of scrubbed deal tables in front of a vast open hearth, and there's a second log fire in the renovated lounge. Well kept Brakspears PA, SB, and Old and Mild tapped from casks down six cellar steps and served through doorways. There are some plain benches at the front of the white stone building, and from the three-acre garden, with its picnic-table sets, you can walk straight into Chilterns beech woods. *(Recommended by Jane and Calum, Derek Brown, Joan Olivier, David Warrellow, TBB, J Charles, Gordon and Daphne, Alison Hayward, Nick Dowson, Lyn and Bill Capper; more reports on the new regime please)*

Brakspears   Licensees Paul and Lisa Clerehugh   Real ale   Meals and snacks Children in eating area   Jazz Sun lunchtime   Open 12–3, 6–11; 11–11 Sat

SWINBROOK   SP2712 Map 4

Swan

Back road 1 mile N of A40, 2 miles E of Burford

Close to the River Windrush and its bridge, this wisteria-covered, 17th-century pub has simple antique furnishings and a woodburning stove in the flagstoned bar, with a lounge area at the back, and a small dining room to the right of the main entrance; shove-ha'penny, dominoes and cribbage. Lunchtime bar food includes prawn and stilton toasted sandwich, tasty salmon and prawn sandwiches, and main dishes such as flaked white fish and prawns in a sauce topped with mushroom, potato and cheese or home-made steak and kidney pie (£3.80), with evening dishes in the dining room like poussin (£5.80) and scallops and prawns in a brandy sauce (£5.95); Morlands Bitter and Wadworths 6X on handpump. There are old-fashioned benches outside by the fuchsia hedge, making the most of this idyllic spot. *(Recommended by Gordon and Daphne, Chris Raisin, B Lambert, B Williams, John Kent, Elizabeth Lloyd, J Charles, EML, Mr and Mrs P B Dowsett, Prof and Mrs Keith Patchett)*

Free house   Licensee H J Collins   Real ale   Meals and snacks   Dining room (bookings only) tel Burford (0993) 822165   Open 11.30–2.30, 6–11

TADPOLE BRIDGE   SP3203 Map 4

Trout

Back road Bampton–Buckland, 4 miles NE of Faringdon

The side lawn here, with its small fruit trees, pretty hanging baskets and flower troughs, and moorings for customers, makes the most of its upper Thameside setting; you can also fish on a 1 3/4 mile stretch of the river (the pub sells day tickets), and there's a caravan and camping site for five. The little L-shaped, flagstoned bar has attractive pot plants on the window sills and mantlepiece, and a good pubby atmosphere. Bar food includes sandwiches (from 75p; toasted from 90p), sausage and egg (£1.90), ploughman's (from £2.50), lasagne (£3), ratatouille or moussaka (£3.30), gammon (£4.50), steak (£5.90), and puddings (from £1.25); regular summer barbecues, and a garden hut selling soft drinks, ice creams and so forth. Gibbs Mew Salisbury and Chudleys on handpump; darts, dominoes, shove-ha'penny, piped music and Aunt Sally. The pub was taken over early in 1990 by the previous landlord's brother-in-law, so we wouldn't anticipate any major changes. *(Recommended by Joan Olivier, EML, Lyn and Bill Capper; reports on the new regime please)*

Free house   Licensees Mick and Maureen Bowl   Real ale   Meals and snacks Restaurant tel Buckland (036 787) 382   Children in restaurant and eating area   Open 11.30–2.30, 6–11

WATLINGTON   SU6894 Map 4

Chequers ⊗

2 1/4 miles from M40, junction 6; Love Lane – B4009 towards Watlington, first right turn in village

A delightful, rambling place cosily tucked away in a back alley, this serves highly praised and genuinely interesting food – toasted sandwiches (£2), ploughman's (from £2.80), pâté (£3.50), tagliatelle with a vegetable sauce (£4), prawn curry, pork fillet in herbs and cream or steak and kidney pie (£5), gammon steak (£6), pasta with fresh prawns (£7), veal T-bone valdostana (£8.60), and steaks (from £9.20); good home-made puddings. In the quietly relaxing, red-carpeted bar there's a low panelled oak settle and character chairs such as a big spiral-legged carving chair around a few good antique oak tables, rugs, red-and-black shiny tiles in one corner, and of course low oak beams in a ceiling darkened to a deep ochre by the candles which they still use; steps on the right lead down to an area with more tables. Brakspears PA and SB on electric pump, and a pale grey cat. The notably pretty garden has picnic-table sets under apple and pear trees, and sweet peas, roses, geraniums, begonias, as well as rabbits. The cheese shop in Watlington itself is recommended. *(Recommended by David Wallington, P C Russell, Henry Midwinter, Chris Raisin, Graham Doyle; more reports please)*

Brakspears   Licensee John Valentine   Real ale   Meals and snacks   Open 11.30–2.30, 6–11

WYTHAM   SP4708 Map 4

White Hart

Village signposted from A34 ring road W of Oxford

Swathed in creepers, this 17th-century, food-oriented pub has an attractively presented and reasonably priced self-service cold table – very popular, particularly on a Sunday – ranging from pastrami salad (£3.95) to turkey and cranberry pie (£4.40), a summer lunchtime barbecue in the walled rose garden, with dishes such as trout (£5.25), lamb with rosemary (£6.25) and venison steak (£7.45), and hot dishes in the evening such as chicken Kiev (£6.20), red mullet in orange and thyme or lemon sole (£6.25), and salmon en croûte (£6.50); the area around the food servery is no-smoking. The flagstoned, partly panelled and atmospheric bar has a fine relief of a heart on the iron fireback, a shelf of blue and white plates, wheelback chairs, and high-backed black settles built almost the whole way round its cream walls; well kept Ind Coope Burton, Tetleys and Wadworths 6X on handpump. *(Recommended by Dick Brown, Joan Olivier, P J and M L Davies, Caroline Wright, P L Knight, Sheila Keene, David Goldstone, Roy Gawne)*

Ind Coope (Allied)   Licensees Rob Jones and Carole Gibbs   Real ale   Meals and snacks   Children in dining room and conservatory   Open 11–2.30(3 Sat), 6–11; closed 25 Dec

Lucky Dip

Besides the fully inspected pubs, you might like to try these Lucky Dips recommended to us and described by readers (if you do, please send us reports):

☆ Abingdon [The Bridge; SU4997], *Nags Head*: Very friendly pub with free Sun bar nibbles, good bar food, well kept Watneys-related real ales on handpump; lovely views looking up the Thames from tables on terrace; bedrooms comfortable and good value, with good breakfasts *(A L Willey)*

☆ Abingdon [St Helens Wharf; SU4997], *Old Anchor*: Characterful Morlands pub in tucked-away riverside location with good mix of customers, flagstoned back bar with little shoulder-height serving hatch, little front bar looking across Thames, bigger lounge and lovely little panelled dining room overlook the carefully clipped bushes of almshouse gardens; Morlands on handpump, usual range of bar food running up to steaks *(Ian Phillips)*

Adderbury [Aynho Rd; SP4635], *Plough*: Well decorated friendly pub with attractive furnishings, helpful efficient staff, and good reasonably priced bar food *(Mr and Mrs T Kenny)*; [Tanners Lane, off Hornhill Rd (signed to Bloxham) towards W end of village], *White Hart*: Old-fashioned seats, pictures, log fire and heavy beams in the small bar; has had decent food in the bar and restaurant and well kept Hook Norton, but opening became unpredictable spring 1990 and sale reported to be impending *(A T Langton, Ian Phillips, J P Cinnamond, Ian Phillips, LYM; more news please)*

Appleton [SP4401], *Plough*: Gently refurbished, with bar food (not Mon, no cooked food Tues), Morlands Bitter and Mild on handpump, live music Fri *(Joan Olivier)*

Ascott under Wychwood [SP3018], *Swan*: Stone, oak-beamed Cotswold village pub with Morrells Graduate on handpump, lunchtime bar food such as cod and home-made pasty *(John and Joan Wyatt)*

☆ Asthall [just off A40 3 miles on Oxford side of Burford; SP2811], *Maytime*: Popular up-market food pub in cosy old Cotswold-stone building with close-set tables; wide choice of dishes, reasonably priced Sun lunch, Morrells Varsity and Wadworths 6X, prompt friendly service; in tiny hamlet — views of Asthall Manor and watermeadows from big car park; bedrooms set attractively around striking courtyard *(Sidney and Erna Wells, Mr and Mrs P B Dowsett, BB)*

Bampton [Bridge St; SP3103], *Romany*: Friendly atmosphere and service, wide choice of good reasonably priced

home-cooked bar food, restaurant; good value bedrooms *(Marjorie and David Lamb)*

Banbury [Parsons St; off Market Pl; SP4540], *Reindeer*: Simple good value bar food from sandwiches through pasta to steaks, well kept Hook Norton and unobtrusive piped Radio-1 in traditional male-oriented bar of much-refurbished pub with Italian bar staff and long history; its 'gallows' inn-sign spanning street is one of only half a dozen left *(Neil Tungate, LYM)*; [Banbury Cross], *Whately Hall*: Plush hotel rather than pub, but the peaceful panelled lounge has well kept Courage Directors and Hook Norton Best and maybe bar food; also good if pricy restaurant *(Joan and Michel Hooper-Immins)*

☆ Barford St Michael [Lower St; SP4332], *George*: Rambling thatched 17th-century pub, very pretty, with modernised open-plan beamed bar, well kept Adnams, Badger Tanglefoot and Wadworths 6X, home-cooked bar food (not Mon evening), log fires, Aunt Sally, blues band Mon — the inn-sign now shows Lowell George *(LYM)*

☆ Begbroke [A34 Oxford—Woodstock; SP4613], *Royal Sun*: Clean and attractively decorated open-plan stone-built pub with good choice of reasonably priced food served very quickly, Ind Coope Burton on handpump, friendly quick service, tables out on terrace and in small garden; pleasant surroundings though on trunk road *(Mrs H A Green, Joy and Peter Heatherley)*

☆ Benson [Brook St; SU6191], *Farmers Man*: Doing well under efficient and friendly new licensees, with pleasant atmosphere, well kept Brakspears ales, good value food *(Gordon Theaker, N S Holmes)*

☆ Benson, *Three Horseshoes*: Friendly unspoilt local with well kept Brakspears and a weekly guest beer, wide choice of good value food, big garden *(Gordon Theaker, Jane and Calum Maclean)*

☆ Bix [A423; SU7285], *Fox*: Well kept creeper-clad brick pub with particularly friendly licensees, fireside armchairs in beamed and panelled carpeted lounge bar, wood-floored farmers' bar with another log fire, darts and fruit machine, good variety of hot and cold bar food from sandwiches and popular soup upwards, well kept Brakspears, picnic-table sets in good-sized garden behind, friendly dog called Henry *(Lyn and Bill Capper, Joan Olivier)*

Bletchingdon [B4027 N of Oxford; SP5017], *Blacks Head*: Very friendly and cosy village pub with well kept Halls, good value bar food inc some unusual home-cooked food and excellent sausage sandwiches; open fire *(Margaret Dyke)*

☆ Blewbury [Chapel Lane; off Nottingham Fee — narrow turning N from A417; SU5385], *Red Lion*: Well kept Brakspears real ales and bar food from sandwiches and ploughman's to salads and changing hot dishes, often highly spiced, in downland village pub with beams, quarry tiles and big log fire; tables on back lawn; children in small restaurant *(Col A H N Reade, H J Stirling, LYM)*

Bodicote [Goose Lane; off A423 S of Banbury; SP4537], *Plough*: Village pub notable for the beers it brews — BB, Boilermaker, Porter, Major and No 9; bar food, darts, dominoes, bar billiards and juke box, friendly black cat called Sid *(Matt Pringle)*

Brightwell [signed from A4130 2 miles W of Wallingford; SU5790], *Red Lion*: Friendly 14th-century low-beamed bar with big open fire, bar food inc filled baked potatoes and meat salads, tables on terrace; handy for Railway Museum, Didcot and Wittenham Clumps *(Joan Olivier)*

Broadwell [SP2503], *Five Bells*: Small but comfortable 16th-century coaching inn with lounge bar, restaurant and big garden; attentive staff, bar food *(Joan Olivier)*

☆ Burcot [SU5695], *Chequers*: Pretty black and white thatched pub with tables among roses and fruit trees on neatly kept roadside lawn; smartly comfortable lounge bar with pretty gallery, well kept real ales on handpump, good range of good value food though service can slow down on busiest lunchtimes, friendly and popular licensees; piano Fri and Sat evenings; OK for wheelchairs, parking good *(Nick Holmes, Dawn and Phil Garside, David and Diane Livesley, BB)*

☆ Burford [High St], *Bull*: Comfortable settees as well as Windsor chairs and so forth in beamed and panelled reconstructed bar with good if somewhat hotelish atmosphere and a wide range of food that's been imaginative if not cheap; well kept Ruddles Best on handpump, good choice of wines by the glass, piped music, restaurant; children welcome; open all day summer; bedrooms *(Simon Collett-Jones, George S Jonas, G and M Brooke-Williams, LYM)*

Burford [High St], *Highway*: Attractive character, good value bar food, friendly family service, restaurant Fri and Sat; good value bedrooms, with original timbers but modern facilities *(Colin and Evelyn Turner)*

Cane End [A4074 N of Reading; SU6680], *Fox*: Good choice of food such as tasty stuffed aubergines with garlic bread; separate area for drinkers *(Mr and Mrs D A P Grattan)*

Caulcott [SP5024], *Horse & Groom*: Quiet and characterful country pub with promising food *(John and Margaret Estdale)*

☆ Charlbury [SP3519], *Bell*: Small 17th-century hotel, clean and smart, with comfortable bedrooms often used by people at nearby conference centres, quiet and civilised flagstoned bar with stripped stone walls and enormous open fire, bar lunches (not Sun) inc good sandwiches, well kept Wadworths real ales, decent restaurant;

children in eating area; bedrooms *(Hope Chenhalls, Paul Harrop, R N Haygarth, LYM)*

Charlbury [Sheep St], *Bull*: Cosy, clean and smart stone-walled lounge with high-backed settles and log-effect gas fire; has had Bass and Worthington on handpump, pleasant reasonably priced wines, bar food, friendly service, but changed hands in summer 1990 *(Mike O'Driscoll)*; [Sheep St], *Farmers*: Pleasant old stone pub with good variety of places to eat, inc spacious beamed cottage room for families; delightfully presented freshly cooked pies inc vegetarian ones, good choice of puddings, generous helpings, good service; tables in courtyard *(Lady Mary Wood)*; [Market St], *White Hart*: Large stone village local with friendly welcome and relaxing atmosphere; basic bar with pews, settles, benches, stone fireplace, Adnams and Hook Norton, darts, lounge with dining area *(Mike O'Driscoll)*

☆ Chazey Heath [Woodcote Rd; A4074 Wallingford—Reading; SU6977], *Pack Horse*: Well kept and attractive old pub with big log fire in simply furnished lounge bar, well kept Gales ales and country wines, good value home-cooked bar food inc vegetarian dishes (and bargain half-shoulder of lamb if you book the day before), sizeable back garden with play area and fairy-lit barbecue terrace, family room, Shetland ponies and boxers *(B Colyer, BB)*

Chazey Heath [Woodcote Rd; as above], *Pack Saddle*: Engagingly 1950s-ish in a disjointed way, with alligator skins, African spears and masks, old rifles, Spanish bullfighting pictures, tartan-blanket carpet, nostalgic pop music, welcoming cheery atmosphere, well kept Gales ales, country wines, basic food; pool in lounge bar *(Ian Phillips, BB)*

☆ Checkendon [OS Sheet 175 map reference 666841; SU6683], *Black Horse*: Great atmosphere in truly old-fashioned unspoilt three-room free house, well kept Brakspears tapped from the cask in a back room, 1950s armchairs, friendly licensees — two elderly sisters; lunchtime opening can be erratic, antiquated gents' *(Richard Sanders, Col A H N Reade, Alison Hayward, Nick Dowson)*

Checkendon [OS Sheet 175 map reference 663829], *Four Horseshoes*: Old, thatched and beamed, with spacious lounge and bar, very welcoming atmosphere, friendly landlord, well kept Brakspears, huge helpings of good cheap food; piped music may be loud; summer barbecues *(David Warrellow)*

☆ Chipping Norton [High St; SP3127], *Crown & Cushion*: Attractively laid out bar with some stripped stone and flagstones, comfortable brocaded seats and a civilised, old-fashioned feel; bar food from sandwiches or ploughman's through omelettes to steak, well kept Donnington, Wadworths IPA and 6X and guest beers, tables in sheltered garden with sun-trap terrace, subdued piped music; bar food restricted Fri/Sat evenings; restaurant has been closed Sun lunchtime; children welcome; bedrooms *(S V Bishop, Lyn and Bill Capper, Michael and Alison Sandy, LYM)*

☆ Chipping Norton [High St], *Blue Boar*: Large, comfortable bar divided into several areas by arches and pillars, with long flagstoned conservatory behind; wide range of well priced food, Courage Directors and Marstons on handpump, good cider, pleasant atmosphere, big restaurant (organist sometimes) *(Michael and Alison Sandy, P R Davis)*

Chipping Norton, *Fox*: Good value bar food from home-made soup or big filled baked potatoes up in comfortable old rambling lounge with Hook Norton real ales, antique oak settles, open fire; upstairs restaurant (can be used for lunchtime bar food); children welcome; bedrooms *(Dave Braisted, LYM)*

Cholsey [SU5886], *Waterloo*: Good bar food under new regime — skittle alley's now a restaurant *(B Colyer)*

Claydon [SP4550], *Sun Rising*: Pleasantly run Cotswold stone pub, functionally modernised, with well kept Hook Norton; historic preserved granary nearby *(John C Baker)*

☆ **Clifton** [B4031 Deddington—Aynho; SP4831], *Duke of Cumberlands Head*: Warmly welcoming thatched stone pub with big lounge, lovely fireplace and simple furnishings; well kept real ales, good wines, friendly service, good freshly home-made bar food — familiar things with one or two more continental touches from the French landlady, cosy restaurant; ten minutes' walk from canal *(Mike O'Driscoll, Prof J C Mann, Mr and Mrs C H Stride)*

Clifton Hampden [SU5495], *Plough*: Ancient low-ceilinged thatched local, not smart inside but small and cosy, with friendly licensee, Ushers ales, bar food from sandwiches up, children's play area; said to be haunted by a benign presence that upturns empty glasses *(R C Gandy, R Houghton, BB)*

☆ **Crawley** [OS Sheet 164 map reference 341120; SP3412], *Lamb*: Splendid 18th-century pub with thick stone walls, low beams (some ornamental), heavy oak timbers and big inglenook fireplace, step up to two smaller areas for family meals; Witney Glenny and Hook Norton, Australian wines; wide choice of bar food (not Sun evening) from sandwiches through authentic Malaysian curry or Indonesian chilli beef to steak; darts, quiet pop music; teetotal landlord drives locals home for donation to charity *(Frank Cummins)*

☆ **Crays Pond** [B471 nr junction with B4526, about 3 miles E of Goring; SU6380], *White Lion*: Bar with open fire, darts and piped music, low-ceilinged lounge, attractive conservatory extension; friendly licensee, well kept real ales, wide range of well presented bar food (not Tues evening), big garden with play area *(Lyn and Bill Capper, Barbara M McHugh)*

☆ **Crowell** [B4009, 2 miles from M40 junction 6; SU7499], *Catherine Wheel*: Old brick-and-flint pub with attractive oldish furnishings inc pews and a grandfather clock; nice welcome, good service, well kept Bass and ABC, pleasant locals *(R Houghton)*

☆ **Crowmarsh** [A423; SU6189], *Queens Head*: Run by a French family, with particularly good value straightforward bar food in spacious low-beamed bar with open fires, piped music and friendly atmosphere, Watneys-related real ales on handpump,

decent wines; good French dishes in handsome galleried medieval-style restaurant, garden *(Joan Olivier, Michael Mortimer)*

Cumnor [Abingdon Rd; SP4603], *Vine*: Good reasonably priced food inc delicious salads in pretty pub with pleasant atmosphere and friendly, helpful service; nice garden *(Mr and Mrs Graham Stable)*

Cuxham [SU6695], *Half Moon*: Attractive medieval Brakspears pub with big garden, play area and pets' corner, in pretty streamside village; new licensees hoping to preserve its old character, while widening range of food to run from sandwiches to steaks (maybe even afternoon teas with all-day opening); traditional pub games; children welcome *(Joan Olivier, LYM; more reports please)*

☆ **Deddington** [off A423 (B4031) Banbury—Oxford; SP4361], *Kings Arms*: Thriving, bustling atmosphere in 16th-century inn's pleasant black-beamed stone-walled L-shaped cottage bar with prompt welcoming service, well kept Marstons Burton and Pedigree on handpump, interesting wine list, good variety of reasonably priced bar food from good sandwiches and ploughman's to substantial dishes such as pork chop with hot sauce, rabbit pie, gammon marinaded in cider and served with peaches, a variety of fish, and children's food *(Mr and Mrs D Norton, Michael Player, J Forster)*

Deddington [Oxford Rd], *Holcombe*: Friendly licensees in 17th-century inn with low-beamed stripped-stone bar, well kept Hook Norton Best and fresh, well presented bar food; bedrooms large and comfortable (triple-glazed at the front) *(P Baker)*

Denchworth [SU3891], *Fox*: Comfortable, clean and very warm thatched pub in quiet and pretty village, good, straightfoward bar food *(Mr and Mrs P B Dowsett)*

Dorchester [SU5794], *Fleur du Lys*: Attractive timbered building with friendly welcome, imaginative bar food, Brakspears and Morlands ales, morning coffee and old brick fireplace in moderate-sized bar with restaurant section; garden and car park through old coach arch *(Stan Edwards, Nigel Gibbs)*

Duns Tew [SP4528], *White Horse*: Flagstones, beams and thick stripped stone walls in former 16th-century farmhouse with two bars and well kept Courage Directors and Hook Norton *(Gwyneth and Salvo Spadaro-Dutturi)*

☆ **Enslow** [Enslow Bridge; off A4095 about 1 1/2 miles SW of Kirtlington; SP4818], *Rock of Gibraltar*: Rambling stone-built canalside pub with cosy nooks in spacious split-level bar, beams, stonework, open fire, bargee-style colourful paintwork; comfortable atmosphere, games area downstairs overlooking big garden with barbecue, Watneys-related real ales on handpump, bar food; children's adventure playground *(Mike O'Driscoll)*

☆ **Enstone** [SP3724], *Crown*: Stripped-stone beamed bar with log fire in brass-fitted stone fireplace, antique furnishings inc stone seats in latticed windows with velvet curtains; wide choice of good bar food (honest ploughman's and beef casserole recommended), attractive dining area, friendly staff, well kept Hook Norton Best and Whitbreads on handpump; good value bedrooms *(John and Karen Day, Frank Gadbois)*

☆ **Enstone** [A34 Chipping Norton--Woodstock], *Harrow*: Pleasant and friendly 16th-century inn with public bar and much refurbished lounge, real ales and ciders, efficient service, good bar food from well filled rolls through help-yourself salads to steaks *(Lyn and Bill Capper, Gordon Smith, TOH, Bernard Phillips)*

☆ **Eynsham** [Newlands St; SP4309], *Newlands*: Pleasant, friendly atmosphere in flagstoned inglenook bar with stripped early 18th-century pine panelling; good reasonably priced food inc produce from their own smokery at reasonable prices, Halls Harvest on handpump, decent wine, log fire, fairly unobtrusive piped music *(Mrs Pamela Dumenil, Edward Hibbert)*

☆ **Faringdon** [Market Pl; SU2895], *Crown*: Well kept real ales such as Hook Norton, Glenny Wychwood, Morlands and Theakstons, decent bar food, friendly staff, flagstones, panelling, varnished wooden tables and as a rule plenty of space, roaring log fires in winter and lovely courtyard for summer; children welcome; bedrooms *(Patrick Godfrey, Dr and Mrs B H Colman)*
Faringdon [Coxwell; 1 1/2 miles SW towards Swindon on A420], *Plough*: Good range of beers such as Arkells and Wadworths 6X, wide choice of good food; back restaurant; children in family extension *(P J and M L Davies)*

☆ **Fifield** [A424; SP2318], *Hunters Lodge*: Isolated but warm and friendly spacious stone inn, dating partly from 13th century, half-mile from pretty village; big helpings of bar food (lunchtime rolls and fresh chilli con carne recommended), well kept Donnington beers, tasteful refurbishments, warm welcome — especially from the dog; comfortably renovated clean bedrooms *(Joan Olivier, Dave Braisted)*
Finstock [SP3616], *Plough*: Friendly pub in small village with well kept beers, especially the Hook Norton, and consistently good food — Wed is steak night; clean and comfortable *(Sarah Bradbrook)*

☆ **Forest Hill** [SP5807], *White Horse*: Quiet and relaxed atmosphere in clean, friendly and well run village local with lots of china hanging from joists of small and simple lounge bar, dining room on left, some stripped stonework, good value bar food (cooked to order by the manageress's son, so may be delays at busy times) inc excellent filled home-baked crusty rolls (particularly popular with spicy sausages), soup with croutons, fine ploughman's, four-egg omelettes, decent main dishes from fennel baked with pasta to salmon poached with herbs, venison and steaks; particularly well kept Morrells Bitter and Varsity; tables on small terrace; handy for Oxfordshire Way path *(Margaret Dyke, Mr and Mrs P B Dowsett, TBB, Maureen Hobbs, BB)*
Fringford [SP6028], *Butchers Arms*: Remote village pub, well kept beer, food inc good pâté, friendly service, boules and seats outside *(Dr Paul Kitchener)*
Garsington [off B480 SE of Oxford;

SP5702], *Plough*: Popular Courage pub with friendly atmosphere, wide variety of fairly priced bar food, terrace and garden with play area *(Joan Olivier)*

☆ **Godstow** [SP4708], *Trout*: It's the marvellous position that makes this creeper-covered medieval pub particularly popular in summer, with a lovely terrace by a stream clear enough to watch the plump trout, and peacocks in the grounds — one of the nicest summer spots in England; extensively commercialised inside, but pleasant enough in winter, with log fires, flagstone and board floors; big snack room extension with children's area, garden bar and decent if pricey restaurant; Bass and Charrington real ale, piped music; very popular in summer — and current reports suggest that bar food value is fair enough *(Miss E Waller, Dr John Innes, R C Gandy, LYM)*
Goosey [SU3591], *Pound*: Popular in previous editions for its attractive stripped-brick bar, well kept real ales, good value bar food and character Welsh landlord; but put up for sale by Morlands summer 1990 *(News please)*
Goring [SU6080], *Miller of Mansfield*: Armchairs in large cosy bow-windowed bar, public bar on right divided from main bar by large brick fireplace with log-effect gas fire; well kept Courage Best and Directors, good bar food from sandwiches up inc good filled baked potatoes, back restaurant; children welcome *(Steve Huggins)*; [Cleeve; off B4009 about a mile towards Wallingford], *Olde Leatherne Bottle*: Overlooking a quiet stretch of the Thames from an extremely attractive unspoilt setting, this formerly unpretentious pub has now become an upmarket restaurant *(J M M Hill, LYM)*
Gosford [Gosford Hill; A43 Oxford—Bicester; SP4912], *Kings Arms*: Friendly old beamed country pub with unobtrusive piped music, modern restaurant in keeping with style; good bar food inc filled French bread, tables out on terrace *(Joan Olivier)*

☆ **Great Milton** [The Green; SP6202], *Bell*: Small, tastefully extended and really welcoming cottagey old country pub with good choice of well kept real ales inc Marstons Pedigree and Uley Old Spot, and good choice of home-made food; relaxed atmosphere and clean lavatories *(Richard Houghton, Mr and Mrs Peiffer)*
Great Milton [The Green; SP6202], *Bull*: Whitewashed 16th-century stone local with big stone fireplace in cosy lounge, warm relaxing atmosphere, well kept Morrells, some emphasis on good varied bar food from ploughman's to steaks, restaurant; public bar with darts and fruit machine *(Mike O'Driscoll, Richard Houghton)*
Hailey [Whiteoak Green; the one nr Witney; SP3414], *Bird in Hand*: Impressive renovation of an old country pub with stone walls, old beams and real log fire; moderately priced bar meals, attentive service; bedrooms *(P B Dowsett)*
Headington [London Rd; SP5407], *White Horse*: Large bars extensively and comfortably refurbished with exposed brickwork, beamery and partitions; has been praised for well kept Morrells beers,

reasonably priced bar food served all day and prompt service, but no recent reports *(News please)*

☆ Henley [Market Pl; SU7882], *Argyll*: Well run pub with long tartan-carpeted lounge, Highland pictures; popular lunchtime food (only roasts Sun), well kept Morlands ales, seats on back terrace, handy parking behind; nr GWG68 *(LYM)*

☆ Henley [Riverside], *Little White Hart*: Friendly and unpretentious, in nice spot right on the river, with good value food and well kept Brakspears; bedrooms *(Lindsey Shaw Radley, David Warrellow)*

Henley [Bell St], *Bell*: Small friendly bar, no-smoking room and dining room; well kept Brakspears, good value food inc ploughman's and roast with up to five veg; no parking *(David Young)*; [West St], *Row Barge*: Friendly atmosphere, well kept Brakspears, good value bar food, garden *(P J Woodall)*

☆ Hook Norton, *Pear Tree*: Welcoming honest village local with famously friendly licensees, open fire, two small and unpretentious bars, well kept Hook Norton ales from brewery a stroll away, freshly cut sandwiches (may not be available if busy, as it tends to be on summer weekends — though there's then plenty of room in the big garden, with a children's play area); one pleasant bedroom with shower; a beer drinker's paradise *(R A Gomme, Su and Andy Jones, Jonathan and Jane Hagger, J S Clements, Joy and Peter Heatherley)*

Islip [B4027; SP5214], *Red Lion*: Most readers find the wide choice of food, all cooked to order, well presented and good value, and report good service; Halls ales, decent wine, cosy bar with fantastic collection of drinking vessels, pleasant barn conversion behind with separate bar, skittle alley and dining area; lavatories for the disabled; garden *(H J Stephens, Robert M Deeley)*; *Swan*: Pretty country village pub, attractively refurbished, with one long bar, well kept Morrells on handpump, reasonably priced bar food, restaurant, tables outside *(Derek and Sylvia Stephenson, BB)*

Kidlington [A423 Banbury Rd; towards Thrupp; SP4914], *Wise Alderman*: Pleasant pub below road level by canal; bar food inc good filled baked potatoes, Halls beers *(Dave Braisted)*

Langford [SP2402], *Crown*: Friendly, clean and cosy pub with log fires, barrel chairs, lots of brassware, toby jugs and clay pipes; Bass and Hook Norton, over 60 whiskies, wide range of good home-made bar food from sandwiches and soup to steak and kidney pie and steaks (closed Mon lunchtimes) *(Miss M Mutch)*

Leafield [Lane End; SP3115], *Spindleberry*: Very comfortable with wide choice of beer, good bar and restaurant menus, big car park *(Mr and Mrs P B Dowsett)*

☆ Letcombe Regis [follow Village Only sign as far as possible; SU3784], *Sparrow*: Unpretentious plain village-edge pub below prehistoric Segsbury hill-fort, relaxed if sometimes rather noisy atmosphere, well kept Morlands Bitter and Mild, simple cheap lunchtime food from soup and sandwiches to fry-ups (not Sun); service may

sometimes be slow; tables, swings and climbing-frame in safely fenced garden *(L Walker, LYM)*

Lewknor [SU7198], *Old Leathern Bottle*: Lovely country pub in small village with bustling atmosphere, well kept Brakspears and good bar food, generously served, such as barbecue ribs, stir-fried chicken with oyster sauce or curry; friendly efficient service *(Roger and Lynda Pilgrim)*

Little Coxwell [A420 Oxford—Swindon; SU2793], *Plough*: Very friendly recently redecorated roadside inn with well kept beer *(Dr and Mrs A K Clarke)*

Long Hanborough [A4095; SP4214], *Bell*: Quaint furnishings with old treadle machine tables and stools like upholstered tree strumps; well kept Morrells, range of home-made wines on tap, good value bar food *(Margaret Dyke)*

☆ Long Wittenham [SU5493], *Machine Man*: Good atmosphere, friendly and welcoming landlord — after a couple of hours strangers feel like popular regulars; several changing well kept real ales, maybe home-made cider, bar food *(David Fowles, A T Langton)*

Longworth [SU3899], *Blue Boar*: Convivial, popular pub, log fires, welcoming and informal atmosphere, wide range of well prepared and generously served bar food *(Richard Fawcett)*

☆ Lower Assendon [B480; SU7484], *Golden Ball*: Excellent, unspoilt pub with well kept Brakspears, cosy and welcoming atmosphere, consistently good food inc fine home-made pies, log fire *(Richard Houghton, B H Pinsent)*

Marsh Baldon [SU5699], *Seven Stars*: Very friendly and welcoming atmosphere, good food in formidably large helpings; by green of attractive village *(Col A H N Reade)*

☆ Marston [Mill Lane, Old Marston — OS Sheet 164 map reference 520090; SP5208], *Victoria Arms*: Notable above all for its position, as its big attractive garden with good robust play area and picnic-table sets runs down to the River Cherwell, where there is a quay for punts; spacious single-floor extension with rugs on bare boards, wood and leather seats, Victorian prints and farm tools; original flagstoned and stone-built core now mainly an eating area; good range of real ales — Badger Tanglefoot and Wadworths IPA, 6X, Farmers Glory and winter Old Timer; loudish piped music, children welcome *(Joan Olivier, Ian Phillips, Edward Hibbert, Michael and Alison Sandy, Miss E Waller, BB)*

Marston [Church Lane, Old Marston; SP5208], *Bricklayers Arms*: Has emerged from enormously costly refurbishment as Victorian-style pub on several levels, with stylish hardwood furnishings and fittings, lots of pictures, glass panelling to divide room; friendly atmosphere, popular at lunchtime for wide range of standard food from sandwiches to main meals, Tetleys and Wadworths 6X on handpump, good facilities for the disabled; open all day, with afternoon teas *(Joan Olivier)*

☆ Middle Barton [SP4325], *Carpenters Arms*: Colour-washed, thatched village inn with open-plan bar, well kept Halls Harvest on handpump, friendly and obliging staff, good choice of reasonably priced lunchtime food served generously; bedrooms *(John and Joan Wyatt)*

Middleton Stoney [SP5323], *Jersey Arms*: Old inn with big log fires and good food in friendly beamed and panelled bar and restaurant; bedrooms large and well furnished, one with four-poster *(Henry Midwinter)*

Milton [the one nr Didcot; SU4892], *Admiral Benbow*: Small friendly pub with friendly and obliging new licensees, well kept Morrells ales, reasonably priced simple bar food, quiet atmosphere; garden; by entrance to 17th-century Manor (open Sun afternoons Easter—Oct) *(A T Langton)*

Minster Lovell [B4070 Witney—Burford; SP3111], *White Hart*: Cotswold stone pub with large, attractively laid-out beamed bar, settles, comfortable chairs, hanging plates; polite welcome, good service, Courage Directors and Best, attractive food from ploughman's up; has been open all day *(Mike O'Driscoll)*

☆ **Murcott** [SP5815], *Nut Tree*: Immaculate white thatched pub with duckpond and interesting garden; particularly good range of drinks from Glenny Wychwood Best and a guest such as Burton Bridge kept under light carbon dioxide blanket to worthwhile whiskies and wines, welcoming service, good if not cheap bar food — particularly magnificent sandwiches and Scotch steaks *(Joan Olivier, Mr and Mrs G Sparrow, Charles Gurney, Sir Nigel Foulkes, LYM)*

Nettlebed [High St; SU6986], *Bull*: Low-beamed carpeted bar with unobtrusive piped music, wide choice of food from ploughman's up inc children's helpings, log fire, no fruit machine or darts, log fire; interesting memorabilia, well kept Brakspears, folk club Mon; restaurant; bedrooms *(Lyn and Bill Capper)*

Newbridge [A415 7 miles S of Witney; SP4101], *Maybush*: Low-beamed bar in small, unassuming Thames-side Morlands pub with waterside terrace and moorings; good local atmosphere, good range of decent bar food, cheerful efficient service; can be smoky *(David Young, Gordon Theaker)*

Northmoor [off A415; SP4202], *Dun Cow*: Simple little family-run pub with lovely gardens *(Dr and Mrs A K Clarke)*

☆ **Nuffield** [SU6687], *Crown*: Doing well after recent renovation, with lots of character, good reasonably priced food, well kept Brakspears, roaring winter log fires *(D Mackay, P M Johnson, Jane and Calum Maclean)*

Osney [Bridge St; SP5005], *Hollybush*: Well run pub with cosy lounge bar, separate panelled room and restaurant; fresh flowers, unobtrusive music, Courage Best and Directors, bar food, occasional live music; children welcome *(Jonathan Long)*; *Watermans Arms*: Useful for boat users — they let you take glasses outside *(RCL)*

☆ **Oxford** [Alfred St], *Bear*: A lot of atmosphere packed into this series of three little low-ceilinged and partly panelled rooms — as are over 7,000 ties (and it sometimes seems almost as many tourists, not to mention the students); student-priced home-made bar food such as sandwiches, omelettes and steak and kidney pie, well kept Ind Coope Burton and Tetleys from

centenarian porcelain handpumps on pewter-topped counter, tables outside; open all day summer *(A J Young, Wayne Brindle, Steve and Carolyn Harvey, Ian Phillips, Simon Collett-Jones, Dr John Innes, LYM — more news of this nice pub please)*

☆ **Oxford** [St Giles], *Eagle & Child*: Long and narrow pub, attractively refurbished, and doing well under new licensees; two four-person panelled snugs either side of the entrance, each with its own fireplace; further tiny area on right just before bar (itself small); modern extension beyond bar with open ceiling joists, leading to no-smoking conservatory and finally a small, pretty terrace; tends to feel least cramped early in the week, and much enjoyed by readers for its friendly old-fashioned feel, also simple, well prepared and reasonably priced basic bar food such as good doorstep sandwiches, pizzas and filled baked potatoes; well kept Ansells, Halls Harvest and Wadworths 6X on handpump, piped classical music, newspapers provided *(P L Knight, Dr and Mrs A K Clarke, Ian Phillips, RCL, Dr John Innes, BB)*

☆ **Oxford** [Holywell St], *Kings Arms*: A student favourite, very full and lively in term-time; large and basic, with one main room (quite warehousey), two more comfortable and smaller ones at the back, no-smoking room just inside the Parks Rd entrance; good range of well kept real ales, coffee, dictionary provided for crossword buffs, decent bar food — no attempt to hurry you *(RCL, Liz and Ian Phillips, D L Evans)*

☆ **Oxford** [Binsey Lane; narrow lane on right leaving city on A420, just before Bishops Depository], *Perch*: Spacious thatched pub fronted by lovely riverside meadows, under new licensee; bare stone walls, flagstones, high-backed settles as well as more modern seats, log fires, bar food, Arkells, Wadworths 6X and Allied real ales (drinks not cheap); big garden, play area, landing stage; piped music may be loud; no dogs; children allowed in eating area *(Mrs Lili Lomas, Joan Olivier; more reports on new regime please)*

☆ **Oxford** [North Parade], *Rose & Crown*: Small unspoilt traditional pub with authentic Oxford feel, but hospitable and not too studenty; bar food from toasted sandwiches to exotic food with middle eastern specialities, well kept Halls and Ind Coope Burton; character landlord, plenty of reference books for crossword buffs *(Michael Quine, Richard Messer, RCL)*

☆ **Oxford** [Broad St], *White Horse*: Small, busy one-roomed pub below street level, sandwiched between parts of Blackwells bookshop; lots of signed local team photographs, oars on exposed beams, other nick-nacks, well kept real ales, reasonable bar food, oak furniture *(Dr John Innes, Wayne Brindle, BB)*

Oxford [Water Eaton Rd], *Cherwell*: Open-plan even rather clinical decor in new pub replacing one demolished, very relaxed slightly up-market atmosphere; pleasant young staff, interesting bar food inc Yorkshire-pudding style pizzas in winter, vegetarian quiches in summer; upstairs restaurant in tasteful blue; overlooks riverside meadow *(Tim Brierly)*; [39 Plantation Rd — first left after Horse & Jockey going N up Woodstock Rd], *Gardeners Arms*: Friendly open-plan pub with mock beams, old local photographs, antique plates and brasses, simple wooden furnishings, home-made bar food, garden room; Morrells real ales, darts, dominoes *(G C Saunders, LYM)*; [Friars Entry], *Gloucester Arms*: Just behind Oxford Playhouse, lots of theatrical photographs; snugs, nooks, nice atmosphere, coal-effect gas fires, cheapish food, rather loud piped music *(Anon)*; *Head of the River*: Civilised well renovated pub close to the river, can get touristy *(Wayne Brindle)*; [off High St], *Wheatsheaf*: Traditional pub with friendly staff, well kept Morrells on handpump, moderately priced lunchtime food in undergraduate quantities *(R A Gomme)*; [272 Woodstock Rd], *Woodstock Arms*: Quiet, neat little lounge, bar with bar billiards and fruit machines, not usually too crowded, even at busy times; obliging service, Morrells beer and good value, simple bar food; garden *(Mike O'Driscoll)*

☆ Play Hatch [Foxhill Lane; SU7476], *Shoulder of Mutton*: Unspoilt little country pub with old-fashioned roses, a real well, horses in the meadows beyond; a lovely oak settle sits at right angles to the well-used fire, friendly locals, Courage beers; we've not yet had reports on the new regime here *(Ian Phillips, Sheila Keene; news please)*

Pyrton [SU6896], *Plough*: Modest local in small village with real ales such as Adnams and Fullers, good carefully presented food, open fire, friendly civilised service, quiet atmosphere, unobtrusive piped music *(Marjorie and David Lamb)*

☆ Radcot [Radcot Bridge; A4095 2 1/2 miles N of Faringdon; SU2899], *Swan*: Unpretentious inn, delightful in summer for its riverside lawn, with Thames boat trips from pub's camping-ground opposite — the boat has a powered platform to bring wheelchairs aboard; well kept Morlands Bitter, Best and Mild, log fire, straightforward food, piped pop music, pub games; children in eating area; bedrooms clean and good value, with hearty traditional breakfast *(PBD, LYM)*

Rotherfield Peppard [Gallowstree Rd; SU7181], *Greyhound*: Charming old beamed pub with splendid tubs and baskets of flowers; nicely and simply restored, with collections of walking sticks, milk jugs, old plates and pictures; delicious home-made dish of day like pheasant casserole, Wethereds beers; tables in garden *(Geoffrey Medcalf, Richard Purser)*

☆ Russells Water [up track past duck pond; village signposted from B481 S of junction with B480; SU7089], *Beehive*: Old-world pub doing well under current regime, with interesting decor and furnishings, big woodburning stove in inglenook, subdued red lighting, well kept Brakspears, Flowers Original, Marstons Pedigree and Wadworths 6X, good home-made food inc imaginative dishes (not Sun evening or Mon), pleasant staff; tables on rose-fringed terrace or under fairy-lit arbour, restaurant; children in family room *(Mr and Mrs G A Evans, Mr and Mrs Graham Dyer, Tony and Lynne Stark, RH, LYM)*

☆ Satwell [just off B481, 2 miles S of Nettlebed; follow Shepherds Green signpost; SU7083], *Lamb*: Sensitively refurbished 16th-century low-beamed farm cottage with tiled floors, friendly licensees, huge log fireplace, well kept Brakspears, traditional games, bar food from sandwiches up *(Joan Olivier, LYM)*

Shilton [SP2608], *Rose & Crown*: Friendly low-beamed 14th-century Cotswold stone pub with decent straightforward bar food from sandwiches to steaks, Courage beers (not cheap), piped music, fruit machine, darts, small garden; close to Cotswold Wildlife Park *(Joan Olivier)*

☆ Shiplake [A4155 towards Play Hatch and Reading — OS Sheet 175 map reference 746768; SU7476], *Flowing Spring*: Well kept Fullers ales and decent bar food from sandwiches and baked potatoes to attractively priced evening dishes such as beef and basil lasagne, in three cosy but unpretentious rooms of friendly, multi-level, countrified pub with open fires and floor-to-ceiling windows overlooking the water meadows; aristocratic black cat, big attractive garden, occasional jazz and Morris dancing *(John Hayward, Ian Phillips, LYM)*

Shrivenham [SU2388], *Prince of Wales*: Pleasant, relaxing atmosphere; maybe Morris dancers *(Ewan McCall, Roger Huggins, Tom McLean)*

☆ Sibford Gower [SP3537], *Wykham Arms*: Impressive reasonably priced food such as shark steak, pheasant, venison, chicken rolled with prawns, in recently rethatched free house with low-beamed lounge (one table formed by glass over old deep well) and smaller bar; well kept Hook Norton, Flowers and Fremlins, decent wines, welcoming landlord and staff; small lawn with tables, slide and swings *(Sir Nigel Foulkes, Su Jones, Joy and Peter Heatherley)*

☆ Sonning Common [Blounts Court Rd; just off B481 Reading—Nettlebed, NE of centre; SU7080], *Butchers Arms*: Leon Banks, who laid down such a successful formula for the Old Crown at Skirmett (Bucks) and then brought his warm personality and adventurous approach to good value food to this 1930s pub, has now moved on — to the Red Lion at Chelwood Gate in Sussex; but this is still well worth knowing for its garden, well equipped for families; Brakspears real ales, bar food, restaurant; bedrooms *(LYM)*

☆ Souldern [SP5131], *Fox*: Delightful Cotswold stone pub with Flowers, Hook Norton and Sam Smiths real ales, good value bar food, particularly good friendly German landlady — her schnitzel is as good as any found by one reader in three years stationed in W Germany; comfortable bedrooms, good breakfasts *(Roy Bamford, Rich and Leslie Smith)*

Stanton St John [B4027 skirting village; SP5709], *George*: Attractive Cotswold stone village pub, well kept Marstons Pedigree and Burton on handpump, friendly landlord and customers, lunchtime bar food from good sandwiches up; big garden *(Anon)*

☆ Steventon [The Causeway; central westward turn off main rd — village signed off A34;

SU4691], *North Star*: Attractive unspoilt pub, tiled passage leading to main bar with built-in settles forming snug, steam-engine pictures, interesting local horsebrasses; open fire in parlourish lounge, simple dining room; Morlands Mild, Bitter and Best straight from casks in a side tap room, cheap weekday lunchtime bar food, cribbage; tables on side grass *(Gordon and Daphne, LYM)*

☆ **Steventon**, *Cherry Tree*: Seven well kept ales inc Hook Norton, Wadworths IPA and 6X, good value quickly served straightforward food, pleasant beams-and-brickwork decor; piped pop music can be intrusive *(John Tyzack, M Morgan, H and P Jeffery)*

Steventon, *Fox*: Good atmosphere and food in well kept pub, doing well under current regime *(A T Langton)*

Stoke Row [Kingwood Common; 1 mile S of Stoke Row, signposted Peppard and Reading — OS Sheet 175 map reference 692825; SU6784], *Grouse & Claret*: Attractive if by no means cheap free house in nice setting, with several cosy and intimate nooks; well kept Morlands Best, Ruddles County, bar food, attentive service; piped music *(Sheila Keene, ND)*

☆ **Stonor** [SU7388], *Stonor Arms*: Carefully refurbished upmarket village pub with flagstoned bar, open log fires and good bar food inc onion and thyme soup, excellent rare beef, more sophisticated dishes, and puddings such as sponge with chocolate sauce; bedrooms *(Harry Stirling, Lyn and Bill Capper)*

☆ **Sutton Courtenay** [Appleford Rd (B4016); SU5093], *Fish*: Tastefully modernised pub with award-winning young chef-patron — limited choice of particularly good imaginative food with quality fresh ingredients and upmarket leanings (priced to match — but good value considering the quality); well kept Morlands and other beers, good wines; only booked restaurant meals Sun lunchtime *(A T Langton, Mrs S Boreham)*

Tackley [SP4720], *Gardiners Arms*: Popular pub with good atmosphere, friendly and chatty staff; public bar with darts and piped pop music (can be loud), lounge bar comfortably carpeted with settles, chairs, coal-effect gas fire, brasses on wall; well kept Allied real ales, efficiently served well presented good value bar food inc bargain two-course steak meal with wine Sun—Thurs; a few picnic-table sets on grass by car park; handy for Rousham House *(Lyn and Bill Capper, Joan Olivier, Margaret and Douglas Tucker, Tim Brierly)*

☆ **Thame** [Cornmarket; SP7005], *Abingdon Arms*: Self-effacing little pub with bare brickwork, old beams, open fireplace, nicely polished tables and truly warm welcome; newspapers and magazines in rack, chatting locals, Adnams and Theakstons real ales and good collection of bottled beers; bar food inc good seafood platter, fine doorstep sandwiches, filled baked potatoes, good main dishes with al dente vegetables *(Ian Phillips, Patrick Godfrey)*

Thame [High St], *Rising Sun*: Good choice of food in big helpings, friendly welcome, well kept Marstons and Wadworths, lively atmosphere *(Patrick Godfrey)*

☆ **Thrupp** [SP4815], *Boat*: Friendly canalside local with Morrells ales, good bar snacks, bar billiards, pleasant surroundings, garden; can get busy *(TRA, MA, Comus Elliott)*

Thrupp, *Jolly Boatman*: Pleasant canalside local *(Comus Elliott)*

Tiddington [SP6504], *Fox*: Neat and attractive low-beamed stone-walled pub, large softly lit comfortable lounge with big fire; lively and friendly atmosphere, efficient service, well kept Allied real ales, good standard bar food, closely attentive service *(Mike O'Driscoll, Gwen and Peter Andrews)*

Toot Baldon [village signed from A423 at Nuneham Courtenay, and B480; SP5600], *Crown*: Friendly village pub, popular at lunchtime for good food — the pudding called toot sweet is splendid; benches and tables out on terrace *(Marjorie and David Lamb)*

Towersey [Chinnor Rd; SP7304], *Three Horseshoes*: Flagstones, old-fashioned furnishings and good log fire make for a warm country atmosphere; well kept ABC real ale with a guest such as Beechwood, bar food, piped music, small restaurant, function room in medieval barn; biggish garden with playthings among fruit trees; children allowed at lunchtime *(LYM)*

Uffington [SU3089], *Fox & Hounds*: Limited space in small two-roomed local with beams and brasses; good atmosphere, friendly jack russell, wide choice of hot and cold bar food at reasonable prices; picnic-table sets outside *(Lyn and Bill Capper)*

☆ **Wantage** [Mill St; past square and Bell, down hill then bend to left; SU4087], *Lamb*: Friendly and snugly comfortable family-run low-beamed and timbered pub with choice of attractively furnished seating areas, well kept Morlands, popular nicely presented freshly cooked bar food, good play area *(Stuart Ballantyne, Barbara M McHugh, LYM)*

Wantage [87 Grove St, just off mkt sq], *Abingdon Arms*: Friendly atmosphere, traditional bar games, well kept Morlands, hot and cold bar food, garden *(David Gass)*

☆ **Warborough** [The Green South; just E of A329, 4 miles N of Wallingford; SU5993], *Six Bells*: Low-ceilinged thatched pub with particularly well kept Brakspears, country furnishings, big fireplace, antique photographs and pictures, fairly priced good simple bar food; tables in back orchard, cricket green in front, boules in summer; children in eating area *(Pat Jones, LYM)*

Warborough [A329], *Cricketers*: Friendly comfortably modernised old village local, well kept Morlands on handpump, welcoming landlord *(Michael Mortimer)*

Wendlebury [signposted from A421 Oxford—Bicester; SP5619], *Red Lion*: Old stone building with low beams, oak parquet floor, reasonably priced bar food from fresh sandwiches up, inc basket meals and children's dishes; games room with pool table and fruit machine; garden with play area, animal sculptures and maybe a peacock; big car park *(Joan Olivier)*

☆ **West Hendred** [Reading Rd; off A417 — OS Sheet 174 map reference 447891; SU4488], *Hare*: Well kept Morlands in two-bar local with good welcome for strangers, popular bar food inc good sandwiches, soups, burgers and specials *(A T Langton, Sarah Bradbrook)*

☆ **Woodstock** [Market St; SP4416], *Feathers*: Traditional hotel with beautiful period furniture of all ages; stuffed birds, fish, watercolours and oils on walls — all of bygone days; food in sedate older-fashioned garden bar interesting, well priced and worth waiting for (smoked goose, game terrine, baked ham, salads all recommended); busy at lunchtime, with tourists and locals; bedrooms *(G and M Brooke-Williams)*

Woodstock [Park St], *Bear*: Handsome, atmospheric and comfortable partly medieval market-town hotel; well kept real ales, civilised bar food, expert service; good if not cheap bedrooms *(Comus Elliott)*; [A34 leading out], *Black Prince*: Good atmosphere, well kept beer inc mind-crippling strong ales, and prompt food service — not cheap, but good range inc ploughman's and Mexican dishes, and helpings plentiful *(B D Gibbs, PLC)*; *Punch Bowl*: Comfortable small-town pub with well kept Wadworths 6X and good food inc some interesting dishes *(Jason Caulkin)*; *Woodstock Arms*: Friendly service, reasonably priced simple bar food, lots of artificial flowers; bedrooms *(Syd and Wyn Donald)*

☆ **Woolstone** [SU2987], *White Horse*: Picturesque partly thatched 16th-century pub in lovely isolated spot, concentrating on quick food service now; two big open fires in spacious beamed and partly panelled bar, well kept Arkells BB, Morrells Varsity and Wadworths 6X on handpump, children allowed in side eating area; restaurant, clean lavatories; now has four bedrooms *(HNJ, PEJ, M J Dyke, Henry Midwinter, T Galligan)*

☆ **Wroxton** [Church St; off A422 at hotel — pub at back of village; SP4142], *North Arms*: Thatched stone pub in lovely village, with attractive sheltered garden, simple, comfortable modernised lounge and dining area; recently taken over by Banks's and then sold by them to Morrells — after an uncertain start it's now doing very promisingly under a friendly new young tenant/chef and his bride; good value wholesome bar food such as home-made goulash, evening restaurant; well kept Morrells Graduate on handpump, darts, dominoes, quiz evenings, summer folk music; the grounds of Wroxton College opposite make a beautiful pre-lunch walk *(Paul Corbett, I R Hewitt, Miss L Y Taylor)*

Wroxton [A422 2 miles W], *New Inn*: Long, spacious bar with central log fire, exposed stone at either end, friendly staff, bar food (or Sun lunch) in dining area *(Paul Corbett)*

Shropshire

The county's landlords and landladies seem to put that little extra into running their pubs, that brings a combination of friendliness, comfortably clean surroundings and smooth service. Pubs currently doing particularly well here include the ancient Royal Oak at Cardington (good atmosphere), the Woodbridge at Coalport (lovely Severnside position – a new main entry), the Sun at Clun (promising new chef), the Stables at Hope (good food in one of the most attractive pubs in the Marches), the pleasantly laid out Crown at Hopton Wafers, the Green Dragon at Little Stretton, the civilised Talbot in Much Wenlock (good food; the unassuming George & Dragon there has decent food, too), the delightful family-run Wenlock Edge Inn on Wenlock Edge (its combination of good food and charming surroundings and atmosphere wins it a star award this year), the canalside Willey Moor Lock near Whitchurch (increasingly popular for food) and the Plough at Wistanstow (besides particularly good beer brewed here, it gains a food award this year). The New Inn at Ironbridge deserves a special mention; this quaint new entry is actually a part of the Blists Hill open air museum – well worth a visit as a working re-creation of a late 19th-century industrial community. Notably promising entries among the Lucky Dips at the end of the chapter include the Feathers at Brockton, Pheasant at Linley, Red Lion at Llanfair Waterdine, Blacksmiths Arms at Loppington, Wheatsheaf in Ludlow, Gaskell Arms in Much Wenlock, Bell at Tong and Old Town Hall Vaults in Whitchurch; Shrewsbury has a good clutch of decent pubs. Pub prices in the area are quite low, with food generally good value (snack bargains at the Hollyhead in Bridgnorth, the Royal Oak at Cardington and the Ragleth at Little Stretton; notably cheap main dishes in the Lion of Morfe at Upper Farmcote and, as we've said, the Willey Moor Lock); the Three Tuns in Bishops Castle, brewing its own beers in a striking Victorian tower brewery, stands out for cheap drinks, but drinks prices in the county's free houses are generally a few pence lower than the national average – and than in pubs here tied to the national brewing combines.

BISHOPS CASTLE SO3289 Map 6
Three Tuns

Salop Street

The many-storied Victorian brick brewhouse across the yard from this unspoilt and family run pub is unique among pub breweries for its traditional tower layout, with the various stages of the brewing process descending floor by floor (it's a Grade I listed building). From it comes the XXX Bitter, Mild, and an old-fashioned dark somewhat stoutish ale called Steamer; brewery tours can be arranged. The quaint public bar has a welcoming atmosphere, and home-made bar food includes soup (£1.25), baps, filled baked potatoes (from £1.25), hot beef and ham in French bread (£2.50), ploughman's or burger (from £2.50), ratatouille and cheese, chilli con carne and pitta bread or cottage pie (£2.85), lasagne (£3.75), steaks (from £7.60), and puddings such as fruit crumble, treacle tart or carrot cake (from £1.20). Hall's and Weston's ciders; malt whiskies. Darts, shove-ha'penny, dominoes and cribbage. There's a garden and terrace, with a large selection of plants for sale. (Recommended by TOH, Dave Braisted, J Penford, Sue Holland, Dave Webster, Nick Dowson, Alison Hayward, Richard and Dilys Smith, BHP, Gwen and Peter Andrews)

Own brew   Licensee Jack Wood   Real ale   Meals and snacks   Children welcome Open 11.30–2.30, 6.30–11; 11.50–5, 6.30–11 summer Fri, Sat and Bank Hols

BRIDGNORTH   SO7293   Map 4

Hollyhead 🏠

Hollybush Road; opposite station

For 200 years this cheerful and unassumingly well kept pub has been a licensed house. The rambling, alcovy lounge has several areas with one or two hunting prints, swirly-plastered timbered walls, oak beams and joists, and logs burning in the big stone fireplace; by the counter there are low chunky elm tables, with high-backed modern winged settles and wheelback chairs around sturdy dining tables elsewhere. A separate, similarly furnished but smaller bar on the left has darts, dominoes, fruit machine and piped music. Simple good value bar food includes filled rolls (70p), home-made chilli con carne (£2.95), plaice or vegetarian lasagne (£3.25), home-made steak and kidney pie (£3.45), gammon steak (£4.95), sirloin steak (£5.95), with children's dishes (£1.50); they do new potatoes as an alternative to chips. Well kept Courage Best and Hook Norton Best on handpump, with regular changing guest beers like Marstons Pedigree, Timothy Taylors Landlord and Wadworths 6X; friendly, attentive service. There are tables under cocktail parasols in a suntrap roadside courtyard, as well as brown-painted slatted railway benches – appropriate enough, with the headquarters of the Severn Valley steam railway across the road. Breakfasts are good. (Recommended by G B Pugh, W H Bland, G M K Donkin)

Free house   Licensees David Wilson and Steven Mellish   Real ale   Meals and snacks (12–2, 5.30–9)   Restaurant   Children in eating area of bar   Mon night disco   Open 12–2.30, 5.30–11; 11–11 Sat   Bedrooms tel Bridgnorth (0746) 762162; £16/£28

CARDINGTON   SO5095   Map 4

Royal Oak

Village signposted off B4371 Church Stretton–Much Wenlock, pub behind church; also reached via narrow lanes from A49

Very much a focus for the village, this ancient pub has people arriving by foot and horse, as well as car. There are rambling corners, gold plush, red leatherette and tapestry seats solidly capped in elm, low beams, old standing timbers of a knocked-through wall, hops draped along the bar gantry, and a vast inglenook fireplace with its roaring winter log fire, cauldron, black kettle and pewter jugs. Good value, home-made lunchtime bar food includes soup (£1.50), sandwiches (£1.30, toasties £2), ploughman's (£2.50) and at least seven dishes – served without vegetables – such as macaroni cheese (£2), meaty or vegetarian lasagne (£2.60), and steak and kidney or fidget pie or quiche (£2.80), with evening dishes like chicken curry or chilli con carne (£3.60), scampi (£4.50), gammon and egg (£5.25), and rump steak (£5.85); no chips at lunchtime. Well kept Marstons Pedigree and Wadworths 6X on handpump, with Bass and Springfield, also on handpump, kept under light blanket pressure. Besides darts, dominoes and cribbage in the main bar, a brightly lit upstairs room has pool, a fruit machine, space game, and juke box. Tables beside roses in the front court look over to hilly fields, and a mile or so away, from the track past Willstone (ask for directions at the pub), you can walk up Caer Caradoc Hill which has magnificent views. (Recommended by Helen and Wal Burns, Mike and Wendy Proctor, M Box, A G Roby, G T Jones, Paul McPherson, Gordon Mott, James and Marion Seeley)

Free house   Licensee John Seymour   Real ale   Meals and snacks (12–2, 7–8.30) Children welcome lunchtime; only if eating in evening   Open 12–2.30, 7–11; closed Mon lunchtime Nov–March excluding school hols   One self-contained double bedroom tel Longville (069 43) 266; £19.50S/£29.50S

COALPORT SJ7002 Map 4
Woodbridge

Turn off A442 S of Telford at Coalport 1/2, Broseley 3 signpost

In a gorgeous spot above the River Severn, this tall building looks down over well spaced rustic benches on steepish waterside lawns to the ash woods on the opposite bank. The softly lit main bar has some carpeting on its quarry tiles, a big red cloth bow window seat for the view, and plenty of other seats below its joists and beams – which are hung liberally with copper and brass bygones. There are Victorian prints, stuffed birds, old bottles and china, lots of modern brass wall clocks, and a snug low-raftered back area with bookshelves and a coal fire. A simple little side bar has the same view, as do the many tables on a side terrace, with a barbecue. Decent bar food at lunchtime includes soup (£1), burger or hot dog (£1), sandwiches (from £1.15), ploughman's (£2.50), a cold table (£3), chilli con carne (£3.50), steak and kidney pie (£4) and daily specials (around £3.50), with evening dishes like pizza (£2.50), scampi (£3.50), home-made pies (£4), and good steaks; Courage Directors on handpump; darts, fruit machine, rather loud piped pop music. An indication of the pub's age is that the present elegant bridge – of iron, not wood – dates back nearly 200 years. *(Recommended by Comus Elliott, G M K Donkin, J Penford, TOH)*

Courage Licensee Sean Brennan Real ale Meals and snacks Open 11.30–3, 6–11; all day Sat in summer Restaurant (not Sun evening) Children welcome Bedrooms tel *Telford (0952) 882054; £15/£30*

CLUN SO3081 Map 6
Sun

High Street; B4368 towards Clunton

In a quiet village, this small Tudor local has a lounge bar – opening on to a sheltered back terrace with tables among pots of geraniums and other flowers – with beams, sturdy wall timbers, some attractive old tables, one or two high-backed winged settles, built-in cushioned wall benches, a carved antique oak armchair, and hop bines around the beams. The L-shaped public bar has traditional settles on its flagstones, an enormous open fire, and dominoes, cribbage, chess, backgammon and tippet; there's a friendly Scotty dog (not always around). As we went to press, a new chef was just about to start working here and hopes to do specials such as chicken breast stuffed with peaches with a brandy and cream sauce, gammon with an orange and lemon sauce and vegetarian cashew nut paella or Mexican bean pot (from around £5.50), as well as more straightforward food likes sandwiches (from £1), home-made soup (£1.50), garlic and herb mushrooms (£2.50), and lasagne, scampi, plaice and so forth. Well kept Banks's Bitter and Mild and Woods Special on handpump. *(Recommended by David Fowles, Colin Laffan, Caroline and Colin, Sue Holland, Dave Webster, Nick Dowson, Alison Hayward, Ninka Sharland)*

Free house Licensee Keith Small Real ale Meals and snacks Restaurant Children in eating area of bar Open 11–3 (4 Sat), 6–11 Bedrooms tel *Clun (058 84) 277; £18/£34(£36B)*

HOPE SJ3401 Map 6
Stables ⊘

Drury Lane, Hopesgate; pub signposted off A488 S of Minsterley, at the Bentlawnt 3/4, Leigh 1 3/4 signpost – then take first right turn

A delightful little cottagey pub with a particularly homely atmosphere and set in utterly unspoilt countryside above the Hope Valley. The black-beamed L-shaped bar, with logs burning in the imposing stone fireplace, has hunting prints of varying ages and degrees of solemnity, well chosen china, and comfortably cushioned or well polished wooden seats around attractive oak and other tables; in a back room (with copper-topped cask tables) are some big prints of butterflies and herbs. Promptly served, the lunchtime home-made bar food changes day by day, with filled rolls (from £1), excellent soup (£1.20), a mixture of local cheeses and salad (£2.75), smoked salmon quiche (£3.20), good stilton and mushroom crumble (£3.95), and venison, red wine and mushroom casserole (£5); evening dishes such as smoked chicken and walnut salad or mushrooms in cream, cheese and nutmeg (£2.50), minted lamb and almonds on rice (£3.90), fresh dressed Cromer crab salad (£4.20), spicy tandoori chicken (£4.50), and fresh poached salmon with a light cucumber sauce (£6.25), with good puddings like ginger and orange log, bread and butter pudding or yoghurt and blackcurrant cream (£1.50); vegetables are fresh. On Thursday to Saturday evenings, the cottagey dining room is open (only four tables, so booking's worth while). Well kept Ansells Dark Mild, Ind Coope Burton, Marstons Pedigree, and Woods Special on handpump, with farm ciders in summer, decent wines and spirits (they do a good kir, buck's fizz or black velvet, and Pimms), and half-a-dozen malt whiskies. On summer Sunday evenings when they have a boules knock-out they do barbecues with fresh sardines, grilled prawns and leg of lamb with fresh herbs and garlic; darts, shove-ha'penny, cribbage, dominoes; several cats (Winge is the characterful ginger tom) and Corrie and Kelly the gruffly friendly mother-and-daughter cream-coloured labradors. There's a lovely view from the front tables, over rolling pastures to the Long Mountain; behind, you look over the Hope Valley to the Stiperstones. A good place to take children at lunchtime. *(Recommended by Andrew Stephenson, R C Morgan, A G Roby, Frank Cummins)*

Free house   Licensees Denis and Debbie Harding   Real ale   Meals and snacks (12–1.30, 7–8.30; not Mon)   Restaurant tel Worthen (0743) 891344   Children welcome lunchtime   Open 11–2.30, 7–11; closed Mon

HOPTON WAFERS   SO6476 Map 4

Crown 🍴 ⊘

A4117

The courteous staff go out of their way to make visitors feel welcome in this substantial and attractive creeper-covered stone building. The spreading bar has a variety of furnishings that include flowery cushions on the black settles, silver band instruments hanging from the beams, oil paintings, fresh flowers, and a large inglenook fire as well as a woodburning stove; unobtrusive piped music. Bar food includes sandwiches (from £1.25, open sandwich with egg and prawns £3.95), soup (£1.50), ploughman's (from £2.50), mushrooms with stilton and cream (£2.65), cauliflower cheese topped with diced bacon (£2.95), salads (from £3.50), lambs liver, bacon and onion casserole (£3.95), chicken curry (£4.25), steak and kidney pie (£4.50), seafood gratin (£4.95), sirloin steak (£7.50), and puddings like hot syrup sponge or lemon cheesecake (from £1.35); specials such as sautéed black pudding with an apple and mustard sauce (£3.75) or supreme of Wye salmon with orange butter (£5.45), and children's dishes (£1.95); it does get very busy. Well kept Flowers Original, Jolly Roger Severn Bore, Marstons Pedigree and Woods Bitter on handpump. There are tables under cocktail parasols on the terraces and in the streamside garden, with plenty of tubs of bright flowers; also, an adventure playground. *(Recommended by PLC, C J McFeeters, W H Bland, Mrs Joy Davis, Stephen and Alison Parker, Brian Jordan, R C Parker, Mrs P Moran, Martin Oxley, Mr and Mrs E J Rees, Ninka Sharland)*

Free house   Licensees Howard and Polly Hill-Lines   Real ale   Meals and snacks (12–2, 7–10)   Restaurant   Children in eating area of bar   Open 11–3, 6–11 Bedrooms tel Cleobury Mortimer (0299) 270372; £35B/£42B

IRONBRIDGE   SJ6903 Map 4

New Inn

Blists Hill Museum: follow brown museum signs from M54 exit 4, or A442; then Blists Hill itself signposted

Where else can you still get a pint of Bitter for tuppence-ha'penny? This is a real pub, formerly in Walsall and moved here with other late Victorian buildings to make up a most unusual open-air museum – a whole working community that reproduces life a century or so ago (see the Northumbria chapter for the other example, up at Beamish). Obviously – the museum entrance fee is £4.50, or £6 to include several other museums in the area – you wouldn't come here only for the pub, but the whole site makes an appealing half-day visit, with shops, all sorts of working tradesmen (tinsmith, cobbler, blacksmith, candlemaker among others), sawmill, ironworks, tileworks and so forth. From most you can buy things, using either modern money or Victorian pricing and money exchanged at the bank. The tradesmen and 'inhabitants' wear period clothes, and explain what they're doing. The pub is a little red-brick corner building, very simple inside – gas lamps, shiny black and brown paint, sawdust on the floorboards, rows of pewter and china tankards, and virtually no ornamentation beyond a few period advertisements; well kept Springfield Bitter and Highgate Mild on handpump, and Bulmer's cider; shove-ha'penny, alley skittles and table skittles. Upstairs is a decorous club room, serving teas and snacks including excellent sandwiches, filled baked potatoes, ploughman's, good pasties from the antique bakery, salads, lasagne or chicken in white wine sauce (from £1 to £3.50). The back yard has some slatted old benches with appropriate noises off – the muted clatter of nearby iron and tin working, burbles from the pigeon coop, and the excitement of the hens when one of the white-costumed girls from the pub comes out to fling some greens over the wire. Even the lavatories have period fittings. (*Recommended by Patrick and Mary McDermott, Mrs Y M Healey, T Galligan, D W Crossley*)

M & B (Bass)   Licensee Brian Morris   Real ale   Lunchtime snacks and afternoon teas (upstairs)   Restaurant tel Ironbridge (0952) 453522   Children in eating area of bar and in restaurant   Open 11–5.30 (4 winter); can be hired evenings; closed 25 and 26 Dec

LITTLE STRETTON   SO4392 Map 6

Green Dragon

Ludlow Road; village well signposted from A49

This welcoming creeper-covered white house is in a lovely setting for walkers. The well kept carpeted lounge bar has a relaxed, pleasant atmosphere, and green plush banquettes and stools around the well spaced polished dark tables. Good value well presented bar food, served efficiently, includes soup (£1.20), filled rolls or sandwiches (£1.25), smoked haddock and tomato in creamy cheese sauce (£2.15), ploughman's (£2.85), broccoli bake (£4.10), salads (from £4.15), home-made steak and kidney pie (£4.25), halibut (£5.75), steaks (from £6.65), and puddings like meringues or home-made fruit pie (from £1.50). Well kept Manns, Ruddles County and Woods on handpump; maybe unobtrusive piped music. There are picnic-table sets under cocktail parasols on the lawn of a prettily planted garden. (*Recommended by T Galligan, M Watson, Mrs A Turner, G T Jones, Kevin Fields, Nick Dowson, Alison Hayward, Paul McPherson*)

Free house   Licensees Roy and Christine Jones   Real ale   Meals and snacks (not summer Sun evenings)   Restaurant tel Church Stretton (0649) 722925   Children in restaurant   Open 11.30–2.30, 6–11; closed 25 Dec

Ragleth

Ludlow Road; village well signposted from A49

This attractive place is reputed to have spent its 16th-century days as a ropeworks, and it's one of the oldest brick pubs in the county. The comfortable bay-windowed lounge bar has an unusual curved corner, an oak-topped bar counter, built-in seats, and a good winter fire. There's a huge inglenook fireplace and a brick-and-tiled-floor in the public bar, as well as darts, dominoes, fruit machine, space game and juke box. Reasonably priced, home-made bar food includes home-made soup (£1.50), prawn sandwiches or filled French bread (£2.50), filled baked potatoes (from £2.20), cottage pie (£2.65), delicious ploughman's (from £2.65), salads (from £3.25), vegetarian dishes (around £3.95), freshly grilled plaice

(from £4.65), and steaks (from £5.50), with daily specials like pork stir-fry or steak
and kidney pie (£4.25), and puddings like home-made cheesecake or chocolate and
brandy mousse (£1.75); good three-course Sunday roast lunch (£7.50). They do
Indian, Italian and Chinese evenings in the restaurant. Well kept Bass, John Smiths
Bitter and Wadworths 6X on handpump. Tables on the lawn (where there's a tulip
tree) look across to an ancient-seeming thatched and timbered church (actually
built in this century). The pub is near *Good Walks Guide* Walk 102, and close to
Long Mynd (a spacious heather-and-bracken plateau owned by the National
Trust, with fine views). *(Recommended by G T Jones, NWN, Mike Tucker, Nick Dowson,
Alison Hayward, Dr P Webb, KC, Paul McPherson, Mr and Mrs M D Jones; more reports
please)*

*Free house   Licensees Harford and Marion Ransley   Real ale   Meals and snacks
Restaurant tel Church Stretton (0694) 722711   Children in one bar   Open 11–2.30,
6–11; closed 25 Dec*

LUDLOW   SO5173   Map 4

Church 🛏

Church Street, behind Buttercross; best chance of parking is in Broad Street

There's been some sort of inn here for seven centuries, though for much of that
time it's been anything from a blacksmith's to a druggist's. A stub wall divides the
calm and airy bar into two, comfortably cushioned beige wall banquettes loop
around the alcoves, and attractively engraved old song title-pages, botanical prints,
paintings by local artists and so forth hang on its cream walls. Good value bar food
includes soup (95p), home-made quiche (£2.95), scampi (£3.50), fresh trout
(£3.95), lasagne (£4.25), steak pie (£4.50) and rump steak (£5.50), with
sandwiches at lunchtime. Well kept Ruddles Best and County, and Websters
Yorkshire on handpump, with guests like Bass or Charles Wells IPA. The
bedrooms by the walk next to the red sandstone church would be the quietest.
*(Recommended by Gordon and Daphne, A Cook, John and Bridget Dean, N P Hopkins,
K and E Leist, Philip King, Nick Dowson, Alison Hayward)*

*Free house   Licensees Brian and Carol Hargreaves   Real ale   Meals and snacks
Restaurant   Children in eating area and restaurant   Open 11–3, 6–11   Bedrooms
tel Ludlow (0584) 872174; £25B/£38B*

MUCH WENLOCK   SJ6200   Map 4

George & Dragon

High St

The front bar in this busy, unassuming town pub, popular with locals, has the
biggest pub collection of water jugs in England – about a thousand hang from the
beams; there's also lots of bottle labels and beer trays, some
George-and-the-Dragon pictures, old brewery and cigarette advertisements, a few
antique settles as well as conventional furnishings, and a couple of attractive
Victorian fireplaces (with coal-effect gas fires). It can get smoky. At the back, the
quieter snug old-fashioned rooms have black beams and timbering, little decorative
plaster panels, tiled floors, a stained-glass smoke room sign, a big
George-and-the-Dragon mural as well as lots of smaller pictures (painted by local
artists), and a little stove in a fat fireplace. A good choice of bar food at lunchtime
includes sandwiches, home-made soup (£1.50), ploughman's with home-made
chutney (from £2.25 – watch out if it's the chilli chutney), home-made pâté
(£2.75), lentils and vegetable gratin (£3), fisherman's pie or chicken in a lemon and
tarragon sauce (£3.50), fresh trout stuffed with prawns, mushroom and ginger or
lamb curry (£3.75), and puddings like home-made sherry trifle (£1.50); evening
meals are served in Eve's Kitchen, with starters such as Stilton and pear pâté
(£2.25), and main courses such as lambs liver (£6.50) or the house speciality, duck
(£8.50). Well kept Hook Norton Best, Marstons Pedigree and guest beers on
handpump; friendly service; music from vintage wireless. *(Recommended by Neil and
Anita Christopher, Chris Raisin, A M J Chadwick; more reports please)*

Free house   Licensee Eve Nolan   Real ale   Lunchtime meals and snacks   Evening restaurant tel *Much Wenlock (1952) 727312; closed Sun and Mon   Older children in restaurant if well behaved   Open 11–2.30, 6–11; winter evening opening 7*

Talbot 🍺

High Street

Just up the road from our other entry, but with quite a different appeal, this very neatly kept and rather smart old pub has a welcoming and relaxed atmosphere. Several opened-together carpeted areas have walls decorated with prints of fish, and with shives, tuts, spices and other barrel-stoppers, comfortable green plush button-back wall banquettes around highly-polished tables, lovely flowers, low ceilings, and two big log fires (one in an inglenook decorated with a hop bine). Good, attractively presented home-made bar food at lunchtime includes soup (£1.50), filled baked potatoes (from £2.25), ploughman's (from £2.65), home-made quiche (£3.95), omelettes (from £3.95), home-made steak and kidney pie with first class pastry (£4.50), locally produced sirloin steak (£6.75), and specials like cauliflower cheese with smoked bacon (£3.75), moussaka (£3.95) and fish and prawn pie (£4.25); evening dishes such as garlic mushrooms (£2.25), prawns and quail eggs (£3.25), beef goulash (£6.95), pork with plum sauce (£7.25) or scampi provençal (£7.95), and popular puddings like bread and butter pudding or blackberry and apple pie (£1.95). They do a roast Sunday lunch (best to book). Ruddles Best and Websters Yorkshire on handpump, good value wines and good coffee; piped music. Through the coach entry, there are white seats and tables in an attractive sheltered yard. *(Recommended by Colin Laffan, Mrs Y M Healey, Mike and Wendy Proctor, Neil and Anita Christopher, Steve Goodchild, Roy Bromell, Paul McPherson; more reports please)*

Free house   Licensee Timothy Lathe   Real ale   Meals and snacks (not 25 Dec) Restaurant   Well behaved children allowed (no babies or prams)   Open 10.30–2.30, 6–11; closed 25 Dec   Bedrooms tel *Much Wenlock (0952) 727077; £30B/£50B*

NORTON   SJ7200 Map 4

Hundred House 🍺 🛏

A442 Telford–Bridgnorth

Plenty of space in this carefully refurbished pub is filled with interesting – even elegant – furnishings. There are several more or less separate areas with old quarry tiles at either end and modern hexagonal ones in the main central part, which has high beams strung with hop-bunches and cooking pots. Steps lead up past a little balustrade to a partly panelled eating area, where stripped brickwork looks older than that elsewhere. Handsome fireplaces have log fires or working Coalbrookdale ranges (one has a great Jacobean arch with fine old black cooking pots), and around sewing-machine tables are a variety of interesting chairs and settles with some long colourful patchwork leather cushions. Food – served all day – starts with breakfast (from 8.30am, English £4.95) and includes afternoon tea (2.30pm–6pm), as well as baps (from £1.50, bacon and mushroom £2.50), soup (£2), ploughman's (from £3), savoury pancake (£3.25), vegetarian savoury nut roast or rice pilaf with apricots, raisins and pine nuts, home-made lasagne or grilled local gammon with egg or pineapple (£5), steak and kidney pie (£5.95), and steaks (from £7.25); puddings such as treacle tart, profiteroles or home-made ices and sorbets, and children's dishes (£2.25). If the restaurant is very busy on a Saturday night, they may well stop doing bar meals then, but would tell customers before they order. Well kept Chesters Mild, Flowers Original, Marstons Pedigree, and Robinsons Old Tom on handpump, with Heritage (light and refreshing, not too bitter) and the stronger Ailrics Old Ale at the moment brewed for them by a small brewery; over 50 wines. Darts, shove-ha'penny, dominoes, cribbage and fruit machine; no dogs; seats out in a neatly kept and prettily arranged garden. The village bowling green is next to the inn. *(Recommended by Wayne Brindle, J P Day, Kevin Fields, Mike and Wendy Proctor, S May, David and Flo Wallington)*

Free house   Licensees Henry, Sylvia and David Phillips   Real ale   Meals and snacks

*(8.30–10pm)   Restaurant   Children welcome away from bar   Open 11–11
Bedrooms tel Norton (095 271) 353; £55B/£65B*

PULVERBATCH   SJ4202   Map 6

White Horse

From A49 at N end of Dorrington follow Pulverbatch/Church Pulverbatch signposts,
and turn left at eventual T-junction (which is sometimes signposted Church
Pulverbatch); OS Sheet 126 map reference 424023

Several interconnected snug areas in this rambling pub have black beams and
heavy timbering, unusual fabric-covered high-backed settles as well as brocaded
banquettes on its Turkey carpet, sturdy elm or cast-iron-framed tables, an open
coalburning range with gleaming copper kettles, and a collection of antique
insurance plaques, big brass sets of scales, willow-pattern plates, and pewter mugs
hanging over the serving counter; there's even a good Thorburn print of a grouse
among the other country pictures. Well kept Flowers Original, Marstons Pedigree
or Whitbreads Best on handpump, several decent wines by the glass, and 105 malt
whiskies. The wide choice of bar food includes sandwiches (their toasted roast beef
and melted cheese is popular, jumbo steak £3.15), tasty cullen skink as a soup
(£1.10), burgers (from £1.50), omelettes (from £1.80), ploughman's (from £1.95),
chicken chasseur (£4.25), hot vegetarian platter (£4.50), a popular fry-up (£4.95),
home-made curries, well hung steaks (from £5.95), children's dishes, and daily
specials. Darts, juke box, friendly efficient service. The quarry-tiled front loggia
with its sturdy old green leatherette seat is a nice touch. The entrance is around the
back of the pub. *(Recommended by Colin Laffan, Brian and Anna Marsden)*

*Whitbreads   Licensee James MacGregor   Real ale   Meals and snacks (till 10pm)
Children welcome   Open 11.30–3, 7–11*

UPPER FARMCOTE   SO7792   Map 4

Lion of Morfe

Follow Claverley 2 1/2 signpost off A458 Bridgnorth–Stourbridge

The traditional core of this country pub is the wallpapered public bar, popular
with the strong-accented locals, which has wood-backed wall seats on the red tiles
and a game trophy over the small coal fire; the carpeted pool room with its big
black kitchen range is also much used. Altogether smarter, the brown-carpeted
lounge bar has pink plush button-back built-in wall banquettes in curving bays,
and a good log fire; it opens into the conservatory – no-smoking, with cushioned
cane chairs and around glass tables on the red-tiled floor. Attractively priced bar food
includes sandwiches (from 85p, steak £1), filled baked potatoes (£1), ploughman's
(£2), home-cooked hot dishes such as curry (£2.25), steak and kidney pie or
chicken surprise (£2.40), and evening dishes such as tomato and herb quiche
(£3.50), grilled trout (£5.50), and steaks (from £6.50); daily specials. Well kept
Banks's on electric pump and Woods Special on handpump; darts, pool, dominoes
and fruit machine on the public side; friendly service. There are picnic-table sets
under cocktail parasols on a terrace, and a lawn spreading out into an orchard
with a floodlit boules piste. *(Recommended by Richard and Dilys Smith; more reports
please)*

*Free house   Licensees Bill and Dinah Evans   Real ale   Meals (not Fri–Sun evenings)
and snacks   Children in eating area   Folk club Sat fortnightly   Open 11.30–2.30
(3.30 Sat), 7–11*

WENLOCK EDGE   SO5796   Map 4

Wenlock Edge Inn   ★   ⊘   ⇌

Hilltop; B4371 Much Wenlock–Church Stretton, OS Sheet 137 map reference 570962

Extremely friendly licensees who make a point of drawing visitors into
conversations, a thoughtful and interesting choice of drinks, and imaginative

home-cooked food, all in lovely surroundings, earn this well run inn a star this year. Two cosy low-ceilinged bar rooms have a door in between them. The one on the right has a shelf of high plates, a big woodburning stove in its large inglenook, and leads into a little dining room. The room on the left has pews that came from a Methodist chapel in Liverpool, a fine oak bar counter, and an open fire. The licensee's interested in local ghosts and Chinese horoscopes. Using fresh ingredients and worth waiting for, the bar food includes soup (mainly vegetarian) such as tomato and red pepper or mushroom (£1.30), pasta salad (£2.90 starter, £5.25 main course), prawns in seafood sauce (£2.95 starter, £5.50 main), ploughman's (£3.70), home-baked ham (£3.90), chicken and apricot quiche with around 10 different salad vegetables with it (£4), fresh fish such as poached salmon, mackerel or trout (£5.60), evening rump steak (£7.75, Tues–Sat), and dishes of the day such as Elizabethan pork casserole, Wedgie pie, beef and South Shropshire venison, chicken breasts with apricots and cider sauce, and Shrewsbury lamb (all around £5.50); attractive puddings such as lemon pudding (the most delicious one reader has ever tasted), fruit crumbles or pies or raspberry meringue (£1.60); no chips. Well kept Tetleys, Shipstones, and Wem Best on handpump, interesting whiskies, decent wines by both glass and bottle, and no music – unless you count the deep-throated chimes of Big Bertha the fusee clock. There are some tables on a front terrace and the side grass. The building is in a fine position just by the Ippikins Rock viewpoint and there are lots of walks through the National Trust land that runs along the Edge. (*Recommended by Christian Leigh, David Williams, Cyril Burton, Gwen and Peter Andrews, Miss G Matthews, Mrs K Clark, Andrea McWilliams, Mike and Wendy Proctor, Mr and Mrs J M Elden, Paul McPherson, John and Christine Rees, M J Penford, Paul and Margaret Baker, Colin Dowse, Annette and John Kenny*)

Free house   Licensee Stephen Waring   Real ale   Meals and snacks (not Mon except Bank Holidays)   Restaurant   Children in restaurant (not under 10 if after 8pm Sat) Open 11.30–2.30 (3 Sat), 6–11; closed Mon lunchtime except Bank Holidays; closed 25 Dec   Twin bedroom tel Much Wenlock (074 636) 403; £28S/£38S; more bedrooms planned

WHITCHURCH   SJ4947   Map 7

Willey Moor Lock

Pub signposted off A49 just under two miles N of Whitchurch

To get to the front door of this low fairylit pub, you have to cross the footbridge over the Llangollen Canal and the rushing sidestream by the lock. Several neatly decorated carpeted rooms have brick-based brocaded wall seats, stools and small chairs around dimpled copper and other tables, crisp black-and-white paintwork, low ceilings, a decorative longcase clock, a shelf of Toby jugs, and two winter log fires. Popular, good value bar food includes winter home-made soup, good freshly cut sandwiches (from £1.20), home-made steak and kidney pie or lasagne (£2.40), a vegetarian dish (£2.50), salads (from £2.50), and scampi (£3.95), deep-fried chicken (£3.60), salads (from £3.75), their speciality fish and chips (£4), gammon (£5.50), large mixed grill (£5.80), lots of big steaks (from £6), puddings (from £1.10), and children's menu (£1.50); food stops one hour before closing, subject to seasonal variations. They hope to have a new dining area by the time this book is published. Well kept Marstons Pedigree, McEwans 70/-, and weekly guest beers on handpump; several dogs and cats, and a goat. From the white tables under cocktail parasols on the terrace you can watch the colourful narrowboats. (*Recommended by Carol and Richard Glover, J D Cranston, Kate and Robert Hodkinson, Chris Raisin, Capt F A Bland, Neil and Elspeth Fearn, Laurence Manning*)

Free house   Licensee Mrs Elsie Gilkes   Real ale   Meals and snacks   Children in eating area   Open 11–3, 6–11; may close some weekday lunchtimes in winter

WISTANSTOW   SO4385   Map 6

Plough ⊗

Village signposted off A49 and A489 N of Craven Arms

Good value, home-made food in this popular own-brew pub includes particularly tasty carrot and orange soup, fresh grilled sardines (£3), ploughman's with three English cheeses or pâté (£2.95), lasagne or prawn curry (£3.50), and good steak and kidney or chicken pies (£3.95) at lunchtime; evening meals might include lamb à la Grecque (£5.25), duck in orange sauce (£5.95), halibut with prawns in a cream and sherry sauce or fresh salmon (£6), rump steak (£6.95) and there's an attractive show of home-made puddings. The brewery is actually separate, an older building right by the pub, and the beers are among the best from any brewery – Woods Parish, Special, the strong Wonderful and the seasonal Christmas Cracker. They keep two farm ciders, there's a fine display cabinet of bottled beers and quite a few wines. The decor is rather a surprise for a Shrophire village pub. Its lounge bar is high-raftered and airy, with high tables and chairs in the bay windows, green velvet curtains, and many tables spread over its swirly-patterned carpet. The games area has darts, pool, dominoes, cribbage, fruit machine, space game and juke box; there may be piped music. There are some tables under cocktail parasols outside. (Recommended by Colin Laggan, John and Joan Wyatt, Paul McPherson, James and Marion Seeley, Richard and Dilys Smith)

Own brew   Licensee Robert West   Real ale   Lunchtime snacks and meals (not Mon evening, except Bank Hols)   Children welcome   Open 11.30–2.30, 7–11

Lucky Dip

Besides the fully inspected pubs, you might like to try these Lucky Dips recommended to us and described by readers (if you do, please send us reports):

All Stretton [SO4695], *Yew Tree*: Friendly and obliging staff, good value straightforward bar food (R and E Harfield)
☆ **Aston Munslow** [OS Sheet 137 map reference 512866; SO5187], *Swan*: Ancient pub with several bars, log fires, pool room, well kept Bass and other real ales, good bar food, garden; lane beside leads to twelfth-century White House (open summer) (D W Crossley)
Baystonhill [A49 Shrewsbury—Hereford; SJ4908], *Compasses*: Attractive, friendly pub by old village common; well kept Bass, pleasant service, naval memorabilia; big garden with summer barbecues (Spencer Roberts)
Birdsgreen [A442 Kidderminster—Bridgnorth; SO7785], *Royal Oak*: Pleasant enlarged pub with restaurant and good value bar snacks; Banks's beers, garden behind (Dave Braisted)
Bishops Castle [High St; SO3289], *Boars Head*: Well modernised, nice old pub with pleasant atmosphere, real ale, reasonably priced bar food; bedrooms recently added (C T and J M Laffan)
Bridges [between the Long Mynd and Stiperstones; SO3996], *Horseshoe*: Attractive old pub in lovely spot, clean and bright, with Marstons Pedigree on handpump, Westons cider, good home-made bar food at moderate prices; interesting windows; children's room (D C Bail)
☆ **Bridgnorth** [Stn; A458 towards Stourbridge, opp the Hollyhead; SO7293], *Railwaymans Arms*: Part of the Severn Valley steam railway terminus (car-parking fee is refundable against either your train ticket or what you spend in the pub); very basic, bustling re-creation of 1940s station bar, with simple snacks, coal fire, fine range of well kept real ales inc Bathams, Timothy Taylors Landlord, Woods Parish and good Milds; children welcome (E J Alcock, Richard Sanders, Gordon Mott, LYM)

Bridgnorth [High St], *Swan*: Attractive old half-timbered pub, comfortable, with good beer and food (Richard Sanders)
☆ **Brockton** [SO5894], *Feathers*: Country pub doing well under new licensees, with wide choice of good well presented bar food inc children's dishes, warm welcome, and well kept real ales; huge set of bellows from local smithy as one table, pretty little covered back terrace (P J Mathews, Paul Denham and Nicola Brown-Denham, LYM)
Cheswardine [Soudley; SJ7228], *Wheatsheaf*: Country local with good family atmosphere, bar food — a nice place to stay (Mrs M H Shropshire)
☆ **Claverley** [High St; off A454 Wolverhampton—Bridgnorth; SO7993], *Crown*: Ancient pub in one of the county's prettiest villages; heavy beams, open fires, good home-made bar food (not Sun—Wed evenings), well kept Banks's Bitter, pleasant service, comfortable furnishings, particularly good family garden with play area, summer children's bar and barbecues; dogs allowed, long Sat opening; children allowed in eating area (LYM)
☆ **Coalport** [Salthouse Rd; nr Mawes Craft Centre, over footbridge by chinaworks museum — OS Sheet 127 map reference 693025; SJ6903], *Boat*: Simple brick-built pub prettily placed by the water in a nice part of the Severn Gorge — easiest approach is by footbridge from china museum side as the road itself is a rough track; cosy inside, with welcoming service, coal fire, generous helpings of basic bar food, well kept Banks's on electric pump, darts; summer barbecues on tree-shaded lawn (E J Alcock, Comus Elliott, BB)
☆ **Corfton** [B4368 Much Wenlock—Craven Arms; SO4985], *Sun*: Good value simple home cooking from soup and burgers through gammon and pies to steaks and a monumental mixed grill, with children's dishes and a bargain Sunday lunch

(especially cheap for children) served till lateish in the evening, in pleasant lounge bar and lively and cheery locals' bar — also new restaurant; tables on terrace and in good-sized garden with good play area in retired tractor; piped music *(John Mills, Mr and Mrs J Kirby, BB)*

Cound [A458 Shrewsbury—Much Wenlock; SJ5605], *Cound*: Large hotel with refurbished bar and big garden with fine views of River Weaver; good Bass; bedrooms *(Chris Raisin)*

Diddlebury [SO5185], *Sun*: Consistently good generous bar food, pleasant accommodating landlord *(L Mayall)*

☆ **Ellesmere** [Birch Rd; SJ4035], *White Hart*: Ancient black and white pub with some claim to be the oldest in Shrops, with very reasonably priced bar food, well kept Marstons ales inc Border, friendly landlord and locals *(P Lloyd, Miss K Bamford, Chris Raisin)*

Ellesmere [1 Birch Rd; SJ4035], *Millies*: Superb, out-of-the-way little wine bar (included because it does have a real ale), with intimate decor, Royal Doulton china on walls, crystal collection in cabinet; good food (tandoori sausages recommended) and service *(Carol and Richard Glover)*

Harmer Hill [SJ4822], *Bridgewater Arms*: Good food and real ales in spacious bar with central servery, restaurant, seats out in front and in small garden; big car park *(Kate Drakes)*

Hodnet [SJ6128], *Bear*: 16th-century smartly refurbished hotel, clean as a new pin, with good range of reasonably priced imaginative food and well kept John Smiths in big main bar; restaurant with small no-smoking area, cocktail bar with unusual sunken garden in former bear pit; opp Hodnet Hall gardens; four bedrooms, not large but comfortable *(MP, P J Taylor)*

☆ **Ironbridge** [Wharfage; SJ6704], *Malt House*: Large, long room with well kept Davenports and surprisingly good food — good value considering the generous helpings; across road from Severn, with rather industrial view; useful for tourists *(Mrs Y M Healey, Mr and Mrs J H Adam)*

Ironbridge, *Olde Robin Hood*: Good home-made food in carpeted lounge with comfortable pink plush seats, handsome collection of clocks and brasses; handy for the museums *(Ken and Barbara Turner)*; *Swan*: Cosy pub with good beer, simple food *(T Galligan)*

Leebotwood [A49 Church Stretton—Shrewsbury; SO4898], *Pound*: Has been praised for pleasant atmosphere, well kept beer, above-average bar food and helpful licensee, but no recent reports *(News please)*

Lilleshall [just off A518 2 miles SW of Newport; SJ7315], *Red House*: Spacious, well equipped and popular, with well kept real ales such as Boddingtons or Wilsons, good lunchtime bar food, restaurant *(A T Langton)*

☆ **Linley** [pub signed off B4373 N of Bridgnorth; SO6998], *Pheasant*: What a shame we hear so little of this welcoming and relaxed country pub — squeezed out of the main entries this year by all those reports we get on other more frequently visited places; honest food (not Sun if busy) from sandwiches and a good ploughman's through gammon with their own free-range eggs to cheap steaks, an inventive choice of real ales and attractive surrounding countryside make this quite a lure *(LYM — more reports please)*

Little Wenlock [SJ6507], *Huntsman*: Free house with friendly licensee and bar staff, well kept Davenports Wem, good food in bar and restaurant *(Colin Dowse)*

Llanfair Waterdine [village signposted from B4355; turn left after bridge; SO2476], *Red Lion*: Rambling lounge bar with good log fire in impressive fireplace, and cosy little black-beamed tap room, in attractive old riverside inn with seats out among roses in front, more on back lawn; licensees who took over a few months ago have been winning praise for their food; Marstons Pedigree on handpump; comfortable bedrooms; closed Tues lunchtime *(K and G Jackson, LYM; more reports on the new regime please)*

☆ **Llanyblodwel** [village and pub signposted off B4396; SJ2423], *Horse Shoe*: Delightfully quaint if rather rough-and-ready black-and-white timbered Tudor inn in pretty spot by the River Tanat (where they have a mile of trout fishing), much enjoyed by readers who don't expect airs and graces; rambling low-beamed rooms, simple furnishings both traditional and more modern, limited choice of basic food from sandwiches to steaks, pub games, piped music, tables outside; the high-Victorian village church is well worth seeing; children in eating area till 9; two simple but cheap bedrooms *(Paul McPherson, Gordon and Daphne, LYM)*

Longden [SJ4406], *Tankerville Arms*: Friendly and welcoming, with imaginative bar food inc evening buffets (not Mon or Sat), game specialities as well as steaks and so forth Tues–Sun evenings, carvery Sun lunches (evening too); immaculate ladies' *(Kate Drakes)*

☆ **Longville** [B4371 Church Stretton—Much Wenlock; SO5494], *Longville Arms*: Well kept Bass and M&B Springfield and bar food from sandwiches, soup, baked potatoes and ploughman's to ham and eggs or lasagne, in plainly modernised big-windowed pub with sturdy elm or cast-iron-framed tables, leatherette banquettes and woodburning stoves in left-hand bar, plusher furniture inc some nice old oak tables in right-hand one; picnic-table sets and play area in neat garden; closed Tues lunchtime; children welcome; good value bedrooms *(Ted and Pat Samuels, BB)*

☆ **Loppington** [signed off B4397 W of Wem; SJ4729], *Blacksmiths Arms*: Neat thatch, heavy beams, inglenook fireplace, country decorations and a couple of neatly comfortable side rooms, with good value home-made bar food from sandwiches and filled baked potatoes to steaks (VAT goes on the bill), Bass on handpump, good choice of malt whiskies, pretty garden with play area; children welcome; closed Mon lunchtime, restaurant; only a relative lack of recent reader reports drops this to the Dips this year *(Mike and Wendy Proctor, Paul*

McPherson, LYM — more reports please)

☆ Ludlow [Lower Bridge St; SO5175], Wheatsheaf: Good traditional atmosphere in attractively refurbished and tastefully furnished 17th-century pub spectacularly built into medieval town gate; friendly new owners doing wide range of good bar food, with well kept Bass, M&B and Ruddles County on handpump, choice of farm ciders; attractive oak-beamed bedrooms (Helen and Wal Burns, Nick Dowson, Alison Hayward, John and Bridget Dean)

☆ Ludlow [Bull Ring/Corve St], Feathers: Famous for exquisitely proportioned and intricately carved timbered frontage, and a fine hotel inside — Jacobean panelling and carving, period furnishings; for the decent bar food or a casual drink you may well be diverted to a plainer more modern side bar; efficient pleasant service, well kept Flowers Original and Wadworths 6X; artistically presented food in restaurant; bedrooms comfortable, if not cheap (Gwen and Peter Andrews, Paul McPherson, Dr P Webb, LYM)

☆ Ludlow, Blue Boar: Attractive, cosy rooms with pleasant prints, photographs and Ludlow Festival posters, good buffet; bedrooms impressively big, with good breakfasts (Nick Dowson, Alison Hayward, Dave Braisted)

Ludlow [between Buttercross and St Laurence's Church], Rose & Crown: Small and brightly lit, with friendly landlord, good filling bar food, orange juice squeezed to order and cheap (Caroline Wright)

Market Drayton [High St; SJ6734], Corbet Arms: More hotel than pub, but with bar food inc buffet lunch that's popular with older people, and those at the sales held in their two halls; comfortable bedrooms (Mrs M H Shropshire); [Shropshire St], Sandbrook Vaults: Lively 16th-century beamed pub with authentic Tudor frontage; good value and quality range of lunchtime meals — very popular for these, especially on market day; pleasant staff (Helen J Graham)

Meole Brace [A49 roundabout just S of Shrewsbury — OS Sheet 126 map reference 490106; SJ4810], Brooklands: Large comfortable bar with Davenports beers and good straightforward attractively priced bar food from filled baps and ploughman's to steaks, inc children's menu (not after 8) (Neil and Anita Christopher)

☆ Much Wenlock [A458; SO6299], Gaskell Arms: Picturesque pub with good popular bar food at reasonable prices, open fire and banknote collection in cosy relaxing lounge; good service, well kept Courage Best and Directors on handpump, piped music, good restaurant; fruit machine in lobby (Chris Raisin, P Corris, A J Woodhouse)

☆ Munslow [B4368 Much Wenlock—Craven Arms; SO5287], Crown: Attractive old building in pleasant countryside with variety of tables and chairs in split-level beamed lounge with flagstones, bare stone walls, bottle collection, snug, bread oven, original cupboards and doors; eating area has small tables around central oven chimney — generous helpings of decent home-made food; reasonably priced Bass, Marstons Mild and Wadworths 6X (Nick Dowson, Alison Hayward)

Neenton [B4364 Bridgnorth—Ludlow; SO6488], Pheasant: Attractively placed free house with generous helpings of reasonably priced standard food; restaurant — give them 24 hours' notice if you want a 3-course meal (Brian Barefoot)

☆ Newcastle [B4368 Clun—Newtown; SO2582], Crown: Spacious well furnished pub with pleasant decor; nicely presented good value food inc some interesting dishes, friendly attentive licensees, wide choice of well kept beer; tables outside, great scenery nearby (Dr M V Roman)

☆ Newport [SJ7519], Bridge: Small, friendly pub with decent bar food from good ham sandwiches up, separate restaurant, attentive staff; satisfactory bedrooms, good parking (M J St John, A M Dudley-Evans, G B Pugh)

Norbury [SO3693], Sun: Ancient welcoming place opposite church in remote village; lovely building, good food (G T Jones)

Onibury [SO4579], Hollybush: Small, friendly and neatly kept, with quiet and homely atmosphere — almost a blend of tearoom and pub; very good fresh home-made food in generous helpings, immaculate ladies'; children welcome (Miles Kington)

Pant [A483 Oswestry—Welshpool; SJ2723], Cross Guns: Pleasant and welcoming with good choice of well served food (F A Noble)

☆ Pipe Gate [A51 Nantwich—Stone; SJ7441], Chetwode Arms: Friendly family pub, clean and comfortably refurbished, with wide choice of good bar food, attractively priced good carvery, evening restaurant; unusual real ales such as St Austells (Paul and Margaret Baker, Mr Armitt)

Quatford [just off Bridgnorth—Kidderminster rd; SO7491], Danery: Well kept M&B beer, decent reasonably priced straightforward bar food (Sue Braisted)

☆ Shifnal [High St; SJ7508], White Hart: Tastefully restored, comfortable and cosy village pub, particularly well kept Allied real ales, consistently good bar food inc good specials (Bob Alton, Mr and Mrs J H Adam)

Shifnal [Market St], Star: Attractively refurbished by new owners, with log fire and stripped-pine furniture; imaginative menu inc venison sausage, hot avocado with stilton, smoky bacon with squid; well kept real ales such as Boddingtons, Devenish Steam, Marstons Pedigree (Bob Alton)

☆ Shrewsbury [Wyle Cop; follow City Centre signposts across the English Bridge], Lion: Grand old inn with distinguished history, cosy oak-panelled bar and sedate series of high-ceilinged rooms opening off, comfortably refurbished by THF; obliging staff, Bass under light carbon dioxide blanket, bar food — which may be served in the restaurant if it's not busy; children welcome; bedrooms comfortable (Colin Dowse, LYM)

☆ Shrewsbury [16 Castle Gates], Castle Vaults: Black and white pub concentrating on good value Mexican food (they do English dishes too), with well kept Border, Marstons Pedigree and Robinsons on handpump; bedrooms (Graham Gibson, Nick Dowson, Alison Hayward)

☆ Shrewsbury [New St; leaving centre via Welsh Bridge/A488 turn into Port Hill Rd], Boat House: Comfortably modernised pub worth knowing for its quiet Severnside position, with river views from the long quiet lounge bar, tables out on a sheltered terrace and rose lawn; Whitbreads-related real ales, usual bar food, afternoon teas, summer barbecues; lavatories due for attention; open all day, by footbridge over to park *(Brian Barefoot, Wayne Brindle, M A Watts, LYM)*

Shrewsbury [Princess St], *Golden Cross*: Scenic and attractive hotel dating from 1428, lovely bar popular with college students, a single cheap lunchtime dish, three well kept beers on handpump; four reasonably priced and good value bedrooms *(Frank W Gadbois)*; [Mardol], *Kings Head*: 15th-century timber-framed pub, carefully restored; popular with trendy young people weekend evenings *(Nick Dowson, Alison Hayward)*; [central, nr St Julians Craft Centre], *Old Post Office*: Tastefull renovated post office with old post box inside, dark beams, well kept Marstons Pedigree on handpump, good hot and cold bar food; tables in cobbled yard *(Catherine and Andrew Brian)*; [St Marys Place], *Yorkshire House*: Attractive panelling, beams and brasses (the best kept in a leaded-light wall cupboard); Wem Bitter on electric pump, hot and cold lunchtime food *(Graham Gibson)*

☆ **Stiperstones** [village signposted off A488 S of Minsterley — OS Sheet 126 map reference 364005; SO3697], *Stiperstones*: Folksy little friendly modernised lounge bar with leatherette wall banquettes, lots of brasware on ply-panelled walls, well kept Woods Parish on handpump, darts in plainer public bar, restaurant; at least in summer has been open all day, with good simple food inc good salads and maybe local whinberry pie right through till 10pm; picnic-table sets outside; on GWG100 *(BB)*

☆ **Tong** [A41 towards Newport, just beyond village; SJ7907], *Bell*: Friendly service, welcoming atmosphere, olde-worlde stripped brickwork, large family room, small dining room, pleasant back conservatory extension and big garden with views of countryside nr Weston Park; busy at lunchtime for good choice of generous decent hot food at reasonable prices, also cold table and good value Sun lunch; well kept Banks's real ales, no dogs; big car park *(T Henwood, Dave Braisted, Richard Fawcett)*

Upper Affcot [A49 S of Church Stretton; SO4486], *Travellers Rest*: Well placed free house, spaciously modern and well furnished, with wide range of beer, good hot food and good service — welcoming and attentive owners obviously enjoy their work; unobtrusive fruit machine and pool table; four ground-floor bedrooms, with own bathrooms *(Peter and Shirley Jobling)*

☆ **Upton Magna** [Pelham Rd; SJ5512], *Corbet Arms*: Big L-shaped lounge bar with armchairs by log fire, good range of popular reasonably priced food, well kept Banks's ales, darts and juke box in smaller public bar, friendly staff who remember return visitors; handy for Attingham Park (NT), busy at weekends *(Mike Tucker)*

Welshampton [A495 Ellesmere—Whitchurch; SJ4335], *Sun*: Friendly village inn — worth the 1/2 mile walk from Llangollen Canal; well kept Davenports, reasonably priced food, big back garden *(Chris Raisin)*

☆ **Whitchurch** [St Marys St; SJ5341], *Old Town Hall Vaults*: Charming and friendly 18th-century pub with well kept Marstons Border Mild and Pedigree on handpump, good value home-cooked lunchtime and evening food, friendly staff, refined rather than hearty atmosphere — piped Tchaikowsky; the birthplace of Sir Edward German *(G T Jones, Chris Raisin, Graham Gibson)*

Woore [London Rd; SJ7342], *Falcon*: Refurbished pub in small, busy village; good helpings of well prpared reasonably priced food *(M A and W R Proctor)*

Somerset and Avon

One of the country's prime areas for fine pubs, this: a good clutch of new main entries here includes the warmly welcoming George at Abbots Leigh (good value food), the quaintly old-fashioned Highbury Vaults in Bristol (tied to Smiles, an interesting newish small brewery), the civilised Poulett Arms at Hinton St George (decent food), the determinedly traditional Old Crown at Kelston, the cottagey Rose & Crown at Stoke St Gregory (a pub which local readers confess to having kept to themselves), the well run Half Moon at Stoke St Mary (good for a quiet family meal), the charmingly placed Blue Ball at Triscombe up in the Quantocks and the thrivingly warm-hearted White Hart at Trudoxhill. Other pubs currently doing notably well here include, for food, the Ashcott Inn at Ashcott, the Boars Head at Aust (particularly useful for the M4), the outstandingly well run Crown at Bathford (why don't more pubs do cheap children's helpings of main dishes – as they do here – instead of just having a kids'-ghetto-menu of fish fingers and the like?), the Wheatsheaf on its steep hillside at Combe Hay, the attractively laid out Strode Arms at Cranmore, the Bull Terrier at Croscombe (particularly well liked by readers, and a nice place to stay), the New Inn just down the lane from an interesting cider farm at Dowlish Wake, the civilised Haselbury Inn at Haselbury Plucknett, the thriving Hood Arms at Kilve (another good place to stay), the homely Three Horseshoes at Langley Marsh, the Notley Arms at Monksilver (a great reader favourite), the interestingly placed Anchor at Oldbury-upon-Severn, the cosily traditional Royal Oak at Over Stratton, the ancient and unusual Pack Horse at South Stoke (nothing fancy, but remarkably cheap), and the ever-interesting Crossways at West Huntspill (good for the M5). The area's pub food is generally attractively priced, with the higher than average poportion of around one in three pubs here hitting our targets of under £1 for bargain snacks and/or under £3 for at least some decent main dishes. The cheapest food bargains we found were at the Highbury Vaults in Bristol, followed closely by the Pack Horse at South Stoke – and it's worth noting that pubs here where the food is specially good are just as likely to have low prices as pubs where it's more run-of-the-mill. Drinks prices here are in general closely in line with the national average, though we found pubs tied to small breweries in the area tended to work out a few pence cheaper than either free houses or pubs tied to the big national combines. We found the best deals on drinks at the Malt Shovel at Bradley Green, Anchor at Oldbury-upon-Severn, White Hart at Trudoxhill and Highbury Vaults in Bristol: in all, the bargain beers were local brews – brewed at the pub itself in the case of the White Hart. Among the Lucky Dip entries at the end of the chapter, pubs showing particular current promise include the Swan at Bathford, Red Cow at Brent Knoll, Ring o' Bells at Compton Martin, Anchor at Exebridge, Inn at Freshford, White Hart at Littleton upon Severn, Olde Kings Arms at Litton, Royal Oak at Luxborough, Lord Nelson at Marshfield,

Queens Head at Milborne Port, Cottage at Nether Stowey, George at Nunney, Volunteer at Seavington St Michael and Burcott Inn at Wookey.

ABBOTS LEIGH (Avon)   ST5473 Map 2

George

3 miles from M5 junction 19; Pill Road (A369 towards Bristol)

Friendly and refreshingly unpompous, this single longish room has a good log fire at either end, lots of harness and saddlery decorating the darkening cream walls, horsebrasses and some stirrups on the beams, flowers in the windows, and brocaded cushions on the pews for tables along the walls; besides these, there are a couple more tables against the bar counter that lines most of the back wall. Good value home-made bar food includes impressive sandwiches (from £1.70, fresh crab £1.90), tasty tuna and tomato pâté (£1.75), good soups such as spicy carrot and coriander or cream of stilton (from £1.95), ploughman's with a good selection of cheeses, mushrooms in an oregano and chilli sauce (£1.95), potato and ham or vegetarian gratin (£4.85), steak and kidney pie (excellent flaky pastry, £5.25) and fish pie (£4.95), with puddings such as strawberry brûlée (£1.95); a tray of unusual bottled sauces includes fresh orange vinaigrette. Well kept Courage, Courage Best and Directors and a guest on handpump; quick and obliging service; subdued piped music (Vivaldi on our visit). A sheltered terrace and garden has picnic-table sets. The pub has two collies, Eric and Ernie. *(Recommended by A Borkowski, Barry and Anne; more reports please)*

Courage   Licensees Mike and Elaine Meredith   Real ale   Lunchtime meals and snacks   Children over 14 allowed   Open 11.45–2.30ish, 6–11; Sat 11–3, 6(7 winter)–11

ALMONDSBURY (Avon)   ST6084 Map 2

Bowl

1 1/4 miles from M5, junction 16 (and therefore quite handy for M4, junction 20; from A38 towards Thornbury, turn first left signposted Lower Almondsbury, then first right down Sundays Hill, then at bottom right again into Church Road

This pretty white cottage by the village church has lovely flowering tubs, hanging baskets and window boxes, and some picnic-table sets across the quiet road (the back garden is now a kitchen extension). Inside, the long neatly kept beamed bar has a big winter log fire at one end and a woodburning stove at the other, blue plush-patterned modern settles, pink cushioned stools and mate's chairs, elm tables, walls stripped to bare stone, and quite a few horsebrasses. Good home-made bar food includes sandwiches (£1.15; toasties from £1.25), soup (£1.40), ploughman's (£2.35), burgers (from £1.95), mushrooms in garlic sauce (£2.25), salads (from £3.35), omelettes (from £3.45), quiche (£3.45), cottage pie (£3.95), chilli beef with croûtons (£4.25), cold honeyroast ham (£4.55), steak and kidney pie (£4.65), puddings (£1.45), and daily specials; grills and steaks Sunday evenings. Well kept Courage Bitter, Best and Directors on handpump, some enterprising bottled beers, good value wines, tea or coffee; efficient, friendly service even when busy. Fruit machine, piped music. The little restaurant is very attractive. *(Recommended by Peter Adcock, Carol Mason, Margaret Dyke, Mark Jackson, Louise Mee, Stan Edwards, Mr and Mrs S Cowherd, Richard Parr)*

Courage   Licensee John Alley   Real ale   Meals and snacks (12–2, 6–9.45; not 25 Dec)   Restaurant; not Sun evening   Children welcome   Open 11–3, 6–11; closed 25 Dec evening   Bedrooms tel Almondsbury (0454) 612757; £34.50B/£57B; cheaper weekend rates

APPLEY (Somerset)   ST0621 Map 1

Globe

Hamlet signposted from the network of back roads between A361 and A38, W of B3187 and W of Milverton and Wellington; OS sheet 181 map reference 072215

The chatter of locals fills the simple beamed front room in this unspoilt 500-year-old country pub, the atmosphere is relaxed, and there are pictures of magpies, benches and a built-in settle, and bare wood tables on the brick floor. The back room has a pool table, and yet another room has easy chairs and other more traditional ones. An entry corridor leads to a serving hatch where Cotleigh Tawny (a local brew) and a guest beer such as Boddingtons are on handpump. Generous helpings of bar food include filled rolls, home-made soup such as pea and marrow (£1.50), ploughman's (from £2.95), chilli con carne (£2.95), good salads such as home-cooked ham (from £3.50), and lamb curry (£3.95); darts, pool, alley skittles, and fruit machine. The hilly pastures which surround this maze of twisting lanes are very pretty, and there are seats, climbing frame and swings outside in the garden; the path opposite leads eventually to the River Tone. (*Recommended by Roger and Jenny Huggins, Katie Verner, Gordon Woodcock, Chris Raisin, Graham Doyle*)

Free house   Licensees A W and E J Burt, R and J Morris   Real ale   Meals and snacks (not Mon lunchtime)   Restaurant tel Greenham (0823) 672327; open Tues–Sat evenings, though they do Sun lunch   Children in eating area of bar and restaruant Open 11–3, 6.30–11; closed Mon lunchtime, except Bank Hols

ASHCOTT (Somerset)   ST4337 Map 1

Ashcott Inn ✿

A39 about 6 miles W of Glastonbury

Now a firm favourite with readers after an unstable patch under several different licensees, this food-oriented pub has good oak and elm tables, some interesting old-fashioned seats among more conventional ones, beams, stripped stone walls, and a gas-effect log fire in its sturdy chimney. Imaginative bar food includes filled baps (from £1.10), a meaty or vegetable soup (£1.45), smokie (£2.45), ploughman's (from £2.60), home-made cottage pie (£2.85), creamy fish pie (£3.95), moussaka, vegetable lasagne or stilton and broccoli bake (£4.95), steaks (from £8.70) and around six different fresh fish dishes each day (from Dartmouth or Port Isaac) such as monkfish and prawns with pine kernels and a walnut dressing, steamed brill on a red pepper coulis, turbot with a sauté of avocados and prawns, and plaice, lemon sole and so forth (from around £6); puddings like steamed ginger pudding, treacle tart or meringues with clotted cream (from £1.75). Well kept Flowers Original and Marstons Pedigree on handpump, and quite a few wines; darts, shove-ha'penny, a fruit machine, alley skittles and piped classical music. There are seats on the terrace, and a pretty walled garden. (*Recommended by Maj and Mrs I McKillop, R W Stanbury, S V Bishop, Ted George, Mrs D A Talbot, Tom Bowen*)

Heavitree (who no longer brew)   Licensees Mr and Mrs Robert Porter   Real ale Meals and snacks (12–2, 6.30–9.30)   Restaurant tel Ashcott (0458) 210282; closed Sun evening   Well behaved children allowed   Open 11–2.30, 5.30–11

nr ASHILL (Somerset)   ST3217 Map 1

Square & Compass

Windmill Hill; turn off A358 at Stewley Cross Garage

A rather out-of-the-way country pub (but all the more pleasant to find for that), this has a comfortable and cosy little bar with upholstered window seats, and an open fire in winter; there's an extra room for eating. Bass, Exmoor Bitter and Gold on handpump; darts, shove-ha'penny and piped music. Bar food includes sandwiches, home-made soup, ploughman's, filled baked potatoes, home-made lasagne and chilli con carne, and honey-roasted ham with egg or pineapple; also, vegetarian dishes and a children's menu. Outside on the grass there are picnic-set tables, a swing, climbing frame and bright blue hay wagon. There's also a touring caravan site. *(Recommended by Shirley Pielou, S J Curtis; more up-to-date reports please)*

Free house   Licensees Fred and Eileen Balm   Real ale   Meals and snacks   Restaurant tel *Hatch Beauchamp (0823) 480467   Children in eating area and restaurant   Open* *12–2.30(3 Sat), 7–11*

AUST (Avon)   ST5789   Map 2
Boars Head

1/2 mile from M4, junction 21; village signposted from A403

The small rooms in this friendly village pub have some walls stripped back to the dark stone, old-fashioned high-backed winged settles in stripped pine, well polished country kitchen tables and others made from old casks, big rugs on dark lino, and decorative plates hanging from one stout black beam; the log fire in the main fireplace may, in summer, have a bunch of dried flowers in the opening of its former side bread oven. In another room with a woodburning stove there's a little parakeet, and a pair of gerbils, and a third room has dining tables. Popular bar food includes home-made soup (£1.40), triple sandwiches (from £1.95), ploughman's (from £2.25), pâté (£2.50), cauliflower cheese and bacon or lasagne (£3.80), lots of omelettes (from £4.40), a cold buffet with a tremendous spread of help-yourself salads (from £4.50, seafood platter £11.15), puddings such as home-made ice-cream or filled crêpes (from £1), and a blackboard showing daily specials and filled baked potatoes; children's helpings are available on request. Well kept Courage Best on handpump. There's a medieval stone well in the pretty and sheltered garden, and a touring caravan site. *(Recommended by Pamela and Merlyn Horswell, William D Cissna, Jon Wainwright, M C Howells, B H Stamp, Drs M and K Parier, Dr P McCarthy, Helena and Arthur Harbottle, David Heath, Stan Edwards, Dr R M Beard, Jacqueline Davis)*

Courage   Licensee Charles Broome   Real ale   Meals and snacks (not Sun) *Restaurant* tel *Pilning (045 45) 2278; only open Thurs, Fri and Sat evenings   Children in two family rooms till 9.30pm   Open 11–2.30(3 Sat), 6–11*

AXBRIDGE (Somerset)   ST4255   Map 1
Lamb

The Square

This ancient place serves a decent range of home-made bar food that includes soup (£1), sandwiches, samosas with mint yoghurt (£1.80), ploughman's (from £2.20), prawn chowder (£2), tripe and onions or cauliflower and broccoli cheese (£2.30), filled potato shells (£2.40), steak in ale pie (£3.50), gammon with egg and pineapple (£4.80) and rump steak (£6.50), with specials such as vegetarian stuffed tomato and cottage pie; children's menu (£1). An old-fashioned glazed partition divides the entrance hall from a big rambling bar full of heavy beams and timbers in butter-coloured plasterwork, and there are red leatherette wall seats and small settles, with a coal-burning stove in one great stone fireplace, and a collection of tools and utensils including an unusual foot-operated grinder in another. Butcombe, Wadworths 6X and Valances (from a brewery in Sidmouth) on handpump from a bar counter built largely of bottles; locally-made wine, and Thatcher's cider. Sensibly placed darts, table skittles, shove-ha'penny, dominoes, cribbage, alley skittles, fruit machine, an aquarium, and piped music. Though the sheltered back garden's not big, it's prettily planted with rock plants, shrubs and trees; starlings in the square have learned to imitate the aviary's cockatiels. The pub is in a notably attractive market square, and faces a striking medieval house. *(Recommended by Lyn and Bill Capper, Drs M and K Parier, J G Thorpe, Dr and Mrs A K Clarke)*

Butcombe   Licensees Simon Whitmore and Max Wigginton   Real ale   Meals and snacks (not 25 or 26 Dec)   Children in eating area of bar until 9pm   Open 11–2.30(3 Sat), 6.30–11   Bedrooms tel *Axbridge (0934) 732253; £16(£22B)/£40B*

BARROW GURNEY (Avon)   ST5367   Map 2

Princes Motto

Barrow Street; B3130 – linking A38 and A370 SW of Bristol

Very much an unchanging, unpretentious and traditional local, it's also the sort of place where strangers immediately feel they fit in. From the snug room by the bar, with a sentimental engraving of *Farewell to Nelson* over its log fire, steps lead up to an unusually long and narrow room behind. This has cosy winged high-backed settles at one end, and darts, shove-ha'penny, cribbage, and a fruit machine towards the other; there are lots of horsebrasses on the beams. They specialise in Bass, but also do Boddingtons, Butcombe, and Marstons Pedigree on handpump, with Bass and Wadworths 6X tapped from casks behind the bar. Good value bar snacks consist of filled rolls, toasted sandwiches and ploughman's, and there may be nibbles. Picnic-table sets on the back grass have rustic views. *(Recommended by Peter Adcock, Steve and Carolyn Harvey; more reports please)*

Free house   Licensee Paul Bryant   Real ale   Lunchtime snacks   Open 11–2.30, 6–11

BATHFORD (Avon)   ST7966   Map 2

Crown ★ ⊘

2 Bathford Hill; signposted off A363 Bath–Bradford-on-Avon

Behind the handsomely classical facade of this substantial pub, they've created a really warm and relaxed chatty atmosphere. Four or five room areas spread around the central well manned bar, with a pleasant variety of furnishings from sensible tables and chairs for people who want to eat to Lloyd-Loom-style chairs, large armchairs and comfortable button-back leather settees. There are rugs on stripped and polished floorboards, prints, old photographs and mounted butterflies on the attractively decorated walls, china, stoneware and so forth on Delft shelves, houseplants (even a sizeable palm), and careful lighting. Generously served home-made bar food includes filled rolls (from £1.50), big toasted sandwiches and filled baked potatoes with unusual fillings like bacon and banana (from £2.25), soup (£1.95), ploughman's with good cheeses (£3.95), chicken satay (£4.25), lentil nut casserole (£4.75), chicken tikka in pitta bread (£5.50), tasty steak pie (£6.25), trout (£6.50), and chicken Kiev (£7.25). They do half portions of several things for children (at less than half price), and nice puddings (£2.50); Sunday brunch. Well kept Ruddles Best and Ushers Best, decent wines including New Zealanders, non-alcohol cocktails, good cafetière coffee with fresh cream; kind service, rack of newspapers and lots of magazines, very unobtrusive piped music, good log fire; dominoes, cribbage and fruit machine. The no-smoking garden room on the left, with old nursery pictures among others, opens on to a terrace with tables under cocktail parasols; there's a small garden beyond its low retaining wall. *(Recommended by Marianne and Lionel Kreeger, Mrs Carol Mason, D Heath, Michael Badcock, Paolo Spyropoulos, B R Woolmington, Roger Cunningham, Deborah Frost, BKA, Mrs Joan Harris)*

Ushers (Watneys)   Licensees Gregg and Angela Worrall   Real ale   Meals and snacks (not Mon lunchtime, served till 9.30 Sun–Thur, 10 Fri and Sat)   Children in garden room and burgundy room   Open 11–2.30, 6.30–11; closed 25–26 Dec

BLAGDON (Avon)   ST5059   Map 2

New Inn

Church Street, off A368

The two warm and individualistic rooms of the bar here have some antique settles – one with its armrests carved as dogs – as well as little russet plush armchairs, mate's chairs and so forth. Big logs burn in both stone fireplaces, the beams are decorated with horsebrasses and some tankards, and decorations include advertisements for Slades now-defunct ales from Chippenham. Bass and Wadworths IPA and 6X on handpump, darts, shove-ha'penny, fruit machine and piped music. There's an elderly black labrador, and a plump cat (no dogs allowed in the garden). Bar food includes sandwiches (from £1.25, toasties from £1.60, open salad ones from £2.95), home-made soup (£1.25), ploughman's (from £2.60), filled baked potatoes (£2.80), salads (from £3.70), home-made steak and kidney pie (£2.85), platter of Scotch beef (£4.25), and evening grills like gammon with pineapple (£4.75), and steaks (from £6.65); there's a 30p charge for cheques under £10. Picnic-table sets on the grass behind look down over the fields to wood-fringed Blagdon Lake, and to the low hills beyond. Note they don't allow children in the bar. (*Recommended by Miss M Byrne, M W Barratt; more reports please*)

Wadworths   Licensee M K Loveless   Real ale   Meals and snacks   Open 11–2.30, 7–11

BRADLEY GREEN (Somerset)   SS0434   Map 1

Malt Shovel 🍺

Pub signposted from A39 W of Bridgwater, near Cannington; though Bradley Green is shown on road maps, note that if you're booking the postal address is Blackmoor Lane, Cannington, Bridgewater, Somerset TA5 2NE

Decidedly remote, this atmospheric little country pub has a main bar with some modern elm country chairs and little cushioned casks, window seats, sturdy modern winged high-backed settles around wooden tables, and a black kettle standing on a giant fossil by the woodburning stove; there's also a tiny snug with red-hessian walls. Butcombe, Wadworths 6X and one guest ale on handpump, and Lane's and Rich's ciders; separate skittle alley. Good value food includes lunchtime sandwiches (from 70p, crusty French rolls from 90p) and ploughman's (from £2.30), as well as filled baked potatoes (from £2.50), smoked haddock cheesy bake (£3), salads (from £3.50), home-made pies such as steak and kidney (£3.25) or chicken and mushroom (£3.75), gammon and pineapple or egg (£3.75), chicken kiev (£5.75) and steaks (from £6.95); also, starters and puddings chalked up on a blackboard, and children's meals on request (£1.50); occasional summer barbecues. The family room opens on to the garden, where there are picnic-table sets (an adjoining field may be used by touring caravans). West of the pub, Blackmore Farm is a striking medieval building. Comfortable bedrooms. (*Recommended by Drs M and K Parier, R C Blatch, JM, PM, Mr and Mrs J Grebbell, Richard Gibbs, Caroline Raphael*)

Free house   Licensees Robert and Frances Beverley   Real ale   Meals and lunchtime snacks   Restaurant   Children in family room and restaurant   Open 11.30–2.30(3 Sat), 6.30–11; winter evening opening 7   Bedrooms tel Combwich (0278) 653432; £16.50(£25B)/£25(£30B); family room £36

BRENDON HILLS (Somerset)   ST0334   Map 1

Raleghs Cross

Junction of B3190 Watchet–Bampton with the unclassified but good E-W summit road from Elworthy to Winsford

The spacious bar here has little red leatherette armchairs around the tables, button-back banquettes along the strip-panelled walls, a good collection of photographs of the old mineral railway, and open fires in cool weather. Bar food, brought to your table, includes sandwiches (from £1), soup (£1.10), pear and walnut starter or pâté (£1.50), ploughman's (£2.75), omelettes (from £3.25), liver and bacon (£3.95), gammon and pineapple, local trout or curries (£4.75), mixed grill (£7.50), steak (16oz T-bone 7.95), and puddings such as pavlova or apple pie (from £1.50); summer cream teas, and children's menu (£1.50). Well kept Flowers Original and Exmoor Bitter on handpump; gentle piped music; some of the tables in the bar are no-smoking. On exceptionally clear days this isolated long white house has views right over the Bristol Channel to Wales. You can walk from the spacious lawns to Clatworthy Reservoir, or, from the road about a mile west, down the track of the railway that used to take iron ore from the mines here to Watchet harbour. Whippet racing is held here on Sundays in summer. (*More reports please*)

*Free house Licensees Roy and Wendy Guppy Real ale Meals and snacks
Restaurant Children in restaurant and family room Open 11–11 July–Sept; 11–2.30,
6–11 the rest of the year Bedrooms tel Washford (0984) 40343; £25B/£36B*

BRISTOL (Avon) ST5872 Map 2
Highbury Vaults

St Michaels Hill, Cotham; main road out to Cotham from inner ring dual carriageway

One of the handful of pubs tied to the local Smiles brewery, this has all their beers
well kept on handpump at attractive prices, as well as Brains SA and interesting
changing guests such as Cotleigh Old Buzzard and Uley Pigor Mortis, and Long
Ashton farm cider. It's a classic corner pub, a lock-up for condemned men in its
early Georgian days; though completely refurbished two or three years ago, you'd
think it had always been this way. There's a cosy and crowded front bar (which is
no-smoking), with the corridor beside it leading through to a long series of little
rooms – wooden floors, green and cream paintwork, old-fashioned furniture and
prints, including lots of period Royal Family engravings and lithographs in the
front room. A nice terrace garden has tables built into a partly covered flowery
arbour; not large, but a pleasant surprise for the locality. Bargain bar food includes
filled rolls (45p), chick-pea salad (£1.60), chilli con carne, vegetable curry, lamb
and aubergine casserole and prawn risotto (all £1.80); friendly informal service,
darts, bar billiards, cribbage, dominoes and piped music (often interesting R&B).
*(Recommended by Peter Adcock, Barry and Anne, Paul Oakley, Drs M and K Parier, Michael
Cochrane, Martin Smietanko, Samantha Taylor)*

*Smiles Licensees John Payne and Timothy Gilroy Real ale Meals and snacks (12–2,
6–9) Open 12–11, but may close for an hour or so mid-afternoon if quiet*

CATCOTT (Somerset) ST3939 Map 1
King William

Village signposted off A39 Street–Bridgewater

Handy for the M5, this cottagey pub serves good bar food – sandwiches (from
90p), home-made soup (£1.40), filled baked potatoes (from £1.95), ploughman's
(from £1.95), salads (from £2.95), quiche (£3.10), beef curry (£3.30), home-made
seafood pie (£3.60), veal in a vermouth sauce (£6.95), duckling in orange sauce
(£8.75), and puddings (from 95p); friendly service. Traditional furnishings include
kitchen and other assorted chairs, brown-painted built-in and other settles,
window seats, stone floors with a rug or two, and Victorian fashion plates and
other old prints. One of the big stone fireplaces has had its side bread oven turned
into a stone grotto with kitsch figurines. Bass, Eldridge Pope Dorchester and Royal
Oak and Palmers BB on handpump, with Wilkin's farm cider; darts, dominoes,
fruit machine, and piped music. A large extension at the back includes a
skittle-alley and a well. *(Recommended by Ted George; more reports please)*

*Free house Licensee Michael O'Riordan Real ale Meals and snacks (12–2, 7–10)
Children welcome Open 11.30–3, 6–11*

CHISELBOROUGH (Somerset) ST4614 Map 1
Cat Head

Village signposted off B3165 between A3088 and A30 W of Yeovil

Surrounded by small hills, this creeper-covered old place, now under friendly new
licensees, has chairs and settles in Italian tapestry coloured to blend with the
honey-coloured velvet curtains, a flagstone floor, a big solid fuel stove, and an
old-fashioned atmosphere. Bar food includes sandwiches (from 80p), filled baked
potatoes (from £1.15), ploughman's or salads (from £2.20), vegetable terrine
(£2.30), steak and kidney pie (£2.90), gammon (£3.80), vegetable crumble (£3.90),
steak (from £6.50), and trout with parsley butter (£7.80); puddings (from £1.50).
Gibbs Mew Wiltshire and Premium and occasional guests on handpump; sensibly

placed darts, dominoes, cribbage, fruit machine, juke box, and piped music. There's a separate skittle alley, and seats outside in an attractive garden. Note they no longer do bedrooms. *(Recommended by Chris Raisin, Mr and Mrs G Turner; more reports on the new regime please)*

Gibbs Mew   Licensees Derek and Janet Burkey   Real ale   Snacks (sandwiches available during opening hours) and meals (normal food times)   Restaurant   Children in restaurant and eating area of bar   Open 11.30–3(4.30 Sat), 6.30–11

CHURCHILL (Avon)   ST4560 Map 1

Crown

Skinners Lane; in village, turn off A368 at Nelson Arms

There's an attractive range of well kept real ales in this atmosperic old cottage, including a nice light but well hopped bitter brewed for the pub by Cotleigh, as well as Cotleigh Tawny, Felinfoel Double Dragon, Fullers London Pride, Marstons Pedigree, Oakhill Farmers, Stout (under some top pressure), and Titanic – four on handpump, with others tapped from casks at the back; Gales country wines. The small and local stone-floored and cross-beamed room on the right has built-in wall benches, a wooden window seat, and an unusually sturdy settle; the left-hand room has a slate floor, and a woodburning stove, and some steps past the big log fire in a big stone fireplace lead to more sitting space. Lunchtime bar food includes a good home-made soup, sandwiches, wholesome ploughman's with real lumps of butter and a pickle tray (£1.95), baked potatoes, and steak and kidney pudding. There are picnic-table sets on a smallish back lawn; near the start of *Good Walks Guide* Walk 1. *(Recommended by William Pryce, Graham Bush, Steve and Carolyn Harvey, Dorothy and Charles Morley, Peter Adcock, P Miller, M Rowlinson, Drs M and K Parier, WTF)*

Free house   Real ale   Meals and snacks   Open 11–2.30, 6–11

CLAPTON IN GORDANO (Avon)   ST4773 Map 2

Black Horse

4 miles from M5 junction 19; A368 towards Portishead, then B3124 towards Clevedon; village signposted in North Weston, then in village turn right at Clevedon, Clapton Wick signposted

The little flagstoned front garden here is exceptionally pretty in summer with a mass of flowers in tubs, hanging baskets and flowerbeds, and some old rustic tables and benches, with more to one side of the car park and in the secluded children's play area with its sturdy wooden climber, slide, rope ladder and rope swing. Inside, the atmosphere is very relaxed and friendly, and the partly flagstoned and partly red-tiled main room has winged settles and built-in wall benches around narrow, dark wooden tables, pleasant window seats, amusing cartoons and photographs of the pub, and a big log fire with stirrups and bits on the mantlebeam. A window in an inner snug is still barred from the days when this room was the petty-sessions jail; high-backed settles – one a marvellous carved and canopied creature, another with an art nouveau copper insert reading *East, West, Hame's Best* – lots of mugs hanging from its black beams, and lots of little prints and photographs. There's also a simply furnished children's room, just off the bar, with high-backed corner settles and a gas fire; darts, dominoes, cribbage and table skittles. Bar food includes ploughman's and hot dishes such as beef cobbler, home-roasted ham, liver and bacon casserole, vegetable pie and so forth; free roast potatoes on the bar, Sunday lunchtime. Well kept Courage Bitter and Best and a guest tapped from the cask, and farm cider; cheerful, efficient service. Paths from here lead up Naish Hill or along to Cadbury Camp. *(Recommended by Helena and Arthur Harbottle, Jon Wainwright, Peter and Rose Flower, Roger Huggins, Drs M and K Parier, Mrs Isobel May, Lindy May, William Stapley, Genie and Brian Smart, David and Valerie Hooley, EML, D and B Carron)*

Courage   Licensee Tom Shaw   Real ale   Lunchtime meals and snacks (not Sun) Children in family room   Occasional Morris dancers in summer   Open 11–3, 6–11; may open all day in school hols

COMBE HAY (Avon)   ST7354 Map 2

Wheatsheaf Ⓟ

Village signposted from A367 or B3110 S of Bath

In a lovely spot, this country village pub is perched on the side of a steep wooded valley, with tables on the spacious sloping lawn that look down past the enterprising plunging garden to the church and ancient manor stables. Inside, the pleasantly old-fashioned rooms have low ceilings, brown-painted settles, pews and rustic tables, a very high-backed winged settle facing one big log fire, old sporting and other prints, and earthenware jugs on the shelf of the little shuttered windows. A wide choice of very good food includes dishes like home-made soup (£1.75), magnificent Stilton ploughman's (£2.50), pork and cider pâté (£2.75), garlic mushrooms (£2.85), vegetable chilli (£3.25), hot-pot, squid or prawn vinaigrette when available, gammon steak with pineapple, loin of pork (£5.10), and a selection of fish specials like scallops in white wine (£4), lovely cheddar baked lemon sole or sole stuffed with asparagus and mushrooms (£4.75), Scotch salmon (£5.75), and whole fresh crab or lobster, with grouse in season, maybe shot by the landlord himself; summer barbecues. Well kept Courage Best and a guest tapped from the cask; courteous, friendly staff (and dogs); shove-ha'penny. (*Recommended by Peter Adcock, GB, Barry and Anne, Nigel Gibbs, Sandra Cook, B H Hill, Tony and Lynne Stark, James Cane, Peter and Rose Flower, M B P Carpenter*)

Courage   Licensee M G Taylor   Real ale   Meals and snacks   Restaurant tel Bath (0225) 833504   Children welcome   Open 11–2.30, 6.30–11; 11–11 Fri and Sat

CRANMORE (Somerset)   ST6643 Map 2

Strode Arms ★ Ⓟ

West Cranmore; signposted with pub off A361 Frome–Shepton Mallet

Run with real care and love, this 15th-century former farmhouse has charming country furnishings, fresh flowers and pot plants, remarkable old locomotive engineering drawings and big black-and-white steamtrain murals in a central lobby, good bird prints, a grandfather clock on the flagstones, newspapers to read, and pretty views through the stone-mullioned windows down to the lively village duckpond. Well kept Bunces Best, Oakhill, Wadworths IPA and 6X and a weekly changing guest beer on handpump, an interesting choice of decent wines by the glass, quite a few ports, good log fires (in handsome fireplaces), shove-ha'penny, fruit machine, unobtrusive piped music. Generous helpings of really good home cooking include sandwiches (from 85p), ploughman's (from £2.25), filled baked potatoes (from £2.50), steak and kidney and other home-made pies (£3.50), juicy ham and eggs (£3.50), scallops with bacon (£3.65), sliced smoked duck breast (£4.55), nut cutlet (£4.75), breast of chicken with cheese and a white wine sauce (£6.25), avocado and seafood platter (£5.95), steaks (from £7.75), with game in winter; puddings such as home-made meringue with raspberries, ice-cream, nuts and cream or treacle tart (from £1.25); daily specials and Sunday roast are chalked up on a blackboard; service stays pleasant under pressure. There's a front terrace with some benches and a back garden. On the first Tuesday of each month, there's a vintage car meeting. Handy for the East Somerset Light Railway. (*Recommended by Dr F Peters, R M Morgan, P M Bisby, Dr J E Gore, Brig J S Green, R W Stanbury, S V Bishop, John and Joan Wyatt*)

Free house   Licensees Rodney and Dora Phelps   Real ale   Meals and snacks (till 10pm Fri and Sat; not Sun evening Oct–Feb and limited for rest of year)   Cottagey restaurant tel Cranmore (074 988) 450; not Sun evening   Children in restaurant Open 11.30–2.30, 6.30–11

CROSCOMBE (Somerset)   ST5844 Map 2

Bull Terrier ★ Ⓟ 🛏

A371 Wells–Shepton Mallet

Consistently popular with readers for the warmth of its welcome, this is actually one of Somerset's oldest pubs. Wholesome bar food includes sandwiches (from £1.05; toasted from £1.25), soup (£1.25), ploughman's (from £2.15), salads (from £3.35), spaghetti bolognese (£3.25), home-made Indian spiced beans (£3.60), home-made Brazil nut loaf (£3.95), excellent home-made steak and kidney pie (£3.95), Barnsley chop (£4.95), trout and almonds (£5.25), steaks (from £8.45), and home-made specials like ginger chicken with noodles, red hot beef or lamb Shrewsbury; lovely puddings such as fudge cake with hot butterscotch sauce (£1.50). The lounge ('Inglenook') bar has attractively moulded 15th-century beams, cushioned wooden wall seats and wheelback chairs around neat glossy tables, a red carpet on its flagstone floor, pictures on its white walls, and a log-effect gas fire in a big stone fireplace with a fine iron fireback. A communicating ('Snug') room has more tables with another gas-effect log fire, and there's a third in the parquet-floored 'Common Bar', by the local noticeboard; there's also a family room. A wide choice of drinks includes well kept Butcombe, Greene King Abbot, Palmers IPA and Bull Terrier Best Bitter (a strongish beer brewed for the pub) on handpump, and farmhouse cider and several wines both by the glass and by the bottle; they also have an off sales price list. Dominoes, cribbage, chess, draughts and maybe piped music. Originally called the Rose & Crown, it changed its name in 1976 and is a regular calling place for owners/breeders of Bull Terriers. *(Recommended by B and J Derry, Gethin Lewis, Roger Huggins, Brig J S Green, T C and A R Newell, K H Frostick, Duncan and Lucy Gardner, Mike Tucker, J B Greenhalgh, Peter and Rose Flower, Dr F Peters, Margaret and Douglas Tucker)*

Free house   Licensees Stan and Pam Lea   Real ale   Meals and snacks (till 10, Fri and Sat evenings; not Sun evenings or Mon Nov–Mar)   Children in family room   Open 12–2.30, 7–11; closed Mon Nov–Mar   Bedrooms tel Wells (0749) 343658; £17/£36B

DOULTING (Somerset)   ST6443 Map 2

Poachers Pocket

Follow Chelynch signpost off A361 in village, E of Shepton Mallet

The atmosphere in this neatly kept little pub is especially warm and friendly, and there are some black beams, one or two settles, small wheelback or captain's chairs, gundog pictures on the white walls, a crackling log fire in the end stripped-stone wall, and flagstones by the bar counter (though it's mainly carpeted); the extension has created a lot more bar space. Popular bar food includes pâté (£1.25), sandwiches (from £1.20), ploughman's (from £2.40), home-made quiche (£2.95), cauliflower cheese or home-cooked ham (£3.25), tasty home-made steak and kidney pie (£3.30), scampi (£3.50), and pan-fried steak (£4.95); an evening charcoal grill serves a selection of lamb cutlets (£4.95), pork chops or gammon steak and pineapple (£5.25) and steaks (from £6.95); puddings like sherry trifle (£1.25) or pineapple pavlova (£1.60). Well kept Butcombe Bitter, Oakhill Farmers and Yeoman on handpump, farm ciders and good tea. *(Recommended by Tony and Lynne Stark, Peter and Rose Flower, M J B Pearson, Dr F Peters, Klaus Leist)*

Free house   Licensees Mike and Joyce Mock   Real ale   Meals and snacks (11.3–1.45, 6.15–9.45; not Mon lunchtime)   Children in eating area   Open 11.30–2.30, 6.15–11; closed Mon lunchtime

DOWLISH WAKE (Somerset)   ST3713 Map 1

New Inn 😊

Village signposted from Kingstone – which is signposted from A303 on W side of Ilminster, and from A3037 just S of Ilminster; keep on past church – pub at far end of village

It's rare to find a smallish pub that seems bound to please everyone, but this friendly and cosy village pub really should do just that. It's spotlessly clean, and the old-fashioned furnishings include a mixture of chairs, high-backed settles, attractive sturdy tables, dark beams which are strung liberally with hop bines, and a stone inglenook fireplace with a woodburning stove. The Swiss landlady does the cooking: as well as bar food including sandwiches (from £1.35), soup (£1.35), good ploughman's (£2), spicy sausage (£2.50), ham and egg (£2.75), omelettes (from £2.95) and sirloin steak (£6.75), she's praised for dishes such as squid or soft roes (£2.50), seafood salad (£3.75), raclette (£4.50), duck and pigeon breast (£7.95), whole shoulder of lamb (£9.75), and puddings like delicious apple and blackberry pancake with blackberry ice-cream; no credit cards. Besides well kept Butcombe, Wadworths 6X and Theakstons Old Peculier on handpump, and a decent choice of whiskies, there's a selection of Perry's ciders. These come from just down the road, and the thatched 16th-century stone cider mill is well worth a visit for its collection of wooden bygones and its liberal free tastings (you can buy the half-dozen different ciders in old-fashioned earthenware flagons as well as more modern containers; it's closed on Sunday afternoons). There may be piped music, and in a separate area they have darts, shove-ha'penny, dominoes, cribbage, table skittles as well as alley skittles and a fruit machine. There's a rustic bench in front of the stone pub, which is decorated with tubs of flowers and a sprawl of clematis. *(Recommended by Bernard Phillips, C P Scott-Malden, Richard Dolphin, K R Harris, David Wallington, Graham and Glenis Watkins, EML, Dr Stewart Rae, Robert and Vicky Tod, PLC, Ted George, Chris Raisin, David Shillitoe)*

Free house   Licensees Therese Boosey and David Smith   Real ale   Meals and snacks (table bookings tel Ilminster (0460) 52413; not Sun evening winter)   Children in family room   Open 11–2.30, 6–11; may open all day Sat if trade demands

DUNSTER (Somerset)   SS9943 Map 1

Luttrell Arms 🍺

A396

Until 1779, this 15th-century Gothic Hall was known as The Ship; now a comfortably modernised THF hotel, it still has a pubby atmosphere in the back bar where there are old settles as well as more modern furniture, bottles, clogs and horseshoes hanging from the high beams, and a stag's head and rifles on the walls. Ancient black timber uprights glazed with fine hand-floated glass, full of ripples and irregularities, separate the room from a small galleried and flagstoned courtyard. Bar snacks include sandwiches, a cold buffet, plaice and a speciality mixed grill, as well as unusual evening meals; well kept Bass and Exmoor Bitter on handpump. In the gardens there are cannon emplacements dug out by Blake in the Civil War when – with Praise God Barebones and his pikemen – he was besieging the Castle for six months. The town, on the edge of Exmoor National Park, is pretty. *(Recommended by W and S Rinaldi-Butcher, Richard Gibbs, H W and A B Tuffill)*

Free house (THF)   Real ale   Meals and snacks   Restaurant   Open 11–2.30, 6–11 Bedrooms tel Dunster (0643) 821555; £67B/£89B

EAST LYNG (Somerset)   ST3328 Map 1

Rose & Crown

A361 about 4 miles W of Othery

There's an unchanging atmosphere in this pub; its open-plan lounge bar is traditionally furnished, with stacks of old *Country Lifes* on a bow window seat by an oak drop-leaf table, a corner cabinet of glass, china and silver, a court cabinet, beams, and a winter log fire in a modernised fine old stone fireplace; piped music. Well kept Butcombe, Palmers IPA and Eldridge Pope Royal Oak on handpump. Freshly prepared food includes good crusty sandwiches (95p; steak £2.50), soup (£1.30), pâté (£1.65), ploughman's (from £2), ham and egg (£2.75), omelettes (£3.95), salads (£3.75), scampi or trout (£4.10), mixed grill or duck (£7.90), steaks (from £7.50), and puddings (£1.65). The prettily planted back garden (largely hedged off from the car park) has picnic-table sets, and there's also a full skittle alley. *(Recommended by Richard Dolphin, Hilary Roberts, Patrick Young)*

Free house   Licensee P J Thyer   Real ale   Meals and snacks (12–2, 7–10)

Restaurant tel Taunton (0823) 69235; not Sun lunchtime   Children in eating area of bar   Open 10.30–2.30, 6.30–11

EXFORD (Somerset)   SS8538 Map 1

White Horse 🛏

B3224

Unusually for the area, this is a tall building, creeper-covered, with its top storey half-timbered. The more-or-less open-plan bar has Windsor and other country kitchen chairs, a high-backed antique settle, scrubbed deal tables, hunting prints, photographs above the stripped pine dado, and a good winter log fire. Home-cooked bar food includes filled rolls (from 90p), sandwiches (from £1.10), ploughman's (from £2.55), macaroni cheese (£2.95), lasagne (£3.95), steak and kidney pie (£4), venison pie (£4.25), steaks (from £6.95), and lobster (around £9.65); the traditional puddings (£1.30) are popular; some of the tables in the eating area are no-smoking. Bass, Cotleigh Tawny, Exmoor Bitter and Gold tapped from the cask, with Worthington on handpump; sensibly placed darts, tables outside. Though the old coach road climbs from here up over Exmoor, the attractive village itself is sheltered – pretty in summer, with the river running past the inn. *(Recommended by T J Maddison, Sarah Vickers, T Galligan and others; more reports please)*

Free house   Licensees Peter and Linda Hendrie   Real ale   Meals and snacks (12–2.30, 6.30–9.30)   Children in eating area of bar   Open 11–11 Whitsun–end Oct; 12–3, 5.30–11 rest of the year   Bedrooms tel Exford (064 383) 229; £32.20B/£64.40B; children under 14 free if sharing with parents

FAULKLAND (Somerset)   ST7354 Map 2

Tuckers Grave

A366 E of village

The smallest pub in the *Guide*, this unspoilt farm cottage pub has a flagstoned entry that opens into a tiny room with casks of well kept Bass and Butcombe Bitter on tap and Cheddar Valley cider in an alcove on the left. Two old cream-painted high-backed settles face each other across a single table on the right, and a side room has shove-ha'penny. There's a skittle alley, and seats outside. Food is limited to ploughman's. *(Recommended by Peter Adcock, Bob Eardley, Roger Huggins, R W Stanbury, Jon Wainwright, Nick Dowson, Alison Hayward)*

Free house   Licensees Ivan and Glenda Swift   Real ale   Children welcome   Open 11–2.30, 6–11

HASELBURY PLUCKNETT (Somerset)   ST4710 Map 1

Haselbury Inn ✑

A3066 E of Crewkerne

The wide choice of bar food in this well kept and inviting place includes soup (£1.20; game £1.50), home-made pâté or ploughman's with five cheeses (£2.80), good pasta dishes such as spaghetti bolognese or lambs kidneys and bacon fettucini (£3.60), beef curry (£4), coq au vin (£6.50), charcoal-grilled steaks (from £7), guinea fowl (£7.50), local trout (£8), large Dover sole (£12), and daily specials like moules marinières in season (£3.80), Hungarian goulash (£3.80), or king prawns (£4.50); also, puddings such as apple strudel or raspberry and redcurrant pie (from £2), and a barbecue menu (from £2.80); you can also choose anything from the à la carte menu; vegetables are fresh, sauces home-made. In one half of the neatly kept bar, chintz armchairs and sofas relax around the fire and television set; in the other, candlelit wooden tables have unusually heavy red-cushioned cask seats – there's a fire down here, too; also plants in the windows, fresh or dried flowers, and a restrained collection of bric-a-brac on the rather lofty beams; piped music. Well kept Boddingtons, Butcombe Bitter, Exmoor Best, Wadworths 6X and

Charles Wells Bombardier on handpump or tapped from the cask, and a good range of wines and other drinks, including espresso coffee. Evening meals in the attractive back restaurant should probably be booked on Fridays and Saturdays. There are picnic-table sets on the side grass. The blue and yellow macaw has now gone to a rest home. *(Recommended by Mr and Mrs H Hearnshaw, Mr and Mrs J R Hulley, Chris Raisin; more reports please)*

Free house   Licensee James Pooley   Real ale   Meals and snacks   No-smoking restaurant tel Crewkerne (0460) 72488   Open 12–2.30, 7–11; closed Mon

HINTON ST GEORGE (Somerset)   ST4212 Map 1

Poulett Arms

Village signposted off A30 W of Crewkerne; and off Merriott road (declassified – former A356, off B3165) N of Crewkerne

The emphasis here is on the front dining lounge – a handsome room with big black beams, stripped masonry, maroon plush chairs (and a couple of high-backed settles), matching velvet curtains, imposing stone fireplace, a few pistols and brasses, and two cosy smaller rooms opening off, one with a big disused inglenook fireplace. It can be very busy mid-evening. As this is largely a retirement village, the smaller back drinking bar seems more of a sideline, despite its comfortable armchairs and the friendliness of the licensees – and Burton, their cream labrador. Good bar food includes sandwiches (from £1.20), home-made soup (£1.25), avocado mousse (£1.65), ploughman's (£2.75), lasagne (£3.75), particularly good steak and kidney pie (£3.95), trout (£4.95), steaks (from 8oz sirloin £7.95) and dishes of the day such as Cumberland sausage with egg and chips (£2.75), cottage pie (£2.95), nut roast (£5.25) and chestnut patties in red wine (£5.75). Well kept Ushers Best and Founders and Ruddles County on handpump; fruit machine, cribbage, dominoes, maybe unobtrusive piped music. The prettily planted back garden has some white tables under cocktail parasols, near a real rarity – a massive pelota wall; there's also a skittle alley, with darts and table skittles. We've not yet had reports on the bedrooms. *(Recommended by Richard Dolphin, Fiona Easeman, Chris Raisin, Nicholas Kingsley)*

Leased from Grand Metropolitan (Watneys)   Licensees Ray and Di Chisnall   Real ale   Meals and snacks   Children in family room   Open 11.30–3, 7–11   Bedrooms tel Crewkerne (0460) 73149; £20B/£40B

KELSTON (Avon)   ST7067 Map 2

Old Crown

Bitton Road; A431 W of Bath

Carefully restored and preserved to make the most of its traditional features, this is a fine antidote to the gutted antiquing – imported beams, timbers and bookshelves – that's become such a fashion with some brewery architects. In one or other of its row of four small rooms you'll find polished flagstones, interesting carved settles, cask tables, candlelight, beams strung with hops, lovely tableau photographs, and logs burning in an ancient open range (we'd guess another attractive fireplace, which now has a log-effect gas fire, is on their list of planned restorations). Well kept Bass, Butcombe, Smiles Best and Exhibition (summer; Wadworths Old Timer instead in winter) and Wadworths 6X on handpump, and Mendip cider; no machines or music – just shove-ha'penny and dominoes. Bar lunches include a good beef casserole, and run from sandwiches through salads to other hot dishes; there are sometimes summer barbecues in the neat, sheltered back garden, which has picnic-table sets. The car park's over quite a fast road. *(Recommended by Carol Mason, Steve and Carolyn Harvey, William Pryce, Roger Huggins, Tony Hodge, Lisa Wilson)*

Free house   Licensees Richard Jackson and Michael Steele   Real ale   Meals and snacks (lunchtime, not Sun)   Restaurant Thurs–Sat evening tel Bath (0225) 23032; children may be allowed here, but not in pub   Open 11.30–2.30, 6–11

KILVE (Somerset)   ST1442   Map 1

Hood Arms

A39 E of Williton

The carpeted main bar in this village inn, run by enthusiastic and attentive
licensees, is straightforwardly comfortable and there's a woodburning stove in the
stone fireplace (decorated with shining horsebrasses on their original leathers). It
leads through to a little cosy lounge with red plush button-back seats. Well kept
Flowers Original and Marstons Pedigree on handpump, several malt whiskies, and
they do tea and coffee; attentive service; dominoes, cribbage, alley skittles and
gentle piped music. Lunchtime home-made bar food, popular as ever with readers,
includes sandwiches (from 85p), soup (£1.40), pâté or good ploughman's (£2.25),
substantial salads (from £2.50), hot daily specials such as country-style chicken,
steak and kidney pie, haddock and broccoli mornay or National Trust pie (all
£3.75), and tasty puddings (from £1.30); in the evenings the main bar takes on
much more the style of a restaurant, with full meals. A sheltered back terrace, by a
garden with a prettily planted old wall behind, has white metal and plastic seats
and tables. *(Recommended by Sue North, Peter Burton, E G Parish, Dr and Mrs Tanner, R
and E Harfield, Mrs K J Betts)*

*Free house   Licensees Robbie Rutt and Neville White   Real ale   Meals and snacks
(12–2, 6.30–10)   No-smoking restaurant Wed–Sat evenings   Children over 7 in
restaurant only   Open 11–2.30, 6–11; closed 25 Dec   Bedrooms tel Holford (027
874) 210; £30B/£50B*

LANGLEY MARSH (Somerset)   ST0729   Map 1

Three Horseshoes ★ ⊗

Village signposted off A361 from Wiveliscombe

The back bar in this popular red sandstone pub has low modern settles, polished
wooden tables with plants, dark red wallpaper, a piano, a local stone fireplace,
banknotes papering the wall behind the bar and planes hanging from the ceiling;
the lively front room has sensibly placed darts, shove-ha'penny, table skittles,
dominoes, cribbage, fruit machine and piped music; separate skittle alley; the pub
alsatian is called Guinness. The range of well kept real ales is wide and often
unusual, typically including Badger Tanglefoot, Bass, Butcombe Best, Eldridge
Pope Hardy, maybe King & Barnes, Palmers IPA, Ringwood, Wadworths 6X and
Youngs on handpump or tapped from the cask; the guest ales change continually,
and they serve Perry's farmhouse cider from the cask. Entirely fresh home-made
food from a constantly changing and imaginative menu includes baps (from
£1.15), vegetable and lentil soup (£1.55), ploughman's (from £1.90), pheasant and
liver pâté or garlic mushrooms (£2), salads, courgette and mushroom bake (£3.60),
leek croustade (£3.75), Somerset fish pie with perfect pastry or chicken and
mushroom pie (£4), sliced lamb and cashew nuts (£4.45), and spiced beef in ginger
(£4.75); most of the vegetables come from their garden (no chips or fried food),
and the butter comes in little pots; puddings include good mincemeat, apple and
brandy pancakes or cheesecake with cherry topping. You can sit on rustic seats on
the verandah or in the sloping back garden, with a climbing frame, swing and slide,
a view of farmland. In fine weather there are usually vintage cars outside. No dogs.
*(Recommended by John Tyzack, A M J Chadwick, Alan P Carr, R W Stanbury, Mr and Mrs
Norman Edwardes, Peter Hall, Mrs Ann Spice, John and Tessa Rainsford, C P Scott-Malden)*

*Free house   Licensee J Hopkins   Real ale   Meals and snacks   Small restaurant
tel Wiveliscombe (0984) 23763   Well behaved children allowed away from bar
Singalongs Sat evenings and occasional spontaneous 'fiddle/squeeze box' sessions with
local Morris Dancing musicians   Open 12–2.30, 7–11*

MONKSILVER (Somerset)   ST0737   Map 1

Notley Arms ★ ✪

B3188

A particular point with this place is the way it's kept its charm – and a vast amount of support from readers – in spite of coming in just a few years from a tucked-away backwater of an inn into an award-winning place that's practically a household word now in the area. The L-shaped bar has beams, small settles and kitchen chairs around the plain country wooden and candle-lit tables, Old Master and other prints on the black-timbered white walls, a couple of woodburning stoves, and a warm atmosphere; dominoes and alley skittles, well reproduced classical music, and a bright little family room; dogs welcome. Regular dishes on the ever-popular menu include soup (£1.10), sandwiches (from 90p), filled baked potatoes (from £1.75), excellent ploughman's (from £2), shepherd's purse (wholemeal pitta bread generously filled with garlicky lamb and salad, £2.50), home-made pasta or vegetarian curry (£3.25), salads (local cured ham £3.75, generous prawn mayonnaise, delicious smoked mackerel), superb Chinese-style pork with stir-fry vegetables (£4.50), and correctly cooked vegetables; lots of interesting specials, and puddings like treacle tart or home-made ice-creams (£1.25), and evening extras such as fresh local trout (£5) and sirloin steak (£7). Well kept Ushers Best and Ruddles County on handpump, and country wines such as oak leaf or raspberry; efficient staff. The neatly kept cottage garden runs down to a swift clear stream. (*Recommended by PLC, Mr and Mrs E Patterson, Pete and Mary Fintelley, Steve and Carolyn Harvey, T H G Lewis, Dr J E Gore, Mr and Mrs J D Cranston, A M J Chadwick, P Miller, Cynthia Pollard, Mr and Mrs Morgan, Russell and Christina Jones, J D Cranston, Steve Dark*)

Ushers (Watneys)   Licensee Alistair Cade   Real ale   Meals and snacks   Children in eating area   Open 11–2.30, 6–11; closed 25 Dec and first two weeks of Feb

MONTACUTE (Somerset)   ST4916   Map 2

Kings Arms

A3088 W of Yeovil

The atmosphere in this early Georgian inn is civilised yet friendly, and the lounge bar is comfortably furnished with grey-gold plush seats, soft armchairs, chintz sofas, a high curved settle, and towards the front – where part of the walls are stripped back to the handsome masonry – plush seats around tables. Popular bar food includes soup with home-made bread (95p), a generous buffet, and daily specials such as steak and kidney pie, chicken chasseur or ham and asparagus bake (£3.80 or £4.45); best to book for Sunday lunch (when people tend to dress smartly); smoking is discouraged in the eating areas. Bass and Gibbs Mew Wiltshire tapped from the cask; good wines and farm cider. The village includes the stately Elizabethan mansion of the same name, and behind the hotel the wooded St Michael's Hill is owned by the National Trust. (*Recommended by Dr and Mrs Frank Wells, D K and H M Brenchley, D I Baddeley, Alan P Carr, Mrs A Crowhurst, Cdr G F Barnett, Mrs E M Thompson, R W Stanbury, A M Kelly, Steve Huggins*)

Free house   Licensee S D Price   Real ale   Meals and snacks (12–2, 7.30–10)   Children welcome   Restaurant   Open 11–3, 6–11; closed 25 Dec and 26 Dec   Bedrooms tel Martock (0935) 822513; £42B/58B

NORTON ST PHILIP (Somerset)   ST7755   Map 2

George

A366

This simply furnished and thoroughly historic pub – it's been functioning for nearly 600 years – has massive stone walls, high mullioned windows, and a fine half-timbered and galleried back courtyard, with an external Norman stone stair-turret. Inside there are leather seats, square-panelled wooden settles, plain old tables, wide bare floorboards, and lofty beams hung with harness, copper preserving pans, and a magnificent pair of bellows; a long, stout table serves well kept Bass, and Wadworths IPA and 6X on handpump. Bar food includes filled rolls, soup, ploughman's, filled baked potatoes or lasagne (£2.40), and a couple of daily specials such as pheasant casserole (from £3.50). A panelled lounge is furnished with antique settles and tables. Off the courtyard is the cellar Dungeon Bar (opened only at busy times – weekends say), named to recall the men imprisoned there after the rebel Duke of Monmouth had been defeated. A stroll over the meadow behind the pub leads to an attractive churchyard around the medieval church. (*Recommended by Mrs A M Viney, Janet Hill, Les Rae, Gwen and Peter Andrews, Lynn Sharpless, Bob Eardley, Peter Adcock, Roger Huggins, H K Dyson, Len Beattie, Tony and Lynne Stark, Carol Mason, Mr and Mrs D M Norton, William Pryce, Barry and Anne, Tony Gayfer, R W Stanbury, D J Milner, W Bailey; more reports please*)

Wadworths Licensee M F Moore Real ale Meals and snacks (12–2, 7–10) Children in restaurant and two other rooms Restaurant tel Faulkland (037 387) 224 Open 11–2.30, 6–11; 11–11 Sat

OLDBURY-UPON-SEVERN (Avon) ST6292 Map 2

Anchor ⊘

Village signposted from B4061

The beamed lounge in this popular food pub is comfortably furnished with cushioned window seats, a curved high-backed settle facing an attractive oval oak gateleg table, winged seats against the wall, easy chairs, and a big winter log fire. The bar menu changes daily, with an emphasis on substantial, good value main meals: quiche (£2.50), cauliflower cheese (£2.70), Yorkshire pudding filled with roast beef (£3.60), beef in ale pie or lasagne (£3.20), locally made pork and garlic sausages (£3.25), prawn curry (£4.05), beef stroganoff (£4.85), particularly good charcoal grilled steaks (£6.25), and enterprising puddings such as rhuburb crumble, blackcurrant supreme, fruit sponge and so forth (from £1.15); friendly waitress service; best to get there early if you want a seat. Bass tapped from the cask, with Butcombe, Hook Norton Best, Marstons Pedigree and Theakstons Best on handpump; over 70 malts, including Sheep Dip; darts, shove-ha'penny and cribbage. You can sit outside in the garden in summer. St Arilda's church nearby is interesting, on its odd little knoll with wild flowers among the gravestones (the primroses and daffodils in spring are lovely), and there are lots of paths over the meadows to the sea dyke or warth which overlooks the tidal flats. (*Recommended by Michael Watts, Patrick Godfrey, J Warren, Jon Wainwright, Margaret Dyke, Tony Ritson, E and P Parkinson, Russell and Christina Jones, Helena and Arthur Harbottle, Barry and Anne*)

Free house Licensees Michael Dowdeswell and Peter Riley Real ale Meals and snacks Restaurant tel Thornbury (0454) 413331 Children in dining room Open 11.30–2.30, 6.30–11; 11.30–3, 6–11 Sat

OVER STRATTON (Somerset) ST4315 Map 1

Royal Oak ⊘

Village signposted from former A303 Yeovil–Ilminster through Seavington St Michael, which itself is signposted off A303 at E end of new Ilminster bypass

Decorations and furnishings in the cosy, extended dark-flagstoned bars of this popular thatched food pub are simple but careful, and the atmosphere is old-fashioned and relaxed. There are scrubbed deal farmhouse kitchen tables, a mixture of similar or dining chairs, pews and settles, candles in bottles, plants in the windows, some hop bines, and a stuffed pheasant. The beams have been prettily stencilled with an oakleaf and acorn pattern, the walls are stripped to bare stonework or attractively ragrolled red, and log fires burn, even in summer; maybe unobtrusive piped music. Bar food includes home-made soup, salads, filled baked potatoes, deep-fried brie (£3.50), game sausages (£3.95), squid platter with lemon mayonnaise (£4.25), garlic-fried or roast sesame chicken (£6.50), fresh stuffed trout or prawn and asparagus pancake (£7.25), and seafood platter (£12.50); good children's dishes (from £1.50). Well kept Boddingtons, Butcombe Bitter and Wadworths 6X on handpump, lots of malt whiskies and an extensive wine list. There are lots of picnic-table sets on a floodlit reconstituted-stone terrace sheltered by the back wings of the building, with more on a further sheltered gravel terrace with a barbecue; the play area is large and well equipped – there's even a big trampoline. (*Recommended by Helena and Arthur Harbottle, George Allardyce, D I Baddeley, John and Pat Smyth, Cdr G F Barnett, A M J Chadwick, Pat Woodward, R J Walden, Chris Raisin, David Wallington, Richard R Dolphin*)

Free house   Licensees Derek and Claire Blezard   Real ale   Meals and snacks (12–2, 7–10)   Restaurant tel Ilminster (0460) 40906   Children in restaurant   Open 12–2.30, 7(6.30 Sats)–11; closed 25 and 26 Dec

PORLOCK (Somerset)   SS8846 Map 1

Ship ★ 🛏

A39

The extended garden (actually almost higher than the thatched roof) at the back of this partly 13th-century village cottage has lovely views of the sea and moor; there's also a children's play area. Inside, the characterful low-beamed front bar, popular with the friendly locals, has a sought-after window-ledge seat, traditional old benches on the tiled and flagstoned floor, hunting prints on the walls, and an inglenook fireplace at each end. The carpeted back lounge has plush red banquettes, a Gothic settle, and a chimney seat. Well kept Bass, Cotleigh Old Buzzard, Courage Best and a weekly guest beer on handpump from an air-conditioned cellar; Perry's cider. Bar food – given the inn's other distinct charms, not the main thing here – includes home-made soup (£1), venison sausages, and main dishes such as pheasant casserole, beef in Guinness or haddock and prawn bake (all £3.50). Shove-ha'penny, dominoes, cribbage, bar billiards, and fruit machine, a separate pool room (which has sensibly placed darts too, in winter), and a full skittle alley. We should stress that the stay award is primarily for the charming *simplicity* of the bedrooms. (*Recommended by P Miller, Klaus Leist, B and J Derry, Andrea and Guy Bradley, R Gray, Andy Hick, F A Noble, Carol Mason, Pamela and Merlyn Horswell, W A D Hoyle, David Goldstone, Vic and Reba Longhorn, WHBM, Steve Dark, P J Hanson, G W Warren, T J Maddison, Sarah Vickers, Virginia Jones, Henry Midwinter, David Young, I T and S Hughes, George Berry*)

Free house   Licensee C M Robinson   Real ale   Meals and snacks   Children in eating area of bar   Restaurant; closed Sun evening   Open 10.30–3(2.30 winter), 5.30–11 Bedrooms tel Porlock (0643) 862507; £11.50(£18.50B)/£31(£35B)

SHEPPERDINE (Avon)   ST6295 Map 4

Windbound

From B4061 just N of Thornbury turn off at Oldbury signpost, then right at Shepperdine signpost, then next left into Shepperdine Lane; some maps and signposts spell it Sheperdine

The downstairs bar here – below the level of the sea dyke – has dining chairs and straight-backed small settles forming booths around the tables, one or two local watercolours and prints with the wicker fish-traps on its walls, and a good winter fire. Ind Coope Burton, Tetleys, Wadworths 6X and a guest beer on handpump, farm ciders such as Addlestone's, and quite a few sherries and bourbons. Bar food includes soup (95p), sandwiches, ploughman's, salads (from £3.75), a vegetarian dish (£3.75), tagliatelli carbonara or chicken enchilada (£5.25), steaks (from £7.50), daily specials and puddings (£1.75); children's menu (£1.95), Sunday lunch (£4.50), afternoon teas from June–September, and barbecues in fine weather. Darts, cribbage, fruit machine, piped music and a separate skittle alley. On the sheltered fairy-lit lawn outside this extended pub there are picnic-table sets among brightly coloured summer flowers, swings and slides, and more seats up on the dyke. You can walk along the banks of the Severn estuary to Sharpness, and the spacious upper dining lounge has extensive views over the Severn Estuary to the hills beyond. (*Recommended by R F Warner, Gwen and Peter Andrews; more reports please*)

Halls (Allied)   Licensees Nigel and Josephine Wright   Real ale   Meals and snacks
Restaurant tel Thornbury (0454) 414343   Children welcome   Country and Western
1st Sun of month, middle-of-road music in restaurant Sat evening   Open 11–3(4 Sat),
6–11; 11.30–2.30, 7–11 in winter; closed Mon lunchtime Jan–Easter

SOUTH STOKE (Avon)   ST7461 Map 2

Pack Horse

Village signposted opposite the Cross Keys off B3110, leaving Bath southwards – just
before end of speed limit

Now entering its sixth century, this former priory and three-gabled stone house has
two rooms on both floors and a central alleyway leading to the church (which was
used for carrying the dead to the cemetery). This entrance corridor – still a public
right of way to the church – takes you to a central space by the serving bar where
you get your well kept Courage Best and Wadworths 6X on handpump and choice
of ciders. Outstandingly good value bar food includes home-baked cider ham in
rolls (60p), home-made pasties or sausage plait (80p), several ploughman's (from
£1.75), and basket meals (from £1.40; scampi £1.80); friendly staff. The main
room has antique oak settles (two well carved), leatherette dining chairs and
cushioned captain's chairs on the quarry-tiled floor, a heavy black beam-and-plank
ceiling, a cheery log fire in the handsome stone inglenook, some Royalty pictures, a
chiming wall-clock, rough black shutters for the stone-mullioned windows (put up
in World War I), and a good local atmosphere; rather fine shove-ha'penny slates
are set into two of the tables, and there are darts, dominoes, and cribbage. There's
another room down to the left. The spacious back garden looks out over the stolid
old church and the wooded valley. (Recommended by Peter and Rose Flower, M J B
Pearson, Chris Raisin, Graham Doyle, Roger Huggins, R W Stanbury, Ron Gentry, Carol
Mason)

Courage   Licensee Colin Williams   Real ale   Meals and snacks   Open 11–11, but
may close in afternoon if quiet

STANTON WICK (Avon)   ST6162 Map 2

Carpenters Arms 🛏️

Village signposted off A368, just W of junction with A37 S of Bristol

This long and low tiled-roof country inn has a big log fire in the central area, by
the serving counter, and a prettily stocked aquarium. It's red-carpeted throughout,
with stripped stone walls, fresh flowers on the heavy tables, and red-cushioned
wall pews and other seats; there's a plump and rather aloof ginger cat. Diners are
encouraged to step down into a snug inner room (lightened by mirrors in arched
'windows'), or to go round to the sturdy tables angling off on the right (where a
pianist may be quietly vamping his way through Hoagy Carmichael and other old
favourites on Friday and Saturday nights). Note that most of these tables get
booked at weekends. The food ordering counter is round here: the wide choice of
popular and good value food includes home-made soup (£1.25), filled baked
potatoes (from £1.35), lots of starters like pâté (£2.25), ploughman's (from £2.65),
grilled fresh sardines (£2.75) or devilled kidneys (£3.65), several vegetarian dishes
such as ratatouille au gratin (£2.65), fresh plaice fillet (£5.25), several
home-cooked cold roasts with salad (£5.25) and steaks (from £7.85); specials like
fresh asparagus or monkfish provençale, and home-made puddings (from £1.50).
Well kept Bass, Butcombe, Smiles and Wadworths 6X on handpump, and a good
wine list, strong on medium priced well-made wines. The bedrooms are attractively
furnished, and breakfasts are good. There are picnic-table sets on the front terrace.
(Recommended by Steve Dark, Michele and Andrew Wells, Angus and Rosemary Campbell,
Roger Huggins, Paul Evans, William Pryce)

Free house   Licensee Nigel Pushman   Real ale   Meals and snacks (12–2.15, 7–10)
Restaurant; closed Sun evenings   Children in eating area of bar   Pianist 5 nights a
week   Open 11–3, 5–11   Bedrooms tel Compton Dando (0761) 490202;
£39.50B/£46.50B

STAPLE FITZPAINE (Somerset)   ST2618 Map 1
Greyhound

Village signposted from A358 Taunton–Ilminster at Hatch Beauchamp; or (better road) from Shoreditch on B3170, just after crossing M5 S of Taunton

This popular creeper-covered country pub has flagstone floors, simple antique furnishings, and log fires in attractive inglenooks. There are some seats outside in front of the pub among troughs of flowers, with more in the gravelled stable yard behind; also, a children's play area with a Wendy House and slide and a barbecue. Popular bar food includes home-made soup (£1.25), pâté (£2.45), ploughman's (£2.95), lasagne (£3.95), scampi (£4.95), and evening charcoal grills like kebabs (£5.45), gigot of lamb or medallions of pork (£5.95), and steaks (£7.95), with home-made puddings such as treacle tart (£1.95) or profiteroles (£2.45), Friday evening fish specials, and Sunday lunch (£3.95). Well kept Exmoor Bitter, Flowers IPA and Original and Marstons Pedigree on handpump, and lots of country wines and a fair number of malt whiskies; piped classical music. Just to the south you can walk in the hillside woods of Neroche Forest, which has a signposted nature trail. (*Recommended by Mr and Mrs P J Barrett, Dr D M Forsyth, Patrick Young, PLC, Carol and Robin Tullo, T C W Moody, A B Barton, Mr and Mrs C Moncreiffe*)

Free house   Licensees Steven Watts and Mrs Audrey Watts   Real ale   Meals and snacks (12–2, 7–10)   Children welcome   Restaurant tel Hatch Beauchamp (0823) 480227   Jazz or Rythmn and Blues Thurs evenings, Folk 2nd and last Fri of month Open 11–3, 5.30–11

STOGUMBER (Somerset)   ST0937 Map 1
White Horse

From A358 Taunton–Williton, village signposted on left at Crowcombe

This delightful little village local has a long room with settles and cushioned captain's chairs around the heavy rustic tables on its patterned carpet, a coal fire in cool weather, and a red-tiled floor at one end with old-fashioned built-in settles. A side room has sensibly placed darts and a fruit machine; shove-ha'penny, dominoes, cribbage, space game and piped music, as well as a separate skittle alley. Good, quickly served food includes sandwiches (from 80p; toasted from 90p), home-made soup (£1), salads or ploughman's (from £1.90), omelettes (£2.20), vegetable curry (£2.60), Somerset pork (£3.50), steak and kidney pudding (£3.70), chicken with Stilton sauce (£5.10), trout (£5.20) and steaks (from £7.20); puddings such as home-made ice-creams or apple crumble (from £1) and three-course Sunday lunch (£7.20); helpful, attentive service. Well kept Cotleigh Tawny and Exmoor Bitter on handpump and Lane's cider. The garden behind is quiet except for rooks and lambs in the surrounding low hills; opposite the front of the pub is the 12th-century red stone church. (*Recommended by John Tyzack, J F and M Sayers, Gwen and Peter Andrews, K R Harris, E G Parish, WHBM, Alan Carr*)

Free house   Licensee Peter Williamson   Real ale   Meals and snacks (11–2, 6–10.30) Restaurant (closed Sun evening)   Children in restaurant   Open 11–2.30, 6–11 Bedrooms tel Stogumber (0984) 56277; /£32B

STOKE ST GREGORY (Somerset)   ST3527 Map 1
Rose & Crown ✪

Woodhill; follow North Curry signpost off A378 by junction with A358 – keep on to Stoke, bearing right in centre and right again past church

This 17th-century cottage is cosily decorated in a pleasantly romanticised stable theme inside, with stripped stonework, dark wooden loose-box partitions for some of the interestingly angled nooks and alcoves, lots of brasses and bits on the low beams and joists, and appropriate pictures including a highland pony carrying a stag. There's an 18th-century glass-covered well in one corner. It's well known locally for particularly good value food, such as sandwiches, ploughman's (£2.50), pint of prawns (£3.35), omelettes (£4), other hot dishes such as tandoori chicken, seafood platter, grilled kidneys and liver and bacon (£4.35), chicken casseroled in farm cider (£4.95) and home-made puddings with local clotted cream. One small dining area is no-smoking. Well kept Eldridge Pope Thomas Hardy and Royal Oak and Exmoor on handpump, Taunton cider, decent wines, unobtrusive piped music, helpful staff; skittle alley. There are picnic-table sets under cocktail parasols by an apple tree on the sheltered front terrace; we've not yet heard from readers who've stayed in the bedrooms here. (*Recommended by Richard Dolphin, John and Phyllis Maloney, Graham Tayar*)

Free house   Licensees Ron and Irene Browning   Real ale   Meals and snacks Restaurant   Children in eating area and restaurant   Open 11–2.30, 6–11   Bedrooms tel North Curry (0823) 490296; £17.50/£32

STOKE ST MARY (Somerset)   ST2622   Map 1
Half Moon

2 3/4 miles from M5 junction 25; A358 towards Ilminster, then first right, then right in Henlade

Extensively modernised, this substantial village pub is open-plan, but careful attention to giving each of its five neat main areas individual furnishings and decor has kept a good deal of character. The overall impression is of clean, roomy comfort, with a warmly friendly atmosphere. Consistently good bar food includes sandwiches (from 95p), soup (95p), starters such as mussels au gratin (£1.95), light basket meals (from £1.95), ploughman's (£2.50), steak and mushroom pie or ham and leek casserole (£3.25), several vegetarian dishes (£3.25), meat salads (from £3.50), 8oz gammon (£4.50), trout or lemon sole filled with smoked ham and cheese (£4.75), steaks (from 8oz sirloin £6.50), specials such as liver and onions (£3.25) or chicken curry (£3.50), a good variety of children's dishes (from £1.50) and lots of knickerbocker-glory-style puddings (from £1.25); three areas, one no-smoking, are laid out as restaurant. Well kept Flowers IPA, Marstons Pedigree and Whitbreads Castle Eden on handpump, decent coffee; friendly and efficient staff, maybe faint piped radio. There are picnic-table sets on the well kept lawn, more tables on a small gravel terrace. (*Recommended by Shirley Pielou, Richard Dolphin*)

Whitbreads   Licensee Pat Howard   Real ale   Meals and snacks (12–2, 6.30–10) Restaurant tel Taunton (0823) 442271   Children in eating area and restaurant   Open 11–2.30, 6–11

TINTINHULL (Somerset)   ST4919   Map 2
Crown & Victoria

Farm Street; from village, which is signposted off A303, follow signs to Tintinhull House

There are old-fashioned high-backed chairs, Windsor chairs, low modern settles, and a couple of easy chairs by the big winter log fire in this stone pub. Bar food includes sandwiches (from 95p), lasagne (£2.95), scampi (£3.50), gammon (£3.95) and steaks (from £5.95). Butcombe and Youngs Special on handpump, with Burrow Hill cider; bar billiards, table skittles, alley skittles, dominoes, cribbage, fruit machine, trivia and piped music. The big lawn behind the pub has cocktail parasols, white chairs, swings and a goldfish pool set in a rockery; there's a children's play area. Tintinhull House with its beautiful gardens is close by. (*Recommended by A M Kelly, F A and J W Sherwood, A M Kelly, Mrs E M Thompson, R Blatch; more up-to-date reports please*)

Free house   Licensee Gordon Perry   Real ale   Meals and snacks (not Sun)   Children in eating area of bar   Open 11–11; may close in afternoon if quiet

TORMARTON (Avon)   ST7678   Map 2
Compass

Under 1 mile from the M4 junction 18; A46 towards Stroud, then first right turn

The upper bar of this well run, busy roadhouse has stone walls, red plush chairs,

614 *Somerset and Avon*

red leatherette stools and cushioned settles, and is popular with locals; the lower bar – more set out for eating – has a glass cold food display cabinet, and leads out to the nicest room, the light and spacious conservatory. This has orange or green garden chairs around wooden-slatted tables, flowers and shrubs, and a vigorous climbing vine. Bar food includes soup (£1.35), sandwiches (from £1.95), cheese with a cottage loaf (from £2.75), home-made cheese flan (£3.55), home-cooked meats (from £3.75), fresh poached salmon or dressed crab (£5.45), and hot specials such as good seafood cassoulette (£4.45). Archers Village, Bass and Wadworths 6X on handpump, country wines, and several malt whiskies; darts, dominoes, cribbage, fruit machine and piped music. Outside, the crazy-paved terrace has bright flowers and some picnic-table sets. Badminton and Dodington are close by. *(Recommended by Mr and Mrs D A P Grattan, Mrs M Price, Dr Stephen Hiew, Len Beattie, Michael and Alison Sandy, Roger Huggins, Tom McLean, Ewan McCall, Helena and Arthur Harbottle, Patrick Godfrey, John Fazakerley, Stan Edwards)*

Free house   Licensee P Monyard   Real ale   Meals and snacks (11–10.30, though limited menu in afternoon)   Restaurant; closed Sun lunchtime   Children in eating area and conservatory   Open 11–11   Bedrooms tel Badminton (045421) 242/577; £47.50B/£59.90B

TRISCOMBE (Somerset)   ST1535 Map 1
Blue Ball

Village (and pub) signposted off A338 Taunton–Minehead

Up on the edge of the Quantocks, this cottagey little thatched country pub has barely more than half a dozen tables in its neat brown-beamed bar, one tucked under the mantlebeam of what used to be a monumental brick and stone fireplace. The atmosphere is particularly relaxed and unhurried out of season, with sporting prints on the white walls, and piped light classical music – excerpts from *Peer Gynt* and so on. A new conservatory relieves the seasonal pressure on space; it can get very busy in summer. Quickly served bar food includes sandwiches (£1.20), good soups (£1.25), starters such as deep-fried brie with mango chutney (£1.65), ploughman's (£2.25), beef and stilton pasty (£2.65), savoury pancakes (from £2.85), venison sausages (£3), vegetable lasagne (£3.85), pork and prune stew (£4.15), some evening and Sunday lunch additions such as scampi (£4.20) and 8oz rump steak (£6.50), and puddings including sweet pancakes (more on the lines of flapjacks or giant dropscones than crêpes, from £2.25). Well kept Cotleigh Tawny and Exmoor on handpump, with another beer from those breweries, or Ind Coope Burton or Youngs Special, as a guest beer; decent wines and coffee, farm cider, polite service; dominoes (and there's a skittle alley). Cassian the wolfhound isn't supposed to be in the bar, but has been known to slip in if he hears a crisp packet rustle. There are picnic-table sets on the narrow terraced lawns built into this steep and peaceful slope, looking across to the Brendon Hills; chickens and goslings may hope to share your meal. It's good walking country. *(Recommended by Shirley Pielou, Dewi Jones, G A Gibbs, P Bacon, Mrs M G S Finch, Gethin Lewis)*

Free house   Licensee Gary Little   Real ale   Meals and snacks   Well behaved children allowed in eating area   Open 11–2.30, 6–11; winter evening opening 7

TRUDOXHILL (Somerset)   ST7443 Map2
White Hart

Village signposted off A361 Frome–Wells

Rob and Julie Viney of this pub liked Bishops Best, brewed in Wellington, so much that when the microbrewery went out of business in 1987 they bought it, keeping the beer in production under the name Ash Vine. The equipment's now been installed here, and that original strongly flavoured light Bitter has now been joined by a stronger mid-brown beer, well hopped with a good lingering dry finish, called Tanker after the nickname of Len Lock – a previous landlord here. They arrange brewery visits, and also have Butcombe, a guest beer such as Hoskins & Oldfields

EXS, cheap Thatcher's farm ciders on handpump, and good country wines. There's a thriving, relaxed atmosphere in the long stripped-stone bar, really two room areas, attractively carpeted, with beams supporting broad stripped ceiling boards. Mostly, it's table seating, with a couple of easy chairs by the big log fire on the right (there's a second at the other end), and some seats in the red velvet curtained windows. A very wide choice of popular bar food includes sandwiches (from 90p, steak £2.40), soup (£1.05), ploughman's (from £2.20), ham and egg (£3.20), lasagne or steak and kidney pie (£3.50), vegetarian dishes such as stilton and celery pie (£3.50), beef curry (£3.75), seafood platter (£4.10), steaks from 8oz rump (£6.20), dishes of the day such as turkey cordon bleu (£4.95) and a bumper mixed grill (£6.55), and children's dishes (from £1.60). Sunday lunch is £5.85 (£4.50 for children); darts, maybe unobtrusive piped music. There are picnic-table sets on a sheltered side lawn. *(Recommended by Nigel Gibbs, Sandra Cook, R and E Harfield, R W Stanbury, Andy Hick, Ted George)*

Own brew   Licensees Doug Warren and Dawn Charlton   Real ale   Meals and snacks (served till 10.30)   Restaurant tel Frome (0373) 84324   Children in eating area and restaurant   Open 12(11.30 Sat)–2.30, 7(6.30 Sat)–11

WELLOW (Avon)   ST7458 Map 2

Fox & Badger

Village signposted on left on A367 SW of Bath

The flagstone-floored bar in this lively stone-built pub has flowers on the tables, seats built into snug alcoves, small winged settles with cushions to match the curtains, a handsome fireplace, and a pleasantly chiming clock. Reasonably priced, wholesome bar food includes sandwiches and main dishes such as vegetarian meals, home-made lasagne, chilli con carne, Cumberland sausage, trout, steak and so forth; Sunday roast lunch with a choice of two roasts. Well kept Butcombe Bitter, Ruddles Best and Ushers Best on handpump. The cosy carpeted public bar has shove-ha'penny, darts, dominoes, cribbage, trivia, juke box and fruit machine, and there's also a free skittle alley. The inn-sign is rather striking, showing the two animals in Regency dress. *(Recommended by Barry and Anne, Peter and Rose Flower, B H Pinsent, Tony and Lynne Stark, Steve and Carolyn Harvey)*

Ushers (Watneys)   Licensees Kevin and Maxine Spragg   Real ale   Meals and snacks Restaurant tel Bath (0225) 832293   Children welcome   Open 11–3, 6–11

WEST HUNTSPILL (Somerset)   ST3044 Map 1

Crossways 🍴

2 ¾ miles from M5 junction 23 (A38 towards Highbridge); 4 miles from M5 junction 22 (A38 beyond Highbridge)

Really popular food in this spacious, lively place includes various home-made soups (£1.30), sandwiches (from £1.50), chicken liver pâté (£2.30), ploughman's (from £2.60), tasty prawns by the half-pint (£2.60), salads (from £4.20), quiches (from £3.90), vegetarian curried nut roast (£2.50), broccoli, chicken and ham mornay or super local faggots with marrowfat peas (£3.50), home-made lasagne or home-baked steak and kidney or lamb and apricot pies (£4.20), excellent gammon with egg or pineapple (£5.30), grilled fresh trout or poached salmon (around £4.50), and steaks (from £6.40). The home-made puddings are good and served with double cream – treacle tart, bitter sweet chocolate pudding or lemon cheesecake (all £1.50). The main part of the bar has good winter log fires, dining room chairs, a mixture of settles, and seats built into one converted book fireplace. At one end there's more of a dining room, prettily decorated with old farm machinery engravings, Albert and Chic cartoons (chiefly about restaurants), and 1920ish hunting prints, as well as neat red seats, and a brass colonial fan in its dark ceiling (Friday and Saturday bistro menu here). The other end has an area with big winged settles making booths, and there's a family room with bamboo-back seats around neat tables; cribbage, pinball, dominoes, fruit machine and skittle alley. Well kept Butcombe Bitter, Flowers IPA and Original, and Eldridge Pope Royal

Oak on handpump, with a changing guest beer such as Cotleigh Old Buzzard, and good wines; friendly, prompt service. There are picnic-table sets among fruit trees in quite a big garden.   *(Recommended by Tom Evans, Ted George, Robert and Vicky Tod, Gethin Lewis, TBB, W F Coghill, P Miller, C F Walling, Richard R Dolphin, Patrick Freeman, Peter Morwood, Diane Duane, K J Betts, Peter Watkins, Pam Stanley, W C M Jones, Dr Keith Bloomfield, John and Pat Smyth, Tessa Stuart, Lynne Sheridan, Bob West, Dr and Mrs K J Lower, Elisabeth Kemp, Drs M and K Parier, Mr and Mrs Peter Woods)*

Free house   Licensees Michael Ronca and Tony Eyles   Real ale   Meals and snacks (12–2, 6.30–9.30)   Fri and Sat evening bistro   Children in eating area of bar and family room   Jazz weekend in marquee in garden, weekend 22–23 June   Open 11–3, 5.30(6 Sat)–11; closed 25 Dec   Bedrooms tel Burnham-on-Sea (0278) 783756; £19.50B/£32.50B

WINSFORD (Somerset)   SS9034 Map 1

Royal Oak 🍺

Village signposted from A396 about 10 miles S of Dunster

The lounge bar in this magnificently thatched Exmoor inn is cosy and partly panelled, with a cushioned big bay-window seat looking across the road towards the village green and foot and packhorse bridges over the River Winn; which joins the Exe here; a notably enjoyable atmosphere. Also, Windsor armed chairs and cushioned seats on the red carpet, horse brasses and pewter tankards hanging from the beam above the attractively panelled bar counter, and a splendid iron fireback in the big stone hearth (with a log fire in winter). Another similarly old-fashioned bar has good brass, copper, wall prints and darts. Bar food includes soup (£1), cold meat sandwiches (around £1.50), ploughman's (from £3), home-made pork, liver and orange pâté or home-made vegetarian quiche (£3.50), game pie or home-baked soft bap with minute steak (£4.95), a hot or cold daily special (£4.95), and puddings; big breakfasts for residents. Well kept Flowers IPA and Original on handpump; friendly staff. Customers in the 17th century were regularly plundered by the Exmoor highwayman Tom Faggus on his strawberry roan, in exploits which R D Blackmore, a frequent visitor, worked into *Lorna Doone*. There are plenty of nearby walks – up Winsford Hill for magnificent views for example, or over to Exford.   *(Recommended by P J Hanson, T J Maddiston, Sarah Vickers, Rona Murdoch, Richard Gibbs, Klaus Leist, N W Acton, W A D Hoyle)*

Free house   Licensee Charles Steven   Real ale   Meals and snacks   Restaurant; not Sun evening   Children in back bar only   Open 11–2.30, 6–11   Bedrooms tel Winsford (064 385) 455; £50B/£100B

WITHYPOOL (Somerset)   SS8435 Map 1

Royal Oak 🍺

Village signposted off B4233

Tucked down below some of the most attractive parts of Exmoor, this busy country village inn has a cosy beamed lounge bar with a stag's head and several fox masks on its walls, comfortable button-back brown seats and slat-backed chairs, and a log fire in a raised stone fireplace; another quite spacious bar is similarly decorated. A wide range of good bar snacks includes sandwiches (from 90p, giant filled rolls from £1.50, steak and onions £2.80), filled baked potatoes (from £1.50), home-made soup (£1.30), ploughman's (from £2.60), good home-cooked ham (£3.50; £4 with two eggs), two large sausages (a choice of pork and garlic, pork and herb, venison and bacon or spicy tomato – £3.50), good steaks (from £4.75) and large tasty Mediterranean prawns with garlic mayonnaise (£7.50). Well kept Ruddles County and Ushers Best on handpump, several vintage brandies, quite a few malt whiskies, and unusual wines; cheerful, pleasant service. Outside on the terrace there are wooden benches and tables with parasols. Just up the road, there are grand views from Winsford Hill and tracks lead up among the ponies into the heather past Withypool Hill. The River Barle runs through the village itself, with pretty bridleways following it through a wooded combe further upstream. For guests, they can arrange for salmon and trout fishing, riding (stabling also), clay pigeon shooting, rough shooting, hunting, sea fishing from a boat and trips to see wild red deer. (*Recommended by Ann and David Stranack, WTF, Mr and Mrs Morgan, WHBM, P Miller, Klaus Leist, T J Maddison, Sarah Vickers, John and Ruth Roberts, T Galligan, W and S Rinaldi-Butcher, R Gray, Mrs K J Betts*)

Free house Licensee Michael Bradley Real ale Meals and snacks Restaurant Children in restaurant in evening Occasional jazz or Country and Western Sun in winter Open 11–2.30, 6–11; closed 25 and 26 Dec Bedrooms tel Exford (064 383) 506; £27(£40B)/£44(£60B)

WOOLVERTON (Somerset)   ST7954   Map 2

Red Lion

A36, at N end of village on E side of road

Three hundred years ago, this attractively extended pub was a farm. The main area has lots of comfortably cushioned seats around decent elm tables, and an expanse of parquet flooring with oriental-style rugs. One older part has beams, flagstones, old panelling, cushioned farmhouse chairs, and a winged high-backed settle by the big stone hearth with a log-effect gas fire. Generous helpings of popular food include rolls (from £1.20), ploughman's (from £2.10), lots of interestingly filled baked potatoes (from £2.20, prawn, ham and asparagus £3.15), original salad bowls such as garlic croutons, walnuts, ham and cheese (£3.50), egg, tomato, smoked sausage, mushrooms and garlic croûtons (£3.55), or tuna, prawns, avocado, pineapple, sweetcorn and orange dressing (£3.85), chicken Korma (£5.75), a truly substantial seafood platter (£5.80), and daily specials; you can eat outside, under the trees. Consistently well kept Bass, Wadworths IPA and 6X on handpump, with mulled wine in winter; good service. (*Recommended by J Mann, R W Stanbury, Roger Huggins, Len Beattie, Tony and Lynne Stark, Charlie Salt, Lynn Sharpless, Bob Eardley*)

Wadworths Licensee Barry Lander Real ale Meals and snacks (12–2.30, 7–10) Children welcome Open 12–11

Lucky Dip

Besides the fully inspected pubs, you might like to try these Lucky Dips recommended to us and described by readers (if you do, please send us reports):

Ashcott, Somerset [ST4337], *Pipers*: Attractive pub easily accessible from main road; high ceilings with big fans, very comfortable; good food (*Eric Durston*)
Banwell, Avon [ST3959], *Whistling Duck*: Modern well done very rural-theme pub, with well kept Bass; friendly (*Dr and Mrs A K Clarke*)
Barrington, Somerset [ST3818], *Royal Oak*: Welcoming bar with log fire, friendly staff, skittle alley; good value varied and beautifully presented bar food inc specials from magnificent open sandwiches to Japanese dishes; good choice of real ales, guest beers and local country wines; skittle alley; handy for NT Barrington Court which is open Apr–Sept (*Shirley Pielou, Mr and Mrs P J Barrett*)
☆ **Bath**, Avon [Mill Lane, Bathampton (off A36 towards Warminster or A4 towards Chippenham)], *George*: Photogenic canalside pub, busy but spacious, with wide choice of well cooked and quickly served food inc vegetarian dishes, friendly welcome, good log fires, well kept Courage Best and Directors; dining room leads directly off the canal towpath; family room, outside tables

under cocktail parasols, garden bar; can be approached by peaceful 3-mile walk from centre; can get very busy at weekends (*Hazel Morgan, Tony and Lynne Stark, Chris Raisin*)
☆ **Bath** [17 Northumberland Pl; off High St by W H Smith], *Coeur de Lion*: Neat little single-room pub in charming flower-filled pedestrian alley, big etched and stained-glass window, well kept Devenish — perhaps Bath's prettiest pub, especially in summer (*Brian Jones, P Miller, LYM*)
☆ **Bath** [Lower Swainswick; Gloucester Rd (A46); ST7667], *Bladud Arms*: Friendly, simple and unassuming pub notable for its wide choice of pub games, modern and traditional, inc a skittle alley; good range of reasonably priced and well kept real ales such as Bass, Butcombe, Marstons Pedigree, Wadworths 6X and Whitbreads, good value plain lunchtime food (not Sun) (*Roger Huggins, Len Beattie, LYM*)
☆ **Bath** [12 Green St], *Old Green Tree*: Small, sometimes crowded but friendly and rather smart pub with unspoilt panelled bar, lounge and no-smoking room, nice traditional furnishings, paintings; well kept Watneys-related real ales on handpump with

a more interesting choice than usual of other drinks, generously served good food (cold dishes such as crab rolls, ploughman's, seafood avocado particularly recommended) *(H K Dyson, N G Bailey, Helena and Arthur Harbottle, Ted George)*

☆ **Bath** [The Paragon, junction with Guinea Lane], *Star*: Welcoming pub close to main shopping street, with outstanding Bass tapped from the cask at old-fashioned prices, fresh filled rolls; interesting group of small rooms separated by glass and panelling, maybe with locals playing cribbage at the back; popular with local cricket and rugby teams *(W Bailey, Peter and Rose Flower, N Burke)*

Bath [nr Royal Crescent], *Assembly*: Lively student pub with good choice of beers and not too obtrusive rock music *(Tony and Lynne Stark)*; [Abbey Green], *Crystal Palace*: Big sheltered courtyard is chief attraction of lively modernised Georgian pub in fine spot, with Eldridge Pope ales under light top pressure, straightforward bar food cooked to order, good service with plenty of staff, family area in heated conservatory *(Michael and Alison Sandy, Tony and Lynne Stark, LYM)*; [Locksbrook Rd], *Dolphin*: Riverside pub with ample lawns; good food served every day by charming and efficient barmaids; friendly atmosphere, wide range of fine beers *(L G Creed)*; [central], *Grapes*: Lively, friendly pub with well kept Courage Directors *(Brian Jones)*; [Lansdown Hill], *Hare & Hounds*: Pleasant pub in delightful situation with plenty of space in conservatory, long terrace and well kept garden with play area, for enjoying marvellous view over Charlcombe Valley; staff friendly and unusually smart; lavatories good; good food from varied menu inc several vegetarian dishes, well kept Courage; family room, piped music *(J L Cox)*; [North Parade], *Huntsman*: Popular old dining pub, open all day for wide choice of home-made hot and cold dishes, not cheap but good and often interesting; Eldridge Pope beers inc Royal Oak; nr Abbey *(Joan and Michel Hooper-Immins, Carol Mason)*; [St Saviours Rd, Larkhall], *Larkhall*: Well kept Courage in unspoilt old-fashioned local, full of character, with lots of brass and bric-a-brac *(Mrs Carol Mason)*; [Sutton St], *Pultney Arms*: Good pub popular with rugby fraternity — who benefit from the capacious three-sided bar counter; well kept Watneys-related real ales, decent food from giant lunchtime baps to barbecued steaks, some seats on pavement *(BKA, B R Woolmington)*; [Summerlays Pl (A36); opp Pultney Gdns], *Royal Oak*: Well kept Gibbs Mew Mild and Bishops Tipple, good bar food — big bacon rolls, omelette, curry recommended *(G Shannon)*; [Saracen St/Broad St], *Saracens Head*: Spacious beamed bars with Courage ales and good value cold buffet lunches *(H K Dyson)*; [150 London Rd West], *Wagon & Horses*: Large peaceful Courage house, pleasant views of Avon Valley from lounge, good food *(K R Harris)*

☆ **Bathford**, Avon [Kingsdown; pub actually just over the Wilts border — OS Sheet 173 map reference 809670; ST8067], *Swan*: Friendly and attractive pub, held by iron strap to hillside in beautiful countryside; doing well under newish local licensees, with well kept Gibbs Mew beers, decent wines, wide choice of bar food inc interesting specials (weekend booking essential), log fire, gardens front and back *(Mr and Mrs R Vaughan, B R Woolmington, Anne Fleming, Roger Cunningham, Deborah Frost)*

Battleton, Somerset [SS9127], *Caernarvon Arms*: Worth knowing for good food *(Anon)*

Biddisham, Somerset [off A38 Bristol—Bridgwater; ST3853], *New Moon*: Busy but friendly main-road local with standard range of well cooked and reasonably priced bar food, good service *(K R Harris)*

☆ **Bishops Lydeard**, Somerset [A358 towards Taunton; ST1828], *Kingfishers Catch*: Two neat little communicating rooms with wheelback chairs around dark shiny tables, mainly turquoise and blue decor, wide choice of good value honest food from ploughman's (lunchtime only) through stuffed pancakes and so forth to gammon and steaks; while it has a pub licence (and keg Eldridge Pope) it's now really run too much as a cottagey restaurant to be a main entry, though it's well up to standard *(Mrs Ann Spice, Shirley Pielou, G and L Owen, LYM)*

Bishops Lydeard [Mount St; ST1629], *Bird in Hand*: Comfortable local with young and pleasant staff, Ushers on handpump, freshly baked pizzas and tasty sandwiches; garden, car park *(E G Parish)*

Blagdon, Avon [A368; ST5059], *Live & Let Live*: Cosy and cheerful partly panelled back bar with log fire and sporting prints, generous bar food inc good value Sun lunch, well kept Courage Bitter and Best, sensibly placed darts, pool and other pub games; handy for fishing on Blagdon Lake; bedrooms *(Tom Evans, LYM)*; *Seymour Arms*: Pleasant pub concentrating on family atmosphere, with well priced food inc particularly good lemon sorbet, good range of real ales tapped from the cask inc their own Churchill, friendly service, children's area *(Anon)*

Blagdon Hill, Somerset [4 miles S of Taunton; ST2217], *White Lion*: Very pleasant service and comprehensive menu of sandwiches and larger meals — more than one would expect in a small village; simple but pleasant, good log fire *(Shirley Pielou)*

Bleadney, Somerset [ST4845], *Stradlings*: Well kept Scottish & Newcastle beers, splendid very reasonably priced food (children eat free Sun lunchtime), friendly staff, occasional live music; children welcome, with play area in garden *(Dr and Mrs C M Howes)*

☆ **Brent Knoll**, Somerset [ST3350], *Red Cow*: Friendly pub, attractively laid out and currently doing well, with well kept real ales inc Flowers IPA and Marstons Pedigree, good well priced food all week, quick service, well spaced tables, skittle alley, pleasant sheltered garden; notable lavatories *(John Hutson, John Cox, W F Coghill, M W Turner)*

Bridgetown, Somerset [SS9233], *Badgers Holt*: Simply furnished with well served food from shortish menu; obliging friendly staff *(Mrs B M McKay)*

☆ **Bristol** [45 King St], *Old Duke*: The Duke of the sign is Ellington — inside, the ochre walls and ceiling are festooned with jazz posters, besides one or two instruments, and the side stage has good bands (not free) every night, and at Sun lunchtime; usual pub furnishings, decent value simple food, well kept Courage Best and Directors on handpump; in attractive cobbled area between docks and Bristol Old Vic, gets packed evenings *(B R Woolmington, Nigel Gibbs, Sandra Cook, Roger Taylor, Tony and Lynne Stark, D P Ryan, BB)*

☆ **Bristol** [St Thomas Lane, off Redcliff St/Victoria St], *Fleece & Firkin*: Lofty 18th-century wool hall stripped back to flagstones, basic furniture; guest beers and own-brewed ales such as the hefty Old Wolly — owned by Halls (Allied); lunchtime food (not Sun) in gigantic filled baps, pleasant staff, live music Wed–Sat, lively Mon quiz night, children weekends *(Michael Cochrane, R Houghton, LYM)*

☆ **Bristol** [between Sion Pl and Portland St, Clifton; ST5673], *Coronation Tap*: Since refurbishment this low-ceilinged cider house (Courage Best and Directors as well as fat casks of cider, but not spirits or wines) is more palatable to casual visitors, though it's lost some of its distinctively robust character; still lively, it has reasonably priced lunchtime bar snacks (not Sun) *(Brian Jones, Peter Adcock, David Pearman, Carol Mason, Roger Taylor, R W Stanbury, LYM)*

☆ **Bristol**, (Avon) [Prince St], *Shakespeare*: Elegant Georgian house nr docks, very popular for good value bar lunches such as ploughman's and chicken pie, busy early evening too; pleasant partly panelled bar with big windows, rugs on bare boards, open fire, appropriate old prints; fine staircase to upper room, tables out on flagstones of iron-railed raised terrace; well kept Courage Best and Directors, John Smiths and a guest; we've no news yet on the new landlord

Bristol [off Boyce's Avenue, Clifton], *Albion*: Friendly and unpretentiously old-fashioned pub with unusual flagstoned courtyard off cobbled alley, well kept Courage ales tapped from the cask *(Roger Taylor, LYM)*; [15 Small St], *Assize Courts*: Smart, early 17th-century free house close to centre, with older upstairs assembly room where Elizabeth I is said to have dined; piped music, Courage Best and Directors and Wadworths 6X, cheap bar food such as rolls, salads and home-made pies, small garden *(Carol Mason)*; [Prince St], *Bristol Clipper*: Old, beamed pub nr harbour with good, lively atmosphere and well kept ales *(P Miller)*; [Pembroke Rd, Clifton], *Channings Hotel*: Basement bar with wide range of fresh bar food inc daily specials *(T R Norris)*; [15 Cotham Rd South], *Cotham Porter Stores*: Lively cider pub — also well kept keenly priced Courage real ales — with benches along the panelled walls, cheap snacks, sensibly placed darts, dominoes, cribbage *(LYM)*; [North St, Stokes Croft], *Full Moon*: Old, well restored, pleasant atmosphere, lots of electronic games *(Dr and Mrs A K Clarke)*; [Jacobs Wells Rd, Clifton], *Hope*: Opposite the 11th-century Jacobs well; medium-sized public bar, smaller back

lounge and garden; well kept Courage beers, good food — both husband and wife are qualified chefs; parking difficult *(Patrick Godfrey)*; [20 King St, nr Bristol & West building], *Jolly Cobblers*: One of the best in this street of good pubs; well kept Sam Smiths, pleasant atmosphere; has been open all day *(Roger Taylor)*; [Bath Rd, Brislington; ST6171], *Kings Arms*: Well updated, low-beamed pub with well kept Courage ales *(Dr and Mrs Tony Clarke)*; [Kingsdown Parade, High Kingsdown; ST5872], *Kingsdown Vaults*: Friendly, welcoming pub; bar food cooked in sight of customers — big helpings at reasonable prices; Courage beers, video library; wide cross-section of customers *(Patrick Godfrey)*; [Hotwell Rd, Hotwells], *Mardyke*: Odd charm with interesting furniture, games, young friendly staff *(Dr and Mrs A K Clarke)*; [17-18 King St], *Naval Volunteer*: good atmosphere, well kept Courage and locals Butcombe and Smiles — low prices *(Roger Taylor, Tony and Lynne Stark)*; [Lower Guinea St — follow General Hospital sign from inner ring rd], *Ostrich*: Very popular — and in summer busy — pub alongside docks, with waterside seats; well kept Courage *(B R Woolmington, BB)*; [Hotwell Rd, Hotwells], *Plume of Feathers*: Marstons pub on waterfront along from SS *Great Britain*; frequent live music weekends and some evenings; all Marstons beers well kept, inc Owd Rodger *(Patrick Godfrey)*; [up very narrow steep rd off to left at top of Whiteladies Rd], *Port of Call*: Good pub with good value bar food *(David Pearman)*; [Merchants Rd], *Pump House*: Smartly converted imposing and spacious building in redeveloped dock area (now largely residential), charcoal-grey brickwork, tiled floors, high ceilings, well kept Bass, decent wines, good value lunchtime bar food inc a generous ploughman's, cheerful mix of customers; waterside tables *(Gwen and Peter Andrews, LYM)*; [Henbury Rd, Henbury; ST5678], *Salutation*: Elaborately refurbished with lots of solid wood intended to give character, new clocktower in old car park, good outdoor drinking area and children's play area, extended car park; all-day opening — handy for nearby Blaise Castle estate, popular with families; new restaurant, varied bar menu; Bass and Charrington IPA *(Anon)*; [Victoria St], *Shakespeare*: Between shopping centre and railway stn; pleasant staff, reasonably priced meals and snacks, well kept Bass and Courage *(Carol Mason)*; [Park Row], *Ship*: Main bar upstairs with pine tables and chairs; juke box and pool table downstairs; ten changing real ales such as Bass, Badger Tanglefoot, Boddingtons, Smiles Exhibition and Wadworths 6X, and reliable hot and cold lunchtime bar food; short walk from Smiles brewery *(Steve and Carolyn Harvey, Graham Bush)*; [Princess Victoria St, Clifton], *Somerset House*: Well kept Watneys-related real ales, good value bar food in separate area, no juke box but maybe piped pop music *(Patrick Godfrey, Michael Badcock)*; [off Whiteladies Rd, next to Clifton Down rly stn], *Steam Tavern*: Appealing pub in cobbled street with boats on roof and half a car through wall; good atmosphere and Mexican food *(P Miller)*; [57 Whiteladies Rd, Clifton], *Vittoria*: Busy pub with cosmopolitan clientele, good food especially burgers, lively landlord *(Barry and Anne)*

Broomfield, Somerset [ST2231], *Travellers Rest*: Attractive interior, wide range of fresh, well served bar food, garden tables *(Shirley Pielou)*

Brushford, Somerset [SS9225], *Carnarven Arms*: Well kept with welcoming staff, good home-cooked bar food inc good soups, salads, sandwiches, more elaborate dishes such as duck, good puddings; can be crowded at lunchtime; bedrooms comfortable and good value, though some are rather small *(P Spence)*

☆ **Bruton**, Somerset [High St; ST6834], *Castle*: Good solid food value — particularly inc well presented Indian food with proper side dishes, changing choice of well kept real ales, skittle alley with striking mural of part of town, tables in sheltered back garden; welcoming, with courteous service, but can get very full; children in eating area and skittle alley *(LYM)*

☆ **Butleigh**, Somerset [ST5233], *Rose & Portcullis*: Welcoming old pub with pleasant atmosphere, particularly good food attractively served in bars and restaurant, well kept Courage Directors *(Cdr G F Barnett)*

Cannington, Somerset [High St; ST2539], *Kings Head*: Warm and friendly licensees, well kept beer on handpump, good freshly-made food in bar and restaurant; bedrooms nice *(R H Baggaley)*; [Blackmoor Lane], *Malt Shovel*: Large helpings of good food from wide menu, quiet and sensible customers; skittle alley; bedrooms, back camp/caravan site *(Richard Gibbs)*

Carhampton, Somerset [A39 Williton—Minehead; ST0042], *Butchers Arms*: Roadside pub catering well for families, with elaborately equipped play area with two-storey house, helter-skelter, castle and so forth, children's dishes and other decent food; Watneys-related real ales, restaurant *(Steve and Carolyn Harvey, Keith Houlgate)*

Castle Cary, Somerset [South St; ST6332], *Countryman*: Nice little pub in attractive market town, with several real ales inc the local Oakhill Farmers, bar food, pleasant garden behind *(K Baxter)*; *George*: Old inn with cosy bar, nice open fire, good food, friendly service; bedrooms *(R J Entenman)*; [Fore St], *White Hart*: Real ale, bar food, family facilities *(Dr and Mrs A K Clarke)*

☆ **Charlton Adam**, Somerset [just off A37 about 3 m N of Ilchester; ST5328], *Fox & Hounds*: Wide choice of good freshly cooked reasonably priced food inc children's menu in partly 16th-century pub with big family room, well equipped playground outside *(Mrs P C Clark)*

Charlton Horethorne, Somerset [ST6623], *Kings Arms*: Small, very friendly village local with short choice of well presented, good quality and value food *(John Nash)*

Charlton Musgrove, Somerset [ST7229], *Smithy*: Smiling welcome and truly home-made food at very reasonable prices, with small restaurant behind bar; log fire, skittle alley *(Maj and Mrs J V Rees)*

Chelston, Somerset [Hockholler; handy for M5 junction 26 — A38 2 miles E of Wellington; ST1621], *Blackbird*: Pleasant and comfortable with open fire, good choice of home-cooked food, good range of beers *(K R Harris)*

Chipping Sodbury, Avon [ST7282], *Dog*: Generously served good bar food in long open-plan bar with alcoves, Marstons Pedigree and Whitbreads-related real ales *(BKA)*

Clevedon, Avon [ST4071], *Little Harp*: Recently renovated comfortable pub on seafront with good choice of reasonably priced food *(F H Sommer)*

Coalpit Heath, Avon [Henfield Rd; A432 Bristol—Chipping Sodbury; ST6881], *Ring o' Bells*: Good bar meals, friendly helpful service, clean and comfortable bars *(K R Harris)*

Cold Ashton, Avon [A420 Bristol—Chippenham 1/2 mile from A46 junction; ST7572], *White Hart*: Large, popular pub with extensive menu, real ale, lots of brass, comfortable furnishings; they call food ticket numbers out over the piped music; on Cotswold Way *(Mr and Mrs N Christopher)*

☆ **Combe Florey**, Somerset [off A358 Taunton—Williton, just N of main village turn-off; ST1531], *Farmers Arms*: Neatly restored thatched and beamed pub with wide choice of food pleasantly served, good winter log fire, well kept Bass; popular in summer, with plenty of tables outside *(Mr and Mrs P W Dryland, Shirley Pielou, BB)*

Combwich, Somerset [ST2542], *Old Ship*: Attractive pub which has been praised for welcoming and helpful service and wide choice of decent bar food, but no recent reports *(News please)*

Compton, Somerset [B3151 S of Street; ST4933], *Castlebrook*: Old village pub with pleasant bars full of local atmosphere, good food; flowering tubs outside, campsite behind *(K R Harris)*

☆ **Compton Martin**, Avon [A368; ST5457], *Ring o' Bells*: Attractively placed country pub with well kept and reasonably priced real ales such as Butcombe, Exmoor, Marstons Pedigree and Wadworths 6X, good value bar food and fine Sun lunch that takes some finishing; snug traditional area with inglenook log fire, rugs and flagstones, opening into extensive carpeted part with lots of tables — cool and spacious in summer; cigarette card collection in public bar with darts and fruit machine, family room with rocking horse, table skittles and toys, good-sized garden with fruit trees, swings, climber and slide *(William Pryce, Tom Evans, Peter Adcock, Jon Wainwright, BB)*

Creech Heathfield, Somerset [nr M5 junction 25; ST2827], *Crown*: Small 17th-century thatched pub which has been praised for pleasant atmosphere, log fire, wide range of generous bar food and well kept Watneys-related real ales, but no recent reports *(News please)*

Culbone Hill, Somerset [A39 W of Porlock; SS8247], *Culbone Stables*: One of the highest points on Exmoor; comfortable well laid out free house with pleasant atmosphere, good service, Bass on handpump, good bar food; children welcome; bedrooms comfortable (*E G Parish*)

☆ **Ditcheat**, Somerset [village signposted off A37 and A371 S of Shepton Mallet; ST6236], *Manor House*: Most attractive frontage — and great views on the way down from Pye Hill on A37; particularly welcoming relaxed atmosphere in neat and simple communicating rooms, flagstones in public bar, unusual arched doorways, close-set tables, good attractively priced bar food; well kept Butcombe on handpump, open fires if cold; skittle alley, white rabbits by tables on back grass (*Col David Smiley, R C Blatch, BB*)

Donyatt, Somerset [High St; ST3313], *George*: Well run friendly free house with well kept beer and good choice of reasonably priced bar food inc popular bargain Sun lunch (*L A Mills*)

Downside, Somerset [ST6244], *Downside*: Simple, pleasant pub with good, cheap, generous bar food, good service; bedrooms (*J H G Owen*)

Doynton, Avon [High St; ST7173], *Cross House*: Pretty ivy-clad olde-worlde pub in idyllic village, which has been praised for good beer, pleasant bar lunches, but no recent reports (*News please*)

Dundry, Avon [Church Rd; ST5567], *Dundry*: Friendly and popular hilltop pub with views of Bristol; open fire in winter, well kept Courage Best and Directors, good food, especially the oggies, big pleasant garden; children welcome (*Peter Adcock*)

Dunkerton, Avon [ST7059], *Prince of Wales*: Straightforward open-plan pub with bar food inc good pies in partitioned-off eating area, piped music, Wadworths 6X on handpump (*Roger Huggins*)

Dunster, Somerset [West St; SS9943], *Stags Head*: Olde-worlde 15th-century inn on flintstone pavement below castle, with bar food and Watneys-related real ales; bedrooms (*Lynne Sheridan and Bob West*)

East Coker, Somerset [ST5412], *Helyar Arms*: Tastefully extended oak-beamed pub with pleasant staff, good food at very competitive prices in bar and restaurant, real ales; attractive setting (*R Boyd McMurrick*)

☆ **East Harptree**, Somerset [ST5655], *Waldegrave Arms*: Good food such as rabbit and steak pie with proper vegetables in dining room and pleasant lounge with lots of nooks and crannies, welcoming service, separate locals' bar popular with young people; decent wine, good coffee (*E H and R F Warner, Marjorie and David Lamb*)

East Harptree, Somerset [ST5655], *Castle of Comfort*: Ancient Mendip coaching inn, in same friendly family for two generations; wide choice of generous food, good range of real ales; attractively set out rooms in newish wing, but historic old bar unspoilt — treetrunk supports roof beams; pleasant ambience (*Edward J Elsey*)

Easton in Gordano, Avon [Martcombe Rd; A369 about ½ mile from M5 junction 19; ST5276], *Rudgleigh Arms*: Good summer pub, with cricket pitch adjoining its garden; straightforward bar food, Courage Best on handpump, can be very busy at lunchtime (*Paul and Joanna Pearson*)

Enmore, Somerset [ST2434], *Tynte Arms*:

Free house with low beams and open fires, and pleasant dining areas; well kept Whitbreads-related real ales, reasonably priced bar food, friendly service; restored well in car park wall (*B M Eldridge, Shirley Pielou*)

☆ **Evercreech**, Somerset [A371 Shepton Mallet—Castle Cary; ST6438], *Pecking Mill*: Low-ceilinged stone-walled pub with ornate solid fuel stove, long-barrelled rifles and harness on walls giving rustic atmosphere, comfortable furnishings, well kept real ales, good value bar food (not always in evening if restaurant busy), friendly staff; seats outside, live music Thurs (*Ted George, John and Joan Nash, BB*)

☆ **Evercreech** [Evercreech Junction; A371 Shepton Mallet—Castle Cary], *Natterjack*: Large well decorated food pub popular for generous helpings of quickly served good bar food inc children's menu, separate dining area; good atmosphere, Butcombe Bitter, garden, plenty of parking (*R C Blatch, Mrs Carol Mason*)

☆ **Exebridge**, Somerset [SS9224], *Anchor*: Well furnished, clean, comfortable and friendly pub in idyllic spot, doing well under current hard-working licensees (it's their first pub), with wide choice of straightforward bar food, Watneys-related real ales, above-average wines, big riverside garden with plenty of tables; cheerful rather than reliably speedy service; smaller bar with pool table; six comfortable bedrooms, with good nicely served breakfasts (*Gwen and Peter Andrews, J S Evans, R Gray*)

☆ **Exford**, Somerset [SS8538], *Crown*: Comfortable and traditional old pub in peaceful village, well kept local ales, pine furniture, log fire, particularly good bar food, friendly service, attractive garden with stream running through (*P J Hanson, T Galligan, T J Maddison, Sarah Vickers*)

Exford [Sandyway], *Sportsmans Arms*: Wide choice of popular if not cheap bar food, inc some unusual specials; good restaurant, garden (*Steve and Carolyn Harvey*)

Failand, Avon [B3128 Bristol—Portishead; ST5271], *Failand*: Pleasant smallish pub with good food and well kept Courage beer (*Jon Wainwright*)

Farmborough, Avon [ST6660], *Butchers Arms*: Comfortable pub with basic bar, darts and juke box, and quieter lounge; Halls Harvest (*Roger Huggins*)

☆ **Flax Bourton**, Avon [A370 Bristol—Weston-super-Mare; ST5069], *Jubilee*: Popular two-level bar/lounge with good food inc lovely puddings, good log fires, well kept beers, big car park; bedrooms (*Ian Phillips*)

☆ **Freshford**, Somerset [OS Sheet 172 map reference 790600; ST7859], *Inn at Freshford*: Picturesque three-storey stone building with comfortably modernised carpeted bar, lots of pictures and plates, stone serving counter with built-in old bread oven — also milk-maid's yoke, coach-lamps, traps and so forth; obliging licensees, pleasant staff, good range of simple but good bar food in big helpings, imaginative good value restaurant; well kept Watneys-related real ales, separate pool room, picnic-table sets on secluded sloping back lawn with shrubs; quiet countryside by old stone bridge over the Avon, footpath walks *(B R Woolmington, Ron Gentry, Peter and Rose Flower, BB)*

Frome, Somerset [Market Pl; ST7747], *Angel*: 17th-century coaching inn with two cosy bars, children's room and tables in garden; wide choice of attractively priced food inc filling hot dogs, good mackerel fillets and beef casserole; Courage real ales, obliging staff *(Mrs Carol Mason)*

☆ **Glastonbury**, Somerset [High St; ST5039], *George & Pilgrims*: Rambling medieval building most notable for its magnificently restored carved stone frontage — much more straightforward inside, though the front bar has a big open fire and 15th-century traceried stained-glass bay window; bar food, consistently well kept Bass, interesting local sweet wine, children in buffet and good upstairs restaurant; good clean bedrooms *(Mrs K J Betts, Helena and Arthur Harbottle, Carol Mason, Robert and Elizabeth Scott, W and S Rinaldi-Butcher, Richard Dolphin, Tony and Lynne Stark, LYM)*

☆ **Glastonbury** [27 Benedict St], *Mitre*: Good proper pub with straightforward lounge, welcoming landlord, good food with interesting specials, real ale, decent garden; children not sneered at *(Barry and Anne, Malcolm Ramsay)*

Green Ore, Somerset [A39 N of Wells; ST5750], *Plough Boy*: Smart decor, Courage beer, lunchtime and evening bar food (inc Sun), garden *(Mrs Carol Mason)*

☆ **Hardway**, Somerset [off B3081 Bruton—Wincanton at Redlynch; pub named on OS Sheet — OS Sheet 183 map reference 721342; ST7234], *Bull*: Isolated pretty country pub on track nr Alfreds Tower on the Somerset plains, with impressive choice of well presented good bar food in character dining room — the problem that's kept it off our inspection shortlist is that if you don't book or get there later than 12.30 you may not be able to eat even a bar snack; good choice of real ales inc Butcombe and Wadworths 6X, farm cider, delightful atmosphere, cheerful efficient landlords; handy for Stourhead Garden *(R J Entenman, Mrs J Gardner)*

Hatch Beauchamp, Somerset [ST3220], *Hatch*: Lots of copper and brass in carpeted lounge bar with pleasant bow-window seats; Bass, choice of ciders, pool room behind yard *(BB)*

Hawkridge, Somerset [Tarr Steps; SS8632], *Tarr Steps*: Charming converted rectory on hillside overlooking stone-age bridge over trout-filled River Barle; idyllic, timeless atmosphere in quiet hotel bar with well kept Courage Directors; good restaurant; fishing, and rough and clay-pigeon shooting; bedrooms comfortable *(M K C Wills)*

Henstridge, Somerset [A30 Shaftesbury—Sherborne, junction with A357; ST7119], *Virginia Ash*: Very good atmosphere and generous helpings of good food in very popular pub *(D A B and J V Llewelyn)*

Highbridge, Somerset [A38, just S of M5 junction 22; ST3147], *Artillery Arms*: Small pleasant pub with interesting bygones, friendly, helpful staff, good value food,

Courage beers *(K R Harris)*

☆ **Hillesley**, Avon [ST7689], *Fleece*: Attractive pub in small Cotswolds village with well kept Marstons Pedigree and Whitbreads-related real ales, decent wines and interesting collection of malt whiskies; basic old-fashioned bar, busy lounge, friendly service, bar food, no-smoking dining room; beautiful surrounding countryside, close to Cotswold Way; bedrooms *(Peter and Rose Flower, John and Joan Wyatt)*

☆ **Hillfarance**, Somerset [ST1624], *Anchor*: Popular local doing well under current regime, with good range of bar food in two good eating areas and small restaurant, speedy friendly service, good beers, children's play area in garden; lovely rural position *(Shirley Pielou, John Tyzack)*

☆ **Hinton Blewett**, Avon [village signposted off A37 in Clutton; ST5957], *Ring o' Bells*: Simple furnishings and country atmosphere in peaceful low-beamed stone-built village local with good value home cooking (not Sun evening), well kept Wadworths Devizes and 6X on handpump, friendly service; pleasant view from tables in sheltered front yard, pretty flowers in summer — outside and in; children welcome *(Drs M and K Parier, Tony and Lynne Stark, Jon Wainwright, LYM)*

☆ **Hinton Charterhouse**, Avon [B3110; ST7758], *Stag*: Attractively furnished ancient pub with good range of well kept real ales such as Bunces Best, Gibbs Mew Salisbury, Marstons Pedigree and Smiles Exhibition, log fire, often enterprising freshly cooked food at a price but usually worth it, in bar's stripped-stone eating area and restaurant; no piped music; children allowed in well thought out eating area, away from bar but not isolated; tables outside, has been open all day; no longer has bedrooms *(Roger Huggins, Lynn Sharpless, Bob Eardley, Tony and Lynne Stark, LYM)*

Hinton Charterhouse, *Rose & Crown*: Friendly atmosphere in comfortable panelled bar areas, well kept Bass, Marstons Pedigree and Wadworths 6X, restaurant with gallery bar; for sale summer 1990 *(Lynn Sharpless, Bob Eardley; news of new regime please)*

Hinton Dyrham, Avon [nr M4 junction 18; A46 towards Bath, then 1st right; ST7376], *Bull*: Good snacks, restaurant, log fire, no-nonsense management; children not allowed in bar *(Anon)*

☆ **Holton**, Somerset [ST6827], *Old Inn*: Friendly 16th-century inn with beams, ancient flagstones, log fire, masses of keys hanging over bar; good service, friendly atmosphere, real ales and ciders, usual bar snacks and various cooked dishes; can fill up early (especially on Wincanton race days), as popular with locals and RNAS Yeovilton; tables on terrace, restaurant — best to book for Sun lunch *(Lt Cdr G J Cardew, Dr and Mrs A K Clarke)*

☆ **Holywell Lake**, Somerset [off A38; ST1020], *Holywell*: Village pub with pleasant young licensees, above-average decor, very welcoming atmosphere, log fire, good value cold buffet with splendid spread of imaginative salads, sandwiches, interesting changing hot dishes; magnificent evening menu in small dining room; tables in peaceful garden *(Shirley Pielou)*

Horton Cross, Somerset [A303 W of Ilminster; ST3315], *Lamb*: Attractive one-bar pub with friendly staff and generously served appetising home-made food — wise to book; pretty hanging baskets *(Sue Hallam)*

Howley, Somerset [ST2609], *Howley Tavern*: Pleasant old-fashioned pub, off the beaten track, which has been praised for warm welcome, imaginative bar food and well kept real ale, but no recent reports *(News please)*

☆ **Huish Episcopi**, Somerset [A372 E of Langport; ST4326], *Rose & Crown*: The special feature of this architecturally unusual pub is the central flagstoned still room with its impressive racks of casked farm ciders, country wines and Bass and Butcombe real ales — prices are very low; it's been in the same family for over a century, and hasn't changed much, with a pleasantly take-us-as-you-find-us attitude to visitors — indeed there are those who preferred it before they updated some of its decidedly elderly furnishings; cheap simple snacks, pub games, skittle alley, tables outside; George the dog will welcome a bitch but can't abide other dogs *(Chris Raisin, Graham Doyle, LYM)*

Iron Acton, Avon [ST6884], *White Hart*: Good stilton ploughman's and popular for food from its woodburning tandoori-style clay oven *(Barry and Anne)*

Keinton Mandeville, Somerset [off A37; ST5430], *Quarry*: Old quarry-master's house with big clean and tidy front bar, back games room, skittle alley and lovely restaurant; good food, well kept, reasonably priced Oakhill Farmers and Wadworths 6X *(Ted George)*

Keynsham, Avon [Bitton Rd; ST6568], *Lock Keeper*: Worth knowing for the big riverside garden, with weir, lock and marina; Courage Best and Youngers Scotch on handpump *(E H and R F Warner)*

☆ **Knapp**, Somerset [ST2925], *Rising Sun*: Wide choice of good enterprising home-made food in 16th-century pub with stripped beams and stonework, Bass and Exmoor real ales; has been closed Mon and Tues lunchtimes *(Andrew and Michele Wells)*

Limington, Somerset [ST5322], *Lamb & Lark*: Pleasant, unpretentious village pub with homely atmosphere, parrot, well kept Ind Coope Burton and good, simple bar food *(M K C Wills)*

☆ **Littleton upon Severn**, Avon [ST5990], *White Hart*: Interesting and unusually carefully extended building in isolated village with hatch service of well kept ales inc Smiles and Long Ashton farm cider, good busy atmosphere (esp Wed jazz night), limited choice of generous good food, various games inc table football, genial bar staff, log fires; garden *(G and L Owen, Jon Wainwright, Steve and Carolyn Harvey, Dr and Mrs A K Clarke)*

☆ **Litton**, Somerset [off A39 Bath—Wells; ST5954], *Olde Kings Arms*: Atmospheric olde-worlde 15th-century pub in unspoilt setting at bottom of tiny valley next to old cottages and interesting little church; friendly, helpful service, big helpings of reasonable food, two large open fires, well

kept Butcombe, Wadworths 6X and another ale tapped from the cask; pleasant terrace and lovely streamside garden with swings and slides; very quiet midweek lunchtime, but can get busy *(GB)*

Long Sutton, Somerset [A372 E of Langport; ST4625], *Lime Kiln*: Generous helpings of good food, restaurant in former skittle alley, well kept Palmers, reliably good service; good value bedrooms *(Sarah Haines)*; *Devonshire Arms*: Good food, well kept beer and warm Australian welcome *(Cdr G F Barnett)*;

Lopen, Somerset [Lopen Head; ST4214], *Poulett Arms*: Straightforward but spotless roadside pub transformed by warm welcome, well kept Bass and guest beer and big helpings of tremendous value food cooked by landlord's wife; busy at weekends *(Richard Dolphin)*

☆ **Luxborough**, Somerset [S of Dunster on minor rds into Brendon Hills — OS Sheet 181 map reference 983378; SS9837], *Royal Oak*: Off-the-tourist-track village pub on only direct road east and west through narrow pass in the Brendons, old and unspoilt, with stone floors, log fire, beams and inglenooks, and amazing variety of furniture in its three rooms; doing very well under enthusiastic and cheerful new young licensees, with five well kept real ales inc Cotleigh Tawny, Eldridge Pope Royal Oak, Exmoor and Palmers on handpump, and good value food from huge sandwiches through home-made pies and home-cured ham to four-course meals (booking recommended for weekend evenings — busy then, and on Bank Hols); Fri folk nights *(Michael Lloyd, Mrs D M Everard, Bob Smith)*

Lydeard St Lawrence, Somerset [ST1232], *Farmers Arms*: Warm welcome, good well prepared food, well kept beer *(John Tyzack)*

Lydford, Somerset [A37 Shepton Mallet—Yeovil; ST5532], *Bunch of Keys*: Small homely country pub with helpful and pleasant bar staff; straightforward but well cooked and presented food at good prices, Wadworths 6X and Watneys-related real ales *(K R Harris)*

☆ **Lydford on Fosse**, Somerset [A37/B3153; ST5531], *Cross Keys*: Interesting pub with good freshly cooked food, well kept real ales, spotless lavatories *(John and Pat Smyth)*

☆ **Mark**, Somerset [ST3747], *White Horse*: Old-world pub dating back to 17th century, with roomy attractive bars, clean and tidy; wide choice of home-cooked food, well kept Whitbreads-related real ales, good friendly service — but very popular, so may be delays; large attractive garden; children allowed in eating area *(M W Turner, A M Kelly)*

☆ **Marshfield**, Avon [A420 Bristol—Chippenham; ST7773], *Lord Nelson*: Good atmosphere in pleasantly refurbished village pub with beams, open fires, view of old well down in cellar, wide choice of bar food from well filled French sticks to fresh crab, well kept Butcombe, Courage Directors, Marstons Pedigree, Smiles and Wadworths 6X, locals' games bar, ex-stables restaurant done out as cobbled lamplit street where you dine in old carriages or repro Victorian railway carriages; tables in small courtyard *(Carol*

Mason, H K Dyson)

Mayshill, Avon [A432 Coalpit
Heath—Yate; ST6882], *New Inn*:
Attractive, local stone building, friendly and
welcoming staff, unusual range of
home-cooked bar food (K R Harris)

☆ **Midford**, Avon [ST7560], *Hope & Anchor*:
Welcoming local with comfortable L-shaped
open-plan bar, wide range of well kept real
ales such as Bass, Butcombe, Fullers and
Wadworths 6X, good moderately priced
food from bar and restaurant menus — can
also be eaten in bar, popular Sun lunch
(booking advised), quick pleasant service;
passage under road to derelict canal, also
good walks along disused railway line
through beautiful countryside (M J B
Pearson, Roger Huggins)

☆ **Milborne Port**, Somerset [A30 E of
Sherborne; ST6718], *Queens Head*: Good
coaching-inn atmosphere in beamed lounge
with plentiful good value genuine food
under current regime, friendly service, good
choice of well kept real ales and farm ciders,
games in public bar, skittle alley, quiet
restaurant; tables in sheltered courtyard and
garden with unusual playthings; children
welcome (except in bars); three cosy
bedrooms — good value (E Mitchelmore, Mr
and Mrs T A Towers, LYM)

☆ **Milton Clevedon**, Somerset [High St
(B3081); ST6637], *Ilchester Arms*: Friendly
three-storey early 17th-century pub, its
beamed and stripped-brick lounge bar
decorated with old farm tools, glass ale jars
and brasswork; homely and comfortable,
with soft lighting by old-fashioned gas-style
lamps in wall alcoves; wide choice of
reasonably priced food, well kept Palmers
and Wadworths 6X, friendly landlord,
piano, smaller restaurant bar; lovely hill
views from garden and from conservatory
with hanging plants; no food Sun, closed
Mon lunchtime (Mike Tucker, Brig J S Green)

☆ **Minehead**, Somerset [Harbour; SS9746],
Old Ship Aground: Comfortably
modernised and extended olde-worlde
Victorian yachting pub, facing the sea by
lifeboat station; decent bar food running up
to steaks all day, Watneys-related real ales,
friendly atmosphere, tables on terrace;
preserved Victorian pleasure steamers to
Wales and North Devon outside in summer
(John Feehan, Diane Barnes)

Minehead [Blue Anchor Bay], *Blue Anchor*:
Well run split-level hotel bars with warm,
friendly atmosphere, popular for wide
choice of good food inc fresh hake, trout,
steaks and mainly home-made puddings;
smoothly painted beams, fruit machines,
piped music; bedrooms clean, pretty and
comfortable (Mr and Mrs J Wright, Keith
Houlgate)

☆ **Monkton Combe**, Avon [ST7762],
Wheelwrights Arms: Impressive choice of
bar food inc particularly good beef and
smoked salmon sandwiches, and quite
elaborate evening dishes, in small inn well
placed in lovely surrounding countryside;
friendly and attractively laid out bar with
chamber-pot collection and lots of other
bric-a-brac, benches against stripped-stone
walls in front part with big open fire, more
formal eating area, tiny darts room at end,
fruit machine, quiet piped music; Adnams,

Flowers IPA and Original; bedrooms
comfortable and well furnished, though not
cheap, across narrow car-park lane (Peter
and Rose Flower, Mrs M Finch, Dr F Peters, H
K Dyson, G C C Bartlett, LYM)

Montacute, Somerset [ST4916], *Phelips
Arms*: Pleasant, restful atmosphere, food
generally good — though service may not be
speedy (Mrs A Crowhurst)

Nailsea, Avon [West End; ST4670], *Blue
Flame*: Small free house with Bass tapped
from the cask, farm cider, bar food, open
fires, pub games, childrens' room, big
garden (Anon)

☆ **Nether Stowey**, Somerset [Keenthorne —
A39 E of village; not to be confused with
Apple Tree Cottage; ST1939], *Cottage*: Big
helpings of good value simple bar food, well
kept Flowers Original on handpump,
friendly service; comfortable dining lounge
with woodburning stove, aquarium,
interesting pictures; games room with two
pool tables, juke box and machines (children
allowed here); skittle alley, tables on terrace
(WHBM, Lynne Sheridan and Bob West,
LYM)

North Curry, Somerset [ST3225], *Rising
Sun*: Very nice cosy pub with well kept beer
and bar food inc good Sun roasts (G F Scott)

North Petherton, Somerset [Taunton Rd
(A38 towards Bridgwater); ST2932],
Compass: Roadhouse dining pub, once a
farmhouse and barn but now designer-style
comfort; well worth knowing for good value
food inc generous sandwiches and
vegetarian dishes, and well kept Marstons
Pedigree (Tom Evans)

North Wootton, Somerset [ST5641],
Crossways: Fairly big pub with good bar
food, restaurant; bedrooms (Alan and Ruth
Woodhouse)

Norton Fitzwarren, Somerset [ST1925],
Cross Keys: Popular, with good service and
well cooked good value food (John Tyzack);
Victory: Nicely decorated quiet free house
with good beer (John Tyzack)

☆ **Nunney**, Somerset [Church St; village signed
off A361 Shepton Mallet—Frome; ST7345],
George: Extensive rambling and much
modernised open-plan bar with stripped
stone walls, log fire, well kept Bass, Bunces
Best and Benchmark and Butcombe on
handpump, decent wines and good choice of
other drinks, generous helpings of good
value food from good sandwiches up in bar
and restaurant (service can be slow),
afternoon teas; rare 'gallows' sign spanning
road, in quaint village with stream
(vociferous ducks) and ruined castle;
bedrooms quiet, clean and well equipped
(Nigel Gibbs, Sandra Cook, GB, Dr and Mrs A
K Clarke, Tony and Lynne Stark, Ron Gentry,
BB)

Old Down, Avon [off A38
Bristol—Thornbury; ST6187], *Fox*: Homely
little L-shaped, one-room pub with log fire,
simple choice of rolls, pies and pasties, Bass
and Flowers real ales; kept pleasantly
unspoilt by new landlord (Steve and Carolyn
Harvey)

☆ **Old Sodbury**, Avon [Badminton Rd;
ST7581], *Dog*: Very popular pink-stuccoed
pub on Cotswold Way, carefully refurbished
to keep stone and plasterwork and warm,
attractive atmosphere; well kept Flowers

Original and Marstons Pedigree, wide range of good bar food from hot beef sandwiches up, inc lots of fish and seafood; service usually friendly and efficient; juke box can make itself heard; adjoining children's room with big log fire; on Cotswold Way; bedrooms *(John and Norma Loweth, Peter Griffiths, Mr and Mrs N Christopher)*

Oldland, Avon [High St, Oldland Common; ST6771], *Dolphin*: Courage pub with friendly and efficient service, bar meals (not Sat and Sun evenings), restaurant *(Mrs Carol Mason)*

☆ **Panborough**, Somerset [B3139 Wedmore—Wells; ST4745], *Panborough*: Carefully reconstructed 17th-century village pub with friendly atmosphere in several clean, comfortable and attractive rooms, main one with inglenook, beams, lots of brass and copper; good range of generous bar food inc particularly good meat ploughman's, competent service, real ales; very popular weekends; skittle alley, small restaurant, tables in front terraced garden, big car park *(Jenny and Brian Seller, K R Harris)*

Patchway, Avon [Aztec West; handy for M5 junction 16 (and M4 junction 20); ST6182], *Black Sheep*: Good new reproduction-old pub by Thwaites, opposite their Shire Inns hotel; outstanding decor, good food and beer, tables on terrace; very popular with youngish office workers from the business park here *(Hugh Geddes)*

Paulton, Avon [Bath Rd; ST6556], *Somerset*: Small and attractively rustic pub with L-shaped bar, two open fires; well kept Courage, good fresh home-cooked lunchtime and evening bar food inc their own soda bread, big pleasant back garden, smaller one in front; wonderful view over Cam Valley *(James Duthie)*

Pennsylvania, Avon [4 miles from M4 junction 18 — A46 towards Bath; ST7373], *Swan*: Modernised, stone-built row of cottages stepped downhill, decorated to underline tiny village's link with its US namesake; limited but decent bar food, good service, well kept real ales inc Smiles, log fire; live music Tues *(Stan Edwards, Peter and Rose Flower)*

Polsham, Somerset [A39 N of Glastonbury; ST5142], *Camelot*: Large roadside family pub in modern idiom, with good big children's area *(Dr and Mrs A K Clarke)*

Porlock Weir, Somerset [SS8547], *Ship*: Little thatched inn of great potential, in fine spot nr peaceful harbour — a shame its atmospheric original back stone-floored bar is so often closed, so that you have to use the more modern front bar; well kept real ales inc Exmoor, bar food, seats outside; children's room; bedrooms creaky and comfortably characterful, though not cheap, in Ship itself — the pub's run in tandem with neighbouring Anchor Hotel, sharing its reception and usually its restaurant *(WHBM, Steve Dark, LYM)*

Portbury, Avon [1/2 mile from A369 (off M5 junction 19); ST5075], *Priory*: Busy Welcome Inn dining pub — generous helpings of generally good food from sandwiches up, well kept Bass, hard-working staff *(Anon)*

Portishead, Somerset [West Hill; ST4777],

Portishead Bay: Inexpensive food in straightforward bar, well kept Bass, good value bedrooms *(Kenneth Sharp)*; *Royal Oak*: Cleanly refurbished pub doing well under current landlady, with good atmosphere in lounge, good value bar food; skittles, dominoes and jazz twice a week *(Gerald Gilling)*

☆ **Priddy**, Somerset [from Wells on A39 pass hill with TV mast on left, then next left — OS Sheet 183 map reference 549502; ST5450], *Hunters Lodge*: Very unassuming, basic and rather bare isolated walkers' and potholers' inn, much enjoyed by people who expect absolutely no frills, airs or graces; good range of well kept real ales such as Badger, Bass, Butcombe and Oakhill Farmers tapped from casks behind the bar, log fire, flagstones; simple bar food such as faggots with bread, tables in garden; bedrooms clean and adequate for their low price *(William Pryce, Jon Wainwright, P Miller, LYM)*

☆ **Priddy**, Somerset [off B3135; ST5251], *New Inn*: Good low-cost food in busy 15th-century former farmhouse on quiet village green — probably the pub to choose here if you want more cosseting than the Hunters Lodge; good log fire in lovely fireplace, low beams, horsebrasses and so forth; well kept Eldridge Pope Royal Oak and Wadworths 6X, good local cider, friendly service; bedrooms very comfortable and homely *(R D Norman, Andy Hick)*

Priddy, *Queen Victoria*: Good cosy family pub with big garden and family room *(Chris Raisin, Graham Doyle)*

Priston, Avon [ST6960], *Ring o' Bells*: Friendly and welcoming landlady, Badger beers, hand-made seats in carpeted lounge *(Roger Huggins)*

☆ **Ridgehill**, Avon [off B3130 2 miles S of Winford; ST5462], *Crown*: Well kept Wadworths real ales, good affordable food in bar and restaurant, log fires, country views, tables in small back garden; lively at weekends *(D G and J M Moore)*

Rimpton, Somerset [ST6021], *White Post*: Small pub with well kept Butcombe, big helpings of reasonably priced food in small dining area with pretty view over fields, pleasant licensees *(Mrs B Haskins)*

Rode, Somerset [signed off A361 Trowbridge—Frome; ST8153], *Red Lion*: This interesting curiosity with its ancient, rambling low-ceilinged rooms has been full of unusual decorations from old prints to a remarkable collection of advertising signs — an enjoyable main entry in past editions, with log fires, simple bar snacks, well kept real ales, tables outside; but it's been closed in 1990 *(News please)*

Roundham, Somerset [A30 Crewkerne—Chard; ST4209], *Travellers Rest*: Comfortable and cosy main-road pub, welcoming staff, good value home-cooked bar food inc unique choice of puddings *(K R Harris)*

☆ **Rudge**, Somerset [just off A36; ST8251], *Full Moon*: Charmingly unspoilt and old-fashioned simple pub, with massive flagstones in entrance hall, good Butcombe beer, better-than-average food inc sandwiches made with massive freshly cut doorsteps of bread, great choice of children's dishes — with chips *(John C Baker, Dr and Mrs A K Clarke)*

Saltford, Avon [ST6867], *Jolly Sailor*: Recently refurbished pub on bank of River Avon; Courage ales, good bar food, restaurant, garden — and its own island between lock and pub; children welcome *(Peter Adcock)*

☆ **Seavington St Michael**, Somerset [signposted from E side of A303 Ilminster bypass; ST4015], *Volunteer*: Dates from 1500s, but much modernised and comfortable; wide choice of reliably good value food using fresh and often local ingredients (fancy prawns and seafood pie particularly recommended), well kept Badger beers, good local Perry's cider, friendly service *(R F Warner, Bernard Phillips, John and Pat Smyth, BB)*

Shepton Mallet, Somerset [coming in from Bath, L at bottom of slope, L down further slope; ST6243], *Kings Head*: Good friendly pub with well kept Wadworths 6X, good bar food, low prices; table skittles, pool, darts and shove-ha'penny in games room *(P M Slade)*

nr **Shepton Mallet** [right off A37 N just before A37/A367 fork — pub 1 1/2 miles on left], *Wagon & Horses*: Well run civilised pub with good view over Mendips from olde-worlde entrance, interconnecting rooms, large upstairs bar and small restaurant; well kept Courage Directors and Best, bar food *(Ted George)*

☆ **Somerton**, Somerset [Church Sq; ST4828], *Globe*: Popular tastefully refurbished local, comfortable and friendly, good value lunchtime bar food, well kept Bass, large collection of flat-irons; big garden with terrace, skittle alley (the pub team is formidable) *(Mrs Carol Mason, Ian Phillips, J S Wilson)*

☆ **Somerton** [Church Sq], *White Hart*: Smart, clean and well run, with well kept Courage Best and Directors, good value bar food inc imaginative salads and children's helpings in two small eating rooms and airy, spacious and well furnished family room *(Mr and Mrs A Smith, K R Harris, Mrs Carol Mason)*

Somerton [opp Barclays Bank], *Red Lion*: Coaching inn with enlarged panelled bar and lounge on right of inner yard — not yet strong on atmosphere after refurbishment, but good bar food; bedrooms *(S V Bishop)*

Stratton on the Fosse, Somerset [A367 towards Radstock, at junction with B3139; ST6550], *White Post*: Good clean welcoming local, well appointed and comfortable, with Watneys-related real ales, good well priced food *(K R Harris)*

Street, Somerset [1-3 Somerton Rd; the one nr Wells; ST4836], *Street*: Recently renovated former coaching inn, comfortable atmosphere in spacious bar and lounge, good home-cooked food, Bass, orchard with children's play area; big car park *(Eric Durston)*

☆ **Taunton**, Somerset *County*: Attractive lounge in big, bustling THF hotel, reliably good bar lunches, afternoon tea; attractive service, well kept Exmoor ale; good parking for centre — get a token to get out; comfortable bedrooms *(W and S Rinaldi-Butcher, Mr and Mrs J H Adam)*

Taunton [Magdalene St], *Masons Arms*:

Popular old-fashioned free house with genial licensee, no piped music, well kept Exmoor and guest beers, good bar food; good value clean bedrooms *(John and Joan Wyatt)*; [Middleway, Wilton; across Vivary Park from centre], *Vivary Arms*: Good interesting range of lunchtime bar food from sandwiches up, with several fish dishes *(Shirley Pielou)*

Temple Combe, Somerset [ST7022], *Royal*: Friendly local with well kept Badger beer and good cheap lunchtime food *(Tony and Lynne Stark)*

Tickenham, Avon [B3130 Clevedon—Nailsea; ST4571], *Star*: Spacious pub, the light and airy lounge's pine furniture pleasantly worn in now, with wide choice of good if not cheap bar food, generously served with ample vegetables — filled baked potatoes and pies recommended; piped music can be loud *(Tom Evans)*

Timsbury, Avon [North Rd; B3115; ST6658], *Seven Stars*: Pleasantly bright and cheery village local with big woodburning stove, cheap well kept Courage Best and Directors, well reproduced juke box, pub games *(LYM)*

Tockington, Avon [ST6186], *Swan*: Attractive and spacious stone-built timbered pub in quiet village; wide choice of generally well cooked and presented food in bar or dining room, Courage Directors and other beers, tables in garden *(Stan Edwards)*

☆ **Tolldown**, Avon [under a mile from M4 junction 18 — A46 towards Bath; ST7577], *Crown*: Handy motorway stop, with generous helpings of straightforward bar food served efficiently, well kept Wadworths IPA and 6X on handpump, good garden with play area (children also allowed in eating area and restaurant), dominoes, darts and fruit machine, open fires in winter; no longer open all day in summer; bedrooms *(John Knighton, LYM)*

Tytherington, Avon [ST6688], *Swan*: Several bars in big village-centre pub, popular for meals inc good traditional fish and chips; Courage Directors and John Smiths on handpump; not far from M5 and A38 *(John and Joan Wyatt)*

Uphill, Avon [ST3158], *Ship*: Split-level village pub with good bar food, family and games areas with pool and darts, and Flowers on handpump *(P Corris)*

☆ **Upton**, Somerset [OS Sheet 181 map reference 006293; SS9928], *Lowtrow Cross*: Warm welcome in lonely country inn with well kept Cotleigh Tawny, nice low-beamed bar with enormous inglenook, simple good value bar food, skittle alley, provision for children *(LYM)*

☆ **Upton Cheyney**, Avon [signposted off A431 at Bitton; ST6969], *Upton*: Spaciously refurbished creeper-covered stone village pub with splendid Avon Valley views, and somewhat ornate plush Edwardian-style elegance (even rugs on the walls); well kept Bass and Wadworths 6X, good reasonably priced home-cooked bar food (not Sat evening, Sun or Mon) inc grills, succulent stuffed mushrooms and tasty steak and kidney pie, restaurant; closed Sun evening, Mon; big car park *(Tom Evans, AMK)*

☆ **Upton Noble**, Somerset [ST7139], *Lamb*:

Small, comfortable bar with well kept beer and good value bar food, Sun roasts; small restaurant with extensive views beyond big garden; closed Mon *(P K Jones)*

☆ **Vobster**, Somerset [Lower Vobster; ST7049], *Vobster*: Well kept sensibly priced Bass, Ushers and Wadworths and generous helpings of good value food in spacious, comfortable lounge and restaurant of pub reopened in mid-80s after 15-year closure; friendly and enthusiastic staff, tables outside, good walking area *(James B Duthie)*
Walton, Somerset [ST4636], *Royal Oak*: Well appointed, clean small pub with open fire, good bar food from sandwiches up, well kept Courage ales on handpump *(Mr and Mrs Harry McCann)*
Wambrook, Somerset [off A30 SW of Chard; ST2907], *Cotley*: Completely rural pub, clean and comfortable, in small, quiet village; warm welcome, plenty of space, good range of good value food inc vegetarian dishes, well kept Badger and Wadworths 6X; lovely walking area *(K R Harris)*

☆ **Waterrow**, Somerset [A361 Wiveliscombe—Bampton; ST0425], *Rock*: Genuinely welcoming pub in small valley village, with log fire, copper and brass in bar, couple of steps up to civilised lunchtime dining room with dark polished tables, doubling as smart evening restaurant; good range of beers, decent coffee, wide choice of food from breakfast through bar snacks and meals to full dinners; good value bedrooms with own bathrooms *(Gwen and Peter Andrews, Michael and Alison Sandy, D C and R J Deeming)*
Wellington, Somerset [High St; ST1320], *Kings Arms*: Locally very popular, with well kept Ushers, big helpings of good food; bedrooms really good value, considering their very low price *(Alastair and Alison Riley)*

☆ **Wells**, Somerset [High St; ST5545], *Star*: Attractively old-fashioned bar, part no-smoking, off narrow cobbled yard (tables under the hanging baskets), with beams, dark panelling, cosy atmosphere of shoppers dropping in, bar food such as steak and kidney pie, ham and egg, salads, steak, well kept real ales such as Bass and Butcombe or Wadworths 6X on handpump, piped music, fruit machine; gingham-tablecloth dining room leads off; small restaurant; bedrooms comfortable, with appropriate furnishings inc four-posters *(S V Bishop, Janet Hill, Les Rae, Andy Hick, P and R Woods, M K C Wills, BB)*

☆ **Wells** [St Thomas St], *Fountain*: Friendly and comfortable, with good value food pleasantly served — especially in restaurant, popular for Sun lunch; well kept Courage Directors, farm cider, piped music *(Mr and Mrs J H Adam, P and R Woods)*
Wells [Market Pl], *Crown*: Good atmosphere in pleasant old multi-level coaching inn with interesting William Penn connection and close to cathedral; magnificent fireplace behind bar, well kept Wadworths ales tapped from the cask, good variety of decent if not cheap bar food *(Gwen and Peter Andrews, P and R Woods)*

☆ **Wells** [High St], *Kings Head*: Old Courage pub with deal tables in flagstoned front bar;

two-level main bar area beyond; good lunchtime food and Courage Best and Directors on handpump; attracts young people in evening, with loud music then *(P Corris, K W J Wood)*

☆ **West Buckland**, Somerset [nr M5 junction 26; A38 Wellington—Taunton; ST1720], *Blackbird*: Partly 16th-century, pleasant, welcoming and quiet, with well kept Watneys-related real ales, reliable food from sandwiches to lobster thermidor inc good Sun lunch; skittle alley, pleasant garden with unusual statue; bedrooms *(Audrey and Roger Adcock)*

☆ **West Harptree**, Avon [B3114, out of village towards Chew Lake; ST5657], *Blue Bowl*: Popular and efficiently run dining pub with wide choice of good value meals inc massive range of puddings; lots of bookable tables in a row of communicating rooms, with attractive family room around corner; well kept Courage Best and Directors and John Smiths on handpump, friendly ginger cat, tables out on terrace and safely fenced lawn, surrounded by fields; bedrooms good value, with good breakfasts *(Mrs M Mills, BB)*
West Hatch, Somerset [ST2820], *Farmers Arms*: Welcoming new landlord has restored all the old beams and fireplaces, put in good Exmoor, Marstons Pedigree and Whitbreads Pompey Royal, and introduced three fixed-price menus at different price levels — fish a speciality; very promising indeed *(Richard Dolphin)*
West Hay, Avon [OS Sheet 172 map reference 435425; ST4663], *Bird in Hand*: Welcoming small country free house with real ales inc Exmoor, reasonable bar food *(M E Wellington)*
West Monkton, Somerset [ST2728], *Monkton*: peaceful spot; reasonably priced bar food (you need a real appetite to tackle their doorstep sandwiches)

☆ **West Pennard**, Somerset [A361 E of Glastonbury; ST5438], *Red Lion*: Three neat dining areas opening off small flagstoned and black-beamed core with log fire in big stone inglenook; wide choice of bar food inc good children's menu (there's another log fire in the stripped-stone family area); Ash Vine (carrying the pub's name), Badger Tanglefoot and Butcombe on handpump, maybe piped radio; bedrooms comfortable and well equipped, in neatly converted side barn *(BB)*

☆ **Weston Super Mare**, Avon [seafront, N end; ST3261], *Claremont Vaults*: Friendly, comfortable and well decorated pub with good views over the sea, two piers and Brean Down through the gaps left by heavily swagged velvet curtains; well kept Bass and Charrington, good choice of tasty lunchtime bar food (hot rather than cold plates would make it even better); helpful staff, relaxing atmosphere, piped music; evening live music in season *(Brian Barefoot, Peter Woods, P Corris, E H and R F Warner)*
Weston Super Mare, *Grove*: Nr seafront with several levels and bar areas inc library alcove and spiral staircase to rooftop bar area; good choice of ales, tempting food, lots of plants *(John Holmes)*
Westonzoyland, Somerset [Main Rd; ST3534], *Sedgemoor*: Small, cosy pub, Royalist base before Battle of Sedgemoor;

good atmosphere, interesting memorabilia inc Monmouth's declaration of his illegitimacy; Flowers IPA, bar food inc several vegetarian dishes, pleasant friendly service *(John Cox)*

Wheddon Cross, Somerset [junction A396/B3224, S of Minehead; SS9238], *Rest & Be Thankful*: Modern comfortable furnishings in two-room bar with log fire, aquarium and piped music, usual bar food, well kept Watneys-related real ales, also tea, hot chocolate and so forth; communicating games area, skittle alley, buffet bar; children allowed in restaurant, with children's dishes *(T J Maddison, Sarah Vickers, LYM)*

Whitchurch, Avon [Court Farm Rd; ST6167], *Baccy Jar*: Good atmosphere in attractive lounge of unusually pleasant estate pub *(Dr and Mrs Tony Clarke)*

Whitfield, Avon [Buckover; A38/B4461, N of Bristol; ST6690], *White Horse*: L-shaped bar with quieter part through ironwork gate, Bass and Theakstons on handpump with a guest beer such as Marstons Pedigree, decent food such as ploughman's, home-made quiche, roast meats, cheerful atmosphere, garden with fine views, outside lavatories; bedrooms *(Gwen and Peter Andrews)*

Wickwar, Avon [B4060 N of Chipping Sodbury; ST7288], *Buthay*: Very comfortable pub dating from 1760, with friendly and helpful staff; Flowers Original, Martsons Pedigree and Wadsworths 6X, good choice of wines, bar food up to steaks at candlelit tables; piped music, fruit machines, garden *(Carol Mason)*

☆ **Widcombe**, Somerset [OS Sheet 193 map reference 222160; ST2216], *Holman Clavel*: Comfortably modernised Whitbreads pub named after its massive holly chimney-beam, good bar food, helpful service, nice country atmosphere; handy for Blackdown Hills and Widcombe Bird Garden *(BB)*

Winsley, Avon [B3108 W of Bradford-on-Avon; ST7961], *Seven Stars*: Recently gutted and handsomely refurbished to make the most of its stripped stonework and snug alcoves, with Watneys-related real ales, good, fairly priced food, decent piped music, tables in garden; attractive village *(Mrs Joan Harris)*

☆ **Winterbourne Down**, Avon [Down Rd, Kendleshire; just off A432 Bristol–Yate, towards Winterbourne; ST6679], *Golden Heart*: Refurbished but keeps its good

atmosphere (and inglenook fireplace), with decent reasonably priced bar food inc good toasted sandwiches and stilton ploughman's, friendly staff, pleasant country view from restaurant; children's room, good gardens front and back, play area; immaculate new lavatories *(Barry and Anne, M A Watts, Dr and Mrs Tony Clarke)*

☆ **Wookey**, Somerset [B3139; ST5245], *Burcott Inn*: Friendly, pleasant and popular unspoilt country local with well kept Butcombe and a couple of guest beers such as Cotleigh on handpump, at reasonable prices; good choice of wine and bar food from doorstep sandwiches through good specials to dishes such as venison with garlic courgettes, friendly service, attractively cottagey scrubbed-table decor; children allowed in restaurant with dark wood furniture, walled garden *(Richard Houghton, John Fazakerley)*

Wookey, [ST5145], *Ring o' Bells*: Pleasant beamed country pub with well kept Bass, Charrington IPA and an interesting guest beer, decent wine by glass, good home-made bar food from sandwiches up, friendly service, open fire, small restaurant area; juke box, fruit machine *(Helena and Arthur Harbottle)*

Wootton Courtney, Somerset [SS9343], *Dunkery*: Locally popular for good choice of food from ploughman's up, inc fine mixed grill and Dunkery Munchies — crispy granary bread topped with toasted prawns and stilton; well kept Exmoor tapped from the cask, pool table, tables in big front garden, good views of the Beacon; service may be slow when busy; good value bedrooms *(Harold and Naydene Snodgrass)*

Worle, Avon [ST3562], *Lamb*: Small Courage pub in big development area which has kept its country atmosphere; friendly and lively, with good value home-cooked food *(K R Harris)*

☆ **Wrington**, Avon [High St; 2½ miles off A370 Bristol—Weston, from bottom of Rhodiate Hill; ST4662], *Plough*: Friendly, rural atmosphere, wide choice of tasty home-made food, good service, well kept beer *(Sybil Baker, Dr and Mrs A K Clarke)*

Yate, Avon [Wellington Rd; ST7283], *Farmhouse*: Split-level bar refurbished in old-fashioned style, with stripped brickwork and lots of beams *(Dr and Mrs A K Clarke)*

Staffordshire   *see* Derbyshire

Suffolk

Suffolk's great strength is in country pubs rather than town pubs.
One town here does have a remarkable number of good pubs,
though: Southwold. The Crown here has some of the best pub food in
East Anglia, in a smart yet relaxed atmosphere – currently doing
particularly well, under a new manager. Several pubs here in the
Lucky Dip section are well worth a visit, too: among them the Swan,
a hotel recently bought back and extensively refurbished by Adnams,
is looking particularly strong. All the really good Southwold pubs are
tied to Adnams, whose brewery is in the town. This brewer's good
influence spreads throughout the county, in that our prices survey
showed that its tied pubs tend to charge less than average for drinks
(they often have better than average wines, too); the cheapest beer
prices (and best wines) were actually at the Crown itself. We found
that drinks prices at Tolly pubs were also lower than the local and the
national averages. This regional chain is part of the Brent Walker
property group. Its beers have been brewed up in the north by
Camerons (another Brent Walker company), though some Brent
Walker pubs seem currently to be selling high-priced national beers
instead. But the Ipswich brewery which used to supply the pubs when
Tolly was independent is now to reopen after a buy-out by members
of the former management – so Tolly pubs will again be selling locally
brewed beers, and this is likely to help to hold prices here down.
Greene King, the other main regional operator, also tends to be priced
lower than the national average, another factor helping to keep drinks
prices here down. Food prices are around the national average; the
Ship at Dunwich (an atmospheric pub, doing so well currently that
it's now in the running for one of our star awards) and Swan at
Hoxne (an interestingly restored ancient building) stood out for
serving better-than-average food at low prices. Both beat our targets
of under £1 for bargain snacks and under £3 for decent main dishes.
The Bell at Clare (also doing well at the moment, with a new
conservatory and terrace and redeveloped garden) also had bargain
main dishes; the attractively placed Butt & Oyster near
Chelmondiston and neatly kept Dobermann at Framsden both had
notably cheap sandwiches – so did the Victoria at Earl Soham, whose
own-brewed beers were the cheapest we found in Suffolk,
undercutting the county average by nearly 15p a pint. Changes to
note here include a popular new chargrill restaurant at the Bull at
Barton Mills, a new landlord at the handsomely placed White Hart at
Blythburgh (he's doing much of the cooking himself – promising), the
Pickerel at Ixworth (popular cooking changes here include more
concentration on fish), ambitious new licensees at the Bell at Kersey
(lots of improvements planned; already the food's looking really
promising), new bedrooms at the beautifully placed Ramsholt Arms
at Ramsholt, the Plough at Rede's increasing tendency towards
becoming a (good) dining pub, our granting of a food award to the
well run Four Horseshoes at Thornham Magna, and a new

conservatory, with extensive improvements to the garden, at the civilised Crown at Westleton. Other pubs here currently doing particularly well include the attractive Peacock at Chelsworth, the cosy Beehive at Horringer (its imaginative cooking goes from strength to strength), the marvellously traditional Kings Head at Laxfield (doing horse-drawn carriage rides now), the Ship at Levington (good food, about as home-made as you can get – with its own smokery), the lively Jolly Sailor at Orford, the Kings Head there (good fresh fish), and the rather smart Angel at Stoke by Nayland (particularly good food). Two Trust Houses here – the Crown at Framlingham and Bull at Long Melford – both have good companionable bars, besides being handsome places to stay; a third, the Swan at Lavenham (in the Lucky Dip section at the end of the chapter) is in the same class. Though none of the Lucky Dip entries here have this year stood out as obvious candidates for promotion to the main entries, given the very strong competition from existing entries of such character and still-developing appeal, lots of them are clearly well worth knowing. The Bury St Edmunds area seems specially well favoured, with the Masons Arms and Nutshell there both doing well, and the Six Bells at Bardwell, Bell at Mildenhall, Fox at Pakenham and White Horse at Whepstead all in easy reach. Other notable Dips include the Ship at Blaxhall, three Queens Heads (at Blyford, Bramfield and Brandeston), Cock at Clare, Queens Head at Erwarton, Ferry Boat at Felixstowe Ferry, Volunteer at Saxtead Green, Plough & Sail at Snape and Cat & Mouse at Wetheringsett.

BARTON MILLS TL7173 Map 5

Bull ⇨

Just off A11 Newmarket–Thetford

The comfortably modernised rambling bar, partly candlelit at night, is opposite the main hotel entrance: big fireplaces, beams and joists showing through the plasterwork, old and more recent panelling, various cosy alcoves – one with attractive antique sporting prints on a Delft shelf – gold plush button-back built-in wall banquettes, and matching stools and studded seats. Well kept Adnams Southwold, Bass, Charringtons IPA and a guest beer on handpump, with a good selection of decent wines – particularly whites; on Sundays, they may set out cheese cubes, nuts and crisps. Bar food includes home-made soup, sandwiches (from £1.25), ploughman's (£2.75), a salad bar with quiche or cold meats (£2.25) or cold pies (£2.95), scampi or gammon (£3.75), 14oz T-bone steak (£9.95), and a daily special (from £3.25). A new grill room has been opened this year with chargrilled steaks and fish served on sizzler plates. Dominoes, cribbage, fruit machine, trivia and piped music. The pretty 17th-century coachyard has a pigeon loft above its neatly converted high-doored stables. *(Recommended by J P Cinnamond, John Day)*

Free house   Licensees Mark and Terry Rumsey   Real ale   Meals and snacks (noon–10 Mon–Sat)   Restaurant   Children in eating area of bar   Open 11–11   Bedrooms tel Mildenhall (0638) 713230; £25B/£40B

BLYTHBURGH TM4575 Map 5

White Hart

A12

There has been a building on this spot above the marshes for over 800 years – it was originally an ecclesiastical courthouse for the priory, and has been an inn since at least 1548. The big open-plan bar has some lovely curved oak beams, a fine Stuart staircase, Elizabethan woodwork, and log fires at each end. Between the bar and dining room there's a large circular open fire. As it's placed on the busy A12, it does cater efficiently for the volume of visitors you'd expect. A new licensee was taking over as we went to press, and hopes to add some new dishes once he's settled in (he does a lot of the cooking himself): soup (£1.45), filled baked potatoes (from £2.85), lasagne (£3.95), lots of fresh local fish (from £3.95), various pies such as chicken and mushroom, steak and kidney or fish (£4.25), and vegetarian dishes like leek croustade; if you want a table in summer, it's best to turn up early. Well kept Adnams Bitter, Broadside and winter Old on handpump; decent wines; table skittles, dominoes and cribbage. The spacious lawn behind has a pétanque pitch. One of East Anglia's grandest churches is down the lane on the other side of the main road. *(Recommended by J P Cinnamond, T Nott, Geoff Halson, Klaus and Elizabeth Leist, M J Morgan; more reports please)*

Adnams   Licensee Don Williamson   Real ale   Meals and snacks   Restaurant tel *Blythburgh (050 270) 217   Children in eating area and restaurant   Open 10.30–2.30, 6–11; 11–11 Fri and Sat; closed evening 25 Dec*

nr CHELMONDISTON   TM2037 Map 5

Butt & Oyster

Pin Mill – signposted from B1456 SE of Ipswich

From the seats in the big bay window of this old bargeman's pub or from the many solid tables and chairs by the water, there's a fine view of the ships coming down the river from Ipswich, and it's interesting to see the long lines of moored black sailing barges. The small, half panelled smoke room has high-backed and other old-fashioned settles on the tiled floor, and is decorated with model sailing ships; spare a glance for the most unusual carving of a man with a woman over the mantelpiece. Good, popular bar food includes sandwiches (from 75p; not on Saturday or Sunday lunchtimes when there's a buffet), ploughman's (from £2), salads, home-made pies and quiches (around £3.50), and four changing home-made daily specials like lamb casserole, cod mornay, cottage pie or Milanese pasta (all £3.50); Camerons Bitter and Strongarm and Tolly Bitter and Mild on handpump with Old Strong in winter tapped from the cask; darts, shove-ha'penny, table skittles, dominoes and cribbage. A good time to visit the pub would be when the annual Thames Barge race is held (end June/beginning July). *(Recommended by Mrs P J Pearce, RCL, Martin and Jane Bailey; more reports please)*

Tolly (Brent Walker)   Licensees Dick and Brenda Mainwaring   Real ale   Meals and snacks (12–2, 7–10)   Children in two separate rooms   Open 11–11; 12–3, 7–11 in winter; closed 25 and 26 Dec evening

CHELSWORTH   TL9848 Map 5

Peacock ★ ⇌

The Street; B1115

Just over the bridge from the rich parkland of Chelsworth Hall, this elegantly restored 14th-century inn has a splendid stone inglenook fireplace in the large beamed bar, which is divided into several areas by a partly open timbered partition. The cosy inner lounge has some exposed Tudor brickwork and is decorated with local paintings which are for sale (there is a craft shop behind the garden). Home-made bar food includes vegetable soup (£1.50), sandwiches (from £1.50), ploughman's (£2.60), chicken curry (£4.50), salads (from £4.50), gammon with pineapple or eggs (£5), scampi (£5.25), steaks (from £8), puddings (£2.25), and daily specials like seafood or steak and mushroom pies or trout cleopatra. Well kept Adnams, Greene King IPA and Abbot and Mauldons on handpump, and sometimes there are nibbles such as stuffed olives or nuts on the tables. Pleasant staff; darts, piped music, and maybe a friendly Jack Russell. *(Recommended by Mr and Mrs J M Elden, J P Cinnamond, John Evans, Frank W Gadbois, Barbara and Norman Wells, R C Gandy, Gwen and Peter Andrews, P Miller; more reports please)*

Free house   Licensees Mrs L R Bulgin and A F Marsh   Real ale   Meals and snacks (till 10pm)   Children in eating area   Jazz Fri evenings, pianist Sun evenings   Open 11–3, 6–11; closed 25 Dec   Bedrooms tel Bildeston 740758; £28/£38

CLARE   TL7645 Map 5

Bell

A comfortable, light and airy conservatory has been built onto this attractive timbered hotel, with sofas and armchairs prettily covered in a burgundy Laura Ashley paisley; there's also a new back terrace, and the garden has been completely redeveloped. The rambling lounge bar has panelling and woodwork around the open fire, splendidly carved black beams, armchairs on the green carpet and local notices on the hessian walls. Another room leads off, and to eat you go through to the Leggers Bar with masses of prints – mainly to do with canals – on its walls: food here includes soup (£1.25), pasta with a choice of sauces (£2.25 starter, £3.50 main course), pizzas (from £2.50), curries (from £3.50), salads (from £4.25), scampi (£4.95), and steaks (from £5.95), and specials like excellent haddock mornay; toasted sandwiches in the comfortable lounge bar. Well kept Nethergate Bitter and Old Growler on handpump, various malt whiskies, and quick service; fruit machine, trivia and piped music. Several other striking buildings in the village include the remains of the priory and the castle (which stands on prehistoric earthworks). (*Recommended by J P Cinnamond, Derek and Sylvia Stephenson; more reports please*)

Free house   Licensees Brian and Gloria Miles   Real ale   Meals and snacks (till 10 on Fri and Sat evenings)   Restaurant (not Sun evening)   Children welcome   Open 11–3, 5–11; 11–11 Sat   Bedrooms tel Clare (0787) 277741; £32.50(£40B)/£49.95(£55B)

CRETINGHAM   TM2260 Map 5

Bell

Some 20 years ago, this buff-washed tiled building was converted from 15th-century cottages. The comfortably modernised lounge bar has exposed beams, standing timbers of a knocked-through wall, a large old fireplace, and a wall tapestry. Well presented, good bar food includes soup (£1.25), ploughman's (from £2.45, they also do vegetarian cheese), vegetarian lasagne or vegetable curry (£2.65), home-made steak in stout or chicken and ham pies (£3.25), chargrilled meats like gammon (£3.75), steaks (£5.75) and venison (£6.25), and puddings such as apple and cinnamon pie or treacle and walnut tart (£1.75). Popular Sunday roast lunch (£7.45), summer barbecues, and children's helpings; they'll do free birthday cakes for celebrations if given advance notice. Well kept Adnams, Greene King Abbot and a regular guest beer on handpump; piped jazz. The quarry-tiled public bar has darts, shove-ha'penny, dominoes and cribbage. On the sheltered grass in front there are rustic tables and seats, with more on another lawn by rose bushes and a fine old oak tree on the corner; there's also a secluded children's play area with play-frame and their own tables and chairs. The local harriers meet here each New Year's Day. (*Recommended by Donald Rice, C H Stride; more reports please*)

Free house   Licensees Ron Blackmore, Tim and James Yeo   Real ale   Meals and snacks   Restaurant tel Earl Soham (072 882) 419   Children welcome   Open 11.30–2.30, 6.30–11

DUNWICH   TM4770 Map 5

Ship

Always busy with a good mix of locals and visitors, this friendly, atmospheric inn has a main bar with a woodburning stove (cheerfully left open in cold weather), cushioned wall benches, pews and captain's chairs, wooden tables with candles, a dusky ochre ceiling, and a tiled floor. Reasonably priced, tasty, home-made bar food includes lovely soup (90p), ploughman's or cottage pie (£2.50), lasagne (£3), and excellent fresh local fish such as plaice (£3.50), with evening dishes like garlic mushrooms (£2.25), home-made pâté (£2.50), hot home-cooked ham with peach and brandy sauce (£6), fish of the day or sirloin steak (£6.75), and vegetarian dishes. Well kept Adnams Bitter, Broadside and Old, and Greene King Abbot on handpump, and James White farm cider (very strong) at the handsomely panelled bar counter. The public bar area has darts, dominoes, cribbage, fruit machine, space game and piped music. The conservatory has bunches of grapes on the vine, there's a well kept garden with an enormous fig tree, and a sunny back terrace. On current form this pub seems clearly in the running for a star award – we'd be glad of your views on this. *(Recommended by Alison and Tony Godfrey, C J Parsons, Mrs S Burrows-Smith, Klaus and Elizabeth Leist, A T Langton, Nick Dowson, Alison Hayward, Derek and Sylvia Stephenson, RCL, Geoff Halson, David Pearman, Jason Caulkin, P Leeson and friends, Ian and Joanna Chisholm, Heather Sharland)*

Free house   Licensees Stephen and Ann Marshlain   Real ale   Snacks (lunchtime) and meals   Evening restaurant   Children welcome (not in Ship Bar)   Open 11–3, 6–11 (winter evening opening 7); closed evening 25 Dec   Bedrooms tel Westleton (072 873) 219; £16/£32, not Christmas/New Year

EARL SOHAM   SM2363 Map 5

Victoria ★

A1120 Stowmarket–Yoxford

Unless you're in the know, it would be easy to drive straight past this friendly and relaxing little country pub. The furnishings are nicely chosen – kitchen chairs and pews, plank-topped trestle sewing-machine tables and other simple country tables with candles, tiled or board floors, stripped panelling, an interesting range of pictures of Queen Victoria and her reign, a piano, and open fires. Reasonably priced, the good home-made food includes sandwiches (from 75p), home-made soup (£1.25), ploughman's (from £2.15), delicious chilli con carne (£2.75), vegetarian lasagne (£3.25), pork with apple and cider (£3.50), and beef curry (£3.75). The very good home-brewed beer (they do a take-away service too) includes a bitter, a mild called Gannet, another called Victoria and a stronger ale called Albert; you can visit the brewery. Darts, shove-ha'penny, dominoes and cribbage; seats out in front and on a raised back lawn. The pub is close to a wild fritillary meadow at Framlingham and a working windmill at Saxtead. *(Recommended by Klaus and Elizabeth Leist, Comus Elliott, Gwen and Peter Andrews, J P Cinnamond, RCL, Geoff Halson, P Miller, John Baker, Nigel Gibbs)*

Own brew   Licensees Clare and John Bjornson   Real ale   Meals and snacks   Children in back bar only   Impromptu folk music   Open 11.30–2.30 (till 3 Sat), 5.30–11

FRAMLINGHAM   TM2863 Map 5

Crown 🛏

Market Hill

Perhaps the best place to sit in the cosy bar of this bustling, friendly little black-and-white Tudor inn is at the old windows overlooking the unusual sloping triangular market place (market day is Saturday, when nearby parking may be difficult). This room is popular with locals: high heavy beams, one or two settles (including an antique carved one), dark green plush armed seats, and a log fire. The comfortable lounge has wing easy chairs beside the fire, and there are more seats in the hall. Bar food includes home-made soup (£1.25), sandwiches (from £1.50), ploughman's (£2.95), steak and kidney pie (£4.50), and a daily special (£4.50). Adnams and Everards Tiger on handpump; piped music. Coaches once clattered through what is now a prettily planted flagstoned courtyard (with a cheerful winter flowering cherry). *(Recommended by D S Cottrell, Heather Sharland, Gwyneth and Salvo Spadaro-Dutturi; more reports please)*

Free house (THF)   Real ale   Meals and snacks   Restaurant   Children in restaurant   Open 11–2.30, 6–11   Bedrooms tel Framlingham (1728) 723521; £65B/£75B

FRAMSDEN   TM1959 Map 5

Dobermann

The Street; pub signposted off B1077 just S of its junction with A1120 Stowmarket–Earl Soham

A central fireplace divides the rooms of this very neatly kept and cheerfully-run thatched pub – its log fire open to both sides. On one there's a big sofa (a favourite with Lottie, the tabby cat), a couple of chintz wing armchairs, and by the big window a refectory table. The other side has a mix of chairs, plush-seated stools and winged settles around scrubbed rustic tables. Photographs of and show rosettes won by the owner's dogs decorate the white walls. Popular bar food includes sandwiches (from 95p, maybe hot beef £1.70), home-made soup (£1.60), sausage in a basket (£1.95), ploughman's (from £3.30), gammon and sausage (£5.50), home-made chicken and mushroom or steak and kidney pies (£5.75), and trout in wine and almonds or popular chicken breast St Etienne (£6.50). Well kept Adnams Bitter and Broadside, Greene King IPA, and a guest beer such as Charles Wells Bombardier all on handpump, with a decent choice of spirits and malt whiskies; shove-ha'penny, dominoes, cribbage, and maybe piped Radio 1. They play boules outside, where there are picnic-table sets by trees and a fairy-lit trellis, with summer barbecues. *(Recommended by Alison Hayward, Nick Dowson, John Whitehead, John Baker; more reports please)*

Free house   Licensee Susan Frankland   Real ale   Meals and snacks (till 10pm)   Open 11.30–2.30, 7–11   Bedrooms tel Helmingham (047 339) 461; £15l£20

HORRINGER   TL8261 Map 5

Beehive ✿

A143

Radiating from the central servery, the rambling little rooms here have carefully chosen dining and country kitchen chairs, one or two wall settles around solid tables, stripped panelling or brickwork, some very low beams in some of the furthest and snuggest alcoves, picture-lights over lots of 19th-century prints, and a woodburning stove; there's a couple of quiet dogs including an aloof borzoi. Very good, often unusual food includes home-made soup (£1.20), sandwiches (from £1.25, fillet steak £4.25), ploughman's or mushrooms in a creamy tarragon sauce on light pastry (£2.50), cheese and broccoli bake (£3.25), bacon roly poly with onion gravy (£3.50), thinly sliced honey-roasted goose breast (£3.95), Arbroath smokies (£4.50), a plate of hors d'oeuvres with smoked salmon, pâté, salami, prawns, avocado and so forth (£5.50), local venison steak in a rich claret sauce (£6.95), puddings such as butterscotch meringue (£1.75), and specials like hot buttered asparagus (£3.50) and whole lobster salad (£12.50). Well kept Greene King IPA and Abbot on handpump and decent house wines. A most attractively planted back terrace has picnic-table sets, with more seats on a raised lawn. *(Recommended by M Rising, John Baker, John Matthews, Nigel Paine)*

Greene King   Licensee Gary Kingshott   Real ale   Meals and snacks (not Sun evening)   Table bookings tel Horringer (028 488) 260   Children welcome   Open 11.30–2.30, 7–11

HOXNE   TM1777 Map 5

Swan

Off B1118; village signposted off A140 S of Diss

The extensive lawn behind this Grade II listed, carefully restored Elizabethan inn is used for croquet – a nice place to sit in summer on the hand-made elm furniture, sheltered by a willow and other trees and its shrub-covered wall; if you are eating outside, rather than use a tannoy, they press a buzzer and then prop up scoreboard-type numbers on the roof to indicate your ticket number. Inside, the front bar has two solid oak bar counters, a deep-set inglenook fireplace with an armchair on either side and a long bench in front of it, and heavy oak floors; you

can see the ancient timber and mortar of the walls. A fire in the back bar divides
the bar area and snug, and the dining room has an original wooden fireplace.
Good home-made bar food includes burger (from 85p), soup such as carrot and
coriander (£1.25), sandwiches (£1.30, good ham), ploughman's (from £1.95), a
choice of omelettes (£2.50), pancakes filled with mushrooms and cheese (£2.65),
plate of salamis with black olives (£3.25), steaks (from £5.35), daily specials such
as chicken liver and pork pâté (£1.75), chicken and asparagus au gratin (£2.75),
lamb brochettes with pineapple and a lime sauce (£4.95), and puddings like
banana and raisin scrunch or lemon cheesecake (from £1.75). Sunday winter roast
lunch (3 courses £8.95) or summer cold table (£5.95). Well kept Adnams tapped
from the cask and Greene King Abbot on handpump, decent wines, and
half-a-dozen malt whiskies; pool, shove-ha'penny, dominoes, and juke box. The
pub is close to the site of King Edmund's Martyrdom on 20 November 870.
(Recommended by Gwen and Peter Andrews, Nick Dowson, Alison Hayward, Chris Beecham,
Mr and Mrs E J Smith; more reports please)

Free house   Licensees Tony and Frances Thornton-Jones   Real ale   Meals and snacks
(not Sat–Mon evenings)   Restaurant Wed–Sat evenings and Sun lunchtime tel Hoxne
(037 975) 275   Children in eating area of bar   Open 12–2.30, 7–11; closed 25 Dec

HUNDON TL7348 Map 5
Plough

Brockley Green; on Kedington road, up hill from village

A new restaurant and bedroom extension has been finished this year, the gardens
have been landscaped, and a big new terrace with pergola and ornamental pool has
been constructed. There's a double row of worn old oak timbers to mark what
must have been the corridor between the two rooms of the neatly-kept and friendly
carpeted bar, most walls are stripped back to bare brick and decorated with
striking gladiatorial designs for Covent Garden by Leslie Hurry (who lived nearby),
and there are low side settles with Liberty-print cushions, spindleback chairs, and
sturdy low tables. Good bar food includes sandwiches (from £1.25), home-made
soup (£1.35), filled French bread (from £1.50), ploughman's (from £2.65), devilled
whitebait in paprika (£2.75), salads (from £3.25), vegetarian or seafood pasta
dishes (£3.95), steaks (from £5.95), daily specials such as dressed crab, fresh
salmon or steak and kidney pie (from around £4.25), and puddings like
home-made apple pie or strawberry pavlova (from £1.95); on Tuesdays they hold
seafood evenings with four starters and six main courses (from £3.95-£15 for
lobster). Well kept Greene King IPA, Nethergate, a delicious house beer brewed by
Mauldons ('Furrowed Brew'), and a guest beer on handpump; choice of wines;
shove-ha'penny, dominoes and cheerful piped music. There's a terrace and a
redesigned garden. It's also a certified location for the Caravan Club, with a
sheltered site to the rear for tourers. (Recommended by Gwyneth and Salvo
Spadaro-Dutturi; more reports please)

Free house   Licensee David Rowlinson   Real ale   Meals and snacks (11–2, 7–9.30
Mon–Sat; 11–2, 7–9 Sun)   Partly no-smoking restaurant   Children welcome   Open
11–11; 11–3, 6–11 Sat; 12–2.30, 7–11 in winter   Bedrooms tel Hundon (0440) 86789;
£32.50B/£40B

IXWORTH TL9370 Map 5
Pickerel

Village signposted just off A143 Bury St Edmunds–Diss

Several small rooms – leading off the central servery – have cushioned chairs and
pews, attractive brickwork, moulded Elizabethan oak beams, panelling that varies
from ancient to 18th-century, and big fireplaces. Good bar food includes
home-made soup (£1.25), filled French bread (from £1.15), ploughman's (from
£2.75 – they also do vegetarian cheddar), mushroom and nut stroganoff or
battered haddock (£3.25), fish pie or gammon and pineapple (£3.95), smoked
halibut (£5.95), chargrilled venison steak (£6.25) or sirloin steak (£6.95), and daily

specials; 3-course Sunday lunch (£6.95), and they plan game dishes in season. The pretty two-roomed dining room has stripped pine tables and dressers, stripped pine dado, blue patterned wallpaper and a high shelf of plates, and there's a small back sun lounge facing a sway-backed Elizabethan timbered barn across the old coach yard. Well kept Greene King Abbot and IPA on handpump, and reasonable house wines; fruit machine, piped music. On a goodish stretch of grass under a giant sycamore are some picnic-table sets. Incidentally, people who remember the pub from a couple of years ago may be interested to know that we've tracked down Kirsten Burge – at the Drewe Arms, Broadhembury, down in Devon. *(Recommended by R M Savage, Maureen and Pat Campbell, John Baker, Charles Bardswell, David Cardy)*

Greene King   Licensee Martin Fincham   Real ale   Meals and snacks (till 10pm) Restaurant tel Pakenham (0359) 30398   Children in restaurant and eating area of bar Jazz July and August, and plan regular live music   Open 11–2.30, 5.30–11

KERSEY   TL9944 Map 5

Bell

Village signposted off A1141 N of Hadleigh

New licensees have taken over this fine timbered building with its jettied upper floor, and as we went to press they were planning a conservatory for family eating, and hoping to add more bedrooms. Doors off a worn brick-tiled corridor open into a bar and lounge which are divided by a brick and timber screen decorated with copper and brassware. The low-beamed public side has simple seating on its tiled floor and a log fire, and the lounge side has comfortable red plush button-back banquettes, latticed windows, and a swirly red carpet. Bar food includes sandwiches (from £1.25), home-made soup (£1.50), ploughman's (£2.85), salads (from £2.85, dressed Cromer crab £4.95, half a Scottish lobster £7.95), vegetarian dishes such as Mediterranean crêpe with fresh ratatouille (£3.95) or hazelnut and mushroom pie (£4.45), home-made chilli, burger or lasagne (all £4.25), home-made steak and kidney pie (£4.95), gammon steak with peach, pineapple or egg (£5.25), and steaks (from £6.95). Sold on a rotational basis, the three handpumps here may serve Adnams Best, Batemans XXXB, Boddingtons, Felinfoel Double Dragon, Flowers Original, Greene King, Mansfield Old Baily, Marstons Pedigree, Sam Smiths, Wadworths 6X, and Websters Yorkshire; around a dozen malt whiskies; dominoes, cribbage, fruit machine and piped music. Out on the sheltered back terrace and under a fairy-lit side canopy, there are white cast-iron tables and chairs. They are listed as a certified location for the Caravan Club (up to 3 units). *(Recommended by Barbara and Norman Wells, Geoff Halson, Mrs L Saumarez Smith, P Miller, John Evans; more reports please)*

Free house   Licensees Alex and Lynne Coote   Real ale   Meals and snacks Restaurant   Children in resaurant and eating area of bar   Open 11–3 (5 summer Sats), 6–11; winter evening opening 7; closed Tues evenings Feb and Mar   Bedrooms tel Ipswich (0473) 823229; £15/£38B

LAXFIELD   TM2972 Map 5

Kings Head ★

Behind church, off road toward Banyards Green

Decidedly unspoilt and warmly friendly, this newly repainted and thatched Tudor pub has an open fire in the old-fashioned, tiled-floor front room, cosily surrounded by a high-backed built-in settle; a couple of other rooms have pews, old seats, scrubbed deal tables, some interesting prints on the walls, and a quietly ticking clock. Well kept Adnams Extra, Blackawton Forty-Four, Mauldons Suffolk Punch and Black Adder, Wadworths 6X, and James White's farmhouse cider are tapped from casks in a back room; cards, Scrabble, and bagatelle. Bar food includes sandwiches, home-made soup such as Stilton and cauliflower, vegetarian meals (from £3.25), beef and pigeon casserole (£4.95), rich seafood stew (£5.25), chicken Kiev or steaks (from £5.95), and home-made puddings; Sunday lunch (£5.95).

Friday evening is traditionally 'kipper night' with oak-smoked kippers (£1.95); four-course evening meals if booked two days in advance. Going out past the casks in the back serving room, you find benches and a trestle table in a small yard. From the yard, a honeysuckle arch leads into a sheltered little garden and the pub's own well kept and secluded bowling, badminton and croquet green; occasional Morris dancers on summer weekends. They plan special lunches and dinners in their candlelit dining room to coincide with horse-drawn carriage rides. *(Recommended by Nick Dowson, Alison Hayward, Klaus and Elizabeth Leist, P A and J B Jones, Gwen and Peter Andrews; more reports please)*

Free house   Licensee Nicholas Lockley   Real ale   Meals and snacks   Restaurant Children welcome   Traditional music/jazz/blues/folk Thurs, Fri, Sat and Sun evenings Open 11–3, 6–11   Bedrooms planned tel Ubbeston (098 683) 395; /£27B

LEVINGTON   TM2339 Map 5

Ship

Gun Hill; village signposted from A45, then follow Stratton Hall sign

Busy at weekends and on summer evenings, this engaging traditional pub has ship prints and photos of sailing barges, beams, benches built into the wall, and upholstered small settles (some of them grouped round tables, as booths). The middle room has an energetic and talkative green parrot called Billy, a marine compass set into the serving counter which has a fishing net slung over it, a big black round stove, and casks of well kept Tolly Bitter and Original; there's a no-smoking area. All home-made, the good, popular bar food might include ploughman's (from £2.25), sausages in cider sauce or mushroom stroganoff (£3.25), salads (from £3.25), prawn risotto or vegetarian nut roast (£3.75), honey-curried chicken, steak and kidney pie or wholemeal lasagne (£3.95), and interesting puddings such as bread pudding made with Guinness, a special spotted dick (called wet nellie) or summer fruit pudding (£1.95); they home-smoke their own meat and fish including prawns and sausages. Benches out in front look over the quiet lane to the distant water. *(Recommended by John Baker, Richard Marjoram, John Tyzack)*

Tolly   Licensee Mrs Wenham   Real ale   Snacks (lunchtime, limited Sun)   Open 11.30–2.30, 7–11; closed 25 Dec evening

LONG MELFORD   TL8645 Map 5

Bull ⇐

A134

Since 1580, this civilised black and white timbered building has been an inn, though it was originally a medieval manorial great hall. The comfortable front lounge – divided by the remains of an oak partition wall – has big mullioned and leaded windows, lots of oak timbering, a huge brick fireplace with log fire, a longcase clock from Stradbrook, a rack of daily papers, and has been recently refurbished with antique furniture. Supporting the beautifully carved high main beam is a woodwose – the wild man of the woods that figures in Suffolk folk-tales. A more spacious back bar has armed brown leatherette or plush dining seats around antique oak tables, dark heavy beams, and sporting prints on the cream timbered walls; the Mylde lounge is no-smoking. Bar food includes soup (£1.60), sandwiches (from £1.60), ploughman's (£2.50), steak and mushroom or trawlerman's pies or a daily special (all £4.25), scampi (£4.95), and an extensive help-yourself cold buffet (£5.95). Well kept Greene King IPA and Abbot on handpump, and cheerful, helpful staff. There are tables in the paved central courtyard. In 1648 a local man, arguing about Civil War politics, was murdered in a brawl just inside the front door (and buried in the yard of the magnificent church – look for the memorial to Richard Evered). Another murder was committed in 1739 and ghost-hunters hold these reponsible for the old brass and copper supposedly rising out of the fireplace and floating around the ceiling. The Elizabethan Melford Hall and moated Tudor Kentwell Hall are both fine buildings, in attractive grounds. *(Recommended by R M Savage, John Evans, P Meacock, Barbara and Norman Wells, Heather Sharland)*

Free house (THF)   Manager Peter Watt   Real ale   Meals and snacks (lunchtime, limited menu Sun; not 25 Dec)   Restaurant   Children welcome   Open 11–3, 6–11; 11–11 Sat   Bedrooms tel Sudbury (0787) 78494; £65B/£80B

ORFORD   TM4250 Map 5

Jolly Sailor ★

This aptly named smugglers' inn was built mainly from wrecked ships' timbers in the 17th century, and the several cheerful and cosy rooms are served from counters and hatches in an old-fashioned central cubicle. One main room has an uncommon spiral staircase in the corner and is warmed in winter by a good solid fuel stove, another has a flagstoned floor, and a small room is popular with the dominoes and shove-ha'penny players; often, seats are pews. The dining room is no-smoking. There are some curious stuffed 'Chinese muff dogs', about half the size of a chihuahua – said to be Tudor, though no one's sure, and a collection of military badges/shields. Well kept Adnams Bitter on handpump; friendly staff (and dogs); fruit machine, piped music. Bar food includes sandwiches, ploughman's or smoked mackerel (£2.20), scampi (£3.40), steaks (£6.50) and a daily special such as fresh local cod (when available) or beef and vegetable or cottage pies (£2.50); good breakfasts. Tables and chairs in the big garden which also has a children's play area. The pub stands by a busy little quay on the River Ore, opposite Orford Ness and close to marshy Havergate Island, where avocets breed. At weekends, the big car park is often given over to activities such as car boot sales, though the consequent street parking is not popular with locals. There's a caravan for rent. *(Recommended by Caroline and Colin, John Baker, Comus Elliott, Richard Gibbs, Nigel Gibbs, WTF, Derek Patey, Jason Caulkin, Rona Murdoch, Heather Sharland, Gwyneth and Salvo Spadaro-Dutturi)*

Adnams   Licensee Patrick Buckner   Real ale   Meals and snacks (12–1.45, 6.30–8.30)   Children in dining room if eating   Live music some Sat evenings   Open 11–2.30, 6–11   Bedrooms tel Orford (0394) 450243; £15.50/£28

Kings Head ✿

Front Street

The friendly main bar in this predominantly Tudor inn – parts date back 700 years – has carved black oak beams, one or two fine old wooden chairs, comfortable blue leatherette seats and cushioned wall benches grouped around the low tables on its carpet, and an open fire. Very good fresh fish at lunchtime in the bar includes plaice (£2.95), delicious home-made fish pie (£5.50), monkfish and lobster soufflé with shellfish sauce (£5.25), scallops in sherry and mushroom sauce (£5.50), king prawns in garlic butter (£7.60), fresh local lobster (from £7.50); also, home-made soup (£1.65), ploughman's (from £2.25) and home-made pâté (£2.50); home-made puddings such as fruit sorbet or brown bread and honey ice-cream (from £1.50); good breakfasts often include grilled sole or poached whiting. Note though that they don't do sandwiches. Well kept Adnams Bitter, Broadside, Mild and winter Old and Tally Ho on handpump, and quite a few wines; fruit machine. By the historical church, and there are views from the well restored keep of the nearby 12th-century castle. *(Recommended by Caroline and Colin, Richard Gibbs, Nigel Gibbs, Jane Buekett, Jamie Lyons, Ruth Harrison, Mrs H M T Carpenter, Jason Caulkin, Heather Sharland)*

Adnams   Licensee Alistair Shaw   Real ale   Meals and snacks   Evening restaurant (not Sun or Thurs), though they do light lunches weekends, Bank Hols and school hols   Children in restaurant (see restaurant notes)   Open 11–2.30 (till 3 Sat), 6–11   Bedrooms tel Orford (0394) 450271; £20/£34

RAMSHOLT   TM3141   Map 5

Ramsholt Arms

Village signposted from B1083; then take turning after the one to Ramsholt Church

On summer weekends, this beautifully placed pub is very popular with boating people (though if you want to pick up a mooring, it's best to contact the harbour-master before doing so). It's quite isolated by an old barge quay on the River Deben which winds past to the sea, and silent but for the distant noise of gulls, curlews and other waders. Simple furnishings include dark oak, tapestry-upholstered seats, red tiles or parquet flooring, some neatly nautical woodwork, tide tables and charts, and a big picture window. Well kept Adnams Bitter, Batemans XXX and Boddingtons on handpump; lunchtime bar food includes ploughman's (from £2.40), cold carvery in summer (from £4.25), and home-cooked meats and fresh fish, with evening bar snacks like char-grilled burgers (from £3.25), chicken goujons (£4.55), and jumbo scampi (£4.95), and more substantial dishes such as swordfish steak (£6.25), chargrilled steaks (from £6.95), and big mixed grill (£9.50). Sensibly placed darts, cribbage, dominoes, fruit machine; piped music. There's a riverside terrace bar which is open every afternoon from May 14 to August 28, excluding Sundays. (*Recommended by Drs M and K Parier; more reports please*)

Free house   Licensees Liz and St John Girling   Real ale   Meals and snacks   Children in dining room   Steep longish walk down from car park   Open 11–3, 5–11; 11–11 Sat; 11.30–2.30, 7–11 in winter   Bedrooms tel Woodbridge (0394) 411229; £25B/£50B

REDE   TL8055   Map 5

Plough ✿

Village signposted off A143 Bury St Edmunds–Haverhill

Warmly welcoming, with a nice country atmosphere, this pretty pink-washed, partly thatched pub is popular for its home-made food. It's the dishes of the day which earn our food award, and on a typical day, they might be beef in horseradish and cream sauce or braised pork in peanut sauce (£4.50), chicken breast in wine and tomatoes (£4.95), scampi in lobster and parsley sauce (£6.50), fresh fish like delicious lemon sole (£8.50) and Dover sole (£10.50), and veal with Dijon mustard, cream and brandy (£9.50); scrumptious puddings. They do a lot of game in season, such as roast partridge or pheasant casserole. There is a wide choice of other hot bar dishes, ploughman's and salads (outstanding beef and Cromer crab), and the little evening restaurant does things like moules au gratin, chicken stuffed with crab meat and Swiss cheese, poached salmon, and steaks; attentive, caring service. The simple and traditional cosy bar has copper measures and pewter tankards hanging from low black beams, decorative plates on a Delft shelf and surrounding the solid fuel stove in its brick fireplace, and red plush button-back built-in wall banquettes; fruit machine, unobtrusive piped radio. In front of the building are some picnic-table sets, with more in a sheltered cottage garden behind; it's a lovely quiet spot, with not much sound beyond the birds in the aviary (and the surrounding trees) or the burbling white doves in the dovecote. (*Recommended by N S Holmes, Frank W Gadbois, Gwen and Peter Andrews*)

Greene King   Licensees Brian and Joyce Desborough   Meals and snacks (not Sun evenings)   Evening restaurant tel Hawkedon (028 489) 208, Sun lunch   Children in eating area and restaurant   Open 11.30–2.30, 6.30–11

SIBTON   TM3669   Map 5

White Horse

Halesworth Road; village signposted from A1120 Peasenhall–Yoxford

Attractively laid out with old-fashioned furnishings, this pleasant 16th-century inn has cushioned settles and little red plush armchairs, lots of tack, horsebrasses and plates on the yellowing walls, a big rug on the black and red tiled floor, and a woodburning stove. Five steps take you up past an ancient partly knocked-through timbered wall into a carpeted gallery with comfortable armed seats around rustic tables. Bar food includes sandwiches (lunchtimes only), soup, ploughman's (£1.70), jumbo sausage (£1.95), lasagne, rump steak (£5.10), duck à l'orange or lamb Shrewsbury (£5.40), and specials such as seafood pie or gammon, and vegetarian dishes. Well kept Adnams Bitter on handpump and farm cider (summer only); darts, shove-ha'penny, dominoes, cribbage and piped music. Out in the big garden are tables under cocktail parasols, a children's play area and space for caravans. (*Recommended by Peter Burton, Klaus and Elizabeth Leist, Nick Dowson, Alison Hayward, N A Wright*)

Free house   Licensees Tony and Fay Waddingham   Real ale   Meals and lunchtime snacks (12–1.30, 7–9; not Sun evening)   Children in gallery eating area   Open 11.30–2.30, 7 (6.30 summer Sats)–11; closed Mon lunchtime except Bank Hols   Bedrooms tel Peasenhall (072 879) 337; £15S/£28S

SNAPE   TM3959 Map 5

Golden Key ★ ⊘

Priory Lane

On the cream walls of the low-beamed stylish lounge in this quietly elegant pub are some nice pictures – pencil sketches of customers, a Henry Wilkinson spaniel and so forth. The serving end has an open log fire in winter, an old-fashioned settle curving around a couple of venerable stripped tables and a tiled floor, and at the other end there are stripped modern settles around heavy Habitat-style wooden tables on a Turkey carpet, and a solid fuel stove in the big fireplace; a brick-floored side room has some more tables. Home-made food includes soup, sausage, egg and onion pie (£3.95), smoked haddock quiche (£4.25), lemon sole (from £5.95), lobster (from £6.95), daily specials such as excellent steak and mushroom pie (£4.50), and a choice of puddings such as fruit pies or lemon cake (from £1.75); a pity about the UHT cream. Well kept Adnams Bitter and Broadside on handpump, with Old ale and Tally Ho in winter, and James White's cider; friendly staff. The small and sheltered pretty front garden has white tables and chairs on the gravel, and a lovely mass of summer flowers. (*Recommended by J P Cinnamond, J A Gifford, Derek Patey, Jamie Lyons, Ruth Harrison, Derek and Sylvia Stephenson, Heather Sharland, Gwen and Peter Andrews, R M Sparkes*)

Adnams   Licensees Max and Susie Kissick-Jones   Real ale   Meals and snacks   Open 11–3, 6–11, with afternoon and evening extensions during Aldeburgh Festival; closed 25 Dec

SOUTHWOLD   TM5076 Map 5

Crown ⊘ ⇐

High Street

The really special thing at this well run, civilised place is the food. From a menu that changes daily, this might include four or so starters such as tomato and pear soup (£1.50), fresh Cromer crab salad (£2.60), hot goats cheese in filo pastry (£3.20) or baked quail on continental leaves (£3.60), half-a-dozen main dishes like tagliatelle verdi with a rich bolognese sauce (£4.40), lovely poached smoked haddock with poached eggs (£4.50), excellent magret of duck with an apricot and honey glaze or orange and Cointreau sauce (£5.75) or sautéed scallops with fresh herbs (£7.70), and puddings like berries in a sharp fruit jelly with forest fruit sauce, chocolate marquise with cold orange custard or bread and butter pudding with hot sauce Anglaise (£2.50); cheeses are carefully chosen, and breakfasts are good. The 18 wines or so, kept perfectly on a cruover machine, are chosen monthly by Simon Loftus (so always interesting), and the Adnams Bitter, Broadside, winter Old and Tally Ho (Christmas only) on handpump are in superb condition – it's the nearby Adnams brewery's flagship; tea, coffee and herbal infusions; staff are friendly and helpful, even when under pressure. The smart and attractive main carpeted bar has green-grained panelling, plain wooden tables with chairs and long settles that give a slightly churchy feel, Georgian-style brass lamps, and a carved marble and wood fireplace. A smaller back oak-panelled bar with more of a pubby atmosphere, has brassy navigation lamps and a brass binnacle. Shove-ha'penny and cribbage. There are some tables in a sunny sheltered corner outside. (*Recommended by Alison and Tony Godfrey, Helen Crookston, Gwen and Peter Andrews, Robert Gomme, SJC, Audrey and Brian Green, Patrick Young, K A V Read, Martin Richards, T Nott, Jamie Lyons, Ruth Harrison, RCL, Hope Chenhalls, Heather Sharland, Helen Crookston, Nigel Gibbs, A C and S J Beardsley, Quentin Williamson, Jason Caulkin, P Leeson and friends, M K Brown, Nigel Gibbs*)

Adnams   Manager Nick Gardener   Real ale   Meals and snacks (12.30–2, 7.30–9.45)   No-smoking restaurant   Children in eating area and restaurant   Live classical, folk, and jazz   Open 10.30–3, 6–11; closed first week Jan   Bedrooms tel Southwold (0502) 722275; £29B/£46B

STOKE BY NAYLAND   TL9836 Map 5

Angel ⊘ ⇌

B1068 Sudbury–East Bergholt; also signposted via Nayland off A134 Colchester–Sudbury

There's a pleasant, chatty atmosphere in this rather smart dining pub. The main bar area has handsome Elizabethan beams, some stripped brickwork and timbers, local watercolours and older prints, attractive table lamps, a relaxed mixture of furnishings including wing armchairs, mahogany dining chairs, and pale library chairs which, like the tables, are lightly stained to bring out the grain, and a huge log fire. Round the corner is a little tiled-floor stand-and-chat bar – with well kept Adnams Bitter, Bass, and Greene King IPA and Abbot on handpump, decent house wines and good coffee. One room has a low sofa and wing armchairs around its woodburning stove, and Victorian paintings on the dark green walls. The enterprising bar food includes interesting soups (£1.60), ploughman's (£2.50), a popular Greek salad (£2.95), fresh asparagus (£3.50), meat tartlet or ham and mushroom flaky-pastry pie (£4.25), moussaka, boiled gammon and parsley sauce or a daily roast (£4.50), a plate packed with three separate griddled fish (from £5.50), home-made gravadlax (£5.85), or chicken and king prawn brochette (£6.75); vegetables, side-salads and bread are good; get there early if you don't want to wait for a table; efficient service. There are cast-iron seats and tables on a sheltered terrace. (*Recommended by Hope Chenhalls, Mr and Mrs J M Elden, Wm H Mecham, Cynth and Marc Pollard, Gwen and Peter Andrews, Sandra Kempson, Jim Matthews*)

Free house   Licensee Peter Smith   Real ale   Meals and snacks (12–2, 6.30–9; last Sun orders 1.30)   Restaurant (not Sun evening)   Open 11–2.30, 6–11; closed 25 and 26 Dec and 1 Jan   Bedrooms tel Colchester (0206) 263245; £35B/£45B

SUTTON   TM3046 Map 5

Plough

B1083

This tiled white house – surrounded by Sutton Common – has a snug little front room with button-back wall banquettes, and there's a more spacious room round the side. Reliably good bar food includes sandwiches (from 95p, home-baked gammon £1.10), home-made soup (£1.35), cold buffet (from £1.55), ploughman's (from £2.10), burgers (from £2.25), ham and egg (£3.85), scampi (£4.55), and steaks (from £7.10). In the evening a rather grander choice concentrates more on fish, with starters like mixed seafood (£3.45), and main courses such as good plaice (£4.75), grilled halibut steak with prawns or garlic butter (£6.25) or Dover sole (£10.50); daily specials include chicken curry (Tuesday and Thursday, £3.85), chicken piri-piri or steak and Guinness pie (£4.25), fresh crab, and house specialities (24 hours notice, not Saturday) such as roast local pheasant in red wine sauce (£6.95) or chateaubriand (£10.95); friendly service. Courage Best on handpump; jugs of Pimms or sangria (£3.25); darts, dominoes, cribbage, fruit machine and piped music. There are picnic-table sets in front and more by the fruit trees. (*Recommended by David Cardy, Martin Lowy; more reports please*)

Brent Walker (bought from Watneys)   Licensees Mike and Anne Lomas   Real ale Meals and snacks   Restaurant (not Sun evening) tel Shottisham (0394) 411785 Children in eating area and restaurant   Open 11–2.30 (3 Sat), 6.30–11

THORNDON   TM1469 Map 5

Black Horse

Village signposted off A140 and off B1077, S of Eye

Dark low beams, some standing timbers, and quite a bit of stripped brick-and-studwork fill this quietly friendly, 16th-century pub. On one side of its central core are scrubbed ancient red flooring tiles, a wall clock that ticks ponderously between stuffed animal heads above a huge fireplace, and a glass plate in the floor covering an illuminated well about 46 feet deep; the carpeted end has small tapestried settles and country dining chairs around stripped country tables or glossy darker ones. On the other side is a games room with sensibly placed darts, dominoes, cribbage, well lit pool, trivia and juke box. A wide choice of attractively priced bar food includes soup (£1), filled baked potatoes (from £1.05), sandwiches (from £1.15), omelettes (£2.20), vegetarian mushroom and nut fettucini (£3.25), salads (from £3.30), steak and kidney or seafood pies (£3.45), 10oz pork chop (£3.95), and steaks (from 6oz rump £4.25). The restaurant (converted stables, with the stalls taken from a local barn) does a good value three-course Sunday lunch. Courage Best, Greene King Abbot, John Smiths Bitter, and Wadworths 6X on handpump are kept well under light blanket pressure; well reproduced piped music. There are picnic-table sets and some white plastic chairs on the lawn that spreads round to the back, where there are views across open fields. (*Recommended by Nick Dowson, Alison Hayward; more reports please*)

Free house   Licensees Rod and Julia Waldron   Real ale   Meals and snacks Restaurant tel Occold (037 971) 523   Well behaved children allowed in eating area and restaurant   Monthly Sunday evening folk nights   Open 11.30–2.30, 6.30–11

THORNHAM MAGNA   TM1070 Map 5

Four Horseshoes ⊗ ⇐

Off A140 S of Diss; follow Finningham 3 1/4 signpost, by White Horse pub

Known as 'The Shoes', this thatched white pub is very popular indeed with locals from a wide radius – often queueing for the doors to open at lunchtime and in the evening – and with visitors on weekend breaks. The extensive bar is well divided into alcoves and distinct areas, and there are some character seats such as tall Windsor chairs as well as the golden plush banquettes and stools on its spread of fitted Turkey carpet, very low and heavy black beams, country pictures and farm tools on the black-timbered white walls, and logs burning in big fireplaces; there's also an inside well. Generous helpings of very good, tasty food, quickly served by uniformed waitresses, include sandwiches (from £1.10, hot bacon £1.30, home-cured ham and tomato £1.50), soup (£1.25), ploughman's (from £2.25), salads (from £2.90, home-cured ham £3.95), country grill (using their home-made sausages £2.75), vegetable and nut cutlets (£3.90), home-made pies like chicken, ham, mushroom, apricot and walnut or sausage and onion (from £3.95), lasagne (£4.20), fisherman's hot pot (£4.50), well hung steaks (£7.25), puddings such as home-made cheesecake or apple and cinammon pie (£1.85), and children's menu (on request); meat comes from the owners' own butcher's shop and most vegetables from either their own market garden or their greengrocer's shop in Eye. Well kept Adnams Bitter, Ruddles County and Websters Yorkshire on handpump. Picnic-table sets stand by flowerbeds on a sheltered lawn and even more sheltered back terrace. Thornham Country Park nearby has several walks, including the sponsored Horseshoe Country Trail (a lovely pre-breakfast walk) and one suitable for the disabled, as well as a walled herb garden, and a scented garden especially for the blind. The thatched church at Thornham Parva is famous for its ancient wall paintings. *(Recommended by Andrew and Michele Wells, Nick Dowson, Alison Hayward, WTF, Alan and Sharron Tod, Jill Hampton, Brian Metherell, Jamie Lyons, Ruth Harrison, Mike and Jill Dixon and friends, Stephen Goodchild, Mrs A Broderick)*

Free house   Licensees Mr and Mrs K D Avery, Managers Malcolm Moore and Caroline Ruth   Real ale   Meals and snacks (12–2, 7–10.30)   Restaurant   Children welcome Occasional live entertainment in winter   Open 12–2.30, 7 (6.30 Sat)–11; closed 25 Dec   Bedrooms tel Occold (037 971) 777; £36.50B/£49.50B

TOSTOCK   TL9563 Map 5
Gardeners Arms

Village signposted from A45 and A1088

A real village atmosphere fills the lounge bar of this warmly friendly and pretty sand-coloured house. There are low heavy black beams and lots of what used to be called carving chairs (dining chairs with arms) around the black tables. A wide range of good bar food includes sandwiches (from £1), memorable home-made cream of mussel soup (£1.10), ploughman's with home-made granary rolls (from £2.20), steak sandwich (£2.85), salads (from £3, cold salt beef £3.55), gammon and egg (£3.55), with supper dishes (bookings only) like ratatouille with peanuts and cheese topping (£1.75), poached salmon steak with home-made mayonnaise (£6.95) and sirloin steak (£7.25); daily specials on the blackboard and puddings (£1.50). Very well kept Greene King IPA and Abbot on handpump. The lively tiled-floor public bar has darts, pool, shove-ha'penny, dominoes, cribbage, juke box, fruit machine and trivia. There's a terrace and a sheltered lawn – a lovely place to sit at picnic-set tables among roses and other flowers, and watch the local team playing steel quoits on the pitch. *(Recommended by Charles Bardswell, Mr and Mrs G C Dickinson, Richard Fawcett, Nigel Paine; more reports please)*

Greene King   Licensee Reg Ransome   Real ale   Meals and snacks (not Mon or Tues evenings or Sun lunchtime)   Restaurant tel Beyton (0359) 70460: Sun opening 8–10pm   Children in restaurant   Open 11–2.30, 7–11

WALBERSWICK   TM4974 Map 5
Bell

Just off B1387

There's a sizeable lawn here with seats and tables among roses and other flowers, sheltered by a hedge from the worst of the sea winds. Most of the bedrooms look over the sea or the river. The oak-beamed bar rambles attractively around, with curved high-backed settles on well worn flagstones, tankards hanging from oars above the bar counter, tiles and flooring bricks (that were here when this sleepy village was a flourishing port 600 years ago), and a woodburning stove in the big fireplace; to one side is a more conventionally comfortable area decorated with local photographs; maybe two friendly bull-mastiffs. Bar food includes sandwiches (from £1, crab £2), ploughman's (from £2.25), a good choice of help-yourself summer salads (from £3.50, fresh Cromer crab or prawns £4.50), and winter soups, omelettes (from £2.75), and dishes such as steak and kidney pie; good breakfasts. Well kept Adnams Bitter, Broadside and Extra on handpump. Shove-ha'penny, cribbage, fruit machine, space game. *(Recommended by John Townsend, A T Langton, SJC, Charles Bardswell, D J Milner, P Miller, Mrs M Webster, RCL, Gwen and Peter Andrews, Mr and Mrs P A Jones, J H Walker, K Leist)*

Adnams   Licensee Mark Stansall   Real ale   Meals and snacks (lunchtime)   Evening restaurant   Children in small room off bar   Open 11–3.30, 6.30–11; closed evening 25 Dec   Bedrooms tel Southwold (0502) 723109; £25(££27S)/£40(£44S)

WESTLETON   TM4469 Map 5

Crown 🚫 🛏

On B1125 Blythburgh–Leiston

The garden of this quietly friendly, well kept village inn has been extensively landscaped, and a terrace, barbecue area and outside bar added – this is floodlit at night. Inside, the comfortably furnished bar has a growing collection of old photographs and postcards of Westleton, farm tools, pews, stools and settles, a couple of lobster pots at one end, and a good open fire in winter; there's also a smart no-smoking dining conservatory. Good bar food includes sandwiches (from £1), home-made soup (£1.50), ploughman's (from £2.35), salads (from £2.45, quiche £3.45), tasty fresh-caught local fish such as cod, haddock, plaice and sole (from £3.95), steak and kidney pie (£4.25) and sirloin steak (£6.95); lovely puddings such as home-made treacle pudding, spotted dick or apple pie (£1.65); children's dishes (£2.25), barbecue menu with kebabs, swordfish steaks, tandoori chicken and so forth, and as much salad as you want (£5.50, children £2.50), and excellent breakfasts; courteous staff. Well kept Adnams Bitter and Broadside, Badger Best, Greene King Abbot, Marstons Owd Rodger (in winter), Sam Smiths, and Wadworths 6X on handpump, and good dry white wine. Dominoes and shove-ha'penny. There are good walks nearby (the 'Westleton Walks') – perhaps over to our Lucky Dip entry at Eastbridge. Minsmere bird reserve is only a couple of miles away. *(Recommended by David Cardy, Richard Fawcett, RCL, Joy Heatherley, Heather Sharland, Gwen and Peter Andrews; more reports please)*

Free house   Licensees Richard and Rosemary Price   Real ale   Meals and snacks   Evening restaurant (that doubles as an art gallery)   Children in restaurant   Open 11–2.30, 6–11; closed 25 and 26 Dec   Bedrooms tel Westleton (072 873) 273; £37.50B/£50.50B; some have jacuzzis and 4-posters

---

Lucky Dip

Besides the fully inspected pubs, you might like to try these Lucky Dips recommended to us and described by readers (if you do, please send us reports):

Aldeburgh [The Parade; TM4656], *Brudenell*: Comfortable hotel with reasonable bar meals in large bar which has spectacular sea views; pleasant, helpful staff; can get crowded at holiday times; children welcome; nr start GWG120; bedrooms *(Derek Patey)*; [Crabbe St], *Cross Keys*: Busy low-ceilinged 16th-century pub with massive central chimney (and two woodburning stoves) dividing its two bar areas, plain rather utilitarian furnishings, straightforward bar food, well kept Adnams ales (the full range), traditional bar games and fruit machine, tables on back gravel which opens on to promenade and beach; nr start GWG120; children may be allowed in to eat if it's wet *(Joanna and Ian Chisholm, LYM)*

☆ **Aldringham** [TM4461], *Parrot & Punchbowl*: Good food in cosy and popular local with well kept beer and uncommonly wide choice of wines by the glass; dining room meals Fri/weekend — when booking essential; garden has tables and umbrellas — delightful on a sunny day; handy for Aldeburgh Festival *(C J Parsons, J H Walker)*
Badingham [TM3068], *White Horse*: Old-fashioned and well run, with its own neat bowling green, well kept Adnams, cheapish bar food inc summer lunchtime cold buffet, vegetarian and children's dishes as well as usual pub food; nice rambling garden *(LYM)*

☆ **Bardwell** [The Green; TL9473], *Six Bells*: 16th-century free house with pleasantly pubby atmosphere, welcoming log fires, wide choice of good food cooked to order inc fine fish specialities, well kept Adnams and guest beers, extensive wine list, restaurant; games evening Sun, folk music weekly; garden with play area; outbuildings now converted into attractive holiday flatlets *(Terence May, Charles Bardswell, Mr and Mrs Naworynsky)*
Barham [TM1451], *Sorrel Horse*: Large, rambling local with exposed beams; friendly bar staff, well kept Tolly Original, well prepared food *(John C Baker)*
Barningham [TL9676], *Swan*: Small two-roomed pub with good choice of bottled beers, as well as Greene King IPA and Abbot; can get busy early evening 5.30—7pm *(Michael Brookes)*
Bildeston [TL9949], *Crown*: Tudor building, reputedly haunted, with open fire in comfortable and well furnished lounge; well kept Mauldons, good choice of reasonably priced bar food from duck or stilton soup and toasted sandwiches up, extensive restaurant menu *(Simon Reynolds)*

☆ **Blaxhall** [off B1069 S of Snape; can be reached from A12 via Little Glemham; TM3657], *Ship*: Generous bar food in sectioned-off straightforward dining lounge (sandwiches and ploughman's to good steaks), with well kept Tolly and Marstons

Pedigree on handpump, piped music; thriving local atmosphere in low-beamed traditionally furnished public bar with log fire, pool table etc; closed Mon lunchtime except Bank Hols, and except then no food Mon evening; children in eating area; bedrooms (just two) *(Jane Buekett, LYM — more reports please)*

☆ **Blundeston** [from B1074 follow Church Lane, right into Short Lane, then left; TM5197], *Plough*: Handy for Jacobean Somerleyton Hall — smartly modernised Watneys pub which was the home of Barkis the carrier in *David Copperfield (A T Langton, LYM)*

☆ **Blyford** [B1123 Blythburgh—Halesworth; TM4277], *Queens Head*: Cheerful 15th-century thatched and beamed pub, well restored after 1988 fire, with huge fireplace, sturdy built-in oak and pine benches, some antique settles, full range of Adnams beers kept well, several malt whiskies, tables out on lawn; the Honekers who made it very convivial and popular with readers in past editions have now moved to the Queens Head at Bramfield, but first reports on the new landlord's regime (and on his father's cooking — perhaps not as cheap as before, but showing signs of real care) are mostly very promising *(Klaus and Elizabeth Leist, A T Langton, Derek and Sylvia Stephenson, LYM)*

☆ **Boxford** [Broad St; TL9640], *Fleece*: Enterprising home cooking and well kept Tolly in partly 15th-century pink-washed pub with cosy panelled bar on right, more spacious and airy lounge bar with big medieval fireplace, armchairs and some distinctive old seats among more conventional furnishings *(LYM)*

Boxford, *White Hart*: Two-part bar with heavy beams, fireplace and brasses; welcoming landlord, good atmosphere, well kept Allied real ales, home-cooked bar food *(Gwen and Peter Andrews)*

Bradfield St George [Felsham Rd; TL9160], *Fox & Hounds*: Externally, the appearance has been spoilt by unsympathetic modernisation, notably a conservatory stuck on the front; however, there's well kept Greene King IPA, cheerful and friendly staff, well prepared food showing real aspiration, with good veg *(John C Baker)*

☆ **Bramfield** [A144; TM4073], *Queens Head*: Handsomely refurbished high-beamed hall-house, clean and pleasant, with panel of original wattle and daub and large open fire; Adnams Bitter, Old and Broadside on handpump, food in bar and restaurant; the licensees who made the Queens Head at Blyford so popular for its cheerful atmosphere and reasonably priced food moved here in early 1990 — should be a place well worth trying *(News please)*

☆ **Brandeston** [back rd Wickham Market—Earl Soham; TM2460], *Queens Head*: Country pub with spacious open-plan partly panelled bar divided into bays, brown leather banquettes, pews and other seats; good value home-made food, recently renovated family room, well kept Adnams on handpump, helpful staff, big neat garden with good play area; caravan/camp site behind; only reason this nice pub leaves the main entries this year is virtual absence of reader reports; bedrooms *(Comus Elliott, LYM)*

Brundish Street [TM2670], *Crown*: Friendly good value country local with good beer — and maybe an accordionist *(Comus Elliott)*

Bures [TL9033], *Eight Bells*: Good food, well served, in attractive bar with good atmosphere — simple but nice *(N S Holmes)*; [Station Hill], *Swan*: 15th-century village pub with unspoilt public bar, bar food inc good value mixed grill and some imaginative home-made dishes such as vegetarian scotch eggs; friendly locals, log fires *(Richard Goss)*; *Three Horseshoes*: Two bars, games area with pool and darts, good bar food, summer barbecues; children's play area; bedrooms *(Sandra Kempson)*

☆ **Bury St Edmunds** [Whiting St; TL8564], *Masons Arms*: White weatherboarded pub, comfortable and friendly, its busy but relaxing lounge incorporating former next-door cottage, divided from it by the standing timbers which once formed part of wall; quickly and generously served good honest food from sandwiches up, well kept Greene King IPA *(Ian Phillips, John Branford, K A V Read)*

☆ **Bury St Edmunds** [Angel Hill], *Angel*: Thriving country-town hotel with popular food in spacious and comfortable lounge, Regency dining room and cellar grill room (good teas too); relaxed atmosphere, well kept Adnams real ale (not cheap here), cheerful friendly service; bedooms comfortable *(Peter Burton, John C Baker)*

☆ **Bury St Edmunds** [Traverse, Abbeygate St], *Nutshell*: Included as one of the smallest pubs in the country – probably the smallest of all, inside; friendly landlord, well kept Greene King IPA and Abbot on handpump, interesting old banknotes and other memorabilia; attractive corner facade; closed Sun and Holy Days *(R C Gandy, Mr and Mrs P A Jones)*

Bury St Edmunds [Eastgate St], *Fox*: Well kept and clean, with good service, good value bar food inc splendid roast with veg or in French bread; close to centre, but adequate parking *(Bill and Wendy Burge)*; [Station Hill], *Linden Tree*: Greene King beers, good choice of wines, enormous helpings of reasonably priced bar food in conservatory *(Mrs M E Beard)*

Buxhall [Mill Green; village signed off B1115 W of Stowmarket, then L at Rattlesden sign; TM0057], *Crown*: Tucked-away country pub with snug little bar and side room, games in separate public bar, restaurant; bar food, Adnams Broadside and Greene King IPA, open fires, jazz twice a month; children allowed in eating *(LYM — more reports on new regime please)*

Chevington [TL7860], *Greyhound*: Lounge full of memorabilia, well kept Greene King IPA, garden with good facilities for children; bar food excellent, especially the properly prepared Indian dishes — licensees are Indophiles and have travelled widely there, collecting recipes *(John C Baker)*

☆ **Clare** [Callis St; TL7645], *Cock*: Friendly new young licensees doing well here — friendly pubby atmosphere, straightforward comfort in lower bar, some brass on walls and above fireplace, plainer public bar,

evening restaurant down some steps; well
kept Adnams, well served wholesome food
inc Thurs fish and chips to eat there or take
away, plus half-price pint while you wait;
piped music (maybe a bit loud), popular Fri
raffle; open all day Sat *(Gwen and Peter
Andrews, Frank Gadbois, Capt John W Behle)*
Clare [Callis St], *Globe*: Old but deceptively
spacious, with wide choice of cheap food inc
good-sized ploughman's, well presented
steak and kidney pie and lots of puddings
(Margaret and Trevor Errington)
Clopton Corner [Crown Hill; TM2254],
Crown: Always friendly; good, well priced
and presented bar food, much of it
home-made *(Miss V Johnston)*
☆ Coddenham [1 1/4 miles E of junction
A45/A140; TM1354], *Dukes Head*: Simple
stripped-pine village pub with well kept
Tolly ales, good helpings of interesting fresh
food, welcoming service, pin-table in public
bar, seats in steep garden behind; three
bedrooms
Cratfield [TM3175], *Cratfield Poacher*:
Well run beamed free house, carefully
extended and refitted — old pews, lots of
nick-nacks — very popular with young
locals, big on theme parties like Hallowe'en
and New Year; one 'beach' party included
plastic palm trees, real donkey rides, ten tons
of sand *(Nick Dowson, Alison Hayward)*
☆ Dalham [TL7261], *Affleck Arms*: Good
atmosphere in attractive thatched village
pub by stream, log fire in cosy low-beamed
locals' bar, more comfortable and intimate
rambling dining bar on right; friendly
service, bar food, some tables outside *(Frank
W Gadbois, LYM)*
☆ Dennington [TM2867], *Queens Head*:
Stylishly simplified beamed Tudor pub with
good range of real ales, decent bar food;
garden by village church *(LYM)*
Earl Soham [TM2363], *Falcon*: Smartly
kept, faultlessly friendly service, Adnams
real ale; bedrooms *(Comus Elliott)*
☆ East Bergholt [Burnt Oak — towards
Flatford Mill; TM0734], *Kings Head*: Clean
and attractive beamed lounge with fine
corner cupboard, brasses, farm tools and —
as you might guess here — Constable prints,
comfortable seats, coal fire; reasonably
priced home-cooked food from sandwiches
up, well kept Tolly Bitter, Original and
XXXX on handpump, decent coffee,
friendly landlord, piped classical music (but
juke box in uncarpeted public bar); pleasant
garden with flower-decked hay wain *(Gwen
and Peter Andrews, Audrey and Brian Green)*
☆ Eastbridge [TM4566], *Eels Foot*: Simple
local well placed for Minsmere bird reserve,
Sizewell pebble beach (a good place to hunt
semi-precious stones) and heathland walks;
crisp varnish, red leatherette, bright carpet
or linoleum, well kept Adnams, hefty
helpings of basic home-made bar food (no
winter evening meals); tables on quiet front
terrace, children in eating area; pretty
village, at start of GWG122 *(Peter Griffiths,
Gwen and Peter Andrews, S Corrigan, LYM)*
☆ Easton [N of Wickham Market on back rd
to Earl Soham and Framlingham; TM2858],
White Horse: Attractive country furnishings
and open fires in two simple rooms, games
room, well equipped play area and barbecue
in garden; Tolly real ales, good choice of

wines, piped music, bar food, restaurant
*(Gwen and Peter Andrews, LYM; more reports
on the new regime please)*
☆ Erwarton [TM2134], *Queens Head*: Good
home-smoked Suffolk ham and other
genuinely home-cooked food in unassuming
16th-century pub with old-fashioned
furnishings; well kept Tolly (inc Mild and
XXXX), picture window with fine view over
the fields to the Stour estuary; seats in
orchard behind *(Margaret and Trevor
Errington, LYM)*
☆ Felixstowe Ferry [TM3337], *Ferry Boat*:
Well kept Tolly real ales, decent simple bar
food and good atmosphere in neatly kept
17th-century pub close to sand dunes,
Martello Tower and harbour *(Comus Elliott,
LYM)*
Felixstowe Ferry, *Victoria*: Good riverside
pub with decent bar food — now a free
house, with good beer choice *(Comus Elliott)*
Felsham [TL9457], *Six Bells*: Unpretentious
but neatly kept building, part of bar
carpeted (tables, chairs, attractive window
seat, brasses and round brick fireplace), part
tiled (more tables, darts); well kept Greene
King IPA and Abbot, piped Radio 2 *(Gwen
and Peter Andrews)*
Framlingham [TM2863], *White Horse*:
Good popular bar food inc beautiful fresh
seafood and fish; restaurant *(M and W
Williams)*
Glemsford [TL8247], *Black Lion*: New
licensees doing very good well presented pub
food in attractive bar *(N S Holmes)*;
[Egremont St], *Cock*: Front door opens
straight off the street (no pavement) and
down two steps into the saloon bar; lively,
friendly atmosphere, well kept Greene King
IPA — a useful find for the area *(John C
Baker)*
Great Barton [TL8967], *Flying Fortress*:
Well kept Adnams, Greene King and
Mauldons, competent friendly service and
straightforward freshly prepared bar food in
former farmhouse HQ of USAF support
group, on north edge of former Rougham
airfield — the original for the film *Twelve
O'Clock High*; plenty of War World II air
force photographs *(John C Baker)*
☆ Great Glemham [between A12 Wickham
Mkt—Saxmundham and B1119
Saxmundham—Framlingham; TM3361],
Crown: Pleasantly modernised old pub with
beamed lounge rambling around central
chimney with big log fire on one side,
woodburner on the other; friendly landlord,
well kept Adnams and Greene King beers,
good choice of malt whiskies,
straightforward bar food, not Mon evening
— simple dishes such as ploughman's, steaks
and traditional Sun lunch have been
generally enjoyed; seat on neat lawn;
children allowed in eating area and
restaurant; has been open all day Sat; simple
bedrooms *(Patrick Young, John C Baker,
Brian MacIvor, B and J Derry, Caroline and
Colin, LYM)*
Groton [TL9541], *Fox & Hounds*: Typical
Suffolk country pub — small, largely
unspoilt and delightful; good snacks and
excellent salad choice; bar billiards *(Richard
Goss)*
Grundisburgh [TM2250], *Dog*: Recently
extended village pub keeping original

character; good range of well kept beers, good bar food inc traditional puddings *(E B Warrington)*

☆ Haughley [Station Rd; by level crossing towards Old Newton; TM0262], *Railway*: Warm-hearted country pub with plain traditional furnishings, log fire, well kept Adnams, Greene King and Mauldons alternating with beers from further afield, good value simple food (not Mon pm), lots of labrador pictures, friendly Scots landlord; children in neat room at back *(John C Baker, BB)*

☆ Haughley [centre], *Kings Arms*: Lots of dark tables in beamed lounge, log fire, wide choice of good value bar food from sandwiches to tender steaks, well kept Greene King ales, good service and atmosphere, maybe loud but well reproduced piped pop music; pool and other games in comfortable saloon; tables and play house on back lawn *(G R Prest, BB)*

Hitcham [The Street; TL9851], *White Horse*: Good choice of restaurant meals and bar food inc outstanding ploughman's *(T Gondris)*

Holbrook [Ipswich Rd; TM1636], *Compasses*: Popular for good value bar lunches and evening restaurant; well kept beer *(G Smith, Miss A Tress)*

☆ Hollesley [TM3544], *Fox*: Wide choice of well presented good food from filled baked potatoes up in remote but welcoming village pub with comfortable bar, somewhat cluttered with foxes (stuffed, ornaments or pictures); pool room *(K Leist)*

☆ Huntingfield [TM3374], *Huntingfield Arms*: Some concentration now on good range of hot and cold bar food in bar with handsome sectioned-tree-trunk tables and matching hard chairs; Adnams real ale, friendly staff, restaurant; on attractive village green with cross, pump and big horse-chestnut tree with bench around its trunk *(Nick Dowson, Alison Hayward, Jane Palmer)*

Ipswich [Tavern St; TM1744], *Great White Horse*: Popular good value lunchtime food and well kept Courage and Greene King real ales in comfortably well kept pub; bedrooms *(Anon)*; [Henley Rd], *Greyhound*: Done up in old style, with bare boards, antiqued pine, lots of Edwardian prints on the dark walls — lively, popular with a friendly youngish lunchtime crowd for Adnams, Boddingtons, Wadworths and other real ales, and a wide range of lunchtime food such as doorstep sandwiches, good ploughman's and steak and kidney pies; piped music rather loud *(Ian Phillips)*; [St Peters Dock], *Malt Kiln*: Great location for cursorily converted former malt kiln, with seats out on the quayside; popular range of bar food, Mauldons, Tetleys, Theakstons and three guest ales (though many of the young people it's so popular with go for the wide range of lagers and foreign beers); friendly staff, piped music, occasional live jazz or blues *(D Savage, A Martin, A Beale)*

☆ Kersey [The Street; TL9944], *White Horse*: Pretty pink-washed village pub with very friendly atmosphere, real fire in the public bar's open Victorian range, beams and timbering, wooden furniture; has had well kept real ales such as Adnams Extra and Old, Nethergate and perhaps a guest beer,

good choice of well presented home-cooked food inc fine ploughman's and Suffolk ham, and good service, but no reports since lease sold; children allowed in lounge bar — there's also a play area behind car park *(LYM; news please)*

☆ Lavenham [TL9149], *Swan*: Handsome and comfortable Elizabethan hotel, with in its heart a pubby little bar, popular among locals, with leather seats on its tiled floor, well kept Greene King, maybe a dog, and plenty of USAF memorabilia; spacious overflow into numerous communicating but cosy seating areas and alcoves with beams, timbers, armchairs and settees; bar food, afternoon teas and so forth, lavishly timbered restaurant, seats in well kept garden, friendly and helpful staff; a magnet for American and other tourists; children welcome; pleasant if pricey bedrooms *(Mrs E M Thompson, John Evans, Geoff Halson, LYM)*

☆ Lavenham [Market Pl], *Angel*: Promising new tenants making lots of changes, adding Nethergate to the Watneys-related real ales on handpump, and doing good food; worthwhile cellar tour; four comfortably renovated bedrooms *(Frank W Gadbois)*

☆ Lavenham, *Greyhound*: Refreshingly unspoilt and simple despite the tourists, with heavy-beamed narrow lounge, more austerely furnished public bar with polished tables and matching settles, and back dining area (decent food from soup to steaks); well kept Greene King IPA and Abbot on handpump, friendly staff; busy at weekends *(Gwen and Peter Andrews)*

Layham [Upper St; TM0240], *Marquis of Cornwallis*: Big helpings of good straightforward bar food from home-made soup up, good atmosphere, small restaurant *(T Gondris)*

☆ Lidgate [TL7257], *Star*: Attractive old building, partly an old cottage and hardly smart, with welcoming landlord, wide choice of reasonably priced bar food inc home-made specials, large open fire with winter Sun spit-roasts, indoor summer barbecue; lovely garden; children welcome *(Anthony Johnson)*

☆ Long Melford [TL8645], *Crown*: Comfortable, quietly sedate and well kept, with pastel decor, rugwork 'pictures', easy chairs and sofas as well as smaller chairs and cushioned pews; currently on an upswing, with friendly service and good bar food from big filled rolls and ploughman's through plenty of vegetarian dishes full of seasonal vegetables to gammon and so forth; good choice of real ales such as Adnams, Greene King IPA, Mauldons and Nethergate, morning coffee, afternoon tea, tables in walled garden with play area, restaurant open all day Sun; children welcome — nicely furnished back family room; pub has been open all day; bedrooms *(Gwen and Peter Andrews, John C Baker, LYM)*

Long Melford [Hall St], *George & Dragon*: True village local, good beers and wines, straightforward well prepared food; regular live music from blues to folk; garden with summer barbecues; bedrooms simple and comfortable — good value *(Richard Goss)*; *Hare*: Country pub with two bars, friendly service, good value changing bar and restaurant food; children's play area *(Sandra Kempson)*

Market Weston [TL9877], *Mill*: Welcoming, with friendly staff, good choice of real ales inc well kept Nethergate, usual bar food inc good chilli con carne *(John C Baker)*

Martlesham [Main Rd; TM2547], *Red Lion*: Well run Chef & Brewer with plenty of tables in attractive beamed lounge bar, at least six home-made dishes of the day; Watneys Country Carvery restaurant; the red lion is probably a figurehead salvaged from a Dutch man-o'-war sunk at the Battle of Sole Bay *(Dr and Mrs Frank Wells)*

Melton [TM2851], *Horse & Groom*: Very good value quickly served food, pleasant staff, Tolly beers, satellite TV in public bar *(Chris Fluck)*

☆ **Mendham** [TM2782], *Sir Alfred Munnings*: Cheery atmosphere in big open-plan bar of inn under promising new regime, with well kept Adnams, Charles Wells Bombardier and a weekly summer guest beer, bar food inc good value ploughman's and fresh mackerel served by neat waitresses, unobtrusive piped music, restaurant; children welcome, swimming pool for residents; bedrooms *(Gwen and Peter Andrews, LYM)*

☆ **Mildenhall** [Main St; TL7174], *Bell*: Beautiful old inn with pleasant atmosphere, spacious open-plan bar and lounge and attractive dining room; very good choice of bar food, quick friendly service, Adnams IPA and Greene King on handpump *(Frank William Gadbois, K and E Leist)*

☆ **Newmarket** [High St; TL6463], *White Hart*: Comfortable central hotel with racing pictures and open fire in spacious lounge, bar food not cheap but reliable, well kept Tolly, friendly staff, solid back cocktail bar, restaurant; children welcome; bedrooms *(R C Vincent, LYM)*

Newmarket [High St], *Rutland Arms*: A welcome for strangers in well run and comfortable Georgian hotel, with decent food and beer; bedrooms *(Anon)*

Orford [TM4250], *Froize*: Old house with woodburning stove, usual bar food, games room, tables in garden; pony-trekking; bedrooms, camp and caravan site *(Richard Gibbs)*

Pakefield [TM5390], *Jolly Sailors*: Good value carvery in comfortable well kept pub *(M J Morgan)*

☆ **Pakenham** [TL9267], *Fox*: Recently refurbished, bar servery now linking beamed lounge and games room; has had good value food from snacks to unusual speciality main dishes — well above average for the area, with restaurant too up in annexe, but as we went to press we heard it had changed hands; well kept Greene King XX, IPA and Abbot, good friendly local staff, impeccable lavatories, tables in garden with ducks *(John C Baker, Mr and Mrs J Barnes, Charles Bardswell; more reports please)*

☆ **Rattlesden** [TL9758], *Brewers Arms*: Unpretentious village pub reopened by friendly new owners, with well presented varied good value food such as unusual soups, kofti meatballs in cream and coconut sauce, cheese and aubergine balls, fresh pasta; Greene King KK, IPA and Abbot, good choice of spirits, lively public bar

(pool, darts and so forth) *(Simon Reynolds, LYM)*

Rumburgh [TM3481], *Buck*: Free house with two cosy, clean and tidy low-ceilinged bars, nice nick-nacks, well kept Adnams and Mauldons; tables on pleasant back lawn with view over fields *(Nick Dowson, Alison Hayward)*

☆ **Saxtead Green** [B1119, opp old working windmill; TM2665], *Volunteer*: Light and airy lounge bar with reliable and popular bar food (they make their own pasties), Tolly ales, spotless housekeeping; games in simpler public bar, plenty of tables on pretty back terrace with small rockery pool; lovely setting, across green from old working windmill; children allowed in corner bar *(Mrs Olive Way, Nick Dowson, Alison Hayward, LYM — more reports please)*

☆ **Snape** [The Maltings; TM3959], *Plough & Sail*: Right by Snape Maltings complex so can get very full when there are concerts; but carefully modernised, with deliberately rather spartan tiled-floor decor in narrow L-shaped bar with alcoves and small restaurant leading off; good Adnams, interesting bar food inc good salads, welcoming efficient staff, lively atmosphere, open-air chess *(John C Baker, Heather Sharland, Derek and Sylvia Stephenson)*

☆ **Snape** [B1069], *Crown*: Busy, cheery pub with civilised customers, well kept Adnams, no piped music, generally enjoyable food running up to pheasant and lobster; front room supposed to be the model for the Boar in Britten's *Peter Grimes*; tables in sizeable garden; bedrooms well equipped *(Tony Gayfer, Joanna and Ian Chisholm, LYM)*

☆ **Southwold** [Market Pl; TM5076], *Swan*: Recently bought back and completely refurbished by Adnams; comfortable hotel bar with leather banquettes and old pictures, short daily choice of good bar food such as delicious tomato soup with fresh-baked bread, boiled silverside with mange tout and buttered parsnips; efficient service, well kept Adnams and Broadside on handpump and the full range of their bottled beers, also decent wines and malt whiskies; ambitious restaurant; well renovated bedrooms inc garden rooms where (by arrangement) dogs can stay too *(Mr and Mrs P A Jones, T Nott, LYM)*

☆ **Southwold** [Blackshore Quay; from A1095, right at Kings Head — pass golf course and water tower], *Harbour*: Friendly if somewhat rough-and-ready waterside pub among the small black fish-sheds; tiny low-beamed front bar, upper back bar with lots of nautical bric-a-brac — even ship-to-shore telephone and wind speed indicator; fish and chips served in newspaper, other basic bar food (not Tues or Thurs evening, cold things only Sun lunchtime; at peak holiday times the system can tend to seize up for a while); well kept low-priced Adnams Bitter and Broadside, darts, tables outside with play area and animals — can be a bit untidy out here, and the hens and gulls leave their mark *(Heather Sharland, Nigel Gibbs, RCL, LYM)*

☆ **Southwold** [South Green], *Red Lion*: Well kept Adnams ales, good range of snacks and salads (seafood recommended) in pale-panelled bar with fine views over green from big windows, ship pictures, brassware and copper, elm-slab barrel tables; friendly local atmosphere, welcoming family room and summer buffet room, tables outside *(Robert Gomme, Gwen and Peter Andrews, BB)*

☆ **Southwold** [42 East St], *Viscount Nelson*: Low-ceilinged wooden-walled local with plenty of character despite recent refurbishment, doing well under newish landlord; well kept Adnams Bitter, Broadside and Old on handpump, friendly atmosphere, good lunchtime food; just yards from the sea *(Caroline and Colin, Robert Gomme, Mr and Mrs P A Jones)*

☆ **Southwold**, *Kings Head*: Pleasant proper local with good food especially seafood, well kept Adnams, decent house wines and efficient, friendly staff; children welcome — comfortable family room; decent bedrooms in house owned by pub across road *(Gordon Theaker, W J Wonham, Mr and Mrs J E Rycroft)*

☆ **Southwold** [7 East Green], *Sole Bay*: Good value simple lunchtime food (not Sun; local sprats recommended) and particularly well kept Adnams — this cheerful and delightfully relaxed Victorian local, its atmosphere scarcely changing over the years, is just across the road from the brewery, and only a stroll from the sea; tables on side terrace and in yard, with budgerigars *(W T Aird, Mr and Mrs P A Jones, LYM)*

☆ **Sproughton** [Old Hadleigh Rd — from A45 Claydon interchange go through village then left down unmarked dead end; TM1244], *Beagle*: Well kept Adnams, Greene King IPA and Abbot and Mauldons in tastefully if plushly converted row of timber-framed cottages with new back conservatory; popular at lunchtime for good genuine food such as tomato and red pepper soup and real kippers *(John C Baker)*

☆ **Stoke by Nayland** [TL9836], *Crown*: Spacious and well kept series of comfortably modernised room areas in spotless flock-wallpaper dining lounge with good value waiter-served bar food strong on chippy things and children's dishes, well kept Tolly on handpump, restaurant which stays open through Sun afternoon; lovely garden with good play area, big car park; bedrooms *(Jane Palmer, LYM)*

Stradishall [A143; TL7452], *Cherry Tree*: Small country pub notable for its unusually big rustic garden, with very well spaced tables and a sizeable pond — friendly ducks and ducklings, moorhens, a side hen run; two small low-beamed bars have big fireplaces and traditional furniture; bar food is a particular interest of the new licensees; Greene King beers under pressure *(BB)*; *Royal Oak*: Two-bar country pub doing well under welcoming new licensee, good cheap bar food served till 10, well kept Nethergate and Mauldons *(Gwyneth and Salvo Spadaro-Dutturi)*

Stratford St Mary [TM0434], *Anchor*: Fine old pub with friendly landlord, open fire, decent hot food, good garden *(Roger Huggins)*

Sudbury [Newton Green; TL8741], *Saracens Head*: Excellent Danish-influenced menu, particularly in bar; surprisingly quiet, next to golf course; Tolly beers, restaurant

(Richard Goss); [Acton Sq], *Waggon & Horses*: Town-centre local with good traditional atmosphere; comfortable old chairs, first-class snacks, lively company, Greene King beers, pub games encouraged *(Richard Goss)*

Thorington Street [TM0035], *Rose*: Popular for decent choice of good hot food *(Mr and Mrs J M Elden)*

Thurston [Barrells Rd; village signed from A1108 N of Norton, then turn left by S-bend by Bayer Experimental Farm, then first right — OS Sheet 155 map reference 939651; TL9365], *Black Fox*: Particularly well kept Adnams, Greene King IPA and Abbot, Mauldons and occasional guest beers tapped from barrels in a back room and served in gently redecorated parlour; thriving atmosphere, open fire, darts room, frequent sing-songs *(John C Baker)*

Thwaite [A140 S of Diss; TM1168], *Bucks Head*: Village pub with warm welcome and good value straightforward bar food *(M D Hare)*

Trimley St Martin [TM2736], *Hand in Hand*: Popular and welcoming extended local, good pub food — especially steaks *(C H Stride)*

Tunstall [TM3555], *Green Man*: Comfortable and airily modern village inn with pleasant and jovial new landlord; good value bar food, well kept Tolly, pool, juke box and fruit machine in smaller bar; bedrooms *(Chris Fluck, BB)*

Washbrook [TM1042], *Brook*: Warm and cosy village pub with friendly service and good cheap food inc excellent steak cooked just as you ask *(Comus Elliott)*

Wenhaston [TM4276], *Star*: Simple local with sun-trap small lounge, well kept Adnams, games in public bar, bar food, spacious lawn; simple bedrooms *(LYM)*

West Row [TL6775], *Judes Ferry*: New licensees improving this riverside free house, with three well kept changing real ales on handpump, healthy freshly prepared bar food, open fire, waterside tables and chairs *(Frank W Gadbois)*

☆ **Westleton** [TM4469], *White Horse*: Friendly pub with well kept Adnams, good well presented bar food inc a children's menu, garden with climbing frame; has been open all day, handy for Minsmere RSPB reserve *(Joanna and Ian Chisholm)*

Wetherden [TM0062], *Maypole*: Friendly and spacious village local with strikingly beamed and timbered open-plan bar, bar food, well kept Adnams and Wethereds, live music or disco many nights *(LYM)*

☆ **Wetheringsett** [Pages Green — OS Sheet 155 map reference 145652; TM1465], *Cat & Mouse*: 15th-century free house, interesting cross of bar, lounge and farmhouse parlour (family and cat photographs on the wall, lots of chickens, ducks, turkeys, donkeys, ponies outside); friendly licensees, remarkable range of well kept real ales on handpump (generally over a dozen), good bar food (Welsh rarebit recommended), separate dining room, tables outside with streamside barbecues *(John C Baker)*

Whepstead [TL8358], *White Horse*: Rustic fairly remote pub, lounge and eating area well restored with many exposed beams, pleasant atmosphere, roaring log fire, well kept Greene King IPA, good range of unusual bar food inc good value oriental and New World dishes such as superb chicken tikka cooked by landlord's Malaysian wife; Sun free nibbles on bar *(John C Baker, E B Warrington, W T Aird)*

☆ **Woodbridge** [Market Sq; TM2749], *Kings Head*: Spacious bar with blazing log fire in inglenook, scrubbed hardwood tables and chairs, and a good atmosphere; well kept Tolly beers on handpump, good basic bar food such as ploughman's or bangers and mash *(Robert Gomme, Chris Fluck)*

☆ **Woodbridge** [off Market Sq], *Olde Bell & Steelyard*: Unusual olde-worlde pub with steelyard still overhanging the street; quiet lounge bar, livelier public bar, well kept Greene King IPA and Abbot on handpump *(Chris Fluck)*

Woodbridge [Market Sq], *Angel*: Friendly pub with good, buzzing atmosphere, low ceilings, interesting decor and well kept Tolly *(Anon)*; [The Thoroughfare], *Crown*: Reasonably priced bar meals inc particularly good value daily specials, fish and steaks; bedrooms *(M J Morgan)*; [Thoroughfare], *Red Lion*: Pleasant, friendly and helpful staff in fine old listed building with quiet fair-sized lounge bar, small livelier public bar with pool and darts; friendly locals, limited food *(Chris Fluck)*

☆ **Woolpit** [The Street; TL9762], *Bull*: Attractive up-and-coming recently refurbished but unspoilt pub with freshly cooked good food in small dining bar, bigger public bar, restaurant — getting popular at weekends; bedrooms *(Charles Bardswell, Mrs B Van der Gucht)*

☆ **Woolpit** [TL9762], *Swan*: Neatly kept straightforward bar, partly panelled and beamed, with usual bar food inc good steak pie at sensible prices (not Thurs–Sat evenings); well kept Watneys-related real ales; good reasonably priced modern bedrooms in converted outbuildings *(Klaus and Elizabeth Leist, Mr and Mrs G C Dickinson, LYM)*

Surrey

Drinks prices here are the highest in the country, outside London. In general, you pay around 15p more for a drink than in the country at large – 25p to 30p more than you would up in Lancashire, say. This may largely be explained by the control which the national brewing giants have over pubs here. We found a markedly higher proportion of pubs tied to them than among our main entries in other areas. So it may well be that pubs tied to smaller breweries (elsewhere often notable for relatively low prices), let alone free houses, are simply too few in number here to have any real price impact on the market. Indeed, we found these tended to charge as much here as the nationals – it seems to be a case of if you can't beat them, join them. Of the three cheapest pubs we found for drinks here (all still more costly than the overall national average), only one, the Dolphin at Betchworth, is tied to a small brewer (Youngs); the other two, the Olde Six Bells at Horley and White Lion at Warlingham, are both tied to Bass. With food, there are more bargains to be found than in some other home-county areas. We found the Cricketers in Dorking, Skimmington Castle at Reigate Heath and Scarlett Arms at Walliswood met our low-price target of under £1 for decent snacks and under £3 for worthwhile main dishes; the Plough at Blackbrook had basket meals under that price, too. All four of these, incidentally, are particularly good pubs – as we've found elsewhere, it's often the nicest pubs which charge the lowest prices; the Plough is outstanding for wines by the glass, and has been extending its attractive garden. Other pubs doing particularly well here currently include the cottagey King William IV at Albury Heath (a new main entry), the relaxed and friendly Donkey at Charleshill (also new to the Guide), the picturesque old-world Woolpack at Elstead (yet another new entry; good food), the stylish Woodcock at Felbridge (fine seafood), the White Bear at Fickleshole (bulging with character), the very popular and well run Three Horseshoes at Laleham, the unpretentious King William IV at Mickleham (good vegetarian cooking), the congenial Surrey Oaks at Newdigate, the thriving Fox Revived at Norwood Hill, the civilised old Punch Bowl near Ockley (its food seems on an upswing), the Bell at Outwood (notably good all round), the Anchor at Pyrford Lock (making the most of its riverside position for families), the quaint and friendly Kings Head in Shepperton, the old-world Three Horseshoes at Thursley (a friendly newish licensee bringing it up into the main entries), and the companionably busy Fox & Hounds at Walton on the Hill. Among the Lucky Dip entries at the end of the chapter, this year's crop of pubs to watch includes the Three Mariners in Bagshot, Dukes Head at Beare Green, Whyte Harte in Bletchingley, Golden Grove in Chertsey, Cricketers near Cobham, Crowns in Haslemere, Squirrel at Hurtmore and Prince of Wales in Oatlands.

ALBURY HEATH TQ0646 Map 3

King William IV

Little London; off A25 Guildford–Dorking to Albury, first left to Albury Heath; go over railway and take first left to Peaslake; OS Sheet 187 map reference 065468

Marvellously unspoilt – especially for Surrey – this warmly friendly, family-run pub has three small linked rooms with a chatty, very relaxed atmosphere. The main bar has beams in the low ochre ceiling, an enormous basket of dried flowers in the big brick fireplace (with a log fire in winter), a big chunky elm table with a long pew and a couple of stools along a beam over the bar with more over the doorway, several traps and old saws, and an ancient baboon dressed in a jacket and hat in one corner; a tiny room leading off one end has an L-shaped elbow rest with a couple of stools in front of it, a table and settle, and darts, and up a few steps at the other end of the main bar is a simple dining room with gingham-clothed tables, two glass cases with stuffed owls and a piano. Good home-made food includes sandwiches (from £1.30), soups like ham and lentil or stilton and celery (£1.40), salads (from £2.80), generous ploughman's (from £3), cottage pie (£3.60) and other pies like game or beef in red wine (£4), excellent steaks (from £7), and lovely puddings like custard syllabub, strawberry crumble or treacle tart (£1.40); Sunday roast lunch (£4.50), a fresh seafood evening on the first Saturday of the month, and a whole spit-roasted lamb or pig on the third Saturday of the month (£5.50). Well kept Courage Best, Fullers ESB, Tetleys, and Youngs Special on handpump; the friendly Alsatian is called Major. In the neat little front garden are some picnic-table sets under umbrellas and old cast-iron garden furniture. (*Recommended by Ian and Liz Phillips, Hilarie Miles-Sharp*)

Free house Licensees Mike and Helen Davids Real ale Meals and snacks (12–2.30, 7–10) Children welcome Open 11–3, 5.30–11; closed evening 25 Dec

BETCHWORTH TQ2049 Map 3

Dolphin

The Street; A25 W of Reigate, village signposted on left after 2 1/2 miles, at Buckland

A cosy, gaslit village pub, its front bar has scrubbed flagstones, big open fireplaces, kitchen chairs and plain tables; the back saloon bar, also flagstoned, is black-panelled and carpeted, with robust old-fashioned elm or oak tables, and a sonorous longcase clock. Good, plain food includes toasted sandwiches, ploughman's, home-made lasagne or tasty locally caught plaice (£3.50), gammon (£5.75), and steak (£6.50); good steamed puddings; Youngs on handpump. There are some seats in the small laurel-shaded front courtyard, and more beyond the car park, opposite the church. The cat can be lively. (*Recommended by Michael Thomson, TBB, D J Penny, Richard Houghton, MKW, JMW*)

Youngs Licensee A R Johnson Real ale Meals and snacks (not Fri or Sat evenings) Open 11–2.30(3 Sat), 5.30–11

BLACKBROOK TQ1846 Map 3

Plough ✦

On byroad E of A24, parallel to it, between Dorking and Newdigate, just N of the turn E to Leigh

The specials on the bar menu in this popular, white-fronted pub get full marks for imagination – soups such as stilton and onion or tomato and coriander, main dishes like swordfish with vegetables cooked with ginger, paella or pork goulash, and puddings such as bramble crumble; the permanent menu includes ploughman's (£2.45), basket meals (from £2.45), salads (from £2.95, fresh prawn £5.25), plaice (£3.95), ratatouille niçoise or ham steak (£3.95), lasagne (£4.25), prawn curry (£4.95), and steaks (£7.45); in winter they do filled baked potatoes. The airy saloon bar (part of which is no-smoking) has fresh flowers on the tables, and large windows (with more fresh flowers on the sills) that look out onto woods and open fields. Down some steps, the public bar has brass-topped treadle tables, quite a formidable collection of ties as well as old saws on the ceiling, bottles, flat irons, and Tigger the tabby cat (Tess the black labrador puts in an appearance after 10pm); shove-ha'penny, dominoes, cribbage and piped music. Notably well kept King & Barnes Broadwood, Festive, Mild (in summer) and Old Ale (in winter) on handpump. There are 18 wines by the glass, including a wine of the month, and vintage port by the glass; pleasant, friendly staff. You can sit outside on the grass or a small terrace at the back (which in summer is full of tubs of flowers), or at the front under the hanging baskets; the garden has now been extended – to twice its original size, with facilities for barbecues. Just south is a good stretch of attractive oakwood with plenty of paths – and a big pond. *(Recommended by Peter Griffiths, D J Penny, Chris Fluck, TOH, Trevor and Helen Dayneswood, Lindsey Shaw Radley, George Key, Richard Houghton)*

King & Barnes   Licensee Robin Squire   Real ale   Meals and snacks (not Mon evening)   Open 11–2.30, 6–11; weekday winter closing 10.30, closed 25, 26 Dec and 1 Jan

CHARLESHILL   SU8944 Map 2

Donkey

On B3001 Milford–Farnham; as soon as you see pub sign, turn left

The garden behind this attractive little cottage is very pretty, with bright flowerbeds, white garden furniture, a tiny pond, an aviary with cockatiels, a big fairy-lit fir tree, and a children's play area with swings, slide and roundabout. Inside, the two little bars are neatly kept: the saloon is bright and cheerful with lots of polished stirrups, bits, lamps, watering cans, scales and so forth, and prettily-cushioned built-in wall benches and wheelback chairs. The lounge bar has similar seating as well as a lovely old high-backed settle and a couple of unusual three-legged chairs, swords on the walls and beams, lots of highly polished horsebrasses, some powder pouches, a longcase clock, and maybe Fred, the engaging west highland white. A conservatory with blond wheelback chairs and stripped tables, fairy lights and some plants has sliding doors into the garden. Popular home-made bar food includes sandwiches (from £1.20, toasted prawn and cheese £2.20), soup (£1.30), ploughman's (from £2.10), filled baked potatoes (winter only, from £2.20), and four daily specials like a platter of salamis and sausages (£3.25), pork and egg pie (£3.50), and spiced beef pasta bake or fisherman's pie (£4); puddings such as apricot tart or gooseberry cheesecake (£1.50). Well kept Courage Best and Directors on handpump. *(Recommended by John and Heather Dwane, W A Gardiner, P A Barfield, Lyn and Bill Capper)*

Courage   Licensee John Foskett   Real ale   Meals and snacks (not Sun evening; they only do snacks on summer evenings)   Children in conservatory lunchtimes   Open 11–2.30, 6–11; closed evenings 25 and 26 Dec

CHIDDINGFOLD   SU9635 Map 2

Crown 🏠

A3100 S of Guilford, left on to A283 after 6 miles; pub on left towards end of village

The sense of history is strong here – based on a 13th-century hospice for Winchester monks on the pilgrimage to Canterbury, it's the oldest licensed house in Surrey and one of the oldest in the country. Under the fine king-post roof there are oak beams over two feet thick, oak panelling, a magnificently carved inglenook fireplace, massive chimneys, and a cabinet of coins going back some 400 years and found during renovations; the lower back area has a wood cooking fire with a central chimney. Courage Best and Directors, Flowers and Whitbreads Pompey Royal and Strong Country on handpump; fruit machine, piped music. Bar food includes sandwiches (from £1.50), home-made pâté (£1.75), ploughman's (from £1.75), lasagne (£3.25), steak, kidney and mushroom pie (£4.25), assorted cold meat salad (£2.85), and a hot daily special; afternoon teas; they try to keep the food areas no-smoking; the restaurant is panelled and tapestry-hung. Seats outside look across the village green to the interesting church, and there are more tables in a sheltered central courtyard. *(Recommended by Robert and Elizabeth Scott, Margot Styles; more reports please)*

Free house   Licensees Peter Riley and John Lever   Real ale   Meals and snacks   Restaurant   Children in eating area of bar   Open 11–11 (but may vary)   Bedrooms tel Wormley (042 879) 2255; £44B/£55B

Swan

Petworth Road (A283 S)

The walls in the comfortable and spacious bar here are hung with a good many hunting, shooting and fishing pictures and objects, and there are good winter log fires, as well as shove-ha'penny, cribbage, dominoes, fruit machine, trivia and piped music. Friary Meux, King & Barnes Sussex and Tetleys on handpump. Bar food includes soup (£1.30), filled baked potatoes (from £1.25), omelettes (from £1.35), sandwiches (from £1.50), ploughman's (from £1.95), herby grilled sardines (£2.95), steak and kidney pie (£3.75) and steaks (from £6.95). Some seats outside this tile-hung pub. *(Recommended by Adrian Pitts; more reports on the new regime please)*

Friary Meux (Allied)   Licensee Paul Edwards   Real ale   Meals and snacks   Restaurant tel Wormley (042 879) 2073; closed Sun evening   Children in restaurant Open 11–3, 6–11

CHIPSTEAD   TQ2757 Map 3

Well House

3 miles from M25, junction 8; A217 towards Banstead, turn right at second roundabout following Mugswell, Chipstead signpost; can also be reached from A23 just W of Coulsdon

Pleasantly isolated in a country valley, this pub is quiet and comfortable inside, with big low 14th-century beams, inglenook fireplaces, and a few tables and wheelback chairs in the central room (mainly used for standing); a second room has many more tables and tapestried seats, and there are darts in the side room. Bar food includes sandwiches, filled baked potatoes (from £1.80), ploughman's (£2.20), plaice or cod (£3.45), home-made cheese and asparagus quiche (£3.50), steak pie or coronation chicken (£3.75), and puddings; Bass and Charrington IPA on handpump; cribbage, dominoes and fruit machine. The well itself is on the sheltered back terrace (proceeds to charity), and the garden, lively with birds and colourful with flowers in summer, has an old yew coppice with taller trees behind. *(Recommended by R Bennett, C P Scott-Malden, R Bennett, Martin Aust, Mr and Mrs P Wilkins; more reports please)*

Charringtons (Bass)   Licensee W G Hummerston   Real ale   Meals and snacks (lunchtime, not Sun)   Open 11–2.30, 5.30(6 Sat)–11

COLDHARBOUR   TQ1543 Map 3

Plough

Village signposted in the network of small roads around Abinger and Leith Hill, off A24 and A29

At 800 feet, this is the highest pub in south-east England; there are fine views, either from the picnic-table sets by the tubs of flowers in front, or from the peaceful garden, with its terrace, fish pond with waterlilies, and more picnic-table sets; walkers are welcome. The two bars have timbering in the warm-coloured dark ochre walls, stripped light beams, quite unusual little chairs around the tables in the snug red-carpeted room on the left, little decorative plates on the walls and a big open fire in the one on the right – which leads through to the restaurant. The games bar on the left has darts, pool, cribbage, shove-ha'penny, dominoes, and piped music. There's a good range of well kept real ales on handpump – typically Adnams Bitter and Broadside, Badger Best, Batemans XXXB, Buckleys Best, Gibbs Mew Bishops Tipple, Ringwood Old Thumper and Theakstons Old Peculier, with a monthly guest, and country wines and farm cider. Decent, home-made bar food includes soup, quiche (£3.75), cottage or steak and kidney pie (£3.95), vegetable or meaty lasagne (£4.50), curry (£5), steak (£6.95), and puddings. Dogs are allowed if on a lead, but not in the restaurant. *(Recommended by Ian Phillips, D J Penny, Maureen Preston, Jenny and Brian Seller)*

Free house   Licensees Richard and Anna Abrehart   Real ale   Meals and snacks (12–2.30, 7.30–9.30)   Restaurant tel Dorking (0306) 711793   Children in family room and eating area of bar   Open 11.30–3, 6.30–11; may open all day summer Sat or Bank Hol Mon; winter evening opening 7; closed evening 25 Dec

COMPTON   SU9546   Map 2

Harrow

B3000

This up-market, food-oriented pub has quite an equestrian theme – in the main bar there are interesting racing pictures below the ancient ceiling – mostly portraits of horses, jockey caricatures and signed race-finish photographs. Opening off here are more beamed rooms with latched rustic doors, and nice touches such as brass horse-head coat hooks, photographs of the area, and a bas relief in wood of the pub sign. Bar food, often unusual, attractively presented and with prices to match, is listed on several blackboards and typically includes sandwiches such as smoked turkey and avocado or thickly-cut beef (from £2.25), winter soup such as cream of leek (£2.50), baked brie with almonds (£4.50), paella (£5.25), chicken in a hot pepper sauce, Delhi lamb with poppadums and chutney or salmon and broccoli (all £5.50), steak and kidney pie or baked trout with bacon (£5.75), and seafood platter (£14). Well kept Friary Meux Bitter, Ind Coope Burton and Tetleys on handpump; piped music, fruit machine. You can sit outside in summer, round by the car park but looking out to gentle slopes of pasture. In the pretty village the art nouveau Watts Chapel and Gallery are interesting, and the church itself is attractive; Loseley House is nearby too. *(Recommended by Peter Griffiths, R Gray, Philip King, Peter and Susan Maguire, M B Porter, Capt F A Bland)*

Friary Meux (Allied)   Licensees Roger and Susan Seaman   Real ale   Meals and snacks (12–3, 6–10)   Children in eating area of bar till 9pm   Open 11–3, 5.30–11; closed 25 and 26 Dec

DORKING   TQ1649   Map 3

Cricketers

81 South Street; from centre follow signs to Horsham (A2003)

The comfortably modernised, attractive bar in this informal town pub has stripped-and-sealed brick walls decorated with Spy cricketer caricatures and other cricketing pictures, library chairs around cast-iron-framed tables, well cushioned sturdy modern settles, and a central servery with a big modern etched-glass cricketers mirror; there's a log-effect gas fire. The Fullers beers – Chiswick, ESB and London Pride – are well kept on handpump; darts, cribbage, dominoes, and piped music. Really good value, home-made bar food includes sandwiches (from around 80p), filled baked potatoes (£2), quiches, liver and bacon, lamb hot pot or chilli con carne (all £2.20), and steak pie (£2.30). Up steps at the back there's a very pretty little sheltered terrace, interestingly planted with roses, a good red honeysuckle, uncommon shrubs and herbaceous plants, and gently floodlit at night. *(Recommended by Tony Bland, TBB, James A Gear, John Pettit, Lindsay Shaw Radley, S J Rice, Chris Payne, D J Penny, Stephen King)*

Fullers   Licensee Iain Anderson   Real ale   Meals and snacks (not Sat or Sun)   Nearby daytime parking difficult   Open 11–3, 5.30–11

ELSTEAD   SU9143 Map 2

Woolpack ⊗

The Green; on B3001 Milford–Farnham

Cheerfully and efficiently run, this big, busy pub fills up quickly with people keen to enjoy the wide range of interesting bar food. Chalked up on a big board near the food servery, this might include filled baked potatoes (from £2.95), mushrooms in herb and garlic butter (£3.50), baked goat's cheese with garlic and chives or hot camembert with mango liqueur sauce (£3.95), home-made pies such as smoked cod and prawn or chicken and ham (£5.15), delicious lamb with Roman sauce, beef, orange and Guinness casserole or chicken in whisky, ginger and red peppers (£5.50), chicken tikka or pork steak in thyme, schnapps and apricot sauce (£6.50), tuna steak in rich herb and tomato sauce (£7.25), and lovely puddings like creme brûlée, chocolate and fruit scrunch or choux ring filled with cream and bananas; vegetables are good – beetroot in creamy sauce, leeks with crunchy topping and cheesy potatoes. Well kept Friary Meux, Ind Coope Burton, and a monthly guest such as Youngs Bitter tapped from the cask; quite a few wines by the glass and bottle. The long, airy main bar has window seats and spindleback chairs around plain wooden tables, a couple of high-backed settles with weaving shuttles and cones of wool above them, a small brick fireplace at one end with copper pans on the mantlepiece and some pretty china on a shelf above it, and another little fireplace at the other end; the large dog basket tucked into a corner is for Megan the golden retriever. Another large room leads off this with lots of country prints on the walls, and other decorations such as a weaving loom, scales, and brass measuring jugs, and a fireplace with unusual wooden pillars on either side and a lace frill above it; beyond this there's a simply furnished small room with pretty curtains. The family room, with lots of dried flowers hanging from the ceiling and nursery-rhyme murals, leads to the garden with picnic-table sets, a children's play area, and a run with two rabbits. *(Recommended by W A Gardiner, Lyn and Bill Capper, Father Robert Davies, Mr Turrall-Clarke)*

Friary Meux   Licensees Jill and Kevin Macready   Real ale   Meals and snacks Children in family room   Open 11–2.30, 6–11; closed evening 25 Dec and all day 26 Dec

FELBRIDGE   TQ3639 Map 3

Woodcock ⊗

A22 N

Bar food in this spacious and plush roadhouse veers firmly towards fish, delivered fresh from Argyllshire – moules (£3.95), langoustines (from £5.75) and grilled giant prawns with garlic sauce or a plate of mixed shellfish (£6.75); there's also sandwiches (from £1.25), soup (£1.50), ploughman's (from £3.50), a roast of the day (£4.75), steaks (from minute, £5.95), and a cold buffet in summer. The busy little flagstoned entrance bar opens on the left into a quieter carpeted room with unusual furniture from heavily upholstered chairs to finely lacquered oriental benches, interesting prints on the walls, oriental screens, occasional tables (maybe with copies of *Vogue*), a stuffed bird of paradise, attractive table lamps – and lots of candles, in wall sconces and on tables. A handsome black spiral staircase leads up from here into the high eaves, where an almost entirely candlelit gallery has low stools and sprawly cushions around a couple of low tables at one end, a fanciful crowd of decorative fans and parasols, and a flamboyant dressing-table which houses, among lots of other bird images elsewhere, the only woodcock in the place – but this one's a delicate skeleton. This in turn opens into a lovely old-fashioned Victorian dining room with just one long, handsome table, used for bar meals (or you can book the whole room – a nice place for a private party of a dozen or so). On the right of the downstairs core, a few steps take you into a sumptuous Victorian parlour area filled with thickly cushioned chairs, settees and chaises-longues that would do credit to any seraglio; beyond that yet more candles glitter and flicker in the inviting restaurant. Well kept Eldridge Pope Hardy, King & Barnes and Ringwood Old Thumper on handpump, decent wines and spirits;

friendly service, maybe unobtrusive piped music. There are tables under cocktail parasols on the flagstones of a sunken front courtyard. *(Recommended by Alan Skull, L M Miall, Bruce Poynter, A W Peters, Mrs V Newman)*

Free house   Licensees Peter and Valerie Jones   Real ale   Meals and snacks (12.30–2, 7–10)   Restaurant (not Mon lunchtime) tel East Grinstead (0342) 325859   Children welcome   Jazz Sun evening   Open 11–3, 6–11

FICKLESHOLE   TQ3860   Map 3
White Bear

Off A2022 Purley Road just S of its junction with A212 roundabout; at The Willows follow Addington Court Golf Club signpost into Featherbed Lane and keep on

This rambling pub has several, partly 15th-century, dimly lit rooms – some are very cosy and some quite spacious, with low and heavy black beams, quarry tiles and oak parquet, polished flagstones, bay windows inset with stained-glass panels, an attractive variety of seating including some antique settles, and decorations ranging from china on Delft shelves through halberds and pikes to a handsome Act of Parliament clock. There are open fires and solid fuel stoves. Lunchtime bar food includes soup (£1), quiches (from £1.35), ploughman's (from £2.30), salads (from £3.80) and a few hot dishes; three-course Sunday lunch (£7.50), and more substantial evening dishes such as lemon sole (£5.75) and steak (£6.95); pleasant, friendly service. Well kept Bass, Fullers London Pride and ESB on handpump. Darts (winter), three fruit machines, inoffensive piped music. There's a big play area, and a walk-through paddock with hens, ducks, geese and white doves, pheasants and rabbits in big pens, and a Nubian goat; other paddocks have a donkey, ponies and sheep. This whitewashed pub (converted from a row of old cottages) is a pleasing find for the outer fringes of London. *(Recommended by Michael and Andrew Wells, Jenny and Brian Wells, W J Wonham, Helen and Wal Burns, Alan Skull, Ian Phillips, Maureen Preston, P Thorogood)*

Free house   Licensee David Stevens   Real ale   Meals and snacks   Children in eating areas   Open 11–2.30(3 Sat), 6–11

HASCOMBE   TQ0039   Map 3
White Horse

On B2130 S of Godalming

Sitting prettily on the Greensand Way, this foody pub has a cosy inner beamed area with quiet small-windowed alcoves and a woodburning stove, and a light and airy extension. The interesting range of popular bar food includes home-made vegetable soup, sandwiches (from £1.50), whitebait (£2.95), home-made meaty burgers or swordfish steak (£4.25), fresh, interesting salads with vegetables like mange tout or avocado (from £4.25, prawn £6.25), poussin Dijonnais (£4.65), and tasty home-made puddings like treacle tart or fruit crumbles (£2.50); tables tend to get taken quickly at lunchtime. Well kept Friary Meux Bitter, Ind Coope Burton and Gales HSB on handpump; quite a few wines. There are some tables in several places outside – on a little patio by the porch at the rose-draped front, in a bower and under a walnut tree. The National Trust's Winkworth Arboretum, with its walks among beautiful trees and shrubs, is nearby. *(Recommended by Tessa Stuart, P A Barfield, Hilarie Miles-Sharp, Jenny and Brian Seller, T Galligan, Gordon Hewitt, W A Gardiner)*

Friary Meux (Allied)   Licensee Susan Barnett   Real ale   Meals and snacks   Restaurant tel Hascombe (048 632) 258; not Sun evening   Children welcome   Open 11–3, 5.30(6 Sat)–11

HORLEY   TQ2842   Map 3
Olde Six Bells

3 miles from M23 junction 9: from Gatwick turn-off follow A23 towards Redhill and

London, then Horley signpost at roundabout; after 600 yards pub signposted by sharp left turn into Church Road, which is first real left turn

The open-plan bar here has heavy beams, butter-coloured plaster walls and ceiling, a tiled floor and some decorative copper measuring dippers. Bass and Charrington IPA on handpump; shove-ha'penny, dominoes, darts, fruit machine and piped music. The quieter, carpeted upstairs bar has high rafters and heavy wall timbering: you can book tables here for the home-made food, which includes filled French bread (around £2), ploughman's (from £2), vegetable lasagne, turkey and ham pie, or chilli con carne (all £4.50) and salads, with more elaborate evening meals such as lamb marengo, pork normandy or veal korma (all £6.30). Beyond a sheltered back flagstone terrace with jasmine on the wall is a sizeable garden beside the little River Mole. (*Recommended by David and Sarah Gilmore, Lindsey Shaw Radley, Jacquie Mundle; more reports please*)

Charringtons (Bass)   Licensee Bill Watson   Real ale   Meals and snacks   Restaurant tel Horley (0293) 782209; may close over the Christmas period   Children in restaurant   Open 11–11; 11–3 6.30–11 Sat; closed 25 Dec evening

LALEHAM   TQ0568   Map 3

Three Horseshoes

Junction 1 of M3, then W on A308; village signposted on left on B377

This 13th-century, wisteria-covered inn has been used as a coroner's court, post office, and parish vestry – all of which may partly explain its thriving and villagey atmosphere these days. Popular and highly praised bar food includes a wide range of huge baked potatoes with hot or cold fillings (from £2.95, prawns £4.50), as well as an excellent choice of sandwiches (from £1.25, prawn with asparagus £2.25), soup (£1.25), ploughman's (£2.95), salads (from £4.25), and a selection of daily specials such as pork in cider and cream (£3.95), steak and oyster pie (£4.35), or poached salmon; they may also prepare dishes on a more individual basis on request. The modernised open-plan bar is furnished with comfortable burgundy plush seats on the red carpet, lots of big copper pots and pans hanging from beams, interesting cock-fighting prints on the red walls, and blacksmith's tools hanging over the main fireplace. One small alcove has high-backed settles, and there's a conservatory; piped music. Well kept Ruddles Best and County, Websters Yorkshire and a guest beer on handpump; decent wines. In the garden there are some statues and plenty of tables – some under a cleverly rainproofed 'arbour' of creepers. The lane opposite leads down to a stretch of the Thames popular for picnics and sunbathing. (*Recommended by M Rising, Liam Devlin, TOH, Ian Phillips, R B Crail, Peter Griffiths*)

Watneys   Licensee Philip Jones   Real ale   Meals and snacks (noon–9 Mon–Sat, 12–2 Sun)   Restaurant tel Staines (0784) 452617   Children in conservatory   Open 11–11

LEIGH   TQ2246   Map 3

Plough

3 miles S of A25 Dorking–Reigate, signposted from Betchworth (which itself is signposted off the main road); also signposted from South Park area of Reigate; on village green

The Walkers tell us that by the time the *Guide* comes out they'll have left this tiled and white-boarded cottage, to which they've done so much to make it popular with readers; and such is its charm that we feel confident in keeping it in this year. The lounge bar has timbered white walls, and very low beams with protective crash-pads; on the left, the more local bar has a good bow-window seat; maybe darts, shove-ha'penny, dominoes, table skittles, cribbage, fruit machine and so forth. Bar food has included sandwiches, ploughman's, salads, ham and eggs and dishes of the day such as deep-fried fresh cod, home-made steak, oyster and Guinness pie and so forth. King & Barnes Bitter, Festive, Mild and winter Old on handpump. There are picnic-table sets under cocktail parasols in a side garden bordered by a white picket fence. Parking nearby is limited. (*Recommended by W M*

Elliott, J Crawford, Mr and Mrs R P Begg, John Pettit, D W Crossley, Lyn and Bill Capper, David and Sarah Gilmore, Reg Tickner, Mrs P Brown, P L Jackson, Mike Tucker, Jane Palmer, Richard Houghton, D J Penny; more reports please)

King & Barnes   Real ale   Meals and snacks; not Sun, not Mon evening   Restaurant tel Dawes Green (030 678) 348   Open 11–2.30, 6–11; closed evening 25 Dec

Seven Stars

The comfortable saloon bar in this friendly pub has an early 18th-century sign painted on the wall, reading '...you are Wellcome to sit down for your ease pay what you call for and drink what you please', and a 1633 inglenook fireback with the royal coat of arms in the smoke-blackened brick inglenook fireplace; also, lots of racing pictures and horse brasses. The plainer public bar has an alley set aside for darts. Good bar food and well kept Ind Coope Burton and Friary Meux. There may be summer Sunday barbecues in the colourful garden. *(Recommended by Win and Reg Harrington, Jenny and Brian Seller, Lindsey Shaw Radley, D J Penny, Gwen and Peter Andrews; more reports please)*

Ind Coope (Allied)   Real ale   Meals and snacks   Children welcome   Open 10.30–2.30, 6.30–11

MICKLEHAM   TQ1753   Map 3
King William IV

Byttom Hill; short but narrow steep track up hill just off A24 Leatherhead–Dorking, just N of main B2289 village turnoff; OS Sheet 187 map reference 173538

Cut into the hillside, this unpretentious place is a steep climb up from the rough track. There's a snug plank-panelled front bar looking down the hill, and a rather more spacious quite brightly lit back bar with kitchen-type chairs around its cast-iron-framed tables; darts sensibly placed in one corner, shove-ha'penny, cribbage, dominoes, unobtrusive nostalgic piped pop music, and a serviceable grandfather clock. Well kept Adnams, Badger Best, Greene King IPA and Youngs Special on handpump; good log fires. Rather unusual bar food includes filled baked potatoes or ploughman's (around £3), several vegetarian dishes such as tostados with tomato and bean sauce (£3.25) or courgette and mushroom ratatouille (£3.75), salads, chilli con carne or steak and kidney pie (£3.95) and Chinese-style chicken (£4.50); easy-going atmosphere, friendly service. The garden, a popular draw in summer, is mainly brick-tiled, with crazy paving in front, then grass below, and plenty of tables – some in a wooden open-sided shelter. A path leads straight up into the open country. *(Recommended by WFL, John Pettit, Norman Foot, Jane Palmer, TOH, D J Penny, Mrs K J Betts, Roger Taylor)*

Free house   Licensee J E Beynon   Real ale   Meals and snacks (not Sun)   Occasional guitarist in summer   Open 11–2.30, 6–11; winter 12–2.30, 7–10.30(6–11 Fri and Sat); closed 25 and 26 Dec evenings

NEWDIGATE   TQ2042   Map 3
Surrey Oaks

Parkgate Road; A24 S of Dorking, then left on to unmarked road signposted for Beare Green – go through that village and take first left fork

This diminutive country pub has a main lounge with rustic tables lit by lanterns hanging low from fairy-lit lowered beams, and tapestried seats in little partly curtained booths. In the much older part on the right there's a little snug beamed room by a coal-effect gas fire, then a standing area with unusually large flagstones and an open fire. A separate games room has a well lit pool table, darts, shove-ha'penny, dominoes, cribbage, a fruit machine, space game, and juke box; Friary Meux, Ind Coope Burton and King & Barnes on handpump. Bar food includes sandwiches, stilton and celery soup (£1.25), ploughman's (£2.35), filled baked potatoes (£2.45), sausages (£2.55), lasagne, moussaka or chilli con carne (£3.25), an interesting selection of vegetarian dishes such as butter bean and vegetable au gratin or good mung bean and mushroom biriani (all £3.75), and puddings (£1.25); their own free-range duck, hen and goose eggs are for sale at the bar. The substantial, pretty garden outside has a large terrace, a rockery with illuminated pools, fountains and waterfall, and a flock of pure white doves; they also have sheep, a calf, and an aviary of budgerigars, and all sorts of fowls – the source of the eggs. (*Recommended by Alec Lewery, TOH, John Pettit, C T H Wickham, Norman Foot*)

Friary Meux (Allied)   Licensee Colin Haydon   Real ale   Meals and snacks Restaurant (top half no-smoking) tel Newdigate (030677) 200; not Sun evening Children welcome   Middle-of-the-road live music Sun evening   Open 11–3, 6–11

NORWOOD HILL   TQ2343   Map 3
Fox Revived

Leigh–Charlwood back road

Fairly close to Gatwick but comfortably tucked away in remote countryside, this cottagey, bare-boarded place has a front area with shelves of books, kitchen tables, chairs, cushioned pews and an attractive stripped high-backed settle, and decorative mugs on the beams; the back dining area is similarly furnished, and has a woodburning stove in a central brick hearth, a set of sharply contrasty photographs in one alcove, and a pleasantly relaxed atmosphere. Opening off of this is a double conservatory with its own stove, cane chairs and tables on shiny brown tiles, and some big plants; well kept Friary Meux Best, Gales HSB and Ind Coope Burton on handpump, decent wines; daily newspapers. Hearty heaps of good food, served cheerily and with splendid celerity, might include home-made soup (£1.50) or jumbo prawns (£3.95) as starters, with evening main dishes such as fresh fish (from £6.95; Dover sole £10.95) or a hefty half-shoulder of lamb (£7.65); and at lunchtime, giant sausages (£2.25), ploughman's (from £2.50), and open sandwiches; good puddings. Picnic-table sets are spread well through their big garden, which has a retired tractor among its weeping willow, apple and other trees, and backs on to paddocks. Note that they don't allow any children under 14. (*Recommended by Ian and Wendy McCaw, Mrs H M M Tickner, D J Penny*)

Friary Meux (Allied)   Licensee Gary Kidd   Real ale   Meals and snacks (12–2, 7–10) Live music around 2 Sun evenings a month   Open 11–2.30, 5–11; Sat 11–3, 6–11

nr OCKLEY   TQ1439   Map 3
Punch Bowl ★

Oakwoodhill (some maps and signposts spell it Okewoodhill); village signposted off A29 S of Ockley

Surrounded by fields, oak trees and woods (best appreciated from the tables on the several terraces), this partly tile-hung old house has a peaceful, homely bar with lots of beams, polished, big dark flagstones, some timbering, an antique settle among simpler country seats and scrubbed deal tables, and an inglenook fireplace with huge logs smouldering gently on the vast round hearth. Another plainer bar has sensibly placed darts, a juke box and fruit machine. Well kept Badger Best, King & Barnes Sussex and three guest ales on handpump; a good choice of malt whiskies. Bar food includes well filled sandwiches (both the ham and beef are recommended), a good value ploughman's, home-baked ham (£4), chicken curry (£4), and steak and kidney pie (£5). There are two cats – a tabby and an enthusiastic three-legged marmalade one. (*Recommended by D J Penny, Norman Foot, Jenny and Brian Seller, WFL, M Rising, Jane Palmer, TOH, S J Rice, M C Howells*)

Free house   Licensee Robert Chambers   Real ale   Meals and snacks (12–2, 7–10; not Sun–Tues evenings)   Restaurant tel Oakwood Hill (030 679) 249; closed Sun evening Children in restaurant   Open 11–3, 5.30–11

OUTWOOD   TQ3245 Map 3

Bell ★ ⊘

Just beyond the broad village green with its striking white windmill, this popular food pub has a carpeted front bar with low beams, elm and oak tables and chairs, some in Jacobean style, and a vast stone inglenook fireplace; there's another lounge bar at the back. Bar food includes main dishes such as steak and kidney pie (£5.50), plaice or English rack of lamb (£4.95), chargrilled sirloin or rump steak (from £5.50; fillet steak topped with stilton £9.50). They do sandwiches (from £1.50), ploughman's (£2.75) and filled baked potatoes (from £2.95) at lunchtime; also, morning coffee and an all-year barbecue, outdoors in good weather. If you want a table, it's best to book in advance, especially in the evening (when drinking-only space is limited). Well kept Batemans XXXB, Fremlins, King & Barnes Sussex and Festive and Whitbreads Pompey Royal on handpump. In summer, the well-managed garden is a peaceful place to sit among flowers and shrubs on the sheltered lawn and look past its bordering pine trees to the fine view over rolling fields, dotted with oak trees and woods. *(Recommended by W A Gardiner, Comus Elliott, I S Wilson, R E Horner, W J Wonham, P Thorogood, Lindsey Shaw Radley, BKA, Mrs H M M Tickner, R Bennett, Sue Carlyle, Raymond Palmer, M Rising, K Leist, A J Young, Lyn and Bill Capper, R Bennett)*

Free house   Licensees Harry Pam, Diane Davis, John Lane   Real ale   Meals and lunchtime snacks   Open 11–2.30, 6–11; may open longer, summer afternoons

Dog & Duck

From A23 in Salfords S of Redhill take Station turning – eventually after you cross the M23 the pub's on your left at the T-junction; coming from the village centre, head towards Coopers Hill and Prince of Wales Road

The spaciously rambling, cheerful bar areas in this partly tile-hung country cottage have ochre walls and stripped dark beams, comfortable settles and oak armchairs as well as more ordinary seats, rugs on the quarry tiles, a good log fire, and a cheerful, lively atmosphere. Well kept Adnams Best and Broadside, Badger Best and Tanglefoot on handpump; decent wines; newspapers out for customers, maybe shove-ha'penny, ring-the-bull, cribbage, Scrabble, backgammon, chess, trivia and unobtrusive piped music. Bar food includes several ploughman's (£2.50), ham and egg (£3.85), mixed grill (£4.65), dressed crab salad (£4.95), a separate vegetarian menu, and children's dishes. In the evening the choice is more on the lines of soup with a puff pastry lid (£2.75), double egg mayonnaise (£3.85), and guinea fowl with gooseberry sauce or poached fresh salmon (around £8); afternoon teas and Sunday roast lunch. The restaurant area, with another huge fireplace, really only functions separately in the evening – during the day it's more part of the bar it leads off. Picnic-table sets under cocktail parasols on the grass outside look over a safely fenced-off duck pond to the meadows. The village, with its old windmill, is worth the walk. *(Recommended by Sue Corrigan, Raymond Palmer, Lindsay Shaw Radley, TOH, David and Sarah Gilmore, WFL, A J Young; more reports please)*

Badger   Licensee Amanda Buchanan-Munro   Real ale   Meals and snacks (noon–10pm)   Evening restaurant tel Smallfield (034 284) 2964 (all day Sun) Children in restaurant   Open 11–11

PIRBRIGHT   SU9455 Map 2

Royal Oak

Aldershot Rd; A324S of village

Carefully kept, this tile-hung extended Tudor cottage is furnished with wheelback chairs, tapestried wall seats and little dark church-like pews set around neat tables; also, ancient stripped brickwork, heavy beams and timbers, gleaming brasses set around the big low-beamed fireplace, and a rambling series of side alcoves. Lunchtime pub food (using produce from their own garden where possible) includes soup (£1.20), sandwiches (from £1.50; toasted £1.90), ploughman's (£2.60), salads (£4.50), hot dishes such as chilli con carne, lasagne, fish pie or moussaka (all £4.50), and puddings (£1.65). Beers under the new licensees (popular with readers for their relaxed attitude) now include more from the Whitbread stable, with Brakspears, Flowers, Marstons Pedigree and Wethereds as well as Badger Best and Wadworths 6X. In summer the neat gardens are a mass of colour. (*Recommended by David and Christine Foulkes, Simon Collett-Jones, John and Heather Dwane, KC; more reports on the new regime please*)

Whitbreads   Licensees Annette and Anthony Woodbine   Real ale   Lunchtime meals and snacks; may also do food in evening   Open 11–11

PYRFORD LOCK   TQ0458   Map 3

Anchor

Lock Lane; service road off A3 signposted to RHS Wisley Gardens – continue past them towards Pyrford

Alone in the country (but close to the Royal Horticultural Society's gardens – open every day), this open-plan and modern pub is popular for its canalside position – watching the narrowboats go by is a recommended summer evening occupation. The bar, partly carpeted and partly brick-floored, has big picture windows and comfortable furnishings; upstairs is full of narrow-boat memorabilia and is mainly reserved for parents with small children. Bar food includes ploughman's, steak and kidney pie or scampi (£4); Courage Best and Directors and John Smiths on handpump, and lots of bustle and noise from the Tannoy system. Friendly, efficient staff; fruit machine, piped music. Lots of picnic-tables on the big terrace. (*Recommended by W A Gardiner, R N Haygarth, TBB, Dave Braisted, Michael and Alison Sandy, WTF, Roger Huggins, Ian Phillips, S Bentley, Cdr W S D Hendry, Ian Phillips*)

Courage   Licensee Stephen Kerrawn   Real ale   Meals and snacks (12–2, 6–9; not Sat and Sun evenings)   Children in own first-floor room overlooking canal   Open 11–11; 11–3, 6–11 winter

REIGATE HEATH   TQ2349   Map 3

Skimmington Castle ★

3 miles from M25 junction 8: through Reigate take A25 Dorking (West), then on edge of Reigate turn left past Black Horse into Flanchford Road; after ¼ mile turn left into Bonny's Road (unmade, very bumpy track); after crossing golf course fork right up hill

Popular with ramblers and a good number of horse riders (some of whom may tie up at the hitching rail on the nearby bridleway) this old cottage has a small central serving counter with dark simple panelling and a collection of oddly shaped pipes (and a skull among them) dangling over it. Leading off here, the bright main front bar has a miscellany of chairs and tables, shiny brown vertical panelling decorated with earthenware bottles, decorative plates, brass and pewter, a brown plank ceiling, and the uncommon traditional game of ring the bull. The back rooms are partly panelled too – cosy, with old-fashioned settles and Windsor chairs; one has a big brick fireplace with its bread-oven still beside it. A small room down steps at the back has space games, darts, shove-ha'penny, cribbage and dominoes. Friary Meux Best, Ind Coope Burton and King & Barnes Bitter on handpump, and Addlestone's draught cider; the stuffed fox leering out of the crisp packets is commonly known as Derek. Bar food includes local sausages (35p), soup (90p), sandwiches (from £1, cream cheese and prawn with walnuts £1.50, steak roll £1.80), basket meals (from £1.40, scampi £3.30), ploughman's (from £1.50), salads (from £4, smoked salmon £6), gammon steak with egg (£4.50), steaks (from £8) and daily specials; on Sundays food is limited to snacks. There's a crazy-paved front terrace and tables on the grass by lilac bushes – tables at the back have good views over the meadows and the hillocks; paths from here wind into the surrounding wooded countryside. (*Recommended by W A Gardiner, Peter Griffiths, Andrew and Michele Wells, D J Penny, Nigel Gibbs*)

Friary Meux (Allied)   Licensees Andrew and Ann Fisher   Real ale   Meals (lunchtime, not Sun) and snacks   Children in small back room until 9   Open 11–3, 5.30–11

RUNFOLD   SU8747 Map 2

Jolly Farmer

A31 just E of Farnham

There's a warm welcome in this busy open-plan roadside pub, and comfortable furnishings include some massive rough-cut elm tables and chairs as well as more conventionally comfortable seats; the painted vineleaf dado around its cornices is unusual. Popular with businessmen at lunchtime, the bar food includes soup (£1.50), ploughman's (from £2.50), vegetarian dishes (from £3), quiche (£3.50), Madras curry (£4), roast beef (£5.50), and puddings (£2); evening dishes tend to be more ambitious. Courage Best and Directors on handpump, also children's cocktails (and adult ones); maybe nibbles on the bar. Darts, shove-ha'penny, dominoes, cribbage, fruit machine and unobtrusive piped music. At one end of the pub, big windows look out on the back garden and terrace, where there are plenty of tables among some flowers and shrubs, and a good adventure playground. No dogs. *(Recommended by Mr and Mrs Foreman, Mr and Mrs P Wilkins, Jenny and Brian Seller, Michael and Harriet Robinson, Mark Porter; more reports please)*

Courage   Licensee Laurie Richardson   Real ale   Meals and snacks   Restaurant tel Runfold (025 18) 2074   Children in restaurant   Open 11–2.30, 5(5.30 Sat)–11; closed 25 Dec

SHEPPERTON   TQ0867 Map 3

Kings Head

Church Square; E side of B375

There'a a homely feel in the assorted small rooms in this black-shuttered pub, with their dark panelling, oak beams, and oak parquet flooring; one of them has an inglenook fireplace; Courage Best and Directors on handpump and good range of wines. Large helpings of good, plain food include sandwiches, tasty Welsh rarebit to a secret recipe, herby sausages, Shepperton pie or chilli con carne, steak and kidney pie, and scampi. The conservatory has detachable outer walls, removed in summer to give an airy covered area merging with the pretty terrace. The pub looks across to the brick and flint church. *(Recommended by Ian Phillips, Mayur Shah; more reports please)*

Courage   Licensee David Longhurst   Real ale   Meals and snacks (12–2.15, 8–10; not Sun)   Restaurant tel Walton-on-Thames (0932) 221910; closed Sun   Children in eating area   Disco Tues   Open 11–3, 5.30–11; 11–11 Sat

SHERE   TQ0747 Map 3

White Horse

Village signposted on right on A25 3 miles E of Guildford

Watch out for the uneven floors in this fine old half-timbered building – there are no foundations, just salvaged ships' timbers plunged into the ground some 600 years ago. The open-plan main lounge bar has antique oak wall seats, old manuscripts on the walls, massive beams, a huge inglenook fireplace, and elegant Tudor stonework in a second inglenook fireplace through in the Pilgrim's Bar; Ruddles Best and County and Websters Yorkshire on handpump. It can get very busy at weekends. Bar food includes sandwiches (from £1.40, prawn, avocado and mayonnaise £2.50), ploughman's (from £1.95), deep-fried goat's cheese and cranberry sauce (£2.75), steak, kidney and Guinness or sausage, Stilton, leek and tomato pies or fresh trout (all £3.95), and sirloin steak (£6.75). There are seats outside on a sunny cobbled courtyard among carefully planted troughs of flowers and bright hanging baskets; good walking in the beech woods on the road north towards East Clandon. The village is pretty. *(Recommended by Robert and Elizabeth Scott, John Evans, Mr and Mrs J H Adam, Mark Porter, Dick Brown, D J Penny; more reports please)*

Chef & Brewer (Watneys)   Licensee M J Wicks   Real ale   Meals and snacks (not Sun evening) *Children in eating area of bar* *Nearby parking may be difficult* *Open 11.30–2.30(3 Sat), 6–11*

THURSLEY SU9039 Map 2

Three Horseshoes

This distinctly civilised, tile-hung stone pub has a dark and cosy bar, with fine old country furniture, including lovingly polished elm tables, and some Brockbank cartoons (he lived here). Lunchtime bar food, entirely home-made by the licensee, changes pretty much every day, typically including soup (£1.30), sandwiches (from £1.50), ploughman's (£1.85), hot dishes like steak and kidney pie or spaghetti bolognese (£3.95), and cold salmon salad (£5.25); popular Friday and Saturday night dinners (£15). Gales BBB and HSB on handpump. There are tables outside on a big roundel of grass under pine trees at the front, with summer barbecues. *(Recommended by Dr Paul Kitchener, Phil and Sally Gorton, Alan Skull, Jane Clayton; more reports please)*

Gales *Licensee Lorraine Hughes* *Real ale* *Lunchtime meals and snacks (not Sun) Restaurant tel Elstead (0252) 703268* *Open 11–3, 6–11; closed 25 Dec and evening 31 Dec*

WALLISWOOD TQ1138 Map 3

Scarlett Arms

Village signposted from Ewhurst–Rowhook back road; or follow Oakwoodhill signpost from A29 S of Ockley, then follow Walliswood signpost into Walliswood Green Road

The old small-roomed layout is still preserved in this friendly and neatly kept, 16th-century pub. Three communicating rooms have deeply polished flagstones, heavy black oak beams in the low brown ceiling, simple but perfectly comfortable benches, high bar stools with backrests, trestle tables, country prints, and log fires – one is an inglenook; darts, shove-ha'penny, cribbage and dominoes and a fruit machine in a small room at the end. Well kept King & Barnes Bitter, Festive, Mild and winter Old on handpump. Bar food includes sandwiches (from 90p, toasties from £1.20), filled baked potatoes (from £1.10), ploughman's (from £1.90), a bowl of chilli con carne (£2.60), salads (from £2.60), breaded plaice (£3.25), ham and eggs (£3.25), and home-made daily specials. There are old-fashioned seats and tables in the garden; there's also a pub dog. *(Recommended by Chris Payne, C P Scott-Malden, D Hughes, Mr and Mrs R P Begg, Phil and Sally Gorton, D J Penny, WFL, Barbara M McHugh, Stephen Goodchild, Paul Sexton, Sue Harrison, R Caldwell)*

King & Barnes *Licensees David and Pat Haslam* *Real ale* *Meals and snacks* *Open 11–2.30, 5.30–11*

WALTON ON THE HILL TQ2255 Map 3

Fox & Hounds

Walton Street

This comfortable village pub has armed chairs and tables spread around the central bar of the low-ceilinged and partly dark-panelled pub; though the various areas open into one another, it's cosy and friendly, with three good coal fires; a cheerfully thriving atmosphere. A wide choice of bar food includes a string of starters such as pâté, avocado and prawns, popular chargrilled burgers, chilli con carne, vegetarian bake, chicken and ham or steak and kidney pie, gammon or prawn curry and steaks; at lunchtime they add good sandwiches, ploughman's, and sausages, and there are good value specials such as roast lamb, tagliatelle with a spicy cheese sauce, or pork escalope done with brandy and mushrooms; good service. The restaurant area, over on the left of the serving counter, has a separate menu. Bass, Charrington IPA and Highgate Mild on handpump, with quite a decent choice of wines; fruit machine. There are rustic picnic-table sets on a back terrace; if children want to run around, they're supposed to go instead to a freer area beyond the car park, with a timber climber and swing. *(Recommended by Jan and Ian Alcock, TOH, Mr and Mrs P Wilkins; more reports please)*

Charringtons (Bass) Real ale Meals and snacks (noon–10) Open 11–11

WARLINGHAM TQ3658 Map 3
White Lion

B269

On the outer fringes of London, this unspoilt pub is a real surprise. It's based on two 15th-century cottages with tales of a secret passage from behind the fine inglenook fireplace to nearby almshouses. The black-panelled rooms have lots of nooks and crannies, wood-block floors, extremely low beams, deeply aged plasterwork, and high-backed settles by the fine Tudor fireplace. Bar food includes sandwiches, filled baked potaoes (from £1.50), ploughman's (from £2), and steak and kidney pie (£3.50). Bass, Charrington IPA, and Youngs on handpump, and several wines. A side room with some amusing early 19th-century cartoons has darts, fruit machine, trivia and piped music. The well kept back lawn, with its rockery, is surrounded by a herbaceous border. *(Recommended by Peter Griffiths, Tony and Louise Clarke; more reports please)*

Charringtons (Bass) Licensee Ian Andrews Real ale Lunchtime meals and snacks Restaurant tel Warlingham (08832) 4106 Children in eating area of bar Open 11–3, 6–11

Lucky Dip

Besides the fully inspected pubs, you might like to try these Lucky Dips recommended to us and described by readers (if you do, please send us reports):

☆ **Abinger Common** [Abinger signposted off A25 W of Dorking — then R to Abinger Hammer; TQ1145], *Abinger Hatch*: Lovely woodland position nr village pub, with attractive garden areas by duckpond; big log fires in heavy-beamed flagstoned bar with plain furnishings, half a dozen changing well kept real ales on handpump such as Badger Best and Tanglefoot, Gibbs Mew Bishops Tipple, King & Barnes and Wadworths 6X, country wines, limited range of usual bar food, with daily changes; restaurant, children allowed in area partly set aside for them; can get very busy indeed at weekends *(John Pettit, Chris Payne, Lindsey Shaw Radley, Roy McNeill, Dr B A W Perkins, WFL, John Branford, LYM)*

☆ **Addlestone** [off A317 into Weybridge industrial estate; left over bridge then first right — pub about 1/2 mile on left; TQ0464], *Pelican*: Modernised canalside pub, busy at lunchtimes but pleasant and comfortable, with long-serving landlord, well kept Watneys-related real ales on handpump, good choice of cheap hot and cold lunchtime food, waterside views from big conservatory, own moorings; children welcome *(R B Crail, Cdr W S D Hendry, Colin Chattoe, Ian Phillips)*

Addlestone [New Haw Rd, corner A318/B385], *White Hart*: Cheerful local with attractive waterside garden, good value quickly served simple food, well kept Courage real ales, darts, bar billiards, juke box; pianist Sat *(Richard Houghton, LYM)*

☆ **Albury** [TQ0547], *Drummond Arms*: Attractively refurbished, with pretty riverside garden, wide choice of good value food inc Sun roast and decent sandwiches (garlic mushrooms recommended) *(J and H Dwane)*

Alfold [B2133; TQ0334], *Crown*: Cheerful pub with pleasant, friendly service, well kept Courage Directors, home-made bar food (not Sun), several rooms, well kept garden, in quiet village *(John Evans, LYM)*

Ashtead [The Street (A24); TQ1858], *Brewery*: Public bar and lounge with quiet appeal, well kept Allied real ales, good, straightforward bar food, with locally popular Sun roasts; nice garden with lots of tables and children's play area *(R P Taylor)*

☆ **Bagshot** [56 High St; SU9163], *Three Mariners*: Welcoming place, recently extended into old adjoining warehouse, with comfortable main bar, upper gallery and separate pool/darts/music area; lots of genuine old beams, some flagstones though it's mainly carpeted, and mix of kitchen-style chairs; wide choice of good food from separate servery (when this is closed in the evening it leaves rather a dark gap), Courage ales; courteous service, professional clientele, big car park *(Ian Phillips, Simon Collett-Jones, Dr M Owton)*

Banstead [High St; TQ2559], *Woolpack*: Popular, roomy local, welcoming to strangers; pleasantly served good value varied bar food *(John Pettit)*

☆ **Batts Corner** [off A325 S of Farnham at Halfway House, Bucks Horn Oak, towards Rowledge, but bear off left after 3/4 mile — OS Sheet 186 map reference 820410; SU8240], *Blue Bell*: Civilised interestingly extended country pub with wide choice of well kept real ales such as Ballards, Brakspears, Courage and Fullers tapped from the cask, traditional games, simple bar food inc good substantial sandwiches; extensive garden with rolling views and good facilities for children — nowhere for them inside though *(Mr and Mrs P Wilkins,*

W A Gardiner, Derek Patey, LYM)

☆ **Beare Green** [A24 Dorking—Horsham; TQ1842], *Dukes Head*: Pretty pub doing well under current regime, with friendly staff, good atmosphere, decent popular food from sandwiches and baked potatoes to steaks, well kept Allied real ales, pleasant garden (*D J Penny, Stephen Goodchild, TOH, LYM*)

☆ **Betchworth** [TQ2049], *Red Lion*: Pleasant bar, well kept Bass, pretty garden, friendly staff, food well presented and quickly served in eating area with extensive collection of chamber-pots; can book squash court (*TOH*)

Bisley [OS Sheet 175 map reference 949595; SU9559], *Hen & Chickens*: Modernised pub (though the beams are genuinely Tudor), with pleasant efficient management, good lunchtime food; Courage (*WHBM*)

☆ **Bletchingley** [11 High St; 2 1/2 miles from M25 junction 6, via A22 then A25 towards Redhill; TQ3250], *Whyte Harte*: Low-beamed mainly open-plan bars with old prints, big log fire in inglenook fireplace, plush-covered settles on rug and parquet floor, home-made bar food from sandwiches to steaks, welcoming atmosphere, well kept Allied real ales and fair range of wines, seats outside; has been open all day Sat; children in dining room; bedrooms generally cosy and comfortable (*Dr M I Crichton, David Shillitoe, LYM; more reports on new regime please*)

Bletchingley [A25, Redhill side], *Red Lion*: Heavily modernised Tudor pub with warm and cosy atmosphere and reasonably priced bar food (*BHP*); [Little Common Lane; off A25 on Redhill side], *William IV*: Country local, prettily tile-hung and weatherboarded, with well kept Bass and Charrington IPA, lunchtime bar food (not Sun), games in back bar, seats in nice garden with summer weekend barbecues (*LYM*)

Blindley Heath [Tandridge Lane; TQ3645], *Red Barn*: Country pub with spacious and attractive garden; has been enjoyed for lovely inglenook fireplace, nicely furnished library bar, discreet piped music, good service, friendly atmosphere, imaginatively presented bar food and well kept Whitbreads-related real ales, but no reports since complete refurbishment 1990 (*Reports please*)

Bramley [High St; TQ0044], *Jolly Farmer*: Cheerful and lively atmosphere in Watneys pub with two log fires, very wide choice of well presented bar food (service can slow; weekday lunchtime discounts for OAPs), beer mats on ceiling, big restaurant; quite handy for Winkworth Arboretum and Loseley House; bedrooms (*LYM*)

☆ **Brockham** [Brockham Green; TQ1949], *Royal Oak*: Promising new management in relaxed and welcoming small local with open fire, wide range of well prepared and presented straightforward bar food from sandwiches and ploughman's up, well kept Gales HSB, ring the bull; pleasant outlook over green, tables on enclosed lawn with play area; be prepared for children (and dogs) at weekends (*John Pettit, J S Evans, Jenny and Brian Seller*)

Brockham [Brockham Green; TQ1949], *Dukes Head*: Homely village-green setting, considerable concentration on wide choice of good value varied food inc vegetarian dishes — many tables booked; friendly, attentive landlord, Allied real ales on handpump, real log fire at one end and coal-effect gas fire at the other (*Sue Corrigan*)

☆ **Brook** [A286 — OS Sheet 186 map reference 930380; SU9337], *Dog & Pheasant*: Pleasant atmosphere in busy and friendly character pub attractively placed opposite cricket green, with polished walking-sticks decorating low beams; well kept Allied real ales, home-cooked food inc huge filled rolls, shove-ha'penny, restaurant with jazz piano Wed—Sun evenings; seats in garden, front and back (*Phil and Sally Gorton*)

Byfleet [High Rd; TQ0661], *Plough*: Solid comfort, lots of farm tools, brass and copper, cheerful log fire, warm welcome, well kept Courage ales, good basic bar food from sandwiches up, lively dominoes; picnic-table sets in big pleasant garden (*Ian Phillips*)

Camberley [A30 W end of town; SU8759], *Lamb*: Well kept Morlands, welcoming service and good atmosphere in brightly modernised extended pub with pleasant flagstoned conservatory; good choice of bar food (*Richard Houghton*); [A30], *Staff*: Pleasant lounge with well kept beer and reasonable food (*Richard Houghton*)

Caterham [235 Stanstead Rd; Whitehill, Caterham on the Hill; TQ3354], *Harrow*: Busy pub with log fires, good choice of simple bar food; garden nice in summer (*M D Hare*)

☆ **Chertsey** [Ruxbury Rd; St Anns Hill (nr Lyne); TQ0466], *Golden Grove*: Charming old pub on edge of St Anns Woods, with low beam-and-plank ceilings, plank-panelling walls, boarded floors; good choice of reasonably priced home-cooked lunchtime food inc good salads, in generous helpings — there's a separate pine-tabled eating area; well kept Allied and Gales real ales, friendly service; unusually big garden with dogs (and a white goat tethered out of reach), playground for children, wooded pond (*Clem Stephens, Tony Tucker, Ian Phillips, Richard Houghton*)

☆ **Chertsey** [London St (B375)], *Crown*: Lively congenial atmosphere and fast friendly (mainly antipodean) service in big Victorian-style pub, open-plan but still with the feel of separate bars; well kept Youngs, good reasonably priced food from doorstep sandwiches up in back food area, restaurant, lovely big garden behind back with masses of roses, pond, parakeet and budgerigar aviaries; exemplary lavatories (*Ian Phillips, Richard Houghton*)

Chertsey [45 Guildford St (A317)], *George*: Friendly old double-gabled low-beamed pub with reasonably priced simple food, pretty garden behind big car park (but you have to go out through the front and round); mentioned in H G Wells' *War of the Worlds*, said to be haunted (*Dr and Mrs A K Clarke, LYM*)

☆ **Cobham** [Downside Common; from A245 on Leatherhead side follow Downside signpost into Downside Bridge Rd, then bear right at second turn after bridge, then next left — OS Sheet 187 map reference 109585;

TQ1158], *Cricketers*: Very low beams, bowed timbers, warm log fire, dimly lit rustic back bar, tables out in charmingly planted neat garden — lots of atmosphere, and almost always seems to be busy (sometimes too much so), with good bar food inc useful salad counter, well kept Watneys-related real ales (drinks prices high); service efficient except sometimes under the busiest crush; restaurant very popular for Sun lunch, children's area *(R B Crail, Peter Griffiths, Mr and Mrs G Turner, Mr and Mrs P Wilkins, Ian Phillips, David and Eloise Smaylen, P L Jackson, M C Howells, John Branford, John Pettit, MKW, JMW, Andrew and Michele Wells)*

☆ Cobham [Plough Lane], *Plough*: Comfortably modernised low-beamed lounge bar, nice little snug with darts and old deal panelling, cheerful lively atmosphere especially in the evening when it's a popular local young people's meeting place; reasonably priced straightforward popular food, well kept Courage real ales, traditional games in public bar, seats outside the pretty black-shuttered brick house *(MKW, JMW, Ian Phillips, LYM)*

☆ Cobham [Pains Hill/Byfleet Rd], *Little White Lion*: Long, low cottagey pub almost opposite entrance to 18th-century Parishill Park (and by giant new Sainsburys); two or three intercommunicating bars, friendly and comfortable, with well kept real ales and decent choice of food from sandwiches to steaks; tables in small front garden, big car park *(Ian Phillips)*

Chobham [just N of village — OS Sheet 176 map reference 970633; SU9761], *Four Horseshoes*: Decent choice of bar food and Courage ales in village pub facing pump on green triangle of common reached by its own little lane; benches outside *(Ian Phillips)*; [B383 1/2 mile towards Sunningdale, turn right into Red Lion Lane], *Red Lion*: Old country pub, pleasantly renovated and enlarged, with plenty of tables, well kept Allied real ales on handpump, helpful staff; popular at lunchtime for reasonably priced bar food *(R B Crail)*; [High St (4 miles from M3 junction 3)], *Sun*: Low-beamed lounge bar with big inglenook fireplace, good choice of bar food, Courage beers, and restaurant; car park could be bigger *(Ian Phillips, LYM)*

☆ Compton [Withies Lane; SU9546], *Withies*: Carefully extended smart dining pub with immaculate garden, good civilised atmosphere in beamed bar with settles and inglenook, some lunchtime bar snacks, well kept Bass, decent wines; prices not low; children in restaurant *(J S Rutter, John Evans, LYM)*

Cox Green [Station Yard, Baynards Lane; off B2128 just N of Rudgwick — OS Sheet 187 map reference 076349; TQ0934], *Thurlow Arms*: Rather isolated pub nr site of Baynards Station on old Guildford–Horsham railway with good attractively priced food and wide range of beers *(G J Lewis)*

☆ Cranleigh [Smithwood Common — OS Sheet 187 map reference 053410; TQ0638], *Four Elms*: Welcoming beamed pub facing large green and overlooking North Downs, with warm welcome, good atmosphere and

service, good bar food (not Sun), central open fire; seats and summer barbecues in back garden, good walks *(Ian Phillips, Jenny and Brian Seller)*

Cranleigh [SW of village], *Boy & Donkey*: Quiet basic country pub with Courage Directors and Best, range of bar food, Sun lunch; efficient polite landlady, informal garden, unusual inn-sign; very close to Downs Link long-distance footway *(Jenny and Brian Seller)*

Dorking [Horsham Rd; TQ1649], *Bush*: Comfortably refurbished, with tables (and chattering budgerigars) on partly covered terrace, and consistently well kept Fullers London Pride, Harveys BB, Marstons Pedigree, Charles Wells Bombardier *(D J Penny)*

☆ Dunsfold [TQ0036], *Sun*: Elegantly symmetrical 18th-century pub overlooking attractive green, well kept Allied real ales, friendly atmosphere, helpful service, comfortable seats, log fires, and beams; unusually varied good bar food inc interesting if not cheap dishes, casually smart young crowd, and separate cottage dining room; children welcome *(Geoff Wilson, LYM)*

Dunsfold, *Rumpoles*: Well refurbished pub on village green with well kept Watneys-related real ales, bar food inc excellent sandwiches and three-course Sun lunch, pleasant staff *(D J Cooke)*

Eashing [SU9443], *Stag*: Attractive riverside pub by working mill, with several traditionally furnished interconnecting rooms, well kept Tetleys, good range of bar food inc children's dishes, Sun roasts and handsome open sandwiches; small garden, big car park *(Ian Phillips)*

☆ East Clandon [TQ0651], *Queens Head*: Traditionally furnished half-timbered pub with big inglenook fireplace, fine old elm bar counter, relaxed atmosphere and tables outside; straightforward bar food, well kept Allied real ales, decent house wines, friendly staff, piped music *(John Evans, Ian Phillips, TOH, Jason Caulkin, MKW, JMW, LYM)*

East Horsley [A246 Guildford—Leatherhead; TQ0952], *Duke of Wellington*: Good buffet counter, popular at lunchtime; pleasant atmosphere, log fire; handy for good walking country *(Mrs H Tickner, John Pettit)*

East Molesey [Bell Rd; TQ1267], *Bell*: Genuine old beams, remarkably thick walls by fireplaces, pretty porch, even the weather-vane off the church; some recent open-planning has left interesting nooks and crannies; reasonably priced straightforward bar food, Courage beers, large area with piano, garden *(Ian Phillips)*

☆ Effingham [TQ1253], [Orestan Lane], *Plough*: Civilised if not cheap commuter-belt pub (no dogs, children or sleeveless T-shirts), with well kept Youngs beers, good value food (game soup with sherry, mackerel pâté, gammon sandwiches recommended), log fires, pleasant staff, tables in garden with play area; convenient for Polesdon Lacey *(John Pettit, C P Scott-Malden, WFL, TOH, MKW, JMW)*

☆ Ellens Green [TQ1035], *Wheatsheaf*: Very clean and well kept rather modern-feeling pub, popular with regulars for full lunches

— very good choice inc specials such as roast lamb with all the trimmings; also evening meals *(John and Heather Dwane)*

Englefield Green [Northcroft Rd; SU9970], *Barley Mow*: Open-plan beamed bar overlooking cricket green, with straightforward food in one area, well kept Courage Best and Directors, darts, machines, CD juke box; tables on back grass *(Mayur Shah, David Fowles)*; [34 Middle Hill], *Beehive*: Small local, popular with students for its wide choice of well kept real ales — and the friendly licensee's collected a good few rums; big car park *(Mayur Shah, Richard Houghton)*; [Bishops Lane], *Hare & Hounds*: Good location with pleasant seats out on lawn to watch horses ambling by, decent if not cheap food *(IP)*; [Wick Lane], *Sun*: Pleasant open-plan pub handy for Savill Gardens; well kept Courage Best and Directors and John Smiths, good choice of reasonably priced food, polite efficient staff *(Richard Houghton)*

Epsom [West St (junction with High St); TQ2160], *Marquis of Granby*: Comfortable town pub with attractive wooden ceiling in bar, fresh flowers in lounge; very popular at lunchtime for good value bar food, especially sandwiches inc formidable hot salt beef ones; good service *(John Pettit)*

☆ **Esher** [82 High St; TQ1464], *Albert Arms*: Good range of real ales (not cheap) and decent French regional wines in lively Victorian pub/bistro with good value bar food inc interesting pâtés and well kept cheeses, friendly service *(Tony and Lynne Stark, LYM)*

Esher [Weston Green], *Alma Arms*: The look of an 1800 lodge, facing big pond with white church beyond and extensive views over the common (now a golf course); basic bar with bare boards and darts, quiet lounge with neatly set-out Windsor chairs and tables, Courage beer *(Ian Phillips)*; *Bear*: Comfortable bar with good atmosphere, high-backed wooden settles, open fire, no piped music, friendly staff, decent bar food *(Mrs J M Moore)*; [West End La (off A244 towards Hersham, by Princess Alice Hospice)], *Prince of Wales*: Comfortable and spacious, slickly run, with coal-effect gas fire, Watneys-related real ales, bar food, piped music; tables in good-sized garden *(Ian Phillips, Mrs Clare Sack, Mrs A Crowhurst)*; [The Green], *Wheatsheaf*: Consistently good value food with one price for main courses and another for puddings in bar running back from food counter; shame about the piped music and machines *(Ian Phillips, Mr and Mrs G Turner)*

Ewell [45 Cheam Rd; TQ2262], *Glyn Arms*: Rambling series of rooms connected by lobbies and passages, reasonable range of well kept beer, reasonably priced food *(Steve Waters, LYM)*

☆ **Ewhurst** [Pitch Hill; a mile N of village on Shere rd; TQ0940], *Windmill*: The unchangingly good feature of this recently refurbished and extended hillside country pub is the spacious series of lawns dropping down below, with marvellous views to the south; it's handy for good walks (and on GWG55), and does have real ales, but the bar food though home-made and pleasant and summer barbecues are far from cheap (with a ploughman's now approaching £5), and the new light and airy conservatory restaurant may increasingly be a focus of the new owner's attention *(D J Penny, Stephen Goodchild, Michael Badcock; more reports on new regime please)*

Farncombe [SU9844], *Cricketers*: Popular unspoilt pub with imaginative decor inc lots of cricketing pictures; busy in evenings, quieter lunchtime — cafe-like atmosphere Sun lunchtime, with papers available; well kept Fullers, barbecues in summer *(Phil and Sally Gorton)*; [Catteshall; outskirts of Godalming], *Ram*: Known locally as the Cider House as its licence has only recently been extended to include beer and spirits; interesting rural retreat in suburbia, with discreet simple rooms and shaded garden *(WFL, Peter Barnsley)*

Farnham [West St (next to No 20); SU8446], *Wheatsheaf*: Unpretentious, old-fashioned and spacious L-shaped bar with subdued lighting, interesting prints, open fire, comfortable banquettes, wide choice of good generously served traditional bar food inc wonderful summer salads and reasonably priced Sun roasts from side food counter, helpful smiling bar staff; unobtrusive juke box, fruit machine; handy for Farnham Maltings concert hall *(Jane Palmer)*

Felbridge [Wiremill Lane; TQ3639], *Wiremill*: Beautiful lakeside spot, well kept beer, good bar food, good service, piped music; tables outside *(BHP)*

Forest Green [nr B2126/B2127 junction; TQ1240], *Parrot*: Rambling bars in quaint old dining pub full of parrot designs, often in the most unlikely materials; real ales such as Courage Best and Directors on handpump, good bar food, restaurant; lots of room in nice surroundings outside; children welcome, play area *(Gordon Hewitt, Roy McNeill, T Galligan, Mrs H M M Tickner, LYM — more reports please)*

☆ **Frensham** [A287 Farnham—Hindhead — OS Sheet 185 map reference 848421; SU8341], *Mariners*: Small, cosy bar in main-road pub/hotel popular with sailors, walkers and riders (close to Frensham ponds); busy, but service prompt and cheerful; wide choice of two-size pizzas and other Italian dishes, steaks and salads, well kept beer; children welcome, at least in the restaurant, which has pew seating and marine decor; occasional jazz; bedrooms *(KC, R Houghton)*

☆ **Godalming** [SU9743], *Inn on the Lake*: Relaxed friendly atmosphere, well kept Whitbreads-related and guest real ales, comfortable decor and furnishings, nicely presented bar food, log fire — welcoming for families; restaurant, gardens overlooking lake, summer barbecues; bedrooms *(J E Newman, Mrs Jeannette Simpson, John and Heather Dwane)*

Godalming [Ockford Rd; SU9743], *Anchor*: Comfortable, tastefully old-fashioned pub with helpful and obliging staff, good range of varying beers such as Brakspears, Courage Directors and Fullers London Pride, straightforward bar food inc excellent soup and sandwiches; pleasant garden and terrace *(Derek and Sylvia Stephenson)*; [off to right of top end of High St], *Rose & Crown*:

Well kept pub with Watneys-related real ales on handpump and bar food inc good choice of sandwiches and tasty breaded cod *(R B Crail, K and E Leist)*

☆ Godstone [128 High St; under a mile from M25 junction 6, via B2236; TQ3551], *Bell*: Spacious beamed and partly panelled main bar of quite some character, with big fires at each end, comfortable and individual seats; also smaller timbered bar set out more for eating; well kept Allied real ales on handpump, straightforward lunchtime bar food, more main dishes and grills evening, restaurant; prices high; good garden for children; bedrooms *(E G Parish, Roger Taylor, LYM)*

☆ Gomshall [Station Rd; A25 Dorking—Guildford; TQ0847], *Black Horse*: Has been a popular main entry, with pleasantly relaxing chatty atmosphere in its several rooms, but early 1990 Youngs sold it to Whitbreads, who later closed it for complete reburbishment; bedrooms *(LYM — more news please)*

Grafham [Smithbrook; A281 Horsham Rd; TQ0241], *Leathern Bottle*: Well kept King & Barnes in comfortably extended lounge bar *(Phil and Sally Gorton)*

☆ Guildford [Quarry St; SU9949], *Kings Head*: Now the pick of the town's pubs — lots of beams and stripped brickwork in spacious corner pub converted from former cottages, lovely big inglenook, spacious banquettes, lots of intimate nooks and crannies, subdued piped music, well kept Courage Best and Directors, decent wines, good range of good value food, especially pies and ploughman's *(Ian Phillips, Ian and Wendy McCaw, Mark Porter, Simon Collett-Jones)*

Guildford [A25 (A246)], *Clavadel*: Part of a hotel, this is the town's only free house: five well kept beers and traditional cider on handpump, regularly changing, and simple, functional decor *(Matt Pringle)*; [Sydenham Rd], *Rats Castle*: Wide range of interesting moderately priced food — quite a haven away from the High St bustle, though decor not striking *(Liz and Ian Phillips)*; [Chertsey St], *Spread Eagle*: Glitzy-fronted Courage local with two-level bar, well kept Best, Directors and John Smiths on handpump, good lunchtime bar food, jazz Sat lunchtime *(Matt Pringle)*; [2 Quarry St], *Star*: Has been popular for good atmosphere and decor (lots of nooks, crannies, arches and corners, ex-court woodwork, open fires, Allied ales); but closed for refurbishment 1990 *(New please)*; [High St], *Three Pigeons*: Smart pub with wooden walls, bare boards, repro 19th-century plaster ceiling, winding stair up to two-level plusher upstairs bar; stuffed birds, barrels, and chests, Liberty-style decor, Allied beers, good value menu; open all day, at least on Sat; a bad point is that it bans servicemen (and under-21s) *(Matt Pringle, Ian Phillips)*

Hambledon [SU9638], *Merry Harriers*: Impressive collection of chamber-pots hanging from beams, lovely inglenook fireplace, cosy atmosphere, Allied real ales, bar food *(Phil and Sally Gorton)*

☆ Haslemere [B2131 Liphook rd; SU9032], *Crowns*: Busy food pub with interesting dishes such as good vegetarian ones or rabbit with mustard and marjoram; light and airy, with comfortable chairs, prints, fresh flowers; Allied beers, lots of wines, tables outside front and back — only a lack of recent reports keeps it out of the main entries; nr start GWG53 *(LYM)*

Haslemere [High St; SU9032], *White Horse*: Recently refurbished spacious bars with good straightforward bar food served efficiently, inc three lunchtime roasts; well kept Allied real ales, decent wines, nicely furnished restaurant area, tables outside in attractive town centre; bedrooms *(Mrs J A Blanks)*

☆ Hersham [Queens Rd; TQ1164], *Bricklayers Arms*: Friendly atmosphere in well kept and clean pub with good value bar food *(Ian and Wendy McCaw, Mrs Clare Sack)*

Hindhead [SU8736], *Punch Bowl*: As it looks so hotelish outside, it's worth noting that this place so handy for the Greensand Way has a straightforwardly pubby bar with well kept Wadworths Farmers Glory and bar food *(BS, JS)*

☆ Holmbury St Mary [TQ1144], *Kings Head*: Quietly spacious pub in beautiful spot on the Greensand Way, with friendly staff, half a dozen well kept real ales on handpump, sensible helpings of reasonable food and big garden *(Dr R Fuller, Jenny and Brian Seller)*

Horley [TQ2842], *Farmhouse*: 16th-century converted beamed farmhouse with connecting rooms, good friendly atmosphere, well kept Courage Best and Directors and John Smiths on handpump, good range of bar food *(Roger Huggins)*; [42 High St; TQ2842], *Gatwick*: Busy but comfortable, with well kept King & Barnes, generously served bar food *(John Baker)*

Horsell [SU9959], *Plough*: Small Friary Meux pub set back from road; food all week, Gales ESB and King & Barnes *(M Rising)*; [Kettlewell Hill], *Wheatsheaf*: Large pub on the green, popular at lunchtime; bright and airy, with restaurant, piped music even in the lavatories *(P B Godfrey)*

Horsell Common [A320 Woking—Ottershaw; SU9959], *Bleak House*: Warm, friendly pub isolated by surrounding heath, Allied real ales on handpump, food currently well worth trying — particularly hot dishes; garden area some way back *(Ian and Wendy Phillips)*

☆ Hurtmore [Hurtmore Rd; just off A3 nr Godalming, via Priorsfield Rd; SY9545], *Squirrel*: Recently comfortably refurbished, with restaurant at one end of comfortable L-shaped bar, friendly service, good choice of real ales, some 20 wines by the glass, good range of original home-cooked bar food, do-it-yourself stone cooking in restaurant, pleasantly lively rather modern atmosphere; children's play area; bedrooms in carefully converted 17th-century cottages *(John Evans, GSS)*

Irons Bottom [Irons Bottom Rd; off A217; TQ2546], *Three Horseshoes*: Simple friendly country pub, airline decorations, changing well kept real ales, inexpensive and freshly cooked straightforward bar food, new clean lavatories, no piped music, tables outside *(WFL)*

☆ Kenley [Old Lodge Lane; left (coming from London) off A23 by Reedham Stn, then keep on; TQ3259], *Wattenden Arms*: One of very few real country pubs on the outskirts of London (and actually within London's boundary, though by long tradition we list it here under Surrey); cosy and friendly, with dark panelling, traditional furnishings, firmly patriotic decor, well kept Bass and Charrington IPA on handpump, big helpings of reasonably priced bar food (not Sun — and no children), prompt service, seats on small side lawn; good car park *(W J Wonham, Ian and Wendy McCaw, LYM)*

Kenley [Godstone Rd (A22)], *Rose & Crown*: Recently refurbished modern pub with long room on different levels; wooden panels, brass rails, art nouveau lamps and prints, button-back banquettes, wing chairs, chesterfields, curved-back wooden chairs; Allied and Gales real ales, wide choice of interesting and fairly priced well presented food; very large garden; children's area *(Pamela E Roper)*

☆ **Kingswood** [Waterhouse Lane; TQ2455], *Kingswood Arms*: Popular, spacious open-plan bar with several more homely areas within it, and light and airy conservatory dining extension — refreshingly non-smoky; wide choice of good value food from doorstep sandwiches and very filling ploughman's to three-course roast dinners inc good puddings, quickly but matter-of-factly served; Watneys-related real ales, attractive if hilly big garden with swings *(Jane Palmer, R Bennett, Martin Aust)*

☆ **Laleham** [The Broadway; TQ0568], *Feathers*: Beamed lounge with red gingham tablecloths at lunchtime, generous helpings of imaginative bar food inc fine well filled baps, steak sandwiches and good value hot dishes, well kept Courage Best and Directors; tables outside the extended old cottage *(Peter Griffiths, Ian Phillips)*

☆ **Leatherhead** [Chessington Rd; A243 nr M25 junction 9 — OS Sheet 187 map reference 167600; TQ1656], *Star*: Busily cheerful pub with some emphasis on generously served food lunchtime and evening, running up to popular chargrilled steaks; winter log fire, choice of real ales, good parking *(John Pettit)*

Limpsfield [Staffhurst Wood, 2 miles S; S down High St, over A25 at lights, follow minor rd to sign at fork; TQ4148], *Royal Oak*: Under current licensees a pub-seeker's delight, a haven in the middle of nowhere; attractive cottage conversion, tastefully extended, in lovely setting; well kept Allied real ales, decent food (not Tues) *(R J Walden)*

☆ **Lingfield** [Haxted Rd; TQ3843], *Hare & Hounds*: Quiet and homely unspoilt country pub with friendly locals, landlord who does much of the cooking — imaginative, reasonably priced food such as cassoulet, curry, fish, rabbit; walkers (and followers of nearby clay-pigeon shooting) asked to leave their wellies in the porch *(Mrs Jensen, E G Parish)*

☆ **Little Bookham** [Little Bookham Street; TQ1254], *Windsor Castle*: Pleasant dining area in lounge bar of well extended Chef & Brewer family dining pub, good choice of hot and cold dishes inc ploughman's, sturdy roasts, and children's helpings, friendly staff, well kept Watneys-related real ales, tables in huge garden with terrace and popular children's play area *(D P Wilcox, Mr and Mrs*

S Cowherd, WFL)

Long Ditton [5 Portsmouth Rd; TQ1666], *City Arms*: Central bar with old coal-burning kitchen range, brocaded stools and banquettes, separate food area with coal-effect gas fire; warm welcome, comfortable atmosphere, well kept Watneys-related real ales, good range of bar food from sandwiches to steaks inc children's helpings *(Ian Phillips)*

Lower Bourne [SU8544], *Spotted Cow*: Attractive rural pub with Courage ales, good food and service, pleasant lunchtime clientele *(W A Gardiner)*

Martyrs Green [TQ0957], *Black Swan*: Pleasant pub handy for RHS Wisley Gardens, with fine range of real ales inc Badger Tanglefoot, Ringwood Old Thumper and Theakstons Old Peculier; bar food inc sandwiches — not cheap but very good, and served with salad — such as hot beef and prawns with seafood, restaurant, log fire *(Jenny and Brian Seller)*

☆ **Merstham** [Nutfield Rd; off A23 in Merstham, or follow Nutfield Ch, Merstham 2 signpost off A25 E of Redhill — OS Sheet 187 map reference 303514; TQ2953], *Inn on the Pond*: Lots of tables in engagingly furnished and decorated back family conservatory, concrete path past herbaceous border and squash court to sheltered back terrace; front area rambles around central fireplace, with settles, pews, shelves of old books, decent prints; half a dozen well kept real ales on handpump, good choice of hot and cold bar food with big crusty sandwiches, good vegetarian dishes, daily specials and Sun morning breakfast; rather pervasive piped radio; views over scrubland (and the small pond and nearby cricket ground) to the North Downs *(Jane Palmer, TOH, M Carrington, BB)*

Merstham [A23], *Jolliffe Arms*: Straightforward pub with well kept real ale and good ploughman's *(Jenny and Brian Seller)*

☆ **Mickleham** [Old London Rd; TQ1753], *Running Horses*: Warm welcome (for walkers too) in pleasant pub in attractive village nr Box Hill, with bar food inc good sandwiches and fish pie, friendly, helpful staff, useful covered yard with tables and chairs; well kept Allied real ales and Gales HSB *(Jenny and Brian Seller, Paul Sexton, Sue Harrison)*

Mogador [coming from M25 up A217, pass second roundabout then follow signpost off; TQ2452], *Sportsman*: Friendly country pub on edge of Banstead Heath, with lots of character, good beer, bar food inc excellent ploughman's; darts and bar billiards *(John Day)*

☆ **Oatlands** [Anderson Rd, just off main Walton—Weybridge rd; TQ0965], *Prince of Wales*: Most civilised, warm, pleasant and comfortable pub, with several well kept changing real ales, good service, good bar food (sandwiches, liver and bacon, hot-pot all recommended), popular restaurant, HQ for local rowing clubs, and gets very busy in evenings; Sun free bar nibbles *(Ian Phillips, R Houghton)*

Ockham [Cobham Lane; Martyrs Green/Effingham Junction crossrds;

TQ0756], *Black Swan*: Enlarged old pub with impressive range of high-priced beers, good pleasant service, bar food; very popular with young people in the evenings; garden *(WFL, Nick Dowson)*

☆ Ockley [Stane St (A29); TQ1439], *Cricketers Arms*: Flagstones, low oak beams and shinily varnished pine furniture in 15th-century stone village pub with good simple bar food, well kept real ales such as Badger Best, Fullers and King & Barnes, country wines, friendly staff, inglenook log fires, quiet piped music, darts area, small attractive dining room decorated with cricketing memorabilia; seats outside, roses around the door *(Paul Sexton, Sue Harrison, D J Penny, Stephen Goodchild, TOH, LYM)*

Ottershaw [Brox Rd; TQ0263], *Castle*: Pretty pub, warm and comfortable, with farm-tool decor, two roaring open fires and a lot of exposed brickwork; real ales inc several changing guest beers, bar food (not weekends), some seats outside *(Ian Phillips)*

☆ Oxted [towards Broadham Green; TQ3951], *Hay Cutter*: Recently enlarged and improved country pub, but still cosy, with good choice of bar food (on Sun limited to oysters, sausages, jellied eels — and free bar nibbles), well kept Allied real ales, friendly if not brisk service, skittle alley, picnic-table sets in garden; big car park, on Greensand Way *(Jenny and Brian Seller, W J Wonham)*

Oxted [High St, Old Oxted; TQ3951], *Crown*: Pleasant lunchtime atmosphere and friendly welcome in pine-panelled upstairs bar with cosy restaurant, attractive back garden, real ales such as Adnams and Pilgrim, wide choice of moderately priced well served food; nearby parking unlikely in this quaint narrow-street area, and in the evenings loud music, smoke and teenagers may predominate *(W J Wonham)*

Puttenham [just off A31 Farnham—Guildford; SU9347], *Jolly Farmer*: Clean and comfortable if somewhat anonymous Victorian/Laura Ashleyesque rooms, some concentration on Harvester restaurant but bar food too, inc a good choice of ploughman's; well kept Courage Best and Directors; picnic-table sets by car park; children welcome *(S A Mackenzie, Ian and Wendy McCaw, LYM — more reports please)*

Ranmore Common [towards Effingham Forest, past Dogkennel Green — OS Sheet 187 map reference 112501; TQ1451], *Ranmore Arms*: Deep in the country, with friendly licensees, wide range of well kept real ales, good bar food, huge log fire, no piped music, play area in big garden; children welcome *(WFL)*

Redhill [3 Redstone Hill; TQ2650], *Home Cottage*: Large but pleasantly updated and comfortable town pub with varying moods in different small areas, well kept real ales, good service, wide mix of customers *(Dr and Mrs A K Clarke, Ian M Baillie)*; [St Johns], *Plough*: Pleasing interior and exterior, interesting bric-a-brac, friendly service, at least two real ales, enticing food *(Ian M Baillie)*

☆ Ripley [High St; TQ0556], *Ship*: Skilfully extended 16th-century local with low beams, flagstones, cosy nooks, comfortable window seats and log fire in vast inglenook on left; warm welcome from young licensees, good atmosphere, well kept Courage Best and Directors and John Smiths on handpump, wide choice of reasonably priced bar food from sandwiches up, steps up to games area with pool and cribbage; interestingly converted courtyard garden *(E G Parish, Ian Phillips, Paul and Moira Entwistle)*

☆ Ripley [Newark Lane, Pyrford Rd], *Seven Stars*: Typical 1940s open-plan brick pub with lots of red leatherette stools and brocaded banquettes, piped music, darts and fruit machines discreetly tucked round a corner; worth knowing for big helpings of good value weekday bar food (evening choice more limited, and music maybe more prominent; good friendly service, spacious garden, nr River Wey *(Ian Phillips, R N Haygarth)*

Ripley [High St], *Half Moon*: Old and unpretentious, with bar food, good range of real ales, friendly staff *(D J Penny)*; [High St], *Talbot*: Old-world low-beamed inn with two adjoining bars — Nelson connections, some atmosphere, pleasant service, several well kept real ales inc King & Barnes; bedrooms *(John Evans)*

Row Town [off Addlestone—Ottershaw rd, sharp left past church up Ongar Hill — OS Sheet 176 map reference 036633; TQ0363], *Cricketers*: Unpretentious, creeper-covered building with a few picnic tables outside; comfortable rather than smart, with big woodburning stove, bar food inc impressive dishes of the day, Watneys-related real ales (not cheap) *(Ian Phillips)*

Rowledge [Cherry Tree Rd; SU8243], *Cherry Tree*: Attractive pub with big garden, handy for visits to Birdworld and Alice Holt Forest; bar food, Courage ales, restaurant area *(Norman Foot)*; [OS Sheet 186 map reference 822434], *Hare & Hounds*: Good beer, good food (inc good pizzas) and prize-winning garden *(Mr and Mrs Foreman)*

Runfold [A31 Farnham—Guildford; SU8747], *Princess Royal*: Good value lunchtime and evening bar food in generous helpings, from sandwiches and filled rolls upwards *(G M K Donkin)*

Salfords [TQ2846], *Dog & Duck*: Good village inn with wide choice of particularly well kept beers *(Comus Elliott)*

Sendmarsh [Marsh Rd; TQ0454], *Saddlers Arms*: Attractive, friendly and very clean little pub well off beaten track, low beams with lots of horse brasses; cheap standard food inc decent ploughman's, omelettes, Allied real ales, darts; popular, but service copes well *(Ian Phillips)*

Shackleford [Pepperharrow Lane; SU9345], *Cyder House*: Pine chairs, tables and settles, seven real ales such as Gales HSB, Hook Norton, Marstons Pedigree, Ringwood Old Thumper and Fortyniner, Wadworths 6X and Youngs, and two ciders; extensive menu inc children's dishes, maybe subdued piped music, picnic-table sets on back lawn; nice setting, pleasant quiet village *(Lyn and Bill Capper)*

Shamley Green [B2128 S of Guildford; TQ0343], *Red Lion*: Surroundings of some character include handsome settles and other country furniture, antique clocks and interesting pictures, with well kept real ales inc Ind Coope Burton tapped from casks behind the bar, though food can take time to come; lovely views over cricket green *(Jenny and Brian Seller, Sue Corrigan, LYM)*

☆ **Shepperton** [Russell Rd; TQ0867], *Red Lion*: Attractive if sometimes busy Thames-side pub dating back to 17th century, dripping with wisteria; plenty of tables on terrace among fine displays of shrubs and flowers, more on lawn over road with lovely river views and well run moorings; good reasonably priced bar food, restaurant, well kept Courage Best and Directors; licensees take a real pride in what they do; can be busy *(Michael Pritchard, Miss E Waller)*

☆ **Shepperton** [Shepperton Lock, Ferry Lane; turn left off B375 towards Chertsey, 100 yds from Square], *Thames Court*: Large and busy 1930s riverside pub with lots of quiet nooks and corners, panelled walls, roomy mezzanine and upper gallery looking out on to Thames and moorings; relaxed atmosphere, Bass and Flowers IPA, bar food inc Sun hot roast, pleasant service, big garden. Very pleasantly situated place with interesting atmosphere and fairly good food *(Mrs A Crowhurst)*

Shepperton [Church Sq], *Anchor*: Two refurbished bars with olde-worlde atmosphere, polite helpful staff, good food, well kept Eldridge Pope ales; seats in front (no garden), short walk to river; small car park; straightforward bedrooms *(Maureen Preston)*

Shere [Shere Lane; TQ0747], *Prince of Wales*: Quiet relaxed atmosphere in friendly pub with pleasant landlord, plenty of tables, well kept Youngs, nice garden *(Richard Houghton)*

Shortfield Common [SU8342], *Holly Bush*: Very pleasant village pub popular with locals (especially elderly ladies) for good lunch *(Mr and Mrs KJV)*

Smallfield [Plough Rd; TQ3143], *Plough*: Flower-decked pub with horse-brasses in attractive bar; so popular for good fish, particularly cod, that you have to be there early or book *(E G Parish)*

South Godstone [Tilburstow Hill Rd; TQ3648], *Fox & Hounds*: Much modernised, but atmosphere cosy and friendly, with well kept Allied real ales and generous helpings of reasonably priced bar food in relaxing low-beamed bar — old prints, some high-backed settles, simple pleasant garden *(W J Wonham)*

St Johns [Hermitage Rd; SU9857], *Capstans Wharf*: Pleasantly converted from old canalside buildings, and though it calls itself a wine bar can be thought of as a nice little pub with Charrington ales, bar snacks and restaurant *(Ian Phillips)*

☆ **Staines** [124 Church St], *Bells*: Attractive and pleasantly decorated local, comfortable and compact around central fireplace, welcoming atmosphere, well kept Courage Best and Directors, wide range of bar food from burgers and ploughman's up even on Sat; darts and cribbage *(Ian Phillips)*

☆ **Staines** [Moor Lane, The Hythe; south bank, over Staines Bridge; TQ0471], *Swan*: Pleasant Thames-side setting, with sycamore-shaded river terrace partly sheltered by upper balcony; both big bars have good river views; well kept Fullers real ales, usual bar food from sandwiches up (snacks only, evening), carefully restored open fireplaces, piped music, restaurant; busy with young people Fri and Sat evenings; children in eating area, open all day summer; bedrooms *(Mayur Shah, HRM, IP, Hazel R Morgan, Andrew Cooke, Cdr W S D Hendry, LYM)*

Staines [The Hythe; TQ0471], *Anne Boleyn*: Maybe loud music Sat evenings, but at quieter times worth a look as carefully restored 16th-century building, a former hunting lodge said to have been built by Henry VIII for Anne Boleyn; pleasant bar; bedrooms *(Cdr W S D Hendry)*; [Leacroft], *Old Red Lion*: Olde-worlde 17th-century pub overlooking green; warm welcome, well kept beer and wide choice of bar food *(Steve and Jane Mackey)*

☆ **Stoke d'Abernon** [Station Rd (off A245); TQ1259], *Plough*: Homely and comfortable pub with reasonably priced good sensible bar food in airy conservatory eating area; well kept Watneys-related real ales, capacious window seats, coal fire, helpful staff, sizeable garden; big car park *(John Pettit, Ian Phillips, BB)*

Sunbury [64 Thames St; TQ1068], *Magpie*: Lovely spot on Thames, with moorings and river terrace; friendly, with well kept beer, decent ploughman's and hot dishes, unsmart early 60s decor; restaurant and food counter at street level, bar and snug some 15ft lower; open all day; bedrooms *(Ian Phillips)*

☆ **Sutton** [B2126 — this is the Sutton near Abinger; TQ1046], *Volunteer*: Attractive quiet spot, with plenty of well spaced tables in good-sized garden (Tannoy food announcements); good value sandwiches, ploughman's and changing hot dishes, warm welcome, well kept Allied real ales; charmingly intimate low-beamed traditional bar, cosy on winter's evening, with military paintings in their right historical context *(Trevor and Helen Dayneswood, John Kimber)*

Tadworth [Box Hill Rd; TQ2256], *Hand in Hand*: Roomy red-brick Courage country pub handy for Box Hill — popular in summer; extended bar with iron scrollwork, brassware, original paintings, relaxed atmosphere, well kept beers, good simple bar food, Sun lunch, efficient friendly service, fruit machine; big garden sheltered by shrubs and trees, with well spaced tables *(John Pettit)*

☆ **Thames Ditton** [Queens Rd; TQ1567], *Albany*: Consistently pleasant atmosphere, well kept Bass on handpump, three real fires, wide range of good lunchtime bar food in big helpings, friendly staff; clean and spacious, but gets busy in summer, when the river terrace and lawn overlooking Hampton Court grounds are an attractive overflow; restaurant *(Jenny and Brian Seller, TOH, I S Wilson, P Gillbe)*

Thames Ditton [Weston Green], *Cricketers*: Clean and attractive, with warm welcome and homely, friendly atmosphere; wide choice of good value bar food, good service *(Mr and Mrs Dobson and friends)*

☆ **Thorpe** [Thorpe Green; TQ0268], *Rose & Crown*: Well kept pub on one of Surrey's largest village greens; Courage ales and good home-cooked bar food lunchtime and evening, with pleasantly busy atmosphere and good staff; covered in roses, and surrounded by gardens and lawns, with children's playground *(Clem Stephens, Mayur Shah, Richard Houghton)*

☆ **Tilford** [SU8743], *Barley Mow*: Beautiful spot by village cricket green, with riverside garden; consistently good pub with quarry-tiled floor, wall benches, scrubbed tables, open fire in big inglenook, curved bar counter, darts and table skittles; good food and service in small back eating area; well kept Courage ales *(Phil and Sally Gorton, Sue Corrigan, W A Gardiner)*

Tilford Common [SU8742], *Duke of Cambridge*: Very rural, with climbing frames and so forth in long garden, tables on high grassy terrace at one end — so you can keep an eye on the children *(P A Barfield)*

☆ **Walton on the Hill** [Chequers Lane; TQ2255], *Chequers*: Well laid out series of mock-Tudor rooms rambling around central servery, dark ochre walls, dark beams, copper-topped tables, tapestry banquettes, flowers and tropical fish; efficient good value lunchtime food bar, popular though not cheap restaurant, well kept Youngs real ale, friendly service, terrace and neat garden with summer barbecues; traditional jazz Thurs; children in restaurant *(Heather Sharland, Barbara M McHugh, Richard Houghton, LYM)*

Warlingham [Farleigh Rd; TQ3658], *Harrow*: Delightful rural setting, with high-raftered flint-walled barn bar, bar food and good-sized lawns; big car park *(M Desmond)*

☆ **West Clandon** [TQ0452], *Onslow Arms*: Rambling beamed country pub, pricey, often busy but well laid out, with comfortable seating in nooks and corners, open fire, soft lighting, thick carpets; wide choice of well kept real ales inc Brakspears, Courage Directors and Youngs, good straightforward bar food from small food bar, restaurant serving Sun lunches, efficient service, great well lit garden; children welcome *(WFL, John Evans, D J Penny, LYM)*

☆ **West Clandon** [Clandon St; TQ0452], *Bull*: Small country pub with comfortably modernised but cosy split-level bars, well kept beers, decent wine, big helpings of reliable reasonably priced lunchtime home cooking (Sun roasts if booked), friendly landlord; convenient for Clandon Park, good walking country *(John Pettit, Ian and Wendy McCaw)*

West Humble [just off A24 below Box Hill — OS Sheet 187 map reference 170517; TQ1651], *Stepping Stones*: Large pub with terrace and garden with summer barbecue and play area; circular bar inside, with real ale and huge pool table; has been praised for good bar food especially pizzas and help-yourself salads, but no recent reports *(News please)*

Westcott [Guildford Rd (A25); TQ1448], *Cricketers*: Friendly three-bar open-plan local, with almost the atmosphere of a club; half a dozen real ales, food, pool table in sunken area, pleasant staff *(P A Barfield)*

☆ **Weybridge** [Thames St; TQ0764], *Lincoln Arms*: Large oldish pub on river road, comfortably refurbished and extended, with

real ales, log-effect gas fires at either end, genuinely welcoming staff, good mix of customers, unobtrusive piped music; picnic-table sets on back lawn, other tables on little green in front *(Ian Phillips, Cdr W S D Hendry)*

Weybridge [Thames St], *Farnell Arms*: Consistently good bar food cooked by licensee and served by pleasant staff in Victorian pub with modestly priced Watneys-related real ales on handpump; big restaurant particularly good value; gets busy, especially towards end of week *(R B Crail)*; [Bridge Rd], *Queens Head*: Intimate beamed bar with open fire, lots of stripped brickwork, rugby football souvenirs, big separate restaurant and seats outside; has been praised for big helpings of good bar food, friendly atmosphere and well kept Watneys-related real ales, but no recent reports *(News please)*

☆ **Windlesham** [Church Rd; SU9264], *Half Moon*: Plain but popular (particularly with younger people) with active atmosphere, fast service, particularly good choice of ten or so real ales, interesting WWII pictures, straightforward lunchtime food (not Sun); big attractive garden overlooking nearby church and paddock *(Dr R Fuller, Richard Houghton, Dr M Owton)*

☆ **Windlesham** [Chertsey Rd], *Brickmakers Arms*: Small, friendly country pub currently doing particularly well, with Courage ales inc Directors, good separate restaurant, upstairs room with baby alarm; new garden behind with boules and summer barbecues *(Dr M Owton)*

Windlesham [School Rd], *Bee*: Small welcoming open-plan local, Courage Directors, bar food and big garden; has been open all day *(Dr M Owton)*

☆ **Witley** [Petworth Rd (A283); SU9439], *White Hart*: Largely Tudor, with good oak furniture, pewter tankards hanging from beams, inglenook fireplace where George Eliot drank; Watneys-related real ales, traditional games, unobtrusive piped music, straightforward bar food; children in restaurant and eating area, seats outside, playground; village church well worth a visit *(LYM)*

Woking [Arthurs Bridge Rd; TQ0159], *Bridge Barn*: Large canalside Beefeater with restaurant up in the roof beams of the barn and bars with flagstone floors downstairs; very welcoming and cheerful, good value all round; lots of waterside tables *(Liz and Ian Phillips)*; [Maybury], *Maybury*: Tudor-style 20s pub, recently refurbished and expanded, with warm friendly atmosphere, lots of shelves lined with antique bottles, bar food lunchtime and evening, seats outside; big car park *(Ian Phillips)*; [Chertsey Rd, nr rly stn], *Old Stillage*: Pleasant town-centre pub with heavy beams, separate pine-table dining area with decent simple food, well kept Greene King IPA, Marstons Pedigree, Wadworths 6X and Websters Yorkshire, loudish music *(Simon Collett-Jones)*

Wonersh [Blackheath; Sampleoak Lane from Percy Arms, Chilworth St, then left at crossroads; TQ0346], *Villagers*: Popular pub off beaten track with Watneys-related real ales on handpump, good choice of moderately priced bar food, pleasant young service; big car park *(R B Crail)*

☆ **Woodmansterne** [High St; TQ2760], *Woodman*: Homely and easy-going country pub with plenty of room for children to play in splendid garden; often packed inside, with good Bass, Charrington IPA and a guest beer on handpump, comfortable settees and armchairs of some character (if you can get one), decent lunchtime food *(Martin Aust)*

☆ **Worplesdon** [take Worplesdon Stn rd from Guildford—Woking rd; SU9753], *Jolly Farmer*: Fine range of about eight well kept real ales — at a price — inc rarities here, in simply furnished L-shaped beamed bar of isolated country pub, bar food (also far from cheap, especially in the evening), piped music, welcoming staff, big sheltered garden; children in restaurant *(M B Porter, Ian Phillips, LYM)*

Wotton [A25 Dorking—Guildford; TQ1247], *Wotton Hatch*: Busy little low-ceilinged front bar, handsome cocktail bar, traditional games and fruit machine in tiled-floor public bar, well kept Fullers real ales on handpump, bar food, restaurant; tables with play area outside; children allowed in restaurant *(D J Penny, PLJ, S Corrigan, LYM)*

☆ **Wrecclesham** [Sandrock Hill Rd; SU8245], *Sandrock*: Old house converted into open-plan bar with chatty atmosphere, friendly staff, good choice of real ales from the smaller breweries; bar billiards in games bar, garden; parking can be difficult *(R G Watts, David Fowles)*

Wrecclesham [Bat & Ball Lane; off Upper Bourne Lane — itself off Sandrock Hill Rd], *Bat & Ball*: Free house with well kept real ales, good bar food, restaurant with Sun lunch *(Stuart Cunnell)*; *Bear & Ragged Staff*: Quite friendly Courage house with long, low bar and exposed beams; reasonable bar food *(Dr John Innes)*

Sussex

A favourite area for fine pubs, this: newcomers to the Guide this year (or pubs right back on form, and back in these pages after a break) include the civilised George & Dragon at Burpham above Arundel, the unspoilt Royal Oak out in the country at Chilgrove, the very winning Griffin at Fletching (good food, a nice place to stay), the Jack Fullers, an engaging dining pub at Oxleys Green (nice garden and surroundings), the quaint old White Horse at Rogate, and the White Hart by the river Arun at Stopham (with a good fish restaurant). Other pubs on a current upswing here include the Rose Cottage at Alciston (its good food includes local game during winter), the Fountain at Ashurst (tasty food in the lovely 16th-century bar on the right), the Bell at Burwash (enterprising food including lots of fish, in warmly atmospheric surroundings; it wins a food award and a star award this year), the Fox Goes Free at Charlton (good home-made food including lots of fish, under its new licensee), the lively Six Bells at Chiddingly, the old-fashioned Bull at Ditchling (pleases people of widely varying tastes), the Olde White Horse at Easebourne (winning our food award this year), the fine old Three Horseshoes at Elsted (good food; it's been celebrating its 450th birthday this last year), the Gun at Gun Hill (good home cooking in interesting surroundings), the Juggs at Kingston Near Lewes (good food, in a nice pub), the Plough & Harrow at Litlington (up to a dozen guest beers in a week), the Halfway Bridge at Lodsworth (good food, very happily run), the friendly Noahs Ark at Lurgashall, the Rose & Crown in Mayfield (the new licensee is doing notably well at the hard task of keeping up its very high reputation, and changes he's made seem to be working out well), the welcoming Cock near Ringmer (decent fresh cooking), the canalside Sloop near Scaynes Hill (big helpings of good food), the busy and cheerful Golden Galleon near Seaford, the atmospheric and friendly Bull near Ticehurst (its food has been winning many new friends), the Horseguards at Tillington (new licensees have brought it up market; it wins a food award this year), the Richmond Arms at West Ashling (masses of changing real ales, wholesome food), the Cat at West Hoathly, and the New Inn in Winchelsea (a nice place to stay, good hearty food); though separate from its quaint old-fashioned pub side, the restaurant of the Dorset Arms at Withyham deserves a special mention for quality, too. This is quite an expensive county for pubs, with drinks costing 10p to 15p more than the national average, and food prices higher than average as well. So it's particularly worth looking out for the bargains. On the drinks side, our prices survey showed that pubs tied to relatively small local or regional brewers (Harveys and King & Barnes here) tended to work out noticeably cheaper than others. The Blackboys at Blackboys, tied to Harveys, and the Gribble at Oving (a free house selling beers from small breweries, including ones brewed to its own recipes) were the cheapest we found. On food, it's become virtually impossible to find a decent snack under £1 in Sussex: we found good really cheap *sandwiches only at the George & Dragon near Coolham. But we did find bargain main dishes under our £3 target at the Six Bells at Chiddingly (lots of them), Fountain at Ashurst, Anglesey Arms at Halnaker, Noahs Ark at Lurgashall and Three Cups near Punnetts Town. Pubs to watch among the Lucky Dip entries at the end of the chapter – ones that may well have the makings of main entries – include the Market Cross at Alfriston, George in Battle, Black Horse at Binstead, Royal Pavilion in Brighton, Cobden at Cocking, Swan at Fittleworth, Anchor at Hartfield, Sussex Brewery at Hermitage, Foresters at Kirdford, Hope in Newhaven, Star at Normans Bay, Kings Head at Rudgwick, White Hart at Selsfield, Red Lion in Shoreham, Hare & Hounds at Stoughton, Ram at West Firle and Three Crowns at Wisborough Green.*

ALCISTON   TQ5103 Map 3

Rose Cottage ⊘

Village signposted off A27 Polegate–Lewes

A good variety of piping hot, tasty bar food in this well run, cosy little cottage includes home-cooked wild rabbit and pigeon, as well as wholesome soup (£1.50), good ploughman's (£1.85; they also do soup and ploughman's together, £3.50), cold gammon and egg (£3), big salads (from £3, prawn with avocado £5), brie and asparagus quiche (£3.50), first-class home-made pies such as rabbit or steak and kidney (£3.50), lasagne (£3.95), curried nut loaf (£4.20), and steaks (from £7.25); in the evening there are extras like whitebait (£2.25), smoked salmon cornet (£3.75), scampi (£4.25) and half a roast duckling (£8). You can use the restaurant area for bar food at lunchtime. They sell local game and eggs. Well kept Harveys (sold as Beards here) and King & Barnes on handpump. The bar room has cushioned old church pews for the half-a-dozen tables, as well as black joists hung with harness, traps, a thatcher's blade and lots of other black ironware, and on the shelves above its dark panelled dado or in the etched glass windows, there's a model sailing ship, a stuffed kingfisher and other birds. The atmosphere stays relaxed and friendly even when it gets full, there are open fires, and a talking parrot (mornings only). A small low-beamed and parquet-floored area by the bar counter has a wall bench and little side bench; they hope to open a no-smoking room. Pleasant, efficient service; piped music. Outside by the tangle of wisteria are some seats under cover (the supports are from an old barn destroyed by the 1987 hurricane), and there's a small paddock with a goat, chickens, and ducks on a pond. Quite a few enamel signs are attached to the fence surrounding the car park. On Good Friday lunchtimes, there is longrope skipping outside the pub. *(Recommended by Mr and Mrs D W Fisher, Tony Gayfer, John Beeken, Miss P A Barfield, W J Wonham, Jane Palmer, S J A Velate, Geoff Wilson, D A Anderson)*

Free house   Licensee Ian Lewis   Real ale   Meals and snacks (till 10pm)   Small evening restaurant tel Alfriston (0323) 870377; not Sun   Children in eating area and restaurant   Open 11.30–2.30, 6.30–11

ALFRISTON   TQ5103 Map 3

Star ⇌

The wooden pillar in the centre of this ancient inn's elegant bar was once a sanctuary post, putting people who were fleeing from the law under the instant protection of the Church (it belonged to Battle Abbey). In 1516 someone rode a stolen horse here all the way from Lydd in Kent, to avoid prosecution (which could have brought the death penalty). The front of the building is decorated with fine brightly painted medieval carvings, and the striking red lion is known by local people as Old Bill – probably a figurehead salvaged from a 17th-century Dutch shipwreck. Inside, the bar has handsome furnishings that include a heavy oak Stuart refectory table with a big bowl of flowers, antique Windsor armchairs worn to a fine polish, a grandfather clock, a Tudor fireplace, and massive beams supporting the white-painted oak ceiling boards (and the lanterns used for lighting). Lunchtime food includes home-made soup (£1.25), sandwiches (from £1.75), ploughman's (from £2.50), a mixed meat salad (£3.95) and home-made dishes of the day such as chicken casserole or good steak and kidney pie (£3.95); puddings (from £1.35). Bass, John Smiths and Websters Yorkshire on handpump and English wines (drinks prices are very reasonable here, considering the style of the place). *(Recommended by Alec Lewery, WHBM; more reports please)*

Free house (THF)   Manager Michael Grange   Real ale   Meals and snacks Restaurant   Children welcome   Open 11–11   Bedrooms tel Alfriston (0323) 870495; £67B/£94B

ARUNDEL   TQ0107   Map 3

Swan 🏠

High Street

A good choice of well kept real ales on handpump in the L-shaped bar of this friendly inn might include Badger Best and Tanglefoot, Courage Directors, Marstons Pedigree, Theakstons Best and a guest bitter. Red plush button-back banquettes sit on the Turkey carpet, there are red velvet curtains, and the atmosphere is relaxed and informal. Good, reasonably priced bar food, using fresh local produce, includes home-made soup (£1.50), lots of sandwiches (from £1.10, home-cooked beef with horseradish £1.50, chicken, smoked bacon and mayonnaise £2.10, toasties 25p extra), filled baked potatoes (from £2.10), ploughman's (from £2.20), garlic mushrooms (£2.50), vegetarian curry, basket meals (from £2.45), bacon, sausages and eggs (£3.25), home-made burger (£3.55), salads with home-cooked meats and quiche (from £3.60), Barnsley chop with mint sauce (£5.45), and steaks (from £10.50); cappuccino or espresso coffee or a pot of tea (all 60p). Fruit machine, trivia and piped music. *(Recommended by Norman Foot, Sandra Kempson, R F Warner, P J Taylor, D J Devey, Klaus and Elizabeth Leist)*

Free house   Licensees Diana and Ken Rowsell   Real ale   Meals and snacks   Partly no-smoking restaurant   Children in eating area and in restaurant Jazz/rock/1950s/1960s/blues Sun evenings   Open 11–11   Bedrooms tel Arundel (0903) 882314; £42.50B/£55B

ASHURST   TQ1716   Map 3

Fountain

B2135 N of Steyning

On a board outside the entrance to this welcoming, partly sixteenth-century country inn is a list of the well kept beers: Batemans XXXB, Flowers Original, Fremlins, Whitbreads Castle Eden or Pompey Royal and a guest beer such as Wethereds SPA or Winter Royal, and Youngs Special on handpump or tapped straight from the cask. On the right as you go in, there's a charmingly unspoilt room with a couple of high-backed wooden cottage armchairs by the brick inglenook fireplace, a cushioned pew built right around two sides, two antique polished trestle tables, brasses on the black mantlebeam, scrubbed flagstones, and a friendly pub dog. Very good value home-made bar food includes soups like very good fresh tomato with a sprinkling of mint and cream (£1.10), ploughman's (£2.50), and various daily specials such as moussaka, lovely cheese and broccoli flan, home-made sausage curry, tasty steak and kidney pie and pizza (from £2.95), and puddings like delicious apricot crumble (£1.25); candle-lit suppers evenings (booking advisable); cheerful service. A bigger carpeted room (no dogs in this one) has spindleback chairs around its circular tables, a woodburning stove, L-shaped settles, corner cabinets, and darts, shove-ha'penny, dominoes, cribbage and fruit machine. There are two garden areas, one with fruit trees, roses, swings, a see-saw and a tiled-roof weekend barbecue counter, the other with picnic-table sets on gravel by an attractive duckpond. *(Recommended by Frank Cummins, Richard Houghton, TOH, Mayur Shah, I W and P J Muir, Norman Foot)*

Free house   Licensee Maurice Caine   Real ale   Meals and snacks (not Sun or Wed evenings)   Children in eating area lunchtime only   Open 11–2.30, 6–11; closed evenings of 25 and 26 Dec

nr BILLINGSHURST   TQ0925   Map 3
Blue Ship

The Haven; hamlet signposted off A29 just N of junction with A264, then follow signpost left towards Garlands and Okehurst

You can sit outside this remote and friendly country pub at the tree-shaded side tables or on benches in front by the tangle of honeysuckle round the door. Inside, there's an unspoilt front bar served from a hatch, a snug bar down a corridor at the back, and another room furnished with kitchen chairs and post-war Utility tables. Good home-made bar food includes sandwiches (from £1.15), ploughman's (from £2.25), cottage pie (£3.10), cod (£3.40), lasagne (£3.70), and steak and kidney pie or scampi (£4.10). Well kept King & Barnes Bitter tapped from the cask, and Old in winter. A games room has darts, bar billiards, shove-ha'penny, cribbage, dominoes and fruit machine. It can get crowded with young people at weekends. The pub has its own shoot. *(Recommended by Mr Cowell, Paul Smith, David and Sarah Gilmore, Sheralyn Coates, Kevin Ryan)*

King & Barnes   Licensee J R Davie   Real ale   Meals and snacks (not Sun or Mon evenings)   Children in dining area and games room   Open 11–3, 6–11

BLACKBOYS   TQ5220   Map 3
Blackboys

B2192, S edge of village

A lovely series of old-fashioned small rooms in this friendly and partly black-weatherboarded fourteenth-century building are full of interesting odds and ends such as a key collection hanging from the beams, some ancient bottles on a high shelf, Spy cricketer caricatures and other more antique prints, a stuffed red squirrel, a snug armchair by the inglenook fireplace, and so forth. Good waitress-served food includes sandwiches (from £1.40, prawn £2), soup (£1.50), ploughman's or steak sandwich (£2.75), mussels in garlic butter (£3.25), seafood pancakes (£4.95), summer crab salad (£5.95) or lobster salad (from £6.95), steaks (from £5.95), lots of puddings (from £1.80), unusual daily specials like mushrooms in port and Stilton (£1.95), beef with chorizo sausage and cinammon (£4.95) or Calabria chicken (£5.95), with winter game (often shot by the landlord) such as pheasant braised in Calvados and cider (£6.95). Well kept Harveys Armada, PA, BB and in winter XXXX on handpump; darts, shove-ha'penny, dominoes, table skittles, cribbage, fruit machine, space game, and juke box. Seats among flowers and shrubs in front of the pub overlook a pond, and altogether, there's about 16 acres. The back orchard has rustic tables among apple trees, and a children's play area with two wooden castles linked by a rope bridge, has quite a few animals; big well equipped playroom in the barn. *(Recommended by Caroline Wright, M Rising, Alan Skull, Jenny and Brian Seller, Philip and Sheila Hanley, Greg Parston, W P Ford, Mrs E M Thompson)*

Harveys   Licensee Patrick Russell   Real ale   Meals and snacks   Restaurant tel Framfield (0825) 890283   Children in restaurant   Open 11–11

BURPHAM   TQ0308   Map 3
George & Dragon

Warningcamp turn off A27 outside Arundel, then keep on up

Beautifully placed in a quiet hill village clustered prettily around its Norman church, with fine views over Arundel Castle and good walks nearby, this

18th-century pub is attractively decked out with window-boxes in summer. Inside, its open-plan lounge bar is spacious and comfortably furnished – and kept spotless. Besides sandwiches (from £1.60), bar food that's recently been particularly recommended includes specials such as carrot and peanut stroganoff (£4.95) or best end of neck of lamb done with honey and applemint (£5.90), lots of fresh fish such as halibut in dill butter, red snapper, salmon and Dover sole (from around £7), and home-made puddings such as banoffi pie, chocolate mousse with brandy and strawberry meringue (£1.90). Service by the new licensees and their team is friendly and efficient, with well kept Courage Directors, Harveys, Ruddles and guest real ales, decent coffee, and maybe gentle piped classical music. There are tables outside. (*Recommended by David and Karina Stanley, E G Parish, Neil and Elspeth Fearn, P Gillbe, Iain and Penny Muir, P A Barfield*)

Free house   Licensees George and Marianne Walker   Real ale   Meals and snacks (till 10; not Sun evening)   Restaurant tel Arundel (0903) 883131   Well behaved children in eating area and (over 6) restaurant   Open 11–3, 6–11

BURWASH   TQ6724   Map 3

Bell   ★   ⊘

A265 E of Heathfield

Under the current regime the atmosphere's a good deal pubbier than it's been for years – a happy change back to the true character of this mainly 17th-century village inn. The main room is very much a bar, L-shaped, with a big log fire (two if it's cold), lots of mainly rustic artefacts on its ochre Anaglypta ceiling and pink walls, and a mixture of seats – mainly well polished built-in pews and the odd small carved settle. While there's probably quite a gaggle of locals chatting around the bar in the evening, it's chiefly popular for food, especially fresh seafood: not cheap, but a decided cut above average. Whole grilled plaice (£5.60), good trout stuffed with celery and tomato or fresh salmon steaks (£5.80), good fresh dressed crab salad (£6.50), excellent tiger prawns served with strir-fried vegetables (£6.95), and Dover sole (£9.30); other dishes such as sandwiches, chicken tikka, which can make a starter for two or a light main course, (£3.80), beef curry (£4.95), breast of chicken with avocado and stilton (£5.25), fillet of lamb (£6.50), and fillet of beef Wellington (£9.50). The room on the left is broadly similar, but quieter, with collections of cigarette cards and so forth as well as the country implements. Service is quietly friendly and efficient, Harveys, and changing guests like Badger Tanglefoot, Larkins, and Palmers Tally Ho on handpump are well kept, house wines respectable, the choice of malt whiskies fair, and besides darts, shove-ha'penny, table skittles, ring-the-bull and toad-in-the-hole they have an entertaining Victorian slot-machine where a night watchman gets a few surprises when you put in 10p; mulled wine and beer in winter; piped music. The pub, covered with flowers in summer, has seats in front looking over the road to the church, and beyond. The village is very pretty, and near Batemans (Kipling's home); *Good Walks Guide* Walk 67 starts close by. Nearby parking may be difficult. The bedrooms (oak beams, sloping floors) can be recommended, but the bathroom is shared. (*Recommended by J P Cinnamond, D J Milner, Lisa Freedman, Peter and Mona Lynch, H H Richards*)

Beards (who no longer brew)   Licensees Mr and Mrs David Mizel   Real ale   Meals and snacks (not Sun evening)   Restaurant   Children in eating area of bar   Small folk evening last Sun of month   Open 11–2.30 (3 Sat), 6–11   Bedrooms tel Burwash (0435) 882304; £20/£30

BYWORTH   SU9820   Map 2

Black Horse

Signposted from A283

Simple furnishings in this ancient pub include stripped pews, scrubbed tables, bare floorboards, and candles in bottles, and decoration is confined to a collection of old sepia photographs in the back part. In contrast with the simplicity of the decor, there's an elaborate choice of bar food: French onion soup (£2.20), ploughman's (from £2.95), shepherd's pie (£3.50), salads (from £3.65), prawns and courgette au gratin or scallops in garlic (£3.90), lambs kidneys in sherry or beef curry (£5.50), sweet and sour chicken (£5.90), vegetarian dishes, monkfish in cream of mustard sauce (£6.70), and steaks (from £8.99); cheesecake or treacle tart (from £2.30). Well kept Ballards Wassail and Youngs Bitter and Special on handpump; darts. The garden is particularly attractive, dropping steeply down through a series of grassy terraces, each screened by banks of flowering shrubs (but still with a view across the valley to swelling woodland); a bigger lawn at the bottom is set beside a small stream and an old willow. *(Recommended by Peter Woods, John and Heather Dwane, Alec Lewery, Marie Enright, Ian and Wendy McCaw, Hope Chenhalls, T Galligan, Mrs Lili Lomas, G S B G Dudley, Mr and Mrs J H Adam, Stephen Goodchild, Miles Kington, WTF)*

Free house   Licensees Mr and Mrs P Hess   Real ale   Meals and snacks (12–1.45, 7–9.45)   Restaurant tel Petworth (0798) 42424   Children in restaurant if well behaved   Open 11–2.30, 6–11; 11.30–2.30, 6.30–11 in winter

CHARLTON   SU8812 Map 2
Fox Goes Free

Village signposted off A286 Chichester–Midhurst in Singleton, also from Chichester–Petworth via East Dean

Surrounded by wonderful walking country in the heart of Sussex, this very popular and well run 16th-century pub has a relaxed and friendly atmosphere in its several cosy rooms. The main bar has blond wood tables and mate's chairs on the partly carpeted brick floor, elm benches built against its yellowing walls, a small but entertaining hat collection, and a big brick fireplace; a nice little low-beamed snug has a sturdy elm settle and a big inglenook fireplace. The rustic-style extension gives extra eating space for bar lunches, and becomes an evening restaurant. The new licensee has introduced more home-made dishes and quite a lot of fish: soup (£1.75), good sandwiches (from £1.50), filled baked potatoes (from £2.50), various ploughman's (from £3.50), home-made pies like chicken, ham and sweetcorn (£4.25) or steak and mushroom (£4.50), home-made curries or steak sandwich (£4.75), and specials like plaice in white wine (£5.25), fresh crab (£6.50), fresh salmon (around £6.50), and half lobster (£8.50); puddings such as spotted dick or tasty apple pie (£1.80), and children's dishes (£1.95). Well kept if pricey Ballards Wassail, Flowers Original, King & Barnes Bitter, Mild and Festive, Ringwood Old Thumper, and various guest beers on handpump, decent house wines, and a good range of country wines; piped music, fruit machine; they also have darts, dominoes, cribbage and shut-the-box. Tables among fruit trees in the back garden looking up to the downs have a summer soft-drinks servery and safe children's play area with sandpit and swings; the barbecue area can be booked. Handy for the Weald and Downland Open Air Museum. The name comes from the legend that Sussex foxes by working in packs completely bewilder the Charlton Hunt which has been meeting here for 300 years. *(Recommended by Jim and Becky Bryson, Dr M Owton, Jacqueline Davis, Dr B A Perkins, Mrs Lili Lomas, Mr Cowell, T Galligan, Dr A M Rankin, E G Parish, Margaret and Roy Randle, Viv Middlebrook, Norman Foot, Brian and Anna Marsden)*

Free house   Licensee Mark Townley   Real ale   Meals and snacks (12–2, 6–10 Mon–Sat, 12–2, 7–9 Sun)   Restaurant tel (024 363) 461   Children in eating area of bar   Occasional live music around Bank Hols   Open 11–2.30, 6–11

CHIDDINGLY   TQ5414 Map 3
Six Bells ★

If you're after a quiet drink, it might be best to visit this warmly welcoming, old-fashioned pub during the week. Under the low beams, the simple but attractive furnishings include an antique box settle, tall Windsor armchairs, pews, scrubbed or polished tables, some panelling, old engravings, lots of prints and stuffed animals, and a good winter fire. In the back bar there's a pianola with many rolls which can be played with the landlord's permission, and an ancient TV set; a barn-like room has bare floorboards and lots of old tools and machinery in a loft – this is where the live music is held at weekends. Consistently good, very good value home-made food includes French onion soup (a bargain at 60p), tasty cheesy garlic bread (£1.15), landlord's special (£1.25), beef and vegetable or shepherd's pies (£1.60), steak and kidney pie or vegetarian or meaty lasagne (£1.70), huge salads (from £1.70), chilli con carne or spare ribs in barbecue sauce (£2.95), spicy prawns (£3.10), fresh dressed crab salad or garlic prawns (£3.25), with generous banana splits, treacle pie and other puddings (£1.30). Well kept Courage Best and Directors on handpump, with Harveys tapped from the cask (winter only). Darts, dominoes, cribbage. There's a fine collection of enamelled advertising signs in the gents'. Outside at the back, there are some tables beyond a goldfish pond. It's certainly popular with bikers at weekends, but we must stress that Porsche drivers – and even you and me – seem equally at home here. *(Recommended by Simon Velate, Jenny and Brian Seller, Win and Reg Harrington, Lindsey Shaw Radley, Yvonne Woodfield)*

Free house   Licensee Paul Newman   Real ale   Meals and snacks (not Mon)   Small children's room and more room in music bar   Live bands Fri, Sat and Sun evenings, jazz Sun lunchtime   Open 10–2.30, 6–11; closed Mon except Bank Holidays

CHILGROVE   SU8214   Map 2
Royal Oak

Hooksway, which is signposted off B2141 Petersfield–Chichester; OS Sheet 197 map reference 814163

This unspoilt and friendly white cottage tucked away under the downs is actually in Hooksway rather than Chilgrove itself, but Hooksway is not shown on many road maps. The two very simply furnished rooms have sturdy leatherette wall benches, plain deal tables, a brick floor in the lower room, some carpet in the upper one, low faded yellow ceilings and two winter log fires; the new licensee has added a restaurant extension. Well kept Gales HSB, Gibbs Mew Bishops Tipple, Ruddles Best and County, and Websters Yorkshire on handpump. Reasonably priced bar food includes winter soup (£1.20), ploughman's (£2.80), vegetarian tagliatelle (£3.65), steak and kidney pie (£3.95) or venison pie (£4.25), and puddings such as apple pie or banoffi pie (£1.80). Sensibly placed darts, shove-ha'penny, and piped music. There are rustic seats on a small and sunny front terrace, and on grass, and some play equipment for children. *(Recommended by Philip and Trisha Ferris, J E Newman, Mrs Lili Lomas, Alan Skull, Brian Cheshire, Brian and Anna Marsden)*

Free house   Licensee John Lyon   Real ale   Meals and snacks   Restaurant tel East Marden (024359) 257   Children in side room   Open 11–2.30, 6–11; closed Mon Oct–March

nr COOLHAM   TQ1423   Map 3
George & Dragon

Dragons Green; pub signposted off A272 between Coolham and A24

In summer, the big lawn which stretches away behind this old tile-hung cottage is lovely, with lots of rustic tables and chairs well spaced among fruit trees, shrubs and flowers, and a 30-foot play caravan for children. Inside, the bar is small and snug with heavily timbered walls, a partly woodblock, and partly polished tiled and carpeted floor, unusually low and massive black beams (see if you can decide whether the date cut into one is 1677 or 1577), simple chairs and rustic stools, some brass, and a big inglenook fireplace with an early 17th-century grate. The new licensee has kept the bar food prices much as they were last year: sandwiches (from 80p), ploughman's (from £2), salads (from £3), ham and egg (£3.80), home-made steak and kidney pie (£4.20), and cold topside of beef with pickles (£4.25); well kept King & Barnes Sussex, Broadwood and Festive on handpump, with Old Ale in winter. Darts, bar billiards, cribbage, dominoes, fruit machine, and piped music. *(Recommended by Mr and Mrs R P Begg, Hazel Morgan, Gwen and Peter Andrews, Norman Foot; more reports please)*

King & Barnes   Licensee Paul Ross   Real ale   Meals and snacks   Children in eating area of bar   Open 11–3, 6–11

COWBEECH   TQ6114 Map 3

Merrie Harriers

Village signposted from A271

Popular bar food in this busy ex-farmhouse is served on pretty matching china by friendly and efficient waitresses: at lunchtime, sandwiches (from £1.50), home-made soup (£1.60), filled cottage rolls (from £2), ploughman's (from £2.75), vegetarian quiche (£3.95), salads (from £4.50), steak and kidney pie (£4.95), and grilled lemon sole (£7.25), with evening dishes such as salmon mousse or pâté (£2.75), fresh rainbow trout (starter £2.95, main course £5.50), mixed grill (£7), steaks (from 12oz rump £7.95), and puddings like summer pudding or apple pie (£1.50); good, crispy vegetables. This year, they added a Victorian-style dining conservatory (bookings 0323–833108). Flowers Original, Harveys and a guest such as Whitbreads Pompey Royal on handpump; biscuits to nibble on the counter on Sunday morning. The panelled public bar has beams, pewter tankards hanging by the bar counter, a curved high-backed settle by the brick inglenook fireplace, pot plants in the window, and several friendly cats. The communicating lounge has spindle-back chairs around the tables on its flowery carpet. Darts, shove-ha'penny, dominoes, cribbage. Outside the pub is a flower garden and a lawn with a swing and rustic seats. *(Recommended by Colin Laffan, Geoff and Julie Bond, C T and J M Laffan, Dr B A W Perkins, Nancy and Grant Buck)*

Free house   Licensees G M and B J Richards   Real ale   Meals and snacks (not Sun evening)   Open 11–2.30, 6.30–11

nr DALLINGTON   TQ6619 Map 3

Swan 🛏

Wood's Corner; B2096, E of Dallington

This friendly place got its name in 1356 from the heraldic swan on the arms of the French King, captured at the battle of Poitiers by a party which included the local lord of the manor. The main bar has brocaded stools and built-in wooden benches, sturdy wooden tables with little bunches of flowers, well polished horsebrasses on the few beams and timbers in the cream walls, some hanging copper saucepans, and a log fire; the back dining bar is simply furnished but has a marvellous view from its big picture windows. The menu changes day by day, serving mostly home-made dishes: sandwiches, vegetarian dishes (£3.95), prawn au gratin (£4.70), beef stew with dumplings (£4.75), chicken, ham and mushroom pie (£4.80), gammon and onion pudding (£5.95), and puddings like treacle tart or blackberry and apple crumble (£1.50); good breakfasts. On Sundays little dishes of nuts, crisps and Cheddar cheese are put out on the bar counter. Well kept Harveys, King & Barnes Festive and Marstons Pedigree on handpump; decent house wines. Bar billiards, shove-ha'penny, chess, trivia, and unobtrusive piped music. From the picnic-table sets in the neatly kept back flower garden you can see right across the soft country below this ridge to Beachy Head, and from the bedrooms, the night view of the tiny distant lights of Eastbourne is stunning. Good woodland walks nearby, especially in Dallington Forest. *(Recommended by Colin Laffan, K Smurthwaite, K Soutter, David Fowles, David Gaunt, Chris Dyer-Smith, A C Earl, S J A Velate, J M Shaw)*

Free house   Licensees John and Marie Blake   Real ale   Meals and snacks   No-smoking restaurant   Children in bar lobby area and restaurant   Occasional folk nights   Open 11.30–3, 6.30–11   Two bedrooms tel Brightling (042 482) 242; £15/£30

DITCHLING   TQ3215 Map 3

Bull 🛏

2 High St; B2112, junction with B2116

Popular with all ages, this ancient and atmospheric pub is said to get its name from the Papal Bull designating it as a safe house for pilgrims and travellers to the great monastery at Lewes. The heavily beamed main bar is attractively furnished with polished oak chests and settles, handsome elm and mahogany tables, one sturdy central refectory table, dark oak floorboards, a longcase clock, and gundog prints and photographs over the wooden dado. A separate Turkey-carpeted corner bar has simpler, neater furnishings (no dogs allowed there); no less than three inglenook log fireplaces. Good homely bar food, changing day by day, includes fish collected by the landlord direct from the trawlermen along the south coast, and local lamb and beef: sandwiches (from £1), home-made winter soups, cauliflower cheese (£3.50), pies (from £4.10, the turkey or venison and rabbit ones are recommended), half-shoulder of lamb roasted with rosemary, well hung steaks (from £7.95), local game, and a good deal of fresh local fish from cod and mackerel to crab and lobster, and smoked fish from the local smokehouse (from £4.25); huge breakfasts. Well kept Flowers Original, Marstons Pedigree, Whitbreads Best and Pompey Royal on handpump, quite a few wines and malt whiskies, and vintage ports from the handsome linenfold panelling bar counter, and a relaxed atmosphere (no games or piped music). More work has been carried out on the spacious garden and back suntrap terrace where there are picnic-table sets, and the flowering tubs and shrubs are very pretty; from here you can see the South Downs Way and Ditchling Beacon, and the busy but charming old village is a good base for walking; a stroll past the duckpond behind the church takes you up a little hill with a fine view of the South Downs, and the Jack and Jill windmills above Clayton. (*Recommended by Paul Evans, David and Fiona Easeman, Patrick Godfrey, John Knighton*)

Whitbreads   Licensees Ronald and Mary Bryant   Real ale   Meals and snacks (not Sun evening – except for residents)   Restaurant   Children in eating area and restaurant   Open 10.30 (11 Sat)–2.30, 6–11   Three bedrooms tel Hassocks (079 18) 3147; £28.50B/£38.50B

EASEBOURNE   SU8922 Map 2

Olde White Horse ⊗

A272, just N of Midhurst

There's said to be the remains of a tunnel from smuggling days, connecting this neatly kept stone pub to the church. The snug and attractive little modernised lounge has Leech and other sporting prints on its white-painted partly panelled walls, a small log fire, and a friendly atmosphere. The bigger public bar, with wall settles on its woodstrip floor, has darts, dominoes, and cribbage; juke box in the tap room. One seat is the preserve of Guy the cat, even on those busy days when a shooting or polo party's in. Good value food, that changes daily, includes sandwiches (lunchtime only, except Sunday), popular soufflé omelettes using free range local eggs, game pie (using local produce, Fridays) or particularly good steak and kidney with oyster pie, or rich beef curry (all £4.25), fresh fish (Fridays, and on Tuesdays in summer; from £3.95), and excellent puddings such as apple tart with quince, honey, cinnamon and ginger, served with home-made pear sorbet (£1.65); they have regular three-course specials such as celery and stilton sauce with walnuts, leg of lamb stuffed with lightly spiced fresh crab meat, and flummery – whipped cream, honey, lemon and Glayva (£8.95; this menu won them a trade competition). As most food is cooked to order, there may be delays at busy times. Well kept Friary Meux on handpump, a few malt whiskies, and around 40 wines by the bottle. There are tables out in a small courtyard, with more on the sheltered and well tended back lawn. (*Recommended by Mrs W Lait, Mrs J A Blanks, Ian and Wendy McCaw, Mr and Mrs Bob Gollner, James Moller*)

Friary Meux (Allied)   Licensees Alan and Christine Hollidge   Real ale   Meals and snacks *Evening restaurant tel Midhurst (073 081) 3521 (they do Sun lunch) Children over 5 in restaurant Open 11–2.30, 6–11; closed evening 25 Dec*

EASTDEAN TV5597 Map 3

Tiger

Pub (with village centre) signposted – not vividly – from A259 Eastbourne–Seaford

The delightful cottage-lined green makes a perfect setting for this long low white tiled pub with its window-boxes, clematis and roses, big bright painting of a tiger on a branch, and rustic seats and tables on the brick front terrace. Inside, two low-beamed, ochre-walled rooms have low rustic tables, padded seats, housekeeper's chairs, and (in the inner room) antique oak settles – one with a big bowed back and another attractively carved; decorations include photographs of the pub (often with a hunt meeting on the green), Victorian engravings, horsebrasses, pewter measures and china mugs hanging from beams, a big kitchen clock facing the bar, some handbells over the counter, and a stuffed tiger's head. Bar food includes toasted sandwiches in winter (from £1.40), various ploughman's (from £2.20), sausages (£2.50), salads, steak and kidney pie, macaroni cheese or excellent scampi, gammon with pineapple (£5), 8oz sirloin steak (£6), and puddings like jam roly poly. Well kept Courage Best and Directors, and Harveys on handpump; good choice of wines by the glass and hot toddies; fruit machine and piped music. The pub is popular with walkers and is on the *Good Walks Guide* Walk 60; it does get very crowded at peak times, especially in summer. *(Recommended by Norman Foot, John and Joan Nash, P A Barfield, Mr and Mrs S Cowherd, David and Ruth Shillitoe, TBB, S J A Velate, Margaret Dyke)*

Courage Licensee James Conroy Real ale Meals and snacks (12–2, 6–8.30; not Sun evening) Children in dining area Open 10–2.30, 6–11

ELSTED SU8119 Map 2

Three Horseshoes ★

Village signposted from B2141 Chichester–Petersfield; also reached easily from A272 about 2 miles W of Midhurst, turning left heading W

In 1990, this pretty tiled house was 450 years old and they celebrated with a pig roast, Morrismen, a marching band, and a marquee in the garden. The four cosy connecting rooms have simple latch and plank doors, rugs on 16th-century bricks, on tiles or on bare boards, low beams, oak benches, antique high-backed settles, studded leather seats, and good tables (candlelit at night); the deep ochre walls are hung with attractive engravings and old photographs, there are log fires, newspapers on racks and two friendly cream retrievers. Changing food might include soup in winter (£1.50), deep-fried camembert (£2.75), ploughman's with a good choice of cheeses (from £2.75), baked potatoes with interesting fillings (from £3.50), Lancashire hotpot (£3.75), rabbit pie in cider (£4.50), dressed crab from Selsey or steak and kidney pie in Guinness (£4.75), whole plaice or chicken tandoori (£5.25), Mediterranean prawns in garlic butter (£6.50), and peppered steak (£6.75); high-chairs for children and half-helpings. Summer buffet and barbecue on Saturday, Sunday and Bank Holidays. The pretty little rustic dining room with candles in brass holders on its plain wooden tables serves the same food as the bar, though on Friday and Saturday evenings from October–March there's a set menu. Well kept changing ales tapped from the cask might include Adnams, Ballards Best and Wassail, Badger, Batemans, Buckleys, Gales HSB, Gibbs Mew Bishops Tipple and Wiltshire, Harveys, Ringwood Old Thumper, Tetleys, and Wadworths 6X; Churchward's farm cider, Gales country wines, summer Pimms, various liqueur coffees, and several wines; dominoes, cribbage, trivia, shut-the-box, and summer boules. They sell local eggs. The biggish garden has picnic-table sets, a good herbaceous border, rose beds and a pets' corner with a lamb, goat, pigs and ornamental fowl. *(Recommended by John and Chris Simpson, Mrs L Davey, Jacqueline Davis, Mrs Lili Lomas, Mrs V Middlebrook, Bev and Doug Warrick, Roy McIsaac, S L Hughes, K Leist, Paul and Margaret Baker, Norman Foot, Bernard Smalley,*

M Rising, Harriet and Michael Robinson, Brian and Anna Marsden, W A Gardiner, John Evans, A J Skull)

Free house Licensees Ann and Tony Burdfield Real ale Meals and snacks (12–2, 6.30–10) Restaurant tel Harting (0730) 825746 Children in eating area and restaurant Open 10–3, 6–11; 11–11 summer weekends

FLETCHING TQ4223 Map 3

Griffin 🏆 🛏

Village signposted off A272 W of Uckfield

Out in the garden before breakfast, writing, one reader was without asking brought a tray of tea by the cook; typical of the thoughtful, civilised and yet friendly service in this attractive small inn, in a pretty village on the edge of Sheffield Park. Everything seems just right. Despite its four centuries and handsomely moulded oak beams, the bar itself hasn't been given the olde-worlde treatment: just studded black leather dining chairs and other straightforward furniture, squared oak panelling with a little china on its Delft shelf, a big corner fireplace, and the small bare-boarded serving area off to one side – with well kept Harveys BB, King & Barnes, Badger Tanglefoot, Wadworths 6X and a guest beer such as Greene King IPA or Morlands Old Masters on handpump, and good wines. Bar food has a regular core of ploughman's and filled baguettes (from £2.75), several quiches such as stilton and walnut or crab and tomato (£4.25), salads (from £4.25) and chargrilled steaks (from £6.95). It's given distinction by the care and inventiveness (not to mention the fresh ingredients, often local) which go into the eight or so flavoursome specials, changing daily. In the weeks leading up to this edition going to press, these included soups such as watercress, tomato and cucumber, and chilled cucumber and mint (£1.95); fish dishes such as grilled fresh sardines (£3.25), seafood lasagne (£4.50), fishcakes with lemon mayonnaise (£4.50), and poached salmon (£5.95) or seatrout (£6.25); pasta such as cappilletti bolognese or linguine with ham and mushroom sauce (£4.50); meat dishes such as a pretty chicken and vegetable terrine in tomato coulis or crispy chicken pieces in soy sauce (£2.95), grilled guineafowl drumsticks in peach sauce (£4.50), pork and pepper kebabs or chicken tikka (£4.95); and puddings such as Eton mess or queen of puddings (£2.50). The restaurant is rewarding, too, and theme nights (Edwardian dress for the Queen Mother's 90th birthday, say) have been enjoyed. A separate public bar has darts, pool, fruit machine, space game and juke box. Picnic-table sets under cocktail parasols on the back grass have lovely rolling Sussex views; there are more tables on a sheltered gravel terrace, used for dining on warm evenings. Three of the four pretty bedrooms have four-posters. *(Recommended by Miles Kington, Heather Sharland, TOH)*

Free house Licensees Nigel and Bridget Pullan Real ale Meals and snacks Restaurant Children in eating area Piano Fri, Sat Open 11.30–2.30(3 Sat), 6(5.30 Sat)–11; afternoon opening by arrangement

FULKING TQ2411 Map 3

Shepherd & Dog

From A281 Brighton–Henfield on N slope of downs turn off at Poynings signpost and continue past Poynings

A path from the South Downs Way leads into the upper tree-sheltered play lawn at the back of this slate-hung cottage; there's a series of prettily planted grassy terraces, some fairy-lit, and a stream running through washes into a big stone trough. Inside, the partly-panelled walls of the low-ceilinged bar are decorated with shepherds' crooks, harness, stuffed squirrels, mounted butterflies, and blue-and-white plates. A big log fireplace in one stripped wall is hung with copper and brass, and furnishings include an antique cushioned oak settle, stout pegged rustic seats around little gateleg oak tables, and attractive bow-window seats. There's usually a long queue at the food servery unless you get there early: sandwiches (not Sunday, from £1.50, locally smoked salmon £3.95), various ploughman's (from £2.75), and salads (from £4.50), with evening dishes like beef and Guinness pie (£5.45), half Sussex duck (£5.95), and sirloin steak (£6.50). Harveys Festive, Ruddles Best and County, and Websters Yorkshire on handpump; pleasant staff; darts. There are new inside lavatories. Parking is difficult when the pub is busy. *(Recommended by Dr T W Hoskins, Frank Cummins, Frank Gadbois, M C Howells, Gwen and Peter Andrews, Alan Skull, Father Robert Davies, Paul Evans, W J Wonham, Keith Walton, John and Heather Dwane)*

Phoenix (Watneys)   Licensees A Bradley-Hole and S A Ball   Real ale   Meals and snacks (limited Sun evening)   Open 11–2.30 (3 Sat), 6–11

GUN HILL   TQ5614   Map 3

Gun

From A22 NW of Hailsham (after junction with A269) turn N at Happy Eater

Outside this pretty tiled and timbered house – covered with clematis, honeysuckle, hanging baskets and heavy flower tubs – there are tables in the spacious garden, which has swings, fairy-lit trees and flower borders. Brasses and pewter measures hang from the beams, an inglenook fireplace is decorated with brass and copper (other winter fires, too), there are small pictures on the cream walls, and latticed windows with flowery curtains (red ones mark the openings between different rambling room areas). It's mostly carpeted, though there are some 15th-century flooring bricks and tiles; one area, furnished more as a dining room, has attractive panelling. Some of the bar food is still cooked on an ancient Aga in the corner of the bar, and might include soup, lamb and apricot pie (£4), turkey, ham and leek pie (£4.20), smoked haddock pasta (£4.40), fillet steak Wellington (£6.50), and lots of rich puddings; best to get there early. Well kept Charrington IPA and Larkins Sovereign on handpump, a good choice of wines by the glass, and country wines; friendly service, with a good mix of age-groups among the customers. *(Recommended by M A and C R Starling, Simon Velate, Colin Laffan, G Carter)*

Free house   Licensee R J Brockway   Real ale   Meals and snacks (12–2, 6–10)   Children in eating area of bar   Open 11–3, 6–11; closed 25 and 26 Dec   Bedrooms tel Chiddingly (0825) 872361; I£25(£30B)

HALNAKER   SU9008   Map 2

Anglesey Arms

A285 Chichester–Petworth

The right-hand bar of this well run roadside pub has flagstones, stripped deal settles and wall seats around candlelit stripped deal tables, and modern paintings on the cream walls; at the back, there's a rather more dining-roomish carpeted area. Generously served food includes sandwiches (from £1.45), omelettes (from £1.50), toasties (from £1.55), ploughman's (£2.50), salads (from £3.45), fry-up (£3.70), lamb chops (£4.25), steaks (from £5.45), and Mediterranean prawns (£5.95), with blackboard specials like home-made crab pâté (£2.15), home-made broccoli and cheese quiche (£3.95), fresh dressed crab (£4.45) and lobster (from £6.75) when available, and home-made puddings such as apple pie or treacle tart with custard (£1.95); vegetables are extra and service is not included. Sunday roast lunch. Well kept Friary Meux and Ind Coope Burton on handpump, and quite a few wines, especially from Northern Spain. Shove-ha'penny, dominoes, cribbage, fruit machine, yatzee, draughts, backgammon, chess and shut-the-box. There are picnic-table sets on the side grass, and white metal and plastic seats and tables by a fig tree in a sheltered back beer garden. The Weald and Downland Open Air Museum is nearby, and Goodwood is only half-a-mile away. *(Recommended by J H L Davis, Neil and Elspeth Fearn; more reports please)*

Friary Meux (Allied)   Licensees C J and T M Houseman   Real ale   Meals and snacks   Restaurant tel Chichester (0243) 773474   Children in restaurant   Open 11–3, 6–11; closed evenings 24 Dec and 31 Dec, and all day 25 Dec

nr HEATHFIELD   TQ5920   Map 3

Star

Old Heathfield; from B2096 coming from Heathfield, turn right at signpost to
Heathfield Church, Vines Cross and Horam, then right at T-junction and follow lane
round church to the left

Lots of action in the award-winning garden of this beautifully placed ancient pub
includes a changing population of livestock that on our most recent inspection
included a tawny owl as well as a couple of peacocks, various lesser birds, and
some rabbits; at peak times there's a children's drinks kiosk by the hedged-off play
area. There are peaceful views over the oak-lined sheep pastures that roll down
from this ridge in the Weald. Inside, the L-shaped bar has close-set sturdy rustic
furniture on its dark brown patterned carpet, window seats, a couple of tables in
the huge inglenook fireplace, fine heavy black oak beams, and some panelling: get
there early if you want a table. Bar food includes soup (£1.60), ploughman's
(lunchtimes, £2.95), omelettes (lunchtimes, £3.50), home-cooked ham and eggs
(£3.95), salad platters (from £4.95), steak and kidney pie (£4.95), sirloin steak
(£7.95) and daily specials; puddings such as apple pie or banoffi pudding (£2.25);
there is waitress service to the garden. Sunday roast lunch (£5.95). Well kept Gales
HSB, Ruddles Best, and Websters Yorkshire on handpump, and good value wines;
shove-ha'penny, dominoes and maybe unobtrusive piped music, mainly classical.
Parking is often such a struggle that it's best to stop on the far side of the church
and walk through the churchyard. No dogs, though the pub has its own.
*(Recommended by M C Howells, Prof A N Black, Jean and Theodore Rowland-Entwistle,
S J A Velate)*

*Phoenix (Watneys)   Licensees Chris and Linda Cook   Real ale   Meals and snacks
(not Sun or Mon evenings)   Restaurant, one room no-smoking – best to book,
tel Heathfield (043 52) 3570   Children in eating area and restaurant   Parking can be
difficult (if so, park beyond church and walk through churchyard)   Open 11–3, 6–11*

HOUGHTON   TQ0111   Map 3

George & Dragon

B2139

As the wide choice of good food in this half-timbered pub is so popular it can be
difficult finding a seat, unless you get there early. The comfortably modernised bar
has heavy beams, a big fireplace with a handsome iron fireback and clockwork
device for turning a spit, and some attractive old tables; part of it is set aside for
diners, with Windsor chairs round neat tables, and full table service in the
evenings. The food includes sandwiches, smoked haddock in a cheese and parsley
sauce, tagliatelli with a mushroom and ham sauce, vegetarian lasagne or
mushrooms poached in dry white wine and cream and topped with stilton (all
£3.95), rack of lamb coated with mustard, cane sugar and fresh rosemary (£8.95),
and individual beef Wellington (£13.95). Well kept Bass, Boddingtons and
Courage Best on handpump, and English and New World wines. Tables and chairs
on a back terrace and on grass sloping down past a walnut tree and wishing well
give lovely views over the Arun valley. You can join the South Downs Way from
the village (turn left off the side road to Bury). *(Recommended by R Gray, TOH,
K Leist, Dr A M Rankin, Trevor and Helen Dayneswood, Jenny and Brian Seller)*

*Free house   Licensee David Walters   Real ale   Meals and lunchtime snacks (till 10pm
Fri and Sat; closed Mon evening)   Open 11–2.30, 6–11; winter evening closing 10.30;
closed 25 Dec*

KINGSTON NEAR LEWES   TQ3908   Map 3

Juggs

The Street; Kingston signed off A27 by roundabout W of Lewes, and off
Lewes–Newhaven road; look out for the pub's sign – may be hidden by hawthorn in
summer

This quaint fifteenth-century tile-hung cottage, covered with roses in summer, is named for the fish-carriers who passed through between the coast and Lewes. An interesting mix of furnishings in the rambling beamed bar ranges from an attractive little carved box settle, Jacobean-style dining chairs and brocaded seats and other settles to the more neatly orthodox tables and chairs of the small no-smoking dining area under the low-pitched eaves on the right. The cream or stripped brick walls are hung with flower pictures, battle prints, a patriotic assembly of postcards of the Lloyd George era, posters, and some harness and brass. Popular home-cooked bar food includes open sandwiches, taramasalata, ploughman's, a broccoli/sweetcorn/peppers/cheese vegetarian dish or sausages (£2.50), pitta bread with grilled ham, tomato, mushrooms and cheese (£2.95), sirloin steak (£5.95), home-made puddings (from £1.75), a dish of the day such as lovely fresh crab salad, and children's helpings. At Sunday lunchtime the choice is limited to cheese or pâté. Well kept Harveys PA and Armada and King & Barnes Bitter and Festive on handpump; polite service; log fires, darts, shove-ha'penny. There are lots of quite closely set rustic teak tables and benches on the front brick terrace, with more tables under cocktail parasols in a neatly hedged inner terrace, and a timber climber and commando net by two or three more tables out on the grass. *(Recommended by P A Barfield, C R and M A Starling, Hon Mrs A M Viney, Prof S Barnett, Alan Skull, Margaret Dyke)*

Free house   Licensee Andrew Browne   Real ale   Meals and snacks (12–2, 6–9.30; limited Sun lunchtime)   Children in two family areas   Open 11–2.30, 6–11; closed evenings of 25, 26 Dec and 1 Jan

LICKFOLD   SU9225   Map 2

Lickfold Inn ⊗

A huge central brick chimney with big winter log fires divides the elegant open-plan bar in this friendly Tudor inn into cosier areas. There are Georgian settles (most of the seats are antique or well chosen to tone in), heavy oak beams, some handsomely moulded panelling, and herringbone brickwork under rugs. Chalked up on a blackboard, the good bar food might include winter soup (£1.25), sandwiches (weekday lunchtimes only, from £1.50), smoked salmon pâté (£2.50), lasagne, oxtail stew or very popular steak and kidney pie (£4), chicken and mushroom pie (£4.20), Barnsley chop (£4.25), whole local trout (£4.75), steaks (from £6.50), half roast duck (£7), whole Dover sole, and puddings such as home-made ginger pear dumplings or treacle tart (£1.60); good Sunday roast lunches. Well kept Adnams, Badger Best and Tanglefoot, Ballards, Fullers ESB and London Pride, Greene King Abbot, Theakstons Old Peculier (winter only), and Wadworths 6X on handpump; good coffee. Attractively landscaped, the garden has eleven separate sitting areas on six different levels, as well as an outside bar and a barbecue. The surrounding countryside is very attractive, with the National Trust woods of Black Down a couple of miles north, and more woodland to the south. *(Recommended by Mrs Lili Lomas, M Rising, P J Taylor, Gwen and Peter Andrews; more reports please)*

Free house   Licensees Ron and Kath Chambers   Real ale   Meals and snacks (not Sun or Mon evenings)   Open 11–3, 6.30 (7 Sat)–11; 11–2.30, 6.30–10.30 Mon–Thurs in winter; closed Mon evenings

LITLINGTON   TQ5201   Map 3

Plough & Harrow

Off A27 Lewes–Polegate, after Alfriston turn (or can be reached from Alfriston); also signed off A259 E of Seaford

They serve a dozen well kept real ales on handpump a week in this bustling, modernised pub rotating around the three handpumps: Adnams Best, Badger Best and Tanglefoot, Brakspears, Charles Wells Bombardier, Greene King IPA and Abbot, Harveys BB, Larkins Best, Marstons Pedigree, Wadworths 6X, and Youngs Special; several wines. The beamed and carpeted little original front bar has quite a few mirrors giving an illusion of space, and a back eating area is done up as a dining car and decorated with steam railway models, pictures and memorabilia. Get there early if you want a seat (especially at weekends). Bar food, served both inside and outside, includes sandwiches (from £1.35, toasties from £2.25), home-made soup such as turkey broth (£1.95), ploughman's (from £2.85), jumbo sausages (£3.25), quite a few salads (from £3.80, crab £6.80), home-made steak and kidney pie (£4.40), scampi (£5.25), charcoal grilled steaks (from £6.75), and home-made daily specials; there may be delays at busy times. Darts, shove-ha'penny, dominoes, cribbage and evening piped music. The views across the Cuckmere Valley to nearby Alfriston are very pretty, and there are rustic seats by a mass of clematis on the lawn beside the extended back car park; a children's bar serves soft drinks, and there's an aviary. *(Recommended by Gwen and Peter Andrews, M Box, A L Willey, Jane Palmer, A J N Lee)*

Free house   Licensees Roger and Christine Taylor   Real ale   Meals and snacks (till 10pm)   Restaurant tel Alfriston (0323) 870632   Children in restaurant   Live music Fri evening   Open 11–2.30 (3 Sat), 6.30–11

LODSWORTH   SU9223 Map 2

Halfway Bridge ★ ✦

A272 Midhurst–Petworth

Several cottagey rooms ramble around the central bar in this well run and warmly friendly old place. There are various log fires, one in a gleaming kitchen range, another in a remarkably broad old fireplace, flowery-cushioned wall pews, nice oak chairs and a mixture of individual tables on the fitted flowery carpet, and little etchings of old buildings on the walls – which show some timbering. Steps lead down to a pretty country dining room with rose wallpaper between the dark oak ceiling trusses, heavy tables, a dresser, and a longcase clock. Home-cooked bar food includes sandwiches, ploughman's, lots of interesting filled baked potatoes, garlic-stuffed mussels (£3.50), chicken in leeks and garlic (£4.25), steak, kidney and Guinness pie (£4.50), fresh salmon with mint and cucumber mayonnaise (£7.25), and half a roast duck with orange and sherry sauce (£7.95); always at least three fresh vegetables available. Well kept Ballards Best, Flowers Original, Fremlins, Marstons Pedigree and Whitbreads Strong County on handpump, decent wines, pleasant, thoughtful service. There are some sturdy old-fashioned tables on the old brick terrace in front, and more mixed with picnic-table sets on the gently sloping grass, with two or three out behind too. *(Recommended by Ian and Wendy McCaw, John and Heather Dwane, A J Kentish, Mrs J A Blanks)*

Free house   Licensees Sheila and Edric Hawkins   Real ale   Meals and snacks (12–2, 7–10)   Restaurant tel Lodsworth (079 85) 281   Children over 10 in restaurant   Open 11–2.30, 6–11; winter evening hours 6.30–10.30; closed winter Sun evenings

LURGASHALL   SU9327 Map 2

Noahs Ark

Village signposted from A283 N of Petworth; OS Sheet 186 reference 936272

In summer, the hanging baskets outside this interesting old pub are lovely and there are rustic seats and tables on the front grass. The two small bars – one with oak parquet, the other carpeted – have simple but attractive furnishings, warm winter fires, and fresh flowers in summer; the lounge on the left has a big inglenook, as well as comfortable chairs and sporting prints. Good bar food includes sandwiches, toasties such as bacon and mushroom or ham and cheese (£1.75), tasty lasagne or moussaka (£2.85), salads (from £2.75, smoked salmon £4.50), lamb curry or winter steak and kidney pie (£3), lamb cutlets (£3.85), calves liver and bacon (£4.75), and puddings like fruit pudding. Friary Meux Best and King & Barnes Bitter on handpump, and Addlestone's farm cider; friendly service. Sensibly placed darts and bar billiards, also shove-ha'penny, dominoes, and cribbage. *(Recommended by Mrs Lili Lomas, Dr P H Mitchell, Ian and Wendy McCaw, John Knighton)*

Friary Meux (Allied)   Licensee Ted Swannell   Real ale   Meals and snacks (till 10pm, not Sun)   Restaurant tel (042 878) 346   Children in own room and restaurant   Open 11–2.30 (3 Sat), 6–11

MAYFIELD   TQ5827 Map 3

Rose and Crown ★ ⊘ 🛏

Fletching Street; off A267 at NE end of village

This pretty weatherboarded house has a new licensee this year who knew the pub as his local for some years before moving away to open his own bistro. Though he plans to leave the bars very much as they are, the back dining room which has been closed for some time is to be re-opened (and the second chef from the Walnut Tree at Fawley – a main entry in Buckinghamshire and well known for its food – is to join them), and two more bedrooms and possibly an indoor swimming pool with sauna and whirlpool added. The side garden is being converted into a car park, and the trade garden is to be moved to the prettier, flatter back part. The bars ramble around the small central servery, though it's the two cosy little front rooms that are the most atmospheric: low beams, benches built in to the partly panelled walls, an attractive bow window seat, ceiling boards with coins embedded in the glossy ochre paint, and a big inglenook fireplace. Popular bar food might include home-made mushroom and tarragon soup (£1.45), ploughman's (£3.25), tuna and bean bake (£3.45), grilled sardines (£3.65), curried vegetable croûte (£3.95), home-made fish pie (£4.85), hot spicy lamb fillets (£4.95), grilled shark steak (£5.25), and sirloin steak (£6.95); puddings like banoffi pie or fresh strawberry mousse (£1.75). Well kept Adnams Best, Harveys Best and guest beers like Badger Tanglefoot, Exmoor Gold, King & Barnes Bitter, Moorhouses Pendle Witches Brew, Morrells Graduate, Shepherd Neame Master Brew, Tetleys, and Youngs Special on handpump from the small central servery; quite a few malt whiskies, and several wines by the glass; darts, bar billiards, shove-ha'penny and cribbage. There are rustic wooden tables on the front terrace, with more on the lawn beside the building, and lots of hanging baskets and tubs filled with brightly coloured flowers. *(Recommended by T Galligan, M Randa Goddard, Gwen and Peter Andrews, Mrs C Hartley, P Bell, Dr R Wilkins, R Houghton, Alan Skull, Jeremy and Margaret Wallington, Peter and Moyna Lynch, Donald Clay, Bobby Goodale, Patrick Stapley, RAB)*

Free house   Licensee Peter Seely   Real ale   Meals and snacks (12–2.15, 6.30–9.30)   Restaurant   Children in restaurant   Open 11–3, 6–11   Bedrooms tel Mayfield (0435) 872200; £35B/£45B

MIDHURST   SU8821 Map 2

Spread Eagle 🛏

South St

A huge fireplace in the big, atmospheric lounge of this old place has a 1608 fireback (part of the building dates back to 1430), as well as old leather wing armchairs, chesterfields, and wicker settees, massive beams, big leaded windows, oriental rugs on broad boards, and original Victorian caricatures on the timbered ochre walls. Badger Best and Ballards Best on handpump or tapped from the cask, decent wines by the glass, courteous service, shove-ha'penny, dominoes and cribbage. A neat and cheerful barrel-vaulted cellar bar with crisp white paintwork has big oak cask seats or brocaded settles on the tiled floor, and serves home-made soup (£1.50), sandwiches (from £1.30, toasties 30p extra), filled French bread (from £1.80), filled baked potatoes (from £2.60), ploughman's (£2.65) and decent salads (from £3.60); darts in one bay, trivia, well reproduced piped music. *(Recommended by Jacqueline Davis, Sidney Wells, Jim and Becky Bryson, E G Parish)*

Free house   Licensee George Mudford   Real ale   Lunchtime snacks   Restaurant   Children welcome in cellar food bar (lunchtime)   Open 11–2.30, 6–11; closed evening 25 Dec   Bedrooms tel Midhurst (073 081) 6911; £68B/£80B

NUTHURST TQ1926 Map 3

Black Horse

Village signposted from A281 SE of Horsham

You can sit outside in front of this country pub or in the attractive back garden by a little stream, and there are good woodland walks nearby. Inside, the black-beamed bar has a couple of armed Windsor chairs and a built-in settle on the big Horsham flagstones in front of the inglenook fireplace, and one end of the room opens out into other carpeted areas, one of which is the dining room. The new licensees have introduced a different menu: open granary sandwiches (from £1.70), ploughman's (from £2.25), fresh pasta dishes like lasagne, cannelloni and ravioli (£4.50), lamb or chicken curries or very hot chilli con carne (£4.75), and home-made pies like chicken, gammon and mushroom or beef in ale (£4.95), vegetarian dishes, steaks, and Sunday evening barbecues. Well kept Badger, Gales HSB, Ind Coope Burton, King & Barnes Bitter, Tetleys, and Youngs on handpump; Gales country wines. (*Recommended by Norman Foot, Win and Reg Harrington, Katherine Cowherd, G T Rhys, Terry and Nicole Buckland, Klaus and Elizabeth Leist*)

Free house   Licensees Trevor and Karen Jones   Real ale   Meals and snacks   Children in eating area   Live music Mon evenings   Open 11–3, 6–11

OVING SU9005 Map 2

Gribble

Between A27 and A259 just E of Chichester, then should be signposted just off village road; OS Sheet 197 map reference 900050

This lovely old thatched cottage is named after Rosa Gribble who lived here for over ninety years. The heavily beamed bar has timbered bare bricks, a big log fire, wheelback chairs and cushioned pews around the old wooden country tables on its carpet, and a bustling atmosphere. On the left, a family room with more pews and rugs on its oak parquet floor, has bar billiards and darts, and there's a no-smoking and an alcohol-free area; also shove-ha'penny, dominoes, cribbage, and fruit machine, with a skittle alley in a long low building near the car park. Besides Gribble Ale and Reg's Tipple (at the moment brewed for them by the Poole Brewery, though they hope to have their microbrewery operating soon), there's well kept Badger Best and Tanglefoot, Gales HSB and Palmers IPA on handpump; Gales country wines and Inch's farm cider. Bar food includes sandwiches (from £1.10, fresh Selsey crab £2.60, toasties from £1.20), soup (£1.25), ploughman's with five different cheeses or home-baked ham (from £2.50), home-made cottage pie (£2.95), home-made burgers including a vegetarian one (from £2.95), home-baked ham and eggs (£3.50), salads (from £3.75, Selsey crab £4.75), big fresh trout (£5.50, mainly Friday), sirloin steak (£7.50), and puddings like home-made apple and blackberry pie (from £1.75). Three roasts on Sunday, and a few smaller (and cheaper) portions for those with not much appetite; good service. The lavatories have blackboards for graffiti. A small open-sided barn opens on to a garden with rustic seats under the apple trees. (*Recommended by R Gray, John Evans, Alec Lewery, Marie Enright, Dr A M Rankin, Mrs Lili Lomas, Lyn and Bill Capper, Trevor and Helen Dayneswood, Jenny and Brian Seller, M Rising, TOH, Henry Midwinter, Matt Pringle, Peter Griffiths*)

Own brew (pub leased to Badger)   Licensees Connie and James Wells   Real ale Meals and snacks (not Sun evening)   Children in family room   Open 11–2.30, 6–11

OXLEYS GREEN TQ6921 Map 3

Jack Fullers ✪

Follow Brightling signposts from Robertsbridge (off A21 N of Hastings); or take Brightling road off B2096 just W of Netherfield, then fork right at Robertsbridge, Mountfield signpost; or turn off Brightling road 50 yds from church

So popular with diners in the evening that you'll have to book or face a long wait for a table, this tucked-away country pub specialises in individual pies and meat puddings such as gammon and onion, steak or steak and kidney, halibut and prawn (from £3.95); other dishes like salmon mousse or cashew and aubergine bake, and unusual vegetables (extra) – honeyed carrots, cheesy leeks and lots more, served generously (£1.10); old-fashioned steamed puddings (from £2.10) including a summer pudding for two people (£5.95), and daily fish specials like salmon mousse (£4.95), seafood mornay (£5.95), and half lobster (£8.95); all served piping hot. The prices are higher in the evenings and on Saturdays. With candles on the good sturdy tables, flickering firelight and dark corners, there's plenty of atmosphere then – heightened by the almost palpable enjoyment of lots of people tucking in; the room furthest from the entrance is the nicer. At lunchtime it can be much quieter; in summer the beautifully kept and quite extensive garden (with a good few uncommon plants) gives fine views over some of Sussex's least-known countryside. Besides Felinfoel Double Dragon, there are decent French wines, and a quite remarkable collection of English ones – including up to a dozen by the glass; lots of malt whiskies, too; table tennis. Though service is quick rather than immediately affable, there is an underlying considerateness that shows, for example, in the thoughtful way they treat children. This is definitely a pub that grows on one. *(Recommended by S J A Velate, Mrs D M Hacker, M J Harper)*

Free house   Licensee Roger Berman   Real ale   Meals and snacks (not Mon) Restaurant tel Brightling (042 482) 212   Children welcome   Folk club twice monthly   Open 12–3, 7–11; closed Mon, except Bank Hols

nr PUNNETTS TOWN   TQ6220   Map 3
Three Cups

B2096 towards Battle

The quietly friendly bar here has big boughs smouldering in the basket of the large stone and brick fireplace (which has a black mantlebeam dated 1696), attractively contrasting cream or deep red varnished panelling, comfortably cushioned wall seats and stools, some mates' chairs, a few beaten copper platters, one or two beagle photographs, lots of pewter tankards on the low beams by the fire, and two big square bay windows. There's an oak parquet floor by the fire, red-and-white tiles by the door, and wood boards at the far end. Reasonably priced bar food includes sandwiches, filled baked potatoes (from £2), local prize winning giant sausages, cottage pie or lasagne (£2.50), and trout or steak (£5.75). Well kept Courage Best and Directors and John Smiths on handpump; piped music. The family room has darts, bar billiards, table skittles, shove-ha'penny, dominoes, cribbage, fruit machine, and space game. There is a small covered back terrace, seats in the garden beyond, and a safe play area for children (as well as ducks, chickens and geese). Clay pigeon shoots every alternate Sunday (by prior appointment), and three pétanque pitches; they have space for five touring caravans. *(Recommended by Mrs P Brown; more reports please)*

Courage   Licensees Leonard and Irenie Smith   Real ale   Meals and snacks   Children in eating area of bar if eating and in other room   Open 11–3, 6.30–11

nr RINGMER   TQ4412   Map 3
Cock

Off A26, N of Ringmer turn-off

The sizeable fairy-lit lawn outside this white weatherboarded house is attractively planted with fruit trees, shrubs, honeysuckle and clumps of old-fashioned flowers, and there are seats on a terrace. Inside, the bar has winter log fires in its inglenook fireplace, small Windsor chairs under the heavy beams, soft lighting, a good mix of customers, and a welcoming atmosphere; also, two lounges (one is no-smoking), and a black labrador. Waitress-served bar food includes open sandwiches (from £2.75), ploughman's (£2.95), and quite a few main dishes such as home-cooked ham and egg (£3.75), fresh fish (from £4.50), moules marinières (in season, £4.25), and tandoori chicken kebab (£6.25); as the food is freshly prepared to order, there may be delays at peak times. Well kept Bass and Ruddles Best and County on handpump, and a good selection of wines, including monthly specials; eclectic and enjoyable piped music. *(Recommended by John Beeken, Tony Gayfer; more reports please)*

Phoenix (Watneys)   Licensee Brian Cole   Real ale   Meals and snacks (12–2, 7–10) Restaurant tel Ringmer (0273) 812040   Well behaved children in restaurant, lounge and no-smoking lounge   Open 11–3, 6–11, though they may stay open longer in the afternoon if there are customers; closed 25 Dec

RIPE   TQ5010   Map 3
Lamb

Signposted off A22 Uckfield–Hailsham at Golden Cross; and via Chalvington from A27 Lewes–Polegate

The various snug rooms radiating around the island serving bar in this cheerful pub are decorated with a lively, enjoyable mix of furnishings: plush-cushioned pews, 18th-century oak settles, stripped kitchen tables, red hessian wallcoverings above the stripped pine dado, pastel pink velvet curtains, and stripped old joists and masses of pitch-pine. Here there are old song-sheet covers (Polly Perkins of Paddington Green, Did I Remember – the Jean Harlow song, even Red Sails in the Sunset); over there a string of 18th-century cartoons; on the left a big engraving of a farmyard scene by Herring; in a window alcove the tear-jerking Tommy Atkins' Friend; off the bar is a no-smoking area. The little brick-floored dining room is very pretty. Home-made bar food includes good sandwiches and toasties (from £1.10, bacon £1.50), soup (£1.30), ploughman's (from £2.70), ham and two eggs (£2.75), macaroni cheese (£2.95), omelettes (from £3.20), shepherd's pie (£3.30), salads (from £3.30), pork and cider hotpot, meaty or vegetarian lasagne or steak, kidney and Guinness pie (all £3.45), 8oz sirloin steak (£6.50), and a good choice of children's dishes (£2.50). Well kept Courage Best and Directors, Harveys, King & Barnes, and John Smiths on handpump, and some malt whiskies; two or three open fires; darts, cribbage, dominoes, fruit machine, space game, juke box, maybe piped music, and toad-in-the-hole; interesting antique postcards in the gents'. The sheltered back garden has rustic tables and picnic-table sets under cocktail parasols, with a climber and swings. *(Recommended by Alan Skull; more reports please)*

Free house   Licensees P A Wilkins, J R Bentley   Real ale   Meals and snacks (11–2, 6.30–9.30)   Restaurant tel Ripe (032 183) 280   Well behaved children welcome until 8.30, unless dining   Open 11 (12 Mon)–2.30, 6–11; closed evening 25 Dec

ROGATE   TQ5529   Map 3
White Horse

A272 Midhurst–Petersfield

The interesting rambling bar of this old village local has flagstones, stripped oak beams, bare stone walls and a big log fire, with plenty of green plush dining chairs and button-back built-in wall banquettes; broad steps lead down to a rush-matting dining area with sizeable fish in a big aquarium, leather books and flowers on its tables. A changing choice of bar food might include ploughman's (£2.50), curried mince pie (£3.95), Mexican or vegetarian pancake rolls (£3), lasagne (£4.75), beef in ale or steak and kidney pie (£4.95) and pork fillet or prawn and avocado salad (£5.25), with good puddings such as apple and sultana pancake rolls or spotted dick (£1.80). Well kept Ballards, Flowers Original, Marstons Pedigree, Wadworths 6X and Whitbreads Best on handpump, fruit machines, well reproduced piped pop music, friendly staff. Quiet on a weekday lunchtime, it can get enjoyably lively in the evenings. There are some tables in a sheltered corner out behind – serenaded by the occupants of an adjacent aviary. *(Recommended by K Leist, R Groves)*

Free house   Licensees Sheila and Jack Cowlam   Real ale   Meals and snacks   Open 11–2.30, 6–11

ROWHOOK   TQ1234 Map 3
Chequers

Village signposted from A29 NW of Horsham

Popular and enjoyable food at lunchtime here includes home-made soups (£1.50), filled baked potatoes (from £1.95), bacon, lettuce and tomato in French bread (£2.50), pâtés (£3.25), very good stilton ploughman's (£3.50), chicken and onion tagliatelle or mushroom and bacon au gratin (£4.25), home-cooked honeyed ham (£3.95), and home-made puddings (£1.75); in the evening there may be chicken satay (£4.25), chicken breast baked with avocado and garlic or King prawns with garlic butter (£6.95), and steaks (from £8.50); best to book at weekends. They do traditional roasts on Sunday lunchtimes. The snug front bar has black beams in its white ceiling, upholstered benches and stools around the tables on its flagstone floor, and an inglenook fireplace; up a step or two, there's a carpeted lounge with a very low ceiling. Well kept Flowers Original, Marstons Pedigree, and Whitbreads Strong Country on handpump, served from the elaborately carved bar counter; darts, shove-ha'penny, dominoes, cribbage and piped music; friendly service. Some sunny benches outside overlook the quiet country lane, and there are picnic-table sets in the big, peaceful side garden among roses and flowering shrubs, and under cocktail parasols on a crazy-paved terrace. *(Recommended by Norman Foot, M G Richards, John and Heather Dwane, Angela and Colin Smithers)*

Whitbreads   Licensee Gyles Culver   Real ale   Meals and snacks (till 10pm)   Children in overflow eating area   Open 11–2.30 (3 Sat), 6–11; closed evening 25 Dec

RUSHLAKE GREEN   TQ6218 Map 3
Horse & Groom

Village signposted from B2096

Ducks visit this old country pub from the village green opposite, there are doves from a dovecot, and tables on the front lawn. Inside, on the left of the central serving counter, there's an adjoining Saddle Room, and on the right, the beamed and timbered Gun Room with its log fire in the big hearth, is set out for diners. Home-made bar food includes hot roast beef in French bread (£1.95), ploughman's (from £2.50), mussels in white wine and garlic (£3.75), beef and Guinness stew (£4.50), poached salmon (£5.95), steaks (from £5.95), and Mediterranean prawns in white wine and garlic (£7.95). Well kept Harveys BB and King & Barnes Bitter on handpump; dominoes, cribbage, and piped music. *(Recommended by Mr and Mrs Clark, Terry Buckland; more reports please)*

Free house   Licensees Jakki and Alan Perodeau   Real ale   Meals and snacks   Restaurant tel Burwash (0435) 830320   Children in eating area of bar and in restaurant   Open 11–3, 6.30–11 weekdays; 11–11 Sat; closed evening 25 Dec

RYE   TQ9220 Map 3
Mermaid

Mermaid St

Though this beautiful, ancient smugglers' inn, with its black and white timbered facade, dates back mainly to the 15th and 16th centuries, the cellars are some seven hundred years old. The small back bar has hardly changed over the last 65 years – as a picture there shows: interesting antique seats (one of them carved in the form of a goat) around its timbered walls, a huge fireplace with a halberd and pike mounted over it, some 18th-century carving, and a longcase clock. Other rooms have panelling, heavy timbering and wall frescoes. The murderous and wide-ranging Hawkhurst gang used to carouse here, their loaded pistols beside their tankards, and the ghost of a serving girl who loved one of them is said to be seen sometimes, just before midnight. Bar food includes sandwiches, home-made soup, ploughman's and a salad buffet; Bass and Whitbreads on handpump, and their own house wines, ports and sherries. There are seats on a small back terrace. *Recommended by Tony and Alison Sims, Hazel Morgan, Sheila Keene, Jill and Paul Ormrod; more reports please*

*Free house   Licensee M K Gregory   Real ale   Snacks (lunchtime, not winter)
Restaurant   Children welcome   Open 11–3, 6–11, but may be closed, particularly at
lunchtime, in midweek out of season   Bedrooms tel Rye (0797) 223065; £45B/£75B*

nr SCAYNES HILL   TQ3623   Map 3
Sloop

Freshfield Lock; at top of Scaynes Hill turn N off A272 into Church Lane, follow
Freshfield signpost

Handy for the Bluebell steam railway and not far from the great lakeside gardens
of Sheffield Park, this popular and welcoming tile-hung pub has a long carpeted
saloon bar with comforable sofas, armchairs, and cushioned banquettes; there may
be pictures for sale. Generous helpings of good bar food that changes daily, include
filled warm cottage loaves (from £1.95), good smoked salmon soup in winter,
ploughman's (from £2.25), good home-made chicken liver pâté with sherry, filled
baked potatoes (from £2.25), and main dishes that change slightly each day and
are chalked up on five blackboards such as fresh plaice (£3.95), smoked salmon
and prawn quiche with lemon salad or steak in old ale pie (£4.95), pasta dishes,
steaks, and a huge mixed grill (£10.95). Well kept Harveys BB and Armada on
handpump, and 26 country wines; piped music. The simpler, airier public bar has a
small games room – sensibly placed darts, pool, dominoes, cribbage, fruit machine
and space game. By the derelict Ouse Canal, the neat and sheltered garden has
been extended this year, and more tables and chairs added; there's a children's
climbing frame, and more benches in the old-fashioned brick porch. *(Recommended
by Dr Keith Bloomfield, Paul Evans, Bernard Phillips, Theo Schofield, Jason Caulkin, W A
Gardiner)*

*Beards (who no longer brew)   Licensees David and Marilyn Mills   Real ale   Meals
and snacks   Restaurant tel Scaynes Hill (044 486) 219   Children in eating area of
bar   Open 11–3, 6–11*

nr SEAFORD   TV4899   Map 3
Golden Galleon

Exceat Bridge; A259 Seaford–Eastbourne, near Cuckmere

The young licensee in this spacious pub – well organised to cope with masses of
customers – is Italian (his wife's English), and the cheerful summer bustle is slightly
reminiscent of an Italian trattoria. Home-cooked bar food includes starters like
tonno e fagioli and a good few others such as an Italian seafood salad, sweet-cured
herrings or pâté (all around £2–£2.50), fresh local fish (from £4.40), a couple of
daily specials such as lasagne or seafood pasta, gammon (£6.50), pork tenderloin
(£7) and steaks (from 8oz fillet, £8.75), with a good help-yourself salad counter
(from £4), and half-portions of most things for children. Well kept Courage Best
and Directors on handpump, decent wines; friendly service. The Turkey-carpeted
main area has neat rows of dining tables under the high trussed and pitched rafters,
and at one side there's a nice little alcove, snugged in by an open fire; half the
bar/dining area is no-smoking. Outside on the terraces and grass of the sloping
garden are plenty of seats, with a mass of very pretty flowers on the steep front
slope, away from the tables. The view looks out past the road to Beachy Head on
the right, with the Seven Sisters Country Park just over the Cuckmere River; it's a
ten-minute easy walk down to the beach, and there are walks inland to Friston
Forest and the Downs. *(Recommended by C T and J M Laffan, Lesley Jones, Geralyn
Meyler; more reports please)*

*Courage   Licensee Stefano Shaw Diella   Real ale   Meals and snacks (12–2, 6–9)
Open 11–2.30, 6–11; winter evening closing 10.30*

SIDLESHAM   SZ8598   Map 2
Crab & Lobster

Off B2145 S of Chichester, either Rookery Lane N of village (on left as you approach) or
Mill Lane from village centre

The pretty flower-filled little garden at the back of this pub – right by the silted Pagham harbour – looks out across a meadow to the coastal flats. The bar has deep rose pink or blue upholstered wall benches, wildfowl and marine prints on the ochre walls, and a good log fire; there's also a plusher side lounge. The simple, popular food's good value: crab or prawn sandwiches, filled baked potatoes, good toasties such as egg and bacon, delicious moules marinières (£3.50), garlic prawns (£3.80), steak and kidney pie (£3.50), Selsey crab (£4.10), and home-made puddings. Well kept Friary Meux, Ind Coope Burton, and King Barnes Bitter on handpump, and a decent choice of other drinks. *(Recommended by Dr P H Mitchell, Mrs J A Banks, Roger Taylor, M Morgan, Dr J D Bassett, Paul and Margaret Baker)*

Friary Meux (Allied)   Licensee Brian Cross   Real ale   Meals and snacks (not Sun evening)   Open 11–2.30, 6–11

STOPHAM   TQ0218 Map 3
White Hart

A283 towards Pulborough

The bars and restaurant in this honey-coloured stone pub have been redecorated this year to give a lighter, airy feel to them. The three cosy rooms have beams and comfortable furnishings, with an open fire in the bottom bar. Good bar food includes home-made soup (£1.45), sandwiches (from £1.10, fresh prawn £1.80), various platters (from £2.95), home-made fresh pasta dishes (£3.50), savoury quiche (£3.75), home-made fish pie (£4.25), and children's dishes (£1.50); the beamed and candlelit restaurant is said to have the widest choice of fresh fish in the south. Well kept Flowers Original and Whitbreads Strong Country on handpump, and decent wines; darts, cribbage, dominoes, fruit machine, and piped music, and they hold special event evenings. The big lawn has well spaced tables and a play area for children, and there are tree-lined grass walks down by the slow Arun and Rother rivers, where they meet at a graceful seven-arched bridge, built in 1309. *(Recommended by John Knighton, Mr and Mrs G Turner, Mrs Lili Lomas, Brian and Anna Marsden)*

Whitbreads   Licensees Bill Bryce and Lina Collier   Real ale   Meals and snacks Restaurant tel Pulborough (079 82) 3321   Several live entertainment evenings Children in family room   Open 11–2.30, 6–11; winter evening opening 6.30

nr TICEHURST   TQ6830 Map 3
Bull ⚫

Three Legged Cross; coming into Ticehurst from N on B2099, just before Ticehurst village sign, turn left beside corner house called Tollgate (Maynards Pick Your Own may be signposted here)

Though this atmospheric 14th-century pub is popular with locals, visitors are made most welcome, too. Several low-beamed rooms have flagstone, brick or oak parquet floors, kitchen seats, flowery cushions on benches and settles, heavy oak joined tables, and a big central fireplace (which the soft grey tabby heads for); there's also a larger, more modern, light and airy room. Good lunchtime bar food includes home-made Stilton soup (£1.10), sandwiches (from £1, hot gammon £1.25, tasty steak £2.50), good ploughman's (£2.50), bubble and squeak, popular steak and kidney pie, gammon steak with mustard and demerara glaze, excellent venison stew or superb pork, apple and cider casserole (£3.75), delicious chicken tikka, 10oz rump steak (£6), a splendid summer buffet (£4.80), and home-made puddings like apple strudel, summer pudding or hokey-pokey ice-cream with honeycomb in it (£1.50). In the evenings (when they prefer bookings), they do more elaborate meals. Well kept Harveys BB, Shepherd Neame Master Brew, a beer named for the pub, and regularly changing guests on handpump; pleasant friendly staff; darts, dominoes and cribbage. The sheltered garden has old-fashioned seats, fruit trees, and a pool by a young weeping willow – all very pretty, and quiet but for birdsong; there's also a bouncy castle and large playing field for children. *(Recommended by D A Wilcock, Miss C M Davidson, Mrs Christina*

Hartley, Mr and Mrs David Bing, R Houghton, Caroline Hall, R C Morgan, M C Howells, Heather Sharland, Jason Caulkin, David and Ruth Shillitoe, Mrs E M Thompson)

Free house   Licensee Mrs Evelyn Wilson-Moir   Real ale   Meals and snacks (not Sun evening)   Restaurant tel Ticehurst (0580) 200586   Children welcome   Occasional live entertainment Tues evenings   Open 11–3, 6–11

TILLINGTON   SU9621 Map 2

Horseguards ✪

Village signposted from A272 Midhurst–Petworth

The new licensees have turned this neat, friendly pub into much more of a dining place now, with a menu that changes twice daily. At lunchtime there may be home-made soup (£2.20), home-made terrines like avocado and chicken or monkfish and turbot and a salad of mixed seafood (all £3.50), and whole grilled plaice or cod with almonds in nut brown butter (£4.50), with more elaborate evening dishes such as chicken breast or duck with sauces (£6.50 and £8.20 respectively), rack of lamb (£7.45), and lots of fish like big grilled lemon sole, Dover sole or fillets of salmon and scallops in filo pastry with a sauce (from around £6); home-made puddings (£2.20), and Sunday roast beef (£4.95). Badger Best, Wadworths 6X and a beer brewed for the pub on handpump. From the seat in the big black-panelled bow window of the beamed front bar, there's a lovely view beyond the village to the Rother Valley; darts, piped music. There's a terrace outside, and more tables and chairs in a garden behind. The church opposite is 800 years old. *(Recommended by D J Cooke, Mrs Lili Lomas, Norman Foot, Frank Cummins, Keith Walton)*

Free house   Licensees Rex and Janet Colman   Real ale   Meals and snacks   Open 11–3, 6–11; closed 25 Dec

WEST ASHLING   SU8107 Map 2

Richmond Arms

Mill Lane; from B2146 in village follow Hambrook signpost

In just nine years, the enthusiastic licensees of this simple, out-of-the-way and very friendly village pub, will have served five hundred and fifty-six different real ales from their ten handpumps: Brakspears PA, Harveys XX, King & Barnes Festive, Ringwood Old Thumper, Timothy Taylors Landlord, and a regular selection of Northern guest beers – notably Yates from Cumbria. They also have most bottle conditioned English beers, and one of the best ranges of good foreign bottled beers in the south that includes beers from all five Trappist breweries (in summer there are fruity ones such as cherry, raspberry, blackcurrant, peach and mint) from Belgium, and some of the rarer German ales like Munich Weisse beer which has three grains of rice to maintain a creamy head and is served with a wedge of lemon; also, Thatcher's cider. The real food fits in well: besides sandwiches (croque monsieur £2.75), excellent ploughman's, and 5oz steak sandwich (£3.95), there are filled baked potatoes (from £2.25), home-made chilli con carne, curry, lasagne, tuna and mushroom or cottage pie (all £3.50), and steak and mushroom pie (£3.75). Around the central servery are some long wall benches, library chairs and black tables, numbered decoy ducks hang on the wall (which are sometimes raced down the local stream), and there's a fire in winter; bar billiards, shove-ha'penny, dominoes, cribbage, and trivia and fruit machines. The old skittle alley doubles as a function and family room; friendly dog. There's a pergola, and some picnic-table sets by the car park. *(Recommended by David and Sarah Gilmore, Derek and Sylvia Stephenson, Mrs Lili Lomas, M Morgan, Richard Houghton, Alan Skull, John and Christine Simpson, Brian and Anna Marsden)*

Free house   Licensees Roger and Julie Jackson   Real ale   Lunchtime meals and snacks (not Sun lunchtime; evening food if pre-booked in skittle alley)   Children in skittle alley   Open 11–3, 5.30–11

WEST HOATHLY   TQ3632 Map 3
Cat

Village signposted from either A22 or B2028 S of East Grinstead

The small suntrap terrace outside this friendly and peaceful old smugglers' pub has seats among the roses that look across to the church nestling among its big yew trees (if you walk through the churchyard to the far side there's an even better view). The pub is near the start of the *Good Walks Guide* Walk 64. The open-plan rooms of the partly panelled and partly beamed bar are separated by the massive central chimney (note the interesting ancient carving) with its big brick hearth and log-effect gas fire. Nicely presented, if rather pricey, home-made bar food from a menu that changes daily may include sandwiches (from £1.50, home-cooked beef £1.75), good oxtail soup (£1.55), decent ploughman's, tasty grilled sardines, smoked salmon pâté (£3.95), summer salads such as fresh cold salmon (£6.95), whole crab salad (£7.95) or whole lobster (£14.95), and winter hot dishes like beef bourguinon (£6.95), and fillet of sole Bretonne or whole spring chicken Mexican (£7.95). Well kept Harveys BB, and winter Old, and King & Barnes Festive on handpump; courteous service. *(Recommended by S L Hughes, Robert and Elizabeth Scott, Robert A Anderson, David and Sarah Gilmore, Peter Hall, T Galligan, TBB, Ian Phillips)*

Beards (who no longer brew)   Licensee G Burillo   Real ale   Meals and snacks (not Sun evening)   Children in dining room   Open 11–2.30, 6–11; closed evenings 25 and 26 Dec and 1 Jan

WINCHELSEA   TQ9017 Map 3
New Inn ⟾

Just off A259

The pleasantly old-fashioned newly carpeted lounge bar in this 18th-century pub rambles through three rather spacious rooms (one of them is no-smoking) with deep terracotta painted walls, and decorations that include old local photographs, old farm tools, and china, pewter and copper on Delft shelves. There are wall banquettes, settles, sturdy wooden tables, masses of hop bines hanging from the beams, and good log fires. Good, hearty bar food includes sandwiches (not Sunday lunchtime or Bank Holidays), home-made soup (£1.75), garlic mushrooms (£2.50), ploughman's (from £2.50), home-cooked ham and egg (£3.95), mixed nut roast or home-made curry (£4.50), salads (from £4.75), steak and kidney pie with good thick fluffy pastry (£4.95), and steaks (from £7.95); children's meals until 7.30pm (from £1.50), daily specials like local plaice, cod, crab or home-made pies, and puddings like home-made trifle or bread and butter pudding; friendly, efficient waitress service. Well kept Courage Best and Directors on handpump, decent wines by the glass, and around 10 malt whiskies. The wholly separate public bar has darts, well lit pool, cribbage, fruit machine, and unobtrusive piped music. There are picnic-table sets and swings in a neat and good-sized orchard garden, and some of the pretty bedrooms look out on a charming medieval scene, with lime tree and swathes of bluebells around the church opposite. *(Recommended by David Gaunt, H Crookston, W J Wonham, K J Betts)*

Courage   Licensee Richard Joyce   Real ale   Meals and snacks (12–2, 6.30–9.30) Children in no-smoking family area   Open 11–2.30, 6–11; closed 25 Dec and evening 26 Dec   Bedrooms tel Rye (0797) 226252; /£28(£35S)

WINEHAM   TQ2320 Map 3
Royal Oak

Village signposted from A272 and B2116

Picturesque and old-fashioned, this black and white timbered pub seems to have changed very little since one reader's last visit fifteen years earlier. The very low beams above the serving counter are decorated with ancient corkscrews, horseshoes, racing plates, tools and a coach horn, the furniture throughout is fittingly simple, and the enormous inglenook fireplace carries the smoke stains of centuries. Well kept Whitbread Pompey Royal is tapped from casks in a still room, on the way back through to the small snug; darts, shove-ha'penny, dominoes, cribbage; a limited range of bar snacks. There are rustic wooden tables on the grass by a well in front, and on a clear day you can just see Chanctonbury Ring from the window in the gents' (past the caravan site). *(Recommended by T Buckland, IAA; more reports please)*

Whitbreads   Real ale   Snacks (not Sat evening or Sun)   Open 10.30–2.30, 6–10.30; closed 25 Dec and evening 26 Dec

WITHYHAM   TQ4935 Map 3

Dorset Arms

B2110

Set well back from the road (which used to be so muddy in winter that even oxen couldn't pull wagons free), this 16th-century pub has white tables on a brick terrace raised well above the small green; the tree-lined lane past here leads to the village cricket ground. Inside, the unusual raised L-shaped bar has simple furnishings, beams, broad oak floorboards, a stone Tudor fireplace with a winter log fire, and a relaxed atmosphere. Good bar food includes sandwiches (from 85p), huge filled rolls (£2), ploughman's (£1.80), whole avocado pear with curried prawns (£3.75), popular fresh plaice or trout or smoked trout salad (£4), and Scotch smoked salmon (£6), with daily specials such as steak and kidney pie, jumbo sausage and egg, braised steak or venison (from £3); on Sunday lunchtimes they only do rolls and ploughman's (though the restaurant does Sunday lunches £7, children £5). Well kept Harveys BB and XX and winter XXXX on handpump; darts, dominoes, cribbage, fruit machine and piped music. The grave of Vita Sackville-West (whose family owned Buckhurst Park here) is in the nearby church. *(Recommended by Richard Gibbs, Alan Skull, Leo and Pam Cohen; more reports please)*

Harveys   Licensee David Clark   Real ale   Snacks and lunchtime meals   Restaurant tel Hartfield (0892) 770278; not Mon, not Sun evening   Children in restaurant and eating area of bar lunchtimes only   Open 11–11 weekdays; 11–3, 6–11 Sat

---

Lucky Dip

Besides the fully inspected pubs, you might like to try these Lucky Dips recommended to us and described by readers (if you do, please send us reports):

☆ **Adversane**, W Sus [TQ0723], *Blacksmiths Arms*: Attractive old beamed pub, well kept and spacious but cosy, with good value though not cheap varied choice of food, friendly service; restaurant *(G Holliday, Norman Foot, Ron Gentry)*

Alfold Bars, W Sus [B2133 N of Loxwood — OS Sheet 186 map reference 037335; TQ0333], *Sir Roger Tichbourne*: Ancient pub with open fireplace in large public bar, small snug saloon; cheerful staff serving good range of bar meals, well kept King & Barnes; big car park *(Reg Tickner)*

☆ **Alfriston**, E Sus [TQ5103], *Market Cross*: Also known as the Smugglers — low beams, cutlasses over the big inglenook, white-painted panelling, cosier side room, back conservatory, generous bar food from sandwiches to steaks (snacks only, Sun lunchtime), well kept Courage Best and Directors, good choice of wines by the glass, friendly staff, children allowed in eating area and conservatory, tables in garden; charming village; a shortage of recent reports keeps this well run pub out of the main entries this year *(John Knighton, John Hayward, LYM)*

☆ **Alfriston** [High St], *George*: Friendly service and good food in long, spacious and well decorated heavily beamed bar with huge fireplace — inn first licensed in 1397; bar food inc good seafood platter and steaks; bedrooms well regarded *(Alec Lewery)*

☆ **Amberley**, W Sus [off A259; TQ0212], *Black Horse*: Friendly and attractive family-run village pub, up a flight of steps, its beams festooned with sheep and cow bells and other Downland farm equipment; flagstones, well kept Allied real ales, home-cooked bar food inc local shellfish, garden; children in eating area and restaurant, occasional folk music *(Cathy Marsh, P A Barfield, LYM)*

Amberley, W Sus [Houghton Bridge; TQ0212], *Bridge*: Neat open-plan bar with several real ales and good garden with well enclosed play area; has been praised for decent straightforward bar food and friendly staff, but no reports on new regime; bedrooms *(Jenny and Brian Seller, Brian and Anna Marsden)*

☆ **Angmering**, W Sus [TQ0704], *Spotted Cow*: Cheerful welcome, jovial and knowledgeable landlord, good range of drinks inc wines at reasonable prices; food above average, attentively served, roomy garden with good separate play area; dogs allowed, at start of lovely walk to Highdown hill fort *(H C Clifford)*

Apuldram, W Sus [Birdham Rd; SU8403], *Black Horse*: Comfortably modernised and well run 18th-century pub with helpful friendly staff, wide choice of straightforward but reasonably priced food from sandwiches to steaks, and well kept Allied real ales; juke box; character not its strongest point *(Peter Ames)*

☆ **Ardingly**, W Sus [B2028 2 miles N; TQ3429], *Gardeners Arms*: Attractive olde-worlde interior with inglenook fireplace behind its plain facade, busy and compact but not overcrowded — and plenty of space on big lawn; simple range of good food individually cooked and well presented, with good specials; King & Barnes Festive, Theakstons and Watneys-related real ales on handpump; handy for Borde Hill and Wakehurst Place *(Tom Rhys, G Dudley, Norman Foot)*

☆ **Ardingly** [Street Lane], *Oak*: Wide choice of good reasonably priced bar food, Watneys-related and guest real ales on handpump in well run 14th-century building with beams, antique furnishings and lovely log fire in magnificent old fireplace; bright and comfortable restaurant, friendly efficient service; pool table in public bar *(Mrs Blanks, Audrey and Brian Green)*

☆ **Arlington**, E Sus [Caneheath; TQ5407], *Old Oak*: Nice atmosphere with good mix of customers — gets busy Sun; well kept beer tapped from the cask, good reasonably priced food, pleasant garden; children tolerated; big car park *(R Houghton, N Patton)*

☆ **Arlington**, *Yew Tree*: Welcoming, neatly kept and comfortably modernised village local with big garden, usual bar food priced reasonably and well presented, Harveys on handpump, subdued piped music; restaurant *(J Beeken, Comus Elliott, BB)*

☆ **Arundel**, W Sus [Mill Rd — keep on and don't give up!; TQ0107], *Black Rabbit*: Recently extensively renovated big-windowed long bar in lovely location, looking over its sheltered riverside tables to bird-reserve watermeadows and Castle; log fires, lots of spirits as well as Youngers Scotch and IPA, pub games, bar food, airy side restaurant; children in eating and family areas; bedrooms *(Mrs Val Rixon, MCG, Alec Lewery, Marie Enright, Ian and Wendy McCaw, A H Denman, LYM; more reports on the new regime please)*

Arundel, *White Hart*: Central bar serving two cosy lounges with old settles and ancient books; several well kept real ales (not cheap), reasonably priced fresh food and comfortable, separate dining area *(I W Muir)*

Barcombe, E Sus [TQ4114], *Anchor*: It is worth knowing this remote inn (sandwiches in small regulars' bar; restaurant) for its charming gardens and boating on very peaceful river *(LYM)*

☆ **Barns Green**, W Sus [TQ1227], *Queens Head*: Old pub in pretty village, pleasantly modernised with one large but cosy bar, several fires inc huge one in inglenook, separate blackboards of sandwiches/salads,

basket meals and more expensive dishes, piped music, fruit machine; well kept Whitbreads-related real ales, live music evenings, benches in front by quiet road, garden behind *(T Buckland, Norman Foot)*

☆ **Battle**, E Sus [25 High St; TQ7416], *George*: Very friendly welcome in lovely old well run coaching inn with L-shaped bar, part pine-panelled and with pine counter, upmarket atmosphere, well kept Harveys on handpump, good lunchtime bar food inc sandwiches, a daily hot dish and good cold table in restaurant, good teas, well kept Harveys; no music; bedrooms *(S J A Velate, E G Parish, Prof S Barnett, J A H Townsend)*

Beckley, E Sus [TQ8523], *Rose & Crown*: Old coaching inn with plenty of character, good value food and welcoming staff under new regime *(AMC)*

☆ **Berwick**, E Sus [Milton Street; TQ5304], *Sussex Ox*: Marvellous play area and big lawn outside country pub just below downs; can get very busy (and noisy in family room), but good atmosphere, well kept beer, good bar food inc nourishing soups with thick crusty bread, pleasantly simple country furniture to match the brick floor and woodburning stove *(Alan Skull, Lesley Sones, Geralyn Meyler, LYM)*

Berwick [by stn], *Berwick*: Family pub with attractive Perspex-roofed garden bar, which has been well worth knowing for good choice of food and real ales and good children's playground behind, but no recent reports *(LYM; news please)*

Bexhill, E Sus [Polegate rd, W; TQ7407], *Denbigh*: Attractive, nicely placed pub with small bar and dining area; good bar food such as steak and kidney pie and three-course Sun lunch, served by very cheerful landlord; well kept Courage beers on handpump; children welcome and well looked after in dining area *(Alec Lewery)*; [Cooden], *Sovereign*: Self-contained bar of Cooden Beach Hotel, popular with locals; warm and comfortable wtih wide choice of real ales on handpump, good range of bar food, good service; bedrooms *(E G Parish)*

Billingshurst, W Sus [High St (A29); TQ0925], *Olde Six Bells*: Partly 14th-century flagstoned and timbered local with well kept King & Barnes real ales, decent wines, friendly welcome, food, inglenook fireplace, pretty roadside garden; gets busy evenings, particularly Fri/Sat *(JSE, P Thorogood, LYM)*

☆ **Binstead**, W Sus [Binstead Lane; about 2 miles W of Arundel, turn S off A27 towards Binstead — OS Sheet 197 map reference 980064; SU9806], *Black Horse*: Unpretentious pub in quiet country lane, clean and pleasant, with big helpings of reasonably priced bar food inc some unusual dishes, well kept Gales, sensibly placed darts, welcoming landlord, rack of tourist information; sheltered back garden with views over meadows towards coast; bedrooms *(Dr A M Rankin, Sion Hughes)*

☆ **Birdham**, W Sus [B2179 a mile S of village; SU8200], *Lamb*: Attractive, comfortable and spotless, with lots of small rooms, friendly atmosphere, well kept ales inc Harveys, King & Barnes, Tetleys, good reasonably priced choice of wines, interesting fairly priced food inc unusual toasted sandwiches and vegetarian dishes, more choice evenings and weekends; lots of tables out in front and in sheltered back garden — good for children *(Ian Phillips, Peter and Susan Maguire)*

Birdham [A286 SW of Chichester], *Black Horse*: Welcoming with good choice of well kept beer, interesting good value bar food; big car park *(SJC)*

☆ Bodiam, E Sus [TQ7825], *Curlew*: L-shaped bar with stable door giving airy atmosphere when half open; well kept Adnams and King & Barnes on handpump, sensibly priced decent wines, good choice of bottled beers, wide range of generously served food inc interesting daily specials in bar and back dining area *(Patrick Young, S J A Velate, BB)*

☆ Bodle Street Green, E Sus [off A271 at Windmill Hill; has been shut Mon Oct—Easter, opens 7pm; TQ6514], *White Horse*: Cheerfully welcoming country pub, clean and well run, in small tucked-away village; airy and comfortably modernised bar with cushioned wheelback seats and a long shiny settle (favoured by the pub's cat), well kept Harveys and King & Barnes Sussex and Festive on handpump, decent wines and malt whiskies, open fires, good value straightforward bar food from sandwiches and ploughman's to steaks (tables often booked), bar billiards, darts, cheery piped music; some tables outside — a helpful touch for walkers is the OS map framed outside *(J H Bell, BB)*

☆ Bosham, W Sus [High St; SU8003], *Anchor Bleu*: Lovely sea and boat views from waterside pub with usual bar food, low beams, open fires and distinct maritime feel; some tables outside, in attractive unspoilt village; at its best out of season *(Margaret and Roy Randle, LYM)*

Boxgrove, W Sus [SU9007], *Anglesey Arms*: Straightforward pub on edge of Goodwood estate, with popular food — especially good steaks; Allied real ales, good coffee *(Ian Phillips)*

☆ Brighton, E Sus [Castle Sq; TQ3105], *Royal Pavilion*: Efficient service from central food counter — good choice, good value; well laid out series of rooms attractively done up for successful old-fashioned look, inc intimate candlelit winebar area (good big glasses), lots of panelling and points of interest; popular first-floor nightclub *(Hazel Morgan, LYM)*

Brighton [175 Queens Park Rd], *Beaufort*: Bright and spacious simple open-plan pub with warm welcome and comfortable atmosphere; open fire one end, tables the other, generous cheap food *(Christopher Portway)*; [Kings Rd Arches, on beach below prom, between the piers], *Belvedere*: Lively and youthful real-ale pub squashed into long arch below the road, right on the beach; with its similar next-door sister-pub the Fortune of War (lined with marine planking, maybe a bit quieter) has good happy hour, 7-8pm; live music *(BB)*; [Ditchling Rd], *Brunswick Arms*: Large, comfortable pub with framed cigarette cards and liqueur miniatures; friendly, helpful staff *(Patrick Godfrey)*; [15 Black Lion St], *Cricketers*: Lovely old-fashioned local with chatty staff, good cheap bar food *(D Bates, LYM)*; [Little East St], *Dr Brightons*: Lively seafront pub

with changing range of real ales and good bar food; busy in summer months, but quieter moments in winter *(Alec Lewery)*; [13 Marlborough Pl], *King & Queen*: Medieval-style lofty and spacious main hall, straightforward decent food, well kept beer, pool table, good jazz most evenings (when parking tends to be difficult), aviary in flagstoned courtyard *(Andrew Cooke, LYM)*; [Trafalgar St], *Lord Nelson*: Good value unpretentious home cooking (great vegetable soup), well kept Harveys and farm cider, good mix of unaffected customers *(Alan Skull, Alec Lewery)*; [Inner Lagoon, Village Sq, Marina], *Master Mariner*: New but pleasant, with well kept Watneys-related real ales and Watneys Country Carvery restaurant *(Prof S Barnett)*; [Kings Rd], *Old Ship*: Heavily panelled plush seafront hotel bar, with nautical theme and grand piano; comfortable, welcoming and relaxing, good service; no bar food, but restaurant; bedrooms *(Barbara and Norman Wells)*; [Queens Rd], *Royal Standard*: Small bar a couple of minutes from stn, with lots of real ales inc several guests tapped from the cask in separate small room called the Vestry *(Patrick Godfrey)*

Broad Oak, E Sus [A28/B2089, N of Brede; TQ8220], *Rainbow Trout*: Comfortably refurbished, with Fremlins on handpump and good bar food strong on fresh fish *(E J and J W Cutting)*

Brownbread Street, E Sus [TQ6715], *Ash Tree*: Small and unspoilt main bar with big inglenook, small restaurant; two well kept guest beers, bar meals from home-made soup to blackboard specials such as beef stew with parsley dumplings and chinese pork *(Alistair Wood)*

☆ Bucks Green, W Sus [TQ0732], *Fox*: Unspoilt village pub with absolutely no frills — like what pubs used to be; King & Barnes real ales, lunchtime sausages and sandwiches *(Phil and Sally Gorton, Stephen Goodchild)*

☆ Bucks Green, *Queens Head*: Olde-worlde village free house with well kept Badger, Courage Directors and King & Barnes; big pleasantly decorated single bar with log fires, nice atmosphere, friendly owners and extensive choice of good reasonably priced food *(Reg Tickner)*

Burpham, W Sus [off A27 outside Arundel; TQ0308], *Green Man*: Harvester with usual rustic decor and perhaps more atmosphere and style than some, with amiable service and decent food pleasantly served *(D T Taylor, John Evans)*

☆ Burwash, E Sus [TQ6724], *Rose & Crown*: Timbered and beamed local tucked away down side street in quaintly restored village, with wide choice of real ale such as Bass, Charrington IPA and Shepherd Neame; decent wines, good log fire, friendly atmosphere, quite enterprising bar food, restaurant; tables on quiet lawn; nr start GWG67 *(Comus Elliott, BB)*

Burwash Common, E Sus [Stonegate Rd; TQ6322], *Kicking Donkey*: Food (sandwiches and so on) and real ales in country local with benches out in front facing adventure playground and hop garden *(BB)*

☆ Burwash Weald, E Sus [A265 two miles W of Burwash; TQ6624], *Wheel*: Good inglenook log fire in long open-plan carpeted room with green plush button-back banquettes along wall, lots of brasses on its five black beams, nicely framed old local photographs; full range of decent bar food, well kept Harveys and Ruddles Best and County, games bar up a step or two behind, tables outside; lovely walks in valley opposite *(BB)*

☆ **Bury**, W Sus [A29 Pulborough—Arundel; TQ0113], *Black Dog & Duck*: Typical village pub, interesting for its small and very ancient back lounge; main bar more like a games room, full of locals; friendly welcome, Gales HSB, well prepared generous bar food (not Sun or Wed evenings) in small dining room; pleasant garden *(Jenny and Brian Seller, R Bennett, Alan Skull, Iain and Penny Muir)*

☆ **Chalvington**, E Sus [village signposted from A27 and A22; then follow Golden Cross rd — OS Sheet 199 map reference 525099; TQ5109], *Yew Tree*: Isolated country local stripped down to bricks and flagstones inside, with elm seats built into the walls, low beams and inglenook fireplace; straightforward bar food (not Sun), well kept Harveys and Fremlins; popular with young people Fri and Sat evenings, and at other times atmosphere may be dominated by its regulars; attractive little walled terrace, and extensive grounds inc own cricket pitch *(M A and C R Starling, Dr B A W Perkins, BB)*

☆ **Chelwood Gate**, E Sus [A275 S of Forest Row; TQ4129], *Red Lion*: Good quickly served bar food from big filled rolls and ploughman's through cold buffet to hot dishes such as steak and kidney pie or veal and pepper crumble, well kept King & Barnes and Watneys-related real ales on handpump, green plush furnishings, small coal fire, lacy-tablecloth dining room on left; delightful large sheltered garden with well spaced tables and barbecue; children welcome; the latest venture of Leon Banks, who made the Old Crown in Skirmett (Bucks) and Butchers Arms at Sonning Common (Oxon) such a success *(BB)*

Chichester, W Sus [Goodwood Park Hotel, in grounds of Goodwood House; SU8809], *Richmond Arms*: Former coaching inn transformed into stylish county hotel with partly detached pubby part; good meals, nice atmosphere *(E G Parish)*

☆ **Chidham**, W Sus [Cot Lane; off A27 at Barleycorn pub; SU7903], *Old House At Home*: Cottagey old pub in remote, unspoilt farm-hamlet location, with well kept Ballards, Ringwood Best and Old Thumper and a couple of guest beers, farm cider, country wines, welcoming atmosphere, open fire in winter, seats outside in summer; good range of reasonably priced bar food from sandwiches to steaks, inc vegetarian dishes and good specials such as casseroled pheasant; children welcome; nearby walks by Chicester Harbour *(Brian and Anna Marsden, Richard Houghton, Mr Cowell, A G Roby, LYM)*

Chilgrove, W Sus [SU8214], *White Horse*: More restaurant than pub, and a smart one at that, with fine but expensive wines; but they do have good bar lunches inc a good choice of meats, seafood and help-yourself salads at reasonable prices; tables out in front and on green opposite; closed Sun and Mon, and not a place to drop in to just for a drink *(G Holliday)*

☆ **Cocking**, W Sus [A286 Midhurst—Chichester — OS Sheet 197 map reference 878179; SU8717], *Cobden*: Welcoming low-beamed three-roomed 18th-century pub with well cushioned settles and other seats, open fire, generous helpings of good value bar food, well kept Badger Best and Tanglefoot, Ballards and Wadworths 6X, friendly staff; piped music can be rather intrusive; good steady walk from here up to South Downs Way; shut Mon lunchtime *(Jenny and Brian Seller, Frank Cummins)*

☆ **Colemans Hatch**, E Sus [signposted off B2026; or off B2110 opp church; TQ4533], *Hatch*: Basic but welcoming rustic pub with lunchtime sandwiches, cheese rolls and home-made pies, pub games, well kept Larkins and Harveys BB on handpump, no juke box, Ashdown Forest views from tables on bluff of grass by quiet lane; outside lavatories; very busy summer weekends *(Jenny and Brian Seller, Comus Elliott, Richard Gibbs, LYM)*

☆ **Compton**, W Sus [SU7714], *Coach & Horses*: Very friendly Spanish licensees in spotless free house; public bar very traditional (walkers welcome here), second bar by good restaurant modernised but still with the old beams; well kept changing real ales such as Adnams on handpump *(Paul and Margaret Baker, R Houghton)*

Cooksbridge, W Sus [junction A275 with Cooksbridge and Newick rd; TQ3913], *Rainbow*: Attractive low-beamed pub with horse-brasses and old photographs; has been praised for efficient service, well kept beer inc King & Barnes Festive and wide choice of reasonably priced good bar food, but no recent reports *(News please)*

Copsale, W Sus [TQ1725], *Bridge*: Comfortable, rustic local with King & Barnes, bar food inc good home-made soup and scampi *(I W and P J Muir)*

☆ **Cousleywood**, E Sus [TQ6533], *Old Vine*: Busy but attractive low-beamed lounge bar with Fremlins on handpump, wide choice of good bar food in small bistroish dining area, good value restaurant, efficient service *(Peter Neate, R and S Bentley)*

Cripps Corner, E Sus [TQ7721], *White Hart*: Comfortable, roomy and pleasantly redecorated, with warm and friendly atmosphere; several well kept real ales, sensibly priced decent wines, good value bar food (not Sun evening), pleasant staff, garden *(Tom and Mary Farr)*

Crowborough, E Sus [Beacon Rd (A26); TQ5130], *Blue Anchor*: Attractive small old pub with surprisingly spacious eating areas; real ale, reasonably priced home-cooked food, children's play area in garden; up on Crowborough Beacon *(Colin Laffan)*; [Mount Pleasant, off Walshes Rd], *Wheatsheaf*: Genuinely pubby, with log fire in small lounge, two-room public bar *(Philip and Sheila Hanley)*

☆ **Cuckfield**, W Sus [TQ3025], *White Harte*: Popular medieval pub by lychgate to church, with cosy little comfortably modernised but olde-worlde bars, roaring log fire in inglenook, friendly licensees and good value standard pub food; well kept King & Barnes real ales, keen darts teams *(Terry Buckland, W J Wonham, Gwen and Peter Andrews, LYM)*

Cuckfield [South St], *Kings Head*: Straightforward and cosy pub with Harveys and King & Barnes real ales, games bar with murals; notable for its two restaurant areas, run as a separate leased-out operation during the week — good subtle cooking using fresh ingredients; bedrooms modern, with own facilities *(Terry Buckland)*

Dale Hill, E Sus [by Dale Hill golf club; junction A268 and B2099; TQ6930], *Cherry Tree*: Attractive buildings, has been popular for generous helpings of good food, good pleasant service and well kept Youngs ales, but no recent reports *(News please)*

☆ **Danehill**, E Sus [School Lane; off A275 opp the former Crocodile; TQ4027], *Coach & Horses*: Gently updated pub in attractive spot, with friendly young licensees, well kept Harveys, a weekly changing guest beer, decent house wine and good value bar food in dining extension — formerly a small stables *(S D Sizen, Ron Gentry)*

☆ **Dell Quay**, W Sus [SU8302], *Crown & Anchor*: Modernised 15th-century pub on site of Roman quay, yacht-harbour views from bow window and garden, good generous food with local fish dishes, evening restaurant food mostly grills; log fire, plenty of tables outside overlooking water, Watneys-related real ales *(Dr A M Rankin, BB)*

Devils Dyke, W Sus [TQ2511], *Devils Dyke*: Perched on downs above Brighton — very touristy indeed, but well worth visiting for the views, which are staggering both night and day; basic bar food, upstairs carvery, and Bass, Charrington IPA, Harveys, Tetleys and a guest beer on handpump; nr a hang-glider jumping-off point *(Keith Houlgate, Michael and Alison Sandy, LYM)*

Dial Post, W Sus [A24/B2244; TQ1519], *Crown*: Well kept friendly pub doing well under new licensee, with good food in bar and reasonably priced restaurant; Badger beer *(Ron Gentry)*

Donnington, W Sus [Selsey Rd (B2201); SU8502], *Blacksmiths Arms*: Two bars with good atmosphere, decent food, well kept real ales such as Badger, Bass and Ringwood Old Thumper; new restaurant extension, occasional live music, garden *(N E Bushby, W Atkins)*

Duncton, W Sus [set back from A285 N; SU9617], *Cricketers*: Several attractive rooms on different levels, autographed cricket bats, good choice of well prepared bar food, service swift and attentive; well kept Allied and King & Barnes real ales

☆ **Eartham**, W Sus [SU9409], *George*: Country pub with cosy, uncluttered and restful lounge, and bar with games area; six well kept real ales, reasonably priced and generously served bar food, swift and courteous service; separate restaurant *(I W Muir, John Beeken, Mrs Lili Lomas)*

Easebourne, W Sus [SU8922], *Holly Tree*: Popular with locals for good bar and restaurant food, good service *(John and Heather Dwane)*

☆ **East Dean**, W Sus [village signposted off

A286 and A285 N of Chichester — OS Sheet 197 map reference 904129; SU9013], *Star & Garter*: Charmingly placed by peaceful green of quiet village below South Downs, with rustic seats and swing in pretty walled garden; bar food from sandwiches and home-made soup through omelettes and scampi to steaks, well kept Allied real ales, pub games, Bank Hol live music (lunchtime barbecues then); handy for South Downs Way, with pleasant walk to Goodwood; children in eating area *(John Pettit, LYM)*

East Grinstead, W Sus [TQ3938], *Dunnings Mill*: Low-ceilinged three-roomed 16th-century mill cottage built right over stream, with tables in pretty garden; bar food, real ales, friendly service, pleasant restaurant; children welcome; handy for Standen (NT) *(Mr and Mrs K J V, Lindsey Shaw Radley, LYM)*

☆ **Eastbourne** [The Goffs, Old Town; TV6199], *Lamb*: Interesting oak-beamed Tudor building with attractive traditional interior (including a priest hole, 12th-century vaulted crypt used as cellar, tales of secret passages — even a reputed bed-lifting poltergeist); pleasantly quiet at lunchtimes, with well kept beer, good bar food; close to art gallery and Gildredge Park, a mile from seafront *(Bernard Phillips)*

☆ **Eastbourne** [Terminus Rd], *Terminus*: Friendly, old-fashioned and busy town-centre pub with popular lunchtime food and well kept Harveys; tables and chairs out in pedestrian precinct *(Roger Taylor, Alan Skull)*

Eastbourne [Cornfield Terr], *Port Hole*: Very friendly small pub in back road parallel to seafront; well kept Bass, comfortable wooden seats and tables, upstairs restaurant; nr Devonshire Park and Congress Theatre *(Roger Taylor)*; [Terminus Rd], *Sherlock Holmes*: Reasonable food, well kept Bass, spacious rooms inc no-smoking area; very good lavatories, unobtrusive piped music *(Mr and Mrs A P Reeves)*

Eastergate, W Sus [SU9405], *Labour in Vain*: Well kept, basic pub with partly carpeted stone floor, Ballards Wassail, Harveys, Ringwood Old Thumper and Youngs Bitter and Special on handpump, good food; back car park small *(Keith Houlgate)*

Elsted, W Sus [Elsted Marsh; nearer to Midhurst than the Three Horseshoes, same road; SU8119], *Elsted*: Simple country local with straightforward food pleasantly served, warm welcome for families *(Dr R Fuller, HEG)*

Falmer, E Sus [Middle St; TQ3508], *Swan*: About eight well kept real ales in locals' bar and plusher lounge with small drinking area between the two; friendly licensee, good value simple lunchtime food *(Matt Pringle)*

☆ **Findon**, W Sus [TQ1208], *Gun*: Large helpings of good standard food, well presented though not cheap, friendly service, and well kept Marstons Pedigree and Whitbreads-related real ales on handpump in comfortably modernised straightforward pub with attractive sheltered lawn, in quiet village below Cissbury Ring *(Jenny and Brian Seller, P A Barfield, Alan and Ruth Woodhouse, LYM)*

Findon, *Villager*: Interesting pub with well

kept beer and good food *(Paul and Inge Sweetman)*

Fishbourne, W Sus [A27 Chichester—Emsworth; SZ8404], *Bulls Head*: Large 16th-century beamed bar with rustic decor and atmosphere, Watneys-related real ales with guest beers such as King & Barnes on handpump, food in bar and restaurant inc indoor cook-your-own barbecue; good friendly service *(N E Bushby)*

☆ **Fittleworth**, W Sus [Lower St (B2138); TQ0118], *Swan*: Attractive 15th-century Chef & Brewer pub with big inglenook log fire in comfortable lounge, collections of wooden truncheons and of bottle-openers, usual bar food from sandwiches up inc children's dishes but little vegetarian food, friendly service, piped music (even in gents'); landscapes by Constable's brother George in attractive panelled side room; Watneys-related real ales, games inc pool in public bar, well spaced tables on big sheltered back lawn, good walks nearby; open all day Thurs—Sat, children in eating area; bedrooms *(Dave Braisted, Alec Lewery, Marie Enright, WTF, Jenny and Brian Seller, Mrs Lili Lomas, LYM)*

Fletching, E Sus [TQ4223], *Red Lion*: Good country pub with which hasn't gone out of its way to be odiously and unnaturally countrified; good simple food, huge garden *(R Tomlinson)*

Frant, E Sus [A267 S of Tunbridge Wells; TQ5835], *Abergavenny Arms*: Imaginative choice of food, charming staff; very clean *(Anon)*

Gatwick, W Sus [Airport; TQ2941], *Country Pub*: Decent straightforward food, real ale on handpump — and reasonably comfortable, considering the number of people; successful evocation of the atmosphere of a thriving city pub *(Gordon B Mott)*

Glynde, E Sus [TQ4509], *Trevor Arms*: Good walks (nr start GWG61), nice setting, Harveys well kept; gardens packed on sunny lunchtimes — good for children, also trains to watch *(Anon)*

Hammerpot, W Sus [A27 4 miles W of Worthing; TQ0605], *Woodmans Arms*: Very low-ceilinged pub with interesting prints and horsey decor, well kept Allied real ales, massive helpings of usual pub food, friendly welcoming staff, comfortable seats inside and out, spotless lavatories *(Michael Bechley)*

☆ **Handcross**, W Sus [Horsham Rd; TQ2529], *Royal Oak*: Relaxing atmosphere, decent quickly served bar food, friendly staff and well kept Ruddles and King & Barnes in spotless pub with rooms decorated in various themes — aircraft, Falklands memorabilia inc a white ensign from HMS *Intrepid*, Churchill *(TOH, Terry Buckland, Norman Foot)*

☆ **Hartfield**, E Sus [Church St; TQ4735], *Anchor*: Bustling, thriving atmosphere, with good easy mix of drinkers and diners — generous bar food from sandwiches to steak, with emphasis on fish and seafood; prompt cheerful service in rambling beamed bar with half a dozen well kept real ales such as Adnams, Flowers Original and King & Barnes; some seats outside, restaurant (not

Sun evening) children in eating area; nr start GWG62, handy for Ashdown Forest *(Lindsey Shaw Radley, Patrick Godfrey, Paul Sexton, Sue Harrison, Philip and Sheila Hanley, Mrs C Hartley, LYM)*

☆ **Hartfield** [Gallipot St], *Gallipot*: Welcoming pub with well kept Charrington and Flowers, wide range of generous straightforward bar food, good log fire, no music or machines; on GWG62 *(Mr and Mrs P C Clark, J Sams, Lindsey Shaw Radley)*

☆ **Hartfield** [A264], *Haywaggon*: Warm welcome, oak beams, good food in very clean bar and attractive good-value restaurant, quick and attentive service; nr start GWG62 *(Mr and Mrs G Turner, Colin Laffan)*

Hastings, E Sus [All Saints; TQ8109], *Crown*: In old part of town below East Cliff; friendly barmaid, bar food inc toasted sandwiches, Harveys beers *(Dave Braisted)*; [Old Harbour], *Dolphin*: Pleasant with well furnished bar, Ruddles and good value locally caught fish, tables outside overlooking harbour *(Jenny and Brian Seller)*; [14 High St, Old Town], *First In Last Out*: Very popular town pub brewing its own keen-priced beer — nutty Ordinary, wonderful stronger Cardinal; lunchtime food, small back courtyard *(David and Fiona Easeman)*

Heathfield, E Sus [Horam Rd; TQ5821], *Prince of Wales*: Good choice of beers and wines, good value generous lunchtime carvery *(D Kayes-Knight)*

Henfield, W Sus [TQ2116], *George*: Spacious olde-worlde pub in pretty village with friendly staff, big helpings of decent bar food, well kept Gales HSB and Ushers Best; restaurant *(Dr P H Mitchell)*; *White Hart*: Doing well under current regime, with good value lunches in pleasant restaurant section, inc fresh fish *(TOH)*

☆ **Hermitage**, W Sus [36 Main Rd (A259); SU7505], *Sussex Brewery*: Superbly kept Hermitage, Warrior and Wyndhams brewed here, with guest beer such as Badger; basic sawdust-floor bar with rustic furniture, no machines, log fire, friendly bar staff; fair-priced food from sandwiches up, inc fresh local seafood (may take time but worth the wait), pianist Sun night; tiny garden *(Richard Houghton, James Adlington, M Hopton)*

☆ **Heyshott**, W Sus [SU8918], *Unicorn*: Friendly welcome and helpful service in small pub with nice local atmosphere in L-shaped bar; well kept beer and decent bar food generously served, particularly ploughman's with good range of help-yourself salads; restaurant, garden with barbecue; in attractive country at foot of Downs *(J S Evans, R D Norman, Ian and Wendy McCaw)*

☆ **Horsham**, W Sus [Tower Hill; S towards Worthing; TQ1730], *Boars Head*: Comfortable free house with three bars, well kept Eldridge Pope and Wadworths 6X, good variety of bar food, terrace *(Norman Foot, D J P Dutton)*

Horsham [Bearsden; A24 some way N], *Dog & Bacon*: Quiet, attractive cottage-type King & Barnes pub with good lunchtime and evening, pleasant service, good parking *(E G Parish)*; [31 North St], *Hurst Arms*: Pleasant bars with old-style armchairs and well kept Watneys-related real ales with King & Barnes; good reasonably priced food from ploughman's up *(Norman Foot)*

Hurstpierpoint, W Sus [High St; TQ2716], *New Inn*: Old-fashioned local with charming traditional back room, bar billiards in panelled snug, simpler public bar, well kept Bass and Charrington IPA, bar food, good value dining room, good warm atmosphere *(Mr Turrall-Clarke, LYM)*

☆ **Icklesham**, E Sus [TQ8816], *Queens Head*: Popular old beamed country pub with splendid view over Brede to Rye, good atmosphere, good value home-cooked bar food inc children's dishes, John Smiths and other real ales, farm cider, country wines, farm tool collection; small garden with pretty views *(Alec Lewery)*

Icklesham, *Oast House*: Free house with two changing real ales and good bar food, especially local fish *(Gordon Smith)*

☆ **Isfield**, E Sus [TQ4417], *Laughing Fish*: Well kept Harveys and good robust lunchtime and evening bar food in simple modernised village local; small garden, enclosed children's play area *(Alec Lewery, Alan Skull, LYM)*

Keymer, W Sus [TQ3115], *Greyhound*: Old pub with plenty of character, recently very well refurbished; good service, good value food such as beef in ale and moussaka *(Miss M Hunt)*

Kingsfold, W Sus [A24 Dorking—Horsham, nr A29 junction; TQ1636], *Dog & Duck*: Useful stop — fairly extensive menu with good specials and lovely puddings

☆ **Kirdford**, W Sus [TQ0126], *Foresters*: Well run flagstoned bar with bench seats and tables, lounge with stools, upholstered benches and tables, third room suitable for families; well kept King & Barnes, nice atmosphere, limited choice of simple but really tasty bar food prepared well by landlord's wife (inc lots of omelettes; also fresh smoked salmon), quick service; restaurant *(Norman Foot, J H Bell, John and Heather Dwane)*

☆ **Lambs Green**, W Sus [TQ2136], *Lamb*: Cosy though extended plush bar with beams and open fire in welcoming pub with lively atmosphere; wide choice of quickly and generously served food (inc good value Sun roast) and several well kept real ales such as Badger Best, Gales HSB, King & Barnes and Ruddles County; big glass-walled garden room *(Steve Goodchild, David and Sarah Gilmore, Norman Foot, BB)*

☆ **Lavant**, W Sus [Midhurst Rd (A286); SU8508], *Hunters*: Bright, attractive and roomy, with wide choice of attractively presented and reasonably priced bar food, both simple and exotic; well kept beer, nice atmosphere, pleasant restaurant, large, pretty garden; bedrooms *(Shirley Pielou, Dr P H Mitchell)*

Lavant, *Royal Oak*: Good varied food, well kept real ale tapped from the cask, two log fires, very welcoming licensees *(J H L Davis)*

☆ **Lewes**, E Sus [22 Malling St; TQ4110], *Dorset Arms*: Well renovated 17th-century pub with good bar food, especially fresh fish, and well kept Harveys — it's within sight of the brewery; restaurant, outside terraces; children in well equipped annexe

next to main bar; bedrooms *(Keith Walton, Alec Lewery, Alan Skull)*

Lewes [Castle Ditch Lane, Mount Pl], *Lewes Arms*: Thriving friendly local, little changed in the last decade or two, with decent lunchtime snacks, wider weekend choice, well kept Harveys *(David and Fiona Easeman, Alan Skull)*; [Malling St], *Prince of Wales*: Recently refurbished to very high standard, with family room, secluded terrace, tables in garden, well kept Ruddles, good value food, warm and friendly welcome; big car park *(A J Skull)*; [South St], *Snowdrop*: Tucked away at end of long cul-de-sac with nautical decor (and adjoining antique shop); well kept King & Barnes, good bar food strong on seafood, with Mon paella/tapas evenings; juke box may be loud *(Alan Skull)*

☆ **Lindfield**, W Sus [98 High St (B2028); TQ3425], *Bent Arms*: Remarkable collection of interesting furnishings and bric-a-brac, from chinoiserie longcase clock to Afghan Wars wheel-mounted cannon — beef cooked on a spit driven by a model steam-engine (lunchtimes, not Wed or Sun), other bar food from sandwiches to grouse, friendly and efficient food service (but specials may start to run out from 12.30 so get there early), well kept Gales HSB, King & Barnes and maybe Whitbreads Pompey Royal on handpump; attractive garden; children in restaurant and eating area; bedrooms *(T Buckland, LYM)*

Lindfield [Walstead — from A272 Haywards Heath—Lewes take B2111 towards Lindfield, then left into Snowdrop Lane], *Snowdrop*: Popular recently refurbished King & Barnes pub, with good bar snacks, lunches (not Sun) and evening meals — booking advised; service quick and friendly, big car park *(A H Denman)*

☆ **Littlehampton**, W Sus [Wharf Rd; westwards towards Chichester, opp rly stn; TQ0202], *Arun View*: Built out on to harbour edge, with extensive views of river — busy here with seagoing vessels; comfortable banquettes, accurate drawings of barges and ships worked into counter-top, Whitbreads-related real ales on handpump, wide choice of reasonably priced decent bar food, restaurant (wise to book), flower-filled terrace; summer barbecues evenings and weekends *(E G Parish)*

Littleworth, W Sus [TQ1920], *Windmill*: Small, two-bar King & Barnes pub with compact but very cosy saloon bar; cheery welcome, well kept real ales, bar food *(Iain and Penny Muir)*

Lodsworth, W Sus [SU9223], *Hollist Arms*: Small bar, games room with pool, good mix of customers; well kept King & Barnes, decent wines, good range of bar food inc trout caught by landlord *(P J Taylor)*

☆ **Lower Beeding**, W Sus [TQ2227], *Crabtree*: Large pub with public bar, snug and inglenook back bar; well kept King & Barnes, good bar food, attractive dining room, attentive welcoming service *(Norman Foot, Stephen Goodchild)*

Lowfield Heath, W Sus [Charlwood Rd; TQ2740], *Flight*: Pictures and models of aircraft, good food; caters well for children in conservatory with view of planes taking off from Gatwick *(Charles Kingdon)*

☆ **Mayfield**, E Sus [TQ5827], *Middle House*:

Olde-worlde Elizabethan hotel with attentive licensee and staff; chatty bar with lots of locals, well kept Harveys and usually an interesting guest beer on handpump, darts and fruit machines at one end, wide choice of decent food, not cheap, inc lots of different ploughman's and maybe a spit-roast over the open fire; separate morning coffee/afternoon tea area with log-effect gas fire in ornate fireplace, big reddish leather chesterfield, armchairs; pretty back garden with log house, slide, dovecot, picnic-table sets and pleasant views; bedrooms *(BB)*

☆ **Midhurst**, W Sus [Petersfield Rd (A272 just W); SU8822], *Half Moon*: Popular, cheerful and friendly; wide range of good bar food at reasonable prices, restaurant *(J F Deshayes, Jim and Becky Bryson)*

☆ **Midhurst** [South St/Market Sq], *Swan*: Popular town pub with oak-beamed lounge and public bar, three Harveys real ales on handpump, wide and interesting range of bar food, restaurant; bedrooms *(Peter Ames)*
Midhurst [North St], *Angel*: Really a hotel, but good soup and other lunchtime bar snacks, also lovely olde-worlde restaurant behind the three or four bar areas; bedrooms *(John and Joan Calvert)*; [opp Spread Eagle], *Bricklayers Arms*: Opposite, though less grand than, the Spread Eagle; consistently decent food, good beer, pleasant service and a 'young' atmosphere *(K Leist)*; [A286 towards Chichester], *Royal Oak*: Worth knowing particularly for the extensive garden, though the formerly quaint little farmhouse pub is now not so easy to detect under a heavy olde-worlde refurbishment; good range of real ales and bottled beers, ploughman's and so forth; barbecues *(P J Taylor, LYM)*
Milland, W Sus [A3; SU8328], *Fox*: Well kept beer, good reasonably priced bar food (may take time when busy), huge garden with animals and swings *(P A Barfield)*; *Rising Sun*: Good choice of food, interesting collection of jugs around dining room (children allowed here and in family room); well kept Gales, dining room *(Anon)*
Netherfield, E Sus [Netherfield Hill; TQ7118], *Netherfield Arms*: Attentive, friendly licensees, quiet piped music; reasonably priced bar food inc good choice of vegetarian dishes *(Jean and Theodore Rowland-Entwistle)*
New Bridge, W Sus [A272 W of Billingshurst; TQ0625], *Limeburners Arms*: Picturesque pub with simple food, well served in friendly atmosphere; tables on lawn *(R Wilson)*

☆ **Newhaven**, E Sus [West Quay; follow West Beach signs from A259 westbound — OS Sheet 198 map reference 450002; TQ4502], *Hope*: Nice spot just out of town, with big windows looking out on the neck of the busy harbour, and upstairs conservatory room for even better view; well kept Flowers Original and Whitbreads Pompey Royal on handpump, unfussy decor with some simple nautical touches, darts and pool in the airy public bar, tables out on terrace by water; has been very popular for quickly served straightforward but good value food and warmly friendly atmosphere, but too few recent reports to judge effect of new 1990

regime *(G B Pugh, Lesley Jones, Geralyn Meyler, LYM; more reports please)*
Newhaven [High St], *Bridge*: Good value food — particularly the Sun lunch *(Win and Reg Harrington)*

☆ **Normans Bay**, E Sus [TQ6805], *Star*: Extensively modernised family pub by caravan park in remote coastal salt marshes, cushioned chairs in comfortable brick-pillared lounge, timber- effect walls and some paving-slab flooring besides the carpet, wide choice of notably generously and efficiently served food, cheerful atmosphere, piped music, fruit machines, games in children's room, seats on front terrace and in hawthorn-tree streamside garden, play area *(David Crafts, David Gaunt, T G Saul, Colin Laffan, BB)*
Northiam, E Sus [The Green; TQ8224], *Hayes Arms*: Civilised hotel overlooking village green, with big brick inglenook in comfortable if unpubby back heavy-beamed Tudor bar; Adnams tapped from the cask, lunchtime bar food inc rare beef sandwiches and hot dishes; bedrooms *(Anon)*
Nutbourne, W Sus [(the one nr Pulborough); TQ0718], *Rising Sun*: Good atmosphere, friendly staff, good food inc vegetarian dishes *(Cathy Marsh)*

☆ **Nutley**, E Sus [A22; TQ4427], *William IV*: Spacious pub, consistently friendly staff and locals, wholesome generous bar food inc good value sandwiches, well kept King & Barnes and Ushers Best, decent wines, lovely log fires *(B Moran, Jan and Ian Alcock)*
Offham, E Sus [A275 N of Lewes; TQ4012], *Blacksmiths Arms*: Comfortable and friendly, with well kept Harveys, King & Barnes and Shepherd Neame on handpump, log fires, wide choice of well prepared food inc notable home-made steak and kidney pie *(Ronald Hallett)*
Patching, W Sus [junction A27/A280; TQ0806], *Horse & Groom*: Attractive roadside pub in pleasant spot with good service, tasty food and ample parking *(E G Parish)*

☆ **Pett**, E Sus [TQ8714], *Two Sawyers*: Good village pub with friendly staff, good range of great value waitress-served bar food, well kept beer, amiable great dane *(Alec Lewery, Marie Enright)*

☆ **Petworth**, W Sus [A283 towards Pulborough; SU9721], *Welldiggers*: Smart low-ceilinged food pub very popular for its good value restaurant-style meals — hardly a place for just a drink; plenty of tables on attractive lawns and terraces *(J G Klint, LYM)*
Plumpton, E Sus [Ditchling Rd (B2116); TQ3613], *Half Moon*: Popular pub with attractive rustic tables and benches out on terrace and lawn looking towards South Downs; prompt friendly service, well kept Watneys-related real ales, good bar food (not Sun evening) specialising in ploughman's lunches; log fires and woodburner, nice painting of dozens of regulars over servery; evening restaurant *(Brian and Jenny Seller)*

☆ **Poundgate**, E Sus [OS Sheet 199 map reference 493289; TQ4928], *Crown & Gate*: Full of character, friendly staff and customers, wide range of food inc ploughman's and interesting main dishes, well kept Charrington IPA on handpump, sensible prices *(Lisa Freedman, Jenny and Brian Seller)*

☆ **Poynings**, W Sus [TQ2612], *Royal Oak*: Almost opp start of Devils Dyke climb, with decorative beams, stone fireplaces, two woodburning stoves, central servery, pleasant bar staff, well kept King & Barnes Festive and Watneys-related real ales on handpump, good varied bar food from sandwiches up inc good fish; picnic-table sets on attractive raised lawn with play area *(Frank Cummins, G B Pugh)*

☆ **Pulborough**, W Sus [99 Lower St; TQ0418], *Oddfellows Arms*: Attractive, friendly and well kept but rather pricey pub with comfortable open-plan bar divided by huge open fireplace; good food inc good sandwiches with home-cooked meats, particularly fine generously served ploughman's; Flowers Strong Country and Original; garden with children's play area *(Keith Walton)*

Pulborough [London Rd (A29)], *Five Bells*: Attractive main-road pub with interesting bar menu, real ales, and good friendly service; spotless, well appointed, garden, lots of parking space; children welcome *(E G Parish)*

☆ **Ringmer**, E Sus [outside village; A26 Lewes—Uckfield, S of Isfield turnoff; TQ4515], *Stewards Enquiry*: Formerly the Ship, tastefully refurbished by new youngish owner; good choice of food inc vegetarian dishes; good courteous service, reasonable prices, three well kept real ales; some outside tables, play area *(C T Laffan, A L Willey)*

☆ **Ringmer** [B2192, in village], *Anchor*: Pretty pub facing green in well tended large garden, with side pigeon loft and play area; bays of comfortable banquettes in attractive main room, more tables in side room, honest welcome, flowers on tables and good value bar food from sandwiches to steaks; restaurant food above average for small pub, with good choice of wines; King & Barnes and Watneys-related real ales *(C Pilbeam)*

Rotherfield, E Sus [TQ5529], *Kings Arms*: Large bar, friendly service, good choice of reasonably priced bar food inc good liver and bacon, restaurant *(Miss P T Metcalfe)*

Rottingdean, E Sus [High St; TQ3702], *Coach House*: Attractive bow-windowed pub close to sea with sedate atmosphere; real ales, well presented bar food at reasonable prices, restaurant, good service *(E G Parish)*

☆ **Rudgwick**, W Sus [Church St; TQ0833], *Kings Head*: Refurbished pub backing on to lovely old church in attractive small village, always crowded, with pleasant atmosphere, wide choice of generously served good straightforward home-made food at reasonable prices, well kept Whitbreads-related real ales, no piped music; helpful, cheerful service — generally antipodean or S African; landlord now also has Kings Head at Slinfold *(Timothy Galligan, Dr B A W Perkins, Stephen Goodchild, Mr and Mrs Foreman, D J P Dutton)*

☆ **Rudgwick** [nr entrance to Baynards Pk, NW of village], *Thurlow Arms*: Charming pub, closed when Guildford—Horsham rly closed in 60s, reopened as popular free house with

Badger, King & Barnes Broadwood, Marstons Owd Roger and other real ales, good range of food, friendly staff, memorabilia on ceiling; right on Downs Link long distance path *(Jenny and Brian Seller)*

Rusper, W Sus [village signed from A24 and A264 N and NE of Horsham; TQ2037], *Plough*: Generous collection of real ales in 17th-century pub with big inglenook in very low-beamed but smartly refurbished partly panelled bar; civilised if not cheap bar food, fountain in back garden, pretty front terrace; children welcome *(Paul Sexton, Sue Harrison, LYM)*; [off A264 S of Crawley], *Star*: Good atmosphere in unabashed old-school drinking pub with pleasant nooks and alcoves, open fires and well kept Whitbreads Strong Country and Pompey Royal *(Roy Clark)*

Rustington, W Sus [sea rd; TQ0502], *Smugglers Roost*: Attractive, modern locally popular free house with good restaurant; next to pleasant promenade *(E G Parish)*

☆ **Rye**, E Sus [Gun Garden; off A259; TQ9220], *Ypres Castle*: Its position up the hill towards the tower, with view over Rother river-mouth, is the attraction of this friendly pub, with well kept Whitbreads-related real ales, old yachting magazines, local events and art exhibition posters, bar food, piped music *(Hazel Morgan, Alan Skull, Dave Braisted)*

Rye [Military Rd], *Globe*: Straightforward pub with pleasant atmosphere (though, facing E with its back to the cliff, it darkens early in winter), decent bar food inc good sandwiches and ploughman's, kind service, well kept Courage Directors *(Capt R E H King)*; [Landgate], *Queens Head*: Old pub with friendly atmosphere, good food inc fresh local fish and good puddings, Courage ales; bedrooms *(Leo and Pam Cohen)*; [East St], *Union*: Clean and well kept useful pub with good range of relatively modestly priced bar food, real ales such as Flowers, Larkins and Ruddles, fresh flowers *(Sheila Keene, Dave Braisted, David and Diana Livesley)*

Rye Hill, E Sus [TQ9221], *Top o' the Hill*: Light and airy pub with comfortable, attractive bars and dining room; good choice of handpumped real ales, good fairly priced wines, decent choice of home-made food inc good daily roast, pies, and fresh fish — reasonably priced and in generous helpings; lovely atmosphere; bedrooms pretty *(Tom and Mary Farr)*

☆ **Sedlescombe**, E Sus [TQ7718], *Queens Head*: Attractive pub in pretty village with three distinct areas giving chatty bar and quieter corners; spotless, well furnished and decorated; Flowers on handpump, decent coffee, plain lunchtime bar food inc some freshly-made sandwiches, garden *(S J A Velate, WHBM, E G Parish)*

Selsey, W Sus [Albion Rd; SZ8593], *Lifeboat*: Good lunches in beautiful garden, very clean; friendly staff *(A H Denman)*

☆ **Selsfield**, W Sus [Ardingly Rd; B2028 N of Haywards Heath, nr West Hoathly (its postal address); TQ3434], *White Hart*: Doing well under new management; dark oak beams and timbers, big log fire dividing bar in two, well presented bar food, well kept Gales, King & Barnes Sussex and Broadwood and Tetleys; restaurant in sensitively reconstructed 16th-century barn brought here from Wivelsfield, picnic-table sets on side lawn above steep wooded combe; handy for Wakehurst Place and Ingwersen's nursery; on GWG64; children welcome *(Alan Skull, Norman Foot, Chris Fluck, LYM)*

Sharpthorne, E Sus [Horstead Lane; TQ3732], *Ravenswood*: Spacious period bar with handsome panelling in converted Victorian house, with tables outside — extensive grounds, lake, summerhouse; has been praised for good atmosphere, friendly service and Badger Best and Tanglefoot on handpump, but no recent reports *(News please)*; [Station Rd], *Bluebell*: Pleasantly unpretentious pub on Sussex Border Path; wide choice of well kept beer inc unusual guests, bar food inc good value ploughman's *(Jenny and Brian Seller)*

☆ **Shipley**, W Sus [TQ1422], *Countryman*: Two-bar Whitbreads pub with well kept Flowers and Marstons Pedigree, wide choice of good value bar food, restaurant, tables in pleasant garden *(Norman Foot)*
Shipley, *George & Dragon*: Good atmosphere, service, and reasonable choice of food; well kept King & Barnes *(Norman Foot)*

☆ **Shoreham by Sea**, W Sus [Upper Shoreham Rd; TQ2105], *Red Lion*: Lovely old pub with low beams, prompt service by welcoming staff, Watneys-related ales, decent wines, big helpings of good value unfussy bar food from sandwiches to steaks and fine salmon, Sun lunch, pretty sheltered garden with pet chipmunks; river walks, good South Downs views *(I W and P J Muir, S L Hughes)*

☆ **Shortbridge**, E Sus [Piltdown — OS Sheet 198 map reference 450215; TQ4521], *Peacock*: Attractive old pub with big inglenook fireplace, Turkey rugs on oak parquet, heavy beams in ochre ceiling, timbered walls, soft lighting, room on left set more for eating (usual bar food, from sandwiches, filled baked potatoes and ploughman's to home-made hot dishes), real ales such as Boddingtons, Courage Directors, Flowers Original, Harveys Best and Larkins on handpump; sizeable garden with playhouse *(BB)*
Singleton, W Sus [SU8713], *Horse & Groom*: Comfortable, relaxing pub with real fires and big helpings of good food even Sun; within walking distance of Weald and Downland Open Air Museum *(Jim and Becky Bryson)*

☆ **Slinfold**, W Sus [The Street; TQ1131], *Kings Head*: Comfortable two-bar pub with good choice of cheap honest food served generously, separate dining room and children's room, well kept Marstons and Whitbreads-related real ales, tables in garden, big car park; recently taken over by the landlord of the successful Kings Head at Rudgwick *(Stephen Goodchild, Norman Foot)*

☆ **South Harting**, W Sus [B2146; SU7819], *White Hart*: Attractive old pub of some character, more popular than spacious, with big log fire, attentive licensees and staff, proper separate public bar for locals and young people; above-average home-cooked food at only average prices; decent coffee *(Dr P H Mitchell)*
South Harting, *Coach & Horses*: South Downs village pub with open log fires, good food and drink, garden; children's room with toys, big blackboards and coloured chalks *(A J Blackler)*; *Ship*: South-facing and full of sparkle on sunny day; pleasant welcome under new regime with cosy log fire, classical piped music, comfortable benches; well kept beer, good, fresh and well presented food; spotless throughout *(Mrs R C Cussons)*

☆ **Stoughton**, W Sus [signposted off B2146 Petersfield—Emsworth; SU8011], *Hare & Hounds*: Much modernised 17th-century brick-and-flint village pub in heart of South Downs, pine cladding, red leatherette, big open fires in dividing chimney, an airy feel; good home-cooked bar food (served soon after opening), changing well kept real ales such as Boddingtons, Fullers London Pride, Gales and Greene King Abbot, friendly young staff, winter restaurant, back darts room, pretty terrace; children in eating area and restaurant; nr start GWG56 *(A J Blackler, R Houghton, LYM)*
Sutton, W Sus [nr Bignor Roman Villa; SU9715], *White Horse*: Two-bar walkers' pub, very attractive outside, with well kept King & Barnes Sussex and Youngs Special and good bar food *(Jenny and Brian Seller)*

☆ **Tismans Common**, W Sus [TQ0732], *Mucky Duck*: Oak beams, timbers and flagstones in cheery well run country pub with good choice of standard home-cooked bar food, well kept King & Barnes and Tetleys, lively evening atmosphere, play area and garden seats *(R Caldwell, LYM)*

☆ **Trotton**, W Sus [A272 Midhurst—Petersfield; SU8323], *Keepers Arms*: Straightforwardly furnished L-shaped bar angling around into restaurant area, in beamed and timbered tile-hung pub standing on a little rise — country views from its latticed windows and from teak tables on a narrow terrace; real ales such as Badger Best and Tanglefoot, Ballards and Ruddles County on handpump, decent spirits, lots of non-alcoholic drinks, quietly chatty atmosphere, decent straightforward food cooked nicely and served quickly *(Chris Fluck, Steve Goodchild, BB)*
Trotton, *Southdowns*: Obviously a hotel, but separate bar of wider appeal, with very courteous service in comfortable surroundings, food good and not over-priced; a beer brewed for the hotel, and real ales on handpump; bedrooms *(E G Parish)*

☆ **Turners Hill**, W Sus [East St; TQ3435], *Crown*: Rustic bookshelves-and-Staffordshire-china refurbishment, pictures inc Victorian oils, low settees as well as tables with dining chairs, open fire, steps down to recently extended bookable dining area with lofty stripped beams and pitched rafters; well kept Friary Meux Best and Tetleys, wide choice of quickly served bar food from ploughman's through pies and marinated lamb to steaks, soft piped music; tables in garden, and in front; handy for Wakehurst Place, and Standen (NT); two bedrooms *(NAC, Robert and Elizabeth Scott, John Pettit,*

Lindsey Shaw Radley, BB)
Uckfield, E Sus [High St; TQ4721], *Olde Maidens Head*: Hotelish though not upmarket bar of some potential, two parquet-floored partly carpeted rooms separated by staircase, comfortable straightforward furnishings, bar food, piped music, dining room; bedrooms *(Brian C Smith, Patrick Young, BB)*
Upper Beeding, W Sus [A2037; TQ1910], *Rising Sun*: Fairly old pub just off South Downs Way, well laid out inside, with well kept Whitbreads Strong Country and Pompey Royal, bar food inc good ploughman's — not cheap but lavish; pleasant garden *(Jenny and Brian Seller)*
☆ **Upper Dicker**, E Sus [TQ5510], *Plough*: Fine country pub with three separate welcoming rooms, one with log fire in winter, friendly staff, wide choice of well prepared bar food, Watneys-related and King & Barnes real ales, good homely atmosphere — busy in the evenings; sadly, they won't waive their no-table-bookings policy even for someone with a severe disability; children's swings in big garden *(E G Parish)*
Walberton, W Sus [set back from A27 Arundel—Chichester, by B2132 junction — OS Sheet 197 map reference 975067; SU9705], *Royal Oak*: Good roadside pub with spick and span, fresh-looking interior; adequate spaces for snacks (with even a mini-billiard-table) and pleasant restaurant section, both with a good choice of food; Watneys-related real ales *(TOH)*
☆ **Warbleton**, E Sus [TQ6018], *Warbil in Tun*: Very wide choice of food in isolated yet friendly dining pub, with pleasant and efficient staff; good cooking at reasonable prices (the meat is especially good) in cosy beamed L-shaped bar with plum-coloured seating, big log fire, Flowers IPA and Harveys on handpump *(J H Bell)*
☆ **Warnham**, W Sus [Friday St; TQ1533], *Greets*: Incredible 15th-century rambling pub, beautifully restored but retaining its uneven flagstone floor and inglenook fireplace; friendly atmosphere, well kept Flowers and Whitbreads Strong County, imaginative home cooking and pleasant garden *(Alison Anholt-White)*
Warnham [just off A24 Horsham—Dorking], *Sussex Oak*: Olde-worlde big bar and eating area, large fire, darts corner; friendly welcome, warm atmosphere and well kept beer; no food Sat evenings *(Mayur Shah)*
☆ **Washington**, W Sus [just off A24 Horsham—Worthing; TQ1212], *Frankland Arms*: Roomy and welcoming pub with wide range of enjoyable food specialising in pies such as chicken and chestnut, luscious gateaux, several real ales, decent house wines, pleasant, efficient staff; large bar, smaller dining area, games area with pool and darts; tables in garden *(Mrs J A Blanks, Alec Lewery)*
☆ **West Firle**, E Sus [village signed off A27

Lewes—Polegate; TQ4607], *Ram*: Village inn with well kept Harveys, traditional bar games, seats in big walled garden; near a fine stretch of the South Downs with spectacular coastal scenery, and close to Glyndebourne; under new regime (friendly and helpful) the food is rather more sophisticated, though still good value, with free-range pork and so forth; three recently updated bedrooms, with big breakfasts *(PB, HB, N Patton, Tony Gayfer)*
West Itchenor, W Sus [SU8001], *Ship*: Large pub in good position near Chichester Harbour and sailing clubs; bar food and separate restaurant; tables with benches and parasols outside; said to be able to get supplies for yachtsmen (nearest shop is two miles away) *(Hazel R Morgan)*
☆ **West Marden**, W Sus [B2146 2 miles S of Uppark; SU7713], *Victoria*: Pleasant rustic surroundings, well kept Gibbs Mew, decent house wines, constantly changing good home-made food inc generous ploughman's and interesting hot dishes, quick friendly service, restaurant; best to book Fri/Sat *(R Houghton, D D Ash)*
Westergate, W Sus [SU9305], *Olde Stables*: Comfortable and welcoming, largely in modern extension; good range of food such as toasted bacon, cheese and mushroom sandwiches or venison pie *(Ian Phillips)*
Wilmington, E Sus [TQ5404], *Wilmington Arms*: More like a converted private house than a pub, but popular with locals, pleasant and comfortably furnished, and useful for a quiet drink *(PB, HB)*
☆ **Wisborough Green**, W Sus [TQ0526], *Three Crowns*: Comfortable and spotless recently refurbished bar and adjoining dining rooms with oak beams, brick walls, parquet and carpeted floors; well kept Allied real ales, wide choice of reasonably priced bar food inc good Sun roast, good service by pleasant young staff *(Steve Goodchild, C T and J M Laffan, Mike and Sue Wheeler, John and Heather Dwane)*
☆ **Wivelsfield Green**, E Sus [TQ3519], *Cock*: Transformed by new licensees with well kept ales and good value home-made bar food cooked by landlord *(Ron Gentry)*
Worthing, W Sus [Chapel Rd; TQ1303], *Fountain*: Roomy pub with enormous helpings of reasonably priced good food with plenty of fresh vegetables; well kept Bass, good atmosphere, friendly North Country landlord *(Mr and Mrs A P Reeves)*; [High St, Old Tarring], *George & Dragon*: Spacious, busy pub with cosy, friendly atmosphere, decent home-cooked food, Watneys-related real ales, secluded and attractive garden *(Sion Hughes, P Gillbe)*; [80-82 Marine Parade], *Wine Lodge*: Roomy seafront pub with pleasant staff, mixed clientele, Ruddles and Youngers IPA, wine from the barrel, good reasonbly priced bar food generously served; quiet at lunchtime, but has three pool tables and can get packed Fri/Sat evenings, with disco-type music *(D L Johnson)*

Tyne & Wear   *see* Northumbria

Warwickshire   *see* Midlands

West Midlands   *see* Midlands

Wiltshire

Food and drinks prices here are not far off the national average. Beers from the Devizes brewer, Wadworths, are widely sold here, and tend to be reasonably priced; Arkells (Swindon) and Gibbs Mew (Salisbury) are also significant forces in the local market, with Wiltshire (Tisbury) gaining ground. A few even smaller breweries may produce real bargains: they supplied the three cheapest main entries we found for drinks here, the Three Crowns at Brinkworth (tied to Whitbreads, but selling Archers from Swindon more cheaply), the Rising Sun near Lacock (Moles), and the Vine Tree at Norton (a beer brewed specially for them). We found that around one in four pubs met our low-price targets of under £1 for bargain snacks or, more usually, under £3 for main dishes (the Royal Oak at Great Wishford managed both); this is a better proportion than we found in the neighbouring counties of Berkshire, Hampshire and Oxfordshire. Pubs currently doing particularly well here include the Crown at Alvediston (quite recovered from its fire now, and more warmly pubby under a new landlady who used to run a heavy-plant hire company), the friendly Maypole at Ansty, the ancient Talbot at Berwick St John (a new main entry, under welcoming licensees who've bought it out as a free house and are serving more food), the Cross Guns near Bradford on Avon (tastefully extended by good new licensees), the Three Crowns at Brinkworth (good interesting food in attractive surroundings – another new main entry), the unpretentious Red Lion at Castle Eaton (the first pub on the Thames; it's also new to the Guide, with a fine waterside garden), the Compasses at Chicksgrove (food even better under its go-ahead new licensees), the Bear in Devizes (great character), the memorably welcoming unspoilt Horseshoe at Ebbesbourne Wake, the cosy and civilised White Hart at Ford (readers find it ever harder to drag themselves away), the Saracens Head in Highworth (a new main entry), the Lamb at Hindon (particularly enthusiastic reports from readers), the warm-hearted Red Lion in Lacock, the Rising Sun just outside (well worth tracking down), the happy Suffolk Arms in Malmesbury, the very enjoyable Silver Plough at Pitton (its high food prices are fully justified by the outstanding quality), the traditional George & Dragon at Potterne, the Bell at Ramsbury (good new licensee, wider choice of beers, food perhaps even better than before), the Haunch of Venison in Salisbury (lovely atmosphere), the canalside Barge at Seend (splendid refurbishment) and the warmly welcoming Royal Oak at Wootton Rivers (good food). Among the Lucky Dip entries at the end of the chapter, pubs which have been showing notably well in recent months include the Crown at Aldbourne, Red Lion at Axford, Bunch of Grapes in Bradford on Avon, Fox & Goose at Coombe Bissett, Swan at Enford, Village Inn in Liddington, Hatchet at Lower Chute, Old Ship in Mere, Carpenters Arms at Sherston, Black Horse at Wanborough, Red Lion at West Dean, New Inn at Westwood and Bell at Wylye.

ALVEDISTON ST9723 Map 2

Crown 🍺

Village signposted on left off A30 about 12 miles W of Salisbury

This Grade II listed building, magnificently thatched (and with some crowns carved on to the roof), has two open-plan beamed rooms comfortably furnished in greens, pinks and browns, brocaded seats, subdued lighting, and a fire at one end. The extension which opens on to the garden is now permanently the restaurant under the new licensee, and the middle room is now the family room. Bar food includes soup (65p), sandwiches (from £1.20), moules (£2.50), ploughman's (£2.75), and steak and kidney pie, chilli con carne or gammon (all £4.95), Sunday lunch (£4.95) and children's dishes (from £1.25). Eldridge Pope Hardy, Hook Norton and Wadworths 6X on handpump. On different levels around a thatched white well, the attractive garden is nicely broken up with shrubs and rockeries among neatly kept lawns; it faces a farmyard with ponies and other animals, and there's a children's play area. Until recently the pub was known as the Weight for Age; the bedrooms now have four-poster beds. *(Recommended by WFL, Ian Phillips, Trevor and Helen Greenfinches, Gordon and Daphne, Richard Fawcett; more reports on the new regime please)*

Free house   Licensee Mrs Moxam   Real ale   Meals and snacks   Partly no-smoking restaurant   Children welcome   Open 12–2.30, 6–11   Bedrooms tel Salisbury (0722) 780335; £25B/£46B

ANSTY ST9526 Map 2

Maypole

Village signposted from A30 Shaftesbury–Salisbury

Dwarfed by England's tallest maypole (brought from Fonthill Abbey in October 1982, though there have been maypoles here since the 15th century), this white-shuttered brick and flint pub has spindleback chairs, cushioned wall seats and winged settles around tables on the Turkey carpet, dark green hessian walls hung with old local photographs, drawings and hunting prints, and a welcoming, attentive landlord. Popular bar food includes sandwiches (from £1.15, home-cooked ham £1.35), soup (£1.35), filled baked potatoes (from £1.95), ploughman's (from £2.50), lasagne (£3.50), salads (from £3.25, topside of beef £4.75), seafood platter (£4.75), breaded chicken with cream cheese and pineapple filling (£5.25), gammon steak with egg or pineapple (£5.95), trout (£6.25), steaks (from £8.95), and enterprising puddings; Sunday roast (£4.25). Well kept Butcombe, Fullers London Pride and Wadworths 6X on handpump. There are seats in front and in the back garden. The manor house next door has a unique pond that is three feet above the road surface, is 30ft deep in places and stocked with trout for private fishing. The pub is near *Good Walks Guide* Walk 34. *(Recommended by J S Evans, Mayur Shah, Mr and Mrs B E Witcher, J Lyons, R Harrison, Roy McIsaac, R W Stanbury)*

Free house   Licensees Brian and Pat Hamshere   Real ale   Meals and snacks (not Sun evening or Mon)   Restaurant (not Sun evening)   Children over 5 in eating area   Open 11–2.30, 6.30–11; closed Sun evening and Mon, except Bank Holidays (they then close the next day)   Bedrooms tel Tisbury (0747) 870 607; £23B/£40B

BECKHAMPTON SU0868 Map 2

Waggon & Horses

A4 Marlborough–Calne; OS Sheet 173, map reference 090689

The new licensee in this old-fashioned, heavy-stoned and thatched pub has converted the lounge into a dining room; however the rest of the bar is still open-plan, with beams in the shiny ceiling where walls have been knocked through, a large, old-fashioned high-backed settle on one side of the room, with a smaller one opposite, as well as red cushioned Windsor chairs, leatherette stools, and comfortably cushioned wall benches; fruit machine, darts, cribbage, dominoes and CD juke box. Bar food includes home-made soup (£1.25), lots of sandwiches (from £1.10, toasted from £1.15, steak £2.95), home-made pâté (£1.50), ploughman's (from £2.50), vegetable lasagne (£3.50), salads (from £3.75), plaice (£4.95), gammon with pineapple (£5.50), steaks (from £7.75), and puddings like home-made fruit pie (£1.50); children's helpings on request. Well kept Wadworths IPA, 6X, Farmers Glory and in winter Old Timer on handpump. Silbury Hill – a prehistoric mound – is just towards Marlborough, and Avebury stone circle and the West Kennet long barrow are very close too. *(Recommended by R W Stanbury, Roger Cunningham, Deborah Frost, David Backhouse, A Triggle, Peter Woods, Tony and Lynne Stark, A R Sayer, David and Christine Foulkes; more reports please)*

Wadworths   Manager Ian McPhail   Real ale   Meals and snacks   Children in own room   Open 11–3, 6–11; closed evening 25 Dec

BERWICK ST JOHN   ST9323   Map 2

Talbot

Village signposted from A30 E of Shaftesbury

This simply furnished Ebble Valley village pub has a single long bar with heavy black beams and cross-beams, nicely shaped with bevelled corners, as well as cushioned solid wall and window seats, spindleback chairs and a comfortable kitchen armchair in the carpeted end, by a huge inglenook fireplace with a good iron fireback and its bread ovens still intact; at the other end there's a high-backed built-in settle. Bar food – with a wider range under the new licensees – includes soup (£1.20), lunchtime sandwiches (from £1.75) or ploughman's (£2.50), basket meals (from £2.85), macaroni with cheese and bacon (£3.50), steak and kidney pie, curry or lasagne (£3.95), with evening steaks (from £6.95). Adnams, Bass, Badger and Wadworths on handpump. Some tables on the back lawn, with swings for children. *(Recommended by Mr and Mrs B E Witcher; more reports please)*

Free house   Licensees W A and R H Rigby   Real ale   Meals and snacks (not Sun) Open 11.30–2.30(3 Sat), 6.30–11; winter closing 10.30

nr BRADFORD-ON-AVON   ST8060   Map 2

Cross Guns

Avoncliff; pub is across footbridge from Avoncliff Station (first through-road left, heading N from river on A363 in Bradford centre, and keep bearing left), and can also be reached down very steep and eventually unmade road signposted Avoncliff – keep straight on rather than turning left into village centre – from Westwood (which is signposted from B3109 and from A366, W of Trowbridge); OS Sheet 173 map reference 805600

This old-fashioned pub has a large ancient fireplace with a smoking chamber behind it, stone walls, low 17th-century beams, and rush-seated chairs around plain sturdy oak tables. Bar food includes sandwiches (from 75p), home-made pâté, ploughman's (from £1.45), home-made steak and kidney pie (£3.40), various fish dishes including crab, trout and lemon sole, and steaks; well kept Badger Tanglefoot, Ruddles Best and County, Smiles Best and Ushers Best on handpump. Darts, dominoes, cribbage, fruit machine and piped music. In summer its floodlit and terraced gardens are quite a draw – they overlook the wide river Avon and a maze of bridges, aqueducts (the Kennet & Avon Canal) and tracks winding through this quite narrow gorge. *(Recommended by Chris Raisin, B R Woolmington, GB, Roger Huggins, Tony and Lynne Stark, P and R Woods, Ian and Debby Mullins)*

Free house   Licensees Dave and Gwen Sawyer   Real ale   Meals and snacks   Open 11–3, 6.30–11   Bedrooms tel Bradford on Avon (02216) 2335; £14/£28

BRINKWORTH   SU0184 Map 2

Three Crowns 🏆

The Street; B4042 Wootton Bassett–Malmesbury

Unlike some other pubs serving inventive restaurant-quality food, this gives equal attention to humbler, pubbier things: at lunchtime excellent double-decker rolls (from £1.10), fine ploughman's (from £3.95 – not cheap, but a collossal helping) and interesting filled baked potatoes (from £3.95). Main dishes include an excellent steak and kidney pie done with Guinness (£5.95), steaks (from £8.45) and rack of lamb (£9.15), alongside more unusual things such as crisp-flavoured vegetarian crêpes (£6), lamb and mint pie (£6.25), guineafowl (£7.45), monkfish done with prawns and scampi in a vermouth sauce (£8.45), baked bream or a prize-winning dish of sautéed scallops wrapped in bacon and served with a Benedictine cream sauce (£8.95), and a tender and unusual duck flavoured lightly with fresh strawberries (£11.45); occasional pig roasting in the garden. Besides well kept Archers Village, Flowers IPA, Marstons Pedigree and Wadworths 6X on handpump, they have decent spirits and wines including some useful bin-ends. The L-shaped bar, not large, rambles around the servery, giving a series of quiet enclaves without cutting people off from the overall pub atmosphere – relaxed and easy-going, with discreet piped music. Two of the tables are gigantic forge bellows, others are stripped deal, with green-cushioned big pews and blond chairs. The plaster's been partly stripped away from the masonry; there are big landscape prints and other pictures, some horse-brasses on the dark beams, a dresser with a collection of old bottles, log fires; on the right there are sensibly placed darts and a fruit machine. The garden stretches around the side and back, with well spaced tables, a good climber, a beached bumper-car and maybe a summer skittle alley; it looks over a side lane to the village church, and out over rolling prosperous farmland. *(Recommended by Mr and Mrs Peter Woods, E U Broadbent, David and Christine Foulkes, A H Bishop)*

Whitbreads   Licensee A Windle   Real ale   Meals (12–2, 6.30–9.30) and lunchtime snacks   Occasional live music   Open 10–2.30(3 Sat), 6–11

CASTLE EATON   SU1495 Map 2

Red Lion

The Street; village signposted off A419 Swindon–Cirencester

It's the big garden along the bank of the fledgling upper Thames which makes this unpretentious village local so special: well spaced picnic-table sets among lots of willows and poplars, with carefully tended flowers and lighting by old streetlamps, and a neat boules pitch – no dogs. The small, simple lounge on the right has scarcely changed since we first saw it over 30 years ago: simple chairs around a few tables on the parquet floor, a brown dado, big fireplace. On the left a little carpeted snug leads through into a games bar with darts, pool, dominoes, shove-ha'penny, juke box (strong on 60s/70s), space game and fruit machine. A limited bar menu includes sandwiches (from £1), filled rolls (from £1.10), very filling soups such as chicken and ham (£2.60), potted shrimps (£2.90), home-made hot-pot (£2.95) and bangers and mash (£3.30), but given 24 hours' notice they'll cook much more ambitiously – pigeon hot-pot (£5.30), roast gammon knuckle (£5.60), pheasant casserole (£6.95) or wild duck (£8.50); and will try to do anything you ask for. Well kept Courage Best and Directors on handpump, quietly friendly newish licensees. *(Recommended by Ewan McCall, Tom McLean, Roger Huggins, David Backhouse, Jenny and Brian Seller)*

Courage   Licensee Tony Beare   Real ale   Meals and snacks   Children if eating Open 12–3, 6–11, but may open longer on good afternoons

CHICKSGROVE   ST9629 Map 2

Compasses

From A30 5 1/2 miles W of B3089 junction, take lane on N side signposted Sutton

Mandeville, Sutton Row, then first left fork (small signs point the way to the pub, but at the pub itself, in Lower Chicksgrove, there may be no inn sign – look out for the car park); OS Sheet 184 map reference 974294

New licensees (one of them actually the old manager) in this peaceful inn have been well received by readers. Inside, high-backed wooden settles form snug booths around tables on the mainly flagstone floor, the partly stripped stone walls are hung with farm tools, traps and brasses, and there are old bottles and jugs on the beams above the roughly timbered bar counter. The good choice of home-made bar food includes sandwiches, ploughman's, avocado with prawns or smoked trout (£3.20), steak and kidney pudding (£3.50) or pie (£3.75), cod and broccoli bake (£3.75), gravadlax or smoked salmon (£3.95), Sunday roasts (£4.95), and puddings (from £1.75). Well kept Adnams, Wadworths 6X and IPA on handpump; darts, shove-ha'penny, table skittles, dominoes, cribbage and piped music. The big garden and the flagstoned farm courtyard are fine places to sit. They're planning an extension to the bedrooms. (*Recommended by Maureen and Steve Collins, Roy McIsaac, Gordon and Daphne, WHBM, Mrs J A Gardner, Barbara M McHugh; more reports please*)

Free house   Licensees Andrew and Linda Moore   Real ale   Meals and snacks Restaurant; bookings only, Sun   Children welcome   Open 12–3, 7–11   Bedrooms tel Fovant (072 270) 318; £15B/£30B

CORTON   ST9340 Map 2

Dove ★ ⊘

Village signposted from A36 at Upton Lovell, SE of Warminster; this back road on the right bank of the River Wylye is a quiet alternative to the busy A36 Warminster–Wilton

Beautifully kept, this charming cottagey pub has attractive furnishings such as cushioned brick side benches, red bentwood cane chairs on the brick-tiled floor, a cane settle with colourful cushions by a pretty little chest-of-drawers in an alcove under the stairs, and a rug in front of the small log fire. Ruddles County and Ushers Best on handpump and good wines including some New World ones. Bar food, on current reports holding up under the new licensees, includes home-made soup (£1.30; summer gazpacho £2.50), pâté (£1.85), good ploughman's (£3.15), half pint of prawns (£3.50), with more main dishes such as roast quail or fish pie (£3.95), steak and kidney pie (£4.25), an Indonesian dish of beef with spinach and coconut (£4.95), whole plaice (£5.25), and steaks (from £10.25); puddings such as home-made ice creams (from £2). There are rustic seats on the grass behind the stone building, which has dovecots by the climbing roses on its walls, as well as a barbecue area and a children's bar and play area. A new conservatory should have been built by the time you read this. (*Recommended by Tony Gayfer, TBB, B H Pinsent, R W Stanbury, Mrs A Cotterill-Davies, Robert and Elizabeth Scott, Col G D Stafford, James Cane, Mrs P Turner; more reports please*)

Ushers (Watneys)   Licensee Stuart Broadbent   Real ale   Meals and snacks (12–3, 7–10; not Sun evening except on Bank Hols)   Restaurant; closed Sun evening Children in restaurant   Open 11–3.30, 6–11; 11–11 Sat

DEVIZES   SU0061 Map 2

Bear ⇌

Market Place

The Wadworths IPA and 6X on handpump, served from an old-fashioned bar counter with shiny black woodwork and small panes of glass, is consistently well kept in this unchanging ex-coaching inn; it's brewed in the town, and from the brewery you can get it in splendid old-fashioned half-gallon earthenware jars. The big main bar, leading off the central hall, has old prints on the walls, muted red button-back cloth-upholstered bucket armchairs around oak tripod tables, black winger wall settles, fresh flowers here and there, and big logs on the fire in winter. The Lawrence room, down some steps from the main bar and separated from it by an old-fashioned glazed screen, is in a traditional style, with dark oak-panelled walls, a parquet floor, shining copper pans on the mantlepiece above the big open fireplace, and plates around the walls; it's useful for serving food until 10pm, in the evening as well as at lunchtime: salads such as turkey and ham pie with cranberry topping or daily hot dishes such as sausage plait with tomato, cheese and herbs or spicy meat loaf with tomato sauce (all around £3.50); evening extras include ratatouille lasagne (£4.35), a generous mixed grill (£4.65), chicken satay (£6.50) and steaks (from £7); tempting puddings, and a children's menu. Quick snacks such as a good range of sandwiches or rolls (from £1, vegetarian wholewheat crispbread sandwich £1.35, roast sirloin of beef with horseradish £1.75, smoked salmon with capers £3.45, steak £3.45), and ploughman's (from £1.25) are served from the bar, with a wider choice ordered from the Lawrence Room waitress in the evening; freshly ground coffee, Sunday roast lunches, and afternoon teas; helpful service. (*Recommended by P J Taylor, Gwen and Peter Andrews, David Eversley, T J Maddison, Sarah Vickers, William Rodgers, Dr J R Hamilton, D I Baddeley, A R Sayer, Doug Kennedy, David Backhouse, Peter Burton*)

Wadworths   Licensees W K and J A Dickenson   Real ale   Meals (11–2, 7–10, not Sun) and snacks   Restaurant; closed Sun evening   Children in eating area   Open 11–11; closed 25 and 26 Dec   Bedrooms tel Devizes (0380) 722444; £45B/£60B

EBBESBOURNE WAKE   ST9824   Map 2

Horseshoe

On A354 S of Salisbury, right at signpost at Coombe Bissett; village is around 8 miles further on

The tables in this delightfully simple, homely downland pub are usually decorated with fresh flowers from the most attractive little garden where seats look out over the small, steep sleepy valley of the River Ebble. The spotless and carpeted public bar is a friendly parlour, its beams crowded with lanterns, farm tools and other bric-a-brac and there's an open fire. Simple bar food consists of sandwiches (from £1.30), trout pâté (£3.50), and ploughman's (£2.45) with other hot dishes such as home-made soup (£1), steak and kidney pie (£3.75) and lemon sole with crabmeat (£3.95); Sunday lunch (£5.95). Well kept Adnams Bitter, Bunces Best, Wadworths 6X and a guest drawn straight from the row of casks behind the bar; farm cider and malt whiskies, darts and piped music. Booking is advisable for the small restaurant. (*Recommended by Mr and Mrs F Hutchings, Gordon and Daphne, Prof H G Allen, Mrs J A Gardner, Roy McIsaac, JM, PM, R W Stanbury, Sidney Wells,*)

Free house   Licensees Anthony and Patricia Bath   Real ale   Meals (not Mon) and lunchtime snacks   Restaurant (evenings and Sun lunchtime only)   Children in restaurant   Open 12–2.30, 7–11 Mon, 11.30–2.30, 6.30–11 Tues–Sat; winter opening 12–2.30, 7–11   Bedrooms tel Salisbury (0722) 780474; £18B/£30B

EVERLEIGH   SU2054   Map 2

Crown

A342 SE of Devizes and Upavon

Since taking over in 1989 the licensees have substantially restored this fine 17th-century building with its twin 18th-century wings; a new restaurant's been built on downstairs, with a sweeping mahogany staircase, and the bedrooms have been upgraded. The bar area has been opened out – they've knocked through to another room beyond the fireplace, and there's a variety of furniture from wood and leather rocking chairs to comfortable old velvet armchairs; fresh flowers, and watercolours and oils on the walls for sale. Home-cooked bar food includes a substantial soup (£2), filled home-baked rolls (from £2, sirloin steak £4), ploughman's (from £2.75), with a daily selection of dishes such as quail's eggs with celery salt (£2.75), hot peppered mackerel with horseradish (£3), cheese herbies (£3.50), and vegetarian dishes (from £3.50); specialities are seafood in summer and game in winter. Well kept Bass, Wadworths 6X and John Smiths Bitter on electric pump. The spacious walled garden is safe for children; fishing can be arranged for residents. Part of the restaurant is no-smoking. *(Recommended by B and J Derry, David Backhouse, HNJ, PEJ, Doug Kennedy)*

Free house   Licensee Mrs Jacki Chapman   Real ale   Meals and snacks   Restaurant Children over 5 in restaurant   Open 11–3, 6–11   Bedrooms tel Collingbourne Ducis (0264) 850229; £30B/£46B

FORD   ST8374 Map 2

White Hart 🏠

A420 Chippenham–Bristol; follow Colerne sign at E side of village to find pub

One reader found the unhurried, friendly service in this little place very much in keeping with its overall charm. The cosy bar has heavy black beams supporting the white-painted boards of the ceiling, tub armchairs around polished wooden tables, small pictures and a few advertising mirrors on the walls, gentle lighting and a big log-burning stove in the old fireplace that's inscribed 1553. Well kept Badger Best and Tanglefoot, Bass, Fullers ESB and London Pride, Greene King Abbot, Marstons Pedigree, Ruddles County, Smiles Exhibition, Tetleys Bitter and Wadworths 6X on handpump. Good bar food includes sandwiches, home-made pâté, filled baked potatoes (from £2.45), lasagne (£2.85), beef casserole or steak and kidney pie (£3.50), gammon (£3.95), and venison pie (£4.50); hearty breakfasts; piped music. In summer, you can drink outside at the front of the ivy-covered and L-shaped stone building, and there's another terrace behind, by a stone bridge over the By Brook; secluded swimming pool for residents. *(Recommended by W Bailey, Audrey and Brian Green, Dr Sheila Smith, Roger Huggins, M C Howells, P B Rea, Tim Locke, P and R Woods, Nick Dowson, Alison Hayward, A R Sayer)*

Free house   Licensee Bill Futcher   Real ale   Meals and snacks   Restaurant Children in eating area and restaurant   Open 11–3, 6–11; Sat 11–11   Bedrooms tel Castle Combe (0249) 782213; £38.50B/£53B

GIDDEAHALL   ST8574 Map 2

Crown

A420 W of Chippenham; keep your eyes skinned for the pub, as there's no village sign

For the second year running we have to report that this 16th-century listed building is to have a new landlord by the time this edition is published. As readers have so much enjoyed the pub for its unusual and interesting layout and furnishings, we are provisionally keeping it among the main entries – although we cannot yet say what the food will be (in the past it's been good value). The bar is one of the most attractively laid out in the county, full of interesting details: a fluted stone plinth made from the base of an old column, little pillars holding up a velvet-fringed canopy, red plush wall seats (some in curtain-draped alcoves), Victorian ointment posters, two cases of small stuffed birds and a stuffed rough-legged buzzard, a crook and so forth over the mantlepiece, and a couple of wicker armchairs by the big log fireplace. It has had well kept Marstons Pedigree, Moles, Smiles Exhibition, Wadworths 6X and Youngers Scotch and IPA on handpump, although the new landlord's choice may be different. *(Recommended by R W Stanbury, Peter and Rose Flower, Roger Huggins, Gordon Hewitt, Roger Cunningham, Deborah Frost, A R Sayer, Peter Woods, Dr Sheila Smith; more reports please)*

Free house   Real ale   Meals and snacks   Restaurant tel Castle Combe (0249) 782229   Children welcome   Open 11–2.30, 6–11; closed 25 and 26 Dec

GREAT WISHFORD   SU0735 Map 2

Royal Oak

In village which is signposted from A36

The new licensee who took over in early 1990 has substantially revamped this friendly village pub; the floor in the main bar is now stripped back to the wood, and there are cushioned pews, small seats and some easy chairs, beams, tapestry curtains, and in winter a log fire at each end; a newer lounge area has some fishing paraphernalia and there's a cheery family area with sturdy bleached wood tables. Eating arrangements are more flexible – you can order from the restaurant menu in the bar, and vice versa; bar food, from a wide and varying choice on blackboards, includes sandwiches (from 95p), soup (£1.45), ploughman's (from £2.95), regular dishes such as chilli con carne, lasagne and moussaka (from £2.95), several home-made pies (around £5), honey-roast lamb on the bone (£7.45), with lots of fish, game in season and Sunday roasts (which they may also make up into hot sandwiches). Ruddles County and Ushers Best and Websters on handpump, and country wines. The garden behind the pub has swings. *(Recommended by Mrs E M Brandwood, Roy McIsaac, Barry and Anne, Robert and Vicky Tod, Gordon Theaker, Helen Roe, Mr and Mrs C Austin, Gary Scott; more reports on the new regime please)*

Ushers (Watneys)   Licensee Miss Tina King   Real ale   Meals and snacks (12–2, 7–10)   Restaurant tel Salisbury (0722) 790 229   Children welcome   Open 11–2.30, 6.30–11; Fri and Sat evening opening 6   Bedrooms planned

HIGHWORTH   SU2092 Map 2

Saracens Head 🛏️

Market Place

Facing the attractive small market-place, this handsome old brick-faced inn has a big beamed lounge bar that must once have been four separate rooms – and still keeps much of that feel, as the central chimney block stops it being wholly open-plan, and as the original decor of the individual former rooms still makes itself felt. So, with easy chairs by a window looking into the courtyard here, timbered walls covered with pictures and decorative china there, and more formal tables and settles in another oak-panelled area, there's a spacious overall feeling of leisured relaxation – helped by the absence of piped music. A wide choice of good value straightforward bar food includes soup (£1.30), various starters such as Scandinavian spring roll (£1.55), ploughman's (£2.55), several weight-watcher dishes (around £2), lots of vegetarian dishes (from £2.50), basket meals such as fish and chips (£2.60), and more substantial things running up to gammon and egg (£6) and sirloin steak (£8.95). Well kept Arkells BB and BBB on handpump, decent whiskies; good friendly service; fruit machine. There are a few tables in the sheltered courtyard. *(Recommended by Dr and Mrs A K Clarke, Nigel Gibbs, Sandra Cook, Col J A B Darlington, David Backhouse)*

Arkells   Licensees Mr and Mrs Roy Bennett   Real ale   Meals and snacks   Well behaved children may be allowed   Open 11–11; Sat 11–2.30, 6–11   Bedrooms tel Swindon (0793) 762064; £38.50B/£52B

HINDON   ST9132 Map 2

Lamb ★ 🔍

B3089 Wilton–Mere

Consistently popular with readers for its food and overall charm and atmosphere, this pub has a really nice long bar: one end in the lower part has a window seat with a big waxed circular table, spindleback chairs with tapestried cushions, a high-backed settle, brass jugs on the mantlepiece above the small fireplace, and a big kitchen clock; the middle – and main – area has a long polished table with wall benches and chairs, and a big inglenook fireplace. Up some steps, a third, bigger area has lots of tables and chairs. Well kept Wadworths 6X and Youngs on handpump and large choice of malt whiskies. Bar food from a varying menu typically includes soup (£1.40), sandwiches (from £1.50), home-made game pâté (around £3), a large ploughman's (£2.95), fresh mussels (£3.95), venison sausages (£3.95), a popular curry which comes with six side dishes (£4.50), home-made game pie or liver and bacon (£4.50), roast guinea fowl (£6.25), and fish such as sardines (£4.50), red bream (£6.50), halibut (£7.25) and Dover sole (£10.95); sustaining, good value Sunday lunch; service is friendly and helpful.

Shove-ha'penny; no dogs. There are picnic-table sets across the road (which is a good alternative to the main routes west). *(Recommended by Colin Laffan, W A Gardiner, John Evans, Robert and Vicky Tod, S V Bishop, John Townsend, Patrick Young, K Baxter, James Cane, Philip and Sheila Hanley, Mrs P C Clark, Richard Gibbs, Henry Midwinter, Gordon and Daphne, J F and M Sayers, Colin Laffan, P G Giddy, Mrs S A Bishop, Dr and Mrs Tanner, J S Rutter, Patrick Young, Theo Schofield, HEG, Sue Carlyle)*

Free house　Licensees A J Morrison and J Croft　Real ale　Meals and snacks (12–2, 7–10)　Restaurant　Children in eating area　Open 11–11　Bedrooms tel Hindon (074 789) 573; £35B/£40(£55B)

KILMINGTON　ST7736　Map 2
Red Lion

Pub on B3092 Mere–Frome, 2 1/2 miles S of Maiden Bradley

The original, flagstoned part of this 15th-century local has a curved high-backed black settle, red leatherette wall and window seats, photographs on the beams, a deep fireplace with fine old iron fireback and a second, recently exposed large brick fireplace, both with log fires in winter. A newer area has a large window and is decorated with brasses, a large leather horse collar and hanging plates. Bass under light blanket pressure and Butcombe Bitter on handpump, with quickly changing guest beers; sensibly placed darts, dominoes, shove-ha'penny, cribbage and piped music. Bar food includes soup (£1), baked potatoes (from 95p), toasties or sandwiches (from £1.60), ploughman's (from £2.25), hot dishes such as meaty or vegetable lasagne (£2.60), steak and kidney or game pie (£3.25) and salads (£2.60), with, in the evenings ham and egg (£2.75), gammon steak (£3.25) and sirloin steak (£5.95). The black labrador is called Lady. Picnic-table sets in the large garden overlook White Sheet Hill (riding, hang gliding and radio-controlled gliders), which can be reached by a road at the side of the pub. *(Recommended by S V Bishop; more reports please)*

Free house　Licensee Christopher Gibbs　Real ale　Meals and snacks (not Mon and Tues eves or 25 Dec)　Children in eating area till 9　Singer/guitarist every third Thurs evening　Open 11–3, 6.30–11; closed lunchtime 25 Dec　Bedrooms tel Maiden Bradley (098 53) 263; £15/£30

LACOCK　ST9168　Map 2
George

Village signposted off A350 S of Chippenham

This atmospheric old inn has upright timbers in the place of knocked-through walls making cosy corners, a low beamed ceiling, armchairs and windsor chairs, seats in the stone-mullioned windows and flagstones just by the bar; the big central fireplace has a three-foot treadwheel set into its outer breast, originally for a dog to drive the turnspit. Well kept Wadworths IPA, 6X, and in winter Old Timer, on handpump. Bar food includes sandwiches, tasty Wiltshire ham, home-made dishes such as steak and kidney or cheese and onion pie, faggots or vegetarian dishes such as mushroom moussaka or spinach, mushroom and blue cheese crumble, and evening grills such as fresh trout or steaks. There are seats in the back garden, and a bench in front that looks over the main street. *(Recommended by Tony Triggle, Robert and Vicky Tod, Dr Sheila Smith, Nick Dowson, Alison Hayward; more up-to-date reports please)*

Wadworths　Licensee John Glass　Real ale　Meals and snacks　Restaurant tel Lacock (024 973) 263　Children welcome　Open 11–3, 6–11

Red Lion

High Street

This tall, red brick Georgian inn has a long bar divided into separate areas by cart shafts, yokes and other old farm implements, and decorated with branding irons hanging from the high ceiling, and plates, oil paintings, Morland prints, tools, and stuffed birds and animals on the partly panelled walls; old-fashioned furniture includes a mix of tables and comfortable chairs, Turkey rugs on the partly flagstoned floor, and a fine old log fire at one end; good pubby atmosphere. Well kept Wadworths IPA, 6X, in summer Farmers Glory and in winter Old Timer on handpump; good wine by the glass; darts. Popular bar food, from a blackboard that changes daily, includes soups, ploughman's, good duck terrine, and main dishes such as pasta with mushrooms and courgette, smoked mackerel with cream and coarse horseradish (£3.80), giant sausages with mustard (£4.50), free-range chicken with tarragon and white wine (£5.75), and local duck in a brandy and apricot sauce (£6.20); prices may be slightly higher in the evening; good breakfasts. They serve morning coffee from 10am, and an old stable block is used for teas, with fresh home-made scones. The pub is close to Lacock Abbey and the Fox Talbot Museum. The licensee now runs another pub, the Dandy Lion in Bradford on Avon. *(Recommended by Gethin Lewis, Jean Morris, Nick Dowson, Alison Hayward, Gwen and Peter Andrews, Sandra Kempson, John and Joan Wyatt, R W Stanbury, Hugh Saddington)*

Wadworths Licensee John Levis Real ale Meals and snacks (12–2.30, 6.30–10) Children in eating area and must be eating Open 11–3, 6–11 Bedrooms tel Lacock (024 973) 456; l£40(£48B)

nr LACOCK ST9367 Map 2

Rising Sun ★

Bowden Hill, Bewley Common; on back road Lacock–Sandy Lane

Inside this isolated little country pub the open-plan series of three welcoming rooms is refreshingly simple: one has a Victorian fireplace and sensible darts area; another has a mix of old chairs and a couple of basic kitchen tables on the stone floor, flowery cushioned wall benches, antlers on the wall, and dried flowers and plants in the windows; the third has a big case of stuffed birds, a stuffed badger, a grandfather clock, some old woodworking planes, a shotgun on the wall and a few country pictures. Well kept Moles PA, Bitter, 97 and Landlords Choice (brewed by Moles to the landlord's recipe) and Wadworths 6X on handpump, with several uncommon guest beers and Long Ashton cider; friendly service. Bar food includes generous toasties and sandwiches (£1.40), home-made smoked trout pâté (£2.30), ploughman's, and hot dishes such as home-made leek and potato soup with Wiltshire bacon scone (£1.80), garlic mushrooms (£2.10), good pork with bubble and squeak, Wiltshire sausage or macaroni cheese (£2.75), and home-made steak and kidney pie (£3.95). Dominoes, shove-ha'penny, cribbage and other card games; there are two Gordon Setters and a tabby cat. One of the best places to sit is on the two-level terrace outside, from where you can enjoy the magnificent view (especially at sunset) looking out over the Avon valley, some 25 miles or so. *(Recommended by Roger Cunningham, Deborah Frost, Peter Woods, R and E Harfield, Derek and Sylvia Stephenson, David and Christine Foulkes, Nick Dowson, Alison Hayward, Bev and Doug Warrick, Richard Houghton, Tony and Lynne Stark)*

Free house Licensees Roger and Laura Catte Real ale Lunchtime meals and snacks (not Mon or Sun) Children in eating area Folk/country Wed evening Open 12–2.30 (11–3 Sat), 7–11; closed Mon lunchtime

LANDFORD SU2519 Map 2

Cuckoo

Village signposted down B3079 off A36 Salisbury–Southampton; take first right turn towards Redlynch

The friendly little front parlour in this unspoilt haven has lots of bird pictures on the papered walls, rustic seats and spindle-back chairs on its stone floor, and a winter log fire. Three other rooms lead off, one the family room, and one with sensibly placed darts, dominoes and a juke box; maybe piped music. The wide range of well kept real ales, tapped from casks down in a cool lower back room, includes Adnams Broadside, Badger Best and Tanglefoot, Bunces Best, Wadworths IPA, 6X, Farmers Glory and winter Old Timer and a monthly guest; food is confined to fresh filled rolls (from 75p), pies and Cornish pasties (95p), and maybe ploughman's; occasional weekend barbecues. The lawn at the front of this thatched cottage is patrolled by bantam cocks, and there's a pétanque pitch and a big play area with swings and a slide. *(Recommended by Dr and Mrs A K Clarke, WHBM; more reports please)*

Free house   Licensees Derek and Jeane Proudley   Real ale   Snacks   Children in garden bar and back room   Impromptu folk music gatherings Fri and maybe Sat and Sun evenings   Open 11.30–3, 6–11 Mon-Fri; 11.30–11 Sat

LIMPLEY STOKE (Avon)   ST7760   Map 2
Hop Pole

Coming S from Bath on A36, 1300 yds after traffic-light junction with B3108 get ready for sharp left turn down Woods Hill as houses start – pub at bottom; if you miss the turn, take next left signposted Limpley Stoke then follow Lower Stoke signs; OS Sheet 172 map reference 781610

The dark-panelled room on the right here has red velvet cushions for the settles in its alcoves, some slat-back and captain's chairs on its turkey carpet, lantern lighting, and maybe a log fire. The spacious left-hand Avon Bar (with an arch to a cream-walled inner room) also has dark wood panelling, and a log-effect gas fire; the lounge is no-smoking. Bar food under the new licensees (Mr Roberts does the cooking) includes soup (£1.25), smoked trout mousse (£2), salads (from £3.50), vegetarian dishes such as pasta with courgettes in a basil sauce (£4.50), and chicken stuffed with crab and pink peppercorns (£7.50); in the evening there are extra dishes such as steaks (from £6.50) and chicken supreme (£7.50); a lunchtime help-yourself buffet operates on Tuesdays to Saturdays from Easter to September; children's menu (from £1). Courage Best and Directors on handpump; darts, dominoes, cribbage. The large garden has a summer barbecue. The pub dates from the 14th century, when it was a monks' wine lodge. *(Reports on the new regime please)*

Courage   Licensees Susan and Howard Roberts   Real ale   Meals and snacks Children in own room   Open 11–2.30(3 Sat), 6–11

LITTLE BEDWYN   SU2966   Map 2
Harrow

Village signposted off A4 W of Hungerford

A small and welcoming village local, this has three rooms to its bar; the front one's the best for eating in, and has a mixture of country chairs and simple wooden tables on its well waxed boards (one table in the bow window), flowery curtains, pale walls with large-scale local Ordnance Survey maps and a big woodburning stove. The two inner rooms are chattier; decorations include a fine brass model of a bull, and maybe locally done watercolours and photographs for sale. On your way to the lavatories you'll go through what's actually the village post office, with the original Victorian sit-up-and-beg counter. Well kept Hook Norton, Marstons Pedigree and a guest on handpump, with decent wines by the glass and a sensible small selection of malt whiskies. From a regularly changing menu, the well cooked, home-made food includes soup (£1.75), smoked salmon pâté (£2.60), ploughman's (£2.50), curry or chilli con carne (£3.80), cheesy tuna and spinach (£3.95), cidered chicken with mushrooms (£3.95), roast loin of pork with a stilton and tomato sauce (£5.75), and garlic-baked poussin with pepper and onion (£5.95); good puddings (£2); bookings are encouraged, especially on Friday and Saturday evenings and for Sunday lunchtime; part of the eating area is no-smoking. Darts, shove-ha'penny, cribbage, unobtrusive piped music. The long-haired Jack Russell is called Max. There are seats out in the garden, and the pub's a couple of hundred yards from the Kennet & Avon Canal, reopened in the summer of 1990 after much restoration. As we say, the pub is closed on lunchtimes during the week. *(Recommended by D J Clifton, C A Gurney, Prof H G Allen, David Backhouse; more reports please)*

Free house   Licensee Richard Denning   Real ale   Meals and snacks (7–10pm only,
Tues–Sun, 12–2 as well, Sat, Sun and Bank Hols; not Mon except Bank hols)
Restaurant tel Marlborough (0672) 870871   Children over ten allowed   Games night
Mon   Open 5.30–11; 12–2.30, 6–11 Sat; closed weekday lunchtimes except Bank Hols

LOWER WOODFORD   SU1235 Map 2
Wheatsheaf

Leaving Salisbury northwards on A360, The Woodfords signposted first right after end
of speed limit; then bear left

The two main areas of the extensive dining bar are linked by a miniature
footbridge over a little indoor goldfish pond. Various rambling side areas include
one with attractive William Morris wallpaper, and besides cushioned wall seats
there are sturdy pale varnished tables and chairs on parquet or brown carpet. A
substantial choice of bar food includes a good few vegetarian dishes such as
broccoli bake (£3.35), as well as home-made soup (£1.15), ploughman's (from
£2.10), filled baked potatoes (from £2.45), salads (from £2.95), local ham (£3.95),
lasagne or home-made steak and kidney pie (£4.10), and steaks (from 8oz rump,
£6.75); children's dishes (£1.40) and daily specials. Well kept Badger Best and
Tanglefoot on handpump, and a good open fire. The snug separate Cabin Bar,
with cask seats and an inglenook log fire, has darts, cribbage, dominoes and a fruit
machine. There are tall trees around the big walled garden, which has picnic-table
sets, a climber and swings. *(Recommended by J A Simms, Adrian M Kelly, Nigel Paine,
WHBM; more reports please)*

*Badger   Licensees Peter Charlton, Jennifer Falconer   Real ale   Meals and snacks
(12–2, 7–10)   Children in eating area   Open 11–2.30, 6.30(6 Sat)–11; closes 10.30 in
winter*

MALMESBURY   ST9287 Map 2
Suffolk Arms

Tetbury Hill; B4014 towards Tetbury, on edge of town

This comfortably atmospheric, welcoming and softly lit pub has a stone pillar
supporting the beams in the knocked-through bar, leaving a big square room
around the stairs, which climb up apparently unsupported; there are copper
saucepans and warming pans on the stripped stone walls, and comfortable seats
such as a chintz-cushioned antique settle, sofa and easy chairs, captain's chairs, and
low Windsor armchairs; there's also a lounge. Consistently well kept Badger
Tanglefoot, Wadworths IPA and 6X on handpump; pleasant bar staff in long
aprons. Home-made bar food includes sandwiches (from £1.25), smokie (£2.85),
grilled sardines or crab au gratin (£2.95), ploughman's, salads (from £3.45), lamb
noisettes (£5.75) and good steak, with vegetarian dishes and home-made puddings.
The neat lawns outside have some seats. *(Recommended by Mr and Mrs Peter Woods,
Hilary Roberts, R W Stanbury, Mr and Mrs Evelyn Cribb, Chris and Linda Elston, Roger
Huggins)*

*Wadworths   Licensee John Evans   Real ale   Meals and snacks (12–2, 7–10)
Children over 10 in eating area   Open 11–2.30, 6–11*

MARKET LAVINGTON   SU0154 Map 2
Green Dragon

High Street; B3098, towards Upavon

Listed by the Department of the Environment as a building of special architectural
or historical interest, this early 17th-century pub has a rambling bar with fancy
Victorian wallpaper or stripped deal panelling, old kitchen chairs, smart dining
room chairs or massive boxy settles, a Spy cartoon of Sir Henry Irving,
photographs of the town in the old days and Highland views, and corn dollies.
Well kept Wadworths IPA and 6X on handpump and wide range of wines. Darts

and bar billiards in a raised, communicating section, also shove-ha'penny, dominoes and cribbage; classical piped music. Good home-made bar food includes soup (£1.20), sandwiches, ham and eggs, liver and bacon or mixed grill (all £4.50), lasagne or lamb kebab (£4.85), steak and mushroom pie, fresh plaice, and puddings such as lemon cheesecake or chocolate and strawberry gateau (£1.15); they use home-cooked and locally bought meat, and vegetables (when not grown in their garden); prices of some dishes may be slightly more in the evenings. There's a garden fenced off behind the car park. *(Recommended by Dr and Mrs Crichton, Alan Curry, Roy Butler, Alan Curry, Mrs D C Starkey, David Backhouse; more reports please)*

Wadworths   Licensees Gordon and Elaine Godbolt   Real ale   Meals and snacks (12.30–2, 8–9.30; not Sun, not 25 and 26 Dec)   Restaurant (closed Sun) tel Devizes (0380) 813235   Open 11.30–2.30, 6–11; closed evening 25 Dec

NORTON   ST8884 Map 2

Vine Tree ★

4 miles from M4 junction 17; A429 towards Malmesbury, then left at Hullavington, Sherston signpost, then follow Norton signposts; in village turn right at Foxley signpost, which takes you into Honey lane

Remote in spite of the fairly handy motorway, this warm-hearted country pub has three smallish rooms, which open together, with lots of stripped pine, candles in bottles on the tables (the lighting's very gentle), some old settles, ochre or dark green walls, and lively decoration that includes plates and small sporting prints, carvings, hop bines and a mock-up mounted pig's mask – there's a game that involves knocking coins off its nose and ears; well kept Greene King Abbot, Wadworths 6X, a guest beer such as Devenish or Everards Tiger and a beer brewed for them by a Mr Kemp, as well as decent wines. Home-made bar food includes soup, ploughman's (from £2.25), deep-fried courgettes or snails in wine and garlic butter (£2.75), filled baked potatoes (from £2.75), chilli con carne (£3.75), burgers and nutburgers (£3.85), beef kebabs (£5.95), chicken cooked in white wine or gammon (£6.50) and steaks from 10oz rump (£7.75) to 30oz whoppers (£19.95), with game in season; puddings are all home-made and include lemon crunch, trifle and rhubarb and peach pie (from £1.75); the pub has had a food award in the past, but we've removed it this year only because we've been hearing so little about the food here recently – more news please. There are picnic-table sets under cocktail parasols in a vine-trellised back garden with young trees and tubs of flowers, and a well fenced separate play area with a fine thatched fortress and other goodies – they have stables at the back. *(Recommended by Peter and Rose Flower; more reports please)*

Free house   Licensees Ken Camerier and Pete Draper   Real ale   Meals and snacks (12–2, 6.30–10)   Restaurant tel (0666) 837654   Children in eating area of bar and restaurant   Open 12–2.30, 6.30–11; closed Tues

PITTON   SU2131 Map 2

Silver Plough ★ ✇

Village signposted from A30 E of Salisbury

The comfortable front bar in this civilised and food-oriented pub has seats on the Turkey carpet that include half-a-dozen red-velvet-cushioned antique oak settles, one elaborately carved beside a very fine reproduction of an Elizabethan oak table. Its black beams are strung with hundreds of antique boot-warmers and stretchers, pewter and china tankards, copper kettles, brass and copper jugs, Toby jugs, earthenware and glass rolling pins, painted clogs, glass net-floats, coach horns and so forth. The timbered white walls have pictures that include Thorburn and other gamebird prints, original Craven Hill sporting cartoons, and a big naval battle glass-painting. The back bar is broadly similar, though more restrained, with a big winged high-backed settle, cased antique guns, substantial pictures, and – like the front room – flowers on its tables. This decidedly isn't the place for a quick bar snack – though they do a properly simple ploughman's with a handsome choice of cheeses (£3.50) and soup; most of the dishes are substantial and strong on style – for example fresh Dorset mussels or goat's cheese with strawberries and pink peppercorns (£3.95), fresh pasta with beef and stilton (£5.95), guinea fowl in a peach schnapps sauce (£10.95), and halibut with saffron, chives and ginger (£11.95); their particular strengths are fresh fish and seafood, and game in season. Well kept Courage Best and Directors, Flowers, Wadworths 6X and John Smiths on handpump, decent wines, good country wines, and a worthy range of spirits. The separate skittle alley has a fruit machine, and there may be unobtrusive piped music. There are picnic-table sets and other tables under cocktail parasols on a quiet lawn, with an old pear tree. (*Recommended by Gordon Hewitt, John and Christine Simpson, Alan Symes, Celia and David Watt, John Derbyshire, WHBM, N I Pratt, Alan Skull, James Cane, TBB, Gordon and Daphne, Gavin Udall, Joan and John Calvert, T Galligan, Mrs M Morawetz, Angus and Rosemary Campbell*)

Free house   Licensees Michael Beckett, Paul Parnell and Charles Monkfelow   Real ale   Meals and snacks   Restaurant tel Farley (072 272) 266   Well behaved children in skittle alley   Open 11–3, 6–11; closed 25 Dec

POTTERNE   ST9958 Map 2

George & Dragon   🛏

A360 beside Worton turn-off

This 15th-century thatched cottage was built for the Bishop of Salisbury. Of the original hall, you can still see the fireplace and old beamed ceiling – which is decorated with banknotes from around the world, box matches, and colourful toby jugs; furnishings include old bench seating and country-style tables; traditional atmosphere, friendly licensees; well kept Wadworths IPA and 6X on handpump. The usual range of bar food includes a specials board with such dishes as home-made curry or lasagne, devilled kidneys and a selection of pies. A separate room has pool and fruit machine; also, darts, shove-ha'penny, dominoes, and cribbage, and there's a full skittle alley in the old stables. Through a hatch beyond the pool room there's a unique indoor .22 shooting gallery. It opens on a 25-yard shoulder-high tube, broad enough at its mouth to rest your elbows in, but narrowing to not much more than the width of the target. The small bull is an electric bell-push, which rings when hit. After your nine shots (two for practice), you pull a rope which lifts a brush from a whitewash bucket to whiten the target for the next marksman; it's available under licence to visiting rifle clubs. A museum of hand-held agricultural implements has been opened at the pub. There's a pleasant garden and a sun-trap yard with a grapevine. (*Recommended by Gwen and Peter Andrews, Philip King, Mr and Mrs A Smith, David and Christine Foulkes, Mr and Mrs Peter Woods*)

Wadworths   Licensee Roger Smith   Real ale   Meals and snacks (not Mon)   Children in games room   Open 12–2.30, 6.30–11   Bedrooms tel Devizes (0380) 722139; £15.50/£25.50

RAMSBURY   SU2771 Map 2

Bell

Village signposted off B4192 (still shown as A419 on many maps) NW of Hungerford, or from A4 W of Hungerford

Separated by a chimney breast with a woodburning stove, the two bar areas in this well kept and civilised pub have polished tables, fresh flowers, and window settles in two sunny bay windows (one with Victorian stained glass panels); Marstons Burton and Pedigree, Wadworths IPA and 6X and a monthly guest on handpump. Bar food under the new licensee includes home-made soup (£1.80), filled baked potatoes (from £2.30), ploughman's (from £2.75), home-made pâté (£2.85), Cumberland sausages with bubble and squeak (£4.50), beef curry (£4.90), beef and ale or fish pie (£4.95), steak sandwich (£3.50 or £5), and puddings (£2). There are picnic tables on the raised lawn. Roads lead from this quiet village into the downland on all sides. (*Recommended by GB, CH, David Backhouse, Mr and Mrs R Onslow, C A Gurney, Gordon and Daphne, GB Pugh; more reports please*)

Free house   Licensee John Noble   Real ale   Meals and snacks (not Sat evening)
Restaurant tel Marlborough (0672) 20230   Children in room between bar and
restaurant and in eating area   Open 11–3, 6–11

SALISBURY   SU1429 Map 2

The pubs mentioned here are all within a short stroll of one another. The George, which used to be one of the country's finest old inns – Shakespeare probably performed in its yard – has now been rebuilt as a shopping arcade, but its facade is still well worth a look, and an upstairs coffee shop gives some idea of what it used to be like inside

Avon Brewery

Castle St

Popular with the frequenters of the nearby Woolley & Wallis auction rooms, and the law courts, the long narrow bar here is divided by little balustered partitions, and attractively decorated with lots of pictures (often patriotic or military), framed ensigns, cigarette cards, decorative china and frilly wall-lamps. The atmosphere's very companionable, and there's a library of reference books should you need back-up in a discussion. Good lunchtime bar food includes sandwiches (from £1.15, steak £2.20), hot dogs (£1.25), filling soups such as lentil with ham and sausage (£1.30), hot dishes such as home-made steak and kidney pie, vegetarian flan, lasagne or curry (around £3.50); three-course supper menu (£8.95 – please note they don't take reservations). Well kept Eldridge Pope Dorchester, Hardy and Royal Oak and a guest on handpump; quite a few wines by the glass (and the bottle); hospitable service. Fruit and trivia machines, shove-ha'penny, cribbage, a rack of newspapers and classical piped music. The bar broadens out at the back, with darts and a dainty Victorian fireplace. A narrow garden, with fruit trees, roses and hops, runs down to the River Avon. The facade, all mosaic tilework and elegant curves, makes it one of the city's prettiest pubs. *(Recommended by David Nutt, Mr and Mrs Reeves, Don Mulcock, Joan and Michel Hooper-Immins)*

Eldridge Pope   Licensee Duncan Broom   Real ale   Meals and snacks (not Sat evening, not Sun)   Well behaved children welcome till 7.30   Very occasional folk music   Open 11–11 (11–3, 4.30–11 in winter, but still 11–11 Sat)

Haunch of Venison ★

1 Minster Street, opposite Market Cross

The chatty little downstairs bar in this thoroughly ancient and atmospheric place has massive beams in the ochre ceiling, stout red cushioned oak benches built into its timbered walls, genuinely old pictures, a black and white tiled floor, an open fire, an old-fashioned – and as far as we know unique – pewter bar counter with a rare set of antique taps for gravity-fed spirits and liqueurs; a tiny snug opens off the entrance lobby. A quiet and cosy upper panelled room has a small paned window looking down onto the main bar, a splendid fireplace that dates back some 600 years, antique leather-seat settles, and a nice carved oak chair nearly three centuries old. In 1903 workmen found a smoke-preserved mummified hand holding some 18th-century playing-cards in here; it's now behind glass in a small wall slit. Well kept Courage Best and Directors and Wadworths 6X on handpump. Bar food, served in the lower half of the restaurant, includes sandwiches (from £1.15, toasties 20p extra), home-made soup (£1), baked potatoes (from £1.20), ploughman's (from £2.20), home-made pies such as game, ham and mushroom or steak and kidney (from £2.25), savoury pancakes (£3), daily specials such as good chicken curry or peppered beef (£2.50), and puddings (95p); attentive and friendly service. Parts of this building date back to about 1430, when it was the church house for the church of St Thomas, just behind. *(Recommended by Leith Stuart, Mr and Mrs KJV, Klaus and Elizabeth Leist, Ian Phillips, Gary Scott, JM, PM, Jerry and Alison Oakes, Gordon and Daphne, Gordon Mott)*

Courage   Licensees Antony and Victoria Leroy   Real ale   Meals and snacks (not Sun evening)   Restaurant tel Salisbury (0722) 22024; closed Sun evening all year, Mon–Wed evening in Jan and Feb, but may still take bookings   Children in eating area and restaurant   Nearby parking may be difficult   Open 11–11

Kings Arms 🍺

St John Street; the main one-way street entering city centre from S

The dark-panelled bars in this creaky old inn have red leatherette benches built around their walls: one has attractive Windsor arm chairs under its heavy beams, with carving around its fireplace and door; the other, more local, has darts, cribbage, dominoes, fruit machine, space game and piped music. The panelling in the heavily beamed restaurant, which has snug high-backed settles, is considerably older. There is Tudor timbering, and the fireplaces are of the same Chilmark stone as the Cathedral, so may be as old as it. Well kept Ruddles County and Ushers Best on handpump; hospitable staff. Bar food includes soup (£1.95), sandwiches (from £2), ploughman's (£3), hot home-made daily specials (£3.25), and a roast carvery (£4.25); in the evenings they only do snacks, but you can order from the restaurant menu in the bar. *(Recommended by Gordon Mott, Gary Scott; more up-to-date reports please)*

Watneys   Licensee E Webber   Real ale   Meals and snacks   Restaurant   Children welcome   Open 11–2.30, 6–11   Bedrooms tel Salisbury (0722) 27629; £52B/£68B

SANDY LANE   ST9668 Map 2

George

A342 Chippenham–Devizes

This homely and rather splendid Georgian building has a neat, carpeted main bar with comfortable cushioned wall benches, decorative wall beams, horse brasses, old pistols and photographs and a log fire; an arch leads through to the attractive back lounge. Well kept Wadworths 6X and IPA on handpump; fruit machine and piped music; pleasant licensee. Largely home-made food includes soup (£1.50), pâté (£2.20), ploughman's (from £2.80), lasagne, chilli con carne, moussaka or fisherman's pie (all £3.90), gammon (£5.80), steaks (from £7.70), duck with port and orange sauce (£7.80), and puddings. There are wooden benches and tables in front, with picnic table-sets on a side lawn; the pub overlooks a small green just off the main road. *(Recommended by Mary Rayner, John and Tessa Rainsford, John and Pat Smyth, Tony and Lynne Stark, Bev and Doug Warrick, J Charles, A R Sayer)*

Wadworths   Licensees Pam and Terry Allington   Real ale   Meals and snacks (12–2, 7–10)   Children in eating area   Open 11–2.30(3 Sat), 6.30–11

SEEND   ST9461 Map 2

Barge

Seend Cleeve; signposted off A361 Devizes–Trowbridge, between Seend village and signpost to Seend Head

This tiled and stonebuilt peaceful canalside pub, which recently won an award for its fine refurbishment, has, unsurprisingly, a strong bargee theme, perhaps at its best in the intricately painted Victorian flowers which cover the ceilings and run in a waist-high band above the deep green lower walls; more bargee paintwork includes some milkchurn seats among a distinctive mix of other attractive seats, including the occasional small oak settle among the rugs on the parquet floor. There's a pretty Victorian fireplace, big bunches of dried flowers, big sentimental engravings, a well stocked aquarium, and crushed red velvet curtains for the big windows; the atmosphere is busy and sociable; well kept Wadworths IPA and 6X on handpump. Bar food includes soup (£1.25), open sandwiches (from £1.95, prawn £3.50), filled baked potatoes (from £1.95), ploughman's (from £1.95), chilli con carne (£2.50), plaice or haddock (£2.95), lasagne (£3.95), steak and kidney pie (£3.95), steaks (from £7.05), with daily specials and children's menu (£1.50). The neat waterside garden, with moorings by a humpy bridge, has picnic-table sets among former streetlamps; besides a busy bird table, nice touches include the weatherdrake and the good inn sign. *(Recommended by Lord Johnston, C T and J M Laffin, Roger Cunningham, Deborah Frost, Mr and Mrs Peter Woods, B R Woolmington, Gwen and Peter Andrews, Mr and Mrs D A P Grattan)*

Wadworths   Licensee Christopher Moorley Long   Real ale   Meals and snacks (12–2, 7–9.30; evening food till 10 Fri and Sat)   Well behaved children allowed   Open 11–2.30, 6–11

SEMLEY   ST8926 Map 2

Benett Arms 🛏

Turn off A350 N of Shaftesbury at Semley Ind Estate signpost, then turn right at Semley signpost

Separated by a flight of five carpeted steps, the two cosy rooms of the bar in this very friendly and relaxed little village inn have deep leather sofas and armchairs, one or two settles and pews, ornaments on the mantlepiece over the log fire, a pendulum wall clock, carriage lamps for lighting, and hunting prints. Down by the thatched-roof bar servery, the walls are stripped stone; upstairs, there's hessian over a dark panelling dado. Gibbs Mew Premium and Salisbury on handpump and kept under light blanket pressure; good house wines and a wide range of spirits; cribbage and piped music. Bar food includes home-made soup (£1.50), ploughman's (£2.75), omelette (from £3.50), local ham and egg (£3.25), lasagne (£3.40), home-made steak and kidney pie (£3.80), freshwater trout (£3.95), gammon with pineapple (£4.25), scampi (£4.50), and home-made puddings such as apple pie or chocolate mousse with rum (£1.75); children's menu; Sunday roasts; good breakfasts. Dominoes, cribbage and piped music. There are seats outside. Well behaved dogs welcome. *(Recommended by Nigel Paine, B and J Derry, Sandra Kempson, J M Smith, Bernard Phillips, John and Christine Simpson, Mrs J A Gardner, S V Bishop, TBB; more reports please)*

Gibbs Mew   Licensees Annie and Joe Duthie   Real ale   Meals and snacks (12–2, 7–10)   Restaurant (not Sun evening)   Children welcome   Open 11–2.30, 6–11; closed 25 and 26 Dec   Bedrooms tel East Knoyle (074 783) 221; £25B/£39B

UPAVON   SU1355 Map 2

Antelope 🍽 🛏

3 High St; village on junction A345/A342

As we went to press new licensees had recently taken over this 17th-century village inn, and though it's too early to be completely sure, we feel confident enough to maintain its awards. Bar food now includes sandwiches (from £1.45), home-made soup (£1.95), local ham and eggs (£3.25), lots of home-made pies such as steak and kidney or lamb, apple and cider (£4.45), fish such as local trout (£5.25), swordfish or tuna (£5.45), and steaks (from £7.50), with home-made puddings like banoffi pie (£1.95). The attractively simple lounge bar has an interesting antique wheel-driven water pump at one end, a good winter log fire at the other, wall settles around dark tables, stools at the long bar counter, and a little bow-windowed games area with darts, cribbage, dominoes, bar billiards and a couple of fruit machines opening off. Wadworths IPA, Farmers Glory and 6X on handpump, with Old Timer and mulled wine in winter. Outside there are hanging baskets and a vine, and a pets' corner with goats, rabbits and guinea pigs. *(Recommended by Mary Rayner, Kev and Caron Holmes, David Backhouse, S Watkins, J H Walker; more reports on the new regime please)*

Wadworths   Licensees Mervyn and Sandy Parish   Real ale   Meals and snacks   Restaurant   Children in family room   Open 11–2.30 (3 Sat), 6–11   Bedrooms tel Stonehenge (0980) 630206; £17.50/£30

WOOTTON RIVERS SU1963 Map 2

Royal Oak 🏮

Village signposted from A346 Marlborough–Salisbury and B3087 E of Pewsey

The L-shaped dining lounge in this prettily thatched, canalside foody pub has a low ceiling with partly stripped beams, partly glossy white planks, slat-back chairs, armchairs and some rustic settles around good tripod tables, a woodburning stove, and a friendly atmosphere; it's decorated with discreetly colourful plates and small mainly local prints, drawings, watercolours and photographs. The timbered bar on the right is comfortably and similarly furnished, though with fewer tables; it has darts, pool, dominoes, cribbage, fruit machine and juke box. Lots of specials might include horiatiki salad (£3.25), vegetables with savoury dip (£2.25), pan-fried mackerel with gooseberry sauce (£5), particularly good home-made steak and kidney pie (£5.50), and lamb and prune casserole (£7.50), with regular dishes such as soup (£1.25), lunchtime sandwiches (£1.25; open from £2) or ploughman's (from £2.25), basket meals (from £2), a good choice of salads (from £3.75; seafood £8.50), chicken Kiev (£7) and lots of steaks (from £7.50; T-bone £10); puddings (£2); they take table bookings, and people may be quite smartly dressed. Well kept Wadworths 6X tapped from the cask, decent wines (running up to some very distinguished vintage ones), Bloody Marys and jugs of Pimms; warm service. There are tables under cocktail parasols in the back gravelled yard, by the car park. The thatched and timbered village is very attractive. *(Recommended by John and Pat Smyth, David and Ruth Shillitoe, Chris Raisin, A R Sayer, Dr C S Shaw, John Hill, R and E Harfield, Mr and Mrs J D Cranston, David Backhouse, HNJ, PEJ)*

Free house Licensees John and Rosa Jones Real ale Meals and snacks (not Sun evenings Oct–Jun, nor 26 Dec) Children welcome Open 11–3 (3.30 Sat), 6–11; winter evening opening 7 Bedrooms (in adjoining house) tel Marlborough (0672) 810322; £17.50(£20B)/£30(£35B)

Lucky Dip

Besides the fully inspected pubs, you might like to try these Lucky Dips recommended to us and described by readers (if you do, please send us reports):

☆ **Aldbourne** [SU2675], *Crown*: Pleasant, welcoming, and spacious slightly up-market local with huge log fire, quiet piped music and pleasant, helpful licensee; clean and well kept, with interesting collections, quickly served standard range of bar food with several daily specials at reasonable prices, piped music, well kept Watneys-related ales on handpump, tables under cocktail parasols in pleasant courtyard *(Mary Rayner, Mr and Mrs P B Dowsett, HNJ, PEJ, David Backhouse, A Y Drummond)*

☆ **Aldbourne** [The Green (off B4192)], *Blue Boar*: Pretty Tudor village pub with picnic-table sets overlooking green and 14th-century church in one of the prettiest villages in the county; very small and clean bar, stuffed boar's head over attractive inglenook fireplace, just a few seats, genuine atmosphere, well kept Wadworths IPA and 6X on handpump (Ringwood Old Thumper tapped from the cask in winter), pleasant and obliging landlady, limited food *(Mary Rayner, David Backhouse, Mr and Mrs P B Dowsett)*

Amesbury [Church St; SU1541], *Antrobus Arms*: Quiet, comfortable and relaxed with good food, no piped music and beautiful garden with cedar tree; bedrooms *(Peter Burton)*; [High St], *George*: Rambling coaching inn with unusually extensive surviving coach yard; well kept Gibbs Mew

Salisbury, limited range of cheap bar food and quick, friendly service; fruit machine, piped country music, pool in public bar; bedrooms *(Robert Gomme, LYM)*; [Earls Court Rd], *Greyhound*: well cooked and generously served food, friendly service and Watneys-related real ales *(Jenny and Michael Back)*

Ashton Keynes [SU0494], *Plough*: Charming pub with small bar, big lounge and well kept Whitbreads on handpump *(David Backhouse)*

Atworth [Bath Rd (A365); ST8666], *White Hart*: Pleasant spot, friendly landlord and reasonable food; bedrooms *(Roger Cunningham, Deborah Frost)*

Avebury [A361; SU0969], *Red Lion*: Right in the heart of the stone circles — much-modernised and somewhat tourist-oriented comfortable thatched pub with well kept Wadworths 6X and Whitbreads-related real ales on handpump, friendly staff, simple but good food inc steaks in interesting dining room *(David Backhouse, Joan Olivier, LYM)*

☆ **Axford** [SU2370], *Red Lion*: Pleasant flintstone pub with well furnished pine-panelled, wood-floored beamed bar; well kept Archers Village, Marstons Pedigree and Wadworths 6X, friendly informal bar service, good dining room with wide choice of good bar food inc sandwiches, home-made soup and local fish; sunny tables outside with lovely views down over field to River Kennet; bedrooms *(David Backhouse, Mary Rayner, A Y Drummond, HNJ, PEJ, Mrs A Sheard)*

☆ Badbury [very near M4 junction 15 — A345 S; SU1980], *Plough*: Keen, friendly licensee extending both the food and the pleasant old building; well kept Arkells BB, BBB and Kingsdown on handpump, sunny garden looking beyond the road to the Vale of the White Horse *(David Backhouse, R G Ollier, Mr and Mrs F Hardy)*

Badbury [SU1980], *Bakers Arms*: Neat open-plan pub with bar and lounge areas divided by chimney; well kept Arkells BB, BBB and Kingsdown on handpump *(David Backhouse)*

☆ Barford St Martin [junction A30/B3098 W of Salisbury; SU0531], *Green Dragon*: Old-fashioned panelled front bar with big log fire and larger games bar in pub; friendly welcome, reasonably priced good food and well kept Badger beer; bedrooms clean and simple *(Mr and Mrs R C Abbott, Col and Mrs L N Smyth, LYM)*

☆ Biddestone [The Green; ST8773], *White Horse*: Straightforward traditional pub overlooking village duckpond in extremely picturesque village; friendly atmosphere and service, particularly good bar food, Courage ales, small carpeted rooms running one into another, shove-ha'penny, darts and table skittles; tables in garden; bedrooms *(C G Barnett, Roger Cunningham, Deborah Frost, Barry and Anne, Roger Huggins)*

Biddestone, *Biddestone Arms*: Well kept village pub with simple but comfortable lounge, games in public bar, well kept Ushers Best and PA and Wadworths 6X; music may be loud in evenings; swings in fairylit garden *(Roger Cunningham, Deborah Frost, BB)*

Bishops Cannings [SU0364], *Crown*: Small, quiet and friendly Wadworths pub with good home-made food (not Sun evening or Mon) and well kept beer *(David and Christine Foulkes)*

Blunsden [SU1593], *Cold Harbour*: Useful big main-road Chef & Brewer, popular with businessmen for wide choice of good food served generously — but also has outside terrace and good play area for children; well kept Watneys-related real ales, restaurant *(Mr and Mrs P B Dowsett, David Backhouse, P and R Woods)*

Box [A4, Bath side; ST8268], *Northey Arms*: Friendly, relaxed open-plan local with deep red walls, wooden tables, chairs and window seats, homely decor; small range of reasonably priced good home-cooked bar food, restaurant, decent wines, young staff, children welcome; panoramic view of Box valley *(Roger Cunningham, Deborah Frost, ADE)*; [Box Hill; off A4 just W of Box], *Quarrymans Arms*: Pleasant, modernised hilltop pub with home-cooked food running up to steaks, several real ales inc interesting guests, quarrying memorabilia, tables outside; two bedrooms *(Peter and Rose Flower, Roger Cunningham, Deborah Frost)*; *Queens Head*: Good local with lounge and bar, friendly staff and simple, adequate bar food *(Roger Cunningham, Deborah Frost)*

☆ Bradford Leigh [B2109 N of Bradford; ST8362], *Plough*: Pleasant pub, on the up-and-up, with good choice of reasonably priced well cooked food, hard-working licensees, friendly bar staff and dog, well kept Marstons Pedigree, Ushers Best, Wadworths 6X and Websters, good cider; nice seats outside *(B R Woolmington, Jan and Ian Alcock)*

☆ Bradford on Avon [Silver St; ST8261], *Bunch of Grapes*: Converted shop in picturesque steep street, with bars on two levels; friendly atmosphere, big helpings of good interesting reasonably priced food, wide range of well kept and attractively priced beers — usually Smiles, with several guests such as Gales HSB, Goachers and Hook Norton; charming landlord, thoughtful service, spotlessly clean *(Derek and Sylvia Stephenson, John and Joan Wyatt, B R Woolmington, R W Stanbury)*

Bradford on Avon [26 Silver St], *Bear*: Wide choice of bar food from sandwiches to 20 oz rump steak, with good choice of home-made pizzas and vegetarian meals; wide range of drinks inc good range of real ales; bedrooms good value *(M Potter)*

Bremhill [ST9773], *Dumbpost*: Rather basic old country pub with welcoming landlord — and parrot; well kept beer and good low-priced bar food (not Wed); attractive views, garden *(P and R Woods)*

☆ Broad Hinton [High St; off A4361 about 5 miles S of Swindon; SU1076], *Crown*: Big open-plan bar with good value home-cooked bar meals, help-yourself salad bar and restaurant section, well kept Arkells BB, BBB and Kingsdown, attentive landlord, cheerful piped music, unusual gilded inn sign; big car park, bedrooms *(PBD, David Backhouse, LYM)*

Broad Hinton [A4361 Swindon—Devizes; SU1076], *Bell*: Well kept Whitbreads in old country pub, beautifully kept and furnished, good bar food; bedrooms *(David Backhouse)*

Brokerswood [ST8352], *Kicking Donkey*: Remote, spotless and friendly free house with several bars, shining brass-topped tables, gentle piped music, half a dozen real ales, decent wines, reasonably priced bar food, restaurant with two log fires, large terrace; children welcome *(Mr and Mrs S Binstead)*

☆ Bromham [ST9665], *Greyhound*: Two attractively lit bars with lots of atmosphere, amazing assortment of interesting items, even a well; imaginative well cooked and presented bar food, well chosen real ales, friendly enthusiastic landlord; skittle alley, pool and darts; big garden, small intimate restaurant *(Mrs D C Starkey)*

☆ Broughton Gifford [ST8763], *Fox & Hounds*: Traditional pleasantly decorated timbered pub, welcoming licensee, well kept Watneys-related real ales, helpful staff and good varied bar food (not cheap), especially steaks *(Roger Cunningham, Deborah Frost, B R Woolmington)*

Burbage [High St(A346); SU2361], *Bullfinch*: Basic but friendly split-level bar with simple good value bar food, pool table, Wadworths 6X tapped from the cask under light blanket pressure; children welcome; bedrooms *(Keith Walton, David Backhouse)*

☆ Burton [ST8179], *Old House At Home*: Main-street old pub with strong emphasis on ambitious choice of good generously served food; attractive dining recess, log fire, well kept Wadworths real ales (*C Davies, Tony Triggle*)

Bushton [SU0677], *Trotting Horse*: Full of character; well kept Ind Coope Burton, Tetleys, Wadworths 6X and a guest beer on handpump, wide choice of malt whiskies, large helpings of good value food, good service; bedrooms (*David Backhouse*)

☆ **Castle Combe** [signed off B4039 Chippenham—Chipping Sodbury; ST8477], *Castle*: Old-world country inn in beautiful village, with nicely furnished bars, clean and attractive; good food and service, good cream teas; they charge much more pro-rata for halves than for pints; bedrooms (*Peter and Rose Flower, Mrs F B Bromfield*)

Castle Combe, *White Hart*: Pretty stone-built pub with log fire in beamed and flagstoned main bar, useful family room; mixed reports on other aspects (*H K Dyson, Roger Huggins, A R Sayer, Len Beattie, William Rodgers, Tony Gayfer*)

☆ nr **Castle Combe** [The Gibb; B4039 Acton Turville—Chippenham — OS Sheet 173 map reference 838791], *Salutation*: Well restored, popular old pub with well kept Flowers and wide range of good bar food inc interesting and imaginatively cooked daily specials; raftered restaurant, nice hanging baskets; deserves food award (*Patrick Godfrey, John and Pat Smyth*)

☆ **Charlton** [B4040 toward Cricklade; ST9588], *Horse & Groom*: Quiet and civilised pub with welcoming log fire, agreeable and relaxing decor, well kept local real ales, decent wines, bar food, restaurant, tables outside; closed Sun evening, Mon (*Tom McLean, Roger Huggins, Ewan McCall, Dick Brown, LYM; more reports please*)

☆ **Chilmark** [B3089 Salisbury—Hindon; ST9632], *Black Dog*: Comfortably modernised 15th-century pub in attractive village; horse-brasses, equestrian plates, armchairs by the log fire in the lounge, fossil ammonites in the stone of another bar, and games in third bar; well kept Courage Best and Directors on handpump, decent straightforward promptly served bar food (not Mon evening), pleasant newish licensees; children allowed in low-key separate dining room (*S V Bishop, Robert and Elizabeth Scott, Steve Huggins, Nigel Paine, LYM*)

Chilton Foliat [SU3270], *Wheatsheaf*: Friendly pub, good service, small choice of bar food inc good home-made steak and kidney pie and puddings; piped music unobtrusive (*J M Potter*)

Coate [the one nr Devizes; SU0462], *New Inn*: Good village pub with well kept Wadworths IPA, 6X and in winter Old Timer, tapped from the cask (*David Backhouse*)

Collingbourne Ducis [SU2453], *Shears*: Pleasantly — even smartly — refurbished, Whitbreads-related real ales on handpump (*David Backhouse*)

☆ **Coombe Bissett** [Blandford Rd (A354); SU1026], *Fox & Goose*: Friendly, spacious and exceptionally clean open-plan pub with rustic wooden refectory-style tables, coal fires, old prints, hanging chamber-pots and classical piped music; Watneys-related real

ales, good coffee, helpful staff, wide choice of simple but good bar food from sandwiches to steaks, evening restaurant; looks over reedy stream to village green and silver-grey wooden barn; tables in garden with play area (*Ian Phillips, Andrea and Guy Bradley, Tim Brierly*)

☆ **Corsham** [A4, Pickwick; ST8670], *Two Pigs*: Real old-fashioned and friendly drinkers' pub with several changing well kept real ales, welcoming character landlord, sawdust on the (very clean) floor, unusual layout and decoration inc bicycle on the ceiling and tailors' dummy hung overhead, good atmosphere and service; parking a problem, no under-21s (*John Hayward, John Riggs, Peter and Rose Flower*)

Corsham [A4 out towards Chippenham], *Cross Keys*: Cosy atmosphere, well kept beer and friendly barman (*Roger Cunningham, Deborah Frost*)

Cricklade [SU0993], *Kings Head*: Small, friendly pub with well kept Whitbreads PA on handpump, good sherry, popular food, good staff (*David Backhouse, P and R Woods*); *Vale*: Good atmosphere in pleasant, comfortable bar adjoining Georgian hotel; well kept Archers Village, Wadworths 6X and in winter Whitbreads Pompey Royal on handpump, popular food; bedrooms (*David Backhouse*)

Crudwell [A429 N of Malmesbury; ST9592], *Plough*: Pleasant and comfortable after extensive recent refurbishment, raised dining area in converted barn, several other attractive rooms inc pool room; landlord friendly and helpful, food good and reasonably priced; Wadworths 6X and Whitbreads-related real ales, appealing garden (*B R Woolmington*)

☆ **Dauntsey** [Dauntsey Lock; A420 — handy for M4 junctions 16 and 17; ST9782], *Peterborough Arms*: Welcoming licensees, good range of good value and often imaginative food, half a dozen real ales, pool, skittle alley, garden with play area; nice location (*P and R Woods*)

☆ **Derry Hill** [ST9570], *Lansdowne Arms*: Unusual Victorian bar, separate restaurant and busy but friendly atmosphere; good range of consistently good value food inc speciality home-made pies (also sold in their shop in Colne); well kept Wadworths real ales, country wines, garden for children; nr Bowood House (*David and Christine Foulkes, Mr and Mrs D A P Grattan, WHBM*)

☆ **Devizes** [Long St; SU0061], *Elm Tree*: Consistently popular pub with friendly relaxed atmosphere, good food and well kept Wadworths IPA and 6X on handpump; bedrooms (*David Backhouse*)

Devizes [Market Pl], *Black Swan*: Small, pleasant and comfortable central hotel with Wadworths IPA and 6X on handpump; bedrooms (*David Backhouse, Tom McLean, Ewan McCall, Roger Huggins*); [A342 out towards Chirton], *Clock*: Free house with well kept Ushers and Wadworths, reasonably priced food, pleasant staff (*B R Woolmington*); [Nursteed (A342)], *Fox & Hounds*: Attractive thatched pub with lounge and separate games area; well kept Wadworths IPA and 6X on handpump (*David Backhouse*); [Hare & Hounds St], *Hare & Hounds*: Popular pub with particularly well kept Wadworths IPA and 6X on handpump (David Backhouse); [Nursteed Rd], Moonraker: Large 1930s food-oriented pub, comfortable lounge, well kept Wadworths IPA and 6X on handpump, good service (K R Harris, David Backhouse); [Dunkirk Hill], Queens Head: Well kept Wadworths IPA, 6X and in winter Old Timer on handpump, good bar food (David Backhouse); [Maryport St], Three Crowns: Friendly town pub, long, low and softly lit, with well kept Wadworths IPA and 6X on handpump, George I backsword blade (found hidden in ex-stables), seats in small sheltered yard (David Backhouse, BB); [Monday Mkt St], White Bear: Well kept Wadworths IPA and 6X on handpump and good food; bedrooms (David Backhouse)

☆ Dinton [SU0131], Penruddocke Arms: Spacious and comfortable country pub, welcoming atmosphere, well kept real ales, country wines, reasonably priced good bar food, welcoming landlord, good pub games in public bar (J M Watkinson, LYM)

☆ East Chisenbury [SU1452], Red Lion: Unspoilt and basic country village pub where locals in the old-fashioned snug around the big winter fire function as a sort of gardeners' brains trust — a pub for devotees of times past, though they no longer keep real ale; play area on lawn (LYM)

☆ Easton Royal [SU2060], Bruce Arms: Wonderfully unspoilt, basic pub with one room full of elderly easy chairs and amaryllis plants, another just benches and tables; well kept Whitbreads Strong Country, much-loved elderly landlady (J Maloney, David Backhouse, JM, LYM)

☆ Enford [SU1351], Swan: Interesting old thatched village local with big log fireplace in comfortable bar, second bar serving as lunchtime family room, well kept Hop Back GFB and HBS, Wadworths 6X and a guest beer on handpump, relatively low prices for drinks and food; tables in back garden with play area, and in front (R H Inns, David Backhouse, Richard Houghton)

☆ Farleigh Wick [A363 Bath—Bradford; ST8064], Fox & Hounds: Welcoming and clean low-beamed 17th-century stone pub with masses of highly polished old oak tables and chairs, brasses and warm red carpets; Watneys-related real ales, log fire, good bar food from local mushrooms in garlic butter and delicious soups to huge slices of Wiltshire ham and various deep pies such as venison and pheasant or sausage and ham; great garden, big car park; can get packed at weekends (John and Bridget Dean)

Fonthill Bishop [ST9333], Kings Arms: Friendly, welcoming atmosphere, darts and bar billiards, quiet side-room off comfortably refurbished open-plan bar; well kept Wadworths 6X and Worthington BB, beautifully cooked and generously served bar food; children welcome (A J Bell)

Fonthill Gifford [ST9232], Beckford Arms: Friendly old stone local with well kept Wadworths tapped from the cask, great ham and toast, and splendid fire in lounge (Tony and Lynne Stark)

☆ Fovant [A30 Salisbury—Shaftesbury; SU0128], Cross Keys: Quiet 15th-century pub with assortment of antique furniture,

collection of brassware, and open fire in main bar; good friendly staff, very relaxing atmosphere, wide range of tasty, low-priced bar food, unusually good wines, restaurant, afternoon teas; craft fairs 2nd Wed of month; bedrooms old and attractive (Philip King, Paul Corbett)

Froxfield [A4; SU2968], Watermeadow: Refurbished inn, now small hotel with restaurant; tasty and well served food in pleasant bar, friendly reception, good service; bedrooms (James Brown)

☆ Great Bedwyn [SU2764], Cross Keys: Spacious L-shaped open-plan bar in old village pub with comfortable chairs and settles, friendly locals (the young ones can be noisy), pleasant, helpful bar staff; well kept Ma Pardoes, Wiltshire Stonehenge, Old Grumble and Old Devil on handpump, enormous variety of fresh, down-to-earth food quickly served in really big helpings (good value, too); pool table, occasional juke box; bedrooms (HNJ, PEJ, David Backhouse, Chas and Dorothy Morley)

Great Durnford [SU1338], Black Horse: Attractive three-room pub with good bar food from sandwiches up, open fire, pleasant service, good charcoal grills in restaurant, clean lavatories; children have the run of an old London bus (Mr and Mrs George Ffoulkes)

Great Hinton [3 1/2 miles E of Trowbridge; ST9059], Linnet: Two attractive rooms in local with well kept Wadworths, helpful staff, interesting choice of food (B R Woolmington)

☆ Ham [SU3362], Crown & Anchor: Pleasant timbered open-plan bar, neat and smart, with well kept Hook Norton Best and Wadworths 6X on handpump, small restaurant with good range of standard pub food, pleasant friendly staff (Stan Edwards, David Backhouse)

☆ Hannington [SU1793], Jolly Tar: Stone-built village local with good value honest straightforward food at low prices; big log fire and beams with ships' crests in lounge on right — mix of stripped stone and flock wallpaper; well kept Arkells BB, BBB and Kingsdown; games bar; upstairs grill room; good robust play area in biggish garden, tables out in front too; skittle alley (David Backhouse, BB)

☆ Heddington [ST9966], Ivy: Lovely thatched village pub with woodburner in good inglenook fireplace of simple low-beamed bar, timbered walls, well kept Wadworths real ales tapped from the cask, limited bar food such as rolls or pies, children's room; seats outside the picturesque house; ideal for walkers (Roger Huggins, LYM)

Highworth [B4019, a mile W; SU2092], Freke Arms: Popular, warm and comfortable with friendly atmosphere and ample seating in four connecting rooms; Ansells beer, wide range of reasonably priced bar food, subdued piped music, big car park and children's play area (Mr and Mrs P B Dowsett); [Swindon St], Jesmond House: Small, good hotel bar with friendly licensee and well kept Archers Best and ASB on handpump; bedrooms (David Backhouse)

Hilcott [SU1158], Prince of Wales: Good free house with well kept Wadworths IPA, 6X and guest beer on handpump and interesting range of bar food *(David Backhouse)*

☆ **Hindon** [ST9132], *Grosvenor Arms*: Pleasant upgraded old pub with good service and shortish choice of good home-cooked food such as steak and kidney pie, locally caught trout; books, prints, fireplaces, fruit machine, Watneys-related and other real ales such as Wadworths 6X; nice terrace (though Nelson the boxer has outgrown his entertaining antics with the flower-pot); usefully complements the Lamb opposite *(R H Inns, Brian Chambers, Barbara M McHugh, Richard Gibbs)*

Hodson [not far from M4 junction 15, via Chiseldon; SU1780], *Calley Arms*: Recently modernised pub with well kept Badgers Tanglefoot and Wadworths IPA and 6X on handpump *(David Backhouse)*

Holt [ST8662], *Old Ham Tree*: Popular local, relaxed and welcoming, with Marstons Pedigree, Wadworths 6X and other real ales, decent food such as steak and mushroom pie and nr NT 'Garden of Mystery' — The Courts *(B R Woolmington, Tom Evans)*

Honey Street [SU1061], *Barge*: Satisfactorily remodelled pub on canal bank; pleasant pictures, Courage Best and Directors, standard bar food inc good sandwiches; bedrooms *(A Y Drummond)*

Hook [B4041, off A420 just W of M4 junction 16; SU0784], *Bolingbroke Arms*: Pleasant pub with reasonably adventurous choice of decent food, Whitbreads-related real ales *(Dave Braisted)*

☆ **Horningsham** [by entrance to Longleat House; ST8141], *Bath Arms*: Comfortable old pub in pretty village, modernised over the years without losing its charm; good food with plenty of variety inc superb smoked trout, maybe good middle eastern dishes in dining room as well as the French cuisine they aim at; pleasant service; well kept Bass, Wadworths 6X and three other real ales; bedrooms well equipped, clean and comfortable *(John C Baker)*

Horton [SU0463], *Bridge*: Interesting canalside pub, long, with four bars and waterside garden; well kept Wadworths IPA and 6X on handpump *(David Backhouse)*

☆ **Lacock** [ST9168], *Carpenters Arms*: Several rambling cottagey areas in carefully contrived pastiche of old-fashioned pub, with interesting mix of furnishings and decorations; quickly served good standard bar food (no sandwiches), well kept Watneys-related real ales, friendly service, restaurant, children in eating area; has had jazz Mon; open all day summer; bedrooms *(James Cane, Mr and Mrs F E M Hardy, W C M Jones, Mr and Mrs D A P Grattan, S V Bishop, Mrs E M Thompson, LYM)*

☆ **Liddington** [a mile from M4 junction 15; just off A419; SU2081], *Village Inn*: Comfortable and well furnished quiet village pub — quite newly done, but old-looking; well kept Fullers ESB, Marstons Pedigree, Wadworths 6X, Whitbread IPA and guest beers on handpump, Bulmers Traditional cider tapped from the cask, consistently good home-cooked lunchtime bar food, log fire; bedrooms simple but very clean *(K R Harris, David Backhouse, Chris Payne, Peter Woods)*

Lockeridge [signposted off A4 Marlborough—Calne just W of Fyfield — OS Sheet 173 map reference 148679; SU1467], *Who'd A Thought It*: Nice inside, with plush-cushioned seats around pine and wood-effect tables in three carpeted rooms around small bar, friendly landlord, ten or so good reasonably priced dishes of day, well kept Badger Tanglefoot, Wadworths IPA, 6X and in winter Old Timer, log fire; family room, back garden with children's play area, good car park; handy for Avebury or the Sarsen-stone fields *(HNJ, PEJ, David Backhouse)*

Longbridge Deverill [ST8740], *George*: Good choice of bar food in three cosy bars *(R W Stanbury)*

☆ **Lower Chute** [the Chutes signposted via Appleshaw off A342 2 1/2 miles W of Andover; SU3153], *Hatchet*: Neatly kept and increasingly upmarket but friendly low-beamed thatched pub with huge log fire, good range of real ales such as Adnams, Bass, John Smiths and Wadworths 6X; the generally good quickly served bar food runs from baked potatoes, cheese and ham toasties, crab bake and so forth to considerably more expensive dishes — there's also a restaurant; seats on terrace and lawn; children in restaurant *(Gordon and Daphne, Henry Midwinter, P M Wray, William Rodgers, PEJ, HNJ, Laurie Walker, Lynda Cantelo, LYM)*

Lydiard Millicent [SU0985], *Sun*: Local with well kept Flowers tapped from the cask, reasonable choice of well priced bar food, pretty garden *(Peter Woods, David Backhouse)*

☆ **Manton** [High St; SU1668], *Up The Garden Path*: Pleasant modernised and recently extended village local up steep path, with friendly staff, well kept Archers BB, Hook Norton Best and a guest beer such as Wadworths 6X on handpump, popular separate eating area, games room *(Margaret Dyke, Derek and Sylvia Stephenson, David and Christine Foulkes, Richard Houghton, David Backhouse)*

Manton [High St], *Oddfellows Arms*: Good, friendly local with well kept Wadworths 6X, Farmers Glory in summer, and Old Timer in winter *(David Backhouse)*

☆ **Marlborough** [High St; SU1869], *Sun*: Attractively furnished, friendly 16th-century pub, good lively atmosphere in bar on right with black panelling, heavy sloping beams, big fireplace, newspapers to read, well kept Watneys-related real ales; plainer lounge on left, seats in small sheltered back courtyard; simple bedrooms *(Barry and Anne, David Backhouse, Mary Rayner, Chris Payne, LYM)*

☆ **Marlborough** [High St], *Wellington Arms*: Thriving atmosphere in cosy well run pub with lots of commemorative and decorative mugs hanging from ceiling, newspapers on canes, steps down to eating area with wide range of good bar food from soup, good crab pâté and ploughman's to steaks; well kept Marstons Pedigree and Whitbreads Strong County on handpump, tables in courtyard; bedrooms *(HNJ, PEJ, David Backhouse, Chris Payne, Col G D Stafford, BB)*

☆ **Marlborough** [High St], *Green Dragon*: Particularly good town pub with well kept

Wadworths 6X and IPA on handpump and wide choice of lunchtime bar food; bedrooms *(David Backhouse)*

Marlborough [Kingsbury St], *Bentleys*: Pleasant wine bar with well kept Archers BBB on handpump *(David Backhouse)*; [The Parade], *Lamb*: Good lively atmosphere in town-centre local with separate pool room and well kept Wadworths IPA and 6X tapped from the cask under light blanket pressure *(Chris Payne, David Backhouse, David and Christine Foulkes)*; [London Rd], *Roebuck*: Welcoming red-brick pub with comfortable bars, well kept Watneys-related real ales, leanings towards more provision for diners; bedrooms *(F E M Hardy, David Backhouse)*

☆ **Marston Meysey** [SU1297], *Spotted Cow & Calf*: Stone pub, once a farmhouse, in pleasant setting, with well kept Boddingtons, Wadworths 6X and guest beer on handpump, raised stone fireplace; beware US airmen throwing darts underhand; fruit machine and piped music may be rather intrusive; spacious garden *(Ewan McCall, Roger Huggins, Tom McLean, David Backhouse, Mr and Mrs P B Dowsett)*

☆ **Melksham** [Market Pl; ST9063], *Kings Arms*: Restored 16th-century inn, friendly and courteous, with well kept Wadworths; popular lunchtime eating place with imaginative and reasonably priced menu; tables in cobbled courtyard, restaurant; bedrooms well furnished *(B R Woolmington)*

Melksham [Semington Rd], *New Inn*: Small, well done-up and spotless open-plan bar with annex for darts and fruit machine; welcoming atmosphere, well kept Watneys-related real ales, good value bar food, pleasant garden, big car park *(B R Woolmington)*

☆ **Mere** [Castle St; ST8132], *Old Ship*: Interesting 16th-century building with open fire in cosy, friendly hotel bar, obliging service, spacious separate bar across coach entry divided into cosy areas by standing timbers and so forth, log fire here too, bar games; wide choice of bar food such as duck casserole; Badger Best under light blanket pressure; timber-walled restaurant; children allowed in eating area; bedrooms *(Bernard Phillips, Tony and Lynne Stark, Mr and Mrs P W Dryland, Roy McIsaac, Helen Roe, Barbara M McHugh, Robert and Elizabeth Scott, LYM)*

Minety [SU0290], *White Horse*: Nicely refurbished place in lakeside setting that has retained its character; big helpings of normally good food *(Miss E Stanley)*

Monkton Farleigh [ST8065], *Kings Arms*: Fine interesting village local with good atmosphere, splendid landlord, tables in courtyard; reasonably priced food *(Roger Cunningham, Deborah Frost)*

Netheravon [SU1449], *Dog & Gun*: Watneys beers, food till 10, family room, two fruit machines *(J H C Peters)*

☆ **Netherhampton** [SU1029], *Victoria & Albert*: Attractive beamed bars doing well under new licensees, antique furnishings on polished flagstones, well kept Watneys-related real ales, good choice of wines, decent bar food; maybe unobtrusive piped music, fruit machine in side room *(Jerry and Alison Oakes, Brigid Avison)*

Nettleton [ST8178], *Nettleton Arms*: Lovely 16th-century pub which has been popular for good range of tasty bar food at reasonable prices, but we've had no reports since it came on the market last year *(News please)*

Newton Tony [off A338 Swindon—Salisbury; SU2140], *Malet Arms*: Good range of reasonably priced food, friendly atmosphere, Wadworths 6X and Watneys-related real ales *(R Elliott)*

North Newnton [A345 Upavon—Pewsey; SU1257], *Woodbridge*: Modernised pub with spacious bars and well kept Wadworths IPA, 6X and in winter Old Timer on handpump; bar billiards, angling rights and tackle shop; animals in garden; bedrooms *(David Backhouse)*

☆ **Nunton** [SU1526], *Radnor Arms*: Quaint and rustic spacious room with cheerful and efficient service, good wine list, good quite interesting food, well kept Badger ales, lavatory for disabled people; big garden *(Barbara Want, Roy McIsaac)*

Oaksey [ST9893], *Wheatsheaf*: Friendly village local with well kept Whitbreads PA; busy for Thurs open quiz night, pool table in back room *(Ewan McCall, Tom McLean, Roger Huggins)*

Oare [SU1563], *White Hart*: Super local with comfortable lounge and friendly bar; well kept Wadworths on handpump *(David Backhouse)*

☆ **Pewsey** [A345 towards Marlborough; SU1560], *French Horn*: Good canalside food-oriented pub with well kept Wadworths IPA, 6X and in winter Old Timer on handpump, striking elm furniture, open fires, games in public bar *(David Backhouse, JM, PM, P and R Woods)*

Pewsey [Ball Lane (off B3087)], *Coopers Arms*: Rustic thatched pub with great character; has had well kept Watneys-related real ales, but up for sale earlier this year *(David Backhouse)*; [North St], *Royal Oak*: Old and quaint with beamed bars and big fireplace; well kept Wadworths IPA, 6X and in winter Old Timer on handpump *(David Backhouse)*

Purton [High St; SU0887], *Angel*: 18th-century pub with spacious beamed bars and well kept Arkells BB and BBB on handpump *(David Backhouse)*; [B4041 Wootton Bassett—Cricklade], *Ghost Train*: Friendly old stone pub, basic but good value, with Courage Directors on handpump, decent food generously served, well equipped games room, skittle alley, children's play area; big car park *(P and R Woods)*

☆ **Salisbury** [Milford St], *Red Lion*: Mix of antique settles, leather chairs and modern banquettes in small two-roomed panelled bar which opens into spacious old-fashioned hall, where interesting furnishings include amazing longcase clock with skeleton bellringers; well kept Watneys-related real ales and a guest beer — maybe many more in July; lunchtime bar food from sandwiches to cheap hot dishes, stylishly medieval restaurant, loggia courtyard seats; children in eating areas; bedrooms comfortable — a nice place to stay *(JAH, Jerry and Alison Oakes, LYM)*

☆ **Salisbury** [Harnham Rd — at southernmost ring rd roundabout (towards A354 and

A338) an unclassified rd not signposted city centre leads to pub], *Rose & Crown*: Worth a visit for the view — almost identical to that in the most famous Constable painting of Salisbury Cathedral; elegantly restored inn with friendly beamed and timbered bar, popular simple bar food (snacks only, Sun — when the restaurant does good generous lunches), Watneys-related real ales, charming garden running down to River Avon, picture-window bedrooms in smart modern extension as well as the more traditional ones in the original building; bedrooms *(Roy McIsaac, LYM)*

☆ Salisbury [New St], *New Inn*: Creaky-beamed ancient timbered pub with good choice of genuine food carefully prepared and presented, well kept Badger beers *(Celia and David Watt, BB)*

☆ Salisbury [Ivy St/Catherine St], *Cloisters*: Charmingly done up to look old and homely, with low beams, spacious seating, well kept local beers and good choice of food; open all day *(Mark Blundell, Dr and Mrs Tony Clarke)*

Salisbury [Bedwin St], *Arts Centre*: Not a pub, but indeed an arts centre which has kept the impressive stained glass of its ecclesiastical origin; included for its well kept Gibbs Mews and Wiltshire on handpump, simple food inc vegetarian dishes; beer festival early June *(Matthew Pringle)*; [Fisherton St], *Deacons*: Clean, basic free house (possibly converted from shop or house), small front bar and back games room, wooden floorboards and jovial atmosphere; well kept Gales HSB, Ringwood Old Thumper and Wadworths 6X *(D J Penny)*; [nr bus station], *Pheasant*: Old pub comfortably modernised, with well kept Courage *(Dr and Mrs A K Clarke, BB)*; [Ivy St], *Queens Arms*: Really friendly, homely pub with comfortable atmosphere *(Dr and Mrs A K Clarke)*; [corner Ivy St/Brown St], *Star*: Basic local with wooden floors, beams painted with canalboat patterns, pool and darts *(Dr and Mrs A K Clarke)*; [St John St], *White Hart*: THF hotel, rebuilt late 18th century, with good bar snacks, well kept Bass; bedrooms *(Roy McIsaac)*; [New St], *Wig & Quill*: Low-beamed 16th-century building with ornate rugs, subtle lighting, real fire, leather chairs, stuffed birds and low arches to connecting rooms; Adnams and Wadworths, 1940s piped music; open all day Sat, dogs allowed *(Matthew Pringle)*; [Estcourt Rd], *Wyndham Arms*: Basic, modern corner pub with small, cosy room opposite bar and friendly atmosphere; reasonably priced Hop Back beers brewed on premises inc GFB, HBS, winter Entire Stout and summer Lightning, country wines, simple bar food *(Matthew Pringle)*

☆ Seend [ST9461], *Bell*: Welcoming traditional country pub with small lounge and bar, well kept beer and good food from interesting soups and sandwiches to daily specials, prepared by the landlord's daughter; well kept Wadworths IPA and 6X; children in dining area; beautiful sloping garden; 1/4 mile from Kennet and Avon canal *(PW, Tim and Ann Newell, B R Woolmington, Angus and Rosemary Campbell)*

Seend [Strand; A361 nr Keevil — OS Sheet

173 map reference 918597], *Lamb*: Popular eating pub, several rooms knocked together and furnished attractively, food running through salad bar to speciality steaks with wide choice of puddings, pleasant staff, Watneys-related real ales, seats outside *(A J Triggle, LYM)*

Semington [A350 2 miles S of Melksham — OS Sheet 173 map reference 898608; ST8960], *Somerset Arms*: Chintz, artificial flowers and brassware in pleasant if commercial beamed pub rather concentrating on food; Watneys-related real ales; tables out behind *(P and R Woods, Roger Cunningham, Deborah Frost)*

☆ Sherston [B4040 Malmesbury—Chipping Sodbury; ST8585], *Carpenters Arms*: Cosy village pub with scrubbed floors and tables, open fire, area set aside for eating — unusual food running to rabbit, hare and pigeon breast; well kept Whitbreads tapped from the cask, welcoming staff, piped radio; tables in garden *(Roger Huggins, Tom McLean, Ewan McCall)*

Sherston [High St], *Angel*: Clean and polished oak-beamed pub with well kept Flowers; very civil and competent service; varied reasonably priced menu — smoked trout salad very good indeed *(D C Bail)*; [OS Sheet 173 map reference 854859], *Rattlebone*: 17th-century beamed and stone-walled free house with games bar and spacious dining room with big stone fireplace; well kept changing real ales such as Bass and Butcombe on handpump, good choice of lunchtime and evening bar food, pebbled terrace, attractive walled back garden; has been open all day Sat *(Roger Huggins)*

South Wraxall [ST8364], *Longs Arms*: Pleasant, cosy atmosphere in remote refurbished rustic pub, friendly and welcoming landlord, well kept Wadworths, good freshly cooked bar food *(J S Wilson, Roger Cunningham, Deborah Frost)*

St Ediths Marsh [ST9764], *Oliver Cromwell*: Rea ales inc Wadworths 6X and maybe McEwans 80/-; standard food, with good value daily specials in bar or dining room *(B R Woolmington)*

Staverton [B3105 Trowbridge—Bradford-on-Avon; ST8560], *Kings Arms*: Large roadside pub with bar food, lots of tables outside, children's play area; open all day; big car park *(Mrs Carol Mason)*; *Old Bear*: Completely refurbished and extended free house with long, narrow, opened-up room and alcoves created by high-backed benches; well kept beers and good value decent food *(B R Woolmington)*

☆ Stibb Green [SU2363], *Three Horseshoes*: Olde-worlde beams and inglenooks in lovely little pub with well kept Wadworths, farm cider, particularly good food and friendly landlord *(David Backhouse)*

Stockton [just off A36 Salisbury—Warminster, near A303; ST9738], *Carriers*: Refurbished pub in charming location, with bar food and good choice of beer; closed Mon *(R W Stanbury)*

☆ Stourton [Church Lawn; follow Stourhead signpost off B3092, N of junction with A303 just W of Mere], *Spread Eagle*: Included chiefly for its lovely setting at head of Stourhead Lake, and popular with mostly older customers; old-fashioned furnishings, Bass and Charrington IPA kept under light blanket pressure, straightforward bar food inc self-service buffet (good smoked salmon sandwiches), restaurant, benches in back courtyard; bedrooms spacious and comfortable, with good residents' lounge (*Hayward Wane, Derek Patey, Tony and Lynne Stark, GB, Marjorie and David Lamb, John and Betsey Cutler, J M M Hill, Gwen and Peter Andrews, Robert and Elizabeth Scott, LYM*)

☆ **Stratton St Margaret** [A420 out of Swindon; SU1787], *White Hart*: Large, pleasantly modernised and welcoming open-plan pub with plush lounge, popular at lunchtimes for quickly served plentiful hot bar food; well kept Arkells BB and BBB on handpump (*David Backhouse, Mr and Mrs Peter Woods, Dr and Mrs A K Clarke*)

☆ **Swindon** [Prospect Hill; SU1485], *Beehive*: Quaint and lively little triangular pub with wooden floors on different levels, plain wooden counters, stools and benches around wall; quite a social centre in the evening, with lots of characters from kissogram girls through college lecturers and offshore sailing devotees to rock bands; poetry readings and live Irish folk music, well kept Morrells Dark Mild and Varsity on handpump, filled rolls and limited range of hot food at lunchtime (*Brian Jones, David Backhouse, W Bailey*)

Swindon [Emlyn Sq], *Bakers Arms*: Good honest local with Arkells BB and BBB on handpump (*David Backhouse*); [Clifton St], *Clifton*: Good, honest local with Arkells BB and BBB on handpump (*David Backhouse*); [Eastcott Hill], *Duke of Wellington*: Good, honest local with Arkells BB and BBB on tap (*David Backhouse*); [Common Platt; out towards Purton], *Foresters Arms*: Reasonably good Courage house with well kept Courage Best and Directors on handpump (*David Backhouse*); [Emlyn Sq], *Glue Pot*: Good pub in stonebuilt listed building; well kept Archers Village, Best, ASB and guest beer on handpump — the tap for Archers brewery (*David Backhouse*); [Bridge St/Regent St], *Lamb & Flag*: Shopping-centre pub with well kept Arkells BB, BBB and Kingsdown on handpump and adequate food (*David Backhouse*); [Fleet St], *Mail Coach*: Well kept Arkells BB and BBB on handpump, close to shopping centre (*David Backhouse*); [Devizes Rd], *Plough*: Good, honest local with well kept Arkells BB, BBB and Kingsdown on handpump (*David Backhouse*); [Bridge St], *Porters*: Smart, interesting modern bar with Courage Best, Directors and John Smiths on handpump (*David Backhouse*); [Union St], *Prince of Wales*: Good, honest local with well kept Courage Best (*David Backhouse*); [Wootton Basset Rd (main rd in from M4 junction 16)], *Running Horse*: Recently refurbished good big Beefeater with panelling, well kept real ale, quiet, relaxing atmosphere; restaurant area at back and upstairs (Beefeater), garden with children's slide, big car park (*Paul Corbett, David Backhouse*); [Thames Ave, Haydon Wick], *Shield & Dagger*: Busy estate pub with two big bars and lounge; well kept Bass (*David Backhouse*); [Marlborough Rd, Coate; S of

town], *Sun*: Large and modernised with well kept Arkells BB, BBB and Kingsdown on handpump (*David Backhouse*); [Newport St], *Wheatsheaf*: Reasonably good big managed pub with Wadworths IPA, 6X, Farmers Glory and in winter Old Timer on handpump (*David Backhouse, Chris Payne*)

☆ **Teffont Magna** [ST9832], *Black Horse*: Good food with frequently changing specials in pretty pub with comfortable and welcoming lounge; well kept real ales, limited but good value range of wines, more basic public bar; in attractive village (*LYM*)

Upper Chute [SU2954], *Cross Keys*: In open walking country with good views; large, comfortable bar with good choice of beers and wide variety of good food served in nice dining room; Sun lunch (*R and E Harfield*)

☆ **Wanborough** [2 miles from M4 junction 15; Callas Hill, B4507 towards Bishopstone; SU2083], *Black Horse*: Cheerful, unpretentious two-bar country pub, lounge doubling as homely Mon–Sat lunchtime dining room — ample helpings of well priced home-made quiche, gammon etc, fine sandwiches and ploughman's (snacks only, Sun lunchtime), and popular three-egg businessmen's breakfasts; well kept Arkells BB and BBB on handpump, with Kingsdown tapped from the cask in winter, friendly staff; adventure playground, aviary, pets' corner and fine views from the garden (*D W Backhouse, HNJ, PEJ, Virginia Jones, Mr and Mrs B E Witcher, Mr and Mrs P B Dowsett*)

☆ **Wanborough** [Foxhill; from A419 through Wanborough turn right, 1 1/2 miles towards Baydon; SU2381], *Shepherds Rest*: Remote pub where Ridgeway crossed Roman rd, doing well under new licensees, with two pool tables in bright and airy basic public bar, low-beamed lounge with hunting prints and brasses; pleasant welcome, good value plentiful food from soup through vegetarian dishes to meat dishes such as halibut and steaks, well kept Marstons Pedigree and Flowers IPA and Original on handpump; can get very busy, dining room decor rather reminiscent of seaside tearoom; garden now has children's games, slides and swings (*Peter Woods, Mary Rayner, David Backhouse*)

Wanborough [Burycroft, Lower Wanborough], *Cross Keys*: Quaint pub, though not that old, with good toasted sandwiches and well kept Whitbreads (*David Backhouse, Dr and Mrs A K Clarke*); [High St, Lower Wanborough], *Harrow*: Pretty thatched and oak-beamed two-bar pub with pear tree against the wall, seats out by flowers, big open fires; has been popular for well kept Whitbreads-related real ales, farm cider and good home-cooked food, but too few reports since it became a managed Roast Inn in spring 1990 for a clear rating yet (*Mary Rayner, David Backhouse, Mr and Mrs Peter Woods*); [High St, Lower Wanborough], *Plough*: Listed thatched pub recently renovated with one bar divided up by fireplaces; well kept Bass tapped from the cask, Wadworths 6X and Whitbreads on handpump (*David Backhouse*)

Warminster [High St; ST8744], *Old Bell*: Olde-worlde country-town hotel — the time-honoured place to go after shopping; good service, well cooked and presented food inc excellent help-yourself salads and trout, good choice of wines; restaurant *(K R Harris, Maj and Mrs D R C Woods)*

☆ **West Dean** [SU2527], *Red Lion*: Reprieved after 1989 brewery plans to sell it as a private house, this unaffected country inn has a particularly lovely setting, with the tree-sheltered village green running down to a fresh and pretty stream-fed duckpond; simple lounge with easy chairs and open fires, games inc pool in small plain back bar, well kept Whitbreads-related real ales, pleasant atmosphere, good value straightforward bar food inc Sun carvery; tables outside *(Chris Fluck, Ken and Barbara Turner, LYM)*

West Lavington [SU0053], *Bridge*: New licensees have put a lot of effort into this free house: spotlessly kept throughout, brassware and horse harness, bar billiards, piped music, and comfortable atmosphere; Gibbs Mew beer and wide choice of good standard food from mushrooms stuffed with stilton to steaks and king prawns *(J H Mason)*

Westbrook [A3102 about 4 miles E of Melksham; ST9565], *Westbrook*: Big helpings of good value food quickly fill this small and cleanly renovated pub, decorated with farm tools and marathon photographs; Watneys-related real ales on handpump, piped music *(LYM)*

Westbury [Market Pl; ST8751], *Crown*: Pleasant atmosphere, with plenty of local regulars, good straightforward competitively priced food, Wadworths beers; bedrooms *(Mr and Mrs F E M Hardy)*

☆ **Westwood** [ST8059], *New Inn*: Cheerful little pub doing well under newish licensee, with several small rooms knocked into one, lots of beams and brasses, helpful efficient staff, well kept Ushers, and good value hot, plentiful and home-cooked food (fried brie with cranberry sauce, corned beef pie, lasagne, curry all recommended) *(B R Woolmington, Joan Olivier, Mrs D C Starkey, Mrs Joan Harris)*

Whiteparish [Main St; SU2423], *Village Lantern*: Friendly and lively village pub, open-plan with central fireplace and sensibly placed pool and darts, well kept Gibbs Mew ales, good value bar food, well cooked and nicely presented *(Chris Fluck)*

☆ **Wilcot** [SU1360], *Golden Swan*: Ancient steeply thatched village inn, very picturesque, with rustic tables on pretty front lawn; friendly atmosphere in two small rooms with lots of china jugs and mugs hanging from beams, well kept Wadworths IPA and 6X and in winter Old Timer on handpump; bar food, dining room, simple bedrooms *(David Backhouse, BB)*

Wilton [Market Pl; SU0931], *Wiltons*: Welcoming new licensees, attractive redecoration; good sensibly priced food *(J Hill)*

☆ **Winterbourne Monkton** [A361 Avebury—Wroughton; SU0972], *New Inn*: Small and friendly village local with well

kept Adnams, Wadworths 6X and a guest such as Archers on handpump; wide choice of good bar food, full meals in separate restaurant; comfortable bedrooms in adjacent converted barn, with good breakfasts *(Caroline Black, Roger Sealey, David Backhouse)*

☆ **Woodborough** [Bottlesford — OS Sheet 173 map reference 112592; SU1059], *Seven Stars*: Doing well under newish management, with delightfully restored small rooms, pleasant atmosphere, interesting food at slightly upmarket prices, well kept Wadworths 6X and a guest beer on handpump *(Mr and Mrs F Hardy, David Backhouse)*

Woodborough [Honey St], *Barge*: Good canalside pub with well kept Courage Best and Directors on handpump *(David Backhouse)*

Wootton Bassett [High St; SU0682], *Angel*: Recent thorough refurbishment of 16th-century coaching inn, well kept Whitbreads-related ales on handpump, wide choice of reasonably priced food; bedrooms *(David Backhouse)*; [High St], *Borough Arms*: Good atmosphere, well kept Arkells on handpump; bedrooms *(David Backhouse)*; [Wood St], *Five Bells*: Good pub, well kept Whitbreads IPA and Pompey Royal on handpump *(David Backhouse)*; [Station Rd], *Old Nick*: Well kept Archers Headbanger, Ind Coope Burton, Tetleys, Wadworths 6X and winter Old Timer, and a guest beer on handpump *(David Backhouse)*

☆ **Wroughton** [A4361 — handy for M4 junction 16; SU1480], *White Hart*: Thatched pub, formerly a blacksmith's, with large old stone fireplace in spacious smartly kept L-shaped beamed lounge; good choice of straightforward bar food, well kept Badger Tanglefoot, Wadworths IPA, 6X and winter Old Timer on handpump, welcoming service, lively public bar and skittle alley *(Mary Rayner, David Backhouse, Peter Woods)*

Wroughton [High St], *Carters Rest*: Basic pub which has been popular for ten well kept changing real ales and good value, generously served bar food (also restaurant); no reports since it changed hands early 1990 *(Mr and Mrs P G Woods; more news please)*; [A4361], *Fox & Hounds*: Well kept Arkells BB, BBB and Kingsdown on handpump; bedrooms *(David Backhouse)*

☆ **Wylye** [just off A303/A36 junction; SU0037], *Bell*: Village local, clean, comfortable and friendly, with decent choice of reasonably priced good food, well kept Wadworths IPA and 6X on handpump and country wines in heavy beamed front area with some stripped masonry, log fire in huge stone inglenook, wall seats and rustic benches around sturdy tables, piped music; bar loops right round past bar billiards area to dining area filled with tables and stall seating; bedrooms *(Dorothy and Jack Rayner, Denzil T Taylor, Gordon and Daphne)*

Yorkshire

Yorkshire is marvellously rich in beautifully positioned country pubs, often with fine views and generally with a good deal of character. It's also one of the country's best areas for pub bargains. You tend to pay about 10p less for a drink here than in the country at large – nearer 15p less if the pub's tied to a regional or local brewer such as Sam Smiths or Wards, or one of the growing number of pubs brewing their own beers. (We found little difference in prices here between free houses and pubs tied to the big national brewing chains.) There are abundant bargains in Yorkshire pub food. Quite a high proportion of the main entries beat our low-price targets of under £1 for decent snacks or (more often) under £3 for worthwhile main dishes. The most striking bargains for food we found here were at the unpretentiously cottagey Red Lion up in Langthwaite, the old-fashioned Whitelocks in Leeds (probably the best pub there – proving yet again that quality doesn't have to mean high prices), the enterprising Fat Cat in Sheffield (a great range of drinks as well), and a new entry this year, the Staff of Life near Todmorden (brews its own good beers, too). Other new main entries, or pubs back in these pages after a break, include the Ship at Aldborough (doing well under new licensees, with popular food), the Brown Cow in Bingley (great Yorkshire puddings – which are currently on a crest of popularity in lots of other pubs, too), the family-run Malt Shovel at Brearton (interesting food, good drinks, attractive layout), the civilised Fox & Hounds at Carthorpe (its food is nudging towards award level), the New Inn up by the moors at Cropton (brews its own beers, good in other ways too), the comfortable Kings Head in Masham, the Mount Skip perched on its steep hillside near Midgley (doing well under a new licensee), the spacious old Royal Oak in Settle (a comfortable place to stay), the Angel & White Horse right by Sam Smiths' brewery – and dray horses – in Tadcaster, and the cosy Countryman in Winksley. A great many changes across the county include new licensees for the well placed Game Cock at Austwick (friendly people), the delightful old Star at Harome (wider beers choice, good food), the Squinting Cat on the outskirts of Harrogate, the unspoilt Kings Arms at Heath (taken over by the local Clarks Brewery), the genuinely ancient if much refurbished Old Hall in Heckmondwike, the Forresters Arms at Kilburn, the quaint Blacksmiths Arms at Lastingham, the classic Garden Gate in Leeds, the prettily set Fountaine at Linton in Craven, the Queens Arms up in the Dales at Litton, the foody Spite at Otley, and the pretty little Greyhound at Saxton. Other pubs currently doing particularly well here include the remote White Lion up at Cray, the Angel at Hetton (hugely popular for food), the unpretentious Bulls Head at Linthwaite (good imaginative food), the Nags Head at Pickhill (generous good food), the sympathetically refurbished Yorke Arms at Ramsgill, the civilised Sawley Arms at Sawley (interesting food), the lively Frog & Parrot in Sheffield (lots of fish, good own-brewed beer), the quaint Anne Arms *at Sutton, the thriving Buck at Thornton Watlass (lots of developments), and the Old Hall Inn at Threshfield (huge helpings of really imaginative food). Among the Lucky Dip entries at the end of the chapter, pubs showing particularly well recently include the Craven Arms at Appletreewick, Birch Hall at Beck Hole, Golden Cock at Farnley Tyas (but it's up for sale as we go to press), Mallyan Spout at Goathland, Black Horse in Grassington, Cow & Calf at Grenoside on the edge of Sheffield, Hales in Harrogate, Fountain at Ingbirchworth, Tennant Arms at Kilnsey, Yorkshire Lass in Knaresborough, Golden Lion in Leyburn, Windmill at Linton, Hare & Hounds at Stutton and Henry Boons in Wakefield, with lots of possibilities in both Leeds and York. Anyone interested in Yorkshire pubs should know that a local reader who's put us on to several fine pubs there, Barrie Pepper, has just published a good well illustrated book delving into the past – and present – of several hundred of the county's pubs: A Haunt of Rare Souls (Smith Settle, £8.95/£12.95).*

ALDBOROUGH (N Yorks)   SE4166 Map 7

Ship 🍺

Village signposted from B6265 just S of Boroughbridge, close to A1

Seats in the heavily beamed bar of this attractive 14th-century pub look through latticed windows to the ancient village church across the lane; there are also some old-fashioned seats around heavy cast-iron tables, sentimental engravings on the walls, and a coal fire in the stone inglenook fireplace. A quieter back room (decorated with ship pictures) has lots more tables. Reasonably priced home-made bar food includes soup (£1.05), sandwiches (from £1.15, open sandwiches from £1.60), salads (from £2.50), good ploughman's or Yorkshire pudding with meat and onion gravy (£2.95), steak and kidney pie (£3.60), chicken curry (£3.95), gammon with egg or pineapple (£4.95), and steaks (from £5.95); Sunday roast lunch (£5.50). Well kept John Smiths, Tetleys and Theakstons on handpump, and some malt whiskies; dominoes, fruit machine and piped music; summer seats on the spacious grass behind. The Roman town for which the village is famous is mainly up beyond the church. *(Recommended by Paul and Janet Waring, GB, J A Gifford, John N Skeldon, David Boyd, J D Andrews, David and Rebecca Killick, Tony Gayfer)*

Free house   Licensees Duncan and Vicki Finch   Real ale   Meals and snacks Children by prior arrangement   Open 12–2.30, 5.30–11   Bedrooms tel Boroughbridge (090 12) 2749; £24B/£36B

ARNCLIFFE (N Yorks)   SD9473 Map 7

Falcon

Off B6160

Charmingly set on an out-of-the-way moorland village green, this timeless, friendly country pub has been run by the same family for four generations, with a fifth growing up. A small servery at the back taps the Youngers ales from the cask, and there's hatch service to a couple of functional little rooms with heavy settles and cast-iron tables, some old humorous sporting prints, and a fire (if you're lucky enough to get near it); there's also a homely front lounge, and an airy conservatory room behind. Simple bar food includes baked potato with cheese (80p), soup (£1), sandwiches (from £1.10) and good ploughman's (£2.60); enormous breakfasts; dominoes. The pub is on *Good Walks Guide* Walk 151 and stands right by a bridleway leading up to Malham Tarn and beyond. *(Recommended by Lee Goulding, Peter and Rose Flower, Jon Wainwright, Neil and Angela Huxter)*

*Free house   Licensee Robin Miller   Real ale   Lunchtime snacks   Children in
conservatory (lunchtime only)   Open 12–3, 6.30–11 in summer; 12–2, 7–11 in
winter   Bedrooms tel Arncliffe (075 677) 205; £19/£38 (may not be available in winter)*

ASKRIGG (N Yorks)   SD9591   Map 10

Kings Arms ⊘ ⊨

Village signposted from A684 Leyburn–Sedbergh in Bainbridge

Turner stayed at this former Georgian manor house in the early 1800s and the tack
hooks where he would have hung his saddle are still in the back parlour. This very
high-ceilinged room is warmly welcoming, and has a kitchen hatch in the
panelling, hunting prints, a curving wall with high window that shows people
bustling up and down the stairs, a huge stone fireplace, and 19th-century fashion
plates and stag's head; an attractive medley of furnishings includes a fine sturdy
old oak settle. The small low-beamed front bar, with more oak panelling, some
side snugs, and a lovely green marble fireplace, now has period furnishings, and all
the bars have photographs of the filming of James Herriot's *All Creatures Great
and Small* (the inn itself, in the series, is the Drovers Arms). A simply furnished
flagstoned back bar has yet another fire, and a fruit machine, bar billiards and juke
box; also darts, shove-ha'penny, dominoes. Bar food includes lovely home-made
soup (£1.10), well presented club sandwiches (from £2.50), filled baked potatoes,
first-class ploughman's, tasty steak and kidney or chicken, ham and mushroom
pies (£4.25), home-made fish pie (£4.50), gammon and egg (£4.95), steak (£6.95),
and lots of puddings (£1.50); well kept McEwans 80/- and Youngers Scotch and
No 3 on handpump, quite a few malt whiskies, an award-winning wine list
(including interesting champagnes), and filter, espresso and cappuccino coffee, and
speciality teas; good, friendly service. The two-level courtyard has lots of tables
and chairs. During 1991, a new grill room is to be opened, and a new entrance
foyer, reception, no-smoking lounge, meeting rooms and leisure facilities created.
*(Recommended by Mr and Mrs M O Jones, Roy and Nicola Byrne, Kelvin Lawton, Bob Smith,
Sidney and Erna Wells, Barbara and Ken Turner, John Fazakerley, Brian and Genie
Krakowska-Smart, J E Rycroft, Paul McPherson, Alan and Ruth Woodhouse, Lee Goulding,
Roger Bellingham, Henry Midwinter, Paul Newberry, Gary Melnyk, Anthony Fernau)*

*Free house   Licensees Raymond and Elizabeth Hopwood   Real ale   Meals and
snacks   Partly no-smoking restaurants   Children in eating area of bar until 8.30 (or
longer if well behaved)   Open 11–4, 6.30–11; 11–11 summer Sat   Bedrooms
tel Wensleydale (0969) 50258; £35B/£55B*

AUSTWICK (N Yorks)   SD7668   Map 7

Game Cock ⊨

Just off A65 Settle–Kirkby Lonsdale

The simply furnished but cosy back bar in this prettily placed, welcoming inn is
popular with climbers and walkers, and has beams, a good winter fire, well made
built-in wall benches and plain wooden tables, and a few cockfighting prints on the
butter-coloured walls. Bar food includes soup (£1), sandwiches (from £1.10),
crispy crab and vegetable parcels (£2.25), pork satay (£2.50), Cumberland sausage
with gravy (£2.75), jumbo cod (£3.35), gammon with egg or pineapple (£4.60),
and sirloin steak (£7.50). Well kept Thwaites on handpump; darts and dominoes.
There are some seats in a glass-enclosed sun loggia, and outside (where there's also
a children's play area). The crags and screes of the Dales National Park and the
Three Peaks rise above the green pastures around this quiet village of rose-covered
stone houses. *(Recommended by Mrs Hilarie Taylor, Andy and Jill Kassube, David
Warrellow, Dr Thomas Mackenzie, G Dobson, A McK, Alan and Ruth Woodhouse, M A and
W R Proctor, A T Langton, Simon Bates, Paul Newberry)*

*Thwaites   Licensee Jack Kenyon   Real ale   Meals and snacks (not Mon evening in
winter)   Restaurant   Children in restaurant   Open 11–3.30, 6–11   Bedrooms
tel Clapham (046 85) 226; £14.50/£29*

BAINBRIDGE (N Yorks)   SD9390 Map 10

Rose & Crown ⇔

A684

Big windows in the spacious main bar of this friendly old inn – part of a cluster of
solid old stone houses – overlook the wide village green. The beamed and panelled
front bar has antique settles and other old furniture, a butterfly collection, flowers,
a cheerful fire, and Sherry the cockatiel. The public bar has been refurbished this
year. Good bar food includes home-made soup (£1.50), sandwiches (from £1.15,
open sandwiches £3.50), cottage cheese with fruit and nuts (£2.50), coronation
chicken (£2.95), good ploughman's (£3.45), home-made sausages (£4.25),
home-made pie of the day (£4.85), sirloin steak, daily specials, home-made
puddings (£1.50) and children's menu (from £2.20); good generous breakfasts.
John Smiths, Theakstons, and Youngers Scotch on handpump; extensive wine list;
darts, pool, shove ha'penny, dominoes, cribbage, fruit machine, juke box and
piped music. *(Recommended by Mr and Mrs M D Jones, H K Dyson, J E Rycroft, J C
Proud, Henry Midwinter, Mr and Mrs J E Rycroft, Jenny Cantle)*

*Free house   Licensee P H Collins   Real ale   Meals and snacks   Restaurant
Children welcome   Open 11–3, 6–11 weekdays, 11–11 Sat   Bedrooms
tel Wensleydale (0969) 50225; £30B/£52B*

BINGLEY (W Yorks)   SE1039 Map 7

Brown Cow

Ireland Bridge; B6429, just W of junction with A650

They specialise in large Yorkshire puddings at this quiet, friendly pub – served
either with beef, stew or Yorkshire sausage (from £2.75). Other home-made bar
food includes soup, sandwiches (from £1.65), salads (from £2.85), home-cooked
ham and egg (£3.85), mixed grill (£6.95), and puddings like hot fudge cake
(£1.85); 3-course Sunday roast (£7.35). The carpeted open-plan main bar is
divided into smaller and snugger areas, with comfortable easy chairs and captain's
chairs around the black tables, lots of pictures and some brass on the partly
panelled walls, and a high shelf of toby jugs under the dark ceiling. Well kept
Timothy Taylors Best, Ram Tam and Landlord on handpump. A sheltered corner
terrace behind has tables and chairs – some of them sturdy pews – below a steep
bluebell wood. Handy for the flights of locks on the Leeds and Liverpool canal,
and there are several antique shops in the town. *(Recommended by Andy and Jill
Kassube, Dr and Mrs I C Jones, J E Rycroft, Reg Nelson, Brian Jones, Barbara Wensworth)*

*Timothy Taylors   Licensees Mr and Mrs Brian Sampson   Real ale   Meals and snacks
(lunchtimes Mon–Fri and Sun)   Restaurant   Children in eating area and small snug
Traditional jazz Mon   Open 12–3, 7–11   Bedrooms in adjoining cottages tel Bradford
(0274) 569482; £23/£46*

BLAKEY RIDGE (N Yorks)   SE6799 Map 10

Lion ⇔

From A171 Guisborough–Whitby follow Castleton, Hutton le Hole signposts; from
A170 Kirkby Moorside–Pickering follow Keldholm, Hutton le Hole, Castleton
signposts; OS Sheet 100 map reference 679996

During the late 19th-century coal-mining days, the mine here was linked to the
railway at Rosedale by a tramway that ran within yards of the pub – it's now the
course of the Cleveland Way, Coast to Coast path and Lyke Wake walk. At 1325
feet above sea level, this rambling old place is said to be the fourth highest inn in
England and the moorland views in virtually every direction are spectacular. It's
got a lot of character inside; the stripped stone walls are hung with some old
engravings and photographs of the pub under snow (it can easily get cut off in
winter – but there are good fires), and there are lots of small dining chairs on the
Turkey carpet, a few big high-backed rustic settles around cast-iron-framed tables,

a nice leather settee, dim lamps, and beams. Bar food includes soup (£1.05), sandwiches (from £1.25) or ploughman's (£2.95 – both these lunchtime only), steak sandwich (£2.45), home-made steak and mushroom pie, chicken and broccoli lasagne or home-cooked ham and egg (all £3.95), steaks (from £6.25), a vegetarian menu (from £3.95), puddings (£1.40), children's menu (£2.45) and Sunday roasts. Well kept Tetleys and Theakstons Best, Old Peculier and XB on handpump; fruit machine and piped music. *(Recommended by Jill Hampton, Brian Metherell, John and Christine Simpson, Brian and Anna Marsden, Sidney and Erna Wells, Tim and Lynne Crawford, Jane and Niall, Dr and Mrs R J Ashleigh)*

Free house   Licensee Barry Crossland   Real ale   Meals and snacks (served all day) Restaurant (food served all day Sun)   Children welcome   Open 10.30am–11pm; 12–10.30 Sun   Bedrooms tel Lastingham (075 15) 320; £15.50(£21B)/£33(£40B)

BOLTON PERCY (N Yorks)   SE5341 Map 7

Crown

Signposted with Oxton from Tadcaster – first real right turn after crossing the bridge, heading out from centre on York road

Very peaceful indeed on a weekday lunchtime, this tiny, unpretentious and very friendly pub has two simply furnished rooms decorated with brass ornaments, a Delft shelf of fox-hunting plates and a big print of shire horses; the three dogs are called Teal (the spaniel) and Coot and Gipsy (the labradors). As the brewery is just over three miles away the cheap Sam Smiths OB on electric pump is in tip-top condition. Freshly made, good value bar food includes sandwiches (from 80p, toasties from £1), soup (90p), burgers (£1.50), filled Yorkshire pudding (from £2.25), ploughman's, chicken, scampi or home-made steak and kidney pie (all £2.75), children's menu (£1.25), and there are summer barbecues on Saturday evenings. Darts and dominoes. Outside, the biggish terrace (with ornamental pheasants in a row of pens beside it) has picnic-table sets among fruit trees, and a very long wooden cat-walk footbridge that snakes out over a slow dark stream and its bordering nettle flats. The landlord runs the village cricket team and another team in York. *(Recommended by Ben Wimpenny, Syd and Wyn Donald; more reports please)*

Sam Smiths   Licensees Geoff and Angela Pears   Real ale   Meals and snacks Children in eating area and family room   Open 10.30–3 (4 Sat), 6–11

nr BRADFIELD (S Yorks)   SK2692 Map 7

Strines Inn

Strines signposted from A616 at head of Underbank Reservoir, W of Stocksbridge; or on A57 heading E of junction with A6013 (Ladybower Reservoir) take first left turn (signposted with Bradfield) then bear left

This area is one of several known as Little Switzerland, for the steep hills and (here) no less than seven dams, giving attractively shaped and natural-looking reservoirs. The best views from this handsome stone-built inn are from the picnic-table sets outside, though you can peer out of the bar windows. Dating from 1275, it's possibly the second oldest pub in the country. The main bar has black beams liberally decked with copper kettles and so forth, quite a menagerie of stuffed animals, homely red-plush-cushioned traditional wooden wall benches and small chairs, and a coal fire in the rather grand stone fireplace; the atmosphere is friendly and relaxed, with a good mixture of walkers and people who work on the moors – the landlord himself works a thriving hill sheep farm. A room off on the right has another coal fire, hunting photographs and prints, and lots of brass and china, and there's a simply furnished candlelit room on the left, with an upstairs restaurant (Saturday evening, Sunday carvery lunch till 4pm). A wide choice of bar food running up to quite elaborate dishes includes good sandwiches and soup, with a daily special such as roast pork; Whitbreads Castle Eden on handpump, exceptionally good coffee (served from 10.30), decent wines and nearly four dozen malt whiskies; darts and dominoes (winter). *(Recommended by Robin and Christine Harman, Steve Mitcheson, Anne Collins, Dennis D'Vigne)*

Free house   Licensees Ken and Angie Slack   Real ale   Meals and snacks (not Sun evening, except for residents)˜ Restaurant (see above)   Children welcome   Open 11–11; a bit iffy Jan and Feb, as they can get snowed in   Bedrooms tel Sheffield (0742) 81247; £15(£20B)/£30(£40B)

BREARTON (N Yorks)   SE3261 Map 7

Malt Shovel

Village signposted off A61 N of Harrogate

Though it's a new entry here, there's already a strong suggestion that the friendly licensees (it's a family-run concern) are putting this 16th-century village pub well in the running for a Food Award. The wide choice includes delicious vegetarian quiches such as leek and mushroom (£2.75), roast ham with fresh parsley sauce, steak pie, chicken breast or nut roast (£3.75), lasagne (£3.80), popular Trinidad prawn curry (£4.95), salmon with cucumber mayonnaise (£5.95) and lamb steak with mint sauce (£6.50). They have decent wines, and well kept Big End Piston (local), Old Mill, Tetleys, Theakstons Best and XB, and guest ales on handpump. Several rooms radiate from the attractive linenfold oak bar counter; heavy beams, an ancient oak partition wall, sewing-machine and other tables, plush-cushioned seats, lively Nigel Hemming hunting prints, both real and gas fires; shove-ha'penny, darts, cribbage, and dominoes. If the cat who makes friends with you isn't Harry, William, Thomas, Charlie or Sooty, it'll be Scraggs from over the road. There are tables behind, with Saturday summer barbecues, on the terrace and the grass leading to a discreet little caravan site; exemplary lavatories.
(Recommended by Andy and Jill Kassube, Michael Rooke)

Free house   Licensee Leigh Parsons   Real ale   Meals and snacks (not Sun evening, not Mon)   Well behaved children allowed   Open 12–3, 7–11; closed Mon, except Bank Hols

BUCKDEN (N Yorks)   SD9278 Map 7

Buck

B6160

In a glorious setting in upper Wharfedale, this busy stone inn has a modernised and extended open-plan bar with upholstered built-in wall banquettes and square stools around shiny dark brown tables on its carpet – though there are still flagstones in the snug original area by the serving counter, and mainly buttery cream walls (one by the big log fire is stripped to bare stone) that are decorated with local pictures, hunting prints, willow-pattern plates and the mounted head of a roebuck. Popular bar food includes home-made soup (£1.50), toasted sandwiches (£2, steak sandwich £3.75), giant Yorkshire puddings filled with rich onion gravy or home-made smooth chicken liver pâté with cream, brandy and garlic (£2.50), omelettes (from £3.75), ploughman's or vegetarian pasta (£4), baked local trout, topped with prawns and toasted almonds or gammon steak with egg or pineapple (both £5.50), mixed grill (£7 – to suit the heartiest appetite), sirloin steak (from £7.50), and blackboard specials; children's menu (£2.50), traditional Sunday lunch. Well kept Tetleys Bitter, Theakstons Old Peculier and Youngers Scotch and regularly changing guest beer on handpump served by uniformed staff (they only served bottled beer in afternoons); good choice of malt whiskies and decent wines. Dominoes, video game, trivia and occasional piped music. Seats on the terrace and beyond the sloping car park in the shelter of a great sycamore have good views of the surrounding moors. *(Recommended by Janet and Paul Waring, Andy and Jill Kassube, Mr and Mrs M Cockram, Jon and Jacquie Payne, Mr and Mrs K H Frostick, Peter and Rose Flower, David Goldstone, Jenny Cantle, J E Rycroft; more reports please)*

Free house   Licensee Trevelyan Illingworth   Real ale   Meals and snacks   Evening restaurant (mainly for residents)   Children in eating area of bar   Open 11–11 Bedrooms tel Kettlewell (075 676) 227; £24.50B/£49B

BURNSALL (N Yorks)   SE0361   Map 7

Red Lion

B6160 S of Grassington, on Ilkley road; OS Sheet 98, map reference 033613

On the cobbles in front of this pretty stone-built pub, white tables look over the quiet road to the village green (which has a tall maypole) running along the banks of the River Wharfe. Inside, the lively main bar has flowery-cushioned sturdy seats built in to the attractively panelled walls (decorated with pictures of the local fell races), Windsor armchairs, rugs on the floor, and steps up past a solid fuel stove to a back area with sensibly placed darts (dominoes players are active up here, too). The carpeted front lounge bar, which is served from the same copper-topped counter through an old-fashioned small-paned glass partition, has a coal fire. Well kept Tetleys and Theakstons on handpump. *(Recommended by Virginia Jones, J E Rycroft, H K Dyson, Andrew Triggs, Andy and Jill Kassube, John and Christine Simpson, Tim Baxter, Jon Wainwright, Professor S Barnett, Paul Newberry)*

Free house   Licensee Patricia Warnett   Real ale   Snacks   Restaurant   Children welcome until 9pm   Open 11.30–3, 6–11   Bedrooms tel Burnsall (075 672) 204; £24(£32.25B)/£33(£43B)

BYLAND ABBEY (N Yorks)   SE5579   Map 7

Abbey Inn   ✪

The Abbey has a brown tourist-attraction signpost off the A170 Thirsk–Helmsley

A rambling series of rooms in this isolated pub – spectacularly set opposite the Abbey ruins – have been carefully furnished to preserve their old-fashioned character. There are oak and stripped deal tables, settees, carved oak seats, and Jacobean-style dining chairs on the polished boards and flagstones, some discreet stripping back of plaster to show the ex-abbey masonry, big fireplaces, bunches of flowers among the candles, various stuffed birds, cooking implements, little etchings, willow-pattern plates, and china cabinets. In a big back room an uptilted cart shelters a pair of gnomelike waxwork yokels, and there are lots of rustic bygones. Though it's quiet in the early evening it quickly fills up with people after the food (all prepared by the licensee's Norwegian wife), which might include home-made pâté (£2.75), Abbey platter (£3.50), lamb rogan josh or pies like steak and kidney or chicken and leek (£4.50), fillet of pork with yoghurt sauce or breast of chicken with tarragon (£5), venison pie (£5.75), and lots of home-made puddings; it's also popular for Sunday lunch. Well kept Tetleys and Theakstons Best on handpump, interesting wines, efficient food service by neat waitresses, inoffensive piped music. No dogs. There's lots of room outside in the garden. *(Recommended by Mary and Lionel Tonks, Mr and Mrs M Cockram, Andy and Jill Kassube, Patrick Clark, Roger Bellingham, M B Porter, Dr John Innes, Gill and Neil Patrick)*

Free house   Licensees Peter and Gerd Handley   Real ale   Meals and snacks (not Sun evening, not Mon)   Children welcome before 8.30   Open 11–2.30, 6.30–11; closed Sun evening and all day Mon

CADEBY (S Yorks)   SE5100   Map 7

Cadeby Inn   ★

3 miles from A1(M) at junction with A630; going towards Conisbrough take first right turn signposted Sprotborough, then follow Cadeby signposts

At the back of this cheerful stone ex-farmhouse is the main lounge: caps of all 17 County Cricket Clubs, a stuffed fox and pheasant, some silver tankards, a high-backed settle made in the traditional style to fit around one stone-walled alcove, comfortable seats around wooden tables, an open fire in the big stone fireplace and lots of house plants. There's a quieter front sitting room, and decently out of the way, a fruit machine (they also have a separate darts room, an old each-way horse racing machine, shove-ha'penny, dominoes, cribbage, and quiz evenings). Good bar food includes a good lunchtime salad bar, generous carvery or gammon steak (all £3.50), as well as soup and sandwiches, home-made steak and kidney pie (£2.45), and sirloin steak (£4.95); their traditional Sunday lunches are exceedingly popular. Well kept Sam Smiths OB and Museum, John Smiths and Tetleys Bitter on handpump, attractively priced, and over 180 whiskies. There are seats in the front beer garden, and in summer they have barbecues out here. *(Recommended by ILP, Richard Cole, Mary and Lionel Tonks, David and Christine Foulmes, Andy and Jill Kassube, T Nott, Barbara and Norman Wells, Michael and Alison Sandy, Steve Mitcheson, Anne Collins, KC, J A Edwards, J H Walker, Paul Newberry)*

Free house   Licensee Walter William Ward   Real ale   Meals and snacks (12–2, 6–9.30)   Children in eating area of bar   Open 11–11

CARTHORPE (N Yorks)   SE3184 Map 10

Fox & Hounds

Village signposted from A1 N of Ripon, via B6285

The L-shaped bar of this pretty little extended village house leads into an attractive high-raftered restaurant with lots of neatly black-painted farm and smithy tools – and throughout, food is a main focus of attention here. In the bar, it includes thick vegetable soup (£1.60), several starters or snacks such as curried vegetable pancake or smoked salmon pâté (£2.95), steak and kidney pie (£4.50), sweet and sour chicken or honey-roast ham salad (£4.95), chicken breast stuffed with Coverdale cheese in a creamy sauce (£5.95 – very popular), hake with mustard sauce (£7.25), excellent steaks and lamb steaks, and tempting puddings like tipsy trifle, fresh fruit romanoff or sticky toffee pudding with rich butterscotch sauce (from £1.95). They use local fish according to season and local meat and cheeses, and devote a good deal of care to their wines, with a wide choice by the bottle and half-bottle, decent wines by the glass, and some interesting bin-ends; well kept John Smiths on handpump. The cosy bar has dark red plush button-back built-in wall banquettes and chairs, blue patterned wallpaper with matching curtains on brass rails, a couple of nice seats by the larger of its two log fires, plates on stripped beams, and some limed panelling; there are quite a few mistily evocative Victorian photographs of Whitby. Quick happy service, inoffensive piped music, exemplary lavatories. *(Recommended by Peter Race, Tim and Sue Halstead, Mr and Mrs F S Stabler, H Bramwell)*

Free house   Licensee Howard Fitzgerald   Real ale   Meals and snacks (not Mon) Restaurant tel Thirsk (0845) 567433   Children over 4 welcome until 8.30   Open 12–2.30, 7–11 Closed Mon and first week of the year from Jan 1

COXWOLD (N Yorks)   SE5377 Map 7

Fauconberg Arms ★ ⇐

Civilised and comfortably furnished, the two cosy knocked-together rooms of the lounge bar in this well kept old stone inn have cushioned antique oak settles, including one that's handsomely carved and another curved to fit the attractive bay window, an oak porter's chair, Windsor armchairs, matting on the flagstones, gleaming brasses on one beam, and on cold days a log fire in the unusual arched stone fireplace; some of the furniture has squirrels carved into it. Lunchtime bar snacks include soup (£1.50), sandwiches (£1.50), specials like fresh crab (£2.50), and hot dishes such as stew and dumplings or steak and kidney pie (around £3.50); unusual vegetables such as delicious salsify; decent breakfasts. Well kept Tetleys, Theakstons and Youngers Scotch on handpump. At the back, the locals' spacious public bar has a fruit machine and piped music. The broad, quiet village street is pretty, with tubs of flowers on its grass or cobbled verges and the pub is close to Shandy Hall, the home of Laurence Stern the novelist. *(Recommended by Mary and Lionel Tonks, Barbara M McHugh, Mr and Mrs M Cockram, Nick Dowson, Alison Hayward, Andrew and Ruth Triggs, Andy and Jill Kassube, Peter Burton, David and Rebecca Killick, Y Batts, Jane Palmer, Dr John Innes)*

Free house   Licensee Richard Goodall   Real Ale   Lunchtime snacks (not Sun or Mon)   Restaurant (not Sun evening, and closed 2 weeks each Feb and Oct   Children welcome   Open 10.30–11   Bedrooms tel Coxwold (034 76) 214; £24/£40

CRACOE (N Yorks)   SD9760   Map 7

Devonshire Arms

B6265 Skipton—Grassington

This attractive and welcoming pub has low shiny black beams supporting creaky white planks, polished flooring tiles with rugs here and there, green plush cushioned dark pews and built-in wall settles, sturdy rustic or oak tripod tables, and gleaming copper pans round the stone fireplace; above the dark panelled dado are old prints, engravings and photographs, with a big circular large-scale Ordnance Survey map showing the inn as its centre. Good bar food includes decent sandwiches (from £1.50), lovely carrot and orange soup (£1.50), delicious scrambled egg done with smoked salmon (£4), cheese platter (£4.40), salmon pâté or fresh haddock (£4.50), meaty steak and kidney pie (£4.75) and salads (from £5.75); huge breakfasts; well kept Youngers Scotch and No 3 on handpump, decent coffee, friendly and attentive service. A fruit machine is tucked discreetly away by the entrance; darts, maybe unobtrusive piped music. A terrace flanked by well kept herbaceous borders has picnic-table sets. *(Recommended by John and Barbara Moss, H K Dyson, Len Beattie, W Marsh, Andy and Jill Kassube, Mr and Mrs J E Rycroft, G Dobson, Jon Wainwright, Syd and Wyn Donald)*

Youngers (S & N)   Licensee M Jaques   Real ale   Meals and snacks (not Sun evening, not Mon)   Restaurant Tues—Sat evenings   Children welcome until 9   Open 11–3, 6.30–11   Bedrooms tel Cracoe (075 673) 237; £18/£36

CRAY (N Yorks)   SD9379   Map 7

White Lion ★

B6160, Upper Wharfedale N of Kettlewell

This friendly and simply furnished little stone-built pub is the highest in Wharfedale (1,100 feet up by Buckden Pike) and the surrounding countryside is superb. The bar has seats around tables on the flagstone floor, a high dark beam-and-plank ceiling, shelves of china, iron tools and so forth, a lovely open fire (even in summer), and a traditional atmosphere; it's especially cheerful and lively on Tuesday evenings – which is the local dominoes night. Well kept Youngers Scotch and Moorhouses Premier on handpump. Bar food includes particularly good home-made soup, sandwiches (rare or well done beef £1.20, prawn £2.50), Yorkshire pudding with lovely onion gravy (£1.30), locally-made Cumberland sausage (£2.95), battered haddock (£3.50), steak and kidney pie (£3.75), prawn salad (£4.20) and sirloin steak (£7.25); good breakfasts; ring the bull. There are picnic-table sets above the very quiet, steep lane, and great flat limestone slabs (pleasant to sit on) in the shallow stream which tumbles down opposite. It's popular with walkers. *(Recommended by P Corris, R August, A M Neal, Lee Goulding, J and K O'Malley, Andy and Jill Kassube, Jon Wainwright, Peter and Rose Flower, KC, Paul Newberry)*

Free house   Licensee J C Outhwaite   Real ale   Meals and snacks   Children in dining room   Limited parking   Open 11–3, 6–11   Bedrooms tel Kettlewell (075 676) 262; £24.50S/£37S

CRAYKE (N Yorks)   SE5670   Map 7

Durham Ox

Off B1363 at Brandsby, towards Easingwold

Facing the village church at the far end of a broad grass-edge street lined with attractive brick houses, this stylish old inn has an old-fashioned, relaxed lounge bar: antique seats and settles around venerable tables on the flagstoned floor, pictures and old local photographs on its dark green walls, a high shelf of plates and interestingly satirical carvings in its panelling (which are Victorian copies of medieval pew ends), polished copper and brass, and an enormous inglenook fireplace with winter log fires (flowers in summer). Some of the panelling here divides off a bustling public area with a good lively atmosphere and more old-fashioned furnishings; above the Victorian fire grate is a written account of the local history dating back to the 12th century, and on the opposite wall, a large framed print of the original famous Durham ox; friendly dog; darts. Bar food includes sandwiches (£1.50, double deckers £1.75), and changing blackboard dishes such as soup, fresh crab, lasagne, curry, chicken breast stuffed with stilton, fresh grilled haddock, gammon, pork fillet wih apricots and kummel, goujons of mixed fish in season or lobster thermidor; puddings like banoffi pie, chocolate truffle or fruit cheesecake. Well kept Tetleys and Theakstons Best and XB on handpump. The tale is that this is the hill which the Grand Old Duke of York marched his men up. *(Recommended by Mary and Lionel Tonks, Simon J Barber, Virginia Jones, JM, PM, Tim and Sue Halstead)*

Free house   Licensee Ian Chadwick   Real ale   Meals and snacks   Restaurant Children in restaurant and eating area of bar   Open 12–3, 7–11   Bedrooms tel Easingwold (0347) 21506; £20/£30

CROPTON (N Yorks)   SE7588   Map 10

New Inn

Village signposted off A170 E of Pickering

There's nothing in the style of this comfortably modernised village inn to suggest that it's one of the few pubs which brew their own beer. Robustly flavoured, their Two Pints and Special Strong use local well water and even natural finings; they also keep Tetleys Mild and Bitter on handpump. The airy lounge has green plush seats, an aquarium let into one wall, copper and brassware, and a small open fire; a new downstairs family bar, also light and airy, has sturdy cast-iron-framed tables and plush seats, and big french windows opening on to a neat terrace and garden. Substantial helpings of good value bar food include lunchtime sandwiches, soup (£1.50), ploughman's (£2.75), spaghetti bolognese (£3.65), chicken and mushroom pie (£3.95), a good range of vegetarian dishes (up to £4.50), gammon perhaps with an interesting cherry and walnut sauce (£4.50) and T-bone steak (£7.95); they start serving early in the evening – popular with older people in the neighbourhood. There's an elegant Victorian-style small restaurant in burgundy plush. Friendly service; darts, dominoes, fruit machine, space game, pool room, and on our visit piped Paul Simon. *(Recommended by Maggie Goodwin, John Woolley, Brian and Pam Cowling, Mary and Lionel Tonks, Tim and Lynne Crawford)*

Own brew   Licensee Michael James Lee   Real ale   Meals and snacks   No-smoking restaurant   Children in family room   Open 11–3, 5.30–11; 12–2.30, 7–11 in winter; closed evening 25 Dec   Bedrooms tel Wrelton (075 15) 330; £20B/£34B

EAST LAYTON (N Yorks)   NZ1609   Map 10

Fox Hall Inn 🏠

A66, not far from Scotch Corner; inn is on the bypass, not in village

Settles are built in to the panelled bar of this tall roadside inn to make cosy booths around the tables, the walls are decorated with prints covering a wide range of sporting pursuits, and there's a high shelf of plates; the back part is more open, with a big south-facing window (where Sam, the friendly boxer, likes to sit). Good bar food includes sandwiches (not Sunday), home-made soup, home-made pâté (£1.75), crispy mushrooms with garlic mayonnaise or goujons of plaice in batter (£2.25), ploughman's or battered cod (£3.25), steak and kidney pie (£3.75), steaks (from £7.25), honey-roasted duckling (£7.95) and daily specials; Sunday lunch; children's helpings; good service. Well kept Theakstons Best on handpump with Theakstons XB and Old Peculier in summer; good range of malt whiskies and wines; dominoes, cribbage, sensibly placed darts, pool, fruit machine, space game, juke box, and piped music. There's a back terrace with tables and chairs. Down the nearby lane to Ravensworth (which climbs to fine views of the rolling countryside) is a ruined medieval castle. Be careful entering or leaving the pub's car park, as some of the traffic on this road is dangerously fast. Well behaved dogs welcome. *(Recommended by H K Dyson, Mrs E Morgan; more reports please)*

Free house   Licensees Jeremy and Susan Atkinson   Real Ale   Meals and snacks
Evening restaurant, though they do Sun lunch   Children welcome   Open 12–11; 12–3,
7–11 in winter   Bedrooms tel Darlington (0325) 718262; £20B/£30B

EGTON BRIDGE (N Yorks)   N28105 Map 10

Horse Shoe ⇐

Village signposted from A171 W of Whitby; via Grosmont from A169 S of Whitby

Charmingly placed in an Esk-side hamlet, this peaceful place has comfortable seats
and tables on a quiet terrace and lawn beside a little stream with ducks and geese;
a footbridge leads to the tree-sheltered residents' lawn which runs down to the
river. Inside, the walls are decorated with a big stuffed trout (caught near here in
1913), a fine old print of a storm off Ramsgate and other pictures, and there are
high-backed built-in winged settles, wall seats and spindleback chairs around the
modern oak tables, and a log fire. Well kept Malton, Tetleys, and Theakstons Best,
XB and Old Peculier on handpump, and a weekly guest beer; occasional farm
ciders. Darts, dominoes and piped music. A good range of bar food with daily
specials includes home-made soup (£1.20), lunchtime sandwiches (from £1.40),
ploughman's (£2.75), vegetable or meaty lasagne or home-made steak and kidney
pie (£3.95), chicken kiev (£4.20), grilled gammon with egg or pineapple (£4.50),
Japanese prawns with garlic dip (£5.85), and steaks (from £6.95); children's
dishes, and summer barbecues. *(Recommended by Mary and Lionel Tonks, J S M
Whitaker, C J McFeeters, Mike and Wendy Proctor, J Wiltshire, Derek and Sylvia Stephenson)*

*Free house   Licensees David and Judith Mullins   Real ale   Meals and snacks (not 25
Dec)   Restaurant   Children in eating area of bar   Open 11.30–3.30, 6.30–11; closed
evening 25 Dec   Bedrooms tel Whitby (0947) 85245; £20(£25B)/£34(£42B)*

Postgate ⇐

Seats and big umbrellas on a sunny flagstoned terrace outside this friendly pub
look down the hill – this steep twisty valley of the lovely River Esk is one of the
prettiest parts of the moors. The well kept and carpeted lounge bar has upholstered
modern settles and seats in a sunny window, Windsor chairs, a high shelf of cups
and bottles, and an open fire. Good, home-made food from the daily changing
menu might include sandwiches, home-made meat and vegetable broth (£1.50),
chick pea curry (£3.50), vegetarian dishes such as tagliatelli (£3.75), home-made
steak and mushroom pie (£3.95), whole roast poussin (£4.50), and home-made
puddings; summer barbecues. Camerons Lion and Strongarm on handpump. The
public bar has darts (one ladies' team as well as three men's), dominoes (Monday
evening), cribbage, and occasional quiz nights against other local pubs. Salmon or
trout fishing can be arranged, as can boat fishing. *(Recommended by David and
Rebecca Killick, Paul McPherson)*

*Camerons   Licensee David Mead   Real ale   Meals and snacks (12–3, 6–9.30)
Restaurant; not Sun evening   Children welcome   Occasional folk nights   Open
11–11; 11–3, 6–11 in winter   Bedrooms tel Whitby (0947) 85241; £16/£32*

ELSLACK (N Yorks)   SD9249 Map 7

Tempest Arms ★

Just off A56 Earby–Skipton; visible from main road, and warning signs 1/4 mile before

A series of quietly decorated areas in this friendly 18th-century French-run pub
have lots of carefully placed tables, small chintz armchairs, chintzy cushions on the
comfortable built-in wall seats, quite a bit of stripped stonework, and a log fire in
the dividing fireplace; the licensee flies the English flag, the Union Jack, the French
tricolour, and the EEC flag. Good bar food includes fish bought by the landlord
from the Manchester market: moules marinières (£2.50), and halibut, plaice, skate
wings, scallops with a fresh ginger and wine sauce, crab salad or fresh bonito
provençale (from around £4); also, sandwiches (from £1.95, open prawn £2.95,

steak £3.95), soups including good French onion soup (from £1.75), ploughman's (£3.20), liver and onion (£3.50), steak, kidney and mushroom pie, gammon and egg or an appetising low-calorie platter (£4.25), scampi (£4.95) and fresh salmon (£4.50); vegetarian dishes. As you can see this pub aims high with its food, and in past years readers have reported great pleasure with it. In the last few months, though, we simply haven't had enough reports on this aspect and we'd be very grateful for more. Well kept Tetleys Mild and Bitter, Thwaites Bitter and Youngers Scotch on handpump, and good French house wines by the glass or bottle; darts, dominoes, fruit machine and piped music. Tables outside are largely screened from the road by a raised bank. As we went to press, we heard that the licensees are planning an extension for ten bedrooms. *(Recommended by Len Beattie, Roy and Nicola Boyne, Bev and Doug Warrick, Dr Thomas Mackenzie, Ben Wimpenny, Syd and Wyn Donald, Russell and Christina Jones, G C and M D Dickinson, Dennis Royles)*

Free house   Licensee Francis Boulongne   Real ale   Meals and snacks (11.30–2.15, 6.30–10)   Restaurant   Children welcome until 8.30pm   Open 11.30–3, 6.30(7 Sat)–11; closed evening 25 Dec   Bedrooms tel Earby (0282) 842450; £37B/£45B

GOOSE EYE (W Yorks)   SE0340 Map 7
Turkey

High back road Haworth–Sutton-in-Craven, and signposted from back roads W of Keighley; OS Sheet 104 map reference 028406

This friendly, cosy pub has various newly refurbished, snug alcoves with a new wooden bar top, brocaded upholstery, and walls covered with pictures of surrounding areas. Generous helpings of value-for-money food include winter soup, sandwiches, chilli con carne (£2.40), giant Yorkshire pudding with beef stew (£2.50) or roast beef (£2.70), home-made lasagne or steak and kidney pie (£2.50), and ploughman's (£2.80); good, popular steak nights (Wednesday to Saturday evenings – 8oz sirloin £4, 32oz rump £10.50). Big End Piston and Ind Coope Burton on handpump. A separate games area has darts, dominoes, cribbage, table skittles, trivia, juke box and fruit machine. The village is placed at the bottom of a steep valley with high-walled lanes. *(Recommended by Andy and Jill Kassube, Stephen Blencowe)*

Free house   Licensee Harry Brisland   Real ale   Meals and snacks (not Sun or Mon evening)   Children welcome till 9pm   Jazz Tues evening   Open 12–3, 5.30–11; 12–5, 7–11 Sat

HARDEN (W Yorks)   SE0838 Map 7
Malt Shovel

Follow Wilsden signpost from B6429

Spotlessly clean and carefully kept, this pleasant little pub has two small rooms and one with oak-panelling, a beamed ceiling, and an open fire; also, red plush seats built into the walls, kettles, brass funnels and the like hanging from the black beams, horsebrasses on leather harness, and stone-mullioned windows. Simple, but good bar food includes sandwiches (from £1.15), ploughman's (£2.65), steak and kidney pie (£3.25), and salads; well kept Tetleys Bitter on handpump, and efficient service; dominoes. From the other side of the bridge you can walk upstream beside the Harden Beck. *(Recommended by J E Rycroft, T Nott, Ben Wimpenny, Andy and Jill Kassube, Andrew and Ruth Triggs, H K Dyson)*

Tetleys (Allied)   Manager David Biggs   Real ale   Meals and snacks   Open 11.30–3, 5.30–11

HAROME (N Yorks)   SE6582 Map 10
Star ★ ⊗

2 miles south of A170, near Helmsley

Though a new licensee has taken over this civilised and stylish thatched pub, reports from readers happily suggest that little has changed. Cushioned old settles and heavy, deeply polished dark rustic tables sit on the Turkey carpet, a very clean glass cabinet holds képis, fine china and Japanese dolls, the dark bowed beam-and-plank ceiling is hung with a few ancient bottles and glass net floats, and there's a copper kettle on the well polished tiled kitchen range (with a ship in a bottle on its mantlepiece), and a fox mask with little spectacles and a lacy ruff. Lunchtime home-made bar food includes excellent Scotch broth (£1.50), lots of very good, generous sandwiches like chicken or prawn curry, good roast beef, ox tongue, tuna, smoked salmon and so forth (from £1.90), a daily special such as cold curried chicken or steak and oyster pie (£4.95), and puddings like fig and peach crumble or bread and butter pudding (£1.95); there's a coffee loft up in the thatch. Well kept Batemans, Camerons Lion, Theakstons Best and Old Peculier, Tetleys, and Timothy Taylors Landlord on handpump, and some interesting, very good wines; darts, dominoes, and unobtrusive classical music. On a sheltered front flagstoned terrace there are some seats and tables, with more in the garden behind which has an old-fashioned swing seat, fruit trees and a big ash. No animals. Plans are afoot for bedrooms. *(Recommended by W C M Jones, Brian and Anna Marsden, Anthony Sargent, Caroline Gant, Andrew and Ruth Triggs, Anne Marie Stephenson, Fiona Mutch, Peter Race, J P Cinnamond, Margaret and Roy Randle, Syd and Wyn Donald, M B Porter, Henry Midwinter, Patrick Clarke, S V Bishop)*

Free house   Licensee T E Blackburn   Real ale   Lunchtime meals and snacks   Evening restaurant tel Helmsley (0439) 70397, though they do Sun lunch   Children welcome   Open 12–3, 6.30–11

nr HARROGATE (N Yorks)   SE3155 Map 7
Squinting Cat

Whinney Lane, B6162 W of Harrogate; turn at traffic lights down Pannel Ash Rd; at roundabout near sports centre, bear right along Whinney Lane; pub on left after about ¾ mile; OS Sheet 104 map reference 296517

The barn-like beamed extension in this very popular and friendly 18th-century pub has York stone walls (re-fashioned from an old railway bridge) hung with pictures, old grain sacks, barrels, and bottles, pine chairs and tables in one part with re-covered armchairs in another, and nautical wooden pulley systems radiating out from a minstrel's gallery complete with boat. The rambling rooms of the original part have dark oak panelling, beam and plank ceilings, some copper warming pans and horsebrasses, and a stained-glass cat worked into a latticed bow window. The new licensee has introduced a different menu: home-made soups such as stilton and onion (from £1.50), home-made pâtés (from £1.90), sandwiches (from £2, hot roast beef £2.95), winter pies and casseroles, home-made pasta dishes such as tagliatelle with ham and garlic, lasagne or cannelloni fascetta (from £3.25), curry (£3.75), vegetarian pancake or ratatouille au gratin (£3.95), and a cold carvery with home-cooked meats (from around £3.25); summer barbecues (from around £3.25, 33oz steak £17.50). Well kept Tetleys Mild and Bitter on handpump; attentive service; piped music, dominoes and fruit machine. There are tables outside. The North of England Horticultural Society's fine gardens on the curlew moors at Harlow Car are just over the B6162. *(Recommended by Genie and Brian Smart, H K Dyson, Mike Tucker, Gwen and Peter Andrews, Mary and Lionel Tonks, David and Rebecca Killick, Carol and Richard Glover, Steve and Carolyn Harvey, Andy and Jill Kassube, Jon Wainwright, A J Leach, G C and M D Dickinson, Richard and Carol Glover, Paul Newberry)*

Tetleys (Allied)   Licensee David Funnell   Real ale   Meals and snacks   Restaurant tel Harrogate (0423) 565650   Open 11.30–3, 5.30–11, though may open longer in afternoon if demand; closed 25 Dec

HATFIELD WOODHOUSE (S Yorks)   SE6808 Map 7
Green Tree

1 mile from M18 junction 5: on A18/A614 towards Bawtry

Both strangers and regulars feel at home in this well kept, pleasant pub, and there's plenty of room in the comfortably modernised series of connecting open-plan rooms and alcoves: brown leatherette seats and Windsor chairs around the tables, an expanse of Turkey carpet, fresh flowers and a warm atmosphere. Good, reasonably priced bar food includes soup (£1), sandwiches (from £1.10; the open-prawn is recommended), very good ploughman's (£2.50), omelette or vegetarian lasagne (£3), a pint of fresh prawns, fresh haddock or plaice from Grimsby or home-made steak and kidney (£3.45), salads (from £3.30), grilled gammon (£3.75), a lunchtime help-yourself buffet (£4), mixed grill (£4.25), steaks (from £4.50), and puddings such as cherry and apple pie (£1.20); you can eat in the garden. Well kept Darleys and Vaux on handpump; prompt service; piped music. Note that they now do bedrooms. (*Recommended by ILP, T Nott, Genie and Brian Smart*)

Wards (Vaux) Licensee Trevor Hagan Real ale Meals and snacks (12–2.30, 6.30–10; not 25 Dec) Restaurant (evenings and Sun lunch) Children in eating area and restaurant Open 11–3, 6–11 Bedrooms tel Doncaster (0302) 840305; £25/£35

HEATH (W Yorks) SE3519 Map 7
Kings Arms

Village signposted from A655 Wakefield–Normanton – or, more directly, turn off to the left opposite Horse & Groom

Clarks – who only have five pubs, all of them in this area, and who brew real ales in Wakefield – have taken over this characterful old pub. As well as Clarks Bitter, they also serve guests like Tetleys and Timothy Taylors Landlord on handpump. The dark-panelled original bar has plain elm stools and oak settles built into the walls, some heavy cast-iron-framed tables on the flagstones, a built-in cupboard of cut glass, and a fire burning in the old black range (with a long row of smoothing irons on the mantelpiece). A more comfortable extension (with a fitted red carpet, even) has carefully preserved the original style, down to good wood-pegged oak panelling (two embossed with royal arms), and a high shelf of plates; there are also two other small flagstoned rooms and another with its own bar. Good bar food (with changing specials listed on a board) includes soup (£1.40), Yorkshire pudding and gravy (£1.10), sandwiches (from £1.25), excellent ploughman's (from £2.75), garlic mushrooms (£1.75), omelettes (£2.40), home-made steak and kidney pie (£2.95), smoked fish platter (£3.60), and daily specials like tasty black pudding with apple sauce (£2.50) or traditional roasts (£3.50); the tables are cleared and cleaned promptly; dominoes. Picnic-table sets along the front of the pub face the village green and there are several more on a side lawn. (*Recommended by Frank Cummins, Roger Huggins, G R Prest, Maureen and Steve Collin, Andy and Jill Kassube, Michael Rooke, Paul Newberry*)

Clarks Licensees Sheila and John Radley Real ale Meals and snacks (till 10 in evening); all day Sun, not Mon evening Gas-lit restaurant tel Wakefield (0924) 377527; not Sun evening Children in eating area of bar until 8.30 Open 11.30–3.30, 6–11; 11.30–11 summer Fri and Sat; closed evening 25 Dec

HECKMONDWIKE (W Yorks) SE2223 Map 7
Old Hall

New North Road; B6117 between A62 and A638; OS Sheet 104 map reference 214244

Snug low-ceilinged alcoves in this sensitively restored, 15th-century manor house lead off the central part with its high ornate plaster ceiling, and an upper gallery room, under the pitched roof, looks down on the main area through timbering 'windows'. Comfortable furnishings include cushioned oak pews and red plush seats, some with oak backs, on a sweep of Turkey carpet (there are flagstones by the serving counter), the walls are brick or stripped old stone (with pictures of Richard III, Henry VII, Katherine Parr and Priestley), there are lots of oak beams and timbers, and latticed mullioned windows with worn stone surrounds. Good bar food brought to your table by efficient staff includes sandwiches (from £1.20), soup (£1.25), pâté (£1.50), ploughman's (£2.95), scampi (£3.50), steaks (from £6.95), and unusual daily specials (£3.25); salad bar during summer, and nice puddings. Well kept Sam Smiths OB and Museum on handpump; unobtrusive piped music, and darts in a wall cupboard. This was once the home of the Nonconformist scientist Joseph Priestley. *(Recommended by T Nott, Ben Wimpenny, Mary and Lionel Tonks, Andy and Jill Kassube, Ian Robinson)*

Sam Smiths   Licensee Thomas Hancock   Real ale   Meals and snacks   Children in function room   Open 11.30–3, 5.30–11

HELMSLEY (N Yorks)   SE6184   Map 10
Feathers
Market Square

Fronting the market square, this large old inn has a low and cosy original pub part with heavy medieval beams and dark panelling, unusual cast-iron-framed tables topped by weighty slabs of oak and walnut, a venerable wall carving of a dragon-faced bird in a grape vine, a big log fire in the stone inglenook fireplace, and a nice pubby atmosphere. The main inn is a handsomely solid 3-storey stone block with a comfortable lounge bar. Generous helpings of popular bar food include lots of changing specials, as well as soup (£1.25), sandwiches (from £1.50), ploughman's or sausage and egg (£2.25), good garlic mushrooms (£2.50), home-made quiche (£3.50), home-made lasagne or chilli con carne (£3.75), fresh Scarborough haddock in batter (£4), salads (from £4), home-made steak pie (£4.75), gammon with egg or pineapple (£5), steaks (£8.50), and specials like spinach tortellini or good Cumberland sausage (£3.75), sweet and sour prawns (£4.75), and roast duck (£6.50). Well kept Tetleys, Theakstons Old Peculier and Tollys Bitter on handpump, and wines chalked on a blackboard; large choice of wines; efficient service. Darts, dominoes, fruit machine, juke box and piped music. There's an attractive back garden. Rievaulx Abbey (well worth an hour's visit) is close by. *(Recommended by Sidney and Erna Wells, H K Dyson, Peter Race, Sue Corrigan, Tim and Lynne Crawford, Tim Locke, Barbara and Norman Wells, M B Porter, Richard Dolphin)*

Free house   Licensee Jack Feather   Real ale   Meals and snacks   Restaurant Children welcome, but in small lounge between bars when busy and in restaurant Open 10.30–11; 10.30–2.30, 6–11 in winter   Bedrooms tel Helmsley (0439) 70275; £22(£26.50B)/£44(£53B)

HETTON (N Yorks)   SD9558   Map 7
Angel ★ ⊘
Just off B6265 Skipton–Grassington

'Excellent', 'wonderful', 'consistently outstanding' and 'delicious' are just some of the adjectives used by many readers to describe the food at this attractively decorated dining pub. As it's so popular, it gets packed with walkers and families by 1pm (and it can be hard to find a seat quarter of an hour earlier). Imaginatively presented, food might include home-made soup with croûtons (£1.45) or terrific provençal fish soup with aïoli (£1.95), lunchtime sandwiches (from £1.95), lovely home-made terrine in orange jelly and Cumberland sauce, fresh spinach noodles in a garlic and basil sauce and fresh parmesan (£3.45), a plate of pickled, cured and smoked fish, their own home-cured and air dried beef or fillet of baby cod with bearnaise sauce (all £3.95), cold rare roast beef or sugar baked ham (£4.75), breast of chicken stuffed with prawns and smokey bacon (£4.95), ragout of venison with onions, fresh herbs and savoury dumplings (£5.75), calves liver with a Dubonnet sauce (£7.50), and very good puddings like creme brûlée, sticky toffee pudding or summer pudding (from £2.15); also, daily fresh fish specials such as fillet of sole poached in cider and served in a cream sauce with mussels, prawns and mushrooms (£4.50), fresh langoustines grilled with garlic and Gruyere cheese (£5.25), and a melody of seafood – king scallops, langoustines, mussels, salmon, sea bream, sole, monkfish and cod fried with lemon juice or superb seafood platter

(£9.95). Well kept Theakstons Bitter and XB, Timothy Taylors Landlord, and Youngers Scotch on handpump, a decent choice of wines by the glass or bottle (chalked up on a blackboard, and often bin-ends), and quite a few malt whiskies; excellent service. The four rambling rooms have lots of cosy alcoves, comfortable country-kitchen chairs or button-back green plush seats, Ronald Searle wine snob cartoons and older engravings and photographs, standing timbers and panelling, and some beams; there are log fires, a solid fuel stove, and in the main bar a Victorian farmhouse range in the big stone fireplace. Darts and dominoes. Sturdy wooden benches and tables are built on to the cobbles outside this pretty house. *(Recommended by Len Beattie, G D Collier, Margaret White, Mr and Mrs M Cockram, Tim and Sue Halstead, J E Rycroft, Gwen and Peter Andrews, Neville Kenyon, Viv Middlebrook, Olive Carroll, E V Walder, Syd and Wyn Donald, G C and M D Dickinson, David and Flo Wallington)*

Free house Licensee Denis Watkins Real ale Meals and snacks (12–2, 7–10) Restaurant tel Cracoe (075 673) 263; not Sun evening Children in eating area of bar Open 11.30–2.30, 6–10.30 (till 11 Fri and Sat); closed evenings 25 and 26 Dec and 1 Jan

HUBBERHOLME (N Yorks) SD9178 Map 7

George ★

Village signposted from Buckden; about 1 mile NW

Though the licensee here was planning to retire, he has now been joined by his daughter and son-in-law and they are running the pub jointly. The two small and well kept flagstoned bar rooms have simple seats around shiny copper-topped tables, dark ceiling-boards supported by heavy beams, walls stripped back to bare stone, and an open stove in the big fireplace. At lunchtime, cheerful walkers crowd in for food, mainly fresh from the Aga, that includes home-made soup, delicious hefty warm rolls filled with big slices of juicy fresh ham, cheese or bacon (around £1.50), pâté (£2.10), steak and kidney or chicken and ham pie with the lightest of crusts (£3.50), lovely chocolate fudge cake, and evening dishes like salmon in asparagus sauce or venison in red wine and port sauce (£6.90). Very well kept Youngers Scotch and No 3 on handpump, a good choice of malt whiskies, and quite a few wines; darts, dominoes and cribbage. The inn looks out on a lovely swirly stretch of the River Wharfe where they have fishing rights; they still let riverside land in aid of a church charity, and when they do (on the first Monday of the New Year), there's a licensing extension till nearly midnight. Seats and tables look up to the moors which rise all around. This was J B Priestley's favourite pub. *(Recommended by Mary and Lionel Tonks, Gwen and Peter Andrews, Helen and Wal Burns, Andy and Jill Kassube, Lynne Sheridan, Bob West, Ian Whitlock, J E Rycroft, J and K O'Malley, Mr and Mrs K H Frostick, Peter and Rose Flower, Jon Wainwright, Neil and Angela Huxter, Jane and Niall)*

Free house Licensee John Fredrick Real ale Meals and snacks No-smoking evening restaurant Children in eating area of bar Open 11.30–3, 7 (6.30 Sat)–11; closed evening 25 Dec Bedrooms tel Kettlewell (075 676) 223; £32

KILBURN (N Yorks) SE5179 Map 7

Forresters Arms 🛏

Signposted from A170 E of Thirsk

New licensees took over this ex-coaching inn at the beginning of 1990, though the bar staff and food servers have stayed on. Most of the sturdy yet elegant furniture, usually of oak, has the trademark of a little carved mouse sitting, standing or running in some discreet corner of the piece. That's also the source of the fine bar counter and the great slab shelf along the wall of the inner room – lights beneath it throw the stripped stonework into striking relief. This inner room has tables for people eating; the smaller outer bar's chairs are much more for sitting and chatting by the log fire in its unusual rounded stone chimney-breast. Well kept John Smiths and Tetleys Bitter on handpump, a good choice of popular bar food including sandwiches, home-made soup (£1.10), lasagne (£3.50), home-made steak and kidney pie (£3.90), steaks, and puddings (£1.20); cribbage, dominoes, and piped music. White tables on the terrace in front of this stone and brick building look across to pretty village gardens, which are interspersed with planked oak trunks weathering for the Thompson furniture workshop next door. Dogs welcome (James Herriot is in fact their vet). *(Recommended by Stephanie Sowerby, N S and J Dury, N P Hodgson, H K Dyson, Andrew and Ruth Triggs, G Dobson, Jenny Cantle)*

Free house   Licensee Peter Cussons   Real ale   Meals and snacks   Restaurant Children welcome   Open 11–11   Bedrooms tel Coxwold (03476) 386; /£42B

KIRBY HILL (N Yorks)   NZ1406 Map 10
Shoulder of Mutton

Signposted from Ravensworth road about 3 1/2 miles N of Richmond; or from A66 Scotch Corner–Brough turn off into Ravensworth, bear left through village, and take signposted right turn nearly a mile further on

This quietly situated ex-farmhouse shares the crest of a ridge above ruined Ravensworth Castle with a tree-shaded churchyard. Inside on the left, the neat and comfortably modernised bar has a good welcoming atmosphere, plush wall settles around simple dark tables, local turn-of-the-century photographs of Richmond, and an open fire; a communicating entry hallway has a pretty 1880s watercolour of boats in a misty estuary. Decent bar food includes lunchtime sandwiches (from 80p) and ploughman's (£2.50), as well as soup (95p), chicken and bacon or steak and kidney pies (£2.80), moussaka (£3.35), a large plateful of haddock and chips (£3.50), delicious trout with almonds (£3.65), scampi (£3.75), and puddings (from 60p), with evening gammon steak (£4.95) or steak (£5.50); the stripped-stone restaurant is noted for its generous helpings. Well kept Ruddles County, Theakstons Best, and Websters Choice on handpump; darts, dominoes, with pool in a side room and a fruit machine around the back; piped music. The yard behind has picnic-table sets. *(Recommended by Mr and Mrs Bill Muirhead, Mrs R Heaton; more reports please)*

Free house   Licensee Hylton Pyner   Real ale   Meals and snacks (not Mon lunchtime)   Restaurant (not Sun evening)   Children in eating area of bar, restaurant and in pool room   Open 12–3, 7–11; closed Mon lunchtime   Bedrooms tel Richmond (0748) 2772; £15.50(£18B)/£31(£36B)

LANGTHWAITE (N Yorks)   NZ0003 Map 10
Red Lion

Just off the Arkengarthdale road from Reeth to Brough

One of the charming little houses here is this homely and unpretentious little pub. It's kept spick and span, and has comfortably cushioned wall seats, a beam-and-plank ceiling (if you think that one's low, try the burrow-like side snug), flowery curtains, a few decorative plates on a Delft shelf, and a fox mask. They also have carved horn beakers, signed copies of books by Herriot and Wainwright, Ordnance Survey maps, and local paintings and books on the Dales for sale; darts and dominoes. The BBC filmed the bar for an episode in the *All Creatures Great and Small* series. A sensibly short choice of simple good value bar food includes toasted sandwiches (from 90p), various quiches (£1.60), lamb pie (£1.65), cheese or pâté ploughman's (£1.90), curries or casseroles (£2.50), and puddings such as chocolate fudge cake or lemon meringue pie (from 75p); country wines and Merrydown cider. They very helpfully open at 10.30 for coffee on summer Sundays and serve tea and coffee all the time they are open. There are some picnic-table sets out in the tiny village square. Footpaths from here thread their way along the Arkle beck and up the moors on either side. *(Recommended by Tony Bland, Anthony Barnes, Peter and Rose Flower, Alan Hall; more reports please)*

Free house   Licensee Mrs Rowena Hutchinson   Meals and snacks (11.30–2, 6.30–9; 10.30–2, 7–9 Sun)   Children in snug at lunchtime and until 8pm   Open 11–3, 6.30–11; 12–3, 7–10.30 in winter

LASTINGHAM (N Yorks) SE7391 Map 10
Blacksmiths Arms

Off A170 W of Pickering at Wrelton, forking off Rosedale rd N of Cropton; or via
Appleton and Spaunton; or via Hutton-le-Hole

Two hundred years ago it was the church's curate who kept this neat stone inn,
saying he needed the money to eke out his stipend and feed his thirteen children.
The comfortable oak-beamed bar has cushioned Windsor chairs and traditional
built-in wooden wall seats, an attractive cooking range with swinging pot-yards,
some sparkling brass, and a good winter fire. Bar food includes sandwiches, fish
(£2.95), lasagne or beef casserole (£3.25), 4oz steak in a bun (£4.25), and steak
(£6). A simply furnished dining area opens off the main bar, and serves traditional
Sunday roasts, and the new licensees are refurbishing and re-opening the
restaurant. Well kept Ruddles Best and County, Websters Yorkshire and Wilsons
Bitter on handpump; good range of malt whiskies; darts, dominoes, cribbage, fruit
machine and piped music. The countryside all around is lovely and there are tracks
through Cropton Forest. *(Recommended by Andy and Jill Kassube, Eileen Broadbent, Tim
and Lynne Crawford, Derek and Sylvia Stephenson)*

*Free house Licensees Mike and Sheila Frost Real ale Meals and snacks (served all
the time they are open) Restaurant Children in eating area of bar Open 11–11
Bedrooms tel Lastingham (075 15) 247; £15/£30*

LEDSHAM (W Yorks) SE4529 Map 7
Chequers

A mile off A1 N of Pontefract

Good, nicely presented bar food in this busy village pub is worth leaving the
motorway for: soup (90p), sandwiches (from £1.40), excellent ploughman's with
two cheeses and an apple (£2.25), tasty scrambled eggs and smoked salmon
(£2.80), very good chicken and mushroom pancake, lasagne (£3.40), steak pie
(£4.20), and good ham and eggs (£4.55). Small, individually decorated rooms open
off an old-fashioned little central panelled-in servery and have low beams, lots of
cosy alcoves, and log fires; dominoes. Well kept John Smiths, Theakstons Best and
Youngers Scotch and No 3 on handpump; cheerful service. A sheltered two-level
terrace behind the creeper-covered stone village house has tables among roses.
*(Recommended by Andy and Jill Kassube, J D Andrews, Ben Wimpenny, Tim and Sue
Halstead, Dr and Mrs Frank Rackow, Mike and Wendy Proctor, Christopher Knowles-Fitton,
J E Rycroft, William Rodgers, Syd and Wyn Donald, Roger Bellingham)*

*Free house Licensee Chris Wraith Real ale Meals and evening snacks Restaurant
tel (0977) 683135 Children in eating area of bar lunchtime and early evening Open
11–3, 5.30–11; 11–11 Sat; closed Sun*

LEEDS (W Yorks) SE3033 Map 7
Garden Gate ★

37 Waterloo Road, Hunslet; leaving Leeds centre on A61, turn right at traffic lights
signpost 'Hunslet Centre P, Belle Isle 1 1/2, Middleton 3', take first right into Whitfield
Way, first left into Whitfield Drive, then first right and park at rear of pub

Inside this handsome, marvellously preserved Victorian building a high cool
corridor with a tiled floor and panelled in mahogany and deep-cut glass links four
old-fashioned rooms. The finest, on the left as you enter, has a mosaic floor and a
lovely free-flowing design of tiles coloured in subtle tones of buff, cream and icy
green: the bar counter itself, the front of which is made from elaborately shaped
and bowed tiles, has hatch service to the corridor too. Perfectly kept Tetleys Bitter
and Mild on handpump – the brewery is just up the Hunslet Road. Sandwiches,
home-made curries and chilli con carne or filled Yorkshire puddings (£1.80),
lasagne (£2.20) and various pizzas (£2.95); pleasant staff; darts, pool, dominoes
(very popular here), cribbage, trivia, and fruit machine. One reader – a lawyer now
– firmly recommending the pub says we should warn that he and his companions

felt very much out of place wearing a suit and tie straight from work; we wonder if he remembers the more unbuttoned praise he himself heaped on it almost a decade ago when using the first edition of the *Guide*! It's very much a working men's pub and is surrounded by a modern development. *(Recommended by Pete Storey, Andy and Jill Kassube, Tim Halstead, Denis Mann)*

Tetleys (Allied)   Licensee Dennis Ashman   Real ale   Snacks (in the evenings and at weekends, they only serve pizzas)   Open 11–11

Whitelocks ★

Turks Head Yard; gunnel (or alley) off Briggate, opposite Debenhams and Littlewoods; park in shoppers' car park and walk

Even though the wonderfully atmospheric, old-fashioned bar in this lively pub is long and narrow, it never seems to get unpleasantly crowded – even when the shoppers pour in for a quick drink and snack. The fine bar counter is decorated with polychrome tiles, and there are stained-glass windows and grand advertising mirrors, with red button-back plush banquettes and heavy copper-topped cast-iron tables squeezed down one side. Good, reasonably priced lunchtime bar food includes sandwiches, bubble and squeak or sausages (50p), home-made Scotch eggs (70p), home-made quiche (£1), Yorkshire puddings (£1 with fillings), very good meat and potato pie (£1.80), and jam roly poly or fruit pie (75p); when it gets busy you may have to wait for your order, though the staff are very cheerful and pleasant. Well kept McEwans 80/- and Youngers IPA, Scotch and No 3 on handpump; quiz evenings every Tuesday in top bar. At the end of the long narrow yard another bar has been done up in Dickensian style. *(Recommended by Reg Nelson, Pete Storey, J E Rycroft, Mr and Mrs Fraser, Virginia Jones, Drs M and K Parier, Andy and Jill Kassube, Ben Wimpenny, Michael Rooke, P Miller, Steve Waters, J F Thorndike, Roger Taylor, Syd and Wyn Donald, Comus Elliott)*

Youngers (S & N)   Licensee Julie Cliff   Real ale   Meals and snacks (11–7.30; not Sun evening)   Restaurant tel Leeds (0532) 453950; not Sun evening   Children in restaurant   Quiz night Tues   Open 11–11

LEVISHAM (N Yorks)   SE8391   Map 10

Horseshoe

Pub and village signposted from A169 N of Pickering

The collection of walking boots outside this well kept, friendly pub nearly shamed a couple of readers into hiding their shoes and going in in their socks. The bars have been refurbished this year and now have new curtains, carpet, light fittings, and brocaded seat covers; log fire in a stone fireplace, and darts, bar billiards, dominoes and piped music. Decent bar food includes sandwiches, home-made soup (£1.10), ploughman's (£2.75), salads (from £3.25), home-made lasagne (£3.45), fresh Whitby haddock or chicken breast filled with garlic, lemon and parsley butter (£3.75), tasty gammon and egg (£4.25), good fresh local trout (£4.95), steaks (from £5.25), puddings like home-made apple pie (£1.75), and children's menu (£1.75). Well kept Hook Norton, Malton, Old Mill, Tetleys Bitter, Theakstons Best and Timothy Taylors Landlord on handpump; good range of malt whiskies; service is pleasant, quick and efficient. Twice a day each way in spring and autumn, and four times in summer, steam trains of the North Yorks Moors Railway stop at this village. *(Recommended by A M Neal, John and Christine Simpson, Eleanor Wallis, Walter and Susan Rinaldi-Butcher, Tim and Sue Halstead, Derek and Sylvia Stephenson)*

Free house   Licensees Roy and Marjorie Hayton   Real ale   Meals and snacks   Restaurant   Children in eating area of bar   Open 11–3, 6–11   Bedrooms tel Pickering (0751) 60240; £18/£36B

LINTHWAITE (W Yorks) SE1014 Map 7

Bulls Head ✪

31 Blackmoorfoot; Blackmoorfoot signposted from town centre, above A62 W of Huddersfield – head up past school towards moors, and bear right by dam; or from Marsden turn off B6107 towards Blackmoorfoot

Changing from day to day, the very quickly served food in this cheerful pub includes sandwiches, cauliflower on a bed of tagliatelle with sour cream horseradish and paprika sauce or mushrooms with a thyme and sherry sauce and soufflé topping (£2.95), aubergine, potato and salmi gratin or baked courgettes with sweetcorn, bacon and cheese stuffing (£3.20), corned beef, onion and potato pie (£3.50), tuna and prawn pancakes in a creamy spinach sauce, marinated breast of chicken in marmalade, coriander and lemon, and spiced beef with gingered peppers (£3.75), and fresh salmon baked under a herb crust (£3.95). Mondays is their steak 'n' bake night (now copied by several dozen other pubs in the area). The two unpretentious communicating rooms are furnished with sturdy brown-plush-upholstered wall benches and stools around cast-iron-framed tables; the room on the right has Victorian-style wallpaper and a Victorian fireplace, and the one on the left has views from its back windows over Linthwaite to the moors beyond, and a stone fireplace. Well reproduced piped music, a fruit machine, and well kept Boddingtons Bitter and Mild and Stones on handpump; quite a few whiskies. There are picnic-table sets in front of the dark stone pub. *(Recommended by H K Dyson, T Nott, Neville Kenyon, Ben Wimpenny, Connie Pearson)*

Free house   Licensees Stephen and Brenda Head   Real ale   Meals and snacks (11–10; not after 3 Sat; permitted hours Sun)   Children in eating area of bar till 8pm   Open 11–11

Sair

Hoyle Ing, off A62; as you leave Huddersfield this is one of the only left turns in Linthwaite, and the street name is marked, but keep your eyes skinned for it – it burrows very steeply up between works buildings; OS Sheet 110 map reference 101143

Mr Crabtree, who was one of the founders of the West Riding Brewery, brews a remarkable range of very well kept real ales here: the pleasant and well balanced Linfit Bitter, Mild and Special, Old Eli, Leadboiler, a Christmas Ale that has a habit of turning up at the most unseasonable times and the redoubtable Enochs Hammer. He even does stout (English Guineas), a Hoyleingerbrau lager, a low-alcohol real ale, and a cider called Causeway Sider; they may provide lunchtime sandwiches. The quaint cluster of rooms have pews or smaller chairs, rough flagstones in some parts and carpet in others, bottle collections, beermats tacked to beams, big stone fireplaces (in winter almost as many fires as beers), and a happy, chatty atmosphere. The room on the right has darts, shove-ha'penny and dominoes. There's a half-timbered cat mansion for the four cats with lots of rooms and toy mice and birds. The view down the Colne Valley is very striking. *(Recommended by P Corris, Matt Pringle, Ben Wimpenny, Maureen and Steve Collin, Michael Rooke, Steve Waters)*

Own brew   Licensee Ron Crabtree   Real ale   Children in three rooms away from the bar   Open 7–11 only on weekdays, 12–4 too Sat and Bank Hols; otherwise closed weekday lunchtimes

LINTON IN CRAVEN (N Yorks) SD9962 Map 7

Fountaine

On B6265 Skipton–Grassington, forking right

New licensees took over this traditional pub in February 1990, and the bar food now includes soup (£1.15), open sandwiches (from £1.80), home-made pâté (£2.20), large Yorkshire pudding with steak and onion gravy (£2.25), meaty or vegetarian lasagne or hazelnut roast (all £3), scampi (£3.95), gammon with egg or pineapple (from £4.95), salmon steak and parsley sauce (£5.10), and lots of puddings (£1.50); specials like Cumberland sausage or steak and mushroom pie

(£3.95). Well kept Theakstons Best, Old Peculier, and XB on handpump. The interestingly furnished little rooms have a cosy, relaxed atmosphere, and darts, dominoes, cribbage, ring the bull, and fruit machine. The pub looks down over the grass to the narrow stream that runs through this delightful hamlet. *(Recommended by Andy and Jill Kassube, R August, Jon Wainwright, Syd and Wyn Donald, Jenny Cantle; more reports please)*

Free house   Licensees Hanson and Christine Hayes   Real ale   Meals and snacks Children away from bar   Open 11.30–3, 5.30–11

LITTON (N Yorks)   SD9074   Map 7

Queens Arms 🛏

From B6160 N of Grassington, after Kilnsey take second left fork; can also be reached off B6479 at Stainforth N of Settle, via Halton Gill

This 17th-century inn is set in fine scenery – a track behind leads over Ackerley Moor to Buckden, and the quiet lane through the valley leads on to Pen-y-Ghent. Inside on the right, the main bar has a brown beam-and-plank ceiling, stripped rough stone walls, stools around cast-iron-framed tables on its stone and concrete floor, a seat built into the stone-mullioned window, a large collection of cigarette lighters, and a good coal fire. On the left, the red-carpeted room has another coal fire and more of a family atmosphere with varnished pine for its built-in wall seats, and for the ceiling and walls themselves. The new licensees used to run a restaurant and aim to offer a wider choice of food (and eventually build a restaurant extension): lunchtime sandwiches (from £1.50) or ploughman's (£2.65), soup (£1.25), mushroom lasagne (£2.65), rabbit pie (£3.50), and grilled swordfish steak or lemon sole filled with prawns and mushrooms (£5.10); good breakfasts. Well kept Youngers Scotch on handpump; darts, dominoes and piped music. *(Recommended by Ruth Humphrey, Major E G Cox, TRA, MA, Roger Etherington, P Corris, A M Neal, Tim and Sue Halstead, Gary Melnyk, Jon Wainwright, Peter and Rose Flower, Neil and Angela Huxter, Jane and Niall)*

Free house   Licensees Eric and Kaye Davidson   Real ale   Meals and snacks Children welcome   Open 11–3, 6.30–11; all day Sat; closed Mon evening in winter Bedrooms tel Arncliffe (075 677) 208; £18/£30

MASHAM (N Yorks)   SE2381   Map 10

Kings Head 🛏

Market Square

The hanging baskets and window boxes decorating this rather grand stone inn are most attractive – as is the setting which faces the broad partly tree-shaded market square. The two opened-up rooms of the neatly kept, spacious lounge bar have green plush seats around heavy cast-iron-framed tables on the patterned carpet, a big War Department issue clock over the imposing slate and marble fireplace, which is decorated with four tall brass coffee-pots (usefully, they serve coffee before the bar opens), a dark green ceiling, and a high shelf of Staffordshire and other figurines. Home-made lunchtime bar food includes sandwiches or home-made soup (from £1.10), Yorkshire pudding with onion gravy (£1.25), ploughman's (£2.95), steak and kidney (£3.25), Old Peculier casserole (£3.50), chicken Kiev (they make their own, £3.65), and daily specials like curries, rice and pasta dishes (from £2.75); delicious puddings; well kept Theakstons Best, XB and Old Peculier on handpump; fruit machine, dominoes, piped pop music. There are picnic-table sets under cocktail parasols in a partly fairy-lit coachyard. *(Recommended by Eileen Broadbent, G Dobson, David Shillitoe, S V Bishop)*

Theakstons (S & N)   Licensee Colin Jones   Real ale   Lunchtime meals and snacks Evening restaurant   Children welcome lunchtime in bar and in evening restaurant Open 11–11   Bedrooms tel Ripon (0765) 89295; £35B/£50B; 4-poster £60B

White Bear ★

Signposted off A6108 opposite turn into town centre

There's enough bric-a-brac in the busy, traditionally furnished public bar here to fill several antique shops: copper brewing implements, harness, pottery, stuffed animals – including a huge polar bear behind the bar – foreign banknotes, and even an electric shock machine that's supposed to help rheumatism (though it's not always working). As the brewery is only on the other side of town, the Theakstons Best, XB and Old Peculier on handpump is very well kept (the pub is part of Theakstons' old stone headquarters buildings). A much bigger, more comfortable lounge has a Turkey carpet. Bar food includes sandwiches (from 60p), curries (from £3.50), trout (from £3.95), seasonal game dishes like pigeon, rabbit, pheasant and venison (around £3.95), and daily specials like home-cured smoked bacon with an egg (served in a cob, £1.50) or chicken korma (£3.95); no chips. Shove-ha'penny, dominoes, cribbage, fruit machine and juke box. In summer there are seats out in the yard. They've built new lavatories this year. *(Recommended by A M Neal, J D Andrews, J E Rycroft, M Hudson, Andy and Jill Kassube, Nick Dowson, Alison Hayward, Jenny Cantle, Paul Newberry)*

Theakstons (S & N)   Licensee Neil Cutts   Real ale   Meals and snacks (not Sat or Sun evenings)   Children welcome   Live music Sat evenings   Open 11–11   Two bedrooms tel Ripon (0765) 89319; l£25

nr MIDGLEY (W Yorks)   SE0326 Map 7

Mount Skip

Village signposted from Hebden Bridge; or from A646 W of Halifax go straight through village, keeping on high road; OS Sheet 104 map reference 007272

The benches outside this pub take in the view: the ground drops so steeply that the opposite moorland and mill towns below take on a toy-like quality, with the streetlamps turned to twinkling golden necklaces at night. Inside, the modernised bar has a warm fire, copper-topped tables and so forth, and windows well placed for the view. Good value bar food includes soup (80p), sandwiches (from £1), Yorkshire pudding with onion gravy (£1.35) or with various fillings (from £2.30), battered cod (£2.25), chicken breast (£2.50), vegetarian lasagne or chilli or scampi (£2.75), and daily specials such as pork and leek sausage (£1.80) or steak and kidney pie (£2.50). Well kept Timothy Taylors Bitter, Landlord and Golden Best on handpump; darts, pool, dominoes, cribbage, fruit machine and piped music. There are high walks nearby on Midgley Moor and Crow Hill. *(Recommended by A M Neal, Mrs J Keen, Jean and Edward Rycroft)*

Timothy Taylors   Licensees Stephen and Gail Farrell   Real ale   Meals and snacks Restaurant tel Halifax (0422) 842765   Children in family room   Open 12–3, 7–11

MOULTON (N Yorks)   NZ2404 Map 10

Black Bull ⊗

Just E of A1, 1 mile S of Scotch Corner

The main bar in this well run and decidedly civilised place has black beams hung with copper cooking utensils, an antique panelled oak settle, an old elm housekeeper's chair and built-in red-cushioned black settles and pews around the cast-iron tables (one has a heavily-beaten copper top), silver-plate Turkish coffee pots and so forth over the red velvet curtained windows, dark grey carpet squares, and a huge winter log fire; decorations include three nice Lionel Edwards hunting prints, an Edwardian engraving of a big hunt meet, and a huge bowl of lilies. A nice side dark-panelled seafood bar has some high seats at the marble-topped counter. Bar snacks (you must search out someone to take your order – the bar staff just do drinks) includes excellent smoked salmon: sandwiches (£2), pâté (£3), delicious smoked salmon and asparagus quiche (£3.50), and smoked salmon plate (£5); they also do a very good home-made soup served in lovely little tureens

(£1.25), mushrooms in garlic butter (£1.75), lovely fresh salmon sandwiches (£2), avocado and prawns (£3.25), Welsh rarebit and bacon (£3.75), and memorable seafood pancakes (£3.75). In the evening, you can also eat in the polished brick-tiled conservatory with bentwood cane chairs or in the Brighton Belle dining car. Good wine and decent coffee. Service is proper and old-fashioned, though some readers have found it a little unbending. There are some seats under trees in the central court. *(Recommended by Leith Stuart, W H Bland, Stephanie Sowerby; more reports please)*

Free house   Licensee Audrey Pagendam   Meals and snacks (12–2, 6.45–10.15; not Sun, snacks only Sat lunch)   Restaurants tel Barton (0325) 377289; closed Sun Children welcome   Open 12–2.30, 6–10.30 (11 Fri and Sat); closed 23–31 Dec

NEWHOLM (N Yorks)   NZ8611   Map 10
Beehive

Village signposted from A171

Inside this cosy and very pretty old thatched pub the two friendly rooms have heavy black beams in the low ceilings, comfortable benches built into the walls, rather narrow rustic tables, lots of horse brasses, and some less common curios on ship-in-bottle lines. Well kept McEwans 80/- and Youngers Scotch on handpump, and food includes good local seafood; the restaurant upstairs has nice dormer windows in the tiled roof, and there are seats on the grass outside. *(Recommended by Mike and Wendy Proctor, Margaret and Roy Randle, Jan and Ian Alcock)*

McEwans (S & N)   Real ale   Meals and snacks   Restaurant tel Whitby (0947) 602703   Open 11–3, 6.30–11

NEWTON ON OUSE (N Yorks)   SE5160   Map 7
Dawnay Arms

Village signposted off A19 N of York

On either side of the entrance to this Grade II listed building are comfortable and spacious red-carpeted room areas. The left-hand room has red plush button-back wall banquettes built into bays and a good log fire in the stone fireplace. On the right there's a good deal of beamery and timbering and green plush wall settles and brown plush chairs around wooden or dimpled copper tables. Popular bar food includes home-made soup (£1.25), sandwiches (£1.45, this includes chips), ploughman's (£3.50), vegetarian mushroom and nut fettucini or chilli (£4.25), fisherman's platter (£4.50), lots of steaks (from £7.50), and daily specials like fillet of pork Normandy with an apple and cider sauce (£5.45), chargrilled swordfish with herb butter and prawns (£5.94), fillet of salmon with a lobster and white wine sauce (£6.95), and roast duckling with a cherry and cointreau sauce (£7.25). Well kept John Smiths and Tetleys and maybe Ind Coope Burton on handpump, decent house wines and good sherry; alcove with darts, fruit machine and trivia; maybe unobtrusive piped music; friendly service. The Ouse swirls past the moorings at the bottom of the neatly kept lawn, and there are picnic-table sets and other tables on the terrace, with a children's play-house and see-saw. *(Recommended by Roger Bellingham, Tim and Anne Halstead)*

Free house   Licensees John and Angela Turner   Real ale   Meals and snacks (12–2, 6.45–9.45; not Mon lunchtime)   Restaurant tel Linton-on-Ouse (034 74) 345 Children in eating area and restaurant   Open 11.30–2.30, 6.30–11; closed Mon lunchtime

NUNNINGTON (N Yorks)   SE6779   Map 7
Royal Oak

Church Street; at back of village, which is signposted from A170 and B1257

The popular food here is served with cloth napkins and it's the home-made daily specials that receive the most praise: ham and mushroom pasta (£3.95), steak and kidney casserole with herb dumpling or breast of chicken in orange and tarragon (£4.95), and seafood crumble (£5.50). Other good food includes sandwiches (£2, not Sun lunchtime), home-made soup (£1.40), ploughman's (from £2.95), salads (from £3.75), meaty or vegetarian lasagne (£3.95), chicken curry (£4.25), and gammon with egg or pineapple (£5.25). Theakstons Bitter on handpump, with Old Peculier kept under light top pressure. The high black beams are strung with earthenware flagons, copper jugs and lots of antique keys, one of the walls is stripped back to the bare stone to display a fine collection of antique farm tools, and there are open fires and a warm, cheerful atmosphere. The carefully chosen furniture on the Turkey carpet includes kitchen and country dining chairs or a long pew around the sturdy tables, and a lectern in one corner. Near the car park there are a couple of tables on a little terrace with a good view. Handy for a visit to Nunnington Hall (National Trust). *(Recommended by Ruth and Andrew Triggs, J A Snell, Jan and Ian Alcock, D E Nicholls, Peter Race, Barbara and Ken Turner)*

Free house   Licensee Anthony Simpson   Real ale   Meals and snacks (not Mon lunchtime)   Restaurant tel Nunnington (043 95) 271   Children over 5 welcome Open 11.45–2.30, 6.30–11; closed Mon lunchtime

nr OTLEY (W Yorks)   SE2047   Map 7
Spite

Newall-with-Clifton, off B6451; towards Blubberhouses about a mile N from Otley, and in fact just inside (N Yorks)

New licensees took over this comfortable and well kept country pub as we went to press in summer 1990. The plain white walls are hung with some wildfowl prints and a collection of walking sticks, there are wheelback chairs and plush or leatherette stools around the orderly tables, and a good log fire as well as central heating. Bar food includes sandwiches (from £1.20), soup (£1.25), ploughman's or salads (£3), home-made steak pie (£3.25), roast turkey, beef or lamb (£3.50), and puddings (£1.50). Beautifully kept Websters Yorkshire and Choice, and maybe a guest beer; dominoes and unobtrusive piped music. The neat, well-lit little rose garden has white tables and chairs. *(Recommended by Mary and Lionel Tonks, Andy and Jill Kassube, Mr Pickering, Gwen and Peter Andrews, Carol and Richard Glover, Drs M and K Parier, Mr and Mrs J E Rycroft, Roger Bellingham, Russell and Christina Jones)*

Websters (Watneys)   Licensees Jeremy and Debby Hollings   Real ale   Meals and snacks (12–2, 7–8.30); not winter Sun evening   Restaurant tel Otley (0943) 463063;   Open 11–11; 11–3, 5.30–11 in winter; closed evening 25 Dec

nr PATELEY BRIDGE (N Yorks)   SE1966   Map 7
Half Moon

Fellbeck; B6265 3 miles E

The spacious open-plan bar here has a Delft shelf on the cream walls, light-wood country kitchen chairs and a spread of russet plush button-back built-in wall banquettes around decent wooden tables, and some easy chairs and a big sofa by the entrance, near a fat free-standing woodburning stove. Well kept Timothy Taylors Landlord, Theakstons Best and Youngers Scotch on handpump; big helpings of simple but properly home-cooked bar food such as sandwiches (from 90p; the Wensleydale cheese ones are good), home-made soup (£1), ploughman's (£2.50), omelettes (from £2.80), haddock (£2.95), home-made steak and kidney pie (£3.25), fresh chicken kiev (£3.75), gammon (£4.25) and sirloin steak (£5.95). A back area has darts, pool, dominoes, pinball, and piped music; there's a caravan park behind the pub. The bedrooms are in well equipped modern chalets. *(Recommended by D A Wilcock, Miss C M Davidson, David and Rebecca Killick, Steve and Carolyn Harvey)*

Free house   Licensees David and Sheila Crosby   Real ale   Meals and snacks Children welcome   Open 12–3, 6.30–11; 12–11 Sat   Bedrooms tel Harrogate (0423) 711560; £20B/£30B

PENISTONE (S Yorks) Map 7

Cubley Hall

Mortimer Road; outskirts, towards Stocksbridge

Converted into a stylish and popular pub in 1983, this former grand Edwardian villa has a spreading bar with panelling or red and gold flock wallpaper, an elaborately plastered pink and cream ceiling, mosaic tiling or Turkey carpet, vast brass chandelier, and plenty of red plush chairs, stools and button-back built-in wall banquettes. Leading off this spacious main area are two snug rooms and a side family sun lounge which gives a nice view beyond the neat tree-sheltered formal gardens to pastures in the distance; there's a second children's room, too. A wide choice of good value bar food served efficiently by neat waitresses includes noted chip butties (80p), home-made soup (95p), sandwiches (from £1.05, steak £1.50), meaty or vegetarian lasagne (£3.10), salads or omelettes (from £3.50), plaice (£3.60), steaks (from £5.85), puddings (£1.25), and children's menu (£2.10); specials such as hot and spicy ribs (£4.15), cod mornay (£4.25) or tuna bake (£4.50), and Sunday lunch (£3.95, children £2.90). Well kept Ansells Best, Arrols 80/-, Ind Coope Burton, and Tetleys on handpump, lots of malt whiskies and other spirits, a fair choice of wines, and good coffee; cribbage, dominoes, fruit machines, space game, trivia, and piped music. A barn has been converted into a function room with exposed oak beams, stone walls and arches, half-panelled walls, and real ales. There are tables out on the terrace, and the attractive garden has a good children's play house. *(Recommended by Derek and Sylvia Stephenson, Michael Rooke, W P P Clarke, SJC)*

Free house   Licensee John Wigfield   Real ale   Meals and snacks (12–2, 7–10) Children in two rooms for them   Open 11–3, 6–11

PICKHILL (N Yorks)   SE3584 Map 10

Nags Head ⊗

Village signposted off A1 N of Ripon, and off B6267 in Ainderby Quernhow

The ingredients for the bar food here are bought carefully, and they have a changing choice of about 20 dishes depending wholly on what looked good – maybe only a couple of helpings of some things (but their definition of a helping is pretty massive): mushrooms stuffed with ham and stilton (£3.45), deep fried mussels in batter, hot roast sirloin of beef sandwich (£3.75), a vegetarian pasta dish, beautifully presented hors d'oeuvres as a starter (£3.55) or main course (£5.50), steak and kidney pie (£5.25), fresh crab salad (£6.50), skate wings with herb and garlic butter (£6.50), and grilled whole Dover sole (£10.55); they will do sandwiches. Well kept Bass, Tetleys, Theakstons Best, XB and Old Peculier, and Youngers Scotch on handpump, over 40 malt whiskies, and over 100 decent wines, including some by the glass. On the left, the busy, friendly tap room is decorated with jugs, coach horns, ale-yards and so forth hanging from the beams, and masses of ties hanging as a frieze from a rail around the red ceiling, and it's comfortably furnished with muted pastel red plush button-back built-in wall banquettes around dark tables. One table's inset with a chessboard, and they also have darts, shove-ha'penny, dominoes, cribbage, a silenced fruit machine and faint piped music in here, with pool in a separate room. A smarter bar with deep green plush banquettes and a carpet to match has pictures for sale on its neat cream walls. Creaky-boarded bedrooms, huge breakfasts. *(Recommended by M Hudson, W H Bland, Tim and Sue Halstead, PLC)*

Free house   Licensees Raymond and Edward Boynton   Real ale   Meals and snacks (12–2, 6–10)   No-smoking restaurant tel Thirsk (0845) 567391; not Sun evening Well behaved children allowed in eating area   Open 11–3, 5–11   Bedrooms tel Thirsk (0845) 567570; £27B/£40B

RAMSGILL (N Yorks)   SE1271   Map 7

Yorke Arms 🛏

Take Nidderdale rd off B6265 in Pateley Bridge; or exhilarating but narrow moorland drive off A6108 at N edge of Masham, via Fearby and Lofthouse

Some sympathetic refurbishments have taken place in the bars of this ex-shooting lodge, and more antiques have been added to the two or three heavy carved Jacobean oak chairs and a big oak dresser laden with polished pewter; one room has been converted into a residents' lounge but they hope to open out the public bar slightly in the near future; open log fires. Bar food includes soup (£1.20), sandwiches (from £1.25, open from £1.75), filled baked potatoes (from £1.75), ploughman's (from £2.50), mini grill (£3.75), salads (from £3.75), seafood pasta in white wine sauce (£3.95), pan fried trout with almonds and grapes (£4.95), sirloin steak (£6.75), and puddings (from £1.75). The inn's public rooms are open throughout the day for tea and coffee, and shorts are served in cut glass. Dominoes and cribbage. You can walk up the magnificent if strenuous moorland road to Masham, or perhaps on the right-of-way track that leads along the hill behind the reservoir, also a bird sanctuary. *(Recommended by J E Rycroft, Anthony Fernau, Paul Newberry)*

Free house   Licensees Peter and Pauline Robinson   Meals and snacks   No-smoking restaurant   Children in eating area and restaurant   Open 11–11   Bedrooms tel *Harrogate (0423) 75243; £34B/£50B*

REDMIRE (N Yorks)   SE0591   Map 10

Kings Arms

Wensley–Askrigg back road: a good alternative to the A684 through Wensleydale

With small windows looking south to the fells, this unpretentious and spotlessly kept thick-walled old pub has a long bar with simple furnishings: a long soft leatherette wall seat and other upholstered wall settles, red leatherette cafe chairs or dark oak ones, round cast-iron tables, and a fine oak armchair (its back carved like a mop of hair); lots of interesting photographs include those of local filming for *All Things Great and Small*, old local scenes (including folk-singers recording here in three-piece suits), of the licensee's RAF squadron, and of his steeplechasing friends such as John Oaksey. Home-made bar food includes sandwiches (from £1), home-made soup (£1.45), excellent pâté in lovely brown terrine pot (£2.45), very good omelettes (£2.95), meaty or good vegetarian lasagne or scampi (£3.95), grilled local trout (£4.15), steak and kidney pie (£4.35), venison in red wine (£7.45), and steaks (from £7.45); Sunday roast lunch (£4.25, best to book). There's also a dining conservatory with good views of the Dales. Well kept John Smiths and Theakstons Best with guests like Tetleys, Theakstons XB and Websters Yorkshire on handpump, 53 malt whiskies, and good Rombouts coffee; cheerful, obliging service. The pit bull terrier is called Bess. Darts (under fluorescent light at one end), pool, trivia machine, dominoes, backgammon, chess and juke box or piped music. There are tables and chairs in the pretty garden, which has a superb view across Wensleydale; fishing nearby. Handy for Castle Bolton where Mary Queen of Scots was imprisoned. *(Recommended by Sidney and Erna Wells, Mrs R Heaton, Stephanie Sowerby, KC, Jenny Cantle; more reports please)*

Free house   Licensees Roger and Terry Stevens   Real Ale   Meals and snacks Restaurant   Children in restaurant only   Sing-alongs every fourth Fri   Open 11–3.30, 6–11   Two bedrooms tel *Wensleydale (0969) 22316; £15/£25*

RIPPONDEN (W Yorks)   SE0419   Map 7

Old Bridge 🔧

Priest Lane; from A58, best approach is Elland Road (opposite Golden Lion), park opposite the church in pub's car park and walk back over ancient hump-backed bridge

On weekday lunchtimes, this well kept and carefully restored medieval house does a popular cold meat buffet which always has a joint of rare beef, as well as spiced ham, quiche, Scotch eggs and so on (£6, with a bowl of soup and coffee). In the evenings, and at lunchtime on Saturdays (when you may have to wait some time for your food), good tasty filling snacks include mushrooms parisienne (£2), steak and kidney pie (£3.25), and sticky toffee pudding (£1.50), with frequently changing specials like delicious smoked haddock pancakes, falafel and raita (£2) or fillet of beef tagine (£4); they will cut fresh sandwiches. Well kept Ruddles County, Timothy Taylors Bitter and Best, and Youngers on handpump. The three communicating rooms, each on a slightly different level, have comfortable furnishings that include rush-seated chairs, oak settles built into the window recesses of the thick stone walls, antique oak tables, a few well-chosen pictures and a big woodburning stove; some of the plasterwork has been stripped away to show the handsome masonry and ceilings have been removed to show the pitched timbered roof. The pub has a good restaurant, across the very pretty medieval bridge over the little river Ryburn. *(Recommended by Mary and Lionel Tonks, Mr and Mrs J E Rycroft, Andy and Jill Kassube, Christopher Knowles-Fitton, Syd and Wyn Donald)*

Free house   Licensee Ian Beaumont   Real ale   Meals and snacks (till 10pm); not Sat evening, not Sun   Restaurant tel Halifax (0422) 822295; open Mon–Sat evenings only; closed Sun   Children in eating area of bar until 5.30   Open 11.30–3.30, 5.30–11; 11.30–11 summer Sat

ROBIN HOODS BAY (N Yorks)   NZ9505 Map 10

Laurel

Village signposted off A171 S of Whitby

At the bottom of a scree of fishermen's cottages at the heart of one of the prettiest and most unspoilt fishing villages on the North East coast, this cosy white pub has a good local atmosphere. The friendly beamed main bar is decorated with old local photographs, Victorian prints and brasses, and has an open fire. Well kept Tetleys Bitter, Theakstons Old Peculier, Tolly Bitter on handpump, with many guest beers; darts, shove-ha'penny, table skittles, and cribbage. In summer, the hanging baskets and window boxes are lovely; *Good Walks Guide* Walk 160 is close by. The self-catering flat above the bar is enticing, and there's also a cottage; tel Whitby (0947) 880400. Please note, they don't do food. *(Recommended by John and Chris Simpson, Brian Barefoot, Mike and Wendy Proctor, Jane and Niall)*

Free house   Licensee Martin Tucker   Real ale   Children in family room   Open 11.30–3 (4 Sat), 6–11

ROSEDALE ABBEY (N Yorks)   SE7395 Map 10

Milburn Arms 🏠

The easiest road to the village is through Cropton from Wrelton, off the A170 W of Pickering

The bar in this splendidly positioned 18th-century pub has been relocated, using the old cellar to give more space: traditional pub furniture and re-upholstered banquettes, lots of sentimental engravings *(The Poor Poet, The Pensionist)* by Karl Spitzweg, sporting prints with an emphasis on rugby and cricket, and new wall and table lamps; partly no-smoking. There's a new back bar, the family room has become a restaurant, and the main entrance has had the beams and original dressed stone exposed. Popular home-made food includes lunchtime wholemeal buns (from £1.30), soup (£1.50), ploughman's (£2.75), smoked trout pâté (£2.95), good mariners hotpot (£3.25), spicy vegetable tagliatelle or fresh vegetable gratin (£3.95), calves liver, onion and bacon (£4.75), beef or chicken curry (£4.90), rabbit pie with Madeira (£5.25), venison pie with green ginger wine (£6.25), sirloin steak (£7.90), and puddings like treacle tart or hot sticky toffee sponge (from £1.75). On Sunday there's also a range of cold meats, fish (the crab is excellent), quiche and cheese with salads, and roast lunch. Well kept Theakstons Best, XB and Old Peculier, and Youngers Scotch on handpump, around 30 malt whiskies, 15 cognacs, over 130 wines (8 by the glass) kept fresh by a vacuum system, and fresh ground coffee. Unobtrusive piped classical music at lunchtime, jazz/blues in the evening; sensibly placed darts, winter pool table, shove-ha'penny, dominoes, cribbage, and fruit machine in a separate balconied area with more tables, up a few steps; seats outside. *(Recommended by John and Christine Simpson, BKA, Brian and Anna Marsden, Gary Melnyk, S V Bishop)*

Free house   Licensee Stephen Colling   Real ale   Meals and snacks   No-smoking restaurant   Well behaved children allowed in eating area of bar at lunchtime and early evening   Open 11–2.30, 6–11; winter opening times 11.30 and 6.30; closed 25 Dec Bedrooms tel Lastingham (075 15) 312; £31B/£50B

White Horse 🛏

Above village, 300 yards up Rosedale Chimney Bank – the exhilarating 1-in-3 moorland road over Spaunton Moor to Hutton-le-Hole

From the windows of the cosy beamed bar in this isolated stone inn (and from the picnic-table sets on the stone front terrace) there are fine views of the high surrounding countryside – the inn itself has 11 acres. Inside, there are captain's chairs, red plush cushioned pews salvaged from a church in Wakefield, wooden tables, a welcoming log fire and fox masks, a stuffed heron and peregrine falcon, various antlers and horns, and a reindeer skin. Good, generously served bar food includes home-made soup (£1.20), sandwiches (from £1.30), ratatouille au gratin (£2.80), ploughman's (£3.20), salads (from £3.75), grilled trout (£3.95), nut roast or home-made pies (£4.30), two local woodpigeon cooked in a game sauce (when available, £5.50), and sirloin steak (£6.80), with children's dishes (from £2.20), puddings like home-made brandy snaps and cream (from £1.50) and Sunday roast lunch (£4.50, children £3). Well kept John Smiths and Tetleys on handpump, good choice of malt whiskies and wines by the bottle; darts, dominoes and piped music. *(Recommended by Jill Hampton, BKA, Brian Metherell, Tim and Lynne Crawford, Paul Newberry)*

Free house   Licensees Howard and Clare Proctor   Real ale   Meals and snacks (12–2, 7–10)   Restaurant   Children in bar if eating till 8.30   Varied live entertainment throughout the year   Open 11.30–3, 6.30–11; 11.30–11 summer Sats; 12–3, 6.30–11 in winter; closed 25 Dec   Bedrooms tel Lastingham (075 15) 239; £30B/£50B

SAWLEY (N Yorks)   SE2568 Map 7

Sawley Arms 🍷

Village signposted off B6265 W of Ripon

A series of small and cosy Turkey-carpeted rooms in this civilised place have comfortable furnishings ranging from small softly cushioned armed dining chairs and greeny gold wall banquettes to the wing armchairs down a couple of steps in a side snug; also, log fires, unobtrusive piped piano music, passe-temps, and an engaging Burmese cat; a small area is reserved for non-smokers. Interesting home-made food includes soups such as celery and apricot, fennel or mushroom with cumin, all made with proper stock, good sandwiches, ham, spinach and almond pancake (£2.90), good ravioli, splendid salmon mousse (£3.20), tasty ham and celery pâté, home-baked ham, steak pie with a fine buttercrust pastry (£4.50; one reader thought it the best he'd ever tasted), salads, steaks, and puddings like chocolate brandy mousse or strawberry marquise; there may be a bit of a wait at peak times. Decent house wines (the beers are keg), and courteous service. The pub is handy for Fountains Abbey (the most extensive of the great monastic remains – floodlit on late summer Friday and Saturday evenings, with a live choir on the Saturday). An attractive and well kept small garden has two or three old-fashioned teak tables. *(Recommended by J D Andrews, Syd and Wyn Donald, Gwen and Peter Andrews, Mr and Mrs M Cockram, Mrs V Middlebrook, Tim and Lynne Crawford)*

Free house   Licensee Mrs June Hawes   Meals and snacks (not Sun evening, not Mon, except Bank Hols)   Restaurant tel Ripon (0765) 86642   Children over 9 only   Open 11.30–3, 6.30–11; closed Mon, except Bank Hols

SAXTON (N Yorks)   SE4736   Map 7

Greyhound

Village signposted off B1217 Garforth–Tadcaster; so close to A1 and A162 N of Pontefract

By the handsome, stonebuilt church, this little tiled white-painted cottage is quite unspoilt – and the very picture of a traditional village pub; as we went to press we heard that a new licensee was to move in, so we're keeping our fingers crossed that things don't change much. Inside, the companionable locals' favourite place is on the left – a cosy and chatty tap room, with a coal fire burning in the Victorian fireplace in the corner, ochre Anaglypta walls and a dark panelled dado; well kept Sam Smiths OB tapped from casks behind the counter. From here a corridor takes you past a small snug with a sturdy mahogany wall settle curving round one corner, other traditional furniture, fancy shades on the brass lamps, and browning Victorian wallpaper; down at the end is another highly traditional room, with darts, shove-ha'penny, table skittles, cribbage, dominoes, and small television. The pub is bright in summer with a climbing rose, passion flower and bedding plants, and there's a couple of picnic-table sets in the side courtyard. Close to Lotherton Hall Museum. *(Recommended by Andy and Jill Kassube, Matt Pringle, J C Proud)*

Sam Smiths   Licensee Mrs Janette Romans   Real ale   Sandwiches (lunchtime) Children welcome   Open 11–3, 6–11; all day Sat

SETTLE (N Yorks)   SD8264   Map 7

Royal Oak   ⊘   ⇐

Market Place; town signposted from A65 Skipton–Kendal

The ground floor of this well kept and substantial low stone inn is virtually one huge room, yet enough walls have been kept to divide it into decent-sized separate areas. Throughout there's dark squared oak or matching oak-look panelling, with a couple of elegantly carved arches and more carving above the fireplaces. Plenty of tables (some dimpled copper, but most wood) are spread over the flowery maroon carpet; lights vary from elaborate curly brass candelabra through attractive table lamps and standard lamps with old-fashioned shades to unexpectedly modernist wall cubes. There's a pleasantly relaxed atmosphere, and the staff are welcoming and helpful. A wide choice of good value bar food includes soup (£1.20), sandwiches (from £1.55, interesting Danish open ones from £1.75, hefty French bread from £2.85), ploughman's (£2.65), shepherd's pie (£2.85), salads (from £3), half a dozen vegetarian dishes such as pasta carbonara (£3.20), venison sausages with Cumberland sauce (£3.25), seafood vol-au-vent (£4.20), steak and kidney pie (£4.35), children's dishes (£1.90) and good puddings (hot tip is a puff pastry and raisins concoction they serve hot with cream and call Fat Rascals – £1.40). Well kept Boddingtons, Flowers IPA and Whitbreads Castle Eden on handpump; some road noise (absurdly heavy quarry lorries cut through the attractive small town – they should certainly be kept out). *(Recommended by Anne Morris, Margaret and Roy Randle, Brian Horner, M J Whitehouse, Peter Race, C A Holloway, J E Rycroft)*

Whitbreads   Licensees Brian and Sheila Longrigg   Real ale   Meals and snacks (till 10; also teas and high teas 3.30–5.30)   Children in eating area of bar   Open 11–3, 6–11; 11–11 Sat   Bedrooms tel Settle (072 92) 2561; £34.50B/£60B

SHEFFIELD (S Yorks)   SK3687   Map 7

Fat Cat

23 Alma St

This chatty, friendly pub is interestingly set in the heart of an industrial conservation area, though it's the wide range of well kept real ales and foreign bottled beers (particularly Belgian ones) that's the main draw: Marstons Pedigree, Merrie Monk and Owd Rodger, Timothy Taylors Landlord, Theakstons Old Peculier, and five interesting guest beers on handpump. At the time we went to press, they were hoping to have opened their own micro-brewery. There were also country wines, several organically grown wines and farm cider. Cheap bar food includes soup (90p), big sandwiches (from 90p), good vegetarian chilli, ploughman's, pork and pasta casserole, spinach and mushroom lasagne or cauliflower in mustard sauce (all £1.80), puddings (60p), and Sunday lunch (£2); vegan dishes always available; efficient service, cribbage, dominoes. The two small downstairs rooms have simple wooden tables and grey cloth seats around the walls, with a few advertising mirrors and an enamelled placard for Richdales Sheffield Kings Ale; the one on the left is no-smoking and both have coal fires. Steep steps take you up to another similarly simple room (which may be booked for functions), with some attractive prints of old Sheffield; there are picnic-table sets in a fairylit back courtyard. Kelham Island Industrial Museum is close. *(Recommended by A M Neal, Frazer and Louise Smith, Steve Mitcheson, Anne Collins, Matt Pringle, John Day, Richard Sanders)*

Free house   Licensee Stephen Fearn   Real ale   Meals and snacks (lunchtime) Children allowed upstairs if not booked, lunchtime and until 8   Open 12–3, 5.30–11; closed 25 Dec

Frog & Parrot

Division Street, corner of Westfield Terrace

In a splendidly spacious cage here (though he's allowed to fly free on occasions) is a blue and yellow macaw, and there's also a tank of large frogs. The atmosphere is chatty and relaxed and furnishings include high stools at elbow-height tables, bare boards, a lofty brown ceiling and huge windows, though one side (with an old neatly blacked kitchen range in a brick chimney-breast) is carpeted, and an area up a few steps has blue plush button-back built-in wall banquettes (this part is no-smoking, as is the area next to the parrot). Up here, you can see down into the basement brew house where they produce the pub's speciality – Roger and Out, a hefty 1125OG ale (at nearly 17% alcohol about five times the strength of an ordinary bitter), which they sell in 1/3 pint glasses, restricting customers to one pint a session. The other beers here are Old Croak (by contrast very light and easy-to-drink), Reckless and Conqueror, with occasional commemorative strong ales. As well as cheap bar food that includes soup (95p), burgers (from 96p), Yorkshire puddings with onion gravy (£1.35), omelettes made with three free-range eggs (from £1.95), vegetable stir-fry or chilli con carne (£2.75), and roast beef (£3.25); there's also a range of 40 different types of fish every day – from haddock, ling, herring, cod and plaice to halibut, salmon, red mullet and swordfish, served in a variety of ways (£2.95-£5.10). Fruit machine, video game, piped music. *(Recommended by Steve Waters, Steve Mitcheson, Anne Collins, Jon Wainwright, J L Thompson; more reports please)*

Own brew/Whitbreads   Licensee Roger Nowill   Real ale   Meals and snacks (lunchtime, not Sun)   Restaurant tel Sheffield (0742) 721280   Sun evening jackpot quiz   Open 11–11; closed Sun lunchtime

SICKLINGHALL (N Yorks)   SE3648 Map 7
Scotts Arms

Leaving Wetherby W on A661, fork left just before hospital

This is undoubtedly a place where you go to eat, though there are some interesting things to look at while you're doing so. As well as a big inglenook fireplace, there's a curious sort of double-decker fireplace with its upper hearth intricately carved, and on a shelf in the corner of the bar is a working model of a two-foot high traditional Scotsman constantly raising and lowering his glass. The bar is more-or-less open plan but keeps some sense of its original rooms with stubs of the old dividing walls left, and there are seats built into cosy little alcoves cut into the main walls. Bar food includes good home-made soup (£1.35), sandwiches (from £1.25), big ploughman's (from £2.75), filled French sticks (from £3.25), large, fried haddock (from £3.50), good steak, kidney and mushroom pie or scampi (£3.75), and daily specials such as gammon with egg or pineapple. Well kept Theakstons Old Peculier, and Youngers IPA and No 3 on handpump; darts, fruit machine, video game, juke box and unobtrusive piped music, and down steps a separate room has pool and another fruit machine. There are tables outside in summer, and a children's play area with slide, climbing frame and wooden animals. *(Recommended by Robert and Lesley Fawthrop, T Nott, David Oakes, GB, Mrs V Middlebrook, Tony and Penny Burton, Andy and Jill Kassube, Roy Bromell, S V Bishop, Lyn and Bill Capper)*

S & N   Licensee Carl Lang   Real ale   Meals and snacks   Restaurant tel Wetherby (0937) 62100 (Tues–Sat evenings)   Children in eating area of bar and restaurant Open 11.30–3, 5.30–11

SOWERBY BRIDGE (W Yorks)   SE0623 Map 7

Moorings

Off Bolton Brow (A58) opposite Java Restaurant

At the junction of the Rochdale Canal and Calder & Hebble Canal, this attractively converted ex-canal warehouse has a spacious beamed bar with stone walls, bare floorboards, big windows, a grain hopper, grain sacks and old pulley wheels; there's an eating area up some steps. The lounge bar is pleasantly furnished with rush-seated stools, tile-top tables and fabric-covered seats built against the stripped stone walls (which are decorated with old waterways maps and modern canal pictures), and the big windows and very high ceiling give a relaxed and airy atmosphere. A lobby leads to a no-smoking family room alongside, similarly furnished. Good, reasonably priced bar food includes home-made soup (95p), filled granary cobs (from 95p), help-yourself salads (from £2.25), chicken tikka with yoghurt or spinach and mushroom lasagne (£2.95), their delicious own recipe Cumberland sausage with spicy beans (£3.10), vegetarian nutburger (£3.25), fresh haddock fillets (from £3.50), home-cooked pie (£4.95), gingered beef casserole (£5.50), stir-fry pork (£6.25), steaks (from £7.50), puddings like apple pie (from £1.10), and children's meals (in the family area, £1.80); service does get pushed when busy. Besides well kept Moorhouses Bitter, McEwans 80/-, Theakstons XB, Youngers Scotch and a regularly changing guest beer on handpump, there is a range of 30 foreign bottled and canned beers, and they import more than 40 Belgian bottle-conditioned real ales (there's a menu with full descriptions), and Dutch Lineboom; also, over 80 malt whiskies (including 7 Irish), reasonably priced house wines, and cocktails – including children's specials; they do tea and coffee. Dominoes and piped music. Tables out on a terrace with grass and small trees. Part of the canal has been reopened and there's now a circular walk; other old canal buildings here house a boat chandlery and canal hire company. *(Recommended by Steve and Maureen Collins, Andrew and Ruth Triggs, Mr and Mrs P A Jones, P A Crossland, D A Cawley, Andy and Jill Kassube, Syd and Wyn Donald, David Oakes, Michael Rooke, Steve Mitcheson, Anne Collins, Derek and Sylvia Stephenson)*

Free house   Licensees Ian Clay and Andrew Armstrong   Real ale   Meals and snacks Restaurant tel Halifax (0422) 833940   Children in family room till 8.30   Open 11.30–3, 5(6 Sat, 7 Mon)–11; closed 25 Dec

SPROTBROUGH (S Yorks)   SE5302 Map 7

Boat

2 ¾ miles from M18 junction 2; A1(M) northwards, then A630 towards Rotherham, then first right, signposted Sprotbrough, by Texaco garage; immediate left after crossing river

A big enclosed brick-paved courtyard outside this busy ex-farmhouse has picnic-table sets, and you can wander round to watch the barges and water-bus on the River Don (as the embankment's quite high you don't see much from the bar); a short walk upstream leads to a nature reserve with hides. Inside, the three room areas are furnished with green-grey plush cushioned wall settles, captains' and wheelback chairs and stools around dark cast-iron tables, prints of bygone scenes, a rack of guns, big cases of stuffed birds, a couple of longcase clocks, and the odd bronze; there are open fires in rather portentous stone fireplaces, latticed windows, and dark brown beams. Bar food includes rabbit casserole or steak and kidney pie (£2.95), very good salad, roasts (£3.50), and halibut or swordfish (£4.50); well kept Courage Directors, John Smiths Bitter and Magnet on handpump, farm cider, and some malt whiskies; fruit machine, noticeable piped music. *(Recommended by Wayne Brindle, ILP, K Leist, GB, Tony Gayfer, Steve Mitcheson, Anne Collins)*

John Smiths (Courage)   Licensee Barrie Wastnage   Real ale   Meals (12–2, 6–9) Restaurant tel Doncaster (0302) 857188 Tues–Sat evening, Sun lunch   Children in restaurant   Open 11–3, 6–11; 11–11 summer Sats

STANSFIELD MOOR (W Yorks)   SD9227   Map 7

Sportsmans Arms

Hawks Stones, Kebcote; on the old packhorse road between Burnley and Hebden Bridge, high above Todmorden; OS Sheet 103 map reference 928273

Isolated but very welcoming, this 17th-century place has a comfortable mix of old and new furnishings such as big heavy russet plush settles facing the open fire in the back area, with mustard-coloured leatherette seats elsewhere, beams hung with mugs and horsebrasses, a few Toby-jugs and other decorative china on a high shelf, and swords, knives, assegais, heavy-horse harness; also, fresh flowers in the stone hearth and on some of the tables, some dark squared panelling and stone-mullioned windows with pot plants on the stone sills. The colour photographs of show horses and of a pony and trap are a clear clue to the licensee's interests. Good quality bar food includes sandwiches (from £1.10), sausage and egg (£2.50), steak pie (£3.25), gammon (£3.50), and sirloin steak (£5.75). Well kept Ruddles County, and Websters Yorkshire and Choice on handpump, with quite a few decent malt whiskies; darts, pool, and fruit machine. Walkers welcome and dogs too, if on a lead. *(Recommended by Len Beattie; more reports please)*

Free house   Licensee Jean Greenwood   Real ale   Meals and snacks (till 10pm) Evening restaurant tel Todmorden (0706) 813449   Children welcome   Open 12–2.30, 7–11 (midnight supper licence); closed Mon–Fri lunchtimes in winter

STARBOTTON (N Yorks)   SD9574   Map 7

Fox & Hounds

B6160 Upper Wharfedale rd N of Kettlewell; OS Sheet 98, map reference 953749

Outside this pretty and beautifully placed stone-slab-roofed inn there are sturdy tables and benches in a sheltered corner where you can look out to the hills all around this little hamlet. The bar has an antique settle and other solid old-fashioned furniture on the flagstones, saddles and country bric-a-brac, high beams supporting ceiling boards, and a big stone fireplace (with an enormous fire in winter). Lunchtime bar food includes very good home-made carrot and orange soup (£1), sandwiches, ploughman's, and giant Yorkshire pudding with onion gravy (£1.95); the dining room is no-smoking. Well kept Theakstons Best, XB, and Old Peculier and Youngers Scotch on handpump; board games and dominoes. *(Recommended by Mary and Lionel Tonks, Andy and Jill Kassube, Carol and Richard Glover, Mr and Mrs K H Frostick, J E Rycroft, A P Hudson, Jon Wainwright, Jenny Cantle, Richard Fawcett)*

Free house   Licensee Mrs Pam Casey   Real ale   Evening meals and lunchtime snacks   Children in small side room at lunchtime   Open 12–3 (2.30 Wed–Fri), 7–11; Nov–May closed Tues lunchtime and all day Mon   Bedrooms tel Kettlewell (075 676) 269; l£40S

SUTTON (S Yorks)   SE5512   Map 7

Anne Arms ★

From A1 just S of Barnsdale Bar service area follow Askern, Campsall signpost; Sutton signposted right from Campsall

Generous helpings of remarkably good value, very tasty home-made food in this cosy creeper-covered stone house include a fresh roast every day, their speciality rabbit pie, braised pork chops with apple sauce and stuffing, poached salmon, fresh haddock, Barnsley chops with mint sauce (all £2.75), and puddings like home-made fruit pies (£1). John Smiths Magnet on handpump, excellent service. An interesting and profuse collection of ornaments consists of latticed glass cases thronged with china shepherdesses and the like, a throng of Toby jugs collected over many years, oak dressers filled with brightly coloured plates, fruit plates embossed with lifesize red apples, lots of colourful five-litre and smaller Bavarian drinking steins, and wooden figures popping out of a Swiss clock when it chimes the quarter-hours. A separate room is filled with brass and copper, and there's a Victorian-style conservatory. *(Recommended by Mrs R M Morris, Mrs B Y Lockwood, Mr and Mrs D W Fisher, Wayne Brindle)*

John Smiths (Courage)   Licensees John and Irene Simm   Real ale   Meals and snacks Children in buffet room/snug   Open 11–3, 6–11

SUTTON HOWGRAVE (N Yorks)   SE3279   Map 7
White Dog

Village signposted from B6267 about 1 mile W of junction with A1

By a peaceful green with field maples and sycamores, this pretty village cottage has two main rooms furnished with comfortably cushioned Windsor chairs and flowers on the polished tables. On one side of the black-beamed bar there's an open kitchen range with a welcoming fire in cool weather; friendly cat. Good bar lunches include French onion soup (£1.30), sandwiches (from £1.50), mariner's hotpot (£3.50), salads (from £3.50), omelettes (from £3.75), fish pie or chicken and mushroom casserole (£4.30), venison pie (£4.50), and puddings (£1.85); small selection of New World wines. In summer, the upper windows are almost hidden by the flowers in the window boxes and two clematis, and there are picnic-table sets among flowerbeds on the grass. *(Recommended by Fiona Mutch, Graham and Karen Oddey, Syd and Wyn Donald, J E Rycroft)*

Free house   Licensees Basil and Pat Bagnall   Lunchtime meals and snacks (not Mon) No-smoking restaurant tel Melmerby (076 584) 404; Tues–Sat evenings, bookings only   Children in restaurant at licensees' discretion   Open 12–2.30, 7–11; closed Sun evening, all day Mon, 25 Dec and 1 Jan

TADCASTER (N Yorks)   SE4843   Map 7
Angel & White Horse

1 Bridge Street

Popular with business people at lunchtime and locals in the evening, this atmospheric pub is the tap for the Sam Smiths Brewery, and from the bar you can see the team of grey shire horses peering out of their stalls across the neat yard. They do brewery tours at arranged times: tel Tadcaster (0937) 832225. Remarkably cheap and well kept Sam Smiths OB and Museum. The open-plan series of rooms have fine oak panelling with unusually well made solid furniture to match, photographs of past brewery workers and above a handsome stone fireplace is a striking oil painting of a dappled grey shire horse. Good value bar food includes sandwiches, various pies and daily specials (£2.65), and roast beef with Yorkshire pudding (£2.75); darts, dominoes and piped music. *(Recommended by Jan and Ian Alcock, Maureen and Steve Collin, Eileen Broadbent, T Nott, Gordon Mott)*

Sam Smiths   Licensee Alan Rhodes   Real ale   Lunchtime meals and snacks Restaurant tel Tadcaster (0937) 835470   Children in restaurant at lunchtime   No nearby daytime parking   Open 11–2.30, 5 (7 Sat)–11

THORNTON WATLASS (N Yorks)   SE2486 Map 10

Buck 🏵 🛏

Village signposted off B6268 Bedale—Masham

Without straying too far from the village pub image, the friendly and enthusiastic licensees are carefully improving the facilities here – the bedrooms now all have en-suite bathrooms, an entrance is being opened up from the small bar to the dining room to create an eating area attached to the bar, the front of the pub is to be tidied up, and their garden with its play equipment is being made much use of. The pleasantly traditional right-hand bar (which they hope will be less crowded once the dining room can be used as an overflow) has handsome old-fashioned wall settles, cast-iron-framed tables, a high shelf packed with ancient bottles, and several mounted fox masks and brushes (the Bedale hunt meets in the village). At lunchtime, bar food includes home-made soup (£1.30), Cumberland sausage made to their own recipe (£1.75), a cold platter (£3.25), and lasagne (£4.25), with evening dishes like Whitby cod (£4), steak and kidney pie (£4.25), chicken chasseur (£4.50), baked avocado and prawn au gratin (£4.95), gammon and eggs (£5.25), and fresh salmon (£5.95); smaller helpings for OAPs and children; well kept Tetleys and Theakstons Best and XB on handpump, and around 50 malt whiskies. A bigger plainer bar has darts, pool, cribbage, and piped music. The low stone building looks past a grand row of sycamores to the village cricket green (they have a team), and has two quoits pitches in the garden (with league matches on summer Wednesday evenings, practice Sunday morning and Tuesday evening), trout fishing on the Ure, and a children's play area. *(Recommended by Mary and Lionel Tonks, Kelvin Lawton, Ian Ornes, Stephen and Alison Parker, J Leslie Anthony, Janice Diamond, Angela Lockett, Richard Gibbs, J D Andrews, H Bramwell, Allen Sharp, Gary Melnyk)*

Free house   Licensees Michael and Margaret Fox   Real ale   Meals and snacks (11.30–2, 6.30–9.30)   Restaurant   Children welcome (at licensees' discretion) up to 9pm; not in function room Sat or Sun evenings   Organ singalong and dancing Sat, organ/country and western Sun evening   Open 11–2.30 (3 Sat), 6–11, all day for cricket matches and so forth   Bedrooms tel Bedale (0677) 22461; £18S/£35

THRESHFIELD (N Yorks)   SD9763 Map 7

Old Hall 🏵

B6265, just on the Skipton side of its junction with B6160 near Grassington

It's the back part of this friendly place – dating back to Tudor times and the oldest inhabited building in Wharfedale – which gives the inn its name. The three communicating rooms have simple, unfussy decorations such as old Cadburys advertisements and decorative plates on a high Delft shelf, cushioned pews built into the white walls, a high beam-and-plank ceiling hung with pots, and a tall well blacked kitchen range. Huge helpings of imaginative bar food that changes daily and uses fresh, seasonal ingredients might include hot beef sandwich (£1.50), mussels baked in garlic breadcrumbs and cheese (£2.50), peach and prawns in a spicy mayonnaise (£2.75), steak pie, seafood lasagne, beef bourguignonne or good Persian lamb curry with cream and almonds (all £5), best end of lamb marinated in honey, onion, turmeric, cumin and chilli and served with a chopped fruit salad or pork brochette with an orange and ginger sauce and saffron rice (£5.25), roast monkfish with garlic or tasty halibut and prawn bake (£5.95), very good mixed grill (£7.95), winter game dishes, a big seafood platter (to order, £13.50), and puddings such as strawberry flan or chocolate roulade (£1.75). Well kept Timothy Taylors Bitter and Landlord, and Youngers Scotch on handpump. Darts, dominoes, fruit machine, maybe piped pop music. A neat side garden, partly gravelled, with young shrubs and a big sycamore has some tables and an aviary with cockatiels and zebra finches; a conservatory is planned. This is of course a fine base for Dales walking, and the inn is on *Good Walks Guide* Walk 150. Please note that they no longer do bedrooms. *(Recommended by Andy and Jill Kassube, Joan and John Calvert, Graham Bush, Margaret White, Gwen and Peter Andrews, Syd and Wyn*

Donald, A M Neal, Jane Buekett, Tim and Sue Halstead, Mr and Mrs M Tarlton, S Barnett, Jon Wainwright, P Bramhall)

Free house   Licensees Ian and Amanda Taylor   Real ale   Meals and snacks (12–2, 6.30–10)   Restaurant   Children in eating area and conservatory   Open 11–3, 5.30–11

nr TODMORDEN (W Yorks) Map 7
Staff of Life

Burnley Road, Knotts; A646 out of centre – after the built-up area ends with an imposing mill and viaduct, keep eyes skinned for car park on right, which is 90 yards walk from pub itself

Warmly welcoming and cheerful, this odd pub is formed from two or three cottages cut into the steep hillside. Its special pride is the range of interesting and well kept beers from its own brewery which you pass on the right coming out of Todmorden: delicately hopped Robinwood Bitter, XB and in winter – nothing delicate about this one – Old Fart; they also have guest beers such as Timothy Taylors Bitter and Landlord; also, farm ciders, malt whiskies, fruit wines and foreign bottled beers. The bar on the right has lots of bedpans on its mainly plastered walls, some horsebrasses on the beams, and a coal fire. On the left, a two-level simply furnished lounge has Turkey carpet on its flagstones, seats including a colourfully upholstered wall settle, more bedpans, giant mounted insects, a reindeer's head over the open fire, and lots of stripped stonework. Very good value freshly cooked bar food includes sandwiches (from 95p), basket meals (from £1.50), a fiery kebab in pitta bread (£1.85), vegetarian dishes (from £1.85), home-made chilli con carne (£1.95), curries (from £2.20), gammon and eggs (£3.75), a phenomenal fry-up (£5) and chargrilled steaks (from 10oz rump, £5); the upstairs restaurant specialises in fish. Darts, dominoes and juke box. There are picnic-table sets and a couple of rustic benches on a flagstoned roadside terrace. *(Recommended by Syd and Wyn Donald, Lee Goulding, Barbara Wensworth, Steve and Maureen Collins, Andrew Stephenson, Michael Rooke)*

Own brew   Licensee Freddie Sleap   Real ale   Meals and snacks (currently not weekday lunchtimes)   Restaurant (not Sun)   Children in eating area of bar until 8.30 Open 12–3, 7–11; closed Mon lunchtimes   Bedrooms tel Todmorden (0706) 812929; £18B/£30B

WATH-IN-NIDDERDALE (N Yorks)   SE1467 Map 7
Sportsmans Arms 🕮   🛏

Nidderdale rd off B6265 in Pateley Bridge; village and pub signposted over hump bridge on right after a couple of miles

In a charming valley setting, this friendly 17th-century country inn serves very good bar lunches: a selection of fresh fish such as moules marinières (£3.50), fresh dressed crab (£3.75), Scarborough woof sautéed in butter with prawns, almonds and capers (£4.25), fresh local trout cooked in brown butter with roasted almonds and capers (£5), and fillet of lemon sole caprice (£5.25); also, home-made soup (£1.80), chicken liver pâté or locally-made or continental cheese ploughman's (£3.20), French baguette filled with chicken waldorf in a mild curry flavoured mayonnaise (£4.20), rolled Spanish omelette (using their own free range eggs (£4.50), prawns in wholemeal bread with a tomato-flavoured mayonnaise (£4.95), and puddings or tremendous range of cheese; 3-course restaurant Sunday lunch. To get the best of the young chef's excellent cooking, you should really stay overnight and enjoy a good leisurely dinner. The bar has been completely redecorated and refurbished this year with elegant curtains and fabrics in pinks and blues; open fire, dominoes. There's a very sensible and extensive wine list, good choice of malt whiskies and attentive service. Benches outside. *(Recommended by Fiona Mutch, Joan and John Calvert, Syd and Wyn Donald, Jane and Niall)*

Free house   Licensee J R Carter   Lunchtime meals and snacks (not Sun)   Evening restaurant (not Sun evening)   Children welcome   Open 12–3, 7–11; closed evenings 24, 25 and 26 Dec and 1 Jan   Bedrooms tel Harrogate (0423) 711306; £25(£27S)/£40(£45B)

WELBURN (N Yorks) SE7268 Map 7
Crown & Cushion

Village signposted from A64 York–Malton

A growing collection of nearly 500 water jugs decorates the two connecting rooms of the lounge bar in this pleasant old stone pub. There are also little pictures between strips of black wood on the cream walls, high shelves of plates, wheelback chairs and small cushioned settles around wooden tables, and open fires in winter. Bar food includes soup (£1.50), good sandwiches (from £1.50), pâté (£1.90), ploughman's (£3.25), salads (from £3.25, the York ham is good), haddock, lasagne or steak and kidney pie (£3.95), fresh local trout (£4.25), gammon with pineapple (£4.95), steaks (from £7.20) and daily specials on a blackboard; Sunday roast (£5.95). Well kept Camerons Bitter and Strongarm on handpump. Darts, dominoes and fruit machine in the public bar; piped music. The neatly landscaped back garden has a terrace with tables and chairs. Castle Howard and Kirkham Abbey are close by. (*Recommended by Anne Phelan, Jean and Edward Rycroft, Robert Kimberley, Tim and Sue Halstead, J C Proud, Philip and Sheila Hanley, S V Bishop*)

Camerons   Licensee David Abbey   Real ale   Meals and snacks (not Mon in winter) Restaurant tel Whitwell on the Hill (065 381) 304   Children in eating area of bar and restaurant   Open 11.30–2.30, 6.30–11; winter evening opening 7

WENTWORTH (S Yorks) SK3898 Map 7
George & Dragon

3 miles from M1 junction 36: village signposted from A6135; can also be reached from junction 35 via Thorpe; pub is on B6090

The pleasantly rambling bar here has an assortment of old-fashioned seats and tables, blue plates on the walls, and steps that split the front area into separate parts; there's also a lounge (back by the little games room) with an ornate stove. Bar food includes sandwiches, venison burger (£1.25), meat and potato pie (£2.25) and salads; very good Sunday roast lunch (£3.95). A wide range of well-kept ales includes Oak Wobbly Bob, Timothy Taylors Bitter, Landlord and winter Porter and Ram Tam, Tetleys Bitter, Theakstons Old Peculier and three different guest beers each week on handpump; also Symonds cider. Dominoes, cribbage, fruit machine, trivia and piped music. There are benches in the front courtyard. (*Recommended by Mary and Lionel Tonks, Andrew Turnbull, M C Howells, Andy and Jill Kassube, Derek and Sylvia Stephenson, David Warrellow, Michael Rooke, Tony Tucker, J A Edwards, Paul Newberry*)

Free house   Licensee Steve Dickinson   Real ale   Lunchtime meals and snacks Children in eating area of bar at lunchtime   Live folk/jazz   Open 12–3, 7–11

WIDDOP (W Yorks) SD9333 Map 7
Pack Horse

The Ridge; from A646 on W side of Hebden Bridge, turn off at Heptonstall signpost (as it's a sharp turn, coming out of Hebden Bridge road signs direct you around a turning circle), then follow Slack and Widdop signposts; can also be reached from Nelson and Colne, on high, pretty road; OS Sheet 103, map reference 952317

Set high on the moors and miles from anywhere, this friendly, traditional walkers' pub has warm winter fires, sturdy furnishings, and window seats cut into the partly panelled stripped stone walls that take in the view. Good, straightforward bar food includes sandwiches (from £1, double decker from £2, open sandwiches on French bread from £2.50), cottage hotpot or ploughman's (£2.95), salads (from £3.50), gammon with two eggs or home-made steak and kidney pie (£4), steaks (from £5.75), and specials such as curry or vegetable lasagne (£3.25) or beef in ale (£4.50); lots of fancy puddings. Be prepared for a wait on summer weekends, when it's crowded. Well kept Theakstons XB, Thwaites, Timothy Taylors, and Youngers IPA and guests on handpump, and decent malt whiskies. There are seats outside. (*Recommended by Len Beattie, Simon Bates, Michael Rooke*)

Free house   Licensees Ron Evans and Andrew Hollinrake   Real ale   Meals and snacks (till 10 in evening; not winter Mon or Tues evenings, see note below)   Children welcome until 9   Open 12–3, 7–11; closed lunchtimes Oct–end April

WIGHILL (N Yorks)   SE4746 Map 7

White Swan   ★

Village signposted from Tadcaster; also easily reached from A1 Wetherby bypass – take Thorpe Arch Trading Estate turnoff, then follow Wighill signposts; OS Sheet 105 map reference 476468

The central bar serves a small lobby as well as several attractively furnished separate rooms in this welcoming, relaxed village pub. A back room has small sporting prints, a dark oil painting, a longcase clock, leather bucket seats and a curly-armed mahogany settle, a settee, and – as in all the other rooms – a coal fire. Lunchtime bar snacks include giant rolls filled with rare beef, prawns or ham (from £2.20), home-made steak pie (£2.40), and lasagne or chilli con carne (£2.75); evening dishes range from scampi and fishermans pot (£5.95) to large steaks (from £8.95, 32oz T-bone £11); good, reasonably priced three-course roast Sunday lunch in winter (£7.50). Well kept Stones, Tetleys and Theakstons on handpump; piped music. French windows from an extension lead onto a patio area overlooking the garden where there are lots of seats. *(Recommended by Andy and Jill Kassube, T Nott, Mr and Mrs M Cockram, Ruth Humphrey, TBB, J C Proud, Mrs B Y Lockwood, Tim and Sue Halstead, GB)*

Free house   Licensee Mrs Rita Arundale   Real ale   Evening meals (Thurs–Sat) and lunchtime snacks   Children in three rooms   Open 12–3, 6–11; closed 25 Dec evening

WINKSLEY (N Yorks)   SE2571 Map 7

Countryman

Village signposted off B6265 W of Ripon

Handy for Fountains Abbey and Studley Royal, this civilised and welcoming 18th-century pub can get busy in summer; it's much more of a warm-hearted local in winter – when the crack darts teams return to the fray. Down stairs from the car park, the stone-walled and heavily beamed main bar has dark brown plush seats, dimpled copper tables, a good log fire even in summer, a rack of newspapers and relaxing piped music. Good bar food in generous helpings includes vegetarian dishes, pork chop (£3.50), haddock, pork in cider and cream or steak and kidney pie (£3.75), swordfish (£4.25), salmon or duck (£5.50), a huge mixed grill (£8.75) and tasty puddings; well kept Ruddles Best, Theakstons Best and Old Peculier and Websters Yorkshire on handpump, decent whiskies, good coffee. A simple, cheerful and spacious upstairs family room has pool and another log fire, and there are some picnic-table sets on a small fairylit front terrace, with more behind. *(Recommended by Mr and Mrs E F P Metters, Tim Baxter, D Lermon, H Bramwell)*

Free house   Licensee Mark James   Real ale   Meals and snacks   Restaurant tel Ripon (0765) 83323   Children in family room   Open 12–3, 6.30–11; closed Mon lunchtime

WORMALD GREEN (N Yorks)   SE3065 Map 7

Cragg Lodge

A61 Ripon–Harrogate, about half way

Probably the widest collection of malt whiskies in Britain – maybe the world – is housed in this comfortably modernised dining roadhouse. There are over 700, including a dozen Macallans going back to 1937 (£2.30 – a remarkable bargain, smooth as silk yet glowing with deep character). They have 16 price bands, between 80p and £7, depending on rarity – with a 17th 'by negotiation' for their unique 1919 Campbelltown. Not being too single-minded, they also have well kept John Smiths Bitter, Tetleys Bitter and Mild (in summer), and Theakstons Best, XB and Old Peculier on handpump, several distinguished brandies, and mature vintage port by the glass; friendly service. The big open-plan bar has Mouseman furniture as well as little red plush chairs around dark rustic tables, a dark joist-and-plank ceiling, horse brasses and pewter tankards hanging from side beams, and a coal fire. Good, well presented bar food at lunchtime includes sandwiches (from 80p), home-made soup (90p), game and liver pâté (£1.40), ploughman's (£2), vegetarian dishes (£2.75), curry (£2.90), salads (from £2.90), gammon with egg or pineapple or country-style chicken (£3.95), steaks (from £5.95), and a daily roast; in the evenings, there's a larger, more elaborate menu (main courses from around £4.50). Home-made puddings such as cheesecake (£1.25), children's meals (£1.30), and morning coffee and snacks from 10am. Dominoes, cribbage, shove-ha'penny, fruit machine and piped music. There are picnic-table sets under cocktail parasols on the side terrace, with more in a sizeable garden. (*Recommended by Peter Burton, John Munro, Dr T H M Mackenzie, Mike Turner, Andy and Jill Kassube, R F Plater, T Nott*)

Free house   Licensee Garfield Parvin   Real ale   Meals and snacks (11.30–2, 6–9.30; till 10 Fri and Sat)   Restaurant   Children in eating area of bar   Open 11.30 (11 Sat)–3, 6–11   Bedrooms tel Ripon (0765) 87214; £15(£27B)/£28(£38B)

YORK (N Yorks)   SE5951 Map 7

Black Swan

Peaseholme Green; inner ring road, E side of centre; the inn has a good car park

Built over five hundred years ago for a family of rich merchants who included York's Lord Mayor and, later, Queen Elizabeth's jeweller, this interesting building was quite plain and plastered until complete restoration before the last war revealed the splendid timbered and jettied facade and original lead-latticed windows in the twin gables. The warmly chatty, black-beamed back bar has wooden settles along the faded cream walls, some cushioned stools and copper-topped tables, and a throne-like cushioned seat in the vast brick inglenook, where there's a coal fire in a grate with a spit and some copper cooking utensils; the fish above the door in the opposite corner was caught in 1942. The cosy panelled front bar, with its little serving hatch, is similarly furnished but smaller and more restful. The crooked-floored hall that runs along the side of both bars has a fine period staircase (leading up to a room fully panelled in oak, with an antique tiled fireplace). Good bar food served by cheerful staff includes attractively presented sandwiches (from £1.40), home-made soup, ploughman's (£3), a generous helping of excellent home-made Yorkshire pudding filled with beef stew (£3.20), and puddings such as treacle pudding (£1.20). Well kept Bass and Stones on handpump; also, fruit wines; dominoes, fruit machine and maybe half pint piped Radio 2. (*Recommended by RCL, Brian and Anna Marsden, Stan Edwards, S V Bishop; more reports please*)

Bass   Licensee Robert Atkinson   Real ale   Lunchtime meals and snacks   Children welcome   Folk night Thurs, other live music Sun   Open 11–11   Bedrooms tel York (0904) 625236; /£35B

Kings Arms

King's Staithe; left bank of Ouse just below Ouse Bridge; in the evening you should be able to get a parking space right outside, turning down off Clifford Street; otherwise there's a 1/4 mile walk

This white painted, black beamed riverside pub gets flooded so often that its 'cellar' is above ground in an adjacent building which used to be a mortuary; a painted board by the entrance to the pub shows how high the floods have been. Inside, there are cushioned stools and wall benches around wooden tables, good thick cushions on stone window seats that look out over the river, bare brick and stone walls, bowed black beams, flagstones, and one wall has a big poster about the Battle of Bosworth; a cosier area up a step at the back on the left has a few prints of Charles I, Edward VI, and Henry VIII. Bar food includes sandwiches, ploughman's (£2.20), home-made steak and kidney pie (£3.20), and roast beef and Yorkshire pudding (£3.50); fruit machines, trivia, CD juke box. There's a row of black-painted picnic-table sets on the cobbled riverside terrace – a popular place to sit on sunny days. *(Recommended by Wayne Brindle, F Teare, E H and R F Warner, Peter Race, RCL, S V Bishop)*

Sam Smiths   Licensee I C Webb   Meals and snacks (12–2, 5.30–8.30; not Sat evenings)   Open 11–11

Olde Starre

Stonegate; pedestrians-only street in centre, far from car parks

This is one of York's most touristy pubs – but only because its appeal is so genuine, and at weekends and in the evening there's a warmly local feel. Right in the busy town centre, it's actually quietly tucked away down an alleyway leading to a courtyard with interesting views of the chimneys and tiled roofs of the medieval Shambles – and of course of the Minster itself. Inside, several little rooms lead off the porch-like square hall – one with its own food servery, one with panelling and some prints, and a third with cream wallpaper and dado. Straight ahead is the main bar, with its large servery running the length of the room, green plush wall seats, some diagonal beams on the cream-papered walls, and a large leaded window with red plush curtains at the far end; well kept Ruddles Best and County, and Websters Yorkshire on handpump; fruit machine, juke box, and piped music – don't be put off by the sound levels in the courtyard, it's more quietly reproduced inside. Bar food includes sandwiches, Scottish haddock (£2.90), steak and kidney pie, mince and vegetable pie or lasagne (£3), lamb in cider, sweet and sour pork or beef in beer (£3.40), and roast beef (£4.25); salad and pudding bar, children's menu (£1.65). *(Recommended by F Teare, Hazel R Morgan, Bernard Phillips, Tim and Lynne Crawford)*

Websters (Watneys)   Licensees Bill and Susan Embleton   Real ale   Meals and snacks (11.45–3, 5.30–8)   Open 11–11

Lucky Dip

Besides the fully inspected pubs, you might like to try these Lucky Dips recommended to us and described by readers (if you do, please send us reports):

Aberford, W Yor [SE4337], *Swan*: Good, homely decor with many brasses and fire in front room; well kept Whitbreads Castle Eden and massive choice of good food inc formidable Billy Bunter's special mixed grill; bedrooms *(T Nott and others)*

Acaster Malbis, N Yor [SE5945], *Ship*: Pleasant river trip from York can be combined with simple good value lunch here; bedrooms *(Stan Edwards)*

Addingham, W Yor [SE0749], *Craven Heifer*: Very friendly and welcoming old pub with modern dark green plush furnishings, lots of pictures, Ind Coope Burton, Tetleys and Websters Green Label Mild; standard bar food, log-effect gas fire in snug (best place to mitigate piped music); steep steps from car park *(Syd and Wyn Donald, Gwen and Peter Andrews)*

Ainthorpe, N Yor [NZ7008], *Fox & Hounds*: 16th-century country pub with oak beams, horse brasses, real fires and homely atmosphere; well kept Theakstons, reasonably priced bar food, outside tables; bedrooms *(Eileen Broadbent)*

Airton, N Yor [SD9059], *Victoria*: Bar food inc good ham sandwiches; handy for interesting church, quieter spot than nearby Malham *(R C Watkins)*

Aldborough, N Yor [SE4166], *George & Dragon*: Decent food in comfortable straightforward pub with obliging staff *(Anthony Barnes)*

☆ **Almondbury**, W Yor [bear left up Lumb Lane; village signposted off A629/A642 E of Huddersfield — OS Sheet 110 map reference 153141; SE1615], *Castle Hill*: Perched high above Huddersfield on site of prehistoric hill fort, with terrific views of the moors dwarfing the mill towns; lots of coal fires in the rambling partly panelled bar, sturdy traditional furnishings, well kept Timothy Taylors Best and Landlord and Tetleys, simple bar food (not Sun–Tues evenings), popular Sun lunch *(LYM)*

Ampleforth, N Yor [SE5878], *White Swan*: Friendly staff, soft piped music, darts and two fruit machines; substantial helpings of good food (not that cheap), restaurant, keg beer *(M B Porter)*

☆ **Appletreewick**, N Yor [SE0560], *Craven Arms*: Country pub in beautiful surroundings, currently doing very well, with two cosy bar rooms and small separate dining rooms, roaring fires (one in old iron range), attractive settles and carved chairs, interesting decorations, fine relaxed atmosphere; jovial landlord, well kept Tetleys, Theakstons XB and Old Peculier and Youngers Scotch on handpump, generous helpings of good value bar food inc good ploughman's and steaks, enterprising specials, good service; lovely views across Wharfedale from outside tables, convenient for walkers *(Peter and Rose Flower, Margaret White, Jon Wainwright, Tim Baxter, Tony and Penny Burton, Paul Newberry)*

☆ **Appletreewick**, *New Inn*: Splendid stone

pub in superb spot, with lovely views; simple good food, well kept S&N beers, splendid collection of bottled foreign beers, pub games; garden *(Andy and Jill Kassube, Jon Wainwright, LYM)*

☆ **Aysgarth**, N Yor [SE0088], *George & Dragon*: Attractive pub with pleasant atmosphere in large lounge divided into nooks and crannies; Websters real ale, good value bar food including interesting vegetarian dishes, seafood and Sun roast; friendly licensees, separate pool area *(N Hesketh, Jenny Cantle)*

Bardsey, W Yor [A58; SE3643], *Bingley Arms*: Popular old pub with fine food inc superb salmon pancakes in bar and restaurant, charming terraced garden *(Tony and Penny Burton)*

Barkisland, W Yor [SE0520], *Fleece*: Comfortable character moors-edge pub with good atmosphere, good choice of well kept real ales and bar food; CD juke box in small cellar wine bar, bar billiards in another room, piano restaurant — open till small hours, maybe with disco/bar; trad jazz Sun afternoon, maybe Tues spit-roasts *(Steve Mitcheson, Anne Collins, BB)*

Barnsley, S Yor [Sheffield Rd; start of A61, nr roundabout edge of centre; SE3406], *Manx Arms*: Pleasant, popular partly open-plan town-centre pub serving widest range of real ales we've found here, inc Bass, Stones, Tetleys, Timothy Taylors Landlord and guests; also farm ciders; lunchtime meals (not Sun) *(W P P Clarke, Michael Rooke)*; [nr Northern College, Stainborough — OS Sheet 110 map reference 325038], *Strafford Arms*: Attractive and tastefully furnished substantial stone-built pub in wooded area next to village cricket ground; well kept Courage Directors and John Smiths Bitter and Magnet, popular bar and restaurant meals, tables in pleasant area outside *(W P P Clarke)*

Bawtry, S Yor [Market Pl; SK6593], *Crown*: THF hotel with good restaurant; nice bar with usual good bar meals and very good puddings; well kept Tetleys and John Smiths on handpump, friendly staff, good bedrooms *(Andy and Jill Kassube)*

Beadlam, N Yor [A170 Helmsley—Scarborough; SE6585], *White Horse*: Old, rustic pub with beamed ceiling, welcoming fires in bar and lounge and homely licensees; Youngers No 3 and reasonably priced straightforward bar food inc sandwiches and hot dishes *(E R Thompson)*

☆ **Beck Hole**, N Yor [OS Sheet 94 map reference 823022; NZ8202], *Birch Hall*: Really unspoilt and unusual pub, in two halves separated by the village shop (run by the same young and friendly couple); keg beer and other drinks, sandwiches and hot pies served through a hole in the wall into small room with very simple furniture; lovely dog by bridge over river in beautiful village, in a steep valley near the steam railway and at the end of a delightful gentle walk (GWG159) on the old railway track to Goathland; ancient picture in glass frame on outside wall; up some steep steps at the side is a little garden with a nice view — lovely on a sunny afternoon; close to Thomason Fosse waterfall *(Paul Newberry, Ian Clayton,*

Hilary Thorpe, Roger Bellingham)

Beckwithshaw, N Yor [Church Row; SE2753], *Smiths Arms*: Pleasant Watneys village pub, largely geared towards food — especially in the carvery (booking recommended at weekends), but also bar food *(Andy and Jill Kassube, J E Rycroft)*

Berry Brow, W Yor [Robin Hood Hill; A616 S edge of Huddersfield; SE1314], *Golden Fleece*: Good bar food inc filled Yorkshire puddings and gammon with egg; Stones ales *(David Waterhouse)*

☆ **Biggin**, N Yor [SE5435], *Blacksmiths Arms*: Pleasant welcoming beamed pub with good value food inc superb puddings trolley; John Smiths ale, character landlord *(J C Proud, B Wilson)*

Bingley, W Yor [Otley Rd, High Eldwick; SE1240], *Dick Hudsons*: Not cheap, and food service may slow, but comfortable, with lovely moors views; good place to finish a walk *(Robert and Lesley Fawthrop, Reg Nelson, J E Rycroft)*

☆ **Birstwith**, N Yor [SE2459], *Station*: Welcoming atmosphere in very smartly modernised but cosy lounge of stone-built old railway hotel tucked away deep in a picturesque valley; good value bar lunches, well kept Tetleys, interesting china, friendly staff *(Andy and Jill Kassube)*

Bland Hill, N Yor [Norwood; B6451, 2 miles S of A59 W of Harrogate — OS Sheet 104 map reference 207538; SE2053], *Sun*: Old stone building, good range of ales, simple good value bar food; open all day; children welcome *(David Oakes)*

Bolsterstone, S Yor [off A616, prettiest route just N of Wharncliffe Side — OS Sheet 110 map reference 271968; SK2796], *Castle*: Attractive old stone-built local in small hilltop conservation-area village, almost 1,000 ft above sea level in spectacular surroundings by Ewden Valley and on edge of Peak Park; friendly and welcoming with plenty of atmosphere, good Stones Bitter on electric pump; prize-winning male voice choir rehearses Mon *(W P P Clarke)*

Borrowby, N Yor [A19 Middlesbrough—Thirsk; SE4389], *Wheatsheaf*: Simple, rustic free house in small village; well kept Tetleys, good sandwiches and cold bar food, small garden *(E J Cutting)*

Bradfield, S Yor [Bradfield Dale; just beyond Low Bradfield on Strines rd — OS Sheet 110 map reference 253919; SK2592], *Haychatter*: Attractive and welcoming small stone-built country pub in scenic countryside, kept unspoilt by long-serving landlady; mainly keg beers, but at least one real ale on handpump in summer — weekends only otherwise; closed Mon—Sat lunchtimes *(W P P Clarke)*

☆ **Bradford** [Barkerend Rd; up Church Bank from centre, on left few hundred yds past cathedral; SE1633], *Cock & Bottle*: Notable Victorian decor in well preserved small rooms, good value cheap lunchtime snacks, unusually well kept Tetleys real ales, live music Fri and Sat evenings; down-to-earth atmosphere, no frills *(LYM)*

☆ **Bradford** [Preston St (off B6145)], *Fighting Cock*: Good basic traditional pub with hard benches and bare floors, but pleasant atmosphere, lots of well kept real ales and farm ciders, some foreign beers, coal fires, legendary door-step sandwiches and good pies (can phone order in to be ready when you arrive), interesting customers (J D Shaw, Barbara Wensworth, Reg Nelson)

☆ Bradford [Kirkgate/Ivegate], *Rams Revenge*: Good atmosphere in relaxed and unpretentious pub formed from several different buildings on site of former city gate; old pews, wooden floor, seats in upper gallery, fascinating old clock from the former gate house in back room, fine old Bradford prints; well kept Clarks, Theakstons and guests such as Moorhouses Pendle Witches Brew on handpump, lunchtime bar food, folk music (Mr and Mrs P A Jones, Reg Nelson)

Bradford [Heaton Rd], *Fountain*: Very popular pub, good landlord, choice of well kept beers and good food from fine sandwiches to haddock (Mr and Mrs J E Rycroft); [Thornton Rd], *Great Northern*: Thwaites house with one large room and central bar, upstairs restaurant with wide choice of good value dishes (Tim Baxter); [Easby Rd, nr Univ], *McCrorys*: Popular cellar bar with local blues and folk bands; rather reminiscent of the late 1950s (Reg Nelson); [Frizinghall], *Old Barn*: Tasteful old barn-style pub with friendly atmosphere and occasional free sandwiches (Reg Nelson); [589 Thornton Rd (B6145)], *Red Lion*: Comfortable lounge, good bar lunches inc wide choice of sandwiches, home-made pies and casseroles, well kept Sam Smiths OB; very popular lunchtime with office workers (Andy and Jill Kassube); [28 Kirkgate], *Shoulder of Mutton*: Cosy town-centre pub specialising in cheap fresh food (not Sun), such as corned beef or savoury sausage flan, curries, Old Brewery casserole, big salads, delicious steak and kidney pies; well kept and well priced Sam Smiths, tables outside (Andy and Jill Kassube); [Hallings], *Victoria*: Large THF hotel — worth knowing it has well kept Timothy Taylors on handpump in the bar; good food inc evening carvery, comfortable bedrooms, enormous breakfasts (Mr and Mrs P A Jones)

Bradshaw, W Yor [SE0614], *Rose & Crown*: Attractive old stone pub with good views across moors and hills; well kept Tetleys, good bar food inc gigantic Sun lunch — best to book (Chris Draper)

Bramham, W Yor [The Square; just off A1 2 miles N of A64; SE4243], *Red Lion*: Former Gt North Rd coaching inn, comfortable, warm and well kept, with tasty food (Brian and Genie Krakowska-Smart)

☆ Bramhope, W Yor [SE2543], *Fox & Hounds*: Popular two-bar Tetleys pub with well kept Mild and Bitter, good hot and cold food, efficient landlord; children welcome, open all day, big car park (John C Gould, J E Rycroft)

Bramhope, *Bramhope Post House*: Big hotel in 16-acre rustic garden with *Wuthering Heights* overtones; well kept Websters Yorkshire in big bar, decent food; comfortable bedrooms (John C Gould)

Brompton on Swale, N Yor [SE2299], *Crown*: Spotless pub doing well under new Italian landlord and his wife, both gentle and courteous; he makes his own pasta dishes — tasty lasagne, good home-made

mushroom soup (Mrs A J P Woodhouse)

Burley in Wharfedale, W Yor [Main St; SE1646], *White Horse*: Tiny traditional Yorkshire local, full of character — and people; lots of local memorabilia, real fire, well kept Tetleys and Mild on handpump; no food (Andy and Jill Kassube)

Burniston, N Yor [A171 N of Scarborough; TA0193], *Oak Wheel*: Wide choice of well priced good bar food, stone walls, roaring fires and polite, efficient staff — very cosy; separate restaurant (Mark Castle)

☆ Burnlee, W Yor [Liphill Bank Rd; just off A635 Holmfirth—Manchester — OS Sheet 110 map reference 131078; SE1307], *Farmers Arms*: Classic stone-built pub on narrow back rd reminiscent of *Last of the Summer Wine*; attractive, quite small and popular; good choice of real ales inc Timothy Taylors Landlord, cheap lunchtime and evening bar food inc huge Yorkshire puddings; children welcome (W P P Clarke, Michael Rooke)

Burnt Yates, N Yor [SE2561], *Bay Horse*: Pleasant spot and good if not cheap bar food; bedrooms in motel extension (Peter Race)

☆ Calder Grove, W Yor [just off M1 junction 39; A636 signposted Denby Dale, then first right into Broadley Cut Rd; SE3116], *Navigation*: Well kept Tetleys and simple food in profusely decorated canalside pub with tables outside — very attractively placed for a pub so close to the motorway, though piped music can be loud (Paul Newberry, LYM)

Carlton, N Yor [the one at the foot of the Cleveland Hills — OS Sheet 93 map reference 509044; NZ5104], *Blackwell Ox*: Atmosphere relaxed and friendly in low-beamed lounge overlooking quiet Georgian village street (Denzil T Taylor)

Carlton, N Yor [Wensleydale; SE0684], *Foresters Arms*: Fascinating moorland pub in delightful spot with good, friendly atmosphere, well kept Theakstons and good range of home-made bar food (Anthony Fernau)

Carlton Husthwaite, N Yor [SE5077], *Carlton*: Good cheerful efficient service in friendly village pub with modernised decor, well kept Youngers on handpump, good varied food (even Sun evening) (G C and M D Dickinson)

Carperby, N Yor [SE0189], *Wheatsheaf*: Good atmosphere, well kept handpumped beer, friendly locals, bar food including good sandwiches (KC)

Castleton, N Yor [NZ6908], *Moorlands*: Pleasant split-level hotel bar, wide choice of good bar food at reasonable prices inc Fri evening steak specials and Sun lunch; friendly licensees; bedrooms good value (Horace Hipkiss)

☆ Chapel le Dale, N Yor [SD7477], *Old Hill*: Promising new licensees gently smartening up basic moorland pub, popular with walkers and climbers; big open fire in cosy back parlour, stone floors, old woodwork and partitions with waggon wheels, well kept Tetleys and Theakstons on handpump, wide choice of bar food; juke box can be obtrusive; open all day at least in summer; children welcome; bedrooms clean, cheery but very simple, with good sturdy breakfasts

(Comus Elliott, HKD, David Warrellow, LYM)

Cleckheaton, W Yor [Highmoor Lane; nr M62 junction 26; SE1825], *Old Pack Horse*: Nice busy local, with quiz and fun nights *(Ian Robinson)*

Clifton, W Yor [SE1623], *Old Corn Mill*: Renovated corn mill with attractive smart furnishings; Tetleys beer, reasonable bar snacks; huge car parks *(H K Dyson)*

Cloughton, N Yor [Whitby Rd — OS Sheet 101 map reference 011955; TA0195], *Falcon*: Stone-built pub on edge of Staintondale moor; big open-plan bar with welcoming real fire in winter, good pub food such as fresh crab, steak and kidney pie, well kept Camerons Strongarm and Tetleys *(Andy and Jill Kassube)*

☆ **Cloughton Newlands**, N Yor [TA0196], *Bryherstones*: Very pleasant position and atmosphere, good food and well kept Youngers *(Prof S Barnett, Andy and Jill Kassube)*

Coneysthorpe, N Yor [SE7171], *Tiger*: Fresh, sparkling pub with nice atmosphere, friendly service and wholesome simple food *(Syd and Wyn Donald)*

☆ **Constable Burton**, N Yor [SE1791], *Wyvill Arms*: Comfortably converted and attractively decorated farmhouse with elaborate stone fireplace and fine plaster ceiling in inner room; good value bar food, well kept Theakstons, obliging service *(LYM)*

☆ **Cridling Stubbs**, N Yor [between junctions 33 and 34 of M62 — easy detour; SE5221], *Ancient Shepherd*: Quiet and comfortable refuge from M62/A1/A19, carefully soothing decor, well kept real ales such as Marstons Pedigree and Whitbreads Castle Eden and Trophy on handpump, popular bar food (not Sat lunchtime, nor Sun or Mon), polite efficient service, restaurant; children in eating areas *(T Nott, Bob Smith, Dr James Haworth, LYM)*

Dalton, N Yor [NZ1108], *Travellers Rest*: Old, rustic pub in quiet hamlet; pleasant, warm atmosphere, good range of bar food, friendly service *(Mr and Mrs Fraser)*

Dewsbury, W Yor [Combs Hill, Thornhill; by B6117 S; SE2419], *Alma*: Well run pleasant pub, warm and friendly, with weekday bar lunches and well kept Courage Directors and John Smiths on handpump *(Andy and Jill Kassube)*

Doncaster, S Yor [St Sepulchre Gate W/Cleveland St; SE5703], *Corner Pin*: Cosy, pleasant little pub with John Smiths ales *(J A Edwards)*; [33 Hallgate, nr Odeon], *Hallcross*: Large, tastefully furnished town-centre pub with own microbrewery behind, producing Stocks Best, Select and Old Horizontal on handpump; extensive lunchtime menu *(W P P Clarke)*; [Frenchgate, on edge of central pedestrian precinct], *White Swan*: Front room so far below counter level that you need a high reach for your well kept Wards Sheffield Best; back lounge, bustling local atmosphere, good value bar snacks *(J A Edwards, LYM)*

Drighlington, W Yor [Whitehall Rd (A58 Leeds—Halifax); SE2229], *Valley*: Nice little whitewashed pub with attractive outside drinking area, nr Cockersdale country park; simple reasonably priced food, Sam Smiths on handpump *(Andy and*

Jill Kassube)

☆ **Dunford Bridge**, S Yor [Windle Edge Lane; off A628 — OS Sheet 110 map reference 158023; SE1502], *Stanhope Arms*: Large ex-shooting lodge hotel/pub, attractively isolated on moors at east end of old Woodhead railway tunnel, now being developed as long-distance Peak Park walking/riding/cycling trail; good food inc Thai dishes and well filled rolls lunchtime and evening, well kept John Smiths Bitter and Magnet, friendly atmosphere, small central bar serving several rooms inc a tiny snug; pleasant garden; bedrooms *(W P P Clarke, A G Roby)*

East Keswick, N Yor [Main St; SE3644], *Duke of Wellington*: Big ornate Victorian dining room (no booking) with good value straightforward meals and snacks, generously served (not Mon) *(Tony and Penny Burton, Mr and Mrs M Cockram)*

☆ **East Marton**, N Yor [A59 Gisburn—Skipton; SD9051], *Cross Keys*: Interesting and comfortable old-fashioned furnishings in nicely decorated pub with well kept Watneys-related beers, friendly helpful staff, open fires, children's area (where the food counter is); tables outside, handy for the Leeds & Liverpool Canal *(Brian Jones, Simon Bates, LYM)*

☆ **East Witton**, N Yor [out towards Middleham; SE1586], *Cover Bridge Inn*: Homely and unspoilt old rural pub with massive helpings of good food, well kept Theakstons and friendly welcome *(Nick Dowson, Alison Hayward, Anthony Fernau, David Gaunt, Syd and Wyn Donald)*

East Witton [A6108 Leyburn—Masham], *Blue Lion*: We don't yet know what is to happen to this pub, until now a popular main entry, kept as a quite remarkably unspoilt reminder of the past by Mrs Bessie Fletcher until she died in 1989 — the third generation of her family to run the pub, spanning between them 133 years; it seems likely to be updated *(News please)*

Egton, N Yor [NZ8106], *Horseshoe*: Warm welcome and good open fire in low-beamed moorland village pub popular for fried food and grills *(C Folkers, A Powell, LYM)*; *Wheatsheaf*: Popular village local catering for shooting parties; well kept McEwans, pretty bedrooms *(Eileen Broadbent)*

☆ **Embsay**, N Yor [Elm Tree Sq; SE0053], *Elm Tree*: Open-plan beamed village pub with brasses, old-fashioned prints and log-effect gas fire; friendly staff, good bar food inc giant Yorkshire puddings with various fillings, locals' area with pool table, darts, fruit machine, dominoes and TV; well kept Whitbreads ales, juke box *(Mr and Mrs J E Rycroft)*

☆ **Escrick**, N Yor [SE6343], *Black Bull*: Good comfortable atmosphere, cheerful fire, decent food such as beef casserole, Yorkshire pudding and scampi; can get quite full *(Roger A Bellingham)*

☆ **Fadmoor**, N Yor [SE6789], *Plough*: Friendly landlord in traditionally furnished pub overlooking quiet village green, lunchtime bar food (when it can be very quiet), restaurant meals inc Sun lunch; Watneys-related real ales; comfortable bedrooms *(LYM)*

☆ **Farnley Tyas**, W Yor [OS Sheet 110 map

reference 165128; SE1612], *Golden Cock*:
Dining pub with coloured glass skylights in
false ceiling, painted glass butterflies over
wall lights, marble-look bar and surround,
pink polka-dot plush bar stools and tub
chairs around circular varnished tables with
vases of fresh flowers, toning carpet and
window drapes, green plants on window
ledges, and smart waitresses; has been
popular for good thoughtful food in bar and
restaurant served by smart waitresses, well
kept Bass and Bass Light, and decent wines,
but up for sale summer 1990 *(Frank
Cummins, Paul Wreglesworth, ILP; news
please)*

Fishlake, S Yor [nr M18 junction 6; A614
N, then keep left — OS Sheet 111 map
reference 653132; SE6513], *Old Anchor*:
Smart wall coverings, banquettes and
captain's chairs in open-plan bar with steps
between two main areas, darts and billiards
in new extension; well presented inexpensive
standard food inc children's menu, Wards
and John Smiths from central servery *(T
Nott)*

☆ **Follifoot**, N Yor [OS Sheet 104 map
reference 343524; SE3452], *Lascelles Arms*:
Welcoming pub with many cosy nooks and
blazing fires; generous helpings of simple,
tasty and inexpensive bar food *(Syd and Wyn
Donald)*

☆ **Follifoot**, *Radcliffe Arms*: Well run place
with attractive bar, friendly pleasant
atmosphere and short choice of good food,
good value *(Syd and Wyn Donald, J E
Rycroft)*

Fulneck, W Yor [Bankhouse Lane; SE2132],
Bankhouse: Charmingly decorated with
brass fittings and comfortable chairs; bar
food and good restaurant (book Sats) *(Andy
and Jill Kassube)*

☆ **Galphay**, N Yor [SE2573], *Galphay Inn*:
Good atmosphere and log fire in dining pub
with beautifully cooked food, efficient
welcoming staff, two bars; decent house
wine, Czech beer *(H Bramwell)*

Ganton, N Yor [A64
Malton—Scarborough; SE9977],
Greyhound: Well placed for the
championship golf course; specialises in
good reasonably priced home-cooked food
inc fresh fish, steaks and vegetarian dishes,
fresh vegetables *(Andy and Jill Kassube)*

Gargrave, N Yor [A65 W of village;
SD9354], *Anchor*: Extensive canalside art
deco Chef & Brewer, worth knowing as a
useful family pub with a superb children's
play area and waterside tables outside; usual
bar food served all day at least in summer,
pleasant competent service, Marstons
Pedigree and Whitbreads-related real ales,
prominent piped music; economically run
bedrooms in modern wing *(Denzil T Taylor,
Mr and Mrs Peter Nelson, GA, PA, LYM)*;
Old Swan: Friendly pub with good cheap
and well presented food; lively Sat night
entertainment, with a wealth of local talent
and a guitarist/accordionist with tremendous
stamina *(Bob and Joan Rosier)*

☆ **Gayles**, N Yor [NZ1207], *Bay Horse*: Much
done-up open-plan bar in friendly farm pub
with small open fires, well kept McEwans
80/-, Newcastle Exhibition and Youngers
Scotch on handpump, darts, good value
straightforward food inc good home-cooked

ham and Sun lunch; closed Weds; children
welcome *(J A Snell, BB)*

Giggleswick, N Yor [SD8164], *Black Horse*:
Quaint 17th-century village pub crammed
between churchyard and row of cottages,
straightforward inside, with friendly
atmosphere, well kept Timothy Taylors,
good value food *(Carol and Philip Seddon,
TRA, MA)*; [Brackenber Lane, just off A65
opp stn], *Craven Arms*: Quite large, with
assorted memorabilia, good bar snacks from
hot beef rolls to stew, well kept Tetleys and
Websters Yorkshire on handpump *(Andy
and Jill Kassube)*

Gilling East, N Yor [B1363; SE6177],
Fairfax Arms: Well furnished main bar in
country inn looking up to castle; pleasant
tables out by stream, food lunchtime and
evening, good filled French sticks, well kept
Tetleys *(Andy and Jill Kassube)*

Glaisdale, N Yor [NZ7705], *Anglers Rest*:
Small, friendly pub with well kept
Theakstons, bar food, no music *(Genie and
Brian Smart)*

☆ **Goathland**, N Yor [opp church; NZ8301],
Mallyan Spout: Very comfortable traditional
bar with well kept Malton Bitter, wide
choice of above-average food — much of it
varying daily and inc huge Yorkshire
puddings with interesting fillings; popular
restaurant; nr GWG159; splendid view from
big garden behind; children allowed away
from bar; bedrooms *(Brian and Anna
Marsden, Dr and Mrs Tony Clarke)*

Gomersal, W Yor [Little Gomersal;
SE2026], *Wheatsheaf*: Nice pub tucked
away in corner of village; food attractively
priced *(Ian W Robinson)*

Grange Moor, W Yor [A6142
Huddersfield—Wakefield; SE2216], *Kaye
Arms*: Wide range of bar food from
interesting soups, good beef sandwiches or
ploughman's with home-made chutney to
steaks; lots of whiskies *(D A Wilcock, Miss C
M Davidson)*

Grantley, N Yor [off B6265 W of Ripon;
SE2369], *Grantley Arms*: Good pub food in
very generous helpings; friendly *(PJP)*

☆ **Grassington**, N Yor [Garrs Lane; SE0064],
Black Horse: Good value traditional
home-cooked bar food and well kept Tetleys
and Theakstons Bitter and Old Peculier in
busy but comfortable open-plan modern bar
with darts in separate back room, open fires,
friendly staff, sheltered terrace, small but
attractive restaurant; bedrooms good value,
looking over stone-slab rooftops to the
moors, with maybe a glimpse of the cobbled
square; nr start GWG150 *(Mrs D Neilson,
Andrew Triggs, Tim and Lynne Crawford, H K
Dyson, Dick Brown, BB)*

☆ **Grassington**, N Yor [The Square; SE0064],
Devonshire: Pleasant and popular inn with
interesting big pictures, attractive
ornaments, open fires, good window seats
overlooking attractive sloping village
square; Youngers Scotch and No 3 on
handpump, good range of food in separate
eating area and well furnished dining room,
friendly staff and quick service; nr start
GWG150; bedrooms reasonable, good
breakfasts *(Mrs D Neilson, Andrew Triggs,
George Hunt, H K Dyson, LYM)*

☆ **Great Ayton**, N Yor [High Green; off A173
— follow village signs; NZ5611], *Royal*

Oak: Bustling old unpretentious bar with huge inglenook, beam-and-plank ceiling, aged partly panelled stone walls, traditional furnishings inc antique settles, pleasant views of elegant village green from bay windows; tables in longer room for wide range of generously served food from sandwiches to steaks, Theakstons XB and Youngers No 3 on handpump; service generally friendly; children in eating areas; bedrooms *(Alan and Ruth Woodhouse, GB, LYM)*

☆ **Great Broughton**, N Yor [High St; NZ5405], *Wainstones*: Well kept Bass and Stones on handpump and good home-made bar food inc Sun lunches in smartish bar; efficient service, restaurant; bedrooms *(Roger A Bellingham)*

☆ **Great Ouseburn**, N Yor [SE4562], *Crown*: Large white building with steep steps to main door; heavy-beamed horseshoe-shaped bar with four spacious rooms, particularly friendly staff, huge helpings of good value freshly cooked straightforward food, real ales inc Timothy Taylors Landlord, open fire; big garden *(Jane and Niall, Tim and Sue Halstead)*

Greenhow Hill, N Yor [B6265 Pateley Bridge—Grassington; SE1164], *Miners Arms*: Good choice of generously served bar food at reasonable prices; note that lunchtime serving may stop short of 2; bedrooms *(Margaret White)*

☆ **Grenoside**, S Yor [Skew Hill Lane; 3 miles from M1 junction 35 — OS Sheet 110 map reference 328935; SK3394], *Cow & Calf*: Good high settles in the several rooms of this neatly converted farmhouse, friendly and entertaining landlord, attractively priced home-cooked weekday bar food, well kept Sam Smiths on electric pump; pleasant out in the walled yard, with animals wandering around outside, and splendid views of Sheffield; children in family area, with children's shop in farmyard; only a shortage of reports keeps this out of the main entries *(Paul Newberry, LYM)*

☆ **Grewelthorpe**, N Yor [SE2376], *Hackfall*: Simple L-shaped lounge with brocaded mate's chairs around brown tables, Theakstons Best and XB on handpump, fruit machine, piped pop music, decent bar food; pool in public bar, couple of tables in small back garden; bedrooms warm and cosy *(P Battams, H Bramwell, R S and E M Rayden, BB)*

☆ **Gristhorpe**, N Yor [off A165 Filey—Scarborough; TA0982], *Bull*: Spacious open-plan low-beamed bar with cushioned banquettes, lots of sporting pictures and village scenes; good value bar food inc lunchtime cold buffet; games area; well kept Youngers Scotch and No 3 *(S Barnett, LYM)*

Guiseley, W Yor [Town St; SE1942], *Drop*: Refurbished pub with good really cheap food inc simple weekday lunches, Sat specials, Sun carvery, Tetleys beer *(Andy and Jill Kassube)*

☆ **Gunnerside**, N Yor [SD9598], *Kings Head*: Classic Dales pub with seats out by pretty bridge, reasonable food such as cheese and salami ploughman's, savoury mushrooms, delicious ratatouille lasagne, bacon chops; popular with locals *(KC, Mrs R Heaton)*

Haigh, S Yor [M1 junction 38; SE2912], *Old Post Office*: Former post office with pleasant bars upstairs and down, video games in family room; well kept Tetleys and Whitbreads Castle Eden, good bar food inc giant Yorkshire puddings and roast beef *(Ian Baillie)*

☆ **Halifax**, W Yor [Paris Gates, Boys Lane — OS Sheet 104 map reference 097241; SE0924], *Shears*: Superbly tucked away down narrow cobbled alleys, shut in by towering mills and the bubbling Hebble Brook; very dark inside, with decor reflecting sporting links with local teams, also collection of pump clips and foreign bottles; well kept Taylors, Youngers and unusual guest beers *(Michael Rooke)*

Halifax [Horsfall St], *Big 6*: Simple but welcoming Victorian mid-terrace pub with memorabilia and interesting bottle collection — a trip into the past; lunchtime snacks, well kept Tetleys and Mild *(Andy and Jill Kassube)*; [Huddersfield Rd (A629)], *Jenny Dees*: Clean, spacious and pleasant purpose-built roadside pub with emphasis on food, overlooking former terminus of Halifax Canal; popular, especially at lunchtime, for straightforward bar food from sandwiches up, well kept Bass and Youngers *(Andy and Jill Kassube)*; [Shibden Fold], *Shibden Mill*: Cottagey riverside pub dating back to 17th century, smart inside with good bar lunches such as ploughman's and scampi, popular restaurant, Bass and Tetleys Gold on handpump; deep in the countryside, a picture when floodlit *(Andy and Jill Kassube)*; [12 Old Market], *Union Cross*: Perhaps the town's oldest pub, serving food nearly all day from noon in comfortable and spacious lounge — favourites are Yorkshire puddings; well kept Websters Choice and other Watneys beers *(Andy and Jill Kassube)*

Hardrow, N Yor [SD8791], *Green Dragon*: Worth knowing for its right of access to Britain's highest single-drop waterfall; spacious bar with fruit machines, bar billiards and small juke box; reasonable range of bar snacks; coal fire in old iron range; tourist prices; on GWG147; bedrooms, self-catering units *(LYM)*

Harmby, N Yor [A684 about 1 1/2 m E of Leyburn; SE1389], *Pheasant*: Cheery local with good beer *(Jenny Cantle)*

☆ **Harrogate**, N Yor [1 Crescent Rd; SE3155], *Hales*: Popular and atmospheric unspoilt 18th-century town local close to pump rooms, with gas lighting, comfortable seats, well kept Bass and Stones, simple good value lunchtime bar food; entertaining quiz nights Tues *(John Hayward, Andy and Jill Kassube, J E Rycroft, G T Jones)*

Harrogate [Bilton Lane], *Gardeners Arms*: Small house converted into good pub in lovely peceful setting — totally unspoilt with tiny bar and three small panelled rooms, tables in spacious garden; well kept Sam Smiths (they don't seem to sell the beer from Franklins microbrewery, in the yard) *(Andy and Jill Kassube)*; [Montpellier Terr], *Montpellier Arms*: Local with well kept John Smiths on handpump and good giant Yorkshire puddings with liver and onion gravy, freshly prepared and good value; pleasant, efficient service *(David and Valerie*

Hooley); [31 Tower St], *Tap & Spile:* Basic three-room traditionally furnished pub with wooden floors, lunchtime food such as sandwiches and home-made pies; well kept Camerons and three or four frequently changing beers *(Andy and Jill Kassube);* [6 Cold Bath Rd, across green from main part of town], *William & Victoria:* Reliably good food in interestingly laid out wine bar down stone steps in Victorian house — particularly recommend soups, lamb with rosemary, seafood bake, salmon in cucumber sauce and the puddings; huge wine list with some vintages; great value and atmosphere *(Mrs V Middlebrook)*

☆ **Hartoft End,** N Yor [SE7593], *Blacksmiths Arms:* Very pleasant spaciously extended modernised bars and lounges in attractive surroundings at the foot of Rosedale; nicely furnished, good service, imaginative food — light lunch of soup, sandwiches and an apple, celery and nut crunch; well kept Tetleys on handpump, log fires; bedrooms *(Barbara and Ken Turner)*

☆ **Hartshead,** W Yor [15 Hartshead Lane; not very far from M62 junction 25; SE1822], *Grey Ox:* A bit isolated in winter, but comfortable, with huge helpings of well cooked food, especially giant Yorkshire pudding with beef and vegetables and hefty steaks; well kept Watneys-related real ales, cosy armchairs in front of fire, garden with good views and children's play area *(Alistair Wood, Andy and Jill Kassube)*

Hawes, N Yor [Main St; SD8789], *Board:* One of the two best pubs here, welcoming, with well kept Marstons Pedigree on handpump, reasonably priced lunchtime and evening food; nr start GWG147 *(Len Beattie, P Corris, KC, Mr and Mrs M D Jones);* [High St], *Crown:* The other main contender here: pleasant and friendly, with beams, cottage furniture, hunting prints, brassware, stuffed pheasant, attractive, more rustic tap room with bar billiards, more prints and stuffed birds; well kept Theakstons, open fires, courteous landlord, quickly served good value lunchtime bar food inc big wholemeal bap, seats out on front cobbled forecourt; children away from bar *(John Fazakerley, C and L H Lever, Peter Race, Gwen and Peter Andrews, Len Beattie); White Hart:* Pleasant bar with John Smiths Magnet on handpump, generously served straightforward bar food, open fire and friendly efficient bar staff; plainly furnished dining room; bedrooms *(John Fazakerley, Mr and Mrs C R Douglas, Anne Morris)*

☆ **Haworth,** W Yor [Main St; SE0337], *Fleece:* Friendly flagstoned village pub with well kept Timothy Taylors beers and good wholesome lunchtime food; real fires, great 'alternative comedy' Brontë room, piped disco/pop music *(Charles Hall, Mrs M J Fraser)*

Haworth [Main St], *Black Bull:* Recently smartly refurbished as Brewers Fayre family pub, with wide choice of standard food (the specials are the things to go for, more unusual, with good vegetarian dishes), friendly staff and Whitbreads Castle Eden and Trophy; used to be Branwell Brontë's main drinking place, and the Museum bookshop opposite used to be the druggist where he got his opium; bedrooms good

(Mrs M J Fraser, David and Christine Foulkes); Old Hall: Friendly 16th-century village pub full of atmosphere, with well kept Bass, Stones and Tetleys; bar meals and restaurant good; piped music inoffensive *(Charles Hall);* [West Lane], *Old White Lion:* Another Brontë-country inn with good, reasonably priced restaurant (vegetarian dishes); comfortable bedrooms *(Sandra Kempson);* [well out on Bingley Rd, off A628 in Cross Roads, up Lees Moor — OS Sheet 104 map reference 054381], *Quarry House:* Converted former farmhouse on the open hills high above Bingley, good bar food inc notable warm and filling soups, good steak sandwiches and pies, good home-made puddings, also chilli, moussaka and so forth, and full restaurant menu; well kept Bass on handpump, cricket ground next door *(Andy and Jill Kassube)*

Hebden, N Yor [SE0263], *Clarendon:* Well kept Timothy Taylors and Tetleys, good food — especially generous steaks; friendly service, laconic in typically Yorkshire way; bedrooms *(J D Maplethorpe)*

Hebden Bridge, W Yor [Keighley Rd; A6033, on right towards Keighley; SD9927], *Nutclough House:* Interesting range of beers inc Robinwood Old Fart — very warming after cold evening's walk from station; very cosy, with attractive food; bedrooms *(Maureen and Steve Collin)*

☆ **Helmsley,** N Yor [Market Pl; SE6184], *Black Swan:* Striking Georgian house and adjoining Tudor rectory included primarily as a place to stay; though the small saloon bar on the corner is quite ordinary, the beamed and panelled hotel bar (sharing the same servery, and the well kept real ale) has attractive carved oak settles and Windsor armchairs, and opens into cosy and comfortable lounges with a good deal of character; charming sheltered garden; bedrooms particularly well equipped and comfortable, but expensive *(HKD, BB)*

☆ **Helmsley** [Market Sq], *Crown:* Good friendly atmosphere in simply but pleasantly furnished beamed front bar rambling back to bigger central dining bar with good value lunchtime snacks and home-made scones and biscuits for afternoon teas; friendly and efficient service, well kept beer, roaring fires, tables in sheltered garden behind with covered conservatory area; bedrooms nice *(Sidney and Erna Wells, JM, PM, H K Dyson, BB)*

☆ **Helmsley** [B1257], *Feversham Arms:* Two bars in very pleasant, efficient and welcoming hotel with interesting bar meals concentrating on seafood — very good shellfish; real ale *(Walter and Susan Rinaldi-Butcher, SVB)*

High Green, S Yor [Packhorse La; SK3397], *Pickwick:* Good, honest home cooking at sensible prices *(Mrs E Sugden)*

High Hoyland, S Yor [OS Sheet 110 map reference 273101; SE2710], *Cherry Tree:* Very attractive stone-built village pub; lovely views of Cannon Hall Country Park; bar snacks, well kept John Smiths on handpump *(W P P Clarke)*

Hinderwell, N Yor [NZ7917], *Badger Hounds:* Recently and impressively renovated village local, cheerful atmosphere, well kept Tetleys; quiz night Tues *(R A*

Caldwell)

Holme, W Yor [SE1006], *Fleece*: Homely and friendly with warm welcome for walkers; log fires, well kept Tetleys, good food and service *(Peter Mayo)*

Holmfirth, W Yor [SD1508], *Rose & Crown*: Basic drinkers' pub (more commonly known as 'the Nook') with low bar and flagstone floors, good range of real ales and riverside garden *(Steve Mitcheson, Anne Collins, Michael Rooke)*; [Hinchliffe Mill — A6024, a mile SW], *Shepherds Rest*: Stone village pub with single modestly sized bar, tastefully yet comfortably furnished; well kept Thwaites Mild and Bitter on handpump, lunchtime bar food (not Mon or Tues), pie and mushy peas Fri evening *(W P P Clarke)*

Holywell Green, W Yor [SE0820], *Duke of York*: Charming old-fashioned atmosphere, delicious Yorkshire pudding; outside terrace has a lovely Dales view *(Mrs Marjorie Donchey — whose great-grandfather was once licensee here)*

☆ **Honley**, W Yor [SE1312], *Coach & Horses*: Very creative imaginative bar food, good value from sandwiches and ploughman's up, with friendly service *(John and Jane Horn, Ben Wimpenny)*

Hood Green, S Yor [Stainborough; SE3103], *Stafford Arms*: Large pub dominated by superb old cooking range; well kept John Smiths, good bar food, ample seating on lawn, pub backs on to pretty cricket pitch *(Paul Newberry, Michael Rooke)*

Horsforth, W Yor [Ring Rd; SE2438], *Woodside*: Recently refurbished pub on roundabout; separate big steak restaurant on different levels, with tables partly partitioned off; good generous food, good children's menu *(Tim Baxter)*

☆ **Hovingham**, N Yor [SE6775], *Worsley Arms*: Good value bar food inc superb ploughman's in comfortable lounge with settees and low tables, Tetleys and Theakstons on handpump in neat, plain but well kept locals' back bar with darts and lots of Yorkshire cricketer photographs, especially of 1930s and 40s; nice tables out by stream; pleasant bedrooms, swifts and house-martins nesting under the eaves — a nice place to stay *(S V Bishop, Paul McPherson, BB)*

Hovingham, *Malt Shovel*: Doing well under engaging new licensees, with ambitious food *(Paul McPherson)*

Huddersfield, W Yor [Chapel Hill; SE1416], *Rat & Ratchet*: Fairly rough-and-ready, worth knowing for its wide range of guest beers *(Jon Wainwright)*; [Queensgate], *Yates Wine Lodge*: Large open-plan fairly recently opened new conversion, high ceilings, full of young people at weekends; decent beers, good value wines and ports *(Ben Wimpenny)*

☆ **Hunton**, N Yor [SE1992], *Countrymans*: Attractively and tastefully refurbished; Turkey carpet, stripped stone, open fire with brass and copper, usual furnishings, no-smoking areas, friendly atmosphere, well kept John Smiths, Theakstons and Youngers No 3, substantial straightforward food, good welcoming service — handy for the Dales; music Suns; well equipped bedrooms *(Mr and Mrs D C Leaman, Mr and Mrs C G Crowther, G W H Kerby)*

☆ **Hunton**, [Leyburn Rd], *New Inn*: Unusual combination of typical welcoming local atmosphere with good food inc wide range of vegetarian and German dishes as well as usual choice; decent wines *(Gill and Neil Patrick)*

Hutton le Hole, N Yor [SE7090], *Crown*: Well placed Rye Dale country pub with well kept Camerons, good value well presented bar food inc evening steaks, picturesque setting *(Tim and Lynne Crawford)*

☆ **Ilkley**, W Yor [Stockel Rd; off Leeds—Skipton rd; SE1147], *Ilkley Moor*: Attractively refurbished, with flagstones, open fires and so forth; popular even early in the evening, with well kept Timothy Taylors and Tetleys; good summner bar food inc giant lunchtime Yorkshire puddings *(Pamela and Merlyn Horswell, J A Harrison)*

☆ **Ingbirchworth**, S Yor [Welthorne Lane; off A629 Shepley—Penistone; SE2205], *Fountain*: Neatly kept Wayfarer Inn, with red plush banquettes in spacious Turkey-carpeted lounge, comfortable family room, quite snug front bar, open fires; consistently good bar food from snacks such as pâté or lasagne to big helpings of gammon and egg or steaks, with several daily specials and children's helpings; well kept Tetleys and Mild on handpump, well reproduced pop music, pleasant staff, tables outside with play area *(W P P Clarke, Mr and Mrs R Shaw, Michael Rooke, BB)*

Ingleby Cross, N Yor [NZ4501], *Blue Bell*: Cosy and friendly country local with well kept beer and interesting bar food; simple bedrooms in converted barn, good facilities *(Dr and Mrs R J Ashleigh)*

Jackson Bridge, W Yor [Scholes Rd; SE1607], *White Horse*: Character low-ceilinged small-roomed pub with pool room looking out on to charming waterfall and ducks behind, well kept Bass, basic home-cooked bar food till about 1.30 *(Steve Mitcheson, Anne Collins, P A Crossland, D A Cawley)*

☆ **Keighley**, W Yor [Church Green, North St; SE0641], *Grinning Rat*: Busy real ale pub with bare wooden/flagstoned tap room popular with young people and hikers, and basic lounge; extensive range of ales such as Moorhouses Pendle Witches Brew, Timothy Taylors Landlord, Theakstons XB and Old Peculier, strong farm ciders and interesting bottled beers; good cheap pizzas, CD juke box *(Charles Hall, Mel and Phil Lloyd)*

☆ **Kettlewell**, N Yor [SD9772], *Bluebell*: Strong local flavour and lively atmosphere in busy, unpretentious knocked-through bar; friendly helpful staff, decent bar food from home-cooked ham rolls up, Theakstons Best and Old Peculier, Youngers Scotch and No 3, unusually fairly priced soft drinks, pool room, children's room, tables on good-sized back terrace; bedrooms of typical old-fashioned-pub standard; nr start GWG151 *(Peter and Rose Flower, Jon Wainwright, David Oakes, Joan and John Calvert, LYM)*

☆ **Kettlewell**, *Racehorses*: Relatively sedate open-plan hotel bar, consistently comfortable and well furnished, well kept Theakstons and other real ales, decent sandwiches, other straightforward bar food; nr start GWG151; bedrooms *(Jon*

Wainwright, Joan and John Calvert, Denzil Taylor, S V Bishop, Tony and Penny Burton, BB)

Kettlewell, *Kings Head*: Lively and cheerful local away from the tourist centre, cheap food, well kept Tetleys and Timothy Taylors; pool room, bedrooms *(Dick Brown, BB)*

☆ **Kilnsey**, N Yor [Kilnsey Crag; SD9767], *Tennant Arms*: Tasteful interconnecting rooms with beams, flagstones (sensible for hikers and farmers), open fires (one fireplace made from an ornate carved four-poster), decorated with kukris and other weapons, maps and fish; well kept Tetleys and Theakstons Best and Old Peculier, good value bar food (ploughman's, haddock, chicken, trout, beef and venison pie and children's dishes all recommended), piped music, friendly service and atmosphere; views over spectacular Kilnsey Crag from restaurant, nice spot by River Wharfe; on GWG150; comfortable bedrooms all with private bathrooms *(Peter and Rose Flower, Len Beattie, R F Plater, Dick Brown, Jon Wainwright)*

Kirkby Malham, N Yor [SD8961], *Queen Victoria*: Pleasantly spare decor, Theakstons, good choice of vegetarian dishes, juke box or piped music; bedrooms *(Jon Wainwright)*

☆ **Kirkby Overblow**, N Yor [SE3249], *Star & Garter*: Popular local doing particularly well under welcoming new larger-than-life landlord, cosy atmosphere and generous helpings of good value standard bar meal with dining room for evening meals; well kept Camerons and Everards *(Syd and Wyn Donald, Robert and Lesley Fawthrop)*

☆ **Kirkham**, N Yor [Kirkham Abbey; SE7466], *Stonetrough*: Notable food under new owner, in pleasant pub with separate cosy nooks and crannies, open log fires, warm welcome, Youngers No 3; restaurant has oak tables and old-fashioned kitchen range with fire *(D E Nicholls, J C Proud)*

Kirkheaton, W Yor [Hopton; SE1818], *Freemasons Arms*: Lively open-plan beamed pub with superb views as far as Castle Hill and over Huddersfield from conservatory; comfortable wall banquettes, pictures (some for sale), fruit machine in lounge and separate pool room; well kept Bass and attractively priced lunchtime bar food *(Andrew and Ruth Triggs)*

☆ **Knaresborough**, N Yor [High Bridge, Harrogate Rd; SE3557], *Yorkshire Lass*: Though there's not entire unanimity among readers about the direction taken by this large pub-restaurant, most really enjoy the atmosphere and food (especially loaf-sized Yorkshire puddings, also more exotic dishes), and find it run with flair and imagination; lively decor of 40s bar inc bicycles and Japanese sunshades, comfortable dining room, friendly licensees and staff, well kept Watneys-related real ales and fine riverside position, close to Mother Shipton's Cave with lovely picturesque views from new terrace; mellow live music Fri and Sat, monthly dress-up theme nights, daily newspapers, courtesy bus for customers; bedrooms well equipped and good value *(John Hayward, Bob Easton, Tim and Ann Newell, Fiona Mutch, Beryl and David Bowter)*

Langdale End, N Yor [off A170 at East Ayton; or A171 via Hackness — OS Sheet 101 map reference 938913; SE9491], *Moorcock*: This unusual old place, very simple indeed but a main entry since our first edition, closed late last year and was put up for sale; as we go to press we have not yet heard of its being reopened *(LYM)*

☆ **Ledston**, W Yor [SE4328], *White Horse*: Friendly pub, with well kept real ale and popular lunchtime food — regulars come from miles; in attractive village *(J E Rycroft)*

☆ **Leeds** [9 Burley Rd, junction with Rutland St], *Fox & Newt*: Done up in cheerful Victorian style — colourful paintwork, dark panelling, bare floorboards, lots of nick-nacks inc fairground music-box with dancing puppets, well reproduced but not obtrusive piped music or juke box, and reasonably priced lunchtime bar food; main draw is the range of beers brewed on the premises (a What The Butler Saw machine shows the microbrewery); open all day *(John Thorndike, Steve Waters, Joy Heatherley, LYM)*

☆ **Leeds** [Hunslet Rd], *Adelphi*: Well restored Edwardian woodwork, glass and tiling in several rooms; particularly well kept Tetleys (virtually the brewery tap), good lunchtime bar food at reasonable prices, live jazz Sat *(Andy and Jill Kassube, Dr and Mrs A K Clarke)*

☆ **Leeds** [Kirkgate, by indoor mkt], *Duck & Drake*: Large, basic, cavernous city-centre pub for real ale fans, with at least 16 different beers from all over the country, and enough custom for them to be fresh and well kept; bustling, friendly atmosphere, limited range of good value bar food, good service *(Pete Storey, David Oakes)*

Leeds [Arkwright St; off new Armley Rd], *Albion*: Attractive exterior — the original for the 00-gauge model railway pub; three well restored rooms, separate pool room, well kept Tetleys from superb brass handpumps *(Matt Pringle)*; [Tong Rd, Farnley], *Beulah*: Hilltop spot with good views, warm welcome from friendly licensee, well kept Tetleys on handpump, good bar food inc three-course Sun lunch *(Andy and Jill Kassube)*; [1 Claypit Lane], *Cobourg*: Fine example of a Tetleys city-centre drinking pub — heaving with social activity even at only 6 on Fri; good beer, atmosphere and surroundings *(Comus Elliott)*; [North St (A61)], *Eagle*: Traditional drinking-man's pub with well kept Timothy Taylors, good filling straightforward lunchtime snacks; atmosphere warmest midweek; bedrooms *(Andy and Jill Kassube)*; [Great George St], *George*: Good central well preserved Tetleys drinking pub, welcoming and lively, at its best during the week *(Reg Nelson, Comus Elliott)*; [Headrow], *Guildford Arms*: Busy central pub refurbished to look like turn-of-the-century Paris brasserie with art nouveau theme, Monet prints, jasmine lamps; well kept Tetleys, decent lunchtime sandwiches (though the crowds may have gobbled up all the fresh-carved hot beef by 1.20) *(T Nott, Roger Taylor)*; [Stainbeck Lane, Chapel Allerton], *Mustard Pot*: Popular, newly refurbished with pleasant lounge and comfortable settees; good lunchtime bar food at reasonable prices, pleasant front garden *(Andy and Jill Kassube)*; [Town St, Chapel Allerton (off A61 Harrogate Rd by Police Stn)], *Nags Head*: Whitewashed and recently refurbished but keeping genuine charm; mounting steps outside with small window formerly used to serve horse-mounted customers; big lounge with snob screens on mahogany bar, well kept Sam Smiths, good lunchtime bar food *(Andy and Jill Kassube, BB)*; [Burley Rd], *Queen*: Renovated Victorian pub with good value bar food attracting wide range of customers; well kept Tetleys *(Syd and Wyn Donald)*; [Seacroft Centre], *Sovereign*: Good place to stay *(W F Woodward)*; [Station Rd, Cross Gates], *Station*: Good food *(W F Woodward)*; [Otley Rd, Headingley], *Three Horseshoes*: Pleasant pub with well kept Ind Coope Burton and Tetleys on handpump, wide choice of cheap lunchtime bar food inc filled Yorkshire puddings *(Andy and Jill Kassube)*;

☆ **Leeds** [Gt George St, just behind Town Hall], *Victoria*: Superbly preserved opulent bar with high ceiling, ample alcoved plush seating, etched mirrors, soft lighting, impressive lamp stands extending from the bar which has unusual elephants' trunks supporting its brass rail and thriving welcoming atmosphere, opening into side room and cosy back room; well kept Tetleys, efficient service, lunchtime bar food *(David Oakes, Pete Storey, Michael Rooke, Reg Nelson)* [New Briggate], *Wrens*: Large old-fashioned city-centre pub with lots of bars, passages and nooks and crannies inc no-smoking room; well kept Tetleys inc Premium, dominoes *(Roger Taylor, David Oakes)*

☆ **Leyburn** [Market Pl], *Golden Lion*: Homely bar with benches around big pine tables, comfortable lounge with bottled beer collection around walls; good value generous and wholesome food from efficient food counter (ploughman's, home-made steak and kidney pie, crisp Yorkshire puddings, garlic chicken, fresh fish and children's dishes all recommended); good unusually flavoured Oliver Johns beer brewed here, also Theakstons Best and XB, decent house wines and malt whiskies, friendly staff; evening restaurant; tables outside, with pretty hanging baskets; bedrooms good value — especially the bargain breaks *(John Fazakerley, Mr and Mrs M O Jones, DP and ME Cartwright)*

☆ **Leyburn** [just off Market Pl], *Sandpiper*: Pleasant atmosphere in cosy lounge area with comfortable seats around the fire, and big dining area on far side of the small bar; well kept Theakstons Best, XB and Old Peculier (and they'll even make a ginger-beer shandy), cheerfully helpful and efficient service, moderately priced bar food from sandwiches up, and restaurant; sunny terrace and flower-surrounded floodlit back garden, friendly dogs *(Anne Morris, Jenny Cantle)*

☆ **Linton**, W Yor [SE3947], *Windmill*: Polished charm, good bar food and pleasant atmosphere in carefully preserved small rooms with antique settles, oak beams, longcase clock, well kept Youngers Scotch and No 3 — where the Leeds millionaires go for Sun sherry, not so upmarket weekdays *(J*

E Rycroft, Tim and Sue Halstead, LYM)

Little Ouseburn, N Yor [B6265 S of Boroughbridge; SE4461], *Green Tree*: Pleasant roadside country inn, plush seats throughout, good choice of bar food inc good value Sun lunch, panelled dining room, well kept Timothy Taylors Landlord, Tetleys and guest beers *(Andy and Jill Kassube)*

Lockton, N Yor [A169 N of Pickering; SE8490], *Fox & Rabbit*: Family pub nicely placed on the edge of the moors and doing well under new owners, with well kept real ales, good value simple food inc good steak and kidney pie, seats outside and in sun lounge; children's room *(Eileen Broadbent, LYM)*

Long Preston, N Yor [A65 Settle—Skipton; SD8358], *Maypole*: Good value bar food, good Sun lunch, well kept Hartleys XB and Whitbreads Castle Eden *(Andy and Jill Kassube)*

Low Barugh, S Yor [Dearnehall Rd; B6428; SE3108], *Millers*: Busy and welcoming little pub on site of old watermill with good value food, well kept Tetleys and Timothy Taylors Landlord *(Andy and Jill Kassube)*

Low Marishes, N Yor [SE8277], *School House*: Welcoming pub with simple but good food and good range of beers inc local Malton Brewery and usually guests such as Hook Norton, Old Mill and Taylors Landlord; well kept big garden with barbecue and good play area *(Helen Helsby)*

Low Row, N Yor [SD9897], *Punchbowl*: Recently reopened 17th-century free house in delightful position; well kept Theakstons and other real ales, good food, friendly service; bedrooms adequate *(U W Bankes)*

Lower Bentham, N Yor [SD6469], *Punch Bowl*: Attractive, welcoming and enjoyable village pub overlooking River Wenning; good choice of beers and well presented lunchtime and evening bar food; fishing permits; bedrooms *(K H Frostick)*

Luddenden Foot, W Yor [SE0424], *Travellers Rest*: Popular country local welcoming visitors, overlooking Calderdale Valley (lovely night view); several cosy little rooms, open fire, varied food *(Mrs Marjorie Donchey)*

☆ **Malham**, N Yor [SD8963], *Buck*: In grand scenery nr Malham Cove and Gordale Scar, on the Pennine Way — it's the most prominent pub in the village; well kept Theakstons Best, XB and Old Peculier in big lounge bar with comfortable old furniture, and busy hikers' bar; usual food inc decent ploughman's; nr start GWG152; children's area off main lounge; good value comfortable bedrooms *(Steve Waters, Sidney and Erna Wells, Ben Wimpenny, Len Beattie, Mr N F Calver, Jenny Cantle)*

Malham, *Lister Arms*: Large stone-built pub with Youngers Scotch and IPA on handpump and good helpings of bar food; steak restaurant; bedrooms *(Tim Baxter)*

Malton, N Yor [Commercial St; SE7972], *Cornucopia*: Friendly staff; good food from ambitious, interesting menu at reasonable prices; need to book at weekends *(Frazer and Louise Smith)*

☆ **Mankinholes**, W Yor [SD9523], *Top Brink*: Lively, friendly moorland village pub, popular in evenings, with very good steaks;

quite close to Pennine Way and nice walks to nearby monument on Stoodley Pike; midnight licence extension *(Len Beattie)*

Marsden, W Yor [Manchester Rd (A62); SE0412], *Olive Branch*: Wide choice of good bar food, Bass and Stones beer *(P A Crossland, D A Cawley)*

Marton cum Grafton, N Yor [signed off A1 3 miles N of A59; SE4263], *Olde Punch Bowl*: Comfortable and spacious open-plan heavy-beamed lounge bar well divided by timbers, with neat groups of tables and open fire; Tetleys and Youngers IPA, Scotch and No 3, generous helpings of good straightforward lunchtime bar food, restaurant; games and juke box in public bar, space for caravans; children welcome *(Jane and Niall, Andy and Jill Kassube, LYM)*

Masham, N Yor [Silver St; linking A6168 with Market Sq; SE2381], *Bay Horse*: John Smiths, Theakstons Old Peculier, XB and Best on handpump, good value bar food inc German specialities, good friendly service *(Maggie Goodwin, John Woolley)*

Meltham, W Yor [Blackmoorfoot Rd; B6107; SE0910], *Wills o' Nats*: Popular moorland pub, well kept Tetleys on handpump, good value changing bar food from sandwiches to salmon and stuffed lamb, hard-working staff; lovely views, big side beer garden *(H K Dyson, A Triggs)*

☆ **Mexborough**, S Yor [S of A6023: follow 'waterbus' signs; SE4800], *Ferry Boat*: Old-fashioned with some traditional furnishings, lively friendly atmosphere, good welcome, well kept real ales inc Bass Special and Theakstons, bar food inc filled Yorkshire puddings, hot meal sandwiches, good pie; nr Aire & Calder Navigation canal *(Steve Mitcheson, Anne Collins, Mrs M Lawrence, LYM)*

☆ **Middleham**, N Yor [SE1288], *Black Swan*: Attractive and comfortable olde-worlde pub in superb village with well kept John Smiths and Theakstons and good choice of generous bar food inc good freshly-made sandwiches; quick, helpful service even though busy; pictures and poems reflect the local racehorse-training connection; mind your head at door; attractive bark terrace, restaurant *(Mr and Mrs D C Leaman, Mr and Mrs J E Rycroft)*

Mirfield, W Yor [Dewsbury Rd; SE2019], *Pear Tree*: Welcoming roadside pub with open fires, friendly and efficient licensee, well kept Websters, home-made bar food inc a particularly good steak and mushroom pie, back garden steeply sloping to river *(B D Gibbs)*

Moorthorpe, S Yor [Barnsley Rd — OS Sheet 111 map reference 461111; SE4611], *Mallard*: Conversion of former Moorthorpe station buildings on working station platform with trains thundering 10-15 feet from the rim of your glass; free house with Bass and Tetleys beers, and Copperhead cider; atmosphere pleasant, straightforward new furnishings with lots of old railway photographs; quickly served, reasonably priced standard bar food; family room and good children's playground *(T Nott)*

Muker, N Yor [SD9198], *Farmers Arms*: Friendly welcome, genuine and cosy atmosphere, well kept Theakstons, simple but well prepared bar food, good service; nr start GWG148 *(Dr and Mrs R J Ashleigh)*

Newbiggin, N Yor [A684; SD9692], *Blue Ball*: Quaint unspoiled old pub with original panelling in small interesting rooms; good bar food especially mixed mushrooms in cream sauce, Bass and Tetleys; evening restaurant upstairs *(Helen Helsby)*

Norland, W Yor [Hob Lane; SE0723], *Hobbit*: Pleasant atmosphere, friendly staff, good value food, wide choice of beers at hotelish prices; bedrooms comfortable and well equipped *(H K Dyson)*

North Rigton, N Yor [SE2748], *Square & Compass*: Well kept beer, good food (service may sometimes slow); upmarket evenings and Sun lunchtime *(J E Rycroft)*

Nosterfield, N Yor [SE2881], *Freemasons Arms*: Friendly staff in pleasant pub with Tetleys and Theakstons ales and good value lunchtime bar snacks and evening meals; children welcome *(Alan Kelly)*

Nun Monkton, N Yor [off A59 York—Harrogate; SE5058], *Alice Hawthorn*: Modernised beamed bar with dark red plush settles back-to-back around dimpled copper tables, open fire in big brick fireplace, keen darts players; on broad village green with pond, near River Nidd; *(Jean and Theodore Rowland-Entwistle, BB)*

Oakworth, W Yor [pub well signed on rd from top end of Haworth; SE0439], *Goose*: Good choice of well kept reasonably priced beers; food in restaurant and carvery or in main bar, with waitress service; polite and efficient, warm and friendly staff inc white-aproned bow-tied smiling barman *(Mark Castle)*

Ogden, W Yor [A629 Denholme—Halifax; SE0631], *Moorland*: Long room with central open fire, raised galleries each end — one comfortably seated for drinks and snacks, the other for more substantial food; another area leads off to further dining tables, and there's a billiards room; nicely done out with decorative beams and stonework, plates, copper and brass pans, photographs; well kept Tetleys, Timothy Taylors Landlord and Websters Yorkshire on handpump, decent bar meals (not Sat evening), good service, quiet piped light music, fruit machine, live entertainment Weds; immaculate lavatories *(Frank Cummins)*

☆ **Oldstead**, N Yor [SE5380], *Black Swan*: Friendly inn in beautiful surroundings with pretty valley views from two big bay windows and picnic-table sets outside; engaging licensees (he's an American — and the dog's called Duke), decent bar food inc lots of grills, well kept John Smiths or Tetleys and Youngers IPA or No 3 on handpump, good log fire, rather fuzzy piped music; reasonably priced popular restaurant; children welcome; bedrooms in comfortable modern back extension, with huge breakfasts *(D B Delany, R A Clements, Greg Parston)*

☆ **Osmotherley**, N Yor [SE4499], *Three Tuns*: Small, pleasant pub in honeypot village, well kept McEwans 80/-, Theakstons Old Peculier and Youngers No 3 in clean and tidy small bar, notably good food in small crisp back restaurant — big helpings, v good value *(Walter and Susan Rinaldi-Butcher, Ruth and Andrew Triggs)*

☆ **Osmotherley** [Staddlebridge; A172 towards Middlesbrough, just off its junction with A19 — OS Sheet 99 map reference 444994], *Cleveland Tontine*: Prosperous and attractive cellar bar with big log fire, good food and cheerful service — but prices decidedly in the restaurant bracket now, and at busy times most tables are reserved for diners *(RAB)*

Osmotherley [The Green], *Golden Lion*: Restaurant quality food at pub prices, well kept John Smiths *(E A Turner)*

Ossett, W Yor [Low Mill Rd/Healey Rd; SE2820], *Boons End*: Good range of particularly well kept Clarks beers as well as changing guest beers, in very cosy old stone-fronted pub, with real fires and lots of breweryana; small but good choice of food inc soups, sandwiches, pies, chilli and a hot filling special; hidden away in a light industrial zone *(Andy and Jill Kassube)*

☆ **Oswaldkirk**, N Yor [signed off B1363/B1257 S of Helmsley; SE6279], *Malt Shovel*: Distinctive ancient building, a former small manor house, with interestingly decorated rooms leading off small heavily beamed traditional bar; well kept Sam Smiths, good open fires, straightforward bar food from sandwiches up, piped music, period garden; children welcome; big bedrooms with lovely views; several changes of licensee since Ian Pickering, its very successful tenant, left a couple of years ago make an unqualified recommendation difficult *(John and Chris Simpson, M B Porter, J E Rycroft, Jan and Ian Alcock, JM, PM, M B Porter, A M Neal, Paul McPherson, Brian and Anna Marsden, Virginia Jones, LYM)*

Otley, W Yor [Boroughgate; SE2045], *Bay Horse*: Very old local with low ceilings, wooden beams, and old-fashioned atmosphere; well kept real ales *(Reg Nelson)*; [Bondgate], *Junction*: Carefully renovated in the mid-70s in olde-worlde style, with wooden beams, benches, and interesting curios; well kept real ales and decent atmosphere, best appreciated before the 8.30 rush *(Reg Nelson)*; [Kirkgate], *Whitakers Arms*: Tastefully renovated and extremely lively old pub with good bar service, Tetleys beers, and juke box (not too loud) *(Reg Nelson)*

Oulton, S Yor [Aberford Rd (A642); nr roundabout and Crest Hotel; SE3628], *Bentley Arms*: Roast Inn, decorated with rugby league memorabilia; friendly atmosphere, good bar meals served all day, reasonably priced restaurant *(David Brighouse)*

Outlane, W Yor [A640 Huddersfield—Rochdale; SE0817], *Jack o' Mitre*: Three open-plan bar areas with small dining area, comfortable wall seats around copper-topped tables, two open fires, pool table and fruit machine, brasses and pictures on walls; Watneys-related real ales on handpump, lunchtime and evening bar food *(Andrew and Ruth Triggs)*

Overton, W Yor [204 Old Rd; SE2617], *Reindeer*: Clean and tidy pub with happy and friendly staff and good value food *(Roger Allott)*

☆ **Oxenhope**, W Yor [off B6141 towards Denholme; SE0335], *Dog & Gun*: Busy pub with plenty of character and atmosphere, doing well under current regime; well kept Timothy Taylors Landlord and Tetleys on handpump, good bar food inc sandwiches at reasonable prices and good value Sun lunches; bistro-style restaurant *(Mr and Mrs J E Rycroft)*

Oxenhope [Denholme Rd], *Lamb*: Well kept Websters, friendly staff, reasonably priced bar meals — a typical village pub, with no juke box, inconspicuous fruit machine and real fires; folk music Thurs, occasional quiz nights Sun *(Charles Hall)*; [A6033 Keighley—Hebden Bridge], *Waggon & Horses*: Good ploughman's and other food in moorside pub with fleeces on stripped stone walls *(LYM)*

☆ **Pickering**, N Yor [Market Pl; SE7984], *Bay Horse*: Cosy red plush bar with red curtains, old-fashioned prints and horsey bric-a-brac, heavy beams, big fire, well kept Camerons Bitter, Strongarm and Premium on handpump, bar food from ploughman's through steak and kidney pie to steaks; bigger public bar behind, restaurant upstairs *(Brian and Anna Marsden, Eileen Broadbent, BB)*

☆ **Pickering** [Market Pl; SE7984], *White Swan*: Inviting small plush hotel bar, often quiet enough to hear the airconditioning; friendly staff and locals, good chip-free food, well kept Camerons Bitter and Strongarm; superior bedrooms *(Paul McPherson, Brian and Anna Marsden)*

Pickering [opp North Yorks Moors Rly stn], *Railway*: Old pub renovated, with big quiet lounge, coal-effect fire, big dining area; smaller and busier public bar; food lunchtime and evening with children's dishes; enthusiastic newish landlord, well kept S&N beers *(Brian and Anna Marsden)*

Pickhill, N Yor [SE3584], *Fox & Hounds*: True friendly village local with main bar and small dining room; well kept beer, good bar food inc lavish puddings *(Stan Edwards)*

Potto, N Yor [NZ4704], *Dog & Gun*: Pleasant, roomy pub in small hamlet just N of the moors, open fire in big L-shaped bar with blue plush alcove seating, wide choice of bar food lunchtime and evening inc delicious puddings; evening carvery *(Shirley Pielou)*

☆ **Reeth**, N Yor [B6270; SE0499], *Black Bull*: Cheery beamed L-shaped bar by wide sloping green of old-world village — a lovely spot; well kept McEwans 80/- and Theakstons Best, XB and Old Peculier, reasonably priced bar food, friendly welcome, children allowed till 8.30 if under supervision; public bar with pool and other games; bedrooms pleasant with good facilities, good breakfasts *(John Fazakerley, M J Lawson, E V Walder, Dr and Mrs R J Ashleigh, LYM)*

Reeth, *Buck*: On good form, with good food and service in comfortable bar; bedrooms *(Peter Race)*; [Market Pl], *Kings Arms*: 18th-century free house with homely welcome in oak-beamed lounge, open fire, well kept Theakstons (and tea or coffee), good reasonably priced bar food, restaurant, obliging service; bedrooms *(E R Thompson)*

☆ **Richmond**, N Yor [Finkle St; NZ1801], *Black Lion*: Cosy and welcoming pub with dark decor, well kept Camerons Strongarm and Everards Old Original on handpump, no-smoking lounge, good generous bar food (salads, chicken pie, casseroles, game and steaks all recommended); bedrooms reasonable *(Lorrie Marchington, Andy and Jill Kassube, Dr and Mrs R J Ashleigh)*

Ripon, N Yor [SE3171], *Black Bull*: Old pub on market place (market day Thurs), with pleasant lounge and bar, well kept Theakstons, reasonably priced bar lunches *(Lyn and Bill Capper, Andy and Jill Kassube)*

Robin Hoods Bay, N Yor [The Dock, Bay Town; NZ9505], *Bay*: Well lit, busy pub with warm fire, welcoming staff, good bar food inc good steaks at moderate prices, well kept Camerons and Everards; long walk back up to village car park; bedrooms *(Angela Nowill, Mike and Wendy Proctor)*; [King St], *Olde Dolphin*: 18th-century pub with wide choice of decent food, especially good fresh fish; well kept real ales *(Andy and Jill Kassube, Mike and Wendy Proctor)*

Roecliffe, N Yor [SE3766], *Crown*: Extended pub with good food (good value despite the prices) and service *(Peter Race)*

Rotherham, S Yor [Moorgate Rd; SK4393], *Belvedere*: Tastefully decorated horseshoe-shaped bar with bar food from sandwiches up in area sectioned off, Whitbreads beers, decent choice of wines *(Mrs R M Morris)*

Rufforth, N Yor [Main St; SE5351], *Tankard*: Consistently pleasant pub in sleepy village, attractive open-plan lounge and bar with well kept Sam Smiths, darts, welcoming licensee *(Jon Wainwright)*

☆ **Runswick Bay**, N Yor [NZ8217], *Royal*: Lovely views down over fishing village and bay from big-windowed plain front lounge (with fishtank) and terrace; cheerful and lively atmosphere, well kept John Smiths, welcoming staff, nautical bank bar; decent choice of bar food inc local fresh fish, in very generous helpings *(Prof S Barnett, Mike and Wendy Proctor, LYM)*

Ryther, N Yor [just off B1223 Selby—Tadcaster; SE5539], *Ryther Arms*: Good pub with superb steaks in restaurant — owner a butcher by trade and takes great pride in them *(Ian W Robinson)*

Scalby, N Yor [High St; TA0191], *Nags Head*: Pleasant village pub away from hustle and bustle of Scarborough; warm welcome, usual bar food, well kept Tetleys on handpump *(Andy and Jill Kassube)*

☆ **Scarborough**, N Yor [Cambridge Terrace; TA0489], *Cask*: Decent choice of real ales in lively conversion of big Victorian house, often buzzing with young people *(J A Edwards, LYM)*

Scarborough [Vernon Rd], *Hole in the Wall*: Well kept ales with regular guest beers *(J A Edwards)*

☆ **Scawton**, N Yor [SE5584], *Hare*: Low and pretty pub, much modernised, with a couple of cosy settees, simple wall settles, stools, little wheelback armchairs and wood-effect or trestle tables, and inoffensive piped music; cheerful welcome, well kept Theakstons Best, XB and Old Peculier and McEwans 80/- on handpump, decent straightforward food from sandwiches through steak and kidney pie to big steaks; pool table up steps, seats outside, nice inn-signs; handy for Rievaulx Abbey *(Nick Dowson, Alison Hayward, Carole and John Rowley, BB)*

Scotch Corner, N Yor [a couple of hundred yds up A66 past the big hotel; NZ2205], *Vintage*: Attractive, homely pub with good bar meals from sandwiches to duck (with half-helpings for the elderly), real ale inc Websters Green Label, decent wine cellar; bedrooms *(E R Thompson)*

☆ **Seamer**, N Yor [Main St; TA0284], *Copper Horse*: Wide range of generously served good bar food inc good ploughman's, sandwiches, and some starters big enough for main courses, in old pub in quiet village; beams, brasses, bare stone, part wood-floored and part carpeted, with gold plush bar stools and wooden chairs around cast-iron-framed tables; well kept Youngers IPA, restaurant *(Ian Blackwell, Dr Thomas Mackenzie)*

Settle, N Yor [SD8264], *Golden Lion*: Bright red plush in cheerful high-beamed bar with enormous fireplace, bar, well kept Thwaites ales, games in lively public bar, horses still stabled in coachyard; bedrooms *(LYM)*

Sheffield, S Yor [592 Loxley Rd; SK3687], *Admiral Rodney*: Friendly, roomy pub with good carvery and wide choice of food; very popular for lunches; restaurant *(Mr and Mrs J A Oxley)*; [66 Victoria St, off Glossop Rd], *Bath*: Several rooms around central bar inc one cosy and circular with bar hatch, traditional Sheffield prints; good local with Tetleys on handpump, cheap lunchtime bar food such as meat and potato pie; oldies juke box, friendly atmosphere, quiz night Thurs *(Matt Pringle)*; [Worksop Rd], *Cocked Hat*: Largely open-plan, tasteful dark colours, breweriana and beer bottles; sewing-machine treadle tables, well kept Marstons Burton and Pedigree, lunchtime bar food *(W P P Clarke)*; [Manchester Rd], *Crosspool*: Popular for tasty and reasonably priced meal *(Steve Mitcheson and Anne Collins)*; [Ecclesall Rd], *Devonshire*: Opposite Wards Brewery, with well kept Kirby Strong, Samson, Vaux Bitter and Wards on handpump; refurbished, with partitions dividing bare-boarded front area from plusher back, interesting old Wards brewery memorabilia, dining conservatory; wide choice of decent good value food, open all day *(Matt Pringle)*; [195-199 Carlisle St], *Norfolk Arms*: Large multi-roomed Tetleys pub in steel area, striking exterior and abundant leather and wood inside; strange, roundabout-style bar with well kept beers, two pool rooms and lively Fri singalong *(Matt Pringle)*; [Packhorse Lane, High Green], *Pickwick*: Wide range of lunchtime and evening bar food, generously served at reasonable prices *(Mrs E Sugden)*; [18 Pitt St], *Red Deer*: Friendly, comfortable and tidy local with particularly well kept Tetleys; flowers outside *(Paul Newberry)*; [Solly St], *Red House*: Small backstreet pub, comfortably redecorated but character three-room layout, with well kept Darleys Best and Wards Kirby and Sheffield Best, good lunchtime bar food and live, often spontaneous, folk music *(W P P Clarke)*; [Charles St, handy for stn], *Red Lion*: Busy, well run, refurbished open-plan town pub, very clean and comfortable; efficiently served standard bar food (not Sun) with orders called over Tannoy, well kept Wards beers maybe inc Weizenbier, small conservatory, pleasant landlady *(T Nott, Pete Storey)*; [off Cemetery Rd], *Royal Oak*: Comfortable, welcoming opulent Edwardian pub with heavy flock wallpaper, heavy velvet curtains with fringes and deep banquettes in a variety of side rooms; often shellfish on bar, well kept Whitbreads Castle Eden *(Ian and James Phillips)*; [Charles St], *Yorkshire Grey*: Comfortably done out in the books-and-old-prints style, with well kept Marstons Pedigree and Whitbreads-related real ales and popular lunchtime bar food inc Yorkshire puddings; open all day, handy for Crucible Theatre *(Allan Lloyd)*

Shelf, W Yor [Lane Ends, Denholme Gate Rd (A644 Brighouse—Keighley); SE1029], *Brown Horse*: Smart and popular, with china, copper and well polished brass on the walls, good straightforward lunchtime food, well kept Websters *(Andy and Jill Kassube)*

☆ **Shelley**, W Yor [Roydhouse; SE2112], *Three Acres*: Good range of real ales in pleasant pub with emphasis on wide choice of nicely presented good food inc imaginative dishes as well as steak and kidney pie and so forth — not cheap, but worth it; restaurant, pleasant attentive staff, pianist playing light music; bedrooms *(Roger A Bellingham, Mrs M Whiteley)*

☆ **Shepley**, W Yor [Penistone Rd; SE1909], *Sovereign*: Open-plan, L-shaped dining lounge with beamery, yucca plants and tables neatly set for popular good value freshly cooked unpretentious bar food inc sandwiches, children's dishes, Yorkshire puddings and plenty of other hot dishes, generous salads and steaks; Bass and Stones Best on handpump normally well kept, moderately priced wines, cheerful and efficient waitress service, garden; very busy weekends *(Frank Cummins)*

Sheriff Hutton, N Yor [SE6566], *Highwayman*: Welcoming Tetleys pub over road from historic castle *(J C Proud)*

☆ **Skipton**, N Yor [Canal St; from Water St (A65) turn into Coach St, then left after canal bridge; SD9852], *Royal Shepherd*: Friendly local near canal with big bar, snug and dining room with open fires and old pictures of town and canal, tables outside, games and juke box; children allowed in dining room lunchtime; generously served simple lunchtime food (inc Sun), well kept Whitbreads-related real ales, unusual whiskies, good mix of lunchtime customers *(Pamela and Merlyn Horswell)*

☆ **Slingsby**, N Yor [Railway St; SE7075], *Grapes*: Straightforward but popular good value food and well kept Camerons in stone-built village local with cast-iron-framed tables on patterned carpet, children in room off bar, helpful service; tables in garden behind *(Tim Baxter, Carole and John Rowley, BB)*

☆ **Snape**, N Yor [SE2784], *Castle Arms*: Friendly licensees, comfortable and homely pub with cosy inglenooks and open fires, and enterprising food; keg beer *(Jon Dewhirst)*

☆ **Soyland**, W Yor [OS Sheet 110 map reference 012203; SE0423], *Blue Ball*: Unspoilt but adequately comfortable moorland pub, good range of consistently well kept Theakstons and Timothy Taylors ales and guest beers; straightforward bar food; music room with piano and organ; bedrooms *(G T Jones, Michael Rooke)*

Soyland [Rochdale Rd (A58); about 200 yds downhill from Blue Ball], *New Inn*: Up a cobbled road on a former turnpike, well placed for walks around nearby reservoirs — straightforward, but very welcoming on a bleak winter's day, with usual bar food from sandwiches up, real ales inc Moorhouses and Thwaites *(Andy and Jill Kassube)*

Spennithorne, N Yor [SE1489], *Old Horn*: Small, friendly, 17th-century pub with lunchtime bar food and good evening restaurant; bedrooms good *(Richard Fawcett, Fiona Mutch)*

Sprotbrough, S Yor [Melton Rd; SE5302], *Ivanhoe*: Large mock-Tudor pub overlooking cricket ground; comfortable, smart lounge/dining area with conservatory extension, uniformed waitresses; emphasis on decent food, well kept Sam Smiths OB; children's play area *(Steve Mitcheson, Anne Collins, J A Edwards)*

Stainforth, N Yor [B6479 Settle—Horton-in-Ribblesdale; SD8267], *Craven Heifer*: Small cosy village pub, useful for this walking area, with log fire, reasonably priced bar food inc well filled sandwiches, Thwaites on handpump *(RAF, Andy and Jill Kassube)*; *Royal Oak*: Useful village pub with well kept Thwaites Bitter *(Len Beattie)*

Stainland, W Yor [Stainland Rd; SE0719], *Duke of York*: Cosy hilltop village pub with warm welcome, good bar food — especially Yorkshire puddings with choice of fillings; well kept Tetleys, Timothy Taylors Landlord and weekend guest beers *(Andy and Jill Kassube)*

Stainton, S Yor [SK5594], *Three Tuns*: Smartly refurbished clean pub with good choice of well presented bar food inc good salads and puddings; pool table *(Richard Cole)*

☆ **Staithes**, N Yor [NZ7818], *Cod & Lobster*: Superb waterside setting for friendly local in unspoilt fishing village under dramatic sandstone cliff; well kept Camerons; parking nearby difficult, and the walk up to the top car park is quite steep *(Mike and Wendy Proctor, Eileen Broadbent, LYM)*

☆ **Stanbury**, W Yor [SE0037], *Old Silent*: Popular moorland village inn near Haworth, small rooms packed with bric-a-brac, four real ales, food in bar and restaurant served till late in the evening, friendly staff; good hill views, tables on attractive terrace; bedrooms old-fashioned but well equipped *(Robert Aitken, Anthony Barnes, LYM)*

Stanley, W Yor [Aberford Rd; SE3423], *British Oak*: Wilsons and Websters, good varied home-cooked bar food, good service, attentive licensee, restaurant; good facilities for disabled people, with helpful service for them *(A J Woodhouse)*

Stannington, S Yor [Greaves Lane, Little Matlock; reached via unmade Myers Grove Lane, off Wood Lane nr its junction with B6076 — OS Sheet 110 map reference 312893; SK3088], *Robin Hood*: Stone-built 18th-century inn in Loxley Valley, reputedly near Robin Hood's birthplace; difficult to find (despite encroaching housing estates); lots of attractive rooms; Stones on electric pump; bar snacks; good outdoor area; popular with walkers (W P P Clarke)

☆ **Stapleton**, N Yor [NZ2612], *Bridge*: Exceptionally good food using top-quality fresh ingredients and showing real imagination and delicate preparation; service very pleasant, helpful and efficient, in cosy Victorian pub with heavy brown Anaglypta walls and log-effect gas fire; restaurant; children allowed, with special helpings and prices, if they eat early (K Baxter)

Staveley, N Yor [signed off A6055 Knaresborough—Boroughbridge;SE3663], *Royal Oak*: Has been a popular main entry for welcoming atmosphere (even for children), civilised layout and furnishings, and notably good food; but the former licensees have now moved to the Handsel, Bridge St, Boroughbridge (LYM; reports on new regime please)

Stockbridge, W Yor [SE0742], *Greyhound*: Popular local with good atmosphere, lovely fireplace in cosy back room; several games, friendly little dog called Meg; fishing in area (Mrs Marjorie Donchey)

Stockton on the Forest, N Yor [Main St; off A64 just NE of York; SE6556], *Fox*: Small traditional country inn with good choice of beers; open bar, cosy country atmosphere, small restaurant (good Sun lunch), bar food (A J Woodhouse)

☆ **Stutton**, N Yor [SE4841], *Hare & Hounds*: Popular old stone-built pub with obliging service, pleasant atmosphere, well kept and priced Sam Smiths OB on handpump, good bar food (inc good pies, Yorkshire pudding with lots of dishes) in olde-worlde low-ceilinged lounge or comfortable and well furnished restaurant (worth booking); big car park; children allowed if eating (Noel and Mo Tornbohm, J G Thorpe, Mr and Mrs M D Jones, Andy and Jill Kassube)

☆ **Sutton under Whitestonecliffe**, N Yor [A170 E of Thirsk; SE4983], *Whitestonecliffe*: Beamed roadside pub with John Smiths and Websters on handpump and good value bar meals which can be eaten in attached restaurant; good puddings, good service, open fire in main bar; also side bar and back games room with pool; bedrooms (Andrew and Ruth Triggs, Mr and Mrs F W Sturch)

Swainby, N Yor [NZ4802], *Black Horse*: Busy but welcoming, with popular bar food inc good home-made soup and good value Sun lunch; family room with juke box, darts and so forth (RAF)

Swinton, N Yor [the one nr Malton, at SE7673], *Blacksmiths Arms*: Nice atmosphere in village roadside pub with good value food, decent beer, helpful landlord (David Gaunt)

☆ **Tan Hill**, N Yor [Arkengarthdale (Reeth—Brough) rd, at junction with Keld/W Stonesdale rd; NY8906], *Tan Hill*: Included for its remarkable very remote position completely isolated (and often snowbound) on the moors — Britain's highest pub, and a haven for walkers on the Pennine Way; basic furnishings, no mains electricity (the juke box is powered by a generator), flagstone floors, two big fires,

Theakstons Best, XB and Old Peculier, cheery food, games room, occasional singalong accordion sessions; housekeeping can be rather rough-and-ready, can get very crowded; children welcome; bedrooms basic (PLC, Mr and Mrs D C Leaman, Paul McPherson, Peter and Rose Flower, Len Beattie, G W Cheney, LYM)

☆ **Thirsk**, N Yor [Market Pl; SE4382], *Golden Fleece*: Popular bar in attractive and comfortable THF hotel well used by locals, with well kept real ales, good reasonably priced bar food, eager young staff; can get rather cramped; comfortable bedrooms (Peter Race, Richard Dolphin)

Thoralby, N Yor [SE0086], *George*: Plain, comfortable, traditional local with friendly welcome, well kept Websters and good range of bar food (Richard Fawcett)

☆ **Thornton le Clay**, N Yor [SE6865], *White Swan*: Good value well presented food inc delicious puddings and good Sun lunch in welcoming and attractive L-shaped room with central bar, brasses, tankards and corn dollies hanging from rafters; relaxed atmosphere, good value bar food inc Sun roast lunch; no-smoking area (S V Bishop, Barbara and Ken Turner)

Thorpe Salvin, S Yor [Church St; SK5281], *Parish Oven*: Recently refurbished spacious beamed pub with old cooking range in pleasant lounge; Home and Youngers on handpump, cheap bar food (Andy and Jill Kassube)

☆ **Thruscross**, N Yor [signed from A59 Harrogate—Skipton at Blubberhouses, or off B6255 Grassington—Pateley Bridge at Greenhow Hill; OS Sheet 104 map reference 159587; SE1558], *Stone House*: village Moorland pub with beams, flagstones, stripped stone, dark panelling and good fires; straightforward bar food from sandwiches to steaks, Tetleys Mild and Bitter, traditional games, sheltered tables outside; restaurant (not Sun evening); has been open all day; children welcome (Simon Bates, LYM)

Thunder Bridge, W Yor [village signed off A629 — OS Sheet 110 map reference 188116; SE1811], *Woodman*: Attractive stone-built roadside pub in delightful wooded valley, unusual slated canopy good for summer; well kept Timothy Taylors and other real ales on handpump, bar food, good atmosphere; upmarket restaurant (W P P Clarke)

☆ **Thurlstone**, S Yor [OS Sheet 110 map reference 230034; SE2303], *Huntsman*: Well run old stone-built pub with well kept Wards and maybe other real ales on handpump, friendly atmosphere, lunchtime bar food (W P P Clarke, Michael Rooke)

Topcliffe, N Yor [Long St; SE4076], *Angel*: Modernised 17th-century pub with well kept John Smiths, Tetleys, and Youngers ales on handpump, good bar food, friendly helpful staff; restaurant, big back garden with terrace (and room for a few caravans); river fishing; well equipped bedrooms (Andrew and Ruth Triggs)

Ulley, S Yor [Turnshaw Rd; nr M1 junction 31 — off B6067 in Aston; SK4687], *Royal Oak*: Fairly modern handsome stone building with stable-theme beamed bar, garden lounge and family room; Sam

Smiths, standard bar food inc children's helpings, restaurant; included for its motorway value *(Helena and Arthur Harbottle)*

Upper Hopton, W Yor [Hopton Lane; SE1918], *Travellers Rest*: Smart, cosy and busy hillside pub with very good family facilities; good value bar food, particularly sandwiches but wide choice of other things; well kept Tetleys, collection of toby jugs *(Andy and Jill Kassube, J E Rycroft)*

Upper Poppleton, N Yor [A59 York—Harrogate; SE5554], *Red Lion*: Attractive and spotless olde-worlde bars and dining areas, good lunchtime bar food from sandwiches to roast beef and Yorkshire pudding; bedrooms in extension *(F J Robinson)*

☆ **Wakefield**, W Yor [Westgate; SE3321], *Henry Boons*: Large, attractive Victorian corner pub by rly stn; interesting decor with main open-plan bar actually thatched, full of breweriana such as sacks of hops and malt but comfortably furnished; side room papered with local newspaper cuttings, library for customers, tables with inlaid chess boards (pieces available); well kept Clarks (it's the brewery tap for these beers) as well as Tetleys and Timothy Taylors Landlord on handpump and Addlestone's cider, good choice of bottled foreign lagers, cheap lunchtime bar food; jazz Sat afternoon in second side room *(W P P Clarke, Mr and Mrs P A Jones)*

☆ **Wakefield** [77 Westgate End], *Beer Engine*: Redone with flagstone floors, wood-backed wall seats, fires in Victorian cast-iron fireplaces, old brewery mirrors, real gas lighting — some fittings rescued from defunct pubs; well kept Old Mill, Tetleys, Timothy Taylors Landlord and Ram Tam on handpump, Marstons Owd Rodger tapped from the cask and other guest beers, good value lunchtime bar food Fri and Sat (closed lunchtime Sun-Thurs); darts, fruit machine, loud juke box, TV in third room; seats out in pleasant area behind *(W P P Clarke, Michael Rooke)*

Wakefield, *Star*: Good reasonably priced food — especially fish pie — in friendly and comfortable long room *(Roger Huggins)*

☆ **Warthill**, N Yor [village signed off A64 York—Malton and A166 York—Great Driffield; SE6755], *Agar Arms*: Highly popular specialisation in steaks, all sorts and sizes, in welcoming and prettily placed pub opposite duckpond, with other dishes inc lunchtime sandwiches and children's dishes; softly lit and nicely decorated, with open fires and well kept Sam Smiths on electric pump *(M Suther, Eddie Palker, BB)*

☆ **Weaverthorpe**, N Yor [SE9771], *Star*: Neat litle village inn with pleasant relaxing atmosphere; front lounge, main back lounge, small pool room and restaurant; open fires, well kept Tetleys and Theakstons Bitter and XB, extensive range of upmarket food inc pheasant and so forth, very friendly licensees; bedrooms a little sparse but cheap, and very good value *(J A Edwards)*

Wentbridge, W Yor [off A1; SE4817], *Blue Bell*: Large pub with family room, good choice of real ales, big helpings of bar food, Sun lunches *(Neil and Anita Christopher)*

Wentworth, S Yor [3 miles from M1 junction 36; signed off A6135; SK3898], *Rockingham Arms*: Comfortably furnished main bar with coal fires, hunting pictures and copper-topped tables, good bar food from sandwiches through filled Yorkshire puddings up (not Sun evening), well kept Home and Youngers Scotch, IPA and No 3 on handpump; separate lively Barn Bar with live music Weds-Fri, tables in attractive garden with own well kept bowling green; open all day; only a shortage of recent reports keeps it out of the main entries this year; bedrooms *(Paul Newberry, J A Edwards)*

West Ayton, N Yor [Pickering Rd (A170); SE9985], *Old Forge Valley*: Hard-working newish licensees doing consistently good value bar food from sandwiches to steaks, inc children's dishes; comfortable lounge bar, public bar, pool room, small restaurant; live group most Friday evenings; big garden with children's play area; bedrooms *(John Richards)*

☆ **West Burton**, N Yor [on green, off B6160 Bishopdale—Wharfedale; SE0186], *Fox & Hounds*: Unspoilt, basic local in idyllic Dales village around one long green; small bar with extension, homely welcoming atmosphere, well kept John Smiths on handpump, reasonably priced decent home-cooked bar food inc children's dishes, good service from friendly staff *(Jenny Cantle, NIH, Anthony Fernau)*

West Tanfield, N Yor [A6108 N of Ripon — OS Sheet 99 map reference 268788; SE2678], *Bruce Arms*: Idiosyncratic village pub with mixture of old-fashioned seats around the log fire in its snug front bar, second bar at the back, jaunty decorations, bar food which may take a long while to prepare, well kept John Smiths and Theakstons Best and XB, games, juke box, tables outside (the stables are still in use); restaurant; no bar food Mon, closed Mon lunchtime exc bank hols; children welcome lunchtime *(Lyn and Bill Capper, LYM)*

☆ **West Witton**, N Yor [A684 W of Leyburn; SE0688], *Wensleydale Heifer*: Clean and comfortable lounge and two snug bars, good log fire, pleasant decor, interesting prints, chintz-upholstered furniture — more the feel of a hotel than a pub; pleasant service, well kept John Smiths, good helpings of carefully prepared food inc interesting dishes in stall-style separate bistro or restaurant; attractive bedrooms *(Helen May, Paul McPherson, Mr and Mrs Bill Muirhead)*

Wetherby, W Yor [8 High St; SE4048], *George & Dragon*: Nice little coaching inn next to river with good views, well kept John Smiths and good lunches *(Andy and Jill Kassube)*

☆ **Whitby**, N Yor [Flowergate; NZ9011], *Little Angel*: Clean and friendly local with welcoming licensees, well kept Tetleys, good value food; children allowed if well behaved *(Eileen Broadbent, Mrs R M Morris)*

Whitby [just over bridge to E/Old Whitby], *Dolphin*: Welcoming landlord, good atmosphere, well kept Camerons Bitter, and good food inc seafood pasta and home-made steak pies; quiz nights *(Sue Corrigan)*

Whitwood, W Yor [nr M62 junction 31; back rd towards Altofts and Stanley — OS Sheet 104 map reference 399247; SE3723],

Bridge: Recently built in traditional style using second-hand bricks and high rafters; simple decor, tapestry benches, stools and Windsor chairs; Theakstons and Youngers ales, simple well presented bar food, quick service, separate dining area *(Thomas Nott)*

Whixley, N Yor [SE4458], *Anchor*: Character village local with well kept John Smiths and Tetleys *(J C Proud)*

☆ **Wigglesworth**, N Yor [SD8157], *Plough*: Well run country inn with civilised atmosphere and unusual choice of reliably good food in bright and comfortable bar or big conservatory; friendly, efficient service, well kept Hartleys XB, good value white wine; bedrooms good and well equipped, with big breakfasts *(Prof S Barnett, G W H Kerby)*

Wistow, N Yor [B1223 NW of Selby; SD5935], *Black Swan*: Tetleys on handpump under light blanket pressure in welcoming village pub with bar food strong on fried food *(Simon Reynolds)*

Worsborough, S Yor [village signed off A61, N of M1 junction 36 — OS Sheet 110 map reference 349027; SE3503], *Edmunds Arms*: Attractive stone-built village pub opp historic St Marys Church — scene of July Mystery plays; well kept Sam Smiths Old Brewery on handpump; something for everybody (even Arthur Scargill) in the many rooms, inc live organ music in the concert room *(W P P Clarke)*

Yeadon, W Yor [Well Hill, The Green; SE2141], *Oddfellows*: Long but low-ceilinged pub with traditional atmosphere; well kept Tetleys, lunchtime bar food, pianist and singalong Sat evening *(Andy and Jill Kassube)*

☆ **York** [High Petergate], *Hole in the Wall*: Rambling, friendly open-plan bar with beams, walls stripped back to brick, Turkey carpeting, prints and paintings, two fireplaces; lots of plush red-cushioned stools and settles, wood-topped cast-iron tables; Mansfield beers, good sandwiches, home-made pies and other generously served food; friendly staff, normally quiet piped music; in fact rather spacious — can get busy but rarely overcrowded *(Stan Edwards, Bernard Phillips, Ian M Baillie, Anne Phelan, Roger A Bellingham, Theo Schofield, BB)*

☆ **York** [26 High Petergate], *York Arms*: Many-roomed pub just down from Minster; entrance nearest Minster leads into snug little wood-panelled room on left or refurbished lounge bar; second entrance further down opens into cosier lounge with brown cushioned wall seats, some wood panelling and a brick fireplace at far end; part no-smoking; well kept Sam Smiths OB, good value food lunchtime and early evening from soup and well filled crusty sandwiches to Yorkshire puddings, cheerfully efficient service *(Prof S Barnett, H K Dyson, Tony Bland, G G Calderwood, Tony Tucker, BB)*

☆ **York** [Walmgate], *Spread Eagle*: Narrow, popular pub with main bar area and two smaller ones leading off; lots of old enamel adverts and prints on walls, good regularly changing range of well kept real ales such as Timothy Taylors and Caledonian 80/-, good bar food inc huge sandwiches and luscious Yorkshire puddings served 12-8, friendly staff, good atmosphere, juke box *(David and Ruth Hollands, BB)*

York [9 St Martins Lane, Micklegate], *Acorn*: Busy, friendly pub in old part *(Dr and Mrs Tony Clarke)*; [Goodramgate], *Anglers Arms*: Small friendly pub, nicer in than out, with log fire, plenty of atmosphere, unusual shape and decor; one of its ghosts is said to turn off the beer pumps *(Roy and Helen Sumner)*; [55 Blossom St], *Bay Horse*: Lots of nooks and alcoves in rambling rooms of Victorian local with little concession to the 80s *(Dr and Mrs Tony Clarke, LYM)*; [Tanner Row], *Corner Pin*: Neat, clean and generally attractive pub with tables outside and glassed-in carvery *(Ian M Baillie)*; [Bishophill], *Golden Ball*: Several characterful, unspoiled rooms; good fish and chip shop next door *(Dr and Mrs A K Clarke)*; [Layerthorpe — just outside walls, on road to Heworth, NE of centre], *John Bull*: Carefully neglected decor but apparently genuine 30s memorabilia; friendly publican and wide range of interesting guest beers; not a family pub and gets very crowded *(RCL)*; [Clifton], *Old Grey Mare*: Best meat pie I've had since my grandmother's, and friendly licensee *(Mrs Marjorie Donchey)*; [Merchantgate; between Fossgate and Piccadilly], *Red Lion*: Low-beamed rambling rooms with some stripped Tudor brickwork, relaxed old-fashioned furnishings, well kept John Smiths real ale, basic bar food, tables outside, good juke box or piped music *(LYM)*; [18 Goodramgate], *Royal Oak*: Well kept Camerons, good traditional roast beef, massive ploughman's till 7.30; traditional cosy rooms *(Melvyn Payne)*; [Monkgate], *Tap & Spile*: Imposing late-Victorian brick building just north of city walls, with one big split-level bar — bare boards, green leatherette banquettes round big bay window, dado with flowery wallpaper; upper area divided off by a wood and frosted-glass panel; strong emphasis on wide range of real ales that change regularly — following week's choice listed on blackboard; food from sandwiches and baked potatoes to Yorkshire puddings, bedrooms *(Russell and Christina Jones, BB)*, [Micklegate], *Walkers*: Unusual layout with long bar at back while front area more a eating area; good bar food generously served *(Stan Edwards)*

London

London

Drinks prices in central London are now absurdly high. Our national price survey shows that pubs here now charge about 20p more for a drink than the national average. This average hides even sharper regional inequities – a London drinker is now paying 30p more than a Lancashire one for exactly the same drink. Outside the centre, London pub prices are a few pence lower, and work out much the same as in Surrey and Sussex (still nearly 15p higher than the national average). Here and there, some central London pubs are already charging £1.50 for a pint of beer; bearing in mind the way the £1-a-pint hurdle was cleared so recently, our prediction is that £1.50 will become the normal price of a central London pint by late next year – and that by then a few pubs will even have the gall to be charging £2 a pint. These astronomical London drinks prices make it particularly worth looking for bargains. One small mainly north London chain, J D Wetherspoons, makes a point of having one beer at a special low price – around 20p lower than the local average; this 'loss leader' approach may well become more general. A general lesson is to look for pubs tied to local or regional brewers rather than the national brewing combines which dominate central London. We found that pubs tied to the London brewers Fullers and Youngs (or to some outside breweries such as Greene King which are beginning to get a toe hold in London) averaged about 10p a pint less than the nationals. We also found that pubs brewing their own beer – a handful, but increasing – averaged 10p or 15p a pint less; these too are sources of good value drink. By contrast, on food prices London pubs can give themselves a pat on the back. In some areas outside London it's now virtually impossible to find a decent snack for under £1 or a substantial main dish for under £3. Setting these targets for pub food bargains, we expected to draw a complete blank in London, given its dismal record on drinks prices. In fact we found around one in four London pubs met those targets – a higher proportion than in many other areas. Pubs to mention for bargain snacks or food (at least one or the other) include in central London the Antelope, Old Coffee House, Olde Mitre (cheap sandwiches in a pricey area), and Princess Louise; the Moon Under Water and Olde White Bear (north); the Alma, George and Phoenix & Firkin (south); the Dove, Eel Pie and Windsor Castle (west) and the Grapes and Hollands (east). The general quality of London pub food has been rising noticeably: the Front Page (central), Ship (south), Dove and Sporting Page (west) and Grapes (east – for its fresh fish) are all particularly good. London pubs currently of special note in other ways include, in the centre, the Argyll Arms (a new main entry: spacious and traditional, in a handy spot, with food all day), the Black Friar (lots of life, and lovely art nouveau decor), the bustling and interesting Cittie of York, the George (new licensee doing well, lots of well kept real ales in civilised surroundings), the Glassblower (some refurbishment, food upstairs as well as down now), the relaxing and traditional Lamb, the Museum (open all day on Sunday, for food, under its new licensee), the characterful Olde Cheshire Cheese (a bit more room) and the Princess Louise (showy architecture, plenty of atmosphere); in north London the Compton Arms (like a little country local – with prices to match), the Freemasons (a new entry, handy for Hampstead Heath), and the Moon Under Water (another new entry; one of the J D Wetherspoons pubs – no music or noise, good surroundings and atmosphere); in south London the Alma (stylish and unusual), the Angel (a favourite for river views), the George (a classic coaching inn, preserved by the National Trust), the Horniman (a comfortable newish but solidly traditional riverside pub) and the Ship (but it does get crowded at weekends and on fine summer evenings); in west London, the Dove (outstandingly popular among readers), the Kings Arms (a new main entry in a lovely position, open all day for food on Sundays) and the White Horse (good all round, fine wines and particularly well kept beers); and in east London the memorably unspoilt and genuine Hollands. Several of the Lucky Dip entries at the end of the chapter are attracting a good deal of current attention, too: in central London the Grenadier (SW1), Red Lion (Duke of York St, SW1), Star (SW1) and Salisbury (WC2); north, theMoon Under Water (Enfield – same chain as our Moon Under Water main entry); south, the Market Porter (SE1) and several possibilities in Richmond and Kingston; west, the White Swan (Twickenham); and east, the Town of Ramsgate (E1), Falcon & Firkin (E9) and House They Left Behind (E14).

CENTRAL LONDON

Covering W1, W2, WC1, WC2, SW1, SW3, EC1, EC2, EC3 and EC4 postal districts
Parking throughout this area is metered during the day, and generally in short supply then; we mention difficulty only if evening parking is a problem too

Antelope (Belgravia) Map 13

Eaton Terrace, SW1

Not far from Sloane Square, this pleasantly old-fashioned pub has plenty of standing room round the central bar servery, with settles – old and modern – in the front part; the side room houses the fruit machine. During the week bar food downstairs is limited to large filled baps (from £1.65; prawn or smoked salmon £2.50), with main dishes served in the upstairs wine bar – anything from salads (from £2.50) to grills or salmon cutlets in dill and white wine (£4.50); on a Saturday lunchtime downstairs they also do ploughman's (£2.50), curries (£3.30) and so forth. Well kept Adnams, Benskins, Ind Coope Burton, Tetleys and Wadworths 6X on handpump. It gets lively in the evening. There are a couple of long seats outside, in the quiet street. (Recommended by Dr and Mrs A K Clarke, Andy and Jill Kassube)

Benskins   Licensee Geoff Elliott   Real ale   Meals and snacks   Restaurant tel (071) 730 7781   Children in eating area   Open 11–11

Argyll Arms (Oxford Circus) Map 13

18 Argyll St W1; opp tube side exit

It's a surprise to come across such a traditional place in an area with a real dearth of good pubs – and one which serves substantial helpings of food until the middle of the evening. The most unusual part is the three cubicle rooms at the front of the pub – all oddly angular, and made by wooden partitions with frosted and engraved glass. A long mirrored corridor leads to the spacious back room, with the food counter in one corner; the blackboard menu includes good sandwiches (from £1.75; club £3.25), ploughman's or salads (from £3.50), cottage pie (£3.95) and roast beef (£4.85), with specials such as whole avocado and tuna salad (£3.95) or steak and mushroom pie (£4.50). Adnams Southwold, Boddingtons, Tetleys Bitter and Wadworths 6X on handpump; two fruit machines, piped pop music. The quieter upstairs bar, which overlooks the busy pedestrianised street, is divided into several snugs with comfortable plush easy chairs; swan's neck lamps, and lots of small theatrical prints along the top of the walls. A penned area outside has elbow-height tables. *(Recommended by Ian Phillips, Peter Griffiths, Gary Scott, Prof S Barnett)*

Nicholsons (Allied; run as free house)   Licensee Michael Tayara   Real ale   Meals and snacks (11–8)   Children welcome   Open 11–11; closed Sun

Black Friar (City) Map 13

174 Queen Victoria Street, EC4

The inner back room here has some of the best fine Edwardian bronze and marble art-nouveau decor to be found anywhere. It includes big bas-relief friezes of jolly monks set into richly coloured Florentine marble walls, an opulent marble-pillared inglenook fireplace, a low vaulted mosaic ceiling, gleaming mirrors, seats built into rich golden marble recesses, and tongue-in-cheek verbal embellishments such as Silence is Golden and Finery is Foolish. In the front room, see if you can spot the opium smoking-hints modelled into the fireplace. Bar food includes filled French bread (from £1.70), ploughman's (from £2.70), filled baked potatoes, a varied cold buffet (from £3), and three daily hot specials such as beef in red wine, coq au vin or cranberry lamb stew (around £3.50). Well kept Adnams, Bass, Boddingtons Bitter and Tetleys on handpump; fruit machine. There's a wide forecourt in front, by the approach to Blackfriars Bridge. *(Recommended by G D Collier, Jamie Lyons, Ruth Harrison, Peter Griffiths, Prof S Barnett, David Fowles, Simon Collett-Jones, Michael Bechley, Dr J C Harrison)*

Nicholsons (Allied)   Licensee David McKinstry   Real ale   Lunchtime meals (not Sat or Sun) and snacks (not Fri evening, not Sat or Sun)   Children in eating area of bar Open 11.30–9 weekdays; closed weekends and Bank Hols; winter opening 11.30–3, 4.30–9

Cittie of Yorke (Holborn) Map 13

22 High Holborn, WC1; find it by looking out for its big black and gold clock

There's been a pub here since 1430, though it was reconstructed in Victorian times using 17th-century materials and parts, and the main back room has much of the fabric of the 1695 coffee house which stood here behind a garden. The bar counter is the longest in Britain with vast thousand-gallon wine vats (empty since prudently drained at the start of the Second World War) above the gantry, and a cat-walk running along the top of them. If you get there early enough (it can get packed, particularly with lawyers and judges), you can bag one of the intimate old-fashioned and ornately carved cubicles; there's an unusual big stove – uniquely triangular, with grates on all three sides, and big bulbous lights hanging from the extraordinarily high raftered roof. A smaller, comfortable wood-panelled room has lots of little prints of York and attractive brass lights. There's a lunchtime food counter in the main hall with more in the downstairs cellar bar: ploughman's (£3.25), beef rolls (£2), a good selection of cold dishes (from £3.25), with hot meals such as chilli con carne, curry, lasagne and daily specials (all £3.50). Sam Smiths OB and Museum on handpump; friendly service; darts, fruit machine and piped music. The ceiling of the entrance hall has medieval-style painted panels and plaster York roses. *(Recommended by Wayne Brindle, Andy Hick, Andy and Jill Kassube, Simon Collett-Jones, Brian Jones, Mark Porter, John Evans)*

Sam Smiths   Licensee Stuart Browning   Real ale   Meals and snacks (12–2.30, 5.30–9.30)   Well behaved children welcome if sitting   Open 11.30–11 weekdays; 11.30–3, 5.30–11 Sat; closed Sun

Cross Keys (Chelsea) Map 12

Lawrence St, SW3

Several interconnecting little rooms radiate off the walk-around island serving counter in this friendly and popular Victorian pub. The decor is old-fashioned, there are military prints, a set of Cries of London prints and photographs of old London on the red or cream walls, high ceilings, and an open fire in winter. Good value food includes sandwiches, seven salads, and home-made hot dishes like fish pie, stir-fry beef in oyster sauce, crispy pork or steak en croûte (around £4). Well kept Courage Best and Directors on handpump, good mulled wine, a fine range of Irish whiskies, and quick and efficient service; shove-ha'penny, dominoes, cribbage, trivia and fruit machine. There are tables in a pretty little sunny back courtyard planted with creepers and tubs of brightly coloured flowers. *(Recommended by Robert and Elizabeth Scott, Patrick Stapley, Richard Gibbs)*

Courage   Licensee Arthur Goodall   Real ale   Meals and snacks (not Sun)   Children in eating area   Open 11–11

Front Page ✪ (Chelsea) Map 12

35 Old Church Street, SW3

Light and airy, this popular pub – in an elegant part of Chelsea – has pews and benches around the panelled walls, heavy wooden tables, a wood-strip floor, big navy ceiling fans, huge windows with heavy navy curtains, and an open fire in one cosy area; lighting is virtually confined to brass picture-lights above small Edwardian monochrome pictures. Big blackboards at either end of the pub list the good value and nicely presented food: good soup of the day (£2.30), chicken liver pâté (£3.10), melon and mozzarella salad (£3.50), sausage and mash (£4), steak sandwich (£4.50), smoked salmon with scrambled eggs (£4.70) and salmon fish cakes with hollandaise sauce (£5.70), and puddings like baked bananas (£2). Well kept Boddingtons, Ruddles County and Websters Yorkshire on handpump; decent wines; quick, pleasant service. Fruit machine. Outside, there are big copper gaslamps hanging above pretty hanging baskets. *(Recommended by Dr John Innes, Simon Turner)*

Watneys   Licensees Peter Stevens and Patrick Coghill   Real ale   Meals   Children in eating area of bar   Open 11–3, 5.30(6 Sat)–11; closed 24–26 Dec

George (West End) Map 13

55 Great Portland Street, W1

Popular with BBC regulars, this solid place has a good choice of ten well kept real ales on handpump – typically Adnams Bitter, Everards Tiger, Flowers IPA, Fullers London Pride, Greene King, Marstons Pedigree, Ruddles Best and County, Wadworths 6X and Websters Yorkshire. There are comfortable red plush high chairs at the bar, captain's chairs around traditional cast-iron-framed tables, heavy mahogany panelling, deeply engraved mirrors, equestrian prints, and etched windows. Bar food includes sandwiches (£1.20, baps £1.60), ploughman's (from £1.75), steak and kidney or beef in Guinness pie, sweet and sour pork and lamb casserole (all £3.50), and roast Sunday lunch (£4.50). They do guided tours of the cellar, ending with a cold snack (£3.50). *(Recommended by Simon Collett-Jones, Steve Waters, Peter Grifiths, Dr John Innes; more reports please)*

Free House   Licensee Harry Medlicott   Real ale   Meals and snacks   Open 11–11

Glassblower (Piccadilly Circus) Map 13

42 Glasshouse Street, W1

The main bar, quite popular with tourists, has lots of untreated rough wooden beams with metal wheel-hoops hanging on them, plain wooden settles and stools, and sawdust on gnarled floorboards. An enormous copper and glass gaslight hangs from the centre of the ceiling, flickering gently, and there are more gaslight-style brackets around the walls, as well as lots of beer towels, framed sets of beer mats and bottle tops. A wide range of real ales on handpump includes Adnams,

Brakspears SB, Greene King Abbot and IPA, Ruddles Best and County, Wadworths 6X and Websters Yorkshire. Food includes sandwiches, fish and chips (from £3), ploughman's or sausages (£3.25), salads (from £3.50), daily hot dishes (£3.75), grills (from £4.55); in the upstairs lounge (refurbished this year) there's a carvery (£4.95); fruit and trivia machines, space game, juke box and piped music. There are hanging flower-baskets outside. *(Recommended by John Fazakerley, GCS, M B Porter, Dr and Mrs A K Clarke, I W and P J Muir, Simon Collett-Jones, Tom Hartman, Steve Waters, Peter Griffiths)*

Whitbreads   Manager Ronan McLister   Real ale   Meals and snacks (11–9, not Sun) Children in upstairs lounge   Open 11–11

Kings Arms (Mayfair) Map 12

2 Shepherd Market, W1

In a busy little patch of narrow streets just north of Piccadilly, this lively busy pub has a stripped-down decor of bare timbers and the textured concrete that is the South Bank's hallmark, with a dimly lit galleried upper area. A good choice of well kept real ales includes Ruddles Best, Wadworths 6X and Websters Yorkshire. Bar food includes large sandwiches (£2.65) and hot dishes such as shepherd's pie or sausages in cider (£4.25); CD juke box, trivia, fruit machine. *(Recommended by Andy and Jill Kassube, Quentin Williamson; more reports please)*

Chef & Brewer   Licensee Kevin Beardsley   Real ale   Meals and snacks (all day) Open 11–11 (12–3, 7–11 Sat)

Lamb ★ (Bloomsbury) Map 13

94 Lamb's Conduit Street, WC1

All the way around the U-shaped bar counter in this popular, friendly pub, there are cut-glass swivelling 'snob-screens', as well as traditional cast-iron-framed tables with neat brass rails around the rim, and on ochre panelling lots of sepia photographs of 1890s actresses; a small room at the back on the right is no-smoking. Good bar food includes sandwiches (£1.10, not Sun), ploughman's (£2.25) and salads, as well as hot dishes such as home-made pies or steak and kidney pudding, and daily specials like spinach and prawn crêpe or pork in cider casserole; oyster evenings in season. Consistently well kept Youngs Bitter and Special on handpump, with Warmer in winter; prompt service, and a good mix of customers. There are slatted wooden seats in a little courtyard beyond the quiet room which is down a couple of steps at the back; dominoes, cribbage, backgammon. *(Recommended by Wayne Brindle, Brian Jones, D A Parsons, Steve Waters, R H Inns, Joel Dobris, Peter Griffiths, Andy and Jill Kassube)*

Youngs   Licensee Richard Whyte   Real ale   Meals and snacks (11.45–11)   Open 11–11

Lamb & Flag (Covent Garden) Map 13

33 Rose Street, WC2; off Garrick Street

This popular, friendly place is still much as it was when Dickens described the Middle Temple lawyers who frequented it when he was working in nearby Catherine Street – low ceiling, high-backed black settles and an open fire. The upstairs Dryden Room tends to be less crowded. There's a choice of ten well kept cheeses and eight pâté s, served with hot bread or French bread, as well as pasties, quiche, steak and kidney pie, roast beef baps (Mon - Fri), shepherd's pie, chilli con carne or curry. Very well kept Courage Best and Directors and John Smiths on handpump. Darts in the small front public bar. Dryden was nearly beaten to death by hired thugs in the courtyard outside. *(Recommended by Peter Griffiths, A Y Drummond, Graham Oddey, Ian Phillips, Steve Waters, Peter Maden, Hilary Robinson, David Shillitoe, Dr J L Innes)*

Courage   Real ale   Meals and snacks (12–8 downstairs, not Sun)   Open 11–11; closed 25 and 26 Dec and 1 Jan

Museum Tavern (Bloomsbury) Map 13

Museum Street, WC1

On a corner opposite the British Museum, this old-fashioned Bloomsbury pub has high-backed benches around traditional cast-iron pub tables, old advertising mirrors between the wooden pillars behind the bar, an 'Egyptian' inn sign, and gas lamps above the tables outside. Bar food, served all day, includes ploughman's, cold pies and pasties, with hot dishes such as steak and kidney or shepherd's pie, beef in ale or pork in cider (all around £4.50). Well kept Brakspears, Everards Tiger, Greene King IPA and Abbot, Ruddles County, and Websters Yorkshire on handpump, and a wide range of wines by the glass; piped music. (Recommended by Prof S Barnett, Peter Griffiths, RHI; more reports please)

Free house   Licensee John Keating   Real ale   Meals and snacks (11–9)   Open 11–11, including Sun

Nag's Head (Belgravia) Map 13

53 Kinnerton St, SW1

Near Belgrave Square and Knightsbridge, this tiny pub has a small old-fashioned front area with a wood-effect gas fire in an old cooking range, panelling, and a low ceiling; a narrow passage leads down steps to an even smaller back bar with comfortable seats; piped music, a 1930s What-the-butler-saw machine and one-armed bandit that takes old pennies. Benskins, Ind Coope Burton and Youngs pulled on attractive 19th-century china, pewter and brass handpumps; freshly squeezed orange juice. Food includes sandwiches, filled baked potatoes (from £1.75), salads (from £2.50), quiche or chilli con carne (£2.75), good beef curry (£3.25) and steak and mushroom pie (£3.45); 50p service charge in the evening, when it can get crowded. (Recommended by Gordon B Mott, M D and E M Fowler, Dr and Mrs A K Clarke, John Fazakerley, JA, Mr and Mrs V Webster Johnson Jr)

Benskins (Ind Coope)   Licensee Kevin Moran   Real ale   Meals and snacks (all day) Children in eating area   Open 11–11 (not Mon or Tues); 11–3, 5.30–11 Sat

Old Coffee House (Soho) Map 13

49 Beak Street, W1

This was one of the first pubs in London to pile itself high with bric-a-brac – and has done it most enjoyably. Downstairs is a busy jumble of stuffed pike, stuffed foxes, great brass bowls and buckets, ancient musical instruments (brass and string sections both well represented), a good collection of Great War recruiting posters, golden discs, death-of-Nelson prints, theatre and cinema handbills, old banknotes, even a nude in one corner, and doubtless lots more that we failed to spot. Upstairs, the food room has as many prints and pictures as a Victorian study. Yet even though the place is small you can often find somewhere to sit. Lunchtime bar food includes sandwiches (95p) and home-made hot dishes such as steak and kidney pie, lasagne, chilli con carne and so forth (all £3.25). Well kept Ruddles Best and County and Websters Yorkshire on handpump. (Recommended by Peter Maden, Hilary Robinson, Peter Griffiths, Dr and Mrs A K Clarke)

Watneys   Licensee Barry Hawkins   Real ale   Meals and snacks (lunchtime)   Open 11–11

Olde Cheshire Cheese (City) Map 13

Wine Office Court; off 145 Fleet Street, EC4

The great cellar vaults date to before the Great Fire, though the present building is 17th-century, and over the years Congreve, Pope, Voltaire, Thackeray, Dickens, Conan Doyle, Yeats and perhaps Dr Johnson have visited this bustling, unpretentious place. The small rooms, up and down stairs, have bare wooden benches built into the walls, sawdust on bare boards, and on the ground floor high beams, crackly old black varnish, Victorian paintings on the dark brown walls, and a big open fire in winter. Snacks include filled rolls (£1), and in the downstairs bar ploughman's or hot dishes (£3.50); the steak, kidney, mushroom and game pie in the busy little upstairs restaurant is something of an institution; well kept Sam Smiths Old Brewery and Museum on handpump, friendly service. (*Recommended by Jamie Lyons, Ruth Harrison, Mary and James Manthei, Simon Collett-Jones, Steve Waters*)

Sam Smiths   Licensees Gordon and Debbie Garrity   Real ale Snacks (lunchtime, not Sat or Sun)   Restaurant tel (071) 353 6170/4388   Children welcome   Open 11.30–11; 11.30–3.30, 5.30–11 Sat; closed Sun

Ye Olde Mitre (City) Map 13

Ely Place, EC1; there's also an entrance beside 8 Hatton Garden

This carefully rebuilt pub with its quaint facade carries the same name of an earlier inn built here in 1547 to serve the people working in the palace of the Bishop of Ely, who actually administered the law here. The dark panelled small rooms have antique settles and big vases of flowers; a new room upstairs, mainly used for functions, doubles as an overflow at peak periods. Good bar snacks include filled rolls (60p), Scotch eggs and pork pies (60p), a good selection of sandwiches such as ham, salmon and cucumber or egg mayonnaise (from 85p, toasted £1); well kept Friary Meux, Ind Coope Burton and Tetleys on handpump, reasonably priced for the area. There are some seats with pot plants and jasmine in the narrow yard between the pub and St Ethelreda's church. (*Recommended by Simon Collett-Jones, M B Porter, John Evans, Andy Hick, Andy and Jill Kassube, Joel Dobris*)

Taylor-Walker (Allied)   Licensee Don O'Sullivan   Real ale   Snacks (all day)   Open 11–11; closed Sat, Sun, Bank Hols

Orange Brewery (Pimlico) Map 13

37 Pimlico Road, SW1

As well as a couple of guest beers on handpump in this lively, friendly pub, they brew over 300 gallons a week in the cellars – SW1, a stronger SW2, Pimlico Light and Pimlico Porter. The high ochre walls of the bar are decorated with sepia photographs and some decorative Victorian plates, there's a stuffed fox above a nicely tiled fireplace, and solid armed seats, a chaise longue, and one or two chesterfields on the bare floorboards. The cheery Pie and Ale Shop (open all day in summer) has lots more sepia photographs on the dark stained plank-panelling, plain wooden tables and chairs on pretty black and white tiles, and a shelf full of old flagons and jugs above the counter where they serve a range of home-made food: sandwiches, ploughman's, quiche, and daily hot dishes, all in pie form, such as chicken and leek, steak and stilton or lamb and apricot (all £3.95); roasts on Sunday lunchtime. Fruit machine, trivia machine, juke box. There are seats outside facing a little concreted-over green beyond the quite busy street. (*Recommended by Mrs M E Collins, Peter Griffiths, Roger Taylor, RCL*)

Own brew (though tied to Clifton Inns, part of Watneys)   Licensee Bernadette Cloran   Real ale   Meals and snacks   Children in eating area   Open 12–11

Princess Louise (Holborn) Map 13

208 High Holborn, WC1

The elaborate decor in this old-fashioned gin-palace includes etched and gilt mirrors, brightly coloured and fruity-shaped tiles, and slender Portland stone columns soaring towards the lofty and deeply moulded crimson and gold plaster ceiling; the green plush seats and banquettes are comfortable. The magnificent gents' is the subject of a separate preservation order. People cluster around the enormous island bar servery, eager for the fine range of regularly changing real ales, well kept on handpump. These include Boddingtons, Darleys Best, Greene King IPA and Abbot, Vaux Samson, Wards Best, and a beer brewed for the pub; quick, Antipodean staff in white shirts and red bow ties; fruit machine, piped music. Food, from a separate serving counter still supplied by the original dumb-waiter, includes rolls, sandwiches and hot snacks (from 80p). Upstairs they have a wider range of food such as salads and lunchtime hot dishes, with lasagne, chilli con carne, cannelloni or Lancashire hot-pot (all £3.50); several wines by the glass – including champagne. (*Recommended by Andy Hick, Roger Taylor, Steve*

Waters, Peter Griffiths, Michael and Alison Sandy, Dr J C Harrison, Andy and Jill
Kassube, Brian Jones, M B Porter, Tony and Louise Clarke, Wayne Brindle)

*Free house   Licensee Ian Phillips   Real ale   Meals and snacks   Jazz Sat evening
Open 11–11 (12–3, 6–11 Sat)*

Red Lion (Mayfair) Map 13

Waverton Street, W1

The atmosphere in the little L-shaped bar of this stylish Mayfair pub is almost like
that of a civilised country pub, with small winged settles on the partly carpeted
scrubbed floorboards, old photographs of Sam Smiths' Tadcaster Brewery in the
1920s and London prints below the high shelf of china on its dark-panelled walls.
Good food includes ploughman's, generous sandwiches, salads and hot dishes such
as Cumberland sausage, duck and venison pie or roquefort and leek quiche
(£3.95). Unusually for the area, food is served morning and evening seven days a
week; Ruddles Best and County and Websters Yorkshire on handpump. It can get
crowded at lunchtime. In the gents' there's a copy of the day's *Financial Times* at
eye level.*(Recommended by Andy and Jill Kassube, Freddy Costello)*

*Watneys   Real ale   Meals and snacks (12–2.30, 6–10)   Children in restaurant
Restaurant tel 01 (071)–499 1307   Open 11–3, 5.30–11*

NORTH LONDON

Parking is not a special problem in this area, unless we say so

Clifton (St John's Wood) Map 12

96 Clifton Hill, NW8

The high-ceilinged, bare-boarded bar area in this spacious pub is designed on more
than one level, and the wooden balustrades create the impression of a series of
small rooms; there are Edwardian and Victorian engravings and 1920s comic
prints on the elegant wallpaper, panelling and other woodwork, unusual art
nouveau wall lamps, cast-iron tables, and fine brass and glass ceiling lights;
relaxed, countrified atmosphere. Taylor Walker and Ind Coope Burton and Tetleys
on handpump; shove ha'penny, cribbage. The good range of bar food has included
sandwiches, vegetable pie, beef and Guinness stew with dumplings, salads, shark
steak and so forth, but just as we went to press we heard there'd been a change of
management. Edward VII and Lily Langtree used to come here and there are quite
a few prints of both of them (one signed by the King and his son – who became
George V). A very leafy front terrace has attractive marble-topped tables, and the
glass conservatory in the back courtyard is a lively, local place. *(Recommended by
Joel Dobris, GB, Gary Scott, M B Porter, Peter Griffiths; more reports please)*

*Taylor Walker (Allied)   Managers Mr and Mrs Eddy   Real ale   Meals and snacks
(11–3, 6.30–10.30)   Restaurant tel (071) 624 5233   Children in eating area and
restaurant   Open 11–3, 5–11 (all day Fri and Sat)*

Compton Arms (Canonbury) Map 12

4 Compton Avenue, off Canonbury Lane, N1

There's a good, friendly atmosphere in this diminutive pub, hidden away up a
mews; the gently refurbished, low-ceilinged and cheerful rooms are simply
furnished with wooden settles and assorted stools and chairs, with little local
pictures on the wall. Greene King IPA and Abbot and Rayments BBA on
handpump, and some bar food; dominoes, cribbage. A quiet little crazy-paved
back terrace has benches around cask tables among flowers under a big sycamore
tree. *(Recommended by Peter Griffiths, M B Porter; more reports on the new regime
please)*

*Greene King   Licensee Philip Bulleyment   Real ale   Meals and snacks (all day; not
Sun)   Open 11–11*

Crockers ★ (Maida Vale) Map 12

24 Aberdeen Place, NW8

There's a fine range of real ales in this imposing Victorian pub, including Arkells, Boddingtons, Brakspears, Darleys Thorne, Greene King Abbot, Samson, Wards and Youngs; also Weizenbier from Wards – the only beer in the country brewed from wheat rather than barley. But the major attraction is architectural: the ceiling in the main room is possibly the most elaborately moulded of any London pub; marble pillars support arches inlaid with bronze reliefs, and there's a sweeping marble bar counter, with a vast pillared marble fireplace with a log-effect gas fire; part of this room is no-smoking. A row of great arched and glazed mahogany doors opens into a similarly ornate but more spacious room. Darts, bar billiards, cribbage, dominoes, fruit machine, space game, trivia and juke box are in a less opulent room; also piped music Bar food at lunchtime ranges from sandwiches and home-made Scotch eggs, through ploughman's, to three hot dishes such as steak and kidney pie, lasagne or cornbeef hash (£3.25); in the evening they do vegetarian dishes (£3.40) and grills such as chicken (£4.60) and rump steaks (£5.70); Sunday lunch (£3.95). The pub is not far from Regents Canal towpath. *(Recommended by Mrs M E Collins, GB, CH; more reports please)*

Vaux Licensees Rosalind and Peter Cox Real ale Meals (11.30–2.30, 6–9.45) and snacks (available all day) Children in eating area Occasional piano player Daytime parking meters Open 11–11

Freemasons (Hampstead) Map 12

Downshire Hill NW3

In a peaceful street close to the Heath, this has a large, rambling garden, with a fountain and goldfish pool; there's also a skittle alley, and the only existing lawn billiards court left in England. Inside, the inner lounge has cane-look chairs around the well spaced tables on its patterned blue carpet, Wedgwood plaques, and a coal-effect gas fire. There are plenty of seats including leather Chesterfields in the outer lounge, too, which leads through to what used to be the public bar. Bar food includes filled rolls or ploughman's (from £1.25), lasagne or steak pie (£3.50), and on Sundays roast beef and Yorkshire pudding (£4.50); the eating area is no-smoking at lunchtime. Bass and Charrington IPA on handpump; darts, bar billiards and shove-ha'penny. *(Recommended by Michael and Alison Sandy; more reports please)*

Bass Charringtons Licensee Trevor Pringle Real ale Meals and snacks (12–2.30, 5.30–7.30) Open 12–11; 12–3, 5.30–11 winter

Holly Bush (Hampstead) Map 12

Holly Mount, NW3

There's an unchanging atmosphere in the front bar here, with its real Edwardian gas lamps, its dark and sagging ceiling, brown and cream panelled walls (which are decorated with old advertisements and a few hanging plates), and cosy bays formed by partly glazed partitions. The more intimate back room (named after the painter George Romney) has an embossed red ceiling, panelled and etched glass alcoves, and ochre-painted brick walls covered with small prints and plates. Bar food includes pasties (£1.50), a good range of ploughman's (from £2.20) and hot dishes such as chilli con carne, beef in ale pie or steak and kidney pie (around £3.50); in winter, on the popular jazz evenings, they also serve hot-pots. Benskins and Ind Coope Burton, Tetleys and Youngs on handpump; fruit machine. *(Recommended by Andy Hick, Tony and Lynne Stark, Mike Tucker)*

Taylor-Walker (Allied) Licensee Peter Dures Real ale Meals and snacks (not Sun evening or Mon) Children in eating area Live music Wed, jazz Thurs evening, cabaret Tues evening around twice a month Nearby parking sometimes quite a squeeze Open 11–3 (4 Sat), 5.30–11

Moon Under Water (Barnet) Map 12

148 High Street, Barnet

The *Moon Under Water* was actually thought up by George Orwell as the imaginary name for his ideal pub – principally somewhere lacking in undesirables such as noisy customers and fake inglenooks. This modern realisation certainly succeeds, with, for a busy town pub, a notable lack of background music – really just the welcoming hum of relaxed conversation. The one, wood-panelled bar is long and very narrow – in the main part there's no room for tables, just tall wheelbacks and an elbow shelf opposite the serving counter; lots of mirrors, an Anaglypta ceiling, some stuffed fish in glass cases, and a print of, literally, the moon under water. The front area is wider, with square tables, wheelbacks and an old-fashioned street lamp by the glass front. The more spacious back area has a conservatory feel, with a glass roof with plants hanging down and attractive blue and white tiling set high up in the walls; seating is homely – mainly plain wooden tables with stools and more wheelbacks, and there are lots of bookshelves with an eclectic range of paperbacks (including some Orwell); swan's neck lamps throughout; three fruit machines and a space game (all completely silent). The range of beers on handpump changes pretty much every week – on our visit Greene King Abbot and IPA, Marstons Pedigree and Theakstons XB, with one bargain at under a pound, usually Youngers Scotch. Lunchtime bar food includes cheese or ham salad (£2.50), quiche (£3) and chicken, lasagne or steak and mushroom pie (all £3.20). Picnic-table sets in the garden area at the back. This is one of Wetherspoon's rapidly expanding chain of pubs (see also the White Lion of Mortimer, in this chapter), and there are actually three more with this pub's name – in Enfield, Colindale and Lordship Lane in Tottenham. *(Recommended by R McIntosh, Chris Fluck; more reports please)*

Free house   Licensee Kevin Rees   Real ale   Lunchtime meals and snacks   Open 11–11

Olde White Bear (Hampstead) Map 12

Well Road, NW3

The dimly lit main room in this neo-Victorian pub has wooden stools, cushioned captain's chairs, a couple of big tasselled armed chairs, and a flowery sofa (surrounded by the excrescences of an ornate Edwardian sideboard), as well as lots of Victorian prints and cartoons on the walls, and a tiled gas-effect log fire with a heavy wooden over-mantle. A small central room – also dimly lit – has Lloyd Loom furniture, dried flower arrangements and signed photographs of actors and playwrights. In the brighter end room there are cushioned machine tapestried ornate pews, marble topped tables, a very worn butcher's table and dark brown paisley curtains. Bar food includes sandwiches, and home-made dishes such as beef in beer (£2.75), pork in cider (£2.85), chicken and mushroom or cottage pie (£3.15), and lasagne (£3.40); piped music, trivia machine. Adnams, Ind Coope Burton and Tetleys on handpump and a decent range of malt whiskies. *(Recommended by Leo and Pam Cohen, David Fowles, M B Porter; more reports please)*

Ind Coope   Licensee David Booker   Real ale   Meals (lunchtime) and snacks Children lunchtime if eating   Quiz nights first Mon of the month   Open 12–3, 5.30–11 (all day Sat in summer)

Spaniards Inn (Hampstead) Map 12

Spaniards Lane, NW3

The atmosphere in this civilised old pub is lively and busy – in the evenings the upstairs bar is quieter. The main bar area (lit by candle-shaped lamps in pink shades in the evening) has genuinely antique winged settles, open fires, and snug little alcoves in the low-ceilinged oak-panelled rooms. Bass, Charrington IPA, Greene King IPA and Youngs Bitter on handpump; fruit machine. Home-cooked bar food includes ploughman's, vegetable moussaka or macaroni and broccoli bake (£3.50), savoury mince pies (£3.75), and beef curry (£3.95). The attractive sheltered garden has slatted wooden tables and chairs on a crazy-paved terrace which opens on to a flagstoned walk around a small lawn, with roses, a side arbour of wisteria and clematis, and an aviary. The pub is named for the Spanish ambassador to the Court of James I who is said to have lived here. *(Recommended by Ian Phillips, Tony and Lynne Stark, David Goldstone)*

Charringtons (Bass)   Licensee David Roper   Real ale   Meals and snacks   Children anywhere alcohol is not served   Open 11–11

Waterside (King's Cross) Map 13

82 York Way, N1

The bar in this busy canalside pub is done out in traditional style, with latticed windows, stripped brickwork, genuinely old stripped timbers in white plaster, lots of dimly lit alcoves, spinning wheels, milkmaid's yokes, horse brasses and so on, with plenty of rustic tables and wooden benches; Boddingtons and Greene King Abbot on handpump, as well as wines on draught; fruit machine and trivia machine. Food from a hot and cold counter includes ploughman's (from £2.95), quiche (£3.75), lots of salads (from £3.95), and hot dishes such as turkey and ham pie (£3.95) and poached salmon steak (£5.50). The terrace (where there may be summer barbecues) overlooks the Battlebridge Basin. *(Recommended by Joel Dobris, E G Parish; more reports please)*

Whitbreads   Manageress Mrs Anne Edmunds   Real ale   Meals and snacks (not Sun evening)   Children in eating area   Open 11–11 (12–3, 7–11 Sat)

White Lion of Mortimer (Finsbury Park) Map 13

127 Stroud Green Road, N4

Attractively converted from a garage showroom in 1986, this atmospheric and spacious place has a large etched front window, subdued gaslamp-style lighting throughout, and two full-size Victorian street lamps just inside the entrance. The carved island servery runs the length of the bar, which has cream tilework at the front, lion pictures on the partly panelled walls, and a medley of old tables. The cooking implements down the left-hand side contrast with the horse harness and farm tools on the right, which also has a public telephone with an old copper fireplace as its booth. Some alcoves have an old cast-iron fireplace and plush settees, and there's a relaxing conservatory area at the back, with hanging ivy plants, and a small fountain outside its door. A particular virtue is the emphasis on real ale; the range changes frequently, always with one beer offered at a price few other London pubs could match – Youngers Scotch at 94p, say; there's also typically Greene King IPA and Abbot, Marstons Pedigree and Theakstons XB. Bar food includes sandwiches and hot dishes, including some vegetarian (from £2.25), and Sunday roast lunch (from £3.50); fruit machine and trivia. There are some cast-iron tables on the pavement outside. This is one of a chain of North London pubs set up a few years ago by Tim Martin as a reaction to the state of other establishments in the area – in his view, not enough real ale and too much loud piped music; other Wetherspoons pubs include the Moon Under Water in Barnet, a new main entry this year. *(Recommended by Andy Hick, Gary Scott, Alan Skull, Mugs Vernon, M B Porter)*

Free house   Managers Mr and Mrs Chambers   Real ale   Meals and snacks (12–2, 5.30–8.30)   Open 11–11

SOUTH LONDON

Parking is bad on weekday lunchtimes at the inner city pubs here (SE1), and at the Orange Tree in Richmond; it's usually OK everywhere in the evenings – you may again have a bit of a walk if a good band is on at the Bulls Head in Barnes, or at the Windmill on Clapham Common if it's a fine evening

Alma (Battersea) Map 12

499 York Road

This stylish place is authentically done out as a French cafe-bar, with pin-table and table footer, barmen in tight black waistcoats, a redundant wooden Frigidaire and, inevitably, bentwood chairs around cast-iron-framed tables. There's a lot of ochre and terracotta paintwork, gilded mosaics of the Battle of the Alma, an ornate mahogany chimney-piece and fireplace, bevelled mirrors in a pillared mahogany room divider, and in a side room a fine turn-of-the-century frieze of swirly nymphs. Service is careful and efficient, even when it's very full – which it often is. Besides Youngs Bitter and Special on handpump from the island bar counter, there are usually decent house wines, good coffee, tea or hot chocolate, newspapers out for customers, and bar food that includes sandwiches or French sticks (from 85p), onion soup (£1.95; soup and sandwich £2.50), eggs and bacon (£2.85), a plate of cheeses (£3), moules marinières (£3.95), Lyon sausages (£3.45), lamb chops (£6.30) and steak (£8.55). A thriving local atmosphere. The pub is under the same management as the Ship at Wandsworth (see below). (Recommended by Caroline Hall, Richard Gibbs)

Youngs   Licensees Charles Gotto and Mrs P M Luckie   Real ale   Meals and snacks (12–3, 7–10)   Children in eating area   Open 11–3, 5–11 (11–11 Sat)

Anchor (South Bank) Map 13

34 Park St, Bankside, SE1; Southwark Bridge end

Carefully restored in the 1960s and dating back to about 1750 (when it was rebuilt to replace the earlier tavern), this was probably where Pepys went to watch the Great Fire burning London: 'one entire arch of fire above a mile long, the churches, houses, and all on fire at once, a horrid noise the flames made, and the cracking of houses at their ruine'. There's still a lot of atmosphere these days, and even when it's invaded by tourists it's usually possible to retreat to one of the smaller rooms. The rambling series of rooms has creaky boards and beams, black-panelling, and old-fashioned high-backed settles as well as sturdy leatherette chairs. The Boswell bar has been renamed the Financial Times – their new offices are nearby. Bar food includes sandwiches and ploughman's and a hot dish of the day (£3.95); there's a full restaurant barbecue in summer. Courage Best and Directors on handpump, and a fair selection of wines by the glass and bottle; fruit machine, space game, trivia and piped music. A terrace overlooks the river. (Recommended by Wayne Brindle, Jan and Ian Alcock, Steve Waters, Jamie Lyons, Ruth Harrison, Graham Bush)

Free house   Licensee Andrew Harding   Real ale   Meals and snacks   Restaurant tel (071) 407 1577   Children in restaurant   Open 11–11; closed 25 and 26 Dec and 1 Jan

Angel (Rotherhithe) Map 12

Bermondsey Wall East, SE16

This comfortably modernised, open-plan pub enjoys the distinction of an upstream view of Tower Bridge and the City – the classic perspective which it is now almost impossible to appreciate from anywhere else; certainly it makes it one of London's best riverside pubs. You can also look down the other way to the Pool of London. The bare-boarded balcony, on timber piles sunk into the river, is lit by lanterns at night. Bar food includes ploughman's (£2.70), or cold salad pie (£3.15); Courage Best and Directors on handpump; piped music. Pepys bought cherries for his wife at the jetty here. (Recommended by Roger Huggins, Tom McLean, Ewan McCall; more up-to-date reports please)

THF – but tied to Courage   Licensee Sven Meakin   Real ale   Lunchtime meals and snacks   Restaurant (closed Sun evening) tel (071) 237 3608   Children in eating area Open 11–11; 11–3, 5.30–11 winter

Bulls Head (Barnes) Map 12

373 Lonsdale Road, SW13

The big draw to this riverside pub, just across from the Thames flood wall, is the live music – top-class modern jazz groups every evening, and weekend lunchtime big band sessions (practice on Saturday, concert on Sunday). Though admission to the well equipped music room is £2 to £3 the sound is perfectly clear – if not authentically loud – in the adjoining lounge bar. Alcoves open off the main area around the efficient island servery, which has Youngs Bitter and Special on handpump; darts, bar billiards, dominoes, cribbage, fruit machine and space game in the public bar. Bar lunches include soup with crusty bread, sandwiches, filled French bread, hot roast meat sandwiches, a pasta dish of the day, home-baked pies, and a carvery of home-roasted joints. *(Recommended by David Fowles, Doug Kennedy; more up-to-date reports please)*

Youngs   Real ale   Meals and snacks   Restaurant tel (081) 876 5241   Children in eating area of bar and in restaurant   Jazz nightly and Sunday lunchtime   Nearby parking may be difficult   Open 11–11

Crown & Greyhound (Dulwich) Map 12

73 Dulwich Village

An imposing landmark in the little village on the edge of Dulwich College, and therefore handy for walks through the park, this grand pub has lots of mahogany, etched glass and mirrors inside, with dark green velvet curtains swagged over the big windows looking out on the village road. The most ornate room is on the right, with its elaborate ochre ceiling plasterwork, fancy former gas lamps, Hogarth prints, good carved and panelled settles and so forth. It opens into the former billiards room, where kitchen tables on a stripped board floor are set for the food, which includes doorstep sandwiches or toasties (£1.30), filled baked potatoes (£1.95), lunchtime ploughman's (£2.50), curry (£3.95) and help-yourself salads (quiche £4.25, meats £4.50). A central snug leads on the other side to the saloon – brown ragged walls, upholstered and panelled settles, a coal-effect gas fire in the tiled period fireplace, and Victorian prints. A big two-level back terrace has a good many picnic-table sets under a chestnut tree, with summer weekend barbecues. Fairly quiet on weekday lunchtimes, it can be very busy in the evenings. Well kept Ind Coope Burton, Tetleys and Youngs on handpump; various fruit machines and piped music. *(Recommended by Alan Franck, Michele and Andrew Wells, Mrs J A Blanks)*

Tetley-Walkers (Allied)   Licensees B P Maguire, N A Riding   Real ale   Meals and snacks (12–2.30, 5.30–10.30)   Restaurant tel (081) 693 2466   Children in restaurant   Open 11–3.30, 5.30–11; 11–11 Fri and Sat

George ★ (Southwark) Map 13

Off 77 Borough High Street, SE1

This pub is one of those rare places which exudes genuine historicity and character. It was noted as one of London's 'fair Inns for the receipt of travellers' in 1598, and rebuilt on its original plan after the great Southwark fire in 1676. Jugglers, acrobats, conjurers, animal-trainers, musicians and even Shakespeare's strolling players used to perform here when Southwark was London's entertainment centre; this tradition is maintained in summer, when there may be Morris men dancing or players from the nearby Globe Theatre performing in the courtyard. It is in fact the only coaching inn in London to survive intact, with its tiers of open galleries looking down on the cobbled courtyard; these days it's carefully preserved by the National Trust. The row of ground-floor rooms and bars all have square-latticed windows, black beams, bare floorboards, some panelling, plain oak or elm tables, old-fashioned built-in settles, a 1797 'Act of Parliament' clock, dimpled glass lantern-lamps and so forth. It does of course attract quite a stream of tourists, and we'd recommend as the safest refuge from them the simple room nearest the street, where there's an ancient beer engine (currently not in use) that looks like a cash register. Boddingtons, Greene King Abbot, Fullers and Whitbreads Castle Eden on handpump; bar food includes sausage and beans (£1.75), ploughman's (£2.25), quiche with three salads (£2.50), and home-made steak and mushroom pie (£3). A splendid central staircase goes up to a series of dining rooms and to a gaslit balcony. *(Recommended by Mr and Mrs J M Elden, Comus Elliott, Roger Bellingham, P Thorogood, Steve Waters, Brian Jones, Wayne Brindle)*

Whitbreads   Licensee John Hall   Real ale   Meals and snacks (not Sun pm) Restaurant tel (071) 407 2056   Children in area by wine bar and restaurant   Nearby daytime parking difficult   Globe Players, Morris dancers and Medieval Combat Society during summer   Open 11–11 (12–3, 6–11 Sat); closed 25 & 26 Dec

Greyhound (Streatham) Map 12

151 Greyhound Lane, SW16

The big side conservatory, with dark cushioned cane chairs, tall rubber plants and other plants on its tiles, rattan blinds and a curious row of side-sweeping cane ceiling fans, is quite an oasis for families, and the garden, with lots of picnic-table sets, comes in for hard wear. But the main attraction here is the product of the built-in brewery, a fine range of distinctively flavoured real ales: Special, Pedigree XXX Mild, Streatham Strong, occasional London Stout, a deadly Christmas Ale, and their hefty Streatham Dynamite – which on bank holidays may be replaced by the ambiguous GBH. The brewer, Anna Bridgstock, may be able to arrange guided visits (tel (081) 677 9962). The main bar has an elaborate high rounded-edge ceiling, with a decorative cornice above the pink striped wallpaper; there are pink button-back built-in wall banquettes, bentwood chairs, lots of smallish Victorian prints and quite a battery of fruit machines. A smaller middle bar, with souvenirs of the Streatham Redskins (the local ice-hockey team), has comfortable blue plush sofas, and a games bar on the left has two pool tables, CD juke box and space games. Quietly busy, with a good mix of mainly youngish people. Bar food includes generous salads (from £3.75), several hot dishes such as curry or lasagne (£3.95), and a good range of chargrills from burgers (£2) to steak (£5.50); decent wines, pleasant service. The management changed just as we were going to press. *(Recommended by Andrew Cooke, Andy and Jill Kassube, Peter Griffiths, Hank Hotchkiss; more reports please)*

Own brew (Clifton Inns – Watneys)　Licensee Carol Winton　Real ale　Meals and snacks throughout opening hours, till 10　Children in conservatory　Open 11–11; closed evening 25 Dec

Horniman (Southwark) Map 13

Hays Galleria, Battlebridge Lane

Named after a tea merchant whose firm formerly operated from this wharf, this ambitiously-designed waterside pub has above the bar the set of clocks made for Frederick Horniman's office, showing the time in various places around the world; the former activities here are commemorated by a tea bar serving coffee, chocolate and other hot drinks, and Danish pastries and so forth; there's also a hundred-foot frieze showing the travels of the tea. But the range of stronger beverages is good too, with Adnams, Boddingtons, Ind Coope Burton, Tetleys and Wadworths 6X on handpump. The bar itself is spacious, elegant and neatly kept; the area by the sweeping bar counter is a few steps down from the door, with squared black, red and white flooring tiles and lots of polished wood. Steps lead up from here to various comfortable carpeted areas, with the tables well spread so as to allow for a feeling of spacious relaxation at quiet times but give room for people standing in groups when it's busy. From some parts there are good views of the Thames, HMS *Belfast* and Tower Bridge, as there are from the picnic-table sets outside. Bar food includes filled baps (£1.95) and hot dishes such as steak and kidney pie (£4.25). Fruit machine, trivia machine, maybe piped music. The pub is at the end of a visually exciting development, several storeys high, with a soaring glass curved roof, and supported by elegant thin cast-iron columns; various shops and boutiques open off. *(Recommended by P Miller, Mr and Mrs J M Elden, Wayne Brindle, Richard Gibbs; more reports please)*

Nicholsons/Taylor Walker (Allied)　Licensee Mr Hastings　Real ale　Bar meals and snacks (lunchtime)　Restaurant tel (081) 407 3611; closed Sat　Children in eating area and restaurant　Open 11–11; Sat closing 10 (6 winter), Sun 6

Olde Windmill (Clapham) Map 12

Clapham Common South Side, SW4

On the edge of Clapham Common, this large Victorian inn has a front room dominated by the substantial and heavily manned bar counter, and the domed and spacious main room has big prints of Dutch windmill pictures on the flowery black and brown wallpaper, and clusters of orange leatherette seats, sofas and small armchairs around elegant black tables; Youngs Bitter and Special on handpump; fruit machine and space game. Bar food includes sandwiches, ploughman's, salads (not winter evenings), home-made pizza, chilli con carne, seafood platter, chicken Kiev and sirloin steak. There are courtyards at each end with picnic tables, and one has a colonnaded shelter and tubs of shrubs. The inn can get packed in summer, when it seems to serve not just the pub but half the Common too. *(Recommended by Greg Parston; more reports please)*

Youngs   Licensee Richard Williamson   Real ale   Meals and snacks (not Sun evening)   Restaurant (closed Sun)   Children in restaurant   Open 11–11; closed winter afternoons   Bedrooms tel (081) 673 4578; £31/£40(£45B)

Orange Tree (Richmond) Map 12

45 Kew Road

The spacious cellar bar here is attractively lit and has a wine-barish atmosphere, with old stripped brickwork walls and simple tables on a tiled floor. Bar food, served down here, includes chilli con carne (£3.75), steak and kidney pie (£4.10), beef salad (£4.25), steaks (from £6.45), and fondues (from £9.50 for two). On the ground floor there's a full range of lunchtime sandwiches (from £1), ploughman's (£1.60), sausage and egg, and scampi. The main bar has an embossed ceiling with an unusual fruit and foliage pattern, and there are big coaching and Dickens prints, and the courtly paintings of the seven ages of man by Henry Stacy Marks – presented to the Green Room theatre club here in 1921; upstairs the fringe theatre carries on the histrionic tradition. Youngs Bitter and Special on handpump; fruit machine. *(Recommended by Michael and Alison Sandy, David Fowles; more reports please)*

Youngs   Licensees Don and Chris Murphy   Real ale   Meals and snacks (available all day; not Sun evening)   Restaurant tel (081) 940 0944; not Sun evening   Children in restaurant   Nearby parking difficult   Open 11–11

Phoenix & Firkin ★ (Denmark Hill)

5 Windsor Walk

Perhaps the most striking of the Firkin own-brew pubs originally established by David Bruce (see also under Ferret & Firkin in the West London section, and *passim* in the Lucky Dips), this attractively renovated, palatial Victorian building has a vast lofty pavilion of a bar; the bar counter itself is made from a single mahogany tree, and there's solid wooden furniture on the stripped wooden floor, paintings of steam trains, old seaside posters, Bovril advertisements, old-fashioned station name signs, plants, big revolving fans, and a huge double-faced station clock, originally from Llandudno Junction, hanging by chains from the incredibly high ceiling. At one end there's a similarly-furnished gallery, reached by a spiral staircase, and at the other arches lead into a food room; piped music. The building spans the railway cutting, and you can feel it throb when trains pass underneath. In the evenings it can get packed with a good mixed crowd. Straightforward food includes big filled baps or a portion of pie (£1.50), ploughman's (£2.30), and a daily hot dish (£2.50). The beers include Phoenix, Rail and Dogbolter on handpump, as well as two weekly guest beers kept under light blanket pressure. Outside there are some tables and chairs with parasols, and the steps which follow the slope of the road are a popular place to sit. *(Recommended by Jamie Lyons, Ruth Harrison, Sue Corrigan; more reports please)*

Own Brew   Licensee Simon Fraser   Real ale   Meals and snacks   Well behaved children allowed   Open 11–11

Ship ✿ (Wandsworth) Map 12

41 Jews Row, SW18

This riverside pub is at its best in summer, when you can sample the food from the charcoal barbecue counter on the extensive terrace; changing daily, it includes burger, sausages or chicken, Mediterranean prawns, lamb steak or kingfish, seafood kebab and sirloin steak; other food, served inside, includes sandwiches,

ploughman's, good peppered brie and pork with bubble-and-squeak. The terrace
itself is on two levels, partly cobbled and partly concrete, with picnic table sets,
pretty hanging baskets, brightly coloured flower beds, small trees and its own
summer bar. Inside, most of the main bar is in a conservatory style, with only a
small part of the original ceiling left. It's light and airy with a relaxed, chatty
atmosphere, wooden tables (one a butcher's table), a medley of stools and old
church chairs, and two comfortable leatherette chesterfields on the wooden
floorboards; one part has a Victorian fireplace, a huge clock surrounded by barge
prints, and part of a milking machine on a table, and there's a rather battered
harmonium, old-fashioned bagatelle, and jugs of flowers around the window sills;
Youngs Bitter and Special on handpump. There are occasional theme evenings –
such as a Last Night of the Proms, when people wear evening dress. The basic
public bar has plain wooden furniture, a black kitchen range in the fireplace and
darts, pinball and a juke box. A Thames barge is moored alongside and can be
used for private parties, although she may sail along the East and South coasts
during the summer months. Note that the atmosphere can get somewhat
boisterous at weekends. *(Recommended by Andy and Jill Kassube, Richard Gibbs, G S
B G Dudley, M B Porter, Greg Parston, Ian Phillips)*

*Youngs   Licensee Charles Gotto   Real ale   Meals and snacks (12–10)   You may
have to park some way away   Open 11–11*

White Swan (Richmond) Map 12

25/26 Old Palace Lane

Readers praise the atmosphere in this little rose-covered cottage – exceptionally
friendly and more like that of a village local than a busy London pub. An attractive
place to sit in summer is the conservatory, looking on to the paved garden with its
climbing plants, flowering tubs, flowerbeds and wooden tables and benches;
summer barbecues out here on Tuesday and Thursday evenings. There are copper
pots hanging from the dark beamed ceiling in the open-plan bar, old prints of
London and china plates on the walls, captain's chairs, dark wood tables and plush
banquettes on the green and terracotta patterned carpet. The good range of bar
food includes sandwiches (£1.50), quiche (£2.95), salads (from £2.95), and hot
dishes such as macaroni cheese (£2.95), and fish or steak and kidney pie, chilli con
carne or lasagne (all £3.25). Courage Best and Directors on handpump.
(Recommended by Nigel Williamson, Dave Braisted, Ian Phillips; more reports please)

*Courage   Licensee Anthony Savage   Real ale   Meals and snacks (12–2.30, 5.30–11)
Children in conservatory till 9   Open 11–3, 5.30–11; 11–4, 6–11 Sat*

WEST LONDON

*During weekday or Saturday daytime you may not be able to find a meter very close to
the Anglesea Arms or the Windsor Castle, and parking very near in the evening may
sometimes be tricky with both of these, but there shouldn't otherwise be problems in this
area*

Anglesea Arms (Chelsea) Map 13

15 Selwood Terrace, SW7

This welcoming pub can get very full – particularly in the evenings and at
weekends – when even the outside terrace (which has seats and tables) tends to
overflow into the quiet side street. There's a good range of ales on handpump,
including Adnams, Boddingtons Bitter, Brakspears SB, Eldridge Pope Hardy,
Greene King Abbot, Theakstons Old Peculier and Youngs Special. The bar itself
has central elbow tables, leather chesterfields, faded Turkey carpets on the bare
wood-strip floor, wood panelling, and big windows with attractive swagged
curtains; at one end several booths with partly glazed screens have cushioned pews
and spindleback chairs, and down some steps there's a small carpeted room with
captain's chairs, high stools and a Victorian fireplace. The old-fashioned mood is
heightened by some heavy portraits, prints of London, a big station clock, bits of
brass and pottery, and large brass chandeliers; the atmosphere is relaxed and
cheery. Food from a glass cabinet includes doorstep sandwiches (from £1.50),

ploughman's (£2.70), pies such as turkey and mushroom, steak or broccoli and cheese (all £3.20), and a Sunday roast (£3.95). *(Recommended by Robert and Elizabeth Scott, Andy Hick, Kevin Fields)*

Free House   Licensee Patrick Timmons   Real ale   Meals and snacks   Children in eating area till 7pm   Daytime parking metered   Open 11–3, 5.30(7 Sat)–11; closed 25 and 26 Dec

City Barge (Chiswick)

27 Strand-on-the-Green, W4

The new management in this 15th-century riverside pub has transformed the Old Bar into a lunchtime restaurant during the week; but in the evening its two little low-ceilinged rooms are still the places to head for, with their cushioned wooden seats built into the ochre walls, ancient fireplace raised above the quarry-tiled floor as protection against floods, a really worn old overmantle, and antique decorative mugs behind latticed glass and miniature bottles in a corner cupboard. Upstairs, a more orthodox and more modern carpeted bar – the New Bar – has been modestly refurbished – the central pillars have been removed, so it's quite airy and open plan; lots of standing room, and reproduction maritime painted signs and bird prints. Bar food includes ploughman's (£3), salads (from £3), quiche (£3.25), and lasagne (£4.50); Courage Best and Directors; darts, fruit machine. There's also a warm white-walled conservatory with wooden chairs around cast-iron-framed tables, a few houseplants and plastic ferns. On warm summer evenings people tend to crowd along the towpath outside, with many sitting on the low wall. *(Recommended by J Hampton, B Metherell, Mrs R Green, R Bennett, Andrew Cooke; reports on the new management please)*

Courage   Managers Mr and Mrs Paul Woodhall   Real ale   Meals and snacks (12–3, not Sun)   Restaurant tel (081) 994 2148   Children in conservatory   Open 11–3, 5.30–11 (all day Sat)

Dove ★ ⊘ (Hammersmith) Map 12

19 Upper Mall, W6

This old-fashioned riverside place is in the *Guinness Book of Records* for having the smallest bar room – the front snug, a mere 4'2" by 7'10". The pub is at its best at lunchtime when it's quiet and relaxed; but even when it's full (often predominantly of young people) there's still a good atmosphere. By the entrance from the quiet alley, the main bar has black wood panelling, red leatherette cushioned built-in wall settles and stools around dimpled copper tables, old framed advertisements, and photographs of the pub; very well kept Fullers London Pride and ESB on handpump. Up some steps, a room with small settles and solid wooden furniture has a big, clean and efficiently served glass food cabinet: sausage and beans, filled baked potatoes (from £1.65), salads (from £2.50), shepherd's pie, lasagne or moussaka (£2.95), and around ten daily specials such as chicken chasseur, kidneys in red wine or hot-pot (£3.95). From here, big windows open out on to a smallish terrace with a large vine; the main flagstoned area, down some steps, has lots of teak tables and white metal and teak chairs looking over the low river wall to the Thames reach just above Hammersmith Bridge. There's a manuscript of 'Rule Britannia' on the wall in one of the bars: James Thomson, who wrote it, is said to have written the final part of his less well-known 'The Seasons' in an upper room here, dying of a fever he had caught on a trip from here to Kew in bad weather. *(Recommended by Tony and Lynne Stark, Doug Kennedy, David Goldstone, Patrick Young, P Thorogood, RCL, Simon Collett-Jones, R Bennett)*

Fullers   Licensee Brian Lovrey   Real ale   Meals and snacks (12noon–8)   Open 11–11

Eel Pie (Twickenham) Map 12

9 Church Street

You can sit at the front window of the simply furnished downstairs bar, decorated in Laura Ashley style, and look out to the quiet village street here. There's a good range of very well kept real ales, with Adnams, Badger Best and Tanglefoot, Everards Tiger, Gales HSB, Ridleys and Wadworths 6X on handpump. Bar food includes toasted sandwiches or large granary baps, ploughman's (from £2.50), salads (£2.75), Lancashire hot-pot, chicken curry or steak, kidney and Guinness pie (all £2.95), and lasagne, goulash or moussaka (£3). Darts, fruit machine, piped music; benches outside on the cobbles. It can be very popular at weekends, especially if there's a rugby match taking place. (*Recommended by Ian Phillips, P Miller, Nigel Gibbs, Peter Griffiths, CEO, A C and S J Beardsley, Nigel Williamson, Simon Collett-Jones, Iain Hewitt; more reports please*)

Free house   Licensee Brendan Mallon   Real ale   Meals (not evening or Sun) and snacks (not Sun)   Children in eating area of bar till 6pm   Open 11–11; 11–3, 5.30–11 Sat, and winter Mon and Tues

Ferret & Firkin (Fulham) Map 12

Lots Road, SW10

Just around the corner from the *Guide* offices, this determinedly basic pub has unsealed bare floorboards, traditional furnishings well made from good wood, slowly circulating colonial-style ceiling fans, a log-effect gas fire, tall airy windows, and plenty of standing room in front of the long bar counter – which is curved, to match the green-painted front wall. Well kept own-brew ales include Ferret, Stoat, the notoriously strong Dogbolter, and usually a Bruce's; with 24 hours' notice you can collect a bulk supply. There are also two or three guest beers from other breweries, and a couple of real ciders. A food counter serves heftily filled giant meat-and-salad rolls (£1.75), pies, ploughman's, salads, spare ribs and chilli con carne. The clientele tends to be young, easy-going, and very mixed. The pub is another of the small chain of own-brew pubs started by David Bruce but sold by him a few years ago (see also Phoenix & Firkin, South London); it was also the pub at the centre of Lord Linley's successful libel action against the *Today* newspaper last year. (*Recommended by Ian Phillips, Simon Collett-Jones*)

Own brew   Real ale   Meals (not evening) and snacks   Daytime parking is metered Evening pianist or guitarist   Open 11–11

Kings Arms (Hampton Court) Map 12

Hampton Court Rd; next to Lion Gate

Right on the edge of the grounds of Hampton Court (and particularly convenient for the maze), this imposing, white-painted pub is a popular draw in summer. The lounge bar is mainly given over, on the left, to food, with half-a-dozen large, check-clothed tables with one or two settles, bunches of dried flowers over an old cooking range and walls stripped back to the brick. Bar food, from an efficient servery, includes soup (£1.50), jumbo sausages or ploughman's (£3.25), fettucini with tuna or macaroni cheese and ham (£3.50), moussaka or prawns in garlic (£3.75), salads (from £3.75; poussin £4.50), steak sandwich or tasty kebab (£3.95), and pies such as steak and mushroom or fish (£4.25). A second bar, leading off to the right, has a cosy atmosphere, with black panelling, some seats and tables made from casks, and fine stained glass around the serving counter; well kept Adnams Broadside and Mild, Badger Best and Tanglefoot and Wadworths 6X on handpump. The public bar at the end is properly old-fashioned and notably relaxed, with good games – an old pin-ball machine that takes two-pence pieces (proceeds to the RNLI), bar billiards and a good darts area; sawdust on the floor, dried hops hanging from the beams, a few casks, a fireplace with a stuffed pheasant above it, and some enamel adverts, one for Camp coffee; fruit machine, board games, unobtrusive piped music. There are several picnic-table sets outside by the road. Dogs welcome. (*Recommended by Michael Sandy, Ian Phillips, Richard Houghton, Mayur Shah, V Hooper-Immins*)

Free house   Licensees I Readman and T Buchanan-Munro   Real ale   Meals and snacks (all day)   Upstairs restaurant (party bookings only) tel (081) 977 1729   Open 11–11, including Sun

Old Ship (Hammersmith) Map 12

25 Upper Mall, W6

The three bar areas in this spacious and comfortably modernised open-plan riverside pub are similarly decorated with a clutter of nautical bric-a-brac, including ship pictures and model boats, with racing skiffs, life-belts, rudders and oars on the beams; the wooden-floored end room has pool, fruit machine, space game and CD juke box. Bar food, served in the central area, includes pizzas (£1.20), ploughman's (£2.30), salads (from £3.20) and hot dishes such as lasagne or chicken and ham pie (£3.20); Ruddles County and Best and Websters Yorkshire on handpump. There's a wrought-iron balcony, wooden picnic-table sets and lots of hanging flowers on the terrace overlooking the river. The *Dove* (see above) is a short walk away. *(Recommended by Ollie Raphael, Patrick Young; more reports please)*

Watneys   Licensee Mary McCormack   Real ale   Meals (lunchtime) and snacks (not Sun evening)   Open 11–3, 5.30–11

Sporting Page ⊗ (Chelsea) Map 12
6 Camera Place

A fine, rather smart Chelsea local which seems as if it's always been as it is – but in fact was completely redone when the Front Page people (see Central London section) took it over a few years ago. There are some obvious resemblances in the range of interesting bar food, which here includes soup (£2.20), prawn and melon salad (£3.75), sausage, mash and beans or avocado, mozzarella and tomato salad (£4), steak sandwich (£4.25), smoked salmon with scrambled eggs (£4.10), and good home-made salmon fishcakes (£5.75). Boddingtons, Ruddles County and Websters Yorkshire on handpump; decent house wines, espresso coffee; civilised service. The sturdy, cleanly cut tables around the walls leave plenty of room by the bar, and there's an airy feel from the big windows and light paintwork, with entertaining sporting decorations – old prints of people playing polo, Rugby football, cricket and so forth, and big painted-tile-effect murals of similar scenes; picnic-table sets outside. *(Recommended by Hank Hotchkiss; more reports please)*

Watneys   Real ale   Meals and snacks (12–2.30, 7–10.15)   Children in eating area Open 11–3, 5.30–11; closed 25 and 26 Dec

White Horse (Fulham) Map 12
1 Parsons Green, SW6

Opposite Parsons Green, this busy well run pub has a spacious U-shaped bar with a solid panelled central bar servery manned by a team of efficient barmen in matching dark blue shirts. The main part has big leather chesterfields and plush stools on the green patterned carpet, wooden slatted blinds and brown hessian drapes over the huge windows, half-panelled and caramel-coloured Anaglypta walls with cheerful posters advertising wine tastings here, a central pillar with elbow rests, and a relaxed atmosphere. To one side is a plainer area with leatherette wall banquettes on the wood plank floor, green velvet curtains, a fruit machine, and a glass cabinet with tankards and sporting cups, and over on the other side is a small raised part reserved for non-smokers, a tiled Victorian fireplace with a marble overmantle, and little plush seats and tables set out for eating; dominoes, cribbage, backgammon. A glass food cabinet (with lots of healthy green plants hanging from a skylight above it) dispenses the truly home-made dishes: Scotch egg, pâté, three-cheese ploughman's (£2.40), and cold meats with carefully planned, really fresh salads (from 70p per helping); hot dishes such as Spanish omelette (from £2), Italian meatballs (£4), carrot and feta cheese lasagne (£4.10), steak and kidney pie with pickled walnuts (around £4.50), seafood pasta (£4.90), puddings like apricot sponge with apricot sauce (£1.40), huge weekend breakfasts (£4.50), and Sunday roast lunch (£9.50, best to book). Particularly well kept Adnams Bitter, Bass, Charrington IPA, Highgate Mild, and maybe even Traquair House Ale (brewed by the daughter of the late Laird of Traquair in a stately home in the Scottish borders) on handpump and with some helpful tasting notes; malt whiskies, and a good, interesting and not overpriced wine list (with happy hour discounts), tutored wine and beer tastings, and seasonal festivals – the best known is for strong old ale held on the last Saturday in November. Outside, there are white cast-iron tables and chairs. It does get very crowded on weekend evenings. *(Recommended by Richard Houghton; more reports please)*

Charringtons   Licensee Sally Cruickshank   Real ale   Meals and snacks (12–2.30, 5.30–10, not Sat evening; weekend breakfasts from 11)   Children allowed weekday lunchtimes   Trad jazz Thurs evening   Open 11.30–3, 5–11; 11–3, 7–11 Sat; closed 4 or 5 days over Christmas

Windsor Castle ★ (Holland Park/Kensington) Map 12

114 Campden Hill Road, W8

An attractive summer feature in this splendidly old pub is the big tree-shaded back terrace which has lots of sturdy teak seats and tables on flagstones, knee-high stone walls (eminently sittable-on) dividing them, high ivy-covered sheltering walls, and soft shade from a sweeping, low-branched plane tree, a lime and a flowering cherry. A bar counter serves the terrace directly, as does a separate food stall. The interior consists of a series of little dark-panelled, old-fashioned rooms, with sturdy built-in elm benches, time-smoked ceilings and soft lighting; a snug little pre-war-style dining room opens off the bar. Bar food includes sandwiches (from £1.30), plaice and chips (£2.95), steak and kidney pie (£3.50), and steak (£3.50); Bass and Charrington IPA on handpump; no fruit machines or piped music. Usually fairly quiet at lunchtime, the pub is often packed in the evenings. Note that they don't allow children. *(Recommended by Patrick Young; more reports please)*

Charringtons (Bass)   Licensee Anthony James Owen   Real ale   Meals and snacks (12–2.30, 5.30–10; not Sun evening)   Daytime parking metered   Open 11–11

EAST LONDON

Weekday daytime parking isn't too bad in this area, though you should expect quite a walk to the Dickens Inn; there should be no real problems in the evening or at weekends

Dickens Inn (Dockland) Map 12

St Katharine's Yacht Haven, off St Katharine's Way, E1

An unashamedly touristy pub which benefits from its fine dockland position, this spacious place has timber baulks for pillars and beams, stripped brickwork, worn floorboards, a very long polished brass bar counter, and a subdued atmosphere emphasised by candles in bottles and by the partly glazed wooden partitions which separate it into smaller areas. There's something of a cosmopolitan feel, with clientele ranging from smartly dressed European tourists drinking tea or coffee, through people from the nearby World Trade Centre or the Tower Hotel, to folk who like at least to imagine themselves messing about in boats (the main bar overlooks the lively yacht harbour); Courage Best and Directors, John Smiths and Dickens Own and Olivers, brewed especially for the pub, just over the river in Tooley St; drinks are at central London prices. Hot bar food includes sausages and beans (£3.45), shepherd's pie (£4.75) and steak and kidney pie (£5.45). Doors open out on to the verandah (a mass of window-boxes), and steps lead down to the cobbled waterside terrace, though you can't take food or drink down here. *(Recommended by Robert Lester, Gary Scott, E G Parish)*

Courage   Manager Jon Davidson   Real ale   Meals and snacks   Restaurant tel (071) 488 2208   Open 11–11; may close over Christmas

Grapes (Limehouse) Map 12

76 Narrow Street, E14

Fresh fish is a speciality in this relatively quiet little pub; in the long and narrow bar they serve seafood risotto (£2.95), fish and chips or seafood mornay (£3.20), and fish pie (£3.50); the upstairs fish restaurant (with fine views of the river) is highly praised. The partly-panelled bar, comfortably free of tourists, has lots of prints, mainly of actors, and some elaborately etched windows. Ind Coope Burton, Taylor-Walker Bitter and Tetleys on handpump. The glass-roofed back balcony is one of the most sheltered places for a riverside drink. Dickens used the pub as the basis of his 'Six Jolly Fellowship Porters' in *Our Mutual Friend.(Recommended by Ian Phillips, Peter Griffiths; more reports please)*

Taylor-Walker (Allied)   Licensee Frank Johnson   Real ale   Meals and snacks (not Sat or Sun, not Mon evening)   Restaurant tel (071) 987 4396   Children in restaurant   Open 11–2.30, 5–11; closed 24 Dec–1 Jan

Hollands (Stepney) Map 12

9 Exmouth Street, E1

There's an unchanging atmosphere in this friendly little place – largely because most of the decorations and furnishings are original early-Victorian. The heavy bar counter has swivelling etched and cut glass snob screens, and there are antique mirrors, *Vanity Fair* pictures, Victorian cartoons and photographs, as well as a clutter of trumpets, glass and brass ornaments hanging from the ochre painted and panelled ceiling in the main bar. Through an arched doorway and heavy velvet curtains is the split-level, red-tiled lounge bar, with its panelled and re-upholstered bench seats, old sepia photographs, brass pots hanging from the ceiling and a big Victorian fireplace with large china ornaments on its mantlepiece. Bar food consists of freshly-made sandwiches (from 90p; hot bacon 95p); Wethereds on handpump; darts, hood skittles. The pub was opened early in Queen Victoria's reign by the present landlord's great grandfather. *(More up-to-date reports please)*

Free House   Licensee John C Holland   Real ale   Lunchtime snacks (not Sat or Sun)   Open 11–11

Lucky Dip

Besides the fully inspected pubs, you might like to try these Lucky Dips recommended to us and described by readers (if you do, please send us reports). We have split them into the main areas used for the full reports — Central, North, and so on. Within each area the Lucky Dips are listed by postal district, ending with Greater London suburbs on the edge of that area.

CENTRAL

EC1

[56 Faringdon Rd], *Betsey Trotwood*: Now just the Betsey; green paint, lots of mirrors in one corner, well kept Shepherd Neame Bitter and Best; popular with *Guardian* and other nearby office-workers *(Peter Griffiths)*

[Chiswell St], *Chiswell Vaults*: Subterranean, much-vaulted Whitbreads pub with plenty of space, very generous helpings of food, friendly well trained staff *(Joan Chenhalls, LYM)*

[Farringdon Lane], *City Pride*: Two attractive downstairs rooms (though the rows of books in the overspill room by the bar are tantalisingly out of reach); well kept reasonably priced Chiswick, London Pride and ESB, imaginative good value food, fire in original fireplace, stained-glass windows with pub's name, extra seating for diners upstairs *(Anon)*

[362 St Johns St], *Empress of Russia*: Recently knocked-together Whitbreads pub with late 19th-century Russian theme, comfortable red banquettes and chairs in single semi-circular bar with eating annexe, small but pleasant, with modest pub food all day — a useful retreat *(TN)*

[1 Middle St], *Hand & Shears*: Traditional Smithfield 16th-century pub, often crowded and lively, one of London's least spoilt pubs, still with the feeling of several small rooms

around the central servery (though virtually all the partitions have gone now); marvellously mixed clientele, well kept Courage real ales; open 11.30-11 Mon–Fri, closed weekends mid-afternoon *(Brian Jones, LYM)*

☆ [166 Goswell Rd], *Pheasant & Firkin*: Good value ploughman's and other simple food, well kept own-brewed beers and guests such as Wadworths 6X; wooden stools, benches and tables on bare boards; popular with businessmen *(LYM)*

☆ [Rising Sun Ct; Cloth Fair], *Rising Sun*: Cool, dark and lofty bar with tall tables, high stools and wooden settles, friendly staff, calm atmosphere; well kept Sam Smiths, coal-effect gas fire, good value huge rolls and sandwiches, views of church; narrow room up steep stairs has more food inc ploughman's, steak pie and quiche; highly polished gents' *(Ian Phillips, Mike Tucker, SJC)*

[56 Chiswell St], *St Pauls*: Done up by Whitbreads in country style, attractive decor with farm tools hanging from ceiling, stained pine tables and chairs, bare floorboards; good atmosphere *(Gavin May)*

[Rosoman St], *Thomas Wethered*: Comfortable pub with well kept McMullens — a rarity in London; also low-priced monthly guest beer, good value happy hour 5.30 - 6.30; carvery roast and Sun lunch *(Alan Skull)*

[67 Fenchurch St], *East India Arms*: Well kept Youngs real ales; superb service even when it gets crowded at lunchtime (*David Fowles*)

[Minories; opp Tower of London], *Minories*: New pub in big railway arch, but surprisingly light and spacious; very expensive Wethereds, food from sandwiches up; wine bar and restaurant on different levels (*Ian Phillips*)

EC4

[22 Fleet St], *Cock*: Popular, with well kept real ale and good basic character (*Dr and Mrs A K Clarke*)

[10 Creed Lane], *Davys*: Though more wine bar than pub, this atmospheric cellar bar is worth knowing for sensibly limited choice of good value food from pâté through dressed crab to sirloin steak; bar in front with standing areas, dining area behind, dim lighting, good Rioja and other wines, sherry in enormous glasses; can be noisy with chatter; good service (*John Evans*)

[Charterhouse St], *Fox & Anchor*: Tremendous helpings of good meat (*A W Dickinson*)

[Fleet St], *Old Bell*: Busy city pub, rebuilt by Wren as commissariat for his workers on St Bride's Church (burnt down in 1940 air raid); well worth a visit at lunchtime (*Dr and Mrs A K Clarke*)

☆ [6 Martin Lane], *Old Wine Shades*: More wine bar than pub, one of the City's very few buildings to have escaped the Great Fire of 1666 — heavy black beams, dark panelling, old prints, subdued lighting, old-fashioned high-backed settles, antique tables and dignified alcoves; good value weekday lunchtime traditional bar snacks, a good range of wines (under same ownership as El Vino's); jacket and tie for men, no jeans or jump-suits for women; open weekdays 11.30-3, 5-8 (*G D Collier, LYM*)

[29 Watling St], *Olde Watling*: Well kept Bass and Charrington IPA in heavy-beamed and timbered pub built by Wren in 1662 as a site commissariat for his new St Pauls Cathedral; lunchtime bar food, closes 9.30, closed Sat and Sun (*LYM*)

[Brooks Wharf; High Timber St, off 48 Upper Thames St], *Samuel Pepys*: Two breezy balconies give interesting river views even at low tides — location the big plus; downstairs flagstone bar with loud music, well kept Bass and Charrington IPA, limited choice of bar food, restaurant; found closed summer 1990 — another refurbishment? (*Ian Phillips, Gary Scott, LYM; news please*)

SW1

☆ [Victoria St], *Albert*: Splendidly redecorated and commanding exterior, set off against bleak cliffs of modern glass; spacious but packed weekday lunchtimes, quiet otherwise; popular for efficiently served bar food, comfortably well kept, a Scotland

Yard local and used by some MPs and many civil servants; Watneys-related real ales (*Robert Lester, John Whitehead, BB*)

☆ [104 Horseferry Rd], *Barley Mow*: Comfortable and well kept pub, handy for Royal Horticultural Society's Halls in Vincent Sq, with Watneys-related real ales, good value efficient self-service food counter with three or four hot dishes and wide range of salads, friendly staff, a few pavement tables in side street (*John Fazakerley, BB*)

[62 Petty France], *Buckingham Arms*: Congenial Youngs local close to Passport Office and Buckingham Palace, unusual long side corridor fitted out with elbow ledge for drinkers, cheerful efficient service; good cheap lunchtime food from ploughman's (*Ian Phillips, Mike Tucker, LYM*)

[39 Palace St], *Cask & Glass*: A half-pint pub serving half-pints of Watneys-related beers, sandwiches; one small room overflowing into street in summer — when it's a riot of colour; handy for Queen's Gallery (*John Whitehead*)

[53 Whitehall], *Clarence*: 18th-century free house with gas lighting in and out, sawdust on the floor, old farm tools on the beams; good fun for tourists — and has bar food and seven real ales (*Robert Lester, Dr and Mrs A K Clarke*)

[63 Eaton Terr], *Duke of Wellington*: Friendly Whitbreads pub in elegant street not far from house where Mozart lived; real ales, cheap snacks inc superb sausage ploughman's (*John Tyzack*)

[130 Victoria St], *Duke of York*: Well kept Arkells (*Alan Skull*)

[20 The Broadway], *Feathers*: Opposite London Transport HQ and near New Scotland Yard; gets crowded at lunchtime, but even then you may find a seat upstairs — early evening is the best time for a quiet drink; decent lunchtime snacks, friendly service (*Robert Lester*)

[29 Passmore St], *Fox & Hounds*: Small and cosy with great atmosphere — glowing fire, friendly bar staff and good mix of customers (young couples, old locals and a Chelsea pensioner); toasted sandwiches in evening (*Anon*)

[25 King St], *Golden Lion*: Rather distinguished bow-fronted building, opp Christies auction rooms; downstairs bar may be packed, but seats and tables usually available both in passageway alongside or upstairs in theatre bar (*Ian Phillips*)

☆ [18 Wilton Row], *Grenadier*: Cramped and spartan little mews bar with Watneys-related real ales and a formidable bloody mary from the pewter-topped bar counter, lunchtime corner snack bar, cosy little intimate candlelit restaurant; proud of its connections with the Iron Duke, lots of character (*TBB, Graham Oddey, Simon Collett-Jones, Ian Phillips, John Tyzack, Jamie Lyons, Ruth Harrison, Dr and Mrs A K Clarke, LYM*)

[Little Chester St], *Grouse & Claret*: Quite upmarket pub in elegant area, but prices

counter; main bar oval-shaped, with good choice of real ales inc well kept Greene King Abbot *(Roger Huggins)*

N6

☆ [77 Highgate West Hill], *Flask*: Original core dating back to early 18th-century rebuilding, with old-fashioned features like the little sash-windowed bar servery, panelling, high-backed carved settle; this snug area has been closed on recent lunchtimes though; the upper bar near the dining area, with a new salad bar, is more straightforward; standard pub food, Allied real ales, well behaved children allowed; pleasant terrace, friendly staff *(J P Day, LYM)*

N8

[Park Rd], *Princess Alexandra*: Large but pleasant Watneys pub with three spacious old-fashioned rooms; garden at one end with lots of tables and flowers, light and airy conservatory at other doubling as lunchtime food bar, leading out to terrace tables *(Michael and Alison Sandy)*

N14

[Bourne Hill], *Woodman*: Very small and civilised one-bar Whitbreads pub with warm, friendly and lively atmosphere, well kept Flowers, almost the air of a rural retreat; tables in garden behind *(Hilary Robinson, Peter Maden)*

N20

[Totteridge Village], *Orange Tree*: Spacious pub by duckpond, plush decor, separate restaurant *(LYM)*
[310 Oakleigh Rd N; (A109)], *York Arms*: Watneys-related real ales in bright, clean and friendly two-bar local with lunchtime snacks and nice atmosphere *(Robert Lester)*

NW1

[Marylebone Rd; Baker St Underground Stn], *Moriarty's*: Good beer in great pub, closed for refurbishment as we go to press summer 1990 *(K A Topping)*
[49 Regents Pk Rd], *Queens*: Little changed in the last 30 years or so, typically Victorian — mahogany, stained-glass windows, Victorian prints, secluded corners; Bass beers, reasonable food — highly recommended for a quiet pint *(Mike Tucker)*
[1 Lidlington Pl], *Russell Arms*: Neat modernised and friendly pub with well kept Watneys-related real ales *(Dr and Mrs A K Clarke)*
[59 Parkway], *Spread Eagle*: Has changed little over the years; good Youngs Bitter *(Mike Tucker, Marshall Jones)*

NW3

[14 Flask Walk], *Flask*: Traditional London local in the old part of Hampstead, with well kept Youngs and good food; popular with actors and artists for 300 years — still is *(Miss K Haydon, BB)*
[79 Heath St], *Nags Head*: Has had good choice of well kept real ales with for example Greene King Abbot as well as McMullens; nice and peaceful on weekday lunchtimes, with real home-made soup and good salt beef, ham or cheese sandwiches, friendly staff; very popular with younger people in the evening; sold summer 1990 *(Leo and Pam Cohen, BB; news of the new regime please)*
[Rosslyn Hill], *Rosslyn Arms*: Down-to-earth atmosphere though in a trendy area — used by working men; well kept Courage Best and Directors, friendly atmosphere *(G F Scott)*
[97 Haverstock Hill], *Sir Richard Steele*: Good genuine relaxing atmosphere, well kept beers, attractive decor *(Jonathan Warner, BB)*

NW4

[56 The Burroughs (A504)], *White Bear*: Smartly modernised split-level pub guarded by stuffed polar bear; popular food such as casseroles, pies, quiches and good steaks, well kept Allied beers, tables outside *(Andy and Jill Kassube)*

NW8

[2 St Ann's Terrace], *Duke of York*: Watneys-related real ales on handpump, notably good food *(Joel Dobris)*
[11 Alma Sq; off Hill Rd], *Heroes of Alma*: Good value freshly cooked food and well kept Watneys real ales in friendly little Victorian pub with tables outside *(LYM)*
[2 Allitsen Rd; on corner of Townsend Rd], *New Inn*: Really good value lunchtime food such as salads, fish and chips and cheap steak, in clean well kept pub with John Smiths and other beers; not too crowded, no juke box *(K Rooney)*
[29 Ordnance Hill], *Ordnance Arms*: Notable for massive helpings of really good fish and chips on Fri and Sat nights; lots of military paraphernalia inc design drawings of guns and cannons, part of a heavy machine-gun; some leather chesterfields, well kept Bass and Charrington IPA, modern conservatory area and terrace behind *(Lyn and Bill Capper, LYM)*
☆ [23 Queens Grove], *Rossetti*: Good range of reasonably priced hot and cold lunchtime food inc daily hot specials in unusually Italianate pub with lots of marble and open space, stairway up to cocktail bar and restaurant with mainly Italian food, no piped music or fruit machines, well kept reasonably priced Fullers London Pride and ESB; friendly service, food well priced for London *(Lyn and Bill Capper, LYM)*

BARNET

[133 East Barnet Rd], *Alexandra*: Delicious well priced food, hot and cold, inc good sandwiches, baps and ploughman's *(Mrs*

Rosemary Cunliffe, Chris Fluck)
[Barnet Rd (A411); nr Hendon Wood Lane], *Gate at Arkley*: Civilised and well run pub with comfortable seats, good log fire in winter and lovely secluded garden for summer; good choice of food from sandwiches to hot dishes, and a better choice of whiskies than usual around London *(BB)*

☆ [High St], *Mitre*: Small-roomed friendly tavern, the tap room area of what was an extensive 17th-century inn with Dickens connections; well kept Benskins Best, Ind Coope Burton and Tetleys on handpump, food even on Sun, usually uncrowded; no piped music *(M B Porter, David Fowles, LYM)*

[193 High St], *Monken Holt*: Good home-cooked food and well kept Courage Best and Directors, pleasing olde-worlde interior; handy for Hadley Wood Common *(D S Fowles)*

EDGWARE

[Glengall Rd], *Sparrowhawk*: Lively two-bar pub with Whitbreads Castle Eden on handpump, separate room for functions and discos *(Robert Lester)*

ENFIELD

[179 Hertford Rd; Enfield Highway], *Black Horse*: Large and imposing single-bar Chef & Brewer set back from main road, with sandwiches as well as other food, Watneys-related real ales, live music and family entertainment, seafood stall on forecourt *(Robert Lester)*

[19 Chase Side Pl; off Chase Side], *Cricketers*: Much rebuilt and extended former cottage-style pub with comfortable lounge and basic public bar, lots of cricket ties above counter and other cricket memorabilia; McMullens on handpump *(Robert Lester)*

☆ [Gentlemans Row], *Crown & Horseshoes*: Pleasant atmosphere in pub in attractive area next to canal with lots of ducks — big garden very popular on good summer days; extensive choice of bar food, helpful staff *(Andy Hick, Helen Crookston)*

[320 Baker St; by rly stn], *Enfield Stores*: Watneys-related real ales in smart and lively one-bar pub; juke box may be rather loud *(Robert Lester)*

[5 The Town], *George*: Much-modified former coaching inn with mock-Elizabethan black and white frontage — passage to back bar used to be the coach entry; Bass and Charrington IPA on handpump, old local postcards, good Toby grill-restaurant upstairs *(Robert Lester)*

[Market Pl (A110)], *Kings Head*: Fine 1898 building by Shoebridge & Rising, with original etched glass and ornate woodwork, Ind Coope Burton, Taylor Walker and Tetleys on handpump; busy, particularly on Thurs - Sat market days *(Robert Lester)*

☆ [Chase Side], *Moon Under Water*: Carefully refurbished free house with splendid range

of well kept real ales such as Brains, Greene King Abbot, Marstons Pedigree, Wadworths 6X and Younger IPA; good food, comfortable civilised surroundings *(Robert Lester, R McIntosh)*

[253 Southbury Rd; A110 just W of junction with A10], *Southbury*: Fine example of 1930s brewers' Tudor, big lively locals' bar, comfortable saloon, separate lounge, meals served till 10pm; opp Enfield FC *(Robert Lester)*

[165 High St; A1010 Hertford Rd], *White Hart*: Imposing main-road pub with good public bar, old-style advertising mirrors in comfortable lounge, Ind Coope Burton and Taylor Walker on handpump *(Robert Lester)*

HARROW

[Old Reddings], *Case is Altered*: Old wood, bare glass and so forth; not smart but comfortably worn in, with good atmosphere and surroundings, probably at its best when busy; Allied real ales, pleasant garden with impressive children's area *(Michael and Alison Sandy)*

[West St], *Castle*: Pleasant in early evening (and popular then with couples), nice garden with talkative caged birds *(Philip Harrison)*

HARROW WEALD

☆ [Old Redding; off A409 — OS Sheet 176 map reference 144926], *Case is Altered*: Notably unspoilt country setting, with peaceful views from spreading garden; inside, the atmosphere's more villagey than you might expect from London's suburbs, with a low ceiling, wooden wall benches, olde-worlde prints, well kept Benskins Best and Ind Coope Burton on handpump, friendly service, bar food from sandwiches and cheap burgers to big steaks (only snacks weekends, no food Sun evening); children welcome until 9 *(LYM)*

☆ [Brookshill], *Hare*: Particularly good value bar lunches inc fine open sandwiches, ploughman's and imaginative hot dishes, quickly, generously and pleasantly served; comfortable bar with good atmosphere; space somewhat limited inside, but nice garden *(H W Wilson, A C Morrison)*

NEW BARNET

[Albert Rd], *Builders Arms*: Good atmosphere in lounge of pleasant local — a rare Greene King tied house *(D S Fowles)*

SOUTH

SE1

[Tower Bridge Rd], *Coppers*: Well placed for Tower Bridge Museum and the Design Museum at Butlers Wharf; prints of old paintings of policemen, old local photos, piped music *(Andrew Cooke)*

[Upper Ground; by Blackfriars Bridge], *Doggetts Coat & Badge*: Magnificent Thames views from comfortable three-level modern pub handy for South Bank arts complex; good range of well kept beers such as Arkells, Boddingtons and Wadworths 6X, nice atmosphere with good service even when crowded at lunchtime, wide range of food at a price — some tables reserved for diners *(R Houghton, BB)*

[Bankside], *Founders Arms*: Notable for the almost unobstructed view over the Thames of St Pauls, from the spacious glass-walled modern bar and the big waterside terrace; Youngs Bitter and Special on handpump, green plush banquettes, elbow-rest screens *(RH, LYM)*

[47 Borough Rd], *Goose & Firkin*: Back-to-basics with bare boards, lots of tables and stools, high-backed benches at the tables around the sides; good cheapish popular food, own-brewed Goose and Dogbolter on handpump, with guest such as Theakstons Old Peculier *(Michael and Alison Sandy)*

☆ [5 Mepham St], *Hole in the Wall*: Take-it-as-you-find-it pub with Waterloo suburban trains shaking its railway-arch ceiling, remarkable choice of well kept real ales at low prices, cheap bar food, basic furnishings, very mixed clientele *(Simon Collett-Jones, Alan Skull, R Houghton, David Fowles, A W Dickinson, LYM)*

[9 Stoney St], *Market Porter*: Fine range of real ales with half a dozen well kept guest beers as well as the Market Bitter and Porter brewed on the premises; exuberantly decorated long U-shaped bar — beer barrels, stuffed animals, stags' heads; usual lunchtime bar food from separate servery, restaurant; open all day weekdays; only a relative shortage of recent reports keeps this interesting pub out of the main entries this year *(Steve Waters, M B Porter, Comus Elliott, LYM)*

[Borough High St], *Old Kings Head*: Useful if the nearby George is full *(Dave Braisted)*

☆ [St Mary Overy Wharf; off Clink St], *Old Thameside*: Dark floorboards, bare yellow brickwork and hefty timbers in main river-view bar, dark beams, pews and flagstones in more intimate candlelit lower bar; well kept Boddingtons, Courage Directors, Flowers and another real ale, good generously filled baps etc upstairs, more choice downstairs; waterside terrace by schooner docked in landlocked inlet; views across to the Monument and overweening modern City developments *(Comus Elliott, Peter Griffiths, LYM; more reports please)*

SE3

[1a Eliot Cottages], *Hare & Billet*: Nicely placed opposite pond, lovely views to south and east; comfortable old-look refurbishment, Whitbreads-related and guest real ales, food such as ploughman's, sausage and mash, turkey and ham pie, beef stew, meat salads *(R N Haygarth)*

SE5

[149 Denmark Hill], *Fox on the Hill*: Comfortably refurbished, with good value well presented food in Toby Grill, polite service, good pub atmosphere; decent wines at fair prices, big car park *(E G Parish)*

SE10

[Lassell St], *Cutty Sark*: Attractive white-painted pub looking over Thames to Docklands, with big upper bow window jettied out over the road; long wooden bar counter, rough brick walls, wooden settles, barrel tables, big central wooden staircase, narrow opening to tiny side rooms, low lighting; big food area serving omelettes, steak and kidney pie and so forth; small upstairs restaurant; jazz some nights, occasional Morris men *(Alan Franck)*

[338 Tunnel Av], *Mitre*: Old-fashioned Victorian pub with solid, well upholstered furnishings; adjacent to St Alphege's church and convenient for *Cutty Sark*, RN College, Maritime Museum, Greenwich Theatre etc; good Bass and simple but ample bar snacks — hot salt beef sandwiches a speciality *(Tony Gayfer)*

[Greenwich High St], *North Pole*: Busy London pub, with well kept Wadworths 6X and Whitbreads-related real ales *(Dave Braisted)*

[52 Royal Hill], *Richard I*: Has been particularly enjoyed as ungimmicky, quiet and friendly place with no music, simple tasty food and particularly well kept Youngs; but the tenant who gave it this unpretentious character has now retired and the brewery has put in a manager *(News please)*

[Crane St], *Yacht*: Light wood panelling and portholes instead of windows, photographs of famous yachts, quite cosy patterned grey banquettes and stools on the patterned red carpet, oval central bar; spacious conservatory-like upper room opening on to terrace overlooking river; decent usual bar food *(Heather Sharland)*

SE13

☆ [316 Lewisham High St], *Fox & Firkin*: Spacious and popular, no frills, good beer brewed here and well kept guest beers, straightforward good value food inc big baps with any two of four meats; parking may be difficult *(LYM)*

SE16

☆ [117 Rotherhithe St], *Mayflower*: Carefully restored 18th-century pub with genuine atmosphere in old-fashioned main bar and side room recalling days when Pilgrim Fathers' ship sailed from here in 1611; well kept Bass and Charrington IPA, bar food (not Sat lunchtime or Sun evening), upstairs evening restaurant and wooden jetty overhanging Thames *(Roger Huggins, Tom McLean, Ewan McCall, LYM)*

☆ [118 Lower Rd], *Prince of Orange:*
Different good jazz acts each night and
weekend lunchtimes, with simple but good
value food (especially pizzas), several
Watneys-related real ales, fine collection of
jazz photographs in one of the two smaller
rooms off the main simply furnished bar;
children allowed in eating area; open
evenings, and Sun lunchtime (LYM)

SE17
[Sutherland Sq], *Beehive*: A real locals' local,
with good beer in friendly surroundings and
bar food inc splendid Sat hot beef
sandwiches *(Anon)*

SE18
[15 Thomas St], *Earl of Chatham*: Simple
cheap food, good quick service even when
busy, cheerful mixed clientele; comfortable
inside, conservatory and terrace *(J B
Simpson)*

SE19
[41 Beulah Hill], *Beulah Spa*: After tasteful
refurbishment and extension one of the most
attractive pubs in the area; good carvery,
garden with picnic-table sets *(E G Parish)*
[Biggin Hill; (A233)], *Manor*: Pleasant long,
open-plan lounge bar; nice helpful staff and
well kept beer; bar food (not tried) *(Chris
Fluck)*
[Anerley Hill], *Paxton Arms*: Popular local
attractively and elaborately refurbished by
Allied, with old sporting prints in nicely
painted and carpeted front bars, and
mementoes of Crystal Palace, old
advertisements and ornaments and
head-height books in back bar *(Andrew and
Michele Wells)*
[West Hill], *Royal Albert*: Small and
unpretentious yet warm and friendly, with
congenial and spacious back lounge bar,
well furnished inc antiques; more than 300
jugs of varying sizes and ages hang from the
beams *(Michele and Andrew Wells)*

SE21
[Park Hall Rd], *Alleyns Head*: Good value
lunches and carvery evening meals, willing
service, good pub atmosphere; can get
crowded in evenings *(E G Parish)*

SE22
[522 Lordship Lane], *Grove*: Harvester food
pub currently doing well; tables under
cocktail parasols on roadside terrace, seats
in garden; good for reasonably priced meal
in civilised surroundings, open for food all
day Sun *(E G Parish)*

SE25
[corner Albert Rd/Harrington Rd], *Albert*:
Busy local with strong cricketing traditions,
pool, darts, well kept Courage Best and
Directors and Youngs Special, friendly
service *(R D Osmond)*

SE26
[39 Sydenham Hill], *Dulwich Wood House*:
Comfortably refurbished suburban pub, well
managed, with full range of Youngs real ales
kept well, polite service, good value food *(E
G Parish, Derek R Patey)*

SW4
[38 Old Town], *Prince of Wales*:
Memorable place — bric-a-brac seems to get
thicker every time and it has that organic
quality you miss in designer imitations, with
always something new to see; well kept
Marstons Pedigree and Whitbreads-related
real ales; good value, well cooked, simple
lunchtime dishes, friendly staff *(Peter
Griffiths)*

SW11
☆ [60 Battersea High St], *Woodman*: Not to
be confused with the original Woodman
next door, this busy pub has lots of prints
and a stag's head in its little panelled front
bar, with a long Turkey-carpeted room
decorated with dried flowers, baskets, a
boar's head and even an aged wheelbarrow;
there are brocaded stools and chairs, some
big casks, and log-effect gas fires; well kept
Badger Best and Tanglefoot and Wadworths
6X on handpump, bar billiards, darts and
trivia machine at one end, picnic-table sets
on raised terrace with barbecue area *(J
Hampton, B Metherell, BB)*

SW12
[97 Nightingale Lane], *Nightingale*: Very
popular local, friendly prompt service, well
kept Youngs *(C J Parsons)*

SW13
[2 Castle Barnes], *Red Lion*: Large smartly
restored Victorian pub with fine woodwork
and three connecting rooms — back one
used mostly as a restaurant; decent
reasonably priced bar food, well kept Fullers
(Richard Sanders)
[7 Church Rd], *Sun*: Tastefully expanded,
with good service, and lovely setting on
common; very popular *(Iain Hewitt)*

SW15
☆ [8 Lower Richmond Rd], *Dukes Head*:
Good atmosphere, super position on
Thames (at Boat Race start point), cleaner,
brighter decor and improved food with good
freshly cooked lunchtime choice; well kept
Youngs *(Ian Phillips)*
[Wildcroft Rd], *Green Man*: In popular spot
on the edge of Putney Heath, with cosy main
bar, quiet sitting room, friendly atmosphere,
well kept Youngs Bitter and Special; simple
bar food, barbecues in the pretty, sheltered
garden, with a play area *(LYM)*
[93 Lower Richmond Rd], *Half Moon*: Solid
Youngs pub with spacious saloon and good
beer; a particular attraction is the consistent
programme of live folk, blues and rock

music *(David Fowles)*

SW16

[498 Streatham High Rd], *Pied Bull*: Large three-roomed pub on edge of common, handily placed for the new Sainsburys; big choice of lunchtime food from sandwiches to hot dishes (at least 6 daily); good choice of Youngs beers *(Andy Kassube, Jenny Shephard)*

SW18

[345 Trinity Rd], *County Arms*: Good Victorian decor, generally friendly service, good value filled rolls and other bar snacks; relaxed local atmosphere on weekday lunchtimes, busy weekends — especially when it's warm enough to sit out on the grass by the dual carriageway; well kept Youngs *(BB)*
[Wandsworth High St], *Kings Arms*: Worth knowing about for its attractive garden; Youngs beers *(Anon)*

SW19

[Camp Rd], *Fox & Grapes*: Well run and spacious, with huge beams in high ceiling of main bar, dark wooden furniture on patterned carpet; friendly staff, good choice of fresh-cooked food, with big ploughman's, enjoyable seafood surprise, main dishes served with lots of vegetables; well kept Courage and John Smiths; not at its best on a Saturday evening, crowded Sun lunchtime — unless it's fine enough to sit out on the common *(Brian and Jenny Seller, BB)*
☆ [6 Crooked Billet], *Hand in Hand*: Pretty and ancient exterior, with outside tables on the grass at the edge of Wimbledon Common, U-shaped bar, useful family room; well kept Youngs and maybe Ruddles real ales, Beamish stout; reasonable choice of food from good ploughman's to steaks, real log fires *(Ian Phillips, Iain Hewitt, Peter Griffiths)*
[55 Wimbledon High St], *Rose & Crown*: Comfortably modernised Youngs pub, formerly a coaching inn, with tables in a former coachyard; well kept real ales on handpump, open fires, set of Hogarth's proverb engravings, green plush seats in alcoves, food from buttery *(LYM)*

BARNES

Sun: Country pub in town opp village pond not far from Thames; spacious bar around central servery, with various rooms and snugs, well kept real ales; very busy evenings and lunchtimes *(Nigel Gibbs, BB)*

BEXLEY

[Black Prince Interchange, Southwold Rd (A2)], *Black Prince*: Part of a hotel complex, but reliably good bar meals and service, with generous helpings, well kept Bass and Charrington IPA on handpump, helpful bar staff; bedrooms *(E G Parish)* *Kings Head*:

Popular pub in old part, keeping its village atmosphere; good value bar food inc cheap chilli, well kept Courage *(Dave Braisted)*

CARSHALTON

[High St], *Coach & Horses*: Friendly local, good licensees, well kept Charrington, upstairs restaurant *(Roger Entwistle)*

CHISLEHURST

[Royal Parade], *Bulls Head*: Well kept Youngs and generous helpings of good reasonably priced bar food inc wide range of substantial individually prepared sandwiches as well as shepherd's pie, curries and so forth, in three big and comfortable bars; pleasant staff, restaurant *(M E A Horler)*
Sydney Arms: Good value bar food, big conservatory and pleasant garden — good for children; almost opp entrance to Scadbury Park — lovely country walks *(Des Thomas)*

CROYDON

[65 Leslie Park Rd; off Cherry Orchard Rd], *Builders Arms*: Good value food inc Sun roasts in two comfortable bars with pleasant decor; open all day Fri and Sat *(R Bennett)*
[Southbridge Pl], *Cricketers Arms*: Attractive inside and out, unobtrusive piped music, simple good food, immaculately kept by its two landlords and landladies — and uninfected by lager louts *(Ann and David Stranack)*
[Junction Rd; off Brighton Rd], *Crown & Sceptre*: Small, friendly and popular one-bar pub, clean and nicely furnished; tropical fish usually above fireplace; good Fullers beers, seats outside back and front *(M Desmond)*
[Morland Rd], *Joiners Arms*: Dimly lit comfortable pub with lots of character and brass everywhere; well kept Allied beers, good doorstep steak sandwiches and other food on sensibly limited good menu; friendly and beautifully maintained, with tables in pretty little creeper-clad courtyard *(Ian Phillips, Brian and Jenny Seller)*

CUDHAM

[Cudham Lane], *Blacksmiths Arms*: Delightful country pub, clean and well kept, with good old-fashioned service; good choice of bar food at reasonable prices, two or even three log fires in bar; pleasant walks in neighbourhood, good car parking *(W J Wonham)*

DOWNE

[High St], *George & Dragon*: Recently refurbished in countrified style, with stuffed animals, rural pictures and so forth — done quite well, two bars instead of three; well kept and for the area relatively cheap Charrington IPA, also Bass; good value food, nice spot in small village; popular with walkers *(R J and F J Ambroziak, E G Parish)*
[High St], *Queens Head*: Homely and welcoming, with three compact lounges and

separate children's room; good bar meals at reasonable cost all week, and Friary Meux and Ind Coope Burton on handpump — tea too *(E G Parish)*

KINGSTON

[Eden St], *Applemarket*: Remarkably big inside, with congenial atmosphere, sage green banquettes and scattering of tables and chairs, well kept real ale, pleasant swift service and cheap simple food from sandwiches through ham and eggs to gammon or steak *(Ian Phillips, R Houghton)*

☆ [2 Bishops Hall; off Thames St — down alley behind W H Smiths], *Bishop out of Residence*: Spacious semi-circular bar with double row of banquettes facing river, Edwardian-style wallpaper, Coronation curtains; modern, but well kitted out to take advantage of Thames and bridge views, second bar upstairs with terrace with small cast-iron chairs and tables, picnic-table sets by riverside walk; well kept Youngs real ales, good value bar food inc sandwiches, ploughman's and hot dishes such as chilli or plaice segments; tables on terrace; handy for central Kingston *(Ian Phillips, Jenny and Brian Seller, Michael and Alison Sandy)*

☆ [Canbury Gdns; Lower Ham Rd], *Boaters*: Excellent river views from recently refurbished pub with comfortable banquettes inside and floodlit tables in garden, real ales inc Courage Directors, John Smiths and guests such as Wadworths 6X *(Ian Phillips)*

[88 London Rd; corner Albert Rd], *Flamingo Brewery*: Large Edwardian corner pub with bare boards, back room dominated by enormous brass chandelier, many tables around edges, snugs and corners but lots of standing room too; three good real ales brewed on the premises, with guest beer; good value bar food inc pitta and hummus, ploughman's, salads and several hot dishes such as steak and kidney pie, cheap Sun lunch; Sat night sing-songs; children's room with adventure play area and view into brewery (though used as part of bar on Sat evening) *(Ian Phillips, R Houghton)*

[Riverside; down alley beside Woolworths off the Market Pl], *Gazebo*: Spotless and comfortable Sam Smiths pub with leather settees and low tables, almost all with views across to Hampton Court Park; downstairs sandwiches only; upstairs, with a reasonable range of typical bar food, has a separate entrance; lots of seats on balcony and terrace *(Ian Phillips)*

☆ [Portsmouth Rd], *Harts Boatyard*: Vast inside, with seven or eight dinghies tiered above bar area, place thick with all sorts of boating paraphernalia — even seats in the form of Peggoty-type upturned boats; external appearance would suggest a newly built weatherboarded place based loosely on tradition of Edwardian boat-builder's, but parts of the original building do survive — notably in the cellar; balconies overlooking

Thames and Hampton Court grounds, upstairs Beefeater steak house; bags of character, varied seating in lots of nooks and crannies, lunchtime bar food, Flowers IPA on handpump *(Ian Phillips)*

[58 High St], *Kingston Mill*: Lovely riverside location with good views; attractive old wooden furniture, tiled or wooden floors, walls as brown as a 40s bus shelter; fine range of real ales, imaginative good value food inc a proper ploughman's; conservatory overlooking river has rooftop vine and seats reserved for diners; clichéd old pictures and out-of-reach books at front; loud piped music; popular with the under-25s *(Peter Griffiths)*

[Fairfield Rd Sth; corner Villiers Rd], *Newt & Ferret*: Busy but comfortable and homely, with cases of decorative corks, cellar gear and so forth; well kept Badger Best, Tanglefoot and Old Timer, sandwiches and hot dishes such as liver and bacon, beef hot-pot and steak and kidney pie, jovial landlord *(R Houghton, Ian Phillips)*

LEAVES GREEN

Crown: Large and comfortable recently modernised bar, with well kept Shepherd Neame beers and good food — not cheap, but big helpings; children's room, tables and summer barbecues in garden; a favourite with local businessmen *(R J and F J Ambroziak)*

RICHMOND

[5 Church Court; alley by Owen Owen], *Angel & Crown*: Old building down narrow alley, good atmosphere, well kept Fullers, sturdy and substantial pub food eg Lancs hot-pot, chilli, steak and kidney casserole *(David Fowles)*

☆ [Upper Ham Rd], *Hand & Flower*: Watneys pub with smart tiled verandah opening into very sheltered pretty garden, banks of greenery and an alternative grotto, waterfall and pond; spacious and comfortable lounge leading to lower snugs and eating area with coal-effect gas fire and china on walls; piped pop music; public bar with mynah bird, beams festooned with soccer programmes *(Ian Phillips)*

[345 Petersham Rd; Ham Common], *New Inn*: Recently refurbished popular local in lovely position on Ham Common, with friendly atmosphere, comfortable banquettes and stools, log-effect gas fire in dining area, usual machines, Watneys-related real ale; good choice of main dishes in evening *(P Gillbe, Ian Phillips)*

[3 King St], *Old Ship*: Busy, bustling Youngs pub close to town centre and river; three communicating bars with lively atmosphere — plenty of youngsters and theatre-goers; beers well kept; unmodernised decor with nautical theme; service variable but generally friendly; parking almost impossible *(Richard Houghton)*

[130 Richmond Hill], *Roebuck*:

Outstanding views from big-windowed panelled front parlours, with pine chairs and tables and brocaded banquettes; two intimate snug back areas with big fireplaces, discreet games machines, Youngers real ale; bar food from hot beef sandwiches and ploughman's to salads and standard hot dishes *(Ian Phillips)*

☆ [Petersham Rd], *Rose of York*: Splendid well furnished, clean and spacious panelled pub with softly lit corners, well kept Sam Smiths, good choice of ample lunchtime food, reasonably priced; efficient service from smart staff, discreet alcove for darts and pool; pleasant location, especially in summer, with extended garden *(John Whitehead, Ian Phillips)*

[17 Parkshort; just tucked away from shopping centre], *Sun*: Delightful, traditional pub with sporting pictures in front bar, bar billiards in attractive long back room with tables; seats, tables and flowers outside; Fullers beers *(Peter Griffiths)*

☆ [Cholmondeley Walk; riverside], *White Cross*: Busy pub with deep bay windows overlooking Thames and Richmond Bridge, with big table in each and banquettes all round the window; reasonably priced lunchtime bar food, with overflow to upstairs dining room; well kept Youngs, friendly service, tables outside *(P Gillbe, Ian Phillips, Prof S Barnett)*

SIDCUP
[64 Blackfen Rd], *Jolly Fenman*: Produces own good Fenman Bitter and barley wine-like Explosive, though linked to Watneys; reasonable food *(Dave Braisted)*

THORNTON HEATH
[Pawsons Rd], *Lion*: Wide range of well kept ales such as Adnams, Everards Tiger, King & Barnes Mild, Bitter and Festive and Youngs Special, lots of bottled beers, good food served throughout the day, friendly well organised staff and splendid mix of customers *(R D Osmond)*

[Bensham Gr; corner Beulah Rd], *Lord Napier*: Characteristic corner Youngs pub with well kept real ales, congenial landlord, big popular jazz room opening straight off bar *(Peter Griffiths)*

WEST WICKHAM
[Pickhurst Lane], *Pickhurst*: Busy suburban pub popular for tasty well presented food (not cheap) lunch and evening — it's largely a Barnabys Carvery; Watneys-related real ales, two very big rooms very comfortably furnished with some deep armchairs, pleasant garden; friendly service; can get crowded in the evening, when it's necessary to book ahead for the restaurant *(E G Parish, Ian Phillips)*

WEST

SW6
[Stevenage Rd], *Crabtree*: Large pub with well kept Watneys beers, good home-cooked food and garden leading down to river; music can be noisy; staff very friendly and helpful *(Anon)*

[235 New Kings Rd], *Duke of Cumberland*: Big lavishly restored Edwardian lounge bar opp Parsons Green; well kept Youngs, cheerful at weekend lunchtimes, relaxed for weekday lunchtime food — not usually too busy *(BB)*

[577 Kings Rd], *Imperial Arms*: Enthusiastic regulars highly recommend this Watneys pub for its food and friendly Irish licensees *(Anon)*

[871 Fulham Rd], *Pitcher & Piano*: Bright, clean, modern, young design, simple menu of snacky food, good wine list, great music *(R Tomlinson)*

SW7
[34 Thurloe Pl], *Hoop & Toy*: Well kept Bass and Charrington IPA; handy for the museums — and the Proms *(BKA)*

[44 Montpelier Sq], *King George IV*: Considerate staff, comfortable inside, a few picnic-table sets out, attractive prints; well kept Flowers, good value decent standard food inc excellent sandwiches *(Ian Phillips, BB)*

SW10
[1 Billing Rd], *Fox & Pheasant*: Cosy old-fashioned backstreet pub with welcoming local atmosphere *(BB)*

[Kings Rd], *Worlds End*: Just taken over by small independent chain (Regent Inns), who are making a determined effort to bring this handsomely decorated house up market; comfortable plush seats, Watneys-related and other real ales, bar food *(BB)*

W4
[72 Strand on the Green], *Bell & Crown*: Traditional riverside pub with loads of atmosphere, well kept Fullers Chiswick, ESB and London Pride; rather long and narrow, with conservatory behind and waterside terrace; friendly customers and dogs *(Simon Collett-Jones)*

☆ [15 Strand on the Green], *Bulls Head*: Little rambling rooms with black-panelled alcoves, simple traditional furnishings, well kept Watneys-related ales on handpump, reasonably priced lunchtime food from no-smoking food bar lunchtimes and Thurs–Sat evenings; back games bar; right on Thames, with picnic-table sets by river; children allowed in Perspex-roofed back courtyard area *(LYM)*

[145 Chiswick High Rd], *Pack Horse & Talbot*: Good choice of beers inc bargain guest beer; lunchtime food, crowded with locals in the evenings *(Anon)*

W5

[Hanger Lane], *Fox & Goose*: Large prewar pub with small public bar, spacious lounge divided into three areas, and conservatory; well kept Fullers London Pride and ESB, food served from separate counter *(Richard Sanders)*

☆ [Elm Grove Rd; by Warwick Dene], *Grange*: Well kept Watneys-related real ales, very popular for good Sun roast lunch, tables on terrace behind, fairly slick service; four drinking areas including small lounge, quite separate public bar, bigger lounge on higher level and conservatory with own bar (leading to garden) *(Simon Collett-Jones, Philip Harrison, Ben Wimpenny)*

[33 Haven Lane], *Haven*: Rambling old pub, cosy and friendly, with good food at fair prices in conservatory buffet; friendly service, wide choice of beers and wines; parking a bit of a problem *(P J and S A Barrett, Chris Raisin)*

[33 Haven Lane], *Haven Arms*: Reliably good food, service and atmosphere, well kept Watneys-related real ales *(Graeme Barnes)*

[Church Gdns; off St Marys Rd], *Rose & Crown*: Fairly big pub with separate public bar and lounge; recently built conservatory, big garden (for London) with picnic-table sets; basic but nice bar food; Fullers beers *(J Hampton, B Metherell)*

W6

☆ [2 South Black Lion Lane], *Black Lion*: Very comfortable and cosy, with friendly, efficient staff, nice oil of A P Herbert over fireplace, photographs of Thames barges, tie collection over bar and so forth; good doorstep sandwiches, also hot dishes inc good value curries Wed evening; healthy mix of customers, easy atmosphere, popular with families for Sun roast beef; Watneys-related beer *(Denis Waters, BB)*

[Lower Mall], *Blue Anchor*: Good, honest riverside pub, very popular in summer; decent Courage from lovely brass pumps, good value food — big rolls, steak and kidney pie *(Jamie Lyons, Ruth Harrison, RCL)*

[15 Lower Mall], *Rutland Ale House*: Chef & Brewer with well done old boathouse-style decor, back room done up in library style; good views, Watneys-related real ales *(RCL)*

W7

[Uxbridge Rd], *Viaduct*: Thriving Fullers house with usual good beer; free hot sausage rolls on counter Sun lunchtime, when there's a nice homely atmosphere *(Comus Elliott)*

W8

[1 Allen St; off Kensington High St], *Britannia*: Real haven of comfort and peace, good food, well kept Youngs and nice new indoor 'garden' *(Prof S Barnett)*

[9 Kensington Church St], *Churchill Arms*: Solid and reliable meeting place, comfortable and friendly *(Ian Phillips)*

[71 Palace Gdns Terr], *Gaiety*: Good pastiche of Edwardian pub with attractive posters, good range of food, comfortable well spaced seating; Whitbreads-related real ales *(Dr and Mrs A K Clarke)*

[84 Earls Ct Rd], *Hansom Cab*: Opulently refurbished pub with the cosy feel suggested by its name *(Dr and Mrs A K Clarke)*

[Abingdon Rd], *Henry J Beans*: Run by same firm as the main entry of this name on the Kings Rd, but tied to Charringtons (keg beers); some concentration on food, which is served throughout opening hours seven days a week; fruit machine, juke box; children in area near the back *(Anon)*

[Hillgate St], *Hillgate*: Two communicating bars full of nick-nacks and pictures, lots of intriguing little nooks and corners, nicely mixed clientele, benches outside among lots of plants and greenery; wide range of lunchtime food, sandwiches (very generous), Watneys-related real ales, separate disabled person's lavatory *(Peter Griffiths)*

[25 Earls Ct Rd], *Princess Victoria*: Pleasant place to drop into, clean, with nice friendly atmosphere *(Dr and Mrs A K Clarke)*

☆ [23a Edwardes Sq], *Scarsdale Arms*: Well kept Watneys-related real ales in partly gaslit Chef & Brewer done up in old-fashioned style with winter fires in spacious bar; tree-shaded courtyard, meals and snacks (not Sun), children in eating area *(LYM)*

[13 Uxbridge St], *Uxbridge Arms*: Comfortable, cosy and almost romantically dimly lit, tucked away in smart streets just behind Notting Hill Gate — with clientele to match; well kept real ales such as Adnams, Brakspears, Greene King Abbot, pleasant tables by street *(Peter Griffiths, John Tyzack)*

W9

[93 Warrington Cres], *Warrington*: Well kept Fullers London Pride, reasonable range of beers, lots of ladies in short skirts *(Claire and Dan Reitche)*

[6 Warwick Pl], *Warwick Castle*: Unspoilt straightforward high-ceilinged Victorian local with good sandwiches and well kept Bass and Charrington IPA, close to Little Venice *(LYM)*

W11

[100 Holland Park Ave; corner Clarendon Rd], *Castle*: Recently refurbished D-shaped bar, the larger part with bare boards, magnificent carved bar, bentwood chairs and tables, blue plush seats in alcoves; better than average pub food from sandwiches and baked potatoes up, with attractively priced daily specials; Charrington beers *(Patrick Young)*

☆ [41 Tavistock Cresc], *Frog & Firkin*: Interesting beers brewed here and well kept guest beers, reasonable food including big baps, enjoyable down-to-earth atmosphere with weekend singalongs *(Patrick Young, LYM)*

[95 Portobello Rd], *Portobello Gold*: Good food, Caribbean-style conservatory, Watneys-related real ales, good sound system *(Patrick Young)*

[7 Portobello Rd], *Sun in Splendour*: Jolly, neat pub at entrance to Portobello Rd, well kept Bass and Charrington IPA, bar food *(Dr and Mrs A K Clarke)*

W14

[187 Greyhound Rd], *Colton Arms*: Pleasant village-pub-like atmosphere and well kept Watneys-related real ales and attractive little rose-arbour garden *(M K C Wills)*

[171 North End Rd], *Three Kings*: Busy at weekends with young people from all over; very wide choice of beers, food bar, spacious seating area, simply furnished, with low lighting, mirrors and paintings; parking a problem *(Andrew Cooke)*

BRENTFORD

[Catherine Wheel Rd], *Brewery Tap*: Good atmosphere and well kept low-priced Fullers *(C E Owens)*

☆ [Brook Rd], *Griffin*: Intimate, traditional Fullers local with ebullient French landlady who serves good cheese baguettes on Bastille Day and Beaujolais Nouveau in season; well kept cellar, good real wines *(Caroline Black, Roger Sealey, Jon Wainwright)*

[3 High St], *O'Riordans*: Pleasant inside, with well kept beer which isn't too expensive for London, lunchtime rolls and reasonable choice of evening food, nice atmosphere, welcoming landlord *(Richard Houghton)*

White Horse: Comfortable furnishings in popular Charringtons pub with conservatory and seats outside; weekday home-cooked food *(Miss E Waller)*

HAMPTON

[Hampton Court Rd], *Bell*: Fine views of Thames and Ham meadows from lounge, tables on terrace under chestnut; newly refurbished, fresh and brisk but welcoming with good bar food inc sandwiches, fresh salads, sensibly priced daily specials such as gammon and lasagne, Allied real ales; big car park *(Ian Phillips)*

[Station Approach], *Railway Bell*: Part of attractive row of cottages at right-angle to railway line and probably predating it; small paved garden in front with picnic-table sets; photos and local memorabilia (enormous waterworks nearby) on walls, homely atmosphere, Courage beers, cheap food; good for quiet lunch *(Ian Phillips)*

☆ [70 High St], *White Hart*: Good range of well kept and competitively priced real ales, lunchtime filled rolls and chippy food, friendly service; atmosphere of this beer-drinkers' pub building up as evening progresses; seats out on terrace, not far from Thames, easy parking *(R Houghton, Ian Phillips, C E Owens)*

HAREFIELD

[Coppermill Lane], *Fisheries*: Bright single-bar layout with fresh panelling, good choice of bar food, Benskins Best and Ind Coope Burton; beside Grand Union Canal *(Stan Edwards)*

[Shrubs Rd/Harefield Rd], *Rose & Crown*: Attractive low-ceilinged pub with Benskins Best and Ind Coope Burton on handpump, good choice of efficiently served food; favoured by staff from Harefield Hospital *(Stan Edwards)*

HATTON

[Green Man Lane; 30 yds from A30 crossroads at Bedfont], *Green Man*: Just the place to take someone who's survived a 23-hour flight but wants to 'feel in England' — only two mins from Hatton Cross tube; good value doorstep steak sandwiches, daily roasts, super puddings; seats in garden; strange to think that this used to be remote and isolated in notorious highwaymen's territory (a secret chamber with two chairs was found in the great outside chimney earlier this century) *(Ian Phillips)*

HOUNSLOW

[Hounslow High St], *Chariot*: Pleasantly furnished split-level bar on each floor, well kept Fullers London Pride and ESB; old red phone box inside *(Andrew Cooke)*

ISLEWORTH

[Church St], *London Apprentice*: Long famous for its pretty Thames-side position, this spaciously comfortable Chef & Brewer pub does get very popular in summer and on winter weekends, especially with younger people; several Watneys-related real ales, young friendly staff, help-yourself salads and daily roast, upstairs restaurant (open all afternoon Sun); children welcome; open all day *(A C and S J Beardsley, LYM)*

NORWOOD GREEN

☆ [Tentelon Rd], *Plough*: A surprise for London — a real country-pub atmosphere, though crowded at weekends, with two real fires, church pew in public bar and a bowling green dating to 1349; fairly compact, with four Fullers real ales kept well; good value bar food from sandwiches to gammon and egg or savoury omelette *(Tom Evans, Simon Collett-Jones)*

OSTERLEY

☆ [Windmill Lane; B454, off A4 — called Syon Lane at that point], *Hare & Hounds*: Suburban pub with mature garden with nooks and crannies to suit families of all ages; busy but relaxed atmosphere, ample well cooked standard pub food (ordering/serving system not ideal for busy times), Fullers Chiswick, ESB and London Pride; nr Osterley Park *(A C Morrison, Richard Houghton)*

RUISLIP

[West End Rd, S Ruislip], *Tally-Ho*: Pleasant civilised modernised pub with good bar food and well kept real ales *(Chris Fluck)*

SIPSON

[Sipson Rd; entrance next to Post House], *Plough*: Lovely little pub with well kept Watneys-related real ales and good food; easy parking, and very convenient for M4 junction 4 *(Graham and Glenis Watkins)*

TEDDINGTON

[Broom Rd], *Anglers*: Spacious, with good gardens running down to the Thames at Teddington Lock, pleasant riverside walks, footbridge to Ham Common, big awning-covered terrace; inside has lots of glass-case fish, three big paintings of the pub and lock, Thames and fishing pictures, decent choice of bar food from sandwiches and ploughman's to burgers and salads, Tetleys on handpump, piped music *(Ian Phillips)*
[High St], *Kings Head*: Good comfortable bar with good atmosphere and good value food; bedrooms *(Comus Elliott)*
[Broom Rd/Ferry Rd; close to bridge at Teddington Lock], *Tide End Cottage*: Small, intimate, cosy and friendly, two little rooms united by big log-effect gas fire; back terrace and cabin sauna, lunchtime bar food, Watneys-related real ale; 15 yards from lock and footbridge though no river view, but some tables outside *(Ian Phillips, Comus Elliott)*

TWICKENHAM

[London Rd], *Cabbage Patch*: Unusual inside — general bar area, with fireplace in centre raised to waist-level, and more comfortable seating in quieter areas; in other direction is games room with pool, darts and video games; fair range of attractively priced food, Watneys-related beers *(Mayur Shah)*
[King St], *George*: Large old pub modernised into one very long bar broken up by 18-inch-high platforms with tables and chairs; warm pale brickwork and plaster, usual range of bar food from pine-clad kitchen area, Whitbreads-related real ales; main attraction elevated view down over pavement and busy King St; open all day, closed Sun lunchtime *(Peter Griffiths)*
[45 Richmond Rd], *Mackenzies*: Winebar-ish pub, with good plain food, good choice of wines, live entertainment such as comedy, music and magicians, well kept Watneys-related real ales, children's room and summer barbecue; pleasant and never too crowded *(Su and Andy Jones)*
☆ [Cross Deep], *Popes Grotto*: Spacious and well run Youngs pub with balustraded outer area overlooking stroll-around central core;

helpful staff, good value lunchtime bar food from sandwiches through salads and steak and kidney pie to roast beef carvery, well kept Youngs real ale, good range of other drinks, games in public bar; tables in own garden, and attractive public garden opposite (closed at night) sloping down to Thames; children in eating area *(Simon Collett-Jones, LYM)*
[Twickenham Green], *Prince Albert*: Well kept Fullers ESB and London Pride, wide choice of sandwiches and ploughman's, other lunchtime food, in pub of character and potential, with friendly and hardworking staff *(John Day)* *Prince Blucher*: Cosy bustling bar with good food and beer, interesting decor, friendly atmosphere *(Dr and Mrs A K Clarke)*
☆ [Riverside], *White Swan*: Family pub resolutely preserving its atmosphere, some 10-12 ft above elegant waterside road, with pleasant balcony overlooking river; plain and simple, blazing fire, wholesome lunchtime food — enjoyed best if you're not in a rush, odd dining tables and chairs, minimal decor (style may not appeal to everybody); riverside garden, can be very crowded some evenings *(Ian Phillips, LYM)*

UXBRIDGE

[Hillingdon Hill], *Red Lion*: Quiet and friendly 16th-century pub with traditional low ceiling and period decoration; good choice of beers inc Fullers ESB, good lunchtime food (especially ploughman's); gets very busy evenings *(Robin Hill, Su and Andy Jones)*
[High St; A4007], *Three Tuns*: Small frontage but quite long and deep inside; food bar on left as you enter, with wooden tables and chairs, flagstone bar down some steps with low beams and a fire at the end; couple of cosy tables sectioned off; on right of bar is conservatory with wicker chairs leading to courtyard and terrace; Youngs *(Mayur Shah)*
[Hillingdon Hill], *Vine*: Attractively refurbished, with good licensees, friendly atmosphere, Ind Coope Burton, Tetleys and Youngs on handpump, and good range of food *(Dennis Jones)*

EAST

E1

☆ [269 Whitechapel Rd], *Grave Maurice*: Popular with staff from London Hospital, quietly comfortable long lounge bar with Victorian plush and polish, well kept Watneys-related real ales, friendly local atmosphere — a real oasis for this area; well cooked and lovingly presented food, inc Sat evening *(A L Latham, LYM)*
[36 Globe Rd], *Horn of Plenty*: Good sidestreet local with well kept Watneys-related real ales and plenty of atmosphere *(Robert Lester)*
[105 Globe Rd], *Prince Regent*: Large

modern two-bar pub with attractive pictures in lounge bar, great atmosphere, Watneys-related real ales, character landlady *(Robert Lester)*

[124 Globe Rd], *Prince of Wales*: Small cosy open-plan pub with good atmosphere, pool table, Watneys-related real ale *(Robert Lester)*

☆ [57 Wapping Wall], *Prospect of Whitby*: Rollicking pub, popular with tourists for its old-style decor and cheerful evening live music (not actually much fun if you're musical yourself); beams, panelling and flagstones, well kept Watneys-related real ales, superb river views (much appreciated by the painter Turner) from flagstoned waterside courtyard *(LYM)*

☆ [62 Wapping High St], *Town of Ramsgate*: Long, rather narrow bar with squared oak panelling, green plush banquettes and captain's chairs, bric-a-brac, old Limehouse prints, fine etched mirror of Ramsgate harbour, interesting old-London Thames-side setting; well kept Bass and Charrington IPA, usual bar food, has been open all day; it's only a shortage of reader reports that keeps this nice pub out of the main entries *(Gary Scott, Marjorie and David Lamb, LYM — more reports please)*

E2

[13 Boundary St], *Ship & Blue Ball*: Small Shoreditch pub which was under same ownership as Pitfield Brewery, and notable for the good value interesting beers produced by them — Pitfield, Hoxton Best and Dark Star on handpump, with an unusual bottled London Porter of some distinction; simple post-war decor, good collection of mainly extinct beer-bottle labels strong on stouts and dinner ales, relaxed and chatty atmosphere; we've had no reports since Pitfield joined forces with Wiltshire *(BB; news please)*

E3

☆ [104 Empson St], *Beehive*: Local which has been praised for its charming atmosphere, hospitable licensees, open fire and interesting range of well kept real ales such as Flowers, Greene King Abbot, Pitfield Dark Star and Theakstons Old Peculier, but no recent reports *(News please)*

E4

[420 Hale End Rd], *County Arms*: open plan, big and busy corner pub built solidly in 1908 by Herts & Essex Public House Trust (forerunner of THF), no cheap brass or stained glass; Watneys-related real ales, coffee too, food lunchtime and evening; pool and darts *(Robert Lester)* [51 Sewardstone Rd; A112, by junction with A110 Lea Valley Rd], *Fountain*: Large open-plan pub with welcoming atmosphere, Allied real ales on handpump, darts, Wed disco *(Robert Lester)*

[Kings Head Hill; next to police stn], *Kings Head*: Pleasant and comfortable open-plan pub with children's room, food lunchtime and evening, Allied real ales on handpump; photographs showing the pub in the 1880s *(Robert Lester)*

[Larkshall Rd], *Larkshall*: Comfortable pub with Victorian dining room serving as saloon bar, old bar back salvaged from former Southwark Brewery; well kept Courage Best and Directors on handpump *(RPH)*

☆ [Mott St; off Sewardstone Rd — OS Sheet 177 map reference 384983], *Plough*: Smart, modern roadside pub (just around the corner from its old precursor) with occasional live music Sun; bar billiards and darts in neat public bar, good value food, genuine friendly atmosphere, well kept McMullens Country and AK Mild on handpump *(Robert Lester)*

[Friday Hill], *Sirloin*: Well kept Watneys-related real ales, good choice of well prepared and imaginative food; attractive lunchtime conservatory which doubles as disco in evenings; good garden with play equipment, barbecues in good weather *(S J Breame)*

E8

[512 Kingsland Rd], *Flock & Firkin*: Large square bar with bare floorboards, lots of pew seating, old enamel beer adverts on the walls, bar billiards, fruit and trivia machines; lively and fairly young atmosphere; own-brew beers inc Shepherds Delight and Dogbolter, the usual range of Firkin food *(BB)*

[90 Amherst Rd], *Pembury*: Friendly and lively tastefully refurbished Victorian pub with good Banks & Taylors real ales on handpump, as well as Ruddles; colourful bar staff especially at weekends, bands many evenings, high standard cabaret some Fri evenings — open late then *(Trevor Sizeland)*

E9

☆ [274 Victoria Park Rd], *Falcon & Firkin*: Vast fun room for children in own-brew pub with bare boards, lots of falconry memorabilia, good value cheap food — big filled baps, quiche, ploughman's, Cumberland sausages and daily specials such as cheese and onion pie or chicken and bacon flan; brews include Falcon Ale and Hackney Bitter, as well as interesting guest beers; lively atmosphere, maybe honky-tonk piano, garden *(Robert Lester, M A and W R Proctor)*

E11

[63 New Wanstead; A113], *British Queen Tavern*: Small open-plan pub with typical country-ish atmosphere; beams, display of tankards and brass; Watneys-related real ales *(Robert Lester)*

[31 Wanstead High St], *Cuckfield*: Recently smartly refurbished local, with good atmosphere and Bass and Charrington IPA on handpump *(Robert Lester)*

[Nightingale Lane], *Duke of Edinburgh*: Tudor-fronted building where courts were once held upstairs (landlord said still to be a magistrate); Allied real ales on handpump, three-course lunches in saloon, opens 10 for coffee *(Robert Lester)*

[76 Holly Bush Hill; A11], *Eagle*: Large three-bar listed building with carvery; main bar has decorative Tottenham Hotspurs mirror, Bass beers on handpump *(Robert Lester)*

E13

☆ [140 Balaam St], *Phantom & Firkin*: Attractive exterior of frosted glass and line of old-fashioned red lamps; simple bare-boarded bar around central island servery, with pew seating and lots of old film posters on walls, mainly on phantom-related themes; well kept Palmers BB and their own Spook and Dogbolter, also hot toddies and liqueur coffees; darts, fruit machine, quiet piped music; live music Thurs - Sat; quiet and relaxing mid-week *(Robert Lester, BB)*

E14

☆ [27 Ropemakers Fields; off Narrow St, opp The Grapes], *House They Left Behind*: Renovated to catch the new Docklands feel (and customers) yet keeping a good local base; fine atmosphere, wine-barish at the edges, good value food cooked in front of you, inc Sun lunchtime roasts and ploughman's, Watneys-related real ales, friendly staff, live music Thurs and weekends *(John and Karen Day)*

E17

[757 Lea Bridge Rd; A104], *Chestnut Tree*: Large local with jazz, darts and pool table in public bar; known as Little Wonder in 1840s, rebuilt 1854; original address was Chestnut Walk, but Lea Bridge Rd widened in 1863 and name of pub changed to commemorate old street *(Robert Lester)*

[807 Forest Rd], *College Arms*: Pleasant atmosphere in small Wetherspoons pub with Greene King Abbot, Marstons Pedigree, cheap Youngers Scotch and Wadworths 6X on handpump *(Robert Lester)*

[199 Shernhall St; Walthamstow], *Lord Raglan*: Pleasant open-plan pub with conservatory; first licensed 1855 — named after Crimean War commander — and rebuilt in 1880s; food evenings, pool, darts, Watneys-related beers on handpump *(Robert Lester)*

E18

[Woodford New Rd; A104, corner of Fullers Rd], *Napier Arms*: Large open-plan pub, recently refurbished; lots of crockery on shelves, old prints of singing trios (the landlord exercises his tonsils, too); Bass, Charrington IPA and Greene King IPA on handpump *(Robert Lester)*

[Woodford New Road; A104], *Travellers Friend*: Watneys-related beers on handpump, preserved old-fashioned decor with snob screens, baps and meals *(Christine and Robin Harman)*

BARKINGSIDE

[105 Fencepiece Rd (A123)], *Old Maypole*: Large two-bar pub with spacious lounge bar, three pool tables and darts in carefully restored public bar, Allied real ales on handpump; maypole outside *(Robert Lester)*

BUCKHURST HILL

[24 Lower Queens Rd], *Prince of Wales*: Much altered pub with regular live jazz bands; one spacious bar with modern decor, pool and darts *(Robert Lester)*

DAGENHAM

[New Rd (A13)], *Anglers Retreat*: Main-road pub by Fords with two panelled bars, three pool tables, discos, Charrington IPA *(Robert Lester)*

[Wood Lane; Becontree Heath, A124], *Three Travellers*: Unspoilt 2-bar local on northern fringe of vast housing estate; prints on wall of various forms of travel across the years; lots of plates and crockery on wall and above bar; Allied real ales on handpump *(Robert Lester)*

HORNCHURCH

[189 High St], *Kings Head*: Small beamed and timbered pub with real fire and Watneys-related real ales on handpump; popular with young people *(Robert Lester)*

[Billet Lane], *Queens Theatre*: Though this is a theatre bar rather than a pub, it's comfortable and handy, and has Greene King IPA on handpump *(Robert Lester)*

ILFORD

☆ [553 Ilford High Rd; A118], *Cauliflower*: Large Victorian open-plan pub; good friendly atmosphere, regular live music, Watneys-related real ales *(Robert Lester)*

[Eastern Ave; A12/Horns Rd], *Farmhouse Table*: Formerly the Green Gate, now completely refurbished with a separate restaurant and bar; old books and bottles above bar, Bass beers, good atmosphere *(Robert Lester)*

[645 Cranbrook Rd; Gants Hill, A123], *King George V*: Good, friendly local atmosphere, Courage Best and Directors and John Smiths on handpump *(Robert Lester)*

NOAK HILL

[Noak Hill Rd; nr A12], *Bear*: Very plush and smart, great atmosphere; completely refurbished restaurant and garden, larger drinking area; Charrington IPA and Tolly Original on handpump *(Robert Lester)*

ROMFORD
Morland Arms: Pleasant staff, good simple food at attractive prices *(Derek R Patey)*

WANSTEAD
[High St; opp Underground], *George*: Large open-plan pub, friendly service, Watneys-related real ales in the bar, Berni restaurant upstairs *(Robert Lester)*

WOODFORD
[13 Cross Rd; just S of Manor Rd (B173)], *Crown & Crooked Billet*: Small and friendly pub overlooking village green, good food, Bass and Charrington IPA on handpump *(Robert Lester)*
[70-74 High Rd; South Woodford, A11], *George*: Popular with the young; cooked meals lunchtime, Bass beers, darts and pool; useful for the area *(Robert Lester)*
[735 Chigwell Rd (A113)], *Three Jolly Wheelers*: Plush Mr Toby eatery with a good friendly atmosphere in the bar *(Robert Lester)*

WOODFORD GREEN
[393 High Rd (A104)], *Castle*: Massive popular showpiece almost opp the green, Watneys-related real ales, good food in upstairs Barnabys restaurant *(Robert Lester)*
[High Rd; A104, just before A121 Loughton fork], *Horse & Well*: Attractively refurbished old pub with good atmosphere and well kept Allied real ales on handpump *(Robert Lester)*
[Hale End Rd/Oak Hill], *Royal Oak*: Good atmosphere in comfortable and spacious two-bar pub with bar billiards in saloon, Allied real ales on handpump, disco Wed and Sun *(Robert Lester)*
[Chigwell Rd/Woodford Br], *White Hart*: Charming olde-worlde pub with posters of boxing bouts over the years, Allied real ales on handpump *(Robert Lester)*

Scotland

Scotland

Food in Scottish pubs is generally cheaper than we found in any other area. Around half the main entries met our targets of under £1 for bargain snacks or under £3 for decent main dishes – or often both. This is a higher proportion than we found elsewhere. Many of these low-priced pubs are ones we've rated highly for food quality – it's not just a question of cheap and cheerful. And this year we've noticed many more Scottish pubs turning away from the catering packs and unearthing good local supplies of fresh food – particularly fresh fish. Food is specially good, and good value considering the quality, if not so obviously low-priced, at the Riverside Inn at Canonbie (our highest-rated Scottish pub), the smart Nivingston House at Cleish, the Crinan Hotel overlooking the canal and sea at Crinan, the civilised Tweeddale Arms at Gifford, the entertaining and relaxing Babbity Bowster in Glasgow, the Tormaukin up in Glendevon (more vegetarian dishes now), the Old Howgate Inn at Howgate (interesting open sandwiches), the well run and consistent Burts Hotel in Melrose, the lightly refurbished Killiecrankie Hotel near Pitlochry, the Crown at Portpatrick (doing particularly well at the moment), the Wheatsheaf at Swinton (new sun lounge and children's play area at this notably good-food inn), the Crook at Tweedsmuir (its restaurant is no-smoking), the Morefield Motel in Ullapool (quite outstanding seafood), the Ailean Chraggan at Weem, and a new entry, the Old Thistle at Westruther (very unassuming, but splendid steaks). Skye is becoming a notable centre for genuinely good food – we'd pick out the Ardvasar Hotel at Ardvasar (no-smoking dining room), the Gaelic-speaking Hotel Eilean Iarmain at Isle Ornsay and the civilised and welcoming Skeabost House Hotel at Skeabost. Quite a few changes here include Prince of Wales's new-found security in Aberdeen (it's no longer under threat of demolition in a Next development), the Galley of Lorne in Ardfern's new restaurant, the Loch Melfort Hotel in Arduaine's tie to Scottish & Newcastle (new licensees here are now keeping their own seafood pens), the Fishermans Tavern in Broughty Ferry's new bedrooms, the acquisition of Bennets Bar in Edinburgh by Scottish & Newcastle (as good as ever), the Guildford Arms there turning its gallery into a restaurant, the entry into these pages of I W Frazers Bow Bar in the same city (such a good find that it gains a star award in its first year in the Guide; another Edinburgh pub, the Jolly Judge, finds its way back into these pages on fine form), new licensees making progress at the Crown & Anchor in Findhorn, the real ale now installed at the entertainingly Scottish Inverarnan Inn at Inverarnan, the new eating area at the hospitable Steam Packet in Isle of Whithorn (temptingly priced lobster), friendly new licensees for the Kilmartin Hotel at Kilmartin, some refurbishment of the classic old George in Moniaive by its new licensee, a new chef at the Grant Arms at Monymusk (more seafood), a new bunkhouse for cyclists and walkers at the Gordon Arms at Mountbenger, updating of the bedrooms at the

*Buccleuch Arms in St Boswells, and the Guide debuts of the attractive
Four Marys in Linlithgow, the Granary in Perth (good value food),
the Sheriffmuir Inn up on Sheriffmuir and the Ferry Boat up in
Ullapool – giving that small town no less than three well deserved
main entries. Region by region, pubs of special note in the Lucky Dip
section at the end of the chapter include the Carbeth at Blanefield and
Cross Keys in Kippen (Central); Black Bull in Moffat (Dumfries and
Galloway); Old Inn at Carnock, Ship in Elie and Grange on the edge
of St Andrews (Fife); Fife Arms in Braemar, Thunderton House in
Elgin, Lairhillock near Peterculter and Towie near Turriff
(Grampian); Applecross at Applecross, Lock in Fort Augustus, Old
Inn at Gairloch and Kylesku at Kylesku (Highland); Castle at
Dirleton (Lothian); Kilberry Inn at Kilberry and Tarbert Hotel in
Tarbert (Strathclyde); and Glenview at Culnaknock on Skye. There
are a good many interesting possibilities in both Glasgow and
Edinburgh (where the Grassmarket/Lawnmarket area is beginning to
rival Rose Street as a pub-lover's hunting ground).*

ABERDEEN (Grampian)　NJ9305　Map 11
Ferryhill House Hotel

Bon Accord St (bottom end)

Kept in immaculate condition, the unusually wide choice of real ales and malt
whiskies in this well run small hotel includes Belhaven 80/-, Broughton
Greenmantle, Maclays 80/-, McEwans 80/-, Timothy Taylors Landlord and
Youngers No 3, on handpump or electric pump. The bar food is wide-ranging:
sandwiches, soup (80p), baked potatoes and ploughman's (£2) with main courses
from fried scampi (£3.75) and chicken Kiev (£5) to fillet steak (from £7); daily
changing set lunches (£4), cold buffet (£4.50). The spacious and airy
communicating bar areas have plenty of seating, and there's a fruit machine and
piped music. Outside, neatly kept, sheltered lawns have lots of well-spaced tables;
children's play area. Accommodation is quite a bit cheaper at weekends. *(More
reports please)*

*Free house　Licensee Douglas Snowie　Real ale　Meals and snacks　Restaurant
Children in restaurant　Open 11–11 Mon–Wed, 11–11.30 Thurs–Sat, 12.30–11 Sun
Bedrooms tel Aberdeen (0224) 590867; £28(£36B)/£58(£62B)*

Prince of Wales

7 St Nicholas Lane

Reached down a Dickensianly narrow cobbled alley that twists right underneath
Union Street, this individualistic Aberdonian institution has the longest bar counter
in the city, and a cosy flagstoned area with pews and other wooden furniture in
screened booths, a log-effect gas fire, and a neatly refurbished main lounge. Well
kept Theakstons Old Peculier on handpump, Caledonian 80/- and Youngers No 3
on tall fount air pressure, and two guest beers; sensibly placed darts and fruit
machine. Popular, good value lunchtime food includes soup (70p), filled rolls
(75p), macaroni cheese (£1.80), lasagne, sweet and sour chicken, haddock and
various home-made pies such as steak and kidney, gammon and leek or chicken
and mushroom (all £2.40). *(Recommended by Richard Sanders, Chris Raisin, Roger
Danes, Allan Clarke)*

*Free house　Licensee Peter Birnie　Real ale　Lunchtime meals and snacks (not Sun)
No nearby parking　Open 11–11*

ARDFERN (Strathclyde) NM8004 Map 11
Galley of Lorne

B8002; village and inn—signposted off A816 Lochgilphead—Oban

This informal inn has a main bar with an easy-going assortment of chairs, little winged settles and rug-covered window-seats on its lino tiles, big navigation lamps by the bar counter, and old Highland dress prints and other pictures. Bar food might include home-made soup (£1.20), baked potato with cheese (£2.35), haggis with neeps or French bread filled with fresh salmon or crab (£3.25), moules marinières (£3.95), scampi (£4.75), Loch Craignish king prawns or Hungarian goulash (£4.95), beef stroganoff (£4), home-made puddings and assorted Scottish cheeses; children's helpings. A wide choice of malt whiskies and bin-end wines; darts and fruit machine. The spacious restaurant has a piano and dance floor with easy chairs in the entrance lounge with windows looking out. There are good views from the sheltered terrace of Loch Craignish and the yacht anchorage; the pub is at the start of *Good Walks Guide* Walk 178. *(Recommended by Richard Gibbs, Gordon Smith)*

Free house   Licensee Tim Hanbury   Meals and snacks   Restaurant   Children in eating area of bar   Open 12–2.30, 5–11   Bedrooms tel Barbreck (085 25) 284; £22(£27B)/£40(£44B)

ARDUAINE (Strathclyde)   NM7910 Map 11
Loch Melfort Hotel 🛏

On A816 S of Oban and opp Luing

The light, modern bar in this comfortable hotel is papered with nautical charts and has a pair of powerful marine glasses which you can use to search for birds and seals on the islets and on the coasts of the bigger islands beyond. Low dark brown fabric-and-wood easy chairs surround light oak tables, and there's a freestanding woodburning stove. The new licensees keep their own lobsters, oysters and scallops in creels in the bay, so there's quite an emphasis on seafood. At lunchtime, the bar menu includes home-made soup (£1), toasted sandwiches (£1.20), home-made pâté (£2.20), a pint of prawns (£4.75), locally smoked trout or spare ribs (£3.95), fresh-caught langoustines or quick-fried tiger-tail scampi (£5.95), half a lobster from Luing, cold with salad or grilled with garlic butter (£9.75) and puddings such as home-made banana and walnut gateau (from £1.50); specials might include fresh salmon mousse (£2.75) or home-made crab quiche (£2.95), 20 local Craignish stuffed mussels (£3.75) or vegetable curry (£4.95); there's a seafood buffet on Sundays in the restaurant, and with a little notice they will prepare vegetarian meals and high teas for children. Helpful service; darts and piped music. Wooden seats on the front terrace are a short stroll through grass and wild flowers (where three horses graze) to the rocky foreshore, though from late April to early June the best walks are through the neighbouring Arduaine woodland gardens. Passing yachtsmen are welcome to use their mooring facilities. *(Recommended by Stephanie Sowerby; more reports on the new regime please)*

S & N   Licensees Philip and Rosalind Lewis   Meals and snacks (high season all afternoon)   Restaurant (closed Sun lunchtime)   Children welcome   Open 11–2.30, 5–11; closed Jan/Feb   Bedrooms tel Kilmelford (085 22) 233; £45B/£75B

ARDVASAR (Isle of Skye)   NG6203 Map 11
Ardvasar Hotel ⊘ 🛏

A851 at S of island; just past Armadale pier where the summer car ferries from Mallaig dock

Looking out across the Sound of Sleat to the fierce Knoydart mountains, the bars in this comfortably modernised 18th-century inn include the cocktail bar with crimson plush wall seats and stools around dimpled copper coffee tables on the red patterned carpet, and Highland dress prints on the cream hessian-and-wood walls;

the locally popular public bar with stripped pews and kitchen chairs, and a room off the comfortable hotel lounge with armchairs around its open fire and a huge TV. Friendly and obliging young owners serve good fresh food in the dining room, including local fish and shellfish, and the home-cooked bar food varies day by day. Typically, it might include a good soup (£1), sweet pickled herring platter (£1.80), braised ox tongue with sherry and tomato sauce (£3), fried plaice (£3.50), home-made steak and kidney pie or vegetarian lentil and cheese flan with garlic (£4), seafood pie or roast rib of beef (£4.50), fresh squat lobster tails (£5.50) and puddings such as warm strawberry and orange sponge, raspberry cheesecake or chocolate banana meringue sundae (from £1.30); Tennents 80/- on tall fount. Darts, pool, bar billiards and fruit machine. The far side of the peninsula, by Tarskavaig, Tokavaig and Ord, has some of the most dramatic summer sunsets in Scotland – over the jagged Cuillin peaks, with the islands of Canna and Rhum off to your left. Near the Clan Donald centre. (*Recommended by P Lloyd, Miss K Bamford, A H Doran, Mr and Mrs G Gittings, S J A Velate*)

Free house   Licensees Bill and Gretta Fowler   Real ale   Meals and snacks (12–2, 5–7)   Restaurant (closed Sun lunchtime)   Children in restaurant and eating area of bar   No smoking in bedrooms or dining rooms   Open 11–11 June–Sept; 11–2.30, 5–11 Oct–May; closed 25 Dec, 1 and 2 Jan   Bedrooms tel Ardvasar (047 14) 223; £25B/£50B

BROUGHTY FERRY (Tayside)   NO4630   Map 11

Fishermans Tavern

12 Fort Street; turning off shore road

A wide range of real ales in this small-roomed rambling pub includes Bass, Belhaven 80/-, Flowers, McEwans 70/- and 80/-, Maclays 80/-, Theakstons Best, Timothy Taylors Landlord, and a guest beer that changes weekly on handpump, with Youngers No 3 on tall-fount air pressure; there's also a choice of 37 malt whiskies. The cosy little snug has light pink, soft fabric seating on the brown carpet, basket-weave wall panels and beige lamps; the carpeted back bar has a Victorian fireplace and brass wall lights. Bar food includes sandwiches (from 59p), burgers (£1.40), spicy chicken wings (£1.65) or ploughman's (£1.95), main meals such as curries or chilli or scampi (£2.70) and steak pie or lasagne (£2.85), and three daily specials such as seafood canneloni (£2.85) or veal à l'orange (£3); friendly and professional service. Dominoes, cribbage, and fruit machine. The nearby seafront gives a good view of the two long, low Tay bridges. Note they now do bedrooms. (*Recommended by N J Mackintosh, Celia and David Watt, Alisdair Cuthil*)

Free house   Licensee Robert Paterson   Real ale   Meals and snacks (12–2, 5–7) Children in snug bar until 6   Open 11–midnight   Bedrooms tel Dundee (0382) 75941; £13/£20

CANONBIE (Dumfries and Galloway)   NY3976   Map 9

Riverside ★ ★ ⊘ ⇤

Village signposted from A7

It's the sense of absolute peace and simplicity here, combined with exacting food standards and notably comfortable bedrooms, that so charms readers. The comfortable and restful communicating rooms of the bar have open fires, stuffed wildlife, local pictures, and good, sensitively chosen chintzy furnishings. Well kept Yates and regularly changing guest beers such as Adnams or Ruddles on handpump; they carefully look after a good range of award-winning wines; farm ciders in summer; sympathetic service. Very good bar food includes home-made soups like pea and broccoli or apricot and lentil (£1.50), potted salmon, herring roe mousse, duck liver pâté , chicken and bacon terrine (all £2.95), salads such as smoked salmon quiche, cider roast ham or hot cheese pudding (all £4.25), with main dishes such as filleted fresh herrings with leeks and smoked bacon (£3.55), a vegetarian dish like leek and tomato croustade or mushroom stroganoff on brown rice (£3.55), ham and mushroom pie with parsley sauce (£4.25), home-made duck sausages with brown lentil gravy or beef in beer with home-made pasta (£4.55), deep fried goujons of fresh salmon with watercress hollandaise or home-cooked confit of duck (£5.25), sirloin steak with oyster mushrooms (£7.25); puddings such as spiced brown bread and butter pudding with toffee sauce or baked rhubarb cheesecake with rhubarb and orange sauce (all £1.50). The food shows lots of careful small touches, like virgin olive oil for salad dressings and they are concentrating more now on finding supplies of 'organic' foods such as undyed smoked fish, wild salmon and naturally-fed chickens; they also have an award-winning range of cheeses; thoughtful as well as substantial breakfasts. In summer – when it can get very busy – there are tables under the trees on the front grass. Over the quiet road, a public playground runs down to the Border Esk (the inn can arrange fishing permits). *(Recommended by Timothy Galligan, Heather Sharland, John and Ruth Roberts, Stephanie Sowerby, Paul Wreglesworth, Peter Burton, PLC, John Townsend, Simon Ward, Syd and Wyn Donald, David and Flo Wallington, C J McFeeters, A C and S J Beardsley, Drs M and K Parier, John Gillett, Dr T H M Mackenzie)*

Free house   Licensee Robert Phillips   Real ale   Meals and snacks (Mon–Sat lunchtime, and Sun evening)   Children welcome (all ages in bar, from 8 yrs in restaurant)   No-smoking restaurant (closed Sun)   Open 11–2.30, 6.30–11; closed Sun lunchtime, 25 and 26 Dec, 1 and 2 Jan, 2 weeks Feb, 2 weeks Nov   Bedrooms tel Canonbie (038 78) 71512 or 71295; £30B/£60B

CARBOST (Isle of Skye)   NG3732   Map 11

Old Inn

This is the Carbost on the B8009, in the W of the central part of the island

This friendly old stone inn, beside the sea loch and popular with climbers down from the fiercely jagged peaks of the Cuillin Hills, is simply furnished with red leatherette settles, benches and seats, and there are bare floorboards, walls part-whitewashed and part-stripped stone, and a peat fire; a second bar is panelled. Popular bar meals include sandwiches, home-made soup (90p), ploughman's (£2.85), haddock (£3) or fresh salmon salad (£4), and home-made puddings such as apple crumble; darts, pool table (not available in summer), dominoes, cribbage, a number of board games, piped traditional music and the occasional ceilidh; malt whiskies, including the local Talisker – there are guided tours round the distillery, with free samples, most days in summer. *(Recommended by Alan and Ruth Woodhouse, J Marshall, M Shinkfield, Roger Danes, M S Hancock, Graham Bush, P Lloyd, Miss K Bamford)*

Tennents (Bass)   Licensee Deirdre Cooper   Meals and snacks (12–2, 5.30–10) Children in eating area of bar till 9   Occasional live music   Open 11–12; Sat 11–11.30; winter 11–2.30, 5–11   Bedrooms tel Carbost (047 842) 205; £12.50/£25

CAWDOR (Highland)   NH8450   Map 11

Cawdor Tavern

Just off B9090; Cawdor Castle signposted from A96 Inverness–Nairn

The right-hand public bar has an imposing pillared serving counter, elaborate wrought-iron wall lamps, chandeliers laced with bric-a-brac such as a stuffed mongoose wrestling a cobra, banknotes pinned to joists, a substantial alabaster figurine – not at all what you'd expect from a little Highland village pub. But then this is just a couple of minutes' drive from the Castle. And it was the Castle which furnished the squared oak panelling and chimneybreast in the lounge, a substantial Turkey-carpeted room with green plush button-back built-in wall banquettes and bucket chairs, a Delft shelf with toby jugs and decorative plates (chiefly game), small tapestries, attractive sporting pictures. Sandwiches and home-made bar food such as lasagne, steak pie and fricassées; well kept McEwans 80/- and Theakstons Best on handpump, well over a hundred malt whiskies and some rare blends, a good choice of wines and decent coffee. Darts, pool, cribbage, dominoes, fruit machine in the public bar; piped music; no dogs. There are tables on the front terrace, with tubs of flowers, roses, and creepers climbing the supports of a big awning; summer Saturday barbecues roughly once a fortnight. The restaurant is now a function room but is used for extra seating when very busy. *(Recommended by Dr John Innes, Neil and Angela Huxter; more reports please)*

Free house   Licensee T D Oram   Real ale   Meals and snacks (not before 12.30)
Children welcome   No dogs   Open 11–11 (11.30 Sat)

CLEISH (Tayside)   NT0998 Map 11

Nivingston House ⊘ ⇔

1 1/2 miles from M90 junction 5; follow B9097 W until village signpost, then almost immediately inn is signposted

Looking out over a lawn sweeping down to shrubs and trees, with hills in the distance, the relaxing L-shaped bar in this civilised country house hotel has rust-coloured comfortable seats against sumptuous lotus-plant wallpaper. Interesting bar snacks might include delicious tomato and orange soup (£1.40), home-made pâté with oatcakes (£3.65), fine tagliatelle with smoked mackerel, mushrooms and parmesan cheese (£3.85), venison burger (£3.95), salad with fruit and Crowdie cream cheese or home-smoked trout with caper and horseradish sauce (£4.25), minute steak (£4.95), and specialities such as the croque Nivingston (French bread baked with ham, cheese, prawns and garlic, £4.65). Belhaven on handpump and good choice of malt whiskies. Outside, there are picnic-table sets below the gravel drive. *(Recommended by Mr and Mrs J H Adam, G R Pearson, T Nott; more reports please)*

Free house   Licensee Allan Deeson   Real ale   Meals and snacks (not evenings)
Children welcome   Restaurant   Open 12–3, 6–12   Bedrooms tel Cleish Hills (057 75) 216; £50B/£75B

CRAMOND (Lothian)   NT1876 Map 11

Cramond Inn

Cramond Glebe Road; signposted from A90 on way out W from Edinburgh

The Firth of Forth is only a short walk away from this friendly, busy old pub in an attractively renovated fishing village. Back in its original place near the main door, the bar has brown button-back wall banquettes, wheelback chairs and little stools, ceiling joists and an open fire. Five tall fonts dispense Caledonian 80/-, Marstons Pedigree and Thwaites under light blanket pressure; reasonably priced spirits are measured in 1/4 gill. Bar food includes home-made soup (£1.10), filled baked potatoes (from £1.60), home-made vegetable lasagne (£2.50), ploughman's (from £2.85), chilli con carne (£2.95), home-made pie of the day (£3.30), deep fried goujons of sole (£4.50) and steaks (from £6); puddings (£1.10). The pub's car park has some fine views out over the Forth; a small side terrace has seats and tables. Be careful not to get cut off if you cross the causeway to the island. *(Recommended by Andy and Jill Kassube, Chris Raisin; more reports please)*

*Sam Smiths   Licensee Mr A Dobson   Real ale   Lunchtime snacks and meals
Restaurant (closed Sun evening)   tel Edinburgh (031) 336 2035   Children in eating area of bar and restaurant at lunchtime only   Open 11–2.30, 5–11(midnight Fri), 11–midnight Sat*

CRINAN (Strathclyde)   NR7894 Map 11

Crinan Hotel ⊘ ⇔

A816 NE from Lochgilphead, then left on to B841, which terminates at the village

You can look down over the busy entrance basin of the Crinan Canal from the picture window in the stylish cocktail bar here, and watch the fishing boats and yachts wandering out towards the Hebrides. Seats in the cosy carpeted back part and the tiled front part are comfortable, and the decor includes sea drawings and coastal waters forecast is chalked on a blackboard. The simpler public bar has the same marvellous views and there's a side terrace with seats outside. Good bar food includes home-made soup (£1.50), Arbroath smokies or freshly baked flan (£3.50), grilled fillet of Loch Awe trout (£3.75), Loch Sween mussels (£3.95), locally smoked salmon (£8.50) and other locally caught fresh fish; large wine list. You can get sandwiches from their coffee shop or Lazy Jack's. The smart top floor evening restaurant and associated bar, where jacket and tie are needed, look out to the islands and the sea. *(Recommended by Rodney Collins, Gary Melnyk)*

Free house Licensee Nicholas Ryan Lunchtime meals Children welcome Evening restaurant (closed Sun and Mon) Pianist Open 11–2.30, 5–11; closed 25 Dec Bedrooms tel Crinan (054 683) 235; £75B

DUMFRIES (Dumfries and Galloway) NX9776 Map 9

Globe

High St; up a narrow entry at S end of street, between Timpson Shoes and J Kerr Little (butcher), opposite Marks & Spencer

An inn since 1610, this old stone house has a little museum devoted to Burns in the room that he used most often, and on the wall of the old-fashioned dark-panelled Snug Bar there's a facsimile of a letter (now in the J Pierpoint Morgan Library in New York): 'the Globe Tavern here... for these many years has been my Howff' (a Scots word meaning a regular haunt). Upstairs, one bedroom has two window panes with verses scratched by diamond in Burns' handwriting (though not the touching verse he wrote for Anna Park the barmaid here, who had his child). McEwans 80/- on handpump, very reasonably priced and low-alcohol beers. A big plain public bar at the back has dominoes, a fruit machine, trivia and piped music. Good value simple bar food includes home-made soup or filled rolls (70p), quiche and salads, a three-course lunch at £3.50, and apple pie (70p). By the way, there's another pub of the same name in Market Street. *(Recommended by Robert and Fiona Ambroziak)*

Free house Licensee Mrs Maureen McKerrow Real ale Lunchtime meals and snacks (not Sun) Restaurant tel Dumfries (0387) 52335; closed Sun Children in eating area and restaurant Nearby daytime parking difficult; car park 5 mins away Open 11–11

EDINBURGH (Lothian) NT2574 Map 11

The two main areas for finding good pubs here, both main entries and Lucky Dips, are around Rose St (just behind Princes St in the New Town) and along or just off the top part of the Royal Mile in the Old Town. In both areas parking can be difficult at lunchtime, but is not such a problem in the evenings.

Abbotsford

Rose St; E end, beside South St David St

Quite an institution for generations of Edinburgh people, this pleasantly formal place has a heavily panelled Victorian island bar counter served by dark-uniformed waitresses and a remarkable mixture of customers. There are long deeply polished old tables, leather-cushioned seats and a handsome ceiling (a long way up – the elegantly panelled walls are tall). Good, reasonably priced food includes soup (70p), salads (from £2.50), grilled liver and bacon or haggis and neeps (£2.75), curried chicken or braised oxtail (£3.05), grilled gammon with pineapple (£3.35), rump steak (£3.95), mixed grill (£4.35), and puddings such as apple crumble (90p). Caledonian 80/- and McEwans tapped from the cask, lots of malt whiskies; fruit machine, tucked well away. Beware of the lunchtime crowds. *(Recommended by Richard Sanders, Peter Corris, Bob Timmis, Roger Huggins)*

Free house Licensee Colin Grant Real ale Lunchtime meals and snacks (not Sun) Restaurant tel Edinburgh (031) 225 1894 Open 11–2.30, 5–11; closed Sun

Athletic Arms

Angle Park Terrace; on corner of Kilmarnock Rd (A71)

Because it was frequented by the grave diggers from the nearby graveyard, this very busy and quite unpretentious pub – the manager calls it old-fashioned with old-fashioned ideas – is known locally as 'The Diggers'. A team of red-jacketed barmen work hard at the gleaming row of tall air-pressure fonts to keep the throng of mainly young and very thirsty customers supplied with McEwans 70/- and 80/- in tip-top condition; filled rolls and pies (from 45p). Opening off the central island servery there are some cubicles partitioned in glossy grey wood with photographs of Hearts and Scotland football teams – a side room is crowded with enthusiastic dominoes players. *(Recommended by Peter Corris, Peter Watkins, Pam Stanley, Richard Sanders)*

S & N Manager Mr Farmer Real ale Snacks Open 11–2.30, 5–10.30

Bannermans Bar

212 Cowgate

This cellar-like bar up in the Old Town (and deep under some of its tallest buildings) has a warren of little brightly-lit rooms with musty brick barrel-vaulted ceilings, massive bare stone walls and flagstones; it's furnished with old settles, pews and settees around barrels, red-painted tables and a long mahogany table. The front part has wood panelling and pillars, and rooms leading off have theatrical posters and handbills. A remarkably wide range of customers enjoy the well kept Caledonian 70/-, McEwans 80/-, Theakstons BB and Old Peculier and Youngers No 3, all on handpump; malt whiskies. Filled rolls are served all day and at lunchtime there's also a full menu of meals and snacks such as soup (60p), filled baked potatoes (£1.70), ploughman's (£2), vegetarian moussaka (£2.20) and a pork or beef dish. Dominoes, backgammon, draughts and cards. The back area, with tables and waitress service, open when busy, is no-smoking. *(Recommended by Richard Sanders, Ralph A Raimi, Ian and Sue Brocklebank, Andy and Jill Kassube)*

S & N Licensee Jo Frood Real ale Meals (lunchtime; Sun breakfast only, 12.30–2) and snacks (all day) Live band Mon–Thurs, fiddler Sun Children allowed till 8pm Open 11–12 Mon–Thurs and Sat, 1am Fri, 12.30–2.30, 6.30–11 Sun

Bennets Bar

8 Leven St; leaving centre southwards, follow Biggar, A702 signpost

There are all sorts of treasures in this splendid Victorian bar: art nouveau stained-glass windows, arched and mahogany-pillared mirrors surrounded by tilework cherubs, Florentine-looking damsels and Roman warriors, and high elegantly moulded beams supporting the fancy dark maroon ceiling; red leather seats curve handsomely around the marble tables and there are old brewery mirrors. The long bar counter serves over 120 malt whiskies – the largest range in Edinburgh – including the pub's own blend of whisky from the barrel, as well as well kept Caledonian 70/-, McEwans 80/- and Theakstons under air pressure. Bar food includes filled rolls, soup (75p), vegetarian dishes such as ratatouille pie (£2.30), rigatoni (£2.50), beef curry or a chicken and bacon dish (£2.60) or fresh fried haddock (£2.75) with puddings such as mandarin sponge or crème caramel (95p). *(Recommended by Richard Sanders; more reports please)*

S & N Licensee Mr Wright Real ale Meals (lunchtime, not Sun) and snacks Children in lounge only Open 11–11 Mon–Weds, 11–midnight Thurs–Sat, 7–11 Sun

Cafe Royal Circle Bar

West Register St

Originally a showroom for the latest thing in Victorian gas and plumbing fittings, this handsome bar has a series of highly detailed Doulton tilework portraits of Watt, Faraday, Stephenson, Caxton, Benjamin Franklin and Robert Peel (in his day famous as the introducer of calico printing). The big island bar counter with hand-carved walnut gantry (a replica of the Victorian original) serves Caledonian 70/-, McEwans 80/-, Youngers No 3 and weekly guest beer from air pressure tall founts and Theakstons BB on handpump; a good choice of whiskies. Simple bar food includes soup (70p), pies or filled rolls (both from 60p), made to order pizzas (from £2.10) and chilli or lasagne (£2.50); fruit machine and trivia machine. *(Recommended by Gary Scott, Roger Huggins, Roger Danes)*

Free house   Licensee Billy Robertson   Real ale   Snacks (12–7)   Oyster bar tel *Edinburgh (031) 556 1884   Children in oyster bar   Open 11–11 Mon–Fri, 11–12 Sat, 6.30–11 Sun; closed 25 Dec and 1 Jan*

Guildford Arms

West Register Street

The snug little Gallery Bar has now become a restaurant and gives a dress-circle view of the main bar (notice the lovely old mirror decorated with two tigers on the way up). Under this gallery a little cavern of arched alcoves leads off the well preserved Victorian main bar. Its chief glory is the crusty plasterwork extending up from the walls, carefully painted in many colours. Other well preserved features include lots of mahogany, scrolly gilt wallpaper, big original advertising mirrors and heavy swagged velvet curtains for the arched windows. But this is no museum piece: the atmosphere is lively and welcoming, with the feeling that plenty is going on. Good basic pub food includes soup (70p), Waldorf salad (£1), pâté (£1.15), a salad bar (from £1.15), jumbo sausage (£2.45), ploughman's or chicken and ham vol au vent (2.75), roast chicken or home-made steak pie (£2.85), scampi (£3.25) and puddings (all £1.10). Well kept Bass, Belhaven 60/- and 80/-, Caledonian 70/- and 80/-, Harviestoun 80/- and Old Manor and Orkney Raven, all on handpump, friendly staff; fruit machine and lively piped music. *(Recommended by Richard Sanders, S V Bishop, Gary Scott, Roger Huggins, Patrick and Mary McDermott, David and Christine Foulkes, Andy and Jill Kassube)*

Free house   Licensee David McPherson Stewart   Real ale   Meals and snacks (lunchtime, not Sundays)   Restaurant tel *031 556 4312 (closed on Sun)   Occasional jazz festivals   Open 11–11 Mon–Thurs, 11–12 Fri–Sat*

I W Frazers Bow Bar ★

80 Victoria Street

Superbly redesigned to catch the essence of the traditional Edinburgh bar, this handsome place in its fine West Bow site below the Castle has no games or music – just relaxed chat, and the clink of glasses. The rectangular room has sturdy leatherette wall seats and heavy narrow tables on its lino floor, cafe-style bar seats and a brass rail around the solid mahogany serving counter, red Anaglypta ceiling and cream Anaglypta walls with a brown panelled dado. Aside from a nice antiqued photograph of the present bar staff in old-fashioned clothes (and moustaches), decorations consist mainly of a fine collection of appropriate enamel advertising signs and handsome antique trade mirrors. Careful details include the umbrella stand by the period gas fire, a (silent) prewar radio and big pendulum clock, and a working barograph. The grand carved mahogany gantry has a splendid array of malts including lots of Macallan variants and 'cask strength' whiskies, with a fine collection of vodkas and, particularly, rums. Impressive banks of prewar tall founts by Aitkens, Mackie & Carnegie, and Gaskell & Chambers dispense well kept Bass, Caledonian 60/-, 70/-, 80/- and Merman, the new Deuchars IPA, Fullers London Pride, Ind Coope Burton, Tetleys, Timothy Taylors Best, Golden Best and Landlord and Wadworths IPA and 6X; they serve filled rolls and toasties, hot pies and bridies. Service is quick and helpful. *(Recommended by Andy and Jill Kassube, JM, PM)*

Free house   Licensee Ian Whyte   Real ale   Snacks   Open 11–11.15; closed Sun

Jolly Judge

James Court; by 495 Lawnmarket

In a courtyard just off the Royal Mile, this cosy tavern is part of one of the Old Town's original buildings. There are fruits and flowers painted on the low beam-and-board ceiling that are typical of 16th-century Scottish houses (a collection of foreign banknotes pinned to a beam near the bar has started), and a 1787 engraving commemorates Burns' triumphant stay in nearby Lady Stair's

Close that January. The atmosphere is relaxed and cosy, with captain's chairs around the cast-iron-framed tables on the carpet, and quickly served small local steak or mince pies (90p) and filled rolls (from 75p); the hot meals include dishes such as lasagne, chilli or curries (all about £2.95); Caledonian 80/- and Ind Coope Burton on handpump, and a regularly changing range of malt whiskies; space game, dominoes in winter and unobtrusive background music. (*Recommended by David and Christine Foulkes, Graham Bush*)

Free house   Licensee Mr De Vries   Real ale   Lunchtime meals (not Sun) and snacks (all day, possibly Sun)   Children in eating area of bar (12–3 only)   Open 11–3, 5–11 Mon–Thurs, 11–12 Fri and Sat, 6.30–11 Sun

Peacock

Newhaven; Lindsay Road

Interesting photographs on the wall of this 18th-century place give some idea of what Newhaven used to be like before the new development (named after the pub) and other modern changes set in here. The main lounge is plushly comfortable, with lots of ply panelling and cosy seats, and the back room is well kept and cheerfully decorated with trellises and plants to seem like a conservatory (it leads on out to a garden). Lunchtime bar food includes home-made soup (70p), salads (£1.95), home-made steak pie (£2.45), fresh haddock (£2.95), good value carvery (3 courses £7.95) and Sunday roast lunch (£3.95); in the evening, when dishes are more expensive, it's best to book (tel Edinburgh (031) 552 5522). Well kept McEwans 80/- under air pressure on tall font; malt whiskies; background music. The family room is no-smoking. (*More reports please*)

Free house   Licensee Peter Carnie   Real ale   Meals and snacks   Children welcome in coffee lounge or family/garden room   Open 11–11; closed 26 Dec and 1 Jan

Sheep Heid

Duddingston; Causeway

The garden behind this old-fashioned ex-coaching inn is a pretty place, with a goldfish pond and fountain, hanging baskets and clematis on the sheltering stone walls of the house, and a skittle alley – it's one of the very few pubs in Scotland that plays alley skittles; barbecues in fine weather – you can cook your own if you feel inclined. The main room has turn-of-the-century Edinburgh photographs, a fine rounded bar counter, seats built against the walls on the Turkey carpet, Highland prints and some reproduction panelling; the atmosphere is warm and relaxing and there's a good mix of customers. Tables in a side room are given some privacy by elegant partly glazed screens dividing them. Bar food includes soup, soused herring salad, mince pie, ploughman's, and sirloin steak. Tennents 80/- on handpump; dominoes, fruit machine, TV and piped music. The little village is lovely, and getting to the pub is a pleasant expedition, past Holyroodhouse, Arthur's Seat and the little nature reserve around Duddingston Loch.
(*Recommended by W F Coghill, Gary Scott, T M McMillan, Ralph A Raimi, S V Bishop*)

Tennents (Bass)   Real ale   Snacks and meals   Children in restaurant   Restaurant tel 031–661–1020; closed Sun   Open 11–11

FINDHORN (Grampian)   NJ0464 Map 11
Crown & Anchor

Coming into Findhorn, keep left at signpost off to beach and car park

Several real ales in this lively and friendly old stone inn include Brakspears PA, Courage Directors, Tennents 80/- and Wadworths 6X with occasional guest beers such as Adnams, Badger, Fullers, Theakstons and Timothy Taylors; they also have draught ciders (rare around here), over 110 foreign beers and a good choice of spirits, including over 100 malt whiskies. The lively public bar has an unusually big arched fireplace, old photographs of the area on the walls, and games (darts, dominoes, cribbage, fruit machine, trivia and juke box); the comfortable lounge bar is decorated with lots of pictures. Bar food includes sandwiches, soup and local smoked mackerel (£1.60) or haddock (£2.90), with specials such as home-made chilli con carne, curry, lasagne and vegetarian dishes (£3) and steak (from £5.95), with puddings such as lemon syllabub (£1.70). The inn still looks down to the jetty where Highlanders would have stayed before taking ship for Edinburgh or even London – people staying have the use of its boats – and sandy beaches are only a few moments' stroll away. *(Recommended by Ian Baillie; more reports please)*

Free house   Licensees George and Heather Burrell   Real ale   Meals and snacks (11–9.45 Mon–Sat, 12–9.45 Sun)   Children in eating area of bar until 9   Folk and country Sun evening   Open 11–11; Fri and Sat closing 11.45   Bedrooms tel Findhorn (0309) 30243; £18.50/£25

GIFFORD (Lothian)   NT5368   Map 11
Tweeddale Arms ⊘ ⇐

High Street

Facing an attractive long wooded green and the avenue to Yester House, this old white inn is a civilised place with a wide choice of good food. The comfortably relaxed lounge has big Impressionist prints on the apricot coloured walls (there are matching curtains to divide the seats), modern tapestried settles and stools on its muted red patterned carpet and brass lamps. Changing daily, the food includes soup (90p), sandwiches (from £1.85), omelettes (£3.50), lamb Madras, steak and kidney pie or deep fried haddock (£3.75), cold gammon salad (£3.95), scampi (£4.15), roasted spring chicken and bacon (£4.25), cold poached Tay salmon (£4.50), and home-made puddings like tropical fruit torte (from £1.75). The gracious dining room has unusual antique wallpaper. McEwans 80/- under air pressure on tall fonts; charming, efficient service. Darts, pool, dominoes, cribbage, fruit machine, and piped music. The tranquil hotel lounge is a lovely place to sit over a long drink; there are antique tables and paintings, chinoiserie chairs and chintzy easy chairs, an oriental rug on one wall, a splendid corner sofa and magazines on a table. The B6355 southwards from here over the Lammermuirs, and its right fork through Longformacus, are both fine empty moors roads. *(Recommened by Mr and Mrs Norman Edwardes, S V Bishop, T Nott, Roger A Bellingham, G Milligan)*

Free house   Licensee Chris Crook   Real ale   Lunchtime meals and snacks (on request in evenings)   Children welcome in lounge   Restaurant   Open 11.30–11 Mon–Thurs, till midnight Fri–Sat; closed (possibly) 1 Jan evening   Bedrooms tel Gifford (062 081) 240; £45B/£55B

GLASGOW (Strathclyde)   NS5865   Map 11
Babbity Bowster ⊘

16–18 Blackfriars St

In a quiet pedestrian-only street this unusual pub/hotel – in a Robert Adam town house – has an almost continental atmosphere, and one where women on their own seem comfortable. There are pierced-work stools and wall seats around dark grey tables on the stripped boards, an open fire, and fine tall windows. A big ceramic of a kilted dancer and piper on the pale grey walls illustrates the folk song which gives the place its name – *Bab at the Bowster*; also, well lit photographs and big pen-and-wash drawings of Glasgow and its people and musicians; piped Scottish music (and occasional good-value musical dinners with folk like Dougie McLean). Well kept Maclays 70/-, 80/- and Porter on air pressure tall fount, a remarkably sound collection of wines, and even good tea and coffee. Enterprising food, usefully available from 8am till 9pm including morning coffee and afternoon tea, starts with good breakfasts (served 10.30–1 on Sunday mornings) – either a full Scottish one (£2.65, including Ayrshire bacon), or traditionally smoked Loch Fyne kippers (£2.30); after midday, it includes soup (95p), Orkney oatcakes and wheat wafers with a selection of cheeses such as Trukie, a mature cheddar from the Mull of Kintyre, fresh Loch Etive mussels in white wine and onion or vegetarian haggis (£2.45), hot goat's cheese on wholemeal toast (£2.85), stovies (from £2.95), steak pie soaked in Murphys stout (£3.65), sole fillets stuffed with crayfish tails in a seafood sauce (£7.95), beef marinaded in whisky with shallot butter (£8.75) and several dishes of the day; puddings range from chocolate and orange fudge cake to apple strudel with cream. A small terrace has tables under cocktail parasols. *(Recommended by WFL, Geoffrey and Sylvia Donald, Diane Duane-Smyth, Martin Rayner, Nigel Hopkins, Neville Burke, Dorothy and David Young)*

Free house   Licensee Fraser Laurie   Real ale   Meals and snacks (12–9)   Restaurant; closed Sun evening   Children in restaurant   Open 11–midnight (and for breakfast); closed 1 Jan   Bedrooms tel Glasgow (041) 552 5055; £32S/£55S

Bon Accord
153 North Street

There are 14 real ale founts in this simply refurbished and traditionally styled pub, serving Adnams, Belhaven 60/-, 70/-, 80/-, Caledonian Porter, 60/-, 70/-, 80/- and Mermen XXX, Fullers London Pride and ESB, Marstons Pedigree, McEwans 70/-, 80/-, Robinsons, Theakstons BB, XB and Old Peculier, Timothy Taylors BB, Golden Best and Landlord, Wadworths and Youngers No 3; if the landlord isn't too pushed he'll let you sample the beer before you make your choice; now over 100 malt whiskies, too. A wide choice of bar food at lunchtime includes burgers (from £2.65), fish (from £2.25), chilli (£2.75) and steak pie (£2.95) and a three course special (£1.95) which is also served in the evenings along with filled rolls (from 75p); coffee is available all day. There are padded leatherette seats and little rounded-back chairs, the red hessian walls are decorated with City of Culture event posters, beer trays and malt whisky boxes, the floor is partly carpeted, partly quarry-tiled; one side has quiet booth seating. Fruit machine, trivia, Trivial Pursuit and dominoes in a back lobby (a TV in the bar may be on for sport). It can get very busy on weekend evenings. *(Recommended by Tim and Lynne Crawford, Peter Watkins, Pam Stanley; more reports please)*

Free house   Licensee Patrick O'Riordan   Real ale   Meals (limited in evening) and snacks   Restaurant (closed Sun) tel Glasgow (041) 248 4427   Children in restaurant lunchtime only   Occasional live music   Daytime parking restricted   Open Mon–Fri 11–midnight, Sat 11–11.45; closed Sun lunchtime

Pot Still

154 Hope Street

Crammed with almost 300 malt whiskies – helpfully documented – the elegantly pillared and moulded bar gantry of this well run split-level pub includes several different versions of the great single malts in different ages and strengths, far more vatted malts than we knew of (these are blends, but malts only – no grain whisky); they sell by the bottle as well as the glass. It's attractively decorated, with comfortably upholstered banquettes in bays around heavy cast-iron-framed tables, photographs of old Glasgow on red baize walls, and slender pillars supporting the ornately coffered high dark maroon ceiling – with its two raj fans. Bar food, trimmed down under the new licensee, includes soup (75p), deep fried whitebait or deep fried mushrooms (95p), sandwiches (from £1.25), big ploughman's (£2.40), beef stir-fry (£2.85) and home-made lasagne (£2.95). Youngers No 3 on tall fount air pressure. *(Recommended by Ian Baillie; more reports on the new regime please)*

Free house   Licensee John David Hebditch   Real ale   Meals and snacks   Open Mon–Fri 11–12, Sat 11–11.45; closed Suns and Bank Hol Mons

GLENCOE (Highland)   NN1058   Map 11
Clachaig

Inn signposted off A82; OS Sheet 42 map reference 128567

Tucked by a little stream among sycamores and birch trees with the mountains soaring above, this slate-roofed white house shares its isolation with a discreetly tucked-away group of chalets. The back public bar is a biggish plain room kitted out for climbers and walkers (it serves as a mountain rescue post), with a nice big woodburning stove in one stone fireplace and another in an opposite corner to thaw out the winter skiers; the atmosphere's lively and cheerful. On the other side, a big modern-feeling lounge bar has tables with green leatherette cushioned wooden wall seats and spindleback chairs around its edges; decorated with good mountaineering photographs, it's usually quieter but can get very lively on folk nights. Simple but robust bar snacks include bridies and toasties, home-made soup, cheeseburgers and home-made shepherd's pie in summer, with more substantial hot dishes added in winter – curries, gammon, fish, steaks; well kept McEwans 80/- and Youngers Scotch and No 3 on air pressure tall founts, a good range of over 50 malt whiskies; pool in public bar. The friendly landlord is helpful with suggestions for walks. The inn has cheap bunkhouse beds as well as the more orthodox ones in the black clapboarded extension. This 'Outdoor Inn' offers a range of courses and activities such as climbing, walking, skiing, fishing and paragliding. *(Recommended by Heather Sharland, John Whitehead, Steve Waters, Alan Hall, E J Alcock)*

Free house   Licensees Peter and Eileen Daynes   Real ale   Snacks (all day)   Children welcome   Folk music Sat evening; winter lecturers eg Chris Bonnington, and Tues mountain safety talks   Open 11–11   Bedrooms tel Ballachulish (085 52) 252; £14/£32B

GLENDEVON (Tayside)   NN9904 Map 11

Tormaukin 🏛 🛏

A823

Ideally placed for walks over the nearby Ochils or along the River Devon which flows past the front of this cosy and neatly kept inn, and loch and river fishing can be arranged with boats for hire; there are also said to be 90 golf courses within an hour's drive. The bar is softly lit and has plush seats against stripped stone and partly panelled walls; Ind Coope Burton on handpump, a good choice of wines (by the bottle or half-bottle) and malt whiskies, and gentle piped music. Very good bar food, served in the beamed eating area, includes starters such as home-made soup (£1.30), Italian pasta salad (£1.75), spicy char grilled chicken wings (£1.95), home-made smoked fish pâté with oatcakes (£2.40), fresh haddock (£3.85), good home-made venison sausages with port wine sauce (£3.95), salads (from £3.95), baked whole local trout with lemon and parsley butter (£4.25), tagliatelle marinara (£4.50), spicy lamb curry (£4.85), daily specials such as deep fried camembert with fruit coulis (£2.40) and rabbit, apple and elderflower pie (£4.30), and steaks (from £6.40), with more vegetarian dishes such as leek and lentil lasagne or pasta shells in a blue cheese, mushroom and walnut sauce (from £3.95), children's dishes (from £1.40), and puddings such as summer fruit pie or banana rum cheesecake (from £1.75); they serve soup and coffee throughout the day, and the breakfasts are good. Some of the bedrooms are in a converted stable block. *(Recommended by G Smith, Miss A Tress, M Cadenhead, PLC, Celia and David Watt, Mr and Mrs J H Adam)*

Free house   Licensee Marianne Worthy   Real ale   Meals (12–2, 6.30–9.30 Mon–Sat; 12–9.30 Sun)   Children in restaurant and eating area, no young children or babies after 6.30   Restaurant (closed Sun lunchtime)   Open 11–11 Mon–Sat, 12–11 Sun; closed from first Sun after New Year for 2 1/2 weeks   Bedrooms tel Muckhart (025 981) 252; £38B/£53B

HOWGATE (Lothian)   NT2458 Map 11

Old Howgate Inn 🏛

From central Edinburgh, S on A702, then left on to A703 at Hillend; village around 7 miles further on

The white panelled bar in this civilised hotel is airy and pretty with red plush window seats and nests of oak stools, a tiled floor and a stone fireplace; a couple of comfortable sitting rooms have easy chairs and orange-red hessian walls. Interesting bar food includes a wide range of attractively presented, Danish-style open sandwiches (they call them finger pieces): chicken liver pâté with mixed pickle, Danish herring on rye bread, chicken with curry mayonnaise, prawn and lemon mayonnaise, dill-pickled salmon with mustard dressing (small portion £1.75, large portion £3.50); they also do a rib-eye steak sandwich and a hot dish of the day such as sweet and sour pork or omelettes (£4.70). Bass, Belhaven 80/-, McEwans 80/- and Timothy Taylors Landlord on handpump, as well as a weekly guest beer, and frozen aquavit; malt whiskies. There are some slat wood tables on a small back lawn, edged with potentilla and herbaceous borders. *(Recommended by Mr and Mrs J H Adam, S J A Velate, John and Tessa Rainsford, W F Coghill, S V Bishop)*

Free house   Licensees S Walsh and F D Arther   Real ale   Snacks   No-smoking restaurant tel Penicuik (0968) 74244   Children in restaurant   Open 11–2.30, 5–12 Mon–Thurs, 11–12 Fri and Sat

INVERARNAN (Central)   NN3118   Map 11

Inverarnan Inn

A82 N of Loch Lomond

The barstaff in this old drovers' inn wear the kilt, and the friendly bar, a firm favourite with readers, is decorated with a horsecollar and a gun among the Highland paintings on the walls, bagpipes, green tartan cushions and deerskins on the black winged settles, and a stuffed golden eagle on the bar counter. Log fires burn in big fireplaces, there are stripped stone or butter-coloured plaster walls, small windows, red candles in Drambuie bottles if not candlesticks, and cupboards of pewter and china; piped traditional Scottish music. Bar food includes sandwiches (toasties 95p, steak £2.85), a good stags broth (90p), Drovers tart (£1.10), pâté (£1.20), herring with oatmeal (£3.75) and fresh salmon steak (£6). Theakstons on tall fount; a range of good malts – 60 in the gantry and 60 more in stock; peanuts charged by the handful. Lots of sporting trophies (such as a harpooned gaping shark), horns and so forth hang on the high walls of the central hall where there's a stuffed badger curled on a table, and a full suit of armour. Outside, in a field beside the house (also on a small back terrace), there are tables and cocktail parasols, a donkey, pony, and three aggressive geese; a stream runs behind. Worth knowing about, too, as a simple but decent place to stay. *(Recommended by Gary Scott, Alan and Ruth Woodhouse, E J Alcock, Cathy Long, Richard Gibbs, GB, CH)*

Free house   Licensee Duncan McGregor   Real ale   Meals and snacks (12–2, 6–8) Well behaved children allowed   Occasional live music   Open 11–11 Mon–Thurs, 11–midnight Fri and Sat, 12–11 Sunday; closed 25 Dec, 1 Jan   Bedrooms tel Inveruglas (03014) 234; £15/£30

ISLE OF WHITHORN (Dumfries and Galloway)   NX4736   Map 9

Steam Packet 🏠

The fine natural harbour here – sheltered by a long quay – is one of the most attractive in South West Scotland; there are interesting buildings, little shops and always something to watch such as people pottering in their yachts or inshore fishing boats, fishermen mending their nets and boys fishing from the end of the pier. The picture windows from this comfortably modernised inn have superb views and it's naturally a popular place with locals and visitors alike. The low-ceilinged, grey carpeted bar has two rooms: on the right, plush button-back banquettes, brown carpet, and boat pictures; on the left, green leatherette stools around cast-iron-framed tables on big stone tiles, and a woodburning stove in the bare stone wall. Good value bar food includes home-made soup (65p), filled rolls made to order (from 65p; prawn cocktail or steak roll with onions or hot roast only on Sundays £1.50), haggis or jumbo sausage or beefburger (£1.75), fried chicken and bacon (£2.50) or salads (from £2.50; prawn £3.50) and a daily special – fresh fish is the most popular; fresh lobster is usually available from tanks at the back of the hotel – prices vary according to the market price and it's helpful if you can order in advance; one reader found the sea bass in a light tomato sauce particularly memorable. Bar food can be served in the lower beamed dining room, which has a big model steam packet boat on the white walls, excellent colour wildlife photographs, rugs on its wooden floor, and a solid fuel stove, and there's now also a small eating area off the lounge bar; darts, pool and piped music; hospitable service. The garden has white tables and chairs. The bedrooms at the front of the inn have a delightful view of the harbour. Every 1 1/2 to 4 hours there are boat trips from the harbour, and in the rocky grass by the harbour mouth are the remains of St Ninian's Kirk. *(Recommended by D P and M E Cartwright, Peter Burton, David and Flo Wallington)*

Free house Licensee John Scoular Meals and snacks Upstairs restaurant (closed Sun evening) Children welcome Folk music alternate Wed evenings Open 11–11 in summer; 11–2.30, 5–11 winter weekdays Bedrooms tel Whithorn (098 85) 334; £17.50B/£35B

ISLE ORNSAY (Isle of Skye)   NG6912 Map 11

Hotel Eilean Iarmain ★   ⊘   ⇔

Signposted off A851 Broadford–Armadale

An attractive part of Skye this – less austere than the central mountains, and you'll probably see red deer, and maybe otters and seals. The hotel, a sparkling white building and a haunt of the Gaelic-speaking locals (menus and price lists are bi-lingual), has a big and cheerfully busy bar with a swooping stable-stall-like wooden divider that gives a two-room feel: leatherette wall seats, brass lamps and a brass-mounted ceiling fan, good tongue-and-groove panelling on the walls and ceiling, and a huge mirror over the open fire. Bar food includes home-made soup (75p), sandwiches (70p; toasties from 75p), haddock (£3.50), salmon steaks (£7.50), vegetarian dishes (£3), a hot daily special such as casseroled steak or curry (£3.50) and good local fish such as smoked mussels (£1.50). The pretty dining room has a lovely sea view past the little island of Ornsay itself and the lighthouse on Sionnach (you can walk over the sands at low tide). Well kept McEwans 80/- on electric pump, 34 local brands of blended and vatted malt whisky (including their own blended whisky called Te Bheag and a splendid vatted malt called Poit Dhubh, bottled for them but available elsewhere), and a good wine list; darts, dominoes and piped music. Some of the simple bedrooms are in a cottage opposite. *(Recommended by C A Holloway, Genie and Brian Smart, Dr J R Hamilton, Mr and Mrs Tony Walker, S J A Velate, P Lloyd, Miss K Bamford, Roger Danes, Richard Gibbs, Leith Stuart)*

Free house Licensee Sir Iain Noble Real ale Meals and snacks (12.30–2, 6.30–9) Children in eating area and restaurant Occasional folk music Restaurant; not Sun lunch Open 11–2.30, 5.00–12 (11.30 Sat) Bedrooms tel Isle of Skye (047 13) 332; l£46(£50B)

KILCHRENAN (Strathclyde)   NS5285 Map 11

Taychreggan ⇔

B845 7 miles S of Taynuilt

In a beautiful spot, this civilised lochside hotel has an airy bar decorated with local photographs, stuffed birds, salmon flies and rods, and lots of stuffed locally caught fish – some of them real monsters; furnishings include turquoise cloth easy chairs and banquettes around low glass-topped tables. Attractively served lunchtime bar food includes sandwiches (from £1), soup (£1.50), ploughman's (£2.75), deep fried camembert with cranberry sauce (£3.25), smoked Inverawe salmon (£3.75), local Etive prawns (£4.50), hot sandwiches including smoked salmon and scrambled egg on brown bread with salmon roe caviar or 6oz sirloin steak in crusty bread (from £4.50), salads (from £5, fresh prawn £6), meat platter (£6.75) or fish platter (£7.25) and a daily open sandwich menu; home-made puddings (from £1.75). Neatly dressed waiters; the dining room is no-smoking. Arched French windows open from the bar on to a cobbled inner courtyard which has slatted white seats and tables among bright hanging baskets, standard roses, and wisteria and clematis climbing the whitewashed walls. Well kept gardens run down to the water where the hotel has fishing and hires boats on the loch. Some bedrooms overlook the loch. *(Recommended by E J Alcock, Kevin Myers; more reports please)*

Free house   Licensee John Tyrrell   Lunchtime meals and snacks   Restaurant open for non-residents Sun lunch only   Children welcome   Open 12–2.30, 6–11; closed Nov–March   Bedrooms tel Kilchrenan (086 63) 211; £33B/£66B

KILMARTIN (Strathclyde)   NR8398   Map 11

Kilmartin Hotel 🏠

A816 Lochgilphead–Oban

This unassuming white-painted village inn has two snug and softly lit rooms decorated with old Scottish landscape, field sport and genre pictures, and a fine prewar Buchanan whisky advertisement of polo-players; there are spindleback armchairs, a settee, and a variety of settles including some attractive carved ones; some are built into a stripped stone wall snugged under the lower part of the staircase. Bar food, served generously, includes sandwiches or home-made soup (80p), home-cooked gammon salad or smoked salmon quiche (£3.50), minute steak or breaded beef cutlet (£4.50) and venison in blackberry sauce (£7); vegetarian dishes and excellent breakfasts; good service; choice of 80 malt whiskies. Sensibly placed cards, darts, dominoes, maybe piped music. The inn is near the start of *Good Walks Guide* Walk 179. The bedrooms are spacious and good value, but not sumptuously equipped. *(Recommended by Richard Gibbs, Steve Dark, C A Holloway; more reports please)*

Free house   Licensees Keith and Heather Parkinson   Meals and snacks (12–2, 6–9) Restaurant   Children in lounge parlour   Accordion and fiddle Fri and Sat evenings Open 11–11.30 Mon–Fri, 11–12 Sat and Sun   Bedrooms tel Kilmartin (054 65) 244; £15(£20B)/£30(£40B)

KILMELFORD (Strathclyde)   NM8412   Map 11

Cuilfail

A816 S of Oban

Across the road from this Virginia-creeper-covered hotel is a very pretty tree-sheltered garden with picnic-table sets among pieris and rhododendrons (they serve afternoon tea here on request). The pubby bar has stripped stone walls, a stone bar counter with casks worked into it, foreign banknotes on the exposed joists, little winged settles around sewing machine treadle tables on the lino floor and a woodburning stove (open in cold weather). A no-smoking inner eating room has light wood furnishings, and the good choice of imaginative bar food includes soup (including a vegetable one), sweet pickled herring, lentil and peanut pâté (from £1.10-£2.50), with main dishes such as haddock, butterbean and cider casserole, home-made burger, steak and mushroom pie or scampi, almond risotto with peanut sauce, and curry or vegetarian pie (from £2.50-£4.50); there's also a fine selection of daily specials such as Tobermory smoked trout with sweet mustard mayonnaise, avocado pear with raspberry and walnut dressing, game pie or mushroom, leek and courgette en croute, poached salmon steak with an orange hollandaise sauce or pork fillet in a creamy grape and white wine sauce; good home-made puddings. Well kept Youngers No 3 on air-pressure tall fount (and served in jugs if you wish), and a good range of malt whiskies. *(Recommended by Richard Gibbs, Kevin Myers, Mrs R M Morris)*

Free house   Licensee James McFadyen   Real ale   Meals and snacks   No-smoking restaurant   Children in eating area of bar   Open 11–2.30, 5–11; closed Jan and Feb Bedrooms tel Kilmelford (085 22) 274; £23(£27B)/£38(£46B)

KIPPFORD (Dumfries and Galloway)   NX8355   Map 9

Anchor

Overlooking the big natural harbour and the peaceful hills beyond, this waterfront inn has a traditional back bar with varnished panelled walls and ceiling, built-in red plush seats (some of them forming quite high booths around sturdy wooden tables), nautical prints and a coal fire. The lounge bar, mainly for eating, has a tremendous variety of old and new prints on the walls of local granite, and dark blue plush banquettes and stools on the patterned carpet. Good home-made bar food includes filled baked potatoes and basket meals, soup (85p), garlic and brandy pâté (£1.80), good open sandwiches (from £1.95, prawn £3.05), half pint of prawns (£2.15), fresh haddock (£3.35, when available) and steak (£7.25), with at least two daily specials chalked up on a blackboard such as curry, lasagne, sweet and sour pork, steak pie or shellfish mornay (all about £3.15); children's dishes (from £1.30); McEwans 80/- or Theakstons Best on air pressure tall fount; cheerful, helpful staff; piped music. A games room has a juke box, pool table, video machines and satellite television. *(Recommended by David and Flo Wallington, NWN, Fiona Mutch, Robert Wells, D Morrell, G A Worthington, John and Joan Dawson)*

S & N   Licensee Simon B Greig   Real ale   Meals and snacks (12–2, 6–9)   Children welcome   Open 10.30–midnight (10.30–2.30, 6–11 in winter)

LINLITHGOW (Lothian)   NS9976   Map 11
Four Marys

65 High Street; 2 miles from M9 junction 3 (and little further from junction 4) – town signposted

Near the entrance to Linlithgow Palace, where Mary Queen of Scots was born, this has masses of mementoes of her – not just pictures and written records, but a piece of bed curtain said to be hers, part of a 16th-century cloth and swansdown vest of the type she'd be likely to have worn, a facsimile of her death-mask, and of course an explanation of how the pub came by its unique name. The companionable and comfortable L-shaped bar has mainly stripped stone walls, including some remarkable masonry in the inner area; seats are mostly green velvet and mahogany dining chairs around stripped period and antique tables; there are a couple of attractive antique corner cupboards, and an elaborate Victorian dresser serves as a bar gantry, housing several dozen malt whiskies. Enjoyable waitress-served bar food, changing daily, includes good soups such as leek and potato, cream of beetroot or stilton and cauliflower (80p), ploughman's (£3), and eight to ten dishes such as interesting salads (from £3), liver and bacon or lamb casserole (£3.25), chicken curry (£3.50) and haddock or goulash (£3.65); good value Sunday lunch. Well kept Belhaven 70/- and 80/- and two or three interesting guest beers such as Exmoor and Fullers Chiswick on handpump, with a twice-yearly beer festival; friendly and helpful staff; piped pop music on our visit, but we understand this is unusual. *(Recommended by Mr and Mrs J H Adam, Robert Timmis, Ian and Sue Brocklebank)*

Free house   Licensee Gordon Scott   Real ale   Meals and snacks (not Sun evening) Children in eating area   Open 12–2.30, 5–11; 12–11.30 Sat; closed 25 and 26 Dec, 1 and 2 Jan

LOCH ECK (Strathclyde)   NS1391   Map 11
Whistlefield

From A815 along lochside, turn into lane signposted Ardentinny; pub almost immediately to the right

Looking out over the loch and to the hills beyond, this isolated 17th-century house was once a drovers' inn. The low-ceilinged lounge bar has old guns, fishing rods and prints of sea trout and other fish on the bare stone or rough plaster walls, winged pine settles and stools upholstered in green and white tweed on the tartan carpet, and a log fire. A games room has a pool table, video game, fruit machine, dominoes, darts and cards; piped music. McEwans 80/- on air pressure under tall fount, 40 malt whiskies and good value bar food that includes sandwiches (from 75p), soup (95p), filled baked potatoes (from 70p), herring in dill or various ploughman's (£2.50), haddock (£3.50), chilli con carne (£3.75), steak (£8.50), weekly specials such as stovies (£1.25), and home-made puddings (from £1.50). There's a log cabin for hire, fishing boats for rent and fishing permits can be bought; children's play area outside. (*Recommended by E J Alcock; more up-to-date reports please*)

Free house   Licensee Ian Smith   Meals and snacks   Children in eating area and family room   Open 11–2.30, 4–1 Mon–Fri, 12–2.30, 6–12 Sat; may close 2.30–6.30 if quiet Folk group on Fri and Sat evening   Bedrooms tel Strachur (036 986) 250; £15/£30

MELROSE (Borders)   NT5434   Map 9

Burts Hotel ⊘ ⇦

A6091

In perhaps the quietest and most villagey of all the Scottish Border towns, this welcoming, 18th-century inn has a comfortable L-shaped lounge bar with cushioned wall seats and Windsor armchairs on its Turkey carpet, and Scottish prints on the walls. A good range of waitress-served, consistently popular bar food includes soup (£1.20), two pâtés (£2.10), ploughman's (£2.70), cheese and tomato pizza or haddock (£3.50), vegetable lasagne or honey-baked ham (£3.80), rare roast beef salad (£4.20); they do more specials in the evening, such as smoked quails' eggs with watercress and orange salad or salmon and sole roulade with lemon mayonnaise (£2.40), breaded escalope of turkey with stem ginger sauce, grilled lambs' livers with orange and cointreau sauce, baked coley in tomato and cider sauce or vegetable and nut pancakes with spinach sauce (all £4.80); puddings like home-made bread and butter pudding (£1.20); good breakfasts. Belhaven 80/- on electric pump; wide range of malt whiskies and wines; good service; snooker room (residents only). There's a well tended garden, with tables in summer. (*Recommended by John Perry, Syd and Wyn Donald, Gordon Smith, Dr R Fuller, John and Anne McIver, Mr and Mrs D M Norton, Mr and Mrs J E Rycroft, Tim Locke, John Townsend, Prof H G Allen*)

Free House   Licensee Graham Henderson   Real ale   Meals and snacks (12–2, 6–9.30; till 10.30 Fri and Sat)   Children welcome   Restaurant   Open 11–2.30, 5–11 Bedrooms tel Melrose (089 682) 2285; £32B/£56B

MONIAIVE (Dumfries and Galloway)   NX7790   Map 9

George ⇦

From A76 N of Dumfries, left on to B729 at New Bridge, then left on to A702 after 10 miles

Worth quite a detour, the endearing little flagstoned bar in this ancient white stone Covenanters' inn has a most welcoming atmosphere and relaxed, friendly and efficient staff. It's been slightly refurbished under the new licensee, and the butter-coloured timbered walls have good antique Tam O'Shanter engravings, and there are some small seats made from curious conical straight-sided kegs, high backed pew seats upholstered with tapestry, dark-beamed ceiling and open fires in winter; darts, pool, dominoes, fruit machine, trivia and a juke box in the adjacent larger bar. The large airy lounge bar and restaurant at the other end of the building have views over the nearby hills. Decent bar food includes home-made soup (80p), filled rolls (90p), sandwiches (from £1), home-made chicken liver pâté (£2.10), haggis (£2.75), haddock (£2.90), and home-made steak and kidney pie or venison in red wine; a range of malts and selection of wines; piped music in the restaurant. The peaceful riverside village is surrounded by fine scenery. (*Recommended by Mr and Mrs J H Adam, GB, Steve Dark, Paul Wreglesworth, Richard Holloway, Peter Burton, John Gillett*)

Free house   Licensee Marjory Price   Meals and snacks   Children allowed, but not after 9 in public bar   Restaurant (Fri–Sun evenings; Sun lunch)   Occasional music from local traditional Scottish band   Open 11–2.30, 5–11 Mon–Thurs, 11–midnight Fri and Sat, 12.30–11 Sun   Bedrooms tel Moniaive (084 82) 203; £13.50/£27

8200203

MONYMUSK (Grampian) NJ6815 Map 11

Grant Arms

Inn and village sigposted from B993 SW of Kemnay

Below Bennachie, this handsome 18th-century stone inn has exclusive rights to 15 miles of good trout and salmon fishing on the River Don, 11 beats with 29 named pools, and there's a ghillie available. Inside, the lounge bar is divided into two areas by a log fire in the stub wall, and there are some newly upholstered, burgundy armchairs as well as other seats, a patterned carpet and dark panelling, and it is decorated with paintings by local artists, which are for sale. Bar food includes soup (£1.05), sandwiches (£1), grilled lamb cutlets (£5.45), and sirloin steak (£6); there's more seafood this year – fried haddock (£3.70), lemon sole (around £4.30), fresh crab, oysters and lobster, with game in season. The simpler public bar has darts, dominoes, cribbage, fruit machine, space game and piped music; McEwans 80/- and Youngers No 3 on air pressure tall founts. North of the village – spick and span in its estate colours of dark red woodwork and natural stone – the gently rolling wooded pastures soon give way to grander hills. (*Recommended by Peter Burton, Celia and David Watt*)

Free house   Licensee Colin Hart   Real ale   Meals and snacks (12–2.15, 6.30–9.30) Restaurant   Children welcome   Open 11–2.30, 5–11 (11.30 Sat), all day Sun; closed 26 Dec, 1 and 2 Jan   Bedrooms tel Monymusk (046 77) 226; £27(£35B)/£45(£49B)

MOUNTBENGER (Borders)   NT3125 Map 9

Gordon Arms

Junction A708/B709

The cosy public bar in this little hotel has an interesting set of photographs of blackface rams from local hill farms, there's a fire in cold weather and a local 'shepherd song' is pinned on the wall; a hundred and fifty years ago another shepherd poet, James Hogg, the 'Ettrick Shepherd', recommended that this very inn should keep its licence, which Sir Walter Scott, in his capacity as a justice and who also knew the inn, subsequently granted. Bar food includes lunchtime sandwiches (from £1.25), home-made soup (£1.10), lunchtime ploughman's (£1.50), salads (from £4.95), home-made steak pie (£4.50) and fresh Yarrow trout (£4.95), with additional evening dishes such as lamb chops (£4.50), gammon (£4.95) and steaks (from £7.95); children's dishes (from £1.50). Well kept Greenmantle on handpump (brewed in Broughton, near Peebles) and Tennents 80/- on air pressure tall fount; a choice of 46 malt whiskies. A lounge bar serves high teas – a speciality here – and there's a games room with pool, fruit machine and piped music, also dominoes. In addition to the hotel bedrooms, there's a bunkhouse which provides cheap accommodation for hill walkers and cyclists. The pub is a welcome sight from either of the two lonely moorland roads which cross here: both roads take you through attractive scenery, and the B road in particular is very grand – indeed, it forms part of a splendid empty moorland route between the A74 and Edinburgh (from Lockerbie, B723/B709/B7062/A703/A6094). (*Recommended by Mr and Mrs J H Adam, Simon Ward; more reports please*)

Free house   Licensees Mr and Mrs H M Mitchell   Real ale   Meals and snacks (12–2.30, 7–9 and high teas 4–6)   Restaurant   Well behaved children welcome; preferred in lounge   Accordion and fiddle club third Wed every month; folk club third Sat every month   Open 11–11 (11–2.30, 7–11 winter); closed Mon mid-winter Bedrooms tel Yarrow (0750) 82222/82232; £15/£26.50; bunkhouse £4.50

NEWBURGH (Grampian)   NJ9925 Map 11

Udny Arms 🏠

From A92 N of Aberdeen, right on to A975 at Rashiereive; village 3 miles

The lounge bar in this hospitable and well kept place has carefully chosen furniture that includes prettily cushioned stripped pine seats and wooden chairs around plain wooden tables on the grey carpet, and bird prints, salmon flies, and a pictorial map of the River Dee on the cream walls. Lunchtime food in the downstairs bar includes soups (from £1.35), sandwiches (from £1.50; open from £2.50), sausage bake (£2.50), cold roast meats (£3.50); evening food in the upstairs lounge bar is much more restauranty, and there's quite an emphasis on seafood – king prawns or crab claws (£4.95), Shetland salmon steak (£8.95) or scallops (£11.95), and chicken casserole (£8.65); in the afternoon they serve tea and shortbread. Well kept McEwans 80/- served bright on tall fount air pressure, house wines, a selection of malt whiskies and bottled beers, and espresso coffee; friendly staff; piped music and pétanque. A sun lounge has green basket chairs around glass-topped wicker tables. On the sheltered back lawn there are lots of white tables, and from here a footbridge crosses the little Foveran Burn to the nine-hole golf links, the dunes and the sandy beach along the Ythan estuary. There are three good golf courses and Pitmedden Gardens nearby. (*Recommened by Peter Burton; more reports please*)

Free house   Licensees Mr and Mrs Craig   Real ale   Snacks (lunchtime) and meals Children welcome   Open 11–11.30   Bedrooms tel Newburgh (Aberdeen) (035 86) 89444; £46B/£58B

OBAN (Strathclyde)   NM8630   Map 11

Oban Inn

Stafford Street

The downstairs beamed bar in this late 18th-century inn has a lively atmosphere and a good mix of local customers – harbour folk, fishermen, Navy divers, doctors, lawyers and so forth. There are small stools, pews and black winged modern settles on its uneven slate floor, blow-ups of old Oban postcards on its cream walls, and unusual brass-shaded wall lamps. Upstairs, a quieter and more decorous carpeted bar has button-back banquettes around cast-iron-framed tables, some panelling and a coffered woodwork ceiling; besides the real windows overlooking the harbour, it has little backlit arched false windows with heraldic roundels in 17th-century stained glass. Lunchtime bar food includes home-made soup (95p), fresh mussels (£1.20), home-made steak pie or haggis, neeps and tatties or salads (£3.45); it may not always be available during winter. Well kept McEwans 80/- and Youngers No 3 from tall founts, a large selection of whiskies; piped music in lounge bar; live folk music on certain nights in downstairs bar. (*Recommended by Graham and Karen Oddey, E J Alcock, Keith Mills, Jane and Calum Maclean, Alan and Ruth Woodhouse, David and Christine Foulkes, Jim and Becky Bryson, Jon Wainwright, Kevin Myers*)

S & N   Licensee Michael Hewitt   Real ale   Lunchtime meals and snacks (12–2.30) Children in eating area of bar 12–2.30 only   Folk musicians on Sun evenings 9–midnight and impromptu during summer   Open 11–12.45am   Bedrooms currently being refurbished and prices unknown as we went to press tel Oban (0631) 62484

PERTH (Tayside)   NO1123   Map 11

Granary

97 Canal Street; 2 miles from M90 junction 10 – coming in on main road, turn left into Canal Street in centre; pub is in turning off right, just after multi-storey car park

Efficiently served good value bar food in this comfortable pub includes soup (80p), interesting filled baked potatoes such as smoked ham with asparagus (from £1.80) and open sandwiches (from £2.50), ploughman's (£2.40), savoury quiche or lasagne (£2.95), chicken curry or fresh haddock (£3.50), home-made steak and kidney pie (£3.75) and tuna salad niçoise (£4.30), with home-made puddings (£1.50); in the evenings, there's a shorter bar choice, with more concentration on meals upstairs, including starters such as real fish soup (£1.70), and main dishes such as saddle of local lamb (£9.25). Note that bar lunches stop very promptly at 2. There are brocaded chairs around polished brown tables, stripped stone walls, low dark beams – except in one area opened up to roof height, giving the upstairs candlelit restaurant a galleried effect. Horse brasses and harness, some old farm tools and bygones allude to the early 17th-century building's past as a city granary; there are attractive lamps, old stag prints, open fires (and see if you can spot all the hot-cross buns, one for each year they've had the pub). Well kept McEwans 80/- on air pressure tall fount; decent wines; piped country and western. *(Recommended by Melvin D Buckner, G and L Owen, Dr Thomas Mackenzie)*

Free house   Licensees Derek and Jeanette Stoner   Real ale   Meals and snacks till 10 Restaurant tel Perth (0738) 36705   Children allowed if eating   Open 11.30–2.30, 6–11 (12 Sat)

nr PITLOCHRY (Tayside)   NN9458   Map 11

Killiecrankie Hotel 🅟 🛏

Killiecrankie signposted from A9 N of Pitlochry

The popular licensees who took over this comfortable country hotel last year have recently refurbished the bar and conservatory extension with the idea of giving a light, summery feel to the place; the bar now has mahogany panelling, new upholstered seating and mahogany tables and chairs, as well as stuffed animals and some rather fine wildlife paintings; in the conservatory the copper-topped tables have been replaced by light beech tables of a decent size along with upholstered chairs. The whole look is enhanced by some discreet decoration with plants and flowers. Good, well presented lunchtime food includes home-made soup (£1.25), ploughman's (£2.95), open sandwiches (from £3.25, smoked salmon and prawn £4.50), home-cooked smoked Ayrshire ham salad or locally smoked trout with limes and horseradish (£3.50), lightly curried chicken mayonnaise (£3.95) and fresh Tayside salmon mayonnaise (£5.95); evening dishes include a vegetarian dish (£4.25), smokies (£4.50), fresh trout in oatmeal or highland game casserole (£4.95), grilled salmon steak with lime and parsley butter (£5.95) and sirloin steak (£7.50); puddings such as traditional Scottish trifle with raspberries and whisky or Tanoffi pie (£1.75). The spacious grounds back on to the hills and include a putting course and a croquet lawn – sometimes there are roe deer and red squirrels. The views of the mountain pass are splendid. *(Recommended by T Nott, John and Anne McIver, M H Box, R G Bentley, D A Wilcock, Miss C M Davidson, Helen and John Thompson, Ralph A Raimi, John and Tessa Rainsford, Leith Stuart, T W Hoskins, E J Knight)*

Free house   Licensees Colin and Carole Anderson   Meals and snacks (12–2.30, 6.30–9.30)   Children welcome, no infants in evenings   Evening restaurant   Open 12–2.30, 6–11; closed Nov–end Feb   Bedrooms tel Pitlochry (0796) 3220; £32.50B/S/£58(£63B)

PLOCKTON (Highland)   NG8033   Map 11

Plockton Hotel

Village signposted from A87 near Kyle of Lochalsh

Strung out among palm trees along the seashore and looking across Loch Carron to rugged mountains, this is a very pretty village. In its centre this low stone-built house has a comfortably furnished, partly panelled and partly stripped stone lounge bar with green leatherette seats around neat Regency-style tables on a tartan carpet, an open fire, and a ship model set into the woodwork; window seats look out to the boats on the water. Bar food includes home-made soup (85p), filled rolls (from 75p), sandwiches (from 75p, toasties 10p extra), good home-made pâtè, ploughman's or vegetable pancake rolls (£2.50), salads (from £2.95), smoked salmon quiche (£3.40), tasty large local prawns (£3.95), with evening dishes like grilled sirloin steak (£6.95) and fresh wild salmon in season; children's dishes (£1.50), good breakfasts. Tennents 80/- on tall fount air pressure and a good collection of whiskies. The separate public bar has darts, pool, shove-ha'penny, dominoes, cribbage, and piped music; dogs welcome. The village is owned by the National Trust for Scotland; the inn is currently on the market, though we understand that the present popular regime is unlikely to change before well into 1990. *(Recommended by Andrew Hazeldine, E J Alcock, Jim and Becky Bryson, M Cadenhead, P B Dowsett, Mr and Mrs J H Adam)*

Free house   Licensee Alasdair Bruce   Real ale   Meals and snacks (12.30–2, 6.30–8.30; basket meals till 9.30)   Children in eating area of bar   Open 11–2.30, 5–12 (till 11.30 Sat)   Bedrooms tel Plockton (059 984) 250; £16.95S/£33.90S (twin rooms only)

PORTPATRICK (Dumfries and Galloway)   NX0154 Map 9

Crown ★ ⊘ ⇐

A treasure is how one reader describes this delightful little harbourfront pub, under new licensees this year. The rambling old-fashioned bar has lots of little nooks, crannies and alcoves, and interesting furniture includes a carved settle with barking dogs as its arms and an antique wicker-backed armchair. There are shelves of old bottles above the bar counter, a stag's head over the coal fire, and the partly panelled butter-coloured walls are decorated with old mirrors with landscapes painted in their side panels; exceptional service and a really relaxing atmosphere. Food (the fish is caught by the chef) includes sandwiches (from 90p, toasties from £1.05), Danish open (from 90p, crab £2.60, prawn or salmon £3), home-made soup (90p), smoked mackerel (£1.65), ploughman's salad (£2.10), salads (from £2.10, fresh crab or smoked trout £4.35, prawn £5.75, grilled jumbo prawns from £7.70, lobster from £10.75), seafood kebab or moules marinières (£3.05), grilled scallops wrapped in bacon with garlic butter sauce (£3.10), whole grilled jumbo prawns (£4.35); then specials such as beef hot-pot (£3.35), vegetarian pancake (£4.20), chicken and mushroom pancake or whole plaice with toasted almonds (£4.45), scallops in white wine sauce (£5.80), steak (from £7.60), roast duckling with orange and grand marnier sauce (£8.50), crown lobster (from £10.75), fillet steak with half lobster (from £13) and seafood platter (from £14.75); excellent breakfasts. Piped music; sensibly placed darts in the separate public bar, and a fruit machine. An airy and very attractively decorated 1930sish dining room opens through a quiet and attractively planted conservatory area into a sheltered back garden. Seats outside in front – served by hatch in the front lobby – make the most of the evening sun. Unusually attractive bedrooms have individual touches such as uncommon Munch prints. *(Recommended by NWN, Robert and Fiona Ambroziak, David and Flo Wallington, D P and M E Cartwright, Lesley Jones, Geralyn Meyler, Peter Burton, Ray and Gwen Jessop, Ruth Humphrey, George Jonas)*

Free house   Licensee Bernard Wilson   Meals and snacks (12–2, 6–10)   Restaurant   Children welcome   Open 11–11   Bedrooms tel Portpatrick (077 681) 261; £28B/£52B

QUEENSFERRY (Lothian)   NT1278 Map 11

Hawes

South Queensferry; A90 W of Edinburgh

In the quieter, older part of this old inn, there's still something of the atmosphere that made the inn so appealing to R L Stevenson – he used it as a setting in *Kidnapped*, and may even have been moved to start writing the book while staying here. The comfortable, airy lounge bar has a fine view of the Forth stretching out between the massively practical railway bridge and the elegantly supercilious road bridge. An efficient food counter serves soup (£1), four hot dishes which change daily such as chilli con carne, deep fried haddock, pork chop or roast beef (from £2.95) and a cold buffet with unusual salads (£3.15). Well kept Arrols and Ind Coope Burtons are served on tall founts. The small public bar – more popular with younger people – has darts, dominoes, fruit machine and piped music. Tables outside overlook the Forth (where boat trips are available), and a back lawn with hedges and roses has white tables and a children's play area. *(Recommended by S V Bishop, Syd and Wyn Donald)*

Alloa Brewery Co Ltd   Licensee David Burns   Real ale   Meals   Children in family room until 8   Restaurant   Open 11–11   Bedrooms tel Edinburgh (031) 331 1990; £31/£45

SELKIRK (Borders)   NT4728 Map 10
Queens Head
28 West Port

The big open-plan, low-beamed lounge bar in this cheerful and well-run town pub
has been recently refurbished by the new owners: navy blue banquettes and
wheelback chairs around copper topped tables on the blue and silver speckled
carpet, a gas-effect coal fire, prints of Sir Walter Scott and his family on the walls
and pretty dried flower arrangements; the red carpeted, simpler public bar has
sensibly placed darts, dominoes, a fruit machine, trivia and juke box. Home-made
bar food includes soup (85p), sandwiches (from 90p, toasties from 95p), steak and
kidney pie, lasagne, haddock, various salads and vegetarian dishes such as lentil
and bean bake (all £3.35) and scampi (£3.45); children's dishes. The Border
country around Selkirk, with gentle hills rising to rounded heather tops, is
particularly beautiful; nearby Bowhill is a stately home in lavish grounds. No dogs
in the lounge. *(Recommended by David Waterhouse, Mr and Mrs J H Adam; more reports
please)*

*Free house   Licensees Eric and Ruth Paterson   Meals and snacks (12–2.30, 5–9.30;
Sunday teas 5.30–8.30)   Children welcome   Open 11–11 (midnight Fri and Sat);
closed afternoons winter*

SHERIFFMUIR (Central)   NN8202 Map 11
Sheriffmuir Inn

Signposted off A9 just S of Blackford; and off A9 at Dunblane roundabout, just N of end
of M9; also signposted from Bridge of Allan; OS Sheet 57 map reference 827022

A wonderful surprise by the single-track road over this sweep of moorland,
uninhabited except for the sheep, cattle and birds: a really civilised and
comfortable pub, open all day in summer. The neat L-shaped bar has pink plush
stools and button-back built-in wall banquettes on a smart pink patterned carpet,
polished tables, olde-worlde coaching prints on its white walls, artificial flowers in
the windows that look out over the moors, and a woodburning stove in a stone
fireplace. A wide choice of lunchtime bar food includes soup (£1.10), toasties
(£1.15), starters such as pâté with oatcakes (£2.15), ploughman's (£2.35),
cheeseburger (£3.25), lasagne (£3.45), salads such as tuna (£3.70), home-made
steak pie (£3.95) and sirloin steak (£7.25, with various puddings (around £1.80);
in the evenings there are more main dishes, no snacks apart from starters. Well
kept Tetleys on handpump, good choice of whiskies, decent coffee; friendly, neatly
uniformed staff, unobtrusive well reproduced piped 1960s music. There are tables
and a play area outside the white-painted house – an inn since 1615. We've not yet
heard from readers who've stayed here, but the very high standard of housekeeping
is a promising sign. *(Recommended by Miss C Haworth, Carol and Richard Glover, Len
Beattie)*

*Free house   Licensees Peter and Sue Colley   Real ale   Meals and lunchtime snacks
(from 6 evening)   Restaurant   Children welcome   Open 12–11; closed 2.30–5 winter
weekdays   Bedrooms tel Dunblane (0786) 823285; £29/£35*

SHIELDAIG (Highland)   NG8154 Map 11
Tigh an Eilean 🍴

Village signposted just off A896 Lochcarron–Gairloch

In a gorgeous position at the head of Loch Shieldaig, this grey-shuttered white
house looks over forested Shieldaig Island to Loch Torridon and then the sea
beyond – at certain times of summer, straight down the path of the late-setting sun.
The basic bar at the side (used by locals, some speaking Gaelic) has red brocaded
button-back banquettes in bays, with picture windows looking out to sea and three
picnic-table sets in a sheltered front courtyard. Quickly served, simple bar food
includes soup (85p), sandwiches (95p), macaroni cheese or lasagne (£2.95),

home-made steak and kidney pie (£3.25) and fresh salmon salad (£4.95) with weekly specials such as chicken in white wine or highland rabbit (£3.25); puddings such as pavlovas or profiteroles (all 95p); children's dishes half price; darts, dominoes and fruit machine. The residents' side is quite a contrast, with easy chairs, books and a well stocked help-yourself bar in the neat and prettily decorated two-room lounge, and an attractively modern comfortable dining room specialising in good value local shellfish, fish and game. Like the public rooms, the front bedrooms have the view. The well kept hotel, which is small and friendly, has private fishing and can arrange sea fishing. *(Recommended by Joan and John Calvert, J A B Darlington, E J Alcock)*

Free house   Licensee Mrs E Stewart   Meals and snacks (not Sun evening)   Evening restaurant summer only   Children in bar till 8.30   No dogs   Open 11–11 summer; winter 11–2.30, 5–11; meals only Sun lunchtime and closed Sun evening summer; closed all day Sun winter, 25 Dec evening and all day 1 Jan   Bedrooms tel Shieldaig (052 05) 251; £23/£44(£48.50B)

SKEABOST (Isle of Skye)   NG4148 Map 11

Skeabost House Hotel ★   ⊘   ⊨

A850 NW of Portree, 1 1/2 miles past junction with A856

In pleasant grounds at the head of Loch Snizort – perhaps Skye's best salmon river, with private fishing – this very civilised and friendly small hotel has a high-ceilinged bar with a new pine counter, red brocade seats on its thick red carpet and some in a big bay window which overlooks a terrace (with picnic-table sets) and the neatly kept lawn; this doubles as a putting course and runs down to the loch, bright with bluebells on its far side. The spacious and airy no-smoking lounge has an attractively laid out buffet table with good home-made soup, generously filled sandwiches or rolls, lots of salads (vegetarian £3, cold meats from £4.05, fresh salmon £4.75), a hot dish of the day, and puddings; lots of malt whiskies. A fine panelled billiards room leads off the stately hall; there's a wholly separate public bar with darts, pool and juke box (and even its own car park). The grounds around the hotel include a bog-and-water garden under overhanging rocks and rhododendrons, and a nine-hole golf course. The village Post Office here has particularly good value Harris wool sweaters, blankets, tweeds and wools. *(Recommended by S J A Velate, Mr and Mrs G Gittings, K and G Oddey, J A B Darlington)*

Free house   Licensee Iain McNab   Meals and snacks (not Sun)   Evening restaurant Children welcome   Open 11–2.30, 5–11; closed end Oct–1 March   Bedrooms tel Skeabost Bridge (047 032) 202; £27(£33B)/£52(£62B)

nr SPEAN BRIDGE (Highland)   NN2281 Map 11

Letterfinlay Lodge Hotel ⊨

7 miles N of Spean Bridge on A82

Set well back from the road, this secluded and genteel family-run country house has attractive grounds running down through rhododendrons to the jetty and Loch Lochy. The spacious modern bar, with comfortable brown plush seats clustered around dark tables, has a long glass wall giving splendid lochside views over to the steep forests on the far side; there's a games area to one side with darts, pool, dominoes, cribbage and a space game. Good and popular lunchtime food is served buffet-style, and includes home-made soup (£1), sandwiches (£1.30), smoked rainbow trout with horseradish sauce (£1.90), main courses such as salads (from £3.25), fried fresh fillets of Aberdeen lemon sole (£3.50), roast haunch of Lochaber venison or grilled Scottish lamb cutlets (£3.75), poached fresh-run Loch Ness salmon (£4.75) or grilled Aberdeen Angus sirloin steak (£6.25) and puddings (£1.50); excellent breakfasts. Good, chilled wines (including Scottish wines from Moniack); friendly, attentive service. Opening off one side of the main bar is an elegantly panelled small cocktail bar (with a black-bow-tied barman) furnished with button-back leather seats, old prints, and a chart of the Caledonian Canal; malt whiskies, piped music. On the side gravel, there are a couple of white tables under cocktail umbrellas. Fishing and perhaps deerstalking can be arranged, there are shower facilities for customers on boating holidays, and a small caravan club; dogs welcome. *(Recommended by S J A Velate, Linda Sewell, David and Christine Foulkes, Joan and Tony Walker, Mark Shinkfield, Joy Marshall, Mr and Mrs J H Adam)*

Free house   Licensee Ian Forsyth   Lunchtime meals and snacks (available all day) Children welcome   Restaurant; closed Sun lunch   Open 11–1am weekdays, till 11.30 Sat; closed Nov–Feb   Bedrooms tel Speanbridge (0397 81) 622; £23(25B)/£46(£50B)

ST BOSWELLS (Borders)   NT5931   Map 10

Buccleuch Arms

A68 just S of Newtown St Boswells

Opposite the village green and next to the cricket ground, this Victorian sandstone inn has a quiet, genteel atmosphere. The bar has reproduction Georgian-style panelling, pink plush seats, elegant banquettes, velvet curtains and something of a hunting theme; there may be dishes of nuts and other nibbles on the bar; the alcove is no-smoking. The public bar is now called the Salmon Room and is used for functions. Imaginative bar food (changed monthly) includes soup (£1.05), sandwiches, mushrooms in garlic butter (£1.25), chicken liver and whisky pâté (£1.50), ploughman's (£2.25), cold meat platter with salad (£3.50), scampi (£3.75), sugar-baked gammon with pineapple (£3.95) and sirloin steak (£7.25); daily specials such as lasagne, spaghetti bolognese or sweet and sour pork (£3.50); they serve sandwiches all day, do afternoon teas, and occasional speciality food nights such as Caribbean or Moroccan. Tables outside in the garden; close to *Good Walks Guide* Walk 162.   *(Recommended by David Waterhouse, John and Anne McIver, Prof H G Allen, Leith Stuart, S V Bishop, Graham and Karen Oddey)*

Free house   Licensee Mrs Lucy Agnew   Meals and snacks (12–2, 6–9 Mon–Thurs; 12–2, 6–10 Fri–Sat   Restaurant   Children welcome   Open 11–11; Sun 12.30–11 Bedrooms tel St Boswells (0835) 22243; £33B/£60B

ST MARY'S LOCH (Borders)   NT2422   Map 9

Tibbie Shiels Inn 🏠

The cosy back bar in the original old stone part of this isolated and beautifully situated old inn has well cushioned black wall benches or leatherette armed chairs, and a photograph of Tibbie Shiels herself: wife of the local mole-catcher and a favourite character of Age of Enlightenment Edinburgh literary society. Waitress-served lunchtime bar food includes home-made soup (80p), sandwiches (85p, toasties 95p), ploughman's (£1.80), home-made chilli con carne (£2.50), chicken curry (£2.80), home-baked gammon (£3), 4oz rump steak (£3.70) or tasty local trout (£3.75); a wide range of vegetarian meals including cashew nut loaf with tomato and herb salad, mushroom and hazelnut crumble or bulghur wheat and walnut casserole (all £3.30); in the evening the menu is slightly more elaborate with starters such as marinated Yarrow trout with dill and mustard sauce or oak smoked mutton marinated in port or avocado mousse with prawns (all £1.80), and main courses such as gammon in a puff pastry parcel with mushrooms (£5), escalope of veal with cream and ginger wine sauce (£6) or chicken in peanut butter sauce with garlic (£6.50), salmon in cream and white wine sauce or venison cooked in blackberry wine sauce (£7), steaks (from £7.65); there are home-baked scones, cakes and shortbread at high tea. Well kept Belhaven 70/- and Greenmantle on handpump; lots of malt whiskies. There's a no-smoking dining area off the main lounge; darts, dominoes and piped music. The Southern Upland Way – a long-distance foot path – passes close by, the Grey Mares Tail waterfall is just down the glen, and the loch is beautiful (with day members to the sailing club welcome, and fishing free to residents; it's very peaceful – except when low-flying jets explode into your consciousness). The bedrooms are comfortable and good value. *(Recommended by Willy Hendrikx, S J A Velate, Mrs R M Morris, A McK, Mark Shinkfield, Joy Marshall, Steve Dark)*

Free house   Licensees Jack and Jill Brown   Real ale   Meals and snacks (12–2.30,

3.30–8.30) *Children welcome Restaurant No-smoking in small 16 seat eating
area Open 11–11; closed Monday and 1 Nov–28 Feb Bedrooms tel Selkirk (0750)
42231; £14/£28*

STRACHUR (Strathclyde) NN0901 Map 11

Creggans 🛏

A815 N of village

The view from the white tables in front of this elegant small hotel looks over the
sea loch to the hills on the far side; close by is the spot where Queen Mary of Scots
landed in 1563. Inside, there's a similar view from the comfortable and attractively
decorated tweedy lounge, with extra seats in a conservatory, and a public bar given
more life by the locals who still use it – pool, darts, dominoes, a fruit machine and
space game. Popular and quite restauranty bar food includes bacon roll (£1.30),
home-made soup (£1.50), toasted sandwiches (from £1.60), ploughman's (£2.75),
a choice of home-made pâté s or terrines (£2.90), home-made burgers including a
venison one (£3.35), spiced beef and pickle or seafood salad (£4.15), local oysters
(£4.95 the half-dozen), lamb cutlets (£5.75), Loch Fyne trout in oatmeal (£5.80),
langoustines (£8.95), 8oz sirloin steak (£9.95), and daily specials. McEwans 80/-
on tall fount, and a good selection of malt whiskies, including their own vatted
malt. You can walk for hours on the owners' land; deerstalking as well as fishing
and ponytrekking may be arranged for residents. *(Recommended by E J Alcock, Cathy
Long, Jon Wainwright, Mrs E M Brandwood)*

*Free house Licensee Sir Fitzroy Maclean Meals and snacks (lunchtime; 6.30–9 winter
only) Children welcome Restaurant Open 11–12.30; Sat 11–1am Bedrooms
tel Strachur (036 986) 27; £35(£40B)/£70(£80B)*

SWINTON (Borders) NT8448 Map 10

Wheatsheaf 🎯 🛏

A6112 N of Coldstream

Everyone who's recommended this attractive small sandstone hotel, facing the long
village green, has particularly praised the outstanding bar food, and that's what
virtually all the customers are here for. Alan Reid, the chef/patron, is particularly
strong on fish such as devilled whitebait (£2.75), Danish herring with dill and
sherry (£2.80) or smoked Tweed salmon (£4.95) as hors-d'oeuvre, smoked fish
brioche (£3.65), prawn curry (£4.35), Scottish seafood stew (£6.70), sautéed tiger
prawns with garlic (£7.95) or 16oz Dover sole meunière (£9.85). A wide choice of
other dishes, generously served, includes soup (90p), sandwiches (from 90p),
deep-fried brie with real ale pickle (£2.65), spinach pancake (£2.85), roast
gammon salad (£2.90), half a dozen snails in garlic butter (£2.95), lasagne (£3.35),
vegetarian stroganoff (£3.45) or lamb curry (£3.90), tagliatelli in seafood and
cream sauce or spaghetti carbonara (£3.95), sautéed lambs' sweetbreads with
marsala (£4.80), sirloin steak (£7.65), and a good many puddings such as summer
pudding with cream or apple and cinnamon cheesecake (from £1.25). Booking is
advisable, particularly from Thursday to Saturday evening. The main area has
sporting prints and plates on the bottle-green wall covering, an attractive long oak
settle and some green-cushioned window seats as well as the wheelback chairs
around the tables, and a stuffed pheasant and partridge over the log fire; a small
lower-ceilinged part by the counter has pubbier furnishings, and small agricultural
prints on the walls – especially sheep. Well kept Greenmantle and Greenmantle
80/- on air pressure tall fount; decent range of malt whiskies, 36 good wines and
coffee; warmly welcoming friendly service. A quite separate side locals' bar has
darts, pool, dominoes and fruit machine. There's a new no-smoking front
conservatory with a vaulted pine ceiling and walls of local stone, and a play area
for children in the garden. *(Recommended by W A Wright, Syd and Wyn Donald, Mr and
Mrs M D Jones, Mrs B Crosland, Alan Hall, Mr and Mrs M O Jones)*

Free house Licensee Alan Reid Real ale Meals and snacks (11.30–2.15, 5.30–10;

not Mon)   Restaurant   Children welcome   Open 11–3, 5.30–11 (11.30 Sat; 6–11 winter); closed Mon, 25 Dec, 1 Jan and middle 2 weeks Feb   Bedrooms tel Swinton (089 086) 257; £20/£32

TARBERT (Strathclyde)   NR8467   Map 11

West Loch Hotel 🛏

A83 1 mile S

The cocktail bar in this quiet modernised country inn has brown cloth upholstered easy chairs, little basket-weave chairs, and photographs of Tarbert; it opens into a lounge with Liberty-print easy chairs, a log/peat fire and piped classical music. The small public bar has a woodburning stove and old fishing photographs. Good bar food includes Scotch broth (90p), venison sausages (£2.95), black pudding and apple pancake (£3.50), tripe and onions or rabbit casserole (£3.75), good salads, phyllo parcels of leek and cheese (£4.10), smoked salmon and scrambled duck eggs (£4.50), local seafood in a light curry mayonnaise (£4.60), grilled Argyll quail with orange wine butter (£4.95), and puddings (£1.75); set evening meals including local fish and game; friendly service. (*Recommended by Dr T H M Mackenzie, Richard Whitehead, Christa Grosse, D M Bednarowska*)

Free house   Licensee Mrs Sandy Ferguson   Meals and snacks (12–2, 6.30–7.30)   Restaurant   Children welcome   Open 12–2, 5–11   Bedrooms tel Tarbert (088 02) 283; £16/£32

TAYVALLICH (Strathclyde)   NR7386   Map 11

Tayvallich Inn ✿

B8025, off A816 1 mile S of Kilmartin; or take B841 turn-off from A816 two miles N of Lochgilphead

Looking over the lane and the muddy foreshore to the very sheltered yacht anchorage, the small bar in this simple pub has cigarette cards and local nautical charts on brown hessian walls, exposed ceiling joists, and pale pine upright chairs, benches and tables on its quarry-tiled floor; sliding glass doors open on to a concrete terrace furnished with picnic-table sets (which shares the same view). Bar food veers attractively towards local seafood, especially shellfish; at lunchtime it includes home-made soup (£1.10), ploughman's (£2.75), burgers (from £3), mussels marinières (£3.30), Cajun blackened chicken (£4), seafood croûte (£5), whole jumbo prawn salad or smoked salmon (£5.50), Sound of Jura clams meunières or grilled sirloin steak (£7.50); vegetarian dishes such as sweet and sour vegetables (£3.50); dinner includes more elaborate dishes such as octopus vinaigrette (£1.25), half a dozen local oysters (£3.30), stir-fried chicken (£5.50), clams with ginger and walnuts (£6.80) and steaks (from £7), half a lobster mayonnaise or thermidor (£12 with prior notice). Decent house wines, darts. (*Recommended by Kevin Myers; more up-to-date reports please*)

Free house   Licensee John Grafton   Meals and snacks (12–2, 6–9)   Restaurant tel Tayvallich (054 67) 282   Children in eating area and restaurant   Open 11-midnight (1am Sat); 11–2.30, 6–11 Tues–Sun winter; closed Mon, Nov–March

THORNHILL (Central)   NS6699   Map 9

Lion & Unicorn

A873

Beside its own bowling green – which can be used by non-residents – this old-fashioned inn has been in business now for about 300 years. The new licensees have refurbished the two communicating rooms of the bar, and there's a log-burning stove in the lounge. Bar food now includes soup (£1.30), ploughman's (£2), pizza (£2.50), a large cold meat salad (£2.95), haddock or scampi (£3.25), chicken Kiev (£3.50) and steak and kidney pie (£3.75), and two daily specials such as vegetable bake (£2.95) or chicken in orange and rosemary (£3.75); they plan to introduce a children's menu, but at the moment they reduce the usual price of main meals; home-made puddings such as strawberry pavlova, hot chocolate fudge cake or apple pie (£1.50); maybe Greenmantle real ale; friendly service. The public bar has darts, dominoes, cards, a fruit machine and piped music; there's a family room off the lounge bar. The restaurant is in the original part of the building which dates from 1635 and contains the original massive fireplace (six feet high and five feet wide). *(Recommended by Carol and Richard Glover, Fiona Mutch, Janet and John Towers; more reports on the new regime please)*

Free house   Licensees Mr and Mrs Johnstone   Meals and snacks (all day)   Evening restaurant   Children in large room adjacent to lounge bar   Ceilidh folk night Sat about once a month   Open 11–midnight Mon–Thurs and Sat, till 1am Fri, 12–12 Sun; winter 11–11 Mon–Thurs and Sat, 11–12 Fri, 11–11 Sun   Bedrooms tel Thornhill (078 685) 204; £15/£27.50   **0204**

TWEEDSMUIR (Borders)   NT0924 Map 9

Crook ⊘ ⇌

A701 a mile N of village

The back bar in this ex-drovers' halt is warm and comfortable, with flagstones, local photographs, simple furniture, Greenmantle on handpump and a good choice of malt whiskies; one very thick wall, partly knocked through, has a big hearth with a log-effect gas fire. It opens into a big airy lounge with comfortable chairs around low tables, and beyond that is a sun lounge. A separate room has darts, pool, dominoes, cribbage, fruit machine and space games. Bar food includes sandwiches, soup (95p), home-made chicken liver pâté or cruicket eggs (boiled egg on bed of ham and Scottish mustard mayonnaise), (both £2.25), with main courses that include baked potatoes with various fillings (£1.75), ploughman's (£2.75), omelettes (from £2.95), salads or home-made pepperoni pizza (£1.75), scampi or curried beef (£3.95), chicken in a rich mushroom and onion sauce (£4.45); home-made puddings like Gaelic coffee meringues and apple pie (£1.50). There are various art-deco features and both the lavatories have superb 1930s tiling and cut design mirrors. There are tables on the grass outside, with a climbing frame and slide, and across the road the inn has an attractive garden, sheltered by oak trees; maybe pétanque here in summer. Trout fishing permits for about 30 miles fishing on the Tweed and its tributaries are available from the pub at about £5 a day. Burns wrote his poem 'Willie Wastles Wife' here. *(Recommended by Paul Wreglesworth, John and Joan Wyatt, Dr R H M Stewart; more reports please)*

Free house   Licensee Stuart Reid   Real ale   Meals and snacks (12–2, 7–9; 12–9 Sat and Sun)   No-smoking restaurant   Children welcome   Open 11–11, 11–12 Sat Bedrooms tel Tweedsmuir (089 97) 272; £26B/£40B

UDDINGSTON (Strathclyde)   NS6960 Map 11

Rowan Tree

60 Old Mill Road; in Uddingston High Street, turn into The Cut, which takes you into Old Mill Road with the pub almost opposite. 1 mile from M73 junction 6; leaving M73 from S, turn sharp right immediately at end of motorway, virtually doing a U-turn (permitted here) into A721, then following B7071 into village

Towering behind the high, heavily panelled serving counter in the bar of this old-fashioned town pub are tall tiers of mirrored shelves, as well as gas-style chandeliers, Edwardian water fountains on the bar counter, interesting old brewery mirrors, and two coal fires. The shinily panelled walls have built-in bare benches divided by elegant wooden pillars which support an arch of panelling, which in turn curves into the embossed ceiling; there's also a lounge. Good, generously served, simple bar food includes sandwiches, soup (50p), home-made steak pie (£2), fried haddock (£2.20), lasagne (£2.30) and chicken chasseur or scampi (£2.40); Maclays 70/-, 80/- and Porter on air pressure tall fount. Darts, dominoes, fruit machine, trivia and piped music. *(Recommended by Ben Wimpenny, Niall and Jane)*

Maclays   Licensee George Tate   Real ale   Lunchtime meals and snacks (not Sun)
Disc jockey with Golden Oldies Thurs and Sat, folk club Fri   Open 11–11.45

ULLAPOOL (Highland)   NH1294 Map 11
Ceilidh Place

West Argyle Street

Unusual for the region, this airy and stylish cafe-bar has bentwood chairs and one
or two cushioned wall benches among the rugs on its varnished concrete floor,
spotlighting from the dark planked ceiling, attractive modern prints and a big
sampler on the textured white walls, piped classical or folk music, magazines to
read, Venetian blinds, houseplants, and mainly young upmarket customers, many
from overseas. Though the beers are keg they have decent wines by the glass (and
pineau de charentes), some uncommon European bottled beers, an interesting
range of high-proof malt whiskies and a choice of cognacs that's unmatched
around here. The side food bar – you queue for service – does a few hot dishes
such as vegetable pie (£2.45), vegetarian or meat curries (£2.85) or beef and
vegetable hotpot (£2.95), with enterprising fresh salads. There's a very up-to-date
woodburning stove, and they have dominoes. The hotel, which has an attractive
conservatory dining room, includes a bookshop. The white house, in a quiet side
street above the small town, has climbing roses and other flowers in front, where
tables on a terrace look over the other houses to the distant hills beyond the
natural harbour. *(Recommended by Dr R Fuller, Russell Hafter; more reports please)*

*Free house   Licensee Mrs Jean Urquhart   Meals and snacks (10–10 summer, 10–6
winter)   No-smoking restaurant (closed Sun lunchtime)   Children in eating area only
Frequent live entertainment – traditional jazz and classical music, poetry and drama
Open 11–2.30, 5–11 (Sun 12.30–2.30, 6.30–11)   Bedrooms tel Ullapool (0854) 2103;
£30(£40B)/£52(£70B)*

Ferry Boat

Shore Street

The big windows of this simple, genuine two-room bar – with curtain-frills top and
bottom – look out to the tall hills beyond the anchorage with its bustle of yachts,
ferry boats, fishing boats and tour boats for the Summer Isles. There are quarry
tiles by the corner serving counter, patterned red carpet elsewhere, with
brocade-cushioned seats around dimpled copper tables; a stained glass door hangs
from the ceiling. The quieter inner room has a coal fire, a Delft shelf of copper
measures and willow-pattern plates. Well kept McEwans 80/- on air-pressure tall
fount, a decent choice of whiskies, good value straighforward bar lunches,
unobtrusive piped pop music, fruit machine, and the warmest pub atmosphere we
found in the town – a relaxed mix of locals and visitors. *(Recommended by A C Lang,
Heather Sharland, Dr T W Hoskins, Jim and Becky Bryson)*

*Free house   Licensee Richard Smith   Real ale   Meals and snacks (lunchtime only,
summer, but also 6–8.30 winter)   Evening restaurant (closed winter)   Open 11–11
June–Sept, 11–2.30, 5–11 rest of year; closed 18 Dec–10 Jan   Bedrooms tel Ullapool
(0854) 2366; £18.50(£29.50B)/£32(£45B)*

Morefield Motel ✪

North Road

Our most northerly main entry, this motel in a new estate on the outskirts of the
small town draws people from far and wide for the exceptional fresh fish and
seafood served in its bar and restaurant. The owners, ex-fishermen and divers, have
first-class sources; the bar food, served with a generosity that overwhelms people
used to southern ideas of seafood value-for-money, changes seasonally, and in high
season might include grilled mussels (£1.95), fresh prawns and mushrooms cooked
in garlic butter (£3.65), and freshly smoked salmon from Achiltibuie (£3.75) as
starters, then side fillet of jumbo haddock (£3.50), scampi tails or haddock baked
in cheese sauce (£4.25), grilled salmon, or sole (£5.95), prawn thermidor (£6.25)

or shellfish supreme – sliced scallops, prawn tails and mussels in a seafood sauce (£6.95) or salmon poached in wine and topped with prawns in seafood sauce (£7.50), and a high-heaped platter of fresh seafood which we've never heard of anyone finishing (£9.95). There are other dishes such as soup (95p), haggis or fresh home-made chicken liver pâté (£1.95), steak pie or chilli con carne (£3.75), curries (from £3.95), chicken chasseur or beef stroganoff (£4.50) and steaks (from £6.95), with puddings (from £1.30). The lounge bar is squarely modern, with dark brown plush button-back built-in wall banquettes, colourful local scenic photographs, and a pleasant brisk atmosphere; in winter (from November to March) the diners tend to yield to local people playing darts or pool, though there's bargain food then, including a three-course meal for £2.95. Keg beer (what else, this far north), but a very good range of 85 malt whiskies, decent wines and friendly tartan-skirted waitresses; piped pop music, fruit machine. There are tables on the terrace. The bedrooms are functional. (*Recommended by Russell Hafter, R Goodger, Joan and John Calvert, Ian Baillie, Brian and Pam Cowling*)

Free house   Licensee David Smyrl   Meals and snacks (12–2, 5.30–9.30)   Evening restaurant   Children in eating area   Open 11–11   Bedrooms tel Ullapool (0854) 2161; £20B/£35B

WEEM (Tayside)   NN8449 Map 11

Aileen Chraggan 🏅

B846

The comfortable modern lounge in this friendly inn has long plump plum-coloured banquettes, and Bruce Bairnsfather First World War cartoons on the red and gold Regency striped wallpaper. Big picture windows look across the flat ground between here and the Tay to the mountains beyond that sweep up the Ben Lawers (the highest in this part of Scotland). Well presented and tasty bar food includes soup (£1.25), pâté (£2.25),smoked fillet of beef or fresh haddock (£3.25), scampi or chicken casserole (£4.50), moules marinières, steak and kidney pie or a half dozen Loch Fyne oysters (£5.25), salmon salad (£5.95), a fine Loch Etive prawn platter (£7.50) and steaks (from £8.50); puddings such as home-made lemon cheesecake or chocolate mousse. Winter darts, dominoes and piped music; malt whiskies. There are tables on the large terrace outside. (*Recommended by Dr T H M Mackenzie, Mrs Pauline Spence*)

Free house   Licensee Alastair Gillespie   Meals and snacks   Children welcome   Open 11–11 (12.30–2.30, 6.30–11 in winter); closed 25 and 26 Dec, and 1, 2 and 3 Jan Bedrooms tel Aberfeldy (0887) 20346; £21.50B/£43.50B

WESTRUTHER (Borders)   NT6450 Map 10

Old Thistle 🏅

B6456 – off A697 just SE of the A6089 Kelso fork

The food award is for the evening steaks – fine local Aberdeen Angus, hung and cooked to perfection (from 8oz sirloin £6.50; larger sizes, also rump, fillet and T-bone). Other food is more what you'd expect from such an unpretentious village local: soup (80p), salads (from £3.50), gammon, scampi and decent home-made lasagne (£3.75), with haddock (£3.50) and steak and egg (£4.75) added at lunchtime. The tiny, quaint bar on the right has some furnishings that look as if they date back to the inn's 1721 foundation – the elaborately carved chimney piece, an oak corner cupboard, the little bottom-polished seat by the coal fire. There are some fine local horsebrasses. A simple back room with whisky-water jugs on its black beams has darts, pool, dominoes, fruit machine and space game, and there's a small, plain room with one or two tables on the left. These three rooms are the real core of the village, full of life in the evenings, with farmers, fishermen, gamekeepers and shepherds down from the hills – and maybe breaking into song when Andrew strikes up on the accordion. There's also a more conventionally comfortable two-room lounge with flowery brocaded seats, neat tables and a small coal fire, leading into the restaurant. Friendly young licensees; piped music. (*Recommended by Syd and Wyn Donald*)

Free house   Licensee David Silk   Meals and snacks (12–2.30, 5–9; not Mon)
Restaurant   Children welcome   Open 11–11; winter 11–2.30, 5–11   Bedrooms
tel *Westruther (057 84) 275; £14B/£25B*

Lucky Dip

Besides the fully inspected pubs, you might like to try these Lucky Dips recommended to us and described by readers (if you do, please send us reports):

BORDERS

Ancrum [off A68 Jedburgh—Edinburgh; NT6325], *Cross Keys*: Quiet, friendly pub with Belhaven 60/- on handpump, as well as Arrols, Drybroughs and Tetleys, and games room; no lunchtime food but staff will do filled rolls or toasties on request; nice back garden *(Mr and Mrs M O Jones)*
Clovenfords [off A72 Selkirk—Innerleithen, on N side; NT4536], *Thornielee House*: Converted farmhouse overlooking River Tweed and road; modern extension has bar with well kept Broughton ales and good bar food lunchtime and evening; adjacent restaurant, nearby caravan park; bedrooms comfortable, with tasty breakfasts *(Col and Mrs L N Smyth)*
Innerleithen [Traquair Rd; NT3336], *Traquair Arms*: Very friendly pub with interesting choice of good food, especially Finan savoury and vegetarian dishes; comfortable lounge bar, friendly service, well kept Greenmantle and the local Traquair on handpump — superb in small quantities; bedrooms *(A McK, Mr and Mrs M O Jones)*
Jedburgh [Abbey Dr; NT6521], *Carters Rest*: Modernised pub with friendly service, Youngers ales and good food at reasonable prices *(W A Harbottle)*
Kelso [signposted off A698 4 miles S; NT7334], *Sunlaws House*: Superb food — at a price — using local produce in handsome and interesting Library bar of classy country-house hotel; bedrooms *(Syd and Wyn Donald)*; *Waggon*: Pleasant atmosphere and surroundings; good choice of good value lunchtime bar food inc children's dishes *(Mr and Mrs A Johnston)*
Kirk Yetholm [NT8328], *Border*: Right at the end of the Pennine Way — free half pint if you've walked all 270 miles for it; good atmosphere, food and beer *(Len Beattie)*
☆ **Lauder** [Market Pl; A68; NT5347], *Eagle*: Interesting serving counter like Elizabethan four-poster in lounge bar, games in public bar, limited range of decent bar food, well kept McEwans 70/-, summer barbecues in old stableyard, children welcome, open all day; bedrooms *(Mr and Mrs M D Jones, LYM)*
Lauder, *Black Bull*: Plank-panelled bar of 17th-century inn with wide choice of bar food; open all day; children welcome *(LYM)*
Melrose [NT5434], *George & Abbotsford*: Spacious, comfortable, well furnished bar with varied good food, carefully presented; McEwans beers; bedrooms *(Prof H G Allen)*
Oxton [A697 Edinburgh—Newcastle; NT5053], *Carfraemill*: Handily placed for the hill roads through the Borders, substantial red sandstone hotel with spaciously refurbished period-style bar, bar

food; now under same management as Buccleuch Arms, St Boswells; bedrooms *(BB)*
West Linton [High St; NT1551], *Linton*: Comfortable two-room lounge bar with Theakstons Best on handpump, bar food, local atmosphere *(S J A Velate)*

CENTRAL

☆ **Ardeonaig** [S side of Loch Tay; NN6635], *Ardeonaig*: Hotel in lovely setting where burn flows down into loch; nice bar, pubby atmosphere, good food; bedrooms good *(Cathy Long)*
Blanefield [West Carbeth; A809 Glasgow—Drymen, just S of B821; NS5579], *Carbeth*: Unusual pine-panelled bar with high fringe of tartan curtains, woodburner one end, log fire the other; fires in smarter lounge and family room too; generous helpings of bar food running up to steaks, sometimes Whitbreads-related real ales, lots of tables outside, live music Wed/Fri, open all day 7 days; bedrooms *(Ian Baillie, Fiona Mutch, LYM)*
Brig o Turk [A821 Callander—Trossachs; NN5306], *Byre*: Converted from old byre, high rafters with modern carved faces on beam ends, tractor-seat bar stools, friendly service; McEwans on air pressure tall founts, good bar food, restaurant, spotless lavatories; open all day; children welcome; bedrooms *(Roger Danes)*
Callander [Bridge St; NN6208], *Bridgend House*: Superb lounge with leather armchairs, waitress service, well kept Broughton Greenmantle; bedrooms *(R G Ollier; more reports on bar food please)*; [(just outside)], *Lade*: Good food inc fine home-made soup, poached salmon, duck, pheasant, venison and chicken; nr start GWG164 *(Mrs E M Brandwood)*; *Myrtle*: Straightforward pub, but under newish licensees food far from that — interesting dishes with special care over presentation and good choice of vegetarian dishes; worth booking at busy times *(J Towers)*; *Waverley*: Excellent, reasonably priced bar lunches, children welcome in lounge bar *(Cathy Long)*
nr Crianlarich [down 10-mile single-track rd; NN3825], *Cozac Lodge*: Beautiful but remote spot, friendly welcome and good food, service and views *(Peter Jones)*
Dollar [Chapel Pl; NS9796], *Strathallan*: Great bar with pool, darts, fruit machine and juke box, quick and friendly service, well kept beers and good food; bedrooms comfortable and inexpensive; *(Elaine and Lyn Hamilton)*
☆ **Drymen** [NS4788], *Salmon Leap*: Comfortable 18th-century inn with L-shaped lounge and bar, good log fires and stove, bric-a-brac, stuffed fish and so forth;

food inc home-made pies, vegetarian dishes, children's helpings; S&N beers, lots of malt whiskies; *(Peter Watkins, Pam Stanley, M J Morgan, Cathy Long, Frank Cummins, LYM more reports please on service and bedrooms)*
Drymen, *Buchanan Arms*: Welcoming, friendly pub with well kept beer and well cooked bar food, quickly served; children welcome *(D P Cartwright);* [The Square], *Winnock*: Attractively placed hotel with fine choice of malts, good if not specially cheap bar meals, friendly service, pleasing atmosphere and Theakstons on handpump; bedrooms *(Ian Baillie)*
☆ **Killearn** [Main St (A875); NS5285], *Old Mill*: Simple bar food in quietly friendly village pub with rustic cushioned built-in settles and wheelback chairs around neat dark tables, open fire, piped music; open all day summer; fine views of Campsie Fells from behind; children in eating area and garden room *(LYM)*
Kinlochard [NN4502], *Altskeith*: Useful stop on the way north — bedrooms comfortable and good value, if rather pink and peachy, with wonderful views of Ben Lomond and the Loch across the road; pub side less obviously appealing *(Neil and Angela Huxter)*
☆ **Kippen** [NS6594], *Cross Keys*: Comfortable and friendly lounge with stuffed birds, wildfowl prints, well kept McEwans 80/-, decent waitress-served bar food, log fire; pool and militaria in public bar; McEwans and Greenmantle on handpump, good bar food, children's room and small restaurant area *(Roger Danes, LYM)*
☆ **Polmont** [Gilston Crescent; under a mile from M9 junction 7; A803 towards Polmont, then left; NS9378], *Whyteside*: Friendly and well run Victorian hotel with extensive comfortably furnished open-plan bar — most notable for its 300-plus whiskies, dozens of other spirits, over 60 bottled beers and well kept Archibald Arrols 70/- and Ind Coope Burton on handpump; children in eating area (not after 7.30), restaurant; organ music some nights; bedrooms *(LYM)*
☆ **Stirling** [Easter Cornton Rd, Causewayhead; off A9 N of centre; NS7993], *Birds & the Bees*: Interestingly furnished ex-byre, dimly lit and convivial, with Arrols 70/- and 80/-, Harviestoun 80/-, Maclays 80/- and Youngers IPA on handpump, reasonably priced bar food, loud piped music, live bands most weekends, restaurant; open all day till 1am — very popular with young people, reliably well run; children welcome *(Russell Hafter, LYM)*
Stirling [Castle Wynd], *Portcullis*: Beside castle, overlooking town and surroundings; friendly service, pleasant atmosphere and reasonable, though limited, bar food; spacious bar with open fire and good choice of whiskies *(G and L Owen)*; [91 St Mary's Wynd; from Wallace Memorial in centre go up Baker St, keep right at top], *Settle*: Early 18th-century, restored to show beams, stonework, great arched fireplace and barrel-vaulted upper room; bar games, snacks till 7, Belhaven 70/- and 80/- on handpump, open all day *(M Cadenhead, Len Beattie, LYM)*; [4 Melville Terr], *Terraces*: Comfortable lounge bar with Renoir prints,

pleasant and attentive service, Tennents ale, good bar food at reasonable prices; bedrooms *(T Nott)*;
[nr castle], *Tolbooth*: Bar and restaurant; meal excellent, atmosphere good *(M Cadenhead)*

DUMFRIES AND GALLOWAY

☆ **Auchencairn** [about 2 1/2 miles off A711; NX7951], *Balcary Bay*: Bar and hotel feature in smuggling tales; very pleasant, with good bar food; bedrooms *(NWN)*
Auldgirth [just E of A75, about 8 miles N of Dumfries; NX9186], *Auldgirth*: Old whitewashed stone inn, comfortable lounge in side annexe with brasses, plates and pictures and varied bar food; bedrooms *(Anon)*
Bargrennan [NX3576], *House O'Hill*: Good bar lunches in renovated hotel at entrance to Glen Trool; fishing in River Cree and lochs, handy for Southern Upland Walkway; bedrooms *(D P and M E Cartwright)*
☆ **Creebridge** [Minnigaff; NX4165], *Creebridge House*: Country-house hotel in compact grounds with simple but comfortable public bar, friendly atmosphere, well kept Broughton ale and excellent bar lunches — busy even in October, get there early or the good scampi and bargain Dover sole may be sold out *(W C M Jones, Fiona Mutch)*
☆ **Dalbeattie** [1 Maxwell St; NX8361], *Pheasant*: Particularly useful for serving bar food till 10 in its comfortable upstairs lounge/restaurant, with the lunchtime choice maybe inc Galloway beef and Solway salmon, and omelettes to steaks in the evening; lively downstairs bar, children welcome, open all day till midnight summer; bedrooms *(LYM)*
Drummore [NX1336], *Queens*: Coastal village inn overlooking Luce Bay, the most southerly hotel in Scotland and fairly handy for Logan Gardens and Mull of Galloway; bar food, separate games room, fishing parties arranged; bedrooms reasonably priced *(F S and N P Grebbell, BB)*
Dumfries [Mabie Forest; well signed off New Abbey rd, a few miles out; NX9776], *Mabie House*: Family-run hotel with bay-windowed lounge bar off large panelled hall with big winter fire, varied good value bar meals inc good puddings; big garden where drinks served in summer; jazz Sun evening, two-day jazz festival Aug; bedrooms *(MH)*; [Lovers Lane], *Station*: Very unpretentious small pub, railway-theme lounge with illuminated layout of nearby Quintinshill yards of sad WW1 memory; decent bar food inc good tuna salad (oddly listed under vegetarian dishes); attentive pleasant staff, good cool beer *(Anon)*
Eskdalemuir [NY2597], *Hart Manor*: Desolate, hilly spot; cosy atmosphere, friendly licensee, Greenmantle and good, varied, home-cooked food inc speciality puddings in pleasant dining room overlooking valley; bedrooms *(Janet Rogerson)*
☆ **Gatehouse of Fleet** [High St], *Angel*: Listed building with friendly, warm and cosy

lounge bar, good value bar food, tasty dinner menu, McEwans ales; family run; bedrooms *(NWN)*

☆ **Gatehouse of Fleet** [NX5956], *Murray Arms*: Carefully rebuilt small 17th-century hotel with strong Burns connections; good buffet, usually with well kept real ales such as Broughton or Youngers, variety of mainly old-fashioned comfortable seating areas, games in quite separate public bar; open all day for food in summer; children welcome *(D W Huebner, LYM)*

Glencaple [NX9968], *Nith*: Hotel on shore of Nith estuary, nautical decorations in spacious and comfortable lounge, McEwans, varied bar food inc super smoked salmon sandwiches, pleasant quick service; bedrooms *(Anon)*

Kirkcowan [NX3260], *Craighlaw Arms*: Doing well under friendly and enthusiastic new landlord, with good value home-cooked food; bedrooms *(M Brooks)*

☆ **Kirkcudbright** [Old High St; NX6851], *Selkirk Arms*: A hotel since 18th century, but quiet modern decor in cosy and comfortable partly panelled lounge with good local flavour; decent bar food, restaurant, evening steak bar, tables in spacious garden with summer live music (and a 1481 font); salmon and trout fishing; children in restaurant and lounge; good value bedrooms, good service *(Tim Locke, LYM)*

Langholm [NY3685], *Eskdale*: Plain hotel bar, popular with locals; clean tablecloths on all bar tables, generous helpings of tasty bar food; bedrooms *(Syd and Wyn Donald)*

☆ **Moffat** [1 Churchgate; NT0905], *Black Bull*: Several bar areas inc pubby public bar with railway memorabilia, plush softly lit cocktail bar (not always open out of season), simply furnished tiled-floor dining room and side games bar; bar food from filled rolls and sandwiches up (soups, fish and shepherd's pie — maybe strong on potato—haggis, goulash, bacon hotpot all recommended); juke box may be loud; children welcome; open all day all week; bedrooms comfortable, with hearty breakfasts *(Hazel Morgan, Dr T H M Mackenzie, E J and A E Alcock, P Lloyd, Miss K Bamford, G A Worthington, KC, Steve Waters, A McK, G Smith, Miss A Tress, Cdr J W Hackett, LYM; more reports please)*

☆ **Moffat** [High St], *Balmoral*: Fine central village pub, consistently good, with decent simple food quickly served in comfortable peaceful bar *(M H Box, John and Chris Simpson)*

Moffat [High S], *Moffat House*: Beautiful house with spacious and comfortable lounge bars — grand, restful and clubby, with good if pricey bar food from sandwiches up; well kept McEwans 70/-; bedrooms very good *(Mr and Mrs J H Adam, Neil and Angela Huxter)*; [High St], *Star*: Comfortable, welcoming lounge/bar (not smoky) with plush button-back seats, well piped Scottish music, attractive prints, friendly quiet service; good choice of bar food, rather brightly lit dining room; bedrooms *(Genie and Brian Smart)*

☆ **nr Moffat** [hotel signposted off A74], *Auchen Castle*: Superb location with spectacular hill views, peaceful

country-house hotel with delicious bar food, decent wines, good choice of malt whiskies, good service; trout loch in good-sized grounds; bedrooms *(Mr and Mrs Norman Edwardes)*

Port Logan [NX0940], *Port Logan*: Doing particularly well under current regime, with good live music Sun evenings provided by licensee and friends; good bar food, very reasonable prices *(L E Sculthord)*

☆ **Stranraer** [George St; NX0660], *George*: Elegant and comfortable lounge bar with good value bar food, huge log fireplace, friendly staff; also wine bar/bistro with world-wide choice of bottled beers; open all day; children welcome; bedrooms most comfortable *(LYM)*

Twynholm [Burn Brae; NX6654], *Burnbank*: Basic village inn with cheerful licensees and cheap food; closed Mon lunchtime; fine nearby coast and countryside; bedrooms *(Richard Holloway, LYM)*; [18 Main St], *Star*: Pleasant village pub with McEwans 80/-, good collection of miniature whiskies all around the bar shelves as well as wide range for sale, and good bar food running up to steaks; open all dat Fri/Sat *(Andrew Triggs)*

FIFE

Aberdour [Manse St; NT1985], *Fairways*: Good value changing home-cooked food and friendly licensees in small hotel; recently refurbished bedrooms with good views over Firth of Forth to Edinburgh *(Mike and Mandy Challis)*; *Woodside*: Original art nouveau ceiling in upper Clipper Bar — glass canopy with panelling rescued from RMS *Orantes* when she was broken up in the nearby yards; pleasant lounge, good bar food, willing service; bedrooms *(T Nott)*

☆ **Anstruther** [High St; NO5704], *Smugglers*: Wide range of good value straightforward bar food (fresh scampi and mixed grill recommended) in friendly old inn with cheerful decor and service; rambling and attractive upstairs lounge bar, busy downstairs games bar with real ales and whiskies, summer barbecues on pretty terrace, popular restaurant; children allowed in eating area; bedrooms small but clean *(Alastair Campbell, John and Ann Prince, LYM)*

☆ **Anstruther** [High St], *Dreel*: Cosy and friendly old building in attractive position, with garden overlooking Dreel Burn, locally popular for well kept ale and reasonably priced well cooked and presented bar food inc local seafood and barbecues; open fire, pool area, tables outside *(Alastair Campbell, G Allen)*

Anstruther [Bankwell Rd], *Craws Nest*: Good if not cheap bar food inc freshly caught haddock in straightforward lounge; Scottish-style entertainment in summer; bedrooms *(Rosalind Russell)*

☆ **Carnock** [6 Main St; A907 Dunfermline—Alloa; NT0489], *Old Inn*: Good food inc children's helpings at neatly spaced tables of tidy low-beamed lounge in cottage-style pub, especially mushrooms in beer batter with garlic dip, home-made pâté with oatcakes, hebridean steak (with melted

Orkney cheese), splendid pies and puddings; well kept Maclays 60/-, 70/-, 80/- and Porter, bar with pool table well out of way; children welcome *(Andy and Jill Kassube)*
Craigrothie [NO3710], *Kingarroch*: Small but unusual pub with good bar food *(Mr and Mrs N W Briggs)*
☆ **Crail** [4 High St; NO6108], *Golf*: Village inn with plenty of atmosphere in bustling little public bar, rather more restrained if not exactly smart lounge; limited choice of simply presented but tasty bar food (Scotch broth and local fish recommended), well kept McEwans 80/-, good range of malt whiskies, cheerful barman, coal fire; bedrooms clean and comfortable though basic, with good breakfasts *(W F Coghill, Ian Baillie)*
Crail, *Marine*: Bar overlooking sea in lovely old fishing village; meals can be served outside in good weather; bedrooms *(Mrs J Hamilton)*
Crossford [A994 W of Dunfermline; NT0686], *Pitfirane Arms*: Small friendly bar, comfortable lounge and separate eating area; homely atmosphere, McEwans 80/- and Youngers No 3, popular bar food *(Roger Huggins)*
Cupar [NO3714], *Oastlers Close*: Well kept, good atmosphere, decent food *(Mr and Mrs N W Briggs)*
☆ **Elie** [harbour; NO4900], *Ship*: In lovely position by sandy harbour bay, basic and unspoilt, with old-fashioned furnishings, some panelling and beams; the newish licensees are bringing its furniture and decor up to date with the intention of preserving its character, and have already done up the waterside garden, with its own bar and barbecues in summer; soup or filled rolls lunchtime, well kept Belhaven 80/-; children may be allowed in back room, has been open all day (afternoon closure Sun) *(LYM — reports please)*
☆ **Falkland** [NO2507], *Covenanter*: Attractive, spotless pub with good food and delightful welcoming service; well kept Tennents 70/- on tall fount pressure, straightforward bar food; children in bistro bar; nr start GWG165, in beautiful old village with magnificent NT palace; bedrooms good *(Michael Bechley, Leith Stuart)*
Kirkcaldy [Coast Rd; NT2791], *Harbour*: Food good and reasonably priced — everything cooked from fresh *(P G Burgess)*
Limekilns [Halketts Hall; off A985; NT0783], *Ship*: Friendly and comfortable lounge with superb views over the Forth; mainly nautical decor; bar lunches, well kept Belhaven 70/- and 90/- and guest beers such as Broughton Special *(Andy and Jill Kassube)*
Lundin Links [Leven Rd; NO4002], *Old Manor*: Elegant hotel overlooking the links, included for its Bunters Bar — in separate building; plainly but sensibly furnished and similarly decorated, with interesting choice of fairly priced food; bedrooms *(Ian Baillie)*
North Queensferry [NT1380], *Ferry Lodge*: Almost a service area off the motorway, complete with craft shop; possible to have a civilised drink, but more of an eating house really; bedrooms *(Roger Huggins)*
Pittenweem [NO5403], *Larrochmhor*: Small two-table dining room at front cosy and bright; limited menu inc good home-made

soup and fresh local prawns, also filled rolls, sandwiches and hamburgers *(Dr J M Jackson)*
☆ **St Andrews** [Grange Rd — a mile S; NO5116], *Grange*: Good atmosphere in fine old building on outskirts; spotlessly clean small bar with decent wine; under current regime the food is particularly good in bar and in restaurant, which has changing set-price meals lunchtime and evening, with interesting dishes such as avocado with raspberry vinaigrette and baked halibut with lobster and brandy sauce *(Mr and Mrs N W Briggs, A D Kucharska)*
☆ **St Andrews** [40 The Scores], *Ma Bells*: Seafront pub by golf course, with popular downstairs bar full of students during term-time, and locals and tourists the rest of the year; well kept Greenmantle and Watneys-related real ales, over 75 different bottled beers inc all the Trappists, lots of malt whiskies; open all day, with reasonably priced bar food served through till 6pm, hot pies in the evening; piped music, games *(Alisdair Cuthil, Dr T H M Mackenzie)*
St Andrews [Strathkinness Low Rd], *Rufflets*: Lovely place to stay and a favourite of Jack Nicklaus and his family; under same ownership as the Grange *(Mrs N W Biggs)*; [32 Bell St], *St Andrews Wine Bar*: Included for small but comfortable cellar bar below the wine bar; good Belhaven 70/- and 80/- and interesting food *(N J Mackintosh)*; [St Mary's Pl; corner of Bell St], *Victoria*: Airy cafe-bar with student-and-shoppers atmosphere during the day, good value fruit juices as well as McEwans 80/-, a few tables on sunny little roof terrace; open all day, maybe loud pop music in the evenings; children welcome *(Alastair Campbell, RCL, LYM)*
Strathmiglo [NO2110], *Strathmiglo*: Under current regime food really good, inc genuinely fresh vegetables and homemade pies; service obliging *(JV, LYM)*
Upper Largo [NO4203], *Largo*: Food helpings would satisfy Desperate Dan — and cheap too!; bedrooms *(Rosalind Russell)*

GRAMPIAN

Aberdeen [Crown St; NJ9305], *Brentwood*: Comfortable lounge bar with well kept Flowers, Wethereds and Whitbreads Castle Eden and popular bar food running up to steaks; bedrooms *(Trevor Stearn)*; [6 Little Belmont St], *Camerons*: Solid stone-built extended former coaching inn, with many rooms inc original snug bar, and wide choice of well kept real ales such as Belhaven 80/-, McEwans 80/- and Whitbreads Castle Eden; open all day *(Richard Sanders)*; [Dee St], *Gabriels*: Lofty converted chapel turned into showy and enjoyable bar; nightclub behind has most elaborate sound and lights system *(LYM)*
Banchory [NO6995], *Tor na Coille*: Welcoming hotel with imaginative bar lunches inc four different kinds of home-baked rolls; Theakstons Best; bedrooms *(Mrs E Higson)*
☆ **Braemar** [NO1491], *Fife Arms*: Clean and comfortable spacious lounge in big Victorian hotel with entirely appropriate attractive

decor; very friendly, efficient service and good value cold buffet with fine range of salads, also good hot dishes; nr start GWG166; children welcome *(Russell Hafter, Niall and Jane, G R Pearson)*

Cabrach [A941; NJ3827], *Grouse*: Well run family pub in fine spot, with masses of whiskies, souvenirs and cafeteria, open all day, handy stop on Braemar—Dufftown hill rd; bedrooms *(LYM)*

Craigellachie [NJ2845], *Fiddich*: Tiny fishing pub in pretty spot on banks of River Fiddich, at its confluence with River Spey, virtually unchanged over past 40 years with old bar and fireplace intact; good choice of malt whiskies *(Alastair Lang)*

☆ **Elgin** [Thunderton Pl; NJ2162], *Thunderton House*: Busy and popular 17th-century town-centre pub, sympathetically refurbished, with fast and friendly service, real ale and wide range of good value bar food from filled rolls and baked potatoes to cheap steaks; children's room *(Mary and James Manthei, Leith Stuart)*

Fochabers [NJ3458], *Gordon Arms*: Real ale and decent bar food in comfortable well kept bars; can arrange fishing for residents; bedrooms *(LYM)*

Gardenstown [take street to left down rd past Free Church; turn left when you see harbour; NJ7964], *The Hotel*: Small hotel in fishing village with tiny bar serving limited range of decent food inc fresh fish; drive here is spectacular; bedrooms *(M Cadenhead)*

Kincardine o Neil [NO5999], *Gordon Arms*: Fine food, friendly staff, well kept beer, good log fire; bedrooms *(J Perry)*

Newmachar [NJ8819], *Begkies Neuk*: Pleasant, neatly kept lounge with wide choice of well cooked food, quick service, good beer *(I S Thomson)*

Pennan [just off B9031 Banff—Fraserburgh; NJ8465], *Pennan*: Impressively placed right by the sea in tiny fishing village — scenes from the film *Local Hero* were shot here; very friendly welcome, helpful service, good evening steaks and seafood; basic bedrooms *(Steve Dark)*

☆ **nr Peterculter** [off B979 a mile N of Netherley and 4 miles S of Peterculter; pub down side rd, INN written on roof clearly visible from main rd; NO8493], *Lairhillock*: Real rustic pub with warm welcome, even when crowded; stone and panelled beamed bar is best room, with horse tack, dark wood fittings, brass lamps, real fire, built-in wall settles, assorted tables and chairs and country-view bay window; more straightforward lounge with central canopy fire; well kept McEwans 80/- and interesting guest beers such as Raven (from Orkney) or Mitchells, wide choice of good interesting bar food, unusually imaginative for the region; good if not cheap raftered barn restaurant, cosy with its own log fire — and pianist; four bedrooms *(Chris Raisin, Allan Clarke)*

Potarch [just off A93 5 miles W of Banchory; NO6097], *Potarch*: Cosy, pleasant tartan-carpeted bar beautifully placed by River Dee, with copper-topped tables and good, friendly service; real ales and good bar suppers, also fresh salmon and steaks in restaurant; bedrooms *(Mrs E Higson)*

☆ **Stonehaven** [Shorehead; open 11-11 inc Sun; NO8786], *Marine*: Popular pub set in row of houses with superb harbour view; lively, friendly atmosphere with young customers, juke box and pool table in room past bar, and lounge and dining room upstairs; McEwans 80/- and guest beers such as Timothy Taylors Landlord, good value bar food, coffee and tea; open all day; bedrooms *(Trevor Stearn, Allan Clarke, Chris Raisin)*

Stonehaven [Shorehead], *Ship*: Also overlooks harbour; plain bar with small room off to right with pool table, and back lounge with cosy built-in seating and eating area; well kept McEwans 80/- and Youngers No 3, simple bar food such as rolls and scampi *(Chris Raisin)*

☆ **nr Turriff** [Auchterless; A947 5 miles S; NJ7250], *Towie*: Stylish upmarket comfort, good friendly atmosphere — more restaurant than pub, but aside from the beautifully prepared restaurant dishes (not cheap but unvaryingly good value, using fresh ingredients), there is well presented bar food from soup and pâté through burgers and vegetarian dishes to steaks done on sizzle-plate, with plentiful chips and salads; quietly efficient service, no smoking or music in dining area; good choice of wines; handy for Fyvie Castle (NT) and Delgatie Castle (traditional archery meet first Sat July); children welcome; bedrooms *(Janet and John Towers, Bernard Phillips)*

HIGHLAND

Achiltibuie [Altandhu; NB9812], *Am Fuaran*: Good, basic, friendly pub in wild setting overlooking Summer Isles; good value small blackboard menu with local prawns, salmon etc; visiting entertainers, pool table and friendly locals *(Linda Sewell)*; *Summer Isles*: Warm and friendly welcome, well furnished public rooms, masses of flowers and tasteful local watercolours; delicious food, good soups, main courses with a touch of nouvelle cuisine; good lamb and salmon, superb stawberry shortcake, and enormous array of most unusual cheeses; bedrooms comfortable, though the cheapest are not lavish *(Moira and John Cole)*

☆ **Applecross** [NG7144], *Applecross*: Where else could you be distracted from your venison-burger by reasonably priced locally caught lobster, crab, cod, monkfish and oysters, plus a view of Skye to make you weep with delight? On a good day sit outside and enjoy the happy mix of visitors and locals; friendly welcome, good choice of beers, bar billiards, open all day at least in summer; at the end of a wonderful scenic drive *(Joan and Tony Walker, P B Dowsett)*

Auldearn [NH9155], *Covenanters*: Tidy, welcoming pub with oak tables and chairs in spacious bar, with pool and darts being quietly played at one end, subdued lighting and piped music; food enjoyable, McEwans beers; attractive old village; pleasantly modern bedroom block *(Alan and Margaret Twyford)*

Aultguish [NH3570], *Aultguish*: Isolated highland inn near Loch Glascarnoch with comfortable attractive lounge; bar food; children welcome; bedrooms *(Ian Baillie,*

LYM)

Aviemore [Loch Alvie; B9152, 2 miles S; NH8609], *Lynwilg*: Large, pleasant old hotel looking over fields to Loch Alvie, comfortable bar with hunting prints and ski-ing information, good range of whiskies, McEwans *(Roger Danes); Olde Bridge*: Warm and inviting with friendly staff and good, imaginative food *(Mrs A Hamilton); Red McGregors*: Useful for families, with decent fast food, welcome for children, games machines and video juke box; 30 bedrooms *(Anon)*

Badachro [B8056 by Gair Loch; NG7773], *Badachro*: Peacefully charming pub with relaxed atmosphere in small bar, glorious garden *(Ian Baillie)*

Ballachulish [NN0858], *Ballachulish*: Basic hotel bar but pleasant lounge with glorious view across Loch Leven to the hills of Ardgour, well kept Arrols 70/-, good food served until 10pm; bedrooms *(Ian Baillie)*

Banavie [off A830 N of Fort William; NN1177], *Moorings*: Mainly hotel with dining room catering to local businessmen, but also wine bar — attractive room panelled with wood from old Edinburgh Bank and catering for yachtsmen passing through nearby Caledonian Canal; Scottish beers and dozens of vintage wines; good bar food from kitchens separate from hotel's, charming local waitresses; bedrooms *(Cdr W S D Hendry)*

Carrbridge [NH9022], *Dalrachney Lodge*: Cosy Highland hotel with warm and friendly bar, log fire in ornate wooden fireplace set in cosy inglenook, good bar meals and dinners; bedrooms *(Robbie Pennington)*

Dalwhinnie [NN6384], *Loch Ericht*: Modern Scandinavian-style hotel with comfortable and welcoming lounge bar; limited but interesting food and good views, inc the waterfall just behind the bar; bedrooms *(Russell Hafter)*

Dornie [8 Francis St; NG8827], *Loch Duich*: Overlooking lovely Eileen Donan Castle (floodlit at night), locally popular pub part has short selection of dishes from main restaurant menu, served in room with just a couple of tables — rather like sitting at private banquet; very accommodating staff; bedrooms *(E J Alcock)*

Drumbeg [B869 Lochinver—Kylescu; NC1233], *Drumbeg*: Remote fishermen's hotel with unassuming bar, friendly mix of locals and visitors, inexpensive plain lunchtime bar meals, 180 single malts, pool tables; evening restaurant; bedrooms *(Neil and Angela Huxter)*

Dulnain Bridge [A938 1/2 mile W of village; NH9925], *Muckrach Lodge*: Secluded Victorian former shooting lodge, now a hotel, notable for its good bar lunches inc amazing sandwiches, interesting local cheeses and formidable puddings such as sticky toffee or Carribean chocolate pot; friendly service, good beers; bedrooms with hearty breakfasts *(Leith Stuart)*

Durness [NC4067], *Sango Sands*: A welcome oasis with cafe, restaurant and family room with darts and pool *(Alastair Lang)*

☆ **Fort Augustus** [NH3709], *Lock*: A proper pub, so a real rarity up here; at the foot of Loch Ness, run by character ex-Merchant sailor, with lots of atmosphere — can get packed evenings with locals and boating people, especially in season as it's opp first lock on Fort Augustus flight of locks on Caledonian Canal; big fire, plain but wholesome bar food with lots of chips, soft Scottish piped music, Scottish beers *(Cdr W S D Hendry, Ben Wimpenny, Cathy Long)*

☆ **Fort William** [off A82 bypass, N end of town; NN1174], *Nevis Bank*: Friendly, bright and warming atmosphere in genteel lounge bar, courteous service, well kept Youngers IPA and No 3, decent bar food; pool in more basic bar bar; bedrooms *(J A Edwards)*

Fort William, *Ben Nevis*: Beams and timbers, loch views, well kept Youngers No 3, cheap bar food, friendly competent staff, video juke box (and disco lights); good value food in nice upstairs restaurant *(A C Lang, Mary and James Manthei)*

☆ **Gairloch** [Fish Harbour; just off A832 near bridge; NG8077], *Old Inn*: Good choice of good value bar food, friendly service, well kept McEwans 80/-, a good few malts, unusually wide range of crisps etc; dimpled copper tables and so forth in two small and rather dark rooms of comfortable lounge, neat and clean public bar with pool table and games, picnic-table sets attractively placed out by stream, splendid beach nearby; open all day; bedrooms *(Steve Waters, J A B Darlington, R Blatch, A C Lang, Graham Bush, Peter Watkins, Pam Stanley, BB)*

Garve [A832; NH3961], *Garve*: Small, quiet, comfortable bar in pleasant 1950sish hotel — a useful stop up here; friendly service, good food served quickly and efficiently; bedrooms *(Ian Baillie)*

☆ **Glencoe** [off A82 E of Pass; NN1058], *Kingshouse*: Alone in a stupendous mountain landscape, with simple bar food inc children's dishes, well kept McEwans 80/-; choose your bar carefully — the climbers' one at the back has very basic furnishings, loud pop music, pool and darts, the genteel modernised central cocktail bar has cloth banquettes and other seats around wood-effect tables; open all day; good value bedrooms in inn itself, and in cheaper dormitory-style bunkhouse *(Philip Whitehead, Mr and Mrs J H Adam, Alan Hall, BB)*

☆ **Glenelg** [unmarked rd from Shiel Bridge (A87) towards Skye — inn tucked away by bend at road junction and easily missed; NG8119], *Glenelg*: Overlooking Skye across own beach and sea loch; friendly beamed and panelled bar with open fire even in summer, high-backed settles, small but imaginative bar menu, and intimate restaurant beautifully furnished and decorated; drive to inn involves narrow steep roads with spectacular views of Loch Duich — there's a short summer ferry crossing from Skye, too; bedrooms *(WAH, E J Alcock)*

Grantown on Spey [High St; NJ0328], *Tyree*: Pine-panelled walls, comfortable plush furnishings, good home-cooked food — even the vegetables are cooked just right; bedrooms *(Janet Rogerson)*

Invermoriston [NH4117], *Glenmoriston*

Arms: Lots of malt whiskies in cosy lounge of inn not far from Loch Ness, fishing and stalking by arrangement; also cheery stables bar; bedrooms *(Mary and James Manthei, LYM)*

Inverness [Church St; NH6645], *Criterion*: Three bars, the most interesting of which is the old-fashioned lounge/ diner; pleasing atmosphere and framed copies of old advertisements; straightforward bar food *(Ian Baillie)*; [41 Haugh Rd], *Haugh*: Friendly pub, very much a local, just off centre not far from River Ness, with panelled bar, keg beers, cheap basic lunchtime food such as soup and mince and tatties at low prices, huge collection of beer mats, friendly landlord, juke box (may be loud); bedrooms in attached Castle Brae hotel *(Graham Bush)*

nr **Inverness** [Stoneyfield; A96 E of Inverness], *Coach House*: Pretty stone-built former coach house looking back over the farmland around Culloden; simply furnished but spacious bar on right leading out to back terrace, McEwans 80/-, piped music; neatly plush lounge bar opening into spacious restaurant; nice little breakfast room, neat residents' lounge; bedrooms *(BB)*

Kinlochbervie [NO2256], *Kinlochbervie*: On hillside with superb views over little fishing port and Atlantic; public bar is simple but pleasant and lounge bar is opulent; limited choice of food, no real ales; single-storey bedroom block *(Ian Baillie)*

☆ **Kylesku** [A894; S side of former ferry crossing; NC2234], *Kylesku*: Glorious coastal surroundings and short choice of particularly good bar food — especially fresh local seafood inc fish, scallops, delicious mussels, large prawns in garlic butter, also sandwiches and soup; friendly staff, happy mix of locals and visitors, restaurant; five comfortable and peaceful bedrooms *(Neil and Angela Huxter, D Goodger)*

Lairg [13 miles N on A836; NC5224], *Crask*: Short choice of good reasonably priced bar food inc good local prawns, haggis, good salads, four puddings, in comfortably restored inn with no piped music, good atmosphere, helpful staff and log fire; bedrooms *(KC)*

☆ **Lewiston** [NH5029], *Lewiston Arms*: Small friendly public bar with games and lots of locals, decorous well kept lounge used mainly by residents and restaurant diners, Youngers No 3, good filling bar food, attractive garden; handy for Loch Ness (nr ruined Urquhart Castle) and Glen Coiltie, with nice drive up to Glen Affric and back; bedrooms *(Cathy Long, LYM)*

Lochailort [NM7682], *Lochailort*: Plain rather rough-and-ready bar and second room with big windows on to road, but cheery landlord, good atmosphere and decent bar food inc excellent fresh salmon sandwiches; bedrooms *(S J A Velate)*

Lybster [ND2436], *Portland Arms*: 19th-century inn with two modernised bars, large residents' lounge, restaurant; good service, huge helpings of good food; nr spectacular cliffs and stacks, with local golf and pony-trekking; shooting and fishing can be arranged; reasonably priced bedrooms *(Hazel Church)*

Mallaig [side street up hill from harbour; NM6797], *Tigh-a-Chlachain*: Red leather settles, sea charts and pool table; welcoming bar staff, relaxed atmosphere, mixed crowd, wide range of malts and good value bar food; open all day *(Gary Scott)*

Melvich [NC8765], *Melvich*: Lovely spot with beautiful views of sea and coastline; friendly staff, leisurely atmosphere, peat fires and good food *(D A Wilcock, Miss C M Davidson)*

☆ **Nairn** [Viewfield St; NH8856], *Clifton House*: Charming and distinguished small hotel, wonderfully civilised, with delightfully furnished and sumptuously decorated lounge, delectable bar lunches made from the freshest and finest ingredients, fine restaurant, good wines and interesting spirits; was our highest-rated main entry in Scotland, until its evolution into what's clearly no longer a pub even by our elastic definition; comfortable bedrooms *(LYM)*

Nairn, *Newton*: Well appointed and well run floodlit hotel, with good value bar food inc soup, starters and main dishes such as venison casserole served till relatively late for the area; welcoming service; bedrooms *(M B P Carpenter)*

North Kessock [NH6548], *North Kessock*: Good bar food from sandwiches and ploughman's up; bedrooms *(Hazel Church)*

Poolewe [Corriness Guest House; NB8580], *Choppys*: Not a pub (really restaurant with bar), but worth knowing for good plain bar food cooked to order, inc home-made soup and sandwiches as well as generous hot dishes; the simple modern bar has pool; friendly licensee; bedrooms in guest house behind; handy for magnificent Scottish NT gardens at Inverewe — as are the other places mentioned here *(Keith Mills, Mrs E M Brandwood, BB)*; *Poole House*: Hotel in lovely setting with good service and good value bar suppers — good soup and fried haddock eaten at tables by lochside; bedrooms *(Mrs E M Brandwood)*; *Poolewe*: Plainly furnished bar and communicating lounge with big helpings of decent bar food served noon–8.30, well kept McEwans 80/-, good malt whiskies, piped folk music (live too, often), log fire; open all day; bedrooms *(BB)*

Scrabster [Harbourside; restaurant and bar of Scrabster Hotel; ND0970], *Upper Deck*: Decent food inc fresh fish and steaks (nothing vegetarian), with bar in one of the dining rooms — often busy in the evening *(Hazel Church, MD)*

☆ **Shiel Bridge** [NG9318], *Kintail Lodge*: Fairly simple hotel worth knowing for good well prepared food (inc children's helpings) such as home-made lentil soup, baked herring, wild salmon; good collection of malt whiskies; good value large bedrooms *(Genie and Brian Smart, M Cadenhead)*

Talladale [A832 Kinlochewe—Gairloch; NG8970], *Loch Maree*: Transformed by new owners; public rooms pleasant, bar food decent, bedrooms beautifully appointed with luxurious bathrooms *(Moira and John Cole)*

☆ **Tomatin** [NH8029], *Tomatin*: Newly decorated, clean and well run, good atmosphere, friendly staff and keenly priced bar food; seats outside; children welcome

(Mrs A Hamilton, Neil and Angela Huxter)
Wick [ND3551], *Rosebank*:
Straightforward bars but super food inc
genuinely home-made soups and good fresh
local salmon and seafood; bedrooms *(Hazel
Church)*

LOTHIAN
Aberlady [A198 towards Edinburgh;
NT4679], *Waggon*: Well run and friendly,
view over the salt-flats and Firth to Fife from
big windows in the airy if somewhat
incongruous high-ceilinged back extension,
attractive front family room, decent bar
food, well kept McEwans 80/- (a better
choice than the white wine); restaurant; nr
GWG175 *(G Milligan, LYM)*
Balerno [22 Main St (off A70); NT1666],
Grey Horse: Traditional Scottish bar, quiet
lounge, well kept Belhaven 80/- *(Andy and
Jill Kassube)*; [off Marchbank Rd, off A70
SW of Edinburgh], *Kestrel*: Pleasant
food-oriented bar with good starters and
main courses; good service *(Andy and Jill
Kassube)*
☆ **Cramond Bridge** [A90; NT1875], *Cramond
Brig*: Good family stop with bar food all
day, on main A90 N of Edinburgh; well kept
McEwans 80/-, restaurant *(LYM)*
☆ **Dirleton** [village green; NT5184], *Castle*:
Pleasant unpretentious but comfortable
lounge, generous helpings of well presented
food inc well filled sandwiches, well kept
McEwans 80/-, friendly service and
atmosphere; restaurant; attractive spot, nr
GWG175; bedrooms *(S V Bishop, Dr M I
Crichton, William D Cissna, T Nott)*
Dirleton [NT5184], *Open Arms*: Fine
position facing castle, with pleasant
atmosphere and good bar food and service
— a nice place to stay; bedrooms attractive
if not cheap *(Mrs N W Biggs)*
☆ **Edinburgh** [Jamaica St West; off India St],
Kays: Charming mock-up of Victorian
tavern with cosy mix of casks and red plush,
and small rooms off; particularly well kept
Belhaven 70/- and 80/-, Youngers IPA and
No 3 on handpump and an uncommon
guest beer such as Batemans or Fullers
London Pride tapped from the cask, cheap
and simple bar food, prompt courteous
service; open all day but closed Sun; children
in quiet panelled back room *(John Gould,
LYM)*
☆ **Edinburgh** [55 Rose St], *Rose Street
Brewery*: Worth visiting for Auld Reekie
80/- and potent 90/-, brewed here using malt
extract yet with a good deal of character;
downstairs
low-beams-boards-and-flagstonessaloon
with loud but well reproduced pop music
from its CD juke box and live music some
evenings, also comfortable partly panelled
upstairs lounge (only downstairs open all
day); bar food — ploughman's and shark
steak recommended; good service; the beers
are now sold in quite a few other tied Allied
pubs here *(P Corris, Roger Huggins, Barbara
Wensworth, Bob Timmis, BB)*
Edinburgh [100 Rose St], *Auld Hundred*:
Done up with peach plush furnishings and
stripped stone — more comfortable now
than older readers will remember it, though

perhaps with less atmosphere *(Peter Corris,
BB)*; [18-20 Grassmarket], *Beehive*: Good
range of well kept real ales in civilised
comfortable lounge with enjoyable
atmosphere, good value food inc fine salmon
and meat salads noon–6pm, upstairs
restaurant *(Ralph A Raimi, LYM)*; [12
Grassmarket], *Black Bull*: Newish pub
popular with University students,
flamboyantly decorated with red flock
wallpaper and brass lamps; see-through
front facade, good atmosphere, tiers leading
up to bar serving well kept McEwans and
Theakstons tapped from the cask, wide
choice of malts, 70/- and 80/-, good bar food
(bread heated in antique oven), juke box,
live jazz Tues *(John Gould)*; [basement of
Howard Hotel, 32-36 Gt King St], *Claret
Jug*: Has been a popular main entry, but has
now been reabsorbed into the hotel —
effectively ceasing to exist in the form we've
known it; [142 Dundas St], *Clarks*: Well
kept Youngers IPA in old-style Scottish bar,
good filling rolls *(BB)*; [Rose St, corner of
Hanover St], *Daddy Milnes*: Basic bar with
good atmosphere and photographs of
former Edinburgh literary set who
congregated here *(WTA)*; [435
Lawnmarket], *Deacon Brodies*: Snugly
refurbished old building, fun for tourists,
commemorating highwayman
Jekyll-and-Hyde town councillor who was
hanged on the scaffold he designed, with
leather armchairs, pictures and fireplace in
upstairs room; downstairs bar has settles
and a younger image and customers— as
well as a lifesize periwigged figure of Brodie;
decent bar food *(T Nott, Graham Bush, BB)*;
[Royal Mile — up towards castle], *Ensign
Ewart*: Olde-worlde with Scottish country
piped music and good lively atmosphere; Ind
Coope beers and Auld Reekie 80/- from
Rose Street Brewery pub, limited range of
tasty food with friendly service *(Barbara
Wensworth)*; [Grassmarket], *Fiddlers*: Period
feel with ornate wooden shelves behind bar,
violins on walls and atmosphere similar to
some London pubs; second bar with pool
(Graham Bush); [152 Rose St], *Kenilworth*:
Fine Edwardian pub with ornate ceiling,
carved woodwork, etched mirrors and
windows; central bar serving Auld Reekie
80/-, Ind Coope Burton, and Tetleys real ales
on handpump (at a price); lunchtime food *(P
Corris)*; [Rutland St], *L'Attache*: Basement
bar with empty bottles and clocks on walls,
vaults with decorated gates, and snug
alcoves — one with a leather wing chair; live
folk or jazz, daytime food; keg beers
(Graham Bush); [437 Gorgie Rd, about ³/₄
mile W of Tynecastle], *Luckies*: Pleasant
decor in compact main lounge and
restaurant area; good value food, well kept
McEwans 80/-, handy for Hearts ground;
children welcome *(Ian M Baillie)*; [Cockburn
St], *Malt Shovel*: Cramped bar counter with
good choice of well kept real ales inc lots of
guests such as Belhaven, Boddingtons and
Fullers ESB; good bar food in separate area,
friendly if slightly pressurised service *(Roger
Danes)*; [Trinity Cres, Newhaven — off
Starbank Rd], *Old Chain Pier*: Attractively
restored old pier building jutting right out
over the Forth with marvellous water views,
friendly, good piped music, cosy upper

gallery, well kept real ales, bar food *(LYM)*; [Princes St], *Overseas Club*: The best bet on Princes St itself — super light bar lunches, fantastic views of castle, good friendly atmosphere *(Syd and Wyn Donald)*; [202 Rose St], *Scotts*: Restrained modernisation in pleasantly traditional pub (old hands who still know it as Ma Scotts hope it doesn't get TOO respectable!), low lighting, old-fashioned efficient service, Tetleys — not cheap *(LYM)*; [11 St Vincent St], *St Vincent*: Boasts one of longest continuous licences in city, dating back to 1830s; well looked after with low beams, 19th-century bar mirror, friendly service and no piped music; well kept Maclays, Auld Reekie 90/- and Tetleys on handpump; open all day Thurs–Sat *(Andrew Cottle)*; [Mortonhall Park, 30 Frogston Rd E; NT2668], *Stables*: Nicest feature is the lovely cobbled stone stable quadrangle outside this cheerful recent conversion — stripped stonework, harness, big open fire, Turkey carpet, dark green leatherette stools and wheelback chairs; open 11–midnight, also breakfasts from 7.30, pizzas all day, other bar food noon to 10, Caledonian 80/- on handpump; very popular with people using the big caravan site here; children welcome — and a water bowl for dogs *(Ian Douglas, BB)*; [67 Laverockbank Rd, by Starbank Gardens], *Starbank*: Marvellous view over the Forth (with a telescope too) in airy bar with fine collection of uncommon whiskies and Belhaven 70/- and 80/-, Greenmantle and Merlin, Maclays 70/- and 80/-, and Timothy Taylors real ales; sheltered back terrace, bar food, restaurant, maybe jazz Mon; open all day, not Sun *(LYM)*; [Fairmilehead (A702); NT2568], *Steadings*: Long, low-ceilinged dining pub with bar at one end, restaurant and food servery at other end on slightly lower level; smart interior, Ind Coope Arrols 70/-, 80/- and Burton, good bar food individually prepared — can take time *(Peter Corris)*; [Drummond St], *Stewarts*: Easy-going traditional bar, open all day, very busy; good value sandwiches, Belhaven 80/- and Youngers IPA, blends own whisky; a particular favourite of Edinburgh traditionalists *(LYM)*; [1 Cumberland St], *Tilted Wig*: Very civilised and well run, with grainy ply-panelling, flowery ceiling, well kept Maclays and Theakstons real ales, back food bar, attractive little sunken garden; open all day *(JM, PM, LYM)*; [42 Bernard St, Leith], *Todds Tap*: Super little pub with log fire and the day's papers in one of its two small rooms, about ten real ales, good choice of whiskies; newspaper pages also pinned up in the gents' *(Peter Adcock)*; [Gt Junction St, Leith], *Waterfront*: Really a wine bar/pub on water of Leith — great fun, with super cheap food inc lots of fishy things such as tuna steaks, smoked prawns etc; good wines *(Syd and Wyn Donald)*; [Grassmarket], *Watermans*: Small but popular refurbished pub, quiet at lunchtimes but lively in evenings with live jazz on Thursdays; well kept Belhaven and Theakstons, house wines, lunchtime salad table, juke box, late closing *(John Gould)*

☆ **Gifford** [NT5368], *Goblin Ha'*: Warmly welcoming licensee, well kept McEwans 80/-, genuine home cooking, quick service;

though the bar's big it's so popular it soon fills — chatty and jolly; boules in good garden; bedrooms *(K M McKelvey)*

☆ **Gullane** [A198; NT4882], *Golf*: Golf's the thing in this friendly easy-going inn with waitress-served good value bar food, restaurant, garden; open all day, nr GWG175; bedrooms *(W D Dickinson, LYM)*

Linlithgow [179 High St; NS9976], *Crown Arms*: Typical simple Scottish town bar; behind intriguing colours of stained glass door lies friendly atmosphere, well kept Greenmantle and Tennents 80/-, clacking of dominoes on wooden tables *(Ian and Sue Brocklebank)*

Queensferry [Hopetoun Rd; NT1278], *Moorings*: Quiet and comfortable with interesting collection of naval memorabilia and good views of Forth Bridge from lounge; good bar food at reasonable prices, children allowed in lounge/family room *(Iain Montgomery)*

Ratho [NT1370], *Bridge*: Extended 18th-century pub by canal, with open fires, own boats (doing trips for the disabled, among others) and waterside garden — play area with mock-up ship and retired tractor; open all day from noon; has been praised for good value food using local fresh ingredients, good choice of wine, but no recent reports *(News please)*

STRATHCLYDE

☆ **Ardentinny** [NS1887], *Ardentinny*: Lovely views of Loch Long from well decorated waterside bars and back terrace, good but somewhat pricey choice of bar food inc fresh fish and vegetables, decent dry white wine, courtesy boat for guests; well placed for Younger Botanic Garden at Benmore; children in eating area; bedrooms; closed Jan/Feb *(Mrs E M Brandwood, LYM)*

Ayr [NS3321], *Caledonian*: Quite central hotel with seaview bedrooms and two bars — worth knowing for good value light meals all day, with reasonably priced drinks and prompt friendly service *(Bernard Phillips)*

Bearsden [Station Rd; NS5471], *Beefeater*: Whitbreads pub-restaurant converted from former railway station with attractive lounge bar full of railway memorabilia; well kept Castle Eden, good bar food *(Ian Baillie)*

Biggar [NT0438], *Elphinstone*: Popular Sun lunchtime with McEwans ale and wide choice of open sandwiches and hot dishes *(Angus and Rosemary Campbell)*

Bothwell [27 Hamilton Rd; NS7058], *Cricklewood*: Popular local with good range of bar food and three Whitbreads-related real ales; bedrooms *(Ian M Baillie)*

Cairndow [NN1810], *Cairndow*: Superb views over Loch Fyne and reasonable choice of good value bar food; Queen Victoria and Keats stayed here; next to gardens with tallest tree in UK; bedrooms *(E J Alcock)*; [just off A83], *Stagecoach*: Old pub with well kept beers, variety of generously served bar food at reasonable prices, friendly staff, pool table and fruit machines, and separate dining room with log fire *(A E Alcock)*

Connel [NM9133], *Falls of Lora*: Well kept hotel on edge of village, across road from Loch Etive: several spacious bar areas with sturdily comfortable cane armchairs, plush banquettes in bays, lots of brass and copper, tubs of plants forming booths, 1920s-style lamps, big watercolour landscapes, and free-standing Scandinavian-style log fire; children allowed; bedrooms comfortable and good value *(BB)*

Eaglesham [Polnoon St; NS5752], *Swan*: Busy pub with McEwans beer and good cheap bar food inc old-fashioned high teas *(Alastair Campbell)*

Gartocharn [A811 Balloch—Stirling; NS4286], *Gartocharn*: Useful stop not far from the S end of Loch Lomond, with leatherette banquettes in modernised saloon, chintzy armchairs in room off, plain public bar (with a couple of shelves of paperbacks) and pool room; tables on neat back terrace, generous helpings of decent bar food, coal fires, attractive service; open all day; bedrooms comfortable and inexpensive *(BB)*

Girvan [Dalrymple St; NX1897], *Kings Arms*: Comfortable kitschy golf bar — serving counter like giant golf ball, everything else has golf theme; also spacious lounge, bar food, real ale, open all day, children welcome; bedrooms *(TL, LYM)*

☆ Glasgow [1256 Argyle St, corner with Radnor St], *Montys*: Pleasantly smart and spacious atmosphere, under friendly newish management; copious dark wood, consistently well kept Belhaven, Greenmantle and other real ales, efficient amiable bar staff, good bar food, pervasive piped music, frequent live entertainment *(Alastair Campbell, Ian Baillie)*

Glasgow [India St, Charing Cross], *Baby Grand*: Continental-style cafe-bar, chatty and clattery with terrazzo or tiled floor, long grey marble counter, well kept McEwans 70/- and 80/- on tall founts, espresso machine, good hot chocolate and decent house wines; attractive bentwood furniture, baby pot palms, wide choice of French bread sandwiches and grills with enterprising specials such as herby mackerel, salt beef hash; jazz Sat evening, open all day *(BB)*; [Byres Rd, Hillhead], *Bonhams*: Almost a wine bar, suiting this studenty/professional area; good value lunch upstairs with gallery overlooking ground floor, olde-worlde decor with interesting articles on wall, good range of imported beers on draught and in bottles; live jazz often on Sun *(Karen Anderson)*; *City Merchants*: Friendly lunchtime service in out-of-the-way bistro/wine bar *(Syd and Wyn Donald)*; [George Sq], *Copthorne*: Lounge bar in city centre with good atmosphere and great decor, though a bit pricey *(Russell Hafter)*; [17 Renfield St], *De Quinceys*: Eye-catching stylish decor — not cheap, but the wide choice of salads is good value *(Ian M Baillie)*; [266 Bath St], *Griffin*: Smartly renovated popular bar with theatrical pictures; cheap bar food *(Ian Baillie)*; [17/19 Drury St, nr Central Stn], *Horseshoe*: Classic big Victorian pub with enormous island bar, lots of mahogany and mirrors, friendly service *(BB)*; [61 Renfield St], *Maltman*: Pleasant and very popular smokeless bar with table service at quieter time, separate back bar for smokers; real ale, varied and tasty bar food; downstairs restaurant prices reflect central location *(Alastair Campbell)*; [241 North St], *Ritz*:

Comfortably refurbished and spacious, with outstanding choice of malt whiskies, good plain bar food, S&N beers *(Ian M Baillie)*; [Highburgh Rd], *Rock*: Good choice of beer and bar food at reasonable prices, attractive Rock Garden section *(Ian Baillie)*; [Bridgegate], *Victoria*: Good atmosphere in unchanging little pub with well kept beer *(Ian M Baillie)*

Gourock [Cardwell Bay; NS2477], *Cardwell*: Nice friendly pub overlooking Firth of Clyde, well stocked bar nicely decorated, with comfortable atmosphere; big family room, extensive menu; well used by business people and visitors *(John Drummond)*

☆ Houston [NS4166], *Fox & Hounds*: Reliable local, three old houses attractively knocked together; clean plush lounge, comfortable seats by fire, attentive bar staff, wolf-whistling mynah, good choice of well kept real ales inc McEwans 70/- and 80/-; livelier bar with video juke box and pool; good popular food which can be eaten in either bar or restaurant; open all day *(Tom McLean, Roger Huggins, Dorothy and David Young)*

Inveraray [NN0908], *Argyll Arms*: Stately old-fashioned hotel overlooking Loch Fyne (especially spacious front conservatory), good choice of bar food and malts, well kept real ale, games in public bar, restaurant; well run, a nice place to stay, and well placed for the Argyll woodland gardens that are at their best in May and early June; open all day *(LYM)*; [Main St E], *George*: Corridor through to chummy stripped-stone bar with tiles, flagstones, exposed joists and log fire; Tennents 80/-, good choice of whiskies, bar games, juke box, food served noon to 9pm; nr GWG 180; children welcome; bedrooms *(Mr and Mrs J H Adam, R G Ollier, LYM)*

☆ Kilberry [B8024; NR7164], *Kilberry*: Unassuming white-washed former post office right off the beaten track, very warmly recommended if you're anywhere near for constantly changing choice of delicious food, cooking in interesting ways using fresh ingredients (traditional Sun lunch, no food Sun evening, closed weekdays Oct—Easter; booking suggested for evening meals); cosy inside, with friendly licensees, interesting bottled beers, and views over the coastal pastures to the nearby sea and the island of Gigha beyond; the coastal drive from Knapdale has glorious sea views *(Alistair H Doran, Kevin Myers)*

Kilchrenan [NN0222], *Kilchrenan*: Formerly derelict, reopened after high-standard restoration with bar fitted out in local pine, adjoining eating area, no TV, darts, music or games; quiet, relaxed atmosphere, good choice of food inc well presented poached salmon, Tennents 80/-, magnificent views of nearby Loch Awe *(Kevin Myers)*

Kilfinan [B8000, Cowal Peninsula; NR9379], *Kilfinan*: Sporting hotel half way down Cowal Peninsula, close to shore of Loch Fyne; small public bar (used by locals) with communicating lounge, good beer and good food; bedrooms *(Paul Wreglesworth)*

Kilmarnock [17 Strand St; NS4238], *Artful Dodger*: Renovated grain store, complete with old pulleys and other gear, decorated with old prints and bills for grain merchant; food good and varied; children welcome *(Mrs A McHallam)*

Kilmory [NR8686], *Kilmory Rest*: Delightful small pub in lovely surroundings, good food and drink served by great husband-and-wife team — a nice place to stay *(Anne Porter)*

Loch Eck [NS1493], *Coylet*: Cosy pub with friendly staff, well kept McEwans 80/-, good value bar food from chicken broth and ploughman's up with plenty of fish, real fires; super views over the loch; bedrooms *(R G Ollier, E J Alcock)*

☆ **Lochaweside** [B840; NN1227], *Portsonachan*: Beautifully placed lochside fishing inn with good service from smartly dressed staff, enormous log fires, loch views from restaurant and library/lounge (lunchtime bar food served here), enlarged hotel bar with fine choice of single malt whiskies, small fishing-minded public bar, waterside gardens, boat hire — residents get first choice; bedrooms simple but large, light and comfortable, with abundant hot water and exceptionally good breakfasts *(A C Lang, Stephanie Sowerby, LYM)*

Lochgair [NR9190], *Lochgair*: Quiet but very friendly, with notably enterprising good food (though they don't let vegetarian fare they'll do something on request); also hotel dining room; bedrooms *(Lidunka Vocadlo)*

Luss [A82 about 3 miles N; NS3593], *Inverbeg*: Handy for its position across rd from Loch Lomond; recent reports suggest that the food (served generously in busy informal lounge and restaurant) is currently on form, as is the service; Caledonian 80/-, games in simple public bar; bedrooms *(Mr and Mrs J H Adam, Ian Baillie, LYM)*

nr Oban [Cologin, Lerags; 3 miles S; NM8526], *Barn*: Down a single-track rd off another single-track rd; good simple food, pool table at lunchtime, numerous roaming pets to amuse children, live entertainment three times a week *(Ian Baillie)*

☆ **Port Appin** [NM9045], *Airds*: Friendly and notably well run inn with lovely shoreside position, particularly good food and charming attentive service; has been a main entry in previous editions but is now solely a hotel/restaurant — very much worth visiting; comfortable and well equipped bedrooms *(LYM)*

Rhu [the one nr Helensburgh; NS2784], *Rosslea Hall*: Hotel bar with decent food inc sandwiches, home-made chicken liver pâté with oatcakes, nice buffet with cold meat and salads — may be a wait; bedrooms *(Syd and Wyn Donald)*

Stair [NS4423], *Stair*: Very friendly welcome from Scottish owners, good cheap bar food, bedrooms clean, comfortable and very reasonably priced, with good huge Scottish breakfasts *(Cathy Long)*

Stewarton [the one N of Kilmarnock; NS4144], *Wardhead Park*: Wide choice of good inexpensive food, very popular with local people; welcoming atmosphere; children welcome *(Mrs A McHallam)*

Straiton [NS3804], *Black Bull*: Small and pleasant, simple and welcoming, with friendly licensees; darts, coal fire in front room, electric in back *(Diane Duane-Smyth)*

☆ **Tarbert** [NR8467], *Tarbert Hotel*: Atmospheric and quaint hotel with lovely outlook over harbour, and very good value evening meals; bedrooms comfortable, with handsome breakfasts *(E J Alcock, Jim and Becky Bryson, Gordon Smith)*

Taynuilt [a mile past village, which is signed off A85; NN0030], *Polfearn*: Newish licensees doing well, with particularly good bar food; bedrooms comfortable, with beautiful views over Loch Etive *(Gordon Smith)*

Tighnabruaich [NR9772], *Royal*: Friendly, lively hotel with two bars — one a cosy dimly lit lounge with open fire and piped music; public bar with local pictures and darts; friendly service, good views of Kyles of Bute and Isale; not cheap; bedrooms *(Lee Goulding)*

☆ **Troon** [Troon Marina; Harbour Rd — from centre go into Temple Hill and keep bearing right; NS3230], *Lookout*: Comfortable plush and wicker-and-bentwood seats in smart first-floor bar of blocky modern building with lively sea and marina views from picture windows, and from barbecue terrace; reasonably priced separate dining area, well kept Greenmantle and Theakstons on electric pump, good espresso coffee, children welcome; open all day summer; sailing, windsurfing and waterskiing can be arranged in the marina *(Jim and Becky Bryson, LYM)*

Troon [Academy St], *Clubhouse*: Spotless upstairs bar with dark decor, interesting old golfing photographs, out-of-the-ordinary choice of good food inc reasonably priced specials, efficient friendly service *(Dorothy and David Young)*

TAYSIDE

Almondbank [just off A85 Perth—Crieff; NO0626], *Almondbank*: Consistently good bar meals — wide choice, all reasonably priced *(NH)*

Auchterarder [towards Gleneagles Hotel; NN9413], *Coll Earn House*: Interesting old house with wood panelling, bar lunches all week — good Sun roast beef; bedrooms *(Mrs J Hamilton)*

Auchterhouse [off A927 NW of Dundee; NO3337], *Old Mansion House*: Pleasant small country hotel, good bar food, good dining room and service; bedrooms *(Mr and Mrs N W Briggs)*

Ballinluig [NN9853], *Ballinluig*: Nice food and friendly efficient service; bedrooms *(G R Pearson)*

Barnhill [13 Panmure Terr; E edge of Dundee; NO4632], *Woodlands*: In small suburb with really good small shops; very good since redecoration, with heated swimming pool — more hotel than pub, but good bar lunches; bedrooms *(Mrs N W Biggs)*

Blairgowrie [Coupar Angus Rd; NO1745], *Altamount House*: In pretty garden and within walking distance of Blairgowrie centre and shops, yet quiet and homely; good bar lunches and nice place to stay for country walks, golf etc; bedrooms *(Mrs N W Biggs)*

Bridge of Cally [NO1451], *Bridge of Cally*:

Beautiful, quiet setting by river with warm welcome and good value food; bedrooms comfortable and well equipped *(P J Evans)*

Broughty Ferry [behind lifeboat stn; NO4630], *Ship*: Behind the lifeboat house, a stone's throw from River Tay; bar and small serving bar downstairs, with tables for bar lunches and suppers upstairs — worth booking to get one by the window; service good and friendly, good choice of food *(Mrs N W Biggs)*

Burrelton [NO1937], *Burrelton Park*: Friendly service in hotel bar with well kept beer and particularly good imaginatively presented bar food, using good ingredients; nice clean bedrooms at a reasonable price *(Anon)*

Crieff [N, signed off A85, A822; open Mar–Dec Mon–Fri till 5.30, also Apr–Oct Sat till 4; NN8563], *Glenturret Distillery*: Not a pub, but the whisky-tasting bar has very good value malt whiskies, full range of other drinks, and good self-service food — the haggis is a treat; terrace overlooks Scotland's oldest distillery, with very good visitors' centre and guided tours; *(T Nott)*; [Oakbank Rd, off A85], *Oakbank*: Pleasantly situated on northern/west outskirts of town — nr the distillery; good range of bar food in extensive tartan lounge *(Mr and Mrs J H Adam)*

Dundee [South Tay St, Old Hawkhill; NO4030], *Tally-Ho*: Popular bar, with lots of stuffed animals; well kept Timothy Taylors Landlord and Youngers No 3, good cheap bar food *(Alisdair Cuthil)*

Fortingall [NN7446], *Fortingall*: Good roast beef lunch inc good horseradish sauce; bedrooms — closed winter *(Mrs J Hamilton)*

Inchture [off A85 Dundee—Perth; NO2829], *Inchture*: Small, pleasant pub/hotel in little village just S of Dundee; good lunchtime bar food, restaurant; ideal travel stop-off; bedrooms *(Peter Adcock)*

Kenmore [NN7745], *Kenmore*: Civilised and quietly old-fashioned small hotel with long landscape poem composed here written in Burns' own handwriting on residents' lounge wall, friendly back bar and lively separate barn bar with well kept Tennents 80/-; decent bar food, restaurant, Tayside gardens, good fishing; nr start GWG185; bedrooms *(Dr T H M Mackenzie, LYM)*

Meikleour [NO1539], *Meikleour*: Friendly pub in lovely village just off the Tay; quiet and homely sometimes, surprisingly lively at others; simple but good food, well kept Maclays *(R McIntosh)*

Perth [South St; NO1123], *Ewe & Lamb*: Small main street pub with bar and upstairs restaurant; good value bar food and quick service; parking 50 yds away by River Tay *(A A Worthington)*

St Fillans [NN6924], *Achray*: Lovely spot overlooking Loch Tay; above-average puddings with superb home-made apple pie; bedrooms — closed winter *(Mrs J Hamilton)*

THE ISLANDS

Arran

Brodick [NS0136], *Islander*: Simple but pleasant hotel bar with Scottish band;

bedrooms *(Jon Wainwright)*

Benbecula

Creagorry [NF7948], *Creagorry*: Has reopened in last year or so after major redevelopment; very pleasant lounge in hotel, with variety of S&N beers; entertaining if rough-and-ready public bar, decent bar food, friendly bar staff; bedrooms *(Alastair Campbell)*

Bute

Rothesay [NS0864], *Black Bull*: Friendly, comfortable three-roomed pub in town centre with good value bar food inc sizzle steaks (evening menu only on Fri and Sat); only pub we know here with real ale — Greenmantle; open 11am–1am *(P LLoyd, K Bamford)*

Coll

Arinagour [NM2257], *Coll Hotel*: Very simple bar on sparse island (sandy beaches/wildlife) with great character, darts, decrepit pool table and basic food; keg beers *(Jon Wainwright)*

Gigha

Gigha [NR6450], *Gigha Hotel*: Has been consistently good over the 17 years the Roebuck family have run it, but we've heard nothing since the whole island was sold, with reports that the Roebucks might be leaving; bedrooms *(Gordon Smith; news please)*

Islay

Port Charlotte [NR2457], *Port Charlotte*: well run, with good atmosphere, reasonable local food; walls covered with nautical charts, underwater photographs, shipwreck salvage; bedrooms *(Paul Wreglesworth)*

Jura

Craighouse [NR5267], *Jura*: Next to the distillery and overlooking Small Isles Bay; good hotel with good enterprising home-cooked food; the island is great for walkers, birdwatchers and photographers; bedrooms *(Paul Wreglesworth)*

Lewis

Ness [NB5261], *Cross*: Friendly, relaxing haven with open peat fire in lounge, substantial evening meals; recently renovated bedrooms *(Mr and Mrs J S Quantrill)*

Mull

Bunessan [NM3821], *Argyll Arms*: Small, friendly, village pub with piped Scottish music and small choice of good food such as smoked salmon pâté or prawn salad *(Angus*

and Rosemary Campbell)
Craignure [NM7136], *Craignure*: Simple and popular well looked after pub with good service and atmosphere, good bar food; handy for Oban ferry; bedrooms *(Jon Wainwright)*
Dervaig [NM4352], *Bellachroy*: Good hotel in sleepy village with traditional basic bar and lounge used more by residents; fine atmosphere and decorations consisting of Mull Rally photos and pennants from various touring clubs of Britain; bedrooms *(Jon Wainwright)*
Tobermory [NM5055], *Mishnish*: Colourful harbourside building with lots of character — a fine place to get to know the locals; loud video juke box, lively atmosphere, friendly service and quick, simple food heated in microwave behind bar; gets packed in summer, particularly when the Western Island Yachting Regatta is on *(Jon Wainwright); Western Isles*: Pleasantly furnished small bar in big hotel with spectacular views across the Sound of Mull; good seasonal atmosphere; bedrooms *(Jon Wainwright)*

Orkney

Dounby [HY2921], *Smithfield*: Pleasant, comfortable lounge bar in friendly family-run hotel, converted barn with small balcony in the eaves; open all day; children welcome; bedrooms *(Mrs Ruth Humphrey)*
Hoy [ND2596], *Hoy*: Lovely setting on beach with seals playing around corner; good, basic and friendly, with longish opening hours for tea and coffee; plenty of good value food with simply cooked fish and shellfish; also an RSPB information centre *(Linda Sewell)*
Stromness [HY2509], *Ferry*: Splendidly run, surprisingly quiet at night; big bar and restaurant menu, with good seafood specials, vegetarian dishes and decent wine; bedrooms spotless and comfortable, with unlimited hot water *(Anon)*

Seil

☆ **Clachan Seil** [island linked to mainland by bridge via B844, off A816 S of Oban; NM7718], *Tigh an Truish*: L-shaped bar built of substantial timber, where it would be a pleasure to be marooned; woodburning stove, prints and oil paintings, wheelback chairs and stools, piano, tartan curtains, bay windows overlooking bridge and mainland; darts, well kept McEwans 80/- and Tennents 80/-, bar food from burgers to dressed crab and local giant prawns with home-made mayonnaise, restaurant; white chairs in small garden and also at side of building; bedrooms *(Robbie Pennington)*

Shetland

Hillswick [HU2977], *Booth*: Friendly service and good food; beware baby seals in the garden; bedrooms *(Denis Mann)*
Lerwick [Docks; HU4741], *Thule*: Rough-and-ready bar full of characters, good atmosphere in upstairs lounge, with

folk music from time to time *(Denis Mann)*

Skye

☆ **Ardvasar** [A851 towards Broadford; NG6203], *Clan Donald Centre*: Not a pub but licensed to sell alcohol and well worth knowing for its reasonably priced well presented tasty food, all cooked here; converted stable block, with candelabra and clan escutcheons, wonderful atmosphere and service; the nature trail and Clan Donald audio-visual history of the Lords of the Isles make for a good visit, with majestic gardens and castle ruins *(P B Dowsett, Genie and Brian Smart)*
☆ **Culnaknock** [13 miles N of Portree on Staffin rd; NG5162], *Glenview*: Attractive white-washed house in lovely position below the Old Man of Storr, with sun-lounge style furniture, comfortable but slightly incongruous in this setting; the special feature is the excellence of the reasonably priced bar and evening restaurant food, home-made (inc the bread and oatcakes), with an inventive approach to traditional tastes and ingredients — honeyed lentil soup with soda scones, brioche filled with egg and smoked salmon, beef in brandy, superb local lobster and scallops, good fresh puddings; bedrooms *(Mary and Bill Parsons, Russell and Christina Jones, A McK, Mrs E M Higson)*
nr Dunvegan [Harlosh; NG2548], *Harlosh*: Idyllically placed hotel on the shores of Lock Caroy with friendly, welcoming and unpretentious atmosphere under helpful newish licensees; restaurant dishes inc superb Scotch broth, good prawn sandwiches, river trout with herb and tomato sauce, good halibut in subtle lemon sauce, good fresh veg; refurbished bedrooms with own bathrooms *(Moira and John Cole)*
Edinbaine [Skye; just off A850; NG3451], *Edinbaine*: In shady nook by babbling brook, former hunting lodge in quiet surroundings; small, family-run with generous helpings of traditional Scottish food; bar floor looks like a ballroom's — seems shame to walk on it *(E J Alcock)*
Isle Ornsay [NG6912], *Duisdale*: Comfortable lounge bar with striped flock wallpaper and deep brown leatherette settles, chairs and stools around dimpled copper-topped tables; ship's wheel on one wall with a smaller one as a light fitting and flags and pennants above the bar give it a nautical atmosphere; bay window at front looks out across croquet lawn/putting green to mainland hills and lovely side garden; appetising bar food; bedrooms *(S J A Velate)*
Portree [Home Farm Rd; NG4843], *Portree House*: Comfortable lounge bar with Tennents 80/- and good food inc smoked trout pâté and oatcakes, local cod, venison in blueberry wine or fresh wild salmon, home-made ice-creams *(Mrs E M Higson)*
Sligachan [A850 Broadford—Portree, junction with A863; NG4830], *Sligachan*: Marvellously placed simple inn, remote in central Skye, its public side recently greatly extended, with fast food and functional decor; plusher more sedate hotel bar with good open fire kept separate for residents; restaurant; bedrooms good value; closed

winter *(Steve Waters, Genie and Brian Smart, S J A Velate, LYM)*

Stein [NG2656], *Stein Inn*: Dark little flagstoned inn given great potential by its position above a quiet sea inlet, with glorious sunsets; traditionally furnished bar with partly panelled stripped stone walls, rather take-us-as-you-find-us; bedrooms *(LYM)*

Uig [Pier; beside Ferry Terminal; NG3963], *Bakur*: Good no-nonsense bar in bungalow-style building right by ferry, pleasant people, usual simple bar food lunchtime and early evening, good choice of whiskies; pool, darts *(Jim and Becky Bryson)*; *Ferry*: Basic bar food, not cheap, in compact lounge with leatherette seats, dimpled copper tables, flock wallpaper, piped music; bedrooms recommendable — comfortable and bright, with lovely views over pier and loch, good breakfasts *(AMcK, S J A Velate, Jim and Becky Bryson, BB)*

Ullinish [NG3138], *Ullinish Lodge*: Not a place to think of as a pub (nondescript lounge bar is accessible only through residents' dining room and separate public bar is very basic), but a nice place to stay considering the relatively low cost; attractive 18th-century building in superb position with fine views to the Cuillins *(S J A Velate)*

South Uist
Lochboisdale [nr ferry dock; NF7919], *Lochboisdale*: Attractive spot, good decor, competent and friendly staff, good food at reasonable prices *(John Laing)*
Pollachar [NF7414], *Pollachar*: 17th-century local with good atmosphere, ex-mariner landlord, piped Gaelic music and lively evenings; evening meals for residents; bedrooms *(Patrick Stapley)*

Wales

Wales

Interesting new entries here include the Black Lion at Abergorlech (a useful find on an attractively forested scenic route), the ancient Courthouse with its unrivalled view of the grandly moated castle in Caerphilly, the Rock & Fountain at Clydach (really interesting food in unexpected surroundings), the well run and relaxing Mountain View near Colwyn Bay, the promising Vine Tree at Llangattock, the marvellously warm-hearted Dragons Head at Llangenny (with what virtually amounts to an unusual subcontracting arrangement for its excellent food), the smart Fox at Penllyn (a foody pub, back in these pages under a new licensee), the canalside Open Hearth near Pontypool (notable real ales, good value food) and the companionable Royal in Usk (very wide choice of food – and the sort of atmosphere that makes you wish it was your local). Other pubs on a current upswing here include the Olde Bulls Head in Beaumaris (lots of character, good food, a splendid policy of stocking dozens of wine bin-ends), the friendly Ty Gwyn at Betwys-y-Coed (another place with loads of character – and good fish dishes), the well run Dinorben Arms at Bodfari (interesting layout, something for everyone – including over a hundred malt whiskies), the civilised Bear in Crickhowell (major refurbishments completed now), the ancient Blue Anchor at East Aberthaw (with a new restaurant), the Old Black Lion in Hay on Wye (notable food – doing particularly well under its current owners), the Walnut Tree at Llandewi Skirrid (more restaurant than pub, quite outstanding Italian cooking), the Queens Head near Llandudno Junction (delicious food), the delightfully tucked-away Leyland Arms at Llanelidan, the Old House at Llangynwyd (very popular food value), the Cerigllwydion Arms at Llanynys (a surprise to find such good food and interesting surroundings in such an out-of-the-way place), the Crown at Llwyndafydd (its new licensees win a food award this year – all home cooking), the Harp at Old Radnor (a charming place to stay), the Ty Coch at Porth Dinllaen (idyllic beach position, closed in winter) and the immaculate Salusbury Arms at Tremeirchion. Quite a few of the Lucky Dip entries at the end of the chapter are also showing particularly well at the moment: in Clwyd, we'd pick out the Hand in Chirk, both Llanarmon D C entries, Red Lion at Llansannan and Sun at Rhewl; in Dyfed, the New Inn at Amroth, Dyffryn Arms at Cwm Gwaun and Pentre Arms at Llangranog; in Glamorgan, the Ty Mawr Arms near Lisvane, Green Dragon at Llancadle, Greyhound at Oldwalls and Bush at St Hilary; in Gwent, the Hostry at Llantilio Crosseny and Beaufort Arms at Monkswood; in Gwynedd, the Britannia in Aberdovey and Kings Head in Llandudno; and in Powys, the Black Lion at Derwenlas and Radnor Arms at Llowes. Our price survey showed that, in general, pub prices in Wales are now a bit lower than the national average – compared with Britain as a whole, you save perhaps 4p or 5p on the price of each drink, and stand a

*rather better chance of finding decent snacks under our bargain target
of £1, and decent main dishes under our £3 target.*

The only area to vote to stay dry on Sundays in the 1989
referendum was Dwyfor – the Lleyn Peninsula. Here, pubs are not
allowed to sell alcohol on that day and generally close (hotels can sell
drinks to their guests, and may stay open for meals). Though the
District of Ceredigion (the west side, between Cardigan and the
mouth of the River Dovey) is no longer dry, many pubs in that area,
used to over a century of enforced Sunday closing, are still opting to
close on Sunday evening. We note in the text any main entry pubs
that we know do close on Sundays.

ABERGORLECH (Dyfed)   SN5833 Map 6

Black Lion

B4310 (a pretty road roughly NE of Carmarthen)

Traditional furnishings in the stripped-stone bar of this 16th-century black and
white pub include high-backed black settles facing each other across the flagstones
by the woodburning stove, plain oak tables and chairs, horsebrasses on the black
beams, and some sporting prints; a pleasant restaurant extension has light-oak
woodwork. Curiously for a pub better known in this heart-of-Wales village as Y
Llow Du, quite a few of the locals seem originally to have come from well over the
border, but it does have a good local atmosphere, with welcoming staff; the newish
landlady is very popular. Bar food includes sandwiches (from 65p) and soup (£1),
filled jacket potatoes (from £1) and ploughman's (from £1.50), home-made steak
and kidney pie (£3.95), salads such as beef (£3.85) or prawn and mayonnaise
(£4.10), grilled local trout (£4.25) and daily specials such as chicken, ham and
mushroom pie (£3.95); afternoon teas in summer with a selection of cakes made
by the licensee's mother; barbecues in the beer garden every Saturday throughout
the summer serving steak, spare ribs, beefburgers, kebabs and lamb chops. Well
kept Felinfoel's Double Dragon on handpump; cribbage, sensibly placed darts,
unobtrusive piped music. Across the quiet road a garden with picnic-set tables and
white metal and plastic seats slopes down to the River Cothi, by an ancient
Roman, high triple-arched bridge; this valley below the Brechfa Forest is beautiful.
The licensee has the fishing rights and the river is good for trout, salmon and sea
trout fishing. The car park is over the road, too (but there's easy step-less access to
the bar and the neatly kept lavatories). There are two dogs, a Jack Russell called
Remy (a lager lout) and an alsatian, Ben, who likes swimming in the river.
(Recommended by Anne Morris)

*Free house   Licensee Mrs Brenda Entwhistle   Real ale   Meals and snacks (not Mons
except Bank Hols); afternoon teas in summer   Restaurant tel Talley (0558) 685 271
Children welcome   Open 11–11, winter 12–3, 7–11   One bedroom with two single
beds; £9.50*

nr ABERYSTWYTH (Dyfed)   SN5882 Map 6

Halfway Inn   ★

Pisgah; A4120 towards Devil's Bridge, 5 3/4 miles E of junction with A487

In April 1990, this interesting pub perched prettily over the Vale of Rheidol once
again got new licensees; it's a great testimony both to the strong character of the
place and to the discreetness of the takeover that its distinctive, even eccentric
charm has survived pretty much intact and such is our confidence that history will
repeat itself that we've kept its star. At the moment you're still trusted to tap your
own interesting beer from the row of half-a-dozen well kept casks (unless you'd
prefer a professional handpump job); Bass and Felinfoel Double Dragon are
always on, and others might include Davenports, Smiles Exhibition, Wadworths

6X and Whitbreads Castle Eden, from a constantly changing range of up to 65 different ales; also a variety of ciders and perry which may be self service or on handpump. The food's kept its distance from chippiness, too: a wide but unfussy choice, including lasagne or steak and mushroom pie (£3.50), chicken curry and rice (£4) and sirloin steak (£7.50). The beamed and flagstoned bar has stripped deal tables and settles between its bare stone walls, with a dining room/restaurant area where tables can be reserved up to 8pm. Darts and pool and piped music, classical at lunchtimes, popular folk and country in the evenings; the new licensees plan to introduce special events such as sheep shearing contests and Welsh choirs. Outside, picnic-set tables under cocktail parasols have fine views of wooded hills and pastures; there's a play area, free overnight camping for customers, a paddock for pony-trekkers, and even free parking and picnic space for visitors – whether or not they use the pub. It gets particularly busy in summer. *(Recommended by F A Owens, Jenny and Brian Seller, Alison and Tony Godfrey, Jerry and Alison Oakes, G T Jones, Mr and Mrs Sumner, Dr Stephen Hiew, Peter Scillitoe, E J Waller)*

Free house   Licensees Bernard and Sylvia Gibbons   Real ale   Meals and snacks (tables can be reserved in dining area until 8pm)   Children welcome   Open 11–3, 7–11; Sun opening 12; closed Sun evenings Oct - mid-May   Bedrooms tel (0970 84) 631, hopefully by late 1990

BEAUMARIS (Anglesey)   SH6076 Map 6

Olde Bulls Head ★ ✦

Castle Street

The lunchtime bar food in this charming partly 15th-century inn has gained an enthusiastic following over the last couple of years. Changing daily, it might include home-made soup (£1.35), sandwiches (from £1.30), good ploughman's (£2.50), hot dishes such as cold poached salmon salad or shredded salad of smoked beef and pastrami (£3.70), casserole of Welsh lamb with leeks (£3.80), braised duck with fresh tarragon (£3.85) or poached fillet of codling with cream and white wine (£3.90), with home-made puddings such as chocolate and orange mousse (from £1.30). The rambling low-beamed bar is interestingly quaint, yet comfortable too, with snug alcoves, low-seated settles, leather-cushioned window seats and a good open fire. Besides copper and china jugs, there's a bloodthirsty crew of cutlasses, a rare 17th-century brass water clock and even the town's oak ducking stool; very well kept Bass on handpump, good comprehensive list of over 100 wines; dominoes and cheerful, friendly service. The entrance to the pretty courtyard is closed by the biggest single hinged door in Britain. *(Recommended by P A Crossland, D A Cawley, Mrs Richards, J E Rycroft, Lord Evans of Claughton, John Heritage, Gordon Theaker, R L Nelson, Jon Wainwright, Gwen and Peter Andrews)*

Free house   Licensee D I Robertson   Real ale   Meals and snacks (lunchtimes only) Restaurant (Sun lunch and evenings)   Children in eating area until 9pm   Every Thurs Beaumaris Folk Club meeting   Open 11–11   Bedrooms tel Beaumaris (0248) 810329; £32.50B/£55B

BETWS-Y-COED (Gwynedd)   SH7956 Map 6

Ty Gwyn ✦ ⇦

A5 just S of bridge to village

Peaceful and cottagey, this relaxed 17th-century coaching inn is protected against the overcrowding that's such an obvious risk even out here on the edge of this popular village both by its diminutive car park and by the terms of its licence – you do have to eat, or stay overnight. Throughout, the furnishings and decorations reflect the fact that the owners run an antique shop next door. The beamed lounge bar has an interesting clutter of unusual antique prints and bric-a-brac, with an ancient cooking range worked in well at one end; there are rugs and comfortable chintz easy chairs on its oak parquet floor. Quickly served bar food includes generous helpings of home-made soup (£1.25), sandwiches, pâté (£2.50), ploughman's (from £2.95), bulghur wheat and walnut casserole (£4.50), lasagne, gammon, fresh plaice, local trout, fresh shark steak or home-made steak and kidney pie (all £4.50), good chicken stuffed with lobster and prawns; fresh king and queen scollops in a thermidor sauce (£6) and sirloin steak (£6.95); children's meals (£1.95), and highchair and toys available; friendly, efficient service. McEwans 80/- on handpump. *(Recommended by J Windle, D P and M E Cartwright, Steve Dark, I T and S Hughes, Frank W Gadbois, A Parsons, KC, Brian Jones, R F Warner, Mr and Mrs Stevens, Lord Evans of Claughton)*

Free house   Licensees Jim and Shelagh Ratcliffe   Real ale   Meals and snacks Restaurant   Children welcome   Open 12–3, 6–11 (anytime for residents)   Bedrooms tel Betws -y-Coed (069 02) 383/787; £16(£25B)/£33(£44B)

BISHOPSTON (W Glam)   SS5789 Map 6

Joiners Arms

50 Bishopston Rd; village signposted from B4436, on the Gower Peninsula

Simple but comfortable, this truly hospitable local has been neatly restored to show off its stripped beams and stonework – underlining the point with quarry tiles, fitted carved oak benches, a massive solid-fuel stove and a copper-topped stone bar counter. But what strikes you most is the unusual spiral staircase. A short choice of good value simple home-made bar food includes filled rolls (from 55p), chilli con carne (from £2), chicken curry (£2.50), chicken pie (£2.60), steak and kidney pie (£2.75) and children's meals (from £1.75); well kept Bass, Worthington BB and Dark and a different guest beer every week such as Felinfoel Double Dragon on handpump; darts, cribbage, dominoes. The white-painted lounge bar is decorated with local paintings. *(Recommended by BHP, M and J Back, S Watkins, Brian Horner, P D Putwain, John and Helen Thompson)*

Free house   Licensees Arthur and Gwyneth Mort   Real ale   Meals and snacks (12–2, 6–8; not Mon evening)   Well behaved children allowed   Nearby parking can be difficult   Organist Sun evening   Open 11–11 (winter 11–3.30, 5.30–11 Mon - Thurs)

BODFARI (Clwyd)   SJ0970 Map 6

Dinorben Arms   ★

From A541 in village, follow Tremeirchion 3 signpost

Coping efficiently with its great popularity, this carefully extended old pub has enough seating areas to give plenty of quiet nooks. As much attention has been paid outside as in: prize-winning, carefully landscaped and prettily planted brick-floored terraces, with lots of tables, have attractive sheltered corners and charming views, and there's a grassy play area which – like the car park – is neatly sculpted into the slope of the hills. Inside, there are beams hung with tankards and flagons, high shelves of china, old-fashioned settles and other seats, and three open fires; there's also a light and airy garden room. Lunchtime bar food includes soup (£1.20), filled French bread (from £1.60), a good value eat-as-much-as-you-like smorgasbord counter, as well as cottage pie or hot-pot (£2.50), pizzas (£3.75), and steak and kidney pie, chicken curry or scampi (£4.25). Evening main courses such as fresh poached salmon (£5), gammon steak (£5.25), shark steak (£5.50), and steaks (from £7.50), and they also do vegetarian meals and children's dishes (£2.50). You choose starters and puddings from an attractive list in the Well Bar, by a glassed-in well which may date back to the seventh century, and there's also an upstairs carvery on Wednesday to Saturday evenings; behind the bar they have Thwaites, over 100 whiskies and many malts and they specialise in liqueur coffees; maybe piped music. *(Recommended by Patrick Godfrey, A M Neal, Mike Tucker, Drs M and K Parier, Neil and Anita Christopher, KC, E G Parish, F A Noble)*

Free house   Licensee Gilbert Hopwood   Real ale   Meals and snacks (12–3, 6–10.15, Sunday lunchtime only smorgasbord)   One no-smoking ground floor restaurant, and 3 other partiallly no-smoking eating rooms tel Bodfari (074 575) 309   Children in garden room and restaurant   Open 12–3, 6–11; closed 25 Dec

BROAD HAVEN (Dyfed)   SM8614   Map 6

Druidstone 🐾 🛏

From village, take coast road N and bear left, keeping on for about 1 1/2 miles, then follow sign left to Druidstone Haven – after another 1/2 mile or so the hotel is a *very* sharp left turn; OS Sheet 157, map reference 862168 (marked as Druidston Villa)

For most readers, the gloriously remote seaside setting and the unusually easy-going friendly informality of this family-run hotel combine to make it enjoyably memorable. The new chef is very interested in medieval food, Chinese, Japanese and Moroccan cooking techniques and the use of herbs, both medicinal and culinary; the result is some very adventurous dishes with an extensive use of fresh herbs and spices. Generously served bar lunches might include tomato and basil soup (£1.10) with home-baked bread, ploughman's (£2), home-made terrine (£2.60), cream cheese and crab strudel (about £4), medieval spiced fruit and duck; chicken underhill – in yoghurt and cream with cashew nuts (about £5) is very popular, as well as curries (about £5.50), and whopping puddings (from £1.80) such as Viennese apple pie or fruit compotes. A seafood quiche turned out to be virtually all lobster, and vegetarian dishes can be imaginative – bean and fresh fennel pie, aubergine and tomato crumble or medieval fruit and vegetable pie, for instance (all about £3.90); Sunday roast (£5.80). Worthington BB is tapped from the cask in a flagstoned cellar bar with a strong folk-club feel, where old sofas and armchairs face a rough but lively mural of the beach below; there's also a wide range of country wines, a good selection of organic wines and many liqueurs and malt whiskies; darts, cards, chess, trivial pursuit and piped music. The rooms above (including simple but spacious bedrooms) have a clifftop view out to sea, and a steep path takes you down to the long and virtually private sandy beach. Outside, there are all sorts of sporting possibilities, from boules through archery to far more strenuous sports. We ourselves look forward to our visits here very much indeed. But we have been taken to task for not mentioning points which, though all part of the picture loved by its devotees, might strike you differently: the autocratic old plumbing, which may decide you've had enough hot water halfway through filling your bath; the very leisurely service; random eccentricities like the old ice-cream container which may be pressed into service to chill white wine (if it's not just served at cellar temperature). And it does help if you like dogs a lot. *(More reports please)*

Free house – club and supper license   Licensee Jane Bell   Real ale   Meals and snacks (12.30–2.30, 7.30–10)   Restaurant   Children welcome   Music weekends four or five times a year   Open 12.30–2.30, 6–10.30 (midnight supper license); closed except for party bookings, Nov, 7 Jan to 9 Feb   Bedrooms tel Broad Haven (0437) 781221; £21/£42

BYLCHAU (Clwyd)   SH9863   Map 6

Sportsmans Arms (Tafarn yr Heliwr)

A543 3 miles S of village

This 400-year-old pub is where the Welsh-speaking people from the surrounding hills come to enjoy the company – not to mention the big helpings of good value bar food such as chicken (£2.95), home-made deep steak pie (£3.90), deep chicken, ham and mushroom pie (£4.25), plaice stuffed with mushrooms and in a wine, cream and prawn sauce (£5.50) and 10oz sirloin steak in a blue cheese sauce (£7.95), with a weekend hot and cold buffet on summer Saturday nights; home-made puddings. It's prepared to order, so there may be a wait if the pub is busy. They do a traditional three-course lunch only on Sundays. The pub – the highest in Wales, and often snowed-up in winter – is spectacularly isolated, with good moorland and forest views. It's comfortable, with both a log fire and a massive woodburning stove to warm the old-fashioned high-backed settles and other more modern seats. Well kept Lees Traditional Bitter on handpump and Best Dark Mild; darts and pool. Nearby Brenig reservoir has sailing, and walks in the forests around it include archaeological trails. *(Recommended by Janet Burd, Andy and Jill Kassube, Mr and Mrs J H Adam, Philip Riding, Lee Goulding)*

[U]Lees   Licensee Ioan Aled Evans   Real ale   Meals (12–2, 7–9.30 winter, 7–10 summer)   Children in eating area   Organist and Welsh singing Sat evening   Open 11–3, 7–11 (Sat summer 6, winter 7); closed Mon and Tues lunchtime

CAERPHILLY (Mid Glam)   ST1484   Map 6
Courthouse

Cardiff Road; one-way system heading N, snugged in by National Westminster Bank – best to park before you get to it

This 14th-century pub's special attraction is the glorious view of the Castle, from the light and airy modern cafe/bar at the back, and from the tables out on the grassy terrace behind – directly over the Castle's peaceful lake. Food in here includes soup (£1.10), big filled rolls (lunchtime), several starters such as breaded mushrooms (£1.95), lunchtime ploughman's (£1.95 – they make their own caerphilly, here at the pub), shepherd's pie, steak and stout pie or lasagne (£2.95), chicken breast in red wine or seafood wellington (£3.50), steak kebab or scampi and prawn provençale (£4.95), 10oz sirloin steak (£7.50), vegetarian dishes (£2.95) and children's dishes (from £1). The long bar has great stone walls, rugs on ancient flagstones, shutters and curtains on thick wooden rails for the small windows, a formidably large stone fireplace, pews, comfortable cloth-upholstered chairs and window seats; it has a raftered gallery at one end, immediately below its heavy stone slab roof. Well kept Courage Best and Directors and John Smiths on handpump, good coffee; fruit machine and piped pop music (even outside). *(Recommended by Keith Walton, M E Hughes; more reports please)*

Courage   Licensee James Jenkins   Real ale   Meals and snacks (12–2.30, 6–9.30) Children in restaurant only   Open 11–11

CARNO (Powys)   SN9697   Map 6
Aleppo Merchant ⇐

A470 Newtown–Machynlleth

Named after the sea captain who retired to open it in 1632, this has been simply but comfortably modernised and recently extended – red plush button-back banquettes around copper-topped tables, stripped stone and brassware in the beamed lounge bar, sofas and easy chairs in a small adjoining lounge, and a public bar with snooker, darts, dominoes, trivia machine and juke box. A wide choice of bar food includes sandwiches (£1.25) and an open prawn sandwich (£2.85), sweet and sour pork (£3.95), fish pie (£4.25), a good steak and kidney pie (£4.95) and steaks (from £7.25); well kept Burton Wood Bitter and Marstons Pedigree and a guest beer on handpump; the licensee tries to stock Welsh spirits, wines and waters; friendly service. *(Recommended by Norman and Kathleen Edwardes, Nick Blackstock, Peter Wakins, Pam Stanley)*

Free house   Licensee John Carroll   Real ale   Meals and snacks   Restaurant Children over 12 in eating area till 9pm   Open 11–3, 6–11 (sometimes Sat afternoons summer)   Bedrooms tel Carno (0686) 420210; £19/£30

CILCAIN (Clwyd)   SJ1865   Map 7
White Horse

Village signposted from A494 W of Mold; OS Sheet 116 map reference 177652

One reader walked five miles to find this homely pub in its delightfully unspoilt hamlet of stone houses. There's a cluster of snug rooms – parlourish in the two by the serving bar at the front, with exposed joists in the low ochre ceiling, mahogany and oak settles, Lloyd Loom chairs, brass, copper and decorative china on a high Delft shelf and around the little inglenook, and even a goldfish tank. Beyond a further little room with a piano (and a grandfather clock awaiting repair), there's one more conventionally furnished with tables and chairs. A separate quarry-tiled bar at the back allows dogs. Home-made food includes filled rolls (from 90p), ploughman's (£2.70), omelettes (from £2.70), steak and kidney pie, curries, lasagne or home-baked ham (£3.90), ham and eggs (£4.80) and 8oz rump steak (£6.20), and also specials such as vegetarian chilli (£3.60), macaroni cheese with leeks and bacon (£3.80), chicken and herb pie or beef goulash (£4.50); puddings like home-made raspberry pie with fresh cream (£1.70). Well kept Ansells, Ind Coope Burton and Sam Powells Bitter and Tetleys on handpump as well as a monthly guest bitter and Addlestone's cider; darts, dominoes, cribbage, fruit machine. There are picnic-table sets at the side, with an attractively naive inn-sign in front of the creeper-covered flower-decked building. *(Recommended by Jenny and Brian Seller, Mr and Mrs J H Adam, P D Putwain, KC)*

Free house   Licensee Peter Jeory   Real ale   Meals and snacks (12–2, 7.30–10) Children in garden only   Open 12–4 (4.30 Sat), 7–11

CILGERRAN (Dyfed)   SN1943 Map 6
Pendre

Village signposted from A478

This pub is an impressive blend of unpretentious comfort with great age – massive 14th-century stonework, broad flagstones; its sympathetic furnishings include armchairs and antique high-backed settles. Good value bar food includes sandwiches (from £1.10), home-made pâté (from £1.50) or filled baked potatoes (£1.40), ploughman's (from £2.25), a late breakfast (£2.75), vegetable and cheese crumble (£3.75), home-made steak and kidney pie (£3.95) and beef or chicken curry with bhajee (£4.50). The public bar has a juke box, darts, pool, and a fruit machine; Bass and Worthington BB on handpump, friendly service. There are seats outside, with an enclosed play area for small children. This end of the village is top of the town (what the pub's Welsh name means); the other leads down to the River Teifi, with a romantic ruined castle on a crag nearby, and coracle races on the Saturday before the August Bank Holiday. Nearby, is a good local wildlife park. *(Recommended by Lynne Sheridan, Jenny and Brian Seller, John Branford)*

Free house   Licensees P T and M O McGovern   Real ale   Meals and snacks Restaurant closed Sun lunchtime tel Cardigan (0239) 614223   Children welcome Open 11.30–3.30, 6–11

CLYDACH (Powys)   SO2213 Map 6
Rock & Fountain ⊗

Old Black Rock Road; take North Clydach signpost off A465 Abergavenny–Brynmawr

Over the last couple of years the new chef-patron – a talented builder, too – has transformed this tucked-away pub into a very comfortable haven of surprisingly good food. Most people eating use the stripped-stone dining room on the right, with crisp table linen, flowers, candles, even a little tinkling fountain flowing from a natural spring; you can also eat in the neat smallish lounge bar, with greyish beige button-back built-in wall banquettes, timbered walls, a coal fire in the stone fireplace – or perhaps in a second little bentwood-chair dining room opening off it (with a red velvet curtain to close off the stone entry arch). The wide choice of food from the bar/bistro menu includes among starters or light snacks mushrooms cooked in garlic, served in a white wine sauce blended with cream or local goat's cheese rolled in oatmeal, fried and served with cranberry sauce (£2.50), battered monkfish with a savoury dip (£3.25), smoked chicken breast served with a pine kernel and honey dressing or scrambled egg with smoked salmon (£3.50); they bake their own garlic bread. Main dishes include vegetarian dishes such as stir-fried cashew nuts and vegetables (£5.95), trout or home-cured bacon with laverbread, oatmeal, cockles and mussels (£6.95), escalope of veal with a cream sauce (£7.95), guineafowl done with muscadet and kiwi fruit (£8.95), various steaks, and dishes of the day such as skate or turbot; puddings such as sherry trifle or apple crumble (from £1.95). Allow at least 20 minutes' cooking time. Ruddles Best and County and Websters Yorkshire on handpump, weekly guest beers such as Uley's Pigor Mortis, a few bottle-conditioned beers, decent wines; a quiet and relaxed atmosphere, with pleasant neatly uniformed staff and, on our visit, piped Simon and Garfunkel; shove ha'penny, cribbage, dominoes, chess and nine men's morris; peaceful views over the valley (the main road's out of sight). There is no public bar – and as the left-hand side is still popular as a local (juke box and all), the atmosphere can sometimes be more heady than you'd expect at a place otherwise so successfully aiming high. We've not yet had readers' reports on the three new bedrooms, but would expect good comfort. *(Recommended by Pamela and Merlyn Horswell, John Hayward, Graham and Glenis Watkins)*

Free house   Real ale   Meals and snacks (roast only Sun), afternoon teas   Restaurant (closed Sunday evening; midnight supper license)   Children welcome   Open 12–3, 7–11, (11–11 Sat)   Bedrooms tel Crickhowell (0873) 830393; £29.50B/£38.50B

COLWYN BAY (Clwyd)   SH8578 Map 6
Mountain View

Mochdre; take service-road into village off link road to A470, S from roundabout at start of new A55 dual carriageway to Conwy; OS Sheet 116 map reference 825785

Surprisingly extensive for the location, this very neatly kept and handsomely modernised pub spreads through several carpeted areas with arched dividing walls, plush seats, quite a few houseplants (and bright window-boxes in the large windows), and big pictures of Conwy Castle and, by the entry, the Aberglaslyn Pass. Bar food includes soup, sandwiches, salmon and broccoli quiche, cold seafood, veal, steak and kidney pie, and lovely puddings. Pleasant, efficient service; well kept Burtonwood Best and Mild on handpump, and a good choice of cocktails; darts, pool, dominoes, juke box and unobtrusive piped music (in the lounge). *(Recommended by KC; more reports please)*

Burtonwood   Real ale   Meals and snacks (not 25 or 26 Dec)   Open 11–3, 5.30–11

COWBRIDGE (South Glamorgan)   SS9974 Map 6
Bear ⇐

Town signposted off A48

This pleasant and neatly kept old coaching inn is still a lively focus for this flourishing part of Glamorgan. On the left, an unusually heavy door opens into a bar with beams, flagstones, panelling, and attractively upholstered stools around cast-iron-framed tables; on the right there's carpet, and comfortable red plush armchairs. Bar food, served from the new bistro area (the lounge is now for residents), includes sandwiches, filled baked potatoes, soup, gammon or curry, steak and kidney pie, and grilled sardines, and there's a separate carvery. Well kept Bass, Brains Bitter and SA, Buckleys Best, Flowers Original, Hancocks HB, Marstons Pedigree and a weekly guest beer such as Hook Norton Old Hooky on handpump; log-effect gas fires, darts, maybe piped music. There's a rambling warren of quiet and comfortable beamed bedrooms, with more in a modern block behind; the breakfasts are good. *(Recommended by Patrick and Mary McDermott; more reports please)*

Free house   Licensee J B Davies   Real ale   Meals and snacks (not Sat evenings) Restaurant   Children in eating area   Open 11.30–3 (3.30 Sat), 5.30–11   Bedrooms tel Cowbridge (0446) 774814; £39B/£44B

CRESSWELL QUAY (Dyfed)   SN0406 Map 6
Cresselly Arms

Village signposted from A4075

If the tides are right, this fine old creeper-covered pub can be reached by boat. The main rooms have almost the feel of a sitting room full of friends: red-and-black flooring tiles, a high beam-and-plank ceiling hung with lots of pictorial china, built-in wall benches, kitchen chairs and simple tables, an open fire in one room and a working Aga in another. A third red-carpeted room is more conventionally furnished, with red-cushioned mate's chairs around neat tables. Well kept and attractively priced Hancocks HB is tapped straight from the cask into glass jugs; sandwiches only; friendly service, fruit machine, dominoes. Outside, picnic-set tables look out over the beautiful creek. *(Recommended by W Bailey; more reports please)*

Free house Licensees Maurice and Janet Cole Real ale Sandwiches (only 11–3, not Sun) Children in garden only Open 11–3.30, 5–11

CRICCIETH (Gwynedd)   SH5038   Map 6

Prince of Wales

The Square; A497

The Lleyn Peninsula is not specially well served with good pubs, making this well kept and comfortable place all the more welcome. The food's good value, too: at lunchtime, filled rolls (70p), prawn sandwiches or ploughman's or sausage and egg (£2.25), lasagne verdi (£2.75), vegetable lasagne (£2.85), home-baked ham or steak and kidney pie or chicken curry (£3.25); in the evening it's meals rather than snacks, with main dishes such as beef curry or spare ribs (£3.50), grilled gammon steak (£3.75), chicken and ham tortellini verdi (£4.25), vegetable au gratin or lasagne (£4.50), fillet of trout (£4.95) and sirloin steak (£6.25). The spacious, modern open-plan bar, pleasantly redecorated recently, has cosy separate areas and alcoves, some nice panelling, attractive local and countryside prints, and open fires (one in a pretty tiled fireplace). Boddingtons and well kept Whitbreads Castle Eden on handpump; cribbage, dominoes and fruit machine. There's a piano for any customer who feels up to setting in motion impromptu sing-songs.
(Recommended by Kit Read, Sue Holland, Dave Webster, R L Nelson; more reports please)

Whitbreads Licensee Chris Johnson Real ale Meals and lunchtime snacks (not Sun) Country and western or light pop music Tues evening Children in eating area, before 8pm, only Open 11–3, 6–11 (all day Sat, summer); closed Sun

CRICKHOWELL (Powys)   SO2118   Map 6

Bear ★ ⊘ ⇌

Brecon Road; A40

The heavily beamed lounge in this friendly and very civilised old coaching inn is packed with antiques including a fine oak dresser filled with pewter and brass, a longcase clock and interesting prints. Spread among the rugs on the oak parquet floor are lots of little plush-seated bentwood armchairs, along with handsome cushioned antique settles and, up by the great log fire, a big sofa and leather easy chairs. A window seat looks down the old market square. Snacks range from substantial sandwiches (from about 80p) and home-made soup (£1.25), through pâté such as chicken livers and pink peppercorn (£1.95) and ploughman's (£2.95), to garlic mushrooms with sherry and cream (£2.75) or seafood avocado (£3.95); main dishes include fresh salmon fishcakes (£3.95), spaghetti with tuna and prawns in a garlic and cream sauce, spicy chicken or rabbit casserole (£4.95), parsnip and cashew nut bake (they hope to widen their range of vegetarian dishes), and evening steaks (from £7.95), with a good choice of often original puddings (£1.95); efficient service. Bar food is served willingly until much later in the evening than usual for Wales. There are now three restaurants, two serving an à la carte menu with main courses that concentrate on Welsh produce (at about £11), and the other, a bistro, serving a cheaper range of French and English dishes such as fresh salmon or home-made steak and kidney pie (£5.25). Well kept Bass, Ruddles County and Best and Websters Yorkshire on handpump; malt whiskies, vintage and late-bottled ports. The back bedrooms – particularly in the new block – are the most highly recommended; the extensions mean there are now 27 bedrooms. *(Recommended by Jenny and Brian Seller, David and Sandy Roe, G D and J A Amos, Gordon Theaker, John and Chris Simpson, P B Dowsett, R C Morgan, Joy Heatherley, Anne Morris, E W B and M G Wauton, Michael and Alison Sandy, G R Pearon, E J Waller, John and Helen Thompson, Mr and Mrs J H Adam, John Hayward, John Honnor)*

Free house   Licensee Mrs Judy Hindmarsh   Real ale   Meals and snacks (till 10 evening)   Restaurant (closed Sun)   Children in eating area   Open 11–3, 6–11 Bedrooms tel Crickhowell (0873) 810408; £35–45B/£45–55B

DINAS (Dyfed)   SN0139   Map 6

Sailors Safety

From A487 in Dinas Cross follow Bryn-henllan 1/2, Pwll Gwaelod 1 signpost

On the edge of an isolated cove below windswept Dinas Head, this 16th-century pub has a no-nonsense medley of big scrubbed deal tables, pews and whisky-keg seats on its red tiles. The lively nautical decor includes its pride – the elaborate brass-inlaid counter, carved for the pub nearly seventy years ago. A brighter side bar has pool, a fruit machine, space game and video juke box, and there's a tiny French restaurant next door. Bar food such as sandwiches (from 85p, fresh crab £1.25), Welsh cawl (£1.75), ploughman's (£2.25), quiche (£2.25), salads (from £2 – fresh crab £3.50), home-made curry or lemon sole (£3.50), fresh scallops (£4.50) and steaks (from £7.50), with children's dishes (£1.25). Well kept Bass, Buckleys, Felinfoel Double Dragon and Ind Coope Burton from handpump or straight from the cask and a decent range of malt whiskies. Outside, seats huddle among the dunes that protect the pub itself; the cliff walks from here are very exhilarating. *(Recommended by W Bailey, Mr and Mrs Sumner, G T Jones, Ian Evans)*

Free house   Licensee Langley Forrest   Real ale Meals and snacks all day summer, 12–2, 7–9 winter   Evening restaurant tel Dinas Cross (034 86) 207   Children welcome   Ceilidh band every 4 weeks, disco every Sat   Open 11–11

EAST ABERTHAW (South Glamorgan)   ST0367   Map 6

Blue Anchor ★

B4265

All the way round the central servery in this pretty thatched and creeper-covered pub is a warren of low-beamed rooms wriggling through massive stone walls and low doorways. It's mainly carpeted, with seats and tables worked into a series of chatty little alcoves, though the more open front bar has an old lime-ash floor, with antique oak seats built into the stripped stonework by the inglenook fire (there seem to be open fires everywhere). The new restaurant – due to open as we went to press – also has one, as well as stone walls three feet thick and a beamed ceiling. Brains Dark and SA, Buckleys Best, Marstons Pedigree, Theakstons Old Peculier and Wadworths 6X are kept carefully at a controlled temperature, and served by handpump. Good value bar food includes sandwiches, faggots and peas (£2.40), home-made steak and kidney pie or home-made beef curry (£2.50), roast lamb (£3) and salads such as fresh crab or fresh salmon (£3.25). Rustic seats shelter among tubs and troughs of flowers outside, with more stone tables on a newer terrace. From here a path leads to the shingly flats of the estuary. The pub can get packed in the evenings and on summer weekends. *(Recommended by Gwyneth and Salvo Spadaro-Dutturi, John and Chris Simpson, Cathy Long, JMC, Patrick and Mary McDermott, Gary Scott)*

Free house   Licensee J Coleman   Real ale   Meals and snacks   Restaurant tel Barry (0446) 750 329 (closed Sunday evening)   Children in own room until 8pm   Open 11–11

GLASBURY (Powys)   SO1739   Map 6

Harp 🏠

A438 just N of village turn-off

The airy games bar, with pine kitchen tables on its wood floor, makes the most of the pub's position above the River Wye, with a good view from its big picture windows; pool, shove-ha'penny, dominoes, cribbage, quoits, juke box and sitting space game. The red-carpeted lounge has small red-cushioned Windsor chairs around dark tables, and a log fire in its stripped-stone end wall; sensibly placed darts in here. Bar food includes filled rolls and sandwiches (from 80p), burger (85p), home-made soup (£1), filled baked potato (£1.50), steak and kidney or chicken and mushroom pie (£2), ploughman's (from £2), lasagne, chicken curry or hot-pot or chilli con carne (£2.75), scampi (£3.25), salads (from £3.50) and a choice of vegetarian dishes such as aubergine and mushroom lasagne (£2.75); puddings such as home-made treacle tart (from 80p); children's portions available by arrangement; they warn of delays at busy times, though the service remains friendly. Flowers IPA and Original and Robinsons Best on handpump, Rombouts coffee. At the price, the centrally heated, no-smoking bedrooms are a real bargain; a cot is available; children under ten reduced prices. There are tables out on a crazy-paved terrace, with grass sloping down to the water. (*Recommended by Anthony Nelson-Smith, Helen and John Thompson, Brian and Anna Marsden, Owen Barder, Eleanor Grey, Keith Walton*)

Free house   Licensees David and Lynda White   Real ale   Meals and snacks (12–2.30, 7–10 in summer; not Dec 25)   Children very welcome   Open 11–3 (4 Sat), 6–11 (winter evening opening 6.30); closed evening 25 Dec   Bedrooms tel Glasbury (049 74) 373; £12.50(£15S)/£23(£25S)

HAVERFORDWEST (Dyfed)   SM9515   Map 6

Bristol Trader

Old Quay, Quay St; coming into town from A40 E, keep left after crossing river and take first left turn

In a lovely position by the river, this pub has been open for 600 years. Much modernised now, with green plush wall banquettes and stools around neat little round tables, and more tables up a couple of steps at one quieter end, it has the deep-down friendliness that often marks really old pubs, however much they've changed. Popular home-made bar food – they grow some of the ingredients themselves – includes sandwiches (from 80p), ploughman's (from £1.85), steak and kidney pie (£2.45) and in summer local oak-smoked mackerel (£2.50), salads (from £2.65), chicken (£2.70), curries or lasagne (£2.75), scampi (£3.10) and gammon (£3.50); well kept Ind Coope Burton on handpump and a decent range of malt whiskies; a CD juke box is kept low at lunchtimes. The pub enjoys a lovely position by the river. (*Recommended by Barry and Anne, Richard and Ann Jenkins*)

Free house   Licensee Michael Roach   Real ale   Meals and snacks (lunchtime only) Well behaved children welcome, also separate area   Open 11–3, 5–11; Fri and Sat 11–11; closed evening 25 Dec

HAY ON WYE (Powys)   SO2342   Map 6

Old Black Lion ⊘ ⇌

26 Lion St

The wide choice of reasonably priced, home-made food in this neatly kept and warmly welcoming inn might include soup with home-made wholemeal bread (£1.65), filled baked potatoes (£2.15), pâté with hazelnuts and whisky (£2.45), burgers (£2.65), ploughman's (from £2.65), home-made faggots (£3.85), lasagne (£3.95), a cold table (from £3.95), a better-than-average, recently enlarged selection of vegetarian dishes including neat laver-cake burgers and nut roast with their own horseradish sauce (£4.95), and steaks (from £7.75); recently introduced pork (£4.95) and lamb chops (£5.95) are very popular with walkers; they use fresh local ingredients. The puddings can be very choice indeed – if their Tia Maria meringue is on, don't miss it, and they plan to introduce such old-fashioned puddings as spotted dick. Sunday lunch (£6.45 per person) includes home-made soup, roast sirloin or pork and sherry trifle. They also do lavish breakfasts including special menus 'for salmon fishermen' and 'for all romantics'. Besides well kept Bass and Flowers Original on handpump (the cellar's air-conditioned) they have four malts and Old Irish Black Bush, an extensive, good value wine list and decent coffee. The low-beamed and partly black-panelled bar has recovered the poise that goes so well with this bookish town, its steep and twisty streets lined with antiquarian bookshops. There are tables on a sheltered back terrace. The pleasant bedrooms have been made very comfortable; the inn has Wye fishing rights and can arrange pony-treking, as well as pony trekking, golf, and the hire of a mountain bike. *(Recommended by Revd Wills, Mrs A M Stephenson, Mrs M Mills, Jamie Lyons, Ruth Harrison, Mrs Robert Jones, D and B Carron, WHBM, Mrs D M Hacker, Sheila Keene)*

Free house   Licensees John and Joan Collins   Real ale   Meals and snacks Restaurant   Children welcome   Open 11–3, 6–11   Bedrooms tel Hay-on-Wye (0497) 820841; £16.50/£33.50(£37.50B)

KENFIG (Mid Glamorgan)   SS8383   Map 6
Prince of Wales

2 1/4 miles from M4 junction 37; A4229 towards Porthcawl, then right when dual carriageway narrows on bend, signposted Maudlam, Kenfig

In the 12th century this was an important port with a castle, but over the next four or five hundred years a series of sandstorms engulfed it under the dunes which now stretch around here. The pub itself, just about the only survivor, still preserves the aldermen's mace upstairs (where, uniquely, they also hold Sunday school). The friendly main bar has a good deal of stripped stone, with an open fire, small storm windows, heavy settles and red leatherette seats around a double row of close-set cast-iron-framed tables. Well kept Bass, Butcombe Bitter, Camerons Strong Arm, Felinfoel Double Dragon, Fullers London Pride, Marstons Pedigree, Morells Varsity, Robinsons Old Tom, Theakstons Old Peculier and Wadworths 6X, Worthington Dark Mild and BB all on tap/gravity – the best choice of ales in this area. Bar food is very simple, but home-made, quickly served and very cheap: pasties, sandwiches and rolls filled to order (from around 55p: the home-roasted meat is well done), faggots (from 85p), cheese and potato pie or cottage pie (£1.10), steak and onion pie (£1.20) or lasagne (£1.40) – prices don't include potatoes or vegetables), they now also do basket meals (from £1.75); the fresh eggs from their own hens are worth knowing about. Dominoes, cribbage and card games. The pub, close to Kenfig Nature Reserve, sells fishing permits during opening hours. *(Recommended by John Nash; more reports please)*

Free house   Licensee Jeremy Evans   Real ale   Meals and snacks (all day)   Children in small lounge (daytime only)   Spontaneous music in side room   Open 11.30–4, 6–11

LITTLE HAVEN   SM8512   Map 6
Swan

This is one of the prettiest coastal villages in west Wales, lining a broad sandy cove sheltering between low hills. And this pub, perched on one side just above the beach, is beautifully placed for the view – especially if you can get a seat in the bay window, or if it's fine enough to sit out on the low sea wall in front. The two communicating rooms, with a winter open fire, are traditionally furnished with comfortable high-backed settles and Windsor chairs; the walls – partly stripped back to the original stonework – are decorated with old prints. Bar food includes soup (£1.10), ploughman's (£2), pâté (£2.25), crab and mayonnaise bake (£2.75), sardine, spinach and egg bake (£2.95), chicken curry or ham salad (£3.50), locally smoked salmon (£4.50) or fresh local crab (£4.95), specials like moules marinières, sliced smoked duck breast or bean goulash, and a selection of home-made puddings (£1.45); Felinfoel Double Dragon and Worthington BB on handpump from the heavily panelled bar counter. Mr Davies, who bought the pub a couple of years ago, is no stranger to it – he used to work here before taking over the Ship at Solva. *(Recommended by Barry and Anne, Geoff Wilson; more reports please)*

James Williams (who no longer brew)   Glyn and Beryl Davies   Real ale   Meals and snacks   Tiny restaurant tel Broad Haven (0437) 781256; open Sun evenings on Bank Hols only   Children in garden only   Open 11–3, 6–11; closed evening 25 Dec

LLANBEDR-Y-CENNIN (Gwynedd)   SH7669   Map 6
Olde Bull

Village signposted from B5106

This 16th-century pub has a jaunty clutter of furniture and furnishings in its knocked-through rooms: antique settles (some elaborately carved), a close crowd of cheerfully striped stools, brassware, photographs, even Prussian spiked helmets. Massive low beams and good log fires (one in an inglenook) add to the cosy feel. Well kept Lees Bitter and Mild on handpump from wooden barrels, and lots of malt whiskies. A wide choice of straightforward food such as soup (85p), burger (90p), sandwiches (from 90p, toasties from £1.20), cheesy baked potato (£1.10), bacon and egg flan or home-made pie (£2.20), salads (from £3.50) and grills (10oz sirloin, £7); darts, dominoes, cribbage, fruit machine, trivia machine and piped music. Outside, a barbecue area which can be covered, free to parties of 20 up to 150 people and the pub will provide music, coloured lighting and disco lights. There are tables out on a terrace by the car parks; standing nearby gives you a sweeping view down over the Vale of Conwy to the mountains beyond. Dogs (except for guide dogs) have to be left in cars. *(Recommended by Mr and Mrs M Cockram, Jon Wainwright; more reports please)*

Lees   Licensees Phillip and Brenda De Ville Forte   Real ale   Meals and snacks (12–3, 6.30–9.45)   Restaurant [U]tel[U] Colwyn Bay (0492) 69 508/69 359   Well behaved children welcome   Electric organ on certain nights   Open 12–3, 6.30–11

nr LLANBERIS (Gwynedd)   SH5860   Map 6
Pen-y-Gwryd

Nant Gwynant; at junction of A498 and A4086, ie across mountains from Llanberis – OS Sheet 115 map reference 660558

High in the mountains of Snowdonia on a lonely windswept road junction, this essentially homely and comfortable place has its heart in the friendly smoke room: climbing mementoes – signatures of the 1953 Everest team, who trained here, among the many others on the bar ceiling, a collection of boots that have done famous climbs, and more climbing equipment. There's also the rugged log-cabin of the slate-floored climbers' bar (which doubles as a mountain rescue post), a hatch where you order bar food, and the dining room where residents sit down together for the hearty and promptly served evening meal (check on the time when you book); clean and sensible rather than luxurious bedrooms. At lunchtime, there are good robust helpings of home-made food such as sandwiches, ploughman's using home-baked French bread (£1.80), quiche Lorraine (£2), cold meat or pâté salad or a home-made pie of the day (£2.50). They serve sherry from their own solera in Puerto Santa Maria; darts, pool, bar billiards and shove-ha'penny for residents (who have a charmingly furnished, panelled sitting room too). The Edwardian bath and shower on the first floor is well worth a look. But of course the real reason for coming here is the magnificent surrounding mountain countryside – like precipitous Moel-siabod beyond the lake opposite, which you can contemplate from a snug little room with built-in wall benches and sturdy country chairs. *(Recommended by Dr John Innes, Drs G N and M G Yates, Gwen and Peter Andrews; more reports please)*

Free house   Licensees Mr and Mrs C B Briggs, Mr and Mrs B C Pullee   Meals and snacks (lunchtime)   Restaurant (evening)   Children welcome, except residents' bar   Open 11–10.30 (11 Sat); no drinks on Suns; closed early Nov to New Year, open weekends only Jan and Feb   Bedrooms tel Llanberis (0286) 870211/768; £16(£20B)/£32(£40B)

LLANDEWI SKIRRID (Gwent)   SO3416   Map 6
Walnut Tree   ★   ⊘

B4521

Though there are a couple of token bar stools – and people using them for just a drink are treated kindly – this is decidedly a place to eat. Food quality matches top restaurant standards; though prices are high for a pub, they're a good deal lower than what you'd expect to pay for similar quality in a restaurant. Particular strengths include fresh fish and shellfish, local lamb, game, home-cured meats, interesting fruity and/or herby sauces (orange with coriander has been one successful combination), prettily dressed salads, uncommon cheeses (Welsh and Italian), and the awesome range of imaginative puddings. They offer nearly 20 first courses that you might perhaps think of as snacks (from around £5), and even more main dishes (from around £13). They don't accept credit cards. The small white-walled bar has some polished settles and country chairs around the tables on its flagstones, and a log-effect gas fire. It opens into an airy and relaxed dining lounge with rush-seat Italianate chairs around gilt cast-iron-framed tables. The attractive choice of wines is particularly strong in Italian ones (they import their own); the house wines by the glass are particularly good value, as is the coffee. Service is efficient and friendly. There are a few white cast-iron tables outside in front. *(Recommended by Lynne Sheridan, Bob West, Mr and Mrs M Wall, John Bowdler, N P Hopkins, Pamela and Merlyn Horswell, Gary Melynk, J D Cranston, Frank Cummins, MKW, Paul McPherson, Henry Midwinter)*

Free house   Licensee Ann Taruschio   Meals and snacks (12–2.30, 7–10.30) Restaurant tel Abergavenny (0873) 2797   Children welcome   Open 12–4, 7–11; closed Sun and Mon, 2 weeks in Feb and 4 days at Christmas

LLANDRINDOD WELLS (Powys)   SO0561 Map 6
Llanerch

Waterloo Road; from centre, head for station

Very relaxed and friendly, this 16th-century inn serves good value simple bar food such as home-made soup (£1), filled baps (£1), baked potatoes (from 80p), ploughman's (£1.95), omelettes (from £2), vegetarian pancakes (£2.50), chicken curry (£2.75), steak, kidney and mushroom pies (£2.95), salads (from £3.25), mixed grill (£6) and steaks (from £6.50). The squarish beamed main bar has old-fashioned settles snugly divided by partly glazed partitions; in summer the big stone fireplace is richly decorated with copper and glass. Well kept Bass, Hancocks HB and Robinsons Best on handpump; fruit machine and trivia machine, piped music; separate pool room, with darts, dominoes, cribbage. There are more orthodox button-back banquettes in communicating lounges, and tables out on the back terrace which has a summer bar and leads on to a garden (where you can play boules in summer) and play area; there's an orchard in front, too. *(More reports please)*

Free house   Licensee John Leach   Real ale   Meals and snacks (12–2, 6–9) Restaurant   Children welcome   Open 11.30–3 (Sat 3.30), 6–11; winter afternoon closing 2.30   Bedrooms tel Llandrindod Wells (0597)82 2086; £17(£20B)/£30(£36B)

nr LLANDUDNO JUNCTION (Gwynedd)   SH7883 Map 6
Queens Head ⊗

Glanwydden; heading towards Llandudno on A546 from Colwyn Bay, turn left into Llanrhos Road as you enter the Penrhyn Bay speed limit; Glanwydden is signposted as the first left turn off this

Behind the little quarry-tiled public bar of this welcoming and well kept pub is a spacious and comfortably modern lounge bar with brown plush wall banquettes and Windsor chairs around neat black tables, divided by a white wall of broad arches and wrought-iron screens. Generous helpings of beautifully prepared home-made food include good soups such as chicken and spinach (£1.25), home-made pâté s such as smoked salmon (£2.45), mussels sautéed in garlic butter, topped with smoked cheese (£3.75), home-made lasagne or lovely quiches (£4.25), salads (from £4.25), seafood vol au vent (£4.75), chicken Kiev or gammon steak (£5.50), Mediterranean prawns (£6.50) or sirloin steak (£6.75), with additional evening dishes like noisettes of lamb with a fresh plum sauce (£5.95), veal in blue cheese and port sauce (£6.50) or 10oz rump steak (£7.50). Fish and seafood is always a good bet here, as are the puddings, a huge range, from traditional bread and butter pudding or treacle tart to more exotic orange and grand marnier trifle (£1.70). Well kept Ansells Mild, Burton and Tetleys on handpump or tapped from the cask, a decent selection of malts, and good coffee maybe served with a bowl of whipped cream; warm winter log fires, pleasant service – even when things get very busy. There are some tables out by the car park. *(Recommended by J R Smylie, Mr and Mrs M Cockram, Mr and Mrs B Hobden, KC, H Geddes)*

Ansells   Licensee Robert Cureton   Real ale   Meals and snacks   Open 11–3, 6.30–11

LLANELIAN YN RHOS (Clwyd)   SH8676 Map 6

White Lion

Village signposted from A5830 (shown as B5383 on many maps) and B5381 S of Colwyn Bay

This picturesque old place has two distinct parts, each with its own personality, linked by a broad flight of steps. Up at the top is a neat and very spacious dining area, while down at the other end is a traditional old bar, with antique high-backed settles angling snugly around a big fireplace, and flagstones by the counter where they serve well kept John Smiths Magnet from handpump, a good wine list and lots of malt whiskies. Bar food includes home-made soup (£1.10), sandwiches (from £1.40) and filled baps (from £1.85), ploughman's (£2.95), salads (from £2.95) and a wide range of hot dishes such as filled baked potatoes (from £2.10), sausages or black pudding (£2.75), cauliflower au gratin (£3.70) or honey roast ham (£3.95) and meaty or vegetable lasagne (£4.20) or gammon steak (£4.95); they do half-price children's portions on certain dishes and will provide for special dietary needs if they can; dominoes, cribbage and piped music. Outside, an attractive courtyard between the pub and the church has rustic seats by tables under cocktail parasols; it's also used for parking. There's good walking in the pasture hills around. *(Recommended by Dennis Royles, Mr and Mrs J H Adam; more reports please)*

Free house   Licensee Jack Cole   Real ale   Meals and snacks (till 9.30 evening)
Children in garden and eating area   Open 11–3, 6–11; opens 12 winter   Bedrooms tel
Colwyn Bay (0492) 515 807; £20(£25B)/£50(£70B)

LLANELIDAN (Clwyd)   SJ1150 Map 6

Leyland Arms ★ ⊘

Village signposted from A494, S of Ruthin; pub is on B5429 just E of village; OS Sheet 116, map reference 110505

This carefully run, unusual pub is part of a cluster of former farm buildings by a country church, separated by a stretch of quiet fields from the village itself. Furnishings are simple but neatly elegant, with little bunches of flowers on tables, and mugs hanging from the beams of the smaller room by the servery. Very good food might include soup (£1.25), sandwiches, lunchtime ploughman's, kipper pâté or fresh sardines (£2.50), brie parcels in filo pastry (£2.75), various pies, such as steak, mushroom and Guinness, rabbit or game (from £4.95), salmon en croûte (£7) and halibut (£7.50), and when they're available the fresh Parkgate shrimps in a light garlic sauce with chunks of home-made bread have always gone down particularly well with readers; vegetarian dishes (from £3.50). Service is friendly, and there's good coffee (with cream) as well as Boddingtons Bitter; darts, dominoes. There are rustic seats on the grass outside, with a dozy background of bird and animal noises. Booking would be wise if you want a meal. *(Recommended by Curt and Lois Stevens, Janet Bord, KC, Mr and Mrs J H Adam, Dennis Royles, Philip Riding)*

Free house   Licensee Mrs C Topping   Real ale   Meals and snacks (12–2.30, 7–10)
Children in garden and eating area   Open 12–3, 7–11   Bedrooms tel Clawdd Newydd
(082 45) 207; /£20

LLANFRYNACH (Powys)   SO0725 Map 6
White Swan

Village signposted from B4558, just off A40 E of Brecon bypass

This pretty black and white pub has an easy-going, unchanging atmosphere, and a flagstoned lounge bar with plenty of well spaced tables, partly stripped stone walls and a big log fire; it rambles back into a series of softly lit alcoves. The emphasis is very much on food – a wide choice, including soup (£1.65), light dishes such as ploughman's (from £2.65), lasagne or ratatouille au gratin (£3.20), and more substantial dishes such as chicken curry (£4.25), haddock and prawn pie (£5.25), beef and mushroom pie (£6.70), Welsh-style grilled trout with bacon, scampi or baked crab (£6.85) and well hung steaks (from £7.50); puddings such as sherry trifle (from £1.50). They also do children's dishes (£2.35), and more egg cooking than most pubs. Service is friendly and efficient; Brains and Flowers IPA on handpump. Facing the churchyard across a very quiet village lane, there are stone and other tables on an unusual sheltered back terrace, attractively divided by roses and climbing shrubs and overlooking peaceful paddocks.The pub is handy for the Abergavenny–Brecon canal. *(Recommended by John and Ann Prince, Robert Horler, G R Pearson, Joy Heatherley, John and Chris Simpson, Jenny Cantle, Robert and Kate Hodkinson, Mrs D M Everard, DJW, Col A H N Reade, M and P Rudlin)*

Free house   Licensee David Bell   Real ale   Meals and snacks (not Mon, except Bank Holidays)   Children welcome   Open 12–2.30, 7(6.30 Sat)–11; closed Mon lunchtime (except Bank Holidays)

LLANGATTOCK (Powys)   SO2117 Map 6
Vine Tree

A4077; village signposted from Crickhowell

Llangattock is separated from Crickhowell by the River Usk, and tables outside under cocktail parasols give a view of the monumental medieval stone bridge (a short stroll takes you to our Crickhowell main entry, the Bear). Lunchtime ploughman's comes with stilton, cheddar and brie and their own freshly made bread, and other bar food includes starters such as stock-pot soup (£1.15), corn on the cob (£1.60), garlic mushrooms with chilli butter (£2.05) and home-made pâté (£2.10), with main dishes such as chicken cooked in white wine sauce (£4.60), lamb chop with rosemary and garlic (£5.75), fresh salmon (£6.95) and steaks (from £6.95). There are lots of puddings, such as home-made apple pie, cherry strudel or filled pancakes (all at £2.25); their fish comes twice a week from Cornwall, and they use local meat and vegetables. For most space, head for the scrubbed deal tables in the snug back dining area, with decorative plates and Highland cattle engravings on the walls; the body of the bar has soft seats, some stripped stone masonry, and brass ornaments around its open fireplace. Well kept Flowers IPA on handpump and Flowers Original alternates with Marstons Pedigree. *(Recommended by Pamela and Merlyn Horswell; more reports please)*

Whitbreads   Licensee I S Lennox   Real ale   Meals and snacks (12–2.30, 6–10)   Children in eating area only   Open 11–3, 6–11

LLANGENNY (Powys) Map 6
Dragons Head ✿

Village signposted off A40 E of Crickhowell

Mr Way is one of the most welcoming landlords in Wales: we must be thankful that after retiring from the Bridge End in Crickhowell he found he couldn't resist the pleasures of running a good pub, and has now returned to the trade in this delightful spot. What's more, he's arranged for the food here to be done by a fellow refugee from Crickhowell, Stephen Molyneux, who worked at the Bear, and who brings unusual flair to the cooking, with dishes of the day running to delicately flavoured turbot with wild mushrooms (£8.50). Other bar food includes sandwiches, starters (from £1.50-£3.75) such as melon with parma ham or peppered mushrooms, main courses (from £4.20-£7.50) such as home-made lasagne, peppered fillet steak or breast of duck with strawberries and puddings (from about £2.20) such as raspberry pavlova or a very popular brandy snap basket filled, for example, with home-made brown bread ice cream. The cosy L-shaped bar has a couple of old-fashioned housekeeper's chairs by the big log fire, one or two long pews, an attractive antique panelled high-backed settle, comfortable smaller chairs, flowers on the serving counter, houseplants in the windows and lots of miners' lamps hanging from the low beams; it opens into a pretty cottagey dining room, which you have to book. Well kept Bass, Brains and Worthingtons BB on handpump. There are tables out on two lawns, one very sheltered, around an apple tree, with a seat in a little stone summer-house; the beer garden runs alongside a little river; the village and its character hump-backed bridge are tucked into a sheltered valley at the foot of the Black Mountains. *(Recommended by Graham and Glenis Watkins; more reports please)*

Free house   Licensees Ivor and Mary Way   Real ale   Meals and snacks (not Sun evenings or all day Mon)   Restaurant tel Crickhowell (0873) 810350 (not Sun evening or all day Mon)   Children in garden and eating area and restaurant only if eating Open 12–3.30, 6–11 (Sat opening 11.30), may vary in winter

nr LLANGURIG (Powys)   SN9179   Map 6

Glansevern Arms Hotel ⇌

Pant Mawr; A44 Aberystwyth Rd, 4 1/2 miles W of Llangurig; OS Sheets 135 or 136, map reference 847824

Over 1,000 feet up, this quiet and civilised inn is a marvellously remote base for the steep hills and forests of the upper Wye valley. The cosy bar has cushioned antique settles and captain's chairs, an open fire, and china mugs on its high beams, and the comfortable residents' lounge has a good supply of books (this really comes into its own as a place to stay). Besides consistently well kept Bass on handpump, the genial landlord stocks several good malt whiskies and a well balanced wine list. Bar snacks are confined to home-made soup and sandwiches with home-baked and roasted meat or fresh cold salmon during the fishing season (£1.50); the seven-course dinners (booking essential) are excellent value; very good breakfasts for residents. *(Recommended by Lord Evans, Curt and Lois Stevens, Steve Dark, P B Rea, Roger Entwistle, John Davidson)*

Free house   Licensee William Edwards   Real ale   Sandwiches (lunchtime, not Sun) Restaurant (closed Sun evening)   Children in eating area at lunchtime only and restaurant   Open 11–2, 6.30–11   Bedrooms tel Llangurig (055 15) 240; £30B/£47.50B

LLANGYNIDR (Powys)   SO1519   Map 6

Red Lion ⇌

Upper village, off B4558 (the quiet alternative to the A40 Crickhowell–Brecon)

Comfortably up-market, this creeper-covered old stone inn has fox-brown leather armchairs, red-plush-cushioned settles, antiques and pictures in the old-fashioned bay-windowed bar. The emphasis is on daily specials, with such dishes as asparagus, ham and cheese bake, lamb chops with garlic, rosemary and marsala or pork chop Wellington (£5.50) and a chicken dish named after the village. The selection is similar to what's served in the restaurant, but often at much cheaper prices. Well kept Bass, Greene King Abbot and HB on handpump, and a decent range of malt whiskies; shove ha'penny, friendly and kindly service, and piped music. The sheltered garden outside is beautifully kept. The bedrooms are attractively decorated, and breakfast is said to be a real treat. *(Recommended by Robert Horler, Robert and Kate Hodkinson, Mrs V A Middlebrook, Mrs M Price, Mr and Mrs Hart, P D Putwain, Jenny and Brian Seller, John Honnor, MKW, JMW)*

Free house   Licensee Ellie Lloyd   Real ale   Meals and snacks (12–2, 6.30–9.30; not

*Mon or Sun evenings winter)   Restaurant (closed Mon and Sun evenings)   children in
eating area only   Open 11–3, 6–11   Bedrooms tel Bwlch (0874) 730223;
£27.50(£30)/£45(£50B)*

LLANGYNWYD (Mid Glamorgan)   SS8588   Map 6
Old House

From A4063 S of Maesteg follow signpost 'Llan 3/4' at Maesteg end of village; pub
behind church

Buzzing with locals, this very popular ancient thatched pub is among the oldest in
Wales. Wil Hopkin is said to have written *Bugeilio'r Gwenith Gwyn* here, and
though it's been much modernised there are comfortably traditional touches in the
two thick-walled rooms of its bar – such as the high-backed black built-in settles
and lots of china and brass around the huge fireplace, the shelves of bric-a-brac,
and the decorative jugs hanging from the beams. Generously served, good bar food
includes soup (90p), chicken, ham or pork (£2.70), steak and kidney pie (£2.80),
aubergine lasagne (£3), gammon and eggs (£4.25); it specialises in fresh fish such
as hake or lemon sole (£4.60); children's dishes (from 90p) and puddings such as
raspberry charlotte (£1.20); our preference is for the well hung steak (sirloin
£6.90); they will prepare any meal that's not on the menu. Well kept Flowers IPA
and Original on handpump. An attractive conservatory extension, with six tables
reserved for no smoking, leads on to the garden, which has a good play area;
there's a soft-ice-cream machine for children. *(Recommended by John and Helen
Thompson, John and Joan Nash, Joy Heatherley)*

*Whitbreads   Licensee Mrs W E David   Real ale   Meals and snacks (11–3, 5.30–10)
Restaurant tel Maesteg (0656) 733310; not Sun evening   Children welcome   Open
11–11; 11–4, 6–11 in winter*

nr LLANRWST (Gwynedd)   SH8062   Map 6
Maenan Abbey Hotel 🍴

Maenan; A470 towards Colwyn Bay, 2 1/2 miles N

Standing in beautifully kept, stately grounds, this steep-gabled early Victorian
house has a spacious, welcoming bar with Windsor chairs around the tables on its
oak parquet floor, tall stone-mullioned windows, Websters Choice on handpump,
and maybe Welsh singing on Saturday night; unobtrusive piped music. The elegant
and airy back dining lounge has brocaded chairs, handsome drop-leaf tables, silky
figured wallpaper and lots of house-plants. Under the new licensee, bar food
includes starters such as soup (95p) and devilled mushrooms with hazelnut
mayonnaise (£2.65), sandwiches (from £1.20, toasted from £1.35), a wide range of
ploughman's (from £2.65), main meals such as half roast Caernarfonshire chicken
or farmhouse pie or curry (£4.25), gammon steak (£4.95) and sirloin steak
(£6.95); vegetarian meals, such as mushroom and pepper stroganoff (from £3.95);
children's dishes, with half portions at half prices on request. Outside, there are
plenty of tables, with well kept lawns stretching beyond the terraces among topiary
yews and tall trees; a good side play area has swings and a castle. Fishing on the
River Conwy and nearby lakes, and rough or clay-pigeon shooting. *(Recommended
by Mike Tucker, Janet and John Towers, Sylvia and Len Henderson)*

*Free house   Licensee Richard Scott   Real ale   Meals and snacks   Restaurant
Children welcome   Welsh singing Sat evenings   Open 11–3, 6–11, Sat 11–11, Sat
winter 11–3, 6–11   Bedrooms tel Dolgarrog (049 269) 247; £37B/£54B*

LLANTHONY (Gwent)   SO2928   Map 6
Abbey Hotel

Included for its quite unique and romantic setting. The vaulted crypt bar is part of
what used to be the prior's house, which now stands quite alone in the graceful
ruins of the 12th-century priory – broken arches soar up from lawns and frame

gentle hill views. The bar is basic and simply furnished, but regularly serves well kept Flowers Original and Ruddles County on handpump or tapped from the cask, and also Brains Bitter, SA, Buckleys Bitter and Wadworths 6X on rotation and according to demand, and farm cider. Bar food is simple too, with good home-made soups (£1.95), toasted sandwiches and ploughman's (from £2.95), home-made meaty and vegetarian burgers (£3.25), and casserole (£4.95). On *Good Walks Guide* Walk 201. *(Recommended by Brian and Anna Marsden, D and B Carron, Tim Locke, Drs M and K Parier, Dr Zatouroff, D J Penny, Greg Parston, Paul McPherson, Helena and Arthur Harbottle, M and J Godfrey, Keith Walton, Alan Kilshaw, David and Eloise Smaylen)*

Free house Licensee Ivor Prentice Real ale Meals and snacks Children welcome Live music Open 11–3, 6–11 (all day Sat and holiday periods); closed weekdays Dec–Feb Bedrooms tel Crucorney (0873) 890487; £40(Sun–Thurs)/£45(for weekend from Fri/Sat)

LLANWNDA (Gwynedd)   SH4758 Map 6

Goat ⊗ ⇐

Village (a couple of houses or so) signposted as short loop off A499 just S of junction with A487 S of Caernarfon

It's the lunchtime cold table in the room on the left which earns the food award here – an excellent help-yourself cold table, with well over twenty fresh and attractive dishes laid out on crisp linen (£4 for as much as you like, including starters such as fresh melon in ginger wine and sherry-marinated grapefruit, then over half a dozen fish, several cold meats and freshly baked quiche, and five different cheeses to finish). They also do home-made soup, particularly good sandwiches, ploughman's, and farmhouse grill, and serve breakfasts from 8am–10am; well kept Bass and Boddingtons on handpump, twenty varieties of malt whisky and Scrumpy Jack cider; piped music. The main bar area is at the back, divided into two rooms by the almost circular bar counter, with its old-fashioned small-paned rounded screen complete with serving hatch, and an ancient cash register. The Welsh speakers seem to gravitate to the red leatherette button-back built-in wall banquettes around the four tables on the right; visitors go for the bright red plush chairs by the coal fire on the left. There's also a genteel front room on the right reserved for non-smokers. In the evenings the buffet table's stripped down to reveal a pool table, and the darts board comes into use; also dominoes, fruit machine, juke box. Tables on the sunny front terrace, another under a sycamore down in the garden. *(Recommended by Patrick Godfrey, Mrs Paddy Tilley; more reports please)*

Free house Licensee L Griffith Real ale Meals and snacks (12–2.30, not Sun) Children welcome Open 11–4.15, 5.30–11 (Sat evening opening 6); closed Sun Bedrooms tel Caernarfon (0286) 830256; £15B/£30B

LLANWONNO (Mid Glamorgan)   ST0295 Map 6

Brynffynon

From B4277 Porth–Aberdare in Ferndale, turn off down into valley at S-bend by Commercial Hotel and Rhonddu Independent Chapel; beyond the railway the road doubles so sharply back on itself that you have to go further up the dead-end and do a U-turn before you can continue uphill; also accessible from B4275 in Mountain Ash, and from Pontypridd via B4273 (keep straight on beyond Ynysybwl, bear left a mile later); OS Sheet 170, map reference 028956

Just what's wanted after a walk in the surrounding largely forested hills – a genuinely warm and helpful welcome, well kept real ale, and good value no-nonsense food. This includes cheap pasties, filled baked potatoes and cheeseburgers, a couple of good home-cooked specials such as salmon rissoles or chicken, and a few hot dishes such as curry or lasagne. The high-ceilinged bar on the left (favoured by the locals – and their dogs) serves Flowers IPA from a massively built counter, and has comfortably traditional turn-of-the-century seating and cast-iron tables, not to mention the piano, and the art nouveau mirrored coat stand; darts, TV. The roomy saloon on the right has a juke box and more modern furnishings, and there's a fruit machine in the hall between. A fine place for walkers. *(More reports please)*

Whitbreads   Real ale   Meals and snacks   Children welcome till 9pm   Occasional live music, quiz winter Weds   Open 11.30–4, 6–11 (winter 12.30–4, 6–11)

LLANYNYS (Clwyd)   SJ1063   Map 7

Cerrigllwydion Arms ⊘

Village signposted from A525 by Drovers Arms just out of Ruthin, and by garage in Pentre further towards Denbigh

There's a splendidly friendly atmosphere here, and the rambling building – which dates back nearly 600 years in part – has plenty of character, with old stonework, dark oak beams and panelling, and a cheerful decor with interesting brasses amd other nick-nacks; seats range from green plush to older settles. Careful cooking of good fresh ingredients might include pheasant in season, and food such as soup, sandwiches (weekday lunchtimes), home-made cottage pie (£3.75), fresh fish (from £3.75), asparagus wrapped in ham with a cream sauce or chicken and ham pie (£4.50), and half a fresh duckling (£7.50), with mouth-watering puddings. Well kept Buckleys Best and Marstons Pedigree and a guest beer on handpump, good coffee; darts, dominoes, fruit machine, piped music; efficient service. Across the quiet lane there's a neat garden, with teak tables among fruit trees looking across the fields to low wooded hills; the church is interesting. *(Recommended by KC, Tim Locke, Philip Riding, Mr and Mrs J H Adam)*

Free house   Licensee Steve Spicer   Real ale   Snacks (Tues - Thurs 7–9.30, Fri and Sat 7–10) and meals (not Mon)   Restaurant tel Llanynys (074 578) 247   Children in restaurant   Open 11.30–3, 7–11; closed Mon lunchtime

LLWYNDAFYDD (Dyfed)   SN3755   Map 6

Crown ⊘

Coming S from New Quay on A486, both the first two right turns eventually lead to the village; the side roads N from A487 between junctions with B4321 and A486 also come within signpost distance; OS Sheet 145 map reference 371555

The pretty tree-sheltered garden of this neat white-painted 18th-century pub has picnic-table sets on a terrace above a small pond among shrubs and flowers, with rides and a slide in a play area. The partly stripped-stone bar – friendly and bustling, especially at weekends – has red plush button-back banquettes around its copper-topped tables, and a big woodburning stove. Popular home-made bar food under the new licensee includes decent lunchtime sandwiches and toasted sandwiches, as well as soup (£1.45), liver pâté (£1.95), garlic mushrooms (£2.25), omelettes (£3.30), pizzas (from £3.85), very good chicken curry or steak and kidney pie (£4.45), vegetarian dishes (from £4.70), salads including home-baked ham (from £4.95), good grilled local trout with almonds (£5.75), half honey-roast duck with orange sauce (£7.45) and steaks (from £5.75); puddings such as chocolate gateau (from £1.35), children's dishes (from £1.55), and Sunday roast lunch. Well kept Flowers IPA and Original and various guest beers and a comprehensive wine list; fruit machine and piped music. The side lane leads down to a cove with caves by National Trust cliffs. *(Recommended by Jerry and Alison Oakes, Derek Patey, Sue Holland, Dave Webster, Gordon Smith, Gwen and Peter Andrews)*

Free house   Licensee Keith Soar   Real ale   Meals and snacks (12–2, 6–9; more limited Sun)   Restaurant (lunch and 7–10.30 April–Oct) tel New Quay (0545) 560396   Children in garden and eating area only   Open 12–3, 6–11; closed Sun evening Oct–March

LLYSWEN (Powys)   SO1337 Map 6

Griffin ★ ⊘ ⊨

A470, village centre

We get more warm praise about this old-fashioned inn than almost any other in
Wales: for the superb food, warmly welcoming and genuinely helpful licensees,
and comfortable surroundings. The Fishermen's Bar, decorated as you'd perhaps
expect with old fishing tackle, has large Windsor armchairs, leatherette wall
benches and padded stools around its low tables, and a big stone fireplace with a
good log fire; at lunchtime there's extra seating in the restaurant for bar meals.
These include noted sandwiches with a choice of white or brown bread and fillings
such as sugar-baked ham (£1.50), prawn (£2.75), and thick, tender slices of
salmon, fresh (£3) or smoked (£3.50), as well as home-made soup (£1.95) and
ploughman's with a wide selection of cheeses (£3.75), both with a choice of white
or brown rolls, salads including home-made quiches, fresh salmon and local roast
chicken (from £3.95) main dishes which change daily such as vegetarian crumble
(£4.10), home-made quiches (£4.25), curry (£4.50), delicious mushroom and
asparagus pancakes (£4.95), roast lamb (£5.25), braised pigeon in cider (£5.85),
and rump steak (£8.25); traditional home-made puddings – their most popular
being treacle tart (£2.25). Most days after Easter they serve brook trout and
salmon, caught by the family or by customers in the River Wye – just over the
road; in season there's game such as roast pheasant. Flowers IPA and Marstons
Pedigree on handpump, with a guest beer; quoits played, dogs allowed.
*(Recommended by G R Pearson, Alan and Marlene Radford, PLC, Mrs R Heaton, Canon K
Wills, Mr and Mrs Peter Crane, T R P Rudin, Jamie Lyons, Ruth Harrison, D and B Carron,
Mrs M Mills, Steve Dark, Philip King, M and J Godfrey, MKW, JMW, L G and D L Smith)*

*Free house   Licensees Richard and Di Stockton   Real ale   Meals and snacks (not Sun
evening except for residents)   Restaurant (closed Sunday)   Children welcome   Open
11–3, 7–11   Bedrooms tel Llyswen (0874) 754241; £22.50(£23.50B)/£35(£44B)*

MAENTWROG (Gwynedd)   SH6741 Map 6

Grapes ★ ⊘ ⊨

A496; village signposted from A470

A popular place to eat in this cheerfully busy pub is on the good-sized and
sheltered verandah (with a shellfish counter at one end). This catches the evening
sunshine, and has lovely views over a pleasant back terrace and walled garden;
there's a fountain on the lawn, and magnificent further views. All three bars have
log fires, and there's another in the great hearth of the restaurant, where there may
be spit-roasts. It's also full of stripped pitch-pine – chiefly ecclesiastical salvage, not
just pews and settles but pillars and carvings too. Home-made bar food comes in
great variety – and quantity: filled baps (from 80p), burgers (from £1.75),
ploughman's (from £2.50), fried sliced beef with mushrooms in French bread (£3),
steak and kidney pie or spare ribs or Madras curry (£4) and 10oz steaks (from
£6.75), with specials running to lobster and local salmon; puddings (from £1.50),
vegetarian dishes (from £3.25), and children's helpings (£1.20); good coffee. Quick
friendly service even at the busiest times, reliably well kept Stones on handpump
and decent selection of malts, piped music. Darts and juke box in the public bar,
where there's also an interesting collection of brass blowlamps. Breakfasts are
pretty monumental. *(Recommended by John Towers, DJW, Anthony Sargent, Tom Evans,
Patrick Godfrey, RT, S L Hughes, C M Whitehouse, Steve Dark, A Parsons, Tim and Lynne
Crawford, Philip Riding)*

*Free house   Licensee Brian Tarbox   Real ale   Meals and snacks (12–2.15, 6–9.30)
Restaurant (closed Sun and Mon)   Children in restaurant and patio   Live
entertainment on Sun nights   Open 11–11   Bedrooms tel Maentwrog (076 685)
208/365; £20B/£40B*

MARIANGLAS (Anglesey)   SH5084 Map 6

Parciau Arms

B5110

Attractively decorated rooms radiate out from the high-ceilinged inner bar area, which has local colour photographs on its dark red hessian walls, horsebrasses and leathers, miners' lamps and other bric-a-brac, and a mounted jungle fowl. The main seating area has comfortable rust-coloured plush built-in wall banquettes and stools around elm tables, a big settee matching the flowery curtains, antique coaching prints, and spears, rapiers and so forth on the elaborate chimney-breast over the coal fire. An airy family dining room with little bunches of flowers on the tables has attractive Snaffles calendar cartoons. Good value bar food includes sandwiches (from £1.30, steak £3.50), home-made soup (£1.30), filled baked potatoes or ploughman's (both from £3.25), a big slice of gammon and egg or sweet-pickled herrings (£3.95) or salads (from £3.95), or steak and kidney pie (£4.25), 8oz sirloin steak (£6.95), good children's dishes (from £1.50) and special dishes on request; well kept Ansells, Banks, Ind Coope Burton and Tetleys on handpump with guest beers such as Banks's or Marstons Pedigree, decent wines; darts, pool, fruit machine, background music; good friendly service. There are picnic-table sets on a terrace, with pews and other tables under cocktail parasols in a good-sized garden; it also has a good play area including a pensioned-off tractor, a camel-slide, a climber and a children's cabin with space game. *(Recommended by Jon Wainwright, David Waterhouse; more reports please)*

Free house   Licensee P H Moore   Real ale   Meals and snacks (all day 12–9.30) Children welcome, family cabin in garden   Live entertainment occasionally, children's entertainment Thurs- - Sat lunchtime and evening summer   Open 11–11, Sun 12–3, 7–10.30; closed 25 Dec evening

MOLD (Clwyd)   SJ1962 Map 7

We Three Loggerheads

Loggerheads; A494 3 miles towards Ruthin

Though the careful refurbishments here have created plenty of space combined with a properly pubby atmosphere, the original part, which dates back to the 18th century, is quite snug. On the left a tiled-floor locals' bar has pool, dominoes, shove-ha'penny, table skittles and cribbage. On the right there are owl prints and other country pictures, stuffed birds and a stuffed fox, and lighting by pretty converted paraffin lamps. Steps lead up to the really spacious area: high-raftered, but pillars support a false ceiling holding farm machinery and carts. Here, in an attractive decor of deep greens and pinks, comfortable green cloth banquettes are set around tables in stripped-wood stalls. It's all well kept, with a thriving atmosphere. Bar food includes sandwiches (from £1.20), herb and brandy pâté (£2.65), Greek sausage with pitta bread (£2.95), a choice of ploughman's (£3.25), home-made chilli con carne (£3.45), home-made steak and kidney pie with Guinness (£3.75), tuna fish bake or chicken and mango curry or broccoli and cauliflower gratinée (£3.95), with a huge range of interesting daily specials such as Turkish appetisers or frogs' legs in garlic butter or deep-fried camembert with cranberry sauce (£2.95), broccoli and brie crêpes (£5.25) or Turkish minced lamb kebabs on buttery tagliatelle (£5.95), and many game and fresh fish dishes such as French duck breasts with pink peppercorn and cognac sauce or fresh sea trout with mousseline of salmon with dill, cream and white wine sauce (£8.95); children's dishes and half portions available; well kept Bass on handpump and a good selection of wines and cocktails; loudish juke box, fruit machine and trivia machine. There are white tables and chairs on a side terrace. *(Recommended by Mr and Mrs M Cockram, Mr and Mrs J H Adam, Neil and Anita Christopher, KC)*

Bass   Licensee Gary Willard   Real ale   Meals and snacks (12–2.30, 6–10; closed Sun evening)   Children in eating area and garden   Open 12–3, 5.30–11 (Fri and Sat 12–11); closed evening 25 Dec

MONTGOMERY (Powys)   SO2296 Map 6
Cottage Inn

Pool Road; B4388 towards Welshpool, just off Newtown road

Below the wooded cliffs of ruined but massively imposing Montgomery castle, this traditional place has a friendly and busy atmosphere in its several well kept small rooms, with their mix of carpets, soft lighting, heavy old-fashioned wooden-armed chairs and some dark marine-ply panelling. The cottagey old decorations are happily not overdone. Good bar food, all freshly made, includes soup (£1.25), several other starters from egg mayonnaise (£1.95) to smoked salmon (£3.45), haddock or chicken (£3.95), salads (from £3.95), curry (£4.75), gammon (£4.95) and steaks (from £6.25); prices are lower than this at lunchtime, when they also do sandwiches (from 80p) and ploughman's (from £2.25; the home-made duck pâté and smoked-salmon pâté versions are good). There are plenty of puddings such as home-made apple and blackcurrant tart (£1.25), and in the evenings they do some more expensive dishes such as salmon, and lemon sole (£6.95). Well kept Tetleys Traditional on handpump (they do make a change from time to time), decent wines and good coffee; unobtrusive piped music; good hospitable service. There are picnic-table sets on the neat grass behind. *(Recommended by T Nott, D H W Davies)*

Free house   Licensees Brendan and Pauline Snelson   Real ale   Meals and snacks (12–2, 7–10, closed Monday except Bank Hols)   Restaurant tel Montgomery (0686) 668 348   Children in eating area, restaurant and garden   Open 12–3, 7–11; closed lunchtime Mon except Bank Hols

MORFA NEFYN (Gwynedd)   SH2840 Map 6
Bryncynan

Junction A497/B4412

Refurbished this year, this busy pub serves local seafood in summer, including crab and lobster, as well as home-made soup (£1.20), seafood chowder or home-made chicken liver pâté (£2.25), Mexican avocado dip with tortilla chips or fresh salmon mousse with cream and asparagus sauce (£2.50), vegetarian quiche (£3.95), home-made lasagne or vegetarian savoury stuffed mushrooms (£4.25), whole roast baby chicken (£4.95), gammon (£5.50), veal cordon bleu (£6.50), king prawns (£7.50) and sirloin steak (£8); daily specials such as home-made chicken, leek and mushroom pie (£4.75); children's dishes (£2.25) and puddings such as home-made bread and butter pudding (from £1.30). Service is quick and pleasant even when pushed. Well kept Tetleys and in summer Ind Coope Burton on handpump; dominoes, cards, fruit machine, space game, piped music and a real fire in winter; rustic seats outside. It's very quiet out of season. *(Recommended by Janet Bord; more reports please)*

Wrexham Lager Brewery Co. (Allied)   Licensee Keith Jackson   Real ale   Meals and snacks (not Sun)   Restaurant tel Pwllheli (0758) 720 879   Children in eating area, restaurant and garden, must be out by 9pm   Occasional live music by local singers   Open 11–3, 5.30–11; (11.30–2.30, 7–11 winter); closed Sun

NEVERN (Dyfed)   SN0840 Map 6
Trewern Arms ★ 🍺

B4582 – a useful short-cut alternative to most of the A487 Newport–Cardigan

The heart of this welcoming, extended pub is undeniably the stripped-stone slate-floored bar, its high rafters strung with nets, ships' lamps, ancient farm and household equipment, shepherds' crooks and cauldrons. Aside from a couple of high-backed traditional settles by the big log fire, it's fitted out with comfortable plush banquettes. Generous helpings of reasonably priced bar food include sandwiches (75p), ploughman's (£2.40), cod (£3.50), cold ham or chicken (£3.80), home-made lasagne or steak and kidney pie (£3.85) and steaks (from £6.80), with children's dishes (£1.75); huge breakfasts. Well kept Bass, Flowers IPA and Original, Marstons Pedigree and a guest beer on handpump; piped music; friendly, efficient service. A back games room has sensibly placed darts, table skittles, pool and dominoes, there's also a fruit machine and a video/juke box; beyond is a more spacious lounge. The licensee's parrot, Laura, may be in the bar to wish you good-day in Welsh or English. Across the medieval bridge over the River Nyfer, the pilgrims' church has pre-Christian stones set into its windows, and a Celtic cross. The lawn has tables set among shrubs and trees. *(Recommended by Jenny and Brian Seller, Simon and Ann Ward, Jerry and Alison Oakes, M Badcock, G T Jones, Stephen Dykes)*

Free house   Licensee Mrs Molly Sanders   Real ale   Meals and snacks   Evening restaurant   Children in the main bar   Dinner dances for up to 120 Sat evenings in winter   Open 11–3, 6–11   Bedrooms tel Newport (0239) 820395; £18B/£36B

NOTTAGE (Mid Glam)   SS8178   Map 6

Rose & Crown 🍽

2 miles from M4 junction 37; A4229 towards Porthcawl, then signposted Nottage, Rest Bay

Under new licensees, this comfortable and well kept pub is just a stroll from the seaside. It shows its age in the thickness of the surviving walls that still divide the beamed bar into distinct areas, part flagstoned, part carpeted, with quite a feature made of the log-effect gas fire in the huge fireplace. There are well made traditional-style settles, plusher seats, and in the area on the right tables arranged more for eating: good value bar food includes sandwiches (from 85p) and a steak sandwich (£1.25), ploughman's (from £2.75), pizza (£2.75), plaice (£3.25), trout (£4.50) or gammon (£4.75) and steaks (from £6.50), with children's portions (from £1.95). Well kept Ruddles Best and County and Websters on handpump; malt whiskies; fruit machine, unobtrusive piped music, efficient service. The bedrooms are attractively decorated and equipped. *(More reports please)*

Chef and Brewer (Watneys)   Licensees Mr and Mrs Williams   Real ale   Meals and snacks   Restaurant   Children in eating area and restaurant   Open 11.30–4, 6–11 (all day Sat)   Bedrooms tel Porthcawl (0656) 714850; £38B/£50B

OGMORE (Mid Glam)   SS8674   Map 6

Pelican

B4524

Why do we hear so little of this well run and attractive pub, looking down on the ruins of Ogmore Castle? It does good value, very tasty bar food, such as winter ploughman's, soup (£1.30), jumbo filled rolls (£1),and a choice of hot dishes such as home-made steak and onion pie (£3) and fresh fish (from £3.25), home-made lasagne, curries or chillis (£3.50) and prawns (£3.75); children's dishes (£2). The friendly bar, fairly functional on the left, has tables with pleasantly upholstered seats built into snug alcoves on the right. This part is given an almost luxurious air by its swagged pink curtains, harmonising carpet, curly wrought-iron wall lamps with pretty porcelain shades, and a shelf of decorative china. Well kept Courage Best, Directors and John Smiths on handpump and a decent selection of malt and Irish whiskies; darts, shove ha'penny, table skittles, a fruit machine and unobtrusive piped music. A side terrace has picnic-table sets, with swings beside it. *(Recommended by Cathy Long, John and Helen Thompson)*

Courage   Licensee Amanda Crossland   Real ale   Meals and snacks (12–2.30 Mon-Fri and Sun, all day Sat)   Restaurant (Wed - Sat) tel Southern Down (0656) 880 049   Children in restaurant at lunchtimes where bar snacks can be ordered   Open 11.30–4 Mon–Thurs, 11–11 Fri and Sat

OLD RADNOR (Powys)   SO2559 Map 6

Harp ★ 🛏

Village signposted from A44 Kington–New Radnor just W of B4362 junction

A lovely, peaceful and friendly place to stay – with good walks nearby (near *Good Walks Guide* walk 93). The cosy slate-floored lounge has a handsome curved antique settle and a fine inglenook log fire. The old-fashioned brownstone public bar has high-backed settles, an antique reader's chair and other elderly chairs around yet another log fire; they play table quoits (matches winter Mon, summer Tues), darts (Fri) and tip-it. Well kept Boddingtons, Marstons Pedigree and Woods Special and other guest bitters on handpump or tapped from the cask. Good simple bar food might include sandwiches (from £1), ploughman's with Stilton cut from the whole cheese (from £2.20), baked potato with prawns (£2.95), faggots (£3.20), lasagne (£3.45), chicken curry (£4.65 – very popular) and gammon and egg (£4.85). Evening main dishes in the snug and pretty dining room are mostly about £7. Service is first-class, and breakfasts good. There's plenty of seating outside, under the big oak tree, on the green by the 15th-century turreted church, and on the side grass (where there are plenty of rabbits as well as a play area). New additions include Hansel and Gretel (a goose and gander) and two younger geese. *(Recommended by Ian and Wendy McCaw, Jerry and Alison Oakes, Helen and Wal Burns, Philip King, Alison and Tony Godfrey, Gordon and Daphne, C M Whitehouse, Heleen van der Meulen, Anny Kragt, R J Yates, Alan and Marlene Radford, F A and J W Sherwood, Mr and Mrs A M Campbell, G L W Ritchie)*

Free house   Licensees Robert and Shirley Pritchard   Real ale Meals and snacks (Sun evening by arrangement only; not Tues lunchtime)   Well behaved children welcome Live entertainment every night and Sat lunchtime   Open 12–2.30, 7–11 (closed Tues lunchtime)   Bedrooms tel New Radnor (054 421) 655; £20B/£34B

nr PENARTH (S Glamorgan)   ST1871 Map 6

Captains Wife

Beach Road, Swanbridge, which is signposted off B4267 at Penarth end of Sully

Said to be haunted by the Captain's Wife herself, this attractively located pub has exposed stone walls and Turkey rugs and carpets on its broad bare boards, and several separate areas. Down at one snugly low-ceilinged end plush chairs and a high-backed traditional settle surround an old tile-surrounded kitchen range; towards the back Liberty-print-cushioned seats form stalls around tables under a glossy red plank ceiling; fruit machine, space game and piped music. Brains Bitter, Flowers IPA and Original and a guest beer on handpump from the good long bar counter as well as a wide selection of wines from all over the world and various whiskies; filled rolls (from 65p). If you're hungrier then there are two restaurants attached to the pub, each with their own bar: the Mariners restaurant, and the Smugglers Haunt (reached via a minstrels' gallery); they specialise in charcoal-grilled food, though the Mariners also has lots of fish and seafood. Sitting on the low sea wall in front, you look out to Sully Island. *(Recommended by Patrick and Mary McDermott, Greg Parston, John and Chris Simpson, Mike and Wendy Proctor)*

Free house   Licensee Mr Van Praag   Real ale   Lunchtime snacks (not Sun)   Two restaurants tel Penarth (0222) 530066/530600; Smugglers Haunt open 7 days a week, Mariners closed Sun night, all Mon, and Tues morning   Children in special family section   Open 11.30–11 (11.30–3.30, 5.30–11 winter, except Sat when open all day)

PENDERYN (Powys)   SN9408 Map 6

Red Lion

From A4059 Aberdare–Brecon, turn off up hill at Lamb Inn, and keep left at T-junction; OS Sheet 160, map reference 945085

Stripped stone walls, dark beams hung with flagons, flagstoned floors, traditional furnishings including bare antique settles – sounds austere, even with the two open fires (one in a singularly big fireplace); but the atmosphere's pleasantly cheerful and lively – thanks both to the friendly staff and regular customers, and the good range of fourteen well kept real ales, such as Felinfoel Double Dragon and Everards Old Original, tapped from the barrel; also fifty malt whiskies. They serve a simple range of filled rolls, pies and pasties (70p); dominoes, cribbage. Outside, sturdy seats and tables look down over the valley below, some built into the wall right on the brink of the pasture that drops away so steeply below. There are good forest walks at Cwm Taf – back down the hill, keep straight across the main road at the Lamb. *(Recommended by Tony Ritson; more reports please)*

Free house   Licensees Keith and Beryl James   Real ale   Snacks (may stop after 8pm if very busy)   Children in garden, not encouraged inside, side room and must leave by 8pm   Open Mon - Sat 1–4, 7–11, Sun 12–3, 7–9.30; closed 25 Dec evening

PENLLYN (South Glamorgan)   SS9776 Map 6
Fox

Village signposted from A48

The smallish high-ceilinged bar here has plush seats and a biggish oriental rug on its dark flagstones, stylish dark tables, a coal fire, small prints on the white walls of the outer area, and stripped stone to go with the varnished beams of the inner part. Black and white uniformed waitresses serve the good bar food: sandwiches, home-made soup, ploughman's, black pudding with apple horseradish mayonnaise (£2.75), omelettes, pan fried fresh plaice, good chicken in apricot and cream curry sauce (£4.95), good crab salad, open steak sandwich topped with mushrooms and melted cheese (£4.25), tasty chicken with apricot in a mild curry sauce, and home-made puddings. Well kept Ruddles Best and County on handpump, 40 good value house wines and 15 decent malt whiskies; darts, cribbage, a trivia machine and piped music. There are neatly laid tables on a front terrace under a fairy-lit yew tree. *(Recommended by Dave Braisted, Margaret Dyke, A A Worthington)*

Watneys   Licensee Mr Allgood   Real ale   Meals and snacks (not Sun, when full Sun lunch served)   Evening restaurant tel Cowbridge (044 63) 2352   Children in eating area only   Open 12–3, 6.30–11; closed Sun evening

PENMAENPOOL (Gwynedd)   SH6918 Map 6
George III   ★   🛏

Just off A493, near Dolgellau

Separated from the estuary – where the hotel has fishing rights – by what used to be a shoreside railway (but is now the inn's private drive), this fine 17th-century inn faces waterside meadows with wildfowl and a bird observation tower. There are fine walks in the forested hills around, too, for example up the long ridge across the nearby toll bridge. The most attractive bar is upstairs – a civilised place, beamed and partly panelled, opening into a cosy lounge where armchairs face a big log fire in a stone inglenook; this has an interesting collection of George III portraits. In summer the downstairs bar is the busy place; heavy beams, flagstones, stripped stone walls and long green leatherette seats around plain varnished tables. Darts, shove-ha'penny, cribbage, dominoes and fruit machine. Home-made lunchtime bar food includes soup (£1.10), pâté (£2.50), steak and kidney pie (£3.95), roast spare rib of pork with barbecue sauce (£4.10), smoked trout (£4.60) and grilled Scotch sirloin steak (£8.20); maybe piped classical music. There's simpler food, lunchtime and evening, from Easter till October in the lower bar, such as toasted sandwiches (from £1.10), pizza (£2.35), and a self-service cold buffet (from £3.60); efficient service. The food in the evening restaurant is imaginative. Some bedrooms are in a very comfortable award-winning conversion of what used to be an adjacent station – the railway closed years ago. The hotel can reserve sea-fishing trips from Barmouth. *(Recommended by John and Christine Simpson, Mrs K J Betts, Pamela and Merlyn Horswell, Roger and Judy Tame, J Windle, Mrs K J Betts, Rt Revd D R Feaver, SJW, F A and J W Sherwood)*

Free house   Licensee Gail Hall   Lunchtime meals (Nov - Easter not Sun or Christmas and New Year fortnight), lunchtime and evening snacks Easter - Oct   Restaurant (closed Sun evening and May Day Monday)   Children in restaurant at lunchtime Open 11–3, 6–11   Double bedrooms (not Christmas and New Year fortnight) tel Dolgellau (0341) 422525; £44(from £52B)

PONTYPOOL (Gwent) ST2998 Map 6
Open Hearth

The Wern, Griffithstown; Griffithstown signposted off A4051 S – opposite British Steel main entrance turn up hill, then first right

A fine changing range of real ales unique to the area and reliably good value bar food make this a draw over at least a ten-mile radius. The smallish lounge bar is comfortably modernised in red and grey plush, with a Turkey carpet and big stone fireplace; a back bar, with more space and leatherette seating, looks out on a disused stretch of the Monmouthshire & Brecon Canal which runs above the pub. Food includes soup (£1.05), garlic mushrooms (£1.75), sausage with egg, chips and peas (£1.90), a liver pâté with sherry, cream and herbs (£1.95), ploughman's or cottage pie (£2.30), salads (from £2.50), home-cooked ham (£3.20), plaice (£3.50), popular curries (from £3.50, bahjees and so forth extra), vegetarian dishes (£3.60), steak and kidney pie (£3.95), gammon and egg (£4.25) and steaks (from £5.65); they do their best to suit you if you want something not on the menu, and the downstairs restaurant is something of a local landmark. Bass, Courage BB, Hook Norton BB and London Pride are on handpump all the time and also four guest beers from a range of about 50, such as Ashvine, Felinfoel; decent coffee, cheap tea, friendly and efficient service; cribbage, dominoes, fruit machine and piped music. There are picnic-table sets, boules and swings among shrubs outside. *(Recomm ended by Pamela and Merlyn Horswell, J M Fletcher, M E Hughes, A J Ritson, Dr R Fuller)*

Free house   Licensee G Morgan   Real ale   Meals and snacks (11.30–2.15, 6.30–10.15)   Restaurant (not Sun evening) tel Pontypool (0495) 763 752   Children in eating area and restaurant only, bar snacks served in a separate room for chldren under 14   Open 11.30–3, 6–11 (Sat afternoon closing 4)

PORTH DINLLAEN (Gwynedd) Map 6
Ty Coch

Beach car park (fee) signposted from Morfa Nefyn; 15-minute walk along beach or over golf links

The pub, right on a curve of shallowly shelving beach backed by low grassy hills and the sand-cliffs where the martins nest, overlooks an expanse of water, boats anchored in the foreground, to the shadowy but dramatic hills across the sparkling bay. The pub is appropriately simple, with particularly cheerful service, and bar food such as filled rolls (from 90p; open prawn roll £3.25), baked potatoes (from £1), ploughman's with three cheeses, garlic mussels, home-made pizza, spare ribs, and meat or quiche salads from a cold display (£3.25); decent coffee, a coal fire at each end. Its 17th-century black beams are hung with a mass of mainly nautical bric-a-brac, with more on the walls; the right-hand wall has a lot of RNLI photographs and memorabilia, and there's a Caernarfon grandfather clock. There are tables outside. *(Recommended by N O Cox, R L Nelson; more reports please)*

Free house   Licensee Mrs B S Webley   Lunchtime snacks   Well behaved children allowed   Open 11ish–10.30; open 12–4 Sun July and Aug only, but no alcohol that day; closed end Oct–mid-March but open Christmas Day and New Year if not Sundays   Nearby holiday cottages tel Pwllheli (0758) 720498

RED WHARF BAY (Anglesey) SH5281 Map 6
Ship

Village signposted off B5025 N of Pentraeth

Looking out over ten square miles of treacherous tidal cockle-sands, this long and picturesque white-painted 16th-century house has lots of tables under cocktail parasols on the front terrace, and more rustic tables and picnic-table sets by an ash tree on grass by the side – where the view out past the anchorage is clearer. Inside is quite spacious, with a feeling of age and solidity in the two rooms on either side of the stone-built bar counter. There are long cushioned varnished pews built around the walls, glossily varnished cast-iron-framed tables, and quite a restrained decor including toby jugs, local photographs, attractive antique foxhunting cartoons and coal fires. Enterprising changing bar food includes sandwiches, spinach and mushroom lasagne (£2.70), cold chicken and ham pie or cheese and mushroom quiche (£2.95), seafood pancakes (£3.50) or provençale fish stew (£3.60), braised pigeon or chicken breast in creamy rum and orange sauce (£3.95), home cured gammon (£4.30); children's dishes (£1.70); there may be delays at busy times. The well kept Banks's and Tetleys Mild and Bitter are drawn by handpump with a tight spray to give a northern-style creamy head; they also usually have Kenneallys, a beer brewed for them by the City Arms in Minera and guest beers will be served on a regular basis this year; a wider choice of wines than usual for the area. Pool, darts and dominoes in the back room, and a family room; friendly service; piped music. *(Recommended by P A Crossland, D A Cawley, Jon Wainwright)*

Free house   Licensee Andrew Kenneally   Real ale   Meals and snacks (not Sun and Mon evenings in winter)   Children in family room and garden   Open 11–11 July–Sept, 11–3.30, 7–11 winter

TALYBONT-ON-USK (Powys)   SO1122 Map 6

Star

B4558

People are drawn to this deliberately simple and old-fashioned pub by its wide choice of real ales and ciders – unique for the area. They change regularly, but the list chalked up by the central servery runs to a dozen, such as Felinfoel, Hook Norton, Marstons Pedigree and Owd Rodger, Wadworths 6X and some that are rare around here, with two or three farm ciders such as Wilkin's on handpump too. Several plainly furnished rooms – unashamedly stronger on character than on creature comforts – radiate from this heart, including a brightly lit games area with darts, pool table and fruit machine; also cribbage, juke box, table skittles and cosy winter fires. Bar food includes filled rolls, soup (£1.50), ploughman's (£2.30), giant sausage (£2.50), home-made lasagne (£3.95), chicken in leek and stilton sauce (£4.50) and steak (£6.50); fish dishes such as fresh trout (from £3.95), vegetarian dishes such as cashew and parsnip roast (from £2.95) and also a separate Indian menu with dishes such as chicken tikka marsala. You can sit outside at picnic tables with parasols in the sizeable tree-ringed garden, and the village, with both the Usk and the Monmouth & Brecon Canal running through, is surrounded by the Brecon Beacons national park. *(Recommended by Paul Evans, Geoff Wilson, M and P Rudlin, David Pearman)*

Free house   Licensee Mrs Joan Coakham   Real ale   Meals and snacks (12–2.15, 6.30–9.45)   Children welcome   Live jazz Thurs 8.30   Open 11–3, 6–11 (all day Sat); winter lunchtime opening 12

TREMEIRCHION (Clwyd)   SJ0873 Map 6

Salusbury Arms

Off B5429 up lane towards church

The smallish beamed bar in this immaculate and civilised country pub has thick carpet and richly upholstered seats; some of the timbering in the lower part, which dates back over six centuries and was originally the stables, is said to have come originally from St Asaphs Cathedral. Mostly home-made bar food – carefully prepared from fresh, local ingredients – includes fish and game in season, as well as sandwiches, good soups (£1.20), hot beef in garlic bread (£3), local sausages wrapped in bacon or chicken breast in tarragon sauce (£3.25) and moules marinières (£3.50); they also do a vegetarian dish of the day (£3). Well kept John Smiths on handpump; dominoes, cribbage, some board games and trivia. Meticulous attention to detail extends outside, too, where tables in the pretty gardens are set among flowers, shrubs and a pond with goldfish; there's also an under-cover barbecue and they serve a special charcoal-cooked menu on Friday nights from the Whitsun weekend onwards. *(Recommended by Patrick Godfrey, Philip Riding, KC, E G Parish; more reports please)*

Free house   Licensees Iain and Catherine Craze   Real ale   Meals and snacks (not Mon except Bank Hols)   Restaurant (closed Sun evening) tel Bodfari (074 575) 262   Well behaved children welcome   Open 12–3, 7–11; closed Mon (except Bank Hols)

USK (Gwent)   SO3801 Map 6
Royal

New Market Street (off A472 by Usk bridge)

A good deal of character marks this relaxed and traditional Georgian country-town inn. The open-plan bar is basically two rooms, nicest on the left, with a tall longcase clock, cream-tiled kitchen range flush with the pale ochre back wall, mirrored sideboard, a rug on neat slate flagstones, plates and old pictures on the walls, china cabinets and a homely mix of tables and chairs. Good value bar food includes chilli con carne or vegetable chilli (£4.25), salads such as fresh salmon or Italian vegetable quiche (from £4.25), half a fresh roast chicken or fisherman's platter (£4.50), steak and onion pie (£4.75), grilled ranbow trout fillets with almonds (£5.25), grilled lamb chops or beef in red wine (£5.95) and steaks (from £7.95); there are also lots of cheaper lunchtime specials such as burgers, pasties or sausage with egg and chips (£1.95), home-made steak or ham and chicken pie, apple and brie quiche, boiled ham, haddock or lasagne (£3.50) and fresh salmon salad or 10oz sirloin steak (from £5.95); get there early for Sunday lunch. Particularly well kept Bass, Felinfoel and Hancocks HB on handpump, farm cider, decent wines; open fires, cribbage and dominoes, unobtrusive piped radio – largely masked by chat. There are some seats out in front, facing a cedar. *(Recommended by Gwyneth and Salvo Spadaro-Dutturi, A J Ritson, Graham and Glenis Watkins; more reports please)*

Free house   Licensees Sylvia Casey and Anthony Lyons   Real ale   Meals and snacks (not Sun evening)   Children in eating area only   Open 11–3, 6–11

Lucky Dip

Besides the fully inspected pubs, you might like to try these Lucky Dips recommended to us and described by readers (if you do, please send us reports):

ANGLESEY
Beaumaris [Castle St; SH6076], *Liverpool Arms*: Comfortable and spacious, well divided into smaller alcoves, friendly and locally popular; bar food inc good fresh crab sandwiches; bedrooms *(R L Nelson, Dr and Mrs J R C Wallace)*
Brynrefail [A5025; SH4887], *Pilot*: Pleasant, well decorated pub close to coast; handy for good walks *(Anon)*
Brynsiencyn [Foel Ferry; SH4867], *Mermaid*: On Menai Straits opp Caernarvon Castle, with spacious bar, good choice of reasonably priced food; outside seats *(W M Elliott, J Crawford)*
Llanddona [4 miles NW of Beaumaris; SH5879], *Owain Glendwr*: Clean and friendly newish pub in old stone building; wide choice of good value bar food, Youngers beer *(Paul and Margaret Baker)*
Menai Bridge [Glyngarth; A545, half way towards Beaumaris; SH5572], *Gazelle*:

Outstanding waterside situation looking across to Snowdonia, steep and aromatic sub-tropical garden behind, lively main bar and smaller rooms off popular with yachtsmen, bar food and restaurants, well kept Robinsons Best and Mild; children allowed away from serving bar; bedrooms comfortable *(Jon Wainwright, E J Waller, LYM)*
Pentraeth [SH5278], *Panton Arms*: Open all day, with wide choice of usual bar food inc children's dishes; bedrooms *(D W Waterhouse)*

CLWYD
Abergele [Market St; SH9578], *Harp*: Quaint old market town pub, once the jail, with good range of bar food, bright and friendly atmosphere, Boddingtons and Higsons real ales *(Mr and Mrs J H Adam)*
Afon Wen [SJ1372], *Pwll Gwyn*: Cheery

and attractive beamed Tudor pub, prettily decorated outside with well tended flowers; pleasant restaurant with good food, particularly steaks; comfortable bedrooms *(Sylvia and Len Henderson)*

Babell [SJ1674], *Black Lion*: Friendly, pleasant pub with warm atmosphere, good lunchtime and evening food, wide range of spirits, decent wine (the beer is keg); in a remote spot, but big car park *(Lord Evans of Claughton)*

Bangor Is y Coed [SJ3945], *Royal Oak*: At foot of the old bridge with pleasant terrace; quiet pub with acceptable food and drink *(Neil and Elspeth Fearn)*

Bodelwyddan [A55 Abergele—St Asaph; SJ0076], *Fanol Fawr*: Handsome recently restored 16th-century manor house with comfortable bar area, good atmosphere, well kept Ruddles, imaginative bar food and separate restaurant; bedrooms — cottage accommodation *(Hugh Geddes)*

Bodfari [A541 — OS Sheet 116 map reference 098702; SJ0970], *Downing Arms*: Friendly and welcoming after long walk; cosy bars, well kept Bass, bar food; on Offa's Dyke Path *(Neil and Anita Christopher)*

☆ Chirk [SJ2938], *Hand*: Plushly furnished connecting bars in clean and spacious Georgian coaching inn, limited choice of decent straightforward food inc fresh sandwiches and children's dishes from buttery bar (not so attractive as main bar area), well kept Marstons Pedigree on handpump, welcoming service, games area in public bar; bedrooms *(Jenny and Brian Seller, Dr and Mrs J R C Wallace, Mr and Mrs J H Adam, Chris Raisin, R L Nelson, Pamela and Merlyn Horswell, LYM)*

Chirk [Chapel Lane — OS Sheet 126 map reference 292377], *Plas-y-Waun*: Large lounge bar and fair range of bar food at reasonable prices *(Neil and Anita Christopher)*; [A5 — OS Sheet 126 map reference 291380], *Stanton*: Small pub with recently extended bar giving added eating area for new kitchens; bedrooms comfortable; good breakfasts *(Neil and Anita Christopher)*

☆ Erbistock [village signposted off A539 W of Overton, then pub signposted; SJ3542], *Boat*: Included for its tables out in a pretty partly terraced garden sharing a sleepy bend of the River Dee with a country church — enchanting on a quiet day, though at busy times in summer cars parking and leaving are a distraction; the pub's mainly given over to food, especially in the big summer dining annee, but there is a pleasant small flagstoned bar (used chiefly by people about to eat in the annee or the beamed dining room, and not always open); children welcome, with half-price helpings *(D W Waterhouse, Neil and Angela Huxter, Laurence Manning, Logan Petch, Brian and Anna Marsden, LYM)*

Ffrith [B5101, just off A541 Wrexham—Mold; SJ2855], *Poachers Cottage*: 18th-century pub, open evenings, concentrating on home cooking — she's Danish, and does some Danish dishes; careful choice of reasonably priced wines *(Anon)*

Froncysyllte [A5 E of Llangollen; SJ2741],

Aqueduct: Fairly basic pub, quite homely and very friendly; good Border Bitter, pool table; good views of aqueduct from garden perched on hill *(Chris Raisin)*

Glyn Ceiriog [SJ2038], *Golden Pheasant*: Comfortable country hotel with superb views; bar has stuffed animals, limited choice of good food inc local trout; imaginative dinners in restaurant; bedrooms *(Mrs J Gittings)*

Graianrhyd [B5430; signposted off A494 and A5104; SJ2156], *Rose & Crown*: Small, bright, cosy country pub, hardworking young licensee, well kept Marstons, good range of bar food inc vegetarian dishes *(Mr and Mrs J H Adam)*

Gwernymynydd [SJ2263], *Plas Hafod*: Fine views, lovely grounds, good Sun lunches in classy dining rooms *(Paula Devlin)*

Halkyn [SJ2172], *Britannia*: 500-year-old former farmhouse with real fire and warm welcome; well kept Lees Bitter on handpump, good bar food inc home-made soups and big bacon and mushroom rolls *(Andy and Jill Kassube)*

☆ Hanmer [SJ4639], *Hanmer Arms*: Good reasonably priced food from sandwiches to steaks, good relaxed pub atmosphere in well kept bar, neat and attractive garden, with church nearby making a pleasant backdrop; pretty village; good sensibly priced and well equipped bedrooms in former courtyard stable block *(Neil and Elspeth Fearn, K H Miller)*

Henllan [B5382 nr Denbigh; SJ0268], *Llindir*: Pleasant pub in beautiful countryside; good range of food; real ale *(Mr and Mrs J H Adam)*

☆ Llanarmon D C [SJ1633], *Hand*: Very civilised country inn in outstanding scenery, well run, with good value food (and imaginative meals in restaurant), quick friendly service, comfortably cushioned chairs and sofas, log fire; bedrooms comfortable — a nice place to stay *(Mr and Mrs A M Campbell, John and Jane Horn, Mr and Mrs B Hibbert, LYM)*

☆ Llanarmon D C, *West Arms*: Under same ownership as the Hand, and as clean, tidy and civilised — though the back bar is a popular and often lively meeting place for people from the surrounding hills; interesting lounge bar inc elaborately carved confessional stall as well as sofas, antique settles and so forth; open fires, good bar food, welcoming friendly staff, peaceful atmosphere, lawn running down to River Ceiriog (where residents of both places can fish free); children welcome in both inns *(Janet Burd, LYM)*

Llanasa [SJ1082], *Red Lion*: Lively village-centre pub with bar, lounge, children's room and restaurant; piano and sing-along in lounge; mini-bus service from Prestatyn to bus-in customers; can be very busy *(P Corris)*

☆ Llandegla [SJ1952], *Crown*: Pleasant, welcoming atmosphere in comfortable olde-worlde pub on Offa's Dyke path, good choice of decent straightforward bar food inc vegetarian dishes, well kept Lees real ale, popular restaurant *(Mr and Mrs J H Adam, KC, Neil and Anita Christopher)*

Llandegla, *Plough*: Attractive, busy pub, good bar food, piped music *(KC)*

☆ **Llanferres** [A494 Mold—Ruthin; SJ1961], *Druid*: Small soberly plush lounge with attractive view over valley from bay window, some oak settles as well as plainer more modern furnishings in bigger saloon which also looks over to the hills; well run, with well kept Burtonwood Best, limited choice of good food inc vegetarian dishes, with emphasis on fresh produce, served in dining room; good walking country; bedrooms well furnished, with wide view (*G T Jones, KC, Dennis Royles, Mr and Mrs J H J Medland, BB*)

Llangedwyn [B4396; SJ1924], *Green*: Country inn in attractive surroundings, with fly-fishing rights on the River Tanat and lovely garden; bright and busy inside, with oak settles and prints; has been popular for real welcome, pleasant service, decent wines and good food in bar and restaurant, but no news since put on market last year (*Mrs J Gittings, Carrie Wright; news please*)

☆ **nr Llangollen** [Horseshoe Pass; A542 N — extreme bottom right corner of OS Sheet 116 at overlap with OS Sheet 117, map reference 200454; SJ2242], *Britannia*: Attractive pub based on 15th-century core, though much extended and comfortably modernised, with good views, generous helpings of good food from soup and ploughman's up in bar and restaurant (inc popular bargain OAPs' meals), pleasant efficient staff; gardens, window boxes and hanging baskets are a fine sight; bedrooms clean and good value (*Mr and Mrs D W Payne, Celia and David Watt, Mr and Mrs E H Warner, P A Crossland, D A Cawley*)

Llangollen [2 miles W; SJ2142], *Chain Bridge*: Part of a substantial hotel, this river bar has a big upstairs window overlooking the rapids on the River Dee (floodlit at night), the Chain Bridge over the river and a renovated station with a steam train service to Llangollen; drinks not cheap (*Carol and Richard Glover*) ; [S of bridge], *Royal*: THF hotel with good restaurant and small, quiet and relaxed bar; fairly smart place, decent beer; bedrooms (*Chris Raisin*); [A539, 200 yds E of bridge (N end)], *Sarah Ponsonbys*: Friendly staff and atmosphere, Border Bitter, good reasonably priced food; big back garden (*Chris Raisin*)

☆ **Llannefydd** [SH9871], *Hawk & Buckle*: Cleanly run and comfortably modernised hill-village inn, decent food; good value bedrooms with remarkable views (*Mrs E M Thompson, LYM*)

Llanrhaeadr ym Mochnant [from Oswestry on B4580, just before bend at junction in village; SJ1326], *Hand*: Interesting 16th-century inn with friendly locals and pleasant service; bedrooms comfortable (*J V Dadswell*)

☆ **Llansannan** [A544 Abergele—Bylchau; SH9466], *Red Lion*: Tiny old-fashioned front parlour with antique furnishings in friendly Welsh-speaking 13th-century hill-village local, other more basic bars; well kept Lees real ale, simple food inc children's dishes — they're welcome; seats in garden; bedrooms (*Andy and Jill Kassube, LYM*)

Llansannan, *Saracens Head*: Pleasant atmosphere in nicely furnished pub with good bar food and well kept Robinsons real ale (*Mr and Mrs J H Adam*)

Nannerch [ST1669], *Cross Foxes*: Fine little village local welcoming visitors, small attractive bar and lounge, photographs of pub football team, Youngers Scotch on handpump, nice fireplace (*Jon Wainwright*)

Northop [SJ2569], *Boot*: Clean and friendly pub with pleasant settles, lots of brass and beams; Greenalls Original, lunchtime bar food (*Neil and Anita Christopher*)

Old Colwyn [Abergele Rd; SH8678], *Plough*: Recently refurbished friendly pub with exceptional service in surroundings which reflect the village's history; local male voice choir occasionally break into song, which adds to the atmosphere; well kept Greenalls, menu limited but good value; small garden (*A J Anderton*)

Pentrefoelas [just off A5 SE of Betws-y-Coed; SH8751], *Giler Arms*: Good value bar food inc good vegetarian pie, Welsh-speaking staff and locals, service good (*KC*)

☆ **Pontblyddyn** [A5104, just S of A541 3 miles SE of Mold — OS Sheet 117 map reference 277602; SJ2761], *New Inn*: Friendly local, plain and unpretentious, with remarkable and genuinely home-made steak and kidney pies served with a jug of gravy — excellent pastry; well kept Watneys-related real ales, darts, juke box and two pool tables upstairs; licensee is trained cooper and will make you a barrel in his cellar workshop (*Alan Kilshaw, J P Berryman*)

Rhescyae [SJ1771], *Miners Arms*: Pleasantly decorated straightforward pub with good food and service; bedrooms (*John Davidson*)

Rhewl [A525 Ruthin—Denbigh; SJ1160], *Drovers Arms*: Intimate, friendly and low-beamed, with good food running up to steaks, inc children's dishes, in three eating areas; good beer, pool room and attractive garden (*Brian and Elaine Skehan*)

☆ **Rhewl** [the other one, off A5 W of Llangollen — OS Sheet 125 map reference 176448; SJ1744], *Sun*: Ancient white-washed pub with two pleasantly furnished rooms, one with a piano; wide range of hot and cold food, friendly landlord, well kept Plassey Farmhouse, small garden; close to Llangollen steam railway, on scenic north side of Dee Valley (*Jon Wainwright, Mr and Mrs Beugge, Andy and Jill Kassube*)

Ruabon [Trevor, off A539 W; SJ2742], *Telford*: Youngers pub on northern side of Pont Cysyllte aqueduct across the Dee; popular with bargers from adjacent canal, attractive views (*Jon Wainwright*)

Trofarth [B5113 S of Colwyn Bay; SH8569], *Holland Arms*: Cosy place with good food (*H Geddes*)

DYFED

Aberaeron [Queen St; SN4462], *Prince of Wales*: Cosy lounge bar with mantlepiece and high shelf display; bar food, restaurant with good fish and Welsh steaks (*Dr Stephen Hiew*)

Aberystwyth [Llanbadarn Fawr, just off A44 E; SN6080], *Black Lion*: Cheerful evening atmosphere in well run local with spacious back lounge, games area, well kept Banks's real ales, good value simple food and

splendid play area in big sheltered garden
with summer evening barbecues *(LYM)*
☆ **Amroth** [SN1607], *New Inn*: Unspoilt
16th-century seafront pub with cushioned
wooden chairs and settles and open fires in
three-roomed beamed bar downstairs,
upstairs lounge bar, separate games room
with pool tables and machines; well kept
Felinfoel, Flowers, Pembrokeshire Benfro
and Tetleys ales, wide choice of bar food inc
local shellfish and children's dishes, no piped
music; picnic-table sets out on grass; holiday
flat to let *(Lyn and Bill Capper, B S Bourne)*
Bosherston [SR9694], *St Govans*:
Straightforward decently run pub with
Worthington on handpump, useful for this
interesting stretch of the coast — the
eponymous hermit's chapel overlooking the
sea is worth getting to, as are the nearby
lilyponds; bar food, piped music, bar
billiards, tables on terrace; nr start
GWG190; bedrooms *(Canon and Mrs G
Hollis, LYM)*
Brynhoffnant [A487 Cardigan—Aberaeron;
SN3351], *Brynhoffnant*: Cheerful and
friendly atmosphere, roaring log fire divides
main bar and dining area during winter,
separate pool room; Bass and Buckleys Best
on handpump and good reasonably priced
bar food *(Sue Holland, Dave Webster)*
Burry Port [Stepney Rd; SN4400], *George*:
Comfortably plush lounge bar with good
range of hot and cold food (not sandwiches),
well kept Buckleys, Felinfoel and
Worthington ales, friendly service, discreet
piped music; nr Pembrey Country Park and
Welsh Motor Sports Centre; bedrooms, also
self-catering *(Lyn and Bill Capper)*
Caio [SN6739], *Brunant Arms*: Good family
atmosphere, reasonably priced home-cooked
food inc home-made bread and wonderful
steak and kidney pies; children welcome
(Diana Jerman)
Cardigan [High St; SN1846], *Black Lion*:
Well kept Flowers ale and quickly served bar
food in spacious rambling lounge of
17th-century inn with stately Georgian
facade; bedrooms *(LYM)*
☆ **Carew** [A4075, just off A477; SN0403],
Carew: Simple welcome in traditionally
furnished country pub with well kept
Worthington, snacks, friendly licensee,
pleasant seats outside and play area;
attractive position near river, tidal watermill
and ruined Norman castle; the Celtic cross
by the pub is 9th-century *(LYM)*
Cenarth [SN2641], *White Hart*:
16th-century pub nr pretty stretch of River
Teifi; central bar and two separate rooms,
simple but pleasant furnishings, Courage
Directors, good bar food generously served
(Joy Heatherley)
Cilycwm [SN7540], *Neuadd Fawr*:
Welcoming Welsh-speaking village pub with
home-made food, simple furnishings,
cheerful atmosphere *(BB)*
Cosheston [SN0004], *Cosheston Brewery*:
Pretty, family-run village pub with well kept
Ind Coope Burton, good imaginative food *(E
O Stephens)*
Croesgoch [A487 Fishguard—St Davids;
SM8230], *Square & Compass*: Good varied
reasonably priced bar food *(E W B and M G
Wauton)*
Cross Inn [B4337/B4577 — not the Cross

Inn near Newport; SN5464], *Rhos yr
Hafod*: Friendly and traditionally furnished
Welsh-speaking country pub with well kept
Flowers IPA, good value specials and
popular upstairs restaurant *(LYM)*
☆ **Cwm Gwaun** [Pontfaen; Cwm Gwaun and
Pontfaen signposted off B4313 E of
Fishguard; SN0035], *Dyffryn Arms*: Basic
rough-and-ready village tavern known
locally as Bessie's, run by same family since
1840 and quite untouched by time — plain
deal furniture, well kept Bass and Ind Coope
Burton served by jug through a hatch,
sandwiches, draughts-boards inlaid into
tables; nr start GWG193 *(Brigid Avison,
LYM)*
Cynwyl Elfed [Llandeilo Rd; SN3727],
Bluebell: Small country local with inglenook
and log-burning stove, bar food *(S Watkins)*
Dinas [A487; SN0139], *Freemasons Arms*:
Traditional cottage-style pub, part of a
terrace, well modernised but keeping cosy
character; good range of good home-cooked
food in big helpings, two dining rooms, open
coal fires, real ale *(Simon and Ann Ward,
Wayne Brindle)*; [A487], *Ship Aground*:
Several rooms opening off servery, sea
pictures and ship's brassware, portholes and
low pitched ceiling give boat feel to long side
gallery, softly lit back room; Felinfoel
Double Dragon on handpump, plain good
value bar food inc children's helpings *(BB)*
Dreenhill [Dale Rd (B4327 2 miles S of
Haverfordwest); SM9214], *Masons Arms*:
Friendly cottage pub where visitors are made
to feel as welcome as locals; well kept Bass,
Courage Directors and Worthington BB
tapped from the cask, simple choice of good
nicely presented food; children welcome
(Keith and Ann Dibble)
Eglwyswrw [A487 Newport—Cardigan, at
junction with B4332; SN1438], *Serjeants*:
Antique high-backed settles in snug if basic
bar with heavy black beams and capacious
inglenook, Worthington BB on handpump,
lounge and dining room — and still a Petty
Sessions court on the premises; promising
reports on friendly and helpful new licensees
— and their food; bedrooms clean and
comfortable *(Rolf Kenton, Mrs Joyce Reid,
LYM)*
Felindre Farchog [A487
Newport—Cardigan; listed in previous
editions under the old spelling of Velindre;
SN1039], *Olde Salutation*: Smart and clean
antiqued pub with cheery barmaid,
comfortable matching seats and tables, real
ale on handpump, good value ploughman's,
restaurant; bedrooms, fishing in nearby
River Nevern; big car park *(Jenny and Brian
Seller)*
Felingwmuchaf [SN5024], *Plough*:
Stone-built country free house with pleasant
atmosphere in period bar with comfortable
banquettes and open fire, very friendly
service; excellent cheeses inc local ones, and
good restaurant dishes inc fresh fish and
game *(Richard and Betty Widder)*
Ffairfach [SN6221], *Torbay*: Busy, popular
free house with jugs, brasses and darts
trophies in spacious heavily beamed
quarry-tiled bar, smaller carpeted lounge;
well kept Buckleys, Flowers and
Worthington, good bar food specialising in
seafood *(Joy Heatherley)*

☆ **Fishguard** [Lower Town; SM9537], *Ship*: Well kept Worthington BB and Dark Mild tapped from the cask in nautically-decorated and dimly lit fisherman's local a stroll from old harbour; good if sometimes smoky atmosphere with a welcome for strangers, homely bar food inc filled rolls (though these may run out very early), friendly licensees, rugby talk; children welcome, with toys provided *(Mr and Mrs Sumner, Dr S Fort, LYM)*

☆ **Fishguard** [24 Main St; A487 just E of central roundabout], *Fishguard Arms*: Friendly welcome in tiny terraced pub with well kept Felinfoel Double Dragon, Marstons Pedigree and Worthington BB served by jug at the unusual elbow-high serving counter; lots of rugby photographs, cheap snacks, open fire, traditional games and impromptu music in back games room *(Dr S Fort, LYM)*

Fishguard [Lower Town], *Dinas Arms*: Straightforward hotel/pub with small but friendly bar, welcoming locals, real ale, good value low-priced ploughman's; bedrooms *(Jenny and Brian Seller)*; [Main St], *Globe*: Copper hull of the Black Fox ship used as bar; two open fires and inglenook, real ale, inexpensive bar food *(Mr and Mrs J R Snook)*; [The Square, Upper Town], *Royal Oak*: Where Irish-American Tate and his army of French ex-convicts attempting to invade Britain during Napoleonic Wars signed total surrender after Jemima Nicholas captured them singlehanded with a pitchfork, in 1797 — they still have the table; military prints and pictures, Felinfoel, Tetleys and Worthington on handpump, good bar food (and back restaurant), tables in garden *(Mr and Mrs Sumner)*

Glanaman [A474; SN6713], *Raven*: Newly decorated dining area divided into bar meal section and smarter restaurant part; good well cooked food, Buckleys Mild and Best, friendly service *(M and J Back)*

Haverfordwest [Hill St; SM9515], *Dragon*: Bright, cheery, welcoming pub, nicely furnished, with good Bass and other beers *(Patrick Godfrey)*

Hundleton [SM9600], *Speculation*: Friendly local, decor gently updated, cheap bar food such as burgers, pies, hot-pots, well kept Felinfoel and Worthington *(A J and M Thomasson)*

Jameston [A4139; SS0599], *Swan Lake*: Well kept Bass and good food in old building with tables outside *(John Davidson, Dave Braisted)*

Lampeter [Bridge St; SN5748], *Kings Head*: Friendly local, popular with students, with a welcome for visitors; good value generous food, several well kept real ales; garden; reasonable bedrooms *(Hugh Lervy)*

☆ **Landshipping** [SN0111], *Stanley Arms*: Attractive riverside pub, surprisingly well appointed, with good value well served bar food inc locally caught salmon and other fish, well kept Worthington tapped from the cask; restaurant *(E W B and M G Wauton)*

Letterston [SM9429], *Harp*: Well produced and served food at reasonable prices; salads imaginative, home-cooked steak and kidney pie excellent *(E W B and M G Wauton)*

Little Haven [in village itself, not St Brides hamlet further W; SM8512], *St Brides*: Neat little cottagey pub a short stroll from the sea, with interesting back well — maybe partly Roman; has been popular for well kept Worthington BB on handpump, spick-and-span housekeeping with gleaming collection of interesting brassware, and enterprising bar food — especially local seafood; but we've had no reports since the Gileses left in 1990; bedrooms *(News please)*

Llandeilo [outside — A40 to Carmarthen; SN6222], *Cottage*: Good value food with quick friendly service; keg beers *(S Watkins)*; [nr centre], *Farmers Arms*: Clean, very friendly pub with nice decor, quick efficient service and good ale; generous helpings of bar food from wide choice *(C and L H Lever)*

Llandybie [6 Llandeilo Rd; SN6115], *Red Lion*: Unusually shaped, comfortable bar with local paintings and photographs for sale; well kept Flowers, wide choice of good bar food inc local salmon and fresh vegetables, enormous Sun lunches, restaurant; bedrooms *(Penny and Gwyn Jones)*

Llangadog [Gwynfe; this is the Llangadog up towards Llandovery; SN7028], *Three Horseshoes*: Lovely spot by stream, pleasant licensees, well kept Flowers and good home-made food *(E Kinnersly)*

☆ **Llangranog** [SN3054], *Pentre Arms*: Nice old historic pub on seafront of beautiful fishing village, with good views from its storm-shuttered windows (some alarming photographs show why the shutters are needed); friendly landlord, well kept Buckleys Best on handpump, well chosen jazz or classical piped music, huge helpings of decent bar food, separate bistro (which may be closed in winter), pool room; residents are lulled to sleep by the sound of waves on the beach *(Lord Evans of Claughton, Sue Holland, Dave Webster)*

☆ **Llangranog**, *Ship*: On edge of beach in same picturesque village; good, fresh home-cooked food, imaginatively prepared, inc tasty vegetarian dishes, real ales, friendly atmosphere — doing well under the two young families who now run it; can get busy summer *(Tim and Ann Newell, Mr and Mrs Nash)*

☆ **Llanwnnen** [B4337 signposted Temple Bar from village, on A475 W of Lampeter; SN5346], *Fish & Anchor*: Snug bar with lots of stripped pine, well kept Greenalls on handpump, reasonable food (not Sun) inc interestingly filled baked potatoes, pretty little country dining room, views from garden with good play area; has been closed Sun; children allowed till 9pm if well behaved *(R J Yates, LYM)*

Llanwnnen [village centre], *Grannell*: Recently refurbished free house, pleasant welcome, lots of local character; real ales, good food in bar and restaurant; good value bedrooms *(Simon and Ann Ward)*

Llanwrda [A482, 2 miles towards Lampeter; SN7131], *Hafod Bridge*: Extensively refurbished old free house with warm welcome, charming lounge, food served all day inc breakfast *(Gwen and Peter Andrews)*

Marloes [OS Sheet 157 map reference 793083; SM7908], *Lobster Pot*: Warm welcome from licensee, big pool table, Felinfoel tapped from the cask and good food inc plenty of fish; at start GWG191

(Gwyneth and Salvo Spadaro-Dutturi)
Myddfai [SN7730], *Plough*: Old, beautifully
kept building in fine hill country; small cosy
bar with big log fire in corner; locals mix
happily with visitors, food good value inc
wide choice of starters (eg mussels),
generous main course and lots of puddings
such as pancakes; games room; bedrooms
(Chris and Robert Marshall)
Newport [East St (A487 on E edge);
SN0539], *Golden Lion*: Generous helpings
of food which can be very good, inc very
fresh fish and superb steak, in seaside-town
inn with interesting stripped-stone bar;
children allowed in eating area and own bar;
bedrooms comfortable for the price,
breakfasts huge *(Philip King, LYM); Black
Lion*: Pleasant bar, generally with wide
range of real ales; most bedrooms have sea
view *(G T Jones)*
Nolton Haven [SM8618], *Mariners*:
18th-century inn overlooking a lovely cove
and serving decent meals; bedrooms *(Dennis
D'Vigne)*
Pantgwyn [B4570 5 miles E of Cardigan —
OS Sheet 145 map reference 241458;
SN2446], *Penllwyn-Du*: New, friendly and
obliging licensees re-establishing traditional
rustic pub with pleasantly carved bar, and
separate cosy lounge; good choice of real
ales on handpump inc Courage Directors,
Wadworths 6X and Worthington BB *(Sue
Holland, Dave Webster)*
Pembroke Ferry [at foot of bridge over
estuary; SM9603], *Ferry*: Nice riverside
setting, with restaurant and Sun carvery; has
been praised for good range of decent bar
food (especially imaginative fresh fish
dishes), friendly helpful service and a
welcome for children, but no recent reports
(News please)
☆ **Pont ar Gothi** [6 miles E of Carmarthen on
A40 Carmarthen—Llandeilo; SN5021],
Salutation: Well converted stone buildings in
unremarkable roadside spot; a friendly
jumble of rooms, with a skilful and efficient
landlord, good snacks and rather pricey but
generous main dishes with fish specialities
inc fresh crab, lobster and sewin; Felinfoel
Double Dragon on handpump; restricted
parking; bedrooms large, breakfasts even
larger *(Anne Morris, Martin Thomas)*
Pont ar Gothi, *Cothi Bridge*: Popular bar
food in comfortable bow-windowed plush
lounge overlooking River Cothi, Courage
ale, restaurant, riverside seats outside;
bedrooms *(LYM)*
Pontarsais [A485 Carmarthen—Lampeter;
SN4428], *Stag & Pheasant*: Roadside pub
with clean, well run bar, relaxing
atmosphere, attentive staff, good food and
restaurant *(K R Harris)*
Ponterwyd [A44 about quarter-mile W of
A4120 junction — OS Sheet 135 map
reference 746806; SN7581], *George
Borrow*: Lounges at front and back of bar
with old copper objects; snooker room, bar
food, restaurant; in fine spot by Eagle Falls
and gorge, so gets lots of summer visitors;
children and dogs welcome *(Dr Stephen
Hiew, BB)*
☆ **nr Ponterwyd** [A44 nearly two miles E of
village — OS Sheet 135 map reference
774817], *Dyffryn Castell*: Good value bar
food in lounge bar and dining room, well

kept Marstons Pedigree, John Smiths and
Worthington BB in unpretentious but
comfortable isolated inn dwarfed by the
mountain slopes sweeping up from it;
children very evidently welcome; bedrooms
clean, comfortable and good value *(Dr
Stephen Hiew, G T Jones, LYM)*
Pontfaen [SN0134], *Gelli Fawr*: In
wonderful setting, mix of pub, hotel,
restaurant and self-catering place, with
18-hour service and family atmosphere;
good value food, well kept Felinfoel,
reasonable wines and comfortable bar;
children welcome; bedrooms good value
(David Eversley)
Rhandirmwyn [SN7843], *Royal Oak*: Good
lively bar with lots of families of walkers
and campers eating — usual bar food
running up to decent steaks; good area for
walks; big bedrooms with superb views —
good value *(Barry and Anne)*
☆ **Rhosmaen** [SN6424], *Plough*:
Deep-cushioned comfort and good value bar
food — especially puddings — in dining
lounge with picture-window views, tiled
front bar and separate restaurant; willing
service *(LYM)*
Saundersfoot [Wogan Terrace; SN1304],
Royal Oak: Good spot just above harbour;
locals' bar and comfortable lounge and
dining room, simply but pleasantly
furnished with banquettes and captain's
chairs; unobtrusive piped music, friendly
and efficient staff, well kept Bass and
Worthington and extensive range of good
bar food from sandwiches, ploughman's and
salads to fresh local crab and steaks *(Joy
Heatherley)*
Solva [OS Sheet 157 map reference 806245;
SM8024], *Ship*: Simple, clean and cosy pub
with freshly decorated low-beamed bar,
popular with locals and visitors; well kept
Bass, Felinfoel Double Dragon and
Worthington, simple bar food generously
served and reasonably priced; close to
harbour *(Joy Heatherley)*
☆ **St Davids** [on rd to Porthclais harbour (and
lifeboat); SM7525], *St Nons*: Hotel, but
original bar well used by locals, with lots of
life and cheery staff; decent food with
generous helpings of vegetables, particularly
well kept Bass and Hancocks HB, good
wines; restaurant area now has its own bar;
jazz Sat; big car park; bedrooms airy and
reasonably priced *(Lord Evans of Claughton,
Mrs M Price)*
St Davids [Goat St; SM7525], *Farmers
Arms*: Smallish genuine pub with shortish
choice of good food, well kept Worthington
BB on handpump, tables in pleasant garden
behind with view of cathedral *(Mr and Mrs
Sumner)*
St Dogmaels [SN1645], *Ferry*: Waterside
family dining pub with interesting range of
bar snacks, attentive staff, Brains Bitter and
SA; restaurant (not Mon) *(Jenny and Brian
Seller, LYM)*
Talybont [SN6589], *Black Lion*: Seats in
sheltered back garden behind substantial
stone village inn with comfortably
modernised back lounge, games in and off
front public bar, bar food and restaurant,
Bass real ale; bedrooms *(LYM); [A487],
White Lion*: Public bar with comfortable
lounge behind, Banks's Mild and Bitter and

Hansons Bitter, wide choice of bar food from sandwiches to steaks, friendly service *(M and J Back)*

☆ Templeton [A478; SN1111], *Boars Head*: Good home-cooked food from filled baked potatoes up at reasonable prices in friendly and appealing family-run local, clean and tidy, with lots of atmosphere, well kept Watneys-related real ales and helpful staff; restaurant; children allowed lunchtime *(Kate Lindsay)*

Trapp [OS Sheet 159 map reference 653189; SN6518], *Cennen Arms*: Three bars served from one glassed-in servery with hatch to lounge; 1950sish decor, simple and comfortable, with friendly staff, decent standard bar food inc Sun roasts; handy for Carreg Cennen Castle and craft centre; small garden and terrace with seats; children welcome *(Michael and Alison Sandy, Keith Walton)*

Tregaron [SN6759], *Talbot*: Olde-worlde hotel bars, but with real pub atmosphere; welcoming staff, well kept beer, well presented food; bedrooms *(Gwyneth and Salvo Spadaro-Dutturi)*

☆ Wolfs Castle [A40 Haverfordwest—Fishguard; SM9526], *Wolfe*: Since our first edition has been a popular main entry, reliable for consistently good value food from sandwiches up, in neat red-carpeted lounge, garden room and conservatory-restaurant, with well kept Felinfoel Double Dragon on handpump, games in public bar and tables outside; the Neumanns who've run it all that time have now retired, and though recent reports show that staff are still friendly and helpful it's too soon to say whether the food is measuring up to past standards; children welcome, one twin bedroom; closed Mon lunchtime Sept–Whitsun *(E W B and M G Wauton, Mr and Mrs Sumner, M Badcock; more reports please)*

GLAMORGAN — MID

Bryncethin [SS9184], *Masons Arms*: Pleasant spot, well kept Brains, wide choice of bar food with good, popular sandwiches *(Helen and John Thompson)*

☆ nr Caerphilly [Watford; nr M4 junction 30 via mountain rd from Tongwynlais and Bwlch-y-Cwm — OS Sheet 171 map reference 144846], *Black Cock*: Neat and comfortable blue-plush bar with particularly well kept Bass, good value bar lunches inc very cheap chippy snacks as well as gammon and eggs, well mixed grill, specials such as roast lamb and so forth; sizeable terracd garden among trees with play area and barbecue, restaurant, open fire in pretty tiled fireplace; up in the hills, just below Caerphilly Common *(Dr A P M Coxon, BB)*

Laleston [SS8780], *Oyster Catcher*: Good food, especially fish — as it's freshly prepared can take over half an hour to come; low prices mean it gets very popular — must book Fri/Sat/Sun *(John and Helen Thompson)*

Llangeinor [SS9187], *Llangeinor Arms*: Remote hill-top pub by church with excellent Bristol Channel view from conservatory; two bars with fine collection of antique artefacts and porcelain; real fires, choice of real ales, decent bar food with adjacent 15th-century restaurant; good walks nearby *(John and Helen Thompson)*

Merthyr Tydfil [SO0709], *Crown*: Good food pleasantly served in huge helpings by helpful chef, well kept Flowers on handpump, welcoming to strangers *(J F Thorndike)*

Miskin [quite near M4 junction 34; ST0481], *Miskin Arms*: Warm welcome, and locals are friendly towards strangers; good value bar food such as good steak and kidney pie *(Cathy Long)*

Pen y Fai [SS8982], *Pheasant*: Large, comfortable pub with good atmosphere and welcoming staff; Courage Best and Directors on handpump and popular range of lunchtime bar food inc traditional puddings such as jam roly-poly and spotted dick *(John and Helen Thompson)*

Pontlottyn [just S of Rhymney; SO1105], *Blast Furnace*: Big comfortable two-level room with good value food inc home-made steak and kidney pie and scampi; keg beers; at one end there's a pool table, darts and TV; open all day Sat *(Roger Huggins)*

Pontneddfechan [SN9007], *Old White Horse*: Small pub with Brains SA and good cheap bar food *(Pamela and Merlyn Horswell)*

☆ Rudry, [ST1986], *Maenllwyd*: Comfortably furnished traditional lounge in low-beamed Tudor pub with well kept Youngers IPA, polite service, popular bar food, spacious more recent restaurant extension with midnight supper licence; Sun lunchtimes is popular with the horsey set; children allowed in some areas *(Gwyneth and Salvo Spadaro-Dutturi, LYM)*

Treharris [Quakers Yard; over bridge off A4054 Merthyr Tydfil—Ystrad Mynach; ST0997], *Clantaff*: Clean and welcoming with low ceilings, highly polished tables and brocaded chairs, mining-history plaques around the walls; good generously served bar food such as curry and lasagne *(John and Bridget Dean)*

GLAMORGAN — SOUTH

Cardiff [nr Howells dept store], *Cottage*: Well laid out city-centre pub with well kept Brains Dark and SA at reasonable prices and particularly good lunchtime food such as curry, steak pie, lasagne, ploughman's and salads *(John Thorndike);* [Wharton St], *Glassworks*: Tremendous place rather like French brasserie with pleasant bar area, real ale and good range of bar snacks and restaurant meals *(Geoff Wilson);* [Custom House St], *Golden Cross*: Victorian pub carefully and expensively restored by Brains, and now a show-piece of conservation; much ornate tilework inside and out, cast-iron tables and fireplace, glittering glass, glossy woodwork and scrubbed floors; friendly licensees, Brains real ales and lunchtime bar food — all main dishes home-made; live music Thurs *(Anon)* [Church St], *Old Arcade*: Classic traditional Brains pub, well renovated with plenty of atmosphere, lots of rugby mementoes (less than 300 yds from Arms Park), well kept Brains Dark, Bitter and SA, big helpings of decent bar

food; wide range of customers from students and market traders to lunchtime businessmen; open all day, but back lounge may be closed late afternoon *(Michael Cochrane, A J Ritson)*; [St Marys St], *Philharmonic*: Extraordinary take-us-as-you-find-us place that has remained unchanged over the years — dark, old-fashioned and atmospheric, with high stools and bar-height tables in centre of bar, standard tables and chairs along the walls; good beer — especially Brains SA — and wonderful cheese (a full half pound and half a loaf); a pity about the loud music *(Richard Dolphin, Michael and Alison Sandy)*; [Westgate St], *Queens Vaults*: Old-fashioned city-centre pub with square central bar serving Allied real ales *(Dave Braisted)*; [Newport Rd, Roath], *Royal Oak*: Large Victorian pub with public bar of unspoilt character and many sporting mementoes going back to the turn of the century; noisy, smoky and busy but informal and friendly — to our knowledge the only Brains tied house with SA tapped straight from the cask *(Dr A P M Coxon)*
Craig Penllyn [SS9777], *Barley Mow*: Good value bar meals inc home-made steak and kidney or steak and mushroom pie *(Cathy Long)*
☆ **Dinas Powis**, [Station Rd; ST1571], *Star*: Well decorated and efficiently run village pub with stripped stone walls or panelling and heavy Elizabethan beams; eating areas, two with welcoming fires, and a no-smoking room; friendly licensees, good bar food, well kept Brains ales *(Mrs E P Hird, LYM)*
☆ **nr Lisvane**, [follow Mill Rd into Graig Rd, then keep on; ST1883], *Ty Mawr Arms*: Country pub with three sizeable and comfortable rooms, one with good log fire; good lunchtime food (not Sun), unusually good monthly-changing choice of real ales such as Butcombe, Hook Norton, Robinsons and Smiles, all well kept; friendly service, restaurant, big attractive garden with patrolling ducks and even peacocks and spectacular view over Cardiff to the Severn Estuary — ideal for children *(Michael Cochrane, Tony Ritson, LYM)*
☆ **Llancadle** [village signed off B4265 Barry—Llantwit just E of St Athan — OS Sheet 170 map reference 038685; ST0368], *Green Dragon*: Thatched pub with interesting high-raftered stripped-stone main bar, enterprising choice of spirits, formidable foreign bottled beers, and several guest beers alongside well kept Courage Best and Directors and John Smiths; lots of bric-a-brac; good bar food (not Mon or Sun evenings), tables outside; squeezed out of the main entries this year by a lack of recent reports, but well worth knowing *(Patrick and Mary McDermott, LYM)*
☆ **Llancarfan**, [signposted from A4226; can also be reached from A48 from Bonvilston or B4265 via Llancadle; ST0570], *Fox & Hounds*: Locally popular for attractively presented reasonably priced food (though some things on menu may not be available) and well kept Brains, Felinfoel Double Dragon, Wadworths 6X and a guest beer, in rambling and comfortable bar; good Sun lunch, tables out on terrace in pretty surroundings; children in eating area *(Patrick and Mary McDermott, LYM)*

☆ **Monknash**, [follow Marcross, Broughton signpost off B4265 St Brides Major—Llantwit Major, turn left at end of Water St — OS Sheet 170 map reference 920706; SS9270], *Plough & Harrow*: Unspoilt and untouched isolated country pub, very basic — flagstones, old-fashioned stripped settles, logs burning in cavernous fireplace with huge side bread oven, good value plain food inc filled granary rolls, Flowers IPA and Original and Marstons Pedigree on handpump; pool, juke box and fruit machine in room on left, picnic-table sets on grass outside the white cottage; nr start GWG195 *(Gwyneth and Salvo Spadaro-Dutturi, Cathy Long, BB)*
☆ **Morganstown**, [Ty Nant Rd (not far from M4 junction 32); ST1281], *Ty Nant*: Exceptionally well run and usually busy, with beamed lounge and popular basic bar; consistently well kept real ale, pool table, generous helpings of usual bar food, seats outside *(Dr A P M Coxon)*
Moulton [ST0770], *Three Horseshoes*: Comfortably refurbished old pub, banquettes and upholstered chairs around tables in carpeted lounge, Bass, Batemans, Hancocks HB and Worthington on handpump, nice restaurant up steps from lounge; wide choice of hot and cold bar food, though no sandwiches or ploughman's, reasonable prices — and free help-yourself coffee; children's play area behind *(Lyn and Bill Capper)*
Porthcawl [Newton; SS7277], *Jolly Sailor*: Friendly pub with collection of nautical hardware, well kept Brains beer, good atmosphere and straightforward bar food *(P L Duncan)*
☆ **Sigingstone**, [SS9771], *Victoria*: Beautifully kept pub with antiques, fresh flowers, fast service and very good reasonably priced bar food; out of the way, but always busy *(Vera Davies, Cathy Long)*
☆ **St Hilary**, [ST0173], *Bush*: Thatched village pub nestling behind church, old settles in traditional flagstoned public bar, comfortable low-beamed lounge with warm atmosphere, well kept Bass, Hancocks and Worthington, generous helpings of good bar food inc some Welsh dishes such as laverbread with bacon and boiled ham with parsley sauce, cheerful service, restaurant with long menu in Welsh and English — worth booking weekends *(Pamela and Merlyn Horswell, G T Rhys, D S Morgan, LYM)*
St Mellons [A48; TT2281], *Fox & Hounds*: Well kept clean Brains pub with friendly service and good value bar meals *(Vera Davies)*
Tongwynlais [Merthyr Rd (A4054); ST1482], *Old Ton*: Friendly pub with good Whitbreads beer, under the shadow of Castell Coch *(Tony and Louise Clarke)*

GLAMORGAN — WEST
Alltwen [Alltwen Hill; SN7203], *Butchers Arms*: Comfortable, friendly pub with imaginative food from simple but well cooked menu — not the usual; beers very well kept, with two or three guest ales *(K Shearer)*

Gowerton [by traffic lights junction B4296/B4295; SS5896], *Welcome*: Spacious pub with cheery atmosphere and lots of comfortable plush seats; well kept Buckleys, good value generous bar food with some imaginative dishes, restaurant *(Michael and Alison Sandy)*

Killay [Gower Rd; SS6092], *Commercial*: Comfortably refurbished, pleasant atmosphere, real ales, piped music, good range of reasonably priced bar food *(E J Knight)*

Kittle [SS5789], *Beaufort Arms*: Busy, interesting pub on two levels (nice character on lower level); occasional live music; standard food, quick friendly service *(M Saunders, S Watkins)*

Llangyfelach [B4489 just S of M4 junction 46; SS6498], *Plough & Harrow*: Smoothly comfortable modernised lounge bar with big helpings from food counter, well kept Courage Best and Directors and John Smiths on handpump *(Michael and Alison Sandy, LYM)*

Llanrhidian [SS4992], *Welcome to Town*: Recently refurbished, with open-plan plush seating, piped music and fruit machine; good food, well kept Youngers IPA, friendly service, and lovely position on green which looks down to the marshy foreshore of the Loughor Estuary and its endless cockle sands *(BHP, LYM)*

Mumbles [Newton Rd, Oystermouth; SS6287], *White Rose*: Large and well organised; cheap bar food promptly served *(Pamela and Merlyn Horswell, Michael and Alison Sandy)*

☆ **Oldwalls**, [SS4891], *Greyhound*: Dark-panelled comfortable lounge bar, plenty of tables and well kept Bass, Hancocks HB and interesting guest beers such as Robinsons Old Tom and Wadworths 6X, reasonably priced bar food; further bar, and restaurant very popular at weekends for generous helpings of good local fish such as bass, baby turbot, pollack, grey mullet, flounder, hake, and mussel salad; good coal fire; can get very busy; big tree-shaded garden with pensioned-off tractor and other play objects *(Pamela and Merlyn Horswell, Michael and Alison Sandy, Gwynne Harper)*

☆ **Parkmill** [SS5489], *Gower*: Large, light and airy well organised pub with art deco interior, plenty of tables and wide choice of reasonably priced above-average food inc lasagne, sweet and sour pork, beef carbonade and choice of vegetarian dishes; welcoming service, open Sun evenings in winter too; big car park *(M Saunders, A G Roby, BHP)*

Penclawdd [Berthlwyd; B4295 towards Gowerton; SS5495], *Berthlwyd*: Large, plush, smartly refurbished pub popular with wide range of age groups, giving fine views across Loughor estuary; Courage Best, John Smiths and Felinfoel, attentive staff; open-plan with banquettes around walls at one end, restaurant area at other; some picnic-table sets on lawn by road *(Michael and Alison Sandy)*

Port Talbot [Margam Rd; (A48, nr M4 junction 38); SS7690], *Twelve Knights*: Very spacious and comfortable, with good value home-made hot dishes and well kept Bass; big car park *(Christopher and Heather Barton)*

☆ **Swansea** [Kingsway; SS6593], *Hanbury*: Congenial atmosphere — feels like an old town pub despite post-war development around; very popular for good choice of good value lunchtime food, plenty of dark wood, pictures of old Swansea, showy Edwardian-style lampshades, lots of tables; Watneys beers well kept; full of shoppers *(Michael and Alison Sandy, F E M Hardy)*

Swansea [10 The Strand], *Exchange*: Guineafowl stuffed with cream cheese and a lime and leek sauce, rack of lamb with redcurrant sauce, kiwi fruit and cointreau pudding; good choice of bottled continental lagers, Welsh Brewers beers *(R Johnstone)*

GWENT

☆ **Abergavenny** [Raglan Rd, Hardwick; B4598 (old A40), 2 miles E; SO3212], *Horse & Jockey*: Pleasant, clean and well furnished with good staff and wide range of popualr good value pub food; well kept Bass *(K R Harris, Pamela and Merlyn Horswell, John and Joan Nash)*

Abergavenny [SO3014], *Greyhound*: More of a pub at lunchtime, more restaurant in the evening; very industrious owners, keen to please; good food *(Pamela and Merlyn Horswell)*; [Flannel St], *Hen & Chickens*: Unspoilt pub with friendly atmosphere, good Bass; good food; children welcome at lunchtime *(Gwyneth and Salvo Spadaro-Dutturi)*; [The Bryn; B4598 (old A40), 3 miles SE; SO3310], *King of Prussia*: Two large, warm, clean bars, busy friendly atmosphere, well kept beer inc Courage on handpump, enjoyable food in separate dining area; good car park *(Col D G Stafford)*; [well out on Brecon Rd (A40)], *Lamb & Flag*: Newish very welcoming country pub, overlooked by Sugar Loaf Mountain and at the very north of Gwent, a few miles from Powys; full range of well kept Brains beers, restaurant bright and airy — set Sun lunch well cooked and presented by friendly staff; bedrooms *(Michel Hooper-Immins)*; [Brecon Rd], *Station*: A real pub with few frills but well kept Bass, Brains SA, Davenports and Ushers; plain wood tables, stools, no carpets; lots of locals, good atmosphere, darts *(Gwyneth and Salvo Spadaro-Dutturi)*

Bassaleg [handy for M4 junction 28; A468 towards Caerphilly; ST2786], *Rupperra Arms*: Small, genuine local with welcoming atmosphere and unpretentious food such as filled baked potatoes and home-made chicken and ham pies; decent beer *(R C Morgan)*

Bryngwyn [off old A40 W of Raglan; SO3909], *Cripple Creek*: Good and friendly, popular with locals; small, separate restaurant with decent straightforward food *(Col G D Stafford)*

Caerleon [ST3490], *Bell*: Pleasant and well organised with above-average food and good landlord *(Pamela and Merlyn Horswell)*

Cross Ash [B4521 E of Abergavenny; SO4119], *Three Salmons*: Small, warm and friendly, with a nice locals' corner, good varied menu and several guest beers introduced by new owners (Graham and Glenis Watkins)

☆ **Grosmont**, [SO4024], *Angel*: Carefully modernised 17th-century village local with friendly landlord, reasonably priced straightforward home-cooked food from sandwiches to steaks, hospitable licensees, well kept Buckleys Best and Crown 1041 on handpump, pool table; nice to sit out in the attractive steep single street, next to ancient market hall and nr attractive church; no children; bedrooms (Brian and Anna Marsden, BB)

☆ **nr Grosmont**, [B4347 N — OS Sheet 161 map reference 408254], *Cupids Hill*: Tiny homely pub, alone on very steep hill in pretty countryside; a quaint survivor — not at all olde-worlde, just basic and homely; bottled beers only (stood on sawn-off former bagatelle table with plyboard top), plain old settles by fire, low white ceiling; table skittles, dominoes, cribbage (BB)

Llandogo [SO5204], *Old Farmhouse*: Lovely Wye Valley setting, several bars, pool tables; delicious food inc home-made rolls with good friendly table service in pretty dining room; motel accommodation (Mrs A Sheard); *Sloop*: Welcoming pub with very pleasant landlord; Buckleys, Smiles and Wadworths beers on handpump, and good interesting bar food inc good value Sun lunches; children welcome; bedrooms (Gwyneth and Salvo Spadaro-Dutturi, Tim and Ann Newell)

Llanfihangel Crucorney [village signposted off A465; SO3321], *Skirrid*: Interesting and palpably ancient building, among the oldest pubs in Britain, with parts dating from 1110 — and formerly where sheep stealers were hanged; now a dining pub, with Courage real ales (Neil and Anita Christopher, Cliff and Karen Spooner, John Honnor, LYM)

☆ **Llangwm**, [B4235 S of Raglan; SO4200], *Bridge*: Relaxed atmosphere in well run pub, varnished pews in bright and airy dining extension with very wide choice of good enterprising food, at a price; well kept Bass in separate pubbier bar with beams, nooks, crannies and traditional furnishings; has been closed Sun evening and Mon lunchtime; children in dining area (Gwyneth and Salvo Spadaro-Dutturi, LYM)

Llanishen [SO4803], *Carpenters Arms*: Genuinely warm welcome, relaxing atmosphere, unobtrusive refurbishments, real fire and pool table; guest beers such as Bass and Hook Norton or Brains SA and Robinsons tapped from the cask as well as Brains Dark and Buckleys, good generous food inc Sun lunch, good service, unspoilt location; small garden; children welcome; comfortable bedrooms (Gwyneth and Salvo Spadaro-Dutturi)

☆ **Llantarnam** [Newport Rd; (A4042 N of M4 junction 26); ST3093], *Greenhouse*: Fine old spacious pub with Courage Best, Directors and John Smiths on handpump and exceptionally wide choice of good if not cheap bar food, served quite quickly; good garden and play area (P Corris, C M J Barton)

☆ **Llantilio Crosseny**, [SO3915], *Hostry*: 15th-century beamed pub (one of oldest in Gwent, though with recent extension), in pretty village; welcoming staff, well kept Bass and Smiles, good choice of

home-cooked bar food inc vegetarian dishes, log fire; children allowed in lounge; bedrooms comfortable (Gwyneth and Salvo Spadaro-Dutturi, Neil Christopher)

Llantrisant [Cardiff Rd, Southgate; ST3997], *Pennyfarthing*: Interesting mix of mock Victorian and Edwardian, but tastefully done; something for everyone (Tony and Louise Clarke)

Llanvetherine [B4521 ENE of Abergavenny; SO3617], *Kings Arms*: Delightful black and white 17th-century coaching inn, rather like a French country eating place; good Bass and Hook Norton ales and farm ciders, very good bar snacks, small restaurant area (good value Sun lunch); licensees and staff very obliging; garden with next-door caravan site; good walking country; children welcome (Gwyneth and Salvo Spadaro-Dutturi)

Llanvihangel Gobion [A40 on Usk turning, about 3 1/2 miles from Abergavenny; SO3509], *Chart House*: Smoothly modernised and relaxing pub doing well under current regime, good food in bar and popular restaurant, distant hill views (Pamela and Merlyn Horswell, BB)

☆ **Mamhilad** [3/4 mile N — OS Sheet 171 map reference 308047; SO3004], *Horseshoe*: Pleasant bar with well kept Brains and Felinfoel, lots of malt whiskies, friendly landlord, well cooked and plentiful straightforward inexpensive food, good service and lovely views, particularly from tables by car park over road (Robert and Kate Hodkinson, Gwyneth and Salvo Spadaro-Dutturi)

Mamhilad, *Star*: Quiet pub with obliging licensees, interesting menu — and they'll do you something else if you want it (Pamela and Merlyn Horswell)

Michaelston y Fedw [a mile off A48 at Castleton; ST2484], *Cefn Mably Arms*: Tastefully refurbished pub in attractive village setting, with two bars, warm welcome, well kept Tetleys, good service and food from bar snacks to Sun lunch; restaurant, garden (Margaret and Bill Rogers, Gwyneth and Salvo Spadaro-Dutturi)

☆ **Monkswood**, [SO3503], *Beaufort Arms*: Notable for outstanding food changing daily, inc delicious unusual soups, fresh seafood, game, good choice of vegetarian dishes and puddings; welcoming atmosphere, well kept Courage Directors and Best tapped from the cask, decent wines — even its own cricket pitch; must book Fri/Sat (Gwyneth and Salvo Spadaro-Dutturi, David Gittins)

Monmouth, [Agincourt Sq; SO5113], *Kings Head*: Period building with comfortable bedrooms, which has been popular for open, inviting atmosphere, flowers everywhere, good food in upmarket dining room with attentive service, decent wines, but no recent reports (News please); [The Narth], *Trekkers*: Good home-cooked reasonably priced food served in friendly atmosphere (Jeffrey Hill)

Parkhouse [SO5003], *Parkhouse*: Small, comfortable village pub away from tourist route; two bars, small restaurant, and particularly generous standard food from ploughman's with four different cheeses (Dr John Innes)

Penallt [SO5211], *Boat*: Though it is just inside the Welsh border, we list this fine pub under Redbrook, in the Gloucs section

Raglan [SO4108], *Beaufort Arms*: Pleasant atmosphere in comfortable and roomy hotel bars with piped music, well kept Courage and John Smiths, bar food, good restaurant, helpful and obliging service; children welcome *(Christopher and Heather Barton)*

Rogerstone [ST2688], *Rising Sun*: Comfortably modernised with attractive eating area in conservatory; good value lunchtime and evening bar food; children's room downstairs, outside play area *(Penny and Gwyn Jones)*; [Cefn Rd; nr junction 27 of M4], *Tredegar Arms*: Rather unexpected for the area, with low beams, good food, really friendly hospitality and real ale *(Dr and Mrs A K Clarke)*

☆ Shirenewton, [in village signposted off B4235 just W of Chepstow; ST4893], *Tredegar Arms*: Usual reasonably priced bar food, well kept Hancocks PA, Smiles, Wadworths 6X and guest beers, good choice of malt whiskies, jolly landlady, plenty of brass and chintz; games in public bar, seats outside; children in eating area; good value bedrooms *(Joy Heatherley, Jenny and Brian Seller, C G A Kearney, John and Tessa Rainsford, LYM)*

Shirenewton [on B4235 Chepstow—Usk; ST4893], *Carpenters Arms*: Lots of little rooms, warm and welcoming, good food, wide range of well kept beers inc Bass and Marstons *(Graham and Glenis Watkins)*; *Tan House*: Old tannery with stone walls and beams, warm welcome, well kept beer and good range of well cooked food *(Charles Bardswell)*

St Brides Wentlooge [ST2982], *Church House*: Friendly and informal country pub, interesting tables with old pennies inlaid, well kept Brains Bitter, Dark and SA, cheap, simple bar food (not Sun) and unobtrusive piped music; garden and play area *(Mel and Phil Lloyd, A J Ritson)*; [Beach Rd], *Lighthouse*: Recently refurbished with distinct nautical theme — most of the paintings and fixtures are original, and it doesn't feel newly decorated; spacious lounge with open fire, very good atmosphere, good bar food all week from sandwiches up inc good sweet pancakes, Allied real ales, good service, upstairs restaurant with polished floorboards and nets and so forth hanging from ceiling; very friendly, some entertainment *(J M Fletcher)*

Talycoed [B4233 Monmouth—Abergavenny; SO4115], *Halfway House*: Good straightforward food (not Sun evening) under new licensees, with excellent atmosphere in this polished country pub *(PB, HB)*

☆ Tintern [Devauden Rd; off A446; SO5301], *Cherry Tree*: Unspoilt genuine pub in pretty spot, pleasant licensee, good Hancocks PA and cider tapped from cask; children welcome *(Gwyneth and Salvo Spadaro-Dutturi, PB, HB)*

Tintern [A466 Chepstow—Monmouth], *Moon & Sixpence*: Spotlessly clean, beautifully furnished and stylish (not a place for muddy boots), with well kept Butcombe, friendly service and real, not frozen chips *(John and Pat Smyth, WHBM)*

☆ Trelleck, [B4293 6 miles S of Monmouth; SO5005], *Lion*: Quiet and unpretentious country pub with unusually good and reasonably priced food in pleasant lounge bar *(J F and M Sayers)*

Usk [The Square; SO3801], *Castle*: Friendly pub with good food inc tasty steak and kidney pie, pleasant back garden with children's swing *(Curt and Lois Stevens)*; [Old Market St], *Kings Head*: Interesting food, real ale and decent lounge; bedrooms *(Pamela and Merlyn Horswell)*

GWYNEDD

☆ Aberdovey, [opp Penhelig rly stn; SN6296], *Penhelig Arms*: Carefully refurbished building in fine position overlooking sea, doing well under current regime, with cosy bar, good home cooking and well kept Burton; bedrooms good *(A J Billingham)*

☆ Aberdovey, *Britannia*: Well kept Bass, good bar food and superb view over Dovey estuary to mountains of N Cardigan, with balcony open in summer; hard to imagine a better situation; good food *(Dave Braisted)*

Abergynolwyn [SH6807], *Railway*: Straightforward pub with friendly staff, well kept Tetleys tapped from the cask, good home-prepared food; in tiny ex-mining village in beautiful countryside, convenient for Tal-y-Llyn Railway

Bala [High St; SH9336], *Olde Bulls Head*: Food and Whitbreads real ale in comfortably refurbished bar of oldest inn here; bedrooms *(LYM)*

Bangor [Garth Rd, nr pier; SH5973], *Union*: Multi-roomed pub close to pier and full of nautical bric-a-brac; mixture of Welsh and English speaking customers, good bar meals and snacks, well kept Burtonwood and good service *(Jon Wainwright)*

☆ Beddgelert, [SH5948], *Prince Llewelyn*: Quietly civilised plush hotel bar with raised dining area, simpler summer bar, good value bar food, straightforward but prepared with real care, well kept Robinsons, cheerful and helpful staff, rustic seats on verandah overlooking village stream and hills; nr GWG206; gets busy at peak holiday times; children if eating when not too busy; bedrooms pleasant, with good breakfasts *(Michael and Alison Sandy, Rt Revd D R Feaver, R L Nelson, Drs G N and M G Yates)*

Beddgelert [SH5948], *Tanronen*: Simply furnished main bar, small but pleasant separate lounge bar, well kept Robinsons real ale, decent straightforward bar food inc good value weekly specials and puddings; not a great deal of atmosphere, but friendly, and used by locals as well as tourists; nr GWG206; bedrooms simple but clean — good value *(Michael and Alison Sandy, N P Cox, Gordon Theaker, BB)*

Bethesda [A5; SH6367], *Douglas Arms*: Largish multi-roomed pub with imposing entrance; totally unspoilt but pleasantly furnished; eccentric — everything still priced in old money, though prices have kept up with inflation, eg well kept Marstons Pedigree 19/6; staff feign indignation when asked to translate into modern currency; bar snacks *(W P P Clarke)*

Betws-y-Coed [A5 next to BP garage and Little Chef; SH7956], *Waterloo*: Large, comfortable bar, efficient service, wide choice of consistent bar food inc good salads and local trout; easy parking; bedrooms *(KC)*

Bronaber [A470 Dolgellau—Trawsfynydd; SH7132], *Rhiw-goch*: Old manor house in grounds of old military camp, with ski slope; big dining room with full menu, real ales, food all year; good value, beautiful Snowdonia views; bedrooms in log cabins *(Mr and Mrs J R Snook)*

☆ **Capel Garmon**, [signed from A470 just outside Betwys-y-Coed, towards Llanrwst; SH8255], *White Horse*: Comfortable and cosy, with very friendly homely atmosphere, magnificent views, good value simple home-made food, pleasant staff; in delightful countryside; bedrooms very reasonably priced and well equipped — marvellous breakfast *(KC)*

Conwy [High St; SH7878], *Castle*: Bar in THF hotel, well used by locals; well kept real ales, decent house wines, welcoming staff who deserve top marks for their help to disabled people; interesting building (said to be haunted) with paintings dating to 1800, and parts dating to 1400; good lunchtime bar food *(Michael Bechley)*

☆ **Corris**, [village signposted off A487 Machynlleth—Dolgellau; SH7608], *Slaters Arms*: Reliably good Banks's Bitter and Mild at attractive prices in classic welcoming local with high-backed antique settles and lots of character; open fire in slate inglenook, good value simple bar food, friendly service; interesting ex-slate-mining village, with railway museum and nearby forest walks *(Dr M Owton, LYM)*

Deganwy [SH7880], *Deganwy Castle*: Plushly comfortable lounge in big hotel with fine views, pleasantly pubby rambling back bar with fat black beams, stripped stone, flagstones and lots of nooks and crannies; good choice of bar food, well kept Watneys-related real ales on handpump; bedrooms *(LYM)*

Dinas Mawddwy [SH8615], *Llew Coch*: Traditionally furnished village inn with hundreds of sparkling horse brasses, food inc trout or salmon from River Dovey just behind; well kept Bass and lively Sat evening music; surrounded by plunging fir forests *(LYM)*

Fairbourne [SH6213], *Fairbourne*: Neatly kept and quite spacious bar that would be a credit to many big city suburbs, well kept Bass and McEwans real ale, maybe fudge pork scratchings; grey stone hotel in holiday village near sea; bedrooms *(BB)*

☆ **Ganllwyd**, [SH7224], *Tyn-y-Groes*: 16th-century Snowdonia inn owned by National Trust, oak beams, appropriate furniture, log fires, snug atmosphere, bar food, Victorian restaurant, lots of malt whiskies, good service; fine forest views, salmon and seatrout fishing, sun lounge; bedrooms comfortable *(Kenneth Bowden, LYM)*

☆ **Llanbedrog** [Bryn-y-Gro (B4413); SH3332], *Ship*: Extensively refurbished friendly local with well kept Burtonwood Mild and JBA, lively simple family lounge, good range of popular straightforward food; pretty in summer, with lots of hanging baskets, window boxes and good outside seating area; dry on Sun *(Tim and Lynne Crawford, N P Cox, LYM)*

Llanbedrog *Glyn-y-Weddw*: Good pub with terrace and garden; good variety of food served efficiently and courteously; pleasant atmosphere *(Kit Read)*

☆ **Llandudno**, [Old St; SH7883], *Kings Head*: Friendly and spacious open-plan bar with variety of areas inc bistro-style part for huge range of good food, not cheap but with many dishes unusual for such an otherwise traditional pub; well kept Tetleys and Ind Coope Burton, pool area, interesting position by Great Orme Tramway station *(Richard Fawcett, P A Crossland, D A Cawley, Miss G Matthews, Prof S Barnett)*

Llandudno [West Shore], *Gogarth Abbey*: Fine views across bay to Puffin Island and Anglesey, bar food, open fire, morning coffee, afternoon teas, restaurant, waitress service; bedrooms *(Graham Gibson)*; [Mostyn St], *London*: Good welcoming local with lots of bric-a-brac, Burtonwood Mild and Bitter on handpump, lunchtime bar food (evenings too in high summer), quiz nights, folk music and fancy dress competitions; bedrooms *(Graham Gibson, P A Crossland, D A Cawley)*

Maentwrog [SH6741], *Oakley Arms*: Very roomy even on Sat night; staff pleasant, service excellent, good value standard food *(KC)*

☆ **Porthmadog**, [Lombard St; SH5639], *Ship*: Attractively renovated old local with generally welcoming landlord and regulars, huge open fireplace and comfortable seats in lounge, several well kept real ales inc their fine own-brew Pencai, efficient staff, wide choice of good generous and genuine lunchtime food, well appointed and popular upstairs evening restaurant; pool table in comfortable public bar; children's room *(R L Nelson, Gordon Theaker, John Towers, Anthony Niner, P A Crossland, D A Cawley)*

Rhyd Ddu [A4085 N of Beddgelert; SH5753], *Cwellyn Arms*: Lively stone-built pub with fine Snowdon views and good value food; log fires, friendly staff, a welcome for walkers and children, restaurant, garden with barbecue *(J Windle, Gordon Theaker,)*

Rhydclafdy [SH3235], *Tu Hwnt I'r Afon*: Charming building in pleasant countryside off the main routes, comfortable inside, with friendly landlord, well kept Whitbreads Castle Eden, wide choice of well presented inexpensive bar food *(R L Nelson)*

Tal y Bont [B5106 6 miles S of Conwy, towards Llanrwst; SH7669], *Y Bedol*: Well kept and friendly Vale of Conwy village local, dark beams, winter open fire, well kept Tetleys on handpump, odd little TV room *(Jon Wainwright, BB)*

Tal y Cafn [A470 Conway—Llanrwst; SH7972], *Tal y Cafn*: Handy for Bodnant Gardens, cheerful and comfortable lounge bar with big inglenook, simple but good value bar food from sandwiches up, Greenalls on handpump, seats in spacious garden *(KC, LYM)*

Talsarnau [SH6236], *Caerffynon Hall*: Attractive entrance courtyard with water garden and tables; interesting bar with raised area overlooking sea, good range of good value meals, esp puddings, from buttery bar, well kept Bass and M & B Mild on handpump; bedrooms, and self-catering *(Tim and Lynne Crawford)*

Trefriw [B5106; SH7863], *Fairy Falls*: Worth knowing for reasonable choice of beers and wide range of food, not cheap but generously served *(Jon Wainwright); Princes Arms*: Good bar food, welcoming service, attractive view; bedrooms *(H Geddes)*

☆ Tremadog [SH5640], *Golden Fleece*: Cheerful stone-built inn in attractive village square, with simply furnished rambling beamed lounge bar with unusual arched serving area, nice little snug, games in public bar, tables in sheltered inner courtyard under Perspex roof — even a solarium/sauna; wide choice of food from side food bar, also restaurant meals; Marstons Pedigree tapped from the cask; children in bistro or small room off courtyard; closed Sun *(Tom Evans, RT, Tim and Lynne Crawford)*

Tremadog [The Square], *Union*: Clean and tidy friendly pub with good, generously served and reasonably priced food *(Tim and Lynne Crawford)*

☆ Tyn-y-Groes, [B5106 N of village; SH7672], *Groes*: Good food inc fresh fish under current regime; pleasant atmosphere in rambling series of dimly lit low-beamed medieval rooms with miscellany of furnishings, log fires, friendly and helpful staff, attractive Victorian-style dining room; bedrooms lovely, overlooking valley *(D M Moss, Hugh Geddes, LYM)*

POWYS

Abercrave [SN8112], *Abercrave*: Atmospheric Welsh local with good value bar food, quick, friendly service, wide range of real ales; handy for Dan-yr-Ogof caves *(S Watkins)*

Berriew [SJ1801], *Lion*: In small, sleepy village; old pub with low ceilings; busy trade in lounge and bar, both quite attractive; a lounge window looks out on the churchyard *(Gordon and Daphne)*

Bleddfa [A488; SO2168], *Hundred House*: Grey stone lounge bar with very fine fireplace stacked with huge logs, antlers on wall, most attentive landlord, particularly good home cooking, well kept Marstons Pedigree *(Gwen and Peter Andrews)*

Brecon [SO0428], *Three Horseshoes*: Great attention to detail in cosy pub with good bar food and well kept beer *(P Miller)*

Builth Wells [SO0351], *Caer Beris Manor*: More hotel than pub, but worth knowing for good food such as deep-fried mushrooms and rack of lamb in conservatory eating area, open all day; lovely grounds, long drive; bedrooms *(Mike Tucker)*

☆ Crickhowell [1 1/2 miles NW, by junction A40/A479; SO2118], *Nantyffin Cider Mill*: Popular food pub in handy main-road position, attractive surroundings, enormous log fire in end dining area, good choice of consistent food, ramp provision for disabled people, good parking alongside; keg beers, decent ciders *(Anne Morris, David Williams, PLC, E W B and M G Wauton, Warren Marsh,*

A J Madel, M E Hughes, Col G D Stafford, BB)

Crickhowell [New Rd], *Bridge End*: The Ways who made this popular are now to be found at the Dragons Head, Llangenny — see main entries; [A40 about 3 miles W], *Kestrel*: Pleasant pub with reasonable atmosphere and excellent, reasonably priced bar food generously served *(K W J Wood)*

Cwmdu [A479 NW of Crickhowell; SO1823], *Farmers Arms*: Ideal for pony trekking and walking in Black Mountains; looks very small from outside but plenty of room; pleasant bar staff, Brains beers, bar food, tables in big garden and out in front; cottage-type interior, bedrooms with own bathrooms *(G and S Spadaro-Dutturi)*

☆ Defynnog, [SN9228], *Lion*: Carefully restored roadside pub with good value home cooking, well kept Flowers real ales, pleasant service, good atmosphere, witty and enthusiastic landlord *(M and P Rudlin, LYM)*

☆ Derwenlas [A487 Machynlleth—Aberystwyth — OS Sheet 135 map reference 723992; SN7299], *Black Lion*: Very old beamed cottage pub with huge log fire, friendly service, cottagey furnishings, well kept Marstons Pedigree on handpump, basic choice of decent wines, unobtrusive piped music; good home-cooked bar food inc wide choice of vegetarian dishes in dining area divided off by oak posts and cartwheels; garden up behind (no dogs), with good adventure playground and steps up into woods *(DJW, Mr and Mrs P A Godley, Gordon and Daphne, G T Jones)*

☆ Dolfor [inn signposted up hill from A483 about 4 miles S of Newtown; SO1187], *Dolfor*: Welcoming much modernised inn high in the hills, with easy chairs in beamed lounge opening into neatly modern dining area, generously served good food, well kept Davenports and Tetleys on handpump, unobtrusive piped music, good views from terrace; bedrooms comfortable and good value *(John Davidson, Mrs Y M Healey, LYM)*

Dylife [off B4518 Llanidloes—Llanbrynmair — OS Sheet 135 map reference 863941; SN8694], *Star*: Cheerful free house with bar food running up to steaks, in former 18th-century lead-mining village *(Dr Stephen Hiew)*

Felindre [sometimes spelled Velindre: the one on the hill rd Hay-on-Wye—Talgarth; SO1836], *Three Horseshoes*: Pleasant pub popular with pony trekkers, canoeists and walkers; Courage Best and Directors on handpump, good pub food with wide choice, pleasant service and attractive dining room *(M and J Godfrey)*

Four Crosses [B4393 — OS Sheet 126 map reference 269186; SJ2718], *Four Crosses*: Sparkling clean with many decorative crosses; games and TV room, Burtonwood Bitter, simple bar food *(Neil and Anita Christopher)*

Frankwell [SN9696], *Swan*: Decent, busy town-centre pub with well kept Ansells, Ind Coope Burton and Wadworths 6X; snooker room, garden and restaurant (good fish Thurs–Sat); good value Sun lunch *(Colin Dowse)*

Garthmyl [SO1999], *Nags Head*: Warm cosy atmosphere, friendly licensees and bar staff, and good country cooking inc beautiful sauces and steaks running up to 20oz T-bone (T Sheppard)

☆ **Gladestry**, [SO2355], *Royal Oak*: Unpretentious inn on Offa's Dyke, pleasant and welcoming new licensees, good home-cooked bar food inc fine ham ploughman's, newly refurbished lounge, separate bar; bedrooms sparkling clean, well equipped and good value, with good breakfasts (Mrs J S England)

Glangrwyney [A40 Crickhowell—Abergavenny; SO2416], *Bell*: Pleasant old building with oak beams and open fire; games room, Davenports ales, cheap standard bar food, separate restaurant and friendly, helpful staff; fishing available to residents; comfortable bedrooms (John Hayward)

Hay on Wye [Bear St/Bull Ring; SO2342], *Kilvert*: Small well furnished hotel bar with outside tables overlooking small town square, relaxed atmosphere, friendly smartly dressed barman, well kept Fullers ESB and other real ales on handpump, good bottled beers; bedrooms all with own bathrooms (D J Penny, Patrick Godfrey)

Hundred House [SO1154], *Hundred House*: Wide range of good food inc good vegetarian dishes, served in huge helpings in low-beamed main bar and two further rooms — also children's dishes and popular Sun lunches, even take-aways; closed Mon lunchtime, Tues; no food Mon evening (M E A Horler)

Knighton [OS Sheet 148 map reference 287721; SO2972], *Swan*: Friendly pub popular with walkers on Offa's Dyke Path; Woods Special, good range of usual bar food strong on filled baked potatoes (Neil and Anita Christopher)

Llanbadarn Fynydd [A483 Newton—Llandrindod Wells; SO1078], *New Inn*: Built like an octagonal theatre with bar surrounded by two rooms and well used play room; service friendly and helpful, good value bar food, delightful lawned garden behind (Tom Evans)

Llanbrynmair [junction A470/B4518; SH9003], *Wynnstay Arms*: Lounge recently redecorated and plaster stripped back to superb stone walls and big fireplace; good variety of food well served, well kept Ansells and Powells Samson, friendly service; bedrooms (Brian Jones)

Llandrindod Wells [Temple St; SO0561], *Metropole*: Upmarket bar in good Edwardian hotel on main street; extremely comfortable seating with terrace overlooking street — glassed in from weather and fumes; Flowers and a Watneys-related guest, good bar snacks from new counter and extension; bedrooms (Joan and Michel Hooper-Immins)

Llanfair Caereinion [High St; SJ1006], *Goat*: Public bar and comfortable lounge with settees and easy chairs, workmanlike inglenook fireplace with roaring coal fire; good value hot and cold food, well kept Felinfoel and Hancocks on handpump, friendly service, garden; bedrooms (Brian Jones, Andy and Jill Kassube)

Llangorse [SO1327], *Red Lion*: Friendly landlord, well kept Welsh beers, good value food and attractive position by stream

through village; may be crowded with summer visitors from campsite at nearby Llangorse Lake; bedrooms (Canon K Wills, LYM)

Llangynidr [B4558, Cwm Crawnon; SO1519], *Coach & Horses*: Worth knowing for its sloping canalside lawn, safely fenced — a particular attraction for families; spacious inside, with Watneys-related real ales, open fire, pub games, straightforward bar food, also restaurant; children welcome (K W J Wood, Mr and Mrs J H Adam, LYM)

Llanidloes [A483; SN9584], *Mount*: Friendly, well appointed and peaceful free house with good quickly served food; pleasant terrace (A A Worthington); [Longbridge St], *Unicorn*: Family-run small hotel with helpful and obliging licensees; main bar with Bass and unobtrusive juke box; evening meals in adjoining restaurant; bedrooms, good breakfasts (Andrew Triggs)

Llanwddyn [SJ0219], *Lake Vyrnwy*: Hotel in superb position on hill giving breathtaking panoramic view of reservoir 200 ft below and backdrop of hills, especially from continental-style balcony; well kept Marstons Pedigree, good value sturdy commonsense bar food, afternoon teas, juke box; bedrooms (Robert A Caldwell, Gwen and Peter Andrews)

☆ **Llowes**, [A438 Brecon—Hereford — OS Sheet 161 map reference 192416; SO1941], *Radnor Arms*: Small, modest and very old, with log fire in bar, neat little cottagey dining room, and tables in imaginatively planted garden looking out over fields towards the Wye; particularly wide choice of food from beautifully filled big rye rolls and good soups to good but restaurant-price dishes such as tender duck in apricot sauce and calorific puddings such as hazelnut meringue; most competent attractive service, jovial licensees, well kept Felinfoel Double Dragon and Devenish Newquay Steam, spotless lavatories; closed Sun pm, all day Mon; at weekends it's wise to book (Paul McPherson, PLC, David Wallington)

Llyswen [B4350 towards Builth Wells; SO1337], *Boat*: Simple country pub with charming, spacious garden overlooking River Wye tumbling through steep valley (LYM)

Middletown [A458 Welshpool—Shrewsbury; SJ3012], *Breidden*: Good inexpensive food in well kept pub; Whitbreads beers (Mrs A Turner)

☆ **Montgomery**, [The Square; SO2296], *Dragon*: Pleasant grey stone tiled hall and left-hand bar with stools, settles and tables, prints of local scenes and ducks on walls, an attractive alcove with china, and a warmly welcoming atmosphere; Felinfoel Double Dragon and Vaux Samson on handpump, good food from smoked salmon and cold lamb with mango chutney sandwiches upwards; unobtrusive piped music; restaurant; pleasant very quiet town below ruined Norman castle; bedrooms (Gwen and Peter Andrews, LYM)

Newbridge on Wye [SO0158], *New Inn*: Friendly village inn in upper Wye Valley, cold meats and fish with wide variety of salads at lunchtime, good home cooking in evening restaurant; well kept Flowers IPA, spacious carpeted back lounge with button-back banquettes in big bays, good bookmatch collection in public bar with TV, snug Cabin Bar with cushioned wall benches, welcoming licensees; bedrooms *(BB)*

☆ **Painscastle** [B4594; off A470 Brecon—Builth Wells; SO1646], *Maesllwch Arms*: Friendly village inn up in hills with spacious big-windowed main bar and cosy more traditional public bar; generously served straightforward bar food, cold Flowers Original and a guest beer on handpump, restaurant, children welcome; an attractive area; bedrooms small but comfortable and neat — good value *(M and J Godfrey, Paul S McPherson, John Bowdler, G and M Hollis, Neil and Anita Christopher, LYM; more reports on current regime please)*

☆ **Presteigne**, [SO3265], *Radnorshire Arms*: Picturesque rambling timbered THF inn with decent food in panelled bar, well kept Bass, good service, well spaced tables on sheltered lawn; bedrooms *(David Williams)*

Presteigne, *Royal Oak*: Very small lounge with long narrow restaurant area; food of high standard and good value, from sandwiches and soup through vegetarian dishes to pies and home-made chilli con carne; wider choice in restaurant but still good value; well kept Worthington BB *(Norman and Kathleen Edwardes)*

Rhayader [SN9768], *Crown*: Very handy for Elan Valley Lakes, with Bass, Hancocks and Whitbreads on handpump, and good helpings of bar food *(M and J Back, Patrick Godfrey)*

☆ **Talgarth**, [from S take first turn into town; 50 yds walk from first car park; SO1534], *Radnor Arms*: Has been marvellously preserved old-fashioned tavern with antique settles, roaring log fire in gleaming kitchen range of flagstoned parlour bar and well kept Flowers Original and Whitbreads brought in the jug to your table; no reports since the long-serving landlord's retirement *(LYM; news please)*

Talgarth *Olde Masons Arms:* Oak-beamed bar in cosy hotel just off village square with light-coloured walls giving an airy feel; friendly licensees and staff; bedrooms comfortable and well equipped, with good breakfasts *(Curt and Lois Stevens)*

Three Cocks [A438 Talgarth—Hay-on-Wye; SO1737], *Old Barn*: Long, spacious converted barn with choice of areas for games, quiet chats, drinking well kept Hancocks, or eating generous helpings of simple bar food; seats outside with good play area and barbecues on fine Friday evenings *(LYM)*

Trecastle [SN8729], *Castle*: Comfortably refurbished former coaching inn with simple pleasant bar, tables outside, and wide choice of reasonably priced bar food; bedrooms *(Mr and Mrs J H Adam)*

Welshpool [Raven Sq; SJ2207], *Raven*: Pleasant comfortable rooms, log fire, unobtrusive piped music, fruit machines and separate pool room; friendly staff, Banks's on draught, good helpings of buffet and other straightforward bar food; free local transport if four book restaurant meal *(M A Watts, Neil and Anita Christopher, E H and R F Warner)*

Ystradfellte [SN9213], *New Inn*: Homely pub with attractive bar, plenty of seating, polished brass and friendly licensee and cat; well kept Flowers Original, bar food, good value Sun lunches; handy for Brecon Beacons *(Jenny and Brian Seller)*

Channel Islands

Channel Islands

The islands are still on average clearly cheaper than the mainland for drinks. However, drinks prices have been rising more quickly here than on the mainland in the last two years. Guernsey and Sark prices can now almost be matched by a handful of mainland pubs, and prices on Jersey – though still low by mainland standards – no longer have quite such a clear margin over the mainland's very cheapest places. Of course a difference is that you can drink in very civilised surroundings on the islands at prices which on the mainland would mean a pretty desperate dive. The other special virtue of pubs here is that so many have good fresh seafood – again at prices that strike mainlanders as absurdly low.

The pick of the islands' pubs is currently the Moulin de Lecq (an entertaining converted watermill at Greve de Lecq on Jersey). Other outstanding places include the civilised Hougue du Pommier, inland in Castel on Guernsey; the Dolphin at Gorey on Jersey (good fish on the waterfront); the Rocquaine Bistro on Rocquaine Bay, Guernsey (restauranty, but fine fish and spectacular sea views); Les Fontaines at St John on Jersey (for its distinctively unspoilt pubby back bar); and the bustling Ship & Crown at St Peter Port on Guernsey.

The OS numbers we give after place names in Jersey (except in St Helier) are six-figure map references to the Ordnance Survey official leisure map of Jersey. Please note that a much higher proportion of the Lucky Dip entries here than on the mainland have been personally inspected by us, often proving a clear cut above the usual Lucky Dip run. We've described these more fully than usual – the BB initials signify which they are.

BEAUMONT (Jersey) OS 613498

Foresters Arms

This white-washed, tiled house can lay claim to being the oldest pub on the island – its licence dates from 1717; before that it served as the Parish bakery, and parts of the building are 15th-century. A more unusual claim to fame is the tombstone in the public bar, the result of a bet between a stonemason and an earlier landlord; there are also darts, dominoes, cribbage, space game and juke box here. The main low-beamed bar is quarry tiled, and has cushioned wheelback chairs and black wooden seats built into bays, small windows with heavy curtains in the thick walls, and a winter log fire in the big stone fireplace; there's a good local atmosphere. The carpeted side lounge with lots of shiny black woodwork has blue plush stools and cushioned seats, and in winter a snooker table. In summer bar food is served from a side servery, an includes sandwiches (70p), filled baked potatoes (from £1), ploughman's (£1.70) and some simple hot dishes such as chicken and mushroom or steak and kidney pie (£1.75) and gammon (£2.40), with home-made soup in winter. There are picnic-table sets on the front terrace, just across the road from St Aubins Bay. *(More reports please)*

Ann St   Licensee Colin Veitch   Meals and snacks (lunchtime, not Sun)   Children in lounge   Open 10–11

CASTEL (Guernsey)

Hougue du Pommier 🍺

Route de Hougue du Pommier, off Route de Carteret; just inland from Cobo Bay and Grandes Rocques

This elegant 18th-century hotel, peacefully set on the west coast of the island, serves good bar food, including home-made soup (95p), ploughman's (from £1.90), sandwiches (from £1.40; good open from £2.15), vegetarian dishes (from £2.35), salads (from £3.20) and hot dishes such as omelettes (from £3.05), gammon and egg or steak and kidney pie (£3.25) and rump steak (£4.65), with several children's dishes (from £1.80), a day's special such as grilled whole plaice, and a couple of carvery roasts (from £3.45). The roomy, red-carpeted and oak-beamed bar has leatherette armed chairs around wood tables, old game and sporting prints, hare and stag heads, guns, a stuffed falcon, pewter platters on a high shelf, good brass candelabra, and a nice snug area by a big stone fireplace surrounded by bellows and copper implements. The oak bar counter is attractively carved, with some mellowed oak linenfold panelling; piped music. There are good leisure facilities in the grounds, such as a pitch-and-putt golf course (for visitors as well as residents), a swimming pool in a sheltered walled garden (tables beside it for drinks or bar meals in summer), a tree-shaded courtyard with lots of flowers, and a neat lawn with white tables under fruit trees. The hotel was originally a cider farm. No dogs. *(Recommended by J S Rutter, David Shillitoe, Peter Woods)*

Free house   Licensee J H Henke   Meals and snacks (lunchtime; limited menu Sun) Restaurant; closed Sun evening   Children in eating area and restaurant   Country and Western music Mon and Thurs evening   Open 11–2.30, 6–11.45   Bedrooms tel Guernsey (0481) 56531/53904; £36B/£72B

GOREY (Jersey) OS 714503

Dolphin 🍴

This cheerful water-side pub is most popular at lunchtime for its straightforward but fine selection of local fish, including stuffed clams (£3.40), grilled sardines (£4), moules marinières (£4), local plaice (£4.40), a dozen oysters (£5.30) and scallops poached in white wine (around £7.50). But at other times the preoccupation is likely to be with the splendid setting – nestling beneath the medieval Mont Orgueil castle, the pub faces towards the harbour and the sweep of the bay; it's well worth climbing the steep rise on the opposite side of the harbour for the view. The bar itself has big bow windows over-looking the busy road, cushioned wheelback and mate's chairs around the tables, and brown nets and the odd lobster-pot hung from its high black beams and woodwork; many of the high stools, with comfortable backrests, along the long bar counter are reserved for diners; efficient Spanish or Portuguese staff. *(Recommended by John Evans, Ewan and Moira McCall; more reports please)*

Free house   Manager Mr Viaira   Meals and snacks   Open 10–11

GREVE DE LECQ (Jersey) OS583552 Map 1

Moulin de Lecq

One of the more popular Jersey pubs with readers, this tall black-shuttered pink granite building is well placed on the way down to one of the only north-coast beaches; the valley and nearby coast have pleasant walks. Outside there's still a huge working waterwheel, and inside it's not just children who are fascinated by the way its massive black gears turn perpetually in their stone housing behind the bar, between the neatly ranked bottles and glasses. Though the mill theme does extend to a pretty miller's-daughter costume for the barmaid, this is a thoroughly proper pub, with good bar food; in summer there's a lunchtime cold table with ploughman's (£2.50) and salads (from £3.95, crab or prawn £5.95), as well as home-made soup (£1.10), sandwiches (from £2.50), steak and kidney or fish pie (£3.95), with extra dishes in the evening such as chicken (£4.95) and steaks (from

£5.95); there's also a popular barbecue outside; in winter they serve traditional Jersey dishes such as bean crock, rabbit casserole and beef in red wine. It's also the only pub we know of on the island which serves four real ales: Bass, Guernsey Mild and Bitter and a guest such as Gales or Ringwood, kept well on handpump. There are red plush cushioned black wooden seats against the white-painted walls, little low black chairs and tables, and a huge stone fireplace with a good log fire in cool weather; service is welcoming and helpful. The terrace has picnic-table sets under cocktail parasols, with swings and a climber in the paddock. The licensee ran the Foresters Arms at Beaumont until a couple of years ago. *(Recommended by Dr C S Shaw, John and Karen Day, Jonathan Warner, P Corris, Ewan and Moira McCall, Comus Elliott)*

Ann Street   Licensee Gary Healey   Real ale   Meals and snacks (12–2.30, 6–8) Children in eating area   Occasional Morris dancing and folk music   Open 10(11 winter)–11

ROCQUAINE BAY (Guernsey)

Rocquaine Bistro 🍴

On the west of the island

From the location alone, you can see why this is such a popular place: from the terrace you can look down to the bay, with its sand-brightened water and the vivid sails of the windsurfers dancing across, and beyond to the castle, floodlit at night; at low tide you can walk out to a great rock pool. But the pub has its own virtues too – particularly the substantial range of fresh fish, displayed prominently on crushed ice in the bar so that you can select exactly what you want; dishes include fish soup (£2.75), half a dozen oysters (£4.95), prawn tails in garlic, crab salad (£7.50), lobster thermidor (£13) and a substantial seafood platter (£25). The cool and quarry-tiled bar has pale bentwood and cane chairs, red gingham tablecloths, a lazy brass fan in the dark green ceiling, and big antique engravings on its swirly cream plastered walls; one of the rooms is no-smoking. Decent wines by the glass, half-litre or bottle, bucks fizz, and coffee; piped music. *(Recommended by David and Jane Russell, J S Rutter; more reports please)*

Free house   Licensee Josef Tautscher   Meals and snacks   Restaurant tel Guernsey (0481) 63149   Children welcome   Open 10.30–2.15, 6–11; closed 1 Nov–1 Mar

SARK

Stocks Hotel 🛏

Dixcart Lane

There's an attractive balance between civility and liveliness in the stone-walled snug bar of this comfortable granite house; beneath the beam-and-plank ceiling there are cushioned easy chairs and small settees as well as red leatherette button-back wall banquettes, and stormy sailing ship prints on the walls. Bar food, efficiently served in a separate buffet, includes soup (£1.50), ploughman's (£2.75), quiche (£3.75), burger (£3.95), pasta (£4.25), home-baked pie (£4.73), and steaks (from £5.95), with a good selection of salads; children's menu (£3.25). In summer there are rustic seats by an attractive fine-grit, sheltered courtyard, and, beside the swimming pool, a terrace for which you can book a table. *(Recommended by David Shillitoe; more reports please)*

Free house   Licensees the Family Armorgie   Meals and snacks (12–2.30, 6–8.30) Partly no-smoking restaurant   Children welcome   Open 12–2.30, 6–10; closed Oct–Apr   Bedrooms tel Sark (0481 83) 2001; £20(£23B)/£40(£46B)

ST AUBIN (Jersey) OS 607486

Old Court House Inn 🛏

This 15th-century inn scores highly on virtually every count – from its fine sea views across the tranquil harbour to St Aubin's fort, through its attractive furnishings, to its well-above-average (even by Jersey standards) fish restaurant. The upstairs cocktail bar is elegantly (and cleverly) crafted as the aft cabin of a galleon, with a transom window and bowed varnished decking planks on the ceiling. The main basement bar has cushioned pale wooden seats built against its stripped granite walls, low black beams and joists in a white ceiling, heavy marble-topped tables on a Turkey carpet, a dimly lantern-lit inner room with an internally lit rather brackish-looking deep well, and beyond that a spacious cellar room open in summer and at busy times (when service can falter, and when it can seem as if half the morning's flight from Gatwick are there). Bar food includes soup, lasagne or pâté , salads, moules marinières, dish of the day, and grilled prawns. The front part of the building was originally a merchant's homestead, storing privateers' plunder alongside more legitimate cargo. The bedrooms, individually decorated and furnished, are small but comfortable. *(Recommended by John Evans, John and Karen Day; more reports please)*

Free house   Licensee Jonty Sharp   Meals and snacks (not Sun)   Restaurant Children welcome   Nearby parking may be difficult   Open 11–11   Bedrooms tel *Jersey (0534) 46433; £40B/£80B*

ST HELIER (Jersey)
La Bourse

Charing Cross

This old-fashioned, one-roomed place has 19th-century French coloured cartoons behind a plate of glass on one purple wall, framed junk bonds, and comfortable, red leatherette tall stools at the bar-counter and the ledge opposite it. Bar food includes soup, sandwiches, home-made pâté , pizza, lasagne, escargots and a good selection of seafood; decent juke box. The bar is at its best on a quiet afternoon, when the atmosphere is truly relaxing, with discreetly friendly service. It's placed between the main central multi-storey car-park and the pedestrian-only bazaar territory of King Street, full of people hunting down their holiday duty-free bargains in electronics, cameras, alcohol, scent and, mainly, gold. *(More reports please)*

Free house   Meals and snacks   Upstairs restaurant tel *Jersey (0534) 77966 (closed Sun)   Children in restaurant   Open 11–11*

Lamplighter

Mulcaster Street

For one reader at least the atmosphere here is the most pubby of any of Jersey's watering holes; a particular bonus is the notably well kept real ale (very rare for the area) — Bass on handpump. The decor is in back-to-basics style, but comfortably so, with captain's and kitchen chairs, pews and tables all done out in stripped wood; there's also grainy panelling, heavy timber baulks, real gas lamps on swan's-neck brass fittings, and old newspapers recording historic Jersey moments and photographs of old packet boats on the walls. Bar food includes sandwiches (from 75p), ploughman's (£1.50), sausages (£1.70), shepherd's pie (£1.80), chicken or plaice (£2.20), salads (from £2.30) and scampi (£2.40). The ornamental facade is attractive, with its elegantly arched windows and proudly carved Britannia on top. *(Recommended by Comus Elliott, Andy and Jill Kassube, Alec Lewery)*

Randalls   Licensee David Ellis   Real ale   Meals (lunchtime, not Sat or Sun) and snacks (lunchtime, not Sun)   Children at one end of bar till 8   Open 9am–11; closed 25 Dec evening

ST JOHN (Jersey) OS 620564
Les Fontaines

Le Grand Mourier, Route du Nord

This traditional locals' pub is attractively set on the northernmost tip of the island, where the 300-feet high granite cliffs face the distant French coast. The main bar is clean and carpeted, with plenty of wheelback chairs around neat dark tables, and a spiral staircase up to a wooden gallery under the high pine-raftered plank ceiling. But the place to head for is the distinctive public bar – and particularly the unusual inglenook by the large 14th-century stone fireplace. There are very heavy beams in the low dark ochre ceiling, stripped irregular red granite walls, old-fashioned red leatherette cushioned settles and solid black tables on the quarry-tiled floor, and for decoration antique prints and Staffordshire china figurines and dogs; look out for the old smoking chains and oven by the granite columns of the fireplace. The only problem is finding the place; either look for the worn and unmarked door at the side of the building, or as you go down the main entry lobby towards the bigger main bar slip through the tiny narrow door on your right, which is marked, but barely visibly. Pool, bar billiards, pin-table, shove-ha'penny, three space games, trivia machine, juke box or piped music in the main bar, and darts, dominoes, and cribbage in the original bar. Bar food includes soup (£1), sandwiches (£1), ploughman's (£2.50), burgers (from £1.50), steak and kidney or chicken and bacon pie (£2.50), trout or calamares (£3) and 8oz sirloin steak (£4.50); Bass on handpump, and cheap house wine. *(Recommended by Ewan and Moira McCall; more reports please)*

Randalls   Licensee Malcolm Shaw   Real ale   Meals and snacks (12–2, 6–8.30, not Sun)   Children in eating area   Open 11–11

ST MARTIN (Guernsey)
Auberge Divette

Jerbourg; near south-east tip of island

There are particularly fine views down past St Peter Port to the top of Guernsey (with Herm lying off to the right) from the lawn of this slightly down-market country pub. In the picture-window bar there are dark navy button-back banquettes in bays around low tables; a small carpeted lounge beyond folding doors has more banquettes and bucket seats. There's also a high-ceilinged back public bar, with sensibly placed darts, bar billiards, dominoes and cribbage; piped music. Well kept Guernsey Bitter and LBA Mild on handpump; the good choice of bar food includes sandwiches, ploughman's, bacon, egg, sausage and chips, salads, gammon or scampi, steaks, and children's dishes. *(Recommended by John Knighton, Dr and Mrs A K Clarke)*

Guernsey Brewery   Real ale   Meals and snacks (not Sun)   Children in small side room (after 7) and eating area   Open 10.30–11; closed Sun

ST PETER PORT (Guernsey)
Ship & Crown ◎

Opposite Crown Pier, North Esplanade

Just over the road from the harbour, this very lively old locals' pub has a distinctly nautical theme: it shares a building with the Royal Guernsey Yacht Club, and many of the local ship photographs on the cream Anaglypta walls above the dark maroon built-in seats date from the war years when this was the Naval HQ of the occupying German forces; there are others of local wrecks, sea disasters and RN and passenger liners which have visited the island. The quieter back area has drawings of tall ships; juke box or piped music. Popular bar food includes sandwiches (£1), ploughman's (£2), home-made lasagne (£2.90), home-made steak and mushroom pie (£3), good fresh fish or rump steak (£3.20), and local crab (£7); Guernsey Bitter on handpump, and a decent selection of malts. The pub is family-run – the current licensee took over from his father. *(Recommended by J S Rutter; more up-to-date reports please)*

Guernsey Brewery   Licensee Glen Pontin   Real ale   Meals (lunchtime, not Sun) and snacks (not Sun)   Open 10.30–11; closed Sun

Taylors

The Arcade; behind Town Church, off High Street

The upstairs bar, previously closed for several years, is now a plush eating bar, serving toasted sandwiches (from 90p), open sandwiches (from £1.30), soup (95p), filled baked potatoes (from £1.50), ratatouille (£1.75), seafood mornay or vegetable curry (£2), scrambled egg with smoked salmon or chicken curry (£2.50), and steak sandwich (£3.20). The downstairs bar, recently redecorated, is more in the style of a cafe, with cafe chairs on its bare boards, a bar counter decorated with tulip-style tall brass lamps, a pretty tiled Victorian open fire, and punka fans circling in the high ceiling; a good choice of wines by the glass; piped music or juke box. It's in an area of small smart shops. *(More reports please)*

Guernsey Brewery   Licensee Geof Warren   Meals and snacks   Children upstairs Open 10.30–11; closed Sun

TRINITY (Jersey) OS 669545

Waters Edge Hotel 🛏

Bouley Bay

Although this partly 17th-century building is far more of a very comfortable hotel complex (complete with spacious grounds and a heated swimming pool) than a pub, its bar is popular with visitors and local fishermen. Called the Black Dog in honour of Bouley Bay's ghost, it's decorated in tranquil neutral colours and has mock-Tudor beams, a bare stone fireplace, stripped granite walls, attractive cushioned captain's chairs and wall seats around cast-iron-framed tables on the berber carpet, and a relaxed atmosphere; there's gentle piped background music, and red-bow-tied barmaids in neat uniforms. Bar food includes sandwiches (from £1.25, crab £3.50, steak £4.75), ploughman's (£2.50), salads (from £3), gammon (£3.25), chicken curry (£3.50), and Jersey lobster or crab, priced according to size. Whitbreads under air pressure, and a very good selection of wines. The residents' lounge, like the restaurant, has big picture windows looking out to sea. The back bar, the 'Picnic Hamper', has sea views from tables on its terrace in summer. *(Recommended by Comus Elliott; more reports please)*

Free house   Manager Mr B Oliver   Meals and snacks (lunchtime, not Sun) Restaurant   Children in restaurant   Open 10–11   Bedrooms tel Jersey (0534) 62777; £65B/£90B

Lucky Dip

Besides the fully inspected pubs, you might like to try these Lucky Dips recommended to us and described by readers (if you do, please send us reports):

ALDERNEY

Newtown, *Harbour Lights*: Varied choice of good bar food at very reasonable prices in welcoming, clean and well run hotel/pub in a quieter part of this quiet island; pleasant garden; caters particularly for families with children; well kept Guernsey Bitter; bedrooms *(Donald Godden)*
St Anne [Victoria St], *Georgian House*: Has been praised for relaxing and welcoming, friendly bar with good food, restaurant, and comfortable bedrooms, but no recent reports *(News please)*

GUERNSEY

Castel [Rue Cohu], *Hotel de Beauvoir*: Uncrowded, somewhat clinical surroundings with speedy service and wholesome food — sandwiches and fish and chips fairly priced; beer well kept; no-smoking area in lounge; bedrooms *(J S Rutter)*;   [Cobo Coast Rd],

Rockmount: Verandahed small hotel with thickly cushioned leatherette seats around American-cloth-covered tables in carpeted lounge; generously served seafood bar lunches inc decent crab sandwiches; picture windows overlook attractive beach with windsurfing school in pretty rock channels — and face the sunsets; bedrooms *(J S Rutter, BB)*
Eree Bay, *L'Eree Hotel*: Not much from outside, but inside cosy bar popular with locals and fishermen *(David and Jane Russell)*
Forest [Le Bourg], *Deerhound*: Friendly pub with well kept beer *(Dr and Mrs A K Clarke)*
Grande Havre [Rte de Picquerel; (part of Houmet du Nord Hotel)], *Houmet*: Big picture windows overlook rock and sand beach; cushioned library chairs and heavy rustic oak tables in high-ceilinged saloon with bar billiards, space game and friendly staff; food includes sandwiches, salads,

scampi, rib-eye steak; bedrooms *(BB)*
Kings Mills [Kings Mills Rd], *Fleur du Jardin*: Swings and a rope swing in neat quiet garden with unusual flower tubs, outside pretty steep-tiled inn with square bar — open fire, lots of flowery-cushioned seats around tables, good range of Guernsey beers; popular with young professional people; no recent reports; bedrooms *(News please, BB)*
St Martin [Les Hubits], *Green Acres*: Pleasant surroundings in large country hotel, good, efficient service, well kept Guernsey Bitter; open Sun; bedrooms *(J S Rutter)* ; [Jerbourg], *Idle Rocks*: Under new management, very professional; superb views from delightful lounge bar or terrace; big helpings from extensive bar menu; Whitbreads on draught; bedrooms *(John Knighton, J S Rutter)*; [Forest Rd], *La Trelade*: Reliable bar food in generous helpings, at attractive prices — often good fresh fish such as plaice, hake, conger eel, Dover or lemon sole; other good recent dishes have included cheese and avocado salad, curry, roast beef, chicken supreme with brie; Guernsey Bitter, surroundings comfortable if not particularly individual; children allowed in lounge; comfortable bedrooms *(J S Rutter)*; [La Fosse], *Les Douvres*: Pleasant surroundings but no sea view; good Guernsey beer, fresh sandwiches; bedrooms *(J S Rutter)*; [La Grande Rue], *Queens*: Surprisingly comfortable with consistently beautiful beer and reasonable service; dry Huntsmans pie; bedrooms *(J S Rutter)*
☆ **St Peter Port** [South Esplanade; by bus stn], *Harbour Lights*: Spacious upstairs lounge looking past trees to harbour locally very popular for lunch — neat waitresses bring sandwiches, ploughman's, salads, omelettes, home-made pies and fish; Guernsey Bitter chilled, under pressure; darts in downstairs bar *(P Corris, BB)*
St Peter Port [Albert Pier], *Buccaneer*: Much nicer inside than it looks from out; has been praised for its dim-lit bars with lots of woodwork and alcoves, sea and ship prints, model ships, nautical brassware; food such as quiche, chilli con carne, curries, omelettes, salads — also restaurant with harbour view; well kept Guernsey real ale; pool, darts and space game in bare-board public bar; some seats outside facing harbourside car park; no recent reports *(BB; news please)*; [Rte de Sausmarez], *Fermain*: Attractive locals' pub with masses of interesting foreign banknotes, in good condition, on the dark brown walls of its parquet-floored saloon; also biggish brightly lit public bar with pool, sensibly placed darts, space game *(BB)*; [Rohais Rd (part of St Pierre Hotel)], *Pierrots*: Very smart pricey cocktail bar (happy hour 7-8) in cool greens and browns with dark bentwood cane-seat chairs and broad marble-topped tables, well reproduced pop music, small sunken corner dance floor for live music; opens into airy tiled-floor brasserie, and into broad terrace by neat lawn running down to pretty pool and fountain, with tennis courts beyond; bedrooms *(BB)*; *Salerie*: Lovely friendly atmosphere; well polished brass; Guernsey real ale well kept *(Ron and Audrey Davidson)*

St Sampsons, *English & Guernsey*: Spacious lounge with modern furnishings and French windows from tables to sheltered lawn; also small snug bar, big plain harbourside public bar with darts, pool and side games room with pin-table and space game; decent sandwiches *(Anon, BB)*; *Mariners*: Locals' bar not much changed — 1860s polychrome tiled floor, knotty veneer panelling, sensibly placed darts, cafe seats and leatherette wall benches, local punters watching horse-racing on TV; on harbour *(BB)*; [Les Capelles], *Pony*: Plush lounge done up in shades of brown, with russet plush armchairs and smart booth seats; well kept Guernsey Mild and Bitter; public has two darts boards, space game, TV and juke box (maybe on together); rather rough-and-ready local atmosphere; tables out by front car park *(BB; more reports please)*
St Saviour [Rue de la Perelle; Perelle Bay], *Atlantique*: Pleasant bar with no-smoking area and sea views, good value food — besides daily specials and usual dishes, bargain cheese platter with glass of wine included; well kept Guernsey beers; bedrooms *(J S Rutter, David Shillitoe)*
Vale [Pembroke Bay], *Pembroke*: Somewhere to shelter from the winds of the flat northern end of Guernsey; delicious Bobby ales; bedrooms very comfortable *(Anon)*

HERM
Mermaid: Truly idyllic setting, good Guernsey real ale, usual bar food; delightful, sitting outside and feeding the chaffinches *(J S Rutter, Graham Gibson)*; *Ship*: Pleasant surroundings on fabulous island; first class food, especially seafood, but by no means cheap; comfortable bedrooms *(J S Rutter)*

JERSEY
Bonne Nuit Bay, *Bonne Nuit*: Hotel bar with superb stone fireplace and marvellous views from the terrace over to the French coast; bedrooms *(Ewan and Moira McCall)*
Gorey [steep climb to castle, above], *Castle Green*: Nice to find this country-style Kandalls house after climb from Dolphin; pleasant for Sunday lunchtime drink in the sun, a locals pub *(Anon)*; [just outside], *Seymour*: A proper, decent locals pub with no pretentions to a meal *(Comus Elliott)*
Greve de Lecq [OS map reference 582554], *Prince of Wales*: Huge lounge with seven space games, three well lit pool tables and juke box; has picture windows looking over roof terrace (with tables, aviary of cockatiels and zebra finches) to small pretty sandy bay in pink granite cove; restaurant; live bands; bedrooms *(BB)*
Jersey Airport, *Horizon Bar*: Up in the lift to glass-walled view of the Flying Banana and other uncommon propeller aircraft which buzz around busily; very wide choice of reasonably priced spirits, conventional airport decor *(BB)*
☆ **Le Hocq** [St Clements Coast Rd — OS map reference 685466], *Le Hocq*: The most southerly pub in the British Isles, just over road from interesting rocky sand beach; green plush button-back seats, Turkey carpet, heavy cast-iron-framed tables, ship

pictures on gold Regency wallpaper — very popular for quickly served filled rolls, ploughman's, home-made fish soup served with lashings of garlic bread, fish, burgers, scampi, steaks etc; some tables on front terrace, side lobby with tortoise rocker; pool, darts and space game in tiled public; on a clear day you can see France from the upstairs restaurant and cocktail bar *(Comus Elliott, BB)*

Rozel, *Couperon de Rozel*: Very plush, high quality place, but not cheap; bedrooms *(Comus Elliott)*; *Rozel Bay*: Snug little inn near quiet and pretty bayside village (geese paddle along the pebbly beach); old prints and local pictures above dark brown plush wall seats in small back bar, plain public bar, pool room; Toby jugs over bar, and 'Guinness es bouan por te' says the clock in the local patois; tables out behind by attractive steep terraced gardens *(Comus Elliott, John and Karen Day, BB)*

☆ **St Brelade** [Portelet Bay — OS map reference 603472], *Old Portelet*: Extensive series of bars in stone pub above fine distant-view climb down to sheltered cove; well kept Bass, neatly kept lounge bar, well equipped children's room, buffet dining room with good lunchtime food, upstairs 1920s bar, partly covered flower-bower terrace, spacious garden, pervasive pop music; children welcome *(Andy and Jill Kassube, Comus Elliott, BB)*

☆ **St Brelade** [Ouaisne Bay — OS map reference 595476], *Old Smugglers*: Genuine local atmosphere in friendly and comfortable thick-walled black-beamed pub just above Ouaisne beach and slipway, sensibly placed darts, cosy black built-in settles, little sun porch, well kept Bass on handpump, good value quickly served bar food; the name refers to World War Two smuggling; pretty public gardens further along beach; children in central lounge *(BB, John and Karen Day, Ewan and Moira McCall, Comus Elliott)*

St Brelade [St Ouen road; OS map reference 562488], *La Pulente*: Across road from the island's longest beach; popular with older local people for lunch, with sandwiches, ploughman's, filled baked potatoes (fillings may include scallops and fish), scampi, salads; more main dishes in evening, inc steaks; Bass on handpump; green leatherette armchairs in smallish lounge, sailing ship prints, leatherette-topped tables; fairy-lit side terrace *(BB)*

St Helier [Halkett Sq], *Dog & Sausage*: Comfortable and neatly refurbished town pub, handy for shops; some snug small rooms *(BB, Anon)*; [The Quay; between English and French Harbour — OS map

reference 649478], *La Folie*: Has been praised as a real harbourman's pub — three little rooms with simple seats, lots of brightly varnished woodwork, big pictures of fish and ships, chart, nautical brassware; cheerful and clean; on harbour though no views; no recent reports *(BB, news please)*; [Royal Sq], *Peirsons*: Traditionally furnished old town pub with green plush button-back seats, Turkey carpet, cast-iron-framed tables, old prints, some black panelling; upstairs food bar, downstairs quite busy; in quiet chestnut-shaded square near shops *(Andy and Jill Kassube, BB and others)*; [The Wharf], *Wharf*: Nice decorative pub; bar food helpings not large *(Alec Lewery)*

St Peter [part of small hotel complex near airport — OS map reference 592507], *Mermaid*: Pretty creeper-covered pub, separated by pond and swimming pool from modern hotel; black beams, plank ceiling, Spanish-style cream flooring tiles, some seats cut into thick walls, wheelback chairs around black lacquered tables, big fireplace in end stone wall; darts, juke box, space games, and pool room with pin-table and space game; plain food, functional service; bedrooms *(BB)*; [St Peters Mill — OS map reference 595540], *Windmill*: Popular, neatly rebuilt windmill in attractive setting, with partly galleried lounge bar — cushioned milk churns, pews built into stable-stall-like alcoves, reasonably priced bar food such as sandwiches, salads, fish and chips, steak, country music; pool, juke box and sensibly placed darts in quarry-tiled public bar; restaurant and diners' cocktail bar in mill tower; tables in neat garden *(P Corris, BB)*

Trinity [OS map reference 663539], *Trinity Arms*: Cheery local with spacious and comfortable lounge, rambling quarry-tiled public bar with pool, space game and juke box; keg beers, straightforward bar food, piped music *(BB)*

SARK

Sark, *Bel Air*: Pretty cottage, where the tractors drop you at the end of the steep climb from the jetty; big woodburning stove, plank ceiling, comfortable easy chairs and settees, model ship, boat-shaped counter; old boat pictures in simpler Harbour Bar; darts, piped pop music, tables on terrace *(BB)*; *Mermaid*: A real country local, basketwork chairs and cloth wall seats in lino-floor entrance bar, big and friendly games bar, paperback charity sales, snacks such as sandwiches and ploughman's, keg beers (not too fizzy or chilly), tea and coffee; seats on side terrace; welcoming *(BB)*

Overseas *Lucky Dip*

We're always interested to hear of good bars and pubs (or their local equivalents) overseas. Readers have recently recommended the following (we start with ones in the British Isles, then go alphabetically through other countries). We don't think that the starring system we use in Britain itself appropriate — tell us if you disagree!

IRELAND

Ballinskelligs, *Sigersons Arms*: Good and friendly service, pleasant atmosphere and lovely view; can easily walk down onto Ballinskelligs beach *(Roger Huggins)*
Belfast [Grt Victoria St, opp Europa Hotel], *Crown Tap*: Gas mantles, ornate decoration, booths, and a wonderful atmosphere; good lunchtime meals and locally brewed Hildon ale; one of the best pubs we've ever been to — a unique cultural experience *(Tony and Louise Clarke, D P Herlihy)* ; *Garrick*: Comfortable and well kept, with very good lunchtime food *(David Simpson)*
Bray [turn left, coming from Dublin], *Harbour Bar*: Very lively place with lots of little rooms, nice decorations inc a stuffed moosehead and nautical souvenirs; friendly staff, good Guinness, open fires in lounge *(David and Rebecca Killick)*
Chapeltown [Valentia Island], *Bostons*: Long thin bar with tables running parallel to it; at the end of the room it leads to another with a pool table, TV and a games machine; live music from about 10pm *(Roger Huggins)*
Crawfordsburn [Main St], *Crawfordsburn*: Mainly a hotel (actually Ireland's oldest) but has basic function as a pub; quaint decor with open fire and burning peat; thatched roof, unspoilt interior; small garden at rear open May-Sep weather permitting; good bar food, with local fish often available; bedrooms *(Karen Anderson)*
Dublin [23/25 Upper Grand Canal St], *Kitty O'Sheas*: Well preserved and friendly Victorian pub close to national stadium; splendid place for Guinness if you're prepared to wait; designed now to cater for big numbers of customers with very little seating; live music *(D P Ryan)* ; [Mounttown], *McCormaks*: Good pub *(David and Rebecca Killick)* ; [Park Gate St], *Ryans*: Good pub *(David and Rebecca Killick)*
Galway, *Two Quays*: An interesting high-ceilinged town pub with ochre paintwork, unassuming fixtures and fittings, and a wide ranging clientele *(Phil and Sally Gorton)*
Gap of Dunloe, *Kate Kearneys Cottage*: More of a tourist souvenir shop with somewhere to drink; wonderful scenery with horse and carts ready to take you up through Gap of Dunloe *(Alec Lewery, Anon)*
Glenear, *Climbers*: Lounge still has pulpit in the middle and seats are pews made more comfortable; pool table in bar; friendly staff

(Roger Huggins)
Glengormley, [585 Antrim Rd (A6)], *Crown & Shamrock*: Typical little Irish bar — good place to meet and talk to the locals *(Tony and Louise Clarke)*
Headford, Ireland, *Anglers Rest*: Comfortably furnished and with warm, friendly atmosphere — the best bar in this small market town; lavatories known locally as Heenahans *(Dr M Owton)*
Hillsborough, [21 Main St], *Hillside*: Remarkably close to the relaxed atmosphere of a classic country village pub, quite old and genuine; popular meeting place with cosy atmosphere, friendly service and very good, varied food; village itself is attractive, too, and the pub is one of the few here to keep real ale *(David Simpson, F S and N P Grebbell)* ; *Marquis of Devonshire*: Well kept and comfortable, with a good welcome *(David Simpson)*
Kilkenny, [N10, 2 miles E], *Pike*: Friendly local with a warm welcome for strangers, particularly good food from sandwiches and children's dishes through starters inc good home-made vegetable soup served with a dollop of creme fraiche to a notable chicken Kiev and big sirloin steaks; real fire in lounge, hand-worked hardwoods, comfortable chairs, live Irish music Thurs *(Jody Lynn Nye)*
Kilorglin, *Nicks Piano Bar*: Amazing pub with comfortable bar, bottle green grand piano played most evenings, the music ranging from pop to classics; well kept beer and very good bar food inc lots of seafood dishes *(John Jones)*
Kinvarra, *Tulleys*: The entrance is through an old-fashioned grocer's shop with the back part of the room used as a bar; Guinness served from very high bar counter *(Phil and Sally Gorton)*
Mitchelstown, *Heneberrys*: Very friendly landlord; small-sized snooker table in lounge bar *(Anon)*
Shannon, Ireland [N18 towards Limerick; nr Bunratty Castle;], *Durty Nellys*: Rather vulgar-looking from outside, but atmospheric, with heavy-beamed low ceiling, huge log fires, hidden lights and old-fashioned lamps, rustic decor and elks antlers and other rarities; efficient service, staff as cheerful as clients (on our visit mostly French people and single Irish women); good meal in restaurant; sawdust on floor; close to Bunratty Castle and Shannon airport; pronounced 'Dorrty Nelly's' *(GB, CH, Simon Turner)*

Waterville, *Bay View*: Very friendly staff, basic though good value food such as sausage and chips *(Roger Huggins)* ;
Fishermans: At back of Butler Arms Hotel and owned by the same people; comfortable and relaxing seats, ceiling beams and TV in one corner; picture of their most famous patron (Charlie Chaplin) on wall, along with a complete section of fishing flies; bedrooms *(Roger Huggins)*

Wexford, *Bohemian Girl*: Swivel top bar stools, some barrel tables and a partitioned area in the corner make it all very cosy; charasmatic, friendly licensee and lots of customers of all ages *(Roger Huggins)*

Youghal, *Ahernes*: Very busy place with delicious fresh fish in generous helpings; pianist playing light classics from about 8pm; bar walls lined with awards *(Anon)*

ISLE OF MAN

Ballasalla, [Airport Rd; SC2870], *Whitestone*: Above average, comfortable pub with most efficient service — my order at the bar reached my table before I did *(Janet and John Towers)*

Castletown, [Market Sq; SC2767], *George*: Very comfortable town square hotel with good, home-made food; bedrooms *(Simon Turner)*

Douglas, [North Quay; SC3876], *Bridge*: Really good pub with fresh crab or lobster salad and well kept Okells Castletown; has a no-smoking section *(Simon Turner)*

Douglas, [Drumgold St; known as the Dogs Home; SC3876], *Victoria*: Excellent, panelled pub with ornate ceiling and interesting bar; friendly staff *(Dr and Mrs A K Clarke)*

Glenmaye, [S of Peel — OS Sheet 95 map reference 236798; SC2480], *Waterfall*: The most pleasant and comfortable pub we've found on the island; interesting menu of well cooked food; Castletown Bitter; very beautiful glen; on GWG141 *(John Towers)*

Laxey, [Tram Station — OS Sheet 95 map reference 433846; SC4484], *Mines Tavern*: In lovely woodland clearing where Manx electric railway and Snaefell mountain railway connect; old advertisement and frames tram pictures on walls, home-cooking, and Okells ales; can sit outside and watch Victorian trams *(Quentin Williamson and others)*

Onchan, [Avondale Rd; SC4079], *Archibald Knox*: Very comfortable chairs (pub is popular with older people), Okells ales and standard lunches; can get very smokey *(Simon Turner)*

Peel, [Station Pl; NX2484], *Creek*: Harbourside pub with friendly landlord, Okells ales and good bar lunches *(Simon Turner)*

Port Erin, [Station Rd; SC2069], *Haven*: Next to the steam railway station; bright, clean, wood-panelled place with good value food and Okells Castletown ales *(Quentin Williamson)*

Ramsey, [Market Pl — OS Sheet 95 map reference 454944; SC4594], *Royal George*: Next to harbour and has very comfortable,

modern wall seats and chairs; well kept Okells Castletown ales and food that includes especially good fresh cod *(Simon Turner, Dr C D E Morris)*

Union Mills, Isle of Man [Peel Rd; A1 W of Douglas; SC3578], *Railway*: Basic and bare, but full of character; three albino cats, Castletown and Okells tapped from the cask, dominoes; landlady's beehive hair-style is not to be missed *(Matt Pringle)*

LUNDY

Marisco: Only pub on island, a one-room tavern is attached to the island shop and the social centre of permanent inhabitants (pop. 20) and holidaymakers; reached only by two-hour voyage from mainland; isolated and idiosyncratic; brews island's own ale, the very good Puffin ale; good straightforward food; children welcome; bedrooms tel 0628-82 5920 *(Robert Humphreys, Simon Reed, Brian Barefoot)*

AUSTRALIA

Adelaide [Pultney St; corner with Carrington St], *Earl of Aberdeen*: One of a growing number of own-brew pubs here — the brewery is visible through the end wall, and the Scotch Ale is fairly authentic; pleasant brewery memorabilia on wall, wooden bar counter *(Nick Dowson, Ben Wimpenny)*

Brisbane [Melbourne St; Queensland], *Terminus*: Large pub with several bars and varied clientele, famous $1 Sun meals; even the fights seem leisurely here *(Ben Wimpenny)*

Cairns [Grafton St; Queensland], *Cock & Bull*: Must intend to dine to get a drink — good choice of draught beers inc a keg British guest, Guinness, good bottled beers; good plentiful food, some of it cheap *(Ben Wimpenny)*

Fremantle [64 South Terr; W Australia], *Sail & Anchor*: Well done replica of an English pub; helpful staff take time to explain the different types of beer they do, even giving small free tastes; home of Matilda Bay Brewery, which produces their own four beers and lagers inc a good English-tasting Bitter and heavy Dogbolter *(Richard Houghton, Nick Dowson)*

Melbourne [Flemington Rd; Victoria], *Redback Brewery*: Good home-brewed Bitter (not cheap) in art deco pub, very busy in the evenings with young trendy people; upmarket bar servery; you can view sizeable brewery through side windows; live bands upstairs *(Nick Dowson, Alison Hayward)*

Perth [William St, Northbridge;], *Brass Monkey*: Replica of an English pub, even with English-style beer brewed by Matilda Bay Brewing Co; very friendly staff, and the re-creation of an English pub has been done particularly well *(Richard Houghton)*

Sydney [Royal Sovereign Hotel; Darlinghurst Rd, Darlinghurst], *Darlo Bar*: Busy with good choice of beers, pool table; fewer Scandinavians than in the Rex, say *(Ben Wimpenny)* ; [George St, The Rocks], *Fortune of War*: Good place for a lunchtime swifty, big bar and impressive

beer garden; crowds spill out into the street in the evening *(Ben Wimpenny)* ; [Lower Fort St, The Rocks], *Hero of Waterloo*: Can get very touristy, with good atmosphere and ten beers on tap *(Ben Wimpenny)* ; [Argyle Pl, The Rocks], *Lord Nelson*: Solid stone, with beams and bare floorboards — the city's oldest pub; brews up to five of its own beers, good but pricey; nautical theme, upmarket atmosphere, pine furniture; open all day *(Nick Dowson, Alison Hayward, Ben Wimpenny)* ; [Glenmore Rd, Paddington], *Rose & Crown*: Founded 1850, with fairly English feel — good for a quiet drink; good Hahn *(Ben Wimpenny)*
Wilmington [Main St], *Wilmington*: Very pleasant, with nice staff and friendly locals — one of the few country pubs where women might feel comfortable; serve Coopers Stout, and bottled real ales *(Richard Houghton)*

AUSTRIA
Seefeld, *Britannia*: English-theme pub in the Tyrol — cribbage, dominoes, shove-ha'penny, draught beer, bottled Guinness, good choice of whiskies, simple food inc Heinz beans, express waitress service; even a red telephone box *(Steve Mitcheson, Anne Collins)*
Soll, *Post Hotel*: Interesting old place with tables in curved plastered alcoves, lively bar on right with painted wooden ceiling, restaurant on left, small hausbar beyond *(Graham Bush)*

BARBADOS
St Philip, *Sams Lantern*: Nice relaxed informal atmosphere in small bar on the right, and further drinking area past the restaurant; good martinis and rum-based cocktails, modest but good snack menu such as flying-fish sandwiches, with reasonably priced main dishes in the evening such as grilled chub; wide windows, bright colours and fans make it seem cool; small drinking area outside; just outside the gates of Sam Lords Castle *(J S Evans)*

BELGIUM
Antwerp [Kleine Markt], *Kumulator*: A must if you're interested in beer — they stock 550, either off the shelf or from the cellar; even the English bottled beers include ones that are very rare here (eg Courage Russian Stout) or virtually unobtainable (eg Bass Kings Ale), and the Belgian and other continental ones are quite remarkable *(Graham Gibson)*
Autelbas, *Cafe de la Biff*: Formerly a railway tavern — but the trains have long stopped; well kept Mousel beer from Luxembourg, request for a sandwich au jambon produces massive plate of Ardennes ham; beautifully panelled bar, well kept billiards room *(John C Baker)*
Brussels [Grand Place], *Roi d'Espagne*: Spectacular location — especially when the

square is floodlit; big room with tables around central fire, further tables in gallery upstairs and outside; wide range of beers — and probably the only pub in the world to contain a stuffed horse *(Dr John Innes)*

CANADA
Ashton [Ottawa], *Old Mill*: Very pleasant if a little self-consciously British, run by British couple who do good fish and chips, steak and kidney pie, Cornish pasties, ploughman's and salads; closed Tues *(John Roue)*
Kingston [Princess St; Ontario], *Toucan*: Known as Kirkpatricks, with good Guinness and piped (sometimes live) Irish music; ornate bar and frosted windows in Victorian-style front part, more casual saloon behind; pub food, Canadian and US beers *(Byrne Sherwood)*
Nanaimo [Yellow Point Rd, off Cedar Rd Nanaimo—Ladysmith; Vancouver Island], *Crow & Gate*: Out in the country, half-timbered building with tables by a duck and swan pond; good pub food inc steak and kidney pie (the ploughman's could do with a nippier English cheese, perhaps), wonderful atmosphere, friendly and welcoming owners, good beers inc O'Keefs Extra Old Stock, Toby, St Patricks Stout, Okanagon Spring; evokes a real English country pub *(Stephen R Holman)*
Ottawa [a few miles S, towards Kars and Osgoode], *Swan on the Rideau*: Good English-style pub with civilised atmosphere and British beers such as Gales, Sam Smiths and Ruddles County; food inc ploughman's and steak and kidney pie *(John Roue)*
St Johns [265 Duckworth St; Newfoundland], *Ship*: Good location and pleasant local atmosphere, with no piped music or video games; ship prints and models, small corner bar in dining area, ex-Liverpudlian landlord; Quebec heater-type open fireplace, Harp, Guinness and Smithwicks *(John Roue)*
Toronto [123 Queen St W], *Good Queen Bess*: Fake English pub in Sheraton Hotel — but there's a good atmosphere and interesting beer *(Dr and Mrs A K Clarke)*

DUBAI
Dubai [in Marine Hotel], *Thatchers*: Imported British beers — and imported panelling, beams, mugs, barmaids; it works really well, with great atmosphere, mixing rig workers, air hostesses and embassy diplomats; just right after a hard day in the desert; good value Thai and English food — as authentic as possible a pub for this part of the world *(W Bailey, Marion Bollans)*

GERMANY
Cologne [100 yds from cathedral], *P J Fruhs*: Famous for brewing its own elegant Kolschbier, served from a barrel by the door and delivered by specially dressed waiters; busy and lively big drinking hall with snugs opening off, good restaurant food; everyone smiling *(Graham Bush)* ; [waterfront], *Papa*

Joes: Lively jazz pub *(Graham Bush)*
Gluckstadt [Am Fleth 4], *Millieways*:
English-run bar with darts, smoked
Cumberland sausage, Guinness and bottled
Charles Wells Bombardier as well as more
Continental food, drink and amusements
(Anon)
Heidelberg [main st, below Schloss], *Sepp'l*:
Panelled student pub with lots of college
photographs, liberated road signs, names
and so forth carved by customers on tables,
walls, even the ceiling; Bitburger or
Heidelberger Pils, 'boots of beer' drinking
contests, singalong piano — even English
folk songs *(Graham Bush)*
Remagen Am rhein [Ackermanngasse 7],
Globetrotter: Newish, but atmosphere
already good, with unusually wide choice of
drinks from overproof Wild Turkey to
Guinness; friendly local landlord, English
spoken *(Steve Mitcheson, Anne Collins)*
Rothenburg [Detwang 21], *Gasthof zum
Schwarzenhaus*: Small place where you
share breakfast with farmers having their
first beer of the day, great decor and
atmosphere; good pork (slaughtering done
here); comfortable bedrooms *(Russell Hafter)*
Wiesbaden [Michelsberg 9], *Stortebeker*:
First-class food and prompt service in
scrupulously clean 'pub' in pedestrian
shopping area, maybe free jazz 11am Sun
(even free Sun brunch for small children);
very reasonable prices *(L V Nutton)*
Wincheringen [Trier—Thionville], *Pension
Jung*: Notable toasts and other local food in
genuine inn with wine from the village
vineyard and good locally brewed Caspary
(John C Baker)

GREECE
Santorini [Kamari], *Banana Moon*: Stylish
cocktail bar, rustic and pretty, with old
waggon-wheels built into decor on terrace;
helpful English bar staff, amazing range of
good if pricey cocktails — try their special
made with fresh bananas, banana liqueur,
vodka and cream *(Jo and Neil Davenport)* ;
Hook Bar: Small cosy seafront bar,
nothing fancy but plenty of atmosphere
with dark wood, candles in bottles, old
barrels — one of the cheapest bars on the
island, even if the very friendly barman
doesn't decide he likes your face and then
pours them on the house *(Jo and Neil
Davenport)*

GUATEMALA
Guatemala City [Avenida de las Americas],
Dannys Marisco Bar: Bistro-style place with
inside bar area opening into outside terrace
— pleasant and informal, with youngish
customers *(John Roué)* ; [Avenida de la
Reforma], *El Establo*: Small, cheerful and
friendly library bar full of paperbacks,
nice owners (she's American, he's
European); opens into big nightclub area
behind *(John Roué)*
Panajachel, *Hotel Atitlan*: Candidate for the
best bar view in the world, with glorious
outlook over Lake Atitlan and its ring of
three volcanoes around the southern shore

— ever-changing panorama of water, sky
and mountains; if clouds and mists allow the
sunsets are fabulous; the hotel itself with its
well tailored lawns and gardens is also
outstanding *(John Roué)*

HAWAII
Waikiki [Honolulu/Oahu;], *Irish Rose*:
Take off your sunglasses for this dim but
pleasant and lively bar; sports-oriented, with
lots of TVs *(Ben Wimpenny)* ;
[Honolulu/Oahu], *Seagulls*: Relatively
cheap, but this is not reflected in the
decor or the customers — though it is
popular with backpackers from nearby
hostels *(Ben Wimpenny)*

LUXEMBOURG
Luxembourg [Rue Albert Unden], *George &
Dragon*: Comfortable traditionally
furnished big room with friendly
atmosphere, range of British and other beers
inc the delightful local Bofferding; the local
wines, notably the sparkling, are worth
sampling; appeals to a wide range of tastes
inc the Luxembourg RUFC — the largest
gnomes in international finance *(Thomas
Nott)*

MEXICO
Ensenada [Main St; Baja California],
Hussongs: Spaghetti-western bar with
pavement artist who paints you as you
drink, ramshackle juke box with ancient
repertoire, thousands of customers' visiting
cards *(D P Ryan)*

NEW ZEALAND
Auckland, *Birdcage*: Large but pleasant,
even civilised; just outside the centre, and
open on Sun — though you're supposed to
eat then; decent steinlager *(Ben Wimpenny)* ;
[St Georges Bay Rd/Kenwyn St], *Nags
Head*: Roomy former warehouse, cosily
converted, with six keg beers, bottled real
ale, huge helpings of good lunches and
suppers, good staff, occasional live music
(Mr and Mrs T S C Kucharski) ; [Albert
St/Wyndham St;], *Shakespeare*:
Three-floor pub brewing its own
palatable beers — Falstaff, Barraclough
lager, Macbeths Red Ale, King Lear Old
Ale, Willpower Stout — and Sir Toby
Belch's ginger beer; quite pricey, and
increasingly upmarket as you climb from
the cellar level; top lounge bar has a real
fire in winter, and live music; friendly
staff *(Ben Wimpenny, Mr and Mrs T S C
Kucharski)*
Christchurch [Cathedral Sq], *Warners*:
Strong Irish influence, Guinness, live music
in both contrasting bars *(Ben Wimpenny)*
Milford Sound [South Island;], *Milford*:
Behind the hotel — spectacular location at
the head of the Sound, with dazzling view of
Mitre Peak soaring 5,000 ft straight out of
the water; surprisingly cheap and friendly,
free pool tables, cheap pies *(Ben Wimpenny)*

SINGAPORE

Singapore [19 Tanglin Rd], *Excalibur*: Straightforward, unpretentious and very friendly, popular with locals and Europeans, draught Tiger, good choice of spirits, bottled Belgian Trappist beer (which has travelled well) *(Mr and Mrs T S C Kucharski)*

SPAIN

Fuengirola [Mijas—Alhuarrin mountain rd], *Finca la Motta*: Tiny cobbled bar, hanging vines, little shady courtyards, Sun barbecue, ponies for hire, pups and pet goats — good food, beers, local wine, company and atmosphere, with lots of individualistic regulars *(W Bailey)*
Torremolinos [Parcela C; La Nogalera; C/SKAL S/N Local 2306], *Pink Panther*: Pink decor, with soft mauve seats, keeps a cool feel; small dance floor and really friendly welcome from Judy (from England) and Issac *(V N Carr)*

SWITZERLAND

Basel [Rheingasse 45; Route 8 tram from SBB stn], *Fischerstube*: Own-brew pub serving three Ueli beers — Hell (a lager), Dunkel (brown) and superb Spezial; food also excellent, more Baden-Wurttemberg than Swiss; faultless friendly service, and of course the place is spotless; closed Sun *(John C Baker)*
Cery, *Fleur de Lys*: One of the select few pubs that give their names to railway stations (in this case a halt on the Lausanne—Echallens line); good, basic, freshly prepared food — neither Turist-twee nor French haute cuisine; Boxer beer — perhaps the best in the Suisse Romande *(John C Baker)*

THAILAND

Phuket [Paradise Beach], *Paradise Bar*: Air stirred by old-fashioned ceiling fans, Singha beer by the neck, bar snacks; one of the few bars where a single unchaperoned male is not targeted by the ladies of the town *(G T Jones)*

USA

Alexandria [Union St; Virginia], *Union Ale House*: Good pub with several unusual specially brewed ales *(Paul McPherson)*
Berkeley [1 Bolivar Dr; California], *Golden Gate Brewery*: Unusual among US brew-pubs for its ambitious food; simple decor dominated by glass-wall view of the gleaming microbrewery which produces their own ale, porter and light wheat beer; closed Mon, and lunchtimes *(Anon)* ; [1920 Shattuck Ave], *Triple Rock*: High-ceilinged rather cavernous place with own-brewed light ale and porter, very young owners, rock music *(Joel Dobris)*
Boston [Fanuel Sq; Massachussetts], *Black Rose*: Downtown Irish pub known as the Roisin Dubh; Irish patriot portraits on panelled walls, Guinness as well as domestic and imported beers; live Irish music evenings *(Anon)*
Cape May [Washington Mall; NJ], *Ugly Mug*: Lager served in frozen mugs in this home of the Froth Blowers' Union, who meet here for annual froth-blowing world championships — their hundreds of mugs hang from the ceiling (and are turned towards the sea when they die); great seafood, especially fresh tuna *(Ed Hamill, Mrs Elliott Doncrey)*
Captiva Island [Sanibel; Florida], *Mucky Duck*: Good food, perfect service — nothing too much trouble *(Mrs B Y Lockwood and others)*
Carmel [California], *Bully III*: Very good dependable food, pleasant staff, cricket bats on the wall *(PLC)* ; *Hogs Breath*: Though more a restaurant than an inn is worth a visit; owned by Clint Eastwood *(PLC)*
Chicago [901 West Jackson Bvd], *Tap & Growler*: Good choice of character beers brewed on the premises *(Anon)*
Cleveland [2516 Market Ave; Ohio], *Great Lakes Brewing* Co: Newish brew-pub with big window into brewing room which produces two or three real ales inc a light lager and dark amber beer; simple home-made food *(Anon)*
Clifton [River Rd; nr Route 3; NJ], *Rutts Hutt*: Started as a 1930s road stand — has original knotty pine decor; best hot dogs on the East Coast, cold fresh lager, handy for New York City via Lincoln Tunnel *(Ed Hamill)*
Davis [California], *Back Alley Brewery*: Great own-brewed beer; popular with students — can be noisy *(Anon)* ; [132 E St], *Mansion Cellars*: Wide range of bottled beers inc dozens of imports; tables outside, snacks *(Joel Dobris)* ; *Pistachios*: Serious wine and beer bar with terrace — popular college hang-out; nearly 100 bottled beers inc lots from Europe and the new dry Japanese beers; about three dozen keg beers, again nice many Europeans *(Joel Dobris)* ; [2001 2nd St], *Sudwerk*: Unusual for a brewpub in that it brews German-style — windows into brewery at bar; bar food; closed Mon *(Anon)*
Denver [1634 18th St; junction Wynkoop St; Colorado], *Wynkoop Brewing* Co: Good cross between an English pub and American bar, brewing six decent real ales — four served on handpump, not too cold; in no way a fake 'pub', genuine attempt to provide English-style beers, and food such as shepherd's pie, bangers and mash, chilli con carne; locally very popular *(Brian Jones)*
Epcot [Florida], *Rose & Crown*: Convivial atmosphere, friendly service, good fish and chips in newspaper, enormous helpings, good seating arrangements; not cheap, and you have to tip the barman *(John Evans)*
Fort Lauderdale [2500 NW 62nd St; Florida], *95th Bomb Group*: Overlooking what is now the executive airport, with earphones to listen to flight control transmissions — replica of English farmhouse with WWII memorabilia, Glen Miller music, nice atmosphere, friendly service, fair to good food *(John Evans)*

Hancock [New Hampshire], *Hancock Inn*:
Low beams and booth seating gives
18th-century English pub atmosphere;
snacks, meals and wide choice of bottled
beers *(Stephen McNees)*

Lititz [14 E Main St; Pennsylvania], *General
Sutter*: Good welcome, pleasant relaxing
atmosphere, usual drinks, wide range of
snacks inc good burgers; gents are in for a
shock when they go to the washroom; the
pleasant town has America's oldest bakery
and a chocolate museum; dates back to
1764; bedrooms spacious and airy *(John
Evans)*

Los Angeles [536 East 8th St; Ca], *Gorkys*:
Airy cafe-bar with food inc good Russian
pastries and hot dishes; now brewing its
own beers, inc an Imperial Russian Stout,
and has a branch in Hollywood (1716 N
Cahuenga Bvd); open all day and night *(J
Dobris)*

Muir Beach [from Highway 101 take
Stinson Beach/Highway 1 exit; California],
Pelican: Perfect replica of a British pub,
nothing jarring or out of place, and no Ye
Olde Tea Shoppe feeling: 16th-century
low-beamed Tudor bar, big inglenook
fireplace, cottage pie, rack of lamb and other
English dishes; draught Bass, Courage,
Watneys and Guinness, bottled Belhaven,
Ruddles County and Theakstons Old
Peculier; ; bedrooms with half-tester beds
and old English furnishings *(Alan Franck and
others)*

New Orleans [Bourbon St, Spanish Qtr;
Louisiana], *Ryans Bar*: The live Irish music
a contrast to the surrounding old and new
jazz; Guinness, warm atmosphere, barman
with alternative humour *(D P Ryan)*

New York [40 Thompson St; New York],
Manhattan Brewing Co: Shepherd's pie and
chilli con carne in spacious sawdust-floored
beer hall with copper-topped tables, live
music weekends, and own-brewed beer; also
smart upper restaurant; no recent reports
(Anon) ; [235 11th Ave; New York], *New
Amsterdam Tap Room*: Bentwood chairs
on stripped boards in spacious
lofty-ceilinged ex- warehouse dominated
by twin five-metre copper brewing kettles
producing Amber own-brew — on a very
big scale for an own-brew pub; also food,
local wines; no recent reports *(Anon)* ; [93
South St Seaport; New York], *North
Star*: In the centre of South St Seaport —
a group of restored warehouses and
quays with a couple of full-rigged ships as
background; a good imitation of an
English pub with dark green lincrusta
ceiling, wall mirrors, oak furniture,
handpumps for the Bass and Watneys,
good choice of English bottled beers, and
real English food inc fish and chips, steak
and kidney pie, and delicious bangers and
mash *(Patrick Young)* ; [93 South St
Seaport; New York], *North Star*:
Interesting spot at the southern tip of
Manhattan opposite the end of Wall St;
nice-looking place, with obliging and
friendly staff *(Dr C D E Morris)* ; [93 South
St Seaport; New York], *North Star*: Very
good choice of beers, good atmosphere

and barkeeps *(Duane Klein)*

North Conway [New Hampshire], *Scottish
Lion*: Tartan walls and carpet, varied beer,
good mixed drinks with free munchies; the
restaurant specialises in good Scottish food
(Stephen McNees)

Oakland [California], *Pacific Coast Brewing
Co*: Adventurous own-brewed beers in
rather English-seeming bar (mahogany,
stained glass, darts, ploughman's, pasties);
seats outside *(Anon)*

Orlando [8282 International Dr; Florida],
Darryls: One of a small chain with whacky
atmosphere (you may be seated in a lift or
aloft in the loft); noisy, busy, frantic but
friendly service, good food, a good fun place
with bizarre decor *(John Evans)*

Philadelphia [Head House Sq; 2nd and Pine
Sts; Pennsylvania], *Dickens*: Dickens beer
from Tooley St, London, with Bass and
Guinness on tap, bottled Fullers ESB,
London Pride, Sam Smiths and other English
ales, friendly British pub atmosphere, good
bar food inc Cornish pasties, pate,
ploughman's, toad-in-the-hole, shepherd's
pie, beef and mushroom pie; darts, good
restaurant, shop selling scones and so forth
as well as take-away bar food; remarkably
good English-style chips *(Paul Weinberg)*

Sacramento [1001 R St; California], *Fox &
Goose*: Landlord from Yorkshire, good food
using fresh ingredients and inc English
specialities, serving several types of tea and
coffee as well as a good choice of English
and other beers *(Joel Dobris)*; [2004 Capitol
Ave], *Rubicon Brewing Co*: Pleasant noisy
brew-pub with blonde furniture and hi-tech
industrial- style decor, producing their own
attractive Pale and Amber ales, Steed
summer wheat beer, delicious Summer Stout
and dark steely Ol Moeller; sandwiches,
snacks, salads; popular with people in their
30s; brewery tours by arrangement *(Joel
Dobris)*

San Francisco [3848 Geary; California], *Pat
O'Shea's Mad Hatter*: Busy Irish sports
saloon with good, unusual food and
interesting beers inc draught English beers
and good bottled ones — the Palo Alto
Brewery beers, brewed to English ale recipes,
are always worth looking out for in the Bay
area *(PLC)* ; [Van Ness/Geary], *Tommy's
Joynt*: Imported beers from all over the
world, vary daily, great atmosphere and
conversation (on the macho side),
fantastic cafeteria-style food specialising
in buffalo-meat stew and Sloppy Joes
(PLC)

Santa Rosa [99 6th St; California], *Xcelsior
Brewery*: Not a pub but a small brewery
which can be visited (tel 707-578-1497);
their Acme Beer is brewed additive-free to
Reinheitsgebot purity standard *(Anon)*

Saratoga [Big Basin Rd; California], *English
Pub*: English food such as fish and chips and
steak and kidney pie — even a couple of
cricket teams *(PLC)*

Savanna [Georgia], *Crystal Beer Parlor*:
Archetypal American long bar with fine
Southern hospitality, good beer, fine food
served with freshly baked corn loaves —
seafood gumbo out of this world *(Ed Hamill)*

Seattle [The Market; Wash], *Pikes Place*:

Worth a visit for its collection of British beers — over 40 on last visit *(Cyril Aydon)*
Sunnyvale [next to Hilton Hotel; California], *Rusty Scupper*: Usual range of American beers in pleasant surroundings, food specialising in seafood and inc outstanding gazpacho served in attractive multi-level area; in the heart of Silicon Valley, British voices often heard *(PLC)*
Walnut Creek [850 S Broadway; California], *Devil Mountain Brewery*: Particularly good own-brewed beers in former railway station — the dining room is a Pullman carriage; bar meals *(Anon)*
Washington [1523 22nd St, NW], *Brickskeller*: Amazing choice of beers from nearly 50 countries — claims to be the world's largest range, with dozens each from Britain and Germany and numerous US microbrewery beers; games bar a bit like a successful contractor's rec room, food from burgers to buffalo steaks in bare brick, stone-floored and gingham tablecloth dining-room *(Joel Dobris)*
White River junction [58 South Main St;], *Catamount Brewing* Co: Not a pub but a small brewery which can be toured (at least in summer) 11am Tues-Sat; brews strong and interesting Amber and Gold, to exacting additive-free standards *(Anon)*

VENEZUELA

Caracas [Av Rio de Janeiro; Las Mercedes], *Dog & Fox*: Half-timbered English pub with jettied upper floor, a few hunting prints looking a little lost inside, local cowboys mixing with young Brits, local blue-collar workers and trendier types; loud piped music *(John Roue)*

Special interest lists

Open all day (at least in summer)

We list here all the pubs that have told us they stay open all day, even if it's only on a Saturday. We've included the few pubs which close just for half an hour to an hour, and the many more, chiefly in holiday areas, which open all day only in summer. The individual entries for the pubs themselves show the actual details. A few pubs in England and Wales, allowed to stay open only in the last two or three years, are still changing their opening hours – let us know if you find anything different.

BERKSHIRE
Littlewick Green, Cricketers

BUCKINGHAMSHIRE
Amersham, Kings Arms
Chalfont St Peter, Greyhound
Northend, White Hart
Penn, Crown
Stoke Green, Red Lion
The Lee, Old Swan
West Wycombe, George & Dragon
Worminghall, Clifden Arms

CAMBRIDGESHIRE AND BEDFORDSHIRE
Cambridge, Anchor
Cambridge, Mill
Etton, Golden Pheasant
Fowlmere, Chequers

CHESHIRE
Chester, Falcon
Church Minshull, Badger
Macclesfield, Sutton Hall
Mobberley, Bird in Hand
Ollerton, Dun Cow
Plumley, Golden Pheasant

CORNWALL
Boscastle, Cobweb
Crows Nest, Crows Nest
Lamorna, Lamorna Wink
Lanner, Fox & Hounds
Mousehole, Ship
Mylor Bridge, Pandora
Pelynt, Jubilee
Pendoggett, Cornish Arms
Penzance, Admiral Benbow; Turks Head
Polkerris, Rashleigh
Polperro, Blue Peter
Porthleven, Ship
St Mawes, Rising Sun
St Merryn, Cornish Arms

CUMBRIA
Ambleside, Golden Rule
Barbon, Barbon
Coniston, Sun
Dent, Sun
Elterwater, Britannia
Hawkshead, Kings Arms; Queens Head
Keswick, Dog & Gun
Kirkby Lonsdale, Sun
Langdale, Old Dungeon Ghyll
Little Langdale, Three Shires
Loweswater, Kirkstile
Lowick Green, Farmers Arms
Wasdale Head, Wasdale Head

DERBYSHIRE AND STAFFORDSHIRE
Bamford, Derwent
Birch Vale, Sycamore
Derby, Abbey; Brunswick
Grindleford, Maynard Arms
Monsal Head, Monsal Head
Rowarth, Little Mill
Shardlow, Hoskins Wharf;
Malt Shovel
Shraleybrook, Rising Sun
Wardlow, Three Stags Heads

DEVON
Broadhembury, Drewe Arms
Cockwood, Anchor
Combeinteignhead, Coombe Cellars
Dartmouth, Royal Castle
Exeter, Double Locks; White Hart
Exminster, Turf
Hatherleigh, George;
Tally Ho
Lustleigh, Cleave

Moretonhampstead, White Hart
Newton St Cyres, Beer Engine
Paignton, Inn on the Green
Postbridge, Warren House
Sandy Park, Sandy Park
Stoke Gabriel, Church House
Topsham, Globe
Ugborough, Anchor

DORSET
Abbotsbury, Ilchester Arms
Cerne Abbas, New; Royal Oak
Chesil, Cove House
Chideock, Anchor
Hurn, Avon Causeway
Lyme Regis, Pilot Boat
Osmington Mills, Smugglers
Poole, Angel
Shaftesbury, Ship
West Lulworth, Castle

ESSEX
Bannister Green, Three Horseshoes
Great Baddow, Seabrights Barn
Stock, Hoop

GLOUCESTERSHIRE
Ampney Crucis, Crown of Crucis
Broad Campden, Bakers Arms
Chipping Campden, Noel Arms
Coates, Tunnel House
St Briavels, George
Stanton, Mount

HAMPSHIRE
Beaulieu, Montagu Arms
Droxford, White Horse
Fawley, Jolly Sailor

Langstone, Royal Oak
Linwood, High Corner
Minley, Crown &
Cushion
Romsey, Luzborough
House
Southampton, Red Lion
Wherwell, Mayfly
Winchester, Eclipse;
Wykeham Arms

HEREFORD AND
WORCESTER
Knightwick, Talbot
Worcester, Farriers Arms

HERTFORDSHIRE
Aldbury, Valiant Trooper
Great Offley, Green Man
St Albans, Garibaldi; Goat

HUMBERSIDE
Beverley, White Horse
Hull, Minerva; Olde
White Harte
Skidby, Half Moon

ISLE OF WIGHT
Chale, Clarendon (Wight
Mouse)
Shalfleet, New

KENT
Boughton Aluph, Flying
Horse
Chilham, White Horse
Cobham, Leather Bottle
St Margaret's At Cliffe,
Cliffe Tavern
Staple, Black Pig
Whitstable, Pearsons
Crab & Oyster House

LANCASHIRE
Balderstone, Myerscough
Bilsborrow, Owd Nells
Blacko, Moorcock
Brierfield, Waggon &
Horses
Broadbottom, Station
Burnley, Coal Clough
House
Clayton le Moors, Dunk
Inn
Darwen, Old Rosins
Entwistle, Strawbury
Duck
Haslingden, Duke of
Wellington
Heaton with Oxcliffe,
Golden Ball
Liverpool, Philharmonic
Dining Rooms
Lytham, Captains Cabin

Manchester
Marble Arch; Lass o'

Gowrie; Mark Addy;
Royal Oak; Sinclairs
Oyster Bar; Tommy
Ducks
Slaidburn, Hark to Bounty
Thornton Hough, Seven
Stars
Uppermill, Cross Keys
Wheatley Lane, Old
Sparrow Hawk

LEICESTERSHIRE,
LINCOLNSHIRE AND
NOTTINGHAMSHIRE
Boston, Eagle
Empingham, White Horse
Lincoln, Wig & Mitre
Market Deeping, Bull
Nottingham, Bell; Fellows
Clayton & Morton; Sir
John Borlase Warren
Retford, Market
Stamford, George of
Stamford

MIDLANDS (including
WARWICKSHIRE AND
NORTHANTS)
Brierley Hill, Vine
Himley, Crooked House
Lowsonford, Fleur de Lys
Netherton, Little Dry
Dock
Oundle, Ship
Preston Bagot, Olde Crab
Mill
Southam, Old Mint
Stoke Bruerne, Boat
Stratford upon Avon, Slug
& Lettuce

NORFOLK
Blakeney, Kings Arms
Brancaster Staithe, Jolly
Sailors
Norwich, Adam & Eve
Scole, Scole
Tivetshall St Mary, Old
Ram

NORTHUMBERLAND,
DURHAM etc
Beamish, Shepherd &
Shepherdess; Sun
Blanchland, Lord Crewe
Arms
Durham, Shakespeare
New York, Shiremoor
House Farm
Newcastle Upon Tyne,
Crown Posada; Tap &
Spile; Cooperage
North Shields, Chain
Locker
Piercebridge, George
Tynemouth, Tynemouth

Lodge; Wooden Doll

OXFORDSHIRE
Burford, Mermaid
Faringdon, Bell
Henley-on-Thames, Three
Tuns
Minster Lovell, Old Swan
Newbridge, Rose Revived
Oxford, Turf Tavern
Stoke Row, Crooked Billet

SHROPSHIRE
Bridgnorth, Hollyhead
Iron Bridge, New
Norton, Hundred House

SOMERSET AND AVON
Brendon Hills, Ralegh's
Cross
Clapton in Gordano,
Black Horse
Combe Hay, Wheatsheaf
Exford, White Horse
Norton St Philip, George
South Stoke, Pack Horse
Tintinhull, Crown &
Victoria
Tormarton, Compass
Woolverton, Red Lion

SUFFOLK
Barton Mills, Bull
Blythburgh, White Hart
Chelmondiston, Butt &
Oyster
Clare, Bell
Hundon, Plough
Laxfield, Kings Head
Long Melford, Bull
Ramsholt, Ramsholt Arms

SURREY
Chiddingfold, Crown
Coldharbour, Plough
Horley, Olde Six Bells
Laleham, Three
Horseshoes
Outwood, Dog & Duck
Pirbright, Royal Oak
Pyrford Lock, Anchor
Shepperton, Kings Head

SUSSEX
Alfriston, Star
Arundel, Swan
Ringmer, Cock
Rushlake Green, Horse &
Groom
Withyham, Dorset Arms

WILTSHIRE
Corton, Dove
Ford, White Hart
Highworth, Saracens
Head
Hindon, Lamb

Landford, Cuckoo
Salisbury, Avon Brewery;
  Haunch of Venison

YORKSHIRE
Askrigg, Kings Arms
Blakey Ridge, Lion
Bradfield, Strines
Buckden, Buck
Cadeby, Cadeby
Coxwold, Fauconberg
  Arms
East Layton, Fox Hall
Egton Bridge, Postgate
Helmsley, Feathers
Kilburn, Forresters Arms
Lastingham, Blacksmiths
  Arms
Ledsham, Chequers
Leeds, Garden Gate;
  Whitelocks
Linthwaite, Bulls Head
Litton, Queens Arms
Masham, White Bear
Otley, Spite
Ramsgill, Yorke Arms
Ripponden, Old Bridge
Rosedale Abbey, White
  Horse
Saxton, Greyhound
Settle, Royal Oak
Sheffield, Frog & Parrot
Sprotbrough, Boat
York, Black Swan; Kings
  Arms; Olde Starre

LONDON, CENTRAL
Antelope, SW1
Argyll Arms, W1
Cittie of York, WC1
Cross Keys, SW3
George, W1
Glassblower, W1
Kings Arms, W1
Lamb, WC1
Lamb & Flag, WC2
Museum Tavern, WC1
Nags Head, SW1
Old Coffee House, W1
Olde Cheshire Cheese,
  EC4
Olde Mitre, EC1
Orange Brewery, SW1
Princess Louise, WC1
Red Lion, W1

LONDON, NORTH
Clifton, NW8
Compton Arms, N1
Crockers, NW8
Moon Under Water,
  Barnet
Olde White Bear, NW3
Spaniards, NW3

Waterside, N1
White Lion of Mortimer,
  N4

LONDON, SOUTH
Alma, SW18
Anchor, SE1
Angel, SE16
Crown & Greyhound,
  SE21
George, SE1
Greyhound, SW16
Horniman, SE1
Olde Windmill, SW4
Orange Tree, Richmond
Phoenix & Firkin, SE5
Ship, SW18

LONDON, WEST
Dove, W6
Eel Pie, Twickenham
Kings Arms, Hampton
  Court
Windsor Castle, W8

LONDON, EAST
Dickens, E1
Hollands, E1

SCOTLAND
Aberdeen, Ferryhill
  House;
  Prince of Wales
Ardvasar, Ardvasar
Broughty Ferry,
  Fishermans Tavern
Carbost, Old
Cawdor, Cawdor Tavern
Cramond, Cramond
Dumfries, Globe
Edinburgh, Bennets Bar;
  Cafe Royal; Guildford
  Arms; I W Frazers Bow
  Bar; Peacock; Sheep Heid
Findhorn, Crown &
  Anchor
Gifford, Tweeddale Arms
Glasgow, Babbity
  Bowster; Bon Accord; Pot
  Still
Glencoe, Clachaig
Glendevon, Tormaukin
Howgate, Old Howgate
Inverarnan, Inverarnan
Isle of Whithorn, Steam
  Packet
Isleornsay, Eilean Iarmain
Kilmartin, Kilmartin
Kippford, Anchor
Linlithgow, Four Marys
Monymusk, Grant Arms
Mountbenger, Gordon
  Arms
Newburgh, Udny Arms

Oban, Oban Bar
Portpatrick, Crown
Queensferry, Hawes
Selkirk, Queens Head
Sheriffmuir, Sheriffmuir
Shieldaig, Tigh an Eilean
Spean Bridge, Letterfinlay
  Lodge
St Boswells, Buccleuch
  Arms
St Mary's Loch, Tibbie
  Shiels
Strachur, Creggans
Tayvallich, Tayvallich
Tweedsmuir, Crook
Uddingston, Rowan Tree
Ullapool, Ferry Boat;
  Morefield Motel
Weem, Ailean Chraggan
Westruther, Old Thistle

WALES
Abergorlech, Black Lion
Beaumaris, Olde Bulls
  Head
Bishopston, Joiners Arms
Caerphilly, Courthouse
Clydach, Rock &
  Fountain
Cowbridge, Bear
Criccieth, Prince of Wales
Dinas, Sailors Safety
East Aberthaw, Blue
  Anchor
Haverfordwest, Bristol
  Trader
Llanberis, Pen-y-Gwryd
Llangenny, Dragons Head
Llangynwyd, Old House
Llanrwst, Maenan Abbey
Llanthony, Abbey
Maentwrog, Grapes
Marianglas, Parciau Arms
Nottage, Rose & Crown
Ogmore, Pelican
Penarth, Captains Wife
Porth Dinllaen, Ty Coch
Red Wharf Bay, Ship
Talybont-on-Usk, Star

CHANNEL ISLANDS
Gorey, Dolphin
St Aubin, Old Court
  House
St Helier, La Bourse
St Helier, Lamplighter
St John, Les Fontaines
St Martin, Auberge
  Divette
St Peter Port, Ship &
  Crown;
  Taylors Bar Trinity,
  Waters Edge

No smoking areas

So many more pubs are now making some provision for the majority of their customers – that's to say non-smokers – that for the first time we are this year listing all those which have told us they do set aside at least some part of the pub as a no smoking area, even if it's just part of a dining room. Look at the individual entries for the pubs themselves to see just what they do: provision is much more generous in some pubs than in others.

BERKSHIRE
Cookham, Bel & the Dragon
Knowl Hill, Bird in Hand

BUCKINGHAMSHIRE
Fingest, Chequers
Worminghall, Clifden Arms

CAMBRIDGESHIRE AND BEDFORDSHIRE
Barrington, Royal Oak
Cambridge, Cambridge Blue; Free Press
Holywell, Olde Ferry Boat
Stilton, Bell
Wansford, Haycock

CHESHIRE
Wybunbury, Swan

CORNWALL
Lerryn, Ship
Mylor Bridge, Pandora
Pendoggett, Cornish Arms
Scorrier, Fox & Hounds

CUMBRIA
Bassenthwaite, Pheasant
Casterton, Pheasant
Coniston, Sun
Dent, Sun
Eskdale Green, Bower House
Hawkshead, Kings Arms; Queens Head
Scales, White Horse
Tirril, Queens Head
Ulverston, Bay Horse

DERBYSHIRE AND STAFFORDSHIRE
Derby, Brunswick
Hartington, Jug & Glass
Melbourne, John Thompson
Seighford, Holly Bush
Tutbury, Olde Dog & Partridge
Wardlow, Bulls Head
Wardlow, Three Stags Heads

DEVON
Exminster, Turf
Hatherleigh, George
Haytor Vale, Rock
Holne, Church House
Knowstone, Masons Arms
Lustleigh, Cleave
Lydford, Castle
Lynmouth, Rising Sun
Tipton St John, Golden Lion
Winkleigh, Kings Arms

DORSET
Abbotsbury, Ilchester Arms
Chideock, Anchor
Corfe Castle, Greyhound
East Chaldon, Sailors Return
Lyme Regis, Pilot Boat
Nettlecombe, Marquis of Lorne
Osmington Mills, Smugglers
Powerstock, Three Horseshoes
Sandford Orcas, Mitre
Stoke Abbott, New
West Bexington, Manor

ESSEX
Danbury, Anchor
Great Baddow, Seabrights Barn

GLOUCESTERSHIRE
Bisley, Bear
Bledington, Kings Head
Hyde, Ragged Cot

HAMPSHIRE
Beaulieu, Montagu Arms
Ibsley, Old Beams
Winchester, Wykeham Arms

HEREFORD AND WORCESTER
Brimfield, Roebuck
Ombersley, Crown & Sandys Arms

HERTFORDSHIRE
Ayot St Lawrence, Brocket Arms
Barley, Fox and Hounds

HUMBERSIDE
Stamford Bridge, Three Cups

KENT
Boyden Gate, Gate
Smarden, Bell

LANCASHIRE
Broadbottom, Station
Burnley, Coal Clough House
Goosnargh, Bushells Arms
Manchester, Sinclairs Oyster Bar
Thornton Hough, Seven Stars

LEICESTERSHIRE, LINCOLNSHIRE AND NOTTINGHAMSHIRE
Drakeholes, Griff
Empingham, White Horse
Hallaton, Bewicke Arms
Newark, Old Kings Arms
Scaftworth, King William
Tetford, White Hart
Wellow, Olde Red Lion

MIDLANDS (including WARWICKSHIRE AND NORTHANTS)
Alderminster, Bell
Charlton, Rose & Crown
Lowsonford, Fleur de Lys
Oundle, Ship
Shipston on Stour, White Bear
Twywell, Old Friar

NORFOLK
Blakeney, Kings Arms
Brancaster Staithe, Jolly Sailors
Norwich, Adam & Eve
Ringstead, Gin Trap
Snettisham, Rose & Crown
Tivetshall St Mary, Old

Ram
Wells Next The Sea,
Crown

NORTHUMBERLAND,
DURHAM etc
Longhorsley, Linden Pub

OXFORDSHIRE
Cumnor, Bear & Ragged
Staff
Noke, Plough
Shipton-under-Wychwood,
Lamb
Stanton St John, Star
Wytham, White Hart

SOMERSET AND AVON
Bathford, Crown
Brendon Hills, Ralegh's
Cross
Exford, White Horse
Haselbury Plucknett,
Haselbury
Kilve, Hood Arms
Stoke St Gregory, Rose &
Crown
Stoke St Mary, Half Moon

SUFFOLK
Cretingham, Bell
Hundon, Plough
Levington, Ship
Long Melford, Bull
Orford, Jolly Sailor
Southwold, Crown

SURREY
Blackbrook, Plough

SUSSEX
Alciston, Rose Cottage
Arundel, Swan
Dallington, Swan
Heathfield, Star
Kingston near Lewes,
Juggs
Ripe, Lamb
Seaford, Golden Galleon
Winchelsea, New

WILTSHIRE
Alvediston, Crown
Everleigh, Crown
Limpley Stoke, Hop Pole
Little Bedwyn, Harrow

YORKSHIRE
Askrigg, Kings Arms
Cropton, New
Hubberholme, George
Pickhill, Nags Head
Ramsgill, Yorke Arms
Rosedale Abbey, Milburn
Arms
Sawley, Sawley Arms
Sheffield, Fat Cat; Frog &
Parrot
Sowerby Bridge, Moorings
Starbotton, Fox &
Hounds
Sutton Howgrave, White
Dog
Wormald Green, Cragg
Lodge

LONDON, CENTRAL
Lamb, WC1

LONDON, NORTH
Crockers, NW8
Freemasons Arms, NW3

LONDON, SOUTH
Crown & Greyhound,
SE21

LONDON, WEST
White Horse, SW6

SCOTLAND
Ardvasar, Ardvasar
Canonbie, Riverside
Edinburgh, Peacock
Howgate, Old Howgate
Kilchrenan, Taychreggan
Kilmelford, Cuilfail
Queensferry, Hawes
Skeabost, Skeabost House
St Boswells, Buccleuch
Arms
St Mary's Loch, Tibbie
Shiels
Swinton, Wheatsheaf
Tweedsmuir, Crook
Ullapool, Ceilidh Place

WALES
Bodfari, Dinorben Arms
Llangynwyd, Old House
Llanwnda, Goat

CHANNEL ISLANDS
Rocquaine Bay,
Rocquaine Bistro
Sark, Stocks

Pubs with good gardens

The pubs listed here have bigger or more beautiful gardens, grounds or
terraces than are usual for their areas. Note that in a town or city this might
be very much more modest than the sort of garden that would deserve a
listing in the countryside.

BERKSHIRE
Aldworth, Bell; Four
Points
Hamstead Marshall,
White Hart
Holyport, Belgian Arms
Hurley, Dew Drop
Marsh Benham, Red
House
West Ilsley, Harrow
Wickham, Five Bells
Winterbourne,
Winterbourne Arms

BUCKINGHAMSHIRE
Akeley, Bull & Butcher
Amersham, Queens Head

Bledlow, Lions of Bledlow
Bolter End, Peacock
Chesham, Black Horse
Fawley, Walnut Tree
Fingest, Chequers
Hambleden, Stag &
Huntsman
Hawridge Common, Full
Moon
Lacey Green, Pink & Lily
Little Horwood, Shoulder
of Mutton
Marsh Gibbon,
Greyhound
Northend, White Hart
Penn, Crown
Skirmett, Old Crown

The Lee, Old Swan
West Wycombe, George
& Dragon
Whitchurch, White Swan
Worminghall, Clifden
Arms

CAMBRIDGESHIRE
AND BEDFORDSHIRE
Bolnhurst, Olde Plough
Chatteris, Crafty Fox
Coton, Plough
Eltisley, Leeds Arms
Fowlmere, Chequers
Heydon, King William IV
Horningsea, Plough &
Fleece

Southill, White Horse
Swavesey, Trinity Foot
Wansford, Haycock

CHESHIRE
Alvanley, White Lion
Brereton Green, Bears
Head
Church Minshull, Badger
Goostrey, Olde Red Lion
Lower Peover, Bells of
Peover
Lower Whitley,
Chetwode Arms
Macclesfield, Sutton Hall
Over Peover, Whipping
Stocks
Weston, White Lion

CORNWALL
Helford, Shipwrights
Arms
Manaccan, New
Philleigh, Roseland
Trebarwith, Mill House

CUMBRIA
Barbon, Barbon
Bassenthwaite, Pheasant
Eskdale Green, Bower
House
Grasmere, Wordsworth

DERBYSHIRE AND
STAFFORDSHIRE
Alrewas, George &
Dragon
Birch Vale, Sycamore
Burton on Trent, Albion
Buxton, Bull i'th' Thorn
Grindleford, Maynard
Arms
Grindon, Cavalier
Little Longstone,
Packhorse
Melbourne, John
Thompson
Onecote, Jervis Arms
Shardlow, Hoskins Wharf
Tutbury, Olde Dog &
Partridge

DEVON
Broadhembury, Drewe
Arms
Cornworthy, Hunters
Lodge
Dartington, Cott
Doddiscombsleigh,
Nobody
Exminster, Turf
Haytor Vale, Rock
Sidford, Blue Ball
South Zeal, Oxenham
Arms

DORSET
Chedington, Winyards
Gap
Child Okeford, Saxon
Farnham, Museum
Hurn, Avon Causeway
Nettlecombe, Marquis of
Lorne
Osmington Mills,
Smugglers
Plush, Brace of Pheasants
Sandford Orcas, Mitre
Shave Cross, Shave Cross
Stoke Abbott, New
Tarrant Monkton,
Langton Arms
West Bexington, Manor

ESSEX
Bannister Green, Three
Horseshoes
Castle Hedingham, Bell
Chappel, Swan
Great Baddow, Seabrights
Barn
Great Henny, Swan
Great Yeldham, White
Hart
Hastingwood, Rainbow
& Dove
Mill Green, Viper
Newney Green, Duck
Peldon, Rose
Stock, Hoop
Woodham Walter, Cats

GLOUCESTERSHIRE
Alderton, Gardeners Arms
Amberley, Black Horse
Ampney Crucis, Crown
of Crucis
Great Rissington, Lamb
Gretton, Royal Oak
Kingscote, Hunters Hall
Lechlade, Trout
Lower Lydbrook, Royal
Spring
North Nibley, New
Oddington, Horse &
Groom
Redbrook, Boat
Sapperton, Daneway
Southrop, Swan
Withington, Mill

HAMPSHIRE
Battramsley, Hobler
Bramdean, Fox
Emery Down, New Forest
Fawley, Jolly Sailor
Kings Worthy, Cart &
Horses
Linwood, High Corner
Longparish, Plough
Newtown, Travellers Rest
Ovington, Bush

Petersfield, White Horse
Romsey, Luzborough
House
Steep, Harrow
Stockbridge, Vine
Tichborne, Tichborne
Arms
Timsbury, Bear &
Ragged Staff
Turgis Green, Jekyll &
Hyde

HEREFORD AND
WORCESTER
Bretforton, Fleece
Fownhope, Green Man
Sellack, Loughpool
Woolhope, Butchers Arms

HERTFORDSHIRE
Ayot St Lawrence,
Brocket Arms
Great Offley, Green Man
Newgate Street Village,
Coach & Horses
Puckeridge, White Hart

HUMBERSIDE
South Dalton, Pipe &
Glass

ISLE OF WIGHT
Chale, Clarendon (Wight
Mouse)

KENT
Biddenden, Three
Chimneys
Bough Beech, Wheatsheaf
Chiddingstone, Castle
Cobham, Leather Bottle
Dargate, Dove
Groombridge, Crown
Newnham, George
Ringlestone, Ringlestone
Smarden, Bell
Southfleet, Black Lion
Stowting, Tiger
Ulcombe, Pepper Box

LANCASHIRE
Burnley, Coal Clough
House
Clayton le Moors, Dunk
Darwen, Old Rosins
Haslingden, Duke of
Wellington
Newton, Parkers Arms
Uppermill, Cross Keys
Whitewell, Inn at
Whitewell

LEICESTERSHIRE,
LINCOLNSHIRE AND
NOTTINGHAMSHIRE
Coningsby, Leagate
Drakeholes, Griff

Exton, Fox & Hounds
Newton, Red Lion
Old Dalby, Crown
Scaftworth, King William
Stamford, George of
Stamford
Upton, French Horn

MIDLANDS (including
WARWICKSHIRE AND
NORTHANTS)
Ashby St Ledgers, Old
Coach House
Berkswell, Bear
East Haddon, Red Lion
Eastcote, Eastcote Arms
Ettington, Chequers
Lowsonford, Fleur de Lys
Stratford upon Avon,
Slug & Lettuce
Thorpe Mandeville, Three
Conies
West Bromwich, Manor
House

NORFOLK
Brancaster Staithe, Jolly
Sailors
Brandon Creek, Ship
Letheringsett, Kings Head
Reedham, Ferry
Titchwell, Manor

NORTHUMBERLAND,
DURHAM etc
Blanchland, Lord Crewe
Arms
Greta Bridge, Morritt
Arms
Longhorsley, Linden Pub
Piercebridge, George

OXFORDSHIRE
Beckley, Abingdon Arms
Binfield Heath, Bottle &
Glass
Brightwell Baldwin, Lord
Nelson
Burford, Lamb
Chinnor, Sir Charles
Napier
Clifton Hampden, Barley
Mow
Fyfield, White Hart
Goring Heath, King
Charles Head
Hook Norton, Gate
Hangs High
Maidensgrove, Five
Horseshoes
Minster Lovell, Old Swan
Moulsford, Beetle &
Wedge
Newbridge, Rose Revived
Noke, Plough
Shipton-under-Wychwood,

Shaven Crown
South Leigh, Mason Arms
South Stoke, Perch & Pike
Stanton Harcourt,
Harcourt Arms
Stanton St John, Star
Stoke Row, Crooked Billet
Tadpole Bridge, Trout
Watlington, Chequers

SHROPSHIRE
Bishops Castle, Three
Tuns
Coalport, Woodbridge
Upper Farmcote, Lion of
Morfe

SOMERSET AND AVON
Ashcott, Ashcott
Axbridge, Lamb
Brendon Hills, Ralegh's
Cross
Bristol, Highbury Vaults
Combe Hay, Wheatsheaf
Dunster, Luttrell Arms
Monksilver, Notley Arms
Over Stratton, Royal Oak
Shepperdine, Windbound
South Stoke, Pack Horse
Tintinhull, Crown &
Victoria
Tormarton, Compass
West Huntspill,
Crossways

SUFFOLK
Blythburgh, White Hart
Hoxne, Swan
Laxfield, Kings Head
Rede, Plough
Walberswick, Bell
Westleton, Crown

SURREY
Charleshill, Donkey
Chipstead, Well House
Coldharbour, Plough
Fickleshole, White Bear
Hascombe, White Horse
Horley, Olde Six Bells
Laleham, Three
Horseshoes
Leigh, Seven Stars
Mickleham, King William
IV
Newdigate, Surrey Oaks
Norwood Hill, Fox
Revived
Outwood, Bell; Dog &
Duck
Pirbright, Royal Oak
Pyrford Lock, Anchor
Warlingham, White Lion

SUSSEX
Blackboys, Blackboys

Byworth, Black Horse
Charlton, Fox Goes Free
Coolham, George &
Dragon
Elsted, Three Horseshoes
Fletching, Griffin
Fulking, Shepherd & Dog
Gun Hill, Gun
Heathfield, Star
Houghton, George &
Dragon
Oxleys Green, Jack Fullers
Ringmer, Cock
Rowhook, Chequers
Rushlake Green, Horse &
Groom
Seaford, Golden Galleon
Sidlesham, Crab &
Lobster
Stopham, White Hart
Winchelsea, New
Wineham, Royal Oak

WILTSHIRE
Alvediston, Crown
Bradford-on-Avon, Cross
Guns
Brinkworth, Three
Crowns
Castle Eaton, Red Lion
Chicksgrove, Compasses
Everleigh, Crown
Lacock, Rising Sun
Landford, Cuckoo
Lower Woodford,
Wheatsheaf
Norton, Vine Tree
Seend, Barge

YORKSHIRE
Bolton Percy, Crown
Egton Bridge, Horse Shoe
Harrogate, Squinting Cat
Penistone, Cubley Hall
Threshfield, Old Hall

LONDON, CENTRAL
Cross Keys, SW3
Red Lion, W1

LONDON, NORTH
Freemasons Arms, NW3
Spaniards, NW3
Waterside, N1

LONDON, SOUTH
Crown & Greyhound,
SE21
Ship, SW18
White Swan, Richmond

LONDON, WEST
Dove, W6
Old Ship, W6
Windsor Castle, W8

SCOTLAND
Aberdeen, Ferryhill House
Ardfern, Galley of Lorne
Arduaine, Loch Melfort
Cleish, Nivingston House
Gifford, Tweeddale Arms
Kilchrenan, Taychreggan
Kilmelford, Cuilfail
Newburgh, Udny Arms
Pitlochry, Killiecrankie
Skeabost, Skeabost House
Spean Bridge, Letterfinlay
Lodge
Strachur, Creggans
Thornhill, Lion &

Unicorn
Tweedsmuir, Crook

WALES
Aberystwyth, Halfway
Bodfari, Dinorben Arms
Caerphilly, Courthouse
Crickhowell, Bear
Dinas, Sailors Safety
Llandrindod Wells,
Llanerch
Llanfrynach, White Swan
Llanrwst, Maenan Abbey
Llanthony, Abbey
Llwyndafydd, Crown

Marianglas, Parciau Arms
Nevern, Trewern Arms
Old Radnor, Harp
Tremeirchion, Salusbury
Arms

CHANNEL ISLANDS
Castel, Hougue du
Pommier
Sark, Stocks
St Martin, Auberge
Divette

Waterside pubs

The pubs listed here are right beside the sea, a sizeable river, canal, lake or loch that contributes significantly to their attraction.

BERKSHIRE
Kintbury, Dundas Arms

CAMBRIDGESHIRE
AND BEDFORDSHIRE
Cambridge, Anchor;
Boathouse; Mill;
Holywell, Olde Ferry Boat
Sutton Gault, Anchor
Wansford, Haycock

CORNWALL
Helford, Shipwrights
Arms
Malpas, Heron
Mousehole, Ship
Mylor Bridge, Pandora
Polkerris, Rashleigh
Polperro, Blue Peter
Port Gaverne, Port
Gaverne
Porthleven, Ship
St Mawes, Rising Sun

CUMBRIA
Biggar, Queens Arms
Ulverston, Bay Horse

DERBYSHIRE AND
STAFFORDSHIRE
Consall, Black Lion
Onecote, Jervis Arms
Shardlow, Hoskins
Wharf; Malt Shovel

DEVON
Ashprington, Watermans
Arms
Burgh Island, Pilchard
Combeinteignhead,
Coombe Cellars
Dartmouth, Royal Castle
Dittisham, Ferry Boat

Exeter, Double Locks
Exminster, Turf
Lynmouth, Rising Sun
Torcross, Start Bay
Tuckenhay, Maltsters
Arms

DORSET
Chesil, Cove House
Chideock, Anchor
Lyme Regis, Pilot Boat

ESSEX
Chappel, Swan
Great Henny, Swan
Leigh on Sea, Crooked
Billet

GLOUCESTERSHIRE
Ashleworth Quay, Boat
Lechlade, Trout
Redbrook, Boat
Withington, Mill

HAMPSHIRE
Fawley, Jolly Sailor
Langstone, Royal Oak
Ovington, Bush
Wherwell, Mayfly

HEREFORD AND
WORCESTER
Knightwick, Talbot
Upton upon Severn, Swan
Wyre Piddle, Anchor

HUMBERSIDE
Hull, Minerva

ISLE OF WIGHT
Cowes, Folly
Shanklin, Fishermans
Cottage

KENT
Conyer Quay, Ship
Fordwich, Fordwich Arms
Oare, Shipwrights Arms
Whitstable, Pearsons
Crab & Oyster House

LANCASHIRE
Bilsborrow, Owd Nells
Garstang, Th' owd
Tithebarn
Heaton with Oxcliffe,
Golden Ball
Manchester, Mark Addy
Whitewell, Inn at
Whitewell

MIDLANDS (including
WARWICKSHIRE AND
NORTHANTS)
Lapworth, Navigation
Lowsonford, Fleur de Lys
Netherton, Little Dry
Dock
Old Hill, Wharf
Stoke Bruerne, Boat
Warwick, Saxon Mill

NORFOLK
Brandon Creek, Ship
Reedham, Ferry

NORTHUMBERLAND,
DURHAM etc
North Shields, Chain
Locker
Piercebridge, George

OXFORDSHIRE
Moulsford, Beetle &
Wedge
Newbridge, Rose Revived
Tadpole Bridge, Trout

SHROPSHIRE
Coalport, Woodbridge
Whitchurch, Willey Moor
Lock

SOMERSET AND AVON
Shepperdine, Windbound

SUFFOLK
Chelmondiston, Butt &
Oyster
Orford, Jolly Sailor
Ramsholt, Ramsholt Arms

SURREY
Horley, Olde Six Bells
Pyrford Lock, Anchor

SUSSEX
Stopham, White Hart

WILTSHIRE
Bradford-on-Avon, Cross
Guns
Castle Eaton, Red Lion
Salisbury, Avon Brewery
Seend, Barge

YORKSHIRE
Newton on Ouse,
Dawnay Arms
Sowerby Bridge, Moorings
Sprotbrough, Boat
York, Kings Arms

LONDON, NORTH
Waterside, N1

LONDON, SOUTH
Anchor, SE1
Angel, SE16
Bulls Head, SW13
Horniman, SE1
Ship, SW18

LONDON, WEST
City Barge, W4
Dove, W6
Old Ship, W6

LONDON, EAST
Dickens, E1
Grapes, E14

SCOTLAND
Ardfern, Galley of Lorne
Arduaine, Loch Melfort
Carbost, Old
Crinan, Crinan
Findhorn, Crown &
Anchor
Isle of Whithorn, Steam
Packet
Isleornsay, Eilean Iarmain
Kilchrenan, Taychreggan
Kippford, Anchor
Plockton, Plockton
Portpatrick, Crown
Queensferry, Hawes

Shieldaig, Tigh an Eilean
Skeabost, Skeabost House
Spean Bridge, Letterfinlay
Lodge
St Mary's Loch, Tibbie
Shiels
Strachur, Creggans
Tarbert, West Loch
Tayvallich, Tayvallich
Ullapool, Ferry Boat

WALES
Abergorlech, Black Lion
Broad Haven, Druidstone
Cresswell Quay, Cresselly
Arms
Dinas, Sailors Safety
Little Haven, Swan
Nevern, Trewern Arms
Penarth, Captains Wife
Penmaenpool, George III
Pontypool, Open Hearth
Porth Dinllaen, Ty Coch
Red Wharf Bay, Ship

CHANNEL ISLANDS
Rocquaine Bay,
Rocquaine Bistro
St Aubin, Old Court
House

Pubs in attractive surroundings

These pubs are in unusually attractive or interesting places – lovely
countryside, charming villages, occasionally notable town surroundings.
Waterside pubs are listed again here only if their other surroundings are
special, too.

BERKSHIRE
Aldworth, Bell
Frilsham, Pot Kiln
Hurley, Dew Drop
Littlewick Green,
Cricketers

BUCKINGHAMSHIRE
Bledlow, Lions of Bledlow
Brill, Pheasant
Hambleden, Stag &
Huntsman
Hawridge Common, Full
Moon
Ibstone, Fox
Little Hampden, Rising
Sun
Northend, White Hart
Turville, Bull & Butcher

CAMBRIDGESHIRE
AND BEDFORDSHIRE
Barrington, Royal Oak
Chatteris, Crafty Fox

CHESHIRE
Barthomley, White Lion
Bottom of the Oven,
Stanley Arms
Great Budworth, George
& Dragon
Langley, Leathers Smithy
Lower Peover, Bells of
Peover

CORNWALL
Boscastle, Cobweb
Chapel Amble, Maltsters
Arms
Lamorna, Lamorna Wink
Lerryn, Ship
Morwenstow, Bush

Polperro, Blue Peter
St Breward, Old
Trebarwith, Mill House

CUMBRIA
Bassenthwaite, Pheasant
Biggar, Queens Arms
Boot, Burnmoor
Coniston, Sun
Crosthwaite, Punch Bowl
Dent, Sun
Elterwater, Britannia
Hawkshead, Drunken
Duck; Kings Arms
Langdale, Old Dungeon
Ghyll
Little Langdale, Three
Shires
Loweswater, Kirkstile
Melmerby, Shepherds
Scales, White Horse

Ulverston, Bay Horse
Wasdale Head, Wasdale
Head

DERBYSHIRE AND STAFFORDSHIRE
Alstonefield, George
Brassington, Olde Gate
Consall, Black Lion
Froggatt Edge, Chequers
Grindon, Cavalier
Hardwick Hall, Hardwick
Holmesfield, Robin Hood
Little Hucklow, Old Bulls
Head
Little Longstone,
Packhorse
Monsal Head, Monsal
Head
Over Haddon, Lathkil
Rowarth, Little Mill

DEVON
Branscombe, Fountain
Head
Burgh Island, Pilchard
Countisbury, Exmoor
Sandpiper
East Budleigh, Sir Walter
Raleigh
Exminster, Turf
Haytor Vale, Rock
Holne, Church House
Horndon, Elephants Nest
Horsebridge, Royal
Iddesleigh, Duke of York
Knowstone, Masons Arms
Lustleigh, Cleave
Lydford, Castle
Lynmouth, Rising Sun
North Bovey, Ring of Bells
Peter Tavy, Peter Tavy
Postbridge, Warren House
Rattery, Church House
Sandy Park, Sandy Park
Slapton, Tower

DORSET
Abbotsbury, Ilchester
Arms
Askerswell, Spyway
Branksome Park, Inn in
the Park
Chedington, Winyards
Gap
East Chaldon, Sailors
Return
Farnham, Museum
Osmington Mills,
Smugglers
Plush, Brace of Pheasants
Powerstock, Three
Horseshoes
Rampisham, Tigers Head
Sandford Orcas, Mitre
Worth Matravers, Square

& Compass

ESSEX
Bannister Green, Three
Horseshoes
Belchamp St Paul, Half
Moon
Leigh on Sea, Crooked
Billet
Mill Green, Viper
Purleigh, Bell

GLOUCESTERSHIRE
Amberley, Black Horse
Ashleworth Quay, Boat
Bisley, Bear
Bledington, Kings Head
Brockweir, Brockweir
Chedworth, Seven Tuns
Coates, Tunnel House
Great Rissington, Lamb
Guiting Power, Olde
Lower Lydbrook, Royal
Spring
Nailsworth, Weighbridge
North Nibley, New
Painswick, Royal Oak
Sapperton, Daneway
St Briavels, George
Stanton, Mount
Stow on the Wold,
Queens Head

HAMPSHIRE
Beaulieu, Montagu Arms
Crawley, Fox & Hounds
Emery Down, New Forest
Hamble, Olde Whyte
Harte
Linwood, High Corner
Ovington, Bush
Petersfield, White Horse
Soberton, White Lion
Tichborne, Tichborne
Arms
Vernham Dean, Boot
Winchester, Eclipse

HEREFORD AND WORCESTER
Hanley Castle, Three
Kings
Knightwick, Talbot
Ruckhall Common,
Ancient Camp
Sellack, Loughpool
Weobley, Olde Salutation
Woolhope, Butchers Arms

HERTFORDSHIRE
Harpenden, Three
Horseshoes
Westmill, Sword in Hand

HUMBERSIDE
South Dalton, Pipe &
Glass

ISLE OF WIGHT
Chale, Clarendon (Wight
Mouse)

KENT
Boughton Aluph, Flying
Horse
Chiddingstone, Castle
Chilham, White Horse
Cobham, Leather Bottle
Groombridge, Crown
Lamberhurst, Brown
Trout
Luddenham, Mounted
Rifleman
Newnham, George
Stowting, Tiger

LANCASHIRE
Blacko, Moorcock
Blackstone Edge, White
House
Downham, Assheton
Arms
Entwistle, Strawbury
Duck
Haslingden, Duke of
Wellington
Middleton, Tandle Hill
Tavern
Newton, Parkers Arms
Slaidburn, Hark to Bounty
Tockholes, Royal Arms
Uppermill, Cross Keys
Whitewell, Inn at
Whitewell

LEICESTERSHIRE, LINCOLNSHIRE AND NOTTINGHAMSHIRE
Exton, Fox & Hounds
Glooston, Old Barn
Hallaton, Bewicke Arms
Laxton, Dovecote
Lyddington, Marquess of
Exeter

MIDLANDS (including WARWICKSHIRE AND NORTHANTS)
Himley, Crooked House
Warmington, Plough

NORFOLK
Blickling,
Buckinghamshire Arms
Brancaster Staithe, Jolly
Sailors
Castle Acre, Ostrich
Thornham, Lifeboat

NORTHUMBERLAND, DURHAM etc
Beamish, Sun
Blanchland, Lord Crewe
Arms
Craster, Jolly Fisherman

Eggleston, Three Tuns
Etal, Black Bull
Moorsholm, Jolly Sailor
Romaldkirk, Rose &
Crown

OXFORDSHIRE
Brightwell Baldwin, Lord
Nelson
Burford, Mermaid
Chinnor, Sir Charles
Napier
Christmas Common, Fox
& Hounds
Clifton Hampden, Barley
Mow
Cropredy, Red Lion
Goring Heath, King
Charles Head
Great Tew, Falkland Arms
Hailey, King William IV
Maidensgrove, Five
Horseshoes
Minster Lovell, Old Swan
Oxford, Turf Tavern
Pishill, Crown
Shenington, Bell
Shipton-under-Wychwood,
Shaven Crown
Stoke Row, Crooked Billet
Swinbrook, Swan

SHROPSHIRE
Cardington, Royal Oak
Coalport, Woodbridge
Hope, Stables
Iron Bridge, New
Wenlock Edge, Wenlock
Edge

SOMERSET AND AVON
Appley, Globe
Ashill, Square & Compass
Axbridge, Lamb
Blagdon, New
Brendon Hills, Ralegh's
Cross
Combe Hay, Wheatsheaf
Cranmore, Strode Arms
Exford, White Horse
Stogumber, White Horse
Triscombe, Blue Ball
Winsford, Royal Oak

SUFFOLK
Blythburgh, White Hart
Chelsworth, Peacock
Dunwich, Ship
Kersey, Bell
Long Melford, Bull
Ramsholt, Ramsholt Arms
Sutton, Plough
Walberswick, Bell

SURREY
Blackbrook, Plough

Chiddingfold, Crown
Mickleham, King William
IV
Ockley, Punch Bowl
Outwood, Bell
Reigate Heath,
Skimmington Castle
Shere, White Horse

SUSSEX
Billingshurst, Blue Ship
Burpham, George &
Dragon
Burwash, Bell
Chilgrove, Royal Oak
Dallington, Swan
Ditchling, Bull
Eastdean, Tiger
Fletching, Griffin
Fulking, Shepherd & Dog
Heathfield, Star
Lickfold, Lickfold
Lurgashall, Noahs Ark
Oxleys Green, Jack Fullers
Seaford, Golden Galleon
Sidlesham, Crab &
Lobster
West Hoathly, Cat
Wineham, Royal Oak

WILTSHIRE
Alvediston, Crown
Bradford-on-Avon, Cross
Guns
Ebbesbourne Wake,
Horseshoe
Lacock, Rising Sun
Landford, Cuckoo
Wootton Rivers, Royal
Oak

YORKSHIRE
Arncliffe, Falcon
Askrigg, Kings Arms
Bainbridge, Rose &
Crown
Blakey Ridge, Lion
Bolton Percy, Crown
Bradfield, Strines
Buckden, Buck
Burnsall, Red Lion
Byland Abbey, Abbey
Cray, White Lion
Heath, Kings Arms
Hubberholme, George
Kilburn, Forresters Arms
Kirby Hill, Shoulder of
Mutton
Langthwaite, Red Lion
Lastingham, Blacksmiths
Arms
Levisham, Horse Shoe
Linton in Craven,
Fountaine
Litton, Queens Arms
Masham, Kings Head

Midgley, Mount Skip
Ramsgill, Yorke Arms
Robin Hoods Bay, Laurel
Rosedale Abbey, Milburn
Arms; White Horse
Stansfield Moor,
Sportsmans Arms
Starbotton, Fox &
Hounds
Sutton Howgrave, White
Dog
Thornton Watlass, Buck
Wath-in-Nidderdale,
Sportsmans Arms
Widdop, Pack Horse

LONDON, CENTRAL
Olde Mitre, EC1

LONDON, NORTH
Freemasons Arms, NW3
Spaniards, NW3

LONDON, SOUTH
Crown & Greyhound,
SE21
Horniman, SE1
Olde Windmill, SW4

LONDON, WEST
Kings Arms, Hampton
Court

LONDON, EAST
Dickens, E1

SCOTLAND
Arduaine, Loch Melfort
Crinan, Crinan
Edinburgh, Sheep Heid
Glencoe, Clachaig
Kilchrenan, Taychreggan
Loch Eck, Whistlefield
Mountbenger, Gordon
Arms
Pitlochry, Killiecrankie
Sheriffmuir, Sheriffmuir
St Mary's Loch, Tibbie
Shiels
Strachur, Creggans
Tweedsmuir, Crook

WALES
Abergorlech, Black Lion
Aberystwyth, Halfway
Broad Haven, Druidstone
Bylchau, Sportsmans
Arms
Caerphilly, Courthouse
Cilcain, White Horse
Dinas, Sailors Safety
Kenfig, Prince of Wales
Llanbedr-y-Cennin, Olde
Bull
Llanberis, Pen-y-Gwryd
Llanelidan, Leyland Arms
Llangenny, Dragons Head

Llangurig, Glansevern
  Arms
Llanthony, Abbey
Llanwonno, Brynffynon
Maentwrog, Grapes
Old Radnor, Harp

Penderyn, Red Lion
Penmaenpool, George III
Porth Dinllaen, Ty Coch
Red Wharf Bay, Ship

CHANNEL ISLANDS
Sark, Stocks
St John, Les Fontaines
Trinity, Waters Edge

Pubs with good views

These pubs are listed for their particularly good views, either from inside or from a garden or terrace. Waterside pubs are listed again here only if their view is exceptional in its own right – not just a straightforward sea view, for example.

BERKSHIRE
Chieveley, Blue Boar

BUCKINGHAMSHIRE
Brill, Pheasant
Great Brickhill, Old Red
Lion
Penn, Crown

CHESHIRE
Higher Burwardsley,
Pheasant
Langley, Leathers Smithy
Rainow, Highwayman

CUMBRIA
Cartmel Fell, Masons
Arms
Hawkshead, Drunken
Duck
Langdale, Old Dungeon
Ghyll
Loweswater, Kirkstile
Ulverston, Bay Horse
Wasdale Head, Wasdale
Head

DERBYSHIRE AND
STAFFORDSHIRE
Foolow, Barrel
Monsal Head, Monsal
Head
Over Haddon, Lathkil

DEVON
Burgh Island, Pilchard
Hennock, Palk Arms
Postbridge, Warren House

DORSET
Chedington, Winyards
Gap
West Bexington, Manor
Worth Matravers, Square
& Compass

ESSEX
Purleigh, Bell

GLOUCESTERSHIRE
Amberley, Black Horse
Gretton, Royal Oak
Lower Lydbrook, Royal
Spring
Stanton, Mount
Woodchester, Ram

HAMPSHIRE
Beauworth, Milbury's

HEREFORD AND
WORCESTER
Ruckhall Common,
Ancient Camp
Wyre Piddle, Anchor

HERTFORDSHIRE
Great Offley, Green Man

KENT
Penshurst, Spotted Dog
Ulcombe, Pepper Box

LANCASHIRE
Blacko, Moorcock
Blackstone Edge, White
House
Darwen, Old Rosins
Entwistle, Strawbury
Duck
Mereclough, Kettledrum
Tockholes, Royal Arms
Uppermill, Cross Keys

NORTHUMBERLAND,
DURHAM etc
Eggleston, Three Tuns
Seahouses, Olde Ship
Tynemouth, Wooden Doll

SHROPSHIRE
Hope, Stables

SOMERSET AND AVON
Blagdon, New
Brendon Hills, Ralegh's
Cross

SUFFOLK
Hundon, Plough

Levington, Ship

SUSSEX
Burpham, George &
Dragon
Byworth, Black Horse
Dallington, Swan
Fletching, Griffin
Houghton, George &
Dragon

WILTSHIRE
Lacock, Rising Sun

YORKSHIRE
Blakey Ridge, Lion
Bradfield, Strines
Kirby Hill, Shoulder of
Mutton
Litton, Queens Arms
Midgley, Mount Skip
Rosedale Abbey, White
Horse

LONDON, SOUTH
Angel, SE16

SCOTLAND
Ardvasar, Ardvasar
Crinan, Crinan
Glencoe, Clachaig
Isleornsay, Eilean Iarmain
Pitlochry, Killiecrankie
Sheriffmuir, Sheriffmuir
Shieldaig, Tigh an Eilean
St Mary's Loch, Tibbie
Shiels
Strachur, Creggans
Ullapool, Ferry Boat
Weem, Ailean Chraggan

WALES
Aberystwyth, Halfway
Bodfari, Dinorben Arms
Broad Haven, Druidstone
Bylchau, Sportsmans Arms
Caerphilly, Courthouse
Llanbedr-y-Cennin, Olde
Bull
Llanberis, Pen-y-Gwryd

Old Radnor, Harp
Penmaenpool, George III
Porth Dinllaen, Ty Coch

CHANNEL ISLANDS
Rocquaine Bay,
Rocquaine Bistro
St Aubin, Old Court
House

St Martin, Auberge
Divette
Trinity, Waters Edge

Pubs in interesting buildings

Pubs and inns are listed here for the particular interest of their building –
something really out of the ordinary to look at, or occasionally a building that
has an outstandingly interesting historical background.

BERKSHIRE
Cookham, Bel & the
Dragon

BUCKINGHAMSHIRE
Forty Green, Royal
Standard of England

CORNWALL
Morwenstow, Bush

DERBYSHIRE AND
STAFFORDSHIRE
Buxton, Bull i'th' Thorn
Derby, Abbey

DEVON
Dartmouth, Cherub
Harberton, Church House
Rattery, Church House
Sourton, Highwayman
South Zeal, Oxenham
Arms

HAMPSHIRE
Beauworth, Milbury's
Southampton, Red Lion

HEREFORD AND
WORCESTER
Bretforton, Fleece

HUMBERSIDE
Hull, Olde White Harte

LANCASHIRE
Garstang, Th' owd

Tithebarn
Liverpool, Philharmonic
Dining Rooms

LEICESTERSHIRE,
LINCOLNSHIRE AND
NOTTINGHAMSHIRE
Nottingham, Olde Trip to
Jerusalem
Stamford, George of
Stamford

MIDLANDS (including
WARWICKSHIRE AND
NORTHANTS)
Birmingham, Bartons
Arms
Himley, Crooked House
West Bromwich, Manor
House

NORFOLK
Scole, Scole

NORTHUMBERLAND,
DURHAM etc
Blanchland, Lord Crewe
Arms

OXFORDSHIRE
Fyfield, White Hart

SHROPSHIRE
Iron Bridge, New

SOMERSET AND AVON
Norton St Philip, George

SUFFOLK
Long Melford, Bull

SURREY
Chiddingfold, Crown
Shere, White Horse

SUSSEX
Alfriston, Star
Rye, Mermaid

WILTSHIRE
Salisbury, Haunch of
Venison

LONDON, CENTRAL
Black Friar, EC4
Cittie of York, WC1

LONDON, NORTH
Crockers, NW8

LONDON, SOUTH
George, SE1
Phoenix & Firkin, SE5

LONDON, EAST
Hollands, E1

SCOTLAND
Dumfries, Globe
Edinburgh, Bennets Bar;
Cafe Royal; Guildford
Arms

WALES
Llanthony, Abbey

Pubs that brew their own beer

The pubs listed here brew their own brew on the premises; many others not
listed have beers brewed for them specially, sometimes to an individual recipe
(but by a separate brewer). We mention these in the text.

CORNWALL
Helston, Blue Anchor
Tregatta, Min Pin

CUMBRIA
Cartmel Fell, Masons

Arms
Dent, Sun

DERBYSHIRE AND
STAFFORDSHIRE
Burton-on-Trent, Burton

Bridge Brewery
Melbourne, John
Thompson
Shraleybrook, Rising Sun

DEVON
Ashburton, London
Hatherleigh, Tally Ho
Horsebridge, Royal
Newton St Cyres, Beer
Engine

HERTFORDSHIRE
Barley, Fox and Hounds

HUMBERSIDE
Hull, Minerva

LANCASHIRE
Manchester, Lass o'
Gowrie

LEICESTERSHIRE,
LINCOLNSHIRE AND
NOTTINGHAMSHIRE
Burrough on the Hill,

Stag & Hounds
Leicester, Tom Hoskins
Nottingham, Fellows
Clayton & Morton

MIDLANDS (including
WARWICKSHIRE AND
NORTHANTS)
Brierley Hill, Vine
Langley, Brewery
Netherton, Old Swan

SHROPSHIRE
Bishops Castle, Three
Tuns
Wistanstow, Plough

SOMERSET AND AVON
Trudoxhill, White Hart

SUFFOLK
Earl Soham, Victoria

YORKSHIRE
Cropton, New
Linthwaite, Sair
Sheffield, Frog & Parrot
Todmorden, Staff of Life

LONDON, CENTRAL
Orange Brewery, SW1

LONDON, SOUTH
Greyhound, SW16
Phoenix & Firkin, SE5

LONDON, WEST
Ferret & Firkin, SW10

Pubs close to motorway junctions

The number at the start of each line is the number of the junction. Detailed
directions are given in the main entry for each pub. In this section, to help you
find the pubs quickly before you're past the junction, we give in abbreviated
form the name of the chapter where you'll find them in the text.

M1
15: Stoke Bruerne
(Midlands) 3 3/4 miles
18: Ashby St Ledgers
(Midlands)
4 miles
Crick (Midlands)
1 mile
20: Walcote (Leics etc)
1 1/2 miles
24:
Kegworth (Leics etc)
under a mile
Shardlow
(Derbys/Staffs)
3 1/2 miles
Shardlow
(Derbys/Staffs)
3 1/4 miles
29: Hardwick Hall
(Derbys/Staffs)
4 1/2 miles
36: Wentworth (Yorks)
3 miles

M2
1: Cobham (Kent)
2 1/2 miles
3: Aylesford (Kent)
3 miles
6: Luddenham (Kent)
3 1/2 miles
7: Selling (Kent)
3 1/2 miles

M3
5: Mattingley (Hants)
3 miles
Rotherwick (Hants)
4 miles
7: Dummer (Hants)
1/2 mile

M4
5: Colnbrook (Bucks)
1 1/4 miles
9: Littlewick Green
(Berks)
3 3/4 miles
Bray (Berks)
1 3/4 miles
Holyport (Berks)
1 1/2 miles
12: Stanford Dingley
(Berks)
4 miles
13: Chieveley (Berks)
3 1/2 miles
14: Great Shefford (Berks)
1/3 mile
Wickham (Berks)
3 miles
18: Tormarton
(Somerset/Avon)
1/2 mile
21: Aust (Somerset/Avon)
1/2 mile
37: Kenfig (Wales)
2 1/4 miles
Nottage (Wales)

2 miles

M5
2: Langley (Midlands)
1 1/2 miles
5: Dunhampstead
(Hereford/Worcs)
3 1/2 miles
9: Bredon
(Hereford/Worcs)
4 1/2 miles
16: Almondsbury
(Somerset/Avon)
1 1/4 miles
19: Clapton in Gordano
(Somerset/Avon)
4 miles
23: West Huntspill
(Somerset/Avon)
2 3/4 miles
25: Stoke St Mary
(Somerset/Avon)
2 3/4 miles
28: Broadhembury
(Devon)
5 miles
30: Exeter (Devon)
4 miles
Woodbury Salterton
(Devon)
3 1/2 miles
Topsham (Devon)
2 miles
Topsham (Devon)
2 1/4 miles

M6

2: Withybrook
   (Midlands)
   4 miles
6: Birmingham
   (Midlands)
   2 miles
9: West Bromwich
   (Midlands)
   2 miles
14: Sandon Bank
   (Derbys/Staffs)
   4 1/2 miles
   Seighford
   (Derbys/Staffs)
   3 miles
15: Whitmore
   (Derbys/Staffs)
   3 miles
16: Weston (Cheshire)
   3 1/2 miles
   Barthomley (Cheshire)
   1 mile
   Shraleybrook
   (Derbys/Staffs)
   3 miles
17: Brereton Green
   (Cheshire)
   2 miles
19: Great Budworth
   (Cheshire)
   4 1/2 miles
   Plumley (Cheshire)
   2 1/2 miles
31: Balderstone (Lancs
   etc)
   2 miles
32: Goosnargh (Lancs etc)
   4 miles
40: Stainton (Cumbria)
   3 miles
   Tirril (Cumbria)
   3 1/2 miles
   Askham (Cumbria)
   4 1/2 miles

M9

3: Linlithgow (Scotland)
   2 miles

M11

5: Loughton (Essex)
   2 1/4 miles
7: Hastingwood (Essex)
13: Coton (Cambs/Beds)
   3/4 mile

M18

2: Sprotbrough (Yorks)
   2 3/4 miles
5: Hatfield Woodhouse
   (Yorks)
   2 miles

M23

9: Horley (Surrey)
   3 miles

M25

5: Chipstead (Kent)
   1 1/4 miles
7: Chipstead (Surrey)
   3 1/2 miles
8: Reigate Heath (Surrey)
   3 miles
   Betchworth (Surrey)
   4 miles
18: Flaunden (Herts)
   4 miles

M27

3: Romsey (Hants)
   3 miles
8: Hamble (Hants)
   3 miles

M40

2: Beaconsfield (Bucks)
   1 mile
   Forty Green (Bucks)
   3 1/2 miles
5: Bolter End (Bucks)

4 miles
   Ibstone (Bucks)
   1 mile
6: Watlington (Oxon)
   2 1/4 miles
7: Little Milton (Oxon)
   2 1/2 miles

M55

1: Broughton (Lancs etc)
   3 1/2 miles

M56

10: Lower Whitley
   (Cheshire)
   2 1/4 miles
   Little Leigh (Cheshire)
   4 1/2 miles
14: Alvanley (Cheshire)
   2 1/2 miles

M62

19: Middleton (Lancs etc)
   2 miles

M65

7: Clayton le Moors
   (Lancs etc)
   1/2 mile
12: Brierfield (Lancs etc)
   1/2 mile

M73

6: Uddingston (Scotland)
   1 mile

M90

5: Cleish (Scotland)
   1 1/2 miles
10: Perth (Scotland)
   2 miles

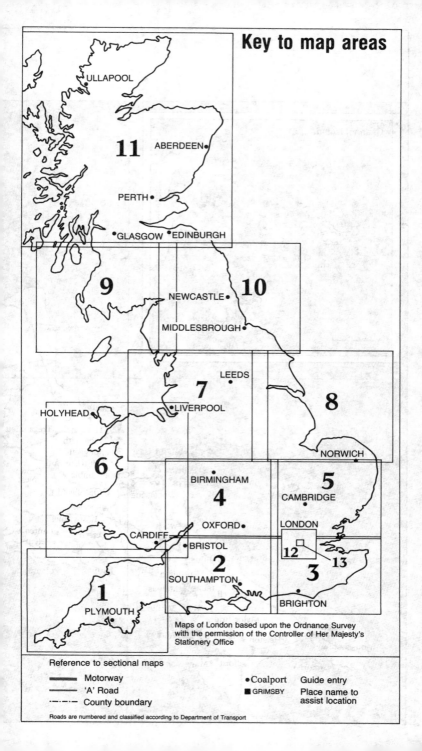

Key to map areas

ULLAPOOL

11 ABERDEEN •

PERTH •

• GLASGOW • EDINBURGH

9 NEWCASTLE • **10**

MIDDLESBROUGH •

HOLYHEAD • LEEDS •

7 LIVERPOOL •

8

NORWICH •

6

BIRMINGHAM •

4 CAMBRIDGE • **5**

OXFORD • LONDON

CARDIFF 12 13

BRISTOL •

2

SOUTHAMPTON • **3**

1 BRIGHTON

PLYMOUTH •

Maps of London based upon the Ordnance Survey
with the permission of the Controller of Her Majesty's
Stationery Office

Reference to sectional maps

▬▬▬	Motorway
───	'A' Road
─·─·─	County boundary

• Coalport   Guide entry
■ GRIMSBY   Place name to
                      assist location

Roads are numbered and classified according to Department of Transport

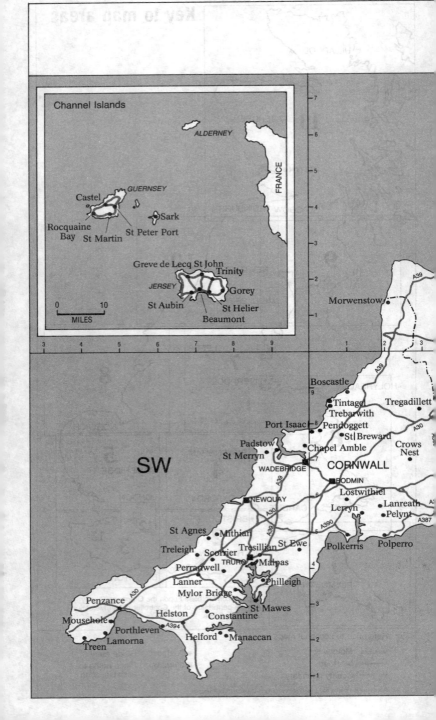

Key to map areas

Channel Islands

ALDERNEY

FRANCE

GUERNSEY

Castel

Rocquaine Bay

St Martin

St Peter Port

Sark

Greve de Lecq St John

Trinity

JERSEY

Gorey

St Aubin

St Helier

Beaumont

0 — 10 MILES

Morwenstow

Boscastle

Tintagel

Tregadillett

Trebarwith

Port Isaac

Pendoggett

St Breward

Crows Nest

Padstow

St Merryn

Chapel Amble

SW

WADEBRIDGE

CORNWALL

BODMIN

Lostwithiel

NEWQUAY

Lerryn

Lanreath

Pelynt

St Agnes

Mithian

Treleigh

Tresillian St Ewe

Scorrier

TRURO

Malpas

Polkerris

Polperro

Perranwell

Lanner

Phleigh

Mylor Bridge

Penzance

St Mawes

Mousehole

Helston

Constantine

Porthleven

Treen

Lamorna

Helford

Manaccan

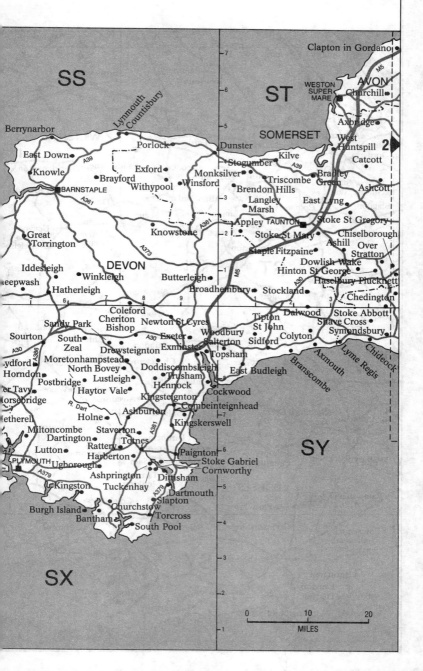

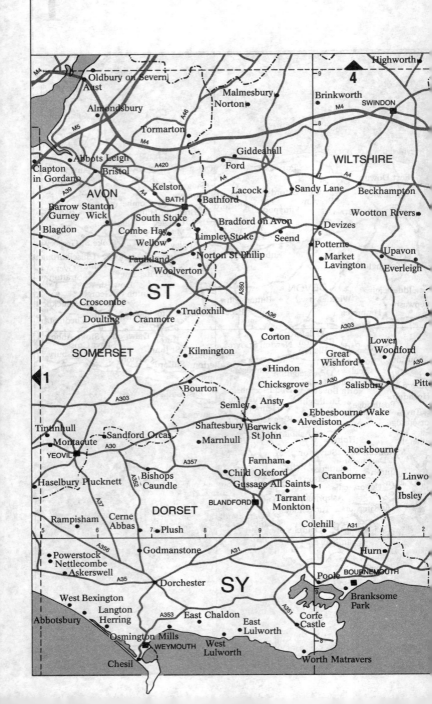

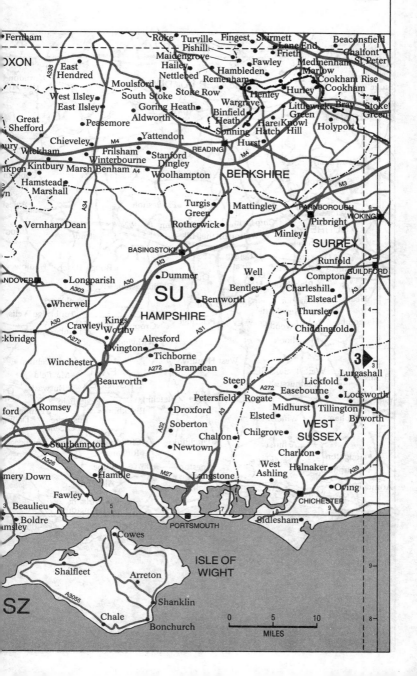

• Fernham

Roke • Turville Fingest Skirmett • Beaconsfield
Pishill • Maidengrove Frieth • Lane End Chalfont St Peter
OXON
East Hendred
Hailey Hambleden Fawley Medmenham
Nettlebed Remenham Marlow Cookham Rise
West Ilsley Moulsford South Stoke Stoke Row Hurley Cookham
East Ilsley Goring Heath Wargrave Henley Littlewick Bray Stoke Green
Great Shefford Peasemore Aldworth Binfield Green Knowl
Chieveley Yattendon Heath Hare Hatch Hill Holyport
Wickham M4 Sonning Hurst
Frilsham Stanford READING
Kintbury Winterbourne Dingley M4
Marsh Benham A4 Woolhampton BERKSHIRE
Hamstead Marshall
A34 Turgis Mattingley FARNBOROUGH M3 6
Green WOKING
Vernham Dean Rotherwick Minley Pirbright
BASINGSTOKE SURREY
M3 Runfold GUILDFORD
ANDOVER Longparish A30 Dummer Well Compton
A303 Bentley Charleshill A3
Wherwell SU Bentworth Elstead
A30 Crawley Kings Thursley
ckbridge Worthy HAMPSHIRE A31 Chiddingfold
A272 Alresford Ovington
Winchester Tichborne Lurgashall 3
A272 Bramdean 3
Beauworth Steep Lickfold
Petersfield A272 Easebourne Lodsworth
ford Romsey Droxford Rogate Midhurst Tillington Byworth
A32 Elsted WEST
Soberton Chilgrove SUSSEX
Southampton Chalton Charlton
A326 Newtown
Hamble M27 West Halnaker
mery Down Langstone Ashling A29
Fawley Oving
Beaulieu CHICHESTER
Boldre 5 7 8 9
msley PORTSMOUTH Sidlesham
Cowes
SZ Shalfleet ISLE OF WIGHT 9
Arreton
A3055 Shanklin 8
Chale 0 5 10
Bonchurch MILES

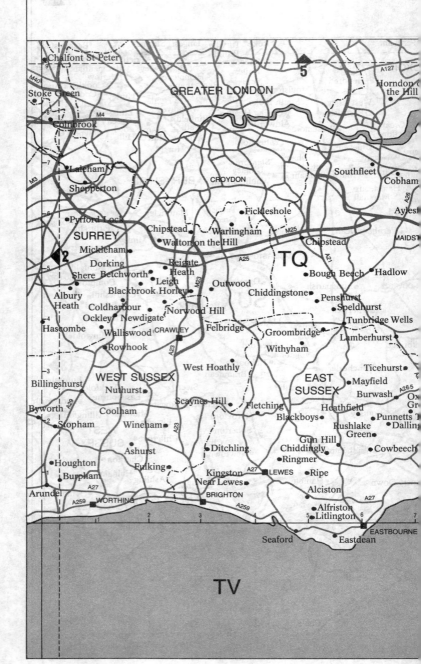

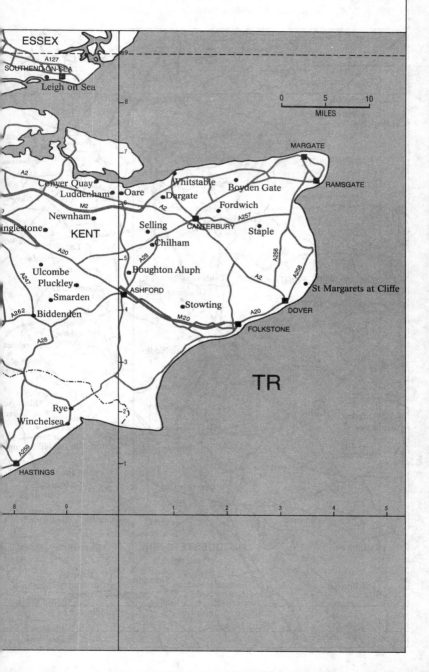

3

ESSEX

A127
SOUTHEND-ON-SEA
Leigh on Sea

0   5   10
MILES

MARGATE

A2
Conyer Quay   Whitstable   Boyden Gate   RAMSGATE
Luddenham   Oare   Dargate   Fordwich
M2
Newnham   A2   A257
nglestone   KENT   Selling   CANTERBURY   Staple
A20   Chilham
A256
A28   Boughton Aluph
A247   Ulcombe   A258
Pluckley   ASHFORD   St Margarets at Cliffe
A262   Smarden   Stowting   A2
Biddenden   M20   A20   DOVER
A28   FOLKSTONE

TR

Rye
Winchelsea

A259
HASTINGS

8   9   1   2   3   4   5

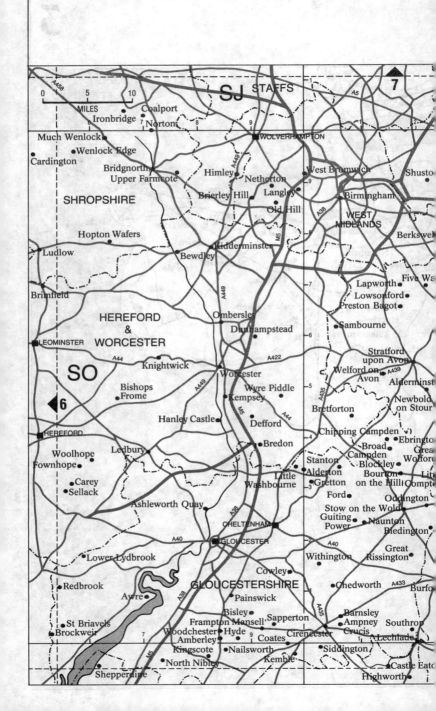

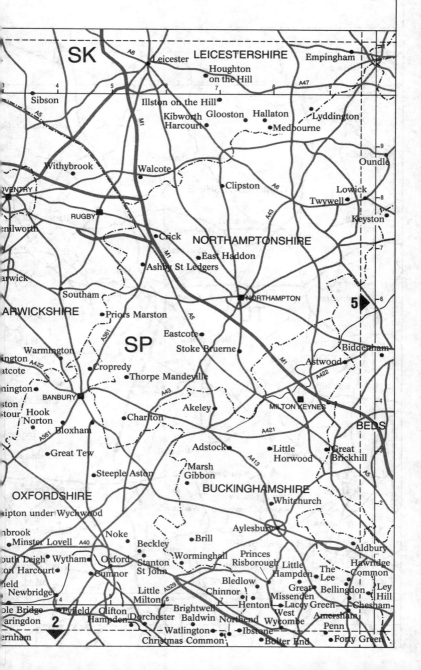

4

SK   A6   Leicester   **LEICESTERSHIRE**   Empingham

Houghton on the Hill   7   A47   8   9

Sibson   Illston on the Hill

A5   Kibworth Harcourt   Glooston   Hallaton   Lyddington

Medbourne   9

Oundle

Withybrook   Walcote   Lowick   8

Clipston   A6   Twywell

COVENTRY   Keyston

RUGBY   7

enilworth   Crick   **NORTHAMPTONSHIRE**

East Haddon   A43

Ashby St Ledgers

arwick   Southam   NORTHAMPTON   **5** ►   6

ARWICKSHIRE   Priors Marston   A5

Eastcote   **SP**   Biddenham

Warmington   Stoke Bruerne   M1

ington   A422   Cropredy   Astwood

atcote   Thorpe Mandeville   A422

mington   A43   4

ston   Hook   BANBURY   Akeley   MILTON KEYNES

tour   Norton   Charlton   **BEDS**

A361   Bloxham   A421

Great Tew   Adstock   Little   Great   3

Horwood   Brickhill   A5

Steeple Aston   Marsh Gibbon   A413

OXFORDSHIRE   **BUCKINGHAMSHIRE**

ipton under Wychwood   Whitchurch   2

nbrook   Noke   Aylesbury

Minster Lovell   A40   Beckley   Brill   Aldbury

outh Leigh   Wytham   Oxford   Worminghall   Princes   Hawridge

on Harcourt   Stanton   Risborough   Little   The   Common

Cumnor   St John   Hampden   Lee

field   Bledlow   Great   Bellingdon   Ley

Newbridge   Little   A329   Chinnor   Missenden   Hill

ole Bridge   Milton   6   Henton   Lacey Green   Chesham

aringdon   4   Tyfield   Clifton   Brightwell   West   Amersham

2   Hampden   Dorchester   Baldwin   Northend   Wycombe   Penn

ernham   Watlington   Ibstone   Forty Green

Christmas Common   Bolter End

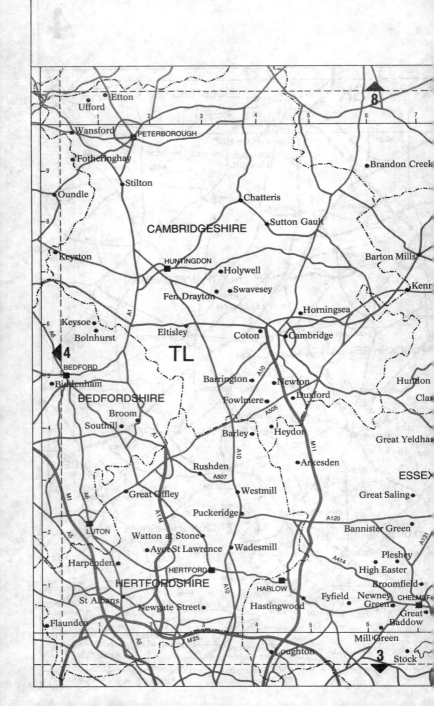

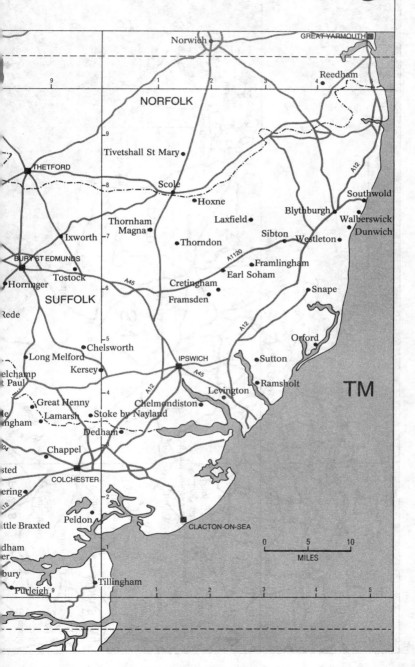

5

Norwich
GREAT YARMOUTH

9

NORFOLK
Reedham

9

Tivetshall St Mary

THETFORD
Scole
Southwold
8
Hoxne
Blythburgh
Walberswick
Thornham   Laxfield
Magna   Sibton   Westleton   Dunwich
Ixworth   7
Thorndon
BURY ST EDMUNDS   Framlingham
Tostock   Earl Soham
Horringer   Cretingham   Snape
SUFFOLK   6   Framsden
Rede
Orford
5
Chelsworth
Long Melford   IPSWICH   Sutton
Kersey
elchamp   TM
t Paul   4
Great Henny   Chelmondiston   Levington
Lamarsh   Stoke by Nayland   Ramsholt
ngham
Dedham
Chappel   3

sted
COLCHESTER
ering
2
Little Braxted   Peldon
CLACTON-ON-SEA
dham
er   0   5   10
bury   MILES
Purleigh 9   Tillingham

1   2   3   4   5

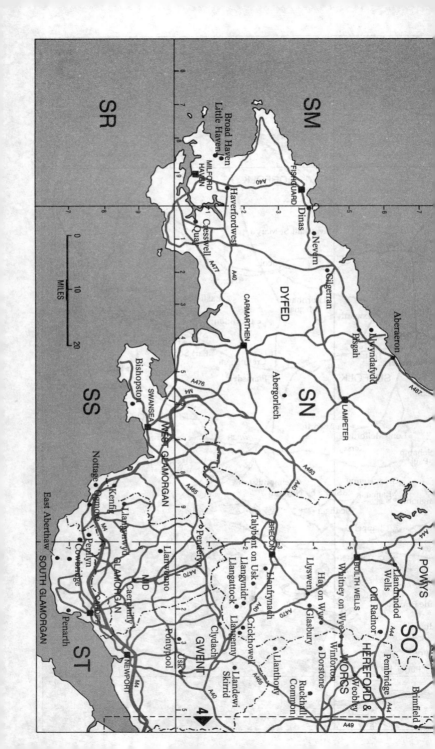

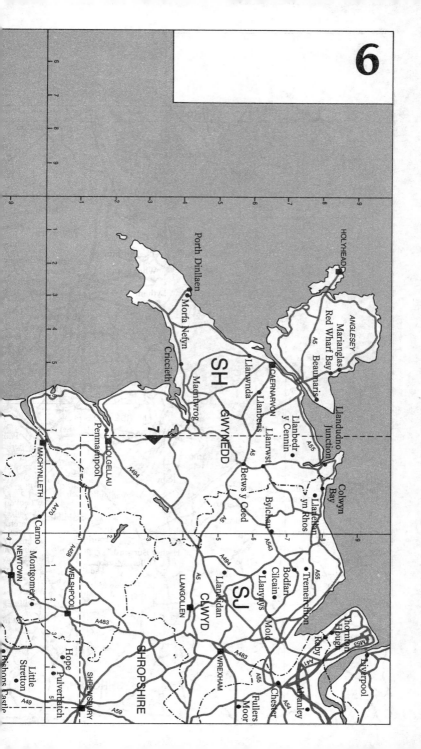

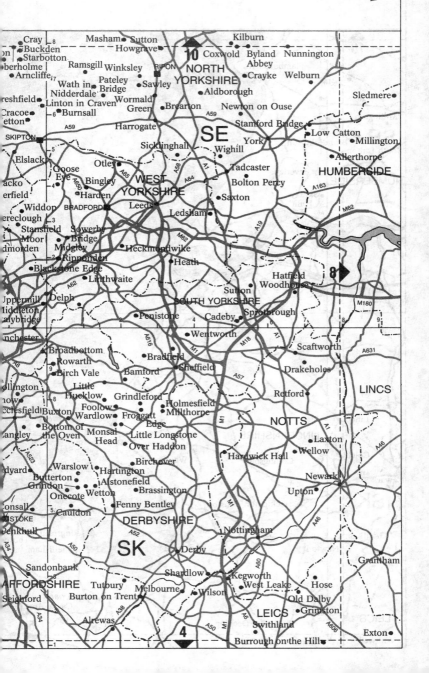

Cray
Buckden
Starbotton
berholme
Arncliffe 17

Masham Sutton
Howgrave

Kilburn

10 Coxwold Byland Nunnington
Abbey
Crayke Welburn

NORTH
YORKSHIRE

Ramsgill Winksley RIPON
Wath in Pateley Sawley
Nidderdale Bridge
Linton in Craven Wormald
Green
Brearton

Aldborough

Newton on Ouse

Sledmere

reshfield
Cracoe
etton
Burnsall

A59

Harrogate

Stamford Bridge

SKIPTON

5

Sicklinghall

A59

SE

Low Catton
Millington

Wighill

York

Elslack

Goose
Eye
Otley
Bingley

Tadcaster

Allerthorpe

HUMBERSIDE

acko
erfield
4

A65

A590
Harden

WEST
YORKSHIRE

A64

Bolton Percy

A163

Widdop
ereclough
3

BRADFORD
Leeds

Saxton

M62

Stansfield Sowerby
Moor Bridge
dmorden Midgley
2 Ripponden
Blackstone Edge
Linthwaite

Ledsham

A19

A62

Heckmondwike
Heath

Uppermill Delph
liddleton
alybridge

SOUTH YORKSHIRE

M62

Hatfield
Woodhouse

8

Sutton

M180

nchester

Penistone

4

Wentworth

Cadeby Sprotbrough

A1

7
8
9

Broadbottom
Rowarth
Birch Vale

A616

M1

M18

Scaftworth

A631

Bradfield
Bamford Sheffield

Drakeholes

LINCS

ollington
nows
cclesfield Buxton
angley

Little
Hucklow Grindleford
Foolow
Wardlow Froggatt
Bottom of Monsal
the Oven Head

A57

Holmesfield
Millthorpe
Edge
Little Longstone
Over Haddon

Retford

M1

NOTTS

A1

Laxton
Wellow

dyard
Butterton
Grindon
onsall
STOKE
enkhull

Warslow Hartington
Alstonefield
Onecote Wetton Brassington

Fenny Bentley

Birchover

Hardwick Hall

Newark

Upton

A46

5 Cauldon

DERBYSHIRE

A52

M1

Nottingham

A34

A50

SK

Derby

A60

Grantham

Sandonbank
AFFORDSHIRE Tutbury
Seighford Burton on Trent

8
Melbourne

Shardlow
Wilson

Kegworth
West Leake

Old Dalby

Hose

A34

Alrewas

A38

A50

M1

4

LEICS
Swithland
Burrough on the Hill

A6
Grimston

A606

Exton

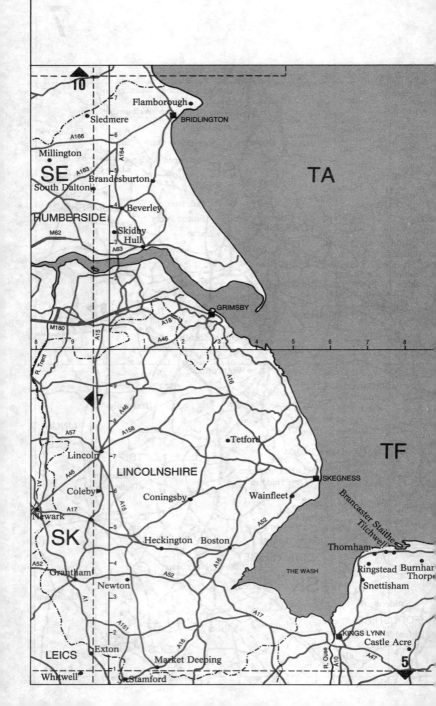

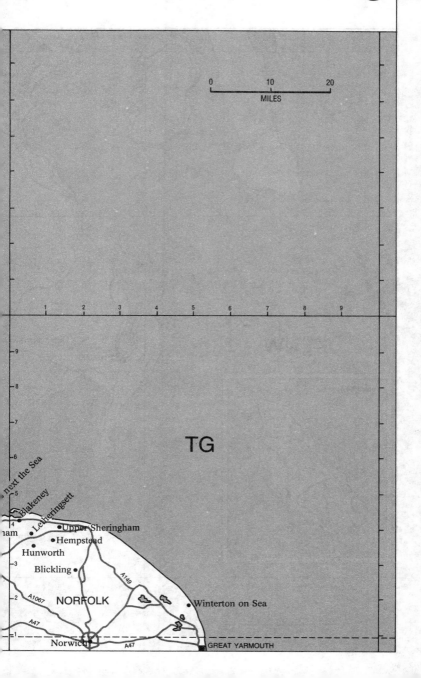

8

0   10   20
MILES

1   2   3   4   5   6   7   8   9

TG

next the Sea
Blakeney
Le Heringsett
Upper Sheringham
Hempstead
Hunworth
Blickling
A149
A1067
NORFOLK
Winterton on Sea
A47
Norwich
A47
GREAT YARMOUTH

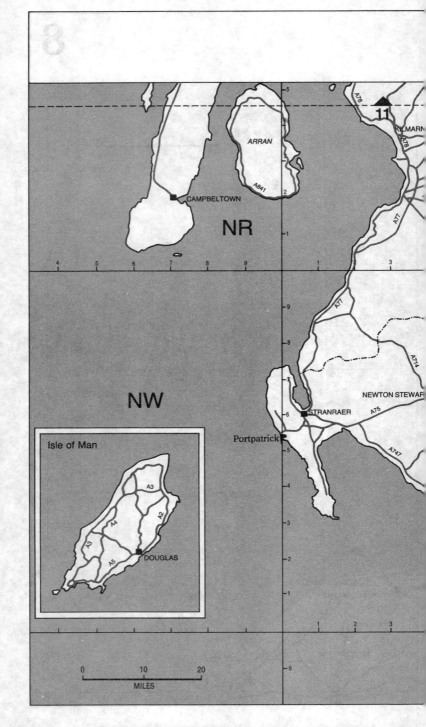

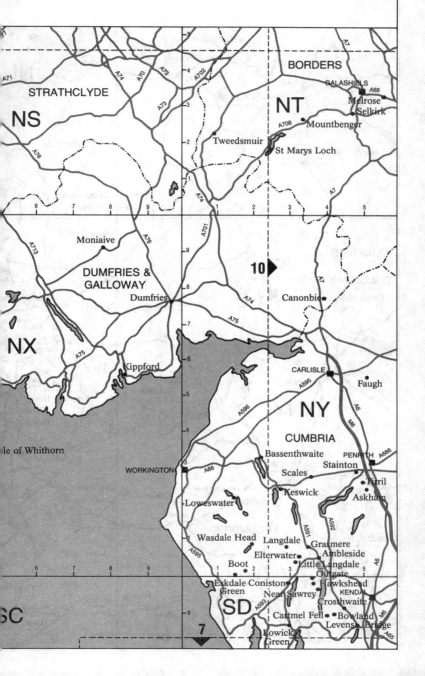

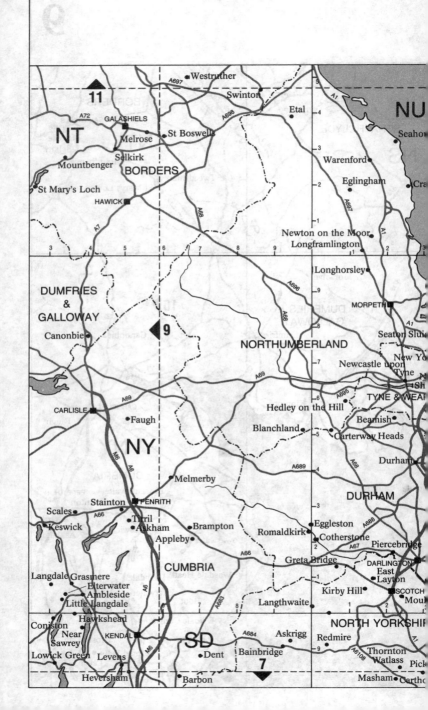

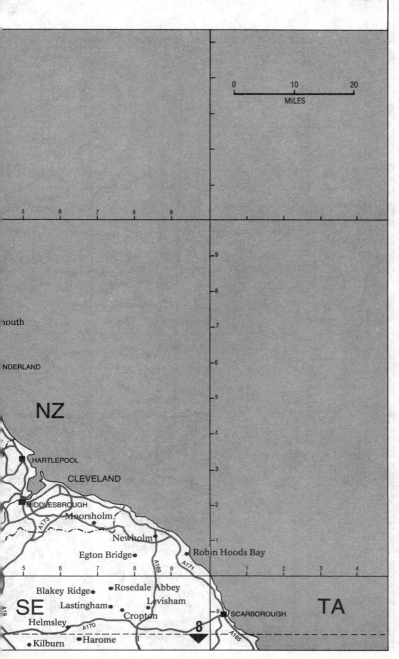

0   10   20
MILES

5   6   7   8   9

NZ

9
8
7
6
5
4
3
2
1

nouth

NDERLAND

HARTLEPOOL

CLEVELAND

MIDDLESBROUGH

Moorsholm

Newholm

Egton Bridge

Robin Hoods Bay

5   6   7   8   9

1   2   3   4

Blakey Ridge   Rosedale Abbey

Lastingham   Levisham

SE   Cropton

Helmsley   A170

Kilburn   Harome

8

SCARBOROUGH

TA

A165

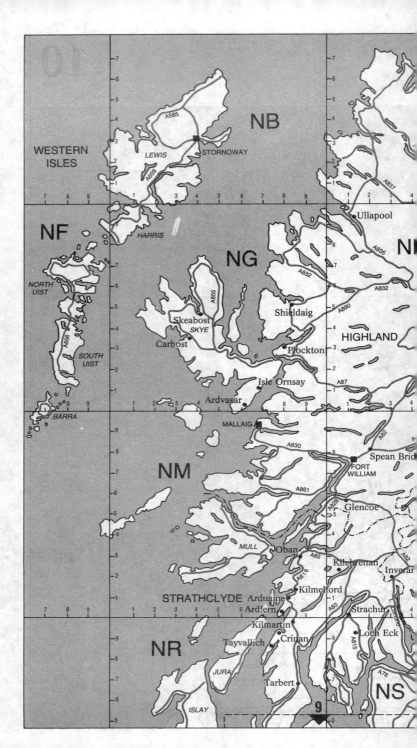

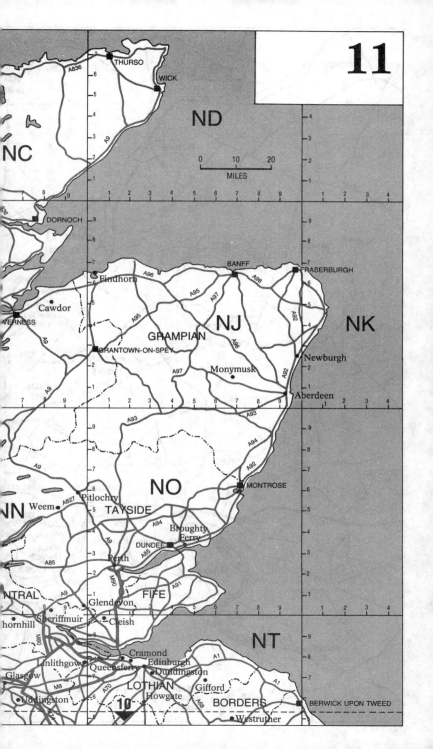

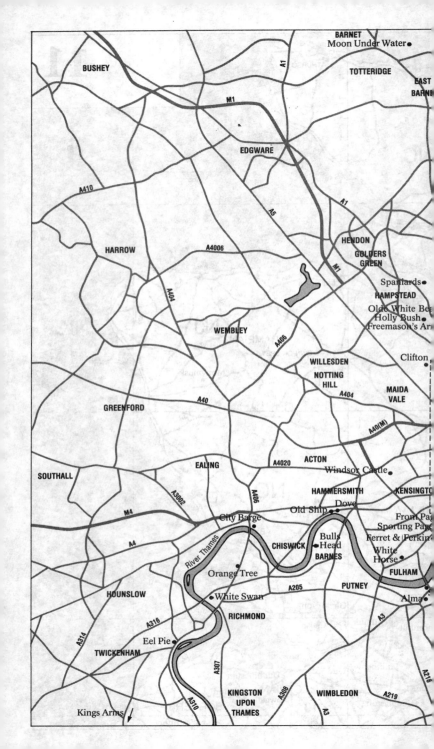

12

A10

A111

EDMONTON

HLEY

M11

A406

TOTTENHAM

WALTHAMSTOW

HORNSEY

A112

A12

GATE

White Lion
of Mortimer

A503

STOKE
NEWINGTON

A1

A11

ompton Arms

A10

A118

WEST HAM

ISLINGTON

See map 13

A124

A13

CITY

Hollands

Dickens
Inn

Grapes

Anchor

Angel

River Thames

GREENWICH

CAMBERWELL

TERSEA

Phoenix & Firkin

LEWISHAM

A2

CLAPHAM

Olde Windmill

A20

A24

A23

Crown & Greyhound

DULWICH

A205

A21

STREATHAM

Greyhound

A215

A231

A23

0   1   2   3
MILES

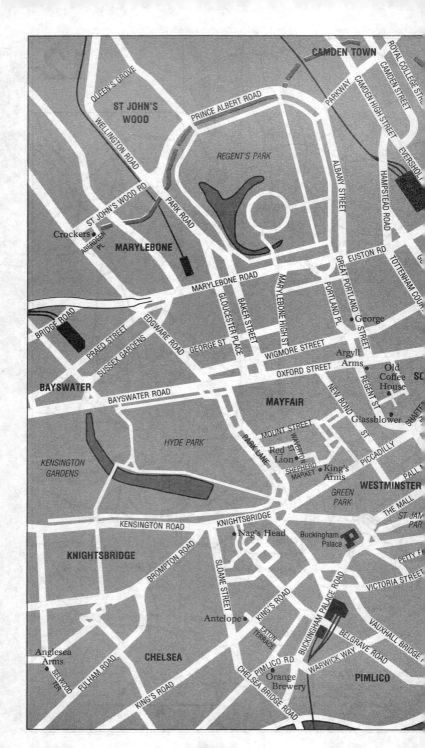

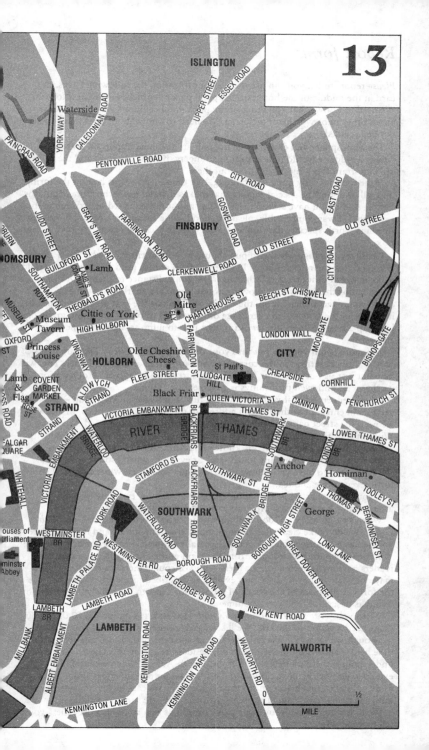

Report forms

Please report to us; you can use the tear-out forms on the following pages, the card in the middle of the book, or just plain paper – whichever's easiest for you. We need to know what you think of the pubs in this edition. We need to know about other pubs worthy of inclusion. We need to know about ones that should not be included.

The atmosphere and character of the pub are the most important features – why it would, or would not, appeal to strangers. But the bar food and the drink are important too – please tell us about them.

If the food is really quite outstanding, tick the FOOD AWARD box on the form, and tell us about the special quality that makes it stand out – the more detail, the better. And if you have stayed there, tell us about the standard of accommodation – whether it was comfortable, pleasant, good value for money. Again, if the pub or inn is worth special attention as a place to stay, tick the PLACE-TO-STAY AWARD box.

Please try to gauge whether a pub should be a main entry or is best as a *Lucky Dip* (and tick the relevant box). In general, main entries need qualities that would make it worth other readers' while to travel some distance to them; *Lucky Dips* are the pubs that are worth knowing about if you are nearby. But if a pub is an entirely new recommendation, the *Lucky Dip* may be the best place for it to start its career in the *Guide* – to encourage other readers to report on it, and gradually build up a dossier on it; it's very rare for a pub to jump straight into the main entries.

The more detail you can put into your description of a *Lucky Dip* pub that's only scantily described in the current edition (or not in at all), the better. This will help not just us but also your fellow-readers to gauge its appeal. A description of its character and even furnishings is a tremendous boon.

It helps enormously if you can give the full address for any new pub – one not yet a main entry, or without a full address in the *Lucky Dip* sections. In a town, we need the street name; in the country, if it's hard to find, we need directions. Without this, there's little chance of our being able to include the pub. And with any pub, it always helps to let us know about prices of food (and bedrooms, if there are any), and about any lunchtimes or evenings when food is not served. We'd also like to have your views on drinks quality – beer, wine, cider and so forth, even coffee and tea.

If you know that a *Lucky Dip* pub is open all day (or even late into the afternoon), please tell us – preferably saying which days.

When you go to a pub, don't tell them you're a reporter for *The Good Pub Guide*; we do make clear that all inspections are anonymous, and if you declare yourself as a reporter you risk getting special treatment – for better or for worse!

Sometimes pubs are dropped from the main entries simply because very few readers have written to us about them – and of course there's a risk that people may not write if they find the pub exactly as described in the entry. You can use the form at the front of the batch of report forms just to list pubs you've been to, found as described, and can recommend.

When you write to *The Good Pub Guide*, FREEPOST, London SW10 0BR, you don't need a stamp in the UK. We'll send you more forms (free) if you wish.

Though we try to answer letters, there are just the two of us, with only part-time help – and with other work to do, besides producing this *Guide*. So please understand if there's a delay. And from June to August, when we are fully extended getting the next edition to the printers, we put all letters and reports aside, taking as much account of their contents as we can, but not answering them until the rush is over (and after our post-press-day late summer holiday).

We'll assume we can print your name or initials as a recommender unless you tell us otherwise.

I have been to the following pubs in The Good Pub Guide *in the last few months, found them as described, and confirm that they deserve continued inclusion:*

PLEASE GIVE YOUR NAME AND ADDRESS ON THE BACK OF THIS FORM

Your own name and address (*block capitals please*)

REPORT on   *(pub's name)*

Pub's address:

☐ YES MAIN ENTRY   ☐ YES *Lucky Dip*   ☐ NO don't include
Please tick one of these boxes to show your verdict, and give reasons and descriptive comments, prices etc:

PLEASE GIVE YOUR NAME AND ADDRESS ON THE BACK OF THIS FORM

☐ Deserves FOOD award   ☐ Deserves PLACE-TO-STAY award   91:1

REPORT on   *(pub's name)*

Pub's address:

☐ YES MAIN ENTRY   ☐ YES *Lucky Dip*   ☐ NO don't include
Please tick one of these boxes to show your verdict, and give reasons and descriptive comments, prices etc:

PLEASE GIVE YOUR NAME AND ADDRESS ON THE BACK OF THIS FORM

☐ Deserves FOOD award   ☐ Deserves PLACE-TO-STAY award   91:2

REPORT on   *(pub's name)*

Pub's address:

☐ YES MAIN ENTRY   ☐ YES *Lucky Dip*   ☐   NO don't include
Please tick one of these boxes to show your verdict, and give reasons and descriptive comments, prices etc:

PLEASE GIVE YOUR NAME AND
ADDRESS ON THE BACK OF THIS FORM

☐ Deserves FOOD award   ☐ Deserves PLACE-TO-STAY award   91:3

REPORT on   *(pub's name)*

Pub's address:

☐ YES MAIN ENTRY   ☐ YES *Lucky Dip*   ☐   NO don't include
Please tick one of these boxes to show your verdict, and give reasons and descriptive comments, prices etc:

PLEASE GIVE YOUR NAME AND
ADDRESS ON THE BACK OF THIS FORM

☐ Deserves FOOD award   ☐ Deserves PLACE-TO-STAY award   91:4

Your own name and address (*block capitals please*)

....

Your own name and address (*block capitals please*)

REPORT on   *(pub's name)*

Pub's address:

☐ YES MAIN ENTRY ☐ YES *Lucky Dip* ☐ NO don't include
Please tick one of these boxes to show your verdict, and give reasons and descriptive comments, prices etc:

PLEASE GIVE YOUR NAME AND
ADDRESS ON THE BACK OF THIS FORM

☐ Deserves FOOD award ☐ Deserves PLACE-TO-STAY award   91:5

. . . .

REPORT on   *(pub's name)*

Pub's address:

☐ YES MAIN ENTRY ☐ YES *Lucky Dip* ☐ NO don't include
Please tick one of these boxes to show your verdict, and give reasons and descriptive comments, prices etc:

PLEASE GIVE YOUR NAME AND
ADDRESS ON THE BACK OF THIS FORM

☐ Deserves FOOD award ☐ Deserves PLACE-TO-STAY award   91:6

. . . .

REPORT on   *(pub's name)*

Pub's address:

☐ YES   MAIN ENTRY   ☐ YES *Lucky Dip*   ☐ NO don't include
Please tick one of these boxes to show your verdict, and give reasons and descriptive comments, prices etc:

PLEASE GIVE YOUR NAME AND
ADDRESS ON THE BACK OF THIS FORM

☐ Deserves FOOD award   ☐ Deserves PLACE-TO-STAY award   91:7

....

REPORT on   *(pub's name)*

Pub's address:

☐ YES   MAIN ENTRY   ☐ YES *Lucky Dip*   ☐ NO don't include
Please tick one of these boxes to show your verdict, and give reasons and descriptive comments, prices etc:

PLEASE GIVE YOUR NAME AND
ADDRESS ON THE BACK OF THIS FORM

☐ Deserves FOOD award   ☐ Deserves PLACE-TO-STAY award   91:8

Your own name and address (*block capitals please*)

. . . .

Your own name and address (*block capitals please*)

REPORT on _____ *(pub's name)*

Pub's address: _____

☐ YES MAIN ENTRY   ☐ YES *Lucky Dip*   ☐ NO don't include
Please tick one of these boxes to show your verdict, and give reasons and descriptive comments, prices etc:

PLEASE GIVE YOUR NAME AND
ADDRESS ON THE BACK OF THIS FORM

☐ Deserves FOOD award   ☐ Deserves PLACE-TO-STAY award   91:9

. . . .

REPORT on _____ *(pub's name)*

Pub's address: _____

☐ YES MAIN ENTRY   ☐ YES *Lucky Dip*   ☐ NO don't include
Please tick one of these boxes to show your verdict, and give reasons and descriptive comments, prices etc:

PLEASE GIVE YOUR NAME AND
ADDRESS ON THE BACK OF THIS FORM

☐ Deserves FOOD award   ☐ Deserves PLACE-TO-STAY award   91:10

REPORT on _____ *(pub's name)*

Pub's address:

_____

☐ YES MAIN ENTRY ☐ YES *Lucky Dip* ☐ NO don't include
Please tick one of these boxes to show your verdict, and give reasons and descriptive comments, prices etc:

☐ Deserves FOOD award ☐ Deserves PLACE-TO-STAY award   91:11

. . . .

REPORT on _____ *(pub's name)*

Pub's address:

_____

☐ YES MAIN ENTRY ☐ YES *Lucky Dip* ☐ NO don't include
Please tick one of these boxes to show your verdict, and give reasons and descriptive comments, prices etc:

☐ Deserves FOOD award ☐ Deserves PLACE-TO-STAY award   91:12

Your own name and address (*block capitals please*)

Pub's address:

☐ YES, MAIN ENTRY ☐ YES, a new DIP ☐ NO, don't include

Please tick one of the boxes to show your verdict, and give reasons and description of comparable prices, etc.

DO NOT USE THIS SIDE OF THE
PAGE FOR WRITING ABOUT PUBS

☐ Deserves FOOD award ☐ Deserves PLACE-TO-STAY award

· ·

Your own name and address (*block capitals please*)

Pub's address:

☐ YES, MAIN ENTRY ☐ YES, a new DIP ☐ NO, don't include

Please tick one of the boxes to show your verdict, and give reasons and description of comparable prices, etc.

DO NOT USE THIS SIDE OF THE
PAGE FOR WRITING ABOUT PUBS

☐ Deserves FOOD award ☐ Deserves PLACE-TO-STAY award

REPORT on   *(pub's name)*

Pub's address:

☐ YES MAIN ENTRY ☐ YES *Lucky Dip* ☐ NO don't include
Please tick one of these boxes to show your verdict, and give reasons and descriptive comments, prices etc:

PLEASE GIVE YOUR NAME AND
ADDRESS ON THE BACK OF THIS FORM

☐ Deserves FOOD award ☐ Deserves PLACE-TO-STAY award   91:13

. . . .

REPORT on   *(pub's name)*

Pub's address:

☐ YES MAIN ENTRY ☐ YES *Lucky Dip* ☐ NO don't include
Please tick one of these boxes to show your verdict, and give reasons and descriptive comments, prices etc:

PLEASE GIVE YOUR NAME AND
ADDRESS ON THE BACK OF THIS FORM

☐ Deserves FOOD award ☐ Deserves PLACE-TO-STAY award   91:14

REPORT on _____ *(pub's name)*

Pub's address:

_____

☐ YES **MAIN ENTRY**   ☐ YES *Lucky Dip*   ☐ NO don't include
Please tick one of these boxes to show your verdict, and give reasons and descriptive comments, prices etc:

PLEASE GIVE YOUR NAME AND ADDRESS ON THE BACK OF THIS FORM

☐ Deserves **FOOD** award   ☐ Deserves **PLACE-TO-STAY** award   91:15

. . . .

REPORT on _____ *(pub's name)*

Pub's address:

_____

☐ YES **MAIN ENTRY**   ☐ YES *Lucky Dip*   ☐ NO don't include
Please tick one of these boxes to show your verdict, and give reasons and descriptive comments, prices etc:

PLEASE GIVE YOUR NAME AND ADDRESS ON THE BACK OF THIS FORM

☐ Deserves **FOOD** award   ☐ Deserves **PLACE-TO-STAY** award   91:16

REPORT on   *(pub's name)*

Pub's address:

☐ YES MAIN ENTRY ☐ YES *Lucky Dip* ☐ NO don't include
Please tick one of these boxes to show your verdict, and give reasons and descriptive comments, prices etc:

PLEASE GIVE YOUR NAME AND
ADDRESS ON THE BACK OF THIS FORM

☐ **Deserves FOOD award** ☐ **Deserves PLACE-TO-STAY award**   91:17

....

REPORT on   *(pub's name)*

Pub's address:

☐ YES MAIN ENTRY ☐ YES *Lucky Dip* ☐ NO don't include
Please tick one of these boxes to show your verdict, and give reasons and descriptive comments, prices etc:

PLEASE GIVE YOUR NAME AND
ADDRESS ON THE BACK OF THIS FORM

☐ **Deserves FOOD award** ☐ **Deserves PLACE-TO-STAY award**   91:18

Your own name and address (*block capitals please*)

DO NOT USE THIS SIDE OF THE
PAGE FOR WRITING ABOUT PUBS

. . . .

Your own name and address (*block capitals please*)

DO NOT USE THIS SIDE OF THE
PAGE FOR WRITING ABOUT PUBS

REPORT on   *(pub's name)*

Pub's address:

□ YES MAIN ENTRY   □ YES *Lucky Dip*   □ NO don't include
Please tick one of these boxes to show your verdict, and give reasons and descriptive comments, prices etc:

PLEASE GIVE YOUR NAME AND
ADDRESS ON THE BACK OF THIS FORM

□ Deserves FOOD award   □ Deserves PLACE-TO-STAY award   91:19

. . . .

REPORT on   *(pub's name)*

Pub's address:

□ YES MAIN ENTRY   □ YES *Lucky Dip*   □ NO don't include
Please tick one of these boxes to show your verdict, and give reasons and descriptive comments, prices etc:

PLEASE GIVE YOUR NAME AND
ADDRESS ON THE BACK OF THIS FORM

□ Deserves FOOD award   □ Deserves PLACE-TO-STAY award   91:20

REPORT on   *(pub's name)*

Pub's address:

☐ YES   MAIN ENTRY   ☐ YES *Lucky Dip*   ☐   NO don't include
Please tick one of these boxes to show your verdict, and give reasons and descriptive comments, prices etc:

PLEASE GIVE YOUR NAME AND ADDRESS ON THE BACK OF THIS FORM

☐ Deserves FOOD award   ☐ Deserves PLACE-TO-STAY award   91:21

....

REPORT on   *(pub's name)*

Pub's address:

☐ YES   MAIN ENTRY   ☐ YES *Lucky Dip*   ☐   NO don't include
Please tick one of these boxes to show your verdict, and give reasons and descriptive comments, prices etc:

PLEASE GIVE YOUR NAME AND ADDRESS ON THE BACK OF THIS FORM

☐ Deserves FOOD award   ☐ Deserves PLACE-TO-STAY award   91:22

Your own name and address (*block capitals please*)

DO NOT USE THIS SIDE OF THE
PAGE FOR WRITING ABOUT PUBS

. . . .

Your own name and address (*block capitals please*)

DO NOT USE THIS SIDE OF THE
PAGE FOR WRITING ABOUT PUBS

REPORT on   *(pub's name)*

Pub's address:

☐ YES MAIN ENTRY ☐ YES *Lucky Dip* ☐ NO don't include
Please tick one of these boxes to show your verdict, and give reasons and descriptive comments, prices etc:

☐ Deserves FOOD award ☐ Deserves PLACE-TO-STAY award   91:23

. . . .

REPORT on   *(pub's name)*

Pub's address:

☐ YES MAIN ENTRY ☐ YES *Lucky Dip* ☐ NO don't include
Please tick one of these boxes to show your verdict, and give reasons and descriptive comments, prices etc:

☐ Deserves FOOD award ☐ Deserves PLACE-TO-STAY award   91:24

Your own name and address (*block capitals please*)

DO NOT USE THIS SIDE OF THE
PAGE FOR WRITING ABOUT PUBS

Your own name and address (*block capitals please*)

DO NOT USE THIS SIDE OF THE
PAGE FOR WRITING ABOUT PUBS

☐ Deserves FOOD award ☐ Deserves PLACE-TO-STAY award

REPORT on   *(pub's name)*

Pub's address:

☐ YES MAIN ENTRY   ☐ YES *Lucky Dip*   ☐ NO don't include
Please tick one of these boxes to show your verdict, and give reasons and descriptive comments, prices etc:

PLEASE GIVE YOUR NAME AND
ADDRESS ON THE BACK OF THIS FORM

☐ Deserves FOOD award   ☐ Deserves PLACE-TO-STAY award   91:25

- -

REPORT on   *(pub's name)*

Pub's address:

☐ YES MAIN ENTRY   ☐ YES *Lucky Dip*   ☐ NO don't include
Please tick one of these boxes to show your verdict, and give reasons and descriptive comments, prices etc:

PLEASE GIVE YOUR NAME AND
ADDRESS ON THE BACK OF THIS FORM

☐ Deserves FOOD award   ☐ Deserves PLACE-TO-STAY award   91:26

Your own name and address (*block capitals please*)

· ·

Your own name and address (*block capitals please*)

REPORT on   *(pub's name)*

Pub's address:

☐ YES MAIN ENTRY ☐ YES *Lucky Dip* ☐ NO don't include
Please tick one of these boxes to show your verdict, and give reasons and descriptive comments, prices etc:

☐ Deserves FOOD award ☐ Deserves PLACE-TO-STAY award   91:27

PLEASE GIVE YOUR NAME AND ADDRESS ON THE BACK OF THIS FORM

....

REPORT on   *(pub's name)*

Pub's address:

☐ YES MAIN ENTRY ☐ YES *Lucky Dip* ☐ NO don't include
Please tick one of these boxes to show your verdict, and give reasons and descriptive comments, prices etc:

☐ Deserves FOOD award ☐ Deserves PLACE-TO-STAY award   91:28

PLEASE GIVE YOUR NAME AND ADDRESS ON THE BACK OF THIS FORM

Your own name and address (*block capitals please*)

Pub's address:

☐ YES Main Entry ☐ YES Shorter Dip ☐ NO don't include
Please tick one of these boxes to show your verdict, and give reasons and any other comments, please tick

DO NOT USE THIS SIDE OF THE
PAGE FOR WRITING ABOUT PUBS

PLEASE GIVE YOUR NAME AND ADDRESS ON THE BACK OF THIS FORM

☐ Deserves FOOD award ☐ Deserves PLACE-TO-STAY award

. . . .

Your own name and address (*block capitals please*)

Pub's address:

☐ YES Main Entry ☐ YES Shorter Dip ☐ NO don't include
Please tick one of these boxes to show your verdict, and give reasons and any other comments, please tick

DO NOT USE THIS SIDE OF THE
PAGE FOR WRITING ABOUT PUBS

PLEASE GIVE YOUR NAME AND ADDRESS ON THE BACK OF THIS FORM

☐ Deserves FOOD award ☐ Deserves PLACE-TO-STAY award

REPORT on   *(pub's name)*

Pub's address:

☐ YES MAIN ENTRY   ☐ YES *Lucky Dip*   ☐ NO don't include
*Please tick one of these boxes to show your verdict, and give reasons and descriptive
comments, prices etc:*

☐ Deserves FOOD award   ☐ Deserves PLACE-TO-STAY award   91:29

REPORT on   *(pub's name)*

Pub's address:

☐ YES MAIN ENTRY   ☐ YES *Lucky Dip*   ☐ NO don't include
*Please tick one of these boxes to show your verdict, and give reasons and descriptive
comments, prices etc:*

☐ Deserves FOOD award   ☐ Deserves PLACE-TO-STAY award   91:30

Your own name and address (*block capitals please*)

DO NOT USE THIS SIDE OF THE
PAGE FOR WRITING ABOUT PUBS

Your own name and address (*block capitals please*)

DO NOT USE THIS SIDE OF THE
PAGE FOR WRITING ABOUT PUBS

REPORT on   *(pub's name)*

Pub's address:

☐ YES MAIN ENTRY ☐ YES *Lucky Dip*   ☐ NO don't include
Please tick one of these boxes to show your verdict, and give reasons and descriptive comments, prices etc:

PLEASE GIVE YOUR NAME AND ADDRESS ON THE BACK OF THIS FORM

☐ **Deserves FOOD award**   ☐ Deserves PLACE-TO-STAY award   91:31

. . . .

REPORT on   *(pub's name)*

Pub's address:

☐ YES MAIN ENTRY ☐ YES *Lucky Dip*   ☐ NO don't include
Please tick one of these boxes to show your verdict, and give reasons and descriptive comments, prices etc:

PLEASE GIVE YOUR NAME AND ADDRESS ON THE BACK OF THIS FORM

☐ **Deserves FOOD award**   ☐ Deserves PLACE-TO-STAY award   91:32

Your own name and address (*block capitals please*)

....

Your own name and address (*block capitals please*)

REPORT on _____ *(pub's name)*

Pub's address: _____
_____

☐ YES MAIN ENTRY ☐ YES *Lucky Dip* ☐ NO don't include
Please tick one of these boxes to show your verdict, and give reasons and descriptive comments, prices etc:

PLEASE GIVE YOUR NAME AND
ADDRESS ON THE BACK OF THIS FORM

☐ Deserves FOOD award ☐ Deserves PLACE-TO-STAY award   91:33

REPORT on _____ *(pub's name)*

Pub's address: _____
_____

☐ YES MAIN ENTRY ☐ YES *Lucky Dip* ☐ NO don't include
Please tick one of these boxes to show your verdict, and give reasons and descriptive comments, prices etc:

PLEASE GIVE YOUR NAME AND
ADDRESS ON THE BACK OF THIS FORM

☐ Deserves FOOD award ☐ Deserves PLACE-TO-STAY award   91:34

REPORT on _____ *(pub's name)*

Pub's address:

_____

☐ YES MAIN ENTRY ☐ YES *Lucky Dip* ☐ NO don't include
Please tick one of these boxes to show your verdict, and give reasons and descriptive comments, prices etc:

PLEASE GIVE YOUR NAME AND
ADDRESS ON THE BACK OF THIS FORM

☐ **Deserves FOOD award** ☐ **Deserves PLACE-TO-STAY award**   91:35

. . . .

REPORT on _____ *(pub's name)*

Pub's address:

_____

☐ YES MAIN ENTRY ☐ YES *Lucky Dip* ☐ NO don't include
Please tick one of these boxes to show your verdict, and give reasons and descriptive comments, prices etc:

PLEASE GIVE YOUR NAME AND
ADDRESS ON THE BACK OF THIS FORM

☐ **Deserves FOOD award** ☐ **Deserves PLACE-TO-STAY award**   91:36